Baseball Prospectus 2010

THE ESSENTIAL GUIDE TO THE 2010 BASEBALL SEASON

WILL CARROLL • CLIFFORD J. CORCORAN • CLAY DAVENPORT

KEN FUNCK • STEVEN GOLDMAN • KEVIN GOLDSTEIN

SHAWN HOFFMAN • JAY JAFFE • CHRISTINA KAHRL

TIM KNIKER • MARC NORMANDIN • JOHN PERROTTO

ERIC SEIDMAN • MATT SWARTZ

GOLDMAN & KAHRL, EDITORS

WILEY

John Wiley & Sons, Inc.

Published by John Wiley & Sons, Inc., Hoboken, New Jersey
Published simultaneously in Canada

For general information about our other products and services, please contact our Customer Care Department within the United States at (800) 762-2974, outside the United States at (317) 572-3993 or fax (317) 572-4002.

Wiley also publishes its books in a variety of electronic formats. Some content that appears in print may not be available in electronic books. For more information about Wiley products, visit our web site at www.wiley.com.

Editorial production by *Marra*thon Production Services. www.marrathon.net

Design by Jane Raese
Set in Utopia

ISBN 978-0-470-55840-9

Printed in the United States of America

10 9 8 7 6 5 4 3 2 1

Contents

Preface

One of the hardest things to get used to in life is the impermanence of everything. People come and go, buildings rise and fall (unless you live in New Jersey, where even something as simple as a new school must clear hurdles that would have hamstrung the builders of the Great Pyramids), and even the seasons themselves are no longer fixed. And yet, here we are at the 15th edition of the Baseball Prospectus annual. Wikipedia tells me that this is the crystal anniversary and that most marriages don't make it this far. Heck, we even outlasted the All-Star Café, financed by some of the very people we write about.

So how do you account for the longevity of the Baseball Prospectus book, which, including this volume, now encompasses over 8,000 pages? Flash back to 1996. Here is how I like to imagine it: a windswept hill, somewhere on the rocky New England coast. Lightning flashes threateningly in the distance. Slowly making their way up to the summit, each arriving from a different direction, are five individuals, all youthful and lean of face: Clay Davenport, Gary Huckabay, Rany Jazayerli, Christina Kahrl, and Joe Sheehan. On that hill, words are spoken, oaths taken, hands joined: Baseball Prospectus was born.

The members of the founding quintet were a dramatically heterogeneous group of personalities, but they did have a few things in common: heterodox thinking; a love of objective truth and the ongoing quest to find it; distaste for myth and a burning desire to debunk it; respect for intelligent thought over reactionary dogma; and a very, very high standard of quality. They would tolerate no sacred cows, even when slaughtering them meant suffering the occasional self-inflicted wound.

Combine these traits with their most important commonality, a love of baseball, and distill it into book form, and you have the 15 volumes of *Baseball Prospectus*. As Huckabay remarked in the introduction to the 1997 edition, "We've put this project together for one simple reason: no member of the authorship group has been happy with any of the available baseball annuals. The ones that claim to be analytical have severely flawed premises, sometimes strange goals, and usually read something like wet plywood. The few that really do have value ... are primarily numbers with very little commentary."

Commentary was and remains a key. The early BP annuals were downright terse compared with the later volumes, but the team, which quickly grew beyond the Fab Five, soon found its voice, moving beyond illustrative statistics and projections to interpretation, explanation, and even disagreement with them and each other—along with the odd digression into history, philosophy, and popular culture. This outpouring of words ultimately resulted in the volume before you, which has more words in it than *Moby Dick* and weighs more than *War and Peace*. The daily output on our Web site, BaseballProspectus.com, surpasses it every few days. We have a lot to say about baseball present, past, and future, and the goal is always more than mere prolixity; every time we pick up our pens, the goal is to say something about an aspect of baseball that you have not heard somewhere else before, to uncover some facet of the game that is not yet part of the discussion in the hidebound mainstream media, which is (with some notable exceptions) still often caught up in old-school thinking about RBI, strikeouts, and starting pitcher win totals. (If they weren't, Jim Rice wouldn't be in the Hall of Fame.)

When I was young and growing up in Reagan's America, baseball was not covered year-round the way it is now, nor in the same depth, not even in season. In the days before the Internet, there were very few avenues to get baseball information: the team broadcast, often compromised and pandering, or the daily beat writer, more concerned with getting quotes than daily analysis—if he told you that Omar Moreno was a great leadoff man, you had to believe him, because there were few competing voices. For the beginning fan, there was the venerable *Baseball Digest*, with its generally happy anecdotes but so completely ignorant of the way the game worked that they once explained how to derive an ERA for a player who had allowed runs but had gotten no outs. The even more venerable *Sporting News* had lost its "Bible of Baseball" identity years before. Bats and balls disappeared from *Sports Illustrated* during the winter and had to compete with other sports even when it was in season. That was initially a problem for ESPN as well, as anyone who ever had to sit through three segments of hockey highlights before getting to the one baseball story on "Sportscenter" can tell you. *Baseball America* and *USA Today Baseball Weekly* each made a game effort to be, separately, aspects of what the *Sporting News* once did all by itself, but were published too infrequently for the fan impatient to know what his or her team was doing to shape its chances for the coming season. Bill James came out with a book once a year, but skipped 1989 and then experimented with various flawed formats before disappearing altogether after 1995.

It was in this relative vacuum that Baseball Prospectus was conceived and brought into being. Since then, a slew of other Web sites have followed, and a few books as well, but BP has retained its place of prominence in what can now be termed an industry. The reason, I think, can be found in the way the books in this series have grown over the years in parallel to the BP Web site. We've never been satisfied to be only statistical analysts or quippy commentators, but we've extended our coverage to every area that baseball touches, all the while keeping in mind the original mission: the search for the home truths hiding behind the game's hoary, Selig-ian façade. In our view, ignorance is not bliss; it's a numbing soporific, and a life unexamined is a life unlived.

In this book, you will find the latest results of that philosophy. Thirty chapters, one for each major-league team, review the issues that determined the outcome of its 2009 season and that will shape its 2010. The heart of these chapters is the capsule discussion of over 60 players per team—what they contribute, what they take away, and the PECOTA projections for what they actually will do in the season to come. Each player comes with his share of numbers, which are fully explained in the statistical introduction that follows this preface.

Note that we often feel free to dispute the numbers when we believe they don't tell the whole story—statistics inform our thinking, but they don't do our thinking for us.

The spirit of inquiry and skepticism that went into this volume has application far beyond baseball. The passionate pursuit of truth, the dispassionate analysis of information, the throwing off of received wisdom handed down by voices now dead and perpetuated by Mommy and Daddy Media—this kind of thinking does not stop at the foul lines, but can be applied to every aspect of our lives, personal, professional, political. This is a baseball book, but what makes it special is the logic that underpins its conclusions. Some will call it a fantasy guide, and it can be used that way, but our ambitions are to give as complete a picture of baseball in 2009-2010 as can be found anywhere, accessible, utilitarian, and entertaining to the fantasy gamer, the casual fan, the baseball professional, and everyone in between, and to do so with the kind of intellectual rigor usually reserved for matters of state. This brings to mind the wonderful line spoken by Gene Hackman in the first *Superman* film: "Some people can read *War and Peace* and come away thinking it's a simple adventure story. Others can read the ingredients on a chewing gum wrapper and unlock the secrets of the universe."

I don't know if the secrets of the universe can be found in this volume, but I know the secrets of baseball sure are. And if you read between the lines, you might find some other stuff, too.

Steven Goldman
New Jersey
January 5, 2010

Statistical Introduction

Eric Seidman, Clay Davenport, and Derek Jacques,

with Fantasy Focus by Marc Normandin

With the rising popularity of statistical analysis and sabermetric research, it has become increasingly clear that a vast disconnect exists among fans. In the blue corner, we have the math-savvy group of fans who majored in the area collegiately or who independently studied various types of statistics. In the red corner stand the more casual fans who are unfortunately intimidated by their opponents because of the misconception that a greater understanding of multivariate probit models is required to parse more meaning out of 21st-century statistics. Fortunately, no matter which of these fraternities offers you a bid, advanced mathematics degrees are not required if you wish to utilize this book to its fullest capacity.

Though Baseball Prospectus prides itself on delivering top-notch analysis while boasting a reputation as a pioneer in statistical research, the careful data descriptions offered in this introduction as well as the supporting text offered throughout the various sections of this book place both of the aforementioned groups on equal footing. Should you conclude that a refresher in statistics—both back-of-the-baseball-card and of the more advanced variety—is needed, continue with this section, as we will introduce key concepts and the bulk of the major statistical concepts. Remember that the goal of creating newer statistics is to model more accurately what occurs on a baseball diamond. Though some of the underlying calculations may induce migraines, understanding the *why* is more important than the *how*, which perfectly segues into the beginning of our journey.

Types of Statistics

Baseball statistics are generally broken down into two major groupings: raw tallies and rates. Raw tallies provide the cumulative total of a particular metric, while the rates group measures the frequency of its occurrence in the form of percentages, averages, or ratios. You might be wondering which is preferable, but the truth is that neither has any sort of advantage without the appropriate context factored in. For instance, Ryan

Howard's raw rookie tally of 22 home runs in 2005 suggests decent pop for a freshman player, but did not necessarily portend an ability to launch 198 home runs—an average of 49.5 per year—over his next four seasons. When it is revealed that Howard's 22 home runs were accrued in a mere 312 at-bats (ABs)—a rate of one dinger per 14.1 ABs—and that he played in just 88 games that season, his raw tally becomes much more impressive.

Then again, solely viewing rates without the accompanying raw totals can conjure up inaccurate assessments of value if observed in a small sample of playing time. If a player were to mimic Howard's home-run rate of one per 14 ABs in a rather minuscule 42 trips to the dish, his impressive rate does not explain much. In fact, even Howard's aforementioned rate could be scrutinized, since the 312 at-bats and 88 games in no way constitute a large enough sample size from which definitive conclusions can be drawn. Bopping homers to the tune of a .567 slugging percentage like Howard did in 2005 does not automatically prorate out to a full season, so you can see how raw tallies and rates can be deceptive if used on their own, even *with* context.

The confluence of raw tallies, rates, and context makes for a delicious blend from which accurate performance assessments can be brewed. Each ingredient has merit on its own, but works much better in conjunction with the others, akin to a "checks and balances" system wherein each component provides clarity lacking from the others. Context in this forum has dealt primarily with playing time, but as we will soon show, it carries more than one meaning and can be incredibly valuable when scaling performance.

FANTASY FOCUS
Sample Size

We know what you're saying, "A statistical intro is all fine and good, but I haven't seen the word 'fantasy' yet—how am I supposed to gain an advantage over my insufferably egotistical league-mates without an assist in that area?" Fear not, dear reader, because we here at Baseball Prospectus have you covered on that score as well. We'll pop in at opportune times to explain a particular stat in more detail in relation to its fantasy twist.

Understanding the context and meaning of both rates and tallies is key to building your roster and shedding dead weight on unsuspecting owners who think they're getting a deal. Take Matt Holliday's time with the St. Louis Cardinals this year. Holliday batted .353, but did so in 270 plate appearances. This followed a .286 batting average with the Athletics, reached in 400 plate appearances. These are two disparate figures that tell different stories, so which one should you trust heading into 2010? There's much more to the tale of Holliday's 2009 than these two figures—some of which we will cover in this intro—but here, at its most basic, you will want to trust the larger sample and adjust from there.

Even 400 plate appearances itself is not a large sample to pull from, so take a look at his career line and performance. Holliday has hit .318 over his career and .313 over the course of both his stops in 2009. It looks as if Holliday has reached this kind of performance often—therefore, on draft day, .313 should be the number that sticks in your mind. This is a rudimentary example, but it's one we can build on throughout this introduction to prep you for this year's draft or auction.

Translating Baseball Performance

Another facet of context, arguably the most important one, involves the environment in which data were accrued. Environments do not necessarily refer to the actual climate or weather in this case, but rather to the conditions of play. Coors Field is a notoriously offense-friendly stadium, affording hitters the opportunity to post more inflated power statistics than in a more pitcher-friendly park. The American and National Leagues differ in quality, due to factors such as the inclusion of designated hitters, making a 3.30 ERA in the junior circuit more valuable than a 3.30 ERA in the senior circuit. If, however, the National League pitcher produced that 3.30 ERA while pitching in Coors Field, the effect of the park and elevation could put him on the same level as his American League doppelgänger in spite of the quality differential. The difference in quality is even greater when you consider a player who spent the year in the International League—or, for that matter, the Pioneer League. The minors have a wider range of league-average performances and parks than do the majors; combine that with widely varying difficulty levels and the possibility of players who are older and more experienced playing in leagues they have no business being in, and seemingly amazing performances can be reduced to nothingness.

Several interfering factors preclude a straight statistical comparison of two players, given the muddled waters of environmental context. For a true comparison of players, every player needs to be analyzed under the same microscopic lens and on the same scale. BP's Clay Davenport is renowned for his work in this specific area, normalizing data across environments. This normalization process works to strip away a good chunk of these outside factors to accurately compare players whose seasonal lines were reliant in one form or another on their environment.

Davenport's humbly monikered Davenport Translations paved the way for an entire family of statistics signified by the "Eq" prefix, which is the abbreviation for "Equivalent." The equivalent statistics adjust player performance to show what the actual data would resemble if amassed in a neutral ballpark—neither overly hitter- or pitcher-friendly—in a major-league season during which an average hitter put up a triple slash line of .265 BA/.335 OBP/.415 SLG. This data can be found on the right side of the statistics card for each player comment in the team chapters.

FANTASY FOCUS
Adjusting for Context

Players move around the league often, through trades, free agency, and waiver claims, which means you need to adjust your own expectations to account for their new environment. Just because a batter hit well in Fenway Park doesn't mean he will put up the same kind of performance in Petco Park, and a pitcher who excels in San Diego is not a guaranteed success back in Boston, either. Why is this? Fenway is one of the friendliest hitter parks, while Petco is actually a time machine that transports the players performing there into the Deadball Era, where offense was nonexistent. Knowing the difference between parks (and leagues as well) is necessary, because you need to assign players the correct value before you pick them up. Jake Peavy had more value when 2009 started, as he was in the National League (the weaker of the two leagues) and in the aforementioned Petco Park for half his starts. Now he's in the American League and pitching in a park that boosts home-run production—homers have been Peavy's Achilles' heel as he has aged and his fastball slows, so he is no longer the frontline ace you may have thought him to be. Conversely, were one of these "Adrian Gonzalez to Boston" rumors finally to resolve in an actual deal, you would pluck him from the middle-of-the-pack first baseman and plop him down near the first few selected at the position.

How do you keep track of who is getting a boost and who is being jobbed by his environment? For hitters, EqA (Equivalent Average) is an essential tool that streamlines performance so that player-to-player comparisons are valid and useful. EqA in-season may not do you much good, as the player is most likely stuck in his surroundings (unless he is traded, in which case you will want to refer to it), but in between seasons and as a tool to help you monitor what a player's true ability level is, EqA deserves a permanent slot in your fantasy utility belt.

Generally speaking, you want to avoid pitchers from places like Colorado or hitters from San Diego unless they have shown themselves capable of dealing with the park's effects—you don't get extra credit for relative performance in your fantasy league, so you need a mind-set different from the one that would build an actual team.

Predicting Future Performance with PECOTA

Having normalized all the data to a universal scale, we have a uniform body of data that allows trend analysis and performance forecasts. Our main tool in this regard is PECOTA (Player Empirical Comparison and Optimization Test Algorithm), a system created by Nate Silver that projects future player performance based on the historical record. PECOTA works by analyzing production metrics like rates and raw tallies; usage metrics involving playing time, career length, and minor-league levels; phenotypic attributes like handedness, height, and weight; and defensive position. For minor leaguers, the player's amateur signing bonus—adjusted for inflation—is added to the mix as a proxy for the scouting community's predraft expectations. With this data, PECOTA identifies as many comparable players as it can to the forecasted player in questions, tracking the career trends of those comparables as a projection component.

Much like the Davenport Translations, PECOTA incorporates park factors, platoon splits, and differences in league quality to more accurately project real-life playing conditions. We'll take Pat Burrell as an example. The senior circuit stalwart had averaged a .254/.385/.504 slash line from 2006 to 2008 before signing a two-year deal as designated hitter (DH) for the Rays. Had Burrell remained with the Phillies, or at least in the National League, his PECOTA projected slash line would have been similar to his previously posted averages, with slight alterations based on rolling park factor numbers and aging, among others. Moving from the relatively friendly confines of the National League and Citizens Bank Park and into the much tougher American League, Burrell was projected to hit just .236/.364/.453 in 2009, signaling a substantial drop-off in perfor-

mance. Unfortunately for the Rays, Burrell could not even muster that meager line, but his projection serves to showcase how several changes—leagues, stadiums, aging, defensive positioning—all work in concert in projections.

FANTASY FOCUS
Foreseeing the Future

Many a fantasy-league champion owes part of its success to PECOTA, as this system's comprehensive and accurate forecasts help owners make the decisions that shape their rosters. But simply taking PECOTA at face value is not enough—as much as we wish it was, the system is not infallible. Saying so may make the baby Jesus Montero cry, but it's true—you need to understand more than just what PECOTA (or any projection system, for that matter) is telling you at its most basic level if you want to have an advantage, especially since all your buddies can go out and buy their own BaseballProspectus.com online subscription and earn the same access to the wealth of knowledge that full-spread PECOTA cards grant.

PECOTA has built-in features that help keep it accurate even if the standard projection falters, as it did for Pat Burrell. Burrell hit .221/.315/.367, which is similar to his 25th-percentile forecast of .211/.338/.389—PECOTA knew Burrell was capable of faltering, as he did, but felt there was less of a chance of that happening than the chance of his reaching his standard, or weighted mean, projection. This information is important to you before the season starts, since, by studying the variance in their 75th, 25th, and weighted mean forecasts—less of a difference means the projection has a high degree of confidence—you can figure out which players are capable of reaching a certain performance level.

The Team Prospectus

The bulk of this book comprises team chapters, with one for each of the 30 major-league franchises. On the first page of each chapter, you will be greeted by a team-specific version as shown in Table 1.

2009 W-L is exactly as it sounds—the straight and unadjusted tally of wins and losses. **Pythag**, which extrapolates to Pythagenpat, tallies wins and losses on an adjusted basis by using the runs scored (**RS/G**) and allowed (**RA/G**) by a team in a season. It is a slight modification of Bill James's Pythagorean record in that Pythagenport uses context-neutral Equivalent Runs scored and allowed as opposed to the actual marks to get a better understanding of teamwide talent instead of numbers either inflated or deflated by the various

ORIOLES PROSPECTUS
2009 W-L: 64-98, 5th in AL East

Pythag	69-93	14th	**Ballpark:** Camden Yards (3-yr. PF: 1025). Not the worst place to pitch, so the upgrades need to come on offense
RS/G	4.6	10th	
RA/G	5.4	14th	
EqA	.253	9th	**2009:** A mixed batch of rookie debuts couldn't get these birds to reach basement-escape velocity
EqBRR	-21.9	14th	
SNWP	.453	14th	
WXRL	6.11	10th	**2010:** Breaking in talent at the corners and the rotation makes them baseball's best fourth-place team
FRAr	5.28	13th	
DE	.682	11th	
PADE	-1.28	10th	**Action Items:** A young shortstop; plenty of Maalox and patience as the talent comes of age
Salary	$67.1	11th	
Attend	1.91	9th	

Table 1. Prospectus Box Sample

factors discussed in prior sections. Comparisons of actual and estimated records are made, since the latter correlates better with performance in the succeeding season.

While runs scored per game traditionally speaks to offensive prowess, **Team EqA** gives us a more advanced measure. Equivalent Average (**EqA**) is a rate statistic that combines all the components of offense, including the stolen-bases facet of baserunning, into a number on the same scale as batting average. For teams, a .260 EqA is league average, a .280 EqA is very good, and a .240 EqA is very poor. Like other Equivalent statistics, EqA is normalized for ballpark and league offensive levels.

Though EqA incorporates certain aspects of success on the basepaths, stolen bases alone do not completely describe how teams fared while on the run. To that end, **EqBRR**, or Equivalent Baserunning Runs, comes to the rescue. Created by Dan Fox, EqBRR measures the number of runs contributed by a player's advancement on the bases above what would be expected given the number and quality of the baserunning opportunities with which the player is presented. The metric is park-adjusted, based on a multiyear run expectancy table, and is the sum of various components: Equivalent Ground Advancement Runs (EqGAR), Equivalent Air Advancement Runs (EqAAR), Equivalent Hit Advancement Runs (EqHAR), Equivalent Other Advancement Runs (EqOAR), and Equivalent Stolen Base Runs

(EqSBR), the last of which works similarly to the parent statistic but focuses solely on stolen base success.

Offense is only half the picture, or course, so we present Support-Neutral Winning Percentage (**SNWP**) for the rotation, and **WXRL** (see next paragraph) and Fair Run Average (**FRA**) for the bullpen. SNWP is similar to the standard winning percentage for pitchers, with the inputs adjusted to determine what a pitcher's win-loss record *should* have looked like had he received league-average support. The statistic is park-adjusted and derived from evaluations on a per-start basis. Comparing the SNWP to the actual winning percentage helps to explain how lucky or unlucky a pitcher was, on the basis of his own efforts in relation to the support received; Wandy Rodriguez, for example, posted a .538 winning percentage in 2009, but his .593 SNWP suggests that his efforts were much better than back-of-the-baseball-card data indicate.

WXRL is a reliever-specific metric that quantifies these pitchers' efforts on a win-expectancy basis, with adjustments for the replacement level and the quality of the opposing lineup. A counting statistic in nature, higher WXRL marks are better, with the data explaining which teams received the greatest or least contributions from their relief corps. This past season, Brad Lidge of the Phillies recorded the worst WXRL of all time for any regular closer.

FRA works similarly to the standard ERA, but assumes that only a league-average amount of bequeathed runners—those left on base upon the pitcher's exit from the game—come around to score. Through this adjustment of the metric, a reliever's contributions are better reflected and not subject to the inherent inflation that could occur if a less competent reliever allows all of his runners to score.

Pitching and defense are often intermingled, and with the data for those toeing the rubber out of the way, next up are two defensive-minded statistics, Defensive Efficiency (**DE**) and Park Adjusted Defensive Efficiency (**PADE**), both of which measure a team's ability to convert balls in play into outs. Raw DE is an invention of Bill James and can be calculated by dividing non-strikeout outs by the non-home-run balls in play, serving as a solid proxy of defensive success. Defense, however, is not solely contingent on the balls-in-play/outs percentage, since the actual fielding environment looms large in whether a batted ball is fielded. To that end, James Click created this park-adjusted form of the popular stat. PADE yields a percentage that gives us an idea of how each team's defense performed against the expected league average, given the team's schedule, the various ballparks in which it played, and how tough the park is, via a defensive park factor, to defend. For instance, Coors Field is notorious for being tough on fielders, and its influence on defensive efficiency is substantial. The Rockies' unadjusted DE bears out this assessment; it is important, but will not tell the entire story.

The final two statistics offered are, again, exactly as they seem. **Salary** refers to the payroll of a team, taken from the *USA Today* database. Last season, the Yankees—surprise, surprise—invested the most money into their personnel, with the Marlins finishing at the bottom of the pile. **Attendance** can have an impact on payroll in the subsequent year and help gauge the interest level of fans as it pertains to home teams. The Yankees and Dodgers led their respective leagues in home attendance this past season.

FANTASY FOCUS
Take Me Out of the Ballpark

Remember the earlier example with Matt Holliday, and his differing batting averages? If you were to look at this section of the team chapter, you would learn that Busch Stadium leans toward pitchers, but that Oakland's canyon-like stadium is one of the worst parks for hitters this side of Petco, thanks to its abundance of foul territory. Holliday's stretch for St. Louis was a combination of good luck on balls in play and getting out of the American League and back to the inferior NL, but getting away from the sepulchral McAfee Coliseum was also key.

The Hitters' Statistics

After an opening essay, each chapter moves on to the player comments. Position players are listed first, in alphabetical order, and each player is listed with the major-league team with which he finished the 2008 season, meaning that free agents who eventually change teams will be listed under their previous employer. As an example, take a gander at Albert Pujols' data in Table 2.

The player-specific sections begin with biographical information before moving on to the column headers and actual data. Other than cups of coffee at the various levels—trimmed out in the interest of space and in accordance with small-sample-size theory—all relevant seasons and partial seasons will be listed. The column headers begin with more standard information like **Year, Team, LVL** (majors or minors, and which level of the minors), **Age** and the raw, untranslated tallies found on the back of a baseball card: **PA** (Plate Appearances), **R** (Runs), **2B** (doubles), **3B** (triples), **HR** (home runs), **RBI** (runs batted in), **BB** (walks), **SO** (strikeouts), **SB** (stolen bases), and **CS** (caught stealing).

Next is Equivalent Baserunning Runs (**EqBRR**), an advanced baserunning statistic developed by Dan Fox; it works to encompass all facets of baserunning and not just stolen base success. EqBRR measures how often extra bases are taken—as well as lost via being thrown out—relative to the average player on hits, outs in play, passed balls, wild pitches, and balks in addition to steals, and translates the results into Equivalent Runs.

Following EqBRR are the triple-slash rate statistics: batting average (**AVG**), On-Base Percentage (**OBP**), and Slugging Percentage (**SLG**). Their "slash" nickname is derived from the occasional presentation of slash-delimitation, such as noting that Longoria hit .272/.343/.531. Each of the three statistics is flawed on its own, but put together, they accurately summarize a hitter's season at the dish. Immediately to their right are the translated equivalent slash-line trio of **EqAVG, EqOBP,** and **EqSLG**. All three of these metrics are scaled to their untranslated brethren as well. As in the Team Prospectus boxes, **EqA** sums up offense in a handy single number scaled to batting average, but this time for the individual player concerned.

The next column in the statistical record is **VORP**, or Value Over Replacement-level Player. What, you may ask, is the replacement level? It is, roughly, "the

Albert Pujols			1B							Bats: R	Throws: R		Height: 6' 3"		Weight: 230		Born: January 16, 1980			Age: 30
YEAR	TEAM	LVL	AGE	PA	R	2B	3B	HR	RBI	BB	SO	SB	CS	EqBRR	AVG	OBP	SLG	EqAVG	EqOBP	EqSLG	EqA	VORP	WARP	DEFENSE

YEAR	TEAM	LVL	AGE	PA	R	2B	3B	HR	RBI	BB	SO	SB	CS	EqBRR	AVG	OBP	SLG	EqAVG	EqOBP	EqSLG	EqA	VORP	WARP	DEFENSE
2007	SLN	MLB	27	679	99	38	1	32	103	99	58	2	6	-1.3	.327	.429	.568	.342	.442	.588	.338	68.4	10.6	150-1B 27
2008	SLN	MLB	28	641	100	44	0	37	116	104	54	7	3	-0.2	.357	.462	.653	.375	.473	.679	.372	91.7	11.7	135-1B 17
2009	SLN	MLB	29	700	124	45	1	47	135	115	64	16	4	-0.4	.327	.443	.658	.348	.454	.699	.368	92.6	12.7	155-1B 23
2010	SLN	MLB	30	658	98	34	1	34	108	100	64	6	5	-0.3	.317	.427	.564	.327	.434	.589	.340	69.1	8.6	147-1B 11

Breakout: 2%   Improve: 29%   Collapse: 12%   Attrition: 12%   MLB: 99%   Comparables: Jeff Bagwell, Jack Clark, Frank Thomas, Derrek Lee

Table 2. Hitter Statistics Example

expected level of performance a team can receive from one or more of the best available players who substitute for a suddenly unavailable starting player at the same position and who can be (or was) obtained with minimal expenditure of team resources." Replacement level tends to be in the neighborhood of 20-25 runs below the value of a starting player, over a full season, which works out to about 30 points of EqA. Below that level, players tend to get washed out of the majors fairly quickly, usable only in the direst of emergencies. VORP is an estimate of how many runs better than that replacement level a player is, combining his rate of performance, playing time, and position.

We've transitioned this year to using a measure of VORP that is based on EqA; this has appeared for years on the BP Web site under the label of "RARP." While the calculation differs, the concept is identical. All players, major- and minor-leaguers both, are evaluated on their fully adjusted EqA (so park effects, league offense, and league difficulty are all accounted for). Replacement level is calculated for each player on the basis of a weighted average of all positions he played.

FANTASY FOCUS
The Replacement Level

The concept of replacement level has less utility in its present form for fantasy players than in real-life analysis, but the ideas behind it are still important to recognize. Replacement level in fantasy is higher than it would be in reality—the rosters are smaller, there are fewer teams, yet the pool of players is the same, which means you can pick the cream of each position's crop and leave the rabble where they belong (i.e., starting for the Royals.)

It's also important to know which positions are scarce and when it's appropriate to select who for what purpose. There are just a few shortstops worth selecting early on in a draft, or for high dollars at auction. After the first three or four are selected, the next eight or so are basically versions of the same player and could be considered having value akin to replacement level. You should just skip out on that position while you fill other needs for a time, since you won't gain anything extra from picking a replacement level player so early on. You may even already do this, which means you accept replacement level whether or not you've learned to call it that.

While VORP considered how a player performs relative to his position as well as the inherent value of staying on the field, it is offensive in nature and excludes fielding ability altogether. To gauge the total contributions of a player, we must turn to the next column, **WARP**, or Wins Above Replacement Player, which encompasses fielding and offense as well as the position of a player into a tidy, singular figure. Pujols' 12.7 WARP in Table 2 tells us that if his entire body of playing time were given to a card-carrying member of the Freely Available Talent Club, the Cardinals would have won approximately 78 games, rather than 91.

The final column, **Defense**, tells us the equivalent number of full games the player played at his position and the number of runs above or below average he was with the glove. In Pujols' case, the 155-1B 23 tells us that in the equivalent of 155 full games, Pujols saved 23 more runs with his glove than did the average first sacker. These figures are derived from play-by-play data; fielders are evaluated on their ability to convert batted balls into outs, to get runners already on base out, and to limit the bases gained by the batter and other runners in the event they can't get an out.

The 2010 line is the PECOTA projection for the player in the upcoming season. Note that the player is projected into the league and park context as indicated by his team abbreviation. All PECOTAs represent a player's projected major-league performance.

The numbers beneath the 2010 forecast line—Breakout, Improve, Collapse, and Attrition—are also a part of PECOTA and estimate the likelihood of changes in performance relative to a player's previously established level of production. Descriptions of each follow:

* **Breakout rate** is the percent chance that a hitter's equivalent runs produced per PA will be at least 20 percent higher than the weighted average of his performance over his most recent seasons.
* **Improve rate** is the percent chance that a hitter's equivalent runs produced per PA will improve *at all* over his baseline performance. A player who is expected to perform just the same as he has in the recent past will have an Improve rate of 50 percent.
* **Collapse rate** is the percent chance that a position player's equivalent runs produced per PA will be at least 25 percent lower than his baseline performance over his past three seasons.
* **Attrition rate** operates on playing time rather than performance. Specifically, it measures the likelihood that a hitter's PAs will decrease by at least 50 percent relative to his established level.
* **MLB** is the percentage of playing time spent in the majors by the player's comparable list.

Breakout rate and Collapse rate can sometimes be counterintuitive for players who have already experienced a radical change in their performance levels.

Moreover, the projected decline in his rate performances might not be indicative of an expected decline in underlying ability or skill, but rather something of an anticipated correction after a breakout season.

The penultimate piece of information, listed just to the right of the hitter's Attrition rate, is called Comparables: the four highest-scoring comparable players as determined by PECOTA. Occasionally, a player's top comparables will not be representative of the larger sample that PECOTA uses. What's more, established major leaguers are compared to other major-leaguers only, while minor-league players may be compared to major-league or minor-league players, with PECOTA strongly preferring the latter. All comparables represent a snapshot of how the listed player was performing at the same age as the current player, so if a 23-year-old hitter is compared to Sammy Sosa, he's actually being compared to a 23-year-old Sammy Sosa, not to the decrepit Orioles version of Sosa or to Sosa's career as a whole.

FANTASY FOCUS
The Breakout

Breakout, Improve, Collapse, and Attrition rates are like the advanced course for PECOTA, as they detail just what PECOTA is thinking when it puts forecasts together. Understanding what this means can be a boon to your team, as you can mentally adjust forecasts and expectations for players you are considering by comparing not just their projected lines, but also the likelihoods that they will reach them. You'll find yourself poring over this information on draft day when you are filling out your roster, and the thorough presentation here for you makes snap decisions that much easier.

The Pitchers' Statistics

After the hitters' comments, pitchers are discussed in each chapter. Table 3 is an example of the data presented for these players.

The first line and the **YEAR**, **TEAM**, **LVL**, and **AGE** columns are the same as in the hitter's example in Table 2. The next set of columns—**W** (Wins), **L** (Losses), **SV** (Saves), **G** (Games pitched), **GS** (Games Started), **IP** (Innings Pitched), **H** (Hits), **BB**, **SO**, **HR**—are the actual, unadjusted cumulative stats compiled by the pitcher during each season.

Next is **GB%**, which is the percentage of all batted balls that were hit on the ground, including both outs and hits. Measuring GB% using just outs can be skewed by having an unusually good (or bad) infield or outfield defense, so we prefer to measure GB% using all batted balls, regardless of whether they result in hits or outs. The average GB% for a major league pitcher in 2007 was about 45 percent; a pitcher with a GB% anywhere north of 50 percent can be considered a good ground-ball pitcher.

BABIP is Batting Average on Balls in Play, a statistic recently popularized by research indicating that pitchers exert a relatively small influence over the outcomes of balls in play (everything except home runs, strikeouts, walks, and times hit by pitch). A high BABIP is most likely due to a poor defense, or bad luck, rather than a pitcher's own abilities, and may be a good indicator of a potential rebound. A typical league-average BABIP is around .295 or .300.

FANTASY FOCUS
The Ball in Play

Ground-ball percentage (GB%) is important when it comes to fantasy. If a pitcher picks up most of his outs via balls in play, you're going to miss out on some strikeouts, a category in most leagues. Then again, if a pitcher picks up a lot of outs and is able to succeed without many strikeouts, then chances are good he will be underrated to a degree and available late, or for low money.

As a stat, GB% goes hand in hand with BABIP, as a pitcher with a high GB% needs a quality defense behind him. A pitcher who puts a lot of balls in play is going to have a

Zack Greinke — Bats: R   Throws: R   Height: 6′ 2″   Weight: 185   Born: October 21, 1983   Age: 26

YEAR	TEAM	LVL	AGE	W	L	SV	G	GS	IP	H	HR	BB	SO	GB%	BABIP	STUFF	WHIP	ERA	SIERA	DERA	EqH9	EqHR9	EqBB9	EqSO9	VORP	SN/WX
2007	KCA	MLB	23	7	7	1	52	14	122	122	12	36	106	37%	.314	17	1.30	3.69	3.76	3.43	8.7	0.8	2.4	7.3	27.4	5.37
2008	KCA	MLB	24	13	10	0	32	32	202¹	202	21	56	183	49%	.308	26	1.28	3.47	3.52	3.53	8.6	0.8	2.2	7.5	44.2	5.74
2009	KCA	MLB	25	16	8	0	33	33	229¹	195	11	51	242	46%	.303	50	1.07	2.16	2.75	2.35	7.2	0.3	1.7	8.5	79.8	9.79
2010	KCA	MLB	26	12	9	0	42	31	197²	195	19	55	179	43%	.317	27	1.26	3.71	3.47	3.70	8.3	0.8	2.3	7.8	39.6	4.80

Breakout: 2%   Improve: 45%   Collapse: 16%   Attrition: 8%   MLB: 100%   Comparables: Jake Peavy, Daisuke Matsuzaka, Pedro Martinez, Camilo Pascual

Table 3. Pitcher Statistics Example

higher BABIP if his defense is porous, especially if they lean toward ground balls over fly balls—Brian Bannister isn't considered a fantasy monster by any stretch of the imagination, but if he played before anything other than the worst defense in the league, he would have considerable value for what he does do right.

Look for pitchers with high or low BABIP marks as you prepare your personal rankings. Some of these players may have experienced a one-year fluctuation due to defense or park effects, and if they are going to rebound (or come back to earth), you will want to know. Some of the best values in the draft come from players that people have given up on—there's a comeback player of the year award for a reason, and recognizing BABIP's role in performance will help you go a long ways toward picking a candidate. On the other hand, someone will always overdraft the one-year wonders. Knowing how to pinpoint who those guys are is just as important as, if not more important than, finding the rebounders.

The next column is **Stuff**, our version of which differs from the scouting term of the same name. Instead of measuring velocity or movement, our Stuff metric is a mathematically formulated shorthand for evaluating demonstrated skills relative to age and level. Thus, the statistic is designed for prospects and not established major-league pitchers. Minor-league hurlers with the talent to become an average big-league starter will score a 10, while excellent prospects exceed the 20 mark, and the absolutely elite score above 30. While several peripheral statistics are utilized in the formula, strikeout rate is by far the most important.

WHIP and **ERA** are common to most fans; WHIP measures the number of walks and hits allowed on a per-inning basis, while ERA prorates runs allowed on a nine-innings basis. Neither is translated or adjusted in any way. **DERA**, however, is translated and adjusts ERA for the quality of the defense playing behind the pitcher, factoring in the ground-ball and fly-ball tendencies of the pitcher for a more granular look at the total impact of defense on his performance. If a pitcher's DERA is lower than his ERA, the assumption is that his performance was hindered by shoddy glovework; on the other hand, a DERA in excess of the ERA indicates that the pitcher's statistics were beautified by slick fielding.

SIERA (Skill Interactive Earned Run Average), a new run-estimation pitching metric created by Matt Swartz and Eric Seidman, builds on the adjustment efforts of DERA by modeling the impact of defense—through the pitcher's ground-ball rate—and its interaction with a pitcher's controllable skills (his walks and strikeouts). SIERA gives us a much better idea of both what should

have been and what is likely to occur in the future, as the pitcher is more likely to be consistent in these aspects of his game than he is to be supported by the same defensive cast performing at the same level of execution. For example, Johan Santana's performance is more accurately reflected under this lens. Though he is prone to the home run, from 2004 through 2007 his low walk rates, high ground-ball rates, and high strikeout rates led to a greater probability that his home runs occurred with no one on base, limiting the damage. In 2008-2009, however, his SIERA was higher than his ERA because each of those components is trending in the wrong direction. For this reason, we would look at his SIERA and conclude that while Santana is still a very good pitcher, his ability to prevent runs now relies more on the defense than before.

The next four columns, all starting with "Eq," are the pitcher's rates of production (hits allowed per nine innings, strikeouts per nine innings, etc.) based on his translated statistics. As with the hitter example above, a pitcher's raw statistics are adjusted and converted to a neutral-park major-league-equivalent performance. We present the translated (or equivalent) rate per nine innings of hits allowed (**EqH9**), walks issued (**EqBB9**), strikeouts recorded (**EqSO9**), and home runs surrendered (**EqHR9**).

A pitcher's **VORP** is the number of extra runs that a replacement-level pitcher would have allowed if he pitched the same number of innings as this pitcher. Slightly different standards are applied for starting and relief pitchers because of the different replacement levels for the two roles.

The final column, **SN/WX**, actually represents two statistics, each of which tell us how many wins the pitcher contributed to his team. We obtain this statistic by applying a concept called "Win Expectation," which gauges the probability of a team's going on to win a game based on the situation—score, men on base, inning, number of outs—at any time. The **WX** is short for **WXRL**, which refers to "**W**ins e**X**pected above **R**eplacement and adjusted for **L**ineup faced" for relief pitchers. For each bullpen appearance, Win Expectation looks at the situation the reliever faced when he entered the game and compares that with the situation when he departs. If a reliever enters a game when his team has an 85 percent chance of winning and leaves with them holding a 95 percent chance, he contributed 0.1 wins. All of these fractional wins are then adjusted for the strength of the actual hitters faced, compared with replacement level, then added up to produce the pitcher's seasonal total of expected wins above replacement adjusted for lineup.

As a metric, WXRL has benefits over other statistics used to evaluate bullpen performance. Because it relies on the Win Expectation framework, it is sensitive to leverage and will assign more value to a reliever who pitches well in a close game than to a reliever who is just as effective in a blowout. Unlike ERA, WXRL rewards a reliever for keeping any inherited runners from scoring—it also punishes a reliever for leaving runners on base for the next pitcher to take care of, regardless of whether or not those runners come around to score. In this way, the reliever's contribution is isolated from that of both the pitcher who preceded him and the one who followed him.

FANTASY FOCUS
Bullpen Help

WXRL has limited uses in fantasy, because of the lack of non-closer relievers in many leagues, but you can still put it to work. Saves will come for any closer as long as he keeps the role, regardless of performance, but if you want a closer who is going to pick up saves *and* pitch effectively for you, then WXRL can help, thanks to its player valuation. If your league counts holds, then it's even more useful, as it can help you sort through the multitude of middle relievers and setup men to find those you should target from year to year. This is an area where everyone needs the help, especially since building a bullpen is something even most major league teams can't do.

The **SN** in this final column is short for **SNLVAR** (**S**upport **N**eutral **L**ineup-adjusted **V**alue **A**dded above **R**eplacement) and measures the performance of starting pitchers. Like WXRL, SNLVAR is based on Win Expectation and is adjusted according to the actual hitters faced and is compared with replacement level. As with hitters, the pitcher's 2010 line and the one below it represent his PECOTA projection for the upcoming season and list his four most comparable pitchers. Breakout, Improve, and Collapse refer to changes in the pitcher's

EqERA, while Attrition refers to a reduction in the pitcher's innings pitched.

FANTASY FOCUS
Mild Starters

Like WXRL, SNLVAR can help you sort through pitchers in the middle of the pack. A starting pitcher could have faced soft lineups all year and racked up some impressive numbers because of it, but any number of factors could change that luck by the next season, such as a new division, league, or team. It's just one more way to recognize potential regression before it occurs—these numbers are also available during the season at BaseballProspectus.com, meaning you can trade off pitchers you expect to fall apart to unwitting owners and play dumb when things go south.

The Managers' Statistics

Each team chapter ends with a manager's comment and data breaking down his tactical tendencies (Table 4). Though it is often difficult to isolate a manager's contributions to a team, comparing specific data modeled after well-documented plays and styles to the league average helps determine what a manager likes to do, even if we are still precluded from translating that information into actual wins and losses.

Following the year, team, and the actual win-loss record, **Pythag +/-** lets us know by how many games the team under- or overperformed its Pythagenpat record. Scioscia's Angels exceeded their projected record by four games and exceeded it in the previous two seasons as well. That isn't necessarily an endorsement of Scioscia—keep in mind that Pythag +/- is a mathematical expression of team performance, not an interpretation of the manager's work, even though it has become commonplace to attribute Actual/Pythag discrepancies to the skipper.

Pitching staff usage follows, first with **Avg PC** report-

MANAGER: MIKE SCIOSCIA

YEAR	TEAM	W-L	Pythag +/-	Avg PC	100+ P	120+ P	QS	BQS	REL	REL w Zero R	IBB	Subs	PH	PH Avg	PH HR	SB2	CS2	SB3	CS3	SAC Att	SAC %	POS SAC	Squeeze	Swing	In Play
2007	LAA	94-68	4	97.4	85	0	85	2	396	245	22	31	101	.250	2	118	47	20	8	48	66.7%	31	3	170	142
2008	LAA	100-62	11	99.6	85	0	87	7	383	249	32	46	74	.182	0	109	38	19	8	46	69.6%	32	3	147	113
2009	LAA	97-65	4	97.1	83	1	70	9	434	269	35	48	79	.308	2	124	57	22	5	64	67.2%	41	4	180	134

Table 4. Manager Statistics Example

ing the average pitch count of his starting pitchers with the subsequent **100+P** and **120+P** offering the number of games in which the starters exceeded certain pitch thresholds. **QS** is the total number of quality starts—a start of at least six innings and with no more than three runs allowed—a manager received from his starting pitchers. **BQS** is Blown Quality Starts, a Baseball Prospectus stat that measures games in which the starter delivered a quality start through six innings before losing it in the seventh inning or later by allowing runs to give him four or more. That said, a BQS is not necessarily an indictment of the manager's abilities or tactics—a number of factors, ranging from excellent offensive support to extremely poor bullpen support, can lead a manager to leave his starter in a game after he has thrown six quality innings. Conversely, the decision by a manager to "bank" quality starts by restricting his starters to only six innings can have downsides as well, as it increases his bullpen's workload and increases the opportunity for the pen to blow a game in which a starter was cruising.

Speaking of bullpen support, the next stats in the manager table tally how many pitching changes a manager made over the course of the season (**REL**) and how many times the reliever called upon didn't allow any runners, his own or inherited, to score (**REL w Zero R**). Bequeathed runners also count against REL w Zero R, meaning that relievers who exit with runners on that subsequently score prevent a manager from "padding" his tally here. Concluding the pitching section, **IBB** is quite simply the number of intentional walks the manager ordered during the given season, which can definitely be a mark of managerial strategy, as long as outliers like Albert Pujols are accounted for.

Managers do more than manage pitchers, however; their usage of a bench can lead to added or lost performance. **Subs** lets us know the number of defensive replacements he employed throughout the regular season, while **PH**, **PH Avg**, and **PH HR** report the offensive statistics of pinch-hitters called upon. We then turn to the so-called small-ball tactics, starting with the running game. The manager's aggressiveness on the bases is broken down by successful steals of second and third base (**SB2, SB3**) and times caught (**CS2, CS3**). We also provide the number of sacrifices a team attempted (**SAC Att**) and their success rate (**SAC %**). Be sure to keep in mind the differences between leagues: National League sacrifice attempts are greatly inflated by the fact that the pitchers hit. To correct for this, we list the number of times a manager got a successful sacrifice from a position player (**POS SAC**), which allows for comparisons between the two leagues. We finish up with **Squeeze**, which counts the number of successful squeeze plays the team executed over the season. Finally, we have a couple of statistics that attempt to measure the manager's hit-and-run tactics. **Swing** is the number of times a hitter swung at a pitch while the runners were in motion, while **In Play** reflects how many times his hitters swung and made contact while those runners were off to the races. Granted, swings on steal attempts does not always translate to hit and run attempts, but managers who greatly deviate from the average can be said to be staunch proponents or opponents of the strategy.

FANTASY FOCUS
The Skipper

You may want to look at a manager's tendencies when the team gets new personnel, as not everyone utilizes the running game in the same manner. Put a burner who picks up 40 steals a year on a club that never runs, and chances are good he won't always have the green light like he did in the past. Conversely, if a high-success-rate basestealer who doesn't run very often goes to a team that doesn't know what a red light means, then its base thievery could pick up. It's a small consideration relative to the many others you need to think of, but having the information won't hurt you.

As we mentioned at the outset of this introduction, no advanced mathematics degree is needed to get the most out of this book, as our comments and analysis on the teams and players incorporates the data and offers a qualitative summary. However, the better you grasp the tools detailed above, the more fun the book becomes. BaseballProspectus.com houses an entire glossary of these statistics (and many more) if you desire more details, and we use this data quite frequently in daily analyses throughout the entire year.

Arizona Diamondbacks

Since 2007, the Diamondbacks have enjoyed a great bullpen, an excellent rotation, and a monster offense. They just haven't managed to have them all in the same season. Their bullpen soared to the top of the league in 2007, but the offense could not hit a lick, generating a paltry .249 EqA. They bolstered the starting rotation in the following season, but experienced drastic, predictable drop-offs in their bullpen's performance. And last year, when the team boasted plenty of power in the lineup, its defense couldn't save runs, and the entire pitching staff took a step backward in preventing them. Timing is everything.

Because they've had their moments in their individual unit performances, expectations were lofty last spring. Dual aces Dan Haren and Brandon Webb looked to lead a formidable rotation featuring live-armed tyro Max Scherzer and league-average innings consumers Doug Davis and Jon Garland. The Chad Qualls–led bullpen appeared strong, and the young, potent offensive nucleus of Justin Upton, Mark Reynolds, Stephen Drew, Conor Jackson, and Chris Young would have another season of experience under their belts, as they moved a year deeper into what should have been their best seasons. PECOTA bought into the hype, projecting a record of 88-74 and a second-place finish behind the Dodgers in a competitive NL West.

The best-laid plans turned out as they often do—badly—this time due to rather unusual items that, were this a balance sheet, would be reported separately to avoid skewing future forecasts. These events also led to an in-season liquidation of dispensable veterans that further biased the team's final tallies, rendering trend discussions based on data worthy of a few dashes from

DIAMONDBACKS PROSPECTUS
2009 W-L: 70-92, 5th in NL West

Pythag	80-82	9th	**Ballpark:** Chase Field (3-yr. PF: 1065). You can't call him 'Bob' any more, but he's still a bandbox.
RS/G	4.4	8th	
RA/G	4.8	14th	
EqA	.253	13th	**2009:** The young power bats didn't deliver enough, the pen wasn't good, and the rotation missed Webb badly
EqBRR	-6.8	10th	
SNWP	.496	8th	
WXRL	2.13	14th	**2010:** The 2007 potential is still there, but youth is becoming non-achieving middle age
FRAr	5.26	15th	
DE	.687	12th	
PADE	-0.66	9th	**Action Items:** Health and production from the lineup, keeping fingers crossed on Webb, Upton, and Young
Salary	$73.5	12th	
Attend	2.13	11th	

a salt shaker. The bad-news parade started on Opening Day. If you can find a more portentous situation than a season-ending injury to the face of the franchise, please let us know, but Brandon Webb labored through a tumultuous outing before exiting with pain in his shoulder in what was his first and last appearance.

So right out of the chute, one of those dual aces was lost for the season, and the replacement combination of Yusmeiro Petit and Billy Buckner failed to pitch up to the level of a Garland, let alone Webb. Without Webb giving the staff some buoyancy, its seventh-best staff ERA of 3.98 in 2008 dropped to 4.42; its aggregate SNVA of 2.96, the 11th-best mark in the sport in 2008, dropped all the way to –1.72; their Fair Run Average dropped from an upper-third 4.45 to a barrel-bottom 4.89 mark; and their walk and strikeout rates, which ranked second in all of baseball, dropped to 11th in the league. Dan Haren could not carry the load on his own, and while the triumvirate of Scherzer, Davis, and Garland exceeded expectations, their efforts were not enough to counteract the loss of an ace starter.

A bad situation turned worse when the Diamondbacks' staff underperformed relative to their abilities as suggested by their controllable skills: strikeouts, walks, and home runs. The D'backs should have been better than they were. It may seem illogical to say that a staff should have been better than it was. In everyday life, things are what they are, and a brick is a brick; it isn't any more or less a brick than its brick-ish attributes would suggest. However, pitchers and pitching staffs are different because so much of what we perceive as immutable results is subject to distortion, and a good season doesn't always look good in the box scores.

Because traditional pitching statistics do a poor job of isolating a pitcher's performance from the context in which it occurred, savvier fans now judge hurlers by run-prevention estimators such as QERA (Quick ERA) or FIP (Fielding Independent Pitching). To these we now add SIERA, a new statistic created by Baseball Prospectus's Matt Swartz and Eric Seidman and designed to supplant QERA as the most accurately modeled run-prevention estimator. SIERA pegs the Snakes' staff as markedly better than their ERA suggests, with a more-than-respectable 3.93 mark.

SIERA, short for Skill Interactive Earned Run Average, builds on the foundation of FIP and QERA, but does a better job of predicting future ERA by more accurately accounting for the way skills within a pitcher's control interact with one another and affect the run environment. (For more on the mathematical underpinnings of SIERA, see www.baseballprospectus.com). It is more accurate than QERA and FIP in predicting subsequent-year park-adjusted ERA and held its own in predicting current-year ERA as well, though it is primarily intended to show what the ERA should look like in subsequent seasons, assuming the controllable skill levels are sustained.

The Diamondbacks play in a bandbox of a ballpark, which was reflected in a park-adjusted ERA that was lower than their unadjusted ERA (4.06 vs. 4.21), but their SIERA shows that they pitched almost as well as the best teams in the league. Their 3.93 mark compiled by club pitchers who threw 40 or more innings pitched ranked right in line with that of the Cardinals, who compiled a much sexier season ERA and were thus much more renowned for their pitching.

This was a clear-cut indicator of Javier Vazquez-itis, more commonly referred to as order of operations syndrome. Order of operations syndrome, or OOPS, refers to pitchers who put together solid marks in the controllable-skills categories but see their ERA rise anyway. For a practical example, consider a hypothetical inning in which a pitcher gets three strikeouts and allows a home run, a walk, and a single. If the sequence of events goes HR-1B-K-K-BB-K, he'll allow one run and strand the runners, but if the sequence is K-K-BB-1B-HR-K, then he serves up a three-run blast. OOPS perpetrators tend to perform worse with ducks on the pond, leading to lower rates of stranding runners in spite of otherwise solid tallies and rates.

For Qualls and Scherzer, the differences above merely prevented good performances from being great, while Petit defined the replacement level in spite of more aesthetically pleasing numbers under the SIERA lens. The Diamondbacks were victimized by injuries,

Table 1. From the Lowest SIERAs . . .

Team	ERA	SIERA	Team	ERA	SIERA
Braves	3.30	3.64	White Sox	4.04	4.03
Yankees	4.08	3.75	Athletics	4.22	4.04
Giants	3.37	3.75	Tigers	4.16	4.07
Cubs	3.65	3.77	Rays	4.34	4.08
Rockies	4.01	3.80	Twins	4.38	4.17
Dodgers	3.36	3.83	Angels	4.34	4.20
Red Sox	4.10	3.84	Mariners	3.63	4.23
Blue Jays	4.30	3.85	Brewers	4.77	4.24
Marlins	4.12	3.85	Reds	4.09	4.29
Cardinals	3.48	3.90	Rangers	4.24	4.30
Phillies	4.16	3.92	Mets	4.55	4.38
D'backs	4.21	3.93	Indians	4.98	4.52
Astros	4.28	3.94	Orioles	5.09	4.57
Padres	4.19	3.98	Pirates	4.53	4.58
Royals	4.58	4.03	Nationals	4.66	4.62

certainly, but the aggregate ERA produced by the aforementioned pitchers proved worse than their SIERA by almost three-tenths of a run, which adds up over the course of a season and could have loomed large had the team actually been competitive. On the bright side, the controllable-skills estimator suggests that a similar approach next season should yield much improved results, especially with runners on the basepaths, a key aspect of their 2010 season to watch, as the team will assuredly enter the spring with high expectations once again.

The pitching staff was not solely at fault for the team's struggles, even though it earned the lion's share of the blame. A managerial change early in the season certainly did not help, even though the controversy surrounding the decision to promote player development operative and former journeyman catcher A. J. Hinch helped divert attention away from the team's shoddy play. Hinch had absolutely no managing experience, but the expectation was that he could develop the necessary skills on the fly in what already figured to be a lost season. Taking over when the team had won just 12 of its first 29 games, he saw the Snakes finish 58-75 under his watch. One seeming advantage for Hinch was that he understood that the young nucleus of offensive performers would be leading the team in the seasons to come, making sure that Justin Upton, whose offensive role had been undefined under Bob Melvin, was consistently penciled into the lineup.

Almost as beneficial, Hinch did not shy away from leaving the name "Eric Byrnes" off the lineup card, despite the three-year, $30 million extension Byrnes signed the year before. Were it not for the unpredictable illness that overtook Conor Jackson, the Diamondbacks

Table 2. The Snakes' Peaks and Valleys

Pitcher	G	GS	IP	ERA	SIERA
Billy Buckner	16	13	77.3	6.40	3.85
Chad Qualls	51	0	52.0	3.64	2.92
Clay Zavada	49	0	51.0	3.35	3.82
Dan Haren	33	33	229.3	3.14	2.90
Doug Davis	34	34	203.3	4.12	4.60
Esmerling Vasquez	53	0	53.0	4.42	4.39
Jon Garland	27	27	167.6	4.29	4.82
Jon Rauch	58	0	54.3	4.14	4.55
Juan Gutierrez	65	0	71.0	4.06	3.84
Leo Rosales	33	0	45.3	4.77	4.23
Max Scherzer	30	30	170.3	4.12	3.44
Yusmeiro Petit	23	17	89.6	5.82	4.30

were primed to send up an offense that might have at least been competitive with the league in several areas and bested it in others. Even with their setbacks, team EqA has improved in baby-steps fashion over the last three seasons, from .249 to .252 to .253, and while that still remains below average, it is quite impressive, given the loss of an on-base luminary. Jackson is not a star, but losing a .370/.450 OBP/SLG player and having to replace him with the .306/.389 of Chad Tracy or .324/.404 of Gerardo Parra hinders offensive output like a kick in the groin.

Pure power made up some of the difference. Mark Reynolds, while continuing to set and break his own strikeout records, mashed 44 home runs. Upton added 26 long balls of his own in 138 games, a figure that prorates to more than 30, had he been healthy enough to play the entire year. Miguel Montero effectively supplanted Chris Snyder as the starting backstop, putting up .294/.355/.478 rates while contributing solid defense, transforming himself from a personal backup into one of the best young catchers in the game. And while Stephen Drew and Chris Young failed to live up to expectations, they did provide some pop. Young may have even hit more than 15 home runs and 28 doubles had he not earned an in-season demotion to Reno.

The greater positive development from the 2009 season was the maturation of the front office. A year earlier, the Diamondbacks were criticized for the late-season "choke" on the way to the division title, a fate that may have been avoided had veteran replacements like Adam Dunn and David Eckstein been imported even a week earlier. Last year, Josh Byrnes and his staff exhibited an understanding of the financial constraints of the franchise and the rather barren nature of the farm system. Byrnes sold high on Tony Pena, extracting power-hitting prospect Brandon Allen from the White Sox.

Felipe Lopez was sent packing in exchange for Cole Gillespie and Roque Mercedes, and his replacement, well-traveled utilityman Ryan Roberts, filled in admirably. They sent both of their Jons packing, with Rauch shipped to the Twins for Kevin Mulvey, and Garland to the Dodgers for infielder Tony Abreu. The Snakes' returns on these deals represent an understanding of how a 74-88 finish with those veterans still on the roster was worse than winding up 70-92 without them.

Can the 2010 season mark the first time in years that the Diamondbacks will fire on all cylinders? If Webb can return to some semblance of his prior self and the decision to trade Scherzer and power lefty Daniel Schlereth in a huge Winter Meetings three-way deal to bring in the unpredictable Edwin Jackson (and strike-thrower Ian Kennedy) into the starting rotation, then they could boast the top 1-2-3 of any rotation in the league, but that depends on Jackson building on last year's breakout season. The lineup still holds promise based on its youth, however long its track record of disappointments might be at this point. If Conor Jackson recovers from a flu-like but longer-lasting illness called Valley Fever (a big if), if Stephen Drew settles between his 2008 and 2009 levels of production, if Justin Upton follows the unique career path he appears to be headed on, if Mark Reynolds counteracts a regression in power with some added plate discipline, and if at long last Chris Young finally lives up to the hype, the Snakes are bound to surprise some folks. Granted, that's a lot of caveats, but the talent to succeed is in place. With a few breaks in Arizona's favor, we could be in line to see an entertaining multiteam race down the stretch in the NL West, as the Snakes try to run with the Rockies and Dodgers.

HITTERS

Brandon Allen **1B** Bats: L Throws: R Height: 6' 2" Weight: 235 Born: February 12, 1986 Age: 24

YEAR	TEAM	LVL	AGE	PA	R	2B	3B	HR	RBI	BB	SO	SB	CS	EqBRR	AVG	OBP	SLG	EqAVG	EqOBP	EqSLG	EqA	VORP	WARP		DEFENSE	
2007	KAN	A	21	561	84	39	5	18	93	39	124	7	4	-2.6	.283	.337	.483	.245	.289	.403	.237	-8.4	-1.8		66-1B	-6
2008	WNS	A+	22	366	57	26	4	15	44	41	83	14	3	-0.6	.279	.372	.527	.246	.322	.450	.265	5.7	0.8		83-1B	1
2008	BIR	AA	22	173	30	6	2	14	31	19	41	3	1	0.7	.275	.358	.614	.259	.328	.551	.288	7.5	0.8		39-1B	-1
2009	BIR	AA	23	274	39	12	3	7	35	30	47	1	2	-3.6	.290	.372	.452	.290	.354	.452	.277	5.1	0.0		57-1B	-5
2009	CHR	AAA	23	61	6	4	0	1	8	0	13	0	0	0.2	.262	.262	.377	.246	.246	.344	.197	-4.0	-0.6		14-1B	-1
2009	RNO	AAA	23	167	33	8	1	12	32	20	25	6	0	0.9	.324	.413	.641	.272	.359	.537	.301	8.2	0.5		35-1B	-4
2009	ARI	MLB	23	116	13	7	0	4	14	12	40	0	0	0.2	.202	.284	.385	.202	.284	.394	.229	-3.7	-0.8		29-1B	-3
2010	ARI	MLB	24	580	74	31	4	23	72	49	145	5	3	-0.8	.256	.321	.458	.253	.318	.446	.258	5.0	0.2		110-1B	-3

Breakout: 20% Improve: 51% Collapse: 5% Attrition: 4%   MLB: 61%   Comparables: Kevin Witt, Travis Hafner, Joey Votto, Scott Thorman

Acquired from the White Sox in July for reliever Tony Pena, Allen's breakout season in the minors has the D'backs envisioning him as their first baseman of the future and a desperately needed power source, but after his big-league showing, many wonder if the future really is now, as he suddenly struck out at an alarming rate and continued to struggle in the Arizona Fall League, where nearly everybody mashes. Allen is agile for his size and has plenty of raw power, but he might need a bit more seasoning at Triple-A to refine his approach.

Bobby Borchering **3B** Bats: S Throws: R Height: 6' 4" Weight: 195 Born: October 25, 1990 Age: 19

YEAR	TEAM	LVL	AGE	PA	R	2B	3B	HR	RBI	BB	SO	SB	CS	EqBRR	AVG	OBP	SLG	EqAVG	EqOBP	EqSLG	EqA	VORP	WARP		DEFENSE	
2009	MSO	Rk	18	93	10	8	1	2	11	5	27	0	0	-1.1	.241	.290	.425	.180	.207	.292	.159	-6.2	-1.8		20-3B	-5
2010	ARI	MLB	19	189	12	12	0	3	15	9	55	0	0	0.0	.208	.247	.324	.208	.247	.322	.184	-8.8	-1.5		40-3B	-5

Breakout: 70% Improve: 81% Collapse: 4% Attrition: 1%   MLB: 0%   Comparables: Bert Adams, Robby Hampton, Shawn Bowman, Carl Holmes

The 16th overall pick in the first round last season, Borchering moved up the draft charts throughout the spring of 2009, and by the time the draft arrived, many thought he was the best high school hitter in the country. A big, switch-hitting third baseman with power and the ability to hit for average, he has true star potential, though this comes with all the risks inherent in 18-year-old prospects. He seemed a bit overwhelmed in his pro debut, but that's nothing to judge on, and in a weak Arizona system, he's already their top positional prospect.

Eric Byrnes **OF** Bats: R Throws: R Height: 6' 2" Weight: 215 Born: February 16, 1976 Age: 34

YEAR	TEAM	LVL	AGE	PA	R	2B	3B	HR	RBI	BB	SO	SB	CS	EqBRR	AVG	OBP	SLG	EqAVG	EqOBP	EqSLG	EqA	VORP	WARP		DEFENSE			
2007	ARI	MLB	31	698	103	30	8	21	83	57	98	50	7	6.6	.286	.353	.460	.282	.349	.449	.282	31.5	5.0		109-LF	8	28-RF	2
2008	ARI	MLB	32	224	28	13	1	6	23	16	36	4	4	-1.4	.209	.272	.369	.214	.277	.369	.218	-5.6	-0.5		47-LF	1		
2009	ARI	MLB	33	258	26	14	1	8	31	12	30	9	3	1.0	.226	.270	.393	.229	.271	.404	.233	-3.4	0.3		43-LF	5	5-RF	1
2010	ARI	MLB	34	319	38	17	3	8	35	27	51	11	4	0.9	.255	.328	.409	.251	.322	.399	.251	3.6	0.6		63-LF	2		

Breakout: 7% Improve: 36% Collapse: 28% Attrition: 29%   MLB: 92%   Comparables: Emil Brown, Kevin McReynolds, Jeffrey Leonard, Reggie Sanders

Since signing a questionable three-year, $30 million extension following the 2007 season, Byrnes has played in just 42 percent of his team's games due to injury or ineffectiveness, hitting a measly .218/.271/.382. For the sake of comparison, Yuniesky Betancourt hit .245/.274/.352 in 2009. Injuries have hindered every facet of his game, sapping his power and speed, and what's left is a 34-year-old corner outfielder who can't do much of anything well. Most Snakes fans would have forgotten he was still a rostered employee if not for the contractual eyesore that is one year and $11.7 million remaining on the books.

Collin Cowgill — OF

Bats: R Throws: L Height: 5' 9" Weight: 195 Born: May 22, 1986 Age: 24

YEAR	TEAM	LVL	AGE	PA	R	2B	3B	HR	RBI	BB	SO	SB	CS	EqBRR	AVG	OBP	SLG	EqAVG	EqOBP	EqSLG	EqA	VORP	WARP	DEFENSE			
2008	YAK	A-	22	95	21	3	1	11	28	12	17	5	0	1.9	.304	.415	.785	.233	.298	.535	.275	4.3	0.7	19-CF	0		
2008	SBN	A	22	231	31	13	3	1	17	25	61	1	0	0.1	.249	.346	.358	.216	.294	.308	.213	-5.9	-1.0	29-LF	2	19-CF	-4
2009	VIS	A+	23	260	39	9	5	6	36	29	49	11	4	-0.6	.277	.373	.445	.226	.300	.343	.231	-2.6	-0.6	37-RF	-2	18-CF	0
2010	ARI	MLB	24	349	39	15	4	8	35	32	91	3	2	0.4	.225	.303	.371	.223	.300	.360	.228	-4.0	-0.7	74-RF	-2		

Breakout: 9% Improve: 32% Collapse: 23% Attrition: 4% MLB: 0% Comparables: John Smith, Robby Hammock, Mike Richardson, Loy McBride

A former fifth-round pick, Cowgill has shown the ability to reach base and rack up extra-base hits, but while his two professional seasons have resembled the major-league production of Conor Jackson, the numbers have been accrued in A-ball. The translation of these numbers, his history of injuries, and an age considered old relative to his levels have frustrated scouts who once saw a skill set reminiscent of Brian Giles. Cowgill is paying the price for a late start to his career, having missed the 2007 college season with a broken hand, then choosing to return to college rather than sign with the A's that same year. This year will determine if he remains a prospect or if the perception of him changes to that of an organizational guy.

Stephen Drew — SS

Bats: L Throws: R Height: 6' 0" Weight: 185 Born: March 16, 1983 Age: 27

YEAR	TEAM	LVL	AGE	PA	R	2B	3B	HR	RBI	BB	SO	SB	CS	EqBRR	AVG	OBP	SLG	EqAVG	EqOBP	EqSLG	EqA	VORP	WARP	DEFENSE	
2007	ARI	MLB	24	619	60	28	4	12	60	60	100	9	0	2.4	.238	.313	.370	.233	.309	.360	.242	11.4	0.4	144-SS	-8
2008	ARI	MLB	25	663	91	44	11	21	67	41	109	3	3	-4.8	.291	.333	.502	.289	.328	.495	.276	39.5	3.5	146-SS	-7
2009	ARI	MLB	26	595	71	29	12	12	65	49	87	5	1	0.3	.261	.320	.428	.262	.318	.424	.259	22.6	2.4	128-SS	-2
2010	ARI	MLB	27	600	75	32	9	16	66	51	97	5	2	-0.3	.265	.330	.447	.260	.325	.429	.260	20.8	2.0	136-SS	-3

Breakout: 5% Improve: 43% Collapse: 10% Attrition: 3% MLB: 98% Comparables: Craig Reynolds, Roy Smalley, Jorge Orta, Tom Foley

Drew was unable to sustain the gaudy .326/.372/.556 line he compiled in the second half of 2008—or any semblance of it, for that matter—winding up with an uninspiring season that barely bested that of Jimmy Rollins. Ironically, the fielding metrics that have pegged him as markedly below average in the past actually approved of his efforts throughout the year. With three full seasons in the books, a talent level hovering around the .270/.326/.445 mark, and below-average defense, our future MVP projection in last year's annual may have been a bit too optimistic. Drew is undoubtedly a useful piece, but at 27 years old, he can no longer be considered a developing prospect.

Evan Frey — OF

Bats: L Throws: L Height: 6' 0" Weight: 170 Born: June 7, 1986 Age: 24

YEAR	TEAM	LVL	AGE	PA	R	2B	3B	HR	RBI	BB	SO	SB	CS	EqBRR	AVG	OBP	SLG	EqAVG	EqOBP	EqSLG	EqA	VORP	WARP	DEFENSE			
2007	YAK	A-	21	277	48	8	6	0	21	27	42	13	10	-1.3	.309	.384	.390	.272	.322	.331	.229	-0.9	-1.0	54-CF	-5		
2008	SBN	A	22	352	54	16	6	0	29	39	38	20	6	-0.1	.327	.401	.417	.293	.355	.375	.261	9.6	0.0	71-CF	-10		
2008	VIS	A+	22	272	44	5	5	3	18	37	46	17	5	1.8	.297	.399	.402	.255	.349	.340	.252	4.9	0.6	56-CF	0		
2009	MOB	AA	23	577	62	21	6	1	52	58	78	31	14	0.5	.267	.348	.338	.250	.316	.317	.229	-3.0	-1.7	108-CF	-11	13-RF	0
2010	ARI	MLB	24	532	59	24	6	3	43	49	92	12	6	0.2	.259	.329	.353	.258	.329	.346	.236	3.0	-0.2	110-CF	-5		

Breakout: 11% Improve: 35% Collapse: 15% Attrition: 13% MLB: 4% Comparables: Troy Thomas, Sherwin Cijntje, Steve Moses, Jim Wawruck

Frey is a speedy, gritty outfielder who combines solid defense up the middle with an ability to work counts. He does not wield a mighty whopping stick by any means and, despite being a good athlete, is lacking in the tools department. Scouts like to compare him to Reed Johnson; maybe they mean this as a compliment, maybe not. Frey's 2008 left Snakes fans thinking he could be their future leadoff hitter, but his disappointing Double-A stint this past season threw cold water on those hopes, making that Johnson comparison—with its attendant destiny as a fourth outfielder—seem more accurate than ever.

Cole Gillespie   OF   Bats: R   Throws: R   Height: 6' 1"   Weight: 205   Born: June 20, 1984   Age: 26

YEAR	TEAM	LVL	AGE	PA	R	2B	3B	HR	RBI	BB	SO	SB	CS	EqBRR	AVG	OBP	SLG	EqAVG	EqOBP	EqSLG	EqA	VORP	WARP	DEFENSE			
2007	BRV	A+	23	522	75	25	3	12	62	72	95	16	8	-0.9	.267	.378	.420	.243	.338	.374	.253	5.8	0.4	122-LF	-3		
2008	HUN	AA	24	550	73	38	4	14	79	75	102	17	1	3.0	.281	.386	.472	.255	.336	.416	.265	12.9	1.3	98-LF	-1	30-RF	-1
2009	BRV	A+	25	51	10	2	3	1	9	7	11	4	0	2.3	.349	.431	.605	.267	.333	.467	.278	1.0	0.1				
2009	NAS	AAA	25	277	29	12	5	7	27	31	56	6	5	0.3	.242	.332	.424	.232	.313	.402	.247	1.4	0.8	72-LF	5		
2009	RNO	AAA	25	170	33	6	4	5	27	27	31	8	0	4.6	.304	.418	.514	.248	.359	.411	.279	7.0	0.6	19-RF	-1	13-LF	1
2010	ARI	MLB	26	453	51	23	5	10	50	51	109	6	3	1.4	.244	.333	.405	.238	.326	.388	.251	5.3	0.6	104-LF	0		

Breakout: 18%   Improve: 34%   Collapse: 21%   Attrition: 13%   MLB: 8%   Comparables: Mike Wolff, Mike Reddish, Tim Tolman, Darren Burton

Imported from the Brewers in the Felipe Lopez deal, Gillespie's claim to fame is the plate discipline that has generated a career .390 on-base percentage in the minors. His solid slugging percentages are largely composed of doubles; Gillespie boasts gap power but little in the way of jimmy-jacks. Though his stolen-base tallies give a hint of his speed, his ability to play center field remains in doubt. Unfortunately, if Gillespie is unfit to play up the middle, he lacks the power to start in a corner. In his favor, plate discipline translates nicely, and an ability to reach base consistently at the major-league level will always be valued. But if he can't improve his defense, he's going to be a bench player. Given his age, the latter outcome is far more likely.

Ruben Gotay   INF   Bats: S   Throws: R   Height: 5' 11"   Weight: 190   Born: December 25, 1982   Age: 27

YEAR	TEAM	LVL	AGE	PA	R	2B	3B	HR	RBI	BB	SO	SB	CS	EqBRR	AVG	OBP	SLG	EqAVG	EqOBP	EqSLG	EqA	VORP	WARP	DEFENSE			
2007	NWO	AAA	24	98	12	7	1	2	13	14	14	1	1	-0.3	.256	.367	.439	.241	.347	.410	.265	3.6	0.3	17-2B	-1		
2007	NYN	MLB	24	211	25	12	0	4	24	16	42	3	3	-0.8	.295	.351	.421	.311	.365	.432	.274	8.7	0.6	33-2B	-3	2-SS	-1
2008	ATL	MLB	25	117	10	5	0	2	8	13	32	1	1	-0.3	.235	.322	.343	.243	.328	.340	.242	-0.4	0.0	7-3B	0		
2009	RNO	AAA	26	479	65	29	2	11	57	102	69	2	4	-5.0	.272	.429	.450	.219	.367	.354	.262	12.5	0.4	64-3B	-4	35-2B	-5
2010	SLN	MLB	27	370	38	17	1	6	35	51	77	2	3	-1.3	.238	.346	.358	.243	.348	.364	.256	8.0	0.7	65-3B	-2		

Breakout: 10%   Improve: 32%   Collapse: 20%   Attrition: 11%   MLB: 32%   Comparables: Brad Mills, Scott Coolbaugh, Brent Gates, Kevin Nicholson

Gotay is currently a sabermetric fave because of a sense that he's been overlooked and stranded in the minors; after all, who doesn't like a "Free Player X!" campaign? And he drew a hundred walks! Now, Gotay did have the misfortune of coming up in the Royals' organization and seems to have caught one unlucky break after another following that brief spin with the Mets in 2007. Keep in mind, however, that his BABIP in that Mets season was an unsustainable .359, that last year he was hitting in hitter-friendly Reno in a circuit increasingly populated by placeholding dreck, and that he's in his prime. Would he make a serviceable platoon starter at second, or even third? Yes, if a team could look past his defense or his struggles against lefties; put him on the Twins in '09, and he'd be the Patient Piranha. Unfortunately, a journeyman's breakthrough requires organizational buy-in *and* his being in the right organization at the right time, because adequate second basemen almost literally do grow on trees, and all you can reasonably bank on is Gotay's on-base percentage against right-handed pitchers. He's been signed by the Cardinals, where he might at last catch a break.

Taylor Harbin   SS   Bats: R   Throws: R   Height: 5' 9"   Weight: 175   Born: February 13, 1986   Age: 24

YEAR	TEAM	LVL	AGE	PA	R	2B	3B	HR	RBI	BB	SO	SB	CS	EqBRR	AVG	OBP	SLG	EqAVG	EqOBP	EqSLG	EqA	VORP	WARP	DEFENSE			
2007	MSO	Rk	21	271	42	15	2	10	42	20	38	5	4	0.0	.276	.341	.477	.215	.266	.351	.213	-4.3	-1.0	54-2B	-3	4-SS	1
2008	SBN	A	22	589	70	40	3	10	85	26	78	3	4	-0.8	.276	.314	.414	.246	.275	.360	.219	-4.5	-0.8	86-2B	2	43-SS	-4
2009	VIS	A+	23	573	70	27	3	14	60	26	91	12	7	-1.4	.259	.305	.401	.209	.243	.305	.188	-18.2	-4.3	96-SS	-14	24-2B	-3
2010	ARI	MLB	24	517	54	28	3	9	56	29	92	4	3	-0.5	.241	.290	.367	.239	.286	.358	.220	-2.6	-1.0	112-SS	-7		

Breakout: 25%   Improve: 50%   Collapse: 14%   Attrition: 9%   MLB: 4%   Comparables: Richard Rembielak, John McDonald, Roberto Deleon, Manny Martinez

Harbin performs well in several different areas, but is by no means special or noteworthy in any of them. He makes decent contact, but lacks the secondary skills needed to truly make an impact. Unfortunately, these skills are unlikely to be developed, and his glove does not play well enough to make up the difference. This would seem to doom him to utility infielder status, with perhaps a Geoff Blum–like upside at best.

Conor Jackson — LF

Bats: R   Throws: R   Height: 6' 2"   Weight: 215   Born: May 7, 1982   Age: 28

YEAR	TEAM	LVL	AGE	PA	R	2B	3B	HR	RBI	BB	SO	SB	CS	EqBRR	AVG	OBP	SLG	EqAVG	EqOBP	EqSLG	EqA	VORP	WARP	DEFENSE		
2007	ARI	MLB	25	477	56	29	1	15	60	53	50	2	2	-0.5	.284	.368	.467	.280	.366	.459	.282	16.4	0.9	98-1B -7		
2008	ARI	MLB	26	612	87	31	6	12	75	59	61	10	2	1.9	.300	.376	.446	.298	.373	.441	.284	24.3	3.3	74-LF 6	65-1B -2	
2009	ARI	MLB	27	110	8	4	0	1	14	11	16	5	0	1.7	.182	.264	.253	.182	.264	.242	.197	-5.3	-1.0	20-LF -2	5-1B -1	
2010	ARI	MLB	28	432	54	23	3	10	57	46	52	5	2	0.6	.279	.364	.435	.277	.359	.431	.272	14.3	1.8	95-LF 2		

Breakout: 13%   Improve: 48%   Collapse: 14%   Attrition: 9%   MLB: 95%   Comparables: Barry Bonnell, Carmelo Martinez, Marty Cordova, Dusty Baker

Jackson missed all but a month of the season after coming down with Valley Fever, which eventually led to a bout with pneumonia. Valley Fever leaves its victims incredibly fatigued, with aches in both the muscles and the joints. Recovery can take up to a year, so don't look at his 2009 numbers as predictive in any way. Jackson's healthy modus operandi is well known: he reaches base at a very solid clip while tallying enough extra-base hits to merit a starting spot somewhere on the diamond. Assuming Jackson is 100 percent in time for spring training—even after recovery, the bug still lingers in the form of residual pain—Jackson should reclaim his post out in left field, providing average defense with his standard .370 on-base percentage and .450 slugging.

Miguel Montero — C

Bats: L   Throws: R   Height: 5' 11"   Weight: 190   Born: July 9, 1983   Age: 26

YEAR	TEAM	LVL	AGE	PA	R	2B	3B	HR	RBI	BB	SO	SB	CS	EqBRR	AVG	OBP	SLG	EqAVG	EqOBP	EqSLG	EqA	VORP	WARP	DEFENSE
2007	ARI	MLB	23	244	30	7	0	10	37	20	35	0	0	-1.2	.224	.292	.397	.222	.288	.387	.238	5.5	-0.1	57-C -5
2008	ARI	MLB	24	207	24	16	1	5	18	19	49	0	0	0.8	.255	.330	.435	.250	.325	.424	.259	7.7	0.7	46-C -1
2009	ARI	MLB	25	470	61	30	0	16	59	38	78	1	2	-1.4	.294	.355	.478	.295	.353	.482	.281	30.6	3.1	104-C -2
2010	ARI	MLB	26	412	55	22	1	16	57	38	73	1	1	-0.7	.267	.343	.466	.266	.341	.452	.269	20.1	2.0	94-C -2

Breakout: 21%   Improve: 57%   Collapse: 7%   Attrition: 9%   MLB: 100%   Comparables: Darrell Porter, Rich Gedman, Mickey Cochrane, Todd Hundley

On his way out the door, Randy Johnson left the Diamondbacks with a ringing endorsement of Montero, formerly the personal catcher of the lanky lefty. After two seasons in which his promise outperformed the results, Montero established himself in 2009 as one of the best all-around catchers in the game. Montero did regress in one aspect of his game, experiencing a decline in walk rate in part due to a higher percentage of swings at pitches out of the strike zone. That he lopped a third off his strikeout rate in spite of this was a good sign, but if he returns to hacking, he will need to exhibit more patience to make up for the resultant decline in batting average.

Reynaldo Navarro — SS

Bats: S   Throws: R   Height: 5' 10"   Weight: 175   Born: December 22, 1989   Age: 20

YEAR	TEAM	LVL	AGE	PA	R	2B	3B	HR	RBI	BB	SO	SB	CS	EqBRR	AVG	OBP	SLG	EqAVG	EqOBP	EqSLG	EqA	VORP	WARP	DEFENSE
2007	MSO	Rk	17	225	21	4	0	1	17	6	41	6	3	0.0	.250	.274	.283	.205	.223	.228	.147	-13.6	-3.6	56-SS -8
2008	MSO	Rk	18	323	42	17	7	2	31	25	77	17	9	-1.9	.258	.323	.385	.200	.248	.277	.182	-10.6	-2.9	70-SS -7
2009	SBN	A	19	493	57	25	5	0	46	27	85	12	4	-1.5	.262	.308	.339	.232	.266	.299	.198	-10.1	-1.6	118-SS -3
2010	ARI	MLB	20	475	45	23	4	3	39	28	104	5	3	-0.3	.238	.286	.326	.234	.280	.315	.205	-8.4	-1.4	114-SS -4

Breakout: 37%   Improve: 62%   Collapse: 14%   Attrition: 7%   MLB: 3%   Comparables: Kevin Davis, Cesar Morillo, Esteban Beltre, Carlos Mendoza

After three seasons, a general trend appears to be emerging in that each of Navarro's positive qualities has an equally frustrating negative. He cannot reach base often enough to utilize his speed, and he cannot field well enough to carry his poor bat. He has plenty of range, but fields sloppily, making many mental mistakes. His gap power has been inconsistent due to a poor approach at the plate. If you dig raw tools, then Navarro is practically shortstop seviche, but right now that's all he is, remaining light-years away from fulfilling his potential.

Augie Ojeda — MI

Bats: S   Throws: R   Height: 5' 9"   Weight: 175   Born: December 20, 1974   Age: 35

YEAR	TEAM	LVL	AGE	PA	R	2B	3B	HR	RBI	BB	SO	SB	CS	EqBRR	AVG	OBP	SLG	EqAVG	EqOBP	EqSLG	EqA	VORP	WARP	DEFENSE	
2007	TUC	AAA	32	118	20	8	0	0	17	10	11	1	0	0.8	.323	.395	.404	.284	.342	.333	.248	2.6	1.3	28-SS 8	
2007	ARI	MLB	32	132	16	2	2	1	12	15	13	1	0	0.7	.274	.354	.354	.265	.344	.345	.252	2.7	0.5	19-2B 3	9-SS -2
2008	ARI	MLB	33	272	27	9	2	0	17	26	24	0	0	1.4	.242	.343	.299	.241	.342	.293	.233	0.7	0.6	32-2B 0	14-SS 2
2009	ARI	MLB	34	309	38	17	3	1	16	32	28	3	1	1.0	.246	.340	.345	.247	.338	.348	.247	5.2	0.3	28-2B 2	27-SS -4
2010	ARI	MLB	35	243	29	11	1	1	21	24	27	1	1	0.6	.258	.345	.334	.257	.343	.337	.237	1.7	0.4	48-2B 2	

Breakout: 5%   Improve: 26%   Collapse: 24%   Attrition: 34%   MLB: 94%   Comparables: Ted Sizemore, Luis Alicea, Jeff Frye, Jamey Carroll

At first glance, Ojeda appears to be a very valuable supersub capable of manning several positions while reaching base at a decent clip. However, at least some of the on-base percentage success is a mirage, the by-product of being bypassed to get to the pitcher. Removing intentional walks drops Ojeda's on-base percentages since 2007 to .338, .334, and .328. Ojeda has slugged only .329 during those same seasons, so there really isn't much offense here at all. Ojeda's defensive versatility has value, but he turned 35 in December, so that's only going to be true for so much longer.

Gerardo Parra   **OF**   Bats: L   Throws: L   Height: 5' 11"   Weight: 195   Born: May 6, 1987   Age: 23

YEAR	TEAM	LVL	AGE	PA	R	2B	3B	HR	RBI	BB	SO	SB	CS	EqBRR	AVG	OBP	SLG	EqAVG	EqOBP	EqSLG	EqA	VORP	WARP	DEFENSE			
2007	SBN	A	20	488	64	25	4	6	57	30	51	24	8	-3.0	.320	.370	.435	.294	.335	.405	.259	8.5	1.9	91-RF	6	15-CF	1
2007	VIS	A+	20	109	11	2	1	2	14	4	17	2	3	-1.0	.284	.303	.382	.252	.266	.350	.212	-2.3	0.0	20-CF	2		
2008	VIS	A+	21	224	26	8	4	2	19	23	31	12	4	-2.3	.301	.381	.413	.255	.327	.350	.242	1.4	0.1	41-CF	-1	8-RF	0
2008	MOB	AA	21	302	35	14	6	4	33	24	34	16	9	-0.7	.275	.341	.419	.253	.303	.377	.240	1.3	-0.2	59-CF	-1	12-RF	-2
2009	MOB	AA	22	130	23	3	1	3	12	22	13	7	4	-0.5	.361	.469	.491	.339	.431	.464	.309	9.4	0.9	22-RF	-1	4-CF	-1
2009	ARI	MLB	22	491	59	21	8	5	60	25	89	5	7	1.0	.290	.324	.404	.294	.325	.410	.252	6.8	0.2	65-LF	-1	37-CF	-4
2010	ARI	MLB	23	582	67	28	7	10	65	43	92	12	8	-1.1	.277	.334	.415	.275	.332	.399	.252	7.2	0.7	120-LF	-1		

Breakout: 17%   Improve: 46%   Collapse: 16%   Attrition: 5%   MLB: 100%   Comparables: Gus Burgess, Troy O'Leary, Brian Kowitz, Curtis Goodwin

Parra drew comparisons to highly regarded prospect Carlos Gonzalez in his initial years as a professional, but has not developed as quickly as scouts projected. He spent most of 2009 in left field, posting slightly above-average defensive marks, with equally below-average range in center. Another of the seemingly dime-a-dozen, vaguely speedy tweener outfielders with little power, Parra may find himself resigned to fourth outfield duty sometime soon. Unfortunately, despite his youth, the cure to many of his offensive woes is increased plate discipline, an incredibly tough skill to develop on the fly at the big-league level.

Mark Reynolds   **3B**   Bats: R   Throws: R   Height: 6' 2"   Weight: 220   Born: August 3, 1983   Age: 26

YEAR	TEAM	LVL	AGE	PA	R	2B	3B	HR	RBI	BB	SO	SB	CS	EqBRR	AVG	OBP	SLG	EqAVG	EqOBP	EqSLG	EqA	VORP	WARP	DEFENSE			
2007	MOB	AA	23	155	28	9	2	6	22	20	32	2	1	0.8	.306	.394	.537	.283	.359	.493	.288	8.5	0.4	31-3B	-3	6-2B	-2
2007	ARI	MLB	23	414	62	20	4	17	62	37	129	0	1	-0.9	.279	.349	.495	.272	.344	.484	.280	18.4	1.8	95-3B	-1		
2008	ARI	MLB	24	613	87	28	3	28	97	64	204	11	2	2.8	.239	.320	.458	.238	.317	.454	.265	18.4	0.5	146-3B	-12		
2009	ARI	MLB	25	662	98	30	1	44	102	76	223	24	9	-4.5	.260	.349	.543	.262	.347	.545	.295	42.7	3.7	126-3B	-3	24-1B	-5
2010	ARI	MLB	26	638	88	29	4	28	88	73	184	10	6	-0.3	.251	.341	.467	.249	.337	.463	.268	22.2	2.0	151-3B	-4		

Breakout: 10%   Improve: 41%   Collapse: 17%   Attrition: 8%   MLB: 100%   Comparables: Doug Rader, Dean Palmer, Matt Williams, Edwin Encarnacion

Reynolds is quite the curious player in that his record-setting whiff tallies are not a huge deal, given the dramatic results when he connects. That said, good fortune from the BABIP Fairy is all that separates him from putting up a .245 batting average and .335 on-base percentage in spite of his ample power supply. It is hard to imagine repeat performances of this past season if he fails to become more disciplined at the plate. His walk rate *has* increased over the last three seasons, but right now, patience and discipline are what separate him from achieving true stardom. When Reynolds broke his own single-season strikeout record, his comment was, "So what?" That's the so what, Mark.

Ryan Roberts   **2B**   Bats: R   Throws: R   Height: 5' 11"   Weight: 190   Born: September 19, 1980   Age: 29

YEAR	TEAM	LVL	AGE	PA	R	2B	3B	HR	RBI	BB	SO	SB	CS	EqBRR	AVG	OBP	SLG	EqAVG	EqOBP	EqSLG	EqA	VORP	WARP	DEFENSE			
2007	SYR	AAA	26	399	46	16	1	12	47	55	85	1	2	-3.5	.249	.355	.409	.233	.327	.378	.250	5.8	-0.6	33-3B	-6	31-2B	-6
2008	OKL	AAA	27	529	71	28	8	10	66	67	78	15	3	3.3	.300	.388	.464	.270	.345	.388	.262	15.3	1.0	55-2B	-1	50-3B	-6
2009	RNO	AAA	28	48	10	1	1	1	10	6	6	7	0	1.5	.310	.396	.452	.256	.333	.395	.271	2.0	0.1	9-2B	-1		
2009	ARI	MLB	28	351	41	17	2	7	25	40	55	7	3	1.7	.279	.367	.416	.283	.369	.427	.276	14.6	1.5	46-2B	-1	15-3B	0
2010	ARI	MLB	29	376	44	18	3	9	37	42	77	5	3	0.4	.255	.343	.400	.253	.338	.390	.254	8.9	0.7	68-2B	-2		

Breakout: 10%   Improve: 46%   Collapse: 18%   Attrition: 16%   MLB: 70%   Comparables: Kelvin Chapman, Jim Pankovits, Riccardo Ingram, Todd Haney

Despite being cut by two previous organizations, Roberts and his versatility may have found a home with the Snakes. Installed at the keystone after the trade of Lopez, Roberts displayed the patience that kept him in farm systems past his prospect expiration date. Defense will never be his calling card, and he is unlikely to manifest even gap power consistently, but the D'backs literally did not miss a beat after trading Lopez, replacing his .364/.412 OBP/SLG with Roberts' .367/.416 OBP/SLG. For a team with financial constraints, this sort of pickup is always welcome, but he's bench-bound by the addition of Kelly Johnson.

Alex Romero — OF

Bats: L Throws: R Height: 6' 0" Weight: 200 Born: September 9, 1983 Age: 26

YEAR	TEAM	LVL	AGE	PA	R	2B	3B	HR	RBI	BB	SO	SB	CS	EqBRR	AVG	OBP	SLG	EqAVG	EqOBP	EqSLG	EqA	VORP	WARP	DEFENSE			
2007	TUC	AAA	23	584	82	32	6	5	66	37	53	12	10	-3.2	.310	.354	.421	.274	.315	.368	.238	-3.1	-0.7	97-RF	-2	16-LF	-1
2008	TUC	AAA	24	186	28	9	2	3	19	11	19	4	3	0.4	.324	.368	.451	.286	.324	.389	.246	1.6	-0.3	25-CF	-5	10-RF	-2
2008	ARI	MLB	24	142	13	8	2	1	12	3	20	4	0	-0.9	.230	.250	.341	.230	.250	.341	.209	-5.3	-0.8	25-RF	-1	5-LF	-1
2009	RNO	AAA	25	317	40	20	3	2	47	32	26	7	4	-1.5	.348	.416	.462	.283	.348	.378	.256	6.0	0.4	33-CF	-9	25-RF	4
2009	ARI	MLB	25	157	14	6	2	1	18	11	23	2	0	-0.3	.248	.306	.338	.248	.306	.338	.229	-2.3	0.0	16-RF	-1	13-LF	1
2010	HOU	MLB	26	427	46	21	3	4	44	30	60	6	4	-0.9	.264	.318	.363	.264	.319	.366	.239	-0.6	-0.1	77-RF	0		

Breakout: 13% Improve: 29% Collapse: 25% Attrition: 17%   MLB: 50%   Comparables: Jake Weber, Jim Wawruck, Shane Costa, Rob Butler

Another seeming archetype on the D'backs roster, Alex Romero is a formerly overhyped prospect with speed decent enough to stretch doubles into triples and to swipe a bag here and there. Unfortunately, the age-old axiom of not being able to steal first base applies; Romero makes little contact and has risible plate judgment. He's a fifth outfielder/defensive replacement at best.

Rusty Ryal — UT

Bats: R Throws: R Height: 6' 2" Weight: 195 Born: March 16, 1983 Age: 27

YEAR	TEAM	LVL	AGE	PA	R	2B	3B	HR	RBI	BB	SO	SB	CS	EqBRR	AVG	OBP	SLG	EqAVG	EqOBP	EqSLG	EqA	VORP	WARP	DEFENSE			
2007	VIS	A+	24	302	46	15	3	11	46	16	47	2	4	-1.1	.301	.354	.496	.249	.287	.386	.231	-1.2	-1.1	38-3B	-3	31-2B	-5
2007	MOB	AA	24	187	18	6	2	6	21	8	42	4	3	-3.0	.238	.291	.405	.220	.257	.347	.208	-4.6	-0.9	25-2B	1	19-3B	-4
2008	MOB	AA	25	509	65	22	4	16	66	35	96	4	4	-0.6	.274	.334	.443	.236	.279	.369	.224	-3.7	1.1	94-2B	12	22-3B	1
2009	RNO	AAA	26	446	65	33	6	17	70	33	94	5	3	-0.9	.290	.347	.527	.234	.288	.424	.243	5.3	0.1	56-2B	-6	29-3B	-1
2009	ARI	MLB	26	68	11	6	2	3	9	6	21	0	0	0.7	.271	.353	.593	.271	.353	.593	.306	4.8	0.5	9-2B	0	5-1B	0
2010	ARI	MLB	27	450	50	23	4	11	48	29	110	3	3	-0.7	.235	.293	.391	.233	.290	.383	.228	-1.0	-0.1	98-2B	0		

Breakout: 10% Improve: 36% Collapse: 28% Attrition: 29%   MLB: 20%   Comparables: Steve Scarsone, George Hinshaw, Gookie Dawkins, Scott Wade

Ryal is a decent power bat capable of manning second or third base who should earn his keep as a pine-riding role player. While we probably shouldn't expect a repeat of his small-sample slugging percentage of nearly .600, his defensive versatility, combination of patience and power, and team-friendly contract status should earn him consistent bench duty.

Chris Snyder — C

Bats: R Throws: R Height: 6' 4" Weight: 245 Born: February 12, 1981 Age: 29

YEAR	TEAM	LVL	AGE	PA	R	2B	3B	HR	RBI	BB	SO	SB	CS	EqBRR	AVG	OBP	SLG	EqAVG	EqOBP	EqSLG	EqA	VORP	WARP	DEFENSE	
2007	ARI	MLB	26	380	37	20	0	13	47	40	67	0	1	-3.6	.252	.342	.433	.246	.339	.418	.264	19.4	3.7	100-C	10
2008	ARI	MLB	27	404	47	22	1	16	64	56	101	0	0	-0.5	.237	.348	.452	.233	.342	.439	.272	22.8	3.6	104-C	8
2009	ARI	MLB	28	202	20	7	0	6	22	32	47	0	0	-2.3	.200	.333	.352	.199	.327	.355	.246	5.4	0.4	49-C	-2
2010	ARI	MLB	29	351	35	15	0	11	50	45	80	0	1	-1.1	.237	.343	.401	.236	.339	.407	.254	11.3	1.6	90-C	3

Breakout: 10% Improve: 41% Collapse: 10% Attrition: 14%   MLB: 90%   Comparables: Gus Triandos, Jason Varitek, Jim Pagliaroni, Joe Oliver

The injury-prone catcher was Pipp'd by Miguel Montero, playing just one-third of the season with a substandard slash line due to a bulging disc in his lower back—a condition that ultimately required surgery. When healthy, Snyder's walks and medium-grade power are assets, but the combination of injury and a lush contract (two years and $11.25 million remaining) have brought him to a career crossroads—he's expensive for a backup, and his injury history and uncertain recovery from microdisc surgery have teams reluctant to bank on him as a starter. He is a better hitter than his career .233/.333/.398 rates suggest, but at this writing, his path to another starting assignment will probably require someone else's getting hurt for a change.

Chad Tracy — 1B

Bats: L   Throws: R   Height: 6' 2"   Weight: 215   Born: May 22, 1980   Age: 30

YEAR	TEAM	LVL	AGE	PA	R	2B	3B	HR	RBI	BB	SO	SB	CS	EqBRR	AVG	OBP	SLG	EqAVG	EqOBP	EqSLG	EqA	VORP	WARP	DEFENSE			
2007	ARI	MLB	27	260	30	18	2	7	35	29	43	0	0	-1.3	.264	.346	.454	.257	.341	.438	.270	7.7	0.8	42-3B	-2	13-1B	1
2008	ARI	MLB	28	292	25	16	0	8	39	16	49	0	0	0.5	.267	.308	.414	.264	.304	.403	.245	-2.1	-0.2	59-1B	0		
2009	ARI	MLB	29	288	29	15	0	8	39	26	38	1	0	-1.9	.237	.306	.389	.233	.299	.377	.241	-6.3	-0.7	56-1B	-2	5-3B	1
2010	ARI	MLB	30	370	38	18	1	10	51	32	63	1	1	-0.8	.257	.326	.412	.255	.324	.399	.249	-0.5	-0.1	73-1B	0		

Breakout: 12%   Improve: 37%   Collapse: 15%   Attrition: 13%   MLB: 84%   Comparables: Robert Fick, Raul Ibañez, Paul Sorrento, John Mayberry

The first-base position is generally reserved for the powerful and mighty or, in a pinch, slick fielders capable of making decent contact and getting on base. Tracy has not fit either of these descriptions since 2006, and even then, he was substandard at the position. Over the last three seasons he has not played more than 98 games in a season, due to a variety of injuries, and has never been on pace for more than 17 home runs. Add in questionable defense, average plate discipline, and a lack of speed, and one has to wonder what Tracy really brought to the table that a prototypical Quad-A player could not have replicated on the cheap. Had the Snakes signed Tracy to his just-expired three-year, $13.25 million contract after his stellar (and, in retrospect, fluke) 2005 season, this might have been an unfair question to ask, but they signed him off his poor 2006, in which he hit .252/.315/.376 on the road. The D'backs bought out Tracy's 2010 option, and the memory of his four-corner versatility—not his bat—will be the quality that gets him his next job.

Justin Upton — RF

Bats: R   Throws: R   Height: 6' 2"   Weight: 205   Born: August 25, 1987   Age: 22

YEAR	TEAM	LVL	AGE	PA	R	2B	3B	HR	RBI	BB	SO	SB	CS	EqBRR	AVG	OBP	SLG	EqAVG	EqOBP	EqSLG	EqA	VORP	WARP	DEFENSE			
2007	VIS	A+	19	150	27	6	2	5	17	19	28	9	4	-0.9	.341	.433	.540	.290	.371	.443	.283	7.7	0.5	28-CF	-4		
2007	MOB	AA	19	306	48	17	4	13	53	37	51	10	7	1.6	.309	.399	.556	.288	.363	.509	.294	19.8	1.8	58-CF	-5	8-RF	0
2007	ARI	MLB	19	152	17	8	3	2	11	11	37	2	0	-0.3	.221	.283	.364	.214	.276	.350	.221	-3.7	-1.0	35-RF	-5		
2008	TUC	AAA	20	68	13	3	1	3	10	7	26	2	0	1.4	.279	.353	.508	.242	.309	.419	.256	0.9	-0.5	12-RF	-5		
2008	ARI	MLB	20	417	52	19	6	15	42	54	121	1	4	-0.8	.250	.353	.463	.247	.348	.458	.272	13.5	0.6	97-RF	-8		
2009	ARI	MLB	21	588	84	30	7	26	86	55	137	20	5	3.2	.300	.366	.532	.302	.365	.537	.301	40.5	5.6	132-RF	10		
2010	ARI	MLB	22	571	77	29	6	21	71	63	133	12	5	0.7	.268	.354	.473	.265	.348	.466	.276	21.9	2.2	127-RF	-2		

Breakout: 12%   Improve: 45%   Collapse: 11%   Attrition: 3%   MLB: 100%   Comparables: Tom Brunansky, Andruw Jones, Juan Gonzalez, Miguel Cabrera

Upton followed his rookie season—one in which he drew comparisons to a young Junior Griffey—with a yearlong coming-out party that was remarkable, given that he is still carded at bars. Players just 21 years of age are deemed promising for an OPS (On Base Percentage + Slugging Percentage) in excess of 800 at the Double-A level; Upton had one above 900 in "The Show." Only 14 players (including Upton) have posted isolated power marks of .230 or higher in a qualifying season before their 22nd birthday. The list includes a slew of current or future Hall of Famers, including Albert Pujols, Alex Rodriquez, Ted Williams, Joe DiMaggio, Jimmie Foxx, and Frank Robinson, so Upton finds himself in rather elite company moving into the 2010 season.

Josh Whitesell — 1B

Bats: L   Throws: L   Height: 6' 1"   Weight: 225   Born: April 14, 1982   Age: 28

YEAR	TEAM	LVL	AGE	PA	R	2B	3B	HR	RBI	BB	SO	SB	CS	EqBRR	AVG	OBP	SLG	EqAVG	EqOBP	EqSLG	EqA	VORP	WARP	DEFENSE	
2007	HAR	AA	25	487	78	23	1	21	74	87	107	6	2	1.0	.284	.425	.512	.245	.363	.422	.276	13.3	1.4	87-1B	-2
2008	TUC	AAA	26	560	86	36	0	26	110	74	136	1	2	-0.2	.328	.425	.568	.280	.367	.456	.284	20.1	0.7	115-1B	-15
2008	ARI	MLB	26	9	1	0	0	1	1	1	2	0	0	-0.1	.286	.444	.714	.286	.444	.714	.359	1.2	0.1		
2009	RNO	AAA	27	274	35	14	1	8	58	40	48	1	1	-1.2	.293	.398	.471	.233	.328	.366	.249	-3.4	-0.2	56-1B	2
2009	ARI	MLB	27	133	7	7	0	1	14	24	29	0	0	0.6	.194	.346	.287	.193	.338	.275	.233	-4.1	-0.6	28-1B	-2
2010	WAS	MLB	28	428	45	19	1	12	54	52	111	1	1	0.0	.232	.335	.387	.236	.336	.387	.260	4.8	0.2	85-1B	-3

Breakout: 6%   Improve: 30%   Collapse: 24%   Attrition: 11%   MLB: 18%   Comparables: Chris Pritchett, Pat Dodson, Gary Burnham, Larry Broadway

Whitesell's minor-league numbers paint a portrait of a Three True Outcomes hitter, one who walks, whiffs, or wallops in a hefty percentage of his plate appearances. Reality might not conform to that perception; he has the reputation of a mistake-punisher, and mistakes occur much less frequently at the major-league level. Whitesell could provide more production than Tony Clark or Chad Tracy, the team's first basemen over the last couple of seasons—but the team wisely let him slip away back to the Nationals during the winter.

Chris Young   CF

Bats: R   Throws: R   Height: 6' 2"   Weight: 200   Born: September 5, 1983   Age: 26

YEAR	TEAM	LVL	AGE	PA	R	2B	3B	HR	RBI	BB	SO	SB	CS	EqBRR	AVG	OBP	SLG	EqAVG	EqOBP	EqSLG	EqA	VORP	WARP	DEFENSE	
2007	ARI	MLB	23	624	85	29	3	32	68	43	141	27	6	0.7	.237	.295	.467	.235	.294	.460	.258	17.3	2.0	142-CF	0
2008	ARI	MLB	24	699	85	42	7	22	85	62	165	14	5	0.8	.248	.315	.443	.248	.312	.438	.258	18.2	2.3	157-CF	3
2009	RNO	AAA	25	63	17	5	1	3	9	9	13	2	2	0.2	.370	.460	.667	.309	.397	.582	.312	5.5	0.6	12-CF	0
2009	ARI	MLB	25	501	54	28	4	15	42	59	133	11	4	-2.1	.212	.311	.400	.216	.311	.402	.250	8.7	0.0	114-CF	-8
2010	ARI	MLB	26	628	83	33	5	25	72	66	143	18	7	-0.1	.242	.327	.451	.240	.322	.447	.260	19.9	2.1	144-CF	-1

Breakout: 13%   Improve: 56%   Collapse: 3%   Attrition: 1%   MLB: 100%   Comparables: Dave Henderson, Terry Moore, Tom Brunansky, Torii Hunter

Chris Young is to PECOTA what Daniel Cabrera is to pitching coaches. No matter how little he produces, the system keeps expecting that Young will figure things out and live up to the performance his attributes and comparables portend. At this point, the Diamondbacks might settle for a comparable of Augie Ojeda. Some will point to Young's strong .263/.351/.508 showing after a recall on August 29th as a sign of things to come, but he hit .278/.343/.508 in the second half of the 2008 season as well. He lacks the center-field defense required to make a .320 on-base percentage playable. Nor does he display the consistent power that would carry one of the corner outfield spots. This will be a make-or-break season for Young, who is increasingly young in name only.

PITCHERS

Bryan Augenstein

Bats: R   Throws: R   Height: 6' 5"   Weight: 225   Born: July 11, 1986   Age: 23

YEAR	TEAM	LVL	AGE	W	L	SV	G	GS	IP	H	HR	BB	SO	GB%	BABIP	STUFF	WHIP	ERA	SIERA	DERA	EqH9	EqHR9	EqBB9	EqSO9	VORP	SN/WX
2007	MSO	Rk	20	0	2	0	10	2	21¹	20	2	7	16	55%	.277	8	1.27	3.37	4.03	6.42	9.3	1.8	4.0	3.5	-2.1	-0.55
2008	SBN	A	21	5	1	0	13	13	87¹	73	2	9	69	61%	.276	22	0.94	2.16	3.19	3.65	9.7	1.0	1.7	4.2	16.3	0.81
2008	VIS	A+	21	2	4	0	9	9	44	57	5	5	30	67%	.354	2	1.41	3.89	3.65	6.15	12.3	1.8	1.8	4.0	-2.9	-0.20
2009	MOB	AA	22	5	0	0	9	9	45²	27	0	8	36	61%	.223	32	0.77	0.99	3.25	1.59	6.2	0.4	1.9	5.5	18.4	1.69
2009	RNO	AAA	22	2	5	0	8	7	36	43	2	7	29	55%	.353	20	1.39	5.50	3.69	5.30	10.1	0.5	2.0	6.1	0.8	-0.29
2009	ARI	MLB	22	0	1	0	7	2	17	23	2	6	6	64%	.323	-20	1.71	7.94	5.29	7.53	11.4	1.0	2.6	2.6	-3.9	-0.40
2010	ARI	MLB	23	5	7	0	27	21	108	116	14	35	62	52%	.298	1	1.40	4.53	4.75	4.79	9.6	1.2	2.7	4.8	8.5	1.87

Breakout: 11%   Improve: 48%   Collapse: 7%   Attrition: 4%   MLB: 59%   Comparables: Kris McWhirter, Garrett Stephenson, Travis Hughes, Tim Dillard

Augenstein throws too many strikes for his own good, a performance attribute that may catch up with him at the major-league level. That's because no matter how good your command or control is, when you are a right-hander sitting in the mid- to upper 80s, you're never going to be much more than serviceable. He doesn't walk anyone, and his bias toward grounders bodes well, but his skill set maxes out at "extra arm."

Michael Belfiore

Bats: R   Throws: L   Height: 6' 3"   Weight: 200   Born: October 3, 1988   Age: 21

YEAR	TEAM	LVL	AGE	W	L	SV	G	GS	IP	H	HR	BB	SO	GB%	BABIP	STUFF	WHIP	ERA	SIERA	DERA	EqH9	EqHR9	EqBB9	EqSO9	VORP	SN/WX
2009	MSO	Rk	20	2	2	0	14	11	58	59	2	13	55	-1%	.328	1	1.24	2.17	3.27	6.37	11.0	1.9	3.6	4.2	-5.1	-0.18
2010	ARI	MLB	21	3	6	0	26	15	75²	93	14	37	40	51%	.316	6	1.71	5.92	5.32	6.22	11.0	1.6	4.0	4.5	-6.0	1.66

Breakout: 21%   Improve: 54%   Collapse: 15%   Attrition: 5%   MLB: 0%   Comparables: Andrew Bausher, Steve Wojciechowski, Brian Carmody, Scott Johnson

A southpaw renowned for throwing 9 ⅔ relief innings in a 25-inning NCAA marathon, Belfiore pitched very well in rookie-level ball this past season, compiling a gaudy 4.2 strikeout/walk ratio. Though he was a reliever in college, the Snakes appear set to develop him as a starter. While Belfiore does not project as an ace, his ability to miss bats and limit free passes should translate as he moves up through the system, and his heater, slider, and changeup are quality offerings. If command and control elude him as the levels of competition become tougher, however, his decent arsenal will become moot.

Blaine Boyer

Bats: R　　Throws: R　　Height: 6' 3"　　Weight: 215　　Born: July 11, 1981　　Age: 28

YEAR	TEAM	LVL	AGE	W	L	SV	G	GS	IP	H	HR	BB	SO	GB%	BABIP	STUFF	WHIP	ERA	SIERA	DERA	EqH9	EqHR9	EqBB9	EqSO9	VORP	SN/WX
2007	RIC	AAA	25	4	3	2	21	12	73^1	76	1	50	62	49%	.352	4	1.72	4.30	4.76	5.81	10.4	0.4	6.3	6.1	-2.4	0.19
2008	ATL	MLB	26	2	6	1	76	0	72	73	10	25	67	49%	.301	-9	1.36	5.87	3.68	6.34	9.3	1.4	2.8	7.0	-6.7	-0.91
2009	SLN	MLB	27	0	0	0	15	0	16^1	14	1	5	9	71%	.241	-15	1.16	4.41	4.23	5.82	7.4	0.5	2.1	3.7	-0.6	-0.08
2009	ARI	MLB	27	0	1	0	30	0	37	39	0	12	18	63%	.307	-9	1.38	2.68	4.77	4.30	9.3	0.0	2.5	3.9	4.9	-0.18
2010	ARI	MLB	28	3	5	0	57	2	63^2	71	7	29	43	53%	.319	-11	1.57	5.02	4.75	5.29	9.9	1.0	3.8	5.6	1.5	-0.05

Breakout: 18%　Improve: 55%　Collapse: 18%　Attrition: 20%　　MLB: 69%　　Comparables: John Verhoeven, Jim Winn, Chad Qualls, Paul Moskau

After two injury-shortened seasons and a 2008 in which he started hot but ran out of fuel, last year Boyer bounced between the Braves and Cards before ending up a member of the Diamondbacks. His 2.68 ERA in 37 innings as a Snake is misleading and the result of a suspiciously nonexistent HR/FB ratio. While he will undoubtedly serve up some gopher balls next season, his strikeout and walk numbers should also return to previously established levels, making Boyer a cost-effective reliever, though not someone to which a team should commit more-than-nominal resources, given the abundant supply of similar, freely available bullpen arms.

Billy Buckner

Bats: R　　Throws: R　　Height: 6' 2"　　Weight: 215　　Born: August 27, 1983　　Age: 26

YEAR	TEAM	LVL	AGE	W	L	SV	G	GS	IP	H	HR	BB	SO	GB%	BABIP	STUFF	WHIP	ERA	SIERA	DERA	EqH9	EqHR9	EqBB9	EqSO9	VORP	SN/WX
2007	WIC	AA	23	1	3	0	4	3	19^1	20	4	6	13	60%	.258	-7	1.34	4.66	4.31	5.26	9.2	2.3	2.7	4.1	0.5	-0.21
2007	OMA	AAA	23	9	7	0	27	15	104^2	108	11	26	83	54%	.309	-8	1.28	3.78	3.78	4.65	10.5	1.5	2.5	5.6	9.2	1.28
2007	KCA	MLB	23	1	2	0	7	5	34	37	5	16	17	50%	.305	-8	1.56	5.29	5.38	4.60	9.8	1.1	4.0	4.6	3.1	0.25
2008	TUC	AAA	24	5	10	0	21	20	116^1	136	9	43	69	54%	.324	-7	1.54	4.95	4.79	5.46	9.8	0.9	3.3	3.8	0.5	-0.23
2008	ARI	MLB	24	1	0	0	10	0	14	16	3	4	11	40%	.325	2	1.43	3.21	4.01	2.77	10.4	1.4	2.1	6.9	3.9	0.09
2009	RNO	AAA	25	9	3	0	18	16	103	91	5	45	96	58%	.298	28	1.32	3.32	3.76	3.39	7.4	0.5	3.9	7.1	24.0	1.60
2009	ARI	MLB	25	4	6	0	16	13	77^1	94	12	29	64	56%	.350	0	1.59	6.40	4.05	6.00	10.8	1.1	2.9	6.7	-4.2	0.50
2010	ARI	MLB	26	7	10	0	40	25	153^1	162	19	63	102	55%	.304	-1	1.47	4.69	4.60	4.93	9.4	1.1	3.4	5.6	9.8	2.07

Breakout: 4%　Improve: 40%　Collapse: 13%　Attrition: 11%　　MLB: 87%　　Comparables: Frank Seminara, Tim Burke, David Pauley, Kelly Downs

Buckner's past two seasons can make your head spin. In 10 appearances during the 2008 campaign, he induced batters to swing at pitches out of the strike zone at a below-average clip, allowing more contact than the league average on those pitches to boot. His ERA? 3.21. In 16 more games in 2009, hitters chased 30 percent of these pitches in a league where batters chased only 25 percent, and he allowed far less contact, a stat amplified by the fact that he threw more pitches out of the zone than in. His ERA? 6.40. Small samples are small samples, and Buckner's true talent level likely lies somewhere in between these two extremes, but a ground-baller with a decent repertoire and the ability to get hitters to chase is a ground-baller who deserves another chance.

Daniel Cabrera

Bats: R　　Throws: R　　Height: 6' 9"　　Weight: 270　　Born: May 28, 1981　　Age: 29

YEAR	TEAM	LVL	AGE	W	L	SV	G	GS	IP	H	HR	BB	SO	GB%	BABIP	STUFF	WHIP	ERA	SIERA	DERA	EqH9	EqHR9	EqBB9	EqSO9	VORP	SN/WX
2007	BAL	MLB	26	9	18	0	34	34	204^1	207	25	108	166	57%	.299	8	1.54	5.55	4.45	5.33	8.7	1.0	4.3	6.6	3.8	2.64
2008	BAL	MLB	27	8	10	0	30	30	180	199	24	90	95	55%	.295	-6	1.61	5.25	5.34	5.03	9.5	1.1	4.0	4.4	9.4	2.42
2009	WAS	MLB	28	0	5	0	9	8	40	48	4	35	16	51%	.293	-20	2.07	5.85	6.56	8.37	9.8	0.8	6.1	2.7	-13.7	-0.71
2009	RNO	AAA	28	0	1	0	4	4	14^2	15	1	10	11	49%	.318	3	1.70	6.14	5.08	5.65	8.8	0.6	6.3	5.7	-0.2	0.07
2009	ARI	MLB	28	0	1	0	6	1	11	11	0	7	7	60%	.314	-16	1.64	6.55	5.12	5.91	9.3	0.0	5.1	5.1	-0.5	0.06
2010	ARI	MLB	29	5	8	0	24	22	118^1	128	15	66	71	55%	.302	-10	1.63	5.43	5.15	5.70	9.6	1.1	4.6	5.0	-2.6	0.76

Breakout: 14%　Improve: 44%　Collapse: 18%　Attrition: 22%　　MLB: 84%　　Comparables: Dave Frost, Joey Hamilton, Mike Morgan, Ed Halicki

Long gone is the flamethrowing strikeout pitcher capable of keeping the ball on the ground. Cabrera barely surpasses 90 mph these days and lacks the requisite stuff to succeed with a below-average fastball and poor control. His strikeout rate has plummeted, but he has not improved in the free-pass department, which only serves to exacerbate the issue. Whatever the cause of his struggles, Cabrera is no longer a major-league-caliber pitcher. Teams need to forget about his mediocre yet potential-laden 2005 season and focus their efforts elsewhere, even if it means looking past the lingering illusion of untapped potential and low asking price.

Doug Davis

Bats: R Throws: L Height: 6' 4" Weight: 215 Born: September 21, 1975 Age: 34

YEAR	TEAM	LVL	AGE	W	L	SV	G	GS	IP	H	HR	BB	SO	GB%	BABIP	STUFF	WHIP	ERA	SIERA	DERA	EqH9	EqHR9	EqBB9	EqSO9	VORP	SN/WX
2007	ARI	MLB	31	13	12	0	33	33	192²	211	21	95	144	55%	.318	10	1.59	4.25	4.60	4.11	9.6	0.8	4.0	6.3	29.3	4.16
2008	ARI	MLB	32	6	8	0	26	26	146	160	13	64	112	55%	.322	12	1.53	4.32	4.39	4.23	9.5	0.6	3.5	6.1	20.5	2.79
2009	ARI	MLB	33	9	14	0	34	34	203¹	203	25	103	146	49%	.291	9	1.50	4.12	4.74	4.05	8.7	0.8	3.9	5.7	32.5	4.22
2010	ARI	MLB	34	8	11	0	32	32	174	189	19	83	119	50%	.315	-1	1.57	4.92	4.79	5.21	9.7	1.0	4.0	5.7	5.7	2.42

Breakout: 1% Improve: 26% Collapse: 17% Attrition: 26%   MLB: 95%   Comparables: Denny Neagle, Bruce Hurst, Frank Viola, Frank Tanana

Davis is a concrete example of how a deceptive delivery and some quality secondary pitches can go a long way toward making up for a below-average fastball for a southpaw. He walks too many hitters relative to his strikeout total, but has proven himself durable—even recovering from cancer to surpass the 200-inning plateau once again—and effective enough to consistently manage an ERA in the low fours. A league-average innings-muncher in every sense of the term, Davis is still a solid third or fourth starter and, at 33 years old, could continue frustrating hitters for years to come.

Kevin Eichhorn

Bats: R Throws: R Height: 6' 0" Weight: 170 Born: February 6, 1990 Age: 20

YEAR	TEAM	LVL	AGE	W	L	SV	G	GS	IP	H	HR	BB	SO	GB%	BABIP	STUFF	WHIP	ERA	SIERA	DERA	EqH9	EqHR9	EqBB9	EqSO9	VORP	SN/WX
2009	MSO	Rk	19	0	2	0	10	0	16	13	1	9	25	-1%	.375	13	1.37	3.37	2.31	5.54	11.1	2.8	7.6	9.0	-0.1	-0.50
2010	ARI	MLB	20	1	4	0	17	0	43²	62	8	29	17	51%	.342	3	2.08	7.58	6.21	7.92	12.6	1.7	5.5	3.3	-11.8	-0.26

Breakout: 23% Improve: 41% Collapse: 28% Attrition: 6%   MLB: 4%   Comparables: Rafael Chaves, Reynaldo Vargas, Eddie McKiernan, Todd Bussa

The Diamondbacks did not take any chances with 2008 third-round pick Eichhorn, the son of former major-league pitcher Mark. With him coming back from nerve transplantation, the organization limited Kevin's action to a mere 10 games in rookie ball as a precaution against additional injury. Scout Darold Brown, who signed the third-round pick, referred to Eichhorn as having a smoke-and-mirrors skill set, suggesting that his average fastball velocity and good curveball will sneak up on hitters and result in a "comfortable ohfer." For this excellent athlete in high school who played shortstop when not on the mound, his 14.1 K/9 in 16 innings of work has to be considered encouraging even if the control needs a bit of work.

Juan Gutierrez

Bats: R Throws: R Height: 6' 2" Weight: 210 Born: July 14, 1983 Age: 26

YEAR	TEAM	LVL	AGE	W	L	SV	G	GS	IP	H	HR	BB	SO	GB%	BABIP	STUFF	WHIP	ERA	SIERA	DERA	EqH9	EqHR9	EqBB9	EqSO9	VORP	SN/WX
2007	ROU	AAA	23	5	10	0	26	25	156	154	17	63	108	51%	.288	-11	1.39	4.15	4.52	5.31	9.4	1.6	3.8	4.7	3.1	0.66
2007	HOU	MLB	23	1	1	0	7	3	21¹	25	3	6	16	40%	.324	2	1.45	5.91	4.21	5.48	10.1	1.3	2.1	5.9	0.0	-0.05
2008	TUC	AAA	24	5	11	0	25	22	116²	152	11	44	87	52%	.362	-15	1.68	6.09	4.40	6.96	11.1	1.1	3.3	4.9	-18.8	-1.26
2009	ARI	MLB	25	4	3	9	65	0	71	67	2	30	66	41%	.316	14	1.37	4.06	3.90	3.80	8.4	0.3	3.2	7.4	13.4	2.68
2010	ARI	MLB	26	3	5	7	57	3	73	76	9	32	52	45%	.305	-7	1.48	4.75	4.64	5.01	9.3	1.1	3.7	6.0	4.0	0.94

Breakout: 33% Improve: 68% Collapse: 10% Attrition: 22%   MLB: 98%   Comparables: Matt Belisle, Tim Layana, Vinnie Chulk, Jerry Dipoto

Acquired in the Jose Valverde deal under the assumption that he could bloom into a key rotation cog, Gutierrez transformed in 2009 from frustrating farmhand starter into relatively reliable reliever. With almost a whiff per frame and a passable walk rate, perhaps Gutierrez can be groomed into the second coming of traded set-up man Tony Pena. Alternatively, if the Snakes decide to move increasingly expensive veteran Chad Qualls midway through the year, expect Gutierrez—who filled in well for Qualls in September—to take over in the closer's role. Gutierrez's success was largely derived from a minuscule HR/FB that is sure to regress and an ability to induce feeble swings out of the zone—an ability that should be sustainable, provided he doesn't fall in love with his 95 mph fastball and keeps mixing in his slider.

Trevor Harden

| | | Bats: B | Throws: R | Height: 6′ 2″ | Weight: 215 | Born: September 1, 1987 | Age: 22 |

YEAR	TEAM	LVL	AGE	W	L	SV	G	GS	IP	H	HR	BB	SO	GB%	BABIP	STUFF	WHIP	ERA	SIERA	DERA	EqH9	EqHR9	EqBB9	EqSO9	VORP	SN/WX
2008	MSO	Rk	20	1	3	2	12	6	42¹	34	2	11	64	48%	.352	38	1.06	1.91	1.63	3.79	9.7	1.7	3.6	7.6	7.2	0.38
2009	SBN	A	21	5	1	0	6	6	37²	28	3	7	31	46%	.248	15	0.93	2.39	3.39	3.74	8.8	2.1	2.7	4.3	6.6	0.25
2009	VIS	A+	21	2	9	0	17	17	91¹	115	11	23	63	41%	.337	-18	1.51	4.43	4.35	7.11	11.9	2.0	3.1	3.4	-15.6	-1.44
2010	ARI	MLB	22	3	8	1	23	22	102²	130	18	44	56	45%	.328	-5	1.70	6.12	5.24	6.42	11.3	1.6	3.5	4.6	-10.5	1.85

Breakout: 4%   Improve: 26%   Collapse: 31%   Attrition: 6%   MLB: 1%   Comparables: Aaron Dean, Joe McCann, Emar Fleming, Mike Welch

It is increasingly difficult to avoid using the term *generic* when describing Harden's tools and potential. He does not miss many bats with his average secondary offerings, and his solid sinker keeps balls on the ground at a decent but not overwhelming clip. A strike-thrower with average controllable skill rates, Harden lacks upside. He could find himself a member of the Snakes' relief corps at some point in the near future, but expectations that he could develop into the next Kevin Slowey or Nick Blackburn should be tempered.

Dan Haren

| | | Bats: R | Throws: R | Height: 6′ 5″ | Weight: 215 | Born: September 17, 1980 | Age: 29 |

YEAR	TEAM	LVL	AGE	W	L	SV	G	GS	IP	H	HR	BB	SO	GB%	BABIP	STUFF	WHIP	ERA	SIERA	DERA	EqH9	EqHR9	EqBB9	EqSO9	VORP	SN/WX
2007	OAK	MLB	26	15	9	0	34	34	222²	214	24	55	192	49%	.287	19	1.21	3.07	3.58	3.54	8.5	1.1	2.0	6.8	48.9	6.45
2008	ARI	MLB	27	16	8	0	33	33	216	204	19	40	206	49%	.303	36	1.13	3.33	3.06	3.31	8.2	0.6	1.5	7.6	52.4	6.13
2009	ARI	MLB	28	14	10	0	33	33	229¹	192	27	38	223	49%	.267	38	1.00	3.14	2.88	3.03	7.2	0.8	1.3	7.6	63.1	6.70
2010	ARI	MLB	29	14	10	0	32	32	212¹	196	22	49	181	49%	.294	27	1.16	3.40	3.46	3.62	8.3	0.9	1.9	7.2	44.3	4.11

Breakout: 6%   Improve: 42%   Collapse: 11%   Attrition: 4%   MLB: 99%   Comparables: Gaylord Perry, Jose Rijo, Roger Clemens, Brandon Webb

Haren turned in his fifth straight season of 33-plus starts and 216-plus innings, all with a fine ERA for a desert-dweller and a league-leading strikeout/walk ratio just shy of 6.0. That he has not yet become a household name serves as a testament to the small markets in which he has played, not the magnitude of his talent. On pure stuff, durability, control, command, track record, age, and contract status, one would be hard-pressed to find five more valuable pitchers in the entire sport. One off-key note on the subject of his durability: since 2006, when he posted a 2.63 ERA down the stretch, Haren has made 34 August and September starts, posting a 5.18 ERA while allowing 263 hits and 33 home runs in 217 ⅓ innings. Normally, small-sample breakdowns such as these can be misleading, but in Haren's case, these stats suggest perhaps that his early-season workloads could be better managed to avoid fatigue at the end of the year.

Wade Miley

| | | Bats: L | Throws: L | Height: 6′ 2″ | Weight: 190 | Born: November 13, 1986 | Age: 23 |

YEAR	TEAM	LVL	AGE	W	L	SV	G	GS	IP	H	HR	BB	SO	GB%	BABIP	STUFF	WHIP	ERA	SIERA	DERA	EqH9	EqHR9	EqBB9	EqSO9	VORP	SN/WX
2008	YAK	A-	21	1	1	0	7	0	11	11	0	5	11	52%	.333	-2	1.45	4.91	3.72	6.97	11.3	0.9	4.4	4.4	-1.7	-0.15
2009	SBN	A	22	5	9	0	21	21	113²	127	8	29	91	60%	.342	-31	1.37	4.12	3.72	6.75	12.5	2.2	3.4	4.2	-13.9	-1.58
2009	VIS	A+	22	1	1	0	3	3	15	18	0	4	11	53%	.360	-7	1.47	4.80	4.07	7.07	11.6	0.6	3.2	3.9	-2.4	-0.29
2010	ARI	MLB	23	3	8	0	19	19	102¹	139	18	47	48	54%	.338	-24	1.81	6.51	5.43	6.86	12.0	1.6	3.8	3.9	-15.4	1.22

Breakout: 16%   Improve: 42%   Collapse: 13%   Attrition: 4%   MLB: 3%   Comparables: Chuck Hensley, Thomas Miller, Derek Root, Daniel Moskos

See Trevor Harden, but add more upside. Miley boasts an average repertoire of pitches capable of getting the job done at times, but his assortment does not even come close to making scouts salivate. His fastball sits in the 88-90 mph range, and he pounds the zone with it, hoping to induce grounders. His secondary pitches—a good slider and an average changeup—should afford him the opportunity to avoid being pigeonholed as a reliever. Miley's upside is that of a fourth or fifth starter, the type of pitcher who fills out a staff but who is by no means a key cog or substantial contributor.

Kevin Mulvey

Bats: R   Throws: R   Height: 6' 2"   Weight: 190   Born: May 26, 1985   Age: 25

YEAR	TEAM	LVL	AGE	W	L	SV	G	GS	IP	H	HR	BB	SO	GB%	BABIP	STUFF	WHIP	ERA	SIERA	DERA	EqH9	EqHR9	EqBB9	EqSO9	VORP	SN/WX
2007	BIN	AA	22	11	10	0	26	26	151²	145	4	43	110	59%	.297	21	1.24	3.32	4.05	4.77	8.6	0.7	2.7	4.7	12.1	0.59
2008	ROC	AAA	23	7	9	0	27	27	148	152	16	48	121	41%	.303	-2	1.35	3.77	4.04	5.34	9.6	1.3	3.1	5.4	2.5	0.51
2009	ROC	AAA	24	5	8	0	24	24	149	153	12	54	113	58%	.308	2	1.39	3.93	4.19	5.60	9.2	1.1	3.5	5.5	-1.6	-0.07
2009	MIN	MLB	24	0	0	0	2	0	1¹	6	0	0	0	0%	.600	-86	4.50	27.00	7.78	27.00	40.5	0.0	0.0	0.0	-3.2	0.01
2009	ARI	MLB	24	0	3	0	6	4	23	23	5	12	18	52%	.269	-5	1.52	7.04	4.57	6.36	8.5	1.5	3.9	6.2	-2.2	-0.20
2010	ARI	MLB	25	7	10	0	33	27	149²	154	17	59	90	40%	.293	0	1.42	4.55	5.00	4.82	9.1	1.0	3.3	5.1	11.3	1.63

Breakout: 7%   Improve: 49%   Collapse: 10%   Attrition: 18%   MLB: 21%   Comparables: Jeff Peterek, Lance Broadway, Ed Wojna, Wally Whitehurst

After acquiring Mulvey as part of the package for Johan Santana, Twins general manager Bill Smith was expected to provide plenty of developmental slack to prove that he got a substantial return for one of baseball's best hurlers. Less than two years later, Mulvey's stock had plummeted to the point that the Twins shipped him to Arizona for Jon Rauch. A severe drop-off in grounders and the subsequent uptick in gopher balls relocated Mulvey from the generic strike-thrower bin into prospect limbo. It's worth the D'backs' while to see if his old ground-balling ways will re-assert themselves, but lacking that attribute, he lacks the abilities to be even a solid bullpen option.

Jarrod Parker

Bats: R   Throws: R   Height: 6' 1"   Weight: 180   Born: November 24, 1988   Age: 21

YEAR	TEAM	LVL	AGE	W	L	SV	G	GS	IP	H	HR	BB	SO	GB%	BABIP	STUFF	WHIP	ERA	SIERA	DERA	EqH9	EqHR9	EqBB9	EqSO9	VORP	SN/WX
2008	SBN	A	19	12	5	0	24	24	117²	113	8	33	117	46%	.312	2	1.24	3.44	3.28	6.41	11.4	1.8	3.5	5.5	-10.8	-0.96
2009	VIS	A+	20	1	0	0	4	4	19	12	0	4	21	55%	.255	18	0.84	0.95	2.47	1.50	6.5	0.5	2.5	6.0	8.0	0.57
2009	MOB	AA	20	4	6	0	16	16	78¹	82	2	34	74	61%	.351	33	1.48	3.68	3.77	4.87	10.8	0.7	4.1	6.5	5.1	0.44
2010	ARI	MLB	21	4	8	0	27	26	111	130	15	53	80	45%	.331	15	1.65	5.56	4.75	5.83	10.4	1.2	3.9	6.0	-4.1	1.77

Breakout: 19%   Improve: 48%   Collapse: 13%   Attrition: 7%   MLB: 13%   Comparables: Tony Ghelfi, Jason Doss, Rick Gorecki, John Roper

All signs pointed toward this 2007 first-rounder developing into a front-of-the-rotation starter. Sadly, Parker's mid-90s heat, three above-average secondary offerings, and his ability to miss bats *and* keep the ball both on the ground and out of the stands will be on hiatus this year, as he underwent Tommy John surgery in October and stands to miss practically all of the 2010 season.

Yusmeiro Petit

Bats: R   Throws: R   Height: 6' 0"   Weight: 255   Born: November 22, 1984   Age: 25

YEAR	TEAM	LVL	AGE	W	L	SV	G	GS	IP	H	HR	BB	SO	GB%	BABIP	STUFF	WHIP	ERA	SIERA	DERA	EqH9	EqHR9	EqBB9	EqSO9	VORP	SN/WX
2007	TUC	AAA	22	8	4	0	17	17	93²	83	11	38	60	27%	.251	9	1.29	4.04	5.31	4.44	7.2	1.2	3.6	4.3	11.1	0.60
2007	ARI	MLB	22	3	4	0	14	10	57	58	12	18	40	35%	.266	12	1.33	4.58	4.57	4.21	8.4	1.4	2.5	5.8	8.2	1.12
2008	TUC	AAA	23	3	3	0	11	11	60	64	7	8	67	38%	.341	23	1.20	4.80	2.42	4.90	9.2	1.2	1.4	7.5	4.0	0.20
2008	ARI	MLB	23	3	5	0	19	8	56¹	45	12	14	42	40%	.206	8	1.05	4.31	4.01	4.19	6.4	1.4	1.9	5.7	8.4	1.18
2009	RNO	AAA	24	0	1	0	5	5	15²	21	4	5	13	41%	.333	-7	1.66	6.89	4.14	6.89	10.5	1.7	2.8	6.1	-2.5	-0.23
2009	ARI	MLB	24	3	10	0	23	17	89²	102	19	34	74	34%	.296	-6	1.52	5.82	4.36	5.60	9.3	1.4	2.8	6.1	-1.1	0.33
2010	SEA	MLB	25	6	6	0	30	21	106²	104	13	38	79	38%	.291	9	1.33	4.16	4.39	4.24	8.5	1.1	2.9	6.0	15.0	1.21

Breakout: 18%   Improve: 62%   Collapse: 11%   Attrition: 24%   MLB: 81%   Comparables: Albie Lopez, Tim Redding, Ty Taubenheim, Ryan Jensen

Petit is probably going to end up serving as a cautionary tale of how minor-league scouting reports truly add context to the numbers. He barely hits 90 mph on the gun and is very hittable in spite of being able to deceive hitters with his windup. His controllable skill set (walks, strikeouts, and home runs) has led to the consistent overestimation of his the run-prevention ability in the majors. Still, Petit is just 24 years old. He may end up earning his keep as a specialist, but he will not be the ace starter his minor-league numbers may have suggested. This figures to be a big year for him; snagged by the Mariners on a waiver claim, he'll have to adapt to pitching in the tougher league, but he'll have the advantages of a fine defense and a bigger ballpark behind him.

Chad Qualls

| | Bats: R | Throws: R | Height: 6' 5" | Weight: 220 | Born: August 17, 1978 | Age: 31 |

YEAR	TEAM	LVL	AGE	W	L	SV	G	GS	IP	H	HR	BB	SO	GB%	BABIP	STUFF	WHIP	ERA	SIERA	DERA	EqH9	EqHR9	EqBB9	EqSO9	VORP	SN/WX
2007	HOU	MLB	28	6	5	5	79	0	82^2	84	10	25	78	64%	.323	7	1.32	3.05	3.37	2.99	9.3	1.1	2.5	7.8	22.2	3.52
2008	ARI	MLB	29	4	8	9	77	0	73^2	61	4	18	71	65%	.279	24	1.07	2.81	3.09	3.21	7.1	0.4	1.9	7.6	18.9	1.90
2009	ARI	MLB	30	2	2	24	51	0	52	53	5	7	45	69%	.304	12	1.15	3.63	3.13	3.65	8.7	0.7	1.0	6.6	10.9	2.00
2010	ARI	MLB	31	4	3	13	67	0	66^1	64	7	20	56	63%	.305	6	1.28	3.83	3.61	4.01	8.6	0.9	2.5	7.0	11.0	1.58

Breakout: 16%   Improve: 37%   Collapse: 24%   Attrition: 5%   MLB: 98%   Comparables: Greg McMichael, Mike Timlin, Jose Mesa, Mike Henneman

Relief pitchers are quite fickle, given the few innings they pitch each season, and definitive statements about their performance based on ERA are quite dodgy. For this reason, it's imperative to evaluate relievers on their "process" more than the outcomes. The prototypical relief pitcher sought by teams will whiff plenty, limit free passes, and keep the ball grounded. Qualls perfectly fits this description, and yet his 3.63 ERA last year is modest, given a career-best 6.4 strikeout/walk ratio and a very high ground-ball rate. He pitched well from the standpoint of controllable skills, but fell prey to OOPS, stranding runners at a below-average rate. Unless your name is Javier Vazquez, this ailment subsides quickly, meaning the only real question mark about Qualls is if the dislocated kneecap that kept him sidelined for the final month of the year will affect his future performance.

Max Scherzer

| | Bats: R | Throws: R | Height: 6' 3" | Weight: 215 | Born: July 27, 1984 | Age: 25 |

YEAR	TEAM	LVL	AGE	W	L	SV	G	GS	IP	H	HR	BB	SO	GB%	BABIP	STUFF	WHIP	ERA	SIERA	DERA	EqH9	EqHR9	EqBB9	EqSO9	VORP	SN/WX
2007	VIS	A+	22	2	0	0	3	3	17	5	0	2	30	60%	.192	16	0.41	0.53	0.29	1.15	5.2	0.6	1.7	9.8	7.6	0.66
2007	MOB	AA	22	4	4	0	14	14	73^2	64	3	40	76	57%	.310	15	1.41	3.91	3.76	5.68	9.0	0.9	4.9	6.3	-1.4	-0.18
2008	TUC	AAA	23	1	1	0	13	10	53	35	2	22	79	57%	.289	38	1.08	2.72	2.14	3.23	6.3	0.5	3.6	9.7	13.4	1.23
2008	ARI	MLB	23	0	4	0	16	7	56	48	5	21	66	49%	.307	32	1.23	3.05	2.93	3.56	7.6	0.6	2.9	9.4	12.0	1.00
2009	ARI	MLB	24	9	11	0	30	30	170^1	166	20	63	174	48%	.308	25	1.34	4.12	3.45	4.48	8.4	0.8	2.8	7.9	19.5	2.69
2010	DET	MLB	25	9	8	0	31	28	153^1	138	15	64	145	54%	.300	24	1.32	4.03	3.68	4.17	8.0	0.8	3.5	8.0	22.6	2.33

Breakout: 21%   Improve: 50%   Collapse: 11%   Attrition: 6%   MLB: 93%   Comparables: Zack Greinke, Josh Beckett, James Shields, Joe Mays

Widely considered one of the best young arms in the game, the 24-year-old Scherzer did not disappoint in 2009, making 30 starts while posting component stats that suggest an ERA closer to 3.44 than his official 4.12 (as per SIERA; see the team essay). Known for his blistering heat and a passion for sabermetrics, Scherzer said that his goal was to be a four-win player last year. Though he fell short by 1.5 WARP, his ability to get strikeouts and keep the ball on the ground bode well moving forward. If he can reduce the rate of free passes issued while sustaining the aforementioned attributes, we're looking at a perennial All-Star and a third potential ace for the Diamondbacks.

Daniel Schlereth

| | Bats: L | Throws: L | Height: 6' 0" | Weight: 210 | Born: May 9, 1986 | Age: 24 |

YEAR	TEAM	LVL	AGE	W	L	SV	G	GS	IP	H	HR	BB	SO	GB%	BABIP	STUFF	WHIP	ERA	SIERA	DERA	EqH9	EqHR9	EqBB9	EqSO9	VORP	SN/WX
2009	MOB	AA	22	0	0	4	21	0	26^2	14	1	16	39	60%	.250	25	1.12	1.01	2.60	1.60	6.4	0.7	5.3	9.9	11.0	1.04
2009	ARI	MLB	22	1	4	0	21	0	18^1	15	1	15	22	57%	.298	18	1.64	5.89	4.00	5.68	7.1	0.5	6.2	9.0	-0.4	-1.09
2010	DET	MLB	24	2	3	1	39	0	46^2	48	6	31	40	48%	.313	-9	1.70	5.62	4.72	5.66	9.0	1.1	5.4	7.2	-0.8	0.90

Breakout: 5%   Improve: 23%   Collapse: 42%   Attrition: 6%   MLB: 62%   Comparables: Thomas Baumgardner, Brad Kilby, Josh Newman, Cesar Jimenez

One of the prized possessions of the farm system, the former first-round pick broke into the bigs as a southpaw specialist when Scott Schoeneweis went out of action. The son of the NFL analyst, Schlereth was stingy with hits but was unsustainably wild. This was also a problem during his brief minor-league apprenticeship, where he posted amazing strikeout numbers (60 in 39 ⅔ innings), but also had trouble throwing strikes (23 walks). Fortunately, he's well short of Brad Pennington territory as far as wildness, and his fastball, which reached 96-98 mph in the minors, showed up. Too many control-free days will limit Schlereth to a relief role, but he could flourish in the bullpen with his skill set and repertoire.

Scott Schoeneweis

Bats: L   Throws: L   Height: 6' 0"   Weight: 190   Born: October 2, 1973   Age: 36

YEAR	TEAM	LVL	AGE	W	L	SV	G	GS	IP	H	HR	BB	SO	GB%	BABIP	STUFF	WHIP	ERA	SIERA	DERA	EqH9	EqHR9	EqBB9	EqSO9	VORP	SN/WX
2007	NYN	MLB	33	0	2	2	70	0	59	62	8	28	41	63%	.292	-19	1.53	5.03	4.55	5.25	9.7	1.4	3.9	5.6	1.6	0.65
2008	NYN	MLB	34	2	6	1	73	0	56²	55	7	23	34	56%	.274	-18	1.38	3.34	4.78	3.89	9.3	1.3	3.3	4.6	9.7	0.01
2009	ARI	MLB	35	1	2	0	45	0	24	29	6	13	14	49%	.280	-29	1.75	7.12	5.36	6.84	9.5	1.8	3.9	4.2	-3.8	-0.40
2010	ARI	MLB	36	1	3	0	40	0	40	47	6	21	23	56%	.315	-20	1.68	5.64	5.11	6.03	10.5	1.3	4.2	4.9	-2.4	0.05

Breakout: 25% Improve: 40% Collapse: 35% Attrition: 33%   MLB: 94%   Comparables: Ken Takahashi, Bob McClure, Rheal Cormier, Paul Lindblad

The lefty specialist struggled last season, serving as a proverbial batting tee for hitters from both sides of the plate. Specialists are particularly difficult to judge, given the especially small sample sizes accrued, but Schoeneweis is certainly a better pitcher than his statistics this past season suggest. At least part of his struggles can be attributed to the untimely death of his wife, which kept him out of action for the latter part of the season. Schoeneweis filed for free agency, suggesting that he will keep playing rather than retire to spend time with his family. If he does return, southpaws with decent sliders are always valued, particularly those who held left-handed batters to .199/.284/.263 from 2005 through 2008.

Bryan Shaw

Bats: B   Throws: R   Height: 6' 1"   Weight: 210   Born: November 8, 1987   Age: 22

YEAR	TEAM	LVL	AGE	W	L	SV	G	GS	IP	H	HR	BB	SO	GB%	BABIP	STUFF	WHIP	ERA	SIERA	DERA	EqH9	EqHR9	EqBB9	EqSO9	VORP	SN/WX
2008	SBN	A	20	0	1	0	11	0	22¹	18	0	6	16	66%	.269	13	1.07	4.03	3.70	7.30	9.3	0.9	3.5	3.5	-4.1	-0.46
2008	MSO	Rk	20	0	1	2	10	0	17¹	24	2	7	17	60%	.386	-2	1.79	6.75	3.77	11.61	13.5	2.7	4.9	3.8	-11.3	-0.59
2009	VIS	A+	21	3	7	0	30	19	107¹	96	7	40	95	61%	.289	4	1.27	4.70	3.71	6.46	8.9	1.4	4.1	4.6	-11.0	-1.73
2010	ARI	MLB	22	4	7	2	34	16	96	103	14	48	53	62%	.293	-1	1.58	5.50	5.02	5.73	9.5	1.3	4.2	4.7	-2.5	0.75

Breakout: 21% Improve: 65% Collapse: 7% Attrition: 10%   MLB: 0%   Comparables: Cory Lidle, Jason Robbins, Al Hulbert, Sean Evans

A former second-round pick out of Long Beach State, Shaw never started a game in his collegiate days, but he began the transition to the rotation in High-A last season. Expectations were high that he could dominate the level with a potent fastball/slider combination, but the results did not bear that out. His peripheral statistics were above average, but Shaw imploded with runners on base, stranding under 60 percent of them in a league with an average of 72 percent. He could succeed in the major leagues as a potential set-up man or closer with mid-90s heat and the filthy slider, but the D'backs are clinging to hopes that he could experience success as a starter. He will need to develop another pitch to get through lineups multiple times, but a fallback projection as a strong set-up man is nothing to fret about.

Cesar Valdez

Bats: R   Throws: R   Height: 6' 2"   Weight: 200   Born: March 17, 1985   Age: 25

YEAR	TEAM	LVL	AGE	W	L	SV	G	GS	IP	H	HR	BB	SO	GB%	BABIP	STUFF	WHIP	ERA	SIERA	DERA	EqH9	EqHR9	EqBB9	EqSO9	VORP	SN/WX
2007	SBN	A	22	7	10	0	25	25	148	130	11	32	106	61%	.270	-6	1.09	3.41	3.77	5.42	9.3	1.7	2.8	3.9	1.2	-0.32
2008	VIS	A+	23	10	3	0	15	15	96	88	5	16	80	57%	.290	12	1.08	2.53	3.38	4.03	8.6	1.1	2.0	5.0	15.1	1.10
2008	MOB	AA	23	3	5	0	12	12	64¹	63	2	23	60	61%	.333	11	1.34	4.06	3.54	5.00	9.8	0.7	3.3	6.3	3.4	0.06
2009	RNO	AAA	24	7	6	0	19	18	96	103	16	30	60	53%	.282	-3	1.39	4.78	4.57	5.05	8.4	1.3	2.8	4.5	4.9	0.04
2010	ARI	MLB	25	6	7	0	26	21	118¹	122	15	44	70	47%	.291	-1	1.41	4.58	4.84	4.81	9.2	1.1	3.1	4.9	9.0	2.01

Breakout: 11% Improve: 50% Collapse: 14% Attrition: 21%   MLB: 10%   Comparables: Tom Filer, J.D. Smart, Mark Holliman, Ismael Ramirez

Valdez succeeds with a modest sinker, thanks to his plus changeup and abilities to control the strike zone and induce grounders. Many wondered how his strikeout-to-walk ratio would fare at Triple-A in 2009, given that the jump from High-A to Double-A in 2008 led to a reduction of the same rate from 5.0 to 2.6. Sure enough, he proved a bit too hittable last season, experiencing a severe drop in strikeouts per nine innings from 8.4 to 5.6 and a decline in his ground-ball rate for the third consecutive season. He projects as a back-end rotation starter or long reliever, but he will need to recoup some of the whiffs and worm-beaters for even that modest projection to come to fruition.

Esmerling Vasquez

Bats: R   Throws: R   Height: 6' 1"   Weight: 175   Born: November 7, 1983   Age: 26

YEAR	TEAM	LVL	AGE	W	L	SV	G	GS	IP	H	HR	BB	SO	GB%	BABIP	STUFF	WHIP	ERA	SIERA	DERA	EqH9	EqHR9	EqBB9	EqSO9	VORP	SN/WX
2007	MOB	AA	23	10	6	0	29	29	165¹	125	11	60	151	49%	.266	10	1.12	2.99	3.60	4.19	8.0	1.2	3.5	5.8	22.1	1.55
2008	TUC	AAA	24	3	6	0	24	15	83	79	11	73	57	38%	.278	-11	1.83	6.72	5.99	7.05	8.3	1.3	7.4	4.4	-14.1	-1.56
2009	ARI	MLB	25	3	3	0	53	0	53	52	4	29	45	45%	.306	0	1.53	4.42	4.49	4.13	8.6	0.5	4.1	6.6	8.1	-1.13
2010	ARI	MLB	26	3	4	0	49	3	66¹	64	8	37	51	41%	.293	-6	1.52	5.03	4.80	5.18	8.5	1.0	4.5	6.4	2.3	0.58

Breakout: 30%   Improve: 54%   Collapse: 13%   Attrition: 22%   MLB: 60%   Comparables: Vinnie Chulk, Courtney Duncan, Tim Mauser, J.D. Smart

A short 26-year-old righty who did not make his major-league debut until this past season, Vasquez sustained a decent semblance of his lower-level strikeout rates, but could not strand runners, allowing 10 of 29 inherited runners to score. The Diamondbacks utilized his services in the rotation throughout the minors, as he combines a 95 mph fastball with a plus changeup and a good-but-not-great slider. The stuff to succeed is certainly there—he induced more swings and less contact than the league average—but he will need to work on locating and sequencing in order to remain, even as the final man in the bullpen.

Brandon Webb

Bats: R   Throws: R   Height: 6' 2"   Weight: 230   Born: May 9, 1979   Age: 31

YEAR	TEAM	LVL	AGE	W	L	SV	G	GS	IP	H	HR	BB	SO	GB%	BABIP	STUFF	WHIP	ERA	SIERA	DERA	EqH9	EqHR9	EqBB9	EqSO9	VORP	SN/WX
2007	ARI	MLB	27	18	10	0	34	34	236¹	209	12	72	194	71%	.285	36	1.19	3.01	3.53	3.14	7.7	0.3	2.4	6.9	61.8	7.31
2008	ARI	MLB	28	22	7	0	34	34	226²	206	13	65	183	72%	.288	32	1.20	3.30	3.45	3.46	7.9	0.4	2.3	6.4	51.3	6.25
2009	ARI	MLB	29	0	0	0	1	1	4	6	2	2	2	76%	.308	-30	2.00	13.50	4.75	13.50	13.5	4.5	4.5	4.5	-3.6	-0.19
2010	ARI	MLB	31	5	6	0	19	17	94²	92	9	35	66	65%	.292	10	1.34	4.07	4.18	4.33	8.7	0.9	3.1	5.8	12.3	1.82

Breakout: 5%   Improve: 35%   Collapse: 32%   Attrition: 32%   MLB: 81%   Comparables: Kevin Appier, Ryan Drese, Cy Blanton, Jake Westbrook

After a Cy Young Award and two straight second-place finishes in the balloting, Webb made a very poor Opening Day start in 2009, and proceeded to miss the remainder of the season after undergoing shoulder debridement surgery. Though the D'backs exercised Webb's 2010 option, his long-term role with the team is an open question and will depend heavily on his comeback this season. Luckily, though symptomatic problems with the labrum are never good, the damage to Webb's shoulder was minimal and he should be fully recovered for next season. When he's healthy, Webb is one of the best pitchers in baseball, with one of the best pitches in the game. Here's hoping that's still true in 2010.

Clay Zavada

Bats: L   Throws: L   Height: 6' 1"   Weight: 195   Born: June 28, 1984   Age: 26

YEAR	TEAM	LVL	AGE	W	L	SV	G	GS	IP	H	HR	BB	SO	GB%	BABIP	STUFF	WHIP	ERA	SIERA	DERA	EqH9	EqHR9	EqBB9	EqSO9	VORP	SN/WX
2008	SBN	A	24	3	1	8	24	0	35¹	6	1	5	54	50%	.093	27	0.31	0.51	0.52	1.60	4.1	1.2	2.0	9.0	13.4	1.61
2009	MOB	AA	25	1	0	0	11	0	17¹	10	2	7	18	44%	.190	1	0.98	2.60	3.29	3.44	6.4	1.6	3.7	6.9	3.9	0.28
2009	ARI	MLB	25	3	3	0	49	0	51	45	5	24	52	33%	.292	11	1.35	3.35	3.85	3.59	7.7	0.7	3.5	7.9	10.9	0.49
2010	ARI	MLB	26	3	3	2	50	0	57¹	48	6	25	50	39%	.273	7	1.27	3.82	4.07	4.03	7.4	1.0	3.6	7.3	9.3	1.54

Breakout: 10%   Improve: 19%   Collapse: 47%   Attrition: 2%   MLB: 59%   Comparables: Robert Dodd, Bill Moloney, Mike Beard, Javier Lopez

Perhaps no other Diamondbacks player was as celebrated this offseason as Zavada, the recipient of the 2009 Robert Goulet Memorial Mustachioed American of the Year Award. Though there are absolutely no studies whatsoever backing this claim, it is our belief that the southpaw's handlebars distracted hitters to the point that it helped his strikeout rate. Zavada could stand to improve his control, and an extreme fly-baller in a bandbox is in no way the ideal recipe for success, but used in short spurts, he represents the type of cost-effective reliever that a team under financial constraints must call upon to get the job done. The only problem is that although Zavada will not be eligible for arbitration until 2011 at earliest, his facial hair will qualify in 2010.

LINEOUTS

Hitters

PLAYER	TEAM	LVL	AGE	PA	R	2B	3B	HR	RBI	BB	SO	SB-CS	EqBRR	AVG/OBP/SLG	EqAVG/EqOBP/EqSLG	EqA	VORP	WARP
C L. Carlin#	RNO	AAA	28	285	45	17	0	7	35	45	55	4-4	-1.4	.321/.430/.481	.253/.354/.363	.256	9.1	1.1
	ARI	MLB	28	21	3	0	0	0	1	3	3	0-0	-0.1	.167/.286/.167	.167/.286/.167	.164	-1.4	-0.5
SS P. Ciriaco	MOB	AA	23	497	56	15	3	4	54	16	71	38-10	1.9	.296/.319/.367	.276/.294/.339	.229	2.1	-0.9
C J. Hester	RNO	AAA	25	355	61	31	5	9	66	22	65	13-3	1.4	.328/.375/.535	.268/.311/.440	.257	12.6	1.5
	ARI	MLB	25	30	4	2	0	1	4	2	7	0-0	-0.2	.250/.300/.429	.250/.300/.429	.249	0.6	0.1
OF M. Krauss*	SBN	A	21	130	14	12	1	2	17	14	21	0-1	-2.7	.304/.377/.478	.271/.331/.424	.262	2.0	-0.3
OF T. Oeltjen*	RNO	AAA	26	488	78	29	14	10	64	31	101	22-8	1.2	.303/.362/.500	.242/.296/.393	.239	-2.2	-0.2
	ARI	MLB	26	73	11	4	1	3	4	1	13	3-1	-0.3	.243/.250/.457	.243/.250/.457	.242	-0.3	0.0
OF A. Pollock	SBN	A	21	277	36	12	3	3	22	16	36	10-4	1.9	.271/.319/.376	.241/.275/.337	.215	-4.9	-1.0
C J. Skelton*	VIS	A+	23	223	28	8	0	4	26	34	51	5-2	-1.4	.236/.359/.348	.193/.294/.267	.210	-4.7	-0.8
	MOB	AA	23	273	34	8	2	0	16	52	40	9-3	-1.1	.182/.341/.238	.173/.305/.227	.204	-4.1	-1.0

At 28 years old and with nothing to offer aside from the mere ability to catch, **Luke Carlin** is likely doomed to the major-league career path of Snakes skipper A. J. Hinch, if even that. ⊘ A very raw shortstop with modest defensive skills, **Pedro Ciriaco** has the ability to swipe bags, which would provide much more impact if he could actually reach base, but his defensive tools alone might get him to the big leagues. ⊘ **John Hester**'s minor-league on-base rates were inflated by unsustainable BABIP marks, but he does possess gap power and the ability to serve as a backup backstop. ⊘ Arizona's second-round pick in 2009, **Marc Krauss** earned mixed reviews in his pro debut. Massive but about as unathletic as they come, he plays a poor left field and will need to absolutely rake to earn a consistent gig in the majors. ⊘ **Trent Oeltjen** finally broke through to the majors after nine years in the bushes and made the most of it, but Reno's park produced the power, and fifth outfielderdom is a tough career path in the age of seven-man pens. ⊘ A budget 2009 first-round pick, **A. J. Pollock** has drawn mixed forecasts. Some see an outfielder capable of being a .280 to .290 hitter with 15 home runs and 20 stolen bases, while others feel that he's no more than a hustling tweener. Stay tuned. ⊘ Though he boasts an innate ability to reach base, **James Skelton**'s wiry frame leaves many wondering where he will settle on the diamond, because it doesn't seem likely to hold up behind the plate.

Pitchers

PLAYER	TEAM	LVL	AGE	W	L	SV	IP	H	HR	BB	SO	GB%	BABIP	STUFF	WHIP	ERA	SIERA	DERA	EqH9	EqHR9	EqBB9	EqSO9	VORP
T. Blackley*	RNO	AAA	26	4	7	3	111^1	133	11	38	101	52%	.357	2	1.54	4.85	3.79	4.88	10.0	0.9	3.1	6.9	7.6
J. Collmenter	VIS	A+	23	8	10	0	145^1	127	8	55	152	47%	.306	-1	1.25	4.15	3.32	5.61	9.0	1.3	4.2	5.8	-1.6
B. Enright	MOB	AA	23	10	9	0	156	171	16	37	103	49%	.309	-16	1.33	3.98	4.27	5.03	11.0	1.7	2.4	4.4	7.6
T. Gordon	ARI	MLB	41	0	1	0	1^2	3	0	3	0	98%	.429	-60	3.60	21.60	6.06	20.25	20.3	0.0	20.3	0.0	-2.2
B. Korecky	RNO	AAA	29	2	1	13	30	26	1	3	25	61%	.287	14	0.97	2.10	3.10	2.58	7.3	0.3	1.2	6.4	9.6
	ARI	MLB	29	0	0	0	6	11	0	4	3	42%	.440	-43	2.50	13.50	6.06	12.00	16.5	0.0	4.5	4.5	-4.3
S. Maine*	MOB	AA	24	3	3	5	47^1	56	2	15	46	50%	.383	-5	1.50	2.66	3.48	3.84	12.3	1.0	3.1	6.9	8.0
	RNO	AAA	24	1	2	2	14^2	13	0	7	15	57%	.302	4	1.36	3.68	3.69	4.11	7.0	0.6	4.1	7.6	2.4
J. Marte	RNO	AAA	25	4	1	2	71^2	68	3	34	63	58%	.307	5	1.42	4.52	4.06	4.31	7.9	0.5	4.1	6.6	9.5
P. McAnaney*	VIS	A+	23	10	8	0	147	162	19	47	146	34%	.347	-27	1.42	4.41	3.48	5.89	11.5	2.2	3.8	5.5	-5.8
R. Mercedes	BRV	A+	22	1	1	6	41^2	26	0	15	45	37%	.248	10	0.98	1.08	3.06	3.08	8.1	0.7	4.3	6.4	10.2
	MOB	AA	22	1	0	1	19	14	2	10	25	57%	.273	15	1.26	3.32	2.94	4.17	7.9	2.0	4.4	8.8	2.7
K. Newby	MOB	AA	24	2	3	4	65^1	67	10	24	48	42%	.282	-33	1.39	3.99	4.46	5.57	10.3	2.3	3.4	4.7	-0.5
J. Norberto*	VIS	A+	22	4	1	2	44^2	36	1	22	59	50%	.340	13	1.30	1.61	2.75	2.47	9.0	0.9	5.4	7.9	13.4
	MOB	AA	22	0	2	2	23^2	29	4	18	30	48%	.385	-4	1.99	7.99	3.90	10.13	13.1	2.8	6.8	8.7	-11.6
W. Roemer	VIS	A+	22	3	1	0	30^2	33	0	13	18	60%	.327	-14	1.50	2.05	4.70	5.08	10.5	1.0	4.8	2.9	1.3
	MOB	AA	22	9	9	0	134^2	132	13	43	98	50%	.291	-3	1.30	4.28	4.23	5.63	10.0	1.6	3.0	4.8	-1.9
L. Rosales	RNO	AAA	28	2	1	3	19^1	12	1	8	12	53%	.200	-6	1.03	1.40	4.69	1.40	5.1	0.5	3.7	4.7	8.8
	ARI	MLB	28	2	1	0	45^1	40	5	12	31	39%	.254	0	1.15	4.76	4.33	4.30	7.4	0.8	2.0	5.3	6.1
L. Septimo*	VIS	A+	23	2	1	6	38^1	29	1	26	44	41%	.295	1	1.43	3.52	3.87	5.05	8.3	1.0	7.1	6.3	1.8
	MOB	AA	23	0	1	3	18^1	20	2	18	25	72%	.383	4	2.07	7.85	3.90	9.68	11.7	2.0	8.2	9.2	-8.2
D. Slaten*	RNO	AAA	29	3	2	9	43^2	41	3	15	40	56%	.309	7	1.28	3.09	3.58	3.38	8.0	0.6	3.2	7.2	10.1
	ARI	MLB	29	0	0	0	6^1	10	1	1	4	59%	.375	-13	1.74	7.11	4.27	6.75	12.2	1.4	1.4	4.1	-0.9
D. Stange	MOB	AA	23	0	4	10	51^2	66	4	15	44	50%	.363	-19	1.57	4.88	3.89	7.11	12.4	1.4	2.7	5.6	-8.9
M. Torra	MOB	AA	25	10	13	0	180	192	24	28	116	45%	.294	-23	1.22	3.75	4.11	5.43	10.8	2.1	1.7	4.3	1.3

Travis Blackley has bounced around four organizations in as many seasons, but he could serve as a lefty specialist if his modest fastball velocity returns. ⊘ **Joshua Collmenter** lacks upside, having just completed a year in High-A as a 23-year-old, but he averages over a whiff per frame and keeps the ball in the yard. ⊘ **Barry Enright** lacks plus stuff but knows how to utilize his skills. Barring vast improvement in his changeup, he is best suited for relief duty. ⊘ **Tom "Flash" Gordon** started the year on the disabled list (DL) and, three games into his return, strained his hamstring covering home plate on a wild pitch, then embarked on a never-ending rehab assignment, and was finally released. Given his age and fragility, it's hard to imagine that Flash will ever again make an impact. ⊘ At 30, **Bobby Korecky** is no longer a prospect, but he could latch onto a bullpen spot if some semblance of his control manifests itself in the bigs. ⊘ A southpaw reliever with very impressive strikeout rates in Double- and Triple-A last season, **Scott Maine** could fight for a bullpen spot with the Cubs, who acquired him for Aaron Heilman in November. ⊘ A big Dominican (6' 6") picked up from the Rangers for Dustin Nippert in March 2008, **Jose Marte** survived the challenge of altitude in Reno well enough to get added to the 40-man roster. ⊘ **Patrick McAnaney** lacks plus velocity but boasts solid command and control; he may wind up being best suited for long relief and spot starts. ⊘ **Roque Mercedes** is a hard-throwing lefty added from the Brewers in the F-Lop exchange, and although he flopped as a starter after being a big-bonus Dominican signing, relief work might get him fast-tracked now that he's on a 40-man. ⊘ It's worth wondering if Rule 5 hysteria has gone too far when **Kyler Newby**, something of a finesse-and-deception righty reliever who let fellow righties slug nearly .500 against him last year, gets protected. ⊘ In the gaggle of hard-throwing lefty Snakelings, **Jordan Norberto**'s fastball might be the one that stands out enough to eventually make him a late-game asset. ⊘ A reputed master of precision control, **Wes Roemer** posted a lower walk rate in Double-A last season, but he'll need to continue that trend to remain successful, given less-than-dazzling stuff. ⊘ **Leo Rosales** posted solid peripherals last season due to a crazy-good changeup, but at his age, he's not going to develop beyond being bullpen filler. ⊘ An outfielder converted to the mound, **Leyson Septimo** has no trouble missing bats, but he offers absolutely no control whatsoever. ⊘ Lacking any standout abilities beyond left-handedness, **Doug Slaten** was snagged by the Nationals via waivers and will try to stick as a secondary southpaw. ⊘ **Daniel Stange** can touch the high 90s with his heat and can mix in a good slider, but he struggled terribly with his location and got hammered after a good start. ⊘ An altered pitching philosophy designed to incorporate more secondary offerings helped **Matt Torra** post a career-best 4.1 strikeout/walk ratio last season.

MANAGER: BOB MELVIN/A. J. HINCH

YEAR	MGR	W-L	Pythag +/−	Avg PC	100+ P	120+ P	QS	BQS	REL	REL w Zero R	IBB	Subs	PH	PH Avg	PH HR	SB2	CS2	SB3	CS3	SAC Att	SAC %	POS SAC	Squeeze	Swing	In Play
2007	B.M.	90-72	11	94.9	68	4	80	7	469	314	38	77	240	.243	12	90	16	18	8	79	69.6%	26	0	118	89
2008	B.M.	82-80	-1	95.8	56	3	94	4	443	292	41	52	257	.226	3	46	16	12	5	97	70.1%	29	1	121	89
2009	B.M.	12-17	0	96.1	11	0	16	2	91	53	3	11	47	.209	3	16	7	5	1	18	50.0%	6	0	25	17
2009	A.J.H.	58-75	-4	99.0	79	0	70	5	392	238	24	25	220	.185	5	68	22	13	9	74	60.8%	24	1	98	66

A former journeyman backup catcher who saw major-league service in parts of seven seasons, Hinch took over the reins from Bob Melvin after the latter's 12-17 start. The director of player development prior to undertaking the skipper's post, Hinch had never managed at any level and rated a good deal of media skepticism because of that. "The lack of experience is overwhelmed by understanding what organizational advocacy is," GM Josh Byrnes answered back. Hinch may have advocated effectively, but his inexperience did show up in his staff handling. Middle of the pack as far as blown quality starts goes, he ranked third among all managers with an average pitch count of 99 per game while finishing in the bottom tier with regards to scoreless relief outings. Still, Hinch performed about as well as anyone could have expected with an injury-depleted club that liquidated several veterans, but he will be tested next season as the high expectations from a healthy and developing team will surely persist.

Atlanta Braves

In January 2007, the Braves traded first baseman Adam LaRoche to the Pirates in exchange for reliever Mike Gonzalez and minor-league shortstop Brent Lillibridge. The deal was straightforward enough: the Braves needed a late-inning reliever and figured that a combination of Scott Thorman, Craig Wilson, and Julio Franco could adequately replace the perpetually adequate LaRoche. As it turned out, the first-base group wasn't up to the task, and the LaRoche-Gonzalez trade ended up setting off a three-year merry-go-round at the position that would ultimately cost the Braves five of their top prospects (several of whom made an impact in the big leagues in 2009) along with a decent chunk of cash. The ride ended this past year with none other than Adam LaRoche back at first base. With exactly zero playoff appearances in between, that chain of events won't quite go down as the best branch on the Braves' decision tree.

In between, of course, the Braves traded the farm for Mark Teixeira, sending five players to Texas in an attempt to close the gap with the Phillies and the Mets. It wasn't a horrible idea, on its face, even considering the players going the other way. Had the Braves won the World Series or even made the postseason during Teixeira's tenure with the team, the deal could have paid off. It didn't, and therein lies the risk: giving up money, or talent, or just about any other asset, can be a zero-sum game. Once it's gone, it's not going to reappear when you need it later. And from that vantage point, the Braves could have been in a much better position heading into 2010.

The 2009 Braves were actually a pretty good team despite missing the playoffs for the fourth straight year.

BRAVES PROSPECTUS
2009 W-L: 86-76, 3rd in NL East

Pythag	88-74	3rd
RS/G	4.5	6th
RA/G	4.0	4th
EqA	.265	4th
EqBRR	-15.7	16th
SNWP	.549	2nd
WXRL	8.33	6th
FRAr	4.18	5th
DE	.687	13th
PADE	-1.12	10th
Salary	$96.7	6th
Attend	2.37	10th

Ballpark: Turner Field (3-yr. PF: 971). The place is getting as comfortable as an old shoe for pitchers

2009: A bad first-half outfield holds back a team with a first-place finish in third-order wins. Feel any better, Braves fans?

2010: A strong rotation needs better run support to send Bobby Cox out with at least a division title

Action Items: Quality work from the new veteran relievers, offense from first base, an outfielder (Heyward?)

They ranked first in the NL East according to BP's third-order standings (which take into account how many runs each team *should* have scored and allowed, as well as the quality of competition), finishing two up on the eventual division champion Phillies, and they placed third in the National League overall. That wasn't a fluke, either: PECOTA had projected them to win 87 games, just one lower than their third-order win total, and one higher than their actual win total.

If it seemed that the Braves weren't quite as good as their record, it's because they spent most of the season chasing their own tail, never mind Philadelphia's. Atlanta lost 40 of its first 74 games and was being handily outscored by its opponents during that time. On June 27th, in a game that would epitomize the first half of the Braves' season, Javier Vazquez pitched 7 ⅔ innings, allowing one run on eight strikeouts and three walks, only to see the effort wasted in a 1-0 loss to Boston. In what would be one of his final games with his hometown team, struggling outfielder Jeff Francoeur went 0 for 3—on seven total pitches.

After that game, the Braves started turning things around. From June 28th on, Atlanta had the third-best record in the NL, trailing only Philadelphia and Colorado, and produced the best run differential in the major leagues, outscoring opponents by 116 runs in its final 88 games. (The Yankees were second, with a 109-run differential.)

Atlanta had righted the ship partly through addition by subtraction. Center fielder Jordan Schafer began the year as the big club's starter, but was sent back down to Triple-A Gwinnett on June 2nd after hitting .204/.313/.287 in just under 200 plate appearances. A day later, the Braves traded three prospects to Pittsburgh for center fielder Nate McLouth, who by dint of sheer unspectacular competence was a major upgrade. Just a few weeks after that, a similar story would play out in right field as well, as Francoeur was mercifully shipped to the Mets for Ryan Church.

With those changes in place, as well as a shift from the struggling Kelly Johnson to the red-hot Martin Prado at second base, the Braves surged through late September, coming within just two games of the wild-card-leading Rockies on the final Monday of the season. The wheels came off in that last week, as the team lost its final six games (four by one run, one by two runs, and one by three runs) to finish seven games behind Philadelphia in the East, and six behind Colorado in the wild-card race. But at the very least, the Braves made their presence known and gave their fans something to cheer about in September.

Considering how close they came, it's hard not to wonder what the team would have looked like had they *not* made the Teixeira trade. In hindsight, it's pretty easy to say that the trade brought the Braves virtually zero long-term value: with Teixeira on board, they fell a few games short of the playoffs in 2007 and fell out of the race quickly in the first half of 2008. Casey Kotchman, who the Braves received from the Angels in exchange for Teixeira, failed to establish himself at first base in his year with the Braves and was traded for the free-agent-to-be La Roche this past July.

For argument's sake, let's say the Teixeira deal had never happened. Obviously, the Braves wouldn't have been much worse off in 2007 and '08, as they could have missed the playoffs just as easily without Teixeira. Had all five players who went to Texas stayed in the Atlanta organization, could they have pushed the Braves over the hump in 2009? And even more importantly, what would they have meant to the franchise going forward?

Neftali Feliz: The Braves' pitching staff was excellent in '09, leading the majors in SIERA (for more on SIERA, check out the book's introduction or the Arizona team essay), but Feliz would have only made it that much better. The righty dominated the minor leagues as a starter and was virtually unhittable in the big leagues as a reliever; Atlanta's bullpen was good, but not so good that it couldn't have used an extra 31 innings with 39 strikeouts against just eight walks and six runs allowed. Looking forward, if Feliz can continue his success in the big leagues as a starter, he alone will make the trade a blowout loss for Atlanta.

Elvis Andrus: Andrus had a better-than-expected rookie year, but he wouldn't have had much of a role with the 2009 Braves. Shortstop Yunel Escobar should be entering the prime of his career, and while Andrus could certainly play second base, his value to the Braves probably would have been as a trade chip. Still, given what we now know about him—his bat played much better than expected last season, to go with an already solid glove—his value is certainly higher now than it was at the time of the Teixeira deal.

Jarrod Saltalamacchia: Salty was never going to be the Braves' catcher, not unless Brian McCann was hit by a truck, and he hasn't panned out as well as the Rangers (or the Braves, at one point) had hoped. Atlanta may have unloaded him at his peak value, and they're probably not losing sleep at night over losing him.

Matt Harrison: Harrison is still a work in progress, and much like Andrus and Saltalamacchia, he wouldn't have had much of a role with the Braves last season. He struggled at the big-league level and hasn't missed many bats at any level over the past couple of years. Whether he becomes a quality major-league starter is still up for debate, but as of now, he's closer to Salty than Feliz.

Beau Jones: Jones spent most of the year at Double-A, and while he has performed well as a reliever over the past couple of seasons, he probably won't ever have the Braves kicking themselves too badly. Guys like Jones are nice to have around, but they're also perfect add-ons in multiplayer trades.

The Braves parted with a solid group, and with hindsight, they would probably love to have them back, but these players would not have put Atlanta in the playoffs last year. The Braves, however, would no doubt be far better off going forward if the Teixeira trade had never happened—Feliz alone makes that an easy decision. They also would have saved about $11 million, which could have been used at a time when the team had a better shot at actually making the postseason.

Frustrating as it may be, the cost is sunk, and the Braves can only try to look forward. Heading into 2010, things are much the same. Atlanta's lineup will feature at least four everyday players already into what is a ballplayer's traditional prime age—McCann (26), Escobar (27), McLouth (28), and Prado (26)—plus a no-doubt Hall of Famer just a season removed from hitting .364 in Chipper Jones, and a potential Rookie of the Year candidate, in the form of outfielder Jason Heyward. However, their decision to settle for retaining Matt Diaz while adding Melky Cabrera via trade and signing veterans Troy Glaus and Eric Hinske to one-year deals seems like a cheap patch job to fix up the lineup..

The bigger question is whether the pitching staff can repeat its outstanding 2009 performance. Javier

Vazquez had a career year, so they elected to trade him when his value was at its highest, dealing the last year of his deal to the Yankees for Melky Cabrera plus pitching prospects Mike Dunn and Arodys Vizcaino. Beyond Vazquez, rookie Tommy Hanson and returning Tommy John'd vet Tim Hudson were terrific as well, while free-agent signee Derek Lowe was decent enough in his first year in Atlanta, albeit well below his previously established level. The biggest wild card might be Jair Jurrjens, who lit up the traditional stat-sheet with a 14-10 record and 2.60 ERA, but his peripherals didn't quite match, as his SIERA was a more pedestrian 4.31.

Altogether, the Braves were fourth in runs allowed, third in ERA, and, as mentioned before, first in SIERA. They'll need to bring some of that mojo back for 2010 if they're going to compete with the Phillies. It would certainly be a fitting end for Bobby Cox, in his final year as Braves manager, if Atlanta could make one more playoff run on the back of its pitching staff, just as they did 14 times from 1991 to 2005.

HITTERS

Garret Anderson — LF

Bats: L   Throws: L   Height: 6' 3"   Weight: 225   Born: June 30, 1972   Age: 38

YEAR	TEAM	LVL	AGE	PA	R	2B	3B	HR	RBI	BB	SO	SB	CS	EqBRR	AVG	OBP	SLG	EqAVG	EqOBP	EqSLG	EqA	VORP	WARP	DEFENSE	
2007	LAA	MLB	35	450	67	31	1	16	80	27	54	1	0	1.0	.297	.336	.492	.292	.331	.487	.278	17.0	2.1	82-LF	2
2008	LAA	MLB	36	593	66	27	3	15	84	29	77	7	4	-4.4	.293	.325	.433	.294	.327	.436	.262	10.1	1.8	77-LF	6
2009	ATL	MLB	37	534	52	27	0	13	61	27	73	1	0	-0.5	.268	.303	.401	.279	.311	.417	.253	5.7	0.7	114-LF	0
2010	ATL	MLB	38	441	44	19	1	12	60	29	67	2	2	-0.5	.257	.308	.393	.267	.314	.406	.248	3.7	0.5	78-LF	1

Breakout: 3%   Improve: 26%   Collapse: 31%   Attrition: 27%   MLB: 97%   Comparables: Paul O'Neill, Ruben Sierra, Ken Griffey Sr., B.J. Surhoff

Anderson was signed as a last-minute (February 22nd), inexpensive stopgap for left field, and the Braves got what they paid for; Anderson was overrated in his prime, so 500 at-bats out of his decline phase didn't help. The Braves paid a higher price than just Anderson's salary, because another February free-agent outfielder like Adam Dunn or Bobby Abreu might have put them in the playoffs. Understandably bitter, the Braves weren't interesting in bringing Anderson back, but after reaching 2,500 career hits, Anderson has his sights set on 3,000, a goal that would require four more years of teams giving him far more playing time than he deserves.

Gregor Blanco — CF

Bats: L   Throws: L   Height: 5' 11"   Weight: 170   Born: December 24, 1983   Age: 26

YEAR	TEAM	LVL	AGE	PA	R	2B	3B	HR	RBI	BB	SO	SB	CS	EqBRR	AVG	OBP	SLG	EqAVG	EqOBP	EqSLG	EqA	VORP	WARP	DEFENSE			
2007	RIC	AAA	23	545	81	18	5	3	35	63	85	23	18	-6.2	.282	.369	.362	.271	.351	.347	.249	8.8	1.8	118-CF	6		
2008	ATL	MLB	24	519	52	14	4	1	38	74	99	13	5	0.7	.251	.366	.309	.266	.377	.324	.260	11.2	0.4	58-LF	-3	56-CF	-4
2009	GWN	AAA	25	397	54	9	1	2	30	50	70	10	3	1.7	.228	.326	.279	.223	.317	.271	.222	-4.3	-0.9	85-CF	-3		
2009	ATL	MLB	25	48	5	0	1	0	1	4	9	2	0	0.4	.186	.255	.233	.182	.250	.227	.188	-3.1	-0.4	8-CF	0		
2010	ATL	MLB	26	434	54	15	3	3	32	52	91	9	5	-0.5	.238	.332	.318	.244	.334	.326	.241	4.6	0.5	96-CF	0		

Breakout: 7%   Improve: 33%   Collapse: 21%   Attrition: 16%   MLB: 60%   Comparables: Sebastien Boucher, Mike Curry, Tony Gwynn, Scott Lusader

After playing 144 games in 2008, Blanco lost the center-field job to Jordan Schafer in the spring and was basically never heard from again, other than a few starts in June, even after Schafer struggled. Blanco's year at Triple-A was exactly as expected—Blanco's good-but-not-great on-base skills represent the sum of his offensive value. By not even giving Blanco a call when rosters expanded in September, the Braves indicated that he's officially in purgatory.

Barbaro Canizares — 1B

Bats: R Throws: R Height: 6' 3" Weight: 210 Born: November 21, 1979 Age: 30

YEAR	TEAM	LVL	AGE	PA	R	2B	3B	HR	RBI	BB	SO	SB	CS	EqBRR	AVG	OBP	SLG	EqAVG	EqOBP	EqSLG	EqA	VORP	WARP	DEFENSE		
2007	RIC	AAA	27	182	24	13	1	3	34	12	28	0	0	-0.8	.344	.390	.491	.315	.354	.455	.280	5.8	0.2	35-1B	-4	
2008	RIC	AAA	28	553	56	28	0	13	67	43	69	1	0	-5.0	.300	.353	.433	.273	.321	.386	.248	-1.7	-1.0	62-1B	-7	
2009	GWN	AAA	29	569	55	31	2	12	79	52	67	2	2	-4.7	.294	.366	.435	.281	.344	.409	.263	1.6	-1.1	88-1B	-11	
2009	ATL	MLB	29	21	1	1	0	0	0	0	6	0	0	0.1	.190	.190	.238	.190	.190	.238	.104	-2.6	-0.5	5-1B	-2	
2010	ATL	MLB	30	486	44	22	1	9	61	39	80	1	1	-1.9	.264	.328	.380	.269	.330	.391	.254	2.1	-0.3	71-1B	-4	

Breakout: 8% Improve: 33% Collapse: 17% Attrition: 16%   MLB: 11%   Comparables: Chan Perry, Brick Smith, Jesse Gutierrez, Luis Lopez

The rare Cuban who signed with little fanfare, Canizares was already 26 when he made his stateside debut for High-A Myrtle Beach, and while he's a career .306 hitter in the minors, he was already pushing 30 when necessity led to a five-game stint in the big leagues. He doesn't have much power, swings at everything, and is an embarrassingly bad defender, so don't be surprised if that ends up being the sum of his major-league service time. At least he gets to live in the land of the free, home of the brave, and all of that swell stuff.

Ryan Church — RF

Bats: L Throws: L Height: 6' 1" Weight: 190 Born: October 14, 1978 Age: 31

YEAR	TEAM	LVL	AGE	PA	R	2B	3B	HR	RBI	BB	SO	SB	CS	EqBRR	AVG	OBP	SLG	EqAVG	EqOBP	EqSLG	EqA	VORP	WARP	DEFENSE				
2007	WAS	MLB	28	530	57	43	1	15	70	49	107	3	2	1.7	.272	.349	.464	.288	.363	.490	.288	28.8	4.7	81-LF	10	37-CF	2
2008	NYN	MLB	29	359	54	14	1	12	49	33	83	2	3	0.7	.276	.346	.439	.292	.358	.464	.278	14.0	2.0	80-RF	3		
2009	NYN	MLB	30	255	26	16	0	2	22	17	36	6	2	0.8	.280	.332	.375	.292	.341	.391	.260	4.9	0.7	53-RF	3	6-CF	-2
2009	ATL	MLB	30	144	20	12	0	2	18	16	22	0	0	0.4	.260	.347	.402	.273	.359	.414	.270	4.8	0.2	19-RF	3	14-CF	-6
2010	PIT	NL	31	431	47	21	1	11	54	41	87	3	3	1.2	.270	.349	.416	.265	.343	.411	.267	12.3	1.7	97-RF	3		

Breakout: 6% Improve: 31% Collapse: 17% Attrition: 16%   MLB: 94%   Comparables: Joe Orsulak, Orlando Merced, Irv Noren, Rick Leach

The Braves lost the challenge trade of Jeff Francoeur to the Mets for Church. While Frenchy gave the Mets a performance (fluke or not) that the Braves were unable to extract from the stubborn outfielder, Church was mediocre at best. He's always been stretched as an everyday outfielder and has problems staying healthy, and making nearly $3 million a year, he was a luxury as a fourth outfielder so he was non-tendered in December.

Matt Diaz — OF

Bats: R Throws: R Height: 6' 1" Weight: 215 Born: March 3, 1978 Age: 32

YEAR	TEAM	LVL	AGE	PA	R	2B	3B	HR	RBI	BB	SO	SB	CS	EqBRR	AVG	OBP	SLG	EqAVG	EqOBP	EqSLG	EqA	VORP	WARP	DEFENSE				
2007	ATL	MLB	29	384	44	21	0	12	45	16	63	0	0	-1.5	.338	.368	.497	.347	.376	.510	.302	25.1	3.4	76-LF	4	2-RF	1
2008	ATL	MLB	30	140	9	2	0	2	14	3	32	4	2	0.8	.244	.264	.304	.252	.271	.311	.202	-5.8	-0.7	33-LF	0		
2009	ATL	MLB	31	425	56	18	4	13	58	35	90	12	5	-2.6	.313	.390	.488	.334	.408	.524	.312	33.8	2.9	60-RF	-6	33-LF	-2
2010	ATL	MLB	32	365	39	16	1	9	43	26	77	6	3	-0.8	.277	.338	.414	.284	.342	.428	.269	11.3	0.9	79-RF	-3		

Breakout: 3% Improve: 25% Collapse: 25% Attrition: 18%   MLB: 94%   Comparables: Brian Jordan, Marty Cordova, Rondell White, Derek Bell

Diaz's 2009 season will be remembered for a brutal base-running gaffe that ended the Braves' long-shot chances at a post-season slot, but the Braves wouldn't even have been in position to make a bid for October without Diaz's hot hitting down the stretch, commencing with the .404/.467/.681 line he put up in August after the Francoeur deal freed him to play every day. Nothing about Diaz's game is pretty. He doesn't run well, is a bad outfielder, doesn't work the count, and has middling power, but he's also a career .310 hitter. Though in a perfect world Diaz would get only 300 at-bats a year as part of a stronger overall outfield, there's still plenty of value here.

Yunel Escobar — SS

Bats: R Throws: R Height: 6' 2" Weight: 200 Born: November 2, 1982 Age: 27

YEAR	TEAM	LVL	AGE	PA	R	2B	3B	HR	RBI	BB	SO	SB	CS	EqBRR	AVG	OBP	SLG	EqAVG	EqOBP	EqSLG	EqA	VORP	WARP	DEFENSE				
2007	RIC	AAA	24	194	20	10	3	2	29	14	27	7	3	1.4	.333	.379	.456	.315	.359	.436	.277	10.7	1.3	45-SS	0		
2007	ATL	MLB	24	355	54	25	0	5	28	27	44	5	3	0.6	.326	.385	.451	.339	.397	.467	.296	25.7	2.8	40-SS	0	18-3B	0
2008	ATL	MLB	25	587	71	24	2	10	60	59	62	2	5	0.9	.288	.366	.401	.302	.376	.420	.275	31.5	5.1	124-SS	12		
2009	ATL	MLB	26	604	89	26	2	14	76	57	62	5	4	0.5	.299	.377	.436	.318	.390	.464	.293	45.0	7.3	134-SS	17		
2010	ATL	MLB	27	617	83	27	4	14	72	60	74	6	5	0.6	.297	.373	.435	.302	.375	.443	.289	40.8	5.0	131-SS	6		

Breakout: 9% Improve: 46% Collapse: 6% Attrition: 3%   MLB: 97%   Comparables: Edgar Renteria, Jim Fregosi, Lou Boudreau, Carney Lansford

There was some talk early in the season that the Braves were looking to move Escobar, as manager Bobby Cox and other franchise leaders had gotten tired of the shortstop's histrionics. He never really was on the block, though, as he's just too talented to give up on, and he rewarded the team's patience with the fourth-highest WARP among shortstops. There's still more power coming as well, as scouts think he can hit upward of 20 bombs a year, while his defense remains rock-solid; he made two errors (count 'em—two) over the last 75 games of the season. With this kind of performance, a team will put up with a little difficulty behavior-wise.

Freddie Freeman   **1B**   Bats: L   Throws: R   Height: 6' 5"   Weight: 220   Born: September 12, 1989   Age: 20

YEAR	TEAM	LVL	AGE	PA	R	2B	3B	HR	RBI	BB	SO	SB	CS	EqBRR	AVG	OBP	SLG	EqAVG	EqOBP	EqSLG	EqA	VORP	WARP	DEFENSE			
2007	BRA	Rk	17	234	24	7	0	6	30	7	33	1	2	-2.6	.268	.295	.379	.237	.255	.325	.196	-12.6	-3.7	49-1B	-5	6-3B	-2
2008	ROM	A	18	540	70	33	7	18	95	46	84	5	5	-5.1	.316	.378	.521	.287	.341	.453	.270	11.3	0.2	120-1B	-10		
2009	MYR	A+	19	297	43	19	0	6	34	26	41	1	4	-2.7	.302	.394	.447	.287	.357	.411	.268	2.5	-0.2	66-1B	-4		
2009	MIS	AA	19	169	15	8	0	2	24	11	19	0	0	-1.1	.248	.308	.342	.248	.294	.340	.227	-6.0	-1.5	40-1B	-6		
2010	ATL	MLB	20	581	64	28	3	15	74	48	102	3	3	-2.6	.269	.339	.422	.277	.343	.435	.270	12.9	0.8	133-1B	-6		

Breakout: 32%   Improve: 60%   Collapse: 12%   Attrition: 1%   MLB: 0%   Comparables: Eric Perry, Lee Stevens, Derrick May, Ben Grieve

Freeman looked like one of the better young hitters around in 2008, when he hit .316/.378/.521 for Low-A Rome as an 18-year-old, but some holes were exposed in his game last year. While a hand injury is something of a mitigating factor, Freeman still hasn't tapped into his raw power and remains an impatient hitter at the plate. First-base prospects can't just be good hitters; they have to be great ones. Most scouts project Freeman as more of a high-average, 20-homer, 50-walk guy, and that's merely average for the position.

Diory Hernandez   **SS**   Bats: R   Throws: R   Height: 6' 0"   Weight: 185   Born: April 8, 1984   Age: 26

YEAR	TEAM	LVL	AGE	PA	R	2B	3B	HR	RBI	BB	SO	SB	CS	EqBRR	AVG	OBP	SLG	EqAVG	EqOBP	EqSLG	EqA	VORP	WARP	DEFENSE			
2007	MYR	A+	23	67	9	8	2	0	9	2	11	2	2	-1.1	.313	.343	.500	.277	.299	.446	.250	1.3	0.2	14-2B	0		
2007	MIS	AA	23	481	50	25	1	7	59	29	68	22	20	-4.3	.307	.370	.418	.294	.343	.396	.254	14.1	0.4	78-SS	-12	33-2B	1
2008	MIS	AA	24	85	8	3	1	2	8	6	8	1	4	-1.5	.286	.341	.429	.266	.314	.405	.245	1.7	-0.3	11-2B	-3	9-SS	-1
2008	RIC	AAA	24	490	46	23	3	5	53	20	73	7	5	-2.8	.288	.317	.383	.269	.298	.358	.229	-0.4	0.8	51-2B	1	35-3B	2
2009	GWN	AAA	25	234	18	16	1	1	32	21	34	8	6	-2.2	.319	.399	.422	.311	.386	.413	.279	13.4	1.5	52-SS	-1		
2009	ATL	MLB	25	93	6	3	0	1	6	6	22	0	1	0.2	.141	.198	.212	.128	.185	.186	.093	-8.5	-0.6	20-SS	1	1-2B	0
2010	ATL	MLB	26	400	36	20	2	6	43	27	74	7	5	-1.7	.258	.315	.368	.262	.318	.375	.244	7.7	0.5	83-SS	-3		

Breakout: 13%   Improve: 44%   Collapse: 19%   Attrition: 13%   MLB: 42%   Comparables: Jeff Forney, Ron Pezzoni, Ira Smith, Ken Pennington

The Braves must have felt like the victims of some kind of bait-and-switch when they called up Hernandez in late May due to a hip injury suffered by Yunel Escobar. With Hernandez hitting .355 at Triple-A at the time of the call, the Braves thought they'd get a guy who could hit, but whose defense at short might fall a little ... short. Instead, he shocked the team with his defensive prowess, but to say he didn't hit a lick would be too kind. The team hopes Hernandez, a .301/.350/.411 hitter in the minors over the last three years, was suffering from first-time jitters and adjusting to not playing every day. He can still turn into a solid bench player.

Jason Heyward   **RF**   Bats: L   Throws: L   Height: 6' 4"   Weight: 220   Born: August 9, 1989   Age: 20

YEAR	TEAM	LVL	AGE	PA	R	2B	3B	HR	RBI	BB	SO	SB	CS	EqBRR	AVG	OBP	SLG	EqAVG	EqOBP	EqSLG	EqA	VORP	WARP	DEFENSE			
2007	BRA	Rk	17	31	1	4	0	1	5	2	4	1	1	-0.7	.296	.355	.556	.286	.323	.536	.287	1.5	0.3	6-RF	0		
2008	ROM	A	18	508	88	27	6	11	52	49	74	15	3	3.9	.323	.388	.483	.295	.352	.434	.275	16.9	2.2	99-RF	0	4-CF	1
2009	MYR	A+	19	214	34	12	0	10	31	21	30	4	0	0.4	.296	.369	.519	.275	.333	.461	.274	7.0	1.1	32-RF	3	8-CF	-1
2009	MIS	AA	19	195	32	13	4	7	30	28	19	5	1	1.2	.352	.446	.611	.345	.421	.607	.339	21.5	3.1	41-RF	5		
2010	ATL	MLB	20	471	67	25	4	16	54	45	79	6	2	1.6	.277	.350	.473	.287	.355	.485	.289	25.9	3.1	93-RF	2		

Breakout: 32%   Improve: 65%   Collapse: 5%   Attrition: 6%   MLB: 7%   Comparables: Derrick May, Tony Tarasco, Carlos Gonzalez, Felix Pie

Despite having had just one full season as a pro under his belt, Heyward spent a surprisingly long time in big-league camp last spring. The reason turned out to be that manager Bobby Cox just liked watching him play so darn much.

Arguably the best position-player prospect in the game, Heyward is a big athlete who possesses the plate discipline of a veteran, the rare combination of raw power and a knack for hard contact, and average speed (if not a bit better than that). He also provides good outfield play and a strong arm. There's really nothing he can't do. This spring, Heyward will get an honest chance to be the Opening Day right fielder. He has face-of-the-franchise potential, and the Braves would love to have a young African American star in a city that is more than 50 percent African American.

Omar Infante   **UT**   Bats: R   Throws: R   Height: 6' 0"   Weight: 180   Born: December 26, 1981   Age: 28

YEAR	TEAM	LVL	AGE	PA	R	2B	3B	HR	RBI	BB	SO	SB	CS	EqBRR	AVG	OBP	SLG	EqAVG	EqOBP	EqSLG	EqA	VORP	WARP	DEFENSE			
2007	DET	MLB	25	178	24	6	1	2	17	9	29	4	1	1.0	.271	.307	.355	.273	.309	.358	.236	0.8	0.0	14-2B	0	9-SS	-2
2008	ATL	MLB	26	348	45	24	3	3	40	22	44	0	1	-3.4	.293	.338	.416	.307	.347	.430	.269	13.0	1.7	26-3B	1	25-LF	-2
2009	ATL	MLB	27	229	24	9	1	2	27	19	28	2	0	1.6	.305	.361	.389	.325	.374	.409	.280	11.6	1.2	22-2B	-2	8-SS	0
2010	ATL	MLB	28	411	52	21	2	6	50	33	62	3	1	-0.1	.287	.347	.398	.291	.349	.404	.269	16.4	1.6	57-2B	-2		

Breakout: 11%   Improve: 42%   Collapse: 8%   Attrition: 6%   MLB: 96%   Comparables: Davey Johnson, Jose Lind, Felix Millan, Dave Cash

If a team plays Infante every day, the holes in his game will be exposed, but he's one of the better bench players around. An excellent fastball hitter who sprays line drives all over the field, Infante can fill in at six positions, can run a bit, and rarely hurts you with fundamental mistakes. He's signed through 2010 with a club option for the following year, and at $4.75 million for the two years, he's a bargain as a playable space-saver on the roster.

Cody Johnson   **LF**   Bats: L   Throws: R   Height: 6' 4"   Weight: 195   Born: August 18, 1988   Age: 21

YEAR	TEAM	LVL	AGE	PA	R	2B	3B	HR	RBI	BB	SO	SB	CS	EqBRR	AVG	OBP	SLG	EqAVG	EqOBP	EqSLG	EqA	VORP	WARP	DEFENSE			
2007	DNV	Rk	18	270	51	18	5	17	57	26	72	7	0	-1.5	.305	.374	.630	.251	.301	.462	.259	4.4	-0.7	50-LF	-9		
2008	ROM	A	19	514	62	26	1	26	89	40	177	8	3	-2.1	.252	.307	.479	.217	.267	.390	.226	-9.8	-3.5	105-LF	-19		
2009	MYR	A+	20	493	59	18	1	32	84	64	171	10	7	-3.9	.242	.345	.517	.217	.303	.442	.254	3.8	-1.4	82-LF	-14	8-RF	-2
2010	ATL	MLB	21	523	52	21	1	24	67	48	179	5	3	-1.1	.217	.291	.418	.224	.294	.430	.249	4.8	-0.4	101-LF	-9		

Breakout: 26%   Improve: 56%   Collapse: 6%   Attrition: 3%   MLB: 3%   Comparables: Van Snider, Chad Whitaker, Kevin King, Greg Blosser

Hitting 32 home runs in High-A is an impressive achievement, but to do so in one of the best pitcher's parks around is borderline remarkable. Johnson has as much pure power as anyone in the game, launching multiple 500-foot shots last year, but that's also the sum of his skills, as he strikes out a rate that would make Mark Reynolds blush and is a laughably bad defensive player in left field. He's in the wrong league for now, and even American League teams won't come calling unless he proves something at the upper levels.

Kelly Johnson   **2B**   Bats: L   Throws: R   Height: 6' 1"   Weight: 205   Born: February 22, 1982   Age: 28

YEAR	TEAM	LVL	AGE	PA	R	2B	3B	HR	RBI	BB	SO	SB	CS	EqBRR	AVG	OBP	SLG	EqAVG	EqOBP	EqSLG	EqA	VORP	WARP	DEFENSE	
2007	ATL	MLB	25	608	91	26	10	16	68	79	117	9	5	0.3	.276	.375	.457	.287	.385	.471	.293	40.6	5.1	128-2B	4
2008	ATL	MLB	26	614	86	39	6	12	69	52	113	11	6	-0.9	.287	.349	.446	.304	.361	.467	.282	34.1	6.0	135-2B	17
2009	ATL	MLB	27	346	47	20	3	8	29	32	54	7	2	-0.3	.224	.303	.389	.239	.312	.412	.253	6.6	1.1	73-2B	3
2010	ARI	MLB	28	556	87	32	9	14	68	61	99	8	6	-0.1	.281	.363	.470	.276	.358	.446	.278	27.5	3.5	121-2B	4

Breakout: 7%   Improve: 47%   Collapse: 8%   Attrition: 9%   MLB: 95%   Comparables: Charlie Gehringer, Rob Wilfong, Adam Kennedy, Felipe Lopez

Remember when Kelly Johnson was good? It really wasn't that long ago. After a 2007 season that had him looking like a future star, Johnson got a bit too power-happy, and last year, the wheels came off as he lost the second-base job to Martin Prado. He's still relatively young, but he was non-tendered to avoid an arbitration-generated raise. He made a canny move to sign with Arizona, where a hitter-friendly park should give him the best possible shot at a comeback campaign.

Brandon Jones · OF

Bats: L Throws: R Height: 6' 1" Weight: 210 Born: December 10, 1983 Age: 26

YEAR	TEAM	LVL	AGE	PA	R	2B	3B	HR	RBI	BB	SO	SB	CS	EqBRR	AVG	OBP	SLG	EqAVG	EqOBP	EqSLG	EqA	VORP	WARP	DEFENSE			
2007	MIS	AA	23	418	58	21	6	15	74	44	84	12	7	0.1	.293	.368	.507	.281	.342	.471	.277	15.9	2.0	89-LF	1		
2007	RIC	AAA	23	191	26	12	1	4	26	17	36	5	0	2.8	.300	.363	.453	.285	.346	.436	.274	6.6	1.3	43-LF	4		
2007	ATL	MLB	23	21	0	1	0	0	4	0	8	0	0	-0.1	.158	.190	.211	.158	.190	.211	.127	-1.9	-0.3	5-LF	-1		
2008	RIC	AAA	24	396	44	24	1	8	52	46	76	9	6	0.7	.260	.343	.405	.244	.326	.376	.248	1.8	0.6	55-LF	2	30-RF	1
2008	ATL	MLB	24	128	16	10	1	1	17	7	28	1	0	0.8	.267	.312	.397	.274	.317	.402	.253	1.1	-0.3	25-LF	-3	4-RF	-1
2009	GWN	AAA	25	443	50	28	2	7	57	50	76	6	3	0.5	.281	.360	.419	.275	.351	.409	.268	10.0	1.4	57-LF	5	21-RF	-3
2009	ATL	MLB	25	17	2	0	0	0	1	4	3	0	0	0.2	.308	.471	.308	.308	.471	.308	.315	0.9	0.1	4-LF	0		
2010	ATL	MLB	26	432	47	20	2	10	53	43	99	5	3	0.7	.240	.318	.378	.250	.324	.390	.250	4.6	0.7	91-LF	1		

Breakout: 7% Improve: 26% Collapse: 25% Attrition: 14%   MLB: 61%   Comparables: Brian Stavisky, Jason Grabowski, Jessie Reid, Everett Graham

Two years ago, Jones was a real prospect, seen as a late-blooming athlete who was finally converting his tools into skills. Two years at Triple-A have represented a pair of steps backward, as Jones's power and speed have ebbed to the point of becoming nonfactors, though he still hits for a bit of average and draws a fair share of walks. As he is now 26, this might be the last year for him even to establish himself as a fourth outfielder.

Chipper Jones · 3B

Bats: S Throws: R Height: 6' 4" Weight: 210 Born: April 24, 1972 Age: 38

YEAR	TEAM	LVL	AGE	PA	R	2B	3B	HR	RBI	BB	SO	SB	CS	EqBRR	AVG	OBP	SLG	EqAVG	EqOBP	EqSLG	EqA	VORP	WARP	DEFENSE	
2007	ATL	MLB	35	600	108	42	4	29	102	82	75	5	1	1.1	.337	.425	.604	.347	.435	.618	.347	73.6	7.7	120-3B	-1
2008	ATL	MLB	36	534	82	24	1	22	75	90	61	4	0	-0.1	.364	.470	.574	.383	.481	.599	.365	74.7	9.1	111-3B	10
2009	ATL	MLB	37	596	80	23	2	18	71	101	89	4	1	-2.2	.264	.388	.430	.280	.395	.455	.297	39.6	4.1	126-3B	-2
2010	ATL	MLB	38	519	70	24	1	17	70	75	77	2	2	-0.2	.289	.392	.462	.297	.395	.477	.305	39.1	4.3	108-3B	1

Breakout: 4% Improve: 20% Collapse: 36% Attrition: 17%   MLB: 98%   Comparables: Rico Carty, Mike Schmidt, Ken Caminiti, Wade Boggs

From 2006 to 2008, Jones hit .342/.435/.592, with at least a 1000 OPS in all three seasons. Last year was a comparative disaster, as all he really did on a positive level was draw a ton of walks, with a career low in home runs and a .202 batting average with just two bombs after the calendar flipped to September (more broadly, Jones hit .316/.434/.500 from April to May and .244/.370/.403 thereafter). Can a player really decline this much, this quickly? Since 1954, only two other players (Norm Cash and Scott Brosius) have seen a 100-point decline in their batting average, so while Jones turns 38 in April and is seemingly always banged up with some kind of ailment, this much of a downturn seems a bit fluky. Still, it was enough for Jones, who is signed through 2012, to be talking of retirement after the 2010 campaign.

Adam LaRoche · 1B

Bats: L Throws: L Height: 6' 3" Weight: 205 Born: November 6, 1979 Age: 30

YEAR	TEAM	LVL	AGE	PA	R	2B	3B	HR	RBI	BB	SO	SB	CS	EqBRR	AVG	OBP	SLG	EqAVG	EqOBP	EqSLG	EqA	VORP	WARP	DEFENSE	
2007	PIT	MLB	27	632	71	42	0	21	88	62	131	1	1	-1.8	.272	.345	.458	.280	.353	.471	.281	21.2	3.4	146-1B	9
2008	PIT	MLB	28	554	66	32	3	25	85	54	122	1	1	-3.0	.270	.341	.500	.285	.352	.525	.292	26.3	2.6	126-1B	-2
2009	PIT	MLB	29	368	46	25	1	12	40	41	81	2	2	0.0	.247	.329	.441	.262	.339	.465	.272	5.4	1.1	86-1B	5
2009	BOS	MLB	29	19	2	2	0	1	3	0	2	0	0	-0.2	.263	.263	.526	.263	.263	.526	.254	-0.1	0.0	4-1B	0
2009	ATL	MLB	29	242	30	11	1	12	40	28	59	0	0	-1.6	.325	.401	.557	.344	.413	.585	.332	20.6	2.4	57-1B	1
2010	ATL	MLB	30	603	68	30	2	22	80	64	134	2	2	-1.1	.263	.344	.450	.272	.348	.461	.280	20.4	2.5	140-1B	2

Breakout: 5% Improve: 35% Collapse: 14% Attrition: 7%   MLB: 97%   Comparables: Leon Durham, Ryan Klesko, Bruce Bochte, Norm Siebern

All of the planets fell into alignment for LaRoche following his arrival in Atlanta, as he hit .325/.401/.557 in 57 games with the Braves. He's historically been a second-half hitter, with a career OPS 132 points higher after the break, and he's always liked playing with Atlanta. Not as good as he looked down the stretch, LaRoche is a solid first baseman who does some good things both offensively and defensively, but his team needs to sit him against strong lefties and to suffer through a good deal of streakiness. The Braves wanted to keep him, but only at a price that represents his true value rather than pay an overinflated bill for two hot months.

Brian McCann — C

Bats: L   Throws: R   Height: 6' 3"   Weight: 230   Born: February 20, 1984   Age: 26

YEAR	TEAM	LVL	AGE	PA	R	2B	3B	HR	RBI	BB	SO	SB	CS	EqBRR	AVG	OBP	SLG	EqAVG	EqOBP	EqSLG	EqA	VORP	WARP	DEFENSE	
2007	ATL	MLB	23	552	51	38	0	18	92	35	74	0	1	-4.2	.270	.320	.452	.276	.326	.459	.267	30.7	3.6	127-C	0
2008	ATL	MLB	24	573	68	42	1	23	87	57	64	5	0	-2.2	.301	.373	.523	.316	.386	.546	.312	58.7	5.8	129-C	-4
2009	ATL	MLB	25	551	63	35	1	21	94	49	83	4	1	-2.9	.281	.349	.486	.299	.361	.511	.295	45.7	4.0	120-C	-6
2010	ATL	MLB	26	575	66	31	1	25	103	56	77	3	1	-1.6	.287	.363	.497	.298	.369	.516	.300	49.2	5.1	131-C	-2

Breakout: 24%   Improve: 62%   Collapse: 2%   Attrition: 3%   MLB: 100%   Comparables: Rich Gedman, Eddie Taubensee, Terry Kennedy, Mike Scioscia

It was a strange start of the year for McCann, who got into the best shape of his career for spring, but then had troubles with his surgically corrected eyes in April (his vision in his left eye was blurred, and it was constantly dry). Corrective lenses compensated for the problem, and he hit like McCann always has from May on (.289/.350/.492). He's a good hitter, maybe even a great one, considering his position, but he's a bit lacking behind the plate, especially against the running game, and the Braves will always need to employ a defensive-minded backup. He had a second Lasik surgery in the offseason, and the glasses will be off in 2010, so get those four-eyes jokes out of your system now.

Nate McLouth — CF

Bats: L   Throws: R   Height: 5' 11"   Weight: 180   Born: October 28, 1981   Age: 28

YEAR	TEAM	LVL	AGE	PA	R	2B	3B	HR	RBI	BB	SO	SB	CS	EqBRR	AVG	OBP	SLG	EqAVG	EqOBP	EqSLG	EqA	VORP	WARP	DEFENSE			
2007	PIT	MLB	25	382	62	21	3	13	38	39	77	22	1	4.2	.258	.351	.459	.267	.360	.474	.293	23.6	1.6	55-CF	-7	12-LF	-1
2008	PIT	MLB	26	685	113	46	4	26	94	65	93	23	3	7.2	.276	.356	.497	.291	.367	.520	.301	51.6	4.4	145-CF	-10	2-LF	0
2009	PIT	MLB	27	195	27	7	1	9	34	21	29	7	0	1.8	.256	.349	.470	.274	.359	.506	.298	14.3	2.4	43-CF	6		
2009	ATL	MLB	27	396	59	20	1	11	36	47	70	12	6	1.0	.257	.354	.419	.276	.367	.452	.281	21.0	1.4	82-CF	-7		
2010	ATL	MLB	28	563	86	28	3	20	69	63	92	21	5	2.5	.261	.354	.454	.270	.358	.467	.289	36.1	3.6	118-CF	-3		

Breakout: 6%   Improve: 35%   Collapse: 11%   Attrition: 3%   MLB: 98%   Comparables: Vada Pinson, Tony Gonzalez, Claudell Washington, Larry Doby

McLouth was overrated with the Pirates—he was the best player on a bad team, but not a star. He's still a great guy to have around, as his biggest strength might be a lack of weaknesses. He has a bit of power and solid on-base skills, and he played an improved center field in 2009. He also really is worthy of his reputation as a great clubhouse player; his max-effort style is infectious, he's a role model to the young players, and he's even fluent in Spanish. McLouth provides value on the stat sheet, but is also an asset in areas we can't really measure in any meaningful way.

Adam Milligan — LF

Bats: L   Throws: R   Height: 6' 3"   Weight: 210   Born: March 14, 1988   Age: 22

YEAR	TEAM	LVL	AGE	PA	R	2B	3B	HR	RBI	BB	SO	SB	CS	EqBRR	AVG	OBP	SLG	EqAVG	EqOBP	EqSLG	EqA	VORP	WARP	DEFENSE	
2009	ROM	A	21	214	28	14	2	10	33	12	43	4	5	-5.7	.345	.393	.589	.287	.326	.475	.269	6.0	0.1	47-LF	-5
2009	DNV	Rk	21	46	9	5	1	2	10	3	7	0	0	-0.3	.439	.500	.756	.326	.370	.535	.303	2.9	0.3	7-LF	-1
2010	ATL	MLB	22	451	41	22	3	12	50	25	117	2	3	-4.5	.243	.296	.401	.252	.302	.414	.243	1.6	-0.5	96-LF	-6

Breakout: 8%   Improve: 23%   Collapse: 33%   Attrition: 0%   MLB: 2%   Comparables: Mike Butia, Scott Seal, John Jensen, Jeremy Dodson

Braves officials are convinced that this is a name that a lot of people are going to hear in 2010. A sixth-round pick in 2008 out of a Tennessee juco, Milligan missed the first half recovering from minor knee surgery, but he was among the best hitters in the Sally League during the second. He's not an athlete, but rather a big, bulky slugger who has plus-plus raw power. He can also hit for average, as he can make hard contact to all fields. Milligan needs to hone his approach a bit, but the bat looks outstanding so far.

Martin Prado — 2B

Bats: R   Throws: R   Height: 6' 1"   Weight: 190   Born: October 27, 1983   Age: 26

YEAR	TEAM	LVL	AGE	PA	R	2B	3B	HR	RBI	BB	SO	SB	CS	EqBRR	AVG	OBP	SLG	EqAVG	EqOBP	EqSLG	EqA	VORP	WARP	DEFENSE			
2007	RIC	AAA	23	443	61	23	3	4	41	34	41	5	4	4.8	.316	.374	.420	.302	.354	.399	.264	15.5	0.9	85-2B	-3	8-3B	-3
2007	ATL	MLB	23	62	5	3	0	0	2	3	6	0	0	0.4	.288	.323	.339	.288	.323	.339	.236	-0.3	0.1	7-2B	0	5-3B	1
2008	ATL	MLB	24	254	36	18	4	2	33	21	29	3	1	-1.2	.320	.377	.461	.338	.391	.478	.299	16.6	2.3	18-3B	4	16-2B	0
2009	ATL	MLB	25	503	64	38	0	11	49	36	59	1	3	-1.7	.307	.358	.464	.326	.373	.493	.291	30.2	3.0	57-2B	-7	30-3B	5
2010	ATL	MLB	26	494	66	27	4	9	52	40	60	3	3	0.4	.302	.363	.440	.308	.367	.445	.285	28.8	2.8	89-2B	-3		

Breakout: 12%   Improve: 49%   Collapse: 5%   Attrition: 4%   MLB: 94%   Comparables: Billy Herman, Yunel Escobar, Ron Oester, Aaron Hill

At this point, with 868 career plate appearances, we can be pretty sure that Martin Prado really is a .300 hitter. He also has gap power, occasionally pops one out, plays a fundamentally sound if unspectacular second base, and can even fill in on the hot corner on the many days that Chipper needs a day off. Prado works as hard as anyone on the team, but he isn't likely to develop further than what he is now—the National League's version of Placido Polanco.

Gerardo Rodriguez — 1B

Bats: R   Throws: R   Height: 6' 1"   Weight: 195   Born: October 25, 1987   Age: 22

YEAR	TEAM	LVL	AGE	PA	R	2B	3B	HR	RBI	BB	SO	SB	CS	EqBRR	AVG	OBP	SLG	EqAVG	EqOBP	EqSLG	EqA	VORP	WARP	DEFENSE	
2007	YAN	Rk	19	101	15	6	0	2	12	7	31	1	2	-0.8	.233	.347	.372	.204	.267	.312	.197	-5.4	-1.2	21-1B	-1
2008	DNV	Rk	20	245	31	11	3	13	49	17	67	1	1	-3.1	.253	.310	.507	.211	.253	.361	.212	-9.9	-2.8	57-1B	-6
2009	ROM	A	21	259	29	9	5	11	42	12	69	4	1	-1.1	.258	.301	.475	.237	.269	.412	.232	-8.2	-1.5	57-1B	-4
2009	MYR	A+	21	242	34	9	2	12	41	15	72	4	1	3.1	.281	.331	.500	.246	.285	.430	.243	-4.7	-1.1	42-1B	-4
2010	ATL	MLB	22	441	42	17	5	13	52	29	139	2	1	0.6	.222	.276	.380	.225	.279	.387	.230	-9.5	-1.5	94-1B	-4

Breakout: 23%   Improve: 52%   Collapse: 23%   Attrition: 9%   MLB: 0%   Comparables: J.J. Johnson, Steve Cordner, Jim Olander, Juan Delarosa

Originally signed by the Yankees, Rodriguez fell victim to a minor-league numbers game with New York. The Braves gave him a new home, and he responded with something of a breakout season at Low-A Rome. Rodriguez's power is very real, coming from a combination of bat speed and raw strength, but there are also some significant holes in his game, namely, a swing-at-anything approach and exceedingly bad defense. The jury is still out here, but at least some of the key elements to make a very good prospect out of him are present.

Dave Ross — C

Bats: R   Throws: R   Height: 6' 2"   Weight: 240   Born: March 19, 1977   Age: 33

YEAR	TEAM	LVL	AGE	PA	R	2B	3B	HR	RBI	BB	SO	SB	CS	EqBRR	AVG	OBP	SLG	EqAVG	EqOBP	EqSLG	EqA	VORP	WARP	DEFENSE	
2007	CIN	MLB	30	348	32	10	0	17	39	30	92	0	0	-1.4	.203	.271	.399	.203	.272	.392	.229	6.2	2.3	94-C	12
2008	CIN	MLB	31	173	17	9	0	3	13	32	36	0	1	-1.5	.231	.381	.366	.235	.382	.375	.270	8.9	1.0	42-C	0
2008	BOS	MLB	31	9	1	0	0	0	0	0	3	0	0	0.1	.125	.125	.125	.125	.125	.125	-.076	-0.9	-0.2	3-C	0
2009	ATL	MLB	32	151	18	9	0	7	20	21	39	0	0	-1.8	.273	.380	.508	.295	.393	.535	.313	15.7	3.3	39-C	10
2010	ATL	MLB	33	245	21	9	0	8	24	30	66	0	0	-0.6	.217	.316	.374	.222	.315	.386	.248	6.8	1.2	60-C	4

Breakout: 11%   Improve: 39%   Collapse: 19%   Attrition: 17%   MLB: 87%   Comparables: Charles Johnson, Rod Barajas, Doug Mirabelli, Damian Miller

Ross might be the current ideal backup catcher. He doesn't hit for average, but he makes up for it with walks and very real power. Defensively, he shuts down the running game, gunning down 19 of 40 attempting base thieves in 2009, and he carries a career rate of 40 percent. Add in that he bats righty while caddying for a lefty regular. Ross is signed through 2010, and the Braves have made no secret of wanting to keep him around even longer.

Jordan Schafer — CF

Bats: L   Throws: L   Height: 6' 1"   Weight: 200   Born: September 4, 1986   Age: 23

YEAR	TEAM	LVL	AGE	PA	R	2B	3B	HR	RBI	BB	SO	SB	CS	EqBRR	AVG	OBP	SLG	EqAVG	EqOBP	EqSLG	EqA	VORP	WARP	DEFENSE	
2007	ROM	A	20	145	16	15	2	5	20	16	31	4	4	-2.9	.372	.441	.636	.311	.372	.515	.296	10.0	1.2	32-CF	0
2007	MYR	A+	20	481	70	34	8	10	43	40	95	19	11	-0.3	.294	.354	.477	.260	.309	.417	.249	7.8	0.8	101-CF	-1
2008	MIS	AA	21	349	46	18	6	10	51	49	88	12	5	-2.2	.269	.378	.471	.247	.335	.425	.264	11.2	0.6	78-CF	-6
2009	GWN	AAA	22	38	6	0	0	2	3	2	10	3	1	-0.4	.229	.263	.400	.229	.263	.400	.233	0.0	0.0	7-CF	0
2009	ATL	MLB	22	195	18	8	0	2	8	27	63	2	1	-1.7	.204	.313	.287	.208	.313	.298	.224	-1.7	-1.5	48-CF	-11
2010	ATL	MLB	23	419	45	19	4	9	34	42	118	8	5	-1.3	.236	.315	.379	.243	.317	.391	.249	8.2	0.6	93-CF	-3

Breakout: 18%   Improve: 40%   Collapse: 15%   Attrition: 9%   MLB: 67%   Comparables: Carlos Gonzalez, Laynce Nix, Peter Bergeron, Terrence Long

Schafer hit a huge home run on the nationally televised Opening Day game, and in retrospect, that was probably the worst thing to happen to him. He got into a slump that he just couldn't get out of, due to a combination of pressing, an inability to make adjustments, and a nagging wrist problem that never went away. Bobby Cox kept him in the lineup for his strong defense before the team acquired McLouth. The hand bothered Schafer even more at Triple-A and finally resulted in season-ending surgery. The Braves still envision a future outfield with Schafer flanked by McLouth and Heyward, and scouts still think he can become a Steve Finley (who took a long time to get going himself) type of talent.

PITCHERS

Manny Acosta

Bats: S   Throws: R   Height: 6' 4"   Weight: 170   Born: May 1, 1981   Age: 29

YEAR	TEAM	LVL	AGE	W	L	SV	G	GS	IP	H	HR	BB	SO	GB%	BABIP	STUFF	WHIP	ERA	SIERA	DERA	EqH9	EqHR9	EqBB9	EqSO9	VORP	SN/WX
2007	RIC	AAA	25	9	3	12	40	0	59²	46	0	35	56	57%	.295	10	1.36	2.26	4.03	3.42	7.8	0.3	5.4	6.8	12.8	1.18
2007	ATL	MLB	25	1	1	0	21	0	23²	13	2	14	22	64%	.200	11	1.14	2.28	3.90	2.42	5.2	0.8	4.8	7.7	7.6	0.64
2008	ATL	MLB	26	3	5	3	46	0	53	48	7	26	31	59%	.255	-19	1.40	3.57	4.92	4.30	8.4	1.4	4.0	4.6	6.9	0.02
2009	GWN	AAA	27	1	3	2	18	0	27¹	21	4	13	25	47%	.239	-7	1.24	2.63	3.96	3.55	8.5	2.1	4.6	6.8	5.5	0.30
2009	ATL	MLB	27	1	1	0	36	0	37¹	45	4	19	32	48%	.350	-11	1.71	4.34	4.40	4.62	10.9	1.0	3.9	6.3	3.6	-0.10
2010	ATL	MLB	29	3	5	2	54	0	60²	63	7	35	44	54%	.308	-12	1.61	4.91	4.82	5.29	9.4	1.0	4.7	5.8	1.4	0.69

Breakout: 13%   Improve: 39%   Collapse: 28%   Attrition: 12%   MLB: 68%   Comparables: Jose Paniagua, Jeff Dedmon, Cris Carpenter, Matt Guerrier

Acosta is one of those guys who drives scouts insane, so we're guessing he has the same effect on the Braves. See him on the right night, and he'll blow hitters away with a mid-90s fastball that gets up to 98 mph, a pretty nice splitter, and a plus slider. Unfortunately, he's so inconsistent from outing to outing, especially when it comes to location, that it's impossible to trust him late in games. So, Acosta is one of those guys, someone who could move to three or four more teams and then finally figure things out and save 30 games five years from now ... or he could just be out of baseball by then.

Jorge Campillo

Bats: R   Throws: R   Height: 6' 1"   Weight: 225   Born: August 10, 1978   Age: 31

YEAR	TEAM	LVL	AGE	W	L	SV	G	GS	IP	H	HR	BB	SO	GB%	BABIP	STUFF	WHIP	ERA	SIERA	DERA	EqH9	EqHR9	EqBB9	EqSO9	VORP	SN/WX
2007	TAC	AAA	28	9	6	0	24	22	149¹	151	11	39	99	43%	.299	2	1.27	3.07	4.33	3.66	8.9	1.2	2.5	4.3	29.6	2.79
2007	SEA	MLB	28	0	0	0	5	0	13¹	18	2	6	9	39%	.356	-16	1.80	6.75	5.01	7.43	11.5	1.4	3.4	5.4	-2.9	-0.15
2008	ATL	MLB	29	8	7	0	39	25	158²	158	18	38	107	45%	.285	0	1.24	3.91	4.20	4.28	9.1	1.1	1.9	5.2	21.0	3.42
2009	ATL	MLB	30	1	0	0	5	0	4¹	7	0	3	3	25%	.467	-27	2.31	4.15	5.89	7.36	17.2	0.0	7.4	4.9	-0.8	-0.27
2010	ATL	MLB	31	4	5	0	26	1	70²	74	9	26	42	44%	.297	-6	1.42	4.51	4.90	4.94	9.6	1.1	3.0	4.8	4.4	1.29

Breakout: 16%   Improve: 49%   Collapse: 27%   Attrition: 29%   MLB: 64%   Comparables: Fernando Arroyo, Chad Durbin, Steve Fireovid, Dave Borkowski

While the World Baseball Classic has been a success in many ways, it hasn't been without its share of civilian casualties. The Braves gave Campillo a shot in 2008 when no one wanted him, and he proved to be a real find, delivering 160 innings of solid baseball by changing speeds and throwing strikes. Then he strained a forearm pitching for Mexico in March 2009, and it all but cost him the season. Campillo was removed from the roster in October, but the Royals, pilot fish of the baseball world, signed him to a minor-league contract.

Buddy Carlyle

Bats: L   Throws: R   Height: 6' 3"   Weight: 210   Born: December 21, 1977   Age: 32

YEAR	TEAM	LVL	AGE	W	L	SV	G	GS	IP	H	HR	BB	SO	GB%	BABIP	STUFF	WHIP	ERA	SIERA	DERA	EqH9	EqHR9	EqBB9	EqSO9	VORP	SN/WX
2007	RIC	AAA	29	5	2	0	9	9	48²	40	5	9	56	51%	.299	26	1.01	2.59	2.32	3.47	8.3	1.4	1.8	8.3	10.2	1.16
2007	ATL	MLB	29	8	7	0	22	20	107	117	19	32	74	40%	.293	-13	1.39	5.21	4.46	5.49	10.0	1.7	2.4	5.6	0.2	1.36
2008	ATL	MLB	30	2	0	0	45	0	62²	52	5	26	59	52%	.280	7	1.24	3.59	3.69	3.86	7.9	0.7	3.4	7.3	11.1	1.26
2009	GWN	AAA	31	3	1	0	12	1	15¹	13	0	1	23	53%	.382	14	0.91	1.76	0.98	2.57	9.6	0.6	0.6	10.3	4.6	0.36
2009	ATL	MLB	31	0	1	0	16	0	21¹	35	5	12	12	44%	.385	-42	2.20	8.86	5.58	9.58	15.2	2.6	4.4	4.4	-9.4	0.05
2010	ATL	MLB	32	3	5	0	31	4	61¹	66	8	25	46	43%	.314	-5	1.48	4.80	4.45	5.25	9.8	1.2	3.3	6.1	1.7	0.78

Breakout: 16%   Improve: 54%   Collapse: 15%   Attrition: 30%   MLB: 68%   Comparables: Reggie Cleveland, Don Lee, Ron Kline, Gil Heredia

The Braves gave Carlyle a chance in 2007 when few others were interested, and he was a serviceable starter in 2007 and then a serviceable reliever in 2008. He wasn't especially good as much as he was better than the other options available, but teams need those catch-me-when-I-fall guys, too. Always a pitcher who depended more on guile than pure stuff, Carlyle was diagnosed with diabetes in May, lost a ton of weight, and was just never the same, having lost a few ticks of velocity and even more movement. Taken off the roster at the end of the season, Carlye will be heading to Japan to see if his junk will stick overseas.

Randall Delgado

Bats: R   Throws: R   Height: 6' 3"   Weight: 165   Born: February 9, 1990   Age: 20

YEAR	TEAM	LVL	AGE	W	L	SV	G	GS	IP	H	HR	BB	SO	GB%	BABIP	STUFF	WHIP	ERA	SIERA	DERA	EqH9	EqHR9	EqBB9	EqSO9	VORP	SN/WX
2008	DNV	Rk	18	3	8	0	14	14	69	63	5	30	81	50%	.339	-9	1.35	3.13	3.08	6.63	12.6	3.0	6.6	5.4	-7.1	-0.71
2009	ROM	A	19	5	10	0	25	25	124	123	9	49	141	55%	.338	-16	1.39	4.35	3.16	7.75	11.7	2.7	5.2	5.7	-27.6	-2.46
2010	ATL	MLB	20	4	10	0	27	27	114¹	146	22	77	88	52%	.347	23	1.95	7.01	5.01	7.57	11.7	1.8	5.5	6.2	-26.3	1.32

Breakout: 18%   Improve: 65%   Collapse: 10%   Attrition: 8%   MLB: 1%   Comparables: Corey Avrard, Freddie Toliver, Jason Doss, Juan Ramirez

Normally, a guy with a 4.35 ERA in Low-A would be lucky to get a quick comment at the end of a team chapter, but Delgado really has a chance to be something special. A 19-year-old Panamanian with oodles of projection, Delgado can run his fastball up to 96 mph and throws strikes with the pitch while also adding some sink and run. His future as a starter or reliever will depend on the development of his breaking ball, but either way, he is one of the best young arms in the system.

Mike Gonzalez

Bats: R   Throws: L   Height: 6' 2"   Weight: 215   Born: May 23, 1978   Age: 32

YEAR	TEAM	LVL	AGE	W	L	SV	G	GS	IP	H	HR	BB	SO	GB%	BABIP	STUFF	WHIP	ERA	SIERA	DERA	EqH9	EqHR9	EqBB9	EqSO9	VORP	SN/WX
2007	ATL	MLB	29	2	0	2	18	0	17	15	0	8	13	40%	.306	2	1.35	1.59	4.57	1.69	8.4	0.0	3.9	6.2	6.8	1.12
2008	ATL	MLB	30	0	3	14	36	0	33²	26	6	14	44	41%	.260	10	1.19	4.28	2.63	5.61	7.5	1.6	3.2	9.6	-0.4	1.08
2009	ATL	MLB	31	5	4	10	80	0	74¹	56	7	33	90	42%	.275	16	1.20	2.42	3.00	3.53	7.2	1.0	3.4	9.0	16.2	2.64
2010	BAL	MLB	32	3	3	10	57	0	56	53	7	24	53	42%	.305	5	1.38	4.27	3.84	4.26	8.1	0.9	3.7	7.9	7.7	1.46

Breakout: 17%   Improve: 43%   Collapse: 23%   Attrition: 12%   MLB: 91%   Comparables: Jesse Orosco, Dave Righetti, Damaso Marte, Eddie Guardado

Finally healthy, Gonzalez had an excellent year out of the bullpen, and the timing is perfect, as it was his pre-free-agency walk year. Gonzalez is the rare left-hander who teams can be comfortable with in the later innings, as his above-average fastball and very good slider mean no real platoon issues. He's a bit of a tightrope walker who rarely puts up 1-2-3 innings, but usually pitches out of trouble. Signed by the Orioles for two years and $12 million, he'll close and should be good at it if he stays healthy, but there's the rub.

Tommy Hanson

Bats: R   Throws: R   Height: 6' 6"   Weight: 210   Born: August 28, 1986   Age: 23

YEAR	TEAM	LVL	AGE	W	L	SV	G	GS	IP	H	HR	BB	SO	GB%	BABIP	STUFF	WHIP	ERA	SIERA	DERA	EqH9	EqHR9	EqBB9	EqSO9	VORP	SN/WX
2007	ROM	A	20	2	6	0	15	14	73	51	6	26	90	43%	.268	36	1.05	2.59	2.59	4.48	8.2	1.9	3.9	7.4	7.6	0.67
2007	MYR	A+	20	3	3	0	11	11	60	53	10	32	64	37%	.287	13	1.42	4.20	3.76	6.25	10.5	3.2	5.5	7.0	-4.5	-0.57
2008	MYR	A+	21	3	1	0	7	7	40	15	0	11	49	28%	.181	37	0.65	0.90	2.13	2.31	5.1	0.5	2.9	8.0	13.1	1.23
2008	MIS	AA	21	8	4	0	18	18	98	70	9	41	114	44%	.257	25	1.13	3.03	3.04	4.41	7.6	1.6	3.7	7.5	11.6	1.35
2009	GWN	AAA	22	3	3	0	11	11	66¹	40	5	17	90	42%	.248	44	0.86	1.49	1.78	2.94	6.9	1.3	2.6	9.5	17.8	1.98
2009	ATL	MLB	22	11	4	0	21	21	127²	105	10	46	116	46%	.275	37	1.18	2.89	3.66	3.18	7.7	0.8	2.8	6.9	32.0	4.64
2010	ATL	MLB	23	10	9	0	33	30	156¹	137	18	70	149	37%	.289	25	1.32	3.99	3.86	4.35	8.0	1.1	3.6	7.8	20.0	3.72

Breakout: 10%   Improve: 45%   Collapse: 17%   Attrition: 14%   MLB: 94%   Comparables: Jason Bere, Wade Davis, Kevin Gross, Jimmy Haynes

Despite a historic showing in the 2008 Arizona Fall League and an outstanding spring, the Braves stuck to their master plan with Hanson, keeping him in Triple-A until June and getting him just short of 130 innings in the big leagues as a rookie. While one can't argue with the results on an individual level, what about the team itself? The Braves were in the playoff hunt in September—how much stronger would the scent of fall baseball have been with 10 more starts from Hanson? He didn't get any better at Triple-A, as his 11 starts for Gwinnett were a waste of time for everyone but Braves bean counters, who got to keep a half-season of service time off Hanson's arbitration clock. Alas, that's the state of baseball today. Hanson will be in the rotation to start 2010, and with an improved changeup and better command within the strike zone, he could move into elite status over the next few years.

Tim Hudson

Bats: R   Throws: R   Height: 6' 1"   Weight: 170   Born: July 14, 1975   Age: 34

YEAR	TEAM	LVL	AGE	W	L	SV	G	GS	IP	H	HR	BB	SO	GB%	BABIP	STUFF	WHIP	ERA	SIERA	DERA	EqH9	EqHR9	EqBB9	EqSO9	VORP	SN/WX
2007	ATL	MLB	31	16	10	0	34	34	224¹	221	10	53	132	71%	.292	20	1.22	3.33	4.01	3.58	9.0	0.4	1.9	4.8	46.5	8.13
2008	ATL	MLB	32	11	7	0	23	22	142	125	11	40	85	66%	.262	15	1.16	3.17	4.15	3.50	8.1	0.8	2.3	4.6	30.6	4.40
2009	ATL	MLB	33	2	1	0	7	7	42¹	49	4	13	30	68%	.338	7	1.46	3.61	3.94	3.79	10.7	0.9	2.5	5.6	7.6	1.02
2010	ATL	MLB	34	6	7	0	24	18	109	113	11	37	62	69%	.296	-2	1.38	4.25	4.35	4.69	9.5	1.0	2.8	4.7	9.8	2.39

Breakout: 7%   Improve: 33%   Collapse: 27%   Attrition: 29%   MLB: 96%   Comparables: Bill Hands, Bill Swift, Joe Horlen, Curt Davis

Hudson is an interesting case. He came back from Tommy John surgery at the end of the year and pitched well on paper, but a look at the game logs shows a pitcher who put up good lines against bad teams, and vice versa. The Braves turned down his $12 million option for 2010, but because Hudson is a Georgia native who enjoyed pitching in Atlanta, the two sides worked out a three-year extension for $28 million instead. Hudson's stuff was still there at the end of the year, and the hope is that as he gets further away from the surgery, his location will return as well.

Jair Jurrjens

Bats: R   Throws: R   Height: 6' 1"   Weight: 200   Born: January 29, 1986   Age: 24

YEAR	TEAM	LVL	AGE	W	L	SV	G	GS	IP	H	HR	BB	SO	GB%	BABIP	STUFF	WHIP	ERA	SIERA	DERA	EqH9	EqHR9	EqBB9	EqSO9	VORP	SN/WX
2007	ERI	AA	21	7	5	0	19	19	112²	112	7	31	94	57%	.312	21	1.27	3.20	3.70	4.16	10.0	0.9	2.8	5.9	15.8	1.40
2007	DET	MLB	21	3	1	0	7	7	30²	24	4	11	13	43%	.215	10	1.14	4.70	5.54	4.40	7.0	1.2	3.0	3.6	3.6	0.70
2008	ATL	MLB	22	13	10	0	31	31	188¹	188	11	70	139	57%	.301	25	1.37	3.68	4.24	4.21	9.0	0.6	2.9	5.6	26.8	3.96
2009	ATL	MLB	23	14	10	0	34	34	215	186	15	75	152	50%	.268	22	1.21	2.60	4.31	3.17	7.8	0.7	2.7	5.3	54.9	7.97
2010	ATL	MLB	24	12	10	0	32	32	192¹	184	19	70	129	60%	.287	9	1.32	3.90	4.34	4.29	8.8	0.9	3.0	5.5	25.9	3.89

Breakout: 11%   Improve: 50%   Collapse: 9%   Attrition: 11%   MLB: 100%   Comparables: Mel Harder, Greg Maddux, Dave Stieb, Rick Wise

It's easy to forget that when the Braves traded Edgar Renteria to the Tigers at the end of the 2007 season, outfielder Gorkys Hernandez (now with the Pirates) was the guy they really wanted. Jurrjens was the secondary player they received in the deal, and now he's a 24-year-old who just finished third in the National League in ERA. Jurrjens always had a slightly above-average fastball and a very good changeup, but he started throwing his solid slider more in 2009, and the mere existence of the pitch was the key to his step forward. He rarely dominates, but he was among the most consistent pitchers in the game, giving up three or fewer runs in 26 of 34 starts, and never more than five. Enjoy him for now, Braves fans, because in three years, he'll be a 27-year-old free agent with Scott Boras as his agent.

Kenshin Kawakami

Bats: R   Throws: R   Height: 5' 10"   Weight: 200   Born: June 22, 1975   Age: 35

YEAR	TEAM	LVL	AGE	W	L	SV	G	GS	IP	H	HR	BB	SO	GB%	BABIP	STUFF	WHIP	ERA	SIERA	DERA	EqH9	EqHR9	EqBB9	EqSO9	VORP	SN/WX
2007	CHU	JPN	32	12	8	0	26	26	167¹	175	18	23	145	—	.312	9	1.18	3.55	3.29	4.84	9.1	1.2	1.5	5.9	12.2	0.70
2008	CHU	JPN	33	9	5	0	20	16	117¹	99	11	25	112	—	.275	21	1.06	2.30	3.11	3.34	7.9	1.1	2.4	7.1	27.3	1.36
2009	ATL	MLB	34	7	12	1	32	25	156¹	153	15	57	105	49%	.284	3	1.34	3.86	4.54	4.30	8.8	1.0	2.8	5.0	20.7	3.06
2010	ATL	MLB	35	7	8	0	25	22	127¹	128	15	42	87	48%	.295	4	1.34	4.24	4.40	4.65	9.2	1.1	2.8	5.6	12.0	1.67

Breakout: 14%   Improve: 32%   Collapse: 23%   Attrition: 16%   MLB: 96%   Comparables: Bump Hadley, Spud Chandler, Marty Pattin, Kevin Tapani

The Braves signed Kawakami to be a solid back-of-the-rotation starter, and in the end, he was just that, no less but also no more, although he garnered the nickname "Dragonslayer" from his teammates for out-pitching Ervin Santana and Roy Halladay. He's a classic Japanese pitcher who mixes a wide-ranging arsenal to keep hitters off their toes. The one drawback is that pitchers who rely on trickery tend to rack up high pitch counts. Still, Kawakami should easily be worth the $13.3 million he'll be paid over the next two years.

Craig Kimbrel

Bats: R   Throws: R   Height: 5' 11"   Weight: 205   Born: May 28, 1988   Age: 22

YEAR	TEAM	LVL	AGE	W	L	SV	G	GS	IP	H	HR	BB	SO	GB%	BABIP	STUFF	WHIP	ERA	SIERA	DERA	EqH9	EqHR9	EqBB9	EqSO9	VORP	SN/WX
2008	ROM	A	20	2	0	4	10	0	12²	6	0	4	26	42%	.333	11	0.79	0.71	0.18	1.59	7.1	0.8	4.0	11.1	4.9	0.65
2008	DNV	Rk	20	1	2	6	12	0	19	5	0	10	27	63%	.122	18	0.79	0.47	2.56	3.38	4.8	1.4	6.3	5.8	4.4	0.22
2009	ROM	A	21	0	0	10	16	0	20	9	0	6	38	48%	.290	18	0.75	0.90	0.57	2.04	7.1	1.0	4.1	10.2	6.8	0.77
2009	MYR	A+	21	0	2	2	19	0	26¹	18	2	28	45	65%	.340	24	1.75	5.47	3.22	8.18	8.7	1.9	10.6	11.0	-7.0	-0.58
2009	MIS	AA	21	2	1	6	12	0	11²	3	0	7	17	42%	.150	11	0.86	0.77	2.44	1.64	4.1	0.8	4.9	9.8	4.7	0.62
2010	ATL	MLB	22	3	4	8	43	0	54²	49	7	45	57	49%	.301	7	1.71	5.23	4.48	5.46	8.0	1.1	6.6	8.3	0.2	1.94

Breakout: 10%   Improve: 26%   Collapse: 43%   Attrition: 7%   MLB: 5%   Comparables: Jake Viano, John Hrusovsky, Dan Miceli, Eddy Rodriguez

On the surface, Kimbrel looks like the Braves' closer of the future. A short righty who is built like a linebacker and pitches without fear, he blows hitters away with a mid-90s fastball than can get up to 98 mph as well as a wipeout slider, and he's certainly shown he can miss bats, with a career total of 159 strikeouts in 95 ⅓ innings for 15 whiffs per nine. The problem is that he often has no idea where his pitches are going, turning every save opportunity into a Maalox moment. He'll begin the year at Triple-A, and if he can harness his command, he'll be in the big leagues in short order. Unfortunately, that's still a pretty big if.

Boone Logan

Bats: R   Throws: L   Height: 6' 5"   Weight: 210   Born: August 13, 1984   Age: 25

YEAR	TEAM	LVL	AGE	W	L	SV	G	GS	IP	H	HR	BB	SO	GB%	BABIP	STUFF	WHIP	ERA	SIERA	DERA	EqH9	EqHR9	EqBB9	EqSO9	VORP	SN/WX
2007	CHA	MLB	22	2	1	0	68	0	50²	59	7	20	35	49%	.317	-1	1.56	4.97	4.62	4.59	9.7	1.1	3.2	5.6	5.2	0.29
2008	CHA	MLB	23	2	3	0	55	0	42¹	57	7	14	42	54%	.376	3	1.68	5.95	3.59	5.86	11.3	1.3	2.5	8.2	-1.7	-0.32
2009	GWN	AAA	24	4	2	2	29	0	35²	26	2	17	39	53%	.273	4	1.21	3.28	3.43	4.59	7.8	1.1	4.6	7.8	3.4	0.24
2009	ATL	MLB	24	1	1	0	20	0	17¹	21	1	9	10	76%	.328	-23	1.73	5.19	4.45	6.11	10.7	0.5	4.1	4.1	-1.2	0.19
2010	NYA	MLB	25	3	5	0	62	0	61	66	8	29	45	51%	.314	-9	1.55	5.12	4.56	5.25	9.6	1.1	3.9	6.3	1.7	0.27

Breakout: 25%   Improve: 45%   Collapse: 15%   Attrition: 15%   MLB: 80%   Comparables: Chris Limbach, Anthony Shumaker, Bill Lee, Mark Yockey

Acquired from the White Sox with Javier Vazquez, Boone was back in Triple-A to begin the year after a rough spring. When he got back to the majors in late June, Bobby Cox used him sparingly, not that his performance warranted much trust. He still has significant potential, as 6-foot-5 lefties with his kind of velocity are rare. If he can ever find more consistency with his slider and fastball command, he could be very good, but a sizable number of pitchers you can say that about end up being counted among the community of the disappointed. As a throw-in to the Yankees on the Vazquez deal, he'll have to grow up fast in the AL East, no easy feat.

Derek Lowe

Bats: R   Throws: R   Height: 6' 6"   Weight: 230   Born: June 1, 1973   Age: 37

YEAR	TEAM	LVL	AGE	W	L	SV	G	GS	IP	H	HR	BB	SO	GB%	BABIP	STUFF	WHIP	ERA	SIERA	DERA	EqH9	EqHR9	EqBB9	EqSO9	VORP	SN/WX
2007	LAN	MLB	33	12	14	0	33	32	199¹	194	20	59	147	75%	.288	16	1.27	3.88	3.63	4.23	8.4	0.9	2.4	5.9	27.8	4.71
2008	LAN	MLB	34	14	11	0	34	34	211	194	14	45	147	67%	.280	20	1.13	3.24	3.68	3.77	8.4	0.7	1.7	5.3	39.6	6.73
2009	ATL	MLB	35	15	10	0	34	34	194²	232	16	63	111	66%	.327	-3	1.52	4.67	4.46	5.12	10.7	0.8	2.5	4.3	8.0	3.10
2010	ATL	MLB	37	10	11	0	35	34	181	193	21	60	108	68%	.301	-2	1.40	4.34	4.31	4.82	9.8	1.1	2.7	4.9	13.8	2.92

Breakout: 2%   Improve: 34%   Collapse: 28%   Attrition: 26%   MLB: 97%   Comparables: Scott Sanderson, Kevin Brown, Jon Lieber, Jim Lonborg

Lowe was seen as one of the safer bets coming into the year. He's consistently good to very good, never great, and his four-year, $60 million contract seemed like a reasonable investment, given his historical record of performance and durability. Then the so-called lesser league hit .301 against him. The bigger concern here is that on a scouting level, this doesn't look like a fluke, as he's experienced a small dip in velocity in each of the last two years, and never being a blow-hitters-away type in the first place, his margin for error is getting smaller and smaller. As he turns 37 in June, it will be hard to see him suddenly getting his stuff back, and the last couple of years of that deal could end up being an albatross.

Kris Medlen

Bats: S   Throws: R   Height: 5' 10"   Weight: 175   Born: October 7, 1985   Age: 24

YEAR	TEAM	LVL	AGE	W	L	SV	G	GS	IP	H	HR	BB	SO	GB%	BABIP	STUFF	WHIP	ERA	SIERA	DERA	EqH9	EqHR9	EqBB9	EqSO9	VORP	SN/WX
2007	ROM	A	21	0	1	8	17	0	20²	13	1	3	33	58%	.279	20	0.77	0.87	1.10	2.70	7.2	1.4	1.8	9.0	6.2	0.40
2007	MYR	A+	21	2	0	2	18	0	24	22	1	7	28	53%	.323	19	1.21	1.12	2.77	3.52	9.8	1.2	3.1	7.4	5.1	0.40
2008	MIS	AA	22	7	8	1	36	17	120¹	121	8	27	120	48%	.341	7	1.23	3.52	3.02	4.32	10.4	1.4	2.3	6.7	14.4	1.36
2009	GWN	AAA	23	5	0	0	8	6	37²	20	0	10	44	44%	.238	35	0.80	1.19	2.23	1.93	5.9	0.3	2.6	8.5	13.9	1.59
2009	ATL	MLB	23	3	5	0	37	4	67²	65	5	30	72	48%	.324	12	1.40	4.26	3.49	4.57	8.9	0.8	3.4	7.9	6.9	0.54
2010	ATL	MLB	24	6	5	1	42	7	94¹	92	10	37	82	47%	.307	6	1.37	4.16	3.91	4.56	8.9	1.1	3.3	7.1	9.8	1.90

Breakout: 13% Improve: 40% Collapse: 23% Attrition: 10%   MLB: 53%   Comparables: Ronnie Corona, Shaun Marcum, Buddy Hernandez, Mark Brandenburg

When the Braves needed a starter in late May, it was quite a surprise to see them reach down to Triple-A Gwinnett for Medlen instead of Tommy Hanson, but this should not be taken as a slight to Medlen—he may not be a future star, but he is certainly a keeper in his own right. Miscast as a starter, Medlen was much more effective out of the bullpen, where his fastball climbed into the 91-93 mph range, and he could dispense with his pedestrian breaking ball in favor of his plus changeup. Medlen will never be a closer, but he could be effective as a late-inning reliever for the next decade.

Mike Minor

Bats: R   Throws: L   Height: 6' 3"   Weight: 200   Born: December 26, 1987   Age: 22

YEAR	TEAM	LVL	AGE	W	L	SV	G	GS	IP	H	HR	BB	SO	GB%	BABIP	STUFF	WHIP	ERA	SIERA	DERA	EqH9	EqHR9	EqBB9	EqSO9	VORP	SN/WX
2009	ROM	A	21	0	1	0	4	4	14	10	0	0	17	39%	.323	12	0.71	0.64	1.01	1.54	9.3	0.8	1.5	6.9	5.1	0.39
2010	ATL	MLB	22	2	4	0	19	13	53	67	8	23	24	41%	.322	-11	1.69	5.74	5.68	6.25	11.5	1.5	3.5	3.7	-4.4	2.37

Breakout: 6% Improve: 24% Collapse: 45% Attrition: 1%   MLB: 2%   Comparables: Derek Andersen, Mike Foster, Lenny DiNardo, Jack Taschner

The selection of Minor with the seventh overall pick was one of the more controversial moments of the 2009 draft. The debate didn't concern Minor's talent, but rather the proper moment to take a player like him. Outsized talent Stephen Strasburg aside, a strong case can be made that no pitcher in the draft had a better chance of a lengthy big-league career, but one might also prefer 50 pitchers ahead of him if the criterion were changed to "most likely to pitch in an All-Star Game." Minor represents the classic, conservative selection in the certainty vs. upside argument, as he has the polish of a veteran and plus-plus command of a four-pitch mix, but he doesn't blow anyone away. His ceiling is that of a third or fourth starter, but it's a ceiling he's going to reach quickly, probably beginning his first full season at Double-A. The third side to the Minor question is that good teams such as the Braves rarely get the chance to pick in the single digits, and that's where the stars come from. So the question remains: Did the Braves do the right thing in finding a consistent starter, or did they blow a golden opportunity to find a true impact player?

Peter Moylan

Bats: R   Throws: R   Height: 6' 2"   Weight: 200   Born: February 12, 1978   Age: 32

YEAR	TEAM	LVL	AGE	W	L	SV	G	GS	IP	H	HR	BB	SO	GB%	BABIP	STUFF	WHIP	ERA	SIERA	DERA	EqH9	EqHR9	EqBB9	EqSO9	VORP	SN/WX
2007	ATL	MLB	29	5	3	1	80	0	90	65	6	31	63	70%	.234	12	1.07	1.80	3.90	2.79	6.7	0.6	2.9	5.8	26.2	3.08
2008	ATL	MLB	30	0	1	1	7	0	5²	5	1	1	5	74%	.235	6	1.06	1.59	3.17	1.50	7.5	1.5	1.5	6.0	2.7	0.32
2009	ATL	MLB	31	6	2	0	87	0	73	65	0	35	61	69%	.308	8	1.37	2.84	3.88	3.69	8.3	0.1	3.7	6.4	14.2	1.49
2010	ATL	MLB	32	4	4	0	59	0	59	56	6	26	39	65%	.283	-6	1.38	4.15	4.41	4.55	8.6	0.9	3.6	5.5	6.2	1.18

Breakout: 11% Improve: 38% Collapse: 25% Attrition: 15%   MLB: 92%   Comparables: Bob Locker, Jack Aker, Lindy McDaniel, Donn Pall

The affable Aussie was downright outstanding in 2007, and after missing most of 2008 recovering from Tommy John surgery, he slowly returned to being downright outstanding again, allowing only two runs in his last 32 appearances. His sinker is among the best you'll find, as he faced 309 batters in 2009 without giving up a home run while compiling a ground-ball ratio of nearly 3-to-1, and despite the surgery, he was durable enough to pitch in 87 games. These kind of pitchers get little attention, but they're worth their weight in gold. Given current gold prices and Moylan's 200 pounds, that would be about $3 million to $3.5 million, which is about right, considering that he's arbitration-eligible.

Eric O'Flaherty

Bats: L   Throws: L   Height: 6' 2"   Weight: 220   Born: February 5, 1985   Age: 25

YEAR	TEAM	LVL	AGE	W	L	SV	G	GS	IP	H	HR	BB	SO	GB%	BABIP	STUFF	WHIP	ERA	SIERA	DERA	EqH9	EqHR9	EqBB9	EqSO9	VORP	SN/WX
2007	SEA	MLB	22	7	1	0	56	0	52¹	45	1	20	36	48%	.277	13	1.24	4.47	4.53	4.27	7.0	0.2	3.1	5.5	7.2	0.53
2008	TAC	AAA	23	1	0	2	14	0	16¹	23	1	9	19	59%	.440	4	1.96	4.96	3.61	5.17	13.2	1.1	4.6	8.0	0.6	0.04
2008	SEA	MLB	23	0	1	0	7	0	6²	16	2	4	4	68%	.467	-48	3.00	20.25	5.30	19.29	20.6	2.6	5.1	5.1	-10.7	-0.66
2009	ATL	MLB	24	2	1	0	78	0	56¹	52	2	18	39	57%	.292	1	1.24	3.04	4.23	3.79	8.4	0.3	2.5	5.3	10.4	1.08
2010	ATL	MLB	25	3	4	1	59	0	58	57	6	25	39	58%	.293	-7	1.41	4.52	4.53	4.91	8.9	0.9	3.6	5.5	3.8	0.62

Breakout: 20%   Improve: 41%   Collapse: 20%   Attrition: 10%   MLB: 88%   Comparables: Jay Sawatski, Frank Baumann, Bill Lee, Alex Carbajal

Not bad for twenty thousand bucks, huh? The Mariners tried to sneak O'Flaherty through waivers last November, hoping that concerns about his 2008 injury problems would discourage potential claimants. Instead, the Braves ended up with a shut-down lefty who is good enough against right-handers that he's not solely a LOOGY. A classic sinker/slider reliever who keeps the ball down and has slightly above-average velocity for a southpaw, O'Flaherty is likely to take over Mike Gonzalez's role in 2010.

Todd Redmond

Bats: R   Throws: R   Height: 6' 3"   Weight: 215   Born: May 17, 1985   Age: 25

YEAR	TEAM	LVL	AGE	W	L	SV	G	GS	IP	H	HR	BB	SO	GB%	BABIP	STUFF	WHIP	ERA	SIERA	DERA	EqH9	EqHR9	EqBB9	EqSO9	VORP	SN/WX
2007	LYN	A+	22	7	12	0	25	25	142²	151	13	32	95	38%	.301	-11	1.28	4.54	4.31	6.24	10.2	1.7	2.5	4.0	-11.2	-1.79
2007	ALT	AA	22	1	1	0	3	3	17¹	15	2	3	12	33%	.250	12	1.04	3.12	4.14	3.78	8.6	1.6	1.6	4.3	3.2	0.21
2008	MIS	AA	23	13	5	0	28	27	166¹	164	17	33	133	37%	.296	-7	1.18	3.52	3.73	4.75	9.8	1.8	2.0	5.1	13.3	0.70
2009	GWN	AAA	24	9	6	0	27	24	145	152	21	47	106	32%	.289	-31	1.37	4.41	4.60	6.34	10.7	2.2	3.2	5.1	-13.0	-0.45
2010	ATL	MLB	25	6	9	0	28	21	126¹	140	18	46	77	33%	.305	-9	1.47	4.98	5.11	5.47	10.1	1.4	3.0	5.0	0.4	1.39

Breakout: 9%   Improve: 59%   Collapse: 12%   Attrition: 22%   MLB: 9%   Comparables: Paul Stewart, Nic Ungs, Joe Kucharski, Jim Hunter

Acquired from the Pirates in 2008 for Tyler Yates, Redmond probably would have gotten a chance by now, but the emergence of Medlen and Hanson left him to enjoy the charming Atlanta suburb of Gwinnett off scenic Interstate 85. He's a classic Quad-A pitcher, an emergency starter who survives simply by throwing strikes. He'll probably get somewhere between 10 and 20 big-league starts over the next six years with a number of different organizations.

Jo-Jo Reyes

Bats: L   Throws: L   Height: 6' 2"   Weight: 230   Born: November 20, 1984   Age: 25

YEAR	TEAM	LVL	AGE	W	L	SV	G	GS	IP	H	HR	BB	SO	GB%	BABIP	STUFF	WHIP	ERA	SIERA	DERA	EqH9	EqHR9	EqBB9	EqSO9	VORP	SN/WX
2007	MIS	AA	22	8	1	0	13	13	73¹	63	5	35	71	48%	.299	8	1.34	3.56	3.80	4.81	9.4	1.5	4.5	5.9	5.1	0.30
2007	RIC	AAA	22	4	0	0	6	6	36	25	2	12	39	55%	.256	34	1.03	1.00	2.95	2.44	6.7	0.8	3.1	7.5	11.9	1.22
2007	ATL	MLB	22	2	2	0	11	10	50²	55	9	30	27	53%	.282	-12	1.68	6.22	5.55	6.75	10.0	1.6	4.9	4.4	-6.9	0.30
2008	RIC	AAA	23	1	1	0	8	8	39	31	2	16	38	59%	.276	16	1.21	2.31	3.54	3.05	7.0	0.7	3.8	6.3	10.4	1.16
2008	ATL	MLB	23	3	11	0	23	22	113	134	18	52	78	57%	.321	-19	1.65	5.81	4.65	6.10	11.0	1.6	3.7	5.3	-7.3	0.68
2009	GWN	AAA	24	4	2	0	15	14	66	68	6	24	32	48%	.284	-21	1.39	2.86	5.25	3.96	10.4	1.5	3.7	3.4	10.5	1.48
2009	ATL	MLB	24	0	2	0	6	5	27	27	4	13	21	64%	.287	-9	1.48	7.00	4.24	8.44	9.1	1.4	3.7	5.7	-8.7	-0.18
2010	ATL	MLB	25	5	7	0	26	21	108²	114	13	54	73	49%	.303	-5	1.54	4.91	4.87	5.33	9.6	1.2	4.1	5.5	2.0	1.53

Breakout: 10%   Improve: 41%   Collapse: 15%   Attrition: 19%   MLB: 62%   Comparables: Allen Watson, Derek Lilliquist, Chris Seddon, Mike Rochford

A second-round pick in 2003, Reyes is big, throws left-handed, and gets his fastball up to 95 at times while sitting in the low 90s. Basically, he should be a successful big-league pitcher, but after 40 games with the Braves and nearly 200 innings, his ERA is still over 6.00, and even the Braves don't really have a good answer as to what has gone wrong. Scouts look at Reyes and see a player who has never graduated from thrower to pitcher. He might be out of chances with the organization.

Rafael Soriano

| | | | | Bats: R | | Throws: R | | Height: 6' 1" | | Weight: 220 | | Born: December 19, 1979 | | Age: 30 |

YEAR	TEAM	LVL	AGE	W	L	SV	G	GS	IP	H	HR	BB	SO	GB%	BABIP	STUFF	WHIP	ERA	SIERA	DERA	EqH9	EqHR9	EqBB9	EqSO9	VORP	SN/WX
2007	ATL	MLB	27	3	3	9	71	0	72	47	12	15	70	33%	.198	12	0.86	3.00	2.97	3.30	6.1	1.5	1.6	7.9	17.4	3.78
2008	ATL	MLB	28	0	1	3	14	0	14	7	1	9	16	25%	.200	14	1.14	2.57	3.96	3.29	5.3	0.7	5.3	8.6	3.4	0.41
2009	ATL	MLB	29	1	6	27	77	0	75²	53	6	27	102	34%	.275	26	1.06	2.97	2.24	3.15	6.8	0.8	2.7	9.5	19.7	3.71
2010	TBA	MLB	30	4	3	13	62	0	60²	51	7	23	60	33%	.285	12	1.23	3.62	3.55	3.65	7.3	1.0	3.1	8.1	12.5	1.98

Breakout: 16%   Improve: 36%   Collapse: 28%   Attrition: 6%   MLB: 91%   Comparables: Rich Garces, Justin Speier, Trevor Hoffman, Keith Foulke

It was the same old story for Soriano in 2009. He was healthy, so he pitched extremely well while assuming full-time closing duties in July. He's got pure closer's stuff, with a 92-97 mph fastball and an excellent slider, but he does tend to elevate his pitches in the zone, and his concentration seems to lapse when the game isn't on the line. The Braves always had to cross their fingers that he would stay off the disabled list. He shocked the Braves by reading the market right and accepting arbitration, which got him traded to the Rays and signed there, a bargain and a boon for Tampa Bay, since they now have a closer for a year at $7.5 million.

Julio Teheran

| | | | | Bats: R | | Throws: R | | Height: 6' 2" | | Weight: 150 | | Born: January 27, 1991 | | Age: 19 |

YEAR	TEAM	LVL	AGE	W	L	SV	G	GS	IP	H	HR	BB	SO	GB%	BABIP	STUFF	WHIP	ERA	SIERA	DERA	EqH9	EqHR9	EqBB9	EqSO9	VORP	SN/WX
2008	DNV	Rk	17	1	2	0	6	6	15	18	2	4	17	47%	.390	-4	1.47	6.60	2.92	10.88	16.5	4.5	4.5	5.3	-7.2	-0.56
2009	ROM	A	18	1	3	0	7	7	37²	42	2	11	28	46%	.342	6	1.41	4.78	4.14	7.36	12.5	2.2	4.1	3.3	-6.8	-0.85
2009	DNV	Rk	18	2	1	0	7	7	43²	36	2	7	39	-1%	.288	14	0.98	2.68	3.13	6.94	12.4	2.5	3.3	4.0	-5.7	-0.35
2010	ATL	MLB	19	2	6	0	16	14	64	89	12	33	31	34%	.342	14	1.91	7.79	6.03	8.54	12.9	1.9	4.2	4.0	-21.6	0.85

Breakout: 25%   Improve: 55%   Collapse: 15%   Attrition: 8%   MLB: 0%   Comparables: Robert Hernandez, Lawrence Gonzalez, Tim Dodd, Sandy Diaz

While Teheran's numbers are well short of eye-popping, scouts are absolutely crazy about this kid. Already dialing heat up to 96 mph with his fastball, Teheran is long, extremely thin, and loaded with projection. Despite being a teenager from Colombia with little experience, he's also highly polished for his age, with above-average command and a changeup that is far beyond his years. After two seasons of restrained usage, Teheran will finally pitch for a full season in 2010. Few prospects out there are better bets for a breakout campaign.

Javier Vazquez

| | | | | Bats: R | | Throws: R | | Height: 6' 2" | | Weight: 210 | | Born: July 25, 1976 | | Age: 33 |

YEAR	TEAM	LVL	AGE	W	L	SV	G	GS	IP	H	HR	BB	SO	GB%	BABIP	STUFF	WHIP	ERA	SIERA	DERA	EqH9	EqHR9	EqBB9	EqSO9	VORP	SN/WX
2007	CHA	MLB	30	15	8	0	32	32	216²	197	29	50	213	45%	.288	31	1.14	3.74	3.07	3.46	7.7	1.0	1.9	8.2	49.0	5.40
2008	CHA	MLB	31	12	16	0	33	33	208¹	214	25	61	200	46%	.316	25	1.32	4.67	3.42	4.36	8.7	0.9	2.3	8.0	26.4	3.69
2009	ATL	MLB	32	15	10	0	32	32	219¹	181	20	44	238	49%	.283	34	1.03	2.87	2.62	3.26	7.6	0.9	1.5	8.1	53.9	7.42
2010	NYA	MLB	33	14	11	0	31	31	203²	195	26	54	180	44%	.300	25	1.22	3.85	3.47	3.95	8.5	1.0	2.2	7.5	35.0	3.38

Breakout: 5%   Improve: 41%   Collapse: 17%   Attrition: 15%   MLB: 98%   Comparables: Mike Mussina, Tom Seaver, Don Sutton, Jason Schmidt

On a basic level, Vazquez's ability to deliver what was arguably the best season of his career came down to two simple things: first, he went to the weaker league, and second, he went from a hitter's park to a pitcher-friendly park. There were other things going on as well, especially on a between-the-ears level, as Vazquez responded far better to Bobby Cox's low-key style over Ozzie Guillen's intensity. He's still prone to bad innings on occasion, but that was another improvement over his White Sox years, when he was simply prone to bad games. Vazquez's one remaining year under contract for an $11.5 million deal made him a top trade chip, but an understandably suspicious market limited the Braves' options, and they settled for trading him to the Yankees with Boone Logan for Melky Cabrera, lefty Mike Dunn, and prospect Arodys Vizcaino. How well he fares in the toughest division back in the DH league is a gamble, but at that price one very much worth taking.

LINEOUTS

Hitters

PLAYER	TEAM	LVL	AGE	PA	R	2B	3B	HR	RBI	BB	SO	SB-CS	EqBRR	AVG/OBP/SLG	EqAVG/EqOBP/EqSLG	EqA	VORP	WARP
OF B. Barton	GWN	AAA	27	426	47	17	4	7	46	45	101	17-7	1.3	.266/.354/.390	.243/.325/.361	.245	1.8	-0.6
C C. Bethancourt	DNV	Rk	17	56	10	5	0	2	8	6	16	1-1	-0.7	.260/.339/.480	.212/.268/.308	.199	-1.4	-0.6
	BRA	Rk	17	131	22	9	1	2	19	11	22	7-0	1.8	.284/.344/.431	.264/.305/.397	.248	3.2	-0.3
UT C. Burke	SDN	MLB	29	89	8	5	0	1	5	6	16	4-1	0.4	.207/.270/.305	.220/.281/.305	.221	-0.4	-0.7
	GWN	AAA	29	309	39	19	2	3	32	22	46	13-2	1.5	.285/.351/.401	.273/.331/.385	.255	8.2	0.7
INF B. Conrad#	GWN	AAA	29	469	66	25	0	12	64	53	108	13-1	4.8	.269/.358/.422	.249/.330/.383	.257	10.9	0.3
	ATL	MLB	29	58	7	1	2	2	8	3	14	0-0	0.7	.204/.259/.407	.204/.259/.407	.230	-1.3	0.1
OF R. Gorecki	GWN	AAA	28	416	57	27	6	9	49	34	73	14-7	1.6	.286/.351/.464	.269/.329/.428	.260	9.2	1.5
	ATL	MLB	28	27	6	0	0	0	3	1	12	1-0	0.8	.200/.222/.200	.200/.222/.200	.156	-1.9	-0.3
SS B. Hicks	MIS	AA	23	534	63	25	4	10	48	53	131	17-1	3.1	.237/.319/.373	.234/.299/.366	.238	9.0	0.6
SS M. Jones	DNV	Rk	22	282	50	18	6	4	27	26	55	19-4	0.7	.258/.337/.430	.211/.265/.301	.201	-5.0	-1.7
UT G. Norton#	ATL	MLB	36	97	3	2	0	0	7	20	20	0-0	0.3	.145/.330/.171	.156/.330/.182	.202	-5.4	-0.6
C C. Sammons	GWN	AAA	26	328	34	12	0	9	37	20	61	7-0	-0.3	.214/.266/.344	.209/.257/.329	.209	-2.7	-0.8
	ATL	MLB	26	12	1	0	0	0	0	1	3	0-0	0.0	.182/.250/.182	.182/.250/.182	.130	-0.7	0.2
OF J. Sucre	ROM	A	21	176	14	15	0	1	18	6	17	1-4	0.3	.325/.352/.432	.298/.318/.386	.240	1.5	0.8
	MYR	A+	21	206	17	8	1	5	20	8	33	3-1	0.1	.259/.286/.386	.237/.262/.343	.207	-2.9	0.1
OF M. Young*	MIS	AA	26	571	81	22	10	4	33	94	59	42-16	4.4	.289/.421/.407	.269/.366/.365	.263	16.0	0.6

Outfielder **Brian Barton** got into one big-league game last year and was caught stealing, but he's one semester away from a degree in aerospace engineering, so he'll be fine. ⊘ Teenage catcher **Christian Bethancourt** has shown impressive power for his age and is worth keeping an eye on. ⊘ After he hit the dramatic home run to knock the Braves out of the playoffs in 2005, **Chris Burke**'s nomadic career landed him in Atlanta. Expect more moves. ⊘ **Brooks Conrad** spent years putting up big numbers in the minors—until 2009—and he still hasn't found a defensive home in the infield. ⊘ Outfielder **Reid Gorecki** finally reached the big leagues at the age of 28, so he can cross that off his bucket list as he prepares for another year at Triple-A. ⊘ **Brandon Hicks** is a good defensive shortstop with above-average power for the position—it's too bad he can't hit a lick. ⊘ A fourth-round pick last June, shortstop **Mycal Jones** has all the tools in the world, but his bat has a long way to go. ⊘ After a bit of a resurgence in 2008, perennial 25th man **Greg Norton** wore out his welcome in 2009 by hitting like a pitcher. ⊘ **Clint Sammons** has been catching at the upper levels of the Braves' system for three years, getting the occasional call to the big leagues. He shouldn't expect much more than that. ⊘ Venezuelan outfielder **Jesus Sucre** sprays line drives all over the field, but with zero secondary skills, his future lies as a bench outfielder, if even that. ⊘ Now 27, **Matt Young** is a 5-foot-8 guy who draws a lot of walks and steals a lot of bases, which might get him a cup of coffee at some point.

Pitchers

PLAYER	TEAM	LVL	AGE	W	L	SV	IP	H	HR	BB	SO	GB%	BABIP	STUFF	WHIP	ERA	SIERA	DERA	EqH9	EqHR9	EqBB9	EqSO9	VORP
B. Brownlie	GWN	AAA	28	5	2	0	56²	60	7	17	47	48%	.308	-12	1.36	4.13	3.89	5.03	10.9	2.0	3.0	5.9	2.8
K. Cofield	MIS	AA	22	10	5	0	140²	122	9	89	87	52%	.259	-11	1.50	3.90	5.36	6.13	9.3	1.5	5.5	3.8	-9.4
E. Cordier	MYR	A+	23	7	8	0	121	115	13	74	88	50%	.284	-26	1.56	3.87	4.94	5.79	10.0	2.2	6.2	4.1	-3.6
D. Hale	DNV	Rk	21	2	1	1	16	7	0	5	12	-1%	.159	-12	0.75	1.12	3.98	4.91	6.8	1.2	4.3	2.5	1.0
L. Hyde*	MYR	A+	24	3	1	1	22¹	13	0	9	28	36%	.245	7	0.99	1.21	2.70	2.25	6.1	0.8	4.1	7.4	7.9
J. Lyman	MIS	AA	22	5	7	0	86²	70	3	43	76	51%	.269	4	1.30	3.12	4.17	4.95	8.6	1.0	4.4	5.6	5.1
	GWN	AAA	22	0	2	0	11	11	0	10	11	40%	.324	11	1.91	4.91	5.10	5.73	9.8	0.0	8.2	6.5	-0.3
S. Marek	MIS	AA	25	3	3	2	39¹	40	2	29	31	44%	.295	-24	1.75	5.72	5.24	8.89	10.1	1.1	6.1	4.7	-15.1
V. Nunez	GWN	AAA	34	3	2	5	83¹	69	7	37	79	42%	.272	-5	1.27	2.16	3.87	3.29	8.6	1.4	4.3	6.7	19.5
J. Ortegano*	MYR	A+	21	4	5	0	69²	56	4	19	59	47%	.264	15	1.08	3.49	3.63	4.88	8.1	1.4	3.0	4.9	4.5
	MIS	AA	21	5	2	0	47²	46	2	15	42	44%	.308	27	1.28	2.83	3.74	4.76	10.1	1.0	3.0	5.8	3.7
E. Osuna*	MYR	A+	21	3	6	0	72²	82	4	14	56	41%	.325	7	1.32	4.33	3.89	6.15	10.8	1.3	2.3	4.2	-5.1
	MIS	AA	21	4	4	0	77¹	74	7	21	49	37%	.271	1	1.23	3.72	4.64	5.77	10.2	1.8	2.6	3.9	-2.2
J. Parr	GWN	AAA	23	1	1	0	30	34	5	5	20	39%	.302	-11	1.30	5.40	4.18	6.43	11.9	2.6	1.9	4.8	-2.9
	ATL	MLB	23	0	0	0	14	17	1	5	12	52%	.340	-1	1.57	5.79	4.07	5.83	10.4	0.6	2.5	6.1	-0.5
C. Rohrbough*	MYR	A+	22	6	8	0	117	129	12	48	100	43%	.329	-25	1.51	5.77	4.16	7.63	11.3	2.1	4.3	4.9	-26.0
L. Valdez	GWN	AAA	24	5	4	27	71¹	66	4	19	75	51%	.304	1	1.19	3.28	3.05	5.66	9.3	1.0	2.6	7.2	-1.2
J. Venters*	MIS	AA	24	4	4	0	65¹	60	2	35	40	64%	.290	-7	1.45	2.76	4.82	4.45	10.0	0.9	5.0	3.9	7.0
	GWN	AAA	24	4	7	0	91¹	103	7	42	58	59%	.322	-23	1.59	5.62	4.80	7.60	11.6	1.3	4.6	4.5	-19.8

Considered the best college pitching prospect back in his Rutgers days, **Bobby Brownlie** seemingly loses a tick of velocity every year, but he throws strikes, changes speeds, and might someday get a chance as a last guy in the pen. ⊘ Standing 6-foot-5 while slinging a solid fastball/curve combination, **Kyle Cofield** isn't going anywhere until he starts striking out more batters than he walks, as opposed to the reverse. ⊘ Acquired from the Royals three years ago for Tony Pena Jr., **Erik Cordier** was once a highly touted arm, but his stuff is far from what it used to be after a series of arm injuries. ⊘ While it was certainly the right call, it took a lot of chutzpah for the Braves to release **Tom Glavine** in order to give his anticipated job to Tommy Hanson, but Glavine's stuff in minor-league rehab starts wasn't big-league-ready, making it a bit of a sad, probable end to a Hall of Fame career. ⊘ The club's third-round pick in June, righty **David Hale** is a raw product, but a phenomenal athlete who has touched 98 mph in the past. If the whole baseball thing doesn't work out, he should be fine after majoring in operations research and financial engineering at Princeton. ⊘ Reliever **Lee Hyde** made an impressive return from Tommy John surgery in 2009; he could get a shot at a middle relief role by the end of the year. ⊘ A second-round pick in 2005, power righty **Jeff Lyman** has had little success in harnessing his stuff, whether starting or relieving. ⊘ When he was acquired from the Angels in the Teixeira deal of '08, the Braves thought **Stephen Marek** could develop into a nice bullpen arm, but he fell apart mechanically last year and started walking the ballpark. ⊘ *Have Arm, Will Travel*, **Vladimir Nunez**'s autobiography, should be arriving in bookstores soon. ⊘ **Jose Ortegano** is left-handed, throws strikes, and had a very good changeup, and his name is vaguely reminiscent of a popular spice. That's enough to put up some nice numbers in the minors, but rarely a package that leads to big-league success. ⊘ **Edgar Osuna** is basically the exact thing Ortegano is, except he's a Mexican with a curveball instead of a Venezuelan with a change. ⊘ Swingman **James Parr** throws strikes and throws fairly hard, but he has yet to find a dependable second pitch and lost time to elbow woes. ⊘ Arguably the most disappointing prospect in 2009, the Braves were expecting a breakout from lefty **Cole Rohrbough**, but instead got an ERA approaching 6.00 as everything about his game went backward. ⊘ Righty **Luis Valdez** was born in Sabana Grande de Palenque in the Dominican Republic, which is just downright fun to say and also more interesting than anything we could add about his middle-of-the-road pitching. ⊘ Southpaw **Jonny Venters** gets a lot of ground balls, but is also quite hittable due to a lack of velocity; his control isn't all that hot, either.

MANAGER: BOBBY COX

YEAR	TEAM	W-L	Pythag +/−	Avg PC	100+ P	120+ P	QS	BQS	REL	REL w Zero R	IBB	Subs	PH	PH Avg	PH HR	SB2	CS2	SB3	CS3	SAC Att	SAC %	POS SAC	Squeeze	Swing	In Play
2007	ATL	84-78	-5	89.2	43	2	78	5	527	346	89	36	288	.213	3	60	25	4	3	77	71.4%	16	2	110	82
2008	ATL	72-90	-6	89.0	41	1	70	6	545	357	80	38	288	.265	8	53	20	5	4	108	63.9%	36	2	130	102
2009	ATL	86-76	-6	95.3	66	2	94	3	488	334	59	49	249	.243	3	56	24	2	2	136	69.9%	44	0	96	78

With the Braves entering a bit of a rebuilding process, it seemed like the perfect time for Cox, now approaching 70, to hand over the reins to Terry Pendleton, who most see as the next Atlanta manager. Yet, as the Yankees showed with Joe Torre, it's hard to fire a legend—a more organic transition goes down a lot easier, so the Braves met Cox halfway, agreeing to bring him back for 2010 while also announcing that it will be his last year before moving into the front office in one of those Tommy Lasorda–type consulting roles. Cox's résumé is truly worthy of the Hall of Fame. While too many think of him as the guy who just won a single World Series in countless tries, he enters the year fourth on the all-time win list and is tied with Joe Torre for first all-time, with 15 postseason appearances, including his remarkable run from 1991 to 2005 with a team that he helped construct as its general manager. Cox will hardly be remembered as a brilliant tactician; in the course of overmanaging his bullpen, he hands out intentional walks like there's an end-of-year bonus attached to them. But what Cox does extremely well is evaluate and manage talent, the kind of thing that is impossible to measure on any programmatic level. Even in 2009, Javier Vasquez's best career season was attributed to Cox, and the manager's inability to win of late is attributable more than anything else to the change of ownership from this generation's Daddy Warbucks to a floundering media company.

Baltimore Orioles

For too many years, Orioles fans have been calling out in the night like the biblical prophet Habakkuk (late of the Mount Vernon neighborhood), "How long, O Lord?" With 12 straight losing seasons and 27 years and counting since their last World Series appearance, the answer has not been forthcoming. The Birds' return to October baseball is not yet assured, but for the first time in many years, there is reason for hope. Professionals are again in charge, as in the days of Harry Dalton, Frank Cashen, and Hank Peters, and the farm system has brought forth a promising crop of youngsters for the first time since Mike Mussina came forth from Williamsport, if not since a Ripken Jr. rose in Havre de Grace. There are even hints that ownership, which has drawn off dollars from a once-generous payroll, is again ready to spend. The reply received to Habakkuk's question, that the "time . . . will come. Even if it tarries, wait for it still; for it will surely come without delay," can now be applied to the Orioles.

The Orioles last won the World Series in 1983. In the 26 years that have elapsed since then, they have had seven winning seasons. In 1989, they finished two games out in what was a rare soft period for the American League East. In 1996, managed by Solonic manager Davey Johnson, they won the AL wild card, with 88 wins. The next season, they won the division. Those seasons aside, even in the good years they were not competitive. The 1996 and 1997 seasons were outliers, islands in a sea of misery that extends back to 1986. The Orioles have had 12 consecutive losing seasons, but this franchise has been in search of a plan for over a quarter of a century.

The Orioles are not the first team to fall into such a deep hole, even in the age of the great correctives to competitive failings like integrated rosters, a worldwide talent net, the farm system, free agency, and the amateur draft. Consigning the famous examples of the Phillies in the 1930s and '40s, the postwar Browns/Orioles, the Kansas City A's, and the era-straddling colossus that was the long Indians slump of roughly 1960 to 1993 to the mists of prehistoric times leaves several non-expansion "lost teams" of recent vintage (see Table 1).

The roughly contemporaneous experiences of the Brewers and Expos/Nationals provide the best comparison with the post-Johnson Orioles, though at first, this trio would seem to be a superficially assembled congeries based on similarity of record and length of their struggles, for the Orioles are perceived to be big spenders and the Brewers and Ex-Nats notoriously penurious. This is only partly true. The Expos were a ward of the state, while the Brewers were a ward of the Selig family, and in both cases, the clubs were the baseball equivalent of inmates in dire Dickensian orphanages. However, a common misunderstanding about the Orioles is that they continue to spend with the big boys. If you take a spin by Table 2, note the drop in the Orioles' payroll rank after 2000.

Indeed, in recent years, the Orioles have been closer to the AL median payroll than the top, and often below the median at that. The days of lavish acquisition, of Roberto Alomar, Rafael Palmeiro, and Randy Myers, are long gone. Characteristic of the new, cheaper brand of birds, the Oriole free-agent signings prior to the 2009 season included dollar-store types such as Cesar Izturis, Mark Hendrickson, Gregg Zaun, and Ty Wigginton, though the O's were reportedly competitive on

ORIOLES PROSPECTUS
2009 W-L: 64-98, 5th in AL East

Pythag	69-93	14th
RS/G	4.6	10th
RA/G	5.4	14th
EqA	.253	9th
EqBRR	-21.9	14th
SNWP	.453	14th
WXRL	6.11	10th
FRAr	5.28	13th
DE	.682	11th
PADE	-1.28	10th
Salary	$67.1	11th
Attend	1.91	9th

Ballpark: Camden Yards (3-yr. PF: 1025). Not the worst place to pitch, so the upgrades need to come on offense

2009: A mixed batch of rookie debuts couldn't get these birds to reach basement-escape velocity

2010: Breaking in talent at the corners and the rotation makes them baseball's best fourth-place team

Action Items: A young shortstop; plenty of Maalox and patience as the talent comes of age

Table 1. The Great Depressives: Long-Haul Losers of Modern Times

Team	Years	Record	Win%	Average	Best	Worst	L ≥ 100	≥ .500	Managers
Tigers	1989-2005 (17)	1147-1540	.427	69-93	85-77 (1993)	43-119 (2003)	4	2	6
Pirates	1993-2009 (17)	1166-1518	.434	70-92	79-83 (1997)	62-100 (2001)	1	0	5
Expos/Nats	1997-2009 (13)	922-1183	.438	71-91	83-79 (2001/2)	59-103 (2009)	2	3	5
Brewers	1993-2004 (12)	825-1051	.440	71-91	80-82 (1996)	56-106 (2002)	1	0	5
Orioles	1998-2009 (12)	855-1087	.440	71-91	79-83 (1998)	63-98 (2001)	0	0	5
Cubs	1973-1983 (11)	779-943	.452	73-89	81-81 (1977)	64-98 (1980)	0	0	8
Royals	1995-2009 (15)	1218-1466	.454	74-88	83-79 (2003)	56-106 (2005)	4	1	5
Mets	1970-1983 (14)	1004-1198	.456	74-88	83-73 (1972)	63-99 (1979)	0	6	7
Braves	1970-1981 (12)	856-1019	.457	74-88	88-74 (1974)	61-101 (1977)	1	3	5

Table 2. Waiting for Book Magwitch: Payroll Rankings of the Poutine/Beer/Crabcake Trio

	Expos/Nats		Brewers		Orioles	
Slump Year	Season	Payroll Rank (NL)	Season	Payroll Rank	Season	Payroll Rank (AL)
1	1997	13	1993	13 (AL)	1998	1
2	1998	16	1994	14 (AL)	1999	2
3	1999	16	1995	14 (AL)	2000	2
4	2000	14	1996	12 (AL)	2001	7
5	2001	16	1997	13 (AL)	2002	8
6	2002	16	1998	12 (NL)	2003	6
7	2003	13	1999	11 (NL)	2004	9
8	2004	14	2000	13 (NL)	2005	6
9	2005	13*	2001	12 (NL)	2006	7
10	2006	10	2002	11 (NL)	2007	7
11	2007	15	2003	16 (NL)	2008	10
12	2008	14	2004	16 (NL)	2009	9
13	2009	13	–	–	–	–

*First year in DC.

Mark Teixeira. Unless one considers Aubrey Huff or Ramon Hernandez a major free agent, the Orioles have been out of the big-bucks signing business since they inked Miguel Tejada to a six-year, $72 million contract in December 2003. The Orioles haven't gone the way of the Marlins and embraced an all-consuming, choking austerity, but they can no longer be counted among baseball's most lavish organizations. Having found that they could not compete solely through amassing a collection of veterans, the O's seemed to scale back their expectations and wait for the farm system to deliver.

That has proved to be a long wait indeed, but what other recourse did they have? The aforementioned Brewers may provide a clue as far as what's to come. They crawled out of the black caldera of their pit with a .500 record in 2005, their first .500 record since 1992. After a year of retrenchment, they broke through to 90 wins and a playoff appearance in 2008. Their 80-82 record last year raises the possibility that the 2007-2008 renaissance will prove to be little more than a fleeting

uptick in a much greater malaise, much as the Orioles' 1997-1998 momentarily obscured the organization's rotten structure. Still, the Brewers' slow rise from 56-106 in 2002 to 90-72 is a legitimate accomplishment, no matter how fleeting their subsequent time with respectability.

Unfortunately, there is no magical lesson in the Brewers' rebuilding except the most basic of all: draft well and have some luck. The Brewers' core talent came to them in a tight run of drafting beginning in 2001, as perspicacious selections in the first and second rounds netted them J. J. Hardy, Manny Parra, Prince Fielder, Richie Weeks, Yovani Gallardo, catcher Angel Salome (who has a chance to contribute at the major-league level as soon as this spring), Ryan Braun, Will Inman (later traded to the Padres for veteran reliever Scott Linebrink), Mat Gamel, and Matt LaPorta. If there was anything unusual about the Brewers' player development effort in creating the 2008 club, it was that the club almost completely lacked any international signees. None of the key players were from the Dominican Republic or other Latin baseball sources. Instead, the players who didn't come through the draft were either lower-level free-agent signings or trade acquisitions. This is also an indication that a competitive club can be built almost exclusively with canny drafting, inexpensive free-agent signings, and targeted trades. Former free agents on the 2008 Brewers were Mike Cameron, Jeff Suppan, Jason Kendall, Russell Branyan, Craig Counsell, Gabe Kapler, Dave Riske, and Eric Gagne; the remainder of the team, including almost the whole of the bullpen, was assembled through trades.

In contrast, until quite recently the Orioles' drafting effort has been among the shoddiest in baseball. *Baseball America* awards a retrospective letter grade to every draft, and while it rated the team's 2007 draft an A, it also considered only one Orioles draft going back to 1998 worthy of a grade above C, that of 2002. Two drafts, 1998 and 2000, rated Fs, and two others, 2004 and 2006, were given a D grade.

The reason for this is not difficult to see; before the professionals were handed the keys, the Orioles simply missed in draft after draft. It's hardly worth listing the deservedly obscure souls who collected Baltimore bonus money in those years. Suffice it to say that the Orioles had many opportunities to bolster the organization, such as 1999, when they had seven picks scattered between the first round and the first-round supplemental phase. They missed on six of seven, coming away only with Brian Roberts, who was selected with the last of those picks, and lucked out even there—Roberts was not projected by scouts to become the kind of player who could hit .290 and whack 50 doubles a year. The following year was a complete miss. Serviceable major-league infielder Mike Fontenot came in the 2001 draft, but he was dealt away for the ghost of Sammy Sosa, and no one else of lasting worth was selected. The 2002 draft was more successful if only because five players, the best of whom was right-hander John Maine, actually made the majors, though Maine was quickly traded (with Jorge Julio, and for Kris Benson, an inexplicable move), and two other desperately needed pitching prospects, Adam Loewen and Hayden Penn, crashed on takeoff.

There was a burp for the better with the 2003 draft. Nick Markakis was selected with the seventh overall pick in the first round, the Orioles' first talent worthy of being taken in that spot since Mike Mussina in 1990. Unfortunately, 2004 was another weak draft. Outfielder Jeff Fiorentino was rushed to the big leagues and flopped, while pitcher Kevin Hart was swapped to the Cubs for the forever fungible Freddie Bynum before ever donning an ornithologically correct cap in the majors, leaving 2009 rookie right-hander Brad Bergesen to salvage the draft. It was the 2004 draft that cost longtime scouting director Tony DeMacio his job (although last October, he was named the Braves' director of scouting, reuniting him with 1999 Orioles general manager Frank Wren). He was replaced by Joe Jordan, who previously was the national cross-checker for the Marlins.

Under Jordan, the Orioles have begun to turn around their performance in the amateur draft. The jury is still out on 2005's first-round pick, Brandon Snyder, a first baseman who finished 2009 struggling at Triple-A after a breakout campaign at Double-A Bowie, but first-round supplemental pick Garrett Olson was sufficiently intriguing to the Cubs that he netted the Orioles intriguing outfielder Felix Pie, who finally solidified a place for himself in the majors with a .290/.346/.497 second half. Second-rounder Nolan Reimold has emerged as a solid starter in left field. There is still hope for third-rounder Brandon Erbe to survive injury and emerge as a major-league pitcher, and 13th-round right-hander David Hernandez joined the major-league rotation in the second half and made eight quality starts in 19 tries, despite a home-run rate that will require correction if he's to thrive.

The 2006 draft was a step backward, and it's not yet clear that the Orioles will get anything of value from it. First-round pick Billy Rowell has been a four-star disaster, hitting only .259/.326/.393 in 375 games as a pro and moving from third base to right field despite his inability to carry either position offensively. Lefty pitcher Zach Britton, the third-round pick, will have to continue the progress he made in 2009, posting a 2.70 ERA as a 21-year-old at High-A Frederick, to salvage the draft—he certainly has more upside than righty Jason Berken, the sole member of the class to make the majors so far.

Fortunately, the 2007 and 2008 drafts were 180 degrees removed from the struggles of 2004 or 2006. Even if first-round pick Matt Wieters is the only player the Orioles get out of their 2007 haul, the draft will have to be marked down as a successful one. But right-hander Jake Arrieta's fastball should ensure that the team sees even more of a return, while 2008 first-round pick Brian Matusz has already taken his place in the rotation.

The combination of Jordan's good work in the draft and the more pragmatic approach to rebuilding the roster emphasized by president of baseball operations Andy MacPhail has led to the reversal of some of owner Peter Angelos's most self-destructive policies. For many years, the Orioles were unwilling to trade veterans for prospects, but recent deals have already made a decisive difference to the organization's outlook. The February 2008 trade of Erik Bedard to the Mariners brought emerging star center fielder Adam Jones, top right-handed starting pitcher prospect Chris Tillman, prospective reliever Kam Mickolio, and veteran lefty short man George Sherrill, who the Orioles converted into a closer, vastly improving his value. Sherrill was subsequently dispatched to the Dodgers, who sent back two solid prospects in third baseman Josh Bell, currently ranked by BP as the second-best prospect in the organization, and right-hander Steve Johnson.

There is, of course, no guarantee that any of these young players will take hold in Baltimore, but the very fact that many of them have already landed bayside is a triumph, given the futility of the team's player development effort in both the recent and the distant past. In 2009 alone, the Orioles debuted Wieters, Reimold, Bergesen, Berken, Hernandez, Matusz, and Tillman. In bringing along so many pitchers, the Orioles may already have gotten through the hard part, the portion of rebuilding their team that the Brewers, their most recent antecedent in the digging out of Sheol, have yet to conquer. The Brewers have the hitters, but the pitching department has not developed in the same way.

The Orioles still have much work to do, or the recent turnaround of the farm system might be sufficient only to break their long losing streak but not boost them into contention. Even if the young starting pitchers mature to best expectations, the Orioles haven't fully developed a support structure. The 2009 offense scored only 4.57 runs per game—league average was 4.82—and ranked toward the bottom of the league in such important categories as walks, isolated power, and on-base percentage. While Wieters still profiles as an impact hitter and Adam Jones may yet blossom into further prowess, the outlines of a top offense are simply not on hand at present. Roberts, Markakis, and Reimold are unlikely to add much in the way of offensive capacity, given their ages and performance histories. Brandon Snyder and Josh Bell may eventually serve to plug up the infield corners, but Snyder's bat may not serve at first, and Bell's glove may not answer at third. A shortstop who can field and make an offensive contribution is nowhere in sight. In the highly competitive environment of the AL East, the Orioles team that unseats the Yankees, Red Sox, or Rays won't have the luxury of punting on production at too many positions.

The establishment of an offense is all the more delicate a proposition because the Orioles also have work to do on the defensive side of the ball. The 2009 club ranked 20th in Park-Adjusted Defensive Efficiency, and as the Braves demonstrated as long ago as 1991 and the Rays showed as recently as 2008, shoring up a team's defense can result in almost miraculous improvements for the pitching staff. One of those hoary old baseball clichés you often hear about is what an unforgivable sin it is to give the opposition extra outs, but it has the virtue of being true. Despite Adam Jones's Gold Glove, the O's have a long way to go. In-house options for the corners such as Snyder and Bell are not good gloves,

and Roberts has never been an exceptional defender. Whatever Luke Scott hits, the Orioles would arguably reap an outsized benefit from jettisoning his contract; this would free designated hitter for Reimold and allow the defensively excellent Felix Pie to patrol left field.

At the same time that MacPhail and company are attempting to master the offense and the defense, the bullpen awaits them. The Orioles ranked 21st in wins added by the bullpen (WXRL) and ended the season with their closer wearing Dodger blue. Signing Mike Gonzalez gives them an obvious closer, but the rest of the pen's wide-open. As the Rays showed over the last two years, a bullpen can go from rags to riches and back again in the blink of an eye; fixing up a relief staff isn't necessarily the most difficult task before the O's, but it is the most unpredictable.

History is full of teams that mastered one aspect of the game but not the other, to their detriment. Quite often, good offensive units lack the pitching to carry them into contention, but the opposite is occasionally true as well. We need look back no further than the 2009 Mariners for an example of a team that led the league in ERA but couldn't piece together enough offense to get beyond 85 wins. After adding veteran Kevin Millwood to front their talented young rotation, the Orioles could finally hatch the next generation of great Bird pitchers and could find the other aspects of team building that have eluded them. These assets are perishable, and they won't wait. The moment that owner Angelos reopens his purse is crucial; MacPhail has suggested that Angelos is willing, but there are probably too many holes to fill in one shopping spree.

MacPhail has said that his fowl need to emulate fish, pointing to the Rays' great leap forward as the model for the Orioles. He is probably premature in offering this as a possibility for 2010, but for the first time in years, such a prophecy does not invite outright derision. Thus is the Habakkuk of Baltimore answered: not now, but maybe soon.

HITTERS

Robert Andino SS

Bats: R   Throws: R   Height: 6' 0"   Weight: 170   Born: April 25, 1984   Age: 26

YEAR	TEAM	LVL	AGE	PA	R	2B	3B	HR	RBI	BB	SO	SB	CS	EqBRR	AVG	OBP	SLG	EqAVG	EqOBP	EqSLG	EqA	VORP	WARP	DEFENSE	
2007	ABQ	AAA	23	644	85	25	13	13	50	40	129	21	13	-3.3	.278	.322	.428	.222	.266	.340	.211	-7.3	-2.0	136-SS	-9
2007	FLO	MLB	23	13	0	1	0	0	0	0	2	0	0	0.0	.385	.385	.462	.385	.385	.462	.299	0.6	0.1		
2008	ABQ	AAA	24	204	28	14	3	6	26	18	31	9	5	-0.5	.287	.356	.497	.228	.292	.380	.235	3.1	0.4	42-SS	0
2008	FLO	MLB	24	68	7	2	0	2	9	4	23	0	0	1.5	.206	.254	.333	.206	.254	.333	.204	-2.4	0.0	10-2B 1 1-SS 1	
2009	BAL	MLB	25	215	31	7	0	2	10	15	47	3	3	0.7	.222	.274	.288	.228	.279	.284	.199	-4.8	-1.1	54-SS -3 4-2B -1	
2010	BAL	MLB	26	354	41	14	3	7	25	24	81	9	6	-0.2	.238	.292	.362	.231	.287	.349	.215	-3.4	-0.6	77-SS	-2

Breakout: 17%   Improve: 42%   Collapse: 17%   Attrition: 20%   MLB: 63%   Comparables: Kent Anderson, Jeff Forney, Andre Robertson, Gus Polidor

The Orioles traded Hayden Penn for Andino at the end of spring training; Penn was out of options, so was Andino, and the Orioles were about to be stuck with using the aged Chris Gomez as their utility player (again). The thinking went that Andino would give them a competent fielding backup shortstop, albeit one who has never been even a league-average hitter in any league in which he's played in as a pro. Unfortunately, Cesar Izturis's appendectomy gave Andino extended regular playing time, and he did just as badly as you'd expect; Oriole management was "pleased" with his performance. Puh-leeze.

Michael Aubrey 1B

Bats: L   Throws: L   Height: 6' 0"   Weight: 195   Born: April 15, 1982   Age: 28

YEAR	TEAM	LVL	AGE	PA	R	2B	3B	HR	RBI	BB	SO	SB	CS	EqBRR	AVG	OBP	SLG	EqAVG	EqOBP	EqSLG	EqA	VORP	WARP	DEFENSE	
2007	KIN	A+	25	59	15	5	0	5	11	6	7	0	0	-1.2	.400	.492	.800	.340	.397	.623	.332	5.6	0.7	8-1B	0
2007	AKR	AA	25	221	22	11	0	7	34	10	35	0	0	0.3	.248	.290	.403	.219	.252	.343	.204	-10.7	-2.2	31-1B	-7
2008	AKR	AA	26	112	14	10	1	2	16	8	12	0	0	0.8	.282	.330	.456	.238	.277	.371	.224	-3.2	-0.4	16-1B	0
2008	BUF	AAA	26	309	29	18	0	7	37	16	40	0	0	-1.6	.281	.328	.418	.260	.304	.385	.240	-3.8	-0.6	33-1B	-1
2008	CLE	MLB	26	50	2	0	0	2	3	5	5	0	0	-1.3	.200	.280	.333	.200	.280	.333	.220	-1.9	-0.3	11-1B	-1
2009	COH	AAA	27	228	27	16	1	5	29	9	25	1	1	-1.4	.292	.322	.448	.272	.300	.423	.249	-3.1	-0.9	34-1B	-4
2009	NOR	AAA	27	179	14	13	0	3	23	11	13	1	1	-0.7	.287	.324	.421	.285	.318	.412	.254	-1.2	-0.3	12-1B	-1
2009	BAL	MLB	27	95	12	7	0	4	14	5	10	0	0	-0.4	.289	.326	.500	.289	.326	.489	.277	1.7	0.3	22-1B	1
2010	BAL	MLB	28	449	46	23	1	12	55	27	67	1	1	-1.0	.261	.311	.406	.256	.306	.393	.235	-7.1	-1.1	61-1B	-2

Breakout: 6%   Improve: 33%   Collapse: 26%   Attrition: 14%   MLB: 18%   Comparables: Tony Brown, Gary Burnham, Pete Dalena, Mike Robertson

Aubrey has missed so much time with injuries over the years that it's almost impossible to know just what the former 11th overall pick of 2003 is really capable of doing. He started the season in Cleveland's system, joined the Orioles in a minor trade, and moved up after Aubrey Huff was traded away (league rules require the O's to maintain a one-Aubrey quota at all times). He actually hit better in Baltimore—raw, untranslated—than he had in either Norfolk or Columbus, which isn't a good betting position for the future. The void that is Oriole first base gives him a chance to prove himself, a chance he wouldn't be likely to get anywhere else.

Josh Bell 3B

Bats: S   Throws: R   Height: 6' 3"   Weight: 235   Born: November 13, 1986   Age: 23

YEAR	TEAM	LVL	AGE	PA	R	2B	3B	HR	RBI	BB	SO	SB	CS	EqBRR	AVG	OBP	SLG	EqAVG	EqOBP	EqSLG	EqA	VORP	WARP	DEFENSE	
2007	GRL	A	20	438	65	21	3	15	62	39	109	5	1	0.0	.289	.354	.470	.252	.311	.408	.248	2.9	-1.2	88-3B	-13
2007	SBR	A+	20	79	4	2	1	2	9	3	19	0	0	-0.5	.173	.203	.307	.158	.177	.289	.145	-6.6	-1.6	17-3B	-7
2008	SBR	A+	21	220	34	12	2	6	21	31	56	4	2	-0.9	.273	.373	.455	.241	.332	.387	.255	2.8	-0.1	32-3B	-4
2009	CHT	AA	22	391	47	30	2	11	52	50	70	3	5	-3.9	.296	.386	.497	.275	.348	.458	.276	17.2	2.0	89-3B	-1
2009	BOW	AA	22	127	18	5	0	9	24	11	28	0	0	0.3	.289	.346	.570	.276	.323	.543	.287	6.8	0.1	25-3B	-6
2010	BAL	MLB	23	469	57	22	2	18	59	42	118	3	2	-0.9	.254	.323	.440	.247	.318	.421	.249	6.8	0.1	95-3B	-6

Breakout: 17%   Improve: 46%   Collapse: 12%   Attrition: 6%   MLB: 12%   Comparables: Elvis Corporan, Wilson Betemit, Mark Merchant, Scott Spiezio

Coming to the Orioles in the George Sherrill deal, Bell immediately became the third baseman of the future, a future that could arrive sometime this year. His bat is ready, with the kind of power you'd expect from a third baseman, yet the Orioles aren't in a hurry to install him right away, as Bell does still have issues. He has worked hard on his fielding, improving from atrocious to just plain bad, and while he is a switch-hitter, he hasn't been able to figure out lefties at all, hitting .193/.282/.259 in 156 plate appearances against left-handers in 2009; if he doesn't iron that out, he might eventually have to be platooned.

Jeff Fiorentino   OF

Bats: L   Throws: R   Height: 6' 1"   Weight: 185   Born: April 14, 1983   Age: 27

YEAR	TEAM	LVL	AGE	PA	R	2B	3B	HR	RBI	BB	SO	SB	CS	EqBRR	AVG	OBP	SLG	EqAVG	EqOBP	EqSLG	EqA	VORP	WARP	DEFENSE			
2007	BOW	AA	24	496	68	18	4	15	65	44	89	8	4	0.8	.282	.346	.445	.265	.318	.404	.252	7.9	0.1	82-CF	-4	29-LF	-2
2008	NOR	AAA	25	267	25	12	1	2	25	34	52	7	3	-0.5	.268	.361	.355	.264	.352	.346	.253	4.2	0.4	40-CF	3	20-LF	-4
2009	NOR	AAA	26	422	70	26	5	12	67	48	62	13	6	0.6	.312	.387	.510	.304	.375	.497	.296	26.0	3.0	79-RF	4	15-CF	-4
2009	BAL	MLB	26	75	8	1	0	0	8	8	16	2	0	0.5	.281	.351	.297	.286	.351	.302	.250	1.2	0.1	12-CF	-2	6-LF	2
2010	BAL	MLB	27	441	53	20	3	10	56	43	90	7	3	0.3	.262	.334	.398	.256	.328	.385	.245	2.2	0.5	97-RF	2		

Breakout: 5%   Improve: 35%   Collapse: 27%   Attrition: 10%   MLB: 28%   Comparables: Terrmel Sledge, Tom Grant, Everett Graham, Jason Grabowski

Fiorentino lucked into some extended major-league playing time when Adam Jones couldn't come back from his ankle sprain. He had a great year at Norfolk, primarily because he hit left-handers as well as right-handers for the first time in his life. A fine defensive outfielder with not quite enough offense, he's a free-agent tweener, liable to spend the next several years on the Triple-A/major-league borderline.

Pedro Florimon Jr.   SS

Bats: S   Throws: R   Height: 6' 2"   Weight: 165   Born: December 10, 1986   Age: 23

YEAR	TEAM	LVL	AGE	PA	R	2B	3B	HR	RBI	BB	SO	SB	CS	EqBRR	AVG	OBP	SLG	EqAVG	EqOBP	EqSLG	EqA	VORP	WARP	DEFENSE	
2007	DEL	A	20	418	50	14	1	4	34	28	107	16	6	3.0	.197	.257	.272	.190	.236	.253	.173	-17.8	-3.7	106-SS	-12
2008	DEL	A	21	305	28	18	1	0	19	27	97	13	2	-0.6	.223	.298	.297	.204	.267	.262	.191	-7.3	-1.1	82-SS	-2
2009	FRD	A+	22	486	76	32	5	9	68	42	107	26	9	2.0	.267	.336	.428	.239	.295	.380	.239	8.7	1.2	113-SS	1
2010	BAL	MLB	23	456	49	20	3	7	43	36	128	12	4	0.6	.223	.288	.334	.217	.283	.318	.209	-6.7	-1.0	117-SS	-2

Breakout: 31%   Improve: 66%   Collapse: 17%   Attrition: 12%   MLB: 2%   Comparables: Lee May, Ozzie Chavez, Brandon Chaves, Steven Johnson

This skinny shortstop got himself back onto prospect lists with a dramatically improved 2009, but we're still skeptical. All of the gain came in April and May, when he hit .308/.377/.589; for the rest of his year, he reverted to .228/.289/.304, in line with the disappointing Delmarva player we saw the last two years. He does have great range and a strong arm, but makes a ton of errors—no shortstop in High-A or above made more.

Tyler Henson   3B

Bats: R   Throws: R   Height: 6' 1"   Weight: 190   Born: December 15, 1987   Age: 22

YEAR	TEAM	LVL	AGE	PA	R	2B	3B	HR	RBI	BB	SO	SB	CS	EqBRR	AVG	OBP	SLG	EqAVG	EqOBP	EqSLG	EqA	VORP	WARP	DEFENSE			
2007	ABE	A-	19	289	44	18	4	5	31	22	68	20	2	3.6	.289	.353	.449	.253	.300	.396	.245	6.5	-0.2	63-SS	-8		
2008	DEL	A	20	541	71	25	3	11	62	25	121	20	3	2.7	.265	.310	.392	.247	.283	.357	.224	-7.5	-0.7	118-3B	2		
2009	FRD	A+	21	509	68	31	2	8	71	38	125	18	6	1.5	.267	.329	.396	.235	.284	.345	.222	-7.5	-0.6	67-3B	2	45-LF	1
2010	BAL	MLB	22	485	53	22	2	10	53	31	129	10	3	1.6	.244	.297	.368	.237	.292	.357	.221	-6.6	-0.6	107-3B	1		

Breakout: 25%   Improve: 55%   Collapse: 18%   Attrition: 13%   MLB: 2%   Comparables: Paul Fryer, Corey Smith, J.J. Johnson, Jim Olander

Henson is a prospect for one reason: he's a great athlete. He's fast. He's strong. He has a great arm. It's just that his baseball skills are not so great. He has no pitch recognition, so he's always chasing what the pitcher chooses and not making them come to him. Resultantly, he strikes out a ton, doesn't walk, and doesn't get to translate his strength into power. Defensively, he's got range to go with his arm, but accumulating error totals have moved him from shortstop to third base to left field.

Rhyne Hughes   1B   Bats: L   Throws: L   Height: 6′ 2″   Weight: 175   Born: September 9, 1983   Age: 26

YEAR	TEAM	LVL	AGE	PA	R	2B	3B	HR	RBI	BB	SO	SB	CS	EqBRR	AVG	OBP	SLG	EqAVG	EqOBP	EqSLG	EqA	VORP	WARP	DEFENSE
2007	VRO	A+	23	373	65	24	1	12	57	35	62	1	1	-0.4	.329	.392	.515	.288	.344	.450	.273	8.8	1.0	87-1B -1
2007	MNT	AA	23	91	12	4	1	2	15	9	23	0	1	-0.6	.295	.378	.449	.272	.333	.420	.259	0.7	0.3	20-1B 2
2008	MNT	AA	24	450	57	27	1	14	52	46	112	2	1	-0.7	.268	.356	.448	.237	.304	.384	.239	-5.7	-2.1	86-1B -12
2009	MNT	AA	25	259	31	11	0	15	46	25	80	4	0	1.9	.252	.340	.500	.221	.288	.413	.243	-5.1	-1.7	56-1B -9
2009	DUR	AAA	25	230	31	22	2	7	26	12	69	0	0	0.0	.313	.361	.533	.288	.332	.498	.278	4.8	0.5	41-1B -1
2009	NOR	AAA	25	81	9	2	1	3	7	7	22	0	0	-2.8	.264	.346	.444	.260	.341	.438	.269	0.8	0.1	14-1B 0
2010	TBA	MLB	26	486	55	25	2	14	52	38	142	1	1	-0.4	.240	.308	.399	.237	.304	.381	.237	-6.3	-1.1	101-1B -3

Breakout: 10% Improve: 25% Collapse: 29% Attrition: 11%   MLB: 3%   Comparables: Gabriel Martinez, Greg Smith, Steven Michael, Jeff Kenaga

The player received from the Rays for Gregg Zaun, Hughes is already 26 and so isn't likely to be much more than a temporary prospect. He's making the most of it, although his strikeout/walk ratio suggests that minor-league mashing may be the extent of his upside. He gets very good marks for his defense, however, and he leans pretty heavily towards platoonability in his righty/lefty splits. And with the competition at first base initially limited to the oft-injured Aubrey and the unglovely Scott, maybe he has a window of opportunity. All in all, he was a worthwhile add-on for six weeks of Zauntime.

Cesar Izturis   SS   Bats: S   Throws: R   Height: 5′ 9″   Weight: 190   Born: February 10, 1980   Age: 30

YEAR	TEAM	LVL	AGE	PA	R	2B	3B	HR	RBI	BB	SO	SB	CS	EqBRR	AVG	OBP	SLG	EqAVG	EqOBP	EqSLG	EqA	VORP	WARP	DEFENSE		
2007	CHN	MLB	27	207	15	11	0	0	8	13	16	3	0	1.7	.246	.298	.304	.241	.293	.288	.214	-2.4	-0.4	51-SS -2		
2007	PIT	MLB	27	130	16	3	2	0	8	6	3	0	3	-1.3	.276	.310	.333	.285	.318	.341	.222	-0.7	-0.3	23-SS -2	6-3B 0
2008	SLN	MLB	28	454	50	10	3	1	24	29	26	24	6	-2.0	.263	.319	.309	.275	.327	.320	.239	8.8	2.1	112-SS 8	2-3B 1
2009	BAL	MLB	29	412	34	14	4	2	30	18	38	12	4	-2.6	.256	.294	.328	.259	.297	.329	.223	0.8	1.2	106-SS 8		
2010	BAL	MLB	30	380	42	16	2	2	26	24	34	11	5	-0.7	.281	.333	.358	.275	.329	.354	.234	3.1	0.6	96-SS 2		

Breakout: 15% Improve: 40% Collapse: 21% Attrition: 15%   MLB: 90%   Comparables: Jose Uribe, Nick Punto, Aaron Miles, Omar Vizquel

The Orioles wanted one thing from Izturis when they got him—defense—and that is exactly what they got. Izturis had the second-best Fielding Runs Above Average in the AL, at +7, despite missing a month with appendicitis, an illness that hampered him for another month after he returned. Offensively, he almost exactly defined the "replacement-level hitter" for a shortstop, although it's easy to imagine a few more stolen bases without the surgery. Izturis is under contract for 2010 and is essentially unopposed as the Orioles' shortstop, but he shouldn't be a regular player after that.

Adam Jones   CF   Bats: R   Throws: R   Height: 6′ 2″   Weight: 210   Born: August 1, 1985   Age: 24

YEAR	TEAM	LVL	AGE	PA	R	2B	3B	HR	RBI	BB	SO	SB	CS	EqBRR	AVG	OBP	SLG	EqAVG	EqOBP	EqSLG	EqA	VORP	WARP	DEFENSE		
2007	TAC	AAA	21	469	75	27	6	25	84	36	106	8	7	1.8	.314	.382	.586	.287	.350	.525	.289	29.0	3.8	93-CF 4	8-RF -1
2007	SEA	MLB	21	71	16	2	1	2	4	4	21	2	1	2.0	.246	.300	.400	.262	.314	.415	.249	0.9	0.0	13-LF 1	4-CF -2
2008	BAL	MLB	22	514	61	21	7	9	57	23	108	10	3	0.8	.270	.311	.400	.276	.316	.411	.253	10.4	3.7	125-CF 21		
2009	BAL	MLB	23	519	83	22	3	19	70	36	93	10	4	0.6	.277	.335	.457	.280	.337	.451	.271	20.8	3.2	114-CF 7		
2010	BAL	MLB	24	534	78	24	5	19	72	38	113	10	5	0.9	.282	.343	.464	.273	.338	.447	.264	18.4	2.6	121-CF 5		

Breakout: 15% Improve: 53% Collapse: 10% Attrition: 5%   MLB: 100%   Comparables: Ellis Burks, Rondell White, Carlos Beltran, Matt Kemp

There is superstar talent here, but we still have to wait for it all to come together. Jones enjoyed an outstanding start to the season, but his midsummer was marred by injuries, first back spasms and then a bad ankle sprain. He missed the end of 2008 due to foot problems, so he is building an unwelcome injury résumé. He won a Gold Glove for his excellent defense, his power improved nicely over the prior year, and he made progress in strike-zone control. On the downside, he still hasn't figured out left-handed pitching, an unusual problem for a right-handed hitter, and his strike-zone judgment is still poor.

Nick Markakis — RF

Bats: L   Throws: L   Height: 6' 2"   Weight: 195   Born: November 17, 1983   Age: 26

YEAR	TEAM	LVL	AGE	PA	R	2B	3B	HR	RBI	BB	SO	SB	CS	EqBRR	AVG	OBP	SLG	EqAVG	EqOBP	EqSLG	EqA	VORP	WARP	DEFENSE
2007	BAL	MLB	23	710	97	43	3	23	112	61	112	18	6	0.2	.300	.362	.485	.299	.362	.490	.289	36.3	5.0	158-RF 8
2008	BAL	MLB	24	697	106	48	1	20	87	99	113	10	7	-2.6	.306	.406	.491	.309	.410	.501	.309	50.2	7.1	155-RF 13
2009	BAL	MLB	25	711	94	45	2	18	101	56	98	6	2	2.0	.293	.347	.453	.296	.349	.449	.277	26.8	2.9	159-RF -1
2010	BAL	MLB	26	726	103	40	2	26	108	78	107	13	7	-0.1	.303	.381	.493	.296	.373	.477	.286	35.4	4.2	155-RF 3

Breakout: 17%   Improve: 48%   Collapse: 1%   Attrition: 2%   MLB: 100%   Comparables: Tony Oliva, Steve Kemp, Babe Herman, Terry Puhl

Signed to a six-year deal in January, Markakis went out and had his worst season yet as an Oriole. A big part of that was a near-total collapse in September (.236/.311/.330), when he could be forgiven for just wanting to get the season over with and get on with watching Ravens games, like everyone else in Baltimore. More troubling, though, are the drops in steals and defense (although Markakis still led AL right fielders, with 13 assists), which suggest a drop in speed. He did hit 40 doubles for the third straight year, and the list of players who had three 40-double seasons by their age-25 seasons is very impressive: Joe Medwick, Albert Pujols, Lou Gehrig, Joe Cronin, Stan Musial, Carl Yastrzemski, Don Mattingly, Dick Bartell, Hal Trosky, and Red Kress, along with David Wright and Hanley Ramirez.

Lou Montanez — OF

Bats: R   Throws: R   Height: 6' 2"   Weight: 200   Born: December 15, 1981   Age: 28

YEAR	TEAM	LVL	AGE	PA	R	2B	3B	HR	RBI	BB	SO	SB	CS	EqBRR	AVG	OBP	SLG	EqAVG	EqOBP	EqSLG	EqA	VORP	WARP	DEFENSE	
2007	BOW	AA	25	135	24	2	0	3	11	10	16	3	2	0.1	.339	.398	.430	.315	.361	.379	.262	3.9	0.0	31-CF -4	
2007	NOR	AAA	25	241	27	11	0	7	26	22	35	1	3	-0.3	.259	.332	.410	.265	.328	.419	.257	3.5	-0.3	32-LF -1	27-RF -5
2008	BOW	AA	26	501	90	32	5	26	97	36	63	4	4	2.0	.335	.385	.601	.293	.331	.487	.277	18.7	2.0	85-LF -2	13-RF 0
2008	BAL	MLB	26	117	18	6	1	3	14	4	20	0	0	-0.3	.295	.316	.446	.295	.316	.446	.264	2.6	-0.4	20-LF -5	3-RF -1
2009	NOR	AAA	27	48	8	3	0	0	3	5	9	3	0	0.2	.429	.500	.500	.372	.449	.442	.324	4.2	0.5	10-RF 0	
2009	BAL	MLB	27	91	5	5	0	1	6	5	16	0	1	-1.8	.183	.244	.280	.185	.247	.272	.182	-5.9	-0.4	15-LF 3	
2010	BAL	MLB	28	298	38	15	1	8	35	19	54	2	1	0.0	.276	.330	.422	.269	.325	.411	.248	2.4	0.2	55-LF -1	

Breakout: 8%   Improve: 34%   Collapse: 31%   Attrition: 22%   MLB: 41%   Comparables: Gary Ward, Mike Edwards, Bob Pate, Robert Perez

Montanez hit .340 in spring training, then hit .429 at Norfolk over the first three weeks, and was called up to Baltimore and given a chance to unseat a struggling Felix Pie in left field. He didn't hit much better than Pie had, and then he tore two ligaments in his thumb making a diving catch before he'd gone many rounds in the fight for playing time. By the time he returned three months later, not only had Pie righted himself, but Nolan Reimold had come up from behind and blown right past him, too. He's a former prospect who had resurrected his career with a knockout 2008, but looks to have reburied it in 2009.

Melvin Mora — 3B

Bats: R   Throws: R   Height: 5' 11"   Weight: 200   Born: February 2, 1972   Age: 38

YEAR	TEAM	LVL	AGE	PA	R	2B	3B	HR	RBI	BB	SO	SB	CS	EqBRR	AVG	OBP	SLG	EqAVG	EqOBP	EqSLG	EqA	VORP	WARP	DEFENSE
2007	BAL	MLB	35	527	67	23	1	14	58	47	83	9	3	-0.9	.274	.341	.418	.274	.342	.418	.266	14.4	2.7	118-3B 9
2008	BAL	MLB	36	570	77	29	2	23	104	37	70	3	7	0.4	.285	.342	.483	.290	.346	.497	.280	26.2	3.3	120-3B 3
2009	BAL	MLB	37	496	44	20	0	8	48	34	60	3	3	-9.1	.260	.321	.358	.263	.323	.363	.240	3.3	-0.2	119-3B -4
2010	BAL	MLB	38	423	45	18	1	12	59	33	64	3	3	-1.3	.270	.335	.417	.262	.330	.395	.248	5.4	0.7	98-3B 1

Breakout: 9%   Improve: 26%   Collapse: 34%   Attrition: 31%   MLB: 97%   Comparables: Vinny Castilla, Carl Furillo, Al Simmons, Gary Gaetti

The Orioles decided not to exercise their $8 million option on Mora after the season, one of the easiest decisions any front office made this winter; if anything, it was a little surprising that he remained an Oriole to the end of the season. Mora was a player in serious decline when he gave us a nice surprise in 2008, allowing a little hope there was still something in the tank—but no. By July he was regularly sitting in place of Ty Wigginton, and he responded to being benched by complaining about a "lack of respect" from management; he should have been more worried about the lack of respect from opposing pitchers. His -9.1 base-running mark was the worst in baseball.

Felix Pie — OF

Bats: L Throws: L Height: 6' 2" Weight: 170 Born: February 8, 1985 Age: 25

YEAR	TEAM	LVL	AGE	PA	R	2B	3B	HR	RBI	BB	SO	SB	CS	EqBRR	AVG	OBP	SLG	EqAVG	EqOBP	EqSLG	EqA	VORP	WARP	DEFENSE			
2007	IOW	AAA	22	250	51	9	5	9	43	19	40	9	6	3.4	.362	.410	.563	.325	.369	.498	.290	15.6	1.4	49-CF	-2	4-RF	-2
2007	CHN	MLB	22	194	26	9	3	2	20	14	43	8	1	2.8	.215	.271	.333	.215	.271	.328	.219	-2.7	0.8	48-CF	10		
2008	IOW	AAA	23	368	57	20	5	10	55	23	54	11	7	2.1	.287	.336	.466	.268	.312	.418	.251	6.6	-0.1	79-CF	-8		
2008	CHN	MLB	23	93	9	2	1	1	10	7	29	3	0	0.3	.241	.312	.325	.241	.312	.325	.236	0.1	0.0	22-CF	0		
2009	BAL	MLB	24	281	38	10	3	9	29	24	58	1	3	-0.8	.266	.326	.437	.271	.330	.438	.260	5.7	1.6	35-CF	4	31-LF	3
2010	BAL	MLB	25	375	53	17	4	11	48	30	78	8	4	1.2	.261	.323	.425	.256	.318	.412	.246	6.0	0.7	86-CF	1		

Breakout: 11% Improve: 31% Collapse: 20% Attrition: 7% MLB: 97% Comparables: Terrence Long, Jacoby Ellsbury, Angel Pagan, Nate McLouth

Pie (acquired in a January trade for Garrett Olson) left spring as the Orioles' primary left fielder, but quickly played himself out of a job. Once Nolan Reimold was called up and produced, Pie became almost forgotten, collecting just 70 at-bats over three months from May through July, but he came on strong after Jones got hurt in August. There's still talent here, which is why his name comes up in trade rumors as somebody's center fielder of the immediate future, but his is a mixed bag of gifts: Pie has great speed, yet he's a lousy baserunner, he still can't hit lefties with an M1 Abrams battle tank, and he is almost mystically anticharismatic, so uninspiring to his managers that they happily forget he exists.

Nolan Reimold — LF

Bats: R Throws: R Height: 6' 4" Weight: 205 Born: October 12, 1983 Age: 26

YEAR	TEAM	LVL	AGE	PA	R	2B	3B	HR	RBI	BB	SO	SB	CS	EqBRR	AVG	OBP	SLG	EqAVG	EqOBP	EqSLG	EqA	VORP	WARP	DEFENSE			
2007	BOW	AA	23	203	30	15	0	11	34	17	47	2	3	-1.5	.306	.365	.565	.280	.330	.513	.278	7.8	0.6	45-RF	-3		
2008	BOW	AA	24	586	87	29	3	25	84	63	82	7	3	-0.1	.284	.367	.501	.262	.329	.441	.266	14.5	1.0	126-RF	-7	5-LF	1
2009	NOR	AAA	25	130	21	11	0	9	27	18	25	6	1	-0.9	.394	.485	.743	.382	.469	.727	.380	20.8	1.9	25-LF	-4		
2009	BAL	MLB	25	411	49	18	2	15	45	47	77	8	2	0.4	.279	.365	.466	.283	.367	.459	.287	18.9	1.6	83-LF	-4		
2010	BAL	MLB	26	441	56	21	1	19	58	41	87	5	3	-0.3	.274	.347	.473	.265	.343	.453	.267	12.7	1.1	96-LF	-3		

Breakout: 10% Improve: 33% Collapse: 14% Attrition: 10% MLB: 100% Comparables: Joe Mather, Mike Diaz, Jason Dubois, Wes Chamberlain

We liked Reimold a lot last year, but he surpassed our expectations. After a ridiculously hot start at Norfolk, Reimold came up in May, shoved Pie out of the left-field picture, and kept on hitting. He did eventually hit the wall in July and August, in part due to accumulating leg injuries, the most serious being a 25 percent tear of his Achilles tendon that he played through, seeking surgery after the season. The power is genuine; the downside is that he was a 25-year-old rookie, so there isn't as much potential growth as you'd expect from a guy who just got here.

Brian Roberts — 2B

Bats: S Throws: R Height: 5' 9" Weight: 175 Born: October 9, 1977 Age: 32

YEAR	TEAM	LVL	AGE	PA	R	2B	3B	HR	RBI	BB	SO	SB	CS	EqBRR	AVG	OBP	SLG	EqAVG	EqOBP	EqSLG	EqA	VORP	WARP	DEFENSE	
2007	BAL	MLB	29	716	103	42	5	12	57	89	99	50	7	8.8	.290	.377	.432	.288	.377	.430	.290	46.5	6.7	150-2B	12
2008	BAL	MLB	30	704	107	51	8	9	57	82	104	40	10	1.6	.296	.378	.450	.301	.384	.458	.295	49.0	5.6	150-2B	1
2009	BAL	MLB	31	717	110	56	1	16	79	74	112	30	7	1.8	.283	.356	.451	.286	.358	.446	.282	38.7	4.0	152-2B	-3
2010	BAL	MLB	32	682	100	38	4	14	63	80	107	36	9	2.0	.287	.372	.436	.281	.369	.420	.274	30.6	3.5	147-2B	2

Breakout: 8% Improve: 35% Collapse: 11% Attrition: 10% MLB: 100% Comparables: Frankie Frisch, Ray Durham, Bill Doran, Pee Wee Reese

Another year, another 30 steals, another 50 doubles (joining Stan Musial, Paul Waner, and Tris Speaker as the only players to have three 50-double seasons). Prior to the season, Roberts signed a contract extension that will keep him a Bird through 2013, when he'll be 35. Signing any player through age 35 is a risk, but Roberts has been as healthy and consistent as is possible. Players of comparable age and performance who are active this decade include Miguel Tejada, Derek Jeter, and Ray Durham, all of whom held reasonable value from the ages of 32-35.

Luke Scott — DH

Bats: L   Throws: R   Height: 6' 0"   Weight: 210   Born: June 25, 1978   Age: 32

YEAR	TEAM	LVL	AGE	PA	R	2B	3B	HR	RBI	BB	SO	SB	CS	EqBRR	AVG	OBP	SLG	EqAVG	EqOBP	EqSLG	EqA	VORP	WARP	DEFENSE				
2007	HOU	MLB	29	425	49	28	5	18	64	53	95	3	1	-0.1	.255	.351	.504	.261	.358	.514	.292	22.6	3.2	90-RF	6	2-LF	0	
2008	BAL	MLB	30	536	67	29	2	23	65	53	102	2	2	0.2	.257	.336	.472	.258	.338	.474	.275	17.7	3.1	95-LF	9			
2009	BAL	MLB	31	506	61	26	1	25	77	55	104	0	0	-1.1	.258	.340	.488	.258	.340	.481	.278	12.2	1.3	23-LF	0	7-1B	-1	
2010	BAL	MLB	32	474	56	24	2	21	63	52	96	2	2	-0.2	.259	.343	.472	.251	.336	.449	.265	12.5	1.7	70-LF	3			

Breakout: 7%   Improve: 33%   Collapse: 19%   Attrition: 17%   MLB: 96%   Comparables: Henry Rodriguez, Ricky Ledee, Geoff Jenkins, Mike Greenwell

Scott spent most of the year as the Orioles' DH; after Huff was traded, the team intended to give Scott most of the first-base opportunities, but he instead logged outfield time after Reimold and Jones both went down. The Orioles would love for him to become at least adequate at first base, as it would help fill what is currently a gaping void with a capable everyday hitter (he hits lefties fine and thus doesn't need platooning) while keeping the DH slot free for Matt Wieters' day off or the minor injury case of the week. Since Scott's professional experience at first base consists of 10 games this past year and four Carolina League games in 2002, the jury is still very much out. Still, Orioles first basemen hit an aggregate .262/.318/.411 last year, so if at first you don't succeed, try Scott again.

Brandon Snyder — 1B

Bats: R   Throws: R   Height: 6' 2"   Weight: 210   Born: November 23, 1986   Age: 23

YEAR	TEAM	LVL	AGE	PA	R	2B	3B	HR	RBI	BB	SO	SB	CS	EqBRR	AVG	OBP	SLG	EqAVG	EqOBP	EqSLG	EqA	VORP	WARP	DEFENSE				
2007	DEL	A	20	501	63	23	3	11	58	44	107	0	2	-3.0	.283	.354	.422	.257	.312	.372	.239	-6.6	-0.8	63-1B	0			
2008	FRD	A+	21	476	70	33	2	13	80	29	83	3	2	-0.9	.315	.358	.490	.283	.318	.432	.259	4.2	0.0	81-1B	-3	6-3B	-1	
2009	BOW	AA	22	233	24	19	1	10	45	27	45	0	1	-0.1	.343	.421	.597	.316	.379	.563	.312	14.2	2.2	55-1B	4			
2009	NOR	AAA	22	297	36	18	2	2	43	24	64	3	1	3.0	.248	.316	.355	.247	.311	.354	.238	-6.3	-0.7	50-1B	0	7-3B	1	
2010	BAL	MLB	23	506	58	25	2	13	68	38	116	2	1	-0.2	.268	.328	.417	.261	.324	.403	.246	-2.2	-0.2	90-1B	0			

Breakout: 16%   Improve: 43%   Collapse: 12%   Attrition: 2%   MLB: 3%   Comparables: Juan Tejeda, Brock Peterson, Charlie Hayes, Corey Kapano

The former first-round pick (in 2005) was having a breakout year in Bowie, but reverted to form at Triple-A. Snyder is a first baseman without much home-run pop, which means he needs to excel at the other things to have value. He does do some things well, but none excellently. He hits for a decent average, racking up some doubles by driving balls to the gaps, and his fielding is roughly average. That's just not good enough to compete in the majors, especially not at first base. Garrett Atkins may prove too large a stumbling block for him.

Justin Turner — INF

Bats: R   Throws: R   Height: 5' 11"   Weight: 180   Born: November 23, 1984   Age: 25

YEAR	TEAM	LVL	AGE	PA	R	2B	3B	HR	RBI	BB	SO	SB	CS	EqBRR	AVG	OBP	SLG	EqAVG	EqOBP	EqSLG	EqA	VORP	WARP	DEFENSE				
2007	DYT	A	22	516	70	25	4	10	59	39	72	12	8	-1.6	.311	.374	.446	.277	.328	.392	.251	10.7	0.0	95-2B	-10	9-SS	-1
2008	SAR	A+	23	151	23	8	1	0	11	12	19	3	1	0.2	.316	.384	.390	.286	.342	.357	.247	2.1	-0.4	30-2B	-6		
2008	CHT	AA	23	323	45	14	1	8	42	33	54	2	1	0.9	.289	.359	.432	.260	.317	.385	.248	5.7	-0.7	70-2B	-12		
2009	NOR	AAA	24	441	54	28	0	2	43	34	37	9	4	1.2	.300	.362	.388	.301	.359	.393	.268	17.0	1.6	78-2B	-3	14-SS	0
2009	BAL	MLB	24	22	2	0	0	0	3	4	3	0	0	0.9	.167	.318	.167	.167	.318	.167	.189	-1.1	-0.1	4-3B	0		
2010	BAL	MLB	25	432	52	20	1	8	44	34	71	4	3	0.3	.271	.334	.385	.265	.331	.377	.240	4.1	-0.1	90-2B	-5		

Breakout: 9%   Improve: 36%   Collapse: 18%   Attrition: 12%   MLB: 23%   Comparables: Marco Scutaro, Derrell Baker, Dustin Carr, Jeff Berblinger

Turner was one of three players (with the unlamented Ryan Freel and Brandon Waring) that the Orioles got from the Reds for Ramon Hernandez. Turner doesn't profile as more than a utility player in the majors, and even in that role, he's scraping replacement level. His only plus skill is hitting for average; his only other pluses come in the nonskill categories of attitude and willingness to play wherever he's needed. He does have a pronounced platoon split, so perhaps he can carve out a role for himself as a kind of modern-day Garth Iorg, spelling Josh Bell against left-handers.

Matt Wieters — C

Bats: S Throws: R Height: 6' 5" Weight: 230 Born: May 21, 1986 Age: 24

YEAR	TEAM	LVL	AGE	PA	R	2B	3B	HR	RBI	BB	SO	SB	CS	EqBRR	AVG	OBP	SLG	EqAVG	EqOBP	EqSLG	EqA	VORP	WARP	DEFENSE
2008	FRD	A+	22	280	48	8	0	15	40	44	47	1	2	-1.6	.345	.448	.576	.311	.398	.496	.306	23.2	3.5	47-C 6
2008	BOW	AA	22	250	41	14	2	12	51	38	29	1	0	0.3	.365	.460	.625	.349	.428	.581	.338	30.2	3.6	44-C 1
2009	NOR	AAA	23	163	25	9	2	5	30	20	30	0	0	-0.7	.305	.387	.504	.296	.374	.486	.295	11.1	1.1	27-C -2
2009	BAL	MLB	23	385	35	15	1	9	43	28	86	0	0	-3.7	.288	.340	.412	.289	.340	.411	.262	15.3	1.7	84-C 1
2010	BAL	MLB	24	512	63	22	2	16	68	52	100	1	1	-1.4	.294	.367	.459	.286	.361	.443	.273	26.1	3.0	97-C 1

Breakout: 7% Improve: 35% Collapse: 23% Attrition: 2% MLB: 93% Comparables: Jarrod Saltalamacchia, Sherman Obando, Charles Johnson, Steve Decker

No, Wieters didn't break every rookie record that existed, and he didn't meet the numbers we (and others) had projected for him. Before you get too caught up in disappointment, keep in mind that he did hit .308 after his first month, and he hit for a .262 EqA as a 23-year-old catcher, something that only Brian McCann, Joe Mauer, and Russ Martin have done in the last 10 years. And those players averaged hitting 40 points higher in their second seasons than they did in their rookie campaigns. Wieters didn't walk nearly as much as expected, symptomatic of someone who's pressing, and the decreased selectivity could also explain the power drop. We still expect big things from him, even if he doesn't sign autographs for five thousand people using only two fishes and five loaves of bread.

Ty Wigginton — UT

Bats: R Throws: R Height: 6' 0" Weight: 225 Born: October 11, 1977 Age: 32

YEAR	TEAM	LVL	AGE	PA	R	2B	3B	HR	RBI	BB	SO	SB	CS	EqBRR	AVG	OBP	SLG	EqAVG	EqOBP	EqSLG	EqA	VORP	WARP	DEFENSE
2007	TBA	MLB	29	417	47	21	0	16	49	28	73	1	4	-2.0	.275	.329	.458	.285	.338	.473	.272	15.3	0.4	36-2B -7 29-3B -3
2007	HOU	MLB	29	187	24	12	0	6	18	13	40	2	0	0.5	.284	.342	.462	.292	.348	.464	.283	8.7	1.0	43-3B 0
2008	HOU	MLB	30	429	50	22	1	23	58	32	69	4	6	-2.8	.285	.350	.526	.301	.361	.552	.295	28.4	2.6	74-3B -4 28-LF 0
2009	BAL	MLB	31	436	44	19	0	11	41	23	57	1	2	-3.7	.273	.314	.400	.276	.317	.400	.246	-1.7	-1.7	38-1B -3 36-3B -10
2010	BAL	MLB	32	459	52	19	1	19	53	33	82	3	4	-1.4	.276	.336	.459	.267	.331	.438	.258	4.0	0.0	90-1B -4

Breakout: 10% Improve: 31% Collapse: 20% Attrition: 21% MLB: 91% Comparables: Ron Coomer, Kevin Millar, Kevin Young, Mike Blowers

The Orioles signed Wigginton for two years last February, expecting a lefty-masher who could platoon with Luke Scott at DH and fill in all around the infield. What they didn't account for was how much of his value over the last several years had been tied to righty-friendly home parks in Houston (he had a .322 EqA in Minute Maid Park) and Tampa (.288 EqA at home); his road stats (.254 over that time) turned out to be far more predictive of what he'd do in Baltimore. While he is willing to play almost every position on the field, he doesn't play any of them that well, adding up to a negative WARP.

PITCHERS

Matt Albers

Bats: L Throws: R Height: 6' 0" Weight: 205 Born: January 20, 1983 Age: 27

YEAR	TEAM	LVL	AGE	W	L	SV	G	GS	IP	H	HR	BB	SO	GB%	BABIP	STUFF	WHIP	ERA	SIERA	DERA	EqH9	EqHR9	EqBB9	EqSO9	VORP	SN/WX
2007	ROU	AAA	24	2	3	0	9	9	53	50	6	22	43	61%	.293	-4	1.36	3.74	3.99	5.20	9.3	1.6	4.0	5.7	1.6	0.39
2007	HOU	MLB	24	4	11	0	31	18	110²	127	18	50	71	56%	.301	-18	1.60	5.86	4.84	5.79	9.8	1.4	3.5	5.1	-3.6	1.94
2008	BAL	MLB	25	3	3	0	28	3	49	43	4	22	26	55%	.253	-7	1.33	3.49	5.14	3.61	7.4	0.6	3.5	4.4	10.2	0.99
2009	NOR	AAA	26	1	0	0	10	0	12²	19	1	5	12	72%	.400	-17	1.89	5.68	3.78	8.88	13.5	1.4	3.6	6.4	-4.8	-0.10
2009	BAL	MLB	26	3	6	0	56	0	67	80	3	36	49	59%	.352	-4	1.73	5.51	4.72	5.06	10.1	0.3	4.2	5.9	3.2	0.79
2010	BAL	MLB	27	4	6	0	42	3	80²	89	11	38	52	56%	.310	-9	1.57	5.25	4.79	5.27	9.4	1.1	4.1	5.5	2.1	0.89

Breakout: 21% Improve: 46% Collapse: 13% Attrition: 26% MLB: 82% Comparables: Joe Grahe, Willie Fraser, Naohisa Sugiyama, Mark Grant

Albers hurt his shoulder in 2008 and elected to go through a rehab program rather than surgery. He was intermittently effective, logging a 2.38 ERA through June and July, then giving up two or more runs in five of seven August outings before being sent back to Norfolk, where he continued to be abused by the opposition. Albers is emphatically not suited to be a LOOGY, although an anomalous split line in 2008 led the Orioles in that direction.

Jake Arrieta

Bats: R   Throws: R   Height: 6' 4"   Weight: 225   Born: March 6, 1986   Age: 24

YEAR	TEAM	LVL	AGE	W	L	SV	G	GS	IP	H	HR	BB	SO	GB%	BABIP	STUFF	WHIP	ERA	SIERA	DERA	EqH9	EqHR9	EqBB9	EqSO9	VORP	SN/WX
2008	FRD	A+	21	6	5	0	20	20	113	80	7	51	120	49%	.262	25	1.16	2.87	3.38	4.28	8.1	1.2	4.6	7.0	14.1	1.02
2009	BOW	AA	22	6	3	0	11	11	59	45	4	23	70	38%	.287	20	1.15	2.59	2.88	4.53	8.9	1.5	3.8	8.1	5.9	0.93
2009	NOR	AAA	22	5	8	0	17	17	91²	97	9	33	78	50%	.324	1	1.42	3.93	3.97	5.34	10.6	1.7	3.6	6.1	1.6	0.43
2010	BAL	MLB	24	6	9	0	27	26	128¹	139	19	65	100	38%	.317	1	1.60	5.51	4.72	5.51	9.3	1.2	4.4	6.6	-0.1	2.48

Breakout: 4%   Improve: 33%   Collapse: 20%   Attrition: 4%   MLB: 14%   Comparables: John Van Benschoten, Erik Schullstrom, Rod Imes, Bryan Bullington

Arrieta has arguably the best fastball in the system, sitting at 92-96 mph with a little natural boring action. He's a big, strong guy, maintains his velocity late into games, and isn't at all afraid to challenge hitters. His secondary pitches are all works in progress; that leads to an overreliance on his fastball, and Triple-A hitters punished him for it. Fundamentally, Arrieta has a tendency to overthrow and flatten out his slider, his curveball and change are average at best, and he has trouble commanding anything but his fastball. He'll be ticketed for Norfolk again, but he could easily come up sometime in 2010.

Danys Baez

Bats: R   Throws: R   Height: 6' 1"   Weight: 235   Born: September 10, 1977   Age: 32

YEAR	TEAM	LVL	AGE	W	L	SV	G	GS	IP	H	HR	BB	SO	GB%	BABIP	STUFF	WHIP	ERA	SIERA	DERA	EqH9	EqHR9	EqBB9	EqSO9	VORP	SN/WX
2007	BAL	MLB	29	0	6	3	53	0	50¹	50	8	29	29	61%	.262	-21	1.57	6.44	5.18	5.87	8.2	1.2	4.6	4.6	-2.1	0.15
2009	BAL	MLB	31	4	6	0	59	0	71²	59	8	22	40	72%	.232	1	1.13	4.02	4.24	3.96	6.6	0.7	2.4	4.5	12.4	0.66
2010	PHI	MLB	32	3	4	1	52	0	51¹	47	6	23	30	44%	.263	-8	1.35	4.44	5.06	4.67	8.2	1.0	3.7	4.8	4.7	0.21

Breakout: 19%   Improve: 47%   Collapse: 19%   Attrition: 21%   MLB: 91%   Comparables: Pete Mikkelsen, Juan Acevedo, Matt Karchner, Masafumi Hirai

Another success story for Tommy John surgery, Baez bounced back to pre-2007 injury form. He didn't get what he wanted, though, which was to either start or close, being relegated to a middle-inning role for most of the season. His BABIP was a whopping 17 hits better than his team, the second-best number in the AL (Matt Guerrier, Twins, was -20), and a strong indicator of regression next year. Wish the Phillies luck with him.

Brian Bass

Bats: R   Throws: R   Height: 6' 2"   Weight: 215   Born: January 6, 1982   Age: 28

YEAR	TEAM	LVL	AGE	W	L	SV	G	GS	IP	H	HR	BB	SO	GB%	BABIP	STUFF	WHIP	ERA	SIERA	DERA	EqH9	EqHR9	EqBB9	EqSO9	VORP	SN/WX
2007	ROC	AAA	25	7	3	1	37	10	103¹	96	8	24	80	60%	.287	-1	1.16	3.48	3.70	4.58	9.2	1.0	2.3	5.5	10.1	0.71
2008	MIN	MLB	26	3	4	1	44	0	68¹	84	11	22	32	71%	.311	-27	1.55	4.87	4.69	5.31	10.7	1.6	2.6	3.9	1.4	0.69
2008	BAL	MLB	26	1	0	0	5	4	21	14	1	9	13	59%	.217	2	1.10	4.71	4.67	5.23	5.7	0.4	3.5	5.2	0.6	0.66
2009	BAL	MLB	27	5	3	0	48	0	86¹	106	11	44	54	71%	.332	-15	1.74	4.90	4.66	4.74	10.3	0.9	4.0	5.0	7.3	-0.42
2010	BAL	MLB	28	4	6	0	43	0	82¹	94	11	31	47	65%	.313	-11	1.52	5.21	4.59	5.29	9.9	1.1	3.2	4.8	1.9	0.53

Breakout: 16%   Improve: 41%   Collapse: 17%   Attrition: 12%   MLB: 73%   Comparables: Jeff Shaw, John Verhoeven, Mark Guerra, Ricky Stone

In something of a throwback to the days when middle relievers carried heavy workloads, Bass was the Orioles' long-relief man. Like his forebears of yore, he was as thoroughly unimpressive as you'd expect from someone who spent the whole year in that role. He does at least throw a decent sinker, racking up the ground balls. He also throws a couple of pretty poor breaking pitches, a slider and curve that have a tendency to get drilled; despite the high ground-ball rate, he still gives up an average-plus number of home runs. With the young pitchers the Orioles have coming, Bass was non-tendered for good reason.

Brad Bergesen

Bats: L   Throws: R   Height: 6' 2"   Weight: 215   Born: September 25, 1985   Age: 24

YEAR	TEAM	LVL	AGE	W	L	SV	G	GS	IP	H	HR	BB	SO	GB%	BABIP	STUFF	WHIP	ERA	SIERA	DERA	EqH9	EqHR9	EqBB9	EqSO9	VORP	SN/WX
2007	DEL	A	21	7	3	0	15	15	94¹	75	3	17	73	64%	.260	21	0.98	2.19	3.40	4.04	8.9	1.1	2.3	4.1	14.3	1.23
2007	FRD	A+	21	3	6	0	10	10	56¹	78	4	9	35	56%	.368	-4	1.54	5.75	4.20	7.26	13.5	1.5	2.0	3.7	-10.4	-1.16
2008	FRD	A+	22	1	1	0	4	3	17¹	15	2	6	15	71%	.265	9	1.21	2.08	3.42	3.86	9.4	1.7	3.3	5.5	3.0	0.28
2008	BOW	AA	22	15	6	0	24	23	148	143	11	27	72	56%	.269	-4	1.15	3.22	4.59	4.69	9.7	1.4	1.9	3.0	12.6	1.46
2009	NOR	AAA	23	1	1	0	2	2	11	6	0	3	9	58%	.194	11	0.82	2.45	3.70	3.97	4.8	0.0	2.4	5.6	1.9	0.20
2009	BAL	MLB	23	7	5	0	19	19	123¹	126	11	32	65	60%	.283	18	1.28	3.43	4.64	3.38	8.3	0.7	2.0	4.2	29.3	3.52
2010	BAL	MLB	24	6	9	0	26	23	131¹	149	19	41	63	56%	.300	-7	1.44	4.92	4.98	4.93	9.7	1.2	2.7	4.1	8.3	2.50

Breakout: 8%   Improve: 53%   Collapse: 19%   Attrition: 21%   MLB: 91%   Comparables: Jose Bautista, Joe Mays, Chance Douglass, Andrew Good

We weren't high on Bergesen last year, despite his strong 2008 performance at Bowie, and that was due to his low strikeout rate. He was nevertheless called up after just two starts in Norfolk—necessity getting the better of discretion—and merely wound up as the Orioles' best pitcher in 2009. Even though he still didn't get many strikeouts, Bergesen's sinker/changeup/slider combo has allowed him to avoid hard contact; he's consistently put up better BABIP marks than his team. His season was cut short in July, when a line drive hit him in the shin so hard that, even two months later, he wasn't able to run. With all winter to heal, he's expected to be fully ambulatory by spring training and take his place in the rotation as the unit's overachiever who earned it.

Jason Berken

Bats: R   Throws: R   Height: 6' 0"   Weight: 175   Born: November 27, 1983   Age: 26

YEAR	TEAM	LVL	AGE	W	L	SV	G	GS	IP	H	HR	BB	SO	GB%	BABIP	STUFF	WHIP	ERA	SIERA	DERA	EqH9	EqHR9	EqBB9	EqSO9	VORP	SN/WX
2007	FRD	A+	23	9	9	0	27	26	151	160	12	49	124	52%	.322	-14	1.38	4.53	3.91	6.43	10.7	1.6	3.4	5.2	-14.6	-1.92
2008	BOW	AA	24	12	4	0	26	25	145²	141	9	38	125	47%	.306	-1	1.23	3.58	3.63	5.45	10.1	1.2	2.6	5.6	0.7	0.63
2009	NOR	AAA	25	2	0	0	5	5	25²	19	1	6	16	56%	.240	8	0.97	1.05	4.15	1.66	7.0	0.7	2.2	4.4	10.4	1.08
2009	BAL	MLB	25	6	12	0	24	24	119²	164	19	44	66	47%	.341	-15	1.74	6.54	5.12	6.07	11.2	1.1	2.8	4.4	-7.6	0.40
2010	BAL	MLB	26	5	9	0	31	26	129¹	153	21	53	76	46%	.316	-11	1.59	5.76	5.01	5.74	10.1	1.3	3.6	5.0	-3.5	1.39

Breakout: 6%   Improve: 41%   Collapse: 17%   Attrition: 24%   MLB: 74%   Comparables: Wade Taylor, Manny Aybar, Chris Rauth, Joshua Geer

Bowie's 2008 rotation—Tillman, Bergesen, Hernandez, and Berken—became the first quartet from one team to each make 10 starts in Double-A one year and 10 starts in the majors the next. Surprisingly, Berken, who was actually sent back to Bowie to start the season, was the one who made the most major-league starts. He had bad luck; his ERA was more than a run higher than it should have been. He suffered through a nine-game losing streak, was demoted to the bullpen without ever pitching a game in relief, and was always on the edge of being sent back to Triple-A, but he hung in there. He throws four pitches, but none of them very well.

Zach Britton

Bats: L   Throws: L   Height: 6' 2"   Weight: 172   Born: December 22, 1987   Age: 22

YEAR	TEAM	LVL	AGE	W	L	SV	G	GS	IP	H	HR	BB	SO	GB%	BABIP	STUFF	WHIP	ERA	SIERA	DERA	EqH9	EqHR9	EqBB9	EqSO9	VORP	SN/WX
2007	ABE	A-	19	6	4	0	15	15	63²	64	1	22	45	63%	.307	12	1.35	3.68	4.09	6.49	10.4	1.2	3.7	3.3	-6.6	-0.42
2008	DEL	A	20	12	7	0	27	27	147¹	118	9	49	114	67%	.255	3	1.13	3.12	3.65	6.56	10.4	2.1	4.2	3.8	-15.3	-0.25
2009	FRD	A+	21	9	6	0	25	24	140	123	6	55	131	72%	.294	24	1.27	2.70	3.36	5.25	9.3	1.1	4.1	5.7	3.7	0.01
2010	BAL	MLB	22	4	8	0	28	24	110¹	130	17	54	61	58%	.314	-2	1.68	6.00	5.12	6.03	10.1	1.3	4.3	4.7	-6.5	1.75

Breakout: 12%   Improve: 44%   Collapse: 13%   Attrition: 13%   MLB: 5%   Comparables: Tom Bolton, Steve Garrison, Ed Riley, John Koronka

Britton's sinker is among the best in the entire minor leagues, reliably coming home at 89-92 mph with a powerful dropping action; his 72 percent adjusted ground-ball/fly-ball ratio led all pitchers with 80-plus innings, majors or minors. He can get the fastball to giddyup to 95 mph if he's willing to sacrifice movement, and he has a solid slider. Mechanically clean with an easy, repeatable delivery, Britton nevertheless still has work to do. His changeup is poor, no more than a show-me pitch right now, and he has trouble controlling his pitches, working too far down in the zone and leaving the sinker too low. He'll begin 2010 in Double-A, working out his problems while the pitching class that graduated in 2009 does its devoirs in the majors.

Brandon Erbe

Bats: R   Throws: R   Height: 6' 4"   Weight: 180   Born: December 25, 1987   Age: 22

YEAR	TEAM	LVL	AGE	W	L	SV	G	GS	IP	H	HR	BB	SO	GB%	BABIP	STUFF	WHIP	ERA	SIERA	DERA	EqH9	EqHR9	EqBB9	EqSO9	VORP	SN/WX
2007	FRD	A+	19	6	8	0	25	25	119¹	127	14	62	111	48%	.325	-3	1.58	6.26	4.15	8.55	10.9	2.1	5.1	5.9	-38.1	-3.14
2008	FRD	A+	20	10	12	0	28	28	150²	120	21	50	151	39%	.256	18	1.13	4.30	3.31	5.77	9.0	2.1	3.5	6.6	-4.1	-0.76
2009	ABE	A-	21	0	1	0	4	4	13²	13	3	2	11	46%	.244	-14	1.10	4.61	3.52	10.32	15.1	7.9	3.2	4.0	-6.1	-0.40
2009	BOW	AA	21	5	3	0	14	14	73	44	5	35	62	45%	.198	24	1.08	2.34	4.22	4.69	6.8	1.4	4.3	5.3	6.4	0.97
2010	BAL	MLB	22	5	8	0	25	25	111²	124	20	55	81	40%	.309	13	1.60	5.73	4.87	5.70	9.5	1.4	4.3	6.1	-2.5	1.26

Breakout: 19%   Improve: 56%   Collapse: 10%   Attrition: 19%   MLB: 8%   Comparables: Ryan Tucker, Dan Gabriele, Chaz Roe, Eric Hurley

The live-armed Erbe's fastball usually runs at 91-94 mph and can occasionally reach 96. He's got a hard slider that rates plus, and he's improved his changeup to average. What he absolutely cannot do is pitch from the stretch: his empty/runners-on split in the minors has been about the same as the difference between Alexei Ramirez and Manny Ramirez, a .259/.334 chasm that has held him back. There's also been talk of switching him to relief for his entire career, because he's got a complex, unrepeatable delivery, a history of arm trouble, and much better heat than off-speed stuff—but he's still a starter for now.

Jeremy Guthrie

Bats: R   Throws: R   Height: 6' 1"   Weight: 195   Born: April 8, 1979   Age: 31

YEAR	TEAM	LVL	AGE	W	L	SV	G	GS	IP	H	HR	BB	SO	GB%	BABIP	STUFF	WHIP	ERA	SIERA	DERA	EqH9	EqHR9	EqBB9	EqSO9	VORP	SN/WX
2007	BAL	MLB	27	7	5	0	32	26	175^1	165	23	47	123	51%	.270	13	1.21	3.70	4.14	3.72	8.0	1.1	2.2	5.8	34.5	4.31
2008	BAL	MLB	28	10	12	0	30	30	190^2	176	24	58	120	51%	.259	14	1.23	3.63	4.50	3.62	7.8	1.0	2.4	5.2	39.9	5.51
2009	BAL	MLB	29	10	17	0	33	33	200	224	35	60	110	42%	.286	-1	1.42	5.04	4.99	4.74	9.0	1.2	2.3	4.4	17.3	2.97
2010	BAL	MLB	31	10	10	0	34	33	179^1	189	24	56	101	47%	.292	2	1.36	4.49	4.78	4.51	9.1	1.1	2.7	4.8	19.8	2.54

Breakout: 0%   Improve: 38%   Collapse: 22%   Attrition: 20%   MLB: 99%   Comparables: Pat Hentgen, Andy Ashby, Ray Washburn, Freddie Fitzsimmons

Guthrie missed most of September 2008 with shoulder fatigue (or an impingement, depending on the source, but there's a pretty big difference). Since then, he hasn't been the same pitcher, getting beaten up in the final game of 2008, smacked around in the World Baseball Classic, slapped silly in spring training, and finally whomped upon in the season. His fastball went from a plus pitch to a minus, and without that pitch working, his changeup won't work, either. His ground-ball percentage dropped precipitously, and he led the league in both homers allowed and losses. With so many young pitchers ready for takeoff, the pressure on Guthrie to hold his job will be enormous.

Mark Hendrickson

Bats: L   Throws: L   Height: 6' 9"   Weight: 240   Born: June 23, 1974   Age: 36

YEAR	TEAM	LVL	AGE	W	L	SV	G	GS	IP	H	HR	BB	SO	GB%	BABIP	STUFF	WHIP	ERA	SIERA	DERA	EqH9	EqHR9	EqBB9	EqSO9	VORP	SN/WX
2007	LAN	MLB	33	4	8	0	39	15	122^2	142	15	29	92	53%	.322	-2	1.39	5.21	3.99	5.11	9.9	1.1	1.9	6.0	5.4	1.26
2008	FLO	MLB	34	7	8	0	36	19	133^2	148	17	48	81	49%	.298	-12	1.47	5.45	4.79	5.58	10.0	1.2	2.9	4.6	-1.1	0.39
2009	BAL	MLB	35	6	5	1	53	11	105	116	16	33	61	56%	.290	-8	1.42	4.37	4.70	4.46	8.9	1.1	2.4	4.6	12.4	1.21
2010	BAL	MLB	36	4	5	0	40	10	84	96	12	29	51	48%	.314	-8	1.49	5.03	4.72	5.08	9.9	1.1	3.1	5.1	3.9	0.43

Breakout: 15%   Improve: 45%   Collapse: 14%   Attrition: 25%   MLB: 92%   Comparables: John Candelaria, Bill Krueger, Terry Mulholland, Jerry Reuss

The much-maligned Hendrickson was a serviceable bullpen arm for the Orioles last year, working mostly in long relief and occasionally starting. Again, he proved much better out of the pen (3.44 ERA, vs. 5.40 as a starter), but teams keep giving him first-inning chances. The tall lefty turned free agent after the season and will look for another swingman job, very possibly right back in Baltimore.

David Hernandez

Bats: R   Throws: R   Height: 6' 3"   Weight: 215   Born: May 13, 1985   Age: 25

YEAR	TEAM	LVL	AGE	W	L	SV	G	GS	IP	H	HR	BB	SO	GB%	BABIP	STUFF	WHIP	ERA	SIERA	DERA	EqH9	EqHR9	EqBB9	EqSO9	VORP	SN/WX
2007	FRD	A+	22	7	11	0	28	27	145^1	139	16	47	168	37%	.324	-2	1.28	4.95	2.90	6.41	10.1	1.9	3.4	7.6	-13.8	-1.60
2008	BOW	AA	23	10	4	0	27	27	141	112	10	71	166	39%	.296	12	1.30	2.68	3.28	4.43	8.8	1.3	4.6	8.0	15.7	1.76
2009	NOR	AAA	24	3	2	0	11	11	57^1	42	5	18	79	45%	.289	26	1.05	3.30	2.03	4.83	7.7	1.5	3.1	9.7	4.1	0.68
2009	BAL	MLB	24	4	10	0	20	19	101^1	118	27	46	68	32%	.284	-17	1.62	5.42	5.25	4.83	9.3	1.9	3.5	5.3	7.8	1.52
2010	BAL	MLB	25	6	9	0	32	29	139	150	22	64	116	35%	.318	4	1.54	5.28	4.48	5.29	9.3	1.2	4.0	7.1	3.3	2.10

Breakout: 13%   Improve: 43%   Collapse: 15%   Attrition: 21%   MLB: 82%   Comparables: Boof Bonser, Mark Clark, Bob Sebra, Joe Slusarski

Could this have been the same David Hernandez who, two years in a row, led his league in strikeouts? He was well on his way to doing it again in Norfolk last year; Tommy Hanson was the only pitcher in Triple-A keeping up with him. True, that old version of Hernandez was always an extreme fly-ball pitcher, and this guy had the lowest ground-ball percentage in the league while still handing out home runs like they were business cards. We did caution last year that he relied on a form of deception that might not fool major leaguers. The major-league strikeouts never materialized, and Hernandez was lucky his ERA wasn't another run higher; he's been tateriffic all along. His actual homers-allowed figures were manageable in the minors, but major-league hitters hit a lot more homers than minor leaguers, so being below league average will kill you faster in the majors than it would in the minors; it's a very nonlinear effect in the case of extreme fly-ball pitchers.

Rich Hill

	Bats: L	Throws: L	Height: 6' 5"	Weight: 205	Born: March 11, 1980	Age: 30

YEAR	TEAM	LVL	AGE	W	L	SV	G	GS	IP	H	HR	BB	SO	GB%	BABIP	STUFF	WHIP	ERA	SIERA	DERA	EqH9	EqHR9	EqBB9	EqSO9	VORP	SN/WX
2007	CHN	MLB	27	11	8	0	32	32	195	170	27	63	183	43%	.271	25	1.19	3.92	3.53	3.84	8.0	1.0	2.6	7.9	35.5	4.90
2008	DAY	A+	28	1	2	0	3	3	12¹	12	0	11	14	0%	.364	-6	1.86	8.03	4.48	17.18	12.3	0.8	9.0	7.4	-14.3	0.97
2008	IOW	AAA	28	2	4	0	7	7	26	22	4	28	32	42%	.295	11	1.92	5.88	4.66	7.02	9.0	1.8	9.0	8.3	-4.2	-0.20
2008	CHN	MLB	28	1	0	0	5	5	19²	13	2	18	15	37%	.208	6	1.58	4.12	5.88	4.12	6.4	0.9	7.3	5.9	3.0	0.68
2009	NOR	AAA	29	1	1	0	3	3	13¹	5	1	9	14	49%	.143	12	1.05	1.35	3.94	2.19	4.4	1.5	6.6	8.0	4.5	0.49
2009	BAL	MLB	29	3	3	0	14	13	57²	68	7	40	46	40%	.337	-1	1.87	7.80	5.20	7.33	9.9	0.9	5.4	6.3	-11.9	0.00
2010	BAL	MLB	30	5	6	0	25	20	98¹	97	12	50	88	40%	.310	11	1.50	4.82	4.26	4.87	8.5	1.0	4.5	7.6	6.8	1.35

Breakout: 8%   Improve: 47%   Collapse: 15%   Attrition: 16%   MLB: 72%   Comparables: Greg Mathews, John Smiley, Ken Kravec, Donovan Osborne

Rich Hill was out of options and was picked in a minor trade from the Cubs before spring training with the hope that the curveballer could recapture his 2007 magic. He battled elbow problems all through the spring and into the season, not playing until May. He gave the O's three lousy months before going under the knife for a torn labrum; Hill thought the labrum was torn all season long, possibly even sometime in 2008. The one thing that's certain is that the 27-year-old who walked only 63 men in 195 innings in 2007 has been replaced by a 30-year-old who put 58 freebies aboard in 77 innings over two seasons. A free agent at press time, Hill might get picked up by a team hoping that he could rehab his way to old glories, though it's not clear if he'll be ready to pitch at the start of spring training.

Jim Johnson

	Bats: R	Throws: R	Height: 6' 5"	Weight: 230	Born: June 27, 1983	Age: 27

YEAR	TEAM	LVL	AGE	W	L	SV	G	GS	IP	H	HR	BB	SO	GB%	BABIP	STUFF	WHIP	ERA	SIERA	DERA	EqH9	EqHR9	EqBB9	EqSO9	VORP	SN/WX
2007	NOR	AAA	24	6	12	0	26	25	148	164	15	48	109	56%	.315	-23	1.43	4.07	4.21	5.78	11.1	1.8	3.0	4.8	-4.4	0.07
2008	BAL	MLB	25	2	4	1	54	0	68²	54	0	28	38	64%	.255	9	1.19	2.23	4.72	2.34	6.8	0.0	3.3	4.7	23.6	3.31
2009	BAL	MLB	26	4	6	10	64	0	70	73	8	23	49	62%	.300	0	1.37	4.11	4.23	3.66	8.6	0.8	2.6	5.7	14.3	2.49
2010	BAL	MLB	27	3	5	7	55	1	71²	80	10	28	45	60%	.309	-9	1.50	5.06	4.57	5.08	9.5	1.1	3.3	5.3	3.4	1.25

Breakout: 14%   Improve: 50%   Collapse: 18%   Attrition: 18%   MLB: 69%   Comparables: Matt Belisle, Aaron Small, Dan Wheeler, Mark Eichhorn

Johnson's 2008 season ended in August due to shoulder trouble, and he might have been better off had he missed September 2009 as well; he entered with a 3.12 ERA and left with a 4.11. He set up Sherrill for the first two-thirds of the season, then took over as closer when Big George was traded away, picking up eight saves while blowing four. That's a poor ratio, but the explanation looks more like simple fatigue than closer stress. Johnson doesn't have overpowering closer stuff, and the team would prefer to get a more "typical" free-agent closer and let Johnson go back to setting up.

Steven Johnson

	Bats: R	Throws: R	Height: 6' 1"	Weight: 200	Born: August 31, 1987	Age: 22

YEAR	TEAM	LVL	AGE	W	L	SV	G	GS	IP	H	HR	BB	SO	GB%	BABIP	STUFF	WHIP	ERA	SIERA	DERA	EqH9	EqHR9	EqBB9	EqSO9	VORP	SN/WX
2007	GRL	A	19	3	6	0	18	16	81²	90	2	40	65	30%	.341	0	1.59	4.85	4.81	8.25	10.8	1.1	5.3	4.1	-23.4	-1.60
2008	GRL	A	20	9	2	0	13	13	73	59	4	25	57	49%	.264	25	1.15	2.34	4.02	4.14	8.8	1.6	4.2	3.9	10.0	0.67
2008	SBR	A+	20	3	6	0	11	11	52	68	9	21	55	30%	.388	-5	1.71	7.10	3.67	10.03	14.1	3.5	4.6	6.4	-23.5	-1.35
2009	SBR	A+	21	8	4	1	18	16	96²	94	14	42	102	34%	.320	-20	1.41	3.82	3.55	6.22	11.6	3.2	5.1	5.7	-6.8	-0.61
2009	CHT	AA	21	1	1	0	2	2	10²	8	1	3	15	36%	.280	11	1.03	1.69	1.97	5.06	7.6	1.7	2.5	9.3	0.5	0.06
2009	BOW	AA	21	3	2	0	7	7	38	24	3	17	37	26%	.219	20	1.08	2.84	4.01	4.25	7.5	1.5	4.3	6.3	5.0	0.61
2010	SFN	MLB	22	4	9	0	28	24	119	134	19	65	85	30%	.315	7	1.67	5.76	5.31	6.15	10.1	1.4	4.6	5.9	-8.6	1.72

Breakout: 23%   Improve: 66%   Collapse: 7%   Attrition: 19%   MLB: 8%   Comparables: Jay Peterson, Brian Brown, Chris Reed, Adam Eaton

Johnson was brought home in the Sherrill deal—his dad started 14 games for the "Why Not?" Orioles of 1989, when Steven was just two. The son works high in the zone, giving up lots of flies, and in the wrong homer-happy ballpark, he's in for a world of hurt. His fastball is good; his off-speed stuff not so much. Grabbed by the Giants in the Rule 5 draft, he's a long shot to stick at the back of their bullpen.

Chris Lambert

Bats: R   Throws: R   Height: 6' 1"   Weight: 205   Born: March 8, 1983   Age: 27

YEAR	TEAM	LVL	AGE	W	L	SV	G	GS	IP	H	HR	BB	SO	GB%	BABIP	STUFF	WHIP	ERA	SIERA	DERA	EqH9	EqHR9	EqBB9	EqSO9	VORP	SN/WX
2007	SFD	AA	23	0	2	0	5	5	26¹	24	5	8	17	44%	.250	-6	1.22	3.42	4.48	4.44	9.2	2.2	3.0	4.4	2.9	0.34
2007	MEM	AAA	23	1	4	0	28	4	57²	74	10	29	50	48%	.358	-32	1.79	7.49	4.36	8.31	12.5	2.5	4.8	5.9	-17.1	-1.59
2008	TOL	AAA	24	12	8	0	26	26	149¹	143	7	48	124	45%	.302	8	1.28	3.50	3.91	4.82	8.9	0.8	3.0	5.2	11.0	1.52
2008	DET	MLB	24	1	2	0	8	3	20²	31	3	7	15	40%	.373	-9	1.84	5.66	4.65	7.06	12.0	1.2	2.5	5.8	-3.8	-0.37
2009	TOL	AAA	25	6	7	0	21	21	126²	121	8	31	106	37%	.297	10	1.20	3.55	3.77	4.72	9.1	1.0	2.4	5.9	10.7	1.32
2009	DET	MLB	25	0	1	0	2	0	6²	12	3	6	4	29%	.391	-32	2.70	14.85	6.63	14.21	15.6	2.8	7.1	5.7	-6.1	-0.24
2009	NOR	AAA	25	1	2	0	3	3	11²	18	3	3	9	31%	.395	-14	1.80	6.94	4.30	7.84	16.5	4.4	2.6	6.1	-2.7	-0.13
2009	BAL	MLB	25	0	0	0	4	0	5²	8	2	1	7	51%	.375	6	1.59	4.76	2.54	4.50	10.5	3.0	1.5	9.0	0.7	-0.03
2010	BAL	MLB	27	5	9	0	39	17	123	145	19	48	85	40%	.326	-6	1.57	5.41	4.71	5.39	10.1	1.2	3.4	5.8	1.5	1.34

Breakout: 13%   Improve: 50%   Collapse: 11%   Attrition: 11%   MLB: 30%   Comparables: Chris Baker, Edward Valdez, John Leister, Greg Beck

His starring role in *Highlander* now years in the past, Lambert was claimed off waivers from the Tigers in August with the idea that he could fill in during September while the Orioles shelved their real prospects to keep their innings down. Lambert had hit the wall himself, though, and only made four relief appearances in Orioles drag. He's improved his command enough that he might be able to hold a back-end rotation spot, but probably not with this team.

Luis Lebron

Bats: R   Throws: R   Height: 6' 1"   Weight: 172   Born: March 15, 1985   Age: 25

YEAR	TEAM	LVL	AGE	W	L	SV	G	GS	IP	H	HR	BB	SO	GB%	BABIP	STUFF	WHIP	ERA	SIERA	DERA	EqH9	EqHR9	EqBB9	EqSO9	VORP	SN/WX
2007	DEL	A	22	1	2	5	46	0	55¹	48	1	55	86	34%	.385	14	1.86	5.04	3.65	7.43	10.9	1.1	10.0	9.2	-10.6	-1.49
2009	FRD	A+	24	2	3	11	28	0	33	20	2	20	52	37%	.277	21	1.21	3.00	2.35	4.06	7.3	1.5	6.1	10.2	4.9	-0.32
2009	BOW	AA	24	1	0	9	24	0	27¹	8	3	13	39	41%	.104	16	0.77	1.98	2.11	2.98	4.6	2.1	4.2	9.5	7.2	1.06
2010	BAL	MLB	25	2	5	6	53	0	53¹	60	9	45	53	34%	.343	-16	1.96	6.43	5.00	6.46	9.6	1.2	7.2	8.4	-5.7	0.20

Breakout: 25%   Improve: 51%   Collapse: 20%   Attrition: 15%   MLB: 5%   Comparables: Josh Kranawetter, Landon Stockman, Jeremy Schmidt, Adalberto Mendez

Lebron missed most of 2008 after Tommy John surgery, but he came back strong, very strong. Always a hard thrower, he had velocity that came all the way back up to the 96-98 mph range. Even better, his slider was sharper than before, and he showed a usable changeup for the first time. He was good enough at Frederick to be invited to the Carolina League all-star game, but after his promotion to Bowie, he was untouchable, holding Eastern League batters to a .093 average. He picked up 20 saves along the way, becoming a possible internal solution to the team's closer problem. Arguments against his future closerdom: he still walks too many, and too many of the few hits he does allow are homers.

Radhames Liz

Bats: R   Throws: R   Height: 6' 2"   Weight: 185   Born: June 10, 1983   Age: 27

YEAR	TEAM	LVL	AGE	W	L	SV	G	GS	IP	H	HR	BB	SO	GB%	BABIP	STUFF	WHIP	ERA	SIERA	DERA	EqH9	EqHR9	EqBB9	EqSO9	VORP	SN/WX
2007	BOW	AA	24	11	4	0	25	25	137	101	13	70	161	40%	.268	7	1.25	3.22	3.32	4.70	8.0	1.7	4.7	7.9	11.6	1.25
2007	BAL	MLB	24	0	2	0	9	4	24²	25	3	23	24	27%	.310	9	1.95	6.93	5.56	6.93	8.5	1.1	7.5	7.8	-4.0	-0.53
2008	NOR	AAA	25	3	7	0	15	15	87	77	6	32	85	39%	.300	6	1.25	3.62	3.55	4.84	8.7	1.2	3.5	6.2	6.0	0.64
2008	BAL	MLB	25	6	6	0	17	17	84¹	99	16	51	57	38%	.312	-15	1.78	6.72	5.45	6.62	10.2	1.5	4.8	5.7	-10.4	0.56
2009	BOW	AA	26	4	1	0	8	8	48	46	1	14	39	44%	.313	4	1.25	2.62	3.87	4.77	10.4	0.8	2.8	5.3	3.6	0.55
2009	NOR	AAA	26	0	3	0	17	6	44¹	56	2	12	37	40%	.372	-11	1.53	5.68	3.96	7.23	12.1	0.9	2.8	5.7	-8.1	-0.22
2010	SDN	MLB	27	5	7	0	31	14	103	101	13	57	83	41%	.299	-4	1.54	4.96	4.67	5.59	9.4	1.2	4.4	6.6	-1.1	1.17

Breakout: 9%   Improve: 53%   Collapse: 11%   Attrition: 25%   MLB: 29%   Comparables: Jeff Peterek, Ezequiel Astacio, Greg Bargar, Shawn Sedlacek

Liz didn't make the Oriole rotation out of spring, and the team sent him to Norfolk to convert to short relief, a move that had been anticipated for years. The only thing this succeeded in doing was messing up his head and his mechanics; he had to go back down to Bowie for five weeks and rejoin the rotation to get his groove back. He'd gotten frequent mention in some kind of "change of scenery" deal, but the Padres claimed Liz on waivers in November, so Bud Black will get a chance to practice some of his old pitching coach skills on this former top prospect. Certainly, Petco will do its share to help a pitcher whose fly-ball inclinations have led to too many home runs allowed in the majors.

Brian Matusz

Bats: L   Throws: L   Height: 6' 5"   Weight: 200   Born: February 11, 1987   Age: 23

YEAR	TEAM	LVL	AGE	W	L	SV	G	GS	IP	H	HR	BB	SO	GB%	BABIP	STUFF	WHIP	ERA	SIERA	DERA	EqH9	EqHR9	EqBB9	EqSO9	VORP	SN/WX
2009	FRD	A+	22	4	2	0	11	11	66²	56	5	21	75	54%	.293	22	1.15	2.16	2.89	3.95	9.2	1.4	3.4	7.0	10.8	0.63
2009	BOW	AA	22	7	0	0	8	8	46¹	31	2	11	46	49%	.250	32	0.91	1.55	2.88	2.76	7.9	1.1	2.6	6.8	12.9	1.29
2009	BAL	MLB	22	5	2	0	8	8	44²	52	6	14	38	36%	.333	25	1.48	4.63	4.02	4.30	9.6	1.0	2.4	6.8	6.0	0.85
2010	BAL	MLB	23	7	9	0	29	28	143	157	22	54	106	39%	.314	9	1.48	5.02	4.48	5.02	9.4	1.2	3.4	6.3	7.7	3.12

Breakout: 10%   Improve: 20%   Collapse: 37%   Attrition: 0%   MLB: 79%   Comparables: Colin Charland, Mike Jeffcoat, Pete Filson, Jeremy Sowers

The Orioles' first-round pick in 2008 and the first pitcher taken that year, Matusz is as polished as any pitching prospect in the game. After a shaky first month, he raced through the system to make his major-league debut in August, pitching just enough to keep his rookie eligibility for 2010. He's a very intelligent pitcher, working both sides of the plate, hitting locations, mixing his pitches, and making adjustments. His stuff is above average but not quite elite: a 90-92 mph fastball that can reach 94, an outstanding changeup that is a true big-league swing-and-miss offering, and two quality breaking balls in his curve and slider. The latter two can go flat on him at times, but he's well placed to start 2010 in the rotation.

Cla Meredith

Bats: R   Throws: R   Height: 6' 0"   Weight: 190   Born: June 4, 1983   Age: 27

YEAR	TEAM	LVL	AGE	W	L	SV	G	GS	IP	H	HR	BB	SO	GB%	BABIP	STUFF	WHIP	ERA	SIERA	DERA	EqH9	EqHR9	EqBB9	EqSO9	VORP	SN/WX
2007	SDN	MLB	23	5	6	0	80	0	79²	94	6	17	59	81%	.342	-5	1.39	3.50	3.40	4.48	11.3	0.9	1.8	5.9	8.6	0.59
2008	SDN	MLB	24	0	3	0	73	0	70¹	79	6	24	49	74%	.329	-17	1.46	4.09	3.86	4.61	11.0	1.2	2.8	5.3	6.5	0.00
2009	SDN	MLB	25	4	2	0	35	0	36²	47	1	13	20	63%	.357	-18	1.64	4.17	4.75	5.01	12.1	0.5	2.8	3.9	1.9	-0.77
2009	BAL	MLB	25	0	0	0	29	0	28²	26	3	12	17	70%	.274	-8	1.33	3.77	4.46	3.29	7.9	0.7	3.3	4.9	6.7	0.70
2010	BAL	MLB	27	3	5	0	71	0	69²	84	9	24	41	69%	.327	-13	1.55	5.17	4.40	5.22	10.3	1.1	3.1	5.0	2.2	0.15

Breakout: 16%   Improve: 44%   Collapse: 15%   Attrition: 12%   MLB: 93%   Comparables: Hipolito Pichardo, Roger McDowell, Jim York, Jim Acker

Meredith's acquisition from the Pad people (for Oscar Salazar) was a tip that George Sherrill was about to be traded, as the O's were bolstering the bullpen for an impending departure. Unfortunately, Meredith continued his downward trend in 2009. His failure to add a complement to his fastball/slider routine is catching up to him, as more players adapt to his unorthodox delivery—note how his strikeout rate has declined in consecutive seasons while his walk rate has risen in three straight seasons.

Kam Mickolio

Bats: R   Throws: R   Height: 6' 9"   Weight: 255   Born: May 10, 1984   Age: 26

YEAR	TEAM	LVL	AGE	W	L	SV	G	GS	IP	H	HR	BB	SO	GB%	BABIP	STUFF	WHIP	ERA	SIERA	DERA	EqH9	EqHR9	EqBB9	EqSO9	VORP	SN/WX
2007	WTN	AA	23	3	1	2	18	0	29²	24	0	12	27	35%	.293	-2	1.21	1.82	3.93	3.38	8.0	0.6	3.9	5.5	6.6	0.11
2007	TAC	AAA	23	3	3	1	14	0	24	19	3	10	28	45%	.271	7	1.21	3.75	3.07	4.75	7.6	1.9	3.8	7.6	2.0	-0.27
2008	BOW	AA	24	2	1	1	28	0	38¹	39	2	22	40	62%	.333	-9	1.59	4.70	3.85	6.20	10.5	1.0	5.1	6.8	-2.9	-0.47
2008	NOR	AAA	24	1	0	2	17	0	20	13	0	9	23	55%	.245	3	1.10	1.80	3.24	3.70	6.1	0.4	3.9	7.0	4.1	0.88
2008	BAL	MLB	24	0	1	0	9	0	7²	8	0	4	8	41%	.333	4	1.57	5.87	3.96	5.40	8.6	0.0	4.3	7.6	0.1	-0.53
2009	NOR	AAA	25	3	3	0	35	0	43²	32	4	16	52	36%	.267	5	1.10	3.50	2.78	5.04	7.5	1.5	3.4	8.4	2.2	0.55
2009	BAL	MLB	25	0	2	0	11	0	13²	11	0	7	14	53%	.289	11	1.32	2.63	3.75	2.57	7.1	0.0	3.9	7.7	4.6	0.03
2010	BAL	MLB	26	3	4	1	52	0	62¹	60	8	30	51	39%	.295	0	1.43	4.66	4.42	4.69	8.3	1.0	4.1	6.9	5.6	0.59

Breakout: 13%   Improve: 51%   Collapse: 18%   Attrition: 16%   MLB: 59%   Comparables: Steve Hoeme, Matt Turner, Timothy Lahey, Terry Bross

Mickolio joined the Orioles in the Erik Bedard trade and is a hulking giant of a pitcher with the stuff to match: a high-90s fastball and a hard slider. Splitting time between Baltimore and Norfolk, he twice ran into trouble, first starting the season and again finishing it, finally ending the year on the DL with a dead arm. In between, however, he was outstanding. He figures to get consideration for the vacant closer's role, but could also work as a righty setup man. You do want him starting his own innings; his stuff suffers in the stretch position.

Jim Miller

Bats: R   Throws: R   Height: 6' 1"   Weight: 200   Born: April 28, 1982   Age: 28

YEAR	TEAM	LVL	AGE	W	L	SV	G	GS	IP	H	HR	BB	SO	GB%	BABIP	STUFF	WHIP	ERA	SIERA	DERA	EqH9	EqHR9	EqBB9	EqSO9	VORP	SN/WX
2007	BOW	AA	25	2	3	4	30	0	38²	26	0	25	49	38%	.289	17	1.32	2.79	3.42	3.77	7.3	0.5	5.8	8.5	7.1	0.71
2007	NOR	AAA	25	1	2	3	22	0	27²	25	3	16	30	39%	.289	-6	1.48	4.23	3.91	5.10	9.2	2.0	4.9	6.9	1.2	0.01
2008	BOW	AA	26	0	1	0	7	0	13	11	1	5	17	52%	.323	11	1.23	3.46	2.68	4.38	9.5	1.5	3.6	8.8	1.5	0.03
2008	NOR	AAA	26	3	5	10	49	0	67	50	4	22	79	42%	.277	8	1.07	3.09	2.67	4.02	7.5	1.0	3.0	7.5	10.7	0.31
2008	BAL	MLB	26	0	2	1	8	0	7²	9	0	5	8	54%	.360	4	1.83	1.17	4.26	3.24	9.7	0.0	4.3	7.6	2.1	-0.30
2009	NOR	AAA	27	4	4	17	54	0	64²	64	3	19	59	36%	.321	-1	1.28	2.64	3.65	3.48	9.6	0.9	2.9	6.4	13.9	-0.18
2010	BAL	MLB	28	3	4	7	54	0	66	69	9	29	54	41%	.314	-2	1.48	4.94	4.29	4.97	9.0	1.1	3.8	6.9	3.9	0.63

Breakout: 8%   Improve: 37%   Collapse: 30%   Attrition: 12%   MLB: 17%   Comparables: *Jeromy Palki, Pat Flury, Steve Reed, Don Strange*

Miller closed for Norfolk all season, never getting The Call despite the revolving door in Baltimore's pen. He pitched well, but gives up too many baserunners to maintain an ERA this low. His big bugaboo is that left-handed hitters rocked him for 100 more points of EqA than righties. Miller was removed from the 40-man roster and cleared waivers, so he should probably renew the lease on his Norfolk apartment.

Troy Patton

Bats: B   Throws: L   Height: 6' 1"   Weight: 185   Born: September 3, 1985   Age: 24

YEAR	TEAM	LVL	AGE	W	L	SV	G	GS	IP	H	HR	BB	SO	GB%	BABIP	STUFF	WHIP	ERA	SIERA	DERA	EqH9	EqHR9	EqBB9	EqSO9	VORP	SN/WX
2007	CCH	AA	21	6	6	0	16	16	102¹	96	10	33	69	50%	.272	14	1.26	2.99	4.43	3.91	9.1	1.5	3.1	4.4	17.5	1.03
2007	ROU	AAA	21	4	2	0	8	8	49	44	5	11	25	36%	.250	9	1.12	4.59	4.96	5.23	8.2	1.5	2.3	3.2	1.4	0.45
2007	HOU	MLB	21	0	2	0	3	2	12²	10	3	4	8	28%	.189	13	1.11	3.55	5.10	4.15	6.9	2.1	2.8	4.8	1.9	0.17
2009	BOW	AA	23	6	2	0	11	11	63¹	50	6	18	47	43%	.245	3	1.07	1.99	4.09	3.78	8.6	1.3	2.8	4.6	11.6	1.07
2009	NOR	AAA	23	1	3	0	9	9	44²	62	12	14	26	38%	.333	-40	1.70	6.45	5.05	8.23	14.3	4.2	3.3	4.2	-12.4	-1.06
2010	BAL	MLB	24	4	7	0	20	17	86¹	99	14	33	45	26%	.301	-11	1.53	5.46	5.85	5.44	9.8	1.3	3.4	4.4	0.6	1.34

Breakout: 9%   Improve: 49%   Collapse: 15%   Attrition: 16%   MLB: 28%   Comparables: *Chris Narveson, John Koronka, Tony Mounce, Abe Alvarez*

Patton's comeback from shoulder surgery looked good at Bowie, good enough to earn a promotion to Triple-A, but his already marginal velocity took a step backward, leaving even less of a margin for error. Double-A hitters were figuring him out as the season went on—monthly splits show increasing ERAs and decreasing strikeouts—and Triple-A hitters lit into him like piranhas on a bloody, drowning cow. If the Orioles and Patton are lucky, it was just residual weakness from the surgery; if it's permanent, he's what's for dinner.

Wilfredo Perez

Bats: L   Throws: L   Height: 6' 0"   Weight: 145   Born: August 12, 1984   Age: 25

YEAR	TEAM	LVL	AGE	W	L	SV	G	GS	IP	H	HR	BB	SO	GB%	BABIP	STUFF	WHIP	ERA	SIERA	DERA	EqH9	EqHR9	EqBB9	EqSO9	VORP	SN/WX
2007	DEL	A	22	5	3	5	27	8	81	53	3	28	108	59%	.272	17	1.00	1.67	2.32	3.01	8.2	1.3	3.7	7.7	20.6	1.45
2008	FRD	A+	23	2	4	2	26	0	56¹	44	5	30	69	61%	.295	9	1.31	2.88	3.07	4.12	9.1	1.6	5.3	8.2	7.9	0.14
2008	BOW	AA	23	0	0	1	16	0	23¹	16	1	8	23	52%	.254	5	1.03	2.31	3.32	3.32	7.5	0.8	3.3	6.6	5.2	0.66
2009	BOW	AA	24	2	0	7	24	0	26¹	12	1	22	29	54%	.190	12	1.29	1.37	4.18	2.74	5.8	1.1	7.3	7.3	7.6	0.68
2010	BAL	MLB	25	3	4	1	35	0	58¹	59	8	29	48	51%	.306	-1	1.51	4.95	4.33	5.03	8.7	1.1	4.5	7.0	3.0	1.53

Breakout: 13%   Improve: 28%   Collapse: 36%   Attrition: 11%   MLB: 10%   Comparables: *Mike Bumatay, Rusty Kilgo, Jesse Carlson, Al Drumheller*

Perez is an unheralded, undersized southpaw who has excelled since moving to relief in 2007, holding runners to a .182/.276/.270 line over the last three years. His 2009 season was cut short in June, when he had bone chips removed from his elbow, which is a concern as he already has a Tommy John surgery in his past. Short and skinny almost to a fault, he throws a fastball more notable for its movement than its velocity.

Chris Ray

Bats: R   Throws: R   Height: 6' 3"   Weight: 225   Born: January 12, 1982   Age: 28

YEAR	TEAM	LVL	AGE	W	L	SV	G	GS	IP	H	HR	BB	SO	GB%	BABIP	STUFF	WHIP	ERA	SIERA	DERA	EqH9	EqHR9	EqBB9	EqSO9	VORP	SN/WX
2007	BAL	MLB	25	5	6	16	43	0	42²	35	5	18	44	45%	.273	11	1.24	4.43	3.48	4.22	7.2	1.1	3.4	8.4	6.1	-0.13
2009	NOR	AAA	27	0	1	1	8	0	12	5	0	4	13	44%	.185	11	0.75	2.25	2.73	2.78	4.0	0.0	3.2	7.9	3.4	0.08
2009	BAL	MLB	27	0	4	0	46	0	43¹	64	8	23	39	50%	.392	-16	2.01	7.27	4.41	6.60	12.2	1.2	4.1	7.1	-5.4	-0.99
2010	TEX	MLB	28	2	4	7	48	0	50²	56	8	23	38	45%	.316	-9	1.55	5.15	4.57	5.26	9.8	1.1	3.7	6.3	1.3	-0.09

Breakout: 18%   Improve: 41%   Collapse: 19%   Attrition: 6%   MLB: 69%   Comparables: *Jose Santiago, Jay Powell, Larry Sherry, Bob Wickman*

Ray missed all of 2008 following Tommy John surgery and did not appear to be fully recovered in 2009. His fastball was a couple of miles per hour off where it was presurgery, and his slider was flat. He endured some epic beatings (13 of his 36 runs came in outings where he failed to retire more than one batter), not to mention a demotion to Norfolk to straighten himself out, a trip to the DL with shoulder tendinitis, and complaints of arm fatigue. He did put together a strong August (17 IP, 2.12 ERA), allowing an optimist to think he just needs to get healthy to be the old Chris Ray once again. Kicked to the Rangers in the Millwood trade, where the park won't help him.

Dennis Sarfate

Bats: R   Throws: R   Height: 6' 4"   Weight: 225   Born: April 9, 1981   Age: 29

YEAR	TEAM	LVL	AGE	W	L	SV	G	GS	IP	H	HR	BB	SO	GB%	BABIP	STUFF	WHIP	ERA	SIERA	DERA	EqH9	EqHR9	EqBB9	EqSO9	VORP	SN/WX
2007	NAS	AAA	25	2	7	4	45	1	61²	61	6	47	68	56%	.344	-5	1.75	4.52	4.13	5.99	10.7	1.6	7.2	8.0	-3.1	-0.53
2007	HOU	MLB	25	1	0	0	7	0	8¹	5	0	1	14	64%	.313	8	0.72	1.08	0.74	1.13	6.8	0.0	1.1	11.3	3.9	0.45
2008	BAL	MLB	26	4	3	0	57	4	79²	62	8	62	86	40%	.276	20	1.56	4.74	4.40	4.84	6.9	0.8	6.3	9.0	5.8	-0.39
2009	NOR	AAA	27	1	1	0	12	0	12²	13	4	2	13	30%	.273	-8	1.18	6.39	2.91	8.10	11.6	4.6	1.5	7.7	-3.4	-0.49
2009	BAL	MLB	27	0	1	0	20	0	23	21	3	14	20	42%	.286	-1	1.52	5.09	4.64	5.16	7.9	0.8	4.8	7.1	0.9	0.17
2010	BAL	MLB	29	2	4	1	51	0	57¹	61	8	36	53	41%	.329	-8	1.69	5.83	4.48	5.87	9.1	1.1	5.5	7.9	-2.3	-0.01

Breakout: 17%   Improve: 59%   Collapse: 20%   Attrition: 16%   MLB: 52%   Comparables: Rocky Cherry, Todd Wellemeyer, Ryan Houston, Joey McLaughlin

A hard-throwing righty, Sarfate has endured some odd injuries the last two years, including a broken clavicle in 2008 (that he pitched through!) and a circulatory problem in his hand that left him literally numb. He did pitch better when he finally made it back to start September, but not so much better that he'll be considered for anything more than a middle-relief role in the coming season.

Chris Tillman

Bats: R   Throws: R   Height: 6' 5"   Weight: 195   Born: April 15, 1988   Age: 22

YEAR	TEAM	LVL	AGE	W	L	SV	G	GS	IP	H	HR	BB	SO	GB%	BABIP	STUFF	WHIP	ERA	SIERA	DERA	EqH9	EqHR9	EqBB9	EqSO9	VORP	SN/WX
2007	WIS	A	19	1	4	0	8	8	33	31	1	13	34	41%	.313	18	1.33	3.55	3.53	7.61	10.1	1.1	4.3	5.7	-7.4	-0.27
2007	HDS	A+	19	6	7	0	20	20	102²	107	12	48	105	45%	.322	27	1.51	5.26	3.80	6.34	9.1	1.3	4.3	6.3	-9.6	-1.37
2008	BOW	AA	20	11	4	0	28	28	135²	115	10	65	154	42%	.303	36	1.33	3.18	3.35	4.58	9.2	1.3	4.4	7.6	13.0	1.68
2009	NOR	AAA	21	8	6	0	18	18	96²	85	5	26	99	47%	.302	34	1.15	2.70	3.07	4.05	8.6	1.0	2.6	7.1	15.0	1.62
2009	BAL	MLB	21	2	5	0	12	12	65	77	15	24	39	42%	.302	12	1.55	5.40	4.98	4.85	9.8	1.7	3.0	4.9	4.6	0.76
2010	BAL	MLB	22	7	9	0	31	31	145	156	21	65	110	35%	.311	20	1.52	5.11	4.73	5.13	9.2	1.2	3.9	6.4	5.9	2.23

Breakout: 8%   Improve: 45%   Collapse: 11%   Attrition: 15%   MLB: 81%   Comparables: Pat Hentgen, Pat Mahomes, Daniel Cortes, John Habyan

Tillman's arrival was eagerly anticipated in Baltimore, and he made his debut the same day that George Sherrill—who had come to the organization with him from Seattle in the Bedard trade—was dealt off to Los Angeles. His long, skinny frame is absolutely loaded with potential, and what he has now is already pretty darned good. His fastball clocks in at 92-94 mph with a boring-in action, his power curveball is a true swing-and-miss offering, and his changeup is solid. He does tend to pitch up in the zone and tired noticeably in September, losing velocity and adding more than a run to his ERA with his last five outings. Note that he cut his walk rate way down in the minors last year, one of the big items on his to-do list; just 22 this April, one of the best pitching prospects out there is still evolving.

Koji Uehara

Bats: R   Throws: R   Height: 6' 2"   Weight: 190   Born: April 3, 1975   Age: 35

YEAR	TEAM	LVL	AGE	W	L	SV	G	GS	IP	H	HR	BB	SO	GB%	BABIP	STUFF	WHIP	ERA	SIERA	DERA	EqH9	EqHR9	EqBB9	EqSO9	VORP	SN/WX
2007	YOM	JPN	32	4	3	32	55	0	62	47	4	4	66	—	.265	21	0.82	1.74	2.23	2.54	7.5	0.7	0.7	7.5	19.9	1.71
2008	YOM	JPN	33	6	5	1	26	12	89²	90	11	16	72	—	.292	-3	1.18	3.81	3.58	5.28	9.3	1.3	2.1	5.9	2.2	1.21
2009	BAL	MLB	34	2	4	0	12	12	66²	71	7	12	48	34%	.302	17	1.24	4.05	4.10	3.90	8.6	0.8	1.3	5.7	12.1	1.92
2010	BAL	MLB	35	4	3	7	38	6	67¹	72	9	17	46	41%	.306	2	1.32	4.18	4.27	4.22	9.2	1.1	2.2	5.8	9.6	1.22

Breakout: 10%   Improve: 30%   Collapse: 29%   Attrition: 17%   MLB: 88%   Comparables: Mike Ryba, Bill Hands, Doug Jones, Pete Appleton

Uehara's pure stuff is less than impressive, beginning with a fastball that only clocks in at 86-88 mph. What is impressive is how many things he can do from there. He cuts the fastball in two ways to produce different movement and also has a splitter that dives into the ground; an occasional slider; and a very slow, wide curve, and all of them are thrown with impeccable control. We had two worries about Uehara entering the season: that he wouldn't have the stamina to start regularly after working mainly in relief the last couple of years in Japan, and that he might suffer a recurrence of the leg injuries that forced him to the bullpen in the first place. Both fears came true, but it was a torn elbow tendon that ended his season. He should be fully healed by spring and is expected to work only in relief.

LINEOUTS

Hitters

PLAYER	TEAM	LVL	AGE	PA	R	2B	3B	HR	RBI	BB	SO	SB-CS	EqBRR	AVG/OBP/SLG	EqAVG/EqOBP/EqSLG	EqA	VORP	WARP
CF M. Angle*	FRD	A+	23	553	78	17	4	1	32	59	72	40-12	3.0	.289/.370/.347	.257/.323/.306	.230	-1.1	-1.1
	BOW	AA	23	32	6	1	0	0	1	4	5	2-0	1.0	.357/.438/.393	.310/.375/.345	.267	1.1	0.4
OF X. Avery*	DEL	A	19	509	55	15	8	2	36	27	111	30-10	-4.3	.262/.306/.340	.239/.274/.308	.204	-14.3	-3.7
OF K. Hudson*	DEL	A	22	456	61	8	2	0	21	49	85	31-16	2.1	.284/.365/.314	.254/.320/.273	.216	-10.9	-2.9
C C. Joseph	FRD	A+	23	412	50	23	2	12	60	26	64	2-1	-1.5	.284/.337/.450	.250/.293/.392	.236	6.8	-0.4
C C. Moeller	NOR	AAA	34	125	7	6	0	0	10	5	22	0-1	-0.2	.203/.242/.254	.193/.226/.235	.143	-6.8	-1.5
	BAL	MLB	34	100	6	8	1	2	10	7	16	0-0	-0.8	.258/.313/.438	.261/.313/.432	.260	4.4	-0.2
3B S. Moore*	NOR	AAA	25	136	19	7	0	7	21	8	22	1-0	-0.3	.252/.316/.480	.250/.309/.460	.262	3.1	0.3
3B B. Waring	FRD	A+	23	543	70	35	2	26	90	51	121	5-3	-2.4	.273/.354/.520	.237/.301/.427	.250	0.7	-1.3

Matt Angle is one of those high-energy center-field grinders who plays the game right, but scouts aren't convinced that his on-base skills are enough to mitigate a complete lack of power. ⊘ The Orioles drafted **Xavier Avery** in 2008's second round as a pure tools bet, hoping he'd be able to translate some of them into baseball skills. One year later, they're still hoping. ⊘ A second-round pick in 2009, **Mychal Givens** is one of those toolsy high school shortstops who will either rocket up prospect lists over the next few years, or never get out of A-ball. ⊘ If you think Matt Angle has no power, you should see **Kyle Hudson**, who had 10 extra-base hits in 117 games; he's also the fastest player in the system. ⊘ Catcher **Caleb Joseph** had a bit of a breakout year in the Carolina League; he doesn't do anything exceptionally well, but he is rather solid across the board, enough to make him a nice little catching prospect. ⊘ **Chad Moeller** spent the year backing up either Gregg Zaun or Wieters, and when both of them were Orioles, he was a Tide. He hit about as well as a Moeller can last year, but threw out only two of 25 basestealers. ⊘ **Scott Moore** missed his chance to fill in for a slumping Mora when, for the second year in a row, Moore tore thumb ligaments early and missed the rest of the season. ⊘ An 11th-round pick to whom the O's gave nearly a million dollars, **Michael Ohlman** has huge power, but there are a lot of questions about his ability to stay behind the plate long-term. ⊘ **Brandon Waring** led the Orioles organization in home runs, but was old for his leagues, is a defensive liability, and comes with a strikeout/walk ratio that has been banned for human use in more than 20 countries.

Pitchers

PLAYER	TEAM	LVL	AGE	W	L	SV	IP	H	HR	BB	SO	GB%	BABIP	STUFF	WHIP	ERA	SIERA	DERA	EqH9	EqHR9	EqBB9	EqSO9	VORP
A. Castillo*	NOR	AAA	33	2	3	13	52	49	2	17	54	52%	.329	3	1.27	2.77	3.26	4.74	9.3	0.7	3.3	7.3	4.1
	BAL	MLB	33	0	0	0	12	12	0	4	8	60%	.333	-1	1.33	2.25	4.31	2.45	9.0	0.0	2.5	5.7	3.7
S. Henn*	ROC	AAA	28	1	1	6	38²	37	3	16	45	43%	.315	6	1.37	2.33	3.19	4.65	8.4	0.9	3.6	8.2	3.7
	MIN	MLB	28	0	3	0	11¹	9	2	8	9	49%	.233	-8	1.50	7.15	4.99	6.55	7.4	1.6	5.7	6.5	-1.3
	BAL	MLB	28	0	0	0	3	6	0	4	6	0%	.667	3	3.33	9.00	3.97	9.00	18.0	0.0	9.0	15.0	-1.2
J. Hoey	BOW	AA	26	2	6	0	48	48	4	32	47	31%	.333	-15	1.67	4.50	4.60	6.70	11.7	1.7	6.3	6.7	-5.7
D. Pauley	NOR	AAA	26	9	12	0	152¹	171	15	45	108	56%	.322	-18	1.42	4.37	4.25	6.02	10.9	1.6	2.9	4.9	-8.3
A. Simon	BAL	MLB	27	0	1	0	6¹	8	5	2	3	34%	.167	-26	1.58	9.95	5.57	8.53	9.9	5.7	2.8	4.3	-2.1
C. Spoone	FRD	A+	23	0	2	0	14¹	17	3	14	12	52%	.326	-17	2.16	9.42	5.39	12.46	13.2	3.5	9.7	4.8	-10.1
	ORI	Rk	23	0	1	0	12¹	9	1	2	11	-1%	.267	-19	0.89	4.38	2.87	8.20	12.5	3.9	2.9	4.8	-2.8
C. Thall*	BOW	AA	23	2	2	1	60¹	48	3	28	55	51%	.263	-9	1.26	2.69	3.97	4.27	8.7	1.1	4.2	5.9	7.9
J. Walker*	BAL	MLB	37	0	0	0	12¹	19	5	0	9	44%	.350	-6	1.54	5.11	3.59	5.25	12.8	3.0	0.0	6.0	0.3

Alberto Castillo has held left-handed hitters to a .191 EqA over the last two years, better than Tim Lincecum; right-handers cranked at a .289 clip, worse than Russ Ortiz. ⊘ The Orioles took a risk in the 2009 draft by giving lefty **Cameron Coffey** a bonus just south of $1 million, despite the fact that he just had Tommy John surgery. Still, 6-foot-

5 teenage lefties who can get it up to 95 mph don't exactly grow on trees. ⊘ **Sean Henn** was working as a Triple-A LOOGY when he was claimed on waivers from the Twins; he worked only three innings for the O's before the season ended, then was claimed on waivers by the Jays. Major-league lefties have hit .305/.386/.516 off him in 146 plate appearances. ⊘ **Jim Hoey** could hit 100 mph two years ago, but struggled at Bowie after missing all of 2008 after a shoulder surgery. ⊘ **David Pauley** has spent the last four years at Triple-A, and even the Orioles never got desperate enough to call him up last year—although they did really, really think about it. ⊘ Minor league journeyman **Alfredo Simon** made the Oriole rotation out of spring training, but lasted just two starts before hitting the Tommy John operating table and missing the rest of the season. ⊘ The 2009 season was the first slow step for former top prospect **Chorye Spoone** on the comeback trail from a 2008 shoulder surgery. ⊘ **Chad Thall** has some serious LOOGY potential, holding lefties to a tidy .199 translated EqA over the last two seasons, mostly at Bowie. ⊘ When LOOGYs allow left-handed hitters an EqA over .400, as **Jamie Walker** did in 2009, they get released and no one picks them up.

MANAGER: DAVE TREMBLEY

YEAR	TEAM	W-L	Pythag +/-	Avg PC	100+ P	120+ P	QS	BQS	REL	REL w Zero R	IBB	Subs	PH	PH Avg	PH HR	SB2	CS2	SB3	CS3	SAC Att	SAC %	POS SAC	Squeeze	Swing	In Play
2007	BAL	40-53	2	94.0	43	1	38	2	279	149	29	24	62	.190	0	76	29	16	3	38	52.6%	19	2	83	63
2008	BAL	68-93	-4	92.6	64	0	56	9	492	265	44	37	117	.218	3	69	32	12	3	42	64.3%	26	2	147	117
2009	BAL	64-98	-4	93.2	64	0	52	6	483	287	45	30	98	.225	2	59	34	16	3	21	61.9%	11	0	130	106

Trembley will be staying for another season, as the Orioles picked up his 2010 option despite yet another September swoon—the O's had to win their last four games to finish 10-20 after September 1st, following up on marks of 5-20 in 2008 and 10-19 in 2007. Those records include losing streaks of 13 games this past year and 10 in '08. Trembley was charged with nurturing and developing a wave of young players, as 15 percent of Oriole plate appearances and 40 percent of their innings came from rookies. He was patient to a fault, as young players (notably Berken and Hernandez) were given extended chances to prove themselves, beyond the point that most teams would have pulled them, although it's not as if the Orioles had many choices. Pie was the only player really given up on during the season, yet he was replaced by another rookie (Reimold) who simply outplayed him, and subsequently was given another chance later in the year. Upper management has recognized that Trembley's job, up until now, has been about demolishing the old team and building a new foundation; with that in place, they're going to expect a few more wins.

Boston Red Sox

The first decade of the 21st century was the most successful in Boston Red Sox history since the second decade of the 20th century. In the just-completed decade's final seven years, the Red Sox made the postseason six times, won two world championships (tying the Yankees for the most in the decade and ending an 86-year title drought), and, in two other seasons, made it as far as the seventh game of the American League Championship Series. Their regular-season record in the decade was second in all of baseball, behind only that of the rival Yankees.

All of that success came in the wake of the January 2002 sale of the team to an ownership group headed by John Henry. The sale was part of a controversial arrangement in which Henry, who had been the owner of the Marlins, sold that team to Jeffrey Loria, who had been the owner of the Montreal Expos, with Major League Baseball taking over stewardship of the failing Expos franchise. At the time, Commissioner Bud Selig was accused of sacrificing two teams (amid murmurs of contraction) to create a superpower capable of challenging the Yankees, who had won five of the previous six American League pennants and four of the last six World Series. Eight years later, that criticism seems as valid as ever. The Expos moved to Washington, DC, after the 2004 season. The Marlins, after a surprising World Series win in 2003, again sold off their championship players and became something of a new Expos, a team constantly trading talent in an effort to avoid paying more than the major-league minimum for all but one or two signature players. The Red Sox, meanwhile, did indeed provide worthy foes for the Yankees over the remainder of the decade, winning two titles before the Yankees won another.

RED SOX PROSPECTUS
2009 W-L: 95-67, 2nd in AL East

Pythag	90-72	3rd	**Ballpark:** Fenway Park (3-yr. PF: 1045). With the Monster looming, it's still a hitter's park
RS/G	5.4	3rd	
RA/G	4.5	3rd	
EqA	.267	3rd	**2009:** The best team in baseball—besides the Yankees, or Angels, or Phillies, or...
EqBRR	-0.2	6th	
SNWP	.507	7th	
WXRL	11.28	2nd	**2010:** Even in a transition year, they could win the AL Wild Card, but will they sort out the left side of the diamond?
FRAr	4.17	2nd	
DE	.679	13th	
PADE	-1.10	9th	**Action Items:** Getting/keeping offense at third and left to carry Papi's last hurrah
Salary	$121.7	2nd	
Attend	3.06	3rd	

Say what you want about conspiracies, but that last fact is to the great credit of Henry's administration. It's easier to tear a team down than to build one up, and we can now see in retrospect that the vast majority of the Red Sox' 86-year drought that was, in its later years, credited to the Curse of the Bambino was largely due to mismanagement. The work of the new front office was all the more impressive, given that it actually wound up building two almost entirely distinct championship teams in a six-year span, where previous ownerships and management teams had failed for decades. Now, as we enter the second decade of the new millennium, they are faced with the possibility of having to build a third.

In Henry, the Red Sox acquired an owner with deep pockets but also a progressive intelligence that helped make the Red Sox not just one of baseball's richest teams, but one of its best run, a combination that has proven to be every bit as enabling as the cronyism and institutionalized racism of the Yawkey years was crippling. That's not to say that Henry took over a terrible team. When Henry and company took over, the club boasted an impressive trio of stars in ace Pedro Martinez, slugger Manny Ramirez, and shortstop Nomar Garciaparra. The Sox also had a handful of other players who would play key roles in the team's coming success, specifically catcher Jason Varitek and deposed closer Derek Lowe, knuckleballer Tim Wakefield, and right fielder Trot Nixon. All of those players had been acquired by outgoing general manager Dan Duquette, with the exception of Nixon, who was the team's first-round pick in 1993, the team's final year under general manager Lou Gorman.

In Henry's first year at the helm, with Mike Port serving as interim GM, the Red Sox moved Lowe back into the rotation and signed Johnny Damon to play center field. That November, after flirting with Billy Beane, they named Port's permanent replacement, 28-year-old Ivy Leaguer Theo Epstein, whom Larry Lucchino had brought over from the Padres, where the young Epstein had been director of baseball operations.

In a single offseason, Epstein fleshed out the team with a variety of low-cost moves. He traded a pair of nonprospects for offense-first second baseman Todd Walker, signed free-agent third baseman Bill Mueller, signed David Ortiz (who had been nontendered by the Twins), claimed right-hander Bronson Arroyo off waivers from the Pirates, and bought first baseman Kevin Millar from Loria's Marlins. Of those five, Millar was the most expensive ($5.3 million over two years), while Mueller's strong work at the hot corner allowed Epstein to trade incumbent Shea Hillenbrand to Arizona for closer Byun-Hyung Kim at the end of May. The Red Sox battled the Yankees down to the 11th inning of Game Seven of the ALCS, the deepest Boston had been in the postseason since their heartbreaking loss to the Mets in the 1986 World Series.

Epstein made a similar move in the ensuing offseason when he replaced Walker with Mark Bellhorn via a minor deal with the Rockies. But having gotten within a few outs of the World Series in 2003 by using his wits to expand upon the Sox' existing assets, Epstein turned to Henry's wallet to put his team over the edge in 2004. He brought in free agent closer Keith Foulke and swung a lopsided deal with the Diamondbacks for disenchanted ace Curt Schilling. Then, at the trading deadline, he shocked his fan base by trading a sulking and injured Garciaparra in a four-team deal for a pair of outstanding glove men in Expos shortstop Orlando Cabera and Twins first baseman Doug Mientkiewicz. That same day, the Red Sox made a minor deal for speedy Dodgers outfielder Dave Roberts, who would help the Sox slip out of the Yankees' noose three outs away from being swept in the ALCS and race toward an improbable and franchise-altering World Series victory.

As remarkable as that title run was, it was all the more so for the 2004 Red Sox' being less the team Epstein had hoped to build than a stopgap hodgepodge. Of the Red Sox who saw action in the ALCS and World Series in 2004, only Nixon had been acquired by the team as an amateur. The youngest man in the starting lineup was Ortiz, at 29, and the 27-year-old Arroyo was the only significant member of the pitching staff under 30.

Having just built the first world champion Red Sox team in 86 years, Epstein quickly set about rebuilding it. Pedro Martinez, Derek Lowe, and Orlando Cabrera left as free agents and were replaced by Matt Clement, David Wells, and Edgar Renteria. Poor returns from those deals as well as an injury-plagued season from Schilling led to a first-round exit in the playoffs in 2005. The next year, Boston missed the playoffs entirely, but Epstein's team was just beginning to take shape. A blockbuster deal that sent the Marlins shortstop prospect Hanley Ramirez for 26-year-old ace Josh Beckett and third baseman Mike Lowell drew most of the attention and proved to be a solid return on a homegrown prospect, but other homegrown stars began to emerge. In 2006, Jonathan Papelbon, drafted in the fourth round in 2003, claimed the closer job at age 25; Kevin Youkilis, a product of Duquette's last draft in 2001, took over first base in his age-27 season; and 22-year-old lefty Jon Lester, a second-round pick in 2002, made his major-league debut, as did another 22-year-old, a scrappy little second baseman, a second-round pick from 2004 named Dustin Pedroia.

Pedroia won the Rookie of the Year Award in 2007 as a rebuilt Red Sox team surged to another title with the help of free agents J. D. Drew in right field, Daisuke Matsuzaka in the rotation, and Hideki Okajima in the bullpen. This 2007 team forms the core of the 2010 Red Sox, but with the Yankees ascendant, the challenge is that Epstein must rebuild again before it can claim another title.

The coming season seems certain to be the final year in Boston for thirtysomethings Ortiz, Varitek, and Lowell: Ortiz is big-bodied and his production has fallen off considerably; Varitek is being relegated to backup duty; Lowell, once a spectacular fielder, has been rendered immobile by hip surgery. Epstein was already working on the problem last year, acquiring superstar Victor Martinez to replace Varitek from Cleveland, but Martinez will also become a free agent after this next season, as will Beckett. The following offseason will bring free agency for Papelbon and Drew, and it will also probably mark the likely retirement for Wakefield.

To deal with this aging core and responding to the failings of last year's club and its early exit from the playoffs, Epstein moved aggressively to shore up the team's bid for further post-season glory in 2010 and 2011. To match the Yankees' hoarding of power arms, he signed the best hurler on the market, Angels ace John Lackey, for five years and $82.5 million. Lackey should give the Sox a top trio alongside Jon Lester and Beckett that can go toe-to-toe with the Yankees' Sabathia, Burnett, and Vazquez. It also provides the club with another nice amount of depth, allowing them to see who can help them most from among Clay Buchholz, Matsuzaka, and Wakefield in the last two slots.

The GM addressed the club's woeful defense just as adroitly, by reaching for the checkbook and inking short-term deals with quality defenders who are simultaneously key complementary players to the lineup. Mike Cameron was signed to play center for two years at $15.5 million, shortstop Marco Scutaro's on hand for two years for $12.5 million, and third-base whiz Adrian Beltre should be picking it for at least 2010 at $10 million. That's a new third of the lineup, not counting V-Mart. The upshot is that Jacoby Ellsbury's been shunted to left (or trade bait status). Contenders also need depth, and Epstein addressed that by adding Jeremy Hermida, a power bench bat for the corners in case Ortiz or Ellsbury struggle, or if Drew gets injured. Shoring up the lineup and the rotation also acquires development time for emerging young hitters Josh Reddick and Ryan Kalish, as well as hurlers Junichi Tazawa and Michael Bowden. Whether these prospects end up being bargaining chips or big parts of the 2012 club will depend on their progress.

Meanwhile, this new blend of established stars and a short-term assemblage of veterans will do what it can to mount the Sox's bid for a third title. It's perhaps just as well that Epstein's leaned so heavily on free agency to cure what immediately ails the club, because there are questions of how heavily they can rely on some current key players. Beckett's injury history suggests he might not be retained, while Youkilis is another bulky late-bloomer like Ortiz, and might not have a peak much longer than Papi's five-year run.

Another nagging thought is that though the Red Sox have made the postseason in six of the last seven years, winning two World Series along the way, they've won their division just once in that span. In four of those six postseason years, they've won exactly 95 games, which is impressive on its face, but problematic when one considers that 95 wins have been enough to win the AL East just once in the last eight seasons (ironically, in that season the Red Sox won 95 games but lost the division in a tiebreaker to the 95-win Yankees). The wild card proved to be a reliable route to the postseason for the Red Sox in the past decade, but given the amount of work Epstein has on his plate simply to keep the team from slipping from its current level, and how accustomed the Hub fan base has come to winning, one wonders just how much room he has for error.

HITTERS

Brian Anderson   **CF**   Bats: R   Throws: R   Height: 6' 2"   Weight: 220   Born: March 11, 1982   Age: 28

YEAR	TEAM	LVL	AGE	PA	R	2B	3B	HR	RBI	BB	SO	SB	CS	EqBRR	AVG	OBP	SLG	EqAVG	EqOBP	EqSLG	EqA	VORP	WARP	DEFENSE			
2007	CHR	AAA	25	223	29	8	2	8	31	19	47	3	2	-1.3	.255	.318	.435	.243	.300	.416	.247	1.7	0.4	35-CF	2		
2007	CHA	MLB	25	19	3	1	0	0	2	7	0	0	0.4	.118	.211	.176	.118	.211	.176	.114	-2.1	-0.3	1-LF	0		
2008	CHA	MLB	26	193	24	13	0	8	26	10	45	5	1	2.0	.232	.272	.436	.233	.274	.433	.243	1.5	-0.2	50-CF	-2		
2009	CHR	AAA	27	46	6	1	1	2	5	2	16	0	1	-0.1	.279	.311	.488	.256	.289	.465	.246	0.4	-0.1	9-CF	-1		
2009	CHA	MLB	27	210	25	9	0	2	13	20	49	3	6	-2.3	.238	.322	.319	.243	.327	.330	.223	-1.8	0.1	49-CF	3	3-RF	0
2009	PAW	AAA	27	90	9	4	0	4	8	7	22	0	2	-1.5	.200	.281	.400	.185	.258	.370	.213	-1.7	0.0	17-CF	2		
2009	BOS	MLB	27	21	7	0	0	2	5	3	5	0	0	0.6	.294	.381	.647	.294	.381	.647	.325	2.3	0.1	5-RF	-1	1-LF	0
2010	KCA	MLB	28	329	41	14	1	11	37	26	81	4	4	-0.5	.242	.306	.408	.235	.302	.395	.231	0.3	0.1	71-CF	1		

Breakout: 10% Improve: 48% Collapse: 14% Attrition: 3%   MLB: 61%   Comparables: Ernie Young, Ryan Thompson, Ken Gerhart, Dustan Mohr

With a .227/.290/.370 career line, Anderson simply hasn't hit since being installed as the starting center fielder of the defending world champion White Sox in 2006. At age 28 and now a free agent, he may already be out of opportunities, but as a poor man's Kapler or Baldelli wannabe, he might land on another 200 plate appearances somewhere. Naturally, the Royals were interested.

Lars Anderson   1B

Bats: L   Throws: L   Height: 6' 4"   Weight: 215   Born: September 25, 1987   Age: 22

YEAR	TEAM	LVL	AGE	PA	R	2B	3B	HR	RBI	BB	SO	SB	CS	EqBRR	AVG	OBP	SLG	EqAVG	EqOBP	EqSLG	EqA	VORP	WARP	DEFENSE
2007	GRN	A	19	533	69	35	3	10	69	71	112	2	4	-2.8	.288	.385	.443	.247	.328	.374	.247	-2.2	-1.6	110-1B -11
2007	LNC	A+	19	47	13	2	0	1	9	11	9	0	0	0.1	.343	.489	.486	.297	.426	.432	.309	2.9	0.3	8-1B 0
2008	LNC	A+	20	358	58	19	1	13	50	46	64	0	0	-1.6	.317	.408	.513	.256	.343	.415	.266	5.5	0.1	70-1B -5
2008	PME	AA	20	163	27	13	0	5	30	29	43	1	0	-0.1	.316	.436	.526	.290	.393	.464	.299	8.5	0.5	21-1B -4
2009	PME	AA	21	512	50	23	0	9	51	63	114	2	0	0.0	.233	.328	.345	.223	.303	.328	.224	-19.4	-3.8	95-1B -12
2010	BOS	MLB	22	530	61	28	1	13	60	61	132	1	1	-0.7	.246	.335	.395	.244	.331	.381	.246	-2.3	-0.8	101-1B -5

Breakout: 18%   Improve: 57%   Collapse: 14%   Attrition: 6%   MLB: 3%   Comparables: Joey Votto, Kila Kaaihue, Steve Cox, Chris Weinke

The top prospect in the Red Sox' system entering 2009 (and our 17th overall in last year's top 50), Anderson had hit .304/.404/.480 across three levels in his first two professional seasons, but during his repeat of Double-A, a back injury caused him to struggle for the first time in May. Despite a rebound in June, prospect hunters were already asking "What happened to Lars?" when he hit the All-Star break batting .272/.366/.413. A deeply intelligent and sensitive young man, Anderson didn't handle the doubters well and suffered a complete collapse in the second half, batting .154/.250/.208 after the break. He looked stiff and unathletic, perhaps due to the residual effects of the back or simply because he was pressing. Either way, he has a lot to prove in 2010, but no longer has that number-one-prospect tag to live up to.

Rocco Baldelli   OF

Bats: R   Throws: R   Height: 6' 4"   Weight: 200   Born: September 25, 1981   Age: 28

YEAR	TEAM	LVL	AGE	PA	R	2B	3B	HR	RBI	BB	SO	SB	CS	EqBRR	AVG	OBP	SLG	EqAVG	EqOBP	EqSLG	EqA	VORP	WARP	DEFENSE	
2007	TBA	MLB	25	150	16	6	0	5	12	9	35	4	1	0.8	.204	.268	.358	.204	.268	.372	.224	-2.5	-0.6	18-CF -3	
2008	TBA	MLB	26	90	12	5	0	4	13	7	25	0	0	-1.0	.262	.344	.475	.275	.356	.512	.285	4.2	0.4	3-RF 0	
2009	BOS	MLB	27	164	23	4	1	7	23	11	37	1	0	0.2	.253	.311	.433	.253	.311	.433	.253	1.3	-0.1	26-RF -2	6-CF 0
2010	BOS	MLB	28	284	35	11	1	12	37	22	70	3	1	0.0	.238	.309	.425	.232	.305	.410	.243	0.9	0.0	31-RF -1	

Breakout: 15%   Improve: 49%   Collapse: 8%   Attrition: 6%   MLB: 77%   Comparables: Wes Chamberlain, Jim Tatum, Ryan Thompson, Terry Harper

The sample size is small enough to be meaningless, but given that Baldelli suffers from channelopathy and thus has difficulty recovering from strenuous activity, it's interesting to note how well he performed as an in-game replacement last year (.310/.394/.586 in 33 plate appearances, including 5-for-14 as a pinch-hitter) compared with his performance as a starter (.240/.290/.397 in 37 games). In the bigger picture, Baldelli twice hit the DL and sat out the postseason, all because of leg injuries (hamstring, ankle contusion, hip flexor), and struggled against right-handed pitching (.193/.258/.431), both of which continued career-long trends. Since he is now 28 years old, his value already seems limited to being a right-handed pinch-hitter and defensive replacement, which suggests a move to the National League.

Jason Bay   LF

Bats: R   Throws: R   Height: 6' 2"   Weight: 205   Born: September 20, 1978   Age: 31

YEAR	TEAM	LVL	AGE	PA	R	2B	3B	HR	RBI	BB	SO	SB	CS	EqBRR	AVG	OBP	SLG	EqAVG	EqOBP	EqSLG	EqA	VORP	WARP	DEFENSE
2007	PIT	MLB	28	614	78	25	2	21	84	59	141	4	1	-2.2	.247	.327	.418	.254	.334	.428	.266	15.6	0.5	138-LF -11
2008	PIT	MLB	29	459	72	23	2	22	64	59	86	7	0	2.2	.282	.375	.519	.301	.388	.554	.314	38.3	2.3	103-LF -16
2008	BOS	MLB	29	211	39	12	2	9	37	22	51	3	0	0.4	.293	.370	.527	.290	.368	.519	.301	14.1	0.6	47-LF -8
2009	BOS	MLB	30	638	103	29	3	36	119	94	162	13	3	1.2	.267	.384	.537	.262	.380	.517	.304	44.2	4.7	144-LF 0
2010	NYN	MLB	31	635	94	28	2	28	95	76	149	9	2	0.3	.261	.358	.475	.264	.359	.476	.291	35.8	3.2	146-LF -6

Breakout: 8%   Improve: 45%   Collapse: 10%   Attrition: 6%   MLB: 100%   Comparables: Dwight Evans, Jesse Barfield, Jim Rice, Bernard Gilkey

Setting aside his 2007 season, during which he was playing on two bad knees, Bay has been remarkably consistent throughout his major-league career. Without 2007, his career line in the majors is .286/.385/.539, with on-base and slugging percentages nearly matching what he did in 2009. Outside of '07, Bay has never slugged below .522 in the majors, and since 2005, he's mixed in a small bit of high-percentage basestealing (59-for-66, or 89 percent). Yet, while his bat and baserunning have recovered from that one bad season, his fielding never has. Left field is at the far left side of the defensive spectrum, but Bay has been bad enough over the last three years that it would profit his team to make him a relatively youthful DH, which is, of course, impossible on the 2010 Mets, who signed him to a four-year, $66 million contract. Given Bay's consistency at the plate, he should at least continue to produce at the plate deep into his thirties.

Chris Carter   1B   Bats: L   Throws: L   Height: 6' 0"   Weight: 230   Born: September 16, 1982   Age: 27

YEAR	TEAM	LVL	AGE	PA	R	2B	3B	HR	RBI	BB	SO	SB	CS	EqBRR	AVG	OBP	SLG	EqAVG	EqOBP	EqSLG	EqA	VORP	WARP	DEFENSE			
2007	TUC	AAA	24	561	74	39	3	18	84	50	68	2	0	-6.6	.324	.383	.521	.285	.342	.449	.273	14.5	0.0	82-1B	-9	20-LF	-6
2007	PAW	AAA	24	52	6	1	0	1	4	4	7	0	0	-0.8	.234	.308	.319	.229	.302	.313	.218	-1.8	-0.1	12-1B	1		
2008	PAW	AAA	25	522	65	25	2	24	81	41	84	0	0	-2.7	.300	.356	.515	.279	.332	.476	.275	16.8	1.2	73-LF	-7		
2008	BOS	MLB	25	20	5	0	0	0	3	2	5	0	0	-0.1	.333	.400	.333	.333	.400	.333	.268	0.4	0.0				
2009	PAW	AAA	26	478	50	25	0	16	61	42	63	0	0	-4.0	.294	.358	.465	.278	.338	.441	.269	9.3	0.4	43-RF	-6	14-LF	0
2009	BOS	MLB	26	6	0	0	0	0	1	0	4	0	0	0.0	.000	.000	.000	.000	.000	.000	-.163	-1.0	0.0				
2010	NYN	MLB	27	466	47	22	1	15	57	39	84	1	0	-2.0	.257	.323	.418	.267	.332	.428	.260	9.9	0.6	71-RF	-5		

Breakout: 8%   Improve: 37%   Collapse: 23%   Attrition: 12%   MLB: 17%   Comparables: Jacob Cruz, Matt Watson, Paul McAnulty, Raul Ibañez

One of the players to be named later sent to the Mets in the Billy Wagner trade, Carter was winding up as another Bailey/Bates type, a solid minor-league bat in danger of becoming a Quad-A player. Tossed to an organization that gets worked up over Danny Murphy, he now resembles a platoon prospect (he slugged .502 vs. Triple-A righties) with a small shot at playing time at first base and the outfield corners. Not to be mistaken with the A's Chris Carter, this one doesn't have a big-time upside.

J. D. Drew   RF   Bats: L   Throws: R   Height: 6' 1"   Weight: 200   Born: November 20, 1975   Age: 34

YEAR	TEAM	LVL	AGE	PA	R	2B	3B	HR	RBI	BB	SO	SB	CS	EqBRR	AVG	OBP	SLG	EqAVG	EqOBP	EqSLG	EqA	VORP	WARP	DEFENSE			
2007	BOS	MLB	31	552	84	30	4	11	64	79	100	4	2	-0.1	.270	.373	.423	.259	.366	.413	.274	17.3	2.6	120-RF	7	3-CF	-1
2008	BOS	MLB	32	456	79	23	4	19	64	79	80	4	1	2.0	.280	.408	.519	.274	.406	.507	.313	35.2	3.5	99-RF	-3		
2009	BOS	MLB	33	539	84	30	4	24	68	82	109	2	6	-2.0	.279	.392	.522	.275	.389	.508	.299	33.3	4.3	122-RF	5		
2010	BOS	MLB	34	487	71	25	3	16	60	73	101	3	4	0.0	.258	.373	.453	.255	.370	.435	.276	18.0	2.1	110-RF	1		

Breakout: 7%   Improve: 40%   Collapse: 9%   Attrition: 15%   MLB: 99%   Comparables: Duke Snider, Bill Nicholson, Charlie Maxwell, Billy Williams

Drew reliably misses 20-plus games a year, but he's also reliably productive when he plays. The only seasons in which his production dipped in the just-completed decade were 2002, when, like Bay in '07, he had problems with both knees, and 2007, when he was understandably distracted by the medical problems of his infant son. In the other eight seasons, he hit .293/.404/.530, which (again like Bay) resembles what he did in 2009. Still, as Drew enters his mid-thirties, one wonders how long he can prevent those annual aches and pains, such as the inflammation in his left shoulder that sent him under the knife for a minor clean-up in November, from becoming chronic. Fortunately for the Red Sox, his contract expires after 2011, and Josh Reddick or Ryan Kalish should be ready to replace him.

Jacoby Ellsbury   CF   Bats: L   Throws: L   Height: 6' 1"   Weight: 185   Born: September 11, 1983   Age: 26

YEAR	TEAM	LVL	AGE	PA	R	2B	3B	HR	RBI	BB	SO	SB	CS	EqBRR	AVG	OBP	SLG	EqAVG	EqOBP	EqSLG	EqA	VORP	WARP	DEFENSE			
2007	PME	AA	23	83	16	10	2	0	13	6	7	8	1	1.6	.452	.518	.644	.400	.458	.573	.350	10.7	1.6	18-CF	3		
2007	PAW	AAA	23	401	66	14	5	2	28	32	47	33	6	4.8	.298	.360	.380	.278	.335	.357	.253	7.5	0.3	66-CF	-2	12-LF	-2
2007	BOS	MLB	23	127	20	7	1	3	18	8	15	9	0	3.0	.353	.394	.509	.336	.378	.483	.311	9.8	1.1	16-LF	0	12-CF	0
2008	BOS	MLB	24	609	98	22	7	9	47	41	80	50	11	7.9	.280	.336	.394	.279	.336	.395	.263	16.3	3.9	61-CF	7	39-LF	3
2009	BOS	MLB	25	691	94	27	10	8	60	49	74	70	12	5.3	.301	.355	.415	.298	.351	.404	.276	31.9	2.4	147-CF	-10		
2010	BOS	MLB	26	684	107	36	8	10	62	52	83	55	13	4.1	.297	.358	.428	.297	.358	.421	.271	29.2	3.1	136-CF	0		

Breakout: 20%   Improve: 65%   Collapse: 3%   Attrition: 4%   MLB: 94%   Comparables: Steve Finley, Juan Pierre, Coco Crisp, Johnny Damon

Ellsbury became Boston's full-time center fielder in 2009 and was exposed as a problematic defender. His is a classic case of speed and some highlight-reel dives distracting from bad routes, bad jumps, bad positioning, and a bad arm. Ellsbury can't do much about the arm, but he's young enough, fast enough, and athletic enough to make up some ground on the rest with good coaching. With Cameron replacing him in center, as Ellsbury's batting-average-dependent production won't carry a corner. True, if you add his franchise-record-tying 70 steals into his total bases (while subtracting his mere 12 times caught from his total bases and hits), his slugging percentage leaps up to .508, while his on-base percentage hangs at a league-average .334, but unless you're Rickey Henderson or Tim Raines, stealing 70 bases is not a sustainable skill. Only three players in the modern era have stolen 70 or more bases more than three times in their careers (Vince Coleman was the third); Ellsbury is unlikely to add his name to that list. Jim Rice thinks Ellsbury has Hall of Fame potential, which is true if you work under the assumption that the standards will continue to erode, thanks to the induction of players like Jim Rice.

Luis Exposito   C

Bats: R   **Throws:** R   **Height:** 6' 3"   **Weight:** 210   **Born:** January 20, 1987   **Age:** 23

YEAR	TEAM	LVL	AGE	PA	R	2B	3B	HR	RBI	BB	SO	SB	CS	EqBRR	AVG	OBP	SLG	EqAVG	EqOBP	EqSLG	EqA	VORP	WARP	DEFENSE
2007	GRN	A	20	32	3	0	0	0	2	2	5	0	0	-0.1	.233	.281	.233	.194	.242	.194	.134	-1.7	-0.4	9-C -2
2008	GRN	A	21	204	34	8	1	11	31	12	42	1	1	-1.4	.283	.328	.508	.244	.284	.420	.238	2.0	-0.2	33-C -4
2008	LNC	A+	21	239	31	13	2	10	37	9	47	0	1	-1.2	.301	.331	.509	.241	.268	.404	.227	1.0	0.8	44-C 6
2009	SLM	A+	22	319	28	24	1	6	45	23	49	3	1	0.9	.271	.329	.424	.252	.298	.391	.239	5.6	-0.3	69-C -8
2009	PME	AA	22	97	14	5	0	3	12	4	27	1	2	-0.2	.337	.371	.489	.301	.330	.430	.259	3.6	0.0	20-C -4
2010	BOS	MLB	23	353	39	19	1	11	42	22	76	1	1	-0.4	.251	.301	.411	.247	.297	.396	.234	4.6	0.2	70-C -2

Breakout: 26%   **Improve:** 53%   **Collapse:** 20%   **Attrition:** 12%   **MLB:** 3%   **Comparables:** Frank Kneuer, Gary Gill, Dan Conway, Dan Walters

Despite a disappointing performance in his repeat of High-A, Exposito is an offense-first catcher, which almost automatically makes him a prospect; he zotzed up his credentials by raking in his brief Double-A debut. He should return there this year at age 23, and if he shines, the post-V-Mart future after 2010 beckons.

Tim Federowicz   C

Bats: R   **Throws:** R   **Height:** 5' 10"   **Weight:** 213   **Born:** August 5, 1987   **Age:** 22

YEAR	TEAM	LVL	AGE	PA	R	2B	3B	HR	RBI	BB	SO	SB	CS	EqBRR	AVG	OBP	SLG	EqAVG	EqOBP	EqSLG	EqA	VORP	WARP	DEFENSE
2008	LOW	A-	20	148	14	6	0	1	15	19	24	10	3	-0.1	.244	.338	.315	.214	.291	.260	.204	-2.5	-0.1	29-C 2
2009	GRN	A	21	247	34	19	0	10	34	15	42	1	0	-1.1	.345	.393	.562	.299	.336	.468	.274	12.8	1.3	46-C -2
2009	SLM	A+	21	197	18	13	0	4	24	5	22	1	0	-1.6	.257	.276	.390	.239	.255	.346	.209	-3.8	-0.2	36-C 2
2010	BOS	MLB	22	384	37	19	0	11	44	26	70	3	2	-0.9	.259	.312	.402	.256	.310	.390	.237	6.1	0.7	73-C 1

Breakout: 22%   **Improve:** 46%   **Collapse:** 13%   **Attrition:** 3%   **MLB:** 3%   **Comparables:** Danny Sheaffer, Joel Galarza, Juan Brito, Carlos Hernandez

A seventh-round pick in the 2008 draft out of the University of North Carolina, Federowicz crushed in the Sally League in his first full-length professional season before running ashore in High-A. The trouble is that a 21-year-old from a top college program is supposed to crush in the Sally League. In a system filled with future backup catchers, Federowicz could distinguish himself with a strong repeat of High-A this year, but he could also get lost in the shuffle rather quickly should he struggle again.

Reymond Fuentes   CF

Bats: L   **Throws:** L   **Height:** 6' 0"   **Weight:** 160   **Born:** February 12, 1991   **Age:** 19

YEAR	TEAM	LVL	AGE	PA	R	2B	3B	HR	RBI	BB	SO	SB	CS	EqBRR	AVG	OBP	SLG	EqAVG	EqOBP	EqSLG	EqA	VORP	WARP	DEFENSE
2009	RSX	Rk	18	159	16	6	2	1	14	7	24	9	5	-1.5	.290	.331	.379	.253	.278	.327	.212	-4.5	-1.9	29-CF -5
2010	BOS	AL	19	300	22	15	2	3	20	15	59	5	3	0.0	.254	.297	.354	.254	.296	.348	.216	-3.9	-1.0	56-CF -5

Breakout: 35%   **Improve:** 60%   **Collapse:** 20%   **Attrition:** 3%   **MLB:** 0%   **Comparables:** John Matulia, Eddie Williams, Ben Candelaria, Daniel Stryffeler

Carlos Beltran's cousin was seen as the best player in Puerto Rico three weeks before the 2009 draft, then rocketed up to the 28th overall pick after coming stateside for some predraft workouts. Fuentes doesn't have his cousin's power, but he can hit for average, burn up the basepaths, and play a very good center field. The total package bears considerable resemblance to that of Jacoby Ellsbury, complete with a similar aversion to ball four. Some felt that Fuentes was overdrafted due to the last-minute hype, but they were largely silenced by his strong debut in the Gulf Coast League.

Alex Gonzalez — SS

Bats: R   Throws: R   Height: 6' 0"   Weight: 200   Born: February 15, 1977   Age: 33

YEAR	TEAM	LVL	AGE	PA	R	2B	3B	HR	RBI	BB	SO	SB	CS	EqBRR	AVG	OBP	SLG	EqAVG	EqOBP	EqSLG	EqA	VORP	WARP	DEFENSE	
2007	CIN	MLB	30	430	55	27	1	16	55	24	75	0	1	1.0	.272	.325	.468	.272	.326	.466	.268	19.7	2.9	98-SS	5
2009	CIN	MLB	32	270	16	12	0	3	26	15	36	0	1	-1.4	.210	.258	.296	.212	.258	.294	.196	-6.1	-0.8	65-SS	-2
2009	BOS	MLB	32	159	26	10	0	5	15	5	29	2	0	0.4	.284	.316	.453	.279	.312	.429	.260	5.8	0.4	41-SS	-3
2010	TOR	MLB	33	338	38	16	0	11	39	24	61	1	1	0.0	.250	.311	.407	.256	.314	.402	.245	6.7	0.7	83-SS	0

Breakout: 10%   Improve: 40%   Collapse: 16%   Attrition: 19%   MLB: 96%   Comparables: Rich Aurilia, Ricky Gutierrez, Mike Lansing, Rafael Ramirez

Gonzalez returned from a year lost to a compression fracture in his left knee to turn in one of the worst hitting seasons in the career of a bad hitter. You can't blame his May oblique strain or the elbow chips he had removed from his right elbow in June. In his 19 games after returning from the surgery, he hit just .197/.261/.279. He finally came around a bit after a mid-August trade to Boston, but still drew just five walks in his 44 games with the Sox. Boston loves Gonzalez because he played a legitimately outstanding shortstop there in 2006, but that was a peak performance, and no defensive work can excuse a career .294 on-base percentage. The Sox declined Gonzalez's option, allowing the Blue Jays to sign him to a one-year deal—a move that really should have been blocked by the commissioner's office, given that Gonzalez's bat should preclude him from starting, and the Jays already had eight years of the *other* Alex Gonzalez, so adding another one is just going to confuse everybody.

Nick Green — INF

Bats: R   Throws: R   Height: 6' 0"   Weight: 180   Born: September 10, 1978   Age: 31

YEAR	TEAM	LVL	AGE	PA	R	2B	3B	HR	RBI	BB	SO	SB	CS	EqBRR	AVG	OBP	SLG	EqAVG	EqOBP	EqSLG	EqA	VORP	WARP	DEFENSE			
2007	TAC	AAA	28	313	52	15	6	16	46	21	67	4	3	-2.9	.337	.385	.600	.279	.325	.483	.271	14.2	1.0	28-SS	-5	23-2B	0
2007	IND	AAA	28	106	9	6	0	5	20	2	28	1	2	-1.3	.245	.264	.451	.233	.252	.388	.217	-1.8	-0.5	8-LF	-1	6-2B	1
2008	SWB	AAA	29	431	41	15	2	12	50	26	102	3	2	2.5	.233	.285	.373	.219	.265	.335	.209	-6.5	-1.5	60-SS	-3	28-2B	-2
2009	BOS	MLB	30	309	35	18	0	6	35	20	69	1	4	1.1	.236	.303	.366	.237	.304	.358	.230	2.1	0.8	73-SS	5	7-2B	-2
2010	LAN	NL	31	361	35	15	2	9	40	23	92	2	2	-0.2	.232	.289	.371	.239	.297	.387	.233	2.8	0.2	72-SS	-1		

Breakout: 16%   Improve: 47%   Collapse: 17%   Attrition: 24%   MLB: 84%   Comparables: Ron Washington, Shane Halter, Craig Shipley, Angel Berroa

Early-season injuries to Jed Lowrie and Julio Lugo made Nick Green Boston's shortstop by default. A solid start to the season (he hit .292/.347/.453 through June 23rd) plus some dreadful fielding by Lugo after his return (seven errors in 32 games) kept Green in the lineup until Gonzalez's arrival, creating a hole in the otherwise formidable Boston attack, as Green stopped hitting entirely after that June 23rd cutoff (.134/.225/.237 until Gonzalez replaced him). Green acquitted himself well in the field, but his defense in his other major-league stints has received poor marks, leaving little to recommend him other than a strong chin.

Ryan Kalish — OF

Bats: L   Throws: L   Height: 6' 1"   Weight: 205   Born: March 28, 1988   Age: 22

YEAR	TEAM	LVL	AGE	PA	R	2B	3B	HR	RBI	BB	SO	SB	CS	EqBRR	AVG	OBP	SLG	EqAVG	EqOBP	EqSLG	EqA	VORP	WARP	DEFENSE			
2007	LOW	A-	19	104	27	4	1	3	13	16	12	18	3	2.3	.368	.471	.540	.330	.408	.495	.311	8.8	0.5	22-CF	-6		
2008	GRN	A	20	420	51	16	1	3	32	53	76	18	4	2.9	.281	.376	.356	.247	.329	.306	.233	-2.6	-1.3	51-RF	-8	41-CF	0
2008	LNC	A+	20	82	6	6	0	2	14	8	23	1	0	0.3	.233	.305	.397	.203	.268	.338	.216	-2.2	-0.4	18-RF	-1		
2009	SLM	A+	21	143	21	5	2	5	21	26	20	7	3	0.5	.304	.434	.513	.275	.389	.442	.290	7.0	1.0	20-RF	1	4-CF	0
2009	PME	AA	21	437	63	19	4	13	56	42	87	14	3	4.8	.271	.341	.440	.256	.316	.415	.255	8.1	0.3	46-CF	-5	43-LF	1
2010	BOS	MLB	22	511	61	25	3	11	52	52	106	13	3	2.3	.255	.334	.397	.254	.332	.387	.249	9.6	0.5	98-CF	-5		

Breakout: 18%   Improve: 45%   Collapse: 8%   Attrition: 4%   MLB: 13%   Comparables: Otis Green, Rod Myers, Kelly Johnson, Anthony Webster

Kalish takes his walks and is a high-percentage basestealer (60 steals at 82 percent in 289 minor-league games), but his power disappeared in 2008 following surgery to remove the hamate bone in his right wrist in late 2007. Fortunately, he rebounded nicely in 2009, hitting .302/.384/.561 with 10 home runs in the second half. If he can build on that this year, concerns over his ability to stick in center will be moot. If not, his position could be the difference between his being a star center fielder with 20/20 potential, or a left-handed Gabe Kapler.

Casey Kotchman   **1B**   Bats: L   Throws: L   Height: 6' 3"   Weight: 215   Born: February 22, 1983   Age: 27

YEAR	TEAM	LVL	AGE	PA	R	2B	3B	HR	RBI	BB	SO	SB	CS	EqBRR	AVG	OBP	SLG	EqAVG	EqOBP	EqSLG	EqA	VORP	WARP	DEFENSE	
2007	LAA	MLB	24	508	64	37	3	11	68	53	43	2	4	-6.3	.296	.372	.467	.295	.372	.469	.287	20.4	2.9	117-1B	6
2008	LAA	MLB	25	398	47	24	0	12	54	18	23	2	1	-4.8	.287	.327	.448	.288	.329	.449	.266	6.6	2.1	96-1B	11
2008	ATL	MLB	25	175	18	4	1	2	20	18	16	0	0	-1.3	.237	.331	.316	.243	.337	.322	.239	-2.0	-0.6	40-1B	-3
2009	ATL	MLB	26	336	28	20	0	6	41	32	28	0	0	-3.8	.282	.354	.409	.295	.363	.419	.276	5.5	1.3	78-1B	6
2009	BOS	MLB	26	95	9	3	0	1	7	7	14	1	0	0.2	.218	.284	.287	.218	.284	.276	.203	-5.3	-0.2	21-1B	3
2010	SEA	AL	27	515	59	25	2	15	71	51	49	2	2	-2.7	.284	.363	.444	.281	.357	.434	.277	14.9	2.1	122-1B	4

Breakout: 18%   Improve: 47%   Collapse: 8%   Attrition: 4%   MLB: 100%   Comparables: Sean Casey, Steve Cox, John Olerud, Sid Bream

Charged with replacing Mark Teixeira, Kotchman slugged .378 over parts of two seasons with the Braves. He's an outstanding defensive first baseman and has walked more than he has struck out in his three full major-league seasons. Entering his age-27 campaign, he's already at risk for slipping into a Mientkiewiczian backup role. Kotchman needs to find his power stroke to salvage his career as a starter, and will get that chance with the defense-minded Mariners. Don't be surprised if, like Sean Casey, he continues to disappoint.

George Kottaras   **C**   Bats: L   Throws: R   Height: 6' 0"   Weight: 185   Born: May 16, 1983   Age: 27

YEAR	TEAM	LVL	AGE	PA	R	2B	3B	HR	RBI	BB	SO	SB	CS	EqBRR	AVG	OBP	SLG	EqAVG	EqOBP	EqSLG	EqA	VORP	WARP	DEFENSE	
2007	PAW	AAA	24	334	32	22	0	9	39	32	71	1	1	-1.3	.241	.316	.408	.232	.301	.387	.241	8.9	-0.3	82-C	-12
2008	PAW	AAA	25	462	63	18	0	22	65	64	110	0	0	0.7	.243	.348	.456	.226	.327	.416	.259	14.0	0.9	71-C	-7
2009	PAW	AAA	26	30	1	3	0	0	0	6	6	0	0	0.1	.292	.433	.417	.250	.400	.375	.283	1.2	0.1	4-C	0
2009	BOS	MLB	26	107	15	11	0	1	10	11	25	0	0	-1.0	.237	.308	.387	.239	.308	.370	.244	2.4	-0.3	28-C	-4
2010	MIL	MLB	27	321	33	14	0	9	34	34	88	1	1	-0.2	.220	.306	.369	.223	.308	.373	.238	5.6	0.2	64-C	-4

Breakout: 6%   Improve: 29%   Collapse: 34%   Attrition: 13%   MLB: 26%   Comparables: Tim DeCinces, Mark Leonard, Jessie Reid, Scott Hatteberg

Kottaras was welcomed into the fraternity of backup catchers in 2009, serving as Jason Varitek's caddy, chasing after Tim Wakefield's knuckleball, and watching whatever small shot he had at a starting job go up in smoke with the Red Sox' acquisition of Victor Martinez. He then saw his backup job vanish when Varitek picked up his player option for 2010. After asking for and receiving his release, Kottaras signed on with Milwaukee, where he will battle for a chance to be the "veteran" caddy to rookie Angel Salome if the Brew Crew punts on the innumerable veteran receivers on this year's market. If Kottaras is able to match his career Triple-A line (.239/.331/.424) in the majors, he'll be a viable starter, albeit an unexceptional one (the average major-league catcher hit .254/.321/.396 in 2009).

Che-Hsuan Lin   **CF**   Bats: R   Throws: R   Height: 6' 0"   Weight: 180   Born: September 21, 1988   Age: 21

YEAR	TEAM	LVL	AGE	PA	R	2B	3B	HR	RBI	BB	SO	SB	CS	EqBRR	AVG	OBP	SLG	EqAVG	EqOBP	EqSLG	EqA	VORP	WARP	DEFENSE			
2007	RSX	Rk	18	200	33	10	6	4	22	17	42	14	3	-0.9	.263	.330	.457	.225	.271	.374	.227	-2.1	-1.0	28-CF	-1	14-RF	-2
2007	LOW	A-	18	50	7	2	0	0	3	5	10	3	2	-1.1	.163	.265	.209	.156	.224	.200	.142	-3.7	-0.5	11-CF	1		
2008	GRN	A	19	415	60	13	6	5	37	43	62	33	7	2.1	.249	.342	.359	.220	.299	.315	.223	-5.1	-2.0	77-CF	1	9-RF	-1
2009	SLM	A+	20	562	75	23	2	7	54	66	75	26	11	1.3	.265	.355	.365	.243	.318	.333	.237	2.0	-2.0	126-CF	-19		
2010	BOS	MLB	21	491	59	21	3	7	43	47	81	17	7	0.6	.241	.319	.354	.239	.318	.341	.230	0.2	-0.5	109-CF	-4		

Breakout: 34%   Improve: 57%   Collapse: 14%   Attrition: 12%   MLB: 2%   Comparables: Larue Baber, Derek Shumpert, Jason Johnson, Shaun Boyd

An example of how far-ranging Sox scouting has gotten, this toolsy 21-year-old Taiwanese center fielder led Chinese Taipei in hitting in the World Baseball Classic (WBC), albeit in all of two games played. Otherwise, Lin's bat has yet to impress, though he does show improving plate discipline and good speed and he's graded an outstanding defender in center by scouts.

Mike Lowell   3B

Bats: R   Throws: R   Height: 6' 3"   Weight: 210   Born: February 24, 1974   Age: 36

YEAR	TEAM	LVL	AGE	PA	R	2B	3B	HR	RBI	BB	SO	SB	CS	EqBRR	AVG	OBP	SLG	EqAVG	EqOBP	EqSLG	EqA	VORP	WARP	DEFENSE	
2007	BOS	MLB	33	653	79	37	2	21	120	53	71	3	2	-6.3	.324	.378	.501	.314	.369	.488	.293	37.4	5.3	149-3B	10
2008	BOS	MLB	34	468	58	27	0	17	73	38	61	2	2	-5.7	.274	.338	.461	.271	.335	.456	.271	16.7	3.7	105-3B	15
2009	BOS	MLB	35	484	54	29	1	17	75	33	61	2	1	-2.7	.290	.337	.474	.286	.333	.459	.271	18.0	1.8	101-3B	-1
2010	BOS	MLB	36	411	42	21	1	13	68	33	59	2	2	-1.9	.271	.334	.434	.267	.331	.422	.254	8.0	1.2	92-3B	3

Breakout: 9%   Improve: 22%   Collapse: 31%   Attrition: 39%   MLB: 95%   Comparables: Cal Ripken, Doug DeCinces, Matt Williams, Ken Boyer

Lowell's last two seasons were nearly identical, with one tremendous exception: his defense. He managed to remain one of the game's best-fielding third basemen in 2008 despite tearing the labrum of his right hip in June, but in 2009, after the hip was surgically repaired, he was a statue, ranking dead last in Ultimate Zone Rating (UZR) among American League third-sackers. As a result, Kevin Youkilis started nearly a third of the team's games at the hot corner, and the Sox have been chasing first basemen in anticipation of moving Youkilis to the hot corner full-time after Lowell's contract expires following the 2010 season. As for Lowell, he has hit .283/.335/.432 away from Fenway over the last two seasons. Unless he can make a miraculous recovery in the field, his career as a starter will end when he leaves the Sox.

Jed Lowrie   SS

Bats: S   Throws: R   Height: 6' 0"   Weight: 180   Born: April 17, 1984   Age: 26

YEAR	TEAM	LVL	AGE	PA	R	2B	3B	HR	RBI	BB	SO	SB	CS	EqBRR	AVG	OBP	SLG	EqAVG	EqOBP	EqSLG	EqA	VORP	WARP	DEFENSE			
2007	PME	AA	23	408	61	31	7	8	49	65	58	5	3	1.0	.297	.410	.501	.277	.377	.467	.291	27.7	2.0	84-SS	-11		
2007	PAW	AAA	23	177	21	16	1	5	21	12	33	0	1	-2.2	.300	.356	.506	.284	.333	.481	.275	9.4	2.0	31-SS	8	7-2B	-1
2008	PAW	AAA	24	234	35	14	2	5	32	31	43	1	0	-0.7	.268	.359	.434	.251	.339	.412	.266	10.7	0.5	47-SS	-7		
2008	BOS	MLB	24	306	34	25	3	2	46	35	68	1	0	-2.6	.258	.339	.400	.253	.336	.393	.263	11.0	1.2	43-SS	-1	27-3B	1
2009	PAW	AAA	25	83	9	3	0	3	8	13	13	0	0	0.5	.176	.313	.353	.174	.310	.333	.234	0.7	0.1	17-SS	0		
2009	BOS	MLB	25	76	5	2	0	2	11	6	20	0	0	-0.2	.147	.211	.265	.149	.211	.269	.164	-3.7	-0.1	19-SS	2	1-3B	0
2010	BOS	MLB	26	379	47	25	3	7	48	43	81	2	1	-0.6	.247	.334	.405	.243	.331	.389	.249	8.6	0.8	82-SS	-2		

Breakout: 7%   Improve: 29%   Collapse: 24%   Attrition: 17%   MLB: 52%   Comparables: Jeff Forney, Delwyn Young, Jim Tracy, Mike Howard

Lowrie suffered a sprain and a nondisplaced fracture in his left wrist in May 2008 while with Triple-A Pawtucket, but played through the pain, earning his way to the majors and ultimately winning the Opening Day shortstop job in 2009. Some call that dedication or determination; we call it stupid. Lowrie never let the wrist heal properly, and after collecting just one hit in the Sox' first five games in 2009, he hit the DL, ultimately undergoing wrist surgery that kept him out until after the All-Star break. After returning, he picked up seven more hits before landing back on the DL in August due to nerve damage in the wrist. When he returned in September, Alex Gonzalez had taken over at shortstop. Lowrie got just three more starts, went hitless in all three, and is unlikely to ever get his job back this year. Playing through pain is typically praised in our macho sporting culture, but it's often a very selfish act that can prove detrimental to both the player and his team.

Victor Martinez   C

Bats: S   Throws: R   Height: 6' 2"   Weight: 210   Born: December 23, 1978   Age: 31

YEAR	TEAM	LVL	AGE	PA	R	2B	3B	HR	RBI	BB	SO	SB	CS	EqBRR	AVG	OBP	SLG	EqAVG	EqOBP	EqSLG	EqA	VORP	WARP	DEFENSE				
2007	CLE	MLB	28	645	78	40	0	25	114	62	76	0	0	-1.8	.301	.374	.505	.297	.370	.501	.298	52.5	6.3	116-C	4	25-1B	-1
2008	CLE	MLB	29	294	30	17	0	2	35	24	32	0	0	-0.7	.278	.337	.365	.283	.342	.374	.253	8.3	1.3	50-C	5	9-1B	-1
2009	CLE	MLB	30	435	56	21	1	15	67	51	51	0	0	-1.0	.284	.368	.464	.295	.377	.471	.294	25.6	1.8	49-C	-7	44-1B	-1
2009	BOS	MLB	30	237	32	12	0	8	41	24	23	1	0	-0.4	.336	.405	.507	.332	.401	.483	.308	17.6	1.6	29-C	-2	21-1B	-2
2010	BOS	MLB	31	582	67	29	1	20	90	58	72	1	0	-0.7	.283	.361	.459	.280	.359	.439	.274	30.5	3.3	126-C	0		

Breakout: 9%   Improve: 32%   Collapse: 21%   Attrition: 7%   MLB: 98%   Comparables: Earl Battey, Jorge Posada, Del Crandall, Alan Ashby

Martinez made a full recovery from his injury-plagued 2008 season, turning in a 2009 season that was almost a dead match for his overall performance at the plate since 2004 with 2008 taken out (.302/.377/.483). Curiously, his production at Fenway, both career and in '09, is a tick below that. His health and production last year might well be part due to his having a career-high 66 starts at first base, where he has shown good hands and adequate range. Having picked up his option, the Sox want Martinez to spend most of his time behind the plate in 2010. It will be interesting to see if his position, and his ballpark, put a damper on his production, or if his bat and his arm (just 14 percent of opposing basestealers caught in '09, only 11 percent with Boston) force the team to reconsider.

Yamaico Navarro SS Bats: R Throws: R Height: 5' 11" Weight: 170 Born: October 31, 1987 Age: 22

YEAR	TEAM	LVL	AGE	PA	R	2B	3B	HR	RBI	BB	SO	SB	CS	EqBRR	AVG	OBP	SLG	EqAVG	EqOBP	EqSLG	EqA	VORP	WARP	DEFENSE			
2007	LOW	A-	19	253	36	10	1	5	37	22	52	12	6	0.0	.289	.357	.409	.259	.310	.375	.240	2.5	-0.4	39-SS	-6	16-3B	1
2008	GRN	A	20	361	46	14	4	7	54	29	73	3	2	0.2	.280	.341	.412	.245	.298	.356	.230	2.4	-0.3	59-SS	-7	11-2B	1
2008	LNC	A+	20	196	33	13	2	4	23	12	30	3	2	-0.4	.348	.393	.508	.273	.316	.393	.246	5.1	-0.5	41-SS	-10		
2009	SLM	A+	21	102	10	9	0	4	17	6	12	2	2	-1.5	.319	.373	.543	.302	.343	.500	.281	6.2	0.3	22-SS	-4		
2009	PME	AA	21	152	16	6	2	2	11	14	28	5	1	-0.4	.185	.270	.304	.174	.243	.283	.186	-4.5	-0.1	38-SS	4		
2010	BOS	MLB	22	402	46	20	2	8	46	30	83	4	3	-0.5	.253	.313	.387	.250	.312	.375	.233	3.1	-0.2	86-SS	-5		

Breakout: 19% Improve: 50% Collapse: 16% Attrition: 12%   MLB: 4%   Comparables: Teuris Olivares, Rudy Pemberton, Juan Delgado, Damon Hollins

Navarro had strong showings at the plate in partial seasons at High-A in both 2008 and 2009, hitting .338/.386/.520 in the two stints combined, but he pancaked upon being promoted to Double-A last year. He's just 22 and a solid defender at shortstop, a position the Red Sox have long struggled to fill, but he'll need his bat to come around at the upper levels to stay ahead of Jose Iglesias's outstanding defensive work.

David Ortiz DH Bats: L Throws: L Height: 6' 4" Weight: 230 Born: November 18, 1975 Age: 34

YEAR	TEAM	LVL	AGE	PA	R	2B	3B	HR	RBI	BB	SO	SB	CS	EqBRR	AVG	OBP	SLG	EqAVG	EqOBP	EqSLG	EqA	VORP	WARP	DEFENSE	
2007	BOS	MLB	31	667	116	52	1	35	117	111	103	3	1	-2.1	.332	.445	.621	.317	.435	.603	.341	68.3	7.2	5-1B	-1
2008	BOS	MLB	32	491	74	30	1	23	89	70	74	1	0	-1.8	.264	.369	.507	.256	.365	.490	.292	22.5	2.5		
2009	BOS	MLB	33	627	77	35	1	28	99	74	134	0	2	-2.4	.238	.332	.462	.234	.327	.447	.266	4.0	0.5	4-1B	0
2010	BOS	MLB	34	561	75	30	1	25	89	80	107	2	1	-1.0	.259	.368	.479	.254	.363	.460	.281	18.8	2.1	3-1B	0

Breakout: 2% Improve: 28% Collapse: 17% Attrition: 15%   MLB: 96%   Comparables: Jason Giambi, Kent Hrbek, Fred McGriff, Lee Stevens

Ortiz went from zero to hero last year, hitting .185/.284/.287 through June 1st, with just one homer in 208 plate appearances, and .264/.356/.548 with 27 dingers in 419 PAs thereafter. That four-month run was better than his injury-shortened 2008 season, but not by much, and his first two months can't be entirely discounted. Ortiz has largely stopped hitting lefties and hit just .223/.323/.415 on the road over the past two seasons. None of this comes as a surprise, and with Papi entering the final year of his contract, it's not even all that poorly timed. Still, Ortiz's five-year peak was so brilliant that it's not much fun watching him climb down the other side of the mountain.

Dustin Pedroia 2B Bats: R Throws: R Height: 5' 9" Weight: 180 Born: August 17, 1983 Age: 26

YEAR	TEAM	LVL	AGE	PA	R	2B	3B	HR	RBI	BB	SO	SB	CS	EqBRR	AVG	OBP	SLG	EqAVG	EqOBP	EqSLG	EqA	VORP	WARP	DEFENSE	
2007	BOS	MLB	23	581	86	39	1	8	50	47	42	7	1	0.0	.317	.380	.442	.309	.374	.436	.282	31.4	4.6	129-2B	8
2008	BOS	MLB	24	726	118	54	2	17	83	50	52	20	1	3.6	.326	.376	.493	.322	.372	.490	.298	53.5	8.4	154-2B	20
2009	BOS	MLB	25	714	115	48	1	15	72	74	45	20	8	-0.7	.296	.371	.447	.293	.368	.439	.280	37.4	4.7	152-2B	5
2010	BOS	MLB	26	676	110	45	3	16	71	64	51	16	4	0.5	.311	.383	.474	.306	.380	.456	.288	39.9	4.9	150-2B	6

Breakout: 15% Improve: 45% Collapse: 4% Attrition: 5%   MLB: 100%   Comparables: Billy Herman, Edgardo Alfonzo, Dave Cash, George Kell

In his follow-up to his MVP season, Pedroia lost 30 points of batting average and an additional 15 points of slugging and saw his success rate on the bases drop to 71 percent. That's more an indication of how good he was in 2008 than anything else. That he shed so little power is a good sign, particularly as the drop was largely the result of a likely fluky poor showing against lefties. Meanwhile, his strikeout/walk ratio jumped off the charts, as he drew 1.6 walks for every strikeout, thereby maintaining his on-base percentage despite the drop in average. He was also good in the field, even ranking second among AL second basemen in UZR for the second year in a row. Still shy of his natural peak, Pedroia has affirmed his status as one of the game's elite talents.

Josh Reddick   OF   Bats: L   Throws: R   Height: 6' 2"   Weight: 180   Born: February 19, 1987   Age: 23

YEAR	TEAM	LVL	AGE	PA	R	2B	3B	HR	RBI	BB	SO	SB	CS	EqBRR	AVG	OBP	SLG	EqAVG	EqOBP	EqSLG	EqA	VORP	WARP	DEFENSE			
2007	GRN	A	20	403	60	17	6	18	72	26	51	8	5	0.1	.306	.352	.531	.266	.304	.441	.254	4.7	0.3	86-RF	1	6-CF	-3
2008	GRN	A	21	58	7	4	2	0	9	5	8	2	1	-0.3	.340	.397	.491	.296	.345	.444	.268	1.5	0.0	12-RF	-2		
2008	LNC	A+	21	331	60	11	8	17	57	17	49	9	1	3.0	.343	.375	.593	.277	.308	.471	.264	7.9	0.8	59-RF	-2	8-CF	1
2008	PME	AA	21	132	22	4	2	6	25	12	25	3	1	-0.1	.214	.290	.436	.192	.258	.383	.222	-1.6	-0.4	31-CF	-2		
2009	PME	AA	22	287	47	17	3	13	29	30	62	5	5	0.8	.277	.352	.520	.261	.324	.487	.271	12.1	1.3	58-CF	-1		
2009	PAW	AAA	22	79	1	0	2	0	6	6	13	0	1	-2.8	.127	.190	.183	.127	.190	.183	.100	-7.9	-0.4	8-CF	1	6-RF	3
2009	BOS	MLB	22	62	5	4	0	2	4	2	17	0	0	-0.3	.169	.210	.339	.169	.210	.322	.181	-4.2	-0.3	9-LF	2	4-RF	0
2010	BOS	MLB	23	425	55	21	5	14	51	32	88	5	3	0.1	.249	.308	.437	.247	.305	.426	.245	6.3	0.5	86-CF	-2		

Breakout: 19%   Improve: 44%   Collapse: 17%   Attrition: 11%   MLB: 30%   Comparables: Randy Byers, Brad Gennaro, Osvaldo Sanchez, Ralph Bryant

Reddick was showing an improved approach at the plate in his repeat of Double-A when he was called up to the majors at the end of July, at which point he instantly fell back into some bad habits. An athletic outfielder with an outstanding arm and good power at the plate, he's in line to inherit right field from J. D. Drew upon the latter's free agency. But to realize that potential, he'll need some time back in Triple-A to refocus on his plate discipline and getting good pitches to hit against upper-level pitchers.

Anthony Rizzo   1B   Bats: L   Throws: L   Height: 6' 3"   Weight: 220   Born: August 8, 1989   Age: 20

YEAR	TEAM	LVL	AGE	PA	R	2B	3B	HR	RBI	BB	SO	SB	CS	EqBRR	AVG	OBP	SLG	EqAVG	EqOBP	EqSLG	EqA	VORP	WARP	DEFENSE	
2008	GRN	A	18	87	9	6	0	0	11	3	15	0	0	0.3	.373	.402	.446	.310	.341	.357	.246	-0.5	-0.4	19-1B	-3
2009	GRN	A	19	274	40	21	0	9	42	25	60	2	1	-2.8	.298	.365	.494	.251	.309	.402	.246	-4.3	-0.7	58-1B	-1
2009	SLM	A+	19	229	23	16	0	3	24	25	39	2	0	-1.6	.295	.371	.420	.278	.343	.385	.260	-0.2	-0.3	52-1B	-2
2010	BOS	MLB	20	470	51	25	0	12	53	40	107	3	1	-1.7	.263	.330	.409	.262	.328	.399	.247	-1.3	-0.4	104-1B	-2

Breakout: 31%   Improve: 67%   Collapse: 12%   Attrition: 0%   MLB: 0%   Comparables: Steve Dunn, Mike Darr, Paul O'Neill, Nick Castaneda

Rizzo's full-season debut in 2008 was cut short in May by limited-stage classical Hodgkin's lymphoma. With the disease in remission in 2009, he hit his way up to High-A while still in his teens and, after taking a handful of games to get his bearings, hit .306/.379/.451 there from July 1st through the end of the season. Rizzo's youth and large frame suggest there's more power to come, which he'll need if he's to make it as a major-league first baseman. He has some work to do on his approach at the plate lest he be exposed at the upper levels. Happily, he has time.

Jason Varitek   C   Bats: S   Throws: R   Height: 6' 2"   Weight: 230   Born: April 11, 1972   Age: 38

YEAR	TEAM	LVL	AGE	PA	R	2B	3B	HR	RBI	BB	SO	SB	CS	EqBRR	AVG	OBP	SLG	EqAVG	EqOBP	EqSLG	EqA	VORP	WARP	DEFENSE	
2007	BOS	MLB	35	518	57	15	3	17	68	71	122	1	2	-3.6	.255	.367	.421	.245	.358	.406	.269	28.1	4.2	120-C	8
2008	BOS	MLB	36	483	37	20	0	13	43	52	122	0	1	-3.2	.220	.313	.359	.218	.313	.363	.236	9.3	2.0	117-C	7
2009	BOS	MLB	37	425	41	24	0	14	51	54	90	0	0	-1.5	.209	.313	.390	.204	.308	.375	.243	10.5	1.0	104-C	-2
2010	BOS	MLB	38	333	28	14	1	9	34	40	83	1	1	-1.0	.217	.317	.368	.215	.316	.351	.231	3.4	0.5	81-C	2

Breakout: 8%   Improve: 29%   Collapse: 34%   Attrition: 39%   MLB: 91%   Comparables: Gregg Zaun, Ron Hassey, Greg Myers, Chad Kreuter

Varitek has hit an aggregate .222/.316/.382 in three of the last four seasons. Last year, he added an inability to catch opposing basestealers, throwing out just 13 percent of them (against a league average of 25 percent). It was no surprise that the Sox declined his $5 million club option or that he picked up his $3 million player option. As a result, he'll be the backup catcher this season, most likely serving as Josh Beckett's caddy and catching games against the odd lefty starter, as his last remaining positive at the plate seems to be some power from the right side.

Ryan Westmoreland   CF   Bats: L   Throws: R   Height: 6' 2"   Weight: 195   Born: April 27, 1990   Age: 20

YEAR	TEAM	LVL	AGE	PA	R	2B	3B	HR	RBI	BB	SO	SB	CS	EqBRR	AVG	OBP	SLG	EqAVG	EqOBP	EqSLG	EqA	VORP	WARP	DEFENSE
2009	LOW	A-	19	267	38	15	3	7	35	38	49	19	0	2.0	.296	.401	.484	.260	.337	.404	.264	1.6	0.4	7-LF 1
2010	BOS	MLB	20	382	39	21	1	9	39	38	98	9	2	1.5	.245	.322	.391	.242	.321	.384	.243	1.0	0.2	10-LF 1

Breakout: 11%   Improve: 29%   Collapse: 21%   Attrition: 0%   MLB: 1%   Comparables: Joe Hamilton, Danny Larson, Andy Van Slyke, Andrew Lambo

The best raw talent in the organization, five-tool high school stud Westmoreland dropped to the fifth round of the

2008 draft due to signability concerns, then underwent minor shoulder surgery that November (which could have had something to do with the 19-strikeout perfect game he threw in his final high school start). After rehabbing for the first half of 2009, Westmoreland finally made his pro debut in the short-season New York-Penn League. He initially lived up to his billing, displaying power and patience as a designated hitter and stealing 19 bases in 60 games without being caught, but his season ended early due to a broken left collarbone suffered in a collision with an outfield wall. He'll start in the Sally League this year and could move quickly, though how his arm has recovered from the shoulder surgery remains a mystery.

Kevin Youkilis   **1B**   Bats: R   Throws: R   Height: 6' 1"   Weight: 220   Born: March 15, 1979   Age: 31

YEAR	TEAM	LVL	AGE	PA	R	2B	3B	HR	RBI	BB	SO	SB	CS	EqBRR	AVG	OBP	SLG	EqAVG	EqOBP	EqSLG	EqA	VORP	WARP	DEFENSE				
2007	BOS	MLB	28	625	85	35	2	16	83	77	105	4	2	4.8	.288	.390	.453	.279	.384	.443	.289	26.3	4.1	123-1B	8	12-3B	2	
2008	BOS	MLB	29	621	91	43	4	29	115	62	108	3	5	-0.4	.312	.390	.569	.308	.386	.563	.312	45.3	5.8	110-1B	1	28-3B	4	
2009	BOS	MLB	30	588	99	36	1	27	94	77	125	7	2	1.3	.305	.413	.548	.299	.408	.521	.317	44.6	5.5	73-1B	2	56-3B	6	
2010	BOS	MLB	31	594	82	35	2	22	86	67	107	4	3	1.0	.283	.379	.488	.277	.375	.467	.287	23.7	2.9	134-1B	2			

Breakout: 2% Improve: 32% Collapse: 12% Attrition: 7% MLB: 100% Comparables: John Jaha, Bob Watson, Jeff Conine, Paul Konerko

Youkilis isn't much fun to watch for non–Red Sox fans. He's an ugly, sweaty, man-beast with a pale, bald pate and a fondness for overgrown facial hair, he's got one of the game's most irritating batting stances, and he's a grade-A red-ass who takes particular exception to being pitched inside while standing on top of home plate (most recently trying to Oddjob Rick Porcello with his batting helmet following an HBP). He's also one of the game's most valuable players. Not only is he among the majors' most productive hitters and best defensive first basemen, but he can also jump across the diamond and provide solid defense at the hot corner and even fill in at the outfield corners in a pinch. The Red Sox know his bat would play even better further right on the defensive spectrum, thus their continued pursuit of Adrian Gonzalez, but for now they'll have to settle for having one of the best all-around first basemen in baseball.

PITCHERS

Daniel Bard   Bats: R   Throws: R   Height: 6' 4"   Weight: 195   Born: June 25, 1985   Age: 25

YEAR	TEAM	LVL	AGE	W	L	SV	G	GS	IP	H	HR	BB	SO	GB%	BABIP	STUFF	WHIP	ERA	SIERA	DERA	EqH9	EqHR9	EqBB9	EqSO9	VORP	SN/WX
2007	GRN	A	22	3	5	0	17	17	61²	55	3	56	38	43%	.281	-13	1.80	6.42	6.11	8.29	9.0	1.3	9.0	3.3	-17.7	-1.58
2007	LNC	A+	22	0	2	0	5	5	13¹	21	2	22	9	65%	.365	-23	3.22	10.12	6.54	15.65	12.9	1.8	12.9	3.1	-16.5	-0.94
2008	GRN	A	23	1	0	0	15	0	28	12	1	4	43	62%	.224	25	0.57	0.64	1.03	1.44	6.1	1.1	2.2	9.0	11.3	0.69
2008	PME	AA	23	4	1	7	31	0	49²	30	3	26	64	66%	.252	17	1.13	1.99	2.82	3.26	6.7	1.1	4.6	9.0	11.7	0.54
2009	PAW	AAA	24	1	0	6	11	0	16	6	2	5	29	66%	.190	14	0.69	1.12	0.82	1.88	5.7	1.9	3.1	11.3	5.8	0.96
2009	BOS	MLB	24	2	2	1	49	0	49¹	41	5	22	63	50%	.303	23	1.28	3.65	2.85	3.84	7.0	0.7	3.4	9.8	9.3	0.24
2010	BOS	MLB	25	3	4	5	57	0	62²	55	6	40	59	50%	.293	0	1.52	4.69	4.33	4.80	7.6	0.9	5.5	8.0	4.8	0.80

Breakout: 28% Improve: 66% Collapse: 13% Attrition: 11% MLB: 72% Comparables: Jeff Stevens, Jim Adamczak, Rick Steed, Mark Lowe

Bard famously can hit 100 mph with his fastball, but the pitch is fairly straight; the key to his success is actually his slider, which at its best is a dominating out pitch, generating both ground balls and swinging strikes. We say "at its best" because Bard spent most of 2009 tinkering with how and when he threw the pitch. Early in the season, he threw a slower, curvelike slider. Later on, he switched to a harder, cutterlike slider, and he seemed to ease off that pitch after a rough August (7.36 ERA, 1.81 WHIP, four of his five homers allowed in the majors). The twist is, he also struck out 14.7 men per nine innings in August, evidence that he might have been onto something with the revamped slider after all. Bard will also mix in a sinker and a changeup, but it's the slider that will determine whether he emerges as Papelbon's successor over the next two years.

Josh Beckett

| | | | | Bats: R | | | Throws: R | | Height: 6' 5" | | Weight: 220 | | Born: May 15, 1980 | | | Age: 30 | |

YEAR	TEAM	LVL	AGE	W	L	SV	G	GS	IP	H	HR	BB	SO	GB%	BABIP	STUFF	WHIP	ERA	SIERA	DERA	EqH9	EqHR9	EqBB9	EqSO9	VORP	SN/WX
2007	BOS	MLB	27	20	7	0	30	30	200²	189	17	40	194	52%	.304	36	1.14	3.27	3.08	3.20	8.5	0.6	1.6	8.2	50.5	6.38
2008	BOS	MLB	28	12	10	0	27	27	174¹	173	18	34	172	48%	.315	33	1.19	4.03	3.02	3.82	8.8	0.7	1.6	8.3	32.2	5.04
2009	BOS	MLB	29	17	6	0	32	32	212¹	198	25	55	199	56%	.290	33	1.19	3.86	3.34	3.66	7.5	0.7	2.0	7.5	44.2	5.63
2010	BOS	MLB	30	12	9	0	31	31	191²	191	20	49	166	51%	.314	24	1.26	3.83	3.53	3.94	8.7	0.9	2.2	7.3	33.2	3.54

Breakout: 3%   Improve: 34%   Collapse: 17%   Attrition: 12%   MLB: 99%   Comparables: Roger Clemens, Kevin Appier, Jim Beattie, Paul Derringer

Post-season stats amount to a short-sample split just like any other "clutch" statistic; the larger the sample, the closer they trend toward a player's overall performance. Beckett built a reputation as a great post-season pitcher because his first two postseasons followed his two best regular seasons (which was no coincidence): he posted a 1.73 ERA, 0.74 WHIP, and a 5.9 K/BB ratio as his teams went 8-2 in his 10 appearances in the 2003 and 2007 postseasons. Over the past two Octobers, though, he's posted a 7.71 ERA and 1.62 WHIP while the Red Sox have gone 1-3 in his four post-season starts. That doesn't mean he has lost it. Beckett is still one of the league's elite starters and is a good bet to remain so in this, his walk year.

Michael Bowden

| | | | | Bats: R | | | Throws: R | | Height: 6' 3" | | Weight: 215 | | Born: September 9, 1986 | | | Age: 23 | |

YEAR	TEAM	LVL	AGE	W	L	SV	G	GS	IP	H	HR	BB	SO	GB%	BABIP	STUFF	WHIP	ERA	SIERA	DERA	EqH9	EqHR9	EqBB9	EqSO9	VORP	SN/WX
2007	LNC	A+	20	2	0	0	8	8	46	35	1	8	46	44%	.281	44	0.93	1.37	2.68	2.16	7.4	0.6	2.1	6.6	16.2	1.09
2007	PME	AA	20	8	6	0	19	19	96²	105	9	33	82	38%	.331	16	1.43	4.28	4.04	5.59	10.7	1.5	3.4	5.7	-0.9	0.11
2008	PME	AA	21	9	4	0	19	19	104¹	72	5	24	101	44%	.245	41	0.92	2.33	2.97	3.36	6.9	0.9	2.2	6.5	23.8	2.03
2008	PAW	AAA	21	0	3	0	7	6	40	40	5	5	29	45%	.287	23	1.12	3.37	3.67	4.18	10.0	1.4	1.4	4.8	5.5	0.51
2008	BOS	MLB	21	1	0	0	1	1	5	7	0	1	3	19%	.389	5	1.60	3.60	5.24	3.86	13.5	0.0	1.9	5.8	0.9	0.18
2009	PAW	AAA	22	4	6	0	24	24	126¹	106	11	47	88	35%	.257	8	1.21	3.13	4.70	4.00	8.7	1.2	3.7	5.1	19.6	2.36
2009	BOS	MLB	22	1	1	0	8	1	16	23	3	6	12	53%	.370	-1	1.81	9.56	4.43	8.27	11.6	1.1	2.8	6.1	-5.0	-0.14
2010	BOS	MLB	23	7	8	0	32	27	131	139	18	48	87	36%	.302	6	1.43	4.63	4.79	4.75	9.2	1.1	3.2	5.6	11.0	2.72

Breakout: 3%   Improve: 40%   Collapse: 18%   Attrition: 15%   MLB: 38%   Comparables: Wade Davis, Andy Hawkins, Julio Valera, Anthony Swarzak

A solid right-handed starter who, prior to September, was twice brought up for bullpen depth during series against the Yankees and then tanked his second major-league start at the end of September, Bowden will probably return to Triple-A in April, again hoping that a rotation spot opens up. He's not much more than a back-end starter who throws strikes—having lost some break on his curve last year, he has increasingly pitched to contact at the upper levels. He's good insurance to have on hand, but he's unlikely to become a fixture in the Boston rotation.

Clay Buchholz

| | | | | Bats: L | | | Throws: R | | Height: 6' 3" | | Weight: 190 | | Born: August 14, 1984 | | | Age: 25 | |

YEAR	TEAM	LVL	AGE	W	L	SV	G	GS	IP	H	HR	BB	SO	GB%	BABIP	STUFF	WHIP	ERA	SIERA	DERA	EqH9	EqHR9	EqBB9	EqSO9	VORP	SN/WX
2007	PME	AA	22	7	2	0	16	15	86²	55	4	22	116	47%	.271	48	0.89	1.77	1.83	2.52	6.7	0.9	2.5	9.2	27.1	2.50
2007	PAW	AAA	22	1	3	0	8	8	38²	32	5	13	55	57%	.300	33	1.16	3.96	2.21	5.40	8.2	1.4	3.1	9.9	0.4	0.07
2007	BOS	MLB	22	3	1	0	4	3	22²	14	0	10	22	44%	.255	21	1.06	1.59	3.57	2.32	5.9	0.0	3.8	8.4	7.5	1.03
2008	PME	AA	23	1	0	0	2	2	15	7	0	1	18	61%	.206	15	0.53	1.80	1.67	3.07	4.9	0.6	0.6	8.0	4.0	0.34
2008	PAW	AAA	23	4	2	0	9	9	43²	36	3	17	43	48%	.295	14	1.21	2.47	3.45	3.29	9.1	0.9	3.9	7.0	9.7	1.10
2008	BOS	MLB	23	2	9	0	16	15	76	93	11	41	72	56%	.355	5	1.76	6.75	4.16	6.75	10.8	1.1	4.3	7.9	-10.6	0.00
2009	PAW	AAA	24	7	2	0	17	16	99	67	4	30	89	58%	.230	22	0.98	2.36	3.42	3.40	7.1	1.0	3.0	6.6	21.9	1.99
2009	BOS	MLB	24	7	4	0	16	16	92	91	13	36	68	64%	.279	16	1.38	4.21	4.21	3.76	7.8	1.0	2.9	5.9	18.4	2.53
2010	BOS	MLB	25	10	8	0	33	33	164²	154	18	64	140	53%	.296	19	1.33	3.99	3.92	4.10	8.2	0.9	3.3	7.2	25.6	3.14

Breakout: 9%   Improve: 45%   Collapse: 13%   Attrition: 10%   MLB: 73%   Comparables: Matt Garza, John Maine, Jose Guzman, Doug Drabek

A heralded pitching prospect who threw a no-hitter in his second major-league start, Buchholz looked ready to conquer the league entering the 2008 season, but found himself back in the minors by June and back in Double-A after posting an 8.29 ERA in a return to the majors in July and August. Buchholz didn't get his next shot until after the All-Star break last year, but soon after returning, he ran off a stretch in August and September in which he made nine quality starts in 10 tries and posted a 2.37 ERA while his team went 8-2 in his starts. That made him Boston's third starter in the postseason, and it guarantees him a spot in the 2010 rotation. After doing nothing but dominating in the minors, it seems Buchholz has finally arrived for real.

Paul Byrd

Bats: R   Throws: R   Height: 6' 1"   Weight: 190   Born: December 3, 1970   Age: 39

YEAR	TEAM	LVL	AGE	W	L	SV	G	GS	IP	H	HR	BB	SO	GB%	BABIP	STUFF	WHIP	ERA	SIERA	DERA	EqH9	EqHR9	EqBB9	EqSO9	VORP	SN/WX
2007	CLE	MLB	36	15	8	0	31	31	192¹	239	27	28	88	44%	.309	-6	1.39	4.59	4.88	4.67	10.4	1.3	1.2	3.7	17.9	2.60
2008	CLE	MLB	37	7	10	0	22	22	131	146	23	24	56	45%	.276	-11	1.30	4.53	5.06	4.63	9.5	1.6	1.5	3.5	12.6	2.66
2008	BOS	MLB	37	4	2	0	8	8	49	58	8	10	26	40%	.309	1	1.39	4.78	4.81	4.37	10.6	1.3	1.7	4.6	5.9	0.67
2009	BOS	MLB	38	1	3	0	7	6	34	47	4	11	11	44%	.333	-16	1.71	5.82	5.89	5.11	11.0	0.8	2.6	2.6	1.5	0.59
2010	BOS	MLB	39	4	7	0	19	17	86²	111	14	24	36	41%	.321	-17	1.55	5.43	5.43	5.52	11.0	1.4	2.3	3.5	-0.2	0.83

Breakout: 4%   Improve: 29%   Collapse: 30%   Attrition: 32%   MLB: 93%   Comparables: Lew Burdette, Bob Forsch, Ray Starr, Scott Sanderson

Byrd opted not to sign with a team following the 2008 season, preferring instead to sell himself as a midseason reinforcement after spending a rare spring with his family. He finally hooked on with the Red Sox in August, made four preparatory starts in the minors, in which he walked one man in 18 innings, then returned to the majors with six shutout innings against the Blue Jays on August 30th. That was as good as it got; Byrd posted a 7.07 ERA in September and was dropped from the rotation in the last week of the season. Byrd is a fly-ball pitcher who can't strike anyone out and whose offerings are raw meat for hungry lefties. He thought about retiring during his extended offseason last year, and AL batters gave him further cause over this winter.

Manny Delcarmen

Bats: R   Throws: R   Height: 6' 2"   Weight: 205   Born: February 16, 1982   Age: 28

YEAR	TEAM	LVL	AGE	W	L	SV	G	GS	IP	H	HR	BB	SO	GB%	BABIP	STUFF	WHIP	ERA	SIERA	DERA	EqH9	EqHR9	EqBB9	EqSO9	VORP	SN/WX
2007	PAW	AAA	25	3	2	0	20	0	29¹	28	1	14	37	41%	.346	10	1.43	3.37	3.05	4.50	9.3	0.6	4.3	8.7	3.2	-0.47
2007	BOS	MLB	25	0	0	1	44	0	44	28	4	17	41	52%	.214	17	1.02	2.05	3.59	2.16	5.8	0.6	3.1	7.8	16.2	1.64
2008	BOS	MLB	26	1	2	2	73	0	74¹	55	5	28	72	55%	.251	23	1.12	3.27	3.51	3.17	6.5	0.5	3.0	8.0	19.5	1.42
2009	BOS	MLB	27	5	2	0	64	0	59²	64	5	34	44	49%	.309	-4	1.64	4.53	4.93	4.43	8.6	0.6	4.4	5.8	7.4	0.34
2010	BOS	MLB	28	4	4	1	68	0	67¹	63	6	29	53	47%	.294	1	1.37	4.22	4.31	4.35	8.2	0.8	3.7	6.6	8.6	0.62

Breakout: 9%   Improve: 26%   Collapse: 36%   Attrition: 8%   MLB: 88%   Comparables: Jose Paniagua, Joey McLaughlin, Dave Smith, Larry Sherry

Delcarmen opened the 2009 season as the Red Sox' secondary set-up man behind Hideki Okajima, but he suddenly lost the plate in late July, walking 17 men in his final 22 innings while giving up five home runs, posting an 8.59 ERA and struggling with random losses in velocity. Then, in early October, he hurt his back when his Hummer hit a median while he was trying to avoid another car, in an accident that caused him to be left off the post-season roster. With Bard ascendant, Delcarmen will enter camp having to earn his way back into high-leverage duty.

Felix Doubront

Bats: L   Throws: L   Height: 6' 2"   Weight: 166   Born: October 23, 1987   Age: 22

YEAR	TEAM	LVL	AGE	W	L	SV	G	GS	IP	H	HR	BB	SO	GB%	BABIP	STUFF	WHIP	ERA	SIERA	DERA	EqH9	EqHR9	EqBB9	EqSO9	VORP	SN/WX
2007	GRN	A	19	3	7	0	11	11	42¹	63	8	17	22	54%	.348	-24	1.89	8.93	5.13	12.30	13.7	2.8	4.1	2.4	-31.2	-2.27
2007	LOW	A-	19	1	3	0	8	8	35	41	2	11	25	45%	.325	4	1.49	5.66	4.39	8.51	12.4	1.9	3.5	3.5	-11.1	-0.79
2008	GRN	A	20	12	8	0	23	23	115¹	115	9	24	118	44%	.331	9	1.21	3.67	2.91	5.64	11.0	1.8	3.0	5.7	-1.6	-0.45
2008	LNC	A+	20	1	1	0	3	3	14	15	1	4	20	40%	.412	13	1.36	3.86	1.92	4.15	11.1	1.4	3.5	9.7	1.9	0.24
2009	PME	AA	21	8	6	0	26	26	121	119	8	52	101	48%	.303	12	1.41	3.35	4.21	5.50	9.8	1.3	3.9	5.3	0.0	0.28
2010	BOS	MLB	22	4	8	0	27	23	101²	126	17	45	62	40%	.328	0	1.68	6.08	5.17	6.19	10.7	1.4	3.9	5.2	-7.7	1.23

Breakout: 12%   Improve: 48%   Collapse: 10%   Attrition: 16%   MLB: 6%   Comparables: John Grabow, Tom Bolton, Ben Van Ryn, John Koronka

There's a lot to like about this skinny Venezuelan lefty, which makes it frustrating that he hasn't been better thus far in his professional career. He walked a few too many men in his Double-A debut last year, but otherwise turned in solid but again unspectacular work. The good news is that he's still fairly young and spins a nice change to complement a solid sinker, and there's nothing wrong with having a decent young left-handed starter lurking in Triple-A, particularly given how fragile the Boston rotation proved to be in 2009.

David Hunter Jones

| | | | | | | | | Bats: L | | Throws: L | | Height: 6' 4" | | Weight: 235 | | Born: January 10, 1984 | | | Age: 26 | |

YEAR	TEAM	LVL	AGE	W	L	SV	G	GS	IP	H	HR	BB	SO	GB%	BABIP	STUFF	WHIP	ERA	SIERA	DERA	EqH9	EqHR9	EqBB9	EqSO9	VORP	SN/WX
2007	LNC	A+	23	4	1	0	24	0	47	35	2	21	40	46%	.262	1	1.19	2.11	4.07	3.15	7.3	0.8	4.3	5.5	11.6	1.03
2007	PME	AA	23	2	1	2	23	0	42¹	35	3	16	43	35%	.286	3	1.20	3.19	3.47	4.35	8.3	1.1	3.6	6.9	5.1	0.03
2008	PME	AA	24	0	1	4	13	0	22²	21	0	4	26	59%	.333	19	1.10	1.19	2.53	1.64	9.0	0.4	1.6	7.8	9.4	0.86
2008	PAW	AAA	24	7	2	8	35	0	50²	55	3	14	50	38%	.347	-2	1.36	3.02	3.34	3.97	11.1	0.8	2.8	6.8	8.1	1.18
2009	PAW	AAA	25	4	3	2	36	0	53	45	7	24	39	35%	.242	-20	1.30	4.25	4.84	5.26	8.6	1.6	4.2	5.3	1.4	0.44
2009	BOS	MLB	25	0	0	0	11	0	12²	16	3	7	9	35%	.302	-21	1.82	9.24	5.33	8.04	9.0	1.3	3.9	5.1	-3.9	0.17
2010	FLO	MLB	26	3	4	1	44	0	65²	67	8	32	47	38%	.299	-7	1.50	4.71	4.90	5.02	9.3	1.1	3.8	5.8	3.5	1.45

Breakout: 13%   Improve: 37%   Collapse: 31%   Attrition: 8%   MLB: 21%   Comparables: Brad Kilby, Scott DeWitt, Anthony Shumaker, Matt Yourkin

Traded to the Marlins in the Jeremy Hermida deal, David Hunter Jones is a big lefty who made 11 garbage-time appearances in the majors last year, giving up at least one run in seven of them. Jones also struggled in Triple-A, particularly in the second half of the season, posting career-worst walk, strikeout, and home-run rates. Though he has shown a reverse split in the past, his platoon splits in 2009 were conventional, and major-league righties owned him, suggesting he's a LOOGY at best.

Casey Kelly   RHP/SS

| | | | | | | | | Bats: R | | Throws: R | | Height: 6' 3" | | Weight: 194 | | Born: October 4, 1989 | | | Age: 20 | |

YEAR	TEAM	LVL	AGE	PA	R	2B	3B	HR	RBI	BB	SO	SB	CS	EqBRR	AVG	OBP	SLG	EqAVG	EqOBP	EqSLG	EqA	VORP	WARP	DEFENSE	
2008	RSX	Rk	18	106	10	5	0	1	9	6	34	1	0	0.9	.174	.230	.258	.137	.174	.196	.086	-10.0	-2.1	21-SS	0
2009	RSX	Rk	19	31	4	1	0	2	6	3	10	1	0	0.2	.217	.293	.473	.172	.226	.276	.166	-2.8	-0.6		
2009	GRN	A	19	150	18	7	1	1	10	16	39	0	1	-0.9	.224	.305	.313	.181	.245	.268	.176	-4.0	-0.6	20-SS	-1

YEAR	TEAM	LVL	AGE	W	L	SV	G	GS	IP	H	HR	BB	SO	GB%	BABIP	STUFF	WHIP	ERA	SIERA	DERA	EqH9	EqHR9	EqBB9	EqSO9	VORP	SN/WX
2009	GRN	A	19	6	1	0	9	9	48¹	32	0	9	39	58%	.237	37	0.85	1.12	3.28	3.30	7.8	1.0	2.9	3.9	10.7	0.76
2009	SLM	A+	19	1	4	0	8	8	46²	33	4	7	35	53%	.221	24	0.86	3.09	3.49	4.95	7.6	1.6	1.9	4.3	2.7	0.18
2010	BOS	MLB	20	8	7	0	27	27	127²	126	18	44	64	55%	.270	29	1.33	4.23	4.96	4.33	8.5	1.2	3.0	4.2	16.7	3.28

Breakout: 6%   Improve: 28%   Collapse: 32%   Attrition: 1%   MLB: 1%   Comparables: Kyle Winters, Jimmy Jones, Toby Nivens, Blake Hawksworth

The Red Sox' first-round pick in the 2008 draft, Kelly spent his first pro season as a slick-fielding, weak-hitting shortstop, then debuted in 2009 as a legitimate pitching prospect. Kelly dominated in nine Sally League starts, then continued to pitch well for High-A Salem before reaching his mandated innings limit and returning to shortstop (where he again failed to impress at the plate, hitting .222/.302/.340 in 182 plate appearances). Kelly throws strikes with a low-90s fastball with good movement, an excellent curve, and a developing change, all of which could be plus pitches, though some scouts worry that none will emerge as a true out pitch. Either way, expect him to remain on the mound going forward.

Jon Lester

| | | | | | | | | Bats: L | | Throws: L | | Height: 6' 2" | | Weight: 190 | | Born: January 7, 1984 | | | Age: 26 | |

YEAR	TEAM	LVL	AGE	W	L	SV	G	GS	IP	H	HR	BB	SO	GB%	BABIP	STUFF	WHIP	ERA	SIERA	DERA	EqH9	EqHR9	EqBB9	EqSO9	VORP	SN/WX
2007	BOS	MLB	23	4	0	0	12	11	63	61	10	31	50	38%	.279	8	1.46	4.57	4.65	4.35	8.7	1.2	4.1	6.7	7.9	1.22
2008	BOS	MLB*	24	16	6	0	33	33	210¹	202	14	66	152	56%	.297	25	1.27	3.21	4.15	3.16	8.7	0.5	2.6	6.3	53.0	6.74
2009	BOS	MLB	25	15	8	0	32	32	203¹	186	20	64	225	59%	.313	41	1.23	3.41	2.95	3.13	7.6	0.7	2.5	9.0	53.7	6.56
2010	BOS	MLB	26	11	10	0	34	34	190¹	192	20	68	152	54%	.309	17	1.36	4.14	4.02	4.25	8.7	0.9	3.1	6.8	26.4	3.69

Breakout: 4%   Improve: 39%   Collapse: 17%   Attrition: 11%   MLB: 97%   Comparables: Justin Thompson, Jamie Moyer, Tom Glavine, Bob Knepper

Just as he did in 2008, Lester got off to a bit of a rough start in 2009. He flipped the switch in late May and cruised the rest of the way, going 12-3 with a 2.31 ERA over his final 22 starts, 19 of them quality starts. Lester's overall numbers were balanced by an uptick in his opponents' batting average on balls in play and a return to normal from what had been a favorable rate of home runs per fly ball in 2008, but his strikeout rate, which is far less dependent on luck, increased dramatically. Lester struck out 10 men in a game just once in his first 66 major-league starts, including the postseason, then did it five times in those final 22 starts of 2009. There's a reason he started Game One of the ALDS over Beckett: Lester is Boston's ace.

Daisuke Matsuzaka

Bats: R   Throws: R   Height: 6' 0"   Weight: 185   Born: September 13, 1980   Age: 29

YEAR	TEAM	LVL	AGE	W	L	SV	G	GS	IP	H	HR	BB	SO	GB%	BABIP	STUFF	WHIP	ERA	SIERA	DERA	EqH9	EqHR9	EqBB9	EqSO9	VORP	SN/WX
2007	BOS	MLB	26	15	12	0	32	32	204²	191	25	80	201	46%	.299	23	1.32	4.40	3.59	4.04	8.6	0.9	3.2	8.4	32.4	5.23
2008	BOS	MLB	27	18	3	0	29	29	167²	128	12	94	154	43%	.258	34	1.32	2.90	4.27	2.96	6.8	0.5	4.5	7.8	47.1	6.25
2009	BOS	MLB	28	4	6	0	12	12	59¹	81	10	30	54	40%	.380	2	1.87	5.76	4.38	5.03	11.3	1.0	3.9	7.3	3.2	0.85
2010	BOS	MLB	29	7	9	0	28	28	141	144	17	67	121	41%	.315	11	1.50	4.84	4.28	4.97	8.9	1.0	4.1	7.2	8.3	2.59

Breakout: 7%   Improve: 31%   Collapse: 22%   Attrition: 24%   MLB: 93%   Comparables: Alex Ferguson, Wade Miller, Charlie Robertson, Francisco Cordova

Matsuzaka's 2008 season was full of red flags—his heavy reliance on clutch pitching and stranded baserunners, his low BABIP, and an average of less than six innings per start, itself due in part to his averaging of 4.05 pitches per plate appearance—but no one saw his disastrous 2009 coming. After pitching Japan to its second World Baseball Classic championship, Matsuzaka lasted just 6 ⅓ innings over two starts before landing on the DL with a shoulder sprain. After returning in late May, he posted a 7.22 ERA in six starts before again landing on the DL with shoulder trouble. Matsuzaka fired a missive at the Red Sox in July, complaining to a Japanese paper about the restrictions on his training regimen and claiming that his ethnicity required him to train differently, pointing to the lack of enduring Stateside success among his countrymen. The Sox, who have received high marks from us and from their American pitchers for the quality of their training and strengthening techniques, claimed that Matsuzaka returned from the WBC out of shape and that he partly blamed the tournament for his struggles. After working to find a middle ground while he rehabbed in Florida, Matsuzaka returned with four strong outings down the stretch (2.22 ERA, three quality starts) looking much like his old self, which suggests he should enter 2010 with as much hope for continued success as he had coming out of 2008.

Hideki Okajima

Bats: L   Throws: L   Height: 6' 1"   Weight: 195   Born: December 25, 1975   Age: 34

YEAR	TEAM	LVL	AGE	W	L	SV	G	GS	IP	H	HR	BB	SO	GB%	BABIP	STUFF	WHIP	ERA	SIERA	DERA	EqH9	EqHR9	EqBB9	EqSO9	VORP	SN/WX
2007	BOS	MLB	31	3	2	5	66	0	69	50	6	17	63	50%	.238	23	0.97	2.22	3.27	2.16	6.6	0.7	2.0	7.6	25.5	4.57
2008	BOS	MLB	32	3	2	1	64	0	62	49	6	23	60	39%	.256	18	1.16	2.61	3.60	2.50	6.9	0.7	2.9	8.0	21.0	1.40
2009	BOS	MLB	33	6	0	0	68	0	61	56	8	21	53	33%	.276	9	1.26	3.39	4.03	2.96	7.4	0.9	2.6	6.9	17.6	3.03
2010	BOS	MLB	34	3	3	1	56	0	55¹	53	6	19	46	39%	.298	5	1.31	3.97	4.00	4.02	8.2	0.9	3.1	7.0	9.1	1.68

Breakout: 8%   Improve: 30%   Collapse: 42%   Attrition: 16%   MLB: 94%   Comparables: Joe Hoerner, Pete Richert, Jeff Williams, Ricardo Rincon

Despite the increase in ERA and slight dip in strikeout rate, Okajima was much more effective last year than he had been in 2008, when he blew eight save opportunities and allowed 52 percent of his inherited runners to score. Last year, those figures dropped to just two blown saves and 16 percent of inherited runners scoring, much closer to his 2007 record. The slight increase in home-run rate was due to just two more home runs and a dip to league average in home runs per fly ball, and the ERA increase was due in part to a correction in BABIP. Okajima posted a 1.78 ERA and 1.03 WHIP in 27 save situations in '09. The only red flag here is that for the first time in the States, he struggled against righties (.309/.386/.520).

Jonathan Papelbon

Bats: R   Throws: R   Height: 6' 4"   Weight: 225   Born: November 23, 1980   Age: 29

YEAR	TEAM	LVL	AGE	W	L	SV	G	GS	IP	H	HR	BB	SO	GB%	BABIP	STUFF	WHIP	ERA	SIERA	DERA	EqH9	EqHR9	EqBB9	EqSO9	VORP	SN/WX
2007	BOS	MLB	26	1	3	37	59	0	58¹	30	5	15	84	33%	.216	39	0.77	1.85	1.46	1.79	5.3	0.6	2.0	10.3	23.7	5.26
2008	BOS	MLB	27	5	4	41	67	0	69¹	58	4	8	77	57%	.293	34	0.95	2.34	2.33	2.91	7.4	0.4	0.9	9.0	20.1	3.38
2009	BOS	MLB	28	1	1	38	66	0	68	54	5	24	76	30%	.278	30	1.15	1.85	3.17	1.86	6.4	0.5	2.7	8.8	28.5	6.18
2010	BOS	MLB	29	5	3	32	63	0	62¹	49	5	19	66	41%	.284	21	1.08	3.04	2.88	3.16	6.9	0.8	2.5	9.0	16.2	3.08

Breakout: 14%   Improve: 38%   Collapse: 30%   Attrition: 14%   MLB: 99%   Comparables: Keith Foulke, Troy Percival, Dick Radatz, Lee Smith

Despite his AL Division Series meltdown, Papelbon remains one of the most dominant closers in baseball. If the Red Sox are hoping Bard will emerge to replace him in anticipation of Papelbon's free agency after the 2011 season, it's motivated purely by finance. Save for his increased walk rate, which was hardly alarming, nothing about Papelbon's 2009 season suggests the Sox can expect anything less than continued dominance from their closer going forward.

Ramon Ramirez

Bats: R   Throws: R   Height: 5' 11"   Weight: 190   Born: August 31, 1981   Age: 28

YEAR	TEAM	LVL	AGE	W	L	SV	G	GS	IP	H	HR	BB	SO	GB%	BABIP	STUFF	WHIP	ERA	SIERA	DERA	EqH9	EqHR9	EqBB9	EqSO9	VORP	SN/WX
2007	CSP	AAA	25	4	0	0	25	0	27²	18	2	16	35	54%	.254	22	1.23	2.28	3.13	3.25	5.5	0.7	5.2	9.4	6.9	0.37
2007	COL	MLB	25	2	2	0	22	0	17¹	21	2	6	15	38%	.352	-4	1.56	8.31	4.07	7.53	10.4	0.5	2.6	7.3	-3.9	-0.08
2008	KCA	MLB	26	3	2	1	71	0	71²	57	2	31	70	54%	.286	24	1.23	2.64	3.61	2.66	7.0	0.3	3.4	8.1	22.4	2.35
2009	BOS	MLB	27	7	4	0	70	0	69²	61	7	32	52	42%	.262	5	1.33	2.84	4.66	2.96	6.9	0.6	3.5	5.9	20.1	1.46
2010	BOS	MLB	28	4	4	0	64	0	63²	57	6	28	52	47%	.284	3	1.33	3.91	4.21	4.06	7.9	0.8	3.8	6.8	10.2	0.97

Breakout: 11%   Improve: 29%   Collapse: 33%   Attrition: 10%   MLB: 85%   Comparables: Tim Scott, Scott Strickland, Jeff Brantley, Tim Mauser

Acquired from the Royals for Coco Crisp, Ramon "Ram-Ram" Ramirez appeared to replicate his solid 2008 season in 2009. A closer look reveals that a dip in BABIP masked a correction in his home-run rate and a dip in his strikeout rate. Ramirez also got by with some impressive clutch pitching (opponents hit .193/.290/.295 with runners in scoring position), and his 2.73 home ERA masked the fact that opponents hit .285/.363/.477 against him at Fenway. All of that suggests he could be in for a rocky 2010.

Takashi Saito

Bats: L   Throws: R   Height: 6' 2"   Weight: 215   Born: February 14, 1970   Age: 40

YEAR	TEAM	LVL	AGE	W	L	SV	G	GS	IP	H	HR	BB	SO	GB%	BABIP	STUFF	WHIP	ERA	SIERA	DERA	EqH9	EqHR9	EqBB9	EqSO9	VORP	SN/WX
2007	LAN	MLB	37	2	1	39	63	0	64¹	33	5	13	78	46%	.207	36	0.72	1.40	1.89	1.45	4.9	0.7	1.7	9.3	27.9	5.85
2008	LAN	MLB	38	4	4	18	45	0	47	40	1	16	60	48%	.331	28	1.19	2.49	2.53	2.89	8.1	0.2	2.7	9.4	13.5	1.87
2009	BOS	MLB	39	3	3	2	56	0	55²	50	6	25	52	39%	.289	12	1.35	2.43	4.01	2.33	7.4	0.6	3.5	7.6	19.7	0.18
2010	ATL	MLB	40	3	3	14	51	0	50²	44	5	22	50	43%	.298	8	1.30	3.73	3.59	4.06	7.9	0.8	3.4	8.1	8.1	1.59

Breakout: 11%   Improve: 27%   Collapse: 40%   Attrition: 15%   MLB: 96%   Comparables: Al Worthington, Russ Springer, Larry Andersen, Mike Timlin

Of the five make-good contracts the Red Sox handed out last winter (to Baldelli, Saito, John Smoltz, Brad Penny, and Josh Bard), only Saito's sort of paid off. That's encouraging news for the experimental procedure Saito underwent, in which platelet-rich plasma was injected into his pitching elbow to treat a partially torn ulnar collateral ligament (UCL) that otherwise might have led to Tommy John surgery. Still, Saito wasn't the same pitcher he had been for the Dodgers. He sported an extreme reverse split, saw most of his peripherals head in the wrong direction, and allowed 61 percent of his inherited runners to score, a tendency that caused Terry Francona to restrict him to low-leverage situations—34 of his 56 appearances came with the Sox either up or down by four or more runs. Despite this, and given that Saito was a 39-year-old switching to the tougher league with a questionable elbow, he was better than the Sox had any right to expect. Signed by the Braves for a year and at least $3.2 million, a risky move.

Junichi Tazawa

Bats: R   Throws: R   Height: 6' 0"   Weight: 175   Born: June 6, 1986   Age: 24

YEAR	TEAM	LVL	AGE	W	L	SV	G	GS	IP	H	HR	BB	SO	GB%	BABIP	STUFF	WHIP	ERA	SIERA	DERA	EqH9	EqHR9	EqBB9	EqSO9	VORP	SN/WX
2009	PME	AA	23	9	5	0	18	18	98	80	8	26	88	46%	.268	16	1.08	2.57	3.41	3.79	8.4	1.5	2.6	5.9	17.6	1.49
2009	PAW	AAA	23	0	2	0	2	2	11¹	7	0	1	6	57%	.212	10	0.71	2.38	4.04	3.92	7.0	0.0	0.9	4.4	1.8	0.25
2009	BOS	MLB	23	2	3	0	6	4	25¹	43	4	9	13	25%	.386	-9	2.05	7.46	5.90	7.09	13.5	1.0	2.7	4.1	-4.7	-0.07
2010	BOS	MLB	24	6	8	0	29	24	125	141	18	45	80	37%	.314	-4	1.49	5.08	4.86	5.19	9.8	1.2	3.1	5.4	4.4	2.32

Breakout: 7%   Improve: 30%   Collapse: 27%   Attrition: 7%   MLB: 70%   Comparables: Tobi Stoner, Felipe Paulino, Dave Gumpert, Shaun Marcum

Japanese-born Tazawa made his professional debut with Double-A Portland last year and pitched well enough in that and two subsequent Triple-A starts to get an early-August call to "The Show." His major-league debut came at the end of a 15-inning scoreless duel with the Yankees and saw him give up a walk-off home run to Alex Rodriguez. Things didn't get much better from there, and he hit the DL in early September with a groin strain and a 7.46 ERA. He should start the year in Triple-A, where he'll battle Bowden to be the first in line to fill any holes that open up in the major-league rotation.

Billy Wagner

														Bats: L		Throws: L		Height: 5' 11"		Weight: 205		Born: July 25, 1971		Age: 38

YEAR	TEAM	LVL	AGE	W	L	SV	G	GS	IP	H	HR	BB	SO	GB%	BABIP	STUFF	WHIP	ERA	SIERA	DERA	EqH9	EqHR9	EqBB9	EqSO9	VORP	SN/WX
2007	NYN	MLB	35	2	2	34	66	0	68^1	55	6	22	80	41%	.285	22	1.13	2.63	2.74	2.91	7.5	0.9	2.6	9.3	19.6	3.73
2008	NYN	MLB	36	0	1	27	45	0	47	32	4	10	52	38%	.237	19	0.89	2.30	2.50	3.52	6.5	1.0	1.7	8.2	10.4	1.45
2009	NYN	MLB	37	0	0	0	2	0	2	0	0	1	4	0%	.000	2	0.50	0.00	0.27	0.00	0.0	0.0	4.5	9.0	1.2	0.05
2009	BOS	MLB	37	1	1	0	15	0	13^2	8	1	7	22	46%	.280	13	1.10	1.98	1.96	2.70	6.1	0.7	4.1	11.5	4.1	0.31
2010	ATL	MLB	38	3	2	11	41	0	40^1	34	4	15	43	39%	.297	12	1.22	3.43	3.23	3.76	7.7	0.9	3.0	8.6	7.8	1.14

Breakout: 14% Improve: 30% Collapse: 35% Attrition: 15%   MLB: 97%   Comparables: Tony Fossas, Mike Remlinger, Tom Burgmeier, Jim Brewer

Wagner spent most of 2009 rehabbing from September 2008 Tommy John surgery, then was flipped to the Red Sox for a pair of players to be named later (who became Chris Carter and Eddie Lora) after two dominant relief innings for the Mets in late August. The trade served no tangible benefit for the Sox, who gained no ground in their division and were quickly dispatched in the ALDS, with Wagner coughing up a pair of runs along the way, but it allowed Wagner to leverage the Sox into dropping his 2010 option. After proving in September that he could still pitch like his old self, Wagner put himself in position to land a well-paying closing job with the Braves in 2010, getting a one-year, $6.75 million deal with a club option for 2011 to join the Bobby Cox farewell tour.

Tim Wakefield

														Bats: R		Throws: R		Height: 6' 2"		Weight: 210		Born: August 2, 1966		Age: 43

YEAR	TEAM	LVL	AGE	W	L	SV	G	GS	IP	H	HR	BB	SO	GB%	BABIP	STUFF	WHIP	ERA	SIERA	DERA	EqH9	EqHR9	EqBB9	EqSO9	VORP	SN/WX
2007	BOS	MLB	40	17	12	0	31	31	189	191	22	64	110	44%	.282	5	1.35	4.76	4.87	4.55	9.2	0.9	2.8	5.0	19.4	4.02
2008	BOS	MLB	41	10	11	0	30	30	181	154	25	60	117	41%	.239	15	1.18	4.13	4.66	4.06	7.4	1.0	2.6	5.4	28.9	4.56
2009	BOS	MLB	42	11	5	0	21	21	129^2	137	12	50	72	41%	.292	12	1.44	4.58	5.23	4.00	8.5	0.6	3.0	4.4	22.0	2.69
2010	BOS	MLB	43	6	8	0	23	22	112^2	120	15	45	63	41%	.295	-4	1.47	4.99	5.18	5.12	9.3	1.1	3.4	4.7	4.8	1.62

Breakout: 13% Improve: 31% Collapse: 25% Attrition: 37%   MLB: 91%   Comparables: Charlie Hough, Don Sutton, Gaylord Perry, Early Wynn

All-Star Game selections are funny things. Wakefield made his first All-Star team last year at age 42, despite a season largely indistinguishable from any of the six before it. Wakefield had a 4.31 ERA in mid-July, nearly a dead match for his career mark of 4.33. He also had an 11-3 record because he received 6.2 runs of support in his first 17 starts. Wakefield hit the DL with a herniated disc just before the break and made just one more start before September. Three poor outings upon his return weren't encouraging, and after the knuckleballer's October surgery, the Sox killed his perpetual option, bringing him back as rotation insurance on a front-loaded two-year deal with a base of just $5 million.

LINEOUTS

Hitters

PLAYER	TEAM	LVL	AGE	PA	R	2B	3B	HR	RBI	BB	SO	SB-CS	EqBRR	AVG/OBP/SLG	EqAVG/EqOBP/EqSLG	EqA	VORP	WARP
3B M. Almanzar	GRN	A	18	203	13	7	0	3	17	9	53	0-0	0.6	.207/.261/.293	.187/.222/.259	.155	-15.3	-2.1
	LOW	A-	18	243	29	7	3	1	29	16	52	1-2	-2.5	.230/.288/.302	.197/.239/.250	.162	-14.8	-4.4
1B J. Bailey	PAW	AAA	30	271	34	7	0	10	27	35	51	2-0	-0.2	.262/.362/.424	.240/.332/.378	.254	0.7	0.2
	BOS	MLB	30	91	14	3	2	3	9	10	21	0-0	0.2	.208/.330/.416	.208/.330/.416	.256	-0.1	0.0
1B A. Bates	PME	AA	25	232	41	13	0	7	39	17	49	1-0	0.8	.340/.405/.505	.282/.332/.418	.261	4.3	-0.5
	PAW	AAA	25	302	28	10	0	5	18	22	59	0-0	-1.2	.213/.285/.305	.204/.272/.292	.198	-18.9	-2.4
	BOS	MLB	25	12	2	2	0	0	2	1	4	0-0	0.1	.364/.417/.545	.364/.417/.545	.319	0.9	0.1
C D. Brown	PAW	AAA	27	333	22	13	0	2	23	37	74	0-0	1.1	.264/.345/.329	.238/.315/.292	.219	0.1	-0.2
	BOS	MLB	27	4	1	0	0	1	1	1	0	0-0	0.0	.333/.500/1.333	.333/.500/.999	.459	1.3	0.1
SS R. Dent	GRN	A	20	411	59	24	3	6	48	49	112	17-5	1.4	.252/.350/.391	.218/.299/.332	.228	0.1	0.7
	SLM	A+	20	44	6	4	0	0	3	0	10	1-0	1.5	.268/.279/.366	.238/.250/.310	.197	-1.0	-0.4
LF C. Duncan*	PAW	AAA	28	94	8	3	0	2	10	7	20	0-0	1.1	.188/.255/.294	.174/.234/.267	.171	-6.8	-1.4
	SLN	MLB	28	304	25	15	2	5	32	41	67	0-1	-0.5	.227/.329/.558	.241/.338/.383	.254	3.1	-0.6
OF J. Gathright*	CHN	MLB	28	15	2	0	0	0	0	1	6	1-2	-1.2	.214/.267/.214	.214/.267/.214	.152	-1.4	-0.3
	NOR	AAA	28	362	49	11	2	0	20	27	41	24-7	-0.8	.329/.386/.376	.316/.366/.353	.260	8.9	1.1
	BOS	MLB	28	17	7	0	0	0	0	1	2	1-0	0.8	.313/.353/.313	.313/.353/.313	.250	0.0	0.0
SS D. Gibson	LOW	A-	19	303	54	15	4	0	25	39	42	28-5	3.9	.290/.395/.380	.257/.334/.338	.244	5.6	0.3
CF P. Hissey*	GRN	A	19	425	50	13	6	0	37	39	88	22-9	-3.5	.279/.356/.347	.241/.302/.297	.217	-7.8	-1.0
3B W. Middlebrooks	GRN	A	20	427	53	25	3	7	57	48	123	7-4	-2.3	.265/.349/.404	.221/.294/.331	.221	-6.6	-2.0
OF D. Nava#	SLM	A+	26	130	18	12	1	1	13	18	21	0-2	-0.4	.339/.434/.495	.270/.341/.400	.258	2.2	-0.7
	PME	AA	26	144	25	10	1	4	23	25	12	0-0	1.0	.364/.479/.568	.328/.421/.496	.316	11.4	1.0
C M. Wagner	PME	AA	25	188	21	18	0	3	23	28	26	1-0	-2.4	.301/.410/.477	.281/.367/.431	.283	11.7	2.1
	PAW	AAA	25	168	12	12	0	3	20	11	29	0-0	-0.2	.214/.268/.351	.206/.260/.335	.207	-2.8	-0.3
MI C. Woodward	TAC	AAA	33	197	24	12	1	1	15	19	30	4-0	1.4	.299/.369/.397	.270/.332/.360	.248	5.0	1.1
	SEA	MLB	33	74	7	1	0	0	5	5	15	1-0	0.3	.239/.288/.254	.239/.288/.254	.202	-2.2	0.0
	PAW	AAA	33	37	1	0	0	0	0	5	7	0-1	-0.3	.129/.250/.129	.125/.243/.125	.109	-3.0	-0.3
	BOS	MLB	33	16	0	0	0	0	0	2	4	0-0	-0.1	.083/.313/.083	.083/.313/.083	.167	-0.8	-0.2

A toolsy, teenage Dominican third baseman, **Michael Almanzar** hasn't hit above rookie ball and isn't being helped by the Sox' aggressive promotions. ⊘ **Jeff Bailey** spent the second half of his 20s as an emergency bat in the system, and has hit .228/.340/.434 in his limited big-league opportunities; designated for assignment in September, he signed with the Snake. ⊘ A 2006 third-round pick and a career .286/.381/.455 hitter in the minors, **Aaron Bates** could be the new Bailey, though he has yet to hit above Double-A. ⊘ **Dusty Brown** has a good arm and takes walks, but he's an aging fourth-stringer on the catching depth chart. ⊘ A supplemental first-round pick out of high school in 2007, **Ryan Dent** is a fleet-footed shortstop who will take a walk, but has yet to show much power and might have to slide over to second base—not a good place to be a prospect in this organization. ⊘ Acquired from the Cards for Julio Lugo, **Chris Duncan** went straight to Triple-A due to a total lack of production dating back to April and was eventually released. After major neck surgery the previous winter, he could be done. ⊘ The prototypical speedy slap hitter, **Joey Gathright** is seeing his major-league opportunities dry up as he approaches 30. ⊘ A second-round pick in 2008, **Derrik Gibson** has speed, great plate discipline, good instincts, and a hard-nosed approach, but he has no power to speak of, and his arm might force him to move from shortstop to second base. ⊘ Teen phenom **Peter Hissey** kept his head above water in a full-season league, and scouts love his tools, prompting Kevin Goldstein to name him the system's sleeper on his winter Top 11 Prospects list on BaseballProspectus.com. ⊘ A Cuban defector who signed a big-league contract worth $8.2 million over four years, 20-year-old **Jose Iglesias** is an outstanding defensive shortstop, but serious doubts exist about his bat; he should begin 2010 at High-A Salem. ⊘ A good defensive third baseman, **Will Middlebrooks** improved at the plate in his first full pro season, but is still a long way from ready. ⊘ A college product who spent 2007 in the independent leagues, **Daniel Nava** made his pro debut at High-A in 2008 and has raked at every level since. He's already 27, but a career .354/.450/.558 hitter who bested those marks in Double-A in the second half has to be taken seriously. ⊘ After a dreadful Double-A showing in 2008, **Mark Wagner** raked while repeating the level last year, but fell flat on his face upon being promoted to Triple-A. At the least, he could eke out a big-league career as a backup with his strong work behind the plate. ⊘ Veteran futilityman **Chris**

Woodward is a .242/.298/.369 career hitter in the majors; Boston's claim on him from Seattle in August is evidence of how desperate the team felt about its shortstop situation late last year.

Pitchers

PLAYER	TEAM	LVL	AGE	W	L	SV	IP	H	HR	BB	SO	GB%	BABIP	STUFF	WHIP	ERA	SIERA	DERA	EqH9	EqHR9	EqBB9	EqSO9	VORP
F. Cabrera	PAW	AAA	27	0	3	22	52²	40	3	22	51	43%	.257	4	1.18	1.71	3.69	2.54	7.7	0.9	3.9	7.0	16.9
	BOS	MLB	27	0	0	0	5¹	7	0	4	8	51%	.467	6	2.06	8.44	3.38	7.15	11.1	0.0	4.8	11.1	-1.0
S. Fife	GRN	A	22	0	3	0	36²	32	1	4	35	55%	.292	5	0.98	2.70	2.83	5.35	10.2	1.3	2.1	4.8	0.6
	SLM	A+	22	3	2	0	50²	58	7	10	51	60%	.340	0	1.34	4.44	3.06	6.18	12.2	2.5	2.5	6.1	-3.6
K. Gabbard*	LOW	A-	26	2	1	0	21¹	19	0	15	15	52%	.322	-11	1.59	2.53	5.13	4.68	12.7	1.7	9.4	3.9	1.5
	PME	AA	26	0	4	0	13	26	2	28	12	68%	.490	-32	4.15	20.77	6.62	27.00	19.9	2.8	17.8	5.7	-30.3
J. Lopez*	BOS	MLB	31	0	2	0	11²	20	1	9	5	71%	.404	-33	2.49	9.26	5.71	8.63	14.3	0.8	6.0	3.8	-4.2
	PAW	AAA	31	1	1	0	39²	35	2	13	23	70%	.275	-15	1.21	3.18	4.23	4.13	9.3	0.8	3.3	4.3	5.5
M. McBeth	PAW	AAA	28	2	3	3	67	43	5	30	66	34%	.229	6	1.09	2.69	3.76	3.30	6.9	1.0	4.3	7.3	15.3
S. Pimentel	GRN	A	19	10	7	0	117²	135	12	29	103	39%	.345	-36	1.39	3.82	3.62	7.44	14.0	2.9	3.7	4.5	-21.8
D. Richardson*	PME	AA	25	2	2	4	63¹	42	2	40	80	39%	.274	15	1.29	2.70	3.36	4.08	7.3	0.9	5.6	8.5	9.6
	PAW	AAA	25	0	0	0	10²	8	1	2	16	20%	.333	9	0.94	1.69	0.95	1.93	9.6	1.0	1.9	10.6	3.7
	BOS	MLB	25	0	0	0	3¹	3	0	1	0	31%	.231	-32	1.20	0.00	8.13	0.00	7.4	0.0	2.5	0.0	2.2
K. Weiland	SLM	A+	22	7	9	0	132²	119	4	57	112	59%	.298	4	1.33	3.46	3.97	5.41	9.5	1.0	4.5	4.9	1.3
A. Wilson	LOW	A-	22	0	1	0	36	10	0	7	33	48%	.116	9	0.47	0.50	2.81	2.32	4.6	1.1	2.7	4.6	11.7
C. Zink	PAW	AAA	29	6	15	0	135¹	134	10	93	47	44%	.274	-21	1.68	5.59	6.64	6.71	10.3	1.1	6.8	2.4	-16.7

Once seen as a future closer in the Indians' system, **Fernando Cabrera** landed with the Red Sox last year, where he continued to dominate in the minors but struggled to find the big-league strike zone; he seems locked in as a Quad-A guy. ∅ A 2008 third-round pick out of the University of Utah, **Stephen Fife** put up some great rates in his first year of full-season ball, but looked hittable in High-A despite his 5.1 strikeout/walk ratio. He's likely to be a reliever in the long run. ∅ Traded to Texas in the ill-fated Eric Gagne deal, oft-injured **Kason Gabbard** was bought back by the Sox in April, only to land back on the DL. ∅ A Rule 5 pick out of the Angels' system, Mexican righty **Miguel Gonzalez** pitched well in 5 ⅔ innings of winter ball in 2008, but otherwise hasn't pitched since 2007, because of knee and elbow injuries; he'll be 26 in May. ∅ Side-armer **Javier Lopez** gave the Sox two and a half seasons of solid LOOGY-dom before earning a demotion last May. ∅ Plucked off waivers from the Reds in August 2008, hard-throwing **Marcus McBeth** pitched well, save for his typically inflated walk rate. ∅ Dominican starter **Stolmy Pimentel** has shown good command in the low minors and is very projectable at age 20, despite underwhelming overall numbers. ∅ Big lefty **Dustin Richardson** moved into the bullpen at Double-A last year and set career highs in his strikeout and walk rate, dominating both lefties and righties. After limiting his walks in a brief Triple-A stint, he got a late-September call-up, but his wildness returned in the Arizona Fall League. ∅ A 2008 third-round pick out of Notre Dame, **Kyle Weiland** pitched well in his full-season debut last year, flashing low-90s heat; he may eventually head to the pen. ∅ Undrafted **Alex Wilson** put up video-game numbers in his pro debut, and his fastball/slider combination is impressive, but he has yet to pitch in a full-season league; if he makes the majors, he'll be just the second player born in Saudi Arabia to do so. ∅ As you've no doubt heard, **Charlie Zink** throws the knuckler; now that he's 30, the good pitching is supposed to commence, right? Right?

MANAGER: TERRY FRANCONA

YEAR	TEAM	W-L	Pythag +/-	Avg PC	100+ P	120+ P	QS	BQS	REL	REL w Zero R	IBB	Subs	PH	PH Avg	PH HR	SB2	CS2	SB3	CS3	SAC Att	SAC %	POS SAC	Squeeze	Swing	In Play
2007	BOS	96-66	-7	97.9	68	4	81	9	451	323	20	43	83	.203	0	83	20	13	4	54	55.6%	30	3	149	100
2008	BOS	95-67	-2	95.9	69	1	78	9	466	298	17	52	60	.236	2	99	32	21	2	48	58.3%	27	0	114	90
2009	BOS	95-67	0	99.1	80	3	80	3	463	309	24	41	84	.205	0	106	35	19	4	32	59.4%	17	0	131	97

Francona is as inoffensive as managers come. He doesn't impose his will on the game, generally letting his players play to their strengths, but he isn't asleep at the wheel, either. He has had a great run of success for a franchise desperate for such a stretch and is always respectful of both his players and his opponents, putting himself almost beyond reproach. The back half of his rotation collapsed on him last year, but he still eked out the team's usual allotment of quality starts. He let his better starters go longer into games than in recent years without abusing them, and he still managed to greatly reduce his staff's number of blown quality starts and keep his bullpen's workload at the same level as 2008, almost to the inning. Burdened with a brutal team defense, he didn't overreact by making constant defensive replacements, preferring instead to keep his best bats in close games rather than make the modest defensive upgrades his bench would allow. As we noted last year, his only real weakness seems to be a soft spot for Jason Varitek; Tek made 28 starts after the acquisition of Victor Martinez, despite hitting .134/.220/.216 in those games. Those starts came largely at the expense of Mike Lowell (via Martinez's moving to first base and Youkilis's moving to third), who hit .280/.344/.455 over the same span. Having picked up his player option, Varitek is supposed to be a bench player this year, but one wonders if a small hot streak by the captain might convince Francona to increase his playing time against the skipper's better judgment.

Chicago Cubs

Ah, heartbreak. Wrigleyville knows it only too well. With the first-time achievement of consecutive division titles under the Cubs' collective belt, and with the time since their last World Series win moving into its second century, there was still considerable optimism about the team's shot at a division-title three-peat. After consecutive three-and-out Division Series embarrassments, general manager Jim Hendry still had a club that had every reason to contend: a rotation stocked with veteran talent, a lineup that had ranked first in the National League in runs scored and second in Equivalent Average. With no truly dominant ballclub in the senior circuit to contend with, it was easy to believe that a few tweaks and another spin could produce a better set of circumstances and post-season matchups in 2009.

As we now know, Jim Hendry's Hot Stove shopping before the 2009 season came to grief too many times over. Unfortunately, the track record for Hendry's bolder strokes has been mixed of late, and his scorecard with big-ticket free agents has been disconcertingly bad. The Cubs haven't been shy about affording premium talent, having re-upped Carlos Zambrano, Derrek Lee, and Aramis Ramirez to contracts now in the eight-figure range for average annual value, and were similarly lavish with free-agent add-on Ted Lilly. The huge deals handed to Alfonso Soriano before 2007 and Kosuke Fukudome in 2008 were sources of regret, almost from the moment they were signed.

Because of the expenses already on board, as well as the decision to reward Ryan Dempster for his best-ever season with a four-year, $52 million deal (representing a $7 million raise for 2009 alone), Hendry had already reached the point of having to balance financial con-

CUBS PROSPECTUS
2009 W-L: 83-78, 2nd in NL Central

Pythag	82-79	8th	**Ballpark:** Wrigley Field (3-yr. PF: 1043). In or out, whichever way the winds may blow, a helpmate to hitters
RS/G	4.4	9th	
RA/G	4.2	5th	
EqA	.254	12th	**2009:** Dueling albatrosses Soriano, Bradley, and Zambrano vie to see who's worth less for more
EqBRR	-14.1	15th	
SNWP	.523	5th	
WXRL	9.0	5th	**2010:** It's a weak division, but everyone's getting old or fat, except the guys who are old **and** fat, and good luck with that
FRAr	4.40	10th	
DE	.701	4th	
PADE	2.26	3rd	**Action Items:** The Ungame with Milton Bradley means nobody wins; who's Jenny Craig?
Salary	$134.8	2nd	
Attend	3.17	4th	

siderations and the relative immobility of huge contracts against any changes to the division-winning roster. Affordable opportunities to improve were available in what turned out to be a buyer's market, especially for outfielders, but instead of considering the merits of a Bobby Abreu, Hendry looked at his team's lineup and went hunting for something that wasn't there, an outfield bat from the left side that he could put in the middle of the order, addressing the lineup's right-handed tilt.

Consider the three calculated risks Hendry took in reshaping the 2008 Cubs. First, he decided to let the ever-popular closer Kerry Wood slip away as a free agent, electing instead to trade a hard-throwing prospect (Jose Ceda) to the Marlins for the last year of Kevin Gregg's arbitration eligibility before free agency. The difference netted the club $5.8 million in 2009 payroll expenses (using Wood's first year with the Tribe for $10 million against Gregg's $4.2 million). Gregg was a utility pitcher who had started, closed, and done everything in between and could serve as a placeholder or rival for Carlos Marmol until the latter could claim the closer's role for himself. That wound up being a disaster, as Gregg's advanced gopheritis produced a shocking spike in his home-run/fly-ball percentage, jumping from 3.4 percent of all flies to 12.6; also shocking was Marmol's equally desperate struggle to find the strike zone. However, the team's overall Fair Runs Average for its relievers remained stable, dropping from 4.52 (and eighth in the NL) to 4.40 (10th). It really wasn't a good pen in either year, but in a broader sense, Hendry's attempted fix didn't really make matters worse. We'll return to this in a moment.

The second risk was the decision to deal away the last year of contractual control of Mark DeRosa for Indian trinkets so seedy they may be a long time sprouting down on the farm. It's been speculated that Hendry was collecting goodies the Padres favored in an attempt to make a play on Jake Peavy, but the real upshot was that the deal saved the club $5.5 million in 2009 payroll. Discarding DeRosa led to all sorts of attendant roster errors—notably signing Aaron Miles and Joey Gathright to add speed and switch-hitting and hustle and all sorts of indefinable qualities that nobody's been able to find in their batting records. Employing that pair cost $3 million, so the net savings weren't all that substantial, and the effect on the offense was toxic.

The third risk was the presumed master stroke. Hendry thought he'd finally catch his white whale and add a premium bat from the left side: Milton Bradley, signed just days after the Cubs ditched DeRosa. No less than with Ahab, this didn't go so well. Bradley became the first player in more than 20 years to have his team attempt to move him from regular DH duty to playing the outfield regularly in the NL (the Phillies' attempt with Mike Easler in 1987 lasted weeks, hardly an inspiring precedent). Bradley gave the outfield his best shot, but as Joe Sheehan has noted, Bradley's career has been a matter of getting only two out of three things at once: health, productivity at the plate, and playing the outfield, but never all three at once. Add in the problems Bradley seems to run into with management almost everywhere he's played, and the decision to bet on all three at once with a three-year, $30 million deal was a regrettable gamble built on the wishcast that his 2008 bust-out as a regular DH was somehow translatable. When the Cubs got relative health from him (he played in 124 of the team's first 145 games) and outfielding but not batsmanship, they matched Bradley sulk for sulk over their mutual predicament. Finally, they almost gleefully suspended him with two weeks left in the season for some relatively mild comments about the organization's unhappy history of failure. The mutual disgust between the parties made Hendry's whale of last winter his white elephant; dumping him on the Mariners brought the fat and expensive Carlos Silva and enough financial wiggle room to add Marlon Byrd to play center.

Taken together, the decisions to trade away DeRosa and bring in Bradley exacerbated the problems of an offense with more than its share of challenges. Geovany Soto flailed early and got hurt midyear, Aramis Ramirez was injured and absent for most of May and all of June, Alfonso Soriano struggled to contribute at the plate while dealing with injuries to both knees before finally getting shut down in August, and Mike Fontenot wilted, overexposed in everyday play. Unlike 2008, there wasn't a Jim Edmonds lying around on the major-league discard pile to repair best-laid plans gone awry, and without DeRosa's multiple gloves available to be plugged into one or more of the holes, the Cubs were left to sort through an odd assemblage of bats (Jake Fox, Micah Hoffpauir, and, eventually, Jeff Baker), gloves (Andres Blanco and Sam Fuld), and "other" (Miles) to patch things up. Consider the performance of the team's various lineup positions, the regulars at those positions during the last three years, and the sum of their contributions (see Table 1).

Since a .260 EqA is definitively average, you can see what this says about their offensive effort. The weak offense had a fatal and deceptive interaction with the bullpen: the fewer runs scored put the bullpen that much more on the spot, because the club played tighter games. Whereas the Cubs could afford to get by with a mediocre pen in 2008, that mediocrity made for an easy target for blame in 2009, obscuring the more fundamental problem, which was the offense's climb back down to inadequacy.

Now, it should be apparent that Hendry hasn't settled for bad offense. Rather, it's just that many of his elective decisions have reliably failed to fix the problem. There's a difference between sensibly re-upping a Derrek Lee or an Aramis Ramirez and handing out multiyear deals at eight figures per annum for substars like Soriano or Fukudome or Bradley. The arrival of Geovany Soto behind the plate was eagerly anticipated, but Ryan Theriot's emergence as a useful everyday shortstop was a happy accident from a development point of view, since there was considerable doubt he'd be able to handle short as an everyday player. Last year's injuries compounded the problems with so many merely playable regulars, especially because deleting DeRosa forced a less useful collection of options onto the field.

The other takeaways from these problems provide news both good and bad for 2010. The good news is that while the Cubs will never have a DeRosa back to fix their problems, you can't anticipate or plan around a comprehensive injury stack like last year's. Production from Cubs catchers, third basemen, and left fielders will all improve, with relatively healthy seasons from Soto, Ramirez, and Soriano. Second base might even settle into a nice platoon between Fontenot and Jeff Baker, which might return Fontenot to his past status as a dangerous part-time player. The bad news is that the key players in this offense are all a year older, with Lee, Ramirez, Soriano, Fukudome, and even Bradley moving deeper into their 30s, further from their peak years, and

Table 1. *Plus ça change ... :* **Cubs Offensive Performance by EqA**

Spot	2007	2008	2009
C	.235 (Barrett, Kendall)	.280 (Soto)	.241 (Soto, Hill)
1B	.304 (Lee)	.282 (Lee)	.314 (Lee)
2B	.262 (DeRosa, Fontenot)	.289 (De Rosa, Fontenot)	.238 (Fontenot, Baker, Miles)
3B	.294 (Ramirez, DeRosa)	.297 (Ramirez, DeRosa)	.276 (Ramirez, Fox)
SS	.234 (Theriot, Izturis)	.264 (Theriot)	.253 (Theriot)
CF	.248 (Jones, Pie)	.281 (Edmonds, Johnson)	.274 (Fukudome, Johnson)
RF	.269 (Jones, Floyd)	.270 (Fukudome, DeRosa)	.271 (Bradley, Fukudome)
LF	.287 (Soriano)	.285 (Soriano, DeRosa)	.258 (Soriano, Fox)
Total	.259	.274	.259
NL Rank	13th	2nd	12th

Table 2. The 10 Best Cubs Rotations, 1972-2009

Rank	Year	SNWP	Heroes (SNWP > .520)
1	2003	.551	Mark Prior, Kerry Wood, Carlos Zambrano, Matt Clement
2	2004	.545	Zambrano, Prior, Wood, Clement, Greg Maddux, Glendon Rusch
3	1970	.542	Milt Pappas, Fergie Jenkins, Ken Holtzman, Bill Hands
4	2008	.540	Ryan Dempster, Zambrano, Ted Lilly, Rich Harden
5	1972	.537	Burt Hooton, Hands, Jenkins, Rick Reuschel, Pappas
6	1969	.533	Hands, Jenkins
7	1992	.526	Maddux, Mike Morgan
8t	2009	.523	Lilly, Randy Wells, Zambrano
8t	2001	.523	Wood, Jon Lieber
10	2007	.521	Zambrano, Lilly, Rich Hill, Sean Marshall

Theriot and Fontenot both turning 30 as well. The only regular aged 27 or younger is the hefty Soto. So, expecting significant improvement in light of their past performances is going to be a bit of a wish-cast.

While Lee and Ramirez have been true star-level hitters at their positions, Soriano and Fukudome are not, and whatever the Cubs get out of Theriot and the second basemen won't be at that level, either. To improve this offense beyond a midpack unit, the Cubs are stuck with a pair of propositions: Soto has got to be really, really good again, and Byrd has to deliver at the plate. Fukudome's bat profiles better in center than right, but most of the available defensive metrics cast doubt on the suggestion that he could handle the position effectively. That argues for adding someone in center, especially when the Cubs already employ Soriano as a heart-attack-inducing left fielder. And happy accidents like winding up with Jim Edmonds in 2008 aside, Hendry's unfortunate history when it comes to spending money on outfielders looks like it has another chapter in Byrd.

While Hendry has been busily beavering away on lineup issues, what might be overlooked is that this team has been enjoying a golden age of starting pitching. Using staffwide Support-Neutral Winning Percentage, we can measure how well starting pitchers improved their team's shot at winning ballgames. In the era of divisional play (1969 to the present), we find that the Cubs have gotten the benefit of six of their 10 best starting staffs in the last nine seasons (see Table 2).

From a historical point of view, you can glean several interesting factoids from this list: the unhappy proposition that the team wasted a good chunk of Greg Maddux's pre-Braves career by failing to give him m/any quality teammates, for example, and the noteworthy absence of the 1984 team (which finished with a .500 SNWP). Instead, there are three clear groups. At the head of the class, there's the 2001-2004 team that was anchored by Mark Prior and Kerry Wood (with Zambrano just entering into the mix)—cue the attendant weeping and gnashing of teeth. That's followed by the team that, in the aftermath of 1969's historic upset by the Mets, was unhappily curdling and killing hope.

And then there's the present team, the one that relies on Zambrano, Lilly, and Dempster and has gotten assists from other, less-famous contributors—Rich Harden, Rich Hill, and now Randy Wells. How secure is the current crew's claim to modest fame, and can they add a fourth season to that top 10? That's not quite so clear. Dempster lost ground from his walk year to his first on his new deal, but he was still an asset, contributing a .500 SNWP and quality starts through his first six innings in 20 of 31 starts. Wells is going to have to show some staying power, a subject on which there's some doubt. Much depends on whether Zambrano can reverse his steady decline as he adds age, bulk, an indifference to conditioning, and/or a navel-gazing fascination with his hitting exploits. From his career-high SNWP of .607 in 2004, he's lost ground in campaign after campaign, all the way down to last year's full-season low of .525.

This leaves Hendry with a tough proposition. Where last winter seemed to be a case of figuring out which little wrinkles needed smoothing out so that the Cubs could take their best shot with a veteran team, this year's club has hope instead of cash to invest in its lineup, as well as a bullpen that's still not doing it any real favors. If Wells turns back into a pumpkin, and if Zambrano continues to shed starts instead of pounds, the rotation becomes an additional question mark that could leave the team brawling with the Reds, Astros, and Brewers with little at stake beyond title-free positions in the NL Central standings. The Cubs can hope that the Cardinals come back to the pack, just as the Cubs themselves did last year, but the clock is running out on this assemblage of aging talent. If Hendry can't deliver another contender in the first year under new ownership, a rebuild with the organization's crop of prospects bodes ill for anything but a long period back out of contention.

HITTERS

Jeff Baker · UT

Bats: R   Throws: R   Height: 6' 2"   Weight: 210   Born: June 21, 1981   Age: 29

YEAR	TEAM	LVL	AGE	PA	R	2B	3B	HR	RBI	BB	SO	SB	CS	EqBRR	AVG	OBP	SLG	EqAVG	EqOBP	EqSLG	EqA	VORP	WARP	DEFENSE			
2007	COL	MLB	26	159	17	2	2	4	12	13	40	0	0	-1.0	.222	.296	.347	.215	.289	.340	.221	-4.4	-0.8	11-1B	-2	10-RF	1
2008	COL	MLB	27	333	55	22	1	12	48	26	85	4	0	-1.4	.268	.322	.468	.265	.316	.456	.268	10.6	1.5	41-2B	1	14-1B	0
2009	COL	MLB	28	24	0	0	1	0	3	1	7	1	0	0.1	.130	.167	.217	.130	.167	.217	.123	-2.5	-0.1				
2009	CHN	MLB	28	224	27	15	1	4	21	17	46	0	0	0.0	.305	.362	.448	.310	.362	.448	.283	11.7	2.2	41-2B	6	9-3B	1
2010	CHN	MLB	29	381	50	19	2	10	43	32	93	2	0	-0.7	.257	.323	.412	.256	.322	.413	.253	8.7	1.3	61-2B	3		

Breakout: 19%   Improve: 52%   Collapse: 10%   Attrition: 9%   MLB: 90%   Comparables: Jeff Kent, Wes Chamberlain, Russ Davis, Junior Spivey

Earl Weaver would have gotten a lot of use out of Baker. A player with good pop against lefties and a solid glove in the corners and at the keystone, Baker is ideally cast as the short side of a second-base platoon and in the NL is additionally useful as the first man off the bench for most any double switch. Start him every day, however, and Baker's poor plate discipline and struggles against righties become a liability. Hopefully, Piniella sticks with asking him to do what he's good at.

Andres Blanco · MI

Bats: S   Throws: R   Height: 5' 10"   Weight: 190   Born: April 11, 1984   Age: 26

YEAR	TEAM	LVL	AGE	PA	R	2B	3B	HR	RBI	BB	SO	SB	CS	EqBRR	AVG	OBP	SLG	EqAVG	EqOBP	EqSLG	EqA	VORP	WARP	DEFENSE			
2007	OMA	AAA	23	107	8	2	0	0	8	5	12	0	0	-0.3	.196	.231	.216	.184	.219	.204	.137	-7.1	-1.0	21-SS	-1	6-2B	0
2008	IOW	AAA	24	330	30	8	2	1	36	15	31	9	3	-0.3	.285	.327	.336	.271	.307	.317	.224	1.4	-0.7	82-SS	-7		
2009	IOW	AAA	25	258	30	17	2	6	29	17	28	6	1	1.0	.304	.353	.474	.295	.336	.453	.274	13.7	1.6	52-SS	-2	7-3B	1
2009	CHN	MLB	25	138	15	8	0	1	12	8	14	0	2	-0.6	.252	.303	.341	.254	.304	.349	.222	-0.7	0.5	25-2B	2	10-SS	2
2010	CHN	MLB	26	322	31	15	1	5	35	21	43	4	2	0.0	.267	.322	.376	.267	.319	.377	.241	5.1	0.4	79-SS	-2		

Breakout: 17%   Improve: 44%   Collapse: 26%   Attrition: 12%   MLB: 100%   Comparables: Augie Ojeda, Danny Bravo, Milko Jaramillo, Luis Figueroa

Defense isn't just Blanco's calling card; it's his meal ticket, lifeline, and fairy godmother rolled into one. Don't let two good months in Des Moines fool you—Blanco's career minor-league line of .256/.318/.326 tells you all you need to know about his bat, but in the field, he's as slick and nimble as they come on either side of the bag. A contender like the Cubs will gladly use him as a defensive backup in their middle infield, but someday, Blanco's glove could earn him a full-time job helping boost the confidence of a rebuilding team's young rotation.

Milton Bradley · DH/DL/RF

Bats: S   Throws: R   Height: 6' 0"   Weight: 225   Born: April 15, 1978   Age: 32

YEAR	TEAM	LVL	AGE	PA	R	2B	3B	HR	RBI	BB	SO	SB	CS	EqBRR	AVG	OBP	SLG	EqAVG	EqOBP	EqSLG	EqA	VORP	WARP	DEFENSE	
2007	OAK	MLB	29	75	6	4	0	2	7	8	14	2	1	-1.3	.292	.373	.446	.292	.373	.431	.290	3.8	0.6	14-CF	0
2007	SDN	MLB	29	169	31	5	1	11	30	23	27	3	1	-1.2	.313	.414	.590	.340	.441	.639	.351	21.7	2.7	36-LF	3
2008	TEX	MLB	30	509	78	32	1	22	77	80	112	5	3	-1.8	.321	.436	.563	.324	.440	.567	.337	50.4	5.5	18-RF	2
2009	CHN	MLB	31	473	61	17	1	12	40	66	95	2	3	-3.4	.257	.378	.397	.263	.379	.404	.276	16.7	2.5	102-RF	5
2010	SEA	MLB	32	455	62	19	1	17	56	66	93	4	3	-1.4	.277	.395	.467	.276	.390	.462	.297	27.6	3.2	64-RF	2

Breakout: 8%   Improve: 34%   Collapse: 16%   Attrition: 11%   MLB: 98%   Comparables: J.D. Drew, Bobby Abreu, Ken Singleton, Reggie Smith

As *The Life of Brian* makes clear, when you anoint the unwilling as your messiah, things usually end badly. The Cubs apparently thought they were buying a slugging outfielder whose potent switch-hitting would help balance their lineup and lead them to the promised land. A decade's worth of evidence, however, shows that while Bradley will always provide good at-bats and get on base, he only slugs, plays the outfield, or hits right-handed pitching intermittently, and leaders don't play for seven teams in nine years. A slow start for both Bradley and the team begat near-instant resentment against the player whose signing was linked to the trade of fan favorite Mark DeRosa. Bradley recovered to hit .282/.405/.429 from May through August—numbers perfectly consistent with his career rates. Ever willing to pour vinegar on the media's baking soda, Bradley's late-season assertion of a pervasive negativity surrounding the organization and his unpopularity in the clubhouse sealed his fate. Jim Hendry had little choice this winter but try to give him away in trade. Absent a few missing home runs, Bradley was his normal, often difficult self, and a wiser team that understands what he is and what he isn't will probably get great value from him in 2010.

Kyler Burke RF
Bats: L   Throws: L   Height: 6' 3"   Weight: 205   Born: April 20, 1988   Age: 22

YEAR	TEAM	LVL	AGE	PA	R	2B	3B	HR	RBI	BB	SO	SB	CS	EqBRR	AVG	OBP	SLG	EqAVG	EqOBP	EqSLG	EqA	VORP	WARP	DEFENSE			
2007	FTW	A	19	243	24	7	1	1	21	26	73	3	1	-0.5	.211	.305	.268	.202	.280	.257	.191	-12.0	-2.3	59-RF	-7		
2007	BOI	A-	19	259	35	11	1	10	41	24	63	1	3	-2.0	.254	.340	.446	.212	.268	.364	.218	-7.1	-1.7	55-RF	-3		
2008	PEO	A	20	144	12	5	1	2	8	11	34	3	0	-1.0	.206	.278	.305	.194	.250	.291	.187	-7.7	-0.7	30-RF	1	3-1B	1
2008	BOI	A-	20	280	46	18	2	7	41	28	70	6	3	-0.5	.261	.336	.437	.218	.264	.346	.214	-8.2	-0.6	65-RF	5		
2009	PEO	A	21	555	93	43	3	15	89	78	99	14	2	1.0	.303	.405	.505	.278	.359	.444	.280	23.4	2.1	67-RF	-3	26-CF	-2
2010	CHN	MLB	22	542	64	26	2	14	61	54	140	3	2	-0.6	.232	.313	.380	.233	.309	.373	.239	-0.5	-0.2	113-RF	-1		

Breakout: 27% Improve: 57% Collapse: 12% Attrition: 6%   MLB: 10%   Comparables: Greg Blosser, Chris Lubanski, Josh Kroeger, Tito Nanni

"Killer" Burke's first full season in A-ball was a revelation, earning him the organization's player of the year award and reminding scouts why the Padres made him a supplemental first-round pick out of a Tennessee high school back in 2006. The toolsy outfielder paced the Midwest League in doubles, hit more than a few homers, drew walks, and showcased a cannon arm tailor-made for right field. If the improved plate discipline and power can be repeated in 2010—a big if, given that even after his season, Burke's career rates stand at .255/.347/.407 in 404 games—he could muscle his way far up the prospect charts.

Starlin Castro SS
Bats: R   Throws: R   Height: 6' 1"   Weight: 160   Born: March 24, 1990   Age: 20

YEAR	TEAM	LVL	AGE	PA	R	2B	3B	HR	RBI	BB	SO	SB	CS	EqBRR	AVG	OBP	SLG	EqAVG	EqOBP	EqSLG	EqA	VORP	WARP	DEFENSE			
2008	CUB	Rk	18	215	33	11	5	3	22	14	33	6	5	-2.9	.311	.364	.464	.265	.298	.387	.235	1.4	1.0	20-SS	3	19-2B	1
2009	DAY	A+	19	387	45	17	3	3	35	19	41	22	11	0.0	.302	.340	.391	.270	.303	.355	.231	3.0	0.7	91-SS	3		
2009	TEN	AA	19	122	11	6	3	0	14	10	12	6	0	-0.1	.288	.347	.396	.265	.314	.372	.247	2.8	0.6	29-SS	2		
2010	CHN	MLB	20	515	50	26	4	5	46	30	71	12	5	-0.9	.264	.310	.364	.263	.308	.363	.234	4.2	0.8	124-SS	3		

Breakout: 16% Improve: 41% Collapse: 27% Attrition: 1%   MLB: 1%   Comparables: Joaquin Arias, Hector Made, Lenny Faedo, Julio Lugo

The Cubs challenged the 19-year-old Castro with an assignment to High-A Daytona, and the young shortstop responded by winning the MVP trophy at the FSL all-star game. To give him a taste of humility, the organization promoted him to Double-A, and Castro just reduced his strikeouts, increased his walk rate, and improved his on-base, slugging, and fielding percentages. He had an exceptional stint in the Arizona Fall League, and it's safe to say that in 2009, Castro improved his stock as much as any other prospect around. A solid defender with good speed, he is expected to develop more power as he fills out. Much of his value is tied up in batting average, and if the power never arrives, he'll have to improve his walk rate to escape the bottom third of the order. Those will be significant challenges, but right now, he has momentum in his favor.

Tyler Colvin OF
Bats: L   Throws: L   Height: 6' 3"   Weight: 190   Born: September 5, 1985   Age: 24

YEAR	TEAM	LVL	AGE	PA	R	2B	3B	HR	RBI	BB	SO	SB	CS	EqBRR	AVG	OBP	SLG	EqAVG	EqOBP	EqSLG	EqA	VORP	WARP	DEFENSE			
2007	DAY	A+	21	262	38	24	3	7	50	10	47	10	4	0.0	.306	.336	.514	.270	.297	.464	.257	7.0	0.7	61-CF	-1		
2007	TEN	AA	21	257	34	11	2	9	31	5	54	7	1	2.3	.291	.313	.462	.261	.277	.406	.235	-0.1	0.1	44-CF	3	12-RF	-2
2008	TEN	AA	22	602	68	27	11	14	80	44	101	7	4	0.0	.256	.312	.424	.228	.271	.375	.225	-9.0	-1.1	65-LF	2	54-CF	0
2009	DAY	A+	23	129	18	5	2	1	10	13	27	3	1	0.0	.250	.326	.357	.217	.285	.304	.212	-5.6	-0.7	10-LF	0		
2009	TEN	AA	23	330	51	13	7	14	50	16	57	5	1	0.1	.300	.334	.524	.282	.311	.487	.269	9.8	0.7	62-RF	-3	8-LF	-1
2009	CHN	MLB	23	20	1	0	0	0	2	2	5	0	0	0.1	.176	.250	.176	.176	.250	.176	.161	-1.2	0.1	5-CF	2		
2010	CHN	MLB	24	477	53	23	7	13	60	30	103	5	3	0.5	.245	.295	.413	.246	.293	.406	.240	-0.2	-0.4	96-RF	-3		

Breakout: 14% Improve: 36% Collapse: 18% Attrition: 13%   MLB: 7%   Comparables: Jeremy Dodson, Joe Deberry, Ralph Bryant, Robin Jennings

Colvin's second pass through the Southern League was a mixed bag. Half-full thinkers will see the increased slugging percentage and note that the former first-round pick finally developed the home-run power his size and swing have long suggested. Meanwhile, the half-empty set will retort that Colvin's move from center to right may have upped the offensive ante beyond what he can be expected to produce. Colvin's walk rate and power production remain inversely proportional, and the product of that unique formula is more likely to be a bench player than a starting corner outfielder.

Ryan Flaherty

Ryan Flaherty   **2B**   Bats: L   Throws: R   Height: 6' 3"   Weight: 200   Born: July 27, 1986   Age: 23

YEAR	TEAM	LVL	AGE	PA	R	2B	3B	HR	RBI	BB	SO	SB	CS	EqBRR	AVG	OBP	SLG	EqAVG	EqOBP	EqSLG	EqA	VORP	WARP	DEFENSE			
2008	BOI	A-	21	245	39	19	2	8	26	24	51	4	2	-1.2	.297	.369	.511	.239	.283	.396	.232	2.4	-0.1	51-SS	-3		
2009	PEO	A	22	543	81	24	5	20	81	50	98	7	6	-4.3	.276	.344	.470	.246	.298	.396	.239	3.5	0.6	53-2B	3	39-SS	-1
2010	CHN	MLB	23	483	55	22	3	13	49	38	116	2	2	-1.7	.238	.300	.389	.240	.297	.387	.234	2.1	0.5	88-2B	3		

Breakout: 17%   Improve: 44%   Collapse: 16%   Attrition: 7%   MLB: 2%   Comparables: Kevin Garner, Travis Hanson, Van Snider, Larry Ray

A former sandwich pick out of Vanderbilt in the 2008 draft, Flaherty overcame a slow start in his full-season debut to display an impressive power bat. Athletic and strong-armed, he's not rangy enough as a shortstop, but he projects nicely as an offense-first second baseman.

Mike Fontenot

Mike Fontenot   **2B**   Bats: L   Throws: R   Height: 5' 8"   Weight: 170   Born: June 9, 1980   Age: 30

YEAR	TEAM	LVL	AGE	PA	R	2B	3B	HR	RBI	BB	SO	SB	CS	EqBRR	AVG	OBP	SLG	EqAVG	EqOBP	EqSLG	EqA	VORP	WARP	DEFENSE			
2007	IOW	AAA	27	231	46	17	4	6	34	16	32	3	1	2.1	.336	.384	.540	.299	.343	.453	.273	10.8	1.2	20-SS	1	18-2B	-2
2007	CHN	MLB	27	260	32	12	4	3	29	22	43	5	4	0.7	.278	.336	.402	.279	.338	.399	.255	6.6	1.0	52-2B	4		
2008	CHN	MLB	28	284	42	22	1	9	40	34	51	2	0	-0.3	.305	.395	.514	.303	.391	.504	.307	22.7	2.6	55-2B	0		
2009	CHN	MLB	29	419	38	22	2	9	43	35	83	4	1	-1.3	.236	.301	.377	.239	.300	.385	.239	2.3	1.5	59-2B	4	40-3B	5
2010	CHN	MLB	30	411	50	21	3	10	48	40	79	4	2	0.2	.265	.340	.418	.266	.337	.412	.262	13.1	1.6	86-2B	1		

Breakout: 11%   Improve: 37%   Collapse: 15%   Attrition: 18%   MLB: 94%   Comparables: Grady Hatton, Lonny Frey, Mickey Morandini, Todd Walker

Fontenot was Ryan Theriot's double-play partner at LSU, and naming him the Opening Day second baseman brought shouts of "*et toi*" from those who expected the lefty to help balance the lineup's right-ward tilt and reproduce his 2008 numbers on a larger scale. Unfortunately, his BABIP had been an unsustainable .355, and when it dropped 70 points, his batting average, on-base, and slugging percentages plummeted with it. As is often the case, the truth lies between his '08 high and '09 low; when spotted well, Fontenot is a decent hitter with surprising pop who plays solid defense, but he's stretched as an everyday player. Expect him to bounce back, but as the last player into this season's Super Two arbitration pool, Fontenot is in line for a raise at exactly the wrong time, coming off what is probably the worst season of his career.

Jake Fox

Jake Fox   **4C**   Bats: R   Throws: R   Height: 6' 0"   Weight: 210   Born: July 20, 1982   Age: 27

YEAR	TEAM	LVL	AGE	PA	R	2B	3B	HR	RBI	BB	SO	SB	CS	EqBRR	AVG	OBP	SLG	EqAVG	EqOBP	EqSLG	EqA	VORP	WARP	DEFENSE			
2007	TEN	AA	24	388	60	23	1	18	60	17	72	6	2	-3.4	.284	.327	.504	.251	.284	.432	.244	0.4	0.5	35-1B	3	17-LF	3
2007	IOW	AAA	24	108	18	7	0	6	19	5	23	2	0	0.5	.283	.343	.535	.260	.315	.460	.266	2.5	-0.1	13-RF	0	6-LF	-2
2007	CHN	MLB	24	15	3	2	0	0	1	1	2	0	0	0.0	.143	.200	.286	.143	.200	.214	.156	-1.3	-0.3				
2008	TEN	AA	25	459	76	29	1	25	79	46	73	4	2	-2.8	.307	.397	.580	.262	.327	.471	.272	12.3	0.6	47-1B	-4	35-LF	-4
2008	IOW	AAA	25	120	17	10	1	6	26	2	31	3	0	0.6	.222	.242	.479	.203	.223	.398	.211	-5.3	-0.7	25-1B	0		
2009	IOW	AAA	26	194	44	14	3	17	53	21	31	2	1	-4.8	.409	.495	.841	.367	.443	.740	.371	27.3	2.8	31-1B	-1	6-RF	-1
2009	CHN	MLB	26	241	23	12	0	11	44	14	47	0	0	-2.5	.259	.311	.468	.260	.307	.470	.268	6.6	0.5	22-3B	-2	16-LF	0
2010	OAK	MLB	27	419	53	20	1	17	62	30	88	3	1	-1.8	.252	.318	.447	.253	.318	.445	.258	3.5	0.3	62-1B	0		

Breakout: 4%   Improve: 36%   Collapse: 23%   Attrition: 16%   MLB: 75%   Comparables: Lloyd McClendon, Tony Brewer, Steve Stanicek, Mike Reddish

An uninspiring walk rate and bad defense at every position has always overshadowed Fox's flat-out ability to hit. But when Aramis Ramirez injured his shoulder in May and the Cubs' offense sputtered, the organization could no longer ignore Fox's video-game Triple-A numbers and gave him a shot. An instant fan favorite, the Indiana native raked (.311/.345/.592) through July before the league figured him out (.212/.280/.354) down the stretch, numbers bad enough to give one pause. He's an emergency-only option behind the plate and a leather liability in the outfield or at third, and he doesn't really have enough bat for first base or DH. Rather than keep him as a four-corners reserve (or even five), the Cubs packaged him with Aaron Miles to the A's to clear roster space in December; Oakland may make him their everyday third baseman, defense be damned.

Kosuke Fukudome   CF   Bats: L   Throws: R   Height: 6' 0"   Weight: 185   Born: April 26, 1977   Age: 33

YEAR	TEAM	LVL	AGE	PA	R	2B	3B	HR	RBI	BB	SO	SB	CS	EqBRR	AVG	OBP	SLG	EqAVG	EqOBP	EqSLG	EqA	VORP	WARP	DEFENSE			
2007	CHU	JPN	30	348	64	22	0	13	48	69	66	5	2	0.0	.294	.443	.520	.292	.411	.412	.295	16.3	1.9				
2008	CHN	MLB	31	590	79	25	3	10	58	81	104	12	4	2.6	.257	.359	.379	.257	.355	.375	.263	12.3	1.6	123-RF	6	7-CF	-4
2009	CHN	MLB	32	603	79	38	5	11	54	93	112	6	10	-3.3	.259	.375	.421	.267	.377	.430	.278	27.5	5.0	101-CF	6	29-RF	10
2010	CHN	MLB	33	531	69	25	2	11	53	74	103	6	6	-0.1	.256	.366	.392	.257	.359	.383	.265	18.7	2.1	91-CF	1		

Breakout: 2%   Improve: 30%   Collapse: 18%   Attrition: 13%   MLB: 94%   Comparables: Bobby Murcer, Fred Lynn, Kenny Lofton, Charlie Maxwell

While the $26.5 million owed to Fukudome for the next two seasons isn't the worst contract on the Cubs' books, it's certainly not a cause for celebration. Moved to center field to make room for Bradley, Fukudome hit a few more gappers and drew a few more walks than in his disappointing 2008 debut, putting up numbers that made him a league-average player at his new position. The Cubs weren't happy with his defense in center and will move him back to right for 2010, a position where his glove is unquestioned but his bat is a liability. Now 33 and entering his third season in the States, his on-base skills give him value at the top of the order, but Fukudome isn't going to develop a corner outfielder's power.

Sam Fuld   OF   Bats: L   Throws: L   Height: 5' 10"   Weight: 185   Born: November 20, 1981   Age: 28

YEAR	TEAM	LVL	AGE	PA	R	2B	3B	HR	RBI	BB	SO	SB	CS	EqBRR	AVG	OBP	SLG	EqAVG	EqOBP	EqSLG	EqA	VORP	WARP	DEFENSE			
2007	TEN	AA	25	392	56	23	2	2	27	41	38	10	3	1.7	.290	.372	.388	.254	.320	.337	.237	0.1	1.1	57-CF	5	20-RF	4
2007	IOW	AAA	25	63	13	4	1	1	2	9	5	2	0	2.1	.269	.397	.442	.245	.365	.396	.274	2.0	0.6	6-RF	3	5-LF	0
2008	TEN	AA	26	397	48	16	3	5	48	50	40	7	8	-2.3	.271	.366	.381	.228	.297	.306	.215	-7.1	-1.8	81-CF	-8		
2008	IOW	AAA	26	76	11	3	0	1	4	8	12	3	2	-0.8	.222	.310	.317	.215	.292	.292	.212	-1.8	0.0	13-CF	2		
2009	IOW	AAA	27	370	62	17	10	2	33	38	24	23	5	4.8	.284	.358	.415	.269	.333	.386	.256	8.4	1.5	78-CF	4		
2009	CHN	MLB	27	115	17	6	1	1	2	17	10	2	1	1.3	.299	.409	.412	.306	.414	.418	.294	6.3	0.4	18-CF	-7	9-LF	4
2010	CHN	MLB	28	455	58	21	5	4	37	48	58	8	5	1.1	.248	.332	.354	.252	.331	.354	.241	5.0	0.5	93-CF	-1		

Breakout: 12%   Improve: 33%   Collapse: 24%   Attrition: 20%   MLB: 30%   Comparables: Ryan Fleming, Chris Prieto, Kenneth Baker, Skip Schumaker

A heady player who sports an economics degree from Stanford, nothing gets past Fuld—he made contact with 93.7 percent of the pitches at which he offered, the highest rate in baseball, and took a hack at an extremely low 14.2 percent of pitches out of the zone. That approach results in a good walk rate, and when combined with decent speed and big-league defense in center, you have yourself a likable reserve outfielder—sort of an effective Reed Johnson with a much lighter paycheck. Already overloaded with big contracts, the Cubs will take their bargains wherever they can find them.

Koyie Hill   C   Bats: S   Throws: R   Height: 6' 0"   Weight: 190   Born: March 9, 1979   Age: 31

YEAR	TEAM	LVL	AGE	PA	R	2B	3B	HR	RBI	BB	SO	SB	CS	EqBRR	AVG	OBP	SLG	EqAVG	EqOBP	EqSLG	EqA	VORP	WARP	DEFENSE	
2007	IOW	AAA	28	162	22	16	0	2	24	11	23	1	1	2.2	.322	.364	.470	.285	.321	.391	.248	3.7	0.4	28-C	0
2007	CHN	MLB	28	105	7	4	0	2	12	8	18	0	0	-0.6	.161	.231	.269	.161	.229	.258	.175	-3.3	0.0	26-C	2
2008	IOW	AAA	29	412	56	24	2	17	64	40	77	3	2	-2.3	.275	.350	.492	.241	.302	.398	.243	8.8	0.9	89-C	-1
2008	CHN	MLB	29	22	0	1	0	0	1	0	12	0	0	-0.1	.095	.095	.143	.143	.143	.190	-.131	-2.6	-0.4	5-C	-1
2009	CHN	MLB	30	284	26	12	2	2	24	27	78	0	0	1.3	.237	.312	.324	.236	.309	.323	.225	1.9	1.5	70-C	9
2010	CHN	MLB	31	280	27	13	1	5	32	25	69	1	1	0.1	.236	.306	.355	.235	.303	.356	.228	2.1	0.4	63-C	1

Breakout: 22%   Improve: 47%   Collapse: 29%   Attrition: 17%   MLB: 36%   Comparables: Damon Berryhill, Mandy Romero, Eric Fox, Joe Kmak

When Geovany Soto went down with a torn oblique in early July, Hill moved into the starting lineup and worked without a net, starting 28 straight games—including both ends of a doubleheader before the All-Star break—and working all but three innings behind the plate until Soto returned. It was a display of rugged backstoppery that, added to his earlier rehab from a table-saw mishap that resulted in the severing and reattachment of several digits, give him ample bragging rights at future lodge meetings of the International Brotherhood of Backup Catchers. His bat has less interesting things to say, and while his defense and ability to switch-flail will keep him on the roster, his best offensive seasons will be no better than Soto's worst.

Micah Hoffpauir   1B/OF   Bats: L   Throws: L   Height: 6' 3"   Weight: 215   Born: March 1, 1980   Age: 30

YEAR	TEAM	LVL	AGE	PA	R	2B	3B	HR	RBI	BB	SO	SB	CS	EqBRR	AVG	OBP	SLG	EqAVG	EqOBP	EqSLG	EqA	VORP	WARP	DEFENSE			
2007	IOW	AAA	27	342	56	24	0	16	73	24	34	2	1	1.1	.319	.365	.552	.287	.327	.468	.271	8.2	0.9	65-1B	1	10-LF	-2
2008	IOW	AAA	28	313	63	34	2	25	100	17	46	2	0	0.3	.362	.393	.752	.320	.345	.609	.310	22.9	2.2	55-1B	-5	8-LF	1
2008	CHN	MLB	28	80	14	8	0	2	8	6	24	1	0	0.0	.342	.400	.534	.342	.400	.507	.315	5.5	0.4	5-1B	-1	4-RF	0
2009	IOW	AAA	29	90	12	4	0	3	13	6	12	2	0	-0.6	.217	.267	.373	.190	.233	.298	.185	-6.5	-0.6	15-1B	0	4-RF	2
2009	CHN	MLB	29	257	28	12	1	10	35	20	46	1	0	0.6	.239	.300	.427	.244	.300	.440	.251	-0.3	0.2	21-RF	0	19-1B	2
2010	CHN	MLB	30	361	44	20	1	13	60	26	65	2	1	0.2	.267	.325	.449	.268	.323	.443	.262	4.7	0.5	69-1B	-1		

Breakout: 5%   Improve: 30%   Collapse: 22%   Attrition: 18%   MLB: 39%   Comparables: Lee Stevens, D.T. Cromer, Mike Lamb, Kevin Grijak

After winning the 2008 Willie Keeler award with a major-league leading .489 BABIP, Hoffpauir's rate stats cratered when his batted balls reversed polarity and became attracted to, rather than repulsed by, fielders' gloves. But you, gentle reader, expected this, knowing that such a rate was unsustainable, just as you know that last year's .258 is likely to improve. Hoffpauir's profile as a bench power source, backup first baseman, and emergency outfielder is unchanged and should keep him playing the game for money into his early 30s.

Brett Jackson   CF   Bats: L   Throws: R   Height: 6' 2"   Weight: 210   Born: August 2, 1988   Age: 21

YEAR	TEAM	LVL	AGE	PA	R	2B	3B	HR	RBI	BB	SO	SB	CS	EqBRR	AVG	OBP	SLG	EqAVG	EqOBP	EqSLG	EqA	VORP	WARP	DEFENSE	
2009	BOI	A-	20	106	14	1	1	1	15	17	20	2	1	-0.2	.330	.443	.398	.247	.333	.312	.232	-0.5	-0.9	20-CF	-5
2009	PEO	A	20	128	30	5	1	7	17	11	32	11	1	1.2	.295	.383	.545	.265	.328	.470	.273	5.6	0.6	27-CF	-1
2010	CHN	MLB	21	410	51	15	3	12	38	42	109	9	4	1.0	.244	.328	.400	.245	.324	.387	.252	9.3	0.4	83-CF	-5

Breakout: 17%   Improve: 48%   Collapse: 14%   Attrition: 0%   MLB: 1%   Comparables: Curtis Pride, Todd Dunwoody, Paul Sorrento, Jeff Key

Few gypsy curses carry more menace than to be prophesied a "Cubs outfield prospect." Those three simple words derailed the careers of Ryan Harvey, Corey Patterson, Brooks Kieschnick, and countless others before them; the last homegrown outfielder to hit 15 home runs or post a .270 EqA for the Cubs in consecutive seasons was Billy Williams. Jackson is hoping to break that hex, so far with encouraging results. A true center fielder with speed, power potential, and an unnerving propensity to whiff, the 2009 first-rounder out of Berkeley was viewed as more of a project than a finished college product, but Jackson signed quickly and showed surprising polish during his first swing through the low minors. He reduced his strikeout rate from "terrifying" to "mildly disturbing," played plus defense, drew walks, stole bases at a high success rate, and discovered his power stroke in Peoria. It was all the Cubs could have hoped for in his debut, and if Jackson continues to make consistent contact, he could be special.

Reed Johnson   OF   Bats: R   Throws: R   Height: 5' 10"   Weight: 180   Born: December 8, 1976   Age: 33

YEAR	TEAM	LVL	AGE	PA	R	2B	3B	HR	RBI	BB	SO	SB	CS	EqBRR	AVG	OBP	SLG	EqAVG	EqOBP	EqSLG	EqA	VORP	WARP	DEFENSE			
2007	TOR	MLB	30	307	31	13	2	2	14	16	56	4	2	-0.5	.236	.305	.320	.241	.307	.325	.225	-5.3	-0.8	56-LF	-1	8-RF	0
2008	CHN	MLB	31	374	52	21	0	6	50	19	68	5	6	-1.3	.303	.358	.420	.306	.358	.417	.268	12.6	2.0	63-CF	-2	14-LF	6
2009	CHN	MLB	32	186	23	10	2	4	22	13	27	2	1	0.2	.255	.330	.412	.259	.333	.416	.260	4.6	0.5	34-CF	-1	4-RF	0
2010	CHN	MLB	33	289	36	14	1	5	31	21	52	3	3	-0.2	.267	.342	.382	.264	.338	.381	.251	6.1	0.6	61-CF	-1		

Breakout: 12%   Improve: 44%   Collapse: 19%   Attrition: 16%   MLB: 92%   Comparables: Jerry Morales, Jim Landis, Billy Hatcher, Jason Michaels

Johnson continued his career-long assault on the sinister, pounding lefties to the tune of .324/.403/.500 last year, but he missed two months with a broken foot, during which time the Cubs grew intimate with cheaper date Sam Fuld, who is younger, faster, and better defensively. Johnson's got that gritty/gutty thing going for him, what with the high kneesocks and wall-banging outfield demeanor, and runs almost well enough to keep from being a major liability in center. A free agent bound for a pay cut, he'll be some other city's blue-collar favorite in 2010.

Derrek Lee — 1B

Bats: R   Throws: R   Height: 6' 5"   Weight: 245   Born: September 6, 1975   Age: 34

YEAR	TEAM	LVL	AGE	PA	R	2B	3B	HR	RBI	BB	SO	SB	CS	EqBRR	AVG	OBP	SLG	EqAVG	EqOBP	EqSLG	EqA	VORP	WARP	DEFENSE	
2007	CHN	MLB	31	650	91	43	1	22	82	71	114	6	5	-5.6	.317	.400	.513	.315	.399	.504	.305	39.3	3.9	143-1B	-3
2008	CHN	MLB	32	698	93	41	3	20	90	71	119	8	2	-2.6	.291	.361	.462	.292	.360	.459	.282	24.5	3.3	149-1B	5
2009	CHN	MLB	33	615	91	36	2	35	111	76	109	1	0	0.8	.306	.393	.579	.311	.394	.585	.323	46.3	4.4	137-1B	-6
2010	CHN	MLB	34	581	72	29	2	19	74	66	107	4	3	-1.1	.279	.365	.455	.279	.362	.454	.280	19.3	2.0	129-1B	-1

Breakout: 3%   Improve: 25%   Collapse: 21%   Attrition: 13%   MLB: 98%   Comparables: Joe Adcock, Boog Powell, Eric Karros, George Scott

After an offseason that saw many fans clamoring for a larger slice of Micah Hoffpauir at first base, D-Lee's power surge was one of the team's few pleasant surprises. Whether due to a changed approach or a rediscovered ability to square up on the ball with regularity, Lee raised his fly-ball rate to 45 percent—by far a career high—with many of those balls causing bleacher bums to drop their Old Styles and reach for a souvenir. Still an asset with the glove and still hitting with an undiminished batting eye, Lee should be the least of the team's worries going into the last year of his contract, even if a few more of those extra fly balls start dying at the track.

Hak-Ju Lee — SS

Bats: L   Throws: R   Height: 6' 2"   Weight: 170   Born: November 4, 1990   Age: 19

YEAR	TEAM	LVL	AGE	PA	R	2B	3B	HR	RBI	BB	SO	SB	CS	EqBRR	AVG	OBP	SLG	EqAVG	EqOBP	EqSLG	EqA	VORP	WARP	DEFENSE
2009	BOI	A-	18	304	56	14	2	2	33	31	50	25	8	0.9	.330	.399	.420	.258	.311	.324	.229	1.2	-1.1	60-SS -8
2010	CHN	MLB	19	449	47	20	2	3	35	39	98	12	5	0.7	.244	.309	.327	.247	.309	.326	.224	-0.4	-0.7	91-SS -6

Breakout: 22% Improve: 43% Collapse: 21% Attrition: 0%   MLB: 0%   Comparables: Mike White, Dion James, Eddie Williams, Tony Longmire

Young shortstops are often longer on promise than production, but Hak-Ju Lee's minor-league debut featured plenty of both. The consensus top prospect in the Northwest League displayed the plus speed and terrific defensive range scouts had expected, but Lee's lefty bat spoke volumes about his upside as well, as he hit for average and showed gap power while drawing enough walks to hit at the top of the order. Still a teenager, Lee is long and lean and might develop more power as he matures. Even if he doesn't, he should still be an asset both in the field and at the plate.

Aaron Miles — INF

Bats: S   Throws: R   Height: 5' 8"   Weight: 185   Born: December 15, 1976   Age: 33

YEAR	TEAM	LVL	AGE	PA	R	2B	3B	HR	RBI	BB	SO	SB	CS	EqBRR	AVG	OBP	SLG	EqAVG	EqOBP	EqSLG	EqA	VORP	WARP	DEFENSE		
2007	SLN	MLB	30	449	55	16	1	2	32	25	40	2	1	2.9	.290	.328	.348	.298	.336	.354	.246	8.7	-1.5	67-2B -12	34-SS -10
2008	SLN	MLB	31	408	49	15	2	4	31	23	37	3	3	0.3	.317	.355	.398	.331	.368	.412	.270	16.9	1.7	56-2B -4	19-SS 1
2009	IOW	AAA	32	91	8	4	0	0	8	2	14	1	2	0.0	.253	.267	.299	.239	.253	.273	.173	-4.6	-0.9	11-2B -1	6-3B 0
2009	CHN	MLB	32	170	17	7	1	0	5	8	21	3	0	1.5	.185	.224	.242	.189	.228	.245	.162	-11.3	-1.4	28-2B -1	5-SS -1
2010	OAK	MLB	33	337	43	15	1	3	25	22	42	3	2	0.7	.277	.325	.361	.280	.327	.365	.236	2.0	-0.2	68-2B -4	

Breakout: 13% Improve: 38% Collapse: 19% Attrition: 18%   MLB: 85%   Comparables: Jimmy Brown, Luis Castillo, Johnny Ray, Marty Barrett

One of the most ill-advised signings of the previous offseason, Miles is an aging middle infielder with no power or speed, a low walk rate, and the ability to play several positions at a slightly below-average level, all at the bargain price of two years and $4.9 million. While Miles may certainly again hit an empty .317, it's hard to picture him as anything other than a nonroster invitee once he stops living off Jim Hendry's largesse. Miles was traded to Oakland with Jake Fox; after the Bobby Crosby experience, the A's are already used to the sounds of silence from a utility-man's bat.

Aramis Ramirez — 3B

Bats: R   Throws: R   Height: 6' 1"   Weight: 215   Born: June 25, 1978   Age: 32

YEAR	TEAM	LVL	AGE	PA	R	2B	3B	HR	RBI	BB	SO	SB	CS	EqBRR	AVG	OBP	SLG	EqAVG	EqOBP	EqSLG	EqA	VORP	WARP	DEFENSE	
2007	CHN	MLB	29	558	72	35	4	26	101	43	66	0	0	-1.5	.310	.366	.549	.306	.362	.538	.300	37.3	5.6	122-3B	12
2008	CHN	MLB	30	645	97	44	1	27	111	74	94	2	2	-3.1	.289	.380	.518	.289	.377	.517	.300	44.4	4.3	142-3B	-4
2009	CHN	MLB	31	342	46	14	1	15	65	28	43	2	1	-2.7	.317	.389	.516	.322	.392	.528	.307	27.5	2.2	76-3B	-6
2010	CHN	MLB	32	499	65	26	2	19	82	49	71	2	1	-1.2	.289	.369	.485	.289	.368	.488	.290	29.1	3.2	112-3B	0

Breakout: 8%   Improve: 40%   Collapse: 19%   Attrition: 2%   MLB: 96%   Comparables: Don Money, Larry Parrish, Ken Boyer, Mike Lowell

A penchant for nagging injuries and a lack of great athleticism have always inspired questions as to how well Ramirez will age, but as he's moved into his 30s, his bat has remained remarkably consistent. A dislocated shoulder kept him out of the lineup for two months and provided the first long, sour note of a disappointing season at Wrigley, but he returned as strong as ever, crushing lefties and holding his own against righties. A-Ram has been the best hitter on the winningest Cubs teams since Leo the Lip spent his days scowling in the home dugout, yet he never seems to be counted among the Cub greats. Only 32, he'll continue to put up cookie-cutter seasons into the near future and change that perception.

Bobby Scales — UT

Bats: S   Throws: R   Height: 6' 0"   Weight: 185   Born: October 4, 1977   Age: 32

YEAR	TEAM	LVL	AGE	PA	R	2B	3B	HR	RBI	BB	SO	SB	CS	EqBRR	AVG	OBP	SLG	EqAVG	EqOBP	EqSLG	EqA	VORP	WARP	DEFENSE		
2007	PAW	AAA	29	499	64	28	8	11	57	50	94	14	3	2.8	.294	.373	.472	.266	.335	.415	.264	11.8	-0.3	31-1B -1	30-2B -6	
2008	IOW	AAA	30	457	94	20	2	15	59	59	90	7	5	2.0	.320	.415	.499	.269	.350	.394	.262	11.5	-0.1	63-2B -8	13-1B 0	
2009	IOW	AAA	31	360	41	15	1	5	39	46	61	8	8	-3.9	.278	.379	.382	.257	.344	.343	.244	0.6	0.4	39-3B -1	24-1B 1	
2009	CHN	MLB	31	138	15	8	2	3	15	11	32	0	0	0.5	.242	.312	.411	.242	.312	.411	.251	1.5	0.3	13-LF 1	8-2B 0	
2010	CHN	MLB	32	463	55	22	3	8	44	49	108	5	4	0.2	.251	.338	.377	.251	.335	.380	.250	6.8	0.7	65-3B -1		

Breakout: 17%   Improve: 43%   Collapse: 22%   Attrition: 16%   MLB: 10%   Comparables: Stuart Pederson, Eric Fox, Mike Brumley, Bill Selby

A switch-hitting multipositional reserve, Scales made his major-league debut last season at the age of 31, getting his first hit off Tim Lincecum. As a player, Scales gets on base (with a career minor-league OBP of .376), has developed decent power for a middle infielder, and can do Aaron Miles' job, whatever that might be, at a fraction of the cost, though it's not likely he'll be given that chance. As a human interest story, Scales reminds fans of the joy to be had in seeing someone's long-held dreams come true—and as a substitute high school teacher, Scales reminds you not to pull that same crap you tried on Mr. Chillsworth last week, because he's onto you and he's not gonna stand for it.

Alfonso Soriano — LF

Bats: R   Throws: R   Height: 6' 1"   Weight: 180   Born: January 7, 1976   Age: 34

YEAR	TEAM	LVL	AGE	PA	R	2B	3B	HR	RBI	BB	SO	SB	CS	EqBRR	AVG	OBP	SLG	EqAVG	EqOBP	EqSLG	EqA	VORP	WARP	DEFENSE		
2007	CHN	MLB	31	617	97	42	5	33	70	31	130	19	6	0.0	.299	.337	.560	.298	.337	.552	.292	36.3	7.4	119-LF 24	11-CF 3	
2008	CHN	MLB	32	503	76	27	0	29	75	43	103	19	3	-0.6	.280	.344	.532	.279	.340	.527	.291	28.3	3.9	104-LF 7		
2009	CHN	MLB	33	522	64	25	1	20	55	40	118	9	2	-1.6	.241	.303	.423	.243	.302	.429	.251	5.3	0.3	112-LF -2		
2010	CHN	MLB	34	483	59	22	2	18	50	40	113	10	5	-0.3	.252	.319	.433	.251	.317	.435	.256	8.2	1.4	103-LF 4		

Breakout: 7%   Improve: 25%   Collapse: 23%   Attrition: 26%   MLB: 98%   Comparables: George Foster, Hank Bauer, Ellis Burks, Gerald Williams

Accurate predictions are better than inaccurate ones, but bring little joy when they involve droughts, earthquakes, or self-inflicted injuries. Jim Hendry's signing of Soriano to an eight-year megacontract brought on a rousing chorus of "you'll shoot your eye out" from most analysts, and we've just witnessed the first painful ricochet. A sore knee that required late-season surgery may account for some portion of Soriano's decline below his 10th percentile PECOTA forecast for 2009, but a steady diet of breaking balls was at least as much to blame—only Ryan Howard saw fewer heaters among NL regulars. When Fonsie can't turn on fastballs and make hard contact, he's a player with no on-base skill, average speed and power, and an indifferent defensive approach highlighted by an apparent belief that Wrigley's outfield wall is covered with poison ivy. In return for that package, the Cubs get to write checks worth $90 million through 2014. Unless batting guru Rudy Jaramillo, the club's new hitting coach, can somehow game the "new trick/old dog" paradigm, the ending is going to be even worse than anyone thought.

Geovany Soto — C

Bats: R   Throws: R   Height: 6' 1"   Weight: 225   Born: January 20, 1983   Age: 27

YEAR	TEAM	LVL	AGE	PA	R	2B	3B	HR	RBI	BB	SO	SB	CS	EqBRR	AVG	OBP	SLG	EqAVG	EqOBP	EqSLG	EqA	VORP	WARP	DEFENSE	
2007	IOW	AAA	24	449	75	31	3	26	109	53	94	0	0	-2.9	.353	.424	.652	.315	.384	.567	.316	44.8	4.5	70-C -2	20-1B -4
2007	CHN	MLB	24	60	12	6	0	3	8	5	14	0	0	-0.3	.389	.433	.667	.389	.433	.648	.353	9.0	1.3	14-C 2	
2008	CHN	MLB	25	563	66	35	2	23	86	62	121	0	1	-3.9	.285	.364	.504	.286	.362	.499	.291	43.3	5.5	128-C 5	
2009	CHN	MLB	26	389	27	19	1	11	47	50	77	1	0	-1.8	.218	.321	.381	.221	.319	.387	.250	12.6	1.4	90-C 1	
2010	CHN	MLB	27	435	45	23	1	15	66	48	98	1	1	-1.4	.262	.348	.445	.261	.345	.450	.271	22.1	2.5	97-C 1	

Breakout: 13%   Improve: 38%   Collapse: 21%   Attrition: 17%   MLB: 92%   Comparables: Terry Steinbach, Bobby Estalella, Gus Triandos, Shanty Hogan

Following his magical 2008 Rookie of the Year campaign, Soto suffered an *annus horribilis* that included a positive drug test at the World Baseball Classic (WBC), an April shoulder injury that seemingly affected his power, a torn oblique that cost him July, and offensive production that sank near his 10th percentile PECOTA forecast. His off-season flirtation with the demon weed and a notably rounder physique led to grumblings about a lack of dedication—and while that may be true, it's not the whole story. The usual gremlin, BABIP, was hard at work, plummeting 80 points to a .251 mark that was fourth-lowest in the league. Soto's walk and strikeout rates actually improved, and while he swapped a few line drives for ground balls (possibly due to the injury), that would only account for a portion of his precipitous drop. A combination of better luck, good health, improved conditioning, and plus skills behind the dish make him an excellent bet to regain his place among the ranks of the league's best backstops.

Ryan Theriot SS Bats: R Throws: R Height: 5' 11" Weight: 175 Born: December 7, 1979 Age: 30

YEAR	TEAM	LVL	AGE	PA	R	2B	3B	HR	RBI	BB	SO	SB	CS	EqBRR	AVG	OBP	SLG	EqAVG	EqOBP	EqSLG	EqA	VORP	WARP		DEFENSE			
2007	CHN	MLB	27	597	80	30	2	3	45	49	50	28	4	1.3	.266	.326	.346	.264	.324	.342	.246	12.1	2.9		96-SS	7	26-2B	6
2008	CHN	MLB	28	661	85	19	4	1	38	73	58	22	13	-0.2	.307	.387	.359	.311	.389	.361	.268	31.1	3.0		141-SS	-4		
2009	CHN	MLB	29	677	81	20	5	7	54	51	93	21	10	-1.5	.284	.343	.369	.290	.346	.376	.256	24.2	3.5		146-SS	5		
2010	CHN	MLB	30	639	84	26	3	5	49	63	72	20	10	-0.1	.285	.359	.366	.283	.355	.365	.257	20.0	2.3		138-SS	1		

Breakout: 11% Improve: 37% Collapse: 12% Attrition: 9%   MLB: 100%   Comparables: Scott Fletcher, Steve Sax, Ted Sizemore, Johnny Temple

Theriot isn't a star, but continues to provide league-average shortstop production at a bargain price. However, knocking five home runs in May, more than he had in any previous whole season, may have been the worst thing that could have happened to him, as he started pulling the ball and hitting more fly balls, lowering his batting average, walk rate, and on-base percentage in the process. What he gave away at the plate he made up for with a surprisingly adept glove and better judgment on the basepaths, recording a career-high WARP as a result. His .266/.331/.303 second-half line is a cause for concern, and with true shortstops Starlin Castro and Hak-Ju Lee in the pipeline, his days on the left side are numbered, but for right now, Theriot isn't part of the problem.

Josh Vitters 3B Bats: R Throws: R Height: 6' 3" Weight: 200 Born: August 27, 1989 Age: 20

YEAR	TEAM	LVL	AGE	PA	R	2B	3B	HR	RBI	BB	SO	SB	CS	EqBRR	AVG	OBP	SLG	EqAVG	EqOBP	EqSLG	EqA	VORP	WARP		DEFENSE
2007	CUB	Rk	17	32	0	0	0	0	2	1	9	0	0	0.0	.067	.094	.067	.065	.091	.065	.000	-4.4	-1.1		4-3B -1
2008	BOI	A-	18	277	38	25	2	5	37	13	45	1	3	-5.6	.328	.365	.498	.271	.292	.402	.237	-0.2	-0.2		57-3B -1
2009	PEO	A	19	288	42	12	1	15	46	7	42	4	0	-2.1	.316	.351	.535	.290	.309	.475	.266	9.1	0.3		59-3B -7
2009	DAY	A+	19	196	21	7	2	3	22	5	23	2	1	0.0	.238	.260	.344	.211	.230	.311	.180	-10.6	-2.1		40-3B -6
2010	CHN	MLB	20	445	51	25	2	13	52	19	79	2	2	-1.8	.267	.303	.430	.266	.299	.433	.246	5.0	0.1		91-3B -4

Breakout: 44% Improve: 73% Collapse: 9% Attrition: 4%   MLB: 3%   Comparables: Pedro Roman, Jim Tatum, Ed Larregui, Alex Liddi

Two seasons since being tabbed as the third overall pick in the draft, the 20-year-old Vitters has accomplished a lot. Always known as a natural hitter, he blew through Peoria, exhibiting both burgeoning power and the ability to post a high average before suffering a hand injury and struggling in his High-A debut. A few questions remain, however, most notably his walk rate and ability to stay at the hot corner. He drew only 12 free passes all season, but scouts attribute that to his ability to hit anything thrown near him—Vitters' plate coverage rivals that of the Belgian waffle special at Arizona Charlie's. The Cubs remain convinced his future is at third base, but many scouts aren't so sure. There's little question Vitters will be a major-league hitter, but if he has to move across the diamond and doesn't draw a few more walks, a .300/.340/.500 line at first base will make him something less than an elite player.

PITCHERS

Chris Archer

Bats: R   Throws: R   Height: 6' 2"   Weight: 165   Born: September 26, 1988   Age: 21

YEAR	TEAM	LVL	AGE	W	L	SV	G	GS	IP	H	HR	BB	SO	GB%	BABIP	STUFF	WHIP	ERA	SIERA	DERA	EqH9	EqHR9	EqBB9	EqSO9	VORP	SN/WX
2007	IDN	Rk	18	1	7	0	12	11	52²	56	4	21	48	0%	.333	-17	1.46	5.64	3.92	12.03	13.7	2.7	4.9	4.5	-33.4	-1.63
2008	LKC	A	19	4	8	0	27	27	115¹	92	8	84	106	56%	.269	-8	1.53	4.29	4.47	7.10	9.9	1.9	8.4	5.0	-18.2	-1.42
2009	PEO	A	20	6	4	0	27	26	109	78	0	66	119	56%	.288	17	1.32	2.81	3.68	5.64	9.6	1.0	6.9	5.9	-1.4	0.34
2010	CHN	MLB	21	3	8	0	29	27	101¹	116	15	81	70	34%	.320	15	1.94	6.73	5.94	6.84	10.0	1.3	6.4	5.7	-15.0	1.53

Breakout: 22%   Improve: 63%   Collapse: 9%   Attrition: 12%   MLB: 4%   Comparables: Carl Hanselman, Brian Barber, Brian Edmondson, Ryan Tucker

Sent over from the Tribe as part of the Mark DeRosa haul, Archer took a big step forward in 2009 and could be a real steal. A projectable right-hander armed with a heavy fastball that Midwest League hitters continually pounded into the ground, Archer has clearly big-league stuff that helped him increase his strikeouts and prohibit any home runs all season. His sky-high walk rate shows that control is still a major problem, although he did improve on his 2008 Sally League numbers. The continuation of that trend will determine whether his eventual destination is the bullpen, but either way, Archer has the kind of stuff you can easily picture in Cubbie blue.

Mitch Atkins

Bats: R   Throws: R   Height: 6' 3"   Weight: 225   Born: October 1, 1985   Age: 24

YEAR	TEAM	LVL	AGE	W	L	SV	G	GS	IP	H	HR	BB	SO	GB%	BABIP	STUFF	WHIP	ERA	SIERA	DERA	EqH9	EqHR9	EqBB9	EqSO9	VORP	SN/WX
2007	DAY	A+	21	8	7	0	20	20	115	99	14	31	88	0%	.261	12	1.13	3.13	3.90	6.81	8.7	1.9	3.0	5.0	-15.6	0.00
2007	TEN	AA	21	1	1	0	7	4	26	30	5	11	18	40%	.301	-6	1.58	5.54	4.86	7.48	11.7	2.6	4.0	4.0	-5.4	-0.59
2008	TEN	AA	22	9	6	0	18	18	110	107	14	27	88	46%	.282	3	1.22	3.76	3.79	5.48	9.4	1.7	2.4	5.2	0.2	0.08
2008	IOW	AAA	22	8	1	0	10	10	54¹	48	11	23	44	32%	.243	-1	1.31	4.47	4.54	5.21	8.5	2.4	3.8	5.3	1.7	0.69
2009	IOW	AAA	23	8	12	0	27	27	146¹	164	26	52	127	41%	.314	-37	1.48	6.58	4.02	7.90	11.5	2.7	3.4	6.0	-37.1	-2.46
2009	CHN	MLB	23	0	0	0	2	0	2	1	0	0	0	39%	.143	-26	0.50	0.00	6.55	0.00	4.5	0.0	0.0	0.0	1.2	0.00
2010	CHN	MLB	24	5	10	0	30	25	131¹	148	23	56	87	26%	.308	-9	1.55	5.56	5.31	5.74	10.0	1.5	3.5	5.5	-3.5	1.32

Breakout: 18%   Improve: 57%   Collapse: 13%   Attrition: 19%   MLB: 9%   Comparables: Gary Knotts, Anthony Lerew, Michael Wuertz, Rick Bauer

The organization's 2008 Pitcher of the Year when he won 17 games across two levels, Atkins saw the wheels come off in his second spin through the PCL. His so-so stuff, featuring a low-90s fastball, curve, and change, has always left little margin for error, and as his ERA and home-run tallies will attest, he spent most of the year coloring outside the lines. Atkins may still turn up at the back end of a major-league rotation, but if he's in yours, you're probably not a contender.

Justin Berg

Bats: R   Throws: R   Height: 6' 3"   Weight: 230   Born: June 7, 1984   Age: 26

YEAR	TEAM	LVL	AGE	W	L	SV	G	GS	IP	H	HR	BB	SO	GB%	BABIP	STUFF	WHIP	ERA	SIERA	DERA	EqH9	EqHR9	EqBB9	EqSO9	VORP	SN/WX
2007	TEN	AA	23	7	7	0	27	26	140	157	4	69	69	63%	.323	-20	1.61	4.95	5.07	6.79	11.7	0.8	4.7	2.9	-18.3	-0.99
2008	TEN	AA	24	0	3	0	5	5	28¹	29	1	11	10	71%	.277	-17	1.41	3.49	4.93	5.14	9.6	0.6	3.5	1.9	1.1	0.10
2008	IOW	AAA	24	4	6	0	27	16	90¹	91	11	48	49	70%	.281	-30	1.54	5.68	4.69	6.86	9.7	1.6	4.7	3.4	-12.9	-0.57
2009	IOW	AAA	25	6	2	0	37	0	55²	41	2	29	35	73%	.235	-8	1.26	2.43	4.32	3.42	7.2	0.8	4.7	4.2	12.5	0.34
2009	CHN	MLB	25	0	0	0	11	0	12	10	0	1	7	60%	.263	5	0.92	0.75	3.86	0.77	7.7	0.0	0.8	4.6	6.1	0.07
2010	CHN	MLB	26	2	5	0	47	4	66¹	77	9	38	28	64%	.304	-28	1.74	6.14	5.53	6.42	10.4	1.2	4.7	3.5	-6.8	0.67

Breakout: 20%   Improve: 54%   Collapse: 16%   Attrition: 25%   MLB: 19%   Comparables: Carl Dale, Len Picota, Matt Peterson, Jim Johnson

A 43rd-round pick of the Yankees whose previous claim to fame was being traded straight up for Matt Lawton, Berg is a ground-ball machine who saw his big-league dreams come true last August when he worked 12 effective innings for the Cubs' pen. Pitching entirely in relief for the first time but still not missing many bats, Berg put up the best numbers of his career for an Iowa club that did its best to match him up against right-handed hitters—good thing, too, since he posted a 1.85 WHIP versus lefties. Add in a career 1.04 K/BB ratio in the upper minors, and Berg's future at best involves a one-way ticket to ROOGY-ville.

Esmailin Caridad

| | | | | | | | | | | | | Bats: R | | Throws: R | | Height: 5′ 10″ | | Weight: 195 | | Born: October 28, 1985 | | Age: 24 |

YEAR	TEAM	LVL	AGE	W	L	SV	G	GS	IP	H	HR	BB	SO	GB%	BABIP	STUFF	WHIP	ERA	SIERA	DERA	EqH9	EqHR9	EqBB9	EqSO9	VORP	SN/WX
2008	DAY	A+	22	6	4	0	14	13	69¹	64	3	17	38	0%	.279	-7	1.17	4.41	4.60	7.74	10.5	1.2	2.9	3.4	-15.3	0.04
2008	TEN	AA	22	7	3	0	14	14	82²	67	15	21	50	51%	.209	-2	1.06	3.16	4.41	4.04	7.7	2.2	2.3	3.8	13.2	1.05
2009	IOW	AAA	23	5	10	0	25	25	131²	139	17	46	114	37%	.307	-18	1.41	4.17	4.02	5.56	10.6	2.1	3.3	6.0	-0.9	0.24
2009	CHN	MLB	23	1	0	0	14	0	19¹	15	0	3	17	33%	.294	18	0.93	1.40	3.14	2.04	8.2	0.0	1.5	7.6	6.8	0.50
2010	CHN	MLB	24	6	9	0	35	24	135²	151	21	56	80	27%	.302	-10	1.52	5.22	5.56	5.44	9.9	1.4	3.4	4.9	0.9	1.97

Breakout: 7%   Improve: 38%   Collapse: 12%   Attrition: 6%   MLB: 41%   Comparables: Sam Lecure, Mike Bovee, Dax Winslett, Tim Meeks

Sometimes the journey is more interesting than the destination. Caridad's path to Wrigley, where he impressed in a late-season call-up, included six years in the Japanese development leagues prior to signing with the Cubs. Caridad doesn't have overwhelming stuff, using his low-90s heater to set up his more effective curveball and change, but so far, the diminutive righty has gotten more out of mixing pitches and changing speeds than you might expect. The organization likes his flexibility and could use him as a swingman and spot starter—think Sean Marshall, but with a release point on the other side of his body and a foot lower.

Chris Carpenter

| | | | | | | | | | | | | Bats: R | | Throws: R | | Height: 6′ 4″ | | Weight: 215 | | Born: December 26, 1985 | | Age: 24 |

YEAR	TEAM	LVL	AGE	W	L	SV	G	GS	IP	H	HR	BB	SO	GB%	BABIP	STUFF	WHIP	ERA	SIERA	DERA	EqH9	EqHR9	EqBB9	EqSO9	VORP	SN/WX
2008	BOI	A-	22	4	2	0	10	6	32	32	2	22	24	62%	.300	-22	1.69	4.22	4.69	8.31	11.0	2.1	6.2	3.6	-9.5	-0.73
2009	PEO	A	23	4	3	0	15	15	73²	55	4	33	60	59%	.251	-20	1.19	2.44	4.02	4.85	10.0	2.1	5.3	4.1	4.6	0.55
2009	DAY	A+	23	2	1	0	5	5	25	15	1	8	33	63%	.241	24	0.92	1.44	2.30	3.75	7.1	1.1	3.8	8.3	4.7	1.19
2009	TEN	AA	23	0	3	0	7	7	32	30	0	11	25	60%	.306	1	1.28	4.78	4.02	6.60	9.4	0.6	3.2	5.3	-3.8	-0.31
2010	CHN	MLB	24	4	7	0	27	24	103¹	114	15	59	62	60%	.302	-14	1.67	5.62	5.10	5.83	9.7	1.3	4.6	5.0	-3.8	1.91

Breakout: 19%   Improve: 43%   Collapse: 16%   Attrition: 9%   MLB: 4%   Comparables: Jaime Cocanower, Brian Bass, Carlos Fisher, Dennis Dove

No, not *that* Chris Carpenter, although there are superficial similarities: this Chris Carpenter also features electric stuff, a great pitcher's build, and an injury history penned by Tolstoy. A two-time survivor of elbow surgery, Carpenter flashes mid-90s heat, a usable slider, and improving command across three levels, but more importantly, he managed to stay healthy through 130 innings of rotation work last year. The Northsiders have seen more than their fair share of promising power arms get lost along the way, but there's lots to like here.

Andrew Cashner

| | | | | | | | | | | | | Bats: R | | Throws: R | | Height: 6′ 6″ | | Weight: 185 | | Born: September 11, 1986 | | Age: 23 |

YEAR	TEAM	LVL	AGE	W	L	SV	G	GS	IP	H	HR	BB	SO	GB%	BABIP	STUFF	WHIP	ERA	SIERA	DERA	EqH9	EqHR9	EqBB9	EqSO9	VORP	SN/WX
2008	BOI	A-	21	1	1	0	6	4	16¹	19	1	19	16	46%	.375	-4	2.33	4.96	5.48	9.30	13.8	2.4	10.2	4.8	-6.3	-0.42
2009	DAY	A+	22	0	0	0	12	12	42	31	1	15	34	51%	.250	6	1.10	1.50	3.96	2.75	8.0	0.9	4.1	4.8	12.0	1.06
2009	TEN	AA	22	3	4	0	12	12	58¹	45	0	27	41	56%	.253	11	1.23	3.39	4.56	5.46	7.5	0.5	4.1	4.5	0.2	0.29
2010	CHN	MLB	23	3	6	0	24	21	82	85	10	49	45	43%	.289	-9	1.63	5.43	5.71	5.62	9.2	1.1	4.9	4.5	-1.1	1.66

Breakout: 13%   Improve: 40%   Collapse: 25%   Attrition: 12%   MLB: 2%   Comparables: Cody Evans, Jason Fernandez, Rod Henderson, Myron Gardner

Graduating from college closer to professional starter is as likely a career change as moving from chartered accountancy to lion taming, but the Cubs' bet on Andrew Cashner just might pay off. With a fastball that sits in the mid-90s and occasionally touches 98, a frequently devastating slider, and an improving changeup, Cashner no doubt has the goods to top a major-league rotation. A strained oblique and understandable caution limited him to 100 innings in High-A and Double-A, leading to a dominating Arizona Fall League assignment that saw him improve his sometimes shaky command. Cashner has the highest upside of any Cubs arm since the Prior/Zambrano days, and he'll be one of the most watched prospects of the 2010 season.

Ryan Dempster

Bats: R   Throws: R   Height: 6' 2"   Weight: 215   Born: May 3, 1977   Age: 33

YEAR	TEAM	LVL	AGE	W	L	SV	G	GS	IP	H	HR	BB	SO	GB%	BABIP	STUFF	WHIP	ERA	SIERA	DERA	EqH9	EqHR9	EqBB9	EqSO9	VORP	SN/WX
2007	CHN	MLB	30	2	7	28	66	0	66²	59	8	30	55	59%	.271	1	1.33	4.72	4.11	4.48	8.1	0.8	3.7	7.0	7.4	2.67
2008	CHN	MLB	31	17	6	0	33	33	206²	174	14	76	187	52%	.280	31	1.21	2.96	3.70	3.21	8.0	0.5	2.9	7.3	51.2	6.60
2009	CHN	MLB	32	11	9	0	31	31	200	196	22	65	172	54%	.302	18	1.30	3.64	3.76	4.11	9.2	0.8	2.5	6.8	30.0	3.60
2010	CHN	MLB	33	9	10	11	52	26	167¹	165	18	64	133	53%	.303	9	1.37	4.21	4.11	4.41	8.8	1.0	3.2	6.6	20.2	3.08

Breakout: 4%   Improve: 38%   Collapse: 17%   Attrition: 10%   MLB: 97%   Comparables: Daisuke Miura, Tom Candiotti, Kevin Gross, Bob Bruce

There was some understandable hand-wringing when the Cubs inked Dempster to a four-year, $52 million deal after his first healthy and effective season in a major-league rotation since the Clinton administration, but so far, so good. The affable Canuck logged 200 innings (pausing only for a broken toe), saw small reductions in his strikeout and walk rates, let a few more fly balls leave the yard, lost a smidge of velocity, got more mileage out of his slider, and generally duplicated his 2008 production. There is likely to be some settling of contents as Dempster enters his mid-30s, but nothing he did this year raises any warning flags, and as he's currently outperforming his contract, some future lack of production has already been paid for. With Zambrano's health and headspace in question, Lilly entering his walk year with a fresh scar on his shoulder, and Wells's future an open question, Dempster is clearly the rotation's anchor, if not its ace. Who would have predicted this three years ago?

John Gaub

Bats: R   Throws: L   Height: 6' 2"   Weight: 200   Born: April 28, 1985   Age: 25

YEAR	TEAM	LVL	AGE	W	L	SV	G	GS	IP	H	HR	BB	SO	GB%	BABIP	STUFF	WHIP	ERA	SIERA	DERA	EqH9	EqHR9	EqBB9	EqSO9	VORP	SN/WX
2008	LKC	A	23	1	1	2	34	0	64	44	3	32	100	36%	.315	9	1.19	3.37	2.07	5.99	9.3	1.4	6.1	9.4	-3.1	-0.23
2009	TEN	AA	24	3	1	4	26	0	28²	19	3	17	40	41%	.262	13	1.26	2.83	2.85	4.72	7.5	1.6	5.2	9.8	2.4	0.48
2009	IOW	AAA	24	1	1	1	26	0	31¹	17	1	16	40	44%	.232	19	1.05	1.72	2.84	2.37	5.9	0.6	4.5	8.9	10.5	0.55
2010	CHN	MLB	25	2	4	1	37	0	57	58	7	36	53	41%	.322	-3	1.65	5.23	4.46	5.43	9.1	1.1	5.1	7.7	0.4	1.11

Breakout: 15%   Improve: 35%   Collapse: 19%   Attrition: 3%   MLB: 9%   Comparables: Al Osuna, Bobby Bevel, Eddie Camacho, Steve Mumaw

More swag from the DeRosa trade, lefty reliever John Gaub's eye-opening 2009 campaign saw the former University of Minnesota closer dominate in his first taste of the high minors. Gaub's offerings aren't overpowering, but a deceptive delivery and late movement have helped his low-90s fastball and plus slider give hitters fits, striking out 12.9 batters per nine innings in his short career. Effective against both righties and lefties, Gaub projects as more than a LOOGY, and even if he doesn't break camp with the big club, he should be toeing the rubber in Wrigley before the year is out.

Tom Gorzelanny

Bats: L   Throws: L   Height: 6' 2"   Weight: 210   Born: July 12, 1982   Age: 27

YEAR	TEAM	LVL	AGE	W	L	SV	G	GS	IP	H	HR	BB	SO	GB%	BABIP	STUFF	WHIP	ERA	SIERA	DERA	EqH9	EqHR9	EqBB9	EqSO9	VORP	SN/WX
2007	PIT	MLB	24	14	10	0	32	32	201²	214	18	68	135	45%	.305	13	1.40	3.88	4.56	3.79	8.6	0.8	2.7	5.3	38.6	5.31
2008	IND	AAA	25	3	1	0	7	7	35	28	1	4	33	48%	.281	18	0.91	2.06	2.75	3.65	8.1	0.5	1.4	5.9	6.9	0.91
2008	PIT	MLB	25	6	9	0	21	21	105¹	120	20	70	67	43%	.301	-25	1.80	6.66	5.54	6.47	9.9	1.8	5.3	4.8	-11.2	0.62
2009	IND	AAA	26	4	3	0	15	15	87	73	3	30	85	49%	.297	18	1.18	2.48	3.40	3.96	8.1	0.8	3.4	6.7	14.2	1.52
2009	PIT	MLB	26	3	1	0	9	0	8²	6	0	4	7	57%	.240	-9	1.15	5.19	4.15	5.50	6.0	0.0	3.0	6.0	0.0	0.27
2009	CHN	MLB	26	4	2	0	13	7	38¹	39	6	13	40	48%	.306	10	1.36	5.63	3.33	5.65	9.0	1.2	2.5	7.8	-0.7	1.02
2010	CHN	MLB	27	6	9	0	30	25	136	142	16	62	88	47%	.302	-1	1.50	4.73	4.87	4.96	9.2	1.1	3.7	5.4	8.2	2.12

Breakout: 9%   Improve: 44%   Collapse: 17%   Attrition: 23%   MLB: 84%   Comparables: Alex Kellner, Greg Mathews, Matt Young, Jim Abbott

A prominent data point in support of the Verducci Effect, Gorzelanny's breakthrough 2007 season came at a cost when the young left-hander made six September starts for a Pirates squad that was going nowhere. He tossed 34 ⅓ completely unnecessary innings and in quick succession lost his last three starts, a couple of ticks off his fastball, confidence in his slider, the health of his elbow, the ability to throw strikes, and a spot in the Pirates' rotation. His disastrous 2008 campaign led to Triple-A banishment, but time heals many wounds, and Gorzelanny was able to pick up the pieces in Indianapolis before moving to Chicago at midseason. His fastball is back in the low 90s, and his strikeout rate and a 3.47 SIERA (combined) hint at a pitcher whose stuff has returned. Penciled in as the fifth starter in 2010, Gorzelanny is a good bet to pitch better than that and, in the process, to reclaim the promising career he almost lost.

John Grabow

Bats: L   Throws: L   Height: 6' 2"   Weight: 205   Born: November 4, 1978   Age: 31

YEAR	TEAM	LVL	AGE	W	L	SV	G	GS	IP	H	HR	BB	SO	GB%	BABIP	STUFF	WHIP	ERA	SIERA	DERA	EqH9	EqHR9	EqBB9	EqSO9	VORP	SN/WX
2007	PIT	MLB	28	3	2	1	63	0	51^2	56	6	19	42	55%	.313	-3	1.45	4.53	4.09	4.33	8.8	1.0	2.9	6.3	6.9	0.75
2008	PIT	MLB	29	6	3	4	74	0	76	60	9	37	62	47%	.239	0	1.28	2.84	4.35	2.97	6.6	1.2	3.7	6.1	21.8	3.26
2009	PIT	MLB	30	3	0	0	45	0	47^1	43	4	28	41	42%	.291	-3	1.50	3.42	4.57	3.76	8.3	0.8	4.6	6.6	9.0	1.93
2009	CHN	MLB	30	0	0	0	30	0	25	19	1	12	16	49%	.240	-7	1.24	3.24	4.90	3.24	6.8	0.4	3.6	5.0	6.3	1.14
2010	CHN	MLB	31	3	4	1	62	0	61^1	59	7	30	44	47%	.290	-6	1.46	4.58	4.74	4.77	8.5	1.0	4.0	5.8	5.0	1.49

Breakout: 13% Improve: 34% Collapse: 32% Attrition: 18%   MLB: 93%   Comparables: Mike Stanton, Alan Embree, Craig Lefferts, Paul Lindblad

Perhaps the most anonymous member of last year's US entry in the WBC, Grabow is a perfectly serviceable lefty reliever, which is another way to of saying he is perfectly fungible—or at least he would be in a perfect world, but in this one, lefty relievers of a certain age develop a beguilingly attractive patina that turns big-market GMs into collectors who throw unreasonable amounts of money at them. Brought over from Pittsburgh along with Gorzelanny at midseason, re-upping the usually effective but rarely dominant Grabow became Jim Hendry's first off-season priority; the lefty was quickly re-signed to a two-year contract. He may be a safer bet as your second lefty than, say, Neal Cotts, but that doesn't mean it's money well spent.

Kevin Gregg

Bats: R   Throws: R   Height: 6' 6"   Weight: 240   Born: June 20, 1978   Age: 32

YEAR	TEAM	LVL	AGE	W	L	SV	G	GS	IP	H	HR	BB	SO	GB%	BABIP	STUFF	WHIP	ERA	SIERA	DERA	EqH9	EqHR9	EqBB9	EqSO9	VORP	SN/WX
2007	FLO	MLB	29	0	5	32	74	0	84	63	7	40	87	29%	.260	19	1.23	3.54	3.85	3.36	6.0	0.7	3.8	8.1	20.4	3.59
2008	FLO	MLB	30	7	8	29	72	0	68^2	51	3	37	58	49%	.247	7	1.28	3.41	4.38	3.83	6.7	0.4	4.2	6.4	12.9	1.14
2009	CHN	MLB	31	5	6	23	72	0	68^2	60	13	30	71	42%	.260	0	1.31	4.72	3.60	4.78	7.9	1.4	3.2	7.9	5.6	0.39
2010	CHN	MLB	32	4	4	17	65	0	64^1	57	7	32	57	39%	.286	3	1.37	4.11	4.19	4.27	7.8	1.0	4.0	7.5	8.8	0.99

Breakout: 17% Improve: 45% Collapse: 18% Attrition: 22%   MLB: 98%   Comparables: Ted Power, Kyle Farnsworth, Jay Witasick, Matt Karchner

Brought in from the Marlins as the proven closer every serious contender thinks it needs, Gregg had a season that was entirely undone by the gopher ball. His Wrigleyville walk and strikeout rates are similar to his breakout 2007 numbers in South Florida, but the home-run rate is a disaster. Surprisingly, 11 of those 13 jacks were surrendered to right-handed hitters, while lefties only slugged .314 against him—a reverse platoon split unique in his career. Gregg's velocity was also down a little, causing him to throw significantly more sliders to keep righties off his fastball. He also saw his fastball's movement go dead in a five-homer August—all of them to right-handers. Put all that together, and—presto!—you're no longer a proven closer. To be a reliever is to be the victim of small sample sizes, so there's no reason to think Gregg can't bounce back and put up solid numbers—any more than there was reason to expect him to produce dominant numbers in the first place.

Angel Guzman

Bats: R   Throws: R   Height: 6' 3"   Weight: 200   Born: December 14, 1981   Age: 28

YEAR	TEAM	LVL	AGE	W	L	SV	G	GS	IP	H	HR	BB	SO	GB%	BABIP	STUFF	WHIP	ERA	SIERA	DERA	EqH9	EqHR9	EqBB9	EqSO9	VORP	SN/WX
2007	CHN	MLB	25	0	1	0	12	3	30^1	32	2	9	26	57%	.337	13	1.35	3.56	3.70	3.30	10.0	0.6	2.5	7.5	7.0	0.39
2008	CHN	MLB	26	0	0	0	6	1	9^2	10	1	4	10	44%	.321	6	1.45	5.59	3.63	5.59	9.3	0.9	2.8	8.4	-0.1	0.17
2009	CHN	MLB	27	3	3	1	55	0	61	41	8	23	47	54%	.199	5	1.05	2.95	4.08	2.95	6.0	1.0	2.8	5.9	17.3	2.67
2010	CHN	MLB	28	3	3	0	46	0	55	50	5	21	43	53%	.286	4	1.29	3.86	4.13	4.04	8.1	0.9	3.1	6.5	8.9	1.19

Breakout: 14% Improve: 43% Collapse: 17% Attrition: 12%   MLB: 87%   Comparables: Elias Sosa, John Wasdin, Bob Grim, Dan Wheeler

Finally. For years, Guzman was the well-informed Cubs fan's version of Mr. Snuffleupagus—the minor-league pitching star who was always talked about but who disappeared before the crowd could see him. Having survived the arm surgery trifecta (labrum, forearm, and elbow) with his swing-and-miss stuff intact, Guzman spent the summer as Lou Piniella's least-heartburn-inducing bullpen option. His unsustainably low BABIP won't be repeated, but now that everyone has witnessed his mid-90s heat and nasty slider, you can expect Guzman to be a visible member of the late-inning cast. If Carlos Marmol struggles to find the plate, Guzman should be next in line to try to join the Big-C Closer Club.

Rich Harden

Bats: L   Throws: R   Height: 6' 1"   Weight: 195   Born: November 30, 1981   Age: 28

YEAR	TEAM	LVL	AGE	W	L	SV	G	GS	IP	H	HR	BB	SO	GB%	BABIP	STUFF	WHIP	ERA	SIERA	DERA	EqH9	EqHR9	EqBB9	EqSO9	VORP	SN/WX
2007	OAK	MLB	25	1	2	0	7	4	25²	18	3	11	27	47%	.254	22	1.13	2.45	3.25	2.63	6.8	1.1	3.8	9.0	7.7	1.08
2008	OAK	MLB	26	5	1	0	13	13	77	57	5	31	92	31%	.286	40	1.14	2.34	2.90	2.60	7.3	0.7	3.3	9.6	23.9	3.79
2008	CHN	MLB	26	5	1	0	12	12	71	39	6	30	89	32%	.210	45	0.97	1.77	2.72	2.27	5.4	0.6	3.3	9.3	25.6	3.19
2009	CHN	MLB	27	9	9	0	26	26	141	122	23	67	171	43%	.289	21	1.34	4.09	3.12	4.55	8.1	1.2	3.6	9.4	14.8	2.73
2010	TEX	MLB	28	8	8	0	23	23	141²	125	16	63	144	40%	.296	30	1.33	4.03	3.61	4.06	7.8	0.9	3.7	8.6	22.6	3.33

Breakout: 5%   Improve: 32%   Collapse: 26%   Attrition: 13%   MLB: 98%   Comparables: Marty Pattin, Darren Dreifort, Mark Portugal, Tom Sturdivant

For the second straight year, Harden used his devastating fastball/changeup combination to lead the majors in strikeout rate among pitchers with 140 or more innings pitched. The surprising part of that sentence isn't the strikeouts; it's the innings—never before has Harden pitched that much in successive seasons, and the Cubs deserve credit for keeping their fragile investment on the mound as much as they did. A few more home runs than usual and a career-high BABIP caused some ERA inflation, but Harden's stuff remains as dominating as ever. His ideal destination was as a contender that doesn't need many innings from him to reach the postseason, but that can afford to pay him like a full-time starter. The Rangers decided that might be them, banking on Mike Maddux's ability to coach and coax a big year from Harden on an incentive-laden $7.5 million year-plus-option deal.

Aaron Heilman

Bats: R   Throws: R   Height: 6' 5"   Weight: 225   Born: November 12, 1978   Age: 31

YEAR	TEAM	LVL	AGE	W	L	SV	G	GS	IP	H	HR	BB	SO	GB%	BABIP	STUFF	WHIP	ERA	SIERA	DERA	EqH9	EqHR9	EqBB9	EqSO9	VORP	SN/WX
2007	NYN	MLB	28	7	7	1	81	0	86	72	8	20	63	54%	.250	5	1.07	3.03	3.92	3.68	7.7	0.9	1.9	5.8	17.4	0.62
2008	NYN	MLB	29	3	8	3	78	0	76	75	10	46	80	49%	.308	-9	1.59	5.21	4.03	5.78	9.3	1.3	4.7	7.8	-2.4	-0.40
2009	CHN	MLB	30	4	4	1	70	0	72¹	68	9	34	65	47%	.289	0	1.41	4.11	4.07	4.10	8.7	1.0	3.7	7.1	11.1	-0.13
2010	ARI	MLB	31	3	4	0	68	0	66²	68	8	29	53	48%	.309	-4	1.46	4.59	4.29	4.79	9.0	1.0	3.6	6.7	5.3	0.02

Breakout: 14%   Improve: 45%   Collapse: 26%   Attrition: 15%   MLB: 93%   Comparables: Tyler Yates, Justin Speier, Paul Reuschel, Tim Worrell

The "Free Aaron Heilman Committee" (Aaron Heilman, Treasurer) must have been exultant when the veteran reliever was traded via Seattle to his native Chicagoland, but any dreams of his moving back into the rotation were dashed when Sean Marshall won the Cubs' fifth starter spot out of spring training. Heilman improved somewhat on his dismal 2008 numbers, but with a twist: while left-handed hitters bore the pitchforks and torches that drove him from New York, in 2009 it was righties who knocked him around. Arbitration eligible, Heilman was dealt to the D'backs in November for minor-leaguers Scott Maine and Ryne White. No doubt he'll continue to talk about moving back to the rotation, even on his fourth team, but the Snakes intend to let him continue to be what he has been—a mediocre relief pitcher with declining stuff.

Jay Jackson

Bats: R   Throws: R   Height: 6' 1"   Weight: 195   Born: October 27, 1987   Age: 22

YEAR	TEAM	LVL	AGE	W	L	SV	G	GS	IP	H	HR	BB	SO	GB%	BABIP	STUFF	WHIP	ERA	SIERA	DERA	EqH9	EqHR9	EqBB9	EqSO9	VORP	SN/WX
2008	PEO	A	20	2	2	0	6	1	24	22	3	5	37	45%	.388	20	1.12	3.00	1.26	4.81	13.3	3.7	3.2	9.6	1.5	0.07
2008	DAY	A+	20	2	0	0	4	3	17	11	0	7	21	0%	.282	15	1.06	1.59	2.66	5.58	8.2	0.6	4.1	8.2	-0.1	1.29
2009	DAY	A+	21	2	2	0	7	7	38¹	31	3	4	46	51%	.295	35	0.91	1.64	2.01	4.08	9.4	1.8	1.5	7.6	5.6	1.06
2009	TEN	AA	21	5	5	0	16	16	82²	73	7	39	77	44%	.287	13	1.35	3.70	3.98	4.67	9.0	1.5	4.2	6.3	7.3	0.53
2010	CHN	MLB	22	4	8	0	23	21	109¹	124	18	51	90	38%	.327	19	1.60	5.48	4.47	5.68	10.1	1.4	3.8	6.9	-2.1	2.45

Breakout: 8%   Improve: 30%   Collapse: 35%   Attrition: 6%   MLB: 5%   Comparables: Sean Watson, Brian Conroy, Josh Towers, Glenn Carter

Armed with a fastball that touches 95 and two usable breaking pitches, Jackson posted solid numbers in his first taste of the upper minors. Like most live-armed pitching prospects, he'll need to improve his command and consistency, and not just on the mound but in the clubhouse, as evidenced by a brief demotion to Daytona for breaking team rules. If Jackson can manage that, as well as overcome the "short right-hander" bias and improve on a 1.3 strikeout/walk ratio against lefties, he could become a mid-rotation starter—but that's a lot of ifs.

Ted Lilly

Bats: L   Throws: L   Height: 6' 1"   Weight: 190   Born: January 4, 1976   Age: 34

YEAR	TEAM	LVL	AGE	W	L	SV	G	GS	IP	H	HR	BB	SO	GB%	BABIP	STUFF	WHIP	ERA	SIERA	DERA	EqH9	EqHR9	EqBB9	EqSO9	VORP	SN/WX
2007	CHN	MLB	31	15	8	0	34	34	207	181	28	55	174	39%	.261	23	1.14	3.83	3.74	3.74	7.8	1.0	2.1	7.0	40.2	5.57
2008	CHN	MLB	32	17	9	0	34	34	204²	187	32	64	184	38%	.270	17	1.23	4.09	3.70	4.03	8.4	1.2	2.5	7.1	33.3	4.56
2009	CHN	MLB	33	12	9	0	27	27	177	151	22	36	151	36%	.261	25	1.06	3.10	3.47	3.36	7.8	0.9	1.5	6.7	41.5	5.13
2010	CHN	MLB	34	10	9	0	31	31	175	172	21	52	138	37%	.299	17	1.28	3.91	4.03	4.11	8.7	1.1	2.4	6.6	27.0	3.08

Breakout: 4%   Improve: 32%   Collapse: 9%   Attrition: 24%   MLB: 98%   Comparables: Jimmy Key, Bruce Hurst, Don Mossi, Jerry Koosman

Often overshadowed by his more famous or exuberant rotation mates, Lilly has quietly become the Cubs' best starter. His 5.1 SNLVAR paced the 2009 club, as does his total of 15.2 through the first three years of his Cubs career. An extreme fly-ball pitcher prone to the home run, the diminutive lefty has found success in Wrigley by keeping his walks down and his strikeouts up—essentially the Fergie Jenkins plan. Lilly's fastball never touches 90, but he throws it inside, and by mixing in a slider, a change, and a big looping curve, he can use it to break bats. Off-season shoulder surgery will delay the start of his upcoming walk year beyond Opening Day, but that shouldn't affect his production or the entertainment value that watching him work provides.

Carlos Marmol

Bats: R   Throws: R   Height: 6' 2"   Weight: 180   Born: October 14, 1982   Age: 27

YEAR	TEAM	LVL	AGE	W	L	SV	G	GS	IP	H	HR	BB	SO	GB%	BABIP	STUFF	WHIP	ERA	SIERA	DERA	EqH9	EqHR9	EqBB9	EqSO9	VORP	SN/WX
2007	IOW	AAA	24	4	1	0	8	7	41	30	4	12	48	35%	.257	22	1.02	3.95	2.75	4.28	6.6	1.3	2.6	7.9	5.6	0.57
2007	CHN	MLB	24	5	1	1	59	0	69¹	41	3	35	96	32%	.259	37	1.10	1.43	2.60	1.51	6.1	0.3	4.1	10.4	30.3	3.76
2008	CHN	MLB	25	2	4	7	82	0	87¹	40	10	41	114	32%	.169	30	0.93	2.68	2.66	3.04	4.6	0.8	3.7	9.6	23.9	4.98
2009	CHN	MLB	26	2	4	15	79	0	74	43	2	65	93	39%	.252	35	1.46	3.41	4.10	3.48	5.9	0.2	6.7	9.8	16.5	3.67
2010	CHN	MLB	27	5	4	6	75	0	80	61	7	46	82	37%	.270	12	1.33	3.85	3.97	3.99	6.8	0.8	4.6	8.6	13.5	2.73

Breakout: 7%   Improve: 26%   Collapse: 37%   Attrition: 14%   MLB: 96%   Comparables: Jeff Reardon, Steve Bedrosian, Cecilio Guante, Mark Littell

Carlos Marmol couldn't throw a ball straight if he tried, and while the ridiculous movement he generates keeps batters from putting balls in play, it creates baserunners in other ways. Marmol struggled to throw either his fastball or his slider over the plate, walking or plunking 23 percent of the batters he faced. He also struck out 27 percent, making his 2009 season one of the most contact-averse in history, but the spike in his walk rate reduced his Adjusted Runs Prevented total from 2008's league-leading 26.0 to a decidedly pedestrian 7.9. Finally handed the ninth-inning keys in mid-August after Kevin Gregg blew one too many saves, Marmol enters the season as the incumbent closer, but he will have to earn back the organization's confidence.

Sean Marshall

Bats: L   Throws: L   Height: 6' 7"   Weight: 220   Born: August 30, 1982   Age: 27

YEAR	TEAM	LVL	AGE	W	L	SV	G	GS	IP	H	HR	BB	SO	GB%	BABIP	STUFF	WHIP	ERA	SIERA	DERA	EqH9	EqHR9	EqBB9	EqSO9	VORP	SN/WX
2007	IOW	AAA	24	2	0	0	4	4	24²	17	2	8	15	51%	.208	3	1.01	1.82	4.51	2.59	5.9	1.1	3.0	4.1	7.9	0.78
2007	CHN	MLB	24	7	8	0	21	19	103¹	107	13	35	67	54%	.285	5	1.37	3.92	4.53	4.21	9.3	0.9	2.7	5.4	14.7	2.70
2008	IOW	AAA	25	1	1	0	7	7	31²	26	2	6	25	52%	.261	7	1.01	3.41	3.56	4.11	7.9	0.9	1.8	5.0	4.7	0.52
2008	CHN	MLB	25	3	5	1	34	7	65¹	60	9	23	58	48%	.276	6	1.27	3.86	3.79	3.74	8.4	1.0	2.8	7.1	12.7	1.59
2009	CHN	MLB	26	3	7	0	55	9	85¹	91	10	32	68	60%	.309	-3	1.44	4.32	4.04	4.41	9.7	0.9	2.9	6.2	10.2	1.79
2010	CHN	MLB	27	4	6	0	40	16	88¹	92	10	36	57	51%	.302	-3	1.44	4.47	4.68	4.74	9.2	1.0	3.4	5.4	7.5	1.60

Breakout: 6%   Improve: 32%   Collapse: 20%   Attrition: 20%   MLB: 84%   Comparables: Dennis Bennett, Steve Avery, Gary Lucas, John Candelaria

Marshall earned the fifth starter's role during spring training, but he pitched his way back to the bullpen by June. No matter—he put up solid numbers in relief and is carving out a nice career as a swingman/situational lefty/managerial security blanket. Marshall relies on a potpourri of breaking balls thrown at different speeds to help keep hitters off his upper-80s fastball, a deceptive mix aided by the incongruity of Marshall's solid 6-foot-7 build. Survival often requires adaptability, and Marshall has that in spades.

David Patton

Bats: R   Throws: R   Height: 6' 3"   Weight: 175   Born: May 18, 1984   Age: 26

YEAR	TEAM	LVL	AGE	W	L	SV	G	GS	IP	H	HR	BB	SO	GB%	BABIP	STUFF	WHIP	ERA	SIERA	DERA	EqH9	EqHR9	EqBB9	EqSO9	VORP	SN/WX
2007	MOD	A+	23	5	5	1	49	0	67²	73	6	34	59	47%	.333	-26	1.58	4.52	4.27	5.62	11.8	1.8	5.0	5.3	-0.8	-1.31
2008	MOD	A+	24	4	5	4	50	0	73²	74	8	28	87	52%	.342	-22	1.38	3.54	2.98	4.70	11.3	2.3	4.3	7.3	5.9	-0.18
2009	CHN	MLB	25	3	1	0	20	0	27²	31	4	19	23	64%	.307	-9	1.81	6.83	4.59	6.83	9.6	0.9	5.0	6.2	-4.3	-0.27
2010	CHN	MLB	26	2	5	1	41	1	54²	68	9	32	36	48%	.337	-23	1.83	6.37	5.17	6.67	11.3	1.5	4.8	5.6	-7.1	0.29

Breakout: 16%   Improve: 42%   Collapse: 22%   Attrition: 16%   MLB: 45%   Comparables: John Trautwein, Mario Iglesias, John Sutherland, Dean Weese

A Rule 5 draftee, Patton had knocked around the foothills of the Rockies system for five years, never getting past High-A Modesto. The Cubs obviously saw something in his fastball/slider combo that they liked, taking him north out of spring training and letting him throw some low-leverage innings before a case of roster-crunch groin kept his name on the 25-man but his body rehabbing in the bus leagues. After a few dozen nondescript big-league innings, Patton's fortune reads "Ask Again Later."

Jeff Samardzija

Bats: R   Throws: R   Height: 6' 5"   Weight: 220   Born: January 23, 1985   Age: 25

YEAR	TEAM	LVL	AGE	W	L	SV	G	GS	IP	H	HR	BB	SO	GB%	BABIP	STUFF	WHIP	ERA	SIERA	DERA	EqH9	EqHR9	EqBB9	EqSO9	VORP	SN/WX
2007	DAY	A+	22	3	8	0	24	20	107¹	142	8	35	45	0%	.344	-31	1.65	4.95	5.38	7.55	12.8	1.5	3.6	2.5	-22.5	-0.70
2007	TEN	AA	22	3	3	0	6	6	34¹	33	8	9	20	46%	.234	-8	1.22	3.41	4.63	4.77	9.8	2.7	2.5	3.3	2.7	0.06
2008	TEN	AA	23	3	5	0	16	15	76	71	6	42	44	37%	.273	-14	1.49	4.86	5.62	5.82	9.2	1.2	4.8	3.7	-2.6	-0.31
2008	IOW	AAA	23	4	1	0	6	6	37¹	32	5	16	40	54%	.300	16	1.29	3.13	3.28	3.57	9.0	1.9	4.0	7.7	7.3	0.69
2008	CHN	MLB	23	1	0	1	26	0	27²	24	0	15	25	48%	.289	6	1.41	2.28	4.27	3.81	7.9	0.0	4.1	7.0	5.3	0.37
2009	IOW	AAA	24	6	6	0	18	17	89	98	12	27	71	46%	.317	-23	1.40	4.35	4.00	5.35	11.2	2.2	2.9	5.6	1.4	0.39
2009	CHN	MLB	24	1	3	0	20	2	34²	46	7	15	21	54%	.333	-26	1.76	7.53	4.94	7.28	12.2	1.6	3.4	4.8	-6.7	-0.45
2010	CHN	MLB	25	4	8	0	44	17	110¹	129	16	53	64	32%	.315	-18	1.65	5.56	5.63	5.79	10.4	1.3	3.9	4.8	-3.5	1.13

Breakout: 15%   Improve: 61%   Collapse: 10%   Attrition: 19%   MLB: 62%   Comparables: Andrew Kown, Roger Mason, Ben Burlingame, Ross Ohlendorf

Remember that FM transmitter you bought to play your iPod in the car, the one you paid early-adopter prices for, the one you kept telling yourself was a good buy, even though static would bleed into your New Wave Ultramix twice per commute and you'd risk your life futzing with the tuner in search of a clear channel? That's Jeff Samardzija. Four years after the Cubs sprayed him with the money hose to keep the former Notre Dame wideout from working weekends in the fall, there's precious little to show he was worth the investment. Considering his loud but straight fastball, inconsistent secondary stuff, and unremarkable strikeout rate, no amount of squinting makes him resemble a major-league starter. Regardless, he will come to camp aiming for a rotation spot and will get a long look—because, you know, he was a good buy.

Jeff Stevens

Bats: R   Throws: R   Height: 6' 2"   Weight: 205   Born: September 5, 1983   Age: 26

YEAR	TEAM	LVL	AGE	W	L	SV	G	GS	IP	H	HR	BB	SO	GB%	BABIP	STUFF	WHIP	ERA	SIERA	DERA	EqH9	EqHR9	EqBB9	EqSO9	VORP	SN/WX
2007	KIN	A+	23	3	2	0	15	0	35	18	2	9	37	47%	.193	7	0.77	2.31	2.74	4.77	6.3	1.4	2.7	6.8	2.7	0.62
2007	AKR	AA	23	3	1	2	34	0	48¹	40	4	16	65	44%	.313	16	1.16	3.17	2.27	3.86	8.5	1.3	3.1	9.3	8.5	0.44
2008	AKR	AA	24	5	1	1	17	0	28²	19	2	11	37	53%	.270	16	1.05	2.51	2.47	3.17	7.3	1.0	3.7	9.0	7.0	0.91
2008	BUF	AAA	24	0	3	5	19	0	29²	19	3	16	44	33%	.271	21	1.18	3.94	2.41	4.61	7.0	1.3	5.1	9.8	2.8	-0.02
2009	IOW	AAA	25	1	3	2	42	0	57²	35	1	25	61	46%	.238	14	1.04	2.03	3.32	2.97	6.1	0.5	3.9	7.4	15.7	1.37
2009	CHN	MLB	25	1	0	0	11	0	12²	14	2	8	9	40%	.308	-12	1.74	7.11	5.29	6.57	10.2	1.5	5.1	5.8	-1.5	-0.08
2010	CHN	MLB	26	3	4	1	47	0	65	60	8	35	58	41%	.295	2	1.47	4.52	4.29	4.62	8.1	1.1	4.3	7.5	6.4	1.45

Breakout: 15%   Improve: 30%   Collapse: 31%   Attrition: 9%   MLB: 30%   Comparables: Gary Mielke, Jim Mann, Keith Fleming, Brian Wood

he most seasoned of the three arms shipped over from Cleveland in exchange for Mark DeRosa, Stevens was up-and-down in his major-league debut, but terrific in the Iowa pen. His low-90s fastball, curve, and slider aren't eye-popping pitches individually, but he manages to miss plenty of bats—he has a career rate of 11.3 K/9 in the upper minors. Forecasting young relievers can be a fool's errand, but this one definitely has a chance.

Randy Wells

Bats: R Throws: R Height: 6' 5" Weight: 235 Born: August 28, 1982 Age: 27

YEAR	TEAM	LVL	AGE	W	L	SV	G	GS	IP	H	HR	BB	SO	GB%	BABIP	STUFF	WHIP	ERA	SIERA	DERA	EqH9	EqHR9	EqBB9	EqSO9	VORP	SN/WX
2007	IOW	AAA	24	5	6	2	40	9	95^2	100	11	41	101	50%	.333	-10	1.47	4.52	3.52	5.33	9.4	1.4	3.9	7.2	1.7	-0.82
2008	IOW	AAA	25	10	4	0	27	19	118^2	127	15	34	102	47%	.310	-13	1.36	4.02	3.75	5.28	10.1	1.6	2.6	5.5	2.9	1.17
2008	CHN	MLB	25	0	0	0	3	0	4^1	0	0	2	1	62%	.000	-24	0.46	0.00	5.61	0.00	0.0	0.0	4.5	2.3	2.4	0.11
2009	IOW	AAA	26	3	0	0	5	5	26	19	1	7	21	60%	.250	11	1.00	2.77	3.56	3.47	7.3	0.7	2.6	5.5	5.6	0.58
2009	CHN	MLB	26	12	10	0	27	27	165^1	165	14	46	104	53%	.288	15	1.28	3.05	4.41	3.59	9.2	0.7	2.2	5.0	34.3	4.61
2010	CHN	MLB	27	7	10	0	38	24	149^2	159	19	56	102	49%	.305	1	1.43	4.59	4.51	4.82	9.4	1.1	3.0	5.7	11.3	2.31

Breakout: 7% Improve: 45% Collapse: 14% Attrition: 13% MLB: 63% Comparables: Nick Blackburn, Doug Brocail, Chien-Ming Wang, Rick Ramos

The happiest story of a gloomy season, Wells seemingly went from a former Rule 5 pick returned to sender to a Rookie of the Year candidate in the time it takes to say "gamer." The converted catcher stepped into the Cubs' rotation in early May and acted as if he were born there, allowing two or fewer runs in nine of his first 11 starts, and three or fewer in 77 percent of his starts on the year. Never overpowering, Wells mixes his sub-90 fastball, slider, and change with great aplomb, avoids free passes, and keeps the ball in the yard. There are a few caution flags going forward: his strikeout rate dropped, lefties gave him trouble, and the Verducci Effect is in play, though the team generally limited his pitch counts. Wells has continually exceeded expectations, and while it's hard to see him as an ace, it's even harder to picture him falling flat.

Carlos Zambrano

Bats: S Throws: R Height: 6' 5" Weight: 255 Born: June 1, 1981 Age: 29

YEAR	TEAM	LVL	AGE	W	L	SV	G	GS	IP	H	HR	BB	SO	GB%	BABIP	STUFF	WHIP	ERA	SIERA	DERA	EqH9	EqHR9	EqBB9	EqSO9	VORP	SN/WX
2007	CHN	MLB	26	18	13	0	34	34	216^1	187	23	101	177	54%	.269	20	1.33	3.95	4.25	3.88	8.0	0.8	3.8	6.9	38.1	5.75
2008	CHN	MLB	27	14	6	0	30	30	188^2	172	18	72	130	53%	.270	15	1.29	3.91	4.46	3.90	8.5	0.7	3.1	5.5	32.9	4.81
2009	CHN	MLB	28	9	7	0	28	28	169^1	155	10	78	152	52%	.300	25	1.38	3.77	4.02	4.05	8.6	0.4	3.6	7.1	26.9	3.87
2010	CHN	MLB	29	9	10	0	30	30	173^2	168	17	77	133	51%	.297	13	1.41	4.25	4.38	4.44	8.6	0.9	3.6	6.4	20.4	2.91

Breakout: 6% Improve: 47% Collapse: 11% Attrition: 14% MLB: 96% Comparables: Brad Penny, Brian Moehler, Freddy Garcia, Jeff Suppan

You can't accuse Big Z of being a snooze. When the Cubs win, Zambrano's shtick (which involves mound petulance, hairstyle experiments, batting-practice power displays, and unending chatter) is usually viewed as entertaining. When they lose, his antics are viewed as selfish, distracting, and detrimental to the ballclub. Whether he's a savvy self-promoter or a cotton-headed muggins is beside the point; mostly, he's a very good starter being paid like an ace who can't keep his ample posterior on the mound. This year, it wasn't a dead arm that cost him innings, but back spasms blamed on poor conditioning, and a hamstring injury suffered, in true Z fashion, while beating out a bunt single. When healthy, he was effective, trading a few fastballs for splitters, which led to more walks and more strikeouts, while a random drop in his home-run rate helped lower his ERA. To this point, and against seemingly high odds, Zambrano's arm has remained firmly attached to his body, but if he expects to keep this up into his 30s and through the end of his contract in 2013, Zambrano will need to take things a little more seriously.

LINEOUTS

Hitters

PLAYER	TEAM	LVL	AGE	PA	R	2B	3B	HR	RBI	BB	SO	SB-CS	EqBRR	AVG/OBP/SLG	EqAVG/EqOBP/EqSLG	EqA	VORP	WARP
OF J. Adduci*	TEN	AA	24	534	63	21	4	4	51	58	76	35-12	-2.1	.300/.377/.388	.275/.337/.356	.248	6.4	0.4
SS D. Barney	TEN	AA	23	284	30	12	0	3	32	23	33	5-1	0.0	.317/.368/.401	.302/.342/.384	.259	10.1	0.2
	IOW	AAA	23	229	25	12	1	0	17	13	32	4-1	3.2	.264/.304/.330	.257/.294/.313	.216	-1.2	-0.3
C W. Castillo	TEN	AA	22	339	27	16	0	11	39	15	71	1-0	-1.7	.232/.275/.386	.216/.251/.352	.205	-3.2	0.1
C S. Clevenger*	TEN	AA	23	89	12	4	3	1	10	10	8	0-0	0.9	.364/.443/.532	.338/.404/.500	.309	8.1	1.3
	IOW	AAA	23	251	21	12	1	0	26	15	31	4-3	-0.4	.265/.309/.326	.258/.296/.313	.214	-2.7	-0.8
CF B. Guyer	DAY	A+	23	305	40	16	3	2	32	24	34	23-2	0.0	.347/.407/.453	.307/.354/.405	.272	10.1	0.5
	TEN	AA	23	205	22	12	2	1	14	10	33	7-5	-2.8	.190/.236/.291	.177/.212/.276	.165	-12.6	-2.5
RF J. Ha	BOI	A-	18	258	31	15	0	2	37	6	31	5-5	-2.1	.242/.264/.327	.195/.209/.267	.150	-21.0	-4.1
MI D. LeMahieu	PEO	A	20	168	19	4	2	0	30	12	22	2-2	0.2	.316/.371/.368	.295/.335/.340	.240	1.8	0.2
C C. Robinson	IOW	AAA	25	331	37	22	3	2	48	13	44	9-3	1.0	.326/.345/.435	.314/.330/.417	.261	12.3	1.2
3B J. Rosa	PEO	A	21	169	17	13	0	4	32	9	27	2-1	-3.6	.301/.337/.464	.280/.308/.408	.249	0.7	0.0
	DAY	A+	21	260	16	19	2	2	33	11	65	2-1	0.0	.220/.254/.339	.198/.227/.304	.179	-17.9	-3.1
2B T. Thomas	TEN	AA	22	497	66	24	1	11	41	50	106	13-13	-3.2	.251/.341/.389	.238/.310/.369	.237	2.2	-1.5
2B L. Watkins*	BOI	A-	19	318	48	14	2	0	29	27	31	14-7	-1.5	.326/.389/.391	.259/.304/.307	.219	-4.7	-2.9

Canadian **James Adduci** wound up on the 40-man roster this winter; four years younger than Sam Fuld and equally equipped with the little man's suite of offensive talents, in time he may get to do unto Fuld what Fuld's done unto Reed Johnson. ⊘ **Darwin Barney** owns a good shortstop's glove, a bad shortstop's bat, and a phone likely to ring if the Cubs need some short-term middle infield help. ⊘ **Welington Castillo** has a solid defensive rep (he threw out 44 percent of stolen-base attempts) and some thunder in his bat, but a hacktastic approach is undermining his chances to be anything more than a backup catcher on a second-division team. ⊘ Continuing his pattern of mastering a league on the second try, **Steve Clevenger** raked in the Southern League only to hit an empty .265 in the PCL; on-base skills and a lefty bat mean he'll be given every opportunity to fulfill his backup catcher destiny. ⊘ Speedy center fielder **Brandon Guyer** has shown he can hit, slug, and post solid OBPs, but never all three at once. Improved synchronicity would make him a real prospect. ⊘ **Jae-Hoon Ha** was a big disappointment in Boise and will have to show more tools than "youth" if he wants to be more than a blip on anyone's prospect radar. ⊘ The Cubs enjoy middle infielders with a little Cajun spice, and LSU's **D. J. LeMahieu** certainly fits the bill, but to really stand out in an organization rife with middle infield prospects, he'll need to show the power his 6-foot-4 frame promises. ⊘ Canadian backstop **Chris Robinson** threw out just 19 percent of stolen-base attempts, but he hit a career-high .326 with a few doubles at Iowa; unless he develops more power or more patience, his updated batting profile will read "*mostly* harmless." ⊘ **Jovan Rosa** flunked his first High-A test, but the corner infielder again showed gap power back at Peoria. He'll need to make more consistent contact and launch a few over the fence if he wants to move up the prospect ladder. ⊘ **Tony Thomas** crushed lefties in his Double-A debut, flailed badly against righties, made outs on the basepaths, and struggled defensively. He'll go as far as his bat takes him, but there's still lots of work to do. ⊘ His glove is definitely a work in progress, but **Logan Watkins** makes contact, hits line drives, and uses his plus speed to great advantage, producing a high batting average, a solid OBP, and absolutely no power.

Pitchers

PLAYER	TEAM	LVL	AGE	W	L	SV	IP	H	HR	BB	SO	GB%	BABIP	STUFF	WHIP	ERA	SIERA	DERA	EqH9	EqHR9	EqBB9	EqSO9	VORP
N. Cotts*	IOW	AAA	29	1	1	1	12^{2}	7	1	6	11	40%	.188	-9	1.03	2.84	4.16	3.75	6.0	1.5	4.5	6.0	2.3
	CHN	MLB	29	0	2	0	11	14	3	9	9	63%	.333	-16	2.09	7.36	4.96	6.75	11.8	2.5	6.8	6.8	-1.5
R. Dolis	DAY	A+	0	3	9	0	99^{2}	78	4	53	75	57%	.263	-9	1.31	3.79	4.47	5.69	8.9	1.2	5.9	4.6	-1.9
C. Huseby	PEO	A	21	4	5	18	54	43	3	10	73	55%	.308	8	0.98	1.83	1.91	3.44	10.8	2.0	2.6	7.3	11.0
M. Mateo	TEN	AA	25	3	6	6	97^{1}	97	9	43	70	48%	.290	-24	1.44	4.07	4.65	5.25	9.8	1.5	3.9	4.7	2.6
J. Mathes*	IOW	AAA	27	12	8	0	129^{1}	150	11	14	51	63%	.303	-21	1.27	3.62	4.64	4.78	11.2	1.5	1.3	2.5	9.8
B. Parker	TEN	AA	24	0	0	3	12^{1}	8	0	8	19	69%	.348	11	1.30	1.46	2.47	2.45	8.2	0.8	5.7	10.6	3.7
	IOW	AAA	24	2	3	22	51	36	3	27	58	59%	.260	7	1.24	3.00	3.39	4.17	7.2	1.1	4.7	7.8	7.4

Neal Cotts has produced one good season out of eight and is now a 30-something coming back from Tommy John surgery, but lefties with his velocity almost always get another chance. ⊘ A stringy Dominican with a nifty sinker,

Rafael Dolis found Florida's heavy air and a tightly managed workload to his liking, but we'll see if he sticks to starting and survives the jump to Double-A now that he's on the 40-man. ⊘ Looking to redeem three years of injury and wildness, former bonus baby **Chris Huseby** shifted his 6-foot-7 frame to the Peoria bullpen and found instant success; if his improved command sticks, look out. ⊘ Warning: the intermittent presence of **Marcos Mateo** on the 40-man roster should in no way be construed as an endorsement of his ability to contribute at the major-league level. ⊘ Lefty **J. R. Mathes** posted a solid ERA with low walk and strikeout rates in his third season at Iowa; type that sentence into Babelfish, and it'll return "not a prospect." ⊘ Despite a name befitting a *Murder, She Wrote* character, **Blake Parker** owns a closer's repertoire, complete with high walk and strikeout rates. If things break right, he could be in the bullpen mix as soon as this year. ⊘ **Dae-Eun Rhee** achieved his 2009 goal of making it back to the mound after Tommy John surgery; 2010 will show us how his fastball/changeup combination will play.

MANAGER: LOU PINIELLA

YEAR	TEAM	W-L	Pythag +/−	Avg PC	100+ P	120+ P	QS	BQS	REL	REL w Zero R	IBB	Subs	PH	PH Avg	PH HR	SB2	CS2	SB3	CS3	SAC Att	SAC %	POS SAC	Squeeze	Swing	In Play
2007	CHN	85-77	-3	95.0	69	6	81	3	478	323	46	85	257	.208	6	78	24	8	9	64	75.0%	28	4	126	98
2008	CHN	97-64	-3	96.0	72	3	83	5	478	298	45	48	271	.198	5	66	27	20	7	109	59.6%	21	3	173	142
2009	CHN	83-78	-2	96.6	69	2	91	6	480	314	46	72	272	.222	5	49	30	7	2	95	68.4%	33	2	143	106

The 66-year-old Piniella is no longer described as "fiery," but he remains one of the game's better skippers. Beyond his occasional histrionics, Lou's talent has always been finding a way to mix and match the talent he is given, putting players in the best position for them to succeed. This season was no different, except more often than not in 2009 those players failed. Handed Kevin Gregg in the offseason, Piniella named him the closer over the objection of many fans, knowing full well that an effective Marmol would be more valuable pitching out of late-inning logjams and working multiple frames. Yet both players struggled, and Marmol was forced to take over ninth-inning duties. Alfonso Soriano's early-season slump gave Piniella the cover he needed to move the mercurial slugger down in the order where he belonged, yet Soriano never pulled out of his tailspin. Mark DeRosa's multi-positional flexibility, which Piniella had used to great advantage, was especially missed when A-Ram's injury forced Piniella to write the names Miles and Blanco into his lineup more often than he would have liked, and required him to buy into the mirage of Jake Fox as a big-league third baseman. With one year left on his contract, Piniella remains a good bet to optimize his team's chances to win, but managers can only manage—their players have to play.

Chicago White Sox

There's an old saying that if you're being chased by a bear, you don't have to run faster than the bear—you just have to run faster than your friends. Teams that buy this way of thinking can wind up limiting their possibilities to keeping up with the Joneses. Rather than build the best teams possible and expend the effort and money that it might take, it is somewhat easier to restrict your ambitions to exceeding only what your closest rivals have going for them, of settling for being the strongest of weaklings in a soft division. It's been easy to ascribe that mediocrity—of limited talent and equally limited ambition—to the AL Central, the division that seems to exist to provide a fourth dance partner every October, ready for first-round elimination. After all, the division has required a one-game playoff to pick that lucky loser in both of the last two seasons. Although the five battling bantams from the AL Central have delivered as many world championships in the last decade as has the AL West (one apiece), the perception is that picking the American League's last playoff team has all the thrills of a midget wrestling championship, just without the dignity. Between the good-fundamentals Twins that aren't good fundamentally, the defensively overhauled Tigers that weren't a great defensive team, and the Indians' seemingly innate capacity to underwhelm, this is a division gifted with its share of teams that take their modest ambitions for getting squashed in the postseason pretty seriously. We could thank the Royals for providing tragicomic relief.

Distinct from that muck are the vaulting ambitions to be found on Chicago's South Side, home of the division's sole world champ since the AL Central was invented, and where gambling for stakes high and low is a form of organizational management. It's that very ambition—to win, to try, *to take a chance*—about the White Sox that can really be very charming. The White Sox don't always win, and they won't. They may be living off of the glory of 2005, but they've definitely invested themselves in trying to win without availing themselves of the standard shabby, self-pitying bleats about how they're limited by geographic or economic determinism. In a sports world virtually wallpapered over in gray, polite men chiseling away at fractions of value and mouthing the easy assertions of sensible asset management, the Sox gamble at a chance for something more. In this age of paralysis by analysis and prim, perfunctory press conferences, bless them for their daring.

While Kenny Williams doesn't get books written about him—indeed, the idea that he was ever flayed in a best-seller for getting Miguel Olivo for Chad Bradford seems increasingly meaningless in retrospect*—the organization he guides has discrete strengths that allow it to keep making runs at post-season play. What these virtues lack in sabermetric sexiness they more than make up for in having enduring value. Some fads come and go: on the free-agent market, or what people will pay for, or what becomes the must-have element to win. In contrast, the Sox stick with a few classics and live *and* die by them: shop for blue-chip talent at red-tag prices, go for star power, and do things your own way.

---

*Through 2009, Olivo's career WARP total is 9.2, while Bradford's is 13.8. Olivo is four years younger and a good bet to match Bradford in career value when all is said and done. Add in position scarcity—it's easier to find a temporarily useful right-handed reliever than an employable catcher—and really, what *was* the fuss about?

WHITE SOX PROSPECTUS
2009 W-L: 79-83, 3rd in AL Central

Pythag	80-82	10th	**Ballpark:** U.S. Cellular Field (3-yr. PF: 1037). Tasty opportunities down both baselines, producing power for pull hitters
RS/G	4.5	12th	
RA/G	4.5	2nd	
EqA	.249	12th	**2009:** Sometimes a roll of the dice leaves you crapped out in-season and tapped out for free agents
EqBRR	-9.2	13th	
SNWP	.525	2nd	
WXRL	6.21	9th	**2010:** Becks at second and full-season doses from Peavy and Rios equals... victory?
FRAr	4.71	10th	
DE	.690	7th	
PADE	-0.40	6th	**Action Items:** A leadoff man, an outfielder, health and production from the newbies, nothing that upsets Ozzie too much
Salary	$96.1	6th	
Attend	2.28	6th	

Shopping for blue-chip prospects is one of the most basic, obvious things that every team will say it's in the business of doing—like Jell-O, there's always room. But why actually go to all the trouble of cooking up your own and putting it in the mold and hoping it sets in time? Why not go straight for premade? Whether as a matter of need forced by a run of bad drafts earlier in the decade or as a matter of heartfelt faith, Kenny Williams' crew follows this credo of kleptocracy assiduously, looking for the guys whose blue has faded and wangling a way to put them in pale hose. Consider the provenance of some of the key assets of the 2009 Sox:

Closer Bobby Jenks was a troubled triple-digit wild man the Angels drafted in the fifth round of 2000. Despairing he'd ever manage several forms of control, on and off the mound, they tried to pass him through waivers after the 2004 season; Kenny Williams knew a freebie with upside potential and snagged him off waivers before Jenks had even turned 24.

Matt Thornton was the 22nd overall selection of the 1998 draft, by the Mariners. It was a bad time to be in that organization—they could identify and slag young pitching talent better than anybody. Thornton tried starting for years, had Tommy John surgery, hurt his shoulder, and struggled through a wild, jacktastic 2005 season in the M's pen that disgusted Bill Bavasi enough to deal him for the immortal Joe Borchard after the year, in an exchange of perceived first-round washouts. Call it scouting or luck, but the Sox subsequently got the benefit of one of the hardest-throwing lefty relievers in the game. The Mariners got a guy who'd played quarterback at Stanford.

Gavin Floyd was the fourth overall pick of the 2001 draft, drafted behind Joe Mauer, Mark Prior, and Dewon Brazelton. He'll have more enduring value than two of those three, but very little of it for the Phillies' benefit—he posted a 6.73 ERA in 19 starts across fragments of three seasons before the Sox traded the last year of contractual control of Freddy Garcia for him and Gio Gonzalez after 2006. That the Chief blew out his arm shortly thereafter can be considered kismet; Floyd would make just 17 more starts in the minors before graduating to "The Show" to stay in his age-24 season.

A top Texas high-school phenom, John Danks was the ninth overall pick of 2003 draft, by the Rangers. He was nabbed by the Sox before his 22nd birthday after 2006 and before ever throwing a big-league pitch for the Rangers, in a package that boiled down to Danks for Brandon McCarthy. Danks never went back to the minors once the Sox got hold of him. This coup gave the Sox six years of contractual control with one of the best young power lefties in baseball.

Carlos Quentin was the 29th overall pick of that same 2003 draft, by the D'backs. He made his way up through the system and made a splashy second-half big-league debut in 2006, slugging .530, but he struggled in his sophomore campaign. GM Josh Byrnes responded by re-signing Eric Byrnes for three years and $30 million in August 2007, squeezing Quentin out of a future in Phoenix. Williams brought him to the South Side for young slugger Chris Carter, whom the Snakes promptly bundled into the package used to get Danny Haren from the A's. Everyone can feel pretty good about that exchange chain—except for the part involving Eric Byrnes.

Next up might be Tyler Flowers, a 2005 draft-and-follow by the Braves whose career's late start was made later still by a positive PED (performance-enhancing drug) test shortly after signing in 2006. He was the key to the four-player package received from the Braves for the enigmatic Javier Vazquez. Questions about Flowers' ability to remain behind the plate seem to have been answered in the affirmative, and while the Braves can feel good about two years of Vazquez, Flowers' career as a slugging backstop seems assured.

What comes through with all these examples is that Williams consistently got in on these guys early, before their upside came to the fore and they were potentially unattainable; as a result, his team will get to enjoy the best years of their careers. For all of the talk about stasis in the trade market, it's clear that Williams is more than happy to treat the rest of the industry as a warehouse stocked with players his club might be able to turn around. That was especially important during the mid-Aughties, when the club's draft record went flat as they went through a bad patch of risk-averse, low-upside college talent selections. But here again, the Sox broke with that previous marketwide standard of "genius" and went back to going for high-risk, high-reward upside with their first-round picks, selecting power lefty Aaron Poreda in 2007, fast-rising infielder Gordon Beckham in '08, and tool-time tyro Jared Mitchell from LSU in '09. Add in an aggressive push to get in on Cuban talent as it arrives, netting themselves a ready-now Alexei Ramirez and a ready-later Dayan Viciedo, and it's clear that the Sox aren't afraid of getting burned buying in a pool that has had more than its share of overhyped duds.

That same boldness characterizes the Sox's willingness to go after big-money veterans. Getting two years and two months of Jose Contreras for two months of Esteban Loaiza was a scouting coup in 2004. Before 2006, Williams got four years of Jim Thome at almost 50 percent off the sticker price for two years of Aaron

Rowand (and eventual Type A pick compensation), plus Gio Gonzalez (whom he got back in the subsequent Garcia deal) and Disappearin' Dan Haigwood. Thome delivered 14.1 WARP in almost four full seasons for the Sox; Rowand managed 4.8 for the Phillies. Not every risk works, of course; Williams took on the expensive end of Nick Swisher's long-term extension with the A's, accepting a $24.55 million four-year expense for a three-player package featuring the ubiquitous Gio Gonzalez. When Swisher melted in the face of high expectations, Williams didn't mope: he got the money back by flipping Swisher's last three years (at $21.05 million) to the Yankees for spare parts.

Seen through that lens, last year's big moves were examples of Williams' doubling down to see if he could squeeze in another title in a transition year. He already has a core of young talent he can win with in the years to come, and he had a number of established veterans, many from the '05 team, with their deals ending after '09 or '10. Rather than play it safe, he dealt four young arms—including Poreda—to the Padres to get the next three years of a then-injured Jake Peavy. While it wasn't certain that Peavy could help a club that was just a game and a half back of the Tigers at the July deadline, it was a move made to get a quality ace-level starter at $52 million through 2012. The price was steep, but one that might be worth it in light of what anyone might have to pay for this winter's best, and good luck getting an ace to accept a three-year deal. The downside is that Peavy is coming from pitcher-friendly Petco in the weaker league to the homer-happy Cell in the adults' circuit, but that's why they're called risks.

Bolder beyond the point of foolhardiness was the decision to put in a waiver claim on Alex Rios in early August. The Jays barely had to think twice about offloading nearly $60 million owed to Rios through 2014, but here again, for the Sox there's an element of upside with a former first-round draft pick (19th overall in '99). Though Rios is headed out of his anticipated peak seasons and his bat doesn't profile well in a corner, he can play in center, and there are no young center fielders just knocking around on the market you really want. Taken together, these seem like huge risks, especially given the expense. However, with so much young talent on the roster making below-market wages because of the club's rapacious willingness to make a deal, they're risks the Sox may prove able to afford.

Obviously, the new pair didn't generate a successful title defense down the stretch in '09. A 2-8 swing through Boston, New York, and Minnesota at the end of August killed off their bid. Rios wound up giving the South Side an instant double dose of outfield disap-

pointment—whether he was the roster zombie that bit Jermaine Dye or vice versa is really somewhat academic. Peavy didn't debut until the bitter end, after Floyd had to be shut down and when the season was already lost. In the end, the Sox were in no position to rally to catch the Tigers, let alone keep up with the Twins on their 16-4 closing run to earn and win last year's division-deciding one-game playoff. But with both Peavy and Rios added for the long haul and with the team's talent core more properly anchored by the futures of Beckham, John Danks, and Floyd, they're still equipped to make a run at the American League Central in 2010.

This brings us to the last quality that makes the Sox one of the game's most interesting teams. Taking their cue from Frank Sinatra, they do things their way. Dealing for young prospects down on their luck or playing for high stakes in trades can help propel you into the postseason, but it's also important to line up the support staff that makes these disparate sources of talent function. Time and again, the Sox have taken chances on players other people are convinced might break down physically, whether that's Thome, Konerko, or Dye in the lineup or Contreras, Garcia, or Bartolo Colon in the rotation, but they do so knowing they have the benefit of one of the best training staffs in baseball, headed up by Herm Schneider. Where many teams fret over setting player's positions lest they upset people, the Sox look at talent and potential challenges, whether it's making Alexei Ramirez a shortstop after breaking him in as a second baseman, moving Gordon Beckham to third out of need before returning him to second for '10, or working hard with Flowers to make him a better backstop.

The question now is whether the Sox will settle for the offense they have in place after trading away Thome in August and dropping their option on Dye. The need for a true leadoff hitter was apparent, but the market wasn't loaded with options, so Williams picked up Juan Pierre cheaply in what looks like a Podzilla Lite solution. Williams struck early, acquiring Mark Teahen—another former top draft pick—from the Royals for the reliably disappointing Josh Fields and replaceable scrapper Chris Getz, a move that will allow him to shift Beckham back to second. Teahen's slated for the hot corner, where his bat certainly profiles as employable, but the moves did little to add OBP to a lineup that needs it. In 2009, the Sox yet again ranked among MLB's leaders in the "Guillen Number," tying the Yankees for third in scoring 41 percent of their runs on homers and trailing only the Phillies (45.1 percent) and the Rangers (42.1 percent). But if they fail to find ways to add baserunners to the attack, the club may again have to follow that same power-reliant formula, as has been the case from 2005 onward.

Happily, while the team has retained its dependence on power hitting, the fulcrum of the club's near-term future remains its rotation—again, just as in its title year. Last season, the unit delivered a league-leading 94 quality starts through the first six innings, allowing three runs or less. That was without the benefit of Peavy or a full season of Garcia. Add those two to a unit that already had Floyd and John Danks lined up behind veteran workhorse Mark Buehrle, and you have no obviously skippable fifth starter.

Power in the lineup and top-quality starting pitching were two of the keys to that 2005 title, but the third element the Sox benefited from then and will need to reestablish in '10 is top-shelf defense, especially if the OBP issue isn't addressed and big leads become infrequent luxuries. That eventual up-the-middle combo of Flowers, Ramirez, Beckham, and Rios certainly will help keep nigh-mythical Ozzieball on the shelf, but

whether it turns into a good defensive combo is a different proposition. Omar Vizquel is being brought in to be an unofficial shortstop coach and infield Jedi master (CGI Yoda edition) for Ramirez's benefit, and they might shunt Rios to right and bring in a center fielder to net a clear defensive gain.

Taken in total, you've got a team that does things differently—but it's still a right way of going about it, one that other teams might want to study as busily as they do more modern models of management. Through the work of Kenny Williams and his front-office crew, the team has been rebuilt in relatively short order with the canny acquisition of other people's goodies and the odd high-yield recent draft pick or two. Whether Peavy and Rios prove to be the right talents in 2010 to put them over the top remains to be seen, but when you're a gambling team hooked on risk and used to rewards, sometimes, you really do just have to roll the dice. The Sox have reliably asserted that they play to win, but when you retool as quickly, quietly, and effectively with other people's talent as they have, you can afford to dare.

HITTERS

Cole Armstrong   C   Bats: L   Throws: R   Height: 6' 3"   Weight: 220   Born: August 24, 1983   Age: 26

YEAR	TEAM	LVL	AGE	PA	R	2B	3B	HR	RBI	BB	SO	SB	CS	EqBRR	AVG	OBP	SLG	EqAVG	EqOBP	EqSLG	EqA	VORP	WARP	DEFENSE
2007	WNS	A+	23	316	35	17	0	12	39	23	69	1	1	-3.6	.288	.342	.474	.246	.287	.386	.232	5.2	-0.2	69-C -7
2007	BIR	AA	23	79	2	6	0	1	12	3	20	0	0	-2.1	.239	.273	.366	.233	.266	.342	.215	0.3	0.3	20-C 2
2008	BIR	AA	24	234	27	17	0	6	31	10	31	0	1	-0.8	.252	.293	.413	.242	.274	.372	.220	0.4	-0.2	53-C -2
2008	CHR	AAA	24	145	12	12	0	2	17	5	27	0	0	-0.6	.275	.310	.406	.266	.301	.388	.238	3.1	0.5	36-C 1
2009	CHR	AAA	25	261	28	13	0	10	32	12	51	0	0	-1.2	.252	.287	.427	.239	.272	.397	.229	2.2	-0.2	61-C -4
2010	CHA	MLB	26	267	24	11	0	8	29	17	63	0	1	-1.1	.231	.285	.368	.235	.286	.365	.215	-1.3	-0.3	63-C -1

Breakout: 13% Improve: 38% Collapse: 27% Attrition: 21% MLB: 8% Comparables: Troy Rusk, Dwight Lowry, Jeff Smith, Ray Ortiz

Armstrong has done yeoman's work at the upper levels as a guy with power and good defense, but even with the advantage of swinging lefty, his bat is barely backup-worthy in the big leagues. This is his second season on the 40-man, and with Tyler Flowers in-system, he'll need to do something even just to stake a claim to backing up the big kid.

Gordon Beckham   3B   Bats: R   Throws: R   Height: 6' 0"   Weight: 185   Born: September 16, 1986   Age: 23

YEAR	TEAM	LVL	AGE	PA	R	2B	3B	HR	RBI	BB	SO	SB	CS	EqBRR	AVG	OBP	SLG	EqAVG	EqOBP	EqSLG	EqA	VORP	WARP	DEFENSE	
2008	KAN	A	21	63	11	2	0	3	8	5	7	0	1	-0.4	.310	.365	.500	.271	.317	.407	.244	1.4	0.2	13-SS 0	
2009	BIR	AA	22	166	23	17	0	4	22	14	24	1	0	0.9	.299	.366	.497	.305	.354	.503	.290	11.7	1.5	29-SS 1	4-2B 0
2009	CHA	MLB	22	430	58	28	1	14	63	41	65	7	4	1.5	.270	.347	.460	.271	.348	.452	.274	18.3	2.0	100-3B 0	
2010	CHA	MLB	23	513	67	28	1	16	69	48	83	7	4	0.8	.272	.348	.445	.273	.345	.437	.266	16.7	2.0	113-3B 1	

Breakout: 12% Improve: 42% Collapse: 14% Attrition: 1% MLB: 100% Comparables: Ron Hunt, Ken Keltner, Dale Berra, Bob Bailey

Beckham needed just 59 minor-league games to reach the big leagues, and it's not like he was rushed—he actually earned his call by hitting .326/.378/.526 between Double-A and Triple-A early in the year. While his performance in the big leagues was excellent for a rookie, keep in mind that he did that while basically learning a new position on the job. He'll do that again this year, as he's slated to move back into the middle infield to play second base, but his skill set works even better there, and his bat will be even more valuable up the middle. Players who move this quickly tend to be stars, and there's an excellent chance that when you visit The Cell three years from now, you'll be greeted by a sea of No. 15 jerseys.

Ramon Castro			C									Bats: R		Throws: R		Height: 6′ 3″		Weight: 260		Born: March 1, 1976			Age: 34
YEAR	TEAM	LVL	AGE	PA	R	2B	3B	HR	RBI	BB	SO	SB	CS	EqBRR	AVG	OBP	SLG	EqAVG	EqOBP	EqSLG	EqA	VORP	WARP	DEFENSE
2007	NYN	MLB	31	157	24	6	0	11	31	10	39	0	0	-3.0	.285	.331	.556	.301	.344	.587	.302	15.6	1.5	37-C	-2
2008	NYN	MLB	32	157	15	7	0	7	24	13	34	0	0	-0.8	.245	.312	.441	.252	.318	.462	.263	7.3	0.9	39-C	1
2009	NYN	MLB	33	87	5	5	0	3	13	8	16	0	0	-0.3	.253	.322	.430	.266	.333	.468	.267	4.3	1.0	21-C	4
2009	CHA	MLB	33	84	8	3	0	4	12	8	23	0	0	-0.5	.184	.262	.382	.184	.262	.382	.219	0.3	-0.1	25-C	-1
2010	CHA	MLB	34	208	22	8	0	10	33	19	51	0	0	-0.9	.245	.318	.446	.243	.313	.435	.254	6.9	0.8	53-C	1

Breakout: 11%   Improve: 35%   Collapse: 25%   Attrition: 17%   MLB: 92%   Comparables: Damian Miller, Ernie Lombardi, Tony Eusebio, Lance Parrish

For a while, we had a brief "Free Player X" movement for Castro, but that was based on one crazy year in 2007; one would think that the statheads who started such a movement would know something about small sample sizes. Castro is what he is, a career .233 hitter with a touch of power by the standards of his position—in other words, a backup catcher, and he's injury-prone, to boot. The only thing "free" attached to him is that he filed for free agency after the season, taking the first step on his journey to nomadic mid-30s backstopping.

Jordan Danks			CF									Bats: L		Throws: R		Height: 6′ 5″		Weight: 205		Born: August 7, 1986			Age: 23
YEAR	TEAM	LVL	AGE	PA	R	2B	3B	HR	RBI	BB	SO	SB	CS	EqBRR	AVG	OBP	SLG	EqAVG	EqOBP	EqSLG	EqA	VORP	WARP	DEFENSE
2008	KAN	A	21	45	10	4	1	2	7	4	14	1	0	-0.5	.325	.400	.625	.293	.370	.585	.312	4.1	0.5	10-CF	0
2009	WNS	A+	22	138	25	11	2	3	21	18	32	5	1	-0.4	.322	.409	.525	.273	.350	.463	.279	6.9	0.1	29-CF	-6
2009	BIR	AA	22	330	50	12	1	6	20	37	73	7	3	-0.3	.243	.337	.356	.241	.317	.350	.238	1.3	0.3	65-CF	0 4-LF 1
2010	CHA	MLB	23	383	55	17	2	10	32	37	100	4	2	-0.4	.240	.319	.386	.241	.319	.381	.239	3.5	0.1	82-CF	-2

Breakout: 17%   Improve: 42%   Collapse: 16%   Attrition: 2%   MLB: 5%   Comparables: Roy Johnson, Troy Neel, Brad Snyder, Kevin Garner

John's younger brother is a big, athletic outfielder who got off to a tremendous start at High-A, but pancaked once promoted to play at the upper levels. In his defense, he was dealing with hand and wrist issues during the second half of the year, and scouts still do like the tools; he's a solid center fielder with a bit of speed and a good approach. Nevertheless, the argument over Danks' power potential remains controversial. Like former White Sox prospect Ryan Sweeney, at 6-foot-4 and 210 pounds Danks *looks* like he should hit for power—but he doesn't. Boilerplate qualifiers like "Power is the last thing to come" apply, but sometimes, it never arrives. That one tool will be the difference between just a regular career for Danks or a very good one.

Jermaine Dye			RF									Bats: R		Throws: R		Height: 6′ 5″		Weight: 245		Born: January 28, 1974			Age: 36
YEAR	TEAM	LVL	AGE	PA	R	2B	3B	HR	RBI	BB	SO	SB	CS	EqBRR	AVG	OBP	SLG	EqAVG	EqOBP	EqSLG	EqA	VORP	WARP	DEFENSE
2007	CHA	MLB	33	561	68	34	0	28	78	45	107	2	1	-1.7	.254	.317	.486	.249	.314	.480	.268	14.4	0.8	130-RF	-7
2008	CHA	MLB	34	645	96	41	2	34	96	44	104	3	2	-1.4	.292	.344	.541	.289	.343	.539	.292	36.0	2.3	147-RF	-15
2009	CHA	MLB	35	574	78	19	1	27	81	64	108	0	2	-0.2	.250	.340	.453	.249	.338	.442	.268	15.4	1.3	126-RF	-4
2010	CHA	MLB	36	533	65	23	1	24	69	50	101	1	2	-0.5	.250	.326	.454	.250	.322	.441	.258	10.2	0.7	123-RF	-4

Breakout: 5%   Improve: 28%   Collapse: 23%   Attrition: 26%   MLB: 97%   Comparables: Dave Winfield, Dale Murphy, Dante Bichette, Joe Carter

In his five years with the White Sox, Dye averaged 33 home runs a year with an 869 OPS, but he finally began to look like an aging player in 2009. He's downright slow now, but it was the speed of his bat that was the real concern, as a player who once crushed fastballs was now consistently behind them. He hit a miserable .179/.293/.297 after the break, often looking like the guy at work who never gets enough sleep. Chicago paid him a $1 million buyout to avoid bringing him back for $12 million, so he'll be elsewhere in '10. Dye will probably chug along, slowly petering out over the next three years or so, but his decade-long run as one of those consistently good but rarely great players is over.

Josh Fields — 3B

Bats: R　Throws: R　Height: 6' 1"　Weight: 220　Born: December 14, 1982　Age: 27

YEAR	TEAM	LVL	AGE	PA	R	2B	3B	HR	RBI	BB	SO	SB	CS	EqBRR	AVG	OBP	SLG	EqAVG	EqOBP	EqSLG	EqA	VORP	WARP	DEFENSE				
2007	CHR	AAA	24	249	28	14	0	10	37	39	60	8	5	-1.7	.283	.394	.498	.269	.373	.476	.291	14.3	1.1	53-3B	-3	4-SS	-2	
2007	CHA	MLB	24	418	54	17	1	23	67	35	125	1	1	-2.6	.244	.308	.480	.240	.306	.480	.263	10.4	0.9	78-3B	0	20-LF	-2	
2008	CHR	AAA	25	318	41	15	3	10	35	37	98	8	2	0.0	.246	.341	.431	.233	.322	.398	.253	4.1	0.6	57-3B	1			
2008	CHA	MLB	25	35	3	1	0	0	2	3	17	0	0	0.1	.156	.229	.188	.156	.229	.188	.132	-3.1	-0.5	7-3B	-1			
2009	CHR	AAA	26	114	15	5	0	5	13	13	22	1	2	-1.1	.265	.357	.469	.253	.339	.444	.263	3.3	0.1	25-3B	-3			
2009	CHA	MLB	26	268	29	5	2	7	30	25	76	2	3	-2.0	.222	.301	.347	.226	.305	.351	.225	-4.7	-0.3	48-3B	3	11-1B	0	
2010	KCA	MLB	27	419	47	17	1	17	53	43	115	4	3	-1.2	.236	.317	.419	.231	.314	.406	.241	2.3	0.2	90-3B	-1			

Breakout: 5%　Improve: 37%　Collapse: 18%　Attrition: 7%　MLB: 70%　Comparables: Gabe Alvarez, Earl Snyder, Alan Cockrell, Jared Sandberg

When Fields hit 23 home runs in 2007, it seemed as if he might just have a shot at a legitimate big-league career, but he was passed by Beckham while failing to replicate that power at either the major- or minor-league level over the last two years. The Mark Teahen deal sent Fields to the Royals in November and might give him a new lease on life, but it's also upped the challenge significantly, as he'll probably be moved to first base or a corner outfield slot. It's a golden opportunity with a new organization, but as he's now 27 years old, it also might be the last one he gets.

Tyler Flowers — C

Bats: R　Throws: R　Height: 6' 4"　Weight: 245　Born: January 24, 1986　Age: 24

YEAR	TEAM	LVL	AGE	PA	R	2B	3B	HR	RBI	BB	SO	SB	CS	EqBRR	AVG	OBP	SLG	EqAVG	EqOBP	EqSLG	EqA	VORP	WARP	DEFENSE				
2007	ROM	A	21	445	65	34	2	12	70	49	74	3	4	-5.6	.298	.378	.488	.273	.337	.433	.266	9.3	-0.2	64-1B	-6	14-C	-5	
2008	MYR	A+	22	520	72	32	1	17	88	98	102	8	7	-6.4	.288	.427	.494	.269	.386	.440	.289	32.8	3.6	85-C	-3			
2009	BIR	AA	23	317	54	18	2	13	43	57	76	3	0	-0.8	.302	.445	.548	.284	.401	.525	.315	30.7	3.7	63-C	1			
2009	CHR	AAA	23	119	13	10	0	2	13	10	32	0	0	-1.2	.286	.364	.438	.283	.356	.434	.274	6.3	0.1	28-C	-6			
2009	CHA	MLB	23	20	3	1	0	0	0	3	8	0	0	0.2	.188	.350	.250	.188	.350	.250	.229	-0.2	-0.1	3-C	-1			
2010	CHA	MLB	24	465	58	22	2	15	60	62	114	2	2	-2.3	.258	.363	.438	.257	.357	.422	.271	23.4	2.2	86-C	-3			

Breakout: 15%　Improve: 34%　Collapse: 20%　Attrition: 7%　MLB: 22%　Comparables: Josh Phelps, Javier Ortiz, Kevin Brown, Josh Willingham

Flowers was the big prospect received from Atlanta in the Javier Vazquez deal, and we mean that literally, as he tips the scales at somewhere around 250 pounds. His power and patience at the plate are rare for a catcher, and he continued to show both in 2009, but the real story of the year was his improved defense, as the White Sox got him to do what the Braves never could—buy into being a catcher and working on it. Once seen as a surefire bet for first base, Flowers went from a nightmare behind the plate to a solidly average receiver, and his prospect status grew significantly because of it. He probably needs to wait out the last year of A. J. Pierzynski's contract, but he'll be an above-average big-leaguer in the end, making up for a low batting average and tons of strikeouts by hitting 20 home runs a year and drawing plenty of walks.

Chris Getz — 2B

Bats: L　Throws: R　Height: 6' 0"　Weight: 185　Born: August 30, 1983　Age: 26

YEAR	TEAM	LVL	AGE	PA	R	2B	3B	HR	RBI	BB	SO	SB	CS	EqBRR	AVG	OBP	SLG	EqAVG	EqOBP	EqSLG	EqA	VORP	WARP	DEFENSE				
2007	BIR	AA	23	319	40	10	2	3	29	36	30	13	7	0.9	.299	.382	.381	.290	.358	.374	.260	9.7	0.1	67-2B	-9			
2008	CHR	AAA	24	457	60	24	1	11	52	41	53	11	4	1.5	.302	.366	.448	.283	.344	.418	.266	17.0	2.2	61-2B	6	26-SS	-5	
2008	CHA	MLB	24	7	2	0	0	0	1	0	1	1	1	0.1	.286	.286	.286	.286	.286	.286	.196	-0.3	0.0	3-2B	0			
2009	CHA	MLB	25	415	49	18	4	2	31	30	54	25	2	6.2	.261	.324	.347	.259	.321	.340	.248	7.0	0.8	101-2B	0			
2010	KCA	MLB	26	394	50	19	3	6	37	38	50	12	4	1.5	.281	.355	.397	.268	.340	.377	.254	9.4	1.0	86-2B	-1			

Breakout: 5%　Improve: 33%　Collapse: 18%　Attrition: 12%　MLB: 76%　Comparables: Warren Morris, Brian Kowitz, Jeff Treadway, Jim Wawruck

It's a pretty simple equation for middle infielders: if you're an athlete, you play shortstop; if you're "scrappy," you play second base. Getz is about as scrappy as they come, and that probably causes him to be overrated; when you watch him play, it's hard not to like him. He's very good defensively around the bag and he did steal bases effectively, but at the plate, he's powerless and lacks the on-base skills to make up for it. A lot of Royals fans were thrilled to get him in the Mark Teahen trade, but at this point, Royals fans are impressed whenever they see a carbon-based life form in powder-blue pants.

Paul Konerko — 1B

Bats: R   Throws: R   Height: 6' 2"   Weight: 220   Born: March 5, 1976   Age: 34

YEAR	TEAM	LVL	AGE	PA	R	2B	3B	HR	RBI	BB	SO	SB	CS	EqBRR	AVG	OBP	SLG	EqAVG	EqOBP	EqSLG	EqA	VORP	WARP	DEFENSE
2007	CHA	MLB	31	636	71	34	0	31	90	78	102	0	1	-3.3	.259	.351	.490	.251	.346	.480	.280	21.5	2.5	138-1B 2
2008	CHA	MLB	32	514	59	19	1	22	62	65	80	2	0	-2.4	.240	.344	.438	.236	.344	.436	.272	11.4	1.5	111-1B 2
2009	CHA	MLB	33	621	75	30	1	28	88	58	89	1	0	-4.2	.277	.353	.489	.274	.350	.472	.283	15.9	1.9	128-1B 1
2010	CHA	MLB	34	542	59	21	1	23	72	70	91	1	1	-1.5	.253	.357	.451	.251	.350	.432	.272	13.0	1.5	117-1B 1

Breakout: 6%   Improve: 35%   Collapse: 20%   Attrition: 19%   MLB: 96%   Comparables: Cecil Fielder, Kevin Millar, Andy Thornton, Todd Zeile

While the five-year, $60 million contract that the White Sox gave Konerko following the club's 2005 World Series title is hardly offensive, it does seem like one of those deals that was more of a payment for what a player has done as opposed to what he's going to do. Konerko had just one very good year (2006) during the deal; otherwise, he's been your everyday, run-of-the-mill first baseman with a decent batting average, a decent number of walks, and some power. That combination of skills was enough for Konerko to rank eighth among American League first baseman in VORP. He's neither much of an asset nor a liability at this point. This year will probably be his last with the White Sox; possessing the dreaded "old player" skill set, the soon-to-be 34-year-old isn't going to get any better as he ages.

Mark Kotsay — 1B

Bats: L   Throws: L   Height: 6' 0"   Weight: 205   Born: December 2, 1975   Age: 34

YEAR	TEAM	LVL	AGE	PA	R	2B	3B	HR	RBI	BB	SO	SB	CS	EqBRR	AVG	OBP	SLG	EqAVG	EqOBP	EqSLG	EqA	VORP	WARP	DEFENSE		
2007	OAK	MLB	31	226	20	14	0	1	20	19	20	1	1	-0.5	.214	.279	.296	.215	.280	.298	.203	-6.0	-1.0	53-CF -3		
2008	ATL	MLB	32	345	39	17	3	6	37	25	34	2	3	-0.5	.289	.340	.418	.301	.351	.439	.268	12.3	0.8	78-CF -5		
2008	BOS	MLB	32	91	6	8	1	0	12	7	11	0	1	-0.3	.226	.286	.345	.226	.286	.333	.215	-2.9	-0.5	17-RF -1	4-1B -1
2009	BOS	MLB	33	79	4	2	0	1	5	4	12	2	1	0.1	.257	.291	.324	.257	.291	.324	.216	-2.9	-0.5	14-1B 1	3-CF -1
2009	CHA	MLB	33	127	12	7	0	3	18	11	9	1	1	-1.6	.292	.349	.434	.286	.341	.411	.267	1.5	0.1	18-1B -1	6-RF 0
2010	CHA	MLB	34	239	23	11	1	4	26	22	28	1	2	-0.5	.263	.330	.382	.263	.328	.371	.240	-2.5	-0.3	48-1B 0		

Breakout: 9%   Improve: 42%   Collapse: 20%   Attrition: 34%   MLB: 86%   Comparables: Scott Hatteberg, Amos Strunk, Doug Mientkiewicz, Willard Marshall

Once Chicago's extremely slim playoff chances finally slipped into oblivion, Ozzie Guillen suddenly spent a lot of time talking to the media about how much he wanted Kotsay back in 2010. Rarely does a bench player generate this much attention, and Kenny Williams wasted no time in giving Kotsay a $1.5 million deal, which is about what a reserve first baseman/outfielder with little power is worth these days. Kotsay should be a lesson to young players: most 34-year-olds with diminished skills would be lucky to have a big-league job, but Kotsay is such a great guy to have around that he's been able to extend his career by years—and his bank account by several million.

Brent Lillibridge — UT

Bats: R   Throws: R   Height: 5' 11"   Weight: 190   Born: September 18, 1983   Age: 26

YEAR	TEAM	LVL	AGE	PA	R	2B	3B	HR	RBI	BB	SO	SB	CS	EqBRR	AVG	OBP	SLG	EqAVG	EqOBP	EqSLG	EqA	VORP	WARP	DEFENSE		
2007	MIS	AA	23	237	31	8	3	3	17	20	60	14	7	0.3	.275	.355	.387	.255	.321	.354	.240	3.9	0.5	52-SS 0		
2007	RIC	AAA	23	355	47	14	2	10	41	20	59	28	5	8.6	.287	.331	.436	.277	.316	.434	.264	15.0	1.3	84-SS -4		
2008	RIC	AAA	24	403	46	18	7	4	39	33	90	23	7	0.3	.220	.294	.344	.209	.278	.326	.219	0.2	-0.1	91-SS -1		
2008	ATL	MLB	24	85	9	6	1	1	8	3	23	2	0	1.4	.200	.238	.338	.213	.250	.350	.206	-0.8	-0.3	21-SS -1		
2009	CHR	AAA	25	283	34	9	4	3	24	29	57	17	1	1.7	.252	.339	.358	.238	.321	.339	.245	5.9	0.2	48-SS -2	18-CF -2
2009	CHA	MLB	25	112	9	2	0	0	3	14	26	6	3	0.5	.158	.273	.179	.158	.273	.179	.178	-5.4	-0.6	16-2B 2	9-CF -1
2010	CHA	MLB	26	379	42	16	3	8	36	33	88	15	5	1.7	.229	.302	.363	.232	.302	.355	.229	1.4	0.0	86-SS -1		

Breakout: 9%   Improve: 46%   Collapse: 23%   Attrition: 23%   MLB: 88%   Comparables: Jeff Forney, George Hinshaw, Vince Holyfield, Mark Davis

The bloom is off the rose. When he was coming up through the minors, Lillibridge looked like a shortstop with patience, speed, and a little bit of pop, but his numbers at the upper levels slipped, and his performances in a series of major-league opportunities have been nothing short of disastrous. He's 26 now. Rarely do players his age suddenly turn things around, and the signing of Omar Vizquel sends a clear message as to how the White Sox feel about him.

Christian Marrero — 1B

Bats: L Throws: L Height: 6' 1" Weight: 185 Born: July 30, 1986 Age: 23

YEAR	TEAM	LVL	AGE	PA	R	2B	3B	HR	RBI	BB	SO	SB	CS	EqBRR	AVG	OBP	SLG	EqAVG	EqOBP	EqSLG	EqA	VORP	WARP	DEFENSE			
2007	GRF	Rk	20	313	53	21	6	12	63	36	43	3	2	1.9	.305	.383	.561	.245	.313	.426	.256	2.0	-0.1	50-1B	-3	6-LF	0
2008	KAN	A	21	505	53	29	5	10	61	54	89	11	5	-2.6	.273	.355	.431	.242	.312	.376	.243	-2.1	-0.9	65-RF	-2	55-1B	-3
2009	WNS	A+	22	241	35	15	1	7	34	11	44	2	3	-0.9	.314	.357	.482	.278	.311	.426	.250	1.7	0.1	30-LF	0	24-RF	-1
2009	BIR	AA	22	257	28	15	1	11	40	18	50	1	1	-2.8	.301	.340	.520	.292	.320	.502	.278	7.6	-0.1	33-1B	-9	27-RF	0
2010	CHA	MLB	23	459	49	23	3	14	60	39	102	3	2	-1.1	.249	.316	.421	.252	.317	.415	.247	3.1	0.2	93-RF	-1		

Breakout: 20% Improve: 44% Collapse: 18% Attrition: 6% MLB: 6% Comparables: Daniel Stryffeler, Mike Robertson, Jason Herrick, Tony Brown

Marrero has put up good numbers in the minors, but to make it as a first-base prospect, your numbers have to be better than good, and Marrero's attempts to cut it in the outfield came up short. To the positive, he's young and he made a clean jump to Double-A, but he needs to do more to avoid winding up as a Brandon Allen–style bargaining chip.

Jared Mitchell — CF

Bats: L Throws: L Height: 6' 0" Weight: 195 Born: October 13, 1988 Age: 21

YEAR	TEAM	LVL	AGE	PA	R	2B	3B	HR	RBI	BB	SO	SB	CS	EqBRR	AVG	OBP	SLG	EqAVG	EqOBP	EqSLG	EqA	VORP	WARP	DEFENSE	
2009	KAN	A	20	139	13	12	2	0	10	23	40	5	3	-1.1	.296	.417	.435	.235	.341	.336	.245	1.7	-0.6	34-CF	-7
2010	CHA	MLB	21	286	20	14	1	1	13	37	85	4	2	-1.1	.228	.328	.304	.230	.326	.307	.223	-1.9	-1.0	68-CF	-7

Breakout: 28% Improve: 53% Collapse: 16% Attrition: 0% MLB: 0% Comparables: Jonathan Slack, Shane Peterson, Tony Sheffield, Chris Testa

Mitchell saved his best for last; too bad it came after the draft. The 23rd overall pick last June, he might have made himself another million if the draft had been a week later, as he earned Most Outstanding Player honors at the College World Series right after his selection. No college player could match Mitchell's tools and athleticism, but for a guy coming off three years at a major program, he's still very raw, as he spent more time focusing on football than baseball during his first two years at LSU. The swing-and-miss in his game is a very real concern, but no player in the White Sox system can match his ceiling.

Brent Morel — 3B

Bats: R Throws: R Height: 6' 1" Weight: 220 Born: April 21, 1987 Age: 23

YEAR	TEAM	LVL	AGE	PA	R	2B	3B	HR	RBI	BB	SO	SB	CS	EqBRR	AVG	OBP	SLG	EqAVG	EqOBP	EqSLG	EqA	VORP	WARP	DEFENSE	
2008	GRF	Rk	21	71	11	0	2	0	3	6	7	7	0	2.9	.375	.437	.438	.299	.338	.328	.244	0.5	-0.4	15-3B	-3
2008	KAN	A	21	192	26	6	2	6	24	16	28	5	2	0.7	.297	.359	.459	.263	.318	.400	.251	2.7	-0.1	46-3B	-4
2009	WNS	A+	22	526	82	33	1	16	79	38	66	25	9	1.9	.281	.335	.453	.249	.295	.397	.241	3.3	0.7	122-3B	2
2010	CHA	MLB	23	483	59	22	2	13	55	37	78	11	4	0.8	.258	.318	.405	.260	.317	.400	.245	4.9	0.4	113-3B	-2

Breakout: 18% Improve: 55% Collapse: 18% Attrition: 4% MLB: 2% Comparables: Todd Brown, Mike Gulan, Clayton Byrne, Aarom Baldiris

Morel is not a high-profile prospect by any means, not as a third-rounder who has consistently put up good-but-not-great numbers in the minors. Similarly, nothing about his game blows anyone away, but he makes consistent hard contact with gap power—at times a bit more—he runs well for his size, and he plays a solid third base. The sum is greater than the parts because of how few weaknesses there are in his game, and while there is little impact potential, he looks like a future big-leaguer.

Jayson Nix — 2B

Bats: R Throws: R Height: 5' 11" Weight: 185 Born: August 26, 1982 Age: 27

YEAR	TEAM	LVL	AGE	PA	R	2B	3B	HR	RBI	BB	SO	SB	CS	EqBRR	AVG	OBP	SLG	EqAVG	EqOBP	EqSLG	EqA	VORP	WARP	DEFENSE			
2007	CSP	AAA	24	483	80	33	2	11	58	31	79	24	8	4.7	.292	.342	.451	.241	.289	.369	.232	0.3	1.7	103-2B	15	5-3B	-1
2008	COL	MLB	25	65	2	2	0	0	2	7	17	1	0	0.5	.125	.234	.161	.125	.234	.161	.130	-4.7	-0.1	16-2B	4		
2008	CSP	AAA	25	303	63	21	2	17	51	27	64	11	5	-0.6	.303	.373	.591	.248	.312	.456	.262	10.3	1.4	62-2B	1		
2009	CHA	MLB	26	290	36	11	0	12	32	28	64	10	2	-0.4	.224	.308	.408	.220	.304	.398	.250	5.0	1.8	46-2B	9	13-SS	-1
2010	CHA	MLB	27	352	46	16	1	11	39	31	76	10	4	0.7	.238	.313	.398	.239	.311	.387	.242	4.1	1.0	76-2B	5		

Breakout: 17% Improve: 41% Collapse: 18% Attrition: 14% MLB: 63% Comparables: Dan Uggla, Steve Lombardozzi, John Valle, Ryan Roberts

Picked up off Colorado's scrap heap, Nix was competing for the everyday second base job in spring training, but a strained quad and a solid performance by Chris Getz limited him to bench duty at five positions once he returned.

Nix has some value, as he's a defensive whiz at second, can play on the left side of the infield in a pinch, and beats up left-handers, nailing them for eight home runs in 135 PAs last year. As long as Nix's manager picks the right spots for him, he can help.

A. J. Pierzynski   C

Bats: L   Throws: R   Height: 6' 4"   Weight: 240   Born: December 30, 1976   Age: 33

YEAR	TEAM	LVL	AGE	PA	R	2B	3B	HR	RBI	BB	SO	SB	CS	EqBRR	AVG	OBP	SLG	EqAVG	EqOBP	EqSLG	EqA	VORP	WARP	DEFENSE
2007	CHA	MLB	30	509	54	24	0	14	50	25	66	1	1	-1.9	.263	.309	.403	.259	.305	.399	.243	15.1	2.2	119-C 4
2008	CHA	MLB	31	570	66	31	1	13	60	19	71	1	0	-1.6	.281	.312	.416	.280	.311	.415	.251	19.4	1.6	127-C -4
2009	CHA	MLB	32	535	57	22	1	13	49	24	52	1	1	-1.3	.300	.331	.425	.296	.327	.416	.257	20.4	1.9	124-C -3
2010	CHA	MLB	33	495	52	21	1	14	49	29	65	1	1	-0.8	.276	.324	.419	.277	.323	.411	.249	13.6	1.4	116-C 0

Breakout: 13% Improve: 40% Collapse: 17% Attrition: 18%   MLB: 97%   Comparables: Mike Scioscia, Terry Kennedy, Greg Myers, Johnny Edwards

Consistency and catching rarely go together, which is why a guy like Pierzynski might be more valuable than he looks. In the last six years, he's never slugged lower than .403 or higher than .436, while his on-base percentages have only ranged from .308 to .333. Just as importantly, he stays healthy, with no major time lost during the stretch, a pretty remarkably achievement for a catcher. In the end, he's an average offensive catcher with a below-average arm, but his teammates love him, and he could be back as Tyler Flowers' backup after his current contract expires at the end of the year.

Scott Podsednik   OF

Bats: L   Throws: L   Height: 6' 2"   Weight: 190   Born: March 18, 1976   Age: 34

YEAR	TEAM	LVL	AGE	PA	R	2B	3B	HR	RBI	BB	SO	SB	CS	EqBRR	AVG	OBP	SLG	EqAVG	EqOBP	EqSLG	EqA	VORP	WARP	DEFENSE
2007	CHA	MLB	31	235	30	13	4	2	11	13	36	12	5	0.4	.243	.299	.369	.244	.300	.371	.236	-1.7	0.4	52-LF 5
2008	COL	MLB	32	181	22	8	1	1	15	16	28	12	4	1.2	.253	.322	.333	.259	.328	.340	.240	-0.2	-0.2	23-CF -2 3-LF 0
2009	CHA	MLB	33	587	75	25	6	7	48	39	74	30	13	1.5	.304	.353	.412	.305	.353	.409	.265	16.8	2.6	69-LF 5 45-CF 1
2010	KCA	AL	34	472	52	21	4	5	36	39	65	18	10	-0.5	.278	.344	.378	.264	.327	.359	.242	0.8	0.2	92-LF 1

Breakout: 9% Improve: 31% Collapse: 24% Attrition: 20%   MLB: 93%   Comparables: Darryl Hamilton, Vada Pinson, Rusty Greer, Rick Miller

With their perpetual need for a center fielder and the injury to Carlos Quentin, the White Sox signed Podsednik after he was cut by the Rockies. While he's a bit short defensively up the middle, Podsednik had his best year at the plate since his 2003 rookie campaign. Despite a batting average on the empty side due to a lack of power and walks, he did an admirable job in filling what was a gaping hole in the club's roster. Signed by the Royals for top o' the order duties and perhaps center, he joins Getz and Fields among the aggrieved ex-Sox in KC.

Carlos Quentin   LF

Bats: R   Throws: R   Height: 6' 2"   Weight: 220   Born: August 28, 1982   Age: 27

YEAR	TEAM	LVL	AGE	PA	R	2B	3B	HR	RBI	BB	SO	SB	CS	EqBRR	AVG	OBP	SLG	EqAVG	EqOBP	EqSLG	EqA	VORP	WARP	DEFENSE
2007	TUC	AAA	24	135	30	12	1	4	27	9	14	0	1	-0.5	.348	.430	.574	.308	.385	.487	.298	7.8	0.7	26-RF -2
2007	ARI	MLB	24	263	29	16	0	5	31	18	54	2	2	-1.4	.214	.298	.349	.215	.295	.342	.227	-4.8	-0.1	65-RF 4
2008	CHA	MLB	25	569	96	26	1	36	100	66	80	7	3	2.7	.287	.394	.571	.286	.393	.572	.318	48.5	5.3	128-LF 0
2009	CHA	MLB	26	399	47	14	0	21	56	31	52	3	0	-0.3	.236	.323	.456	.231	.320	.440	.264	8.6	-0.1	85-LF -9
2010	CHA	MLB	27	531	80	22	1	26	88	56	78	4	3	0.1	.265	.371	.492	.263	.366	.477	.287	26.7	2.7	122-LF -2

Breakout: 15% Improve: 49% Collapse: 9% Attrition: 6%   MLB: 96%   Comparables: Richard Hidalgo, Conor Jackson, Juan Gonzalez, Wil Cordero

If 2008 was a dream season, '09 was nothing short of a nightmare for Quentin. After hitting seven home runs in his first 12 games, Quentin bruised a hand in late April and suffered a bruised heel in May, and that turned into plantar fasciitis, a condition that bothered him for the rest of the year and still had him seeing specialists after the season had ended. Oh, yes—his right knee was sore as well. While some pointed to Quentin's weight as an issue, the bigger concern is that this is a player in his late 20s with a number of debilitating health issues; what happened in '08 looks like a lightning/bottle situation that may never repeat itself.

Alexei Ramirez — SS

Bats: R Throws: R Height: 6' 3" Weight: 185 Born: September 22, 1981 Age: 28

YEAR	TEAM	LVL	AGE	PA	R	2B	3B	HR	RBI	BB	SO	SB	CS	EqBRR	AVG	OBP	SLG	EqAVG	EqOBP	EqSLG	EqA	VORP	WARP	DEFENSE			
2007	PdR	CBA	25	403	65	13	4	20	68	48	37	6	3	0.0	.335	.437	.574	.289	.357	.488	.287	16.4	2.5				
2008	CHA	MLB	26	509	65	22	2	21	77	18	61	13	9	-0.1	.290	.317	.475	.291	.319	.479	.265	20.0	2.0	114-2B	-2	7-CF	1
2009	CHA	MLB	27	606	71	14	1	15	68	49	66	14	5	0.6	.277	.333	.389	.276	.332	.382	.254	20.3	1.7	146-SS	-6		
2010	CHA	MLB	28	544	69	21	2	21	78	45	76	10	6	0.1	.272	.337	.448	.274	.334	.437	.262	20.3	2.0	98-SS	-2		

Breakout: 7% Improve: 38% Collapse: 14% Attrition: 12% MLB: 88% Comparables: Brendan Harris, Rich Aurilia, Dave Concepcion, Julio Lugo

A slow start made Ramirez a focal point for Chicago's early struggles, but he recovered, hitting at least .280 in every month after April and batting .286/.342/.405 from May on. Despite the disappointing season, he has above-average power for the position, and he worked hard with the coaching staff to develop a better approach—make that, "an approach," the result of which was a walk rate that nearly tripled for the Cuban. While Ramirez is 29 and not likely to experience much in the way of growth, he's still a valuable piece of the puzzle. Although the final numbers weren't up to the standard set in his rookie campaign, there's still plenty of room for optimism.

C. J. Retherford — 2B

Bats: R Throws: R Height: 5' 10" Weight: 190 Born: August 14, 1985 Age: 24

YEAR	TEAM	LVL	AGE	PA	R	2B	3B	HR	RBI	BB	SO	SB	CS	EqBRR	AVG	OBP	SLG	EqAVG	EqOBP	EqSLG	EqA	VORP	WARP	DEFENSE	
2007	GRF	Rk	21	299	53	30	4	13	48	24	45	2	3	-4.1	.318	.389	.613	.250	.303	.438	.253	4.4	0.6	61-3B	-1
2008	WNS	A+	22	519	66	28	1	16	71	37	78	11	6	-1.3	.295	.350	.464	.265	.308	.400	.247	5.2	0.0	118-3B	-5
2009	BIR	AA	23	526	70	46	4	10	76	30	70	3	3	-3.8	.297	.340	.473	.295	.327	.469	.271	21.7	2.9	120-2B	2
2010	CHA	MLB	24	483	56	27	2	13	57	33	87	3	2	-0.9	.259	.314	.416	.261	.313	.408	.244	6.6	0.8	111-2B	1

Breakout: 12% Improve: 27% Collapse: 27% Attrition: 11% MLB: 9% Comparables: Justin Turner, Charles Poe, Adam Riggs, Keith Williams

Undrafted out of college, Retherford kept getting moved up one level by the White Sox every year, and he keeps hitting, to the point where scouts now see him as a legitimate prospect. Sure, he's small and he's slow, but he's a natural, instinctual hitter who tied for the minor-league lead with 46 doubles. He can punish mistakes, including a moon shot that gave his team the lead for good in the Arizona Fall League title game. All skills and zero tools could be enough for at least a utility career and maybe even a few years as a second-division starter.

Alex Rios — CF

Bats: R Throws: R Height: 6' 5" Weight: 215 Born: February 18, 1981 Age: 29

YEAR	TEAM	LVL	AGE	PA	R	2B	3B	HR	RBI	BB	SO	SB	CS	EqBRR	AVG	OBP	SLG	EqAVG	EqOBP	EqSLG	EqA	VORP	WARP	DEFENSE			
2007	TOR	MLB	26	711	114	43	7	24	85	55	103	17	4	2.0	.297	.354	.498	.296	.354	.502	.291	38.4	5.6	140-RF	10	18-CF	1
2008	TOR	MLB	27	686	91	47	8	15	79	44	112	32	8	1.5	.291	.337	.461	.299	.344	.476	.281	32.2	4.1	92-RF	5	59-CF	0
2009	TOR	MLB	28	479	52	25	2	14	62	31	78	19	3	0.4	.264	.317	.427	.272	.324	.433	.267	13.2	1.9	102-RF	1	7-CF	2
2009	CHA	MLB	28	154	11	6	0	3	9	6	29	5	2	-0.3	.199	.229	.301	.199	.229	.295	.186	-7.3	-1.1	32-CF	-3	8-RF	0
2010	CHA	MLB	29	626	82	34	4	20	74	52	105	18	7	0.6	.274	.339	.451	.275	.337	.444	.265	16.7	2.2	144-RF	3		

Breakout: 6% Improve: 35% Collapse: 8% Attrition: 6% MLB: 97% Comparables: Juan Encarnacion, Joe Carter, Moises Alou, Tom Brunansky

As surprising as the Jake Peavy trade was, Kenny Williams' claiming Rios in August wins the award for the most shocking transaction of 2009. With Williams hoping that the talented outfielder simply needed a change of scenery to get things going again, Rios responded by not even getting his batting average above the Mendoza line, and the club is stuck with him for six more years at a cost of more than $80 million. Rios is young enough to figure things out again, but the most galling aspect of his performance might not be the stat line; it's the gaggle of scouts who see a player who just doesn't give a damn.

Dayan Viciedo — 3B

Bats: R Throws: R Height: 6' 0" Weight: 225 Born: March 10, 1989 Age: 21

YEAR	TEAM	LVL	AGE	PA	R	2B	3B	HR	RBI	BB	SO	SB	CS	EqBRR	AVG	OBP	SLG	EqAVG	EqOBP	EqSLG	EqA	VORP	WARP	DEFENSE	
2007	VCI	CBA	18	369	39	14	3	8	35	49	52	2	4	0.0	.252	.377	.399	.209	.292	.331	.220	-11.8	-1.8		
2008	VCI	CBA	19	214	41	5	1	10	38	28	27	2	1	0.0	.294	.403	.503	.230	.305	.382	.240	-2.6	-0.4		
2009	BIR	AA	20	540	72	20	0	12	78	23	89	5	2	-1.8	.280	.317	.391	.280	.307	.391	.243	3.7	0.0	114-3B	-4
2010	CHA	MLB	21	503	64	19	2	15	67	40	106	3	2	-0.4	.253	.320	.403	.254	.317	.393	.243	4.1	0.4	52-3B	-1

Breakout: 32% Improve: 58% Collapse: 7% Attrition: 5% MLB: 7% Comparables: Edwin Encarnacion, Tom Evans, Paul Konerko, Jim Bishop

One of the biggest prizes of last year's international crop, this Cuban defector won a $10 million deal as a teenager, and he responded with a nondescript showing at Double-A. It's easy to see what the White Sox liked about Viciedo, as his bat speed is exceptional, he has plenty of raw power, and his arm is strong, but all of those things were covered in several layers of fat, as it seems that Viciedo's favorite thing about not living in Cuba is easy access to milkshakes and cheeseburgers. Cubans often struggle both on and off the field during their first year in los Estados Unidos, and the White Sox are hoping that's the case here.

Dewayne Wise CF Bats: L Throws: L Height: 6' 1" Weight: 195 Born: February 24, 1978 Age: 32

YEAR	TEAM	LVL	AGE	PA	R	2B	3B	HR	RBI	BB	SO	SB	CS	EqBRR	AVG	OBP	SLG	EqAVG	EqOBP	EqSLG	EqA	VORP	WARP	DEFENSE		
2007	LOU	AAA	29	222	34	11	7	7	20	8	56	8	2	1.2	.251	.284	.473	.233	.260	.419	.231	-1.4	-0.3	29-CF	0	15-RF -1
2008	CHR	AAA	30	222	39	14	3	9	23	22	32	15	7	-0.9	.319	.402	.565	.286	.362	.485	.286	11.0	1.7	34-RF	4	11-CF -1
2008	CHA	MLB	30	143	20	4	2	6	18	8	32	9	0	3.0	.248	.293	.450	.242	.288	.445	.264	3.8	0.8	16-CF	2	15-LF 0
2009	CHA	MLB	31	153	17	8	3	2	11	3	27	4	5	-1.1	.225	.262	.366	.234	.270	.369	.212	-4.6	-0.1	24-CF	1	16-RF 3
2010	PHI	MLB	32	275	34	14	4	7	23	19	62	7	4	0.4	.245	.305	.412	.248	.305	.419	.245	4.4	0.6	56-CF	1	

Breakout: 9% Improve: 36% Collapse: 16% Attrition: 23% MLB: 57% Comparables: Eric Bullock, Gary Varsho, David Newhan, Mitchell Page

On July 23rd, Wise made the catch of the year. It wasn't the pure best catch you'll ever see, but it involved a long run, a bang into a wall, and a juggle. More important was the circumstance, as it maintained Mark Buehrle's perfect game in the ninth inning. Defense is why Wise is in the big leagues in the first place. He runs well and can play all three outfield positions, but he can't hit lefties at all, while the evidence of his ability to do anything against right-handers is sketchy at best. He'll compete for a back-of-the-bench job in Phillies camp this spring, but whether he makes it or not, he'll always have that catch.

PITCHERS

Mark Buehrle Bats: L Throws: L Height: 6' 2" Weight: 230 Born: March 23, 1979 Age: 31

YEAR	TEAM	LVL	AGE	W	L	SV	G	GS	IP	H	HR	BB	SO	GB%	BABIP	STUFF	WHIP	ERA	SIERA	DERA	EqH9	EqHR9	EqBB9	EqSO9	VORP	SN/WX
2007	CHA	MLB	28	10	9	0	30	30	201	208	22	45	115	51%	.287	14	1.26	3.63	4.51	3.38	8.6	0.9	1.8	4.8	47.0	5.86
2008	CHA	MLB	29	15	12	0	34	34	218²	240	22	52	140	59%	.312	14	1.34	3.79	4.24	3.91	9.5	0.8	1.9	5.5	37.8	5.25
2009	CHA	MLB	30	13	10	0	33	33	213¹	222	27	45	105	53%	.282	8	1.25	3.84	4.73	3.63	9.1	0.9	1.7	4.1	43.0	5.79
2010	CHA	MLB	31	11	12	0	>32	32	194	204	24	55	106	54%	.292	1	1.33	4.26	4.68	4.48	9.6	1.0	2.3	4.6	21.9	3.28

Breakout: 4% Improve: 35% Collapse: 16% Attrition: 14% MLB: 98% Comparables: Charlie Leibrandt, Terry Mulholland, Nate Robertson, Paul Minner

It's hard to make sense of how Buehrle does it. His command is excellent, but not historically so, and one would think it would have to be at that level to make up for his kind of stuff—we're talking about a guy whose fastball often sits in the mid-80s. While he has location and deception in his favor, no amount of trickery should make him a consistently above-average or better starter, and the fact that he occasionally throws a no-hitter or a perfect game is almost even more shocking. In the end, Buehrle is an anomaly, the kind of player we can certainly enjoy, but not learn much from.

D. J. Carrasco Bats: R Throws: R Height: 6' 1" Weight: 215 Born: April 12, 1977 Age: 33

YEAR	TEAM	LVL	AGE	W	L	SV	G	GS	IP	H	HR	BB	SO	GB%	BABIP	STUFF	WHIP	ERA	SIERA	DERA	EqH9	EqHR9	EqBB9	EqSO9	VORP	SN/WX
2007	TUC	AAA	30	5	14	0	34	22	137¹	185	16	60	103	57%	.360	-24	1.78	6.68	4.49	7.74	11.1	1.3	3.9	5.0	-34.6	-3.40
2008	CHR	AAA	31	2	1	1	8	1	25	24	0	7	24	66%	.333	9	1.24	2.88	3.21	3.80	9.5	0.4	2.7	6.5	4.5	0.10
2008	CHA	MLB	31	1	0	0	31	0	38²	30	2	14	30	60%	.262	9	1.14	3.96	4.00	3.58	6.9	0.5	2.9	6.7	8.0	1.08
2009	CHA	MLB	32	5	1	0	49	1	93¹	103	5	29	62	55%	.319	7	1.41	3.76	4.42	3.58	9.6	0.4	2.4	5.4	19.8	0.37
2010	CHA	MLB	33	4	7	0	45	0	85²	95	11	40	55	62%	.313	-12	1.58	5.29	4.69	5.53	10.1	1.1	3.8	5.4	-0.3	0.10

Breakout: 13% Improve: 48% Collapse: 23% Attrition: 20% MLB: 78% Comparables: Anthony Telford, Salomon Torres, Brian Boehringer, A.J. Sager

Carrasco is rubber-armed enough for the middle-relief role, but he does have his issues. With a 90-92 mph fastball and solid slider, Carrasco has decent enough stuff, and his low three-quarters arm angle makes him hell on right-handers, who had a sub-.300 on-base percentage and just one homer in 203 at-bats against him. Unfortunately, lefties teed off a bit, hitting him at a .317/.392/.463 that argues for him to be spotted carefully with a close lead or mop-up when down by a lot—which is exactly how Ozzie did use him.

Bartolo Colon

Bats: R   Throws: R   Height: 5' 11"   Weight: 245   Born: May 24, 1973   Age: 37

YEAR	TEAM	LVL	AGE	W	L	SV	G	GS	IP	H	HR	BB	SO	GB%	BABIP	STUFF	WHIP	ERA	SIERA	DERA	EqH9	EqHR9	EqBB9	EqSO9	VORP	SN/WX
2007	LAA	MLB	34	6	8	0	19	18	99¹	132	15	29	76	45%	.357	-7	1.62	6.34	4.20	6.01	11.2	1.3	2.3	6.2	-5.6	0.48
2008	BOS	MLB	35	4	2	0	7	7	39	44	5	10	27	43%	.302	9	1.38	3.92	4.35	4.84	9.4	0.9	2.0	5.6	2.9	0.40
2009	CHA	MLB	36	3	6	0	12	12	62¹	69	13	21	38	53%	.277	-4	1.44	4.19	4.72	5.30	9.2	1.4	2.5	4.8	1.4	0.98
2010	CHA	MLB	37	3	5	0	17	12	64¹	74	10	24	39	48%	.312	-8	1.52	5.21	4.84	5.43	10.4	1.2	3.1	5.0	0.5	0.83

Breakout: 4%   Improve: 31%   Collapse: 27%   Attrition: 40%   MLB: 85%   Comparables: Dave Burba, Denny Galehouse, Al Benton, Boom-Boom Beck

Given one more shot, Colon had a handful of decent starts in April and May, but his conditioning got the better of him again, leading to knee and elbow problems. By the time June arrived, Colon's velocity slipped into the mid-80s. After a long time on the shelf, the White Sox released him in September without his getting another chance to pitch. Since winning the 2005 Cy Young Award, Colon has pitched just 257 innings with a 5.18 ERA. This looks like the end of the line.

John Danks

Bats: L   Throws: L   Height: 6' 1"   Weight: 200   Born: April 15, 1985   Age: 25

YEAR	TEAM	LVL	AGE	W	L	SV	G	GS	IP	H	HR	BB	SO	GB%	BABIP	STUFF	WHIP	ERA	SIERA	DERA	EqH9	EqHR9	EqBB9	EqSO9	VORP	SN/WX
2007	CHA	MLB	22	6	13	0	26	26	139	160	28	54	109	41%	.309	8	1.54	5.50	4.39	5.13	9.6	1.5	3.1	6.5	5.8	0.79
2008	CHA	MLB	23	12	9	0	33	33	195	182	15	57	159	51%	.293	33	1.23	3.32	3.81	3.13	8.0	0.6	2.3	6.9	50.7	6.50
2009	CHA	MLB	24	13	11	0	32	32	200¹	184	28	73	149	50%	.267	17	1.28	3.77	4.27	3.56	7.9	1.0	2.9	6.1	42.9	5.48
2010	CHA	MLB	25	11	10	0	32	32	192²	186	24	69	147	48%	.291	14	1.32	4.15	4.17	4.31	8.8	1.0	2.9	6.3	25.4	2.89

Breakout: 9%   Improve: 40%   Collapse: 15%   Attrition: 6%   MLB: 100%   Comparables: Jose Rosado, Jim Abbott, Don Gullett, Ray Sadecki

Danks's numbers from 2008 to 2009 weren't markedly different, other than a home-run rate that suddenly doubled, thanks to his giving up 12 big flies in his last eight starts. Danks doesn't turn 25 until a couple of weeks into the '10 season, and he's still more of an unbridled stallion as opposed to a thoroughbred. He's usually good, but when he's bad, he's very bad, getting clocked for five or more runs six times. He might still be three to five years away from his best season.

Octavio Dotel

Bats: R   Throws: R   Height: 6' 0"   Weight: 215   Born: November 25, 1973   Age: 36

YEAR	TEAM	LVL	AGE	W	L	SV	G	GS	IP	H	HR	BB	SO	GB%	BABIP	STUFF	WHIP	ERA	SIERA	DERA	EqH9	EqHR9	EqBB9	EqSO9	VORP	SN/WX
2007	KCA	MLB	33	2	1	11	24	0	23	24	3	11	29	54%	.344	17	1.52	3.91	3.18	3.75	8.6	1.1	3.8	10.1	4.7	0.55
2007	ATL	MLB	33	0	0	0	9	0	7²	5	1	1	12	9%	.250	8	0.78	4.70	0.78	5.87	7.0	1.2	1.2	10.6	-0.3	0.18
2008	CHA	MLB	34	4	4	1	72	0	67	52	12	29	92	41%	.267	18	1.21	3.76	2.53	4.13	6.8	1.3	3.4	10.2	10.5	1.22
2009	CHA	MLB	35	3	3	0	62	0	62¹	54	7	36	75	41%	.313	21	1.44	3.32	3.42	3.32	7.8	0.7	4.6	9.9	14.8	1.58
2010	CHA	MLB	36	3	3	3	54	0	53²	46	7	25	60	42%	.298	11	1.33	4.03	3.31	4.14	7.8	0.9	3.8	9.3	8.1	0.76

Breakout: 15%   Improve: 42%   Collapse: 25%   Attrition: 9%   MLB: 94%   Comparables: Tom Gordon, Juan Berenguer, Marc Kroon, Rich Gossage

The White Sox drew a lot of criticism for giving Dotel a two-year deal prior to the 2008 season, but he delivered two solid years setting up by mitigating his control issues with a continuing ability to miss bats. He's still a far cry from his dominating days earlier in the decade, but his heat sits at 92-94 mph and the slider is still wicked. He's one of those Type A free agents who might have to wait a while for the market to settle out.

John Ely
Bats: R   Throws: R   Height: 6' 1"   Weight: 200   Born: May 17, 1986   Age: 24

YEAR	TEAM	LVL	AGE	W	L	SV	G	GS	IP	H	HR	BB	SO	GB%	BABIP	STUFF	WHIP	ERA	SIERA	DERA	EqH9	EqHR9	EqBB9	EqSO9	VORP	SN/WX
2007	GRF	Rk	21	6	1	0	13	12	56	55	6	14	56	51%	.325	6	1.23	3.86	3.08	5.67	10.8	2.2	3.4	5.4	-0.9	-0.10
2008	WNS	A+	22	10	12	0	27	27	145¹	142	18	46	134	54%	.305	-4	1.29	4.71	3.53	5.75	10.2	1.9	3.3	6.0	-3.7	-1.07
2009	BIR	AA	23	14	2	0	27	27	156¹	140	9	50	125	57%	.289	-5	1.22	2.82	3.87	5.18	9.7	1.5	3.1	5.2	5.2	1.02
2010	LAN	MLB	24	6	10	0	28	26	131	145	20	52	85	45%	.307	-8	1.50	5.02	4.77	5.50	10.0	1.4	3.5	5.4	0.1	2.15

Breakout: 4%   Improve: 40%   Collapse: 9%   Attrition: 7%   MLB: 8%   Comparables: Scott Arnold, Ryan Nye, Heath Rollins, Nelson Figueroa

Ely nearly won the Southern League triple crown in 2009, leading the circuit in strikeouts, tying for the league lead in wins, and finishing second in ERA, yet scouts don't believe in him. First, Birmingham is a wonderful place to pitch (his road ERA was a still-respectable 3.21). Second, Ely is a bit of a finesse pitcher, dialing up to just 88-91 mph with his fastball, none of his secondary offerings truly stand out, and he just doesn't have the control to succeed as he moves up. He's a prospect, but nothing close to what the numbers suggest. Packaged with Jon Link to LA for Juan Pierre, Ely's lost in their crowd of farm arms.

Gavin Floyd
Bats: R   Throws: R   Height: 6' 5"   Weight: 230   Born: January 27, 1983   Age: 27

YEAR	TEAM	LVL	AGE	W	L	SV	G	GS	IP	H	HR	BB	SO	GB%	BABIP	STUFF	WHIP	ERA	SIERA	DERA	EqH9	EqHR9	EqBB9	EqSO9	VORP	SN/WX
2007	CHR	AAA	24	7	3	0	17	17	106²	93	9	35	96	45%	.284	12	1.20	3.12	3.64	3.85	8.7	1.2	3.1	6.5	18.6	1.41
2007	CHA	MLB	24	1	5	0	16	10	70	85	17	19	49	49%	.305	-9	1.49	5.27	4.31	5.01	10.0	1.9	2.2	5.7	3.9	0.87
2008	CHA	MLB	25	17	8	0	33	33	206¹	190	30	70	145	47%	.256	14	1.26	3.84	4.40	4.19	7.6	1.1	2.7	5.8	30.5	3.76
2009	CHA	MLB	26	11	11	0	30	30	193	178	21	59	163	56%	.284	26	1.23	4.06	3.73	3.84	8.1	0.8	2.4	6.9	35.2	5.12
2010	CHA	MLB	27	11	10	0	32	30	179¹	168	22	65	133	50%	.282	14	1.30	4.10	4.24	4.23	8.5	1.0	3.0	6.2	25.4	2.47

Breakout: 4%   Improve: 41%   Collapse: 8%   Attrition: 15%   MLB: 97%   Comparables: Brett Tomko, Scott Baker, Dan Haren, Don Cardwell

The difference between Floyd's 17-8 2008 season and his 11-11 campaign last year is really just in the won-lost record. His hits and walk rates were nearly identical, while he actually upped his strikeout numbers a bit, and his quality start percentage was higher than the year before—he was simply hit harder in his losses. To judge his 2009 season as a disappointment is unfair. If Floyd deserves fault, it's that he started poorly, with a 7.71 ERA in his first eight starts, and finished cold. In between, he had 100 midseason innings with an ERA of 2.24. Floyd is a solid midrotation starter for now, but there's still the possibility of more. Hip soreness may have contributed to his poor finish (he was shut down in mid-September), but he's still just 27, and about five times a year, his plus fastball and even better curve come together and he looks like the stud many thought he would be when he was the best high school pitcher in the 2001 draft.

Freddy Garcia
Bats: R   Throws: R   Height: 6' 4"   Weight: 240   Born: June 10, 1975   Age: 35

YEAR	TEAM	LVL	AGE	W	L	SV	G	GS	IP	H	HR	BB	SO	GB%	BABIP	STUFF	WHIP	ERA	SIERA	DERA	EqH9	EqHR9	EqBB9	EqSO9	VORP	SN/WX
2007	PHI	MLB	32	1	5	0	11	11	58	74	12	19	50	46%	.348	0	1.60	5.90	3.96	5.57	11.1	1.7	2.7	7.1	-0.5	0.59
2008	DET	MLB	33	1	1	0	3	3	15	11	3	6	12	46%	.205	11	1.13	4.20	4.15	4.20	6.0	1.8	3.0	6.6	2.2	0.36
2009	CHA	MLB	34	3	4	0	9	9	56	56	4	12	37	53%	.295	18	1.21	4.34	4.13	3.85	8.7	0.5	1.6	5.4	10.1	1.40
2010	CHA	MLB	35	3	4	0	16	0	57²	64	8	20	40	47%	.315	0	1.45	4.86	4.44	5.15	10.2	1.2	2.9	5.7	2.3	0.87

Breakout: 19%   Improve: 44%   Collapse: 29%   Attrition: 19%   MLB: 84%   Comparables: Jason Johnson, Tanyon Sturtze, Don Larsen, Hideki Irabu

Garcia's surgically repaired shoulder was slow to heal. After a brutal spring training and a pair of poor starts in Triple-A, the Mets just flat-out released him, leading to another opportunity to pitch for fellow Venezuelan Ozzie Guillen. The White Sox were as cautious with Garcia as the Mets were reckless, signing him in June and bringing him along slowly; he didn't join the big-league rotation until mid-August. He pitched well, with seven quality starts in nine chances (and an eighth was blown after the sixth inning). Chicago's decision to include a cheap 2010 option for $1 million plus $2 million in incentives looks like a steal, especially with pitching prices likely to prove recession-proof.

Lucas Harrell

Bats: S   Throws: R   Height: 6' 2"   Weight: 205   Born: June 3, 1985   Age: 25

YEAR	TEAM	LVL	AGE	W	L	SV	G	GS	IP	H	HR	BB	SO	GB%	BABIP	STUFF	WHIP	ERA	SIERA	DERA	EqH9	EqHR9	EqBB9	EqSO9	VORP	SN/WX
2008	KAN	A	23	1	1	0	3	3	10²	13	0	4	7	68%	.351	-27	1.59	5.91	4.19	7.65	12.6	0.9	4.5	2.7	-2.4	-0.24
2008	BIR	AA	23	3	3	0	11	10	54²	56	3	19	34	56%	.306	-14	1.37	3.46	4.52	6.31	10.5	1.2	3.2	3.7	-4.5	0.32
2009	BIR	AA	24	8	3	0	14	14	80¹	78	4	32	51	70%	.302	-16	1.37	3.25	4.29	5.91	10.5	1.4	3.9	4.1	-3.3	0.11
2009	CHR	AAA	24	4	1	0	11	11	65²	58	3	37	42	64%	.282	7	1.45	3.29	4.82	3.98	8.4	0.7	5.5	4.7	10.3	0.80
2010	CHA	MLB	25	4	8	0	23	22	104²	120	15	62	54	58%	.304	-20	1.74	5.96	5.46	6.11	10.3	1.2	4.8	4.3	-7.1	1.56

Breakout: 12%   Improve: 46%   Collapse: 25%   Attrition: 13%   MLB: 4%   Comparables: Jason Scobie, Chance Chapman, Matt Wright, Robert Williams

Harrell pitched well for both upper-level affiliates in 2009, and if all goes according to plan, he should see the big leagues at some point in 2010. He doesn't miss a lot of bats, but he's a ground-ball machine with his 89-92 mph sinker. His changeup is good, his slider not so much, and most scouts see a bullpen role for him in the end. The skill set is enough for him to have some minor success there.

Dan Hudson

Bats: R   Throws: R   Height: 6' 4"   Weight: 220   Born: March 9, 1987   Age: 23

YEAR	TEAM	LVL	AGE	W	L	SV	G	GS	IP	H	HR	BB	SO	GB%	BABIP	STUFF	WHIP	ERA	SIERA	DERA	EqH9	EqHR9	EqBB9	EqSO9	VORP	SN/WX
2008	GRF	Rk	21	5	4	0	14	14	69²	52	6	22	90	50%	.284	6	1.06	3.36	2.38	5.24	9.3	2.2	4.0	6.2	1.8	-0.08
2009	KAN	A	22	1	2	0	4	4	22	15	0	2	30	60%	.300	20	0.77	1.23	1.58	3.60	8.6	0.9	1.8	7.2	4.2	0.38
2009	WNS	A+	22	4	3	0	8	8	45	31	3	13	49	51%	.252	24	0.98	3.40	2.82	4.86	7.8	1.3	3.2	6.9	3.0	0.08
2009	BIR	AA	22	7	0	0	9	9	56¹	37	1	10	63	41%	.269	38	0.83	1.60	2.20	2.87	7.3	0.7	1.9	7.5	15.1	1.48
2009	CHR	AAA	22	2	0	0	5	5	24	22	1	9	24	30%	.313	23	1.29	3.00	3.71	4.05	8.5	0.8	3.5	7.3	3.8	0.35
2009	CHA	MLB	22	1	1	0	6	2	18²	16	3	9	14	28%	.236	10	1.34	3.37	5.15	3.72	7.0	0.9	3.7	6.1	3.8	0.28
2010	CHA	MLB	23	7	8	0	30	28	135	132	20	59	109	40%	.292	14	1.41	4.65	4.34	4.74	8.7	1.2	3.6	6.7	11.4	3.35

Breakout: 2%   Improve: 25%   Collapse: 27%   Attrition: 1%   MLB: 44%   Comparables: Matt Garza, Clint Wickensheimer, Ryan Baerlocher, Rich Lacko

The minor leagues' breakout pitcher of the year, Hudson began 2009 as a relatively nondescript fifth-rounder out of Old Dominion, but he finished it in the big leagues, pitching at every full-season stop along the way. Hudson's command and control were always quite good, but some mechanical tweaks found him suddenly sitting at 93-95 mph with his fastball, changing him from afterthought into Cinderella. There's still work to be done, as his breaking ball can be inconsistent and he works up in the zone, but he should start 2010 in the majors, probably beginning the year as a reliever until a need in the rotation arises.

Bobby Jenks

Bats: R   Throws: R   Height: 6' 3"   Weight: 275   Born: March 14, 1981   Age: 29

YEAR	TEAM	LVL	AGE	W	L	SV	G	GS	IP	H	HR	BB	SO	GB%	BABIP	STUFF	WHIP	ERA	SIERA	DERA	EqH9	EqHR9	EqBB9	EqSO9	VORP	SN/WX
2007	CHA	MLB	26	3	5	40	66	0	65	45	2	13	56	58%	.243	28	0.89	2.77	3.24	2.42	5.7	0.3	1.7	7.2	22.2	2.58
2008	CHA	MLB	27	3	1	30	57	0	61²	51	3	17	38	65%	.261	10	1.10	2.63	4.15	2.40	7.2	0.3	2.3	5.3	20.7	4.70
2009	CHA	MLB	28	3	4	29	52	0	53¹	52	9	16	49	57%	.283	7	1.27	3.71	3.55	3.56	8.3	1.2	2.3	7.3	11.7	1.83
2010	CHA	MLB	29	4	3	34@B:64	1		64	53	7	21	49	60%	.264	8	1.16	3.37	3.86	3.50	7.6	0.8	2.6	6.4	14.2	2.12

Breakout: 16%   Improve: 42%   Collapse: 28%   Attrition: 10%   MLB: 99%   Comparables: Jose Valverde, Jose Jimenez, Esteban Yan, Antonio Alfonseca

The offseason on the South Side had plenty of drama before the postseason even ended, as Jenks and general manager Kenny Williams traded barbs about what went wrong in 2009, with Williams pointing the finger at Jenks's bulging waistline. While this was possibly some politicking for what could be an acrimonious arbitration hearing, the White Sox don't necessarily need that much ammo—Jenks clearly isn't the pitcher he was as recently as two years ago. Neither radar guns (nor scales) lie, and what was once a 96-98 mph fastball that could touch 100 is now 92-95, making Jenks, on a pure stuff level, more of a set-up man.

Scott Linebrink

| | | | | | | | | | | | | | Bats: R | | Throws: R | | Height: 6′ 2″ | | Weight: 215 | | Born: August 4, 1976 | | Age: 33 |

YEAR	TEAM	LVL	AGE	W	L	SV	G	GS	IP	H	HR	BB	SO	GB%	BABIP	STUFF	WHIP	ERA	SIERA	DERA	EqH9	EqHR9	EqBB9	EqSO9	VORP	SN/WX
2007	SDN	MLB	30	3	3	1	44	0	45	41	9	14	25	46%	.234	-26	1.22	3.80	4.84	3.98	9.2	2.7	2.5	4.4	7.3	2.12
2007	MIL	MLB	30	2	3	0	27	0	25¹	27	3	11	25	59%	.343	5	1.50	3.55	3.64	4.56	9.5	1.1	3.6	8.0	2.6	-0.29
2008	CHA	MLB	31	2	2	1	50	0	46¹	41	8	9	40	45%	.256	9	1.08	3.69	3.35	3.47	7.3	1.3	1.5	7.1	10.5	2.01
2009	CHA	MLB	32	3	7	2	57	0	56	70	9	23	55	42%	.361	-2	1.66	4.66	3.84	4.79	10.9	1.1	3.2	7.8	4.4	-1.15
2010	CHA	MLB	33	3	4	1	56	0	55¹	61	9	22	44	44%	.319	-7	1.50	5.00	4.26	5.14	9.9	1.3	3.2	6.6	2.2	0.53

Breakout: 9%   Improve: 38%   Collapse: 34%   Attrition: 8%   MLB: 88%   Comparables: Justin Speier, Ricky Bottalico, Carl Willis, Dave Veres

One of the most consistent seventh- or eighth-inning-men around, Linebrink continued in that role for the first four months of the year before collapsing and ending the season with his worst numbers since his rookie campaign. The good news (or bad, depending on how you look at it) is that whatever went wrong, it seems to be mental, as his scouting reports remained the same and his peripheral numbers were fine. Expect a return to form.

Jhonny Nunez

| | | | | | | | | | | | | | Bats: L | | Throws: R | | Height: 6′ 3″ | | Weight: 185 | | Born: November 26, 1985 | | Age: 24 |

YEAR	TEAM	LVL	AGE	W	L	SV	G	GS	IP	H	HR	BB	SO	GB%	BABIP	STUFF	WHIP	ERA	SIERA	DERA	EqH9	EqHR9	EqBB9	EqSO9	VORP	SN/WX
2007	HAG	A	21	4	6	0	23	22	106²	97	10	48	86	43%	.273	0	1.36	4.05	4.39	5.78	8.8	1.7	4.5	4.3	-3.2	-0.52
2008	POT	A+	22	2	8	0	21	17	81	88	11	21	82	46%	.338	-15	1.35	5.22	3.17	7.02	12.0	2.6	2.9	6.5	-12.5	-0.85
2008	TRN	AA	22	1	0	0	8	0	19¹	16	2	6	26	36%	.304	18	1.14	1.86	2.22	3.50	10.0	2.0	3.0	9.0	4.0	0.82
2009	BIR	AA	23	3	0	3	26	0	46¹	38	3	21	57	39%	.318	5	1.27	2.14	2.91	3.54	9.6	1.7	4.3	8.4	9.2	0.94
2009	CHR	AAA	23	2	0	1	16	0	24¹	19	3	5	22	37%	.254	7	0.99	3.33	3.20	3.77	7.5	1.6	2.0	6.8	4.4	-0.05
2009	CHA	MLB	23	0	0	0	7	0	5²	10	1	2	3	37%	.391	-22	2.12	9.53	5.48	8.25	15.0	1.5	3.0	4.5	-1.8	0.01
2010	CHA	MLB	24	3	5	0	46	2	73²	77	11	36	59	37%	.307	-6	1.53	5.28	4.61	5.45	9.5	1.3	4.0	6.6	0.4	1.35

Breakout: 20%   Improve: 67%   Collapse: 9%   Attrition: 9%   MLB: 28%   Comparables: Garvin Alston, Todd Burns, Kyle Jackson, Juan Morillo

While Nunez struggled during his big-league debut, scouts still think he could be a nice bullpen piece. Part of the package received from the Yankees for Nick Swisher, Nunez is already in his fourth organization, but he's managed steady growth all along the way, relying primarily on a fastball/slider combination, the former sitting at 92-94 mph and reaching as high as 96. Nunez will get a long look this spring for a more permanent role, but it could come down to a numbers game as much as his talent and readiness.

Jake Peavy

| | | | | | | | | | | | | | Bats: R | | Throws: R | | Height: 6′ 1″ | | Weight: 195 | | Born: May 31, 1981 | | Age: 29 |

YEAR	TEAM	LVL	AGE	W	L	SV	G	GS	IP	H	HR	BB	SO	GB%	BABIP	STUFF	WHIP	ERA	SIERA	DERA	EqH9	EqHR9	EqBB9	EqSO9	VORP	SN/WX
2007	SDN	MLB	26	19	6	0	34	34	223¹	169	13	68	240	51%	.273	37	1.06	2.54	2.94	2.95	7.4	0.7	2.5	8.3	61.7	9.31
2008	SDN	MLB	27	10	11	0	27	27	173²	146	17	59	166	45%	.279	13	1.18	2.85	3.45	3.28	8.5	1.4	2.8	7.1	40.9	6.08
2009	SDN	MLB	28	6	6	0	13	13	81²	69	7	28	92	45%	.300	19	1.19	3.97	2.91	4.60	8.6	1.3	2.8	8.2	7.9	1.62
2009	CHA	MLB	28	3	0	0	3	3	20	11	1	6	18	53%	.200	20	0.85	1.35	3.33	1.37	5.0	0.5	2.3	7.3	9.0	1.04
2010	CHA	MLB	29	10	9	0	27	27	162	152	21	59	141	46%	.293	21	1.30	4.07	3.81	4.18	8.4	1.1	3.0	7.3	23.8	3.89

Breakout: 8%   Improve: 40%   Collapse: 17%   Attrition: 16%   MLB: 97%   Comparables: Bret Saberhagen, Mort Cooper, Bill Lohrman, Tex Carleton

One of Kenny Williams' most admirable traits is that he keeps his mouth shut as well as any general manager in the business. The rumor mill is a 24/7 operation in today's digital age, and the signal-to-noise ratio is downright embarrassing at times. If one goes back into the multigigabyte-sized archives from July 2009, one thing is clear—no one saw the Jake Peavy deal coming. While Peavy's three starts at the end of the year did little to tell us if he's ready for a 200-inning workload again, he sure looked good. The White Sox are on the hook for at least $52 million for the next three years, and one gets the feeling that the deal will end up being a bargain or a bust, with very little room for something in between.

Tony Pena

Bats: R   Throws: R   Height: 6' 2"   Weight: 220   Born: January 9, 1982   Age: 28

YEAR	TEAM	LVL	AGE	W	L	SV	G	GS	IP	H	HR	BB	SO	GB%	BABIP	STUFF	WHIP	ERA	SIERA	DERA	EqH9	EqHR9	EqBB9	EqSO9	VORP	SN/WX
2007	ARI	MLB	25	5	4	2	75	0	85¹	63	8	31	63	51%	.232	13	1.10	3.27	4.21	3.42	6.4	0.6	3.0	6.3	19.5	4.16
2008	ARI	MLB	26	3	2	3	72	0	72²	80	5	17	52	52%	.318	3	1.33	4.33	4.08	4.25	9.5	0.6	1.8	5.7	10.1	1.56
2009	ARI	MLB	27	5	3	1	37	0	34	41	3	11	26	50%	.339	-4	1.53	4.24	4.21	4.85	10.2	0.5	2.4	6.0	2.5	0.30
2009	CHA	MLB	27	1	2	1	35	0	36	40	4	9	29	54%	.310	4	1.36	3.75	3.87	3.74	9.2	0.7	1.9	6.3	7.3	0.17
2010	CHA	MLB	28	4	4	2	71	0	72¹	70	8	24	48	49%	.287	-2	1.30	4.12	4.42	4.33	8.8	0.9	2.8	5.6	9.4	1.30

Breakout: 15%   Improve: 38%   Collapse: 22%   Attrition: 14%   MLB: 93%   Comparables: Bob Wickman, Hipolito Pichardo, Hal Reniff, Jose Santiago

The White Sox traded away a nice first-base prospect in Brandon Allen in order to add Pena to their bullpen, but one wonders if they also put themselves on the hook for the same kind of frustration that Arizona dealt with for years. It's not that Pena is bad, not by any measure; it's just that he tends to leave observers wondering why he isn't even better. With a 93-96 mph fastball and a slider that is excellent at times, Pena should at least be a reliable set-up type, but his heater can be a little too true, and there are just too many days when he has so little that it's hard to trust him in the late innings. Someone needs to coin a single word that means "annoyingly mercurial" and apply it to Pena. How about *fickleflustering? Variagrating? Changeraging?*

Clevelan Santeliz

Bats: R   Throws: R   Height: 6' 0"   Weight: 190   Born: September 1, 1986   Age: 23

YEAR	TEAM	LVL	AGE	W	L	SV	G	GS	IP	H	HR	BB	SO	GB%	BABIP	STUFF	WHIP	ERA	SIERA	DERA	EqH9	EqHR9	EqBB9	EqSO9	VORP	SN/WX
2007	KAN	A	20	1	4	0	27	0	37²	40	4	27	37	49%	.327	-4	1.78	6.69	4.47	9.29	10.4	2.0	6.9	5.4	-15.3	-1.99
2007	WNS	A+	20	2	1	0	14	0	14²	10	3	9	18	34%	.226	13	1.30	4.30	3.45	5.06	8.1	2.7	6.1	8.8	0.6	-0.12
2008	WNS	A+	21	3	6	0	15	15	68	55	8	48	60	49%	.261	8	1.51	4.90	4.64	6.93	8.7	1.9	6.9	5.7	-10.0	-0.87
2008	BIR	AA	21	0	1	0	10	0	16¹	14	2	8	6	33%	.240	-24	1.35	4.41	6.46	5.52	9.2	2.5	4.3	1.8	0.0	-0.51
2009	BIR	AA	22	4	0	10	40	0	56¹	43	2	35	52	42%	.279	6	1.38	0.96	4.39	2.70	8.5	1.0	5.6	6.1	16.1	1.23
2010	CHA	MLB	23	2	5	3	55	0	58²	64	10	40	42	41%	.305	-15	1.77	6.17	5.39	6.15	9.5	1.3	5.6	5.9	-4.2	0.30

Breakout: 22%   Improve: 52%   Collapse: 17%   Attrition: 16%   MLB: 3%   Comparables: Willie Eyre, Scott Eggleston, Matt Skrmetta, Derrek Nunley

One of those little guys with a big arm, Santeliz turned into a very real prospect in 2009 by finishing the year with a sub-1.00 ERA, having allowed earned runs in just two of his last 26 appearances. His mid-90s fastball can get up to the 97-98 range at times, his slider is effective enough considering his velocity, and last year, he added a splitter that provides some movement to the mix. After an equally impressive showing over the winter in his native Venezuela, Santeliz is a long shot to make the big-league club this spring, but it might not take much longer after that.

Charles Shirek

Bats: R   Throws: R   Height: 6' 3"   Weight: 205   Born: October 25, 1985   Age: 24

YEAR	TEAM	LVL	AGE	W	L	SV	G	GS	IP	H	HR	BB	SO	GB%	BABIP	STUFF	WHIP	ERA	SIERA	DERA	EqH9	EqHR9	EqBB9	EqSO9	VORP	SN/WX
2008	KAN	A	22	6	6	0	22	21	112	112	8	25	82	57%	.289	-14	1.22	3.54	3.88	5.59	10.2	1.7	2.9	3.5	-1.1	-0.50
2009	WNS	A+	23	8	1	0	11	11	65	63	0	16	44	61%	.300	0	1.22	3.88	3.97	5.39	10.0	0.7	2.8	4.0	0.8	-0.22
2009	BIR	AA	23	6	4	0	15	14	90¹	97	8	17	32	57%	.287	-31	1.26	3.39	5.10	5.60	11.3	2.1	2.1	2.0	-0.9	-0.03
2010	CHA	MLB	24	5	9	0	22	22	120¹	147	21	45	45	53%	.303	-24	1.59	5.75	5.57	5.94	11.0	1.4	3.0	3.1	-5.8	1.70

Breakout: 10%   Improve: 52%   Collapse: 17%   Attrition: 8%   MLB: 3%   Comparables: Matt Guerrier, Eric Brown, Chuck Stanhope, Bill King

Shirek puts both scouts and stat folks in a bit of a conundrum. He gets a lot of ground balls and throws a ton of strikes, but can one really succeed with a strikeout rate straight out of the 1940s? It's hard to walk less than two per nine innings while still compiling a strikeout/walk ratio of less than two to one, but even more difficult to succeed that way. For every Chien-Ming Wang type who manages to make this approach work for a few years, there are dozens more who are completely undone by the sheer number and variety of balls in play they allow. Smoke, meet mirror.

Matt Thornton

| | | | | Bats: L | | Throws: L | | Height: 6' 5" | | Weight: 245 | | Born: September 15, 1976 | | Age: 33 |

YEAR	TEAM	LVL	AGE	W	L	SV	G	GS	IP	H	HR	BB	SO	GB%	BABIP	STUFF	WHIP	ERA	SIERA	DERA	EqH9	EqHR9	EqBB9	EqSO9	VORP	SN/WX
2007	CHA	MLB	30	4	4	2	68	0	56¹	59	4	26	55	54%	.340	8	1.51	4.79	3.81	4.26	9.0	0.5	3.7	8.2	7.7	0.08
2008	CHA	MLB	31	5	3	1	74	0	67¹	48	5	19	77	58%	.261	32	1.00	2.67	2.66	2.46	6.1	0.5	2.3	9.2	22.9	1.49
2009	CHA	MLB	32	6	3	4	70	0	72¹	58	5	20	87	54%	.298	32	1.08	2.74	2.49	2.51	7.3	0.5	2.1	9.4	23.8	4.31
2010	CHA	MLB	33	4	3	2	63	0	62¹	53	7	23	63	53%	.293	13	1.23	3.61	3.31	3.71	7.7	0.8	3.0	8.4	12.4	1.19

Breakout: 15% Improve: 44% Collapse: 25% Attrition: 7%   MLB: 97%   Comparables: Arthur Rhodes, Brian Fuentes, John Bale, Damaso Marte

One of baseball's hardest throwing left-handers, Thornton has put up back-to-back outstanding seasons, and with two years left on a contract that pays him $5.25 million, he's arguably the best bullpen bargain in baseball. Getting away from who has saved this and who is a proven closer that, Thornton is a better pitcher on both a scouting and a statistical level than Bobby Jenks, and while a reversal in roles might ruffle some feathers, it could also lead to more wins.

Carlos Torres

| | | | | Bats: R | | Throws: R | | Height: 6' 2" | | Weight: 195 | | Born: October 22, 1982 | | Age: 27 |

YEAR	TEAM	LVL	AGE	W	L	SV	G	GS	IP	H	HR	BB	SO	GB%	BABIP	STUFF	WHIP	ERA	SIERA	DERA	EqH9	EqHR9	EqBB9	EqSO9	VORP	SN/WX
2007	WNS	A+	24	0	2	3	19	0	36¹	33	0	10	41	56%	.351	9	1.18	3.72	2.73	4.68	9.9	0.8	3.0	8.0	3.0	0.01
2007	BIR	AA	24	2	2	1	36	0	56	57	3	22	59	47%	.348	-12	1.41	3.70	3.37	5.16	10.5	1.2	3.8	6.4	2.0	-0.52
2008	BIR	AA	25	9	5	0	21	17	101¹	86	4	29	93	51%	.297	6	1.13	3.20	3.39	4.61	9.0	1.1	2.8	6.0	9.2	1.05
2008	CHR	AAA	25	0	0	0	8	1	19²	23	2	11	19	62%	.356	-6	1.73	4.58	4.01	5.06	11.6	1.4	5.3	6.3	0.9	-0.17
2009	CHR	AAA	26	10	4	1	23	20	128	96	4	56	130	54%	.275	30	1.19	2.39	3.50	3.14	7.1	0.6	4.2	7.4	32.4	2.64
2009	CHA	MLB	26	1	2	0	8	5	28¹	30	5	17	22	48%	.298	-2	1.66	6.04	4.87	5.56	9.2	1.3	4.8	6.4	-0.2	0.15
2010	CHA	MLB	27	6	8	1	43	16	124	125	16	59	100	44%	.303	2	1.48	4.80	4.42	4.96	9.1	1.1	3.9	6.7	7.5	2.03

Breakout: 13% Improve: 42% Collapse: 23% Attrition: 12%   MLB: 32%   Comparables: Mark Clemons, Cliff Speck, Chris Seelbach, Donne Wall

A bit of a late bloomer, Torres has achieved a lot of success in the minors as a starter, but his future probably lies in the middle of a bullpen. He doesn't offer much in the way of velocity, but changes his grip and release point to sink or cut the ball and to add or subtract velocity. It's a bit of a tightrope walk, but he's good at it.

LINEOUTS

Hitters

PLAYER	TEAM	LVL	AGE	PA	R	2B	3B	HR	RBI	BB	SO	SB-CS	EqBRR	AVG/OBP/SLG	EqAVG/EqOBP/EqSLG	EqA	VORP	WARP
INF W. Betemit#	CHR	AAA	27	286	36	19	0	11	49	21	73	2-0	0.0	.241/.294/.441	.228/.276/.403	.235	-3.7	0.3
	CHA	MLB	27	50	2	5	0	0	3	5	13	0-0	-0.1	.200/.280/.311	.200/.280/.289	.207	-2.3	-0.6
SS E. Escobar#	KAN	A	20	514	64	10	7	3	41	29	91	20-6	0.7	.256/.300/.328	.226/.262/.288	.195	-12.0	-3.4
OF S. Gartrell	BIR	AA	25	412	72	20	4	19	70	46	99	6-0	2.7	.285/.371/.521	.254/.320/.449	.264	9.3	-1.0
	CHR	AAA	25	121	14	11	1	4	19	7	29	0-2	0.0	.265/.314/.487	.254/.303/.465	.253	1.3	-0.7
C M. Gonzalez	BRI	Rk	18	173	24	15	1	4	19	16	25	2-1	-1.6	.311/.385/.503	.268/.324/.395	.252	4.9	0.0
C J. Phegley	KAN	A	21	214	27	9	0	9	33	11	40	1-1	-0.4	.224/.277/.408	.194/.234/.328	.192	-5.5	-0.6
OF J. Shelby	BIR	AA	23	493	64	32	3	10	49	49	77	30-9	1.2	.243/.323/.402	.242/.305/.398	.247	5.2	1.7
OF T. Thompson	BRI	Rk	18	93	8	3	1	0	10	4	33	2-0	0.3	.188/.247/.247	.170/.204/.227	.137	-7.3	-1.9

The Sox hoped **Wilson Betemit** could be their supersub in the infield, but his bat had him playing that role at Triple-A—and not well. He'll be in the Royals' camp this spring. ⊘ **Eduardo Escobar** is a toolsy, slick-fielding Venezuelan shortstop, but the bat has a long way to go. ⊘ Outfielder **Stefan Gartrell** is a huge man with plenty of raw power; that's about the sum of his skills, but he's on the 40-man and trying to become the first-ever 945th overall selection in a draft to make the majors. ⊘ Sox officials think Venezuelan catcher **Miguel Gonzalez** is the biggest sleeper in the system, a teenage backstop with power and solid catch-and-throw skills. ⊘ A supplemental first-round pick last June, **Josh Phegley** has the power and patience rarely found in a catcher, but many scouts think he has no chance to stay at the position. ⊘ **John Shelby III** was seen as a potential fourth outfielder coming into the year, but he hit the metaphorical wall at Double-A. ⊘ A second-round pick in 2009, outfielder **Trayce Thompson** is the son of Mychal, the first overall pick in the 1978 NBA draft; while Trayce offers plenty to dream on, he's as raw as sushi.

Pitchers

PLAYER	TEAM	LVL	AGE	W	L	SV	IP	H	HR	BB	SO	GB%	BABIP	STUFF	WHIP	ERA	SIERA	DERA	EqH9	EqHR9	EqBB9	EqSO9	VORP
D. Holmberg*	BRI	Rk	17	2	2	0	40	40	5	18	37	0%	.307	-15	1.45	4.72	3.94	9.32	13.5	4.3	6.8	4.1	-14.1
B. Hynick	CSP	AAA	24	10	9	0	155	153	17	48	92	48%	.276	4	1.30	3.83	4.68	4.48	8.3	1.0	2.8	4.3	17.4
N. Jones	KAN	A	23	2	0	1	18²	8	0	9	25	47%	.216	10	0.91	2.41	2.49	3.86	6.1	1.1	6.1	7.2	3.0
	WNS	A+	23	2	1	0	49¹	44	4	13	43	46%	.286	-11	1.16	3.65	3.53	4.76	9.7	1.6	3.0	5.4	3.7
J. Link	CHR	AAA	25	1	2	13	56¹	55	5	27	66	53%	.340	4	1.46	3.99	3.27	4.70	9.6	1.2	4.5	8.7	4.8
S. Luis	WNS	A+	25	5	4	14	56	50	11	23	79	47%	.300	-15	1.30	4.34	2.43	6.79	10.0	2.7	4.2	9.0	-7.6
H. Mabee	WNS	A+	23	4	1	8	32¹	32	1	15	23	70%	.310	-18	1.45	3.06	4.08	4.60	10.7	0.9	4.9	4.3	2.9
	BIR	AA	23	2	2	1	29²	22	0	13	22	64%	.250	-15	1.18	3.34	4.18	6.67	7.4	0.6	3.7	4.3	-3.8
J. Marquez	CHR	AAA	24	2	8	0	45²	72	12	22	27	45%	.366	-52	2.06	9.85	5.32	11.13	14.8	3.1	4.5	4.1	-27.3
B. Omogrosso	BIR	AA	25	7	2	0	73	67	4	40	64	49%	.306	-9	1.47	4.19	4.34	6.82	10.0	1.5	4.9	5.7	-9.9
J. Rasner	WNS	A+	22	4	7	1	127²	115	11	42	98	49%	.279	-11	1.23	4.72	4.06	6.38	9.8	1.5	3.6	4.7	-11.5
D. Remenowsky	KAN	A	23	7	3	24	63¹	40	3	16	109	38%	.319	8	0.88	1.99	0.78	4.26	8.8	1.8	3.7	9.6	7.7
S. Rodriguez*	BRI	Rk	21	2	0	4	27	18	0	17	42	0%	.333	11	1.30	1.33	2.50	3.22	10.1	1.6	8.5	7.7	5.6
S. Sauer	KAN	A	22	6	5	0	142	163	4	19	123	65%	.357	-16	1.28	3.36	3.19	6.02	12.5	1.5	2.4	4.2	-7.4
W. Whisler*	CHR	AAA	26	10	12	0	152²	165	10	56	77	57%	.299	-9	1.45	4.01	5.05	5.35	9.7	1.0	3.5	3.5	2.4
	CHA	MLB	26	0	0	0	1¹	0	0	3	2	51%	.000	1	2.25	13.50	6.26	13.50	0.0	0.0	20.3	13.5	-1.2
R. Williams*	CHR	AAA	33	3	0	1	36²	31	3	11	40	51%	.277	6	1.15	3.44	3.02	4.58	7.7	1.0	2.9	7.5	3.8
	CHA	MLB	33	0	1	0	17²	13	2	12	22	57%	.268	18	1.42	4.58	3.56	4.00	6.5	1.0	5.0	10.0	3.0

A 2009 draft pick out of a Florida high school, left-hander **David Holmberg** is known more for his polish than stuff, but his kind of polish is rarely found in a teenager. His nickname should be "The Hat." ⊘ Acquired from the Rockies in the Jose Contreras deal, righty **Brandon Hynick** is a pure finesse righty, but he's pretty darn good at it, as any ERA under 4.00 at Triple-A Colorado Springs is impressive. ⊘ **Nathan Jones** is a bit of a project who has been slow to develop, but he's tall and long and can touch 98 mph with his fastball. ⊘ Reliever **Jon Link** has above-average stuff and can rack up strikeouts, especially right-handers (more than 32 percent of the time); with just a slight improvement to his control, he could help as early as this year. ⊘ **Santo Luis** is a tall righty with power stuff and a career strikeout rate of over 12 per nine, but he's also 25 years old and has never pitched above A-ball. ⊘ **Henry Mabee** generates a lot of grounders, but that might be his only skill. Mabee it will be enough to get him to the big leagues, and mabee not. ⊘ Initially seen as one of the big prizes in the Nick Swisher deal, right-hander **Jeffrey Marquez** continued to have problems staying healthy, and even when he was, his stuff had deteriorated to the point of pure dreadful. ⊘ **Brian Omogrosso**'s path to the big leagues as a swingman type who can start or relieve while keeping the ball down was postponed by midseason shoulder surgery. ⊘ **Jacob Rasner** has the size and stuff to keep scouts intrigued, but his performances have yet to impress. ⊘ **Dan Remenowsky** put up some crazy-stupid numbers at Low-A, but he's a pure command guy whose fastball sits in the upper 80s. ⊘ As a 6-foot-6 teenage lefty who can get his fastball up to 97 mph, **Santos Rodriguez** has tremendous potential, but for now, he's much more of a thrower than a pitcher. ⊘ A former first-round pick who never hit much as an infielder, **Sergio Santos** moved to the mound in 2009 and showed mid-90s heat in the Arizona Fall League, earning him a spot on the 40-man roster. ⊘ **Stephen Sauer** walked only 19 batters over 142 innings in his full-season debut; his stuff is marginal at best. ⊘ **Wes Whisler** made his big-league debut on Sabermetrics Night at the Cell in 2009, but most think that will be his sole career highlight. ⊘ Having not pitched in the majors since 2005 while moving across four organizations, **Randy Williams** spent the last two months of the season earning big-league paychecks and proving once again that being left-handed is an awesome thing.

MANAGER: OZZIE GUILLEN

YEAR	TEAM	W-L	Pythag +/−	Avg PC	100+ P	120+ P	QS	BQS	REL	REL w Zero R	IBB	Subs	PH	PH Avg	PH HR	SB2	CS2	SB3	CS3	SAC Att	SAC %	SAC	POS Squeeze	Swing	In Play
2007	CHA	72-90	6	100.7	99	2	82	12	463	258	50	31	100	.227	3	75	38	3	6	61	67.2%	36	0	128	108
2008	CHA	89-74	-1	97.3	72	4	86	9	463	286	42	49	75	.281	2	54	29	13	4	47	59.6%	25	1	128	98
2009	CHA	79-83	-1	95.1	62	0	85	9	415	246	41	35	105	.106	2	105	45	6	3	49	69.4%	30	1	139	113

Guillen is certainly an iconoclast. In an age where managers pay their dues and give boring, politically correct answers to every question, Ozzie took a different path, refusing to manage in the minor leagues and insisting on doing everything his way. After winning the first World Series title for his two-team city in nearly a century, he's pretty much untouchable. That's good, because his often-brutal honesty walks the edge of danger in a game that has become a little too corporate and milquetoast for its own good. As a tactician, he always wanted to play "Ozzieball," which involved a lot of bunting, running, and manufacturing runs, but the strategy never really matched well with what has usually been an old, slow roster. Over the years he's learned to adjust, and as far as most strategies go, he's now the middle of the road. As an individual, he's anything but.

Cincinnati Reds

Nineteen years removed from their last world championship, 14 years removed from their last playoff berth, and nine years removed from their last winning season, the Cincinnati Reds entered the 2009 season as a popular sleeper pick.

The previous year had been an important one for the franchise. Walt Jocketty, architect of the Cardinals teams of the past decade and the A's farm director leading up to their late-1980s dynasty, had replaced Wayne Krivsky as general manager in April 2008, taking over a team flush with exciting young talent. That season, 24-year-old first baseman Joey Votto, a second-round pick from the Jim Bowden era, overcame new manager Dusty Baker's infamous reluctance to break in young players and finished second in the Rookie of the Year voting. Right fielder Jay Bruce, a first-rounder from the Dan O'Brien era, had a rocky rookie campaign but still hit his age in homers (21), establishing himself in Baker's lineup as well. On the mound, 24-year-old Edinson Volquez, acquired by Krivsky from the Rangers along with lefty reliever Daniel Ray Herrera for his winning Rule 5 lottery ticket Josh Hamilton, emerged as a potential ace, while 22-year-old Dominican righty Johnny Cueto, an O'Brien-era signing, showed potential as well. Adding those four plus toolsy rookie outfielder Chris Dickerson (a middle-rounds Bowden selection), and the lingering potential of O'Brien's other first-round pick, pitching prospect Homer Bailey, to a team centered on 27-year-old second baseman Brandon Phillips, 26-year-old Edwin Encarnacion, veteran workhorse starters Aaron Harang and Bronson Arroyo, and big-money closer Francisco Cordero gave the Reds the look of an exciting young team that was starting to coalesce.

REDS PROSPECTUS
2009 W-L: 78-84, 4th in NL Central

Pythag	71-91	13th
RS/G	4.2	11th
RA/G	4.5	8th
EqA	.251	14th
EqBRR	-9.2	12th
SNWP	.491	9th
WXRL	11.5	2nd
FRAr	3.96	3rd
DE	.705	3rd
PADE	0.64	4th
Salary	$73.6	11th
Attend	1.75	14th

Ballpark: Great American Ball Park (3-yr. PF: 1002). There are few worse places to pitch than the Gap, or uglier

2009: Injuries and bad taste in free agents hurt the lineup; a strong rotation suffers as Dusty-ball plates dustbunnies

2010: Slack-bat choices up the middle leave the lineup weak; the Reds hope the division's the same way to contend

Action Items: Swapping out veterans; who wants to be the Ohio Astros?

The Reds won just 74 games in 2008, but there were many reasons to expect improvement heading into 2009. Beyond the continued development of the aforementioned youngsters, Cincinnati had ample opportunity for upgrades at shortstop, catcher, and particularly in center field. Heading into 2008, the Reds appeared to catch a break when a knee injury to Alex Gonzalez gave the shortstop job to a superior offensive player in Jeff Keppinger, but Keppinger suffered a knee injury of his own that May and was a liability on both sides of the ball for the rest of the season. Behind the plate, the 2008 Reds had a trio of backups, with Paul Bako, one of Baker's players in Chicago in 2003 and 2004, ultimately winning the bulk of the playing time from Dave Ross and Javier Valentin despite coming to the park every day without a glove or bat to contribute to the cause. Meanwhile, failed Cubs prospect Corey Patterson was given 82 starts in center by his former Cubs manager, despite having Neifi'd his way to a jaw-droppingly awful .200/.235/.338 in those games.

With Gonzalez returning to shortstop for 2009, the Reds figured they would at least make up ground defensively and perhaps get a few extra long balls as icing. To fill the catching hole, Jocketty took advantage of the Orioles' anticipation of Matt Wieters' arrival by trading for veteran Ramon Hernandez, and for center field, he pounced on nontendered Rockie Willy Taveras, giving the speedster a two-year deal worth $6.5 million. The moves did significantly improve the Reds' defense (see Table 1), which jumped from last in the National League in Defensive Efficiency in 2008 to third-best in 2009, but that was undermined by the performance of those three at the plate. A slow-healing Gonzalez was significantly worse with the bat than even the injured Keppinger, thus keeping his total contribution below replacement level. Hernandez didn't hit and missed most of the second half with a sore knee of his own, a situation that again resulted in a modest upgrade to rookie Ryan Hanigan. Meanwhile, Taveras was, amazingly, as destructive a force as Patterson, hitting .242/.277/.282 while making 95 starts in center, 81 of which also saw him hitting leadoff. (Why not start nearly 75 percent of your games with an out, right?) By season's end, Gonzalez was back in Boston and all three positions were in the hands of rookies, two of whom had seen major-league action in 2008. Even good-field/no-hit shortstop Paul Janish and thumpless catcher Hanigan represented upgrades on both sides of the ball.

Table 1. You're with Me, Leather

Position	2008 VORP	2008 FRAA	Total Runs	2009 VORP	2009 FRAA	Total Runs	Change
C	3.34	-6	-2.66	6.34	9	15.34	+9.00
SS	14.40	-18	-3.60	-3.39	12	8.61	+12.21
CF	2.64	1	3.64	-1.14	26	24.86	+21.22

As great as those missed opportunities for improvement at those three positions were, there was little reason to expect much better given Jocketty's solutions. Far more devastating to the team's fortunes were the struggles of the aforementioned young players and the injuries that tore through the roster. Jay Bruce had a few hot weeks early in the season, but fell into a self-perpetuating slump by mid-May and broke his right wrist just before the All-Star break, earning a two-month stay on the disabled list. Chris Dickerson struggled in a platoon role early in the season, fell out of favor with Baker, and then severely sprained his ankle in late August, effectively ending his season. Cueto had an ugly stretch of a dozen starts midseason, after which he hit the DL with shoulder inflammation. Set-up man Jared Burton followed a similar path, struggling for three months before being shelved with shoulder fatigue. Votto raked but missed some time early in the year due to an inner-ear infection and depression stemming from his father's death, leaving first base in the hands of Hernandez and exposing the team's alarming lack of depth. Encarnacion collapsed at the plate and was as awful in the field as ever, prompting Jocketty to finally give up and ship him to Toronto at the trading deadline, thereby acquiring Scott Rolen for the second time this decade. Harang looked primed for a return to form after pitching first in bad luck, but was again inconsistent until an appendectomy sent him home for the year. The most devastating blow the Reds suffered in 2009, however, was the loss of Volquez to Tommy John surgery after just nine starts, and injury that not only beheaded their 2009 rotation, but also leaves them without an effective Volquez for the coming season and could well derail Volquez entirely from the track he was on as a potential staff ace.

A few things did go right for the Reds in 2009. Despite his early-season medical issues, Votto was among the most productive hitters in the majors when healthy, which he was for the entire second half. Center-field prospect Drew Stubbs arrived in mid-August to mercifully displace Taveras, finally giving the Reds a center fielder who can contribute at the plate and improving on Taveras's already strong defense in the process. Nick Masset came over from the White Sox at the 2008 deadline in the trade that ended the Ken Griffey Jr. era, and he turned in a strong, if somewhat lucky season setting up Cordero. After two years of growing pains and attitude problems, top pitching prospect Bailey improved his conditioning and mechanics and emerged as the pitcher the Reds had been waiting for, going 6-1 with a 1.70 ERA over his final nine starts.

If Bailey remains dedicated, he should more than replace Volquez in the rotation, but that's only partial consolation, as the 2010 Reds rotation could have included both youngsters with innings-eaters Arroyo and Harang behind them. Now, it's just Bailey, who is sure to endure more growing pains (at least until Aroldis Chapman arrives), and the offseason was littered with rumors of one of the two veteran starters being traded to provide the team with salary relief. Jocketty said in December that the team's 2010 payroll would remain at its 2009 (and 2008) level, but arbitration raises and back-loaded contracts mean that $74 million will buy less in the coming season than it did a year ago. As we went to press, the Reds had $66 million committed to just 10 players, with $46.5 million going to veterans Harang, Arroyo, Rolen, and Cordero. Even if the remaining 25 men on the roster all earned the minimum, the Reds' payroll would already be at $72 million. Add arbitration for set-up men Burton and Masset and standard raises for pre-arbitration players such as Votto, Bruce, Cueto, and company, and the Reds maxed out their 2010 payroll less than two weeks after the World Series, when Jocketty inexplicably re-signed Ramon Hernandez for $3 million, burbling about his veteran intangibles.

Asked over the winter about rumors, Arroyo posited that the first few months of the coming season would be do or die for the current roster. Arroyo explained his thinking to MLB.com's Mark Sheldon: "If you re-sign Ramon for a year, why then go in the other direction? If we were saving, we could have easily had Hanigan catching 130 games next year. ... In my mind, there was no reason to get Rolen if we're turning around and moving guys without waiting to see what happens. I think they'll give us four months to see if we can compete in the division. We need to have a good April, May, and June."

That's a short leash for a team that has no hope of seeing Volquez until July at the earliest. Still, with that significant exception, the potential the Reds held entering the 2009 season is still there. Votto is a stud. Bruce hit .326/.426/.652 in his brief return from his wrist injury in September, providing hope in 2010 that a proper breakout will follow this season. To a lesser degree, the same goes for Cueto, who posted a 3.63 ERA in five Reds wins over his six starts after returning from the DL, as

well as Burton (2.35 ERA and 3.2 K/BB in 22 appearances after returning from the DL in early August). Stubbs has solved center field. Rolen represents a couple of wins' worth of value over Encarnacion. Bailey gave Reds fans a lot to dream on down the stretch, and the six-year, $30.25 million commitment to Cuba's Aroldis Chapman might provide additional excitement and hope. All that leaves are holes at shortstop, where Janish's bat is quite simply unacceptable, and in left field.

Competing in the NL Central with the Cubs climbing down and the Cardinals likely to come back to the pack helps matters. Still, there's a lot of wishful thinking going on here, just as there was a year ago. The Reds might be scrambling and rescrambling to remain relevant, but they're working with a short deck.

HITTERS

Yonder Alonso — 1B

Bats: L Throws: R Height: 6' 2" Weight: 215 Born: April 8, 1987 Age: 23

YEAR	TEAM	LVL	AGE	PA	R	2B	3B	HR	RBI	BB	SO	SB	CS	EqBRR	AVG	OBP	SLG	EqAVG	EqOBP	EqSLG	EqA	VORP	WARP	DEFENSE	
2009	SAR	A+	22	201	21	13	0	7	38	24	30	0	1	-1.0	.303	.383	.497	.279	.351	.447	.275	3.2	0.0	41-1B	-3
2009	CAR	AA	22	121	12	11	0	2	14	14	15	1	0	-1.2	.295	.372	.457	.287	.347	.454	.278	2.5	0.4	27-1B	1
2010	CIN	MLB	23	333	30	18	0	9	46	35	61	1	1	-1.0	.261	.338	.414	.263	.338	.414	.260	3.5	0.3	70-1B	0

Breakout: 21% Improve: 42% Collapse: 14% Attrition: 1% MLB: 3% Comparables: Don Ross, Bob Tumpane, John Urick, Todd Helton

A big-hitting first-base prospect in an organization that already boasts a 26-year-old stud first-sacker, the Cuban-born Alonso is blocked in the bigs, but just as they were when they drafted him seventh overall out of the University of Miami in 2008, the Reds are hoping Alonso's bat will force its way into their lineup, anyway, most likely by pushing Joey Votto to left field. If that's going to happen, Alonso will need to solve lefty pitching and show some more pop. When Votto was 22, he slugged .547 with 22 home runs at Double-A. Alonso, meanwhile, slugged just .395 in the hitters' paradise that is the Arizona Fall League. That came after suffering a broken hamate bone in late July, but depending on your outlook, the injury could increase concern rather than dissuade it.

Wladimir Balentien — OF

Bats: R Throws: R Height: 6' 2" Weight: 215 Born: July 2, 1984 Age: 25

YEAR	TEAM	LVL	AGE	PA	R	2B	3B	HR	RBI	BB	SO	SB	CS	EqBRR	AVG	OBP	SLG	EqAVG	EqOBP	EqSLG	EqA	VORP	WARP	DEFENSE			
2007	TAC	AAA	22	544	77	24	4	24	84	54	105	15	4	2.8	.291	.362	.509	.273	.339	.458	.275	18.6	1.8	106-RF	-5	5-LF	1
2008	TAC	AAA	23	275	49	20	0	18	55	32	49	3	4	-2.9	.266	.354	.584	.248	.325	.504	.275	10.9	1.2	24-LF	2	19-CF	-3
2008	SEA	MLB	23	260	23	13	0	7	24	16	79	0	1	-0.9	.202	.250	.342	.207	.255	.343	.208	-8.3	-1.5	33-RF	-1	25-CF	-4
2009	SEA	MLB	24	170	18	10	0	4	13	13	43	1	0	0.6	.213	.271	.355	.221	.276	.364	.222	-3.6	0.2	38-LF	5	3-RF	0
2009	CIN	MLB	24	125	12	7	1	3	11	15	27	1	1	0.5	.264	.352	.427	.279	.365	.441	.277	4.3	0.9	17-LF	3	12-RF	0
2010	CIN	MLB	25	410	46	18	1	15	50	40	102	5	3	0.0	.243	.320	.421	.245	.319	.424	.254	6.1	1.3	78-LF	6		

Breakout: 10% Improve: 42% Collapse: 11% Attrition: 7% MLB: 74% Comparables: Ozzie Timmons, Glenn Wilson, Brian Anderson, Ben Petrick

A 25-year-old corner outfield prospect with big-time power and improving plate discipline but a few too many holes in his swing, the hot-headed Balentien wore out his welcome with the new Mariners administration alarmingly quickly. Just 130 games into his major-league career, he was designated for assignment and flipped to the Reds for a minor-league reliever who was subsequently lost on waivers after the season. True, Balentien hit just .209/.260/.359 in those 130 games with the M's, but he perked up upon arrival in the much friendlier hitting environment in Cincinnati and should be in the mix for the left-field job in camp.

Jay Bruce

RF   Bats: L   Throws: L   Height: 6' 3"   Weight: 205   Born: April 3, 1987   Age: 23

YEAR	TEAM	LVL	AGE	PA	R	2B	3B	HR	RBI	BB	SO	SB	CS	EqBRR	AVG	OBP	SLG	EqAVG	EqOBP	EqSLG	EqA	VORP	WARP	DEFENSE			
2007	SAR	A+	20	298	49	27	5	11	49	24	67	4	4	-1.4	.325	.379	.586	.276	.326	.496	.275	12.8	1.4	49-CF	-2	18-RF	1
2007	CHT	AA	20	74	10	7	1	4	15	8	20	2	1	-0.1	.333	.405	.652	.299	.365	.597	.309	6.3	0.5	11-CF	-1	4-RF	-1
2007	LOU	AAA	20	204	28	12	2	11	25	15	48	2	2	-1.3	.305	.358	.567	.287	.338	.543	.289	12.4	1.9	40-CF	3	9-RF	1
2008	LOU	AAA	21	201	34	9	5	10	37	12	45	8	1	-1.0	.364	.393	.630	.342	.370	.598	.319	19.0	2.7	26-CF	1	10-RF	2
2008	CIN	MLB	21	452	63	17	1	21	52	33	110	4	6	-0.1	.254	.314	.453	.262	.319	.465	.261	10.4	0.1	66-RF	-8	32-CF	1
2009	CIN	MLB	22	387	47	15	2	22	58	38	75	3	3	0.0	.223	.303	.470	.234	.311	.494	.266	10.3	2.2	90-RF	9		
2010	CIN	MLB	23	518	73	26	5	27	73	45	126	6	5	-0.5	.267	.333	.513	.268	.333	.501	.280	23.4	2.7	115-RF	1		

Breakout: 15% Improve: 53% Collapse: 5% Attrition: 5%   MLB: 100%   Comparables: Eric Anthony, Mel Hall, Harold Baines, Nick Markakis

Bruce was our top prospect in the 2008 annual, and his power is undeniable, but after 839 MLB plate appearances, his ability to get on base or to hit lefties is in doubt. Bruce had a nice 19-game run from mid-April to early May, but an ensuing slump led him to tinker with his swing to the point that his mechanics fell apart almost completely. Bruce hit just .177/.250/.370 over a three-month span through July 11, at which point he broke his right wrist while making a sliding catch. The time off might have been just what he needed, as he raked in his late-September return (.326/.426/.652 in 54 PAs). He still has a lot to prove, but he'll be just 23 this season, so he has time to prove it.

Zack Cozart

SS   Bats: R   Throws: R   Height: 6' 1"   Weight: 185   Born: August 12, 1985   Age: 24

YEAR	TEAM	LVL	AGE	PA	R	2B	3B	HR	RBI	BB	SO	SB	CS	EqBRR	AVG	OBP	SLG	EqAVG	EqOBP	EqSLG	EqA	VORP	WARP	DEFENSE			
2007	DYT	A	21	201	28	7	2	2	18	11	36	3	1	-0.5	.239	.288	.332	.220	.259	.317	.200	-4.4	-0.9	45-SS	-2	6-2B	-1
2008	DYT	A	22	464	57	20	6	14	49	24	77	3	3	0.6	.280	.330	.457	.245	.283	.385	.231	4.7	0.6	101-SS	0		
2009	CAR	AA	23	541	72	29	2	10	59	63	87	10	2	3.9	.262	.360	.398	.253	.331	.387	.255	15.8	2.3	116-SS	3		
2010	CIN	MLB	24	472	53	21	3	10	43	37	99	4	2	0.8	.237	.304	.371	.241	.305	.370	.234	4.0	0.5	108-SS	0		

Breakout: 11% Improve: 34% Collapse: 23% Attrition: 10%   MLB: 6%   Comparables: Jeff Bannon, Erick Almonte, Tim Olson, Eddie Zosky

An outstanding defensive shortstop drafted out of Ole Miss in 2007's second round, Cozart not only survived the leap to Double-A last year, but made considerable gains in his plate discipline in the process, posting a 1.4 K/BB ratio with a strikeout every 6.2 plate appearances after posting a 3.2 K/BB with a K every 5.3 plate appearances in his first two pro seasons. He also stole 10 bases in 12 tries, all of which made his inability to repeat his 2008 power surge less problematic.

Chris Dickerson

OF   Bats: L   Throws: L   Height: 6' 3"   Weight: 225   Born: April 10, 1982   Age: 28

YEAR	TEAM	LVL	AGE	PA	R	2B	3B	HR	RBI	BB	SO	SB	CS	EqBRR	AVG	OBP	SLG	EqAVG	EqOBP	EqSLG	EqA	VORP	WARP	DEFENSE			
2007	CHT	AA	25	123	11	4	1	1	11	7	31	7	2	-0.4	.272	.325	.351	.231	.268	.308	.203	-3.4	-0.9	29-CF	-4		
2007	LOU	AAA	25	416	58	11	6	13	44	52	131	23	5	2.1	.260	.361	.435	.249	.341	.416	.268	13.6	0.8	57-CF	-5	27-LF	-3
2008	LOU	AAA	26	414	65	16	9	11	53	54	102	26	7	4.2	.287	.384	.479	.262	.354	.428	.275	16.9	2.4	66-CF	3	18-RF	-1
2008	CIN	MLB	26	122	20	9	2	6	15	17	35	5	3	-0.4	.304	.413	.608	.320	.426	.621	.331	13.0	1.8	21-LF	2	5-CF	1
2009	CIN	MLB	27	299	31	13	3	2	15	39	66	11	3	-1.9	.275	.370	.373	.289	.379	.391	.278	11.6	2.1	28-LF	2	19-CF	6
2010	CIN	MLB	28	405	47	17	5	9	39	47	118	11	5	0.5	.244	.337	.396	.245	.336	.394	.256	7.0	0.8	75-LF	0		

Breakout: 14% Improve: 37% Collapse: 20% Attrition: 13%   MLB: 57%   Comparables: Fred Lewis, Brant Brown, Curtis Pride, Jeromy Burnitz

Dickerson entered 2009 with a chance to seize the left-field job, but started off cold and lost his share of the platoon to Laynce Nix by early May. Fighting for playing time thereafter, he hit for average and showed off his on-base and base-stealing abilities, hitting .305/.394/.406 in 218 plate appearances with 11 steals in 12 attempts from May 13th to August 23rd. On the latter date, he severely sprained his ankle trying to beat a pickoff throw at first base, essentially ending his season. Dickerson will be in the mix for playing time in left again this spring, but he'll be 28 soon after Opening Day and may have to resign himself to a career as a toolsy part-timer at all three outfield positions.

Daniel Dorn — OF

Bats: L   Throws: L   Height: 6' 2"   Weight: 190   Born: July 20, 1984   Age: 25

YEAR	TEAM	LVL	AGE	PA	R	2B	3B	HR	RBI	BB	SO	SB	CS	EqBRR	AVG	OBP	SLG	EqAVG	EqOBP	EqSLG	EqA	VORP	WARP	DEFENSE			
2007	SAR	A+	22	387	49	21	1	12	66	32	69	3	1	-0.2	.281	.359	.456	.256	.320	.418	.257	6.0	0.0	74-LF	-6	12-RF	0
2007	CHT	AA	22	109	20	6	1	8	21	15	23	1	0	0.8	.311	.422	.667	.290	.385	.602	.323	9.9	1.2	14-LF	0		
2008	CHT	AA	23	388	64	21	2	21	60	42	84	1	0	0.5	.277	.367	.539	.250	.320	.474	.269	10.3	0.9	53-LF	1	19-1B	-2
2009	LOU	AAA	24	396	45	21	1	14	47	30	78	2	1	-1.0	.275	.337	.457	.265	.324	.446	.264	5.7	0.9	56-LF	0	24-1B	2
2010	CIN	MLB	25	386	45	19	1	14	50	34	95	2	1	0.0	.245	.318	.430	.246	.318	.423	.256	6.4	0.6	78-LF	-1		

Breakout: 5%   Improve: 28%   Collapse: 22%   Attrition: 15%   MLB: 6%   Comparables: John Vander Wal, Jim Bennett, Stanley Davis, Ryan Church

A late-round pick out of Cal State Fullerton in 2006, Dorn doesn't do much other than hit righties a little, but he does that well enough that he might have a career as a lefty platoon player or bench weapon able to bounce between left field and first base.

Juan Francisco — 3B/LF

Bats: L   Throws: R   Height: 6' 2"   Weight: 180   Born: June 24, 1987   Age: 23

YEAR	TEAM	LVL	AGE	PA	R	2B	3B	HR	RBI	BB	SO	SB	CS	EqBRR	AVG	OBP	SLG	EqAVG	EqOBP	EqSLG	EqA	VORP	WARP	DEFENSE	
2007	DYT	A	20	562	69	21	4	25	90	23	161	12	6	-3.7	.268	.301	.463	.241	.269	.406	.230	-6.9	-1.6	116-3B	-6
2008	SAR	A+	21	541	71	34	5	23	92	19	123	1	2	-1.0	.277	.303	.496	.250	.270	.438	.239	-0.5	-2.2	105-3B	-18
2009	CAR	AA	22	464	64	26	2	22	74	20	91	6	2	-4.0	.281	.317	.501	.269	.297	.479	.261	13.3	-0.4	102-3B	-17
2009	LOU	AAA	22	99	17	5	1	5	19	4	24	0	0	-0.5	.359	.384	.598	.337	.364	.565	.309	8.4	1.0	21-3B	0
2009	CIN	MLB	22	25	4	1	0	1	7	3	7	0	0	0.3	.429	.520	.619	.429	.520	.619	.399	3.6	0.6	3-3B	1
2010	CIN	MLB	23	545	63	26	4	20	78	26	157	4	2	-1.4	.244	.284	.428	.245	.284	.420	.240	2.6	-0.4	113-3B	-7

Breakout: 16%   Improve: 42%   Collapse: 19%   Attrition: 8%   MLB: 8%   Comparables: Scott Moore, Brad Gennaro, Mark Ryal, Juan Williams

Francisco has a ton of power, but there's not much else to recommend him. He won't take walks, he struck out 442 times in 447 minor-league games, he can't hit lefties, and, outside of a strong arm, he's not particularly adept in the field, in part because of his struggles with his weight. Still, that power is awfully alluring and helped him race through the Reds' system in 2009, debuting in Double-A to start the year and slugging .518 between Carolina and a brief stint in Triple-A Louisville before making the most of a cup of coffee after rosters expanded.

Todd Frazier — 2B

Bats: R   Throws: R   Height: 6' 3"   Weight: 215   Born: February 12, 1986   Age: 24

YEAR	TEAM	LVL	AGE	PA	R	2B	3B	HR	RBI	BB	SO	SB	CS	EqBRR	AVG	OBP	SLG	EqAVG	EqOBP	EqSLG	EqA	VORP	WARP	DEFENSE			
2007	BIL	Rk	21	186	29	6	5	5	25	18	22	3	3	-0.1	.319	.409	.512	.262	.328	.393	.252	4.5	-0.4	34-SS	-7		
2008	DYT	A	22	127	25	10	0	7	20	15	28	4	2	-0.6	.321	.402	.598	.270	.339	.487	.278	6.4	0.9	16-SS	0	4-1B	1
2008	SAR	A+	22	414	62	20	3	12	54	41	84	8	4	-0.2	.281	.357	.451	.256	.319	.405	.252	8.6	0.5	55-SS	-2	15-1B	-1
2009	CAR	AA	23	500	59	40	2	14	68	42	67	7	8	-5.0	.290	.350	.481	.278	.326	.461	.267	13.5	1.5	73-LF	3	23-2B	-4
2009	LOU	AAA	23	69	9	5	0	2	9	6	12	2	0	0.6	.302	.362	.476	.286	.348	.444	.278	3.3	0.8	15-2B	3		
2010	CIN	MLB	24	513	60	26	2	16	58	46	109	5	3	-1.1	.255	.325	.425	.259	.325	.425	.257	9.3	1.2	95-LF	2		

Breakout: 15%   Improve: 41%   Collapse: 16%   Attrition: 12%   MLB: 10%   Comparables: Todd Brown, Wes Chamberlain, Ozzie Timmons, Matt Holliday

Drafted as a shortstop in the first supplemental round in 2007, New Jersey native and Rutgers product Todd Frazier has been a true utility man in his first two full seasons of pro ball, appearing at all four infield positions and in left field. Wherever he has played, he has hit, compiling a .296/.367/.491 career line and capping his 2009 season with a strong showing in Triple-A, where he was primarily used as a second baseman. Not strong enough defensively to stick at short, Frazier remained at the keystone in an instructional league and will enter camp at the position. It's a good fit, given his offensive profile, which isn't enough to carry a corner in the major leagues but which would make him a valuable second sacker. He'll be blocked by Brandon Phillips there, of course, but it's quite possible that the Reds will trade Phillips to suppress payroll, thus handing the position to Frazier.

Jonny Gomes   OF

Bats: R   Throws: R   Height: 6′ 1″   Weight: 225   Born: November 22, 1980   Age: 29

YEAR	TEAM	LVL	AGE	PA	R	2B	3B	HR	RBI	BB	SO	SB	CS	EqBRR	AVG	OBP	SLG	EqAVG	EqOBP	EqSLG	EqA	VORP	WARP	DEFENSE			
2007	TBA	MLB	26	394	48	20	2	17	49	35	126	12	4	1.1	.244	.322	.460	.251	.329	.481	.274	12.4	1.0	29-RF	0	21-LF	-3
2008	DUR	AAA	27	123	19	11	0	2	14	12	32	0	1	-0.3	.252	.341	.411	.229	.309	.349	.231	-2.0	0.0	12-LF	2		
2008	TBA	MLB	27	177	23	5	1	8	21	15	46	8	1	0.5	.182	.282	.383	.188	.288	.409	.245	-0.7	-0.5	14-RF	-3	4-LF	-1
2009	LOU	AAA	28	147	18	10	1	9	27	12	36	4	1	-1.4	.282	.361	.580	.263	.333	.534	.286	7.0	0.2	17-LF	-2	12-RF	-3
2009	CIN	MLB	28	314	39	17	0	20	51	26	85	3	1	-0.1	.267	.338	.541	.278	.344	.569	.298	19.6	1.7	30-RF	-4	28-LF	-1
2010	CIN	MLB	29	465	57	21	2	22	65	48	135	8	4	0.0	.242	.335	.467	.243	.332	.467	.272	16.4	1.5	68-LF	-2		

Breakout: 17%   Improve: 45%   Collapse: 7%   Attrition: 5%   MLB: 91%   Comparables: Pete Incaviglia, Preston Wilson, Ernie Young, Richard Hidalgo

Stop us if you've heard this one before: Gomes has big-time power but struggles against same-handed pitching, strikes out too much, is a brutal fielder, and has seen his patience at the plate erode in recent seasons. Last year, he overcame the first to slug .539 against righties and to work his way into the Reds' outfield picture in the wake of Bruce's wrist injury. As he did down the stretch last year, Gomes might fit a left-field platoon somewhere (the Reds non-tendered him), but he's not a long-term solution and, at 29, is unlikely to be a long-term major leaguer.

Ryan Hanigan   C

Bats: R   Throws: R   Height: 6′ 0″   Weight: 195   Born: August 16, 1980   Age: 29

YEAR	TEAM	LVL	AGE	PA	R	2B	3B	HR	RBI	BB	SO	SB	CS	EqBRR	AVG	OBP	SLG	EqAVG	EqOBP	EqSLG	EqA	VORP	WARP	DEFENSE	
2007	CHT	AA	26	247	30	14	1	3	27	41	30	0	2	-0.5	.299	.420	.426	.257	.352	.357	.256	10.1	0.9	55-C	-3
2007	LOU	AAA	26	150	16	5	0	1	9	14	15	0	0	-0.3	.252	.333	.315	.237	.308	.290	.218	0.2	1.0	31-C	8
2007	CIN	MLB	26	11	3	1	0	0	2	1	2	0	0	0.8	.300	.364	.400	.300	.364	.400	.256	0.2	0.0		
2008	LOU	AAA	27	311	37	14	0	4	35	25	39	1	0	-2.4	.324	.392	.419	.303	.365	.383	.268	15.1	2.3	71-C	4
2008	CIN	MLB	27	98	9	2	0	2	9	10	9	0	0	0.3	.271	.367	.365	.271	.367	.365	.264	4.3	0.7	26-C	2
2009	CIN	MLB	28	293	22	6	1	3	11	37	31	0	0	-1.4	.263	.361	.331	.269	.363	.336	.255	10.7	2.0	75-C	6
2010	CIN	MLB	29	309	32	12	1	4	25	33	44	1	1	-0.4	.260	.352	.357	.265	.353	.361	.252	9.3	1.3	74-C	2

Breakout: 8%   Improve: 29%   Collapse: 22%   Attrition: 13%   MLB: 64%   Comparables: Bud Bulling, Carlos Ruiz, A.J. Hinch, Greg Olson

Hanigan is not a particularly exciting player, but he deserves better than he's gotten from the Reds. Last year, he clearly outproduced Ramon Hernandez, a catcher four years his senior, but the Reds opted to bring back Hernandez for his "veteran experience," despite the fact that he will cost them nearly four times as much as Hanigan for the 2010 season. Hernandez has more power than Hanigan, but that's not saying much. Hanigan, on the other hand, is considerably better at getting on base and, in his brief major-league career, has walked more than he's struck out. He has also thrown out an impressive 40 percent of opposing basestealers. Hanigan would be a backup on a good team, but he shouldn't have to lose playing time to the rapidly aging Hernandez.

Chris Heisey   OF

Bats: R   Throws: R   Height: 6′ 0″   Weight: 200   Born: December 14, 1984   Age: 25

YEAR	TEAM	LVL	AGE	PA	R	2B	3B	HR	RBI	BB	SO	SB	CS	EqBRR	AVG	OBP	SLG	EqAVG	EqOBP	EqSLG	EqA	VORP	WARP	DEFENSE			
2007	DYT	A	22	414	60	24	2	9	46	25	57	19	5	1.9	.289	.350	.436	.256	.303	.381	.239	-1.0	0.0	88-LF	2	10-CF	-1
2007	SAR	A+	22	49	6	1	0	1	5	4	6	3	1	0.4	.349	.396	.442	.318	.367	.409	.275	1.8	-0.2	9-LF	-4		
2008	SAR	A+	23	515	77	31	7	7	51	57	69	27	2	7.5	.287	.381	.438	.258	.333	.393	.259	9.9	0.9	75-RF	-3	36-CF	1
2008	CHT	AA	23	82	11	6	1	2	10	3	15	5	0	1.2	.316	.341	.494	.287	.305	.463	.265	2.8	0.3	18-CF	0		
2009	CAR	AA	24	314	54	18	2	13	40	34	34	13	1	3.3	.347	.426	.572	.327	.388	.541	.313	27.5	2.4	66-CF	-7		
2009	LOU	AAA	24	271	37	17	1	9	37	14	43	8	2	-1.4	.278	.323	.465	.272	.316	.463	.268	8.9	1.1	26-CF	1	22-LF	-1
2010	CIN	MLB	25	527	65	27	3	13	52	42	95	11	4	2.1	.262	.329	.414	.267	.330	.419	.258	15.0	1.4	115-CF	-2		

Breakout: 8%   Improve: 34%   Collapse: 12%   Attrition: 8%   MLB: 12%   Comparables: Chris Aguila, Mike Berger, Ben Francisco, Chris Denorfia

A 17th-round pick out of Messiah College in 2006, Heisey hardly had "prospect" written all over him as he entered pro ball, but a big age-24 season has significantly raised his profile. After a brief taste of Double-A in 2008, Heisey crushed there last year, earning a promotion to Triple-A, where he cooled off considerably, but not so much that he looked overmatched. A high-percentage basestealer (86 bags at 84 percent in 3 ½ minor-league seasons) with some pop, a solid plate approach (1.6 K/BB career with a strikeout every 7.5 plate appearances), and a hard-nosed approach to the game, Heisey seems likely to grind out a major-league career as a fourth outfielder or second-division starter.

Sean Henry — OF

Bats: R Throws: R Height: 5' 10" Weight: 180 Born: August 18, 1985 Age: 24

YEAR	TEAM	LVL	AGE	PA	R	2B	3B	HR	RBI	BB	SO	SB	CS	EqBRR	AVG	OBP	SLG	EqAVG	EqOBP	EqSLG	EqA	VORP	WARP	DEFENSE		
2007	SLU	A+	21	504	59	26	7	11	57	42	73	18	11	-7.4	.293	.355	.456	.267	.321	.420	.256	9.2	-1.0	73-LF	-12	39-CF -6
2007	CHT	AA	21	67	9	3	0	1	2	6	11	1	1	-0.4	.241	.333	.345	.217	.288	.317	.213	-1.2	-0.4	12-CF	-2	
2008	SAR	A+	22	46	6	3	1	0	7	3	7	4	0	0.1	.293	.370	.415	.262	.326	.381	.257	0.6	-0.2	9-LF	-2	
2008	CHT	AA	22	454	66	22	6	11	62	42	75	16	7	-1.3	.285	.361	.455	.259	.319	.403	.252	4.6	-0.2	47-RF	-1	44-LF -3
2009	CAR	AA	23	469	66	22	1	11	38	40	66	23	9	3.7	.271	.341	.407	.260	.315	.392	.248	3.5	-0.4	57-RF	-5	33-CF -2
2010	CIN	MLB	24	470	52	21	3	11	45	39	92	10	5	-0.8	.247	.314	.389	.250	.314	.389	.243	1.6	-0.1	98-RF	-3	

Breakout: 17% Improve: 36% Collapse: 24% Attrition: 5% MLB: 5% Comparables: Winston Ficklin, Alex Ochoa, Phil Avlas, Manny Martinez

Acquired from the Mets for Jeff Conine late in the 2007 season, Henry is a small infielder turned outfielder the Reds are hoping might have a future as a supersub, with solid all-around skills despite doing no one thing particularly well.

Ramon Hernandez — C

Bats: R Throws: R Height: 6' 0" Weight: 235 Born: May 20, 1976 Age: 34

YEAR	TEAM	LVL	AGE	PA	R	2B	3B	HR	RBI	BB	SO	SB	CS	EqBRR	AVG	OBP	SLG	EqAVG	EqOBP	EqSLG	EqA	VORP	WARP	DEFENSE	
2007	BAL	MLB	31	409	40	18	0	9	62	36	59	1	3	-2.6	.258	.333	.382	.259	.334	.383	.251	15.2	0.7	96-C	-5
2008	BAL	MLB	32	507	49	22	1	15	65	32	62	0	0	-3.5	.257	.308	.406	.260	.312	.410	.251	17.0	0.6	118-C	-7
2009	CIN	MLB	33	331	25	13	1	5	37	33	34	1	0	-3.1	.258	.336	.362	.267	.341	.382	.257	8.4	1.3	50-C 2	28-1B 1
2010	CIN	MLB	34	315	30	13	1	8	44	28	48	1	1	-1.2	.260	.336	.399	.265	.337	.404	.255	10.6	1.0	75-C	-1

Breakout: 16% Improve: 47% Collapse: 21% Attrition: 17% MLB: 96% Comparables: Bengie Molina, Damian Miller, Mike Matheny, Dan Wilson

Once an underrated catching asset for the A's and Padres, Hernandez has hit .258/.324/.387 over the last three seasons, which just barely matches the low standard of the average big-league backstop. He has also surpassed 111 games played just twice in his last six seasons. Last year, he made just 53 starts behind the plate, in part due to his filling in for Joey Votto at first base, and in part due to the bum knee, which required an arthroscopic cleanup, essentially costing him the second half beyond a few season-ending starts. Though Hanigan more than doubled his VORP total in fewer plate appearances last year, Hernandez was bought back by the allegedly cost-cutting Reds via a $3 million deal with a $3.25 million option that vests with 120 games played in the coming season—this, after they spent $1 million to buy out his original 2010 option. Walt Jocketty cited that old straw man, "veteran influence," when announcing the deal, but one wonders if he isn't just trying to justify the loss of the two infield prospects he sent to the O's for Hernandez the previous offseason.

Paul Janish — SS

Bats: R Throws: R Height: 6' 2" Weight: 190 Born: October 12, 1982 Age: 27

YEAR	TEAM	LVL	AGE	PA	R	2B	3B	HR	RBI	BB	SO	SB	CS	EqBRR	AVG	OBP	SLG	EqAVG	EqOBP	EqSLG	EqA	VORP	WARP	DEFENSE	
2007	CHT	AA	24	391	46	21	2	1	20	50	54	10	3	-0.2	.244	.358	.330	.221	.312	.295	.223	-0.8	-0.3	67-SS 0	13-2B -2
2007	LOU	AAA	24	227	20	8	1	3	19	14	31	2	0	0.2	.221	.278	.317	.211	.264	.304	.202	-4.2	-1.0	55-SS	-4
2008	LOU	AAA	25	365	45	20	1	7	42	26	71	2	0	1.4	.252	.324	.387	.241	.305	.367	.238	6.4	1.4	88-SS	5
2008	CIN	MLB	25	89	5	2	0	1	6	7	18	0	0	0.1	.188	.270	.250	.188	.270	.250	.182	-2.8	0.1	23-SS	3
2009	CIN	MLB	26	292	36	21	0	1	16	26	40	2	0	0.7	.211	.296	.305	.216	.298	.305	.221	-0.5	1.3	66-SS	15
2010	CIN	MLB	27	379	40	18	1	5	30	35	72	2	1	0.3	.225	.306	.329	.230	.307	.333	.223	-0.9	0.2	90-SS	3

Breakout: 25% Improve: 50% Collapse: 28% Attrition: 23% MLB: 74% Comparables: Tim Bogar, Freddie Benavides, Tony Walker, Josh Wilson

As poor a hitter as Janish is, he's that good with the glove, enough so that he was able to keep his head above replacement level last year (note the difference between his VORP and WARP totals above, as WARP includes defense and VORP doesn't). That's fitting, as Janish was very much a replacement player at shortstop last year after Alex Gonzalez was dealt to Boston at the deadline. As such, Janish will serve as a sufficient caddy to whatever solution the Reds find for shortstop for the coming season, but he shouldn't retain the job himself, as he hasn't hit since he was in A-ball.

Laynce Nix   OF

Bats: L   Throws: L   Height: 6' 1"   Weight: 220   Born: October 30, 1980   Age: 29

YEAR	TEAM	LVL	AGE	PA	R	2B	3B	HR	RBI	BB	SO	SB	CS	EqBRR	AVG	OBP	SLG	EqAVG	EqOBP	EqSLG	EqA	VORP	WARP	DEFENSE
2007	NAS	AAA	26	386	60	20	1	24	74	31	104	5	0	0.4	.268	.329	.539	.244	.298	.460	.259	8.8	2.3	59-CF 5 23-RF 5
2008	NAS	AAA	27	420	63	22	3	23	60	36	88	5	3	-1.0	.284	.348	.539	.253	.307	.442	.255	6.9	0.2	42-CF -1 41-RF -5
2009	CIN	MLB	28	337	42	26	1	15	46	22	81	0	1	1.1	.239	.291	.476	.249	.297	.492	.263	6.7	1.1	62-LF 2 7-RF 2
2010	CIN	MLB	29	376	42	19	1	16	48	28	105	2	1	0.1	.233	.296	.438	.235	.296	.427	.248	3.0	0.5	76-LF 1

Breakout: 11%   Improve: 34%   Collapse: 22%   Attrition: 18%   MLB: 39%   Comparables: John-Ford Griffin, Luke Scott, Jason Grabowski, Ryan Radmanovich

Another member of the Reds "Power, but …" team, Nix played in just 39 major-league games from 2006 to 2008 after falling out of favor in Texas. Like his compadres in the Queen City, he won't walk, doesn't hit for average, and can't touch same-handed pitching (.179/.220/.263 against lefties in his big-league career, albeit in just 166 PAs), but he's a valuable defender capable of making positive contributions in all three pastures. Nix, designated for assignment, was brought back on a minor-league deal and figures to be in the mix for a job.

Brandon Phillips   2B

Bats: R   Throws: R   Height: 6' 0"   Weight: 195   Born: June 28, 1981   Age: 29

YEAR	TEAM	LVL	AGE	PA	R	2B	3B	HR	RBI	BB	SO	SB	CS	EqBRR	AVG	OBP	SLG	EqAVG	EqOBP	EqSLG	EqA	VORP	WARP	DEFENSE
2007	CIN	MLB	26	702	107	26	6	30	94	33	109	32	8	1.9	.288	.331	.485	.291	.334	.485	.278	38.1	4.0	153-2B -3
2008	CIN	MLB	27	609	80	24	7	21	78	39	93	23	10	0.9	.261	.312	.442	.269	.317	.453	.261	20.4	2.3	139-2B -1
2009	CIN	MLB	28	644	78	30	5	20	98	44	75	25	9	3.0	.276	.329	.447	.289	.337	.466	.275	31.3	3.3	148-2B -2
2010	CIN	MLB	29	641	89	28	5	26	95	46	98	22	10	1.0	.279	.339	.479	.283	.340	.478	.276	32.0	3.4	148-2B -1

Breakout: 15%   Improve: 51%   Collapse: 5%   Attrition: 4%   MLB: 100%   Comparables: Shawon Dunston, Ryne Sandberg, Alfonso Soriano, Odell Hale

A fine fielder, Phillips' gains at the plate in 2009 were mostly due to a 15-point jump in batting average. He actually gave back some power, but it was an encouraging campaign nonetheless, as his plate approach was the best of his career. At 28, Phillips will never generate significant value from his patience, but even some small improvement could keep him from disaster should his batting average head in the other direction. Prior to 2009, Phillips' K/UBB ratio was 3.4, and he drew an unintentional walk once every 20.9 plate appearances. In 2009, those numbers improved to 1.8 K/UBB and 15.7 PA/UBB. His salary jumps up to $11 million in 2011, the final nonoption year of his contract, making him a player the Reds might choose to trade to suppress payroll, particularly given his trade value and the emergence of Frazier at the keystone.

Scott Rolen   3B

Bats: R   Throws: R   Height: 6' 4"   Weight: 250   Born: April 4, 1975   Age: 35

YEAR	TEAM	LVL	AGE	PA	R	2B	3B	HR	RBI	BB	SO	SB	CS	EqBRR	AVG	OBP	SLG	EqAVG	EqOBP	EqSLG	EqA	VORP	WARP	DEFENSE
2007	SLN	MLB	32	441	55	24	2	8	58	37	56	5	3	1.6	.265	.331	.398	.277	.342	.415	.263	11.5	2.7	106-3B 12
2008	TOR	MLB	33	467	58	30	3	11	50	46	71	5	0	-0.9	.262	.349	.431	.268	.353	.440	.278	20.2	4.4	113-3B 17
2009	TOR	MLB	34	373	52	29	0	8	43	26	42	4	2	3.0	.320	.370	.476	.330	.379	.482	.295	24.6	3.3	87-3B 5
2009	CIN	MLB	34	162	24	7	1	3	24	19	20	1	2	-1.5	.270	.364	.401	.285	.370	.416	.277	6.8	0.8	38-3B 0
2010	CIN	MLB	35	481	59	24	2	11	58	48	74	3	3	0.4	.271	.353	.415	.274	.353	.412	.266	15.5	2.4	117-3B 6

Breakout: 5%   Improve: 35%   Collapse: 16%   Attrition: 15%   MLB: 97%   Comparables: Casey Blake, Matt Williams, Bobby Bonilla, Mike Lowell

The trade that sent Rolen from Toronto to Cincinnati for Edwin Encarnacion and Triple-A relievers Josh Roenicke and Zach Stewart was instigated by Rolen, who asked to be traded closer to his Indiana home for "personal reasons." One wonders if those personal reasons had anything to do with Rolen's meager .239/.376/.388 performance at the Gap, a ballpark that favors right-handed power hitters. Then again, Rolen isn't much of a power hitter anymore. His batting average spike with Toronto over the season's first four months, largely obtained against left-handed pitching, hid the fact that his isolated slugging was again below league average. Over the last three seasons, Rolen has hit just 30 home runs in 1,443 plate appearances with a below-average ISO of .151. Rolen can still pick it at the hot corner and gives the Reds a much-needed boost in on-base percentage, which makes him an upgrade on Encarnacion, but he'll be 35 in 2010 and will cost the Reds $11 million, making him the most expensive regular on a team looking to cut payroll. Assuming he can stay healthy in the early going (a concussion suffered four games into his Reds tenure prompted his only DL stay in 2009), he's almost guaranteed to be flipped again, assuming things are going better at home.

Adam Rosales — INF

Bats: R Throws: R Height: 6' 1" Weight: 195 Born: May 20, 1983 Age: 27

YEAR	TEAM	LVL	AGE	PA	R	2B	3B	HR	RBI	BB	SO	SB	CS	EqBRR	AVG	OBP	SLG	EqAVG	EqOBP	EqSLG	EqA	VORP	WARP	DEFENSE			
2007	SAR	A+	24	300	47	23	5	5	48	31	46	9	2	2.4	.294	.393	.488	.258	.336	.412	.264	4.3	0.5	49-1B	0		
2007	CHT	AA	24	302	51	18	6	13	31	37	66	4	4	4.5	.278	.377	.549	.249	.329	.468	.271	6.6	0.7	57-1B	-1		
2008	LOU	AAA	25	473	70	29	7	11	58	22	82	7	1	1.8	.287	.339	.463	.272	.319	.437	.261	12.5	2.4	60-3B	0	21-SS	4
2008	CIN	MLB	25	30	0	1	0	0	2	1	4	1	0	0.0	.207	.233	.241	.207	.233	.241	.166	-2.3	-0.2	3-3B	0		
2009	LOU	AAA	26	125	27	8	2	5	20	12	15	4	0	1.9	.349	.408	.596	.336	.392	.573	.325	13.4	1.8	11-3B	0	10-SS	2
2009	CIN	MLB	26	266	23	10	1	4	19	26	46	1	2	0.3	.213	.303	.317	.221	.306	.325	.228	-3.3	-0.4	47-3B	-3	9-1B	2
2010	CIN	MLB	27	411	52	21	3	9	42	36	83	4	2	1.5	.250	.328	.399	.255	.329	.403	.253	7.3	0.7	73-3B	-1		

Breakout: 9% Improve: 34% Collapse: 23% Attrition: 19% MLB: 55% Comparables: Les Norman, Craig Stansberry, Tucker Ashford, Jeff Moronko

Drafted as a shortstop in 2005 and moved to first base in 2007, Rosales spent the majority of his time in 2008 and 2009 at third. All that movement tells us that Rosales' primary value is on offense. Indeed, he's a career .299/.353/.490 hitter at Triple-A. The catch is that given an extended trial in the majors last year, he didn't hit a lick, which is problematic for a notional offense-first player who will be 27 in May. The ability to play all four infield positions and left field in a pinch will only go so far.

Drew Stubbs — CF

Bats: R Throws: R Height: 6' 4" Weight: 200 Born: October 4, 1984 Age: 25

YEAR	TEAM	LVL	AGE	PA	R	2B	3B	HR	RBI	BB	SO	SB	CS	EqBRR	AVG	OBP	SLG	EqAVG	EqOBP	EqSLG	EqA	VORP	WARP	DEFENSE			
2007	DYT	A	22	575	93	29	5	12	43	69	142	23	15	-7.7	.270	.364	.421	.232	.312	.352	.235	1.0	-0.1	125-CF	-2		
2008	SAR	A+	23	358	49	21	4	5	38	50	82	27	8	1.8	.261	.366	.406	.226	.313	.350	.240	2.0	-1.6	84-CF	-16		
2008	CHT	AA	23	106	12	8	0	0	9	11	21	3	1	0.4	.315	.400	.402	.271	.340	.344	.245	1.2	0.6	24-CF	4		
2008	LOU	AAA	23	84	14	4	2	2	10	6	20	3	0	-0.3	.293	.354	.480	.276	.337	.461	.276	3.8	0.7	18-CF	2		
2009	LOU	AAA	24	472	57	25	2	3	39	51	104	46	8	3.3	.268	.353	.360	.249	.333	.339	.251	8.6	3.8	98-CF	20	5-LF	1
2009	CIN	MLB	24	196	27	5	1	8	17	15	49	10	4	-1.3	.267	.323	.439	.282	.337	.470	.270	8.3	2.0	41-CF	8		
2010	CIN	MLB	25	597	68	27	3	9	45	60	164	20	8	-0.6	.234	.315	.348	.239	.315	.352	.236	3.2	0.7	133-CF	3		

Breakout: 12% Improve: 40% Collapse: 19% Attrition: 10% MLB: 55% Comparables: Chris Sheff, Chad Alexander, Scott Lydy, Bert Hunter

The eighth pick in the 2006 draft, Stubbs is an otherworldly defensive center fielder and an excellent baserunner with real power—at least at the Gap, where he hit .337/.380/.616 with seven of eight home runs, versus .202/.272/.277 on the road. (Small-sample caveats apply.) Unfortunately, his propensity for strikeouts undermines the rest of his offensive game. He'll take his walks, but not so many that he's viable at the top of the order without learning to hit for a better average, and those better averages won't come until he figures out how to cut down on the Ks. The good news is that he's only 25 and staked his claim to the center-field job in mid-August, meaning he'll have both the time and the opportunity to improve.

Drew Sutton — UT

Bats: S Throws: R Height: 6' 3" Weight: 185 Born: June 30, 1983 Age: 27

YEAR	TEAM	LVL	AGE	PA	R	2B	3B	HR	RBI	BB	SO	SB	CS	EqBRR	AVG	OBP	SLG	EqAVG	EqOBP	EqSLG	EqA	VORP	WARP	DEFENSE			
2007	CCH	AA	24	558	81	28	1	9	53	57	86	24	5	-0.6	.269	.351	.387	.248	.315	.345	.240	1.9	-1.3	89-3B	-6	26-2B	-5
2008	CCH	AA	25	606	102	39	4	20	69	76	98	20	7	2.5	.317	.408	.523	.273	.347	.432	.271	25.2	1.1	94-2B	-12	15-3B	1
2009	LOU	AAA	26	190	32	14	2	5	22	26	39	1	2	-2.1	.261	.381	.471	.250	.363	.450	.278	9.1	1.0	14-SS	-1	12-3B	0
2009	CIN	MLB	26	76	10	4	1	1	9	7	20	0	2	-0.6	.212	.297	.348	.224	.307	.358	.225	-1.5	0.2	4-LF	2	4-2B	-1
2010	CIN	MLB	27	387	48	18	2	7	35	38	87	5	3	-0.1	.242	.323	.369	.244	.322	.370	.242	6.5	0.4	68-SS	-2		

Breakout: 5% Improve: 23% Collapse: 31% Attrition: 16% MLB: 14% Comparables: Dave Rohde, Chase Lambin, Ben Zobrist, Mark Gillaspie

Acquired straight-up for Jeff Keppinger at the beginning of the 2009 season, Sutton looks a lot like Rosales, an older minor-league player who started out up the middle (second base, in Sutton's case, due to a weak arm) and has since diversified to all four infield positions and the outfield corners. A college product (Baylor), Sutton has always been old for his leagues, so his .280/.378/.442 career line in the minors has to be taken with a grain of salt. He also stopped stealing bases last year after swiping 64 the previous three seasons. He has a better eye than Rosales, but is ultimately a less athletic version of the same player.

Willy Taveras   CF

Bats: R   Throws: R   Height: 6' 0"   Weight: 160   Born: December 25, 1981   Age: 28

YEAR	TEAM	LVL	AGE	PA	R	2B	3B	HR	RBI	BB	SO	SB	CS	EqBRR	AVG	OBP	SLG	EqAVG	EqOBP	EqSLG	EqA	VORP	WARP	DEFENSE	
2007	COL	MLB	25	408	64	13	2	2	24	21	55	33	9	1.5	.320	.367	.382	.318	.366	.377	.267	14.0	0.8	79-CF	-6
2008	COL	MLB	26	538	64	15	2	1	26	36	79	68	7	11.7	.251	.308	.296	.250	.306	.295	.241	4.3	0.0	111-CF	-3
2009	CIN	MLB	27	437	56	11	2	1	15	18	58	25	6	3.6	.240	.275	.285	.248	.281	.294	.214	-8.0	1.0	93-CF	16
2010	CIN	MLB	28	434	61	17	2	3	23	30	68	32	9	2.6	.261	.320	.337	.267	.323	.341	.240	4.5	0.6	91-CF	1

Breakout: 18%   Improve: 50%   Collapse: 18%   Attrition: 11%   MLB: 97%   Comparables: Bob Dernier, Chuck Carr, Darren Lewis, Miguel Dilone

You have to hand it to the Reds. Their 2008 center fielder, Corey Patterson, was so bad that they were almost guaranteed to get better at the position after letting Patterson go, yet they went out and spent $6.25 million on a player who turned out to be nearly as awful. Patterson's -19.0 VORP was the second-worst by an everyday player in the majors in 2008 (the one guy below him, Tony Peña Jr., has since defected to pitching, rather obvious, given his contributions to their cause). Taveras's -14.3 VORP in 2009 was the third-worst in the majors (above the ghost of Brian Giles and Ronny Cedeño). Taveras has hit .246/.293/.291 over the last two seasons. He's fast, which pays off on the bases and in the field, but Usain Bolt couldn't outrun that batting line.

Chris Valaika   SS

Bats: R   Throws: R   Height: 6' 1"   Weight: 180   Born: August 14, 1985   Age: 24

YEAR	TEAM	LVL	AGE	PA	R	2B	3B	HR	RBI	BB	SO	SB	CS	EqBRR	AVG	OBP	SLG	EqAVG	EqOBP	EqSLG	EqA	VORP	WARP	DEFENSE			
2007	DYT	A	21	331	38	20	3	10	56	17	72	1	4	-4.4	.307	.353	.493	.268	.305	.431	.252	9.2	-0.1	71-SS	-10		
2007	SAR	A+	21	241	26	9	1	2	23	13	42	0	3	-1.9	.253	.310	.332	.231	.276	.312	.205	-4.6	-1.4	50-SS	-7		
2008	SAR	A+	22	145	20	9	0	7	31	7	28	2	0	0.6	.363	.393	.585	.314	.342	.511	.289	10.1	1.6	29-SS	3		
2008	CHT	AA	22	417	58	19	1	11	50	28	74	7	4	0.1	.301	.352	.443	.271	.312	.394	.245	10.2	0.4	95-SS	-7		
2009	LOU	AAA	23	392	32	20	1	6	36	16	76	1	0	1.7	.235	.271	.344	.229	.263	.341	.210	-4.4	-0.5	76-SS	-2	18-2B	2
2010	CIN	MLB	24	439	43	20	1	10	52	29	104	2	2	-0.6	.239	.297	.368	.244	.299	.378	.228	1.2	-0.3	100-SS	-4		

Breakout: 18%   Improve: 37%   Collapse: 17%   Attrition: 24%   MLB: 6%   Comparables: Mike Davis, Dan Wagner, Manuel Benitez, Alfredo Torres

A third-round pick in 2006, Valaika is a poor defensive shortstop who pancaked at Triple-A in 2009. That combination probably puts him at the back of the line at second base, which means he might not have much of a future in this organization. This could be a crucial year for him.

Joey Votto   1B

Bats: L   Throws: R   Height: 6' 3"   Weight: 220   Born: September 10, 1983   Age: 26

YEAR	TEAM	LVL	AGE	PA	R	2B	3B	HR	RBI	BB	SO	SB	CS	EqBRR	AVG	OBP	SLG	EqAVG	EqOBP	EqSLG	EqA	VORP	WARP	DEFENSE			
2007	LOU	AAA	23	580	74	21	2	22	92	70	110	17	10	-5.5	.294	.381	.478	.285	.364	.466	.285	23.5	1.7	90-1B	-5	34-LF	-4
2007	CIN	MLB	23	89	11	7	0	4	17	5	15	1	0	-2.7	.321	.360	.548	.321	.360	.524	.301	5.0	0.3	15-1B	-1	6-LF	-2
2008	CIN	MLB	24	589	69	32	3	24	84	59	102	7	5	-6.6	.297	.368	.506	.304	.373	.514	.296	30.3	3.7	137-1B	4		
2009	CIN	MLB	25	544	82	38	1	25	84	70	106	4	1	-0.3	.322	.414	.567	.335	.423	.590	.335	48.6	4.8	122-1B	-4		
2010	CIN	MLB	26	591	79	30	1	29	95	67	114	7	5	-2.5	.292	.376	.519	.295	.378	.514	.300	33.8	3.5	133-1B	-1		

Breakout: 16%   Improve: 50%   Collapse: 3%   Attrition: 7%   MLB: 94%   Comparables: Adrian Gonzalez, Justin Morneau, Todd Helton, Wally Joyner

Votto's strong sophomore season is all the more impressive when one considers that he spent the first half of it battling panic attacks and depression stemming from the death of his 52-year-old father in August 2008. Votto hit the DL in mid-May with an inner-ear infection and then, just a week after his return, landed back on the DL with what was obliquely labeled "stress." Despite all that, August was his only poor month, and he finished the year fourth among all qualified major leaguers with a marginal lineup value per game of .397. With a clear head in 2010, he should remain one of the best hitters in the game.

PITCHERS

Bronson Arroyo

Bats: R   Throws: R   Height: 6' 5"   Weight: 195   Born: February 24, 1977   Age: 33

YEAR	TEAM	LVL	AGE	W	L	SV	G	GS	IP	H	HR	BB	SO	GB%	BABIP	STUFF	WHIP	ERA	SIERA	DERA	EqH9	EqHR9	EqBB9	EqSO9	VORP	SN/WX
2007	CIN	MLB	30	9	15	0	34	34	210²	232	28	63	156	41%	.309	13	1.40	4.23	4.29	4.12	8.9	1.0	2.4	6.0	33.0	4.46
2008	CIN	MLB	31	15	11	0	34	34	200	219	29	68	163	48%	.314	7	1.43	4.77	4.04	4.73	9.2	1.2	2.6	6.3	17.1	3.27
2009	CIN	MLB	32	15	13	0	33	33	220¹	214	31	65	127	50%	.265	-1	1.27	3.84	4.67	4.22	9.2	1.3	2.3	4.5	30.5	5.75
2010	CIN	MLB	33	10	11	0	34	34	192²	202	26	65	126	45%	.298	2	1.39	4.54	4.56	4.83	9.5	1.2	2.8	5.3	14.3	2.76

Breakout: 5%   Improve: 37%   Collapse: 17%   Attrition: 13%   MLB: 99%   Comparables: Bob Welch, Steve Trachsel, Jim Lonborg, Charles Nagy

In a season littered with doping revelations about some of the game's top hitters, including his former teammates Manny Ramirez and David Ortiz, Arroyo made headlines in August by bragging to a *USA Today* reporter about the regimen of supplements he takes, which swells to 16 substances on days he pitches and includes some not on Major League Baseball's preapproved list. Arroyo said he has been taking supplements since he was five years old and took androstenedione and amphetamines until they were banned by the league in 2004 and 2006, respectively. The lanky Arroyo says the goal of his regime is less strength than endurance, and the results are clear. Only Mark Buehrle has an active streak of 200-innings seasons longer than Arroyo's five years, and only Dan Haren and Javier Vazquez have streaks of equal length. Arroyo is the only one of those four who doesn't have ace stuff, which makes him the best league-average innings-muncher (or LAIM, for those of you still acronym-hungry) in the game.

Homer Bailey

Bats: R   Throws: R   Height: 6' 4"   Weight: 205   Born: May 3, 1986   Age: 24

YEAR	TEAM	LVL	AGE	W	L	SV	G	GS	IP	H	HR	BB	SO	GB%	BABIP	STUFF	WHIP	ERA	SIERA	DERA	EqH9	EqHR9	EqBB9	EqSO9	VORP	SN/WX
2007	LOU	AAA	21	6	3	0	12	12	67¹	49	4	32	59	49%	.246	26	1.20	3.07	4.05	4.61	7.0	1.0	4.3	6.1	6.4	0.81
2007	CIN	MLB	21	4	2	0	9	9	45¹	43	3	28	28	49%	.280	22	1.57	5.76	5.40	5.58	7.6	0.4	4.9	5.1	-0.4	0.68
2008	LOU	AAA	22	4	7	0	19	19	111¹	118	10	46	96	48%	.332	3	1.47	4.77	4.04	5.77	10.7	1.2	4.0	5.9	-3.1	0.06
2008	CIN	MLB	22	0	6	0	8	8	36¹	59	8	17	18	47%	.372	-20	2.09	7.93	5.53	8.22	13.5	1.7	3.7	3.7	-11.1	-0.66
2009	LOU	AAA	23	8	5	0	14	14	89²	87	10	27	82	49%	.301	7	1.27	2.71	3.56	4.06	9.6	1.5	3.0	6.6	13.6	1.60
2009	CIN	MLB	23	8	5	0	20	20	113¹	115	12	52	86	45%	.300	5	1.47	4.53	4.54	4.89	9.7	1.0	3.6	5.9	7.4	2.51
2010	CIN	MLB	24	8	10	0	34	28	165²	172	22	79	121	42%	.303	1	1.51	4.79	4.72	5.06	9.3	1.1	3.9	5.9	8.2	1.94

Breakout: 24%   Improve: 69%   Collapse: 10%   Attrition: 14%   MLB: 100%   Comparables: Jason Olsen, Chad Durbin, John Thomson, Joe Johnson

In the 2007 annual, we listed Bailey as the "#1A" pitching prospect in the game behind fellow 2004 first-rounder Phil Hughes. Though both have had their struggles since—Hughes largely due to injury, Bailey largely due to attitude—both achieved some sustained major-league success in 2009 at the still-tender age of 23. In Bailey's case, his struggles in 2007 and 2008 prompted him to rededicate himself to his craft, prioritizing his workouts over hunting (seriously) with a focus on simplifying his mechanics, raising his arm angle, repeating his delivery, and mixing his pitches better. That last was aided by his picking up a splitter from Louisville teammate Justin Lehr early in the season. All of that work paid off in Bailey's final nine starts for the Reds, as he went 6-1 with a 1.70 ERA and just two home runs allowed. Given that Hughes' success came in the bullpen, one could argue that Bailey is now the closer of the two to realizing his potential, and with continued diligence this offseason and a live-and-let-live posture toward whitetail deer, he could do just that in 2010.

Jared Burton

Bats: R   Throws: R   Height: 6' 5"   Weight: 230   Born: June 2, 1981   Age: 29

YEAR	TEAM	LVL	AGE	W	L	SV	G	GS	IP	H	HR	BB	SO	GB%	BABIP	STUFF	WHIP	ERA	SIERA	DERA	EqH9	EqHR9	EqBB9	EqSO9	VORP	SN/WX
2007	LOU	AAA	26	1	0	1	10	0	14	11	0	4	13	74%	.306	11	1.07	0.64	2.91	1.42	7.8	0.0	2.8	7.1	5.7	0.53
2007	CIN	MLB	26	4	2	0	47	0	43	28	2	22	36	45%	.228	10	1.16	2.51	4.33	2.83	5.2	0.4	4.2	6.9	12.8	1.28
2008	CIN	MLB	27	5	1	0	54	0	58²	56	6	25	58	58%	.301	9	1.38	3.22	3.64	3.43	7.9	0.7	3.3	7.5	13.9	0.58
2009	LOU	AAA	28	3	0	0	10	0	11	8	0	3	10	44%	.258	5	1.00	0.82	3.40	1.69	6.8	0.0	2.5	6.8	4.5	0.68
2009	CIN	MLB	28	1	0	0	53	0	59¹	61	5	23	45	46%	.298	-6	1.42	4.40	4.39	4.68	9.5	0.8	2.9	5.7	5.5	0.67
2010	CIN	MLB	29	4	4	0	65	0	64	60	6	29	53	50%	.295	0	1.39	4.09	4.20	4.31	8.3	0.8	3.7	6.6	8.4	0.83

Breakout: 9%   Improve: 41%   Collapse: 30%   Attrition: 7%   MLB: 87%   Comparables: Bob Howry, Todd Jones, Jay Powell, Braden Looper

Coming off a latissimus injury in 2008, Burton struggled mightily over the first three months of 2009, allowing more than half of his inherited runners to score and posting a meager 1.5 K/BB. That earned him a demotion on July 1. He returned at the end of the month and gave up five runs in 2 ⅔ innings, after which he was shut down with shoulder fatigue. The rest seemed to do him well, as he returned just two weeks later and, after a poor initial outing, posted a 1.66 ERA and a handsome 3.17 K/BB with 19 Ks in 21 ⅔ innings while allowing just 20 percent of his inherited runners to score. Burton will challenge Nick Masset for the eighth-inning job this year.

Francisco Cordero

Bats: R   Throws: R   Height: 6' 3"   Weight: 240   Born: May 11, 1975   Age: 35

YEAR	TEAM	LVL	AGE	W	L	SV	G	GS	IP	H	HR	BB	SO	GB%	BABIP	STUFF	WHIP	ERA	SIERA	DERA	EqH9	EqHR9	EqBB9	EqSO9	VORP	SN/WX
2007	MIL	MLB	32	0	4	44	66	0	63¹	52	4	18	86	44%	.316	32	1.11	2.98	2.07	3.02	7.3	0.6	2.3	10.0	17.6	3.29
2008	CIN	MLB	33	5	4	34	72	0	70¹	61	6	38	78	45%	.302	15	1.41	3.33	3.61	3.30	7.5	0.8	4.2	8.5	17.4	3.16
2009	CIN	MLB	34	2	6	39	68	0	66²	58	2	30	58	48%	.301	9	1.32	2.16	4.03	2.98	8.7	0.3	3.6	7.0	17.7	2.97
2010	CIN	MLB	35	3	4	26	60	0	59¹	54	6	26	57	45%	.305	5	1.36	3.99	3.72	4.20	8.2	0.8	3.6	7.7	8.6	1.87

Breakout: 13%   Improve: 36%   Collapse: 30%   Attrition: 13%   MLB: 96%   Comparables: Jay Howell, Lee Smith, Roberto Hernandez, Brendan Donnelly

It's a shame that it was a buyer's market for closers this past offseason, because the Reds should have been selling on Cordero. By ERA and save percentage, Cordero had one of his finest seasons in 2009, but he saw a sharp drop in his strikeout rate and was very lucky on home runs (he allowed just two as a minuscule 2.1 percent of his fly balls left the park), and his line-drive rate has been on a steady upward trend over the last few seasons. Add in that he'll be 35 in May and is the second-highest-paid Red in 2010 ($500,000 behind Aaron Harang) and under contract for another $12 million in 2011, and it's clear that now is the time for the Reds to sell.

Johnny Cueto

Bats: R   Throws: R   Height: 5' 10"   Weight: 185   Born: February 15, 1986   Age: 24

YEAR	TEAM	LVL	AGE	W	L	SV	G	GS	IP	H	HR	BB	SO	GB%	BABIP	STUFF	WHIP	ERA	SIERA	DERA	EqH9	EqHR9	EqBB9	EqSO9	VORP	SN/WX
2007	SAR	A+	21	4	5	0	14	14	78¹	72	3	21	72	48%	.299	31	1.19	3.33	3.47	4.97	9.0	0.9	3.0	5.8	4.4	0.14
2007	CHT	AA	21	6	3	0	10	10	61	52	6	11	77	42%	.307	36	1.03	3.10	2.08	4.27	8.7	1.5	1.8	7.9	8.1	0.45
2007	LOU	AAA	21	2	1	0	4	4	22	22	2	2	21	32%	.323	21	1.09	2.05	2.82	2.61	10.0	1.3	0.9	7.0	6.6	0.62
2008	CIN	MLB	22	9	14	0	31	31	174	178	29	68	158	45%	.298	20	1.41	4.81	3.90	4.74	8.5	1.3	3.0	6.9	15.0	2.42
2009	CIN	MLB	23	11	11	0	30	30	171¹	172	24	61	132	46%	.291	4	1.36	4.41	4.22	4.79	9.6	1.3	2.8	6.0	13.1	3.03
2010	CIN	MLB	24	8	10	0	30	30	162	160	21	57	134	48%	.302	12	1.34	4.45	3.94	4.76	9.0	1.1	2.9	6.8	13.4	2.17

Breakout: 14%   Improve: 49%   Collapse: 14%   Attrition: 14%   MLB: 93%   Comparables: Ken Cloude, Scott Bankhead, Brad Radke, Jake Peavy

On the whole, Cueto's sophomore season looked a lot like his rookie campaign, but buried in the middle was an ugly stretch of 12 starts in which he posted an 8.73 RA/9. Cueto made just two quality starts during that stretch while turning in four disaster starts (more runs allowed than innings pitched). He also left the penultimate start of that run after two innings due to tweaking his hip while running the bases. The hip injury proved to be incidental, but after the fourth disaster start, Cueto was placed on the DL with shoulder inflammation. Like Burton, the rest worked, as he went 3-1 with a 3.63 ERA in his final six starts, but Cueto's small stature and emerging pattern of arm aches (he had elbow soreness down the stretch in 2008) is a worrisome combination.

Matthew Fairel

Bats: L   Throws: L   Height: 6' 3"   Weight: 203   Born: July 8, 1987   Age: 22

YEAR	TEAM	LVL	AGE	W	L	SV	G	GS	IP	H	HR	BB	SO	GB%	BABIP	STUFF	WHIP	ERA	SIERA	DERA	EqH9	EqHR9	EqBB9	EqSO9	VORP	SN/WX
2009	DYT	A	21	8	5	0	19	19	110²	98	9	37	107	49%	.294	2	1.22	2.93	3.45	4.45	10.2	2.1	4.1	5.3	11.6	0.07
2009	SAR	A+	21	3	3	0	8	8	50	46	0	19	30	47%	.293	6	1.30	3.24	4.79	5.16	9.7	0.8	4.4	3.4	1.7	-0.14
2010	CIN	MLB	22	5	10	2	28	26	135	157	22	72	82	42%	.314	-1	1.70	5.95	5.36	6.27	10.6	1.4	4.3	4.9	-11.6	2.69

Breakout: 6%   Improve: 27%   Collapse: 22%   Attrition: 2%   MLB: 4%   Comparables: Jorge De La Rosa, Craig Anderson, Ben Norris, Tom Fordham

A draft-eligible sophomore from Florida State in 2008, Fairel was taken in the 35th round by the Reds, but given fifth-round money, he decided he'd seen enough of college. He acquitted himself well in High-A in the latter part of his first pro season last year and could prove to be a solid back-end rotation starter.

Carlos Fisher

Bats: R   Throws: R   Height: 6' 3"   Weight: 210   Born: February 22, 1983   Age: 27

YEAR	TEAM	LVL	AGE	W	L	SV	G	GS	IP	H	HR	BB	SO	GB%	BABIP	STUFF	WHIP	ERA	SIERA	DERA	EqH9	EqHR9	EqBB9	EqSO9	VORP	SN/WX
2007	SAR	A+	24	4	1	0	7	7	41	34	1	7	41	61%	.289	20	1.00	2.20	2.81	3.55	8.2	0.7	2.1	6.4	8.5	0.68
2007	CHT	AA	24	5	9	0	21	21	113¹	127	11	42	94	56%	.336	-18	1.49	4.29	4.02	5.68	11.0	1.5	3.5	5.0	-2.1	-0.18
2008	CHT	AA	25	1	5	8	36	0	50²	52	3	20	46	62%	.314	-10	1.42	3.73	3.77	5.47	9.4	1.1	3.4	5.6	0.2	-0.24
2008	LOU	AAA	25	5	0	0	14	0	17¹	14	0	9	21	66%	.304	14	1.33	1.04	3.16	1.56	7.8	0.5	4.7	7.8	7.6	0.54
2009	LOU	AAA	26	2	0	2	13	0	18	11	0	4	21	59%	.256	17	0.83	2.00	2.35	2.60	6.2	0.5	2.1	8.3	5.6	0.58
2009	CIN	MLB	26	1	1	0	39	0	52¹	50	4	31	48	50%	.324	1	1.55	4.47	4.27	4.53	9.6	0.7	4.8	7.4	5.2	0.64
2010	CIN	MLB	27	3	4	2	51	1	65¹	65	8	30	52	53%	.300	-4	1.46	4.64	4.33	4.93	9.1	1.0	3.8	6.4	4.1	1.01

Breakout: 21%   Improve: 56%   Collapse: 15%   Attrition: 25%   MLB: 44%   Comparables: David Holdridge, Rob Wassenaar, Chris Hook, Dan Wheeler

Called up in late May, sinkerballer Fisher pitched most of his innings in garbage time, which is just as well, as he allowed half of his inherited runners to score on the season and posted a 6.75 ERA as opposing batters hit .280/.370/.473 against him in his last 18 appearances. Left-handed batters saw Fisher particularly well, hitting .337/.402/.410 (righties hit .204/.341/.352; small-sample caveats apply to both). He's not suited for higher-leverage work.

Aaron Harang

Bats: R   Throws: R   Height: 6' 7"   Weight: 275   Born: May 9, 1978   Age: 32

YEAR	TEAM	LVL	AGE	W	L	SV	G	GS	IP	H	HR	BB	SO	GB%	BABIP	STUFF	WHIP	ERA	SIERA	DERA	EqH9	EqHR9	EqBB9	EqSO9	VORP	SN/WX
2007	CIN	MLB	29	16	6	0	34	34	231²	213	28	52	218	46%	.288	33	1.14	3.73	3.21	3.47	7.5	0.9	1.8	7.7	52.8	6.30
2008	CIN	MLB	30	6	17	0	30	29	184¹	205	35	50	153	39%	.307	3	1.38	4.78	3.87	4.63	9.3	1.6	2.1	6.4	18.0	3.21
2009	CIN	MLB	31	6	14	0	26	26	162¹	186	24	43	142	39%	.331	2	1.41	4.21	3.71	4.62	10.9	1.4	2.1	6.8	15.4	3.01
2010	CIN	MLB	32	8	10	0	27	27	158	164	22	47	128	40%	.310	11	1.33	4.35	3.93	4.65	9.5	1.2	2.5	6.6	14.9	2.34

Breakout: 4%   Improve: 33%   Collapse: 21%   Attrition: 25%   MLB: 93%   Comparables: Andy Benes, Steve Renko, Freddy Garcia, Rolando Arrojo

If Harang's 2008 season was a disaster marred by bad luck and bad decisions (specifically, a 63-pitch relief outing on two days' rest that derailed him for nearly three months), his 2009 was just a bummer. Harang was hit harder in 2009, and more of those balls in play fell in for hits. He was unable to establish any start-to-start consistency, and after he strung three solid outings together in August, he was struck with appendicitis and had to undergo a season-ending appendectomy. Approaching his 32nd birthday, he's clearly not a late-blooming ace after all, just a solid, midrotation starter in need of some better luck.

Daniel Ray Herrera

Bats: L   Throws: L   Height: 5' 7"   Weight: 145   Born: October 21, 1984   Age: 25

YEAR	TEAM	LVL	AGE	W	L	SV	G	GS	IP	H	HR	BB	SO	GB%	BABIP	STUFF	WHIP	ERA	SIERA	DERA	EqH9	EqHR9	EqBB9	EqSO9	VORP	SN/WX
2007	BAK	A+	22	2	0	1	7	1	11	14	1	5	11	60%	.371	-1	1.73	3.27	3.78	3.38	11.8	1.7	4.2	5.9	2.5	0.15
2007	FRI	AA	22	5	2	0	34	0	52¹	43	3	20	64	56%	.328	16	1.20	3.78	2.71	4.94	9.1	1.1	3.8	8.9	2.9	-0.07
2008	CHT	AA	23	3	0	0	10	0	17²	12	0	7	10	52%	.235	-13	1.08	2.55	4.82	3.51	6.5	0.5	3.8	3.8	3.7	0.15
2008	LOU	AAA	23	4	4	6	47	0	55	47	4	10	50	56%	.274	4	1.04	2.78	3.17	3.94	8.2	1.0	1.8	5.9	9.3	1.43
2008	CIN	MLB	23	0	0	0	7	0	7¹	10	1	3	8	84%	.391	5	1.77	7.36	3.18	7.63	11.7	1.2	3.5	8.2	-1.8	0.06
2009	CIN	MLB	24	4	4	0	70	0	61²	63	5	24	44	62%	.310	-8	1.41	3.06	4.25	4.47	10.0	0.8	3.1	5.7	6.6	0.71
2010	CIN	MLB	25	3	4	0	58	0	63¹	66	8	27	46	55%	.305	-8	1.47	4.79	4.43	5.06	9.5	1.1	3.4	5.9	3.1	1.00

Breakout: 13%   Improve: 30%   Collapse: 25%   Attrition: 12%   MLB: 76%   Comparables: Joey Vierra, Ed Pruitt, Frederick Farwell, Steve Frey

The throw-in in the Josh Hamilton/Edinson Volquez trade, tiny Texas lefty Herrera spent all of 2009 in the Reds' bullpen as a second LOOGY behind Arthur Rhodes. As one might expect from a small lefty with a low three-quarters delivery, a fastball in the mid-80s, and a breaking ball in the mid-60s, Herrera gets the job done against lefties (.183/.254/.266), but is murdered by right-handers (.361/.423/.529). There's little hope of that split improving, which means it's on the manager to reduce his exposure to right-handers, who actually had more at-bats against him than lefties in 2009.

Mike Leake

| | | Bats: R | Throws: R | Height: 5' 11" | Weight: 160 | Born: November 12, 1987 | Age: 22 |

Did Not Play.

Breakout: 13%   Improve: 30%   Collapse: 25%   Attrition: 12%   MLB: 76%   Comparables: NA

If it wasn't for that Stephen Strasburg guy, Leake would have gotten a lot more attention last spring. Pitching in one of collegiate baseball's toughest conferences for an Arizona State squad that plays in a very hitter-friendly park, Leake went 16-1 with a 1.71 ERA while allowing just 95 hits in 142 innings and compiling a 6.8 K/BB ratio. He's on the small side, but Leake is a fantastic athlete who combines slightly above-average stuff with excellent command. He could move quickly through the system, and though many feel he'll ultimately be no more than a third or fourth starter, there's an outside chance he could be another Tim Hudson.

Sam LeCure

| | | Bats: R | Throws: R | Height: 6' 0" | Weight: 190 | Born: May 4, 1984 | Age: 26 |

YEAR	TEAM	LVL	AGE	W	L	SV	G	GS	IP	H	HR	BB	SO	GB%	BABIP	STUFF	WHIP	ERA	SIERA	DERA	EqH9	EqHR9	EqBB9	EqSO9	VORP	SN/WX
2007	CHT	AA	23	7	5	0	21	21	110	119	12	46	104	45%	.339	-14	1.50	4.17	3.82	5.33	10.8	1.7	3.9	5.9	1.9	-0.17
2008	CHT	AA	24	9	7	0	27	27	155¹	147	12	58	128	43%	.297	1	1.32	3.42	4.07	4.06	9.0	1.3	3.4	5.4	24.0	1.28
2009	LOU	AAA	25	10	8	0	25	25	143¹	143	17	44	125	44%	.306	-7	1.30	4.46	3.74	5.63	10.0	1.6	3.1	6.4	-1.9	-0.07
2010	CIN	MLB	26	5	9	0	27	24	122	135	20	56	86	43%	.310	-7	1.57	5.34	4.78	5.63	10.0	1.4	3.8	5.7	-1.8	1.75

Breakout: 4%   Improve: 37%   Collapse: 20%   Attrition: 17%   MLB: 10%   Comparables: Kevin McGehee, Nick Pereira, Mike York, Hugh Kemp

A fourth-round pick in 2005, LeCure is a fly-ball pitcher with slightly above-average velocity on his fastball, but also below-average movement. In his Triple-A debut in 2009, he posted solid peripherals, but had underwhelming results. He's in line to be a replacement starter in 2010 and could have a future as a fifth starter, but one can expect that, pitching at the Gap, he'll see a drop in his strikeout rate and an increase in his home-run rate, which is a dangerous combination.

Justin Lehr

| | | Bats: R | Throws: R | Height: 6' 2" | Weight: 205 | Born: August 3, 1977 | Age: 32 |

YEAR	TEAM	LVL	AGE	W	L	SV	G	GS	IP	H	HR	BB	SO	GB%	BABIP	STUFF	WHIP	ERA	SIERA	DERA	EqH9	EqHR9	EqBB9	EqSO9	VORP	SN/WX
2007	TAC	AAA	29	7	1	1	27	17	119²	132	8	41	61	53%	.310	-15	1.45	3.99	4.97	4.97	9.7	1.1	3.3	3.2	6.8	0.95
2008	LOU	AAA	30	6	2	1	16	8	64¹	51	5	11	41	58%	.247	4	0.96	2.10	3.90	2.72	7.8	1.1	1.8	4.2	18.5	2.04
2009	LEH	AAA	31	5	2	0	8	7	41²	43	5	16	20	54%	.279	-23	1.42	4.75	5.21	5.88	10.2	1.8	3.7	3.2	-1.7	0.03
2009	LOU	AAA	31	8	1	0	12	11	75¹	57	3	10	40	53%	.236	15	0.89	2.51	4.26	3.36	7.4	0.6	1.4	3.8	16.9	1.46
2009	CIN	MLB	31		5	3	0	11	11	65¹	72	14	28	33	43%	.279-21	1.53	5.37	5.42	5.34	10.5		2.0	3.5		4.0	1.1	0.45
2010	CIN	MLB	32	6	9	0	31	22	133¹	141	19	51	61	56%	.282	-12	1.44	4.74	5.20	5.03	9.6	1.2	3.1	3.7	7.0	2.30

Breakout: 11%   Improve: 45%   Collapse: 13%   Attrition: 18%   MLB: 46%   Comparables: Ray Soff, Walter Silva, Victor Santos, Fernando Arroyo

Veteran journeyman Lehr's biggest contribution to the Reds will probably be having taught Homer Bailey how to throw a splitter. Purchased from the Phillies early last year, Lehr was called up at the end of July and inserted in the rotation. Appearing in the majors for the first time since he posted an 8.62 ERA with the Brewers in 2006, Lehr reeled off four solid starts, including a shutout of the Cubs, then turned back into a pumpkin, posting a 7.32 ERA, a 1.70 WHIP, and a 1.3 K/BB over his final seven starts. Lehr had planned to retire if he didn't make it back to "The Show" last year, and his velocity was down to the mid-80s by season's end. Perhaps he has a future as a pitching coach.

Matt Maloney

| | | Bats: L | Throws: L | Height: 6' 4" | Weight: 220 | Born: January 16, 1984 | Age: 26 |

YEAR	TEAM	LVL	AGE	W	L	SV	G	GS	IP	H	HR	BB	SO	GB%	BABIP	STUFF	WHIP	ERA	SIERA	DERA	EqH9	EqHR9	EqBB9	EqSO9	VORP	SN/WX
2007	REA	AA	23	9	7	0	21	21	125²	117	13	45	115	43%	.286	-1	1.29	3.94	3.77	5.86	9.4	1.5	3.4	6.1	-4.9	-0.33
2007	CHT	AA	23	2	2	0	4	4	28	17	4	3	39	47%	.228	27	0.71	2.57	1.17	3.71	6.8	2.0	1.4	8.8	5.3	0.38
2007	LOU	AAA	23	2	1	0	3	3	17	10	2	6	23	45%	.229	16	0.94	3.18	2.09	3.86	6.6	1.7	3.3	9.4	3.0	0.20
2008	LOU	AAA	24	11	5	0	25	25	140¹	143	18	39	132	45%	.309	-6	1.30	4.68	3.45	5.55	9.9	1.5	2.7	6.2	-0.8	0.29
2009	LOU	AAA	25	9	9	0	22	22	143	143	11	24	125	47%	.311	11	1.17	3.08	3.31	4.28	9.7	1.1	1.8	6.3	18.5	1.74
2009	CIN	MLB	25	2	4	0	7	7	40²	43	9	8	28	39%	.279	0	1.25	4.87	4.14	4.96	10.2	2.1	1.6	5.3	2.3	0.68
2010	CIN	MLB	26	8	9	0	33	26	153	155	21	53	123	43%	.304	8	1.36	4.44	4.05	4.74	9.3	1.2	2.9	6.6	12.9	2.09

Breakout: 20%   Improve: 57%   Collapse: 10%   Attrition: 22%   MLB: 38%   Comparables: J.A. Happ, John Cerutti, Brian McNichol, Dennis Cook

Make LeCure bigger, left-handed, and exchange some velocity for near-pinpoint control, and you get something like Matt Maloney, who was drafted by the Phillies a round earlier in 2005 and acquired by the Reds for Kyle Lohse in 2007. Maloney gave up six home runs in three major-league starts in June of last year, and two more in his first start back in late August, but otherwise pitched well and finished the year with three solid September outings, allowing just one homer and walking only one man in 17 innings. Maloney could excel as a midrotation arm for a team that plays in a pitchers' park, but as a Red, he'll have to work to avoid being victimized by the Gap.

Nick Masset

Bats: R   Throws: R   Height: 6' 4"   Weight: 235   Born: May 17, 1982   Age: 28

YEAR	TEAM	LVL	AGE	W	L	SV	G	GS	IP	H	HR	BB	SO	GB%	BABIP	STUFF	WHIP	ERA	SIERA	DERA	EqH9	EqHR9	EqBB9	EqSO9	VORP	SN/WX
2007	CHR	AAA	25	0	4	0	11	9	45¹	51	6	9	33	50%	.317	-9	1.32	4.57	3.92	5.86	10.9	1.7	1.9	5.2	-1.7	-0.12
2007	CHA	MLB	25	2	3	0	27	1	39¹	52	2	26	21	42%	.352	-18	1.98	7.09	5.96	6.47	11.1	0.5	5.2	4.3	-4.3	0.19
2008	CHA	MLB	26	1	0	1	32	1	44²	55	4	21	32	69%	.354	-7	1.70	4.63	4.39	4.67	11.0	0.6	3.9	6.2	4.0	1.05
2008	CIN	MLB	26	1	0	0	10	0	17¹	16	3	5	11	56%	.265	-4	1.21	2.08	4.27	3.03	8.3	1.7	2.2	5.0	4.5	-0.42
2009	CIN	MLB	27	5	1	0	74	0	76	54	6	24	70	58%	.250	15	1.03	2.37	3.31	2.83	7.2	0.8	2.5	7.4	21.3	2.71
2010	CIN	MLB	28	3	4	0	62	0	67¹	70	7	27	48	55%	.308	-6	1.44	4.46	4.39	4.79	9.4	1.0	3.3	5.9	5.3	0.78

Breakout: 21%   Improve: 52%   Collapse: 16%   Attrition: 12%   MLB: 88%   Comparables: Chad Qualls, Dan Wheeler, Scott Linebrink, Chris Reitsma

Oh, the gifts the BABIP fairy can leave under your pillow. The second-best prospect sent to the White Sox in the Brandon McCarthy trade, the hard-throwing Masset struggled with the Sox, was flipped to Cincy in the Ken Griffey Jr. deal, and excelled as a set-up man last year. Still, a quick look at his opponents' batting averages on balls in play shows that his extreme performances in Chicago and Cincinnati have been largely the result of the defenses behind him—nearly a hundred points lower than with the Sox. The good news for Masset and the Reds is that Nick also improved his strikeout, walk, and line-drive rates in 2009, had a typical percentage of his fly balls leave the park, and, as a slight ground-ball pitcher, is well-suited to the Gap.

Logan Ondrusek

Bats: R   Throws: R   Height: 6' 7"   Weight: 205   Born: February 13, 1985   Age: 25

YEAR	TEAM	LVL	AGE	W	L	SV	G	GS	IP	H	HR	BB	SO	GB%	BABIP	STUFF	WHIP	ERA	SIERA	DERA	EqH9	EqHR9	EqBB9	EqSO9	VORP	SN/WX
2007	SAR	A+	22	7	10	1	31	22	124	131	4	48	86	49%	.324	-9	1.44	4.43	4.51	6.48	10.6	0.9	4.2	4.4	-12.4	-1.03
2008	SAR	A+	23	1	7	1	40	3	79²	93	5	32	58	55%	.331	-32	1.57	4.97	4.45	6.75	11.4	1.5	4.1	4.1	-10.6	-2.00
2009	SAR	A+	24	2	0	0	13	0	18²	7	0	7	12	71%	.140	-16	0.75	0.96	3.76	3.06	4.1	0.5	4.1	3.6	4.8	0.21
2009	CAR	AA	24	2	1	7	24	0	32²	21	0	12	24	58%	.228	-5	1.01	1.65	4.10	2.90	7.0	0.6	3.5	4.9	8.9	1.54
2009	LOU	AAA	24	0	0	12	19	0	20²	16	1	2	11	63%	.242	-5	0.87	1.74	3.94	2.33	7.4	0.9	0.9	3.7	6.8	1.05
2010	CIN	MLB	25	3	4	7	52	1	67¹	70	8	34	42	54%	.296	-13	1.54	5.12	4.96	5.43	9.4	1.1	4.2	5.0	0.6	0.99

Breakout: 23%   Improve: 60%   Collapse: 14%   Attrition: 18%   MLB: 11%   Comparables: Mike Timlin, Mitchell Johnson, John Davis, Jimmy Daspit

A mid-round pick in 2005, this tall, hard-throwing Texan didn't appear to be anything special in his first four pro seasons, which he spent bouncing between starting and relief work. Then last year, he dominated out of the gate in his third go-round in High-A and was nearly as good in Double-A, where he took over the closer's job in June. Ondrusek didn't allow a home run in 51 ⅔ innings between those two levels, and though he did finally give up a lone dinger after being promoted to Triple-A—where he continued to close—he compensated by walking just two men in 20 ⅔ innings. Altogether, he posted a 1.50 ERA in 72 minor-league innings. As great as his season was, there was clearly a lot of luck involved, and while there's some projection in his big frame, deceptive delivery, and hard cutter, he was pitching way above his abilities in 2009—perhaps more than just fatigue was at work in his ugly showing in the Arizona Fall League. Still, he could contribute to the major-league pen yet, albeit further down the depth chart. The size of the correction he experiences this year will tell us a lot.

Micah Owings

Bats: R   Throws: R   Height: 6' 5"   Weight: 220   Born: September 28, 1982   Age: 27

YEAR	TEAM	LVL	AGE	W	L	SV	G	GS	IP	H	HR	BB	SO	GB%	BABIP	STUFF	WHIP	ERA	SIERA	DERA	EqH9	EqHR9	EqBB9	EqSO9	VORP	SN/WX
2007	ARI	MLB	24	8	8	0	29	27	152²	146	20	50	106	46%	.273	13	1.28	4.30	4.41	4.19	8.2	0.9	2.6	5.8	22.1	3.04
2008	ARI	MLB	25	6	9	0	22	18	104²	104	14	41	87	37%	.288	10	1.39	5.93	4.28	5.65	8.4	0.9	3.0	6.5	-1.8	0.65
2009	CIN	MLB	26	7	12	1	26	19	119²	126	18	64	68	40%	.280	-20	1.59	5.34	5.55	5.64	9.8	1.4	4.1	4.3	-1.9	1.29
2010	CIN	MLB	27	5	7	0	25	18	107¹	108	13	49	75	40%	.295	-1	1.46	4.94	4.81	5.24	9.2	1.1	3.7	5.7	3.2	1.12

Breakout: 11%   Improve: 40%   Collapse: 20%   Attrition: 28%   MLB: 84%   Comparables: Clint Hartung, Chris Knapp, Art Mahaffey, Darryl Kile

How many pitchers can you name with an OPS+ better than their ERA+? (Among active pitchers with 100 or more PAs, there's only Owings and Brandon Backe.) Owings is a serviceable fifth starter, but he's now 27 with three years of major-league experience under his belt, and the only trends he's showing are heading in the wrong direction. Meanwhile, he's a career .300/.331/.547 hitter in 184 big-league at-bats. Rick Ankiel hit .285/.328/.535 in 190 plate appearances in his age-27 season *after* spending the better parts of two seasons as a full-time hitter in the minors. Owings isn't nearly as bad a pitcher as Tony Peña Jr. is a hitter, but at a certain point, one has to start playing to one's strengths.

Ramon Ramirez

Bats: R   Throws: R   Height: 5′ 10″   Weight: 170   Born: September 16, 1982   Age: 27

YEAR	TEAM	LVL	AGE	W	L	SV	G	GS	IP	H	HR	BB	SO	GB%	BABIP	STUFF	WHIP	ERA	SIERA	DERA	EqH9	EqHR9	EqBB9	EqSO9	VORP	SN/WX
2007	SAR	A+	24	5	2	1	15	12	73¹	64	5	25	86	46%	.317	6	1.21	4.05	2.79	5.69	9.3	1.5	3.7	7.9	-1.4	-0.02
2007	CHT	AA	24	5	1	1	16	0	31¹	30	3	12	35	47%	.329	-5	1.34	4.60	3.11	5.52	9.8	1.5	3.7	7.1	-0.1	0.01
2007	LOU	AAA	24	1	0	0	5	2	14²	7	0	6	16	54%	.219	13	0.89	0.00	2.93	0.68	5.4	0.0	4.1	8.1	7.1	0.70
2008	CHT	AA	25	2	3	0	11	9	46	41	6	15	52	41%	.297	4	1.22	4.70	2.92	6.25	8.7	1.8	3.0	7.5	-3.7	-0.49
2008	LOU	AAA	25	4	5	1	19	15	99¹	76	8	42	93	51%	.266	9	1.19	3.08	3.67	4.00	7.9	1.1	4.1	6.4	15.4	2.13
2008	CIN	MLB	25	1	1	0	5	4	27	17	3	11	21	49%	.203	16	1.04	2.67	4.12	2.56	5.5	1.0	3.4	6.2	8.6	0.91
2009	LOU	AAA	26	6	7	0	31	20	127¹	122	13	50	78	42%	.273	-19	1.35	4.03	4.96	5.64	9.3	1.4	3.8	4.3	-1.9	-0.08
2009	CIN	MLB	26	0	0	0	11	0	12¹	8	2	4	8	44%	.182	-8	0.97	3.65	4.45	3.86	6.2	1.5	2.3	5.4	2.1	0.26
2010	BOS	MLB	27	7	7	0	45	15	121¹	120	16	57	95	41%	.298	3	1.46	4.64	4.52	4.76	8.6	1.1	4.0	6.6	10.0	1.92

Breakout: 14%   Improve: 46%   Collapse: 8%   Attrition: 21%   MLB: 20%   Comparables: Francisco Oliveras, Jody Treadwell, Les Straker, Joe Whitmer

Save for one rocky outing in late May, Ramirez didn't get a major-league look until rosters expanded. He pitched well enough in those 10 relief outings, but the Reds lost interest in the undersized righty. Claimed off waivers by the Rays in November, he was released less than a month later. Here's hoping he lands anywhere but with the Red Sox, because if we start seeing box scores in which "Ramon Ramirez" is credited with both a win and a save, people are going to start thinking the rules have been changed. On the other hand, it would be fun to see how they deal with names on the back of their away jerseys. The Orioles had this problem in the late 1980s, when they had two Michael Anthony Smiths; they ended up referring to them as "Texas" and "Arkansas," but neither was around long enough to make this a real issue—sort of like this particular RamRam.

Arthur Rhodes

Bats: L   Throws: L   Height: 6′ 2″   Weight: 210   Born: October 24, 1969   Age: 40

YEAR	TEAM	LVL	AGE	W	L	SV	G	GS	IP	H	HR	BB	SO	GB%	BABIP	STUFF	WHIP	ERA	SIERA	DERA	EqH9	EqHR9	EqBB9	EqSO9	VORP	SN/WX
2008	SEA	MLB	38	2	1	1	36	0	22	17	0	13	26	34%	.321	21	1.36	2.86	3.53	3.16	7.2	0.0	5.1	9.7	5.5	1.24
2008	FLO	MLB	38	2	0	1	25	0	13¹	11	0	3	14	27%	.297	13	1.05	0.67	2.95	0.68	7.4	0.0	2.0	8.1	7.1	0.97
2009	CIN	MLB	39	1	1	0	66	0	53¹	37	3	20	48	43%	.238	12	1.07	2.53	3.72	2.82	6.7	0.5	2.9	6.8	15.7	2.62
2010	CIN	MLB	40	3	3	0	46	0	45¹	42	4	22	40	37%	.299	2	1.40	3.93	4.27	4.11	8.1	0.8	3.9	7.1	7.0	1.63

Breakout: 15%   Improve: 30%   Collapse: 36%   Attrition: 9%   MLB: 95%   Comparables: Jesse Orosco, Chris Hammond, John Franco, Mike Stanton

Good lefty relievers can pitch forever. Just look at the career leaders in games pitched: Jesse Orosco and former Reds Mike Stanton and John Franco hold the top three spots, with Dan Plesac ranking sixth. Rhodes is quite a ways down that list (47th), but he's 11th all-time in K/9 among pitchers with 1,000 or more innings pitched, which confirms his status as a "good lefty reliever." In two season since having had his elbow rebuilt via Tommy John surgery, Rhodes has posted a 2.33 ERA and a 1.14 WHIP and struck out 8.9 men per nine innings while holding lefties to a .148/.239/.174 line, also holding his own against righties. As long as he doesn't have to face the Yankees too often, he should remain valuable well into his 40s.

Daryl Thompson

Bats: R **Throws: R** **Height: 6' 0"** **Weight: 180** **Born: November 2, 1985** **Age: 24**

YEAR	TEAM	LVL	AGE	W	L	SV	G	GS	IP	H	HR	BB	SO	GB%	BABIP	STUFF	WHIP	ERA	SIERA	DERA	EqH9	EqHR9	EqBB9	EqSO9	VORP	SN/WX
2007	DYT	A	21	5	0	0	5	5	28	16	1	2	24	35%	.208	26	0.64	0.96	2.69	1.93	6.7	1.1	1.4	4.9	10.2	0.76
2007	SAR	A+	21	9	5	0	22	22	105	106	19	31	97	35%	.296	-21	1.30	3.77	3.61	5.52	10.7	3.0	3.3	6.1	-0.2	0.18
2008	SAR	A+	22	0	2	0	3	3	15²	20	2	7	7	65%	.333	-27	1.72	6.89	5.03	8.68	13.5	2.6	5.1	2.6	-4.9	-0.62
2008	CHT	AA	22	3	2	0	10	10	61¹	44	2	14	56	41%	.261	35	0.95	1.76	3.13	3.26	7.0	0.8	2.2	6.2	14.4	1.46
2008	LOU	AAA	22	5	0	0	7	7	45²	39	4	9	33	51%	.263	17	1.05	2.76	3.81	3.63	8.3	1.0	2.1	4.8	9.0	1.06
2008	CIN	MLB	22	0	2	0	3	3	14¹	20	3	7	6	39%	.327	-13	1.88	6.91	6.03	6.44	11.0	1.8	3.7	3.1	-1.5	0.16
2009	LOU	AAA	23	1	2	0	8	6	28²	34	3	7	8	44%	.279	-32	1.43	6.59	5.88	8.13	10.4	1.2	2.5	1.5	-8.6	-0.50
2010	*CIN*	*MLB*	*24*	*3*	*6*	*0*	*28*	*10*	*77¹*	*85*	*13*	*34*	*50*	*40%*	*.301*	*-12*	*1.54*	*5.36*	*4.99*	*5.65*	*10.0*	*1.5*	*3.5*	*5.2*	*-1.3*	*1.47*

Breakout: 14% **Improve: 49%** **Collapse: 19%** **Attrition: 19%** **MLB: 11%** **Comparables:** *Glenn Carter, Johnny Abrego, Kip Yaughn, Jamie Arnold*

Thompson finally stayed relatively healthy in consecutive seasons in 2007 and 2008 and stormed all the way up to his big-league debut in '08, but his shoulder problems returned at the end of that season and limited him to just 29⅓ innings in 2009. Now 24 and clearly incapable of holding up under a starters' workload, he was outrighted off the 40-man roster in November and cleared waivers. If he manages to pitch his way back to the majors, it will be as a middle reliever.

Pedro Viola

Bats: L **Throws: L** **Height: 6' 1"** **Weight: 185** **Born: June 29, 1983** **Age: 27**

YEAR	TEAM	LVL	AGE	W	L	SV	G	GS	IP	H	HR	BB	SO	GB%	BABIP	STUFF	WHIP	ERA	SIERA	DERA	EqH9	EqHR9	EqBB9	EqSO9	VORP	SN/WX
2007	DYT	A	24	3	1	2	22	0	43¹	29	3	17	49	41%	.250	-6	1.06	1.87	2.98	4.46	8.0	1.6	4.6	6.6	4.5	-0.08
2007	SAR	A+	24	0	1	2	10	0	20	14	0	7	28	26%	.298	19	1.05	0.90	2.13	1.63	7.4	0.5	3.7	9.3	8.3	0.64
2007	CHT	AA	24	0	0	2	14	0	19	12	2	6	17	48%	.196	-4	0.95	0.95	3.54	1.89	6.2	1.4	2.8	5.2	7.6	0.91
2008	CHT	AA	25	4	7	2	52	7	82¹	88	6	36	84	52%	.343	-13	1.51	4.48	3.66	6.05	10.2	1.2	3.8	6.7	-4.9	-1.00
2009	LOU	AAA	26	2	2	8	54	0	49¹	48	7	33	57	46%	.308	-5	1.64	5.47	3.90	6.33	9.7	1.9	6.1	8.2	-4.5	0.14
2009	CIN	MLB	26	0	0	0	9	0	7	7	2	3	5	39%	.250	-15	1.43	5.14	4.70	5.40	9.4	2.7	4.1	5.4	0.1	0.01
2010	*CIN*	*MLB*	*27*	*3*	*5*	*1*	*48*	*1*	*59²*	*61*	*8*	*33*	*51*	*44%*	*.309*	*-7*	*1.57*	*5.11*	*4.48*	*5.37*	*9.3*	*1.2*	*4.5*	*6.8*	*0.8*	*0.82*

Breakout: 21% **Improve: 48%** **Collapse: 17%** **Attrition: 12%** **MLB: 7%** **Comparables:** *Al Drumheller, Josh Newman, Cowboy Helton, Augie Ruiz*

A lanky lefty who was signed as an outfielder by the Giants prior to 2006, only to be dropped when it was discovered he had used a cousin's birth certificate to appear younger than his actual 22 years at the time, Viola was quickly snatched up by the Reds and converted to pitching. After an aborted conversion to starting, Viola made his Triple-A debut last year as a reliever, but struggled, largely due to a huge spike in his walk rate. Things went better in his September cup of coffee in "The Show," where he held lefties to just one hit in 13 at-bats. He has potential as a LOOGY, but that's probably his limit.

Edinson Volquez

Bats: R **Throws: R** **Height: 6' 0"** **Weight: 200** **Born: July 3, 1983** **Age: 26**

YEAR	TEAM	LVL	AGE	W	L	SV	G	GS	IP	H	HR	BB	SO	GB%	BABIP	STUFF	WHIP	ERA	SIERA	DERA	EqH9	EqHR9	EqBB9	EqSO9	VORP	SN/WX
2007	BAK	A+	23	0	4	0	7	7	35¹	27	4	20	38	49%	.258	2	1.33	7.13	3.73	7.68	7.9	1.9	5.3	6.4	-8.2	-0.65
2007	FRI	AA	23	8	1	0	11	11	58¹	46	9	19	62	49%	.253	9	1.11	3.55	3.06	4.39	8.5	2.1	3.3	7.3	6.8	0.42
2007	OKL	AAA	23	6	1	0	8	8	51	25	0	21	66	46%	.229	44	0.90	1.41	2.42	1.94	5.4	0.4	3.9	9.1	19.2	1.93
2007	TEX	MLB	23	2	1	0	6	6	34	34	4	15	29	39%	.303	16	1.44	4.50	4.28	4.24	8.5	1.1	3.4	6.9	4.8	0.57
2008	CIN	MLB	24	17	6	0	33	32	196	167	14	93	206	51%	.299	33	1.33	3.21	3.56	3.46	7.4	0.6	3.7	8.2	44.2	5.27
2009	CIN	MLB	25	4	2	0	9	9	49²	34	6	32	47	52%	.219	16	1.33	4.35	4.30	4.59	6.7	1.1	4.9	7.0	5.1	1.07
2010	*CIN*	*MLB*	*26*	*6*	*6*	*0*	*23*	*21*	*109²*	*97*	*12*	*55*	*99*	*52%*	*.285*	*16*	*1.38*	*4.25*	*4.05*	*4.46*	*8.0*	*1.0*	*4.1*	*7.3*	*12.7*	*2.11*

Breakout: 14% **Improve: 45%** **Collapse: 21%** **Attrition: 23%** **MLB: 78%** **Comparables:** *Omar Olivares, Gary Bell, Chuck Estrada, Les Tietje*

It's all too easy to blame Dusty Baker for the injured arms that litter his path as a major-league manager, but on closer inspection, it's even easier to blame him. Volquez threw 110 or more pitches in six of his last seven starts in 2008, topping out at a career-high 121 pitches. In those six starts, Volquez posted a 5.81 ERA for a Reds team more than 20 games out of first place. Last year, Volquez hit the DL with back spasms in late May and lasted just one inning in his return before heading off for the operating table. The loss is devastating for a Reds team hoping to coalesce around its young talent. Volquez will miss most if not all of 2010 and will return in 2011 as a 27-year-old pitcher with only one full major-league season under his belt. After watching the struggles of Francisco Liriano, a more talented pitcher, last year, we find it difficult to be optimistic about Volquez's ability to return to the front of the rotation.

Kip Wells

Bats: R   Throws: R   Height: 6' 3"   Weight: 205   Born: April 21, 1977   Age: 33

YEAR	TEAM	LVL	AGE	W	L	SV	G	GS	IP	H	HR	BB	SO	GB%	BABIP	STUFF	WHIP	ERA	SIERA	DERA	EqH9	EqHR9	EqBB9	EqSO9	VORP	SN/WX
2007	SLN	MLB	30	7	17	0	34	26	162^2	186	19	78	122	59%	.320	-7	1.62	5.70	4.53	5.96	10.2	1.1	3.8	5.9	-8.4	0.83
2008	CSP	AAA	31	0	3	0	4	4	18^1	32	4	6	15	53%	.418	-20	2.07	8.84	4.21	12.29	14.5	1.4	2.9	5.3	-14.1	-0.68
2008	KCA	MLB	31	0	1	0	10	0	10^1	10	1	11	9	59%	.321	7	2.03	8.71	5.40	8.10	9.0	0.9	9.0	7.2	-2.9	0.18
2008	COL	MLB	31	1	2	0	15	2	27^1	29	3	19	22	67%	.321	-2	1.76	5.27	4.57	5.50	9.0	0.7	5.3	6.3	0.0	0.17
2009	SYR	AAA	32	1	0	0	2	2	11	9	1	2	11	66%	.286	10	1.00	2.45	2.71	3.48	7.8	1.7	1.7	7.0	2.3	0.25
2009	LOU	AAA	32	1	0	0	5	1	14^2	12	2	5	16	78%	.278	12	1.16	3.07	2.78	3.95	8.6	2.0	3.3	7.9	2.4	0.24
2009	WAS	MLB	32	0	2	2	23	0	26^1	23	1	18	18	58%	.275	-8	1.56	6.49	5.08	5.98	7.9	0.3	5.1	5.1	-1.4	0.37
2009	CIN	MLB	32	2	3	0	10	7	46^1	37	5	22	25	52%	.229	-6	1.27	4.66	5.20	4.76	7.5	1.0	3.8	4.2	3.7	0.57
2010	CIN	MLB	33	4	6	1	35	11	84^1	90	11	44	57	62%	.305	-10	1.59	5.23	4.70	5.49	9.6	1.1	4.3	5.4	0.1	0.53

Breakout: 12%   Improve: 46%   Collapse: 25%   Attrition: 35%   MLB: 72%   Comparables: Russ Meyer, Rube Ehrhardt, Jeremy Powell, Ed Whitson

Over the last four seasons, Wells has pitched for seven teams and posted a 5.79 ERA with a 1.62 WHIP. Why he keeps getting opportunities is beyond us. Prior to the Reds, his last three teams released him after less than a full season of work, yet he just keeps catching on. Maybe there's still some first-rounder shine on him somewhere, but we can't see it. He has never struck out twice as many men as he's walked in a season, and over the last two years, he's walked 70 against 74 strikeouts. Even his best season, with the Pirates in 2003, wasn't all that great. He has already been through Pittsburgh, Kansas City, and Washington, so our guess is he splits 2010 between Baltimore and San Diego in his gamewide basements tour.

Travis Wood

Bats: R   Throws: L   Height: 5' 11"   Weight: 166   Born: February 6, 1987   Age: 23

YEAR	TEAM	LVL	AGE	W	L	SV	G	GS	IP	H	HR	BB	SO	GB%	BABIP	STUFF	WHIP	ERA	SIERA	DERA	EqH9	EqHR9	EqBB9	EqSO9	VORP	SN/WX
2007	SAR	A+	20	3	2	0	12	12	46^1	49	6	27	54	32%	.341	20	1.64	4.86	3.76	7.83	11.1	2.3	6.0	7.6	-11.3	-0.93
2008	SAR	A+	21	3	4	0	9	9	46^2	39	2	21	41	49%	.278	20	1.29	2.70	4.04	4.67	8.5	1.2	4.5	5.3	4.1	0.26
2008	CHT	AA	21	4	9	0	17	17	80	91	9	48	58	42%	.323	-8	1.74	7.09	5.12	8.39	10.7	1.6	5.1	4.5	-25.1	-1.78
2009	CAR	AA	22	9	3	0	19	19	119	78	2	37	103	46%	.243	37	0.97	1.21	3.56	2.65	7.3	0.7	2.9	5.9	34.9	3.67
2009	LOU	AAA	22	4	2	0	8	8	48^2	43	4	16	32	50%	.269	10	1.21	3.14	4.43	3.87	8.7	1.2	3.4	4.8	8.2	0.75
2010	CIN	MLB	23	6	8	0	27	26	124^2	123	15	65	85	37%	.289	3	1.51	4.89	5.16	5.14	9.0	1.1	4.3	5.5	4.9	2.27

Breakout: 15%   Improve: 56%   Collapse: 10%   Attrition: 11%   MLB: 7%   Comparables: Benji DeQuin, Bobby M. Jones, Mike Jeffcoat, Brian Householder

This little lefty sinkerballer was as good in his repeat of Double-A last year as he was bad in his first stint there in 2008, the result of better conditioning allowing him to recapture some of the velocity he had lost the year before. That velocity is crucial to the effectiveness of his changeup, which is a legitimate out pitch and the best change in the Reds' organization. His strikeout rate took a tumble after his promotion to Louisville, but he's just 23 and handles righties well, and his ability to keep the ball down and in the park is ideal for the Reds and their stadium. If his repeat of Triple-A goes half as well, Wood could be in the major-league rotation in short order.

LINEOUTS

Hitters

PLAYER	TEAM	LVL	AGE	PA	R	2B	3B	HR	RBI	BB	SO	SB-CS	EqBRR	AVG/OBP/SLG	EqAVG/EqOBP/EqSLG	EqA	VORP	WARP
1B K. Barker*	LOU	AAA	33	417	58	22	3	22	69	54	80	1-1	-0.5	.285/.376/.551	.258/.344/.481	.282	10.2	0.2
	CIN	MLB	33	36	2	3	0	0	3	3	9	0-0	-0.1	.281/.333/.375	.281/.333/.375	.256	-0.3	0.0
OF J. Duran	RDS	Rk	17	174	15	7	4	0	17	8	52	0-0	0.6	.177/.218/.268	.168/.195/.240	.127	-17.2	-4.1
SS M. Gregorius*	SAR	A+	19	74	8	4	0	0	2	1	9	0-0	1.0	.254/.274/.310	.236/.257/.278	.181	-2.5	-0.4
	BIL	Rk	19	225	28	10	1	1	16	12	27	8-6	-1.7	.314/.363/.387	.255/.286/.297	.205	-3.4	-2.3
SS B. Hamilton	RDS	Rk	18	180	19	6	3	0	11	11	47	14-3	1.1	.205/.253/.277	.188/.223/.247	.160	-9.3	-1.5
OF D. McDonald	LOU	AAA	30	304	42	22	7	9	40	16	56	8-3	-0.4	.314/.349/.539	.287/.319/.486	.272	9.5	2.0
	CIN	MLB	30	111	12	6	1	2	10	5	31	1-0	0.7	.267/.306/.400	.276/.315/.410	.251	0.6	-0.1
C D. Mesoraco	SAR	A+	21	357	32	22	1	8	37	35	76	0-1	-2.8	.228/.311/.381	.210/.280/.348	.220	-1.7	-1.2
C C. Miller	CHA	MLB	33	42	5	3	0	0	5	3	9	0-0	-0.2	.205/.262/.282	.205/.262/.282	.187	-1.3	-0.3
	CIN	MLB	33	69	4	1	0	1	10	9	14	0-0	-0.5	.179/.299/.250	.193/.309/.263	.212	0.0	0.1
2B C. Puckett	DYT	A	22	538	76	35	1	19	67	39	138	19-1	0.3	.263/.325/.459	.225/.270/.370	.224	-4.6	-3.7
2B D. Richar*	LOU	AAA	26	181	20	11	1	4	16	10	17	2-3	-1.7	.290/.330/.438	.276/.313/.418	.248	3.4	-0.6
CF Y. Rodriguez	RDS	Rk	16	95	9	2	1	0	2	10	23	5-0	-0.8	.274/.347/.321	.230/.284/.276	.202	-2.6	-0.7
	BIL	Rk	16	193	21	10	2	3	17	9	61	5-2	0.4	.219/.259/.344	.182/.207/.267	.149	-13.5	-3.3
SS M. Rojas	DYT	A	20	527	50	16	3	3	49	35	44	14-8	-1.9	.273/.326/.339	.235/.276/.293	.202	-8.4	-1.6
CF D. Sappelt	DYT	A	22	331	44	14	7	3	25	23	46	26-11	-1.0	.269/.322/.392	.227/.267/.330	.210	-7.9	-0.8
	SAR	A+	22	271	27	10	3	4	21	13	29	21-11	-2.8	.295/.333/.406	.271/.302/.376	.236	1.0	0.3
3B N. Soto	SAR	A+	20	537	53	21	2	11	57	23	95	1-3	-4.9	.248/.282/.362	.227/.257/.335	.203	-20.3	-4.1
C C. Tatum	LOU	AAA	26	233	22	12	0	3	21	17	55	0-0	-1.0	.239/.300/.338	.228/.286/.316	.212	-0.8	0.0
	CIN	MLB	26	77	3	1	0	1	6	7	10	0-0	0.1	.162/.250/.221	.159/.247/.217	.160	-3.4	-0.4

Veteran minor-leaguer **Kevin Barker** hit .292/.370/.417 in 27 pinch-hit appearances down the stretch last year, his first big-league work since 2006. He's a career .262/.350/.466 hitter in Triple-A. ⊘ Dominican outfielder **Juan Duran**'s first season in the States didn't go terribly well, but he was just 17 and incredibly raw. He has a ton of projection as a tall, willowy, right-handed slugger with a whiplike swing. ⊘ A Dutch-born shortstop who just turned 20 in February, **Mariekson Gregorius** is a solid contact hitter who is likely to hit for average, but power, walks, and the ability to remain at shortstop remain to be seen, though he should remain in the infield. ⊘ A second-round pick in 2009, **Billy Hamilton** is a small, speedy, high school shortstop with raw talent and a lot of upside. ⊘ The Orioles' 1997 first-round pick, **Darnell McDonald** got his first extended big-league look last year and hit consistent with his career .277/.337/.420 line in Triple-A. Nearly all of his production came against lefties, and his drop in steals suggests his best skill is slipping away. ⊘ A first-round pick in 2007, **Devin Mesoraco** was clearly overdrafted and, having plumped up as a pro, now looks like a full-on bust. He'll be 22 in June and may have to rely on his strong defense to scratch out a career as a catch-and-throw backup, like **Corky Miller**. ⊘ An eighth-round pick out of college in 2008, **Cody Puckett** is a second baseman with some pop and speed but lacks an approach at the plate, making him a pure mistake hitter unlikely to make it very far. ⊘ The Reds didn't need **Danny Richar** to amount to anything for the Ken Griffey Jr. trade to have been a success, which is good, because he didn't. ⊘ A five-tool center fielder who signed for $2.5 million (a record for a Venezuelan amateur), **Yorman Rodriguez** started his pro career last year at the age of 16. ⊘ Another Venezuelan, shortstop **Miguel Rojas** made his full-season debut last year at age 20. He's unlikely to hit much, but his play in the field is good enough to get him to the majors as a utilityman without much help from his bat. ⊘ A ninth-round pick out of Coastal Carolina University in 2008, center fielder **Dave Sappelt** hit for a bit of average in his full-season debut, but his power and patience were lacking and he was caught far too often on the bases. ⊘ Despite a strong arm, **Neftali Soto** is an offense-first third baseman who will go only as far as his bat takes him, which makes his awful showing at High-A last year, due somewhat to poor conditioning, particularly troubling. ⊘ **Craig Tatum** is cut from the Corky Miller mold; claimed off waivers by the Orioles in November, he will be lucky to scratch out a career as a strong-armed catch-and-throw backup.

Pitchers

PLAYER	TEAM	LVL	AGE	W	L	SV	IP	H	HR	BB	SO	GB%	BABIP	STUFF	WHIP	ERA	SIERA	DERA	EqH9	EqHR9	EqBB9	EqSO9	VORP
D. Buck	CAR	AA	24	2	3	0	37^1	49	1	18	25	67%	.378	-18	1.79	4.82	4.58	7.01	13.8	0.8	4.5	4.5	-5.7
E. Del Rosario	SAR	A+	23	2	1	7	50	40	2	6	33	67%	.247	-9	0.92	1.98	3.55	3.78	8.3	1.3	1.7	3.6	9.1
	LOU	AAA	23	1	0	4	24^2	24	1	6	12	79%	.287	-11	1.22	1.09	3.63	2.74	9.4	0.8	2.3	3.5	7.1
B. Jukich*	LOU	AAA	26	9	6	0	123	125	16	40	106	58%	.304	-15	1.34	4.10	3.76	5.51	10.2	1.8	3.3	6.3	-0.1
M. Lincoln	CIN	MLB	34	1	1	0	23	29	7	19	9	58%	.289	-39	2.09	8.22	6.27	7.98	12.3	2.9	6.5	3.3	-6.1
A. Smit*	SAR	A+	23	0	0	0	12^2	12	1	7	12	52%	.324	-3	1.50	4.26	4.03	6.95	11.5	2.5	6.5	5.7	-1.8
	CAR	AA	23	4	3	0	71	54	9	42	73	38%	.263	-6	1.35	3.04	4.03	4.50	9.3	2.4	5.5	7.3	7.1
J. Smith	CAR	AA	23	5	3	0	73^1	77	4	21	39	60%	.299	-14	1.34	3.44	4.67	5.82	11.0	1.2	2.8	3.3	-2.4
J. C. Sulbaran	DYT	A	19	5	5	0	92^2	94	19	51	100	33%	.311	-36	1.56	5.24	3.94	8.87	12.6	4.1	6.4	6.1	-30.6
M. Thurman*	DYT	A	22	3	0	0	30^2	24	3	11	35	41%	.269	0	1.14	2.93	2.96	4.92	9.2	2.2	4.1	6.4	1.8
	SAR	A+	22	0	2	8	49	30	0	14	47	50%	.229	13	0.90	1.10	3.22	2.87	6.7	0.8	3.3	5.6	13.7
P. Valiquette*	SAR	A+	22	1	1	6	19^2	11	2	9	19	51%	.200	5	1.02	2.29	3.54	3.44	7.4	2.6	5.3	6.4	3.9
	CAR	AA	22	1	1	3	32^2	25	2	20	27	56%	.258	-5	1.38	2.76	4.53	4.75	8.6	1.2	5.3	5.6	2.5

Former Expos first-rounder **Bill Bray** will be battling back from May 2008 Tommy John surgery this season. ⊘ The other minor leaguer from the Dunn trade, **Dallas Buck** was once a highly regarded prospect, but spent most of 2009 working his way back from Tommy John surgery, and he'll be 25 this year. ⊘ **Enerio Del Rosario**'s 2009 season mirrored Logan Ondrusek's, as he dominated across the top three levels; both were added to the 40-man in November, but the stringy Dominican lacks Ondrusek's big frame. ⊘ Acquired from the A's in the Chris Denorfia deal, tall lefty **Ben Jukich** spent his first full season in Triple-A last year and saw his homer rate spike despite otherwise solid peripherals. In the end, he's a reliever at best. ⊘ Successive Tommy John surgeries caused **Mike Lincoln** to sit out three full seasons from 2005 to 2007. He made a miraculous return to the majors in 2008 at age 33, but a mid-June bulging disk in his neck cut his 2009 season short. He'll return on the second year of the contract he earned in '08, but he was never all that special, even when healthy. ⊘ Drafted out of high school in the first supplemental round in 2007, **Kyle Lotzkar** was the top pitching prospect in the Reds' system until a fractured elbow in late 2008 derailed him. That he was just 19 last year allowed the Reds to be cautious when he suffered setbacks in his recovery, but the fact that he never did pitch invites frightening comparisons to fellow British Columbian Adam Loewen, who suffered a similar injury and is now struggling to make it as an outfielder. ⊘ In part due to a history of injuries, Dutch lefty **Alex Smit** didn't get above A-ball until last year, his seventh minor-league season. Though healthy, he still hasn't solved his control problems and projects best as a LOOGY. ⊘ As a sinkerballer adept at keeping the ball in the park, **Jordan Smith** would seem to be in the right organization, but his strikeout rate took a tumble last year. If he makes the majors, it's likely to be as a reliever. ⊘ Florida native **J. C. Sulbaran** has a live arm and drew some brief national attention with a big relief outing for the surprising Dutch team in the World Baseball Classic, but he was extremely inconsistent in his pro debut in the Midwest League. ⊘ Twice drafted by the Blue Jays, lefty reliever **Mace Thurman** finally signed with the Reds out of Baylor in 2008 and made a strong showing in High-A. ⊘ Montreal native **Philippe-Alexandre Valiquette** is a lefty with control problems; he finally reached Double-A after five years in the minors, but the few extra ticks he has on the radar gun got him added to the 40-man instead of Smit. Just 23, Valiquette has potential as a LOOGY or even a full-inning set-up man.

MANAGER: DUSTY BAKER

YEAR	TEAM	W-L	Pythag +/−	Avg PC	100+ P	120+ P	QS	BQS	REL	REL w Zero R	IBB	Subs	PH	PH Avg	PH HR	SB2	CS2	SB3	CS3	SAC Att	SAC %	POS SAC	Squeeze	Swing	In Play
2008	CIN	74-88	3	97.9	80	3	75	3	507	321	40	48	282	.231	5	68	39	17	6	118	61.0%	34	6	136	104
2009	CIN	78-84	3	98.7	89	2	77	3	477	320	36	43	251	.227	4	80	35	15	4	137	73.0%	47	4	122	98

Baker let his starter throw 120 pitches just three times last year, and the starters who went long were veterans Arroyo (123 pitches) and Harang (123 and 120). Still, it was alarming that in Volquez, yet another promising young arm went under the knife for major surgery on Baker's watch. Cueto survived another season, but not without a shoulder-related DL stay, which, in combination with his manager, should be a red flag for 2010. If there's one thing Baker seems to love more than sending young pitchers to the DL, it's maximizing his lineup's potential for making outs; following the Corey Patterson experience with Willy Taveras shows a failure to learn. Worse, Baker batted Taveras leadoff 81 times, sabotaging his lineup. Baker's most frequent number-two hitter was Jerry Hairston Jr. (.305 OBP); once Hairston was in the Bronx and Drew Stubbs pushed Taveras out of the lineup, Baker started batting the Belanger-ish Paul Janish second. True, the Reds didn't have many strong on-base options last year, but Baker repeatedly picked the worst of a weak group for the top of the order. Stubbs seems to have secured the leadoff spot for the coming season, but we're not about to see Baker batting base-cloggers Scott Rolen or Ryan Hanigan second despite relatively high OBPs. If there's one thing to credit Baker with, it was using Micah Owings as a pinch-hitter, but just 16 times seems like another half-step in the right direction.

Cleveland Indians

For the fifth year in a row, PECOTA predicted the Indians to be in contention in the AL Central with at least 85 wins. For the third time in the last four years, they didn't live up to the expectations, which is at least reliability, just of the wrong sort. But in 2009, they underachieved especially well, finishing 21 games below PECOTA's prediction of a division title and a record of 86-76. While you ascribe some of the wipeout to the team's stumble-then-dump response to initial disappointment, there's no way of ducking the obvious: the Indians blew it.

There were causes for concern, beyond the obvious mediocrity of a projected 86-win ballclub. Before the season started, it was obvious that the Indians' greatest vulnerability was their starting rotation. Coming off a Cy Young year, Cliff Lee was a lock as staff ace. Behind him, however, Fausto Carmona was coming off a horrendous year, Carl Pavano was signed to an incentive-laden, make-good contract after pitching in just nine major-league games in the previous three seasons, and the club faced a bushel of possibilities for the fourth and fifth starters. Even with a cast of thousands waiting in the wings and bouncing around relative readiness, the rotation was definitely the club's weakest link.

Thus handicapped, the Indians dug themselves an early hole, consistent with their other down years in 2006 and 2008, this time starting off with a 1-7 record while being outscored 38-62. The bullpen was again horrendous; the Indians finished 2008 last in the league in WXRL, and would rank last again in 2009, and "contributed" a 5.80 ERA and 1.654 WHIP in April. (There is no truth to the rumors that GM Mark Shapiro is in discussions with Universal Pictures for a new disaster

movie franchise: *Bullpen; Bullpen 2: Horrific Boogaloo; Bullpen 3: The Pen and the Pendulum*, etc. It didn't help that the Indians' rotation did not record a quality start until the 10th game. However, the lineup started listing early on as well. Team star Grady Sizemore was nursing an elbow injury throughout the year, so the unit was carried by the consistency of Shin-Soo Choo, a rebound year from Victor Martinez, and a breakout season by Asdrubal Cabrera. Except for a few days in mid-June, when they managed to poke their heads above the plummeting Royals, the Indians were stuck in last place until late July. Though they were spared the humiliation of finishing the season with a worse record than the Royals, after June 20th the Indians never got closer than 10 games behind the Tigers.

Appropriately enough, rather than play out the string with a team already unstrung, the Indians began selling, starting by sending Mark DeRosa to the Cardinals on June 28th in exchange for reliever Chris Perez and a player to be named later (who wound up being hard-throwing righty Jess Todd). From then until the point when the dust cleared in early August, the Tribe had traded four position players (DeRosa, Ryan Garko, Victor Martinez, and Ben Francisco), plus their staff ace (Lee), their third starter (Pavano), and a key piece of their bullpen (Rafael Betancourt).

After the stars were gone and the pressure was off, the Indians did have a nice August (15-12), but ended the season with an awful run in September and October, going 7-25 in a stretch that included an 11-game losing streak. Eric Wedge was told that he would be canned with six games to go, though he was allowed to finish out the season as a lame-duck manager, conclud-

INDIANS PROSPECTUS
2009 W-L: 65-97, 4th (tied) in AL Central

Pythag	74-88	12th	**Ballpark:** Progressive Field (3-yr. PF: 974). Even a friendly park couldn't help this pitching staff
RS/G	4.8	8th	
RA/G	5.3	13th	
EqA	.263	7th	**2009:** The age of Wedge (mis)management ends, but did tearing down bring the talent to win soon?
EqBRR	-3.1	9th	
SNWP	.472	13th	
WXRL	0.51	14th	**2010:** Sizemore healthy and less sulk from Peralta helps, but Pronk's a prob, the rotation's a mess; will Acta-vision fix the pen?
FRAr	5.09	12th	
DE	.681	12th	
PADE	-0.32	4th	**Action Items:** Finding the keepers on the staff, breaking in LaPorta and young catchers
Salary	$81.6	7th	
Attend	1.77	13th	

ing the season with a five-game losing streak, 21 games behind the Tigers and Twins, who tied for the division lead with 86-76 records, the same record that PECOTA had predicted the 2009 Indians would have.

Given that the standard for what it takes to win the Central has been set at "modest," it figures to remain one of the weaker divisions. That's good news for Cleveland, in that the Indians are going to have a much lower summit to climb compared with either the Orioles or Blue Jays in the East, or the Athletics out West. The slope of their climb will be further eased as the Tigers, the biggest spenders in the division, start to strip payroll in response to the region's economic distress. Unfortunately, Cleveland also has been hit hard by the downturn. This worsening economic climate along with the underachieving ballclub have combined to keep the turnstiles unspun at Progressive Field, causing the Indians to drop to 26th in attendance, falling behind even the Royals to become the poorest-drawing team in the division. The days of Jacobs Field sellouts and the Indians being considered a borderline big-market team belong to history, and while the Indians had a small recovery in 2007 because of the division title and a hanger-on effect in 2008, it will be tough for them to get above the bottom third of teams in attendance until they can string several winning seasons together.

Table 1. Leaving the Tribe: Attendance in the Shapiro Years

Year	Win Pct.	Attendance	ML Rank
2001	.562	3,175,523	4
2002	.457	2,616,940	12
2003	.420	1,730,001	24
2004	.494	1,814,401	25
2005	.574	2,013,763	24
2006	.481	1,997,995	25
2007	.593	2,275,916	21
2008	.500	2,169,760	22
2009	.401	1,766,242	26

From 2007 to 2009, attendance has dropped off by 510,000. If we assume that this lost attendance was at Forbes' reported average MLB ticket price of $26, the Indians have lost over $13 million in revenue. This might not be as crippling as it sounds. The strength of Shapiro's administration has been acquiring prospects through trades (or identifying minor-league free agents) that typically translate into solid major leaguers relatively quickly. In the recent past, the Indians have not received much production out of their free-agent additions, save for 2005 (Kevin Millwood, Bob Wickman, Ronnie Belliard, and Bobby Howry). Rather, in the last six years, most of the team's production has come from

players acquired via trade when they were just prospects with other teams (such as Sizemore, Travis Hafner, Lee, Choo, Cabrera, and Jake Westbrook) and, to a lesser extent, homegrown talent in the Indians' farm system (Victor Martinez, CC Sabathia, and Jhonny Peralta).

Table 2. Prospecting for Gold: Source of Indians WARP3, 2004-2009

Year	WARP3 Total	Major Leaguer		Prospect		Amateur	
		Free Agent	via Trade	Free Agent	via Trade	Free Agent	Draft
2004	45.9	0.9	5.5	8.2	19.2	5.3	6.8
2005	68.1	19.4	0.0	5.7	24.6	11.9	6.5
2006	54.6	0.9	-0.1	4.4	29.8	8.6	11.0
2007	61.4	1.4	0.4	6.8	20.2	20.8	11.8
2008	56.2	1.8	3.3	3.1	29.2	8.6	10.2
2009	45.6	6.1	1.9	1.0	27.5	2.0	7.1

In Table 2, the WARP3 that each year's squad generated is categorized on the basis of how the organization acquired the player. For trades and free-agent signings, if the player could still qualify as a rookie when he was traded or signed, he was classified as a prospect. The small value that has come from waiver claims is grouped with the free agents. Only in 2007 did the production from homegrown talent exceed that from those who were acquired as prospects.

One key to this spread of talent is that the four players (Choo, Lee, Cabrera, and Sizemore) with the highest VORP in 2009 were players that Shapiro acquired from other organizations. Lee and Sizemore (along with Brandon Phillips and Lee Stevens) were traded by the Expos back in 2002 for Bartolo Colon and Tim Drew. In two separate deals with the Mariners, Choo and Cabrera were traded in exchange for Ben Broussard and Eduardo Perez, respectively. Along with the four mentioned above, the top two prospects in the Indians system to start the year were also acquired by the Indians via trade in 2008: Carlos Santana (from the Dodgers for Casey Blake) and Matt LaPorta (from the Brewers for CC Sabathia).

Shapiro's skill as a talent miner was on display again in 2009, when he received a major leaguer (Justin Masterson) and 10 prospects, eight of whom were one of their teams' top 11 prospects lists, based on Kevin Goldstein's 2009 pre-season prospect lists for all 30 clubs.

Once the Indians have accumulated the talent, they have a reputation for preparing their players to field multiple positions. There are three main reasons for doing this. First, it keeps the organization from having to scramble and make midseason acquisitions when injury occurs. Second, it keeps a player from being

Table 3. Wampum Returns: Haul from Cleveland Trades, 2009

Player	Traded For	Trading Team	2009 Pre-season Prospect Rank
Chris Perez	DeRosa	Cardinals	#3 (4-star)
Jess Todd	DeRosa	Cardinals	#5 (3-star)
Connor Graham	Betancourt	Rockies	#8 (3-star)
Carlos Carrasco	Lee/Francisco	Phillies	#1 (5-star)
Lou Marson	Lee/Francisco	Phillies	#5 (3-star)
Jason Donald	Lee/Francisco	Phillies	#6 (3-star)
Jason Knapp	Lee/Francisco	Phillies	#10(3-star)
Nick Hagadone	Martinez	Red Sox	#8 (3-star)
Justin Masterson	Martinez	Red Sox	Major Leaguer
Scott Barnes	Garko	Giants	—
Yohan Pino	Pavano	Twins	—

Table 4. Shuffling the Deck: Unique Player-Position Combinations, AL 2009

Team	Position Players Used	Players w/ 100+ Starts at Same Pos.	Players w/ 10+ Starts at Same Pos.	Defensive Efficiency (AL Rank)
Indians	23	2	29	12
Royals	20	3	25	14
Twins	18	3	24	6
Athletics	25	3	24	9
White Sox	21	6	21	7
Mariners	26	5	21	1
Orioles	21	5	19	10
Red Sox	28	6	19	13
Rangers	21	5	19	2
Tigers	22	7	18	5
Yankees	22	6	18	3
Blue Jays	20	6	18	10
Angels	21	6	17	8
Rays	20	6	17	4

blocked. Third, it increases the player's value for trades down the road. This flexibility not only occurs in the minors, but also continues at the top. In his attempt to find the right combination on the field in 2009, Wedge used 148 lineups (as well as 136 in 2008). There were very few fixtures in the field, as the Indians had the fewest 100-plus starts at the same position of all teams in the AL (Peralta had 102 starts at third, and Choo had 121 starts in right). On the flip side, there were 29 player/position combinations in the field with 10 or more starts. This constant juggling of the defensive set was further demonstrated by the fact that 10 Indians played three or more field positions during the year, including 11 different left fielders.

While having that flexibility is a safeguard against injury and allows a manager to exploit better lefty/righty matchups, it can lead to a lack of proficiency afield. The Indians were 12th in the AL in Defensive Efficiency, while the next team with an inclination toward shuffling, the Royals, was dead last. Of the top four teams that did significantly more shuffling than the rest of the league, only the Twins seemed to be able to make it work, finishing in the top half of the league in Defensive Efficiency.

Can the Indians compete in the weak AL Central in 2010? The good news is that their Achilles' heel of the last two seasons began to mend at the end of last year. In the first half, the bullpen had a 5.58 Fair Run Average (a BP metric that calculates runs allowed with inherited runners allowed to score factored in), while in the second half it had a middling 4.49 FRA. Kerry Wood is still a concern in the closer's role, but with the acquisition of Chris Perez, the emergence of Tony Sipp, and the hoped-for comeback of Rafael Perez, the Indians may surprise many with their pen's performance in 2010. As for the offense, Grady Sizemore should bounce back from injury. Jhonny Peralta, having very publicly bick-

ered with Wedge, may be reenergized by a fresh start with a new skipper. One of the keys to the new offense will be Matt LaPorta's ability to return to health and finally make a successful and permanent place for himself in the majors.

However, the real key to the Indians in 2010 will again be the starting rotation. In some ways, it is 2009 all over again, but with even more concerns in that the "ace" and likely Opening Day starter is no longer a Cy Young Award winner but an injury-prone hurler (Jake Westbrook) who hasn't had a big-league start since May 2008. The likely second starter will again be Fausto Carmona, an extra year removed from his breakout 2007. The other three likely starters are David Huff and his 5.61 ERA, Masterson and his platoon issues, and Aaron Laffey, who was shuffled between rotation and bullpen and finished the season with an ERA of 7.39 in his last six games.

If this rough posse gels, then a return to .500 ball and a run at relevance in the lowest of low-standards divisions may not be that far off. If, more probably, it does not, you might anticipate another Indians fire sale in July, as expiring commitments to veterans get swapped out for parts in another round of noncontention. Unfortunately, the Tribe's cupboard of attractive veteran commodities is starting to get relatively bare. If this sounds like a team touching bottom, you're not hearing things, but the real question is how long this latest bad patch will last. Talents such as Carlos Santana and LaPorta might provide the lineup anchors for the next great crop of Tribesmen, but even in the decisively mediocre AL Central, it figures to be a slow climb back.

HITTERS

Michael Brantley   CF   Bats: L   Throws: L   Height: 6' 2"   Weight: 180   Born: May 15, 1987   Age: 23

YEAR	TEAM	LVL	AGE	PA	R	2B	3B	HR	RBI	BB	SO	SB	CS	EqBRR	AVG	OBP	SLG	EqAVG	EqOBP	EqSLG	EqA	VORP	WARP	DEFENSE			
2007	WVA	A	20	255	41	15	1	2	32	31	22	18	6	-0.9	.335	.413	.440	.298	.365	.391	.269	5.9	0.5	30-1B	0	19-LF	-2
2007	HUN	AA	20	223	28	6	1	0	21	29	25	17	3	3.5	.251	.353	.294	.232	.318	.268	.225	-3.9	0.2	48-LF	6		
2008	HUN	AA	21	479	80	17	2	4	40	50	27	28	8	4.8	.319	.395	.398	.298	.357	.370	.262	10.9	2.2	60-CF	9	21-1B	1
2009	COH	AAA	22	528	80	21	2	6	37	59	48	46	5	7.3	.267	.350	.361	.257	.338	.354	.258	13.1	0.3	93-CF	-10	21-LF	-1
2009	CLE	MLB	22	121	10	4	0	0	11	8	19	4	4	-1.9	.313	.358	.348	.330	.375	.366	.254	2.4	0.0	19-CF	-3	7-LF	1
2010	CLE	MLB	23	568	73	25	2	6	48	55	61	26	8	2.3	.270	.344	.359	.275	.349	.364	.256	15.0	1.5	115-CF	-1		

Breakout: 12%   Improve: 46%   Collapse: 12%   Attrition: 11%   MLB: 60%   Comparables: Brandon Watson, Everett Graham, Bruce Fields, Goef Tomlinson

Brantley's first year in the organization after coming over from the Brewers in the Sabathia deal had only one blemish, a dip in batting average, but his 50-point drop from 2008 in Triple-A was discouraging. On the other hand, he dramatically improved both his stolen-base attempts and his success rate, and he was among the youngest position players in the league. He is also starting to see a little boost in his power, and though not a walk machine, he remains perfect in walking more than striking out in every professional season. With Trevor Crowe stalling and LaPorta's likely move to first base, Brantley has a significant chance of getting playing time in left field this year, but team officials would like him to get some more seasoning back at Columbus.

Jordan Brown   1B/OF   Bats: L   Throws: L   Height: 6' 0"   Weight: 205   Born: December 18, 1983   Age: 26

YEAR	TEAM	LVL	AGE	PA	R	2B	3B	HR	RBI	BB	SO	SB	CS	EqBRR	AVG	OBP	SLG	EqAVG	EqOBP	EqSLG	EqA	VORP	WARP	DEFENSE			
2007	AKR	AA	23	558	85	36	2	11	76	63	56	11	2	-5.4	.333	.421	.484	.310	.385	.452	.292	25.1	2.5	92-1B	-3	9-LF	-1
2008	BUF	AAA	24	460	52	30	3	7	51	35	67	3	3	-4.0	.281	.337	.417	.263	.317	.389	.245	-2.9	-0.6	86-1B	-2		
2009	COH	AAA	25	455	65	35	1	15	67	30	64	2	4	-4.6	.336	.381	.532	.320	.364	.508	.292	22.1	1.1	40-LF	2	27-RF	-12
2010	CLE	MLB	26	421	51	23	1	10	50	35	64	3	2	-2.0	.273	.338	.413	.277	.342	.420	.263	10.0	1.2	74-LF	1		

Breakout: 7%   Improve: 27%   Collapse: 24%   Attrition: 15%   MLB: 17%   Comparables: Mark Sweeney, Andy Abad, Brian Stavisky, Vince Sinisi

Brown had a comeback year, winning the International League batting title and reestablishing himself as a possible short-term alternative at first base if LaPorta is not available to start the season. He'll need that opportunity, because he's trying to beat an "organizational player" label as it is. As you can see, he's not someone to work his way aboard for a free pass, managing just 18 unintentionals in 331 plate appearances against right-handers, but with a .196 ISO. That may excite some, but it could also be a few bricks shy of a Gload.

Asdrubal Cabrera   SS   Bats: S   Throws: R   Height: 6' 0"   Weight: 170   Born: November 13, 1985   Age: 24

YEAR	TEAM	LVL	AGE	PA	R	2B	3B	HR	RBI	BB	SO	SB	CS	EqBRR	AVG	OBP	SLG	EqAVG	EqOBP	EqSLG	EqA	VORP	WARP	DEFENSE			
2007	AKR	AA	21	425	78	23	3	8	54	45	42	23	7	1.4	.310	.383	.454	.290	.354	.428	.275	22.4	2.3	90-SS	-3		
2007	CLE	MLB	21	186	30	9	2	3	22	17	29	0	0	2.5	.283	.354	.421	.280	.350	.414	.273	8.5	2.0	36-2B	5	5-SS	3
2008	BUF	AAA	22	152	25	7	1	4	13	7	25	2	2	-3.5	.326	.375	.475	.310	.355	.458	.275	8.4	0.3	29-SS	-5	5-2B	-1
2008	CLE	MLB	22	418	48	20	0	6	47	46	77	4	4	-1.9	.259	.346	.366	.267	.356	.388	.261	14.4	3.5	88-2B	13	17-SS	2
2009	CLE	MLB	23	581	81	42	4	6	68	44	89	17	4	1.9	.308	.361	.438	.321	.373	.450	.286	37.9	3.8	98-SS	-3	28-2B	-1
2010	CLE	MLB	24	592	88	33	4	11	71	55	91	14	5	0.3	.289	.360	.423	.289	.360	.427	.277	31.6	3.2	137-SS	-2		

Breakout: 20%   Improve: 57%   Collapse: 7%   Attrition: 5%   MLB: 85%   Comparables: Tony Fernandez, Derek Jeter, Steve Sax, Alan Trammell

Cabrera exceeded most expectations offensively, hitting his 90th-percentile PECOTA projection, but in terms of overall value, Cabrera's offensive improvement may have come at a price. While he was touted as a solid defender, all the fielding metrics suggest that he was a far-below-average shortstop defensively in 2009. Heading into 2010, Tribe fans may want to prepare for a bit of a drop in his offensive performance. His "breakout" was a direct result of a very high BABIP (.360), some of which was justified by an increase in his line-drive rate (from 15 percent to 20 percent) and hitting the ball on the ground more to utilize his speed. On the other hand, Cabrera has now hit .311/.371/.445 in 193 games, going back to his midseason demotion in 2008, so perhaps the improvement is real enough.

Jamey Carroll — INF

Bats: R   Throws: R   Height: 5' 9"   Weight: 170   Born: February 18, 1974   Age: 36

YEAR	TEAM	LVL	AGE	PA	R	2B	3B	HR	RBI	BB	SO	SB	CS	EqBRR	AVG	OBP	SLG	EqAVG	EqOBP	EqSLG	EqA	VORP	WARP	DEFENSE			
2007	COL	MLB	33	268	45	9	1	2	22	28	34	6	2	2.7	.225	.317	.300	.224	.317	.294	.226	-0.7	0.6	48-2B	3	7-3B	0
2008	CLE	MLB	34	402	60	13	4	1	36	34	65	7	3	1.4	.277	.355	.346	.285	.364	.355	.260	11.6	1.7	65-2B	2	23-3B	2
2009	CLE	MLB	35	358	53	10	2	2	26	36	63	4	2	0.9	.276	.355	.340	.287	.364	.350	.257	8.2	0.6	53-2B	-2	18-3B	-1
2010	LAN	MLB	36	273	37	10	1	2	23	27	57	3	2	0.7	.241	.326	.313	.248	.334	.326	.236	1.6	0.2	59-2B	1		

Breakout: 8%   Improve: 27%   Collapse: 31%   Attrition: 40%   MLB: 96%   Comparables: Willie Randolph, Dom DiMaggio, Luis Alicea, Tony Taylor

After missing the first month of the season with a broken hand that he sustained in the final exhibition game of spring training, Carroll essentially repeated his triple-slash stats from 2008. In another case of the middle class getting squeezed, slightly above replacement-level production at $2.5 million per year seems like money that could be spent somewhere else, so Carroll scrammed for LA, signing a two-year, $3.85 million deal.

Lonnie Chisenhall — 3B

Bats: L   Throws: R   Height: 6' 1"   Weight: 200   Born: October 4, 1988   Age: 21

YEAR	TEAM	LVL	AGE	PA	R	2B	3B	HR	RBI	BB	SO	SB	CS	EqBRR	AVG	OBP	SLG	EqAVG	EqOBP	EqSLG	EqA	VORP	WARP	DEFENSE	
2008	MHV	A-	19	305	38	20	3	5	45	24	32	7	2	-0.4	.290	.355	.438	.257	.308	.391	.243	5.6	0.6	55-SS	-2
2009	KIN	A+	20	432	59	26	2	18	79	37	80	2	1	0.7	.276	.346	.492	.257	.313	.448	.259	9.0	0.1	78-3B	-8
2009	AKR	AA	20	101	13	5	1	4	13	7	16	1	0	-0.2	.183	.238	.387	.170	.218	.362	.199	-3.7	-0.7	23-3B	-2
2010	CLE	MLB	21	500	58	28	2	16	68	37	89	4	2	0.0	.250	.310	.423	.254	.314	.428	.253	9.5	0.5	94-3B	-5

Breakout: 24%   Improve: 53%   Collapse: 6%   Attrition: 1%   MLB: 3%   Comparables: Mat Gamel, Brandon Pico, Otis Green, Troy O'Leary

When the Indians selected Chisenhall with their first-round pick in 2008, it was a bit of a surprise, but one year later, it looks like a steal. Moved to third base for his full-season debut, Chisenhall played the position well, and his downright pretty swing should produce high batting averages and above-average power. After an impressive showing in High-A, he was rewarded with a promotion to Double-A for the last month of the season, where his aggressive approach at the plate betrayed him, but he snapped back in the playoffs, going 14-for-30 in seven games. Chisenhall will start the season back at Double-A, but it would be no surprise if he got a September trial with an eye toward replacing Peralta, whose contract fortuitously expires after this season.

Shin-Soo Choo — RF

Bats: L   Throws: L   Height: 5' 11"   Weight: 200   Born: July 13, 1982   Age: 27

YEAR	TEAM	LVL	AGE	PA	R	2B	3B	HR	RBI	BB	SO	SB	CS	EqBRR	AVG	OBP	SLG	EqAVG	EqOBP	EqSLG	EqA	VORP	WARP	DEFENSE			
2007	BUF	AAA	24	238	34	11	2	3	26	21	40	10	3	1.6	.260	.328	.375	.243	.303	.357	.241	-1.2	-0.1	31-LF	2	9-RF	-2
2007	CLE	MLB	24	20	5	0	0	0	5	2	5	0	1	-0.1	.294	.350	.294	.235	.300	.235	.222	-0.3	0.1				
2008	CLE	MLB	25	370	68	28	3	14	66	44	78	4	3	3.2	.309	.397	.549	.317	.405	.562	.321	32.5	2.8	45-RF	-5	25-LF	-2
2009	CLE	MLB	26	685	87	38	6	20	86	78	151	21	2	3.9	.300	.394	.489	.312	.404	.500	.314	53.7	6.3	123-RF	2	19-LF	0
2010	CLE	MLB	27	568	77	31	3	17	77	65	115	12	6	1.7	.280	.377	.458	.285	.381	.466	.292	32.2	3.4	112-RF	-1		

Breakout: 16%   Improve: 52%   Collapse: 6%   Attrition: 7%   MLB: 93%   Comparables: Bobby Higginson, Jody Gerut, Matt Lawton, Rusty Greer

There was no World Baseball Classic hangover for Choo, despite his elbow issues. Hands down the brightest light in the Indians' lineup last year, Choo was consistent throughout the year, never having an OPS below 790 in any month. He held his own against lefties as well, provided solid defense in right field, and chipped in lots of additional value on the basepaths. Assuming that he gets an expected exemption from compulsory military service from the South Korean government, Choo should be a solid fixture in the outfield, at least until arbitration eligibility places stress on a beautiful relationship.

Trevor Crowe — OF

Bats: S   Throws: R   Height: 6' 0"   Weight: 190   Born: November 17, 1983   Age: 26

YEAR	TEAM	LVL	AGE	PA	R	2B	3B	HR	RBI	BB	SO	SB	CS	EqBRR	AVG	OBP	SLG	EqAVG	EqOBP	EqSLG	EqA	VORP	WARP	DEFENSE			
2007	AKR	AA	23	589	87	26	4	5	50	62	71	28	9	1.0	.259	.341	.353	.240	.311	.327	.232	-2.3	-1.7	99-CF	-11	26-RF	-1
2008	AKR	AA	24	229	45	16	2	4	28	27	29	13	5	2.9	.323	.404	.485	.289	.355	.426	.273	7.8	1.4	22-LF	1	15-CF	3
2008	BUF	AAA	24	164	25	12	2	5	13	15	43	5	2	-0.6	.274	.350	.486	.259	.331	.449	.266	4.5	0.2	21-LF	-3	9-CF	1
2009	COH	AAA	25	219	27	11	1	2	20	30	31	14	7	0.7	.297	.401	.400	.278	.381	.380	.271	7.4	0.3	22-RF	-2	20-CF	-4
2009	CLE	MLB	25	202	22	9	3	1	17	11	39	6	0	1.6	.235	.278	.333	.243	.284	.343	.229	-1.5	-0.6	28-LF	-1	22-CF	-2
2010	CLE	MLB	26	392	51	19	2	5	34	37	71	13	6	0.8	.255	.330	.361	.253	.328	.366	.248	7.0	0.4	75-CF	-3		

Breakout: 11% Improve: 35% Collapse: 21% Attrition: 19%   MLB: 58%   Comparables: Chris Magruder, Mitch Webster, Fernando Perez, R.J. Reynolds

Crowe was on the Opening Day roster after David Dellucci went on the DL with a strained calf muscle, but it was pretty much downhill from there. He never could put it together in the majors in three separate stints, but at least he hit well in Columbus when he wasn't shuttling back and forth, absorbing the picturesque views along I-71. As Brantley has progressed, Crowe's role has diminished to fourth outfielderdom, if even that; a fully healthy Sizemore probably erases his opportunity to stick and Austin Kearns will be in camp.

Jason Donald — MI

Bats: R   Throws: R   Height: 6' 1"   Weight: 190   Born: September 4, 1984   Age: 25

YEAR	TEAM	LVL	AGE	PA	R	2B	3B	HR	RBI	BB	SO	SB	CS	EqBRR	AVG	OBP	SLG	EqAVG	EqOBP	EqSLG	EqA	VORP	WARP	DEFENSE	
2007	LWD	A	22	238	41	9	3	4	30	29	39	2	5	0.6	.310	.409	.447	.285	.360	.391	.266	10.1	1.2	52-SS	0
2007	CLR	A+	22	336	48	22	5	8	41	35	70	3	2	-2.7	.300	.386	.491	.267	.343	.447	.272	16.7	0.6	79-SS	-12
2008	REA	AA	23	414	57	19	4	14	54	47	86	11	2	0.4	.307	.391	.497	.272	.344	.442	.272	22.0	1.2	90-SS	-12
2009	LEH	AAA	24	230	26	15	1	1	16	14	53	6	0	1.6	.236	.297	.332	.230	.288	.330	.223	0.6	0.7	45-SS	5
2009	COH	AAA	24	40	10	2	0	1	1	3	11	1	0	-0.1	.257	.350	.400	.257	.350	.400	.269	1.8	0.3	9-SS	1
2010	CLE	MLB	25	371	45	17	2	8	33	35	93	4	2	0.0	.248	.326	.380	.246	.322	.379	.249	8.9	0.7	83-SS	-3

Breakout: 5% Improve: 31% Collapse: 21% Attrition: 10%   MLB: 5%   Comparables: Gary Cooper, Richard Barnwell, Rod Allen, Kevin Sliwinski

Cleveland may have bought low from the Phillies in picking Donald as part of the return on Cliff Lee. Because of injuries, Donald had a forgettable season in 2009 (a torn meniscus in his knee, a recurring back problem). Up through 2008, Donald had played shortstop exclusively, despite scouting reports that he is a below-average defender and would be better at second. With Rollins a fixture at short, the Phillies played Donald all around the infield, enhancing his value. In 2010, Donald could very easily find himself playing at Progressive Field as the new utilityman, replacing Jamey Carroll while producing similar value. Unfortunately, that might also be his ceiling, in that squished-up Willie Wonka hallway sort of way.

Tim Fedroff — OF

Bats: L   Throws: R   Height: 5' 11"   Weight: 220   Born: February 4, 1987   Age: 23

YEAR	TEAM	LVL	AGE	PA	R	2B	3B	HR	RBI	BB	SO	SB	CS	EqBRR	AVG	OBP	SLG	EqAVG	EqOBP	EqSLG	EqA	VORP	WARP	DEFENSE			
2008	MHV	A-	21	102	12	6	1	0	12	10	20	1	1	0.7	.319	.382	.407	.255	.311	.340	.231	-0.2	-0.7	23-CF	-4		
2009	KIN	A+	22	449	70	23	2	4	39	64	95	13	3	-1.0	.278	.383	.381	.251	.341	.349	.250	5.0	0.3	55-CF	-3	30-LF	0
2010	CLE	MLB	23	412	51	21	2	4	33	45	97	4	2	-0.1	.243	.328	.340	.246	.331	.347	.240	3.8	0.0	82-CF	-4		

Breakout: 17% Improve: 52% Collapse: 12% Attrition: 3%   MLB: 5%   Comparables: Jacob Cruz, David Dellucci, Dustin Majewski, Marvin Lowrance

Despite fighting a hamstring injury all season, Fedroff had a solid season at Kinston this year, which is one of the notoriously tough pitcher's parks in the notoriously tough Carolina League. Especially encouraging, he finished strong, hitting .298/.405/.400 after the break. Coming out of college, he was a nice combination of speed and power, but his power was the kind that only works with metal bats, so he'll need to develop into a top-of-the-order hitter for his career to work out. Still, if he can maintain his patient approach as he rises and refine his play in center field, he might have a future as a leadoff man.

Chris Gimenez — C/UT

Bats: R Throws: R Height: 6' 2" Weight: 200 Born: December 27, 1982 Age: 27

YEAR	TEAM	LVL	AGE	PA	R	2B	3B	HR	RBI	BB	SO	SB	CS	EqBRR	AVG	OBP	SLG	EqAVG	EqOBP	EqSLG	EqA	VORP	WARP	DEFENSE			
2007	KIN	A+	24	332	56	14	1	20	54	50	55	3	2	-4.7	.283	.406	.565	.240	.332	.439	.266	12.7	0.9	42-C	-2	9-1B	-1
2007	AKR	AA	24	123	20	6	0	6	12	9	31	1	0	-0.7	.221	.285	.434	.200	.252	.365	.212	-2.1	-0.5	14-3B	0	11-C	-2
2008	AKR	AA	25	233	46	15	1	6	26	52	33	0	1	0.9	.339	.487	.537	.296	.421	.444	.305	20.0	1.9	49-C	-4	4-1B	0
2008	BUF	AAA	25	229	23	9	1	3	19	23	60	2	1	0.1	.272	.354	.374	.258	.335	.354	.248	7.0	0.8	52-C	0		
2009	COH	AAA	26	157	20	8	0	6	15	15	40	0	0	-0.7	.235	.323	.426	.225	.303	.391	.243	2.6	-0.3	22-C	-4	11-LF	-1
2009	CLE	MLB	26	130	12	2	0	3	7	17	36	1	1	-0.7	.144	.256	.243	.153	.264	.252	.183	-7.6	-1.0	14-1B	0	9-LF	1
2010	CLE	MLB	27	271	33	11	1	7	24	30	66	1	1	-0.7	.235	.323	.373	.232	.320	.371	.246	6.6	0.5	49-C	-2		

Breakout: 7% Improve: 32% Collapse: 29% Attrition: 29% MLB: 44% Comparables: Marty Castillo, Erik Pappas, Alan Cockrell, Tim Spehr

If the Indians merit a designated Ringo Starr type, Gimenez might be that guy, the one who fell into a better gig than expected, and survived. A catcher who plays some first base and outfield because he's asked to, he hasn't mashed since being an older High-A player in 2007, but he's playable behind the plate. The acquisition of Marson and a year-ending 8-for-76 run after the All-Star break has muddled whatever limited future Gimenez had, but with the trade of Kelly Shoppach, he has a shot at a reserve job.

Travis Hafner — DH

Bats: L Throws: R Height: 6' 3" Weight: 240 Born: June 3, 1977 Age: 33

YEAR	TEAM	LVL	AGE	PA	R	2B	3B	HR	RBI	BB	SO	SB	CS	EqBRR	AVG	OBP	SLG	EqAVG	EqOBP	EqSLG	EqA	VORP	WARP	DEFENSE	
2007	CLE	MLB	30	659	80	25	2	24	100	102	115	1	1	-1.4	.266	.385	.451	.260	.382	.446	.289	27.5	3.3	10-1B	2
2008	CLE	MLB	31	233	21	10	0	5	24	27	55	1	1	-2.5	.197	.305	.323	.198	.308	.325	.229	-5.1	-0.6		
2009	CLE	MLB	32	383	46	19	0	16	49	41	67	0	0	0.5	.272	.355	.470	.281	.363	.482	.287	12.2	1.3		
2010	CLE	MLB	33	392	39	15	1	13	50	48	77	1	1	-0.7	.244	.345	.406	.249	.350	.413	.265	6.4	0.7	0-	0

Breakout: 6% Improve: 36% Collapse: 19% Attrition: 22% MLB: 89% Comparables: Henry Rodriguez, Erubiel Durazo, Eddie Robinson, Chili Davis

After annihilating AL pitching for three years, the "old-player skill" wheels on the Hafner bandwagon have been rattling, if they haven't already simply fallen off. In 2009, Pronk did at least improve on his nightmarish 2008 season, but didn't get anywhere close to where he needs to be to justify the $37.5 million guarantee that he has for the next three seasons. The reduced production has come in two flavors: his BABIP has dropped from .333 in his halcyon days to .285, and his percentage of ball-in-play hits that went for extra bases dropped as well. Simply put, he's not getting as many hits as he used to, and those that he does get aren't going for extra bases. As he is now 33, a surge back to his peak years is doubtful, with the best-case scenario being steady league-average production for a DH or first-base type.

Wes Hodges — 3B

Bats: R Throws: R Height: 6' 2" Weight: 180 Born: September 14, 1984 Age: 25

YEAR	TEAM	LVL	AGE	PA	R	2B	3B	HR	RBI	BB	SO	SB	CS	EqBRR	AVG	OBP	SLG	EqAVG	EqOBP	EqSLG	EqA	VORP	WARP	DEFENSE	
2007	KIN	A+	22	450	60	22	3	15	71	44	90	0	0	-0.1	.288	.367	.473	.260	.322	.418	.257	7.8	-0.5	98-3B	-12
2008	AKR	AA	23	573	70	29	3	18	97	52	105	3	1	0.2	.290	.354	.466	.267	.319	.420	.258	12.2	-1.0	125-3B	-21
2009	COH	AAA	24	359	33	24	0	5	38	19	64	8	5	-1.9	.265	.307	.383	.258	.297	.381	.236	-3.8	-2.4	50-3B	-17
2010	CLE	MLB	25	399	41	18	1	9	49	31	95	3	2	-0.4	.250	.311	.375	.247	.309	.377	.240	1.8	-0.6	81-3B	-7

Breakout: 7% Improve: 27% Collapse: 29% Attrition: 15% MLB: 4% Comparables: Tim McWilliam, Gerald Williams, Lou Lucca, Casey McGehee

The steady (if not quick) progression of Wes Hodges hit multiple speed bumps in 2009. He battled a number of injuries, including a sore shoulder in April and a dislocated wrist. The latter affected his defense (his fielding percentage went from an awful .899 in 2008 to an atrocious .852 in 2009) and caused a significant decrease in power at the plate. The immediate need for a third baseman in Cleveland has been temporarily fixed with the move of Peralta to third, though that could open up if Peralta does not bounce back offensively. Even with a bounce back from Peralta in 2010, the presence of Chisenhall could make Hodges the odd man out before he even really gets going.

Matt LaPorta — 1B/LF

Bats: R Throws: R Height: 6' 2" Weight: 210 Born: January 8, 1985 Age: 25

YEAR	TEAM	LVL	AGE	PA	R	2B	3B	HR	RBI	BB	SO	SB	CS	EqBRR	AVG	OBP	SLG	EqAVG	EqOBP	EqSLG	EqA	VORP	WARP	DEFENSE		
2007	WVA	A	22	102	18	8	0	10	27	7	22	0	1	-1.5	.318	.392	.750	.261	.314	.554	.286	4.9	0.6	17-LF	0	
2008	HUN	AA	23	366	56	23	2	20	66	45	63	2	1	0.4	.288	.402	.576	.268	.355	.524	.294	21.0	1.4	70-RF	-8	7-LF -1
2008	AKR	AA	23	67	6	1	0	2	8	4	12	0	0	1.1	.233	.299	.350	.213	.269	.328	.210	-2.3	0.0	15-LF	2	
2009	COH	AAA	24	393	63	23	2	17	60	42	56	1	3	-3.5	.299	.388	.530	.290	.375	.519	.299	21.2	1.3	46-1B	-5	30-LF -4
2009	CLE	MLB	24	198	29	13	0	7	21	12	37	2	0	-0.5	.254	.308	.442	.267	.318	.456	.265	4.5	0.8	29-LF	1	9-RF 0
2010	CLE	MLB	25	473	62	22	1	19	65	45	94	2	2	-0.8	.256	.342	.452	.256	.340	.457	.274	17.6	1.8	92-LF	-1	

Breakout: 9% Improve: 37% Collapse: 21% Attrition: 11% MLB: 89% Comparables: Adam Hyzdu, Bubba Trammell, Jeff Baker, Andy Bevins

Is LaPorta following in the great footsteps of Chase Utley, Mike Lowell, and Alex Rodriguez? Unfortunately, the answer is yes, at least in terms of his requiring hip surgery this winter; he also got the benefit of a simultaneous surgery on his big toe. The prognosis is that he will be out four to six months, which means there's a good chance he will start spring training late and possibly miss the start of the regular season. The main need for the surgery was that the hip hurt LaPorta most when he played first base, a position that he's slated to man in 2010. The good news is that two of the three aforementioned players weren't overly hindered by their recovery, particularly at bat, so LaPorta's main asset should still be intact.

Lou Marson — C

Bats: R Throws: R Height: 6' 1" Weight: 200 Born: June 26, 1986 Age: 24

YEAR	TEAM	LVL	AGE	PA	R	2B	3B	HR	RBI	BB	SO	SB	CS	EqBRR	AVG	OBP	SLG	EqAVG	EqOBP	EqSLG	EqA	VORP	WARP	DEFENSE
2007	CLR	A+	21	457	68	24	1	7	63	52	80	3	1	-2.5	.288	.373	.407	.266	.341	.376	.256	19.0	2.2	106-C -1
2008	REA	AA	22	395	55	18	0	5	46	68	70	3	3	1.2	.314	.433	.416	.284	.387	.377	.276	21.7	2.1	85-C -4
2009	LEH	AAA	23	241	32	13	0	1	24	30	40	3	1	-1.0	.294	.382	.370	.288	.373	.363	.265	11.1	0.9	61-C -4
2009	PHI	MLB	23	20	3	1	0	0	0	3	7	0	0	0.4	.235	.350	.294	.235	.350	.294	.243	0.4	0.3	6-C 2
2009	COH	AAA	23	116	10	5	1	1	9	10	19	1	0	-0.1	.243	.319	.340	.231	.308	.327	.229	1.3	0.3	28-C 1
2009	CLE	MLB	23	52	6	6	0	0	4	7	14	0	0	-0.4	.250	.346	.386	.250	.346	.364	.269	2.5	0.8	14-C 3
2010	CLE	MLB	24	405	47	17	1	6	42	46	86	3	1	-0.4	.256	.344	.358	.255	.341	.355	.253	12.6	1.3	96-C 0

Breakout: 6% Improve: 33% Collapse: 25% Attrition: 12% MLB: 42% Comparables: Leverne Jackson, Kurt Suzuki, Bob Henley, Gary Cooper

Thanks to Shapiro's sharp trading, the Indians have two catching prospects on the verge of sticking. Santana is the far superior hitter, but he could use some time at Triple-A to work on his defensive game. Meanwhile, Marson is as ready as he'll ever be right now. Scouts love Marson's approach at the plate and his ability to handle pitchers behind it. The main concern is the dip in OBP that Marson experienced at Triple-A last year, which hints at the pitfalls in his near-term future. He's picky at the plate but punchless and will end up seeing far more strikes in the majors than he did in the bushes, because experienced pitchers won't hesitate to challenge him. If he can't adjust, then the one leg his offense is standing on will be knocked out from under him, and the "Marson Era," already likely to be brief due to Santana's imminent arrival, will be over that much sooner.

Andy Marte — 1B

Bats: R Throws: R Height: 6' 1" Weight: 205 Born: October 21, 1983 Age: 26

YEAR	TEAM	LVL	AGE	PA	R	2B	3B	HR	RBI	BB	SO	SB	CS	EqBRR	AVG	OBP	SLG	EqAVG	EqOBP	EqSLG	EqA	VORP	WARP	DEFENSE		
2007	BUF	AAA	23	379	47	17	1	16	60	21	64	0	0	0.5	.267	.309	.457	.251	.290	.435	.247	2.7	0.2	84-3B	-1	
2007	CLE	MLB	23	60	3	4	0	1	8	2	9	0	0	0.1	.193	.233	.316	.193	.233	.298	.184	-3.4	-0.5	15-3B	-1	
2008	CLE	MLB	24	257	21	11	1	3	17	14	52	1	2	-1.4	.221	.268	.315	.227	.274	.322	.208	-7.3	0.1	66-3B	8	
2009	COH	AAA	25	326	48	24	1	18	66	22	50	3	0	-0.8	.327	.369	.593	.312	.354	.561	.303	24.8	3.5	72-3B	5	5-1B 0
2009	CLE	MLB	25	175	20	6	1	6	25	14	30	0	0	-0.5	.232	.293	.400	.240	.299	.409	.247	-2.7	-0.5	44-1B	-2	
2010	CLE	MLB	26	423	50	20	1	15	61	31	82	2	1	-0.4	.257	.314	.431	.256	.312	.437	.257	9.7	1.3	103-3B	2	

Breakout: 19% Improve: 43% Collapse: 11% Attrition: 13% MLB: 67% Comparables: Tracy Woodson, Willis Otanez, Pedro Feliz, Mike Bell

A strong four months at Triple-A resurrected Marte's prospect status ... sort of. Maybe he actually learned something, or perhaps after five years at the same level, pitchers took pity. Maybe he's peaking, but in the wrong league, like a busboy in a cougars' night club. Keep in mind, Marte will still only be 26 in 2010; despite how long he's been stalled, he still has his youth. With Peralta owning third base for now, Marte's path heads toward first base and thus toward a role as an infield corners reserve. Given that LaPorta may miss some time in the early part of the season, this does open the door for Marte; he has run into it enough times that you could certainly understand the door's finally giving way through sheer persistence.

Matt McBride   C/LF/1B   Bats: R   Throws: R   Height: 6' 2"   Weight: 215   Born: May 23, 1985   Age: 25

YEAR	TEAM	LVL	AGE	PA	R	2B	3B	HR	RBI	BB	SO	SB	CS	EqBRR	AVG	OBP	SLG	EqAVG	EqOBP	EqSLG	EqA	VORP	WARP	DEFENSE
2007	LKC	A	22	474	66	35	2	8	66	38	54	1	0	0.0	.283	.348	.432	.247	.295	.366	.232	6.2	-0.8	84-C -13
2008	LKC	A	23	44	6	4	0	1	7	5	5	0	0	-0.1	.308	.386	.487	.275	.341	.450	.271	1.0	0.1	
2008	KIN	A+	23	76	9	2	0	0	6	7	9	0	0	0.2	.179	.263	.209	.174	.247	.188	.146	-6.8	-0.9	
2008	IDN	Rk	23	60	13	7	1	2	9	6	5	3	0	-0.1	.380	.483	.680	.309	.367	.509	.298	3.8	0.5	5-C -1
2009	KIN	A+	24	139	24	15	0	6	36	11	15	0	0	0.7	.405	.453	.667	.364	.403	.581	.327	11.1	1.0	22-1B -3
2009	AKR	AA	24	406	48	29	0	12	63	18	42	1	1	0.6	.247	.301	.427	.229	.268	.385	.227	-10.1	-2.3	41-LF 1 16-1B -5
2010	CLE	MLB	25	461	54	25	1	11	60	31	70	1	1	0.3	.256	.317	.393	.255	.315	.395	.247	3.3	0.5	68-LF 1

Breakout: 8%   Improve: 38%   Collapse: 18%   Attrition: 9%   MLB: 2%   Comparables: Chan Perry, Todd Trafton, Bob Parry, Jim Auten

Does McBride have Sheryl Crow on his iPod? He seems to have taken her song "A Change Will Do You Good" to heart, because after moving out from behind the plate to protect a sore shoulder, the first baseman/outfielder smacked the ball at Kinston, which earned him a promotion to Double-A. McBride did some catching in the Arizona Fall League, though this is probably nothing more than just making sure that he can still serve as an emergency catcher should the need arise. It's a shame really, as he'd be a nice prospect if he could play the position; at the other end of the defensive spectrum, he's just another guy.

Beau Mills   1B   Bats: L   Throws: R   Height: 6' 2"   Weight: 220   Born: August 15, 1986   Age: 23

YEAR	TEAM	LVL	AGE	PA	R	2B	3B	HR	RBI	BB	SO	SB	CS	EqBRR	AVG	OBP	SLG	EqAVG	EqOBP	EqSLG	EqA	VORP	WARP	DEFENSE
2007	LKC	A	20	198	32	12	1	5	36	14	38	0	0	0.6	.271	.333	.435	.236	.283	.374	.229	-3.4	-0.8	22-3B -3 16-1B 0
2007	KIN	A+	20	48	7	6	0	1	5	4	8	0	0	-0.9	.275	.375	.500	.262	.333	.429	.266	0.8	0.1	
2007	MHV	A-	20	33	5	2	0	1	3	7	0	0	0.2	.179	.303	.250	.167	.242	.233	.159	-2.7	-0.5	
2008	KIN	A+	21	549	78	34	3	21	90	54	105	2	3	0.1	.293	.373	.506	.272	.337	.450	.269	11.4	0.7	98-1B -6 8-3B 0
2009	AKR	AA	22	564	59	33	1	14	83	31	95	1	2	-1.5	.267	.308	.417	.250	.282	.388	.233	-16.9	-1.9	123-1B 2
2010	CLE	MLB	23	517	58	26	1	15	69	37	109	1	1	-0.3	.249	.308	.398	.252	.312	.404	.244	-3.2	-0.4	102-1B -1

Breakout: 17%   Improve: 50%   Collapse: 17%   Attrition: 5%   MLB: 4%   Comparables: Kevin Barker, Brian Daubach, Travis Ishikawa, Jim Fasano

After a Carolina League MVP season in 2008 that established him as the best first-base prospect in the Indians' system, Mills had a greatly disappointing '09. Even though he made the Eastern League All-Star team, it was somewhat perfunctory, and some of the shine on his prospect status has worn off. Given the plethora of solid-hitting, poor-defense talent in the Indians' system (LaPorta, Nick Weglarz, Hodges), there isn't a clear path to the majors for Mills unless he recaptures the power stroke—which was never much more than merely above-average in the first place.

Jhonny Peralta   3B   Bats: R   Throws: R   Height: 6' 1"   Weight: 210   Born: May 28, 1982   Age: 28

YEAR	TEAM	LVL	AGE	PA	R	2B	3B	HR	RBI	BB	SO	SB	CS	EqBRR	AVG	OBP	SLG	EqAVG	EqOBP	EqSLG	EqA	VORP	WARP	DEFENSE
2007	CLE	MLB	25	647	87	27	1	21	72	61	146	4	4	-2.9	.270	.341	.430	.270	.341	.433	.267	29.1	3.2	149-SS -1
2008	CLE	MLB	26	664	104	42	4	23	89	48	126	3	1	0.3	.276	.331	.473	.282	.337	.485	.279	40.6	4.7	143-SS 1
2009	CLE	MLB	27	645	57	35	1	11	83	51	134	0	2	-4.4	.254	.316	.375	.264	.323	.386	.247	10.3	1.2	102-3B -2 38-SS 2
2010	CLE	MLB	28	643	82	32	2	19	83	60	136	3	3	-1.2	.269	.341	.429	.267	.339	.432	.268	22.3	2.3	145-3B -1

Breakout: 15%   Improve: 57%   Collapse: 7%   Attrition: 6%   MLB: 100%   Comparables: Jeff Kent, Travis Fryman, Pinky Higgins, Ken McMullen

Since 2005, the hot corner has been an offensive black hole for the Indians. A logical change was to have the emerging Asdrubal Cabrera play short and move the increasingly immobile Peralta to third. Unfortunately, Peralta's OPS dropped over 100 points after the move, and it wasn't just a bout of bad luck—his BABIP stayed about the same. For the first time since his rookie season in 2003, he hit more ground balls than flies. When he did hit a fly ball, they only went out of the park 5.6 percent of the time, as compared with his 9.7 percent average over the previous two seasons. These two factors led to the halving of his home-run rate, which makes up for most of his significant drop in OPS. Peralta has never been the most consistent player, but given the gross similarities of his 2007-2008 seasons, any bounce back seems likely to be similar in form—good, but just barely that.

Cord Phelps — 2B

Bats: S   Throws: R   Height: 6' 2"   Weight: 200   Born: January 23, 1987   Age: 23

YEAR	TEAM	LVL	AGE	PA	R	2B	3B	HR	RBI	BB	SO	SB	CS	EqBRR	AVG	OBP	SLG	EqAVG	EqOBP	EqSLG	EqA	VORP	WARP	DEFENSE	
2008	MHV	A-	21	157	24	10	2	2	21	15	22	4	3	-2.5	.312	.376	.454	.269	.318	.386	.245	1.5	-1.3	25-2B	-10
2009	KIN	A+	22	582	72	27	5	4	53	93	97	17	14	-5.7	.261	.386	.363	.245	.350	.338	.249	8.3	0.3	117-2B	-6
2010	CLE	MLB	23	497	52	24	4	5	42	61	99	8	5	-2.8	.246	.341	.350	.246	.339	.351	.248	8.8	0.4	97-2B	-5

Breakout: 13%   Improve: 46%   Collapse: 18%   Attrition: 7%   MLB: 2%   Comparables: Greg Norton, Jeff Patzke, Shawn Livsey, John Palica

A third-rounder out of Stanford in 2008, Phelps led the Carolina League in walks (the second-place finisher had just 74) and finished second in on-base percentage. He was quite polished in the field, only making four errors in 561 chances for a .993 fielding percentage. In other words, he's one of those classic nontoolsy, good-fundamentals types who doesn't offer much in the way of upside. Double-A will be a huge test for him, but even if he passes it, it's hard to see much of a future for him, due to his inability to play on the left side.

Carlos Rivero — SS

Bats: R   Throws: R   Height: 6' 3"   Weight: 210   Born: May 20, 1988   Age: 22

YEAR	TEAM	LVL	AGE	PA	R	2B	3B	HR	RBI	BB	SO	SB	CS	EqBRR	AVG	OBP	SLG	EqAVG	EqOBP	EqSLG	EqA	VORP	WARP	DEFENSE
2007	LKC	A	19	490	59	26	0	7	62	47	84	1	2	-3.0	.261	.332	.369	.235	.294	.321	.218	-2.7	-0.7	111-SS -3
2008	KIN	A+	20	455	46	27	1	8	64	36	84	1	2	-2.2	.282	.342	.411	.265	.313	.377	.241	9.0	-0.6	104-SS -14
2009	AKR	AA	21	546	50	24	2	7	58	50	73	1	0	-7.0	.242	.309	.344	.224	.280	.320	.215	-2.8	-1.6	131-SS -11
2010	CLE	MLB	22	499	51	22	1	11	60	44	99	1	1	-2.1	.250	.317	.373	.248	.315	.371	.242	8.1	0.4	118-SS -5

Breakout: 26%   Improve: 68%   Collapse: 13%   Attrition: 5%   MLB: 6%   Comparables: Sergio Santos, Adam Hyzdu, Danny Clyburn, Trevor Plouffe

Always the kind of guy you'd talk about when discussing the term "upside," Rivero had always been young for his level but finally ran out of alibis last year. Not only did he fail to hit, but he also continued to grow, generating long-term concerns about his ability to play up the middle; if he has to move off shortstop, offensive expectations rise, so either his bat will come around, or this is the last mention of Rivero you'll see in this book.

Carlos Santana — C

Bats: S   Throws: R   Height: 5' 11"   Weight: 190   Born: April 8, 1986   Age: 24

YEAR	TEAM	LVL	AGE	PA	R	2B	3B	HR	RBI	BB	SO	SB	CS	EqBRR	AVG	OBP	SLG	EqAVG	EqOBP	EqSLG	EqA	VORP	WARP	DEFENSE	
2007	GRL	A	21	334	32	20	1	7	36	40	45	5	3	-1.4	.223	.318	.370	.205	.288	.332	.218	-0.4	-1.1	64-C -6	5-3B 0
2008	SBR	A+	22	434	88	34	4	14	96	69	59	7	4	0.5	.323	.431	.563	.297	.394	.503	.306	38.3	3.4	75-C -9	
2008	KIN	A+	22	126	34	5	1	6	19	20	24	3	0	1.3	.352	.452	.590	.303	.394	.495	.307	11.3	1.6	24-C 2	
2009	AKR	AA	23	535	91	30	2	23	97	90	83	2	2	2.1	.290	.413	.530	.270	.375	.493	.298	38.9	4.2	92-C -3	
2010	CLE	MLB	24	509	74	26	2	15	71	68	94	3	2	0.5	.253	.356	.425	.252	.355	.427	.275	28.1	2.7	94-C -3	

Breakout: 8%   Improve: 30%   Collapse: 15%   Attrition: 5%   MLB: 11%   Comparables: Mitch Meluskey, J.D. Closser, Koyie Hill, Warren Newson

For the second consecutive season, Santana garnered MVP honors in his league (California in 2008, Eastern in 2009), leading in both slugging and OPS. Santana's bat might play in the bigs right now, given both his great power and his refined plate judgment. However, the converted third baseman still has some work to do behind the plate (2009 was only his third year behind the dish), but his arm is plus and he receives fairly well. Before an off-season broken hamate put his 2009 power production at temporary risk, it was his lack of experience that had held him back. He needs to get a better feel for calling games, working with scouting reports, and improving his English. Dominican amateurs play so few actual baseball games, focusing more on tools and showcases, that it leaves them a bit behind the eight-ball when it comes to experience-sharpened instincts. The Indians may have a catcher in front of Santana, but the back of his jersey might as well say HUMAN PLACEHOLDER instead of MARSON, as he's going to be pushed aside as soon as Santana makes a good showing at Triple-A. Sandy Alomar Jr. holds the career record for home runs by an Indians catcher with 91; that's not going to last, even with Santana's winter injury putting his power production on pause in the early going.

Kelly Shoppach   C   Bats: R   Throws: R   Height: 6' 0"   Weight: 220   Born: April 29, 1980   Age: 30

YEAR	TEAM	LVL	AGE	PA	R	2B	3B	HR	RBI	BB	SO	SB	CS	EqBRR	AVG	OBP	SLG	EqAVG	EqOBP	EqSLG	EqA	VORP	WARP	DEFENSE	
2007	CLE	MLB	27	177	26	13	0	7	30	11	56	0	0	0.0	.261	.310	.472	.262	.312	.469	.265	9.6	1.6	47-C	3
2008	CLE	MLB	28	403	67	27	0	21	55	36	133	0	0	0.6	.261	.347	.517	.268	.353	.536	.295	33.3	3.3	98-C	-1
2009	CLE	MLB	29	327	33	14	0	12	40	33	98	0	0	-1.4	.214	.335	.399	.223	.345	.409	.266	14.9	1.2	76-C	-2
2010	TBA	MLB	30	364	46	15	0	15	46	35	115	0	1	-0.2	.234	.332	.427	.234	.332	.425	.256	12.6	1.4	93-C	0

Breakout: 5%   Improve: 40%   Collapse: 15%   Attrition: 7%   MLB: 100%   Comparables: Ron Karkovice, Ozzie Virgil, Chris Hoiles, Mike Macfarlane

After two solid seasons, Shoppach's production dropped off precipitously. A notorious hacker, Shoppach actually improved his strikeout and walk rates, but his BABIP dropped to .280 after having three consecutive years above .350, suggesting a possible rebound in 2010. The Rays seemed to think so, snagging the arbitration-eligible catcher in a November deal for a player to be named later. Shoppach did somewhat find himself in the second half, batting .241/.353/.431 in 39 games. Small-sample caveats apply to those rates, as in fact they apply to his whole season, given limited and erratic playing time—Eric Wedge almost never gave him more than two consecutive days in the starting lineup. He should easily outhit Dioner Navarro, but the Rays might miss the latter's throwing arm.

Grady Sizemore   CF   Bats: L   Throws: L   Height: 6' 2"   Weight: 200   Born: August 2, 1982   Age: 27

YEAR	TEAM	LVL	AGE	PA	R	2B	3B	HR	RBI	BB	SO	SB	CS	EqBRR	AVG	OBP	SLG	EqAVG	EqOBP	EqSLG	EqA	VORP	WARP	DEFENSE	
2007	CLE	MLB	24	748	118	34	5	24	78	101	155	33	10	7.5	.277	.390	.462	.276	.391	.466	.296	51.3	6.8	156-CF	10
2008	CLE	MLB	25	745	101	39	5	33	90	98	130	38	5	5.0	.268	.374	.502	.272	.379	.511	.307	59.7	6.7	151-CF	2
2009	CLE	MLB	26	503	73	20	6	18	64	60	92	13	8	-1.5	.248	.343	.445	.262	.356	.464	.277	22.3	3.2	91-CF	6
2010	CLE	MLB	27	653	97	30	4	27	76	88	122	24	8	1.8	.262	.373	.478	.268	.379	.486	.296	47.0	5.4	133-CF	3

Breakout: 16%   Improve: 56%   Collapse: 4%   Attrition: 2%   MLB: 100%   Comparables: Lloyd Moseby, Andy Van Slyke, Rick Monday, Carlos Beltran

Last season was one to forget. Sizemore attempted to play through the pain of elbow inflammation and an unstable abdominal wall, struggled, and was finally shut down in early September. Despite that, Tribe fans should be happy for four reasons: Sizemore's numbers still helped put them third in the AL in OPS from center field; when he was at his closest to healthy in July and August, his production was perfectly in line with his career numbers; his secondary rate stats (like BB%, XBH%, and HR/FB) were near his career numbers, and only his BABIP was down 50 points off his career average; and finally, the Indians are expecting full recoveries from the arthroscopic elbow and abdominal surgery just as he's entering his theoretical peak age-27 season. If he can stay healthy, all indications are that he will return to form in 2010.

Wyatt Toregas   C   Bats: R   Throws: R   Height: 5' 11"   Weight: 200   Born: December 2, 1982   Age: 27

YEAR	TEAM	LVL	AGE	PA	R	2B	3B	HR	RBI	BB	SO	SB	CS	EqBRR	AVG	OBP	SLG	EqAVG	EqOBP	EqSLG	EqA	VORP	WARP	DEFENSE	
2007	AKR	AA	24	324	36	16	0	6	39	27	45	3	1	-1.1	.250	.317	.370	.230	.285	.326	.219	2.5	1.0	82-C	6
2008	AKR	AA	25	186	22	9	0	12	35	17	20	0	1	-1.0	.296	.371	.574	.257	.317	.467	.266	8.9	1.5	42-C	4
2008	BUF	AAA	25	178	15	8	0	2	25	15	32	2	0	0.6	.219	.301	.310	.203	.276	.272	.197	-2.8	-0.3	47-C	0
2009	COH	AAA	26	229	22	10	0	7	29	16	43	0	1	-1.7	.284	.336	.433	.268	.319	.397	.249	7.0	0.3	56-C	-5
2009	CLE	MLB	26	60	1	1	0	0	6	6	12	0	0	-0.6	.176	.267	.196	.180	.267	.200	.176	-1.7	-0.2	17-C	0
2010	CLE	MLB	27	265	22	11	0	6	34	21	51	1	1	-0.5	.242	.312	.361	.241	.308	.359	.236	3.9	0.5	68-C	1

Breakout: 21%   Improve: 42%   Collapse: 30%   Attrition: 23%   MLB: 39%   Comparables: Gary Bennett, Alberto Castillo, Javi Herrera, Blake Barthol

The best defensive catcher in the Indians' organization, Toregas lacks the bat of even a Marson, never mind Santana. He might start the season as the big-league club's reserve catcher while Santana matures in Columbus's wine cellar, but once Santana pushes Marson to the bench, Toregas will probably be out of a job. His long-term future is likely to be as some other organization's catcher caddy.

Luis Valbuena INF

Bats: L   Throws: R   Height: 5' 10"   Weight: 200   Born: November 30, 1985   Age: 24

YEAR	TEAM	LVL	AGE	PA	R	2B	3B	HR	RBI	BB	SO	SB	CS	EqBRR	AVG	OBP	SLG	EqAVG	EqOBP	EqSLG	EqA	VORP	WARP	DEFENSE			
2007	WTN	AA	21	505	55	23	3	11	44	48	83	10	6	0.4	.239	.311	.378	.220	.281	.343	.221	-4.0	-1.2	121-2B	-6		
2008	WTN	AA	22	277	43	12	2	9	40	31	37	8	4	-2.6	.304	.381	.483	.274	.338	.423	.264	9.9	0.7	67-2B	-4		
2008	TAC	AAA	22	246	41	9	0	2	20	28	32	10	4	-0.5	.302	.383	.373	.286	.357	.336	.251	5.1	0.6	58-2B	0		
2008	SEA	MLB	22	54	6	5	0	0	1	4	11	0	0	-0.2	.245	.315	.347	.245	.315	.327	.243	0.7	-0.3	14-2B	-3		
2009	COH	AAA	23	95	15	4	2	3	13	16	13	3	3	-1.8	.321	.436	.538	.304	.421	.519	.310	8.4	1.1	11-2B	0	6-SS	0
2009	CLE	MLB	23	398	52	25	3	10	31	26	83	2	3	-0.5	.250	.298	.416	.262	.308	.425	.249	8.4	1.0	74-2B	-2	23-SS	2
2010	CLE	MLB	24	500	64	24	2	12	45	46	89	9	5	-0.8	.252	.322	.389	.255	.325	.396	.249	9.8	0.8	121-2B	-3		

Breakout: 20%   Improve: 53%   Collapse: 10%   Attrition: 3%   MLB: 100%   Comparables: Jon Nunnally, Brian Kowitz, Troy O'Leary, David Newhan

When the music finally stopped on the Indians' game of infield musical chairs, Valbuena found himself at second base. Or maybe second base found him—Valbuena's range is so bad that the bag is more likely to go to him than the other way around. Some fielding statistics compare him unfavorably to the notably statuesque Alberto Callaspo of the Royals. Valbuena's strength has been the bat; in the minors, Valbuena was more notable for his willingness to take the odd walk than his ability to hit the ball for extra bases, but this seemed to reverse itself in the majors. The Indians have had four starting second basemen over the last four seasons (Ron Belliard, Josh Barfield, Asdrubal Cabrera, and Valbuena). Valbuena's OBP will have to come up for him to avoid losing out to whoever is behind Door Number Five. (Mark Grudzielanek, perhaps? No, really, he'll be in camp.)

Nick Weglarz LF

Bats: L   Throws: L   Height: 6' 3"   Weight: 245   Born: December 16, 1987   Age: 22

YEAR	TEAM	LVL	AGE	PA	R	2B	3B	HR	RBI	BB	SO	SB	CS	EqBRR	AVG	OBP	SLG	EqAVG	EqOBP	EqSLG	EqA	VORP	WARP	DEFENSE
2007	LKC	A	19	532	75	28	0	23	82	82	129	1	1	-1.7	.276	.395	.497	.242	.342	.413	.264	11.5	-0.4	103-LF -15
2008	KIN	A+	20	454	68	20	5	10	41	71	78	9	5	1.8	.272	.396	.432	.256	.359	.392	.266	9.8	0.5	74-LF -6
2009	AKR	AA	21	427	69	17	2	16	65	75	78	2	3	-0.3	.227	.377	.431	.210	.336	.391	.257	4.5	0.7	75-LF 1
2010	CLE	MLB	22	501	66	21	2	17	58	68	114	2	2	0.0	.235	.347	.407	.239	.350	.417	.266	13.8	1.1	90-LF -4

Breakout: 18%   Improve: 57%   Collapse: 7%   Attrition: 2%   MLB: 11%   Comparables: Ricky Ledee, Matt Winters, Ben Grieve, Dee Brown

Despite a drop in his batting average to just .227 (caused mostly by an abysmal 5-for-59 start in April), "Big Red" was praised by the Indians' organization for one key stat, his walk percentage, a patient-to-a-fault 17.6 percent. Along with top prospect Carlos Santana, he led Double-A Akron to an Eastern League championship. Unfortunately, as wonderful as the walks were, Weglarz's average and so-so power display made for his second disappointing year in a row. Even after he got over the slow start, he hit only .257, and that just doesn't leave much on which to hang a big-league translation. His ability to recapture some of his former prospect cred in the Arizona Fall League was cut short when the stress fracture in his leg that had slowed him in August was reaggravated, causing him to be shut down. A rod was inserted in his leg, but Weglarz is expected to be ready for spring training. He needs to start mashing, because the bat is the only tool of note.

PITCHERS

Scott Barnes

Bats: L   Throws: L   Height: 6' 3"   Weight: 175   Born: September 5, 1987   Age: 22

YEAR	TEAM	LVL	AGE	W	L	SV	G	GS	IP	H	HR	BB	SO	GB%	BABIP	STUFF	WHIP	ERA	SIERA	DERA	EqH9	EqHR9	EqBB9	EqSO9	VORP	SN/WX
2008	AUG	A	20	3	2	0	6	6	32²	15	0	7	41	33%	.205	30	0.67	1.38	1.83	2.97	5.9	0.9	2.7	7.1	8.5	1.04
2009	SJO	A+	21	12	3	0	18	18	98	82	7	29	99	42%	.292	2	1.13	2.85	3.16	5.11	10.5	2.1	3.6	5.3	3.8	0.51
2009	KIN	A+	21	0	0	0	3	3	12²	14	1	6	10	28%	.333	7	1.58	2.13	4.86	3.18	12.7	1.6	4.8	4.8	2.9	0.24
2009	AKR	AA	21	2	2	0	6	6	31²	35	7	14	29	31%	.318	2	1.55	5.68	4.24	7.62	12.4	3.2	4.4	6.7	-6.7	-0.64
2010	CLE	MLB	22	5	9	0	28	25	117	139	19	56	85	35%	.329	7	1.66	5.84	4.97	6.25	10.7	1.5	4.0	6.0	-9.8	2.68

Breakout: 10%   Improve: 34%   Collapse: 25%   Attrition: 4%   MLB: 7%   Comparables: Kurt Birkins, Kevin Andersh, Butch Henry, Kevin Morton

Little did the Indians expect that no more monkeying around with General Garko would bring them a prospect as worthwhile as Barnes, but when Brian Sabean locks in, what's a team to do? Barnes may well end up another of the

Tribe's seemingly limitless supply of low-velo lefties, but he can dial his heat into the low 90s at times, and he supports it with a plus change and a quality curve. An eighth-round pick out of St. John's in 2008, he's moving up fast, and in the right organization to make something of it.

Fausto Carmona

Bats: R   Throws: R   Height: 6' 4"   Weight: 230   Born: December 7, 1983   Age: 26

YEAR	TEAM	LVL	AGE	W	L	SV	G	GS	IP	H	HR	BB	SO	GB%	BABIP	STUFF	WHIP	ERA	SIERA	DERA	EqH9	EqHR9	EqBB9	EqSO9	VORP	SN/WX
2007	CLE	MLB	23	19	8	0	32	32	215	199	16	61	137	72%	.280	24	1.21	3.06	3.94	3.14	8.1	0.7	2.4	5.3	54.9	6.98
2008	CLE	MLB	24	8	7	0	22	22	120²	126	7	70	58	74%	.294	2	1.62	5.44	4.99	5.74	8.9	0.5	4.7	4.0	-3.2	1.63
2009	COH	AAA	25	1	3	0	5	5	33	32	5	6	27	79%	.273	10	1.15	3.55	3.18	4.05	8.4	1.9	1.9	5.7	5.4	0.31
2009	CLE	MLB	25	5	12	0	24	24	125¹	151	16	70	79	66%	.319	-11	1.76	6.32	4.90	6.40	10.1	1.1	4.3	4.8	-12.8	0.23
2010	CLE	MLB	26	9	10	0	29	29	164	165	17	68	94	71%	.289	-1	1.42	4.50	4.41	4.93	9.2	1.0	3.6	4.8	10.4	2.20

Breakout: 8%   Improve: 38%   Collapse: 15%   Attrition: 17%   MLB: 88%   Comparables: Scott Erickson, Ismael Valdez, Jason Jennings, Brad Penny

The plan for a title in 2009 required a rebound season from Carmona, ideally something approaching his 2007 performance. Instead, his -12.8 VORP was the second-worst single-season mark among all pitchers whose team allowed them 20 starts. In the middle of the year, he was sent down, where he pitched effectively (2.72 ERA and only 1.4 BB/9), and his postreturn numbers did show some improvement (5.29 ERA, 43 K, and 29 BB in 64 ⅔ IP). Improvement is relative, obviously. Because of experience and a fugitive wish that there is upside to be rediscovered, Carmona has an inside track on a job in the starting rotation, but he will be on a pretty short leash.

Carlos Carrasco

Bats: R   Throws: R   Height: 6' 3"   Weight: 215   Born: March 21, 1987   Age: 23

YEAR	TEAM	LVL	AGE	W	L	SV	G	GS	IP	H	HR	BB	SO	GB%	BABIP	STUFF	WHIP	ERA	SIERA	DERA	EqH9	EqHR9	EqBB9	EqSO9	VORP	SN/WX
2007	CLR	A+	20	6	2	0	12	12	69²	49	8	22	53	48%	.218	16	1.02	2.84	3.98	3.98	8.2	2.3	3.6	4.8	10.7	0.99
2007	REA	AA	20	6	4	0	14	13	70¹	65	9	46	49	36%	.264	3	1.58	4.86	5.52	6.22	9.5	1.7	5.9	4.5	-5.4	-0.21
2008	REA	AA	21	7	7	0	20	19	114²	109	13	45	109	50%	.308	11	1.34	4.32	3.66	5.19	9.7	1.6	3.7	6.7	3.7	-0.07
2008	LEH	AAA	21	2	2	0	6	6	36²	37	1	13	46	47%	.353	37	1.36	1.72	2.78	4.10	8.9	0.5	3.1	7.7	5.8	0.82
2009	LEH	AAA	22	6	9	0	20	20	114²	118	14	38	112	51%	.315	2	1.36	5.18	3.51	6.81	10.2	1.8	3.3	6.9	-16.1	-0.93
2009	COH	AAA	22	5	1	0	6	6	42¹	31	3	7	36	44%	.233	31	0.90	3.19	3.27	4.08	6.1	1.0	1.7	5.9	6.8	0.25
2009	CLE	MLB	22	0	4	0	5	5	22¹	40	6	11	11	67%	.405	-20	2.28	8.87	5.23	8.65	16.0	2.5	4.2	4.2	-7.5	-0.62
2010	CLE	MLB	23	8	10	0	32	28	157	163	22	68	117	38%	.303	7	1.47	4.84	4.62	5.26	9.4	1.3	3.7	6.3	4.1	1.89

Breakout: 13%   Improve: 48%   Collapse: 15%   Attrition: 12%   MLB: 33%   Comparables: Kevin Gross, Victor Santos, Shawn Boskie, Steven Shell

One of the many prizes in the Cliff Lee trade, Carrasco will be competing for a spot in the rotation. The problem beyond his control is that with all the acquisitions that the Indians made this year, there will be a lot of competition. He didn't help his case with an awful September call-up, as his tendency to turn bad innings into game-losing nightmares continued. The scouting consensus is that he's got a complete but not overly spectacular arsenal; at 23, he still has time for further development, especially given his moving, low-90s fastball and plus changeup.

Kelvin De La Cruz

Bats: L   Throws: L   Height: 6' 5"   Weight: 187   Born: January 8, 1988   Age: 22

YEAR	TEAM	LVL	AGE	W	L	SV	G	GS	IP	H	HR	BB	SO	GB%	BABIP	STUFF	WHIP	ERA	SIERA	DERA	EqH9	EqHR9	EqBB9	EqSO9	VORP	SN/WX
2007	IDN	Rk	19	3	0	0	3	3	18	7	1	2	20	0%	.150	16	0.50	0.50	1.99	2.20	6.1	2.2	1.7	5.5	6.0	0.45
2007	MHV	A-	19	2	4	0	12	12	54¹	41	5	34	53	47%	.269	7	1.38	3.98	4.12	6.17	10.0	2.5	6.8	5.8	-3.5	-0.36
2008	LKC	A	20	8	4	0	18	18	95²	71	2	34	96	57%	.275	30	1.10	1.69	3.24	3.53	9.1	1.1	4.4	5.7	18.6	1.49
2008	KIN	A+	20	3	2	0	8	8	29¹	35	1	25	36	47%	.395	21	2.05	6.44	4.18	8.10	12.4	1.0	7.9	7.3	-8.2	-0.49
2009	KIN	A+	21	2	0	0	2	2	12	6	1	2	19	41%	.217	11	0.67	1.50	0.78	2.38	7.1	1.6	2.4	9.5	3.9	0.30
2010	CLE	MLB	22	3	5	0	26	6	63¹	65	9	39	47	37%	.302	5	1.64	5.51	5.17	5.93	9.4	1.2	5.2	6.2	-3.1	1.57

Breakout: 15%   Improve: 48%   Collapse: 20%   Attrition: 19%   MLB: 4%   Comparables: Kasey Richardson, Tony Guerrero, Andy McCormack, Mariano Gomez

A great start to the season came to naught, as De La Cruz had tightness in his throwing forearm and was sidelined for most of the year. He's probably stuck with a possible do-over at Kinston for 2010, but when healthy, De La Cruz had a fastball that sat around 91 and a strong curve, with a long, lean body that offers tons of projection. We'll see what's left when he gets back on the hill, but team officials are confident he'll be on everyone's prospect lists 12 months from now.

Jeanmar Gomez

Bats: R   Throws: R   Height: 6' 4"   Weight: 190   Born: October 2, 1988   Age: 21

YEAR	TEAM	LVL	AGE	W	L	SV	G	GS	IP	H	HR	BB	SO	GB%	BABIP	STUFF	WHIP	ERA	SIERA	DERA	EqH9	EqHR9	EqBB9	EqSO9	VORP	SN/WX
2007	LKC	A	18	11	7	0	27	27	140²	152	19	46	94	49%	.301	-7	1.41	4.80	4.45	6.63	11.4	2.3	3.7	3.7	-16.2	-1.22
2008	KIN	A+	19	5	9	0	27	27	138¹	154	14	46	110	51%	.328	-7	1.45	4.55	4.07	6.08	11.7	2.0	3.5	4.8	-8.3	-1.00
2009	KIN	A+	20	2	2	0	4	4	24	17	2	5	15	61%	.217	22	0.92	2.62	3.89	4.09	8.2	1.6	2.5	3.7	3.4	0.22
2009	AKR	AA	20	10	4	0	22	22	123¹	117	11	40	109	51%	.296	22	1.27	3.43	3.70	5.04	10.1	1.5	3.2	6.0	5.9	0.42
2010	CLE	MLB	21	6	10	0	29	29	136	158	21	58	82	43%	.314	18	1.59	5.52	5.07	6.01	10.6	1.4	3.7	5.1	-7.7	2.10

Breakout: 17%   Improve: 48%   Collapse: 9%   Attrition: 9%   MLB: 10%   Comparables: Rich Yett, Javier Vazquez, Blaine Mull, Justin Germano

Being the third wheel of the Latin Trifecta of Indian prospect pitchers (with Rondon and De La Cruz), the 21-year-old Gomez saw his stock rise dramatically this year. His Akron Aeros campaign included a perfect game in May against Trenton and being named the Eastern League Pitcher of the Year. Each year in the organization, his strikeout rate has consistently risen, while he has maintained a respectable walk rate. Proving himself at Double-A was a huge step, but he's one of those pitchers who does many things good, but nothing great, as with three average pitches and plus command, his ceiling is somewhere around "big-league fourth starter." Expect a promotion to the Columbus rotation for 2010.

Connor Graham

Bats: R   Throws: R   Height: 6' 6"   Weight: 235   Born: December 30, 1985   Age: 24

YEAR	TEAM	LVL	AGE	W	L	SV	G	GS	IP	H	HR	BB	SO	GB%	BABIP	STUFF	WHIP	ERA	SIERA	DERA	EqH9	EqHR9	EqBB9	EqSO9	VORP	SN/WX
2007	TRI	A-	21	1	0	0	6	4	19	23	2	6	18	52%	.368	3	1.53	2.37	3.54	4.50	13.2	2.6	3.7	4.8	1.9	0.38
2008	ASH	A	22	12	6	0	26	26	147¹	99	3	83	138	53%	.246	21	1.24	2.26	4.01	4.21	7.5	1.0	6.4	5.3	19.4	1.40
2009	MOD	A+	23	7	4	0	16	16	80¹	68	2	41	87	50%	.304	2	1.36	3.14	3.58	5.22	9.2	1.1	5.5	5.5	2.3	0.17
2009	AKR	AA	23	1	3	0	8	7	38¹	40	3	25	39	64%	.343	6	1.70	4.93	3.99	6.06	11.4	1.5	6.1	7.1	-2.2	-0.37
2010	CLE	MLB	24	6	8	0	25	25	121	123	15	81	80	49%	.294	-10	1.69	5.34	5.35	5.77	9.3	1.2	5.8	5.6	-3.6	2.74

Breakout: 8%   Improve: 41%   Collapse: 12%   Attrition: 8%   MLB: 10%   Comparables: Pat Leahy, Adam Russell, Brooks Brown, Erik Schullstrom

Without even seeing a photograph, one can get a good mental picture with just a few numbers: his height and weight, plus 9.6 K/9 and 5.0 BB/9. These numbers scream intimidating power pitcher, albeit one with some control issues, and that's exactly what we have. Acquired from Colorado for Rafael Betancourt during the 2009 fire sale, he throws a mid-90s fastball with some sink and a slider. A closer in college, Graham has yet to find either a third pitch or good command. With all the other recently acquired young arms in the system, Graham seems a candidate for the pen. Given the sorry state of the major-league relief corps, this would probably put him on the fast track.

Nick Hagadone

Bats: L   Throws: L   Height: 6' 5"   Weight: 230   Born: January 1, 1986   Age: 24

YEAR	TEAM	LVL	AGE	W	L	SV	G	GS	IP	H	HR	BB	SO	GB%	BABIP	STUFF	WHIP	ERA	SIERA	DERA	EqH9	EqHR9	EqBB9	EqSO9	VORP	SN/WX
2007	LOW	A-	21	0	1	0	10	10	24¹	14	1	8	33	55%	.250	22	0.90	1.85	2.10	2.86	7.8	1.6	3.7	7.8	6.4	0.74
2009	GRN	A	23	0	2	0	10	10	25	13	0	14	32	65%	.236	6	1.08	2.52	2.92	4.84	7.3	1.2	6.9	6.9	1.6	0.38
2009	LKC	A	23	0	1	0	5	5	14²	8	0	5	21	55%	.286	12	0.89	2.45	1.85	4.38	8.0	0.7	5.1	8.8	1.5	0.13
2010	CLE	MLB	24	3	4	0	29	12	50²	50	6	32	40	54%	.299	-7	1.60	5.12	4.74	5.44	8.8	1.1	5.3	6.5	0.3	2.05

Breakout: 15%   Improve: 40%   Collapse: 23%   Attrition: 10%   MLB: 5%   Comparables: Ryan Edell, Jeff Wilson, Brian Matz, Carlos Sencion

A key part of the V-Mart trade, Hagadone missed most of the 2008 season with Tommy John surgery. In his 15 Sally League starts across both systems, he impressed, showing both the good (a 93-98 mph fastball is unusual power for a lefty, plus he has good sinking movement) and the bad (control issues). Hagadone is a rare talent who has only given up one home run in 79 ⅓ minor-league innings, but his health, lack of command, and the absence of a solid third pitch have some scouts already projecting him as a reliever. That's one heck of a back-up plan, though, as we're talking about a guy with Billy Wagner's arsenal and about eight more inches of height to angle it from.

T. J. House

Bats: R **Throws: L** **Height: 6′ 2″** **Weight: 215** **Born: September 29, 1989** **Age: 20**

YEAR	TEAM	LVL	AGE	W	L	SV	G	GS	IP	H	HR	BB	SO	GB%	BABIP	STUFF	WHIP	ERA	SIERA	DERA	EqH9	EqHR9	EqBB9	EqSO9	VORP	SN/WX
2009	LKC	A	19	6	11	0	26	26	134¹	127	8	49	109	50%	.300	-2	1.31	3.15	4.01	5.88	11.6	2.1	5.0	4.1	-4.9	-0.92
2010	CLE	MLB	20	4	10	0	28	27	117	151	21	66	62	48%	.328	8	1.85	6.69	5.58	7.17	11.6	1.7	4.8	4.4	-21.7	1.93

Breakout: 14% Improve: 47% Collapse: 16% Attrition: 0%   MLB: 2%   Comparables: Luis Galindez, Trevor Reckling, Benj Sampson, Ryan Rodriguez

A 16th-round prep pick out of Mississippi who had planned on college ball at Tulane until the Indians made him an over-slot offer he couldn't refuse, "Dr." House has a heavy, low-90s fastball and a slider that acts more like a slurve. In his first full pro season, the 19-year-old House was put in Low-A ball and performed well for someone so young, which made him one of the Indians' better pitching prospects in the low minors. He'll probably start the season at High-A Kinston, and he might soon be better known than his TV counterpart, at least in Drew Carey country.

David Huff

Bats: L **Throws: L** **Height: 6′ 2″** **Weight: 190** **Born: August 22, 1984** **Age: 25**

YEAR	TEAM	LVL	AGE	W	L	SV	G	GS	IP	H	HR	BB	SO	GB%	BABIP	STUFF	WHIP	ERA	SIERA	DERA	EqH9	EqHR9	EqBB9	EqSO9	VORP	SN/WX
2007	KIN	A+	22	4	2	0	11	11	59²	57	4	15	46	44%	.290	1	1.21	2.72	3.90	4.93	10.3	1.6	2.7	4.7	3.5	0.42
2008	AKR	AA	23	5	1	0	11	10	65²	44	5	14	62	56%	.228	25	0.88	1.92	3.03	3.07	6.9	1.1	2.1	6.4	17.0	1.52
2008	BUF	AAA	23	6	4	0	16	16	80²	68	8	15	81	51%	.278	20	1.03	3.01	2.86	3.81	8.1	1.2	1.8	6.7	14.7	1.39
2009	COH	AAA	24	5	1	0	7	7	39¹	35	5	16	32	44%	.273	0	1.30	4.35	4.17	4.78	7.9	1.7	3.8	6.0	3.0	0.13
2009	CLE	MLB	24	11	8	0	23	23	128¹	159	16	41	65	44%	.317	-9	1.56	5.61	5.18	5.29	10.4	1.1	2.5	3.9	3.0	1.92
2010	CLE	MLB	25	9	9	0	30	27	148	153	19	50	93	41%	.294	0	1.38	4.41	4.72	4.78	9.4	1.2	2.9	5.3	11.8	2.57

Breakout: 3% Improve: 33% Collapse: 25% Attrition: 8%   MLB: 97%   Comparables: Greg Mathews, Glenn Dishman, Dave Gassner, Blaine Beatty

Despite not joining the starting rotation until mid-May and having a dreadful ERA, Huff got a staff-leading 11 wins, thanks to strong run support. The most concerning aspect of Huff's year was that despite being a relatively consistent 8.1 K/9 pitcher in the minors, he managed only 4.6 K/9 in the majors, living down to scouting reports that suggested that his middling fastball meant that he was just the latest lefty off the Laffey/Sowers assembly line. Huff is supposed to have more upside than those two pitch-to-contact types, but there's still little or no projection to Huff's stuff; what you see is what you get, and that means that it's down to minor adjustments that hopefully pay off in outsized improvements.

Jason Knapp

Bats: R **Throws: R** **Height: 6′ 5″** **Weight: 215** **Born: August 31, 1990** **Age: 19**

YEAR	TEAM	LVL	AGE	W	L	SV	G	GS	IP	H	HR	BB	SO	GB%	BABIP	STUFF	WHIP	ERA	SIERA	DERA	EqH9	EqHR9	EqBB9	EqSO9	VORP	SN/WX
2008	PHL	Rk	17	3	1	0	7	6	31	26	1	12	38	39%	.329	27	1.23	2.61	2.78	4.73	11.1	2.0	5.1	6.8	2.3	-0.02
2009	LWD	A	18	2	7	0	17	17	85¹	63	3	39	111	45%	.309	18	1.20	4.01	2.75	7.51	9.7	1.8	5.9	6.8	-16.6	-1.11
2009	LKC	A	18	0	0	0	4	4	11²	10	0	8	12	25%	.303	-4	1.54	5.40	4.66	11.39	10.1	0.8	8.4	5.1	-7.0	-0.46
2010	CLE	MLB	19	4	7	0	21	21	94	103	14	63	77	39%	.320	37	1.76	6.16	5.02	6.65	10.0	1.4	5.7	6.8	-12.0	1.44

Breakout: 16% Improve: 58% Collapse: 15% Attrition: 4%   MLB: 1%   Comparables: Jairo Heredia, Royal Thomas, Ricardo Aramboles, Doug Salinas

The Indians were happy to take Knapp as part of the return on Cliff Lee—this, despite being aware of his biceps tendinitis, not to mention intractable mechanical problems of the kind that have led the U.S. space program to be surpassed in engineering efficiency by the South-Central New Jersey Star Trek Model-Builders Club. Their own doctors found "loose bodies" in his throwing shoulder, which required surgery; this was carried out successfully and he is expected to be ready for spring training. A big kid and hard thrower who can touch 99 mph, Knapp is a strikeout pitcher whose secondary offerings have already come a long way. His command is still coming along as well, but for now, job one is to keep him on the mound for an entire season.

Aaron Laffey

Bats: L   Throws: L   Height: 6' 0"   Weight: 180   Born: April 15, 1985   Age: 25

YEAR	TEAM	LVL	AGE	W	L	SV	G	GS	IP	H	HR	BB	SO	GB%	BABIP	STUFF	WHIP	ERA	SIERA	DERA	EqH9	EqHR9	EqBB9	EqSO9	VORP	SN/WX
2007	AKR	AA	22	4	1	0	6	6	35	29	2	7	24	71%	.257	15	1.03	2.31	3.62	4.01	8.0	1.1	2.1	4.5	5.6	0.62
2007	BUF	AAA	22	9	3	0	16	15	96¹	89	5	23	75	68%	.291	27	1.16	3.08	3.51	3.86	8.7	0.8	2.2	5.5	17.0	1.60
2007	CLE	MLB	22	4	2	0	9	9	49¹	54	2	12	25	72%	.317	14	1.34	4.56	4.27	4.47	9.7	0.4	2.1	4.4	5.4	0.86
2008	BUF	AAA	23	6	2	0	11	11	61²	72	2	18	47	59%	.347	5	1.46	4.38	4.03	5.20	10.9	0.6	2.9	5.0	2.0	0.13
2008	CLE	MLB	23	5	7	0	16	16	93²	103	10	31	43	58%	.294	-1	1.43	4.23	5.10	4.78	9.5	1.0	2.6	3.8	7.4	2.07
2009	CLE	MLB	24	7	9	1	25	19	121²	140	9	57	59	56%	.318	-6	1.62	4.44	5.39	4.66	10.0	0.7	3.8	3.9	11.0	2.01
2010	CLE	MLB	25	7	9	0	27	25	134²	143	14	52	71	56%	.297	-6	1.45	4.64	4.97	5.07	9.7	1.0	3.3	4.4	6.5	1.82

Breakout: 9%   Improve: 38%   Collapse: 18%   Attrition: 15%   MLB: 79%   Comparables: Zach Duke, Greg Hibbard, Butch Henry, Dave Fleming

How often is your bullpen so bad that you need to move your second-most-effective starter there to shore it up? That's what happened with the Indians when they made Laffey a temporary reliever to provide some stability after he went 2-0 with a 4.09 ERA in his first four starts. As the old saying goes, this was robbing Peter to pay Paul, or more appropriately, stealing from Bert Blyleven to enrich Ernie Camacho, and one of the traditional signs of a manager in over his head. Laffey pitched well in sporadic work (six games in a little over two weeks) before heading to the DL with a right oblique strain, which sidelined him through the first week of July. While solid throughout most of the year, he finished poorly in September, when he went 0-6; in that stretch, his ERA jumped from 3.36 to 4.44. Despite the poor ending, he has the highest SNLVAR of any returning starter, giving him the closest thing any incumbent Indian has to a claim on a rotation spot.

Jensen Lewis

Bats: R   Throws: R   Height: 6' 3"   Weight: 210   Born: May 16, 1984   Age: 26

YEAR	TEAM	LVL	AGE	W	L	SV	G	GS	IP	H	HR	BB	SO	GB%	BABIP	STUFF	WHIP	ERA	SIERA	DERA	EqH9	EqHR9	EqBB9	EqSO9	VORP	SN/WX
2007	AKR	AA	23	2	0	1	24	0	39	27	2	13	49	41%	.281	19	1.03	1.85	2.37	3.44	7.4	1.0	3.2	8.8	8.4	0.83
2007	BUF	AAA	23	1	0	1	10	0	13	5	1	4	12	32%	.129	9	0.69	1.38	3.41	2.08	3.5	0.7	2.8	6.2	4.9	0.64
2007	CLE	MLB	23	1	1	0	26	0	29¹	26	1	10	34	34%	.316	26	1.23	2.15	2.96	2.40	7.5	0.3	2.7	9.3	10.3	0.64
2008	BUF	AAA	24	1	2	1	11	0	20	16	2	8	18	35%	.241	-9	1.20	3.60	4.07	5.23	7.0	1.3	3.5	5.7	0.6	-0.45
2008	CLE	MLB	24	0	4	13	51	0	66	68	8	27	52	40%	.300	-4	1.44	3.82	4.44	3.87	8.8	1.1	3.3	6.4	12.0	1.73
2009	COH	AAA	25	1	0	0	12	0	18²	13	0	7	28	45%	.351	17	1.07	0.00	1.74	0.53	7.4	0.5	3.7	10.6	9.4	0.71
2009	CLE	MLB	25	2	4	1	47	0	66¹	62	13	29	62	43%	.274	-6	1.37	4.61	3.91	4.64	8.2	1.8	3.4	7.2	6.3	-0.10
2010	CLE	MLB	26	5	5	3	63	0	77¹	73	9	32	65	41%	.295	1	1.36	4.13	4.14	4.54	8.6	1.0	3.6	7.1	8.2	1.03

Breakout: 13%   Improve: 33%   Collapse: 22%   Attrition: 11%   MLB: 79%   Comparables: Cecilio Guante, Jorge Julio, Ron Davis, Stan Belinda

With the addition of Kerry Wood, Lewis was removed from the closer's role (which he had won through the process of elimination in 2008) and repositioned as a set-up man. Unfortunately, his 5.93 ERA through May 5th marked the end of his use in almost any high-leverage situation, and he was optioned back to Triple-A to make room for Jose Veras in late June. He returned to the Indians and posted a 4.00 ERA for the rest of the season, but only worked in trash-time situations: in 19 appearances after the All-Star break, only twice did he pitch when the Indians had a lead (and those were 10-run and eight-run leads). Lefties had no trouble with his fastball/changeup combo, slugging .609 off him, but he remained reasonably effective against same-side hitters. Only 26 this year, and gifted with a viable strikeout rate, he'll have a chance to start fresh with a new manager this spring.

Scott Lewis

Bats: S   Throws: L   Height: 6' 0"   Weight: 195   Born: September 26, 1983   Age: 26

YEAR	TEAM	LVL	AGE	W	L	SV	G	GS	IP	H	HR	BB	SO	GB%	BABIP	STUFF	WHIP	ERA	SIERA	DERA	EqH9	EqHR9	EqBB9	EqSO9	VORP	SN/WX
2007	AKR	AA	23	7	9	0	27	25	134²	135	13	34	121	36%	.317	-1	1.25	3.68	3.53	4.52	10.2	1.5	2.6	6.2	13.6	1.06
2008	AKR	AA	24	6	2	0	13	13	73¹	62	2	9	61	39%	.279	21	0.97	2.33	3.25	3.39	8.3	0.6	1.4	5.6	16.5	1.80
2008	BUF	AAA	24	2	2	0	4	4	24	19	2	4	21	33%	.258	16	0.96	2.62	3.24	3.52	7.4	1.2	1.6	5.9	5.1	0.53
2008	CLE	MLB	24	4	0	0	4	4	24	20	4	6	15	40%	.222	9	1.08	2.62	4.50	3.33	7.0	1.5	1.8	5.2	5.9	0.85
2009	CLE	MLB	25	0	0	0	1	1	4¹	7	2	1	3	31%	.357	-3	1.85	8.31	4.62	6.75	15.8	4.5	2.3	6.8	-0.6	-0.09
2010	CLE	MLB	26	5	4	0	26	9	75²	77	10	24	55	35%	.298	3	1.33	4.23	4.42	4.62	9.3	1.2	2.7	6.0	7.4	1.75

Breakout: 19%   Improve: 53%   Collapse: 19%   Attrition: 22%   MLB: 29%   Comparables: Oscar Rivera, Chris Peters, Dennis Moeller, Rob Henkel

The injury bug bit Lewis yet again. He's been effective when healthy, compiling a 2.71 ERA in 84 minor-league starts.

He missed significant time in 2004-2005 with Tommy John surgery, and then only managed 21 starts in 2008; elbow pain in '09 limited him again. He'll get consideration for a starting spot in '10, but needs to convince the front office that he has the endurance to last an entire season, or at least longer than it takes to sit through the commercials and trailers before the movie starts.

Justin Masterson

Bats: R   Throws: R   Height: 6' 6"   Weight: 250   Born: March 22, 1985   Age: 25

YEAR	TEAM	LVL	AGE	W	L	SV	G	GS	IP	H	HR	BB	SO	GB%	BABIP	STUFF	WHIP	ERA	SIERA	DERA	EqH9	EqHR9	EqBB9	EqSO9	VORP	SN/WX
2007	LNC	A+	22	8	5	0	17	17	95^2	103	4	22	56	63%	.307	6	1.31	4.33	4.28	5.11	9.7	0.8	2.4	3.5	4.0	-0.45
2007	PME	AA	22	4	3	0	10	10	58	49	4	18	59	76%	.288	26	1.16	4.34	2.86	5.25	8.4	1.1	3.1	7.0	1.5	0.21
2008	PME	AA	23	1	3	0	8	8	38^1	37	0	16	37	71%	.327	8	1.38	4.23	3.49	6.03	9.4	0.5	3.9	6.3	-2.2	-0.15
2008	BOS	MLB	23	6	5	0	36	9	88^1	68	10	40	68	65%	.243	15	1.22	3.16	4.14	2.99	6.9	0.8	3.7	6.7	23.9	2.80
2009	CLE	MLB	24	1	7	0	11	10	57^1	56	5	35	52	62%	.315	14	1.59	4.55	4.27	5.03	8.6	0.8	5.0	7.2	2.9	0.95
2009	BOS	MLB	24	3	3	0	31	6	72	72	7	25	67	61%	.314	16	1.35	4.50	3.61	4.09	8.2	0.6	2.7	7.6	11.4	1.42
2010	CLE	MLB	25	8	8	0	39	21	134^2	128	13	55	98	65%	.291	6	1.36	4.28	4.15	4.67	8.7	1.0	3.5	6.1	12.5	1.98

Breakout: 9%   Improve: 50%   Collapse: 13%   Attrition: 13%   MLB: 87%   Comparables: Ben Rivera, John Lackey, Freddy Garcia, Joey Hamilton

In Boston, a starter with a 4.50 ERA means you're heading to the bullpen, while in Cleveland, it means you're in contention to start Opening Day. Masterson's left/right splits were again extreme; in 2009, righties struggled (.203/.289/.302) and lefties excelled (.323/.407/.470). His Achilles' heel is his walk rate, but he was especially hurt in 2009 by BABIP as the good luck of 2008 deserted him. If he maintains his walk and strikeout rates, then a relatively normal BABIP would put him around a 3.90 ERA without any additional improvements, and that's good enough to make him the answer to the prayers of Tribe fans.

Tomo Ohka

Bats: S   Throws: R   Height: 6' 1"   Weight: 200   Born: March 18, 1976   Age: 34

YEAR	TEAM	LVL	AGE	W	L	SV	G	GS	IP	H	HR	BB	SO	GB%	BABIP	STUFF	WHIP	ERA	SIERA	DERA	EqH9	EqHR9	EqBB9	EqSO9	VORP	SN/WX
2007	TOR	MLB	31	2	5	0	10	10	56	68	10	22	21	53%	.293	-25	1.61	5.79	5.64	6.05	11.3	1.7	3.3	3.1	-3.3	0.66
2008	CHR	AAA	32	5	11	0	28	20	135^2	146	23	35	112	47%	.298	-18	1.33	4.18	3.80	5.18	10.3	1.8	2.5	5.4	4.7	0.27
2009	COH	AAA	33	3	3	0	9	9	52^2	53	6	9	26	39%	.283	-4	1.18	3.42	4.79	3.74	8.9	1.5	1.8	3.5	9.6	0.61
2009	CLE	MLB	33	1	5	0	18	6	71	77	18	19	31	47%	.252	-26	1.35	5.96	5.22	5.49	9.1	2.3	2.0	3.4	0.1	-0.26
2010	CLE	MLB	34	5	8	0	24	16	104^1	125	17	36	51	48%	.310	-20	1.54	5.35	5.16	5.88	11.0	1.5	3.0	4.2	-4.5	0.59

Breakout: 11%   Improve: 48%   Collapse: 17%   Attrition: 18%   MLB: 60%   Comparables: R.A. Dickey, Luis Rodriguez, John Wasdin, Steve Fireovid

Ohka reemerged after spending all of 2008 in the minors, unable to crack the White Sox' rotation. He got a new lease on big-league life after injuries and ineffectiveness opened up opportunities for many of the pitchers in Columbus. With an inability to strike anyone out and a homer rate that reflects more cookies than Mrs. Fields could cook up, Ohka is likely to resort to signing a minor-league contract with a different team for the fourth year in a row.

Chris Perez

Bats: R   Throws: R   Height: 6' 4"   Weight: 225   Born: July 1, 1985   Age: 24

YEAR	TEAM	LVL	AGE	W	L	SV	G	GS	IP	H	HR	BB	SO	GB%	BABIP	STUFF	WHIP	ERA	SIERA	DERA	EqH9	EqHR9	EqBB9	EqSO9	VORP	SN/WX
2007	SFD	AA	21	2	0	27	39	0	40^2	17	3	28	62	36%	.197	36	1.11	2.43	2.73	3.12	5.3	1.2	6.2	10.4	10.3	2.40
2007	MEM	AAA	21	0	1	8	15	0	14	6	2	13	15	70%	.148	13	1.36	4.50	4.09	4.97	5.0	2.1	8.5	7.8	0.7	0.22
2008	MEM	AAA	22	1	1	11	26	0	25^1	18	3	12	38	56%	.294	23	1.18	3.20	2.25	3.75	7.9	1.5	4.1	10.1	4.7	0.54
2008	SLN	MLB	22	3	3	7	41	0	41^2	34	5	22	42	41%	.271	9	1.34	3.46	3.87	3.98	7.7	1.3	4.2	7.7	6.9	0.48
2009	SLN	MLB	23	1	1	1	29	0	23^2	17	3	15	30	43%	.255	13	1.35	4.18	3.42	4.88	7.1	1.1	4.9	9.0	1.7	0.52
2009	CLE	MLB	23	0	1	1	32	0	33^1	24	5	12	38	44%	.253	18	1.08	4.32	2.84	4.08	6.8	1.4	2.8	9.3	5.1	-0.30
2010	CLE	MLB	24	4	4	13	64	0	63^1	52	8	34	67	42%	.284	5	1.37	4.32	3.72	4.66	7.5	1.1	4.7	8.9	5.9	1.56

Breakout: 15%   Improve: 35%   Collapse: 31%   Attrition: 11%   MLB: 89%   Comparables: Mike Jackson, Antonio Osuna, Mark Wohlers, Kurt Knudsen

The main return for Mark DeRosa, Perez was and is a prized commodity. He has a devastating fastball/slider combination, with his heater averaging around 94 mph. When you consider his peripherals, it seems as if he should be able to do better than a league-average ERA. The problem is pitching out of trouble—if Perez doesn't have a perfect inning, the opposition puts up crooked numbers against him. In his 32 appearances with the Indians, 25 were scoreless, but in the other seven, five of them were multirun outings in which he wasn't able to pitch a full inning. If he can learn how to pitch out of the big inning, he could be the main set-up guy and just a heartbeat away from closing.

Rafael Perez

Bats: L   Throws: L   Height: 6' 3"   Weight: 195   Born: May 15, 1982   Age: 28

YEAR	TEAM	LVL	AGE	W	L	SV	G	GS	IP	H	HR	BB	SO	GB%	BABIP	STUFF	WHIP	ERA	SIERA	DERA	EqH9	EqHR9	EqBB9	EqSO9	VORP	SN/WX
2007	BUF	AAA	25	3	3	0	8	7	46²	53	3	11	31	56%	.333	-1	1.37	3.66	4.17	5.77	10.9	0.8	2.3	4.7	-1.3	-0.36
2007	CLE	MLB	25	1	2	1	44	0	60²	41	5	15	62	60%	.234	28	0.92	1.78	2.88	2.20	5.7	0.7	1.9	8.2	22.5	3.24
2008	CLE	MLB	26	4	4	2	73	0	76¹	67	8	23	86	68%	.304	20	1.18	3.54	2.78	3.64	7.8	1.0	2.4	9.2	15.5	2.56
2009	COH	AAA	27	1	0	3	16	0	21²	23	0	5	23	56%	.371	16	1.29	0.83	2.93	1.71	9.4	0.4	2.1	7.7	8.8	0.61
2009	CLE	MLB	27	4	3	0	54	0	48	66	5	25	32	65%	.367	-24	1.90	7.31	4.80	6.99	11.9	0.9	4.2	5.3	-7.9	-1.19
2010	CLE	MLB	28	4	5	2	63	0	73¹	74	8	27	58	60%	.309	-1	1.38	4.27	4.01	4.64	9.2	1.0	3.1	6.5	7.0	1.01

Breakout: 11%   Improve: 39%   Collapse: 28%   Attrition: 13%   MLB: 78%   Comparables: Scott Stewart, Terry Forster, Mark Guthrie, Greg Cadaret

In a bullpen that resembled the cast of *The Poseidon Adventure*—only with no Gene Hackman to lead them to safety—Perez was the biggest disappointment as far as nonsurvivors. After 2007 and 2008, Perez seemed like one of the few pitchers they could count on, but he started horribly, recording only five strikeouts against his first 62 batters, with his slider visibly declining from its formerly elite status. Lefties had hit only .222/.300/.299 against him in '08, but took their revenge, hitting .412/.480/.588 in '09. He pitched well during two refresher trips to Triple-A, but continued to get fried extra-crispy in his big-league return engagements. In the absence of an injury, he might seem like a good candidate to bounce back, but it's going to have to be a pretty high bounce to get him back to where he was.

Anthony Reyes

Bats: R   Throws: R   Height: 6' 2"   Weight: 230   Born: October 16, 1981   Age: 28

YEAR	TEAM	LVL	AGE	W	L	SV	G	GS	IP	H	HR	BB	SO	GB%	BABIP	STUFF	WHIP	ERA	SIERA	DERA	EqH9	EqHR9	EqBB9	EqSO9	VORP	SN/WX
2007	SLN	MLB	25	2	14	0	22	20	107¹	108	16	43	74	41%	.277	-8	1.41	6.04	4.75	6.01	9.0	1.4	3.2	5.5	-6.1	0.50
2008	SLN	MLB	26	2	1	1	10	0	14²	16	2	3	10	42%	.304	-8	1.30	4.91	4.14	5.14	10.3	1.3	1.9	5.1	0.6	0.39
2008	CLE	MLB	26	2	1	0	6	6	34¹	31	2	12	15	50%	.259	4	1.25	1.83	5.33	1.99	7.7	0.5	2.9	3.7	13.3	1.78
2009	CLE	MLB	27	1	1	0	8	8	38¹	40	5	23	22	42%	.282	-12	1.64	6.57	5.69	6.40	8.8	1.2	4.7	4.4	-3.9	0.10
2010	CLE	MLB	28	4	5	0	24	13	75²	78	10	31	48	45%	.293	-5	1.44	4.78	4.84	5.23	9.4	1.2	3.6	5.3	2.3	1.15

Breakout: 16%   Improve: 43%   Collapse: 26%   Attrition: 32%   MLB: 65%   Comparables: Art Mahaffey, Stan Williams, Kenta Asakura, Josh Hancock

After Reyes lost the last few weeks of 2008 to a sore elbow, the problem returned just eight starts into 2009. His velocity dropped in each of his starts, and in his final appearance, he was having trouble feeling the ball and had no idea where it was going. The hopeful solution to his problems is reconstructive surgery to his ulnar collateral elbow. The surgery will sideline him at least until midseason, but possibly for the entire 2010 campaign; the Tribe nontendered him in December, but re-signed him to a minor-league deal.

Hector Rondon

Bats: R   Throws: R   Height: 6' 3"   Weight: 180   Born: February 26, 1988   Age: 22

YEAR	TEAM	LVL	AGE	W	L	SV	G	GS	IP	H	HR	BB	SO	GB%	BABIP	STUFF	WHIP	ERA	SIERA	DERA	EqH9	EqHR9	EqBB9	EqSO9	VORP	SN/WX
2007	LKC	A	19	7	10	0	27	27	136	143	13	27	113	46%	.315	1	1.25	4.37	3.59	6.41	11.1	1.8	2.5	4.8	-12.8	-1.09
2008	KIN	A+	20	11	6	0	27	27	145	130	12	42	145	42%	.299	21	1.19	3.60	3.22	4.88	9.7	1.7	3.1	6.2	9.3	0.45
2009	AKR	AA	21	7	5	0	15	13	72	60	3	16	73	41%	.297	32	1.06	2.75	2.89	3.71	9.0	0.9	2.3	7.2	13.2	1.03
2009	COH	AAA	21	4	5	0	12	12	74¹	83	8	13	64	41%	.333	20	1.29	4.00	3.46	4.98	9.8	1.4	1.7	6.1	4.2	0.17
2010	CLE	MLB	22	8	10	0	30	28	140	149	19	49	97	35%	.304	16	1.41	4.70	4.68	5.14	9.7	1.3	3.0	5.9	5.6	2.40

Breakout: 10%   Improve: 48%   Collapse: 9%   Attrition: 9%   MLB: 24%   Comparables: Tony Ghelfi, Tyler Clippard, Brad Radke, Pat Hentgen

Featuring a combination of quality stuff and plus command, Rondon can touch 95 mph with his fastball, but walked more than two batters just once in 27 appearances in 2009. After impressing in the first half of his age-21 season at Double-A, Rondon didn't embarrass himself in a second-half intro to Triple-A, so he's surviving the fast track. Although he's immediately in contention for a starting spot in the rotation come 2010—it's a pulse-optional battle royale—the likely scenario is that he'll be back at Columbus to work on his secondary offerings. Since he's so often around the plate, he needs better breaking stuff to change batters' eye levels. Given his age, the Indians see no need to rush him to the majors.

Tony Sipp

				Bats: L		Throws: L		Height: 6' 0"		Weight: 190		Born: July 12, 1983			Age: 26						

YEAR	TEAM	LVL	AGE	W	L	SV	G	GS	IP	H	HR	BB	SO	GB%	BABIP	STUFF	WHIP	ERA	SIERA	DERA	EqH9	EqHR9	EqBB9	EqSO9	VORP	SN/WX
2008	AKR	AA	24	0	3	1	16	0	21²	19	4	7	32	44%	.319	12	1.20	3.74	1.86	5.75	9.7	2.2	3.1	10.2	-0.6	-0.53
2009	COH	AAA	25	1	0	1	12	0	17	17	1	6	22	18%	.356	14	1.35	3.71	2.79	4.50	9.0	1.1	3.2	9.0	1.9	0.56
2009	CLE	MLB	25	2	0	0	46	0	40	27	5	25	48	46%	.244	18	1.30	2.92	3.46	3.40	6.1	1.1	5.0	9.3	9.2	0.96
2010	CLE	MLB	26	3	4	0	46	0	51	47	6	27	49	34%	.305	1	1.46	4.38	4.19	4.74	8.4	1.1	4.5	8.0	4.3	0.69

Breakout: 15%   Improve: 30%   Collapse: 39%   Attrition: 7%   MLB: 57%   Comparables: Bill Landis, J.J. Munoz, Tyler Johnson, Tim Christman

When Rafael Perez went Krakatoa, the Indians called upon Sipp to provide some help. The Pascagoula, Mississippi, native led the pen in WXRL, which isn't saying much. Despite a high walk rate, he was effective against both lefties and righties, holding the latter to a .179 batting average. He doesn't throw hard, but his deceptive delivery seems to have carried over from the minors, which isn't always the case with pitchers of this type. This bodes well for him being a solid set-up man and perhaps even future closer material, as he's likely to show better command in his second full year back from Tommy John surgery. However, note his low BABIP, a warning sign of eruptions to come.

Joe Smith

				Bats: R		Throws: R		Height: 6' 2"		Weight: 210		Born: March 22, 1984			Age: 26						

YEAR	TEAM	LVL	AGE	W	L	SV	G	GS	IP	H	HR	BB	SO	GB%	BABIP	STUFF	WHIP	ERA	SIERA	DERA	EqH9	EqHR9	EqBB9	EqSO9	VORP	SN/WX
2007	NYN	MLB	23	3	2	0	54	0	44¹	48	3	21	45	78%	.349	9	1.56	3.45	3.47	3.61	10.1	0.6	3.9	8.0	9.2	0.51
2008	NYN	MLB	24	6	3	0	82	0	63¹	51	4	31	52	71%	.261	0	1.29	3.55	3.86	4.24	7.6	0.7	3.9	6.2	8.8	1.68
2009	CLE	MLB	25	0	0	0	37	0	34	30	4	13	30	64%	.274	2	1.26	3.44	3.72	3.97	7.7	1.1	2.9	6.9	5.8	0.84
2010	CLE	MLB	26	3	4	0	57	0	56²	55	6	24	44	69%	.298	-4	1.39	4.32	3.96	4.76	8.9	0.9	3.7	6.6	4.6	0.90

Breakout: 11%   Improve: 30%   Collapse: 23%   Attrition: 14%   MLB: 95%   Comparables: Ron Davis, Bob Apodaca, Cecilio Guante, Turk Farrell

After being sidelined with a viral infection in spring training, Smith had a rocky start in April; then again, the Tribe had more rocky Aprils than Bullwinkle's spring dance card. Smith then lost all of May to a sprained rotator cuff, but came back strong in June, with a 2.60 ERA in his next 27 ⅔ IP. Then a sprained left knee shelved him for the season in late August. Smith still seems to be the ROOGY he was with the Mets, as he again showed an extreme split (right-handed batters, .198/.271/.344; left-handed batters, .355/.412/.581). A healthy Smith would be one of the key pieces toward making Tribe skippers less squirrelly about their bullpens.

Jeremy Sowers

				Bats: L		Throws: L		Height: 6' 1"		Weight: 180		Born: May 17, 1983			Age: 27						

YEAR	TEAM	LVL	AGE	W	L	SV	G	GS	IP	H	HR	BB	SO	GB%	BABIP	STUFF	WHIP	ERA	SIERA	DERA	EqH9	EqHR9	EqBB9	EqSO9	VORP	SN/WX
2007	BUF	AAA	24	4	5	0	15	15	96²	112	6	24	61	50%	.316	-1	1.41	4.10	4.46	5.80	10.3	0.8	2.3	4.2	-3.2	-0.77
2007	CLE	MLB	24	1	6	0	13	13	67¹	84	10	21	24	42%	.303	-20	1.56	6.42	5.77	6.08	10.6	1.3	2.5	2.9	-4.4	0.47
2008	BUF	AAA	25	4	3	0	10	10	60²	56	4	17	43	46%	.287	8	1.20	2.08	4.13	2.83	8.8	0.9	2.7	4.7	17.0	1.60
2008	CLE	MLB	25	4	9	0	22	22	121	141	18	39	64	52%	.301	-12	1.49	5.58	4.96	5.99	10.0	1.3	2.5	4.3	-6.6	0.82
2009	COH	AAA	26	2	2	0	6	6	37¹	36	2	9	27	44%	.283	11	1.21	2.89	4.12	3.29	7.7	0.7	2.3	4.9	9.4	0.72
2009	CLE	MLB	26	6	11	0	23	22	123¹	134	11	52	51	44%	.287	-5	1.51	5.25	5.79	4.86	9.1	0.8	3.3	3.2	8.8	1.50
2010	CLE	MLB	27	8	10	0	30	28	148²	160	17	61	67	49%	.291	-12	1.48	4.79	5.45	5.18	9.7	1.1	3.5	3.7	5.2	1.35

Breakout: 7%   Improve: 37%   Collapse: 12%   Attrition: 22%   MLB: 78%   Comparables: Neal Heaton, John Koronka, Rick Honeycutt, Mike Maroth

With nothing but tarnish covering the shine of being a high first-round pick, it's time to reassess Sowers' career. Despite getting his fastball back into the low 90s, he simply does not have the ability to strike out enough hitters at the major-league level ... or does he, at least in the right circumstances? When looking at the splits, one can see the issues. In 396 career PAs against righties, he has recorded only 27 strikeouts, versus 42 walks. Facing lefties, he's struck out 24 and walked 10 in just 149 PAs. The latter is still not a great rate, but it might be salvageable, and with all of the new arms coming up, one of the few remaining options may be to turn Sowers into a lefty specialist.

Jess Todd

Bats: R Throws: R Height: 5' 11" Weight: 210 Born: April 20, 1986 Age: 24

YEAR	TEAM	LVL	AGE	W	L	SV	G	GS	IP	H	HR	BB	SO	GB%	BABIP	STUFF	WHIP	ERA	SIERA	DERA	EqH9	EqHR9	EqBB9	EqSO9	VORP	SN/WX
2007	BAT	A-	21	4	1	0	16	7	58¹	48	2	14	69	51%	.317	19	1.06	2.78	2.43	4.92	9.2	1.4	2.9	6.8	3.4	0.31
2008	PMB	A+	22	3	0	1	7	4	27¹	18	0	7	35	51%	.277	25	0.91	1.65	2.17	3.68	7.7	0.7	2.8	7.7	5.2	0.46
2008	SFD	AA	22	4	5	0	17	16	103	79	12	24	81	56%	.244	16	1.00	2.97	3.61	3.90	7.8	1.5	2.4	5.5	17.0	1.45
2008	MEM	AAA	22	1	1	0	4	4	22²	19	4	11	20	52%	.250	9	1.32	3.97	4.08	4.43	8.4	2.5	4.2	5.9	2.5	0.27
2009	MEM	AAA	23	4	2	24	41	0	49	39	3	13	59	45%	.290	16	1.06	2.20	2.44	3.02	8.1	1.1	2.5	8.1	13.1	2.39
2009	CLE	MLB	23	0	1	0	19	0	20²	31	3	7	18	42%	.394	-5	1.84	7.40	4.10	6.64	12.9	1.3	2.6	6.9	-2.7	-0.13
2010	CLE	MLB	24	5	6	10	42	7	89²	85	11	33	70	40%	.290	4	1.32	4.24	4.22	4.60	8.6	1.1	3.2	6.6	9.0	2.42

Breakout: 20% Improve: 47% Collapse: 18% Attrition: 8% MLB: 73% Comparables: Chin-Hui Tsao, Scott Strickland, Jim Waring, Ricky Bottalico

The player to be named later in the DeRosa deal, Todd has used a cut fastball to absolutely dominate right-handed hitters, holding them under .200 in his minor-league career. A starter until last year, he's a bit undersized to pitch 200 innings a year and so was moved to the pen. He closed for Memphis and showed good control and an improved strikeout rate. Lefties weren't fooled by him at all in his brief time in the majors, going 20-for-49 with four homers. Appropriately, the Indians are content to try him in a set-up role to spot him against right-handers, which is probably his ultimate role.

Jose Veras

Bats: R Throws: R Height: 6' 5" Weight: 235 Born: October 20, 1980 Age: 29

YEAR	TEAM	LVL	AGE	W	L	SV	G	GS	IP	H	HR	BB	SO	GB%	BABIP	STUFF	WHIP	ERA	SIERA	DERA	EqH9	EqHR9	EqBB9	EqSO9	VORP	SN/WX
2007	NYA	MLB	26	0	0	2	9	0	9¹	6	0	7	7	53%	.222	-5	1.39	5.79	5.15	5.59	5.6	0.0	5.6	5.6	-0.1	0.37
2008	NYA	MLB	27	5	3	0	60	0	57²	52	7	29	63	47%	.298	13	1.40	3.59	3.57	3.38	7.5	0.9	4.0	8.9	13.9	1.03
2009	NYA	MLB	28	3	1	0	25	0	25²	23	5	14	18	44%	.234	-17	1.44	5.96	5.08	5.47	7.9	1.7	4.1	5.5	0.1	-0.16
2009	CLE	MLB	28	1	2	0	22	0	24²	19	3	14	22	47%	.242	-5	1.34	4.38	4.35	5.40	6.5	1.1	4.3	6.8	0.3	-0.06
2010	CLE	MLB	29	3	3	3	57	0	56²	50	6	27	51	47%	.286	2	1.35	4.24	4.02	4.58	7.9	0.9	4.2	7.6	5.8	0.96

Breakout: 14% Improve: 51% Collapse: 26% Attrition: 13% MLB: 75% Comparables: Bill Koch, Juan Salas, Travis Hughes, Todd Jones

Well, beggars can't be choosers. In return for what was basically the major-league minimum, the Indians got exactly replacement-level bullpen help. Given the state of their bullpen in June, that was actually an improvement. When comparing his peripherals in his time with the Indians against his 2008 "breakout" season with the Yankees, he actually pitched better in most stats save one, his strikeout rate. He had a lower WHIP and a significantly lower BABIP. The one blemish was that his strikeout rate was down almost 20 percent. If he can bring that back up, somebody might have a bargain on their hands, but then the whole problem with Veras is that he and Mr. Consistency have never been introduced, causing four organizations (now that the Indians nontendered him in December) to give up on him despite good stuff.

Jake Westbrook

Bats: R Throws: R Height: 6' 3" Weight: 215 Born: September 29, 1977 Age: 32

YEAR	TEAM	LVL	AGE	W	L	SV	G	GS	IP	H	HR	BB	SO	GB%	BABIP	STUFF	WHIP	ERA	SIERA	DERA	EqH9	EqHR9	EqBB9	EqSO9	VORP	SN/WX
2007	CLE	MLB	29	6	9	0	25	25	152	159	13	55	93	63%	.304	9	1.41	4.32	4.50	4.33	9.2	0.8	3.0	5.1	19.2	3.35
2008	CLE	MLB	30	1	2	0	5	5	34²	33	5	7	19	65%	.262	7	1.15	3.12	4.26	3.34	8.3	1.3	1.6	4.5	8.1	0.98
2010	CLE	MLB	32	4	4	0	16	3	65²	71	8	28	37	57%	.303	-7	1.51	4.77	4.93	5.18	9.9	1.0	3.6	4.7	2.3	0.97

Breakout: 13% Improve: 50% Collapse: 15% Attrition: 24% MLB: 71% Comparables: Dennis Lamp, Mark Petkovsek, Dave Wickersham, Ron Kline

After Tommy John surgery in June 2008 (with a September 2008 hip surgery thrown in just for kicks), Westbrook's return wasn't anticipated until midseason in 2009 at the earliest. Instead, he had multiple setbacks due to elbow pain and was forced to miss the entire year, save for some rehab work at Double-A. In the first two years of his contract, the Indians have paid $20 million for five big-league starts; with $11 million on the line for 2010, there are no guarantees that Westbrook will pitch for the Indians again. However, there is one guarantee: Mark Shapiro has said that if Westbrook is healthy, he will be the 2010 Opening Day starter. Way to motivate that rehab, Mr. Shapiro.

Alex White

Bats: R	Throws: R	Height: 6' 3"	Weight: 200	Born: August 29, 1988	Age: 21

Did Not Play.

Breakout: 13%   Improve: 50%   Collapse: 15%   Attrition: 24%   MLB: 71%   Comparables: NA

White entered the spring as one of the top college pitchers in the draft, but he didn't quite live up to expectations, which dropped him to the middle of the first round. Some scouts aren't really sure what to make of him, as he has two plus pitches in his 92-95 mph fastball and darting split pitch, but that unique combination leaves some to wonder if he isn't just a power reliever in the end. He's going to miss bats, we just don't know in which role, yet. Knowing that 200 innings are more valuable than 75, Cleveland will begin his career in the High-A rotation.

Kerry Wood

Bats: R	Throws: R	Height: 6' 5"	Weight: 210	Born: June 16, 1977	Age: 33

YEAR	TEAM	LVL	AGE	W	L	SV	G	GS	IP	H	HR	BB	SO	GB%	BABIP	STUFF	WHIP	ERA	SIERA	DERA	EqH9	EqHR9	EqBB9	EqSO9	VORP	SN/WX
2007	CHN	MLB	30	1	1	0	22	0	24¹	18	0	13	24	40%	.281	16	1.27	3.33	3.96	3.23	7.2	0.0	4.6	8.4	6.0	0.03
2008	CHN	MLB	31	5	4	34	65	0	66¹	54	3	18	84	46%	.311	31	1.09	3.26	2.35	3.15	7.8	0.4	2.2	9.7	17.1	2.03
2009	CLE	MLB	32	3	3	20	58	0	55	48	7	28	63	41%	.293	9	1.38	4.25	3.47	3.96	7.6	1.1	3.9	8.7	9.5	0.82
2010	CLE	MLB	33	3	4	16	52	2	51²	47	5	22	50	42%	.306	5	1.34	4.12	3.69	4.53	8.4	0.9	3.6	8.2	5.6	0.82

Breakout: 10%   Improve: 41%   Collapse: 37%   Attrition: 9%   MLB: 91%   Comparables: Jeff Russell, Jim Gott, Rich Gossage, Carl Willis_NoPara

In his first season in the junior circuit, Wood saw his ERA jump a full run from his 2008 All-Star season in the weaker league. The two main reasons were a doubling of his walk rate from 2.4 BB/9 to 4.6 and a bump in his home-run rate. Also, the new league may have picked up on something in Wood's delivery—in 2009, the league was 10-for-10 in stolen-base attempts on Wood (tying Jonathan Papelbon for most stolen bases against a closer), whereas in 2008, only one stolen base was attempted. Wood was much improved in the second half of the season, albeit in just 24 ⅓ innings, because of few opportunities and a bout of shoulder stiffness. The Indians will pay him $10.5 million this year, then must face an $11 million team option that vests if Wood finishes 55 games. Just a guess, but they'll probably think hard about moving him if he starts closing in on that number.

LINEOUTS

Hitters

PLAYER	TEAM	LVL	AGE	PA	R	2B	3B	HR	RBI	BB	SO	SB-CS	EqBRR	AVG/OBP/SLG	EqAVG/EqOBP/EqSLG	EqA	VORP	WARP
RF A. Abreu	LKC	A	19	265	36	16	4	7	30	11	68	3-3	1.2	.305/.351/.488	.250/.283/.393	.231	-4.3	-0.9
2B J. Barfield	COH	AAA	26	319	27	15	0	3	35	8	48	5-3	-0.3	.252/.271/.331	.239/.258/.307	.195	-11.8	-0.9
3B J. Brito	MHV	A-	21	107	16	7	2	0	18	14	15	0-1	-1.9	.333/.419/.456	.295/.358/.389	.266	3.2	0.5
	IDN	Rk	21	155	36	12	8	3	25	18	26	2-1	0.0	.366/.439/.642	.275/.329/.430	.262	3.9	-0.2
INF T. Graffanino	COH	AAA	37	286	39	24	0	6	40	17	46	3-0	2.0	.264/.311/.425	.246/.287/.383	.235	-1.3	-0.2
OF S. Head*	COH	AAA	25	304	28	16	0	6	31	17	34	1-2	-2.9	.246/.291/.368	.235/.278/.345	.217	-10.2	-1.6
2B J. Kipnis*	MHV	A-	22	129	19	8	3	1	19	15	18	3-3	-0.5	.306/.388/.459	.265/.318/.376	.244	0.2	-0.4
DH N. Recknagel	LKC	A	23	399	46	21	4	13	67	49	73	2-4	-3.5	.280/.379/.482	.227/.304/.360	.234	-11.3	-2.0
	KIN	A+	23	97	10	5	0	1	8	6	17	0-1	-0.1	.233/.281/.322	.217/.258/.293	.189	-7.0	-1.1
MI J. Rodriguez	AKR	AA	24	131	18	4	0	0	12	23	30	2-3	-2.0	.295/.426/.333	.255/.369/.282	.241	0.7	-0.3
INF N. Romero#	AKR	AA	24	134	13	4	0	0	8	12	19	3-1	0.9	.209/.292/.243	.193/.260/.218	.173	-7.3	-0.2
	COH	AAA	24	284	34	10	1	1	27	21	27	10-4	-0.3	.254/.313/.313	.241/.299/.300	.218	-2.1	-1.7
OF D. Webb#	LKC	A	23	525	69	17	12	7	57	40	110	35-9	3.2	.289/.351/.420	.235/.282/.333	.218	-11.4	-1.9
	COH	AAA	23	33	3	4	0	0	6	2	7	1-0	-0.3	.367/.394/.500	.333/.364/.467	.293	2.2	0.4

Rangy Dominican **Abner Abreu** has some of the best raw power in the system and was on the verge of a breakout before injuries struck; that breakout could come this year. ⊘ **Josh Barfield** has been terminally wounded by his inability to control the strike zone and is milling around on the Hairston career path toward a utility role. ⊘ **Jesus Brito** turned some heads this year with a 998 OPS between two levels, but his bat is his only plus tool, his power ceiling is questionable, and he may not stick at third. ⊘ Not every utilityman hangs around forever, because for **Tony Graffanino**, the end is near. ⊘ A sore knee sustained in spring training caused a big drop in **Stephen Head's** numbers, putting a huge dent in his future. ⊘ A second-round pick last June, **Jason Kipnis** looked like a well-rounded prospect as an outfielder, but the Tribe is hoping he can be even more valuable with a conversion to second base. ⊘ **Nate Recknagel** might be the Indians' next version of Ryan Garko, but who asked for a Garko sequel? Recknagel, whose name is an anagram for "Carnage Elk Ten," happens to be something of a Carnage Elk on defense, which caused him to spend much of the season as a DH. ⊘ Middle infielder **Josh Rodriguez** lost most of the season due to a hamstring injury. He has shown great plate discipline (12.1 percent walk rate), but his age is an issue, his defense on the left side falls a bit short, and this will be the year he needs to make the jump. ⊘ **Niuman Romero** can play all four infield positions consistently, which earned him a surprise September call-up; if he wants to stay up, he'll need to spend some time in the cage, as he has never had an OPS higher than 753 in the minors. ⊘ Possible leadoff hitter **Donnie Webb** led the Sally League with 12 triples, though his strikeout rate was high for a college player in Low-A.

Pitchers

PLAYER	TEAM	LVL	AGE	W	L	SV	IP	H	HR	BB	SO	GB%	BABIP	STUFF	WHIP	ERA	SIERA	DERA	EqH9	EqHR9	EqBB9	EqSO9	VORP
E. Berger*	KIN	A+	23	7	8	0	110^1	93	4	45	100	43%	.286	-1	1.25	2.45	3.85	4.37	9.4	1.1	4.3	5.3	12.8
	AKR	AA	23	3	1	0	33^2	32	1	16	33	40%	.326	12	1.43	2.67	3.89	4.60	10.3	0.9	4.6	6.9	3.1
R. Edell*	AKR	AA	25	4	1	0	89^1	82	8	19	91	41%	.306	7	1.13	2.32	2.88	3.54	10.0	1.5	2.3	7.1	18.0
	COH	AAA	25	0	6	0	46^2	68	7	15	37	39%	.379	-22	1.78	6.36	4.33	7.19	12.6	1.9	3.1	5.4	-8.7
M. Gosling*	ROC	AAA	28	7	1	1	35	33	2	17	43	42%	.348	12	1.43	4.37	3.13	4.81	8.8	0.8	4.5	9.1	2.6
	COH	AAA	28	0	3	0	32^1	45	5	7	30	49%	.404	-2	1.61	5.29	3.39	6.30	13.2	2.1	2.4	6.9	-2.7
	CLE	MLB	28	0	0	0	25	30	5	11	13	35%	.294	-24	1.64	5.04	5.72	4.97	9.9	1.8	3.6	3.9	1.5
Z. Jackson*	COH	AAA	26	4	8	0	99^2	128	13	33	67	55%	.345	-31	1.62	6.05	4.51	7.33	11.2	1.7	3.2	4.6	-19.7
	CLE	MLB	26	0	0	0	8^2	14	2	4	10	51%	.414	0	2.08	9.35	3.75	9.64	13.5	1.9	2.9	8.7	-4.3
J. Judy	AKR	AA	23	4	3	11	49^1	35	2	18	63	55%	.287	16	1.07	3.10	2.54	4.34	7.9	1.0	3.5	8.9	6.0
M. Kobayashi	COH	AAA	35	2	2	1	19^1	28	4	7	11	34%	.369	-30	1.81	4.66	5.30	5.09	13.8	2.5	3.6	4.1	0.8
	CLE	MLB	35	0	0	0	9^2	12	2	4	4	36%	.294	-32	1.66	8.38	6.03	7.45	10.2	1.9	2.8	2.8	-2.1
C. Lofgren*	AKR	AA	23	3	1	0	42^2	24	1	15	31	44%	.193	12	0.91	1.48	4.23	2.61	5.9	0.7	3.3	4.8	13.3
	COH	AAA	23	6	10	0	98^1	94	15	33	62	36%	.257	-11	1.29	5.31	4.91	6.22	8.1	1.8	3.1	4.3	-7.9
A. Perez	LKC	A	19	5	4	0	83	69	9	24	76	56%	.263	-7	1.12	3.04	3.38	6.13	10.7	2.8	4.1	4.7	-5.1
	KIN	A+	19	1	2	0	31^1	32	1	9	31	51%	.348	27	1.31	2.87	3.24	4.18	11.6	1.0	3.2	6.1	4.1
Y. Pino	NBR	AA	25	5	1	0	62	61	4	16	64	42%	.329	-3	1.24	3.19	3.08	4.53	10.0	1.4	2.6	6.8	6.4
	ROC	AAA	25	2	2	0	51	37	5	11	44	36%	.232	19	0.94	2.82	3.44	3.69	6.5	1.3	2.2	6.3	10.1
	COH	AAA	25	2	0	0	14	12	0	2	14	39%	.316	13	1.00	1.29	2.62	1.69	7.4	0.0	1.4	7.4	5.6
Z. Putnam	KIN	A+	21	2	0	0	24	22	1	5	23	53%	.313	15	1.12	4.12	3.07	6.23	10.4	1.2	2.5	5.8	-1.8
	AKR	AA	21	4	2	2	56^2	59	2	18	57	64%	.341	12	1.36	4.13	3.25	5.62	10.9	0.8	3.0	6.9	-0.7
E. Stiller	AKR	AA	24	8	3	0	69^2	56	2	30	68	32%	.274	-1	1.23	3.23	3.93	4.81	8.3	0.8	3.8	6.5	5.3
R. Swindle*	NAS	AAA	25	3	1	2	43^2	30	1	13	41	46%	.248	11	0.98	1.03	3.34	1.81	6.8	0.6	2.8	6.4	17.4
	MIL	MLB	25	0	0	0	6^2	12	3	4	8	57%	.429	-23	2.40	16.20	3.89	16.20	16.2	4.1	4.1	9.4	-7.9
J. Tomlin	AKR	AA	24	14	9	0	145	149	21	27	125	41%	.304	-21	1.21	4.16	3.43	6.09	11.1	2.2	2.0	5.9	-8.8

A 2008 pick out of the University of Arizona, **Eric Berger** continues to quickly climb through the Indians' system due to a 2.42 ERA in 182 ⅓ career innings. The secret of his success has been a good strikeout rate and keeping the ball in the park (only seven career homers allowed). ⊘ Chunky lefty **Ryan Edell** was an eighth-round pick in 2005; a good move and strike-throwing skill aren't enough to combat fly-ball tendencies and merely OK stuff. ⊘ **Mike Gosling**'s walk rates and mediocre results against lefties make any kind of LOOGY work impossible, dooming him to the same future as the great auk, the moa, and the newspaper. ⊘ Despite the big-league club's desperate need for help, **Zach Jackson** got one start, signaling that the Indians saw his proper place as falling somewhere between Triple-A and the Great Pacific Garbage Patch before just trading him to Toronto. Not every southpaw gets a million chances, especially not in an organization that boasts more mediocre lefties than a meeting of the House Progressive Caucus. ⊘ If there are relief prospects, **Josh Judy** is one of them; he's had a midseason promotion every year with the Indians, and with his velocity creeping into the 93-94 mph range, there's a possibility he may be in the pen sometime in 2010. Suggested nicknames include "Judge," "Punch," or "Daughter." ⊘ **Masahide Kobayashi** was cut from the 40-man roster after a disastrous beginning and has since taken this Indians no-win scenario back to Japan as a free agent. ⊘ After eight solid starts at Akron, homers and hittability hurt **Chuck Lofgren**'s chances to reestablish himself as a prospect, but that didn't stop the Brewers from snagging him from the Tribe in the Rule 5 draft. ⊘ Former top prospect **Adam Miller**'s problematic middle finger on his pitching hand has limited him to less than 93 innings over two years; he's had a fourth off-season surgery on it this winter, throwing his future into even greater doubt. ⊘ **Alexander Perez** had an impressive year at Low-A, but the control is better than the stuff, and he gives up the long ball a little too often. ⊘ The player to be named later in the Pavano trade, last year **Yohan Pino** rebounded after two shaky seasons in Double-A. He could provide future benefits as a middle reliever. ⊘ The Tribe's bullpen woes created some panic down below, as they briefly converted **Zach Putnam** to relief work in 2009; he'll be back to starting at Double-A and has the stuff to fit in the back end of a good rotation. ⊘ Undrafted reliever **Erik Stiller** has risen through the ranks, adding muscle to get his fastball to top out at 94 mph. If he can make the leap, he'll have an Old Nassau mini-reunion with fellow Princeton alum Mark Shapiro and director of baseball ops Mike Chernoff. ⊘ **R. J. Swindle** was the subject of dizzying transaction madness in 2009, getting designated, claimed, designated, and claimed by the Brewers, Rays, and Indians; a pitcher with a below-speed-limit curve and great peripherals, Swindle faces his last hurdle, which is to reproduce his lower-level success as a situational southpaw. ⊘ After relieving in '08, **Josh Tomlin** was exclusively used as a starter in '09 and saw his ERA go up a run due to a declining strikeout rate.

MANAGER: ERIC WEDGE

YEAR	TEAM	W-L	Pythag +/-	Avg PC	100+ P	120+ P	QS	BQS	REL	REL w Zero R	IBB	Subs	PH	PH Avg	PH HR	SB2	CS2	SB3	CS3	SAC Att	SAC %	POS SAC	Squeeze	Swing	In Play
2007	CLE	96-66	4	95.9	69	1	89	9	395	248	42	58	116	.272	4	66	40	6	1	43	74.4%	30	0	136	98
2008	CLE	81-81	-5	94.8	60	1	79	10	397	231	28	31	111	.237	2	73	26	3	3	58	74.1%	42	0	133	90
2009	CLE	65-97	-7	94.5	65	2	70	7	444	256	31	19	63	.231	0	71	29	13	2	54	72.2%	35	0	138	107

If one had to pick a single word to describe the Eric Wedge era, it would be "underachievement." In only one year (the division-winning 2007 campaign) did Wedge's Indians outperform their Pythagorean win expectancy, with the club winding up a total of 30 games below that during his seven-year tenure. Wedge's tenure was characterized by the annual slow start; his Indians had a .495 win percentage overall, but that breaks down to a .432 winning percentage in April and .506 the rest of the time. As a tactician, he was notable for a slow hook; even in the bullpen meltdown seasons of 2008 and 2009, Wedge was near the bottom of the league in relievers used. When Manny Acta comes to town, the bullpen should be prepared to punch the clock more often, as he has led the majors in relievers used since 2007, though some of his high totals are probably due to Washington's starting pitching (and the interchangeable cast of thousands in the Nats' pen). Wedge and Acta were similar in their relatively sparse use of the stolen base, with both managers finishing in the bottom third, though in the latter's case, both the low totals and his team's poor success rate suggest that he understood that if his Nationals couldn't run well, they might as well not run often. One potential benefit of the Acta hiring that you won't see in the box scores is his ability to connect with Latino players. Some of the biggest disappointments from last year (Carmona, Rafael Perez, and Peralta) as well as the next group of key prospects (Santana, Rondon, and Carrasco) are from Latin America, and they may benefit from the lack of a language barrier between them and the manager.

Colorado Rockies

The Rockies made their third playoff appearance as a franchise, which may not sound like much, but a second trip to October in three years suggests that baseball in Denver has achieved some semblance of normality. As recently as 2003, the Society for American Baseball Research was devoted to the topic of whether a team could win "at altitude." A number of hypotheses for altitude-adjusted player usage patterns were suggested, and none of the ideas—cool or kooky or anywhere in between—were adopted. Frankly, they probably promised as little success as the "great changeup experiment" that involved signing Mike Hampton and Denny Neagle and then losing money and ballgames.

General manager Dan O'Dowd, the man who was hired a decade ago on the premise that he knew how to adapt to baseball in Denver, has instead stood the concept on its head after hundreds if not thousands of man-hours spent researching the issue. Rather than going on and on about how to adapt to their environment, the Rockies have instead risen to the challenge of what it takes to win within baseball's competitive ecology. The Rockies aren't stuck on the symptoms of baseball played at altitude, the way much of the research community is. They've done the homework, and after so much navel gazing, they have finally become an organization that fields a team that wins ballgames—*anywhere*. A reflection of that was last season's 41-40 record on the road, the first time that Colorado's ballclub finished above .500 away from Coors Field, besting the previous high set by the pennant-winning Rockies of 2007 (39-42). Nor was that sort of modest success at all fluky—the Rockies' split of 340 runs scored on the road against 336 allowed should have given them exactly what they wound up with.

That total of runs scored on the road isn't good, though, since it ranked just 10th in the league. Still, it suggests what it is that made the Rockies win in 2009, and what makes their present core of talent the best in franchise history and a model for future playoff appearances: tremendous pitching combined with a defense that kills run-scoring, qualities that work everywhere, even in a park where every inning can give rise to rallies.

As you'll find in a table in the D'backs' chapter, that kind of performance contributes to a teamwide SIERA (Skill Interactive Earned Run Average) of 3.80 for the pitching staff, which ranked fifth in the major leagues. The linchpin of that staff success over the course of the season was the best rotation in franchise history. Using starting pitcher performance through the first six innings and total runs allowed (not earned runs) as the standard for quality starts, last year's Rockies team finished first in the major leagues, getting quality starts from their rotation through a game's first six innings in 99 games. The MLB-wide average last year was just under 50 percent of all ballgames; in the National League, it was higher, at 51.4 percent, while in the AL, starting pitchers allowed three runs or less in 48.1 percent of their ballgames. For the Rockies, it was a rotation-wide quality that produced a league-leading tally, meaning that the rotation was delivering winnable ballgames more often than any other team in baseball (see Table 1).

ROCKIES PROSPECTUS
2009 W-L: 92-70, 2nd in NL West

Pythag	90-72	2nd	**Ballpark:** Coors Field (3-yr. PF: 1073). Why not soak the balls in blue cheese? Balls take wing, so it's still a hot spot for hitters
RS/G	5.0	2nd	
RA/G	4.4	7th	
EqA	.265	5th	
EqBRR	7.2	2nd	**2009:** An even better pitching-and-defense club rebounded from an early slump after getting the skipper axed
SNWP	.519	6th	
WXRL	6.42	11th	
FRAr	4.85	13th	**2010:** The D plus a multi-pony outfield and the best rotation in franchise history should contend
DE	.689	10th	
PADE	0.48	5th	**Action Items:** An outfield pecking order, a second or third baseman to help on O, an effective pen
Salary	$75.2	10th	
Attend	2.67	8th	

Table 1. The Five Horsemen of the Rockolypse

Starter	GS	QS	BQS	5+/3*	SNWP
Jimenez	33	24	4	0	.580
Marquis	33	21	1	0	.534
De La Rosa	32	17	0	4	.526
Hammel	30	13	1	4	.483
Cook	27	15	1	3	.524
Others	7	2	0	0	.484
Total	**162**	**92**	**7**	**10**	**.528**

*Five-plus innings pitched but less than six; three runs allowed or less

Consider as well how the Rockies got their men. Ubaldo Jimenez and Aaron Cook are products of their player-development effort, as is Jeff Francis, who would have been in the rotation if not for a torn labrum. Jorge De La Rosa was the product of a scrap-heap swap with the Royals the year before, Jason Marquis was acquired for pennies on the dollar in a mutual dump of veterans with the Cubs (for Luis Vizcaino), and Jason Hammel was a distressed property available from the Rays late in the spring because he was out of options and their staff was already jam-packed. In short, three of five rotation regulars were *not* the product of big-time investments; they were nifty pickups from the less glamorous end of the player pool. Admittedly, this unit was not so much a product of any guiding strategy as it was a matter of contingent events, but credit O'Dowd's crew for getting better results than anyone expected from any of the three add-ons beyond Jimenez and Cook.

If a top-to-bottom rotation capable of delivering quality work was to some extent a happy accident, one of the key elements of that success was not—the team's defense. The original edition of Rocktober was particularly defense-dependent, winding up second in the majors in PADE (Park-Adjusted Defensive Efficiency). In 2008, the team fell back to 23rd, but in 2009 rebounded up to seventh. Perhaps the single largest factor in the rise and fall and rebirth of Rockies defense was a full season of a healthy Troy Tulowitzki at shortstop, but the eventual decisions to entrust larger roles to Seth Smith and Carlos "CarGo" Gonzalez in the outfield, to make Clint Barmes the everyday second baseman, and to get Garrett Atkins off third base all contributed measures of defensive improvement. As well-worn as the truism that pitching and defense win games is, the important factor is that nothing about altitude prevents the Rockies from enjoying those benefits the same as with any other ballclub.

Which brings us to the other happy lessons from the 2009 season for the Rockies. Their early-season struggles, stumbling to an 18-28 record in the first seven weeks of the season, and the resultant decision to fire Clint Hurdle, was a normal reaction. The decision to plug in Jim Tracy, an experienced former skipper who'd been brought in as the bench coach, was subsequently hailed as inspired. (It was one of the few in-season managerial switches in baseball history, along with the exchange of Billy Martin for Bob Lemon in 1978, that produced exactly the desired result.) But you'd be hard-pressed to find any in-game tactical masterstrokes that were so different between Hurdle and Tracy that produced the club's 74-42 streak under Tracy. This lack of tactical distinction too easily contributes to the usual assertion by the performance analysis community that managers don't make that much of a difference. Setting aside the absurdity of the suggestion—as in any field of history, soft or human factors always play a role—the key decisions that Tracy made more effectively than Hurdle are not in the realm of tactics. While the willingness to squeeze or leave a starter out there a little longer is an important distinction, the real difference in the two men lies in an area of agency that much of managerial analysis ignores: *picking who plays.*

Tracy helped himself and his ballclub best by not being attached to who Garrett Atkins used to be, or by not being hung up on an expectation that Ryan Spilborghs somehow deserved to play every day because it was his turn, or by not being wed to the goofy notion that asking Ian Stewart to play second or an outfield corner was somehow a sensible thing to do. Instead, Tracy pushed Spilborghs back into a part-time role he's much better suited for, put Stewart at third most of the rest of the way, left second base to Clint Barmes, and leaned more heavily on Seth Smith and then also Carlos Gonzalez in the outfield. Tracy wasn't winning ballgames by dugout wizardry; he was winning them with his lineup cards.

Tracy wasn't alone in providing in-season improvements in selecting who got playing time. Dan O'Dowd did his part as well in shoring up the bullpen for the stretch run, adding Rafael Betancourt and Joe Beimel and later Jose Contreras to fortify a relief crew already improved by the decision to employ Franklin Morales there instead of in the rotation. Losing Alan Embree and Manuel Corpas no doubt added impetus, but as the example of the 2003 Marlins reminds us, throwing together a functional bullpen with only a month or two of action left to go is no impediment to success; nor does it require a club to bid for the best. Betancourt's track record as a premium reliever made him a relatively high-yield target, but seeing value in Contreras and renting Beimel were sensible bits of detail work to make sure that the club wouldn't be handicapped by a reliance on the Foggs and Peraltas in key situations. O'Dowd's addition of Jason Giambi to provide bench sock at the big-league minimum also provided a reminder of the increasing adaptability of clubs when it comes to making sure that their post-season benches aren't necessarily the same collection they carry through the regular season's six-month slog. Taken together, talent management and roster manipulation are further symptoms of creeping normalcy, as an organization moves into dealing with straightforward propositions about what works and stops spinning its wheels trying to be unique.

So, we've dispensed with this whole "how to win at altitude" issue, but there's still the more basic question—are the Rockies set up to keep winning? As tough as the National League West might be, the Rockies are the organization doing things the right way when it comes to stocking its roster via player development, pointed trading, and effective additions via free agency and the free talent pool. So there's every reason to expect that they should continue to run with the Dodgers' big-budget bids, let alone the Giants' "Lincecum and Cain and then feel pain" or the Snakes' slippery slither toward reliable disappointment. The lineup is relatively young, providing a collection of talents who make for adept fielders as well as offensive contributors. A bounce-back season from Chris Iannetta and the location of a better everyday option than Barmes at second should provide them with an eight-deep lineup capable of scoring everywhere, home or road. Because of the

team's control of CarGo, Smith, and Dexter Fowler and its having already locked in Tulowitzki, the Rockies have a collection of affordable talents that creates the opportunity for them to investigate short-term options at the keystone or the hot corner. Whether or not they consequently elect to trade Brad Hawpe to add that upgrade at second or third base presents an interesting possibility for a team that isn't in a position where it has to make a move, but can instead deal from outfield depth as a matter of choice.

Yes, the purple shadow of more Rocktobers is with us. The fundamental keys—their rotation and defense—are already in place, at least for as long as they can count on the likes of Ubaldo Jimenez up front and Tulo at short. Jimenez is arguably already the best starting pitcher in franchise history, and the team's rotation situation might get better without significant revisions to the roster, because swapping a recovered Jeff Francis for Marquis should mean that the team is still in a position to count on a quality quintet. Sure, Hammel or De La Rosa might be hard to count on, given their relatively sparse track records for reliably good work, but a healthy Francis is a better bet to deliver on Marquis 2009-level quality in 2010 than is Marquis himself. In the wrestling match of the National League playoff picture, these are elements to win with, in Denver or anywhere else, and they make for a franchise that has finally outgrown the existential fascinations of its early years.

HITTERS

Nolan Arenado 3B Bats: R Throws: R Height: 6' 1" Weight: 205 Born: April 16, 1991 Age: 19

YEAR	TEAM	LVL	AGE	PA	R	2B	3B	HR	RBI	BB	SO	SB	CS	EqBRR	AVG	OBP	SLG	EqAVG	EqOBP	EqSLG	EqA	VORP	WARP	DEFENSE
2009	CAS	Rk	18	225	28	15	0	2	22	16	18	5	2	0.5	.300	.351	.404	.238	.276	.300	.202	-7.2	-1.9	49-3B -4
2010	COL	MLB	19	405	38	19	0	6	34	26	49	3	2	0.0	.267	.318	.366	.262	.313	.358	.229	-2.3	-0.7	90-3B -4

Breakout: 43% Improve: 72% Collapse: 6% Attrition: 0%   MLB: 0%   Comparables: Travis Fryman, Wilton Veras, Damian Rolls, Jerry Salzano

The Rockies' 2009 second-round pick made a solid debut in the Pioneer League, overcoming a slow start to hit for average and to display a good approach and doubles power as a teenager. A prep shortstop converted to third base, he has the tools to stay at the hot corner, and the organization loves his makeup and expects him to develop 25-30 home-run power. Stay tuned.

Garrett Atkins 3B/1B Bats: R Throws: R Height: 6' 3" Weight: 215 Born: December 12, 1979 Age: 30

YEAR	TEAM	LVL	AGE	PA	R	2B	3B	HR	RBI	BB	SO	SB	CS	EqBRR	AVG	OBP	SLG	EqAVG	EqOBP	EqSLG	EqA	VORP	WARP	DEFENSE	
2007	COL	MLB	27	684	83	35	1	25	111	67	96	3	1	-1.7	.301	.367	.486	.293	.360	.471	.286	34.4	1.9	146-3B -16	4-1B 1
2008	COL	MLB	28	664	86	32	3	21	99	40	100	1	1	-0.3	.286	.328	.452	.286	.325	.447	.265	16.5	1.2	89-3B 0	59-1B -6
2009	COL	MLB	29	399	37	12	1	9	48	41	58	0	0	-1.3	.226	.308	.342	.228	.308	.341	.230	-4.3	-0.3	65-3B 2	14-1B -1
2010	BAL	MLB	30	570	71	25	1	21	94	50	84	2	1	-0.5	.283	.348	.456	.275	.344	.437	.264	17.1	1.6	126-3B -3	

Breakout: 15% Improve: 49% Collapse: 5% Attrition: 4%   MLB: 99%   Comparables: Todd Zeile, Mike Lowell, Jim Fregosi, Joe Crede

Each year since his 2006 breakout, Atkins has seen his rate stats gradually erode, and in 2009, we witnessed the landslide. He saw fewer fastballs this year, he swung at four percent fewer pitches in the zone, his line-drive rate plummeted along with his BABIP, and fewer fly balls left the yard. While part of his decline may be random chance, there's some evidence to support the whispers that his swing is messed up. Combine all that with an indifferent glove and a career .252/.324/.411 line outside Colorado, and Atkins doesn't sport the look of an undervalued victim of chance poised for a comeback. He'll hold down an infield corner for the Orioles at least initially in 2010, but the end could be Fonzie Bichette–level ugly.

Clint Barmes　2B/UT

Bats: R　Throws: R　Height: 6' 0"　Weight: 210　Born: March 6, 1979　Age: 31

YEAR	TEAM	LVL	AGE	PA	R	2B	3B	HR	RBI	BB	SO	SB	CS	EqBRR	AVG	OBP	SLG	EqAVG	EqOBP	EqSLG	EqA	VORP	WARP	DEFENSE
2007	CSP	AAA	28	477	68	20	6	11	44	22	52	8	6	0.1	.299	.364	.451	.240	.297	.345	.225	-0.3	0.6	87-SS 7 5-CF -2
2007	COL	MLB	28	39	5	3	0	0	1	1	13	0	0	1.3	.216	.237	.297	.216	.237	.297	.175	-2.1	-0.2	4-SS 0 2-2B 0
2008	COL	MLB	29	417	47	25	6	11	44	17	69	13	4	2.3	.290	.322	.468	.289	.321	.462	.267	17.9	2.7	54-2B 1 32-SS 5
2009	COL	MLB	30	604	69	32	3	23	76	31	121	12	10	0.0	.245	.294	.440	.247	.293	.443	.248	11.3	3.0	129-2B 8 12-SS 5
2010	COL	MLB	31	506	58	26	6	12	52	30	84	8	6	0.7	.262	.317	.417	.253	.308	.399	.242	5.9	1.0	108-2B 3

Breakout: 9%　Improve: 33%　Collapse: 16%　Attrition: 13%　　MLB: 85%　　Comparables: Ron Coomer, Alex Gonzalez, Ronnie Belliard, Bret Boone

Like most players, Barmes can succeed in the right situation—the problem is, that situation is maddeningly specific. Having proven he can't hit right-handed pitching (.248/.288/.384 for his career) or on the road (.222/.262/.351), all that's left is torturing lefties at Coors. Given his ability to play shortstop, Barmes profiles best as a middle-infield reserve and pinch-lefty-masher, but the Rockies plan to sign him for two years and play him at the keystone every day. Do you know how hard it is to hit 23 homers at a premium position and still produce a VORP of only 11.3? That should give you a solid picture of the rest of his offensive game. Chicks may dig the long ball, and infield defense is a big part of the Rockies' master plan, but with Eric Young Jr. ready and willing to bring his table-setting speed game to "The Show," paying millions to watch Barmes knock a few out from the bottom of the order seems like a misallocation of resources.

Charles Blackmon　CF

Bats: L　Throws: L　Height: 6' 2"　Weight: 185　Born: July 1, 1986　Age: 23

YEAR	TEAM	LVL	AGE	PA	R	2B	3B	HR	RBI	BB	SO	SB	CS	EqBRR	AVG	OBP	SLG	EqAVG	EqOBP	EqSLG	EqA	VORP	WARP	DEFENSE
2008	TRI	A-	21	321	42	21	5	2	33	16	37	13	7	-1.7	.338	.390	.466	.296	.325	.411	.254	5.5	0.1	50-CF -5
2009	MOD	A+	22	616	87	34	7	7	69	39	83	30	13	3.6	.307	.370	.433	.275	.321	.371	.245	4.5	-1.2	109-CF -15
2010	COL	MLB	23	546	59	31	4	6	49	33	87	10	5	0.6	.275	.326	.385	.271	.321	.373	.238	4.3	-0.2	95-CF -6

Breakout: 14%　Improve: 44%　Collapse: 24%　Attrition: 7%　　MLB: 4%　　Comparables: Ricky Lemon, Stanley Younger, David Francia, Tommy Gregg

Call him "Black and Blue." A former pitcher who's still quite raw as a position player, Blackmon has been plunked 29 times in his short minor-league career, producing high OBPs despite a low walk rate. He's a fine athlete with the tools to stay in center, but at 23, the former Georgia Tech star remains a *masala* of skills—a little power, a little speed, a little Ron Hunt—that fall short of a satisfying dish. Right now, he looks like a fourth outfielder.

Dexter Fowler　CF

Bats: S　Throws: R　Height: 6' 4"　Weight: 175　Born: March 22, 1986　Age: 24

YEAR	TEAM	LVL	AGE	PA	R	2B	3B	HR	RBI	BB	SO	SB	CS	EqBRR	AVG	OBP	SLG	EqAVG	EqOBP	EqSLG	EqA	VORP	WARP	DEFENSE
2007	MOD	A+	21	299	43	7	5	2	23	44	64	20	11	0.4	.273	.397	.367	.246	.347	.320	.243	3.0	0.4	61-CF 0
2008	TUL	AA	22	505	92	31	9	9	64	65	89	20	8	4.6	.335	.431	.515	.291	.376	.450	.286	28.0	2.2	105-CF -10
2008	COL	MLB	22	27	3	0	0	0	0	0	5	0	1	-0.1	.154	.185	.154	.154	.185	.154	-.077	-3.2	-0.4	6-CF 0
2009	COL	MLB	23	518	73	29	10	4	34	67	116	27	10	7.3	.266	.363	.406	.269	.363	.412	.273	22.2	0.6	110-CF -15
2010	COL	MLB	24	482	68	26	8	7	42	61	106	17	8	2.4	.270	.368	.421	.260	.356	.393	.267	17.7	1.4	102-CF -5

Breakout: 16%　Improve: 54%　Collapse: 9%　Attrition: 12%　　MLB: 100%　　Comparables: Willie McGee, Gerald Young, Brian McRae, Jerome Nelson

Fowler managed to leap the yawning canyon between the Texas League and the NL with ease and without the benefit of a rocket-powered X-1 Skycycle. Instead, the young center fielder relied on good wheels and an advanced batting eye to get on base and work himself into the Rookie of the Year conversation. Defensive metrics show him playing a subpar center, but he has the speed and work ethic to eventually become an asset with the glove—and he'll need to be, since he doesn't have power enough for a corner. He'll steal bases, but won't get on base enough to be an elite table-setter, which makes him less than an All-Star but more than a useful cog.

Jason Giambi 1B
Bats: L Throws: R Height: 6' 3" Weight: 235 Born: January 8, 1971 Age: 39

YEAR	TEAM	LVL	AGE	PA	R	2B	3B	HR	RBI	BB	SO	SB	CS	EqBRR	AVG	OBP	SLG	EqAVG	EqOBP	EqSLG	EqA	VORP	WARP	DEFENSE
2007	NYA	MLB	36	303	31	8	0	14	39	40	66	1	0	-3.3	.236	.356	.433	.233	.354	.423	.274	7.5	0.8	14-1B -1
2008	NYA	MLB	37	565	68	19	1	32	96	76	111	2	1	-1.8	.247	.373	.502	.246	.373	.503	.299	30.7	2.4	101-1B -9
2009	OAK	MLB	38	328	39	13	0	11	40	50	72	0	0	0.0	.193	.332	.364	.198	.335	.369	.254	-2.3	-0.4	50-1B -1
2009	COL	MLB	38	31	4	1	0	2	11	7	8	0	0	-0.1	.292	.452	.583	.292	.452	.583	.343	3.0	0.4	4-1B 1
2010	COL	MLB	39	333	33	12	0	14	47	46	76	1	1	-0.9	.227	.356	.417	.225	.348	.414	.261	3.7	0.3	46-1B -1

Breakout: 4% Improve: 31% Collapse: 25% Attrition: 35% MLB: 96% Comparables: Fred McGriff, Rafael Palmeiro, Johnny Mize, Ken Griffey Jr.

As exciting as the thought of rekindling past glory can be, reunions usually disappoint, and Giambi's return to Oakland was like watching old classmates argue their way through an endless, drunken game of H-O-R-S-E. Brought in to help add thunder to a moribund A's attack, the former MVP suffered through an injury-plagued and ineffective season before earning his August release. Still able to draw walks and launch the occasional home run, Giambi no longer hits for average, hitting .248 from 2003 to 2008, and he finally sank below the Mendoza line last year. A few big hits during his late-season stint with the Rockies may stoke the interest of AL clubs looking to catch lightning in a bottle, but if Giambi wants to continue playing, his springs will soon be sponsored by the letters N, R, and I.

Hector Gomez SS
Bats: R Throws: R Height: 6' 2" Weight: 180 Born: March 5, 1988 Age: 22

YEAR	TEAM	LVL	AGE	PA	R	2B	3B	HR	RBI	BB	SO	SB	CS	EqBRR	AVG	OBP	SLG	EqAVG	EqOBP	EqSLG	EqA	VORP	WARP	DEFENSE
2007	ASH	A	19	576	89	34	8	11	61	29	120	20	10	-3.3	.266	.309	.421	.217	.252	.339	.204	-10.7	-1.2	121-SS 1
2009	MOD	A+	21	368	39	21	4	7	46	15	68	10	4	1.2	.275	.310	.423	.244	.269	.355	.219	-3.9	-1.8	66-SS -11
2010	COL	MLB	22	356	39	18	4	7	33	20	78	5	3	-0.4	.248	.295	.391	.239	.285	.365	.226	0.4	-0.2	72-SS -2

Breakout: 36% Improve: 59% Collapse: 16% Attrition: 10% MLB: 3% Comparables: Doug Bearden, Gus Polidor, Ronny Cedeño, Malvin Matos

After losing a year to Tommy John surgery, Gomez continues to have trouble staying on the field, so he's still more projection than production. He's a true shortstop with soft hands, a strong arm, and surprising pop, but like countless middle-infield prospects before him, he doesn't make enough contact or draw enough walks to inspire confidence or provide offensive value. If he can fix that, he may be more than a utility infielder, but time's a-wastin'.

Carlos Gonzalez OF
Bats: L Throws: L Height: 6' 1" Weight: 200 Born: October 17, 1985 Age: 24

YEAR	TEAM	LVL	AGE	PA	R	2B	3B	HR	RBI	BB	SO	SB	CS	EqBRR	AVG	OBP	SLG	EqAVG	EqOBP	EqSLG	EqA	VORP	WARP	DEFENSE
2007	MOB	AA	21	499	63	33	3	16	75	32	103	9	5	-0.4	.286	.330	.476	.267	.303	.439	.254	6.4	0.2	92-RF -4 22-CF -1
2007	TUC	AAA	21	48	9	5	0	1	11	6	6	1	0	-1.3	.310	.396	.500	.279	.354	.442	.279	2.3	0.2	11-CF -1
2008	SAC	AAA	22	189	23	9	1	4	28	16	35	1	1	-1.2	.283	.344	.416	.274	.328	.383	.248	2.1	0.0	31-CF -4 11-RF 2
2008	OAK	MLB	22	316	31	22	1	4	26	13	81	4	1	1.4	.242	.273	.361	.249	.280	.375	.226	-2.8	1.2	59-CF 9 18-RF 4
2009	CSP	AAA	23	223	43	12	7	10	59	22	32	6	3	-0.9	.339	.418	.630	.291	.367	.536	.298	16.3	1.1	46-CF -7
2009	COL	MLB	23	317	53	14	7	13	29	28	70	16	4	2.7	.284	.353	.525	.282	.347	.521	.293	20.1	2.9	35-CF 4 33-LF 2
2010	COL	MLB	24	510	67	28	6	16	70	41	109	11	4	0.0	.269	.331	.454	.264	.324	.445	.259	15.1	1.7	117-CF 0

Breakout: 17% Improve: 58% Collapse: 10% Attrition: 10% MLB: 83% Comparables: Kelly Johnson, Matt Joyce, Robin Jennings, Ralph Bryant

Very few things provide as much glee as a plan coming to fruition. Gonzalez came over as part of the Matt Holliday haul, and the toolsy outfielder finally started to deliver on his immense promise, providing typical fireworks in Colorado Springs before slugging his way onto the NL scene. A terrific fielder with enough arm for right and enough range for center, CarGo has always had light-tower power but now exhibits an improved approach, working deeper counts and upping his walk rate to league average. His bat translates well to ballparks closer to the earth's core, he hangs in well against lefties, and he has started to convert his speed into stolen bases. With Fowler set in center, Gonzalez should become an All-Star in right, teaming with Seth Smith to give the Rockies a highly productive outfield that costs peanuts—just the way Dan O'Dowd planned it.

Brad Hawpe — RF

Bats: L   Throws: L   Height: 6' 3"   Weight: 205   Born: June 22, 1979   Age: 31

YEAR	TEAM	LVL	AGE	PA	R	2B	3B	HR	RBI	BB	SO	SB	CS	EqBRR	AVG	OBP	SLG	EqAVG	EqOBP	EqSLG	EqA	VORP	WARP	DEFENSE
2007	COL	MLB	28	606	80	33	4	29	116	81	137	0	2	-4.3	.291	.387	.539	.281	.380	.517	.301	38.3	3.3	137-RF -7
2008	COL	MLB	29	569	69	24	3	25	85	76	134	2	2	-1.8	.283	.381	.498	.280	.376	.491	.294	31.3	0.3	131-RF -27
2009	COL	MLB	30	588	82	42	3	23	86	79	145	1	3	0.6	.285	.384	.519	.285	.380	.518	.301	38.4	2.7	135-RF -12
2010	COL	MLB	31	560	68	29	2	21	84	75	134	1	2	-0.9	.268	.371	.471	.264	.362	.461	.278	22.2	1.6	129-RF -7

Breakout: 7%   Improve: 33%   Collapse: 12%   Attrition: 6%   MLB: 99%   Comparables: Geoff Jenkins, Paul O'Neill, Jeromy Burnitz, Kirk Gibson

Timing is everything, and Hawpe picked the worst possible time for a slump—during a pennant race and when there are younger, cheaper options available to do your job. After he bopped his way to his first All-Star appearance, a .240/.370/.442 line in the second half caused Jim Tracy to lose confidence in his veteran, dropping him down in the order and reducing his playing time. Look at those numbers, though—if that's a massive dropoff (and it was), Hawpe is still a quality bat. Despite a strong arm, his defense is best described as "statuesque," he's about to turn 31, and he's due for a $2 million raise. While he should continue to draw walks and hit home runs for years to come, he won't be doing it with the Rockies for much longer.

Todd Helton — 1B

Bats: L   Throws: L   Height: 6' 2"   Weight: 210   Born: August 20, 1973   Age: 36

YEAR	TEAM	LVL	AGE	PA	R	2B	3B	HR	RBI	BB	SO	SB	CS	EqBRR	AVG	OBP	SLG	EqAVG	EqOBP	EqSLG	EqA	VORP	WARP	DEFENSE
2007	COL	MLB	33	682	86	42	2	17	91	116	74	0	1	-5.5	.320	.434	.494	.306	.424	.468	.313	45.3	5.3	148-1B 3
2008	COL	MLB	34	361	39	16	0	7	29	61	50	0	0	-3.5	.264	.391	.388	.260	.385	.373	.275	8.7	1.4	80-1B 3
2009	COL	MLB	35	645	79	38	3	15	86	89	73	0	1	-3.7	.325	.416	.489	.325	.411	.489	.311	36.5	4.3	144-1B 2
2010	COL	MLB	36	538	58	27	1	12	66	85	69	0	1	-2.1	.286	.402	.428	.281	.392	.421	.283	18.3	2.1	120-1B 1

Breakout: 9%   Improve: 28%   Collapse: 23%   Attrition: 30%   MLB: 100%   Comparables: Wally Joyner, Mark Grace, George Brett, Fred McGriff

Whew. After back problems bit his 2008 season in half and sapped much of his already-waning power, Colorado's on-base machine stayed in the lineup and put up numbers that are spot-on matches for 2007. Not coincidentally, the Rockies were again playing baseball in mid-October. While a .306 EqA is mundane for a first baseman, it's still plenty nice for a hitter in his decline phase. Colorado still owes him $35-plus million over two years, money beyond his likely value, but thanks to Helton's renaissance, not the franchise-crippling obligation some feared it might become.

Chris Iannetta — C

Bats: R   Throws: R   Height: 6' 0"   Weight: 225   Born: April 8, 1983   Age: 27

YEAR	TEAM	LVL	AGE	PA	R	2B	3B	HR	RBI	BB	SO	SB	CS	EqBRR	AVG	OBP	SLG	EqAVG	EqOBP	EqSLG	EqA	VORP	WARP	DEFENSE
2007	CSP	AAA	24	63	8	3	0	1	7	7	6	0	0	-0.4	.296	.397	.407	.255	.349	.345	.250	2.0	0.2	14-C 0
2007	COL	MLB	24	234	22	8	3	4	27	29	58	0	0	-1.4	.218	.330	.350	.214	.329	.342	.240	6.2	0.7	55-C 0
2008	COL	MLB	25	407	50	22	2	18	65	56	92	0	0	-0.6	.264	.390	.505	.263	.387	.497	.301	35.5	4.0	94-C 1
2009	COL	MLB	26	350	41	15	2	16	52	43	75	0	1	-0.5	.228	.344	.460	.228	.340	.467	.274	20.4	2.7	86-C 2
2010	COL	MLB	27	422	51	19	4	16	66	53	88	0	1	-0.6	.251	.367	.462	.242	.357	.443	.275	22.5	2.5	104-C 0

Breakout: 20%   Improve: 46%   Collapse: 12%   Attrition: 3%   MLB: 100%   Comparables: Mike Napoli, Bill Freehan, Bobby Estalella, John Buck

Front offices and fans continue to slowly accept that batting average is not a particularly compelling statistic, but there is a limit, and when Rockies broadcasts continued to flash ".222" under Iannetta's name, he gradually lost playing time to Yorvit Torrealba's more appealing digits. Regardless, Iannetta's power and patience made him a valuable offensive contributor even in a down year, with an EqA that not only beat Torrealba's but was fifth in the NL among the backstop set. A 60-point drop in BABIP was part luck and part approach; Iannetta's fly-ball rate spiked, hinting at a player who spent too much time swinging for the fences. With Iannetta reinstated to the starting lineup and entering his age-27 season, look for him to reward the team's confidence in him with a season more like his 2008 breakout.

Michael McKenry   C   Bats: R   Throws: R   Height: 5' 10"   Weight: 200   Born: March 4, 1985   Age: 25

YEAR	TEAM	LVL	AGE	PA	R	2B	3B	HR	RBI	BB	SO	SB	CS	EqBRR	AVG	OBP	SLG	EqAVG	EqOBP	EqSLG	EqA	VORP	WARP	DEFENSE		
2007	ASH	A	22	485	79	35	1	22	90	66	84	8	9	-0.4	.287	.392	.539	.228	.315	.397	.246	11.8	1.8	84-C	3	
2008	MOD	A+	23	472	59	28	1	18	75	55	101	2	4	-2.5	.257	.360	.468	.226	.313	.383	.244	10.6	1.9	95-C	5	
2009	TUL	AA	24	417	52	25	1	12	50	54	69	2	2	-4.1	.279	.376	.455	.245	.325	.396	.252	14.5	1.6	100-C	-1	
2010	COL	MLB	25	391	41	18	1	10	43	42	92	2	2	-1.0	.233	.321	.380	.228	.315	.368	.235	5.5	0.7	81-C	1	

Breakout: 8%   Improve: 32%   Collapse: 27%   Attrition: 13%   MLB: 4%   Comparables: Mike Wolff, Kevin Cash, Giuseppe Chiaramonte, Lloyd McClendon

McKenry is an outstanding defensive catcher whose future depends on the development of his bat, and last year was a nice step forward. Always a patient hitter with decent power, McKenry significantly lowered his strikeout rate and saw a commensurate increase in batting average, making his profile more and more like that of a possible MLB starter. At the very least, his glove should guarantee some sort of a career.

Omar Quintanilla   MI   Bats: L   Throws: R   Height: 5' 9"   Weight: 190   Born: October 24, 1981   Age: 28

YEAR	TEAM	LVL	AGE	PA	R	2B	3B	HR	RBI	BB	SO	SB	CS	EqBRR	AVG	OBP	SLG	EqAVG	EqOBP	EqSLG	EqA	VORP	WARP	DEFENSE				
2007	CSP	AAA	25	393	54	30	4	3	43	31	65	3	1	2.7	.319	.380	.454	.263	.321	.364	.243	4.5	0.4	46-SS	0	26-2B	-1	
2007	COL	MLB	25	75	6	4	0	0	5	5	15	0	0	0.7	.229	.280	.286	.229	.280	.286	.195	-2.1	-0.6	18-2B	-3			
2008	CSP	AAA	26	91	18	4	0	1	8	16	11	3	0	0.0	.329	.451	.425	.263	.374	.342	.268	4.0	0.0	14-SS	-3	5-2B	-1	
2008	COL	MLB	26	234	28	17	0	2	15	15	46	0	0	4.3	.238	.288	.348	.235	.284	.333	.220	-1.3	-0.4	32-SS	0	24-2B	-3	
2009	COL	MLB	27	69	7	2	0	0	2	8	27	0	0	-0.4	.172	.273	.207	.169	.269	.203	.178	-3.4	-0.2	9-2B	0	5-SS	0	
2010	COL	MLB	28	323	36	17	1	3	24	28	69	2	1	1.4	.245	.316	.342	.240	.309	.331	.223	-2.1	-0.6	69-2B	-3			

Breakout: 17%   Improve: 43%   Collapse: 25%   Attrition: 11%   MLB: 40%   Comparables: Mike Rouse, Jim Steels, Bobby Hill, Kevin Koslofski

The former Longhorn star spent the entire season as Colorado's primary middle-infield reserve and managed only 69 plate appearances, which tells you all you need to know about his bat (you would never guess that Omar is a career .312/.374/.450 minor-league hitter). With Barmes on hand to slide over to short when necessary, and Young set to strap on the club's utility belt, Quintanilla became a redundancy. He still has a major-league glove and could wind up at the end of somebody's bench.

Seth Smith   LF   Bats: L   Throws: L   Height: 6' 3"   Weight: 215   Born: September 30, 1982   Age: 27

YEAR	TEAM	LVL	AGE	PA	R	2B	3B	HR	RBI	BB	SO	SB	CS	EqBRR	AVG	OBP	SLG	EqAVG	EqOBP	EqSLG	EqA	VORP	WARP	DEFENSE				
2007	CSP	AAA	24	505	68	32	6	17	82	39	73	7	3	-0.6	.317	.381	.528	.263	.323	.425	.259	8.7	-0.6	96-RF	-10	21-CF	-4	
2007	COL	MLB	24	8	4	0	1	0	0	0	1	0	0	0.1	.625	.625	.875	.625	.625	.875	.492	2.2	0.2					
2008	CSP	AAA	25	303	55	16	2	10	53	46	46	11	0	4.2	.323	.426	.524	.263	.360	.412	.279	11.5	1.1	37-LF	0	26-RF	-2	
2008	COL	MLB	25	123	13	7	0	4	15	15	23	1	0	-1.4	.259	.350	.435	.259	.350	.417	.270	3.7	0.4	10-RF	-2	5-CF	1	
2009	COL	MLB	26	387	61	20	4	15	55	46	67	4	1	0.2	.293	.378	.510	.292	.373	.509	.299	22.7	3.3	71-LF	6			
2010	COL	MLB	27	376	45	19	2	11	50	41	67	5	2	0.4	.268	.354	.437	.264	.347	.430	.264	9.4	1.3	76-LF	2			

Breakout: 7%   Improve: 44%   Collapse: 14%   Attrition: 12%   MLB: 69%   Comparables: David Murphy, Gabe Gross, Brad Hawpe, Rusty Greer

The Rockies' player development staff has shown a recent knack for not just building outfielders, but also shipping them to Coors fully assembled. Smith is the latest model to come off the line, built on the Brad Hawpe chassis but with an upgraded glove and a less pronounced platoon split. The decision to play Smith in left most days played a large role in the Rockies' midseason turnaround, and while he's not exactly young, he is exactly cheap—meaning it's time to start editing those "We'll Miss You, Brad" video compilations. Smith is not a star, but should be a valuable contributor for a few years before being replaced by a younger, cheaper version of himself.

Ryan Spilborghs   LF   Bats: R   Throws: R   Height: 6' 1"   Weight: 190   Born: September 5, 1979   Age: 30

YEAR	TEAM	LVL	AGE	PA	R	2B	3B	HR	RBI	BB	SO	SB	CS	EqBRR	AVG	OBP	SLG	EqAVG	EqOBP	EqSLG	EqA	VORP	WARP	DEFENSE			
2007	CSP	AAA	27	145	25	7	1	5	17	18	19	4	3	0.2	.323	.410	.516	.260	.345	.394	.259	3.0	-0.3	19-LF	-4	9-CF	-2
2007	COL	MLB	27	300	40	14	1	11	51	28	45	4	1	-0.3	.299	.363	.485	.294	.359	.473	.286	16.0	2.0	36-CF	2	14-RF	0
2008	COL	MLB	28	275	38	14	2	6	36	38	41	7	4	-2.3	.313	.407	.468	.313	.404	.464	.300	16.8	0.5	19-LF	-4	16-RF	-3
2009	COL	MLB	29	393	55	24	3	8	48	34	79	9	5	1.0	.241	.310	.395	.243	.309	.401	.245	1.6	-0.5	47-LF	2	22-RF	-4
2010	COL	MLB	30	400	56	20	3	11	56	45	71	7	5	-0.3	.273	.358	.439	.266	.351	.423	.265	10.3	0.9	60-LF	-2		

Breakout: 12%   Improve: 43%   Collapse: 15%   Attrition: 8%   MLB: 96%   Comparables: Cleon Jones, Hank Bauer, Dan Gladden, Steve Henderson

The veteran fourth outfielder set career highs in games and plate appearances, and not surprisingly, his production suffered and he struggled to fulfill his prime directive: punish lefties. Spilborghs provides solid defense in the corners, won't embarrass himself in center, and can steal the odd base. In a crowded outfield picture stuffed with younger, more exciting talents, Spilborghs will never be a starter, but he can still play a useful role.

Ian Stewart   3B   Bats: L   Throws: R   Height: 6' 3"   Weight: 205   Born: April 5, 1985   Age: 25

YEAR	TEAM	LVL	AGE	PA	R	2B	3B	HR	RBI	BB	SO	SB	CS	EqBRR	AVG	OBP	SLG	EqAVG	EqOBP	EqSLG	EqA	VORP	WARP	DEFENSE			
2007	CSP	AAA	22	474	72	23	2	15	65	49	92	11	2	3.5	.304	.379	.478	.252	.325	.388	.253	6.5	0.1	105-3B	-6		
2007	COL	MLB	22	46	3	4	0	1	9	1	17	0	0	0.0	.209	.261	.372	.209	.261	.349	.213	-1.9	0.3	5-3B	4		
2008	CSP	AAA	23	298	65	15	6	19	57	34	66	7	2	0.8	.280	.372	.607	.229	.313	.469	.266	9.1	0.6	62-3B	-4		
2008	COL	MLB	23	304	33	18	2	10	41	30	94	1	1	-0.9	.259	.349	.455	.256	.343	.447	.271	11.2	1.6	60-3B	2	10-2B	1
2009	COL	MLB	24	491	74	19	3	25	70	56	138	7	4	1.1	.228	.322	.464	.228	.318	.461	.266	16.9	1.7	94-3B	6	17-2B	-5
2010	COL	MLB	25	482	63	22	2	18	64	52	123	6	3	0.7	.239	.329	.427	.235	.321	.420	.251	7.9	0.9	108-3B	0		

Breakout: 7%   Improve: 43%   Collapse: 13%   Attrition: 8%   MLB: 95%   Comparables: Mike Pagliarulo, Scott Moore, Scott Cooper, Keith Hughes

Stewart's ascension to the starting lineup had less to do with any improvement on his part than with Garrett Atkins' case study in self-immolation, but there it is—he's the Rockies' third baseman now. There are benefits, of course: Stewart is younger, is left-handed, and has more raw power and a better glove than Atkins, plus he's cheaper. And by giving him an everyday job, the Rockies can stop their mad experiments with him at second and in the outfield. Ideally, Stewart would have made his bones by, say, making more contact, solving left-handed pitching, or getting on base at an acceptable level—the sort of things that would make him a developing star, rather than an amorphous nebula of persisting potentiality.

Yorvit Torrealba   C   Bats: R   Throws: R   Height: 5' 11"   Weight: 200   Born: July 19, 1978   Age: 31

YEAR	TEAM	LVL	AGE	PA	R	2B	3B	HR	RBI	BB	SO	SB	CS	EqBRR	AVG	OBP	SLG	EqAVG	EqOBP	EqSLG	EqA	VORP	WARP	DEFENSE	
2007	COL	MLB	28	443	47	22	1	8	47	34	73	2	1	0.4	.255	.323	.376	.252	.321	.365	.242	12.7	2.5	104-C	7
2008	COL	MLB	29	261	19	17	0	6	31	12	44	0	4	-4.1	.246	.293	.394	.245	.291	.384	.232	3.7	0.2	65-C	-2
2009	COL	MLB	30	242	27	11	1	2	31	21	42	1	1	0.7	.291	.351	.380	.290	.346	.379	.257	10.0	0.8	61-C	-3
2010	COL	MLB	31	303	30	15	1	6	37	25	51	1	2	-0.5	.264	.333	.394	.259	.328	.376	.243	6.4	0.7	75-C	0

Breakout: 15%   Improve: 41%   Collapse: 24%   Attrition: 9%   MLB: 95%   Comparables: Terry Steinbach, Jim Essian, Jim Sundberg, Odell Hale

The veteran reserve backstop endured a roller-coaster season that included the June kidnapping and subsequent safe release of his 11-year-old son back home in Venezuela. After taking a month off to get over the trauma, Torrealba posted a .322/.373/.392 second-half line and took over for a struggling Chris Iannetta down the stretch and in the playoffs. The offensive value of this solid defensive catcher with marginal power depends on the vagaries of safeties dropping in. Last season's career high .291 batting average was the result of an unrepeatable .355 BABIP; thus the Rockies wisely bought out his option, knowing that Iannetta is the starter, Miguel Olivo's a better alternative, and that minor-league options Michael McKenry and Wilin Rosario may soon be ready.

Troy Tulowitzki | SS | Bats: R | Throws: R | Height: 6' 3" | Weight: 205 | Born: October 10, 1984 | Age: 25

YEAR	TEAM	LVL	AGE	PA	R	2B	3B	HR	RBI	BB	SO	SB	CS	EqBRR	AVG	OBP	SLG	EqAVG	EqOBP	EqSLG	EqA	VORP	WARP	DEFENSE	
2007	COL	MLB	22	682	104	33	5	24	99	57	130	7	6	0.5	.291	.359	.479	.286	.356	.468	.278	39.5	8.9	152-SS	37
2008	COL	MLB	23	421	48	24	2	8	46	38	56	1	6	-1.1	.263	.332	.401	.262	.329	.397	.248	11.7	1.8	97-SS	4
2009	COL	MLB	24	628	101	25	9	32	92	73	112	20	11	0.8	.297	.377	.552	.298	.374	.554	.305	57.4	6.6	146-SS	2
2010	COL	MLB	25	613	93	31	6	26	96	66	97	8	7	0.2	.295	.377	.516	.288	.370	.498	.288	39.9	5.2	140-SS	8

Breakout: 19% Improve: 73% Collapse: 1% Attrition: 2% MLB: 100% Comparables: Derek Jeter, Cal Ripken, Jim Fregosi, Chris Speier

It's easy to cherry-pick seasonal turning points, but on D-day, Tulowitzki's batting line sat at .216/.306/.377. Afterward, he hit a downright Pujolsian .332/.410/.629, and not coincidentally the Rockies went 70-38 the rest of the way. That blur you saw was a young star taking his game to the next level. Tulo set career highs in each major rate stat, drawing more walks and displaying easy power that's no high-altitude mirage. In the field, he has good range and a cannon arm, and he even managed to steal 20 bases, though he'll need to improve his success rate. Only 25 and under team control at a bargain salary through 2014 (including a team option), he's the heart of a talented young core that will keep the Rockies competitive for years to come.

Tim Wheeler | CF | Bats: L | Throws: R | Height: 6' 4" | Weight: 205 | Born: January 21, 1988 | Age: 22

YEAR	TEAM	LVL	AGE	PA	R	2B	3B	HR	RBI	BB	SO	SB	CS	EqBRR	AVG	OBP	SLG	EqAVG	EqOBP	EqSLG	EqA	VORP	WARP	DEFENSE	
2009	TRI	A-	21	309	44	13	3	5	35	29	60	10	4	-1.8	.256	.332	.381	.207	.260	.295	.194	-11.2	-1.6	61-CF	2
2010	COL	MLB	22	402	42	19	2	6	33	34	101	5	3	-1.2	.231	.298	.344	.227	.291	.338	.215	-5.6	-0.5	80-CF	1

Breakout: 50% Improve: 76% Collapse: 9% Attrition: 6% MLB: 0% Comparables: J.T. Hall, Jason Wuerch, John Vindivich, Mark Steffens

Wheeler didn't exactly light it up in his pro debut the way you'd hope a supplemental first-rounder would. A big, athletic kid who just plain looks like a ballplayer, Wheeler has solid tools but no breathtaking ones. The organization expects him to stay in center, but if he doesn't, he might not have the arm for right, and he'll have to develop a lot more power than he's shown to start in a corner. It's early, of course, but there are already a few obstacles to be negotiated.

Eric Young Jr. | 2B/CF | Bats: S | Throws: R | Height: 5' 10" | Weight: 180 | Born: May 25, 1985 | Age: 25

YEAR	TEAM	LVL	AGE	PA	R	2B	3B	HR	RBI	BB	SO	SB	CS	EqBRR	AVG	OBP	SLG	EqAVG	EqOBP	EqSLG	EqA	VORP	WARP	DEFENSE			
2007	MOD	A+	22	613	113	29	11	8	63	46	105	73	18	3.5	.291	.359	.430	.269	.322	.379	.252	14.1	1.5	126-2B	-2		
2008	TUL	AA	23	476	74	24	4	3	33	61	77	46	16	2.6	.290	.391	.392	.260	.347	.351	.254	10.8	1.4	92-2B	4	4-CF	-3
2009	CSP	AAA	24	552	118	21	10	7	43	56	79	58	14	10.5	.299	.387	.430	.256	.339	.370	.257	14.7	3.7	105-2B	14	10-CF	2
2009	COL	MLB	24	61	7	1	0	1	1	4	12	4	4	0.1	.246	.295	.316	.246	.295	.316	.211	-2.5	-0.5	5-2B	0	4-CF	-2
2010	COL	MLB	25	551	78	26	7	7	38	50	102	30	12	2.8	.264	.339	.385	.256	.330	.364	.248	9.9	1.4	115-2B	3		

Breakout: 9% Improve: 34% Collapse: 8% Attrition: 4% MLB: 22% Comparables: Henry Mateo, Chone Figgins, Quilvio Veras, Keith Miller

Eric Young Jr. is a slap-happy speedster who hits for average, draws walks, steals bases by the bushel, and plays subpar defense at second and in the outfield—in short, he's a carbon copy of his father, and Clint Barmes' reverse-doppelgänger. Young wintered in the Dominican working on his positional flexibility and is slated to break camp as a utilityman. A switch-hitter with somewhat better numbers from the left side, he makes for an interesting platoon partner at the keystone and, if he isn't a disaster in the field, could wind up taking over there sooner than you might expect.

PITCHERS

Joe Beimel

Bats: L Throws: L Height: 6' 3" Weight: 215 Born: April 19, 1977 Age: 33

YEAR	TEAM	LVL	AGE	W	L	SV	G	GS	IP	H	HR	BB	SO	GB%	BABIP	STUFF	WHIP	ERA	SIERA	DERA	EqH9	EqHR9	EqBB9	EqSO9	VORP	SN/WX
2007	LAN	MLB	30	4	2	1	83	0	67^1	63	1	24	39	55%	.287	2	1.29	3.88	4.74	3.73	8.1	0.1	2.8	4.7	13.0	2.26
2008	LAN	MLB	31	5	1	0	71	0	49	50	0	21	32	48%	.316	-3	1.45	2.02	4.80	2.27	9.4	0.2	3.4	4.9	17.1	1.35
2009	WAS	MLB	32	1	5	1	45	0	39^2	38	3	15	24	37%	.271	-9	1.34	3.40	5.06	3.65	8.2	0.7	2.9	4.4	8.4	-0.06
2009	COL	MLB	32	0	1	0	26	0	15^2	19	2	4	11	40%	.333	-5	1.47	4.02	4.29	4.02	10.3	1.1	1.7	5.7	2.6	0.15
2010	COL	MLB	33	2	4	0	52	0	51^1	55	5	21	29	43%	.307	-10	1.50	4.72	5.15	4.82	9.3	0.9	3.4	4.7	3.9	0.68

Breakout: 22% Improve: 42% Collapse: 26% Attrition: 15%   MLB: 83%   Comparables: Scott Radinsky, Scott Eyre, Aaron Fultz, Steve Kline

Looking for a new start on the East Coast, Beimel became a different pitcher after signing a one-year deal with the Nationals—and most of the changes weren't for the better. In his Dodger years, the veteran lefty had relied heavily on his high-80s sinker to produce high ground-ball rates and keep the ball in the park, but last year, he threw 17 percent fewer sinkers, replacing them with curves and changeups. Consequently his ground-ball rate plummeted, his homer rate spiked, and he was less effective. Used as a LOOGY after getting traded to the Rockies, Beimel had best remember his core competency if he wants to remain an important cog in a big-league pen.

Matt Belisle

Bats: R Throws: R Height: 6' 3" Weight: 230 Born: June 6, 1980 Age: 30

YEAR	TEAM	LVL	AGE	W	L	SV	G	GS	IP	H	HR	BB	SO	GB%	BABIP	STUFF	WHIP	ERA	SIERA	DERA	EqH9	EqHR9	EqBB9	EqSO9	VORP	SN/WX
2007	CIN	MLB	27	8	9	0	30	30	177^2	212	26	43	125	48%	.326	7	1.44	5.32	4.18	4.93	9.8	1.1	1.9	5.8	11.3	1.81
2008	LOU	AAA	28	5	1	4	26	1	38	43	1	11	27	69%	.331	-14	1.42	4.26	3.97	6.03	10.6	0.5	2.7	4.6	-2.2	0.37
2008	CIN	MLB	28	1	4	0	6	6	29^2	47	4	6	14	65%	.364	-13	1.79	7.28	4.69	7.40	12.5	1.2	1.5	3.5	-6.6	-0.48
2009	CSP	AAA	29	1	1	9	33	4	58^1	58	2	15	47	62%	.324	8	1.25	3.09	3.62	3.17	8.9	0.5	2.4	6.3	14.3	1.43
2009	COL	MLB	29	3	1	0	24	0	31	35	6	5	22	48%	.293	-6	1.29	5.52	3.94	5.68	9.4	1.4	1.1	5.4	-0.6	0.38
2010	COL	MLB	30	4	6	3	34	13	91^2	102	11	30	59	63%	.316	-1	1.45	4.63	4.33	4.71	9.6	1.1	2.7	5.5	8.1	0.99

Breakout: 20% Improve: 62% Collapse: 10% Attrition: 20%   MLB: 72%   Comparables: Mike Morgan, Mike Thurman, Tim Leary, Storm Davis

You could say Belisle is nothing special, a Quad-A pitcher with mediocre stuff, but of course he's one of only several hundred people on earth talented enough to pitch intermittently in the major leagues. So there's that. The Rockies DFA'd him twice during his nondescript Coors debut, so it was a bit of a surprise when they patted him on the head, gave him a small raise, and brought him back for 2010.

Rafael Betancourt

Bats: R Throws: R Height: 6' 2" Weight: 200 Born: April 29, 1975 Age: 35

YEAR	TEAM	LVL	AGE	W	L	SV	G	GS	IP	H	HR	BB	SO	GB%	BABIP	STUFF	WHIP	ERA	SIERA	DERA	EqH9	EqHR9	EqBB9	EqSO9	VORP	SN/WX
2007	CLE	MLB	32	5	1	3	68	0	79^1	51	4	9	80	27%	.240	39	0.76	1.47	2.42	1.56	5.6	0.5	0.9	8.3	34.0	6.96
2008	CLE	MLB	33	3	4	4	69	0	71	76	11	25	64	33%	.311	-5	1.42	5.07	3.97	4.98	9.2	1.4	2.8	7.3	4.1	0.73
2009	CLE	MLB	34	1	2	1	29	0	30^2	25	3	15	32	33%	.278	8	1.30	3.52	3.78	4.11	7.0	0.9	3.8	8.2	4.7	0.84
2009	COL	MLB	34	3	1	1	32	0	25^1	17	1	5	29	31%	.254	26	0.87	1.78	2.31	1.75	6.0	0.4	1.4	8.8	10.7	1.00
2010	COL	MLB	35	4	3	1	62	0	61	55	6	19	52	30%	.290	9	1.22	3.54	3.97	3.63	7.8	0.9	2.6	7.3	12.7	1.82

Breakout: 11% Improve: 36% Collapse: 31% Attrition: 15%   MLB: 91%   Comparables: Jeff Reardon, Akinori Otsuka, Eric Plunk, Lindy McDaniel

After a subpar 2008, the usually reliable Betancourt rediscovered his mojo and worked his way back up the bullpen pecking order to become a primary set-up man, first with the Tribe and then in Colorado after a midseason trade. The Rockies valued his good work in stabilizing their injury-depleted pen but not enough to pick up his $5 million option. They did, however, offer arbitration, which Betancourt accepted. The main risk was not in offering Betancourt a ticket to an automatic range, but that he is an extreme fly-ball pitcher who was undone in his one bad season by a high home-run rate—not exactly a good fit for thin air.

Rex Brothers

Bats: L   Throws: L   Height: 6' 0"   Weight: 205   Born: December 18, 1987   Age: 22

YEAR	TEAM	LVL	AGE	W	L	SV	G	GS	IP	H	HR	BB	SO	GB%	BABIP	STUFF	WHIP	ERA	SIERA	DERA	EqH9	EqHR9	EqBB9	EqSO9	VORP	SN/WX
2009	ASH	A	21	0	0	0	9	0	10^2	6	1	3	10	63%	.200	8	0.84	3.37	3.03	4.66	6.5	1.9	3.7	4.7	0.9	-0.22
2009	TRI	A-	21	2	0	0	8	0	10^2	10	0	5	18	49%	.476	8	1.41	3.37	1.75	5.40	14.0	1.1	6.5	10.8	0.1	0.00
2010	COL	MLB	22	1	4	0	41	0	44^1	57	7	28	30	56%	.345	-9	1.91	6.53	5.10	6.50	10.9	1.4	5.1	5.8	-4.9	0.70

Breakout: 15% Improve: 39% Collapse: 28% Attrition: 0%   MLB: 1%   Comparables: Paul Stabile, Arthur Hammond, Blake Allen, Jeff Twitty

A sandwich pick in the 2009 draft, Brothers is a hard-throwing lefty with mid-90s heat and a sharp-breaking power slider. The Rockies moved him straight to the pen, where his closer-level stuff was overpowering in his short-season debut. He'll probably start the year as Modesto's closer, and if he keeps his walk rates low, he'll move quickly.

Taylor Buchholz

Bats: R   Throws: R   Height: 6' 4"   Weight: 220   Born: October 13, 1981   Age: 28

YEAR	TEAM	LVL	AGE	W	L	SV	G	GS	IP	H	HR	BB	SO	GB%	BABIP	STUFF	WHIP	ERA	SIERA	DERA	EqH9	EqHR9	EqBB9	EqSO9	VORP	SN/WX
2007	COL	MLB	25	6	5	0	41	8	93^2	105	8	20	61	52%	.318	5	1.33	4.23	4.22	4.06	9.9	0.6	1.8	5.6	14.7	1.01
2008	COL	MLB	26	6	6	1	63	0	66^1	45	5	18	56	42%	.220	20	0.95	2.17	3.61	2.83	5.4	0.5	2.1	6.6	20.3	2.49
2010	COL	MLB	28	3	4	0	38	3	60^2	64	7	21	36	45%	.301	-4	1.40	4.42	4.76	4.50	9.2	1.0	2.7	5.0	6.7	0.88

Breakout: 12% Improve: 36% Collapse: 22% Attrition: 12%   MLB: 81%   Comparables: Bob Howry, Todd Coffey, Jay Powell, Bob James

A former starter who has found great success in the pen, Buchholz suffered a sore elbow in spring training and spent several months on the much-prescribed and occasionally successful "strengthening program" before finally undergoing Tommy John surgery in June. He's scheduled for a midseason return to the mound; expect his command, and thus his effectiveness, to return at some nonspecific point after that, most likely 2011.

Jhoulys Chacin

Bats: R   Throws: R   Height: 6' 1"   Weight: 168   Born: January 7, 1988   Age: 22

YEAR	TEAM	LVL	AGE	W	L	SV	G	GS	IP	H	HR	BB	SO	GB%	BABIP	STUFF	WHIP	ERA	SIERA	DERA	EqH9	EqHR9	EqBB9	EqSO9	VORP	SN/WX
2007	CAS	Rk	19	6	5	0	16	16	92	85	5	26	77	62%	.296	15	1.21	3.13	3.44	5.13	9.1	1.5	3.6	4.2	3.6	-0.27
2008	ASH	A	20	10	1	0	16	16	111^1	82	3	30	98	66%	.260	35	1.01	1.86	3.21	3.52	8.1	1.1	3.4	5.0	22.5	1.14
2008	MOD	A+	20	8	2	0	12	12	66^1	61	3	12	62	67%	.317	31	1.10	2.31	2.89	3.54	10.0	1.2	2.4	5.7	13.0	1.25
2009	TUL	AA	21	8	6	0	18	18	103^1	87	10	35	86	62%	.263	16	1.18	3.14	3.74	4.58	8.7	1.6	3.2	6.2	10.1	1.08
2009	CSP	AAA	21	1	2	0	4	4	14^1	11	2	13	11	78%	.237	9	1.67	3.77	4.56	4.61	6.6	1.3	7.9	5.9	1.4	0.36
2009	COL	MLB	21	0	1	0	9	1	11	6	1	11	13	55%	.217	11	1.55	4.91	4.36	4.91	4.9	0.8	7.4	9.0	0.7	0.02
2010	COL	MLB	22	6	9	0	31	26	140	145	18	64	91	58%	.296	15	1.49	4.89	4.72	4.97	8.9	1.1	3.7	5.5	8.2	3.23

Breakout: 11% Improve: 52% Collapse: 14% Attrition: 9%   MLB: 34%   Comparables: Terry Taylor, Urbano Lugo, Tom Kramer, Leonard Damian

The club's top pitching prospect, Chacin made the jump to Double-A at the tender age of 21, and his five-pitch arsenal baffled enough hitters to earn him an 11-inning look-see in the big club's pen. There his command deserted him, and while the organization will forgive some adrenaline-rush wildness, his increased walk rate and fewer strikeouts in his high-minors debut are a little more troubling. Still, Chacin's sinking fastball brings that ground-pounding goodness the Rockies adore, and he'll be given every opportunity to straighten things out in the PCL before fulfilling his midrotation destiny.

Jose Contreras

Bats: R   Throws: R   Height: 6' 4"   Weight: 255   Born: December 6, 1971   Age: 38

YEAR	TEAM	LVL	AGE	W	L	SV	G	GS	IP	H	HR	BB	SO	GB%	BABIP	STUFF	WHIP	ERA	SIERA	DERA	EqH9	EqHR9	EqBB9	EqSO9	VORP	SN/WX
2007	CHA	MLB	35	10	17	0	32	30	189	232	21	62	113	49%	.326	1	1.56	5.57	4.80	5.50	10.2	0.8	2.6	4.9	-0.1	1.16
2008	CHA	MLB	36	7	6	0	20	20	121	130	12	35	70	58%	.294	12	1.36	4.54	4.59	4.23	9.0	0.7	2.3	4.8	17.3	2.71
2009	CHR	AAA	37	3	1	0	5	5	33^1	19	2	16	27	58%	.195	13	1.05	2.70	4.17	3.76	5.3	0.8	4.5	5.8	6.3	0.61
2009	CHA	MLB	37	5	13	0	21	21	114^2	121	11	45	89	56%	.304	13	1.45	5.42	4.29	5.71	9.0	0.6	3.0	6.1	-2.8	0.89
2009	COL	MLB	37	1	0	0	7	2	17	20	2	8	17	52%	.367	15	1.65	1.59	3.79	1.62	10.3	1.1	3.8	8.1	7.2	0.97
2010	COL	MLB	38	6	9	0	29	26	143	163	17	56	85	54%	.317	-3	1.53	5.00	4.82	5.12	9.9	1.0	3.2	5.1	6.1	1.25

Breakout: 4% Improve: 36% Collapse: 18% Attrition: 22%   MLB: 93%   Comparables: Steve Renko, Masato Yoshii, Tom Candiotti, Mike Morgan

The former Cuban exile, Evil Empire washout, and World Series hero had an eventful season, stumbling badly out of the gate in April, dominating in June, and then pitching his way out of the White Sox rotation with a series of gruesome outings in August. Picked up by the Rockies for a song, Contreras seemingly rediscovered his fastball and his confidence while tossing 17 effective innings for Colorado, mostly out of the pen. Now he's a free agent, and the Rockies think they've fixed him and are looking to re-sign him to a bargain contract and use him as a power arm in the pen. Contreras' stuff has never left him, but his maddening inconsistency and tendency to allow big innings make him a bad bet to provide much help.

Aaron Cook

Bats: R   Throws: R   Height: 6' 3"   Weight: 215   Born: February 8, 1979   Age: 31

YEAR	TEAM	LVL	AGE	W	L	SV	G	GS	IP	H	HR	BB	SO	GB%	BABIP	STUFF	WHIP	ERA	SIERA	DERA	EqH9	EqHR9	EqBB9	EqSO9	VORP	SN/WX
2007	COL	MLB	28	8	7	0	25	25	166	178	15	44	61	68%	.285	5	1.34	4.12	4.86	4.29	9.5	0.6	2.2	3.2	21.8	2.95
2008	COL	MLB	29	16	9	0	32	32	211¹	236	13	48	96	66%	.308	13	1.34	3.96	4.55	3.86	9.3	0.4	1.8	3.7	38.0	3.80
2009	COL	MLB	30	11	6	0	27	27	158	175	19	47	78	65%	.295	4	1.41	4.16	4.60	4.03	9.4	0.8	2.3	3.9	25.5	3.57
2010	COL	MLB	31	8	10	0	28	28	167	186	18	52	69	67%	.297	-6	1.42	4.47	4.86	4.61	9.7	1.0	2.5	3.5	16.4	2.14

Breakout: 3%   Improve: 40%   Collapse: 19%   Attrition: 17%   MLB: 97%   Comparables: Duane Pillette, Omar Olivares, Bryn Smith, Ray Washburn

A helpful reminder that strikeouts aren't everything, Cook gives up a lot of hits but doesn't walk anyone and relies on his 90 mph sinker to get ground balls, which the Rockies' top-notch infield defense turns into outs. A strained shoulder kept him on the shelf for most of September, but he came back strong to win his last two starts and should come into 2010 healthy. Such a low strikeout rate leaves little margin for error—a few more lucky hits or a defensive slump will play havoc with Cook's ERA—but odds are he'll continue to soak up innings and be a solid midrotation starter.

Manny Corpas

Bats: R   Throws: R   Height: 6' 3"   Weight: 170   Born: December 3, 1982   Age: 27

YEAR	TEAM	LVL	AGE	W	L	SV	G	GS	IP	H	HR	BB	SO	GB%	BABIP	STUFF	WHIP	ERA	SIERA	DERA	EqH9	EqHR9	EqBB9	EqSO9	VORP	SN/WX
2007	COL	MLB	24	4	2	19	78	0	78	63	6	20	58	65%	.259	17	1.06	2.08	3.70	2.21	7.2	0.5	2.2	6.5	27.5	4.20
2008	COL	MLB	25	3	4	4	76	0	79²	93	7	23	50	58%	.326	-3	1.46	4.52	4.41	4.07	9.7	0.6	2.3	5.0	12.7	-0.32
2009	COL	MLB	26	1	3	1	35	0	33²	44	3	7	24	56%	.369	-4	1.51	5.88	4.01	5.29	11.7	0.6	1.7	5.8	0.8	-0.50
2010	COL	MLB	27	4	4	6	71	0	70	71	7	24	47	56%	.301	-2	1.36	4.16	4.37	4.31	8.9	0.9	2.8	5.6	9.3	0.84

Breakout: 19%   Improve: 43%   Collapse: 19%   Attrition: 13%   MLB: 96%   Comparables: Rawly Eastwick, Randy Moffitt, Gary Ross, Max Leon

Corpas lost the spring closer tryout and all the future riches this entails to Huston Street and then suffered through an ineffective and injury-riddled season that ended with surgery to remove bone chips from his elbow. Expected to be back healthy and in the bullpen mix, Corpas has boring stuff—that is to say, his low-90s fastball bores down and generates a lot of ground balls with low walk and strikeout rates. It's also not exciting in an acid-spitting bullpen leviathan sort of way, so while a reduction from last year's .366 BABIP should help Corpas regain the bullpen utility he's previously enjoyed, he'll never be an elite reliever.

Matt Daley

Bats: R   Throws: R   Height: 6' 2"   Weight: 175   Born: June 23, 1982   Age: 28

YEAR	TEAM	LVL	AGE	W	L	SV	G	GS	IP	H	HR	BB	SO	GB%	BABIP	STUFF	WHIP	ERA	SIERA	DERA	EqH9	EqHR9	EqBB9	EqSO9	VORP	SN/WX
2007	TUL	AA	25	2	6	0	43	10	95¹	83	12	22	84	37%	.257	-8	1.10	3.49	3.56	4.53	8.5	1.5	2.3	5.8	10.1	-0.14
2008	CSP	AAA	26	4	6	1	60	0	62¹	56	6	33	61	41%	.289	1	1.43	3.75	4.05	3.79	7.6	0.9	4.4	6.9	12.0	-0.35
2009	COL	MLB	27	1	1	0	57	0	51	43	6	18	55	43%	.285	16	1.20	4.24	3.12	3.91	7.5	0.9	2.7	8.5	9.0	0.26
2010	COL	MLB	28	3	4	0	65	0	64	64	8	25	54	41%	.308	1	1.39	4.48	4.06	4.55	8.7	1.1	3.2	7.2	6.8	0.56

Breakout: 8%   Improve: 40%   Collapse: 31%   Attrition: 14%   MLB: 44%   Comparables: Brian Sanches, John Costello, Tim Barrett, Craig Pippin

Daley was summoned from the minors in late April to help clean up an injury-riddled and ineffective Rockies pen and wound up staying for the party, logging 51 solid innings and making the post-season roster. As an undrafted free agent who worked his way up the system, Daley has stuff that's underwhelming, but he makes the most of it, striking out more than a man per inning during his debut and eventually gaining Tracy's trust as the default seventh-inning option down the stretch. As much as we like to root for a Humble Shoeshine Boy, a more extensive menu of bullpen options and a league that's learning his tricks mean that a repeat performance isn't likely.

Jorge De La Rosa

Bats: L   Throws: L   Height: 6' 1"   Weight: 210   Born: April 5, 1981   Age: 29

YEAR	TEAM	LVL	AGE	W	L	SV	G	GS	IP	H	HR	BB	SO	GB%	BABIP	STUFF	WHIP	ERA	SIERA	DERA	EqH9	EqHR9	EqBB9	EqSO9	VORP	SN/WX
2007	KCA	MLB	26	8	12	0	26	23	130	160	20	53	82	46%	.325	-11	1.64	5.82	4.90	5.34	10.4	1.2	3.3	5.2	2.2	1.41
2008	COL	MLB	27	10	8	0	28	23	130	128	13	62	128	53%	.319	20	1.46	4.92	3.81	4.73	8.4	0.7	3.7	7.8	11.1	2.00
2009	COL	MLB	28	16	9	0	33	32	185	172	20	83	193	51%	.308	26	1.38	4.38	3.55	4.29	8.1	0.7	3.4	8.2	24.9	4.09
2010	COL	MLB	29	8	10	0	31	30	157^2	165	18	72	131	50%	.319	12	1.50	4.68	4.23	4.75	9.0	1.0	3.7	7.0	13.1	1.90

Breakout: 4%   Improve: 32%   Collapse: 9%   Attrition: 15%   MLB: 97%   Comparables: Sterling Hitchcock, Bob Ojeda, Terry Mulholland, Joe Shaute

A former baseball vagabond, De La Rosa has floated through five, six, or seven organizations, depending on whether you count Mexican League outfits and whether being acquired by "Grover Cleveland" Garagiola on two nonconsecutive occasions makes Arizona count as one or two. Through it all, he has consistently flashed swing-and-miss stuff, with mid-90s lefty heat and three solid off-speed offerings, but something has clicked for him in Colorado. Projected to help out at the back of the rotation, De La Rosa had a breakout year, striking out more than a batter per inning, lowering his walk rate, and going 4-0 with a 2.97 ERA during the Rockies' stretch run. While not a devoted worm-killer like the other Rockies starters, De La Rosa gets more ground balls than some, and the Rockies have wisely protected his arm with low inning and pitch counts in his first full season in the rotation. It looks as if his talent has finally translated to production, and his wanderin' days are through.

Samuel Deduno

Bats: R   Throws: R   Height: 6' 1"   Weight: 156   Born: July 2, 1983   Age: 26

YEAR	TEAM	LVL	AGE	W	L	SV	G	GS	IP	H	HR	BB	SO	GB%	BABIP	STUFF	WHIP	ERA	SIERA	DERA	EqH9	EqHR9	EqBB9	EqSO9	VORP	SN/WX
2007	MOD	A+	23	1	1	0	2	2	11	9	1	7	8	43%	.242	-11	1.45	6.55	5.18	7.59	8.4	1.7	5.9	4.2	-2.5	-0.24
2007	TUL	AA	23	5	8	0	21	21	124	120	13	66	121	70%	.303	-2	1.50	5.44	3.76	7.65	9.7	1.4	4.8	6.6	-28.8	-2.26
2009	TUL	AA	25	12	4	0	24	24	133	94	3	72	123	64%	.264	24	1.25	2.57	3.83	3.88	7.5	0.7	4.9	7.1	22.3	1.88
2010	COL	MLB	26	4	6	0	21	16	94	93	11	57	77	39%	.305	6	1.60	5.12	4.83	5.14	8.5	1.0	5.0	6.9	3.8	1.09

Breakout: 14%   Improve: 56%   Collapse: 12%   Attrition: 18%   MLB: 8%   Comparables: Paul Fletcher, Mark Parker, Brent Schoening, Wilton Chavez

Coming off a year lost to elbow surgery, Deduno returned to the Texas League and picked up right where he left off. The slight right-hander throws a mid-90s heater with whiffle-ball action and two sharp breaking pitches, all of which miss bats and the strike zone with similarly high frequency. He'll start the year in the Colorado Springs rotation, but his future is in the bullpen, and if the big club needs a live arm, he'll be in the conversation.

Alan Embree

Bats: L   Throws: L   Height: 6' 2"   Weight: 200   Born: January 23, 1970   Age: 40

YEAR	TEAM	LVL	AGE	W	L	SV	G	GS	IP	H	HR	BB	SO	GB%	BABIP	STUFF	WHIP	ERA	SIERA	DERA	EqH9	EqHR9	EqBB9	EqSO9	VORP	SN/WX
2007	OAK	MLB	37	1	2	17	68	0	68	67	5	19	51	38%	.297	1	1.26	3.97	4.16	3.76	8.9	0.8	2.3	6.0	12.9	3.39
2008	OAK	MLB	38	2	5	0	70	0	61^2	59	8	30	57	48%	.295	-7	1.44	4.96	4.05	5.15	9.1	1.3	3.9	7.5	2.4	0.31
2009	COL	MLB	39	2	2	0	36	0	24^2	28	3	12	12	46%	.301	-26	1.62	5.84	5.56	5.92	10.0	0.7	3.7	4.1	-1.1	0.46
2010	COL	MLB	40	1	3	2	39	0	38	45	5	18	26	43%	.330	-14	1.66	5.68	4.92	5.81	10.3	1.3	3.9	5.8	-1.3	0.66

Breakout: 16%   Improve: 37%   Collapse: 35%   Attrition: 29%   MLB: 92%   Comparables: Mike Stanton, Mike Remlinger, Chris Hammond, Tom Burgmeier

Did you know Embree was on the brink of his big-league debut when "Bohemian Rhapsody" was the number one song in America? Okay, so it was the *Wayne's World* re-release in 1992, but Embree has been pumping portside gas for a long time, although the end may finally be near. While he can still bring the heat, Embree's short stint in Colorado featured a halving of his strikeout rate and twice as many walks before a line drive broke his leg and forced season-ending surgery. Colorado declined his option, and while he may still get another chance to work his LOOGY magic, his services are no longer in high demand.

Josh Fogg

Bats: R   Throws: R   Height: 6' 0"   Weight: 205   Born: December 13, 1976   Age: 33

YEAR	TEAM	LVL	AGE	W	L	SV	G	GS	IP	H	HR	BB	SO	GB%	BABIP	STUFF	WHIP	ERA	SIERA	DERA	EqH9	EqHR9	EqBB9	EqSO9	VORP	SN/WX
2007	COL	MLB	30	10	9	0	30	29	165²	194	23	59	94	48%	.308	-1	1.53	4.94	4.97	4.84	10.1	0.9	2.8	4.8	12.0	2.45
2008	CIN	MLB	31	2	7	0	22	14	78¹	97	17	27	45	41%	.300	-24	1.58	7.58	5.05	7.19	9.8	1.7	2.5	4.2	-15.3	-0.49
2009	CSP	AAA	32	3	1	0	8	8	40¹	44	8	17	16	49%	.265	-24	1.51	5.80	5.68	5.74	9.0	1.6	3.8	2.7	-1.1	-0.40
2009	COL	MLB	32	0	2	0	24	1	45²	32	7	20	27	49%	.189	-5	1.14	3.74	4.94	3.66	5.8	1.0	3.3	4.6	9.5	-0.29
2010	COL	MLB	33	3	6	0	23	15	80¹	93	11	36	41	47%	.310	-15	1.60	5.85	5.38	5.93	10.0	1.2	3.6	4.3	-3.8	0.46

Breakout: 11%   Improve: 39%   Collapse: 27%   Attrition: 41%   MLB: 77%   Comparables: Armando Reynoso, Jack Kramer, Bob Porterfield, Dave Johnson

Fogg returned to the mountains of Colorado after a disastrous season with the Reds and, for the first time in his career, posted a sub-four ERA. If you think that makes him an asset or that pitching out of the pen has made him more effective, then you don't know Fogg. Despite the respectable ERA, the former subpar innings sponge still doesn't strike anyone out and has walked more batters than ever, and his run-prevention numbers are built on the quicksand foundation of a league-low BABIP.

Jeff Francis

Bats: L   Throws: L   Height: 6' 5"   Weight: 205   Born: January 8, 1981   Age: 29

YEAR	TEAM	LVL	AGE	W	L	SV	G	GS	IP	H	HR	BB	SO	GB%	BABIP	STUFF	WHIP	ERA	SIERA	DERA	EqH9	EqHR9	EqBB9	EqSO9	VORP	SN/WX
2007	COL	MLB	26	17	9	0	34	34	215¹	234	25	63	165	52%	.316	17	1.38	4.22	4.05	3.91	9.6	0.8	2.4	6.6	37.6	5.52
2008	COL	MLB	27	4	10	0	24	24	143²	164	21	49	94	51%	.305	6	1.48	5.01	4.58	4.65	9.2	1.0	2.6	5.1	13.8	1.74
2010	COL	MLB	29	4	5	0	24	3	80¹	87	10	30	56	48%	.312	2	1.46	4.64	4.48	4.72	9.4	1.1	3.0	5.9	7.0	1.16

Breakout: 23%   Improve: 47%   Collapse: 23%   Attrition: 26%   MLB: 79%   Comparables: Billy Hoeft, Pete Richert, Paul Mirabella, Billy Traber

Francis missed all of 2009 following shoulder surgery, but is said to be on schedule for a spring return. After letting Jason Marquis walk, the Rockies are counting on Francis to move back into the starting rotation, although the emergence of Jimenez and De La Rosa and the continued effectiveness from Cook mean he won't have to be the staff's ace as far as production. With a fastball that sits in the upper 80s, Francis still posts good strikeout rates and is yet another ground-ball pitcher who will benefit from the Rockies' excellent infield defense. That is, if he's healthy—if the words "labrum" and "rotator cuff" send a chill down your spine, you're not alone.

Christian Friedrich

Bats: R   Throws: L   Height: 6' 3"   Weight: 210   Born: July 8, 1987   Age: 22

YEAR	TEAM	LVL	AGE	W	L	SV	G	GS	IP	H	HR	BB	SO	GB%	BABIP	STUFF	WHIP	ERA	SIERA	DERA	EqH9	EqHR9	EqBB9	EqSO9	VORP	SN/WX
2008	ASH	A	20	0	1	0	3	3	12	14	2	7	15	46%	.343	12	1.75	7.50	3.53	9.64	12.3	2.3	6.2	6.9	-5.4	-0.41
2008	TRI	A-	20	2	1	0	8	8	36	31	2	8	50	40%	.337	32	1.08	3.25	1.79	5.71	10.9	2.2	2.8	7.5	-0.7	-0.12
2009	ASH	A	21	3	3	0	8	8	45¹	35	2	15	66	55%	.340	33	1.10	2.18	1.94	4.31	9.3	1.6	4.5	8.6	5.2	0.07
2009	MOD	A+	21	3	2	0	14	14	74¹	59	3	28	93	41%	.306	19	1.17	2.54	2.68	4.13	9.2	1.3	4.3	6.7	10.5	0.78
2010	COL	MLB	22	4	8	0	24	24	109¹	126	16	58	91	38%	.335	19	1.68	5.71	4.61	5.79	9.9	1.3	4.4	7.1	-3.5	2.55

Breakout: 9%   Improve: 44%   Collapse: 18%   Attrition: 4%   MLB: 7%   Comparables: Benjamin Snyder, Alberto Blanco, Mike Jeffcoat, Tony Sipp

The former number one pick marches onward, leaving trails of strikeout victims in his wake. Friedrich's curveball may be the best in the minors, while his low-90s fastball is more than just a show-me pitch. His changeup is a work in progress, but he'll need it against righties as he moves up in class, and that may determine whether he's a second starter in "The Show" or something a little less. If he can survive this year's jump to Double-A with his peripherals intact, watch out.

Jason Hammel

Bats: R   Throws: R   Height: 6' 6"   Weight: 220   Born: September 2, 1982   Age: 27

YEAR	TEAM	LVL	AGE	W	L	SV	G	GS	IP	H	HR	BB	SO	GB%	BABIP	STUFF	WHIP	ERA	SIERA	DERA	EqH9	EqHR9	EqBB9	EqSO9	VORP	SN/WX
2007	DUR	AAA	24	4	5	0	13	13	76¹	61	3	28	75	52%	.282	22	1.17	3.42	3.44	4.17	8.1	0.6	3.3	7.1	10.8	1.17
2007	TBA	MLB	24	3	5	0	24	14	85	100	12	40	64	43%	.331	-9	1.65	6.14	4.69	5.34	9.3	1.4	3.8	6.0	1.6	0.98
2008	TBA	MLB	25	4	4	2	40	5	78¹	83	11	35	44	54%	.283	-22	1.51	4.60	5.10	5.03	10.1	1.4	3.7	4.7	3.9	1.22
2009	COL	MLB	26	10	8	0	34	30	176²	203	17	42	133	54%	.326	14	1.39	4.33	3.97	4.42	9.8	0.7	1.8	5.9	21.3	2.42
2010	COL	MLB	27	7	9	0	40	25	146²	159	17	56	104	53%	.316	3	1.47	4.71	4.42	4.82	9.4	1.0	3.1	6.0	11.0	1.57

Breakout: 8%   Improve: 35%   Collapse: 12%   Attrition: 17%   MLB: 93%   Comparables: Tommy Greene, Dustin Moseley, Jeff Russell, Chris Reitsma

Coming over from the Rays at the end of spring training when Jeff Niemann beat him out for the final rotation spot, Hammel turned out to be a godsend in Denver. Already getting the ground balls that pitching coach Bob Apodaca insists on, he cut his walk rate in half and increased his strikeouts, finally realizing the production his minor-league numbers have hinted at. Hammel complements his heavy low-90s fastball with a grab bag of mediocre secondary stuff—essentially the fifth starter's toolkit. Already 27, he's not a breakout candidate, but he's a good bet to remain a cheap and valuable back-end starter.

Matt Herges Bats: L Throws: R Height: 6' 0" Weight: 210 Born: April 1, 1970 Age: 40

YEAR	TEAM	LVL	AGE	W	L	SV	G	GS	IP	H	HR	BB	SO	GB%	BABIP	STUFF	WHIP	ERA	SIERA	DERA	EqH9	EqHR9	EqBB9	EqSO9	VORP	SN/WX
2007	CSP	AAA	37	2	1	1	32	0	35¹	24	2	10	33	56%	.247	14	0.96	1.27	3.19	1.59	5.8	0.5	2.6	7.1	14.8	1.62
2007	COL	MLB	37	5	1	0	35	0	48²	34	4	15	30	56%	.211	6	1.01	2.96	4.40	2.87	5.9	0.6	2.4	5.2	14.2	2.01
2008	COL	MLB	38	3	4	0	58	0	64¹	79	5	24	46	47%	.346	-5	1.60	5.04	4.53	4.98	10.2	0.6	2.9	5.7	3.7	-0.77
2009	CLE	MLB	39	2	1	0	21	0	25¹	24	3	6	18	57%	.262	0	1.18	3.55	4.04	3.25	7.5	1.0	1.7	5.5	6.6	0.48
2009	CSP	AAA	39	3	2	0	13	0	18¹	13	1	4	14	52%	.226	4	0.93	1.96	3.73	2.17	5.8	0.5	1.9	5.3	6.9	0.31
2009	COL	MLB	39	1	0	0	9	0	9¹	10	2	2	8	60%	.286	4	1.29	2.89	3.52	3.72	8.4	1.9	1.9	6.5	1.9	0.14
2010	KCA	MLB	40	3	3	1	57	0	56	58	6	23	35	52%	.300	-7	1.45	4.54	4.79	4.58	8.8	1.0	3.4	5.4	5.7	0.82

Breakout: 14% Improve: 35% Collapse: 31% Attrition: 18%   MLB: 88%   Comparables: Gerry Staley, Al Worthington, Steve Reed, Joe Heving

At this point, Herges' paychecks rely less on his stuff than on the memories of strangers, when GMs who remember seeing him get a few big outs a few Septembers ago take a flyer on him to fill out their bullpen. Then when the GM realizes he'd be better off giving those few low-leverage innings to that kid in the Texas League with the big fastball and the anarchy symbol on his backside, Herges gets his walking papers. Lather, rinse, repeat.

Ubaldo Jimenez Bats: R Throws: R Height: 6' 4" Weight: 200 Born: January 22, 1984 Age: 26

YEAR	TEAM	LVL	AGE	W	L	SV	G	GS	IP	H	HR	BB	SO	GB%	BABIP	STUFF	WHIP	ERA	SIERA	DERA	EqH9	EqHR9	EqBB9	EqSO9	VORP	SN/WX
2007	CSP	AAA	23	8	5	0	19	19	103	110	9	62	89	55%	.332	10	1.67	5.85	4.44	6.14	9.2	0.9	5.4	6.4	-7.2	-0.84
2007	COL	MLB	23	4	4	0	15	15	82	70	10	37	68	55%	.258	22	1.30	4.28	4.18	4.55	7.3	0.8	3.6	6.9	8.7	1.85
2008	COL	MLB	24	12	12	0	34	34	198²	182	11	103	172	62%	.299	27	1.43	3.99	4.09	3.92	7.7	0.4	4.0	6.9	35.0	4.24
2009	COL	MLB	25	15	12	0	33	33	218	183	13	85	198	61%	.280	35	1.23	3.47	3.67	3.40	7.3	0.4	3.0	7.1	51.1	5.99
2010	COL	MLB	26	11	10	0	34	34	199¹	184	17	94	159	63%	.294	19	1.40	4.06	4.15	4.16	8.0	0.8	3.9	6.8	29.6	2.96

Breakout: 4% Improve: 46% Collapse: 10% Attrition: 14%   MLB: 98%   Comparables: Ron Darling, Mark Gubicza, Wade Miller, Mike Moore

Jimenez has always had the stuff—a fastball that tickles the century mark and solid off-speed offerings—to be an elite major league starter, but this year, we saw Jimenez graduate from thrower to pitcher. He remains an extreme ground-ball pitcher, which is a particularly valuable skill in Colorado, while managing to significantly reduce his walk rate and amp up his strikeouts. Better command allowed him to pitch deeper into games, tossing 20 more innings in one less start than in 2008. Only 26 on Opening Day and with every needle moving in the right direction, Jimenez looks set to start a run of pitcher seasons unlike any other in club history.

Shane Lindsay Bats: R Throws: R Height: 6' 1" Weight: 205 Born: January 25, 1985 Age: 25

YEAR	TEAM	LVL	AGE	W	L	SV	G	GS	IP	H	HR	BB	SO	GB%	BABIP	STUFF	WHIP	ERA	SIERA	DERA	EqH9	EqHR9	EqBB9	EqSO9	VORP	SN/WX
2008	ASH	A	23	1	2	0	6	6	24¹	30	1	12	26	44%	.403	-5	1.73	5.55	3.72	7.59	13.9	1.3	5.9	6.3	-5.0	-0.50
2008	MOD	A+	23	2	3	0	10	10	47¹	33	1	34	56	46%	.278	16	1.42	3.99	3.82	6.70	7.7	0.8	7.3	7.1	-5.9	-0.23
2009	TUL	AA	24	3	1	1	22	0	27²	12	0	19	36	42%	.200	26	1.12	2.60	3.34	3.25	4.9	0.3	5.9	9.4	6.9	0.41
2010	COL	MLB	25	2	4	0	34	0	52²	51	6	40	48	43%	.310	-4	1.73	5.33	4.85	5.30	8.3	1.0	6.1	7.7	1.1	0.71

Breakout: 23% Improve: 51% Collapse: 22% Attrition: 9%   MLB: 6%   Comparables: Tom Paskievitch, Carlos Alvarado, Joey Newby, Todd Stephan

Lindsay has filthy stuff, featuring mid-90s heat and a nasty breaking ball that have helped him rack up 12.5 K/9 for his minor-league career. But injuries have derailed his progress and moved him to the bullpen, where he's just now reached the high minors. Lindsay hands out walks like Halloween candy, though the club hopes it's just a matter of more work before he finds his command. If it's right, he'll become a late-inning bullpen asset; if not, he'll be just another cautionary tale.

Jason Marquis

Bats: L   Throws: R   Height: 6' 1"   Weight: 210   Born: August 21, 1978   Age: 31

YEAR	TEAM	LVL	AGE	W	L	SV	G	GS	IP	H	HR	BB	SO	GB%	BABIP	STUFF	WHIP	ERA	SIERA	DERA	EqH9	EqHR9	EqBB9	EqSO9	VORP	SN/WX
2007	CHN	MLB	28	12	9	0	34	33	191²	190	22	76	109	58%	.268	5	1.39	4.60	4.87	4.83	8.8	0.8	3.1	4.7	14.4	3.21
2008	CHN	MLB	29	11	9	0	29	28	167	172	15	70	91	53%	.283	3	1.45	4.53	5.08	4.45	9.4	0.7	3.3	4.3	19.2	2.38
2009	COL	MLB	30	15	13	0	33	33	216	218	15	80	115	64%	.287	13	1.38	4.04	4.66	4.05	8.7	0.5	2.8	4.2	34.7	4.44
2010	WAS	MLB	31	11	12	0	34	33	188¹	188	19	72	96	59%	.282	-3	1.38	4.18	4.95	4.70	9.3	0.9	3.3	4.3	16.8	2.20

Breakout: 2%   Improve: 46%   Collapse: 20%   Attrition: 18%   MLB: 98%   Comparables: Kirk McCaskill, Jim Colborn, Omar Olivares, Howie Fox

Through 10 seasons and four organizations, from flame-throwing prospect to veteran innings sponge, one thing has remained constant: if you want to play post-season baseball, make sure Jason Marquis is on your roster. As is, he's been a rotation regular on a playoff team for six straight seasons. When he was pried loose from Chicago in exchange for Luis Vizcaino, the Rockies ignored his low strikeout rate and gambled that the veteran's ground-ball tendencies would play well in Coors. The bet paid off handsomely when Marquis won 11 games before the break and made his first All-Star appearance, before (perhaps predictably) he faded down the stretch. Priced out of Denver as a free agent, Marquis took his five-pitch repertoire and above-average bat to DC to play solid citizen for the kiddie corps' benefit—for $15 million over two years of course, not just warm fuzzies.

Tyler Matzek

Bats: L   Throws: L   Height: 6' 3"   Weight: 185   Born: October 19, 1990   Age: 19

Did Not Play.

Breakout: 2%   Improve: 46%   Collapse: 20%   Attrition: 18%   MLB: 98%   Comparables: NA

Colorado's first-round pick in last year's draft, Matzek was considered the top prep lefty available and dropped to the Rockies due to signability concerns. Matzek is said to have a deep arsenal for a teenager, with a plus fastball and slider, a usable curve, and an occasional changeup. Of course, that's all just talk; we'll know more after he faces a few professional hitters. Between here and the big leagues, there be dragons.

Franklin Morales

Bats: L   Throws: L   Height: 6' 0"   Weight: 170   Born: January 24, 1986   Age: 24

YEAR	TEAM	LVL	AGE	W	L	SV	G	GS	IP	H	HR	BB	SO	GB%	BABIP	STUFF	WHIP	ERA	SIERA	DERA	EqH9	EqHR9	EqBB9	EqSO9	VORP	SN/WX
2007	TUL	AA	21	3	4	0	17	17	95²	77	8	45	77	50%	.262	24	1.28	3.48	4.30	4.63	8.4	1.2	4.4	5.5	8.6	0.60
2007	CSP	AAA	21	2	0	0	3	3	17	20	1	13	16	43%	.422	14	1.94	3.71	4.69	4.08	11.9	0.6	7.5	8.2	2.3	0.17
2007	COL	MLB	21	3	2	0	8	8	39¹	34	2	14	26	65%	.269	37	1.22	3.43	4.25	3.14	7.7	0.2	2.8	5.6	10.1	1.36
2008	CSP	AAA	22	10	5	0	21	21	110¹	108	14	82	83	51%	.298	10	1.72	5.47	5.16	5.54	8.7	1.0	6.4	5.5	-0.4	0.21
2008	COL	MLB	22	1	2	0	5	5	25¹	28	2	17	9	51%	.286	-10	1.78	6.39	6.31	5.64	8.9	0.7	5.1	2.7	-0.4	0.21
2009	CSP	AAA	23	2	2	0	8	8	41¹	39	4	19	37	46%	.304	13	1.40	3.48	4.06	3.71	8.3	0.9	4.3	7.0	7.9	0.92
2009	COL	MLB	23	3	2	7	40	2	40	38	4	23	41	33%	.309	10	1.52	4.50	4.17	4.65	8.2	0.7	4.2	8.0	3.9	1.35
2010	COL	MLB	24	5	6	3	35	18	97¹	95	11	57	71	41%	.293	0	1.56	4.82	5.05	4.89	8.4	1.0	4.8	6.1	6.6	1.81

Breakout: 14%   Improve: 48%   Collapse: 15%   Attrition: 19%   MLB: 100%   Comparables: Josh Outman, Bobby M. Jones, Jon Lester, Bob Baldrick

Tabbed as the fifth starter out of spring training, Morales went down in late April with a strained shoulder that kept him on the shelf or tuning up in the PCL until July. When he returned, the lefty flamethrower moved to the pen and thrived, even doing solid ninth-inning work when Huston Street suffered a September bout of bicep tendinitis. His fastball, which had suffered a dramatic drop in velocity during earlier rotation stints, was again touching 95, and while his walk rate is still troubling, he finally started whiffing prodigious numbers of major-league hitters. Morales' future is as a reliever, and if he continues to improve his command, it'll be a bright one.

Greg Reynolds

Bats: R   Throws: R   Height: 6' 7"   Weight: 225   Born: July 3, 1985   Age: 24

YEAR	TEAM	LVL	AGE	W	L	SV	G	GS	IP	H	HR	BB	SO	GB%	BABIP	STUFF	WHIP	ERA	SIERA	DERA	EqH9	EqHR9	EqBB9	EqSO9	VORP	SN/WX
2007	TUL	AA	21	4	1	0	8	8	50²	32	2	9	35	60%	.211	37	0.81	1.42	3.67	2.53	6.4	0.8	1.9	4.7	15.8	1.45
2008	CSP	AAA	22	1	3	0	13	13	63¹	84	4	22	37	64%	.364	-1	1.67	4.26	4.56	5.16	11.7	0.7	3.2	4.1	2.3	0.42
2008	COL	MLB	22	2	8	0	14	13	62	83	14	26	22	50%	.303	-22	1.76	8.13	5.83	7.55	10.5	1.5	3.2	2.7	-14.7	-0.50
2010	COL	MLB	24	2	5	0	21	5	61²	72	9	27	27	52%	.305	-17	1.61	5.48	5.51	5.57	10.1	1.2	3.6	3.7	-0.5	0.80

Breakout: 26%   Improve: 50%   Collapse: 20%   Attrition: 15%   MLB: 100%   Comparables: Justin James, Mike McClendon, Joel Gilmore, Dustin Robinson

Famously taken as the second overall pick in 2006—just ahead of Evan Longoria—the oft-injured Reynolds tossed just four Triple-A innings before a shoulder impingement and eventual surgery shut him down for the year. He's expected to be healthy for spring training, though he's not expected to be particularly good; a complete inability to get professional hitters to swing and miss means he really doesn't have a big-league future.

Esmil Rogers

Bats: R Throws: R Height: 6' 1" Weight: 150 Born: August 14, 1985 Age: 24

YEAR	TEAM	LVL	AGE	W	L	SV	G	GS	IP	H	HR	BB	SO	GB%	BABIP	STUFF	WHIP	ERA	SIERA	DERA	EqH9	EqHR9	EqBB9	EqSO9	VORP	SN/WX
2007	ASH	A	21	7	4	0	19	18	117^2	125	6	42	90	47%	.320	13	1.42	3.75	4.25	5.34	9.8	1.1	3.8	4.4	2.0	-0.82
2008	MOD	A+	22	9	7	0	25	25	143^2	146	9	45	116	48%	.315	-7	1.33	3.95	3.94	5.60	10.6	1.5	3.6	4.6	-1.4	-0.19
2009	TUL	AA	23	8	2	0	15	15	94^1	87	2	19	83	46%	.310	25	1.12	2.48	3.34	3.55	9.4	0.7	2.1	6.7	19.2	1.57
2009	CSP	AAA	23	3	5	0	12	11	60^2	77	9	35	46	55%	.351	-10	1.85	7.42	4.78	7.32	11.1	1.4	5.2	5.6	-11.9	-1.14
2009	COL	MLB	23	0	0	0	1	1	4	3	0	2	3	61%	.273	3	1.25	4.50	4.27	4.91	7.4	0.0	4.9	7.4	0.2	0.06
2010	COL	MLB	24	6	9	0	28	24	135^2	157	17	63	83	43%	.320	-7	1.62	5.34	5.11	5.47	10.0	1.1	3.8	5.2	0.5	2.04

Breakout: 13% Improve: 49% Collapse: 19% Attrition: 15%   MLB: 9%   Comparables: Matt Crouch, Joe Turek, Howard Farmer, Mike Oquist

A converted shortstop, Rogers whips surprising mid-90s heat and a good curve out of his slight frame, and managed to work his way up to a major-league cup of coffee while still just learning how to pitch. He exhibited terrific command at Tulsa, but struggled somewhat in the PCL, so he's not a finished product. He's close, though, and should became an inexpensive back-end rotation option sooner rather than later.

Greg Smith

Bats: L Throws: L Height: 6' 2" Weight: 190 Born: December 22, 1983 Age: 26

YEAR	TEAM	LVL	AGE	W	L	SV	G	GS	IP	H	HR	BB	SO	GB%	BABIP	STUFF	WHIP	ERA	SIERA	DERA	EqH9	EqHR9	EqBB9	EqSO9	VORP	SN/WX
2007	MOB	AA	23	5	3	0	12	12	69^2	64	7	14	62	48%	.295	4	1.12	3.36	3.26	4.76	9.5	1.7	2.1	5.6	5.3	0.38
2007	TUC	AAA	23	4	2	0	10	10	52^1	61	4	18	34	46%	.339	-2	1.51	3.78	4.58	4.50	10.1	0.9	3.2	4.5	5.6	0.65
2008	OAK	MLB	24	7	16	0	32	32	190^1	169	21	87	111	39%	.256	0	1.35	4.16	5.33	4.30	8.4	1.2	3.8	4.9	24.5	4.78
2009	MOD	A+	25	1	0	0	2	2	11^2	11	1	4	7	57%	.278	-21	1.29	3.86	4.52	5.91	10.1	1.7	4.2	2.5	-0.5	-0.14
2009	CSP	AAA	25	1	2	0	7	7	29^2	34	5	11	15	52%	.299	-21	1.52	7.28	5.11	7.06	9.7	1.6	3.5	3.8	-5.0	-0.49
2010	COL	MLB	26	3	6	0	24	11	76^2	86	11	35	45	44%	.306	-9	1.58	5.21	5.20	5.29	9.6	1.2	3.8	5.0	1.8	1.16

Breakout: 18% Improve: 48% Collapse: 18% Attrition: 30%   MLB: 69%   Comparables: Dennis Moeller, Dave Walsh, Curt Young, Guy Normand

The short leg of the stool Colorado received in the Holliday heist, Smith spent the season dealing with shoulder problems and posted unimpressive numbers across three levels. The Rockies are giving him a mulligan and expect him to compete for a big-league job this year, perhaps in the rotation. But Smith walks too many and whiffs too few to profile as much more than a situational lefty, and since the club has a vacancy there, if he's healthy, he might just stick.

Huston Street

Bats: R Throws: R Height: 6' 0" Weight: 200 Born: August 2, 1983 Age: 26

YEAR	TEAM	LVL	AGE	W	L	SV	G	GS	IP	H	HR	BB	SO	GB%	BABIP	STUFF	WHIP	ERA	SIERA	DERA	EqH9	EqHR9	EqBB9	EqSO9	VORP	SN/WX
2007	OAK	MLB	23	5	2	16	48	0	50	35	5	12	63	46%	.252	27	0.94	2.88	2.14	3.46	6.4	1.1	2.0	9.2	11.5	2.35
2008	OAK	MLB	24	7	5	18	63	0	70	58	6	27	69	45%	.283	11	1.21	3.73	3.49	3.72	8.0	0.9	3.2	8.1	13.4	2.12
2009	COL	MLB	25	4	1	35	64	0	61^2	43	7	13	70	48%	.240	28	0.91	3.06	2.40	3.02	5.9	0.7	1.6	8.8	17.3	4.11
2010	COL	MLB	26	4	3	24	67	0	66	58	7	22	62	45%	.291	13	1.21	3.40	3.42	3.49	7.7	0.9	2.7	8.1	14.7	2.07

Breakout: 14% Improve: 36% Collapse: 27% Attrition: 16%   MLB: 100%   Comparables: Bob Apodaca, Rawly Eastwick, Steve Kealey, Ugueth Urbina

The most famous player Colorado received for a year of Matt Holliday, Street has been a professional closer since the day he arrived, fully formed and riding a clamshell, out of the University of Texas, so it was somewhat surprising that he had to win a closer duel with Manny Corpas to take the ninth-inning reins. Street was the anchor in an often roiling bullpen, notching the highest save percentage of his career and—more importantly for his future—reversing a few troubling statistical trends. Walks plunged, strikeouts surged, and he even managed his first-ever reverse platoon split, holding lefties to an anemic .167/.227/.265 line. One of several prominent closers to suffer Post-Season Implosion Syndrome this fall, Street's season ended on a sour note, but he reestablished himself as a solid second-tier closer and set himself up for a nice payday going into his final arbitration season.

Casey Weathers

Bats: R   Throws: R   Height: 6' 1"   Weight: 200   Born: June 10, 1985   Age: 25

YEAR	TEAM	LVL	AGE	W	L	SV	G	GS	IP	H	HR	BB	SO	GB%	BABIP	STUFF	WHIP	ERA	SIERA	DERA	EqH9	EqHR9	EqBB9	EqSO9	VORP	SN/WX
2007	ASH	A	22	0	1	2	13	0	13²	6	2	7	19	53%	.154	13	0.95	4.61	2.54	5.40	4.7	2.0	4.7	8.8	0.1	-0.35
2008	TUL	AA	23	2	1	2	44	0	44¹	34	1	28	54	56%	.308	15	1.40	3.05	3.45	4.18	8.1	0.6	5.8	8.4	6.2	-0.34
2010	COL	MLB	25	2	4	0	34	0	45	52	6	27	29	52%	.323	-17	1.77	6.03	5.19	6.03	9.9	1.2	4.9	5.5	-2.6	0.09

Breakout: 11%   Improve: 29%   Collapse: 28%   Attrition: 13%   MLB: 4%   Comparables: Steve Gajkowski, Doug Thompson, Andy Shipman, Scott Medvin

The Rockies' top pick in 2007, Weathers spent his summer rehabbing from Tommy John surgery and should be ready to start back down that old prospect road. A classic power closer with a fastball that breaks radar guns and with a nasty slider, Weathers has walked 5.6 men per nine in his short minor-league career; if just getting healthy is at the top of the to-do list, improving his command should be right below it. Regardless, it's hard to see a pitcher with this kind of arm not becoming a bullpen beast, and Weathers stands a good chance to become The Monster That Ate Huston once the Rockies' current closer prices himself out of Colorado.

LINEOUTS

Hitters

PLAYER	TEAM	LVL	AGE	PA	R	2B	3B	HR	RBI	BB	SO	SB-CS	EqBRR	AVG/OBP/SLG	EqAVG/EqOBP/EqSLG	EqA	VORP	WARP
OF C. Garner	TUL	AA	24	440	65	25	4	16	64	23	78	13-5	-1.0	.288/.342/.492	.254/.295/.429	.249	3.9	-0.3
SS M. McCoy	CSP	AAA	28	572	102	27	5	2	52	80	70	40-6	7.5	.307/.405/.400	.253/.342/.320	.249	8.4	0.5
OF M. Miller	CSP	AAA	26	589	83	39	8	9	98	51	78	4-1	2.3	.319/.380/.476	.265/.322/.389	.251	4.9	-1.0
OF M. Murton	CSP	AAA	27	424	72	27	1	12	79	39	52	12-2	1.4	.324/.389/.499	.268/.328/.408	.260	7.7	0.1
	COL	MLB	27	56	7	5	0	1	6	4	14	2-0	0.0	.250/.304/.404	.250/.304/.385	.250	-0.4	-0.1
UT C. Nelson	TUL	AA	23	122	21	5	2	4	17	12	21	5-2	-1.3	.280/.355/.477	.255/.320/.427	.260	5.0	-0.3
C W. Rosario	MOD	A+	20	222	17	12	2	4	33	10	55	2-1	-2.0	.266/.297/.404	.238/.260/.345	.212	-2.4	-0.2

Cole Garner has been a slow-developing organizational soldier, but his Double-A debut was an unqualified success. ⊘ After earning his first cup of coffee, reduced-scale grinder Mike McCoy was claimed on waivers and will be taking his cut-rate Cangelosi impression to Toronto. ⊘ Matt Miller isn't going to develop more power at the age of 27, and with the Rockies outfield suddenly younger than he is, he'll need to change organizations to get a sniff of the bigs. ⊘ Memo to Matt Murton: Getting on base is nice, but if you only do it so much and you can't go deep regularly in Colorado Springs, it's no wonder you're with the Hanshin Tigers in 2010. ⊘ Oft-injured top pick Chris Nelson got off to a good start in his second attempt to improve his defense and master Double-A, but a bum wrist ended his year before he could rekindle his prospect flame. ⊘ Despite a rough year in Modesto, the organization believes in Wilin Rosario's offensive potential and strong arm, though he needs to improve behind the dish.

Pitchers

PLAYER	TEAM	LVL	AGE	W	L	SV	IP	H	HR	BB	SO	GB%	BABIP	STUFF	WHIP	ERA	SIERA	DERA	EqH9	EqHR9	EqBB9	EqSO9	VORP
A. Alburquerque	DAY	A+	23	1	0	2	34²	26	4	14	44	61%	.272	3	1.15	2.08	2.68	4.26	9.1	2.3	4.5	8.2	4.4
	TUL	AA	23	1	3	0	26¹	23	0	13	31	66%	.343	14	1.37	3.76	3.14	5.11	9.1	0.4	4.4	9.1	1.1
A. Eaton	BAL	MLB	31	2	5	0	41	56	9	19	28	41%	.341	-13	1.83	8.56	5.02	7.61	11.1	1.5	3.6	5.4	-9.8
	CSP	AAA	31	4	3	0	79¹	81	4	16	50	54%	.298	13	1.22	3.18	4.23	3.83	8.7	0.6	1.9	4.6	14.6
	COL	MLB	31	1	0	0	8	9	1	8	7	35%	.320	7	2.12	5.62	5.80	5.40	9.7	1.1	7.6	6.5	0.1
E. Escalona	MOD	A+	22	2	0	0	32²	25	3	7	34	41%	.262	-2	0.98	2.48	2.77	3.90	8.7	2.1	2.7	5.4	5.3
	TUL	AA	22	1	2	4	36²	33	5	11	32	39%	.262	3	1.20	2.45	3.80	3.63	9.0	2.0	2.8	6.3	7.5
R. Flores*	CSP	AAA	33	0	2	0	31²	37	2	11	33	54%	.368	2	1.52	4.26	3.40	5.60	10.3	0.9	3.2	7.8	-0.4
	COL	MLB	33	0	1	0	12	14	2	2	14	45%	.353	12	1.33	5.25	2.51	5.11	9.5	1.5	1.5	8.8	0.5
J. Nicasio	ASH	A	22	9	3	0	112	110	6	23	115	54%	.325	1	1.19	2.41	2.95	5.26	10.2	1.6	3.0	5.3	2.8
J. Peralta	CSP	AAA	33	6	0	4	36²	31	3	11	32	33%	.264	5	1.15	2.45	3.83	2.77	7.0	0.7	2.7	6.3	11.3
	COL	MLB	33	0	3	0	24²	27	3	12	22	36%	.329	-5	1.58	6.20	4.37	5.84	9.5	0.7	3.6	6.9	-0.9
J. Rincon	DET	MLB	30	1	0	0	10¹	12	2	6	10	36%	.323	-3	1.74	5.23	4.43	5.06	10.1	1.7	4.2	7.6	0.5
	CSP	AAA	30	1	0	3	17¹	8	1	7	22	39%	.200	17	0.87	1.56	2.47	1.62	4.3	0.5	3.8	9.7	7.2
	COL	MLB	30	3	2	0	26¹	18	2	20	25	62%	.235	2	1.44	7.52	4.33	7.09	6.1	0.7	5.7	7.4	-4.7
C. Roe	TUL	AA	22	7	3	0	117	105	7	43	77	49%	.274	9	1.26	3.15	4.56	4.28	9.1	1.1	3.5	4.8	14.9

Slight Dominican **Al Alburquerque** infuriates batters and copyeditors alike; he was added to the organization from the Cubs in the Jeff Baker trade and boasts a nice sinker/slider mix. ⊘ Formerly famous free agent **Adam Eaton** was bad in Baltimore and Colorado, and his biggest contribution to a major-league team was his finally coming off the Phillies' books. ⊘ Not to be mistaken for a minor Saxon king from long before the battle of Hastings, Venezuelan **Edgmer Escalona** gets by with high strikes, but might find the going harder at altitude against more advanced competition. ⊘ Former La Russa plaything **Randy Flores** provided 12 mediocre innings spread over 27 games, so the Rockies decided to renew his LOOGY license. ⊘ They say teenager **Alving Mejias** has "advanced pitchability," but six walks and no homers in 72 innings (in the Dominican Summer League)—that has the makings of a career, in any league. His stateside debut will be closely watched. ⊘ A little old for the Sally League, **Juan Nicasio** nonetheless impressed by posting a ridiculous K/BB ratio in a notorious hitter's park; he might surprise. ⊘ **Joel Peralta** has enjoyed modest success in the majors as a rubber-armed ROOGY, but Denver is a tough spot for a guy who has allowed all lefties to slug .560 against him in his career. ⊘ Years removed from his Metrodome heyday, **Juan Rincon** couldn't stick with the Tigers or Rockies and won't stick anywhere until he stops handing out free passes. ⊘ **Chaz Roe** cut down on the gopher balls during his second swing through Tulsa, but he'll need to walk fewer batters and strike out a few more for the organization to take his prospectdom more seriously.

MANAGER: CLINT HURDLE/JIM TRACY

YEAR	TEAM	W-L	Pythag +/–	Avg PC	100+ P	120+ P	QS	BQS	REL	REL w Zero R	IBB	Subs	PH	PH Avg	PH HR	SB2	CS2	SB3	CS3	SAC Att	SAC %	POS SAC	Squeeze	Swing	In Play
2007	C.H.	90-73	-2	90.5	51	0	74	3	529	348	61	52	283	.216	4	98	31	2	0	124	66.9%	37	2	142	104
2008	C.H.	74-88	1	92.3	53	0	67	4	484	310	49	43	250	.239	4	116	34	25	3	130	69.2%	41	0	108	82
2009	C.H.	19-28	-3	92.9	20	0	26	1	136	79	12	16	74	.302	2	25	13	6	2	31	67.7%	8	0	52	48
2007	J.T./PIT	68-94	0	92.6	48	1	73	8	495	289	55	35	238	.231	9	62	27	6	2	84	71.4%	22	4	112	86
2009	J.T.	73-42	4	95.9	55	5	66	6	347	225	39	50	182	.281	3	66	36	9	2	85	64.7%	30	3	102	75

Hurdle managed to survive five straight losing seasons at the start of his tenure, but when the Rockies regressed after their 2007 Rocktober playoff appearance, there was finally enough evidence for an even-handed evaluation. Loyal, affable, and well-liked, Hurdle undermined his position over the years by frequently overmanaging his charges—too many bunts and intentional walks, too many pitching and lineup changes, too much of a spotlight on the oldest guys. After the 18-28 start that got Hurdle hurdled, newly installed bench coach Jim Tracy was handed the reins. The Rockies were a talented, underachieving bunch, and Tracy immediately decided the best approach would be to sort out their roles and let them play. He reworked an injured and ineffective bullpen, lending permanence to Huston Street in the closer role and Franklin Morales as a valuable set-up man. He installed Ian Stewart and Clint Barmes as everyday infield starters to improve the defense and worked Carlos Gonzalez and Seth Smith into the outfield rotation. None of this was revolutionary, but once these questions were settled, the Rockies responded to Tracy's "light fuse, get away" approach and launched themselves into contention and an eventual wild-card berth. As much as we like to applaud managers for their tactical brilliance, sometimes it's the application of fundamental personnel management techniques that realizes the largest gains in the win column.

Detroit Tigers

Since winning a pennant in 2006, the Tigers were supposed to be back and matter and all that good stuff. They were heavy hitters during the ensuing offseasons, spending Mike Ilitch's money as if he were printing it like so many Little Caesars coupons, trying to keep up with his other major plaything, their corporate cousins in hockey, the annually contending, no-expense-is-too-much Red Wings. Yet, for their troubles in the last three years, the Tigers have won exactly nothing other than a moderate tally of regular-season contests. Now, the club may finally be ready to make a stronger course correction, instead of settling for the frantic, often expensive tacking of recent seasons.

The nonachievements in the years since their pennant weren't for lack of trying. The 2007 team won 88 games, enough to have tied or won the title in either of the next two seasons, but that squad was stuck looking up at what proved to be the division's last Indians' summer. The adaptive response was to trade for Miguel Cabrera and Edgar Renteria (and Dontrelle Willis) and just settle affairs by scoring a thousand runs in 2008, except that they didn't score a thousand runs, let alone regain the division title; they instead fell into last place, behind even the Royals, the very definition of ignominy.

If *that* masterstroke didn't work, why not find answers with a lurch into the latest fashion? It's a well-worn proposition by now, but after the Rays' rocketing from worst to first in defense from 2007 to 2008, maybe a similar adoption of the latest fad as far as "discovering" undervalued assets would provide the key to victory. If defense was the way to win and employing Edgar Renteria at short had been a losing proposition,

then there was no better way to get au courant than to pick up some prêt-à-porter defensive help.

Fundamental to all these calculations was Dave Dombrowski's attempt to leverage a legacy of big-ticket contracts signed when the economy seemed to be en route to permanent expansion. The worst of these deals was the $90 million certain to be paid out to Magglio Ordonez though 2010 on a deal signed in February 2005, an average annual value (AAV) of $15 million, but there's more to regret in terms of outlays from the pizza baron's coffers (see Table 1).* Much of the team's budget was tied into two groups of big-budget signings: the trio of deals handed out as rewards for key players from the 2006 team before the 2007 season (to Jeremy Bonderman, Brandon Inge, and Carlos Guillen) and the next winter's wave of four, handed to the two arbitration-eligible Marlins added in trade (Dontrelle Willis and Miguel Cabrera) and two home-grown products (Nate Robertson and Curtis Granderson). Combined, the big bucks were due a little more than $88 million in 2009, and even with Placido Polanco due for free agency after the year, the remaining eight were due $97.6 million.

That's great for these nine, of course. It might also be cause to evaluate Dombrowski's sense of checkbook management, but any judgment must be defined in the context of what he was brought in to do, which was to dig the franchise out of the pit into which Randy Smith

---

TIGERS PROSPECTUS
2009 W-L: 86-77, 2nd in AL Central

Pythag	79-84	11th
RS/G	4.6	11th
RA/G	4.6	5th
EqA	.251	11th
EqBRR	-3.3	10th
SNWP	.517	3rd
WXRL	7.56	8th
FRAr	4.66	9th
DE	.695	5th
PADE	0.02	3rd
Salary	$115.1	3rd
Attend	2.57	4th

Ballpark: Comerica Park (3-yr. PF: 1027). Even, wide-open spaces produce a generally neutral environment

2009: A division-title run came up short, witnessed by fewer fans in the buckle of the Rust Belt

2010: Dealing Granderson won't add fannies in a year of waiting for contracts to expire, breaking in kids

Action Items: A ready-now CF; finding suckers for the end of deals, even if salary-eating's required; rounding out the pen

---

* It might become $105 million if they don't cut or trade him before his 2011 option for $15 million more vests, and he has a no-trade clause.

Table 1. Tiger Budget, Burning Bright: Detroit's 2009 Big-Money Contracts

Player	Signed	Total	AAV	Period
Ordonez	2/05	$90M	$15.0M	2005-10, vesting 2011 option for $15M
Polanco	8/05	$18.4M	$4.6M	2006-09
Bonderman	12/06	$38.0M	$9.5M	2007-10
Inge	12/06	$24M	$6.0M	2007-10
Guillen	3/07	$48M	$12.0M	2008-11
Willis	12/07	$29M	$9.67M	2008-10
Robertson	1/08	$21.25M	$7.1M	2008-10
Granderson	2/08	$28.25M	$5.65M	2008-13, 2014 club option for $13M/$2M buyout
Cabrera	3/08	$152.3M	$19.04M	2008-15

Table 2. Robbing Peter and Paul: What Did Change Bring?

Position	2008 EqR	2008 FRAA*	2009 EqR	2009 FRAA*	Net Runs Gained/Lost
C	70	10	51	16	+13
3B	95	4	69	6	-24
SS	75	-17	55	-3	-6
LF	80	7	75	4	-8

*We're using what has been labeled FRAA2 (Fielding Runs Above Average, adjusted for league difficulty) on the BP.com site.

had assiduously ditched it. The early phase of the project was not pretty, given the 100-loss humiliations of 2002 and 2003, but a quick turnaround had always been unlikely, considering that Detroit wasn't on the short list of desirable destinations for free agents. Getting Ivan Rodriguez, Fernando Vina, and Rondell White to sign for the 2004 season set a new tone, letting the market know that the Tigers were in the business of paying top dollar. The subsequent major commitments were consistent with Dombrowski's work in the 1990s with the Marlins—he was not simply building up an organization; he was building it to win.

As a result, this wasn't a roster with a lot of wiggle room. Having gone so deeply in on these guys without having won, and having traded for Willis and Cabrera to win, and not winning, the club could do little more through at least 2010. This team had to make do with this core. Going gaga for gloves might be swell, but it would have to be done on the cheap. Enter the decisions to acquire Adam Everett for short and Gerald Laird for catching chores, shunting Inge back to the hot corner and Guillen to left field. The cost was relatively light, a couple of arms for Laird, plus the modest expense to employ him and Everett. As a proposition, it seemed to suggest improvement, getting a catcher who wanted to catch, a significantly upgraded left side of the infield, and Guillen to a position he could handle.

Of course, these things are swell to do on paper, but a funny thing happened during the execution: the Tigers improved in the field, but not so much that it made that big a difference. The 2008 Tigers were 18th in the majors in Park Adjusted Defensive Efficiency (PADE), and the 2009 Tigers were 10th—nice, but hardly as epic as the Rays' huge one-season turnaround. The price paid in runs on offense, with so many punchless wonders, was steep, as the attack went from being tied for third in the AL to 11th in team EqA. To better appreciate the loss

of offense versus the gains on defense, consider an apples-to-apples comparison of Equivalent Runs and Fielding Runs Above Average (see Table 2).

There was, of course, variation in the performances of the other parts not reflected here—Cabrera at first, Polanco at second, Granderson in center, and Ordonez (and help) in right—which colors the overall picture. Still, totting up the full losses and gains says the Tigers wound up losing a net of two wins from the sum of the offensive and defensive contributions from their position players from 2008 to 2009. Much of that was Inge's bat, but you could also hone in on the two offensive wins they lost at shortstop in exchange for merely adequate performance afield at short.

The Tigers weren't the only team that deliberately tried to ape the Rays and improve their defense; it's just that they didn't wind up being anywhere close to one of the biggest improvers on this score. Rather, the biggest improvements between 2008 and 2009 were made by the Mariners, Rangers, and Reds, whose swings between seasons all rated better than four percent improvements via PADE, still well short of the Rays' seven percent swing between seasons, but also dwarfing the Tigers' modest gain of half a percentage point in PADE. Moreover, these sorts of improvement afield are no more permanent than normal season-to-season variations in hitting or pitching; the Rays' historic jump from 30th in PADE in 2007 to 3rd in 2008 was followed by a slide back down to 15th in 2009, with much the same personnel.

Nevertheless, adding defensive-oriented vets was a reasonable but transient bid to try to make something of the commitments already made. The Tigers were limited, though, by the inescapable financial dead weight of the deals with three-fifths of a rotation, a steeply declining right fielder, and a positionless player like Guillen. As gambles go, in the broad strokes it very nearly worked, not because of the effort expended on that end of the team, but because of the significantly improved rotation. Justin Verlander enjoyed his best season, and Rick Porcello proved ready far sooner than expected, but perhaps the biggest single gain the team made was grabbing Edwin Jackson from the Rays in a trade for outfield prospect Matt Joyce. The move was greeted with derision by many analysts, but Dombrowski had the last laugh when Jackson, long one of the game's least predictable talents, wound up among the game's best starters in a breakout campaign.

Put all that together, and the Tigers could have reasonably expected to make it into the postseason, as a 16-12 September was among their better months. Timing is everything, though, especially in the Pamplona-cum-Lilliput Running of the Munchkins that is the AL Central. The Twins had their 11-1 stretch to get back into the race, the White Sox played spoiler at season's end, and the now de rigueur one-game playoff became necessary, so Dombrowski's bid to get another flag out of this collection of talent came up short.

To the organization's credit, they didn't mope about it. Whatever mistakes have been made, they were made after 2006 and before 2008, and the team has to live them down through 2010, when Bonderman, Willis, Guillen, Robertson, Inge, and perhaps also Ordonez all come off the books. The organization gets to consider its options more effectively after that point, but with attendance in extra-depressed Detroit last year plummeting more than 700,000, the bottom line is especially problematic at present. With an eye on both that and the less cash-strapped future, Dombrowski made a point of changing gears at the Winter Meetings, trading Jackson with his value spiking to get younger blue-chip talent to sustain the club beyond this last run with the old gang. A three-way deal with the Yankees and the Diamondbacks gave the Tigers young right-hander Max Scherzer and power lefty reliever Daniel Schlereth from the Snakes, and center-field prospect Austin Jackson and extra lefty Phil Coke from the Yankees, while costing them Edwin Jackson and Curtis Granderson.

The move is certain to be controversial for years to come, not least because the Tigers traded two fine young veteran players who might be significant assets for years to come. Granderson is a wonderful player to watch, and an African American star in Detroit has additional value. There's a very good chance that both traded Tigers will end up having more career value than what Detroit got back. But even if you take the new and improved Edwin Jackson as a permanent fact, he was only under club contractual control for two more sea-

sons (and was certain to get raises via arbitration). Scherzer seems likely to give the Tigers a solid one-for-one swap in terms of quality help in the rotation for years beyond their control of Edwin Jackson, and adding Schlereth gives the bullpen another flame-thrower in what might become a pen packed with power arms. In addition, Granderson's merits are balanced with a few warts. If Austin Jackson eventually winds up becoming part of the next good Tigers team as its everyday center fielder, there's not much cause for regret, although he'll have competition in-house.

For a team with something of a balloon payment yet to make as far as its 2010 payroll, this wasn't the worst adaptation, and they've potentially added three key contributors that they'll control for roughly 17 player-seasons, in exchange for two they had under control for six or seven years at considerably greater cost. The question now is whether they just took themselves out of the AL Central race. Given the general weakness of the division, the answer is "not necessarily." Even if they go with rookies Scott Sizemore at second, Alex Avila behind the plate, and Austin Jackson (or Casper Wells) in center, they could still be a .500 team on the strength of a rotation built upon Verlander, Scherzer, and Porcello, and a .500 team is almost automatically a contender in the AL Central.

This certainly isn't the worst way to give the veterans a glory ride en route to futures in other organizations. If things start to slip away at the end of July, Dombrowski can start advertising a rent-a-vet initiative for any of the big contracts on short time, offering to pay the balance of the deals just to get some talent back by way of trade. That might sound dubious, but Ordonez and Guillen are only a year removed from useful seasons, and Robertson might finally be healthy enough to be a rotation regular again.

If this does wind up being a rebuild beyond 2010's final spin with the expensive old-timers, the challenge will be for the Tigers to continue the improvements in the player development program already initiated under scouting director David Chadd. With a sweet tooth for high-upside power arms, the accelerated arrivals of Porcello and Ryan Perry seem likely to be duplicated. It certainly isn't quite the desperation situation the organization has endured in other transitional periods, whether we're talking about the mishaps of the Smith or the Schembechler regimes.

HITTERS

Alex Avila   C   Bats: L   Throws: R   Height: 5' 11"   Weight: 210   Born: January 29, 1987   Age: 23

YEAR	TEAM	LVL	AGE	PA	R	2B	3B	HR	RBI	BB	SO	SB	CS	EqBRR	AVG	OBP	SLG	EqAVG	EqOBP	EqSLG	EqA	VORP	WARP	DEFENSE	
2008	WMI	A	21	244	21	14	0	1	22	27	41	0	1	-3.5	.305	.383	.385	.284	.350	.358	.252	6.1	0.8	42-C	0
2009	ERI	AA	22	387	52	23	1	12	55	52	77	2	1	-2.0	.264	.365	.450	.239	.325	.407	.255	13.0	1.8	80-C	2
2009	DET	MLB	22	72	9	4	0	5	14	10	18	0	0	-0.6	.279	.375	.590	.279	.375	.574	.313	6.9	0.4	17-C	-3
2010	DET	MLB	23	418	44	19	1	12	51	48	92	1	1	-1.8	.244	.330	.399	.247	.332	.399	.248	11.3	1.2	84-C	0

Breakout: 18%   Improve: 38%   Collapse: 14%   Attrition: 3%   MLB: 100%   Comparables: Bob Helsom, Billy McMillon, Mike Martin, Eric Helfand

Avila is the son of the Tigers' assistant GM, but taking him in the fifth round of 2008 was no act of nepotism. He's a legitimate ballplayer, one who reached the majors in his first full pro season. He features good plate discipline, decent power, and a quick release against baserunners. He's also slower than the DMV, has a good-sized platoon split, and is likely to be close to his ceiling right now. Gerald Laird is considered too good defensively (and too expensive, having reached arbitration) to waste on the short side of a platoon, but with Dusty Ryan gone and Laird still untraded at this writing, it appears that that just might be the case to open the season.

Brennan Boesch   OF   Bats: L   Throws: L   Height: 6' 6"   Weight: 210   Born: April 12, 1985   Age: 25

YEAR	TEAM	LVL	AGE	PA	R	2B	3B	HR	RBI	BB	SO	SB	CS	EqBRR	AVG	OBP	SLG	EqAVG	EqOBP	EqSLG	EqA	VORP	WARP	DEFENSE	
2007	WMI	A	22	542	52	19	4	10	86	23	81	15	4	-2.2	.267	.297	.378	.241	.267	.336	.210	-18.9	-2.2	113-RF	1
2008	LAK	A+	23	461	46	17	8	7	64	36	90	3	5	-3.1	.249	.310	.379	.223	.271	.336	.211	-14.9	-4.4	104-RF	-21
2009	ERI	AA	24	571	89	26	7	28	93	33	127	11	2	4.0	.275	.318	.510	.239	.274	.434	.242	-1.0	-0.4	122-RF	-2
2010	DET	MLB	25	501	53	20	4	11	65	30	121	4	2	-0.2	.228	.278	.358	.233	.281	.365	.212	-13.7	-1.9	109-RF	-4

Breakout: 13%   Improve: 39%   Collapse: 24%   Attrition: 14%   MLB: 5%   Comparables: Brent Bowers, J.T. Hall, B.J. Barns, Jamie Ogden

After hitting just 22 home runs in his first three years, the gigantic Boesch finally tapped into his power at Double-A, topping that total in just this one Erie season. He has a long way to go, though, because between a swing more hole-y than the pope and a swing-at-anything approach less discriminating than Tila Tequila, there are issues that go beyond mere ironing out.

Miguel Cabrera   1B   Bats: R   Throws: R   Height: 6' 4"   Weight: 240   Born: April 18, 1983   Age: 27

YEAR	TEAM	LVL	AGE	PA	R	2B	3B	HR	RBI	BB	SO	SB	CS	EqBRR	AVG	OBP	SLG	EqAVG	EqOBP	EqSLG	EqA	VORP	WARP	DEFENSE		
2007	FLO	MLB	24	680	91	38	2	34	119	79	127	2	1	-3.3	.320	.401	.565	.326	.407	.571	.326	66.7	5.9	147-3B	-11	
2008	DET	MLB	25	684	85	36	2	37	127	56	126	1	0	-2.5	.292	.349	.537	.292	.349	.540	.297	37.6	3.2	135-1B	-8	13-3B -1
2009	DET	MLB	26	685	96	34	0	34	103	68	107	6	2	-2.3	.324	.396	.547	.321	.393	.533	.311	40.3	4.7	147-1B	3	
2010	DET	MLB	27	703	94	32	1	40	125	80	119	3	2	-1.4	.302	.385	.551	.298	.379	.531	.307	45.8	4.8	154-1B	-1	

Breakout: 13%   Improve: 50%   Collapse: 10%   Attrition: 4%   MLB: 100%   Comparables: Derrek Lee, Paul Konerko, Mark McGwire, Joe Adcock

Cabrera was a solid, productive player for the Tigers last year. The trouble is that his contract is elite-level compensation, not solid and productive. The Tigers have made a series of missteps with their long-term contracts, signing players to salaries beyond the range of production they had already demonstrated, counting on either the players to improve or the market to grow to the point that what was an inflated salary shrinks relative to the cost of newer contracts. By moving to first and coming down from .330 EqAs to .310, Cabrera is now a 4-5 WARP player who's being paid like an 8-10 WARP player. We wouldn't be at all surprised to see him bust out for a .340 season one year, which will get him back up into the elite range, but that won't happen every year.

Brent Dlugach   SS   Bats: R   Throws: R   Height: 6' 4"   Weight: 195   Born: March 3, 1983   Age: 27

YEAR	TEAM	LVL	AGE	PA	R	2B	3B	HR	RBI	BB	SO	SB	CS	EqBRR	AVG	OBP	SLG	EqAVG	EqOBP	EqSLG	EqA	VORP	WARP	DEFENSE	
2007	ERI	AA	24	78	12	4	3	1	7	6	25	1	1	-0.5	.292	.346	.472	.247	.295	.397	.237	1.0	-0.3	20-SS	-4
2009	TOL	AAA	26	517	58	36	4	9	59	39	137	5	3	-1.2	.294	.349	.446	.271	.324	.418	.257	17.8	2.7	117-SS	5
2010	DET	MLB	27	348	36	18	3	6	35	28	98	2	2	-0.5	.246	.309	.386	.245	.306	.375	.234	3.0	0.4	81-SS	0

Breakout: 14%   Improve: 40%   Collapse: 22%   Attrition: 16%   MLB: 9%   Comparables: Rod Hobbs, Jake Wald, Mike Manfre, Kelly Dransfeldt

Dlugach missed almost all of 2007 and 2008 after tearing his labrum while diving for a grounder in the hole. It was a nice surprise to see that he retained both the pop in his bat and his outstanding defensive skills after so much downtime. Given his age, there's no projectability here; not only can Dlugach not be counted upon to improve, but since so much of his value is tied up in defense, he's more likely to start sliding downward. Performance-wise, there's no reason to expect much difference between Dlugach and Adam Everett, but Dlu is six years younger and at least a million bucks cheaper. That's a significant advantage for a team looking to pare costs.

Adam Everett			SS							Bats: R		Throws: R		Height: 6' 0"		Weight: 180		Born: February 2, 1977			Age: 33	
YEAR	TEAM	LVL	AGE	PA	R	2B	3B	HR	RBI	BB	SO	SB	CS	EqBRR	AVG	OBP	SLG	EqAVG	EqOBP	EqSLG	EqA	VORP	WARP	DEFENSE
2007	HOU	MLB	30	236	18	11	1	2	15	14	31	4	2	-1.7	.232	.281	.318	.236	.285	.323	.214	-2.2	0.4	59-SS 5
2008	MIN	MLB	31	150	19	6	1	2	20	12	15	0	0	0.8	.213	.278	.323	.216	.280	.328	.224	0.3	0.5	41-SS 3
2009	DET	MLB	32	390	43	21	0	3	44	22	61	5	2	2.4	.238	.288	.325	.238	.288	.328	.221	0.3	-0.3	106-SS -3
2010	DET	MLB	33	288	33	13	1	4	36	23	44	3	2	0.3	.248	.312	.356	.248	.310	.351	.228	0.7	0.2	80-SS 1

Breakout: 19% Improve: 56% Collapse: 13% Attrition: 19%   MLB: 89%   Comparables: Mike Bordick, Mike Lansing, John McDonald, Rafael Bournigal

Everett was brought in as a temp, a cheap, short-term solution for shortstop, and sometimes, you get exactly what you pay for. Everett was a good example of what BP's Jay Jaffe called a Replacement-Level Killer in our book *It Ain't Over*—a contending team fills a position with a noncontributing nonentity who arguably ends up costing the team a title. Everett's slight bat has been buoyed in the past by outstanding defense, but shoulder and ankle injuries have eroded those skills. He can't hit righties at all (.189 EqA), and he disappeared in the second half (.160 EqA after July 1st). Nevertheless, the temp will get to make a one-year encore at Comerica, because the Tigers care more about the "cheap" part than the "contending" part of getting replacement-killed.

Curtis Granderson			CF							Bats: L		Throws: R		Height: 6' 1"		Weight: 185		Born: March 16, 1981			Age: 29	
YEAR	TEAM	LVL	AGE	PA	R	2B	3B	HR	RBI	BB	SO	SB	CS	EqBRR	AVG	OBP	SLG	EqAVG	EqOBP	EqSLG	EqA	VORP	WARP	DEFENSE
2007	DET	MLB	26	676	122	38	23	23	74	52	141	26	1	6.9	.302	.361	.552	.298	.358	.551	.305	55.4	7.9	144-CF 14
2008	DET	MLB	27	629	112	26	13	22	66	71	111	12	4	5.9	.280	.365	.494	.283	.369	.505	.294	41.4	5.6	133-CF 9
2009	DET	MLB	28	710	91	23	8	30	71	72	141	20	6	1.9	.249	.327	.453	.249	.327	.448	.266	25.7	3.5	155-CF 6
2010	NYA	MLB	29	665	104	27	10	28	68	73	131	16	4	2.4	.268	.351	.491	.267	.347	.486	.280	35.2	4.4	143-CF 5

Breakout: 9% Improve: 47% Collapse: 6% Attrition: 6%   MLB: 99%   Comparables: Andy Van Slyke, Steve Finley, Lloyd Moseby, Vada Pinson

Granderson made it to 30 home runs, but he was waning with the season—his monthly OPS declined every month after May, sliding from 849 to 725. The park factors say that Detroit was an antilefty park last year, and Granderson was buried in home games. More troubling was how he disappeared against lefties, opening up a .297/.172 right/left EqA split that finally even Jim Leyland noticed, moving Granderson down in the order against lefties in September. He had an even more extreme split in 2007 (.307/.168) and bounced back fine in 2008, so it isn't the end of the world. Now that Granderson has been swapped to the Yankees, even with the new park's quickly minted reputation as a homer-happy home, his new team should be prepared for the possibility that he'll need a platoon mate.

Carlos Guillen			LF							Bats: S		Throws: R		Height: 6' 1"		Weight: 215		Born: September 30, 1975			Age: 34	
YEAR	TEAM	LVL	AGE	PA	R	2B	3B	HR	RBI	BB	SO	SB	CS	EqBRR	AVG	OBP	SLG	EqAVG	EqOBP	EqSLG	EqA	VORP	WARP	DEFENSE
2007	DET	MLB	31	630	86	35	9	21	102	55	93	13	8	-0.2	.296	.357	.502	.294	.356	.501	.287	40.4	3.0	120-SS -14 20-1B 2
2008	DET	MLB	32	489	68	29	2	10	54	60	67	9	3	0.8	.286	.376	.436	.288	.379	.441	.287	24.7	3.2	84-3B 4 18-1B 0
2009	DET	MLB	33	322	36	10	3	11	41	39	56	1	3	-0.1	.242	.339	.419	.243	.339	.409	.260	2.5	0.6	36-LF 2
2010	DET	MLB	34	372	45	16	3	11	49	43	63	4	3	0.1	.263	.353	.430	.263	.351	.417	.266	10.1	1.3	72-LF 2

Breakout: 5% Improve: 32% Collapse: 23% Attrition: 24%   MLB: 92%   Comparables: Jerry Mumphrey, Kevin McReynolds, Carl Everett, Gary Matthews

Guillen struggled out of the gate and eventually hit the DL with a shoulder injury that kept him out until late July and deprived him of the ability to hit right-handed long after that. He did hit well after he returned, batting .262/.371/.503 in 57 games, so he is a good bet to return to form in 2010. On the other hand, this is the second straight season in which he has missed significant time to injury, he's at an age where those things just get more common, and he's going to have to continue to hit at a very high level for his bat to stand out now that he's been pushed to the outfield.

Aubrey Huff   DH   Bats: L   Throws: R   Height: 6' 4"   Weight: 235   Born: December 20, 1976   Age: 33

YEAR	TEAM	LVL	AGE	PA	R	2B	3B	HR	RBI	BB	SO	SB	CS	EqBRR	AVG	OBP	SLG	EqAVG	EqOBP	EqSLG	EqA	VORP	WARP	DEFENSE			
2007	BAL	MLB	30	603	68	34	5	15	72	48	87	1	1	1.8	.280	.337	.442	.279	.337	.443	.268	12.2	0.6	47-1B	-3	14-3B	-3
2008	BAL	MLB	31	661	96	48	2	32	108	53	89	4	0	-2.3	.304	.360	.552	.306	.362	.556	.306	44.2	4.6	31-3B	-3	22-1B	0
2009	BAL	MLB	32	480	51	24	1	13	72	41	74	0	6	-3.9	.253	.321	.405	.255	.322	.400	.248	-6.7	-1.0	94-1B	-2		
2009	DET	MLB	32	117	8	6	0	2	13	10	13	0	0	-1.3	.189	.265	.302	.189	.265	.292	.198	-7.4	-0.9				
2010	SFN	NL	33	574	58	28	2	17	74	49	89	1	2	-1.7	.265	.331	.423	.268	.334	.434	.260	6.3	0.6	65-1B	-1		

Breakout: 8%   Improve: 37%   Collapse: 14%   Attrition: 17%   MLB: 94%   Comparables: Tino Martinez, Eddie Robinson, Sid Bream, Hal Morris

Huff was horrid in 2009, finishing dead last in the majors with a -14 VORP. For the Orioles, empty offense didn't matter; for the Tigers, trading for this "bat" in the middle of a pennant race was a disaster. He was hitting decently, in line with his 2005-07 performances, through early July; after a groin strain that never put him on the DL, his offense fell completely apart and his power all but disappeared. There's a good chance he'll return to being a .260-.270 EqA guy, but when you're limited to DH, that's worth essentially nothing. The Giants signed him to play first base, continuing a recent tradition of sub-par offense at the position.

Brandon Inge   3B   Bats: R   Throws: R   Height: 5' 11"   Weight: 190   Born: May 19, 1977   Age: 33

YEAR	TEAM	LVL	AGE	PA	R	2B	3B	HR	RBI	BB	SO	SB	CS	EqBRR	AVG	OBP	SLG	EqAVG	EqOBP	EqSLG	EqA	VORP	WARP	DEFENSE			
2007	DET	MLB	30	577	64	25	2	14	71	47	150	9	2	0.3	.236	.312	.376	.233	.309	.375	.243	2.3	2.2	147-3B	16		
2008	DET	MLB	31	407	41	16	4	11	51	43	94	4	3	-2.4	.205	.303	.369	.206	.307	.378	.241	6.3	2.2	55-C	3	36-3B	7
2009	DET	MLB	32	637	71	16	1	27	84	54	170	2	5	-2.3	.230	.314	.406	.230	.316	.400	.247	8.7	1.7	155-3B	7		
2010	DET	MLB	33	558	60	21	2	18	69	54	140	4	4	-0.8	.230	.317	.392	.227	.311	.380	.240	2.7	1.0	140-3B	6		

Breakout: 12%   Improve: 37%   Collapse: 19%   Attrition: 12%   MLB: 98%   Comparables: Gary Gaetti, Billy Johnson, Damion Easley, Steve Buechele

Inge played most of the season with a partially torn tendon in one knee, with inflammation or worse in the other as well; in November he had surgery on both knees, which must have made for a stay-at-home Thanksgiving. Inge had a surprisingly good first half, hitting 20 home runs before the All-Star game. After that, the pain in the knees started getting to him, yet he refused to come out (nobody wants to risk an angry Inge). Points for toughness, but as a hobbled player, he couldn't hit (.186/.259/.279 after the break) or field (assists per game dropped 20 percent after July 1st). The total stat line is almost exactly what was expected.

Cale Iorg   SS   Bats: R   Throws: R   Height: 6' 2"   Weight: 190   Born: September 6, 1985   Age: 24

YEAR	TEAM	LVL	AGE	PA	R	2B	3B	HR	RBI	BB	SO	SB	CS	EqBRR	AVG	OBP	SLG	EqAVG	EqOBP	EqSLG	EqA	VORP	WARP	DEFENSE	
2008	LAK	A+	22	431	61	15	7	10	47	35	111	22	11	-3.3	.251	.329	.405	.234	.295	.373	.234	5.5	-0.6	93-SS	-11
2009	ERI	AA	23	532	57	17	3	11	41	32	149	13	7	0.9	.222	.274	.336	.203	.245	.309	.192	-14.7	-1.8	122-SS	0
2010	DET	MLB	24	433	47	16	3	11	38	31	122	9	5	-0.6	.218	.279	.357	.216	.275	.348	.213	-4.7	-0.8	98-SS	-2

Breakout: 23%   Improve: 45%   Collapse: 19%   Attrition: 11%   MLB: 2%   Comparables: Jim Auten, Chuck Abbott, Will Pennyfeather, Martin Rivero

Iorg entered 2009 as the Tigers' top position-playing prospect, but while his defense was fine, his strike-zone judgment was nonprospect bad, calling into question whether he was rushed to Double-A. Whether he has a future left, or just a mighty big dent in it, remains to be seen, but there aren't a lot of positives to take from getting stomped.

Gerald Laird   C   Bats: R   Throws: R   Height: 6' 1"   Weight: 225   Born: November 13, 1979   Age: 30

YEAR	TEAM	LVL	AGE	PA	R	2B	3B	HR	RBI	BB	SO	SB	CS	EqBRR	AVG	OBP	SLG	EqAVG	EqOBP	EqSLG	EqA	VORP	WARP	DEFENSE	
2007	TEX	MLB	27	448	48	18	3	9	47	30	103	6	2	2.1	.224	.278	.349	.222	.278	.353	.222	5.1	1.9	112-C	11
2008	TEX	MLB	28	381	54	24	0	6	41	23	63	2	4	1.1	.276	.329	.398	.284	.337	.412	.256	15.0	1.5	85-C	0
2009	DET	MLB	29	477	49	23	2	4	33	40	68	5	0	2.0	.225	.306	.320	.224	.307	.315	.228	5.8	2.8	122-C	13
2010	DET	MLB	30	437	54	19	2	9	45	37	80	4	3	0.9	.246	.322	.372	.244	.320	.364	.237	7.0	1.2	111-C	4

Breakout: 14%   Improve: 45%   Collapse: 15%   Attrition: 7%   MLB: 99%   Comparables: Dan Wilson, Jason LaRue, Bob Boone, Henry Blanco

Texas was overflowing with catchers, and the Tigers were anxious to get Inge out from behind the plate, so Laird was dealt to the Motor City. As we worried about last year, the Tigers overused him. Jim Leyland had no confidence in any of his backups until Avila came up in August, so Laird wound up leading the AL in games caught and wore down badly as the season dragged on. While his inability to hit right-handed pitching is a good reason to limit his use, his defense is a good reason to keep him out there as more than just the short side of a platoon.

Jeff Larish 1B/3B | Bats: L | Throws: R | Height: 6' 2" | Weight: 200 | Born: October 11, 1982 | Age: 27

YEAR	TEAM	LVL	AGE	PA	R	2B	3B	HR	RBI	BB	SO	SB	CS	EqBRR	AVG	OBP	SLG	EqAVG	EqOBP	EqSLG	EqA	VORP	WARP	DEFENSE	
2007	ERI	AA	24	556	71	25	2	28	101	87	108	6	2	-0.5	.267	.390	.515	.231	.338	.426	.266	9.2	0.4	120-1B -6	
2008	TOL	AAA	25	440	49	20	2	21	64	50	109	0	1	1.5	.250	.341	.477	.245	.330	.459	.269	9.0	1.8	92-1B 7	8-3B -1
2008	DET	MLB	25	111	12	6	0	2	16	7	34	2	2	-0.5	.260	.306	.375	.269	.315	.404	.238	-0.6	-0.6	9-3B -4	4-1B 0
2009	TOL	AAA	26	257	38	13	0	6	26	42	56	2	2	1.0	.265	.397	.412	.252	.377	.388	.272	3.7	0.3	50-1B 0	4-3B -1
2009	DET	MLB	26	90	13	3	1	4	7	15	25	0	1	0.2	.216	.344	.446	.216	.344	.446	.269	1.0	0.2	8-1B 1	
2010	DET	MLB	27	431	45	17	1	14	52	52	112	2	2	0.3	.228	.326	.391	.230	.326	.391	.244	-2.6	-0.3	89-1B 0	

Breakout: 3%　Improve: 24%　Collapse: 31%　Attrition: 10%　　MLB: 42%　　Comparables: Bob Tumpane, Jessie Reid, Tom Grant, Phil Stephenson

Larish made the team out of spring training, but he only got a rental on that last roster spot; he wound up being sparingly used in Detroit and was readily yo-yoed to Toledo whenever Leyland wanted an extra pitcher. He could be a productive bat if given a chance. Instead, he's stuck behind a fixture in Cabrera in a park that kills left-handed power. He tried to play through a wrist injury with the Mud Hens and eventually had season-ending surgery; he's better than his final line.

Magglio Ordonez RF | Bats: R | Throws: R | Height: 6' 0" | Weight: 215 | Born: January 28, 1974 | Age: 36

YEAR	TEAM	LVL	AGE	PA	R	2B	3B	HR	RBI	BB	SO	SB	CS	EqBRR	AVG	OBP	SLG	EqAVG	EqOBP	EqSLG	EqA	VORP	WARP	DEFENSE
2007	DET	MLB	33	678	117	54	0	28	139	76	79	4	1	-2.0	.363	.434	.595	.358	.430	.590	.340	72.4	8.6	137-RF 6
2008	DET	MLB	34	623	72	32	2	21	103	53	76	1	5	-8.0	.317	.376	.494	.320	.379	.503	.296	36.2	2.7	128-RF -12
2009	DET	MLB	35	518	54	24	2	9	50	51	65	3	1	-1.1	.310	.376	.428	.308	.375	.422	.280	18.3	1.9	89-RF -1
2010	DET	MLB	36	499	56	25	1	15	76	52	73	2	2	-1.5	.295	.370	.457	.293	.365	.448	.279	20.7	2.2	98-RF -1

Breakout: 5%　Improve: 26%　Collapse: 26%　Attrition: 32%　　MLB: 98%　　Comparables: Moises Alou, Carl Furillo, Al Smith, Sid Gordon

For much of the season, Ordonez was the subject of a contract-inspired drama: if he were to reach 457 plate appearances, his $18 million option for 2010 would vest. He did, despite a season where his power vanished, he was benched for a week, and initially returned to the lineup as a platoon player. Perhaps the rest did him good, because while the power stayed away, he did hit .381 over the final two months and was just about the only Tiger keeping the offense afloat. Still, he could hit .381 all season, and if the power doesn't come back, he still won't be worth 18 megabucks.

Placido Polanco 2B/3B | Bats: R | Throws: R | Height: 5' 10" | Weight: 195 | Born: October 10, 1975 | Age: 34

YEAR	TEAM	LVL	AGE	PA	R	2B	3B	HR	RBI	BB	SO	SB	CS	EqBRR	AVG	OBP	SLG	EqAVG	EqOBP	EqSLG	EqA	VORP	WARP	DEFENSE
2007	DET	MLB	31	641	105	36	3	9	67	37	30	7	3	0.9	.341	.388	.458	.340	.387	.459	.292	42.3	5.1	135-2B 3
2008	DET	MLB	32	629	90	34	3	8	58	35	43	7	1	2.9	.307	.350	.417	.310	.354	.422	.272	27.4	2.4	135-2B -7
2009	DET	MLB	33	675	82	31	4	10	72	36	46	7	2	1.3	.285	.331	.396	.285	.331	.389	.254	15.0	3.4	144-2B 14
2010	PHI	MLB	34	597	80	30	3	8	57	39	47	5	3	0.8	.290	.346	.400	.291	.345	.400	.260	17.9	2.1	131-2B 2

Breakout: 8%　Improve: 37%　Collapse: 26%　Attrition: 26%　　MLB: 95%　　Comparables: Orlando Cabrera, Mark Loretta, Johnny Temple, Alvin Dark

Gold Glove–winner Polanco was healthy all year, but posted the second-worst EqA of his career, and he had to rally to do even that, hitting .318 over the final two months. His EqA has dropped two years in a row; players of his age, who played regularly during the previous three years, only have one chance in four of reaching their three-year average EqA in their following year (in Polanco's case, .267, only a couple of points above average for a second baseman). Nonetheless, the Phillies jumped on Polanco early in the offseason, signing him to a three-year deal (with a mutual option for a fourth) to replace Pedro Feliz as their third baseman. Polanco did have some mildly bad luck on balls in play, so perhaps he's in line for a rebound, but even if he returns to his career rates of .303/.348/.414, that's not special production by the standards of major-league third basemen, who have averaged .268/.338/.433 over the last three years. If Polanco can't get his on-base percentage back into the .350 range, the Phillies are going to find themselves trying to continue their current run of pennant winners with an aging, ineffective singles hitter at the hot corner.

Ryan Raburn — UT

Bats: R Throws: R Height: 6' 0" Weight: 185 Born: April 17, 1981 Age: 29

YEAR	TEAM	LVL	AGE	PA	R	2B	3B	HR	RBI	BB	SO	SB	CS	EqBRR	AVG	OBP	SLG	EqAVG	EqOBP	EqSLG	EqA	VORP	WARP	DEFENSE			
2007	TOL	AAA	26	373	60	21	3	17	64	51	73	12	4	2.5	.292	.394	.540	.283	.373	.512	.299	25.8	2.7	45-CF	0	39-LF	-3
2007	DET	MLB	26	148	28	12	2	4	27	8	33	3	0	2.2	.304	.340	.507	.299	.336	.496	.286	7.5	1.0	10-RF	2	8-2B	0
2008	DET	MLB	27	199	26	10	1	4	20	16	49	3	1	2.4	.236	.298	.368	.238	.299	.365	.237	-0.4	-0.2	14-LF	1	13-2B	-2
2009	TOL	AAA	28	56	11	3	0	5	9	7	13	2	1	0.5	.255	.357	.638	.229	.321	.521	.277	2.4	0.4	10-CF	1		
2009	DET	MLB	28	291	44	11	2	16	45	26	60	5	4	0.2	.291	.359	.533	.292	.360	.519	.291	15.7	1.7	48-LF	2	5-RF	-1
2010	DET	MLB	29	462	67	23	3	18	69	48	106	8	4	1.5	.261	.342	.466	.257	.335	.448	.270	15.0	1.6	73-LF	0		

Breakout: 9% Improve: 25% Collapse: 13% Attrition: 7%   MLB: 89%   Comparables: Scott Hairston, Ryan Spilborghs, Gary Ward, Bernard Gilkey

Raburn didn't earn a roster spot last spring—in fact, the team was trying to trade him—but he'll have one in 2010, barring a complete collapse. He can respectably impersonate a fielder at any position, which is valuable enough in these occasional days of 13-man pitching staffs, but he is a legitimate hitter. He socked 16 homers in essentially half-time play, and his minor-league history says he's not as much of a platoon hitter as his .314/.245 left/right EqA split last year says; its not hard to see him graduating to a full-time role.

Wilkin Ramirez — OF

Bats: R Throws: R Height: 6' 2" Weight: 190 Born: October 25, 1985 Age: 24

YEAR	TEAM	LVL	AGE	PA	R	2B	3B	HR	RBI	BB	SO	SB	CS	EqBRR	AVG	OBP	SLG	EqAVG	EqOBP	EqSLG	EqA	VORP	WARP	DEFENSE	
2007	LAK	A+	21	343	48	7	4	10	41	20	86	28	6	4.2	.273	.315	.414	.245	.283	.379	.234	-3.1	-0.3	77-LF	1
2007	ERI	AA	21	133	15	3	1	2	14	8	38	6	2	-0.8	.215	.273	.306	.195	.242	.285	.187	-7.7	-1.4	17-LF	-4
2008	ERI	AA	22	482	74	24	7	19	73	43	138	26	12	0.4	.303	.371	.522	.265	.324	.448	.264	10.6	0.2	100-LF	-9
2008	TOL	AAA	22	38	2	1	0	0	0	1	11	1	0	0.3	.083	.132	.111	.083	.132	.139	.000	-4.8	-0.7	9-LF	-1
2009	TOL	AAA	23	481	69	18	6	17	51	41	143	33	10	3.9	.258	.326	.445	.248	.314	.431	.258	7.1	0.2	93-LF	-6
2009	DET	MLB	23	13	6	0	1	1	3	1	3	0	0	-0.1	.364	.385	.818	.364	.385	.818	.360	1.8	0.2		
2010	DET	MLB	24	476	58	18	3	16	52	36	144	18	7	1.3	.234	.297	.403	.230	.292	.385	.237	-1.4	-0.5	96-LF	-3

Breakout: 9% Improve: 40% Collapse: 20% Attrition: 13%   MLB: 10%   Comparables: Yamil Benitez, Stoney Briggs, Dennis Hood, Tyrone Woods

Ramirez is a perennial prospect due to his tremendous athleticism and tools, but he very nearly got relegated to one-line status because he can't stop striking out so damn much. That's not the only raw-edged component in his game—he also makes his share of mistakes on the bases and in the field. With old men in the outfield corners and Curtis Granderson in pinstripes, raw may be no roadblock to a big-league job this spring, but if you thought Curtis Maybin needed seasoning last season with the Marlins, you can imagine how much paprika it'll take in this instance.

Dusty Ryan — C

Bats: R Throws: R Height: 6' 4" Weight: 220 Born: September 2, 1984 Age: 25

YEAR	TEAM	LVL	AGE	PA	R	2B	3B	HR	RBI	BB	SO	SB	CS	EqBRR	AVG	OBP	SLG	EqAVG	EqOBP	EqSLG	EqA	VORP	WARP	DEFENSE			
2007	LAK	A+	22	168	17	0	0	7	22	18	52	0	1	-2.6	.214	.310	.359	.196	.280	.324	.213	-1.4	-0.4	32-C	-2		
2008	ERI	AA	23	338	46	17	2	15	50	38	95	2	1	0.4	.253	.340	.476	.228	.302	.422	.249	8.7	0.7	65-C	-4	7-1B	1
2008	TOL	AAA	23	81	12	7	2	2	13	6	27	0	0	-0.7	.315	.370	.548	.311	.366	.541	.303	7.2	0.8	17-C	0		
2008	DET	MLB	23	50	6	2	0	2	7	5	13	0	0	0.2	.318	.380	.500	.318	.380	.500	.304	4.7	0.8	14-C	2		
2009	TOL	AAA	24	235	25	8	1	10	35	29	64	2	0	-1.0	.257	.359	.455	.246	.343	.438	.272	13.0	1.2	60-C	-3		
2009	DET	MLB	24	30	1	1	0	0	4	4	12	0	1	-0.4	.154	.267	.192	.154	.267	.192	.152	-1.5	-0.2	9-C	0		
2010	SDN	MLB	25	314	32	11	1	10	36	34	102	1	1	-0.7	.216	.306	.377	.227	.311	.397	.253	10.4	1.0	72-C	-1		

Breakout: 18% Improve: 40% Collapse: 21% Attrition: 10%   MLB: 60%   Comparables: David Wallace, Colt Morton, Chris Hatcher, Kevin Richardson

Ryan has lit up the minors the last two years, but due to defensive concerns, the Tigers weren't ready to turn the reins over to him in 2009; instead they traded for Laird and kept Ryan down to start in Toledo rather than sub in Detroit. He battered Triple-A pitching yet again, but flopped badly in a midseason call-up and then watched Alex Avila succeed in his place. Traded to the Padres, he'll compete with Nick Hundley for playing time.

Ramon Santiago   SS

Bats: S   Throws: R   Height: 5' 11"   Weight: 175   Born: August 31, 1979   Age: 30

YEAR	TEAM	LVL	AGE	PA	R	2B	3B	HR	RBI	BB	SO	SB	CS	EqBRR	AVG	OBP	SLG	EqAVG	EqOBP	EqSLG	EqA	VORP	WARP	DEFENSE			
2007	TOL	AAA	27	402	40	19	4	3	30	16	61	8	9	-5.1	.263	.309	.362	.257	.294	.349	.223	-0.3	1.0	89-SS	9		
2007	DET	MLB	27	74	10	5	1	0	7	1	10	3	0	0.0	.284	.324	.388	.284	.324	.373	.257	2.3	0.7	21-SS	3		
2008	TOL	AAA	28	33	3	2	0	0	3	2	7	0	0	-0.7	.214	.313	.286	.207	.281	.276	.200	-0.5	-0.6	8-SS	-5		
2008	DET	MLB	28	156	30	6	2	4	18	22	17	1	0	1.1	.282	.411	.460	.285	.413	.455	.306	12.8	0.7	26-SS	-5	13-2B	-1
2009	DET	MLB	29	296	29	6	2	7	35	17	57	1	2	-2.7	.267	.318	.385	.266	.317	.382	.245	6.2	0.6	56-SS	0	18-2B	-1
2010	DET	MLB	30	335	41	14	2	6	34	25	59	3	2	-1.4	.259	.326	.382	.259	.325	.378	.242	5.4	0.6	85-SS	0		

Breakout: 12%   Improve: 34%   Collapse: 19%   Attrition: 16%   MLB: 85%   Comparables: Jose Uribe, Kazuo Matsui, Domingo Cedeno, Bud Harrelson

Whatever fairy dust gave Santiago an eagle eye in 2008 vanished like so many Michigan jobs in 2009, as he reverted to his typical no-hit form. He plays a role that virtually every team in baseball has, but in this case, it's not as much "backup" as "redundancy"; there's hardly any difference between Santiago and Everett in the type of player they are. The team could do better to exploit what little difference there is by starting him more often against righties.

Scott Sizemore   2B

Bats: R   Throws: R   Height: 6' 0"   Weight: 185   Born: January 4, 1985   Age: 25

YEAR	TEAM	LVL	AGE	PA	R	2B	3B	HR	RBI	BB	SO	SB	CS	EqBRR	AVG	OBP	SLG	EqAVG	EqOBP	EqSLG	EqA	VORP	WARP	DEFENSE			
2007	TOL	AAA	27	402	40	19	4	3	30	16	61	8	9	-5.1	.263	.309	.362	.257	.294	.349	.223	-0.3	1.0	89-SS	9		
2007	DET	MLB	27	74	10	5	1	0	7	1	10	3	0	0.0	.284	.324	.388	.284	.324	.373	.257	2.3	0.7	21-SS	3		
2008	TOL	AAA	28	33	3	2	0	0	3	2	7	0	0	-0.7	.214	.313	.286	.207	.281	.276	.200	-0.5	-0.6	8-SS	-5		
2008	DET	MLB	28	156	30	6	2	4	18	22	17	1	0	1.1	.282	.411	.460	.285	.413	.455	.306	12.8	0.7	26-SS	-5	13-2B	-1
2009	DET	MLB	29	296	29	6	2	7	35	17	57	1	2	-2.7	.267	.318	.385	.266	.317	.382	.245	6.2	0.6	56-SS	0	18-2B	-1
2010	DET	MLB	25	496	61	26	3	11	42	52	91	9	4	-1.0	.256	.338	.402	.253	.333	.385	.254	11.7	1.4	105-2B	1		

Breakout: 2%   Improve: 25%   Collapse: 16%   Attrition: 10%   MLB: 12%   Comparables: Jed Hansen, Mark Bradley, Steven Tolleson, Dave Matranga

The Tigers had a well-laid plan to let Polanco go as a free agent (mission accomplished) and give his job to Sizemore, but have to be concerned with how the latter will recover from a broken ankle in the Arizona Fall League. Sizemore is an offense-first second baseman who has hit everywhere he's played, relying on outstanding hand-eye coordination and a quick, compact stroke. He's a doubles machine and should hit 15-20 homers. He plays with a quiet intensity; scouts love his makeup. He only has average speed and can be sloppy on defense, neither of which will be helped by the ankle injury.

Ryan Strieby   1B

Bats: R   Throws: R   Height: 6' 5"   Weight: 235   Born: August 9, 1985   Age: 24

YEAR	TEAM	LVL	AGE	PA	R	2B	3B	HR	RBI	BB	SO	SB	CS	EqBRR	AVG	OBP	SLG	EqAVG	EqOBP	EqSLG	EqA	VORP	WARP	DEFENSE			
2007	WMI	A	21	519	65	23	2	16	76	63	78	6	5	-2.9	.253	.347	.422	.233	.314	.379	.245	-3.6	-1.5	112-1B	-9		
2008	LAK	A+	22	478	65	19	7	29	94	46	101	0	1	-0.5	.278	.352	.563	.255	.316	.500	.273	11.9	0.7	92-1B	-6		
2009	ERI	AA	23	362	64	18	1	19	58	57	80	2	0	-2.5	.303	.427	.565	.271	.377	.500	.299	17.3	1.2	64-1B	-1	16-LF	-6
2010	DET	MLB	24	439	56	19	2	19	67	47	101	2	1	-1.0	.253	.337	.464	.247	.329	.447	.268	8.5	0.6	94-1B	-3		

Breakout: 19%   Improve: 39%   Collapse: 12%   Attrition: 7%   MLB: 11%   Comparables: Brandon Sing, Brock Peterson, Eddie Vargas, Mark Higgins

A pure masher, Strieby has established himself as a classic slugging first baseman. He has steadily improved his game as he has risen through the minors, maintaining his power despite hamate problems—problems with that wrist bone often kill power. Still, Strieby has not one but two problems: the first is that he doesn't have any useful skills except hitting, and the second is Miguel Cabrera. The two combine to explain why Strieby played some left field last year despite not even being able to play an adequate first; the Tigers want to find someplace for a bat like this to play.

Marcus Thames — DH

Bats: R   Throws: R   Height: 6' 2"   Weight: 220   Born: March 6, 1977   Age: 33

YEAR	TEAM	LVL	AGE	PA	R	2B	3B	HR	RBI	BB	SO	SB	CS	EqBRR	AVG	OBP	SLG	EqAVG	EqOBP	EqSLG	EqA	VORP	WARP	DEFENSE			
2007	DET	MLB	30	284	37	15	0	18	54	13	72	2	1	-0.1	.242	.278	.498	.238	.275	.494	.256	2.8	0.9	31-LF	1	22-1B	2
2008	DET	MLB	31	342	50	12	0	25	56	24	95	0	3	-1.5	.241	.292	.516	.241	.295	.521	.267	8.7	0.7	55-LF	-2	5-1B	0
2009	TOL	AAA	32	54	6	0	0	2	6	5	14	0	0	0.0	.245	.315	.367	.240	.309	.360	.235	-1.5	-0.2				
2009	DET	MLB	32	294	33	11	1	13	36	29	72	0	2	-2.2	.252	.323	.453	.250	.320	.438	.263	1.6	-0.1	14-LF	-2		
2010	DET	MLB	33	304	34	11	0	16	43	26	84	1	1	-0.6	.231	.299	.447	.226	.291	.424	.246	2.0	0.2	40-LF	-1		

Breakout: 5%   Improve: 29%   Collapse: 24%   Attrition: 29%   MLB: 94%   Comparables: Gorman Thomas, Joe Rudi, Johnny Lindell, Tony Armas

Thames is as one-dimensional a player as you'll find in the majors, and that dimension is the home run. After missing almost two months with a strained rib, Thames had two months to shine as the team's primary DH. That lasted until Carlos Guillen came off the DL and claimed the DH slot for himself. With the reduced playing time, Thames lost his stroke, failing to hit a home run in his last 29 appearances of the season (84 PAs). Thames is a free agent at this writing, one who still should have some appeal as part of a DH/pinch-hitting package (with five home runs in 55 career pinch-hit at-bats, he carries a .636 slugging percentage in the role), provided he can rediscover his one dimension.

Clete Thomas — OF

Bats: L   Throws: R   Height: 5' 11"   Weight: 195   Born: November 14, 1983   Age: 26

YEAR	TEAM	LVL	AGE	PA	R	2B	3B	HR	RBI	BB	SO	SB	CS	EqBRR	AVG	OBP	SLG	EqAVG	EqOBP	EqSLG	EqA	VORP	WARP	DEFENSE			
2007	ERI	AA	23	599	97	30	6	8	53	59	110	18	11	-2.8	.280	.359	.405	.252	.320	.361	.240	3.9	0.7	122-CF	2	4-LF	0
2008	TOL	AAA	24	333	44	18	2	9	45	37	88	29	11	-1.0	.247	.333	.416	.241	.323	.405	.255	7.3	-0.3	75-CF	-10		
2008	DET	MLB	24	133	7	9	1	1	9	14	26	2	0	-1.1	.284	.366	.405	.287	.369	.409	.277	5.2	0.7	16-LF	1	13-CF	1
2009	TOL	AAA	25	205	27	17	1	1	17	26	49	18	3	1.5	.291	.390	.417	.266	.361	.390	.273	7.1	0.3	29-RF	1	14-CF	-6
2009	DET	MLB	25	310	46	13	3	7	39	33	77	3	0	2.0	.240	.324	.385	.240	.324	.382	.250	2.3	1.1	56-RF	8	16-LF	-1
2010	DET	MLB	26	471	56	23	3	8	44	49	118	13	6	-0.2	.236	.318	.362	.240	.321	.369	.235	-2.3	0.3	100-RF	5		

Breakout: 9%   Improve: 36%   Collapse: 17%   Attrition: 12%   MLB: 81%   Comparables: Rob Mackowiak, Jeromy Burnitz, Ron Calloway, Jeff Salazar

Thomas is a speedy backup outfielder, a generic example of a type so numerous they deserve their own taxonomic scheme, complete with Latinate classification: *velox susicivus upilio opilio*. He's shown a tendency to go on streaks of hot and cold hitting—pitchers are able to build a book on him, and he's slow (or unable) to react. His natural swing is long, requiring him to constantly fight to keep it compact and avoid racking up Ks. He did manage to elevate himself into a platoon role in right for a while, when he was hot and Magglio was not, but we don't expect such chances to present themselves again; he's more of an injury replacement.

Casper Wells — CF

Bats: R   Throws: R   Height: 6' 2"   Weight: 210   Born: November 23, 1984   Age: 25

YEAR	TEAM	LVL	AGE	PA	R	2B	3B	HR	RBI	BB	SO	SB	CS	EqBRR	AVG	OBP	SLG	EqAVG	EqOBP	EqSLG	EqA	VORP	WARP	DEFENSE			
2007	ONE	A-	22	288	46	18	11	9	47	18	64	8	7	-0.8	.265	.323	.523	.219	.257	.404	.224	-6.0	-1.8	31-RF	0	28-LF	-5
2008	WMI	A	23	211	30	7	0	10	26	22	39	17	5	1.3	.240	.351	.447	.206	.288	.349	.227	-3.6	-0.1	46-RF	3		
2008	ERI	AA	23	313	60	18	6	17	53	30	66	8	3	1.9	.289	.376	.589	.253	.328	.491	.276	13.9	1.8	57-CF	-4	18-RF	5
2009	ERI	AA	24	367	52	18	4	15	41	43	103	8	8	-2.0	.260	.369	.489	.231	.319	.420	.254	7.7	0.7	82-CF	-2		
2010	DET	MLB	25	383	48	16	3	13	43	34	103	7	3	0.1	.228	.311	.410	.225	.306	.398	.244	5.3	0.4	87-CF	-2		

Breakout: 10%   Improve: 44%   Collapse: 16%   Attrition: 10%   MLB: 6%   Comparables: Alan Cockrell, Ozzie Canseco, Chris Jones, Troy Afenir

The film major from Towson State is an injury-prone, bulky outfielder with good power and a complete tools set (including a strong arm). Wells swings and misses a little too often at the plate to profile as a regular, but a strong platoon split may make him useful as a lefty-basher off the bench, and it might be a role he can handle without breaking down, à la Thames.

PITCHERS

Jeremy Bonderman

Bats: R   Throws: R   Height: 6' 2"   Weight: 220   Born: October 28, 1982   Age: 27

YEAR	TEAM	LVL	AGE	W	L	SV	G	GS	IP	H	HR	BB	SO	GB%	BABIP	STUFF	WHIP	ERA	SIERA	DERA	EqH9	EqHR9	EqBB9	EqSO9	VORP	SN/WX
2007	DET	MLB	24	11	9	0	28	28	174^1	193	23	48	145	54%	.319	11	1.38	5.01	3.80	5.01	9.7	1.1	2.2	6.9	9.4	2.56
2008	DET	MLB	25	3	4	0	12	12	71^1	75	9	36	44	50%	.291	1	1.56	4.29	5.12	4.48	8.8	1.0	4.0	5.2	8.1	1.35
2009	TOL	AAA	26	1	4	1	14	3	34	40	4	7	26	43%	.330	-11	1.38	4.24	3.92	5.37	11.3	1.7	2.2	5.5	0.5	0.28
2009	DET	MLB	26	0	1	0	8	1	10^1	16	4	8	5	45%	.343	-33	2.32	8.71	6.32	8.10	13.5	2.7	6.3	3.6	-2.9	-0.22
2010	DET	MLB	27	4	5	0	19	12	83^2	93	12	32	61	46%	.320	1	1.50	4.93	4.42	5.12	9.9	1.1	3.2	6.1	3.5	0.85

Breakout: 18%   Improve: 47%   Collapse: 16%   Attrition: 27%   MLB: 81%   Comparables: Mike Wood, Omar Olivares, Paul Rigdon, Rick Aguilera

Looking back to 2006-07, Bonderman lived and died by his slider. It was his best pitch, and he threw it something like a third of the time. That's a lot—there are quite literally no pitchers who throw sliders more often than that. Some pitches are inherently harder on the arm than others—curves, screwballs, sliders, split-fingers, even spitballs from the Deadball Era—and pitchers who rely on them too heavily tend to have just a couple of years of dominance before the damage catches up to them. It isn't clear from Bonderman's struggles this season whether he's still injured but fixable, or healthy and permanently damaged, but the strong likelihood is that he'll never be able to throw the slider that well or that often ever again. That seems likely to make him just another pitcher, and not a particularly good one.

Eddie Bonine

Bats: R   Throws: R   Height: 6' 5"   Weight: 220   Born: June 6, 1981   Age: 29

YEAR	TEAM	LVL	AGE	W	L	SV	G	GS	IP	H	HR	BB	SO	GB%	BABIP	STUFF	WHIP	ERA	SIERA	DERA	EqH9	EqHR9	EqBB9	EqSO9	VORP	SN/WX
2007	ERI	AA	26	14	5	0	25	25	154^2	159	13	24	73	58%	.280	-8	1.18	3.90	4.59	5.30	10.0	1.2	1.7	3.0	3.2	0.00
2008	TOL	AAA	27	12	4	0	17	17	106^1	107	10	18	69	60%	.287	-4	1.18	4.15	3.98	5.18	9.2	1.4	1.7	4.0	3.6	0.69
2008	DET	MLB	27	2	1	0	5	5	26^2	36	3	5	9	61%	.337	-10	1.54	5.40	5.16	5.79	11.9	1.1	1.4	2.8	-0.8	0.16
2009	TOL	AAA	28	4	5	0	17	17	102	112	9	16	51	62%	.300	-12	1.25	4.41	4.44	5.79	10.5	1.3	1.7	3.5	-3.1	-0.04
2009	DET	MLB	28	1	1	0	10	4	34^1	40	7	12	19	69%	.311	-10	1.51	4.46	4.53	4.50	10.7	1.7	2.8	4.8	3.6	0.51
2010	DET	MLB	29	5	8	0	23	20	115^2	135	17	35	50	67%	.302	-13	1.47	5.05	4.79	5.24	10.3	1.2	2.5	3.7	3.3	1.29

Breakout: 9%   Improve: 49%   Collapse: 20%   Attrition: 17%   MLB: 26%   Comparables: Jeff Heathcock, Kennie Steenstra, Larry Luebbers, Mike Rowland

For someone who has resort to the knuckleball, Bonine has a good fastball; by any *relevant* standard, however, it's not good. He does his best with what he has, keeping the ball down and limiting free passes, but he's just not capable of missing bats. Don't get too excited, ye knuckler enthusiasts waiting for someone to keep the pitch alive once the inevitable end claims Tim Wakefield: Bonine does throw a sort of hard knuckleball, but just once in a while as a show-me pitch, not as a regular offering; he relies on a pretty standard fastball/slider/change arsenal.

Casey Crosby

Bats: R   Throws: L   Height: 6' 5"   Weight: 200   Born: September 17, 1988   Age: 21

YEAR	TEAM	LVL	AGE	W	L	SV	G	GS	IP	H	HR	BB	SO	GB%	BABIP	STUFF	WHIP	ERA	SIERA	DERA	EqH9	EqHR9	EqBB9	EqSO9	VORP	SN/WX
2009	WMI	A	20	10	4	0	24	24	104^2	70	3	48	117	54%	.270	22	1.13	2.41	3.17	5.14	8.8	1.5	5.4	6.2	3.6	0.74
2010	DET	MLB	21	3	7	0	22	22	87	98	14	56	55	51%	.308	17	1.76	6.05	5.36	6.09	9.8	1.3	5.3	5.3	-5.7	2.45

Breakout: 17%   Improve: 33%   Collapse: 27%   Attrition: 3%   MLB: 1%   Comparables: Micah Bowie, Tom Marx, Andy Pettitte, James Houser

Crosby has barely had a pro career, missing almost all the time since being drafted in 2007 to Tommy John surgery. He came back last year hurling 93-97 mph fastballs, a hard down-biting curveball, and a mediocre change. Like many other TJ survivors, his control was shaky, but it improved as the season went on. Teams didn't hit him for average (.195) or power (three home runs) all year, so once he got his control back he was totally dominant. Crosby was on very tight pitch counts last year due to the injury; the team may loosen up a little as he advances—or they could go a different route, transforming him into a power reliever. With his stuff, Crosby has got definite closer potential despite being left-handed.

Casey Fien

Bats: R   Throws: R   Height: 6' 2"   Weight: 195   Born: October 21, 1983   Age: 26

YEAR	TEAM	LVL	AGE	W	L	SV	G	GS	IP	H	HR	BB	SO	GB%	BABIP	STUFF	WHIP	ERA	SIERA	DERA	EqH9	EqHR9	EqBB9	EqSO9	VORP	SN/WX
2007	WMI	A	23	6	1	6	39	0	61	55	4	10	77	36%	.321	-5	1.07	3.10	2.04	6.12	10.2	1.7	2.2	7.2	-4.0	0.79
2008	ERI	AA	24	3	3	12	40	0	45²	38	5	12	42	29%	.266	-1	1.09	2.96	3.53	3.71	8.0	1.2	2.5	6.4	8.7	0.35
2008	TOL	AAA	24	2	0	1	12	0	15	14	2	4	17	39%	.316	5	1.20	2.40	2.72	3.21	9.6	1.9	2.6	7.7	3.6	0.36
2009	TOL	AAA	25	2	1	14	42	0	58	51	5	15	66	40%	.315	7	1.14	3.41	2.61	4.42	9.0	1.3	2.7	8.5	6.5	0.79
2009	DET	MLB	25	0	1	0	9	0	11¹	13	2	6	9	34%	.306	-15	1.68	7.94	4.94	7.71	10.0	1.5	3.9	6.2	-2.9	-0.33
2010	DET	MLB	26	3	4	3	50	0	641	69	9	25	50	33%	.312	-5	1.45	4.93	4.51	5.15	9.6	1.3	3.2	6.6	2.5	1.29

Breakout: 22% Improve: 44% Collapse: 21% Attrition: 9%   MLB: 29%   Comparables: Marty Mason, Josh Roenicke, Danny Rueckel, Jeff Pierce

Fien (pronounced like "fiend" without the *d*, not like "fine") is a reasonably good-looking relief prospect, projecting primarily as a middle-innings guy, if there are prospects for that. He was a starter in college and doesn't have the stuff to close, so you don't want to limit him to just one inning. He has a decent fastball, the home-run rate of someone who has trouble keeping the ball down, and a very large on/empty split, suggesting problems throwing from the stretch. He struggled his first two months in Toledo (.323/.370/.548), but came on very strong (.197/.246/.303) thereafter.

Alfredo Figaro

Bats: R   Throws: R   Height: 6' 0"   Weight: 175   Born: July 7, 1984   Age: 25

YEAR	TEAM	LVL	AGE	W	L	SV	G	GS	IP	H	HR	BB	SO	GB%	BABIP	STUFF	WHIP	ERA	SIERA	DERA	EqH9	EqHR9	EqBB9	EqSO9	VORP	SN/WX
2007	LAK	A+	22	0	2	0	5	4	22²	26	0	6	6	62%	.310	-23	1.41	4.76	5.30	6.65	10.4	0.8	2.9	1.2	-2.8	-0.24
2007	ONE	A-	22	4	2	0	11	11	53¹	56	1	16	40	62%	.325	-6	1.35	3.37	3.90	5.23	11.4	1.1	3.5	4.0	1.4	-0.13
2008	WMI	A	23	12	2	0	19	19	123	99	0	30	96	57%	.273	3	1.05	2.05	3.68	4.28	9.5	0.9	3.2	4.0	15.0	0.86
2008	LAK	A+	23	0	5	0	6	5	29¹	37	2	12	23	45%	.368	-18	1.67	4.91	4.38	9.23	13.7	1.7	4.4	4.8	-10.9	-0.90
2009	ERI	AA	24	6	3	0	16	11	80	67	8	23	69	51%	.262	3	1.12	3.60	3.61	4.87	8.3	1.4	2.8	6.0	5.4	0.14
2009	DET	MLB	24	2	2	0	5	3	17	23	3	10	16	36%	.377	4	1.94	6.35	4.58	6.35	11.6	1.1	4.8	7.4	-1.6	-0.07
2010	DET	MLB	25	4	7	0	27	17	103¹	118	15	47	59	47%	.309	-12	1.59	5.43	5.16	5.59	10.1	1.2	3.8	4.9	-1.0	1.47

Breakout: 13% Improve: 44% Collapse: 19% Attrition: 17%   MLB: 100%   Comparables: Paul Byrd, Jake O'Dell, Shawn Purdy, Jeffrey Andrews

Figaro is either "skinny" or "wiry," depending on your level of optimism for him; either way, it brings into doubt his ability to remain a starting pitcher. A cousin of Fernando Rodney, he has a pretty good fastball that can occasionally reach 95, and could be expected to do that more consistently in short relief. He started two midseason games for Detroit before a sprained wrist sidelined him for two months; all of his relief appearances followed that DL stint.

Armando Galarraga

Bats: R   Throws: R   Height: 6' 4"   Weight: 180   Born: January 15, 1982   Age: 28

YEAR	TEAM	LVL	AGE	W	L	SV	G	GS	IP	H	HR	BB	SO	GB%	BABIP	STUFF	WHIP	ERA	SIERA	DERA	EqH9	EqHR9	EqBB9	EqSO9	VORP	SN/WX
2007	FRI	AA	25	9	6	0	23	22	127²	122	14	47	114	49%	.304	-10	1.32	4.02	3.80	4.96	10.1	1.6	3.7	6.2	7.1	0.87
2007	OKL	AAA	25	2	2	0	4	4	24²	23	1	11	21	51%	.293	2	1.38	4.74	4.16	5.36	8.9	0.7	4.1	5.5	0.4	0.04
2007	TEX	MLB	25	0	0	0	3	1	8²	8	2	7	6	42%	.240	-7	1.73	6.23	5.74	5.19	8.3	2.1	6.2	5.2	0.3	-0.11
2008	TOL	AAA	26	2	0	0	2	2	12	7	1	1	11	59%	.194	12	0.67	2.25	2.66	3.09	5.4	1.5	0.8	6.2	3.1	0.34
2008	DET	MLB	26	13	7	0	30	28	178²	152	28	61	126	51%	.236	15	1.19	3.73	4.33	3.80	7.0	1.2	2.7	5.7	34.4	4.00
2009	DET	MLB	27	6	10	0	29	25	143²	158	24	67	95	48%	.298	-7	1.57	5.64	4.92	5.25	9.6	1.2	3.7	5.4	4.0	1.63
2010	DET	MLB	28	6	8	0	28	23	130¹	135	18	59	88	48%	.296	0	1.48	4.84	4.76	4.98	9.1	1.1	3.8	5.6	7.6	1.70

Breakout: 10% Improve: 36% Collapse: 26% Attrition: 21%   MLB: 88%   Comparables: John Maine, Phil Regan, Charles Hudson, Kip Wells

Galarraga's fall from grace was one of the easiest and most widespread predictions made last spring, all based on his ridiculously low BABIP in 2008. He's got a good, hard slider that he throws way too often (ponder the fate of Bonderman); he came down with elbow problems in August and tried to pitch through them in September with predictable results. Since the slider is his only major league-quality offering, expect him to keep using it at every opportunity. Don't be surprised if he misses more time.

Edwin Jackson

Bats: R   Throws: R   Height: 6' 3"   Weight: 210   Born: September 9, 1983   Age: 26

YEAR	TEAM	LVL	AGE	W	L	SV	G	GS	IP	H	HR	BB	SO	GB%	BABIP	STUFF	WHIP	ERA	SIERA	DERA	EqH9	EqHR9	EqBB9	EqSO9	VORP	SN/WX
2007	TBA	MLB	23	5	15	0	32	31	161	195	19	88	128	51%	.341	2	1.76	5.76	4.67	5.65	9.4	1.1	4.3	6.2	-2.9	1.59
2008	TBA	MLB	24	14	11	0	32	31	183^1	199	23	77	108	43%	.302	-10	1.51	4.42	5.12	4.40	10.6	1.3	3.5	5.1	21.0	4.34
2009	DET	MLB	25	13	9	0	33	33	214	200	27	70	161	45%	.276	18	1.26	3.62	4.19	3.60	8.2	0.9	2.6	6.1	44.4	6.23
2010	ARI	MLB	26	9	12	0	33	33	188	199	23	81	128	48%	.305	2	1.49	4.66	4.69	4.92	9.4	1.1	3.6	5.7	12.1	2.55

Breakout: 6%   Improve: 42%   Collapse: 14%   Attrition: 15%   MLB: 100%   Comparables: Ron Darling, Rick Wise, Jason Schmidt, Jon Garland

Jackson was sensational, a serious Cy Young candidate, for the first 3 ½ months of the season, before coming back to earth a bit in August and September. He was reportedly tipping his slider, which is a pretty big deal, considering it is his best pitch. Still, without any improvement after time spent specifically working on that, it sounds like an excuse for fatigue. Jackson didn't do much that was different last year beyond throwing his slider a little more often, and he had a significant amount of favorable luck in both his runs and his hits allowed; without that, it would look like a typical Jackson season. Sending him to the easier league but a tougher park should help him some, and if tipping's an issue, perhaps he's better off in a new (unfamiliar) league and his new coaches will be able to iron out the issue.

Brandon Lyon

Bats: R   Throws: R   Height: 6' 1"   Weight: 195   Born: August 10, 1979   Age: 30

YEAR	TEAM	LVL	AGE	W	L	SV	G	GS	IP	H	HR	BB	SO	GB%	BABIP	STUFF	WHIP	ERA	SIERA	DERA	EqH9	EqHR9	EqBB9	EqSO9	VORP	SN/WX
2007	ARI	MLB	27	6	4	2	73	0	74	70	2	22	40	48%	.281	6	1.24	2.68	4.84	2.70	8.2	0.1	2.5	4.5	22.8	4.43
2008	ARI	MLB	28	3	5	26	61	0	59^1	75	7	13	44	43%	.338	-5	1.48	4.70	4.08	4.67	10.5	0.7	1.6	5.8	5.6	1.22
2009	DET	MLB	29	6	5	3	65	0	78^2	56	7	31	57	58%	.226	11	1.11	2.86	4.24	2.63	6.3	0.6	3.2	6.0	24.6	2.03
2010	HOU	MLB	30	4	4	10	67	0	66^2	66	7	22	44	49%	.290	-4	1.32	4.00	4.49	4.30	8.9	0.9	2.9	5.3	8.9	1.59

Breakout: 13%   Improve: 34%   Collapse: 26%   Attrition: 16%   MLB: 94%   Comparables: Randy Moffitt, Cal Koonce, Dave Smith, Jeff Shaw

Pre-season publications were torn trying to choose between advocating Rodney or Lyon for the closer's role, with some kind of time-share being widely expected. After Lyon gave up five homers and 12 runs in 12 spring innings and three runs to blow a save in his first real outing, Leyland had seen enough to play the Decider, and Lyon never got another real chance to finish games. He threw his slider a lot more often than he has in the past, at the expense of his fastball. That can explain the bounces in both walk rate (up, bad) and BABIP (down, good) and why it took him until June to get going. Signed by Houston to a three-year, $15 million deal, he's a good bet to fall backward in 2010; note his BABIP, which is going to spring forward like a lion pouncing on a wounded gazelle—and the gazelle's name is Brandon.

Zach Miner

Bats: R   Throws: R   Height: 6' 3"   Weight: 200   Born: March 12, 1982   Age: 28

YEAR	TEAM	LVL	AGE	W	L	SV	G	GS	IP	H	HR	BB	SO	GB%	BABIP	STUFF	WHIP	ERA	SIERA	DERA	EqH9	EqHR9	EqBB9	EqSO9	VORP	SN/WX
2007	TOL	AAA	25	1	4	0	11	8	51^2	43	4	22	33	58%	.253	-14	1.26	4.88	4.58	6.38	8.5	1.3	3.9	4.3	-4.8	-0.08
2007	DET	MLB	25	3	4	0	34	1	53^2	56	3	22	34	61%	.306	-3	1.45	3.02	4.60	3.50	9.2	0.5	3.4	5.3	11.7	0.35
2008	DET	MLB	26	8	5	0	45	13	118	118	10	46	62	52%	.281	0	1.39	4.27	5.10	4.12	8.4	0.7	3.1	4.3	18.1	2.89
2009	DET	MLB	27	7	5	1	51	5	92^1	101	11	45	62	55%	.311	-9	1.58	4.29	4.82	4.35	9.8	0.9	3.9	5.6	11.5	1.40
2010	DET	MLB	28	4	5	0	52	5	82	85	9	36	52	53%	.299	-7	1.48	4.72	4.81	4.88	9.2	1.0	3.7	5.3	5.7	0.85

Breakout: 15%   Improve: 48%   Collapse: 19%   Attrition: 25%   MLB: 88%   Comparables: Dallas Green, Jeff Dedmon, Joe Haynes, Brad Hennessey

The man who wasn't there, Miner has found a home in the long-relief/emergency starter portion of the Tigers bullpen, earning praise from his managers for his performances, but not any kind of promotion to a better role; that means they don't quite believe what they're saying, however polite. Miner is an average performer across the board, throwing four unexceptional pitches, with no exploitable splits and nothing to get you to notice he's been in the game.

Fu-Te Ni

Bats: L   Throws: L   Height: 6' 0"   Weight: 170   Born: November 14, 1982   Age: 27

YEAR	TEAM	LVL	AGE	W	L	SV	G	GS	IP	H	HR	BB	SO	GB%	BABIP	STUFF	WHIP	ERA	SIERA	DERA	EqH9	EqHR9	EqBB9	EqSO9	VORP	SN/WX
2009	TOL	AAA	26	3	0	0	24	0	34²	31	4	9	32	41%	.287	0	1.15	2.60	3.34	3.34	8.9	1.7	2.5	6.7	7.8	0.16
2009	DET	MLB	26	0	0	0	36	0	31	20	3	11	21	36%	.200	1	1.00	2.61	4.64	2.37	5.6	0.6	3.0	5.6	10.5	0.15
2010	DET	MLB	27	3	3	0	58	0	57	56	7	21	39	41%	.286	-3	1.36	4.32	4.61	4.37	8.5	1.1	3.1	5.8	7.2	0.35

Breakout: 5%   Improve: 18%   Collapse: 51%   Attrition: 2%   MLB: 49%   Comparables: Steve Mingori, Mike Gallo, Stan Clarke, Derek Stroud

Ni was one of the foremost pitchers in Taiwan, leading the league in strikeouts in 2008. He became a free agent when his team folded, a not uncommon happening in the American minors during the Great Depression and earlier. The Tigers signed him and let him play in the World Baseball Classic (or else he may have started the season in Detroit). He's a well-polished lefty with good control, a fairly weak fastball that tops out at 89 mph, a changeup, and a hard curve, all thrown sidearm. Lefties stand about as much chance against him as a November turkey does of making it to December, hitting .113 in 62 at-bats.

Ryan Perry

Bats: R   Throws: R   Height: 6' 4"   Weight: 200   Born: February 13, 1987   Age: 23

YEAR	TEAM	LVL	AGE	W	L	SV	G	GS	IP	H	HR	BB	SO	GB%	BABIP	STUFF	WHIP	ERA	SIERA	DERA	EqH9	EqHR9	EqBB9	EqSO9	VORP	SN/WX
2008	LAK	A+	21	1	2	4	12	0	11²	15	0	7	12	50%	.385	4	1.89	3.86	4.20	6.17	12.3	0.8	5.4	5.4	-0.9	-0.49
2009	TOL	AAA	22	1	0	3	8	0	13²	13	1	4	12	60%	.293	10	1.24	2.63	3.61	3.38	8.8	1.4	2.7	6.1	3.1	0.42
2009	DET	MLB	22	0	1	0	53	0	61²	56	7	38	60	50%	.293	13	1.52	3.79	4.21	4.04	8.1	0.7	4.8	7.9	10.0	0.85
2010	DET	MLB	23	3	5	2	51	0	59¹	59	7	33	45	48%	.301	-4	1.56	5.11	4.72	5.25	8.9	1.0	4.6	6.5	1.6	0.48

Breakout: 9%   Improve: 34%   Collapse: 31%   Attrition: 14%   MLB: 100%   Comparables: Jason Burch, Gabe Molina, Jeff Hirsch, Ken Smith

Perry is a pure flamethrower, capable of reaching 100 mph on a generous gun. The Tigers' first-round pick in 2008, he impressed Leyland in the spring and made the team despite having less than 15 innings of pro experience. The fairy tale story doesn't keep going; despite pitching well overall, he did have problems with his control and finding a reliable non-fastball pitch and ultimately made a few trips to Toledo for remedial work. Tiger officials salivate about having him as their closer. He may yet be a little too raw for the job in 2010, but he's already busted timing expectations.

Rick Porcello

Bats: R   Throws: R   Height: 6' 5"   Weight: 200   Born: December 27, 1988   Age: 21

YEAR	TEAM	LVL	AGE	W	L	SV	G	GS	IP	H	HR	BB	SO	GB%	BABIP	STUFF	WHIP	ERA	SIERA	DERA	EqH9	EqHR9	EqBB9	EqSO9	VORP	SN/WX
2008	LAK	A+	19	8	6	0	24	24	125	116	7	33	72	67%	.270	15	1.19	2.66	4.18	5.21	9.6	1.4	3.0	3.2	3.8	0.38
2009	DET	MLB	20	14	9	0	31	31	170²	176	23	52	89	65%	.277	25	1.34	3.96	4.64	3.90	8.9	1.0	2.4	4.3	29.9	4.46
2010	DET	MLB	21	7	9	0	30	29	148	157	20	56	73	59%	.287	19	1.44	4.83	5.00	4.99	9.4	1.1	3.2	4.1	8.4	2.46

Breakout: 8%   Improve: 44%   Collapse: 21%   Attrition: 3%   MLB: 100%   Comparables: Jon Garland, Buddy Carlyle, Bronson Arroyo, Kyle Hartshorn

Porcello is another in a line of recent, high-draft pitchers whose minor-league numbers are completely useless for analysis. He wasn't pitching as best he could, but was instead working on a specific program designed to develop all his pitches and to teach him to pitch efficiently, and definitely *not* using the same style of pitching he would use in a major-league game. He relies on a sinking two-seam fastball that reaches 92 mph and a four-seamer than touches 95, plus a curveball, slider, and change, all with good control. He was a surprise pick to make the team out of spring training, but fully deserved it—other than a hiccup around the All-Star break, he was solid and consistent. The worry shifts toward keeping his pitch counts and innings in check, as he's only 21.

Clay Rapada

Bats: R   Throws: L   Height: 6' 5"   Weight: 200   Born: March 9, 1981   Age: 29

YEAR	TEAM	LVL	AGE	W	L	SV	G	GS	IP	H	HR	BB	SO	GB%	BABIP	STUFF	WHIP	ERA	SIERA	DERA	EqH9	EqHR9	EqBB9	EqSO9	VORP	SN/WX
2007	IOW	AAA	26	7	2	17	55	0	55¹	55	4	25	50	50%	.336	-7	1.45	3.58	3.95	4.24	9.4	1.1	4.4	6.5	7.2	0.71
2008	TOL	AAA	27	0	1	2	28	0	35	32	2	14	45	44%	.341	8	1.31	2.31	2.71	3.21	9.1	1.1	3.7	8.3	8.6	0.51
2008	DET	MLB	27	3	0	0	25	0	21¹	19	0	14	15	56%	.297	0	1.55	4.22	5.06	4.29	7.7	0.0	5.1	6.0	2.8	0.26
2009	TOL	AAA	28	4	2	5	42	0	45²	50	1	17	47	47%	.371	3	1.47	2.76	3.42	3.69	10.8	0.4	3.8	7.6	8.6	0.17
2009	DET	MLB	28	0	0	0	3	0	3¹	4	1	2	2	64%	.273	-23	1.80	5.40	5.11	5.40	10.8	2.7	5.4	5.4	0.0	-0.13
2010	TEX	MLB	29	2	4	5	51	0	49²	56	6	27	40	49%	.332	-9	1.68	5.55	4.58	5.50	9.8	1.1	4.4	7.0	0.0	0.59

Breakout: 15%   Improve: 45%   Collapse: 18%   Attrition: 17%   MLB: 33%   Comparables: Dave Lynch, Bill Earley, Tom McGraw, Jerry Don Gleaton

Rapada's value is mainly as a LOOGY, but Detroit had plenty of lefty arms for the pen—Seay, Nate Robertson for much of the year, plus Ni later on—so he spent the year pitching an inning at a time for Toledo. Given that he barely breaks the mid-80s with his fastball, he's done extremely well for himself, but he's fringy enough not to have any roster spots reserved for him. The Rangers felt he'd fit, however, acquiring Rapada in December for "future considerations"—a player, cash, or hey, you gonna eat that?

Nate Robertson

| | | | | | | | | | | | | | | | | Bats: R | Throws: L | Height: 6' 2" | | Weight: 225 | Born: September 3, 1977 | | Age: 32 |

YEAR	TEAM	LVL	AGE	W	L	SV	G	GS	IP	H	HR	BB	SO	GB%	BABIP	STUFF	WHIP	ERA	SIERA	DERA	EqH9	EqHR9	EqBB9	EqSO9	VORP	SN/WX
2007	DET	MLB	29	9	13	0	30	30	177²	199	22	63	119	51%	.308	3	1.47	4.76	4.55	4.60	9.8	1.0	2.8	5.5	17.7	2.89
2008	DET	MLB	30	7	11	0	32	28	168²	218	26	62	108	54%	.341	-11	1.66	6.35	4.69	5.91	11.1	1.2	3.0	5.4	-7.6	0.62
2009	TOL	AAA	31	1	1	0	5	5	19	19	1	4	21	46%	.367	17	1.21	1.89	2.56	4.24	10.6	1.1	2.1	8.5	2.4	0.65
2009	DET	MLB	31	2	3	0	28	6	49²	59	4	28	35	47%	.333	-10	1.75	5.44	5.06	5.31	10.3	0.5	4.3	5.6	1.1	0.41
2010	DET	MLB	32	5	8	0	30	21	116²	133	15	49	76	48%	.319	-5	1.56	5.15	4.80	5.23	10.0	1.1	3.5	5.4	3.5	0.88

Breakout: 8%   Improve: 46%   Collapse: 21%   Attrition: 25%   MLB: 92%   Comparables: Atlee Hammaker, Chris Hammond, Darren Oliver, Terry Mulholland

Robertson was terrible all spring; he not only lost out on the rotation slot he coveted, but also was essentially a second LOOGY, working behind Seay. He continued being awful, eventually going under the knife in June with a 7.71 ERA. Doctors pulled four "fatty masses" out of his elbow, and without them, he came back to throw 29 innings with a 3.77 ERA as a starter. He's yet another Tiger pitcher with an overblown salary at $10 million for 2010, but the postsurgery performance gives some plausible hope that he can earn a decent fraction of that.

Fernando Rodney

| | | | | | | | | | | | | | | | | Bats: R | Throws: R | Height: 5' 11" | | Weight: 220 | Born: March 18, 1977 | | Age: 33 |

YEAR	TEAM	LVL	AGE	W	L	SV	G	GS	IP	H	HR	BB	SO	GB%	BABIP	STUFF	WHIP	ERA	SIERA	DERA	EqH9	EqHR9	EqBB9	EqSO9	VORP	SN/WX
2007	DET	MLB	30	2	6	1	48	0	50²	46	5	21	54	54%	.293	12	1.32	4.26	3.44	4.39	7.7	0.9	3.3	8.4	6.5	0.43
2008	DET	MLB	31	0	6	13	38	0	40¹	34	3	30	49	52%	.301	22	1.59	4.91	3.86	4.39	7.1	0.6	5.8	9.6	5.2	-0.05
2009	DET	MLB	32	2	5	37	73	0	75²	70	8	41	61	66%	.284	0	1.47	4.40	4.29	4.16	8.2	0.7	4.3	6.6	11.1	4.71
2010	LAA	MLB	33	3	4	14	58	0	59²	56	7	33	52	54%	.296	-2	1.49	4.74	4.29	4.93	8.3	1.0	4.7	7.4	3.8	1.15

Breakout: 8%   Improve: 38%   Collapse: 31%   Attrition: 15%   MLB: 87%   Comparables: Jim Hughes, Jim Mecir, Luis Vizcaino, Shinya Okamoto

Despite a shaky spring of his own, Rodney was the beneficiary of Lyon's even shakier performance and won the closer's job. He held on all year, although not without a fair bit of excitement, but blew only one save, reserving his worst pitching for nonsave situations. He throws hard enough (95+) for a typical closer, but he never dominates, giving up enough runs that he shouldn't be treated as anything more than a slightly above-average pitcher—there's no closer's mystique here. Over the last four years, he's given up more than twice as many runs (6.71) on the road than in Comerica (3.10). Nonetheless, the Angels signed him to a two-year contract, giving them a wild and woolly setup man to go with their wild and woolly closer.

Cody Satterwhite

| | | | | | | | | | | | | | | | | Bats: R | Throws: R | Height: 6' 4" | | Weight: 205 | Born: January 27, 1987 | | Age: 23 |

YEAR	TEAM	LVL	AGE	W	L	SV	G	GS	IP	H	HR	BB	SO	GB%	BABIP	STUFF	WHIP	ERA	SIERA	DERA	EqH9	EqHR9	EqBB9	EqSO9	VORP	SN/WX
2008	LAK	A+	21	0	0	2	17	0	18¹	16	0	12	22	34%	.320	4	1.53	4.42	3.80	6.62	9.2	0.5	6.1	7.1	-2.2	-0.39
2009	ERI	AA	22	4	6	12	34	0	49¹	46	5	27	52	49%	.308	1	1.48	3.47	3.78	4.79	9.6	1.3	5.0	7.5	3.7	-0.47
2010	DET	MLB	23	2	4	6	38	0	46²	52	6	28	36	38%	.323	-9	1.70	5.51	5.01	5.71	9.9	1.2	5.0	6.5	-1.1	0.15

Breakout: 14%   Improve: 47%   Collapse: 24%   Attrition: 9%   MLB: 1%   Comparables: Todd Erdos, Steve Connelly, Joe Borowski, Greg Johnson

Satterwhite was a 2008 second-round pick who fits the recent Tiger template of big guys who throw hard. He unleashes mid-90s fastballs with a bit of tailing action and can push it up to 97 mph when he reaches back for a bit more. His hard slider has plenty of bite, and he creates deception with an exaggerated delivery. His delivery has a lot of moving parts, though, and he has problems throwing strikes at times. He was shut down at the end of the year with shoulder soreness, leading to more questions about his mechanics. On most teams, he'd be a Future Closers of America member, but Perry is clearly ahead of him right now; Satterwhite is still a good late-inning prospect.

Bobby Seay

Bats: L   Throws: L   Height: 6' 2"   Weight: 235   Born: June 20, 1978   Age: 32

YEAR	TEAM	LVL	AGE	W	L	SV	G	GS	IP	H	HR	BB	SO	GB%	BABIP	STUFF	WHIP	ERA	SIERA	DERA	EqH9	EqHR9	EqBB9	EqSO9	VORP	SN/WX
2007	DET	MLB	29	3	0	1	58	0	46¹	38	1	15	38	42%	.278	14	1.14	2.33	3.91	2.27	7.3	0.2	2.6	6.9	16.4	2.22
2008	DET	MLB	30	1	2	0	60	0	56¹	59	4	25	58	46%	.350	12	1.49	4.47	3.62	4.07	9.3	0.5	3.6	8.6	8.8	1.18
2009	DET	MLB	31	6	3	0	67	0	48²	46	3	17	37	48%	.291	3	1.29	4.25	4.23	3.88	8.3	0.4	2.8	6.1	8.7	1.26
2010	DET	MLB	32	3	3	0	53	0	52	48	4	24	41	44%	.294	2	1.38	3.96	4.39	4.10	8.1	0.8	3.7	6.7	8.1	1.02

Breakout: 14%   Improve: 39%   Collapse: 20%   Attrition: 11%   MLB: 95%   Comparables: Matt Thornton, Damaso Marte, Chuck McElroy, Jesse Orosco

The long-ago first-round pick faced an average of three batters per game—typical LOOGY numbers—yet he doesn't really dominate lefties, so he should yield that role to Ni in the coming year, becoming a standard reliever instead. Seay went almost two months through midseason without allowing a run, half of it in one- or two-batter chunks. Even at that torrid pace, he wears down in September.

Jacob Turner

Bats: R   Throws: R   Height: 6' 5"   Weight: 210   Born: May 21, 1991   Age: 19

Did Not Play.

Breakout: 14%   Improve: 39%   Collapse: 20%   Attrition: 11%   MLB: 95%   Comparables: NA

Turner was perhaps the top high school arm in the 2009 draft; the Tigers took him with the ninth pick overall and signed him at the deadline with a major-league deal and a $4.7 million bonus. He is the very model of a modern major-league pick: big, mechanically sound, and in possession of excellent stuff led by a fastball that goes as high as 98 mph, a good curve, and a change. He gets favorably compared to Justin Verlander, and you may recall Verlander reached the majors in his pro debut season.

Justin Verlander

Bats: R   Throws: R   Height: 6' 5"   Weight: 200   Born: February 20, 1983   Age: 27

YEAR	TEAM	LVL	AGE	W	L	SV	G	GS	IP	H	HR	BB	SO	GB%	BABIP	STUFF	WHIP	ERA	SIERA	DERA	EqH9	EqHR9	EqBB9	EqSO9	VORP	SN/WX
2007	DET	MLB	24	18	6	0	32	32	201²	181	20	67	183	44%	.279	27	1.23	3.66	3.72	3.69	7.7	0.8	2.6	7.3	41.1	5.69
2008	DET	MLB	25	11	17	0	33	33	201	195	18	87	163	43%	.296	19	1.40	4.84	4.36	4.78	8.2	0.7	3.4	6.7	16.1	3.23
2009	DET	MLB	26	19	9	0	35	35	240	219	20	63	269	41%	.319	41	1.17	3.45	2.72	3.42	8.2	0.6	2.1	9.2	54.5	7.35
2010	DET	MLB	27	12	11	0	35	35	208	196	21	74	179	42%	.301	22	1.30	3.99	3.87	4.15	8.4	0.8	2.9	7.2	31.2	3.33

Breakout: 2%   Improve: 40%   Collapse: 12%   Attrition: 17%   MLB: 100%   Comparables: Javier Vazquez, Dennis Leonard, Jack McDowell, Dan Haren

Verlander had a breakthrough season, with career bests in wins, ERA, strikeouts, innings—pretty much anything worth having career bests in. While most breakthrough seasons are the result of slightly better-than-average luck, Verlander was, if anything, unlucky, yielding 16 more hits and five more runs than the stats support. PITCHf/x tells us his fastball picked up two mph, averaging near 96 last season. We love all that. What we don't love is that in the drive for the pennant, he wound up leading the league in pitches thrown by about almost 10 percent, with the highest season pitch count in the last four years. If Verlander also breaks down, it can be put more directly on management's shoulders—Bonderman was always a risk, and Willis's issues aren't all with his arm—and, because of his excellence, it would be that much more tragic.

Jarrod Washburn

Bats: L   Throws: L   Height: 6' 1"   Weight: 195   Born: August 13, 1974   Age: 35

YEAR	TEAM	LVL	AGE	W	L	SV	G	GS	IP	H	HR	BB	SO	GB%	BABIP	STUFF	WHIP	ERA	SIERA	DERA	EqH9	EqHR9	EqBB9	EqSO9	VORP	SN/WX
2007	SEA	MLB	32	10	15	0	32	32	193²	201	23	67	114	42%	.284	1	1.38	4.32	4.93	4.51	8.5	1.2	2.8	4.6	21.6	3.55
2008	SEA	MLB	33	5	14	1	28	26	153²	174	19	50	87	41%	.303	-7	1.46	4.69	5.01	4.87	9.7	1.3	2.6	4.5	10.7	2.82
2009	SEA	MLB	34	8	6	0	20	20	133	109	11	33	79	41%	.242	17	1.07	2.64	4.57	2.91	8.1	0.8	2.0	4.8	36.9	5.31
2009	DET	MLB	34	1	3	0	8	8	43	51	12	16	21	49%	.275	-18	1.56	7.33	5.28	6.59	10.0	2.1	2.9	4.0	-5.2	-0.21
2010	DET	MLB	35	7	10	0	27	27	148²	159	20	54	82	39%	.293	-2	1.43	4.76	5.15	4.84	9.4	1.2	3.0	4.7	10.9	2.04

Breakout: 5%   Improve: 35%   Collapse: 11%   Attrition: 20%   MLB: 96%   Comparables: Jim Rooker, John Tudor, Larry Gura, Hank Aguirre

Washburn pitched well over his head all season for Seattle, especially during a well-timed July hot streak that enabled the Mariners to deal him for Luke French and prospect Mauricio Robles. His regression to (and past) career norms after going to Detroit was immediate; he only gave the Tigers two quality starts out of eight before missing most of September due to knee injuries that had bothered him all year and that required surgery in October. Burned that badly, the Tigers wanted nothing more to do with him and let him walk as a free agent.

Dontrelle Willis

| | | | | | | | | | | Bats: L | | Throws: L | | Height: 6' 4" | | Weight: 225 | | Born: January 12, 1982 | | Age: 28 |

YEAR	TEAM	LVL	AGE	W	L	SV	G	GS	IP	H	HR	BB	SO	GB%	BABIP	STUFF	WHIP	ERA	SIERA	DERA	EqH9	EqHR9	EqBB9	EqSO9	VORP	SN/WX
2007	FLO	MLB	25	10	15	0	35	35	205¹	241	29	87	146	56%	.318	-1	1.60	5.17	4.58	5.19	9.3	1.2	3.3	5.5	7.4	2.09
2008	DET	MLB	26	0	2	0	8	7	24	18	4	35	18	49%	.219	6	2.21	9.37	6.77	8.51	6.3	1.1	11.5	6.3	-8.1	-0.04
2009	TOL	AAA	27	1	2	0	5	5	24¹	22	1	17	15	64%	.284	-6	1.60	4.81	5.20	5.76	8.7	0.8	6.8	4.4	-0.6	-0.08
2009	DET	MLB	27	1	4	0	7	7	33²	37	4	28	17	66%	.300	-8	1.93	7.49	5.74	6.68	9.8	0.8	6.5	4.1	-4.3	0.19
2010	DET	MLB	28	3	6	0	21	12	69	78	11	39	42	55%	.309	-14	1.69	5.93	5.16	6.04	10.0	1.2	4.7	5.2	-4.2	0.39

Breakout: 18%   Improve: 41%   Collapse: 25%   Attrition: 37%   MLB: 61%   Comparables: Greg Mathews, Chris Nabholz, Vaughn Eshelman, Horacio Ramirez

Willis was about as lost as a baseball player could be in 2009, forced to deal with anxiety disorders in a public spotlight while wretched performances and a large contract ($10 million in 2009, $12 million in 2010) created a different kind of anxiety in the front office. He hasn't pitched well since 2006, which was long before any anxiety issues came to the fore—although they can simmer, undiagnosed, for a long time, so it is at least possible they are the root cause—and he has lost velocity and all semblance of control. There are big problems here, and sadly, there's no reasonable case to be made to expect improvement.

Joel Zumaya

| | | | | | | | | | | Bats: R | | Throws: R | | Height: 6' 3" | | Weight: 210 | | Born: November 9, 1984 | | Age: 25 |

YEAR	TEAM	LVL	AGE	W	L	SV	G	GS	IP	H	HR	BB	SO	GB%	BABIP	STUFF	WHIP	ERA	SIERA	DERA	EqH9	EqHR9	EqBB9	EqSO9	VORP	SN/WX
2007	DET	MLB	22	2	3	1	28	0	33²	23	3	17	27	40%	.213	12	1.19	4.28	4.56	4.02	5.7	0.8	3.9	6.5	5.7	0.90
2008	DET	MLB	23	0	2	1	21	0	23¹	24	3	22	22	42%	.313	8	1.97	3.47	5.27	4.56	8.7	1.1	7.2	7.6	2.5	-0.51
2009	DET	MLB	24	3	3	1	29	0	31	34	5	22	30	40%	.319	2	1.81	4.94	4.68	4.78	9.3	1.1	5.3	7.6	2.6	-0.67
2010	DET	MLB	25	3	4	1	45	0	502	47	6	30	39	42%	.281	-6	1.51	4.75	4.86	4.91	8.3	1.0	5.0	6.5	3.3	0.00

Breakout: 14%   Improve: 36%   Collapse: 29%   Attrition: 16%   MLB: 90%   Comparables: Eddy Rodriguez, Gene Pentz, Brian Bruney, Yoshihiro Suzuki

When his shoulder is right, Zumaya showed he can still bring triple-digit heat. Getting it right and keeping it right after reconstructive surgery in 2008 is proving to be a challenge. He was only right for about eight weeks last year, from mid-April to mid-June, before popping something in his shoulder and heading out for another surgical consult with Dr. Andrews. He should be ready by spring, and it's thought that there was no further damage; with the closer situation wide open, he's a very high-risk, high-reward play.

LINEOUTS

Hitters

PLAYER	TEAM	LVL	AGE	PA	R	2B	3B	HR	RBI	BB	SO	SB-CS	EqBRR	AVG/OBP/SLG	EqAVG/EqOBP/EqSLG	EqA	VORP	WARP
SS A. Ciriaco	LAK	A+	22	470	55	17	5	11	59	20	89	15-4	0.9	.262/.296/.397	.246/.274/.373	.224	1.5	0.1
RF B. Clevlen	TOL	AAA	25	531	61	26	5	16	64	42	139	10-1	-0.1	.265/.328/.441	.249/.309/.417	.252	6.9	1.4
3B M. Hessman	TOL	AAA	31	548	58	30	3	23	77	65	171	3-1	-1.0	.217/.324/.442	.202/.299/.392	.241	2.7	0.6
UT D. Kelly*	TOL	AAA	29	420	57	20	6	6	40	43	51	27-4	1.7	.331/.404/.465	.308/.376/.424	.283	19.8	1.9
	DET	MLB	29	62	8	3	1	0	3	4	10	1-0	0.1	.250/.311/.339	.250/.311/.339	.234	-0.7	0.0
SS G. Nunez#	WMI	A	21	514	82	16	10	5	40	25	62	45-25	-5.6	.315/.360/.425	.285/.317/.382	.243	11.7	2.4
C D. Sardinha	DET	MLB	30	34	1	1	0	0	3	0	16	0-0	0.0	.097/.091/.129	.133/.121/.167	-.111	-3.5	-0.3
	TOL	AAA	30	135	10	7	0	3	16	11	34	0-0	-0.8	.178/.250/.314	.175/.241/.292	.188	-3.2	-0.4
OF D. Scram*	ERI	AA	25	517	75	23	8	20	70	63	121	9-2	-0.3	.252/.342/.476	.214/.288/.385	.237	-3.6	-0.8
C M. Treanor	DET	MLB	33	14	0	0	0	0	0	1	4	0-0	0.0	.000/.071/.000	.077/.143/.077	-.187	-1.6	-0.5

Shortstop **Audy Ciriaco** is a plus defender with very good all-around tools, including above-average power for the position, but his bat just hasn't developed. ⊘ **Brent Clevlen** has to be regarded as a former prospect, as it becomes ever more apparent that he has no pitch-recognition skills. ⊘ **Mike Hessman** has spent the last five years as Toledo's third baseman, averaging 29 home runs and 149 strikeouts with a .225 average—before translation, folks.

He escaped to ... Buffalo (if it can be called escape), joining the Mets on a minor-league deal. ⊘ **Don Kelly** is a speedy veteran who can play just about anywhere and parlayed a well-timed hot streak at Triple-A (fueled by a BABIP 80 points above his career average) into a month of big-league playing time. ⊘ Tiny **Gustavo Nunez** is an outstanding defensive shortstop who sprays the ball around and runs like the wind; his batting average will always be empty, so the question is, can he get it high enough to deliver value? ⊘ **Dane Sardinha** spent two months as the Tigers' backup catcher, but was such an anemic presence he could have been cast as a vampire victim; let's call his time on the roster the 60 days of night. He signed a minor-league deal with the Phillies. ⊘ With the best trolley-dodger's name possible, minor-league slugger **Deik Scram** has at least that much going for him, but it'll take more than that to skiddoo to "The Show." ⊘ Injuries limited **Matt Treanor** last season; it would seem that his sports hernia operation in the 2008-2009 offseason didn't fix the problem, so the surgery had to be repeated. The Brewers signed him to a minor-league contract.

Pitchers

PLAYER	TEAM	LVL	AGE	W	L	SV	IP	H	HR	BB	SO	GB%	BABIP	STUFF	WHIP	ERA	SIERA	DERA	EqH9	EqHR9	EqBB9	EqSO9	VORP
D. Below*	LAK	A+	23	1	4	0	28^2	22	4	14	38	50%	.269	9	1.26	3.14	2.82	5.13	9.6	3.4	5.5	8.2	1.1
	ERI	AA	23	1	0	0	11^1	7	1	6	7	51%	.176	-7	1.15	1.59	5.07	3.86	6.2	1.5	4.6	3.9	2.1
B. Brown	ERI	AA	24	5	0	0	36^2	32	1	8	13	50%	.258	-5	1.09	2.21	5.24	2.94	8.6	0.5	2.4	2.1	9.6
	TOL	AAA	24	3	13	0	112^2	120	9	55	48	55%	.287	-21	1.55	4.71	5.63	6.04	10.0	1.3	4.7	2.8	-6.5
F. Dolsi	TOL	AAA	26	4	3	10	51^2	49	2	19	31	62%	.283	-17	1.32	3.83	4.61	5.76	8.8	0.7	3.6	4.1	-1.4
	DET	MLB	26	1	0	0	10^2	13	0	4	3	70%	.325	-25	1.59	1.69	5.40	4.35	11.3	0.0	2.6	2.6	1.3
J. Gayhart	WMI	A	22	5	3	3	45^2	24	2	15	49	52%	.198	3	0.85	1.97	2.92	3.93	6.8	1.7	3.8	5.7	7.4
	LAK	A+	22	0	0	0	11^2	5	0	0	10	40%	.167	11	0.43	0.77	2.32	1.64	4.9	0.8	0.8	4.9	4.7
	ERI	AA	22	1	1	0	28^1	32	0	18	20	50%	.348	-9	1.76	4.45	5.14	6.41	11.5	0.7	5.7	4.7	-2.7
B. Jensen	ERI	AA	25	5	5	12	53^2	48	8	18	59	40%	.288	-4	1.23	3.19	3.07	4.09	9.1	1.9	3.1	7.7	8.1
J. Kibler*	ERI	AA	22	6	9	0	161^2	168	14	68	87	53%	.293	-10	1.46	4.06	5.08	5.58	10.3	1.3	4.0	3.6	-1.3
L. Marte	ERI	AA	22	5	8	0	105^1	106	18	28	84	43%	.281	-7	1.27	4.02	3.89	5.75	9.9	2.0	2.6	5.4	-2.8
J. Rainwater	ERI	AA	24	2	1	2	41^2	33	1	14	32	51%	.267	-3	1.13	2.59	4.05	3.97	7.9	0.7	3.2	5.2	6.7
	TOL	AAA	24	1	3	3	29^2	34	3	11	22	62%	.310	-26	1.52	5.76	4.28	9.30	10.5	1.5	3.3	4.8	-12.7
J. Sborz	ERI	AA	24	1	2	0	25	16	3	13	29	39%	.232	8	1.16	2.52	3.29	3.99	6.8	1.5	4.6	8.4	4.0
T. Weber	LAK	A+	24	4	4	0	67^2	54	6	11	40	61%	.235	-17	0.96	2.13	3.97	3.99	8.9	2.3	2.2	3.2	10.4
	ERI	AA	24	7	3	0	75^1	78	7	18	44	47%	.298	-10	1.27	4.06	4.51	5.39	10.4	1.3	2.5	4.0	0.9
R. Weinhardt	LAK	A+	23	1	1	3	31^2	24	2	10	40	55%	.282	5	1.07	0.85	2.51	2.73	8.8	1.8	3.6	7.6	9.1
	ERI	AA	23	0	1	2	31^1	28	0	16	32	49%	.315	7	1.40	2.30	3.84	3.23	9.1	0.6	4.7	7.0	7.7
A. Wilk*	WMI	A	21	2	1	0	36^1	30	2	2	33	45%	.280	21	0.88	1.49	2.65	3.34	10.0	1.9	1.4	4.7	7.8
	ONE	A-	21	2	0	0	37^1	23	0	5	34	38%	.230	24	0.75	1.45	2.83	3.18	7.4	1.1	2.4	4.5	8.8

Duane Below was the Tigers' minor league pitcher of the year in 2007, but had to get TJ surgery just two starts after being promoted to Double-A. ⊘ **Brooks Brown** was traded to Detroit so the D'backs could keep Rule 5 pick James Skelton, but hasn't shown enough velocity to handle the upper minors. ⊘ Undersized **Freddy Dolsi** serves up mid-90s fastballs with regularity, but he hasn't come up with anything to reliably retire left-handed hitters or a working off-speed pitch. DFA'd in December, he was claimed by the White Sox. ⊘ **Jared Gayhart** was a college outfielder who rarely took the mound, but the 13th-round pick made an encouraging switch to full-time relief work, reaching Double-A in his first full pro year with a plus-fastball/slider combination. ⊘ **Brett Jensen** is a tall, side-arming righty who came back strong after losing most of 2008 to an elbow injury. ⊘ **Jon Kibler** was the Tigers' minor league pitcher of the year in 2008, but his already marginal strikeout numbers dropped further after a two-level promotion to Erie. Fortunately, he can always fall back on the family cookie business. ⊘ **Luis Marte** excited everyone with the way he pitched in early 2008, but the pint-sized righty came down with elbow trouble and hasn't been the same since. ⊘ Nabbed in the second round of the 2009 draft, **Andy Oliver** is the rare power lefty with reliable mid-90s heat on a moving fastball, and he dominated during his debut in the AFL this winter. He might climb to Double-A and move fast as a reliever, but a better slider and change could leave him starting. ⊘ **Josh Rainwater** did a little bit of everything—starter, closer, setup, long relief, customer service—for Erie and Toledo, pitching very well before imploding in the season's final month. ⊘ **Jay Sborz** has had problems staying healthy throughout his career, but he's still a big guy who throws hard, and he showed enough at Double-A to get added to the 40-man roster. ⊘ Once a Twins prospect, **Brad Thomas** pitched well enough in Japan and Korea to get a major-league deal from the Tigers to take Rapada's place as the third lefty in a two-lefty pen. ⊘ Strike-throwing Cornhusker **Thad Weber** was snagged in 2008's 16th round and did well before last year's arrival at Double-A; he's organizational material until he proves otherwise. ⊘ **Robbie Weinhardt**'s fastball/breaking ball combination isn't good enough for big-league closing, but he still could help the Detroit bullpen as early as mid-2010. ⊘ **Adam Wilk** was an 11th-round pick last year who put up gaudy numbers in his pro debut; surprisingly for a low-minor lefty, he was much better against right-handers.

MANAGER: JIM LEYLAND

YEAR	TEAM	W-L	Pythag +/–	Avg PC	100+ P	120+ P	QS	BQS	REL	REL w Zero R	IBB	Subs	PH	PH Avg	PH HR	SB2	CS2	SB3	CS3	SAC Att	SAC %	POS SAC	Squeeze	Swing	In Play
2007	DET	88-74	-2	94.8	65	1	66	4	441	261	41	67	77	.246	2	86	25	16	4	42	73.8%	30	5	157	127
2008	DET	74-88	-4	94.9	68	2	63	12	440	237	63	66	66	.254	2	58	24	5	5	42	71.4%	27	0	148	122
2009	DET	86-77	5	97.1	72	13	68	5	437	266	42	78	122	.221	3	63	29	8	2	71	74.6%	51	4	158	126

Leyland has his one ring as a Fish skipper, and after the Bonds-less aftermath he suffered in Pittsburgh, the melted-down Marlins he stuck with in '98, and then a quick fail-and-bail season in Denver in '99, we'll have to see if he can wait out a preplanned setback season with this year's strange brew of inexpensive kitties and overpaid old toms. In some ways, he was more tactically active last year, but employing Gerald Laird and Adam Everett has a way of putting the sac bunt on the options menu, and it wasn't until September that it occurred to him to drop Curtis Granderson from the leadoff slot against lefties. He worked Verlander hard by current standards down the stretch, but never pushed him to 130 pitches and avoided asking too much of Porcello. Leyland also enjoyed the benefit of a miraculously good year from a dubious cast in the pen. Whether, like Sparky Anderson, he gets a free pass forever and eventually packs it in himself remains to be seen, but he and Dombrowski go back decades, they're both signed through 2011, and it seems more likely that they're a package as long as Ilitch wants to afford them.

Florida Marlins

The Marlins' new ballpark may or may not usher in a new era of consistently competitive baseball in Miami, an age in which the team takes its obligations to its fans seriously. Either way, it may not come in time to save Hanley Ramirez from becoming the new Ernie Banks. The invocation of the famous "Mr. Cub" is not meant to suggest that Ramirez will adopt an ever-present smile and a "Let's play two" eagerness for the game—Dan Uggla would surely scoff at such a notion—but that he may soon join Banks as a shortstop-cum-island of greatness in an unnaturally becalmed and toxic sea of surrender.

During his peak years of 1955-1961, Banks, the first African American Cub, starred at short for one of the most miserable, most ineptly run, and most poorly attended franchises in the majors. Banks made his big-league debut before a crowd of 2,703. A more typical Cubs crowd of the period was closer to 8,000-10,000, but even that was good for no better than sixth or seventh in the league. During these years, Banks hit .294/.359/.579. He hit over 40 home runs five times, twice leading the National League, made the All-Star team every year, and won a Gold Glove and two MVP Awards. His EqA was over .300 in all those seasons.

Despite his excellence, he never came close to playing for a winner in any of these seasons, indeed did not play on a winner from his debut until 1963 (when the Cubs went 82-80) because it was his misfortune to come of age at a time when the Cubs were suffering from neglect by disengaged owner P. K. Wrigley and incompetent general manager Wid Mathews. Not only was Banks the best player on the Cubs, but he was often the only player on the Cubs. In 1955, Banks was worth

9.7 wins above replacement; the Cubs as a whole were worth 20.3. In 1959, Banks produced 11.2 WARP; the rest of the team combined had a WARP of 19.9. The 1960 Cubs generated 17.9 WARP as a team. Banks supplied more than half, 9.1 WARP, by himself.

This is the fate that awaits Hanley Ramirez, though for different reasons than those that doomed Banks to years of irrelevance. The Cubs suffered because ownership didn't care and team executives had no clue. The Marlins are the old Cubs' mirror image: general manager Larry Beinfest clearly has a clue and more, and ownership clearly cares—but not about winning. Discussions about Major League Baseball's revenue-sharing policies initiated by Scott Boras this past offseason have refocused attention on the sheer implausibility of the Marlins' needing to maintain a player payroll of between $15 million and $37 million, roughly the range of salaries that the Marlins have suffered to pay since the 2005 team's $60.4 million was downsized to $14.9 million for 2006. The Marlins have been stuck near the bottom of the league since Wayne Huizenga gutted the team prior to the 1998 season, and they have shown no signs of rising. But even given the Marlins' mediocre attendance of 1.46 million in 2009, the second-worst in the majors (Oakland finished last), or their three last-place finishes before that, attendance would subsidize roughly 75 percent of the Marlins' $37 million payroll, the major league's lowest.* This figure does not include any of their current in-stadium revenue, however meager, or payments in the form of revenue sharing, ad-

MARLINS PROSPECTUS
2009 W-L: 87-75, 2nd in NL East

Pythag	83-79	7th	**Ballpark:** Land Shark Stadium (3-yr. PF: 1018). Neutral; 'moist' is best for brownies, not a place that's been named for underpants and beer
RS/G	4.8	5th	
RA/G	4.7	10th	
EqA	.264	7th	
EqBRR	0.6	5th	**2009:** Daring the world to care, mostly stocking the roster with HanRam and spares
SNWP	.476	13th	
WXRL	8.32	7th	
FRAr	4.44	11th	**2010:** More of the same; if Johnson and Uggla get dealt, can they avoid too many Bonifacios?
DE	.685	15th	
PADE	0.23	7th	
Salary	$36.8	16th	**Action Items:** Keep the plausibility angle going until the next revenue-sharing check is cashed
Attend	1.46	16th	

---

*Assuming an average ticket price of approximately $19.

205

vanced media, or local or national television rights payments. Prior to the 2009 season, *Forbes* estimated the Marlins' operating income at a major-league-best $43.7 million. It is possible that in starving the Marlins and simply providing Official Major League Baseball to the Miami market, Jeff Loria may have created baseball's biggest cash cow. Even if this estimation proves to be overstated (we will never know), it is clear that even without all the relevant numbers available, the Marlins' extreme austerity beggars credulity.

While some commentators have projected a *Christmas Carol*–like change of heart on Loria's part after the new ballpark arrives, with the payroll rising back to the $60 million neighborhood of 2005, this is by no means a sure thing or even something to be hoped for. First, the Marlins will provide $155 million toward the completion of the new park, and that represents debt that will have to be serviced with more urgency than any playoff aspirations. Second, the big revenue-sharing checks the Marlins currently receive are likely to shrink somewhat, given the new ballpark and presumably greater ticket sales, and while it is unlikely that exchanging a welfare check for a new ballpark represents a net loss for the Marlins, they will see a reduction of income in that sense. Finally, a $60 million payroll will not make Marlins' expenditures consistent with those of the Mets ($139 million in 2009), Phillies ($128 million), or Braves ($98 million).

Thus, the concept of a consistently competitive, committed Marlins team rising with the new ballpark is probably a chimera. In the meantime, two seasons remain before that magical day comes to pass, two more years for Island Hanley to take root like one of those palm-shaped, artificial archipelagos being constructed in the waters off Dubai. To see this happening, one must first dispense with the hot starts the Marlins had in 2008 and 2009. In the former season, the Marlins spent 42 days in first, going 30-20 in their first 50 games and maintaining the division lead through the end of May before concluding the season with a 54-57 record that was more appropriate to their offensive and defensive qualities. In 2009, the Marlins opened with a stunning 11-1 record, but this was a distortion caused by a trick of scheduling: six of those 11 games were against the Nationals at their worst. From then on, the Marlins were a pedestrian 76-74 team. Consistent with that sort of mediocrity, overall they scored 772 runs and allowed 766, figures worthy of a record of 83-79, according to BP's third-order wins.

The National League East will not always be as forgiving as it has been over the last five years. With the exception of the 97-65 Mets of 2006, the division has been winnable by teams with as few as 89 wins and no more than 93. When that day dawns, the time of the Marlins as even momentary competitors for post-season play will be over, their ability to post .570 winning percentages against divisional opponents, as the Marlins have done over the last two seasons, eroded by stiffer competition. Even the NL wild card, which has required between 88 and 92 wins over the last five seasons, may remain just out of reach.

The foregoing addresses merely the exterior pressures represented by improved intradivision competition. It doesn't cover the primary difficulty involved in building an enduringly competitive Marlins club: its frequent downsizing of the roster. Not even Connie Mack held as many fire sales as the Marlins have in their short history. After the 2005 season, the Marlins scattered much of their roster, not only dealing veterans like Paul Lo Duca, Carlos Delgado, Luis Castillo, and Mike Lowell, but also trading Josh Beckett, then only 26, whose sin was being arbitration eligible. This gave the Marlins a roster with an average age of 25 years and forestalled additional bleeding of the roster until after the 2007 season, when arbitration-eligible players Miguel Cabrera and Dontrelle Willis were shipped to the Tigers. Another purge took place following the 2008 season, when Mike Jacobs, Josh Willingham, Kevin Gregg, and Scott Olsen were dealt away as a function of their arbitration eligibility. Even journeyman righty Joe Nelson, who had put up a 2.00 ERA in 2008, was nontendered.

Having already declined to participate in the free-agent system, the Marlins are also opting out of salary arbitration. As a process, salary arbitration is often a lose/lose proposition for management—no player takes a pay cut as a result of the hearings; only the degree of increase is in contention. But the Marlins have completely abandoned the process, which means that they will fail to create the kinds of compromise contracts that reward young players for avoiding arbitration and free agency. So instead of the usual six-year span that most teams enjoy with their players before free agency kicks in (even then, teams retain the option to re-sign them), a young Marlin's career can be restricted to two to three years.

The Marlins entered the 2009-10 offseason with 12 players eligible for major raises through arbitration. Two players, Jeremy Hermida and Matt Lindstrom, were traded. Two others, Ricky Nolasco and Reynel Pinto, agreed to one-year contracts. What remained was the cream of the starting rotation, Josh Johnson, the always promising but rarely healthy Anibal Sanchez, second baseman Dan Uggla, closer-of-the-moment Leo Nunez, and outfielder Cody Ross. The

Marlins have already vowed to rid themselves of Uggla, and Johnson seemed to place himself on the trading front lines when he refused to accept a conservative (and, it is tempting to say, a merely face-saving gesture for ownership) three-year contract offer. The fate of the rest of the arbitration crew is unknown at this writing, but if past practice is any guide, by Opening Day, they could be playing anywhere from New York to Los Angeles to Astrakhan—in short, anywhere they are likely to get paid, a vast list that doesn't include Miami, Florida. The January agreement among the Marlins, MLB, and the Players Association that the Marlins "have assured the Union and the Commissioner's Office that they plan to use [revenue sharing] proceeds to increase player payroll annually as they move toward the opening of their new ballpark," apparently designed to avert a grievance, is vague enough to promise little beyond, perhaps, something more than the current desultory efforts to retain Johnson and Uggla.

If the bulk of these players move on—and there is no guarantee that those who have survived the winter will last through the trading deadline—Land Shark Stadium is going to be a very lonely place for Hanley Ramirez, the only Marlin of note signed to a long-term contact. In May 2008, Ramirez signed a six-year contract with the Marlins, which stuck him with the Fish through 2014. His 2010 salary of $7 million may even be low enough to keep him in Florida for now (he notably does not have no-trade protection), though Loria will be obligated to spend another $26 million if he wants to keep his star shortstop through the opening of the new ballpark in 2012.

Some of the departing Marlins will be replaced by newly arriving talent, of course. Chris Coghlan arrived from the farm system to give the Marlins a leadoff man to replace the execrable Emilio Bonifacio last year, and Sean West showed promise in the starting rotation. Cameron Maybin, still only 23 this year, may yet establish himself as a major-league center fielder. There is still hope that first baseman Logan Morrison will be an impact player in the bigs, and outfielder Mike Stanton is one of the most intriguing prospects in all of the minor leagues, perhaps the consistent 40-home-run threat the team has never had.

Yet even these players will may not come fast enough, or in sufficient numbers, to prop up a team that will not come to a long-term agreement with more than one player. Due to the presence of Josh Johnson, Uggla, Nolasco and, until he was traded, Miguel Cabrera, Ramirez has had a supporting cast far superior to that enjoyed by Ernie Banks at his peak, but isolation is creeping up on him. Just 26, he should still be in his prime when the new ballpark opens and the Marlins' ownership supposedly suddenly discovers largess, munificence, and an appreciation of Miami baseball fans equal to its appreciation of Miami baseball taxpayers. At this stage, believing in that seems an act of blind faith and naïveté. Leopards don't change their spots, fish don't change their fins, and a franchise that has been run on the cheap far in excess of actual necessity is going to use its new ballpark as a means of further self-enrichment first and as a vehicle toward competitiveness second. Sorry, Hanley.

HITTERS

Alfredo Amezaga — UT

Bats: S   Throws: R   Height: 5' 10"   Weight: 180   Born: January 16, 1978   Age: 32

YEAR	TEAM	LVL	AGE	PA	R	2B	3B	HR	RBI	BB	SO	SB	CS	EqBRR	AVG	OBP	SLG	EqAVG	EqOBP	EqSLG	EqA	VORP	WARP	DEFENSE			
2007	FLO	MLB	29	448	46	14	9	2	30	35	52	13	7	-1.3	.262	.324	.357	.276	.337	.371	.249	8.3	1.7	72-CF	9	14-SS	-2
2008	FLO	MLB	30	337	41	13	5	3	32	19	47	8	2	1.1	.264	.312	.367	.272	.319	.374	.244	4.5	0.9	51-CF	0	14-SS	2
2009	FLO	MLB	31	75	6	3	0	0	5	5	16	1	1	-1.2	.217	.267	.261	.217	.267	.261	.183	-3.3	0.0	9-CF	1	5-SS	1
2010	FLO	MLB	32	220	25	9	3	2	18	18	34	5	3	-0.2	.263	.330	.369	.263	.326	.367	.244	3.0	0.5	43-CF	2		

Breakout: 12%   Improve: 33%   Collapse: 22%   Attrition: 25%   MLB: 89%   Comparables: Jose Macias, Mike Felder, Taylor Douthit, Tony Scott

When the Icelandic saga of the Marlins' center fielders is written (the *Chuckie Carr sögur*), Amezaga will be shown to have heroically but somewhat pointlessly bridged the roughly two-year period between Reggie Abercrombie's faceplant and the elevation of Cody Ross. The heroic part is that Amezaga did a fine job defensively, despite having been almost exclusively an infielder to that point. The pointlessness comes in because he hit all of .260/.323/.346 in the role, which isn't really helping. Amezaga missed most of the season after microfracture surgery on his left knee; Ross had center field and Emilio Bonifacio had his utility job while Amezaga was nontendered. He will probably never again be a regular, nor should he be, though we probably don't have to worry about that, as there's only one Marlins organization.

John Baker · C

Bats: L   Throws: R   Height: 6' 1"   Weight: 210   Born: January 20, 1981   Age: 29

YEAR	TEAM	LVL	AGE	PA	R	2B	3B	HR	RBI	BB	SO	SB	CS	EqBRR	AVG	OBP	SLG	EqAVG	EqOBP	EqSLG	EqA	VORP	WARP	DEFENSE	
2007	ABQ	AAA	26	303	35	15	0	8	41	28	58	2	0	-0.6	.285	.360	.430	.226	.295	.332	.222	1.7	-0.4	70-C	-5
2008	ABQ	AAA	27	221	35	14	1	6	31	24	34	1	2	0.8	.321	.398	.497	.253	.324	.379	.248	5.7	0.7	48-C	0
2008	FLO	MLB	27	233	32	14	0	5	32	30	48	0	0	0.7	.299	.392	.447	.310	.397	.447	.298	18.6	1.5	56-C	-5
2009	FLO	MLB	28	423	59	25	0	9	50	41	89	0	0	-1.8	.271	.349	.410	.277	.352	.424	.270	21.9	0.9	97-C	-11
2010	FLO	MLB	29	388	44	16	1	9	46	38	85	1	1	-0.1	.251	.333	.381	.252	.332	.378	.248	10.3	0.7	91-C	-4

Breakout: 7%   Improve: 35%   Collapse: 26%   Attrition: 13%   MLB: 68%   Comparables: Scott Hatteberg, Chad Kreuter, Mike Maksudian, Bob Brenly

The average major-league catcher hit .254/.321/.396 last year. The Marlins got .276/.350/.419 out of the Baker/Ron Paulino platoon, so they were very quietly ahead of the game. Baker's batting slid from 2008, with a drop in his line-drive rate leading to a drop in batting average on balls in play just as night follows day or the placement of a quality science-fiction TV show on Friday night leads to cancellation. Baker would be an acceptable placeholder for a more offense-oriented catcher if not for his defensive weaknesses—his throwing isn't quite Jason Varitek–level bad, but his 20 percent caught-stealing rate was nonetheless in the lower echelon of starting catchers.

Emilio Bonifacio · 3B/2B/PR

Bats: S   Throws: R   Height: 5' 10"   Weight: 195   Born: April 23, 1985   Age: 25

YEAR	TEAM	LVL	AGE	PA	R	2B	3B	HR	RBI	BB	SO	SB	CS	EqBRR	AVG	OBP	SLG	EqAVG	EqOBP	EqSLG	EqA	VORP	WARP	DEFENSE			
2007	MOB	AA	22	596	84	21	5	2	40	38	105	41	13	6.1	.285	.333	.352	.262	.302	.327	.226	-0.1	0.0	75-2B	3	55-SS	-3
2007	ARI	MLB	22	27	2	1	0	0	2	4	3	0	1	0.1	.217	.333	.261	.217	.333	.261	.207	-0.8	-0.3	5-2B	-2		
2008	TUC	AAA	23	402	49	18	5	1	29	27	64	17	8	-2.0	.302	.348	.387	.272	.312	.341	.233	0.4	0.2	70-2B	1	10-LF	0
2008	ARI	MLB	23	12	3	1	0	0	2	0	5	1	0	0.3	.167	.167	.250	.167	.167	.250	.152	-1.1	-0.1				
2008	COH	AAA	23	36	9	2	0	0	3	4	4	4	2	-0.3	.452	.500	.516	.419	.472	.484	.326	3.7	0.2	8-2B	-2		
2008	WAS	MLB	23	174	26	5	5	0	12	14	41	6	4	1.0	.248	.305	.344	.256	.310	.359	.234	0.9	-0.9	37-2B	-9		
2009	FLO	MLB	24	509	72	11	6	1	27	34	95	21	9	2.5	.252	.303	.308	.261	.310	.319	.228	-1.6	0.1	80-3B	1	15-SS	-1
2010	FLO	MLB	25	511	68	21	5	3	32	40	101	17	8	1.1	.259	.317	.343	.259	.314	.338	.232	-1.5	-0.1	105-3B	1		

Breakout: 15%   Improve: 43%   Collapse: 11%   Attrition: 13%   MLB: 93%   Comparables: Terry Pendleton, Nelson Liriano, Eric Fox, Lou Collier

You know the Silver Sluggers, the annual award given to the best hitter at each position? No, Bonifacio didn't get one of those, but if there were an Iron Oxide award—that is, a Rusty Slugger—Bonifacio would have taken the prize for third basemen, having been the worst hitter in the majors (as per VORP) to play regularly at the position. He was badly miscast both at a run-producing position and as a leadoff man; it's a problem when your leadoff hitter bats .218/.284/.275 against right-handers. Heck, it's a problem when your number eight hitter does it. Bonifacio did finally lose the leadoff job with the arrival of Chris Coghlan, and his playing time disappeared when the acquisition of Nick Johnson pushed Jorge Cantu to third base. He received just 66 plate appearances over the rest of the season, spotting at short or center and pinch-running. He should have some value continuing in the role of a speedy 25th man—assuming the Marlins don't again decide to cripple their offense by overrating a minor talent; they averaged 4.5 runs a game with Bonifacio leading off, 4.9 with Coghlan at the top, and that adds up fast.

Jorge Cantu · 1B/3B

Bats: R   Throws: R   Height: 6' 3"   Weight: 200   Born: January 30, 1982   Age: 28

YEAR	TEAM	LVL	AGE	PA	R	2B	3B	HR	RBI	BB	SO	SB	CS	EqBRR	AVG	OBP	SLG	EqAVG	EqOBP	EqSLG	EqA	VORP	WARP	DEFENSE			
2007	TBA	MLB	25	65	4	1	0	0	4	5	16	0	0	0.1	.207	.277	.224	.207	.277	.224	.183	-4.2	-0.6	6-1B	-1		
2007	CIN	MLB	25	68	8	8	0	1	9	7	10	0	0	-1.2	.298	.382	.491	.304	.382	.482	.302	3.9	0.3	12-1B	-1		
2008	FLO	MLB	26	685	92	41	0	29	95	40	111	6	2	3.0	.277	.327	.481	.286	.333	.490	.278	29.3	2.7	120-3B	-8	32-1B	4
2009	FLO	MLB	27	643	67	42	0	16	100	47	81	3	1	-1.2	.289	.345	.443	.297	.350	.453	.277	17.7	1.0	95-1B	-1	40-3B	-7
2010	FLO	MLB	28	582	68	29	1	21	87	46	97	3	2	-0.1	.282	.348	.459	.283	.343	.455	.274	15.2	1.7	120-1B	1		

Breakout: 14%   Improve: 54%   Collapse: 7%   Attrition: 6%   MLB: 91%   Comparables: Ryan Garko, Shea Hillenbrand, Frank Thomas, Pat Tabler

Cantu was at his best when he was first up in an inning, hitting .330/.412/.470 in such situations. Yet because of Marlins fifth-place hitters, in particular Jeremy Hermida and Uggla, Cantu became a very minor statistical oddity, the 40th player in history to drive in 100 or more runs in a season without crossing the plate even 70 times. Cantu is no on-base machine and is a poor baserunner to boot, but he didn't quite deserve a place with noted sluggardly sluggers like Luke Easter '51 and Dave Kingman '84. In any case, the 100 RBI are a bit misleading, representative of

Cantu's having come to bat with the most baserunners on of any player in baseball. Cantu was miscast as a first baseman/cleanup hitter, but with the acquisition of Nick Johnson, he slid over to third base, where his bat profiles better even if his glove makes grown men weep. Only 28, he'll continue to be a corner stopgap until his next low-average year whittles his OBP away to nothing.

Brett Carroll — OF

Bats: R Throws: R Height: 6' 0" Weight: 190 Born: October 3, 1982 Age: 27

YEAR	TEAM	LVL	AGE	PA	R	2B	3B	HR	RBI	BB	SO	SB	CS	EqBRR	AVG	OBP	SLG	EqAVG	EqOBP	EqSLG	EqA	VORP	WARP	DEFENSE			
2007	CAR	AA	24	117	9	13	0	3	12	12	20	0	2	-2.5	.270	.359	.490	.250	.322	.423	.257	2.0	0.5	21-RF	2	8-CF	0
2007	ABQ	AAA	24	346	60	21	6	19	70	18	69	0	4	0.3	.314	.361	.597	.255	.301	.474	.258	7.2	1.6	39-RF	7	34-CF	0
2007	FLO	MLB	24	53	10	1	0	0	2	3	15	0	0	0.8	.184	.231	.204	.184	.231	.204	.137	-4.1	-0.6	9-CF	-1	3-RF	0
2008	JUP	A+	25	78	10	2	0	2	9	6	22	1	0	0.3	.169	.231	.282	.151	.192	.219	.119	-8.0	-1.2	7-RF	-1		
2008	ABQ	AAA	25	75	18	5	0	9	23	8	18	1	1	0.0	.418	.480	.896	.324	.387	.647	.328	8.2	0.5	16-CF	-4		
2008	FLO	MLB	25	18	5	0	1	0	1	1	6	0	0	0.9	.059	.111	.176	.059	.111	.176	-.126	-2.7	-0.2	3-RF	1	1-LF	0
2009	NWO	AAA	26	112	16	3	1	5	12	8	23	0	1	-1.1	.233	.295	.427	.221	.277	.385	.224	-2.2	0.2	18-RF	4	4-LF	0
2009	FLO	MLB	26	158	18	8	2	3	18	11	33	0	0	1.7	.234	.306	.383	.239	.310	.387	.245	0.1	1.3	36-RF	8	4-LF	1
2010	FLO	MLB	27	291	34	13	2	8	35	23	73	1	2	0.1	.233	.304	.389	.234	.301	.394	.235	-1.3	0.4	63-RF	5		

Breakout: 10% Improve: 34% Collapse: 18% Attrition: 23%   MLB: 64%   Comparables: Les Norman, Matt Mieske, John Fishel, Joe Gaetti

Carroll is a hustling defensive outfielder with a strong arm, but his bat just doesn't play and never has. Even at Triple-A, where he has hit well in 133 games over three seasons (.311/.364/.602), he has drawn only 34 walks in 533 PAs. While he has some power, there can only be one Jeff Francoeur, and Carroll isn't him. Right-handers eat him for breakfast, and with his .257 career OBP against left-handers, they have him for lunch. Plans for dinner have yet to be determined, but they could involve Pat Venditte. It's also tough to make a career as a fourth outfielder when you're stretched in center field.

Chris Coghlan — LF/2B

Bats: L Throws: R Height: 6' 1" Weight: 195 Born: June 18, 1985 Age: 25

YEAR	TEAM	LVL	AGE	PA	R	2B	3B	HR	RBI	BB	SO	SB	CS	EqBRR	AVG	OBP	SLG	EqAVG	EqOBP	EqSLG	EqA	VORP	WARP	DEFENSE			
2007	GRB	A	22	360	60	26	4	10	64	47	43	19	4	1.6	.325	.419	.534	.267	.344	.425	.269	14.5	0.7	75-2B	-9		
2007	JUP	A+	22	148	17	5	3	2	18	15	19	5	1	1.8	.200	.277	.331	.197	.264	.318	.210	-2.8	-0.5	31-2B	-1		
2008	CAR	AA	23	565	83	32	5	7	74	67	65	34	10	2.1	.298	.396	.429	.275	.352	.394	.265	19.7	1.2	114-2B	-10	9-3B	0
2009	NWO	AAA	24	110	21	9	1	3	22	12	10	9	1	1.6	.344	.418	.552	.351	.418	.557	.332	12.2	1.3	13-2B	-1	10-3B	0
2009	FLO	MLB	24	565	84	31	6	9	47	53	77	8	5	0.5	.321	.390	.460	.333	.398	.473	.299	34.6	2.9	116-LF	-7		
2010	FLO	MLB	25	583	75	33	4	11	70	60	86	13	5	1.3	.284	.362	.425	.284	.362	.427	.273	20.4	1.8	121-LF	-4		

Breakout: 14% Improve: 46% Collapse: 6% Attrition: 6%   MLB: 100%   Comparables: Andre Ethier, Terrence Long, Tommy Dunbar, Derek Lee

The Marlins have experienced enough variation in the performances of their primary leadoff men—from Todd Dunwoody's .292 OBP of 1998 to Luis Castillo's .418 of 2000—that they should have known better than to mess around with Bonifacio, but NL Rookie of the Year Coghlan rescued them from that error in judgment. Coughlin was a supplemental first-round pick out of Ole Miss in 2006, and his combined performance between Triple-A and the majors suggests either a great leap forward that scouts didn't anticipate or an early, not-to-be-repeated peak. It's more likely the latter, because his .365 BABIP probably will drop faster than Lehman Brothers. The other bad news is that Coghlan was very much the transplanted infielder in left field. Should he, as expected, return to second base or third, Coghlan's bat should nevertheless play very nicely, leaving the Fish a heck of a lot better off than they were when they put their faith in Bonifacio.

Scott Cousins — OF

Bats: L Throws: L Height: 6' 2" Weight: 190 Born: January 22, 1985 Age: 25

YEAR	TEAM	LVL	AGE	PA	R	2B	3B	HR	RBI	BB	SO	SB	CS	EqBRR	AVG	OBP	SLG	EqAVG	EqOBP	EqSLG	EqA	VORP	WARP	DEFENSE			
2007	GRB	A	22	472	69	25	0	18	74	38	92	16	7	2.3	.292	.358	.480	.240	.290	.378	.232	-5.1	-1.5	86-RF	-9	16-CF	2
2008	JUP	A+	23	211	35	9	2	9	29	20	47	11	3	-0.5	.304	.370	.513	.267	.322	.446	.263	5.1	0.4	27-RF	0	13-CF	-2
2008	CAR	AA	23	103	15	7	1	1	9	10	28	4	1	-0.8	.264	.350	.396	.234	.301	.362	.233	-1.0	0.0	17-RF	2	5-CF	-1
2009	JAX	AA	24	533	60	31	11	12	74	42	107	27	9	1.9	.263	.323	.448	.256	.301	.430	.252	8.7	0.9	86-CF	2	22-RF	-2
2010	FLO	MLB	25	452	46	20	4	11	51	34	121	8	4	0.5	.237	.299	.384	.239	.299	.388	.234	1.8	0.2	94-CF	0		

Breakout: 6% Improve: 32% Collapse: 18% Attrition: 8%   MLB: 4%   Comparables: Sean Ross, Oreste Marrero, Jason Robertson, Jalal Leach

A two-way player in college, the Marlins made Cousins a full-time outfielder. The move has yielded mixed returns so far. On the plus side, Cousins is a rangy outfielder with a strong arm, speed, and some power. On the other hand, he'll be making his Triple-A debut in his age-25 season, doesn't control the strike zone, and batted only .225/.294/.388 against his fellow left-handers. His physical skills should allow him to carve out a career in the majors, but it's going to take some serious late bloomin' for Cousins to be an acceptable starter.

Alejandro De Aza   **OF**   Bats: L   Throws: L   Height: 6' 0"   Weight: 175   Born: April 11, 1984   Age: 26

YEAR	TEAM	LVL	AGE	PA	R	2B	3B	HR	RBI	BB	SO	SB	CS	EqBRR	AVG	OBP	SLG	EqAVG	EqOBP	EqSLG	EqA	VORP	WARP	DEFENSE			
2007	FLO	MLB	23	158	14	8	2	0	8	6	37	2	0	0.9	.229	.261	.313	.234	.265	.310	.209	-4.3	-1.1	34-CF	-6		
2009	NWO	AAA	25	307	45	21	5	8	34	27	53	11	5	1.6	.300	.370	.506	.297	.358	.495	.286	14.7	0.0	24-CF	-11	23-RF	-5
2009	FLO	MLB	25	27	6	1	0	0	3	5	5	0	0	0.9	.250	.385	.300	.250	.385	.300	.272	0.7	-0.1	3-CF	0	1-LF	-1
2010	CHA	MLB	26	279	35	15	3	6	25	23	61	4	3	0.9	.256	.321	.401	.259	.322	.407	.243	3.6	-0.4	49-CF	-7		

Breakout: 5%   Improve: 34%   Collapse: 24%   Attrition: 11%   MLB: 34%   Comparables: Stuart Pederson, McKay Christensen, Peter Bergeron, Alan Cartwright

After missing the entire 2008 season due to ankle surgery, De Aza failed to find a place with the Marlins last year. However, he did well enough at New Orleans to provoke a waiver claim by the White Sox, who have been looking for help in center field roughly since Judge Landis banned Happy Felsch. The subsequent acquisition of Juan Pierre could put him in a minor reserve role or keep him off the roster altogether.

Matt Dominguez   **3B**   Bats: R   Throws: R   Height: 6' 2"   Weight: 180   Born: August 28, 1989   Age: 20

YEAR	TEAM	LVL	AGE	PA	R	2B	3B	HR	RBI	BB	SO	SB	CS	EqBRR	AVG	OBP	SLG	EqAVG	EqOBP	EqSLG	EqA	VORP	WARP	DEFENSE	
2007	JAM	A-	17	38	3	2	0	1	4	1	12	0	0	-0.1	.189	.211	.324	.162	.184	.270	.134	-3.3	-0.6	10-3B	0
2008	GRB	A	18	381	59	16	0	18	70	28	68	0	1	-2.4	.296	.354	.499	.247	.298	.406	.242	2.1	-1.9	88-3B	-18
2009	JUP	A+	19	429	49	25	1	11	53	38	68	1	0	-3.1	.262	.333	.420	.252	.312	.396	.247	5.8	0.7	102-3B	0
2009	JAX	AA	19	114	10	7	0	2	9	14	24	0	0	-3.9	.186	.292	.320	.190	.274	.300	.205	-3.2	-0.4	28-3B	0
2010	FLO	MLB	20	506	59	25	1	17	66	44	105	0	1	-2.6	.250	.319	.419	.250	.313	.420	.251	8.3	0.4	122-3B	-5

Breakout: 43%   Improve: 71%   Collapse: 12%   Attrition: 3%   MLB: 2%   Comparables: Greg Toler, Pedro Roman, Brian Richardson, Alex Liddi

Dominguez was the Marlins' first-round pick (12th overall) in their strong 2007 draft (Mike Stanton was their second-rounder). He made it up to Double-A as a teenager, but didn't hit well there, and he carried his struggles over to the Arizona Fall League this winter. Dominguez might be the best defensive third baseman in the minors, but his bat remains unproven. The power he showed in 2008 might have been a product of his home park, and the lack of follow-up in 2009 can only be partly attributed to the pitcher-friendly environment of the Florida State League. Dominguez is quite young, so there's no reason to rush to judgment. Much will be revealed when he returns to Double-A, so don't get on the Marlins for selecting Dominguez over Jason Heyward (taken by the Braves at 14th overall) *too* much—not yet.

Ross Gload   **1B/OF**   Bats: L   Throws: L   Height: 6' 1"   Weight: 190   Born: April 5, 1976   Age: 34

YEAR	TEAM	LVL	AGE	PA	R	2B	3B	HR	RBI	BB	SO	SB	CS	EqBRR	AVG	OBP	SLG	EqAVG	EqOBP	EqSLG	EqA	VORP	WARP	DEFENSE			
2007	KCA	MLB	31	346	37	22	3	7	51	16	39	2	2	-0.3	.287	.318	.441	.286	.315	.447	.259	3.3	0.7	76-1B	3	6-LF	0
2008	KCA	MLB	32	418	46	18	1	3	37	23	39	3	4	-2.3	.273	.317	.348	.276	.321	.349	.235	-7.0	-1.7	98-1B	-9	7-LF	1
2009	FLO	MLB	33	259	33	10	2	6	30	23	30	0	0	1.1	.261	.329	.400	.270	.333	.422	.259	0.3	0.2	33-1B	2	5-RF	-1
2010	PHI	MLB	34	281	30	13	1	5	32	22	39	2	2	-0.2	.264	.326	.378	.268	.326	.388	.244	-1.6	-0.2	63-1B	-1		

Breakout: 6%   Improve: 35%   Collapse: 22%   Attrition: 27%   MLB: 94%   Comparables: Frank Catalanotto, Todd Walker, Mickey Vernon, Joe Kuhel

In 176 career pinch-hit plate appearances, Gload has hit .300/.358/.425; teammate Helms has hit .289/.362/.462 in 303 career pinch-hit plate appearances. That is kind of neat; it's hard to find one pinch-hitter who achieves success with any regularity, but the Marlins employed two of them. Gload hit .318/.418/.455 when pinch-hitting in 2009; the major league averages in the role were .225/.315/.353. Unfortunately, at all other times, Gload was even more futile than he was in 2008. His ability to make contact and lash line drives seems to confer some advantages in one-off matchups, but regular play exposes his limitations, so to say that the less you see of him, the more valuable Gload is should not be taken as a put-down. Having had his option declined by the Marlins, Gload signed a two-year deal to replace Matt Stairs on the Phillies' bench. The presence of Ryan Howard should function to restrict Gload to an appropriate number of plate appearances.

Brett Hayes   C

Bats: R   Throws: R   Height: 6' 1"   Weight: 200   Born: February 13, 1984   Age: 26

YEAR	TEAM	LVL	AGE	PA	R	2B	3B	HR	RBI	BB	SO	SB	CS	EqBRR	AVG	OBP	SLG	EqAVG	EqOBP	EqSLG	EqA	VORP	WARP	DEFENSE	
2007	JUP	A+	23	75	10	3	1	1	11	9	10	2	3	-1.1	.338	.413	.462	.328	.395	.448	.288	5.6	0.8	16-C	1
2007	CAR	AA	23	295	22	16	0	3	31	18	51	2	0	2.9	.234	.280	.326	.220	.259	.300	.194	-4.5	-2.2	71-C	-14
2008	CAR	AA	24	194	19	8	0	6	18	10	43	1	4	-1.2	.232	.275	.376	.207	.242	.315	.188	-5.2	-1.0	47-C	-3
2008	ABQ	AAA	24	126	21	3	1	5	17	4	23	1	1	0.4	.293	.331	.466	.239	.274	.385	.227	1.3	-0.2	32-C	-3
2009	NWO	AAA	25	353	27	15	0	4	37	20	66	2	0	0.1	.240	.281	.324	.243	.279	.317	.213	-1.3	-0.2	85-C	0
2009	FLO	MLB	25	12	5	1	0	1	2	0	4	0	0	0.3	.273	.333	.636	.273	.333	.636	.315	0.7	0.1		
2010	FLO	MLB	26	302	27	11	1	6	30	21	71	1	1	0.2	.226	.285	.338	.227	.280	.341	.212	-2.2	-0.6	73-C	-3

Breakout: 15%   Improve: 32%   Collapse: 35%   Attrition: 27%   MLB: 5%   Comparables: Omir Santos, Jeffrey Howell, Jim Horner, Tommy Adams

The Marlins' second-round pick in 2005, Hayes has played in 393 minor-league games and batted .249/.303/.367. That translates to "horrifically bad" at the major-league level, but here he is, on the 40-man roster. Hayes is excellent defensively and has the kind of personality that one imagines will make him a manager in about 10 years. Given these attributes and the normal shortage and/or uneven distribution of catchers—Wil Nieves and Koyie Hill got extensive playing time last year, after all—Hayes may be able to carve out a career for himself. He simply can't hit, however.

Wes Helms   3B/1B

Bats: R   Throws: R   Height: 6' 4"   Weight: 220   Born: May 12, 1976   Age: 34

YEAR	TEAM	LVL	AGE	PA	R	2B	3B	HR	RBI	BB	SO	SB	CS	EqBRR	AVG	OBP	SLG	EqAVG	EqOBP	EqSLG	EqA	VORP	WARP	DEFENSE				
2007	PHI	MLB	31	308	21	19	0	5	39	19	62	0	0	-0.6	.246	.297	.368	.247	.297	.366	.234	-2.4	-0.1	49-3B	2	11-1B	-1
2008	FLO	MLB	32	278	28	11	0	5	31	17	65	0	0	0.3	.243	.299	.347	.249	.302	.349	.232	-3.3	-0.6	37-3B	0	24-1B	-2
2009	FLO	MLB	33	234	18	11	0	3	33	13	54	1	1	-0.3	.271	.318	.364	.280	.325	.369	.245	0.6	0.5	41-3B	1	4-1B	2
2010	FLO	MLB	34	292	24	11	0	6	41	23	70	1	0	-0.1	.246	.315	.356	.245	.311	.350	.234	-0.4	0.0	61-3B	1		

Breakout: 11%   Improve: 45%   Collapse: 25%   Attrition: 21%   MLB: 85%   Comparables: Charlie Hayes, Leon Roberts, Jeff Conine, Ed Sprague

Helms used to hit left-handers rather well, but hasn't done much with them recently, hitting just .272/.329/.406 against them over the last two seasons. That might seem like something worth keeping, but last year the *average* major-league right-handed hitter hit .268/.341/.430 against southpaws. Helms can still field competently at first and third, and he did hit .347/.429/.408 in 56 plate appearances as a pinch-hitter, an occupation at which he's had unusual durability and competence. As for what Helms does when asked to actually start, well, let's just say the whole package was not worth five percent of the entire Marlins payroll.

Jeremy Hermida   RF

Bats: L   Throws: R   Height: 6' 3"   Weight: 210   Born: January 30, 1984   Age: 26

YEAR	TEAM	LVL	AGE	PA	R	2B	3B	HR	RBI	BB	SO	SB	CS	EqBRR	AVG	OBP	SLG	EqAVG	EqOBP	EqSLG	EqA	VORP	WARP	DEFENSE				
2007	FLO	MLB	23	484	54	32	1	18	63	47	105	3	4	-3.9	.296	.369	.501	.308	.380	.516	.299	29.7	3.7	111-RF	3		
2008	FLO	MLB	24	559	74	22	3	17	61	48	138	6	1	0.4	.249	.323	.406	.256	.328	.417	.258	9.3	1.2	123-RF	2		
2009	FLO	MLB	25	491	48	14	2	13	47	56	101	5	2	-4.1	.259	.348	.392	.267	.352	.405	.266	12.7	1.9	70-RF	5	38-LF	-1
2010	BOS	MLB	26	563	73	28	2	22	70	60	122	5	4	-1.4	.275	.359	.468	.273	.357	.455	.273	19.7	2.3	126-RF	1		

Breakout: 24%   Improve: 55%   Collapse: 0%   Attrition: 4%   MLB: 100%   Comparables: Ben Grieve, Babe Herman, Garret Anderson, Harold Baines

Boston might have made a very canny move in picking up Hermida, though he is widely viewed as a disappointment a Florida, an unmotivated kid who threw his career into reverse after what seemed like a breakthrough season in 2007. For all the negativity directed toward his weak defense and his perceived bad attitude, there are hints that there is more to this player than meets the eye. Hermida has been badly handicapped by Dolphin Stadium, hitting a hopeless .253/.328/.393 at home but a more robust .276/.359/.476 on the road. He has also struggled against left-handers, hitting only .237/.321/.376 against them, versus .274/.351/.441 against righties. Filter out his two handicaps, and you get a Hermida who hits .288/.369/.484. The latter figure is the one that the Red Sox hope to see and build on, given that Hermida will be only 26 this year.

Nick Johnson   1B

Bats: L   Throws: L   Height: 6' 3"   Weight: 235   Born: September 19, 1978   Age: 31

YEAR	TEAM	LVL	AGE	PA	R	2B	3B	HR	RBI	BB	SO	SB	CS	EqBRR	AVG	OBP	SLG	EqAVG	EqOBP	EqSLG	EqA	VORP	WARP	DEFENSE	
2008	WAS	MLB	29	147	15	8	0	5	20	33	25	0	0	0.5	.220	.415	.431	.220	.411	.440	.303	8.1	1.0	34-1B	1
2009	WAS	MLB	30	424	47	16	2	6	44	63	66	2	2	-2.1	.295	.408	.402	.311	.417	.427	.298	17.3	1.8	92-1B	-1
2009	FLO	MLB	30	150	24	8	0	2	18	36	18	0	2	-2.3	.279	.477	.413	.295	.480	.438	.331	11.3	1.2	29-1B	-1
2010	NYA	MLB	31	466	60	19	1	11	59	81	75	2	3	-1.5	.279	.421	.423	.276	.413	.415	.294	21.4	2.3	103-1B	0

Breakout: 6%   Improve: 35%   Collapse: 7%   Attrition: 5%   MLB: 98%   Comparables: Boog Powell, Greg Brock, John Mayberry, Kent Hrbek

The Marlins must have rated themselves suckers after they picked up Johnson to bolster their surprising post-season candidacy only to watch him sit for 21 of 59 possible games due to hamstring problems and a bout of the flu. Hey, caveat emptor—this is what Johnson does. As we've often said at BP, staying healthy is a skill, and it's one that Johnson doesn't have. What Johnson did do surprisingly well, given that he missed almost 290 games from 2007 to 2008, is get on base. The old power was absent, his range afield has declined, and the only guy he might beat in a race around the bases is Carlos Lee, but Nick the Stick can still smack line drives for singles and his terrific batting eye remains sharp. He ranked second in the NL in OBP and stands 10th among active players in that category (2,500 or more PAs). The Yankees signed Johnson to a one-year contract to serve as their DH, but even minimal exertion and a sterile environment might not keep him on the field for 150 games.

Cameron Maybin   CF

Bats: R   Throws: R   Height: 6' 4"   Weight: 205   Born: April 4, 1987   Age: 23

YEAR	TEAM	LVL	AGE	PA	R	2B	3B	HR	RBI	BB	SO	SB	CS	EqBRR	AVG	OBP	SLG	EqAVG	EqOBP	EqSLG	EqA	VORP	WARP	DEFENSE			
2007	LAK	A+	20	350	58	14	5	10	44	43	83	25	6	1.2	.304	.393	.486	.261	.341	.432	.272	13.9	0.0	69-CF	-14		
2007	DET	MLB	20	53	8	3	0	1	2	3	21	5	0	1.1	.143	.208	.265	.143	.208	.265	.189	-2.6	-0.2	9-LF	-1	3-CF	2
2008	CAR	AA	21	459	73	15	8	13	49	60	124	21	7	3.7	.277	.375	.456	.249	.330	.405	.258	11.4	1.4	101-CF	0		
2008	FLO	MLB	21	36	9	2	0	0	2	3	8	4	0	2.1	.500	.543	.563	.500	.543	.563	.404	6.5	1.1	7-CF	3		
2009	NWO	AAA	22	343	44	18	8	3	39	38	58	8	2	1.4	.319	.399	.463	.304	.375	.442	.286	18.3	3.5	72-CF	11		
2009	FLO	MLB	22	199	30	12	2	4	13	17	51	1	3	0.5	.250	.318	.409	.258	.325	.433	.253	4.3	0.8	47-CF	2		
2010	FLO	MLB	23	496	68	23	5	12	45	57	134	15	5	1.7	.254	.342	.411	.254	.335	.410	.262	16.4	1.8	108-CF	0		

Breakout: 10%   Improve: 43%   Collapse: 14%   Attrition: 10%   MLB: 100%   Comparables: Adam Jones, Steve Hosey, Alonzo Powell, Javier Ortiz

Eternal prospect Maybin won the starting job in center in spring training, but lasted just 26 games, hitting .202/.280/.310 and striking out in 33 percent of his plate appearances. After a slow start at New Orleans, Maybin was socking the ball with consistency by June, but with Cody Ross doing well in center and Chris Coghlan getting an extended trial in left, the Marlins opted to let Maybin marinate in the Big Muddy's muck. Upon finally returning in September, he batted .293/.353/.500 in 104 plate appearances, cutting the strikeouts to a manageable 19 percent, a figure that would allow him to put enough balls in play to hit for a decent average. Maybin underwent surgery on a partially torn labrum in his left (nonthrowing) shoulder, but is expected to have recovered in time for spring training to take up everyday duties in center.

Jai Miller   OF

Bats: R   Throws: R   Height: 6' 4"   Weight: 195   Born: January 17, 1985   Age: 25

YEAR	TEAM	LVL	AGE	PA	R	2B	3B	HR	RBI	BB	SO	SB	CS	EqBRR	AVG	OBP	SLG	EqAVG	EqOBP	EqSLG	EqA	VORP	WARP	DEFENSE			
2007	CAR	AA	22	473	54	26	2	14	58	55	127	12	5	-1.1	.261	.354	.438	.241	.318	.396	.251	8.4	0.8	109-CF	0	4-LF	-2
2008	ABQ	AAA	23	498	67	22	5	19	56	52	133	20	6	2.5	.267	.349	.472	.219	.294	.373	.238	-1.7	-1.1	84-RF	-2	28-CF	-6
2009	NWO	AAA	24	390	55	24	2	16	52	38	106	6	3	-0.6	.289	.360	.510	.279	.342	.494	.282	18.4	1.1	50-RF	-2	40-CF	-7
2010	FLO	MLB	25	434	45	20	2	12	42	44	130	7	3	0.1	.230	.313	.384	.230	.306	.379	.242	0.7	-0.1	102-RF	-2		

Breakout: 7%   Improve: 30%   Collapse: 29%   Attrition: 10%   MLB: 5%   Comparables: Stoney Briggs, Brent Clevlen, Mario Encarnacion, Alan Cockrell

Sometimes, it seems as if Miller has been in the minors longer than the Marlins have existed, but in truth it has only been seven years. He didn't hit at all for the first four of those seasons, but the former three-sport high school star only recently began figuring out how to apply his skills to baseball. Miller has legitimate power and the ability to play center field, but his control of the strike zone remains shaky and his present upside is something out of the sketchier sections of the Corey Patterson catalog. Still, a Corey Patterson comparison is something of a personal triumph, given how long Miller had to last to get there.

Logan Morrison   1B   Bats: L   Throws: L   Height: 6' 2"   Weight: 215   Born: August 25, 1987   Age: 22

YEAR	TEAM	LVL	AGE	PA	R	2B	3B	HR	RBI	BB	SO	SB	CS	EqBRR	AVG	OBP	SLG	EqAVG	EqOBP	EqSLG	EqA	VORP	WARP	DEFENSE
2007	GRB	A	19	513	71	22	2	24	86	48	96	2	2	-2.2	.267	.343	.483	.221	.284	.382	.231	-10.9	-3.6	111-1B -19
2008	JUP	A+	20	555	71	38	1	13	74	57	80	9	3	-3.5	.332	.402	.494	.318	.375	.472	.292	25.3	2.0	118-1B -9
2009	JAX	AA	21	343	48	18	2	8	47	63	46	9	4	0.3	.277	.411	.442	.276	.385	.445	.289	11.0	1.9	73-1B 5
2010	FLO	MLB	22	484	56	25	1	15	62	49	96	4	3	-1.1	.268	.345	.432	.268	.346	.433	.266	8.5	0.5	104-1B -4

Breakout: 15% Improve: 50% Collapse: 13% Attrition: 5%   MLB: 6%   Comparables: Matt Winters, Mike Carp, Travis Ishikawa, Troy O'Leary

While the Marlins employed Nick Johnson at the major-league level, they had a potential doppelgänger down on the farm, a duplicate right down to the injury bug—Morrison missed about two months nursing a fractured wrist. At least Morrison's walk total speaks to his more positive Johnsonian qualities. This was a huge jump in patience; Morrison had taken only 105 walks in his previous 258 games, and we'll have to see if it sticks. It had better, because his home-run power has ebbed since he poked those 24 homers at Greensboro, and if he's going to succeed at first base, he's either going to have to remember how to launch a few or else continue to be awfully patient.

Ronny Paulino   C   Bats: R   Throws: R   Height: 6' 2"   Weight: 245   Born: April 21, 1981   Age: 29

YEAR	TEAM	LVL	AGE	PA	R	2B	3B	HR	RBI	BB	SO	SB	CS	EqBRR	AVG	OBP	SLG	EqAVG	EqOBP	EqSLG	EqA	VORP	WARP	DEFENSE
2007	PIT	MLB	26	494	56	25	0	11	55	33	79	2	2	-1.0	.263	.314	.389	.272	.323	.404	.249	18.4	1.9	122-C -1
2008	PIT	MLB	27	130	8	5	0	2	18	11	24	0	0	0.0	.212	.277	.305	.212	.277	.297	.208	-1.4	-0.4	29-C -1
2009	FLO	MLB	28	266	24	10	1	8	27	25	48	1	0	-0.2	.272	.340	.423	.279	.343	.438	.270	14.0	2.1	65-C 3
2010	FLO	MLB	29	341	34	16	1	10	41	33	69	1	1	-0.4	.264	.337	.418	.264	.329	.411	.259	13.0	1.5	81-C 0

Breakout: 14% Improve: 47% Collapse: 10% Attrition: 12%   MLB: 90%   Comparables: Toby Hall, Rod Barajas, Ramon Hernandez, Joe Oliver

Paulino might have found his best destiny as the short half of the Marlins catching platoon. Paulino has hit only .252/.305/.347 against right-handers on his career, but he's a whole other guy against southpaws, hitting .333/.392/.485 with 13 home runs in 390 at-bats, and as you know from reading the Wes Helms comment, that's actually pretty good. He's also the half of the platoon with John Baker that can throw, and since Kyle Skipworth isn't coming quickly and Brett Hayes isn't coming at all, Paulino should get to prosper in the role.

Bryan Petersen   OF   Bats: L   Throws: R   Height: 6' 0"   Weight: 200   Born: April 9, 1986   Age: 24

YEAR	TEAM	LVL	AGE	PA	R	2B	3B	HR	RBI	BB	SO	SB	CS	EqBRR	AVG	OBP	SLG	EqAVG	EqOBP	EqSLG	EqA	VORP	WARP	DEFENSE	
2007	JAM	A-	21	240	27	13	1	5	24	18	53	11	2	-0.1	.250	.318	.389	.210	.255	.335	.207	-8.8	-3.9	42-RF -14	6-CF -1
2008	GRB	A	22	345	60	10	2	19	58	38	74	15	6	0.6	.301	.381	.541	.243	.311	.410	.252	6.6	0.3	77-CF -4	
2008	JUP	A+	22	175	23	5	0	3	12	15	29	7	1	2.0	.265	.339	.355	.258	.316	.333	.235	-0.8	0.3	19-RF 2	14-CF 1
2008	CAR	AA	22	44	5	2	0	1	10	5	6	1	2	-1.1	.351	.409	.486	.316	.364	.447	.282	1.8	0.2	10-RF 0	
2009	JAX	AA	23	494	64	15	7	7	49	50	66	13	12	-0.8	.297	.368	.413	.298	.354	.415	.268	13.4	0.4	91-LF -12	9-CF 2
2010	FLO	MLB	24	463	54	19	3	12	47	38	103	8	5	0.1	.255	.322	.399	.256	.323	.398	.248	3.7	-0.3	98-LF -6	

Breakout: 18% Improve: 51% Collapse: 12% Attrition: 10%   MLB: 7%   Comparables: Ross Gload, Adam Seuss, Xavier Paul, Kenny Lofton

A 2007 fourth-rounder, Petersen has evolved dramatically in his short minor-league career. In his first season and a half of play, which comprise his stints at Jamestown and Greensboro, he struck out 127 times in 585 plate appearances (roughly 22 percent) while hitting 24 home runs. Then, almost as if he met Joe Sewell on the road to Jupiter, he greatly curtailed the strikeouts—in 713 plate appearances since reaching High-A, Petersen has whiffed just 101 times (14 percent). The trade-off for this improved contact-hitting was that the home runs went away as well, with Petersen hitting just 11 since his transformation. Fortunately, he can play center field, so offensive expectations are less than if he were restricted to a corner. Petersen ransacked the Arizona Fall League, hitting .379/.412/.600, something that should raise his profile quite a bit.

Hanley Ramirez SS

Bats: R Throws: R Height: 6' 3" Weight: 200 Born: December 23, 1983 Age: 26

YEAR	TEAM	LVL	AGE	PA	R	2B	3B	HR	RBI	BB	SO	SB	CS	EqBRR	AVG	OBP	SLG	EqAVG	EqOBP	EqSLG	EqA	VORP	WARP	DEFENSE	
2007	FLO	MLB	23	706	125	48	6	29	81	52	95	51	14	2.3	.332	.386	.562	.351	.404	.588	.323	79.9	7.9	146-SS	-7
2008	FLO	MLB	24	693	125	34	4	33	67	92	122	35	12	2.8	.301	.400	.540	.316	.410	.564	.321	76.8	9.1	146-SS	6
2009	FLO	MLB	25	652	101	42	1	24	106	61	101	27	8	2.8	.342	.410	.543	.354	.417	.563	.327	75.0	7.6	141-SS	-5
2010	FLO	MLB	26	659	109	36	3	27	81	77	102	30	13	1.3	.321	.409	.535	.320	.401	.533	.315	64.0	6.7	142-SS	-1

Breakout: 10% Improve: 37% Collapse: 5% Attrition: 8% MLB: 100% Comparables: Derek Jeter, Alex Rodriguez, Nomar Garciaparra, David Wright

When a shortstop has a season that would fit on the back of Honus Wagner's baseball card, you know he's arrived. The NL batting title winner may not be the best hitter in baseball—that would have to be Albert Pujols—but if he were a better defender at shortstop, you could make a strong argument that he's the best all-around *player* or that he should be considered in tandem with Joe Mauer for the title. This may be overstating Ramirez's defensive short-comings; he has improved. We're talking about a shortstop approaching average here, not Derek Jeter '03—and Jeter was a legitimate MVP candidate even with range problems that far exceeded Ramirez's. Contractually, the Marlins are in an interesting place—Ramirez is signed through 2014, and for a player of his talents, he's inexpensive, making $7 million this year. After that, he gets into real, superstar-level money, bouncing up to $11 million in 2011 and $15 million in 2012, the same year their new ballpark is scheduled to open. No doubt the Marlins would prefer Ramirez to carry their limited fan base into the new park. However, this is the most penurious franchise in baseball, and it's going to be very difficult to field a complete team and carry an $11 million Ramirez if the team payroll is going to stay south of $40 million.

Cody Ross OF

Bats: R Throws: L Height: 5' 9" Weight: 205 Born: December 23, 1980 Age: 29

YEAR	TEAM	LVL	AGE	PA	R	2B	3B	HR	RBI	BB	SO	SB	CS	EqBRR	AVG	OBP	SLG	EqAVG	EqOBP	EqSLG	EqA	VORP	WARP	DEFENSE			
2007	FLO	MLB	26	197	35	19	0	12	39	20	38	2	0	1.6	.335	.411	.653	.349	.426	.674	.351	26.3	2.9	27-CF	-3	12-RF	2
2008	FLO	MLB	27	506	59	29	5	22	73	33	116	6	1	-0.6	.260	.316	.488	.270	.322	.502	.277	23.3	3.7	97-CF	9	17-RF	1
2009	FLO	MLB	28	604	73	37	1	24	90	34	122	5	2	-0.9	.270	.321	.469	.279	.327	.480	.273	24.7	1.6	96-CF	-9	50-RF	-1
2010	FLO	MLB	29	532	67	29	2	24	82	44	113	4	2	0.0	.272	.343	.490	.273	.339	.486	.279	27.9	3.0	122-CF	-1		

Breakout: 11% Improve: 39% Collapse: 6% Attrition: 5% MLB: 98% Comparables: Joe Medwick, Aaron Rowand, Jim Rice, Tommie Agee

Sold to the Marlins back in 2006, Ross eventually rescued center field from a cadre of pretenders who nearly succeeded in making "the Juan Pierre years" seem synonymous with "the Joe DiMaggio era." Unfortunately, he also had to rescue it from Cameron Maybin, at least for the time being. As a free-talent pickup, Ross was a thorough win for the Marlins, but that doesn't mean he's without faults. Ross is a slow starter (his bat takes April off), he's impatient, and he does most of his dirty work against lefties (.291/.354/.610 career vs. .253/.309/.429 against right-handers), and a guy the *Sun Sentinel* called a "bald, stubby castoff" has about the range you would imagine from that description. Ross is reaching the phase of his career where he's going to become expensive relative to his talents, but will probably stick in a wide-open Marlins outfield for now, probably heading to right to replace Hermida.

Gaby Sanchez 1B/3B

Bats: R Throws: R Height: 6' 2" Weight: 225 Born: September 2, 1983 Age: 26

YEAR	TEAM	LVL	AGE	PA	R	2B	3B	HR	RBI	BB	SO	SB	CS	EqBRR	AVG	OBP	SLG	EqAVG	EqOBP	EqSLG	EqA	VORP	WARP	DEFENSE			
2007	JUP	A+	23	547	89	40	3	9	70	64	74	6	6	2.7	.279	.369	.433	.265	.341	.405	.261	5.8	0.0	98-1B	-6	7-3B	0
2008	CAR	AA	24	557	70	42	1	17	92	69	70	17	8	-5.6	.314	.404	.513	.284	.354	.449	.277	19.5	2.8	66-1B	3	59-3B	1
2008	FLO	MLB	24	8	0	2	0	0	1	0	2	0	0	0.0	.375	.375	.625	.375	.375	.625	.332	0.7	0.1				
2009	NWO	AAA	25	370	55	11	0	16	56	41	44	5	0	-0.3	.289	.374	.475	.287	.360	.454	.284	14.8	0.5	41-1B	-4	40-3B	-7
2009	FLO	MLB	25	23	2	0	0	2	3	2	3	0	0	-0.1	.238	.304	.524	.238	.304	.524	.279	0.7	0.1				
2010	FLO	MLB	26	448	53	23	1	12	54	47	79	4	3	-0.5	.264	.346	.416	.265	.340	.415	.263	6.0	0.5	94-1B	-2		

Breakout: 13% Improve: 32% Collapse: 18% Attrition: 16% MLB: 19% Comparables: Tim Belk, Robb Quinlan, Alejandro Freire, Jason Phillips

The Marlins' handling of Sanchez was less than adroit. They went into the season with Bonifacio and Cantu manning the infield corners. As far as it goes, Sanchez is a prospect with a limited ceiling, but with his excellent eye and ability to cream left-handers, he had more of a chance of contributing to an upset division win than Bonifacio, who could have been replaced by Cantu at any time during the season (as he was after the Nick Johnson acquisition). Instead, Sanchez's time in the majors was spent on the bench, as Fredi Gonzalez gave him exactly one start.

Michael Stanton RF Bats: R Throws: R Height: 6' 5" Weight: 205 Born: November 8, 1989 Age: 20

YEAR	TEAM	LVL	AGE	PA	R	2B	3B	HR	RBI	BB	SO	SB	CS	EqBRR	AVG	OBP	SLG	EqAVG	EqOBP	EqSLG	EqA	VORP	WARP	DEFENSE	
2007	JAM	A-	17	35	2	1	0	1	2	3	15	0	0	0.2	.067	.147	.200	.065	.118	.194	.040	-4.5	-0.8	9-RF	0
2008	GRB	A	18	540	89	26	3	39	97	58	153	4	2	0.3	.293	.381	.611	.247	.324	.486	.273	19.3	1.8	63-RF -5	43-CF 0
2009	JUP	A+	19	210	27	9	3	12	39	28	45	2	2	-0.3	.294	.390	.578	.281	.365	.546	.302	13.7	1.2	37-RF -5	4-CF 1
2009	JAX	AA	19	341	49	15	2	16	53	31	99	1	1	-1.0	.231	.311	.455	.231	.293	.440	.251	2.6	1.2	73-RF	7
2010	FLO	MLB	20	560	76	27	3	34	87	58	161	2	2	-0.2	.247	.331	.517	.247	.324	.509	.279	24.6	2.6	116-RF	-1

Breakout: 44% Improve: 74% Collapse: 6% Attrition: 3% MLB: 4% Comparables: Luis Mateo, Chad Hermansen, Jim Presley, Terry Mayo

You're going to hear a lot about Stanton's strikeouts, which is an amazingly short-sighted thing to focus on with a teenager who has shown this kind of power. There just aren't a lot of kids his age playing at Double-A, and some pitch-recognition problems aren't surprising, given his relative inexperience—Stanton could be in college now instead of a couple of steps away from the majors. If the Marlins don't rush Stanton to "The Show" because they've dealt away every player who makes more than the minimum, Stanton should start the season back at Double-A and try to adjust to more advanced pitching. When he does, his walk rate should skyrocket, as pitchers aren't going to want to pitch to this guy. Stanton's AFL season was cut short by a sore back, but the problem should be resolved by spring training. P.S.: What is it about folks with the surname Stanton naming their kid Mike? This Mike Stanton will be the third in major league history.

Dan Uggla 2B Bats: R Throws: R Height: 5' 11" Weight: 200 Born: March 11, 1980 Age: 30

YEAR	TEAM	LVL	AGE	PA	R	2B	3B	HR	RBI	BB	SO	SB	CS	EqBRR	AVG	OBP	SLG	EqAVG	EqOBP	EqSLG	EqA	VORP	WARP	DEFENSE
2007	FLO	MLB	27	728	113	49	3	31	88	68	167	2	1	2.2	.245	.326	.479	.254	.333	.494	.280	40.5	2.5	155-2B -19
2008	FLO	MLB	28	619	97	37	1	32	92	77	171	5	5	1.0	.260	.360	.514	.271	.367	.531	.297	45.6	4.9	143-2B -2
2009	FLO	MLB	29	668	84	27	1	31	90	92	150	2	1	1.7	.243	.354	.459	.253	.358	.477	.285	38.4	4.3	157-2B -1
2010	FLO	MLB	30	644	94	31	1	29	88	82	155	3	3	0.8	.251	.357	.467	.250	.348	.463	.280	33.3	3.2	149-2B -4

Breakout: 9% Improve: 36% Collapse: 10% Attrition: 4% MLB: 99% Comparables: Damion Easley, Ron Cey, Don Money, Harmon Killebrew

Last year we wrote, "Every year has been a surprise with Uggla." This year's surprise was an assault on the record books; Uggla became the fastest second baseman to reach 100 home runs, and he also was the first second baseman in the history of the game to hit 30 home runs in three consecutive seasons. Four other second basemen have had three 30-homer seasons, but none of them ever did it three times in a row or had a fourth such season. When Uggla was notified of the record, he told the *Palm Beach Post*, "It's something to be proud of, but I don't really know what to think or what to make of it right now." That was ironic, since many observers feel the same way about Uggla, with his streakiness, his high-strikeout approach, and his shaky glove-work at the keystone. After going cold in the second half of 2008, he opened 2009 the same way, batting just .218/.317/.428 through the end of May. He hit .258/.370/.473 thereafter, consonant with his career rates. His higher walk rate last year is reflective of being pitched carefully due to his place in the batting order (he was usually followed by Ross or Hermida) rather than any new-found patience and will probably regress in this arbitration-eligible player's new home.

PITCHERS

Burke Badenhop Bats: R Throws: R Height: 6' 5" Weight: 220 Born: February 8, 1983 Age: 27

YEAR	TEAM	LVL	AGE	W	L	SV	G	GS	IP	H	HR	BB	SO	GB%	BABIP	STUFF	WHIP	ERA	SIERA	DERA	EqH9	EqHR9	EqBB9	EqSO9	VORP	SN/WX
2007	LAK	A+	24	10	6	0	23	23	135^1	130	5	34	78	60%	.283	0	1.21	3.13	4.36	4.76	8.7	1.0	2.7	3.4	10.8	0.54
2007	ERI	AA	24	2	0	0	3	3	18^2	8	1	3	12	64%	.137	13	0.59	1.45	3.48	2.21	4.4	1.0	1.5	4.4	6.7	0.51
2008	FLO	MLB	25	2	3	0	13	8	47^1	55	7	21	35	63%	.316	-10	1.61	6.08	4.37	6.18	10.5	1.3	3.4	5.7	-3.6	-0.36
2009	FLO	MLB	26	7	4	0	35	2	72	71	5	24	57	63%	.306	7	1.32	3.75	3.86	3.88	8.8	0.6	2.5	6.1	12.7	1.20
2010	FLO	MLB	27	5	5	0	32	15	81	81	9	31	48	61%	.285	-3	1.37	4.32	4.63	4.61	9.0	1.0	3.1	4.8	8.0	1.14

Breakout: 14% Improve: 44% Collapse: 17% Attrition: 24% MLB: 52% Comparables: Chad Qualls, Chris Reitsma, Matt Belisle, Zach Miner

It was a relatively healthy season for the sinker-balling Badenhop, who missed a good chunk of 2008 with shoulder tendinitis. It was also a relatively successful one, as he pitched well in mostly trash-time relief. The conversion to the pen allowed Badenhop to up his strikeout rate past anything he had been able to sustain as a starter in the high minors. That increase, combined with his ground-ball tendencies and solid control, combine to make him the (so far) most accomplished player the Marlins received in the Miguel Cabrera/Dontrelle Willis deal. Not bad for a throw-in.

Kiko Calero

Bats: R   Throws: R   Height: 6' 1"   Weight: 210   Born: January 9, 1975   Age: 35

YEAR	TEAM	LVL	AGE	W	L	SV	G	GS	IP	H	HR	BB	SO	GB%	BABIP	STUFF	WHIP	ERA	SIERA	DERA	EqH9	EqHR9	EqBB9	EqSO9	VORP	SN/WX
2007	OAK	MLB	32	1	5	1	46	0	40²	46	3	21	31	35%	.336	-13	1.65	5.75	4.96	5.45	10.4	0.7	4.3	6.1	0.2	0.18
2008	OAK	MLB	33	0	0	0	5	0	4²	3	0	3	7	15%	.300	5	1.29	3.86	2.97	5.79	5.8	0.0	5.8	11.6	-0.1	0.04
2009	FLO	MLB	34	2	2	0	67	0	60	36	1	30	69	34%	.254	29	1.10	1.95	3.28	2.07	5.7	0.2	3.8	8.9	22.4	1.74
2010	FLO	MLB	35	3	4	0	53	0	51²	48	5	29	45	33%	.297	-2	1.49	4.40	4.65	4.61	8.4	0.9	4.5	7.0	5.1	0.37

Breakout: 18%   Improve: 43%   Collapse: 24%   Attrition: 10%   MLB: 81%   Comparables: Aurelio Lopez, Ricky Bottalico, Doug Henry, Jim Mecir

Credit Calero for coming back after hitting bottom, having spent 2008 getting thrashed in the sticks after shoulder problems dropped him out of Oakland's plans. His 5.4 hits allowed per nine innings was top six in baseball (50 IP and up), and despite fly-ball tendencies, he allowed just one home run. Despite his effectiveness, his manager didn't use him in too many tight situations. Calero is a free agent at this writing; his shoulder, which put him on the DL once in 2009, probably dooms him to a series of make-good contracts from here until the end of his career.

Brendan Donnelly

Bats: R   Throws: R   Height: 6' 3"   Weight: 250   Born: July 4, 1971   Age: 38

YEAR	TEAM	LVL	AGE	W	L	SV	G	GS	IP	H	HR	BB	SO	GB%	BABIP	STUFF	WHIP	ERA	SIERA	DERA	EqH9	EqHR9	EqBB9	EqSO9	VORP	SN/WX
2007	BOS	MLB	35	2	1	0	27	0	20²	19	0	5	15	32%	.288	4	1.16	3.05	4.38	3.21	8.1	0.0	1.7	6.0	5.3	0.63
2008	CLE	MLB	36	1	0	0	15	0	13²	20	2	10	8	43%	.367	-28	2.20	8.56	5.94	7.90	12.5	1.3	5.9	4.6	-3.6	0.39
2009	ROU	AAA	37	2	0	6	24	0	25²	21	0	7	23	51%	.296	6	1.09	1.75	3.41	2.63	8.3	0.4	2.6	6.4	7.7	1.20
2009	FLO	MLB	37	3	0	2	30	0	25¹	22	1	9	25	38%	.309	12	1.22	1.78	3.44	2.92	8.0	0.4	2.9	7.7	7.1	1.15
2010	FLO	MLB	38	2	3	2	39	1	39	41	4	16	25	39%	.308	-9	1.46	4.72	4.89	5.04	9.5	1.0	3.2	5.3	2.0	1.17

Breakout: 18%   Improve: 36%   Collapse: 32%   Attrition: 25%   MLB: 85%   Comparables: Dixie Howell, Roberto Hernandez, Ted Power, Jim Corsi

Trying to come back from Tommy John surgery, Donnelly passed through two organizations before signing with the Marlins in July. Aside from a short DL stay due to a calf strain, his time in teal was almost without blemish. Donnelly turns 39 in July, and there's no telling how much he has left, but he's been surprising people since making the majors at 30.

Kyle Gunderson

Bats: R   Throws: R   Height: 6' 3"   Weight: 215   Born: January 31, 1985   Age: 25

YEAR	TEAM	LVL	AGE	W	L	SV	G	GS	IP	H	HR	BB	SO	GB%	BABIP	STUFF	WHIP	ERA	SIERA	DERA	EqH9	EqHR9	EqBB9	EqSO9	VORP	SN/WX
2007	NAT	Rk	22	0	1	4	14	0	18²	14	1	6	9	54%	.224	-23	1.07	0.48	4.89	1.82	7.3	1.6	3.6	2.1	7.1	0.50
2008	HAG	A	23	4	2	8	34	0	55¹	38	4	9	42	54%	.213	-9	0.85	2.60	3.55	3.75	6.8	1.5	2.2	3.8	10.5	1.29
2008	POT	A+	23	1	0	0	6	0	12¹	10	1	3	10	63%	.265	-2	1.05	1.46	3.32	2.38	8.7	1.6	2.4	4.8	3.9	0.07
2009	JUP	A+	24	1	3	14	38	0	40¹	39	1	11	36	63%	.314	-19	1.24	3.12	3.43	5.03	11.3	1.2	3.4	5.2	1.9	-0.31
2010	FLO	MLB	25	3	4	3	42	0	57	59	8	23	26	56%	.278	-16	1.45	4.83	5.25	5.18	9.6	1.3	3.4	3.8	2.0	1.62

Breakout: 5%   Improve: 21%   Collapse: 44%   Attrition: 10%   MLB: 4%   Comparables: Bradley Stone, Aaron Hartsock, Jeremy Ward, Tad Powers

Logan Kensing was spectacularly mishandled by the Marlins, rushed to the majors from High-A for no particular reason, then bounced up and down when he wasn't recovering from Tommy John surgery. Finally, like gangsters who have wrung every possible penny from a front, they burned the building for the insurance money—that is, they dealt Kensing to the Nationals for Gunderson. A 2007 48th-round pick out of Rice, Gunderson has closed at the lower levels, but there's nothing to particularly recommend him for more than fringe work.

Brad Hand

Bats: L   Throws: L   Height: 6' 2"   Weight: 185   Born: March 20, 1990   Age: 20

YEAR	TEAM	LVL	AGE	W	L	SV	G	GS	IP	H	HR	BB	SO	GB%	BABIP	STUFF	WHIP	ERA	SIERA	DERA	EqH9	EqHR9	EqBB9	EqSO9	VORP	SN/WX
2008	MRL	Rk	18	2	0	0	9	7	32²	25	0	11	34	73%	.294	10	1.10	2.48	2.81	7.69	9.7	1.3	4.4	4.7	-7.0	-0.13
2008	JAM	A-	18	1	2	0	3	3	15	11	0	10	12	69%	.268	13	1.40	3.00	4.20	5.06	8.1	1.4	7.4	4.1	0.6	-0.04
2009	GRB	A	19	7	13	0	26	26	127²	130	12	66	122	48%	.324	-14	1.54	4.86	4.02	7.97	11.2	2.2	6.6	5.1	-31.3	-3.16
2010	FLO	MLB	20	3	9	0	26	24	106¹	127	18	80	71	61%	.324	19	1.95	6.87	5.29	7.02	10.7	1.5	5.8	5.4	-17.9	0.98

Breakout: 24%   Improve: 48%   Collapse: 8%   Attrition: 3%   MLB: 0%   Comparables: Joe Torres, Mark Sims, Nate Cromwell, Al Leiter

Still very young, Minnesotan Hand was selected by the Marlins in the second round of the 2008 draft. The lefty has typical lefty velocity, which is to say that he sits around 89-90, and his calling card is a curve. He's still trying to get a (pardon the pun) Hand-le on his command, control, and mechanics, but then he was only in his first full season. If the Marlins can curtail their propensity for jumping pitchers from the playpen to the big leagues and give Hand time to develop, they might get a usable back-end starter.

Daniel Jennings

Bats: L   Throws: L   Height: 6' 3"   Weight: 190   Born: April 17, 1987   Age: 23

YEAR	TEAM	LVL	AGE	W	L	SV	G	GS	IP	H	HR	BB	SO	GB%	BABIP	STUFF	WHIP	ERA	SIERA	DERA	EqH9	EqHR9	EqBB9	EqSO9	VORP	SN/WX
2008	JAM	A-	21	1	4	0	13	13	58²	79	2	18	62	57%	.418	1	1.65	3.53	3.28	6.58	14.0	1.5	3.9	5.2	-6.4	-0.92
2009	GRB	A	22	1	2	0	34	0	49¹	42	1	21	54	63%	.315	-1	1.28	2.74	3.15	5.42	9.6	1.2	5.5	6.1	0.4	-0.73
2009	JUP	A+	22	0	0	6	8	0	11²	5	0	4	13	52%	.200	10	0.77	0.00	2.64	0.90	6.3	0.9	4.5	7.2	5.1	0.63
2010	FLO	MLB	23	2	4	2	51	1	58	68	8	40	39	60%	.327	-19	1.86	6.13	5.14	6.41	10.7	1.3	5.4	5.5	-5.8	0.50

Breakout: 20%   Improve: 50%   Collapse: 25%   Attrition: 9%   MLB: 5%   Comparables: Pat Clements, Bob Baxter, Jeff Edwards, Anthony Shelby

A 2008 ninth-rounder, Jennings rocketed up three levels last year, propelled by a sinker/slider combo that resulted in an excellent strikeout rate and lots of grounders, as just one home run allowed in 62 ⅔ IP should suggest. He doesn't blow anyone away and his control still needs a bit of refinement, so don't envision a future closer, but nonetheless, he could be a solid bullpen contributor in the very near future.

Josh Johnson

Bats: L   Throws: R   Height: 6' 7"   Weight: 230   Born: January 31, 1984   Age: 26

YEAR	TEAM	LVL	AGE	W	L	SV	G	GS	IP	H	HR	BB	SO	GB%	BABIP	STUFF	WHIP	ERA	SIERA	DERA	EqH9	EqHR9	EqBB9	EqSO9	VORP	SN/WX
2007	FLO	MLB	23	0	3	0	4	4	15²	26	1	12	14	70%	.455	5	2.43	7.47	4.64	8.90	13.8	0.6	6.3	6.9	-5.9	-0.19
2008	FLO	MLB	24	7	1	0	14	14	87¹	91	7	27	77	57%	.332	19	1.35	3.61	3.62	3.63	10.0	0.8	2.5	7.0	17.2	2.50
2009	FLO	MLB	25	15	5	0	33	33	209	184	14	58	191	55%	.290	33	1.16	3.23	3.42	3.27	7.9	0.6	2.1	7.1	51.3	6.57
2010	FLO	MLB	26	11	10	0	26	26	179²	176	19	59	142	62%	.302	15	1.31	3.96	3.87	4.29	9.1	0.9	2.6	6.5	24.1	3.56

Breakout: 7%   Improve: 44%   Collapse: 6%   Attrition: 4%   MLB: 94%   Comparables: Ed Halicki, Pete Vuckovich, Gaylord Perry, Dave Goltz

Johnson finally threw off the still-smoldering wreckage of Joe Girardi's Marlins stint. He posted the best strikeout and walk rates of his career, and even made his first All-Star team. At this writing, it is unclear if the Marlins will be able to sign him to a long-term deal, in which case the arbitration-eligible pitcher will probably be in the wind by the time you read this. Reasons for an acquiring team to exercise caution: by virtue of his two injury-afflicted years, Johnson experienced a big jump in his workload, and fatigue might be an issue, especially as his ERA increased every month of the season, rising from 2.60 in April to 4.11 in September. By that month, the Marlins were clearly trying to limit his innings. Let's hope both for Johnson's sake and for that of the team that spends its prospects in support of the Marlins' mingy habits that they acted soon enough to avert another injury.

Chris Leroux

Bats: L   Throws: R   Height: 6' 6"   Weight: 210   Born: April 14, 1984   Age: 26

YEAR	TEAM	LVL	AGE	W	L	SV	G	GS	IP	H	HR	BB	SO	GB%	BABIP	STUFF	WHIP	ERA	SIERA	DERA	EqH9	EqHR9	EqBB9	EqSO9	VORP	SN/WX
2007	GRB	A	23	2	3	0	46	0	71²	72	6	29	76	53%	.330	-13	1.41	4.14	3.42	5.52	10.4	1.5	4.3	6.5	-0.1	-1.14
2008	JUP	A+	24	6	7	1	57	0	74	60	6	26	78	44%	.286	-29	1.16	3.65	3.18	6.58	10.3	2.3	4.0	6.4	-7.9	-1.55
2009	JAX	AA	25	5	3	2	46	0	60	59	0	17	55	57%	.333	-4	1.27	2.70	3.46	4.34	11.0	0.5	2.8	6.1	7.1	0.44
2009	FLO	MLB	25	0	0	0	5	0	6²	11	0	4	2	60%	.379	-47	2.25	10.80	6.04	10.29	14.1	0.0	3.9	2.6	-3.7	0.00
2010	FLO	MLB	26	3	5	0	54	0	62²	72	9	31	45	48%	.324	-16	1.64	5.59	4.78	5.97	10.5	1.3	4.0	5.8	-3.3	0.28

Breakout: 23%   Improve: 49%   Collapse: 21%   Attrition: 18%   MLB: 18%   Comparables: Chris Young, Talley Haines, Dave Johnson, Tristan Crawford

Leroux jumped from Double-A to the majors, but his chance to impress was hindered by right shoulder inflammation. This is nothing new—Leroux's career was significantly delayed by Tommy John surgery just prior to his being drafted in 2005. He retains good stuff, however, working with a low- to mid-90s fastball and a slider. There was absolutely nothing wrong with his Double-A numbers, and the abuse he took in the bigs probably resulted from the confluence of inexperience and pain. He remains on the 40-man roster and should get another chance to contribute this year.

Matt Lindstrom

Bats: R   Throws: R   Height: 6' 4"   Weight: 210   Born: February 11, 1980   Age: 30

YEAR	TEAM	LVL	AGE	W	L	SV	G	GS	IP	H	HR	BB	SO	GB%	BABIP	STUFF	WHIP	ERA	SIERA	DERA	EqH9	EqHR9	EqBB9	EqSO9	VORP	SN/WX
2007	FLO	MLB	27	3	4	0	71	0	67	66	2	21	62	52%	.327	18	1.30	3.09	3.56	3.33	8.0	0.3	2.5	7.3	16.4	1.61
2008	FLO	MLB	28	3	3	5	66	0	57¹	57	1	26	43	52%	.322	1	1.45	3.14	4.44	3.21	9.4	0.2	3.8	5.9	13.9	2.16
2009	FLO	MLB	29	2	1	15	54	0	47¹	54	5	24	39	48%	.329	-12	1.65	5.89	4.49	6.28	9.9	0.9	3.8	6.2	-4.2	1.79
2010	HOU	MLB	30	3	3	5	59	0	58¹	59	6	23	45	46%	.307	-3	1.42	4.33	4.33	4.55	9.0	0.9	3.4	6.3	6.1	1.27

Breakout: 12% Improve: 42% Collapse: 16% Attrition: 14%   MLB: 83%   Comparables: Jerry Johnson, Aaron Heilman, Travis Harper, John Habyan

Lindstrom's season was a turkey along the lines of *Battlefield Earth*. His ERA was a turgid 6.52 when he went on the DL with a sprained elbow in late June, missing five weeks. Two horrifically bad outings in which he allowed a total of 11 runs in one inning helped disfigure his numbers, but he was only moderately effective before the injury and didn't pitch at all well after coming back. He may never have been healthy, as he rushed into action for the World Baseball Classic and then was slowed by a strained rotator cuff, though the Marlins chose not to disable him at that time. The Marlins have envisioned Lindstrom as a closer for years, and with his great stuff, he ought to get a chance to try again when he's physically sound. Arbitration eligible, he was dispatched to the Astros, where there happens to be an opening in the closer department.

Cristhian Martinez

Bats: R   Throws: R   Height: 6' 1"   Weight: 160   Born: March 6, 1982   Age: 28

YEAR	TEAM	LVL	AGE	W	L	SV	G	GS	IP	H	HR	BB	SO	GB%	BABIP	STUFF	WHIP	ERA	SIERA	DERA	EqH9	EqHR9	EqBB9	EqSO9	VORP	SN/WX
2007	GRB	A	25	9	5	0	18	18	97	97	16	18	74	50%	.279	-22	1.19	4.08	3.74	5.87	9.9	2.2	2.3	4.4	-3.8	-0.75
2008	GRB	A	26	4	1	0	8	8	44¹	44	2	9	14	54%	.264	-21	1.20	4.67	5.22	5.87	8.7	1.2	2.7	1.0	-1.8	-0.69
2008	JUP	A+	26	2	7	0	20	19	109¹	117	7	16	78	52%	.308	-29	1.22	3.79	3.84	6.84	11.8	1.9	2.0	3.9	-15.1	-0.96
2009	JAX	AA	27	9	3	0	17	16	104	96	7	22	62	57%	.276	-18	1.13	2.94	4.26	5.01	10.6	1.7	2.2	3.9	5.0	0.81
2009	FLO	MLB	27	1	1	0	15	0	26¹	27	2	8	18	63%	.298	-5	1.33	5.13	4.11	5.30	8.9	0.7	2.4	5.1	0.6	-0.04
2010	FLO	MLB	28	5	8	0	24	17	103²	119	16	37	47	50%	.297	-17	1.50	5.16	5.29	5.54	10.4	1.4	2.9	3.7	-0.4	1.27

Breakout: 13% Improve: 46% Collapse: 21% Attrition: 20%   MLB: 35%   Comparables: Wilton Chavez, Larry Shikles, Jared Gothreaux, Tom Dixon

Rule 5'd away from the Tigers in 2006, the year after he underwent Tommy John surgery, Martinez excelled in his first season at Double-A and got the call to the Marlins when the entire bullpen was hit by fatigue and injury at the same time. He augments a so-so fastball with a slider, change, and sinker. His strikeout numbers have always been middling, but he induces grounders and (in the minors, at least) rarely issues a walk, with an average of 1.8 free passes per nine innings. Primarily a starter, Martinez is a nice story but seems unlikely to succeed in a role requiring extended exposure, given the ease with which batters make contact.

Dan Meyer

Bats: R   Throws: L   Height: 6' 3"   Weight: 220   Born: July 3, 1981   Age: 28

YEAR	TEAM	LVL	AGE	W	L	SV	G	GS	IP	H	HR	BB	SO	GB%	BABIP	STUFF	WHIP	ERA	SIERA	DERA	EqH9	EqHR9	EqBB9	EqSO9	VORP	SN/WX
2007	SAC	AAA	25	8	2	0	21	21	115¹	103	12	51	105	41%	.290	-7	1.34	3.28	3.95	3.97	9.4	1.8	4.3	6.3	18.2	2.16
2007	OAK	MLB	25	0	2	0	6	3	16¹	20	2	9	11	26%	.316	-25	1.78	8.82	5.74	10.06	10.6	1.1	4.2	5.3	-8.6	-0.50
2008	SAC	AAA	26	10	5	0	22	20	122²	113	10	52	109	43%	.293	-4	1.35	4.48	4.00	5.32	9.1	1.3	3.8	5.7	2.4	0.74
2008	OAK	MLB	26	0	4	0	11	4	27²	35	6	14	20	31%	.319	-25	1.77	7.48	5.25	8.95	11.7	2.3	3.9	5.9	-10.6	-0.64
2009	FLO	MLB	27	3	2	2	71	0	58¹	47	7	21	56	35%	.255	8	1.17	3.09	3.62	3.58	7.0	0.9	2.7	7.2	12.6	1.71
2010	FLO	MLB	28	4	5	2	48	10	84²	87	11	43	67	40%	.307	-5	1.53	4.90	4.62	5.15	9.4	1.2	3.9	6.5	3.3	1.31

Breakout: 12% Improve: 44% Collapse: 16% Attrition: 21%   MLB: 57%   Comparables: Russ Swan, Micah Bowie, Justin Hampson, Scott Sauerbeck

Five years on, it's clear the Tim Hudson trade won't go down as one of Billy Beane's best, but at least Meyer, a key part of that deal, finally broke through—just not for the A's and not as a starter, but rather as one of the Marlins' set-up relievers. In this he was generally effective, earning enough trust to be momentarily anointed the closer during an injury crunch, though he faded down the stretch. Batters had a hard time making solid contact with Meyer's slider, resulting in a low line-drive rate, and thus a low BABIP that just might sustain this year. A nice salvage job on a waiver claim.

Andrew Miller

Bats: L   Throws: L   Height: 6' 6"   Weight: 210   Born: May 21, 1985   Age: 25

YEAR	TEAM	LVL	AGE	W	L	SV	G	GS	IP	H	HR	BB	SO	GB%	BABIP	STUFF	WHIP	ERA	SIERA	DERA	EqH9	EqHR9	EqBB9	EqSO9	VORP	SN/WX
2007	DET	MLB	22	5	5	0	13	13	64	73	8	39	56	58%	.327	13	1.75	5.62	4.51	5.55	9.9	1.0	4.8	7.0	-0.4	0.85
2008	FLO	MLB	23	6	10	0	29	20	107¹	120	7	56	89	52%	.336	2	1.64	5.87	4.45	6.22	10.2	0.6	4.1	6.3	-8.5	0.36
2009	FLO	MLB	24	3	5	0	20	14	80	85	7	43	59	57%	.306	-1	1.60	4.84	4.67	5.51	9.1	0.7	4.0	5.5	-0.1	0.18
2010	FLO	MLB	25	6	8	0	30	23	116	119	12	62	88	55%	.310	1	1.57	4.88	4.60	5.11	9.3	0.9	4.2	6.2	5.0	1.12

Breakout: 12%   Improve: 47%   Collapse: 10%   Attrition: 10%   MLB: 83%   Comparables: Andy Hassler, Chris Haney, Steve Trout, Joe Lazor

More than ever, waiting for Miller to capitalize on the talents that made him the sixth overall pick in the 2006 draft seems like an exercise in futility. He often struggled, and despite a couple of minor-league stints (one on rehab after an oblique strain), Miller again failed to establish himself. After the season, he went to the AFL to work on improving his mechanics, which is a bit like going to Antarctica to work on raising your body temperature. Heading into his age-25 season, he's still young enough to sort himself out, and he deserves some understanding in light of the way he was rushed through the minors. But the '06 draft is starting to look pretty distant, and if Miller doesn't come through soon, expectations need to be adjusted from "untapped talent" to "another journeyman looking to catch lightning in a bottle." That day isn't here yet, but it's bearing down on Miller like one of his runaway fastballs.

Ricky Nolasco

Bats: R   Throws: R   Height: 6' 2"   Weight: 220   Born: December 13, 1982   Age: 27

YEAR	TEAM	LVL	AGE	W	L	SV	G	GS	IP	H	HR	BB	SO	GB%	BABIP	STUFF	WHIP	ERA	SIERA	DERA	EqH9	EqHR9	EqBB9	EqSO9	VORP	SN/WX
2007	FLO	MLB	24	1	2	0	5	4	21¹	26	3	9	11	36%	.307	-13	1.64	5.48	5.62	6.04	9.3	1.2	3.2	4.0	-1.4	0.06
2008	FLO	MLB	25	15	8	0	34	32	212¹	192	28	42	186	42%	.271	20	1.10	3.52	3.37	3.64	8.2	1.2	1.6	6.7	43.6	5.61
2009	NWO	AAA	26	1	1	0	2	2	15	12	0	3	12	43%	.279	14	1.00	2.40	3.51	3.14	7.5	0.6	1.9	5.0	3.8	0.39
2009	FLO	MLB	26	13	9	0	31	31	185	188	23	44	195	45%	.317	22	1.25	5.06	2.97	5.15	9.0	1.0	1.8	7.9	7.3	2.32
2010	FLO	MLB	27	11	10	0	31	31	182	177	22	50	149	45%	.298	18	1.25	3.82	3.74	4.14	8.9	1.1	2.2	6.8	27.5	2.29

Breakout: 10%   Improve: 47%   Collapse: 10%   Attrition: 7%   MLB: 96%   Comparables: Adam Eaton, David Cone, Burt Hooton, Eric Rasmussen

After his breakthrough 2008 campaign, Nolasco seemed ready to take his place at the forefront of the Marlins' rotation. Instead, he was pounded in eight of his first nine starts. When the Rays ripped him for eight runs in two innings on May 22nd, the erstwhile ace found himself an unhappy resident of the Big Easy. Two refresher starts later, Nolasco was back. His remaining 22 turns were redolent of '08, with an ERA of 3.82 and 15 quality starts. Nolasco's recovery climaxed in his final start of the season, as he whiffed 16 Braves, including nine in a row—the third modern-era pitcher to strike out nine straight. (Tom Seaver got 10 consecutive Padres on a notably low-visibility day in 1970.) As it's not certain what caused Nolasco to go so badly off the tracks, we can't be sure that it won't happen again, but more ace-quality performances seem just as likely, if not more so. One of the club's arbitration-eligible players still with the Marlins at press time, Nolasco could be pitching anywhere on the planet by the time you read this, depending on what the letters in Jeff Loria's alphabet soup spell out at contract time.

Leo Nunez

Bats: R   Throws: R   Height: 6' 1"   Weight: 175   Born: August 14, 1983   Age: 26

YEAR	TEAM	LVL	AGE	W	L	SV	G	GS	IP	H	HR	BB	SO	GB%	BABIP	STUFF	WHIP	ERA	SIERA	DERA	EqH9	EqHR9	EqBB9	EqSO9	VORP	SN/WX
2007	KCA	MLB	23	2	4	0	13	6	43²	44	8	10	37	35%	.283	13	1.24	3.92	3.70	3.89	8.4	1.4	1.8	7.0	7.9	0.83
2008	KCA	MLB	24	4	1	0	45	0	48¹	45	2	15	26	41%	.272	-2	1.24	2.98	5.05	3.24	7.8	0.4	2.4	4.4	12.2	0.38
2009	FLO	MLB	25	4	6	26	75	0	68²	59	13	27	60	43%	.243	-5	1.25	4.06	3.97	4.20	7.5	1.6	3.0	6.6	10.1	1.45
2010	FLO	MLB	26	4	4	8	52	1	61¹	57	7	22	43	42%	.277	-1	1.29	3.95	4.49	4.23	8.4	1.0	2.9	5.8	8.7	0.98

Breakout: 8%   Improve: 30%   Collapse: 22%   Attrition: 23%   MLB: 92%   Comparables: Bob Apodaca, Steve Ridzik, Bill Stafford, Hiroyuki Kobayashi

Some orthodox sabermetricians argue that "anyone can close," while traditional baseball men say that a pitcher requires "a closer's mentality" to save games. The former underrate the human element, and the latter underestimate the number of pitchers with the fortitude to pitch under pressure. The correct formulation, as Nunez is the latest to prove, is "Not every pitcher can close, but most can." Nunez became the Fishy closer in June, when Lindstrom was shut down with elbow problems. Though he had never earned a save in five years in the majors, Nunez didn't go to pieces in the role. He was hardly Mariano Rivera, but he was sufficient, saving 24 games in 28 chances, an average rate. Nevertheless, this is an experiment the Marlins might not get away with again, as Nunez's home-run rate (1.7 per nine innings) has the potential to mean souvenirs for the bleacher creatures at the worst possible times.

Hayden Penn

Bats: R   Throws: R   Height: 6′ 3″   Weight: 200   Born: October 13, 1984   Age: 25

YEAR	TEAM	LVL	AGE	W	L	SV	G	GS	IP	H	HR	BB	SO	GB%	BABIP	STUFF	WHIP	ERA	SIERA	DERA	EqH9	EqHR9	EqBB9	EqSO9	VORP	SN/WX
2007	NOR	AAA	22	2	1	0	4	4	21	26	2	5	20	55%	.381	16	1.48	5.14	3.34	6.16	13.3	1.9	2.4	6.6	-1.4	0.01
2008	NOR	AAA	23	6	7	0	21	21	99^2	110	14	35	65	57%	.299	-30	1.45	4.79	4.50	5.91	10.5	2.1	3.4	3.9	-4.3	-0.06
2009	NWO	AAA	24	2	4	0	14	13	70	71	9	26	62	42%	.300	-20	1.39	4.11	3.92	5.24	10.3	2.6	3.5	5.9	1.9	0.50
2009	FLO	MLB	24	1	0	0	16	1	22	30	3	20	27	67%	.397	-1	2.27	7.77	4.18	10.46	11.4	1.1	6.5	8.7	-13.0	-0.36
2010	FLO	MLB	25	3	6	0	30	17	82^1	95	14	39	59	51%	.318	-12	1.62	5.51	4.67	5.86	10.5	1.5	3.8	5.9	-3.3	0.85

Breakout: 17%   Improve: 44%   Collapse: 18%   Attrition: 17%   MLB: 100%   Comparables: Tony Peguero, Doug Kline, Christopher Willsher, Tim McDowell

In the course of a few years, Penn has gone from coveted Orioles phenom to fringe player with the Fish, having been acquired for Robert Andino in April in an exchange of players out of options. Tried as a reliever, Penn was flogged into a frothy meringue, prompting the Marlins to successfully pass him through waivers to New Orleans in June. He was vaguely-sorta-kinda successful in the Crescent City—after further whippings in July, he closed out the season with a 2.32 ERA in his final seven starts, spanning 42 ⅔ IP. This was enough to convince the Marlins that some of that prospect-y sheen still legitimately clung to Penn, and they added him back onto the 40-man after the season. Refraining from issuing ball four remains the major obstacle in his quest to stick.

Renyel Pinto

Bats: L   Throws: L   Height: 6′ 4″   Weight: 215   Born: July 8, 1982   Age: 27

YEAR	TEAM	LVL	AGE	W	L	SV	G	GS	IP	H	HR	BB	SO	GB%	BABIP	STUFF	WHIP	ERA	SIERA	DERA	EqH9	EqHR9	EqBB9	EqSO9	VORP	SN/WX
2007	FLO	MLB	24	2	4	1	57	0	58^2	45	7	32	56	45%	.264	10	1.31	3.68	4.02	3.49	6.5	1.1	4.4	7.9	12.6	1.03
2008	FLO	MLB	25	2	5	0	67	0	64^2	52	9	39	56	50%	.244	-4	1.41	4.45	4.48	4.41	7.4	1.3	4.8	6.6	7.8	1.64
2009	FLO	MLB	26	4	1	0	73	0	61^1	53	4	45	58	48%	.295	10	1.60	3.23	4.58	3.63	8.0	0.6	5.6	7.3	12.6	0.65
2010	FLO	MLB	27	4	5	0	69	0	68	62	8	42	59	46%	.287	-3	1.52	4.54	4.56	4.68	8.1	1.0	4.8	7.0	6.2	0.88

Breakout: 12%   Improve: 42%   Collapse: 32%   Attrition: 8%   MLB: 91%   Comparables: Dave LaRoche, Mitch Williams, Ken Patterson, Pete Filson

Pinto has upped his walk rate in consecutive seasons, which is hard to do when you started at 4.9 per nine innings. Last year he reached 6.6, which he somehow survived—even elbow inflammation didn't set him back much more than the minimum. Pinto isn't properly utilized as a lefty spot reliever, as the wildness means you can't be sure who he's going to pitch to—left-handed hitters had a .413 on-base percentage against him last year. He has also had a reverse split the last two years, with lefties hitting a robust .268/.393/.454 compared with .207/.325/.292. As such, Pinto is best used as a long man who has some breathing room to work around his own wildness, and that's largely how Fredi Gonzalez utilized him, giving him an inning or more to play with about 60 percent of the time. However he's used, Pinto is a time bomb: all it will take to double his ERA is that walk rate and a run of bad luck on balls in play.

Brian Sanches

Bats: R   Throws: R   Height: 6′ 0″   Weight: 195   Born: August 8, 1978   Age: 31

YEAR	TEAM	LVL	AGE	W	L	SV	G	GS	IP	H	HR	BB	SO	GB%	BABIP	STUFF	WHIP	ERA	SIERA	DERA	EqH9	EqHR9	EqBB9	EqSO9	VORP	SN/WX
2007	OTT	AAA	28	2	3	16	36	1	47^1	57	5	8	52	45%	.377	-3	1.37	4.75	2.70	6.07	11.2	1.6	1.8	7.4	-2.9	0.63
2007	PHI	MLB	28	1	1	0	12	0	14^2	13	6	12	9	54%	.175	-19	1.70	5.52	5.75	6.14	7.4	3.1	6.8	4.9	-1.0	0.03
2008	COH	AAA	29	2	1	13	32	0	33^2	24	2	9	45	31%	.289	19	0.98	2.41	1.93	2.78	7.2	0.8	2.5	8.9	9.8	1.33
2008	WAS	MLB	29	2	0	0	12	0	11	16	2	5	14	51%	.389	-10	1.91	7.36	4.19	7.36	13.1	1.6	3.3	7.4	-2.3	-0.76
2009	NWO	AAA	30	1	1	4	16	0	17^2	13	1	4	22	32%	.279	13	0.96	2.04	2.12	3.71	7.4	1.1	2.1	8.5	3.4	-0.27
2009	FLO	MLB	30	4	2	0	47	0	56^1	50	5	26	51	34%	.281	6	1.35	2.56	4.24	2.92	7.9	0.8	3.5	6.8	16.3	0.74
2010	FLO	MLB	31	3	4	9	59	0	62^2	63	8	27	56	40%	.312	-2	1.43	4.65	4.05	4.98	9.2	1.1	3.5	7.2	3.6	0.74

Breakout: 16%   Improve: 49%   Collapse: 30%   Attrition: 16%   MLB: 69%   Comparables: Scott Proctor, Joel Peralta, Scott Atchison, Rich DeLucia

Soft-tossing Brian Sanches has been kicking around the minors since 1999. His splitter gave him a swing-and-miss pitch despite his lack of fastball, but wildness had always thwarted him in the majors. His walk rate was much improved last year, though you can't see it in the numbers, because manager Gonzalez ordered him to pass eight hitters, one of the highest single-pitcher totals in the majors. Sanches was also helped by subsequent relievers, who succeeded in stranding the runners he left on base (or was ordered to put aboard). Officially, Sanches allowed only 2.88 runs per nine, but his Fair Run Average was 3.70. Sanches had some truly electric outings, and it is to be hoped that 2009 represented a Crash Davis type finally arriving rather than a flash in the pan. Gonzalez could help secure the former by just letting him pitch.

Anibal Sanchez

Bats: R Throws: R Height: 6' 0" Weight: 180 Born: February 27, 1984 Age: 26

YEAR	TEAM	LVL	AGE	W	L	SV	G	GS	IP	H	HR	BB	SO	GB%	BABIP	STUFF	WHIP	ERA	SIERA	DERA	EqH9	EqHR9	EqBB9	EqSO9	VORP	SN/WX
2007	FLO	MLB	23	2	1	0	6	6	30	43	3	19	14	46%	.354	-12	2.07	4.80	6.04	4.60	11.2	0.9	4.9	3.4	3.1	0.37
2008	FLO	MLB	24	2	5	0	10	10	51^2	54	7	27	50	44%	.311	5	1.57	5.57	4.13	5.76	9.5	1.2	4.0	7.2	-1.5	0.19
2009	FLO	MLB	25	4	8	0	16	16	86	84	10	46	71	48%	.290	8	1.51	3.87	4.49	3.95	8.6	0.9	4.1	6.2	15.0	2.13
2010	FLO	MLB	26	5	7	0	17	17	104	106	12	53	76	47%	.303	3	1.53	4.85	4.73	5.13	9.3	1.0	4.1	6.0	4.3	1.58

Breakout: 12% Improve: 43% Collapse: 18% Attrition: 13% MLB: 80% Comparables: Joe Horlen, Satoru Kanemura, Hiroki Kuroda, Bob Apodaca

Shoulder problems cost this former labrum case a good chunk of the season, as what the Marlins initially treated as a transient sprain developed into a long-term problem that required extensive rest and rehab before he could return. When he finally did reemerge, having been absent from all but one game from early May to late August, his control was unsurprisingly wobbly, but on the whole, he was unhittable, holding batters to a .212 average with a resultant 2.68 ERA in 50 ⅓ innings. Coming up on the fourth anniversary of Sanchez's September 2006 no-hitter, we're still waiting for him to put in a full season in the majors and pitch as well as he has in shorter stints. Holding your breath in anticipation of that joyous event is not recommended by Baseball Prospectus.

Ryan Tucker

Bats: R Throws: R Height: 6' 2" Weight: 190 Born: December 6, 1986 Age: 23

YEAR	TEAM	LVL	AGE	W	L	SV	G	GS	IP	H	HR	BB	SO	GB%	BABIP	STUFF	WHIP	ERA	SIERA	DERA	EqH9	EqHR9	EqBB9	EqSO9	VORP	SN/WX
2007	JUP	A+	20	5	8	0	24	24	138^1	142	6	46	104	48%	.313	8	1.36	3.71	4.21	5.54	10.5	1.4	3.6	4.4	-0.6	-0.02
2008	CAR	AA	21	5	3	0	25	12	91	64	2	37	74	46%	.241	35	1.11	1.58	4.12	2.38	7.1	0.6	3.5	5.2	30.9	2.82
2008	FLO	MLB	21	2	3	0	13	6	37	46	8	23	28	46%	.325	-7	1.86	8.27	5.02	7.98	11.3	2.0	4.9	5.9	-10.1	-0.44
2009	NWO	AAA	22	1	2	0	4	4	15^2	18	1	14	7	37%	.304	-24	2.04	8.04	6.97	9.10	10.6	1.2	7.6	2.3	-6.1	-0.33
2010	FLO	MLB	23	4	6	0	23	13	772	81	10	40	48	39%	.295	-5	1.56	5.17	5.32	5.52	9.6	1.2	4.2	5.0	-0.1	1.43

Breakout: 13% Improve: 42% Collapse: 19% Attrition: 13% MLB: 40% Comparables: Ken Chenard, Ronnie Richardson, Julio Rangel, Kane Davis

It was a lost year for Tucker, a 2005 supplemental first-rounder, who missed most of the season after knee surgery. The great insight of Ray Kroc at the founding of the McDonald's chain was that variety equals inefficiency. Alas, the opposite is true in baseball, and Tucker's mid-90s fastball remains his only plus pitch. As such, though he's been a starter thus far, a date with the bullpen seems an inevitability. Even then, he's going to have to find a consistent off-speed pitch if he's going to be a dependable asset.

Rick VandenHurk

Bats: R Throws: R Height: 6' 5" Weight: 195 Born: May 22, 1985 Age: 25

YEAR	TEAM	LVL	AGE	W	L	SV	G	GS	IP	H	HR	BB	SO	GB%	BABIP	STUFF	WHIP	ERA	SIERA	DERA	EqH9	EqHR9	EqBB9	EqSO9	VORP	SN/WX
2007	CAR	AA	22	2	2	0	9	9	53^2	42	5	21	61	38%	.280	22	1.17	3.52	3.03	4.68	8.8	1.4	3.8	7.2	4.6	0.16
2007	ABQ	AAA	22	2	0	0	2	2	12	6	3	4	14	43%	.130	12	0.83	2.25	2.44	2.31	3.9	1.5	3.1	8.5	4.1	0.29
2007	FLO	MLB	22	4	6	0	18	17	81^2	94	15	48	82	35%	.342	3	1.74	6.83	4.31	6.31	9.7	1.6	4.7	8.0	-7.4	0.20
2008	CAR	AA	23	3	3	0	10	10	55^1	49	8	19	55	43%	.279	1	1.23	4.23	3.39	6.11	9.3	2.1	3.1	6.7	-3.5	-0.41
2008	ABQ	AAA	23	2	1	0	4	4	17^2	13	3	11	21	48%	.238	18	1.36	4.08	3.54	4.91	5.9	1.0	4.9	8.3	1.2	0.04
2008	FLO	MLB	23	1	1	0	4	4	14	20	1	10	20	40%	.463	14	2.14	7.71	3.53	7.53	13.2	0.6	5.7	10.7	-3.2	0.14
2009	NWO	AAA	24	5	2	0	11	11	59^2	43	3	16	51	35%	.237	12	0.99	2.87	3.72	3.66	7.0	1.1	2.4	5.5	12.1	1.20
2009	FLO	MLB	24	3	2	0	11	11	58^2	57	11	21	49	30%	.269	5	1.33	4.30	4.30	4.30	8.4	1.5	2.7	6.2	8.0	1.23
2010	FLO	MLB	25	6	7	0	24	22	1102	106	14	59	95	34%	.297	8	1.49	4.75	4.58	4.97	8.6	1.1	4.2	6.9	6.5	1.35

Breakout: 11% Improve: 49% Collapse: 7% Attrition: 18% MLB: 100% Comparables: Turk Wendell, Matt Wise, Alfredo Aceves, Justin Orenduff

Normally, one can't talk about Henricus without mentioning that he's one of a handful of Netherlands-born players to reach the majors. It's always Bert Blyleven this, Win Remmerswaal that, and William the Silent, Prince of Orange, during rain delays. VandenHurk's season was nearly a case of, as the Dutch say, *uitstel is afstel*—postponement equals cancellation. He disappeared from Marlins camp to pitch in the World Baseball Classic, then developed a sore elbow when he returned. He didn't make it back to the majors until July and was inconsistent after that. Mixing in more off-speed pitches than he had in the past, VandenHurk got strikeouts and lowered his walk rate to something manageable, but continued to have a real problem with the home run—his extreme fly-ball tendencies are going to have to be corrected if he's going to achieve any sort of consistency. *Hoop doet leven,* Henricus.

Chris Volstad

Bats: R   Throws: R   Height: 6' 8"   Weight: 225   Born: September 23, 1986   Age: 23

YEAR	TEAM	LVL	AGE	W	L	SV	G	GS	IP	H	HR	BB	SO	GB%	BABIP	STUFF	WHIP	ERA	SIERA	DERA	EqH9	EqHR9	EqBB9	EqSO9	VORP	SN/WX
2007	JUP	A+	20	8	9	0	21	20	126	152	8	37	93	61%	.340	-7	1.50	4.50	4.05	7.09	12.1	1.8	3.2	4.2	-21.1	-1.81
2007	CAR	AA	20	4	2	0	7	7	42²	41	4	10	25	62%	.270	23	1.20	3.16	4.26	4.87	9.7	1.5	2.4	3.3	2.9	0.53
2008	CAR	AA	21	4	4	0	15	15	91	86	0	30	56	65%	.292	24	1.27	3.36	4.26	4.43	9.3	0.5	3.0	3.8	10.4	0.65
2008	FLO	MLB	21	6	4	0	15	14	84¹	76	3	36	52	60%	.271	37	1.33	2.88	4.66	3.19	8.1	0.3	3.3	4.7	21.7	3.11
2009	FLO	MLB	22	9	13	0	29	29	159	169	29	59	107	59%	.289	1	1.43	5.21	4.41	5.39	9.5	1.6	2.9	5.2	1.9	1.56
2010	FLO	MLB	23	8	11	0	31	29	159¹	172	21	62	88	59%	.297	-3	1.47	4.75	4.85	5.12	9.9	1.2	3.1	4.5	6.7	2.02

Breakout: 13%   Improve: 50%   Collapse: 11%   Attrition: 11%   MLB: 100%   Comparables: Jamey Wright, Nate Minchey, Mark Gubicza, Josh Johnson

Volstad seemed to continue his fine rookie season in April, but there were warning signs of the breakdown of command that would destroy his season. The sinkerballer's strikeouts were up, but he was walking 3.6 batters per nine and his home-run rate was high for a pitcher whose forte is supposed to be getting batters to pound the ball into the ground. He muddled along, mixing strong starts with poor ones, and even pitching a shutout against the Giants on July 8th. At the end of the month, his ERA stood at 4.35, disappointing given his 2008 results, but livable, especially coming from a 22-year-old whose fastball only averages 91. At that point, Volstad went into freefall, losing his release point; his ERA in his final seven starts was 9.45, with seven home runs allowed in 26 ⅔ IP. A one-start demotion at the end of August achieved nothing. Volstad clearly has ability, but a ground-ball pitcher without his sinker is like a stripper without nipples. Bringing Volstad's sinker back to earth where it belongs will be job one for new pitching coach Randy St. Claire.

Sean West

Bats: L   Throws: L   Height: 6' 8"   Weight: 200   Born: June 15, 1986   Age: 24

YEAR	TEAM	LVL	AGE	W	L	SV	G	GS	IP	H	HR	BB	SO	GB%	BABIP	STUFF	WHIP	ERA	SIERA	DERA	EqH9	EqHR9	EqBB9	EqSO9	VORP	SN/WX
2008	JUP	A+	22	6	5	0	21	20	100²	79	3	60	92	53%	.287	4	1.38	2.41	4.20	4.58	9.7	1.2	6.3	5.6	9.0	0.68
2009	JAX	AA	23	7	3	0	12	11	64	68	12	28	65	43%	.311	-35	1.50	4.78	3.73	7.22	13.2	4.0	4.2	6.8	-11.1	-0.58
2009	FLO	MLB	23	8	6	0	20	20	103¹	115	11	44	70	43%	.307	2	1.54	4.79	4.82	5.14	9.6	0.9	3.2	5.1	4.2	1.25
2010	FLO	MLB	24	5	10	0	33	29	134²	152	20	82	98	45%	.320	-12	1.74	5.87	5.06	6.11	10.2	1.3	4.8	5.9	-9.1	1.67

Breakout: 10%   Improve: 45%   Collapse: 9%   Attrition: 4%   MLB: 100%   Comparables: Sean Marshall, James Happ, Bob Strube, John Shea

West wasn't pitching especially well at Double-A when he got the call to take a spot in the Marlins' rotation, so it's not surprising that results were mixed—young lefties notoriously struggle with their command, and that's without being less than 30 starts removed from labrum surgery. West was consistently inconsistent and was optioned back down in mid-July with an ERA of 4.91. Lack of depth forced a rapid recall, but West was hardly improved by the experience, giving up 62 hits in 48 ⅓ IP after coming back. Though left-handed hitters couldn't touch West in the minors—lefties facing him in 2008 didn't manage a single extra-base hit in 105 plate appearances—the southpaw swingers at the major-league level treated him harshly. He also had a big case of road jitters, with a 6.47 ERA away from home. West remains one of the most intriguing pitchers in the Marlins' possession, but required more developmental time than he received in 2009. With luck, he'll still be able to build on the experience he did get, mixed though it was.

Tim Wood

Bats: R | Throws: R | Height: 6' 1" | Weight: 185 | Born: November 16, 1982 | Age: 27

YEAR	TEAM	LVL	AGE	W	L	SV	G	GS	IP	H	HR	BB	SO	GB%	BABIP	STUFF	WHIP	ERA	SIERA	DERA	EqH9	EqHR9	EqBB9	EqSO9	VORP	SN/WX
2007	JUP	A+	24	0	2	0	17	0	26	24	1	8	26	59%	.311	-11	1.23	3.81	3.23	6.39	9.5	1.5	3.3	5.8	-2.4	-0.45
2008	JUP	A+	25	5	2	1	27	1	40	25	1	15	22	60%	.207	-22	1.00	1.80	4.60	3.72	7.2	1.0	4.0	3.0	7.2	1.11
2008	CAR	AA	25	2	1	0	12	0	20¹	20	2	6	15	68%	.286	-19	1.28	5.75	3.63	7.32	9.6	1.4	2.7	4.6	-4.0	-0.03
2009	NWO	AAA	26	1	2	0	31	0	39²	42	1	17	37	51%	.339	-7	1.49	3.18	3.89	4.31	10.0	0.7	4.0	6.1	5.1	0.30
2009	FLO	MLB	26	1	0	0	18	0	22¹	22	2	10	16	55%	.294	-6	1.43	2.82	4.52	3.27	9.0	0.8	3.3	5.7	5.4	-0.04
2010	FLO	MLB	27	2	3	0	39	0	49	51	6	23	31	59%	.294	-11	1.51	4.76	4.82	5.11	9.4	1.1	3.7	5.1	2.1	0.79

Breakout: 10% Improve: 46% Collapse: 31% Attrition: 16%   MLB: 62%   Comparables: Mike Cather, Kevin Cameron, Paul Josephson, Daniel Brown

Wood was drafted way back in 2002, and his ascent was slowed by injuries and a late conversion to the bullpen. He was deployed mostly in low-leverage long relief, with seven of 18 appearances coming with the Marlins ahead or behind by long scores. He throws a hard sinking fastball; despite good velocity and an evolving slider, Wood's approach hasn't thus far yielded a lot of strikeouts. On most teams, he wouldn't be much of a threat to graduate into a higher-leverage role, but in the wild world of the Marlins, where players can be dealt for asking for more gruel, he could wake up one day as the most experienced pitcher on the staff.

LINEOUTS

Hitters

PLAYER	TEAM	LVL	AGE	PA	R	2B	3B	HR	RBI	BB	SO	SB-CS	EqBRR	AVG/OBP/SLG	EqAVG/EqOBP/EqSLG	EqA	VORP	WARP
OF G. Burns*	JUP	A+	22	553	64	20	7	4	35	64	163	37-15	-0.9	.242/.335/.339	.220/.300/.318	.224	-4.7	-0.2
OF I. Galloway	GRB	A	19	359	44	24	3	3	30	12	89	15-9	0.2	.268/.293/.382	.218/.240/.320	.192	-15.3	-3.0
UT A. Gonzalez	NWO	AAA	27	404	45	11	0	8	43	48	79	8-2	1.1	.259/.351/.358	.250/.329/.331	.238	5.4	-0.1
OF T. Hickman*	GRB	A	21	109	14	9	1	7	19	17	27	2-2	-0.9	.322/.440/.678	.255/.358/.521	.292	6.0	0.5
	JUP	A+	21	84	5	4	0	1	4	14	33	0-0	0.6	.129/.274/.229	.125/.250/.208	.160	-5.9	-1.1
OF J. Raynor	NWO	AAA	25	503	63	24	2	6	36	42	121	19-8	0.9	.257/.327/.360	.244/.306/.343	.230	-7.2	-1.2
C K. Skipworth*	GRB	A	19	286	28	14	1	7	37	18	91	1-2	-1.5	.208/.263/.348	.175/.220/.279	.164	-13.3	-3.6
INF J. Smolinski	GRB	A	20	322	50	25	0	7	31	38	45	2-5	-4.9	.283/.379/.448	.233/.314/.358	.235	-1.0	-1.6
OF S. Stonecipher	JAM	A-	19	159	20	11	1	2	12	11	31	4-0	-0.5	.264/.318/.396	.223/.261/.338	.209	-6.1	-1.5

Greg Burns is very fast and will take a walk every once in awhile, but he has massive problems making contact, problems that did not improve sufficiently, given that he repeated High-A. ⊘ **Isaac Galloway** has a center fielder's tool kit, but he and the strike zone need to become better acquainted if he's going to develop. Youth is on his side, but with 16 walks in 570 pro plate appearances, he has a long, long way to go. ⊘ **Andy Gonzalez** yo-yoed from New Orleans to Miami whenever a minor injury created a momentary need on the big-league club. ⊘ Still very raw three years after being drafted, **Tom Hickman** raked in the Sally League but was overwhelmed at High-A Jupiter, and not just by pitchers; he twice hit the restricted list with dreaded "personal issues." ⊘ **John Raynor** looked like a sleeper prospect after strong seasons in 2007 and 2008, but he pancaked at Triple-A, with his power, walk rate, and stolen bases plunging. Rule 5'd to the Pirates, his speed alone might allow him to make the roster as an extra outfielder. ⊘ Forgive the easy pun, but with batting rates of .208/.263/.345 in 113 career games, **Kyle Skipworth** might be worth skipping. However, the 2008 first-rounder has youth, strong defense, and all the right physical tools on his side, so patience is warranted. ⊘ Drafted by the Nats, **Jake Smolinski** headed south in the Willingham/Olsen trade. He missed quite a bit of time the last two years recovering from every injury this side of being mauled by a lion, but he has good pop for a middle infielder—*if* he's a middle infielder. His defense at second base was fringy, so the Marlins moved him to third base, where he fielded .879. ⊘ "Dude, really, the guy's name is **Sequoyah Stonecipher**! A 14th-round pick in '09, shares a birthday with Christina ... we *have* to include him in the book!"

Pitchers

PLAYER	TEAM	LVL	AGE	W	L	SV	IP	H	HR	BB	SO	GB%	BABIP	STUFF	WHIP	ERA	SIERA	DERA	EqH9	EqHR9	EqBB9	EqSO9	VORP
J. Allison	JUP	A+	24	7	9	0	139^1	151	13	30	71	45%	.291	-60	1.30	3.68	4.79	6.55	12.9	2.8	2.9	2.6	-14.5
L. Ayala	MIN	MLB	31	1	2	0	32^1	38	4	8	21	50%	.333	-7	1.42	4.18	4.34	4.55	10.6	1.2	2.1	5.3	3.2
	FLO	MLB	31	0	3	0	7^2	12	1	6	7	46%	.407	-15	2.35	11.74	5.02	11.25	13.5	1.1	5.6	6.8	-5.1
J. Buente	JAX	AA	25	0	1	1	22	17	1	11	23	73%	.286	0	1.27	2.45	3.29	3.82	9.4	1.4	4.5	7.2	3.7
	NWO	AAA	25	5	1	1	61	59	6	32	56	63%	.303	-17	1.49	3.39	3.97	4.27	9.9	2.0	4.8	6.1	7.9
K. Harvey	JUP	A+	25	6	7	1	72	67	3	34	54	49%	.292	-33	1.40	4.37	4.54	7.34	11.1	1.7	5.5	4.2	-13.2
J. Koronka*	NWO	AAA	28	4	10	0	128^2	159	17	43	77	45%	.321	-52	1.57	4.83	4.86	6.37	12.2	2.6	3.1	3.8	-11.8
	FLO	MLB	28	0	2	0	7^1	11	4	7	4	40%	.269	-38	2.45	11.05	6.53	13.50	12.4	4.5	6.8	3.4	-7.1
J. Rosario	GRB	A	23	2	0	0	21	24	3	6	14	40%	.300	-26	1.43	5.14	4.51	8.32	11.3	2.7	4.1	3.2	-6.3
	JUP	A+	23	8	7	0	109	90	4	25	91	39%	.267	-10	1.06	3.14	3.64	5.82	9.7	1.4	2.8	4.6	-3.6
B. Sinkbeil	NWO	AAA	24	2	8	0	83	106	9	44	52	64%	.342	-51	1.81	6.07	4.84	8.01	12.7	2.2	4.9	4.0	-21.9
G. Taylor*	JAX	AA	25	8	7	0	126^2	115	9	54	71	53%	.265	-31	1.33	3.69	5.04	6.33	10.3	1.8	4.0	3.4	-10.7
	FLO	MLB	25	0	2	0	11	16	0	12	5	39%	.356	-25	2.55	8.18	7.15	10.88	12.0	0.0	7.5	3.0	-7.2
E. Villanueva	JUP	A+	22	9	12	0	158	159	10	18	110	42%	.295	-21	1.12	3.47	3.82	6.03	11.8	2.1	1.8	3.8	-8.4

Pursuing the Josh Hamilton path to redemption got **Jeff Allison** through a season of so-so starting work in Jupiter. Lacking the velocity of his high school days, when he was considered the best prep arm in the draft, he now looks like an 11th or 12th guy. That doesn't seem like much, but given that not long ago, Allison was more avidly pursuing self-destruction than pitching, it's actually quite a lot. ⊘ Signed as a free agent in July after having been released by the Twins, **Luis Ayala** personally destroyed the Marlins' dark horse campaign to unseat the Phillies and was released. Pitching for four teams in the last two seasons, Ayala has gone 3-15 with a 5.68 ERA. ⊘ Groundballin' **Jay Buente** is a Hoosier added to the 40-man after doing good work in the AFL on top of last season; his Zephyrs-leading five intentional walks suggest he's already part of Fredi Gonzalez's friend-and-family cell package. ⊘ **Jose Ceda** and his upper-90s fastball were shelved for the entirety of 2009 by a torn labrum. ⊘ As a hitter, 2005 second-rounder **Kris Harvey** washed out, but Bryan Harvey's son throws low-90s heat, so a conversion to pitching began in '08; after a good first half he wore down to deliver a mixed first full season in '09. He's a project, but one already on the 40-man. ⊘ The 18th overall pick of 2009's draft, **Chad James** could prove to be a steal for the Marlins, as hard-throwing lefties are usually off the board by the second half of the first round. ⊘ Journeyman **John Koronka** joined the Marlins on the rebound from Japan and got called up when a hot start at New Orleans happened to coincide with Anibal Sanchez's injury; he was soon deselected for Sean West. ⊘ **Henry Owens'** comeback from shoulder surgery was delayed by a 50-game PED suspension. He didn't show much control in the few games that he worked, and it remains to be seen if this late-blooming former catcher can get back on the big-league beam. ⊘ **Scott Proctor** spent the year recovering from Tommy John surgery, in his case, also known as the "Joe Torre Gave Me Too Much Lovin'" operation. He'll try to come back on a Braves minor-league contract. ⊘ **Jose Rosario** is a generic Dominican with decent stuff and command, but whose secondary stuff needs work. Use only as directed, batteries not included. ⊘ **Brett Sinkbeil** was chosen with the 19th overall pick in 2006, and it's increasingly likely that in that moment, he hit his career peak. The ground-ball pitcher was somewhat more effective after a move to the pen, but he'll never justify that pick. ⊘ **Graham Taylor** had been making a desultory climb through the Marlins' system, when Andrew Miller's April trip to the DL produced an improbable promotion for the standard-issue slow-stuff, groundballing lefty. Predictably mashed into slurry, he's no longer on the 40-man. ⊘ **Elih Villanueva**, a 2008 27th-rounder, doesn't have much in the way of a fastball, but oh, can he locate, making one wonder about his 11 hit batsmen and the definition of "purpose pitch."

MANAGER: FREDI GONZALEZ

YEAR	TEAM	W-L	Pythag +/−	Avg PC	100+ P	120+ P	QS	BQS	REL	REL w Zero R	IBB	Subs	PH	PH Avg	PH HR	SB2	CS2	SB3	CS3	SAC Att	SAC %	POS SAC	Squeeze	Swing	In Play
2007	FLO	71-91	0	91.0	50	3	48	7	560	375	60	54	284	.213	7	83	25	22	7	92	78.3%	24	4	135	90
2008	FLO	84-77	3	93.6	46	2	70	5	510	337	66	80	248	.211	7	69	25	7	2	80	61.3%	15	4	122	89
2009	FLO	87-75	5	92.6	44	1	72	3	529	346	60	74	278	.280	8	66	28	9	6	106	66.0%	26	3	127	92

In February 2009, the Marlins gave manager Fredi Gonzalez a two-year contract extension. By October, the team was publicly flirting with Bobby Valentine. "As we looked at the performance at things that happened, games that went one way, games that went another way, there is no question we felt we should have been a playoff team," said club president and goodwill ambassador David Samson. In the interim, Gonzalez's team outplayed its projected winning percentage by four games, posting 87 victories on the majors' lowest payroll. Clearly, expectations are set to extra-picky. That is not to say that Gonzalez lacks faults. He loves the intentional walk so much that he shakes hands with only four fingers, having called for 185 freebies in his three seasons of skippering, the second most in the majors after Bobby Cox (Cox's use of the intentional walk is a mania, not a tactic). Conversely, Gonzalez has sacrificed with his nonpitchers fewer than any single manager of the last three years, so he's 1-for-2 on opposition-enabling strategies. However, Gonzalez could have bunted twice a game and still not wasted as many outs as he did by choosing Emilio Bonifacio as his leadoff man, an act of offensive self-emasculation comparable only to Dusty Baker's embrace of Willy Taveras. Regardless of how bleeping fast Bonifacio is or how much minor-league seasoning Chris Coghlan required, Gonzalez should have acted sooner and more decisively; when Coghlan did arrive, he dropped Bonifacio all the way down in the order—to number two.

Houston Astros

As Rachel Phelps, the Harridan owner of the Cleveland Indians in the film *Major League* might have said, if you're not going to be good, you may as well be really, really bad. The Astros, unfortunately, have been somewhere in between for the past four years: not quite good enough to be a contender, not quite bad enough to stock up on high draft picks and rebuild a farm system that has been in dire need of that rebuilding. Although they nominally competed for a playoff spot with 86 wins in 2008, PECOTA saw right through it, projecting the team to win 70 games in '09—and coming oh so close to their actual Pythagenpat record.

Right on cue, the 2009 Astros were thoroughly mediocre or worse in just about every way, shocking just about nobody beyond the team's offices. The biggest problem of all was that few of their players actually underperformed expectations. Lance Berkman, Hunter Pence, Carlos Lee, Kazuo Matsui, Geoff Blum, and Jeff Keppinger were all within just a few points of their PECOTA-projected EqAs, while Michael Bourn and Miguel Tejada far exceeded theirs. In fact, the only player who received 200 or more plate appearances and who underperformed his PECOTA-projected EqA by more than 10 points was Ivan Rodriguez, who was eventually traded to the Rangers in August.

The story is generally similar for the pitchers, although they wound up doing slightly *better* than their predicted performance. Roy Oswalt didn't quite match his projection, but Wandy Rodriguez blew his away. Mike Hampton, Brian Moehler, and Russ Ortiz—who were, amazingly enough, the team's 3-4-5 starters coming into the season—produced about what you would expect, combining for a 5.44 ERA in over 350 innings. If

anything, the Astros got more surprisingly good performances from their pitchers—particularly out of the bullpen—than surprisingly bad ones. Relievers Jose Valverde, LaTroy Hawkins, Jeff Fulchino, and Alberto Arias all beat their projections, while starter Felipe Paulino put up solid peripherals (3.80 SIERA) that far outpaced his ugly 6.27 ERA.

In other words, the Astros were what they should have been, and that says just as much about the front office's roster construction as it does about the guys on the field, including former manager Cecil Cooper, who ultimately took the fall in mid-September. After all, it was the front office that chose to enter the season with Blum and Keppinger, Rodriguez, and Matsui playing regularly at three lineup positions, and this group's combined performance was barely above replacement level. Not to mention the 400-plus at-bats they gave to below-replacement-level veterans like Darin Erstad, Jason Michaels, and, later, Chris Coste.

This is what happens when you resist the idea of having to tear down and start over with a team that's not good enough to contend. Thanks to those choices, among others, the Astros have found themselves adrift, stuck in the dead ground between competing for the playoffs and competing for a top draft pick. Since reaching its first World Series in 2005, Houston has averaged 79 wins over the past four years, and those wins haven't come cheap: the Astros have sported higher-than-average payrolls in three of those seasons, including a bloated $103 million figure in 2009.

Plenty of research has shown just how bad Houston's situation really is. In our book *Baseball Between the Numbers,* Nate Silver demonstrated that there's not that

ASTROS PROSPECTUS
2009 W-L: 74-88, 5th in NL Central

Pythag	67-95	15th
RS/G	4.0	14th
RA/G	4.8	12th
EqA	.256	11th
EqBRR	-0.8	7th
SNWP	.488	10th
WXRL	5.78	12th
FRAr	4.63	12th
DE	.676	16th
PADE	-2.46	16th
Salary	$103.0	4th
Attend	2.52	9th

Ballpark: Minute Maid Park (3-yr. PF: 981). Despite its design quirks and the Crawford Boxes in left, it's somewhat neutral

2009: Ed Wade's kamikaze run misses the target, leaving the team short of long-term talent and short-term exploits

2010: Shuffling towards the inevitable foundation-blasting rebuild

Action Items: Getting the nerve to explore offers for Berkman, Oswalt; setting horizons higher than mediocrity

much added benefit, in terms of revenue, from winning 80 games instead of 65:

> The most sensitive part of [a team's record]—what we'll call the sweet spot—is between 86 and 93 wins. Winning 90 games rather than 89, for example, improves a team's chances of making the playoffs by about 13 percent. ... The 70th win or the 105th win, which have no discernible impact on a team's playoff chances, are worth only about $600,000. But the 90th game won, right at the peak of the sweet spot, is worth nearly $3.5 million all on its own.

There's also the issue of payroll, of course: it costs more to build an 80-win team than a 65-win team, so it's almost always more profitable to field a 65-win team. This cash can then be saved for when the team is actually competitive and could use that last extra boost.

Shawn Hoffman attempted to quantify this on BaseballProspectus.com last year, building on the work of Silver and the late Doug Pappas. The result was PER, or Payroll Efficiency Rating, which evaluates front offices by the return they get on their payroll dollars. Part of this is their expected revenue intake—which is determined using Silver's marginal revenue curve, the team's third-order winning percentage, and market size—but also includes the value they can expect to receive in the following year's draft. Turning to the data in terms of one-year and four-year PER-formances (sorry, folks) shows the expected return—that is, the bang for their buck—for a team in an average-sized market, depending on how many games they win (see Tables 1 and 2).

Here's how the calculations are done: first, you find expected revenue, based on the team's third-order winning percentage and how big its market is. The more games they win, and the bigger the market, the higher the team's expected revenue will be. The Astros compiled 68 third-order wins, which, in their market, should generally create around $62 million in marginal revenue. Then, you divide that by what their marginal revenue should have been, had they won exactly as many games as their payroll would have predicted. Since the Astros spent $103 million on payroll in 2009, they should have won around 85 games, which would have produced around $75 million in marginal revenue. The result is a .82 PER, or a mark that's about 18 percent below average.

As it turns out, without even factoring in the added costs, winning 60 games can bring more value than winning 75 and is about the same as winning 80. As expected, the Astros have fared pretty poorly in these rankings over the past four years, never finishing above

Table 1. Bang for the Buck: 2009 Top and Bottom Five in Team Payroll Efficiency Ratings (PER)

Rk	Team	PER
1	Tampa Bay Rays	1.88
2	Los Angeles Dodgers	1.84
3	Colorado Rockies	1.43
4	Boston Red Sox	1.37
5	St. Louis Cardinals	1.28
— —		
26	Milwaukee Brewers	0.93
27	Detroit Tigers	0.84
28	Houston Astros	0.82
29	Chicago Cubs	0.80
30	New York Mets	0.72

Table 2: For a Few Dollars More: Cumulative Top and Bottom Five in PER, 2006-2009

Rk	Team	PER
1	Tampa Bay Rays	1.43
2	Toronto Blue Jays	1.35
3	Colorado Rockies	1.28
4	Cleveland Indians	1.24
5	Minnesota Twins	1.22
— —		
26	Chicago Cubs	0.93
27	San Francisco Giants	0.92
28	Chicago White Sox	0.91
29	Houston Astros	0.88
30	Seattle Mariners	0.82

23rd, and bottoming out in 2009 with a 28th-place finish, ahead of only the Cubs and Mets—both of whom expected to contend, and both of whom saw injuries undermine those bids for contention. Even worse, looking at the cumulative four-year standings, the Astros are the second-worst in all of baseball, just ahead of the Seattle Mariners (thank *you*, Bill Bavasi) and within shouting distance of only the White Sox, Giants, Cubs, and Mets.

Not surprisingly, those teams have a lot in common. For one thing, they've all had some reasonable measure of success lately—the Mets, Cubs, and White Sox have all won their division in the past five years, whereas the Astros and Giants both won pennants earlier in the decade. They've also had their share of embarrassments. The 2008 Mariners were history's first $100 million payroll/100-loss team in baseball history, while the 2009 Cubs and Mets had two of the top five highest payrolls of all-time among teams that didn't make the postseason.

Also, subjective as it may be, none of these franchises—aside from perhaps the Jack Zduriencik–led

Mariners—have the reputation of having fully embraced statistical analysis and sabermetrics. That's not necessarily a death knell—the Twins and Dodgers both rank very high on the PER standings, and neither team is known for being among the industry's most stats-savvy outfits—but the top of the list is far more populated by "new school" teams than is the bottom of the list.

Coincidence or not, the teams on the bottom have generally had two fatal flaws: overpaying for top talent and filling in at the margins with replacement-level players. (This includes platoon players, the bench, bullpen, and so forth.) Houston is a prime example of the perils of that formula for team-building. We've already discussed the bevy of near- or sub-replacement-level hitters that received significant playing time in 2009, but the Astros also managed to whiff on the high end; their two highest-paid players weren't Lance Berkman and Roy Oswalt, as one might expect, but Carlos Lee and Miguel Tejada. Both Miggy and C-Lee have their virtues, and they played decently enough in '09, at least relative to expectations, but neither is worth the inflated salaries the Astros were paying them, which combined to make up about a third of the team's total payroll. (Tejada's deal is finally over, but Lee is still on board for another three years.)

These are mistakes that the teams at the top of the PER rankings have generally avoided—or at least, haven't made nearly as often. These teams are generally small-market clubs that had, at some point, torn it all down and started from scratch (for example, the Rays, Twins, Rockies, and Indians) or larger-market teams that have developed a number of homegrown players to go with their bigger-name acquisitions (such as the Red Sox and Dodgers).

The Astros are somewhere in the middle in terms of market size and earning potential. And perhaps befitting that standing, they've been stuck between the two most common approaches to roster construction: either go for it all, or tear it all down. Since their pennant-winning club of '05, they've tried to continue being all-in, and to do that, it's important to have a solid base to build around first. The Astros may actually have had this; Berkman, Oswalt, Pence, Lee, and Rodriguez are a decent enough group, especially in the weaker league. Unfortunately for them, and thanks to a poor farm system and, at best, spotty decision making in regard to the major-league roster, Houston hasn't been able to put together a competitive team around that core. Of course, the Astros could also take the second approach and tear down their roster, but a significant amount of short-term pain comes from that, and really, the Astros have enough pieces that it's not entirely necessary.

The early part of the Astros' offseason certainly doesn't give much hope that they've changed course. They signed third baseman Pedro Feliz to a one-year contract, which doesn't improve the offense one jot. They paid $15 million for the next three years of Brandon Lyon, a fungible reliever with lifetime 4.20 ERA coming off a .229 BABIP-fueled "successful" season. They did make a more reasonable deal to shore up the bullpen by dealing from an organizational strength (nonprospects) to acquire an arbitration-eligible mediocre closer, Matt Lindstrom, from the Marlins, but even this move indicates a belief that they're just a few wins away from contention.

One way or another, Ed Wade and company need to start hashing out a more realistic plan, because going for it the last two years hasn't gotten them anywhere. Fielding one mediocre team after another doesn't serve any purpose, and the team's fans have certainly taken notice: attendance declined for the third straight year in 2009, a full 17 percent off of its post–World Series level. It's certainly a salvageable situation, because there are some good players already in place and the fans have shown they'll support a winning team. But the Astros desperately need to find cheaper and better talent and to stop throwing away money on declining veterans.

Whether Wade is the general manager who can find that kind of talent is anyone's guess. He's the man who talked his way into the job by stressing that the club could win now, and much of his actions and reactions have been to add former Phillies. If he fails to find something more, the Astros are little better than a zero-gravity gas giant: however much hot air they blow around that solid core, however much they spin, in the end, what they're left with is a rock.

HITTERS

Jose Altuve — 2B

Bats: R   Throws: R   Height: 5' 5"   Weight: 148   Born: May 6, 1990   Age: 20

YEAR	TEAM	LVL	AGE	PA	R	2B	3B	HR	RBI	BB	SO	SB	CS	EqBRR	AVG	OBP	SLG	EqAVG	EqOBP	EqSLG	EqA	VORP	WARP	DEFENSE	
2008	GRV	Rk	18	152	26	9	3	2	21	8	26	8	2	0.6	.284	.320	.433	.224	.253	.315	.198	-4.6	-1.3	38-2B	-3
2009	TCV	A-	19	87	13	5	0	0	7	8	10	7	2	-0.2	.250	.337	.316	.213	.276	.262	.194	-3.1	-0.5	19-2B	0
2009	GRV	Rk	19	208	45	20	2	3	18	26	16	21	4	2.0	.324	.408	.508	.258	.325	.387	.252	4.1	0.7	42-2B	0
2010	HOU	MLB	20	351	41	17	4	3	28	28	57	9	4	-0.1	.244	.306	.349	.246	.306	.350	.232	0.5	-0.1	79-2B	-1

Breakout: 25% Improve: 56% Collapse: 26% Attrition: 7%   MLB: 0%   Comparables: Gary Cates, Nelson Pedraza, Carlos Porte, Shane Letterio

Altuve is a pint-sized second baseman who was good enough to spark some Rafael Belliard comparisons last summer; he'll have to fill out a bit if he wants to be compared to David Eckstein. Unlike Belliard, however, Altuve can't really handle short, which means he won't have much use on a big-league team unless he can hit well enough to play second every day. Don't count on it, but root for him—if he makes it, he'd be the shortest middle infielder since Freddie Patek in the '70s.

Jay Austin — CF

Bats: L   Throws: L   Height: 5' 11"   Weight: 170   Born: August 10, 1990   Age: 19

YEAR	TEAM	LVL	AGE	PA	R	2B	3B	HR	RBI	BB	SO	SB	CS	EqBRR	AVG	OBP	SLG	EqAVG	EqOBP	EqSLG	EqA	VORP	WARP	DEFENSE
2008	GRV	Rk	17	235	31	4	2	0	14	19	70	14	6	0.5	.198	.277	.236	.164	.221	.187	.127	-19.3	-5.4	51-CF -11
2009	LEX	A	18	435	49	22	6	1	33	31	78	23	13	-2.3	.267	.320	.360	.243	.287	.329	.215	-7.5	-2.8	96-CF -16
2010	HOU	MLB	19	483	46	21	5	2	30	37	119	10	5	-0.8	.231	.290	.315	.230	.288	.314	.212	-8.0	-2.0	107-CF -10

Breakout: 47% Improve: 72% Collapse: 14% Attrition: 6%   MLB: 0%   Comparables: Engel Beltre, Miguel Negron, Juan Williams, Darran Hall

A second-round pick in 2008, Austin is still very raw, but he's about as athletic as anyone in the Astros' system (for what that's worth). He's very fast and is solid defensively in center, which should give him a leg up on Houston's other outfielders if he can develop any kind of offensive game. His numbers should get a superficial boost if he ends up at Lancaster this year, but he's still a ways off.

Lance Berkman — 1B

Bats: S   Throws: L   Height: 6' 1"   Weight: 220   Born: February 10, 1976   Age: 34

YEAR	TEAM	LVL	AGE	PA	R	2B	3B	HR	RBI	BB	SO	SB	CS	EqBRR	AVG	OBP	SLG	EqAVG	EqOBP	EqSLG	EqA	VORP	WARP	DEFENSE			
2007	HOU	MLB	31	668	95	24	2	34	102	94	125	7	3	-3.6	.278	.386	.510	.285	.394	.520	.308	44.6	4.3	118-1B	0	25-RF	-5
2008	HOU	MLB	32	665	114	46	4	29	106	99	108	18	4	2.4	.312	.420	.567	.325	.427	.588	.336	66.4	10.2	148-1B	25		
2009	HOU	MLB	33	562	73	31	1	25	80	97	98	7	4	-2.4	.274	.399	.509	.292	.409	.543	.318	38.6	4.6	129-1B	3		
2010	HOU	MLB	34	563	78	26	2	24	83	83	108	9	5	-0.5	.278	.390	.490	.279	.389	.489	.302	32.9	4.1	127-1B	5		

Breakout: 3% Improve: 31% Collapse: 16% Attrition: 7%   MLB: 100%   Comparables: Jeff Bagwell, Eddie Murray, George Brett, Rafael Palmeiro

Berkman keeps on keeping on. His offensive numbers were down a bit from a monster '08 (in large part due to hitting .162 in April; he batted .295 thereafter), and he spent some time on the DL with a strained calf, but the result was a typically Berkmanesque season. He's not the type of player who will usually age well—he's always had old-player skills, despite his 2008 spike in stolen bases—but he's also better than the great majority of players in that category. He has one guaranteed year left on a six-year contract, but the Astros also hold a $15 million club option for 2011. Considering how much they're paying Carlos Lee, that seems like an easy choice.

Geoff Blum — INF

Bats: S   Throws: R   Height: 6' 3"   Weight: 205   Born: April 26, 1973   Age: 37

YEAR	TEAM	LVL	AGE	PA	R	2B	3B	HR	RBI	BB	SO	SB	CS	EqBRR	AVG	OBP	SLG	EqAVG	EqOBP	EqSLG	EqA	VORP	WARP	DEFENSE			
2007	SDN	MLB	34	370	34	21	1	5	33	32	52	0	0	1.1	.252	.319	.367	.264	.331	.385	.251	7.6	1.7	54-2B	5	10-SS	1
2008	HOU	MLB	35	356	36	14	1	14	53	21	54	1	2	-1.2	.240	.287	.418	.248	.289	.424	.246	2.7	1.1	68-3B	6	5-2B	0
2009	HOU	MLB	36	427	34	14	1	10	49	33	61	0	1	-2.1	.247	.314	.367	.258	.321	.384	.247	5.0	0.0	94-3B	-4	7-1B	0
2010	HOU	MLB	37	309	24	13	1	7	36	26	54	1	1	-0.3	.244	.314	.372	.245	.313	.371	.239	1.3	0.2	65-3B	0		

Breakout: 6% Improve: 31% Collapse: 22% Attrition: 41%   MLB: 94%   Comparables: Cal Ripken, Frank Thomas, Ken Boyer, Brooks Robinson

Blum wasn't exactly an inspiring choice as the lead half of a third-base platoon, and he lived up (or down, as it may be) to PECOTA's muted expectations. He's a versatile player who can switch-hit and field several positions, and his defense at third is decent enough (while our system didn't love him last year, others have him as near average). That won't make up for his replacement-level bat, however—as a starting third baseman, Blum makes a fine utility infielder. The decision to sign Feliz means he should slip back into his better role, as the Astros re-signed him for 2010 with a mutual option for 2011.

Brian Bogusevic — OF

Bats: L Throws: L Height: 6' 3" Weight: 215 Born: February 18, 1984 Age: 26

YEAR	TEAM	LVL	AGE	PA	R	2B	3B	HR	RBI	BB	SO	SB	CS	EqBRR	AVG	OBP	SLG	EqAVG	EqOBP	EqSLG	EqA	VORP	WARP	DEFENSE			
2008	CCH	AA	24	145	21	10	2	3	20	16	24	8	1	0.6	.371	.447	.556	.313	.380	.461	.292	11.7	0.5	19-CF	-5	12-RF	-1
2009	ROU	AAA	25	581	68	25	3	6	53	53	118	22	3	4.4	.271	.342	.365	.251	.315	.333	.234	-2.4	-0.2	73-LF	8	56-CF	-7
2010	HOU	MLB	26	440	42	20	2	6	37	40	108	9	3	1.6	.242	.314	.347	.244	.314	.344	.235	-2.1	0.4	99-LF	5		

Breakout: 10% Improve: 29% Collapse: 18% Attrition: 11%   MLB: 11%   Comparables: Pedro Swann, Brian Stavisky, Ray Ortiz, Jalal Leach

In his first season as a full-time outfielder, Bogusevic disappointed, putting up pedestrian numbers at Round Rock. He also spent much of his time in left field instead of center, but that can be partly explained by having defensive whiz Yordany Ramirez as a teammate. Bogusevic has had a crazy career path—he was a first-round pick in 2005 and spent three years pitching before returning to the outfield in 2008—so there are all sorts of ways that this story could play out. At this point, his 2008 line looks more like a BABIP-induced fluke than an indication of Bogusevic's true talent, but he has plenty of tools and is heading into his prime. He'll probably be turning to Triple-A, and the Astros will have their fingers crossed, hoping for a breakout.

Michael Bourn — CF

Bats: L Throws: R Height: 5' 11" Weight: 180 Born: December 27, 1982 Age: 27

YEAR	TEAM	LVL	AGE	PA	R	2B	3B	HR	RBI	BB	SO	SB	CS	EqBRR	AVG	OBP	SLG	EqAVG	EqOBP	EqSLG	EqA	VORP	WARP	DEFENSE	
2007	PHI	MLB	24	133	29	3	3	1	6	13	21	18	1	4.0	.277	.348	.378	.277	.348	.378	.279	5.6	0.9	24-LF 1	6-CF 0
2008	HOU	MLB	25	514	57	10	4	5	29	37	111	41	10	2.0	.229	.288	.300	.238	.295	.309	.227	-4.1	-0.1	114-CF	3
2009	HOU	MLB	26	678	97	27	12	3	35	63	140	61	12	15.0	.285	.354	.384	.305	.369	.414	.282	36.4	4.7	150-CF	5
2010	HOU	MLB	27	578	83	23	7	6	32	54	118	44	11	4.7	.267	.338	.371	.269	.338	.371	.259	17.5	2.1	130-CF	2

Breakout: 18% Improve: 45% Collapse: 10% Attrition: 4%   MLB: 100%   Comparables: Steve Finley, Omar Moreno, Juan Pierre, Mickey Rivers

Bourn had a terrible 2008, hitting so poorly that his terrific defense in center field only partly redeemed his season. Many questioned whether he could ever become a decent everyday player, but Bourn showed his upside in 2009. By merely being adequate offensively, he became one of the most valuable players in the National League. It's not difficult to see what changed—his BABIP jumped over 70 points, to .366. Combined with an unchanged strikeout rate and similar power number, you'd expect regression in 2010; nevertheless, not all players regress equally, and a speed player has certain advantages so that, if he keeps his rate in the .320s or .330s with a walk rate around nine percent, he'll be a very valuable player going forward.

Jason Castro — C

Bats: L Throws: R Height: 6' 3" Weight: 210 Born: June 18, 1987 Age: 23

YEAR	TEAM	LVL	AGE	PA	R	2B	3B	HR	RBI	BB	SO	SB	CS	EqBRR	AVG	OBP	SLG	EqAVG	EqOBP	EqSLG	EqA	VORP	WARP	DEFENSE	
2008	TCV	A-	21	162	10	9	0	2	12	22	32	0	2	-1.3	.275	.383	.384	.228	.313	.303	.219	-1.3	-0.7	26-C	-3
2009	LNC	A+	22	243	27	20	1	7	44	30	41	1	1	-1.7	.309	.399	.517	.243	.321	.393	.251	5.8	1.6	43-C	7
2009	CCH	AA	22	268	38	11	1	3	29	25	35	2	1	-2.7	.293	.362	.385	.270	.326	.361	.243	5.6	0.2	57-C	-4
2010	HOU	MLB	23	436	40	19	1	8	44	45	89	2	2	-1.9	.245	.326	.359	.245	.325	.364	.241	8.7	1.0	83-C	0

Breakout: 30% Improve: 45% Collapse: 20% Attrition: 8%   MLB: 2%   Comparables: John Baker, Bryce Terveen, Emerson Frostad, Darrin Fletcher

Castro didn't have a great full-season debut, but it wasn't particularly bad, either. His numbers at Double-A are a bit more indicative than those from Lancaster—he has decent contact skills and should be able to put up acceptable on-base percentages, but he's not going to be an impact power bat anytime soon. That might sound like a disappointment, considering he was the 10th overall pick in the draft two years ago, but the rap on him hasn't really changed: Castro has always been projected to become an average everyday catcher, nothing more. With the Astros' catching situation still in flux, he could get a shot at the spot at some point in 2010.

Koby Clemens   C

Bats: R   **Throws: R**   **Height: 5' 11"**   **Weight: 193**   **Born: December 4, 1986**   **Age: 23**

YEAR	TEAM	LVL	AGE	PA	R	2B	3B	HR	RBI	BB	SO	SB	CS	EqBRR	AVG	OBP	SLG	EqAVG	EqOBP	EqSLG	EqA	VORP	WARP	DEFENSE		
2007	LEX	A	20	484	65	21	0	15	56	53	112	8	2	-4.3	.252	.344	.412	.227	.300	.356	.234	-3.7	-1.6	99-3B	-10	
2008	SLM	A+	21	458	54	29	5	7	52	61	99	1	4	-1.4	.268	.369	.423	.244	.328	.372	.247	9.0	0.3	76-C	-7	
2009	LNC	A+	22	492	74	45	6	22	121	51	109	4	1	-1.0	.345	.419	.636	.263	.327	.465	.271	19.8	0.2	62-C	-16	12-LF -3
2010	HOU	MLB	23	476	47	23	2	11	55	49	122	2	1	-1.1	.239	.322	.383	.241	.322	.386	.247	12.4	0.6	85-C	-7	

Breakout: 15%   **Improve: 47%**   **Collapse: 13%**   **Attrition: 12%**   **MLB: 7%**   **Comparables: Mike Napoli, Pat Bryant, Harry McCulla, Jason Dewey**

Clemens spent most of his year raking at High-A Lancaster, but a number of caveats attend that performance. His offensive numbers were backed by a ridiculously high .425 BABIP, which isn't sustainable in this or any other universe, and he was doing it in one of the best hitter's parks in perhaps the best hitter's league in the country. On the positive side, his strikeout rate remained manageable, and he continued to walk at a pretty good clip. He'll have to prove the power was real, and his defense at catcher still needs a lot of work. Double-A should be a good test for him, but if he passes it, he could end up giving Castro a run for his money.

Chris Coste   C/1B

Bats: R   **Throws: R**   **Height: 6' 1"**   **Weight: 215**   **Born: February 4, 1973**   **Age: 37**

YEAR	TEAM	LVL	AGE	PA	R	2B	3B	HR	RBI	BB	SO	SB	CS	EqBRR	AVG	OBP	SLG	EqAVG	EqOBP	EqSLG	EqA	VORP	WARP	DEFENSE			
2007	REA	AA	34	116	14	5	0	5	31	5	13	0	0	0.0	.287	.319	.472	.234	.256	.351	.210	-1.5	-0.3	19-C	-1	6-1B	0
2007	OTT	AAA	34	102	8	5	0	0	10	10	14	0	0	0.6	.233	.317	.289	.217	.294	.261	.199	-4.1	-0.6	16-1B	0	6-C	-1
2007	PHI	MLB	34	137	15	3	0	5	22	4	20	0	0	0.7	.279	.311	.419	.277	.309	.408	.251	4.7	0.4	27-C	-1		
2008	PHI	MLB	35	305	28	17	0	9	36	16	51	0	1	-2.8	.263	.325	.423	.269	.329	.422	.260	12.5	1.3	69-C	0		
2009	PHI	MLB	36	118	12	8	0	2	8	14	27	0	0	0.1	.245	.342	.382	.252	.347	.398	.261	3.7	0.1	24-C	-2		
2009	HOU	MLB	36	112	3	5	0	0	10	8	28	0	0	-0.1	.204	.259	.252	.204	.259	.252	.179	-6.0	-0.8	16-C	-2	13-1B	2
2010	NYN	MLB	37	228	18	9	0	5	25	16	47	0	0	-0.1	.236	.304	.353	.240	.305	.351	.232	2.6	0.2	51-C	-1		

Breakout: 11%   **Improve: 33%**   **Collapse: 33%**   **Attrition: 27%**   **MLB: 82%**   **Comparables: John Flaherty, Frank Thomas, Damian Miller, Eddie Perez**

The game's most famous indy leagues graduate had a pretty good first half with the Phillies, filling in for an injured Carlos Ruiz for most of April. Then the team chose Paul Bako as its backup, because of defensive concerns, and placed Coste on waivers in July. Claimed by the Astros, he shared the catching chores after Pudge Rodriguez was sent to the Rangers, and Coste also subbed for Berkman at first. The wheels came off, as that .252 slugging percentage attests, but that shouldn't surprise—Coste may have only four years in the majors, but he arrived late. He signed a one-year deal with the Mets that guaranteed him a spot on the 40-man, but not necessarily a job in the majors.

Collin DeLome   OF

Bats: L   **Throws: R**   **Height: 6' 2"**   **Weight: 195**   **Born: December 18, 1985**   **Age: 24**

YEAR	TEAM	LVL	AGE	PA	R	2B	3B	HR	RBI	BB	SO	SB	CS	EqBRR	AVG	OBP	SLG	EqAVG	EqOBP	EqSLG	EqA	VORP	WARP	DEFENSE			
2007	TCV	A-	21	273	31	17	6	6	28	23	65	9	2	0.3	.300	.374	.494	.245	.297	.403	.242	0.6	-0.9	33-CF	-2	11-LF	-4
2008	LEX	A	22	252	41	9	6	12	36	18	71	7	2	-0.3	.261	.329	.513	.233	.286	.422	.243	0.6	-0.6	34-LF	-4	17-CF	-2
2008	SLM	A+	22	267	40	14	3	10	35	17	57	7	2	3.1	.232	.305	.443	.217	.271	.398	.232	-3.8	-0.9	49-LF	-4		
2009	CCH	AA	23	522	79	18	10	20	61	37	141	15	8	-0.9	.255	.323	.465	.232	.287	.424	.242	1.9	-0.5	79-LF	1	38-CF	-7
2010	HOU	MLB	24	472	51	20	6	14	47	32	139	6	3	0.4	.229	.290	.403	.230	.290	.407	.238	-1.0	-0.5	96-LF	-3		

Breakout: 19%   **Improve: 41%**   **Collapse: 16%**   **Attrition: 10%**   **MLB: 2%**   **Comparables: Van Snider, Ralph Bryant, Steve Murphy, Joe Deberry**

In an organization short on prospects, somebody has to get hung with the label, lest people just wander out into the Texas sun and wait until the absence of air-conditioning kills them. DeLome does more than his part as far as contributing his name to the lifesaving conversation—he has some tools, with a strong arm, blazing speed, and tremendous bat speed. The jump to Double-A was hard on him, however, as pitchers exploited his long swing and pull-happiness. He won't wind up as a center fielder, so the bat has to come around for him to steer the conversation toward "prospect in any organization."

Darin Erstad   OF/1B

Bats: L   Throws: L   Height: 6' 2"   Weight: 220   Born: June 4, 1974   Age: 36

YEAR	TEAM	LVL	AGE	PA	R	2B	3B	HR	RBI	BB	SO	SB	CS	EqBRR	AVG	OBP	SLG	EqAVG	EqOBP	EqSLG	EqA	VORP	WARP	DEFENSE			
2007	CHR	AAA	33	52	3	0	0	0	2	5	14	0	0	0.0	.128	.212	.128	.125	.192	.125	.000	-5.5	-0.8	9-CF	-1		
2007	CHA	MLB	33	345	33	13	1	4	32	28	44	7	2	0.8	.248	.310	.335	.247	.311	.331	.231	-2.9	0.2	42-CF	2	20-1B	3
2008	HOU	MLB	34	342	49	16	0	4	31	14	68	2	3	1.2	.276	.309	.363	.283	.314	.370	.236	-1.3	0.7	34-CF	5	23-LF	2
2009	HOU	MLB	35	150	13	8	2	2	11	14	31	0	2	0.3	.194	.268	.328	.200	.273	.333	.207	-7.8	-0.8	11-1B	0	7-LF	0
2010	HOU	MLB	36	172	17	7	0	2	15	14	35	1	2	0.2	.239	.302	.321	.238	.300	.332	.215	-5.9	-0.5	28-1B	1		

Breakout: 11%   Improve: 27%   Collapse: 28%   Attrition: 38%   MLB: 91%   Comparables: Scott Hatteberg, Ted Kluszewski, Barney McCosky, Mike Aldrete

Onward rolls the replacement-level train, with Erstad as one of the team's biggest offensive offenders. To be fair, Houston shouldn't have expected much else. Erstad's offensive value is entirely wrapped up in his batting average, which bottomed out in 2009. He can still run down flies in the outfield and plays a decent enough first base, but he's now 10 years past his peak, and the arrow is not only pointing down, but it's flaccid. Expect a modest dead-cat bounce in 2010, but anyone who offers Erstad more than the minimum and an NRI has made a sucker's bet.

Jonathan Gaston   OF

Bats: L   Throws: R   Height: 6' 0"   Weight: 210   Born: November 13, 1986   Age: 23

YEAR	TEAM	LVL	AGE	PA	R	2B	3B	HR	RBI	BB	SO	SB	CS	EqBRR	AVG	OBP	SLG	EqAVG	EqOBP	EqSLG	EqA	VORP	WARP	DEFENSE			
2008	TCV	A-	21	236	18	11	1	2	25	25	65	0	2	-1.5	.193	.292	.285	.167	.242	.247	.163	-17.2	-3.4	40-RF	-2		
2009	LNC	A+	22	607	119	31	15	35	100	71	164	14	4	3.3	.278	.367	.598	.224	.300	.443	.255	7.2	-1.3	68-LF	-11	48-RF	-8
2010	HOU	MLB	23	539	62	24	5	16	60	51	156	4	3	0.6	.215	.295	.386	.216	.295	.393	.235	-2.8	-1.2	102-LF	-8		

Breakout: 18%   Improve: 49%   Collapse: 13%   Attrition: 4%   MLB: 1%   Comparables: David Mattle, Jeff Key, Brian Simmons, Roosevelt Brown

Gaston put up some huge numbers at Lancaster—whoever the JetHawks are affiliated with, this becomes a bit of a chapter-wide theme—and while he gets mixed reviews from scouts and wasn't exactly young for High-A ball, there was more substance to his line than there was for, say, Clemens. Gaston led the Cal League in home runs and extra-base hits, while throwing in a 12 percent walk rate. He strikes out way too much, in about 27 percent of his PAs, which could hurt him as he moves into the high minors, and there are plenty of baseball people who are reserving judgment until they see him hit at Double-A. For a seventh-round pick who was terrible in his pro debut, 2009 was certainly a nice surprise, but 2010 will be a much greater test.

Chris Johnson   3B

Bats: R   Throws: R   Height: 6' 3"   Weight: 220   Born: October 1, 1984   Age: 25

YEAR	TEAM	LVL	AGE	PA	R	2B	3B	HR	RBI	BB	SO	SB	CS	EqBRR	AVG	OBP	SLG	EqAVG	EqOBP	EqSLG	EqA	VORP	WARP	DEFENSE			
2007	LEX	A	22	277	37	14	0	8	44	17	38	3	4	-1.6	.259	.304	.408	.227	.261	.331	.204	-9.1	-1.5	29-3B	0	19-SS	-2
2007	SLM	A+	22	240	24	11	0	6	38	8	41	1	0	-0.6	.263	.292	.393	.246	.266	.355	.216	-5.9	-1.1	53-3B	-3	2-1B	0
2008	CCH	AA	23	358	43	24	0	12	58	20	61	5	0	-0.3	.324	.364	.506	.296	.330	.460	.271	13.1	1.0	82-3B	-5		
2008	ROU	AAA	23	107	10	2	1	1	9	5	25	0	0	-0.7	.218	.252	.287	.206	.234	.275	.169	-6.5	-0.9	26-3B	-1		
2009	ROU	AAA	24	412	48	20	5	13	42	21	90	2	1	-0.9	.281	.323	.461	.264	.301	.429	.249	6.6	0.0	100-3B	-7		
2009	HOU	MLB	24	23	1	0	0	0	1	1	6	0	0	0.0	.091	.130	.091	.136	.174	.136	-.166	-3.7	-0.6	5-3B	-1		
2010	HOU	MLB	25	472	47	20	2	13	57	28	107	2	1	-0.6	.252	.299	.397	.254	.300	.398	.239	1.8	-0.1	106-3B	-3		

Breakout: 15%   Improve: 54%   Collapse: 7%   Attrition: 4%   MLB: 13%   Comparables: Brennan King, Ed Smith, Chris Saunders, Chris Truby

The biggest thing Johnson has going for him is the Astros' organizational lassitude. In most systems, he would hardly get a second look, but the Astros are so thin on position-playing prospects that Johnson tends to stand out. He gets good reviews defensively, but his offensive numbers have been propped up by his home ballparks, as well as a symptomatic string of high BABIPs. Johnson could have had a shot at winning the third-base job this spring, but the limit of the Astros' love of their own was reflected in their signing Pedro Feliz to a one-year deal, probably forcing a Round Rock repeat for Johnson.

Jeff Keppinger   INF

Bats: R   Throws: R   Height: 6' 0"   Weight: 180   Born: April 21, 1980   Age: 30

YEAR	TEAM	LVL	AGE	PA	R	2B	3B	HR	RBI	BB	SO	SB	CS	EqBRR	AVG	OBP	SLG	EqAVG	EqOBP	EqSLG	EqA	VORP	WARP	DEFENSE			
2007	LOU	AAA	27	261	31	15	1	2	18	23	14	1	1	-1.6	.368	.424	.469	.348	.397	.446	.295	15.8	2.2	19-3B	0	19-2B	3
2007	CIN	MLB	27	276	39	16	2	5	32	24	12	2	1	1.5	.332	.400	.477	.335	.404	.475	.302	21.4	2.7	44-SS	-1	9-3B	2
2008	CIN	MLB	28	502	45	24	2	3	43	30	24	3	1	0.7	.266	.310	.346	.270	.311	.348	.235	6.4	-0.7	99-SS	-11	8-3B	-1
2009	HOU	MLB	29	344	35	13	3	7	29	27	33	0	2	-2.4	.256	.320	.387	.269	.329	.409	.254	7.6	0.3	58-3B	-3	16-2B	-3
2010	HOU	MLB	30	499	57	25	2	8	50	42	37	3	2	-0.6	.293	.357	.412	.295	.358	.418	.269	17.6	1.8	91-3B	-1		

Breakout: 14%   Improve: 38%   Collapse: 7%   Attrition: 5%   MLB: 97%   Comparables: Joe Randa, Mark Loretta, Chris Stynes, George Kell

Needing a right-handed hitting third baseman to replace Boone, the Astros shipped off a player to be named (Drew Sutton) to Cincinnati for Keppinger, who had fallen out of favor with the Reds. Always a lefty-lasher (.341/.391/.495 in his career), he also faced a few righties last season, thanks to injuries to Blum and Matsui. As a contact hitter extraordinaire, Keppinger is what he is, and while he certainly has some value as a bench player, he's not an everyday solution at any position.

Carlos Lee   LF

Bats: R   Throws: R   Height: 6' 2"   Weight: 240   Born: June 20, 1976   Age: 34

YEAR	TEAM	LVL	AGE	PA	R	2B	3B	HR	RBI	BB	SO	SB	CS	EqBRR	AVG	OBP	SLG	EqAVG	EqOBP	EqSLG	EqA	VORP	WARP	DEFENSE	
2007	HOU	MLB	31	697	93	43	1	32	119	53	63	10	5	-3.6	.303	.354	.528	.313	.362	.543	.300	46.3	3.6	152-LF	-13
2008	HOU	MLB	32	481	61	27	0	28	100	37	49	4	1	-1.7	.314	.368	.569	.326	.376	.586	.316	41.3	3.3	103-LF	-10
2009	HOU	MLB	33	662	65	35	1	26	102	41	51	5	3	-7.3	.300	.343	.489	.317	.355	.514	.292	37.6	2.2	144-LF	-17
2010	HOU	MLB	34	573	65	26	1	25	100	46	61	4	3	-2.0	.299	.359	.497	.301	.358	.498	.290	31.8	2.7	127-LF	-6

Breakout: 2%   Improve: 28%   Collapse: 17%   Attrition: 19%   MLB: 98%   Comparables: Dante Bichette, Rondell White, Brian Jordan, Jim Rice

Halfway through his gargantuan six-year contract, Lee has actually been a pleasant surprise, in a funny kind of way: his combined EqA since coming to Houston is .302, which is the best three-year stretch of his career. Of course, that might just go to show how ridiculous his contract was in the first place. Never a good left fielder to begin with, Lee has seen his defense take a turn for the worse in Houston, and it isn't likely to get any better as he ages. He's also one of the least-effective baserunners in the biz (worst in the NL, according to EqBRR). That he's produced as well and as consistently as he has offensively is certainly a plus, but in terms of overall value, he was closer to Randy Winn and Scott Podsednik in 2009 than to Matt Holliday and Ryan Braun. It's not likely to get any better.

Tommy Manzella   SS

Bats: R   Throws: R   Height: 6' 2"   Weight: 190   Born: April 16, 1983   Age: 27

YEAR	TEAM	LVL	AGE	PA	R	2B	3B	HR	RBI	BB	SO	SB	CS	EqBRR	AVG	OBP	SLG	EqAVG	EqOBP	EqSLG	EqA	VORP	WARP	DEFENSE	
2007	SLM	A+	24	251	28	13	0	0	24	19	30	5	2	-0.3	.238	.305	.296	.212	.259	.247	.177	-9.9	-1.4	55-SS	-1
2007	CCH	AA	24	254	35	12	3	1	15	19	40	10	2	2.4	.289	.343	.382	.270	.316	.356	.240	3.7	-0.6	58-SS	-9
2008	CCH	AA	25	249	27	11	5	4	34	17	35	4	4	-3.4	.299	.346	.446	.262	.300	.384	.238	4.5	-1.0	53-SS	-13
2008	ROU	AAA	25	247	19	15	1	0	15	17	39	0	4	-2.5	.219	.273	.294	.203	.249	.260	.168	-10.3	-0.7	61-SS	5
2009	ROU	AAA	26	580	68	31	5	9	56	40	99	12	3	-2.6	.289	.339	.417	.266	.311	.375	.241	10.8	0.8	129-SS	-4
2009	HOU	MLB	26	5	0	0	0	0	0	0	4	0	0	-0.1	.200	.200	.200	.200	.200	.200	.064	-0.7	-0.1		
2010	HOU	MLB	27	506	49	23	4	5	41	37	105	5	3	-1.1	.242	.299	.339	.244	.299	.340	.223	-1.1	-0.5	116-SS	-4

Breakout: 20%   Improve: 43%   Collapse: 21%   Attrition: 16%   MLB: 7%   Comparables: Brian Keck, Brandon Wilson, Jake Wald, Kelly Dransfeldt

The Astros claim to be over the Miguel Tejada experience (or the expense of it) and have been posturing this winter with the position that Manzella is the antidote. That's great news if you're Tommy Manzella, of course; the 2005 third-rounder out of Tulane had been on an incrementally upward path toward the majors with no guarantee of arriving. Athletic and strong-armed, he should be a defensive asset at short, and while he showed more pop last year, he's also already headed into his age-27 season. Manzella is a good-glove placeholder headed for the eighth slot in the order on a good team, but the Astros won't hold up their end of that proposition.

Kazuo Matsui   2B

Bats: S   Throws: R   Height: 5′ 10″   Weight: 185   Born: October 23, 1975   Age: 34

YEAR	TEAM	LVL	AGE	PA	R	2B	3B	HR	RBI	BB	SO	SB	CS	EqBRR	AVG	OBP	SLG	EqAVG	EqOBP	EqSLG	EqA	VORP	WARP	DEFENSE	
2007	COL	MLB	31	453	84	24	6	4	37	34	69	32	4	6.8	.288	.342	.405	.282	.337	.393	.265	16.9	3.9	96-2B	16
2008	HOU	MLB	32	422	58	26	3	6	33	37	53	20	5	4.1	.293	.354	.427	.308	.365	.448	.282	24.1	1.7	91-2B	-9
2009	HOU	MLB	33	533	56	20	2	9	46	34	85	19	3	2.7	.250	.302	.357	.263	.312	.376	.247	8.8	1.5	125-2B	4
2010	HOU	MLB	34	469	61	22	4	8	42	40	82	17	7	2.1	.265	.329	.387	.265	.328	.385	.253	10.8	1.4	104-2B	2

Breakout: 11% Improve: 37% Collapse: 17% Attrition: 25%   MLB: 92%   Comparables: Omar Vizquel, Frankie Frisch, Tony Taylor, Bill Doran

In his six seasons in the bigs, Matsui's offensive production has always come and gone with his batting average, as he's never been able to find the pop he had in Japan, leaving him prone to the whims of the most volatile of offensive stats. That didn't work out so well in 2009, as his average fell 43 points. If nothing else, his strikeout rate wasn't abnormally high (only 0.3 percent higher than his career mark), and his walk rate didn't completely fall off the map. He also set a career high in games played and plate appearances, which is a moral victory in itself. But the Astros probably would have been better off had they given his 335 plate appearances in the first two slots in the order to someone else, Matsui having put up a .287 OBP there. Expect something of a bounce back in the last year of his deal, but nothing to get overly excited about.

Jason Michaels   OF

Bats: R   Throws: R   Height: 6′ 0″   Weight: 205   Born: May 4, 1976   Age: 34

YEAR	TEAM	LVL	AGE	PA	R	2B	3B	HR	RBI	BB	SO	SB	CS	EqBRR	AVG	OBP	SLG	EqAVG	EqOBP	EqSLG	EqA	VORP	WARP	DEFENSE			
2007	CLE	MLB	31	295	43	11	1	7	39	20	50	3	4	-0.8	.270	.324	.397	.271	.324	.406	.250	2.3	0.6	55-LF	1	13-RF	1
2008	CLE	MLB	32	67	3	4	0	0	9	4	13	1	1	0.3	.207	.258	.276	.211	.258	.281	.203	-2.7	0.2	11-LF	3	5-RF	1
2008	PIT	MLB	32	254	25	9	1	8	44	23	52	1	0	-0.2	.228	.300	.382	.241	.312	.395	.245	0.6	-0.4	28-RF	-4	14-LF	-3
2009	HOU	MLB	33	152	17	12	1	4	16	16	38	1	2	-0.5	.237	.322	.430	.250	.333	.463	.265	2.7	0.3	12-CF	0	10-LF	-1
2010	HOU	MLB	34	198	20	9	1	4	26	19	46	1	2	-0.2	.235	.314	.365	.237	.314	.362	.236	1.1	0.1	39-CF	0		

Breakout: 10% Improve: 31% Collapse: 36% Attrition: 35%   MLB: 94%   Comparables: Sam Chapman, Bobby Thomson, Jim Fregosi, Merv Rettenmund

Michaels used to be a valuable bench player for a good team (one Ed Wade happened to be the GM of); he's now a reasonably valuable bench player for a bad team. His defensive versatility is still an asset, but over the last two seasons, he's received 473 plate appearances and batted .228/.301/.382. As he's now 34, there are younger, cheaper, more potent options who can do what he can ... Except in Houston, which found it necessary to re-sign him.

Jiovanni Mier   SS

Bats: R   Throws: R   Height: 6′ 2″   Weight: 175   Born: August 26, 1990   Age: 19

YEAR	TEAM	LVL	AGE	PA	R	2B	3B	HR	RBI	BB	SO	SB	CS	EqBRR	AVG	OBP	SLG	EqAVG	EqOBP	EqSLG	EqA	VORP	WARP	DEFENSE	
2009	GRV	Rk	18	229	32	7	6	7	32	30	45	10	5	-2.3	.276	.380	.484	.213	.293	.337	.225	1.0	-1.5	49-SS	-10
2010	HOU	MLB	19	390	36	14	5	8	37	39	102	6	4	0.0	.227	.308	.365	.227	.306	.360	.236	4.0	-0.5	85-SS	-9

Breakout: 34% Improve: 57% Collapse: 14% Attrition: 0%   MLB: 0%   Comparables: Brian Costello, Jose Zambrano, Ronnie Hall, Rob Lemle

Mier was the Astros' first-round pick in last June's draft. He was picked more for his defense than his bat, as he's been billed as a potential Gold Glover at shortstop, and he lived up to advance notices in his limited action. He signed very early and got to spend the summer with Houston's rookie-league team, hitting well enough not to raise any red flags. Expect the Astros to take it slow with him, as he'll be 19 when the season starts and he still has a lot of filling out to do. If he can become even a slightly above-average hitter, the Astros will be very happy.

Hunter Pence   RF

Bats: R   Throws: R   Height: 6′ 4″   Weight: 210   Born: April 13, 1983   Age: 27

YEAR	TEAM	LVL	AGE	PA	R	2B	3B	HR	RBI	BB	SO	SB	CS	EqBRR	AVG	OBP	SLG	EqAVG	EqOBP	EqSLG	EqA	VORP	WARP	DEFENSE			
2007	ROU	AAA	24	106	17	11	1	3	21	10	15	2	0	0.3	.326	.387	.558	.302	.358	.521	.298	7.4	1.1	18-CF	0	6-RF	2
2007	HOU	MLB	24	484	57	30	9	17	69	26	95	11	5	-0.2	.322	.360	.539	.334	.372	.556	.305	38.6	4.0	93-CF	-3	13-RF	1
2008	HOU	MLB	25	642	78	34	4	25	83	40	124	11	10	-0.8	.269	.318	.466	.282	.329	.482	.269	18.8	4.3	154-RF	18		
2009	HOU	MLB	26	647	76	26	5	25	72	58	109	14	11	-1.4	.282	.346	.472	.302	.362	.503	.287	33.3	3.5	156-RF	-2		
2010	HOU	MLB	27	647	82	32	6	26	91	52	120	13	10	-0.4	.294	.353	.500	.294	.353	.499	.286	33.5	4.1	153-RF	4		

Breakout: 16% Improve: 56% Collapse: 7% Attrition: 4%   MLB: 98%   Comparables: Alex Rios, Juan Encarnacion, Bob Allison, Gary Matthews

Pence is one of the few position players to come out of the Astros system that can actually play. He saw a big jump in his walk rate in '09, fixing what had been his biggest offensive weakness. Even more impressive, he did so while chopping a bit off his strikeout rate as well. He may not match his rookie numbers anytime soon—they were backed by a fluky BABIP—but he's a solid everyday right fielder and should be for the near future.

Humberto Quintero C   Bats: R   Throws: R   Height: 5' 9"   Weight: 215   Born: August 2, 1979   Age: 30

YEAR	TEAM	LVL	AGE	PA	R	2B	3B	HR	RBI	BB	SO	SB	CS	EqBRR	AVG	OBP	SLG	EqAVG	EqOBP	EqSLG	EqA	VORP	WARP	DEFENSE	
2007	ROU	AAA	27	188	22	12	1	5	22	4	21	0	2	-0.9	.333	.355	.497	.307	.326	.447	.262	8.8	1.8	45-C	6
2007	HOU	MLB	27	57	2	2	0	0	1	2	13	0	0	-1.4	.226	.281	.264	.226	.281	.264	.187	-1.1	0.0	17-C	1
2008	ROU	AAA	28	124	13	2	2	3	18	5	15	0	2	-1.2	.237	.274	.364	.210	.242	.311	.183	-3.4	-0.3	30-C	1
2008	HOU	MLB	28	183	16	6	0	2	12	6	34	0	0	0.0	.226	.270	.298	.229	.272	.294	.201	-2.4	0.7	51-C	6
2009	HOU	MLB	29	168	11	8	1	4	14	7	41	0	0	0.3	.236	.286	.376	.248	.298	.389	.234	3.3	1.3	48-C	6
2010	HOU	MLB	30	233	20	10	1	4	20	11	47	0	1	-0.5	.247	.296	.357	.248	.295	.364	.224	0.9	0.5	63-C	3

Breakout: 19%   Improve: 47%   Collapse: 29%   Attrition: 12%   MLB: 63%   Comparables: Vance Wilson, Todd Greene, Orlando Mercado, Mike Redmond

For the second straight year, Quintero got a shot at being the Astros' starting catcher, and for the second straight year, he proved that he's a catch-and-throw backup. He's never going to be a good enough hitter to play every day (in 589 career PAs, he's at .232/.275/.325), but he did throw out 12 of 26 attempted basestealers, following up on a solid 44 percent mark in his long minor-league career; in another life, he'd have made a fine fourth Molina. The Astros must find a better everyday alternative. As is, it's been a depressing run at the position; the last Houston catcher to do anything like solid offensive work in a season of more than 120 games was Craig Biggio—in 1991.

Miguel Tejada SS   Bats: R   Throws: R   Height: 5' 9"   Weight: 215   Born: May 25, 1974   Age: 36

YEAR	TEAM	LVL	AGE	PA	R	2B	3B	HR	RBI	BB	SO	SB	CS	EqBRR	AVG	OBP	SLG	EqAVG	EqOBP	EqSLG	EqA	VORP	WARP	DEFENSE	
2007	BAL	MLB	33	568	72	19	1	18	81	41	55	2	1	-0.6	.296	.357	.442	.292	.354	.439	.275	28.8	2.5	120-SS	-6
2008	HOU	MLB	34	666	92	38	3	13	66	24	72	7	7	-0.5	.283	.314	.415	.293	.323	.427	.254	23.3	3.7	153-SS	8
2009	HOU	MLB	35	673	83	46	1	14	86	19	48	5	2	-0.9	.313	.340	.455	.330	.354	.477	.284	44.6	6.1	155-SS	8
2010	HOU	MLB	36	540	62	25	1	13	67	31	66	3	4	-0.3	.282	.333	.415	.284	.334	.417	.257	17.5	2.1	124-SS	1

Breakout: 8%   Improve: 26%   Collapse: 26%   Attrition: 35%   MLB: 96%   Comparables: Riggs Stephenson, Melvin Mora, Joe Randa, Royce Clayton

All things considered, Tejada's two years in Houston could have been a lot worse. He actually had a terrific season in 2009, which not-so-coincidentally was a contract year. That doesn't make the original decision to trade for him look any smarter. It's not that the players the Astros handed over have made such a big impact. The Astros also got nearly what they paid for in performance. Still, just because you made out good on a bad bet doesn't mean you should do it again. Emptying the wallet on that last-piece-of-the-puzzle that isn't actually the last piece is exactly the type of mistake mid- and small-market teams need to avoid. That money won't just reappear when the team needs it later. Tejada wasn't offered arbitration, so he also won't be leaving any first-round draft picks behind as a legacy. Given his age, it wouldn't be a surprise to see him at third base for somebody this year.

J. R. Towles C   Bats: R   Throws: R   Height: 6' 2"   Weight: 190   Born: February 11, 1984   Age: 26

YEAR	TEAM	LVL	AGE	PA	R	2B	3B	HR	RBI	BB	SO	SB	CS	EqBRR	AVG	OBP	SLG	EqAVG	EqOBP	EqSLG	EqA	VORP	WARP	DEFENSE	
2007	SLM	A+	23	115	14	3	2	0	11	12	15	3	5	-1.5	.200	.339	.278	.184	.276	.235	.190	-2.0	-0.5	26-C	-2
2007	CCH	AA	23	257	47	12	2	11	49	23	35	9	4	1.4	.324	.425	.551	.310	.388	.513	.304	22.4	2.2	46-C	-4
2007	ROU	AAA	23	50	5	0	0	0	2	4	7	2	4	-1.2	.279	.354	.279	.273	.347	.273	.216	0.3	-0.3	12-C	-3
2007	HOU	MLB	23	44	9	5	0	1	12	3	1	0	1	-0.2	.375	.432	.575	.375	.432	.550	.332	5.5	0.7	11-C	1
2008	ROU	AAA	24	192	28	8	2	7	28	13	31	4	3	-0.7	.304	.370	.500	.281	.339	.433	.265	9.3	0.9	45-C	-2
2008	HOU	MLB	24	171	10	5	0	4	16	16	40	0	0	-0.4	.137	.250	.253	.136	.249	.245	.178	-5.4	-0.6	46-C	0
2009	ROU	AAA	25	178	23	12	1	4	22	22	27	3	0	0.4	.276	.386	.455	.262	.362	.430	.280	9.9	1.2	40-C	0
2009	HOU	MLB	25	53	7	2	0	2	3	3	16	0	0	0.1	.188	.250	.354	.184	.245	.347	.211	-0.4	-0.4	13-C	-2
2010	HOU	MLB	26	301	35	13	2	7	37	27	60	3	3	-0.3	.246	.330	.390	.245	.327	.390	.251	9.2	0.8	71-C	-2

Breakout: 10%   Improve: 29%   Collapse: 28%   Attrition: 13%   MLB: 67%   Comparables: Ray Montgomery, Dave Valle, Terry McGriff, Jeff Forney

Towles is a fun player to have around. Not for Houston, which has lost a win or two just by putting him in the lineup, but for the statheads. He's a puzzle, and a genuinely interesting one. His career BABIP in the majors is now .218; in the minors, it's .336. Eventually, one would think, something's gotta give. Had his BABIP with the Astros been even .280 (still well below league average), with all of the extra hits being singles, his career line would be .233/ .317/.376—still not great, but manageable enough that Towles would almost certainly be heading into camp as the team's starting catcher. He needs to manage the strike zone better, but perhaps more importantly, he needs to simply hit the ball with more authority—the average hitter smacks a line drive about 19 percent of the time, and those drives form the bulk of his hits. In his brief career, Towles' line-drive percentage is only 13 percent. His minor-league production suggests an offensive skill set far better than that of most catchers. Given that and the Astros' options, he's worth another shot.

PITCHERS

Alberto Arias

Bats: R   Throws: R   Height: 5′ 11″   Weight: 155   Born: October 14, 1983   Age: 26

YEAR	TEAM	LVL	AGE	W	L	SV	G	GS	IP	H	HR	BB	SO	GB%	BABIP	STUFF	WHIP	ERA	SIERA	DERA	EqH9	EqHR9	EqBB9	EqSO9	VORP	SN/WX
2007	CSP	AAA	23	2	2	0	10	3	26^1	32	1	8	15	61%	.356	-9	1.52	3.76	4.47	4.07	11.1	0.7	3.0	4.4	3.9	0.37
2008	CSP	AAA	24	3	4	0	30	0	45^2	50	3	16	41	66%	.346	-1	1.45	4.73	3.61	4.77	9.7	0.6	3.2	6.5	3.6	-0.71
2008	COL	MLB	24	0	0	0	12	0	13^2	12	1	4	5	75%	.244	-15	1.17	2.63	4.35	2.63	7.2	0.7	2.0	2.6	4.4	0.00
2008	ROU	AAA	24	1	0	1	8	3	23^2	21	0	5	15	74%	.284	1	1.10	1.52	3.55	1.99	8.3	0.4	2.0	4.0	8.9	0.84
2008	HOU	MLB	24	1	1	0	3	2	8	11	0	6	8	83%	.458	7	2.12	6.75	3.93	6.75	13.5	0.0	6.1	8.6	-1.0	0.36
2009	ROU	AAA	25	2	2	0	4	3	16^1	14	1	10	15	64%	.289	2	1.47	3.86	4.10	5.46	8.6	1.1	5.7	6.3	0.1	0.18
2009	HOU	MLB	25	2	1	0	42	0	45^2	49	1	19	39	68%	.333	4	1.49	3.35	3.88	4.12	9.0	0.2	3.1	6.1	7.2	0.72
2010	HOU	MLB	26	3	4	0	43	0	67	72	8	29	44	65%	.307	-9	1.50	4.90	4.48	5.16	9.6	1.0	3.5	5.3	2.5	0.82

Breakout: 10%   Improve: 32%   Collapse: 24%   Attrition: 13%   MLB: 58%   Comparables: Bob Apodaca, Mark Williamson, Tim Drummond, Carlos Reyes

Arias had a good season, although it wasn't without its fits and starts. He was taken to the hospital in June after being hit in the face by a ball in warm-ups, and his season eventually ended early due to knee surgery. But despite those setbacks, the smallish Arias worked his game, inducing ground ball after ground ball and posting solid K/BB numbers. His velocity was up a bit from 2008, and he used his breaking stuff far more than in the past—his leaving Colorado Springs probably had something to do with that. He won't be a dominant reliever unless he can miss a few more bats, but he should remain an effective spare part for the Astros in 2010.

Yorman Bazardo

Bats: R   Throws: R   Height: 6′ 2″   Weight: 220   Born: July 11, 1984   Age: 25

YEAR	TEAM	LVL	AGE	W	L	SV	G	GS	IP	H	HR	BB	SO	GB%	BABIP	STUFF	WHIP	ERA	SIERA	DERA	EqH9	EqHR9	EqBB9	EqSO9	VORP	SN/WX
2007	TOL	AAA	22	10	6	0	23	21	136^2	134	8	43	69	59%	.285	-3	1.30	3.75	4.77	5.42	9.9	1.1	3.0	3.3	1.1	1.20
2007	DET	MLB	22	2	1	0	11	2	23^2	19	2	5	15	52%	.239	14	1.01	2.28	4.20	2.66	6.8	0.8	1.5	5.3	7.5	0.32
2008	TOL	AAA	23	4	13	0	25	22	130	177	19	44	75	62%	.359	-48	1.70	6.72	4.65	7.90	13.4	2.2	3.4	3.7	-31.8	-2.71
2009	ROU	AAA	24	9	6	0	23	20	135	121	15	32	80	61%	.259	-6	1.13	3.20	4.23	3.94	8.8	1.6	2.3	4.2	21.9	2.05
2009	HOU	MLB	24	1	3	0	10	6	32	37	2	22	17	52%	.313	-19	1.84	7.87	5.76	8.51	9.5	0.5	5.1	3.8	-11.1	-0.34
2010	HOU	MLB	25	6	10	0	35	23	134	152	19	62	66	58%	.301	-17	1.59	5.41	5.24	5.70	10.1	1.3	3.9	4.1	-3.0	1.24

Breakout: 10%   Improve: 50%   Collapse: 11%   Attrition: 26%   MLB: 100%   Comparables: Virgil Vasquez, Marc Kaiser, David Pauley, Craig Stammen

Bazardo got his shot in the rotation when Hampton and Oswalt broke down late in the year, but he didn't make much of it, walking more men than he struck out and failing to record a quality start in six attempts. He'll only be 26 next year, so there's still time for something to click, but if Bazardo is going to have a career, it's looking more and more as if it will be as a reliever. And remember, he's not just Yorman Bazardo, he's everybody's Bazardo.

Doug Brocail

Bats: L   Throws: R   Height: 6' 5"   Weight: 250   Born: May 16, 1967   Age: 43

YEAR	TEAM	LVL	AGE	W	L	SV	G	GS	IP	H	HR	BB	SO	GB%	BABIP	STUFF	WHIP	ERA	SIERA	DERA	EqH9	EqHR9	EqBB9	EqSO9	VORP	SN/WX
2007	SDN	MLB	40	5	1	0	67	0	76²	66	8	24	43	48%	.240	-14	1.17	3.05	4.80	4.03	8.1	1.3	2.5	4.3	12.4	1.81
2008	HOU	MLB	41	7	5	2	72	0	68²	63	8	21	64	47%	.289	3	1.22	3.93	3.48	4.03	8.6	1.1	2.4	7.3	10.9	1.58
2009	HOU	MLB	42	1	0	0	20	0	17²	21	4	13	9	52%	.293	-24	1.92	4.58	5.94	4.58	10.2	2.0	5.6	3.6	1.8	0.16
2010	HOU	MLB	43	2	4	0	41	0	40²	45	6	16	25	49%	.305	-13	1.50	4.98	4.81	5.27	9.8	1.3	3.3	5.0	1.0	0.55

Breakout: 12%   Improve: 38%   Collapse: 32%   Attrition: 41%   MLB: 85%   Comparables: Mike Timlin, Don McMahon, Roberto Hernandez, Terry Mulholland

Coming off a solid two-year stretch, Brocail hit a big speed bump last year, spending most of the season on the DL and struggling with his command when he was healthy. If he wanted to hang up his spikes now, he'd have plenty to be proud of—over 600 big-league appearances in 15 seasons, plus countless returns from arm injuries, not to mention a 2006 angioplasty. The Astros declined his option for 2010, but the man's got more comebacks in him than a cat, and he's easier on the furniture.

Tim Byrdak

Bats: L   Throws: L   Height: 5' 11"   Weight: 195   Born: October 31, 1973   Age: 36

YEAR	TEAM	LVL	AGE	W	L	SV	G	GS	IP	H	HR	BB	SO	GB%	BABIP	STUFF	WHIP	ERA	SIERA	DERA	EqH9	EqHR9	EqBB9	EqSO9	VORP	SN/WX
2007	TOL	AAA	33	1	0	0	17	0	24¹	22	3	8	30	51%	.322	8	1.23	2.59	2.59	3.43	10.1	2.0	3.2	8.9	5.1	0.59
2007	DET	MLB	33	3	0	1	39	0	45	38	3	26	49	44%	.292	14	1.42	3.20	3.80	4.24	7.5	0.6	4.5	8.9	6.4	0.81
2008	HOU	MLB	34	2	1	0	59	0	55¹	45	10	29	47	50%	.235	-10	1.34	3.90	4.31	4.03	7.6	1.6	4.1	6.6	8.9	1.09
2009	HOU	MLB	35	1	2	0	76	0	61¹	39	10	36	58	45%	.188	0	1.22	3.23	4.19	3.43	5.6	1.6	4.3	6.9	14.5	-0.09
2010	HOU	MLB	36	3	4	0	52	0	51	49	7	28	46	47%	.298	-4	1.50	4.68	4.26	4.85	8.4	1.2	4.5	7.3	3.7	0.55

Breakout: 21%   Improve: 38%   Collapse: 40%   Attrition: 27%   MLB: 91%   Comparables: Bob McClure, Jeffrey Williams, Dae-Sung Koo, Ricardo Rincon

Byrdak has carved out something of a career for himself as a situational lefty, but those low ERAs owe a lot to his low BABIP, the lowest mark in baseball among pitchers with 60-plus innings last year, and he was among the leaders in 2008 as well. If he is used carefully, his strikeout rates are pretty solid, but he walks too many guys and doesn't keep the ball on the ground enough—cardinal sins for a lefty at Minute Maid Park. Don't expect this tightrope act to continue much longer, but for a guy who at one point went almost five years between big-league appearances, it should all be gravy at this point, anyway.

Jeff Fulchino

Bats: R   Throws: R   Height: 6' 5"   Weight: 250   Born: November 26, 1979   Age: 30

YEAR	TEAM	LVL	AGE	W	L	SV	G	GS	IP	H	HR	BB	SO	GB%	BABIP	STUFF	WHIP	ERA	SIERA	DERA	EqH9	EqHR9	EqBB9	EqSO9	VORP	SN/WX
2007	ABQ	AAA	27	6	2	0	16	16	88	108	13	39	55	45%	.318	-13	1.67	5.83	5.03	5.92	10.2	1.1	3.9	4.3	-4.1	-0.66
2008	OMA	AAA	28	3	4	5	25	5	61¹	71	2	27	53	54%	.361	-12	1.60	4.84	4.10	6.05	11.3	0.6	4.0	5.7	-3.6	-0.09
2008	KCA	MLB	28	0	1	0	12	0	14	21	2	8	12	60%	.388	-15	2.07	9.00	4.55	8.59	12.3	1.2	4.3	6.8	-5.0	-0.44
2009	HOU	MLB	29	6	4	0	61	0	82	70	7	27	71	53%	.276	9	1.18	3.40	3.70	3.71	7.4	0.9	2.5	6.5	16.2	1.17
2010	HOU	MLB	30	3	5	1	47	1	69¹	73	8	33	49	54%	.310	-8	1.54	4.82	4.64	5.14	9.5	1.1	3.9	5.8	2.8	0.57

Breakout: 20%   Improve: 57%   Collapse: 19%   Attrition: 17%   MLB: 61%   Comparables: David Weathers, Kyle Snyder, Ted Power, Tyler Walker

Claimed off waivers from the Royals in December '08, the Kerfeldian ginormous Fulchino turned in a surprisingly solid season out of the pen. He bounced between Houston and Round Rock several times during the early parts of the season, but finally stuck after being recalled in mid-May. Keep in mind, 2009 was Fulchino's first year as a full-time reliever—if he can repeat that performance going forward, the Astros might have found a hidden gem.

Sam Gervacio

Bats: R   Throws: R   Height: 6' 0"   Weight: 170   Born: January 10, 1985   Age: 25

YEAR	TEAM	LVL	AGE	W	L	SV	G	GS	IP	H	HR	BB	SO	GB%	BABIP	STUFF	WHIP	ERA	SIERA	DERA	EqH9	EqHR9	EqBB9	EqSO9	VORP	SN/WX
2007	SLM	A+	22	1	3	18	39	0	55¹	42	1	15	80	44%	.323	25	1.03	2.44	1.82	3.84	8.5	0.9	2.9	9.2	9.7	0.84
2007	CCH	AA	22	3	2	0	13	0	22²	15	1	11	24	43%	.264	12	1.15	1.99	3.41	3.27	7.4	0.9	4.8	7.8	5.1	0.84
2008	CCH	AA	23	2	5	5	47	0	65¹	69	8	26	82	44%	.365	-5	1.45	4.13	2.84	5.52	10.3	1.7	3.8	8.6	-0.1	-1.63
2009	ROU	AAA	24	2	2	0	39	0	52¹	43	5	21	58	44%	.277	-2	1.22	4.82	3.23	5.75	8.0	1.4	3.7	7.7	-1.4	0.00
2009	HOU	MLB	24	1	1	0	29	0	21	16	1	8	25	68%	.313	20	1.14	2.14	2.67	2.29	7.3	0.5	3.2	9.6	7.0	0.26
2010	HOU	MLB	25	4	5	3	59	0	72	72	9	32	69	40%	.317	2	1.44	4.57	3.88	4.81	8.8	1.1	3.7	7.7	5.5	0.99

Breakout: 17%   Improve: 54%   Collapse: 9%   Attrition: 7%   MLB: 65%   Comparables: Heath Haynes, Julian Heredia, Jesse Chavez, Gabe Molina

Gervacio had a terrific big-league debut, bringing his odd sidearm-ish delivery to Houston's bullpen for good in mid-August. On the surface, the results don't look like a fluke: he has consistently struck out more than a batter per inning and walked about 3.5 per nine over several levels. Still, many scouts question his sustainability: Is he getting guys out with his stuff, or his freak delivery? Will hitters catch up to him once they've seen him multiple times? Can his body hold up with that kind of motion? Stay tuned to this channel for breaking news.

Mike Hampton

Bats: R   Throws: L   Height: 5' 10"   Weight: 195   Born: September 9, 1972   Age: 37

YEAR	TEAM	LVL	AGE	W	L	SV	G	GS	IP	H	HR	BB	SO	GB%	BABIP	STUFF	WHIP	ERA	SIERA	DERA	EqH9	EqHR9	EqBB9	EqSO9	VORP	SN/WX
2008	ATL	MLB	35	3	4	0	13	13	78	83	10	28	38	61%	.287	-10	1.42	4.85	4.89	5.18	9.9	1.3	2.9	3.9	2.6	0.96
2009	HOU	MLB	36	7	10	0	21	21	112	128	13	46	74	61%	.320	-7	1.55	5.30	4.51	5.65	9.9	1.1	3.2	5.0	-1.9	0.89
2010	HOU	MLB	37	4	7	0	23	18	87²	103	12	37	51	62%	.318	-12	1.60	5.29	4.79	5.58	10.5	1.2	3.5	4.7	-0.8	0.91

Breakout: 8%   Improve: 41%   Collapse: 14%   Attrition: 10%   MLB: 96%   Comparables: Ed Lopat, Kenny Rogers, Jim Rooker, Harvey Haddix

For Hampton, the only surprise was that he made it all the way to August. After 21 starts—almost as many as he had made from 2005 to 2008 combined—Hampton's shoulder finally gave out. He suffered a full tear of the rotator cuff, along with some damage to the labrum. His performance was about as expected, better than that ugly ERA, but not quite good enough to generate any serious hopes for a player who will have missed three of the previous five seasons by the time 2011 rolls around. If we ever see Hampton on a major-league mound again, that will be an accomplishment in its own right.

LaTroy Hawkins

Bats: R   Throws: R   Height: 6' 5"   Weight: 215   Born: December 21, 1972   Age: 37

YEAR	TEAM	LVL	AGE	W	L	SV	G	GS	IP	H	HR	BB	SO	GB%	BABIP	STUFF	WHIP	ERA	SIERA	DERA	EqH9	EqHR9	EqBB9	EqSO9	VORP	SN/WX
2007	COL	MLB	34	2	5	0	62	0	55¹	52	6	16	29	73%	.264	-4	1.23	3.42	4.20	3.08	8.2	0.7	2.3	4.5	14.5	0.29
2008	NYA	MLB	35	1	1	0	33	0	41	42	3	17	23	56%	.300	-12	1.44	5.71	4.93	5.22	8.8	0.7	3.4	4.8	1.2	-0.41
2008	HOU	MLB	35	2	0	1	24	0	21	11	0	5	25	47%	.224	21	0.76	0.43	2.18	1.50	5.1	0.0	1.7	8.6	9.3	1.68
2009	HOU	MLB	36	1	4	11	65	0	63¹	60	7	16	45	55%	.280	0	1.20	2.13	4.02	2.45	8.2	1.2	1.9	5.3	21.1	1.68
2010	MIL	MLB	37	3	3	2	54	0	54¹	51	5	19	33	59%	.280	-5	1.30	3.89	4.53	4.31	8.7	0.9	2.9	4.9	7.2	0.65

Breakout: 20%   Improve: 44%   Collapse: 34%   Attrition: 22%   MLB: 92%   Comparables: Jim Corsi, Clay Carroll, Tim Worrell, Steve Reed

One of Wade's brag-worthy pickups, the durable Hawkins has had a minor renaissance since arriving in Houston. He wasn't as good as that 2.13 ERA would make him seem, but he posted his highest K/BB rate since 2004 and made his most appearances since 2005. And if there's ever a time to catch a break, it's in a walk year. At 37, he probably wasn't worth a multiyear deal, but the Brewers gave him a two-year contract for $7.5 million, hoping he could fill the bill as Trevor Hoffman's set-up man. We'll see if propinquity reinspires Wrigleyville's loathing.

Chia-Jen Lo

Bats: R   Throws: R   Height: 5' 11"   Weight: 181   Born: April 7, 1986   Age: 24

YEAR	TEAM	LVL	AGE	W	L	SV	G	GS	IP	H	HR	BB	SO	GB%	BABIP	STUFF	WHIP	ERA	SIERA	DERA	EqH9	EqHR9	EqBB9	EqSO9	VORP	SN/WX
2009	LNC	A+	23	1	0	1	12	0	25¹	10	1	13	36	50%	.196	23	0.91	1.78	2.30	2.70	4.6	1.2	5.4	8.5	7.3	0.54
2009	CCH	AA	23	0	2	2	30	0	39	30	1	20	39	49%	.274	7	1.28	2.31	3.85	3.49	7.4	0.7	4.4	7.0	8.6	0.58
2010	HOU	MLB	24	3	4	0	39	0	61	58	7	35	51	44%	.296	-3	1.53	4.85	4.57	5.08	8.4	1.1	4.8	6.9	2.8	1.73

Breakout: 4%   Improve: 15%   Collapse: 59%   Attrition: 2%   MLB: 5%   Comparables: Kevin Lynch, Mike Soper, Jeff Montgomery, Brennan Garr

The rare Far East add-on for the Astros is a sign of progress as far as Wade's willingness to start casting a wider net to shore up the farm system. A Taiwanese import who had starred on his country's Olympic squad, Lo made a solid stateside debut using an effective mix of low-90s heat, a sinker, and a few flavors of breakers and followed up his summer with a nice turn in the AFL. He needed to move fast, but he has so far, which gives him a shot at making the majors in 2010 if he continues to sling strikes at the upper levels.

Jordan Lyles

Bats: R | Throws: R | Height: 6' 4" | Weight: 185 | Born: October 19, 1990 | Age: 19

YEAR	TEAM	LVL	AGE	W	L	SV	G	GS	IP	H	HR	BB	SO	GB%	BABIP	STUFF	WHIP	ERA	SIERA	DERA	EqH9	EqHR9	EqBB9	EqSO9	VORP	SN/WX
2008	GRV	Rk	17	3	3	0	13	13	49²	44	4	10	64	47%	.315	14	1.09	3.99	2.20	6.65	10.5	2.4	3.4	6.0	-5.8	-0.62
2009	LEX	A	18	7	11	0	26	26	144²	134	5	38	167	45%	.342	6	1.19	3.24	2.67	5.76	11.8	1.9	3.9	6.0	-3.6	-0.85
2010	HOU	MLB	19	4	10	0	28	28	122²	150	22	60	91	43%	.336	29	1.71	6.19	4.74	6.53	11.0	1.6	4.1	6.1	-14.1	2.34

Breakout: 22% Improve: 66% Collapse: 11% Attrition: 3%   MLB: 1%   Comparables: Pat Mahomes, Storm Davis, John Mitchell, Edwin Correa

If there was any Astros prospect to get excited about last year, it was Lyles, who dominated Lexington in his full-season debut. A supplemental first-round pick in 2008, Lyles has a plus fastball and plus command, and it showed last season, as his K/BB rate approached 4.5. Even scarier: his ERA probably should have been about a run lower, as his defense beat him more often than the opposing hitters did. He'll have a couple of tough assignments ahead in Lancaster and Corpus Christi, but at 19, he has plenty of time.

Brian Moehler

Bats: R | Throws: R | Height: 6' 3" | Weight: 235 | Born: December 31, 1971 | Age: 38

YEAR	TEAM	LVL	AGE	W	L	SV	G	GS	IP	H	HR	BB	SO	GB%	BABIP	STUFF	WHIP	ERA	SIERA	DERA	EqH9	EqHR9	EqBB9	EqSO9	VORP	SN/WX
2007	HOU	MLB	35	1	4	1	42	0	59²	67	8	17	36	59%	.301	-11	1.41	4.07	4.49	4.02	9.7	1.2	2.3	4.9	9.8	-0.02
2008	HOU	MLB	36	11	8	0	31	26	150	166	20	36	82	49%	.287	-8	1.35	4.56	4.70	4.84	9.7	1.2	1.9	4.1	11.1	3.07
2009	HOU	MLB	37	8	12	0	29	29	154²	187	21	51	91	53%	.315	-11	1.54	5.47	4.76	5.79	10.1	1.3	2.5	4.3	-5.1	1.34
2010	HOU	MLB	38	6	9	0	40	22	126²	152	18	43	63	52%	.315	-17	1.53	5.16	5.06	5.50	10.7	1.3	2.8	4.1	0.0	0.98

Breakout: 9% Improve: 37% Collapse: 24% Attrition: 26%   MLB: 94%   Comparables: Mike Morgan, Cal McLish, Bob Forsch, Tim Belcher

Surely, most of you have skipped ahead by now to start reading about Roy Oswalt, or maybe the Royals, no? I mean, if Moehler's on your fantasy team, how deep is your league? Scuffy's your basic bit of veteran back-end rotation filler, better than his 2009 ERA, but not quite as good as his 2008 mark. He's probably worth having around, but not if he's going to push Bud Norris or Felipe Paulino out of the rotation. The Astros picked up his modest $3 million option for 2010, so he'll get at least one more go-round. At 38, he may very well be looking at his last.

Bud Norris

Bats: R | Throws: R | Height: 6' 0" | Weight: 195 | Born: March 2, 1985 | Age: 25

YEAR	TEAM	LVL	AGE	W	L	SV	G	GS	IP	H	HR	BB	SO	GB%	BABIP	STUFF	WHIP	ERA	SIERA	DERA	EqH9	EqHR9	EqBB9	EqSO9	VORP	SN/WX
2007	LEX	A	22	2	8	0	22	22	96²	85	8	41	117	55%	.316	1	1.30	4.75	2.99	6.52	9.8	1.7	4.5	7.2	-10.2	-0.76
2008	CCH	AA	23	3	8	0	19	19	80	89	8	31	84	51%	.365	-3	1.50	4.05	3.43	5.28	10.8	1.6	3.8	7.2	1.8	0.32
2009	ROU	AAA	24	4	9	0	19	19	120	104	6	53	112	52%	.293	15	1.31	2.62	3.83	3.68	8.5	0.9	4.1	6.7	23.3	1.99
2009	HOU	MLB	24	6	3	0	11	10	55²	59	9	25	54	42%	.316	5	1.51	4.53	3.89	4.66	9.3	1.6	3.4	7.2	5.2	1.26
2010	HOU	MLB	25	6	9	0	32	29	135	139	18	65	113	37%	.311	4	1.51	5.01	4.45	5.26	9.1	1.2	4.0	6.8	3.7	2.49

Breakout: 16% Improve: 44% Collapse: 9% Attrition: 20%   MLB: 76%   Comparables: Ron Mathis, Sam Lecure, Jeff Hartsock, Turk Wendell

Norris's debut was spectacular, given the modest expectations that attend most Astros prospects, as he started 10 games for the Astros in the final two months. He really turned on the jets in September, allowing just four runs in 23 innings pitched in his last four starts of the season, striking out 24 and walking six. Despite his lack of height and his chunky build, he has, thanks to a mid-90s fastball and an improving slider, put up solid K/BB numbers throughout his minor-league career. Rather than settle for genetic destiny as an undertall hurler, he has worked on his delivery to multiply the number of angles at which he comes at hitters, improving the tilt on his slider, and making his fastball that much more effective. He should be locked into a rotation spot starting now, regardless of the current master plan for world domination from the front office.

Roy Oswalt

Bats: R | Throws: R | Height: 6' 0" | Weight: 185 | Born: August 29, 1977 | Age: 32

YEAR	TEAM	LVL	AGE	W	L	SV	G	GS	IP	H	HR	BB	SO	GB%	BABIP	STUFF	WHIP	ERA	SIERA	DERA	EqH9	EqHR9	EqBB9	EqSO9	VORP	SN/WX
2007	HOU	MLB	29	14	7	0	33	32	212	221	14	60	154	62%	.307	22	1.33	3.18	4.04	3.23	8.9	0.6	2.2	5.8	53.9	6.86
2008	HOU	MLB	30	17	10	0	32	32	208²	199	23	47	165	58%	.285	16	1.18	3.54	3.68	3.98	8.7	1.1	1.8	6.1	34.6	5.49
2009	HOU	MLB	31	8	6	0	30	30	181¹	183	19	42	138	51%	.298	14	1.24	4.12	3.87	4.14	8.6	1.0	1.7	5.7	27.2	4.63
2010	HOU	MLB	32	11	11	0	32	31	189²	193	22	52	130	58%	.298	9	1.29	4.09	4.14	4.38	9.1	1.0	2.3	5.6	23.6	3.58

Breakout: 1% Improve: 36% Collapse: 12% Attrition: 8%   MLB: 100%   Comparables: Andy Ashby, Bob Porterfield, Dutch Leonard, Mike Boddicker

Oswalt reached the 30-start plateau for the sixth straight reason, but a degenerative disc in his back took a toll on him, particularly in the second half. As a result, his ERA topped 4.00 for the first time, and when the season ended, the Astros were seriously concerned about his health for 2010. On the bright side, his peripherals were pretty much in line with his 2007 and 2008 seasons, and he did manage to get through virtually the entire season before being shut down in late September. He'll have to become very serious about conditioning and stretching in order to stay on the field, but if he does, you can expect he'll provide additional reminders for the reason that not every right-hander has to stand 6-foot-4 to be a quality big-leaguer.

Felipe Paulino

Bats: R　Throws: R　Height: 6' 2"　Weight: 180　Born: October 5, 1983　Age: 26

YEAR	TEAM	LVL	AGE	W	L	SV	G	GS	IP	H	HR	BB	SO	GB%	BABIP	STUFF	WHIP	ERA	SIERA	DERA	EqH9	EqHR9	EqBB9	EqSO9	VORP	SN/WX
2007	CCH	AA	23	6	9	0	22	21	112	103	6	49	110	38%	.303	9	1.36	3.62	3.82	5.00	9.1	1.0	4.0	6.5	6.1	0.22
2007	HOU	MLB	23	2	1	0	5	3	19	22	5	7	11	60%	.274	-11	1.53	7.11	4.76	6.52	9.8	2.3	2.8	4.7	-2.2	0.28
2009	ROU	AAA	25	2	1	0	7	7	34²	30	1	23	29	61%	.282	8	1.53	3.12	4.54	3.80	8.1	0.5	5.8	5.8	6.5	0.68
2009	HOU	MLB	25	3	11	0	23	17	97²	126	20	37	93	48%	.361	-21	1.67	6.27	3.80	6.66	11.5	2.0	2.9	7.2	-12.4	0.36
2010	HOU	MLB	26	4	7	0	33	6	101	113	14	49	74	46%	.321	-8	1.61	5.23	4.70	5.56	10.1	1.2	4.0	6.0	-0.7	1.08

Breakout: 25%　Improve: 49%　Collapse: 23%　Attrition: 14%　　MLB: 67%　　Comparables: Carlos Torres, Steve Finch, Russell McDonald, Jim Gutierrez

Paulino is an interesting case. That hideous ERA was caused more by an outlandishly high balls in play average than by Paulino himself; add in a high rate of fly balls becoming home runs, and what you have is either a remarkably unfortunate pitcher or the Cookie Monster's best-ever enabler. As a starter, Paulino's peripherals were good: 87 innings pitched, 81 strikeouts, 29 walks. A converted shortstop with liquid flame for heat and a power curve, he missed almost all of 2008 with a plethora of arm problems and he only pitched 35 career innings at Triple-A, so there's not much else to go by. Don't be fooled by the record and the runs allowed; the book on Paulino has yet to be written, but the raw material is a great start, and not just for cookie dough.

Wandy Rodriguez

Bats: R　Throws: L　Height: 5' 11"　Weight: 180　Born: January 18, 1979　Age: 31

YEAR	TEAM	LVL	AGE	W	L	SV	G	GS	IP	H	HR	BB	SO	GB%	BABIP	STUFF	WHIP	ERA	SIERA	DERA	EqH9	EqHR9	EqBB9	EqSO9	VORP	SN/WX
2007	HOU	MLB	28	9	13	0	31	31	182²	179	22	62	158	48%	.293	15	1.32	4.58	3.84	4.64	8.5	1.1	2.7	6.9	17.5	4.14
2008	HOU	MLB	29	9	7	0	25	25	137¹	136	14	44	131	46%	.310	16	1.31	3.54	3.51	4.38	9.1	0.9	2.5	7.3	16.9	3.39
2009	HOU	MLB	30	14	12	0	33	33	205²	192	21	63	193	51%	.302	22	1.24	3.02	3.44	3.45	8.2	1.0	2.4	7.1	45.9	6.91
2010	HOU	MLB	31	10	10	0	31	31	177¹	179	21	61	136	48%	.303	11	1.35	4.23	4.13	4.47	9.0	1.1	2.9	6.3	20.2	3.28

Breakout: 6%　Improve: 36%　Collapse: 17%　Attrition: 12%　　MLB: 100%　　Comparables: Kenny Rogers, Earl Whitehill, Jimmy Key, Larry French

Sometimes, it all just comes together. Rodriguez has drastically improved in each of the last four seasons, as all of his major statistical categories (K/9, BB/9, ERA, SIERA, or FIP) keep moving in the right directions. He was without question the Astros' best starter last year—including Oswalt—and one of the 10 best in the National League. If there's been a change in his repertoire, it's that he's become more reliant on his curveball in recent years, but the biggest differences seem simply to be better control and improved sequencing. Corporate Juice Beverage Ballpark is always going to be tough on lefties, but there's no reason to think that Rodriguez shouldn't be a frontline starter again in 2010.

Chris Sampson

Bats: R　Throws: R　Height: 6' 1"　Weight: 190　Born: May 23, 1978　Age: 32

YEAR	TEAM	LVL	AGE	W	L	SV	G	GS	IP	H	HR	BB	SO	GB%	BABIP	STUFF	WHIP	ERA	SIERA	DERA	EqH9	EqHR9	EqBB9	EqSO9	VORP	SN/WX
2007	HOU	MLB	29	7	8	0	24	19	121²	138	20	30	51	57%	.285	-14	1.38	4.59	5.05	4.36	9.8	1.5	2.0	3.5	15.1	2.35
2008	HOU	MLB	30	6	4	0	54	11	117¹	118	8	23	61	61%	.287	-2	1.20	4.22	4.39	4.76	9.1	0.6	1.6	4.0	9.3	2.82
2009	HOU	MLB	31	4	2	3	49	0	55¹	66	2	21	33	61%	.333	-11	1.57	5.04	4.67	5.38	10.0	0.3	2.9	4.3	0.7	0.79
2010	HOU	MLB	32	4	5	1	57	4	75²	86	10	26	34	58%	.301	-18	1.48	4.83	5.12	5.21	10.3	1.1	2.9	3.6	2.4	1.06

Breakout: 12%　Improve: 48%　Collapse: 20%　Attrition: 28%　　MLB: 89%　　Comparables: Vern Ruhle, Bruce Dal Canton, Frank Hiller, Mark Petkovsek

For the first time in his career, Sampson was a full-time reliever. It's not a bad role for him—he generally throws strikes and keeps the ball on the ground regardless of when he comes into the game, but his strikeout rate is a bit more respectable as a reliever. His former rubber-armed rep is belied by his making a trip to the DL around the All-

Star break, and his walk rate jumped; the Astros lost their patience and sent him down in August, but if he can bring his free passes back down to previous levels, and if the defense behind him can turn a few more balls in play into outs, he could resume being a middle-relief sponge, bound for whatever branch campus of the Hall of Utility is named for Gene Nelson.

Ross Seaton

Bats: L   Throws: R   Height: 6' 4"   Weight: 190   Born: September 18, 1989   Age: 20

YEAR	TEAM	LVL	AGE	W	L	SV	G	GS	IP	H	HR	BB	SO	GB%	BABIP	STUFF	WHIP	ERA	SIERA	DERA	EqH9	EqHR9	EqBB9	EqSO9	VORP	SN/WX
2009	LEX	A	19	8	10	0	24	24	136²	137	11	39	88	41%	.289	-29	1.29	3.29	4.50	7.29	12.0	2.8	4.1	2.8	-24.1	-1.30
2010	HOU	MLB	20	3	9	0	22	22	107¹	147	22	56	36	43%	.322	3	1.88	7.24	6.30	7.65	12.2	1.8	4.3	2.8	-25.6	1.42

Breakout: 22%   Improve: 67%   Collapse: 11%   Attrition: 7%   MLB: 0%   Comparables: Michael McClain, Jake Dittler, Steven Shell, J.M. Gold

Seaton was a third-round pick in 2008, one the Astros felt was worth an above-slot $700,000 bonus. He's a big, projectable righty, but he didn't get many strikeouts at Lexington. He wasn't bad, as his other numbers attest, but whereas Lyles, his younger teammate, blew away hitters to the tune of 10.4 K/9, Seaton settled for just 5.8. His velocity is still a bit below average, and he'll need to start using his curve or slider as an out pitch if he wants to put hitters away. He'll probably head to Lancaster, which usually isn't a fun assignment for pitch-to-contact guys.

Polin Trinidad

Bats: L   Throws: L   Height: 6' 3"   Weight: 170   Born: November 19, 1984   Age: 25

YEAR	TEAM	LVL	AGE	W	L	SV	G	GS	IP	H	HR	BB	SO	GB%	BABIP	STUFF	WHIP	ERA	SIERA	DERA	EqH9	EqHR9	EqBB9	EqSO9	VORP	SN/WX
2007	LEX	A	22	6	8	0	23	23	131¹	118	16	35	120	48%	.283	-10	1.16	4.18	3.41	5.21	9.9	2.3	3.2	5.4	3.8	-0.36
2007	SLM	A+	22	2	1	0	4	4	25²	23	4	3	23	35%	.268	15	1.01	2.81	3.10	4.56	9.9	3.0	1.5	5.7	2.5	0.48
2008	SLM	A+	23	4	2	0	10	10	62	46	2	11	34	43%	.228	5	0.92	2.32	4.41	3.41	7.4	0.9	2.0	3.0	13.8	0.98
2008	CCH	AA	23	6	5	0	18	18	107¹	109	13	21	75	44%	.287	-4	1.21	3.61	4.02	4.44	9.1	1.6	2.1	4.4	12.4	0.57
2009	CCH	AA	24	7	5	1	13	12	82²	87	7	10	53	46%	.304	-4	1.17	2.94	3.97	4.60	10.4	1.6	1.4	4.7	7.8	0.44
2009	ROU	AAA	24	6	5	0	13	12	87¹	90	18	25	59	42%	.262	-28	1.32	4.53	4.44	5.28	9.8	2.6	2.6	4.5	2.1	0.24
2010	HOU	MLB	25	6	10	0	33	26	139²	154	22	46	79	36%	.298	-9	1.43	4.90	5.07	5.18	9.9	1.4	2.8	4.7	4.9	2.65

Breakout: 5%   Improve: 42%   Collapse: 20%   Attrition: 23%   MLB: 13%   Comparables: Gary Rath, Rick Krivda, John Courtright, Robert Rohrbaugh

Trinidad is a Dominican (no Tobago TBNL) gifted with excellent control, as he's walked less than two men per nine in his minor-league career. Whether that will translate to the big leagues is another story—he doesn't miss a lot of bats, and his ground-ball rates aren't as high as you'd like for a finesse lefty heading to Minute Maid Park. However, he's been pitching to contact all along, rolling with the outcomes, so if there's one thing that could be improved, it's sharpening his off-speed stuff. He'll head back to Round Rock to start the year, but don't be surprised to see him in Houston's rotation at some point.

Jose Valverde

Bats: R   Throws: R   Height: 6' 4"   Weight: 255   Born: July 24, 1979   Age: 30

YEAR	TEAM	LVL	AGE	W	L	SV	G	GS	IP	H	HR	BB	SO	GB%	BABIP	STUFF	WHIP	ERA	SIERA	DERA	EqH9	EqHR9	EqBB9	EqSO9	VORP	SN/WX
2007	ARI	MLB	27	1	4	47	65	0	64¹	46	7	26	78	41%	.258	27	1.12	2.66	2.82	2.64	6.3	0.7	3.2	9.6	20.5	4.34
2008	HOU	MLB	28	6	3	44	74	0	72	62	10	23	83	40%	.281	11	1.18	3.37	2.85	3.59	7.9	1.2	2.5	8.7	15.4	2.74
2009	HOU	MLB	29	4	2	25	52	0	54	40	5	21	56	41%	.259	14	1.13	2.33	3.31	2.62	6.6	0.8	3.0	7.8	17.1	2.94
2010	HOU	MLB	30	4	4	37	62	0	60²	51	6	26	62	40%	.292	11	1.27	3.78	3.49	3.94	7.5	0.9	3.5	8.4	10.5	2.13

Breakout: 14%   Improve: 34%   Collapse: 29%   Attrition: 3%   MLB: 96%   Comparables: Armando Benitez, Rich Gossage, Troy Percival, Dick Radatz

Like Hawkins, Valverde timed his luck perfectly, putting up his best ERA in six years right before hitting the free-agent market. In reality, Valverde actually slipped a bit last year, as his SIERA suggests. His strikeout rate was down and his walk rate was up, but those were canceled out by a fortuitously low BABIP. He's still a pretty good closer in a world that values pretty good closers as worthy of eight-figure salaries (a pity no royalty for inventing the save goes to the estate of the late Jerome Holtzman), and he's managed to work a reputation for fragility into the background, even with last year's trip to the DL with a calf problem in June.

Wesley Wright

| | | | | | | | | | | Bats: R | Throws: L | | Height: 5' 11" | | Weight: 160 | | Born: January 28, 1985 | | Age: 25 |

YEAR	TEAM	LVL	AGE	W	L	SV	G	GS	IP	H	HR	BB	SO	GB%	BABIP	STUFF	WHIP	ERA	SIERA	DERA	EqH9	EqHR9	EqBB9	EqSO9	VORP	SN/WX
2007	JAX	AA	22	6	2	2	30	1	61¹	45	4	31	68	47%	.265	6	1.24	2.49	3.43	3.76	8.0	1.4	4.6	6.6	11.4	0.24
2007	LVG	AAA	22	1	2	0	14	1	16²	28	4	18	18	43%	.471	-3	2.76	9.18	5.16	11.53	14.6	2.3	9.6	7.9	-10.7	-0.92
2008	HOU	MLB	23	4	3	1	71	0	55²	45	8	34	57	45%	.252	2	1.42	5.01	4.09	5.56	7.5	1.3	4.6	7.6	-0.4	0.70
2009	ROU	AAA	24	2	1	0	13	1	19	13	0	10	18	60%	.255	4	1.21	3.32	3.86	3.86	6.8	0.5	4.8	6.8	3.4	0.32
2009	HOU	MLB	24	3	4	0	49	0	44²	53	9	25	47	44%	.358	-10	1.75	5.44	3.92	5.40	10.8	2.1	4.4	8.1	0.5	-0.13
2010	HOU	MLB	25	3	5	0	61	0	62²	64	8	35	57	45%	.317	-6	1.59	5.17	4.34	5.34	9.0	1.2	4.6	7.3	1.1	0.37

Breakout: 19%   Improve: 40%   Collapse: 16%   Attrition: 11%   MLB: 90%   Comparables: Jesus Pena, Luis Arroyo, Dave Meads, Ricardo Jordan

It was a very up-and-down season for Wright, and not just because he spent much of it traveling from Houston to Round Rock and back. On the positive side, he decreased his walk rate, improving on the biggest weakness in his game. On the not-so-positive side, he spent a month on the DL after being rushed to the hospital with dehydration in late July, and he continued to get beaten senseless by the long ball. The latter problem isn't going away: he's a left-handed fly-ball pitcher in a stadium where left-handed fly-ball pitchers go to die. There's still plenty of potential here, but he'll need to find a way to keep the ball on the ground if he wants to have a long future in Houston.

LINEOUTS

Hitters

PLAYER	TEAM	LVL	AGE	PA	R	2B	3B	HR	RBI	BB	SO	SB-CS	EqBRR	AVG/OBP/SLG	EqAVG/EqOBP/EqSLG	EqA	VORP	WARP
OF R. Abercrombie	ROU	AAA	28	557	64	28	6	11	52	29	159	26-10	-2.3	.271/.314/.412	.229/.266/.340	.212	-16.9	-1.5
UT A. Boone	HOU	MLB	36	14	0	0	0	0	0	0	2	0-0	-1.2	.000/.071/.000	.077/.143/.077	-.210	-3.5	-0.4
INF M. Kata#	ROU	AAA	31	244	22	10	1	2	22	12	25	8-0	1.5	.269/.313/.348	.248/.284/.326	.218	-4.0	-1.6
	HOU	MLB	31	52	2	1	0	0	5	0	5	1-0	0.7	.200/.212/.220	.180/.192/.200	.140	-5.3	-0.2
LF A. Locke	CCH	AA	26	558	81	31	3	20	109	46	84	2-2	-1.3	.338/.389/.531	.284/.324/.433	.261	10.5	0.1
INF E. Maysonet	ROU	AAA	27	217	21	11	0	1	14	26	39	3-0	0.2	.235/.330/.310	.219/.301/.276	.211	-3.7	-0.2
	HOU	MLB	27	79	9	2	0	1	7	5	19	0-0	-0.6	.290/.333/.362	.300/.342/.371	.258	1.7	0.4
OF Y. Ramirez	ROU	AAA	24	477	41	22	1	11	47	11	64	14-8	-3.0	.256/.275/.381	.241/.259/.359	.211	-11.9	1.3
1B M. Saccomanno	ROU	AAA	29	539	67	23	5	15	67	34	87	5-0	-0.3	.278/.329/.436	.251/.294/.377	.235	-13.8	-3.2
INF J. Smith*	ROU	AAA	31	285	32	6	2	6	28	13	83	11-2	0.7	.198/.242/.305	.184/.219/.270	.170	-16.5	-1.1
	HOU	MLB	31	27	1	0	0	0	1	0	9	0-0	-0.1	.000/.000/.000	.080/.077/.240	-.213	-6.6	-0.8
OF T. Steele	LNC	A+	22	208	41	11	8	5	40	9	40	8-6	-1.2	.345/.385/.562	.273/.303/.424	.247	1.6	0.2
SS W. Sutil	CCH	AA	24	536	77	21	0	1	37	44	42	19-13	-1.2	.273/.348/.324	.255/.313/.306	.222	0.5	-1.7
2B J. Vallejo#	FRI	AA	22	89	13	3	1	0	10	4	14	7-1	1.5	.289/.318/.349	.274/.295/.333	.229	-0.5	-0.3
	OKL	AAA	22	334	32	7	5	2	28	22	73	3-2	-2.5	.233/.282/.307	.221/.266/.288	.193	-11.6	-1.9

Reggie Abercrombie walked in over five percent of his plate appearances for the first time in nine years. ⊘ Originally signed to be Blum's platoon partner at third, **Aaron Boone** underwent heart surgery last March, after doctors determined he needed his aortic valve removed. He fought his way back, but retirement's expected. How you remember him probably depends on where you're from; he could marry a Kennedy, and he still wouldn't be welcome in Boston. ⊘ **Matt Kata** briefly made it back to the big leagues, but spent most of his year hacking away at Round Rock. ⊘ Far too old to be a prospect, Dodgers refugee **Andrew Locke** went 20/20 in homers and GDPs in his first year at Double-A. ⊘ **Edwin Maysonet** had three big-league stints in '09, and can play all four infield positions—or all eight nonpitcher positions, as Cecil Cooper claimed—which isn't quite enough to stick. ⊘ **Yordany Ramirez** gets great marks for his outfield defense, but hits like Rey Ordonez on Valium. ⊘ **Mark Saccomanno** continues to play just well enough to keep his gig in Round Rock, a city named by *Money* magazine as the "seventh-best American city to live in," which has to be nice for him after three seasons there. ⊘ **Jason Smith** led the league in DFA/Hit ratio, as he was designated for assignment twice before getting a hit; he'll be 33 in July, so every opportunity is a break for him from here on out. ⊘ Athletic **T. J. Steele** put up huge numbers at Lancaster—shocking, we know—in an injury-shortened season. He'll have to prove himself next year, but he's an outstanding glove type with fourth outfielder possibilities. ⊘ If Tommy Manzella comes up short at short, Venezuelan **Wladimir Sutil** is a step behind with his brand of aggressive ineffectiveness. ⊘ **Jose Vallejo** was the player to be named in the Pudge swap; he has lots of glovely qualities, but none of them involve hitting.

Pitchers

PLAYER	TEAM	LVL	AGE	W	L	SV	IP	H	HR	BB	SO	GB%	BABIP	STUFF	WHIP	ERA	SIERA	DERA	EqH9	EqHR9	EqBB9	EqSO9	VORP
F. Abad*	LNC	A+	23	4	6	6	82²	78	8	8	79	34%	.304	-4	1.04	4.14	2.77	5.11	8.5	1.5	1.6	5.2	3.5
	CCH	AA	23	0	1	0	14	12	1	3	13	49%	.275	14	1.07	3.21	3.21	5.27	8.6	1.3	2.0	6.6	0.4
B. Backe	HOU	MLB	31	0	0	0	13	21	5	6	10	35%	.364	-27	2.08	10.38	4.87	10.38	13.8	3.5	3.5	5.5	-7.1
T. Bushue	AST	Rk	18	1	0	0	22¹	18	2	5	19	0%	.258	19	1.03	2.42	3.42	4.66	10.2	3.7	3.7	4.2	1.8
R. Corcoran	SEA	MLB	29	2	0	0	19	25	2	17	6	71%	.354	-28	2.21	6.16	6.22	5.79	14.3	1.1	8.3	2.8	-0.5
	ROU	AAA	29	0	0	0	19²	24	0	7	11	61%	.353	-23	1.58	4.12	4.74	6.14	11.8	0.5	3.4	3.9	-1.3
C. Daigle	ROU	AAA	28	4	3	5	55²	61	3	25	53	52%	.349	-7	1.54	2.91	3.89	3.63	10.6	1.0	4.1	6.8	11.1
E. Englebrook	CCH	AA	27	2	0	9	25²	19	2	9	16	58%	.224	-18	1.09	3.16	4.42	4.93	7.3	1.5	3.3	4.4	1.6
B. James	CCH	AA	25	2	10	0	107²	127	10	62	55	58%	.315	-38	1.76	6.69	5.42	8.06	11.4	1.7	5.1	3.4	-29.4
W. Lopez	CCH	AA	25	4	5	0	110¹	133	8	13	69	62%	.331	-18	1.32	4.73	3.95	5.83	11.4	1.4	1.4	4.3	-3.9
	HOU	MLB	25	0	2	0	19¹	32	4	8	9	66%	.373	-35	2.07	8.38	5.07	9.61	13.7	1.8	3.2	3.2	-9.0
M. Nevarez	HIC	A	22	1	4	9	35	22	1	15	50	48%	.269	4	1.06	2.83	2.37	5.29	8.1	1.4	5.3	7.8	0.8
B. Sadler	FRE	AAA	27	5	3	0	55²	64	4	29	51	48%	.357	-2	1.67	5.34	4.21	5.77	11.0	1.0	4.8	6.6	-1.6
H. Villar	LEX	A	22	3	4	5	90	80	6	18	109	52%	.319	-21	1.09	2.60	2.35	5.92	11.5	2.5	3.2	6.3	-3.7

Fernando Abad survived the Lancaster experience with strike-throwing precision and a willingness to work inside, so even with his fly-ball tendencies, he might be the perfectly prefabricated southpaw for Minute Maid. ⊘ Always a bit overrated, **Brandon Backe** finally ran out of chances, getting DFA'd in June; he has either been injured, ineffective, or both for at least four years running, and he'll be trying to come back from a partially torn rotator cuff. ⊘ **Tanner Bushue** was Houston's second pick in last year's draft; he's a big, projectable righty, but was generally considered an overdraft. He won't turn 19 until June, so this one's just getting started. ⊘ Ground-baller **Roy Corcoran** had a decent year for the Mariners in 2008, but he struggled last year and didn't exactly light up the PCL when the Astros put him in Round Rock. ⊘ **Casey Daigle**, AKA Mr. Jenny Finch, had his second straight solid season as a Triple-A reliever. As the 12th guy out of the bullpen, you could do a lot worse than to be married to Jenny Finch. ⊘ Added to the 40-man roster after six seasons in the bushes, sinkerballer **Evan Englebrook** is 6-foot-8 and … well, he's 6-foot-8, and fear of the Rule 5 draft is such that all sorts get put on the 40-man. ⊘ Sinkerballer **Brad James** avoided injuries to put in his third consecutive poor showing at Double-A, which should finally push him to the pen. ⊘ **Wilton Lopez** throws strikes and gets lots of ground balls, but his strikeout rate could depress Judd Apatow. ⊘ Part of the payment for Pudge, **Matt Nevarez** throws hard, which is what you could say about him when he was drafted five years ago, before injuries cost him all of 2006 and 2007; last year marked his full-season debut, and he's seen as closer-worthy. ⊘ **Billy Sadler** throws hard and has pretty good stuff, but still has no conception of how to throw strikes. ⊘ Short Dominican **Henry Villar**—on the theory everyone under 6 feet is short—had an outstanding full-season debut, showing off a nice power assortment to pitch his way onto the 40-man.

MANAGER: CECIL COOPER/DAVE CLARK

YEAR	MGR	W-L	Pythag +/-	Avg PC	100+ P	120+ P	QS	BQS	REL	REL w Zero R	IBB	Subs	PH	PH Avg	PH HR	SB2	CS2	SB3	CS3	SAC Att	SAC %	POS SAC	Squeeze	Swing	In Play
2008	C.C.	86-75	9	90.0	45	1	67	4	488	325	53	69	252	.233	7	103	46	10	5	90	63.3%	32	2	125	92
2009	C.C.	70-79	6	91.6	50	3	68	3	449	275	53	43	237	.209	1	99	33	8	8	89	69.7%	33	0	117	85
2009	D.C.	4-9	1	85.8	3	0	3	0	48	32	3	4	28	.077	0	4	2	0	1	6	66.7%	3	0	9	7

Cooper was the victim of his own good luck. The Astros won 86 games in 2008, beating just about any reasonable expectation. The team was never actually that good; it should have been somewhere in the mid-70s, based on its run differential. Drayton McLane and Ed Wade probably never knew that, though, and fully expected the team to compete for a playoff spot in 2009, even with replacement-level talent making up almost half the roster. Having been dealt an impossible hand, Cooper inevitably took the fall, officially getting the axe on September 22. He'll be replaced by long-time Red Sox bench coach Brad Mills, who will be going from a powerful, laissez-faire offense to one that needs every last run squeezed out of it. Expect him to be a bit less bunt-happy than Cooper but far more active than his old boss, Terry Francona. He'll need some luck, but hopefully not so much as to raise the always trigger-happy McLane's expectations beyond reality.

Kansas City Royals

There's one figure that sticks out in every recap of the Royals 2009 season: 18-11. That was the Royals' record at the end of the day on Thursday, May 7th. They were in first place, three games up on the Tigers, and were on a six-game winning streak that included two-game sweeps over the White Sox and the Mariners at home. This was the largest first-place lead that the Royals had enjoyed since August 17, 2003. Desperate fans were already starting to think playoffs, examining the Tigers' schedule to determine which team had the advantage and wondering if they had the minor-league pieces to make a play for Roy Halladay at the trade deadline.

As the Royals boarded the plane that evening for a West Coast trip, they also appeared to have the top pitching staff in the league, with Gil Meche and Zack Greinke providing a formidable one-two punch. Joakim Soria was still money in the bank, though struggling to stay healthy enough to get in the game. Given that Kyle Farnsworth had already blown three games, some were thinking that the Royals should have been up even more. With the Royals' great run at the end of 2008, they were an impressive 36-19 since September 1, 2008. No other team in the AL Central was above .500, and only the Dodgers had a better record since that date in all of baseball.

Fans starved of success could be forgiven for small-sample enthusiasm (many a miserable team has found it within itself to put together a winning month) and for believing that maybe, just maybe, the Royals had found the winning combination. The next immediate step was a weekend series against the struggling Angels at the Big A, but a series win seemed likely since Meche and Greinke would start the first two games. But then Meche lost, and the next day Greinke lost a 1-0 duel against Joe Saunders. On Sunday, thanks in part to Jamey Wright's implosion in the seventh, the Royals suffered their first sweep of the season. They proceeded to win only *two* of their next thirty-four series.

During that subsequent four-month stretch, many of Dayton Moore's questionable off-season moves were scrutinized further. Moore had traded two top relievers from the previous year, Ramon Ramirez and Leo Nunez, for Mike Jacobs and Coco Crisp. In 2009, Ramirez and Nunez had a combined 29.0 VORP (and +2.837 WXRL) with the Red Sox and Marlins, respectively, and were paid $856,000. Jacobs and Crisp had a combined 0.4 VORP for the Royals and were paid $9.36 million total. To replace Ramirez and Nunez, the Royals decided they needed to resort to the free-agent market, picked up Farnsworth and Juan Cruz (2.4 VORP but a -1.574 WXRL), and paid them $6.5 million. Looking at that circle of deals in isolation, the Royals paid a net of $15 million more to get substantively worse, by 26.2 VORP. It gets worse when one compares how well Nunez and Ramirez pitched in high-leverage situations to Farnsworth's meltdowns, because that would have had an even greater impact, but after a few million and a few wins' worth of value out the window, who's counting?

Moore pulled off one of the biggest midseason head-scratchers when he traded Dan Cortes, one of the Royals' top preseason pitching prospects, for Yuniesky Betancourt, the underachieving Mariners shortstop with a liberally overcompensatory contract. To be fair, Cortes was struggling with his control and had just been charged with disorderly conduct, but the Dayton Moore honeymoon was now officially over. For his first

ROYALS PROSPECTUS
2009 W-L: 65-97, 4th (tied) in AL Central

Pythag	70-92	13th	**Ballpark:** Kauffman Stadium (3-yr. PF: 1026). Lovely and unique, and slightly hitter-friendly for everything but homers
RS/G	4.2	13th	
RA/G	5.2	12th	
EqA	.246	13th	**2009:** With added veterans, their ambitions exceeded their grasp; another menu of Greinke or beatings
EqBRR	-8.8	12th	
SNWP	.501	10th	
WXRL	2.39	13th	
FRAr	5.34	14th	**2010:** That grasp thing? They have arms aplenty, but their reach hasn't improved yet
DE	.675	14th	
PADE	-1.69	12th	
Salary	$70.5	9th	**Action Items:** Young pitchers must turn the corner; sort out the infield and finding a CF
Attend	1.8	12th	

two years, despite an occasional tiff here and there, Moore had the benefit of a happy marriage with the Royals' fan base. In this third year, the gloves came off.

When Moore became the Royals' general manager in 2006, it was the baseball equivalent of those teen comedies where the plain Jane goes to the prom with the homecoming king; he had that air of being way too attractive for his current dance partner. Hired by arguably one of the worst-run franchises of the last 20 years, Moore was considered one of the top GM candidates in the industry and had even been wooed by the much more popular Boston Red Sox—baseball's ultimate stuck-up cheerleader franchise—when Theo Epstein was temporarily not their general manager. When Moore came to town, he said all the right things that made knees buckle and fans swoon. In one of his first interviews with the Kansas City media, he talked about Country Club Plaza, the part of town where he wanted the World Series Championship parade to be, and sent away underachievers like Ambiorix Burgos, Andy Sisco, Mike MacDougal, and Jeremy Affeldt, clearing out the teasing friends and acquaintances that provided potential good times, but really only caused emotional duress.

It was a promising start given the inertia that had held back the franchise for years, but by year three, the warning signs of a failed relationship were obvious to all:

Warning Sign 1: The two of you bicker in public a great deal. In general, fans had been excited about Dayton Moore and, to a lesser extent, Trey Hillman. With consistent improvement every year of Moore's tenure, fans expected that it was going to continue; with the 10-game drop in the Royals won-loss record in 2009, even wishful thinking fell by the wayside. Overly sensitive Royals management (including Moore and Hillman) fired back at the Royals' own fans, complaining that the people didn't "trust the Process" and were too focused on their own "instant gratification."

Warning Sign 2: You don't trust one another, and you feel suspicious. In another bizarre turn of events, the Royals front office was enraged when BP cofounder and eternal Royals optimist Rany Jazayerli wrote a harsh criticism of the Royals' medical staff, and specifically head trainer Nick Swartz. Jazayerli pointed out a disturbing trend at work in 2009: numerous Royals who were seemingly only slightly hurt were told to rest for a few days, went back on the field, and were quickly sent to the DL with serious injuries. The Royals boycotted Jazayerli's radio show on a local KC station, not allowing

any of their staff to appear, and threatened to cut off other members of the media who did. The Royals eventually relented, but the damage had been done.

Warning Sign 3: You can't agree on goals and values. In an interview to justify the trade for Betancourt, Moore said that he didn't really understand many of the newer defensive statistics and that it is obvious who is good and who isn't when you watch baseball every day. Despite previous statements touting the importance of on-base percentage, the trades for Jacobs and Betancourt and a contract extension to Miguel Olivo seemed hypocritical. This created a feeling that the statistics revolution in baseball had completely bypassed the Royals and that they were decades behind other teams. Former *Kansas City Star* columnist Joe Posnanski expressed the dilemma of many Royals fan when he wrote of the difficulty of rooting for a team whose organizational philosophy seems totally against what you believe.

Warning Sign 4: You fight about money. For any franchise that does not make the playoffs, there will always be grumbling from fans about salaries being paid to certain players. In Kansas City, however, many complained about another money issue: ticket prices. Despite not even sniffing the postseason in 23 years, the Royals had the third-highest percentage increase (13.3 percent) in average ticket prices, trailing only the Yankees and Mets, teams that had moved into completely new stadiums.

Warning Sign 5: You no longer have fun together. Even though the Royals had three 100-loss seasons in recent memory, 2009 was perhaps the most arduous season yet from a fan perspective. Expectations were for a possible division title in the very weak AL Central, or at least meaningful games in September for the first time in six years. By the end of June, the Royals were out of it again, with the only two really interesting stories being Zack Greinke's run at a Cy Young Award and the emergence of Billy Butler as a possible star.

In the end, can this marriage be saved? Does a troubled marriage between the Royals and their fans even matter? It will if fans stop coming to the ballpark in the coming years. For all of the Royals' disappointments this past season, all will be forgiven if the team can show progress and get back on the track that Moore had been on previously. Like a spouse apologizing after a bitter squabble, Moore has belatedly admitted that what happened in 2009 didn't work, that it wasn't only the injuries, and maybe "the Process" needed some tweaking. Golly, talk about being the last one to notice.

To that end, there are three major areas where the Royals need to make drastic improvements to even be close to competing for a division title: the bullpen, the offense, and the defense. The Royals could even use some improvement in the starting rotation (who couldn't?), but with Greinke, a possible rebound by Meche, and a collection of interesting kids on the way, this area seems less crucial than the others.

The Royals bullpen's Fair Run Average of 5.78 was last in the American League. With one of the best closers in the game, the bullpen woes are solely in setup and middle relief, where no one did well. In Farnsworth and Cruz, the Royals have two expensive pieces that will, unfortunately, be fixtures. The problem is that beyond Carlos Rosa, there isn't a lot of talent in the high-minors.

The bullpen picture is bleak, but the prospects for a short-term turnaround by the offense are even darker. At three of the nine lineup positions, the Royals were last in OPS in the American League (designated hitter, right field, and shortstop) and second to last at another

(center field). Two of those positions are probably set in 2010 with relatively large, immovable contracts (Jose Guillen in right field and Yuniesky Betancourt at shortstop). Unless Moore shows an ability to get these off the books via a trade, or a willingness to absorb these sunk costs and move on, the Royals' offense is likely to be in the bottom third, where it has been since 2004.

Moore's stated emphasis is now to bring in as many "zero-to-three [major-league service] players" into the mix as possible, demonstrated by trading away Mark Teahen for Chris Getz and Josh Fields. Given how far they need to go and how much they need to improve, the probability that the Royals will be a contender in the still weak AL Central seems unlikely. At the end of 2010, however, $26.2 million will come off the payroll, with Guillen, Farnsworth, David DeJesus, Cruz, and Willie Bloomquist departing, which should set the Royals up to be bigger spenders for 2011. The real question is whether enough lessons have been learned in year three of "the Process" to suggest they'll spend it wisely. This far in, it's worth wondering if there are only scars where expectations once survived.

HITTERS

Mike Aviles SS Bats: R Throws: R Height: 5' 9" Weight: 195 Born: March 13, 1981 Age: 29

YEAR	TEAM	LVL	AGE	PA	R	2B	3B	HR	RBI	BB	SO	SB	CS	EqBRR	AVG	OBP	SLG	EqAVG	EqOBP	EqSLG	EqA	VORP	WARP	DEFENSE			
2007	OMA	AAA	26	581	78	27	6	17	77	30	59	5	5	-0.8	.296	.332	.463	.267	.299	.397	.240	5.7	1.4	52-SS	3	47-3B	4
2008	OMA	AAA	27	227	42	21	6	10	42	11	23	3	0	0.0	.336	.370	.631	.301	.330	.528	.287	15.0	3.7	32-2B	9	19-SS	7
2008	KCA	MLB	27	441	68	27	4	10	51	18	58	8	3	4.5	.325	.354	.480	.328	.357	.486	.285	29.7	4.3	84-SS	11	13-2B	-1
2009	KCA	MLB	28	127	10	3	1	1	8	4	26	1	0	1.7	.183	.208	.250	.185	.210	.252	.154	-6.8	-0.6	31-SS	1		
2010	KCA	MLB	29	381	49	22	3	10	45	22	53	4	2	0.8	.283	.326	.448	.278	.323	.431	.251	9.9	1.6	78-SS	5		

Breakout: 13% Improve: 41% Collapse: 15% Attrition: 12%   MLB: 56%   Comparables: Kevin Polcovich, John McDonald, Ramon Martinez, Alvaro Espinoza

One of the Royals' keys to a successful 2009 was not to have Aviles regress too much, since very few expected him to maintain his 2008 numbers, let alone improve on them. With a tendency to step in the bucket and an unhealthy appetite for the shoulder-level fastball, Aviles' 2009 season started worse than anyone expected. Only later did he reveal to club officials that a strained right forearm (incurred during the World Baseball Classic when he played for Puerto Rico) was slowing down his bat. After hopes that it would improve with rest were disappointed, he was shut down in early June. Club officials say that a healthy Aviles can compete for a job, but with Yuniesky Betancourt clogging up the infield, his best hope is that he can push the defensively stiff Alberto Callaspo off second base.

Yuniesky Betancourt SS Bats: R Throws: R Height: 5' 10" Weight: 195 Born: January 31, 1982 Age: 28

YEAR	TEAM	LVL	AGE	PA	R	2B	3B	HR	RBI	BB	SO	SB	CS	EqBRR	AVG	OBP	SLG	EqAVG	EqOBP	EqSLG	EqA	VORP	WARP	DEFENSE	
2007	SEA	MLB	25	559	72	38	2	9	67	15	48	5	4	0.7	.289	.308	.418	.296	.314	.427	.254	16.8	0.9	147-SS	-9
2008	SEA	MLB	26	590	66	36	3	7	51	17	42	4	4	-3.0	.279	.300	.392	.291	.311	.410	.248	16.7	-0.3	150-SS	-20
2009	SEA	MLB	27	245	15	10	1	2	22	10	18	3	1	-1.0	.250	.278	.330	.257	.284	.333	.221	0.3	-0.9	61-SS	-7
2009	KCA	MLB	27	263	25	10	5	4	27	11	26	0	2	-1.6	.240	.269	.370	.241	.269	.367	.220	-0.3	-1.4	69-SS	-11
2010	KCA	MLB	28	514	63	29	3	10	58	25	50	4	4	-0.8	.285	.321	.419	.279	.316	.405	.240	7.5	0.0	135-SS	-7

Breakout: 16% Improve: 42% Collapse: 10% Attrition: 10%   MLB: 97%   Comparables: Jack Wilson, Rafael Ramirez, Bucky Dent, Johnny Logan

By July, the Royals found themselves comfortably in 30th place in terms of offensive production from their short-stops. Their solution? Poach the starting shortstop from the team that was 29th, trading top prospect Dan Cortes to do so. It wouldn't be so bad if Betancourt provided a defensive spark, but the numbers reliably say he's a below-average shortstop—even though Moore and his crew insist that he's one of the best. The Royals got aggregate production of .222/.251/.319 from their shortstops in 2009. It should be better than that this year, but not so much that you'll notice.

Jeff Bianchi · MI

Bats: R   Throws: R   Height: 6' 0"   Weight: 175   Born: October 5, 1986   Age: 23

YEAR	TEAM	LVL	AGE	PA	R	2B	3B	HR	RBI	BB	SO	SB	CS	EqBRR	AVG	OBP	SLG	EqAVG	EqOBP	EqSLG	EqA	VORP	WARP	DEFENSE			
2007	BUR	A	20	403	43	19	0	2	36	25	72	15	4	0.7	.247	.296	.315	.239	.279	.300	.208	-6.8	-1.1	79-SS	0	5-2B	-2
2008	WIL	A+	21	431	57	34	5	10	61	20	95	13	4	0.2	.255	.290	.442	.244	.271	.400	.233	0.4	0.9	75-2B	8	12-SS	-1
2009	WIL	A+	22	245	32	12	2	4	28	20	47	12	2	0.9	.300	.360	.427	.280	.332	.404	.260	9.7	1.1	59-SS	-1		
2009	NWA	AA	22	297	42	17	1	5	42	19	58	10	4	-0.3	.315	.356	.441	.270	.305	.391	.244	5.9	1.1	60-SS	3		
2010	KCA	MLB	23	480	55	26	2	8	53	31	107	10	3	0.3	.257	.307	.378	.249	.301	.366	.227	0.9	0.1	104-SS	0		

Breakout: 22%   Improve: 50%   Collapse: 20%   Attrition: 9%   MLB: 4%   Comparables: Joe Mikulik, Juan Castro, Charles Poe, Carlos Garcia

The 50th overall pick in the 2005 draft, Bianchi showed huge promise in his first two seasons in rookie ball despite missing significant time with back and shoulder injuries, but the limited playing time made it hard to draw conclusions. After last year's split between Wilmington and Northwest Arkansas, we know what that conclusion is: utility infielder. After a move to second base due to reduced arm strength from a shoulder injury, he returned to shortstop in 2009, but that assignment may be temporary, as his range is borderline and his plate judgment remains a serious impediment to projecting much in the way of offense. A future on the bench looms ahead, but probably not until 2011.

Willie Bloomquist · UT

Bats: R   Throws: R   Height: 5' 11"   Weight: 195   Born: November 27, 1977   Age: 32

YEAR	TEAM	LVL	AGE	PA	R	2B	3B	HR	RBI	BB	SO	SB	CS	EqBRR	AVG	OBP	SLG	EqAVG	EqOBP	EqSLG	EqA	VORP	WARP	DEFENSE			
2007	SEA	MLB	29	188	28	3	0	2	13	10	35	7	5	0.2	.277	.321	.329	.291	.333	.337	.236	0.7	-0.5	16-2B	-3	15-3B	-1
2008	SEA	MLB	30	192	32	1	0	0	9	25	29	14	3	1.1	.279	.377	.285	.293	.393	.299	.268	6.2	0.8	18-CF	2	11-SS	-3
2009	KCA	MLB	31	468	52	11	8	4	29	27	73	25	6	2.9	.265	.308	.355	.268	.310	.356	.241	3.7	0.6	37-RF	1	27-SS	1
2010	KCA	MLB	32	324	44	11	2	3	20	27	57	14	7	0.8	.265	.328	.345	.261	.324	.341	.228	-3.8	-0.4	48-RF	1		

Breakout: 4%   Improve: 22%   Collapse: 26%   Attrition: 22%   MLB: 96%   Comparables: Darren Lewis, Eric Owens, Chad Curtis, Brian Hunter

Bloomquist apologists have long said that success would come if he just got more regular playing time. The Royals, Pollyannas of the horsehide, were willing to oblige, but the needle didn't budge. Bloomquist's "power" came back from his historic brown-out of 2008, as he had the highest slugging percentage of his career. Unfortunately, this new "swing for the fences" approach dropped his OBP to its lowest point in four years. Given his ability to play adequate defense at any position in the field besides catcher and pitcher, he can be a valuable asset in limited doses, but there's just no excuse for showing fans this much of him.

John Buck · C

Bats: R   Throws: R   Height: 6' 3"   Weight: 220   Born: July 7, 1980   Age: 29

YEAR	TEAM	LVL	AGE	PA	R	2B	3B	HR	RBI	BB	SO	SB	CS	EqBRR	AVG	OBP	SLG	EqAVG	EqOBP	EqSLG	EqA	VORP	WARP	DEFENSE	
2007	KCA	MLB	26	399	41	18	0	18	48	36	92	0	1	-0.2	.222	.308	.429	.220	.306	.428	.253	16.3	1.9	104-C	3
2008	KCA	MLB	27	418	48	23	1	9	48	38	96	0	3	-2.9	.224	.304	.365	.225	.305	.366	.236	7.7	0.1	107-C	-4
2009	KCA	MLB	28	202	16	12	4	8	36	13	55	1	1	-1.6	.247	.299	.484	.247	.299	.484	.261	7.4	-0.1	42-C	-7
2010	TOR	MLB	29	352	35	15	2	13	46	33	90	1	1	-0.8	.232	.315	.418	.233	.314	.409	.250	10.5	1.0	89-C	-1

Breakout: 13%   Improve: 43%   Collapse: 11%   Attrition: 8%   MLB: 91%   Comparables: Chris Widger, Nelson Santovenia, Jody Davis, Gus Triandos

It has been a long time since the Carlos Beltran trade in 2004. Civilizations have risen and fallen, whole solar systems have fallen into collapsing suns, and the Royals have waited for John Buck to figure out how to hit. He has stubbornly hovered around replacement level, albeit with a little pop in his bat. There has been a steady decrease in his ability to throw out runners; from 2004 to 2006, he averaged 32 percent caught stealing, but that has gradually fallen, down to 16 percent in 2009. Nontendered after the Royals signed Jason Kendall, Buck was on the market for about 49 seconds before the Blue Jays signed him to a one-year, $2 million contract, placeholding behind the plate, at least until J. P. Arencibia shows that he's ready.

Billy Butler · 1B

Bats: R   Throws: R   Height: 6' 1"   Weight: 240   Born: April 18, 1986   Age: 24

YEAR	TEAM	LVL	AGE	PA	R	2B	3B	HR	RBI	BB	SO	SB	CS	EqBRR	AVG	OBP	SLG	EqAVG	EqOBP	EqSLG	EqA	VORP	WARP	DEFENSE			
2007	OMA	AAA	21	256	40	10	1	13	46	43	32	1	0	-3.9	.291	.412	.542	.266	.380	.478	.298	14.5	0.8	25-LF	-5	22-1B	-3
2007	KCA	MLB	21	360	38	23	2	8	52	27	55	0	0	-1.5	.292	.347	.447	.287	.344	.445	.270	8.5	0.6	9-1B	1	5-LF	-3
2008	OMA	AAA	22	115	18	6	1	5	13	14	7	0	0	0.2	.337	.417	.564	.311	.383	.505	.301	6.5	0.4	21-1B	-3		
2008	KCA	MLB	22	478	44	22	0	11	55	33	57	0	1	-0.5	.275	.324	.400	.278	.328	.410	.254	1.3	-0.4	29-1B	-5		
2009	KCA	MLB	23	672	78	51	1	21	93	58	103	1	0	-6.4	.301	.362	.492	.301	.362	.484	.289	22.0	1.8	142-1B	-6		
2010	KCA	MLB	24	679	80	33	2	25	95	66	95	1	1	-2.2	.288	.360	.470	.282	.355	.459	.271	15.4	1.3	92-1B	-3		

Breakout: 15% Improve: 55% Collapse: 10% Attrition: 5%   MLB: 100%   Comparables: Paul Konerko, Aramis Ramirez, Adrian Beltre, Ryan Zimmerman

The conventional wisdom was that if the Royals' offense was going to produce enough runs to be competitive, both Butler and Gordon would need to have breakout years. One out of two ain't bad. Butler started off slowly (.193/.324/.246 as of April 27), but then the hits came, and after the All-Star break, he hit .314/.385/.540. The 50 doubles/20 homer combo he rolled up has only been achieved by five other players his age or younger—Hank Greenberg, Albert Pujols, Alex Rodriguez, Grady Sizemore, and Miguel Cabrera. His defense is still well below average (a huge improvement over 2008), but hopefully, the days when the Royals sacrificed first-base offense for defense went out with Tony Muser.

Alberto Callaspo · 2B

Bats: S   Throws: R   Height: 5' 9"   Weight: 180   Born: April 19, 1983   Age: 27

YEAR	TEAM	LVL	AGE	PA	R	2B	3B	HR	RBI	BB	SO	SB	CS	EqBRR	AVG	OBP	SLG	EqAVG	EqOBP	EqSLG	EqA	VORP	WARP	DEFENSE			
2007	TUC	AAA	24	261	48	15	2	5	30	28	17	1	2	-0.2	.341	.406	.491	.301	.364	.419	.275	13.3	0.5	33-SS	-5	17-2B	-4
2007	ARI	MLB	24	156	10	8	0	0	7	9	14	1	1	-0.1	.215	.265	.271	.215	.265	.264	.186	-7.3	-0.9	13-3B	0	8-SS	2
2008	KCA	MLB	25	234	21	8	3	0	16	19	14	2	1	-0.6	.305	.361	.371	.307	.362	.368	.264	7.7	0.5	41-2B	-5	9-SS	1
2009	KCA	MLB	26	634	79	41	8	11	73	52	51	2	1	-0.9	.300	.356	.457	.301	.356	.447	.279	30.9	2.5	141-2B	-9	11-3B	-1
2010	KCA	MLB	27	523	65	30	4	8	55	46	47	3	2	-0.4	.297	.361	.428	.288	.352	.413	.261	16.0	1.3	108-2B	-5		

Breakout: 10% Improve: 50% Collapse: 11% Attrition: 4%   MLB: 90%   Comparables: Orlando Hudson, Bill Doran, Donnie Hill, Brian Roberts

Callaspo made the team despite a poor spring, but when Gordon went down and Mark Teahen went back to third, Callaspo got his chance and made the most of it. A nice addition to his game was rediscovered power he'd flashed in the minors; he had gone homerless in his first 441 big-league at-bats. He had some rather extreme splits, doing most of his work at home and against lefties. Despite his offensive breakthrough, his poor range afield has encouraged the Royals to look for another alternative at the keystone, perhaps moving Callaspo into a utility role.

Coco Crisp · CF

Bats: S   Throws: R   Height: 6' 0"   Weight: 180   Born: November 1, 1979   Age: 30

YEAR	TEAM	LVL	AGE	PA	R	2B	3B	HR	RBI	BB	SO	SB	CS	EqBRR	AVG	OBP	SLG	EqAVG	EqOBP	EqSLG	EqA	VORP	WARP	DEFENSE	
2007	BOS	MLB	27	591	85	28	7	6	60	50	84	28	6	8.5	.268	.330	.382	.261	.324	.377	.253	12.4	3.8	137-CF	19
2008	BOS	MLB	28	409	55	18	3	7	41	35	59	20	7	1.1	.283	.344	.407	.282	.345	.411	.266	14.2	1.1	99-CF	-3
2009	KCA	MLB	29	215	30	8	5	3	14	29	23	13	2	2.8	.228	.336	.378	.229	.338	.374	.262	6.5	0.7	47-CF	-1
2010	OAK	MLB	30	425	60	19	4	8	43	44	63	17	6	2.2	.264	.342	.402	.265	.342	.399	.259	12.6	1.7	102-CF	3

Breakout: 7% Improve: 44% Collapse: 9% Attrition: 13%   MLB: 97%   Comparables: Brian McRae, Tony Scott, Stan Javier, Eddie Milner

Acquired from the Red Sox for reliever Ramon Ramirez, Crisp hit well in April (.247/.371/.494), while the rest of the offense was in the doldrums. Perhaps here, at last, was one of the few Royals actually delivering some much-needed OBP. Sadly, Crisp's place in the revolution would be short-lived, as right shoulder pain killed his production, eventually resulting in a diagnosis of a torn labrum that required season-ending surgery; he later had the same procedure on his left shoulder. The Royals declined his $8 million club option for 2010; the A's signed him to a one-year deal with a club option for 2011. He had to pass a physical to do so, but whatever the state of his health, it has been a long time since Crisp did anything interesting on offense, hitting .266/.331/.389 in 417 games since 2005.

David DeJesus   LF   Bats: L   Throws: L   Height: 6' 0"   Weight: 190   Born: December 20, 1979   Age: 30

YEAR	TEAM	LVL	AGE	PA	R	2B	3B	HR	RBI	BB	SO	SB	CS	EqBRR	AVG	OBP	SLG	EqAVG	EqOBP	EqSLG	EqA	VORP	WARP	DEFENSE	
2007	KCA	MLB	27	703	101	29	9	7	58	64	83	10	4	3.0	.260	.351	.372	.257	.348	.371	.257	17.3	1.4	152-CF	-4
2008	KCA	MLB	28	577	70	25	7	12	73	46	71	11	8	-0.4	.307	.366	.452	.313	.372	.460	.283	27.5	3.8	57-CF -3 54-LF	12
2009	KCA	MLB	29	627	74	28	9	13	71	51	87	4	9	-2.5	.281	.347	.434	.286	.352	.431	.267	16.7	4.4	137-LF	20
2010	KCA	MLB	30	604	80	28	8	10	69	60	77	8	7	0.0	.291	.374	.429	.276	.357	.412	.266	15.9	3.0	132-LF	11

Breakout: 7%   Improve: 42%   Collapse: 10%   Attrition: 10%   MLB: 97%   Comparables: Joe Orsulak, Mark Kotsay, Gene Woodling, Luis Gonzalez

After an incredibly slow start, DeJesus turned it up in the second half (.316/.390/.462) to repair his season. He doesn't have the range or the arm for center, but is a solid defensive left fielder, which led to an ill-conceived Gold Glove campaign by the Royals front office—this may seem like small beer for a front office to concern itself with, but season-ticket renewal campaigns have got to be based on *something*. Given his incredibly club-friendly contract, DeJesus is usually near the top of the list in terms of baseball's best bargains—and if he'd won that Gold Glove, he would no doubt be an international celebrity.

Johnny Giavotella   2B   Bats: R   Throws: R   Height: 5' 8"   Weight: 185   Born: July 10, 1987   Age: 22

YEAR	TEAM	LVL	AGE	PA	R	2B	3B	HR	RBI	BB	SO	SB	CS	EqBRR	AVG	OBP	SLG	EqAVG	EqOBP	EqSLG	EqA	VORP	WARP	DEFENSE	
2008	BUR	A	20	310	50	18	2	4	26	25	34	10	7	2.6	.299	.355	.421	.276	.322	.378	.246	4.9	-0.3	67-2B	-8
2009	WIL	A+	21	561	84	24	8	6	52	66	54	26	9	3.3	.258	.351	.380	.253	.328	.371	.250	10.5	1.0	131-2B	-2
2010	KCA	MLB	22	516	72	27	5	6	45	46	66	11	5	1.8	.266	.333	.386	.260	.329	.377	.240	5.1	0.2	120-2B	-3

Breakout: 11%   Improve: 30%   Collapse: 15%   Attrition: 3%   MLB: 8%   Comparables: Chuck Knoblauch, Joe Jester, Scott Fletcher, Luis Alicea

The stumpy Giavotella was a surprise second-round choice in 2008. The Royals felt there was a chance he would turn into a Dustin Pedroia–style grinder. A lot of teams have taken this same chance with gritty, fundamentally sound college infielders over the last few years, but we still have only one Pedroia. Giavotella has a good eye at the plate and has the defensive basics down pat, but will have to hit enough to start if he's going to make it, as his inability to play on the left side closes off the utilityman's path.

Alex Gordon   3B   Bats: L   Throws: R   Height: 6' 1"   Weight: 220   Born: February 10, 1984   Age: 26

YEAR	TEAM	LVL	AGE	PA	R	2B	3B	HR	RBI	BB	SO	SB	CS	EqBRR	AVG	OBP	SLG	EqAVG	EqOBP	EqSLG	EqA	VORP	WARP	DEFENSE	
2007	KCA	MLB	23	600	60	36	4	15	60	41	137	14	4	-1.1	.247	.314	.411	.244	.311	.408	.251	6.3	0.4	128-3B -3 17-1B	1
2008	KCA	MLB	24	571	72	35	1	16	59	66	120	9	2	3.4	.260	.351	.432	.261	.354	.435	.276	23.4	1.6	132-3B	-8
2009	KCA	MLB	25	189	28	6	0	6	22	21	43	5	0	2.5	.232	.324	.378	.233	.326	.374	.254	3.9	0.2	46-3B	-2
2010	KCA	MLB	26	539	67	28	3	16	57	59	110	11	5	1.0	.263	.354	.432	.253	.342	.427	.261	14.0	1.3	126-3B	-2

Breakout: 20%   Improve: 51%   Collapse: 8%   Attrition: 7%   MLB: 100%   Comparables: Eric Chavez, Hank Blalock, Eric Hinske, Robin Ventura

Many predicted Gordon to have a breakout year in 2009, as there has been steady improvement since his horrible two-month start in 2007. He homered in his first at-bat, but promptly went 1-for-20 immediately after, at which point he was shelved with a tear in his hip's labral cartilage. He returned in July without completing the full course of rehab starts in the minors, struggled, and was sent back down to the minors. His September recall was more successful (.279/.359/.471). With Gordon now 26, it seems increasingly likely that the second coming of George Brett will have to be one of Gordon's eventual successors; if Gordon is going to achieve even a rudimentary echo of the great number 5, he will need to work on hitting southpaws to avoid platooning, as his career slash line against them is a disheartening .217/.288/.365.

Jose Guillen   RF   Bats: R   Throws: R   Height: 6' 0"   Weight: 210   Born: May 17, 1976   Age: 34

YEAR	TEAM	LVL	AGE	PA	R	2B	3B	HR	RBI	BB	SO	SB	CS	EqBRR	AVG	OBP	SLG	EqAVG	EqOBP	EqSLG	EqA	VORP	WARP	DEFENSE	
2007	SEA	MLB	31	658	84	28	2	23	99	41	118	5	1	-0.6	.290	.353	.460	.299	.360	.476	.287	31.0	3.1	144-RF	-3
2008	KCA	MLB	32	633	66	42	1	20	97	23	106	2	1	-1.8	.264	.300	.438	.266	.303	.446	.253	6.4	1.0	60-RF 4 42-LF	-1
2009	KCA	MLB	33	312	30	8	0	9	40	22	50	1	0	-1.7	.242	.314	.367	.243	.315	.361	.240	-1.9	-1.3	57-RF -7 4-LF	-2
2010	KCA	MLB	34	369	38	17	1	11	51	25	70	2	1	-0.5	.265	.330	.423	.258	.323	.406	.247	2.7	0.2	73-RF	-1

Breakout: 9%   Improve: 30%   Collapse: 30%   Attrition: 34%   MLB: 94%   Comparables: Hubie Brooks, Emil Brown, Andy Pafko, Del Ennis

The second year of Guillen's contract started with his missing a portion of spring training because he pulled out an ingrown toenail by himself, moved on to his telling the media that he "sucks" midyear, and involved his partially tearing his lateral collateral ligament while putting on his shin-guard before an at-bat, costing him 10 weeks on the DL. Ironically, that was tame compared with the previous year. Now that he's 34 with obviously diminished skills, fans should not expect a rebound, so it's just one year and $12 million to go—with these kinds of busted investments on the book, it's surprising the Royals weren't in line for TARP money.

Luis Hernandez   SS

Bats: S   Throws: R   Height: 5' 10"   Weight: 180   Born: June 26, 1984   Age: 26

YEAR	TEAM	LVL	AGE	PA	R	2B	3B	HR	RBI	BB	SO	SB	CS	EqBRR	AVG	OBP	SLG	EqAVG	EqOBP	EqSLG	EqA	VORP	WARP	DEFENSE			
2007	BOW	AA	23	393	42	15	6	0	37	18	50	6	5	0.2	.242	.276	.316	.231	.260	.296	.194	-10.3	-0.8	89-SS	4		
2007	BAL	MLB	23	71	5	2	0	1	7	1	10	2	2	-0.7	.290	.300	.362	.290	.300	.362	.228	-0.5	0.1	16-SS	2		
2008	NOR	AAA	24	216	18	7	0	0	11	8	27	2	2	-0.9	.185	.216	.220	.184	.215	.209	.123	-14.9	-2.7	54-SS	-7		
2008	BAL	MLB	24	91	9	1	0	0	3	7	11	2	0	-1.1	.241	.295	.253	.244	.299	.256	.215	-0.4	0.0	25-SS	-1	2-2B	1
2009	OMA	AAA	25	223	24	10	0	1	26	16	17	1	3	-2.2	.303	.356	.369	.296	.342	.355	.244	4.5	0.2	44-SS	-1	10-2B	-2
2009	KCA	MLB	25	81	4	1	0	0	4	4	18	1	0	0.1	.205	.256	.219	.208	.260	.222	.173	-3.6	0.1	16-SS	5	4-2B	-1
2010	KCA	MLB	26	346	36	14	2	2	33	20	51	3	3	-0.7	.260	.305	.334	.251	.297	.323	.209	-4.9	-0.5	86-SS	1		

Breakout: 23% Improve: 43% Collapse: 26% Attrition: 14%   MLB: 79%   Comparables: Link Jarrett, Edgar Caceres, Milko Jaramillo, Irving Falu

Some people collect comic books, Depression glass, or original Maxfield Parrish pages from *Colliers*. The Royals collect impotent shortstops. In 2009, the same organization had Hernandez, Betancourt, and Tony Pena Jr., and it's understood that a collector in Detroit might be willing to sell them an original Ray Oyler and a slightly mildewed Ed Brinkman if they can just meet his price. For 32 days, both Hernandez and Pena were on the 25-man roster. On July 3rd, both were in the lineup in "support" of Zack Greinke—it's a credit to Greinke's sense of professionalism that he didn't just walk off the field (not a fanciful thought; other pitchers have done so under similar circumstances). Hernandez is a career .249/.297/.320 hitter in the minors and has a solid but unspectacular glove. Due to the Royals' lack of depth and seriousness, he may still find himself as organizational filler come 2010.

Eric Hosmer   1B

Bats: L   Throws: L   Height: 6' 4"   Weight: 215   Born: October 24, 1989   Age: 20

YEAR	TEAM	LVL	AGE	PA	R	2B	3B	HR	RBI	BB	SO	SB	CS	EqBRR	AVG	OBP	SLG	EqAVG	EqOBP	EqSLG	EqA	VORP	WARP	DEFENSE	
2009	BUR	A	19	327	31	17	2	5	49	44	68	3	2	-2.3	.254	.352	.382	.224	.303	.328	.225	-12.2	-2.2	57-1B	-6
2009	WIL	A+	19	107	9	2	2	1	10	9	22	0	0	0.2	.206	.280	.299	.202	.262	.273	.184	-8.0	-0.9	26-1B	1
2010	KCA	MLB	20	404	35	19	3	6	51	41	90	2	1	-1.0	.242	.321	.363	.232	.307	.347	.228	-8.9	-1.3	76-1B	-2

Breakout: 51% Improve: 73% Collapse: 15% Attrition: 3%   MLB: 0%   Comparables: Reed Olmstead, Paul Chmiel, Mike Snyder, Logan Morrison

Hosmer had a disappointing, confusing full-season debut. Scouts viewed him as having perfect power and an above-average glove. Those things are still true, even though he showed nothing with the bat last year. After a slow start, he did start to pick it up a little at Burlington, but for some unknown reason, the Royals promptly promoted him to Wilmington, where he struggled mightily. Hosmer lost over a week due to an inability to get the right prescription glasses and was eventually shut down for Lasik surgery to correct his vision, and all involved hope that this was the root of his struggles. It's too early to say that the Royals made another first-round error in spending the third overall pick of the 2008 draft on Hosmer, but the pressure will be on him to hit when he returns to Wilmington.

Tug Hulett   INF

Bats: L   Throws: R   Height: 5' 10"   Weight: 185   Born: February 28, 1983   Age: 27

YEAR	TEAM	LVL	AGE	PA	R	2B	3B	HR	RBI	BB	SO	SB	CS	EqBRR	AVG	OBP	SLG	EqAVG	EqOBP	EqSLG	EqA	VORP	WARP	DEFENSE			
2007	OKL	AAA	24	595	95	31	2	11	67	64	114	20	4	-2.5	.275	.359	.406	.256	.333	.366	.252	13.8	0.8	104-2B	-6	18-SS	-3
2008	TAC	AAA	25	400	71	22	5	14	47	49	73	10	5	-0.5	.298	.380	.518	.272	.345	.443	.274	19.5	1.7	43-SS	-4	36-2B	-1
2008	SEA	MLB	25	56	2	1	0	1	2	5	17	0	0	-1.5	.224	.309	.306	.224	.309	.306	.230	-1.4	-0.1	2-SS	0	2-2B	0
2009	OMA	AAA	26	442	62	27	4	11	53	58	79	9	2	1.5	.291	.384	.473	.276	.359	.438	.278	19.9	2.0	57-2B	-2	16-RF	-1
2009	KCA	MLB	26	19	4	0	0	0	1	1	6	0	0	0.5	.111	.158	.111	.111	.158	.111	-.121	-2.6	-0.3	2-2B	0		
2010	BOS	MLB	27	433	54	23	2	8	41	42	103	7	3	-0.4	.244	.321	.376	.242	.319	.366	.236	2.3	0.1	82-2B	-2		

Breakout: 5%   Improve: 24% Collapse: 31% Attrition: 13%   MLB: 18%   Comparables: Stuart Pederson, Mike Fontenot, Mike Hart, Joe Inglett

For the third season in a row, the well-traveled Hulett hit well at Triple-A, but his performance failed to secure more than a handful of plate appearances with the big-league club. The Royals tried him at five different positions in the eight games where he was on the field, which suggests a potential role as a super-utility guy akin to the Great Bloomquist, a player whose versatility is an end unto itself. The Royals, already having the original model under contract for another year, sold Hulett to the Red Sox in November. He'll get a chance to claim a bench spot, but he'll have a hard time sticking in these days of short major-league benches.

Mike Jacobs   **DH**   Bats: L   Throws: R   Height: 6' 3"   Weight: 215   Born: October 30, 1980   Age: 29

YEAR	TEAM	LVL	AGE	PA	R	2B	3B	HR	RBI	BB	SO	SB	CS	EqBRR	AVG	OBP	SLG	EqAVG	EqOBP	EqSLG	EqA	VORP	WARP	DEFENSE	
2007	FLO	MLB	26	460	57	27	2	17	54	31	101	1	2	-1.8	.265	.317	.458	.275	.328	.471	.267	8.5	0.5	101-1B	-3
2008	FLO	MLB	27	519	67	27	2	32	93	36	119	1	0	-1.3	.247	.299	.514	.252	.301	.521	.273	13.2	-0.2	104-1B	-15
2009	KCA	MLB	28	478	46	16	1	19	61	41	132	0	0	-2.7	.228	.297	.401	.230	.299	.394	.240	-10.8	-1.2	13-1B	0
2010	KCA	MLB	29	484	58	23	3	21	69	43	110	1	1	-1.0	.254	.322	.464	.246	.312	.455	.253	1.7	-0.2	73-1B	-3

Breakout: 17%   Improve: 54%   Collapse: 9%   Attrition: 4%   MLB: 94%   Comparables: Paul Sorrento, Dave Revering, Greg Walker, Rico Brogna

Note to whoever manages Jacobs in 2010: he should never start against a left-handed pitcher. Given 111 plate appearances against same-side pitchers in 2009, he "hit" .178/.252/.248, and his career line of .221/.269/.374 against them provides ample evidence that Jacobs is platoon material at best—although it's not clear he's even that. While Kila Ka'aihue rotted in Omaha along with his .400 OBP and minuscule salary, Jacobs' sub-replacement performance was consistent with his previous weak work and revealed Dayton Moore's supposed turn toward an OBP-oriented lineup to be an utter sham. He was waived in December, and given his weak hitting and exceedingly poor defense, it's difficult to envision a regular role for him.

Kila Ka'aihue   **1B**   Bats: L   Throws: R   Height: 6' 3"   Weight: 230   Born: March 29, 1984   Age: 26

YEAR	TEAM	LVL	AGE	PA	R	2B	3B	HR	RBI	BB	SO	SB	CS	EqBRR	AVG	OBP	SLG	EqAVG	EqOBP	EqSLG	EqA	VORP	WARP	DEFENSE	
2007	WIL	A+	23	253	28	8	0	9	42	35	38	1	0	-1.9	.251	.360	.420	.225	.308	.349	.237	-3.8	-0.4	33-1B	1
2007	WIC	AA	23	288	37	13	0	12	40	41	40	0	0	-0.4	.246	.359	.447	.227	.324	.394	.251	0.1	0.1	35-1B	1
2008	NWA	AA	24	376	64	11	0	26	79	80	41	3	2	-1.6	.314	.463	.624	.272	.402	.510	.312	25.5	2.1	69-1B	-8
2008	OMA	AAA	24	139	27	4	0	11	21	24	26	0	0	0.5	.316	.439	.640	.291	.403	.556	.320	10.9	1.4	25-1B	1
2008	KCA	MLB	24	24	4	0	0	1	1	3	2	0	0	-0.1	.286	.375	.429	.286	.375	.429	.284	0.8	0.1	2-1B	0
2009	OMA	AAA	25	555	83	27	1	17	57	102	85	0	1	-1.4	.252	.392	.433	.241	.366	.400	.273	7.9	0.5	117-1B	-4
2010	KCA	MLB	26	496	61	19	1	17	57	75	89	1	1	-0.8	.247	.364	.418	.238	.350	.413	.261	5.8	0.5	87-1B	-1

Breakout: 8%   Improve: 33%   Collapse: 25%   Attrition: 22%   MLB: 17%   Comparables: Ben Broussard, Joe Koshansky, Bob Tumpane, Pat Dodson

On October 30, 2008, Ka'aihue should have signed a 12-month lease on an apartment in Omaha. That was the day the Royals traded for Mike Jacobs, which was the equivalent of a vote of no-confidence in Ka'aihue and which signaled that he would have to prove that his 2008 season was no fluke to get a crack at a major-league job. This was a tall order—no one can maintain a pace of hitting 2.5 times as many homers as doubles, and the season was unprecedented in Ka'aihue's career. So he did not repeat the feat, although he did top 100 walks for the second year in a row. The Royals desperately need a massive injection of players with Ka'aihue's selectivity, but they may not need him, as little suggests that he's going to hit with enough consistency for the walks to have value. The end of Jacobs' term with the Royals means an open spot at DH, but the big Hawaiian will have to fight his way past Guillen and Josh Fields for at-bats. He's on the same career path as Justin Huber, putting up good numbers in the Royals' system without getting a shot or quite convincing anyone that he deserves one.

David Lough   **OF**   Bats: L   Throws: L   Height: 6' 0"   Weight: 180   Born: January 20, 1986   Age: 24

YEAR	TEAM	LVL	AGE	PA	R	2B	3B	HR	RBI	BB	SO	SB	CS	EqBRR	AVG	OBP	SLG	EqAVG	EqOBP	EqSLG	EqA	VORP	WARP	DEFENSE			
2007	BNC	Rk	21	92	15	6	0	2	12	4	13	6	1	0.4	.337	.380	.477	.292	.323	.404	.252	1.7	0.3	17-CF	0		
2008	BUR	A	22	543	76	21	11	16	62	35	70	12	11	-1.4	.268	.329	.455	.242	.287	.389	.232	-3.3	-1.2	63-CF	-3	59-LF	-4
2009	WIL	A+	23	250	28	15	2	5	30	12	34	6	4	-3.3	.320	.370	.473	.306	.343	.441	.269	5.9	0.7	31-RF	3	13-LF	-3
2009	NWA	AA	23	253	41	13	2	9	31	12	30	13	4	1.8	.331	.371	.517	.308	.341	.488	.280	11.3	0.9	21-LF	-1	18-RF	0
2010	KCA	MLB	24	428	51	23	5	10	43	26	69	7	4	-0.6	.276	.327	.437	.263	.312	.416	.249	3.8	0.7	86-RF	3		

Breakout: 8%   Improve: 41%   Collapse: 18%   Attrition: 9%   MLB: 3%   Comparables: Jay Davis, Anthony Webster, Jeff Kenaga, Bruce Fields

Lough is a free swinger with good speed that still hasn't been fully utilized on the basepaths. His high average last year covered up a low walk rate that will need to improve as he moves up. Though a gamer, if Lough can't turn up his offensive game, he could fall into permanent fourth-outfielderdom, a tweener whose glove shuts him out of center and whose bat can't carry a corner. Slated to begin the season at Triple-A, he should be on the short list for a big-league call-up; we'll see whether Omaha or Kansas City has the last Lough.

Mitch Maier   CF   Bats: L   Throws: R   Height: 6' 2"   Weight: 205   Born: June 30, 1982   Age: 28

YEAR	TEAM	LVL	AGE	PA	R	2B	3B	HR	RBI	BB	SO	SB	CS	EqBRR	AVG	OBP	SLG	EqAVG	EqOBP	EqSLG	EqA	VORP	WARP	DEFENSE			
2007	OMA	AAA	25	596	75	29	5	14	62	33	89	7	2	1.4	.279	.320	.428	.255	.291	.376	.234	-1.7	0.6	82-CF	6	31-RF	0
2008	OMA	AAA	26	383	57	24	1	9	41	29	42	12	3	0.0	.316	.366	.470	.288	.331	.402	.258	9.7	2.0	84-CF	7		
2008	KCA	MLB	26	97	9	1	1	0	9	2	18	0	2	0.1	.286	.316	.319	.286	.316	.319	.221	-1.3	0.0	24-CF	1	2-RF	0
2009	OMA	AAA	27	60	8	3	0	2	10	8	8	1	1	0.0	.314	.400	.490	.288	.367	.442	.280	2.8	0.6	8-CF	2	4-RF	0
2009	KCA	MLB	27	397	42	15	3	3	31	43	76	9	2	0.9	.243	.333	.331	.245	.334	.330	.244	3.5	1.6	67-CF	6	20-RF	4
2010	KCA	MLB	28	435	50	20	3	6	40	36	74	7	3	0.4	.263	.329	.369	.252	.316	.359	.233	1.4	0.6	94-CF	4		

Breakout: 8% Improve: 28% Collapse: 31% Attrition: 15%   MLB: 64%   Comparables: Dan Grunhard, Mark Ryal, Jason Conti, Bruce Dostal

Though he was slated to be organizational depth at Triple-A, injuries let Maier spend almost the entire season in the majors. Despite his defensive abilities (including 11 outfield assists, 10 while playing center), his replacement-level offensive production still had the front office scrambling for even worse alternatives like Ryan Freel and Josh Anderson. Those of us who have anxieties, who must resort to drugs like Paxil and Xanax to calm the clamoring, crazy voices in our minds, would very much like a bottle of whatever it is that lets you live in a problem-free world where Anderson and Freel are seen as improvements. On a better team, Maier could be a valuable fourth outfielder, but given their lack of center fielders (something the signing of Scott Podsednik does little to change), the Royals may again require more than he's able to give.

Mike Moustakas   3B   Bats: L   Throws: R   Height: 6' 0"   Weight: 195   Born: September 11, 1988   Age: 21

YEAR	TEAM	LVL	AGE	PA	R	2B	3B	HR	RBI	BB	SO	SB	CS	EqBRR	AVG	OBP	SLG	EqAVG	EqOBP	EqSLG	EqA	VORP	WARP	DEFENSE			
2007	IDA	Rk	18	47	6	4	1	0	10	4	8	0	0	-0.4	.293	.383	.439	.233	.298	.349	.226	-0.3	0.1	7-SS	1		
2008	BUR	A	19	549	77	25	3	22	71	43	86	8	4	-0.1	.272	.337	.468	.249	.301	.410	.245	8.0	0.9	59-3B	1	56-SS	-2
2009	WIL	A+	20	530	66	32	2	16	86	32	90	10	6	1.5	.250	.297	.421	.240	.278	.389	.229	-3.1	0.5	121-3B	7		
2010	KCA	MLB	21	512	63	27	3	15	65	37	93	4	3	0.3	.260	.316	.421	.251	.305	.415	.240	2.5	0.6	112-3B	2		

Breakout: 26% Improve: 63% Collapse: 7% Attrition: 5%   MLB: 3%   Comparables: Tom O'Malley, Brandon Pico, George Cecchetti, Blake DeWitt

Going into last season, Hosmer and Moustakas ranked one-two among Royals prospects, and ranked 18th and 21st among the top 100 prospects in the game. Neither is likely to be spoken of so reverently in the near future, given their highly disappointing seasons, but it's still premature to call them busts. Wilmington's Frawley Stadium is tough, and Moustakas did hit .292/.331/.473 on the road. What's more, his seemingly low 16 home runs were the most by a Wilmington player since 1999, though this may be as much due to the weak talent the Royals have sent there as to the ballpark. Still, a big part of the problem was Moustakas's weak plate judgment, which had him hitting in too many pitcher's counts. He still displays some of the best bat speed in the minors, and his arm is so strong that even routine 5-3 tosses are a threat to crack the sound barrier (many scouts would like to see him take that 80 arm behind the plate). Likely to start the season in the hitter-friendly environment of the Texas League, he'll have to hit to avoid becoming the latest victim of the Royals' Midas-in-Reverse touch.

William Myers   C   Bats: R   Throws: R   Height: 6' 3"   Weight: 190   Born: December 10, 1990   Age: 19

YEAR	TEAM	LVL	AGE	PA	R	2B	3B	HR	RBI	BB	SO	SB	CS	EqBRR	AVG	OBP	SLG	EqAVG	EqOBP	EqSLG	EqA	VORP	WARP	DEFENSE	
2009	IDA	Rk	18	80	18	7	1	4	14	9	15	2	0	-1.2	.426	.488	.735	.292	.338	.444	.274	3.0	0.5	9-C	0
2010	KCA	MLB	19	292	30	15	2	8	32	21	67	2	1	0.0	.246	.299	.406	.242	.296	.395	.229	2.6	0.3	18-C	0

Breakout: 19% Improve: 37% Collapse: 29% Attrition: 2%   MLB: 0%   Comparables: Javier Gonzalez, Cesar Diaz, Orlando Mercado, Werner Lajszky

This third-round selection in the 2009 draft might have been the Royals' first-rounder had there not been signability concerns. When he was still on the board in the third round, the Royals cannily figured they would turn their pick into the talent equivalent of a first-rounder by making Myers an offer they knew he wouldn't refuse, $2 million. He made an immediate splash and was named the Pioneer League's top prospect despite only 80 plate appearances. It's still not certain that he can remain behind the plate, as he's very raw defensively, so wait and see.

Miguel Olivo   C   Bats: R   Throws: R   Height: 6' 0"   Weight: 220   Born: July 15, 1978   Age: 31

YEAR	TEAM	LVL	AGE	PA	R	2B	3B	HR	RBI	BB	SO	SB	CS	EqBRR	AVG	OBP	SLG	EqAVG	EqOBP	EqSLG	EqA	VORP	WARP	DEFENSE	
2007	FLO	MLB	28	469	43	20	4	16	60	14	123	3	2	0.6	.237	.262	.405	.243	.269	.416	.230	8.7	1.3	111-C	3
2008	KCA	MLB	29	317	29	22	0	12	41	7	82	7	0	-1.0	.255	.278	.444	.255	.278	.451	.249	7.4	2.2	55-C	10
2009	KCA	MLB	30	416	51	15	5	23	65	19	126	5	2	-1.0	.249	.292	.490	.252	.295	.483	.261	17.1	2.4	96-C	1
2010	COL	NL	31	385	37	17	3	15	50	20	102	4	2	-0.2	.243	.289	.430	.239	.284	.415	.234	5.3	0.8	85-C	2

Breakout: 12%   Improve: 30%   Collapse: 18%   Attrition: 10%   MLB: 99%   Comparables: Ron Karkovice, Jason LaRue, Brian Johnson, Rod Barajas

Royals catchers hit an aggregate .279/.310/.504 last season, leading the majors in home runs at the position (31). For better and for worse, Olivo, with his trademark combination of power and impatience, was a big part of that. The backstops' combined .261 EqA tied for ninth in the majors. You'd think a team like the Powder-Blue Pushovers would take whatever small victories happen to fall into their laps, but they tore the position down this winter, nontendering Buck and declining Olivo's $3.3 million option, choosing instead to sign rotting scow Jason Kendall to a reported two-year, $6 million deal. But hey, the team saved $2.3 million over what Olivo and Buck would have cost, and that's what's important. Right? *Right?* The Rockies signed Olivo to serve as a backup/impediment to Chris Iannetta.

Jordan Parraz   RF   Bats: R   Throws: R   Height: 6' 3"   Weight: 210   Born: October 8, 1984   Age: 25

YEAR	TEAM	LVL	AGE	PA	R	2B	3B	HR	RBI	BB	SO	SB	CS	EqBRR	AVG	OBP	SLG	EqAVG	EqOBP	EqSLG	EqA	VORP	WARP	DEFENSE			
2007	LEX	A	22	530	69	28	3	14	76	47	89	33	10	2.0	.281	.364	.446	.246	.307	.371	.239	-2.1	-1.9	108-RF	-10	11-CF	-4
2008	SLM	A+	23	504	82	31	3	6	42	64	79	21	10	-0.6	.289	.399	.419	.266	.351	.372	.258	8.9	0.3	68-RF	0	36-CF	-7
2009	NWA	AA	24	269	35	17	3	7	42	29	25	4	8	-3.8	.358	.451	.553	.331	.403	.513	.306	19.0	2.1	61-RF	-1		
2009	OMA	AAA	24	53	6	6	0	0	5	4	14	0	2	0.1	.298	.358	.426	.271	.333	.375	.240	-0.1	0.0	13-RF	0		
2010	KCA	MLB	25	455	51	23	2	8	45	40	89	9	5	-0.4	.264	.341	.392	.258	.335	.380	.244	2.0	0.0	102-RF	-2		

Breakout: 8%   Improve: 39%   Collapse: 19%   Attrition: 9%   MLB: 4%   Comparables: Jack Ayer, Jerry Salzano, Bill Ortega, Josh Rabe

Despite producing at every level in the Astros organization, Parraz moved up relatively slowly; it was difficult to evaluate him because he was always quite old for his levels. Scouts credit his athleticism, arm, plate discipline, gap power, and speed (though he needs to clean up his baserunning). The Royals snagged this sleeper for failed pitching prospect Tyler Lumsden after the 2008 season, and while Parraz will be the starting right fielder in Omaha this season, he could see time in Kansas City, especially when the inevitable Guillen injury occurs.

Brayan Pena   C   Bats: S   Throws: R   Height: 5' 11"   Weight: 210   Born: January 7, 1982   Age: 28

YEAR	TEAM	LVL	AGE	PA	R	2B	3B	HR	RBI	BB	SO	SB	CS	EqBRR	AVG	OBP	SLG	EqAVG	EqOBP	EqSLG	EqA	VORP	WARP	DEFENSE			
2007	RIC	AAA	25	370	42	20	2	6	48	19	38	5	7	-5.0	.301	.341	.423	.284	.319	.405	.247	4.3	-0.8	30-C	-8	20-1B	-2
2007	ATL	MLB	25	33	2	0	0	1	3	0	3	0	1	-0.3	.212	.212	.303	.212	.212	.303	.154	-2.1	0.0	7-C	2		
2008	OMA	AAA	26	266	33	17	1	6	31	26	17	7	3	-3.7	.303	.376	.462	.275	.340	.396	.258	9.7	0.3	44-C	-5	5-3B	-1
2008	ATL	MLB	26	15	3	1	0	0	0	1	2	0	0	-0.2	.286	.333	.357	.286	.333	.357	.249	-0.1	0.0				
2009	OMA	AAA	27	98	11	6	1	4	18	4	9	2	1	-1.2	.307	.354	.534	.289	.323	.467	.267	2.5	-0.2	8-LF	-4	5-C	0
2009	KCA	MLB	27	183	17	10	0	6	18	12	18	0	0	-0.6	.273	.318	.442	.274	.318	.427	.260	3.1	0.5	24-C	0		
2010	KCA	MLB	28	297	31	17	1	6	34	20	33	3	3	-1.7	.281	.335	.417	.272	.326	.407	.246	7.2	0.6	45-C	-2		

Breakout: 10%   Improve: 35%   Collapse: 29%   Attrition: 16%   MLB: 69%   Comparables: Paul Lo Duca, Riccardo Ingram, Carlos Ruiz, Javier Valentin

Pena has thrown out 30 percent of baserunners in his major- and minor-league career, though his receiving abilities are as bad as advertised; he averaged nearly one wild pitch or passed ball per game in 2009. This is something of a handicap for a catcher. Still, he did enough hitting from the left side of the plate in 2009 (.282/.321/.495) to provide value in spite of his weaknesses. The six home runs that Pena hit represent either a change in hitting philosophy or an incredible fluke—he hit only 25 round-trippers in 654 minor-league games. With the Olivo-Buck purge, Pena is presently first in line to back up Kendall, but in the near future, he'll have to fight the defensively gifted Manny Pina to keep his job.

Tim Smith · OF

Bats: L   Throws: L   Height: 6' 3"   Weight: 225   Born: June 14, 1986   Age: 24

YEAR	TEAM	LVL	AGE	PA	R	2B	3B	HR	RBI	BB	SO	SB	CS	EqBRR	AVG	OBP	SLG	EqAVG	EqOBP	EqSLG	EqA	VORP	WARP	DEFENSE			
2007	SPO	A-	21	96	18	5	0	1	9	11	16	1	2	-0.4	.284	.396	.383	.241	.313	.310	.218	-1.4	-0.9	19-CF	-3	3-RF	-1
2008	CLN	A	22	538	67	25	4	13	70	33	81	21	9	-1.6	.300	.359	.450	.267	.310	.388	.244	-0.7	-1.9	67-LF	-17	12-RF	2
2009	BAK	A+	23	138	18	5	0	4	19	10	20	7	1	-0.4	.333	.413	.475	.286	.341	.381	.257	1.8	-0.4	30-LF	-5		
2009	FRI	AA	23	160	22	9	0	3	32	14	21	8	1	0.6	.309	.380	.439	.301	.358	.427	.278	5.8	0.7	26-LF	0	4-RF	0
2010	TEX	MLB	24	401	43	18	1	9	49	29	75	7	3	-0.4	.262	.324	.390	.264	.326	.388	.236	-1.7	-0.9	71-LF	-6		

Breakout: 16%   Improve: 47%   Collapse: 13%   Attrition: 7%   MLB: 7%   Comparables: Kurt Bierek, Barry Jones, Robin Jennings, Richard Lane

In return for the talented but troubled pitcher Danny Gutierrez, the Royals acquired Smith and catcher Manny Pina from the Rangers. Smith is a solid all-around hitter with no standout skill. Despite his big frame, he has deceptively good speed and uses it well. Since he throws lefty, he's relegated to left field, but that fits in well with Lough in center and Parraz in right—Omaha will have a very athletic outfield in 2010.

Mark Teahen · 3B

Bats: L   Throws: R   Height: 6' 3"   Weight: 210   Born: September 6, 1981   Age: 28

YEAR	TEAM	LVL	AGE	PA	R	2B	3B	HR	RBI	BB	SO	SB	CS	EqBRR	AVG	OBP	SLG	EqAVG	EqOBP	EqSLG	EqA	VORP	WARP	DEFENSE			
2007	KCA	MLB	25	608	78	31	8	7	60	55	127	13	5	3.1	.285	.353	.410	.280	.350	.408	.265	13.4	0.8	130-RF	-6	6-1B	-1
2008	KCA	MLB	26	623	66	31	4	15	59	46	131	4	3	-1.8	.255	.313	.402	.257	.316	.406	.249	4.1	-0.1	85-RF	-4	30-LF	3
2009	KCA	MLB	27	571	69	34	1	12	50	37	123	8	1	-1.3	.271	.325	.408	.272	.325	.400	.256	10.7	-0.3	99-3B	-8	29-RF	-5
2010	CHA	MLB	28	584	66	28	4	12	54	52	126	8	4	0.0	.259	.330	.396	.262	.330	.396	.246	6.6	0.2	125-3B	-5		

Breakout: 12%   Improve: 47%   Collapse: 9%   Attrition: 6%   MLB: 96%   Comparables: B.J. Surhoff, Ken Oberkfell, Steve Lyons, Jack Howell

If you want an example of why the World Baseball Classic is evil, consider patriotic Canadian-American Teahen, who blew off his obligations in Royals camp—where he was supposed to be learning how to play second—to play the hot corner for Team Canada. As far as its relevance to helping the Royals win games, this was one step removed from leaving camp to take cello lessons from Yo-Yo Ma. Injuries rendered the defection moot, as Gordon's trip to the DL ended the keystone experiment after three games (in which he looked awful to boot). Teahen spent the rest of the season plying his trade at third and right field, two positions for which his bat isn't an asset; as AL second basemen batted .275 /.336/.428, his bat wouldn't have played well there, either. In November, the White Sox, an organization famous for its poor taste in third basemen (there's even a book about it, *Who's On 3rd*, by Richard Lindberg), dealt Chris Getz and Josh Fields for Teahen and cash, and then granted Teahen a three-year extension to be the exemplar of their hot-corner legacy through 2012. We're now three years removed from the 2006 campaign where he relearned how to pull the ball and gave glimmers of hope; at this point, he's just a placeholder, and not a good one.

PITCHERS

Brian Bannister

Bats: R   Throws: R   Height: 6' 2"   Weight: 210   Born: February 28, 1981   Age: 29

YEAR	TEAM	LVL	AGE	W	L	SV	G	GS	IP	H	HR	BB	SO	GB%	BABIP	STUFF	WHIP	ERA	SIERA	DERA	EqH9	EqHR9	EqBB9	EqSO9	VORP	SN/WX
2007	OMA	AAA	26	1	1	0	4	4	20²	16	4	4	14	60%	.207	-3	0.97	2.61	3.78	5.26	7.8	2.3	1.8	4.6	0.5	0.38
2007	KCA	MLB	26	12	9	0	27	27	165	156	15	44	77	48%	.261	13	1.21	3.87	5.03	3.65	7.8	0.7	2.1	3.9	34.0	4.66
2008	KCA	MLB	27	9	16	0	32	32	182²	215	29	58	113	46%	.308	-5	1.49	5.76	4.72	5.60	10.0	1.3	2.5	5.1	-2.0	1.65
2009	OMA	AAA	28	0	1	0	3	3	13	12	1	1	8	76%	.268	2	1.00	3.46	3.29	3.91	8.5	1.4	0.7	4.3	2.2	0.34
2009	KCA	MLB	28	7	12	0	26	26	154	161	15	50	98	56%	.291	14	1.37	4.73	4.54	4.78	8.4	0.7	2.4	5.0	12.6	2.34
2010	KCA	MLB	29	8	9	0	30	30	161¹	174	18	51	88	48%	.301	3	1.39	4.45	4.85	4.41	9.0	1.0	2.6	4.7	19.5	1.86

Breakout: 7%   Improve: 51%   Collapse: 6%   Attrition: 16%   MLB: 95%   Comparables: Todd Stottlemyre, Jack Fisher, Kyle Lohse, Jeff Suppan

Bannister was optioned to Omaha at the end of spring training in favor of Sidney Ponson and Horacio Ramirez before getting his recall in late April. Always thinking, Bannister changed his approach in 2009, eschewing rising four-seam fastballs in favor of a cutter designed to induce more grounders. This worked quite well for a while, as Bannister's ground-ball rate shot up and he generated a 3.59 ERA through his start of August 7th, a seven-inning shutout of

Tampa Bay. That was when disaster struck, as Bannister was slammed for a 9.29 ERA in six starts before being shut down with shoulder fatigue. Bannister's intelligent approach to the game makes him an easy guy to root for, but at 29, he still hasn't put together a successful 30-start season in the majors. If a pitcher can *think* his way to effectiveness, Bannister is that guy. Perhaps this will be the year.

Roman Colon

Bats: R   Throws: R   Height: 6' 6"   Weight: 225   Born: August 13, 1979   Age: 30

YEAR	TEAM	LVL	AGE	W	L	SV	G	GS	IP	H	HR	BB	SO	GB%	BABIP	STUFF	WHIP	ERA	SIERA	DERA	EqH9	EqHR9	EqBB9	EqSO9	VORP	SN/WX
2007	ERI	AA	27	2	0	1	5	1	10²	11	3	5	10	43%	.276	-14	1.50	5.91	4.02	6.75	10.8	2.7	4.5	6.3	-1.4	-0.18
2008	NWA	AA	28	2	0	1	10	0	17	18	1	4	8	43%	.288	-27	1.29	5.29	5.01	6.21	9.7	1.1	2.2	2.7	-1.3	0.11
2008	OMA	AAA	28	5	5	1	23	10	95	109	15	27	62	51%	.313	-29	1.43	4.64	4.39	5.28	11.3	1.9	2.7	4.4	2.2	0.75
2009	OMA	AAA	29	2	3	2	13	0	25¹	27	1	8	26	38%	.356	5	1.38	2.84	3.30	3.70	10.0	0.7	3.0	7.0	4.9	0.22
2009	KCA	MLB	29	2	3	0	43	0	50¹	50	7	22	29	47%	.269	-12	1.43	4.83	5.15	4.30	8.1	1.1	3.3	4.6	6.9	-0.01
2010	KCA	MLB	30	2	5	0	36	0	64²	81	10	27	35	47%	.328	-17	1.68	5.72	5.23	5.70	10.6	1.3	3.5	4.6	-1.4	0.88

Breakout: 18% Improve: 44% Collapse: 28% Attrition: 14%   MLB: 38%   Comparables: Jim Czajkowski, Wes Wilkerson, Jim Ed Warden, Dale Mohorcic

The Royals have so many former Braves pitchers that it wouldn't be a surprise to see Tom Glavine on the rubber one of these days. The Royals acquired Colon in 2007 after an off-field incident made him persona non grata with the Tigers. He put up some decent numbers in Omaha in 2009 before receiving a call to join the ailing bullpen. He was ineffective in general terms (his 4.82 Fair Run Average was below average) and effective by Royals standards (it was the third-best in the Royals pen). There is little to recommend him—indeed, there may be *less* to recommend him— over any of 100 other relievers looking for a big-league job.

Aaron Crow

Bats: R   Throws: R   Height: 6' 3"   Weight: 195   Born: November 11, 1986   Age: 23

Did Not Play.

Breakout: 18% Improve: 44% Collapse: 28% Attrition: 14%   MLB: 38%   Comparables: NA

Drafted by the Nationals with the ninth overall pick of the 2008 draft, Crow didn't sign and ended up going to the Royals in 2009 at 12th overall, losing some of the bonus money the Nats offered in the process, but gaining a major-league contract. In the year between the two selections, he took some time off, pitching some independent league ball in the spring, and his stuff was still good but not nearly as sharp as it had looked in college. Now a year older and a year further away from free agency, Crow is still a power arm with good velocity and a good slider. He'll be expected to move up quickly, and at his age, he almost has to if he's going to make up for his lack of pro experience.

Juan Cruz

Bats: R   Throws: R   Height: 6' 2"   Weight: 145   Born: October 15, 1978   Age: 31

YEAR	TEAM	LVL	AGE	W	L	SV	G	GS	IP	H	HR	BB	SO	GB%	BABIP	STUFF	WHIP	ERA	SIERA	DERA	EqH9	EqHR9	EqBB9	EqSO9	VORP	SN/WX
2007	ARI	MLB	28	6	1	0	53	0	61	45	7	32	87	37%	.290	25	1.26	3.10	2.62	3.69	6.9	0.7	4.1	10.8	12.3	0.82
2008	ARI	MLB	29	4	0	0	57	0	51²	34	5	31	71	33%	.276	28	1.26	2.61	2.92	2.70	6.5	0.7	4.9	10.4	15.6	1.12
2009	KCA	MLB	30	3	4	2	46	0	50¹	46	6	29	38	25%	.276	-5	1.49	5.72	5.47	5.31	7.7	0.9	4.5	6.1	1.1	0.06
2010	KCA	MLB	31	3	3	1	57	1	55²	54	6	29	55	30%	.319	5	1.50	4.65	4.18	4.55	7.9	1.0	4.4	8.4	5.8	0.52

Breakout: 12% Improve: 36% Collapse: 39% Attrition: 9%   MLB: 92%   Comparables: Frank LaCorte, Jason Frasor, Scott Bankhead, Don Elston

For reasons that remain obscure, the Royals sacrificed their second-round draft choice to sign Cruz as spring training began. He pitched well in April, then was relentlessly savaged over the next three months (opponents hit .273/.378/.468) before he was shut down with a shoulder strain. Cruz returned roughly seven weeks later, but didn't pitch enough (just 3 ⅔ innings) to support any conclusions about future effectiveness. Even at his best, Cruz is wild, averaging nearly five walks per nine innings during his career, and with his strikeout rate cut nearly in half last season, he just didn't miss enough bats to survive all those baserunners. One season and the inevitable buyout remain before he concludes his KC run.

Kyle Davies

Bats: R   Throws: R   Height: 6' 2"   Weight: 205   Born: September 9, 1983   Age: 26

YEAR	TEAM	LVL	AGE	W	L	SV	G	GS	IP	H	HR	BB	SO	GB%	BABIP	STUFF	WHIP	ERA	SIERA	DERA	EqH9	EqHR9	EqBB9	EqSO9	VORP	SN/WX
2007	ATL	MLB	23	4	8	0	17	17	86	92	12	44	59	48%	.294	-9	1.58	5.76	4.94	6.22	9.7	1.3	4.1	5.5	-6.9	0.97
2007	KCA	MLB	23	3	7	0	11	11	50	63	10	26	40	40%	.331	-6	1.78	6.66	4.76	6.49	10.5	1.6	4.0	6.5	-5.6	0.08
2008	OMA	AAA	24	6	2	0	11	11	57²	47	4	21	38	47%	.254	-1	1.18	2.03	4.51	3.89	8.0	1.0	3.3	4.3	9.7	1.24
2008	KCA	MLB	24	9	7	0	21	21	113	121	10	43	71	45%	.307	8	1.45	4.06	4.82	4.11	9.4	0.7	3.1	5.4	17.1	2.59
2009	OMA	AAA	25	4	2	0	8	8	46¹	47	3	14	44	48%	.328	11	1.32	2.14	3.44	4.16	9.5	1.2	2.8	6.7	6.6	0.54
2009	KCA	MLB	25	8	9	0	22	22	123	122	18	66	86	51%	.286	4	1.53	5.27	4.88	4.82	8.4	1.0	4.3	5.7	9.1	2.05
2010	KCA	MLB	26	7	10	0	32	32	156	174	19	74	100	48%	.314	-1	1.58	5.10	4.95	5.03	9.3	1.0	3.9	5.5	8.2	1.83

Breakout: 7%   Improve: 46%   Collapse: 16%   Attrition: 20%   MLB: 93%   Comparables: Skip Lockwood, Kyle Lohse, Matt Keough, Kan Ohtake

With an excellent September in 2008 and probably the best showing of any Royals pitcher in spring training, Davies had a stranglehold on the third spot in the rotation to start the season. His first start, seven innings of shutout ball against the White Sox, ended up being his sole season highlight; by mid-June, he had an ERA of 5.76 and was exiled to Omaha. Recalled in August, Davies was bombed in his first start back, but again finished strong, putting up a 3.48 ERA over his final six starts. He has the gifts to be a solid middle-rotation guy, but tends to nibble instead of just trusting his stuff. He'll be in the rotation mix again, but now that he's in his arbitration years, only improvement over full seasons will guarantee tendered contracts.

Daniel Duffy

Bats: L   Throws: L   Height: 6' 2"   Weight: 185   Born: December 21, 1988   Age: 21

YEAR	TEAM	LVL	AGE	W	L	SV	G	GS	IP	H	HR	BB	SO	GB%	BABIP	STUFF	WHIP	ERA	SIERA	DERA	EqH9	EqHR9	EqBB9	EqSO9	VORP	SN/WX
2007	ROY	Rk	18	2	3	0	11	9	37¹	24	0	17	63	41%	.324	35	1.10	1.45	1.69	4.24	8.2	1.3	4.9	8.5	4.9	0.45
2008	BUR	A	19	8	4	0	17	17	81²	56	4	25	102	33%	.274	34	0.99	2.20	2.35	4.50	8.5	1.6	3.8	6.9	8.2	0.68
2009	WIL	A+	20	9	3	0	24	24	126²	108	6	41	125	44%	.297	17	1.18	2.98	3.30	5.41	10.1	1.5	3.6	5.8	1.2	0.91
2010	KCA	MLB	21	5	8	0	26	26	115	128	16	54	83	35%	.318	22	1.58	5.21	4.92	5.20	9.4	1.2	4.0	6.2	3.8	2.86

Breakout: 11%   Improve: 44%   Collapse: 11%   Attrition: 6%   MLB: 8%   Comparables: John Bohnet, Arthur Rhodes, Chris Myers, Matt Ford

Along with Michael Montgomery and Tim Melville, this 2007 third-rounder gives the Royals three pitchers who have both the projection and the performance to warrant genuine excitement. Duffy is a step below Montgomery and Melville on a stuff level, with his best pitch a curve to go with an average-to-tick-above heater. While the M&M boys have a chance to be second or third starters, Duffy projects as more of an eventual fourth man. Of course, when we say "number four," we're talking about major-league teams—on the Royals, anyone else's number four is actually a number two, anyone else's number two is actually a number one, and Zack Greinke exists in a class by himself.

Kyle Farnsworth

Bats: R   Throws: R   Height: 6' 4"   Weight: 235   Born: April 14, 1976   Age: 34

YEAR	TEAM	LVL	AGE	W	L	SV	G	GS	IP	H	HR	BB	SO	GB%	BABIP	STUFF	WHIP	ERA	SIERA	DERA	EqH9	EqHR9	EqBB9	EqSO9	VORP	SN/WX
2007	NYA	MLB	31	2	1	0	64	0	60	60	9	27	48	29%	.283	-8	1.45	4.80	4.77	4.80	8.4	1.2	3.5	6.5	4.8	1.18
2008	NYA	MLB	32	1	2	1	45	0	44¹	43	11	17	43	44%	.283	1	1.35	3.65	3.58	3.35	8.4	2.1	3.1	8.2	10.3	2.06
2008	DET	MLB	32	1	1	0	16	0	16	27	4	5	18	27%	.469	7	2.00	6.75	3.33	7.04	15.3	2.3	2.3	10.0	-2.6	-1.08
2009	KCA	MLB	33	1	5	0	41	0	37¹	43	3	14	42	46%	.370	13	1.53	4.58	3.24	4.62	9.7	0.5	2.8	8.8	3.7	-1.55
2010	KCA	MLB	34	3	4	0	57	0	55	63	8	23	49	36%	.340	-2	1.56	5.01	4.14	4.89	9.4	1.2	3.5	7.6	3.7	0.21

Breakout: 15%   Improve: 41%   Collapse: 38%   Attrition: 16%   MLB: 80%   Comparables: Kerry Ligtenberg, Rick White, Bob Howry, Guillermo Mota

Farnsworth is probably the worst clutch pitcher in the game; more than a year after he was traded out of the Bronx, you could still see "Anyone But Farnsworth" T-shirts around Yankee Stadium. In late-and-close situations, he allowed opposing hitters to hit .500 (19-for-38). In high-leverage situations, they hit .548 (17-for-31). In tie games, they hit .625 (10-for-31). Somehow, he held batters to less than a homer per nine innings after being a meatball machine over most of the rest of his career, and in games in which the margin was four or more runs in either direction, no one could touch him. But in every way that mattered, he was sacked, reduced to rubble, and the ground sown with salt. Why did the Royals sign him? No one knows. What did they hope to accomplish? Likewise a mystery. Why did they choose to devote six percent of their 2009 payroll to this well-known arsonist? Your guess is as good as ours. Will they get any value out of his last year on the roster prior to the obligatory buyout of his 2011 option? What do *you* think?

Zack Greinke

				Bats: R			Throws: R		Height: 6' 2"		Weight: 185		Born: October 21, 1983			Age: 26		

YEAR	TEAM	LVL	AGE	W	L	SV	G	GS	IP	H	HR	BB	SO	GB%	BABIP	STUFF	WHIP	ERA	SIERA	DERA	EqH9	EqHR9	EqBB9	EqSO9	VORP	SN/WX
2007	KCA	MLB	23	7	7	1	52	14	122	122	12	36	106	37%	.314	17	1.30	3.69	3.76	3.43	8.7	0.8	2.4	7.3	27.4	5.37
2008	KCA	MLB	24	13	10	0	32	32	202¹	202	21	56	183	49%	.308	26	1.28	3.47	3.52	3.53	8.6	0.8	2.2	7.5	44.2	5.74
2009	KCA	MLB	25	16	8	0	33	33	229¹	195	11	51	242	46%	.303	50	1.07	2.16	2.75	2.56	7.2	0.3	1.7	8.5	79.8	9.79
2010	KCA	MLB	26	12	9	0	42	31	197	195	19	55	179	43%	.317	27	1.26	3.71	3.47	3.70	8.3	0.8	2.3	7.8	39.6	4.80

Breakout: 2% Improve: 45% Collapse: 16% Attrition: 8%   MLB: 100%   Comparables: Jake Peavy, Daisuke Matsuzaka, Pedro Martinez, Camilo Pascual

The eagle has landed. In terms of the gap between Greinke's ability to prevent runs and the league average, the Cy Young winner's 2009 ranks as one of the 30 best of the modern era, and one of the top 15 of the postwar period. While not quite of the same level of dominance as Pedro, Maddux, or Clemens at their peaks, this is as close as anyone has come in some time. The question is, what does he do for an encore? There is one indication that a little (but just a little) luck may have been at work last season: with no one on base, opponents had an OPS of 696, while with men on, teams had an OPS of 493. You'd expect this type of split to even out, resulting in a slightly higher ERA. Greinke is signed through 2012; his 2010 salary will be a manageable $7.25 million, but his payout jumps to $13.5 million in 2011. Over the past three seasons, the Royals have averaged about $65.3 million in total payroll. If they remain consistent in this regard, about 21 percent of their player outlay would go to Greinke alone.

Luke Hochevar

				Bats: R			Throws: R		Height: 6' 5"		Weight: 205		Born: September 15, 1983			Age: 26		

YEAR	TEAM	LVL	AGE	W	L	SV	G	GS	IP	H	HR	BB	SO	GB%	BABIP	STUFF	WHIP	ERA	SIERA	DERA	EqH9	EqHR9	EqBB9	EqSO9	VORP	SN/WX
2007	WIC	AA	23	3	6	0	17	16	94	110	13	26	94	45%	.348	-6	1.45	4.69	3.35	6.53	11.0	1.7	2.7	6.8	-10.5	-1.10
2007	OMA	AAA	23	1	3	0	10	10	58	53	11	21	44	43%	.253	-10	1.28	5.12	4.26	5.76	9.4	2.3	3.5	5.3	-1.6	0.14
2007	KCA	MLB	23	0	1	0	4	1	12²	11	1	4	5	64%	.244	-7	1.18	2.13	5.07	2.84	7.1	0.7	2.8	3.6	3.7	0.06
2008	OMA	AAA	24	1	1	0	3	3	17¹	11	2	6	12	78%	.188	1	0.98	2.60	3.36	3.97	6.4	1.6	3.2	4.2	2.9	0.31
2008	KCA	MLB	24	6	12	0	22	22	129	143	12	47	72	59%	.305	4	1.47	5.51	4.82	5.26	9.5	0.8	2.9	4.7	3.4	1.23
2009	OMA	AAA	25	5	1	0	8	8	48	41	2	12	36	73%	.285	15	1.10	1.50	3.39	2.52	8.1	0.8	2.4	5.2	14.8	1.59
2009	KCA	MLB	25	7	13	0	25	25	143	167	23	46	106	55%	.321	2	1.49	6.55	4.23	6.00	9.7	1.1	2.5	6.0	-7.9	0.29
2010	KCA	MLB	26	8	10	0	34	32	162²	184	21	60	106	55%	.317	2	1.50	4.91	4.55	4.85	9.4	1.1	3.1	5.6	11.7	1.29

Breakout: 11% Improve: 48% Collapse: 10% Attrition: 16%   MLB: 81%   Comparables: LaTroy Hawkins, Jason Schmidt, Brett Tomko, Kip Wells

As with Bannister, Hochevar went into exile at the end of spring training so that the Royals could have their dalliance with Sir Sidney Ponson; Hochevar pitched well in the sticks and was back in mid-May. Getting a fix on the 2006 first overall draft pick remains difficult. He had some terrific starts, including an 80-pitch complete-game three-hitter against the Reds and a 13-strikeout, no-walk game against the Rangers. He also had just too many games where his line was destroyed by a single big inning: in his wins, Hochevar had an ERA of 2.49, against 10.88 in his losses, a larger-than-normal disparity. His ERA rose by the month, climaxing with a 9.38 for six September starts, but even amid the devastation, he pulled off a three-hit shutout of the White Sox. In Hochevar's defense, we should add that the Royals' indifferent fielding doesn't do his ground-ball-oriented approach any favors, but that's small consolation, given the 2006 first-rounders the Royals could have picked: Evan Longoria (no. 3), Clayton Kershaw (no. 7), Tim Lincecum (no. 10), Max Scherzer (no. 11), and so on.

Dusty Hughes

				Bats: L			Throws: L		Height: 5' 10"		Weight: 187		Born: June 29, 1982			Age: 28		

YEAR	TEAM	LVL	AGE	W	L	SV	G	GS	IP	H	HR	BB	SO	GB%	BABIP	STUFF	WHIP	ERA	SIERA	DERA	EqH9	EqHR9	EqBB9	EqSO9	VORP	SN/WX
2007	WIC	AA	25	6	2	1	25	16	108	98	5	45	77	40%	.280	1	1.32	3.08	4.68	4.12	8.3	0.8	3.8	4.7	16.3	0.81
2008	NWA	AA	26	5	2	3	20	4	52²	47	3	16	43	45%	.299	-2	1.20	2.91	3.77	3.56	9.2	0.9	3.2	5.6	10.3	0.91
2008	OMA	AAA	26	3	2	0	12	11	55¹	65	8	25	36	43%	.324	-25	1.63	5.04	4.94	5.66	11.7	1.7	4.2	4.4	-0.9	0.18
2009	OMA	AAA	27	3	3	1	34	11	87¹	79	6	41	76	45%	.297	-6	1.37	3.50	4.14	4.12	8.7	1.2	4.3	6.1	12.7	0.70
2009	KCA	MLB	27	0	2	0	8	1	14	13	2	8	15	56%	.306	7	1.50	5.14	3.81	5.14	7.7	1.3	4.5	8.4	0.6	0.33
2010	KCA	MLB	28	3	6	0	33	10	80²	90	11	39	49	41%	.309	-10	1.61	5.45	5.23	5.44	9.5	1.1	4.2	5.3	0.5	1.46

Breakout: 13% Improve: 43% Collapse: 18% Attrition: 22%   MLB: 14%   Comparables: Mark Bowden, Travis Baptist, Paul Gibson, Francisley Bueno

One of the many organizational soldiers at Omaha, Hughes was rewarded with a September call-up and a spot start against the White Sox. A swingman since 2006 Tommy John surgery, Hughes doesn't have a blazing fastball (it's a high-80s pitch that can occasionally touch the low 90s), but he does effectively mix it with a plus changeup and decent curveball. He pitched well enough to compete for a bullpen spot to start 2010, possibly as a lefty spot-reliever.

Victor Marte

Bats: R   Throws: R   Height: 6′ 2″   Weight: 227   Born: November 8, 1980   Age: 29

YEAR	TEAM	LVL	AGE	W	L	SV	G	GS	IP	H	HR	BB	SO	GB%	BABIP	STUFF	WHIP	ERA	SIERA	DERA	EqH9	EqHR9	EqBB9	EqSO9	VORP	SN/WX
2007	HRO	JPN	26	0	1	0	17	0	17^1	28	2	10	13	—	.406	-21	2.19	8.31	4.97	9.00	14.8	1.1	5.8	5.3	-6.6	1.63
2009	NWA	AA	28	2	1	4	13	0	22	15	1	5	17	46%	.226	0	0.91	2.45	3.69	3.38	6.3	0.8	2.1	5.5	5.0	0.29
2009	OMA	AAA	28	1	4	4	26	0	42^1	35	0	20	36	56%	.280	-1	1.30	2.13	4.13	3.51	7.4	0.4	4.0	5.5	9.4	0.33
2009	KCA	MLB	28	0	0	0	8	0	12	13	2	12	7	55%	.297	-12	2.08	8.25	6.20	7.71	9.3	1.5	7.7	4.6	-2.9	-0.04
2010	KCA	MLB	29	2	4	3	32	0	52	61	6	26	27	52%	.317	-16	1.68	5.45	5.42	5.40	9.8	1.1	4.2	4.3	0.6	0.64

Breakout: 18%   Improve: 57%   Collapse: 17%   Attrition: 19%   MLB: 18%   Comparables: Rob Stanifer, Jason Bullard, Kenny Greer, Robert Marquez

A product of the Hiroshima Toyo Carp's Dominican academy, Marte was purchased by the Royals after he spent three seasons in Japan. A nonroster invitee to Royals camp, he was initially assigned to Double-A but quickly moved up to Omaha after just two months and continued to impress with his heavy fastball, which allowed him to keep the ball in the park. Marte has been referred to as "effectively wild," but he was only the latter in the majors, and his fastball isn't the only thing about him that's heavy. Still, he showed enough to figure in the 2010 bullpen mix.

Gil Meche

Bats: R   Throws: R   Height: 6′ 3″   Weight: 220   Born: September 8, 1978   Age: 31

YEAR	TEAM	LVL	AGE	W	L	SV	G	GS	IP	H	HR	BB	SO	GB%	BABIP	STUFF	WHIP	ERA	SIERA	DERA	EqH9	EqHR9	EqBB9	EqSO9	VORP	SN/WX
2007	KCA	MLB	28	9	13	0	34	34	216	218	22	62	156	52%	.296	19	1.30	3.67	4.14	3.64	8.5	0.8	2.3	6.0	44.4	5.45
2008	KCA	MLB	29	14	11	0	34	34	210^1	204	19	73	183	43%	.303	25	1.32	3.98	3.86	3.79	8.4	0.7	2.8	7.2	39.7	4.96
2009	KCA	MLB	30	6	10	0	23	23	129	144	17	58	95	56%	.311	6	1.57	5.09	4.53	4.90	9.1	0.9	3.5	5.8	8.8	1.87
2010	KCA	MLB	31	9	9	0	29	29	164^2	174	18	62	116	47%	.311	11	1.44	4.41	4.48	4.37	8.9	0.9	3.2	6.0	20.7	2.37

Breakout: 5%   Improve: 43%   Collapse: 22%   Attrition: 15%   MLB: 96%   Comparables: Steve Renko, Chris Bosio, Darryl Kile, Aaron Sele

After two years of better-than-expected performances, the pitcher with the biggest contract in franchise history finally lived down to his pre-Royals rep as fragile and ineffective. Battling back spasms and then a dead arm, he was finally done in by a managerial assassination attempt: after two poor outings at the end of June, after which Meche complained of a dead arm, Hillman left him out for 121 and 114 pitches in consecutive starts. He pitched only one more time before going on the DL with a bad back. He returned 33 days later, pitched four bad outings in August to increase his ERA from 4.50 to 5.09, and was then shut down for the rest of the season with shoulder inflammation. Like Don Corleone, Meche has survived the hit, but we won't know until the season starts whether he'll go on, albeit in enfeebled fashion, make a full recovery, or see Sollozzo make another attempt on his life.

Tim Melville

Bats: R   Throws: R   Height: 6′ 5″   Weight: 210   Born: October 9, 1989   Age: 20

YEAR	TEAM	LVL	AGE	W	L	SV	G	GS	IP	H	HR	BB	SO	GB%	BABIP	STUFF	WHIP	ERA	SIERA	DERA	EqH9	EqHR9	EqBB9	EqSO9	VORP	SN/WX
2009	BUR	A	19	7	7	0	21	21	97^1	89	10	43	96	44%	.298	-15	1.36	3.79	3.71	7.66	11.1	2.8	5.2	5.3	-20.7	-1.24
2010	KCA	MLB	20	3	8	0	24	24	100^1	123	18	60	70	43%	.331	29	1.82	6.48	5.20	6.36	10.2	1.6	4.9	5.9	-9.6	1.09

Breakout: 35%   Improve: 80%   Collapse: 3%   Attrition: 4%   MLB: 0%   Comparables: J.M. Gold, Luis Rodriguez, Glenn Spagnola, Marshall Jones

Melville is one of the main catches resulting from the Royals' new drafting scheme of going over-slot for early-round talents who drop in the draft due to perceived signability issues. In Melville's case, they were able to snag a top arm in the fourth round, pressing him not only with dough but also with the chance to work from home, as the pitcher is a Missouri native. A big-bodied right-hander (his weight understates his size), Melville can get his fastball up to 94 mph and possesses a good breaking ball, but his changeup needs work and his command is just OK. Of course, he's only 20 years old, so he has time to mature.

Michael Montgomery

Bats: L   **Throws: L**   **Height: 6' 5"**   **Weight: 180**   **Born: July 1, 1989**   **Age: 20**

YEAR	TEAM	LVL	AGE	W	L	SV	G	GS	IP	H	HR	BB	SO	GB%	BABIP	STUFF	WHIP	ERA	SIERA	DERA	EqH9	EqHR9	EqBB9	EqSO9	VORP	SN/WX
2008	ROY	Rk	18	2	1	0	12	9	42²	31	2	12	34	62%	.257	15	1.01	1.69	3.38	3.65	8.5	2.4	3.9	3.6	7.6	0.42
2009	BUR	A	19	2	3	0	12	12	58	42	1	24	52	61%	.268	19	1.14	2.17	3.65	4.65	8.6	1.2	4.9	4.7	4.9	0.47
2009	WIL	A+	19	4	1	0	9	9	52	38	0	12	46	42%	.252	32	0.96	2.25	3.41	4.29	7.9	0.7	2.5	4.8	6.8	0.53
2010	KCA	MLB	20	6	8	0	28	26	124²	132	18	55	66	55%	.287	27	1.50	5.02	5.12	5.02	9.0	1.3	3.8	4.5	6.7	3.45

Breakout: 8%   Improve: 27%   Collapse: 21%   Attrition: 4%   MLB: 1%   Comparables: Larry Wimberly, Chuck Lofgren, John Bohnet, Justin Thompson

After an outstanding year, Montgomery has established himself as the top prospect in the Royals' system. The 36th overall pick in 2008's supplemental first round, Montgomery is a smart, heady kid with smooth, effortless mechanics and a fastball that sits in the low 90s (touching 94). Of all the pitchers the Royals are developing, Montgomery has the most star potential—a bit short of ace level, but star potential nonetheless.

Carlos Rosa

Bats: R   **Throws: R**   **Height: 6' 1"**   **Weight: 185**   **Born: September 21, 1984**   **Age: 25**

YEAR	TEAM	LVL	AGE	W	L	SV	G	GS	IP	H	HR	BB	SO	GB%	BABIP	STUFF	WHIP	ERA	SIERA	DERA	EqH9	EqHR9	EqBB9	EqSO9	VORP	SN/WX
2007	WIL	A+	22	2	1	0	4	4	23	18	0	3	15	58%	.254	14	0.91	0.39	3.72	1.90	8.9	0.8	1.7	3.8	8.5	0.81
2007	WIC	AA	22	6	6	1	21	17	97	101	8	43	70	57%	.313	-2	1.48	4.36	4.47	5.15	9.9	1.2	4.2	4.9	3.5	0.16
2008	NWA	AA	23	4	2	0	8	8	45	30	2	7	42	52%	.243	28	0.82	1.20	2.80	2.25	6.9	0.9	1.7	6.4	15.2	1.38
2008	OMA	AAA	23	4	3	0	11	11	50²	51	3	12	44	59%	.331	9	1.24	4.09	3.39	4.66	10.3	1.0	2.3	6.0	4.3	0.93
2009	OMA	AAA	24	2	8	7	43	0	71	69	6	32	80	59%	.337	-5	1.42	4.56	3.27	5.61	9.6	1.5	4.1	8.0	-0.9	-1.05
2009	KCA	MLB	24	0	0	1	7	0	10²	10	1	3	4	51%	.257	-16	1.22	3.37	5.36	3.05	7.8	0.9	2.6	3.5	2.8	0.07
2010	KCA	MLB	25	4	6	3	39	12	85²	96	11	39	59	52%	.319	-4	1.57	5.09	4.68	5.01	9.3	1.2	3.7	6.0	4.7	1.47

Breakout: 13%   Improve: 51%   Collapse: 18%   Attrition: 22%   MLB: 24%   Comparables: Brian Holton, Woody Williams, Paul Quinzer, Tom Wegmann

In 2009, fastball/slider pitcher Rosa boosted the ho-hum strikeout rate he had as a starter into something eye-popping as a reliever at Omaha. With the new focus on relieving, his fastball jumped from 94 mph to 97. Unfortunately, he was less effective overall, mainly from issuing more walks. When a pitcher is converted from starting to relieving, he's told to "just let it fly." Rosa let it fly to excess, perhaps, not worrying as much about command as much as he should have. He'll get another chance to make good this season.

Joakim Soria

Bats: R   **Throws: R**   **Height: 6' 3"**   **Weight: 185**   **Born: May 18, 1984**   **Age: 26**

YEAR	TEAM	LVL	AGE	W	L	SV	G	GS	IP	H	HR	BB	SO	GB%	BABIP	STUFF	WHIP	ERA	SIERA	DERA	EqH9	EqHR9	EqBB9	EqSO9	VORP	SN/WX
2007	KCA	MLB	23	2	3	17	62	0	69	46	3	19	75	42%	.250	37	0.94	2.48	2.73	2.39	5.6	0.4	2.2	8.8	24.1	4.90
2008	KCA	MLB	24	2	3	42	63	0	67¹	39	5	19	66	47%	.207	30	0.86	1.60	3.07	1.68	5.0	0.5	2.3	8.2	28.4	5.65
2009	KCA	MLB	25	3	2	30	47	0	53	44	5	16	69	44%	.300	30	1.13	2.21	2.33	2.14	7.1	0.7	2.3	9.5	20.4	4.90
2010	KCA	MLB	26	5	3	43	72	0	70²	54	6	22	68	43%	.267	20	1.08	2.98	3.28	3.00	6.5	0.7	2.6	8.3	19.6	3.76

Breakout: 18%   Improve: 37%   Collapse: 28%   Attrition: 15%   MLB: 100%   Comparables: Rawly Eastwick, Gregg Olson, Ugueth Urbina, Bruce Sutter

Hillman's usage of Soria in 2009 is Exhibit A in the trial against using closers in relatively low-leverage situations. Of his 47 appearances this year, only 16 times did he come into the game either facing a tie or with the Royals ahead by one run, and another 11 times, he arrived with the Royals ahead by two runs. Yet there were nine times when the Royals had a lead going into the eighth (plus an additional five times in the seventh), but couldn't get it to Soria and eventually lost. In defense of Hillman, for the first six weeks of the season, Soria battled through some sore shoulder issues, allegedly caused by a lack of work from the World Baseball Classic. After a stint on the DL at the end of May, Soria came back and put up great numbers for the third year in a row, cementing his status as a top closer. The Royals have locked him up until 2011 with club options through 2014 at very nice prices, especially if he maintains his current level.

Robinson Tejeda

Bats: R   Throws: R   Height: 6' 3"   Weight: 230   Born: March 24, 1982   Age: 28

YEAR	TEAM	LVL	AGE	W	L	SV	G	GS	IP	H	HR	BB	SO	GB%	BABIP	STUFF	WHIP	ERA	SIERA	DERA	EqH9	EqHR9	EqBB9	EqSO9	VORP	SN/WX
2007	TEX	MLB	25	5	9	0	19	19	95¹	110	17	60	69	35%	.308	-12	1.78	6.61	5.41	6.59	9.6	1.5	5.0	5.8	-11.7	-0.23
2008	TEX	MLB	26	0	0	0	4	0	6	5	1	5	4	22%	.211	-14	1.67	9.00	6.78	8.10	5.4	1.4	5.4	5.4	-1.9	-0.53
2008	KCA	MLB	26	2	2	0	25	1	39¹	22	3	19	41	35%	.204	20	1.04	3.20	3.61	3.55	4.8	0.7	3.9	8.7	8.5	0.95
2009	KCA	MLB	27	4	2	0	35	6	73²	43	4	50	87	34%	.231	37	1.26	3.54	3.83	3.24	4.9	0.4	5.3	9.4	18.8	2.02
2010	KCA	MLB	28	3	5	0	40	3	69	67	8	38	62	36%	.308	5	1.52	4.75	4.42	4.67	8.1	1.0	4.6	7.7	6.4	0.63

Breakout: 17% Improve: 44% Collapse: 19% Attrition: 13%   MLB: 86%   Comparables: Joaquin Benoit, Seth McClung, Dennis Sarfate, Rocky Biddle

Tejeda sometimes appears to be a little bit better than his hard-earned journeyman status suggests, and he had one of those tantalizing runs in the second half of last season. Over a stretch of 13 games spanning July 31st to September 20th, he was almost literally unhittable, pitching 38 ⅔ innings, allowing 14 hits and three runs (0.70 ERA) while walking 14 and striking out 45. Given that the last four appearances were starts, the Royals had visions of finding that elusive third starter behind Greinke and Meche. Unfortunately, the before and after parts of the picture were not nearly so pretty, as Tejeda's chronic control problems involved 35 walks and 27 runs allowed in 35 innings. Nevertheless, the ineffectiveness of Hochevar and Davies means Tejeda will be given another shot to make the back end of the rotation.

Blake Wood

Bats: R   Throws: R   Height: 6' 4"   Weight: 225   Born: August 8, 1985   Age: 24

YEAR	TEAM	LVL	AGE	W	L	SV	G	GS	IP	H	HR	BB	SO	GB%	BABIP	STUFF	WHIP	ERA	SIERA	DERA	EqH9	EqHR9	EqBB9	EqSO9	VORP	SN/WX
2007	BUR	A	21	2	1	0	7	7	35²	32	3	14	26	39%	.274	-1	1.29	3.03	4.53	4.50	10.4	2.3	4.5	3.9	3.6	0.16
2008	WIL	A+	22	3	2	0	10	10	57¹	32	3	15	63	45%	.225	30	0.82	2.67	2.50	3.83	6.8	1.4	3.0	7.1	9.6	0.85
2008	NWA	AA	22	5	7	0	18	18	86²	96	7	32	76	47%	.341	-1	1.48	5.30	3.93	6.59	11.0	1.3	3.6	5.8	-9.9	-0.68
2009	NWA	AA	23	2	8	0	17	13	78²	92	8	28	49	56%	.337	-25	1.53	5.83	4.58	6.97	11.9	1.9	3.5	4.6	-11.6	-1.56
2010	KCA	MLB	24	3	7	0	24	21	89¹	109	14	42	58	43%	.332	-11	1.70	5.93	5.02	5.89	10.3	1.3	3.9	5.6	-3.9	1.33

Breakout: 15% Improve: 46% Collapse: 12% Attrition: 15%   MLB: 5%   Comparables: Jose Veras, Greg McMichael, Mike Iglesias, Matt Lorenzo

Wood drives scouts (and probably the Royals) crazy, because if you catch him on the right day, he looks like a future big-league starter, whereas on other days, he leaves observers wondering if he's even qualified to pitch at Double-A. Assets include a plus-velocity fastball, a solid curve, and an above-average changeup, but he's just maddeningly inconsistent. Every team keeps guys with Wood's kind of physical tools around, hoping they'll get it, but few do.

Jamey Wright

Bats: R   Throws: R   Height: 6' 5"   Weight: 230   Born: December 24, 1974   Age: 35

YEAR	TEAM	LVL	AGE	W	L	SV	G	GS	IP	H	HR	BB	SO	GB%	BABIP	STUFF	WHIP	ERA	SIERA	DERA	EqH9	EqHR9	EqBB9	EqSO9	VORP	SN/WX
2007	OKL	AAA	32	2	1	0	3	3	16¹	21	2	3	11	78%	.339	-6	1.47	4.41	3.50	6.61	12.1	1.7	1.7	4.6	-1.9	-0.07
2007	TEX	MLB	32	4	5	0	20	9	77	72	6	41	39	61%	.276	0	1.47	3.62	5.23	3.71	8.1	0.6	4.5	4.4	14.7	1.79
2008	TEX	MLB	33	8	7	0	75	0	84¹	93	5	35	60	72%	.325	2	1.52	5.12	4.18	5.31	8.9	0.4	3.3	5.8	1.9	0.20
2009	KCA	MLB	34	3	5	0	65	0	79	73	8	44	60	73%	.281	0	1.48	4.33	4.29	5.01	7.7	0.7	4.3	6.2	4.3	0.92
2010	KCA	MLB	35	3	5	0	54	0	71²	77	8	35	40	68%	.302	-12	1.56	5.03	4.74	5.03	9.1	0.9	4.0	4.8	3.7	0.53

Breakout: 16% Improve: 46% Collapse: 25% Attrition: 20%   MLB: 91%   Comparables: Tanyon Sturtze, David Weathers, Guillermo Mota, Roger Mason

Wright was initially an afterthought, but he pitched himself into a more prominent role with a hot April. Then Lautrec, god of small sample sizes, smote Wright and the rest of his season was as unremarkable as the bulk of his previous career. Sadly, even after he again proved he was at best midgame mop-up relief, Hillman still assumed he had Soria Lite and overused him in high-leverage situations. Then again, given that the Royals' pen bore more than a passing resemblance to the fiery pits of Mount Doom, it's not as if the skipper had many options.

LINEOUTS

Hitters

PLAYER	TEAM	LVL	AGE	PA	R	2B	3B	HR	RBI	BB	SO	SB-CS	EqBRR	AVG/OBP/SLG	EqAVG/EqOBP/EqSLG	EqA	VORP	WARP
RF C. Aldridge*	OMA	AAA	30	385	48	20	4	22	71	24	86	0-1	-1.0	.316/.361/.582	.270/.309/.479	.265	7.1	-0.5
CF J. Anderson*	DET	MLB	26	175	22	4	4	0	16	8	22	13-2	-0.4	.242/.282/.315	.242/.282/.303	.223	-4.3	-0.2
	KCA	MLB	26	123	20	3	0	1	8	5	21	12-3	1.0	.237/.268/.288	.246/.276/.297	.213	-2.6	0.1
CF J. Dyson*	BUR	A	24	75	14	2	1	0	5	5	14	9-4	1.8	.343/.397/.403	.261/.292/.304	.213	-1.5	-0.5
	NWA	AA	24	283	38	7	4	0	14	27	54	37-6	0.7	.258/.331/.319	.230/.289/.281	.218	-4.8	-0.7
UT I. Falu#	OMA	AAA	26	532	64	19	5	2	40	52	35	12-5	0.2	.269/.342/.344	.257/.321/.326	.233	0.9	0.2
UT R. Freel	BAL	MLB	33	20	2	0	0	0	1	5	4	0-0	0.1	.133/.350/.133	.133/.350/.133	.205	-0.7	-0.1
	CHN	MLB	33	32	1	0	0	0	1	2	7	1-0	-0.3	.143/.226/.143	.138/.219/.138	.133	-2.3	-0.4
	KCA	MLB	33	49	8	2	0	0	3	4	12	0-0	0.2	.244/.306/.289	.244/.306/.289	.213	-1.2	-0.2
INF M. Lisson	NWA	AA	25	158	20	4	0	2	17	14	29	4-3	1.1	.206/.287/.279	.184/.247/.248	.178	-6.6	-1.3
	OMA	AAA	25	366	34	23	0	12	43	19	89	7-4	-1.6	.236/.282/.410	.227/.267/.385	.223	-0.7	0.0
C M. Pina	FRI	AA	22	355	36	17	1	8	42	19	58	1-0	-3.8	.259/.313/.393	.247/.287/.375	.231	4.8	0.0
CF D. Robinson#	WIL	A+	21	571	72	19	5	5	47	35	90	69-23	-1.1	.239/.290/.324	.234/.275/.313	.213	-10.8	-0.8
1B R. Shealy	OMA	AAA	29	108	15	7	0	0	12	18	25	0-0	-0.4	.345/.454/.425	.300/.398/.356	.279	2.1	0.3
OF S. Thorman*	OMA	AAA	27	405	45	12	2	19	63	21	66	5-3	-3.8	.297/.346/.496	.275/.317/.441	.259	6.9	0.0

Journeyman outfielder (and, yes, Braves castoff) **Cory Aldridge** had a great year at Omaha, but it didn't earn him a September cuppajoe. ⊘ With no power and a .313 OBP in his first 519 MLB plate appearances, **Josh Anderson** provides very little offense; most fielding stats suggest that he's an above-average center fielder, but his value is as a defensive replacement and pinch runner. He was nontendered in December; the Reds signed him to a minor-league contract. ⊘ **Jarrod Dyson** is an athletic outfielder whose performances suggest he'll be one of the most athletic guys—on the bench. ⊘ Who needs a Bloomquist when organizational soldier **Irving Falu** can play six positions *and* switch-hit? ⊘ **Ryan Freel** is the last refuge of the incompetent. ⊘ **Mario Lisson** has been protected on the 40-man after strong years in the Royals' hitter-unfriendly low-minors affiliates, but when he escaped the parks, he also escaped A-ball pitching; he's now two years removed from the last time he hit. ⊘ Good-field/no-hit catcher **Manny Pina** should eventually figure into the team's reserve backstop plans. ⊘ A second stint at Wilmington didn't improve **Derrick Robinson**'s numbers; he still has blazing speed, and scouts remain intrigued by his tools, but Double-A will make or break him. ⊘ Three years ago, **Ryan Shealy** was seen as one of Dayton Moore's first trading coups; after turning 30 this year, the fragile Shealy now seems an organizational soldier at best. ⊘ Former Braves hand **Scott Thorman** is more likely to invent a method of faster-than-light travel than he is to take ball four, and was granted free agency at year's end.

Pitchers

PLAYER	TEAM	LVL	AGE	W	L	SV	IP	H	HR	BB	SO	GB%	BABIP	STUFF	WHIP	ERA	SIERA	DERA	EqH9	EqHR9	EqBB9	EqSO9	VORP
J. Abreu	WIL	A+	24	3	2	12	21^1	8	1	14	28	35%	.167	10	1.03	1.69	3.15	3.43	5.5	1.4	6.4	7.8	4.5
	NWA	AA	24	2	2	4	20^1	19	3	22	25	42%	.308	7	2.02	5.75	4.73	7.52	9.3	2.2	8.9	8.9	-4.6
J. Bale*	KCA	MLB	35	0	1	1	28^1	34	3	18	24	52%	.344	-8	1.84	5.72	4.72	5.28	9.9	0.6	5.0	6.5	0.7
B. Chen*	OMA	AAA	32	4	2	0	82	57	8	23	69	42%	.224	9	0.98	3.40	3.64	4.14	6.7	1.6	2.6	5.8	12.0
	KCA	MLB	32	1	6	0	62^1	74	12	25	45	37%	.321	-8	1.59	5.78	4.74	5.33	9.9	1.5	3.2	5.8	1.2
L. Coleman	WIL	A+	23	3	1	1	14^1	8	0	3	16	38%	.229	5	0.77	1.26	2.33	3.71	6.8	0.7	2.7	6.8	2.6
L. DiNardo*	OMA	AAA	29	10	5	2	151^2	139	5	38	127	67%	.300	18	1.17	3.32	3.44	4.08	8.5	0.7	2.4	5.7	23.1
	KCA	MLB	29	0	3	0	21^1	41	2	15	8	65%	.429	-30	2.62	10.12	5.97	10.76	16.5	0.8	5.5	3.0	-12.5
C. Hayes	NWA	AA	26	3	0	3	36^2	33	1	6	17	73%	.260	-10	1.06	0.98	4.00	3.50	8.0	0.8	1.8	3.0	8.0
	OMA	AAA	26	1	6	3	49	67	2	7	24	58%	.357	-20	1.51	4.59	4.60	5.48	12.1	0.8	1.5	3.2	0.1
J. Lamb*	IDA	Rk	18	3	1	0	41^1	33	4	11	46	0%	.282	14	1.06	3.70	2.71	6.56	9.7	2.7	4.0	5.4	-4.3
	BRL	Rk	18	2	2	0	27^1	24	4	9	25	0%	.263	-6	1.21	3.95	3.63	7.52	12.3	3.9	5.0	4.2	-5.2
A. Lerew	NWA	AA	26	10	6	0	152	164	14	55	101	51%	.305	-18	1.44	4.09	4.57	5.54	10.3	1.6	3.4	4.6	-0.6
	KCA	MLB	26	0	1	0	13^1	14	4	8	7	31%	.233	-17	1.65	4.05	6.25	4.50	8.4	1.9	4.5	3.9	1.6
S. Ponson	OMA	AAA	32	2	1	0	33	34	2	5	19	73%	.317	4	1.18	2.18	3.72	2.76	10.1	1.2	1.8	4.3	8.9
	KCA	MLB	32	1	7	0	58^2	79	6	25	32	59%	.351	-13	1.77	7.36	5.07	6.67	11.2	0.8	3.4	4.4	-7.6
T. Sample	BRL	Rk	20	4	2	1	50^2	34	2	20	44	0%	.227	9	1.07	2.84	3.90	6.50	9.2	2.0	5.6	3.6	-5.0
D. Waechter	OMA	AAA	28	1	1	1	18^2	22	0	1	10	54%	.333	-13	1.23	4.82	4.19	5.65	10.3	0.5	1.0	3.4	-0.3
	KCA	MLB	28	0	0	0	5^1	9	2	3	3	47%	.350	-31	2.25	8.44	5.58	7.94	12.7	3.2	4.8	4.8	-1.5
Y. Yabuta	KCA	MLB	36	2	1	0	14	29	3	7	9	35%	.448	-35	2.57	13.50	5.48	11.66	16.6	1.2	3.7	4.9	-10.0
	OMA	AAA	36	2	1	0	45^2	39	5	17	53	40%	.293	2	1.23	3.55	2.94	4.26	8.3	1.8	3.5	8.1	6.1

Not all the traffic is one-way: no sooner had slow-developing Dominican righty **Juan Abreu** managed to reach Double-A than he escaped the Royals' system to sign a big-league contract with the Braves as a minor-league free agent. ⊘ After a season ruined by a dead arm and a losing bout with a door, **John Bale** got off to an even worse start in 2009 when he lost 25 pounds from a hyperactive thyroid; he was waived in December. ⊘ **Henry Barrera** is a power pitcher who needs to get past a stretch of 2009 arm problems. ⊘ **Bruce Chen** delivered sub-replacement, back-end rotation filler most clubs have in abundance, but seems in short supply here; rather than hop to his 12th organization, he reupped with the Royals on a minor-league contract. ⊘ Like Crow, **Louis Coleman** was someone the Nationals drafted in 2008 but didn't sign, only to have the Royals get him the next year; his stuff isn't that good, but it's solid. ⊘ Journeyman **Lenny DiNardo** somehow posted the lowest SNLVAR and VORP of any Royals pitcher, doing so in just five starts in September. ⊘ Soft-tossing submariner and uber-blogger **Chris Hayes** continued to dazzle in the first half of the year at Double-A, but slipped in the second half at Omaha; he retains a small chance of making it. ⊘ If not for a car accident, **John Lamb** might have been a 2008 first-rounder; with a fine combo of size and stuff, he's pitched like one since signing. ⊘ Another castoff from the Braves' system, **Anthony Lerew** lost most of the 2007-2008 period to Tommy John surgery and the ensuing rehab. ⊘ In one fell swoop, injury wiped out both **Julio Pimental**'s 2009 season and his status as a top pitching prospect in the system; he'll be lucky to pitch in 2010 as he recovers from Tommy John surgery. ⊘ Solid outings for the Dutch team in the World Baseball Classic were enough to fool Moore into thinking that **Sidney Ponson** had something to offer; Moore wasn't the only sucker—since 2004, Ponson has pitched 121 games for six teams, putting up a 5.82 ERA. ⊘ A 2008 third-rounder, **Tyler Sample** is a physically intimidating (6-foot-7, 245 pounds) specimen who has been brought along slowly because of his inexperience. He has as much upside as any pitcher in the system, but is far from achieving it. ⊘ Last year, we predicted **Doug Waechter** would be a prime example of the volatility of relief pitchers; luckily for the Royals, he was never healthy enough to do much damage, and he underwent season-ending labrum surgery in August. ⊘ Moore hasn't taken heat for dishing out a two-year, $6 million contract for **Yasuhiko Yabuta**, perhaps because the Farnsworth signing gives critics more than enough ammunition.

MANAGER: TREY HILLMAN

YEAR	TEAM	W-L	Pythag +/−	Avg PC	100+ P	120+ P	QS	BQS	REL	REL w Zero R	IBB	Subs	PH	PH Avg	PH HR	SB2	CS2	SB3	CS3	SAC Att	SAC %	POS SAC	Squeeze	Swing	In Play
2008	KCA	75-87	4	98.2	73	2	76	2	438	277	15	52	71	.270	1	58	32	21	6	57	56.1%	28	0	122	97
2009	KCA	65-97	0	97.6	74	4	70	8	425	212	28	53	90	.207	2	79	27	8	1	64	59.4%	37	3	118	95

When Hillman was given the reins of the Royals, he said that he wanted to merge Japanese small-ball with American-style baseball. In 2008, the Royals had the fifth-most attempted sacrifices in the American League, despite a fundamentally atrocious success rate; in 2009, Hillman again finished fifth in the AL in sacrifice attempts, despite an equally poor success rate. You would think that at some point, like General Currie's standing up to Field Marshal Haig's order to make another charge at Passchendaele, someone in the organization might call attention to the senseless butchery. This underscores Hillman's main weakness as a manager: he does not adjust his decisions according to his players' strengths and weaknesses. In other words, he doesn't put his players in a position to succeed. More disturbing during these two years are the long stretches of poor play, during which it has sometimes seemed as if Hillman had lost the team. Since Dayton Moore's job is secure through 2014 with his contract extension, if the Royals don't improve at least by the time Greinke's contract runs out in 2012 (or sooner), you can anticipate that Hillman's brand of baseball will make him the fall guy for the franchise's continued woes.

Los Angeles Angels of Anaheim

From the 30,000-foot view, the 2009 Angels' season looked a lot like those of recent years: they drew more fans than did any other AL team except the Yankees, won the AL West by a comfortable margin with a nucleus featuring John Lackey, Chone Figgins, and other homegrown talents, then were bounced from the playoffs prior to reaching the World Series. Though they didn't win a world championship, they retained their place among the game's most successful franchises, both on the field and at the gate. Same old, same old.

A closer look reveals a few key distinctions between the 2009 Angels and their predecessors. From the outset of the season, the departures of Garret Anderson and Francisco Rodriguez, two of the small handful of players remaining from the team's 2002 world championship, created an air of transition from what has become the Angels' brand of baseball under Mike Scioscia—the primacy of contact skills, batting average, and baserunning ahead of power and patience, and the certainty of a strong late-inning relief crew. While the Angels continued to beat opponents, they did so in different fashion. Their offense set a franchise record with 883 runs scored, a total second only to the Yankees, while the team allowed 761 runs, more than any other Angels club since 2000, Scioscia's first year as manager.

Even in winning with a different blend of offense and pitching than before, the 2009 club shared a unique distinction with its predecessors: significant overachievement relative to its Pythagenpat record. The Angels exceeded their first-order Pythagenpat projection—their expected win total based on runs scored and runs allowed—for the sixth year in a row, the game's longest

active streak, and the third-longest of the past decade, behind the 2000-2007 Expos/Nationals and the 2000-2006 Yankees.

Furthermore, the 2009 club became the first in history to exceed its *third-order* Pythagenpat projection—its expected win total based on the combination of events on the field (hits, walks, total bases, stolen bases, and outs of all kinds, as well as those of their opponents), all adjusted for park, league, and quality of competition—by at least 10 games for two consecutive years, and by at least eight games for three straight years. The 2008 Angels actually shattered the record for such overachievement, outdoing their expected record by a whole 16 wins, while the 2007 club did so by 8.1 wins.

We often talk of teams that over- or underperform their projected records as "lucky" or "unlucky," but it's a mistake to chalk up the entirety of such discrepancies to luck. They generally stem from an irregular distribution of runs; overachieving teams tend to win most of the close games but get blown out a few times, losses that distort their run differentials. The Angels were 27-18 (.600) in one-run games, the league's second-best winning percentage, but they were 2-5 in games decided by 10 or more runs, so at the extremes, they were outscored by 26 runs despite going 29-23.

A major factor in outperforming one's projected record is having relatively more success in higher-leverage situations, such as hitting well with runners in scoring position or being especially stingy in late-game relief. Since 1954, the correlation between a team's cumulative WXRL and its third-order discrepancy is .42, by far the highest of any of our offensive, defensive, or pitching metrics. As bullpen usage has become increas-

ANGELS PROSPECTUS
2009 W-L: 97-65, 1st in AL West

Pythag	87-75	4th
RS/G	5.5	2nd
RA/G	4.7	9th
EqA	.266	4th
EqBRR	1.3	5th
SNWP	.511	4th
WXRL	8.57	7th
FRAr	4.80	11th
DE	.689	8th
PADE	-0.92	8th
Salary	$113.7	4th
Attend	3.24	2nd

Ballpark: Angel Stadium (3-yr. PF: 1023). Still in Anaheim, the Big A cuts into homers

2009: Overcame the Adenhart tragedy and blew by their expected record—again

2010: Lack of Lackey and Figgins makes fending off threats from Texas and Seattle that much harder

Action Items: Shoring up the staff, Kendry's '09 must be real, Brandon Wood's time must be now

ingly more codified via matchup specialists and one-inning closers, the correlation has increased; since 1996, the first full season since the strike, it has risen to .48. By comparison, the latter-day correlations for our other win-expectancy-based stats are .20 for SNLVAR (our starting pitching stat) and .38 for WX (our hitter stat).

The Angels' consistent overachievement is the result of repeated success in those higher-leverage situations, particularly via the bullpen. While they only placed seventh in the AL in WXRL in 2009 (more on this below), they've been regulars near the top of the league rankings in recent years (see Table 1).

Table 1. Wind Under Angels' Wings: Pen Performance in Anaheim, 2000-09

Year	W-L	D3*	WXRL	AL Rank
2000	82-80	0.5	9.9	5
2001	75-87	-5.3	7.3	7
2002	99-63	-2.6	12.8	2
2003	77-85	-4.6	10.9	3
2004	92-70	0.8	13.0	4
2005	95-67	6.7	13.5	1
2006	89-73	-1.8	14.2	2
2007	94-68	8.1	10.7	6
2008	100-62	16.0	13.3	3
2009	97-65	10.2	8.6	7

*D3: The difference between the expected third-order Pythagenpat-projected record and actual record.

That's a testament not only to the talent on hand, including Rodriguez and longtime top set-up man Scot Shields, but also to Scioscia's seemingly innate ability to run a bullpen and the front office's ability to corral a stable full of live arms, many of them on the cheap. While they haven't been as consistent with the bat for as long, the Angels have finished in the AL top three in hitter WX in each of the past three years.

For awhile, it looked as though the bullpen would actually topple the 2009 Angels; during April, their relievers posted a 7.83 Fair Run Average and a league-worst -1.6 WXRL while taking seven of the team's losses in a 9-12 month. The bigger story during April, however, was the rotation, which began the year with both Lackey and Ervin Santana on the DL, but soon faced an even bigger loss: top pitching prospect Nick Adenhart had overcome a dismal 2008 to earn a rotation spot with a strong spring, but hours after the 22-year-old tossed six shutout innings in the season's third game, he was fatally injured when the car in which he was riding was struck by a drunk driver.

The tragedy indelibly marked the season, and while a makeshift rotation—swingman Dustin Moseley, journeyman Shane Loux, et al.—held things together behind Jered Weaver and Joe Saunders until the big guns could heal, in the end Weaver (3.75 ERA, .565 SNWP) and Lackey (3.83, .540) were the only two starters to make at least 10 starts with an SNWP above .500. Thirty-year-old rookie Matt Palmer (3.93, .489) had a reasonably strong stint in the rotation, but Saunders (4.60, .481) and Santana (5.03, .466) came nowhere near matching their 2008 breakouts. The team did get a notable late-season reinforcement when general manager Tony Reagins shipped three prospects to Tampa Bay for Scott Kazmir just as the lefty got his groove back.

As for the bullpen, in the wake of Rodriguez's departure, Reagins signed former Rockies closer Brian Fuentes to a two-year, $17.5 million contract. He was erratic all season, with Fair Run Averages above 5.00 in four out of six months, including April. Neither Shields nor Jose Arredondo (both of whom had finished in the league's top 20 in WXRL in 2008) were very good, either, and top lefty Darren Oliver was briefly pulled into the decimated rotation before suffering a triceps strain. Justin Speier pitched so poorly that the team released him, eating more than a third of his $18 million deal. The pen eventually rounded into shape, thanks to Oliver's recovery and the emergence of rookies Kevin Jepsen and Jason Bulger as high-leverage options. Both men helped to cover for the loss of Shields, who needed surgery to alleviate patellar tendinitis. From May 1st to the end of the season, the Angels' bullpen ranked second in the league in WXRL, behind the Yankees, a much more characteristic performance.

Just as the pitching staff endured transition, the offensive attack differed markedly from past Angels' clubs. The departure of late-2008 acquisition Mark Teixeira left a gaping hole in the lineup as far as both power and patience were concerned, but 26-year-old Cuban defector Kendry Morales, who'd done little in three partial years with the Angels, clubbed 34 homers and finished second in the league in slugging percentage (.569). A fully healthy Juan Rivera took over left field from the departed mainstay, Anderson, and hit .287/.332/.478 with 25 homers himself. Such power was all the more productive with a healthy Figgins drawing a league-leading 101 walks atop the lineup, and Bobby Abreu, who signed as a free agent for a mere $5 million plus incentives in mid-February, adding another 94 walks (third in the league) and a .390 OBP, primarily from the second or third spot in the order. Abreu's showing went a long way toward offsetting a subpar season from Vlad Guerrero (.295/.334/.460 in 100 games, and only two afield, during one of which he suffered a hamstring injury).

Furthermore, strong seasons from Erick Aybar and Maicer Izturis (the latter at Howie Kendrick's expense) led to a lineup so deep that the top 11 players in plate appearances posted OBPs within two points of the AL average (.334), helping the Angels place in the league's top four in all three triple-slash stats as well as EqA. This marked the first time they'd cracked the upper half of the league in slugging since 2002, and in EqA since 2004 (see Table 2).

Table 2. Paradise Found: Angels Offensive Rates and AL Rankings, 2000-09

Year	AVG	Rank	OBP	Rank	SLG	Rank	EqA	Rank
2000	.280	5	.352	7	.472	1	.266	4
2001	.261	11	.327	9	.405	12	.250	11
2002	.282	1	.341	4	.433	6	.266	4
2003	.268	9	.330	9	.413	8	.258	7
2004	.282	2	.341	6	.429	10	.265	5
2005	.270	7	.325	9	.409	9	.256	8
2006	.274	9	.334	10	.425	8	.256	10
2007	.284	3	.345	3	.417	9	.260	8
2008	.268	7	.330	11	.413	9	.253	10
2009	.285	1	.350	3	.441	4	.266	4

Overall, the team led the majors in scoring going into September before the Yankees passed them. Even so, they still surpassed the 1979 squad's franchise record during the season's final week. Meanwhile, the Angels retained their trademark aggressiveness on the basepaths, ranking second in the league in stolen-base attempts (211); even if they weren't terribly successful (-6.98 EqSBR), they ran away with the major-league lead in hit advancement runs (10.68) for the second time in four years.

The Angels enter 2010 with more transition in store, as the sluggish economy will likely compel them to maintain a payroll similar to last year's $113 million Opening Day mark. Figgins signed a four-year, $36 million deal to become a Mariner, John Lackey has become a Red Sock for five years and $82.5 million, and Oliver has departed as a free agent, as have two players who provided little bang for the buck in 2009 due to injuries, Guerrero ($15 million) and Kelvim Escobar ($10 million for one start). With Weaver, Saunders, Aybar, Kendrick, and Jeff Mathis all reaching arbitration for the first time, Mike Napoli for the second, and Kazmir, Rivera, Santana, and Abreu (who signed a two-year, $19 million extension) all due substantial raises, Reagins' wiggle room has been severely reduced.

Given those circumstances, it's no surprise the Impaler was a goner, joining Figgins in exile. Replacing that pair in the lineup will end up adding power from each side of the plate, however: the decision to add Hideki Matsui as their new DH adds lefty balance and power, and to replace Figgins at third, they have a strong in-house candidate in Wood, who has managed to tame his long swing while running out of minor-league options during his Triple-A apprenticeship. For Wood, the time is now; for Matsui, it's a matter of living up to the standard for ex-Yankee excellence at the plate set by Abreu, having signed a similar make-good, one-year deal (for $6.5 million). Taken together, these additions might mean the Angels will become even less of a small-ball lineup.

Replacing Lackey atop the rotation, on the other hand, is no small matter and threatens the team's shot at a successful title defense. As we go to press, it remains to be seen if the Angels will wind up trying to repeat what they did in acquiring Kazmir and add another starter already inked to a multiyear deal, or if they decide to get in on any one of the less-exciting free agents available on the market. It would help their financial flexibility to make either kind of deal if they could unload some of the $23 million remaining on Gary Matthews Jr.'s contract. Then again, it would also help if Little Sarge simply disappeared into witness protection.

At least matters are improving on the prospect front. After two years without a top 30 pick in the draft due to free-agent signings, the Angels went a long way toward restocking a below-average system with five picks in the first 48, including top prospect Mike Trout. Beyond Wood, they don't have much in the way of substantial ready help beyond the hope that the pitchers who took poundings at the back of the 2009 rotation—Sean O'Sullivan, Anthony Ortega, Trevor Bell—improve enough to emerge as back-end options in the rotation. That's a significant problem, given the strength of the prospects on hand for the Rangers, who already threatened the Angels' AL West supremacy by leading the division for most of the first half of 2009.

Indeed, the Angels find themselves in a reinvigorated division, as both the sale of the Rangers out from under the control of the financially troubled Tom Hicks and the further maturation of Jack Zduriencik's master plan in Seattle pose dire threats. The Halos do retain considerable advantages over both in terms of their attendance base (even with a three percent decline, they drew over one million more fans than either team did in 2009), the game's third-most lucrative cable contract, and one of its cleanest ledgers, debtwise. So while the team may be tightening its belt in the short term, its long-term outlook suggests it will not only remain competitive, but maintain its place among the game's marquee franchises.

HITTERS

Bobby Abreu   **RF**   Bats: L   Throws: R   Height: 6' 0"   Weight: 210   Born: March 11, 1974   Age: 36

YEAR	TEAM	LVL	AGE	PA	R	2B	3B	HR	RBI	BB	SO	SB	CS	EqBRR	AVG	OBP	SLG	EqAVG	EqOBP	EqSLG	EqA	VORP	WARP	DEFENSE	
2007	NYA	MLB	33	699	123	40	5	16	101	84	115	25	8	0.0	.283	.369	.445	.282	.370	.445	.284	31.0	2.9	149-RF	-5
2008	NYA	MLB	34	684	100	39	4	20	100	73	109	22	11	-0.8	.296	.371	.471	.300	.377	.481	.290	35.4	3.1	147-RF	-7
2009	LAA	MLB	35	667	96	29	3	15	103	94	113	30	8	-1.4	.293	.390	.435	.294	.389	.428	.292	34.4	3.2	121-RF -6 10-LF 1	
2010	LAA	MLB	36	626	86	29	3	16	89	80	110	17	10	-0.3	.273	.367	.426	.272	.365	.418	.269	18.6	1.7	132-RF	-3

Breakout: 3%   Improve: 31%   Collapse: 16%   Attrition: 20%   MLB: 98%   Comparables: Brian Giles, Brady Anderson, Raul Ibanez, B.J. Surhoff

Blanching at the prospect of upping his $16 million salary of 2008, the Yankees declined to offer Abreu arbitration, and the buyer's market for corner outfielders forced him to wait until February to receive a one-year deal with a $5 million base salary from the Angels. They got more than they bargained for, as Abreu provided a much-needed dash of plate discipline, posting his highest OBP since 2006 and the team's second-highest walk total since 2001; Chone Figgins walked even more often, and the two table-setters helped the team set a franchise record for runs scored. Alas, Abreu offset his keen batting eye with a career low in isolated power, and his defense remained rather ghastly, though FRAA holds him in higher esteem than do other systems. Unless one of those two areas improves, his two-year, $19 million extension isn't much better than a break-even proposition, with the potential to look worse if the third year vests amid further decline.

Alexia Amarista   **2B**   Bats: S   Throws: R   Height: 5' 8"   Weight: 150   Born: April 6, 1989   Age: 21

YEAR	TEAM	LVL	AGE	PA	R	2B	3B	HR	RBI	BB	SO	SB	CS	EqBRR	AVG	OBP	SLG	EqAVG	EqOBP	EqSLG	EqA	VORP	WARP	DEFENSE	
2008	ANG	Rk	19	236	46	6	4	2	21	29	20	22	14	-2.6	.332	.416	.431	.257	.316	.327	.228	-2.0	-0.6	21-CF -2 12-RF 1	
2009	CDR	A	20	557	84	39	10	4	49	50	61	38	20	-1.6	.319	.390	.468	.281	.336	.412	.260	16.1	2.5	118-2B	4
2010	LAA	MLB	21	496	56	33	5	4	37	37	63	14	8	-0.7	.276	.334	.399	.277	.336	.401	.248	8.7	1.2	109-2B	2

Breakout: 32%   Improve: 57%   Collapse: 15%   Attrition: 5%   MLB: 0%   Comparables: Eddie Tanner, Jose Guillen, Jose Gualdron, Francisco Burgos

This pint-sized Venezuelan put up impressive numbers in his first taste of full-season ball, winning the Midwest League batting title, placing in the top five in OBP, doubles, and triples, and being voted the circuit's top defensive second baseman by managers. Amarista has a nice blend of gap power, plate discipline, contact skills, and speed, but he doesn't get much love from scouts or prospect hounds because of his size (which is closer to 5-foot-6) and lack of physical projection. Still, if he continues to hit, he'll play his way onto prospect lists and into the Angels' plans.

Erick Aybar   **SS**   Bats: S   Throws: R   Height: 5' 10"   Weight: 170   Born: January 14, 1984   Age: 26

YEAR	TEAM	LVL	AGE	PA	R	2B	3B	HR	RBI	BB	SO	SB	CS	EqBRR	AVG	OBP	SLG	EqAVG	EqOBP	EqSLG	EqA	VORP	WARP	DEFENSE	
2007	LAA	MLB	23	211	18	5	1	1	19	10	32	4	4	-0.9	.237	.279	.289	.238	.280	.290	.201	-6.3	-0.9	36-2B 1 9-SS -1	
2008	LAA	MLB	24	375	53	18	5	3	39	14	45	7	2	3.8	.277	.314	.384	.279	.316	.384	.248	10.7	1.1	88-SS	-1
2009	LAA	MLB	25	556	70	23	9	5	58	30	54	14	7	1.4	.312	.353	.423	.314	.355	.422	.269	27.4	3.0	133-SS	-2
2010	LAA	MLB	26	496	69	23	5	7	56	31	60	12	7	1.2	.290	.344	.407	.290	.344	.404	.254	13.9	1.4	118-SS	-1

Breakout: 22%   Improve: 56%   Collapse: 4%   Attrition: 7%   MLB: 99%   Comparables: Omar Vizquel, Rafael Furcal, Curtis Wilkerson, Spike Owen

Aybar's sudden evolution from offensive liability into modest asset may have owed something to freedom both from nagging injuries and from uncertainty regarding his starting status, but luck played a part as well. His BABIP rose from .311 in 2008 to .338 last year, despite a line-drive rate that didn't budge from a sub-league-average 15.4 percent, and ground-ball, fly-ball, and pop-up rates moving in the wrong directions for an expected increase—these aren't hard-won infield singles he's benefiting from. Yes, Aybar's unintentional walk rate increased, but only to a still-weak 5.2 percent, and his isolated power rose just four points. While there's still growth possible as he enters his age-26 season, don't be surprised to find Aybar's performance leveling off when the hits that dropped in last year don't do so again in 2010.

Peter Bourjos — CF

Bats: R   Throws: R   Height: 6' 1"   Weight: 175   Born: March 31, 1987   Age: 23

YEAR	TEAM	LVL	AGE	PA	R	2B	3B	HR	RBI	BB	SO	SB	CS	EqBRR	AVG	OBP	SLG	EqAVG	EqOBP	EqSLG	EqA	VORP	WARP	DEFENSE	
2007	CDR	A	20	270	37	9	6	5	29	20	53	19	9	-1.2	.274	.335	.426	.253	.302	.390	.243	3.0	1.2	61-CF	7
2008	RCU	A+	21	545	83	29	10	9	51	19	96	50	10	1.9	.295	.326	.444	.262	.288	.390	.239	3.1	0.1	116-CF	-2
2009	ARK	AA	22	504	72	16	14	6	51	49	77	32	12	2.0	.281	.354	.423	.272	.331	.419	.261	15.4	2.8	109-CF	8
2010	LAA	MLB	23	455	52	22	6	9	40	31	91	16	7	0.6	.252	.308	.397	.252	.307	.390	.237	3.1	0.6	102-CF	2

Breakout: 7%   Improve: 40%   Collapse: 22%   Attrition: 13%   MLB: 4%   Comparables: Angel Ramirez, Dante Powell, Brian Hunter, Kash Beauchamp

A 10th-round 2005 pick out of Scottsdale, Bourjos is considered the system's best athlete, known for outstanding speed, a strong arm, and excellent instincts—your basic leadoff-hitting center fielder in the making. The big knock on him coming into the year was a lack of patience; he walked in just 4.8 percent of his personal appearances in 2007 and 2008. He doubled his walk rate in 2009, and while improved pitch recognition played a part, a June wrist injury that required post-season surgery may have contributed as well. He hit .316/.368/.454 with a 7.1 percent walk rate prior to the injury, .253/.350/.398 with a 12.3 percent rate after. He'll start the year at Triple-A, but with Torii Hunter signed through 2012, and 2009 first-rounder Mike Trout now the system's best prospect, Bourjos' shot at a regular job may be in another organization altogether.

Angel Castillo — RF

Bats: R   Throws: R   Height: 6' 3"   Weight: 190   Born: June 7, 1989   Age: 21

YEAR	TEAM	LVL	AGE	PA	R	2B	3B	HR	RBI	BB	SO	SB	CS	EqBRR	AVG	OBP	SLG	EqAVG	EqOBP	EqSLG	EqA	VORP	WARP	DEFENSE			
2007	ANG	Rk	18	140	19	4	1	4	23	19	39	5	0	-0.2	.252	.364	.403	.205	.279	.323	.212	-4.4	-0.7	29-RF	1		
2008	ORM	Rk	19	296	53	20	3	14	47	18	85	7	2	-0.1	.281	.345	.533	.225	.267	.379	.221	-6.8	-2.7	63-RF	-10		
2008	CDR	A	19	48	3	4	0	0	4	0	12	1	1	0.4	.133	.170	.222	.130	.149	.217	.068	-5.8	-0.4	4-RF	2	4-LF	1
2009	CDR	A	20	453	56	20	1	12	61	29	111	16	2	1.2	.242	.315	.389	.215	.265	.332	.214	-13.6	-1.8	102-RF	-1		
2010	LAA	MLB	21	443	49	21	1	13	52	27	118	5	2	0.5	.226	.285	.380	.224	.282	.363	.221	-8.4	-1.2	99-RF	-3		

Breakout: 39%   Improve: 64%   Collapse: 15%   Attrition: 2%   MLB: 0%   Comparables: Ron Shepherd, Mike Mallory, Timmie Morrow, Brant Alyea

Castillo had an unimpressive year even by the standards of a 20-year-old in the Midwest League. Though his strike-out and walk rates did improve slightly over 2008, he struggled to make contact, whiffing in nearly a quarter of his plate appearances, and his line-drive rate plummeted, eroding his batting line. Right-handers simply ate him alive (.225/.300/.345), though he more than held his own against lefties (.290/.357/.520). Scouts continue to like his raw power, speed, and defense, but he won't get anywhere without better command of the strike zone.

Hank Conger — C

Bats: S   Throws: R   Height: 6' 0"   Weight: 205   Born: January 29, 1988   Age: 22

YEAR	TEAM	LVL	AGE	PA	R	2B	3B	HR	RBI	BB	SO	SB	CS	EqBRR	AVG	OBP	SLG	EqAVG	EqOBP	EqSLG	EqA	VORP	WARP	DEFENSE	
2007	CDR	A	19	320	33	20	0	11	48	21	48	9	4	-3.6	.290	.336	.472	.265	.305	.425	.252	11.0	0.3	68-C	-9
2008	RCU	A+	20	318	47	20	2	13	75	14	55	2	1	-1.3	.303	.333	.517	.268	.296	.446	.253	2.1	-0.1	9-C	-3
2009	ARK	AA	21	524	61	20	3	11	68	55	68	4	2	-3.4	.295	.369	.424	.286	.345	.416	.266	19.1	1.5	86-C	-7
2010	LAA	MLB	22	450	50	22	1	16	66	35	80	3	2	-1.9	.274	.332	.445	.270	.329	.427	.258	16.7	1.4	65-C	-4

Breakout: 17%   Improve: 54%   Collapse: 14%   Attrition: 10%   MLB: 7%   Comparables: Phil Ouellette, Al Pardo, Donnie Scott, Troy O'Leary

While few question this 2006 first-rounder's ability to hit from either side of the plate, the bigger issue is whether he can remain behind it. Limited to just 91 games at catcher from 2006 through 2008 due to back, shoulder, and other injuries, he nearly equaled that total during a healthy but uneven 2009. While he threw out 30 percent of basesteal-ers, he also demonstrated his rawness by making 14 errors, airmailing far too many balls into center. Meanwhile, his unintentional walk rate more than doubled and his strikeout rate dropped, but his isolated power fell considerably as well, particularly when catching (.293/.357/.399 in 364 PAs) as opposed to playing DH (.299/.386/.492 in 159 PAs). Still, it's solid progress; with another healthy season, a roster spot could be within his grasp.

Terry Evans   **RF**   Bats: R   Throws: R   Height: 6' 3"   Weight: 205   Born: January 19, 1982   Age: 28

YEAR	TEAM	LVL	AGE	PA	R	2B	3B	HR	RBI	BB	SO	SB	CS	EqBRR	AVG	OBP	SLG	EqAVG	EqOBP	EqSLG	EqA	VORP	WARP	DEFENSE			
2007	SLC	AAA	25	507	70	40	4	15	75	26	119	24	9	2.1	.316	.352	.512	.259	.294	.409	.243	1.7	0.3	59-RF	4	46-CF	-3
2007	LAA	MLB	25	13	3	0	0	1	2	2	4	0	0	0.1	.091	.231	.364	.091	.231	.364	.205	-0.6	-0.1	3-RF	0		
2008	SLC	AAA	26	200	31	12	0	4	21	20	60	6	5	-0.1	.270	.345	.408	.230	.299	.320	.222	-4.4	-0.7	38-RF	-1		
2009	SLC	AAA	27	592	104	33	6	26	90	40	146	28	5	4.7	.291	.341	.520	.242	.287	.419	.246	1.9	-1.2	100-RF	-10	18-CF	-2
2009	LAA	MLB	27	7	2	0	0	0	1	0	2	0	0	0.4	.286	.286	.286	.286	.286	.286	.195	-0.4	0.1	1-RF	1		
2010	LAA	MLB	28	474	54	23	2	13	50	32	134	11	6	1.3	.231	.287	.383	.228	.284	.367	.223	-8.2	-1.1	97-RF	-1		

Breakout: 6%   Improve: 36%   Collapse: 32%   Attrition: 17%   MLB: 10%   Comparables: Dante Powell, Chris Hatcher, Chris Sheff, Alan Cockrell

Evans rebounded from a shoulder strain that cost him more than half of 2008, hitting more homers than any Angels minor-leaguer except for Sean Rodriguez and stealing bases at an excellent clip. Even so, his plate discipline is lacking, and once the air is let out of his Salt Lake stats, the translations don't offer a great deal of hope that he could hold down a big-league corner job. He's organizational depth in an organization that has plenty of depth at his position, thanks.

Chone Figgins   **3B**   Bats: S   Throws: R   Height: 5' 8"   Weight: 180   Born: January 22, 1978   Age: 32

YEAR	TEAM	LVL	AGE	PA	R	2B	3B	HR	RBI	BB	SO	SB	CS	EqBRR	AVG	OBP	SLG	EqAVG	EqOBP	EqSLG	EqA	VORP	WARP	DEFENSE			
2007	LAA	MLB	29	503	81	24	6	3	58	51	81	41	12	7.5	.330	.393	.432	.333	.395	.435	.295	30.4	2.3	95-3B	-5	10-RF	-3
2008	LAA	MLB	30	520	72	14	1	1	22	62	80	34	13	7.7	.276	.367	.318	.282	.375	.324	.258	11.0	2.1	102-3B	7	7-2B	0
2009	LAA	MLB	31	729	114	30	7	5	54	101	114	42	17	3.9	.298	.395	.393	.302	.399	.395	.283	37.3	7.2	150-3B	26		
2010	SEA	MLB	32	635	95	27	4	4	49	84	110	36	16	3.3	.290	.385	.374	.292	.383	.378	.272	24.3	3.2	132-3B	5		

Breakout: 11%   Improve: 42%   Collapse: 9%   Attrition: 6%   MLB: 97%   Comparables: Omar Vizquel, Luis Castillo, Jim Gilliam, Billy Werber

Talk about a walk year: in the final season of his contract, Figgins burnished his credentials as an elite leadoff hitter by leading the AL in bases on balls and ranking second in both times on base and runs scored, third in steals, and fourth in pitches per plate appearance. It was no fluke; his walk rate has improved in six straight years, his P/PA in three straight, but his 2007-2008 injuries concealed those advances. His defense, which was good in 2008, was off-the-charts outstanding across the major systems; he led all third basemen in FRAA and Plus/Minus runs saved (+30) while placing third in UZR (+16.7). The only ding on his performance was a league-leading caught-stealing total, but even with his -3.35 EqSBR, you can see that his overall baserunning was a plus. In all, his season priced him out of the suddenly cost-conscious Angels' range—perhaps not the worst thing in the world as he heads into his mid-30s—but his four-year, $36 million deal from the Mariners was nonetheless a reasonable one.

Vladimir Guerrero   **DH**   Bats: R   Throws: R   Height: 6' 3"   Weight: 235   Born: February 9, 1975   Age: 35

YEAR	TEAM	LVL	AGE	PA	R	2B	3B	HR	RBI	BB	SO	SB	CS	EqBRR	AVG	OBP	SLG	EqAVG	EqOBP	EqSLG	EqA	VORP	WARP	DEFENSE	
2007	LAA	MLB	32	660	89	45	1	27	125	71	62	2	3	-2.1	.324	.403	.547	.316	.397	.537	.313	49.3	5.3	105-RF	-1
2008	LAA	MLB	33	600	85	31	3	27	91	51	77	5	3	-1.7	.303	.365	.521	.301	.363	.519	.296	34.1	3.9	94-RF	1
2009	LAA	MLB	34	407	59	16	1	15	50	19	56	2	1	-0.9	.295	.334	.460	.295	.334	.449	.269	3.7	0.3		
2010	TEX	AL	35	483	58	23	1	18	66	44	58	2	2	-1.3	.287	.357	.472	.279	.346	.452	.269	9.8	1.1	—	

Breakout: 3%   Improve: 27%   Collapse: 23%   Attrition: 17%   MLB: 91%   Comparables: Mike Lowell, Matt Williams, Brian Jordan, Dante Bichette

A mid-April pectoral strain may have marked Guerrero's crossing into baseball middle age. Despite his previous back woes, he had actually been rather durable from 1998 to 2008, averaging 150 games and serving just one lengthy DL stint and two minimal ones. This time around, however, he lost nearly six weeks to the pec problem plus four additional weeks to a calf and lower hamstring injury sustained while playing right field for just the second time all season. Limping off the DL in early August with four homers and a .291/.323/.413 line, he impaled at a .300/.347/.498 clip with 11 homers the rest of the way, four of them—including his milestone 400th homer—in his first week back. The bottom line was still career lows in virtually every key category from a player who increasingly looks like a full-time DH. The Rangers signed him to fill that role in January. He's a career .394/.471/.705 hitter at the Ballpark; alas, he no longer gets to face Rangers pitching.

Torii Hunter   CF

Bats: R   Throws: R   Height: 6' 2"   Weight: 225   Born: July 18, 1975   Age: 34

YEAR	TEAM	LVL	AGE	PA	R	2B	3B	HR	RBI	BB	SO	SB	CS	EqBRR	AVG	OBP	SLG	EqAVG	EqOBP	EqSLG	EqA	VORP	WARP	DEFENSE
2007	MIN	MLB	31	650	94	45	1	28	107	40	101	18	9	0.1	.287	.334	.505	.291	.338	.518	.283	36.4	3.5	148-CF -4
2008	LAA	MLB	32	608	85	37	2	21	78	50	108	19	5	3.2	.278	.344	.466	.278	.345	.471	.280	29.7	1.8	133-CF -12
2009	LAA	MLB	33	506	74	26	1	22	90	47	92	18	4	0.6	.299	.366	.508	.301	.366	.501	.296	34.4	4.0	110-CF 2
2010	LAA	MLB	34	497	66	25	1	19	75	43	91	12	6	0.6	.273	.341	.460	.269	.338	.443	.266	18.6	1.8	111-CF -2

Breakout: 3%   Improve: 29%   Collapse: 21%   Attrition: 19%   MLB: 97%   Comparables: Dante Bichette, Mike Cameron, Glenallen Hill, Jim Rice

When Hunter was available, he was effective, setting career highs in batting average, OBP, and EqA while posting his highest slugging percentage since 2002. Alas, he lost five weeks to a groin injury and hit just .289/.341/.422, with a 41/13 K/UBB ratio on returning in mid-August. Helped by his strongest defensive showing in years, he still wound up with his highest WARP total since 2001, but even so, it's arguable that his performance justified his $17.5 million salary. Worse, he's still got three years on that deal at similarly steep pre-recession rates as he settles into his mid-30s. For all his considerable charm, he's likely to develop into one of the game's most overpaid players. Ouch.

Maicer Izturis   INF

Bats: S   Throws: R   Height: 5' 8"   Weight: 170   Born: September 12, 1980   Age: 29

YEAR	TEAM	LVL	AGE	PA	R	2B	3B	HR	RBI	BB	SO	SB	CS	EqBRR	AVG	OBP	SLG	EqAVG	EqOBP	EqSLG	EqA	VORP	WARP	DEFENSE		
2007	LAA	MLB	26	374	47	17	2	6	51	33	39	7	1	2.3	.289	.349	.405	.287	.349	.410	.267	12.5	0.4	51-3B -5	35-2B -1	
2008	LAA	MLB	27	321	44	14	2	3	37	26	27	11	2	3.6	.269	.329	.362	.270	.332	.360	.253	8.7	2.2	50-SS 8	21-2B 1	
2009	LAA	MLB	28	437	74	22	3	8	65	35	41	13	5	4.5	.300	.359	.434	.302	.360	.432	.277	20.5	1.3	64-2B -2	25-SS -5	
2010	LAA	MLB	29	506	72	23	3	10	73	48	55	13	5	2.1	.282	.355	.411	.281	.353	.399	.262	16.0	1.7	111-2B 0		

Breakout: 12%   Improve: 41%   Collapse: 15%   Attrition: 2%   MLB: 98%   Comparables: Quilvio Veras, Bump Wills, Terry Pendleton, Jerry Browne

Utility infielders don't get much better than Izturis. Though his 2008 injury woes settled the Angels' long-running shortstop drama in Erick Aybar's favor, Izturis carved out significant playing time in 2009 by taking over second base upon Howie Kendrick's demotion. Izturis retained the long half of a platoon even after Kendrick's return, starting 40 of the team's 53 games against righties from July 4th onward. His defense at the keystone measured slightly below average according to FRAA, but UZR (+6.6) and Plus/Minus (+3) viewed him more favorably; the systems all agree that his defense at shortstop has certainly slipped. How exactly he fits into the Angels' 2010 picture is unclear, but Izturis provides enough in the way of contact skills, plate discipline, punch, speed, and, of course, versatility to be a significant asset.

Howie Kendrick   2B

Bats: R   Throws: R   Height: 5' 10"   Weight: 200   Born: July 12, 1983   Age: 26

YEAR	TEAM	LVL	AGE	PA	R	2B	3B	HR	RBI	BB	SO	SB	CS	EqBRR	AVG	OBP	SLG	EqAVG	EqOBP	EqSLG	EqA	VORP	WARP	DEFENSE
2007	LAA	MLB	23	353	55	24	2	5	39	9	61	5	4	2.3	.322	.347	.450	.322	.347	.456	.271	15.3	2.5	85-2B 6
2008	LAA	MLB	24	361	43	26	2	3	37	12	58	11	4	2.6	.306	.333	.421	.310	.336	.422	.265	12.9	2.3	87-2B 6
2009	SLC	AAA	25	87	11	6	1	2	11	7	12	4	2	0.3	.346	.414	.526	.304	.368	.468	.282	4.6	0.4	19-2B -1
2009	LAA	MLB	25	400	61	21	3	10	61	20	71	11	4	-0.5	.291	.334	.444	.295	.338	.445	.267	14.4	2.6	90-2B 8
2010	LAA	MLB	26	498	71	30	3	11	63	26	83	11	6	1.0	.299	.345	.447	.297	.344	.438	.264	17.2	2.4	116-2B 5

Breakout: 18%   Improve: 55%   Collapse: 8%   Attrition: 6%   MLB: 96%   Comparables: Aaron Hill, Craig Biggio, Dave Cash, Tony Taylor

Though he stayed healthy and set a career high in plate appearances, Kendrick came no closer to that long-predicted batting title. On the contrary, an early slump (.231/.281/.355 with a 9.9 percent line-drive rate through June 11th) forced the Angels to send him to Triple-A to iron out his swing. When he returned in early July, he found himself platooning with Maicer Izturis, and no matter how hot Kendrick got—his line-drive rate nearly tripled, to 26 percent—he couldn't reclaim the full-time job. He started 28 of the team's 30 remaining games against lefties, hitting .371/.391/.562, but just 17 of 43 against righties (including five turns at DH) despite a .333/.383/.505 showing. As special as Kendrick's bat speed is, his minimal secondary batting contributions make him a drag on the offense if the hits aren't falling, and on balance, he's not much more than a league-average second baseman, albeit one whose defense helps his case a bit—a particularly important consideration on this club.

Jeff Mathis   C

Bats: R   Throws: R   Height: 6' 0"   Weight: 200   Born: March 31, 1983   Age: 27

YEAR	TEAM	LVL	AGE	PA	R	2B	3B	HR	RBI	BB	SO	SB	CS	EqBRR	AVG	OBP	SLG	EqAVG	EqOBP	EqSLG	EqA	VORP	WARP	DEFENSE	
2007	SLC	AAA	24	273	39	14	2	5	26	17	45	3	1	2.0	.244	.295	.376	.202	.251	.306	.194	-5.3	-0.2	58-C	4
2007	LAA	MLB	24	195	24	12	0	4	23	15	49	0	1	-1.0	.211	.276	.351	.207	.272	.343	.221	1.7	0.3	53-C	0
2008	LAA	MLB	25	328	35	8	0	9	42	30	90	2	2	-1.8	.194	.275	.318	.193	.276	.321	.214	-0.6	0.8	89-C	6
2009	LAA	MLB	26	272	26	8	0	5	28	22	73	2	3	-2.5	.211	.288	.308	.213	.290	.302	.213	-1.5	0.5	74-C	4
2010	LAA	MLB	27	321	38	12	0	9	40	27	75	2	2	-0.5	.224	.298	.360	.220	.295	.348	.220	-0.1	0.2	86-C	2

Breakout: 34%   Improve: 53%   Collapse: 18%   Attrition: 16%   MLB: 88%   Comparables: Ozzie Virgil, Brad Ausmus, Yorvit Torrealba, Mike Heath

You wouldn't know it if all you saw was the ALCS, but let's not mince words: Mathis can't hit lefties or righties, in a box, with a fox, in a house, or with a mouse. Of the 45 catchers with at least 200 plate appearances last year, only an ailing Dioner Navarro had a lower EqA. Out of 823 hitters with at least 800 plate appearances in the post-strike era, only 19 have worse EqAs than Mathis; he's in the 97th percentile for craptacularity. Sure, his overall defensive numbers are above average, but his skills at pitch calling and pitch blocking don't offset the damage he does with the bat. According to MLVr and Fielding Rate, the difference between the Angels' two backstops comes out to .405 runs of offense per game in favor of Mike Napoli, and .15 runs per game on defense in favor of Mathis. You do the math.

Gary Matthews Jr.   OF

Bats: S   Throws: R   Height: 6' 3"   Weight: 225   Born: August 25, 1974   Age: 35

YEAR	TEAM	LVL	AGE	PA	R	2B	3B	HR	RBI	BB	SO	SB	CS	EqBRR	AVG	OBP	SLG	EqAVG	EqOBP	EqSLG	EqA	VORP	WARP	DEFENSE			
2007	LAA	MLB	32	579	79	26	3	18	72	55	102	18	4	4.0	.252	.323	.419	.249	.321	.418	.260	16.4	0.9	129-CF	-8		
2008	LAA	MLB	33	477	53	19	3	8	46	45	95	8	3	-1.6	.242	.319	.357	.245	.323	.362	.243	0.3	-0.5	38-RF	2	35-LF	-4
2009	LAA	MLB	34	360	44	19	2	4	50	40	74	4	1	3.0	.250	.336	.361	.251	.336	.359	.249	4.3	-1.4	49-CF	-14	24-RF	-2
2010	LAA	MLB	35	366	42	15	2	9	42	38	78	7	2	0.7	.238	.321	.377	.235	.319	.361	.239	3.1	-0.1	72-CF	-4		

Breakout: 8%   Improve: 40%   Collapse: 26%   Attrition: 27%   MLB: 91%   Comparables: Michael Tucker, Brian Jordan, Jeffrey Leonard, Dante Bichette

Whether it's the loss of his performance enhancers or simply the aging process, Little Sarge hasn't come close to matching his 2006 production. Bobby Abreu's arrival and Juan Rivera's rebound further marginalized him, to the point where he started less than half his team's games for the first time since 2004. Not helping matters were his atrocious defensive numbers across the major systems, particularly in center field. These numbers threaten to turn him from the game's most expensive fourth outfielder into its priciest fifth outfielder. A change of scenery is in order, but the Angels will have to eat a good chunk of his remaining $23.5 million to make it happen.

Kendry Morales   1B

Bats: S   Throws: R   Height: 6' 1"   Weight: 225   Born: June 20, 1983   Age: 27

YEAR	TEAM	LVL	AGE	PA	R	2B	3B	HR	RBI	BB	SO	SB	CS	EqBRR	AVG	OBP	SLG	EqAVG	EqOBP	EqSLG	EqA	VORP	WARP	DEFENSE			
2007	SLC	AAA	24	275	42	20	1	5	37	15	30	0	2	-3.4	.341	.385	.486	.284	.327	.401	.252	0.2	-0.3	42-1B	-3		
2007	LAA	MLB	24	126	12	10	0	4	15	6	21	0	1	-2.7	.294	.333	.479	.286	.325	.471	.269	2.2	0.5	14-1B	1	2-RF	1
2008	SLC	AAA	25	340	46	19	0	15	64	19	43	1	3	-1.3	.341	.376	.543	.284	.318	.438	.258	2.6	0.3	60-1B	0	5-RF	0
2008	LAA	MLB	25	66	7	2	0	3	8	4	7	0	1	-1.2	.213	.273	.393	.213	.273	.393	.225	-1.8	-0.2	7-RF	0	5-1B	0
2009	LAA	MLB	26	622	86	43	2	34	108	46	117	3	7	-5.5	.306	.355	.569	.307	.355	.557	.298	27.7	3.7	143-1B	5		
2010	LAA	MLB	27	537	67	27	1	24	85	38	88	2	4	-2.7	.285	.339	.492	.280	.336	.474	.270	12.2	1.4	106-1B	1		

Breakout: 14%   Improve: 49%   Collapse: 11%   Attrition: 5%   MLB: 83%   Comparables: Ryan Garko, Shea Hillenbrand, Bob Hamelin, Paul Sorrento

One of PECOTA's biggest whiffs in 2009 was its weighted mean projection for Morales: -0.2 WARP on a .253/.295/.389 line. Save for a few dozen walks, Morales' final numbers wound up much closer to those of the man he replaced, Mark Teixeira, than to that paltry line, validating—at least in the short term—the Angels' decision to skip offering a nine-figure contract to the departing free agent, preferring their Cuban import. Morales' projection was so grim because he hadn't produced in his big-league opportunities (.249/.302/.408 in 407 PAs) and because his performances in one of the minors' most hitter-friendly environments only translated to three half-seasons of .250-ish EqAs. To be fair, no competing projection system foresaw the breakout, either; Bill James' was the most optimistic, at .327/.456 OBP/SLG. Obviously, the Angels' scouts and coaches saw far beyond the numbers, but credit Morales for adjusting to big-league pitching and making solid contact far more often than he had in the past. Even if PECOTA suggests a major regression, this is one case where you're better off letting go of those numbers.

Mike Napoli   C

Bats: R   Throws: R   Height: 6' 0"   Weight: 215   Born: October 31, 1981   Age: 28

YEAR	TEAM	LVL	AGE	PA	R	2B	3B	HR	RBI	BB	SO	SB	CS	EqBRR	AVG	OBP	SLG	EqAVG	EqOBP	EqSLG	EqA	VORP	WARP	DEFENSE	
2007	LAA	MLB	25	263	40	11	1	10	34	33	63	5	2	1.8	.247	.351	.443	.243	.350	.436	.277	16.9	1.6	68-C	-2
2008	LAA	MLB	26	274	39	9	1	20	49	35	70	7	3	0.0	.273	.374	.586	.276	.377	.600	.314	29.3	2.2	70-C	-6
2009	LAA	MLB	27	432	60	22	1	20	56	40	103	3	3	-0.2	.272	.350	.492	.273	.350	.488	.282	26.3	2.2	85-C	-6
2010	LAA	MLB	28	409	57	18	1	24	64	49	99	7	4	0.4	.263	.364	.518	.255	.359	.486	.288	28.7	2.8	97-C	-3

Breakout: 17%   Improve: 52%   Collapse: 7%   Attrition: 2%   MLB: 100%   Comparables: Johnny Bench, Gary Carter, Johnny Romano, Lance Parrish

As a player, Mike Scioscia was an excellent defender, and as a manager, he does not suffer fools wearing the tools of ignorance. Despite Napoli's ability to mash, his defensive limitations have always dimmed his stature in his skipper's eyes. Coming off shoulder surgery, he nabbed a higher percentage of basestealers than in 2008 (22 percent, up from 17 percent) and set a career high in starts, but he was prone to what his manager termed "defensive funks" with his pitch selection and sloppy setup. The struggles may have carried over into his hitting; soon after his most public airing-out in August, Napoli slid into a 3-for-45 offensive funk. Given his skills as a hitter, the Angels might be better served treating him as an everyday DH/backup backstop, but such a plan is virtually unprecedented—only two catchers (one an injured Carlton Fisk in 1979) have caught more than 30 games in a season while serving as DH more frequently—and the scheme loses its value if it results in more at-bats for Jeff Mathis.

Chris Pettit   OF

Bats: R   Throws: R   Height: 6' 0"   Weight: 190   Born: August 15, 1984   Age: 25

YEAR	TEAM	LVL	AGE	PA	R	2B	3B	HR	RBI	BB	SO	SB	CS	EqBRR	AVG	OBP	SLG	EqAVG	EqOBP	EqSLG	EqA	VORP	WARP	DEFENSE				
2007	CDR	A	22	266	47	24	1	9	41	23	41	17	4	2.3	.346	.429	.579	.311	.372	.508	.300	17.6	1.6	37-LF	-1	14-CF	-3
2007	RCU	A+	22	307	54	20	2	9	54	36	48	13	3	5.8	.309	.395	.502	.278	.350	.429	.273	11.4	0.9	32-LF	0	31-CF	-3
2008	ARK	AA	23	251	27	12	2	6	26	16	39	5	2	-3.2	.248	.320	.401	.231	.289	.371	.232	-3.2	-1.2	50-RF	-6	4-LF	-1
2009	SLC	AAA	24	414	70	30	3	8	58	31	62	18	2	3.7	.321	.383	.482	.279	.337	.418	.266	9.2	0.5	68-LF	-6	7-RF	1
2009	LAA	MLB	24	7	2	0	0	0	0	0	1	0	0	0.2	.286	.286	.286	.286	.286	.286	.195	-0.4	0.0	2-RF	0		
2010	LAA	MLB	25	407	50	22	2	10	47	32	78	9	3	1.5	.262	.328	.412	.259	.325	.397	.250	4.3	0.2	82-LF	-2		

Breakout: 2%   Improve: 22%   Collapse: 24%   Attrition: 10%   MLB: 4%   Comparables: Marty Castillo, Jack Peel, Manny Martinez, Michael Senne

You have to admire Pettit's resilience. A 19th-round pick out of Loyola Marymount in 2006, he has clawed his way up the ladder, winning the organization's Minor League Player of the Year honors in 2007 and overcoming a 2008 marred by a broken foot with a strong AFL showing that helped push him to Triple-A to start 2009. He set a blistering pace at Salt Lake City, hitting .367/.415/.556 through June 3rd, but a broken hamate bone cost him seven weeks, and he hit just .269/.354/.400 after returning, though he earned a September call-up. Pettit lacks a plus tool beyond his bat, and he's got only gap power, but he also has no glaring weaknesses. Despite the Angels' crowded outfield, Pettit can handle center field in a pinch and throw well enough to play right, which could put him in the mix for a big-league roster spot at some point in 2010.

Juan Rivera   LF

Bats: R   Throws: R   Height: 6' 2"   Weight: 225   Born: July 3, 1978   Age: 31

YEAR	TEAM	LVL	AGE	PA	R	2B	3B	HR	RBI	BB	SO	SB	CS	EqBRR	AVG	OBP	SLG	EqAVG	EqOBP	EqSLG	EqA	VORP	WARP	DEFENSE				
2007	SLC	AAA	28	65	4	8	0	0	17	3	6	0	0	0.5	.262	.292	.393	.210	.242	.290	.183	-3.9	-0.8	7-RF	-3	4-LF	0
2007	LAA	MLB	28	44	3	1	0	2	8	1	4	0	0	0.1	.279	.295	.442	.279	.295	.442	.249	0.1	0.0	6-RF	1		
2008	LAA	MLB	29	280	31	13	0	12	45	16	33	1	1	0.0	.246	.282	.438	.248	.282	.437	.249	0.6	-0.1	34-LF	0	13-RF	-2
2009	LAA	MLB	30	572	72	24	1	25	88	36	57	0	1	-3.4	.287	.332	.478	.288	.332	.468	.273	18.7	2.3	116-LF	1	5-RF	0
2010	LAA	MLB	31	432	51	21	1	19	72	30	52	1	1	-0.8	.282	.333	.481	.276	.328	.457	.267	12.3	1.4	84-LF	0		

Breakout: 19%   Improve: 46%   Collapse: 10%   Attrition: 16%   MLB: 91%   Comparables: Tracy Jones, Raul Ibanez, Daryle Ward, Johnny Lindell

Rivera celebrated his new three-year, $12.75 million deal by rebounding from an injury-shortened 2007 and a recuperating 2008 to post career highs in several key counting stats. Taking over as the Halos' left fielder, he showed more patience and considerably more pop than Garret Anderson (.288/.322/.445, 2005-2008). Even so, Rivera's EqA was five points below that of the average left fielder, and if he was a terror against lefties (.333/.385/.645 in 156 PAs), he was filler against righties (.271/.313/.418), a problem exacerbated by the roster's dearth of lefty-hitting outfielders. Oddly, while Rivera's FRAA suggests he was basically an average left fielder, as he's been for most of his career, both Plus/Minus (+15 runs) and UZR (+12.7) placed him among the majors' best, thanks to suddenly improved range deep in the outfield. It's tough to believe he's the new Tris Speaker out there, but at the very least, he's not the new Bobby Abreu.

Freddy Sandoval — INF

Bats: S | Throws: R | Height: 6' 1" | Weight: 200 | Born: August 16, 1982 | Age: 27

YEAR	TEAM	LVL	AGE	PA	R	2B	3B	HR	RBI	BB	SO	SB	CS	EqBRR	AVG	OBP	SLG	EqAVG	EqOBP	EqSLG	EqA	VORP	WARP	DEFENSE			
2007	ARK	AA	24	563	84	32	6	11	72	67	78	21	11	0.6	.305	.392	.468	.281	.353	.412	.269	17.3	1.6	122-3B	-4		
2008	SLC	AAA	25	587	92	45	2	15	88	47	74	6	3	-0.9	.335	.389	.514	.281	.329	.416	.260	12.5	1.4	76-3B	8	20-2B	-4
2009	SLC	AAA	26	303	46	16	5	6	46	26	39	12	3	2.4	.300	.360	.458	.253	.307	.384	.242	-0.2	-0.1	44-3B	1	13-1B	-2
2010	LAA	MLB	31	432	51	21	1	19	72	30	52	1	1	-0.8	.282	.333	.481	.276	.328	.457	.267	12.3	1.4	84-LF	0		

Breakout: 19%   Improve: 46%   Collapse: 10%   Attrition: 16%   MLB: 91%   Comparables: Tracy Jones, Raul Ibanez, Daryle Ward, Johnny Lindell

A switch-hitting infielder short on secondary skills, Sandoval is merely organizational depth in the flesh for the Angels. His luck isn't too hot, either—had he not been injured at the time of Kendrick's swoon, he might have gotten a look, but as it was, a late-May wrist sprain required surgery, costing him three months. A dogged rehab effort earned him a September call-up, but whatever big-league future he has will more likely be with another outfit.

Mike Trout — CF

Bats: R | Throws: R | Height: 6' 1" | Weight: 200 | Born: August 7, 1991 | Age: 18

YEAR	TEAM	LVL	AGE	PA	R	2B	3B	HR	RBI	BB	SO	SB	CS	EqBRR	AVG	OBP	SLG	EqAVG	EqOBP	EqSLG	EqA	VORP	WARP	DEFENSE	
2009	ANG	Rk	17	187	29	7	7	1	25	18	28	13	2	1.1	.360	.418	.506	.263	.310	.374	.240	1.4	-1.0	38-CF	-7
2010	LAA	MLB	18	175	6	3	0	1	4	14	24	0	0	0.7	.205	.268	.245	.202	.265	.234	.161	-13.4	-1.5	0-	0

Breakout: 74%   Improve: 79%   Collapse: 12%   Attrition: 5%   MLB: 0%   Comparables: Ed Larregui, Greg Jackson, Jim Presley, Jose Iglesias

The Angels tabbed this heavily scouted New Jersey prepster with the 25th pick of the 2009 draft after he showed polish under the predraft spotlight, this despite a reputation for rawness. Despite not turning 18 until the midpoint of his season, Trout tore up the Arizona League, demonstrating good strike-zone judgment and gap power while flashing outstanding speed and getting good jumps in center field. He walked away with *Baseball America*'s top prospect honors for the circuit while drawing raves for his makeup. He got a late-season taste of Cedar Rapids, where he'll start the 2010 season.

Mark Trumbo — 1B

Bats: R | Throws: R | Height: 6' 4" | Weight: 220 | Born: January 16, 1986 | Age: 24

YEAR	TEAM	LVL	AGE	PA	R	2B	3B	HR	RBI	BB	SO	SB	CS	EqBRR	AVG	OBP	SLG	EqAVG	EqOBP	EqSLG	EqA	VORP	WARP	DEFENSE			
2007	CDR	A	21	516	57	27	2	14	76	34	98	10	8	-2.8	.272	.326	.427	.246	.291	.382	.233	-9.9	-1.8	112-1B	-5		
2008	RCU	A+	22	438	70	28	2	26	68	26	67	7	3	0.6	.283	.329	.553	.248	.289	.461	.253	0.7	0.0	96-1B	-1		
2008	ARK	AA	22	134	13	7	1	6	25	7	29	1	2	-1.2	.276	.311	.496	.256	.286	.440	.247	-0.7	-0.3	28-1B	-2		
2009	ARK	AA	23	581	54	35	3	15	88	37	100	6	3	-6.5	.291	.333	.452	.279	.314	.434	.257	-1.2	0.1	109-1B	1	10-RF	1
2010	LAA	MLB	24	569	57	30	2	20	78	37	119	4	4	-1.7	.259	.309	.436	.255	.306	.420	.245	-3.1	-0.5	123-1B	-1		

Breakout: 19%   Improve: 46%   Collapse: 8%   Attrition: 7%   MLB: 2%   Comparables: Troy Hughes, Brock Peterson, Stan Royer, Billie Merrifield

Trumbo finally broke out in 2008, taking a big step toward justifying the $1.425 million bonus he received in 2004, a record for an 18th-round pick. He started slowly in 2009 (.231/.278/.379 with a 21 percent strikeout rate through May), but the benefits of a shortened swing and improved pitch recognition began to pay off; he hit .319/.360/.486 with a 16 percent strikeout rate the rest of the way. That's good news, considering that Trumbo's bat is his ticket to "The Show"; he's slow, unathletic, and lacking in plate discipline and defensive range, but he does have plus-plus power.

Reggie Willits — OF

Bats: S   Throws: R   Height: 5' 11"   Weight: 185   Born: May 30, 1981   Age: 29

YEAR	TEAM	LVL	AGE	PA	R	2B	3B	HR	RBI	BB	SO	SB	CS	EqBRR	AVG	OBP	SLG	EqAVG	EqOBP	EqSLG	EqA	VORP	WARP	DEFENSE			
2007	LAA	MLB	26	518	74	20	1	0	34	69	83	27	8	-0.8	.293	.391	.344	.293	.392	.350	.274	18.5	2.6	58-LF	7	26-CF	-2
2008	LAA	MLB	27	136	21	4	0	0	7	21	26	2	1	1.4	.194	.321	.231	.198	.326	.236	.220	-3.6	-0.6	15-LF	-1	10-RF	-1
2009	SLC	AAA	28	280	40	10	1	1	27	34	44	11	4	0.4	.261	.351	.325	.219	.299	.273	.214	-7.1	-0.9	34-CF	0	8-LF	0
2009	LAA	MLB	28	92	16	2	0	0	6	5	17	5	1	2.3	.213	.256	.237	.203	.247	.228	.196	-4.4	-0.7	15-LF	-2	4-RF	0
2010	LAA	MLB	29	339	48	13	2	2	28	40	64	11	5	0.6	.251	.342	.330	.252	.344	.325	.236	1.9	0.1	56-CF	-1		

Breakout: 14% Improve: 49% Collapse: 19% Attrition: 16%   MLB: 58%   Comparables: Gerald Young, Willie Harris, Mike Brumley, John Cangelosi

Since his breakout rookie campaign in 2007, a slew of injuries and a crowd of healthy outfielders have conspired to limit Willits largely to pinch-running and defensive replacement duties. The real culprit is Willits' own lack of power; between Salt Lake and Anaheim, his translated slugging percentage for 2008-2009 was just .255—so low it doesn't pay for pitchers to do anything but pound the strike zone against him, neutralizing the impact of his plate discipline. Unless he can show some muscle amid his limited opportunities—particularly against righties, given Juan Rivera's struggles—he'll remain a spare part.

Bobby Wilson — C

Bats: R   Throws: R   Height: 6' 0"   Weight: 220   Born: April 8, 1983   Age: 27

YEAR	TEAM	LVL	AGE	PA	R	2B	3B	HR	RBI	BB	SO	SB	CS	EqBRR	AVG	OBP	SLG	EqAVG	EqOBP	EqSLG	EqA	VORP	WARP	DEFENSE			
2007	ARK	AA	24	204	24	9	0	6	27	22	26	5	3	-2.2	.271	.348	.420	.249	.314	.368	.240	4.4	1.1	42-C	5	4-1B	0
2007	SLC	AAA	24	141	15	13	1	3	22	8	18	1	0	1.0	.295	.336	.477	.241	.279	.383	.229	2.4	-0.6	36-C	-8		
2008	SLC	AAA	25	298	33	20	0	4	45	29	45	0	0	-2.9	.312	.386	.435	.263	.329	.346	.241	5.4	1.2	57-C	5	9-1B	0
2009	SLC	AAA	26	381	38	19	1	8	55	22	56	0	0	0.7	.271	.316	.398	.231	.272	.337	.210	-6.4	-0.9	72-C	0	13-1B	-1
2009	LAA	MLB	26	6	0	1	0	0	0	0	1	0	0	0.0	.200	.200	.400	.200	.200	.400	.213	0.0	0.0	3-C	0		
2010	LAA	MLB	27	324	28	14	1	7	43	24	56	1	1	-0.6	.250	.307	.371	.246	.305	.356	.227	1.9	0.3	75-C	0		

Breakout: 17% Improve: 41% Collapse: 30% Attrition: 16%   MLB: 12%   Comparables: Alberto Castillo, Mike Amrhein, Tony Kounas, Henry Blanco

The limitations of the Mathis/Napoli tandem prompted the Angels to carry Wilson as a third catcher intermittently, basically wasting a bench spot and a few round-trip plane fares. Prior to September, he was recalled from Triple-A three times, playing all of three innings in three weeks; hell, Scioscia could have done that himself. In any event, this high school teammate of Casey Kotchman has methodically climbed the organizational ladder because he's sound on both sides of the ball. One shouldn't ding his 2009 Triple-A showing too badly in light of the impact of repeated cases of forced idleness. He did throw out 38 percent of base thieves, and he really couldn't be a worse hitter than Mathis, though he's no major improvement, either.

Brandon Wood — 3B

Bats: R   Throws: R   Height: 6' 3"   Weight: 190   Born: March 2, 1985   Age: 25

YEAR	TEAM	LVL	AGE	PA	R	2B	3B	HR	RBI	BB	SO	SB	CS	EqBRR	AVG	OBP	SLG	EqAVG	EqOBP	EqSLG	EqA	VORP	WARP	DEFENSE			
2007	SLC	AAA	22	488	73	27	1	23	77	45	120	10	1	4.8	.272	.338	.497	.229	.293	.408	.245	4.9	-0.8	73-3B	-7	32-SS	-5
2007	LAA	MLB	22	33	2	1	0	1	3	0	12	0	0	0.0	.152	.152	.273	.152	.152	.273	.110	-3.4	-0.4	9-3B	0		
2008	SLC	AAA	23	448	82	21	2	31	84	45	104	6	5	-0.6	.296	.375	.595	.246	.319	.473	.267	21.0	-0.3	88-SS	-25	13-3B	1
2008	LAA	MLB	23	157	12	4	0	5	13	4	43	4	0	1.0	.200	.224	.327	.200	.224	.320	.197	-5.1	-1.1	22-SS	-4	21-3B	-1
2009	SLC	AAA	24	428	65	28	4	22	72	36	80	1	1	1.1	.293	.353	.557	.254	.311	.477	.266	16.1	1.0	46-3B	2	44-SS	-9
2009	LAA	MLB	24	46	5	1	0	1	3	3	19	0	0	-1.2	.195	.267	.293	.195	.267	.293	.198	-1.8	-0.3	5-3B	-1	4-SS	-1
2010	LAA	MLB	25	474	58	21	2	20	61	39	120	5	2	0.8	.239	.305	.435	.234	.301	.409	.245	5.0	0.3	107-3B	-2		

Breakout: 19% Improve: 44% Collapse: 14% Attrition: 9%   MLB: 100%   Comparables: Wade Rowdon, Mike Blowers, Gerald Williams, Aaron Boone

Stuck again in Salt Lake City with another case of the Mormon Tabernacle Choir blues, Wood has made genuine headway in taming his long swing during three years of Triple-A. Last year saw his lowest strikeout rate (18.7 percent) and best K/UBB ratio (2.4), and while fewer balls left the yard, his line-drive and pop-up rates moved in the right directions. Crowded out of the Angels' infield, he has seen his star dimmed since walloping 43 homers at Rancho Cucamonga in 2005, particularly given his major-league flailing (.192/.222/.313 with a 74/7 K/BB ratio in 236 PAs). Still, his name continues to surface in every Angels-related blockbuster scenario, and between Chone Figgins' departure and his being out of options, he figures to spend 2010 on someone's big-league roster.

PITCHERS

Jose Arredondo

Bats: R   Throws: R   Height: 6' 0"   Weight: 175   Born: March 30, 1984   Age: 26

YEAR	TEAM	LVL	AGE	W	L	SV	G	GS	IP	H	HR	BB	SO	GB%	BABIP	STUFF	WHIP	ERA	SIERA	DERA	EqH9	EqHR9	EqBB9	EqSO9	VORP	SN/WX
2007	RCU	A+	23	2	4	4	28	0	35	46	5	11	34	48%	.369	-26	1.63	6.43	3.60	8.64	13.2	2.2	3.2	5.7	-11.6	-1.71
2007	ARK	AA	23	0	1	10	23	0	25	16	2	12	28	41%	.233	3	1.12	2.52	3.30	4.50	6.8	1.1	4.5	7.5	2.7	0.67
2008	SLC	AAA	24	1	1	10	15	0	17	12	2	4	15	64%	.227	6	0.94	2.12	3.18	2.16	5.9	1.1	2.2	6.5	6.2	1.32
2008	LAA	MLB	24	10	2	0	52	0	61	42	3	22	55	57%	.239	22	1.05	1.62	3.60	2.21	5.9	0.4	2.8	7.4	22.3	2.88
2009	SLC	AAA	25	1	1	1	19	0	20²	13	1	14	24	38%	.255	17	1.31	2.18	3.81	3.15	5.8	0.4	5.8	9.0	5.2	0.19
2009	LAA	MLB	25	2	3	0	43	0	45	47	6	23	47	51%	.325	3	1.56	6.00	3.77	5.32	8.9	1.0	3.9	8.3	0.9	0.52
2010	LAA	MLB	26	4	4	3	64	0	671	62	8	30	53	46%	.285	1	1.37	4.24	4.34	4.37	8.2	1.0	3.8	6.7	8.5	1.22

Breakout: 21%   Improve: 50%   Collapse: 19%   Attrition: 7%   MLB: 100%   Comparables: Ramon Ramirez, Steve Ontiveros, Bob Apodaca, Matt Whiteside

Arredondo came out of nowhere as a rookie in 2008, cracking the league's top 20 in WXRL and looking like the Angels' closer of the future. Alas, his 2009 was a complete disasterpiece, due in part to injuries—a strained hip flexor in March and a UCL (ulnar collateral ligament) sprain in late June (suffered during his Triple-A stint)—which caused his average fastball velocity to drop by about 1.5 mph. His BABIP and ground-ball and HR/FB rates all moved in the wrong direction (the HR/FB rate doubled from seven to 14 percent), but much of it was simply regression; his SIERA barely budged, suggesting that Arredondo's sophomore jinx owed much to things he couldn't control. Barring further injury, he's a good candidate to rebound, but the Angels nontendered him in December rather than wait to see it.

Trevor Bell

Bats: L   Throws: R   Height: 6' 2"   Weight: 180   Born: October 12, 1986   Age: 23

YEAR	TEAM	LVL	AGE	W	L	SV	G	GS	IP	H	HR	BB	SO	GB%	BABIP	STUFF	WHIP	ERA	SIERA	DERA	EqH9	EqHR9	EqBB9	EqSO9	VORP	SN/WX
2007	CDR	A	20	8	4	0	21	21	115¹	136	8	23	90	52%	.341	-5	1.38	4.14	3.79	6.94	12.2	1.7	2.6	4.2	-17.1	-1.34
2008	CDR	A	21	1	0	0	3	2	17	13	0	4	13	51%	.295	14	1.00	2.12	3.54	3.62	9.9	0.7	3.3	4.6	2.9	0.17
2008	RCU	A+	21	6	8	0	36	12	100¹	106	8	39	80	64%	.316	-9	1.45	4.22	3.98	6.30	10.3	1.6	4.2	4.5	-8.4	-1.32
2009	ARK	AA	22	4	3	0	11	11	68²	54	1	20	51	56%	.256	23	1.08	2.23	3.97	4.16	7.8	0.7	2.7	5.0	9.9	0.96
2009	SLC	AAA	22	3	4	0	11	11	71¹	67	5	15	38	54%	.274	15	1.15	3.15	4.52	3.56	8.4	0.8	2.1	4.0	14.8	1.12
2009	LAA	MLB	22	1	2	0	8	4	20¹	40	3	11	14	45%	.451	-16	2.51	9.74	5.21	10.02	16.5	0.9	4.4	5.7	-10.4	-0.88
2010	LAA	MLB	23	6	9	0	35	21	1262	146	20	51	71	47%	.309	-8	1.56	5.40	5.08	5.57	10.3	1.2	3.5	4.8	-1.0	1.42

Breakout: 8%   Improve: 52%   Collapse: 16%   Attrition: 18%   MLB: 44%   Comparables: Tim Crews, Ed Martel, Dan Denham, Randy Veres

Oh, the perils of child stardom. The grandson of one of the original *Bozo the Clown* actors, Bell starred in commercials during his youth, gaining further fame when *Baseball America* anointed him the country's top 14-year-old in 2001. Alas, Bell's velocity as a prospect has receded since, and he's now a command-and-control type who backs up a low-90s fastball with a solid slider and changeup. He didn't miss many bats at Double-A or Triple-A, but got his share of popups and a good deal of help from his defense. Bell was recalled in August; his stuff didn't play so well at the big-league level, as batters scorched him for a 26 percent line-drive rate.

Jason Bulger

Bats: R   Throws: R   Height: 6' 4"   Weight: 210   Born: December 6, 1978   Age: 31

YEAR	TEAM	LVL	AGE	W	L	SV	G	GS	IP	H	HR	BB	SO	GB%	BABIP	STUFF	WHIP	ERA	SIERA	DERA	EqH9	EqHR9	EqBB9	EqSO9	VORP	SN/WX
2007	SLC	AAA	28	5	2	10	49	0	52²	51	4	24	81	59%	.382	21	1.42	3.76	2.30	3.87	8.8	0.9	4.1	10.7	9.5	0.93
2007	LAA	MLB	28	0	0	0	6	0	6¹	5	0	3	8	56%	.357	6	1.26	2.84	2.75	3.18	7.9	0.0	4.8	11.1	1.5	-0.03
2008	SLC	AAA	29	4	0	16	37	0	43	25	0	22	75	55%	.333	37	1.09	0.63	1.67	0.89	6.9	0.4	4.7	11.4	20.6	3.73
2008	LAA	MLB	29	0	0	0	14	0	16	15	3	9	20	45%	.308	10	1.50	7.31	3.34	6.61	8.3	1.7	4.4	9.9	-2.0	0.48
2009	LAA	MLB	30	6	1	1	64	0	65²	46	7	30	68	52%	.250	18	1.16	3.56	3.42	3.25	6.2	0.8	3.7	8.6	15.9	1.78
2010	LAA	MLB	31	4	4	8	62	0	612	55	7	30	67	51%	.311	10	1.39	4.09	3.48	4.19	7.9	0.9	4.2	9.2	9.0	2.06

Breakout: 15%   Improve: 40%   Collapse: 27%   Attrition: 9%   MLB: 90%   Comparables: Jim Kern, Heath Bell, Brad Lidge, Mike Timlin

Eight years after being the Diamondbacks' first-round pick, Bulger finally made good at the major-league level, helping the Angels' bullpen pick up the slack for the injured and/or ineffective Scot Shields and Jose Arredondo. Bulger has always been able to pump his fastball in the mid-90s, but a newfound consistency throwing strikes with his breaking balls worked him into Scioscia's good graces. Bombed for a 12.13 Fair Run Average in low-leverage duty in April, he yielded just a 1.78 FRA and 5.4 hits per nine the rest of the way. His leverage score climbed each month, and he finished with the staff's lowest line-drive rate (11.7 percent). Such dominance insures that he'll be in the mix for important innings in 2010.

Ryan Chaffee
Bats: R   Throws: R   Height: 6' 2"   Weight: 190   Born: May 18, 1988   Age: 22

YEAR	TEAM	LVL	AGE	W	L	SV	G	GS	IP	H	HR	BB	SO	GB%	BABIP	STUFF	WHIP	ERA	SIERA	DERA	EqH9	EqHR9	EqBB9	EqSO9	VORP	SN/WX
2009	CDR	A	21	8	8	0	23	23	116^1	84	6	65	121	68%	.271	-8	1.28	4.33	3.51	7.26	9.6	1.8	6.4	5.8	-19.9	-1.70
2010	LAA	MLB	22	3	7	0	25	22	94^1	101	15	63	70	67%	.306	7	1.74	6.19	4.67	6.33	9.5	1.3	5.7	6.3	-8.7	1.17

Breakout: 23% Improve: 58% Collapse: 10% Attrition: 2%   MLB: 2%   Comparables: Roger Pavlik, Mark Leiter, Ryan Mattheus, Jason Secoda

A 2008 third-rounder out of a Florida juco, Chaffee didn't debut professionally until 2009 due to a broken bone in his foot. He made a tantalizing showing at Cedar Rapids, striking out over one hitter per inning and at one point going 13 straight starts without allowing a homer. He may have run out of gas down the stretch; the 26 earned runs he yielded over his final 22 innings ballooned his ERA from 2.86 to 4.33. Chaffee offers a low-90s fastball with late movement, a plus changeup, and an assortment of breaking balls that feature different release points but which can also compromise his command; his 16 hit batsmen led the league, and his 16 wild pitches placed third.

Tyler Chatwood
Bats: R   Throws: R   Height: 5' 11"   Weight: 175   Born: December 16, 1989   Age: 20

YEAR	TEAM	LVL	AGE	W	L	SV	G	GS	IP	H	HR	BB	SO	GB%	BABIP	STUFF	WHIP	ERA	SIERA	DERA	EqH9	EqHR9	EqBB9	EqSO9	VORP	SN/WX
2008	ANG	Rk	18	1	2	0	11	11	38	25	1	36	48	58%	.296	14	1.61	3.08	3.87	5.17	10.1	2.0	10.6	6.9	1.1	-0.08
2009	CDR	A	19	8	7	0	24	24	116^1	99	3	66	106	56%	.306	2	1.42	4.02	4.10	6.98	10.8	1.4	6.6	5.2	-16.3	-1.23
2010	LAA	MLB	20	3	9	0	28	28	107	130	19	88	78	54%	.333	24	2.03	7.16	5.39	7.29	10.7	1.4	7.0	6.2	-21.2	2.07

Breakout: 13% Improve: 53% Collapse: 13% Attrition: 7%   MLB: 1%   Comparables: Freddie Toliver, Kevin Coker, Rick Balabon, Jason Doss

Little man, big arm. Chosen in the second round of the 2008 draft (number 74 overall) as the Angels' top pick, Chatwood drew inevitable comparisons to Roy Oswalt due to his diminutive size and combination of a mid-90s fastball and a knee-buckling curve. Impressive enough in his pro debut in 2008, he bypassed the Pioneer League and made a solid showing at Cedar Rapids, missing bats and producing ground balls. Command was an issue, particularly earlier in the year; he walked 6.1 per nine before the break, but just 4.3 after, and luckily, his strikeout rate didn't waver. He'll have plenty of time to continue ironing out his command as he climbs the ladder.

Kelvim Escobar
Bats: R   Throws: R   Height: 6' 1"   Weight: 230   Born: April 11, 1976   Age: 34

YEAR	TEAM	LVL	AGE	W	L	SV	G	GS	IP	H	HR	BB	SO	GB%	BABIP	STUFF	WHIP	ERA	SIERA	DERA	EqH9	EqHR9	EqBB9	EqSO9	VORP	SN/WX
2007	LAA	MLB	31	18	7	0	30	30	195^2	182	11	66	160	50%	.299	30	1.27	3.40	3.93	3.32	7.9	0.5	2.7	6.7	46.9	6.35
2009	LAA	MLB	33	0	1	0	1	1	5	4	0	4	5	57%	.308	5	1.60	3.60	4.51	3.60	7.2	0.0	5.4	7.2	1.1	0.14
2010	NYN	MLB	34	4	5	0	14	3	68	63	7	27	52	50%	.285	10	1.31	3.94	4.22	4.37	8.6	0.9	3.3	6.2	8.6	1.52

Breakout: 13% Improve: 47% Collapse: 29% Attrition: 17%   MLB: 75%   Comparables: Chris Carpenter, Jim Barr, Freddy Garcia, Tanyon Sturtze

For their $28.5 million, the Angels wound up with Escobar's career year and two years of nothing but shoulder miseries. Thanks to his dogged effort to rehab from July 2008 labrum surgery, initial Cactus League reports abounded with hopeful news about Escobar reaching the mid-90s without pain and possibly returning to the big leagues by May instead of by the All-Star break. Alas, the particular progression of his arm troubles (elbow, then shoulder) didn't bode well, and his shoulder couldn't even hold up beyond a single big-league appearance in June. The Mets signed him to a one-year deal and intend to let him compete for the bullpen set-up role; if that doesn't work out, there's always his seminar, "Form and Frangibility: The Dignified Disabled Pitcher."

Brian Fuentes

Bats: L   Throws: L   Height: 6' 4"   Weight: 230   Born: August 9, 1975   Age: 34

YEAR	TEAM	LVL	AGE	W	L	SV	G	GS	IP	H	HR	BB	SO	GB%	BABIP	STUFF	WHIP	ERA	SIERA	DERA	EqH9	EqHR9	EqBB9	EqSO9	VORP	SN/WX
2007	COL	MLB	31	3	5	20	64	0	61¹	46	6	23	56	42%	.245	16	1.12	3.08	3.76	3.45	6.6	0.6	2.9	7.6	14.0	0.37
2008	COL	MLB	32	1	5	30	67	0	62²	47	3	22	82	41%	.297	33	1.10	2.73	2.36	2.91	6.5	0.3	2.7	9.7	18.2	3.52
2009	LAA	MLB	33	1	5	48	65	0	55	53	6	24	46	39%	.292	2	1.40	3.93	4.36	3.58	8.1	0.8	3.4	6.7	11.8	2.56
2010	LAA	MLB	34	3	3	19	54	0	53²	48	6	21	47	39%	.289	6	1.28	4.01	3.93	4.17	8.1	0.9	3.3	7.5	8.0	1.30

Breakout: 14%   Improve: 42%   Collapse: 36%   Attrition: 13%   MLB: 90%   Comparables: Damaso Marte, Jesse Orosco, Jerry Don Gleaton, Joe Hoerner

In reclaiming the Rockies' closer job in 2008, Fuentes set career bests for ERA, strikeouts, and homer rate, so moving to a more pitcher-friendly park via his two-year, $17.5 million deal certainly didn't figure to hurt his cause. While he did lead the majors in saves, Fuentes put the lie to the value of that stat by finishing just 20th in the AL in WXRL. His fastball velocity decreased after spiking in 2008, his strikeout rate fell by 57 percent, and righties punished him at a .261/.358/.428 clip, up from .211/.290/.306 the year before. The Angels might want to mind his workload in 2010, as Fuentes has a $9 million option for 2011 that's based on his finishing 55 games, two fewer than he finished last year.

Kevin Jepsen

Bats: R   Throws: R   Height: 6' 3"   Weight: 215   Born: July 26, 1984   Age: 25

YEAR	TEAM	LVL	AGE	W	L	SV	G	GS	IP	H	HR	BB	SO	GB%	BABIP	STUFF	WHIP	ERA	SIERA	DERA	EqH9	EqHR9	EqBB9	EqSO9	VORP	SN/WX
2007	RCU	A+	22	1	5	3	44	0	53²	61	2	38	50	60%	.371	-9	1.84	4.19	4.44	5.42	12.1	1.1	6.8	5.7	0.4	-0.93
2008	ARK	AA	23	2	1	11	25	0	31²	22	0	18	35	69%	.282	14	1.26	1.42	3.30	2.10	7.2	0.6	5.4	7.2	11.3	1.59
2008	SLC	AAA	23	1	3	2	15	0	23	17	3	12	21	67%	.237	5	1.26	2.35	3.73	3.22	6.4	1.2	4.4	6.4	5.6	0.42
2008	LAA	MLB	23	0	1	0	9	0	8¹	8	0	4	7	54%	.320	0	1.44	4.32	4.24	5.40	8.6	0.0	4.3	6.5	0.1	0.15
2009	SLC	AAA	24	1	0	2	14	0	18	30	4	16	20	80%	.419	-15	2.56	9.00	4.25	11.84	14.2	1.9	7.1	7.6	-13.4	-0.96
2009	LAA	MLB	24	6	4	1	54	0	54²	63	2	19	48	62%	.363	7	1.50	4.94	3.75	4.81	10.1	0.3	2.9	7.3	4.1	1.69
2010	LAA	MLB	25	3	5	3	64	0	68²	75	9	39	50	62%	.316	-13	1.65	5.38	4.63	5.58	9.7	1.1	4.8	6.3	-0.6	1.05

Breakout: 15%   Improve: 37%   Collapse: 19%   Attrition: 6%   MLB: 97%   Comparables: Jim Davins, Steve Wapnick, Jeremy Accardo, Juan Padilla

A 2002 second-round pick whose upward progress was slowed by a torn labrum, Jepsen broke camp with the big club, but lower-back spasms caused him to elevate his pitches, and he went on the DL having surrendered 16 baserunners and 12 runs in 4 ⅔ innings. He was still shaky though June, but he worked his way into high-leverage duty with a 2.93 ERA and a 42/14 K/BB ratio in 43 innings from July 1st onward; his 2.3 WXRL over that span would have cracked the league's top 25. Jepsen can dial his fastball into the high 90s, and both that pitch and his cutter get exceptional movement. He's the frontrunner to be the team's top righty set-up man in 2010.

Scott Kazmir

Bats: L   Throws: L   Height: 6' 0"   Weight: 190   Born: January 24, 1984   Age: 26

YEAR	TEAM	LVL	AGE	W	L	SV	G	GS	IP	H	HR	BB	SO	GB%	BABIP	STUFF	WHIP	ERA	SIERA	DERA	EqH9	EqHR9	EqBB9	EqSO9	VORP	SN/WX
2007	TBA	MLB	23	13	9	0	34	34	206²	196	18	89	239	45%	.333	37	1.38	3.48	3.16	3.53	7.7	0.8	3.5	9.2	45.6	5.63
2008	TBA	MLB	24	12	8	0	27	27	152¹	123	23	70	166	36%	.265	17	1.27	3.49	3.48	3.61	7.9	1.5	3.8	9.0	31.1	5.15
2009	TBA	MLB	25	8	7	0	20	20	111	121	15	50	91	41%	.309	0	1.54	5.92	4.47	5.80	9.8	1.1	3.5	6.4	-3.8	1.44
2009	LAA	MLB	25	2	2	0	6	6	36¹	28	1	10	26	25%	.257	24	1.05	1.73	4.58	2.02	6.6	0.3	2.3	5.8	13.8	1.
2010	LAA	MLB	26	10	10	0	32	32	179¹	174	23	72	160	39%	.303	19	1.37	4.32	3.95	4.43	8.6	1.0	3.5	7.7	21.3	3.20

Breakout: 7%   Improve: 41%   Collapse: 14%   Attrition: 9%   MLB: 100%   Comparables: Don Gullett, Curt Simmons, Fernando Valenzuela, Mickey Lolich

Kazmir was the Rays' ace once upon a time, but the team outgrew him in its evolution to contender status. Perhaps he'd have been dealt regardless, but when he racked up a 7.69 ERA through his first nine starts and then missed five weeks with a quad strain, one could understand Tampa Bay's determination to find a window to deal him, given his declining performance and the weight of the remaining contract ($22.5 million, including a 2012 option buyout). Fortunately, Kazmir rebounded on returning from the DL, and to a team with a hole in its rotation as the waiver deadline neared (as well as some long-term uncertainty regarding John Lackey's future), his late-summer string of five quality starts out of six made him look like a worthwhile gamble. Kazmir ran up a sterling ERA, and while his strikeout rate continued to fall, his walk and homer rates plummeted even more precipitously as he produced a plethora of popups (13.2 percent, nearly double the league average). The good news going forward is that the restoration of Kazmir's slider into his repertoire alleviated some concerns about his elbow and that even if he's less dominating than in 2007, his final 17 starts (3.63 ERA, 82/31 K/BB ratio in 101 ⅔ innings) were more than merely serviceable.

Michael Kohn

Bats: R   Throws: R   Height: 6' 2"   Weight: 200   Born: June 26, 1986   Age: 24

YEAR	TEAM	LVL	AGE	W	L	SV	G	GS	IP	H	HR	BB	SO	GB%	BABIP	STUFF	WHIP	ERA	SIERA	DERA	EqH9	EqHR9	EqBB9	EqSO9	VORP	SN/WX
2008	ORM	Rk	22	2	0	0	16	0	23¹	11	1	11	44	46%	.270	21	0.94	1.93	1.21	3.00	7.3	1.7	5.6	9.4	5.8	0.35
2009	CDR	A	23	4	1	6	28	0	37	20	1	12	60	39%	.292	17	0.86	2.19	1.13	3.69	8.2	1.4	4.0	9.9	6.4	0.54
2009	RCU	A+	23	2	0	3	22	0	28²	13	0	14	43	26%	.255	21	0.94	0.94	1.95	1.80	6.1	0.7	5.4	9.0	10.3	0.98
2010	LAA	MLB	24	3	4	3	46	0	53¹	54	8	30	52	35%	.320	-1	1.59	5.08	4.24	5.14	8.9	1.2	4.8	8.4	2.1	2.09

Breakout: 4%   Improve: 18%   Collapse: 52%   Attrition: 6%   MLB: 7%   Comparables: Todd Pennington, Fred Rath, Steve Wapnick, Chris Schroder

A 13th-round 2008 pick out of College of Charleston, Kohn is a pure relief prospect whose deceptively short arm action—derived from his days as an infielder—gives hitters the impression that his mid-90s fastball is on top of them even more quickly. Having only devoted himself to full-time pitching as a pro, Kohn is still very raw, and his slider remains a work in progress. Nonetheless, he's racked up astronomical strikeout numbers; through 87 pro innings, he's averaging 14.9 strikeouts per nine while allowing just 4.4 hits per nine. He's likely to be ticketed for Double-A Arkansas to start the year; if his stuff translates to the high minors, Angel opponents may soon be feeling the wrath of Kohn.

John Lackey

Bats: R   Throws: R   Height: 6' 6"   Weight: 245   Born: October 23, 1978   Age: 31

YEAR	TEAM	LVL	AGE	W	L	SV	G	GS	IP	H	HR	BB	SO	GB%	BABIP	STUFF	WHIP	ERA	SIERA	DERA	EqH9	EqHR9	EqBB9	EqSO9	VORP	SN/WX
2007	LAA	MLB	28	19	9	0	33	33	224	219	18	52	179	53%	.301	28	1.21	3.01	3.72	3.21	8.2	0.7	1.9	6.5	56.8	7.00
2008	LAA	MLB	29	12	5	0	24	24	163¹	161	26	40	130	53%	.288	13	1.23	3.75	3.76	3.62	8.7	1.4	2.0	6.7	33.2	4.84
2009	LAA	MLB	30	11	8	0	27	27	176¹	177	17	47	139	56%	.299	24	1.27	3.83	3.87	3.86	8.5	0.7	2.1	6.3	32.4	4.17
2010	BOS	MLB	31	12	11	0	31	31	194¹	195	22	53	143	53%	.301	16	1.28	4.01	3.99	4.12	8.7	0.9	2.3	6.2	29.8	3.59

Breakout: 5%   Improve: 38%   Collapse: 13%   Attrition: 10%   MLB: 98%   Comparables: A.J. Burnett, Freddy Garcia, Erik Hanson, Kevin Millwood

For the second season in a row, Lackey opened the year on the DL; this time an elbow strain shelved him until mid-May. He was erratic during his first month, putting up a 6.61 ERA through his first six starts. Luckily for the Angels, he settled into his typical groove, compiling a 3.23 ERA with a tidy 3.1 K/BB ratio while averaging 6.9 innings per start for the rest of the year. Unable to work out a contract extension prior to the season, he hit the winter market as the top starter available. Bigger questions about arm health dogged A. J. Burnett last winter and he did just fine, so it was no surprise when Lackey got a virtually identical five-year deal for $82.5 million with the Red Sox in the latest salvo of the AL East's arms race.

Dustin Moseley

Bats: R   Throws: R   Height: 6' 4"   Weight: 215   Born: December 26, 1981   Age: 28

YEAR	TEAM	LVL	AGE	W	L	SV	G	GS	IP	H	HR	BB	SO	GB%	BABIP	STUFF	WHIP	ERA	SIERA	DERA	EqH9	EqHR9	EqBB9	EqSO9	VORP	SN/WX
2007	LAA	MLB	25	4	3	0	46	8	92	97	7	27	50	55%	.304	-2	1.35	4.40	4.73	3.94	9.1	0.7	2.4	4.6	15.4	1.34
2008	SLC	AAA	26	7	10	0	20	20	116²	150	23	34	83	58%	.339	-17	1.58	6.94	4.19	6.73	11.1	1.5	2.7	4.9	-15.5	-1.78
2008	LAA	MLB	26	2	4	0	12	10	50¹	70	6	20	37	58%	.372	-5	1.79	6.79	4.46	6.12	12.2	0.9	3.2	6.1	-3.4	-0.30
2009	LAA	MLB	27	1	0	0	3	3	14²	20	3	3	8	45%	.333	-1	1.57	4.30	4.72	4.30	11.7	1.2	1.8	4.3	2.0	0.22
2010	LAA	MLB	28	4	6	0	30	9	80¹	92	11	29	45	51%	.310	-10	1.51	5.13	4.92	5.33	10.3	1.1	3.1	4.8	1.5	0.41

Breakout: 19%   Improve: 62%   Collapse: 17%   Attrition: 24%   MLB: 60%   Comparables: Renie Martin, Tom Hausman, Frank Pastore, Bryan Clutterbuck

Throughout Moseley's career, batters have hit .275/.336/.414 when facing him for the first time in a game, and .365/.401/.556 thereafter. Nonetheless, hope sprung eternal when he gave the Angels two good starts amid their April tribulations. The fun didn't last, as Moseley soon wound up on the DL due to the inflammation of a nerve running from his neck to his elbow and then needed surgery to repair a torn hip labrum in August. Non-tendered by the Halos, he should be ready in time for camp with somebody, but unless doctors implanted some mid-90s velocity, he's unlikely to turn a corner.

Sean O'Sullivan

Bats: R   Throws: R   Height: 6' 1"   Weight: 220   Born: September 1, 1987   Age: 22

YEAR	TEAM	LVL	AGE	W	L	SV	G	GS	IP	H	HR	BB	SO	GB%	BABIP	STUFF	WHIP	ERA	SIERA	DERA	EqH9	EqHR9	EqBB9	EqSO9	VORP	SN/WX
2007	CDR	A	19	10	7	0	25	25	158^1	136	6	40	125	52%	.273	22	1.11	2.22	3.79	4.81	8.8	1.2	3.0	4.2	11.6	0.77
2008	RCU	A+	20	16	8	0	28	25	158	167	8	50	111	53%	.311	22	1.37	4.73	4.31	6.29	10.0	1.2	3.5	3.8	-13.4	-1.28
2009	ARK	AA	21	1	2	0	3	3	18^2	21	1	0	14	56%	.328	17	1.12	5.30	3.30	6.75	11.4	1.6	0.5	5.2	-2.4	-0.29
2009	SLC	AAA	21	6	4	0	14	13	69	74	9	20	48	44%	.294	18	1.36	5.48	4.36	5.54	9.3	1.3	2.6	5.0	-0.3	0.04
2009	LAA	MLB	21	4	2	0	12	10	51^2	60	12	16	29	45%	.284	9	1.47	5.92	4.92	5.25	9.5	1.7	2.4	4.5	1.5	0.54
2010	LAA	MLB	22	7	10	0	30	26	144	154	21	55	77	39%	.291	8	1.46	4.99	5.27	5.15	9.5	1.2	3.3	4.6	5.6	1.95

Breakout: 8%   Improve: 50%   Collapse: 11%   Attrition: 13%   MLB: 100%   Comparables: Roy Smith, Yorman Bazardo, Arnold Gooch, Kyle Lohse

Once considered the nation's top prep pitching prospect, O'Sullivan lost some velocity, slipped to the third round of the 2005 draft, and remade himself as a finesse pitcher. He's adept at setting up hitters with a three-pitch arsenal consisting of a 90 mph fastball with good movement, a plus curve, and an average changeup, but he lacks a true out pitch. The Angels' rotation injuries fast-tracked him to the majors in mid-June despite just 13 starts and a 5.82 ERA above A-ball, and for a while, O'Sullivan stayed afloat, with a 3.72 ERA through his first five starts. Yo-yoed back and forth between Salt Lake and Anaheim, he was torched for 20 runs in 14 ⅔ innings in August, serving as a reminder that he'll need seasoning before becoming a viable rotation regular. Expect to see him back at some point in 2010.

Darren Oliver

Bats: R   Throws: L   Height: 6' 2"   Weight: 200   Born: October 6, 1970   Age: 39

YEAR	TEAM	LVL	AGE	W	L	SV	G	GS	IP	H	HR	BB	SO	GB%	BABIP	STUFF	WHIP	ERA	SIERA	DERA	EqH9	EqHR9	EqBB9	EqSO9	VORP	SN/WX
2007	LAA	MLB	36	3	1	0	61	0	64^1	58	5	23	51	54%	.275	7	1.26	3.78	4.08	3.89	7.4	0.7	2.9	6.3	11.8	1.42
2008	LAA	MLB	37	7	1	0	54	0	72	67	5	16	48	53%	.284	9	1.15	2.87	4.11	2.83	8.2	0.5	1.8	5.7	20.8	2.26
2009	LAA	MLB	38	5	1	0	63	1	73	61	5	22	65	51%	.286	19	1.14	2.71	3.52	2.50	7.4	0.5	2.4	7.4	23.5	2.99
2010	TEX	MLB	39	4	4	0	57	0	60	57	6	22	41	52%	.286	0	1.32	4.09	4.41	4.13	8.5	0.9	2.9	6.0	9.1	1.22

Breakout: 11%   Improve: 30%   Collapse: 38%   Attrition: 20%   MLB: 99%   Comparables: Chris Hammond, Hank Aguirre, Tom Burgmeier, Bob Patterson

As banged up as the Angels' staff was in April, things might have gotten worse had their attempt to press Oliver into rotation duty not been thwarted by the lefty's triceps strain. Upon returning in early May, Oliver anchored a bullpen reeling from injuries and departures and wound up leading the club in WXRL and posting his highest strikeout rate since 1994. Late in life, the former starter has become an exceptional reliever better suited to multi-inning work than to LOOGYdom, thanks to a reverse platoon split (.233/.304/.317 vs. righties from 2007 to 2009, .257/.303/.415 vs. lefties). He'll be an asset in the Ranger's bullpen in 2010.

Anthony Ortega

Bats: R   Throws: R   Height: 6' 0"   Weight: 170   Born: August 24, 1985   Age: 24

YEAR	TEAM	LVL	AGE	W	L	SV	G	GS	IP	H	HR	BB	SO	GB%	BABIP	STUFF	WHIP	ERA	SIERA	DERA	EqH9	EqHR9	EqBB9	EqSO9	VORP	SN/WX
2007	RCU	A+	21	7	11	0	28	28	163^1	157	17	68	127	47%	.288	2	1.38	4.02	4.33	5.15	9.8	1.7	4.1	4.5	5.9	0.06
2008	ARK	AA	22	9	7	0	22	22	135	124	11	49	83	51%	.270	-2	1.28	3.73	4.66	5.17	8.7	1.4	3.5	3.7	4.7	0.50
2008	SLC	AAA	22	5	0	0	6	6	39^1	46	2	6	22	54%	.314	12	1.32	2.52	4.40	3.15	9.7	0.7	1.6	3.6	10.4	0.89
2009	SLC	AAA	23	2	1	0	4	4	18^2	30	5	6	5	52%	.347	-39	1.93	9.64	5.89	10.25	14.0	2.5	3.0	1.5	-9.5	-0.69
2009	LAA	MLB	23	0	2	0	3	3	12^2	19	4	6	7	57%	.333	-20	1.97	9.24	5.23	9.69	12.5	2.1	3.5	4.2	-6.1	-0.33
2010	LAA	MLB	24	3	6	0	25	10	80^2	96	14	40	40	48%	.305	-22	1.68	6.30	5.53	6.39	10.5	1.4	4.2	4.1	-8.0	1.27

Breakout: 15%   Improve: 50%   Collapse: 19%   Attrition: 23%   MLB: 8%   Comparables: Larry Lamonde, Joel Moore, Jeffrey Stottlemyre, Stan Kyles

Ortega won the Angels' Minor League Pitcher of the Year award, thanks to a breakout 2008 in which he pitched down in the zone more consistently and generated more ground balls, but the follow-up didn't go so well. After battling forearm and elbow problems during spring training, he was pummeled both at Salt Lake City and during his brief major-league trial as well. Shortly after returning to Triple-A, he was sidelined—for the year, as it turned out—due to elbow inflammation. A pitch-to-contact type whose upside is as a fourth or fifth starter, Ortega throws a low-90s fastball, but just an average curve, and he lacks a consistent out pitch.

Matt Palmer

Bats: R   Throws: R   Height: 6' 2"   Weight: 200   Born: March 21, 1979   Age: 31

YEAR	TEAM	LVL	AGE	W	L	SV	G	GS	IP	H	HR	BB	SO	GB%	BABIP	STUFF	WHIP	ERA	SIERA	DERA	EqH9	EqHR9	EqBB9	EqSO9	VORP	SN/WX
2007	FRE	AAA	28	11	8	0	29	25	150	155	17	51	98	50%	.296	-15	1.37	4.32	4.53	5.11	9.9	1.5	3.3	4.5	6.1	0.88
2008	FRE	AAA	29	6	10	0	26	25	142	138	11	72	143	57%	.323	8	1.48	4.18	3.77	4.57	9.3	1.0	4.5	6.8	14.2	1.47
2008	SFN	MLB	29	0	2	0	3	3	12²	17	1	13	3	54%	.333	-25	2.37	8.53	7.23	8.76	12.4	0.7	8.0	2.2	-4.5	-0.17
2009	LAA	MLB	30	11	2	0	40	13	121¹	105	12	55	69	60%	.255	5	1.32	3.93	4.90	3.69	7.5	0.8	3.7	4.7	23.8	2.38
2010	LAA	MLB	31	5	8	0	34	18	106 1	115	15	49	64	55%	.299	-10	1.55	5.38	4.94	5.54	9.7	1.2	3.9	5.1	-0.4	1.56

Breakout: 15%   Improve: 39%   Collapse: 17%   Attrition: 26%   MLB: 55%   Comparables: Rod Bolton, Mark Petkovsek, Rick Lysander, Don Welchel

A 30-year-old rookie who spent seven years in the Giants' chain, Palmer landed in the right place at the right time for the Angels. He stepped into their decimated rotation in late April, notched wins in his first five starts, and went 9-1 despite a 4.66 ERA in that role, thanks to 7.2 runs per game of offensive support. His ERA was a respectable 2.74 out of the bullpen, though his strikeout and walk rates were considerably worse. Palmer doesn't miss many bats; he's a ground-baller who uses a sinker, cutter, and curve to get by with a little help from his leather-wielding friends. He won't go 11-2 again, but he's an adequate utility pitcher.

Trevor Reckling

Bats: L   Throws: L   Height: 6' 2"   Weight: 205   Born: May 22, 1989   Age: 21

YEAR	TEAM	LVL	AGE	W	L	SV	G	GS	IP	H	HR	BB	SO	GB%	BABIP	STUFF	WHIP	ERA	SIERA	DERA	EqH9	EqHR9	EqBB9	EqSO9	VORP	SN/WX
2007	ANG	Rk	18	3	1	2	9	5	36	33	2	7	55	50%	.373	32	1.11	2.75	1.50	4.41	11.9	2.3	2.8	8.2	3.9	-0.05
2008	CDR	A	19	10	7	0	26	26	152¹	137	8	59	128	57%	.297	4	1.29	3.37	3.90	5.85	10.6	1.5	4.7	4.6	-5.2	-0.69
2009	RCU	A+	20	1	2	0	3	3	19	9	2	3	16	56%	.149	18	0.63	0.95	3.03	2.25	5.0	2.0	2.0	4.5	6.5	0.49
2009	ARK	AA	20	8	7	0	23	23	135¹	118	4	75	106	55%	.295	29	1.43	2.93	4.51	4.35	9.4	0.9	5.2	5.6	15.8	1.50
2010	LAA	MLB	21	5	10	0	26	26	137 2	157	22	74	83	48%	.309	20	1.68	5.89	5.25	6.02	10.1	1.3	4.7	5.2	-8.0	2.73

Breakout: 10%   Improve: 43%   Collapse: 10%   Attrition: 5%   MLB: 11%   Comparables: Doug Million, Benj Sampson, Clayton Kershaw, Nick Bierbrodt

A seventh-round 2007 pick out of a Newark Catholic high school, Reckling has fast become one of the organization's elite pitching prospects. Raw, but possessing outstanding athleticism, he offers three plus pitches: a low-90s fastball with significant sink and a good changeup, plus a drop-off-the-table curve that some consider the system's best, although hitters often lay off it while waiting for it to fall out of the zone. He barely unpacked at Rancho before traveling to the Travelers, and he held his own as the league's youngest starter, wriggling out of jams caused by his high walk rate thanks to his ability to avoid contact and generate grounders. He'll need to improve his command of his secondary stuff to take the next developmental step.

Rafael Rodriguez

Bats: R   Throws: R   Height: 6' 1"   Weight: 175   Born: September 24, 1984   Age: 25

YEAR	TEAM	LVL	AGE	W	L	SV	G	GS	IP	H	HR	BB	SO	GB%	BABIP	STUFF	WHIP	ERA	SIERA	DERA	EqH9	EqHR9	EqBB9	EqSO9	VORP	SN/WX
2007	ARK	AA	22	0	6	0	46	1	71¹	79	6	30	42	56%	.312	-23	1.53	4.16	4.89	5.47	11.2	1.4	4.1	3.8	0.2	-0.81
2008	ARK	AA	23	2	4	11	42	0	53¹	46	3	11	48	60%	.291	4	1.07	1.86	3.14	2.50	8.4	1.1	2.1	5.9	16.8	2.22
2008	SLC	AAA	23	2	0	0	9	0	14¹	20	2	6	8	77%	.367	-25	1.81	6.28	4.28	6.75	12.8	1.4	4.1	4.1	-1.9	-0.10
2009	SLC	AAA	24	1	0	3	22	0	34	27	3	10	23	64%	.255	-1	1.09	1.85	3.96	2.01	7.5	0.9	2.9	5.2	12.1	1.32
2009	LAA	MLB	24	0	1	0	18	0	30²	47	4	9	10	69%	.355	-27	1.83	5.58	5.20	5.72	12.9	0.9	2.3	2.6	-0.8	-0.34
2010	LAA	MLB	25	3	5	2	50	0	67	80	10	29	32	60%	.313	-22	1.63	5.66	5.16	5.88	10.8	1.2	3.7	4.2	-2.9	1.24

Breakout: 13%   Improve: 33%   Collapse: 26%   Attrition: 14%   MLB: 52%   Comparables: Ryan Brewer, Travis Minix, Lino Rivera, Joe Hudson

Signed to the biggest bonus paid by the Angels to a Dominican prospect, Rodriguez took seven seasons honing his control. Once a heat-thrower, he has evolved into a sinker/slider ground-baller who pounds the lower strike zone. When he's not getting pounded himself, that is—something that happened all too often during five separate stints with the big club in 2009. Opponents batted .356/.396/.538 against Rodriguez, lashing line drives on 25 percent of the balls they put into play, and they put a lot of them into play. Unless he rediscovers some way to get batters to miss the ball once in a while, Rodriguez is doomed to the margins.

Ervin Santana

Bats: R   Throws: R   Height: 6' 2"   Weight: 185   Born: December 12, 1982   Age: 27

YEAR	TEAM	LVL	AGE	W	L	SV	G	GS	IP	H	HR	BB	SO	GB%	BABIP	STUFF	WHIP	ERA	SIERA	DERA	EqH9	EqHR9	EqBB9	EqSO9	VORP	SN/WX
2007	SLC	AAA	24	2	1	0	5	5	32¹	39	4	10	32	40%	.368	14	1.52	5.01	3.49	4.97	10.2	1.1	2.8	7.4	1.9	-0.08
2007	LAA	MLB	24	7	14	0	28	26	150	174	26	58	126	39%	.324	-3	1.55	5.76	4.24	5.53	9.8	1.5	3.1	6.8	-0.4	1.60
2008	LAA	MLB	25	16	7	0	32	32	219	198	23	47	214	44%	.289	34	1.12	3.49	3.07	3.43	7.8	0.9	1.7	8.0	50.5	6.09
2009	LAA	MLB	26	8	8	0	24	23	139²	159	24	47	107	46%	.317	3	1.47	5.03	4.25	4.76	9.8	1.2	2.7	6.2	11.3	2.01
2010	*LAA*	*MLB*	*27*	*9*	*10*	*0*	*29*	*29*	*164²*	*171*	*23*	*55*	*126*	*41%*	*.305*	*11*	*1.37*	*4.60*	*4.19*	*4.72*	*9.2*	*1.1*	*2.9*	*6.6*	*14.3*	*1.99*

Breakout: 6%   Improve: 39%   Collapse: 11%   Attrition: 15%   MLB: 96%   Comparables: Kirk McCaskill, Reggie Cleveland, Ian Snell, Pat Hentgen

Santana failed to match his breakout 2008 performance or to begin living up to the four-year, $30 million extension he signed last February, in no small part because he sprained his ulnar collateral ligament in early March. He made just six starts through June and was bombed for a 7.47 ERA; according to PITCHf/x, his average fastball velocity in that span was down 3.3 mph from 2008. His ERA remained in Boeing territory as late as August 11, but as his velocity returned, he closed out the season making eight quality starts out of 10. Nonetheless, his strikeout and walk rates fell and rose, respectively, and his homer rate soared, which was a result of the confluence of more balls in play, a higher fly-ball rate, and worse-than-average luck on home runs per fly ball (15.5 percent, compared with an MLB average of 13 percent). The Angels can hope that a healthy Santana can build on his 2008 showing, but that was the year way out of line with his career numbers, not 2009.

Joe Saunders

Bats: L   Throws: L   Height: 6' 3"   Weight: 210   Born: June 16, 1981   Age: 29

YEAR	TEAM	LVL	AGE	W	L	SV	G	GS	IP	H	HR	BB	SO	GB%	BABIP	STUFF	WHIP	ERA	SIERA	DERA	EqH9	EqHR9	EqBB9	EqSO9	VORP	SN/WX
2007	SLC	AAA	26	4	7	0	14	14	86¹	89	10	20	84	50%	.313	19	1.26	5.11	3.22	5.11	8.3	1.0	2.1	6.9	3.8	-0.44
2007	LAA	MLB	26	8	5	0	18	18	107¹	129	11	34	69	54%	.330	6	1.52	4.44	4.53	4.19	10.1	0.9	2.5	5.3	15.6	1.74
2008	LAA	MLB	27	17	7	0	31	31	198	187	21	53	103	52%	.266	12	1.21	3.41	4.77	3.50	8.3	0.9	2.2	4.4	42.9	5.78
2009	LAA	MLB	28	16	7	0	31	31	186	202	29	64	101	56%	.286	0	1.43	4.60	4.88	4.42	9.1	1.1	2.7	4.4	22.3	2.85
2010	*LAA*	*MLB*	*29*	*10*	*11*	*0*	*30*	*30*	*177*	*186*	*22*	*56*	*99*	*52%*	*.292*	*2*	*1.36*	*4.44*	*4.76*	*4.60*	*9.4*	*1.0*	*2.7*	*4.8*	*17.7*	*2.20*

Breakout: 3%   Improve: 34%   Collapse: 14%   Attrition: 10%   MLB: 98%   Comparables: Nate Robertson, Denny Neagle, Jarrod Washburn, Paul Minner

Saunders took up residence in Regression City in 2009, an unhappy metropolis where many of the inhabitants are the previously successful, reminiscing about life's peaks while suffering through its valleys. Though he put together a career year in 2008, it didn't take much to see that Saunders' meager strikeout rate suggested his performance was unsustainable. Not only did his BABIP rise 20 points, but his rate of homers per fly balls also skyrocketed, from 10.7 percent to 16.2 percent, the league's fourth-highest rate among ERA qualifiers. He compounded those already-serious problems with a walk rate that increased by 29 percent over 2008. It could have been much worse, as various ERA estimators suggested an ERA close to 5.00. At least he showed up for work, which counted for something on a staff where just three pitchers made more than 23 starts.

Scot Shields

Bats: R   Throws: R   Height: 6' 1"   Weight: 180   Born: July 22, 1975   Age: 34

YEAR	TEAM	LVL	AGE	W	L	SV	G	GS	IP	H	HR	BB	SO	GB%	BABIP	STUFF	WHIP	ERA	SIERA	DERA	EqH9	EqHR9	EqBB9	EqSO9	VORP	SN/WX
2007	LAA	MLB	31	4	5	2	71	0	77	62	7	33	77	51%	.276	15	1.23	3.86	3.55	3.83	7.0	0.8	3.5	8.3	14.1	2.62
2008	LAA	MLB	32	6	4	4	64	0	63¹	56	6	29	64	58%	.296	12	1.34	2.70	3.61	3.88	7.9	0.7	3.7	8.5	11.3	3.37
2009	LAA	MLB	33	1	3	1	20	0	17²	16	1	15	12	43%	.273	-6	1.75	6.62	5.88	6.38	7.4	0.5	6.4	5.4	-1.8	-0.52
2010	*LAA*	*MLB*	*34*	*3*	*4*	*1*	*51*	*0*	*50²*	*45*	*6*	*24*	*44*	*47%*	*.287*	*2*	*1.37*	*4.28*	*4.13*	*4.41*	*8.0*	*0.9*	*4.0*	*7.4*	*6.1*	*1.14*

Breakout: 18%   Improve: 38%   Collapse: 32%   Attrition: 18%   MLB: 87%   Comparables: Jim Hughes, Brian Boehringer, Hal White, Yasuhiko Yabuta

Save for a 2003 detour into the rotation, Shields spent the better part of the 2002-2008 seasons as one of the game's most reliable relievers; only eight pitchers compiled higher WXRLs, and all of them spent multiple seasons closing. Patellar tendinitis got the best of Shields last year, sending the Angels' bullpen into further disarray after the departure of Francisco Rodriguez. Diagnosed in early May, Shields tried to pitch through it, mostly without success, and then opted for season-ending surgery in June. He's expected to be healthy by spring training, and he'll get every chance to resume his usual role.

Justin Speier   Bats: R   Throws: R   Height: 6' 4"   Weight: 205   Born: November 6, 1973   Age: 36

YEAR	TEAM	LVL	AGE	W	L	SV	G	GS	IP	H	HR	BB	SO	GB%	BABIP	STUFF	WHIP	ERA	SIERA	DERA	EqH9	EqHR9	EqBB9	EqSO9	VORP	SN/WX
2007	LAA	MLB	33	2	3	0	51	0	50	36	6	12	47	37%	.233	17	0.96	2.88	3.23	2.79	6.1	1.1	2.0	7.7	15.1	1.96
2008	LAA	MLB	34	2	8	0	62	0	68	69	15	27	56	44%	.269	-12	1.41	5.03	4.25	5.01	8.5	1.8	3.1	6.6	3.8	-0.22
2009	LAA	MLB	35	4	2	0	41	0	40	44	7	15	39	44%	.316	2	1.47	5.17	3.73	4.68	9.1	1.3	2.8	7.6	3.8	0.44
2010	LAA	MLB	36	3	3	0	56	0	55¹	53	8	21	44	41%	.289	0	1.34	4.41	4.20	4.50	8.5	1.1	3.2	6.8	6.1	0.65

Breakout: 15% Improve: 46% Collapse: 18% Attrition: 14%   MLB: 86%   Comparables: Steve Reed, Dick Tidrow, Moe Drabowsky, Jason Grimsley

It says something for the evolution of front office smarts that teams no longer hand out the kind of sweetheart four-year, $18 million deal that Speier received in November 2006, but unfortunately for the Angels, they were behind the curve. They never got a full season out of Speier, an extreme fly-baller who was at least effective when available in 2007. He worked his way into Scioscia's doghouse in 2008, thanks to the AL's highest homer rate among pitchers with at least 60 innings, and his continuing Farnsworthian gopher tendencies—culminating with a trio of homers in a four-batter span on August 7th—led the Angels to cut bait, swallowing nearly $7 million. Given that a team signing him is only on the hook for the major-league minimum, somebody will give Speier a shot; for his sake, we hope they've got an XXL ballpark.

Rich Thompson   Bats: R   Throws: R   Height: 6' 1"   Weight: 180   Born: July 1, 1984   Age: 25

YEAR	TEAM	LVL	AGE	W	L	SV	G	GS	IP	H	HR	BB	SO	GB%	BABIP	STUFF	WHIP	ERA	SIERA	DERA	EqH9	EqHR9	EqBB9	EqSO9	VORP	SN/WX
2007	ARK	AA	22	2	3	0	21	3	49¹	34	5	14	50	42%	.234	18	0.97	2.01	3.05	3.54	7.3	1.5	2.9	6.9	10.2	0.49
2007	SLC	AAA	22	3	0	1	16	0	24²	17	2	6	32	42%	.263	25	0.93	2.19	2.09	2.52	5.8	0.7	2.2	9.4	8.3	0.44
2008	SLC	AAA	23	1	0	0	10	0	13¹	12	1	9	11	45%	.282	-6	1.57	4.05	4.88	4.05	8.1	0.7	5.4	5.4	2.1	-0.01
2009	SLC	AAA	24	3	1	0	29	0	43¹	41	7	11	51	38%	.298	11	1.20	3.12	2.64	4.09	8.2	1.4	2.3	8.6	6.9	0.21
2009	LAA	MLB	24	0	0	0	13	0	19¹	27	6	7	21	40%	.368	5	1.76	5.12	3.49	4.58	11.9	2.3	2.7	8.7	2.0	-0.02
2010	LAA	MLB	25	3	4	0	41	1	63²	64	10	24	57	41%	.305	4	1.38	4.69	3.82	4.78	8.9	1.2	3.3	7.7	5.1	1.01

Breakout: 19% Improve: 45% Collapse: 27% Attrition: 11%   MLB: 100%   Comparables: David Patton, Mark Chapman, Gary Buckels, Jose Rodriguez

Australia's delegate to the Angels' pitching staff served three stints with the big club in 2009, the longest of which lasted six weeks but featured three separate occasions in which he went at least seven days without pitching. Thompson entered all but one game with the Angels down by at least three runs; they lost every game. He had trouble keeping the ball in the park, having now allowed 10 homers in 28 big-league innings. Low 90s fastball/solid curve combo or no, this is how you get stuck pitching mop-up 7,500 miles from home.

Jordan Walden   Bats: R   Throws: R   Height: 6' 5"   Weight: 220   Born: November 16, 1987   Age: 22

YEAR	TEAM	LVL	AGE	W	L	SV	G	GS	IP	H	HR	BB	SO	GB%	BABIP	STUFF	WHIP	ERA	SIERA	DERA	EqH9	EqHR9	EqBB9	EqSO9	VORP	SN/WX
2007	ORM	Rk	19	1	1	0	15	15	64¹	49	3	17	63	55%	.271	17	1.03	3.08	3.03	5.37	8.6	1.5	3.5	4.9	0.9	0.55
2008	CDR	A	20	4	6	0	18	18	107¹	80	3	32	91	66%	.259	25	1.04	2.18	3.40	4.42	8.8	1.1	3.7	4.7	11.6	1.00
2008	RCU	A+	20	5	2	0	9	9	49	42	4	24	50	60%	.284	24	1.35	4.04	3.62	6.41	8.6	1.7	5.0	5.9	-4.8	-0.16
2009	ARK	AA	21	1	5	0	13	13	60	72	4	29	57	47%	.376	1	1.68	5.25	4.03	7.24	13.0	1.6	4.6	6.9	-10.6	-0.19
2010	LAA	MLB	22	4	7	0	24	23	99¹	108	15	49	66	49%	.302	10	1.58	5.35	4.91	5.47	9.6	1.2	4.2	5.6	0.3	2.24

Breakout: 11% Improve: 56% Collapse: 13% Attrition: 17%   MLB: 6%   Comparables: Cliff Brantley, Doug Brocail, Ron Richardson, Stuart Pomeranz

Walden entered the year as the Angels' top pitching prospect, ahead of the late Nick Adenhart in the eyes of many. When he is healthy, his fastball sits at 93-95 mph and can touch 98 while featuring excellent sink, making him both a strikeout pitcher and a ground-ball machine, although his secondary stuff is a work in progress. In 2009, his velocity was off and his ground-ball percentage dropped, as forearm troubles shelved him in May and ended his season in mid-July. Nonetheless, he did put together one tantalizing stretch in June: five starts with a 2.05 ERA and a 33/8 K/BB ratio in 30 ⅔ IP. Assuming no further arm troubles, he'll probably return to Arkansas to begin working his way back.

Jered Weaver

Bats: R   Throws: R   Height: 6' 7"   Weight: 205   Born: October 4, 1982   Age: 27

YEAR	TEAM	LVL	AGE	W	L	SV	G	GS	IP	H	HR	BB	SO	GB%	BABIP	STUFF	WHIP	ERA	SIERA	DERA	EqH9	EqHR9	EqBB9	EqSO9	VORP	SN/WX
2007	RCU	A+	24	1	0	0	2	2	11	5	1	3	12	44%	.160	11	0.73	0.82	2.57	1.69	5.1	1.7	2.5	6.8	4.5	0.41
2007	LAA	MLB	24	13	7	0	28	28	161	178	17	45	115	40%	.312	12	1.39	3.91	4.33	3.90	9.2	0.9	2.2	5.8	28.9	4.22
2008	LAA	MLB	25	11	10	0	30	30	176^2	173	20	54	152	39%	.298	20	1.28	4.33	3.83	4.13	8.6	0.9	2.4	7.1	26.6	4.25
2009	LAA	MLB	26	16	8	0	33	33	211	196	26	66	174	37%	.278	23	1.24	3.75	4.02	3.52	7.8	0.9	2.4	6.6	46.8	6.17
2010	LAA	MLB	27	11	10	0	32	32	1871	185	22	58	132	38%	.292	13	1.30	4.06	4.39	4.20	8.8	1.0	2.7	6.0	27.1	3.26

Breakout: 2%   Improve: 38%   Collapse: 12%   Attrition: 15%   MLB: 99%   Comparables: Josh Beckett, Dan Haren, Scott Baker, Jack McDowell

Amid the Angels' rotation chaos, Weaver emerged as the staff savior, carrying a 2.08 ERA through his first 13 starts, thanks to a string of six straight homerless appearances. He couldn't maintain that torrid pace, though; he put up a 5.01 ERA the rest of the way as the ball flew out of the yard at a rate of 1.4 HR/9. Still, he set career highs and led the team in innings, strikeouts, and SNWP, finishing ninth in the league in the last measure (.565). The key to Weaver's success is popups galore; his 15.5 percent pop-up rate led the majors in 2009 and was double the MLB average. It's a great skill to have (the major-league batting average on popups was a microscopic .019), and it helps compensate for his having the lowest ground-ball rate of any ERA qualifier. Weaver isn't quite staff ace material, but as a frontline pitcher who's still three years away from free agency, he's worth every penny.

LINEOUTS

Hitters

PLAYER	TEAM	LVL	AGE	PA	R	2B	3B	HR	RBI	BB	SO	SB-CS	EqBRR	AVG/OBP/SLG	EqAVG/EqOBP/EqSLG	EqA	VORP	WARP
1/3 M. Brown	SLC	AAA	26	447	57	27	0	13	69	45	92	5-5	-2.2	.245/.333/.415	.209/.287/.350	.222	-16.9	-3.3
C R. Budde	SLC	AAA	29	307	32	16	1	7	31	31	73	1-1	0.7	.223/.304/.366	.183/.254/.290	.188	-9.4	-0.9
CF C. Fuller#	RCU	A+	22	544	89	18	4	9	48	71	127	30-8	2.6	.232/.341/.350	.203/.293/.292	.217	-10.1	-4.3
OF R. Grichuk	ANG	Rk	17	256	47	13	10	7	53	9	64	6-4	1.2	.322/.352/.551	.230/.249/.374	.214	-6.9	-2.5
OF R. Lopez	CDR	A	23	420	61	18	0	11	67	40	52	5-7	-2.9	.271/.365/.415	.229/.291/.322	.218	-13.1	-3.3
LF J. Moore*	RCU	A+	22	516	61	20	12	11	58	34	144	17-13	-2.0	.279/.330/.443	.234/.277/.349	.218	-12.6	-2.4
4C R. Quinlan	LAA	MLB	32	120	13	5	0	2	14	5	30	1-1	0.0	.243/.275/.339	.243/.275/.330	.211	-5.3	-0.6
SS A. Romine#	RCU	A+	23	555	68	13	9	1	36	51	83	26-11	-2.2	.278/.351/.349	.240/.298/.295	.215	-3.7	0.4
2B J. Segura	ORM	Rk	19	177	33	10	4	3	21	11	11	11-3	0.6	.346/.392/.512	.269/.301/.383	.239	1.5	0.4

For a guy who had already aged his way into organizational depth territory, **Matt Brown**'s stock fell even further last year as injuries sapped his production at Triple-A; he signed a minor-league deal with the Rangers. ⊘ The fretting over Napoli's acumen with the tools of ignorance is such that the Angels carry fourth catcher **Ryan Budde** on the 40-man as a "break glass if you've already called up Bobby Wilson" re-insurance policy. ⊘ A switch-hitting outfielder with range, speed, patience, and little else, **Clayton Fuller** is developing into the next Reggie Willits. ⊘ Texas high school outfielder **Randal Grichuk** didn't look like a first-rounder until private workouts just before the 2009 draft; the Angels made him their top pick at number 24. His power is a plus, but he struggles with pitch recognition, and he's a below-average runner and defender. ⊘ Dominican third baseman **Luis Jimenez** didn't get a chance to build on 2008's .331/.361/.630 and Pioneer League-leading 15 homers, because he missed 2009 due to a torn labrum that required surgery. ⊘ **Roberto Lopez** shredded as an Orem Owl with a .400/.480/.667 season in 2008, but at 22, he was old for his level. Though he didn't tear up Midwest League pitching, he boosted his stock by taking up catching. ⊘ A four-sport standout in high school, **Jeremy Moore** has made slow progress since being drafted in the sixth round in 2005. Though his strike-zone judgment remains questionable, his line-drive rate increased dramatically last year, so he bears watching. ⊘ Once upon a time, **Robb Quinlan** was a moderately useful lefty-mashing corner man, but the last time he managed a 700 OPS against southpaws, the Republicans controlled Congress. ⊘ **Andrew Romine**, the brother of Yankees catching prospect Austin, is an above-average defender with an outstanding arm. A speedy switch-hitter, he has decent on-base skills but minimal power. ⊘ Though a broken finger shortened his season, **Jean Segura** drew acclaim from manager Tom Kotchman as Orem's best position player. He's the type of speedy contact hitter the Halos love, but defensively, he's limited to second base.

Pitchers

PLAYER	TEAM	LVL	AGE	W	L	SV	IP	H	HR	BB	SO	GB%	BABIP	STUFF	WHIP	ERA	SIERA	DERA	EqH9	EqHR9	EqBB9	EqSO9	VORP
J. Bachanov	ANG	Rk	20	4	0	0	28^2	26	0	4	47	0%	.394	25	1.05	3.14	1.06	5.29	12.8	1.8	3.3	7.7	0.6
B. Cassevah	ARK	AA	23	3	7	4	73^1	64	2	37	45	75%	.273	-17	1.38	3.68	4.22	6.13	9.1	0.9	4.6	4.2	-4.8
D. Herndon	ARK	AA	23	5	6	11	65^1	70	9	14	35	65%	.289	-39	1.29	3.03	4.27	4.53	12.0	2.9	2.3	3.7	6.4
T. Kehrer*	ORM	Rk	21	3	3	0	55	57	6	22	57	0%	.333	-21	1.44	4.75	3.49	9.03	12.9	3.2	5.7	4.9	-18.6
S. Loux	SLC	AAA	29	1	2	0	25	24	2	14	13	75%	.286	-11	1.52	3.96	4.65	4.30	9.0	0.8	5.1	3.9	3.1
	LAA	MLB	29	2	3	0	58^1	84	4	19	19	58%	.356	-21	1.77	5.86	5.60	5.73	12.4	0.5	2.5	2.7	-1.5
F. Martinez Mesa	ANG	Rk	19	3	2	0	60^2	45	1	36	92	0%	.321	8	1.34	3.26	2.63	7.82	10.8	2.2	8.1	6.9	-13.5
T. Mendoza	ARK	AA	21	7	7	0	128^2	130	10	31	86	41%	.289	4	1.25	3.36	4.31	5.33	10.4	1.8	2.4	4.5	2.3
	SLC	AAA	21	2	1	0	21^2	18	3	11	10	49%	.227	5	1.34	2.91	5.61	3.48	7.4	1.3	4.8	3.5	4.6
B. Mosebach	ARK	AA	24	2	0	6	26^1	12	0	9	16	63%	.164	-3	0.80	0.34	4.20	1.07	5.0	0.4	3.2	3.9	12.5
	SLC	AAA	24	2	2	7	40^1	33	1	18	31	64%	.283	0	1.26	2.23	4.08	2.63	7.9	0.5	4.3	6.0	12.0
G. Richards	ORM	Rk	21	3	1	0	35^1	37	0	4	30	0%	.352	6	1.16	1.53	3.19	2.88	12.7	1.5	2.7	3.9	8.6
F. Rodriguez	ARK	AA	25	3	1	4	42^1	20	0	22	52	39%	.204	21	0.99	1.28	3.07	2.34	5.3	0.4	4.5	8.3	14.9
	SLC	AAA	25	1	1	0	37	44	5	23	25	38%	.333	-23	1.81	7.54	5.45	7.97	11.1	1.3	5.7	5.1	-9.6
W. Smith*	CDR	A	19	10	5	0	115	109	11	24	95	46%	.287	-14	1.16	3.76	3.57	7.19	11.4	2.5	2.9	4.4	-19.3

A 2007 supplemental first-rounder, **Jon Bachanov** didn't throw a professional pitch until 2009, due to Tommy John surgery; although he pitched exclusively in relief, the Angels view him as a starter once he builds up arm strength. ⊘ **Bobby Cassevah**'s ground-ball rate got him snagged by the A's in the Rule 5 draft, but his extreme problems with lefties suggest ROOGYdom at best. ⊘ The most surprising selection of the Rule 5 draft, **David Herndon** is a big strike-thrower (standing 6-foot-5), but his raw stuff is pedestrian; it'll be an upset if the Phillies keep him. ⊘ **Tyler Kehrer** was the last of the Angels' three supplemental first-rounders in 2009. His low-90s fastball can touch 96, but his delivery, command, and secondary stuff are works in progress that put him in the thrower-not-pitcher category, and he is likely to be bullpen bound. ⊘ Once upon a time in the late '90s, **Shane Loux** was a top 10 prospect in the Tigers' system; now he's a palooka at the back of the Angels' staff whom lefties blitzed at a .385/.426/.600 clip in 148 plate appearances. ⊘ After impressing in the Dominican Summer League in 2008, **Fabio Martinez Mesa** dominated stateside, thanks to his mid-90s fastball and plus-plus slider, leading the Arizona Fall League in strikeouts. Scouts like his projectable frame and the potential for his changeup to be a plus pitch as well. ⊘ A fourth-round 2005 pick, **Tommy Mendoza** rebounded from an ugly 2007-2008 stretch, which ended with a 50-game suspension for amphetamine usage. He's got good command, but as a fly-baller who doesn't miss many bats, he'll find that his ceiling is still back-end rotation starter. ⊘ A ground-baller who fell off the Angels' radar after a lousy 2008 in the Arkansas rotation, **Bobby Mosebach** was chosen in last year's Rule 5 draft by the Phillies; upon being returned to the Angels, he switched to the pen and put up strong enough numbers to earn a brief cup of coffee. ⊘ Power college arm **Garrett Richards** often had trouble finding the plate with his mid-90s heat at Oklahoma; taken with the 42nd pick in the 2009 supplemental phase, he ironed out his mechanics and is now considered to have frontline potential. ⊘ Hanging around Double-A ball in your age-25 season and racking up strikeouts on younger hitters isn't an ideal career choice, but it's what **Fernando Rodriguez** was left with after being bombed out of Salt Lake as a reliever. ⊘ A lefty prepster from Santa Monica, **Tyler Skaggs** has a low-90s fastball and a projectable frame that makes scouts salivate; taken in the 2009 supplemental phase (40th overall), he's more of a project than some of the system's other young guns. ⊘ Though hardly as fresh as the Fresh Prince of Bel Air, **Will Smith** is an athletic, projectable lefty who misses bats with an 88-92 mph fastball and a slurvy breaker, both thrown on a steep downward plane, thanks to his 6-foot-5 frame; he overcame a slow 2009 start caused by hamstring and lower-back injuries.

MANAGER: MIKE SCIOSCIA

YEAR	TEAM	W-L	Pythag +/−	Avg PC	100+ P	120+ P	QS	BQS	REL	REL w Zero R	IBB	Subs	PH	PH Avg	PH HR	SB2	CS2	SB3	CS3	SAC Att	SAC %	POS SAC	Squeeze	Swing	In Play
2007	LAA	94-68	4	97.4	85	0	85	2	396	245	22	31	101	.250	2	118	47	20	8	48	66.7%	31	3	170	142
2008	LAA	100-62	11	99.6	85	0	87	5	383	249	32	46	74	.182	0	109	38	19	8	46	69.6%	32	3	147	113
2009	LAA	97-65	4	97.1	83	1	70	9	434	269	35	48	79	.308	2	124	57	22	5	64	67.2%	41	4	180	134

Mike Scioscia is building a Hall of Fame career as a manager. Like Bobby Cox, Tony La Russa, and Joe Torre in his Bronx days, he has become inextricably identified not just with a string of successful teams but with a successful brand of baseball. The 10-year extension he signed last winter only underscores the faith that the Angels have in that brand, even as their cast changes. The 2009 club featured the most robust offense in the franchise's history, but that didn't stop Scioscia from pressing his advantage by implementing his signature running game. The Angels were second in the majors in stolen base attempts and first in hit-and-run plays, although their runners went just 37-for-63 (58.7 percent) when hitters swung and missed in such cases, lowering their overall EqBRR total to 1.3 runs—still fifth in the league, thanks to the team's MLB-leading EqHAR total (10.7 runs). In other words, their aggressiveness on the basepaths—a core component of his offensive philosophy—remains a net positive. Scioscia also managed to apply his stamp to a changing pitching staff, not only to a rotation torn apart by injury and the Adenhart tragedy (a crisis unto itself, where the skipper's blend of leadership and compassion came to the fore) but also to a bullpen that initially struggled, given significant turnover from a successful core. His deft touch with the latter remains a major factor in the Angels' continued success, as does his ability to take advantage of the team's considerable depth while challenging its younger players such as Erick Aybar, Mike Napoli, and Howie Kendrick to fully round their games.

Los Angeles Dodgers

On October 14, 2009, the day before the Dodgers opened the National League Championship Series against the Phillies, an earthquake struck at Chavez Ravine. Though its magnitude on the Richter scale was unavailable, its aftershocks promised to reverberate throughout the 2009-2010 offseason, and well beyond. On that day, the news broke that Dodger owner Frank McCourt and wife Jamie, the team's CEO, had separated, the culmination of a tension-filled season in which the two had rarely been sighted together in public. By month's end, Jamie McCourt had been fired from her job and had filed for divorce, with the messy details of their acrimonious split turned into tabloid fodder.

While the news had nothing to do with the Dodgers' bowing to the Phillies in five games for the second year in a row, it cast a pall over the franchise, and not just because it was a public relations disaster. Over the previous year and a half, the division rival Padres had provided an object lesson in the effects of a baseball owner's divorce on a franchise, particularly under California's community-property law, which necessitated that the involved parties (John and Becky Moores) split the team 50-50. In early November, Frank McCourt asserted the validity of a postnuptial agreement, placing the team in his name and the couple's property in hers—thus raising the possibility that the franchise might not need to be sold—but as that great divorce lawyer Yogi Berra once observed, "It ain't over 'til it's over." Prior to the foreboding signs that emerged as the Hot Stove season kicked off, the irony was that Dodger fans might have had at least some reason to hope the status quo prevailed.

When the McCourts bought the Dodgers in early 2004, interested observers had every reason to be skeptical of the fit. Nearly half a century of Dodger tradition and continuity had already been upset when the franchise changed hands from the O'Malley family to Rupert Murdoch's News Corporation in 1998. The Foxies were brash from the get-go, trading franchise superstar Mike Piazza rather than negotiating a contract extension, toppling longtime general manager Fred Claire, and firing manager Bill Russell, Tommy Lasorda's handpicked successor—and that was just their first three months. During their six seasons of ownership, the NewsCorp Dodgers spent more on payroll than all but the Yankees and Red Sox without netting a single postseason appearance.

The McCourts' highly leveraged purchase of the franchise, its ballpark, and the adjoining real estate instantly called into question the Dodgers' ability to spend with the big boys, particularly when the team bypassed an opportunity to sign free agent Vlad Guerrero just as the sale was being completed. Surprisingly enough, the franchise has actually enjoyed a mini-renaissance on the McCourts' watch, winning three division titles and a wild card, winning a post-season series (two, actually) for the first time since 1988, and advancing to the National League Championship series in consecutive years for the first time since 1977-1978. Furthermore, they've gotten far more bang for the buck than during the NewsCorp Era (see Table 1).

Certainly, the NL West's alignment has been kind to the Dodgers during the McCourts' tenure, allowing the team to capitalize on their large-market resources in a

DODGERS PROSPECTUS
2009 W-L: 95-67, 1st in NL West

Pythag	99-63	1st
RS/G	4.8	4th
RA/G	3.8	2nd
EqA	.272	2nd
EqBRR	-5.2	8th
SNWP	.534	4th
WXRL	13.22	1st
FRAr	3.46	1st
DE	.714	1st
PADE	2.55	2nd
Salary	$100.4	5th
Attend	3.76	1st

Ballpark: Dodger Stadium (3-yr. PF: 946). Chavez Ravine's a friend to the boys on the bump

2009: Manny's excused for PEDs, but a deep staff and Kemp's breakout fuel another division win

2010: Divorce blues force tight belts, but with Colletti's track record, is that bad?

Action Items: Keeping Kershaw and Billingsley healthy, finding power from Martin and Loney, avoiding bad trades

Table 1. A Fox-y Handoff: Dodgers Success Under NewsCorp and the McCourts*

Owner	Win %	Playoff G	Payroll%†	Avg Attendance
NewsCorp (1998-2003)	.524 (11)	0 (19t)	149% (3)	3.08 M (6)
McCourt (2004-2009)	.528 (7)	23 (7)	125% (6)	3.70 M (2)

*Numbers in parentheses are rank among MLB teams.
†Percentage relative to MLB-average payroll.

Table 2. Putting the Joneses Underfoot: NL West Performance

	1998-2003			2004-2009		
Team	Payroll % (Rk)	Top 10	Win %	Payroll% (Rk)	Top 10	Win %
Dodgers	149 (3)	5	.524	125 (6)	5	.528
Giants	105 (13)	2	.574	107 (14)	3	.487
Diamondbacks	128 (7)	5	.539	80 (18)	0	.459
Padres	78 (20)	0	.470	76 (22)	0	.497
Rockies	103 (14)	0	.464	74 (25)	0	.480

*Numbers in parentheses are rank among MLB teams.

division with four other franchises increasingly hamstrung by payroll concerns and unable to field winning teams with consistency (see Table 2).

The Dodgers' payroll relative to the major-league average has fallen by 25 percent, yet only once in the past six years has a rival outspent them (the 2005 Giants), and only three times have they had company from within the division among the game's top 10 payrolls. Their on-field success has mirrored that financial advantage, as the team is the only one in the division with a winning record in that span.

Furthermore, where the McCourts' purchase brought much uncertainty about the future of Dodger Stadium—selling naming rights wasn't out of the question, nor was pressing the city for a new ballpark—their tenure has been marked by an ambitious multiyear renovation of the current park, now the majors' third-oldest, replacing every seat, adding restrooms and concession stands, and generally modernizing the facility. That work, in conjunction with the team's on-field success, has helped the club lead the league in attendance in every year of the McCourts' tenure except 2008, averaging a staggering 3.7 million per year. In 2009, even amid a harsh economic climate that saw the game's attendance decrease by 6.6 percent, the Dodgers' attendance rose 0.8 percent.

Paramount to the McCourts' efforts to rein in costs have been the efforts of the assistant GM for scouting, Logan White, on whose watch the team drafted Chad Billingsley, Clayton Kershaw, Jonathan Broxton, Russell Martin, James Loney, and Matt Kemp. That homegrown nucleus has been the basis of the past two division winners, and its production—while not uniformly excellent—has enabled the team to remain competitive despite several expensive mistakes by general manager Ned Colletti, including Jason Schmidt, Andruw Jones, Juan Pierre, and Nomar Garciaparra.

Indeed, Colletti put together his best season at the helm in the final year of his four-year deal. The team's Opening Day payroll was $18 million less than 2008, thanks in part to his willingness to hunt for bargains.

Though Colletti tripped over himself to re-sign Casey Blake to a three-year, $17.5 million deal in early December, the GM bought three years of Rafael Furcal for just $30 million, nearly 25 percent less than he'd paid for the shortstop's previous deal. Biding his time after those deals, Colletti waited almost until camps opened to fill major gaps in the team's rotation and infield via one-year deals for Randy Wolf ($5 million plus incentives) and Orlando Hudson ($3.38 million plus incentives), and forced Team Boras into blinking and settling for a two-year, $45 million deal for Manny Ramirez, less than half of what the slugger and his agent had sought.

The mix of homegrown and mercenary talents won their first 13 home games, taking sole possession of first place in the NL West for good on April 19th, and finishing with the league's best record and the majors' best run differential. The Dodgers didn't lose three straight games until late July, had just two losing streaks of longer than three games, and spent just one day with a lead of less than two games, that during the season's final weekend, after they had already clinched a playoff berth.

The team did have to surmount one major obstacle. The Dodgers were 21-8 on May 7th, when Ramirez, hitting .348/.492/.641, was handed a 50-game suspension for violating the game's drug policy via an improper prescription for human chorionic gonadotropin, a female fertility drug often used to mask steroid usage. Though the offense's scoring dipped by 18 percent in Ramirez's absence, the slap-happy Pierre earned his keep by hitting .318/.381/.411 as the starting left fielder during that stretch. Ramirez returned to a team with a seven-game lead, half a game larger than at the time of the suspension, and he continued to hit for another three weeks before a Homer Bailey fastball to the wrist cooled him off.

Even with Martin, Loney, and Furcal turning in relatively disappointing years and the offense finishing just 11th in the league in home runs, the team's offense ranked among the league's best. Every Dodger regular save for Furcal put up an OBP north of .350, Hudson earned All-Star honors, Blake had a career year, and both Kemp and Andre Ethier emerged as star sluggers in their own right, becoming the first Dodger hitters to top 20 homers since 2005.

Meanwhile, the rotation and the bullpen ranked among the league's stingiest. The rotation found its groove during Ramirez's absence, with Billingsley pitching his way onto the All-Star squad before stumbling in the second half, Kershaw unveiling a hellacious slider to go with his already-brutal curveball, and Wolf demonstrating a newfound consistency en route to a career year. Amid Hiroki Kuroda's multiple injuries, Colletti scrounged up a motley assortment of back-rotation starters, virtually all of whom outperformed expectations. Jeff Weaver, Eric Milton, Charlie Haeger, Vicente Padilla, and Jon Garland, none of whom began the year on the big club's roster, combined for 28 starts with a 3.28 ERA and a .518 Support-Neutral Winning Percentage (SNWP), better numbers than Kuroda himself could muster. In the bullpen, Broxton paced the circuit in WXRL, with sophomore Ramon Troncoso working his way into manager Joe Torre's good graces and finishing eighth. Free-talent find Ronald Belisario spent time on the leaderboard as well, and George Sherrill was lights out after arriving from Baltimore at the deadline.

Sherrill didn't come for free, costing the Dodgers talent in the form of third baseman Josh Bell, who was ranked as the Dodgers' sixth-best prospect by BP's Kevin Goldstein last winter, and pitcher Steven Johnson, who just missed the top 11. The move continued an ominous trend that points to ownership's short-sightedness and hints at its possible cash-flow problems. In all the Dodgers' key midseason trades over the past two summers, they've given up better prospects in exchange for remaining more or less payroll-neutral, not taking on the bulk of the remaining salary of those acquired at the expense of some of the player development system's sweetest fruit. Blake cost the Dodgers catcher Carlos Santana, who now tops the Indians' prospect list. Ramirez cost them third-base prospect Andy LaRoche; Greg Maddux cost 2007 second-round pick Michael Watt, and Garland cost them Tony Abreu, who once appeared to be their second baseman of the future.

Add to that talent drain the fact that according to *Baseball America,* the Dodgers paid just $8.5 million in signing bonuses over the past two years, the lowest figure among the 30 teams. They've also squandered their long-held advantages in Asia and Latin America: of the 115 international players signed to bonuses of $100,000 or more in 2008, none of them were signed by the

Dodgers. The team bucked that trend with a pair of six-figure bonuses in 2009, but even so, the Dodgers are still underrepresented on the international market.

While that penny-wise pound-foolishness flew under the radars of those outside the industry, the Dodgers' behavior, when it came time to offer arbitration to their free agents on December 1st, made their problems glaringly apparent. The Dodgers didn't offer arbitration to any of their 15 eligible free agents, including Wolf and Hudson, both Type-A free agents, and both of whom were extremely unlikely to return. Colletti explained the nonmoves as "made strictly from a baseball perspective," but his statement had all the credibility of a blindfolded hostage on camera telling the world, "My captors are treating me very well."

By forgoing offers to Wolf and Hudson, the Dodgers sacrificed shots at gaining two first-round picks and two sandwich picks, the values of which were estimated at $9 million and $3 million apiece by Nate Silver back in 2005. Such picks cost significant bonus money, but it's nonetheless alarming that a team would forgo $24 million (or more) in potential future value for the price of maybe $6 million worth of investments in 2010, particularly given that in addition to lowering the payroll by $18 million between Opening Days 2008 and 2009, they shed $30 million more via those 15 free agents and saved another $13 million via Ramirez ($8 million in lost salary due to the suspension, and $5 million less in salary in 2010 than in 2009).

Instead, Colletti braced Dodger fans for a quiet winter devoid of major additions almost from the moment the Dodgers were eliminated. Despite the hash Torre made of his rotation during the postseason, the GM quickly ruled out blockbuster deals for an ace either in trade (Roy Halladay) or via free agency (John Lackey). He'll try to plug the gap left by Wolf's departure with a similar short-term fix or perhaps by taking on a bad contract having shed that of Pierre, and if all else fails, he may turn to youngsters Scott Elbert, Josh Lindblom, and James McDonald as potential options. The same approach will determine the occupant of second base, though again, the club does have viable prospects (Blake DeWitt, Chin-lung Hu, Ivan De Jesus) if it wants to patch the position internally.

The real reason for such inactivity is the unfortunate confluence of the McCourt divorce and the upcoming career milestones of several important members of the roster. Billingsley, Kemp, Kuo, and Loney are all reaching arbitration for the first time; Broxton, Ethier, and Martin for the second time; and Sherrill for the third. All will receive substantial raises over 2009—raises that will offset much of the shed payroll—and longer-term deals to buy out arbitration years are probably out of the question.

Luckily, Colletti has also pledged that the Dodgers won't trade any of those youngsters, viewing the sacrifice of relatively inexpensive cogs as counterproductive—a welcome change from years past in which his public statements regarding such possible trades have made him seem like a drunk waving a loaded gun at his blue-chippers. Particularly since losing Edwin Jackson, Dioner Navarro, and Willy Aybar in 2006, Colletti has restrained himself from pulling the trigger far more often than not and, in doing so, has managed to win while keeping the budget in line and the best assets in house. That (and the good timing of having his best year in his walk year) goes a long way toward justifying the five-year extension he received at season's end. Perhaps just

as importantly, he's still got White and vice president/assistant GM Kim Ng, who interviewed for the Padres' GM job, at his side.

While the Dodgers have the resources to remain in the driver's seat of the NL West, the family drama surrounding the club is unlikely to be settled anytime soon. The good news is that the likelihood of the McCourts' needing to sell grows by the day, particularly since Bud Selig has little appetite for bad public relations involving one of the game's marquee franchises; he'll throw the McCourts no lifelines. So while it's bound to be a winter and perhaps even a full season of discontent, the likelihood that the Dodgers will look toward a less woefully underfinanced ownership down the road should make this storm a bit easier to bear.

HITTERS

Tony Abreu   INF

Bats: S   Throws: R   Height: 5' 11"   Weight: 200   Born: November 13, 1984   Age: 25

YEAR	TEAM	LVL	AGE	PA	R	2B	3B	HR	RBI	BB	SO	SB	CS	EqBRR	AVG	OBP	SLG	EqAVG	EqOBP	EqSLG	EqA	VORP	WARP	DEFENSE			
2007	LVG	AAA	22	253	48	22	5	2	18	14	34	5	0	0.9	.355	.399	.517	.301	.344	.441	.273	11.3	0.8	24-2B	-3	17-SS	-2
2007	LAN	MLB	22	178	19	14	1	2	17	7	21	0	0	0.3	.271	.309	.404	.279	.315	.412	.251	3.4	1.4	22-3B	4	13-2B	4
2009	CHT	AA	24	90	11	4	1	0	5	1	12	0	2	-1.8	.292	.300	.360	.258	.267	.326	.197	-2.8	-0.5	17-2B	0	3-SS	-1
2009	ABQ	AAA	24	236	36	18	3	11	48	12	37	3	1	-3.1	.353	.385	.615	.295	.328	.505	.280	12.7	0.8	32-2B	-6	11-3B	1
2009	LAN	MLB	24	11	0	0	0	0	1	3	2	0	1	-0.4	.250	.455	.250	.250	.455	.250	.261	-0.1	0.1				
2010	ARI	MLB	25	342	44	22	4	6	33	22	59	3	1	-0.9	.275	.327	.422	.271	.321	.413	.252	7.6	0.7	54-2B	-2		

Breakout: 6%   Improve: 28%   Collapse: 18%   Attrition: 4%   MLB: 79%   Comparables: Matt Tolbert, Brooks Conrad, Roy Silver, Dionys Cesar

Abreu's 2007 ended with sports hernia surgery, and he lost most of 2008 to a torn hip labrum, which knocked him out of the running for the second-base job. Hampered by an early-season ankle sprain in '09, he made the most of his time at Albuquerque. Once he and the Dodgers finally settled a grievance over 2007 service time—Colletti publicly doubted his injuries prior to surgery—he was Arizona-bound in the Jon Garland deal. He's Arizona's best in-house candidate for the job at second, as he'll provide some sock while fitting in with its all-too-hacktastic ways.

Pedro Baez   3B

Bats: R   Throws: R   Height: 6' 2"   Weight: 195   Born: March 11, 1988   Age: 22

YEAR	TEAM	LVL	AGE	PA	R	2B	3B	HR	RBI	BB	SO	SB	CS	EqBRR	AVG	OBP	SLG	EqAVG	EqOBP	EqSLG	EqA	VORP	WARP	DEFENSE	
2007	DGR	Rk	19	229	35	14	2	3	39	17	40	3	1	2.7	.274	.341	.408	.243	.285	.352	.225	-3.2	-1.0	53-3B	-2
2008	GRL	A	20	211	23	10	1	1	16	17	45	3	1	-0.4	.178	.244	.259	.169	.223	.249	.164	-13.8	-2.2	55-3B	-4
2008	OGD	Rk	20	268	37	20	1	12	50	18	69	2	2	-0.5	.267	.317	.502	.202	.239	.348	.200	-9.9	-2.0	58-3B	-2
2009	SBR	A+	21	331	48	17	1	10	61	16	84	5	1	0.3	.286	.326	.445	.249	.281	.377	.228	-2.1	-1.0	77-3B	-6
2010	LAN	MLB	22	389	39	18	1	8	47	26	110	3	2	0.0	.215	.268	.338	.221	.275	.356	.213	-8.4	-1.3	93-3B	-3

Breakout: 36%   Improve: 58%   Collapse: 18%   Attrition: 8%   MLB: 2%   Comparables: J.J. Johnson, Tyrone Woods, Bob Hicks, Jim Olander

This toolsy Dominican is considered to have the system's best raw power and strongest arm, but he has struggled to convert those tools into skills thus far. Baez was so overmatched at Low-A in 2008 that he was sent back down to rookie ball. For this reason, it was surprising that the Dodgers decided to jump him to High-A in 2009. His performance at Inland Empire was a mixed bag; he flashed power, but continued his free-swinging ways, striking out in more than a quarter of his plate appearances, and footwork and positioning woes led to defensive difficulties. A July knee injury required surgery, cutting his season short.

Ronnie Belliard   INF   Bats: R   Throws: R   Height: 5' 10"   Weight: 215   Born: April 7, 1975   Age: 35

YEAR	TEAM	LVL	AGE	PA	R	2B	3B	HR	RBI	BB	SO	SB	CS	EqBRR	AVG	OBP	SLG	EqAVG	EqOBP	EqSLG	EqA	VORP	WARP		DEFENSE	
2007	WAS	MLB	32	557	57	35	1	11	58	34	72	3	0	0.9	.290	.332	.427	.303	.345	.442	.273	24.5	2.0	113-2B	-6	5-1B -1
2008	WAS	MLB	33	337	37	22	0	11	46	37	58	3	2	0.0	.287	.372	.473	.296	.378	.488	.292	20.2	1.5	26-2B	-5	24-3B -3
2009	WAS	MLB	34	204	26	7	1	5	22	14	40	2	0	0.6	.246	.296	.374	.257	.304	.385	.243	0.5	0.4	36-2B	2	4-1B 0
2009	LAN	MLB	34	83	13	7	0	5	17	6	16	1	0	0.5	.351	.398	.636	.377	.422	.688	.356	11.6	1.1	10-2B	-2	9-3B 0
2010	LAN	MLB	35	385	40	19	1	10	44	32	72	3	1	0.3	.260	.324	.406	.269	.333	.416	.261	12.4	1.1	73-2B	-2	

Breakout: 3%   Improve: 25%   Collapse: 21%   Attrition: 19%   MLB: 97%   Comparables: Willie Horton, Miguel Tejada, Mark Grudzielanek, Joe Randa

Belliard's magical powers of adequacy appeared to wear off in Washington, but his fortunes turned dramatically with the August 31 waiver deal that sent him west. With Casey Blake aching and Orlando Hudson slumping, Belliard found his way into the lineup and hit like the second coming of Marlon Anderson. To the surprise of no one familiar with Joe Torre's magpie-like lust for shiny objects, Belliard supplanted Hudson in the postseason, starting every game and giving interested observers something to second-guess besides Torre's rotation choices. At this point in his career, Belliard is a handy role player who can provide some pop, but he's nobody's first choice to man second base.

Casey Blake   3B   Bats: R   Throws: R   Height: 6' 2"   Weight: 210   Born: August 23, 1973   Age: 36

YEAR	TEAM	LVL	AGE	PA	R	2B	3B	HR	RBI	BB	SO	SB	CS	EqBRR	AVG	OBP	SLG	EqAVG	EqOBP	EqSLG	EqA	VORP	WARP		DEFENSE	
2007	CLE	MLB	33	662	81	36	4	18	78	54	123	4	5	0.4	.270	.339	.437	.271	.340	.440	.267	19.0	2.5	134-3B	3	6-RF 0
2008	CLE	MLB	34	368	46	24	0	11	58	33	68	2	0	-1.8	.289	.365	.465	.293	.371	.478	.291	20.3	1.7	72-3B	-4	18-1B 0
2008	LAN	MLB	34	233	25	12	1	10	23	16	52	1	0	0.1	.251	.313	.460	.261	.321	.464	.269	7.9	1.3	53-3B	3	
2009	LAN	MLB	35	565	84	25	6	18	79	63	116	3	4	-2.2	.280	.363	.468	.303	.379	.499	.298	40.6	6.0	128-3B	13	
2010	LAN	MLB	36	512	55	23	2	13	62	47	113	2	3	-0.5	.248	.326	.391	.255	.333	.411	.256	11.3	1.5	119-3B	2	

Breakout: 8%   Improve: 20%   Collapse: 26%   Attrition: 37%   MLB: 95%   Comparables: Todd Zeile, Doug DeCinces, Ken Boyer, Sal Bando

Though he ran Andy LaRoche out of town, blocked Blake DeWitt, and cost the Dodgers catching prospect Carlos Santana, Blake otherwise made Ned Colletti look pretty good in the first year of his three-year, $17.5 million deal. Blake set career highs in OBP, EqA, and WARP, the last thanks in part to an outstanding year with the glove. The spike in his hitting was in part due to a career-best performance against lefties (.320/.442/.563) and a platoon split about 200 points of OPS higher than in 2008. Like all too many good things in life, it won't last, though Blake at least does have a good shot at living up to his midlevel contract.

Juan Castro   SS   Bats: R   Throws: R   Height: 5' 11"   Weight: 190   Born: June 20, 1972   Age: 38

YEAR	TEAM	LVL	AGE	PA	R	2B	3B	HR	RBI	BB	SO	SB	CS	EqBRR	AVG	OBP	SLG	EqAVG	EqOBP	EqSLG	EqA	VORP	WARP		DEFENSE	
2007	CIN	MLB	35	98	5	5	0	0	5	4	21	0	0	-0.5	.180	.211	.236	.180	.208	.225	.152	-6.4	-1.3	10-SS	0	7-3B -2
2008	BAL	MLB	36	166	15	6	0	2	16	10	26	0	0	-1.0	.205	.256	.285	.207	.258	.293	.195	-3.7	-0.2	44-SS	3	1-3B -1
2009	LAN	MLB	37	121	18	4	0	1	9	6	25	0	0	-0.8	.277	.311	.339	.283	.317	.336	.237	0.7	-0.3	19-SS	-3	10-2B -1
2010	PHI	MLB	38	147	15	5	0	2	12	9	30	0	0	-0.7	.224	.273	.306	.224	.275	.304	.195	-3.8	-0.5	33-SS	0	

Breakout: 15%   Improve: 34%   Collapse: 28%   Attrition: 32%   MLB: 88%   Comparables: Billy Jurges, Jeff Reboulet, Jose Vizcaino, Dave Concepcion

With Luis Sojo retired and Miguel Cairo otherwise engaged, Torre needed a pet utilityman to fill out his roster, preferably one close to his own age. By his own meager standards, Castro had a fabulous year with the stick, mainly spelling Rafael Furcal. The Dodgers will sleep easily knowing the Phillies are paying more than the minimum to own the regression-laden B-side to this happy little tale.

Ivan De Jesus   SS   Bats: R   Throws: R   Height: 5' 11"   Weight: 182   Born: May 1, 1987   Age: 23

YEAR	TEAM	LVL	AGE	PA	R	2B	3B	HR	RBI	BB	SO	SB	CS	EqBRR	AVG	OBP	SLG	EqAVG	EqOBP	EqSLG	EqA	VORP	WARP		DEFENSE	
2007	SBR	A+	20	502	69	22	3	4	52	57	64	11	6	0.1	.287	.371	.381	.270	.339	.345	.247	11.4	-1.2	115-SS	-22	
2008	JAX	AA	21	560	91	21	2	7	58	76	81	16	2	3.7	.324	.419	.423	.311	.386	.406	.284	34.7	3.3	87-SS	-13	34-2B 6
2010	LAN	NL	23	349	45	16	1	5	33	34	58	4	2	0.7	.274	.350	.376	.280	.356	.385	.265	14.0	0.8	80-SS	-7	

Breakout: 35%   Improve: 53%   Collapse: 16%   Attrition: 17%   MLB: 1%   Comparables: Antonio Perez, Lonny Landry, Yuniesky Betancourt, Juan Fredymond

De Jesus missed virtually the entire season due to a broken tibia sustained while sliding in spring training. After surgery to implant a rod in his leg, he did return for a late-August cameo in complex-league ball. A patient, contact-oriented hitter, he sprays line drives to all fields and offers excellent instincts, steady hands, solid range, and arm strength afield. His assets are enhanced by a basic baseball intelligence inherited from his same-named father, a glove-first shortstop who spent 15 years in the majors. Whether he can stay at short remains the question, but the opening at second base might be his if his breaks come as opportunities, not with crutches.

Anthony Delmonico   C   Bats: R   Throws: R   Height: 6' 0"   Weight: 194   Born: April 27, 1987   Age: 23

YEAR	TEAM	LVL	AGE	PA	R	2B	3B	HR	RBI	BB	SO	SB	CS	EqBRR	AVG	OBP	SLG	EqAVG	EqOBP	EqSLG	EqA	VORP	WARP	DEFENSE	
2008	OGD	Rk	21	167	38	20	0	11	39	18	28	0	0	1.2	.340	.443	.716	.252	.323	.470	.269	6.3	-1.0	30-2B	-13
2009	GRL	A	22	428	53	22	2	9	43	46	86	5	0	-0.2	.285	.383	.430	.250	.321	.359	.242	0.6	-1.1	47-C -6 18-1B -4	
2010	LAN	MLB	23	371	37	18	1	7	30	31	94	2	0	-0.1	.230	.306	.356	.238	.314	.366	.239	6.7	0.3	60-C	-4

Breakout: 10% Improve: 36% Collapse: 23% Attrition: 5%   MLB: 1%   Comparables: Eric Lane, Curtis Thigpen, Joseph Soprano, Joe Roebuck

Delmonico played for his father at the University of Tennessee, transferred to Florida State when the old man got the axe, and was drafted by the Dodgers in the sixth round in 2008. A college shortstop, he was initially converted to second base, then moved behind the plate last year. An overnight success he was not, throwing out just 26 percent of runners, struggling to block pitches in the dirt, and allowing 11 passed balls in 49 games, but he showed progress until a hand injury cut his year short. He was a polished college hitter, and his offense suffered little with the move to catcher, but he'll need to mind the strikeouts.

Blake DeWitt   INF   Bats: L   Throws: R   Height: 5' 11"   Weight: 175   Born: August 20, 1985   Age: 24

YEAR	TEAM	LVL	AGE	PA	R	2B	3B	HR	RBI	BB	SO	SB	CS	EqBRR	AVG	OBP	SLG	EqAVG	EqOBP	EqSLG	EqA	VORP	WARP	DEFENSE	
2007	SBR	A+	21	361	48	29	2	8	46	20	42	2	3	-0.2	.298	.338	.466	.276	.309	.407	.245	2.1	0.3	79-3B	0
2007	JAX	AA	21	187	20	13	1	6	20	7	26	0	1	-0.2	.281	.306	.466	.272	.294	.456	.251	2.4	1.0	43-3B	6
2008	LVG	AAA	22	124	16	4	2	4	18	10	14	1	0	-0.8	.306	.366	.486	.257	.315	.407	.253	2.7	0.0	20-2B -4 5-3B	1
2008	LAN	MLB	22	421	45	13	2	9	52	45	68	3	0	1.9	.264	.344	.383	.272	.349	.390	.265	12.3	2.4	81-3B 12 22-2B -3	
2009	ABQ	AAA	23	407	64	21	9	7	47	48	44	2	2	5.2	.256	.349	.426	.212	.300	.349	.229	-1.1	-1.4	43-2B -7 39-3B -3	
2009	LAN	MLB	23	53	4	3	0	2	4	3	7	0	0	0.0	.204	.245	.388	.204	.245	.367	.225	-1.3	-0.2	8-3B	-1
2010	LAN	MLB	24	471	54	24	3	10	53	39	73	2	2	0.9	.252	.317	.393	.251	.318	.393	.253	8.5	1.3	105-3B	3

Breakout: 13% Improve: 36% Collapse: 20% Attrition: 12%   MLB: 100%   Comparables: Brian Kowitz, Dan Masteller, Joe Kesselmark, Doug Loman

Despite an unimpressive minor-league track record, this 2004 first-rounder was pressed into service in 2008, first at the hot corner, then at second base. Though a midsummer slump led Colletti to trade for Casey Blake, DeWitt held his own as a rookie, even getting the nod ahead of Jeff Kent during the team's late-season run. Colletti's subsequent machinations to re-sign Blake and bring in Orlando Hudson blocked DeWitt, who struggled to find a groove while shuttling between the bench and Albuquerque no less than five times in-season. His unimpressive Triple-A numbers were the product of a .273 BABIP; his walk and extra-base hit rates were more than acceptable. He's young enough to have a future in the majors and may even wind up as the starting second baseman so that the Dodgers can spend elsewhere.

A. J. Ellis   C   Bats: R   Throws: R   Height: 6' 3"   Weight: 230   Born: April 9, 1981   Age: 29

YEAR	TEAM	LVL	AGE	PA	R	2B	3B	HR	RBI	BB	SO	SB	CS	EqBRR	AVG	OBP	SLG	EqAVG	EqOBP	EqSLG	EqA	VORP	WARP	DEFENSE	
2007	JAX	AA	26	430	59	22	2	8	57	60	61	1	4	-3.2	.269	.382	.409	.244	.329	.345	.241	11.6	0.7	103-C	-6
2008	LVG	AAA	27	337	44	17	4	4	59	50	44	0	2	-4.6	.321	.436	.456	.267	.367	.361	.263	15.1	2.1	79-C	3
2009	ABQ	AAA	28	360	48	13	2	0	39	64	44	2	2	-0.3	.314	.438	.375	.254	.367	.295	.249	10.2	0.8	85-C	-4
2009	LAN	MLB	28	10	0	0	0	0	0	1	0	1	0	0	0.0	.100	.100	.100	.100	.100	.100	-.189	-1.5	-0.1	3-C	1
2010	LAN	MLB	29	344	36	14	2	3	38	41	62	1	1	-1.2	.242	.342	.329	.248	.347	.339	.249	9.2	0.9	84-C	-1

Breakout: 11% Improve: 46% Collapse: 26% Attrition: 18%   MLB: 20%   Comparables: Tom Wilson, Doug Mirabelli, Keith McDonald, Andy Dominique

Just as a man who shows up at a barbershop every day will eventually wind up with a haircut, Ellis has hung around the high minors long enough to develop solid on-base skills despite a lack of power, though his OBP is boosted considerably by batting eighth in front of pitchers. The only nonconverted catcher on the roster, he's well regarded defensively, and he threw out 29 percent of basestealers last season. Whatever major-league future he's got probably lies elsewhere, as Torre prefers his backup catchers in the salty veteran flavor.

Andre Ethier RF Bats: L Throws: L Height: 6' 2" Weight: 210 Born: April 10, 1982 Age: 28

YEAR	TEAM	LVL	AGE	PA	R	2B	3B	HR	RBI	BB	SO	SB	CS	EqBRR	AVG	OBP	SLG	EqAVG	EqOBP	EqSLG	EqA	VORP	WARP	DEFENSE			
2007	LAN	MLB	25	505	50	32	2	13	64	46	68	0	4	-1.5	.284	.350	.452	.288	.354	.457	.277	18.3	2.7	87-RF	3	34-LF	2
2008	LAN	MLB	26	596	90	38	5	20	77	59	88	6	3	0.8	.305	.375	.510	.324	.389	.542	.310	46.4	4.5	99-RF	-1	31-LF	-3
2009	LAN	MLB	27	685	92	42	3	31	106	72	116	6	4	0.7	.272	.361	.508	.293	.377	.548	.306	50.5	5.1	150-RF	-4		
2010	LAN	MLB	28	636	86	38	3	25	95	64	96	4	4	0.0	.290	.369	.502	.289	.371	.497	.303	45.5	4.9	147-RF	0		

Breakout: 8%   Improve: 40%   Collapse: 10%   Attrition: 10%   MLB: 100%   Comparables: Willie Crawford, Terry Puhl, Tony Oliva, Trot Nixon

Ethier stepped forward into stardom in 2009, becoming the first Dodger to reach 30 homers since 2004, leading the majors with six walk-off hits, and tying a major-league record previously held by Jimmie Foxx (1940) and Roy Sievers (1957) with his four walk-off homers. He set career highs in every important counting stat, but his rate stats were down from 2008 due to a .194/.283/.345 showing in 187 plate appearances against lefties, compared with .302/.390/.571 against righties. Torre did seem to notice, frequently dropping Ethier lower in the order against southpaws, but Ethier's split has been widening with increased playing time, encouraging platooning him. Like the possibility of Charlie Manuel's benching Ryan Howard against the tougher lefties, such a move won't actually happen.

Rafael Furcal SS Bats: S Throws: R Height: 5' 9" Weight: 195 Born: October 24, 1977 Age: 32

YEAR	TEAM	LVL	AGE	PA	R	2B	3B	HR	RBI	BB	SO	SB	CS	EqBRR	AVG	OBP	SLG	EqAVG	EqOBP	EqSLG	EqA	VORP	WARP	DEFENSE	
2007	LAN	MLB	29	642	87	23	4	6	47	55	68	25	6	4.8	.270	.333	.355	.278	.340	.360	.253	19.2	3.9	135-SS	13
2008	LAN	MLB	30	164	34	12	2	5	16	20	17	8	3	2.8	.357	.439	.573	.385	.463	.601	.350	23.5	2.1	33-SS	-4
2009	LAN	MLB	31	680	92	28	5	9	47	61	89	12	6	1.9	.269	.335	.375	.287	.349	.399	.262	28.2	4.7	141-SS	11
2010	LAN	MLB	32	563	80	25	3	8	43	53	73	14	7	1.8	.278	.347	.384	.284	.353	.393	.265	23.0	2.9	117-SS	4

Breakout: 7%   Improve: 34%   Collapse: 14%   Attrition: 9%   MLB: 98%   Comparables: Omar Vizquel, Bobby Avila, Ray Durham, Dave Bancroft

When Furcal's completely healthy, as in 2006 or early 2008, he flashes near-MVP form. When he's not, as in 2007 and the first five months of 2009, he's a drag on the offense, particularly in the hands of a manager given to writing his name atop the lineup, anyway, and hoping for the best. The Dodgers shelled out a three-year, $30 million deal (plus vesting option) to keep him, but the spark he showed in his late-2008 return from a microdiscectomy was rarely in evidence for most of 2009. Though physically healthy, according to trainer Stan Conte, he struggled to regain confidence in his back, and he hit just .255/.321/.349 with nine stolen-base attempts through August. Finally in baseball shape, he caught fire over the season's last five weeks, batting .330/.400/.491 and carrying that spark into the postseason. While that late showing is cause for optimism, it's balanced by the reality that the Dodgers have gotten just 12 weeks' worth of the star version of their shortstop over the last three years.

Dee Gordon SS Bats: L Throws: R Height: 5' 11" Weight: 150 Born: April 22, 1988 Age: 22

YEAR	TEAM	LVL	AGE	PA	R	2B	3B	HR	RBI	BB	SO	SB	CS	EqBRR	AVG	OBP	SLG	EqAVG	EqOBP	EqSLG	EqA	VORP	WARP	DEFENSE	
2008	OGD	Rk	20	274	45	13	3	2	27	16	29	18	5	4.4	.331	.371	.430	.253	.283	.315	.213	-1.6	-2.5	59-SS	-14
2009	GRL	A	21	601	96	17	12	3	35	43	90	73	25	-2.4	.301	.362	.394	.273	.318	.356	.240	10.9	-0.7	124-SS	-17
2010	LAN	NL	23	349	45	16	1	5	33	34	58	4	2	0.7	.274	.350	.376	.280	.356	.385	.265	14.0	0.8	80-SS	-7

Breakout: 0%   Improve: 0%   Collapse: 0%   Attrition: 0%   Comparables:

The son of reliever Tom Gordon, this fourth-round 2008 pick is an outstanding athlete with blazing speed. In his full-season debut, he shared Midwest League co-MVP honors with teammate Kyle Russell and ranked second in the minors in stolen bases. His ceiling is high enough to draw comparisons to Jimmy Rollins, but he comes with some concerns: he doesn't hit for much power, due to size, and is so incredibly raw from a fundamentals standpoint, particularly in the field, that he may wind up in the outfield. Still, a year with such progress is cause for optimism.

Jamie Hoffmann   RF

Bats: R   Throws: R   Height: 6' 3"   Weight: 220   Born: August 20, 1984   Age: 25

YEAR	TEAM	LVL	AGE	PA	R	2B	3B	HR	RBI	BB	SO	SB	CS	EqBRR	AVG	OBP	SLG	EqAVG	EqOBP	EqSLG	EqA	VORP	WARP	DEFENSE			
2007	SBR	A+	22	495	67	22	7	9	81	47	70	19	7	-2.2	.309	.378	.455	.288	.344	.405	.263	11.9	1.0	66-RF	-4	33-CF	1
2008	JAX	AA	23	544	64	20	3	10	71	54	73	28	9	0.7	.278	.350	.395	.269	.323	.379	.251	4.6	0.4	111-RF	0	7-CF	-1
2009	CHT	AA	24	129	25	9	2	2	16	22	18	5	3	-0.4	.307	.457	.495	.278	.400	.463	.298	7.9	1.2	24-RF	4	4-CF	-2
2009	ABQ	AAA	24	293	44	14	3	8	48	32	37	10	8	-0.6	.284	.360	.455	.238	.311	.379	.239	0.2	-0.8	39-RF	-1	27-CF	-6
2009	LAN	MLB	24	24	2	2	0	1	7	0	5	0	0	0.0	.182	.167	.409	.190	.167	.429	.208	-1.2	0.0	4-RF	1		
2010	NYA	MLB	25	474	55	20	2	11	64	43	82	12	6	-0.4	.261	.332	.399	.261	.331	.393	.248	4.1	0.5	103-RF	0		

Breakout: 8%   Improve: 39%   Collapse: 17%   Attrition: 8%   MLB: 10%   Comparables: Chris Sheff, T.R. Lewis, Tony Walker, Mark Smith

Hoffmann wasn't drafted by any baseball team, but the Minnesota native did get picked by the NHL's Carolina Panthers in 2003. An organizational favorite because of his work ethic and his defensive play, Hoffman made progress with his plate discipline and showed a bit more power, though he profiles as a gap hitter, not a slugger, and as a center fielder, he kills a lot of grass. He got a very brief taste of the bright lights during Manny Ramirez's suspension and made the most of it, collecting a double, a homer, and four RBI in his first start. A curious selection by the Yankees as the first pick in the Rule 5 draft, he improves their penalty-killing unit, if nothing else.

Chin-lung Hu   SS

Bats: R   Throws: R   Height: 5' 11"   Weight: 190   Born: February 2, 1984   Age: 26

YEAR	TEAM	LVL	AGE	PA	R	2B	3B	HR	RBI	BB	SO	SB	CS	EqBRR	AVG	OBP	SLG	EqAVG	EqOBP	EqSLG	EqA	VORP	WARP	DEFENSE			
2007	JAX	AA	23	356	56	30	5	6	34	26	33	12	4	2.7	.329	.380	.508	.317	.359	.489	.288	24.2	2.8	77-SS	-1		
2007	LVG	AAA	23	200	33	10	1	8	28	6	18	3	4	-0.9	.318	.337	.505	.264	.281	.415	.234	1.9	0.0	26-SS	0	17-2B	-2
2007	LAN	MLB	23	31	5	0	1	2	5	0	8	0	0	1.0	.241	.241	.517	.233	.233	.500	.254	0.6	-0.2	8-SS	-3		
2008	LAN	MLB	24	129	16	2	2	0	9	11	23	2	0	2.3	.181	.252	.233	.171	.242	.222	.164	-6.3	0.0	26-SS	5	12-2B	0
2008	LVG	AAA	24	168	21	5	3	1	15	7	19	2	0	-1.5	.295	.323	.385	.253	.279	.323	.212	-1.1	0.0	39-SS	1		
2009	ABQ	AAA	25	544	66	21	5	6	53	25	54	14	5	2.8	.294	.332	.393	.244	.279	.323	.212	-5.0	-0.4	118-SS	0	6-2B	2
2009	LAN	MLB	25	6	2	1	0	0	2	0	2	0	0	0.4	.400	.333	.600	.400	.333	.600	.335	0.7	0.1				
2010	LAN	MLB	26	474	57	23	4	7	42	28	65	6	4	1.1	.256	.303	.375	.264	.310	.388	.241	7.5	0.9	111-SS	0		

Breakout: 21%   Improve: 47%   Collapse: 15%   Attrition: 16%   MLB: 56%   Comparables: Mike Aviles, Esteban Beltre, Chris Bourjos, Julio Cordido

Once a highly regarded prospect, thanks to his acrobatic defense, Hu failed to hit during a brief audition at shortstop during Furcal's absence in 2008. Blurred vision in his right eye was a factor, but even with that problem corrected, his gap power has failed to develop, and his career has been moving backward to the point where his bat appears iffy beyond a utility role. Sure, he might be up to Juan Castro's job, but is that really worth aspiring to?

Orlando Hudson   2B

Bats: S   Throws: R   Height: 6' 0"   Weight: 190   Born: December 12, 1977   Age: 32

YEAR	TEAM	LVL	AGE	PA	R	2B	3B	HR	RBI	BB	SO	SB	CS	EqBRR	AVG	OBP	SLG	EqAVG	EqOBP	EqSLG	EqA	VORP	WARP	DEFENSE	
2007	ARI	MLB	29	601	69	28	9	10	63	70	87	10	2	2.6	.294	.376	.441	.289	.373	.429	.283	33.4	3.8	133-2B	0
2008	ARI	MLB	30	455	54	29	3	8	41	40	62	4	1	0.1	.305	.367	.450	.301	.362	.441	.280	23.4	2.4	102-2B	-2
2009	LAN	MLB	31	631	74	35	6	9	62	62	99	8	1	0.4	.283	.357	.417	.303	.371	.447	.286	36.7	6.1	140-2B	16
2010	LAN	MLB	32	535	61	27	3	10	53	56	86	6	2	0.5	.278	.356	.407	.283	.362	.416	.277	25.9	3.1	122-2B	2

Breakout: 10%   Improve: 35%   Collapse: 11%   Attrition: 9%   MLB: 98%   Comparables: Johnny Ray, Red Schoendienst, Bill Doran, Roberto Alomar

Coming off his second straight season-ending hand injury, Hudson remained a free agent until late February, when the Dodgers snapped him up for a base salary of $3.38 million, thereby sidestepping the issue of whether one of their homegrown infielders could carry the keystone. The move paid quick dividends, as Hudson hit for the cycle in his first home game, batted .332/.407/.469 through May, and made the All-Star team. Alas, Torre wore him down to the nub, starting him in 76 of the team's first 77 games, and while his defense remained above average, Hudson's bat flagged. He hit just .253/.325/.385 from June 1st onward and took the losing of his job to Ronnie Belliard in September lying down; reportedly, he never pressed for a meeting with the manager. Instead, he was practically run out of town on a rail, riding the bench during the postseason and receiving no arbitration offer even when his departure was a forgone conclusion. Still a free agent at press time, he remains a good performer on both sides of the ball and should get a fair shake elsewhere.

Matt Kemp — CF

Bats: R   Throws: R   Height: 6' 2"   Weight: 230   Born: September 23, 1984   Age: 25

YEAR	TEAM	LVL	AGE	PA	R	2B	3B	HR	RBI	BB	SO	SB	CS	EqBRR	AVG	OBP	SLG	EqAVG	EqOBP	EqSLG	EqA	VORP	WARP	DEFENSE			
2007	LVG	AAA	22	174	32	16	3	4	20	10	26	9	2	2.8	.329	.374	.540	.278	.322	.444	.265	4.9	0.7	18-RF	2	18-CF	-1
2007	LAN	MLB	22	311	47	12	5	10	42	16	66	10	5	-0.3	.342	.373	.521	.357	.386	.543	.306	22.1	2.6	69-RF	0	2-CF	1
2008	LAN	MLB	23	657	93	38	5	18	76	46	153	35	11	2.4	.290	.340	.459	.307	.354	.479	.284	34.7	4.4	92-CF	5	54-RF	0
2009	LAN	MLB	24	667	97	25	7	26	101	52	139	34	8	2.6	.297	.352	.490	.322	.372	.526	.304	53.5	7.3	149-CF	11	6-RF	0
2010	LAN	MLB	25	649	93	32	5	22	86	49	136	27	12	1.4	.295	.351	.476	.305	.361	.498	.290	43.3	5.2	148-CF	5		

Breakout: 13%   Improve: 63%   Collapse: 4%   Attrition: 2%   MLB: 100%   Comparables: Andruw Jones, Ellis Burks, Andre Dawson, Vernon Wells

This is exactly what the Dodgers had in mind when they drafted Kemp in 2003, hoping that his raw athleticism would translate into star-caliber play, given enough time. Like Andre Ethier, Kemp set career highs in key counting stats, but unlike Ethier, he also took a small step forward with his rate stats, thanks to a more selective approach at the plate; his pitches per plate appearance rose from 3.72 to 3.96. His showings against righties (.278/.329/.453) and lefties (.362/.429/.616) both improved by about 70 points of OPS; only Albert Pujols, Matt Diaz, and Jayson Werth outhit him against southpaws. Kemp's spike in homers did have an element of luck to it; according to Hit Tracker, he led the Dodgers with four "Lucky Homers," those that would not have cleared the fence on a calm, 70-degree day.

Andrew Lambo — LF

Bats: L   Throws: L   Height: 6' 3"   Weight: 190   Born: August 11, 1988   Age: 21

YEAR	TEAM	LVL	AGE	PA	R	2B	3B	HR	RBI	BB	SO	SB	CS	EqBRR	AVG	OBP	SLG	EqAVG	EqOBP	EqSLG	EqA	VORP	WARP	DEFENSE			
2007	DGR	Rk	18	218	38	15	1	5	32	29	34	1	2	0.0	.343	.440	.519	.297	.367	.448	.282	8.4	1.1	35-RF	-1	13-1B	-2
2008	GRL	A	19	518	58	33	2	15	79	41	110	5	2	-2.8	.288	.346	.462	.262	.311	.410	.249	2.6	-0.9	99-LF	-11	5-1B	1
2008	JAX	AA	19	38	7	2	1	3	12	2	9	0	0	-0.2	.389	.421	.750	.351	.385	.703	.343	4.8	0.8	7-LF	2		
2009	CHT	AA	20	541	70	39	1	11	61	39	95	4	3	-3.3	.256	.311	.407	.238	.281	.377	.228	-7.8	-1.9	125-LF	-8		
2010	LAN	MLB	21	564	65	33	2	16	71	39	130	3	2	-1.6	.255	.307	.418	.254	.309	.414	.255	9.3	0.5	123-LF	-5		

Breakout: 27%   Improve: 56%   Collapse: 13%   Attrition: 2%   MLB: 2%   Comparables: Greg Blosser, Rob Ducey, Otis Green, Chris Lubanski

This 2007 fourth-rounder came into the year considered the best pure hitter in the system, thanks to a combination of bat speed and raw strength. He was also the system's most advanced prospect for his age, reaching Double-A as a 20-year-old and spending 2009 as the league's fourth-youngest hitting prospect. Despite a hot start at Chattanooga (.321/.383/.548 in April), Lambo soon went Arctic, batting just .243/.295/.377 the rest of the way as his plate discipline suffered and his power failed to develop. His odd reverse platoon split persisted, as he batted just .241/.299/.388 against righties. Lacking in speed, athleticism, and defensive ability, Lambo will only go so far as his bat takes him, and right now, that appears to be back to Chattanooga.

James Loney — 1B

Bats: L   Throws: L   Height: 6' 3"   Weight: 220   Born: May 7, 1984   Age: 26

YEAR	TEAM	LVL	AGE	PA	R	2B	3B	HR	RBI	BB	SO	SB	CS	EqBRR	AVG	OBP	SLG	EqAVG	EqOBP	EqSLG	EqA	VORP	WARP	DEFENSE			
2007	LVG	AAA	23	261	28	19	1	1	32	25	48	2	1	-2.3	.279	.345	.382	.234	.299	.319	.220	-7.3	-0.8	33-1B	0	22-RF	1
2007	LAN	MLB	23	375	41	18	4	15	67	28	48	0	1	-1.0	.331	.381	.538	.338	.388	.551	.312	27.0	2.9	87-1B	0		
2008	LAN	MLB	24	651	66	35	6	13	90	45	85	7	4	-0.6	.289	.338	.434	.303	.349	.451	.274	17.4	1.0	153-1B	-7		
2009	LAN	MLB	25	651	73	25	2	13	90	70	68	7	3	-2.7	.281	.357	.399	.299	.370	.427	.278	13.3	2.1	148-1B	5		
2010	LAN	MLB	26	647	73	34	3	18	102	58	90	5	4	-1.1	.296	.361	.457	.296	.363	.452	.289	28.7	3.1	150-1B	0		

Breakout: 20%   Improve: 58%   Collapse: 3%   Attrition: 7%   MLB: 100%   Comparables: Sean Casey, Todd Helton, Kent Hrbek, Justin Morneau

Loney is an enigma, a contact hitter whose textbook line-drive swing and improving plate discipline and defense add up to less than the sum of those parts. Loney continued to manifest a puzzling split, batting a mere .251/.324/.316 with one homer at home compared with .309/.387/.475 with 12 homers on the road. This isn't a new thing; his career OPS at Dodgers Stadium is just 709, compared with 900 elsewhere. The flagging power bodes poorly for Loney's future; since 1954, only three players 25 or younger (Paul Konerko, Bill Skowron, and Jeff Burroughs) lost 100 or more points of slugging percentage over a three-year span, regained significant power in the fourth season, and sustained it into the fifth.

Mark Loretta INF

Bats: R   Throws: R   Height: 6' 0"   Weight: 185   Born: August 14, 1971   Age: 38

YEAR	TEAM	LVL	AGE	PA	R	2B	3B	HR	RBI	BB	SO	SB	CS	EqBRR	AVG	OBP	SLG	EqAVG	EqOBP	EqSLG	EqA	VORP	WARP	DEFENSE			
2007	HOU	MLB	35	511	52	23	2	4	41	44	41	1	2	-4.8	.287	.352	.372	.296	.361	.378	.261	14.9	1.1	54-SS	-5	22-2B	-3
2008	HOU	MLB	36	297	27	15	0	4	38	29	30	0	0	-2.4	.280	.350	.383	.288	.354	.396	.267	9.5	1.1	42-2B	-3	13-3B	2
2009	LAN	MLB	37	204	19	8	0	0	25	20	21	1	1	0.7	.232	.309	.276	.238	.309	.276	.217	-7.4	-0.2	15-3B	3	13-1B	1
2010	LAN	MLB	38	183	17	8	0	2	21	17	21	0	1	-0.6	.260	.331	.341	.268	.341	.356	.244	1.5	0.5	29-3B	3		

Breakout: 11%   Improve: 31%   Collapse: 37%   Attrition: 39%   MLB: 98%   Comparables: Brooks Robinson, Alvin Dark, Carl Furillo, Frankie Frisch

Loretta saw more playing time than any Dodger reserve this side of Juan Pierre, drawing starts at first and third mainly against lefties and serving as the team's most frequent pinch-hitter. In the latter role, he followed a 7-for-10 start with a 7-for-50 finish, but Torre kept calling his number. It all added up to less playing time than he was used to, and he set a career low in EqA by packing about as much punch as a Monty Burns uppercut. This may be the end of the line.

Russell Martin C

Bats: R   Throws: R   Height: 5' 10"   Weight: 210   Born: February 15, 1983   Age: 27

YEAR	TEAM	LVL	AGE	PA	R	2B	3B	HR	RBI	BB	SO	SB	CS	EqBRR	AVG	OBP	SLG	EqAVG	EqOBP	EqSLG	EqA	VORP	WARP	DEFENSE			
2007	LAN	MLB	24	620	87	32	3	19	87	67	89	21	9	-1.7	.293	.374	.469	.307	.387	.486	.296	53.7	7.1	140-C	8		
2008	LAN	MLB	25	650	87	25	0	13	69	90	83	18	6	-0.1	.280	.385	.396	.296	.395	.417	.288	46.2	5.8	139-C	4	8-3B	3
2009	LAN	MLB	26	588	63	19	0	7	53	69	80	11	6	-0.1	.250	.352	.329	.266	.363	.352	.256	22.5	3.8	132-C	9		
2010	LAN	MLB	27	621	74	23	1	14	73	72	87	12	8	-0.3	.272	.363	.394	.279	.372	.411	.275	34.3	4.1	143-C	4		

Breakout: 17%   Improve: 37%   Collapse: 17%   Attrition: 4%   MLB: 100%   Comparables: Brian Downing, Johnny Romano, Ivan Rodriguez, Jason Kendall

The Dodgers seem hell-bent on breaking Martin, who led the majors in innings caught for the second year out of three. Between that and an off-season training regimen that was supposed to slim him down but ended up costing him strength, he had his worst season with the stick, declining by at least 30 points in all three triple-slash categories. Though he maintained some measure of plate discipline—no small thing amid a season-long slump—his power vanished almost completely; he didn't homer until June 20th, reached a .400 slugging percentage in just one month out of six, and posted the majors' sixth-lowest ISO figure among batting title qualifiers. His defense did improve; he caught 31 percent of basestealers and was charged with just three passed balls, but the Dodgers' staff ranked second in the league in wild pitches, and Martin's struggles with blocking balls in the dirt were apparent for all to see in the postseason. He's on the Jason Kendall career path, not exactly a good thing, and with the system bereft of viable replacements, he really needs to rebound to justify his rising salary.

Lucas May C

Bats: R   Throws: R   Height: 6' 0"   Weight: 190   Born: October 24, 1984   Age: 25

YEAR	TEAM	LVL	AGE	PA	R	2B	3B	HR	RBI	BB	SO	SB	CS	EqBRR	AVG	OBP	SLG	EqAVG	EqOBP	EqSLG	EqA	VORP	WARP	DEFENSE	
2007	SBR	A+	22	554	81	25	3	25	89	36	107	5	7	-4.2	.256	.313	.465	.234	.278	.396	.230	1.2	-0.8	76-C	-8
2008	JAX	AA	23	441	54	27	1	13	54	32	112	6	1	1.8	.230	.294	.403	.224	.270	.383	.229	4.0	-1.0	94-C	-13
2009	CHT	AA	24	277	32	18	1	6	32	31	58	3	1	0.7	.306	.390	.468	.262	.329	.406	.259	11.2	1.0	64-C	-3
2010	LAN	MLB	25	349	34	15	1	8	34	25	90	2	2	-0.2	.224	.285	.354	.230	.291	.368	.226	1.9	-0.2	66-C	-3

Breakout: 11%   Improve: 31%   Collapse: 28%   Attrition: 16%   MLB: 2%   Comparables: Mike Wolff, Mike Nipper, Bill Bathe, Ken Ford

For now, May is the top catching prospect in the organization since the trade of Carlos Santana. Originally drafted as a shortstop in 2003, he's three years into his conversion to catching, and while he's strong-armed (thwarting 35 percent of stolen-base attempts), he's still chasing too many balls to the backstop (20 passed balls in 65 games). Repeating in Double-A after a lousy 2008, he improved his plate discipline and contact skills at the expense of power, though a wrist fracture that cost him seven weeks may have been a factor. The Dodgers claim to be particularly pleased with the defensive progress he demonstrated during the September IBAF World Cup and the Arizona Fall League, so perhaps they'll make a bona fide backstop out of him yet.

Xavier Paul — OF

Bats: L Throws: R Height: 6' 0" Weight: 195 Born: February 25, 1985 Age: 25

YEAR	TEAM	LVL	AGE	PA	R	2B	3B	HR	RBI	BB	SO	SB	CS	EqBRR	AVG	OBP	SLG	EqAVG	EqOBP	EqSLG	EqA	VORP	WARP	DEFENSE			
2007	JAX	AA	22	482	64	21	2	11	50	48	112	17	9	-1.1	.291	.366	.429	.267	.331	.394	.254	9.3	-0.6	95-CF	-14	5-RF	-1
2008	LVG	AAA	23	506	82	28	5	9	68	43	96	17	7	-1.6	.316	.378	.463	.270	.327	.378	.250	8.6	-1.2	104-CF	-19		
2009	ABQ	AAA	24	129	13	10	2	2	16	10	22	8	2	-1.8	.328	.378	.500	.271	.320	.415	.257	3.2	-0.2	26-CF	-5		
2009	LAN	MLB	24	16	3	1	0	1	1	2	4	0	1	-0.3	.214	.313	.500	.214	.313	.500	.262	-0.2	0.1				
2010	LAN	MLB	25	385	43	18	2	7	39	32	95	8	4	-0.8	.251	.317	.374	.252	.320	.376	.250	7.6	0.1	80-CF	-7		

Breakout: 8% Improve: 35% Collapse: 17% Attrition: 3% MLB: 8% Comparables: Pedro Swann, Everett Graham, Anthony Webster, Ty Gainey

Paul was the Dodgers' most advanced outfield prospect at the start of the year and was off to a strong start at Triple-A when he was recalled to fill Manny Ramirez's spot. Alas, Paul's stay in the majors lasted just two weeks, as he was sidelined by a staph infection in his knee, which required surgery, and then was lost for the year when he crashed into a wall and sustained microfractures in his ankle. When healthy, Paul is a classic tweener, an outfielder who doesn't play strong enough defense to hold down center on a regular basis but who doesn't hit for enough power to play a corner. He'll probably need someone else's injury or a trade elsewhere to make it in 2010.

Jaime Pedroza — 2B

Bats: S Throws: R Height: 5' 10" Weight: 175 Born: September 12, 1986 Age: 23

YEAR	TEAM	LVL	AGE	PA	R	2B	3B	HR	RBI	BB	SO	SB	CS	EqBRR	AVG	OBP	SLG	EqAVG	EqOBP	EqSLG	EqA	VORP	WARP	DEFENSE			
2007	OGD	Rk	20	239	33	18	1	8	40	14	44	4	4	-3.0	.360	.413	.569	.280	.319	.427	.257	7.5	-0.4	49-SS	-10		
2008	SBR	A+	21	535	78	31	7	9	57	33	120	25	11	-1.8	.290	.342	.441	.255	.300	.384	.239	9.7	-2.5	102-SS	-23	23-2B	-9
2009	GRL	A	22	609	100	33	6	15	78	78	162	36	14	0.6	.260	.361	.433	.225	.303	.352	.232	-1.1	-1.7	121-2B	-13		
2010	LAN	MLB	23	524	56	25	3	10	47	45	142	11	6	-0.4	.233	.304	.359	.239	.311	.366	.238	4.4	-0.5	113-2B	-9		

Breakout: 16% Improve: 47% Collapse: 13% Attrition: 18% MLB: 2% Comparables: Rich Casarotti, Chris Dean, Brian Specht, Angel Santos

Unimpressed by both his plate discipline and his play at shortstop, the Dodgers actually demoted Pedroza despite his superficially solid 2008 showing. Though his strikeout and walk numbers were affected by batting second behind speedster Dee Gordon for most of the season, Pedroza made the most of it, improving his plate discipline and showing more power despite a tough hitting environment. Transitioning to second base full-time, he was rough around the edges. Expect him to progress slowly.

Juan Pierre — OF

Bats: L Throws: L Height: 5' 11" Weight: 180 Born: August 14, 1977 Age: 32

YEAR	TEAM	LVL	AGE	PA	R	2B	3B	HR	RBI	BB	SO	SB	CS	EqBRR	AVG	OBP	SLG	EqAVG	EqOBP	EqSLG	EqA	VORP	WARP	DEFENSE			
2007	LAN	MLB	29	729	96	24	8	0	41	33	37	64	15	13.2	.293	.331	.353	.306	.343	.366	.258	20.1	0.5	158-CF	-15		
2008	LAN	MLB	30	406	44	10	2	1	28	22	24	40	12	2.2	.283	.327	.328	.300	.342	.345	.252	4.1	0.4	70-LF	-1	13-CF	0
2009	LAN	MLB	31	425	57	16	8	0	31	27	27	30	12	0.3	.308	.365	.392	.333	.387	.424	.283	18.6	2.4	72-LF	5	11-CF	-3
2010	CHA	MLB	32	425	61	18	4	2	31	30	32	34	12	2.2	.293	.349	.376	.299	.353	.385	.255	6.6	0.9	90-LF	1		

Breakout: 4% Improve: 29% Collapse: 14% Attrition: 16% MLB: 99% Comparables: Ichiro Suzuki, Lance Johnson, Joe Orsulak, Vince Coleman

The $44 million man actually did a laudable job in 2009, both in the lineup and off the bench. He hit .318/.381/.411 while taking over left field during Ramirez's suspension, helping to keep the offense humming and to provide sanctimonious scribes with a contrast to the dreadlocked one, with his work ethic and untainted urine. Or something—when Rob Dibble is showering you with midseason MVP love, then we're through the looking glass. In any event, Pierre also hit .326/.396/.419 in 51 pinch-hit appearances and wound up with his highest marks since 2004 in all three triple-slash categories. The Dodgers parlayed that performance into a deal to the White Sox where LA swallows $10.5 million of his remaining $18.5 million salary for two prospects; on the South Side, he becomes the leadoff man and center fielder and the instant paragon of Ozzieball's virtue.

Manny Ramirez　　　　LF　　　　Bats: R　Throws: R　Height: 6' 0"　Weight: 200　Born: May 30, 1972　Age: 38

YEAR	TEAM	LVL	AGE	PA	R	2B	3B	HR	RBI	BB	SO	SB	CS	EqBRR	AVG	OBP	SLG	EqAVG	EqOBP	EqSLG	EqA	VORP	WARP	DEFENSE
2007	BOS	MLB	35	569	84	33	1	20	88	71	92	0	0	-2.1	.296	.388	.493	.283	.378	.473	.294	31.3	2.0	112-LF -12
2008	BOS	MLB	36	425	66	22	1	20	68	52	86	1	0	0.2	.299	.398	.529	.291	.393	.519	.309	29.4	3.4	60-LF 2
2008	LAN	MLB	36	229	36	14	0	17	53	35	38	2	0	-0.3	.396	.489	.743	.414	.498	.763	.404	43.7	4.6	49-LF 1
2009	LAN	MLB	37	431	62	24	2	19	63	71	81	0	1	-2.3	.290	.418	.531	.311	.432	.568	.333	43.8	4.4	89-LF -3
2010	LAN	MLB	38	435	52	20	1	15	62	53	87	1	1	-0.6	.266	.366	.442	.274	.374	.461	.289	23.1	2.3	83-LF -2

Breakout: 2%　Improve: 17%　Collapse: 34%　Attrition: 22%　　MLB: 99%　　Comparables: Bob Johnson, Al Kaline, Al Simmons, Rico Carty

Despite the lovefest Ramirez inspired in Mannywood in late 2008, the Dodgers played hardball during his free agency, waiting out Scott Boras, the tepid economy, and the market's glut of corner outfielders into early March before signing Ramirez to a two-year, $45 million deal with an opt-out clause prior to year two. Ramirez resumed his torrid pace once the season opened, batting .348/.492/.641 through May 6, but the honeymoon ended when he was handed a 50-game suspension for a prescription for a female fertility drug often used to mask steroids. Greeted with open arms by most Dodger fans upon returning, Ramirez continued to terrorize pitchers, but his performance took a significant downturn after a Homer Bailey fastball hit his left wrist on July 21st. Manny hit just .255/.380/.448 the rest of the way, his strikeout rate increased from 15 percent of plate appearances to 21 percent, and his BABIP dropped from .369 to .302. That dip, along with a leak implicating him as one of the players on the 2004 survey testing list, chilled the market for his services and led to his choosing not to opt out. Unless he can recapture some of his initial magic, expect reports of his act wearing thin to abound.

Trayvon Robinson　　　　CF　　　　Bats: S　Throws: R　Height: 5' 10"　Weight: 175　Born: September 1, 1987　Age: 22

YEAR	TEAM	LVL	AGE	PA	R	2B	3B	HR	RBI	BB	SO	SB	CS	EqBRR	AVG	OBP	SLG	EqAVG	EqOBP	EqSLG	EqA	VORP	WARP	DEFENSE
2007	GRL	A	19	443	50	9	4	2	31	32	119	22	9	-0.4	.253	.314	.311	.229	.280	.284	.204	-12.2	-3.5	108-CF -17
2008	SBR	A+	20	489	67	20	8	4	42	33	104	22	12	-0.4	.276	.328	.385	.252	.297	.344	.227	-3.9	0.2	102-CF 6
2009	SBR	A+	21	529	82	28	9	15	54	50	125	43	18	-4.8	.306	.375	.500	.257	.316	.398	.250	9.1	-0.7	112-CF -15
2009	CHT	AA	21	70	8	1	2	2	10	10	18	4	2	0.7	.246	.358	.439	.233	.324	.417	.257	1.7	0.3	15-CF 1
2010	LAN	MLB	22	554	59	23	5	8	43	43	145	16	8	-0.9	.239	.301	.349	.245	.308	.359	.235	2.8	-0.2	125-CF -5

Breakout: 20%　Improve: 56%　Collapse: 11%　Attrition: 6%　　MLB: 5%　　Comparables: Jarred Ball, Delwyn Young, Jaisen Randolph, Shane Victorino

A 10th-round pick in 2005 out of LA's Crenshaw High School—Darryl Strawberry's alma mater—Robinson made little progress in converting his tools into baseball skills through his first four minor-league seasons, but he took a huge leap forward last year. His power spiked with a switch to a bigger bat and a newfound ability to recognize pitches he could drive and the counts where he was likely to find them. He also had the green light all year long, hence the increase in stolen bases. Robinson's defensive numbers weren't pretty, but scouts consider him a solid center fielder, albeit one with a fringe-average arm.

Kyle Russell　　　　RF　　　　Bats: L　Throws: L　Height: 6' 5"　Weight: 190　Born: June 27, 1986　Age: 24

YEAR	TEAM	LVL	AGE	PA	R	2B	3B	HR	RBI	BB	SO	SB	CS	EqBRR	AVG	OBP	SLG	EqAVG	EqOBP	EqSLG	EqA	VORP	WARP	DEFENSE
2008	OGD	Rk	22	260	46	13	5	11	46	27	82	4	0	5.1	.279	.365	.534	.206	.264	.339	.215	-7.4	-1.8	54-RF -3
2009	GRL	A	23	563	90	39	7	26	102	72	180	20	2	3.3	.272	.371	.545	.218	.293	.396	.240	-1.3	-0.8	113-RF -2 11-CF -3
2010	LAN	MLB	24	465	44	22	3	12	53	41	164	3	2	1.0	.205	.280	.359	.206	.281	.351	.227	-6.4	-0.9	102-RF -2

Breakout: 16%　Improve: 38%　Collapse: 24%　Attrition: 14%　　MLB: 0%　　Comparables: Andy Brown, Tom Waldrop, Troy Fryman, Doug Frobel

"The Texas Wind Machine" didn't earn his nickname for nothing, as this 2008 third-rounder out of the University of Texas tied for second in the entire minors in strikeouts last year due to his long stroke. Thanks to his strength and pull-conscious approach, he also led the pitcher-friendly Midwest League in homers, total bases, slugging percentage, and RBI and shared co-MVP honors with teammate Dee Gordon. The caveat is that he was old for his level, but he's athletic, with good speed, a strong arm, and above-average defense, not to mention some amount of plate discipline. Sluggers such as Russell Branyan, Kirk Gibson, Ryan Howard, and Derrek Lee all whiffed in 30 percent or more of their plate appearances during a minor-league season, yet went on to major-league success; less happily,

Billy Ashley, Billy Beane, Brad Eldred, and Wily Mo Peña struck out with similar frequency and underwhelmed upon reaching "The Show."

Jim Thome — DH

Bats: L Throws: R Height: 6' 3" Weight: 255 Born: August 27, 1970 Age: 39

YEAR	TEAM	LVL	AGE	PA	R	2B	3B	HR	RBI	BB	SO	SB	CS	EqBRR	AVG	OBP	SLG	EqAVG	EqOBP	EqSLG	EqA	VORP	WARP	DEFENSE
2007	CHA	MLB	36	536	79	19	0	35	96	95	134	0	1	-2.8	.275	.410	.563	.265	.404	.549	.318	40.3	4.4	
2008	CHA	MLB	37	602	93	28	0	34	90	91	147	1	0	-0.8	.245	.362	.503	.240	.360	.496	.291	27.2	3.0	
2009	CHA	MLB	38	417	55	15	0	23	74	69	116	0	0	-5.4	.249	.372	.493	.244	.367	.477	.291	14.1	1.6	
2009	LAN	MLB	38	17	0	0	0	0	3	0	7	0	0	0.0	.235	.235	.235	.235	.235	.235	.135	-1.8	-0.2	
2010	LAN	MLB	39	423	50	15	1	20	61	60	118	1	1	-1.2	.231	.346	.447	.231	.348	.443	.282	15.0	1.7	0- 0

Breakout: 2% Improve: 28% Collapse: 18% Attrition: 23%   MLB: 95%   Comparables: Harold Baines, Dave Parker, Johnny Mize, Frank Thomas

Thome surpassed Mike Schmidt and Reggie Jackson to climb to 12th on the all-time list for homers, but he was well on his way to full-season lows in homers and slugging percentage, even before being traded on August 31st. With even spot appearances at first base out of the question because of his history of back troubles, Thome was touted as the Dodgers' answer to Matt Stairs, a deluxe pinch-hitter who could play DH in the World Series. Alas, plantar fasciitis limited Thome's opportunities and his power, and the team fell short of a pennant. Thome can still produce in a full-time DH role—his .223/.328/.485 line against lefties in 2008-2009 is a vast improvement on the previous three years—but unless he can turn the clock back to 2006, he'll need two seasons to reach 600 homers. A date in Cooperstown probably awaits, nonetheless.

Scott Van Slyke — RF

Bats: R Throws: R Height: 6' 5" Weight: 195 Born: July 24, 1986 Age: 23

YEAR	TEAM	LVL	AGE	PA	R	2B	3B	HR	RBI	BB	SO	SB	CS	EqBRR	AVG	OBP	SLG	EqAVG	EqOBP	EqSLG	EqA	VORP	WARP	DEFENSE
2007	GRL	A	20	390	38	18	1	2	35	27	68	4	4	-2.8	.254	.310	.328	.236	.282	.306	.209	-13.2	-2.2	92-RF -2 7-CF -3
2008	GRL	A	21	76	4	4	0	0	7	12	11	0	0	-0.7	.148	.280	.213	.143	.253	.190	.166	-5.2	-1.1	17-RF -4
2008	SBR	A+	21	192	29	9	2	5	26	11	35	7	4	-2.4	.261	.309	.420	.236	.277	.365	.222	-4.0	-0.5	21-RF 1 13-LF 1
2009	SBR	A+	22	563	75	42	4	23	100	61	128	10	7	-2.4	.294	.373	.534	.255	.321	.434	.259	9.8	1.0	113-RF -3 10-LF 1
2010	LAN	MLB	23	478	44	23	1	9	49	42	116	4	4	-1.6	.228	.298	.349	.235	.306	.363	.231	-4.3	-0.7	108-RF -2

Breakout: 22% Improve: 48% Collapse: 18% Attrition: 14%   MLB: 1%   Comparables: Joe Mather, Jonathan Rivers, Rod Hobbs, Scott Lydy

A 14th-round pick in 2005, the son of former major leaguer Andy Van Slyke bypassed a ride at Ole Miss to join the Dodgers. He made slow progress during his first four minor-league seasons, and both his approach and his physique matured to the point that he broke out in the hitter-friendly California League in 2009, finishing fifth in the league in homers, and 10th in slugging percentage. If he can maintain that power as he moves up to Double-A, the Dodgers might have something.

PITCHERS

Ronald Belisario

Bats: R Throws: R Height: 6' 2" Weight: 240 Born: December 31, 1982 Age: 27

YEAR	TEAM	LVL	AGE	W	L	SV	G	GS	IP	H	HR	BB	SO	GB%	BABIP	STUFF	WHIP	ERA	SIERA	DERA	EqH9	EqHR9	EqBB9	EqSO9	VORP	SN/WX
2007	LYN	A+	24	0	3	4	19	0	34¹	38	5	13	19	61%	.287	-37	1.49	4.46	4.69	5.73	10.6	2.5	3.8	3.0	-0.8	-0.76
2007	ALT	AA	24	1	0	0	18	0	24²	23	4	14	21	49%	.264	-19	1.50	3.28	4.53	4.81	9.2	2.2	5.2	5.5	1.9	0.34
2008	ALT	AA	25	4	4	9	38	0	57	63	5	25	36	59%	.314	-30	1.54	4.74	4.72	5.62	11.1	1.3	4.0	4.0	-0.7	-0.57
2009	LAN	MLB	26	4	3	0	69	0	70²	52	4	29	64	59%	.245	9	1.15	2.04	3.77	3.07	7.4	0.6	3.1	6.7	19.0	0.19
2010	LAN	MLB	27	3	5	2	50	0	60¹	67	8	27	38	59%	.310	-15	1.54	5.17	4.73	5.67	9.9	1.2	3.9	5.3	-1.2	0.39

Breakout: 15% Improve: 40% Collapse: 32% Attrition: 19%   MLB: 62%   Comparables: Mike DeJean, Jim Mecir, Jim Czajkowski, Kurt Archer

A tremendous free-talent find, this 27-year-old Venezuelan had never advanced beyond Double-A, putting up an ugly 4.89 ERA in three stints at that level sandwiched around years lost to Tommy John surgery (2005) and a suspension (2006). The Dodgers plucked him off the scrap heap, and thanks to a mid-90s two-seam fastball, he became one of Torre's workhorses, generating ground balls by the bushel. Despite a few high-leverage hiccups and a month lost to elbow woes, he was sheer hell on righties (.157/.234/.252). As with fellow workhorse Ramon Troncoso, his workload bears watching, but he's yet another reminder that good relievers can be found in unlikely places.

Chad Billingsley

Bats: R Throws: R Height: 6' 1" Weight: 245 Born: July 29, 1984 Age: 25

YEAR	TEAM	LVL	AGE	W	L	SV	G	GS	IP	H	HR	BB	SO	GB%	BABIP	STUFF	WHIP	ERA	SIERA	DERA	EqH9	EqHR9	EqBB9	EqSO9	VORP	SN/WX
2007	LAN	MLB	22	12	5	0	43	20	147	131	15	64	141	49%	.290	24	1.33	3.31	3.75	3.31	7.9	0.9	3.5	7.7	35.3	4.83
2008	LAN	MLB	23	16	10	0	35	32	200²	188	14	80	201	56%	.313	26	1.34	3.14	3.51	3.59	8.8	0.7	3.2	7.6	41.9	5.96
2009	LAN	MLB	24	12	11	0	33	32	196¹	173	17	86	179	51%	.292	10	1.32	4.03	3.87	4.73	9.3	1.0	3.5	7.0	15.9	3.68
2010	LAN	MLB	25	12	11	0	38	30	195²	188	21	76	175	53%	.307	17	1.35	4.01	3.79	4.40	8.7	0.9	3.4	7.4	23.9	3.50

Breakout: 11% Improve: 49% Collapse: 5% Attrition: 7%   MLB: 100%   Comparables: Kevin Appier, Jeremy Bonderman, Kelvim Escobar, John Smoltz

Lofty expectations turned Billingsley's year—bookended by the 2008 NLCS (two early knockouts) and 2009's (bypassed for a start)—into an *annus horribilis* due to its sequence of events. Recovering from a November spiral fracture of his fibula in time to open the season, he earned All-Star honors by reeling off 14 quality starts in his first 19, with a 3.38 ERA and 8.5 K/9. A hyperextended knee and a general lack of stamina undid his second half; he surrendered 16 runs in the nine sixth innings he pitched after the break, didn't record a single out in any seventh inning after July 5, and wound up with a 5.20 second-half ERA, with six quality starts out of 13. By October, he had been marginalized to the point that many pundits expected him to be traded, but the Dodgers view his dip as temporary and he remains a key part of their plans.

Jonathan Broxton

Bats: R Throws: R Height: 6' 4" Weight: 290 Born: June 16, 1984 Age: 26

YEAR	TEAM	LVL	AGE	W	L	SV	G	GS	IP	H	HR	BB	SO	GB%	BABIP	STUFF	WHIP	ERA	SIERA	DERA	EqH9	EqHR9	EqBB9	EqSO9	VORP	SN/WX
2007	LAN	MLB	23	4	4	2	83	0	82	69	6	25	99	55%	.310	29	1.15	2.85	2.59	3.17	7.6	0.7	2.4	9.6	21.0	2.86
2008	LAN	MLB	24	3	5	14	70	0	69	54	2	27	88	49%	.315	27	1.17	3.13	2.62	3.94	7.6	0.3	3.1	9.6	11.6	1.79
2009	LAN	MLB	25	7	2	36	73	0	76	44	4	29	114	56%	.263	31	0.96	2.61	1.90	3.25	6.8	0.6	2.9	10.2	18.3	5.03
2010	LAN	MLB	26	5	4	18	69	0	68²	58	6	24	77	55%	.305	18	1.18	3.22	2.89	3.54	7.6	0.8	3.0	9.3	15.0	1.96

Breakout: 19% Improve: 47% Collapse: 20% Attrition: 11%   MLB: 100%   Comparables: Armando Benitez, Jose Valverde, Bobby Jenks, Esteban Yan

In his first full year as closer, Broxton, a nearly 300-pound man throwing 100 mph fastballs and 88 mph sliders, continued to scare the bejesus out of hitters. Broxton yielded a .165/.247/.232 line and led all relievers in strikeouts and strikeout rate. Torre's willingness to call on him in the eighth inning helped Broxton pace the circuit in WXRL as well. His year wasn't flawless; he allowed his four homers during a midsummer swoon, and a big-toe injury scratched him from the All-Star Game. As in 2008, his year ended with a critical NLCS failure, but there's no reason to think the disappointment will carry over.

Scott Elbert

Bats: L Throws: L Height: 6' 1" Weight: 210 Born: August 13, 1985 Age: 24

YEAR	TEAM	LVL	AGE	W	L	SV	G	GS	IP	H	HR	BB	SO	GB%	BABIP	STUFF	WHIP	ERA	SIERA	DERA	EqH9	EqHR9	EqBB9	EqSO9	VORP	SN/WX
2007	JAX	AA	21	0	1	0	3	3	14	6	0	10	24	23%	.261	13	1.14	3.86	2.23	4.85	6.2	0.7	6.2	10.4	0.9	0.10
2008	JAX	AA	22	4	1	0	25	1	41¹	22	2	20	46	34%	.213	16	1.02	2.40	3.34	3.92	6.2	1.2	4.4	7.2	6.8	0.20
2009	CHT	AA	23	2	3	0	12	11	62¹	59	5	30	87	48%	.362	19	1.43	3.90	2.68	5.57	10.2	1.4	4.3	9.9	-0.4	-0.22
2009	ABQ	AAA	23	2	1	0	8	7	33²	34	2	14	38	61%	.352	23	1.43	3.74	3.21	4.13	9.4	0.6	3.9	8.8	5.0	0.41
2009	LAN	MLB	23	2	0	0	19	0	19²	19	4	7	21	45%	.294	4	1.32	5.03	3.20	5.54	10.1	2.4	2.9	8.2	-0.1	-0.24
2010	LAN	MLB	24	5	6	0	46	10	88²	90	10	42	84	37%	.323	2	1.49	4.69	4.05	5.16	9.2	1.1	4.1	7.8	3.4	0.92

Breakout: 16% Improve: 46% Collapse: 13% Attrition: 8%   MLB: 58%   Comparables: Lenny DiNardo, Ken Holubec, Jason Miller, Bryan Duquette

Chosen about halfway between Jered Weaver and Philip Hughes, this 2004 first-rounder might have long since joined the Dodgers' rotation had labrum woes not cost him good chunks of 2007-08. Working around no less than four call-ups to the Dodgers' bullpen, Elbert whiffed more than a batter per inning at both Chattanooga and Albuquerque, winning the organization's Minor League Pitcher of the Year award. His high-effort delivery generates some concern, but not his stuff—an explosive low- to mid-90s fastball and a power curve. After a rough April (three homers in his first 6 ⅓ big-league innings), he held opponents to a .191/.283/.277 line with one homer. With fellow lefties Kuo and Sherrill in the pen, his quickest path to the majors may be as the fifth starter, but he'll have to convince the team he's durable.

Jon Garland

Bats: R   Throws: R   Height: 6' 6"   Weight: 210   Born: September 27, 1979   Age: 30

YEAR	TEAM	LVL	AGE	W	L	SV	G	GS	IP	H	HR	BB	SO	GB%	BABIP	STUFF	WHIP	ERA	SIERA	DERA	EqH9	EqHR9	EqBB9	EqSO9	VORP	SN/WX
2007	CHA	MLB	27	10	13	0	32	32	208¹	219	19	57	98	47%	.284	9	1.32	4.23	5.07	4.26	8.6	0.7	2.2	3.9	28.9	4.44
2008	LAA	MLB	28	14	8	0	32	32	196²	237	23	59	90	60%	.313	-5	1.51	4.90	5.00	4.84	10.5	1.0	2.4	3.9	14.1	2.34
2009	ARI	MLB	29	8	11	0	27	27	167²	188	19	52	83	51%	.298	3	1.43	4.29	5.02	4.34	9.5	0.8	2.4	3.9	21.6	2.67
2009	LAN	MLB	29	3	2	0	6	6	36¹	37	4	9	26	51%	.287	6	1.27	2.72	4.09	4.42	10.1	1.3	2.0	5.3	4.3	0.83
2010	LAN	MLB	30	10	12	0	31	31	188²	205	21	57	89	53%	.297	-6	1.39	4.34	5.02	4.77	9.8	1.0	2.7	3.9	15.3	2.03

Breakout: 5%   Improve: 41%   Collapse: 11%   Attrition: 12%   MLB: 98%   Comparables: Bob Forsch, Steve Trachsel, Aaron Cook, Jimmy Haynes

All things considered, this LAIM (League-Average Innings-Muncher) didn't fare too badly in the chilly free-agent market of 2008-09, netting $7.25 million from the Snakes for a one-year deal—that's more guaranteed money than Randy Wolf received. Integrating a cut fastball into his repertoire, he got off to a rough start (5.75 ERA through May), but stabilized over the next three months (3.56 ERA). The Dodgers bit on a waiver deal to bolster a shaky rotation in September and then let him go in October. Along with Javier Vazquez and Mark Buehrle, Garland is one of three pitchers to toss at least 190 innings every year since 2002; he's not the equal of that duo, but his dependability will continue to get him work.

Charlie Haeger

Bats: R   Throws: R   Height: 6' 1"   Weight: 220   Born: September 19, 1983   Age: 26

YEAR	TEAM	LVL	AGE	W	L	SV	G	GS	IP	H	HR	BB	SO	GB%	BABIP	STUFF	WHIP	ERA	SIERA	DERA	EqH9	EqHR9	EqBB9	EqSO9	VORP	SN/WX
2007	CHR	AAA	23	5	16	0	24	23	147²	138	16	67	126	42%	.289	-1	1.39	4.08	4.22	5.65	9.3	1.4	4.1	6.1	-2.3	-0.63
2007	CHA	MLB	23	0	1	0	8	0	11¹	17	3	8	1	45%	.304	-47	2.21	7.15	7.46	7.71	12.3	2.3	5.4	0.8	-2.9	-0.13
2008	CHR	AAA	24	10	13	0	28	25	178	167	13	77	117	44%	.280	-4	1.37	4.45	4.85	5.36	9.1	1.0	4.1	4.3	2.6	-0.27
2009	ABQ	AAA	25	11	6	0	22	22	144²	134	16	58	103	48%	.271	10	1.33	3.55	4.52	3.81	8.1	0.9	3.6	5.3	26.9	1.29
2009	LAN	MLB	25	1	1	0	6	3	19	13	4	7	15	50%	.176	-2	1.05	3.32	4.09	3.62	7.2	2.4	2.9	5.8	3.9	0.46
2010	LAN	MLB	26	7	10	0	33	21	145²	149	19	69	96	39%	.293	-5	1.49	5.01	5.05	5.49	9.3	1.2	4.1	5.4	0.2	1.31

Breakout: 8%   Improve: 37%   Collapse: 17%   Attrition: 16%   MLB: 34%   Comparables: Nelson Figueroa, Scott Arnold, Russ Herbert, Kiko Calero

Like wine, cheese, and many of life's other fine things, knuckleballers generally need to age before they're much good. More than three years after debuting with the White Sox, Haeger put together his first major-league-quality start in late August, then followed up with seven shutout innings against the Cubs. The magic ran out just as Garland arrived, and Haeger pitched sparingly in September. Though his command of his signature pitch is improving, Haeger doesn't vary his speeds much, so more than two-thirds of his knucklers sit in the 70-73 mph range, producing less break and less variation than Tim Wakefield's 60-70 mph offerings. Fans of the flutterball can hope he'll be ready to hold down a job by the time Wakefield retires. Haeger will be in the mix for a back-end rotation spot come spring.

Clayton Kershaw

Bats: L   Throws: L   Height: 6' 3"   Weight: 220   Born: March 19, 1988   Age: 22

YEAR	TEAM	LVL	AGE	W	L	SV	G	GS	IP	H	HR	BB	SO	GB%	BABIP	STUFF	WHIP	ERA	SIERA	DERA	EqH9	EqHR9	EqBB9	EqSO9	VORP	SN/WX
2007	GRL	A	19	7	5	0	20	20	97¹	72	5	50	134	51%	.302	37	1.25	2.77	2.71	4.98	8.4	1.5	5.6	8.0	5.2	0.47
2007	JAX	AA	19	1	2	0	5	5	24²	17	4	17	29	46%	.228	23	1.38	3.65	3.74	6.17	8.1	3.1	6.2	6.9	-1.7	0.12
2008	JAX	AA	20	2	3	0	13	11	61¹	39	0	19	59	48%	.239	48	0.95	1.91	3.25	3.56	6.7	0.5	2.9	6.1	12.8	1.40
2008	LAN	MLB	20	5	5	0	22	21	107²	109	11	52	100	58%	.320	37	1.50	4.26	3.92	4.40	9.6	1.1	3.9	7.2	12.8	2.83
2009	LAN	MLB	21	8	8	0	31	30	171	119	7	91	185	44%	.269	50	1.23	2.79	3.54	3.31	7.5	0.5	4.3	8.2	39.6	6.56
2010	LAN	MLB	22	9	9	0	32	31	154²	137	16	75	143	45%	.292	30	1.37	3.94	3.98	4.35	8.1	1.0	4.2	7.7	19.7	3.56

Breakout: 10%   Improve: 51%   Collapse: 11%   Attrition: 9%   MLB: 100%   Comparables: Scott Kazmir, Oliver Perez, Steve Avery, Dontrelle Willis

Kershaw took a major step toward elite status in 2009, posting the NL's lowest hit rate, second-lowest homer rate, and fifth-highest strikeout rate. A key was the incorporation of a slider into his already-impressive arsenal of a mid-90s fastball, knee-buckling curve, and changeup. The two off-speed pitches share the same release point and early flight path, making them difficult for the hitter to distinguish from one another until too late; the new pitch produced significantly more strikes via swings-and-misses as well as fouls than its big-bending sibling. Kershaw's numbers from the point of introducing it on June 4th are eye-popping: 2.04 ERA, 10.2 K/9, 2.3 K/BB, 0.2 HR/9. Walks are still an issue, particularly as they run up his already-limited pitch counts, but he's a bona fide ace in the making.

Hong-Chih Kuo

Bats: L　　Throws: L　　Height: 6' 1"　　Weight: 235　　Born: July 23, 1981　　Age: 28

YEAR	TEAM	LVL	AGE	W	L	SV	G	GS	IP	H	HR	BB	SO	GB%	BABIP	STUFF	WHIP	ERA	SIERA	DERA	EqH9	EqHR9	EqBB9	EqSO9	VORP	SN/WX
2007	LVG	AAA	25	0	1	0	7	5	20	18	2	8	28	43%	.364	19	1.30	3.60	2.28	3.79	8.1	0.9	3.8	10.4	3.6	0.23
2007	LAN	MLB	25	1	4	0	8	6	30¹	35	3	14	27	34%	.337	0	1.62	7.42	4.39	7.11	9.9	0.9	3.5	7.0	-5.6	0.07
2008	LAN	MLB	26	5	3	1	42	3	80	60	4	21	96	52%	.281	33	1.01	2.14	2.48	2.64	7.0	0.6	2.0	8.9	25.4	3.04
2009	LAN	MLB	27	2	0	0	35	0	30	21	2	13	32	52%	.253	9	1.13	3.00	3.34	3.41	7.4	0.6	3.4	8.1	6.7	1.09
2010	LAN	MLB	28	4	4	0	45	0	60	55	6	22	55	45%	.299	8	1.27	3.80	3.62	4.18	8.2	0.8	3.2	7.7	8.8	1.25

Breakout: 18%　Improve: 44%　Collapse: 25%　Attrition: 10%　　　MLB: 86%　　Comparables: Arthur Rhodes, Mark Guthrie, Eddie Guardado, Scott Stewart

Status Kuo: the man with four elbow surgeries (including two Tommy Johns) struggled in April, then missed half the season due to arthritic change in his elbow, wear and tear that requires rest and rehab. Rejoining the Dodgers in late July, he was like a gift from Adephagia-Bing, goddess of gluttony and trade deadline acquisitions, flaying hitters (.188/.266/.271) in 24 ⅔ innings the rest of the way. Alas, his fragility required some restrictions on usage; he never pitched more than an inning, never bridged two innings, and worked back-to-back days just once. Even with such limitations, his capability for dominance merits the Dodgers' continuing to nurse him along.

Hiroki Kuroda

Bats: R　　Throws: R　　Height: 6' 1"　　Weight: 210　　Born: February 10, 1975　　Age: 35

YEAR	TEAM	LVL	AGE	W	L	SV	G	GS	IP	H	HR	BB	SO	GB%	BABIP	STUFF	WHIP	ERA	SIERA	DERA	EqH9	EqHR9	EqBB9	EqSO9	VORP	SN/WX
2007	HRO	JPN	32	12	8	0	26	26	179²	176	20	42	123	—	.285	7	1.21	3.56	4.10	4.36	9.1	1.0	2.5	5.0	21.7	0.61
2008	LAN	MLB	33	9	10	0	31	31	183¹	181	13	42	116	58%	.281	14	1.22	3.73	4.22	4.33	8.7	0.7	1.8	4.7	24.1	4.73
2009	LAN	MLB	34	8	7	0	21	20	117¹	110	12	24	87	58%	.271	6	1.14	3.76	3.79	4.96	9.2	1.2	1.6	5.5	7.0	2.10
2010	LAN	MLB	35	7	8	0	23	23	128	133	16	37	73	54%	.292	0	1.33	4.23	4.61	4.64	9.4	1.1	2.5	4.7	12.2	1.96

Breakout: 15%　Improve: 38%　Collapse: 13%　Attrition: 18%　　　MLB: 94%　　Comparables: Bryn Smith, Daisuke Miura, Rick Reed, Esteban Loaiza

Kuroda was a one-man MASH unit in 2009. The Dodgers' Opening Day starter strained his oblique in his first in-season side session, which sidelined him for nearly two months. He was drilled above his right ear by a line drive on August 15th, sustaining a concussion that cost him three weeks and a herniated disc that shelved him during the NLDS. But he returned in time to inflict considerable neck pain on himself in his NLCS start. Lost amid the litany of Kuroda's injuries was a strong second half (2.98 ERA, 49/12 K/BB ratio), thanks to the work of trainer Stan Conte to patch him up. Kuroda is still a very solid midrotation starter, though at his age, rebounding from injuries won't get any easier.

Josh Lindblom

Bats: R　　Throws: R　　Height: 6' 5"　　Weight: 220　　Born: June 15, 1987　　Age: 23

YEAR	TEAM	LVL	AGE	W	L	SV	G	GS	IP	H	HR	BB	SO	GB%	BABIP	STUFF	WHIP	ERA	SIERA	DERA	EqH9	EqHR9	EqBB9	EqSO9	VORP	SN/WX
2008	GRL	A	21	0	0	0	8	8	29	14	2	4	33	57%	.179	24	0.62	1.86	2.13	3.13	5.9	1.6	2.0	5.9	7.2	0.56
2009	CHT	AA	22	3	5	0	14	11	57¹	55	4	14	46	51%	.293	6	1.20	4.71	3.79	6.51	9.6	1.1	2.4	5.4	-6.2	-0.57
2009	ABQ	AAA	22	3	0	1	20	3	39	34	3	12	36	51%	.284	23	1.18	2.54	3.52	2.58	7.7	0.7	2.8	7.0	12.4	0.69
2010	LAN	MLB	23	6	6	0	30	19	98	91	12	34	69	50%	.278	10	1.27	4.10	4.29	4.50	8.4	1.1	3.0	5.9	10.9	1.76

Breakout: 9%　Improve: 34%　Collapse: 31%　Attrition: 5%　　　MLB: 5%　　Comparables: Joel Gilmore, Sergio Lizarraga, Mike Murphy, Michel Simard

A closer at Purdue, the Dodgers' 2008 second-round pick didn't dominate in the Chattanooga rotation the way he had in his pro debut, but he didn't pitch badly; his ERA was inflated by a .357 BABIP with runners in scoring position. The Dodgers returned him to the bullpen upon promotion to Albuquerque to groom him for a potential late-season call-up that never happened, though he pitched well. Lindblom's 92-94 mph fastball is considered by some the best in the system, thanks to a heavy sink that generates plenty of grounders, and he also offers a power curve and a swing-and-miss splitter that he consistently throws for strikes. If there's a complaint, it's that he needs to make hitters chase more balls out of the zone. If he doesn't break camp in the big-league pen, he'll start at Albuquerque, and he could get a shot as the fifth starter at some point in 2010.

Ethan Martin

Bats: R   Throws: R   Height: 6' 2"   Weight: 195   Born: June 6, 1989   Age: 21

YEAR	TEAM	LVL	AGE	W	L	SV	G	GS	IP	H	HR	BB	SO	GB%	BABIP	STUFF	WHIP	ERA	SIERA	DERA	EqH9	EqHR9	EqBB9	EqSO9	VORP	SN/WX
2009	GRL	A	20	6	8	1	27	19	100	85	4	61	120	43%	.321	5	1.46	3.87	3.56	7.30	10.6	1.7	6.8	6.5	-17.9	-1.26
2010	LAN	MLB	21	4	8	0	29	18	94²	107	15	61	78	40%	.329	12	1.78	6.11	4.93	6.61	10.2	1.4	5.6	6.8	-11.7	1.10

Breakout: 29%   Improve: 63%   Collapse: 13%   Attrition: 8%   MLB: 1%   Comparables: Blake King, Mark Diapoules, Robb Nen, Kyle Sebach

The first high school hurler drafted in 2008 (15th overall), Martin couldn't demonstrate his wares until 2009, because he tore a meniscus during a postdraft minicamp. His pro debut mixed promise with reminders of his rawness; he mostly played third base until his senior year and might have gone in the second round as a hitter. With three plus pitches—an explosive 93-95 mph fastball, a hard curve, and a splitter—Martin put up both the Midwest League's second-highest strikeout rate and its third-highest walk rate, as command of his breaking ball was an issue. He was kept on a short leash and used in tandem with Nathan Eovaldi over the final three months. As much as there is to like here, he needs innings before the Dodgers will have an idea of what they've got.

James McDonald

Bats: L   Throws: R   Height: 6' 5"   Weight: 195   Born: October 19, 1984   Age: 25

YEAR	TEAM	LVL	AGE	W	L	SV	G	GS	IP	H	HR	BB	SO	GB%	BABIP	STUFF	WHIP	ERA	SIERA	DERA	EqH9	EqHR9	EqBB9	EqSO9	VORP	SN/WX
2007	SBR	A+	22	6	7	0	16	15	82	79	8	21	104	36%	.350	10	1.22	3.95	2.28	4.62	10.2	1.9	2.7	7.7	7.4	0.76
2007	JAX	AA	22	7	2	0	10	10	52²	42	5	16	64	42%	.289	17	1.10	1.71	2.52	3.38	8.9	1.8	2.9	7.5	11.6	1.25
2008	JAX	AA	23	5	3	0	22	22	118²	98	12	46	113	38%	.274	-9	1.21	3.19	3.67	4.50	9.2	2.0	3.6	6.2	12.2	1.20
2008	LVG	AAA	23	2	1	0	5	4	22¹	17	3	7	28	32%	.259	23	1.07	3.63	2.57	3.52	6.3	1.2	2.7	8.6	5.1	0.31
2008	LAN	MLB	23	0	0	0	4	0	6	5	0	1	2	25%	.238	-11	1.00	0.00	6.28	0.00	7.5	0.0	1.5	3.0	3.7	0.16
2009	ABQ	AAA	24	1	0	0	6	6	30¹	21	2	14	40	32%	.288	29	1.15	3.26	2.62	3.10	6.8	0.6	4.3	9.9	7.7	0.63
2009	LAN	MLB	24	5	5	0	45	4	63	60	6	34	54	42%	.298	-10	1.49	4.00	4.47	5.22	9.8	1.0	4.3	6.4	1.9	0.70
2010	LAN	MLB	25	5	7	0	37	18	105¹	107	14	46	89	39%	.310	1	1.46	4.77	4.25	5.19	9.2	1.2	3.8	7.0	3.6	2.29

Breakout: 10%   Improve: 44%   Collapse: 19%   Attrition: 23%   MLB: 51%   Comparables: Rick Huisman, Steve Dreyer, Shaun Marcum, Mike Griffin

The Dodgers hoped the two-time winner of their Minor League Pitcher of the Year award would claim the fifth starter's spot in 2009, but McDonald was tarred and feathered in four April starts (13 runs in 13 ⅓ IP). He continued to start during a six-week Triple-A refresher, but pitched exclusively in relief upon returning, with considerable success (2.72 ERA, 8.7 K/9, 3.0 K/UBB). McDonald is known more for deception than power, and his average fastball speed increased from 91 to 93 mph with the move to the pen. He got far more strikes with his 12-to-6 curveball (his best pitch) and changeup, and he generated enough grounders to move out of the "extreme" category of fly-ballers. He's a better fit in the pen as a change of pace from the power arms, but may get another shot at the back end of the rotation.

Aaron Miller

Bats: L   Throws: L   Height: 6' 3"   Weight: 200   Born: September 18, 1987   Age: 22

YEAR	TEAM	LVL	AGE	W	L	SV	G	GS	IP	H	HR	BB	SO	GB%	BABIP	STUFF	WHIP	ERA	SIERA	DERA	EqH9	EqHR9	EqBB9	EqSO9	VORP	SN/WX
2009	GRL	A	21	3	1	0	7	7	30¹	22	3	10	38	39%	.292	17	1.05	2.08	2.33	3.55	10.3	2.8	4.3	7.5	5.5	0.45
2010	LAN	MLB	22	3	8	0	24	24	89¹	116	17	49	66	33%	.347	-3	1.85	6.63	5.16	7.38	12.0	1.9	4.9	6.2	-18.7	3.13

Breakout: 3%   Improve: 18%   Collapse: 44%   Attrition: 0%   MLB: 0%   Comparables: Chris Hancock, Wade LeBlanc, Ryan Edell, Trey Moore

The Dodgers tabbed this fast-rising two-way lefty out of Baylor University as a supplemental first-rounder in 2009. Though Miller spent most of his college career as an outfielder, the Dodgers had followed him as a pitcher since high school. His stuff has improved rapidly upon his committing to the mound; he whiffed plenty of hitters in his pro debut with a 90-94 mph fastball and an excellent hard slider, though his changeup needs refinement. The organization was impressed with his poise as well. Expect him to climb quickly.

Eric Milton

Bats: L   **Throws:** L   **Height:** 6' 3"   **Weight:** 220   **Born:** August 4, 1975   **Age:** 34

YEAR	TEAM	LVL	AGE	W	L	SV	G	GS	IP	H	HR	BB	SO	GB%	BABIP	STUFF	WHIP	ERA	SIERA	DERA	EqH9	EqHR9	EqBB9	EqSO9	VORP	SN/WX
2007	CIN	MLB	31	0	4	0	6	6	31¹	39	4	9	18	36%	.313	-1	1.53	5.17	5.06	5.27	9.5	0.8	2.7	4.6	0.9	0.02
2009	ABQ	AAA	33	3	2	0	7	7	35	29	3	6	27	49%	.255	17	1.00	2.83	3.56	3.12	7.3	0.8	1.6	6.0	9.2	0.67
2009	LAN	MLB	33	2	1	0	5	5	23²	30	2	6	20	33%	.359	6	1.52	3.80	3.99	4.89	12.5	0.8	2.0	6.3	1.6	0.27
2010	LAN	MLB	34	2	3	0	9	0	43	44	5	12	27	27%	.299	4	1.32	4.14	4.95	4.64	9.4	1.0	2.6	5.3	4.1	0.59

Breakout: 18% Improve: 38% Collapse: 24% Attrition: 19%   MLB: 73%   Comparables: Joe Nuxhall, Scott Radinsky, Milt Shoffner, Dan Schatzeder

Along with Jeff Weaver and Shawn Estes, Milton appeared to be part of the Dodgers' spring training "Turn Back the Clock" initiative. Working his way back from 2007 Tommy John surgery, he survived a month-long stint at Albuquerque—normally hell on an extreme fly-baller—and fared well as a fifth starter before back woes set in, ultimately forcing him into season-ending surgery to remove a herniated disc. Milton has just 55 big-league innings since 2006, so it's an open question as to whether he can hold his body together long enough to get another opportunity.

Guillermo Mota

Bats: R   **Throws:** R   **Height:** 6' 6"   **Weight:** 210   **Born:** July 25, 1973   **Age:** 36

YEAR	TEAM	LVL	AGE	W	L	SV	G	GS	IP	H	HR	BB	SO	GB%	BABIP	STUFF	WHIP	ERA	SIERA	DERA	EqH9	EqHR9	EqBB9	EqSO9	VORP	SN/WX
2007	NYN	MLB	33	2	2	0	52	0	59¹	63	8	18	47	52%	.296	-9	1.37	5.76	4.04	5.70	9.6	1.4	2.4	6.2	-1.3	-0.38
2008	MIL	MLB	34	5	6	1	58	0	57	52	7	28	50	50%	.283	-7	1.40	4.11	4.15	4.47	8.8	1.1	3.9	6.8	6.3	0.43
2009	LAN	MLB	35	3	4	0	61	0	65¹	53	6	24	39	42%	.236	-11	1.18	3.44	4.91	3.82	8.2	1.0	2.8	4.4	11.9	0.18
2010	LAN	MLB	36	3	4	0	62	0	62¹	64	8	25	42	47%	.298	-9	1.42	4.45	4.60	4.91	9.3	1.1	3.5	5.7	4.1	-0.06

Breakout: 18% Improve: 51% Collapse: 15% Attrition: 12%   MLB: 88%   Comparables: Stan Bahnsen, Tom Ferrick, Eddie Fisher, Eric Plunk

After a 4 ½-year walkabout, Mota returned to the Dodgers still able to pump his fastball into the mid-90s and still maddeningly inconsistent. He began the year as part of the arson squad before the correction of a mechanical flaw enabled him to put the fire out. From May 22nd through August 2nd—a span of 36 ⅓ innings pitched—he dominated, yielding a 0.50 ERA while holding hitters to a .143 average. Perhaps distracted by success, he apparently neglected personal hygiene; an ingrown toenail cost him half of September, and he was too rusty to make the postseason roster. Those hoping for a continued revival should note that his low BABIP (.244), high rate of allowing inherited runners to score (17 out of 38), and career-worst strikeout rate don't bode well.

Vicente Padilla

Bats: R   **Throws:** R   **Height:** 6' 2"   **Weight:** 220   **Born:** September 27, 1977   **Age:** 32

YEAR	TEAM	LVL	AGE	W	L	SV	G	GS	IP	H	HR	BB	SO	GB%	BABIP	STUFF	WHIP	ERA	SIERA	DERA	EqH9	EqHR9	EqBB9	EqSO9	VORP	SN/WX
2007	TEX	MLB	29	6	10	0	23	23	120¹	146	16	50	71	51%	.319	-9	1.63	5.76	5.01	5.88	10.2	1.1	3.3	4.8	-5.1	0.70
2008	TEX	MLB	30	14	8	0	29	29	171	185	26	65	127	48%	.303	7	1.46	4.74	4.41	4.65	8.7	1.2	3.0	6.1	16.4	2.05
2009	TEX	MLB	31	8	6	0	18	18	108	120	12	42	59	56%	.305	1	1.50	4.92	4.98	4.56	10.1	0.8	3.2	4.6	11.0	2.09
2009	LAN	MLB	31	4	0	0	8	7	39¹	36	4	12	38	52%	.305	16	1.22	3.20	3.30	3.80	9.6	1.2	2.5	7.6	6.9	1.21
2010	LAN	MLB	32	7	9	0	28	27	137²	150	17	55	89	51%	.310	-4	1.49	4.88	4.70	5.36	9.9	1.1	3.5	5.4	2.1	1.21

Breakout: 8% Improve: 44% Collapse: 20% Attrition: 17%   MLB: 96%   Comparables: Pat Rapp, Jeff Suppan, Paul Wilson, Tim Wakefield

Rarely durable enough or average enough to earn the LAIM tag, Padilla wore out his welcome in Texas with his penchant for inciting beanball wars and retreating to the clubhouse midgame to surf the Web. (Who doesn't read BaseballProspectus.com at work?) The Rangers punted in early August, whereupon the Dodgers tabbed him to patch their rotation. The move from a hitter's haven to a pitcher's palace and three weeks of rest seemingly worked wonders; Padilla gained an extra tick of velocity on his fastball and curveball, generating far more strikes with both, and rewarded Torre's decision to ride the hot hand with two stellar post-season starts before the magic ran out in game five of the NLCS. Soon after the season he sustained a minor gunshot wound in his thigh by his target-shooting instructor, no doubt engendering schadenfreude among disgruntled Rangers fans.

Travis Schlichting

Bats: R   Throws: R   Height: 6' 4"   Weight: 190   Born: October 19, 1984   Age: 25

YEAR	TEAM	LVL	AGE	W	L	SV	G	GS	IP	H	HR	BB	SO	GB%	BABIP	STUFF	WHIP	ERA	SIERA	DERA	EqH9	EqHR9	EqBB9	EqSO9	VORP	SN/WX
2008	JAX	AA	23	6	4	0	33	0	59²	58	4	18	49	52%	.305	-14	1.27	3.77	3.86	5.71	10.3	1.4	2.9	5.1	-1.3	-1.39
2009	CHT	AA	24	1	0	1	9	0	13²	7	1	7	12	42%	.167	-10	1.02	0.66	4.24	3.95	5.3	1.3	4.6	5.9	2.4	0.22
2009	ABQ	AAA	24	1	0	0	13	0	12²	8	0	8	7	72%	.211	-11	1.26	1.42	4.75	2.13	5.7	0.0	5.7	4.3	4.7	0.36
2009	LAN	MLB	24	0	0	0	2	0	2²	1	1	5	2	33%	.000	-23	2.25	3.37	8.09	6.00	6.0	3.0	12.0	6.0	-0.2	-0.01
2010	LAN	MLB	25	3	4	0	39	2	55²	59	8	27	35	48%	.297	-15	1.53	5.20	5.01	5.66	9.5	1.2	4.2	5.2	-1.0	0.02

Breakout: 8%   Improve: 29%   Collapse: 31%   Attrition: 10%   MLB: 49%   Comparables: Joe Cotton, Mauro Zarate, Sean Jarrett, Aaron Williams

A fourth-round pick as a third baseman by the Devil Rays in 2003, Schlichting returned to the mound while in the Angels' chain in 2006 (he'd pitched in high school), but didn't emerge as a pitching prospect until reaching the Dodgers' organization. Since then, he's made fast progress, reaching the majors after less than 75 innings of work above rookie- and indie-league ball, thanks to a 90-94 mph sinking fastball and a slider that *Baseball America* considered the organization's best. Alas, his 2009 season was bookended by lower-back woes, but if healthy, he'll get another shot at helping the big club.

George Sherrill

Bats: L   Throws: L   Height: 6' 0"   Weight: 230   Born: April 19, 1977   Age: 33

YEAR	TEAM	LVL	AGE	W	L	SV	G	GS	IP	H	HR	BB	SO	GB%	BABIP	STUFF	WHIP	ERA	SIERA	DERA	EqH9	EqHR9	EqBB9	EqSO9	VORP	SN/WX
2007	SEA	MLB	30	2	0	3	73	0	45²	28	4	17	56	32%	.231	24	0.99	2.36	2.65	2.33	5.2	1.0	2.9	9.1	16.3	1.64
2008	BAL	MLB	31	3	5	31	57	0	53¹	47	6	33	58	32%	.291	11	1.50	4.72	4.11	4.39	7.6	0.8	4.8	8.8	6.7	1.58
2009	BAL	MLB	32	0	1	20	42	0	41¹	34	3	13	39	38%	.272	17	1.14	2.40	3.54	2.14	6.9	0.4	2.4	7.5	15.7	2.78
2009	LAN	MLB	32	1	0	1	30	0	27²	19	1	11	22	51%	.234	5	1.08	0.65	4.08	1.00	7.0	0.3	3.0	6.0	13.5	1.62
2010	LAN	MLB	33	4	3	17	62	0	62	51	5	28	58	36%	.280	9	1.27	3.42	3.95	3.76	7.4	0.8	3.9	7.7	12.0	1.82

Breakout: 14%   Improve: 42%   Collapse: 24%   Attrition: 14%   MLB: 100%   Comparables: Hal Haid, Orlando Pena, Willie Hernandez, Yukinaga Maeda

Rebounding from a late-2008 meltdown with shoulder misery, Sherrill fattened up for the midsummer trade market with four effective months closing for the Orioles. Dealt to the Dodgers, Sherrill stepped into their eighth-inning role ahead of Broxton, rewarding his new employers with lights-out work and his fellow relievers with a reprieve from the Kerlan-Jobe Clinic. For the year, he smothered lefties at a .128/.188/.154 clip, good for the lowest OPS among those facing at least 75 such varmints, but he's serviceable enough against righties (.244/.321/.375) to be used for full innings rather than situational spots. Expect him to be in the mix for more heavy lifting in 2010.

Eric Stults

Bats: L   Throws: L   Height: 6' 0"   Weight: 225   Born: December 9, 1979   Age: 30

YEAR	TEAM	LVL	AGE	W	L	SV	G	GS	IP	H	HR	BB	SO	GB%	BABIP	STUFF	WHIP	ERA	SIERA	DERA	EqH9	EqHR9	EqBB9	EqSO9	VORP	SN/WX
2007	LVG	AAA	27	5	7	0	21	17	89¹	134	12	36	81	40%	.411	-16	1.90	7.56	4.13	7.08	12.1	1.2	3.6	6.4	-15.7	-1.84
2007	LAN	MLB	27	1	4	0	12	5	38²	50	5	17	30	48%	.357	-7	1.73	5.82	4.50	5.63	11.3	1.2	3.5	6.3	-0.6	0.53
2008	LVG	AAA	28	7	7	0	20	20	117²	118	14	35	102	47%	.301	15	1.30	3.82	3.70	3.78	8.2	1.1	2.7	5.9	22.6	1.59
2008	LAN	MLB	28	2	3	0	7	7	38²	38	6	13	30	40%	.274	3	1.32	3.49	4.24	4.31	8.8	1.6	2.6	5.8	5.1	0.91
2009	ABQ	AAA	29	5	4	0	12	11	64	86	5	24	40	55%	.363	-9	1.72	5.20	4.72	5.69	12.1	0.9	3.5	4.7	-1.3	-0.74
2009	LAN	MLB	29	4	3	0	10	10	50	51	3	26	33	42%	.306	-6	1.54	4.86	5.11	5.29	10.4	0.8	4.2	5.1	1.1	0.99
2010	LAN	MLB	30	6	8	0	26	22	113²	128	13	46	77	48%	.322	-6	1.54	4.91	4.65	5.46	10.3	1.1	3.6	5.6	0.5	1.31

Breakout: 9%   Improve: 42%   Collapse: 14%   Attrition: 18%   MLB: 66%   Comparables: Kirt Ojala, Jeff Ballard, Dave LaPoint, Jason Jacome

After three years of only fleeting success trying to crack the rotation, Stults got his best opportunity yet when Kuroda strained his oblique in April. Stults didn't exactly cover himself in glory, but put up a .498 SNWP, despite a high walk rate and just one quality start (a complete-game shutout against the Giants, which barely counts). After spraining his thumb while fielding a bunt, he began an odyssey that included declining performance, a DL stint, and an extended stay in the minors, receiving just one more start. Stults' career big-league numbers (145 innings, with a 4.84 ERA and 6.1 K/9) could probably get him a fifth starter job elsewhere, but they'll probably keep him on the fringes of the Dodgers' rotation picture.

Ramon Troncoso

Bats: R　　Throws: R　　Height: 6′ 2″　　Weight: 200　　Born: February 16, 1983　　Age: 27

YEAR	TEAM	LVL	AGE	W	L	SV	G	GS	IP	H	HR	BB	SO	GB%	BABIP	STUFF	WHIP	ERA	SIERA	DERA	EqH9	EqHR9	EqBB9	EqSO9	VORP	SN/WX
2007	SBR	A+	24	3	1	7	16	0	26	18	0	3	30	69%	.273	15	0.81	1.04	2.14	2.49	6.8	0.7	1.4	6.8	8.5	1.71
2007	JAX	AA	24	7	3	7	35	0	52	52	3	18	39	72%	.310	-20	1.35	3.12	3.74	4.38	10.2	1.3	3.4	4.3	6.0	0.50
2008	LVG	AAA	25	4	0	0	22	0	30²	43	1	16	18	71%	.378	-24	1.92	4.99	4.66	6.38	11.9	0.6	4.5	3.9	-3.0	0.04
2008	LAN	MLB	25	1	1	0	32	0	38	37	2	12	38	71%	.333	9	1.29	4.26	3.12	4.58	9.4	0.5	2.5	7.7	3.7	-0.11
2009	LAN	MLB	26	5	4	6	73	0	82²	83	3	34	55	61%	.305	-5	1.42	2.72	4.46	3.70	10.0	0.5	3.3	5.0	15.8	3.55
2010	LAN	MLB	27	4	5	3	62	0	71²	78	8	28	45	68%	.310	-12	1.48	4.77	4.38	5.27	9.9	1.1	3.4	5.2	1.8	1.80

Breakout: 16%　Improve: 37%　Collapse: 31%　Attrition: 9%　　MLB: 60%　　Comparables: Jim Acker, Justin Lehr, Hipolito Pichardo, Matt Whiteside

After wetting his feet in low-leverage bullpen duty in 2008, Troncoso emerged as a vital cog in '09, working his way into the team's top righty set-up role by Memorial Day, winding up second in the league in relief innings and eighth in WXRL. Thanks to his 93 mph fastball and a heavy sinker, Troncoso generated ground balls galore, and while his strikeout rate receded to a level in line with his track record, he still missed a reasonable number of bats. Note that his untranslated walk rate was inflated by nine intentional passes. A 4.87 ERA over the final two months should serve to remind that, as with many a Torre-driven reliever, Troncoso's workload bears watching, though at this writing, the Dodgers are considering him to be a possible fifth starter.

Cory Wade

Bats: R　　Throws: R　　Height: 6′ 2″　　Weight: 185　　Born: May 28, 1983　　Age: 27

YEAR	TEAM	LVL	AGE	W	L	SV	G	GS	IP	H	HR	BB	SO	GB%	BABIP	STUFF	WHIP	ERA	SIERA	DERA	EqH9	EqHR9	EqBB9	EqSO9	VORP	SN/WX
2007	SBR	A+	24	7	0	6	25	2	66	50	6	17	67	39%	.260	-2	1.02	2.45	3.01	3.09	7.8	1.7	2.7	5.9	16.8	1.67
2007	JAX	AA	24	0	1	0	14	0	33	22	2	11	33	40%	.222	1	1.00	1.36	3.34	2.16	6.8	1.4	3.0	5.7	12.4	0.47
2008	JAX	AA	25	0	0	1	6	0	14²	14	3	1	13	54%	.282	-4	1.02	4.30	2.94	5.54	11.1	3.5	0.7	6.2	-0.1	0.07
2008	LAN	MLB	25	2	1	0	55	0	71¹	51	7	15	51	46%	.222	6	0.93	2.27	3.83	2.93	6.7	1.0	1.7	5.5	19.7	2.73
2009	ABQ	AAA	26	1	1	1	18	0	22²	20	5	7	19	45%	.242	-7	1.19	6.75	3.81	6.45	7.7	1.6	2.8	6.4	-2.4	0.03
2009	LAN	MLB	26	2	3	0	27	0	27²	28	3	10	18	35%	.281	-18	1.37	5.53	4.91	5.93	9.9	1.3	2.6	4.6	-1.3	-0.32
2010	LAN	MLB	27	4	5	1	48	0	69	68	9	24	46	42%	.285	-4	1.32	4.19	4.57	4.55	8.8	1.2	3.0	5.4	7.3	1.64

Breakout: 10%　Improve: 39%　Collapse: 36%　Attrition: 16%　　MLB: 42%　　Comparables: Carlos Reyes, Paul Byrd, Jonah Bayliss, Joe Bateman

The staff's biggest surprise as a rookie in 2008, Wade was a prime candidate to be felled by the Curse of Scott Proctor, a common affliction among pitchers who work their way into Torre's good graces. Battling shoulder soreness in spring training, Wade wound up on the DL with bursitis once Torre called his number four times during the team's first six games. Returning nearly three weeks later, he threw 4 ⅓ innings in the team's next five games, and from there things got ugly: a 6.86 ERA and five blown leads over his next 19 appearances. After spending the second half on the DL and in Albuquerque, he'll compete for a bullpen spot while providing another object lesson in reliever fungibility.

Jeff Weaver

Bats: R　　Throws: R　　Height: 6′ 5″　　Weight: 200　　Born: August 22, 1976　　Age: 33

YEAR	TEAM	LVL	AGE	W	L	SV	G	GS	IP	H	HR	BB	SO	GB%	BABIP	STUFF	WHIP	ERA	SIERA	DERA	EqH9	EqHR9	EqBB9	EqSO9	VORP	SN/WX
2007	SEA	MLB	30	7	13	0	27	27	146²	190	23	35	80	40%	.327	-19	1.53	6.20	4.91	6.09	10.8	1.6	1.9	4.3	-9.8	1.39
2008	NAS	AAA	31	2	4	0	9	9	55	64	9	20	37	47%	.322	-24	1.53	6.22	4.57	7.64	11.7	2.1	3.4	4.4	-12.0	-0.66
2008	BUF	AAA	31	2	2	0	13	4	29²	38	7	10	22	48%	.330	-26	1.62	6.07	4.33	6.67	12.1	2.5	3.2	4.8	-3.7	-0.27
2009	ABQ	AAA	32	1	0	1	5	1	12²	11	1	2	12	53%	.278	13	1.03	3.55	3.00	4.26	7.8	0.7	1.4	7.1	1.7	0.02
2009	LAN	MLB	32	6	4	0	28	7	79	87	7	33	64	50%	.325	-8	1.52	3.65	4.27	4.30	11.1	1.1	3.3	6.1	10.1	1.71
2010	LAN	MLB	33	3	6	0	26	13	79²	98	13	30	46	48%	.326	-18	1.61	5.59	4.96	6.07	11.1	1.4	3.2	4.7	-5.1	0.63

Breakout: 10%　Improve: 46%　Collapse: 25%　Attrition: 32%　　MLB: 67%　　Comparables: Doyle Alexander, Ray Burris, Glenn Abbott, Bobby Bolin

After pitching his way out of the majors in 2007 and putting up ugly numbers in Triple-A in 2008, Weaver reunited with Torre and the Dodgers for what looked like a last stop before Atlantic League oblivion. Injuries opened up work for him as a utility pitcher—spot starting, long relief, mop-up duty, extra-inning cannon fodder—and he turned out to be as handy as a roll of duct tape, finishing seventh in the club in combined win expectancy (SNLVAR + WXRL). Despite averaging just 4.5 innings per start, he put up a 3.13 ERA and a .519 SNWP as a starter, and a 4.02 Fair Run

Average with 7.8 strikeouts per nine as a reliever. Though still fairly helpless against lefties, he'll survive to pitch another year so long as he can miss righty bats.

Chris Withrow

Bats: R   Throws: R   Height: 6' 3"   Weight: 195   Born: April 1, 1989   Age: 21

YEAR	TEAM	LVL	AGE	W	L	SV	G	GS	IP	H	HR	BB	SO	GB%	BABIP	STUFF	WHIP	ERA	SIERA	DERA	EqH9	EqHR9	EqBB9	EqSO9	VORP	SN/WX
2009	SBR	A+	20	6	6	0	19	16	86¹	80	3	45	105	52%	.358	18	1.45	4.69	3.21	6.90	10.7	1.4	5.9	6.6	-11.9	-0.99
2009	CHT	AA	20	2	2	0	6	6	27¹	24	2	12	26	43%	.301	25	1.32	3.95	3.80	5.40	9.4	1.4	4.0	6.8	0.3	0.04
2010	LAN	MLB	21	3	7	0	21	19	80	95	12	46	49	49%	.322	10	1.76	6.03	5.31	6.64	10.8	1.4	5.0	5.1	-10.1	1.24

Breakout: 14% Improve: 42% Collapse: 18% Attrition: 6%   MLB: 4%   Comparables: Felix Montilla, Chris Lugo, Adrian Ramirez, Mike Johnson

A Texas high-schooler taken with the 20th pick in 2007, Withrow totaled just 13 innings in his first two seasons, due to elbow tenderness and a hand injury sustained while snorkeling (ignoring the PLEASE DON'T PET THE BLOWFISH signs, apparently). Finally healthy in 2009, he made up for lost time, ranking fourth in strikeout rate and homer rate among Cal League pitchers with at least 70 innings, though command of his power arsenal—including a fastball that can reach the mid-90s—was occasionally shaky, and an astronomical BABIP inflated his ERA. After blowing that popsicle stand, he made a solid showing in Chattanooga. He's definitely back on the radar, and the Dodgers feel he's got the potential to be a second or third starter.

Randy Wolf

Bats: L   Throws: L   Height: 5' 10"   Weight: 200   Born: August 22, 1976   Age: 33

YEAR	TEAM	LVL	AGE	W	L	SV	G	GS	IP	H	HR	BB	SO	GB%	BABIP	STUFF	WHIP	ERA	SIERA	DERA	EqH9	EqHR9	EqBB9	EqSO9	VORP	SN/WX
2007	LAN	MLB	30	9	6	0	18	18	102²	110	10	39	94	49%	.324	16	1.45	4.73	3.85	4.54	9.3	0.9	3.0	7.2	11.1	1.64
2008	SDN	MLB	31	6	10	0	21	21	119²	123	14	47	105	46%	.313	-9	1.42	4.74	3.97	5.49	10.2	1.6	3.2	6.5	0.1	2.18
2008	HOU	MLB	31	6	2	0	12	12	70²	68	7	24	57	41%	.292	13	1.30	3.57	4.09	4.09	8.8	0.9	2.7	6.2	10.9	1.89
2009	LAN	MLB	32	11	7	0	34	34	214¹	178	24	58	160	46%	.251	8	1.10	3.23	3.96	3.83	8.5	1.3	2.2	5.7	38.1	6.07
2010	MIL	MLB	33	9	11	0	31	31	167¹	171	23	59	124	46%	.299	4	1.37	4.49	4.27	4.95	9.5	1.2	2.9	6.0	10.2	2.61

Breakout: 5% Improve: 42% Collapse: 16% Attrition: 14%   MLB: 96%   Comparables: Jim Rooker, Jesse Petty, Ed Lopat, Ron Guidry

Despite a strong 2008 stretch run in Houston, Wolf had to settle for a one-year, $5 million deal (before incentives) to return to LA. It was money well spent, as he set personal bests for starts, innings, and ERA+ (122) while compiling his highest back-to-back season innings total since 2002-2003. Thanks in no small part to a league-low .254 BABIP (regression alert!), he finished a strong 11th in SNLVAR and tied for fourth in quality starts (24); at one point from late June to late September, he delivered at least six innings in 17 straight starts. Having dispelled some qualms about his fragility, Wolf hit the market as the second-best free-agent starter behind John Lackey, but even given the near certainty of his getting a multiyear deal somewhere, the Dodgers inexplicably didn't offer him arbitration, so they went uncompensated when he signed a three-year, $29.75 million contract with Milwaukee.

LINEOUTS

Hitters

PLAYER	TEAM	LVL	AGE	PA	R	2B	3B	HR	RBI	BB	SO	SB-CS	EqBRR	AVG/OBP/SLG	EqAVG/EqOBP/EqSLG	EqA	VORP	WARP
C B. Ausmus	LAN	MLB	40	107	9	4	0	1	9	5	21	1-0	-1.1	.295/.343/.368	.309/.356/.371	.266	4.6	0.5
1B S. Caseres*	SBR	A+	22	461	61	25	6	15	55	54	116	1-0	-0.7	.260/.360/.468	.235/.316/.387	.247	-6.8	-1.8
OF B. Cavazos-Galvez	OGD	Rk	22	323	59	29	3	18	63	10	43	17-8	-1.7	.322/.353/.618	.225/.244/.370	.210	-10.5	-2.4
C G. Erickson#	OGD	Rk	21	225	40	18	1	5	36	24	36	0-0	-1.3	.305/.378/.482	.222/.276/.319	.208	-2.8	-1.3
OF M. Jones	ABQ	AAA	31	434	72	26	3	35	103	40	102	9-3	-0.3	.297/.364/.651	.233/.293/.489	.261	8.6	0.2
	LAN	MLB	31	15	1	1	0	0	0	0	6	0-0	-0.1	.308/.400/.385	.308/.400/.385	.296	0.7	0.1
INF H. Luna	ABQ	AAA	29	350	59	18	6	17	62	28	52	4-2	0.0	.351/.414/.610	.281/.337/.478	.276	12.4	1.6
4C D. Mientkiewicz*	LAN	MLB	35	20	0	1	0	0	3	1	6	0-0	-0.1	.333/.400/.389	.333/.400/.389	.296	0.7	0.1
OF J. Repko	ABQ	AAA	28	433	70	20	4	16	47	28	81	24-7	4.1	.277/.329/.471	.220/.266/.368	.222	-6.1	-0.9

Due to a failure to communicate, **Brad Ausmus** wound up mentoring Russell Martin on the finer points of hitting, not catching. ⊘ **Steven Caseres** is a strapping, power-hitting lefty with major contact and platoon issues. Aside from an off-the-charts June (.444/.532/.857), he hit just .224/.325/.394. ⊘ The son of former Dodgers reliever Balvino Galvez, **Brian Cavazos-Galvez** led his league in six offensive categories, including homers and slugging percentage, and claimed MVP honors. ⊘ The son of a former minor-league catcher, **Gorman Erickson** is a late-blooming 15th-round 2006 pick with good receiving skills and a solid approach at the plate; he earned Pioneer League all-star honors. ⊘ Well into his 10th minor-league season, masher **Mitch Jones** finally got a cup of coffee—or at least a demitasse of espresso—in the majors. He joined the Braves on a minor-league contract. ⊘ A serviceable utilityman with a career .250 EqA in the majors, **Hector Luna** hasn't seen much of "The Show" over the past few years, because his body has thickened, costing him the range necessary to play shortstop. ⊘ A Torre favorite, **Doug Mientkiewicz** made the Opening Day roster, but soon dislocated his shoulder on a headfirst slide and spent most of the year on the DL. ⊘ **Jason Repko** continues to occupy a spot on the 40-man roster despite just 27 major-league plate appearances since 2006; his continued presence has cost the team more than one Rule 5 pick.

Pitchers

PLAYER	TEAM	LVL	AGE	W	L	SV	IP	H	HR	BB	SO	GB%	BABIP	STUFF	WHIP	ERA	SIERA	DERA	EqH9	EqHR9	EqBB9	EqSO9	VORP
J. Adkins*	CHT	AA	23	6	10	0	138²	144	8	72	81	57%	.297	-16	1.56	4.48	5.13	6.36	10.3	1.1	4.6	3.7	-12.8
A. Bastardo*	SBR	A+	25	6	2	0	75	73	6	23	71	55%	.322	-21	1.28	3.84	3.41	5.64	10.9	2.0	3.8	5.0	-1.1
	CHT	AA	25	6	3	0	72¹	72	6	30	58	56%	.308	-9	1.41	4.23	4.16	6.28	10.3	1.5	3.9	5.6	-5.9
N. Eovaldi	GRL	A	19	3	5	1	96¹	95	2	41	71	46%	.313	4	1.41	3.27	4.50	6.67	11.1	1.4	5.0	3.5	-11.2
J. Guerra	GRL	A	23	3	1	16	41	23	1	15	55	42%	.244	5	0.93	1.54	2.20	2.87	7.4	1.2	4.3	7.4	11.0
	CHT	AA	23	3	1	0	28¹	32	2	16	29	52%	.366	-2	1.69	4.13	3.97	5.81	12.0	1.4	5.1	7.2	-0.9
K. Jansen	SBR	A+	21	0	0	0	11²	14	1	11	19	34%	.481	10	2.14	4.63	3.41	6.30	14.4	2.7	10.8	9.0	-0.9
B. Leach*	CHT	AA	26	0	1	1	13	12	1	8	17	55%	.314	13	1.54	0.69	3.34	2.70	9.4	1.4	4.7	8.8	4.1
	ABQ	AAA	26	2	0	1	18²	17	2	16	20	57%	.306	3	1.77	6.75	4.44	7.85	8.3	1.0	7.4	8.3	-4.8
	LAN	MLB	26	2	0	1	20¹	16	3	12	19	59%	.245	-8	1.38	5.75	4.09	6.18	8.2	1.8	4.6	6.9	-1.5
W. Ohman*	LAN	MLB	31	1	0	1	12¹	12	4	8	7	29%	.229	-29	1.62	5.84	6.24	6.35	10.3	4.0	5.6	4.8	-1.1
J. Redding	GRL	A	21	16	3	0	133	149	9	39	96	49%	.322	-30	1.41	4.60	4.25	7.88	12.4	2.2	3.7	3.4	-32.1
J. Schmidt	LAN	MLB	36	2	2	0	17²	16	1	12	8	28%	.254	-17	1.58	5.60	6.91	6.37	8.7	0.5	5.1	3.1	-1.7

A supplemental 2007 first-rounder who was seen as a polished college lefty, **James Adkins** is shaping up as a bust, all too hittable and lacking in a true out pitch. ⊘ It's tough not to root for a little Venezuelan lefty to grow up to be "Albert the Bastard" at the big-league level, but ground-baller **Alberto Bastardo**'s progress has been slow; his future probably lies in the bullpen. ⊘ Tommy John surgery and a commitment to Texas A&M scared most teams off **Nathan Eovaldi**, but the Dodgers plucked him in the 11th round in 2008; he can pump his fastball into the mid-90s, but his secondary stuff is a work in progress. ⊘ **Javy Guerra** has taken his sweet time climbing the organizational ladder since being a fourth-round pick in '04; he's undersized, and his command lacking, but the Dodgers like his power arsenal and aggressive approach, particularly out of the bullpen. ⊘ The starting catcher on the upstart Netherlands World Baseball Classic squad, **Kenley Jansen** has a cannon-like arm, strong physique, and light hitting (.229/.311/.337 in five seasons), all of which prompted a conversion to the mound. His AFL stint drew raves, as he consistently reached 96-97 mph while demonstrating an improved feel for his slider. ⊘ Injuries to Kuo and Will Ohman opened the door for **Brent Leach** to demonstrate that he could fulfill a LOOGY role with the Dodgers, but lefties clobbered him at a .256/.360/.488 clip. ⊘ A durable LOOGY who averaged 72 games a year from 2005-2008 while holding lefty hitters to .189/.281/.315, **Will Ohman** was expected to fulfill a similar role in LA; instead, he was hit hard, had shoulder and elbow pain, and wound up undergoing surgery to clean up his acromioclavicular (AC) joint in late September. ⊘ A fifth-round 2008 pick, **Jon Michael Redding** is a strike-throwing machine with a moving 92-94 mph fastball and a solid slider; though he tied for the Midwest League lead in wins, he was hittable and had a below-average strikeout rate. ⊘ Additional surgery and painstaking rehab allowed **Jason Schmidt** one final ride, but his shoulder couldn't hold out long enough for him to get the per-inning cost of his three-year, $47 million deal down to $1 million. Expect retirement.

MANAGER: JOE TORRE

YEAR	TEAM	W-L	Pythag +/−	Avg PC	100+ P	120+ P	QS	BQS	REL	REL w Zero R	IBB	Subs	PH	PH Avg	PH HR	SB2	CS2	SB3	CS3	SAC Att	SAC %	POS SAC	Squeeze	Swing	In Play
2007	NYA	94-68	-5	90.8	39	0	75	9	522	326	33	33	98	.221	1	113	35	10	5	52	78.8%	39	1	190	145
2008	LAN	84-78	-3	90.9	47	1	78	3	460	295	58	88	275	.233	2	102	40	24	2	85	75.3%	22	10	143	115
2009	LAN	95-67	-5	93.4	54	2	79	2	526	366	68	32	260	.253	5	104	41	12	7	119	65.5%	32	0	153	125

In his second year at the Dodgers' helm, Torre guided the club to its highest win total since 1985 and to its first back-to-back NLCS appearances since 1977-1978. He deserves credit for demonstrating the same trademark unflappability that enabled him to survive 12 years under George Steinbrenner; his team didn't crumble in the face of losing Ramirez after a hot start. A closer look at Torre's tactics reveals a more mixed bag. His tendency to play the hot hand—Belliard over Hudson, or Padilla over Billingsley—may have cost the team its best shot in the NLCS. His over-reliance on hit-and-run plays—the Dodgers were second in the league in setting runners in motion—cost his team runs, as the team went just 19-for-42 in steals when batters swung and missed, the third-worst rate in the majors. At the same time, Torre nursed a rotation that tied for 23rd in the majors in the number of 100+ pitch outings to the fifth-highest SNLVAR total and ninth-highest quality start total. Showing a willingness to trust the relatively inexperienced arms of Troncoso and Belisario, he also used more relievers than all but two managers and got the majors' second-highest WXRL total. While his history of burning out reliable set-up men is certainly a bit ominous, Torre at least understands when he should have his best arms out on the mound, particularly when he deploys Broxton in the eighth inning à la Mariano Rivera. The bottom line is that Torre's teams have now made the postseason a record-tying 14 consecutive times, and though he's far from perfect, you can't divorce his teams' successes from his work with them.

Milwaukee Brewers

After suffering a dozen straight losing seasons, many of them under the control of a regime seemingly committed to benign neglect, the Milwaukee Brewers have won 80 or more games in four of the last five seasons and are once again a franchise worth paying attention to. Under the stewardship of general manager Doug Melvin since before the 2003 season, the Brewers have committed to building a winner from the ground up through minor-league player development, greatly abetted by the drafting acumen of former scouting director Jack Zduriencik. By slowly adding top-flight amateur talent and eschewing crippling long-term contracts for veterans who wouldn't be around for the eventual flowering of a Brew City renaissance, Milwaukee slowly improved from laughingstock to contender, culminating in a 2008 playoff appearance.

Their 2008 stretch run was a well-considered all-in play. Oft-injured ace Ben Sheets, in his contract year, was healthy and effective, and the Brewers were getting solid rotation efforts from journeyman Dave Bush and inconsistent youngster Manny Parra. At midseason, their young, homegrown offensive core (Prince Fielder, Ryan Braun, J. J. Hardy, Rickie Weeks, and Corey Hart) was hitting on all cylinders, except for Weeks, whose second-half surge would make up for Hart's September fade. The club's top prospect, Matt LaPorta, was a prodigious iron-gloved slugger blocked by Braun and Fielder; consequently, Melvin traded LaPorta for impending free-agent starter CC Sabathia, whose yeoman's work earned him Cy Young votes, and the club even took the unorthodox step of firing longtime skipper Ned Yost with two weeks left in the season, hoping to shake the team out of a late-season slump. It was the

right play, as Milwaukee won 90 games and a seat at the league's final table, but was knocked out in an NLDS showdown with eventual champion Philadelphia.

As frequently happens when you lose such a bet, the Brewers left themselves short-stacked going into 2009. Impressive youngster Yovani Gallardo, who had been lights-out prior to suffering a May knee injury, was on hand to fill one of the rotation slots left open by the departed Sabathia and Sheets, but Melvin would still need to scare up another starter. Eric Gagne, brought in to close, had been a disaster and was only the most famous member of a bullpen in need of a complete makeover. Interim manager Dale Sveum, who had piloted the team down the stretch, was quickly replaced by the more experienced Ken Macha, but there was more turmoil when Zduriencik left to helm the Seattle front office and pitching coach Mike Maddux was hired away by the Rangers. Maddux was an underrated commodity who had repeatedly managed to spin gold, or at least silver, out of the cut-rate pitching straw he had often been handed, and as it turned out, he would be sorely missed.

To cover these holes, Melvin went into the offseason desperately short on spackle. With LaPorta gone, there were few trade chits on hand, and while Zduriencik had left the minor-league larder stocked with his typical collection of offensive talent, a complete dearth of pitching in the upper minors meant that Milwaukee would need to find a starter and bullpen help elsewhere, and at bargain prices. In 2004, the last year of Selig ownership before new owner Mark Attanasio came on the scene, Milwaukee's $27 million payroll was baseball's lowest. As the team improved and atten-

BREWERS PROSPECTUS
2009 W-L: 80-82, 3rd in NL Central

Pythag	74-88	12th
RS/G	4.9	3rd
RA/G	5.1	15th
EqA	.273	1st
EqBRR	-9.5	13th
SNWP	.438	16th
WXRL	8.1	9th
FRAr	4.23	7th
DE	.688	11th
PADE	-1.57	12th
Salary	$80.2	9th
Attend	3.04	6th

Ballpark: Miller Park (3-yr. PF: 968). Bland dome with a hood you can pop, helps pitchers

2009: The pitching beyond Hoffman and Gallardo was a disaster, plus Triple-H flops (Hardy, Hart, Hall)

2010: Reconfigured defense and staff should give the offense chances to win games

Action Items: Betting on renewed health for Weeks and a breakout for Gomez? Yeah, good luck

dance increased, Attanasio plowed money back into the franchise until the Brewers' payroll reached a mid-pack $80 million in 2008, but the economic downturn and the limits imposed by playing in one of baseball's smallest television markets meant Attanasio would have to draw the line there.

With such limited scratch, Melvin had his pick of the old, the infirm, and the stuff-deficient to fill out his staff, and his recent history with free-agent pitchers has been spotty at best. In addition to the $10 million he gambled on Gagne, Melvin decided in 2006 to pay $42 million over four years for a close-up view of Jeff Suppan's slow fade to black, and then committed $13 million for three years of middling reliever David Riske starting in 2007. So fans crossed their fingers when the Brewers inked 41-year-old closer Trevor Hoffman to head the bullpen and the Dave Duncan reclamation project Braden Looper to fill out the rotation, while Melvin crossed his fingers that longtime bullpen coach Bill Castro, now promoted to pitching coach, could keep the questionable back of the rotation producing at a useful level.

The 2009 season started well enough, with the offense scoring runs by the bushel, the patched-over rotation holding up its end, and Hoffman closing things out with a vengeance—the future Hall of Famer converted his first 15 save chances without giving up a run, holding batters to a ridiculous .129/.143/.288 line in the process. Milwaukee took over the NL Central lead in mid-May and worked its way to 10 games over .500 by the end of the month. Then cracks started to appear. Brewers pitching posted monthly ERAs of 5.37, 5.67, and 5.18 from June through August, numbers the still-potent offense couldn't overcome. The rest of the Central was also treading water through much of the summer, and the Crew sniffed first place as late as Independence Day before the weight of its rotation woes dragged it below the .500 mark by mid-August. The club finished at 80-82 and failed to record a third straight winning record for the first time since its early-1980s heyday.

While the pitching was bad in aggregate, giving up more runs than any NL team save the Nationals, the bullpen was actually a bargain. Hoffman provided exceptional work all season, Todd Coffey thrived in the set-up role, and inexpensive options Mitch Stetter and Mark DiFelice provided situational effectiveness. It was the bottom of the rotation that sank the Brewers' season—and the bottom of Milwaukee's rotation includes everyone not named Gallardo. As hoped, the 23-year-old came back from knee surgery to replace Sheets as the staff ace, striking out more than a man per inning

and posting a 4.9 SNLVAR, but Looper joined Suppan as a free-agent disaster. The other rotation holdovers, Bush and Parra, somehow managed to be even worse, with Parra's -24.1 VORP qualifying as the largest self-inflicted wound in all of baseball last year. Despite Gallardo's best efforts, Brewers starters posted a league-worst 8.0 SNLVAR and 5.37 ERA. Some of this can be attributed to a defensive decline, as the Brewers dropped from sixth to 12th in the league in Park Adjusted Defensive Efficiency, but mostly it was just a case of poor pitchers pitching poorly.

The offense wasn't quite able to overcome such a daily dose of mound disaster, but was still good enough to be cast in bronze. The Crew finished third in the league in runs, home runs, walks, on-base percentage, and slugging percentage, led as usual by the slugging duo of Fielder and Braun. Both young superstars set career highs in EqA, VORP, and WARP, and both managed to significantly improve their performance against same-side pitching, eliminating the last perceived weaknesses in their offensive games. Braun is already signed to a very reasonable contract that will keep him in Milwaukee through 2015, but Fielder's shakier 2008 caused management to take a more cautious approach, signing him to a two-year extension through 2010 and leaving him eligible for a huge arbitration payday for 2011, after which he can walk. Fielder may be pricing himself out of Milwaukee, and the decision on what to do with him will be Melvin's biggest challenge.

The other three members of Milwaukee's home-grown batting core took steps backward, however, clouding their futures and, by reflection, that of the franchise. Weeks got off to a terrific start, leading some to think the mercurial second sacker had finally turned the corner, when yet another wrist injury sidelined him for the year. He's two years from free agency and still an enigma. Hart continued a precipitous decline from his 2007 peak and is in danger of losing his starting gig or being traded—fates that have already befallen shortstop J. J. Hardy, who struggled at the plate, was sent down in favor of slick-fielding phenom Alcides Escobar, and was eventually traded to Minnesota for speedy center fielder Carlos Gomez.

The Brewers were able to patch over these struggles last year, but it will be harder to do so going forward. Weeks was initially replaced by rookie Casey McGehee, a rookie with an adept glove who came out of nowhere to eventually elbow struggling third baseman Bill Hall out of town. Now 27, McGehee will come to camp as the starter, but we've probably just seen his career year. He'll be pushed by top prospect Mat Gamel, a good-hit/no-field player whose left-handedness is a rarity in the Brewers' lineup and may be given a look-see in right if Hart can't exorcise the demons in his bat. Craig Counsell and trade deadline acquisition Felipe Lopez provided on-base ability and lineup balance; the combination of Counsell, Lopez, and McGehee, along with improvements by Braun and Hart, helped the Brewers increase their on-base percentage against right-handers from .317 (15th in the NL) to .336 (sixth). Counsell re-signed for 2010, but Lopez is gone, making the need for Gamel's lefty bat even more pressing.

Despite the struggles of Weeks and Hart and the departure of Hardy, it's reasonable to believe that the Brewers will develop cheaper alternatives to replace them. Milwaukee has gotten more production from homegrown batting talent than has any other team in the league. During the 2009 season, amateur players drafted or signed by the Brewers since 2000 produced a total of 25.4 WARP for the big club, with 22.5 WARP coming from position players—the most in baseball (see Table 1). This is not unique to last season, as it was true in 2008 and also in aggregate throughout the decade.

Table 1. Lay on the Brats: 2009 Production from Homegrown Players (drafted 2000-2009)

Top Ten Teams	Total WARP	Batter WARP	Pitcher WARP	Batter WARP %	PA	IP
Red Sox	32.5	14.0	18.5	43%	2071	511
Twins	32.1	19.2	12.9	60%	2225	706
Rockies	31.0	21.3	9.7	69%	4382	264
Giants	31.0	7.3	23.7	24%	2016	728
Dodgers	29.7	16.2	13.5	55%	1987	686
Angels	25.8	13.2	12.6	51%	2469	642
Brewers	25.4	22.5	2.9	89%	2845	375
Phillies	25.3	15.6	9.7	62%	1410	392
Royals	21.0	9.8	11.2	47%	2012	383
Diamondbacks	19.6	16.2	3.4	83%	2915	215

Conversely, it's difficult to believe that the Brewers will develop ready alternatives to help fill out their rotation, as few teams have developed less pitching than Milwaukee. Milwaukee's 2.9 WARP from young homegrown pitchers last year ranked 22nd in the league, their aggregate for the decade ranks 23rd, and there are currently no top pitching prospects in the upper minors, though new scouting director Bruce Seid spent last year's number one on Eric Arnett, the first college pitcher drafted with the Brewers' first pick since Ben Sheets in 1999. The Brewers have hired former A's and Mets pitching coach Rick Peterson to right the ship, and held an organization-wide pitching symposium this offseason, but those are mostly long-term solutions that won't provide much help this year.

Given the dearth of pitching options in the system and their recent failures in the free-agent budget bin, the Brewers decided they needed to shop uptown to fill out the rotation. To afford this, they freed up roughly $12 million by trading Hardy for Gomez, waving good-bye to veteran center fielder Mike Cameron, and installing Escobar and Gomez in the starting lineup. This makes the Brewers faster, cheaper, and younger at two up-the-middle positions, but at a significant cost to the offense. Both Escobar and Gomez are defensive prodigies with speed to burn, but they've shown little power and are only an incremental improvement over Hardy and Cameron in the field. Gomez is young and was once highly touted, but has a career line of .246/.292/.346 in over a thousand major-league plate appearances. Escobar is even younger and shows more promise at the plate, but will need to adjust to big-league pitching. Expecting them to hit enough to keep the Brewers in the top tier of NL offenses may be a wishcast too far, and best left to Brewers fans.

The money saved by ditching Hardy and Cameron went toward signing starter Randy Wolf for a seemingly reasonable roughly $30 million over three years. The veteran lefty is coming off a fine season in Los Angeles, appears to have put his injury woes behind him, and is certainly a cut above the Suppan/Looper class of free-agent starter regrets. The Brewers' rotation is in such dire straits that even replacement-level pitching would be an improvement, so Wolf will make a huge difference slotted in behind Gallardo. Melvin seems to be betting that Wolf's addition will help the team's run prevention significantly more than the arrival of Escobar and Gomez will hurt the offense, but there's a lot of risk in that plan. Wolf is a solid starter, but he's 33 years old, he's not an ace, and he's probably coming off his best season.

All of which leaves the Brewers needing to improve via better production from Parra, Bush, or Suppan—the same plan that led to last year's Vesuvian mound cataclysm. Sure, it could happen, and the offense could keep on keepin' on despite a few extra-out-makers in the lineup, but odds are that Melvin's off-season moves have merely robbed Peter (Vuckovich) to pay Paul (Molitor). Such are the challenges of winning with a small-market franchise: everything needs to come together perfectly if you want to have a big year. Until the Brewers can achieve that rare synchronicity, which is likely to require the development of some homegrown pitching talent, the team will continue to hover around the .500 mark, seemingly too smart to get much worse and too poor to get much better.

HITTERS

Ryan Braun LF

Bats: R Throws: R Height: 6' 1" Weight: 200 Born: November 17, 1983 Age: 26

YEAR	TEAM	LVL	AGE	PA	R	2B	3B	HR	RBI	BB	SO	SB	CS	EqBRR	AVG	OBP	SLG	EqAVG	EqOBP	EqSLG	EqA	VORP	WARP	DEFENSE	
2007	NAS	AAA	23	134	28	12	0	10	22	15	11	4	3	0.7	.342	.418	.701	.319	.393	.622	.323	13.1	1.5	29-3B	0
2007	MIL	MLB	23	492	91	26	6	34	97	29	112	15	5	1.2	.324	.370	.634	.336	.382	.657	.328	53.3	2.2	106-3B	-29
2008	MIL	MLB	24	663	92	39	7	37	106	42	129	14	4	1.3	.285	.335	.553	.297	.344	.574	.300	45.1	5.8	146-LF	8
2009	MIL	MLB	25	708	113	39	6	32	114	57	121	20	6	0.4	.320	.386	.551	.346	.407	.593	.329	72.6	7.2	154-LF	-6
2010	MIL	MLB	26	693	110	37	6	39	119	60	126	20	8	0.6	.298	.369	.562	.306	.373	.572	.313	58.9	6.3	154-LF	1

Breakout: 10% Improve: 44% Collapse: 5% Attrition: 2%   MLB: 100%   Comparables: Al Simmons, Joe Medwick, Del Ennis, Frank Robinson

Here's a scary thought: Braun became a better, more rounded player in 2009 and is just now about to enter his peak. The slugging left fielder led the NL with 203 hits; raised his batting average, walk rate, and OBP; lowered his strikeouts; stole more bases; grounded into fewer double plays; held his slugging percentage steady; and got on base at a high rate against right-handed pitching. His glove in left field is still a work in progress, but he's not a statue out there, and he teamed with Prince Fielder to put up a combined 148.2 VORP, making them the most productive duo in baseball. Braun just turned 26 and will be a Brewer through 2015 at eminently reasonable prices. Pitchers, be afraid. Be very afraid.

Mike Cameron CF

Bats: R Throws: R Height: 6' 2" Weight: 200 Born: January 8, 1973 Age: 37

YEAR	TEAM	LVL	AGE	PA	R	2B	3B	HR	RBI	BB	SO	SB	CS	EqBRR	AVG	OBP	SLG	EqAVG	EqOBP	EqSLG	EqA	VORP	WARP	DEFENSE	
2007	SDN	MLB	34	651	88	33	6	21	78	67	160	18	5	4.3	.242	.328	.431	.263	.349	.463	.279	32.7	2.7	146-CF	-8
2008	MIL	MLB	35	508	69	25	2	25	70	54	142	17	5	-0.8	.243	.331	.477	.257	.341	.502	.283	28.3	3.2	118-CF	2
2009	MIL	MLB	36	628	78	32	3	24	70	75	156	7	3	0.1	.250	.342	.452	.270	.355	.488	.286	36.5	4.7	143-CF	5
2010	BOS	MLB	37	528	69	26	2	20	65	55	137	10	6	0.4	.245	.331	.438	.241	.327	.424	.255	13.2	1.4	123-CF	0

Breakout: 6% Improve: 31% Collapse: 22% Attrition: 21%   MLB: 97%   Comparables: Reggie Sanders, Frank Robinson, Ron Gant, Hank Sauer

At age 37, Cameron continues to play a superlative center field and provides continuing value at the plate, drawing walks, hitting home runs, and posting low batting averages due to a high strikeout rate. How long he can thumb his nose at Father Time is an open question, as a drop in stolen bases and an increase in double plays points to a loss of speed, and his .244/.318/.430 line against righties continues a worrisome trend. Cameron certainly earned his sizable paycheck in Milwaukee, but the acquisition of Carlos Gomez made letting him leave as a free agent easier. The Red Sox signed him to a two-year deal worth between $15 and $16 million with the intention of upgrading their miserable 2009 outfield defense. Since Jacoby Ellsbury plays center field as if he were lost in a hedge maze, the Red Sox will reap huge benefits by letting Cameron push the younger man to left field.

Frank Catalanotto OF

Bats: L Throws: R Height: 6' 0" Weight: 205 Born: April 27, 1974 Age: 36

YEAR	TEAM	LVL	AGE	PA	R	2B	3B	HR	RBI	BB	SO	SB	CS	EqBRR	AVG	OBP	SLG	EqAVG	EqOBP	EqSLG	EqA	VORP	WARP	DEFENSE			
2007	TEX	MLB	33	377	52	20	4	11	44	28	37	2	1	-0.5	.260	.337	.444	.261	.338	.448	.268	9.3	0.9	55-LF	-3	11-1B	1
2008	TEX	MLB	34	278	28	23	1	2	21	20	29	1	1	0.7	.274	.342	.399	.279	.349	.413	.264	4.3	-0.1	25-1B	0	19-LF	-5
2009	MIL	MLB	35	162	18	6	3	1	9	14	23	2	0	0.8	.278	.346	.382	.292	.356	.396	.268	3.6	0.9	26-RF	4	4-LF	0
2010	MIL	MLB	36	233	26	13	2	4	21	21	32	1	1	0.1	.262	.344	.408	.267	.347	.410	.266	6.5	1.1	40-RF	3		

Breakout: 6% Improve: 39% Collapse: 21% Attrition: 29%   MLB: 94%   Comparables: Heinie Manush, Ken Griffey, Jim Eisenreich, Goose Goslin

Frankie the Cat has been a likable player throughout a surprisingly long and productive career, but the end is near. When he was released by Texas at the end of spring training, the Brewers lit on him as a cheap lefty bat to help balance their bench. They were rewarded with a decent OBP against righties, but little else. Catalanotto retains his discriminating eye at the plate, but has little power and no speed and is a defensive liability in the outfield. He's now a free agent with few suitors, but it sure was fun while it lasted.

Craig Counsell — INF

Bats: L   Throws: R   Height: 6' 0"   Weight: 180   Born: August 21, 1970   Age: 39

YEAR	TEAM	LVL	AGE	PA	R	2B	3B	HR	RBI	BB	SO	SB	CS	EqBRR	AVG	OBP	SLG	EqAVG	EqOBP	EqSLG	EqA	VORP	WARP	DEFENSE				
2007	MIL	MLB	36	334	31	12	2	3	24	41	47	4	2	-1.0	.220	.323	.309	.223	.326	.307	.233	-0.3	1.0	33-3B	7	22-2B	-2	
2008	MIL	MLB	37	302	31	14	1	1	14	46	42	3	1	0.9	.226	.355	.302	.234	.359	.310	.251	4.5	1.5	30-3B	-2	21-SS	6	
2009	MIL	MLB	38	459	61	22	8	4	39	42	54	3	4	-0.4	.285	.357	.408	.306	.374	.442	.280	23.6	4.6	45-2B	11	29-3B	1	
2010	MIL	MLB	39	323	36	14	2	3	23	36	57	2	2	-0.1	.239	.336	.340	.244	.341	.344	.245	4.7	0.9	55-2B	4			

Breakout: 6%   Improve: 26%   Collapse: 28%   Attrition: 42%   MLB: 95%   Comparables: Jim Gantner, Ken Williams, Graig Nettles, Dave Concepcion

For years, fans have watched Counsell work himself into that contorted Apple Bonker imitation at the plate and asked themselves how he can hit like that, and until recently the answer has been "he can't." At hitting coach Dale Sveum's urging, Counsell adopted a more conventional approach; the result has been fewer two-hoppers, more gappers, and a career-high EqA last year. A free agent at season's end, Counsell simply re-signed a one-year deal in December. His plus infield defense and patient approach ensure he'll be a valuable reserve even if his offense regresses and a bargain if his improvement at the plate is real.

Kentrail Davis — CF

Bats: L   Throws: R   Height: 5' 9"   Weight: 195   Born: June 29, 1988   Age: 22

Did Not Play

Breakout: 6%   Improve: 26%   Collapse: 28%   Attrition: 42%   MLB: 95%   Comparables: NA

Projected as an early first-round pick in 2009 before a bad sophomore season at the University of Tennessee lowered his stock, Davis fell to the Brewers at the 39th overall pick and signed too late to play. His stocky build, speed, and power potential have drawn numerous Kirby Puckett comparisons, and the organization has been impressed with his work in their instructional league. Doubters fear he won't have the range for center, the arm for right, the on-base skills for the top of the order, or the power to be a run producer. Professional pitchers will soon weigh in with their opinion, and until that happens, everyone's just speculatin' about a hypothesis.

Alcides Escobar — SS

Bats: R   Throws: R   Height: 6' 1"   Weight: 175   Born: December 16, 1986   Age: 23

YEAR	TEAM	LVL	AGE	PA	R	2B	3B	HR	RBI	BB	SO	SB	CS	EqBRR	AVG	OBP	SLG	EqAVG	EqOBP	EqSLG	EqA	VORP	WARP	DEFENSE				
2007	BRV	A+	20	283	37	8	3	0	25	7	35	18	10	-0.6	.325	.345	.377	.307	.324	.352	.238	3.7	0.6	61-SS	1			
2007	HUN	AA	20	245	27	5	4	1	28	11	36	4	3	-1.3	.283	.314	.354	.265	.290	.326	.216	-1.6	-0.2	59-SS	0			
2008	HUN	AA	21	597	95	24	5	8	76	31	82	34	8	5.4	.328	.363	.434	.305	.332	.404	.260	23.7	4.1	125-SS	10			
2009	NAS	AAA	22	487	76	24	6	4	34	32	65	42	10	5.9	.298	.353	.409	.290	.339	.397	.261	20.0	2.9	100-SS	6	7-2B	-2	
2009	MIL	MLB	22	134	20	3	1	1	11	4	18	4	2	2.2	.304	.333	.368	.325	.353	.389	.260	5.1	0.5	34-SS	-1			
2010	MIL	MLB	23	590	76	27	5	7	54	34	98	20	9	2.0	.275	.320	.376	.284	.327	.383	.248	13.4	1.8	134-SS	3			

Breakout: 13%   Improve: 50%   Collapse: 15%   Attrition: 6%   MLB: 57%   Comparables: Luis Mercedes, Carlos Garcia, Brian Hunter, Rusty Tillman

Milwaukee's shortstop of the future has finally arrived, his role cemented by the off-season trade of incumbent J. J. Hardy last fall. Escobar is an exciting talent, a defensive whiz with a flair for the dramatic and the ability to steal 40 bases if he gets enough chances. Alas, there's the rub. As with so many young shortstops, his offensive approach is a work in progress. Speed keeps his BABIP and batting average high, but a subpar walk rate undermines his OBP and may keep him from hitting at the top of the order. Since he is only 23, the organization thinks he still has room to develop better plate discipline and a little more pop, and he'll need to improve against right-handed pitching. Even if that doesn't happen (and it almost never does), his outstanding glove work ensures he'll be an asset, and for a franchise typically loaded with prospects whose best position is "hitter," that's a welcome relief. He's Orlando Cabrera with more speed and a higher batting average, and that's a very good player.

Prince Fielder — 1B

Bats: L   Throws: R   Height: 5' 11"   Weight: 270   Born: May 9, 1984   Age: 26

YEAR	TEAM	LVL	AGE	PA	R	2B	3B	HR	RBI	BB	SO	SB	CS	EqBRR	AVG	OBP	SLG	EqAVG	EqOBP	EqSLG	EqA	VORP	WARP	DEFENSE
2007	MIL	MLB	23	681	109	35	2	50	119	90	121	2	2	-2.8	.288	.395	.618	.292	.399	.622	.330	63.7	6.0	150-1B -8
2008	MIL	MLB	24	694	86	30	2	34	102	84	134	3	2	-7.2	.276	.372	.507	.285	.376	.519	.302	40.8	3.5	154-1B -8
2009	MIL	MLB	25	719	103	35	3	46	141	110	138	2	3	-5.3	.299	.412	.602	.323	.426	.650	.346	75.6	7.2	162-1B -9
2010	MIL	MLB	26	725	109	33	2	51	140	101	136	3	4	-2.7	.290	.402	.601	.291	.402	.590	.333	71.7	7.1	155-1B -4

Breakout: 15%   Improve: 57%   Collapse: 5%   Attrition: 3%   MLB: 100%   Comparables: Jim Thome, Mo Vaughn, Johnny Mize, Fred McGriff

At this point, it should be mandatory to refer to Cecil Fielder as Prince's father rather than describing Prince as Cecil's son, since Prince will have surpassed his dad's career WARP count of 20.9, amassed in a productive 1,470-game career, in a little over half the time. Fielder bounced back from a comparatively pedestrian 2008 to cement his place as the best non-Pujols first baseman in the NL, and like Ryan Braun, he improved virtually every aspect of his game—drawing more walks, mashing lefties as well as righties, and flashing what some metrics and most observers see as a much-improved glove. Unlike Braun, Fielder is not signed up long-term with the Brewers, and now he may have priced himself out of Milwaukee. With Fielder under the team's control for two more years but headed for a huge arbitration payday in 2011, the decision about whether to sign Fielder, trade him, or let him walk may be the toughest one Melvin will ever make.

Mat Gamel — 3B

Bats: L   Throws: R   Height: 6' 0"   Weight: 195   Born: July 26, 1985   Age: 24

YEAR	TEAM	LVL	AGE	PA	R	2B	3B	HR	RBI	BB	SO	SB	CS	EqBRR	AVG	OBP	SLG	EqAVG	EqOBP	EqSLG	EqA	VORP	WARP	DEFENSE
2007	BRV	A+	21	534	78	37	8	9	60	58	98	14	7	-4.0	.300	.378	.472	.278	.347	.440	.272	17.8	-0.7	112-3B -24
2008	HUN	AA	22	572	96	35	7	19	96	55	111	6	7	-0.6	.329	.395	.537	.292	.345	.478	.279	25.9	1.9	126-3B -10
2009	NAS	AAA	23	320	42	18	1	11	48	38	89	1	0	-2.9	.278	.367	.473	.263	.342	.446	.274	13.4	1.4	73-3B -2
2009	MIL	MLB	23	148	11	6	1	5	20	18	54	1	0	0.0	.242	.338	.422	.258	.347	.461	.276	5.7	0.2	22-3B -4
2010	MIL	MLB	24	487	59	26	3	14	59	46	137	4	2	-1.1	.252	.326	.418	.254	.328	.415	.261	13.3	0.8	105-3B -6

Breakout: 9%   Improve: 34%   Collapse: 16%   Attrition: 5%   MLB: 59%   Comparables: Troy O'Leary, Scott Moore, John Vander Wal, Steve DeAngelis

Gamel is the latest prospect to arrive at Miller Park best suited for the "hitter" position, boasting a solid eye, decent power, and left-handedness, all of which can help the Brewers' lineup. The question is, where will he play? If he's left at third base, the acts of butchery he's liable to commit will require Brewers broadcasts again to sport a TV-MA rating, not long after getting the parental blocks removed by exiling Braun's ball-aversion techniques to left field. Gamel's bat could be an upgrade on the degraded version of Corey Hart manning right field, but he has never played the outfield. However this latest round of Positional Plinko turns out, if the Brewers can find a way to work him in, the reward will be 20 home runs and a solid on-base percentage—production well worth the trouble.

Jody Gerut — OF

Bats: L   Throws: L   Height: 6' 0"   Weight: 210   Born: September 18, 1977   Age: 32

YEAR	TEAM	LVL	AGE	PA	R	2B	3B	HR	RBI	BB	SO	SB	CS	EqBRR	AVG	OBP	SLG	EqAVG	EqOBP	EqSLG	EqA	VORP	WARP	DEFENSE	
2008	POR	AAA	30	123	22	9	2	5	18	13	11	4	1	1.2	.308	.382	.570	.282	.341	.464	.277	4.4	0.5	20-RF 0	
2008	SDN	MLB	30	356	46	15	4	14	43	28	52	6	4	-1.6	.296	.351	.494	.328	.379	.544	.304	28.7	3.9	67-CF 6	7-RF 0
2009	SDN	MLB	31	121	17	6	0	4	14	5	22	2	0	2.0	.221	.248	.381	.241	.264	.420	.234	-0.2	0.2	21-CF 4	3-RF -2
2009	MIL	MLB	31	177	23	7	0	5	21	14	21	4	2	-1.9	.236	.299	.373	.255	.316	.398	.246	0.7	-0.4	20-RF 0	13-CF -4
2010	MIL	MLB	32	394	55	20	2	15	49	32	63	6	4	-0.1	.275	.336	.463	.279	.339	.455	.276	19.3	2.4	77-CF 2	

Breakout: 7%   Improve: 36%   Collapse: 16%   Attrition: 15%   MLB: 92%   Comparables: Claudell Washington, Gary Varsho, David Newhan, B.J. Surhoff

Gerut's return from two seasons lost to injury was one of the feel-good stories of 2008, but he got off to a cold start for the Pads in 2009. In a bizarre twist on the old "play me or trade me" line, the Brewers traded for Gerut six weeks into the season and decided not to play him. In his first three months in Milwaukee, Gerut started only seven games despite Corey Hart's struggles and suffered the indignity of having to sit in favor of Frank Catalanotto while Hart was on the DL. Finally given more regular playing time down the stretch, Gerut responded with a .278/.340/.474 line. A fine defensive player and a lefty bat on a roster with a starboard-side lean, he stands a good chance of breaking camp as a spare outfielder as long as the Brewers take the time to find out what he has left instead of studiously ignoring him.

Caleb Gindl   OF

Bats: L   Throws: L   Height: 5' 9"   Weight: 185   Born: August 31, 1988   Age: 21

YEAR	TEAM	LVL	AGE	PA	R	2B	3B	HR	RBI	BB	SO	SB	CS	EqBRR	AVG	OBP	SLG	EqAVG	EqOBP	EqSLG	EqA	VORP	WARP	DEFENSE		
2007	HEL	Rk	18	231	40	22	3	5	42	20	38	4	4	-2.2	.372	.420	.580	.299	.342	.450	.272	7.0	0.8	50-RF	-2	
2008	WVA	A	19	578	86	38	4	13	81	63	144	14	5	0.5	.307	.388	.474	.248	.321	.383	.247	3.3	0.8	116-RF	4	17-CF -1
2009	BRV	A+	20	462	61	15	3	17	71	57	92	18	4	-1.8	.277	.363	.459	.263	.338	.427	.268	12.7	1.6	91-RF	0	6-CF 1
2010	MIL	MLB	21	463	55	24	2	12	56	46	127	7	3	-0.2	.251	.327	.408	.254	.329	.406	.260	9.8	1.1	103-RF	0	

Breakout: 17% Improve: 56% Collapse: 11% Attrition: 3%   MLB: 4%   Comparables: Anthony Collier, Chito Martinez, Xavier Paul, Matt Sulentic

Gindl continues to show his many doubters that he can flat-out play. Spending the year in a pitchers' league, the pint-sized outfielder managed to hit more home runs, steal more bases, and improve both his walk and his strike-out rates. Gindl displays an advanced approach that should help him survive the big jump to Double-A, and the organization loves his attitude and work ethic. His upside is limited not so much by his size as his defensive range and arm, which will probably limit him to left field in the majors, though the organization believes he wouldn't be a disaster in center. The longer he succeeds, the easier it becomes to believe he can channel Frank Catalanotto's career.

J. J. Hardy   SS

Bats: R   Throws: R   Height: 6' 2"   Weight: 190   Born: August 19, 1982   Age: 27

YEAR	TEAM	LVL	AGE	PA	R	2B	3B	HR	RBI	BB	SO	SB	CS	EqBRR	AVG	OBP	SLG	EqAVG	EqOBP	EqSLG	EqA	VORP	WARP	DEFENSE
2007	MIL	MLB	24	638	89	30	1	26	80	40	73	2	3	-1.2	.277	.323	.463	.284	.331	.471	.269	30.6	3.3	143-SS -2
2008	MIL	MLB	25	629	78	31	4	24	74	52	98	2	1	-1.3	.283	.343	.478	.294	.351	.492	.285	43.2	6.2	141-SS 11
2009	NAS	AAA	26	74	7	2	0	4	12	3	9	0	0	0.2	.254	.284	.451	.239	.270	.394	.226	0.0	-0.5	16-SS -4
2009	MIL	MLB	26	465	53	16	2	11	47	43	85	0	1	-0.7	.229	.302	.357	.244	.310	.379	.242	9.7	1.9	107-SS 6
2010	MIN	MLB	27	607	80	26	2	25	78	49	88	1	2	-0.5	.276	.335	.466	.273	.333	.457	.265	24.6	2.9	138-SS 2

Breakout: 11% Improve: 46% Collapse: 4% Attrition: 3%   MLB: 97%   Comparables: Joe Cronin, Puddin' Head Jones, Glenn Wright, Chris Speier

And then there were two. Hardy joined Corey Hart and the injured Rickie Weeks as major disappointments in 2009, leaving Fielder and Braun as the only Brewers in good standing in the Young Slugger Corps. As usual, Hardy played stellar defense and struggled against right-handed pitching, but his power inexplicably evaporated, and he was helpless (.169/.310/.229) against the portsiders he has traditionally punished (.299/.374/.564 career through 2008). Rate stat excavators can point to a low line-drive rate and a drop in his BABIP, but the simple fact is Hardy just didn't make much hard contact. Traded to Minnesota to make room for the much-cheaper Alcides Escobar, Hardy has an outstanding glove that will make him a valuable addition to the Twins' roster, but while he's a good bet to improve on his woeful 2008 numbers, a return to All-Star production with the bat isn't likely, given his career-long struggle to hit right-handers (.256/.309/.401).

Corey Hart   RF

Bats: R   Throws: R   Height: 6' 6"   Weight: 220   Born: March 24, 1982   Age: 28

YEAR	TEAM	LVL	AGE	PA	R	2B	3B	HR	RBI	BB	SO	SB	CS	EqBRR	AVG	OBP	SLG	EqAVG	EqOBP	EqSLG	EqA	VORP	WARP	DEFENSE	
2007	MIL	MLB	25	566	86	33	9	24	81	36	99	23	7	2.8	.295	.353	.539	.305	.361	.550	.302	39.5	5.4	97-RF	7 26-CF 1
2008	MIL	MLB	26	657	76	45	6	20	91	27	109	23	7	3.7	.268	.300	.459	.278	.307	.473	.266	17.1	2.4	153-RF	4
2009	MIL	MLB	27	472	64	24	3	12	48	43	92	11	6	0.8	.260	.335	.418	.281	.352	.452	.274	17.3	2.0	105-RF	1
2010	MIL	MLB	28	574	76	33	6	19	78	44	104	17	7	1.3	.272	.340	.469	.279	.343	.474	.280	25.7	3.1	133-RF	2

Breakout: 9% Improve: 45% Collapse: 5% Attrition: 3%   MLB: 98%   Comparables: Alex Rios, Moises Alou, Richard Hidalgo, Gary Matthews

His 2007 breakout season already fading in the rearview mirror, Hart struggled through another difficult year and continues to look lost at the plate. Many blamed his 2008 collapse on an overly aggressive approach, so at the organization's behest, Hart made adjustments, laying off pitches out of the zone, swinging less, and working deeper counts. His walk rate more than doubled, but his strikeout rate also increased and his isolated power plunged. This new approach was clearly a Faustian bargain, allowing Hart to post a .336 OBP against righties—the best of his career—while leaving him especially punchless (.248/.333/.356) against the lefties he has traditionally feasted on. The cost-conscious Brewers are shopping him, but wherever he lands, his employer might be best served by letting him hack away in search of his lost power stroke.

Adam Heether UT

Bats: R Throws: R Height: 6' 0" Weight: 190 Born: January 14, 1982 Age: 28

YEAR	TEAM	LVL	AGE	PA	R	2B	3B	HR	RBI	BB	SO	SB	CS	EqBRR	AVG	OBP	SLG	EqAVG	EqOBP	EqSLG	EqA	VORP	WARP	DEFENSE		
2007	HUN	AA	25	491	60	27	5	9	62	51	89	2	6	-4.3	.299	.371	.447	.267	.324	.386	.248	4.1	0.9	116-3B	3	
2008	NAS	AAA	26	471	70	31	2	11	51	64	89	11	1	0.4	.272	.383	.446	.253	.347	.392	.265	16.7	1.9	54-SS	2	46-3B -3
2009	HUN	AA	27	45	5	3	0	2	12	1	10	0	0	-0.5	.325	.356	.550	.262	.283	.381	.235	0.7	0.2	7-SS	1	
2009	NAS	AAA	27	452	62	29	1	16	59	59	84	5	1	0.9	.293	.400	.501	.274	.367	.449	.284	23.9	2.0	61-3B	2	15-LF -1
2010	MIL	MLB	28	437	43	22	1	8	42	43	105	3	2	-0.5	.238	.322	.360	.246	.327	.373	.244	3.9	0.5	90-3B	0	

Breakout: 6% Improve: 31% Collapse: 34% Attrition: 19% MLB: 8% Comparables: Geronimo Berroa, George Hinshaw, Larry Littleton, Pat Casey

A nice season for the Sounds earned organizational soldier Heether a spot on the 40-man roster, and while it would be nice if he could hit left-handed, not to mention fly or make world peace, his patience, power, and willingness to play anywhere in the infield makes him a more plausible utility option than if he'd simply been left at third base.

Hernan Iribarren 2B/OF

Bats: L Throws: R Height: 6' 1" Weight: 180 Born: June 29, 1984 Age: 26

YEAR	TEAM	LVL	AGE	PA	R	2B	3B	HR	RBI	BB	SO	SB	CS	EqBRR	AVG	OBP	SLG	EqAVG	EqOBP	EqSLG	EqA	VORP	WARP	DEFENSE		
2007	HUN	AA	23	542	72	23	12	4	53	44	109	18	16	-1.0	.307	.363	.430	.276	.324	.386	.247	9.7	0.4	118-2B	-7	
2008	NAS	AAA	24	397	47	17	3	0	30	28	61	19	8	2.3	.277	.329	.341	.265	.310	.317	.227	-4.7	0.4	53-LF	6	24-2B 3
2008	MIL	MLB	24	15	1	1	0	0	1	1	3	0	0	-0.2	.143	.200	.214	.143	.200	.214	.107	-1.6	-0.2			
2009	NAS	AAA	25	421	46	19	5	3	54	28	63	13	7	2.7	.311	.362	.412	.301	.345	.394	.258	11.0	1.1	96-2B	-2	
2009	MIL	MLB	25	14	1	2	0	0	1	1	5	0	0	0.3	.231	.286	.385	.231	.286	.385	.240	-0.5	0.1			
2010	MIL	MLB	26	415	44	20	4	3	36	30	93	9	5	0.6	.250	.306	.348	.256	.313	.352	.233	1.1	0.0	89-2B	-1	

Breakout: 8% Improve: 37% Collapse: 35% Attrition: 17% MLB: 9% Comparables: Freddie Bynum, Lonnie Maclin, Jason McFarlin, Jim Wawruck

Iribarren continues to slap singles by the boatload in the Pacific Coast League, but his ability to make contact might be his best and only skill. There simply isn't a ton of demand for utility players who can't play shortstop or center well, or hit for power, or steal bases successfully (Iribarren's stolen 50 bases against 31 times caught in Double- and Triple-A). There are groups for people who like to watch others stroke singles; maybe one is managing a team and will take a shine to Iribarren.

Jason Kendall C

Bats: R Throws: R Height: 6' 0" Weight: 205 Born: June 26, 1974 Age: 36

YEAR	TEAM	LVL	AGE	PA	R	2B	3B	HR	RBI	BB	SO	SB	CS	EqBRR	AVG	OBP	SLG	EqAVG	EqOBP	EqSLG	EqA	VORP	WARP	DEFENSE	
2007	OAK	MLB	33	312	24	10	0	2	22	12	27	3	1	-0.7	.226	.261	.281	.227	.261	.282	.193	-4.9	-1.3	80-C	-6
2007	CHN	MLB	33	202	21	10	1	1	19	19	15	0	3	-0.6	.270	.362	.356	.269	.363	.354	.250	7.3	-0.1	48-C	-7
2008	MIL	MLB	34	587	46	30	2	2	49	50	45	8	3	0.4	.246	.327	.324	.253	.331	.330	.238	12.4	3.2	148-C	12
2009	MIL	MLB	35	526	48	19	2	2	43	46	58	7	2	1.0	.241	.331	.305	.256	.340	.322	.243	13.4	0.5	131-C	-6
2010	KCA	MLB	36	432	35	18	1	3	39	38	46	3	3	0.0	.252	.333	.328	.246	.328	.321	.223	1.0	0.0	112-C	-1

Breakout: 11% Improve: 34% Collapse: 35% Attrition: 30% MLB: 92% Comparables: Brad Ausmus, Rick Cerone, Bob Boone, Tony Pena

The offensive bar for catchers is often set very low, but when the best thing to say about yours is "he's not a complete and utter OBP sink," it's time to try another flavor. Major-league position players can't slug .305 and expect to keep their jobs, no matter how much veteran grittiness and defensive intangibles they supposedly provide. With Kendall's caught-stealing percentage down to 20 percent and the Brewers' rotation in shambles, there can't be much of that to brag on, anyway. For reasons that are literally impossible to fathom, the Royals elected to sign this husk of a once-great backstop to a two-year, $6 million contract. Over his last 715 games spanning five seasons, Kendall has hit .261/.336/.321 with eight home runs, and his most notable offensive accomplishment was 71 hit-by-pitches. When small-market teams bellyache about not having the wherewithal to compete, they should be reminded of self-inflicted wounds such as Kendall.

Brett Lawrie   2B

Bats: R   Throws: R   Height: 5' 11"   Weight: 200   Born: January 18, 1990   Age: 20

YEAR	TEAM	LVL	AGE	PA	R	2B	3B	HR	RBI	BB	SO	SB	CS	EqBRR	AVG	OBP	SLG	EqAVG	EqOBP	EqSLG	EqA	VORP	WARP	DEFENSE	
2009	WIS	A	19	423	48	18	5	13	65	41	70	19	11	-1.8	.274	.348	.454	.250	.307	.396	.245	5.3	-0.5	97-2B	-10
2009	HUN	AA	19	53	6	0	1	0	0	0	14	0	2	-0.8	.269	.283	.308	.250	.264	.288	.180	-2.4	-0.2	13-2B	1
2010	MIL	MLB	20	500	49	23	5	12	54	39	109	8	6	-1.4	.241	.305	.386	.248	.308	.390	.242	6.1	0.1	118-2B	-5

Breakout: 22%   Improve: 49%   Collapse: 19%   Attrition: 0%   MLB: 1%   Comparables: Michael Coleman, Harvey Pulliam, Scott Hunter, Ellis Burks

The former Canadian prep star shined in his stateside professional debut, making solid contact and demonstrating terrific power potential for a 19-year-old in the Midwest League. Originally drafted with the thought of putting him behind the plate, Lawrie asked to play second base, and while the reviews of his defense at the keystone are generally poor, the club feels he has the athleticism to stay there. With Escobar and Gamel graduating to the bigs, Lawrie becomes the top hitting prospect in the system, and while many scouts feel his bat will play anywhere, the farther up the defensive spectrum he can stay, the more valuable he'll be. If he can stick in the middle infield, he'll be special.

Felipe Lopez   2B

Bats: S   Throws: R   Height: 6' 0"   Weight: 205   Born: May 12, 1980   Age: 30

YEAR	TEAM	LVL	AGE	PA	R	2B	3B	HR	RBI	BB	SO	SB	CS	EqBRR	AVG	OBP	SLG	EqAVG	EqOBP	EqSLG	EqA	VORP	WARP	DEFENSE			
2007	WAS	MLB	27	671	70	25	6	9	50	53	109	24	9	-3.0	.245	.308	.352	.259	.320	.369	.245	13.7	1.3	104-SS	-1	42-2B	-2
2008	WAS	MLB	28	363	34	20	0	2	25	32	54	4	5	-4.8	.234	.305	.314	.242	.309	.322	.221	-3.5	-0.7	70-2B	-4	6-SS	1
2008	SLN	MLB	28	169	30	8	2	4	21	11	28	4	3	-0.9	.385	.426	.538	.410	.450	.564	.334	19.1	1.1	18-2B	-2	10-3B	-1
2009	ARI	MLB	29	383	44	18	1	6	25	34	59	6	3	-0.9	.301	.364	.412	.303	.363	.416	.272	15.9	2.1	80-2B	3		
2009	MIL	MLB	29	297	44	20	2	3	32	37	41	0	3	-3.5	.320	.407	.448	.346	.428	.488	.310	25.0	2.6	61-2B	-2		
2010	MIL	MLB	30	644	76	31	3	11	57	61	109	11	8	-2.3	.270	.343	.392	.277	.347	.392	.261	20.1	2.0	134-2B	-2		

Breakout: 9%   Improve: 28%   Collapse: 10%   Attrition: 7%   MLB: 98%   Comparables: Jose Offerman, Orlando Hudson, Ken Caminiti, Roberto Alomar

It's amazing how much better you feel right after you've been sick. As soon as Lopez was released from his two-year quarantine in the Nat-atorium back in 2008, he found a home at second base and became a stone-cold on-base machine. Prior to his sojourn in Washington, his OBP had hovered around .350, but higher batting averages and an increased walk rate have pushed him past the magical .400 mark over his last 850 plate appearances. Some of this is doubtless due to a career-high BABIP, but even factoring in some regression, he's valuable at the top of the order. A midseason trade sent Lopez from Arizona to Milwaukee, where his switch-hitting talents were a godsend, but he'll probably be too expensive for the Brewers in 2010. There's reasonable suspicion about him after his awful stretch as a National, but he'll spend the year wearing out pitchers somewhere.

Jonathan Lucroy   C

Bats: R   Throws: R   Height: 6' 0"   Weight: 195   Born: June 13, 1986   Age: 24

YEAR	TEAM	LVL	AGE	PA	R	2B	3B	HR	RBI	BB	SO	SB	CS	EqBRR	AVG	OBP	SLG	EqAVG	EqOBP	EqSLG	EqA	VORP	WARP	DEFENSE
2007	HEL	Rk	21	253	35	18	2	4	39	16	37	0	3	-4.8	.342	.383	.487	.277	.310	.378	.238	2.0	1.0	32-C	4
2008	WVA	A	22	274	45	16	1	10	33	30	39	8	1	2.7	.310	.391	.510	.264	.335	.415	.262	10.2	1.5	47-C	2
2008	BRV	A+	22	272	31	12	1	10	44	28	45	1	2	-2.6	.292	.364	.479	.277	.335	.446	.270	12.6	2.0	48-C	4
2009	HUN	AA	23	506	61	32	2	9	66	78	66	1	1	1.5	.267	.380	.418	.257	.349	.405	.266	21.7	2.4	105-C	-2
2010	MIL	MLB	24	452	48	23	1	9	49	47	85	2	1	0.3	.241	.323	.368	.249	.326	.380	.246	11.5	1.4	82-C	1

Breakout: 6%   Improve: 24%   Collapse: 24%   Attrition: 15%   MLB: 5%   Comparables: Eric Christopherson, Curtis Thigpen, Matt Cimo, Gary Cooper

Lucroy emerged from a successful 2008 season in the low minors, ranking third on the organizational catching depth charts, but when Brett Lawrie chose to drop his mask and shinguards and Angel Salome struggled in Triple-A, Lucroy vaulted to the head of the class. His patient approach (.380 career OBP), gap power, and quick release from behind the plate have always been evident, but a successful year-end stint in the Arizona Fall League convinced most observers that he can be a major-league backstop. Lucroy won't be a star and is years removed from being able to match Kendall's square-jawed veteran crustiness, but he should be able to provide better offensive production at a fraction of the cost starting sometime in 2010. Beyond Salome, Gregg Zaun and George Kottaras are on hand to bridge the time until Lucroy is judged ready, but it won't be long.

Casey McGehee 3B

Bats: R Throws: R Height: 6' 1" Weight: 195 Born: October 12, 1982 Age: 27

YEAR	TEAM	LVL	AGE	PA	R	2B	3B	HR	RBI	BB	SO	SB	CS	EqBRR	AVG	OBP	SLG	EqAVG	EqOBP	EqSLG	EqA	VORP	WARP	DEFENSE				
2007	TEN	AA	24	429	53	26	2	9	54	40	73	1	2	-3.0	.273	.338	.422	.242	.295	.366	.232	2.3	-0.1	48-C	-3	47-3B	0	
2007	IOW	AAA	24	57	3	2	0	1	5	3	10	0	1	-0.5	.173	.228	.269	.154	.211	.250	.147	-4.8	-0.6	10-3B	0	3-1B	0	
2008	IOW	AAA	25	550	68	30	0	12	92	40	89	0	3	-4.1	.296	.345	.429	.278	.319	.383	.247	6.2	0.0	111-3B	-7	12-C	0	
2008	CHN	MLB	25	25	1	1	0	0	5	0	8	0	0	0.0	.167	.160	.208	.167	.160	.208	.084	-2.8	-0.1	5-3B	2			
2009	MIL	MLB	26	394	58	20	1	16	66	34	67	0	2	1.4	.301	.360	.499	.324	.378	.532	.303	30.7	2.6	60-3B	-9	20-2B	2	
2010	MIL	MLB	27	431	50	20	1	11	61	36	85	1	2	-0.9	.254	.318	.390	.263	.323	.400	.248	5.7	0.3	94-3B	-3			

Breakout: 16% Improve: 35% Collapse: 25% Attrition: 15%   MLB: 56%   Comparables: Willis Otanez, Dan Uggla, Marshall McDougall, Joe Randa

When Rickie Weeks went down for the year with a broken wrist in mid-May, McGehee got his first chance at regular playing time in the majors and made the most of it. Always known as a slick glove, the former Cub farmhand used a power stroke unseen in his earlier travails to earn the third-base job and force his way into the Rookie of the Year conversation, all of which was a pleasant surprise. McGehee should rightly enter the season as an everyday player at the hot corner, but with his 2008 power numbers completely out of character and Mat Gamel's more potent bat looking for a position, the Brewers would be wise to keep him on a short leash. McGehee's bad defensive numbers at third belie an excellent reputation, and his solid cameo at the keystone hints at a certain untapped positional flexibility. When the clock strikes midnight and the home runs of 2009 disappear in a puff of regression, as seems likely, McGehee will still have a career as a valuable infield reserve.

Mike Rivera C

Bats: R Throws: R Height: 6' 1" Weight: 230 Born: September 8, 1976 Age: 33

YEAR	TEAM	LVL	AGE	PA	R	2B	3B	HR	RBI	BB	SO	SB	CS	EqBRR	AVG	OBP	SLG	EqAVG	EqOBP	EqSLG	EqA	VORP	WARP	DEFENSE			
2007	NAS	AAA	30	382	37	15	0	19	61	24	71	5	5	-4.8	.215	.270	.421	.184	.230	.325	.189	-10.5	-1.3	74-C	0	16-1B	0
2007	MIL	MLB	30	15	2	0	0	2	3	1	3	0	0	-0.1	.231	.286	.692	.231	.286	.692	.303	1.6	0.3	4-C	0		
2008	MIL	MLB	31	69	8	5	0	1	14	6	10	2	0	-0.1	.306	.377	.435	.323	.391	.435	.295	5.2	0.6	14-C	-1		
2009	MIL	MLB	32	132	10	7	0	2	14	15	32	1	0	-0.9	.228	.326	.342	.237	.333	.360	.248	3.6	0.4	31-C	0		
2010	NYA	MLB	33	203	16	8	0	7	28	16	48	2	1	-1.0	.219	.289	.372	.214	.284	.349	.222	0.3	0.0	47-C	0		

Breakout: 13% Improve: 46% Collapse: 26% Attrition: 13%   MLB: 67%   Comparables: Mike Matheny, Josh Paul, Miguel Ojeda, Tom Wilson

Rivera has spent the last two seasons as a seldom-used backup to the desiccated remains of Kendall, a humiliating job description if ever there was one. Though he was once a well-regarded prospect with burgeoning power and questionable receiving skills, after years of benign neglect it's hard to say what Rivera is now. Nontendered in December, Rivera became a free agent, but the question remains: if he couldn't prove himself more valuable than Jason Kendall, how likely is he to steal playing time from anyone else?

Angel Salome C

Bats: R Throws: R Height: 5' 7" Weight: 200 Born: June 8, 1986 Age: 24

YEAR	TEAM	LVL	AGE	PA	R	2B	3B	HR	RBI	BB	SO	SB	CS	EqBRR	AVG	OBP	SLG	EqAVG	EqOBP	EqSLG	EqA	VORP	WARP	DEFENSE	
2007	BRV	A+	21	276	33	20	0	6	53	12	32	1	0	0.3	.318	.341	.465	.308	.326	.454	.269	11.4	0.0	38-C	-12
2008	HUN	AA	22	411	67	30	2	13	83	33	57	3	2	-5.6	.360	.415	.559	.332	.376	.511	.301	33.5	2.8	76-C	-10
2008	MIL	MLB	22	3	0	0	0	0	0	0	1	0	0	0.0	.000	.000	.000	.000	.000	.000	-.229	-0.7	-0.1		
2009	NAS	AAA	23	314	32	14	2	6	44	22	55	0	0	-1.7	.286	.334	.413	.276	.321	.395	.252	9.4	0.5	69-C	-5
2010	MIL	MLB	24	324	36	18	1	8	50	24	59	1	1	-1.2	.271	.328	.415	.281	.335	.424	.260	12.9	0.9	60-C	-4

Breakout: 11% Improve: 34% Collapse: 16% Attrition: 7%   MLB: 7%   Comparables: Roy Silver, Willie Morales, Carlos Hernandez, Joe Girardi

Nobody expected "Pocket Pudge" to hit .360 again, but Salome's struggles in Nashville were enough to give the organization pause. A series of nagging injuries seemed to bother him, and he struggled all year to make hard contact, which resulted in a greatly increased strikeout rate, reduced walks, and less power. None of this can be explained away by luck, as his BABIP remained reasonably high. Salome sports a strong arm, but the rest of his backstop skills remain works in progress, and while the Brewers believe he'll rise to the challenge and they expect his bat to bounce back, Jonathan Lucroy has moved ahead of him for the time being.

Logan Schafer CF

| | | | | | | | | | | | | | | | Bats: L | Throws: L | | Height: 6' 1" | | Weight: 170 | | Born: September 8, 1986 | | Age: 23 |

YEAR	TEAM	LVL	AGE	PA	R	2B	3B	HR	RBI	BB	SO	SB	CS	EqBRR	AVG	OBP	SLG	EqAVG	EqOBP	EqSLG	EqA	VORP	WARP	DEFENSE
2008	WVA	A	21	196	25	13	2	0	20	8	42	3	8	-1.5	.276	.306	.370	.240	.268	.317	.201	-7.3	-1.2	23-CF -1 9-RF -2
2008	HEL	Rk	21	31	4	0	1	2	8	5	4	1	0	0.2	.240	.355	.560	.185	.281	.370	.233	0.0	0.2	6-CF 1
2009	BRV	A+	22	505	76	31	6	6	58	38	53	16	8	-0.7	.313	.369	.446	.301	.347	.439	.271	19.5	2.6	100-CF 0 4-RF 1
2010	MIL	MLB	23	454	56	25	4	6	48	32	83	6	5	-0.7	.258	.315	.382	.263	.319	.380	.245	6.9	0.8	90-CF 0

Breakout: 8%   Improve: 31%   Collapse: 25%   Attrition: 6%   MLB: 2%   Comparables: Cory Sullivan, Tony Brown, Pedro Valdes, Austin Krum

The Brewers' Minor League Player of the Year, Schafer is a speedy center fielder who showed off consistent gap power and a knack for making contact during his full-season debut. While none of his tools are outstanding, he's a well-rounded player who hangs in well against lefties and has some additional power potential. He'll probably make the jump to Double-A this year, and if some of those doubles start leaving the yard, he could make a rapid climb up the prospect boards.

Rickie Weeks 2B

| | | | | | | | | | | | | | | | Bats: R | Throws: R | | Height: 5' 10" | | Weight: 215 | | Born: September 13, 1982 | | Age: 27 |

YEAR	TEAM	LVL	AGE	PA	R	2B	3B	HR	RBI	BB	SO	SB	CS	EqBRR	AVG	OBP	SLG	EqAVG	EqOBP	EqSLG	EqA	VORP	WARP	DEFENSE
2007	MIL	MLB	24	506	87	21	6	16	36	78	116	25	2	5.1	.235	.374	.433	.240	.379	.444	.293	34.3	2.3	110-2B -13
2008	MIL	MLB	25	560	89	22	7	14	46	66	115	19	5	4.9	.234	.342	.398	.246	.350	.417	.270	23.3	2.8	118-2B 1
2009	MIL	MLB	26	162	28	5	2	9	24	12	39	2	2	-2.2	.272	.340	.517	.293	.358	.558	.297	11.6	1.6	34-2B 2
2010	MIL	MLB	27	537	88	23	7	18	51	72	120	17	5	1.4	.243	.363	.445	.249	.362	.445	.287	32.5	3.3	116-2B -2

Breakout: 9%   Improve: 50%   Collapse: 12%   Attrition: 4%   MLB: 100%   Comparables: Ian Kinsler, Joe Gordon, Edgardo Alfonzo, Ronnie Belliard

It started with his first trip to Miller Park, a September goodwill tour six weeks after he signed his first professional contract to convince fans a bright future was at hand. Six years later, it continues: Rickie Weeks is baseball's biggest tease. That 2003 cup of coffee was followed by 18 months in the high minors, and after Weeks arrived for good in 2005, he has drifted between spectacular, awful, and injured with alarming regularity. He has occasionally been a slugger, more frequently a reliable table-setter, and most frequently not enough of either. Through it all Weeks has shown a dogged determination to overcome every obstacle. He has made himself into a solid defender and seemed to have finally turned the corner with a .283/.415/.528 line down the stretch in 2008, when Milwaukee needed him most. A hot start last year saw him finally do some damage against right-handed pitching before he was felled by yet another wrist injury. It's easy to see the talent that made him the second overall pick back in the day, but two seasons short of free agency, it's time for Weeks to start delivering.

PITCHERS

Eric Arnett

| | | | | | | | | | | | | | Bats: R | Throws: R | | Height: 6' 5" | | Weight: 230 | | Born: January 25, 1988 | | Age: 22 |

YEAR	TEAM	LVL	AGE	W	L	SV	G	GS	IP	H	HR	BB	SO	GB%	BABIP	STUFF	WHIP	ERA	SIERA	DERA	EqH9	EqHR9	EqBB9	EqSO9	VORP	SN/WX
2009	HEL	Rk	21	0	4	0	14	9	34²	33	1	21	35	—	.286	-21	1.56	4.41	4.23	11.19	10.0	2.1	6.7	3.9	-22.1	-1.14
2010	MIL	MLB	22	2	5	0	28	9	51²	58	9	39	30	51%	.298	-15	1.87	6.86	5.76	7.23	10.2	1.5	6.1	4.7	-9.9	-0.19

Breakout: 48%   Improve: 78%   Collapse: 10%   Attrition: 10%   MLB: 0%   Comparables: Kevin Helton, Luis Pardo, Tim Henkenjohann, Sergio Valenzuela

The Brewers' top pick in the 2009 draft out of Indiana University, Arnett is the first college pitcher the Brewers have taken in the first round since Ben Sheets a decade ago. The hulking right-hander signed quickly and managed to make nine starts in the Pioneer league, striking out more than a man per inning but showing little command of his mid-90s fastball or sharp-breaking slider. Arnett is the organization's top pitching prospect by default, but is years away from plugging one of the big-league club's yawning rotation voids.

John Axford

				Bats: R			Throws: R			Height: 6' 5"			Weight: 195			Born: April 1, 1983			Age: 27

YEAR	TEAM	LVL	AGE	W	L	SV	G	GS	IP	H	HR	BB	SO	GB%	BABIP	STUFF	WHIP	ERA	SIERA	DERA	EqH9	EqHR9	EqBB9	EqSO9	VORP	SN/WX
2007	CSC	A	24	0	3	0	13	5	26²	29	2	22	21	56%	.321	-26	1.91	4.39	5.10	8.88	12.6	1.8	8.1	4.1	-9.1	-0.64
2007	TAM	A+	24	0	0	2	5	0	11¹	6	2	7	15	32%	.190	10	1.15	2.38	3.00	5.40	7.2	3.6	6.3	9.0	0.1	-0.11
2007	STA	A-	24	1	1	2	8	0	24¹	13	0	15	30	42%	.232	6	1.15	2.22	3.34	4.70	6.7	0.8	6.3	6.3	2.1	0.13
2008	BRV	A+	25	5	10	0	26	14	95	86	5	73	89	47%	.310	-15	1.67	4.55	4.70	7.64	10.2	1.6	7.7	5.7	-20.4	-1.87
2009	BRV	A+	26	4	1	0	19	0	27²	14	0	16	43	51%	.275	24	1.08	1.63	2.24	3.19	7.5	0.8	6.8	10.1	6.2	0.40
2009	NAS	AAA	26	5	0	0	22	0	33	23	2	19	37	58%	.262	7	1.27	3.55	3.49	4.16	7.5	1.1	5.2	8.0	4.6	0.12
2009	MIL	MLB	26	0	0	1	7	0	7²	5	0	6	9	42%	.263	8	1.43	3.52	4.06	3.38	5.6	0.0	5.6	7.9	1.9	0.14
2010	MIL	MLB	27	3	5	0	43	1	61	61	8	45	53	44%	.309	-12	1.75	5.50	4.91	5.81	9.1	1.2	6.0	7.0	-2.1	0.46

Breakout: 18% Improve: 51% Collapse: 16% Attrition: 22%   MLB: 45%   Comparables: Earl Sanders, Stu Tate, Greg Mix, Colin McLaughlin

A lanky Canadian reliever who worked his mid-90s fastball all the way from High-A to Miller Park in a single season, Axford has posted consistently high strikeout rates throughout his minor-league career. But command has always been his bugbear, and while 2009 saw his lowest walk rates to date, he still handed out a plethora of free passes (five per nine innings). The combination of live arm and small paycheck means he should have a good shot at going north with the big club, but if Axford can't do a better job of avoiding ball four, he won't be there long.

Zach Braddock

				Bats: L			Throws: L			Height: 6' 4"			Weight: 230			Born: August 23, 1987			Age: 22

YEAR	TEAM	LVL	AGE	W	L	SV	G	GS	IP	H	HR	BB	SO	GB%	BABIP	STUFF	WHIP	ERA	SIERA	DERA	EqH9	EqHR9	EqBB9	EqSO9	VORP	SN/WX
2007	WVA	A	19	3	1	0	10	9	47	28	1	15	68	49%	.276	44	0.91	1.15	1.81	1.85	7.0	0.8	3.5	9.1	17.7	1.37
2008	BRV	A+	20	4	7	0	21	11	65¹	55	7	42	80	37%	.302	10	1.48	5.51	3.63	8.40	10.1	2.5	6.4	7.5	-19.3	-1.43
2009	BRV	A+	21	1	1	0	14	0	24²	12	2	4	40	39%	.227	22	0.65	1.09	0.60	2.45	7.8	2.5	2.0	9.8	7.4	0.65
2009	HUN	AA	21	2	1	0	12	0	15²	16	2	3	22	31%	.350	15	1.21	2.87	1.84	6.46	10.6	2.3	1.8	9.4	-1.6	-0.39
2010	MIL	MLB	22	3	4	0	40	5	64	59	9	36	66	39%	.302	14	1.48	4.66	3.93	5.04	8.5	1.2	4.6	8.4	3.3	1.23

Breakout: 17% Improve: 45% Collapse: 19% Attrition: 9%   MLB: 12%   Comparables: Tony Saunders, Garland Kiser, Bob Raftice, Jason Miller

A former starter converted to relief due to recurrent injuries, Braddock has always been able to miss bats with his mid-90s fastball and nasty slider. The move to the pen has worked miracles with his command, as his walk rate plummeted and he posted a gaudy strikeout-to-walk ratio, but the beefy lefty continues to miss time with assorted ailments. If he can stay healthy and continue to eschew the base on balls, Braddock could begin a lengthy and productive stay in the Milwaukee pen before the season is out.

Mike Burns

				Bats: R			Throws: R			Height: 6' 1"			Weight: 210			Born: July 14, 1978			Age: 31

YEAR	TEAM	LVL	AGE	W	L	SV	G	GS	IP	H	HR	BB	SO	GB%	BABIP	STUFF	WHIP	ERA	SIERA	DERA	EqH9	EqHR9	EqBB9	EqSO9	VORP	SN/WX
2007	PAW	AAA	28	4	9	3	35	15	112	125	15	29	80	52%	.306	-22	1.37	4.66	4.15	6.03	10.5	1.6	2.4	4.9	-6.4	-1.71
2008	IOW	AAA	29	8	12	2	37	14	133	150	18	24	101	43%	.317	-21	1.31	4.67	3.81	5.65	10.7	1.7	1.8	4.9	-2.2	-0.06
2009	NAS	AAA	30	8	3	0	14	14	92²	89	9	16	63	51%	.276	-2	1.13	2.62	3.97	3.78	9.3	1.6	1.7	4.5	17.1	1.55
2009	MIL	MLB	30	3	5	0	15	8	51²	60	10	17	39	41%	.313	-16	1.49	5.75	4.30	6.35	10.9	2.0	2.5	5.7	-4.7	-0.55
2010	MIL	MLB	31	5	7	1	39	13	112	128	18	36	67	47%	.307	-13	1.46	5.02	4.71	5.46	10.6	1.4	2.6	4.8	0.4	0.79

Breakout: 16% Improve: 43% Collapse: 15% Attrition: 21%   MLB: 25%   Comparables: Matt Ginter, Anthony Telford, Ciro Licea, Travis Driskill

Minor-league journeyman Mike Burns continued to fill out his NL Central paycheck collection, having already been the property of the Astros, Reds, Pirates, and Cubs before signing with the Crew last January. Burns both added to and benefited from the Brewers' mound woes, managing eight generally poor starts in the bigs while sleeping in much nicer hotels than he would have as a Nashville Sound. With a fastball that doesn't touch 90, he relies on a collection of off-speed junk that will fool some of the PCL most of the time, but most of the NL none of the time. Re-upped to a minor-league contract, Burns will again be an insurance policy that the Brewers desperately hope they won't need to use.

Dave Bush

| | | | | Bats: R | | Throws: R | | Height: 6′ 2″ | | Weight: 205 | | Born: November 9, 1979 | | Age: 30 |

YEAR	TEAM	LVL	AGE	W	L	SV	G	GS	IP	H	HR	BB	SO	GB%	BABIP	STUFF	WHIP	ERA	SIERA	DERA	EqH9	EqHR9	EqBB9	EqSO9	VORP	SN/WX
2007	MIL	MLB	27	12	10	0	33	31	186¹	217	27	44	134	50%	.320	3	1.40	5.12	4.11	4.85	9.8	1.3	1.9	5.8	13.4	2.81
2008	MIL	MLB	28	9	10	0	31	29	185	163	29	48	109	46%	.236	-1	1.14	4.18	4.55	4.57	8.2	1.5	2.1	4.5	18.9	3.61
2009	MIL	MLB	29	5	9	0	22	21	114¹	131	19	37	89	43%	.322	-17	1.47	6.38	4.20	6.69	10.8	1.8	2.5	6.0	-14.6	0.71
2010	MIL	MLB	30	8	10	0	28	27	143¹	149	21	45	95	46%	.294	-1	1.36	4.65	4.46	5.09	9.7	1.3	2.6	5.4	6.6	1.46

Breakout: 13%   Improve: 53%   Collapse: 10%   Attrition: 11%   MLB: 92%   Comparables: Frank Castillo, Victor Santos, Ismael Valdez, Dick Bosman

While it may look as if Bush fell off a cliff last year, it was really just the culmination of a slow, steady decline. When he arrived in Milwaukee, Bush was a ground-ball pitcher with a fastball that touched 90. He kept his walk rate low, threw first-pitch strikes, and let his infield make plays behind him—but four years on, that's not him anymore. His fastball, which he threw less than half the time, now sits at 88, his first-pitch strike percentage has dropped, his line-drive percentage and walk rate have increased, and among NL starters, only Ted Lilly induced fewer ground balls last year. The ingredients that led to Bush's modest success are nowhere to be seen, so new pitching coach Rick Peterson will have his work cut out for him.

Josh Butler

| | | | | Bats: R | | Throws: R | | Height: 6′ 5″ | | Weight: 195 | | Born: December 11, 1984 | | Age: 25 |

YEAR	TEAM	LVL	AGE	W	L	SV	G	GS	IP	H	HR	BB	SO	GB%	BABIP	STUFF	WHIP	ERA	SIERA	DERA	EqH9	EqHR9	EqBB9	EqSO9	VORP	SN/WX
2007	CGA	A	22	5	1	0	13	13	77¹	63	3	20	54	69%	.264	4	1.07	2.33	3.61	4.24	9.3	1.2	3.1	3.9	9.8	0.82
2007	VRO	A+	22	4	3	0	10	9	49¹	51	9	21	34	60%	.286	-18	1.46	4.93	4.42	6.65	10.5	2.8	4.6	4.4	-5.8	-0.49
2008	VRO	A+	23	0	2	0	3	3	17	18	1	5	10	63%	.304	-17	1.35	6.35	4.39	9.19	11.5	1.1	3.4	3.4	-6.4	-0.40
2008	BRV	A+	23	2	8	0	20	20	82¹	86	10	40	63	47%	.306	-42	1.53	5.36	4.59	8.08	11.7	2.8	5.2	4.5	-21.4	-1.51
2009	BRV	A+	24	6	0	0	9	9	51	44	0	23	32	58%	.280	-10	1.31	2.47	4.67	4.90	10.4	0.8	5.2	3.4	3.0	0.31
2009	HUN	AA	24	2	1	0	8	8	41	37	2	13	33	66%	.292	2	1.22	2.85	3.68	4.85	9.0	1.2	3.0	5.3	2.8	0.49
2009	NAS	AAA	24	1	1	0	3	3	15	15	2	1	15	60%	.317	14	1.07	3.60	2.66	4.50	10.3	1.9	0.6	7.1	1.6	0.14
2009	MIL	MLB	24	0	0	0	3	0	4	7	0	6	3	66%	.412	-4	3.25	9.00	6.18	9.64	13.5	0.0	9.6	3.9	-2.1	-0.08
2010	MIL	MLB	25	4	8	0	26	22	98¹	111	15	52	58	54%	.307	-20	1.66	5.97	5.16	6.47	10.5	1.4	4.4	4.7	-10.6	1.59

Breakout: 14%   Improve: 50%   Collapse: 12%   Attrition: 17%   MLB: 39%   Comparables: Steve Buckholz, Scott Taylor, Josh Karp, Robert Theodile

A former second-round pick of the Rays who ping-ponged through five levels last year—including a brief September call-up—Butler uses a low-90s sinker and a decent curve and changeup to keep the ball in the yard and remain effective despite mundane walk and strikeout rates. He should start the year in the Nashville rotation, and while he's not exactly Mr. Excitement, with few other starter candidates in the high minors, the team might very well give Butler his shot later this year.

Todd Coffey

| | | | | Bats: R | | Throws: R | | Height: 6′ 5″ | | Weight: 240 | | Born: September 9, 1980 | | Age: 29 |

YEAR	TEAM	LVL	AGE	W	L	SV	G	GS	IP	H	HR	BB	SO	GB%	BABIP	STUFF	WHIP	ERA	SIERA	DERA	EqH9	EqHR9	EqBB9	EqSO9	VORP	SN/WX
2007	LOU	AAA	26	2	0	1	19	0	27	17	0	5	25	64%	.239	14	0.81	1.33	2.91	2.08	6.2	0.3	1.7	6.6	9.9	1.30
2007	CIN	MLB	26	2	1	0	58	0	51	70	12	19	43	63%	.356	-14	1.75	5.82	4.06	5.63	11.3	1.7	2.9	6.8	-0.7	-0.55
2008	LOU	AAA	27	3	3	2	34	0	39¹	49	4	15	43	64%	.378	-10	1.63	4.35	3.31	5.99	12.0	1.2	3.5	7.0	-2.1	-1.50
2008	CIN	MLB	27	0	0	0	17	0	19¹	25	4	6	8	65%	.309	-25	1.60	6.05	4.95	5.35	10.7	1.9	2.3	3.3	0.3	-0.03
2008	MIL	MLB	27	1	0	0	9	0	7¹	6	0	2	7	76%	.300	7	1.09	0.00	2.92	0.00	7.7	0.0	2.6	7.7	4.3	0.45
2009	MIL	MLB	28	4	4	2	78	0	83²	76	8	21	65	57%	.285	2	1.16	2.90	3.73	3.22	8.6	1.0	2.0	6.0	20.2	2.39
2010	MIL	MLB	29	4	5	1	72	0	72¹	78	9	26	56	61%	.316	-8	1.43	4.75	4.06	5.23	10.0	1.1	3.0	6.2	2.2	0.56

Breakout: 14%   Improve: 40%   Collapse: 28%   Attrition: 8%   MLB: 78%   Comparables: Chad Qualls, Tim Crabtree, Kevin Gregg, Aaron Heilman

Finally freed from pitching in Cincinnati's bandbox when the Reds released him late in the 2008 season, Coffey has quickly become a reliable late-innings weapon in Milwaukee. Built like a fullback, he's throwing harder than ever with a fastball that sits consistently near 95 and a power slider, but a less-than-ideal platoon split keeps him from true dominance. His ground-ball tendencies didn't provide much proof against gopher balls in Cincinnati, but should help immunize him in a more neutral environment. He's already a low-priced asset, and if Rick Peterson can teach him another weapon to use against lefties, he could eventually take over ninth-inning duties.

Yovani Gallardo Bats: R Throws: R Height: 6' 2" Weight: 220 Born: February 27, 1986 Age: 24

YEAR	TEAM	LVL	AGE	W	L	SV	G	GS	IP	H	HR	BB	SO	GB%	BABIP	STUFF	WHIP	ERA	SIERA	DERA	EqH9	EqHR9	EqBB9	EqSO9	VORP	SN/WX
2007	NAS	AAA	21	8	3	0	13	13	77²	53	4	28	110	48%	.287	55	1.04	2.90	2.09	3.80	7.4	0.8	3.4	9.6	14.1	1.81
2007	MIL	MLB	21	9	5	0	20	17	110¹	103	8	37	101	44%	.299	44	1.27	3.67	3.66	3.63	7.8	0.6	2.7	7.3	23.2	3.91
2008	NAS	AAA	22	0	1	0	3	3	15²	20	2	5	18	50%	.419	14	1.60	5.17	2.95	5.79	13.5	1.9	3.2	8.4	-0.4	-0.08
2008	MIL	MLB	22	0	0	0	4	4	24	22	3	8	20	45%	.288	22	1.25	1.87	3.83	2.01	9.3	1.2	2.8	6.9	8.6	1.19
2009	MIL	MLB	23	13	12	0	30	30	185²	150	21	94	204	51%	.275	24	1.31	3.73	3.49	3.94	7.7	1.2	3.9	8.2	31.9	4.86
2010	MIL	MLB	24	10	10	0	27	27	168²	155	19	74	155	50%	.297	19	1.36	4.06	3.85	4.41	8.5	1.0	3.6	7.4	20.4	3.65

Breakout: 10% Improve: 36% Collapse: 14% Attrition: 12% MLB: 97% Comparables: Rob Bell, Roger Clemens, Bob Welch, Fausto Carmona

The lone bright spot in a rotation otherwise full of plague victims, Gallardo had a breakout year and, while there are still improvements to be made, positioned himself as Milwaukee's ace. Gallardo abets his rising low-90s fastball with a big bender and a slider, both of which he can throw for strikes, and a straight change he works in against lefties. The combination causes awkward swings, a low contact rate, and a strikeout rate second only to Tim Lincecum among qualifying NL starters. Still only 24, Gallardo has a high walk rate that is a bit of a concern, but it hasn't been much of a hindrance so far and it gives him some room for improvement. If he can cut down on the free passes and keep making batters look silly, he'll be a perennial All-Star.

Kyle Heckathorn Bats: R Throws: R Height: 6' 6" Weight: 235 Born: June 17, 1988 Age: 22

YEAR	TEAM	LVL	AGE	W	L	SV	G	GS	IP	H	HR	BB	SO	GB%	BABIP	STUFF	WHIP	ERA	SIERA	DERA	EqH9	EqHR9	EqBB9	EqSO9	VORP	SN/WX
2009	HEL	Rk	21	0	1	0	6	5	22¹	30	4	4	15	—	.351	-30	1.52	6.04	4.14	10.61	16.4	4.8	3.4	2.4	-10.6	-0.81
2010	MIL	MLB	22	1	4	0	15	4	44²	71	11	17	18	50%	.361	-24	1.98	7.80	5.62	8.46	14.6	2.2	3.2	3.2	-14.7	0.48

Breakout: 60% Improve: 79% Collapse: 3% Attrition: 3% MLB: 2% Comparables: Todd Miller, Kirby Krueger, Chris Ratliff, Lee Daniels

Blessed with a big body, a power arsenal, and a name that's just plain fun to say, supplemental first-rounder Kyle Heckathorn is a prospect you can dream on. He deals mid-90s heat, flashes a sharp slider, and issued only four walks in his brief debut. Still, despite his impressive stuff, he seemed eminently hittable. He'll need to develop a third pitch to stay in the rotation, and while some scouts feel he's destined for the pen, the pitching-starved Brewers will give him every opportunity to remain a starter. Expect to hear his name more and more in years to come. Heckathorn. *Heckathorn*. Gosh, that's entertaining.

Trevor Hoffman Bats: R Throws: R Height: 6' 0" Weight: 220 Born: October 13, 1967 Age: 42

YEAR	TEAM	LVL	AGE	W	L	SV	G	GS	IP	H	HR	BB	SO	GB%	BABIP	STUFF	WHIP	ERA	SIERA	DERA	EqH9	EqHR9	EqBB9	EqSO9	VORP	SN/WX
2007	SDN	MLB	39	4	5	42	61	0	57¹	49	2	15	44	33%	.270	6	1.12	2.98	4.13	3.45	7.8	0.5	2.0	5.8	13.0	2.97
2008	SDN	MLB	40	3	6	30	48	0	45¹	38	8	9	46	39%	.256	-2	1.04	3.77	2.81	4.05	8.7	2.5	1.7	7.5	7.0	1.75
2009	MIL	MLB	41	3	2	37	55	0	54	35	2	14	48	38%	.228	19	0.91	1.83	3.41	2.08	5.8	0.3	2.0	6.5	20.5	3.36
2010	MIL	MLB	42	3	3	22	46	0	46	44	6	15	33	38%	.283	-1	1.28	3.78	4.34	4.11	8.7	1.1	2.7	5.9	7.1	1.55

Breakout: 9% Improve: 39% Collapse: 35% Attrition: 29% MLB: 93% Comparables: Ellis Kinder, Hoyt Wilhelm, Don McMahon, Rich Gossage

Conventional wisdom insisted that moving Hoffman and his fly-ball tendencies out of Petco would bring nothing but chagrin, but the NL's grand old man had the last laugh. Hoffman bounced back from a subpar 2008 to save 37 games, posted the third-best DERA of his Hall-worthy career, and continued to argue that in his case, a low HR/FB percentage is a skill, not a variable. He remains a joy to watch, mixing his low-velocity fastball with baseball's best changeup, while mixing in a few more sliders this year just for grins. Handing out $8 million to a closer who was conceived prior to the Summer of Love may seem excessive, but for a fan base still suffering from Turnbow-induced nightmares, it's well worth the peace of mind.

Jeremy Jeffress

Bats: R   Throws: R   Height: 6' 0"   Weight: 197   Born: September 21, 1987   Age: 22

YEAR	TEAM	LVL	AGE	W	L	SV	G	GS	IP	H	HR	BB	SO	GB%	BABIP	STUFF	WHIP	ERA	SIERA	DERA	EqH9	EqHR9	EqBB9	EqSO9	VORP	SN/WX
2007	WVA	A	19	9	5	0	18	18	86^1	62	8	44	95	42%	.255	26	1.23	3.13	3.50	5.52	8.1	1.7	5.2	6.6	-0.2	0.21
2008	BRV	A+	20	4	6	0	15	14	79^1	65	5	41	102	57%	.323	33	1.34	4.08	2.97	6.28	9.7	1.8	5.4	8.2	-6.2	-0.39
2008	HUN	AA	20	2	1	0	4	4	14^2	17	2	11	13	42%	.349	11	1.91	5.52	4.97	6.75	12.8	2.0	6.8	6.1	-1.9	-0.05
2009	BRV	A+	21	2	1	0	6	5	33	16	2	22	36	65%	.189	18	1.15	2.18	3.60	5.83	7.4	1.8	7.4	6.8	-1.1	0.03
2009	HUN	AA	21	1	3	0	8	8	27^1	26	1	33	34	62%	.362	14	2.16	7.57	4.68	11.94	10.0	1.0	10.0	8.3	-18.6	-1.07
2010	MIL	MLB	22	3	6	0	20	15	73	73	10	53	70	47%	.315	10	1.72	5.84	4.55	6.23	9.2	1.2	5.9	7.6	-5.9	1.00

Breakout: 23%   Improve: 57%   Collapse: 11%   Attrition: 15%   MLB: 5%   Comparables: Blake King, Don Levinski, Jason Satre, Yadier Pedroso

The former 16th overall pick again started the year trying to command his overpowering stuff, and ended it just trying to get control of his career after his third suspension for marijuana use. Jeffress can punch out hitters with upper-90s gas and a nasty curve, but wildness has hampered his development. His first trip through the Southern League saw him walk more than a man per inning before a merciful demotion to the Florida State League. Then came the 100-game suspension and the inevitable questions as to whether he will ever be able to make good on his immense promise. If he's caught again, he could be banned for life. Jeffress is again undergoing treatment and will miss a little over a month in 2010 before he can again take the mound. He'll then have the rest of the summer to convince the organization that he's worth a spot on the 40-man roster, and if he can show just a modicum of progress, he will be. Jeffress has the type of talent that's too valuable to throw away, but that's really his call.

Braden Looper

Bats: R   Throws: R   Height: 6' 3"   Weight: 235   Born: October 28, 1974   Age: 35

YEAR	TEAM	LVL	AGE	W	L	SV	G	GS	IP	H	HR	BB	SO	GB%	BABIP	STUFF	WHIP	ERA	SIERA	DERA	EqH9	EqHR9	EqBB9	EqSO9	VORP	SN/WX
2007	SLN	MLB	32	12	12	0	31	30	175	183	22	51	87	52%	.277	-5	1.34	4.94	4.96	4.79	9.3	1.2	2.3	4.0	13.7	3.95
2008	SLN	MLB	33	12	14	0	33	33	199	216	25	45	108	54%	.292	-5	1.31	4.16	4.60	4.66	9.9	1.3	1.8	4.1	18.1	3.98
2009	MIL	MLB	34	14	7	0	34	34	194^2	226	39	64	100	53%	.284	-28	1.49	5.22	4.98	5.74	10.4	2.0	2.5	3.8	-5.2	1.21
2010	MIL	MLB	35	8	12	0	33	33	170^2	189	27	53	80	53%	.290	-14	1.42	4.92	5.05	5.39	10.3	1.4	2.6	3.8	2.1	1.84

Breakout: 9%   Improve: 32%   Collapse: 10%   Attrition: 14%   MLB: 98%   Comparables: Bill Gullickson, Masato Yoshii, Mark Leiter, Tim Belcher

A recent graduate of Dave Duncan's Temporary Effectiveness Academy (DD-TEA), Looper was signed to replace Ben Sheets in the Milwaukee rotation. Seriously. It worked, too, as Looper led the NL in three separate categories. One of them, Games Started, is usually a good category to lead, but since the other two were Home Runs Allowed and Earned Runs, watching Looper tote his weighty ERA out to the mound 34 times was an unfortunate thing. Thirty-nine home runs is really a genuinely impressive achievement, whichever side of the ball you're on. Few people expected things to turn out quite this badly, but Looper's walk and homer rates both spiked, and he doesn't whiff enough batters to overcome that. The Brewers declined his option, so it's up to someone else to plug him into the back of their rotation and cross their fingers.

Seth McClung

Bats: L   Throws: R   Height: 6' 6"   Weight: 250   Born: February 7, 1981   Age: 29

YEAR	TEAM	LVL	AGE	W	L	SV	G	GS	IP	H	HR	BB	SO	GB%	BABIP	STUFF	WHIP	ERA	SIERA	DERA	EqH9	EqHR9	EqBB9	EqSO9	VORP	SN/WX
2007	DUR	AAA	26	1	5	5	40	0	58^2	38	3	43	68	53%	.254	20	1.38	1.99	3.85	3.36	6.9	0.8	6.4	8.5	13.4	0.13
2007	NAS	AAA	26	2	0	0	5	3	19	14	2	5	25	51%	.286	18	1.00	1.42	2.04	2.04	8.2	1.5	2.5	9.7	6.8	0.77
2007	MIL	MLB	26	0	1	0	14	0	12	11	0	5	11	60%	.324	2	1.33	3.75	3.77	6.17	8.5	0.0	3.1	7.7	-0.9	0.02
2008	MIL	MLB	27	6	6	0	37	12	105^1	93	10	55	87	50%	.279	2	1.41	4.02	4.40	4.12	8.6	0.9	4.2	6.5	15.6	2.04
2009	MIL	MLB	28	3	3	0	41	2	62	62	11	39	40	45%	.273	-24	1.63	4.94	5.37	5.00	9.4	1.8	4.9	4.9	3.4	0.04
2010	MIL	MLB	29	3	5	1	44	0	69^1	68	8	38	58	48%	.302	-5	1.52	4.87	4.45	5.29	9.1	1.0	4.6	6.7	1.6	0.69

Breakout: 14%   Improve: 51%   Collapse: 26%   Attrition: 12%   MLB: 67%   Comparables: Todd Jones, J.J. Putz, Bob Howry, Rich Loiselle

The numbers of this star pupil of departed pitching coach Mike Maddux took a turn for the worse without his coach's tutelage last year. Walks had been Seth McClung's downfall in Tampa Bay, and they were back with a vengeance last year, while a drop in his strikeout rate resulted in the second-worst strikeout-to-walk ratio in the NL. Due for a raise from the $1.66 million he earned in 2009, he was nontendered, becoming a free agent.

Chris Narveson

Bats: L   Throws: L   Height: 6' 3"   Weight: 205   Born: December 20, 1981   Age: 28

YEAR	TEAM	LVL	AGE	W	L	SV	G	GS	IP	H	HR	BB	SO	GB%	BABIP	STUFF	WHIP	ERA	SIERA	DERA	EqH9	EqHR9	EqBB9	EqSO9	VORP	SN/WX
2007	MEM	AAA	25	3	2	0	9	9	45²	41	6	21	35	38%	.271	-12	1.36	5.72	4.59	6.33	8.9	1.9	4.4	5.3	-3.9	0.01
2008	NAS	AAA	26	6	13	0	28	22	136	140	23	57	125	45%	.299	-27	1.45	5.43	3.92	6.46	10.2	2.1	3.8	6.0	-13.9	-1.05
2009	NAS	AAA	27	4	4	5	26	6	75¹	59	3	26	76	57%	.271	10	1.13	3.70	3.30	5.02	7.6	0.8	3.1	6.8	3.9	0.90
2009	MIL	MLB	27	2	0	0	21	4	47	45	7	16	46	32%	.284	2	1.30	3.83	3.67	4.31	8.6	1.5	2.4	7.1	6.3	0.68
2010	MIL	MLB	28	4	6	1	41	7	90²	97	13	43	71	43%	.313	-8	1.54	5.20	4.53	5.62	9.8	1.3	3.8	6.3	-1.2	1.10

Breakout: 13% Improve: 47% Collapse: 16% Attrition: 23%   MLB: 29%   Comparables: Eric Bell, Jack Taschner, Matt Blank, Tim Birtsas

If it feels as though Narveson has spent a decade spinning his wheels, that's because he has, but it might be that the former Cardinals second-round pick is finally getting some traction. Injuries have plagued him during his years in the bus leagues, but last year he moved to the pen, saw his walk and strikeout numbers move in the right direction, and topped off his first extended major-league stay with four impressive late-season starts. Narveson has fringy stuff, sets up his upper-80s fastball with a big, looping curve and a passable changeup, throws strikes, and suffers recurrent bouts of Gopher Ball Syndrome. With the Brewers desperate for mound help, he may well break camp as a bullpen lefty, but if Rick Peterson can help Narveson channel his inner Zito, it's not crazy to think he could work his way into the back end of the rotation.

Jacob Odorizzi

Bats: R   Throws: R   Height: 6' 2"   Weight: 175   Born: March 27, 1990   Age: 20

YEAR	TEAM	LVL	AGE	W	L	SV	G	GS	IP	H	HR	BB	SO	GB%	BABIP	STUFF	WHIP	ERA	SIERA	DERA	EqH9	EqHR9	EqBB9	EqSO9	VORP	SN/WX
2008	BRR	Rk	18	1	2	0	11	4	20²	18	2	9	19	49%	.258	6	1.31	3.48	3.94	5.26	10.1	3.7	5.0	4.1	0.5	-0.33
2009	HEL	Rk	19	1	4	0	12	10	47	55	3	9	43	—	.356	2	1.36	4.40	3.35	7.62	13.5	2.6	3.5	3.9	-9.7	-0.88
2010	MIL	MLB	20	2	5	0	23	12	56	74	12	28	31	50%	.330	5	1.82	6.99	5.32	7.51	12.2	1.9	4.2	4.5	-12.5	1.07

Breakout: 27% Improve: 60% Collapse: 20% Attrition: 12%   MLB: 0%   Comparables: Vladimir Perez, Wilmer Villatoro, Hubert Crumley, Jimmy Barrett

A projectable right-hander drafted out of an Illinois high school, Odorizzi has been treated with kid gloves, but what he's shown so far has been encouraging. Armed with a sinking low-90s fastball and a developing curve, Odorizzi throws strikes and logged an impressive 4.8 strikeout-to-walk ratio last year. The Brewers think he'll add velocity as he fills out, and they attribute him with top-of-the-rotation potential, but until he starts succeeding in full-season leagues and perfecting his secondary offerings, he'll remain just a twinkle in the development staff's collective eye.

Manny Parra

Bats: L   Throws: L   Height: 6' 3"   Weight: 210   Born: October 30, 1982   Age: 27

YEAR	TEAM	LVL	AGE	W	L	SV	G	GS	IP	H	HR	BB	SO	GB%	BABIP	STUFF	WHIP	ERA	SIERA	DERA	EqH9	EqHR9	EqBB9	EqSO9	VORP	SN/WX
2007	HUN	AA	24	7	3	0	13	13	80²	70	2	26	81	52%	.306	14	1.19	2.68	3.28	4.20	9.2	0.7	3.1	6.2	10.9	0.83
2007	NAS	AAA	24	3	1	0	4	4	26	15	1	7	25	47%	.212	21	0.85	1.73	3.12	2.88	6.1	0.7	2.5	6.5	7.3	0.80
2007	MIL	MLB	24	0	1	0	9	2	26¹	25	1	12	26	37%	.320	14	1.41	3.76	3.89	4.05	8.1	0.3	3.7	7.8	4.3	-0.08
2008	MIL	MLB	25	10	8	0	32	29	166	181	18	75	147	58%	.327	1	1.54	4.39	4.02	4.98	10.3	1.1	3.6	6.8	9.4	2.83
2009	NAS	AAA	26	1	2	0	4	4	24²	16	0	13	19	60%	.225	8	1.18	2.92	4.37	4.38	6.2	0.4	4.7	5.1	3.1	0.39
2009	MIL	MLB	26	11	11	0	27	27	140	179	19	77	116	54%	.349	-19	1.83	6.36	4.55	7.04	11.5	1.4	4.1	6.0	-24.1	-0.04
2010	MIL	MLB	27	8	10	0	31	27	157	169	19	72	113	55%	.314	-3	1.54	4.87	4.56	5.38	10.1	1.1	3.8	5.8	2.1	1.63

Breakout: 9% Improve: 42% Collapse: 11% Attrition: 10%   MLB: 88%   Comparables: Mike Mason, Shawn Estes, Steve Avery, Chris Nabholz

And you thought Looper was bad! On the heels of an encouraging 2008 campaign, Parra was an unmitigated disaster last year, suffering through a June demotion and September neck spasms to throw 140 sub-replacement-level innings and record 11 quality starts out of 27. Parra continues to show off major-league stuff, but he has yet to harness it, walking nearly five batters per nine and suffering a reduced strikeout rate. Shoulder woes have slowed his development, and he underwent another joint cleanup during the offseason, giving Rick Peterson another reason to make fixing the inconsistent lefty his top priority. Parra's episodes of competence and health have become fewer and farther between, so don't hold your breath.

Wily Peralta

Bats: R   Throws: R   Height: 6' 2"   Weight: 225   Born: May 8, 1989   Age: 21

YEAR	TEAM	LVL	AGE	W	L	SV	G	GS	IP	H	HR	BB	SO	GB%	BABIP	STUFF	WHIP	ERA	SIERA	DERA	EqH9	EqHR9	EqBB9	EqSO9	VORP	SN/WX
2008	HEL	Rk	19	1	1	2	15	2	29¹	23	4	8	36	54%	.264	10	1.06	3.07	2.48	5.67	9.3	3.0	3.7	5.7	-0.5	-0.17
2009	WIS	A	20	4	4	1	27	15	103²	91	5	46	118	52%	.315	5	1.32	3.47	3.24	5.70	10.1	1.9	5.0	5.9	-2.1	-0.14
2010	MIL	MLB	21	4	7	0	30	16	99²	108	16	56	75	49%	.308	12	1.65	5.52	4.80	5.92	10.0	1.4	4.6	6.0	-4.7	2.19

Breakout: 13%   Improve: 50%   Collapse: 11%   Attrition: 3%   MLB: 1%   Comparables: Matt Maysey, Josh Rupe, Jason Isringhausen, Brian Tuller

A live-armed Tommy John surgery survivor, Peralta impressed in his full-season debut by striking out more than a man per inning, keeping the ball in the park, and getting more than his fair share of ground-ball outs. Peralta's fastball touches 95, and his slider can be a weapon, but like countless young pitchers before him, he'll need to improve his command and develop a third pitch to be this effective in the bigs.

David Riske

Bats: R   Throws: R   Height: 6' 2"   Weight: 180   Born: October 23, 1976   Age: 33

YEAR	TEAM	LVL	AGE	W	L	SV	G	GS	IP	H	HR	BB	SO	GB%	BABIP	STUFF	WHIP	ERA	SIERA	DERA	EqH9	EqHR9	EqBB9	EqSO9	VORP	SN/WX
2007	KCA	MLB	30	1	4	4	65	0	69²	61	8	27	52	45%	.264	5	1.26	2.45	4.34	2.22	7.4	0.9	3.1	6.3	25.2	1.16
2008	MIL	MLB	31	1	2	2	45	0	42¹	47	6	25	27	31%	.304	-22	1.70	5.31	5.72	5.38	10.5	1.3	4.8	5.0	0.6	0.51
2010	MIL	MLB	33	2	4	1	38	0	42¹	47	5	21	26	42%	.312	-17	1.61	5.22	5.23	5.69	10.3	1.2	4.1	4.8	-0.9	0.45

Breakout: 9%   Improve: 34%   Collapse: 31%   Attrition: 23%   MLB: 72%   Comparables: Marc Valdes, Joe Coleman, Andy Karl, Jim Corsi

Riske has suffered through a series of elbow problems since signing a three-year, $13 million contract with the Brewers prior to the 2008 season. It all culminated last June with Tommy John surgery, which will keep him shelved until this summer at the least. At the time of the deal, Riske was that rarest of birds, a consistently effective middle reliever, which made him seem a reasonable addition for a contending club, but his story is a reminder that every hurler is always one pitch away from injury, and very few relievers are worth a three-year deal. Riske is unlikely to provide much value this season if he gets back on the field at all, and come fall, he'll be looking for another job at a much lower salary.

Mark Rogers

Bats: R   Throws: R   Height: 6' 2"   Weight: 205   Born: January 30, 1986   Age: 24

YEAR	TEAM	LVL	AGE	W	L	SV	G	GS	IP	H	HR	BB	SO	GB%	BABIP	STUFF	WHIP	ERA	SIERA	DERA	EqH9	EqHR9	EqBB9	EqSO9	VORP	SN/WX
2009	BRV	A+	23	1	3	0	23	22	64²	46	2	29	67	56%	.275	0	1.16	1.67	3.37	3.96	9.5	1.3	5.3	6.5	9.5	1.34
2010	MIL	MLB	24	4	7	0	29	25	91	99	13	61	67	49%	.312	-15	1.75	5.76	5.10	6.18	10.0	1.3	5.5	5.9	-6.9	3.03

Breakout: 5%   Improve: 18%   Collapse: 42%   Attrition: 2%   MLB: 8%   Comparables: Brett Laxton, Jason Fronio, Nelson Figueroa, J.D. Durbin

The fifth overall pick in 2004, Rogers returned from two years lost to shoulder woes with his electric stuff mostly intact. Working on a strict pitch count that limited him to fewer than three innings per start, Rogers flashed mid-90s heat and missed plenty of bats, even managing to lower his walk rate from its lofty presurgery heights. Clearly (and perhaps understandably) fatigued during a disastrous AFL campaign, he'll add developing greater endurance and improved command to next year's task list. If those don't improve, his future is in the bullpen, but for now, the Brewers can be happy he has a future at all.

Cody Scarpetta

Bats: R   Throws: R   Height: 6' 3"   Weight: 240   Born: August 25, 1988   Age: 21

YEAR	TEAM	LVL	AGE	W	L	SV	G	GS	IP	H	HR	BB	SO	GB%	BABIP	STUFF	WHIP	ERA	SIERA	DERA	EqH9	EqHR9	EqBB9	EqSO9	VORP	SN/WX
2008	HEL	Rk	19	1	0	0	6	3	20²	18	2	8	31	53%	.364	18	1.26	3.48	2.11	5.60	11.7	2.5	5.1	7.6	-0.2	-0.15
2008	BRR	Rk	19	1	0	0	6	5	15²	8	0	8	27	48%	.320	13	1.02	0.57	1.62	1.38	8.3	1.4	6.2	9.7	5.9	0.48
2009	WIS	A	20	4	11	0	26	18	105	83	5	55	116	50%	.292	5	1.31	3.43	3.53	6.56	9.3	1.9	5.9	5.8	-11.2	-0.56
2010	MIL	MLB	21	4	8	0	27	21	97¹	100	15	60	76	47%	.300	15	1.64	5.59	4.84	5.95	9.4	1.4	5.0	6.2	-4.9	2.17

Breakout: 20%   Improve: 49%   Collapse: 23%   Attrition: 5%   MLB: 4%   Comparables: Jason Sharber, Javier Martinez, Scott Tyler, Luis Rivera

A big right-hander with low-90s velocity and an excellent curveball, Scarpetta struck out more than a batter per inning in his full-season debut. This year the Brewers will hand him a copy of the standard Double-A task list—improved command and a better changeup—and may ask him to lay off the Veal Scarpetta for a while to firm up his "husky" physique, but so far, he's right on schedule.

Ben Sheets

Bats: R Throws: R Height: 6' 1" Weight: 225 Born: July 18, 1978 Age: 31

YEAR	TEAM	LVL	AGE	W	L	SV	G	GS	IP	H	HR	BB	SO	GB%	BABIP	STUFF	WHIP	ERA	SIERA	DERA	EqH9	EqHR9	EqBB9	EqSO9	VORP	SN/WX
2007	MIL	MLB	28	12	5	0	24	24	141¹	138	17	37	106	41%	.281	17	1.24	3.82	4.09	3.67	8.0	1.0	2.1	6.0	29.1	4.19
2008	MIL	MLB	29	13	9	0	31	31	198¹	181	17	47	158	47%	.278	21	1.15	3.09	3.73	3.53	8.5	0.8	1.9	6.1	42.7	6.04
2010	MIL	MLB	31	4	4	0	21	1	74	73	9	25	52	43%	.290	4	1.32	4.10	4.36	4.50	9.2	1.1	2.8	5.7	8.2	1.50
2010	MIL	MLB	31	9	7	0	25	24	139¹	133	15	43	99	45%	.287	11	1.26	3.80	4.23	4.21	8.8	1.0	2.6	5.7	20.0	2.82

Breakout: 8% Improve: 42% Collapse: 25% Attrition: 12% MLB: 95% Comparables: Tim Belcher, Burt Hooton, Chris Bosio, Esteban Loaiza

Sheets missed all of 2009 with a torn flexor tendon and is nobody's property, but we figure we have to put him somewhere, so it'll have to be with his old outfit until the Homestead Homies start holding spring training for the first time in 15 years. The major comparable player in terms of someone who had this surgery (by this surgeon, Dr. James Andrews) was Andy Pettitte in 2004; Pettitte was fine for 2005. The major difference is that Sheets has pitched just one full season in the last five; not that he's Carl Pavano, but it's a risk. Sheets' recovery from this specific procedure should leave him ready for employment when camps open. The potential's there for him to return to being an outstanding front-end starter, with the question being who will provide the right deal.

Chris Smith

Bats: R Throws: R Height: 6' 2" Weight: 200 Born: April 9, 1981 Age: 29

YEAR	TEAM	LVL	AGE	W	L	SV	G	GS	IP	H	HR	BB	SO	GB%	BABIP	STUFF	WHIP	ERA	SIERA	DERA	EqH9	EqHR9	EqBB9	EqSO9	VORP	SN/WX
2007	PME	AA	26	6	9	1	30	14	104	126	10	42	80	45%	.356	-29	1.62	4.41	4.42	5.79	12.1	1.5	3.9	5.2	-3.1	-0.41
2008	PAW	AAA	27	1	5	15	37	4	59¹	54	6	11	52	41%	.286	-3	1.10	3.19	3.30	4.12	9.4	1.3	1.9	6.0	8.5	0.27
2008	BOS	MLB	27	1	0	0	12	0	18¹	18	6	7	13	33%	.231	-15	1.36	7.85	4.78	7.12	8.3	2.5	2.9	5.9	-3.3	0.03
2009	NAS	AAA	28	2	0	17	28	0	42²	31	3	6	49	37%	.275	19	0.87	1.27	2.03	2.03	7.7	1.4	1.6	8.3	15.4	2.76
2009	MIL	MLB	28	0	0	0	35	0	46	41	11	19	35	33%	.227	-19	1.30	4.11	4.67	4.27	8.2	2.3	3.1	5.6	6.3	-0.05
2010	MIL	MLB	29	3	6	7	56	0	71¹	80	11	28	52	41%	.318	-14	1.52	5.29	4.52	5.81	10.5	1.4	3.2	5.9	-2.4	1.02

Breakout: 13% Improve: 48% Collapse: 27% Attrition: 32% MLB: 46% Comparables: Steve Montgomery, Jimmy Rogers, Tony Menendez, Mike James

For the first time in his career, longtime Red Sox farmhand Chris Smith spent much of a summer traveling the country as a member of a big-league bullpen, but he probably shouldn't get used to such pampering. A soft-tosser who would be called "crafty" if he threw left-handed, the mediocre production he provided was based on an unsustainable .241 BABIP that provided cover for a sky-high homer rate and indifferent peripherals. That's a combination with "Highly Flammable" stenciled all over it.

Mitch Stetter

Bats: L Throws: L Height: 6' 4" Weight: 200 Born: January 16, 1981 Age: 29

YEAR	TEAM	LVL	AGE	W	L	SV	G	GS	IP	H	HR	BB	SO	GB%	BABIP	STUFF	WHIP	ERA	SIERA	DERA	EqH9	EqHR9	EqBB9	EqSO9	VORP	SN/WX
2007	NAS	AAA	26	1	0	1	24	0	14²	8	1	5	19	54%	.233	10	0.89	4.30	2.20	5.27	5.9	1.3	3.3	9.2	0.4	0.29
2007	MIL	MLB	26	1	0	0	6	0	5	2	0	2	4	51%	.167	3	0.80	3.60	4.07	3.60	3.6	0.0	3.6	7.2	1.1	0.14
2008	NAS	AAA	27	3	3	0	28	0	29	21	2	7	30	49%	.260	6	0.97	2.48	2.80	3.62	7.6	1.0	2.3	6.9	5.7	0.38
2008	MIL	MLB	27	3	1	0	30	0	25¹	14	2	19	31	43%	.226	22	1.30	3.20	3.76	3.33	5.9	0.7	5.9	9.6	5.9	0.52
2009	MIL	MLB	28	4	1	1	71	0	45	37	4	27	44	41%	.268	0	1.42	3.60	4.27	3.94	7.7	1.0	4.5	7.1	7.9	1.43
2010	MIL	MLB	29	3	3	0	50	0	49	41	5	23	46	45%	.280	5	1.31	3.91	3.84	4.16	7.6	0.9	3.9	7.7	7.3	1.17

Breakout: 18% Improve: 38% Collapse: 21% Attrition: 8% MLB: 68% Comparables: Will Ohman, Doug Slaten, John Grabow, Alan Embree

No need to look at the demographic information under his name to determine Stetter's handedness—his games and innings pitched totals bear the indelible stamp of a situational lefty, and a pretty good one at that. Stetter throws his slider 60 percent of the time, more than any pitcher in the NL, and used it to hold lefties to a feeble .178/.295/.300 line. Righties torched him, however, and he struggled down the stretch, but the Brewers will ride him until he becomes either expensive or ineffective, hopefully several years down the line.

Jeff Suppan

| | | | | | | | | | Bats: R | | Throws: R | | Height: 6' 2" | | Weight: 235 | | Born: January 2, 1975 | | Age: 35 |

YEAR	TEAM	LVL	AGE	W	L	SV	G	GS	IP	H	HR	BB	SO	GB%	BABIP	STUFF	WHIP	ERA	SIERA	DERA	EqH9	EqHR9	EqBB9	EqSO9	VORP	SN/WX
2007	MIL	MLB	32	12	12	0	34	34	206²	243	18	68	114	52%	.318	5	1.50	4.62	4.91	4.50	9.8	0.7	2.6	4.4	23.1	3.17
2008	MIL	MLB	33	10	10	0	31	31	177²	207	30	67	90	53%	.301	-25	1.54	4.96	5.11	5.60	11.1	1.6	3.1	4.0	-1.8	2.39
2009	MIL	MLB	34	7	12	0	30	30	161²	200	25	74	80	57%	.314	-29	1.69	5.29	5.25	5.97	11.3	1.6	3.5	3.7	-8.3	0.98
2010	MIL	MLB	35	7	11	0	30	30	150	175	22	58	69	53%	.305	-20	1.56	5.35	5.29	5.89	10.9	1.3	3.3	3.7	-6.5	1.13

Breakout: 7%   Improve: 31%   Collapse: 12%   Attrition: 17%   MLB: 96%   Comparables: Bill Gullickson, Jack Billingham, Aaron Sele, Mark Leiter

Making a LAIM (League-Average Innings Muncher) your highest-paid player is an odd choice for a small-market team, and when neither half of that sobriquet can be appropriately applied to the pitcher in question, you have a financial disaster on your hands. Nagging injuries and ineffectiveness have reduced Suppan's innings pitched totals, and his walk and strikeout rates are trying their best to intersect. Including his inevitable 2011 buyout, Suppan will earn $14.5 million this season, money that could be better used for Prince Fielder's signing bonus, building a baseball academy in the Far East, or being randomly fired from T-shirt guns into the Miller Park stands. Instead, the Brewers will grit their teeth and hope for a randomly low BABIP to make the pain of his slow, slug-worthy fastballs a little more bearable.

Claudio Vargas

| | | | | | | | | | Bats: R | | Throws: R | | Height: 6' 4" | | Weight: 240 | | Born: June 19, 1978 | | Age: 32 |

YEAR	TEAM	LVL	AGE	W	L	SV	G	GS	IP	H	HR	BB	SO	GB%	BABIP	STUFF	WHIP	ERA	SIERA	DERA	EqH9	EqHR9	EqBB9	EqSO9	VORP	SN/WX
2007	MIL	MLB	29	11	6	1	29	23	134¹	153	23	54	107	39%	.310	-5	1.54	5.09	4.44	4.88	9.4	1.4	3.1	6.3	9.4	1.62
2008	NWO	AAA	30	5	2	0	8	8	43¹	47	5	13	43	44%	.333	-1	1.38	4.36	3.36	5.49	11.4	1.8	2.9	6.4	0.1	0.39
2008	NYN	MLB	30	3	2	0	11	4	37	33	4	11	20	48%	.257	-9	1.19	4.62	4.79	5.01	8.5	1.3	2.6	4.1	1.9	0.74
2009	ABQ	AAA	31	0	0	1	7	0	13	15	3	1	12	71%	.324	12	1.23	3.46	2.80	3.55	9.9	1.4	0.7	7.1	2.7	-0.13
2009	LAN	MLB	31	0	0	0	8	0	11	7	1	4	10	37%	.222	8	1.00	1.64	3.66	1.74	7.0	0.9	2.6	7.0	4.3	0.10
2009	MIL	MLB	31	1	0	0	28	0	30¹	18	2	11	20	46%	.195	-1	0.96	1.78	4.45	2.15	5.5	0.6	2.8	4.9	10.9	2.01
2010	MIL	MLB	32	4	5	0	34	5	73	73	9	28	55	45%	.296	-1	1.38	4.38	4.34	4.81	9.3	1.1	3.2	6.1	5.6	1.07

Breakout: 9%   Improve: 56%   Collapse: 13%   Attrition: 24%   MLB: 75%   Comparables: Don Larsen, Ciro Licea, Mark Leiter, Tim Worrell

Veteran swingman Claudio Vargas started his season on the DL, returned to throw some low-leverage innings in a crowded Dodger pen, and came over to Milwaukee at the end of July. Used exclusively in relief for the first time in his career, Vargas thrived as a Brewers reliever, where his fastball/slider combination was much more effective in small doses. Left-handed hitters have plagued him for years, but that's less of a problem coming out of the pen, where he can be more appropriately spotted. While he was definitely hit-lucky last year and won't put up another sub-2.00 ERA, he can definitely be a useful middle reliever. The Brewers re-signed him to a one-year deal to continue in that role.

Carlos Villanueva

| | | | | | | | | | Bats: R | | Throws: R | | Height: 6' 2" | | Weight: 215 | | Born: November 28, 1983 | | Age: 26 |

YEAR	TEAM	LVL	AGE	W	L	SV	G	GS	IP	H	HR	BB	SO	GB%	BABIP	STUFF	WHIP	ERA	SIERA	DERA	EqH9	EqHR9	EqBB9	EqSO9	VORP	SN/WX
2007	MIL	MLB	23	8	5	1	59	6	114¹	101	16	53	99	38%	.267	6	1.35	3.94	4.29	3.77	7.5	1.2	3.7	6.9	22.1	3.82
2008	MIL	MLB	24	4	7	1	47	9	108¹	112	18	30	93	51%	.294	-10	1.31	4.07	3.71	4.47	9.7	1.6	2.2	6.6	12.2	1.26
2009	MIL	MLB	25	4	10	3	64	6	96	102	13	35	83	48%	.308	-13	1.43	5.34	3.95	5.50	9.7	1.4	2.7	6.4	0.0	-0.53
2010	MIL	MLB	26	6	6	1	57	6	100²	101	13	39	80	45%	.302	-2	1.39	4.43	4.18	4.81	9.3	1.2	3.2	6.4	7.7	1.02

Breakout: 8%   Improve: 40%   Collapse: 17%   Attrition: 10%   MLB: 95%   Comparables: Dave Lemanczyk, Frank Smith, Pedro Astacio, Mark Grant

Villanueva is a junk-balling swingman who for the second year running lobbed fewer fastballs (39 percent) than any NL starter not named Doug Davis. Pressed into the rotation in late July, at a time when Doug Melvin was rifling through his Facebook friends list looking for Jeff D'Amico and Juan Nieves, Villanueva proved yet again that he needs to stay in the bullpen. While his offspeed smoke and mirrors leave hitters posting a .232/.302/.384 career mark the first time through a lineup, their .275/.342/.482 line the second time through proves they can quickly see the magician's hand. Villanueva's durability would make him valuable in a tandem starter arrangement, but that's not about to happen, so he'll continue on as an inexpensive and useful multi-inning reliever.

David Weathers

								Bats: R			Throws: R		Height: 6' 3"		Weight: 235		Born: September 25, 1969			Age: 40

YEAR	TEAM	LVL	AGE	W	L	SV	G	GS	IP	H	HR	BB	SO	GB%	BABIP	STUFF	WHIP	ERA	SIERA	DERA	EqH9	EqHR9	EqBB9	EqSO9	VORP	SN/WX
2007	CIN	MLB	37	2	6	33	70	0	77²	67	4	27	48	42%	.258	9	1.21	3.59	4.80	3.38	6.8	0.3	2.7	4.9	18.9	3.25
2008	CIN	MLB	38	4	6	0	72	0	69¹	76	6	30	46	48%	.310	-6	1.53	3.25	4.79	3.25	9.0	0.8	3.3	5.0	17.7	0.62
2009	CIN	MLB	39	3	3	1	43	0	38	27	7	17	27	47%	.183	-11	1.16	3.32	4.61	3.43	6.4	1.6	3.2	5.3	9.0	0.50
2009	MIL	MLB	39	1	3	0	25	0	24	26	3	11	10	53%	.284	-30	1.54	4.87	5.59	5.79	10.0	1.2	3.5	3.1	-0.7	0.03
2010	MIL	MLB	40	3	4	8	57	0	56²	55	7	26	33	45%	.277	-12	1.43	4.51	5.11	4.89	9.0	1.0	3.7	4.8	3.8	0.82

Breakout: 11%   Improve: 35%   Collapse: 34%   Attrition: 20%   MLB: 93%   Comparables: Jose Mesa, Steve Reed, Masao Kida, Todd Jones

The target of trade deadline rumors every year, Weathers moved from Cincinnati to Milwaukee last August in a futile attempt to revive the Crew's flagging playoff hopes. Stormy's slider has been a bullpen asset for a decade, but while the wheels didn't exactly fall off down the stretch, they certainly showed some wobble. His already low strikeout rate took another hit, his walk and home-run rates rose, and only an unsustainably low .238 BABIP for the year allowed him to stay reasonably effective. The Brewers, saving up for a trip to the Rotation Store, wisely declined his $3.7 million option, and while Weathers is certain to latch on somewhere, he's 40 years old and every indicator is moving in the wrong direction.

LINEOUTS

Hitters

PLAYER	TEAM	LVL	AGE	PA	R	2B	3B	HR	RBI	BB	SO	SB-CS	EqBRR	AVG/OBP/SLG	EqAVG/EqOBP/EqSLG	EqA	VORP	WARP
OF J. Bourgeois	NAS	AAA	27	454	61	18	6	2	41	22	40	36-7	5.1	.316/.354/.401	.301/.333/.375	.253	8.4	0.5
	MIL	MLB	27	40	6	0	0	1	3	3	7	3-0	0.5	.189/.250/.270	.189/.250/.270	.209	-2.2	-0.1
CF L. Cain	WIS	A	23	61	3	4	0	0	3	9	15	0-0	-0.4	.192/.311/.269	.164/.258/.218	.164	-3.5	-0.4
	HUN	AA	23	160	17	6	0	4	15	10	35	3-3	0.1	.214/.277/.338	.203/.252/.311	.195	-6.1	-1.4
2B C. Dykstra	WIS	A	20	113	16	4	1	1	7	12	27	4-2	-0.4	.212/.310/.303	.194/.265/.282	.190	-4.9	-1.3
	HEL	Rk	20	239	35	5	1	5	26	27	50	14-4	0.9	.244/.332/.349	.187/.248/.260	.177	-12.3	-4.4
2B E. Farris	BRV	A+	23	534	68	18	1	7	49	29	46	70-6	9.2	.298/.341/.385	.283/.318/.366	.250	9.8	1.5
3B T. Green*	HUN	AA	22	345	34	15	0	5	43	33	37	0-2	0.3	.258/.330/.356	.252/.308/.351	.233	-1.3	-0.3
OF B. Katin	NAS	AAA	26	506	67	33	6	24	92	35	164	2-0	3.8	.244/.305/.499	.219/.271/.431	.239	-2.4	-1.9
1B B. Kjeldgaard	WIS	A	23	549	65	30	4	20	74	58	172	12-6	-3.9	.250/.342/.458	.210/.275/.349	.218	-20.4	-4.7
1B J. Koshansky*	NAS	AAA	27	531	72	21	3	24	80	64	166	7-4	1.4	.218/.316/.435	.200/.286/.373	.231	-17.4	-2.6
OF C. Patterson*	SYR	AAA	29	283	30	16	1	7	40	13	65	14-5	-1.1	.274/.318/.422	.248/.288/.380	.232	-2.8	-0.1
	NAS	AAA	29	135	24	12	3	5	22	8	25	7-3	-0.3	.331/.366/.597	.294/.326/.508	.277	6.6	0.8
SS J. Prince	WIS	A	21	140	18	5	0	1	10	15	21	12-5	0.8	.221/.307/.287	.206/.271/.254	.191	-3.6	-1.4
	HEL	Rk	21	176	32	5	1	0	8	33	25	26-7	-2.9	.298/.426/.348	.237/.330/.270	.226	1.0	-0.6
OF M. Walla*	BRR	Rk	18	212	18	5	2	2	19	15	82	4-2	-3.8	.199/.283/.280	.157/.203/.227	.132	-19.1	-4.6

Speedster **Jason Bourgeois** had to be kicked to the outfield when he couldn't handle the inner-diamond life; reaching to achieve modest ambitions there, he's 10 years into his pro career, and now that he's an Astro via a winter waiver claim, he's on his sixth organization. ⊘ Toolsy center fielder **Lorenzo Cain** still has not developed the power/speed mojo projected for him after a badly injured knee resulted in a lost season. The acquisition of Carlos Gomez may relegate him to a corner, where his bat probably won't play. ⊘ **Cutter Dykstra** struggled through a disastrous full-season debut that saw him demoted to the Pioneer League and converted to second base; he's way too young to write off, but he'll need to regroup and become a tougher out if he wants to have a career. ⊘ Speedy second baseman **Eric Farris** opened a few eyes by swiping 70 bags and flashing a plus glove in High-A, but will need to get on base more to profile as a prospect. ⊘ A fringy prospect to begin with, third baseman **Taylor Green** struggled with injuries and ineffectiveness in his first taste of the high minors and will need to show power this season to keep people's interest. ⊘ Mighty **Brendan Katin**'s feats of strength involved consistent production at Nashville the last two years, and better health in 2009; being Ryan Braun's college teammate isn't getting him any extra breaks, but as Katin is more a latter-day Mark Brouhard, it shouldn't. ⊘ Large Canadian person **Brock Kjeldgaard** started off as a pitcher, but last year, in just his second season as a hitter, he generated one of the Three True Outcomes—walks, whiffs, or bombs—in 46 percent of his PAs. ⊘ A huge drop in BABIP masked another typically slug-worthy season from ex-Rockie farmhand **Joe Koshanksy**, but rebranding from Todd Helton Insurance to Prince Fielder Insurance isn't getting him any closer to a big-league gig. ⊘ It's always tempting to take a chance on his obvious physical tools, but when **Corey Patterson** is unable to post a decent OBP in Triple-A, why give him a big league job? Signed by the Mariners to a minor-league deal, he'll serve as a cautionary example for the prospects. ⊘ A solid sleeper candidate, former Tulane burner **Josh Prince** led Division I with 48 steals last year, added 38 more in his pro debut, showed enough range to stay at shortstop, and gets on base. ⊘ Hailed as the next Gindl, prep outfielder **Max Walla** won't be able to show off his prodigious power on a bigger stage if he continues to strike out in 40 percent of his PAs.

Pitchers

PLAYER	TEAM	LVL	AGE	W	L	SV	IP	H	HR	BB	SO	GB%	BABIP	STUFF	WHIP	ERA	SIERA	DERA	EqH9	EqHR9	EqBB9	EqSO9	VORP
O. Aguilar	BRV	A+	24	2	1	8	29^2	16	1	9	37	50%	.238	4	0.84	2.12	2.22	4.38	7.7	1.4	3.9	8.1	3.2
—	HUN	AA	24	1	0	6	25^2	36	3	18	33	34%	.412	-20	2.10	7.71	3.92	13.67	13.5	2.1	5.9	8.0	-23.6
E. Anundsen	BRV	A+	21	10	8	0	130^1	101	2	41	118	55%	.277	21	1.09	2.69	3.51	5.90	9.6	1.0	3.8	5.3	-5.2
M. Bowman	WIS	A	22	3	1	0	44	45	1	14	41	47%	.331	-1	1.34	2.66	3.60	5.66	10.7	1.3	3.7	4.6	-0.7
—	BRV	A+	22	5	4	0	87^2	86	5	39	60	45%	.299	-26	1.43	2.57	4.73	6.25	12.1	2.0	5.3	3.9	-6.4
M. DiFelice	MIL	MLB	32	4	1	0	51^2	49	6	15	48	32%	.289	1	1.24	3.66	3.66	3.81	8.7	1.2	2.3	6.8	9.8
T. Dillard	NAS	AAA	25	11	7	0	147^2	162	11	52	64	57%	.298	-23	1.45	4.51	5.20	6.07	10.7	1.4	3.4	2.8	-8.9
—	MIL	MLB	25	0	1	0	4^1	7	1	5	1	69%	.375	-50	2.77	12.46	6.80	13.50	15.8	2.3	9.0	2.3	-3.6
E. Frederickson*	WIS	A	22	3	9	2	97^1	99	5	82	93	51%	.335	-27	1.86	5.27	4.82	8.74	11.5	2.1	9.0	4.7	-31.7
A. Periard	WIS	A	22	0	0	0	11^1	14	0	2	5	59%	.326	-23	1.41	3.18	4.76	5.73	11.5	0.8	2.5	1.6	-0.3
—	BRV	A+	22	3	2	0	31	37	1	13	22	56%	.353	-26	1.61	5.23	4.51	9.17	14.3	1.3	5.0	4.0	-11.0
A. Rivas	BRV	A+	23	13	7	0	133	109	11	43	123	53%	.267	-31	1.14	2.98	3.50	6.10	10.6	2.4	3.9	5.5	-7.9

Omar Aguilar is your standard-issue late-inning relief suspect, with the full accessory package: upper-90s velocity, unreliable breaking ball, and high walk and strikeout rates; he's already 25 and has never succeeded in the high minors, so time is not on his side. ⊘ Unsung ground-ball artist **Evan Anundsen** drew a spotlight with his April no-hitter, then held it by posting a terrific K/BB ratio. Mid-80s heat doesn't often play at higher levels, but at least he has the organization's attention. ⊘ Athletic VMI product **Michael Bowman** had a good year in his full-season debut, but inconsistent command of a mediocre three-pitch assortment suggests limited upside at best. ⊘ Former rotation stalwart **Chris Capuano** is finally ready to attempt his most recent Tommy John surgery comeback, and while the Brewers are unlikely to catch lightning in a bottle, even trapping a firefly in a jar would help. ⊘ A career minor leaguer and indy-league survivor, **Mark DiFelice** briefly revived his career by throwing a darting low-80s cutter almost exclusively, but he tore up his shoulder and figures to miss all of 2010. ⊘ Moved back to the rotation after a successful stint in Nashville's 2008 pen, ground-ball specialist **Tim Dillard** again proved he doesn't miss enough bats when he starts. ⊘ A supplemental first-rounder in 2008, hulking lefty **Evan Frederickson** has shown no ability to repeat his delivery and command his mid-90s heat, making a move to the pen inevitable. ⊘ Shoulder woes limited Quebecois sinkerballer **Alex Periard** to 12 unimpressive starts in the low minors, and he's slowly being eclipsed by prospects with more electric stuff and better results. ⊘ **Amaury Rivas** used his solid fastball/changeup combination to win the organization's Pitcher of the Year award, but he'll need to prove himself in the high minors before prospect mavens can get all hot and bothered.

MANAGER: KEN MACHA

		Pythag	Avg	100+	120+			REL w					PH	PH					SAC		POS		In
YEAR	TEAM	W-L	+/–	PC	P	P	QS	BQS	REL	Zero R	IBB	Subs	PH	Avg	HR	SB2	CS2	SB3	CS3	Att	SAC %	SAC	Squeeze	Swing	Play
2009	MIL	80-82	2	93.8	65	2	61		512	334	60	47	258	.175	1	51	34	17	3	78	74.4%	15	0	133	100

Macha's last managerial gig was with the A's, a job reputed to be similar to that of a Mercury astronaut: you're a gifted pilot at the pinnacle of your career, but the engineers who built the craft you're supposed to fly mostly just want you to sit there and not touch anything. Once he was freed from those controls, you could perhaps forgive him if he decided to put the Brewers through a few barrel-rolls this season, but that didn't happen. Macha couldn't do much with the bad rotation he was handed, but ran a solid bullpen, getting good use out of situational arms like Mitch Stetter and Mark DiFelice. He didn't overmanage Milwaukee's power-based offense, but since he's not a player's manager or fiery, and his communication skills came under attack at the end of his Oakland tenure, his "Leader of Men" stats (not listed above) may be questioned in some quarters. Macha goes into 2010 with one year and a newly added club option left on his contract, so his Milwaukee future probably depends more on whatever rotation pieces Doug Melvin adds than on anything Macha himself does.

Minnesota Twins

Revenge is sweet. A year after losing a division title in a 163rd game, the Twins won one with much the same cast of characters. They didn't beat the White Sox, the team they'd lost to in 2009, but having already avenged themselves on the Sox with a 12-6 record against the South Siders, they could bask in dispensing with the Tigers after catching Detroit from behind.

Doing so with an imperfect team was especially impressive. Superficially, the Twins might seem like a so-called stars and scrubs squad, since you'll find few bigger distinctions between regular or semiregular players in the same lineup than going from Joe Mauer to Alexi Casilla or Nick Punto. It's easy to dwell on the Twins' weaknesses, because they were so glaring. The lineup beyond five key regulars—Mauer, Justin Morneau, Michael Cuddyer, Denard Span, and Jason Kubel—was almost the picture image of replacement-level talent. Despite the promise of better from the starting staff, it endured all sorts of churn, as Scott Baker and Nick Blackburn were the two hurlers who began and ended the year in a unit that cycled through nine guys for the other three rotation slots. The distinctions were just as dramatic in the pen: Joe Nathan was his usual dominating self as the closer, and Matt Guerrier and Jose Mijares became key contributors entrusted with more significant roles, but nobody else shined over the season.

However, getting hung up on the limitations of the back half of the roster obscures two key points for why the Twins won and why they're in a good position to win again. First, they didn't sit still and accept their lot, and full-season data have a great way of obliterating in-season improvements. Span went from being the fourth outfielder to an everyday regular, with the equally frustrating Delmon Young and Carlos Gomez losing at-bats as a result. Minnesota traded for additional help, adding Orlando Cabrera to play shortstop and Jon Rauch to add another useful warm body to the pen. Additional relief help came in the form of Jesse Crain's return to effectiveness once he came back from a month-long midseason demotion. To address a rotation handicapped by the loss of Kevin Slowey for the season plus ineffectiveness from Francisco Liriano (their Opening Day starter), Anthony Swarzak, and Glen Perkins, the Twins traded for Carl Pavano (replacing Perkins) and inserted farmhands Brian Duensing and Jeff Manship for the stretch run, rather than crash and burn with Liriano and Swarzak. The additions may not have been notable for their excellence, but at least general manager Bill Smith didn't sit by and let the season slip away.

The second major key is that the Twins have the merits of their strengths, which might seem like a truism, but their core talent is exceptional for its ability and its relative youth. The quartet of Mauer, Morneau, Span, and Kubel delivered the highest combined WARP that any AL team received from its age 25-29 position players. That's the age range that usually gets shortened to the age-27 peak phenomenon, but going with the wider range describes the more important trend in players' careers: across those five seasons, you're liable to get any one player's best work. Their total WARP of 19.6 was the third-highest total from any such cadre in the American League in the decade, behind the production the 2001 Mariners got from Mike Cameron, Ichiro Suzuki, Carlos Guillen, and David Bell (20.4) and what

TWINS PROSPECTUS
2009 W-L: 87-76, 1st in AL Central

Pythag	83-80	8th	**Ballpark:** HHH Metrodome (3-yr. PF: 999). Say goodbye to the Hefty Bag and hello Target Field—the revolution won't be climate-controlled
RS/G	5.0	4th	
RA/G	4.7	8th	
EqA	.264	5th	
EqBRR	3.8	4th	**2009:** Mauer's might and a big September rally creates a game-163 win
SNWP	.494	11th	
WXRL	10.37	5th	**2010:** Adding Hardy helps even the lineup strikethrowing staff, plus star power = another shot at winning
FRAr	4.22	4th	
DE	.691	6th	
PADE	-1.33	11th	**Action Items:** Offense from 2B and/or 3B, Liriano and Delmon Young must develop
Salary	$65.3	12th	
Attend	2.42	5th	

the 2002 Angels received from Troy Glaus, Darin Erstad, Adam Kennedy, and David Eckstein (21.5). It's a fun coincidence that the 2001 Mariners tied the all-time record for wins while the Angels won the World Series, but it's only that. The Twins depend entirely on their core of players already nestled in their careers' sweet spots, whereas those clubs had other assets contributing toward their greater success.

Of course, the Twins might have won even more games if Mauer hadn't missed April and Morneau the last couple of weeks of the year, but that last fact serves as a reminder that no matter how much we think we know, we can't anticipate every outcome. When Morneau played his last game on September 12 before having to call it a year because of his back problems, the Twins were 70-72. That was just 5 ½ games behind the Tigers, but Morneau was just the latest loss, following that of Joe Crede three weeks before. If the Twins were going to make a run, they'd have to do it with the opposition pitching around Mauer, which they did, 20 times in his 90 plate appearances during the last 20 games.

If, as the saying goes, defeat is an orphan but victory has many fathers, you could forgive the analysis community for asking for a paternity test to explain how the Twins achieved what came next: a 16-4 run in their last 20 games to force the one-game playoff with the Tigers. The rotation certainly didn't step up. Blackburn did, by giving the team four quality starts in his four turns, but the other starters combined for just that many in the other 16 games. The pen slaved away, posting a 2.76 FRA while totaling 2.1 WXRL, with Nathan getting the glory by going 9-for-9 in save opportunities (0.9 WXRL), but Rauch wound up being the critical addition with 0.5 WXRL in lower-profile set-up work. But the real stunner was that the Twins scored 127 runs in these 20 games—sure, Mauer got on base, but Michael Cuddyer mashed eight homers, and Kubel five more. They weren't alone, because relying on some of the season's worst regulars anywhere on any team ended up not hurting the Twins in the least in their last 20 contests: Nick Punto put up a .400 OBP, Delmon Young slugged .600, and Matt Tolbert (!) chipped in a 795 OPS. With so many people on base, Orlando Cabrera plated 17 baserunners. It was somehow appropriate that Alexi Casilla, the worst semiregular on the roster, wound up driving the division-winning blow in the bottom of the 12th of the tie-breaker.

They then got squashed by the Yankees in the ALDS, an unsurprising result, because in the real world, Cinderella usually has to settle for the townhouse and the station wagon, not Prince Charming and the palace. To some extent, the Twins are the American League's answer to the Marlins: OK team, OK success. They're more successful at it, but a lot of that is because of the division they're assigned to. It's a lot easier to contend in the AL Central than in the NL East. While the Marlins can laugh down at teams like the Braves or the Mets for doing less with more, it isn't as if Florida is mounting a challenge of its own; instead, it's more like baseball's existential prank on those who aspire to titles and flags and playoff games.

The key distinction between the Twins and the Fish, however, is that when it comes to attendance, the Twins have a fine record now and an even better record historically. However long it took to wangle a new stadium out of the taxpaying audience, to some extent people have been willing to buy whatever the Twins are selling. We can argue about the atmospherics that go into that acceptance. The Twins' better player-development program translates into a roster that's chock-a-block with homegrown products of varying levels of quality, whereas the Fish are an odd agglomeration of driftwood and talent. The Twins don't automatically discard people for having the impudence of achieving seven-figure salaries. But the Twins have also had previous iterations of Cinderella deliver, having won in 1987 and 1991. Those teams, like this one, had the benefit of a very few outstanding key players and a well-regarded manager; they also have had their share of Puntos. Less optimistically, the Twins have won five of the last nine division titles, yet have less to show for it than the Marlins with their one wild-card trip in the same span. As challenges go, this is no different from the challenge the team of the early Aughties failed to overcome: being good is swell, but if the Twins again fail to leverage that into something more than the thrill of another AL Central flag, it will be a sad thing for a team that has had higher standards and achieved greater things.

If Minnesota is going to enjoy the full benefit of Mauer's walk year—and ideally encourage him to stay—it can't settle for the fact that the division is theirs for the taking. Sure, it makes for a lovely way to christen Target Field in its inaugural season. Attendance should top three million for the first time since 1988, between the new venue and the year-after spike that trails a playoff trip, but new parks don't guarantee attendance, especially if the team has just done something massively demoralizing, like waving good-bye to one of the game's best players.

Happily, it seems as if Smith presides over an organization as serious about its near-term future as the longer term. Last year's holes in the lineup are being filled in. Trading Carlos Gomez and his vaunted future to the Brewers to get two seasons of J. J. Hardy isn't simply a matter of disgust over how badly the Johan

Santana trade turned out; it's a matter of adding a quality player whose value was down at a position where good help is hard to find, and having, in Hardy, a shortstop they'll control for at least two years before free agency. Span's takeover from Gomez in center field makes for a commitment to Young in left for the time being. Although this call has kept the team on slow burn much of the last two years while Matt Garza and Jason Bartlett blossomed with the Rays, it was a long-term investment in Young's bat and upside. And the investment finally seems to have started bearing fruit during the second half of the 2009 season. Last season's one-year spin with Crede may well give way at some point this season to Danny Valencia, barring another veteran pickup, leaving second base as the one slot for Punto, Casilla, Tolbert, and Brendan Harris to figure out which of them is the Little Big Man of the keystone.

The dilemma that isn't being as neatly addressed is the rotation, where implacable faith seems to be the rule of the day. Baker is supposed to be the best of the lot. Brought back early from a spring shoulder injury that may have contributed to his allowing 14 of his total 28 homers in his first nine starts, he settled in, throwing 15 quality starts through the first six innings in his next 24 and posting a 3.67 ERA. Blackburn might be the reigning exemplar of Twins-style strike-throwing finesse, but after a four-start stretch starting in late June when he faced 32.5 batters per turn, even his efficiency appeared overtaxed, and he didn't really hit a good patch again until the late-September run that put the team over the top. The fabulously fragile Pavano promptly accepted an offer of arbitration after putting up his first full season in five years, initially leaving just two slots open to the remaining collection of disappointments. Slowey should be healthy by the time camps open, while Perkins may be in a bad odor after filing (but later resolving) a grievance over his service time. It's hard to imagine a pitcher more disappointing than Liriano. Given that nobody went away over the winter, guys like Duensing, Manship, and Swarzak may just have to queue up and wait for Smith and Ron Gardenhire to make a few tough calls.

Taken collectively, whatever hopes there are for the Twins' defense-dependent staff to keep up with the Tigers' blue-chip trio or the White Sox' division-best quintet should get the benefit of the addition of Hardy at short and the switch to playing outdoors at home, on grass, and in the Minnesota elements. It may not fully equalize matters in the Central's arms race, but it will help, and better balance from the lineup should help as well.

If they can convince Mauer to stick around, he'll be the signature player of a franchise that isn't just going to be a so-called right-way team. The Twins have shown an idiosyncratic aggressiveness in the draft, trusting in the long-term upside possibilities of picks like outfielders Ben Revere, Aaron Hicks, and Angel Morales, while continuing to favor more finished pitchers, like 2009 first-round hurler Kyle Gibson. Whatever their past reputation for parsimony, buying top Dominican prospect Miguel Sano last summer makes it clear they're not merely making the rounds on the player development beat, but they're playing at the high end of the market. In the broad strokes, they've obviously reaped the benefits of this approach. It leaves them missing the greatness of a Santana or a Frank Viola atop the rotation, but if anyone in-house was supposed to be that kind of talent, it was the fragile and frustrating Liriano.

Finally, Smith's unwillingness to merely let it ride last season speaks to something more than the old indifference frequently ascribed to the tenure of the late Carl Pohlad. The family's billionaire scion passed away before last season, but interestingly, his three sons have been the anti-Steinbrenners, with Jim Pohlad riding point and quietly taking on a larger role in extending larger commitments by signing off on multiyear extensions to key players like Cuddyer, Nathan, and Morneau in the spring of 2008 and likewise rewarding Kubel in '09. Can the Pohlad trio do the same with Mauer before he says hello and good-bye to the Twin Cities' faithful in the new house they've built? The Twins' shot at remaining in the AL Central's turgid mix depends on it.

HITTERS

Brian Buscher 3B Bats: L Throws: R Height: 6' 0" Weight: 220 Born: April 18, 1981 Age: 29

YEAR	TEAM	LVL	AGE	PA	R	2B	3B	HR	RBI	BB	SO	SB	CS	EqBRR	AVG	OBP	SLG	EqAVG	EqOBP	EqSLG	EqA	VORP	WARP	DEFENSE	
2007	NBR	AA	26	284	37	19	1	7	37	31	30	2	2	-4.1	.308	.391	.478	.270	.335	.402	.257	4.2	0.3	43-3B	-2
2007	ROC	AAA	26	147	21	7	0	7	22	13	11	1	0	-0.7	.311	.374	.523	.291	.351	.485	.286	6.8	1.0	24-3B	2
2007	MIN	MLB	26	94	8	1	0	2	10	10	16	1	0	-2.6	.244	.323	.329	.244	.323	.329	.241	-0.2	-0.1	23-3B	-1
2008	ROC	AAA	27	214	27	12	0	8	30	20	21	1	2	-1.4	.319	.402	.514	.291	.364	.460	.282	9.2	1.7	36-3B 4	7-1B 1
2008	MIN	MLB	27	244	29	9	0	4	47	19	42	0	2	-0.3	.294	.340	.390	.301	.344	.398	.264	6.7	0.6	58-3B -1	2-1B 0
2009	ROC	AAA	28	89	6	0	0	1	2	11	20	0	1	-0.6	.179	.281	.218	.165	.258	.203	.154	-8.0	-1.0	8-1B -1	4-3B 1
2009	MIN	MLB	28	164	14	3	1	2	12	24	35	0	0	0.0	.235	.360	.316	.235	.360	.316	.252	0.1	-0.1	22-3B -1	8-1B 0
2010	*CLE*	*MLB*	*29*	*336*	*36*	*14*	*1*	*8*	*42*	*33*	*56*	*1*	*1*	*-1.4*	*.258*	*.335*	*.389*	*.262*	*.340*	*.397*	*.255*	*6.8*	*0.8*	*65-3B*	*0*

Breakout: 16% Improve: 40% Collapse: 18% Attrition: 21%   MLB: 46%   Comparables: Matt Franco, Jack Hannahan, Brad Mills, Mark Leonard

Buscher has spent the last two years as the Twins' primary backup at both infield corners, only playing against righties and not showing much power. That's a fairly limited skill set, and the Twins understandably removed Buscher from the 40-man roster after the season. An interesting piece of ephemera: in one of the stranger season-to-season changes you'll see, Buscher's batting average dropped by nearly 60 points last year, yet a sudden spike in his walk rate meant that his on-base percentage went up; Sixto Lezcano from 1984-85 is the only other player to do the same. Buscher is a nonroster invitee with the Indians, where he might form the platoon of gloom with Andy Marte at one corner or the other.

Orlando Cabrera SS Bats: R Throws: R Height: 5' 9" Weight: 185 Born: November 2, 1974 Age: 35

YEAR	TEAM	LVL	AGE	PA	R	2B	3B	HR	RBI	BB	SO	SB	CS	EqBRR	AVG	OBP	SLG	EqAVG	EqOBP	EqSLG	EqA	VORP	WARP	DEFENSE	
2007	LAA	MLB	32	701	101	35	1	8	86	44	64	20	4	4.7	.301	.345	.397	.301	.345	.402	.265	30.3	3.3	150-SS	-1
2008	CHA	MLB	33	730	93	33	1	8	57	56	71	19	6	2.6	.281	.334	.371	.282	.335	.376	.253	24.3	2.7	155-SS	0
2009	OAK	MLB	34	448	41	23	0	4	41	25	39	11	4	2.4	.280	.318	.365	.289	.326	.371	.247	11.7	-0.2	99-SS	-13
2009	MIN	MLB	34	260	42	13	3	5	36	11	32	2	0	3.1	.289	.313	.430	.296	.317	.433	.261	10.3	1.1	55-SS	0
2010	*MIN*	*MLB*	*35*	*616*	*77*	*26*	*2*	*9*	*68*	*45*	*69*	*13*	*6*	*1.9*	*.280*	*.334*	*.383*	*.277*	*.332*	*.378*	*.245*	*11.8*	*1.1*	*136-SS*	*-2*

Breakout: 4% Improve: 28% Collapse: 19% Attrition: 25%   MLB: 98%   Comparables: Alvin Dark, Luis Aparicio, Mike Bordick, Omar Vizquel

Have glove, will travel. Cabrera was signed by the A's in the offseason, as Oakland thought they had a shot at contending in 2009 (whoops). They dealt him at the deadline to Minnesota, which actually *was* contending, thanks to the AL Central's being to playoff possibilities what *MADtv*'s "Lowered Expectations" skit is to dating. Everyone knows what Cabrera is at this point; his offensive performances have been nearly identical for the last four years, he never gets hurt, and he comes with a good rep on D. He's the kind of player where you're sort of happy when you have him, but you're wondering if you didn't settle. The Twins decided that Hardy is a relative dreamboat, so Cabrera will begin 2010 with his seventh team in seven years.

Alexi Casilla 2B Bats: S Throws: R Height: 5' 9" Weight: 180 Born: July 20, 1984 Age: 25

YEAR	TEAM	LVL	AGE	PA	R	2B	3B	HR	RBI	BB	SO	SB	CS	EqBRR	AVG	OBP	SLG	EqAVG	EqOBP	EqSLG	EqA	VORP	WARP	DEFENSE	
2007	ROC	AAA	22	365	53	13	1	3	20	34	50	24	12	-1.2	.269	.345	.344	.252	.322	.326	.234	2.9	-1.6	41-SS -12	41-2B -5
2007	MIN	MLB	22	204	15	5	1	0	9	9	29	11	1	1.5	.222	.256	.259	.223	.258	.255	.198	-5.8	-1.0	48-2B -4	3-SS 0
2008	ROC	AAA	23	121	11	3	0	0	2	18	18	4	3	-0.2	.219	.350	.250	.204	.331	.235	.214	-0.9	-1.0	20-SS -4	9-2B -4
2008	MIN	MLB	23	437	58	15	0	7	50	31	45	7	2	0.4	.281	.333	.374	.289	.342	.384	.260	13.7	1.5	93-2B	-1
2009	ROC	AAA	24	171	21	3	4	2	17	11	23	9	6	-0.8	.340	.379	.449	.314	.355	.423	.266	6.3	0.9	38-2B	1
2009	MIN	MLB	24	256	25	7	3	0	17	22	36	11	0	0.9	.202	.280	.256	.203	.281	.256	.208	-6.2	-1.3	64-2B	-5
2010	*MIN*	*MLB*	*25*	*470*	*60*	*17*	*3*	*6*	*40*	*42*	*68*	*16*	*6*	*0.0*	*.262*	*.333*	*.362*	*.263*	*.332*	*.355*	*.241*	*4.9*	*0.2*	*111-2B*	*-3*

Breakout: 22% Improve: 49% Collapse: 9% Attrition: 8%   MLB: 100%   Comparables: Bryan Little, Brian Roberts, Abraham Nunez, Jeff Carter

For three years, Casilla has been a source of frustration while trying and failing to establish himself. With enough quality work on the farm scene to be a 4-H all-star, Casilla has the numbers and the scouting reports to deserve more chances, but he's pressed every time he's in the majors, while also occasionally getting on Ron Gardenhire's bad side for his effort and attitude. The Twins aren't giving up on him yet, and now that he's got hero status after getting the walk-off hit against the Tigers to put the Twins in the playoffs, he'll get another chance in 2010. It's up to him to avoid joining the Giants' John Patterson in history's dustbin as a one-clutch-hit wonder.

Joe Crede 3B

Bats: R   Throws: R   Height: 6' 2"   Weight: 230   Born: April 26, 1978   Age: 32

YEAR	TEAM	LVL	AGE	PA	R	2B	3B	HR	RBI	BB	SO	SB	CS	EqBRR	AVG	OBP	SLG	EqAVG	EqOBP	EqSLG	EqA	VORP	WARP	DEFENSE	
2007	CHA	MLB	29	178	13	5	0	4	22	10	24	0	1	0.0	.216	.258	.317	.216	.258	.329	.197	-6.8	0.0	44-3B	7
2008	CHA	MLB	30	373	41	18	1	17	55	30	45	0	3	-1.2	.248	.314	.460	.246	.313	.461	.261	9.7	2.0	93-3B	8
2009	MIN	MLB	31	367	42	16	1	15	48	29	56	0	0	-0.3	.225	.289	.414	.229	.292	.416	.243	3.1	1.5	82-3B	10
2010	MIN	MLB	32	299	33	13	1	14	45	25	46	0	1	-0.3	.246	.314	.452	.241	.308	.434	.252	5.2	1.1	73-3B	4

Breakout: 12%   Improve: 42%   Collapse: 21%   Attrition: 18%   MLB: 91%   Comparables: Ed Sprague, Pedro Feliz, Charlie Hayes, Herb Perry

After two years of serious back issues, Crede signed a relatively cheap one-year deal with the Twins, hoping that a healthy, productive year would lead to more money down the road. Instead, it led to another year of back problems, including another surgery at the end of the year. He's now had three straight years of playing fewer than 100 games, and he has hit .232/.293/.413 when available. When he was healthy, he wasn't even that good as a low-average, low-walk, plus-power third baseman with good defense. He's looking for another shot, and it just might be the Twins who come calling again, although at an even cheaper rate this time around.

Michael Cuddyer RF

Bats: R   Throws: R   Height: 6' 2"   Weight: 215   Born: March 27, 1979   Age: 31

YEAR	TEAM	LVL	AGE	PA	R	2B	3B	HR	RBI	BB	SO	SB	CS	EqBRR	AVG	OBP	SLG	EqAVG	EqOBP	EqSLG	EqA	VORP	WARP	DEFENSE			
2007	MIN	MLB	28	623	87	28	5	16	81	64	107	5	0	-0.7	.276	.356	.433	.279	.360	.439	.280	23.8	3.1	138-RF	3	4-1B	0
2008	MIN	MLB	29	279	30	13	4	3	36	25	40	5	1	0.2	.249	.330	.369	.253	.336	.369	.254	2.6	0.3	56-RF	0		
2009	MIN	MLB	30	650	93	34	7	32	94	54	118	6	1	-0.5	.276	.342	.520	.279	.345	.521	.290	32.6	2.3	112-RF	-10	32-1B	-2
2010	MIN	MLB	31	566	76	28	5	20	76	54	100	5	2	-0.1	.271	.348	.463	.269	.346	.455	.271	18.8	1.9	126-RF	-1		

Breakout: 16%   Improve: 46%   Collapse: 14%   Attrition: 8%   MLB: 98%   Comparables: Al Cowens, Eric Byrnes, Richie Zisk, Leon Roberts

One of the players who stepped up in the absence of Justin Morneau, Cuddyer delivered a career year in 2009, finishing sixth in the league in extra-base hits, among them the eight homers he hit in the last 20 games to propel the Twins to the tie-breaker. His value might be a bit overstated, as he absolutely hammers southpaws (15 home runs in 166 at-bats), while being fairly fungible for a corner hitter against righties (.263/.333/.469). Other than the bat, he doesn't offer much in the ways he can beat you; he's an average fielder at unimportant positions and a below-average runner. Don't get us wrong, he's good to have and an above-average starter, but there are some holes in his game, and he's something less than a true star.

Carlos Gomez CF

Bats: R   Throws: R   Height: 6' 4"   Weight: 195   Born: December 4, 1985   Age: 24

YEAR	TEAM	LVL	AGE	PA	R	2B	3B	HR	RBI	BB	SO	SB	CS	EqBRR	AVG	OBP	SLG	EqAVG	EqOBP	EqSLG	EqA	VORP	WARP	DEFENSE			
2007	NWO	AAA	21	157	24	8	2	2	13	15	23	17	4	2.2	.286	.363	.414	.275	.348	.394	.266	5.6	1.0	35-CF	3		
2007	NYN	MLB	21	139	14	3	0	2	12	8	27	12	3	1.4	.232	.288	.304	.242	.295	.306	.232	-1.8	0.3	20-LF	4	15-RF	-1
2008	MIN	MLB	22	614	79	24	7	7	59	25	142	33	11	2.2	.258	.296	.360	.267	.306	.373	.242	4.7	3.1	142-CF	21		
2009	MIN	MLB	23	349	51	15	5	3	28	22	72	14	7	-0.2	.229	.287	.337	.236	.294	.342	.225	-2.6	1.6	95-CF	16		
2010	MIL	MLB	24	488	66	21	6	7	45	36	110	27	11	1.2	.245	.312	.363	.253	.316	.370	.244	7.1	1.7	115-CF	8		

Breakout: 20%   Improve: 57%   Collapse: 13%   Attrition: 3%   MLB: 100%   Comparables: Andre Dawson, Ellis Burks, Juan Encarnacion, B.J. Upton

On the positive side of things, Gomez is just 24 years old, and his tools are still stunning. He's a top-line runner who plays an outstanding center, but ... well, those are the positives. With over 1,000 plate appearances in the majors, his career on-base percentage is still under .300. The Twins had enough of waiting, so they sent him to Milwaukee for Hardy in a trade of players who had frustrated their former employers and worn out their welcomes. Gomez will be the everyday center fielder for the Brewers, and while Milwaukee won't lose a thing defensively going from Mike Cameron to Gomez, they're hoping that the guttering candle of Gomez's potential reaches full flame in their care.

Brendan Harris INF

Bats: R   Throws: R   Height: 6' 1"   Weight: 210   Born: August 26, 1980   Age: 29

YEAR	TEAM	LVL	AGE	PA	R	2B	3B	HR	RBI	BB	SO	SB	CS	EqBRR	AVG	OBP	SLG	EqAVG	EqOBP	EqSLG	EqA	VORP	WARP	DEFENSE
2007	TBA	MLB	26	576	72	35	3	12	59	42	96	4	1	0.6	.286	.343	.434	.291	.349	.441	.274	28.7	0.3	85-SS -16 46-2B -8
2008	MIN	MLB	27	490	57	29	3	7	49	39	98	1	1	1.2	.265	.327	.394	.274	.337	.409	.260	17.3	0.5	52-SS -6 36-2B -2
2009	MIN	MLB	28	453	44	22	1	6	37	29	78	0	2	0.0	.261	.310	.362	.265	.312	.362	.238	3.5	0.1	51-SS 3 35-3B -5
2010	MIN	MLB	29	523	62	28	2	12	54	43	95	2	2	0.3	.278	.342	.416	.276	.341	.410	.256	15.7	1.1	108-SS -5

Breakout: 16% Improve: 56% Collapse: 6% Attrition: 7%   MLB: 96%   Comparables: Rich Aurilia, Alex Gonzalez, Chris Gomez, Deivi Cruz

For the second straight year, Harris entered the year as the team's utility man, but injuries and poor performances propelled him into nearly full-time work, albeit spread across every infield position. As a bench player, he's useful due to his versatility and occasional gap power, but when you give him 400-plus plate appearances, his impatient approach and difficulties hitting good right-handers gets exposed. When you consider the scrubby alternatives in the world of infield sidekicks, the Twins are happy to have him, and they're smart enough to know they don't want him playing this much.

Aaron Hicks CF

Bats: S   Throws: R   Height: 6' 2"   Weight: 170   Born: October 2, 1989   Age: 20

YEAR	TEAM	LVL	AGE	PA	R	2B	3B	HR	RBI	BB	SO	SB	CS	EqBRR	AVG	OBP	SLG	EqAVG	EqOBP	EqSLG	EqA	VORP	WARP	DEFENSE
2008	TWI	Rk	18	204	32	10	4	4	27	28	32	12	2	1.6	.318	.409	.491	.271	.342	.409	.264	6.2	0.3	40-CF -5
2009	BLT	A	19	297	43	15	3	4	29	40	55	10	8	-2.5	.251	.353	.382	.215	.295	.314	.218	-4.4	-1.1	64-CF -5
2010	MIN	MLB	20	360	40	16	2	5	30	36	81	5	4	-1.5	.233	.309	.345	.232	.308	.342	.222	-2.7	-0.6	79-CF -3

Breakout: 38% Improve: 56% Collapse: 19% Attrition: 0%   MLB: 0%   Comparables: Jarred Ball, Gerald Young, Rafael Boitel, Dexter Fowler

The club's first-round pick in 2008, Hicks might not have put up monster numbers in his full-season debut, but the scouting reports were universally glowing. It didn't add up to a great season, but in every game you might see him in, chances were good you'd see something impressive. He's not your classic raw, toolsy player; instead, he has an excellent feel for the strike zone, already plays a fantastic center field, and features an arm that touched 97 mph off the mound in high school. There's raw power in his stroke as well, but he's going to need to learn how to tap into it. If there is one prospect in baseball with the most pent-up energy waiting to explode in 2010, it might be Hicks.

Luke Hughes 3B

Bats: R   Throws: R   Height: 5' 11"   Weight: 200   Born: August 2, 1984   Age: 25

YEAR	TEAM	LVL	AGE	PA	R	2B	3B	HR	RBI	BB	SO	SB	CS	EqBRR	AVG	OBP	SLG	EqAVG	EqOBP	EqSLG	EqA	VORP	WARP	DEFENSE
2007	NBR	AA	22	362	56	18	2	9	43	34	68	4	1	1.6	.283	.356	.438	.264	.327	.407	.257	7.9	1.0	44-2B 3 19-LF -6
2008	NBR	AA	23	319	53	15	3	15	40	28	70	4	1	1.5	.319	.385	.551	.282	.338	.478	.277	14.2	0.3	39-3B -10 17-2B -4
2008	ROC	AAA	23	117	17	7	1	3	21	7	30	2	0	1.2	.283	.325	.453	.264	.308	.434	.259	2.6	0.0	26-3B -3
2009	NBR	AA	24	229	22	15	3	6	36	19	38	1	1	-2.5	.250	.320	.445	.239	.294	.415	.246	2.8	0.2	44-3B -2 7-2B 1
2009	ROC	AAA	24	157	19	8	2	6	28	18	38	2	0	-0.4	.259	.344	.481	.243	.329	.456	.273	5.9	0.9	31-3B 2
2010	MIN	MLB	25	363	45	17	2	11	43	31	86	3	1	0.2	.249	.319	.409	.246	.316	.397	.245	3.7	0.0	72-3B -3

Breakout: 2% Improve: 31% Collapse: 19% Attrition: 12%   MLB: 9%   Comparables: Tony Brewer, Chuckie Canady, Mike Reddish, Jerry Lomastro

Hughes failed to build on his 2008 breakout and might be relegated to Quadruple-A status at this point, and even that might be a reach, since the squat Aussie had to be sent back to Double-A last summer. The Twins' lack of good third-base options probably has Rich Rollins back on their radar, so Hughes may yet have another life with the club.

Jason Kubel DH

Bats: L   Throws: R   Height: 6' 0"   Weight: 210   Born: May 25, 1982   Age: 28

YEAR	TEAM	LVL	AGE	PA	R	2B	3B	HR	RBI	BB	SO	SB	CS	EqBRR	AVG	OBP	SLG	EqAVG	EqOBP	EqSLG	EqA	VORP	WARP	DEFENSE
2007	MIN	MLB	25	466	49	31	2	13	65	41	79	5	0	-3.5	.273	.335	.450	.274	.338	.454	.275	15.2	1.4	79-LF -2
2008	MIN	MLB	26	517	74	22	5	20	78	47	91	0	1	-0.6	.272	.335	.471	.280	.342	.489	.281	19.3	1.7	27-RF -2 15-LF -2
2009	MIN	MLB	27	578	73	35	2	28	103	56	106	1	1	-2.1	.300	.369	.539	.303	.371	.533	.303	32.6	4.0	24-RF -2 23-LF 4
2010	MIN	MLB	28	545	70	29	3	23	90	55	99	2	1	-1.1	.281	.355	.494	.278	.352	.478	.281	24.0	2.4	60-RF -2

Breakout: 10% Improve: 44% Collapse: 11% Attrition: 11%   MLB: 100%   Comparables: Bobby Higginson, Johnny Briggs, Trot Nixon, Warren Cromartie

The Twins' lineup is loaded with some massive platoon splits, and Kubel is one of their paragons of such virtues, slugging .345 with just two homers against southpaws while hitting like an MVP-caliber player against righties, batting .323/.397/.619. All of these players with exploitable weaknesses put Gardenhire in a tough situation. Along with Joe Mauer, Kubel carried the offense at several points in the second half, and his name showed up at the bottom of a few MVP ballots, so it's difficult to say, "Hey Jason, we're going to bench you against lefties." Earl Weaver was a genius, but it's hard to see today's players (and their agents) accepting that kind of strategy, making the job of manager even more challenging than it once was.

Joe Mauer   C   Bats: L   Throws: R   Height: 6' 5"   Weight: 230   Born: April 19, 1983   Age: 27

YEAR	TEAM	LVL	AGE	PA	R	2B	3B	HR	RBI	BB	SO	SB	CS	EqBRR	AVG	OBP	SLG	EqAVG	EqOBP	EqSLG	EqA	VORP	WARP	DEFENSE	
2007	MIN	MLB	24	471	62	27	3	7	60	57	51	7	1	1.1	.293	.382	.426	.295	.384	.433	.287	32.3	4.8	88-C	9
2008	MIN	MLB	25	633	98	31	4	9	85	84	50	1	1	4.1	.328	.413	.451	.336	.420	.464	.312	59.6	7.5	134-C	7
2009	MIN	MLB	26	606	94	30	1	28	96	76	63	4	1	-3.6	.365	.444	.587	.368	.446	.580	.346	77.5	8.8	104-C	2
2010	MIN	MLB	27	608	90	31	2	19	90	82	63	4	2	0.3	.318	.412	.491	.317	.411	.477	.306	51.9	5.9	118-C	3

Breakout: 14% Improve: 51% Collapse: 10% Attrition: 4%   MLB: 100%   Comparables: Terry Kennedy, A.J. Pierzynski, Johnny Edwards, Eddie Taubensee

In 284 career minor-league games, Joe Mauer hit a grand total of nine home runs. Yes, every scout you could find would tell you that one day, he'd hit 25 to 30 a year. He averaged less than 10 per year in his first four full seasons for the Twins, but scouts insisted that he was the ultimate example of why there is the cliché about power being the last tool to develop. In 2009, it finally showed up. Nobody thinks it's a fluke, and he's now easily in the argument for most valuable future career in baseball based on his production, age, and position, a franchise player at a position that has seen only one hitter of his caliber in 50 years—and Mike Piazza lacked Mauer's gifts behind the plate.

Angel Morales   OF   Bats: R   Throws: R   Height: 6' 1"   Weight: 180   Born: November 24, 1989   Age: 20

YEAR	TEAM	LVL	AGE	PA	R	2B	3B	HR	RBI	BB	SO	SB	CS	EqBRR	AVG	OBP	SLG	EqAVG	EqOBP	EqSLG	EqA	VORP	WARP	DEFENSE			
2007	TWI	Rk	17	143	18	6	3	2	15	12	44	11	5	-1.8	.256	.357	.405	.223	.285	.354	.226	-2.6	-2.0	32-RF	-8	5-CF	0
2008	ELZ	Rk	18	218	33	12	1	15	28	26	72	7	2	0.3	.301	.413	.623	.232	.317	.438	.259	5.7	0.8	52-CF	-1		
2009	BLT	A	19	418	63	22	5	13	62	30	104	19	6	-1.6	.266	.329	.455	.230	.276	.382	.229	-4.1	-2.5	51-CF	-11	50-RF	-6
2010	MIN	MLB	20	431	48	20	2	15	46	34	124	7	3	-0.5	.236	.301	.410	.233	.300	.402	.238	3.3	-0.3	106-CF	-6		

Breakout: 26% Improve: 60% Collapse: 14% Attrition: 3%   MLB: 0%   Comparables: Don Brown, Oscar Jiminez, Carl Jones-Pointer, Alex Ramirez

Morales' cumulative numbers might not pop out at you, but it was really a tale of two seasons for him, as he was one of the Midwest League's most dangerous hitters during the second half, bopping at a .317/.372/.533 clip after the All-Star break. In a system loaded with toolsy outfielders, Morales ranks right up there with them. He possesses above-average power and speed, but his plate discipline lags behind, and the overall rawness of his game prevents him from stealing as many bases as one might expect. Likely profiling better as a corner outfielder, especially with the organization's crop of center-field prospects, Morales still has a lot of upside, but also a lot of work to do.

Jose Morales   C   Bats: S   Throws: R   Height: 5' 11"   Weight: 190   Born: February 20, 1983   Age: 27

YEAR	TEAM	LVL	AGE	PA	R	2B	3B	HR	RBI	BB	SO	SB	CS	EqBRR	AVG	OBP	SLG	EqAVG	EqOBP	EqSLG	EqA	VORP	WARP	DEFENSE	
2007	ROC	AAA	24	411	42	25	1	2	37	30	44	1	4	-7.1	.311	.366	.399	.292	.341	.374	.250	12.6	1.9	89-C	3
2008	ROC	AAA	25	208	18	8	1	4	15	8	28	0	1	-2.7	.315	.348	.426	.293	.324	.399	.248	5.4	0.8	44-C	1
2009	ROC	AAA	26	242	30	13	1	2	26	28	27	1	3	-1.6	.336	.413	.436	.310	.384	.404	.276	11.0	0.5	38-C	-7
2009	MIN	MLB	26	134	14	6	0	0	7	14	22	0	0	0.0	.311	.381	.361	.311	.381	.353	.270	3.7	0.4	21-C	-1
2010	MIN	MLB	27	321	32	16	1	4	25	26	49	1	2	-1.9	.278	.341	.384	.275	.338	.371	.245	7.6	0.8	62-C	-1

Breakout: 13% Improve: 36% Collapse: 26% Attrition: 24%   MLB: 71%   Comparables: Brayan Pena, Ed Yacopino, Mark Dalesandro, Ryan Hanigan

We have plenty of evidence at this point that Morales really is a .300 hitter, as he's done it for three straight seasons in the minors while repeating the feat in a series of call-ups with the big boys. He can also draw a fair share of walks, but that's about the sum of his abilities, as there are Little Leaguers with more power, and his arm behind the plate is below average. That combination has the Twins still deciding if they should let him be the backup in 2010, or if they should opt for a more defensive-minded choice to caddy for Mauer.

Justin Morneau   1B

Bats: L   Throws: R   Height: 6' 4"   Weight: 230   Born: May 15, 1981   Age: 29

YEAR	TEAM	LVL	AGE	PA	R	2B	3B	HR	RBI	BB	SO	SB	CS	EqBRR	AVG	OBP	SLG	EqAVG	EqOBP	EqSLG	EqA	VORP	WARP	DEFENSE	
2007	MIN	MLB	26	668	84	31	3	31	111	64	91	1	1	-3.0	.271	.343	.492	.273	.344	.499	.285	25.3	3.9	142-1B	9
2008	MIN	MLB	27	712	97	47	4	23	129	76	85	0	1	-2.6	.300	.374	.499	.307	.381	.512	.303	42.1	4.2	152-1B	-3
2009	MIN	MLB	28	590	85	31	1	30	100	72	86	0	0	0.8	.274	.363	.516	.277	.364	.510	.296	24.7	3.1	121-1B	3
2010	MIN	MLB	29	617	87	32	2	30	115	71	86	1	1	-0.8	.286	.371	.520	.281	.368	.504	.293	29.8	3.4	133-1B	1

Breakout: 17%   Improve: 50%   Collapse: 6%   Attrition: 5%   MLB: 100%   Comparables: Kent Hrbek, Jason Giambi, Boog Powell, David Ortiz

One of the biggest stories for the Twins in 2009 was the late-season loss of Morneau due to back and wrist problems and how the club overcame it, but let's get away from that for a bit, because on a performance level, Morneau's 2006 MVP line looks more and more like an outlier with each passing day. He's been consistently good for the last three years, but rarely great, racking up triple-digit RBI totals because of the opportunities presented to him by the lineup as opposed to truly mashing. His composite line of .282/.360/.501 from 2007-09 is more indicative of his true ability, and while that adds up to an above-average first baseman, it falls short of the impact-player level.

Trevor Plouffe   SS

Bats: R   Throws: R   Height: 6' 2"   Weight: 200   Born: June 15, 1986   Age: 24

YEAR	TEAM	LVL	AGE	PA	R	2B	3B	HR	RBI	BB	SO	SB	CS	EqBRR	AVG	OBP	SLG	EqAVG	EqOBP	EqSLG	EqA	VORP	WARP	DEFENSE			
2007	NBR	AA	21	555	75	37	2	9	50	38	89	12	7	-1.0	.274	.326	.410	.255	.299	.381	.238	7.7	-0.1	121-SS	-9		
2008	NBR	AA	22	249	32	17	3	3	21	16	43	4	2	0.4	.269	.325	.410	.251	.297	.381	.235	2.6	-0.4	45-SS	-4	11-3B	-2
2008	ROC	AAA	22	272	34	17	3	6	39	14	47	1	1	-0.2	.256	.292	.420	.238	.272	.389	.228	-1.2	0.5	32-3B	5	20-2B	-3
2009	ROC	AAA	23	477	53	23	5	10	60	34	68	3	6	-3.2	.260	.313	.407	.246	.298	.392	.238	7.1	1.1	109-SS	2		
2010	MIN	MLB	24	488	58	25	3	12	54	34	90	5	4	-0.6	.250	.305	.396	.248	.303	.388	.234	4.1	0.2	103-SS	-2		

Breakout: 17%   Improve: 42%   Collapse: 15%   Attrition: 14%   MLB: 9%   Comparables: Jack Ayer, Mendy Lopez, Mike Manfre, Kevin Coughlon

The club's first-round pick way back in 2004, Plouffe has been stuck at the upper levels of the Twins' system for three years now, and there's little reason to believe he'll escape anytime soon. While his double-digit power is rare for an up-the-middle player, he's an average-at-best defender who doesn't walk, run, or hit for much of an average. The Twins have toyed at times with the idea of turning him into a utility type, and their lack of confidence in his ever developing into an everyday player was reflected in the trade for J. J. Hardy.

Nick Punto   INF

Bats: S   Throws: R   Height: 5' 9"   Weight: 195   Born: November 8, 1977   Age: 32

YEAR	TEAM	LVL	AGE	PA	R	2B	3B	HR	RBI	BB	SO	SB	CS	EqBRR	AVG	OBP	SLG	EqAVG	EqOBP	EqSLG	EqA	VORP	WARP	DEFENSE			
2007	MIN	MLB	29	536	53	18	4	1	25	55	90	16	6	-0.6	.210	.291	.271	.213	.295	.275	.210	-12.3	-1.1	93-3B	2	24-SS	-1
2008	MIN	MLB	30	377	43	19	4	2	28	32	57	15	6	0.9	.284	.344	.382	.295	.356	.393	.266	15.9	3.0	59-SS	6	24-2B	2
2009	MIN	MLB	31	440	56	15	1	1	38	61	70	16	3	4.3	.228	.337	.284	.234	.340	.287	.242	7.1	0.5	56-2B	-2	55-SS	-1
2010	MIN	MLB	32	389	45	16	2	2	30	43	72	12	6	0.7	.243	.327	.321	.243	.327	.320	.227	-1.3	-0.1	91-2B	0		

Breakout: 12%   Improve: 36%   Collapse: 22%   Attrition: 21%   MLB: 89%   Comparables: Denny Hocking, Mark McLemore, Luis Alicea, Aaron Miles

Punto received the bulk of the playing time at second base when Casilla struggled, while also playing shortstop before the team acquired Orlando Cabrera. He also suffered through the worst offensive year of his career, excusing himself from all offensive obligations except drawing walks. Luckily, he rose to the occasion down the stretch, doing his thing by generating a .406 OBP over the last 30 games. He's the kind of fundamentally sound scrapper who Ron Gardenhire loves having around (perhaps such players remind him of himself), and despite the numbers, his contract ($4 million in 2010) and utility make him a lock for some kind of infield role in 2010.

Wilson Ramos   C

Bats: R   Throws: R   Height: 6' 0"   Weight: 205   Born: August 10, 1987   Age: 22

YEAR	TEAM	LVL	AGE	PA	R	2B	3B	HR	RBI	BB	SO	SB	CS	EqBRR	AVG	OBP	SLG	EqAVG	EqOBP	EqSLG	EqA	VORP	WARP	DEFENSE
2007	BLT	A	19	316	40	17	1	8	42	19	61	1	1	-1.4	.291	.345	.438	.263	.307	.391	.240	4.9	1.7	50-C	9
2008	FTM	A+	20	500	50	23	2	13	78	37	103	0	1	-6.1	.288	.346	.434	.265	.311	.397	.246	7.7	1.3	74-C	3
2009	NBR	AA	21	214	31	16	0	4	29	6	23	0	0	0.1	.317	.341	.454	.309	.327	.449	.265	8.9	1.5	43-C	4
2010	MIN	MLB	22	370	40	18	1	9	48	24	79	0	1	-1.3	.264	.316	.405	.263	.316	.399	.240	7.1	1.1	61-C	3

Breakout: 21%   Improve: 48%   Collapse: 17%   Attrition: 8%   MLB: 6%   Comparables: Joe Oliver, Lou Marson, Chris Cassels, Ryan Luzinski

While a broken finger and some hamstring issues limited him to less than a half-season in 2009, Ramos is still one of the better catching prospects around. His pure hitting skills and power are above average for the position, and he's also a plus defender. His allure only grew with a huge winter in Venezuela, but the biggest question about his future is more a question about Joe Mauer's. Depending on Mauer's willingness to stick around, Ramos is either the Twins' catcher of the future or one of the most obvious trade chips in the game.

Mike Redmond   C

Bats: R   Throws: R   Height: 5' 11"   Weight: 200   Born: May 5, 1971   Age: 39

YEAR	TEAM	LVL	AGE	PA	R	2B	3B	HR	RBI	BB	SO	SB	CS	EqBRR	AVG	OBP	SLG	EqAVG	EqOBP	EqSLG	EqA	VORP	WARP	DEFENSE	
2007	MIN	MLB	36	298	23	13	0	1	38	18	23	0	0	-2.6	.294	.346	.353	.295	.346	.351	.252	7.6	1.6	54-C	6
2008	MIN	MLB	37	137	14	6	0	0	12	5	11	0	0	-0.2	.287	.321	.333	.295	.328	.333	.238	1.7	0.1	28-C	-1
2009	MIN	MLB	38	147	9	5	1	0	7	11	19	0	0	-1.1	.237	.299	.289	.237	.299	.281	.210	-1.2	-0.9	37-C	-6
2010	MIN	MLB	39	121	9	5	0	1	13	9	15	0	0	-0.4	.265	.332	.340	.262	.325	.326	.231	1.1	0.1	25-C	0

Breakout: 13%   Improve: 34%   Collapse: 34%   Attrition: 47%   MLB: 94%   Comparables: Brad Ausmus, Birdie Tebbetts, Elston Howard, Felipe Alou

For a four-year period from 2005 to 2008, Redmond did a fine job as Mauer's primary backup. While he offered a big fat zero in the way of secondary skills, he'd at least hit for average, making Mauer's days off a not-completely value-free proposition at the plate. When the average went away in 2009, Redmond became a massive liability, as his defense took a huge step backward as well: after gunning down 37 percent of basestealers the previous four seasons, he terminated just five of 40 in '09. The Twins have officially cut their ties with him, and he'll probably get no more than a spring invite from another team.

Ben Revere   OF

Bats: L   Throws: R   Height: 5' 9"   Weight: 166   Born: May 3, 1988   Age: 22

YEAR	TEAM	LVL	AGE	PA	R	2B	3B	HR	RBI	BB	SO	SB	CS	EqBRR	AVG	OBP	SLG	EqAVG	EqOBP	EqSLG	EqA	VORP	WARP	DEFENSE			
2007	TWI	Rk	19	216	46	6	10	0	29	13	20	21	9	1.1	.325	.388	.461	.290	.327	.430	.260	6.3	2.2	49-CF	5		
2008	BLT	A	20	374	51	17	10	1	43	27	31	44	13	0.9	.379	.433	.497	.340	.384	.444	.288	21.0	2.3	68-CF	0	8-LF	-2
2009	FTM	A+	21	517	75	13	4	2	48	40	34	45	17	4.3	.311	.372	.369	.295	.345	.352	.250	5.6	0.2	76-CF	-3	18-LF	-1
2010	MIN	MLB	22	487	57	22	5	3	47	37	49	20	8	1.4	.302	.359	.398	.301	.358	.394	.261	14.9	1.5	94-CF	-1		

Breakout: 11%   Improve: 44%   Collapse: 10%   Attrition: 1%   MLB: 6%   Comparables: Carlos Urquiola, Juan Pierre, Wayne Kirby, Lance Johnson

Revere's 2009 season was similar to his full-season debut the year before: he sliced balls all over the field, almost never struck out, and ran like crazy. Not everything remained the same, for better and for worse. The good news is that he showed an improved approach at the plate; the bad news is that much of his game is still messy, as his routes in center field need work and he has yet to figure out how to fully utilize his speed on the basepaths. Some scouts think he's going to fall into double-digit power down the road, but if that doesn't happen, he might just be Juan Pierre ... you know, the good version of Juan Pierre.

Miguel Sano   SS

Bats: R   Throws: R   Height: 6' 1"   Weight: 185   Born: May 1, 1993   Age: 17

Did Not Play.

Breakout: 11%   Improve: 44%   Collapse: 10%   Attrition: 1%   MLB: 6%   Comparables: NA

The Twins made a huge splash on the international market in the summer of 2009, as the best player in Latin America surprised a lot of people by signing with them for a bonus of over $3 million. That's a ton of cash to give to a 16-year-old, but scouts believe that Sano could really turn into something special. At his size and his age, there's no way he'll wind up staying at shortstop, but the Twins paid for his bat, not his glove, and his kind of power is rarely seen in such a young player. If he plays in the big leagues during the 2014 season, even that will be way ahead of schedule, so strap in for a long wait.

Denard Span — CF

Bats: L Throws: L Height: 6' 0" Weight: 205 Born: February 27, 1984 Age: 26

YEAR	TEAM	LVL	AGE	PA	R	2B	3B	HR	RBI	BB	SO	SB	CS	EqBRR	AVG	OBP	SLG	EqAVG	EqOBP	EqSLG	EqA	VORP	WARP	DEFENSE			
2007	ROC	AAA	23	548	59	20	7	3	55	40	90	25	14	2.4	.267	.323	.355	.252	.304	.337	.228	-2.7	0.0	133-CF	3		
2008	ROC	AAA	24	184	32	11	1	3	14	26	36	15	8	-0.5	.340	.434	.481	.316	.410	.449	.294	11.7	1.1	32-CF	-2	7-RF	0
2008	MIN	MLB	24	411	70	16	7	6	47	50	60	18	7	3.5	.294	.387	.432	.308	.401	.453	.295	24.4	3.9	77-RF	11	13-CF	-1
2009	MIN	MLB	25	676	97	16	10	8	68	70	89	23	10	1.6	.311	.392	.415	.319	.398	.422	.288	36.4	3.7	65-CF	-6	49-LF	6
2010	MIN	MLB	26	628	93	27	9	10	68	67	99	25	12	1.2	.289	.372	.421	.289	.371	.410	.271	26.3	2.7	134-CF	-2		

Breakout: 18% Improve: 61% Collapse: 9% Attrition: 6%   MLB: 89%   Comparables: Terrence Long, Mark Kotsay, Kenny Lofton, Bobby Abreu

If somebody deserves the title of Most Underrated Twin, it's Span. His game continued to grow in his second season; beyond his willingness to walk, with some extra-base potential he's not merely some slappy speed type, and he seemed to get better as the season wore on, batting .331/.402/.443 in the second half. He'll become even more valuable in 2010, as the center-field job, a position more suited to his offensive profile, is his following the trading of Carlos Gomez. A .300-hitting leadoff man with walks and good defense? Sign us up. While a .353 BABIP might lead to a reflexive assertion of regression, speed players do a bit better on this score, and if he's walking 10 percent of the time, he'll continue to be the table setter the heart of this order relishes having around.

Matt Tolbert — INF

Bats: S Throws: R Height: 6' 0" Weight: 185 Born: May 4, 1982 Age: 28

YEAR	TEAM	LVL	AGE	PA	R	2B	3B	HR	RBI	BB	SO	SB	CS	EqBRR	AVG	OBP	SLG	EqAVG	EqOBP	EqSLG	EqA	VORP	WARP	DEFENSE			
2007	ROC	AAA	25	477	65	24	7	6	53	37	56	11	3	3.4	.293	.353	.427	.275	.328	.405	.259	14.2	1.0	99-2B	-12	10-3B	5
2008	NBR	AA	26	57	6	3	0	0	6	1	6	3	3	-0.7	.250	.263	.304	.232	.246	.268	.165	-2.6	-0.2	9-SS	1		
2008	MIN	MLB	26	123	18	6	3	0	6	7	19	7	1	2.7	.283	.322	.389	.295	.333	.402	.265	4.8	0.8	10-3B	1	10-SS	0
2009	ROC	AAA	27	251	35	11	6	3	22	14	32	7	4	-0.2	.288	.331	.424	.262	.303	.384	.237	0.9	-0.2	22-2B	-3	14-LF	1
2009	MIN	MLB	27	231	28	7	1	2	19	21	37	6	2	1.6	.232	.303	.308	.235	.305	.311	.228	-1.3	0.1	32-2B	4	20-3B	-2
2010	MIN	MLB	28	393	52	19	4	5	38	30	61	9	3	1.2	.259	.319	.379	.258	.318	.377	.238	3.2	0.1	76-2B	-3		

Breakout: 10% Improve: 33% Collapse: 25% Attrition: 13%   MLB: 32%   Comparables: Bernie Castro, Ramon Santiago, Gerald Young, Jim Steels

The new Rob Wilfong, Tolbert dropped 10 successful sac bunts in the little playing time he got. There are spares, and then there are spares for spares, and the Twins are the type of conservative Minnesotan institution that believes in laying in for the winter by stocking up on switch-hitting infielders who can't hit a lick, because you never know, you might get snowed in during January, and what are you going to live on, Fritos? Tolbert played all four infield positions in 2009, and he has delivered some sock against lefties. That might just be enough for another shot this spring.

Rene Tosoni — OF

Bats: L Throws: R Height: 6' 0" Weight: 194 Born: July 2, 1986 Age: 23

YEAR	TEAM	LVL	AGE	PA	R	2B	3B	HR	RBI	BB	SO	SB	CS	EqBRR	AVG	OBP	SLG	EqAVG	EqOBP	EqSLG	EqA	VORP	WARP	DEFENSE			
2007	ELZ	Rk	20	286	58	13	4	3	31	32	48	13	4	1.0	.301	.407	.428	.257	.329	.348	.244	0.1	-1.5	57-RF	-10	4-CF	1
2008	FTM	A+	21	170	27	7	3	1	19	21	30	3	5	-3.6	.300	.408	.414	.274	.361	.370	.259	3.3	0.0	23-RF	-1	10-CF	-1
2009	NBR	AA	22	490	64	25	4	15	71	45	98	8	8	-1.1	.271	.360	.454	.260	.331	.432	.262	11.4	-0.4	85-RF	-8	27-CF	-7
2010	MIN	MLB	23	404	53	19	3	10	50	37	96	5	4	-1.0	.251	.331	.404	.250	.330	.394	.248	3.3	-0.2	90-RF	-5		

Breakout: 15% Improve: 52% Collapse: 13% Attrition: 8%   MLB: 8%   Comparables: Curtis Pride, Rafael Alvarez, Bruce Fields, Sam Taylor

Tosoni made it to the Futures Game in 2009, and while everything about him screams "future fourth outfielder," just achieving a big-league profile is an upgrade from previous years. His overall line masks his potential value as a platoon-oriented reserve, because beyond good fundamentals in the outfield, the Canadian hit northpaws at a .308/.389/.515 clip, and it's been a long time since the honorary Randy Bush roster spot had a worthwhile claimant.

Danny Valencia 3B

Bats: R   Throws: R   Height: 6' 2"   Weight: 200   Born: September 19, 1984   Age: 25

YEAR	TEAM	LVL	AGE	PA	R	2B	3B	HR	RBI	BB	SO	SB	CS	EqBRR	AVG	OBP	SLG	EqAVG	EqOBP	EqSLG	EqA	VORP	WARP	DEFENSE	
2007	BLT	A	22	271	44	15	0	11	35	28	54	3	3	0.8	.302	.374	.500	.263	.326	.417	.256	3.9	0.6	46-3B	1
2007	FTM	A+	22	250	28	8	2	6	31	16	48	1	0	0.2	.291	.332	.422	.272	.308	.397	.247	1.6	-0.6	56-3B	-7
2008	FTM	A+	23	251	35	19	3	5	44	27	43	2	2	-0.2	.336	.402	.518	.292	.347	.447	.274	9.5	0.8	52-3B	-3
2008	NBR	AA	23	287	40	18	2	10	32	18	70	2	1	2.0	.289	.334	.485	.256	.295	.433	.248	2.6	0.7	56-3B	3
2009	NBR	AA	24	252	44	14	4	7	29	31	40	0	2	-2.6	.284	.373	.482	.268	.341	.451	.271	9.9	1.0	57-3B	-2
2009	ROC	AAA	24	282	35	24	0	7	41	8	37	0	2	-2.5	.286	.305	.454	.275	.294	.439	.248	3.8	-0.2	65-3B	-6
2010	MIN	MLB	25	501	64	24	2	14	58	38	112	2	2	-0.4	.258	.315	.408	.256	.313	.403	.241	3.3	0.1	106-3B	-2

Breakout: 7%   Improve: 35%   Collapse: 14%   Attrition: 11%   MLB: 13%   Comparables: Aaron Boone, Benny Colvard, Mike Berger, Stan Royer

A 19th-round pick in 2006, Valencia has often been seen as no more than an organizational player, but he keeps hitting at every level he's assigned to, and he's now very close to getting a big-league look with a team that has no set third baseman at the big-league level. He does no one thing exceptionally well, but he's solid across the board, hitting for a decent average with a bit of power and solid defense at the hot corner. He's more of a multiyear stopgap than a future star, the kind of player who holds down an everyday job while you try to find something better.

Delmon Young LF

Bats: R   Throws: R   Height: 6' 3"   Weight: 200   Born: September 14, 1985   Age: 24

YEAR	TEAM	LVL	AGE	PA	R	2B	3B	HR	RBI	BB	SO	SB	CS	EqBRR	AVG	OBP	SLG	EqAVG	EqOBP	EqSLG	EqA	VORP	WARP	DEFENSE		
2007	TBA	MLB	21	681	65	38	0	13	93	26	127	10	3	0.3	.288	.316	.408	.294	.321	.418	.257	10.3	0.0	129-RF	1	28-CF -11
2008	MIN	MLB	22	623	80	28	4	10	69	35	105	14	5	-1.9	.290	.336	.405	.298	.344	.417	.266	15.4	1.0	148-LF	-5	
2009	MIN	MLB	23	416	50	16	2	12	60	12	92	2	5	-0.6	.284	.308	.425	.290	.313	.430	.250	3.0	-0.2	89-LF	-4	
2010	MIN	MLB	24	554	67	25	2	15	77	34	103	9	5	-0.4	.290	.340	.432	.287	.336	.425	.259	10.9	0.9	130-LF	-2	

Breakout: 19%   Improve: 57%   Collapse: 10%   Attrition: 3%   MLB: 100%   Comparables: Tommy Davis, Joe Vosmik, Jim Rice, Jose Guillen

If you have written Young off as a bust, you've acted prematurely. Still only 24 years old, Young finally showed some of the form from his top prospect days, batting .302/.322/.502 during the second half of the year, with nine of his 12 home runs coming in his last 42 games. He doesn't walk, and that will always hurt him and lower his overall value, but he could easily be a .300 hitter with 20-25 home runs in 2010, and that kind of performance can go a long way toward making up for a lack of patience. Grab him as a sleeper in your fantasy draft, and thank us later.

PITCHERS

Scott Baker

Bats: R   Throws: R   Height: 6' 4"   Weight: 220   Born: September 19, 1981   Age: 28

YEAR	TEAM	LVL	AGE	W	L	SV	G	GS	IP	H	HR	BB	SO	GB%	BABIP	STUFF	WHIP	ERA	SIERA	DERA	EqH9	EqHR9	EqBB9	EqSO9	VORP	SN/WX
2007	ROC	AAA	25	3	2	1	7	6	42²	34	3	4	41	50%	.274	25	0.89	3.16	2.62	3.94	8.1	0.9	1.1	7.0	6.9	0.66
2007	MIN	MLB	25	9	9	0	24	23	143²	162	15	29	102	39%	.323	9	1.33	4.26	4.09	4.15	10.0	1.0	1.7	5.8	21.1	3.41
2008	MIN	MLB	26	11	4	0	28	28	172¹	161	20	42	141	35%	.284	19	1.18	3.45	3.82	3.42	8.2	1.1	2.0	6.7	39.2	5.74
2009	MIN	MLB	27	15	9	0	33	33	200	190	28	48	162	38%	.276	18	1.19	4.36	3.82	4.10	8.1	1.1	1.9	6.4	31.3	4.56
2010	MIN	MLB	28	12	10	0	32	32	188¹	189	23	47	139	37%	.297	16	1.25	3.94	4.07	4.07	8.8	1.0	2.1	6.2	29.8	3.20

Breakout: 4%   Improve: 39%   Collapse: 11%   Attrition: 8%   MLB: 98%   Comparables: Javier Vazquez, Dave Goltz, Kevin Millwood, Dan Haren

Baker's ERA was up by nearly a full run in 2009, but it was a strange occurrence, as his hit, walk, and strikeout rates were nearly identical to 2008. His home-run rate was up a touch, but a lot of that came in the early going as he hurried back from a spring shoulder problem, allowing 14 taters in his first nine games. Most of his problems came with his runners on/off splits, as with the bases empty, batters hit just .233/.285/.377 against him, but that ratcheted up to .270/.304/.481 once ducks were on the pond. Looking forward, he probably isn't as good as he was in 2008, nor as bad as he was in 2009. The truth lies somewhere in between, and his $14.5 million cost over the next three years should be one of the Twins' best bargains.

Nick Blackburn

Bats: R   Throws: R   Height: 6' 4"   Weight: 225   Born: February 24, 1982   Age: 28

YEAR	TEAM	LVL	AGE	W	L	SV	G	GS	IP	H	HR	BB	SO	GB%	BABIP	STUFF	WHIP	ERA	SIERA	DERA	EqH9	EqHR9	EqBB9	EqSO9	VORP	SN/WX
2007	NBR	AA	25	3	1	0	8	7	38	36	1	7	18	59%	.263	-7	1.13	3.08	4.65	5.59	8.1	0.7	1.9	2.8	-0.4	-0.20
2007	ROC	AAA	25	7	3	0	17	17	110²	96	7	12	57	55%	.251	12	0.98	2.11	4.27	3.21	8.3	0.8	1.2	3.5	27.2	2.33
2007	MIN	MLB	25	0	2	0	6	0	11²	19	2	2	8	33%	.405	-12	1.80	7.71	4.36	8.74	14.3	1.6	1.6	5.6	-4.1	-0.54
2008	MIN	MLB	26	11	11	0	33	33	193¹	224	23	39	96	50%	.305	-3	1.36	4.05	4.77	4.59	10.0	1.1	1.6	4.1	19.3	4.27
2009	MIN	MLB	27	11	11	0	33	33	205²	240	25	41	98	55%	.301	2	1.37	4.03	4.80	4.14	9.8	1.0	1.5	3.8	31.1	4.92
2010	MIN	MLB	28	11	11	0	35	33	190¹	208	23	43	90	51%	.295	-2	1.32	4.27	4.86	4.46	9.7	1.0	2.0	4.0	22.0	2.71

Breakout: 6%   Improve: 36%   Collapse: 8%   Attrition: 11%   MLB: 95%   Comparables: Chien-Ming Wang, Brian Moehler, Jon Garland, Bill Gullickson

Blackburn throws strikes and gets a decent amount of ground balls. Because of those things, he's very efficient, which means that instead of being one of those unspectacular guys who keeps you in the ballgame with six solid innings, Blackburn tends to get you into the seventh. The problem is, he really doesn't have a swing-and-miss offering, and it's nearly impossible for a pitcher to maintain any level of success while striking out less than five batters per nine. The bubble might have already burst, as hitters went off on Blackburn to the tune of .323/.346/.517 after the break, and that's including his season-ending four quality starts to help get the team into postseason action. Just as for every 100 guys who might be Jamie Moyer there's only one Moyer, how many Bob Tewksburys do you think there actually are? Beware.

David Bromberg

Bats: L   Throws: R   Height: 6' 5"   Weight: 241   Born: September 14, 1987   Age: 22

YEAR	TEAM	LVL	AGE	W	L	SV	G	GS	IP	H	HR	BB	SO	GB%	BABIP	STUFF	WHIP	ERA	SIERA	DERA	EqH9	EqHR9	EqBB9	EqSO9	VORP	SN/WX
2007	ELZ	Rk	19	9	0	0	13	11	58¹	45	4	32	81	52%	.318	16	1.32	2.78	2.75	4.80	10.9	2.5	6.9	7.2	3.9	-0.10
2008	BLT	A	20	9	10	0	27	27	150	149	10	54	177	51%	.354	13	1.35	4.44	2.97	6.90	11.3	1.7	4.4	6.7	-21.0	-2.21
2009	FTM	A+	21	13	4	0	27	26	153¹	125	6	63	148	39%	.290	15	1.23	2.70	3.70	4.77	9.6	1.5	4.8	5.8	11.1	0.21
2010	MIN	MLB	22	5	10	0	28	26	127²	147	22	72	100	38%	.325	10	1.72	6.31	4.91	6.49	10.2	1.4	4.9	6.6	-14.0	1.95

Breakout: 12%   Improve: 51%   Collapse: 14%   Attrition: 13%   MLB: 14%   Comparables: Colby Lewis, Dustin McGowan, Rich Monteleone, Chris Carpenter

Over the last three years, Bromberg has led the Appalachian, Midwest, and Florida State Leagues in strikeouts. On the surface, that makes him sound like some kind of overpowering monster, but in reality, he's a pitchability guy, just like most of the Twins' arms. His fastball is average to a tick above, but his delivery has a lot of arms and legs in it to help create deception, and he's willing to use his solid breaking ball and changeup at any point in the count. His big body is built to eat up innings, so put out an extra helping or two when he comes to dinner, but don't expect a flamethrower.

Jesse Crain

Bats: R   Throws: R   Height: 6' 1"   Weight: 215   Born: July 5, 1981   Age: 28

YEAR	TEAM	LVL	AGE	W	L	SV	G	GS	IP	H	HR	BB	SO	GB%	BABIP	STUFF	WHIP	ERA	SIERA	DERA	EqH9	EqHR9	EqBB9	EqSO9	VORP	SN/WX
2007	MIN	MLB	25	1	2	0	18	0	16¹	19	4	4	10	59%	.288	-21	1.41	5.51	4.39	8.16	10.1	2.3	2.3	5.1	-4.7	-0.06
2008	MIN	MLB	26	5	4	0	66	0	62²	62	6	24	50	45%	.299	-1	1.37	3.59	4.21	4.06	8.7	0.9	3.0	6.5	9.9	0.12
2009	ROC	AAA	27	1	0	1	12	0	17²	13	0	8	22	35%	.317	17	1.19	2.55	2.81	3.24	7.0	0.5	4.3	9.7	4.2	0.38
2009	MIN	MLB	27	7	4	0	56	0	51²	48	3	27	43	50%	.296	1	1.45	4.70	4.44	4.50	8.0	0.5	4.2	6.6	5.8	-0.55
2010	MIN	MLB	28	3	4	0	58	0	57¹	60	6	25	43	45%	.311	-5	1.47	4.65	4.46	4.81	9.2	1.0	3.7	6.3	4.4	-0.01

Breakout: 16%   Improve: 41%   Collapse: 18%   Attrition: 12%   MLB: 83%   Comparables: Felix Rodriguez, Matt Whiteside, Brandon Lyon, Hal Reniff

Early-season shoulder troubles rendered Crain so ineffective that he was sent to Triple-A to get healthy and figure things out. This proved to be a great move: upon his return, he limited batters to a .217 batting average without giving up a home run in over 34 innings. What was a 92-94 mph fastball in April and May recovered the 94-97 velocity we've seen in the past, so Crain seems to be over his problems and all systems are go for him to become part of what's shaping up as a fully stocked, quality pen.

R. A. Dickey

Bats: R   Throws: R   Height: 6' 3"   Weight: 220   Born: October 29, 1974   Age: 35

YEAR	TEAM	LVL	AGE	W	L	SV	G	GS	IP	H	HR	BB	SO	GB%	BABIP	STUFF	WHIP	ERA	SIERA	DERA	EqH9	EqHR9	EqBB9	EqSO9	VORP	SN/WX
2007	NAS	AAA	32	13	6	0	31	22	169^1	159	18	60	119	58%	.280	-14	1.29	3.72	4.22	5.12	9.6	1.6	3.5	4.9	6.6	2.38
2008	TAC	AAA	33	2	5	0	7	7	49^2	58	2	8	30	54%	.333	3	1.33	3.44	4.24	4.56	10.2	0.7	1.7	3.7	5.0	0.33
2008	SEA	MLB	33	5	8	0	32	14	112^1	124	15	51	58	54%	.291	-20	1.56	5.21	5.27	4.94	9.5	1.4	3.6	4.1	6.9	1.13
2009	ROC	AAA	34	2	1	0	5	5	33^1	39	1	9	18	49%	.322	-5	1.44	5.13	4.83	5.94	10.0	0.5	2.7	3.8	-1.6	-0.27
2009	MIN	MLB	34	1	1	0	35	1	64^1	74	8	30	42	58%	.316	-12	1.62	4.62	4.81	4.34	9.9	1.0	3.6	5.2	8.3	-0.34
2010	MIN	MLB	35	4	7	0	34	10	92	108	14	39	45	54%	.308	-19	1.60	5.62	5.29	5.81	10.4	1.3	3.7	4.1	-3.1	1.04

Breakout: 7%   Improve: 30%   Collapse: 27%   Attrition: 26%   MLB: 79%   Comparables: Burt Hooton, Pete Walker, Steve Fireovid, Tanyon Sturtze

You have to give Dickey a round of applause. You know the ulnar collateral ligament, the one that gets replaced during a Tommy John procedure? Dickey doesn't have one. He was born that way. When his attempt to be a standard three-pitch mix guy didn't work out, he reinvented himself as a knuckleballer and it was good enough to get him back to the big leagues as a mop-up man for the Twins. Released at the end of the year, he signed a minor-league deal with the Mets.

Brian Duensing

Bats: L   Throws: L   Height: 5' 11"   Weight: 210   Born: February 22, 1983   Age: 27

YEAR	TEAM	LVL	AGE	W	L	SV	G	GS	IP	H	HR	BB	SO	GB%	BABIP	STUFF	WHIP	ERA	SIERA	DERA	EqH9	EqHR9	EqBB9	EqSO9	VORP	SN/WX
2007	NBR	AA	24	4	1	0	9	9	50^2	47	2	7	38	41%	.285	12	1.07	2.66	3.67	3.87	8.5	0.7	1.4	4.9	9.1	0.55
2007	ROC	AAA	24	11	5	0	19	19	116^2	115	13	30	86	54%	.292	-4	1.24	3.24	3.96	4.84	9.8	1.4	2.5	5.3	8.0	0.83
2008	ROC	AAA	25	5	11	0	25	24	138^2	150	16	34	77	55%	.293	-13	1.33	4.28	4.58	5.34	9.9	1.3	2.4	3.6	2.4	-0.05
2009	ROC	AAA	26	4	6	0	13	13	75^1	87	2	19	44	55%	.335	2	1.41	4.66	4.54	5.31	10.4	0.5	2.5	4.1	1.5	-0.05
2009	MIN	MLB	26	5	2	0	24	9	84	84	7	31	53	48%	.291	5	1.37	3.64	4.72	3.67	8.6	0.6	2.9	5.1	16.9	2.06
2010	MIN	MLB	27	7	9	0	34	22	133^2	147	17	45	72	55%	.302	-7	1.44	4.86	4.87	5.08	9.8	1.1	3.0	4.5	6.3	1.58

Breakout: 11%   Improve: 37%   Collapse: 11%   Attrition: 27%   MLB: 46%   Comparables: Mark Thurmond, Eddie Priest, Lance Painter, Scott Sauerbeck

Duensing was seen as an organizational lefty coming into the year, but he joined the Twins for good in July, replaced Francisco Liriano in the rotation at the end of August, and more than held his own in both roles. Like most young arms raised in the Twins' system, Duensing is far from overpowering, but his fastball has enough velocity to set up his changeup, which is a true plus offering; he also mixes in both a curveball and a slider. There's not much of a ceiling here, but he's earned a right to compete for a back-end rotation job this spring.

Kyle Gibson

Bats: R   Throws: R   Height: 6' 6"   Weight: 210   Born: October 23, 1987   Age: 22

Did Not Play.

Breakout: 11%   Improve: 37%   Collapse: 11%   Attrition: 27%   MLB: 46%   Comparables: NA

Gibson was all lined up to be a single-digit pick in June, but then his velocity dropped dramatically in the weeks leading up to the draft, and it was revealed that he had a stress fracture in his pitching forearm. The Twins believe he'll be perfectly healthy to begin 2010, and if this bears out, he's a steal with the 18th overall pick, due to his much-desired combination of plus stuff, size, and command. His health will be an issue until he proves that it's not, but he could be ready for the majors as soon as 2011.

Deolis Guerra

Bats: R   Throws: R   Height: 6' 5"   Weight: 200   Born: April 17, 1989   Age: 21

YEAR	TEAM	LVL	AGE	W	L	SV	G	GS	IP	H	HR	BB	SO	GB%	BABIP	STUFF	WHIP	ERA	SIERA	DERA	EqH9	EqHR9	EqBB9	EqSO9	VORP	SN/WX
2007	SLU	A+	18	2	6	0	21	20	89^2	80	9	25	66	54%	.268	7	1.17	4.01	3.99	5.66	9.0	1.8	3.1	4.6	-1.5	0.09
2008	FTM	A+	19	11	9	0	26	25	130	138	12	71	71	34%	.292	-21	1.61	5.47	5.84	8.26	11.4	2.2	5.6	2.8	-37.0	-2.65
2009	FTM	A+	20	6	8	0	16	15	86^1	95	6	25	57	51%	.311	-2	1.39	4.69	4.41	8.00	12.0	2.0	3.5	3.5	-22.0	-1.82
2009	NBR	AA	20	6	3	0	12	11	62^2	62	4	17	49	44%	.304	19	1.26	5.17	3.96	6.82	9.8	1.4	2.7	4.9	-8.8	-0.64
2010	MIN	MLB	21	5	9	0	29	28	130	155	22	64	64	41%	.307	7	1.69	6.01	5.71	6.15	10.5	1.5	4.2	4.1	-9.4	0.99

Breakout: 18%   Improve: 58%   Collapse: 6%   Attrition: 10%   MLB: 2%   Comparables: Kurt Miller, Rob Woodward, Paul Stewart, Darrell Goedhart

One of the key components of the Johan Santana deal, Guerra was the top pitcher on the international market in 2005, but the stuff he showed back in the day now rarely manifests. He's baffling to scouts, because about once a month, he'll be utterly dominant, with a fastball than gets up to 95 mph and an excellent changeup for his age, but otherwise his velocity tends to sit around average, while his breaking ball is often flat. The good news is that he doesn't turn 21 until mid-April and he at least occasionally shows signs of greatness, so there's some slender cause for optimism still here, unlike the other components received in the deal (Carlos Gomez, Kevin Mulvey, and Philip Humber).

Matt Guerrier

Bats: R   Throws: R   Height: 6' 3"   Weight: 195   Born: August 2, 1978   Age: 31

YEAR	TEAM	LVL	AGE	W	L	SV	G	GS	IP	H	HR	BB	SO	GB%	BABIP	STUFF	WHIP	ERA	SIERA	DERA	EqH9	EqHR9	EqBB9	EqSO9	VORP	SN/WX
2007	MIN	MLB	28	2	4	1	73	0	88	71	9	21	68	53%	.250	11	1.05	2.35	3.75	2.34	7.1	1.0	2.0	6.2	30.5	2.48
2008	MIN	MLB	29	6	9	1	76	0	76¹	84	12	37	59	53%	.305	-18	1.59	5.19	4.53	5.28	9.5	1.5	3.9	6.2	1.9	0.93
2009	MIN	MLB	30	5	1	1	79	0	76¹	58	10	16	47	51%	.211	5	0.97	2.36	4.25	2.55	6.3	1.0	1.6	4.8	25.5	3.61
2010	MIN	MLB	31	4	5	1	68	0	69¹	69	10	23	45	48%	.284	-4	1.32	4.26	4.52	4.37	8.7	1.2	2.8	5.4	8.7	1.29

Breakout: 16%   Improve: 39%   Collapse: 32%   Attrition: 18%   MLB: 93%   Comparables: Tim Burke, Scott Linebrink, Felix Rodriguez, Randy Gumpert

After leading the AL in appearances in 2008, Guerrier repeated the feat in 2009, only this time he also pitched fantastically well in a more significant role. A classic fastball/slider type, Guerrier found a way to maintain his low-90s velocity while suddenly pounding the strike zone, and when you can cut your walk rate, good things tend to happen. He'll probably regress a bit, but he's still part of a great set-up crew for Joe Nathan, with Crain seemingly repaired, Mijares arrived, Jon Rauch added, and Pat Neshek recovering.

Carlos Gutierrez

Bats: R   Throws: R   Height: 6' 3"   Weight: 205   Born: September 22, 1986   Age: 23

YEAR	TEAM	LVL	AGE	W	L	SV	G	GS	IP	H	HR	BB	SO	GB%	BABIP	STUFF	WHIP	ERA	SIERA	DERA	EqH9	EqHR9	EqBB9	EqSO9	VORP	SN/WX
2008	FTM	A+	21	3	1	1	16	0	25²	23	0	7	19	71%	.287	6	1.17	2.10	3.50	3.70	9.2	0.7	3.0	4.1	4.9	0.04
2009	FTM	A+	22	2	3	0	11	10	54²	37	1	22	33	76%	.220	-4	1.08	1.32	3.77	5.08	7.4	1.1	4.4	3.2	2.4	0.52
2009	NBR	AA	22	1	3	0	22	6	52¹	62	6	24	32	69%	.327	-30	1.64	6.19	4.50	7.67	12.0	2.2	4.4	3.9	-11.8	-0.78
2010	MIN	MLB	23	3	6	0	40	6	79²	92	13	40	37	71%	.301	-19	1.67	5.88	4.93	6.02	10.2	1.4	4.4	3.9	-4.6	0.98

Breakout: 15%   Improve: 42%   Collapse: 23%   Attrition: 6%   MLB: 0%   Comparables: Tim Dell, Josh Perrault, Paul Slifko, Charles Fick

Gutierrez was the talk of the Florida State League during the first half of the year, but a promotion to Double-A proved to be too much too soon, as he ran out of gas and pancaked. A closer in college, Gutierrez tired with less than 100 innings under his belt, which almost assures him an eventual return to a relief role, but he could end up as a darn good penman. When Mauer was rehabbing in Fort Myers, he called Gutierrez's sinker the best he's seen at any level, and the pitcher's ridiculous ratio of 4.5 grounders for each fly backs up the assertion. He is the definition of worm-killing machine and could take off once Minnesota puts him in the right role.

Bob Keppel

Bats: R   Throws: R   Height: 6' 5"   Weight: 205   Born: June 11, 1982   Age: 28

YEAR	TEAM	LVL	AGE	W	L	SV	G	GS	IP	H	HR	BB	SO	GB%	BABIP	STUFF	WHIP	ERA	SIERA	DERA	EqH9	EqHR9	EqBB9	EqSO9	VORP	SN/WX
2007	CSP	AAA	25	8	10	0	26	23	138	162	14	60	64	58%	.314	-15	1.61	5.48	5.24	5.91	9.8	0.9	4.0	3.2	-6.2	-0.89
2008	ABQ	AAA	26	9	11	0	28	27	159¹	208	26	57	85	59%	.336	-16	1.66	5.99	4.86	6.12	10.6	1.1	3.2	3.7	-10.8	-2.09
2009	ROC	AAA	27	3	3	1	23	3	55²	51	1	13	28	65%	.275	-2	1.15	2.43	4.47	3.40	8.0	0.3	2.3	3.5	12.7	0.98
2009	MIN	MLB	27	1	1	0	37	0	54	63	4	21	32	58%	.328	-10	1.56	4.83	4.83	4.58	10.2	0.5	3.1	4.8	5.4	0.35
2010	MIN	MLB	28	5	7	0	42	11	99¹	112	13	41	46	62%	.300	-17	1.54	5.17	5.12	5.40	9.9	1.1	3.6	3.9	1.1	0.72

Breakout: 14%   Improve: 54%   Collapse: 17%   Attrition: 20%   MLB: 49%   Comparables: Steve Stemle, Jim Hunter, Kyle Middleton, Kevin Hodges

Pitching for his fifth organization in five years, Keppel finally got consistent big-league work in 2009, but he didn't do enough to guarantee anything more than a chance to compete for a job at the back end of the pen this year. He has always been an arm-strength guy, sitting at 92-95 mph while touching 97, but his command and control waver, and he has yet to find a dependable second pitch. Twelve parsecs may be the record for the Keppel run, but if it doesn't land him in the majors, does it matter? Radar-gun readings can earn opportunities, but results earn tenure, and Keppel isn't there yet.

Francisco Liriano

Bats: L   Throws: L   Height: 6' 2"   Weight: 225   Born: October 26, 1983   Age: 26

YEAR	TEAM	LVL	AGE	W	L	SV	G	GS	IP	H	HR	BB	SO	GB%	BABIP	STUFF	WHIP	ERA	SIERA	DERA	EqH9	EqHR9	EqBB9	EqSO9	VORP	SN/WX
2008	ROC	AAA	24	10	2	0	19	19	118	102	8	31	113	50%	.289	20	1.13	3.28	3.24	3.81	8.3	0.9	2.5	6.4	21.3	1.79
2008	MIN	MLB	24	6	4	0	14	14	76	74	7	32	67	44%	.302	15	1.39	3.91	4.05	4.56	8.5	0.8	3.3	7.1	7.9	1.54
2009	MIN	MLB	25	5	13	0	29	24	136²	147	21	65	122	48%	.319	0	1.55	5.80	4.16	5.57	9.5	1.2	3.8	7.1	-1.0	0.66
2010	MIN	MLB	26	10	10	0	33	29	169¹	172	21	68	133	49%	.304	10	1.42	4.47	4.24	4.63	9.0	1.0	3.5	6.7	16.3	1.80

Breakout: 12%   Improve: 50%   Collapse: 8%   Attrition: 4%   MLB: 91%   Comparables: Chris Capuano, Matt Young, Shawn Estes, Noah Lowry

While medical technology has advanced to the point where Tommy John surgery is often seen as a mere bump in the road for a player's development, it still has its fair share of casualties. Witness Liriano, who burst onto the scene in 2006 with such force that many inside the game thought his potential surpassed that of even Johan Santana, his teammate at the time. Three years later, Liriano has pitched himself out of the rotation, thanks to a 3-5 mph drop in velocity, command that has gone backward, and confidence that is absolutely shot. Still dreaming of what once was, the Twins will give him another shot this spring, so 2010 could be his last chance at avoiding being a sad reminder that no surgery comes with guaranteed results.

Jeff Manship

Bats: R   Throws: R   Height: 6' 0"   Weight: 165   Born: January 16, 1985   Age: 25

YEAR	TEAM	LVL	AGE	W	L	SV	G	GS	IP	H	HR	BB	SO	GB%	BABIP	STUFF	WHIP	ERA	SIERA	DERA	EqH9	EqHR9	EqBB9	EqSO9	VORP	SN/WX
2007	BLT	A	22	7	1	0	13	13	77²	51	4	9	77	66%	.239	28	0.77	1.51	2.46	2.78	7.6	1.3	1.8	5.8	21.6	1.52
2007	FTM	A+	22	8	5	0	13	13	71¹	77	5	25	59	56%	.323	-5	1.43	3.15	3.96	5.95	11.1	1.6	3.7	5.1	-3.4	-0.09
2008	FTM	A+	23	7	3	0	13	13	78²	68	0	20	63	63%	.292	8	1.12	2.86	3.57	5.18	9.2	0.7	2.8	4.7	2.6	0.20
2008	NBR	AA	23	3	6	0	14	14	76²	90	8	24	62	55%	.337	-9	1.49	4.46	3.99	6.33	10.7	1.6	2.9	5.2	-6.9	-0.55
2009	NBR	AA	24	6	4	0	13	13	75²	72	2	20	45	63%	.286	0	1.22	4.28	4.25	5.55	8.9	0.7	2.6	3.6	-0.4	-0.33
2009	ROC	AAA	24	4	2	0	8	8	50¹	53	1	17	30	49%	.319	2	1.39	3.22	4.74	4.63	9.6	0.4	3.4	4.3	4.6	0.39
2009	MIN	MLB	24	1	1	0	11	5	31²	39	4	15	21	57%	.333	-11	1.71	5.68	4.84	5.40	10.5	1.1	3.7	5.1	0.4	0.31
2010	MIN	MLB	25	7	8	0	32	24	129	143	17	50	72	49%	.304	-8	1.49	4.99	4.99	5.18	9.8	1.1	3.3	4.7	4.6	1.93

Breakout: 9%   Improve: 43%   Collapse: 13%   Attrition: 23%   MLB: 44%   Comparables: Tim Meeks, Joe Bitker, Paul Voigt, Mike Oquist

Manship is a stocky strike-thrower who mixes his pitches well, but it's the kind of stuff where scouts worry about the level at which he'll hit a wall. In light of his 2009 season, the big leagues might have been it. His fastball parks at around 90 mph, and nothing about his secondary offerings really stands out, so there's just so little margin for error, which also means little upside. That's probably for the best: even as an ace, it's not likely the Twins could sell a lot of jerseys saying "Manship" on the back. He's likely to be bound for Triple-A as the "sixth starter" who returns to Minnesota when the need arises.

Jose Mijares

Bats: L   Throws: L   Height: 6' 0"   Weight: 230   Born: October 29, 1984   Age: 25

YEAR	TEAM	LVL	AGE	W	L	SV	G	GS	IP	H	HR	BB	SO	GB%	BABIP	STUFF	WHIP	ERA	SIERA	DERA	EqH9	EqHR9	EqBB9	EqSO9	VORP	SN/WX
2007	NBR	AA	22	5	3	9	46	0	61	40	7	48	75	50%	.231	11	1.44	3.54	3.86	4.38	6.8	1.6	6.8	8.2	7.6	-0.11
2008	NBR	AA	23	1	1	2	11	0	15¹	16	2	7	17	38%	.326	1	1.50	2.93	3.53	3.52	9.4	1.8	4.1	7.0	3.4	0.42
2008	MIN	MLB	23	0	1	0	10	0	10¹	3	0	0	5	47%	.103	4	0.29	0.87	3.84	0.87	1.7	0.0	0.0	3.5	5.3	0.65
2009	MIN	MLB	24	2	2	0	71	0	61²	50	7	23	55	40%	.259	10	1.18	2.34	3.85	2.36	7.1	0.9	3.0	7.1	21.3	3.54
2010	MIN	MLB	25	4	4	1	60	0	62²	56	8	30	47	43%	.271	-3	1.38	4.25	4.58	4.43	8.0	1.1	4.1	6.4	7.5	1.45

Breakout: 10%   Improve: 25%   Collapse: 35%   Attrition: 11%   MLB: 71%   Comparables: Brad Kilby, Taylor Tankersley, Daryl Harang, Adam Butler

Somewhere in Venezuela there is a magical place, known as Gordo Synestra. From that magical place come pitchers, fat ones at that, who are made to look even larger because of their incredibly fleshy faces. Once known as the home of Rich Garces, Gordo Synestra has now gifted baseball with Mijares, a lefty doppelgänger of Garces'. Mijares is also an effective pitcher who will still be getting hitters out a decade from now, with plus velocity for a lefty and power breaking stuff. Hopefully he avoids the situational label, because he has the stuff to handle a more expansive role.

Joe Nathan

| | | | | | | | | | Bats: R | | Throws: R | | Height: 6' 4" | | Weight: 225 | | Born: November 22, 1974 | | Age: 35 | |

YEAR	TEAM	LVL	AGE	W	L	SV	G	GS	IP	H	HR	BB	SO	GB%	BABIP	STUFF	WHIP	ERA	SIERA	DERA	EqH9	EqHR9	EqBB9	EqSO9	VORP	SN/WX
2007	MIN	MLB	32	4	2	37	68	0	71²	54	4	19	77	49%	.276	30	1.02	1.88	2.77	1.91	6.8	0.5	2.2	8.7	28.2	5.15
2008	MIN	MLB	33	1	2	39	68	0	67²	43	5	18	74	54%	.235	31	0.90	1.33	2.68	1.87	5.6	0.7	2.1	8.8	27.1	5.30
2009	MIN	MLB	34	2	2	47	70	0	68²	42	7	22	89	46%	.232	32	0.93	2.10	2.22	2.09	5.6	0.8	2.5	9.5	26.2	5.32
2010	MIN	MLB	35	5	3	30	63	0	62	48	5	20	64	48%	.276	19	1.09	3.03	3.06	3.16	6.9	0.8	2.7	8.6	16.1	3.06

Breakout: 10%   Improve: 30%   Collapse: 38%   Attrition: 9%   MLB: 97%   Comparables: Tom Henke, Jay Howell, Kaz Sasaki, Dennis Eckersley

While Nathan fell under the curse that seemed to affect nearly every non-Rivera closer in the postseason, he remains one of the best at his job. He has now extended his run to seven straight healthy, dominant seasons. Although he has lost maybe a tick or so off his fastball since his prime, his improved slider makes up for it, and the Twins should be happy to have him under contract for the next two seasons with an option for a third. Even if Liriano doesn't get turned around, even if Boof Bonser didn't exactly blossom, dealing A. J. Pierzynski to get Nathan into their organization alone would still represent one of the great steals of the last decade.

Carl Pavano

| | | | | | | | | | Bats: R | | Throws: R | | Height: 6' 5" | | Weight: 240 | | Born: January 8, 1976 | | Age: 34 | |

YEAR	TEAM	LVL	AGE	W	L	SV	G	GS	IP	H	HR	BB	SO	GB%	BABIP	STUFF	WHIP	ERA	SIERA	DERA	EqH9	EqHR9	EqBB9	EqSO9	VORP	SN/WX
2007	NYN	MLB	31	1	0	0	2	2	11¹	12	1	2	4	48%	.282	-6	1.24	4.76	5.22	4.91	9.0	0.8	1.6	3.3	0.7	0.16
2008	NYN	MLB	32	4	2	0	7	7	34¹	41	5	10	15	43%	.300	-9	1.49	5.77	5.39	5.45	9.9	1.0	2.3	3.6	0.2	0.31
2009	CLE	MLB	33	9	8	0	21	21	125²	150	19	23	88	52%	.327	-1	1.38	5.37	4.00	5.27	10.4	1.4	1.5	5.6	3.2	2.02
2009	MIN	MLB	33	5	4	0	12	12	73²	85	7	16	59	50%	.332	17	1.37	4.64	3.79	4.38	9.9	0.7	1.7	6.3	9.2	1.06
2010	MIN	MLB	34	6	10	0	26	26	133	168	20	38	84	50%	.338	-8	1.55	5.50	4.53	5.70	11.1	1.3	2.5	5.3	-2.9	1.35

Breakout: 9%   Improve: 39%   Collapse: 26%   Attrition: 15%   MLB: 88%   Comparables: Scott Sanderson, Brian Moehler, Ken Forsch, Mark Leiter

After becoming a bit of a joke in New York after three seasons and just 26 starts on a four-year contract, Pavano found his health waiting for him in Cleveland, where it had been keeping a low profile while recording an album with Santana. Reunited with it, Pavano made 33 starts in 2009, including 12 for the Twins after a midseason trade. He took the surprising step of accepting the Twins' offer of arbitration after looking at the market for a few weeks as a free agent and is a lock for a rotation slot in 2009. He remains a strike-throwing machine with a good changeup, but he's hittable, and even healthy, he isn't a starter who puts you closer to a pennant.

Glen Perkins

| | | | | | | | | | Bats: L | | Throws: L | | Height: 6' 0" | | Weight: 200 | | Born: March 2, 1983 | | Age: 27 | |

YEAR	TEAM	LVL	AGE	W	L	SV	G	GS	IP	H	HR	BB	SO	GB%	BABIP	STUFF	WHIP	ERA	SIERA	DERA	EqH9	EqHR9	EqBB9	EqSO9	VORP	SN/WX
2007	MIN	MLB	24	0	0	0	19	0	28²	23	2	12	20	39%	.266	-1	1.22	3.14	4.67	3.04	7.4	0.7	3.7	6.1	7.3	0.45
2008	ROC	AAA	25	2	1	0	7	6	33¹	28	2	19	27	35%	.260	2	1.41	2.97	4.88	4.54	7.8	0.8	5.1	5.1	3.6	0.44
2008	MIN	MLB	25	12	4	0	26	26	151	183	25	39	74	46%	.304	-15	1.47	4.41	5.03	4.65	10.4	1.6	2.0	4.0	14.2	2.90
2009	MIN	MLB	26	6	7	0	18	17	96¹	120	13	23	45	50%	.314	-9	1.48	5.89	5.01	5.45	10.5	1.0	1.9	3.7	0.6	1.20
2010	MIN	MLB	27	5	8	0	30	20	105	124	16	41	50	45%	.308	-16	1.57	5.35	5.38	5.50	10.4	1.2	3.4	4.1	0.0	1.17

Breakout: 6%   Improve: 35%   Collapse: 25%   Attrition: 18%   MLB: 78%   Comparables: Horacio Ramirez, Mike Caldwell, Trevor Wilson, Pete Falcone

The local product was off to a fine start in 2009, but everything fell apart in the second half as he struggled with shoulder soreness that was finally diagnosed as tendinitis, the official medical term for "His shoulder hurts, but we're not really sure why." If his performance wasn't bad enough, things got really ugly when the club sent Perkins to Triple-A and then shut him down for the season, leaving the lefty to consider filing a grievance for the lost service time that prevented him from becoming arbitration-eligible. They've publicly kissed and made up, but behind the scenes the Twins are looking to make a deal and get him out of town pronto, Golden Gopher pedigree or no.

Jon Rauch

Bats: R   Throws: R   Height: 6' 11"   Weight: 290   Born: September 27, 1978   Age: 31

YEAR	TEAM	LVL	AGE	W	L	SV	G	GS	IP	H	HR	BB	SO	GB%	BABIP	STUFF	WHIP	ERA	SIERA	DERA	EqH9	EqHR9	EqBB9	EqSO9	VORP	SN/WX
2007	WAS	MLB	28	8	4	4	88	0	87¹	75	7	21	71	36%	.267	7	1.10	3.61	3.79	3.81	7.9	0.8	2.0	6.4	16.3	2.98
2008	WAS	MLB	29	4	2	17	48	0	48¹	42	5	7	44	34%	.272	14	1.01	2.98	3.10	3.07	7.6	0.9	1.1	7.1	13.0	1.97
2008	ARI	MLB	29	0	6	1	26	0	23¹	27	6	9	22	37%	.318	-5	1.54	6.56	3.85	6.17	10.0	1.9	3.1	7.3	-1.7	-0.63
2009	ARI	MLB	30	2	2	2	58	0	54¹	57	5	17	35	42%	.294	-4	1.36	4.14	4.63	4.07	8.8	0.7	2.3	5.0	8.8	0.48
2009	MIN	MLB	30	5	1	0	17	0	15²	13	1	6	14	38%	.286	9	1.21	1.72	3.88	1.80	7.8	0.6	3.0	7.2	6.2	0.59
2010	MIN	MLB	31	4	4	6	71	0	70¹	68	8	21	53	35%	.290	3	1.26	3.93	4.19	4.06	8.5	1.0	2.6	6.3	11.3	1.10

Breakout: 18%   Improve: 43%   Collapse: 26%   Attrition: 9%   MLB: 100%   Comparables: Jerry Spradlin, Kevin Gregg, Tyler Yates, Aaron Harang

Acquired from the D'backs for the stretch run, the giant right-hander with the distracting neck tattoos (they're wedding rings, by the way), turned into a major contributor in September. He relies mostly on a 90-92 mph fastball and crisp slider, but his pitches tend to play up because of his size alone creating angles and release points that hitters usually don't see. He's not a stud, but he's a solid middle-relief asset, and with Arizona picking up his 2010 option before trading him away, he is guaranteed at least one more year in the Twins' pen.

Anthony Slama

Bats: R   Throws: R   Height: 6' 3"   Weight: 207   Born: January 6, 1984   Age: 26

YEAR	TEAM	LVL	AGE	W	L	SV	G	GS	IP	H	HR	BB	SO	GB%	BABIP	STUFF	WHIP	ERA	SIERA	DERA	EqH9	EqHR9	EqBB9	EqSO9	VORP	SN/WX
2007	BLT	A	23	1	1	10	21	0	24¹	15	0	9	39	52%	.306	21	0.99	1.48	1.67	2.42	7.7	0.8	4.0	9.7	7.6	0.41
2008	FTM	A+	24	4	1	25	51	0	71	43	0	24	110	57%	.301	25	0.94	1.01	1.69	2.60	7.5	0.7	3.6	9.7	21.1	2.98
2009	NBR	AA	25	4	2	25	51	0	65¹	46	5	32	93	39%	.297	12	1.19	2.48	2.42	3.38	7.9	1.5	4.5	9.7	14.5	1.50
2009	ROC	AAA	25	0	2	4	11	0	15²	11	0	8	19	49%	.306	15	1.21	3.45	3.03	3.68	6.8	0.6	4.9	9.2	3.0	-0.12
2010	MIN	MLB	26	3	4	8	53	0	62²	61	7	34	65	47%	.321	4	1.52	4.70	3.84	4.80	8.4	1.0	4.7	8.6	4.8	2.23

Breakout: 7%   Improve: 19%   Collapse: 44%   Attrition: 5%   MLB: 25%   Comparables: Brian Wood, Jeff Pierce, Jay Tessmer, Josh Roenicke

A 39th-round pick in 2009, Slama has registered 13.3 strikeouts per nine innings in his three pro seasons, but he's anything but the Twins' closer of the future. Instead, he's something of a trick pitcher, not in terms of his stuff, which consists of a 90-92 mph fastball and average slider, but because of his delivery, which features a lot of moving parts that serve to hide the ball until the moment of release. The results have been nothing short of outstanding, but scouts have a hard time projecting him as anything but a middle reliever based on his stuff and his age. He's been especially tough on right-handers, limiting them to .129/.214/.194 at Double-A while striking out an incredible 43 percent of them, and then 53 percent of right-handers in his brief time in Triple-A. Trickster or not, he may offer something exploitable here.

Kevin Slowey

Bats: R   Throws: R   Height: 6' 3"   Weight: 205   Born: May 4, 1984   Age: 26

YEAR	TEAM	LVL	AGE	W	L	SV	G	GS	IP	H	HR	BB	SO	GB%	BABIP	STUFF	WHIP	ERA	SIERA	DERA	EqH9	EqHR9	EqBB9	EqSO9	VORP	SN/WX
2007	ROC	AAA	23	10	5	0	20	20	133²	110	4	18	107	44%	.271	32	0.96	1.89	3.35	2.73	8.0	0.6	1.4	5.6	39.6	3.76
2007	MIN	MLB	23	4	1	0	13	11	66²	82	16	11	47	35%	.296	-7	1.39	4.72	4.21	4.93	10.3	2.2	1.3	5.5	4.4	1.15
2008	MIN	MLB	24	12	11	0	27	27	160¹	161	22	24	123	42%	.290	13	1.15	3.99	3.64	4.06	8.8	1.3	1.2	6.3	25.3	4.28
2009	MIN	MLB	25	10	3	0	16	16	90²	113	15	15	75	37%	.345	5	1.41	4.86	3.67	4.57	10.8	1.3	1.3	6.6	9.3	1.50
2010	MIN	MLB	26	9	9	0	28	28	148²	158	20	33	102	40%	.303	9	1.28	4.18	4.17	4.33	9.4	1.1	2.0	5.8	19.3	2.70

Breakout: 8%   Improve: 40%   Collapse: 15%   Attrition: 19%   MLB: 84%   Comparables: Larry Christenson, Joel Pineiro, Rick Aguilera, Scott Baker

In an organization that collects finesse pitchers as if they'll be used as currency following the apocalypse, Slowey is a high-denomination bill among the singles, but even so, 2009 just didn't work out for him. He began to slide in June (evidenced by the fact that he'd occasionally walk guys) before getting shut down with a never-ending wrist injury that culminated in season-ending surgery. His command and control is as good as you'll find in the business, but it needs to be this good, considering his subpar stuff. The wrist problem probably contributed to his missing in the zone more often, producing that BABIP spike that should come back down, now that he's healthy. Expect him to reestablish himself as a nice midrotation starter in 2010.

Anthony Swarzak   Bats: R   Throws: R   Height: 6' 3"   Weight: 230   Born: September 10, 1985   Age: 24

YEAR	TEAM	LVL	AGE	W	L	SV	G	GS	IP	H	HR	BB	SO	GB%	BABIP	STUFF	WHIP	ERA	SIERA	DERA	EqH9	EqHR9	EqBB9	EqSO9	VORP	SN/WX
2007	FTM	A+	21	0	0	0	3	3	15²	14	0	5	18	28%	.333	15	1.21	2.30	2.94	4.30	9.2	0.6	3.7	7.4	2.0	0.17
2007	NBR	AA	21	5	4	0	15	14	86¹	78	6	23	76	32%	.295	23	1.17	3.23	3.69	4.08	8.9	1.1	2.6	6.0	12.9	1.02
2008	NBR	AA	22	3	8	0	20	20	101²	126	12	37	76	38%	.341	-17	1.60	5.67	4.52	7.22	11.2	1.7	3.3	4.7	-19.1	-1.75
2008	ROC	AAA	22	5	0	0	7	7	45	41	4	14	26	46%	.262	7	1.22	1.80	4.76	3.30	8.5	1.0	2.9	3.7	10.7	1.01
2009	ROC	AAA	23	4	5	0	13	13	79²	79	4	21	45	45%	.292	8	1.26	3.28	4.71	3.93	8.8	0.7	2.6	4.0	13.4	1.07
2009	MIN	MLB	23	3	7	0	12	12	59	76	12	20	34	41%	.320	-12	1.63	6.25	5.06	6.03	11.0	1.7	2.6	4.6	-3.4	0.75
2010	MIN	MLB	24	6	8	0	27	24	129¹	144	18	51	74	34%	.305	-7	1.51	5.13	5.33	5.30	9.8	1.2	3.4	4.8	2.8	1.78

Breakout: 5%   Improve: 38%   Collapse: 14%   Attrition: 11%   MLB: 96%   Comparables: Landon Jacobsen, Todd Redmond, Kennie Steenstra, Bobby Rodgers

It's strange to talk about a power pitcher in this system, but Swarzak is just that, relying on a 92 mph fastball that gets up to 95 and looks like lightning compared with what most Twins hurlers fling when they really let fly. Unfortunately, his substandard second and third offerings meant that big-league hitters teed off on him. There's no obvious job for him in the majors for 2010, and given his limited assortment, the next time we see him in Minnesota, it will probably be as a reliever.

Loek Van Mil   Bats: R   Throws: R   Height: 7' 1"   Weight: 232   Born: September 15, 1984   Age: 25

YEAR	TEAM	LVL	AGE	W	L	SV	G	GS	IP	H	HR	BB	SO	GB%	BABIP	STUFF	WHIP	ERA	SIERA	DERA	EqH9	EqHR9	EqBB9	EqSO9	VORP	SN/WX
2007	ELZ	Rk	22	2	2	0	13	0	24	14	0	17	23	50%	.230	-7	1.29	2.62	4.29	6.12	7.6	1.3	8.0	4.2	-1.5	-0.32
2008	BLT	A	23	2	2	3	28	0	44²	36	5	25	42	47%	.252	-19	1.37	3.22	4.17	6.00	8.8	2.4	6.2	4.9	-2.3	-0.45
2009	FTM	A+	24	0	0	5	25	0	34²	29	3	17	23	38%	.260	-29	1.33	2.86	5.04	4.45	10.1	2.4	5.6	3.9	3.5	-0.44
2010	MIN	MLB	25	2	4	1	38	0	48	51	7	32	25	45%	.285	-23	1.73	5.79	5.88	5.91	9.3	1.3	5.8	4.4	-2.2	0.18

Breakout: 20%   Improve: 57%   Collapse: 16%   Attrition: 9%   MLB: 5%   Comparables: Terry Bross, Derek Aucoin, Jeff Sobkoviak, Greg Johnson

How cool is it that the team with the tallest player in major-league history (Rauch) has a chance in 2010 of adding a bullpen arm that towers over him? Returning from Tommy John surgery in 2009, Van Mil wasted no time in moving back up the ladder by living off his sinker, which is made all the more effective by his height, as the pitch seems to be descending from Everest when he releases it. As it does with nearly any pitcher his height, command comes and goes, but once the towering Dutchman is close to ready and combined with Rauch, the Twins could have a bullpen that, if nothing else, could certainly challenge the Timberwolves in a pick-up game.

LINEOUTS

Hitters

PLAYER	TEAM	LVL	AGE	PA	R	2B	3B	HR	RBI	BB	SO	SB-CS	EqBRR	AVG/OBP/SLG	EqAVG/EqOBP/EqSLG	EqA	VORP	WARP
OF J. Benson	FTM	A+	21	327	46	10	3	5	29	46	74	14-7	-3.4	.285/.414/.403	.255/.361/.371	.263	8.3	0.5
C D. Butera	ROC	AAA	25	333	23	16	1	2	25	22	49	0-1	-1.2	.211/.268/.292	.197/.252/.273	.184	-9.1	-0.3
INF E. De Los Santos#	FTM	A+	22	284	33	11	7	1	23	13	49	11-4	-2.2	.290/.330/.397	.274/.307/.376	.240	4.3	-0.2
2B B. Dinkelman*	NBR	AA	25	542	62	38	2	8	65	55	73	5-6	0.6	.296/.383/.440	.276/.342/.399	.260	13.5	-0.2
1B J. Huber	ROC	AAA	26	506	60	22	2	22	76	51	84	4-3	-4.3	.273/.356/.482	.252/.330/.440	.265	4.6	0.0
OF D. Martin*	ROC	AAA	25	470	58	16	5	5	53	39	92	26-8	3.7	.254/.319/.351	.236/.299/.330	.228	-5.4	-1.4
1B C. Parmelee*	FTM	A+	21	501	61	27	1	16	73	65	109	2-2	-2.5	.258/.359/.441	.244/.329/.408	.259	3.9	-0.4
C J. Pinto	ELZ	Rk	20	230	34	14	2	13	55	19	39	0-1	-3.0	.332/.387/.610	.259/.303/.429	.253	2.2	-0.1
OF J. Pridie*	ROC	AAA	25	546	69	23	5	9	53	19	85	25-7	3.0	.265/.295/.382	.247/.274/.359	.224	-5.2	0.2
C D. Rams	ELZ	Rk	20	72	19	7	1	6	23	8	22	0-0	0.1	.355/.444/.790	.262/.333/.508	.281	2.9	0.5
	BLT	A	20	195	24	14	0	7	23	18	77	0-0	-1.8	.229/.308/.429	.189/.251/.339	.202	-5.4	-0.9
UT S. Tolleson	NBR	AA	25	173	21	10	2	2	13	16	20	6-2	-0.2	.258/.343/.391	.242/.302/.357	.234	1.7	-0.5
	ROC	AAA	25	394	57	17	1	6	27	36	52	7-6	-2.0	.270/.338/.375	.251/.318/.350	.236	0.7	-1.0
OF D. Winfree	ROC	AAA	23	457	48	31	3	14	61	28	88	0-2	-1.3	.273/.317/.460	.258/.302/.444	.253	5.1	-1.0

Outfielder **Joe Benson** has the tools to rank with nearly any outfielder in the system, but they come with plenty of questions about his bat; a second-half comeback from a broken hand helped, but he'll need to show more power. ⊘ **Drew Butera** will compete with Morales for the privilege of backing up Mauer in 2010; Butera is twice the defender but half the hitter, which could strand him in third-catcher limbo. ⊘ **Estarlin De Los Santos** was an intriguing addition to the 40-man roster; he has tools and makes contact, but he's without power or patience at the plate. ⊘ Another one of those scrappy, versatile types who the Twins love, **Brian Dinkelman** had a nice year at Double-A, hitting .302/.388/.454 against right-hand pitchers; he could be a bench player by 2011. ⊘ Tired of Triple-A pay in the states, Aussie **Justin Huber** will make much better money in 2010 with the Hiroshima Carp. ⊘ After a minor breakout in 2008, **Dustin Martin** never got going last year, so 2010 will be a make-or-break season. ⊘ Former first-rounder **Chris Parmelee** has lots of power and patience, but that's also the sum of his skills; he'll need to shine in Double-A to regain his prospect status. ⊘ Venezuelan **Josmil Pinto** obliterated Appy League pitching in 2009, but he's not really a catcher in the long term, so he'll need to keep mashing. ⊘ **Jason Pridie** has speed and the ability to play all three outfield positions, but his bat has stalled at Triple-A and he's not getting any younger; with the fourth outfielder's role open, it's now or perhaps never. ⊘ **Danny Rams** has some of the best power in the system, but he's probably not a catcher in the end, and moving from one end of the defensive spectrum to another is never a good thing. ⊘ Utilityman **Steven Tolleson** finally stayed healthy in 2009, but his bat regressed; his best chance is to become the next Harris/Punto/Tolbert, but the Twins have already collected the set and may not have space on the pine for another. ⊘ **David Winfree** moved to the outfield in 2009, but didn't hit enough to justify more than a future as a bench bat. He joined the Yankees as a minor-league free agent.

Pitchers

PLAYER	TEAM	LVL	AGE	W	L	SV	IP	H	HR	BB	SO	GB%	BABIP	STUFF	WHIP	ERA	SIERA	DERA	EqH9	EqHR9	EqBB9	EqSO9	VORP
B. Bullock	BLT	A	21	3	0	8	26¹	25	0	12	35	30%	.373	7	1.41	2.73	2.95	5.11	10.6	1.1	5.1	7.3	1.1
A. Burnett	FTM	A+	21	2	1	4	22²	14	0	7	26	53%	.246	16	0.93	1.99	2.74	3.74	7.1	0.8	3.3	6.6	4.2
—	NBR	AA	21	1	2	9	55¹	36	2	19	52	44%	.241	18	0.99	1.79	3.42	3.18	6.7	0.9	3.3	6.2	13.5
R. Delaney	NBR	AA	24	1	1	0	36	32	1	6	40	43%	.330	11	1.06	2.00	2.38	3.74	9.1	0.8	1.9	7.5	6.6
—	ROC	AAA	24	7	3	7	47²	43	5	15	38	32%	.270	-9	1.22	4.53	4.23	5.23	8.0	1.3	3.0	5.7	1.4
A. Gabino	ROC	AAA	25	6	4	1	98	80	7	24	64	41%	.252	4	1.06	2.94	4.31	3.57	7.2	1.0	2.4	4.7	20.4
P. Humber	ROC	AAA	26	7	9	0	119²	135	15	45	87	42%	.313	-16	1.50	5.34	4.57	6.54	10.0	1.4	3.5	5.1	-13.7
—	MIN	MLB	26	0	0	0	9	17	1	9	9	51%	.516	3	2.89	8.00	5.16	7.56	18.4	1.1	8.6	8.6	-1.9
S. Hunt	BLT	A	22	0	1	0	17²	15	1	33	18	41%	.298	-2	2.72	10.70	6.85	15.43	9.9	2.2	18.2	5.0	-18.0
—	TWI	Rk	22	0	4	0	15	10	0	25	8	—	.238	-25	2.33	9.60	7.63	15.75	10.5	2.3	20.3	1.5	-13.7
J. Morillo	ROC	AAA	25	6	6	5	67	56	1	51	87	57%	.335	27	1.60	3.90	3.60	4.55	7.9	0.4	7.0	9.5	6.9
B. Pugh	BLT	A	20	4	5	0	85	71	4	47	99	43%	.309	14	1.39	2.86	3.47	4.86	9.2	1.6	6.1	6.4	5.6
K. Waldrop	FTM	A+	23	3	2	3	35	43	0	7	20	68%	.358	-25	1.43	3.09	4.10	5.81	13.4	0.9	2.6	3.2	-1.1
—	NBR	AA	23	2	3	0	55²	51	2	18	30	64%	.272	-13	1.24	1.46	4.55	3.17	8.7	0.8	3.0	3.2	14.0

After he missed all of 2009 recovering from shoulder surgery, **Boof Bonser** was designated for assignment before the Twins dealt him to the Red Sox for marginal minor-leaguer Chris Province. ⊘ A second-round pick last June, **Billy Bullock** is one of those college relievers who could move quickly and settle into a set-up man role within the next two years. ⊘ **Alex Burnett** went from organizational arm to real prospect with a move to the pen, where his fastball/slider combination played up. ⊘ Like most Twins farmhands, **Rob Delaney** succeeds by locating his pitches with pinpoint precision, not on stuff. ⊘ Generic righty **Armando Gabino** got ripped in a pair of big-league appearances in 2009; he is now with the Orioles for 2010. ⊘ Another failure-to-launch prospect from the Johan Santana deal, **Philip Humber** pitched his way out of the picture, getting picked up by the Royals off waivers at year's end. ⊘ A supplemental first-round pick in 2008, **Shooter Hunt** contracted Steve Blass syndrome in his full-season debut, and the Twins are just trying to get him out of the tall weeds at this point. ⊘ A "have arm, will travel" lefty, **Ron Mahay** was a serviceable extra LOOGY down the stretch, and there remain plenty of teams willing to give him another chance. ⊘ **Juan Morillo** keeps bouncing around because of his upper-90s fastball, but he has little command and no second pitch; he's bouncing all the way to Japan for 2010. ⊘ The Twins hope that **Pat Neshek** can return to form as a dominating sidearmer after missing all of 2009 recovering from elbow surgery. ⊘ A little-known 19th-round pick in 2008, **Bruce Pugh** grabbed a lot of attention in 2009 with a 93-94 mph fastball. ⊘ A first-round pick in 2004, big righty **Kyle Waldrop** stalled for a while, but finally showed some signs of life in 2009 after moving to the pen.

MANAGER: RON GARDENHIRE

YEAR	TEAM	W-L	Pythag +/–	Avg PC	100+ P	120+ P	QS	BQS	REL	REL w Zero R	IBB	Subs	PH	PH Avg	PH HR	SB2	CS2	SB3	CS3	SAC Att	SAC %	POS SAC	Squeeze	Swing	In Play
2007	MIN	79-83	-1	93.8	47	0	75	4	436	291	33	40	102	.250	1	94	29	18	1	55	61.8%	29	4	161	134
2008	MIN	88-75	-2	91.8	47	1	81	5	485	312	38	25	108	.247	3	86	37	16	5	85	61.2%	47	7	138	118
2009	MIN	87-76	0	92.4	56	1	76	8	477	301	20	49	83	.303	4	74	28	11	2	80	63.7%	46	4	150	127

Like his predecessor, Tom Kelly, Gardy gets high marks for game management and getting the most out of what he's got. Also like Kelly, he generally keeps his roster active instead of ignoring the last few bodies on the bench. A relative tendency toward the sac bunt isn't that surprising given the number of slack bats in the regular lineup, so it isn't as if he's Gene Mauch reborn, despite his having a designated bunter like Tolbert around. You'd hope he'll take the bat out of Denard Span's hands a bit less frequently (12 sacs, second on the team behind Punto, barely ahead of Tolbert). Despite so many weak hitters, he wasn't especially aggressive pinch-hitting for them, but he was adaptive as the season progressed, sitting Gomez and giving Young that extra chance in the outfield once Span had earned the full-time role. As a staff manager, he's not a slow hook but not notably so relative to his peers, and he's generally reluctant to order up the intentional pass. Running a pen effectively is one of his gifts, as he's willing to make space for a long reliever to keep his tactical options open in tighter games; if there's a complaint, it might be that absolute need down the stretch led to some overuse of Mijares. Like Kelly, he won't be accused of any particular genius, but outstanding competence creates its own rewards and engenders considerable respect.

New York Mets

It really looked as though things couldn't get any worse for the Mets than September 2007. That was when the team blew a seven-game lead with 17 to go. How little we knew; 2007 was just the place where misery began. In the last 2 ½ years, Murphy's Law has completely taken over the Mets' franchise. Injuries, late-season collapses, an apocalyptic economy, botched firings, emotional meltdowns, Ponzi schemes—the list is longer and more diverse than any reasonable person could have ever imagined.

These were supposed to be the Mets' salad days. After posting baseball's best record and running away with the National League East in 2006, the Mets looked stocked for the long haul; they had signed their two young superstars, David Wright and Jose Reyes, to very inexpensive long-term deals and had another potential Hall of Famer, Carlos Beltran, locked down for at least another five years. The economy was doing very well, the team was drawing record crowds at Shea Stadium, Johan Santana was a year away from being brought into the fold, and Citi Field was slowly taking shape behind the old park. For the Mets, as for so many others in the miserable decade that has just closed, utopian dreams dissipated to reveal nightmares, the horn of plenty sputtered and coughed itself shut, and any luck to be found was bad. The Mets hit rock bottom in 2009, going 70-92 despite a $136 million payroll. While a good portion of their problems were self-inflicted, the Mets have also found themselves in the center of some really unusual, not to mention historic and unlikely, circumstances. Let's take a look at the timeline, starting with the team's epic breakdown three years ago:

METS PROSPECTUS
2009 W-L: 70-92, 4th in NL East

Pythag	77-85	10th
RS/G	4.1	12th
RA/G	4.7	9th
EqA	.263	8th
EqBRR	1.9	4th
SNWP	.482	12th
WXRL	4.37	13th
FRAr	4.38	9th
DE	.693	8th
PADE	-1.74	14th
Salary	$149.4	1st
Attend	3.17	5th

Ballpark: Citi Field (1-yr. PF: 972). Pitcher-friendly, and the one thing that didn't get hurt

2009: Epic wave of injuries blots out problems in roster contruction, further big-money mistakes

2010: Will heads roll if nobody gets hurt and they still don't win? Help from the farm's far off, so it's win now or die

Action Items: Reliability from non-Johan starters, power at first base, a catcher, corner outfielders with power

- **September 30, 2007:** Tom Glavine allows seven runs in a third of an inning on the final day of the season, as the Mets complete their historic collapse.
- **June 16, 2008:** The team fires manager Willie Randolph, but only after he makes a cross-country flight to Los Angeles and coaches a win over the Angels. General manager Omar Minaya tells the press it was his decision alone and he wanted to do it as soon as he had made up his mind, but he and the Wilpons are heavily criticized in the press for handling the situation poorly.
- **September 15, 2008:** Lehman Brothers declares bankruptcy, taking the global economy down with it and leaving the financial system on the brink of collapse. That night, Pedro Martinez headlines a 7-2 Mets loss to John Lannan and the Nationals, little realizing the way the rapidly intensifying Great Recession will change the future of their team.
- **September 24, 2008:** With the Mets a game up in the wild-card race in the final week of the season, Minaya receives a four-year contract extension.
- **September 28, 2008:** For the second straight year, the Mets lose to the Marlins on the final day of the season, completing another unlikely collapse. Shea Stadium closes on a solemn note.
- **November 24, 2008:** The US government injects $20 billion into Citigroup, bringing the total federal investment to $45 billion, and guarantees $306 billion of the bank's risky assets. Many people across the country—including some congressional representatives—call for the government to cancel Citi's $400 million naming rights deal with the Mets, although no action is taken.

- **December 11, 2008:** Financial advisor Bernard Madoff is arrested and charged with operating a $60 billion Ponzi scheme. Fred Wilpon is reported to be a major investor, potentially putting his financial fortune—and his ownership of the Mets—in serious jeopardy. There is speculation in the press, vehemently disputed by the team, that the Mets' expenditures may be restricted. That same day, the Mets complete a three-way trade with the Mariners and Indians in which they receive relievers Sean Green and J. J. Putz as well as reserve outfielder Jeremy Reed. The two pitchers will back up single-season saves leader Francisco Rodriguez, signed two days earlier, creating what is projected to be an impregnable bullpen. The rest of the winter is devoted to acquiring inexpensive, second-line talent.

All of this was mere prologue to a season as frustrating and difficult as any in team history, but lacking the joie de vivre, the pleasure that fans could take in the club's mere existence, of 1962. The season was a long, almost literal battle of attrition in which the roster was whittled away like the nursery rhyme *Ten Little Indians:* "One lefty Mets pitcher dozing in the sun / his elbow made a popping sound / and then there were none." Along with the carnage, the Mets also presented more than their share of bizarre sidelights:

- **March 15, 2009:** Recently re-signed lefty Oliver Perez throws 85 pitches in a start for Mexico in the World Baseball Classic, well ahead of the pace he normally would have applied in Mets camp. Perez would make just two starts in 19 days for Team Mexico and was visibly out of shape by the time he returned to Port St. Lucie. Mets staffers would later blame the WBC for the injuries to both Perez and reliever J. J. Putz.
- **May 26, 2009:** Shortstop Jose Reyes is retroactively placed on the DL with a mild calf strain. He is expected to be back with the team on June 5th.
- **May 29, 2009:** The Mets finish the day in first place for the final time in 2009.
- **July 27, 2009:** The team fires vice president of player development, Tony Bernazard, after he took his shirt off and challenged the entire Binghamton Mets team to a fight. At the ensuing press conference, Minaya blamed beat writer Adam Rubin, the reporter who broke the story, claiming that Rubin was trying to get hired by the team. When a stunned Rubin challenged his logic, Minaya backed off. The GM later apologized to Rubin and the Mets' fans, saying that his emotions had gotten the best of him.
- **August 12, 2009:** With the team struggling, the Mets cut ticket prices, some by as much as 50 percent. After the season ends, they announce broad cuts for 2010 tickets as well.
- **August 25, 2009:** Johan Santana is placed on the DL, becoming the 19th Mets player to spend time on the DL in 2009. Of the team's eight Opening Day position players and five original starting pitchers, only Daniel Murphy, Mike Pelfrey, and Livan Hernandez stayed healthy the entire season—and Hernandez completed the season wearing Nationals togs.
- **September 18, 2009:** The Mets lose their 10th game out of 11, falling to 22 games under .500 for the first time in six years.
- **September 30, 2009:** Jose Reyes tears his hamstring, finally ending a four-month rehab try. He joins a parade of teammates heading to the OR.

All in all, not a fun couple of years, and you can bet that the team is just glad it's over, if indeed it is over. Considering the continuing effects of the fiscal crisis and the possibility that Madoff's schemes might still affect the club, not to mention a shattered roster that will not have been much improved by this offseason's work, it still may not be over. Yet, if you look very closely, there are some positives to be found amid the wreckage. First, the Mets were in a surprisingly good position to withstand the economic Pearl Harbor. By early October 2008, the team had already sold out its luxury suites for 2009, having priced much of its inventory at about half or even a third of what the Yankees were selling their boxes in NuYankee for. This may have turned out to be a lifesaving move. And with a smaller capacity and far cheaper single-game prices than those in the Bronx, the Mets actually filled a higher percentage of their seats in 2009 than they did in 2008. As chief operating officer Jeff Wilpon said in March, "I'd rather be opening up a new stadium in this economy than trying to sell seats in the old Shea." It's debatable how long the new park's novelty will let the Mets survive a losing ballclub and a losing economy, but for 2009, the timing couldn't have been better.

There's also some hope down on the farm. Twenty-year-old outfielder Fernando Martinez mashed at Triple-A before a brief stint in the big leagues (which inevitably ended with an extended stay on the DL), as did catcher/bat-control king Josh Thole (179 walks and 170 strikeouts in his pro career). The Mets are also particularly excited about right-hander Jenrry Mejia and first baseman Ike Davis, both of whom could end up in the big leagues if things break right in 2010; Mejia struck out more than a batter per inning as a teenager at Double-A, while Davis hit .298/.381/.524 in his pro debut.

Most importantly, though, the team still has a ton of frontline talent and could easily compete for a playoff spot in 2010. When healthy, Beltran, Wright, Reyes, Santana, and free-agent signee Jason Bay are about as good as any group you'll find, particularly in the National League, and there's no reason the Mets shouldn't be able to build around them competently enough to give the Braves and Phillies a solid run for their money. The big question, of course, is whether they'll all be healthy in 2010. Of that foursome, only Wright has a totally clean bill of health; he suffered a concussion after getting beaned in August, but didn't show any negative effects after he returned in September. Santana should be fine, as well, although bone chips do tend to recur every three to four years.

On the other hand, Beltran and Reyes are still huge question marks. Beltran was having an MVP-type season before his ailing right knee kept him out of the lineup from late June until early September. He returned rather than have microfracture surgery, which not only would have kept him out for the rest of 2009, but also would have eaten up a significant chunk of 2010 as well. It remains to be seen if the athroscopic procedure he underwent in January will alleviate the problem, but it will likely cost him spring training, if not longer.

There's even more uncertainty around Reyes, who was only supposed to be out for a couple weeks, but instead missed almost 4 ½ months. The team's medical staff was ridiculed in the press, but it was really more of a PR issue: had the Mets simply said Reyes was out indefinitely, instead of putting out phantom return dates every couple of weeks, the public perception probably would have been very different. As it was, the situation brought back memories of Reyes's first couple years in the big leagues, when his hamstrings created endless problems, and no one knew quite how to solve them. Eventually, he was forced to relearn how to run with the help of outside trainer Vern Gambetta, and Reyes managed to play in over 150 games for four straight seasons. He'll probably need to get back on a similar regimen if he wants to avoid another calamity-filled season.

There are some other concerns as well. It's impossible to tell whether Oliver Perez is injured or simply broken, and Wright's peripherals (particularly his power and strikeout rate) took a very scary turn in 2009. The Mets played the last few seasons without a net; they lacked the depth to survive a hangnail. In 2009, they got everything *but* the hangnail, and while no team would have been able to endure the onslaught—regardless of the efficacy of their medical staff—the Mets were not adequately prepared to make even the pretense of try-ing. To a large degree, this will still be the case in 2010. The reasons for optimism will be the same as they have been: the frontline talent is still in place, the farm system might spin off a couple of solid pieces, and if the team has good luck where it had bad and good health where it had injury, then Bailout—that is, *Citi* Field could be a much happier place in 2010.

DISASTERPIECE THEATER
The Mets' Injury Picture in 2009

WILL CARROLL

There's very literally no way to take the Mets' 2009 campaign and put it into anything less than a historical context. The alpha and omega of their season were injuries, failures, breakdowns, setbacks ... and that was just the good stuff. In the end, head trainer Ray Ramirez and his staff were faced with the public's looking very hard at what they do, something medical staffs in the game just aren't used to. Were Ramirez and his staff to blame? That's a question that can only be truly answered by people on the inside, but a closer look at what the injuries were and how they happened helps provide a few answers.

First, let's look at these numbers. It's impossible to do for injury stats what BP does for game stats—league, park, and era adjustments, plus the factor of inflation—largely because we lack historical numbers. Even so, it's safe to say that the Mets' losses in dollars and injury cost (a calculation developed to show the "true cost" of the injury, rather than undervaluing underpaid players, and vice versa) is flat-out historic, if not the worst ever. People are surprised that the Mets lost fewer player-days in 2009 than in 2008. In fact, the 2009 Mets were less hurt than four teams from the 2008 season, including their own club, which had 200 more player-days lost.

Instead, the value-based numbers are just stunning, but that's more the form than anything else. While teams like the Rangers, Cardinals, and Yankees lost more player-days in 2008 and managed pretty good seasons all the same, it's easier to compare the 2008 Mets, with 1,645 days lost and $34 million in value lost, to the '09 Mets and their tally of 1,451 days lost but $52 million in value lost. The '08 team collapsed at the end of the season, but they were contenders. The difference between these two teams is their losses of top-level talents, nearly irreplaceable players like Jose Reyes, David Wright, and Carlos Delgado. While "replacement level" is a tough concept, the Mets showed exactly how bad it can affect a team—and how expensive that can be.

For example, before the season, the Mets had already gone out to get Francisco Rodriguez on the open market to replace Billy Wagner. Omar Minaya would probably not have gotten the top closer on the market if Wagner had been available. (Possible, but reasonably unlikely. And J. J. Putz too? Not a chance.) That's an additional $12 million on top of Wagner's salary of nearly $10 million; I don't have to go into any advanced math to explain that this is an unsustainable model for any team. In this, however, the Mets had a way of getting a better-than-replacement-level talent. Danny Murphy might be better than the calculated replacement level, but he's a drop-off, even from an aging Delgado.

Table 1. 2008 Mets Injuries: The Good Old Days?

Player	Position	Type	Body Part	Surgery?	Salary	Days Lost	Salary Lost	% of Payroll Lost	Injury Cost
Moises Alou	LF	Hernia	Groin	Y	$7,500,000	32	$1,304,348	1.0%	$1,008,889
—		Strain	Left Calf	N	$7,500,000	20	$815,217	0.6%	$630,556
—		Strain	Left Calf	N	$7,500,000	113	$4,605,978	3.3%	$3,562,639
Marlon Anderson	UT	Strain	Left Hamstring	N	$1,050,000	18	$102,717	0.1%	$185,000
—		Strain	Left Hamstring	N	$1,050,000	31	$176,902	0.1%	$318,611
Tony Armas Jr.	P	Strain	Abdomen	N	$390,000	85	$180,163	0.1%	$897,222
Ambiorix Burgos	P	Tear	Right Elbow	N	$415,000	184	$415,000	0.3%	$2,887,777.78
Luis Castillo	2B	Strain	Left Hip	N	$6,250,000	54	$1,834,239	1.3%	$1,785,000
Ramon Castro	C	Strain	Right Hamstring	N	$1,975,000	39	$418,614	0.3%	$991,250
—		Strain	Right Quadriceps	N	$1,975,000	36	$386,413	0.3%	$915,000
Ryan Church	OF	Concussion	Head	N	$2,000,000	24	$260,870	0.2%	$1,030,000
—		Concussion	Head	N	$2,000,000	48	$521,739	0.4%	$2,060,000
Orlando Hernandez	P	Unknown	Right Foot	Y	$7,000,000	184	$7,000,000	5.1%	$4,216,667
John Maine	P	Strain	Right Shoulder	N	$450,000	16	$39,130	0.0%	$586,667
—		Bone Spurs	Right Shoulder	N	$450,000	32	$78,261	0.1%	$1,173,333
Pedro Martinez	P	Strain	Left Hamstring	N	$11,813,351	63	$4,044,789	2.9%	$3,150,000
Trot Nixon	OF	Strain	Groin	Y	$390,000	95	$201,359	0.2%	$1,015,972
Angel Pagan	OF	Bruised	Left Shoulder	N	$401,500	142	$309,853	0.2%	$1,538,333
Duaner Sanchez	P	Fracture	Right Shoulder	Y	$850,000	15	$69,293	0.1%	$216,667
Jason Vargas	P	Tear	Left Hip	Y	$394,000	184	$394,000	0.3%	$690,000
Billy Wagner	P	Strain	Left Forearm	N	$10,500,000	60	$3,423,913	2.5%	$3,083,333
Matt Wise	P	Soreness	Right Forearm	N	$1,200,000	42	$273,913	0.2%	$513,333
—		Tendinitis	Right Shoulder	N	$1,200,000	128	$834,783	0.6%	$1,564,444
Total 23 injuries					$137,793,376	1645	$27,691,495	20.1%	$34,020,694

Table 2. 2009 Mets Injuries: The Wages of Ouch

Player	Position	Type	Body Part	Surgery?	Salary	Days Lost	Salary Lost	% of Payroll Lost	Injury Cost
Carlos Beltran	CF	Bruised	Right Knee	N	$18,500,000	78	$7,842,391	5.3%	$9,251,667
Ryan Church	OF	Strain	Right Hamstring	N	$2,800,000	15	$228,261	0.2%	$156,250
Alex Cora	INF	Strain	Right Hand	N	$2,000,000	16	$173,913	0.1%	$68,889
—		Tear	Right Hand	N	$2,000,000	45	$489,130	0.3%	$193,750
Carlos Delgado	1B	Impingement	Right Hip	N	$16,000,000	144	$12,521,739	8.4%	$4,720,000
John Maine	P	Fatigue	Right Shoulder	N	$2,600,000	98	$1,384,783	0.9%	$2,000,833
Jesus Martinez	OF	Inflammation	Right Knee	N	$400,000	85	$184,783	0.1%	$484,028
Ramon Martinez	INF	Fracture	Left Hand	Y	$750,000	121	$493,207	0.3%	$268,889
Jon Niese	P	Tear	Right Hamstring	N	$400,000	57	$123,913	0.1%	$387,917
Fernando Nieve	P	Strain	Right Quadriceps	N	$414,000	74	$166,500	0.1%	$205,556
Angel Pagan	OF	Bone Spurs	Right Elbow	Y	$575,000	42	$131,250	0.1%	$408,333
—		Soreness	Groin	N	$575,000	39	$121,875	0.1%	$379,167
Oliver Perez	P	Tendinitis	Right Knee	N	$12,000,000	66	$4,304,348	2.9%	$1,695,833
—		Tendinitis	Right Knee	N	$12,000,000	38	$2,478,261	1.7%	$976,389
J. J. Putz	P	Bone Spurs	Right Elbow	Y	$5,000,000	119	$3,233,696	2.2%	$3,057,639
Tim Redding	P	Soreness	Right Shoulder	N	$2,250,000	43	$525,815	0.4%	$352,361
Jose Reyes	SS	Tendinitis	Right Calf	N	$5,750,000	134	$4,187,500	2.80%	$19,262,500
Johan Santana	P	Bone Spurs	Left Elbow	N	$20,000,000	42	$4,565,217	3.1%	$3,896,667
Brian Schneider	C	Strain	Back	N	$4,900,000	43	$1,145,109	0.8%	$465,833
Gary Sheffield	OF	Strain	Right Hamstring	N	$400,000	15	$32,609	0.0%	$158,333
Billy Wagner	P	Tear	Left Elbow	N	$10,500,000	137	$7,817,935	5.2%	$3,463,056
Total 21 injuries					$149,373,987	1451	$52,152,234	34.9%	$51,853,889

Just look at the differences between Tables 1 and 2. Quite simply, no team could have survived these types of losses and won. We have to ask whether *this* team could have anticipated the problem; clearly, 2008 wasn't a stellar year from an injury standpoint, but aside from knowing that Wagner would be out the better part of the year (and his relatively speedy rehab pace was one of few bright spots for the Mets), the simple answer is no. Delgado not only had a hip surgery that couldn't have been anticipated, but was also the only player who didn't come back quickly and at level. Reyes did have a history of hamstring injuries, but he'd also more recently had three years without a hint of problem. Beltran had longstanding knee issues, but the Mets had kept him relatively productive, making it tough to see this kind of cliff.

Moreover, take a look at the specific injury issues: players on this team had elbow, hip, hamstring, head, shoulder, groin, and quad problems. In other words, a lot of everything, and there's no pattern, no one thing that stands out, like the great Yankees' Hamstring Epidemic of '08. This is as close to a random listing as there is.

There's only one pattern, and it's the real problem here: the way the injuries were handled in the press. Is it possible that the Mets have more of a PR problem than an injury issue? Casting aside the public-relations nightmare of the Tony Bernazard episode, let's take a look at how the injury to Jose Reyes was handled. When Reyes first injured the leg, it was labeled a calf injury. Reyes tested it with the strength coach, had it looked at by team doctors, and then went out and played through some pain. At this stage, since Reyes had been cleared by both the strength coach and the doctors, it's hard to blame the training staff. It took nearly two weeks for Reyes to end up on the DL, and by then, the damage was done, but there had been little discussion that this was a tendon issue rather than a muscular problem. Over the next few

weeks, various Mets spokesmen, including Jerry Manuel and Minaya, gave progress reports. Reyes himself contradicted Minaya on one occasion, after Minaya had said Reyes was running on a treadmill and taking ground balls. The Mets continued trying to paint a rosy picture, showcasing a workout at Citi Field for the press at the same time knowing that Reyes had pain only when running at near full-go (not during the easy jogging he was doing that day).

By the end of July, Manuel's forecasts of "two weeks" were being ridiculed, as Reyes had made no progress toward a return. Meanwhile, Manuel continued to answer questions with the baseless timetable. Finally, after Reyes made a last-ditch attempt to return, the news broke that he had a completely torn hamstring tendon and would need surgery. Given this information, it's unbelievable that the team ever truly thought Reyes could come back. Medically, a torn hamstring tendon is an easy diagnosis and an injury easily fixed, and the diagnosis could have come as early as May. While there was no need to have the surgery immediately—Reyes had it in October and will be ready for spring training—the obfuscation is what made no sense. Fans in this day and age grasp that injuries, especially traumatic ones like this, are part of the game. By mishandling it, the Mets dug themselves into a gratuitous public-relations hole.

Just by getting back to average or even in improving the player-days lost ratio in the way the team did between '08 and '09, it's easy to anticipate a regression to the mean that would equal several wins for the Mets in the lineup alone. A healthy Reyes is a consistent six-win player, while Beltran could bounce back somewhere near that level, in light of his eight-win '08. While Ramirez and his team on the training staff are clearly on the hot seat, in taking a closer look at the Mets' long litany of issues, we can see that he shouldn't be at the top of the list.

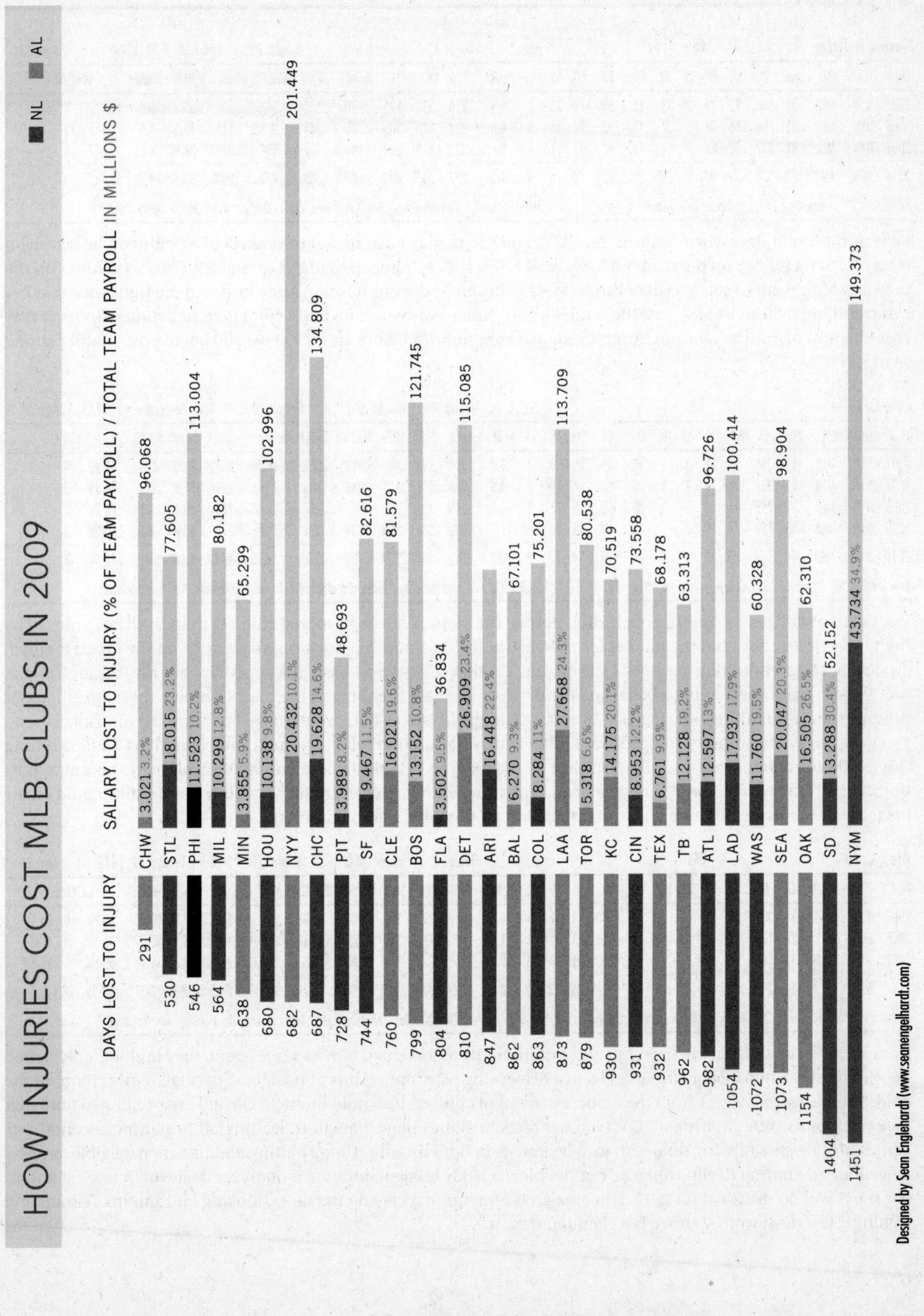

HOW INJURIES COST MLB CLUBS IN 2009

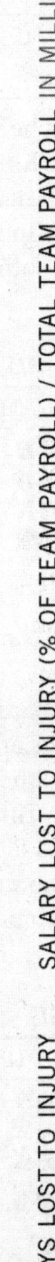

■ NL ■ AL

DAYS LOST TO INJURY   SALARY LOST TO INJURY (% OF TEAM PAYROLL) / TOTAL TEAM PAYROLL IN MILLIONS $

Team	Days	Salary (%)	Total payroll
CHW	291	3.021 3.2%	96.068
STL	530	18.015 23.2%	77.605
PHI	546	11.523 10.2%	113.004
MIL	564	10.299 12.8%	80.182
MIN	638	3.855 5.9%	65.299
HOU	680	10.138 9.8%	102.996
NYY	682	20.432 10.1%	201.449
CHC	687	19.628 14.6%	134.809
PIT	728	3.989 8.2%	48.693
SF	744	9.467 11.5%	82.616
CLE	760	16.021 19.6%	81.579
BOS	799	13.152 10.8%	121.745
FLA	804	3.502 9.5%	36.834
DET	810	26.909 23.4%	115.085
ARI	847	16.448 22.4%	67.101
BAL	862	6.270 9.3%	67.101
COL	863	8.284 11%	75.201
LAA	873	27.668 24.3%	113.709
TOR	879	5.318 6.6%	80.538
KC	930	14.175 20.1%	70.519
CIN	931	8.953 12.2%	73.558
TEX	932	6.761 9.9%	68.178
TB	962	12.128 19.2%	63.313
ATL	982	12.597 13%	96.726
LAD	1054	17.937 17.9%	100.414
WAS	1072	11.760 19.5%	60.328
SEA	1073	20.047 20.3%	98.904
OAK	1154	16.505 26.5%	62.310
SD	1404	13.288 30.4%	52.152
NYM	1451	43.734 34.9%	149.373

Designed by Sean Englehardt (www.seanenglehardt.com)

HITTERS

Carlos Beltran — CF

Bats: S   Throws: R   Height: 6' 1"   Weight: 205   Born: April 24, 1977   Age: 33

YEAR	TEAM	LVL	AGE	PA	R	2B	3B	HR	RBI	BB	SO	SB	CS	EqBRR	AVG	OBP	SLG	EqAVG	EqOBP	EqSLG	EqA	VORP	WARP	DEFENSE
2007	NYN	MLB	30	636	93	33	3	33	112	69	111	23	2	4.5	.276	.353	.525	.289	.364	.547	.306	53.7	6.8	138-CF 7
2008	NYN	MLB	31	706	116	40	5	27	112	92	96	25	3	6.8	.284	.376	.500	.300	.387	.525	.311	60.6	8.5	156-CF 15
2009	NYN	MLB	32	357	50	22	1	10	48	47	43	11	1	-0.7	.325	.415	.500	.346	.431	.534	.329	37.8	4.8	77-CF 6
2010	NYN	MLB	33	530	71	26	2	20	82	62	90	12	4	1.5	.277	.363	.472	.281	.366	.473	.292	35.1	4.3	117-CF 4

Breakout: 3%   Improve: 26%   Collapse: 20%   Attrition: 9%   MLB: 98%   Comparables: Bernie Williams, Carlos Guillen, Rusty Staub, Dusty Baker

Beltran was exemplary when healthy, though the new park may have served to conceal just how good he was, with rates of .354/.448/.585 on the road but "only" .292/.376/.403 at home. He's now a career .290/.368/.548 hitter on the road as a Met; there's a secret Hall of Fame career going on under our noses. A bone bruise in the right knee that began troubling Beltran in May cost the outfielder 70 games between June and September and surgery to fix it may cost him part of April as well, but he has overcome knee injuries before and is a very solid bet to post another strong season.

Luis Castillo — 2B

Bats: S   Throws: R   Height: 5' 11"   Weight: 190   Born: September 12, 1975   Age: 34

YEAR	TEAM	LVL	AGE	PA	R	2B	3B	HR	RBI	BB	SO	SB	CS	EqBRR	AVG	OBP	SLG	EqAVG	EqOBP	EqSLG	EqA	VORP	WARP	DEFENSE
2007	MIN	MLB	31	384	54	11	3	0	18	29	28	9	4	5.0	.304	.356	.352	.308	.362	.363	.258	11.3	0.8	82-2B -4
2007	NYN	MLB	31	231	37	8	2	1	20	24	17	10	2	4.6	.296	.371	.372	.310	.385	.385	.279	11.9	0.3	48-2B -10
2008	NYN	MLB	32	359	46	7	1	3	28	50	35	17	2	3.6	.245	.355	.305	.260	.364	.320	.261	10.7	-0.1	76-2B -12
2009	NYN	MLB	33	580	77	12	3	1	40	69	58	20	6	1.7	.302	.387	.346	.324	.402	.368	.282	29.7	2.5	130-2B -8
2010	NYN	MLB	34	502	70	18	4	3	39	55	54	12	5	2.5	.282	.362	.359	.288	.366	.363	.264	16.8	1.2	112-2B -6

Breakout: 12%   Improve: 36%   Collapse: 20%   Attrition: 22%   MLB: 93%   Comparables: Tom Herr, Mark McLemore, Jim Gilliam, Red Schoendienst

Yes, Castillo's still here, signed through 2011, despite the Mets' best efforts to trade him. Perhaps he'll have moved by the time you read this, but the market for players who hit .300 and still don't put many runs on the board is small, especially since his batting average is so variable. Castillo still gets on base at a good clip, but his legs aren't what they were, so his baserunning has declined and his range afield is a thing of the past. Combine this with a bat that produces almost nothing but singles—16 extra-base hits in 486 at-bats would have embarrassed Joe Tinker—and you have a very iffy property going forward. Citi Field's small amount of foul ground contributed to Castillo's hitting .350/.429/.402 at home against .250/.341/.284 on the road; even if hitting homers was difficult in the new digs, putting the ball in play when everything's fair can help a guy like this. However, the possibility that Castillo could hit for his road rate across a full season of at-bats frightens off potential trading partners.

Alex Cora — MI

Bats: L   Throws: R   Height: 6' 0"   Weight: 200   Born: October 18, 1975   Age: 34

YEAR	TEAM	LVL	AGE	PA	R	2B	3B	HR	RBI	BB	SO	SB	CS	EqBRR	AVG	OBP	SLG	EqAVG	EqOBP	EqSLG	EqA	VORP	WARP	DEFENSE	
2007	BOS	MLB	31	232	30	10	5	3	18	7	23	1	1	0.0	.246	.298	.386	.238	.287	.374	.234	0.9	1.2	34-2B 8	23-SS 1
2008	BOS	MLB	32	179	14	8	2	0	9	16	13	1	1	-1.5	.270	.371	.349	.270	.371	.342	.260	6.7	0.7	43-SS -2	4-2B 1
2009	NYN	MLB	33	308	31	11	1	1	18	25	28	8	3	0.9	.251	.320	.310	.265	.330	.327	.239	4.7	-0.2	53-SS -6	15-2B -1
2010	NYN	MLB	34	218	22	9	2	2	15	17	25	3	2	-0.1	.247	.324	.345	.256	.331	.344	.241	3.3	0.2	53-SS -2	

Breakout: 12%   Improve: 33%   Collapse: 30%   Attrition: 35%   MLB: 87%   Comparables: Craig Reynolds, Amos Strunk, Jim Gantner, Tim McCarver

Cora is known as a highly intelligent player, but when the Mets signed him as a free agent, they undoubtedly hoped he would more often display this intelligence dispensing witty aphorisms at postgame cocktail parties than on the field. "Necessity relieves us from the embarrassment of choice," he would quote to Oliver Perez, failing to note that Perez's earbuds were in. Instead, Cora led the Mets in games played at short, leading off or batting second in 47 games, this despite missing time with torn ligaments in both thumbs. Cora's batting abilities are negligible, and his glove may be starting to slip with age, but the Mets quickly re-signed him to a one-year deal with a vesting option (80 starts will do the trick) for 2011. One imagines him, upon receiving the news, looking up from his Talmud and sighing, "The most worthy crown is a good reputation."

Ike Davis   1B

Bats: L   Throws: L   Height: 6' 5"   Weight: 195   Born: March 22, 1987   Age: 23

YEAR	TEAM	LVL	AGE	PA	R	2B	3B	HR	RBI	BB	SO	SB	CS	EqBRR	AVG	OBP	SLG	EqAVG	EqOBP	EqSLG	EqA	VORP	WARP	DEFENSE	
2008	BRO	A-	21	239	17	15	0	0	17	23	43	0	0	-1.4	.256	.326	.326	.231	.285	.281	.199	-12.0	-3.0	55-1B	-6
2009	SLU	A+	22	255	28	17	3	7	28	31	52	0	2	-1.3	.288	.376	.486	.260	.340	.441	.268	2.1	0.8	61-1B	4
2009	BIN	AA	22	233	30	14	0	13	43	26	60	0	0	1.1	.309	.386	.565	.283	.350	.514	.290	8.0	0.7	49-1B	-2
2010	NYN	MLB	23	459	42	22	1	13	46	43	119	0	1	-0.5	.238	.310	.388	.246	.316	.398	.245	-2.7	-0.4	104-1B	-1

Breakout: 12%   Improve: 42%   Collapse: 15%   Attrition: 4%   MLB: 1%   Comparables: Luis Antonio Jimenez, John Urick, Jim Orsag, Brian Turner

As bad a year as the Mets had, there were a handful of good stories down on the farm, and Davis was one of them. A first-round pick in 2008, Davis was selected for his power bat, but failed to hit a single home run in 215 at-bats during his pro debut, leading some to classify him as a bust. The doomsayers proved to be premature, as Davis slugged his way through both High-A and Double-A to stake his claim on the first-base job that had been cleared out by Carlos Delgado. His arrival in time for the 2011 season is a far more realistic expectation than 2010, as Davis does most of his damage against right-handers, giving him something to work on ... but what a difference a year makes.

Carlos Delgado   1B

Bats: L   Throws: R   Height: 6' 3"   Weight: 265   Born: June 25, 1972   Age: 38

YEAR	TEAM	LVL	AGE	PA	R	2B	3B	HR	RBI	BB	SO	SB	CS	EqBRR	AVG	OBP	SLG	EqAVG	EqOBP	EqSLG	EqA	VORP	WARP	DEFENSE	
2007	NYN	MLB	35	607	71	30	0	24	87	52	118	4	0	-7.6	.258	.333	.448	.267	.339	.457	.276	16.5	1.8	136-1B	-1
2008	NYN	MLB	36	686	96	32	1	38	115	72	124	1	1	-0.2	.271	.353	.518	.283	.360	.538	.300	38.8	4.5	152-1B	2
2009	NYN	MLB	37	112	15	7	1	4	23	12	20	0	0	-0.5	.298	.393	.521	.319	.407	.574	.326	9.1	0.7	25-1B	-2
2010	NYN	MLB	38	382	45	17	1	16	61	36	82	1	1	-1.2	.248	.332	.443	.256	.337	.452	.270	8.4	0.9	88-1B	0

Breakout: 4%   Improve: 24%   Collapse: 25%   Attrition: 18%   MLB: 98%   Comparables: Fred McGriff, Willie Stargell, Jason Giambi, Rafael Palmeiro

Delgado's strong second half in 2008 convinced the Mets to pick up his $12 million option, and he made that decision look good in the early going. Sadly, his hip was on the verge of collapse, with a bone spur and a torn labrum (the latter of which hereby is awarded the first annual Baseball Prospectus Most Popular New Injury citation). Delgado played with pain into early May and then underwent surgery. The rehabilitation was endless, and when Delgado strained an oblique while running, the injury proved fatal to hopes that he would return. A free agent at this writing, Delgado is playing winter ball in the hopes of showing suitors that he can still play. Delgado was not terribly mobile before the injury and should probably be limited to DH duty, but the Mets are reportedly open to bringing him back.

Nick Evans   1B/LF

Bats: R   Throws: R   Height: 6' 3"   Weight: 210   Born: January 30, 1986   Age: 24

YEAR	TEAM	LVL	AGE	PA	R	2B	3B	HR	RBI	BB	SO	SB	CS	EqBRR	AVG	OBP	SLG	EqAVG	EqOBP	EqSLG	EqA	VORP	WARP	DEFENSE			
2007	SLU	A+	21	440	65	25	1	15	54	53	64	3	0	-0.6	.286	.374	.476	.262	.340	.438	.270	9.3	1.5	101-1B	3		
2008	BIN	AA	22	326	52	18	7	14	53	26	64	2	1	-1.2	.311	.365	.561	.282	.328	.492	.276	10.2	0.5	52-1B	1	19-LF	-6
2008	NYN	MLB	22	119	18	10	0	2	9	7	24	0	0	-0.5	.257	.303	.404	.269	.311	.426	.250	1.2	0.0	21-LF	-1		
2009	BIN	AA	23	117	16	9	1	3	9	10	22	2	0	1.4	.276	.350	.467	.262	.319	.439	.261	0.8	-0.3	14-1B	-3	7-RF	0
2009	BUF	AAA	23	261	27	12	3	10	30	23	55	0	0	0.7	.211	.280	.414	.202	.268	.395	.227	-6.5	-0.6	34-LF	1	28-1B	1
2009	NYN	MLB	23	69	5	5	1	1	7	4	20	0	0	0.6	.231	.275	.385	.246	.290	.400	.234	-1.4	-0.4	8-LF	-2	4-1B	0
2010	NYN	MLB	24	475	54	22	4	15	52	41	107	2	1	0.1	.243	.311	.416	.245	.311	.416	.254	1.9	0.3	102-1B	1		

Breakout: 5%   Improve: 26%   Collapse: 14%   Attrition: 7%   MLB: 91%   Comparables: Justin Huber, Wes Bankston, Juan Tejeda, Trey McCoy

One of the Mets' top minor-league performers in 2008, Evans regressed in 2009, and it was a step backward that his career could not really afford. He's got a patina of power and some idea of what he's doing at the plate, but when you are limited athletically to first base and left field, you need a *lot* of power and a *very good* idea at the plate. Just like coffee is for closers, first base is for mashers, and Evans is a long way from getting the Glengarry leads.

Wilmer Flores   SS   Bats: R   Throws: R   Height: 6' 3"   Weight: 175   Born: August 6, 1991   Age: 18

YEAR	TEAM	LVL	AGE	PA	R	2B	3B	HR	RBI	BB	SO	SB	CS	EqBRR	AVG	OBP	SLG	EqAVG	EqOBP	EqSLG	EqA	VORP	WARP	DEFENSE	
2008	BRO	A-	16	32	3	1	0	0	1	1	7	0	0	-0.1	.267	.290	.300	.233	.258	.267	.181	-1.0	-0.2	8-SS	0
2008	KNG	Rk	16	265	36	12	4	8	41	12	28	2	1	0.3	.310	.352	.490	.243	.273	.363	.220	0.1	-1.0	57-SS	-6
2009	SAV	A	17	528	44	20	2	3	36	22	72	3	3	-4.1	.264	.305	.332	.245	.274	.297	.199	-9.7	-2.2	124-SS	-8
2010	NYN	MLB	18	538	47	23	2	7	41	25	89	2	1	-1.3	.251	.292	.348	.256	.296	.348	.224	-0.6	-0.6	125-SS	-5

Breakout: 40%   Improve: 56%   Collapse: 15%   Attrition: 6%   MLB: 0%   Comparables: Jim Kelly, Elvis Andrus, Glenn Williams, Rafael DeLeon

After more than handling the Appalachian League as a 16-year-old in 2008, Flores came into the 2009 season with high expectations. Unfortunately, his showing at Low-A left much to be desired, at least on a statistical level, and while the numbers might not thrill you, his date of birth certainly should, as Flores is younger than most 2009 high-school-based draft picks, few of whom would come close to hitting .264 at this level with a reasonable strikeout rate. There's no way he'll still be a shortstop when all is said and done, as he's getting bigger and slower, seemingly by the month, but don't give up on the bat—taken in context, it's really not that bad.

Jeff Francoeur   RF   Bats: R   Throws: R   Height: 6' 4"   Weight: 220   Born: January 8, 1984   Age: 26

YEAR	TEAM	LVL	AGE	PA	R	2B	3B	HR	RBI	BB	SO	SB	CS	EqBRR	AVG	OBP	SLG	EqAVG	EqOBP	EqSLG	EqA	VORP	WARP	DEFENSE	
2007	ATL	MLB	23	696	84	40	0	19	105	42	129	5	2	-0.2	.293	.338	.444	.302	.346	.455	.274	23.3	5.3	160-RF	23
2008	ATL	MLB	24	652	70	33	3	11	71	39	111	0	1	0.8	.239	.294	.359	.246	.299	.370	.232	-7.6	-1.8	149-RF	-8
2009	ATL	MLB	25	324	32	12	2	5	35	12	46	5	1	-1.3	.250	.282	.352	.257	.287	.368	.230	-3.6	0.5	78-RF	8
2009	NYN	MLB	25	308	40	20	2	10	41	11	46	1	3	-2.7	.311	.338	.498	.330	.353	.528	.291	17.3	1.3	72-RF	-6
2010	NYN	MLB	26	679	83	32	4	19	98	46	117	4	4	-0.6	.276	.333	.431	.279	.335	.430	.266	19.2	2.4	155-RF	3

Breakout: 21%   Improve: 58%   Collapse: 6%   Attrition: 2%   MLB: 100%   Comparables: Tom Brunansky, Carlos Lee, Garret Anderson, Alex Rios

There's nothing wrong with putting balls in play if you're driving them, but Francoeur's overeager approach (his 3.34 pitches seen per plate appearance was the fifth-worst in the NL) meant everything but line drives, which are the foundation of batting average, and an excess of grounders and popups. Unable to correct this tendency in a season and a half, he was dumped on the Mets. Francoeur wasn't any more selective in New York, but he did square up on more balls. His line-drive rate leaped to a career-best 25 percent, a rate that would have ranked in the full-season top 10 (Jason Bartlett led the majors at 27.4 percent). With the Mets thinking about making a multiyear contract offer to him, is he likely to maintain his hitting on a high line-drive rate alone? Perfect data do not exist, but we'll use the numbers we have: going back to 1988, there have been 5,701 seasons of 300 or more plate appearances. Of these, just 264 seasons (4.6 percent) had a line-drive rate of 24.5 percent or higher. Of the 264, only 36 hitters reached that percentage in two or more consecutive seasons, and only three, Mark Grace, Mo Vaughn, and Paul O'Neill, did it in four straight seasons. In short, Francoeur is extremely likely to regress, leaving the Mets with what he was before, an out machine with a good arm.

Reese Havens   SS   Bats: L   Throws: R   Height: 6' 1"   Weight: 195   Born: October 20, 1986   Age: 23

YEAR	TEAM	LVL	AGE	PA	R	2B	3B	HR	RBI	BB	SO	SB	CS	EqBRR	AVG	OBP	SLG	EqAVG	EqOBP	EqSLG	EqA	VORP	WARP	DEFENSE	
2008	BRO	A-	21	97	13	6	2	3	11	11	27	3	1	0.2	.247	.340	.471	.216	.281	.375	.226	-2.6	-0.4		
2009	SLU	A+	22	430	53	19	1	14	52	55	73	3	2	1.4	.247	.361	.422	.223	.319	.373	.245	10.1	1.4	96-SS	1
2010	NYN	MLB	23	369	39	15	1	10	38	40	84	2	1	0.5	.224	.317	.367	.229	.321	.377	.245	7.0	0.8	69-SS	0

Breakout: 17%   Improve: 46%   Collapse: 18%   Attrition: 5%   MLB: 1%   Comparables: Don Robinson, Kevin Garner, Jeff Hunter, Blane Fox

The Mets toyed with making Havens a catcher when they drafted him in the first round, but the scheme was quickly abandoned and he spent all of 2009 at shortstop. Between getting banged up with some minor injuries (quadriceps, hand), Havens showed some unique skills for a middle infielder, particularly above-average power and excellent plate discipline. He doesn't hit for much of an average, and scouts aren't sure he ever will. To add to the troubles, he's just not very fast and probably fits better as a second baseman in the big leagues. Even so, his secondary skills alone should give him some value there.

Anderson Hernandez — MI

Bats: S   Throws: R   Height: 5' 9"   Weight: 170   Born: October 30, 1982   Age: 27

YEAR	TEAM	LVL	AGE	PA	R	2B	3B	HR	RBI	BB	SO	SB	CS	EqBRR	AVG	OBP	SLG	EqAVG	EqOBP	EqSLG	EqA	VORP	WARP	DEFENSE			
2007	NWO	AAA	24	597	84	28	5	5	42	31	82	16	9	1.7	.301	.339	.397	.289	.323	.371	.244	11.7	0.7	108-SS	-9	19-2B	3
2008	NWO	AAA	25	523	57	21	7	5	36	38	95	11	8	0.8	.203	.262	.307	.193	.244	.274	.178	-19.0	-3.7	114-SS	-11	6-2B	0
2008	WAS	MLB	25	91	11	4	0	0	17	10	8	0	0	0.5	.333	.407	.383	.333	.407	.370	.288	4.7	0.1	16-2B	-1		
2009	WAS	MLB	26	255	25	9	2	1	23	20	41	5	3	-0.3	.251	.310	.320	.262	.316	.335	.231	-0.3	-0.3	57-2B	-3		
2009	NYN	MLB	26	149	14	6	2	2	14	13	22	2	2	-0.1	.252	.315	.370	.267	.329	.385	.248	3.6	-0.2	33-SS	-5	6-2B	-1
2010	NYN	MLB	27	436	50	20	5	4	34	32	86	6	5	0.4	.247	.305	.350	.252	.309	.346	.231	0.4	-0.1	98-2B	-1		

Breakout: 18%   Improve: 46%   Collapse: 23%   Attrition: 23%   MLB: 71%   Comparables: Casey Candaele, Bobby DeJardin, Jose Uribe, Andrew Beattie

Hernandez, a guy who can slash line drives and run well, has been in the upper levels of the minors since 2004, but he suddenly found himself as the possessor of a starting second-base job in Washington to begin the 2009 season. Once the Nationals' new baseball administration was put in place by midseason, Hernandez was justifiably out of a job, and when you lose a job to Alberto Gonzalez, that's never a good sign for your career. The Mets picked him up for the stretch run (more like the stretch retreat) when Castillo went down, but there's really no reason for him to be a big-league regular again.

Fernando Martinez — LF

Bats: L   Throws: R   Height: 6' 1"   Weight: 190   Born: October 10, 1988   Age: 21

YEAR	TEAM	LVL	AGE	PA	R	2B	3B	HR	RBI	BB	SO	SB	CS	EqBRR	AVG	OBP	SLG	EqAVG	EqOBP	EqSLG	EqA	VORP	WARP	DEFENSE			
2007	BIN	AA	18	259	32	11	1	4	21	20	51	3	4	-2.9	.271	.336	.377	.250	.305	.350	.227	-1.4	-2.2	57-CF	-18		
2008	BIN	AA	19	385	48	19	4	8	43	27	73	6	2	1.2	.287	.340	.432	.263	.306	.391	.243	3.4	-0.4	82-CF	-7		
2009	BUF	AAA	20	190	24	16	2	8	28	11	33	2	1	-1.2	.290	.337	.540	.277	.325	.514	.279	7.3	0.5	23-LF	-2	14-RF	-1
2009	NYN	MLB	20	100	11	6	0	1	8	5	14	2	0	0.8	.176	.242	.275	.185	.250	.272	.188	-5.2	-0.7	9-LF	-1	7-CF	1
2010	NYN	MLB	21	427	49	22	3	11	41	30	94	5	3	-0.5	.249	.308	.404	.256	.314	.409	.249	3.9	0.0	86-LF	-4		

Breakout: 27%   Improve: 60%   Collapse: 7%   Attrition: 3%   MLB: 100%   Comparables: Tony Longmire, Carlos Gonzalez, Xavier Paul, Jeff Key

Martinez has been the top prospect in the system since the Mets signed him in 2005, at which time he was the best prospect on the international market. His good-but-not-great numbers have always been excused by the fact that he was often three to five years younger than his competition, but regardless, you have to hit at some point. Martinez was finally doing that during the first half of 2009 in Triple-A. When he was called up, his unbridled approach allowed big-league hurlers to make mincemeat out of him, and before he could make adjustments, his knee went pop—which gets at another issue. Constant injuries have limited him to just 303 games in four full seasons. Martinez hasn't exactly had a full apprenticeship, which makes the light-speed push to the big leagues even more curious. Scouts still see special potential in him, but four years after being signed, he has answered few questions.

Daniel Murphy — 4C

Bats: L   Throws: R   Height: 6' 3"   Weight: 210   Born: January 4, 1985   Age: 25

YEAR	TEAM	LVL	AGE	PA	R	2B	3B	HR	RBI	BB	SO	SB	CS	EqBRR	AVG	OBP	SLG	EqAVG	EqOBP	EqSLG	EqA	VORP	WARP	DEFENSE			
2007	SLU	A+	22	559	68	34	3	11	78	42	61	6	3	-0.5	.285	.338	.430	.261	.308	.399	.247	4.3	1.1	131-3B	5		
2008	BIN	AA	23	407	56	26	1	13	67	39	46	14	5	-1.0	.308	.374	.496	.285	.340	.449	.273	15.7	2.4	60-3B	2	18-2B	0
2008	NYN	MLB	23	151	24	9	3	2	17	18	28	0	2	-0.4	.313	.397	.473	.328	.411	.489	.306	10.7	1.5	28-LF	3		
2009	NYN	MLB	24	556	60	38	4	12	63	38	69	4	2	1.8	.266	.313	.427	.281	.325	.454	.265	5.3	0.6	97-1B	5	24-LF	-4
2010	NYN	MLB	25	546	62	30	3	14	71	46	82	5	4	0.0	.264	.328	.420	.273	.336	.430	.262	7.1	1.1	112-1B	3		

Breakout: 16%   Improve: 43%   Collapse: 16%   Attrition: 6%   MLB: 100%   Comparables: Todd Helton, Chad Tracy, Adrian Gonzalez, Tino Martinez

Murphy began the season in left field, a position at which he looks not unlike a novice on his first orienteering expedition; you really haven't experienced baseball at its fullest until you've seen an outfielder stop to take a compass reading before chasing after the ball. With Delgado's demise, he moved over to first base, where he showed far more promise, as often happens when transplanted third basemen (Murphy's minor-league position) move across the diamond. Unfortunately, he wields a light bat for the position: Murphy makes excellent contact, but the downside is that he takes few walks. Combine that with only small gifts in the power department, and you get production far short of first-base expectations. The Mets also found he needed to be platooned, and his performance away from Citi was weak (.238/.304/.358). Murphy did have a stronger second half, hitting .282/.313/.485, which still isn't first-base-worthy, but at least gives hope that he might narrow the gap.

Kirk Nieuwenhuis — OF

| | | | | | | | | | | | | | Bats: L | | Throws: R | | Height: 6′ 3″ | | Weight: 210 | Born: August 7, 1987 | | | Age: 22 |

YEAR	TEAM	LVL	AGE	PA	R	2B	3B	HR	RBI	BB	SO	SB	CS	EqBRR	AVG	OBP	SLG	EqAVG	EqOBP	EqSLG	EqA	VORP	WARP	DEFENSE			
2008	BRO	A-	20	319	34	15	5	3	29	29	70	11	7	0.7	.277	.348	.396	.249	.302	.355	.229	-2.5	-1.7	44-CF	-7	27-RF	-1
2009	SLU	A+	21	547	91	35	5	16	71	53	118	16	4	2.9	.274	.357	.467	.247	.317	.423	.256	11.0	0.8	105-CF	-5		
2009	BIN	AA	21	36	8	3	1	1	2	4	9	1	1	-0.6	.406	.472	.656	.364	.417	.606	.328	3.9	0.3	8-CF	-1		
2010	NYN	MLB	22	536	67	28	3	13	50	47	140	8	5	0.9	.239	.310	.389	.245	.314	.396	.246	8.7	0.4	111-CF	-5		

Breakout: 12%   Improve: 49%   Collapse: 14%   Attrition: 8%   MLB: 10%   Comparables: Tommy Dunbar, Nic Jackson, T.J. Staton, Al Martin

We're the first to admit that we're geeks here at BP. Hell, we wear it like a badge of honor. Come on, though: even if you're not as geeky as us, how can you not love a ballplayer with the nickname "Captain Kirk"? Not only does Nieuwenhuis have a better-than-average chance of sleeping with a green alien princess, but he can also really play; no Mets farmhand took a larger step forward in 2009. Possessing at least average tools across the board, Nieuwenhuis hit his stride during the second half, batting .446 with an insane 62 total bases in his last 15 games for High-A St. Lucie, and he didn't slow down much during his brief stay at Double-A. He's got true 20-20 potential, but again, his tools are merely good, not great, so 30-30 is more than a bit of a reach.

Angel Pagan — OF

| | | | | | | | | | | | | | Bats: S | | Throws: R | | Height: 6′ 2″ | | Weight: 195 | Born: July 2, 1981 | | | Age: 28 |

YEAR	TEAM	LVL	AGE	PA	R	2B	3B	HR	RBI	BB	SO	SB	CS	EqBRR	AVG	OBP	SLG	EqAVG	EqOBP	EqSLG	EqA	VORP	WARP	DEFENSE			
2007	IOW	AAA	25	127	18	4	3	3	9	10	20	6	1	0.5	.250	.310	.414	.222	.278	.342	.221	-2.0	0.1	19-CF	2	6-LF	2
2007	CHN	MLB	25	161	21	10	2	4	21	10	32	4	1	-0.3	.264	.306	.439	.264	.304	.432	.256	2.9	0.3	26-CF	-2	10-RF	1
2008	NYN	MLB	26	105	12	7	1	0	13	11	18	4	0	2.5	.275	.346	.374	.286	.352	.385	.275	3.1	0.3	19-LF	-1		
2009	NYN	MLB	27	376	54	22	11	6	32	25	56	14	7	0.2	.306	.350	.487	.328	.367	.516	.295	25.5	3.7	58-CF	4	17-LF	1
2010	NYN	MLB	28	410	56	22	9	8	42	33	74	14	5	1.2	.280	.338	.452	.282	.341	.444	.276	20.4	2.4	76-CF	1		

Breakout: 14%   Improve: 47%   Collapse: 5%   Attrition: 3%   MLB: 90%   Comparables: Randy Winn, Brian McRae, Jerry Mumphrey, R.J. Reynolds

Pagan was about the best he can be in 2009, as the dimensions of Citi Field favored Pagan's style, which can be summed up as "put it in play and let 'em chase it." He hit .333/.373/.565 at the new ballpark, with six of 11 triples and five of six home runs. As was par for the course with the Mets, elbow surgery kept Pagan on the shelf until May 16th, and he spent the month of June on the DL with a groin strain. When actually playing, Pagan cultivated a reputation for making bonehead plays on the bases and in the field and sometimes found himself in Jerry Manuel's doghouse as a result, but overall, he was an asset in both areas. Pagan's level of power production is unprecedented in his career, but even if he gives some back, he's still a very solid fourth outfielder.

Jeremy Reed — OF

| | | | | | | | | | | | | | Bats: L | | Throws: L | | Height: 6′ 0″ | | Weight: 200 | Born: June 15, 1981 | | | Age: 29 |

YEAR	TEAM	LVL	AGE	PA	R	2B	3B	HR	RBI	BB	SO	SB	CS	EqBRR	AVG	OBP	SLG	EqAVG	EqOBP	EqSLG	EqA	VORP	WARP	DEFENSE			
2007	TAC	AAA	26	628	92	37	5	13	64	47	73	14	9	-2.1	.300	.354	.452	.279	.327	.405	.254	8.3	0.2	91-LF	-8	17-CF	0
2007	SEA	MLB	26	17	2	0	1	0	0	0	3	0	0	-0.2	.176	.176	.294	.176	.176	.294	.139	-1.7	-0.2				
2008	TAC	AAA	27	168	26	11	1	6	21	16	14	6	1	-1.8	.349	.413	.557	.314	.369	.477	.291	9.9	0.6	25-CF	-2	6-RF	-3
2008	SEA	MLB	27	312	30	18	1	2	31	18	38	2	3	0.6	.269	.314	.360	.282	.325	.373	.245	1.5	-0.1	51-CF	0	11-RF	-2
2009	NYN	MLB	28	177	9	6	2	0	9	14	36	0	3	-4.2	.242	.301	.304	.253	.311	.315	.215	-6.1	-0.1	16-LF	2	10-CF	2
2010	NYN	MLB	29	370	40	19	2	5	32	28	59	5	3	-1.1	.261	.320	.373	.272	.330	.389	.246	2.1	0.0	66-LF	-2		

Breakout: 12%   Improve: 44%   Collapse: 18%   Attrition: 11%   MLB: 43%   Comparables: Orlando Palmeiro, Mike Greenwell, Rob Butler, Terrence Long

Now seven years removed from the exciting season when he hit .373 between High-A and Double-A, Reed is now pretty well confirmed as a singles hitter who hits too many ground balls to produce with any consistency in the majors. The Mets used him primarily as a pinch-hitter and outfield defensive replacement. The best you can say of his season is that he posted a .322 OBP in 59 pinch-hit plate appearances. He ceased to hit in the second half and was nontendered after the season, becoming a free agent.

Jose Reyes   **SS**   Bats: S   Throws: R   Height: 6' 1"   Weight: 200   Born: June 11, 1983   Age: 27

YEAR	TEAM	LVL	AGE	PA	R	2B	3B	HR	RBI	BB	SO	SB	CS	EqBRR	AVG	OBP	SLG	EqAVG	EqOBP	EqSLG	EqA	VORP	WARP	DEFENSE	
2007	NYN	MLB	24	765	119	36	12	12	57	77	78	78	21	9.7	.280	.354	.421	.298	.371	.443	.284	50.6	6.2	160-SS	4
2008	NYN	MLB	25	763	113	37	19	16	68	66	82	56	15	8.0	.297	.358	.475	.317	.375	.507	.298	65.3	6.6	157-SS	-5
2009	NYN	MLB	26	166	18	7	2	2	15	18	19	11	2	1.3	.279	.355	.395	.299	.370	.415	.284	10.6	0.8	35-SS	-4
2010	NYN	MLB	27	582	83	28	11	13	52	58	67	43	14	3.3	.293	.364	.462	.295	.366	.457	.292	42.2	4.5	122-SS	-1

Breakout: 6%   Improve: 44%   Collapse: 9%   Attrition: 4%   MLB: 99%   Comparables: Roberto Alomar, Tony Fernandez, Rafael Furcal, D'Angelo Jimenez

Reyes is expected to be fully healthy by spring training, but so much of his value revolves around elite-level speed that there are reasons to be worried about what he has lost to his recent injury. His over-the-top speed is why he hits 18 triples a year instead of eight, and why he steals 60-70 bases a year instead of 30, and even the slightest slowing down would hurt his value significantly.

Omir Santos   **C**   Bats: R   Throws: R   Height: 6' 0"   Weight: 200   Born: April 29, 1981   Age: 29

YEAR	TEAM	LVL	AGE	PA	R	2B	3B	HR	RBI	BB	SO	SB	CS	EqBRR	AVG	OBP	SLG	EqAVG	EqOBP	EqSLG	EqA	VORP	WARP	DEFENSE	
2007	TRN	AA	26	39	4	2	0	0	0	1	8	0	0	0.8	.211	.231	.263	.184	.205	.211	.110	-2.7	-0.2	9-C	1
2007	SWB	AAA	26	182	13	8	0	3	19	10	35	1	1	-3.2	.234	.278	.335	.225	.265	.308	.200	-1.6	-0.9	48-C	-6
2008	NOR	AAA	27	332	31	13	0	1	36	20	57	1	2	-1.2	.269	.328	.323	.265	.315	.315	.224	2.4	-0.3	80-C	-5
2008	BAL	MLB	27	10	0	0	0	0	0	0	2	0	0	0.0	.100	.100	.100	.100	.100	.100	-.163	-1.5	-0.3	3-C	0
2009	NYN	MLB	28	306	28	14	1	7	40	15	44	0	0	-3.0	.260	.296	.391	.274	.305	.413	.249	10.3	0.8	77-C	0
2010	NYN	MLB	29	292	27	12	0	5	35	18	59	1	1	-1.1	.246	.301	.347	.251	.307	.354	.228	2.2	0.0	75-C	-2

Breakout: 18%   Improve: 40%   Collapse: 17%   Attrition: 9%   MLB: 74%   Comparables: Mike DiFelice, Eddie Perez, Dave Van Gorder, Robert Machado

Signed to a minor-league contract, Santos, in an ideal world, would have had little to do but provide organizational depth, but the Mets weren't dealing with anything like an ideal world in 2009. So, he was called up in mid-April when Brian Schneider got hurt. Santos then stuck around after Ramon Castro was traded, working in a loose platoon with the former. The veteran busher revealed no unsuspected talents, but we'll say this for him: he played good defense and hit far better than his career .258/.304/.348 minor-league numbers would have suggested.

Brian Schneider   **C**   Bats: L   Throws: R   Height: 6' 1"   Weight: 195   Born: November 26, 1976   Age: 33

YEAR	TEAM	LVL	AGE	PA	R	2B	3B	HR	RBI	BB	SO	SB	CS	EqBRR	AVG	OBP	SLG	EqAVG	EqOBP	EqSLG	EqA	VORP	WARP	DEFENSE	
2007	WAS	MLB	30	477	33	21	1	6	54	56	56	0	0	-1.9	.235	.326	.336	.241	.331	.345	.245	14.7	1.8	118-C	2
2008	NYN	MLB	31	384	30	10	0	9	38	42	53	0	0	-1.6	.257	.339	.367	.265	.344	.375	.256	14.7	2.6	98-C	8
2009	NYN	MLB	32	194	11	11	0	3	24	18	21	0	0	-0.1	.218	.292	.335	.228	.295	.345	.231	2.7	0.7	50-C	3
2010	PHI	MLB	33	255	17	10	0	5	30	31	39	0	0	-0.4	.252	.346	.361	.253	.343	.372	.251	7.4	1.0	66-C	2

Breakout: 21%   Improve: 51%   Collapse: 23%   Attrition: 25%   MLB: 94%   Comparables: Geno Petralli, Brent Mayne, Milt May, Johnny Roseboro

Schneider entered the year as the top candidate for the everyday catcher's job on a roster without much in the catching department, the best of a series of bad choices. Schneider got banged up in the spring (knee), and then, as with most Mets in 2009, things just piled on from there as he added back problems. In the end, he was limited to 59 depressingly unproductive games. Schneider's loss was Omir Santos' gain (we guess, at least the Mets think so), so he's out of New York. His tour of the NL East will continue in 2010, as he signed with the Phillies. The fact that he's hit .245/.323/.342 total in the last four years and still had multiple teams bidding for his services should convince every parent to go out and buy the kid a catcher's mitt.

Gary Sheffield   OF

Bats: R   Throws: R   Height: 6' 0"   Weight: 215   Born: November 18, 1968   Age: 41

YEAR	TEAM	LVL	AGE	PA	R	2B	3B	HR	RBI	BB	SO	SB	CS	EqBRR	AVG	OBP	SLG	EqAVG	EqOBP	EqSLG	EqA	VORP	WARP	DEFENSE			
2007	DET	MLB	38	593	107	20	1	25	75	84	71	22	5	4.9	.265	.378	.462	.262	.376	.459	.293	27.7	3.1	6-RF	0	6-LF	0
2008	DET	MLB	39	482	52	16	0	19	57	58	83	9	2	0.0	.225	.326	.400	.225	.328	.403	.258	3.7	0.3	5-LF	-1		
2009	NYN	MLB	40	312	44	13	2	10	43	40	46	2	1	0.4	.276	.372	.451	.294	.383	.480	.297	17.6	0.4	41-LF	-9	16-RF	-5
2010	NYN	MLB	41	326	38	12	1	11	40	41	63	5	3	0.7	.238	.340	.407	.242	.343	.406	.265	8.7	0.8	17-LF	-2		

Breakout: 6%   Improve: 27%   Collapse: 21%   Attrition: 33%   MLB: 99%   Comparables: Rickey Henderson, Moises Alou, Bing Miller, Hank Aaron

Sheffield really hates playing without a contract. The mere thought of not being signed for the following year turns him into a seething mess of resentment who is impossible to live with. The Tigers, facing the last year of his contract, ate $14 million just to get away from him, just as the Yankees traded him to the Tigers so they could avoid dealing with Sheff as his previous deal expired. Signed by the Mets on April 5th for what was optimistically termed "depth," Sheffield hit well when healthy enough to play—he frequently sat for the kinds of nagging injuries that come with being 40 and spent time on the DL with a strained hamstring—but was as bad in the outfield as might have been expected, given his age and a glove that wasn't great even when he was young and sprightly. Predictably, he momentarily benched himself in August, when the Mets would not be forced into an extension. Sheffield can still hit enough to help as a DH, but if he can't accept that at 41, he's a year-to-year rental, who wants the aggravation? Heck, Gary, we're all year to year—day to day, even.

Cory Sullivan   OF

Bats: L   Throws: L   Height: 6' 0"   Weight: 180   Born: August 20, 1979   Age: 30

YEAR	TEAM	LVL	AGE	PA	R	2B	3B	HR	RBI	BB	SO	SB	CS	EqBRR	AVG	OBP	SLG	EqAVG	EqOBP	EqSLG	EqA	VORP	WARP	DEFENSE			
2007	CSP	AAA	27	228	29	9	3	1	21	18	44	4	3	-0.6	.262	.324	.350	.210	.265	.276	.188	-9.1	-1.2	50-CF	-1		
2007	COL	MLB	27	153	19	6	1	2	14	9	25	2	0	1.2	.286	.336	.386	.279	.329	.379	.251	2.7	0.1	29-CF	-2		
2008	CSP	AAA	28	419	70	32	3	7	47	31	63	13	7	0.0	.320	.373	.475	.252	.297	.357	.229	-2.4	-1.7	82-CF	-12	5-RF	0
2008	COL	MLB	28	24	3	0	1	0	4	0	5	1	0	0.6	.217	.250	.304	.217	.250	.304	.200	-1.1	-0.4	3-CF	-2	1-RF	0
2009	BUF	AAA	29	320	37	16	0	2	24	29	30	2	2	-0.5	.290	.352	.367	.270	.327	.336	.236	-0.2	-1.2	72-CF	-10		
2009	NYN	MLB	29	157	17	2	5	2	15	19	22	7	1	-0.4	.250	.338	.382	.265	.344	.419	.273	4.7	0.9	26-LF	1	5-CF	0
2010	NYN	MLB	30	410	48	17	3	5	36	32	75	6	3	0.0	.242	.306	.344	.249	.312	.353	.232	0.6	-0.5	88-CF	-5		

Breakout: 17%   Improve: 39%   Collapse: 26%   Attrition: 23%   MLB: 37%   Comparables: Stuart Pederson, Terry Bogener, Jon Weber, Bruce Fields

Signed to a $600,000 deal prior to the season, Sullivan was expected to be a bench outfielder who could hit from the left side and provide great defense, but due to a miserable spring, he began the year in Buffalo instead of the big leagues. He assumed the expected big-league duties in mid-July, when Sheffield went on the DL, but didn't really do much offensively. Not that anyone expected him to do much in the first place—this is a guy who hit one home run in 441 at-bats in Coors Field. The Mets declined to offer him arbitration this winter, but his glove alone will get him a spring look from somebody.

Fernando Tatis   UT

Bats: R   Throws: R   Height: 5' 11"   Weight: 195   Born: January 1, 1975   Age: 35

YEAR	TEAM	LVL	AGE	PA	R	2B	3B	HR	RBI	BB	SO	SB	CS	EqBRR	AVG	OBP	SLG	EqAVG	EqOBP	EqSLG	EqA	VORP	WARP	DEFENSE			
2007	NWO	AAA	32	572	90	31	5	21	67	62	103	8	6	0.1	.276	.359	.485	.246	.318	.401	.251	6.1	0.7	122-3B	0		
2008	NWO	AAA	33	139	18	6	0	12	31	17	23	0	0	-0.4	.242	.345	.592	.210	.300	.468	.259	3.0	0.5	26-3B	1	3-LF	0
2008	NYN	MLB	33	306	33	16	1	11	47	29	59	3	0	0.2	.297	.369	.484	.311	.380	.505	.302	19.9	1.7	32-RF	-3	31-LF	0
2009	NYN	MLB	34	379	42	21	4	8	48	22	54	4	1	1.4	.282	.339	.438	.299	.351	.463	.280	13.6	2.6	34-1B	3	22-3B	3
2010	NYN	MLB	35	358	39	16	2	10	42	33	78	3	2	0.2	.251	.331	.411	.254	.333	.407	.262	4.6	0.8	64-1B	3		

Breakout: 3%   Improve: 30%   Collapse: 19%   Attrition: 24%   MLB: 94%   Comparables: Todd Zeile, Rich Aurilia, Willie Horton, Hubie Brooks

After a remarkable comeback in 2008, injuries once again pressed Tatis into service. While the results weren't equal to what he did the year before, he still performed admirably while playing six positions, including two games at shortstop. (We didn't make that up; the 2009 Mets were really that sad.) In reality, his glove only works at first base, with third and left being "in a pinch" options, and his bat is big league–worthy, but only in a bench player's way, with most of the power coming against lefties. The Mets declined to offer arbitration, making him a free agent. He should bounce around for another few years putting up similar numbers.

Ruben Tejada — INF

Bats: R   Throws: R   Height: 5' 11"   Weight: 165   Born: September 1, 1989   Age: 20

YEAR	TEAM	LVL	AGE	PA	R	2B	3B	HR	RBI	BB	SO	SB	CS	EqBRR	AVG	OBP	SLG	EqAVG	EqOBP	EqSLG	EqA	VORP	WARP	DEFENSE		
2007	MTS	Rk	17	149	13	4	3	0	16	19	16	2	1	-1.2	.283	.401	.367	.248	.327	.310	.235	1.5	0.5	26-SS	3	7-2B -2
2008	SLU	A+	18	555	55	19	4	2	37	41	77	8	5	-0.2	.229	.293	.296	.209	.261	.270	.187	-15.3	-2.8	129-SS	-7	
2009	BIN	AA	19	553	59	24	3	5	46	37	59	19	3	0.2	.289	.351	.381	.271	.321	.361	.244	12.0	-0.3	119-SS	-12	14-2B -3
2010	NYN	MLB	20	604	63	27	4	6	47	45	92	10	4	0.0	.252	.314	.347	.256	.316	.347	.237	7.0	0.1	147-SS	-6	

Breakout: 35%   Improve: 61%   Collapse: 17%   Attrition: 2%   MLB: 3%   Comparables: Reegie Corona, Joaquin Arias, Jesus Lopez, Ricky Magdaleno

In a world filled with toolsy Latin American players, Tejada is unusual, his game revolving more around fundamentals than athleticism. He more than held his own in Double-A at 19, a rare feat indeed, but scouts have trouble blessing him with a big-league projection beyond "solid," and even then they see him at second base rather than shortstop, due to range and arm issues. He doesn't have much power, and more isn't coming. He walks a bit, but is hardly an on-base machine, and while he's going to hit for average, that's about the sum of his skills. Nevertheless, with just a little growth, he could be a .300 hitter. The Mets will gladly take it.

Josh Thole — C

Bats: L   Throws: R   Height: 6' 1"   Weight: 190   Born: October 28, 1986   Age: 23

YEAR	TEAM	LVL	AGE	PA	R	2B	3B	HR	RBI	BB	SO	SB	CS	EqBRR	AVG	OBP	SLG	EqAVG	EqOBP	EqSLG	EqA	VORP	WARP	DEFENSE		
2007	SAV	A	20	458	46	17	0	0	36	61	57	4	4	0.2	.267	.372	.311	.251	.335	.288	.227	-9.2	-2.4	102-1B	-7	11-C -3
2008	SLU	A+	21	402	49	25	2	5	56	45	38	2	1	-3.8	.300	.382	.427	.275	.342	.398	.261	13.0	0.3	70-C	-10	11-1B -1
2009	BIN	AA	22	442	48	29	2	1	46	42	34	8	4	-3.8	.328	.395	.422	.305	.360	.397	.270	20.9	1.3	88-C	-10	
2009	NYN	MLB	22	59	2	2	1	0	9	4	5	1	0	-0.3	.321	.356	.396	.340	.367	.415	.284	4.0	0.0	15-C	-2	
2010	NYN	MLB	23	456	44	23	2	4	48	47	62	3	2	-1.3	.263	.342	.359	.273	.349	.365	.253	14.1	0.8	102-C	-7	

Breakout: 19%   Improve: 49%   Collapse: 15%   Attrition: 9%   MLB: 83%   Comparables: Geno Petralli, Daniel Stryffeler, Steven Clevenger, Jeff Reed

There might not be a player in the minors who plays more within himself than Thole. He knows what he's good at—working the count and rifling balls up the middle for singles—so that's all he every tries to do. The result is a powerless catcher with average-at-best defense, but one who gets on base with the best of them. Expected to begin the year at Triple-A in 2010, Thole is coming off a fantastic winter in Venezuela, where he flirted with .400 (and a .500 OBP). A good spring could expedite his timetable.

David Wright — 3B

Bats: R   Throws: R   Height: 6' 0"   Weight: 215   Born: December 20, 1982   Age: 27

YEAR	TEAM	LVL	AGE	PA	R	2B	3B	HR	RBI	BB	SO	SB	CS	EqBRR	AVG	OBP	SLG	EqAVG	EqOBP	EqSLG	EqA	VORP	WARP	DEFENSE	
2007	NYN	MLB	24	711	113	42	1	30	107	94	115	34	5	2.5	.325	.416	.546	.343	.433	.576	.338	80.7	9.6	158-3B	8
2008	NYN	MLB	25	735	115	42	2	33	124	94	118	15	5	-3.2	.302	.390	.534	.324	.405	.566	.323	72.7	7.8	159-3B	0
2009	NYN	MLB	26	618	88	39	3	10	72	74	140	27	9	5.2	.307	.390	.447	.328	.405	.481	.306	48.6	3.6	140-3B	-14
2010	NYN	MLB	27	665	96	34	2	26	105	85	125	19	7	0.7	.303	.397	.508	.306	.398	.504	.314	57.9	6.1	150-3B	-1

Breakout: 7%   Improve: 42%   Collapse: 12%   Attrition: 6%   MLB: 100%   Comparables: Sal Bando, Pedro Guerrero, Ron Santo, Orlando Cepeda

David Wright was that one Met who was able to disappoint fans despite staying healthy, other than one trip to the DL to recover from a Matt Cain fastball to the ol' noggin'. After the beaning, he set himself up as a pioneer, becoming the first player to wear the new Great Gazoo–style batting helmet. His .307 batting average and .390 on-base percentage were within .003 of his career marks, but he lost 20 home runs. The dimensions of the new park were partly responsible, not only in the effect of the dimensions themselves, but because Wright seemed psyched out by them; he also pressed at times as there were plenty of days where he was the only good hitter in the lineup. Some scouts saw mechanical differences in his swing as well, and space limits the 800 other theories on the power outage. The truth is nobody really knows, and he could hit 30 homers again in 2010 … or not.

PITCHERS

Lance Broadway

Bats: R   Throws: R   Height: 6' 3"   Weight: 190   Born: August 20, 1983   Age: 26

YEAR	TEAM	LVL	AGE	W	L	SV	G	GS	IP	H	HR	BB	SO	GB%	BABIP	STUFF	WHIP	ERA	SIERA	DERA	EqH9	EqHR9	EqBB9	EqSO9	VORP	SN/WX
2007	CHR	AAA	23	8	9	0	26	26	155	155	17	78	108	49%	.292	-9	1.50	4.65	4.81	5.62	9.8	1.4	4.6	4.9	-2.0	-0.08
2007	CWS	MLB	23	1	1	0	4	1	10¹	5	0	5	14	31%	.227	10	0.97	0.87	2.54	1.74	4.4	0.0	3.5	10.5	4.3	0.55
2008	CHR	AAA	24	11	7	0	24	23	145	166	24	44	101	59%	.311	-25	1.45	4.66	4.21	5.91	11.2	1.9	3.0	4.6	-6.3	-0.48
2008	CHA	MLB	24	1	0	0	7	1	14	20	4	5	7	68%	.320	-21	1.79	7.07	4.83	6.28	11.9	1.9	2.5	4.4	-1.2	0.03
2009	CHR	AAA	25	0	2	0	3	3	16	18	2	4	15	67%	.327	7	1.37	5.62	3.41	6.75	10.1	1.7	2.3	6.8	-2.2	-0.28
2009	CHA	MLB	25	0	1	0	8	0	16	19	0	9	9	43%	.328	-17	1.75	5.06	5.63	4.86	10.3	0.0	4.3	4.3	1.2	-0.30
2009	BUF	AAA	25	5	7	0	16	14	84²	101	6	34	41	61%	.319	-22	1.59	6.27	5.13	7.49	11.0	1.0	3.9	3.3	-18.1	-1.52
2009	NYN	MLB	25	0	0	0	8	0	14²	19	0	6	9	68%	.365	-15	1.70	6.75	4.52	6.59	11.9	0.0	3.1	4.4	-1.7	0.13
2010	TOR	MLB	26	5	9	0	34	19	114¹	129	18	55	68	48%	.307	-16	1.61	5.56	5.13	5.87	10.2	1.3	4.1	4.9	-4.7	0.57

Breakout: 17%   Improve: 57%   Collapse: 15%   Attrition: 29%   MLB: 57%   Comparables: Blake Hawksworth, Mike Parisi, Tom Filer, Dave Adam

A first-round pick by the White Sox in 2005, Broadway represented the old draft philosophy on the South Side as a low-ceiling safe pick. His best pitch is a curveball, but he just doesn't have enough of a fastball to really set the pitch up. These kinds of talents tend to hit a wall at some point, and for Broadway, that point was Triple-A. He was consistently battered around in a quartet of big-league opportunities, and the White Sox got a nice one-year backup catching solution in Ramon Castro for him. Broadway's life as a Met was equally short-lived; the Blue Jays signed him off the waiver wire after the season came to an end.

Jeurys Familia

Bats: R   Throws: R   Height: 6' 3"   Weight: 185   Born: October 10, 1989   Age: 20

YEAR	TEAM	LVL	AGE	W	L	SV	G	GS	IP	H	HR	BB	SO	GB%	BABIP	STUFF	WHIP	ERA	SIERA	DERA	EqH9	EqHR9	EqBB9	EqSO9	VORP	SN/WX
2008	MTS	Rk	18	2	2	0	11	11	51²	46	2	13	38	57%	.275	7	1.14	2.79	3.88	5.46	10.5	2.1	3.6	3.3	0.2	-0.22
2009	SAV	A	19	10	6	0	24	23	134	109	3	46	109	52%	.273	14	1.16	2.69	3.90	5.74	9.5	1.6	4.5	3.6	-3.3	-0.35
2010	NYN	MLB	20	5	9	0	25	24	120²	137	20	64	61	52%	.297	30	1.66	5.92	5.48	6.40	10.4	1.5	4.5	4.1	-12.0	2.37

Breakout: 12%   Improve: 55%   Collapse: 14%   Attrition: 8%   MLB: 1%   Comparables: Pedro Pena, Colton Willems, Hayden Penn, Jeff Bumgarner

One of the more exciting young arms in the system, Familia finished third in the Sally League with a 2.69 ERA as a teenager. His low-90s fastball can get up to 95 mph and has a bit of sink, so there's plenty to talk about on a stuff level as well. The issues for now are the usual ones for such a young talent, primarily the need for more development of his secondary pitches. He could turn out to be something really special, or just a nice reliever.

Pedro Feliciano

Bats: L   Throws: L   Height: 5' 10"   Weight: 190   Born: August 25, 1976   Age: 33

YEAR	TEAM	LVL	AGE	W	L	SV	G	GS	IP	H	HR	BB	SO	GB%	BABIP	STUFF	WHIP	ERA	SIERA	DERA	EqH9	EqHR9	EqBB9	EqSO9	VORP	SN/WX
2007	NYN	MLB	30	2	2	2	78	0	64	47	3	31	61	63%	.251	13	1.22	3.09	3.78	3.60	6.8	0.4	3.9	7.3	13.7	2.11
2008	NYN	MLB	31	3	4	2	86	0	53¹	57	7	26	50	58%	.331	-9	1.56	4.05	3.93	4.24	10.4	1.4	4.1	7.2	7.2	0.17
2009	NYN	MLB	32	6	4	0	88	0	59¹	51	7	18	59	66%	.278	6	1.16	3.03	3.12	3.80	8.2	1.2	2.3	7.4	10.9	2.71
2010	NYN	MLB	33	3	4	1	55	0	55	53	6	23	47	61%	.302	-2	1.39	4.35	3.94	4.75	8.9	1.0	3.7	6.9	4.6	1.04

Breakout: 16%   Improve: 42%   Collapse: 21%   Attrition: 12%   MLB: 95%   Comparables: Tug McGraw, Ron Perranoski, Tippy Martinez, Frank DiPino

Feliciano has led the league in appearances in each of the last two seasons, which lets you know he's a LOOGY. He's good at it, limiting left-handed hitters to a .245 on-base percentage, depending primarily on an upper-80s sinker and darting slider. At the same time, he has the rare combination of generating a significant number of ground balls (with a 2.2-to-1 ratio in 2009), while also giving up a surprising number of home runs, due to inconsistent command. He finished the year with 12 straight hitless appearances, and he'll contend for a third straight games-pitched title in 2010.

Nelson Figueroa

Bats: R   Throws: R   Height: 6' 1"   Weight: 205   Born: May 18, 1974   Age: 36

YEAR	TEAM	LVL	AGE	W	L	SV	G	GS	IP	H	HR	BB	SO	GB%	BABIP	STUFF	WHIP	ERA	SIERA	DERA	EqH9	EqHR9	EqBB9	EqSO9	VORP	SN/WX
2007	CHH	MEX	33	8	6	0	19	19	153²	163	13	36	94	—	.302	6	1.30	3.87	4.40	4.38	8.6	1.2	2.5	5.2	18.9	0.17
2008	NWO	AAA	34	4	7	0	20	16	113²	120	15	33	97	48%	.314	-23	1.35	4.43	3.74	5.49	11.2	2.1	2.8	5.6	0.2	-0.15
2008	NYN	MLB	34	3	3	0	16	6	45¹	48	3	26	36	40%	.313	-6	1.63	4.57	4.87	5.32	9.7	0.6	4.5	5.9	0.9	-0.24
2009	BUF	AAA	35	7	5	0	17	17	112	91	5	24	94	44%	.275	27	1.03	2.25	3.43	2.89	7.8	0.7	2.2	6.2	30.8	2.94
2009	NYN	MLB	35	3	8	0	16	10	70¹	80	8	24	59	45%	.327	1	1.48	4.09	4.07	4.29	10.4	1.2	2.6	6.1	9.5	1.76
2010	NYN	MLB	36	7	10	0	28	22	143	149	20	52	99	47%	.299	-1	1.41	4.70	4.48	5.17	9.7	1.2	3.1	5.6	5.2	2.34

Breakout: 11%   Improve: 48%   Collapse: 11%   Attrition: 25%   MLB: 78%   Comparables: Francisco Campos, Kevin Jarvis, Frank Castillo, Woody Williams

The journeyman from Brooklyn has pitched for his hometown team of late, because for the second straight year, injuries gave him far more of an opportunity than he deserved. The scouting term for Figueroa is "a thumber," as he only throws his upper-80s fastball a third of the time while mixing in cutters, sinkers, curves, sliders, and change-ups, really just hoping to win what amounts to a guessing game with hitters. A four-hit shutout on the final day of the season, when the Astros were more interested in their off-season vacation plans than the game, lowered his ERA by more than a half-run. He's not lined up for any significant role in 2010, but he did get kept on the 40-man as we went to press, a big improvement for a man used to bouncing around between nonroster invites.

Sean Green

Bats: R   Throws: R   Height: 6' 6"   Weight: 235   Born: April 20, 1979   Age: 31

YEAR	TEAM	LVL	AGE	W	L	SV	G	GS	IP	H	HR	BB	SO	GB%	BABIP	STUFF	WHIP	ERA	SIERA	DERA	EqH9	EqHR9	EqBB9	EqSO9	VORP	SN/WX
2007	TAC	AAA	28	2	1	1	10	0	17²	13	0	8	10	75%	.241	-15	1.19	2.04	4.07	2.86	6.2	0.5	4.2	3.6	5.1	0.54
2007	SEA	MLB	28	5	2	0	64	0	68	77	2	34	53	74%	.354	0	1.63	3.84	4.08	3.93	9.8	0.3	4.1	6.4	11.5	1.17
2008	SEA	MLB	29	4	5	1	72	0	79	80	3	36	62	74%	.307	4	1.47	4.67	3.99	5.07	8.4	0.3	3.5	6.1	3.9	1.13
2009	NYN	MLB	30	1	4	1	79	0	69²	64	5	36	54	75%	.278	-5	1.44	4.52	3.99	4.78	8.3	0.8	3.8	5.6	5.7	-0.26
2010	NYN	MLB	31	4	5	1	69	0	69	66	6	34	48	71%	.292	-8	1.45	4.38	4.26	4.81	8.8	0.8	4.1	5.6	5.3	0.53

Breakout: 18%   Improve: 45%   Collapse: 30%   Attrition: 17%   MLB: 92%   Comparables: Tyler Yates, Kevin Gryboski, Paul Reuschel, Bob Stanley

Part of the 12-man Mets-Indians-Mariners trade of December 2008, Green was often used as Francisco Rodriguez's set-up man, which is a bit too important a role for someone with Green's abilities. He's a usable arm, to be sure, and he's a low three-quarters, borderline side-armer who gets a ton of ground balls—nice, but a little too hittable while giving up a few too many walks for a late-inning role. He was one of the worst pitchers in baseball to use with runners on, allowing nearly half of his 34 inherited runs to score. With the right roles and responsibilities, Green can be an important part of a big-league bullpen, but the Mets weren't in a position to figure out what that was.

Bradley Holt

Bats: R   Throws: R   Height: 6' 4"   Weight: 194   Born: October 13, 1986   Age: 23

YEAR	TEAM	LVL	AGE	W	L	SV	G	GS	IP	H	HR	BB	SO	GB%	BABIP	STUFF	WHIP	ERA	SIERA	DERA	EqH9	EqHR9	EqBB9	EqSO9	VORP	SN/WX
2008	BRO	A-	21	5	3	0	14	14	72¹	43	3	33	96	45%	.258	11	1.05	1.87	2.55	4.14	8.7	1.9	5.4	6.7	9.5	0.76
2009	SLU	A+	22	4	1	0	9	9	43¹	34	5	13	54	43%	.290	13	1.08	3.12	2.35	5.00	9.5	2.6	3.7	8.1	2.1	0.21
2009	BIN	AA	22	3	6	0	11	11	58	58	9	23	45	40%	.293	-9	1.40	6.21	4.37	7.54	9.8	2.3	3.8	5.1	-12.3	-1.29
2010	NYN	MLB	23	4	8	0	24	22	105	109	17	59	88	41%	.306	2	1.61	5.47	4.63	5.88	9.5	1.4	4.7	6.7	-4.4	1.82

Breakout: 11%   Improve: 47%   Collapse: 9%   Attrition: 6%   MLB: 1%   Comparables: Jason Robbins, Matt Lorenzo, Jeffrey Stevens, Stacey Burdick

A supplemental first-round pick in 2008, Holt obliterated the New York-Penn League in his pro debut and did much the same to the Florida State League in the early going, but he injured his ankle during his first Double-A start and was never the same. The ankle injury doesn't explain away all his struggles; scouts have always been leery of his shallow arsenal. His fastball is a true plus pitch that gets up to 94-95 mph at times, but his curveball, while improving, is still inconsistent at best, and his changeup is well below average. That combination has many projecting a bullpen role for him down the road, but he's going to be given every opportunity to remain a starter.

Ryoto Igarashi

Bats: R   Throws: R   Height: 5' 10"   Weight: 190   Born: May 28, 1979   Age: 31

YEAR	TEAM	LVL	AGE	W	L	SV	G	GS	IP	H	HR	BB	SO	GB%	BABIP	STUFF	WHIP	ERA	SIERA	DERA	EqH9	EqHR9	EqBB9	EqSO9	VORP	SN/WX
2008	YKL	JCL	29	3	2	3	44	0	43²	35	3	6	42	—	.271	11	0.94	2.47	2.82	3.43	7.7	0.9	1.7	7.1	9.7	1.67
2009	YKL	JCL	30	3	2	3	56	0	53²	42	3	20	44	—	.258	-5	1.16	3.19	3.97	4.09	7.8	0.7	4.1	6.0	8.0	1.54
2010	NYN	MLB	31	3	3	2	56	0	56¹	51	7	21	43	47%	.278	-1	1.29	3.94	4.19	4.32	8.4	1.1	3.3	6.3	7.4	0.00

Breakout: 14%   Improve: 41%   Collapse: 30%   Attrition: 7%   MLB: 95%   Comparables: Dyar Miller, Jason Frasor, Vicente Romo, Scott Proctor

Igarashi was once one of the most feared relievers in Japan, with an upper-90s fastball, but Tommy John surgery in 2007 cost him some velocity, and he's now suited to be set-up man. The fastball still combines above-average velocity with good command, and like many Japanese pitchers, a stuttered delivery provides an extra bit of deception. A decent slider is his breaking pitch, and while at 30 he's past his prime, some international scouts think that a $3 million deal for two years could end up being a bargain.

John Maine

Bats: R   Throws: R   Height: 6' 4"   Weight: 200   Born: May 8, 1981   Age: 29

YEAR	TEAM	LVL	AGE	W	L	SV	G	GS	IP	H	HR	BB	SO	GB%	BABIP	STUFF	WHIP	ERA	SIERA	DERA	EqH9	EqHR9	EqBB9	EqSO9	VORP	SN/WX
2007	NYN	MLB	26	15	10	0	32	32	191	168	23	75	180	43%	.275	15	1.27	3.91	3.74	4.15	8.3	1.2	3.2	7.5	28.3	5.62
2008	NYN	MLB	27	10	8	0	25	25	140	122	16	67	122	43%	.266	7	1.35	4.18	4.23	4.67	8.2	1.2	3.7	6.5	12.9	2.85
2009	NYN	MLB	28	7	6	0	15	15	81¹	67	8	38	55	42%	.242	5	1.29	4.43	4.89	4.63	7.5	1.0	3.5	5.0	7.9	1.59
2010	NYN	MLB	29	6	8	0	25	22	128²	127	17	59	99	42%	.294	3	1.45	4.69	4.54	5.09	9.1	1.2	3.9	6.2	5.8	2.13

Breakout: 9%   Improve: 41%   Collapse: 16%   Attrition: 30%   MLB: 94%   Comparables: Adam Eaton, Kelly Downs, Steve McCatty, Bill Voiselle

Maine's strikeout rate dipped in 2009 as he was bothered by shoulder soreness during the first half of the season. The injury initially led to his next start getting pushed back a day, but like most Mets injuries in 2009, it turned into a seemingly endless nightmare. First he was put on the 15-day DL; rehab outings led to more pain, and a final diagnosis of a pinched nerve. There was at least some light at the end of the tunnel; he made it back by the end of the season and looked fairly sharp. He should settle back into his role as a third or fourth starter in 2010.

Jenrry Mejia

Bats: R   Throws: R   Height: 6' 0"   Weight: 162   Born: October 11, 1989   Age: 20

YEAR	TEAM	LVL	AGE	W	L	SV	G	GS	IP	H	HR	BB	SO	GB%	BABIP	STUFF	WHIP	ERA	SIERA	DERA	EqH9	EqHR9	EqBB9	EqSO9	VORP	SN/WX
2008	BRO	A-	18	3	2	0	11	11	56²	42	4	23	52	66%	.257	0	1.15	3.49	3.43	5.92	10.0	2.6	5.0	4.4	-2.3	-0.28
2008	MTS	Rk	18	2	0	0	3	3	15	9	0	3	15	76%	.225	14	0.80	0.60	2.44	1.93	7.1	1.3	3.2	5.1	5.6	0.34
2009	SLU	A+	19	4	1	0	9	9	50¹	41	0	16	44	65%	.279	31	1.13	1.97	3.48	4.91	8.5	0.8	3.6	5.1	3.1	0.31
2009	BIN	AA	19	0	5	0	10	10	44¹	44	2	23	47	70%	.333	34	1.51	4.47	3.53	6.55	9.2	1.0	4.5	6.8	-5.1	-0.42
2010	NYN	MLB	20	5	8	0	23	23	115¹	118	16	59	85	65%	.298	38	1.54	5.09	4.40	5.51	9.4	1.2	4.4	5.9	-0.1	2.04

Breakout: 15%   Improve: 51%   Collapse: 14%   Attrition: 9%   MLB: 1%   Comparables: Jody Johnston, P.J. Bevis, Clint Everts, Joe Roa

The most exciting young arm in the system, Mejia struck out more than a batter per inning at Double-A as a teenager, and his fastball is as exciting as the numbers suggest. Although he is a little undersized, his thick, muscular build provides 92-96 mph fastballs, and he can maintain that velocity all night long. The pitch also has both horizontal and vertical movement, almost dancing as it gets to the plate. Mejia's changeup is advanced for his age; really the only knock against him is occasional control lapses and some real struggles in developing a consistent breaking ball. He has been rushed through the system so far, but the Mets will slow things down a bit in 2010, keeping him at Double-A in the hope that he can find enough beyond the fastball to turn into an impact starter.

Patrick Misch   Bats: R   Throws: L   Height: 6' 2"   Weight: 195   Born: August 18, 1981   Age: 28

YEAR	TEAM	LVL	AGE	W	L	SV	G	GS	IP	H	HR	BB	SO	GB%	BABIP	STUFF	WHIP	ERA	SIERA	DERA	EqH9	EqHR9	EqBB9	EqSO9	VORP	SN/WX
2007	FRE	AAA	25	2	5	1	34	3	66²	54	4	19	74	56%	.301	14	1.09	2.29	2.76	3.61	8.2	0.9	2.9	8.1	13.1	1.59
2007	SFN	MLB	25	0	4	0	18	4	40¹	47	3	12	26	54%	.331	-4	1.46	4.24	4.47	4.46	10.5	0.7	2.5	5.3	4.5	0.06
2008	FRE	AAA	26	6	5	0	20	13	87	101	15	27	56	55%	.305	-24	1.47	5.38	4.49	6.04	10.5	1.8	2.9	4.1	-5.1	-0.89
2008	SFN	MLB	26	0	3	0	15	7	52¹	56	11	15	38	52%	.276	-8	1.36	5.68	4.20	5.48	9.1	1.9	2.2	5.4	0.1	-0.32
2009	FRE	AAA	27	3	0	1	12	1	27	24	1	4	12	61%	.267	-8	1.04	2.00	4.51	2.66	8.2	0.7	1.4	3.2	8.0	1.12
2009	SFN	MLB	27	0	0	0	4	0	3¹	6	0	3	0	76%	.375	-44	2.70	10.80	6.44	10.80	16.2	0.0	8.1	0.0	-2.0	-0.31
2009	BUF	AAA	27	1	2	0	6	4	25¹	27	1	4	21	64%	.325	7	1.22	4.26	3.43	5.58	9.7	0.7	1.8	5.8	-0.2	-0.09
2009	NYN	MLB	27	3	4	0	22	9	59	62	9	19	23	49%	.268	-23	1.37	4.12	5.44	4.16	9.6	1.6	2.5	3.0	8.5	0.79
2010	NYN	MLB	28	5	7	0	44	10	98¹	105	13	37	59	52%	.297	-12	1.44	4.95	4.78	5.40	9.8	1.2	3.2	4.9	1.1	0.99

Breakout: 9%   Improve: 33%   Collapse: 25%   Attrition: 15%   MLB: 46%   Comparables: Greg Mathews, Scott Bailes, Buddy Groom, Lee Hancock

Once seen as nice little late bloomer in the Giants' system, Misch had regressed a bit over the last couple of years. When they designated him for assignment, the Mets, desperate for any living, breathing biped with a working arm, picked him up. After bouncing back and forth between Triple-A and the Mets for a month, he took over Johan Santana's rotation spot when the team's ace was shut down. Misch really didn't do anything to make Mets fan forget their sorrows other than a fluky eight-hit shutout against the Marlins in late September. With a mid-80s fastball and every secondary pitch in the book, Misch is a finesse lefty who doesn't miss bats, and the Mets are hoping that a healthier overall roster in 2010 will reduce him to a back-end bullpen role, if that.

Jon Niese   Bats: L   Throws: L   Height: 6' 4"   Weight: 215   Born: October 27, 1986   Age: 23

YEAR	TEAM	LVL	AGE	W	L	SV	G	GS	IP	H	HR	BB	SO	GB%	BABIP	STUFF	WHIP	ERA	SIERA	DERA	EqH9	EqHR9	EqBB9	EqSO9	VORP	SN/WX
2007	SLU	A+	20	11	7	0	27	27	134¹	151	9	31	110	55%	.340	9	1.35	4.29	3.69	6.61	11.2	1.4	2.7	5.2	-15.4	-0.98
2008	BIN	AA	21	6	7	0	22	22	124¹	118	5	44	112	56%	.316	24	1.30	3.04	3.68	4.54	9.6	0.8	3.3	6.2	12.5	0.84
2008	NWO	AAA	21	5	1	0	7	7	39²	34	4	14	32	59%	.261	21	1.21	3.40	3.91	4.03	9.0	1.7	3.3	5.0	6.2	0.82
2008	NYN	MLB	21	1	1	0	3	3	14	20	2	8	11	56%	.375	6	2.00	7.07	4.72	7.07	12.9	1.3	4.5	5.8	-2.4	0.11
2009	BUF	AAA	22	5	6	0	16	16	94¹	95	7	26	82	63%	.313	20	1.28	3.82	3.57	5.09	9.5	1.0	2.7	6.2	4.1	0.56
2009	NYN	MLB	22	1	1	0	5	5	25²	27	1	9	18	55%	.317	15	1.40	4.21	4.35	4.32	9.7	0.4	2.9	5.4	3.3	0.68
2010	NYN	MLB	23	6	8	0	27	24	125²	131	16	50	90	48%	.304	5	1.44	4.60	4.46	5.00	9.5	1.1	3.3	5.8	7.0	1.84

Breakout: 20%   Improve: 59%   Collapse: 11%   Attrition: 13%   MLB: 47%   Comparables: Ben Van Ryn, Chris Green, Kevin Rogers, John Rocker

With injuries come opportunities, and everything was lined up perfectly for Niese to take that big step forward last year. Unfortunately, he began the year completely out of whack mechanically at Triple-A Buffalo, giving up 48 hits and allowing 34 runs over 31 ⅔ innings in his first seven starts. Once the weather warmed up, he rediscovered his release point and his plus-plus curveball. His addition to the big-league roster in July looked to be a permanent one, until August 5, when he didn't just tear his hamstring, but also completely separated it from the bone; season-ending surgery ensued. He's expected to be fine this spring and to win a spot at the tail end of the rotation, which also happens to be where his ceiling lies.

Fernando Nieve   Bats: R   Throws: R   Height: 6' 0"   Weight: 195   Born: July 15, 1982   Age: 27

YEAR	TEAM	LVL	AGE	W	L	SV	G	GS	IP	H	HR	BB	SO	GB%	BABIP	STUFF	WHIP	ERA	SIERA	DERA	EqH9	EqHR9	EqBB9	EqSO9	VORP	SN/WX
2007	ROU	AAA	24	1	3	0	5	5	21²	30	1	15	13	27%	.387	-18	2.08	6.23	6.22	8.55	13.5	0.9	6.8	4.1	-6.8	-0.24
2008	ROU	AAA	25	2	5	6	36	7	72¹	87	13	27	63	42%	.332	-31	1.58	5.72	4.06	6.46	11.4	2.2	3.3	5.6	-7.5	-0.93
2008	HOU	MLB	25	0	1	0	11	0	10²	17	2	2	12	31%	.455	5	1.78	8.44	2.89	8.55	15.3	1.8	1.8	9.0	-3.4	-0.35
2009	BIN	AA	26	0	1	0	5	4	18¹	16	1	6	19	47%	.313	7	1.20	4.91	3.15	5.45	8.3	1.0	3.1	7.3	0.1	-0.14
2009	BUF	AAA	26	3	0	0	4	4	24¹	18	2	10	23	42%	.254	13	1.15	3.70	3.69	4.30	7.4	1.2	3.9	7.0	3.1	0.17
2009	NYN	MLB	26	3	3	0	8	7	36²	36	4	19	23	37%	.281	-6	1.50	2.95	5.37	3.25	9.0	1.0	4.0	4.8	9.0	1.29
2010	NYN	MLB	27	3	5	3	33	5	67	75	10	31	47	35%	.316	-14	1.58	5.36	4.99	5.94	10.6	1.4	3.9	5.6	-3.3	0.55

Breakout: 14%   Improve: 58%   Collapse: 11%   Attrition: 15%   MLB: 35%   Comparables: Stan Fansler, Jamie Brown, Kevin Towers, Chad Durbin

Once a top prospect for Houston, Nieve never developed as expected, in part due to injuries ranging from a deviated septum to Tommy John surgery, and the Mets picked him up off waivers in the spring. He acquitted himself well, delivering quality starts in his first three trips in the rotation, but that excited Mets fans a bit too much. To be fair, they were looking for anything to be excited about. He scuffled some after that run, and then on July 19th, as if he was succumbing to peer pressure, he tore his right quad and missed the rest of the season. Nieve does have a good fastball, at least in terms of velocity, as he parks it at 92-93 mph while touching 95, but he's a fly-baller who lives in the upper half of the zone, which explains his 24 home runs allowed in 143 ⅔ big-league innings. He'll get a shot at some kind of role this spring, but nothing is guaranteed.

Bobby Parnell

Bats: R   Throws: R   Height: 6′ 4″   Weight: 200   Born: September 8, 1984   Age: 25

YEAR	TEAM	LVL	AGE	W	L	SV	G	GS	IP	H	HR	BB	SO	GB%	BABIP	STUFF	WHIP	ERA	SIERA	DERA	EqH9	EqHR9	EqBB9	EqSO9	VORP	SN/WX
2007	SLU	A+	22	3	3	0	12	12	55¹	56	0	22	62	69%	.364	16	1.41	3.25	3.06	4.62	10.5	0.7	4.2	7.3	5.1	0.26
2007	BIN	AA	22	5	5	0	17	17	88²	98	9	38	74	49%	.322	-2	1.53	4.77	4.24	5.93	10.1	1.4	3.9	5.4	-4.1	-0.64
2008	BIN	AA	23	10	6	0	24	24	127²	126	14	57	91	57%	.289	-16	1.43	4.30	4.50	5.43	9.9	1.6	4.1	4.7	0.9	0.08
2008	NWO	AAA	23	2	2	0	5	4	20¹	25	0	9	23	50%	.403	3	1.67	6.64	3.43	7.91	12.6	0.5	4.2	7.4	-5.2	-0.33
2008	NYN	MLB	23	0	0	0	6	0	5	3	0	2	3	54%	.214	-16	1.00	5.40	4.65	5.79	5.8	0.0	3.9	3.9	-0.1	0.02
2009	NYN	MLB	24	4	8	1	68	8	88¹	101	8	46	74	48%	.331	-13	1.66	5.30	4.49	5.64	10.4	0.9	3.9	6.1	-1.4	-0.12
2010	NYN	MLB	25	5	8	0	44	18	106²	111	12	53	77	50%	.308	-8	1.54	4.97	4.71	5.48	9.7	1.0	4.2	5.8	0.2	1.04

Breakout: 14% · Improve: 52%   Collapse: 12%   Attrition: 24%   MLB: 70%   Comparables: Zach Day, Kelly Downs, Dan Perkins, Edgar Gonzalez

One of the hardest throwers the organization has had in years, Parnell owns a 94-97 mph fastball that touched triple digits a couple of times in 2009, and while the rest of his repertoire lags well behind, that kind of fastball can be enough for a reliever to succeed. Parnell performed adequately, pitching well overall but having some problems with inherited runners. His 2009 stats are distorted by the eight-start look the Mets took with him beginning in August; he had a 7.93 ERA and allowed a .304 batting average. As a reliever, he was at 3.46 and .264, respectively. The Mets wanted him to pitch this winter to advance his conversion to starting, but Parnell refused the assignment and was probably right to do so.

Mike Pelfrey

Bats: R   Throws: R   Height: 6′ 7″   Weight: 230   Born: January 14, 1984   Age: 26

YEAR	TEAM	LVL	AGE	W	L	SV	G	GS	IP	H	HR	BB	SO	GB%	BABIP	STUFF	WHIP	ERA	SIERA	DERA	EqH9	EqHR9	EqBB9	EqSO9	VORP	SN/WX
2007	NWO	AAA	23	3	6	0	14	14	74	74	6	26	56	61%	.297	-4	1.35	4.01	4.06	4.92	9.7	1.4	3.3	4.9	4.6	0.84
2007	NYN	MLB	23	3	8	0	15	13	72²	85	6	39	45	57%	.325	-6	1.71	5.57	5.10	5.61	10.9	0.9	4.4	4.9	-0.9	0.36
2008	NYN	MLB	24	13	11	0	32	32	200²	209	12	64	110	56%	.302	6	1.36	3.72	4.74	4.09	9.9	0.7	2.6	4.3	29.9	5.64
2009	NYN	MLB	25	10	12	0	31	31	184¹	213	18	66	107	57%	.312	-5	1.51	5.03	4.77	5.42	10.4	1.0	2.7	4.3	1.5	2.22
2010	NYN	MLB	26	8	11	0	31	31	174	189	20	67	95	61%	.302	-8	1.47	4.81	4.80	5.35	10.1	1.0	3.3	4.5	2.9	2.32

Breakout: 8%   Improve: 47%   Collapse: 12%   Attrition: 15%   MLB: 93%   Comparables: Bill Wegman, Jon Garland, Jason Schmidt, Jaime Navarro

Well, at least he stayed healthy, leading the '09 squad in starts and innings. Even for all that, Pelfrey has been a massive disappointment, having been seen by some as the best pitcher in the 2005 draft. It's easy to see why scouts like him: he's gigantic, with a sinking 92-94 mph fastball that he can dial up to 97. The problem is that he's forced to throw that pitch nearly 80 percent of the time, as his slider and changeup remain well-below-average offerings. The shallow repertoire renders him hittable, and for a guy with his size, clean arm mechanics, and tons of stamina, a move to the pen would just seem like a waste. There's still some room for improvement here, but his 2009 season is closer to what we can expect going forward, rather than a return to the heights of 2008.

Oliver Perez

Bats: L   Throws: L   Height: 6′ 3″   Weight: 215   Born: August 15, 1981   Age: 28

YEAR	TEAM	LVL	AGE	W	L	SV	G	GS	IP	H	HR	BB	SO	GB%	BABIP	STUFF	WHIP	ERA	SIERA	DERA	EqH9	EqHR9	EqBB9	EqSO9	VORP	SN/WX
2007	NYN	MLB	25	15	10	0	29	29	177	153	22	79	174	34%	.271	15	1.31	3.56	3.92	4.47	8.0	1.2	3.6	7.7	20.2	4.12
2008	NYN	MLB	26	10	7	0	34	34	194	167	24	105	180	33%	.271	6	1.40	4.22	4.39	4.80	8.3	1.3	4.3	7.0	14.8	4.22
2009	NYN	MLB	27	3	4	0	14	14	66	69	12	58	62	32%	.303	-5	1.92	6.82	5.37	6.92	9.9	1.8	6.6	6.9	-10.5	0.00
2010	NYN	MLB	28	5	8	0	23	21	114¹	112	15	63	100	34%	.303	5	1.53	4.94	4.56	5.32	9.0	1.2	4.6	7.1	2.3	1.49

Breakout: 7%   Improve: 39%   Collapse: 18%   Attrition: 30%   MLB: 84%   Comparables: Chris Nabholz, Brandon Claussen, Allen Watson, Greg Mathews

A free agent coming into the 2009 season, Perez had a well-established reputation for being a capricious, mutable pitcher, Cy Young on Monday, Cy Schwartz on Friday. So which team was silly enough to give him a big deal? Why, the Mets, of course, as if Perez's inconsistent ways hadn't already driven them insane. (Maybe that's why they did it.) After he turned down a three-year, $30 million offer, the Mets upped the ante to $36 million. Perez responded by showing up to camp horribly out of shape, claiming to be fatigued after participating in the World Baseball Classic. The regular season began disastrously, with Perez walking 21 batters in 21 ⅔ innings with a 9.97 ERA in his first five starts, soon followed by a two-month DL stint due to knee tendinitis, a mercy that gave Perez a chance to try to fix his mechanical issues. Things weren't really much better upon his return, and he was added to the surgical rolls in August, undergoing a procedure to clean up scar tissue from his patella. Even when healthy, he's rarely worth $12 million a year, and there's little reason to expect this to change now.

J. J. Putz

Bats: R   Throws: R   Height: 6' 5"   Weight: 250   Born: February 22, 1977   Age: 33

YEAR	TEAM	LVL	AGE	W	L	SV	G	GS	IP	H	HR	BB	SO	GB%	BABIP	STUFF	WHIP	ERA	SIERA	DERA	EqH9	EqHR9	EqBB9	EqSO9	VORP	SN/WX
2007	SEA	MLB	30	6	1	40	68	0	71²	37	6	13	82	50%	.197	35	0.70	1.38	2.09	1.54	4.6	0.9	1.5	8.7	31.0	7.48
2008	SEA	MLB	31	6	5	15	47	0	46¹	46	4	28	56	43%	.347	15	1.60	3.88	3.57	3.79	8.7	1.0	4.9	9.5	8.8	-0.46
2009	NYN	MLB	32	1	4	2	29	0	29¹	29	1	19	19	51%	.292	-16	1.64	5.22	5.30	5.55	8.7	0.3	4.8	4.8	-0.2	0.39
2010	CHA	MLB	33	3	3	17	55	1	54	46	5	24	46	46%	.275	6	1.29	3.70	4.08	3.78	7.5	0.9	3.5	7.1	10.3	1.88

Breakout: 6%   Improve: 26%   Collapse: 35%   Attrition: 9%   MLB: 88%   Comparables: Jose Mesa, LaTroy Hawkins, Heathcliff Slocumb, Mike Fetters

After compiling one of the best relief seasons ever in 2007, Putz regressed significantly the following year, but the Mets were convinced that they had the most dominating bullpen combination in the game after trading for him at the Winter Meetings, with Putz ready to set up their new closer, K-Rod, who was himself coming off a record-setting campaign. Unfortunately, this is the Mets' chapter of *Baseball Prospectus 2010*, so if we are writing about a player, chances are good that we're going to talk about an injury, and quite likely, surgery. Had the Mets actually won anything, in the future they would have celebrated the campaign by waiving a bloody shirt. After giving up eight runs over a three-game stretch in June, Putz vanished, having been bundled off to the butcher's to undergo what was termed a "minor" elbow procedure. His subsequent plaints of forearm tightness prevented his return. That's the way it went for the Mets in 2009, each injury not merely what it seemed, but a puzzle box, each subsequent layer revealing further damage and decrepitude. Putz's 2010 option having been declined, the White Sox signed him to a one-year deal to serve as Bobby Jenks insurance.

Tim Redding

Bats: R   Throws: R   Height: 5' 11"   Weight: 225   Born: February 12, 1978   Age: 32

YEAR	TEAM	LVL	AGE	W	L	SV	G	GS	IP	H	HR	BB	SO	GB%	BABIP	STUFF	WHIP	ERA	SIERA	DERA	EqH9	EqHR9	EqBB9	EqSO9	VORP	SN/WX
2007	COH	AAA	29	9	5	0	17	16	89²	110	9	24	63	49%	.345	-19	1.49	5.32	4.23	6.59	12.1	1.5	2.6	4.9	-10.2	-0.40
2007	WAS	MLB	29	3	6	0	15	15	84	84	10	38	47	47%	.277	-8	1.45	3.64	5.22	3.78	9.6	1.3	3.8	4.6	15.5	2.84
2008	WAS	MLB	30	10	11	0	33	33	182	195	27	65	120	44%	.294	-3	1.43	4.95	4.65	4.98	9.5	1.3	2.8	5.2	10.3	3.06
2009	NYN	MLB	31	3	6	0	30	17	120	122	18	50	76	37%	.274	-17	1.43	5.10	5.06	5.35	9.3	1.5	3.2	4.7	1.9	2.01
2010	NYN	MLB	32	5	8	0	27	22	119¹	134	17	49	68	42%	.305	-13	1.53	5.15	5.16	5.66	10.4	1.3	3.5	4.6	-2.1	1.53

Breakout: 5%   Improve: 38%   Collapse: 19%   Attrition: 26%   MLB: 85%   Comparables: Josh Fogg, Armando Reynoso, Jeff Suppan, Mark Gardner

Instead of waiting for everything to go wrong and then getting hurt, Redding decided to start the season on the DL with back and shoulder soreness that lingered throughout the spring. Joining the club in May, Redding made a nearly even number of appearances as both a starter and a reliever, proving to be utterly mediocre in either role. His stuff is substandard, with an 88-90 mph fastball to go along with a second-rate slider and changeup. Though he gave the Mets 120 much-needed innings, the pitching-starved club wasted little time in nontendering him to let him look elsewhere for work.

Francisco Rodriguez

Bats: R   Throws: R   Height: 6' 0"   Weight: 195   Born: January 7, 1982   Age: 28

YEAR	TEAM	LVL	AGE	W	L	SV	G	GS	IP	H	HR	BB	SO	GB%	BABIP	STUFF	WHIP	ERA	SIERA	DERA	EqH9	EqHR9	EqBB9	EqSO9	VORP	SN/WX
2007	LAA	MLB	25	5	2	40	64	0	67¹	50	3	34	90	47%	.299	31	1.25	2.81	2.78	2.71	6.6	0.4	4.0	10.1	21.1	4.31
2008	LAA	MLB	26	2	3	62	76	0	68¹	54	4	34	77	48%	.292	24	1.29	2.24	3.37	2.66	7.0	0.5	4.0	9.4	21.4	5.86
2009	NYN	MLB	27	3	6	35	70	0	68	51	7	38	73	39%	.250	6	1.31	3.71	3.80	4.48	7.0	1.0	4.2	7.8	7.9	1.44
2010	NYN	MLB	28	4	4	33	64	0	63²	54	6	32	65	44%	.293	7	1.34	3.76	3.68	4.08	7.7	0.9	4.3	8.3	10.1	2.37

Breakout: 8%   Improve: 34%   Collapse: 32%   Attrition: 7%   MLB: 95%   Comparables: John Wetteland, Trevor Hoffman, Danny Frisella, Jack Baldschun

Rodriguez was better than he looked in 2009; a couple of five-run outings in the second half of the season completely blew up his ERA, which was 2.41 in his other 68 appearances. Still, the Mets probably figured that he'd be something more than the 75th-best reliever in the game (as ranked by WXRL). Rodriguez just isn't the same pitcher that he was with the Angels. The 94-96 mph fastball is now more often in the 92-94 range, and the power breaking ball that was his out pitch is almost never seen anymore, as Rodriguez has lost nearly all command of it. In his defense, he has found a good changeup in its place, but he's hardly the dominating monster that he once was, and the Mets are paying him a minimum of $26.5 million over the next two years to be that guy, not the current version.

Johan Santana

Bats: L   Throws: L   Height: 6' 0"   Weight: 210   Born: March 13, 1979   Age: 31

YEAR	TEAM	LVL	AGE	W	L	SV	G	GS	IP	H	HR	BB	SO	GB%	BABIP	STUFF	WHIP	ERA	SIERA	DERA	EqH9	EqHR9	EqBB9	EqSO9	VORP	SN/WX
2007	MIN	MLB	28	15	13	0	33	33	219	183	33	52	235	45%	.271	26	1.07	3.33	2.74	3.48	7.5	1.5	1.9	8.7	48.5	6.52
2008	NYN	MLB	29	16	7	0	34	34	234¹	206	23	63	206	45%	.274	20	1.15	2.53	3.54	3.12	8.3	1.0	2.1	6.6	61.2	8.33
2009	NYN	MLB	30	13	9	0	25	25	166²	156	20	46	146	40%	.280	14	1.21	3.13	3.66	3.72	8.6	1.2	2.1	6.5	33.1	4.91
2010	NYN	MLB	31	11	10	0	29	29	182	175	24	54	148	44%	.292	15	1.26	3.96	3.84	4.30	8.8	1.2	2.5	6.6	24.4	3.90

Breakout: 5%   Improve: 32%   Collapse: 21%   Attrition: 18%   MLB: 100%   Comparables: Larry French, Ted Higuera, Hal Newhouser, Ed Lopat

M*E*T*S episode 47.2: for the first two months of the season, Santana was arguably once again the best pitcher in baseball, putting up a 1.77 ERA in 10 starts while striking out 86 in just 66 innings. Things slowly slid from there, as Santana tried to pitch through increasing elbow soreness. His season ended in late August, and the Surgery Fairy visited in September. The good news is that the operation was not drastic, just a simple procedure to remove some bone chips. He'll be healthy in 2010, and he'll be great again.

Brian Stokes

Bats: R   Throws: R   Height: 6' 1"   Weight: 210   Born: September 7, 1979   Age: 30

YEAR	TEAM	LVL	AGE	W	L	SV	G	GS	IP	H	HR	BB	SO	GB%	BABIP	STUFF	WHIP	ERA	SIERA	DERA	EqH9	EqHR9	EqBB9	EqSO9	VORP	SN/WX
2007	TBA	MLB	27	2	7	0	59	0	62¹	90	11	25	35	55%	.359	-31	1.84	7.07	5.03	6.14	11.4	1.7	3.1	4.4	-4.5	-1.21
2008	NWO	AAA	28	10	8	0	23	22	130²	124	7	48	97	49%	.290	-4	1.32	4.41	4.29	5.71	9.6	1.0	3.3	4.6	-2.9	0.73
2008	NYN	MLB	28	1	0	1	24	1	33¹	35	5	8	26	48%	.303	-4	1.29	3.51	3.82	3.69	10.2	1.7	2.0	6.0	6.4	0.12
2009	NYN	MLB	29	2	4	0	69	0	70¹	72	6	38	45	52%	.293	-16	1.56	3.97	5.05	4.20	9.4	0.9	4.1	4.8	10.1	0.64
2010	NYN	MLB	30	4	5	0	69	3	76¹	81	10	32	47	49%	.299	-15	1.48	4.82	4.88	5.31	9.9	1.2	3.6	5.0	1.6	0.48

Breakout: 19%   Improve: 63%   Collapse: 14%   Attrition: 16%   MLB: 79%   Comparables: Jose Mercedes, Carlos Reyes, Barry Latman, Dale Murray

Stokes had an ERA right around league average, and unlike most Mets arms, he stayed healthy all year, but he was about as dependable as the typical home contractor. He began the year with 11 consecutive scoreless appearances, but had a 6.20 ERA for the next two months, followed that up with a 2.39 mark in July and August, and then put a bow on it all with an 8.18 mark from there to the end of the season. He's certainly a live arm, with a 94-96 mph fastball, but he has never quite found a much-needed breaking ball. The lack of a horizontal aspect to his game has allowed southpaws to hit like All-Stars against him, lambasting him at .330/.435/.487 rates in 2009. At best, he's a ROOGY, a role that few teams have room on their rosters to accommodate.

Tobi Stoner

Bats: S   Throws: R   Height: 6' 2"   Weight: 192   Born: December 3, 1984   Age: 25

YEAR	TEAM	LVL	AGE	W	L	SV	G	GS	IP	H	HR	BB	SO	GB%	BABIP	STUFF	WHIP	ERA	SIERA	DERA	EqH9	EqHR9	EqBB9	EqSO9	VORP	SN/WX
2007	SAV	A	22	3	5	0	11	11	57¹	59	1	17	50	51%	.326	3	1.33	3.61	3.71	6.29	10.4	1.0	3.3	4.8	-4.8	-0.16
2007	SLU	A+	22	4	5	0	16	16	82²	90	9	25	57	48%	.308	-19	1.39	4.90	4.34	7.80	10.8	2.0	3.4	4.3	-19.7	-1.25
2008	SLU	A+	23	1	5	0	9	9	52	46	3	9	48	47%	.295	11	1.06	2.60	3.08	4.10	9.3	1.3	2.2	5.8	7.5	0.39
2008	BIN	AA	23	4	6	0	15	15	79	80	7	29	59	42%	.304	-7	1.38	4.33	4.37	5.21	10.2	1.3	3.5	5.0	2.4	0.36
2009	BIN	AA	24	2	2	0	7	7	47	28	5	13	28	44%	.170	1	0.87	2.68	4.50	3.47	5.4	1.5	2.5	3.7	10.5	0.42
2009	BUF	AAA	24	7	7	0	16	16	97²	92	9	34	64	42%	.272	-2	1.29	3.96	4.68	4.74	8.7	1.2	3.3	4.6	8.1	0.67
2009	NYN	MLB	24	0	0	0	4	0	9	9	2	3	5	41%	.269	-14	1.33	4.00	4.92	4.50	10.1	2.3	3.4	4.5	0.9	-0.07
2010	NYN	MLB	25	6	9	0	28	23	125	129	17	51	74	40%	.289	-7	1.44	4.73	5.08	5.18	9.6	1.2	3.5	4.9	4.4	1.82

Breakout: 6%   Improve: 45%   Collapse: 12%   Attrition: 20%   MLB: 12%   Comparables: Steven Kelly, Josh Hancock, Ryan Glynn, J.D. Smart

Stoner became the first player from the 16th round of the 2006 draft to reach the majors, which is far more interesting than anything scouts have to say about him. They're not high on pedestrian fastball, and there aren't great seeds for success in his off-speed offerings. He's on the 40-man, but so is Nelson Figueroa—whoa! Total buzzkill.

LINEOUTS

Hitters

PLAYER	TEAM	LVL	AGE	PA	R	2B	3B	HR	RBI	BB	SO	SB-CS	EqBRR	AVG/OBP/SLG	EqAVG/EqOBP/EqSLG	EqA	VORP	WARP
SS A. Berroa	NYA	MLB	31	24	6	1	0	0	1	0	6	0-0	-1.0	.136/.174/.182	.136/.174/.182	.075	-2.6	-0.2
	NYN	MLB	31	31	4	1	0	0	2	3	6	0-0	0.0	.148/.233/.185	.143/.226/.179	.125	-2.3	0.0
3B S. Bowman	BIN	AA	24	379	42	24	3	9	44	25	101	0-0	0.6	.294/.346/.458	.257/.300/.395	.241	2.4	0.8
OF E. Brown	POR	AAA	34	168	22	13	0	4	22	19	27	2-2	-1.2	.260/.345/.432	.247/.320/.387	.246	-0.1	0.1
	BUF	AAA	34	132	14	7	0	2	13	6	30	0-3	-0.3	.256/.295/.360	.230/.265/.310	.192	-7.7	-1.0
C R. Cancel	BUF	AAA	33	282	25	12	2	2	16	18	29	7-3	-2.5	.248/.297/.333	.227/.272/.308	.206	-2.6	-1.3
1B L. Duda*	BIN	AA	23	467	49	29	1	9	53	61	91	2-2	-1.0	.281/.380/.428	.265/.348/.405	.265	5.8	1.1
3B Z. Lutz	SLU	A+	23	415	46	19	2	11	62	50	72	1-1	-2.7	.284/.381/.441	.250/.332/.386	.252	5.6	0.1
	BIN	AA	23	34	0	1	0	0	2	5	7	0-0	-1.4	.207/.324/.241	.200/.294/.233	.190	-1.4	-0.3
3B J. Marte	SAV	A	18	526	58	21	6	6	41	25	117	5-5	-3.0	.233/.279/.338	.214/.248/.301	.188	-22.4	-4.2
MI R. Martinez	BUF	AAA	36	35	5	1	0	0	1	4	5	0-1	-0.8	.290/.371/.323	.258/.343/.290	.221	-0.1	-0.2
	NYN	MLB	36	44	1	2	0	0	4	1	9	1-0	0.2	.167/.182/.214	.143/.159/.190	.119	-3.4	-0.5
OF C. Puello	KNG	Rk	18	221	37	10	0	5	23	10	51	15-5	1.8	.296/.373/.423	.236/.281/.322	.212	-6.6	-2.7
MI A. Reyes#	BUF	AAA	26	416	43	19	4	3	31	29	46	10-3	-1.9	.282/.336/.377	.264/.316/.356	.238	3.7	0.5
	NYN	MLB	26	18	0	0	0	0	0	1	4	1-0	0.1	.118/.167/.118	.118/.167/.118	-.076	-2.3	-0.4
SS W. Valdez	COH	AAA	31	137	17	1	0	0	6	10	19	5-1	-0.6	.198/.263/.207	.187/.246/.195	.160	-6.7	-1.4
	BUF	AAA	31	126	13	4	0	0	6	7	10	1-1	-0.9	.298/.341/.333	.278/.317/.304	.223	0.1	0.4
—	NYN	MLB	31	95	11	3	2	0	7	8	10	0-1	0.3	.256/.326/.337	.267/.337/.349	.241	1.6	0.0

Desperation, thy name is **Angel Berroa**. He returns to the Dodgers on a minor-league contract; frighteningly, 84 games in 2008 were probably enough for him to become one of Joe Torre's "guys." ⊘ **Shawn Bowman** did enough at Double-A to get added to the 40-man roster, but he still doesn't show enough power or patience to be a factor in the big-league picture. ⊘ **Emil Brown** played three games for the Mets in June; at least that's what we were told. ⊘ Journeyman **Robinson Cancel** appeared in one big-league game during a brief respite from grooming the Triple-A arms; we can probably reuse this comment for the next four years. ⊘ **Lucas Duda** is already overshadowed by Ike Davis, but offers some platoon pop against right-handers, having hit .320/.421/.516 against northpaws. ⊘ **Zach Lutz** has shown a decent amount of power and patience so far in the minors, but he'll need to step it up further to make it as a corner-infield type. ⊘ Another teenage prodigy who was seen as just a tick behind Wilmer Flores going into the year, **Jefry Marte** wasn't ready for Low-A as a 17-year-old, and his scouting reports were not kind. ⊘ The Mets completed their collection of past-prime utility players by giving **Ramon Martinez** 42 bigleague at-bats. ⊘ Dominican teen **Cesar Puello** has loads of tools, but is as raw as a freshly uprooted radish. ⊘ Oh wait, we forgot about **Argenis Reyes**. *He* completes the collection of aging utility scrubs. ⊘ Our mistake—it was **Wilson Valdez** who finished the set. If you walked out on the Mets before the credits rolled, you missed the outtake where they picked up Valdez to serve as a multiposition warm body—hilarious! The Phillies signed him to do the same at Triple-A.

Pitchers

PLAYER	TEAM	LVL	AGE	W	L	SV	IP	H	HR	BB	SO	GB%	BABIP	STUFF	WHIP	ERA	SIERA	DERA	EqH9	EqHR9	EqBB9	EqSO9	VORP
K. Allen	SAV	A	19	9	6	2	125¹	109	8	51	111	61%	.287	-25	1.28	3.45	3.70	6.94	11.0	2.7	5.4	4.1	-17.4
A. Bostick*	BIN	AA	26	3	0	0	17¹	16	1	4	20	67%	.349	15	1.15	2.60	2.44	3.16	9.8	1.1	2.3	8.0	4.1
—	BUF	AAA	26	0	3	3	38²	33	5	18	43	36%	.277	2	1.32	3.26	3.50	4.26	8.3	1.7	4.3	8.1	5.2
R. Carson*	SAV	A	20	8	10	0	131²	139	4	45	90	56%	.313	-13	1.40	3.21	4.32	7.85	11.8	1.8	4.6	2.8	-31.0
E. Dessens	BUF	AAA	38	3	2	11	35	26	2	9	28	51%	.247	2	1.00	2.31	3.65	2.97	7.0	0.8	2.4	5.9	9.4
—	NYN	MLB	38	0	0	0	32²	24	5	10	14	45%	.192	-18	1.04	3.31	5.29	3.38	6.8	1.7	2.3	3.1	7.6
J. Egbert	CHR	AAA	26	6	11	1	108²	132	13	33	78	63%	.325	-22	1.52	5.05	4.20	6.54	10.8	1.5	2.9	4.9	-12.6
—	CHA	MLB	26	0	0	0	2²	8	1	2	0	90%	.467	-94	3.75	27.00	5.67	24.00	24.0	3.0	6.0	0.0	-6.2
D. Gee	BUF	AAA	23	1	3	0	48¹	47	5	16	42	44%	.298	8	1.30	4.10	3.86	4.63	9.3	1.3	3.3	6.2	4.5
E. Kunz	BUF	AAA	23	4	5	1	61	54	8	31	38	71%	.254	-21	1.39	5.02	4.57	5.77	8.6	1.7	4.8	4.5	-1.8
A. Lopez*	POR	AAA	26	0	0	0	31	27	0	13	23	47%	.278	-11	1.29	3.77	4.47	4.79	8.1	0.3	3.8	4.6	2.4
—	BUF	AAA	26	0	2	0	30¹	36	1	13	19	53%	.337	-20	1.62	3.86	4.89	5.68	11.0	0.6	4.0	4.3	-0.6
S. Moviel	SLU	A+	21	4	5	0	64¹	61	1	24	46	46%	.297	4	1.32	3.92	4.49	7.45	9.9	0.9	4.1	4.0	-13.2
E. Niesen*	SLU	A+	23	3	4	0	57²	52	5	16	49	44%	.283	-9	1.18	3.28	3.67	5.72	10.1	2.1	3.4	5.1	-1.3
—	BIN	AA	23	4	7	0	83	75	4	41	85	42%	.308	6	1.40	4.66	3.76	5.85	8.8	1.4	4.5	6.8	-3.1
J. Switzer*	BUF	AAA	29	1	3	4	52	46	4	23	49	51%	.286	-4	1.33	3.29	3.85	4.59	8.3	1.1	4.1	6.7	5.2
—	NYN	MLB	29	0	0	0	3¹	4	1	2	3	56%	.300	-16	1.80	8.10	4.50	8.10	10.8	2.7	5.4	5.4	-1.0
K. Takahashi*	BUF	AAA	40	1	3	0	56²	55	2	23	38	58%	.294	-4	1.38	2.38	4.56	3.93	9.0	0.7	3.9	4.7	9.6
—	NYN	MLB	40	0	1	0	27¹	23	2	14	23	46%	.280	-2	1.35	2.96	4.34	3.08	8.2	0.7	4.1	6.5	7.1

The Mets think righty **Kyle Allen** is one of the system's better sleepers, with a fastball and changeup that already rate as plus. ⊘ **Adam Bostick** looked very good against lefties with a move to the pen, but he'll take his NRI shot at big-league LOOGY-dom with the Royals. ⊘ **Rob Carson** is a projectable lefty with plus velocity who needs to find something else to go with it like the Lone Ranger needs Tonto. ⊘ **Elmer Dessens** misses bats about as often as Oprah misses a meal, but he still pitched well enough to get a minor-league deal to return. ⊘ Picked up off waivers from the White Sox at the end of the year, **Jack Egbert** is a finesse righty and a native of Staten Island, so maybe he'll bring some home cooking around to the clubhouse. ⊘ A strike-throwing, finesse righty, **Dillon Gee** suffered through shoulder issues in 2009; he can't afford to see his stuff regress. ⊘ The team's top pick in 2007, **Eddie Kunz** is a ground-ball machine, but he can't miss bats and can't stay in shape; when the Mets needed all hands on deck in the majors, they had so much faith in him that he never left Buffalo. ⊘ Little lefty **Arturo Lopez** has an average fast-ball and slider, but he's old for a prospect and his stay on the 40-man roster will probably be brief. ⊘ Skyscraping (6-foot-11) **Scott Moviel** is loaded with promise and is light-years away from being good enough for the big leagues. ⊘ **Eric Niesen** is an arm-strength lefty whose fastball sits in the low 90s (touching 94), but his secondary stuff and command need work. ⊘ Once a high-ceiling lefty beset by arm injuries, **Jon Switzer** began the journey-man portion of his career by signing with Houston in December. ⊘ **Ken Takahashi** decided to live his dream of pitching in the United States after an unspectacular career in Japan and proved to be unspectacular for the Mets. Mission accomplished, he's headed back to Japan to rejoin the Hiroshima Carp.

MANAGER: JERRY MANUEL

YEAR	TEAM	W-L	Pythag +/−	Avg PC	100+ P	120+ P	QS	BQS	REL	REL w Zero R	IBB	Subs	PH	PH Avg	PH HR	SB2	CS2	SB3	CS3	SAC Att	SAC %	POS SAC	Squeeze	Swing	In Play
2008	NYN	55-38	0	101.4	56	2	49	2	324	212	37	46	164	.245	2	54	16	16	3	64	57.8%	21	0	90	63
2009	NYN	70-92	-1	95.6	80	2	76	5	511	331	60	50	286	.206	5	105	41	17	1	120	73.3%	49	3	156	136

The Mets signed Manuel to a two-year deal prior to the 2009 season, so like it or not, lachrymose Mets fans, you are stuck with him in 2010 unless things continue to go horribly wrong. While 2009 was an utter nightmare for a num-ber of reasons out of his control, namely, the nonstop injuries, Manuel caused his share of difficulties. He might be fantastic with the media, but his calm, downright jovial demeanor grates on fans. Not that some crazy-ass yelling would have helped; the bigger problem—and it's one that few managers can recover from—is that Manuel lost the team in the second half of the season. The team's play was defined by costly errors, embarrassing baserunning gaffes, and some disturbing quotes from players like David Wright, who had no problem openly discussing how difficult it was to get up for "meaningless games." We can print stat after stat about manager tendencies, but arguably the biggest aspect of the job is getting a consistently good effort, and Manuel failed to do that. If there's one reliable tendency, it's his love of bunting with position players, as nutty in the National League as it was in the AL.

New York Yankees

On December 1, 2009, a little less than a month after the Yankees dispatched the Phillies for their 27th championship, Tommy Henrich, oldest living former Yankee, passed away at the age of 96. Henrich, part of seven of those championship teams, played for the Yankees from the late 1930s through 1950, a time when they were run at peak efficiency. Henrich himself was an example of that efficiency, a minor-league free agent the Yankees were smart enough to grab after the Indians failed to realize what they had.

For many years, the Yankees were run in a way that enabled Henrich's teams to win pennant after pennant: make a profit, but not so much that you don't press your financial advantage. Invest heavily in the farm system, even if you can already blow everyone else out of the water on individual bonuses. Be alert to opportunities presented by poorly run organizations. If the Indians miss on a Henrich, grab him. Branch Rickey thinks Yogi Berra is too ugly to be worth a bid? We're not running a beauty contest here—sign him up. The Orioles want to send you their best young pitcher in return for a midlevel catching prospect and a bunch of organizational players? Can't say yes fast enough. Owner of the Kansas City A's wants to be our bitch? Back up the truck and strip his roster down to its underpants.

The Yankees were run with a ruthless perspicacity for years, the only exception being the organizational racism that restricted them to the best white players they could get, instead of the best players, period. They survived the consequences of this reprehensible handicap long after most other teams began to draw from the wider well of talent, because the Yankees were so well run in other ways. The secret to the great Yankees teams

YANKEES PROSPECTUS
2009 W-L: 103-59, 1st in AL East

Pythag	101-61	1st	**Ballpark:** Yankee Stadium (1-yr. PF: 984). Early flurry of homers gave way to neutrality in the House that Ruthlessness Built
RS/G	5.7	1st	
RA/G	4.7	6th	
EqA	.285	1st	
EqBRR	-6.4	11th	**2009:** Big spending gave the Core Four the right kind of support, scoring a handy WS win
SNWP	.508	5th	
WXRL	15.66	1st	**2010:** Still the class of MLB; Granderson plus a full year of A-Rod should balance out the Captain's comedown
FRAr	4.18	3rd	
DE	.697	3rd	
PADE	-0.39	5th	
Salary	$201.4	1st	**Action Items:** Fend off Father Time, straighten out Joba and Hughes
Attend	3.72	1st	

wasn't just the financial advantage derived from being in New York; it was that they made very few mistakes.

Under a goodly stretch of George Steinbrenner's ownership, half of this formula was forgotten. The monetary advantage became a blunt weapon. Young free agent Tommy Henrich and his .339 minor-league average wouldn't have had a chance of signing with the Yankees, because he wasn't 30 and making seven figures. Rather than grow a team through canny acquisitions, Steinbrenner tried to force the process by accumulating veterans. He and Gabe Paul did this successfully in the 1970s, and as wonderful and entertaining a ride as the 1977-1978 championship teams provided, they conveyed a terrible message to The Boss—that a great team could be summoned up at will. He spent the remainder of the active phase of his ownership trying to buy World Series teams off the shelf. As Graig Nettles once remarked, "Every year is like being traded: a new manager and a whole new team."

Escape from that madness came during the brief interregnum during which general manager Gene Michael was allowed to operate with a free hand as a result of Steinbrenner's "lifetime ban" from July 1990 to March 1993 (for hiring someone to give him dirt on Dave Winfield, one of his own players). It was during that brief bit of Boss-lessness that players like Derek Jeter, Andy Pettitte, Jorge Posada, and Mariano Rivera were developed, safe from the owner's constant pressure to send them spinning off across organized baseball in trade for "ready" veterans. There were some close calls once he returned—he reportedly offered Posada and Rivera to the Reds for David Wells in 1995.

The Boss came back, and the merry-go-round of

GMs spun again, lurching from Michael to Bob Watson to Brian Cashman, who has now served for a remarkable 12 years. Only 31 at the time of his promotion, Cashman has both literally and figuratively grown on the job, but initially Steinbrenner was able to reassert his traditional methods of leadership at the expense of his young GM. The farm system was left to rot, the scouting operation a joke that produced little of use on draft day. Veterans became the team's sole focus, but its tastes weren't discriminating. In large part this was because the dearth of prospects gave them no choice but to buy whatever was on the market, as well as forcing them to let aging vets linger too long. The list of hitters and pitchers ranging from 35 to 41 who got to pad their imminent retirements with Yankee bucks defies listing here; suffice it to say that in the history of the club, 96 hitters age 35 or older have had seasons of 100 or more games, 59 pitchers of that age have started 20 or more games, and 29 have relieved in 40 or more. Forty-eight of these seasons, or over a quarter of them, occurred in the years 2002-2009.

Some of these oldsters were quite good at times. Gary Sheffield hit quite well in 2004 and 2005. Even Jason Giambi's worst seasons had enough walks and home runs to provide production, Randy Johnson's 2005 was one of the best seasons a pitcher in his 40s has ever had, and some of those elderly relief seasons were Mariano Rivera specials. The teams were on the whole very good as well, in terms of winning regular-season games, but always fell short in the playoffs. Some of that was no doubt bad luck, a series of short-series losses that represented nothing more than the cosmic coin coming up heads an unlikely number of times in a row. In a broader sense, though, the teams that defeated the Yankees tended to have rosters that were cheaper and had lower Q-ratings, but had little advantages around the edges. These advantages were magnified in the tense environment of post-season play, particularly in starting pitching and defense.

The 2002 and 2003 Yankees had both terrific offenses and pitching staffs and in that sense were on some level great teams, but were so poor on defense that they were helpless when the opposition put the ball in play. With the exception of 2008, the Yankees have not put together an offense that was less than historically outstanding, all of them having an OPS+ of between 11 and 22 percent better than league average from 2002 to 2009. However, the mass defection of David Wells, Roger Clemens, and Andy Pettitte after the 2003 World Series loss, followed soon afterward by the exiling of Jeff Weaver and Jose Contreras, wiped the pitching staff clean. Cashman found quality replacements impossible to obtain at any price, and the farm system was not yet up to helping.

The struggle for pitching, which culminated in the we-have-no-choice signings of Carl Pavano and Jaret Wright in December 2004, became Cashman's road-to-Damascus moment. For the first time in literally decades, someone in a position of power with the Yankees realized that chasing the game's elder statesmen was both expensive and no surefire formula for success. No doubt the experience of having to watch the younger Theo Epstein carry off two World Series rings for the rival Red Sox, steamrollering over the Yankees in the process, with homegrown talents like Kevin Youkilis, Dustin Pedroia, Jacoby Ellsbury, Jon Lester, and Jonathan Papelbon, also provided an object lesson. Steinbrenner's retirement and the advent of his more reasonable (though sometimes just as blustering) sons Hal and Hank allowed Cashman to put these lessons into practice.

The result is that for the first time in years, the Yankees have operated with a plan that's more detailed than "win now." The 2009 championship was directly founded upon Cashman's decision to avoid a situation the elder Steinbrenner surely could not have resisted, the bidding for Twins ace Johan Santana following the 2007 season. With the farm system finally yielding items of value like Phil Hughes and Joba Chamberlain and confronted by a weak free-agent market in which his best possible decisions would be to re-sign Posada, Rivera, and Alex Rodriguez, Cashman recognized that Santana wouldn't be enough in the short term and would (as happened to the Mets) deprive the Yankees of enough assets to limit future moves. Knowing that the expensive contracts of Giambi, Bobby Abreu, and Mike Mussina would be coming off the books after 2008—granting some relief and flexibility to a payroll that had begun to strain even the Yankees' resources—and looking ahead one year to the 2008-2009 free-agent class, Cashman ultimately demurred on Santana. For the first time in memory, the Yankees didn't try to force 2007's 94-win team into a 100-win season the way a goose is forced to turn its liver into foie gras; the team decided to let the chips fall where they would for a year.

The consequence of that decision was a failure to make the postseason for the first time since 1993, a fate that possession of Santana might well have avoided. Still, the short-term pain allowed Cashman to better heal some of the franchise's long-term wounds. Cashman had saved up his pennies for two of the best buys to become free agents in years: CC Sabathia and Mark Teixeira. At 28 and 29 years old, respectively, these were the rare MVP-caliber free agents in their primes who promised not to age overnight. Cashman took more of a gamble on the oft-injured, erratically performing A. J. Burnett, 32, but a gamble with an important distinction from Pavano-style seppuku signings of years past. Burnett was no pitch-to-contact junkballer whose true abilities could not be separated from that of the fielders behind him; his mid-90s fastball and diving-dolphin curve mean that if he's healthy enough to pitch, batters are going to swing and miss, a talent far more projectable than how many hard-hit grounders are going to find their way into the shortstop's mitt.

Simultaneously, Cashman, alert to the Tommy Henrich possibilities in the world, made a move reminiscent of his predecessor Michael's acquisition of Paul O'Neill when he swapped Wilson Betemit and two minor-league pitchers to the White Sox in return for Nick Swisher. In both cases, the players were talented offensive performers who were despised by their teams due to excessive focus on their weaknesses. Swisher not only replaced the departing Bobby Abreu's offense on a roughly one-to-one basis (Swisher created .225 VORP per game vs. .231 for Abreu, a difference of less than a run over 162 games), but also displaced his glove. Though no Dwight Evans, Swisher was adequate, which was a far cry from the eyes-wide terror with which Abreu greeted a deep fly. With Swisher in right, Teixeira erasing the memory of the execrable Giambi at first, an improved middle infield with a maturing Robinson Cano, and a newly rangy Jeter, the Yankees were able to support their pitching staff for the first time in years, leaping from 25th in Defensive Efficiency to seventh (and from 25th to 13th in PADE).

Finally, significantly, in a nonmove that provides a lesson to every general manager in the business, Cashman did *not* throw money at expensive, name-brand relievers, choosing instead to rely entirely on internal solutions. Even after the initial cast behind Rivera imploded, he did not drop an unnecessary dime on fixes, using a temporary surplus of starters as an excuse to send Phil Hughes to the bullpen and promoting the promising curveball specialist David Robertson to the majors.

Not everything that happened on the way to ring XXVII was the result of a carefully executed plan; the Yankees were also lucky. Veterans apparently in a fatal state of decline gave the team years that were historic, given their ages, especially Posada and Jeter. Hideki Matsui had an exceptional year, considering the state of his knees; Johnny Damon created a new peak season for the second time in two years at the age of 35; and Alex Rodriguez was barely debilitated by surgery to repair his hip labrum.

As the 2010 season dawns, it is apparent that Cashman is trying to walk a tightrope, one eye on the future and the budget, another on the clock ticking off the remaining minutes in the career of his Fab Four veteran core of Jeter, Posada, Rivera, and Pettitte. Rather than try to force something with one of the least exciting free-agent classes in recent memory, he jumped on the possibility of upgrading in center field when the Tigers made Curtis Granderson available as part of a rather dubious downsizing. Taking similar advantage of the Braves' desire to pare payroll, he shipped Melky Cabrera, Michael Dunn, and Arodys Vizcaino south for alumnus Javier Vazquez. Vazquez is coming off the best season of his career and, even if he reverts to his previous American League form (more league-average innings muncher than ace), should provide important stability to a rotation at risk. He helps because of the heavy workload imposed by the successful post-season run and the still uncertain abilities of Hughes and Joba Chamberlain to establish themselves as reliable starters. Vizcaino is a terrific prospect, but a 19-year-old's time is not in the here and now but in the hazy post-Fab future. This move should not be viewed as a concession to traditional Steinbrennarian anxiety, but rather as a necessary bow toward the ephemeral nature of even great teams and players.

Cashman also signed 31-year-old former Yankee Nick Johnson (traded for Vazquez, once upon a time) to a one-year contract to take over at designated hitter and simultaneously bade farewell to age-36 incumbents Damon and Matsui. The latter decision was not based on any evaluation that suggests that the outgoing outfielder-DHs are likely to lose their value in 2010, though some of those shockingly productive veterans are sure to show at least some signs of age this year. Rather, it was done in the knowledge that the players would have wanted at least two years and not overly onerous pay cuts to return. Had Cashman acceded, he would have complicated his plans for the 2010-2011 offseason. Possible fish in the water next winter include Albert Pujols, Victor Martinez, Joe Mauer, Carl Crawford (long rumored to be a secret Cashman crush), Josh Beckett, and Matt Cain, not to mention his own pair of future free agents, Jeter and Rivera.

With the pitching staff returning not only intact but augmented by Vazquez, the Yankees are still in a very good position to repeat, especially if Hughes or Chamberlain takes a step forward in his next crack at starting. But more importantly, by not forcing things in 2010 with an overcommitment to players like Matt Holliday and Jason Bay, players who, given their limitations, promise to hemorrhage value over the life of a long-term contact, Cashman is laying the groundwork for even stronger contenders to come and the possibility of a painless transition out of the age of the great core four. The Yankees are again being run with the intelli-gence of their golden age. If Tommy Henrich is looking down at the Bronx, we can imagine that despite the new ballpark and the million-dollar salaries, he is smiling with recognition.

HITTERS

David Adams   2B

Bats: R   Throws: R   Height: 6′ 2″   Weight: 190   Born: May 15, 1987   Age: 23

YEAR	TEAM	LVL	AGE	PA	R	2B	3B	HR	RBI	BB	SO	SB	CS	EqBRR	AVG	OBP	SLG	EqAVG	EqOBP	EqSLG	EqA	VORP	WARP	DEFENSE				
2008	STA	A-	21	297	45	19	2	4	31	32	57	8	2	3.5	.257	.350	.393	.231	.300	.340	.228	-0.7	-0.9	66-2B	-5			
2009	CSC	A	22	304	32	23	2	0	34	35	49	8	4	-1.3	.290	.385	.394	.263	.336	.344	.244	3.3	1.1	51-2B	1	14-3B	5	
2009	TAM	A+	22	265	37	17	6	7	41	26	39	3	4	0.9	.281	.360	.498	.266	.330	.460	.268	9.3	1.5	56-2B	3			
2010	NYA	MLB	23	503	55	25	3	8	53	47	103	4	3	1.0	.245	.323	.368	.249	.324	.369	.235	2.5	0.2	111-2B	0			

Breakout: 13% Improve: 52% Collapse: 17% Attrition: 4%   MLB: 4%   Comparables: Eric White, Tim Cooper, Tyrone Woods, Darren Burton

A third-round pick out of UVA in 2008, Adams has shown decent pop and selectivity at the lower levels and plays a surprisingly good second base. If he stays at second, he has a future as one of those starters who gives you a little hitting and a little defense, but not a ton of either. Should either aspect fail to come with him to the higher levels, that will be all she wrote. The difficult hitting environment at Trenton looms as his next test.

Melky Cabrera   CF

Bats: S   Throws: L   Height: 5′ 11″   Weight: 200   Born: August 11, 1984   Age: 25

YEAR	TEAM	LVL	AGE	PA	R	2B	3B	HR	RBI	BB	SO	SB	CS	EqBRR	AVG	OBP	SLG	EqAVG	EqOBP	EqSLG	EqA	VORP	WARP	DEFENSE				
2007	NYA	MLB	22	612	66	24	8	8	73	43	68	13	5	-0.2	.273	.327	.391	.274	.328	.396	.254	13.3	2.6	120-CF	8	16-LF	1	
2008	NYA	MLB	23	453	42	12	1	8	37	29	58	9	2	-1.1	.249	.301	.341	.250	.303	.347	.231	-0.7	0.3	109-CF	3	3-RF	1	
2009	NYA	MLB	24	540	66	28	1	13	68	43	59	10	2	0.3	.274	.336	.416	.282	.342	.418	.267	17.8	2.2	90-CF	0	23-LF	2	
2010	ATL	MLB	25	530	60	22	3	11	63	48	67	10	5	-0.6	.269	.340	.400	.274	.342	.411	.267	20.1	2.4	123-CF	2			

Breakout: 20% Improve: 55% Collapse: 9% Attrition: 4%   MLB: 100%   Comparables: Mark Kotsay, Carlos Beltran, George Wright, Reggie Smith

Cabrera's season rates as a triumph, given how far he had fallen in 2008. Brett Gardner won the starting job in center in spring training, but Cabrera waited while Gardner played his way out of the job, then sprang into action, hitting .323/.368/.481 with five home runs in 44 games through the end of May, including a 14th-inning walk-off shot at Yankee Stadium on April 22nd. That blast fixed him as a starter in Girardi's mind, an unfortunate development, as Cabrera reverted to his old form after a minor shoulder injury in late May, hitting just .256/.324/.392 the rest of the way. The whole package can be summed up as league-average defense and slightly below-average hitting. Cabrera would be a valuable fourth outfielder, but he's stretched as a starter, as the Braves are about to discover having acquired him in the Javier Vazquez deal. Bobby Cox would be wise to give many of his at-bats versus southpaws to Matt Diaz, and his power seems likely to evaporate at the Ted. If his acquisition pushes Nate McLouth to left field, a position more in line with his defense abilities, even better.

Robinson Cano   2B

Bats: L   Throws: R   Height: 6′ 0″   Weight: 205   Born: October 22, 1982   Age: 27

YEAR	TEAM	LVL	AGE	PA	R	2B	3B	HR	RBI	BB	SO	SB	CS	EqBRR	AVG	OBP	SLG	EqAVG	EqOBP	EqSLG	EqA	VORP	WARP	DEFENSE	
2007	NYA	MLB	24	669	93	41	7	19	97	39	85	4	5	-2.4	.306	.353	.488	.305	.352	.492	.282	38.3	5.7	157-2B	11
2008	NYA	MLB	25	634	70	35	3	14	72	26	65	2	4	-0.7	.271	.305	.410	.274	.308	.415	.247	10.7	1.8	155-2B	4
2009	NYA	MLB	26	674	103	48	2	25	85	30	63	5	7	0.4	.320	.352	.520	.330	.361	.525	.293	45.6	6.0	156-2B	7
2010	NYA	MLB	27	658	88	36	3	24	90	40	74	3	6	-0.5	.295	.343	.483	.296	.342	.476	.270	27.8	3.4	155-2B	4

Breakout: 12% Improve: 47% Collapse: 13% Attrition: 2%   MLB: 100%   Comparables: Cecil Travis, Jose Vidro, Adam Kennedy, Carlos Baerga

On one level, Cano had a terrific comeback year. On another, he was still struggling, hitting .376 with the bases empty, .255 with men on, and .207 with runners in scoring position. In 2009, 171 players had 200 or more plate appearances with runners on base. On average, these hitters plated 15.1 percent of those runners. Cano drove in only

12.6 percent, a mark that tied him for 141st place—a problem, given that he came up with the ninth-highest tally of men aboard in baseball. Cano's struggles are consistent with his career-long splits: he's a career .331/.363/.528 hitter with the bases empty, .280/.312/.425 with men on, and .256/.291/.398 with runners in scoring position. He's still a fine hitter, but with his hack-at-anything ways in RBI situations, he's also far better at setting the table than cleaning it. Combine this with his solid defense, and you have a flawed but valuable player.

Francisco Cervelli   C   Bats: R   Throws: R   Height: 6' 1"   Weight: 210   Born: March 6, 1986   Age: 24

YEAR	TEAM	LVL	AGE	PA	R	2B	3B	HR	RBI	BB	SO	SB	CS	EqBRR	AVG	OBP	SLG	EqAVG	EqOBP	EqSLG	EqA	VORP	WARP	DEFENSE	
2007	TAM	A+	21	348	34	24	2	2	32	36	59	4	3	-4.5	.279	.387	.397	.257	.346	.370	.255	14.5	2.2	88-C	4
2008	TRN	AA	22	88	8	5	0	0	8	11	14	0	0	0.0	.315	.432	.384	.303	.398	.355	.275	4.1	0.7	16-C	2
2009	TRN	AA	23	64	8	1	0	2	7	6	13	0	0	0.6	.190	.266	.310	.186	.250	.305	.190	-1.4	-0.2	16-C	0
2009	SWB	AAA	23	75	7	5	0	1	7	3	13	0	2	-0.6	.275	.311	.391	.275	.311	.377	.233	1.2	0.2	21-C	0
2009	NYA	MLB	23	101	13	4	0	1	11	2	11	0	3	-1.7	.298	.309	.372	.301	.313	.366	.233	1.3	0.7	27-C	3
2010	NYA	MLB	24	264	25	13	1	3	23	21	51	2	2	-1.2	.250	.325	.353	.251	.325	.348	.231	2.7	0.5	67-C	2

Breakout: 10%   Improve: 37%   Collapse: 26%   Attrition: 12%   MLB: 100%   Comparables: Kurt Brown, Chris Heintz, Alberto Castillo, Clint Sammons

Cervelli is a fun player, an animated and athletic backstop who has thrown well in limited exposure, nailing 10 of 23 stolen-base attempts in 2009. His .298 batting average with nonexistent peripherals probably represents the top of his offensive range; Cervelli didn't hit with any authority in the minors, and what little he did produce came at the lower levels. Due to injuries and calls to the majors, his Double-A and Triple-A experience has been limited to a total of 58 games. Scheduled to take over as second-string catcher, his defense suggests they won't miss Jose Molina much.

Johnny Damon   LF   Bats: L   Throws: L   Height: 6' 2"   Weight: 205   Born: November 5, 1973   Age: 36

YEAR	TEAM	LVL	AGE	PA	R	2B	3B	HR	RBI	BB	SO	SB	CS	EqBRR	AVG	OBP	SLG	EqAVG	EqOBP	EqSLG	EqA	VORP	WARP	DEFENSE			
2007	NYA	MLB	33	605	93	27	2	12	63	66	79	27	3	7.5	.270	.351	.396	.267	.349	.395	.270	17.4	2.4	42-CF	1	30-LF	2
2008	NYA	MLB	34	623	95	27	5	17	71	64	82	29	8	1.7	.303	.375	.461	.306	.380	.467	.293	34.8	4.1	74-LF	6	32-CF	-4
2009	NYA	MLB	35	626	107	36	3	24	82	71	98	12	0	2.9	.282	.365	.489	.290	.372	.495	.298	37.9	4.9	125-LF	5		
2010	NYA	MLB	36	591	86	26	3	17	66	69	88	17	6	2.0	.272	.360	.433	.272	.356	.424	.270	18.7	2.4	97-LF	3		

Breakout: 3%   Improve: 32%   Collapse: 16%   Attrition: 18%   MLB: 98%   Comparables: Raul Ibañez, B.J. Surhoff, Goose Goslin, Paul O'Neill

Damon had become adept at jerking the ball down the short right-field line in Yankee Stadium: 17 of his 24 homers were hit at home, every one of them to right. He hit a still-serviceable .284/.349/.446 in away games, but with a .330 BABIP, the figure is likely to regress. As a result, any team that might pluck Damon from the free-agent pool is likely to get less than it anticipated. Damon's broad-based skill set has aged terrifically well, though he has lost speed both on the bases and in the field. His arm is still useful for lifting forks, pens, and other small items, but it no longer functions to throw out runners; even routine throws back to the infield are depressingly limp. At this stage, he's best suited to a split left-field/DH role as he continues his dark-horse run at 3,000 hits.

Brett Gardner   CF   Bats: L   Throws: L   Height: 5' 10"   Weight: 180   Born: August 24, 1983   Age: 26

YEAR	TEAM	LVL	AGE	PA	R	2B	3B	HR	RBI	BB	SO	SB	CS	EqBRR	AVG	OBP	SLG	EqAVG	EqOBP	EqSLG	EqA	VORP	WARP	DEFENSE			
2007	TRN	AA	23	241	43	14	5	0	17	33	32	18	4	3.1	.300	.392	.419	.293	.371	.399	.278	11.3	1.0	50-CF	-3		
2007	SWB	AAA	23	207	37	4	3	1	9	21	43	21	3	3.4	.260	.343	.331	.255	.332	.332	.249	3.5	1.1	42-CF	6		
2008	SWB	AAA	24	426	68	12	11	3	32	70	76	37	9	1.8	.296	.414	.422	.294	.407	.424	.297	27.8	3.7	72-CF	-1	20-LF	5
2008	NYA	MLB	24	141	18	5	2	0	16	8	30	13	1	2.6	.228	.283	.299	.230	.285	.302	.232	-1.0	0.8	18-CF	5	16-LF	2
2009	NYA	MLB	25	284	48	6	6	3	23	26	40	26	5	4.9	.270	.345	.379	.279	.354	.389	.272	11.3	0.6	70-CF	-5		
2010	NYA	MLB	26	434	67	18	6	4	34	51	79	29	8	2.8	.266	.356	.378	.268	.355	.384	.261	13.4	1.5	98-CF	0		

Breakout: 14%   Improve: 44%   Collapse: 10%   Attrition: 9%   MLB: 70%   Comparables: Mookie Wilson, Kenny Lofton, Alex Sanchez, Joey Gathright

Gardner's 2009 gets an "incomplete." Awarded the starting job in center in camp, the speedster went cold in April and was benched for Melky Cabrera, but recovered his stroke as a sub and part-time starter during May and June, hitting .330/.427/.510 in 120 plate appearances. Girardi began to start him again with greater frequency, but in short order Gardner slumped, then broke his thumb, requiring a six-week timeout. When he returned, he had trouble getting Girardi's attention and didn't hit in the little time he was given, a bout of impotence he carried over to the post-season. Despite these struggles, Gardner's speed on the bases and in the field merits another long look. With Granderson added and Cabrera gone, he might be able to grab a piece of left field, though the Yankees will most likely have upgraded by the time you read this. Even if Gardner doesn't start, he's a valuable reserve.

Jerry Hairston Jr.   UT

Bats: R **Throws:** R **Height:** 5' 10" **Weight:** 185 **Born:** May 29, 1976 **Age:** 34

YEAR	TEAM	LVL	AGE	PA	R	2B	3B	HR	RBI	BB	SO	SB	CS	EqBRR	AVG	OBP	SLG	EqAVG	EqOBP	EqSLG	EqA	VORP	WARP	DEFENSE			
2007	TEX	MLB	31	184	22	7	0	3	16	11	24	5	1	1.6	.189	.249	.289	.185	.244	.293	.203	-5.8	-0.4	15-CF	0	12-2B	0
2008	CIN	MLB	32	297	47	20	2	6	36	23	36	15	3	0.1	.326	.384	.487	.335	.390	.494	.304	24.7	1.9	30-SS	-8	13-CF	1
2009	CIN	MLB	33	340	47	18	1	8	27	21	46	7	3	-0.5	.254	.305	.397	.265	.313	.414	.252	8.0	0.1	31-3B	-4	24-SS	-4
2009	NYA	MLB	33	93	15	5	0	2	12	11	8	0	1	-0.5	.237	.352	.382	.240	.356	.373	.263	2.6	0.5	9-3B	1	7-LF	0
2010	NYA	MLB	34	342	48	16	1	9	39	28	49	8	4	0.1	.266	.338	.413	.264	.335	.407	.254	6.7	0.5	49-3B	-2		

Breakout: 9%   Improve: 45%   Collapse: 23%   Attrition: 28%   MLB: 93%   Comparables: Jerry Royster, Al Smith, Joe Medwick, Tom Brookens

Acquired at the trading deadline, Hairston gave the Yankees a versatile utilityman who was used primarily to give Johnny Damon and Alex Rodriguez time off, but he also served as a pinch-hitter, pinch-runner, and outfielder. Hairston has never been that much of a hitter, but the Yankees got a little something extra with his hot August (.293/.400/.512, two home runs in 51 PAs). His jack-of-all-gloves abilities make him a useful 25th man, but the 98 starts he received in 2009 asked for more than he could provide.

Eric Hinske   4C

Bats: L **Throws:** R **Height:** 6' 2" **Weight:** 235 **Born:** August 5, 1977 **Age:** 32

YEAR	TEAM	LVL	AGE	PA	R	2B	3B	HR	RBI	BB	SO	SB	CS	EqBRR	AVG	OBP	SLG	EqAVG	EqOBP	EqSLG	EqA	VORP	WARP	DEFENSE			
2007	BOS	MLB	29	218	25	12	3	6	21	28	54	3	0	-0.1	.204	.317	.398	.195	.312	.384	.248	-0.1	0.0	31-1B	-1	11-LF	1
2008	TBA	MLB	30	432	59	21	1	20	60	47	88	10	3	0.6	.247	.333	.465	.253	.340	.479	.279	16.2	1.9	38-RF	1	30-LF	0
2009	PIT	MLB	31	126	18	9	0	1	11	17	27	0	0	-1.0	.255	.373	.368	.271	.386	.402	.277	3.7	0.9	13-RF	3	5-1B	1
2009	NYA	MLB	31	98	13	3	0	7	14	10	25	1	0	0.3	.226	.316	.512	.229	.316	.518	.282	4.2	0.0	14-RF	-2	4-3B	-1
2010	ATL	NL	32	363	40	15	1	12	37	43	87	4	2	-0.1	.225	.326	.399	.233	.329	.414	.261	8.0	1.0	60-RF	1		

Breakout: 7%   Improve: 35%   Collapse: 24%   Attrition: 19%   MLB: 94%   Comparables: Dave Clark, Cliff Floyd, Henry Rodriguez, Ken Griffey

Brian Cashman has a long tradition of not holding bench players in high regard, but Hairston and Hinske represented a departure from previous policy. Acquired on June 30th, Hinske homered in his first game as a Yankee and then swatted four more in his next six appearances. He was less effective in sporadic work after that, but seemed happier minding the bench for a contender than he did on a second-division club, and his combined season line (.242/.348/.432) was consistent with his career averages. Hinske signed with the Braves; given the fragility of Troy Glaus and Chipper Jones, as well as the uncertain timing of Jason Heyward's arrival, he could see quite a bit of action.

Austin Jackson   CF

Bats: R **Throws:** R **Height:** 6' 1" **Weight:** 185 **Born:** February 1, 1987 **Age:** 23

YEAR	TEAM	LVL	AGE	PA	R	2B	3B	HR	RBI	BB	SO	SB	CS	EqBRR	AVG	OBP	SLG	EqAVG	EqOBP	EqSLG	EqA	VORP	WARP	DEFENSE			
2007	CSC	A	20	266	33	16	1	3	25	24	59	19	6	-1.3	.260	.336	.374	.236	.294	.326	.223	-2.8	-0.5	56-CF	-1		
2007	TAM	A+	20	284	53	15	6	10	34	22	48	13	5	0.0	.345	.398	.566	.309	.356	.515	.293	18.7	2.8	63-CF	5		
2008	TRN	AA	21	584	75	33	5	9	69	56	113	19	6	-1.6	.285	.354	.419	.273	.331	.395	.256	12.1	1.2	111-CF	-2		
2009	SWB	AAA	22	557	67	23	9	4	65	40	123	24	4	2.5	.300	.354	.405	.289	.342	.399	.264	17.0	1.7	94-CF	-4	24-LF	0
2010	DET	MLB	23	537	65	26	6	10	54	46	124	14	5	0.0	.261	.326	.396	.259	.323	.386	.247	9.3	1.0	112-CF	0		

Breakout: 8%   Improve: 41%   Collapse: 20%   Attrition: 9%   MLB: 6%   Comparables: Lorenzo Cain, Jason Romano, Alonzo Powell, Alex Ochoa

In his first season at Triple-A, the athletic Jackson was two different players. He got off to a hot start in April and May, but cooled after that, hitting .260/.296/.328 in the second half. Home-run power has yet to manifest itself, and his plate judgment took a pigeon-hop backward. That he still managed to hit .300 for the season is a superficially reassuring accomplishment, but when you start knocking bits off his performance to make a major-league translation, you're not left with a whole lot to hang a projection of stardom upon. You have to have faith that Jackson's youth and athleticism will allow for development of skills we don't yet see, like authoritative hitting or top-flight defense. As a putative center fielder, he'll get a bit of extra wiggle room for that evolution to take place, but with the Curtis

Granderson trade, he'll be doing it in the central pasture at Comerica Stadium. The comparisons to Granderson will be unflattering at first and may stay that way.

Derek Jeter — SS

Bats: R Throws: R Height: 6' 3" Weight: 195 Born: June 26, 1974 Age: 36

YEAR	TEAM	LVL	AGE	PA	R	2B	3B	HR	RBI	BB	SO	SB	CS	EqBRR	AVG	OBP	SLG	EqAVG	EqOBP	EqSLG	EqA	VORP	WARP	DEFENSE
2007	NYA	MLB	33	714	102	39	4	12	73	56	100	15	8	2.2	.322	.388	.452	.321	.387	.453	.290	48.7	3.2	147-SS -19
2008	NYA	MLB	34	668	88	25	3	11	69	52	85	11	5	1.1	.300	.363	.408	.304	.367	.413	.274	36.0	3.1	141-SS -9
2009	NYA	MLB	35	716	107	27	1	18	66	72	90	30	5	1.1	.334	.406	.465	.343	.414	.468	.310	65.6	6.0	141-SS -11
2010	NYA	MLB	36	594	67	24	2	11	58	55	95	10	7	0.6	.286	.359	.401	.286	.358	.398	.260	20.0	1.6	125-SS -6

Breakout: 9% Improve: 20% Collapse: 26% Attrition: 37% MLB: 95% Comparables: Dave Concepcion, Mark Grudzielanek, Tommy Davis, Craig Biggio

Only a handful of shortstops 35 or older have had great offensive seasons, and most of them are named Honus Wagner. To the Honuses (or *Honi*) you can now add Jeter, who bounced back from a lackluster 2008 to take third place in the MVP voting and to become the first Yankee to receive *Sports Illustrated*'s Sportsman of the Year citation. The Captain started slowly by his standards, then hit his stride in May, and raked for the rest of the season. New Yankee Stadium helped him rediscover his home-run stroke after a few years of relative dormancy, with 12 of 18 round-trippers coming at home. A new flexibility regimen undertaken prior to last season got the bulk of the credit for reenergizing the veteran shortstop, especially on defense. Jeter now enters the last year of his contract; it is a certainty he'll be re-signed to continue his march to 3,000 (or more) hits with the Yankees. Now all we need to hear are answers involving those three little words "How many years?" How many years will the Yankees give him? How many years does he want to play? How many years can his professionalism, dedication, and training stave off the effects of age?

Corban Joseph — 2B

Bats: L Throws: R Height: 6' 0" Weight: 168 Born: October 28, 1988 Age: 21

YEAR	TEAM	LVL	AGE	PA	R	2B	3B	HR	RBI	BB	SO	SB	CS	EqBRR	AVG	OBP	SLG	EqAVG	EqOBP	EqSLG	EqA	VORP	WARP	DEFENSE	
2008	YAN	Rk	19	183	25	15	2	2	18	20	24	2	5	-2.2	.277	.359	.434	.229	.287	.355	.222	-2.0	-2.0	42-2B -9	
2009	CSC	A	20	436	39	17	8	4	57	49	61	8	5	-2.7	.300	.381	.418	.276	.343	.384	.257	10.2	0.3	55-2B -13	37-3B 5
2010	NYA	MLB	21	438	36	19	3	5	50	45	78	3	2	-1.4	.261	.339	.371	.263	.337	.378	.244	5.7	-0.6	93-2B -11	

Breakout: 8% Improve: 42% Collapse: 14% Attrition: 2% MLB: 1% Comparables: Adrian Cardenas, Brian Hartsock, Nate Spears, Rafael Delima

A 2008 fourth-round prep pick, Joseph's story is very similar to that of David Adams. His modest ability to hit shouldn't be taken for granted in a middle infielder, but his defense at second has been problematic. If you can't field at second and can't hit like a third baseman, you've got nowhere to go but home, which in Joseph's case is Franklin, Tennessee, sight of a famous but utterly useless Civil War battle in which Confederate General John Bell Hood intentionally marched his army under the Union guns. There's a metaphor in there, but it's probably better applied to the Marlins than the Yankees.

Hideki Matsui — DH

Bats: L Throws: R Height: 6' 2" Weight: 210 Born: June 12, 1974 Age: 36

YEAR	TEAM	LVL	AGE	PA	R	2B	3B	HR	RBI	BB	SO	SB	CS	EqBRR	AVG	OBP	SLG	EqAVG	EqOBP	EqSLG	EqA	VORP	WARP	DEFENSE
2007	NYA	MLB	33	633	100	28	4	25	103	73	73	4	2	2.5	.285	.367	.488	.283	.365	.487	.291	33.3	3.5	109-LF -1
2008	NYA	MLB	34	378	43	17	0	9	45	38	47	0	0	-0.5	.294	.370	.424	.292	.370	.423	.278	11.7	1.3	20-LF 1
2009	NYA	MLB	35	526	62	21	1	28	90	64	75	0	1	-0.8	.274	.367	.509	.281	.373	.512	.299	23.6	2.7	
2010	LAA	MLB	36	456	54	19	1	16	67	56	66	1	1	0.2	.272	.364	.445	.269	.359	.437	.272	10.9	1.2	0- 0

Breakout: 7% Improve: 34% Collapse: 24% Attrition: 40% MLB: 94% Comparables: Harold Baines, Cliff Floyd, Eddie Mathews, Goose Goslin

Matsui's fine comeback season culminated in his winning the World Series MVP award. It took considerable care of his knees to keep him in the lineup, with Girardi being careful to give him frequent rest; the results speak for themselves. Matsui remains an excellent all-around hitter. The rare lefty who has almost no platoon issues (.282/.358/.618 against southpaws in 2009, .294/.359/.465 career), he was also one of the few Yankees whose '09 power surge wasn't a gift granted by the new ballpark. Matsui might have been able to play the field in a pinch, but the Yankees saw no reason to risk it; it wasn't as if he was a great outfielder, even on two good legs. Matsui has the kind of skills that should age reasonably well as long as he continues to be handled with the kind of sensitivity the Yankees showed last year. Matsui was signed to a one-year contract to DH for the Angels, where he joins former Yankee Bobby Abreu.

Juan Miranda   1B

						Bats: L		Throws: L		Height: 6' 0"		Weight: 220		Born: April 25, 1983				Age: 27					

YEAR	TEAM	LVL	AGE	PA	R	2B	3B	HR	RBI	BB	SO	SB	CS	EqBRR	AVG	OBP	SLG	EqAVG	EqOBP	EqSLG	EqA	VORP	WARP	DEFENSE
2007	TAM	A+	24	293	35	17	3	9	50	29	60	1	0	-2.5	.264	.348	.464	.228	.297	.386	.240	-3.4	-1.4	66-1B -8
2007	TRN	AA	24	227	29	17	2	7	46	23	46	0	1	0.2	.265	.352	.480	.252	.322	.441	.261	2.5	0.1	28-1B -2
2008	SWB	AAA	25	417	40	22	0	12	52	55	79	2	1	-1.7	.287	.384	.449	.283	.373	.442	.284	14.8	1.4	76-1B -3
2008	NYA	MLB	25	14	2	1	0	0	1	2	4	0	0	-0.1	.400	.500	.500	.400	.500	.500	.365	1.7	0.3	4-1B 1
2009	SWB	AAA	26	502	74	30	2	19	82	55	101	1	0	1.6	.290	.369	.498	.283	.357	.484	.288	15.7	2.0	114-1B 1
2009	NYA	MLB	26	9	2	0	0	1	3	0	4	0	0	-0.1	.333	.333	.667	.333	.333	.667	.321	0.7	0.1	3-1B 0
2010	NYA	MLB	27	474	52	22	2	15	66	51	115	1	1	-0.4	.249	.333	.419	.249	.330	.407	.253	1.7	0.0	96-1B -2

Breakout: 5%   Improve: 30%   Collapse: 24%   Attrition: 8%   MLB: 14%   Comparables: Brian Myrow, Josh Whitesell, Boi Rodriguez, Brian Daubach

The ageless (because he has no official age) Miranda spent his second season at Scranton and continued to provide unexceptional production for a first baseman. Though Brian Cashman suggested in December that Miranda could be the team's 2010 DH (fancifully; Nick Johnson got the job), the role seems beyond him; over the last three seasons, the average AL DH has hit .260/.344/.442. In a peak year, Miranda might match these numbers, but he's unlikely to surpass them. Perhaps some team in need of a lefty pinch-hitter might give him a shot. What is certain is that he has no future with the Yankees and is taking up a 40-man roster spot to no useful purpose.

Jose Molina   C

						Bats: R		Throws: R		Height: 6' 2"		Weight: 235		Born: June 3, 1975				Age: 35					

YEAR	TEAM	LVL	AGE	PA	R	2B	3B	HR	RBI	BB	SO	SB	CS	EqBRR	AVG	OBP	SLG	EqAVG	EqOBP	EqSLG	EqA	VORP	WARP	DEFENSE
2007	LAA	MLB	32	131	9	8	0	0	10	3	30	2	1	-0.8	.224	.242	.288	.226	.244	.282	.183	-3.1	-0.1	37-C 1
2007	NYA	MLB	32	71	9	5	0	1	9	2	13	0	0	-1.2	.318	.333	.439	.323	.338	.431	.266	3.9	1.0	19-C 3
2008	NYA	MLB	33	297	32	17	0	3	18	12	52	0	0	0.1	.216	.263	.313	.218	.264	.320	.207	-2.6	1.6	83-C 12
2009	NYA	MLB	34	155	15	4	0	1	11	14	28	0	0	-0.7	.217	.292	.268	.217	.292	.261	.204	-2.1	0.3	40-C 3
2010	NYA	MLB	35	179	19	8	0	2	15	11	39	0	0	-0.4	.234	.291	.322	.233	.291	.320	.204	-2.5	0.0	50-C 3

Breakout: 21%   Improve: 43%   Collapse: 25%   Attrition: 24%   MLB: 93%   Comparables: Jeff Newman, Mike Matheny, Dan Wilson, Gary Bennett

Nothing about Molina surprises. He could be caught in a hot-tub tryst with two porn starlets and a Dallas Cowboys linebacker and you'd still yawn, because it wouldn't change a thing: he's a glove man who can't hit. In the last two years, he has posted identical 51 OPS+ marks, batting .217/.273/.298 in 452 plate appearances. He accumulated that much playing time because of Posada's various injuries and scheduled days off. Though Molina's good defense stands in direct contrast to Posada's complete immobility behind the plate (so much so that Molina was used as A. J. Burnett's personal catcher during the postseason), the offensive price was too high to pay. Molina is a free agent at press time; the Yankees are ready to turn his job over to Cervelli.

Jesus Montero   C

						Bats: R		Throws: R		Height: 6' 4"		Weight: 225		Born: November 28, 1989				Age: 20					

YEAR	TEAM	LVL	AGE	PA	R	2B	3B	HR	RBI	BB	SO	SB	CS	EqBRR	AVG	OBP	SLG	EqAVG	EqOBP	EqSLG	EqA	VORP	WARP	DEFENSE
2007	YAN	Rk	17	123	13	6	0	3	19	12	18	0	0	-2.4	.280	.366	.421	.241	.301	.366	.234	1.1	-0.7	21-C -5
2008	CSC	A	18	569	86	34	1	17	87	37	83	2	1	-2.3	.326	.376	.491	.306	.348	.447	.273	23.5	2.3	70-C -5
2009	TAM	A+	19	198	26	15	1	8	37	14	26	0	0	-2.5	.356	.406	.583	.333	.376	.552	.309	15.7	0.5	25-C -12
2009	TRN	AA	19	181	19	10	0	9	33	14	21	0	0	-1.4	.317	.370	.539	.324	.368	.541	.303	14.8	1.3	32-C -4
2010	NYA	MLB	20	528	68	27	1	23	84	38	85	1	1	-1.7	.299	.352	.498	.297	.348	.484	.280	32.4	2.9	71-C -6

Breakout: 28%   Improve: 50%   Collapse: 16%   Attrition: 2%   MLB: 0%   Comparables: Torii Hunter, John Buck, Justin Huber, Derek Bell

Montero can flat-out hit and might be ready to hit in the majors now if it weren't for his lack of position. Teams are phobic about grooming young players as designated hitters, but every once in a while, the farm system produces a special hitter, an Edgar Martinez or a Frank Thomas, whose natural, God-given position is DH. Like those fellows, Montero could be propped up in the field from time to time, particularly at first base, but he's clearly not a catcher, at least not right now. Montero is only 20 and could figure out how to catch eventually, perhaps at the same age at which a college-trained catcher might be drafted, but his bat is propelling him forward too fast for his glove to keep up. Obviously, Montero would be more valuable if he could stay behind the plate; the same was true of Carlos Delgado, Paul Konerko, and even Jimmie Foxx. Only a fool is gifted with a hitter with this kind of talent and focuses on the things he *can't* do. The Yankees will send Montero to Triple-A and let him play at catching, do a little gardening around first base, and see if he continues to dominate at the new level, particularly after a fractured finger cost him the end of last season. If he does hit, though, there's no point in holding him back waiting for some revelation of defensive ability that might never come. It was that kind of thinking that kept Edgar Martinez from being a regular until he was 27.

Xavier Nady — RF

Bats: R Throws: R Height: 6' 2" Weight: 215 Born: November 14, 1978 Age: 31

YEAR	TEAM	LVL	AGE	PA	R	2B	3B	HR	RBI	BB	SO	SB	CS	EqBRR	AVG	OBP	SLG	EqAVG	EqOBP	EqSLG	EqA	VORP	WARP	DEFENSE			
2007	PIT	MLB	28	470	55	23	1	20	72	23	101	3	1	0.8	.278	.330	.476	.288	.338	.486	.279	18.5	1.0	84-RF	-5	9-LF	-1
2008	PIT	MLB	29	360	50	26	1	13	57	25	55	1	0	-2.4	.330	.383	.535	.350	.398	.555	.320	31.5	3.6	80-RF	0		
2008	NYA	MLB	29	247	26	11	0	12	40	14	48	1	1	0.2	.268	.320	.474	.268	.320	.474	.269	6.6	0.8	44-LF	3	6-RF	-2
2009	NYA	MLB	30	29	4	4	0	0	2	1	6	0	0	-0.2	.286	.310	.429	.286	.310	.429	.255	0.2	0.0	5-RF	0		
2010	NYA	MLB	31	382	45	18	1	16	57	26	73	2	1	-0.3	.282	.341	.475	.279	.338	.459	.271	12.4	1.2	81-RF	-2		

Breakout: 13% Improve: 43% Collapse: 18% Attrition: 14%   MLB: 88%   Comparables: Jose Guillen, Brian Jordan, Brian Buchanan, Matt Diaz

The Yankees named Nady their starting right fielder coming out of spring training, but in an act of divine providence, he injured his throwing elbow in mid-April. After a long rest and a try at rehabilitation, Nady reinjured the elbow and went down for Tommy John surgery for the second time of his career. Thus were the Yankees saved from a major error in judgment. When healthy, Nady exists in that nebulous area between low-quality starter and high-quality reserve, hewing closer to the latter. The Yankees erred by placing him on the wrong side of the divide when they had better options. Since he's expected to be ready to play during spring training, the role that he's assigned to this year will represent a test of your local GM's perspicacity.

Eduardo Nunez — SS

Bats: R Throws: R Height: 6' 0" Weight: 155 Born: June 15, 1987 Age: 23

YEAR	TEAM	LVL	AGE	PA	R	2B	3B	HR	RBI	BB	SO	SB	CS	EqBRR	AVG	OBP	SLG	EqAVG	EqOBP	EqSLG	EqA	VORP	WARP	DEFENSE	
2007	CSC	A	20	360	36	10	2	1	28	25	42	20	8	-0.4	.238	.293	.290	.222	.265	.263	.188	-11.1	-2.2	89-SS	-7
2007	TAM	A+	20	134	16	5	0	1	13	7	18	9	0	0.2	.285	.336	.350	.264	.306	.320	.231	1.1	-0.1	29-SS	-2
2008	TAM	A+	21	402	45	18	3	6	42	19	48	14	10	-2.7	.271	.305	.383	.251	.279	.360	.223	1.1	-1.1	89-SS	-10
2009	TRN	AA	22	528	70	26	1	9	55	22	63	19	7	3.9	.322	.349	.433	.325	.347	.432	.271	26.4	1.2	118-SS	-17
2010	NYA	MLB	23	481	55	21	1	8	45	26	72	12	5	0.2	.273	.316	.376	.273	.315	.377	.235	4.7	-0.2	112-SS	-6

Breakout: 21% Improve: 53% Collapse: 11% Attrition: 5%   MLB: 4%   Comparables: Carlos Rios, Ronny Cedeño, Pedro Ciriaco, Fred Manrique

Nunez first drew attention in 2005, when he hit .318 as an 18-year-old Low-A-baller playing against strapping college types. Three years went by during which Nunez hit .243/.286/.329. What seemed like a social promotion to Trenton turned into a shot at redemption when Nunez rediscovered how to hit. He picked the right place: Waterfront Park is a tough place to hit .322. He isn't out of the woods yet, because he won't walk, and 33 errors in 120 games means he's probably not a shortstop. If he keeps hitting .300, someone will find a place for him, but if (or when) his BABIP regresses, he has nothing to fall back on.

Ramiro Pena — SS

Bats: S Throws: R Height: 5' 11" Weight: 165 Born: July 18, 1985 Age: 24

YEAR	TEAM	LVL	AGE	PA	R	2B	3B	HR	RBI	BB	SO	SB	CS	EqBRR	AVG	OBP	SLG	EqAVG	EqOBP	EqSLG	EqA	VORP	WARP	DEFENSE			
2007	TRN	AA	21	233	23	7	1	0	10	22	33	7	3	0.7	.252	.332	.297	.246	.313	.285	.218	-0.9	1.0	54-SS	9		
2008	TRN	AA	22	506	57	20	7	2	45	41	86	8	6	-4.5	.266	.330	.357	.265	.315	.347	.235	7.8	0.6	109-SS	-3		
2009	SWB	AAA	23	180	18	9	0	2	9	18	28	5	1	0.1	.231	.310	.327	.236	.314	.338	.236	1.9	1.1	21-SS	6	11-2B	3
2009	NYA	MLB	23	121	17	6	1	1	10	5	20	4	1	0.3	.287	.317	.383	.296	.325	.391	.250	3.1	0.1	16-SS	-3	15-3B	2
2010	NYA	MLB	24	354	38	15	2	3	28	30	69	5	3	-0.6	.248	.313	.334	.250	.314	.342	.221	-1.3	0.0	76-SS	2		

Breakout: 10% Improve: 32% Collapse: 16% Attrition: 14%   MLB: 78%   Comparables: Ricky Baker, Julio Peguero, Javier Guzman, Walt Weiss

Ramiro Pena did a fine job subbing around the infield and picking up the occasional pinch-running assignment. He's a fine defender, particularly at short, but given career minor-league hitting rates of .255/.315/.320, Pena almost certainly hit over his head last year, and his chances of growing into a larger role seem almost nonexistent short of a major injury to Jeter.

Jorge Posada C Bats: S Throws: R Height: 6' 2" Weight: 215 Born: August 17, 1971 Age: 38

YEAR	TEAM	LVL	AGE	PA	R	2B	3B	HR	RBI	BB	SO	SB	CS	EqBRR	AVG	OBP	SLG	EqAVG	EqOBP	EqSLG	EqA	VORP	WARP	DEFENSE	
2007	NYA	MLB	35	589	91	42	1	20	90	74	98	2	0	-7.8	.338	.426	.543	.333	.424	.544	.327	68.5	6.9	124-C	-4
2008	NYA	MLB	36	195	18	13	1	3	22	24	38	0	0	-0.9	.268	.364	.411	.269	.369	.407	.274	8.3	0.0	26-C -6 4-1B	0
2009	NYA	MLB	37	438	55	25	0	22	81	48	101	1	0	-8.0	.285	.363	.522	.291	.368	.529	.301	37.8	3.7	88-C	-3
2010	NYA	MLB	38	348	37	16	1	12	49	41	76	1	1	-2.4	.263	.355	.445	.261	.351	.424	.269	16.7	1.6	70-C	-2

Breakout: 3% Improve: 20% Collapse: 37% Attrition: 36% MLB: 95% Comparables: Chad Kreuter, Ken Boyer, Elston Howard, Rico Carty

Offensively, Posada made a fine recovery from surgery to repair labrum and capsule damage to the shoulder of his throwing arm. His recuperation lasted well into spring training, but once the bell rang, the injury didn't keep him out of the lineup; his sole DL stay came as the result of a hamstring strain. Defense was a different story: Posada's throwing, never great to begin with, snapped back to about his career rate (28 percent caught), but a catcher who was always slow to corral pitches in the dirt now seemed positively frozen each time a ball bent near the ground. Years of catching have also caught up to him on the basepaths, where, to borrow an old line from George Brett, it takes a triple to score him from second. He was the second-worst baserunner in the majors (behind Melvin Mora) according to our Equivalent Baserunning metric. Posada is signed through 2011, and his bat should continue to carry his glove for the nonce—even Posada's .245/.327/.432 away from Yankee Stadium was above-average as catchers go.

Alex Rodriguez 3B Bats: R Throws: R Height: 6' 3" Weight: 225 Born: July 27, 1975 Age: 34

YEAR	TEAM	LVL	AGE	PA	R	2B	3B	HR	RBI	BB	SO	SB	CS	EqBRR	AVG	OBP	SLG	EqAVG	EqOBP	EqSLG	EqA	VORP	WARP	DEFENSE
2007	NYA	MLB	31	708	143	31	0	54	156	95	120	24	4	5.6	.314	.422	.645	.308	.417	.637	.343	84.4	8.9	149-3B -1
2008	NYA	MLB	32	594	104	33	0	35	103	65	117	18	3	2.9	.302	.392	.573	.301	.392	.571	.321	56.0	7.1	127-3B 9
2009	NYA	MLB	33	535	78	17	1	30	100	80	97	14	2	-0.4	.286	.402	.532	.293	.407	.537	.320	49.7	5.7	109-3B 2
2010	NYA	MLB	34	532	82	19	1	31	92	67	102	13	5	1.2	.282	.388	.532	.276	.382	.502	.303	39.4	4.4	115-3B 1

Breakout: 1% Improve: 30% Collapse: 22% Attrition: 13% MLB: 98% Comparables: Mike Schmidt, Jeff Bagwell, Johnny Bench, Harmon Killebrew

A-Rod got the barest consideration in the AL MVP voting, but think of the impact that he had. While Rodriguez was off recovering from hip surgery, the Yankees had 28 games of Cody Ransom, Ramiro Pena, and (unbelievably) Angel Berroa. That motley crew combined to hit .202/.248/.283, and the Yankees went 13-15. Rodriguez came back on May 8th; although he came back slow, he hit .322/.421/.572 over his final 83 games, with the Yankees going 58-25 in those games and 81-41 overall in his starts, a 108-win pace. Talk about absence making the heart grow fonder, but A-Rod raked into November with a .365, six-homer postseason. He's signed for another eight years and crazy amounts of dough, and it's spectacularly unlikely he'll justify every year of the contract, but for the moment, he remains one of the most valuable and essential players in the game.

Austin Romine C Bats: R Throws: R Height: 6' 2" Weight: 210 Born: November 22, 1988 Age: 21

YEAR	TEAM	LVL	AGE	PA	R	2B	3B	HR	RBI	BB	SO	SB	CS	EqBRR	AVG	OBP	SLG	EqAVG	EqOBP	EqSLG	EqA	VORP	WARP	DEFENSE
2008	CSC	A	19	436	66	24	1	10	49	25	56	3	0	-0.8	.300	.344	.437	.282	.319	.403	.250	7.0	0.0	51-C -7
2009	TAM	A+	20	481	61	28	3	13	72	29	78	11	5	-1.6	.276	.322	.441	.258	.297	.414	.245	6.9	0.3	80-C -5
2010	NYA	MLB	21	478	61	23	1	15	60	32	82	3	2	-0.6	.266	.318	.422	.265	.315	.413	.247	12.4	1.0	69-C -3

Breakout: 25% Improve: 51% Collapse: 21% Attrition: 0% MLB: 1% Comparables: Mike Nixon, John Buck, Wilson Ramos, Joe Oliver

Unlike Montero, Romine is a catching prospect who can actually catch, although he's not yet defensively polished. In the short term, he's in for a difficult time offensively, as his best tool is power, a difficult skill to show off at Trenton. However, if the cold Delaware River breezes can teach him to hold back on close pitches instead of swinging at them, he'll have accomplished something more valuable than just hitting home runs. Romine has a very good chance to start in the majors, perhaps as Posada's heir, but he's also the kind of prospect who won't bear being rushed—he needs the reps he'll get at Double-A and Triple-A to refine his game.

Kevin Russo　　2B

Bats: R　Throws: R　Height: 5' 11"　Weight: 190　Born: July 8, 1984　Age: 25

YEAR	TEAM	LVL	AGE	PA	R	2B	3B	HR	RBI	BB	SO	SB	CS	EqBRR	AVG	OBP	SLG	EqAVG	EqOBP	EqSLG	EqA	VORP	WARP	DEFENSE			
2007	TAM	A+	22	414	47	22	3	2	45	15	66	19	6	-3.3	.281	.311	.369	.257	.282	.342	.222	-2.9	1.3	102-2B	14		
2008	TRN	AA	23	298	46	17	3	2	33	23	42	8	3	0.9	.307	.363	.416	.305	.351	.404	.267	9.7	1.9	32-2B	4	25-3B	2
2009	SWB	AAA	24	406	51	18	2	5	31	42	55	13	7	-5.6	.326	.397	.431	.327	.395	.439	.290	25.1	3.0	65-2B	-1	18-3B	0
2010	NYA	MLB	25	390	44	18	2	6	34	31	72	9	4	-1.4	.272	.333	.380	.273	.333	.375	.244	5.2	1.0	87-2B	4		

Breakout: 7%　Improve: 32%　Collapse: 15%　Attrition: 6%　　MLB: 9%　　Comparables: Jeff Berblinger, William Bergolla, Freddy Sanchez, Luis Maza

Teams don't expect to get much out of 20th-round draft picks, but Russo has hit well enough in his minor-league career to suggest he could succeed as a hustling reserve in the majors. The usual caveats for would-be bench infielders apply: Russo isn't a shortstop, and with burgeoning bullpens, it's almost mandatory that a team's reserve infielder be passable there. He has also been frequently injured. One intriguing but possibly trivial aspect of Russo's game is that he has a consistent reverse split throughout his career, not doing much against southpaws. If he can continue to hit .300 against righties while learning to do what seems to come naturally to most right-handers, he could boost himself out of the afterthought category.

Nick Swisher　　RF

Bats: S　Throws: L　Height: 6' 0"　Weight: 215　Born: November 25, 1980　Age: 29

YEAR	TEAM	LVL	AGE	PA	R	2B	3B	HR	RBI	BB	SO	SB	CS	EqBRR	AVG	OBP	SLG	EqAVG	EqOBP	EqSLG	EqA	VORP	WARP	DEFENSE			
2007	OAK	MLB	26	659	84	36	1	22	78	100	131	3	2	1.7	.262	.381	.455	.267	.386	.465	.296	38.7	3.8	54-CF	-9	46-RF	1
2008	CHA	MLB	27	588	86	21	1	24	69	82	135	3	3	1.0	.219	.332	.410	.217	.332	.407	.259	10.1	-0.2	60-CF	-13	52-1B	-1
2009	NYA	MLB	28	607	84	35	1	29	82	97	126	0	0	-0.9	.249	.371	.498	.256	.376	.502	.300	37.7	3.7	118-RF	-4	12-1B	-1
2010	NYA	MLB	29	592	84	24	1	28	80	92	128	2	2	0.3	.248	.370	.470	.244	.364	.447	.282	26.2	2.7	112-RF	-1		

Breakout: 9%　Improve: 39%　Collapse: 5%　Attrition: 5%　　MLB: 98%　　Comparables: Todd Hundley, Reggie Smith, Chili Davis, Tom Tresh

Nick Swisher is not master of his mental domain. Two years ago, he hit only at home, a feat that helped chase him from the White Sox. In 2009, but for a brief September flurry, he confined his hitting to the road. He excels in working pitchers to a full count, even if he's started out the plate appearance at 0-2 (he went to a full count in 22 percent of his PAs, the fifth-highest rate in baseball), but though the team reaps some benefit from his pushing the pitcher's pitch count up, he does little hitting in those situations. Hitting with runners on is also not his bag. As a defender, he's competent but will drop the occasional can of corn because feelings of inadequacy clouded his vision. There are no external reasons for Swisher's inconsistencies. The overall offensive package is still worthwhile, and Swisher is an animated, entertaining player who changes hairstyles so often that his scalp should have its own statistical category, but if you're looking for a frustration-free ballplayer, you've come to the wrong place.

Mark Teixeira　　1B

Bats: S　Throws: R　Height: 6' 3"　Weight: 220　Born: April 11, 1980　Age: 30

YEAR	TEAM	LVL	AGE	PA	R	2B	3B	HR	RBI	BB	SO	SB	CS	EqBRR	AVG	OBP	SLG	EqAVG	EqOBP	EqSLG	EqA	VORP	WARP	DEFENSE	
2007	TEX	MLB	27	335	48	24	1	13	49	45	66	0	0	0.9	.297	.397	.524	.291	.394	.516	.308	21.3	2.5	71-1B	2
2007	ATL	MLB	27	240	38	9	1	17	56	27	46	0	0	-1.0	.317	.404	.615	.329	.417	.638	.340	25.4	2.7	53-1B	-1
2008	ATL	MLB	28	451	63	27	0	20	78	65	70	0	0	-1.2	.283	.390	.512	.296	.398	.529	.314	31.9	5.1	101-1B	13
2008	LAA	MLB	28	234	39	14	0	13	43	32	23	2	0	0.4	.358	.449	.632	.356	.449	.628	.358	28.8	3.6	49-1B	5
2009	NYA	MLB	29	707	103	43	3	39	122	81	114	2	0	-2.5	.292	.383	.565	.298	.389	.565	.318	48.7	5.3	146-1B	0
2010	NYA	MLB	30	659	96	32	2	35	115	86	106	2	0	-0.6	.294	.395	.541	.289	.389	.518	.309	43.3	5.0	143-1B	3

Breakout: 5%　Improve: 35%　Collapse: 11%　Attrition: 6%　　MLB: 99%　　Comparables: Eddie Murray, Lance Berkman, Boog Powell, Todd Helton

Unlike A-Rod, Teixeira received a great deal of respect from MVP voters, finishing second, albeit without receiving a first-place vote. He got them for all the traditional reasons, leading the league in home runs and RBI, as well as for the stability his defense brought to the infield. That last doesn't show up in metrics, perhaps because Teixeira did less throwing than in any other season of his career. (The Yankees had relatively few double-play situations, but even when the staff's high number of strikeouts is taken into account, the Yankees just weren't very good at turning two.) Still, Teixeira's graceful play stood in such vivid contrast to Jason Giambi's butchery that it was easy to believe that the Yankees had benefited from the second coming of Keith Hernandez. Tremendously strong, Teixeira utilizes an unorthodox swing, hitting off his back foot but using his great strength to muscle the ball out of the park. This raises the question of how many home runs he would hit with a more conventional weight transfer and how far they would go—miles, probably.

PITCHERS

Alfredo Aceves

| | Bats: R | Throws: R | Height: 6' 3" | Weight: 220 | Born: December 8, 1982 | Age: 27 |

YEAR	TEAM	LVL	AGE	W	L	SV	G	GS	IP	H	HR	BB	SO	GB%	BABIP	STUFF	WHIP	ERA	SIERA	DERA	EqH9	EqHR9	EqBB9	EqSO9	VORP	SN/WX
2007	MTR	MEX	24	11	5	0	18	18	106¹	96	6	33	70	—	.275	1	1.21	3.64	4.39	4.74	8.6	1.3	3.2	5.3	8.6	1.31
2008	TAM	A+	25	4	1	0	8	8	47	32	1	8	37	49%	.235	11	0.85	2.11	3.43	4.33	6.9	0.8	2.0	4.6	5.8	0.42
2008	TRN	AA	25	2	2	0	7	7	50	37	3	6	35	46%	.243	8	0.86	1.80	3.53	2.82	8.7	1.4	1.4	4.6	13.3	1.24
2008	SWB	AAA	25	2	3	0	10	8	43²	42	6	13	42	47%	.290	-6	1.26	4.12	3.42	5.29	10.2	2.2	2.8	6.0	1.0	0.28
2008	NYA	MLB	25	1	0	0	6	4	30	25	4	10	16	40%	.233	4	1.17	2.40	5.08	2.43	7.0	1.2	2.7	4.6	10.1	1.05
2009	SWB	AAA	26	2	0	0	4	4	23²	18	3	5	18	44%	.211	0	0.97	3.80	3.85	5.51	8.0	2.3	1.9	4.9	0.0	0.12
2009	NYA	MLB	26	10	1	1	43	1	84	69	10	16	69	42%	.249	12	1.01	3.54	3.52	3.62	7.3	1.0	1.5	6.5	17.4	2.66
2010	NYA	MLB	27	6	6	0	37	14	97¹	95	13	33	67	48%	.285	4	1.32	4.34	4.37	4.39	8.7	1.1	2.9	5.8	12.0	2.09

Breakout: 11% Improve: 44% Collapse: 10% Attrition: 20%   MLB: 56%   Comparables: Tim Burke, Mike Grace, Matt Guerrier, Nick Blackburn

This monument to the value of scouting the Mexican League continued to perform well for the Yankees, to the point that he was underexploited. Though "Ace" was a starter in the minors, the Yankees were hesitant to turn to him when the back end of their starting rotation was taking its lumps; when his sole start went badly, he never got another chance. Nor was Aceves used in high-leverage situations, despite his excellent control and the difficulty hitters have had hitting safely against him thus far. The only real knock on him is a league-average homer rate. Another team might see Aceves as a fourth starter, but thanks to the Yankees' newly refined taste in pitching material, he'll continue to be an overqualified middle man.

Jonathan Albaladejo

| | Bats: R | Throws: R | Height: 6' 5" | Weight: 260 | Born: October 30, 1982 | Age: 27 |

YEAR	TEAM	LVL	AGE	W	L	SV	G	GS	IP	H	HR	BB	SO	GB%	BABIP	STUFF	WHIP	ERA	SIERA	DERA	EqH9	EqHR9	EqBB9	EqSO9	VORP	SN/WX
2007	HAR	AA	24	4	3	2	21	0	36²	30	3	15	35	62%	.265	-6	1.23	4.17	3.59	5.38	8.0	1.3	3.8	6.3	0.5	-0.04
2007	COH	AAA	24	3	0	0	15	0	24	14	2	7	21	60%	.194	5	0.87	1.12	3.42	1.54	5.8	1.2	2.7	6.2	10.3	0.46
2007	WAS	MLB	24	1	1	0	14	0	14¹	7	1	2	12	63%	.171	14	0.63	1.88	2.95	1.98	4.6	0.7	1.3	6.6	5.4	0.40
2008	NYA	MLB	25	0	1	0	7	0	13²	15	1	6	13	58%	.368	12	1.54	3.95	3.74	3.46	9.7	0.7	3.5	8.3	2.9	-0.03
2009	SWB	AAA	26	3	0	11	27	0	36	25	4	3	26	69%	.204	-4	0.78	1.75	3.23	2.99	7.5	1.8	1.0	4.9	9.7	1.56
2009	NYA	MLB	26	5	1	0	32	0	34¹	41	6	16	21	65%	.313	-22	1.66	5.24	4.79	5.61	11.0	1.6	3.7	4.8	-0.4	0.17
2010	NYA	MLB	27	3	3	3	48	0	57²	57	8	22	39	60%	.285	-4	1.37	4.54	4.39	4.63	8.8	1.1	3.3	5.7	5.6	0.98

Breakout: 10% Improve: 37% Collapse: 36% Attrition: 13%   MLB: 43%   Comparables: Jose Veras, Jerry Spradlin, Scott Service, Jay Aldrich

Unless there's a lend-lease program for vowels in the offing, Albaladejo may never contribute as much to the Yankees in his extra-relief-guy spins as mop-up mauler Tyler Clippard has already contributed to the Nats. Albaladejo's slider has its moments, but command has come all too infrequently for the big Puerto Rican.

Manuel Banuelos

| | Bats: L | Throws: L | Height: 5' 10" | Weight: 155 | Born: March 13, 1991 | Age: 19 |

YEAR	TEAM	LVL	AGE	W	L	SV	G	GS	IP	H	HR	BB	SO	GB%	BABIP	STUFF	WHIP	ERA	SIERA	DERA	EqH9	EqHR9	EqBB9	EqSO9	VORP	SN/WX
2008	YAN	Rk	17	4	1	0	12	3	42	32	3	13	37	48%	.248	0	1.07	2.57	3.66	4.70	9.6	2.6	4.2	4.2	3.4	-0.19
2009	CSC	A	18	9	5	0	25	19	108	88	4	28	104	45%	.282	0	1.07	2.67	3.22	5.77	10.1	1.9	3.7	4.6	-2.9	-0.29
2010	NYA	MLB	19	4	8	0	25	16	97	111	18	45	54	45%	.301	19	1.61	6.02	5.28	6.06	10.2	1.5	3.9	4.7	-6.0	1.80

Breakout: 25% Improve: 48% Collapse: 22% Attrition: 3%   MLB: 0%   Comparables: Darren Hursey, Efrain Nieves, Kelvin Villa, Ricardo Palma

Though a baseball-loving country, Mexico doesn't export many players to the States. The land south of the Rio Grande can boast a Joakim Soria here, a Fernando Valenzuela there, but despite having nearly four times the population of Venezuela and 10 times that of the Dominican Republic, Mexico's contribution is a pittance in comparison. With Aceves and now Banuelos, the Yankees seem bent on rescuing Estados Unidos Mexicanos from its status as a scouting backwater. The quintessential undersized lefty, Banuelos has good-but-not-great velocity, topping out at 92 mph, but he has an excellent change, an evolving curve, excellent command, and a precocious understanding of the art of pitching. His ceiling isn't high, but it will find him in the majors.

Jeremy Bleich

Bats: L   Throws: L   Height: 6' 2"   Weight: 195   Born: June 18, 1987   Age: 23

YEAR	TEAM	LVL	AGE	W	L	SV	G	GS	IP	H	HR	BB	SO	GB%	BABIP	STUFF	WHIP	ERA	SIERA	DERA	EqH9	EqHR9	EqBB9	EqSO9	VORP	SN/WX
2009	TAM	A+	22	6	4	0	14	14	79^1	79	4	22	56	54%	.300	-8	1.27	3.40	4.11	5.77	10.3	1.6	3.3	3.9	-2.2	-0.36
2009	TRN	AA	22	3	6	0	13	13	65	84	6	34	60	58%	.379	-26	1.82	6.65	4.18	9.96	14.5	2.4	5.0	5.7	-29.5	-1.93
2010	NYA	MLB	23	4	10	0	24	24	113^2	151	24	58	63	50%	.334	-21	1.85	6.98	5.35	7.03	11.8	1.6	4.3	4.7	-19.3	0.61

Breakout: 20%   Improve: 54%   Collapse: 18%   Attrition: 4%   MLB: 5%   Comparables: Zachary Kroenke, Frank Gonzales, Joe Beimel, Joe Savery

Bleich put up an 8.53 ERA in six starts at Trenton last year, which, given the park's generous run-retardant effects (only four parks in organized baseball were friendlier to pitchers), is a bit like being mugged at Petco—it just shouldn't happen. So, as bad as those numbers look, they're actually worse, which is a problem, considering that the Yankees so badly bollixed up the 2008 draft that first-round supplemental pick Bleich (44th overall) was the only one of their first three picks to sign. The southpaw's fastball sits in the low 90s, which is a bit faster than on draft day, perhaps because he's further removed from his 2008 elbow problems. Despite the uptick in velocity, he's not going to overwhelm anyone and has to have command, something that vanished at Trenton.

Brian Bruney

Bats: R   Throws: R   Height: 6' 3"   Weight: 235   Born: February 17, 1982   Age: 28

YEAR	TEAM	LVL	AGE	W	L	SV	G	GS	IP	H	HR	BB	SO	GB%	BABIP	STUFF	WHIP	ERA	SIERA	DERA	EqH9	EqHR9	EqBB9	EqSO9	VORP	SN/WX
2007	NYA	MLB	25	3	2	0	58	0	50	44	5	37	39	28%	.271	-2	1.62	4.68	5.67	4.68	7.7	0.9	5.9	6.5	4.6	-0.25
2008	NYA	MLB	26	3	0	1	32	1	34^1	18	2	16	33	43%	.188	18	0.99	1.83	3.76	1.78	4.1	0.5	3.6	7.6	14.6	1.79
2009	NYA	MLB	27	5	0	0	44	0	39	36	6	23	36	37%	.275	-3	1.51	3.92	4.52	3.66	8.2	1.4	4.6	7.1	8.0	1.65
2010	WAS	MLB	28	3	3	0	58	0	57^2	50	6	32	44	37%	.272	-5	1.42	4.22	4.92	4.68	8.1	0.9	4.6	6.5	5.3	1.15

Breakout: 10%   Improve: 35%   Collapse: 27%   Attrition: 6%   MLB: 81%   Comparables: Todd Jones, Jesus Colome, Jared Burton, Hector Carrasco

Brian Cashman doesn't seem to spend a lot of time thinking about the free-talent possibilities available to his team, one of the reasons that his payrolls have been so high and his benches so weak. Bruney was the rare exception, a wild bullet-thrower signed after the D'backs discarded him. The Yankees got Bruney to work on his weight and control issues, and though he never fully conquered the latter, they got 153 games with a 3.25 ERA over four seasons. Bruney had frequent health issues and tended to get twitchy with runners on, allowing a cumulative 9.6 more inherited runs to score than the average pitcher during his time in New York, but he was otherwise effective. Traded for a Rule 5 pick, outfielder Jamie Hoffmann, Bruney jumps from the back of the Yankees' pen to the front of the Nats'.

A. J. Burnett

Bats: R   Throws: R   Height: 6' 5"   Weight: 230   Born: January 3, 1977   Age: 33

YEAR	TEAM	LVL	AGE	W	L	SV	G	GS	IP	H	HR	BB	SO	GB%	BABIP	STUFF	WHIP	ERA	SIERA	DERA	EqH9	EqHR9	EqBB9	EqSO9	VORP	SN/WX
2007	TOR	MLB	30	10	8	0	25	25	165^2	131	23	66	176	63%	.261	24	1.19	3.75	3.23	3.86	7.6	1.3	3.3	8.8	29.5	4.39
2008	TOR	MLB	31	18	10	0	35	34	221^1	211	19	86	231	58%	.314	26	1.34	4.07	3.39	4.35	8.9	0.8	3.1	8.5	28.0	5.29
2009	NYA	MLB	32	13	9	0	33	33	207	193	25	97	195	50%	.295	16	1.40	4.04	3.92	4.04	8.7	1.0	3.8	7.5	32.9	5.11
2010	NYA	MLB	33	11	11	0	32	32	193	192	25	81	175	54%	.311	18	1.42	4.57	3.85	4.65	8.8	1.0	3.5	7.6	18.1	3.05

Breakout: 6%   Improve: 38%   Collapse: 17%   Attrition: 12%   MLB: 96%   Comparables: Jason Schmidt, Jim Weaver, Kevin Millwood, Kevin Brown

When Burnett, AKA the Comeback Pie-Man, was on, he dominated with a 1.81 ERA. When he was off, he got thumped for a 7.09 ERA. The spread is not all that unusual as far as the disparities between pitchers at their best and worst last year, but seems extreme in Burnett's case because his stuff is just too good for him to be in aggregate just a few ticks above league average. The mid-90s fastball and the biting curve capable of fooling both opposing hitters and Jorge Posada seem to promise more, and quite often they do. He had 21 quality starts in 33 tries, a good success rate. There's just not a lot of middle ground; Burnett comes out of the pen with either no-hitter stuff or absolutely no feel for his pitches. Perhaps the biggest triumph of his season was that he stayed healthy. Four more years to go.

Joba Chamberlain

Bats: R   Throws: R   Height: 6' 2"   Weight: 230   Born: September 23, 1985   Age: 24

YEAR	TEAM	LVL	AGE	W	L	SV	G	GS	IP	H	HR	BB	SO	GB%	BABIP	STUFF	WHIP	ERA	SIERA	DERA	EqH9	EqHR9	EqBB9	EqSO9	VORP	SN/WX
2007	TAM	A+	21	4	0	0	7	7	40	25	0	11	51	57%	.284	36	0.90	2.02	2.13	3.50	7.5	0.5	3.3	8.8	8.0	0.67
2007	TRN	AA	21	4	2	0	8	7	40¹	32	4	15	66	53%	.354	36	1.17	3.35	1.63	4.33	10.2	2.0	3.7	10.9	4.7	0.55
2007	NYA	MLB	21	2	0	1	19	0	24	12	1	6	34	46%	.224	24	0.75	0.37	1.55	0.75	4.9	0.4	1.9	10.1	12.7	1.87
2008	NYA	MLB	22	4	3	0	42	12	100¹	87	5	39	118	59%	.324	45	1.26	2.60	2.92	2.72	7.5	0.4	3.1	9.6	30.7	4.62
2009	NYA	MLB	23	9	6	0	32	31	157¹	167	21	76	133	49%	.313	3	1.54	4.75	4.34	4.99	9.7	1.2	3.8	6.7	8.7	2.30
2010	NYA	MLB	24	9	10	0	49	27	159	156	20	67	150	54%	.312	14	1.40	4.45	3.75	4.54	8.8	1.0	3.5	8.0	17.0	3.42

Breakout: 7%   Improve: 41%   Collapse: 15%   Attrition: 6%   MLB: 98%   Comparables: Bill Gullickson, Kelvim Escobar, Frank Castillo, Mark Prior

What a mess. It's possible that no pitcher in the history of baseball has suffered through as many team-inflicted head games as Chamberlain has. Though not pitching up to expectations, he was nonetheless the club's most successful starter in the early going, posting a 3.89 ERA in 15 starts that were often shortened due to a combination of strikeouts and nibbling eating up the pitcher's strict pitch counts. A couple of rough starts heading into the All-Star break raised anxiety levels, but Chamberlain came roaring out of the hiatus, allowing just two runs in three starts comprising 21 ⅔ innings. At that point, the Yankees initiated the Joba Rules 2.0 to hold the young pitcher to no more than 160 innings on the season, skipping starts and then shortening them, which had the effect of turning Joba's starts into bad relief appearances. From the new rules' imposition onward, his ERA was 7.52, as he was so clearly rattled by the constant threat of being pulled about two minutes into the game and then not pitching again for a week that he was unable to concentrate. If the Joba Rules are in conflict with the goal of developing Chamberlain into a consistently successful major-league pitcher, then it isn't clear what the Yankees are accomplishing. The rules are supposed to be out the window for 2010, but the acquisition of Javier Vazquez is likely to push Chamberlain back to the pen and perhaps to a tacit admission that in their eagerness to spare him injury, the Yankees killed a potentially great starter with kindness.

Phil Coke

Bats: L   Throws: L   Height: 6' 1"   Weight: 210   Born: July 19, 1982   Age: 27

YEAR	TEAM	LVL	AGE	W	L	SV	G	GS	IP	H	HR	BB	SO	GB%	BABIP	STUFF	WHIP	ERA	SIERA	DERA	EqH9	EqHR9	EqBB9	EqSO9	VORP	SN/WX
2007	TAM	A+	24	7	3	0	17	16	99	93	4	37	76	54%	.305	-6	1.31	3.09	4.11	4.60	10.2	1.1	4.1	5.1	8.9	0.74
2008	TRN	AA	25	9	4	0	23	20	118¹	105	7	39	115	49%	.303	-3	1.22	2.51	3.37	4.22	10.2	1.4	3.3	6.4	15.3	1.84
2008	SWB	AAA	25	2	2	0	14	1	17¹	19	0	5	22	49%	.388	5	1.38	4.67	2.56	6.75	11.3	0.5	2.7	8.1	-2.3	0.13
2008	NYA	MLB	25	1	0	0	12	0	14²	8	0	2	14	55%	.222	14	0.68	0.61	2.57	0.63	4.4	0.0	1.3	8.2	7.8	0.82
2009	NYA	MLB	26	4	3	2	72	0	60	44	10	20	49	44%	.215	-2	1.07	4.50	3.88	4.76	6.8	1.4	2.6	6.6	4.9	1.93
2010	DET	MLB	27	3	5	0	60	5	71²	77	10	32	55	49%	.313	-6	1.52	5.00	4.46	5.05	9.4	1.1	3.7	6.4	3.5	1.61

Breakout: 18%   Improve: 45%   Collapse: 14%   Attrition: 14%   MLB: 50%   Comparables: Dave Dravecky, Gabe White, Ryan Karp, Norm Charlton

Getting traded to the Tigers as part of the Granderson deal could be a blessing for Coke. Sure, it's hard to leave behind the big city and the World Series shares, but as a fly-ball pitcher who had five of the seven home runs he allowed at home pulled to Yankee Stadium's very giving right side, he's going to be much happier at Comerica. Coke's home-run rate ranked fourth in the AL among pure relievers with over 50 innings pitched, so any reduction in that rate is going to have a big impact on a pitcher who was otherwise effective, holding lefties to .195/.218/.366. In December, Dave Dombrowski speculated that Coke could get a shot at the rotation, though he wasn't particularly successful as a starter in the minors.

Wilkin De La Rosa

Bats: L   Throws: L   Height: 6' 1"   Weight: 185   Born: February 21, 1985   Age: 25

YEAR	TEAM	LVL	AGE	W	L	SV	G	GS	IP	H	HR	BB	SO	GB%	BABIP	STUFF	WHIP	ERA	SIERA	DERA	EqH9	EqHR9	EqBB9	EqSO9	VORP	SN/WX
2007	YAN	Rk	22	1	0	0	12	0	24	20	0	11	32	42%	.364	6	1.29	2.62	2.57	4.95	11.3	1.4	5.8	7.7	1.2	-0.09
2008	CSC	A	23	7	3	0	29	8	90¹	60	2	39	110	45%	.274	6	1.10	2.29	2.82	4.61	8.2	1.2	5.2	6.7	8.0	0.46
2008	TAM	A+	23	2	1	0	3	3	16¹	12	0	5	15	54%	.267	10	1.04	1.10	3.44	3.45	7.5	0.6	3.4	5.2	3.6	0.40
2009	TAM	A+	24	1	0	0	3	3	14	9	0	4	17	54%	.273	13	0.93	1.29	2.38	2.77	6.9	0.7	3.5	7.6	3.9	0.36
2009	TRN	AA	24	4	5	0	16	16	82²	67	11	41	77	36%	.259	-32	1.31	3.48	4.11	5.53	10.2	3.3	4.9	6.1	-0.3	0.46
2010	NYA	MLB	25	4	6	0	22	13	77¹	83	14	42	56	38%	.301	-7	1.62	5.59	5.06	5.63	9.6	1.4	4.6	6.1	-1.1	1.62

Breakout: 7%   Improve: 34%   Collapse: 25%   Attrition: 8%   MLB: 8%   Comparables: Huck Flener, Brett Price, Brian Forystek, Brian Burres

Former outfielder De La Rosa has taken a right-fielder's arm and applied it to pitching, with a good low- to mid-90s fastball. His story is the same as it ever was: his command and secondary pitches reflect his late conversion and have yet to reach the same level as his fastball. Even though same-side hitters have found him difficult, he's still too wild to use as a spot reliever. He might be that unusual creature, a lefty long man. In yet another example of the wonderful things Trenton can do for a pitcher, De La Rosa had a 2.27 ERA at home and 5.14 on the road.

Michael Dunn

Bats: L   Throws: L   Height: 6' 1"   Weight: 185   Born: May 23, 1985   Age: 25

YEAR	TEAM	LVL	AGE	W	L	SV	G	GS	IP	H	HR	BB	SO	GB%	BABIP	STUFF	WHIP	ERA	SIERA	DERA	EqH9	EqHR9	EqBB9	EqSO9	VORP	SN/WX
2007	CSC	A	22	12	5	0	27	27	144²	136	14	45	138	41%	.307	-20	1.25	3.42	3.41	5.90	11.6	2.3	3.7	5.7	-5.6	-0.23
2008	TAM	A+	23	4	7	1	30	22	124²	124	10	58	118	45%	.324	-22	1.46	4.55	3.92	6.89	10.6	1.9	4.9	5.8	-17.6	-1.52
2009	TRN	AA	24	3	3	2	26	0	53¹	41	3	32	76	48%	.325	7	1.37	3.71	2.81	5.33	9.6	1.7	5.5	9.4	0.9	-0.18
2009	SWB	AAA	24	1	0	0	12	0	20	17	1	14	23	47%	.314	12	1.55	2.25	3.92	3.13	9.2	1.0	6.8	8.2	4.9	0.40
2009	NYA	MLB	24	0	0	0	4	0	4	3	1	5	5	44%	.222	4	2.00	6.75	5.03	6.75	6.8	2.3	9.0	9.0	-0.6	0.00
2010	ATL	MLB	25	3	6	0	36	8	74¹	83	11	43	62	40%	.329	-12	1.70	5.66	4.70	6.12	10.2	1.4	4.7	6.8	-5.1	1.05

Breakout: 16%   Improve: 46%   Collapse: 16%   Attrition: 29%   MLB: 10%   Comparables: Tony Mounce, Rich Hines, Todd Credeur, James Johnson

Another converted outfielder, Dunn picked up a few miles per hour when he moved to the bullpen in 2008, but all semblance of control flew out the window as well. His Arizona Fall League stint was representative: 10 innings, 10 walks, 20 strikeouts. Pitchers like Dunn still manage to get substantial work as LOOGYs, even though their managers never know who they're going to pitch to. Traded to Atlanta in the Vazquez deal, Dunn will compete for a spot in the pen but might have to bide his time in Triple-A.

Chad Gaudin

Bats: R   Throws: R   Height: 5' 10"   Weight: 190   Born: March 24, 1983   Age: 27

YEAR	TEAM	LVL	AGE	W	L	SV	G	GS	IP	H	HR	BB	SO	GB%	BABIP	STUFF	WHIP	ERA	SIERA	DERA	EqH9	EqHR9	EqBB9	EqSO9	VORP	SN/WX
2007	OAK	MLB	24	11	13	0	34	34	199¹	205	21	100	154	61%	.305	3	1.53	4.42	4.41	4.61	9.4	1.1	4.1	6.2	19.4	3.93
2008	OAK	MLB	25	5	3	0	26	6	62²	63	6	17	44	47%	.295	0	1.28	3.59	4.20	4.08	9.3	1.0	2.2	5.8	9.6	1.16
2008	CHN	MLB	25	4	2	0	24	0	27¹	29	5	10	27	39%	.312	-1	1.43	6.26	3.60	6.50	9.7	1.3	3.0	8.0	-3.0	-0.13
2009	SDN	MLB	26	4	10	0	20	19	105¹	105	7	56	105	50%	.323	3	1.53	5.13	3.96	6.30	9.7	0.9	4.1	7.0	-9.2	1.60
2009	NYA	MLB	26	2	0	0	11	6	42	41	7	20	34	48%	.274	1	1.45	3.43	4.44	3.30	8.7	1.5	3.6	6.4	10.4	1.02
2010	NYA	MLB	27	7	9	0	39	22	137	147	20	64	99	50%	.308	-3	1.54	5.18	4.63	5.26	9.5	1.1	3.9	6.1	3.7	1.65

Breakout: 12%   Improve: 44%   Collapse: 8%   Attrition: 19%   MLB: 95%   Comparables: Joel Pineiro, Shohei Tateyama, Moose Haas, Skip Lockwood

The Fireman of Atlantis. Once acquired by the Yankees, Gaudin was continually held in reserve for emergency starts that never had to be made. This was in part understandable, but the failure to give Gaudin a chance meant the preservation of Sergio Mitre in the starting rotation—the Yankees had nothing to lose by giving Gaudin a few more spins. The well-traveled righty retains his fine swing-and-miss slider; the inability to command it is what keeps him on the fringes of major-league pitching staffs.

Phil Hughes

Bats: R   Throws: R   Height: 6' 5"   Weight: 230   Born: June 24, 1986   Age: 24

YEAR	TEAM	LVL	AGE	W	L	SV	G	GS	IP	H	HR	BB	SO	GB%	BABIP	STUFF	WHIP	ERA	SIERA	DERA	EqH9	EqHR9	EqBB9	EqSO9	VORP	SN/WX
2007	SWB	AAA	21	4	1	0	5	5	28²	16	0	8	28	67%	.232	27	0.84	2.20	2.86	3.04	5.7	0.3	2.7	7.1	7.3	0.86
2007	NYA	MLB	21	5	3	0	13	13	72²	64	8	29	58	40%	.268	31	1.28	4.46	4.29	4.42	7.6	0.9	3.2	6.6	8.7	1.59
2008	SWB	AAA	22	1	0	0	6	6	29	34	2	9	31	51%	.364	13	1.48	5.90	3.28	7.07	11.9	1.0	2.9	6.8	-4.9	0.67
2008	NYA	MLB	22	0	4	0	8	8	34	43	3	15	23	45%	.348	6	1.71	6.62	4.88	6.29	10.5	0.8	3.4	5.5	-3.0	0.42
2009	SWB	AAA	23	3	0	0	3	3	19¹	17	2	3	19	51%	.283	18	1.03	1.86	2.83	2.75	9.5	2.0	1.5	7.0	5.5	0.59
2009	NYA	MLB	23	8	3	3	51	7	86	68	8	28	96	40%	.280	26	1.12	3.03	2.90	3.15	7.4	0.7	2.6	8.9	22.0	4.60
2010	NYA	MLB	24	7	5	2	34	19	103¹	95	12	41	90	48%	.291	15	1.32	4.07	3.90	4.13	8.2	0.9	3.2	7.3	15.8	2.52

Breakout: 21%   Improve: 55%   Collapse: 14%   Attrition: 12%   MLB: 100%   Comparables: Stan Williams, Fausto Carmona, Don Cardwell, Lindy McDaniel

Recalled from Scranton when Chien-Ming Wang hit the DL for the first time, Hughes made seven starts, during which Yankee Stadium treated him roughly, with five of the six home runs he allowed during his starting stint allowed there. A blowout in Baltimore upped his road ERA to 5.22, but the peripherals were good: 2.6 walks and 7.8 strikeouts per nine. The Yankees overreacted, pushing Hughes to the pen when Wang made his fleeting return. It was a miscalculation, but one that had the best possible result, as Hughes dominated pitching out of the bullpen, holding hitters to .172/.228/.228 and filling the troublesome eighth-inning "Bridge to Mo-where" role, at least until the postseason, when Hughes experienced some command problems. In the short term, the move to the pen might have been exactly what Hughes needed, but in the long term, limiting him to one-inning appearances would be wasteful. The Yankees realize this, so Hughes will try to rejoin the rotation in spring training, competing with Chamberlain (if he's not bullpen-bound) and Sergio Mitre for the final spot in the rotation.

Ian Kennedy

Bats: R   Throws: R   Height: 6' 0"   Weight: 195   Born: December 19, 1984   Age: 25

YEAR	TEAM	LVL	AGE	W	L	SV	G	GS	IP	H	HR	BB	SO	GB%	BABIP	STUFF	WHIP	ERA	SIERA	DERA	EqH9	EqHR9	EqBB9	EqSO9	VORP	SN/WX
2007	TAM	A+	22	6	1	0	11	10	63	39	2	22	72	35%	.262	32	0.97	1.29	2.67	2.26	7.4	1.0	3.9	8.1	20.0	1.98
2007	TRN	AA	22	5	1	0	9	9	48²	27	2	17	57	47%	.231	31	0.90	2.59	2.60	3.63	6.9	1.0	3.4	8.1	9.3	1.26
2007	SWB	AAA	22	1	1	0	6	6	34²	25	2	11	34	46%	.264	31	1.04	2.08	3.22	2.78	7.5	1.1	3.1	7.0	9.8	1.13
2007	NYA	MLB	22	1	0	0	3	3	19	13	1	9	15	30%	.231	19	1.16	1.89	4.76	2.84	5.7	0.5	3.8	6.6	5.6	0.68
2008	SWB	AAA	23	5	3	0	13	12	69	52	4	17	72	45%	.264	21	1.00	2.35	2.90	3.26	8.0	0.9	2.4	6.6	16.5	2.30
2008	NYA	MLB	23	0	4	0	10	9	39²	50	5	26	27	45%	.333	-8	1.92	8.17	5.40	7.68	10.3	0.9	5.0	5.5	-9.9	-0.39
2009	SWB	AAA	24	1	0	0	4	4	22²	18	0	7	25	49%	.305	21	1.10	1.59	2.84	2.95	8.4	0.4	3.0	7.6	6.0	0.66
2010	ARI	MLB	25	4	4	0	32	2	73¹	64	7	33	68	44%	.292	14	1.33	3.94	3.89	4.12	7.8	0.9	3.8	7.8	11.3	1.99

Breakout: 14%   Improve: 52%   Collapse: 22%   Attrition: 28%   MLB: 50%   Comparables: Tom Wegmann, Carlos Marmol, Doug Bochtler, David Hooten

The 2006 first-rounder pitched himself out of the organization's good graces by eschewing his pinpoint control for nibbling in his 2008 trial, getting hurt, and sometimes acting confused about the goal of his starts—Kennedy didn't seem to care if the team won or lost, so long as he got in a good workout. He redeemed himself by coming back rapidly and effectively from May surgery for the removal of an aneurysm from his pitching arm, continuing to pitch effectively in the Arizona Fall League, striking out 28 against five walks in 29 ⅔ innings. Dealt to the Diamondbacks in the three-way Granderson deal, Kennedy will have to fight his park to succeed (though no more so than had he remained a Yankee), but his low-velocity, pitch-to-spots approach should play better in the senior circuit than it ever would have in the DH league. PECOTA is being conservative; the D'backs expect him to start.

Damaso Marte

Bats: L   Throws: L   Height: 6' 2"   Weight: 215   Born: February 14, 1975   Age: 35

YEAR	TEAM	LVL	AGE	W	L	SV	G	GS	IP	H	HR	BB	SO	GB%	BABIP	STUFF	WHIP	ERA	SIERA	DERA	EqH9	EqHR9	EqBB9	EqSO9	VORP	SN/WX
2007	PIT	MLB	32	2	0	0	65	0	45¹	32	2	18	51	50%	.275	24	1.10	2.38	3.01	2.72	6.0	0.4	3.2	9.1	13.8	1.31
2008	PIT	MLB	33	4	0	5	47	0	46²	38	4	16	47	40%	.274	12	1.16	3.47	3.33	3.35	7.1	0.8	2.7	7.5	11.2	3.11
2008	NYA	MLB	33	1	3	0	25	0	18¹	14	1	10	24	23%	.295	17	1.31	5.40	3.26	4.74	6.6	0.5	4.3	9.9	1.6	0.57
2009	NYA	MLB	34	1	3	0	21	0	13¹	15	3	6	13	36%	.308	-10	1.57	9.45	4.06	8.56	9.9	2.0	3.3	7.2	-4.6	-0.02
2010	NYA	MLB	35	3	3	1	43	0	42²	38	6	18	40	38%	.285	5	1.31	4.09	3.82	4.22	7.9	1.0	3.6	8.0	6.1	1.08

Breakout: 11%   Improve: 42%   Collapse: 25%   Attrition: 18%   MLB: 84%   Comparables: Alan Embree, Arthur Rhodes, Jerry Don Gleaton, Joey Eischen

Marte ended 2008 with elbow soreness, then began 2009 with new wounds, returning from the World Baseball Classic reporting shoulder pain. He was then racked in seven appearances before heading to the DL with left-shoulder tendinitis. Four months of inactivity and rehabilitation ensued, but Marte had time for just 14 appearances and eight innings over the remainder of the season. With all his struggles, lefties went only 3-for-25 against him. He seemed like a new pitcher in the World Series, striking out five batters in 2 ⅔ innings, and looks like a good bet for a solid 2010, assuming Girardi refrains from the overuse that might have caused Marte's problems in the first place.

Zach McAllister

Bats: R   Throws: R   Height: 6' 6"   Weight: 230   Born: December 8, 1987   Age: 22

YEAR	TEAM	LVL	AGE	W	L	SV	G	GS	IP	H	HR	BB	SO	GB%	BABIP	STUFF	WHIP	ERA	SIERA	DERA	EqH9	EqHR9	EqBB9	EqSO9	VORP	SN/WX
2007	STA	A-	19	4	6	0	16	15	71¹	80	3	28	75	54%	.370	0	1.51	5.17	3.43	7.76	12.7	2.0	4.3	5.5	-16.2	-1.20
2008	CSC	A	20	6	3	0	10	10	62¹	59	3	8	53	60%	.299	14	1.07	2.45	3.18	5.81	10.4	1.6	2.0	4.2	-2.0	0.25
2008	TAM	A+	20	8	6	1	15	14	88²	74	6	13	62	50%	.259	34	0.98	1.83	3.75	3.62	8.4	1.5	1.8	4.1	17.4	1.34
2009	TRN	AA	21	7	5	0	22	22	121	98	4	33	96	47%	.266	25	1.08	2.23	3.82	4.17	8.7	1.1	2.7	4.8	16.9	1.82
2010	NYA	MLB	22	6	8	0	26	24	117²	128	18	46	66	43%	.295	8	1.48	5.05	5.09	5.14	9.7	1.2	3.2	4.8	4.7	2.46

Breakout: 8%   Improve: 50%   Collapse: 13%   Attrition: 11%   MLB: 13%   Comparables: Adam Harben, Mitchell Johnson, Matt Peterson, Matt Wright

Despite some late-season arm fatigue, McAllister boosted his standing as a solid prospect by leading the Eastern League in ERA. He doesn't have anything to brag about in the fastball department, sitting around 90 mph, but has a plus slider. His other off-speed pitches are just token offerings, which means that unless McAllister can maintain his strong command, he's going to be heading to the bullpen as a two-pitch middle reliever. For now, he'll head to Triple-A Scranton with the portfolio of a back-end starter and will await an opening, such as perhaps the imposition of the Joba Rules 3.0, which require that Chamberlain be sealed in aspic and not allowed to pitch at all.

Mark Melancon

Bats: R   Throws: R   Height: 6' 2"   Weight: 215   Born: March 28, 1985   Age: 25

YEAR	TEAM	LVL	AGE	W	L	SV	G	GS	IP	H	HR	BB	SO	GB%	BABIP	STUFF	WHIP	ERA	SIERA	DERA	EqH9	EqHR9	EqBB9	EqSO9	VORP	SN/WX
2008	TAM	A+	23	1	0	0	13	0	25¹	26	2	6	20	43%	.308	-13	1.26	2.84	3.83	4.50	10.1	1.9	2.6	4.5	2.7	0.08
2008	TRN	AA	23	6	0	2	19	0	49²	32	3	12	47	65%	.227	6	0.89	1.81	2.98	3.79	7.6	1.4	2.3	6.2	8.8	1.52
2008	SWB	AAA	23	1	1	1	12	0	20	11	1	4	22	55%	.213	14	0.75	2.70	2.43	4.03	6.2	0.9	1.9	7.1	3.1	0.21
2009	SWB	AAA	24	4	0	3	32	0	53	37	3	11	54	63%	.254	7	0.91	2.89	2.81	4.93	7.8	1.1	2.2	7.3	3.1	0.59
2009	NYA	MLB	24	0	1	0	13	0	16¹	13	0	10	10	74%	.260	-7	1.41	3.86	4.70	3.94	7.3	0.0	5.1	5.1	2.8	-0.49
2010	NYA	MLB	25	4	5	0	43	0	70¹	68	10	27	51	57%	.284	0	1.35	4.65	4.28	4.67	8.6	1.1	3.2	6.1	6.5	1.26

Breakout: 10%   Improve: 34%   Collapse: 29%   Attrition: 4%   MLB: 50%   Comparables: Nicholas Evangelista, Brian Rogers, Dan Chergey, Rodney Stevenson

Melancon possesses a low/mid-90s fastball and a wicked curve and has shown excellent control in the minor leagues, walking only two batters per nine. His control deserted him during his three brief major-league auditions—you can add four hit batters to the walks above—as he fell into nibbling. The Yankees showed very little patience, but they might have been smarter to wait a little longer, especially as they'll need to replace Phil Hughes in the late innings this year—right-handers couldn't touch Melancon, hitting .161 against him with no extra-base hits in the majors and .180 in the minors. No one can lift his stuff, which has a pronounced groundward tilt; he has allowed just nine home runs in 172 professional innings.

Sergio Mitre

Bats: R   Throws: R   Height: 6' 3"   Weight: 225   Born: February 16, 1981   Age: 29

YEAR	TEAM	LVL	AGE	W	L	SV	G	GS	IP	H	HR	BB	SO	GB%	BABIP	STUFF	WHIP	ERA	SIERA	DERA	EqH9	EqHR9	EqBB9	EqSO9	VORP	SN/WX
2007	FLO	MLB	26	5	8	0	27	27	149	180	9	41	80	71%	.328	10	1.48	4.65	4.37	4.76	9.5	0.5	2.1	4.2	12.6	1.72
2009	SWB	AAA	28	3	1	0	7	7	45	40	3	5	35	75%	.287	12	1.00	2.40	3.08	3.62	9.7	1.3	1.3	5.5	8.6	0.91
2009	NYA	MLB	28	3	3	0	12	9	51²	71	10	13	32	72%	.333	-16	1.63	6.79	4.23	7.31	12.0	1.5	1.9	4.8	-10.5	-0.58
2010	NYA	MLB	29	4	6	0	20	17	84²	99	12	27	42	47%	.309	-11	1.49	5.34	5.07	5.49	10.4	1.2	2.6	4.2	0.1	0.63

Breakout: 11%   Improve: 40%   Collapse: 9%   Attrition: 27%   MLB: 71%   Comparables: Joey Hamilton, Kelly Downs, Jason Jennings, Don Wengert

One of the reasons the front office became disenchanted with Joe Torre was that it felt he had become so enamored of his "guys" that he was no longer managing them objectively, keeping Bernie Williams in center field for longer than he was effective and failing to communicate to Jeter that his defense needed work. Joe Girardi took a small step down the same road when Mitre was retained in the starting rotation despite repeated poundings, with one quality start in nine tries. After missing time with numerous injuries, including the Tommy John surgery that kept him sidelined for all of 2008, Mitre still gets grounders with his 89-90 mph fastball. Left-handers saw through him like he was wearing pinstriped Saran wrap, going 40-for-95 against him. They say the second year back from having a TJS is when a pitcher really gets his stuff back, but Mitre never really had great stuff, the effective portion of his career coming down to a fluke first half in 2007. Still, he'll be in the mix for the last spot in the rotation.

Hector Noesi

Bats: R   Throws: R   Height: 6' 2"   Weight: 174   Born: January 26, 1987   Age: 23

YEAR	TEAM	LVL	AGE	W	L	SV	G	GS	IP	H	HR	BB	SO	GB%	BABIP	STUFF	WHIP	ERA	SIERA	DERA	EqH9	EqHR9	EqBB9	EqSO9	VORP	SN/WX
2007	CSC	A	20	1	1	0	5	5	20	25	2	8	11	42%	.329	-4	1.65	4.50	5.20	6.25	14.0	2.5	4.5	2.5	-1.5	-0.12
2008	STA	A-	21	1	1	0	5	5	24	20	5	7	31	36%	.273	-2	1.12	3.00	2.28	7.43	13.5	6.3	4.1	6.8	-4.3	-0.23
2008	YAN	Rk	21	2	1	0	9	2	24²	23	2	3	24	38%	.309	6	1.05	3.65	2.74	5.91	11.8	3.0	2.5	5.1	-1.0	-0.26
2009	CSC	A	22	3	4	0	17	11	75²	62	3	11	78	44%	.288	-3	0.96	2.38	2.59	5.01	10.2	1.9	2.5	5.1	3.6	-0.16
2009	TAM	A+	22	3	0	0	9	9	41¹	34	3	4	40	37%	.274	11	0.92	3.92	2.64	5.87	9.2	1.9	1.6	5.6	-1.6	-0.42
2010	NYA	MLB	23	3	6	0	25	17	78¹	97	17	30	51	37%	.322	-8	1.62	5.98	4.93	6.02	11.0	1.7	3.1	5.4	-4.5	1.19

Breakout: 13%   Improve: 52%   Collapse: 12%   Attrition: 8%   MLB: 1%   Comparables: Fernando Zarranz, Tim Harikkala, Mike McDougal, Todd Goergen

A new arrival on the 40-man, Noesi has seen his progress through the Yankees' system be slowed by injuries, including Tommy John surgery and a 50-game suspension for a positive performance-enhancing drug test. He appears to have been worth waiting for: Noesi has a low- to mid-90s fastball, an emerging curve, and exemplary command and control. He needs to show he can survive a grownup's workload; he has pitched a grand total of 192 ⅔ innings in four seasons. A fly-ball pitcher, he'll thrive at Trenton if healthy.

Ivan Nova

Bats: R   Throws: R   Height: 6' 4"   Weight: 210   Born: January 12, 1987   Age: 23

YEAR	TEAM	LVL	AGE	W	L	SV	G	GS	IP	H	HR	BB	SO	GB%	BABIP	STUFF	WHIP	ERA	SIERA	DERA	EqH9	EqHR9	EqBB9	EqSO9	VORP	SN/WX
2007	CSC	A	20	6	8	0	21	21	99¹	121	8	31	54	49%	.331	-23	1.53	4.98	4.87	7.82	13.9	2.0	3.7	2.8	-22.7	-1.54
2008	TAM	A+	21	8	13	0	26	24	148²	168	6	46	109	55%	.347	1	1.44	4.36	4.14	6.68	11.6	1.3	3.5	4.4	-17.7	-1.93
2009	TRN	AA	22	5	4	0	12	12	72¹	65	3	31	47	68%	.279	-2	1.33	2.36	4.30	4.70	9.8	1.3	4.0	3.9	5.9	0.50
2009	SWB	AAA	22	1	4	0	12	12	67	72	4	28	43	57%	.318	-8	1.49	5.10	4.68	6.71	11.4	1.2	4.3	4.4	-8.2	-0.33
2010	NYA	MLB	23	4	8	0	25	23	111²	139	19	55	56	47%	.319	-18	1.74	6.35	5.52	6.43	11.1	1.3	4.1	4.2	-11.6	1.02

Breakout: 19%   Improve: 55%   Collapse: 13%   Attrition: 19%   MLB: 10%   Comparables: Darrell Goedhart, Randy Veres, Ben Rivera, Joe Foote

Ivan Nova made it to the 40-man roster in December, a year after being temporarily hijacked by the Padres in the 2008 Rule 5 draft. He represents the Portrait of the Back-End Starter (or Middle-Reliever) as a Young Man. Nothing in particular stands out about him except for a surname that indicates an exploding star or a particularly tasty form of smoked salmon. He possesses a low-90s fastball, a curve, a change, and not quite enough stuff or command to be more exciting than lox. Imagine it: a fresh-baked bagel, a light spread of cream cheese, and some tangy, salty Nova salmon. Wouldn't that just hit the spot about now?

Andy Pettitte

Bats: L   Throws: L   Height: 6' 5"   Weight: 225   Born: June 15, 1972   Age: 38

YEAR	TEAM	LVL	AGE	W	L	SV	G	GS	IP	H	HR	BB	SO	GB%	BABIP	STUFF	WHIP	ERA	SIERA	DERA	EqH9	EqHR9	EqBB9	EqSO9	VORP	SN/WX
2007	NYA	MLB	35	15	9	0	36	34	215¹	238	16	69	141	55%	.322	13	1.43	4.05	4.43	4.07	9.8	0.6	2.7	5.6	33.2	5.54
2008	NYA	MLB	36	14	14	0	33	33	204	233	19	55	158	60%	.333	17	1.41	4.54	3.91	4.51	9.6	0.8	2.1	6.4	22.3	3.08
2009	NYA	MLB	37	14	8	0	32	32	194²	193	20	76	148	48%	.295	11	1.38	4.16	4.33	4.39	9.1	0.9	3.1	6.1	23.5	4.61
2010	NYA	MLB	38	10	11	0	33	32	180	197	23	64	116	52%	.310	2	1.45	4.70	4.58	4.86	9.8	1.0	3.0	5.5	12.7	2.43

Breakout: 1%   Improve: 29%   Collapse: 14%   Attrition: 18%   MLB: 99%   Comparables: Al Leiter, Chuck Finley, Jerry Koosman, Frank Tanana

The Yankees have had many inner-circle Hall of Famers on offense—Ruth, Gehrig, DiMaggio, Mantle, and so on—but the club has never had a pitcher put together an equivalent career. Many pitchers were excellent for a period of years, but none stuck around long enough to win 300 or even 250 games. Whitey Ford's franchise-record 236 wins have stood for 33 years and aren't falling anytime soon, nor will number two Red Ruffing (231) be heading down the list this year. Third place, though, will be in a constant state of flux, because Andy Pettitte has rejoined the Yankees for another season. The venerable Louisianan put together another season roughly consistent with his career norms, and if his stuff and command weren't quite what they had been in 2008, the improved Yankees defense gave back some of what it had taken away the previous two seasons. He posted a 3.71 ERA on the road versus 4.59 at home, with 14 of his 20 homers allowed coming at the new ballpark, perhaps due to an ill-timed leap in his fly-ball rate. Pettitte seems a safe bet to give the Yankees another year of solid if unspectacular keep-'em-in-the-game pitching.

Mariano Rivera

Bats: R   Throws: R   Height: 6' 2"   Weight: 185   Born: November 29, 1969   Age: 40

YEAR	TEAM	LVL	AGE	W	L	SV	G	GS	IP	H	HR	BB	SO	GB%	BABIP	STUFF	WHIP	ERA	SIERA	DERA	EqH9	EqHR9	EqBB9	EqSO9	VORP	SN/WX
2007	NYA	MLB	37	3	4	30	67	0	71¹	68	4	12	74	62%	.322	26	1.12	3.15	2.81	2.96	8.3	0.5	1.4	8.5	20.1	3.77
2008	NYA	MLB	38	6	5	39	64	0	70²	41	4	6	77	58%	.218	43	0.67	1.40	2.11	1.39	4.8	0.4	0.6	8.6	32.6	6.42
2009	NYA	MLB	39	3	3	44	66	0	66¹	48	7	12	72	68%	.248	27	0.90	1.76	2.50	1.92	6.6	1.0	1.4	8.5	26.1	6.32
2010	NYA	MLB	40	4	3	22	58	0	57¹	50	7	15	54	61%	.287	13	1.14	3.53	3.19	3.59	7.8	0.9	2.1	7.9	12.2	2.96

Breakout: 8%   Improve: 25%   Collapse: 35%   Attrition: 12%   MLB: 97%   Comparables: Larry Andersen, Marv Grissom, Stu Miller, Dennis Eckersley

Rivera has had an entry in every edition of this book. Superlatives we have employed: "something special" (1996); "amazing ... the most important player in baseball" (1997); "completely unhittable" (2000); "the best closer of his generation" (2002); "otherworldly" (2004); "a one-trick pony [but] the best of all time" (2005); "splendid ... like *Fort Apache: The Lead*" (2006); "the by-acclamation Greatest Closer of All Time" (2008); "the closest thing baseball has to Fred Astaire" (2009). Get the picture? The only question is when it will all end. Girardi was very careful to keep Rivera healthy, using him to get more than three outs only a handful of times and for two innings just once during the regular season and then turning him loose during the postseason. Rivera was again brilliant with the season on the line (16 innings, one run). The great man's velocity was down slightly last year, his great control is sometimes just a bit off, but you can't find evidence of either in the results. Rivera's contract is up at the end of the season, but he says he wants to continue. He has shut down everyone else, so why not Father Time?

David Robertson

Bats: R　Throws: R　Height: 5' 11"　Weight: 180　Born: April 9, 1985　Age: 25

YEAR	TEAM	LVL	AGE	W	L	SV	G	GS	IP	H	HR	BB	SO	GB%	BABIP	STUFF	WHIP	ERA	SIERA	DERA	EqH9	EqHR9	EqBB9	EqSO9	VORP	SN/WX
2007	CSC	A	22	5	2	3	24	0	47	25	0	15	67	63%	.248	27	0.85	0.77	1.94	1.94	7.0	0.8	3.5	8.4	17.4	1.16
2007	TAM	A+	22	3	1	1	18	0	33¹	18	0	15	37	60%	.234	15	0.99	1.08	3.04	2.67	6.5	0.6	4.7	7.4	9.5	0.56
2008	TRN	AA	23	0	0	2	9	0	18²	8	0	6	26	49%	.229	17	0.75	0.96	1.73	1.89	5.9	0.5	3.2	9.2	6.7	0.78
2008	SWB	AAA	23	4	0	1	21	0	35	20	1	17	51	57%	.250	22	1.06	2.06	2.40	3.76	6.5	0.5	4.4	9.1	6.7	1.21
2008	NYA	MLB	23	4	0	0	25	0	30¹	29	3	15	36	40%	.338	18	1.45	5.34	3.27	4.80	8.4	0.9	3.9	9.9	2.3	0.83
2009	SWB	AAA	24	0	3	2	8	0	14²	10	0	6	25	48%	.357	13	1.09	1.84	1.42	5.74	8.8	0.7	4.1	11.5	-0.4	0.21
2009	NYA	MLB	24	2	1	1	45	0	43²	36	4	23	63	44%	.320	21	1.35	3.30	2.62	3.68	8.0	0.8	4.1	10.4	8.9	0.22
2010	NYA	MLB	25	4	3	1	49	0	67	59	8	35	66	46%	.295	9	1.41	4.21	3.88	4.24	7.8	0.9	4.3	8.3	9.4	1.54

Breakout: 13%　Improve: 46%　Collapse: 24%　Attrition: 8%　　MLB: 71%　　Comparables: Darrin Chapin, Carlos Guevara, Buddy Hernandez, Steve Olin

Justin Verlander led the AL in strikeout rate with 10 per nine among qualifiers, but in the 40 IP minimum category, Robertson (and his curveball) led with 13. Despite this, Girardi was slow to embrace him, spending almost half his appearances on games in which the team was behind and abandoning him in the postseason, although the manager alibied this lapse by suggesting that the elbow tightness that shelved Robertson in September was still causing problems. Assuming health, Robertson is a front-running candidate for the coveted set-up role, though his command needs to improve before the team will fully trust him.

CC Sabathia

Bats: L　Throws: L　Height: 6' 7"　Weight: 290　Born: July 21, 1980　Age: 29

YEAR	TEAM	LVL	AGE	W	L	SV	G	GS	IP	H	HR	BB	SO	GB%	BABIP	STUFF	WHIP	ERA	SIERA	DERA	EqH9	EqHR9	EqBB9	EqSO9	VORP	SN/WX
2007	CLE	MLB	26	19	7	0	34	34	241	238	20	37	209	52%	.311	30	1.14	3.21	3.26	3.35	8.6	0.8	1.3	7.2	56.4	6.65
2008	CLE	MLB	27	6	8	0	18	18	122¹	117	13	34	123	49%	.311	27	1.23	3.83	3.16	3.88	8.4	1.0	2.2	8.3	21.7	3.35
2008	MIL	MLB	27	11	2	0	17	17	130²	106	6	25	128	58%	.283	42	1.00	1.65	2.92	2.41	7.8	0.4	1.6	7.6	43.6	5.50
2009	NYA	MLB	28	19	8	0	34	34	230	197	18	67	197	50%	.277	29	1.15	3.37	3.65	3.56	7.9	0.7	2.3	6.8	48.5	6.85
2010	NYA	MLB	29	15	10	0	32	32	219²	206	24	55	183	51%	.295	25	1.19	3.66	3.58	3.79	8.4	0.9	2.1	7.1	41.8	4.41

Breakout: 6%　Improve: 44%　Collapse: 13%　Attrition: 5%　　MLB: 99%　　Comparables: Chuck Finley, Aaron Harang, John Lackey, Denny Neagle

A slow first month saw Sabathia struggle with command and post an indifferent strikeout rate, raising the specter of past workloads diminishing another Yankee free-agent signee. That's how free agency often works: the originating team gets the production, the signing team gets the reputation. But Sabathia kicked it into gear after that; if his excellent post-season work is included, from May on, Sabathia went 22-7 with a 2.84 ERA in 34 starts, striking out 7.7 per nine, walking 2.3, and relying on his terrific fastball more than he had in recent years. The huge number of decisions combined with the 266 ⅓ innings the burly southpaw threw between the regular and postseasons (the third straight season he was over 250 innings) suggests Sabathia's workhorse nature. It's not so much that he's abused, as he shows up for every start and works deep into games, averaging just under seven innings and 105 pitches per start. He has handled it before and seems a safe bet to do so again, but this could always be the year that he doesn't.

Romulo Sanchez

Bats: R | Throws: R | Height: 6' 5" | Weight: 260 | Born: April 28, 1984 | Age: 26

YEAR	TEAM	LVL	AGE	W	L	SV	G	GS	IP	H	HR	BB	SO	GB%	BABIP	STUFF	WHIP	ERA	SIERA	DERA	EqH9	EqHR9	EqBB9	EqSO9	VORP	SN/WX
2007	ALT	AA	23	6	3	1	40	0	57²	43	8	17	52	54%	.224	-6	1.04	2.81	3.50	4.39	7.5	1.9	2.9	5.9	6.9	-0.61
2007	PIT	MLB	23	1	0	0	16	0	18	16	2	8	11	57%	.275	-9	1.33	5.00	4.76	4.59	8.1	1.1	3.8	5.4	1.7	0.01
2008	IND	AAA	24	5	1	4	33	0	54²	50	5	19	32	49%	.268	-26	1.26	3.46	4.77	5.29	9.4	1.4	3.4	3.7	1.2	0.51
2008	PIT	MLB	24	0	0	1	10	0	13¹	14	0	6	3	51%	.298	-30	1.50	4.05	6.33	3.91	9.2	0.0	3.6	1.4	2.2	0.10
2009	IND	AAA	25	1	0	0	10	0	12¹	11	1	5	15	61%	.323	4	1.30	4.38	2.92	5.40	9.3	1.5	3.9	8.5	0.1	0.06
2009	SWB	AAA	25	5	5	0	19	13	64²	66	3	34	64	48%	.337	-3	1.55	4.04	4.00	5.64	10.8	1.0	5.0	7.0	-0.9	0.39
2010	NYA	MLB	26	3	5	1	50	0	72	75	11	34	47	47%	.292	-11	1.52	5.36	4.89	5.45	9.3	1.2	3.9	5.5	0.4	0.59

Breakout: 19%   Improve: 44%   Collapse: 23%   Attrition: 17%   MLB: 85%   Comparables: Ryan Halla, Rich Thompson, Austin Coose, Marc Pisciotta

This massive steamer failed to make port with the Pirates and was swapped to the Yankees for the DFA'd Eric Hacker. Sanchez had long ago been consigned to the bullpen by Pittsburgh, but the Yankees pressed him into the rotation at Scranton and he held his own, showing a vastly improved fastball. Sanchez is wild, and his fastball is pretty much all that's worth writing about, but it was enough to get him protected on the 40-man roster this winter. The 9.2 strikeouts per nine Sanchez achieved last year was a career high; if he holds on to his newfound velocity, he's a dark horse candidate for the bullpen.

Jose Valdez

Bats: R | Throws: R | Height: 6' 4" | Weight: 186 | Born: January 22, 1983 | Age: 27

YEAR	TEAM	LVL	AGE	W	L	SV	G	GS	IP	H	HR	BB	SO	GB%	BABIP	STUFF	WHIP	ERA	SIERA	DERA	EqH9	EqHR9	EqBB9	EqSO9	VORP	SN/WX
2007	TAM	A+	24	3	4	3	37	0	59²	54	4	21	60	49%	.301	-11	1.26	2.87	3.38	4.45	9.9	1.5	3.9	6.5	6.5	-0.17
2008	TAM	A+	25	6	2	3	27	0	36	30	4	9	32	59%	.271	-16	1.08	2.75	3.29	4.73	9.2	2.2	3.1	5.6	2.8	0.12
2008	TRN	AA	25	1	0	4	17	0	24¹	17	4	7	23	54%	.213	-10	0.99	2.22	3.26	3.89	9.0	3.3	2.9	6.1	3.9	0.59
2009	TRN	AA	26	1	1	10	34	0	38¹	32	2	23	42	60%	.297	-8	1.43	3.05	3.70	5.50	9.5	1.5	5.5	6.8	0.0	0.35
2009	SWB	AAA	26	2	1	0	9	0	19¹	23	2	10	18	52%	.375	-8	1.71	4.19	4.10	5.29	13.2	2.1	5.3	6.9	0.4	-0.45
2010	HOU	MLB	27	2	4	3	43	0	54¹	60	9	27	41	52%	.316	-13	1.60	5.42	4.55	5.76	10.0	1.4	4.2	6.3	-1.6	0.75

Breakout: 14%   Improve: 45%   Collapse: 30%   Attrition: 13%   MLB: 10%   Comparables: Jack Hardy, Joe Ausanio, Jeff Plympton, Josh Perrault

Valdez had been in the Yankees organization since 2002, but injuries kept him in A-ball until 2008. He throws in the low 90s with deception, but that's a double-edged word, as the deception is created by miserable mechanics, also the cause of the aforementioned injuries. After a terrific showing in the Dominican winter league (including two walks in 21 innings), the Astros signed him to a free-agent contract and will give him a 40-man roster spot and a shot at the back of their bullpen.

Arodys Vizcaino

Bats: R | Throws: R | Height: 6' 0" | Weight: 189 | Born: November 13, 1990 | Age: 19

YEAR	TEAM	LVL	AGE	W	L	SV	G	GS	IP	H	HR	BB	SO	GB%	BABIP	STUFF	WHIP	ERA	SIERA	DERA	EqH9	EqHR9	EqBB9	EqSO9	VORP	SN/WX
2008	YAN	Rk	17	3	2	0	12	6	44	38	5	13	48	39%	.277	2	1.16	3.68	2.99	6.69	11.1	3.6	4.1	5.7	-5.3	-0.63
2009	STA	A-	18	2	4	0	10	10	42¹	34	2	15	52	53%	.294	12	1.16	2.13	2.75	6.93	11.7	2.7	4.9	6.1	-5.9	-0.26
2010	ATL	MLB	19	3	6	0	19	15	76	94	16	42	59	46%	.335	27	1.80	6.41	4.77	6.92	11.3	2.0	4.5	6.3	-12.0	1.02

Breakout: 25%   Improve: 57%   Collapse: 18%   Attrition: 6%   MLB: 0%   Comparables: Marcos Sandoval, Rod Poissant, Tim Scott, Sergio Valdez

The Yankees might someday have had A-Rod and Arodys on the same team, but instead Vizcaino became the key prospect in the Javier Vazquez trade. Vizcaino has terrific velocity for a teen, reaching 95 mph, and a plus curve. Look at the equivalent stats to the right, not his untranslated numbers, because the New York-Penn League is a nice place to pitch. More important are Vizcaino's physical capabilities and his ability to more than hold his own in a league littered with college hitters fresh off campus. Low-A and the injury gauntlet comes next. At least he now will pitch for an organization that has an excellent track record of developing pitchers, a club 100 percent less likely to come up with anything as innovative and pointless as the Arodys Rules. Still, many a great young arm has been shredded before reaching Double-A, so don't look for Vizcaino until you see him coming.

Chien-Ming Wang

Bats: R   Throws: R   Height: 6' 3"   Weight: 225   Born: March 31, 1980   Age: 30

YEAR	TEAM	LVL	AGE	W	L	SV	G	GS	IP	H	HR	BB	SO	GB%	BABIP	STUFF	WHIP	ERA	SIERA	DERA	EqH9	EqHR9	EqBB9	EqSO9	VORP	SN/WX
2007	NYA	MLB	27	19	7	0	30	30	199¹	199	9	59	104	66%	.295	18	1.29	3.70	4.50	3.52	8.8	0.4	2.5	4.5	42.1	6.12
2008	NYA	MLB	28	8	2	0	15	15	95	90	4	35	54	62%	.281	21	1.32	4.07	4.69	3.87	7.7	0.3	2.9	4.7	17.3	2.46
2009	NYA	MLB	29	1	6	0	12	9	42	66	7	19	29	70%	.396	-24	2.02	9.64	4.53	9.18	14.4	1.5	3.8	5.5	-16.6	-0.74
2010	NYA	MLB	30	5	5	0	19	12	83¹	86	10	33	45	64%	.289	-3	1.43	4.59	4.72	4.71	9.3	1.0	3.3	4.6	7.3	1.31

Breakout: 14%   Improve: 48%   Collapse: 19%   Attrition: 29%   MLB: 81%   Comparables: Mike Thurman, Storm Davis, Mike Morgan, Ron Herbel

Wang has had two lost years already, and the bad news is that his time in the wilderness isn't yet over. Having lost more than half of 2008 to a Lisfranc (midfoot) injury, Wang noisily derailed his 2009 with shoulder problems that required season-ending surgery. With rehabilitation efforts having put off the surgery until July, Wang might not be ready to pitch until after Opening Day. The Yankees, wisely deciding not to let a wounded pitcher take them to arbitration, nontendered Wang in December. The result is a scenario in which Wang might not even sign with another club until after a Freddy Garcia–style rehab-and-scones series of brunch auditions for interested clubs. What they'll see is anyone's guess. Wang's velocity was quite good even with the injury; it was lost command that was his undoing. Wang has always been unusual, a hard-throwing, pitch-to-contact, righty sinkerballer, so the form of his recovery is harder to predict than that of a more generic hurler.

LINEOUTS

Hitters

PLAYER	TEAM	LVL	AGE	PA	R	2B	3B	HR	RBI	BB	SO	SB-CS	EqBRR	AVG/OBP/SLG	EqAVG/EqOBP/EqSLG	EqA	VORP	WARP
OF A. Almonte#	CSC	A	20	484	63	14	10	5	56	35	81	36-5	1.8	.280/.333/.391	.257/.301/.355	.234	-1.5	-0.4
SS R. Corona#	TRN	AA	22	368	56	21	2	3	26	56	50	12-4	0.5	.287/.397/.397	.290/.383/.410	.282	19.6	1.5
	SWB	AAA	22	177	13	7	0	3	14	9	20	4-0	0.8	.200/.241/.300	.205/.246/.311	.202	-3.9	-1.1
RF S. Duncan	SWB	AAA	29	527	85	30	1	30	99	64	94	2-0	-1.0	.277/.370/.546	.265/.350/.498	.288	23.2	2.8
OF F. Guzman#	TAC	AAA	28	45	5	2	1	0	3	2	5	4-2	-0.7	.214/.244/.310	.190/.222/.286	.176	-2.4	-0.1
	PAW	AAA	28	231	25	6	2	2	10	13	35	21-7	1.2	.229/.272/.304	.208/.249/.278	.191	-9.7	-0.8
	NOR	AAA	28	79	7	1	1	0	3	5	9	13-0	2.1	.192/.241/.233	.189/.228/.230	.190	-4.0	-0.4
OF N. Medchill*	STA	A-	22	244	42	13	2	14	41	24	66	7-2	-0.9	.278/.350/.551	.227/.276/.387	.229	-3.7	-1.4
OF M. Mesa	CSC	A	22	564	76	24	7	20	74	51	168	18-6	2.2	.225/.309/.423	.206/.268/.340	.212	-16.0	-2.5
INF C. Ransom	NYA	MLB	33	86	11	9	1	0	10	7	25	2-0	0.4	.190/.256/.329	.190/.256/.316	.211	-2.4	-0.6
	SWB	AAA	33	120	24	7	1	3	16	19	22	0-0	0.8	.240/.367/.427	.235/.350/.418	.273	5.2	0.3
2/O D. Sublett*	TAM	A+	23	473	68	24	11	4	41	65	93	11-7	-1.2	.270/.376/.416	.246/.335/.380	.252	8.5	-1.0
1B J. Vazquez	TRN	AA	27	238	30	15	1	13	56	8	45	0-0	-1.0	.329/.357/.578	.275/.297/.441	.251	-2.6	-1.0

Abraham Almonte has a center fielder's tool kit and made some strides in repeating the Sally League, but will need to further refine his strike-zone judgment if he's going to make it. ⊘ **Reegie Corona**'s plate judgment took a small step forward at Trenton and his bat took a giant step back at Scranton. Nonetheless, he claimed a spot on the 40-man this winter. ⊘ The International League MVP, **Shelley Duncan** could provide Cleveland with part of a low-cost DH platoon with his lefty-mashing power. ⊘ The Yankees added **Freddy Guzman** to the post-season roster to be their New Millennium Herb Washington, then discovered that there's a huge opportunity cost to simultaneously carrying a designated pinch-runner and an overstuffed bullpen—your track star ends up not just running, but hitting. ⊘ The system hasn't produced an impact outfielder since Bernie Williams, but **Slade Heathcott**, the Yankees' top pick in 2009, is their latest attempt. He features great raw power and a history of inactivity due to injuries and bad behavior. ⊘ A 2009 11th-rounder out of Oklahoma State, **Neil Medchill** broke short-season Staten Island's record for homers, but it's best not to get too excited—the previous record-holder was Mitch Jones. ⊘ **Melky Mesa** has a name Russ Meyer would have loved and all the tools in the world, but he needs to figure out how to hit something other than fastballs. ⊘ **Cody Ransom** proved his September '08 was a fluke while standing in for the injured A-Rod, though he was injured himself, which landed him on the DL. He has been signed to a minor-league contract with the Phillies. ⊘ Getting moved to center field in the second half might give **Damon Sublett** a new lease on prospectdom, and he hit .290/.387/.451 against right-handers. ⊘ Another product of the Yankees' exploration of the Mexican League, veteran **Jorge Vazquez** slugged over .650 away from a tough Trenton ballpark, but his walk rate makes Shawon Dunston look like Wade Boggs.

Pitchers

PLAYER	TEAM	LVL	AGE	W	L	SV	IP	H	HR	BB	SO	GB%	BABIP	STUFF	WHIP	ERA	SIERA	DERA	EqH9	EqHR9	EqBB9	EqSO9	VORP
A. Brackman	CSC	A	23	2	12	0	106²	106	8	76	103	53%	.325	-55	1.71	5.91	4.40	10.72	12.9	3.1	9.0	4.7	-52.6
C. Garcia	TRN	AA	23	2	0	0	25¹	15	1	17	24	63%	.222	16	1.26	0.71	4.07	1.90	7.2	1.1	6.1	6.1	9.5
A. Horne	CSC	A	26	0	1	0	18	17	1	11	13	53%	.291	-23	1.56	5.50	4.87	9.77	11.5	2.3	7.5	2.9	-7.4
	TRN	AA	26	0	3	0	15¹	25	3	16	13	58%	.386	-40	2.67	11.15	5.48	16.50	17.4	4.2	9.0	4.8	-18.3
	YAN	Rk	26	4	0	0	28¹	23	2	10	22	—	.253	-27	1.16	2.86	4.09	5.36	11.8	3.3	4.8	3.7	0.4
K. Igawa*	SWB	AAA	29	10	8	0	145¹	165	21	40	105	38%	.313	-42	1.41	4.15	4.35	5.96	12.3	2.6	2.8	5.0	-6.8
G. Kontos	TRN	AA	24	1	1	0	20¹	19	0	9	24	41%	.317	10	1.38	2.66	3.33	4.29	9.4	0.4	3.9	6.9	2.8
	SWB	AAA	24	3	4	0	51	44	6	21	39	49%	.253	-12	1.27	3.35	4.35	5.49	9.3	2.0	3.9	5.2	0.0
Z. Kroenke*	SWB	AAA	25	7	1	4	72¹	54	4	30	55	54%	.246	-9	1.16	1.99	4.24	4.03	8.1	1.1	4.2	5.4	10.9
D. Mitchell	CSC	A	22	4	1	0	37	31	1	6	42	61%	.316	11	1.00	1.95	2.36	6.54	10.6	1.7	2.8	5.8	-3.7
	TAM	A+	22	8	6	0	103¹	93	1	38	83	71%	.306	6	1.27	2.87	3.54	5.43	9.6	0.9	4.3	4.7	0.7
D. Phelps	CSC	A	22	10	3	0	112²	117	9	25	90	52%	.320	-48	1.26	2.80	3.67	6.51	13.1	3.1	3.5	3.8	-10.7
	TAM	A+	22	3	1	0	38¹	34	1	6	32	57%	.295	14	1.04	1.17	3.25	3.57	9.4	1.0	2.0	4.8	7.6
E. Ramirez	SWB	AAA	28	1	5	4	51	39	3	16	62	48%	.288	10	1.08	3.18	2.52	4.50	8.4	1.1	3.2	8.6	5.3
	NYA	MLB	28	0	0	0	22	25	6	18	22	41%	.297	-4	1.95	5.73	4.87	5.67	9.8	2.3	6.3	7.4	-0.4
J. Schmidt	TRN	AA	26	8	4	0	83²	57	2	38	96	51%	.275	9	1.14	1.61	3.12	2.73	8.0	0.9	4.3	7.3	23.8
K. Texeira	TRN	AA	23	9	6	2	101¹	90	7	43	88	67%	.284	-23	1.31	2.84	3.73	4.82	10.0	1.8	4.0	5.3	7.1
J. Towers	SWB	AAA	32	7	6	0	101²	89	13	24	55	53%	.247	-26	1.11	2.74	4.57	3.86	9.7	2.3	2.5	3.8	16.7
P. Venditte	CSC	A	24	2	2	20	30²	24	1	2	40	52%	.315	-1	0.85	1.47	1.53	4.33	10.3	1.7	1.7	6.7	3.5
	TAM	A+	24	2	0	2	36²	37	1	9	47	36%	.379	4	1.25	2.21	2.20	4.36	11.2	1.1	3.0	7.9	4.2
K. Whelan	TRN	AA	25	4	0	2	54²	38	1	28	63	53%	.289	7	1.21	2.63	3.22	4.01	8.2	0.7	4.9	7.7	8.1
	SWB	AAA	25	0	0	1	12²	7	0	13	22	57%	.304	12	1.58	2.84	3.12	3.75	6.8	0.8	9.8	11.3	2.3

The most wrong-headed first-round pitching selection since Bill Bene, Tommy John surgery survivor **Andrew Brackman** was healthy enough to completely destroy any remaining illusions about his being a prospect at all—mechanical consistency is no more than a concept. ⊘ **Christian Garcia** has terrific stuff, racking up 9.8 K/9 in a minor-league career going back to 2004, but he's incapable of staying healthy. ⊘ **Alan Horne** had the pitches to succeed in the majors, but hasn't been healthy since 2007, and it's hard to know what he has left or if he can stay off the shelf long enough to use it. ⊘ Under contract through 2011 and due another $8 million, **Kei Igawa** is not the world's worst pitcher, at least not when he's in the minors. ⊘ Tommy John surgery will keep **George Kontos** shelved until sometime after spring training; when healthy, he has back-end-rotation potential with three breaking pitches, the best of which is his slider. ⊘ Low-velocity lefty **Zach Kroenke** is a Rule 5 selection for two years in a row: the Marlins took him in December 2008, and the D'backs took him this time around. The Snakes need south-paws, so Kroenke might stick, but if not, he would have the option of becoming a free agent rather than returning to the Yankees. ⊘ **D. J. Mitchell**, a 2008 10th-rounder the Yankees went over-slot to sign, is an android sent back from the future on a mission to generate ground balls. ⊘ Keep a weather eye on **David Phelps**, a 2008 14th-rounder out of Notre Dame; excellent command has made him a man among boys thus far, which is both a compliment and a condemnation. ⊘ **Edwar Ramirez**'s changeup remains a thing of beauty, but he lacks the command to set it up properly, resulting in what is colloquially referred to as "batting practice." ⊘ Yes, **Josh Schmidt** is a side-armer, and no, no one takes him seriously because of that, but the guy has been crazy-effective and righty hitters can't touch him—that should have some value to someone, somewhere. ⊘ Coming over to the Yankees in the Swisher trade, **Kanekoa Texeira** has a fine slider, but control remains a bridge too far; Rule 5'd to the Mariners in December. ⊘ Journeyman **Josh Towers** took his fine control and lack of strikeout stuff to the Dodgers on a minor-league contract. ⊘ Ambidextrous pitcher **Pat Venditte** has dominated at the lower levels but is still looked on as a novelty. If he falters at all, the naysayers will be confirmed; unfortunately, winter ball gave the doubters another bullet. ⊘ **Kevin Whelan**'s profile is as fixed as the Rock of Gibraltar: he throws hard but has no idea where the ball is going. Effectiveness in spite of that should earn him a shot, though probably not with this organization.

MANAGER: JOE GIRARDI

YEAR	TEAM	W-L	Pythag +/−	Avg PC	100+ P	120+ P	QS	BQS	REL	REL w Zero R	IBB	Subs	PH	PH Avg	PH HR	SB2	CS2	SB3	CS3	SAC Att	SAC %	POS SAC	Squeeze	Swing	In Play
2008	NYA	89-73	1	90.7	44	0	77	4	474	320	37	55	97	.256	4	107	36	11	3	39	79.5%	29	0	173	136
2009	NYA	103-59	6	96.8	79	4	74	4	461	304	28	58	97	.237	3	99	26	12	1	49	63.3%	28	0	145	108

If there was a positive to the disappointing year that was 2008, it was that Girardi, in many ways still a managing neophyte, got a chance to learn on the job. To his credit, he grew up a great deal. By 2009, the paranoia in dealing with the media and the reflexive dishonesty about injuries were gone, replaced by a sunnier public persona. During the regular season, Girardi was an unobtrusive strategist. With seven lefties and switch-hitters in the starting lineup, Girardi didn't have to think too hard about maintaining a platoon advantage on offense. He didn't indulge too much in one-run strategies, his one crutch being the hit-and-run. Girardi sometimes doesn't think far enough ahead, and his major-league-leading use of pinch-runners sometimes came back to bite him when he found himself under-manned late in games (a scenario played out with Freddy Guzman during the postseason). This same failure to think an inning ahead sometimes dogged his pitching moves as well, as he makes changes impulsively and ends up with unfavorable matchups. That said, he's been smart enough not to form attachments to his non-Rivera relievers, rebuilding the bullpen on the fly twice in two seasons, an impressive feat. He managed Rivera's workload carefully, going to the closer in the eighth inning more often than any other manager in baseball, yet eschewing the two-inning appearances to which Torre often resorted (though this changed in the postseason). Some of the old nervous tics returned in October as Girardi reacted to the stress of trying to win a championship, and he overmanaged the Yankees out of at least one game. Still, Girardi matured greatly from 2008 to 2009. His refusal to pick favorites and his facility in constructing pitching staffs marks him as one of the most promising young managers in the game.

Oakland Athletics

I have foresworn myself. I have broken every law I have sworn to uphold.
I have become what I beheld and I am content that I have done right!
—Kevin Costner as Eliot Ness, *The Untouchables* (1987)

The Oakland Athletics are a franchise with two feet solidly in the air. Off the field, the team is moving, albeit very slowly and hesitantly, like an iceberg operating under a court injunction, toward an undisclosed location. On the field, they have one team coming in the form of a terrific collection of young pitching, and another going, as a patchwork collection of position players milling around, waiting to be replaced by younger and better.

Billy Beane had been running a low-wattage, relatively star-free operation since his terrific teams of the early 2000s had to be broken up. But seeing that the 2009 AL West was theoretically there for the taking, he gambled on hauling in a star in the final year of his contract. Beane sent arbitration-eligible closer Huston Street and two young players who had just completed their rookie seasons (outfielder Carlos Gonzalez and southpaw Greg Smith) to the Rockies for Matt Holliday. A career .319/.386/.552 hitter through 2008, Holliday was supposed to provide the impetus to an attack that had finished last in the AL in runs scored, batting average, and slugging percentage. The A's had even tied for last in on-base percentage, supposedly the franchise's trademark. Put all together, their .244 team EqA in 2008 had been among the worst of this century. Seeking to repair that and contend, Beane also signed free agent Jason Giambi to play first base; 38 years old, Giambi was admittedly coming off a generally productive but controversial stay with the Yankees. During spring training, the GM added two other veteran props, signing the peripatetic shortstop Orlando Cabrera and the perpetually injured former great Nomar Garciaparra.

The lineup that the four veterans were supposed to carry was extremely light. The holdovers—catcher Kurt Suzuki, second baseman Mark Ellis, outfielder Ryan Sweeney, and designated hitter Jack Cust—have had their moments, especially Ellis in 2005 and Cust in 2007, but none could be considered a top run-producer. Third base was supposed to be manned by Eric Chavez, the former Gold Glover who had once been one of the top young hitters at his position, averaging .280/.357/.513 from 2000 to 2004, but injuries hadn't allowed him to stay on the field in three years. Even if Holliday could maintain his potency away from Coors Field—a big if, as it turned out—and even if Giambi could recover only a little of the magic that had made him an MVP award winner in green and gold, and even if porcelain dolls Ellis, Garciaparra, and Chavez could play without breaking, the offense still didn't promise to deliver top-drawer production.

As it turned out, the offense didn't deliver. Giambi couldn't lift his batting average over the Mendoza line. Ellis, Chavez, and Garciaparra got hurt, as they are wont to do, and none of the three played well when they were in the lineup. Cust's production dropped off for the second year in a row. Holliday was good (.296 EqA), but he was not the Superman of his Purple Moun-

ATHLETICS PROSPECTUS
2009 W-L: 75-87, 4th in AL West

Pythag	82-80	9th	**Ballpark:** The Coliseum (3-yr. PF: 974). Disfigured remnant of the concrete bowl era helps pitchers with its big foul ground
RS/G	4.7	9th	
RA/G	4.7	10th	
EqA	.253	10th	
EqBRR	12.5	1st	**2009:** The kiddie corps on the mound gave it their best shot, eventually got some offensive support
SNWP	.482	12th	
WXRL	11.13	3rd	**2010:** Consolidation from the pitching, sorting out who's part of the lineup beyond this season
FRAr	3.80	1st	
DE	.683	9th	
PADE	-2.86	13th	**Action Items:** Getting more power from all four corners plus DH; is Pennington an everyday shortstop?
Salary	$62.3	14th	
Attend	1.41	14th	

tains' Majesty phase. Even Scott Hairston, acquired after hitting .299/.358/.533 for the Padres, saw his bat wither after he was acquired on July 28th—the rare instance of someone hitting better in Petco. The team hit just .246/.316/.371 in the first half, and if the A's offense did take off in the season's second chapter, hitting .280/.342/.426, the ultimate irony was that they were a better-hitting team without Holliday, who was dealt to the Cardinals on July 24th. That little surge meant that the A's offense improved overall from its miseries of 2008, but it still wasn't good. The infield was a particular sore point; its unadjusted aggregate rates of .250/.319/.391 were the second-worst in the league. The outfield was comparatively robust, merely fourth-worst. In another irony, the A's led the majors in extra runs gained through baserunning (12.5 EqBRR); our copy of Dante isn't clear on the point, but becoming what you've mocked seems certain to be one of the outermost circles of Hell.

Despite the impoverished offense, there was still hope for the A's because of their pitching staff. The 2008 pitching had been solid, with the bullpen being particularly strong. Though Street had to be sacrificed for Holliday, the club still retained side-arming sensation Brad Ziegler, the hard-throwing Santiago Casilla, and the friable but powerful Joey Devine, who had put himself in line to succeed Street with an overpowering second half. The rotation had been headed up by Justin Duchscherer; but for the hip injury that truncated his season, his transition from relief work had been a tremendous success, with the hurler making the All-Star team and recording a sterling 2.54 ERA.

As with the plans for the offense, much that seemed promising on paper turned out badly in actuality. Elbow pain and assorted subsequent problems kept Duchscherer under wraps the entire season. Devine missed the season as well after undergoing Tommy John surgery. Casilla imploded and earned his December release. Ziegler was good, but no longer held the element of surprise with his delivery and proved to be fairly hittable.

Yet not all was lost. However much the planned pillars of their pitching had crumbled, a new staff arose. It would take its lumps due to inexperience, but on a team awash in disappointment, at least the youth movement was both good and promising. The opening-week quintet was so fresh it still had that new-rotation smell. Of the five initial starters, Dana Eveland, 25 years old, was the most experienced, with 35 major-league starts; Dallas Braden, also 25, was second, with 24 starts. Josh Outman, 24, had made four starts, while Brett Anderson and Trevor Cahill, both 21, were virgins.

The unit was later augmented by two other rookies, 22-year-old Vin Mazzaro and 23-year-old Gio Gonzalez. Of these, Anderson did the most to establish himself as a Cy Future type, while the others showed varying flashes of effectiveness. Outman was quite good before Tommy John surgery swept him away.

Simultaneously, the bullpen was almost magically rebuilt. The Cubs took Michael Wuertz and his back-breaking slider for granted for years; he was dominant in Oakland. Lefty Craig Breslow had bounced from team to team for years without establishing himself. After Beane picked him up from the Twins on waivers and gave him a home, Breslow spent the rest of the season putting away both left- and right-handers. The most propitious development of all was Double-A reliever Andrew Bailey's grabbing hold of the closer's role and keeping it with a nasty cutter, winding up winning the Rookie of the Year Award. As the young pitchers matured and the offense gave them more support, the team performed better, going 40-41 in the second half, though not well enough to overcome a miserable 35-46 start and not well enough to provide real hope for 2010.

Off the field, all was in turmoil as well. The planned relocation of the A's, a process which seemingly began sometime around December 1971, kicked into high gear in 2009, as the team continued its mating ritual with San Jose and Fremont while officials in Oakland tried to smear another layer of lipstick on the team's current hometown with December proposals for four other locations within the city limits. This is nothing new; under Charlie Finley, the A's had flirted with towns from Denver to New Orleans to Washington, DC. Owner Lew Wolff seems bent on escaping the "Mausoleum," however, and the A's are positioned to break a dubious record they share with the Braves for most-often relocated franchise. Their plans for a "ballpark village" in nearby Fremont fell through because of the free-falling housing market and local opposition. (Note to future ballpark planners: do not attempt to locate your stadium in or around anything called a national wildlife refuge.) Wolff opted to spare the endangered Salt Marsh Harvest Mouse and has set his sights on San Jose, approximately 40 miles to the south.

The A's have only occasionally drawn well in Oakland. The great dynasty of the early 1970s only once reached the top five in attendance and failed to make winning pay off; their championship team of 1974 averaged 10,441 fans a game and finished 11th in attendance in a 12-team league. The city was more supportive of the "Bash Brothers" teams of the late 1980s, pushing attendance into the high two millions. That showing proved good enough for a couple of second-place finishes, and one in third place, but this proved to be a short-lived surge that ebbed as soon as the club's success on the field faded. The strong teams of 1999-2006 rose no higher than sixth, and for the last three seasons, the club has been stuck under two million fans per year, falling to 13th in the 14-team league in 2009. The television market is considered the country's sixth-largest, encompassing roughly 2.5 million homes.

In both cases, the A's have to compete with the Giants for a share of local dollars and eyeballs. While Oakland and San Francisco are separate municipalities, their proximity, shrunken by the BART system, makes such distinctions meaningless. In practical terms, the A's and Giants are closer than the Nationals and Orioles, Dodgers and Angels, or the Yankees and Mets. The San Francisco–Oakland metropolitan area is far smaller than the other two-team markets. A move to San Jose would not completely get the A's out of the Giants' shadow—the Giants are arguing, both directly and through proxies, that San Jose is their territory—but it would shrink the direct competition between the clubs for souls who could choose to spend their money on either ballclub. Indeed, these poor, torn individuals may have given all they can, even those in San Jose; consider that the New York metropolitan area, containing approximately 19 million people as of 2008, bought roughly 6.9 million tickets between the Yankees and Mets. Los Angeles, a metropolitan area of 13 million, bought approximately 7 million tickets from the Dodgers and Angels. The Bay Area has a population of 4.3 million and bought the same number of tickets (4.3 million) from the Giants and A's combined. For the Giants to insist on the necessity of their permission and then withhold it might be a boon to both clubs. Were the A's to remove themselves completely from the Bay Area, they might have to settle for a smaller market, but a market they would have all to themselves. Simultaneously, the Giants, the area's original team, would no longer have to compete for market share. Portland, Sacramento, and Orlando, are you ready for your close-ups?

The relocation drama drags on with no resolution in sight. Meanwhile, the team on the field must soldier on. The difficulty the team faces entering 2010 is the result of its Jekyll-and-Hyde farm system, which pumped out enough pitching to restock the starting rotation in 2009 but has failed to furnish the same quality or quantity of position players. The failure of the A's internal development is evident in just how many of their lineups come from sources outside the organization. Homegrown talent for 2010 includes just the catchers—Kurt Suzuki (a 2004 second-round pick) and Landon Powell (their first-rounder that same year)—and shortstop Cliff Pennington (number one in 2005). The rest have come as free-agent signings, waiver claims, or trades.

Beane has avoided any blockbusters this winter, settling for smaller, short-term fixes. Cust was not offered arbitration and seems certain to leave as a free agent. His role may be taken by Jake Fox, the position-less slugger acquired from the Cubs (along with the poison pill of infielder Aaron Miles) in a minor exchange. In December, the A's signed center fielder Coco Crisp to a one-year deal with an option for 2011. Even before his two rotator-cuff surgeries in 2009, Crisp had hit only .271/.330/.390 in three years with the Red Sox, numbers boosted by a very favorable home/road split. Crisp is not a solution to the problem of a light-hitting outfield, being perhaps not even an improvement on journeyman Rajai Davis.

Another deal with a greater long-term impact saw third-base prospect Brett "Walrus" Wallace, prize of the Holliday deal with the Cards, turned around and sent to the Blue Jays for top outfield prospect Michael Taylor, who they had just acquired from the Phillies as part of the Roy Halladay payday. With the potential to be an annual .300 hitter with 20-25 homers, the Brobdingnagian Taylor could be the most dynamic offensive player the A's have had in years, and he should be ready before the 2010 season is out. He should arrive at roughly the same moment as potential 40-homer first baseman Chris Carter, the slugging prospect acquired in the Dan Haren trade. Finally, a full season of Cliff Pennington, who took over at shortstop after Cabrera was traded, should bolster the infield's collective on-base percentage, if nothing else.

The A's are a team in transition, traversing the world's longest tunnel toward a newly competitive team and in a new home. They will arrive at the former sooner, as the pitching staff continues to mature and as the offense adds, well, almost anything of value. As for that other exit, right now Amelia Earhart seems more likely to land, Percy Fawcett more likely to find his way out of the jungle, Gilligan more likely to get off that damned island, than the A's seem likely to find a new home.

HITTERS

Darlc Barton   1B   Bats: L   Throws: R   Height: 6' 0"   Weight: 225   Born: August 16, 1985   Age: 24

YEAR	TEAM	LVL	AGE	PA	R	2B	3B	HR	RBI	BB	SO	SB	CS	EqBRR	AVG	OBP	SLG	EqAVG	EqOBP	EqSLG	EqA	VORP	WARP	DEFENSE			
2007	SAC	AAA	21	604	84	38	5	9	70	78	69	3	4	-3.5	.293	.389	.438	.282	.371	.412	.276	16.6	2.3	111-1B	6	16-3B	-3
2007	OAK	MLB	21	84	16	9	0	4	8	10	11	1	0	0.4	.347	.429	.639	.361	.440	.667	.358	10.9	1.1	18-1B	-1		
2008	OAK	MLB	22	523	59	17	5	9	47	65	99	2	1	1.6	.226	.327	.348	.233	.333	.359	.249	-1.3	-0.3	126-1B	-1		
2009	SAC	AAA	23	313	48	21	1	9	48	45	43	1	0	-0.1	.261	.386	.458	.262	.372	.446	.287	9.2	2.1	65-1B	8		
2009	OAK	MLB	23	192	31	12	1	3	24	26	25	0	2	-2.1	.269	.372	.412	.277	.377	.421	.280	4.2	1.2	47-1B	6		
2010	OAK	MLB	24	541	73	26	3	14	62	66	86	2	2	-0.6	.264	.359	.421	.265	.359	.417	.269	11.0	1.5	123-1B	3		

Breakout: 16% Improve: 50% Collapse: 10% Attrition: 3%   MLB: 100%   Comparables: Billy Jo Robidoux, Chris Carter, Tino Martinez, Ray Brown

Seen as Oakland's first baseman of the future since being acquired for Mark Mulder in 2004, Barton has had a marvelous minor-league career, hitting .293/.408/.455, but the major-league portion just hasn't worked out. Insiders say Barton cruised through the minors on talent alone, and when things got hard at the highest level, he just didn't know how to respond. Bouncing back and forth between Triple-A and the big leagues last year, he finally showed some signs of life during the last six weeks of the season, batting .302/.389/.437 in 37 games, but with Chris Carter coming quickly from behind, he can't afford another setback.

Corey Brown   OF   Bats: L   Throws: L   Height: 6' 2"   Weight: 210   Born: November 26, 1985   Age: 24

YEAR	TEAM	LVL	AGE	PA	R	2B	3B	HR	RBI	BB	SO	SB	CS	EqBRR	AVG	OBP	SLG	EqAVG	EqOBP	EqSLG	EqA	VORP	WARP	DEFENSE			
2007	VAN	A-	21	256	31	18	4	11	48	37	77	5	3	-2.9	.268	.379	.545	.233	.311	.432	.257	5.2	-0.7	36-CF	-4	17-RF	-6
2008	KNC	A	22	351	44	18	2	14	49	41	96	12	0	1.3	.270	.359	.483	.235	.309	.394	.249	4.7	-0.7	72-CF	-11		
2008	STO	A+	22	214	34	9	0	16	34	17	72	4	1	0.9	.260	.322	.551	.226	.284	.452	.248	2.8	0.1	42-CF	-2		
2009	MID	AA	23	281	46	20	4	9	43	27	69	5	2	-1.2	.268	.349	.488	.238	.306	.441	.255	6.4	0.2	62-CF	-5		
2010	OAK	MLB	24	394	41	19	2	14	49	35	121	4	2	-0.4	.230	.303	.410	.230	.302	.405	.242	4.7	0.0	83-CF	-4		

Breakout: 18% Improve: 39% Collapse: 16% Attrition: 8%   MLB: 4%   Comparables: Greg Blosser, John Jensen, Justin Nelson, Ralph Bryant

After hitting 30 home runs in 2008, Brown was hampered by knee problems in '09, which cut into his development time. He remains an intriguing talent with above-average power and speed and the ability to play center field. The decision to sign Coco Crisp will give him time to demonstrate health and effectiveness at Triple-A. There are still the strikeouts to worry about, as he's now totaled 314 in 259 professional games. It's unlikely that he'll ever hit for a high average, but he does enough things well that he should be able to carve out a career in spite of his flaws.

Travis Buck   RF   Bats: L   Throws: R   Height: 6' 2"   Weight: 225   Born: November 18, 1983   Age: 26

YEAR	TEAM	LVL	AGE	PA	R	2B	3B	HR	RBI	BB	SO	SB	CS	EqBRR	AVG	OBP	SLG	EqAVG	EqOBP	EqSLG	EqA	VORP	WARP	DEFENSE			
2007	OAK	MLB	23	334	41	22	5	7	34	39	66	4	1	-0.1	.288	.377	.474	.297	.386	.491	.300	21.3	2.8	57-RF	-1	14-LF	4
2008	SAC	AAA	24	197	28	8	2	2	17	25	34	4	1	2.5	.296	.396	.402	.289	.379	.387	.275	7.2	1.0	20-CF	-2	13-RF	3
2008	OAK	MLB	24	172	16	9	1	7	25	11	38	1	0	-1.8	.226	.291	.432	.232	.297	.452	.257	2.7	0.6	32-RF	1	5-LF	1
2009	SAC	AAA	25	266	37	13	3	5	29	23	44	3	1	0.4	.272	.345	.418	.270	.332	.409	.260	4.3	0.8	50-RF	2		
2009	OAK	MLB	25	115	11	3	0	3	10	10	20	1	1	0.0	.219	.287	.333	.229	.296	.343	.220	-2.7	0.1	24-RF	4	3-LF	-1
2010	OAK	MLB	26	361	43	17	3	11	39	36	77	3	2	0.2	.258	.341	.429	.258	.340	.420	.263	8.7	1.2	72-RF	2		

Breakout: 15% Improve: 46% Collapse: 13% Attrition: 9%   MLB: 85%   Comparables: Raul Ibañez, Gabe Gross, Seth Smith, Laynce Nix

The star that shone so brightly in 2007 has dimmed to the point where it's only viewable on a very clear night on a dark country road. Between the shoulder and oblique problems that waylaid him last year, Buck worked hard to refashion his swing in an attempt to regain what once was, but his numbers regressed, even during his time at Triple-A. Because he hits left-handed, he'll still get some chances, but at this point, his high upside is that he winds up as an extra outfielder.

Adrian Cardenas 2B

Bats: L   Throws: R   Height: 6' 0"   Weight: 185   Born: October 10, 1987   Age: 22

YEAR	TEAM	LVL	AGE	PA	R	2B	3B	HR	RBI	BB	SO	SB	CS	EqBRR	AVG	OBP	SLG	EqAVG	EqOBP	EqSLG	EqA	VORP	WARP	DEFENSE			
2007	LWD	A	19	564	70	30	2	9	79	47	80	19	7	0.8	.295	.354	.417	.276	.323	.376	.248	10.7	0.0	123-2B	-11		
2008	CLR	A+	20	293	44	11	6	4	23	28	42	16	0	2.7	.307	.371	.441	.289	.344	.421	.271	12.2	0.1	64-2B	-12		
2008	STO	A+	20	74	11	1	0	1	10	1	14	1	0	1.7	.278	.297	.333	.247	.267	.301	.198	-2.2	-0.8	12-2B	-5		
2008	MID	AA	20	102	12	4	0	0	7	15	10	0	1	-1.5	.279	.392	.326	.247	.350	.281	.230	1.0	0.0	26-SS	-1		
2009	MID	AA	21	373	56	26	2	3	55	38	44	5	4	1.8	.326	.392	.446	.291	.348	.408	.265	13.0	0.7	39-2B	-4	32-3B	-2
2009	SAC	AAA	21	207	23	15	2	1	24	17	29	3	2	-2.5	.251	.317	.372	.247	.306	.360	.235	0.3	-0.5	34-2B	-5	7-3B	-1
2010	OAK	MLB	22	555	67	28	3	8	61	47	92	8	3	0.5	.270	.334	.382	.271	.335	.382	.248	9.9	0.2	118-2B	-8		

Breakout: 18% Improve: 52% Collapse: 14% Attrition: 9%   MLB: 7%   Comparables: Troy O'Leary, Brandon Pico, Bruce Fields, Anthony Collier

Part of the package received from Philadelphia in 2008's Joe Blanton deal, Cardenas earns universal acclaim for his bat. The problem is that the bat has little in it except a good batting average. Cardenas has an unexciting, acceptable walk rate and slices a good number of doubles, but has little over-the-fence power, while his speed and defense are average at best. If he can keep hitting .300, he'll probably replace Mark Ellis at second base after 2010 (the A's can buy Ellis out of his $6 million 2011 option for a cool $500,000), but unless he finds more in the way of secondary skills, he's not going to make a big impact.

Chris Carter 1B

Bats: R   Throws: R   Height: 6' 4"   Weight: 210   Born: December 18, 1986   Age: 23

YEAR	TEAM	LVL	AGE	PA	R	2B	3B	HR	RBI	BB	SO	SB	CS	EqBRR	AVG	OBP	SLG	EqAVG	EqOBP	EqSLG	EqA	VORP	WARP	DEFENSE			
2007	KAN	A	20	545	84	27	3	25	93	67	112	3	2	-0.5	.291	.383	.522	.253	.328	.429	.262	6.5	0.3	73-1B	-4		
2008	STO	A+	21	596	101	32	4	39	104	77	156	4	0	-3.7	.259	.361	.569	.228	.319	.469	.269	14.7	-0.8	38-3B	-11	38-1B	-7
2009	MID	AA	22	593	108	41	2	24	101	82	119	13	5	-2.3	.337	.435	.576	.291	.377	.510	.301	28.6	2.4	102-1B	-8	5-RF	-1
2009	SAC	AAA	22	58	7	2	0	4	14	3	14	0	1	-0.9	.259	.293	.519	.259	.293	.519	.264	0.8	0.0	6-1B	-1	5-LF	0
2010	OAK	MLB	23	603	79	29	2	27	81	67	159	4	2	-1.3	.246	.335	.462	.246	.333	.455	.269	12.6	0.9	90-1B	-4		

Breakout: 14% Improve: 40% Collapse: 12% Attrition: 9%   MLB: 7%   Comparables: Gary Alexander, Jamie Romak, Nate Espy, Wes Bankston

After leading the minor leagues in total bases in 2008, Carter got off to a solid start at Double-A Midland, but absolutely exploded during the second half of the year, including a 62-for-143 (.434) run with the Rockhounds that finally moved him up to Triple-A, where he slugged four more homers in 13 games. The best power hitter in the system, Carter also became a much better all-around hitter in 2009, significantly cutting down his strikeout rate, so he's nearly ready. The A's briefly dreamed of moving him to the outfield due to the first-base logjam, but trading away Brett Wallace helped open things back up. All Carter may have to do is wait for the next Daric Barton slump for his path to the majors to be clear.

Eric Chavez 3B

Bats: L   Throws: R   Height: 6' 1"   Weight: 220   Born: December 7, 1977   Age: 32

YEAR	TEAM	LVL	AGE	PA	R	2B	3B	HR	RBI	BB	SO	SB	CS	EqBRR	AVG	OBP	SLG	EqAVG	EqOBP	EqSLG	EqA	VORP	WARP	DEFENSE	
2007	OAK	MLB	29	379	43	21	2	15	46	34	76	4	2	-2.6	.240	.306	.446	.245	.311	.454	.262	8.8	1.2	87-3B	2
2008	OAK	MLB	30	95	10	7	0	2	14	6	18	0	0	-0.1	.247	.295	.393	.258	.305	.427	.244	0.4	0.2	15-3B	1
2009	OAK	MLB	31	31	0	1	0	0	1	1	7	0	0	-0.1	.100	.129	.133	.133	.161	.167	-.137	-3.7	-0.4	8-3B	1
2010	OAK	MLB	32	266	27	13	1	10	31	22	56	2	1	-0.7	.234	.298	.413	.235	.299	.405	.240	1.3	0.3	57-3B	1

Breakout: 17% Improve: 35% Collapse: 24% Attrition: 17%   MLB: 60%   Comparables: Mike Davis, Greg Norton, Scott Livingstone, Daryl Boston

Chavez surprised many observers in 2009 with a good showing in spring training—given how many injuries he's had, the mental picture of Chavez resembles less an athlete than Boris Karloff as Frankenstein's monster—but then neck and shoulder issues hit after Opening Day, followed by the discovery of a herniated disk (not Chavez's first), which necessitated another back surgery. He's reportedly on track to be 100 percent this spring, but at this point, nobody is quite sure what 100 percent of Eric Chavez even is anymore, as he's played just 31 games over the past two years and hasn't been at his best since 2004. The only thing Oakland should look forward to from him at this point is his eight-figure salary coming off the books after the season.

Bobby Crosby — INF

Bats: R   Throws: R   Height: 6' 3"   Weight: 205   Born: January 12, 1980   Age: 30

YEAR	TEAM	LVL	AGE	PA	R	2B	3B	HR	RBI	BB	SO	SB	CS	EqBRR	AVG	OBP	SLG	EqAVG	EqOBP	EqSLG	EqA	VORP	WARP	DEFENSE			
2007	OAK	MLB	27	374	40	16	0	8	31	23	62	10	2	2.0	.226	.278	.341	.229	.283	.347	.223	0.1	1.1	91-SS	9		
2008	OAK	MLB	28	605	66	39	1	7	61	47	96	7	3	2.9	.237	.296	.349	.245	.305	.363	.234	8.7	1.8	142-SS	6		
2009	OAK	MLB	29	272	35	10	2	6	29	24	44	2	1	1.8	.223	.295	.357	.229	.300	.360	.236	-2.6	-0.3	33-3B	-2	30-1B	0
2010	PIT	MLB	30	453	52	21	1	10	46	40	74	7	4	1.2	.243	.311	.368	.246	.314	.373	.238	1.5	-0.2	109-3B	-3		

Breakout: 18%   Improve: 50%   Collapse: 8%   Attrition: 6%   MLB: 95%   Comparables: Daryl Spencer, Ed Sprague, Tim Naehring, Puddin' Head Jones

Even in his Rookie of the Year campaign, Crosby wasn't that good, with his 22 home runs masking myriad offensive holes. Once the power dropped a bit and he couldn't stay healthy, he became a nonfactor. Signed by the Pirates (a nonfactor team for a nonfactor player), he'll give Ronny Cedeño some spring competition at short as both infielders try to live down to the legacy of Sammy Khalifa, but Crosby probably has more value as a versatile utility player and latter-day Bill Almon. Considering that he has hit .231/.292/.346 over the last four seasons, he clearly has little enough to offer as a regular.

Aaron Cunningham — OF

Bats: R   Throws: R   Height: 5' 11"   Weight: 195   Born: April 24, 1986   Age: 24

YEAR	TEAM	LVL	AGE	PA	R	2B	3B	HR	RBI	BB	SO	SB	CS	EqBRR	AVG	OBP	SLG	EqAVG	EqOBP	EqSLG	EqA	VORP	WARP	DEFENSE			
2007	WNS	A+	21	306	51	12	5	8	37	34	39	22	8	2.5	.294	.376	.476	.258	.323	.409	.259	5.1	-0.8	36-RF	-6	26-LF	-6
2007	VIS	A+	21	135	25	11	2	3	20	5	23	5	3	-0.4	.358	.386	.553	.296	.318	.432	.258	3.0	0.4	16-CF	2	6-RF	-1
2007	MOB	AA	21	132	25	8	3	5	20	12	27	1	3	-0.1	.288	.364	.534	.273	.333	.488	.272	4.6	0.6	19-RF	2	9-CF	-2
2008	MID	AA	22	401	65	18	6	12	52	38	92	12	4	0.4	.317	.386	.507	.272	.332	.433	.266	12.5	-0.2	59-CF	-17	22-LF	2
2008	SAC	AAA	22	89	21	5	0	5	14	11	16	3	1	0.3	.382	.461	.645	.346	.422	.551	.327	8.7	0.9	16-RF	2	4-CF	-3
2008	OAK	MLB	22	87	7	7	1	1	14	6	24	2	0	-0.4	.250	.310	.400	.262	.322	.412	.257	1.3	0.3	17-LF	1		
2009	SAC	AAA	23	375	62	24	1	11	48	33	74	11	4	-1.1	.302	.372	.479	.289	.352	.454	.277	13.4	1.2	33-LF	0	30-RF	-2
2009	OAK	MLB	23	57	6	2	0	1	6	3	16	0	0	-0.3	.151	.211	.245	.151	.211	.245	.143	-4.7	-0.9	13-RF	-3	2-LF	0
2010	OAK	MLB	24	459	59	22	3	11	47	40	108	9	5	0.1	.251	.323	.399	.252	.322	.397	.247	3.5	0.0	80-RF	-4		

Breakout: 11%   Improve: 27%   Collapse: 29%   Attrition: 13%   MLB: 79%   Comparables: Keith Williams, Mike Humphreys, Harvey Pulliam, Geronimo Berroa

Oakland had high hopes for Cunningham, part of the package received for Dan Haren, and while he's compiled a .317/.389/.510 mark in 103 games at Triple-A thus far, he has yet to establish himself in the big leagues, where he struggled mightily in 2009, albeit in a very brief audition. In many ways, he's a right-handed Travis Buck, a player who can hit for average but might not have enough secondary skills to play in a corner every day. There are many players like Cunningham, who put up solid minor-league numbers, hitting for a good average but not a great one, having fair selectivity without being truly selective, and hitting for modest power without being powerful. Some of them succeed, but with many, the greater difficulty of the major leagues gnaws away at their advantages until they become unplayably ordinary. It's too early to say if this is the case with Cunningham, but it's a possibility.

Jack Cust — DH

Bats: L   Throws: R   Height: 6' 1"   Weight: 230   Born: January 16, 1979   Age: 31

YEAR	TEAM	LVL	AGE	PA	R	2B	3B	HR	RBI	BB	SO	SB	CS	EqBRR	AVG	OBP	SLG	EqAVG	EqOBP	EqSLG	EqA	VORP	WARP	DEFENSE			
2007	POR	AAA	28	100	17	7	0	9	20	19	29	0	0	0.3	.300	.430	.725	.253	.370	.578	.311	7.5	0.5	14-LF	-3		
2007	OAK	MLB	28	507	61	18	1	26	82	105	164	0	2	-3.8	.256	.408	.504	.263	.416	.523	.319	40.6	3.2	43-RF	-10	9-LF	-1
2008	OAK	MLB	29	598	77	19	0	33	77	111	197	0	0	1.5	.231	.375	.476	.241	.385	.504	.302	37.1	3.5	66-LF	-4	4-RF	-1
2009	OAK	MLB	30	612	88	16	0	25	70	93	185	4	1	-0.5	.240	.356	.417	.248	.363	.424	.277	15.1	0.4	45-RF	-11		
2010	OAK	MLB	31	573	73	18	1	28	75	98	186	1	1	-0.4	.237	.370	.455	.235	.366	.442	.283	26.0	2.1	58-RF	-7		

Breakout: 9%   Improve: 35%   Collapse: 13%   Attrition: 7%   MLB: 97%   Comparables: Geoff Jenkins, Henry Rodriguez, Paul O'Neill, Jeromy Burnitz

How one-dimensional is Cust? In 2009, only he and Brandon Inge hit more than 25 homers while failing to slug at least .450. When Cust averaged a home run once every 15 at-bats and walked once every five plate appearances, one could live with his low batting average and all the strikeouts. Pitchers figured out Cust over the years, and many started to challenge him more, knowing that he had no way to beat them other than a walk or a home run. With Cust now seeing more strikes than he was capable of exploiting, he was able to work fewer hitter's counts, with the result that his home-run rate dropped (to less than one per 20 at-bats), as did his walk rate (still excellent, just not insane). With more rounded sluggers in their minors, the A's were seemingly on the cusp of letting Cust go, but surprisingly re-signed him to a one-year deal.

Rajai Davis — CF

Bats: R Throws: R Height: 5' 11" Weight: 195 Born: October 19, 1980 Age: 29

YEAR	TEAM	LVL	AGE	PA	R	2B	3B	HR	RBI	BB	SO	SB	CS	EqBRR	AVG	OBP	SLG	EqAVG	EqOBP	EqSLG	EqA	VORP	WARP	DEFENSE			
2007	IND	AAA	26	239	31	12	4	4	30	21	25	27	9	-2.0	.318	.384	.469	.307	.366	.451	.283	12.2	1.7	26-LF	-1	26-CF	3
2007	PIT	MLB	26	57	6	2	1	0	2	7	3	5	2	-1.0	.271	.357	.354	.292	.375	.375	.269	1.6	0.4	9-CF	1		
2007	SFN	MLB	26	162	26	9	1	1	7	14	25	17	4	3.5	.282	.363	.380	.294	.373	.392	.276	7.3	1.1	33-CF	2	2-LF	0
2008	SFN	MLB	27	19	2	0	0	0	0	1	6	4	0	0.6	.056	.105	.056	.056	.105	.056	.089	-2.3	-0.4	3-CF	-1		
2008	OAK	MLB	27	207	28	5	4	3	19	7	34	25	6	2.6	.260	.288	.372	.272	.299	.385	.253	3.5	0.7	52-CF	3		
2009	OAK	MLB	28	432	65	27	5	3	48	29	70	41	12	8.0	.305	.360	.423	.322	.375	.438	.285	24.1	3.5	96-CF	8	4-RF	-1
2010	OAK	MLB	29	434	61	22	5	5	42	36	70	36	13	2.4	.280	.348	.401	.282	.348	.403	.264	15.3	2.1	100-CF	4		

Breakout: 7% Improve: 34% Collapse: 12% Attrition: 13%   MLB: 91%   Comparables: Ron LeFlore, Vince Coleman, Billy North, Dan Gladden

After years as a bench outfielder, Davis finally wound up with steady playing time in 2009, much of it because he was the only player on the roster with a center fielder's skill set. He ended up delivering a career year, in part due to a .361 batting average on balls in play (itself goosed by 22 infield hits). Davis has little power, and his approach prevents him from working well as a leadoff hitter. He played well enough to earn an encore, but the Coco Crisp signing probably pushes him out of center and perhaps back into a platoon role with Ryan Sweeney.

Grant Desme — OF

Bats: R Throws: R Height: 6' 2" Weight: 205 Born: April 4, 1986 Age: 24

YEAR	TEAM	LVL	AGE	PA	R	2B	3B	HR	RBI	BB	SO	SB	CS	EqBRR	AVG	OBP	SLG	EqAVG	EqOBP	EqSLG	EqA	VORP	WARP	DEFENSE			
2007	VAN	A-	21	53	6	3	0	1	6	6	21	2	2	-0.9	.261	.358	.391	.224	.283	.327	.212	-1.5	-0.1	8-RF	0	4-CF	1
2009	KNC	A	23	288	49	19	2	11	38	21	81	24	0	6.2	.274	.334	.490	.224	.268	.369	.225	-4.8	-1.8	31-CF	-7	21-RF	-1
2009	STO	A+	23	264	49	12	4	20	51	33	67	16	5	2.2	.304	.398	.656	.250	.326	.479	.273	10.4	0.7	42-CF	-3	12-RF	-1
2010	OAK	MLB	24	387	41	18	2	12	39	32	116	9	4	2.4	.228	.295	.396	.228	.293	.393	.235	2.0	-0.3	76-CF	-4		

Breakout: 23% Improve: 53% Collapse: 18% Attrition: 7%   MLB: 4%   Comparables: Preston Wilson, Gerald Williams, Alan Cockrell, Ozzie Canseco

A second-round pick in 2007, Desme faced a career that seemed in danger of being over before it began, as wrist surgery and a bum shoulder limited him to a grand total of 14 games in his first two years. Finally healthy in 2009, Desme exploded, becoming the only 30-30 player in the minors. He followed that up with an MVP showing in the Arizona Fall League, but it's still hard to evaluate him, as his peers, the other college outfielders from the 2007 draft, are in the big leagues or on the brink of making it, and the game has already rendered a verdict on their skills, whereas Desme is simply ready for Double-A and further testing. From a scouting point of view, his power is real and his speed is a plus, though perhaps not so much so that he'll steal 40 bases annually, and it's not clear that he can maintain this level of production with such a high strikeout rate. There are still many questions to be answered, but that's not to say there isn't some excitement as well.

Mark Ellis — 2B

Bats: R Throws: R Height: 5' 11" Weight: 190 Born: June 6, 1977 Age: 33

YEAR	TEAM	LVL	AGE	PA	R	2B	3B	HR	RBI	BB	SO	SB	CS	EqBRR	AVG	OBP	SLG	EqAVG	EqOBP	EqSLG	EqA	VORP	WARP	DEFENSE	
2007	OAK	MLB	30	642	84	33	3	19	76	44	94	9	4	-1.0	.276	.336	.441	.284	.342	.455	.273	30.0	6.5	148-2B	24
2008	OAK	MLB	31	507	55	20	3	12	41	53	65	14	2	1.0	.233	.321	.373	.241	.330	.387	.258	13.7	3.9	114-2B	17
2009	OAK	MLB	32	410	52	23	0	10	61	23	54	10	3	-1.0	.263	.305	.403	.272	.313	.416	.253	9.3	2.1	102-2B	8
2010	OAK	MLB	33	465	56	22	2	13	53	39	69	9	4	-0.2	.266	.333	.420	.268	.334	.418	.258	13.2	2.3	111-2B	8

Breakout: 14% Improve: 42% Collapse: 15% Attrition: 15%   MLB: 98%   Comparables: Phil Garner, Tadahito Iguchi, Rich Aurilia, Connie Ryan

Ellis missed a third of the season with a severe calf strain, but otherwise, there were no surprises (not that an Ellis injury is really an unexpected event), as his batting and slugging averages were both within .004 of his career marks. He's not a great hitter, but at least he's consistent, and he remains a solid fielder, though the calf limited him. He has one more guaranteed year on his deal, but the A's will almost certainly pay the $500,000 buyout on their 2011 club option so as to bring in someone younger, cheaper, and presumably less prone to injuries and absence.

Tommy Everidge   1B/3B

Bats: R   Throws: R   Height: 6' 1"   Weight: 215   Born: April 20, 1983   Age: 27

YEAR	TEAM	LVL	AGE	PA	R	2B	3B	HR	RBI	BB	SO	SB	CS	EqBRR	AVG	OBP	SLG	EqAVG	EqOBP	EqSLG	EqA	VORP	WARP	DEFENSE			
2007	STO	A+	24	539	75	13	3	26	90	66	103	2	2	0.0	.258	.354	.469	.214	.289	.356	.227	-13.6	-3.5	97-1B	-16	4-RF	1
2008	MID	AA	25	607	89	34	0	22	115	55	133	0	0	-0.4	.279	.346	.467	.236	.290	.375	.234	-10.1	-2.1	87-1B	-5	16-3B	-2
2009	MID	AA	26	258	41	18	0	8	53	28	34	0	1	0.1	.306	.380	.489	.257	.314	.397	.246	-0.6	-0.7	27-3B	-5	8-1B	0
2009	SAC	AAA	26	229	39	15	1	12	41	23	34	0	0	-2.9	.368	.428	.632	.343	.397	.583	.326	17.9	1.6	32-1B	-4		
2009	OAK	MLB	26	97	13	6	0	2	7	8	17	0	0	0.3	.224	.302	.365	.226	.305	.357	.238	-2.3	-0.6	19-1B	-3		
2010	OAK	MLB	27	525	60	22	1	15	68	47	120	1	1	-0.4	.236	.309	.382	.238	.309	.382	.235	-8.0	-1.5	89-1B	-5		

Breakout: 9%   Improve: 42%   Collapse: 23%   Attrition: 17%   MLB: 32%   Comparables: Mike Reddish, Alan Griffin, Tim Glass, Domingo Martinez

One of those old-school Oakland types who can hit but who is utterly without tools, Everidge was destroying Pacific Coast League pitching while becoming a fan favorite for his gregarious personality and matching Kruk-esque build. Charming as such things might be, a 2-for-21 slump ended his time in Oakland, and as a first base fill-in who will be 27, playing in a system packed with sluggers, he's rapidly approaching Quadruple-A status.

Nomar Garciaparra   INF

Bats: R   Throws: R   Height: 6' 0"   Weight: 190   Born: July 23, 1973   Age: 36

YEAR	TEAM	LVL	AGE	PA	R	2B	3B	HR	RBI	BB	SO	SB	CS	EqBRR	AVG	OBP	SLG	EqAVG	EqOBP	EqSLG	EqA	VORP	WARP	DEFENSE			
2007	LAN	MLB	33	466	39	17	0	7	59	31	41	3	1	-1.4	.283	.328	.371	.287	.333	.373	.250	1.1	0.1	64-1B	2	40-3B	-2
2008	LAN	MLB	34	181	24	9	0	8	28	15	11	1	1	-0.8	.264	.326	.466	.276	.335	.485	.276	9.7	1.2	27-SS	2	8-3B	-1
2009	OAK	MLB	35	169	17	8	0	3	16	8	28	2	0	1.3	.281	.314	.387	.287	.320	.400	.250	-1.6	-0.3	11-1B	-1	4-3B	0
2010	OAK	MLB	36	136	12	5	0	3	18	11	18	1	1	0.0	.262	.323	.376	.266	.325	.380	.239	-1.5	-0.2	25-1B	0		

Breakout: 6%   Improve: 21%   Collapse: 34%   Attrition: 55%   MLB: 93%   Comparables: Bill Madlock, Rich Aurilia, Bill Skowron, Joe Medwick

Garciaparra has averaged just 84 games a year over the last six seasons, but he usually contributed something when healthy. Sure, he wasn't NO-MAH! anymore, but you could just perceive the shadow of the old batting-title winner at work. That changed in 2009, as Normal looked older and frailer than ever, rarely showing any ability to drive the ball. Pitchers no longer fear to challenge him, which results in anorexic walk rates. We have forever to look at No-mar's career stats and wonder what might have been, but only a little time left to see him play.

Grant Green   SS

Bats: R   Throws: R   Height: 6' 3"   Weight: 170   Born: September 27, 1987   Age: 22

YEAR	TEAM	LVL	AGE	PA	R	2B	3B	HR	RBI	BB	SO	SB	CS	EqBRR	AVG	OBP	SLG	EqAVG	EqOBP	EqSLG	EqA	VORP	WARP	DEFENSE
Did Not Play.																								
2010	OAK	MLB	22	149	5	5	0	0	7	6	21	0	0	0.3	.214	.246	.250	.215	.248	.263	.148	-12.9	-1.4	0- 0

Breakout: 76%   Improve: 80%   Collapse: 13%   Attrition: 9%   MLB: 0%   Comparables: Keith Foley, Hassan Robinson, Tim Vaughn, Kurt Endebrock

If you don't have enough evidence that the A's have abandoned *Moneyball* when it comes to drafting, look no further than Green. Can you really imagine the Oakland organization earlier in the decade selecting a Scott Boras client with its first-round pick, and giving him an over-slot bonus of $2.75 million? That's what the A's did last June, and it could end up being a bargain, as Green looked like a top-three pick before a disappointing spring in college ball dropped him in the draft. Tools-wise, he's a plus defender with power and speed, and while the A's system is one of the deepest in baseball, it's thin at shortstop, giving Green a clear path to the big leagues that could take less than two years to traverse.

Scott Hairston   OF

Bats: R   Throws: R   Height: 6' 0"   Weight: 185   Born: May 25, 1980   Age: 30

YEAR	TEAM	LVL	AGE	PA	R	2B	3B	HR	RBI	BB	SO	SB	CS	EqBRR	AVG	OBP	SLG	EqAVG	EqOBP	EqSLG	EqA	VORP	WARP	DEFENSE			
2007	ARI	MLB	27	199	21	13	1	3	16	19	37	2	0	-1.0	.222	.301	.358	.220	.303	.350	.232	-2.5	-0.1	43-LF	1		
2007	SDN	MLB	27	95	16	5	1	8	20	7	18	0	0	-0.1	.287	.337	.644	.310	.358	.701	.332	10.7	0.9	20-LF	-2		
2008	SDN	MLB	28	362	42	18	3	17	31	28	84	3	1	-0.1	.248	.312	.479	.272	.331	.520	.284	18.5	3.0	42-CF	4	34-LF	3
2009	SDN	MLB	29	216	26	14	1	10	29	17	45	8	1	1.8	.299	.358	.533	.343	.395	.606	.328	23.7	2.8	33-CF	-3	15-LF	4
2009	OAK	MLB	29	248	24	13	1	7	35	8	38	3	2	-2.6	.236	.262	.391	.247	.271	.403	.229	-2.7	0.0	40-LF	3	12-CF	-1
2010	OAK	MLB	30	424	51	22	2	18	51	36	89	5	3	-0.4	.264	.331	.473	.264	.330	.465	.269	13.4	1.8	91-LF	3		

Breakout: 16%   Improve: 43%   Collapse: 15%   Attrition: 12%   MLB: 98%   Comparables: Roy Sievers, Candy Maldonado, Wally Post, Irish Meusel

Hairston seemed to be finally living up to his early-career reputation as a hitting machine early in the season with the Padres, but after the trade to Oakland, he stopped hitting. A variety of leg issues, however, provided a mitigating factor. His 17 home runs tied a career high, and when you consider that he reached that number while playing in two of baseball's nastiest offensive parks, there is still room for optimism here. He may have to compete with Rajai Davis, dislocated from center field with the Coco Crisp signing, for the starting job in left.

Adam Kennedy — 2B/3B
Bats: L Throws: R Height: 6' 1" Weight: 195 Born: January 10, 1976 Age: 34

YEAR	TEAM	LVL	AGE	PA	R	2B	3B	HR	RBI	BB	SO	SB	CS	EqBRR	AVG	OBP	SLG	EqAVG	EqOBP	EqSLG	EqA	VORP	WARP	DEFENSE			
2007	SLN	MLB	31	306	27	9	1	3	18	22	33	6	2	-1.5	.219	.282	.290	.222	.288	.290	.206	-6.6	-1.6	71-2B	-6		
2008	SLN	MLB	32	365	42	17	4	2	36	21	43	7	1	3.3	.280	.321	.372	.290	.328	.382	.252	6.9	0.8	71-2B	-2	6-RF	1
2009	DUR	AAA	33	93	11	4	0	3	9	10	12	2	1	-0.7	.280	.366	.439	.253	.333	.398	.254	1.8	-0.1	16-2B	-3		
2009	OAK	MLB	33	586	65	29	1	11	63	45	86	20	6	2.7	.289	.348	.410	.300	.357	.421	.272	24.4	1.7	77-3B	-3	47-2B	-6
2010	OAK	MLB	34	500	52	20	1	8	51	42	72	11	6	0.7	.264	.331	.363	.265	.331	.365	.242	3.2	0.1	109-3B	-2		

Breakout: 10% Improve: 43% Collapse: 28% Attrition: 24%   MLB: 94%   Comparables: Amos Strunk, Ken Oberkfell, Jim Gantner, Glenn Adams

After he failed to make the Rays' roster out of spring training, Kennedy killed time at Durham until they dealt him to Oakland. He turned into one of Oakland's most valuable performers by sheer adequacy, filling in for the injured Eric Chavez and Mark Ellis while putting together the best year of his career since his 2002 season with the Angels. Kennedy remains the same player he was in his 20s, an infielder who can hit for average while popping a smattering of extra-base hits. His career reinvigorated by his Bay-side stay, he remains a free agent at press time, but one with plenty of suitors.

Eric Patterson — UT
Bats: L Throws: R Height: 5' 11" Weight: 170 Born: April 8, 1983 Age: 27

YEAR	TEAM	LVL	AGE	PA	R	2B	3B	HR	RBI	BB	SO	SB	CS	EqBRR	AVG	OBP	SLG	EqAVG	EqOBP	EqSLG	EqA	VORP	WARP	DEFENSE			
2007	IOW	AAA	24	582	94	28	6	14	65	54	85	24	9	1.3	.297	.362	.455	.272	.333	.410	.261	17.3	0.3	79-2B	-15	23-CF	1
2008	IOW	AAA	25	220	33	16	3	6	28	12	45	11	0	2.7	.320	.358	.517	.282	.315	.427	.263	7.5	1.6	44-2B	6		
2008	CHN	MLB	25	44	5	1	0	1	7	5	12	2	1	0.6	.237	.318	.342	.237	.318	.342	.241	-0.1	-0.5	8-LF	-4		
2008	SAC	AAA	25	124	18	8	2	4	19	9	28	8	2	1.3	.330	.380	.550	.297	.344	.477	.282	7.1	0.7	22-2B	-1	4-CF	0
2008	OAK	MLB	25	104	11	3	0	0	8	12	24	8	0	1.5	.174	.269	.207	.174	.269	.207	.201	-3.4	-0.8	19-2B	-3	7-LF	-1
2009	SAC	AAA	26	530	91	29	11	12	56	52	81	43	6	9.1	.307	.376	.494	.298	.359	.464	.286	29.9	3.0	45-2B	2	26-CF	-2
2009	OAK	MLB	26	110	15	5	1	1	11	14	25	6	1	1.7	.287	.373	.394	.298	.378	.404	.287	5.5	0.4	20-LF	2	3-2B	-2
2010	OAK	MLB	27	542	66	25	5	10	51	46	116	20	6	2.9	.253	.317	.382	.255	.319	.383	.243	7.1	0.5	89-2B	-3		

Breakout: 7% Improve: 26% Collapse: 32% Attrition: 18%   MLB: 45%   Comparables: Terry Bradshaw, Jack Perconte, Eric Bullock, Tim Knight

Patterson is the younger brother of veteran outfielder Corey, and as one scout observed of him, "Half the tools, but twice the ballplayer." The A's have tried for years to develop their own version of Chone Figgins, and they might have finally hit pay dirt. He can play all three outfield positions and can pass at second base; an attempt to expand his options to include third base at Sacramento last season didn't go well. But with four positions and his ability as an above-average runner who knows how to work the count, he could help out immediately, not least because players like this create a lot of roster flexibility.

Cliff Pennington — SS
Bats: S Throws: R Height: 5' 11" Weight: 185 Born: June 15, 1984 Age: 26

YEAR	TEAM	LVL	AGE	PA	R	2B	3B	HR	RBI	BB	SO	SB	CS	EqBRR	AVG	OBP	SLG	EqAVG	EqOBP	EqSLG	EqA	VORP	WARP	DEFENSE			
2007	STO	A+	23	333	50	17	3	6	36	43	54	9	2	0.2	.255	.348	.399	.223	.300	.328	.226	1.1	1.1	66-SS	8		
2007	MID	AA	23	314	41	13	2	2	21	38	35	8	2	2.7	.251	.343	.336	.235	.314	.314	.228	1.5	-0.8	64-SS	-8	5-2B	0
2008	MID	AA	24	244	42	7	2	0	18	39	36	20	1	0.8	.260	.379	.314	.227	.329	.270	.231	1.7	0.2	34-SS	3	17-2B	-3
2008	SAC	AAA	24	294	47	9	3	2	16	54	34	11	5	-2.5	.297	.426	.386	.291	.404	.369	.282	17.0	3.4	46-SS	13	15-2B	-1
2008	OAK	MLB	24	117	14	5	0	0	9	13	18	4	1	0.9	.242	.339	.293	.255	.351	.306	.248	2.0	-0.3	15-2B	-1	7-3B	0
2009	SAC	AAA	25	417	48	22	3	3	40	45	54	27	4	3.8	.264	.345	.367	.261	.333	.356	.253	12.2	1.4	78-SS	1	16-2B	-2
2009	OAK	MLB	25	229	27	11	3	4	21	19	46	7	5	-1.5	.279	.342	.418	.293	.355	.433	.267	10.8	1.2	60-SS	0		
2010	OAK	MLB	26	593	72	26	4	6	48	66	100	16	5	0.7	.251	.337	.353	.253	.338	.354	.245	11.1	1.6	129-SS	3		

Breakout: 13% Improve: 44% Collapse: 15% Attrition: 23%   MLB: 100%   Comparables: Mike Yastrzemski, Matt Tolbert, Elvis Pena, Jeff Forney

Once it became clear that the ship that had carried Bobby Crosby off to the underworld would not be returning him to port and Orlando Cabrera had been dealt to Minnesota, Pennington became the starting shortstop for the last two months of the season. He enters 2010 with little competition for the job. One of those players whose greatest strength might be a lack of weaknesses, Pennington sprays singles to all fields with a contact-oriented approach, yet he draws enough walks as well, while also being a solid, if unspectacular defender. He's the kind of player who can hold the job down and not hurt the team, but Oakland will be looking for something better, waiting for Grant Green to arrive.

Landon Powell   C   Bats: S   Throws: R   Height: 6' 3"   Weight: 250   Born: March 19, 1982   Age: 28

YEAR	TEAM	LVL	AGE	PA	R	2B	3B	HR	RBI	BB	SO	SB	CS	EqBRR	AVG	OBP	SLG	EqAVG	EqOBP	EqSLG	EqA	VORP	WARP	DEFENSE			
2007	MID	AA	25	256	46	9	2	11	39	36	40	1	0	-2.0	.292	.391	.502	.252	.336	.416	.263	12.3	2.0	58-C	4		
2008	SAC	AAA	26	367	42	11	0	15	53	63	85	0	1	-2.5	.230	.360	.417	.210	.322	.345	.240	8.0	0.7	85-C	-2		
2009	OAK	MLB	27	155	19	7	0	7	30	14	36	0	0	-1.5	.229	.297	.429	.236	.303	.429	.253	3.9	1.0	31-C	4	5-1B	0
2010	OAK	MLB	28	268	32	10	1	9	36	31	65	0	0	-1.0	.231	.319	.400	.230	.317	.397	.246	6.5	0.9	62-C	1		

Breakout: 23% Improve: 41% Collapse: 26% Attrition: 10%   MLB: 46%   Comparables: Bobby Hughes, Jason Varitek, Bill Haselman, Scott Hatteberg

Oakland probably feels lucky just to have gotten anything out of former first-round pick Powell (2004), whose minor-league apprenticeship went off track a few times, mostly due to knee surgeries and conditioning issues that had seen Powell's weight push 300 pounds at times. Now at least 260 pounds (don't believe the official weight above), he's still a bit plump, but he turned out to be a nice reserve catcher, provided that what one looks for in a backup was a mix of walks, power, and a plus arm. If he can stay healthy, he could remain in this role for a decade. Smile when you call him "Shanty."

Kurt Suzuki   C   Bats: R   Throws: R   Height: 6' 0"   Weight: 195   Born: October 4, 1983   Age: 26

YEAR	TEAM	LVL	AGE	PA	R	2B	3B	HR	RBI	BB	SO	SB	CS	EqBRR	AVG	OBP	SLG	EqAVG	EqOBP	EqSLG	EqA	VORP	WARP	DEFENSE	
2007	SAC	AAA	23	240	32	9	0	3	27	21	41	0	0	-0.7	.280	.351	.365	.271	.335	.336	.242	5.0	0.7	43-C	1
2007	OAK	MLB	23	248	27	13	0	7	39	24	39	0	0	-0.8	.249	.327	.408	.256	.332	.412	.264	12.7	1.7	60-C	2
2008	OAK	MLB	24	588	54	25	1	7	42	44	69	2	3	-1.6	.279	.346	.370	.289	.356	.382	.261	24.6	3.7	136-C	7
2009	OAK	MLB	25	614	74	37	1	15	88	28	59	8	2	3.9	.274	.313	.421	.282	.320	.430	.260	25.0	3.0	131-C	2
2010	OAK	MLB	26	603	69	28	1	14	77	48	81	4	3	0.1	.276	.344	.408	.278	.345	.406	.259	22.5	2.7	136-C	2

Breakout: 22% Improve: 50% Collapse: 13% Attrition: 8%   MLB: 94%   Comparables: Don Slaught, Spud Davis, Tony Pena, Del Crandall

Analyzing Suzuki's 2009 performance requires something of a balancing act. He became much more comfortable with letting his bat fly, leading to more doubles and more than twice as many home runs, yet his new free-swinging ways cut into his walk rate so much as to leave his offense in roughly the same place. Defensively, he has improved his receiving skills and, in this way, played a big role in the successful development of the young pitchers. Teams ran on him slightly more often, and he gunned out just a quarter of them, marks that may improve as the staff gets more experience. Above-average everyday catchers are hard to come by, and Suzuki is just that and is still only turning 26 to boot.

Ryan Sweeney   RF   Bats: L   Throws: L   Height: 6' 4"   Weight: 215   Born: February 20, 1985   Age: 25

YEAR	TEAM	LVL	AGE	PA	R	2B	3B	HR	RBI	BB	SO	SB	CS	EqBRR	AVG	OBP	SLG	EqAVG	EqOBP	EqSLG	EqA	VORP	WARP	DEFENSE			
2007	CHR	AAA	22	450	50	17	2	10	47	48	71	8	5	-1.5	.270	.348	.398	.254	.327	.378	.248	4.4	2.2	46-CF	1	34-RF	5
2007	CHA	MLB	22	49	5	3	0	1	5	4	5	0	1	0.3	.200	.265	.333	.200	.265	.333	.200	-2.0	-0.1	10-LF	1		
2008	OAK	MLB	23	433	53	18	2	5	45	38	67	9	1	2.7	.286	.350	.383	.296	.360	.398	.272	15.2	2.7	55-RF	10	41-CF	-2
2009	OAK	MLB	24	534	68	31	3	6	53	40	67	6	5	0.9	.293	.348	.407	.305	.358	.417	.268	17.3	3.2	67-RF	6	51-CF	4
2010	OAK	MLB	25	495	62	23	2	10	53	49	77	8	4	0.3	.277	.351	.404	.279	.351	.403	.261	10.9	2.0	101-RF	7		

Breakout: 19% Improve: 45% Collapse: 9% Attrition: 4%   MLB: 100%   Comparables: Derrick May, Dave Nilsson, Garret Anderson, Jeremy Hermida

Sweeney certainly looks the part of a slugging outfielder, a 6-foot-4 athlete with as pretty a swing as you'll find, but the power that was forecast to come from that swing has now generated 12 home runs in 948 big-league at-bats. He's an excellent defensive outfielder, but given his lack of power (and patience, too) plus his troubles hitting lefties, he's simply not enough of a hitter to play every day. He'd be an excellent fourth outfielder on a good team, but Oakland isn't that team yet.

Brett Wallace — 1B/3B

Bats: L   Throws: R   Height: 6' 1"   Weight: 245   Born: August 26, 1986   Age: 23

YEAR	TEAM	LVL	AGE	PA	R	2B	3B	HR	RBI	BB	SO	SB	CS	EqBRR	AVG	OBP	SLG	EqAVG	EqOBP	EqSLG	EqA	VORP	WARP	DEFENSE	
2008	QUD	A	21	177	28	8	1	5	25	17	32	0	0	-2.2	.327	.418	.490	.296	.367	.459	.285	8.6	0.6	37-3B -4	
2008	SFD	AA	21	57	13	5	0	3	11	2	7	0	0	-0.8	.367	.456	.653	.327	.397	.577	.322	5.4	0.4	11-3B -2	
2009	SFD	AA	22	154	22	5	0	5	16	18	34	0	0	-3.2	.281	.403	.438	.246	.344	.388	.259	3.6	0.3	30-3B -1	
2009	MEM	AAA	22	243	22	11	0	6	19	15	42	0	1	-3.4	.293	.346	.423	.295	.342	.420	.263	6.6	0.8	49-3B -1	6-1B 1
2009	SAC	AAA	22	203	32	10	0	9	28	14	40	1	1	-0.4	.302	.365	.505	.293	.350	.478	.282	9.2	0.2	34-3B -8	6-1B 0
2010	TOR	MLB	23	555	69	24	1	19	60	44	119	1	2	-3.4	.270	.339	.436	.274	.344	.437	.265	17.3	1.2	118-3B -6	

Breakout: 18% Improve: 42% Collapse: 13% Attrition: 2%   MLB: 7%   Comparables: Aubrey Huff, Ray Ortiz, Dan Peltier, Ray Brown

Wallace gets a lot of hype as a hitting machine, but when you add up his three stops in the minors last year, you get a line of .293/.367/.455. That's certainly good, especially for a player at Double-A and Triple-A in his first full season, but it's hardly worthy of the attention he gets. Even more troubling is his defense. When Toronto traded Michael Taylor for him as part of the Halladay/Lee off-season orgy, they all but admitted that he's a first baseman. That's a position where mashing is the bare minimum, but the consistently overrated "Walrus" really won't be much of an upgrade over incumbent Lyle Overbay.

Jemile Weeks — 2B

Bats: S   Throws: R   Height: 5' 10"   Weight: 175   Born: January 26, 1987   Age: 23

YEAR	TEAM	LVL	AGE	PA	R	2B	3B	HR	RBI	BB	SO	SB	CS	EqBRR	AVG	OBP	SLG	EqAVG	EqOBP	EqSLG	EqA	VORP	WARP	DEFENSE
2008	KNC	A	21	90	11	3	1	1	8	13	12	6	2	0.5	.297	.422	.405	.273	.371	.377	.268	3.3	-0.5	18-2B -8
2009	STO	A+	22	232	29	9	2	7	31	26	40	5	1	-1.1	.299	.385	.468	.255	.325	.380	.248	3.5	0.4	46-2B 0
2009	MID	AA	22	123	10	5	0	2	13	10	16	4	0	0.7	.238	.303	.343	.213	.267	.306	.212	-2.7	-1.1	27-2B -7
2010	OAK	MLB	23	324	30	14	1	6	30	32	61	4	2	0.0	.243	.321	.363	.243	.321	.366	.237	2.3	-0.4	68-2B -6

Breakout: 14% Improve: 45% Collapse: 21% Attrition: 6%   MLB: 1%   Comparables: Jake Thrower, John Tamargo, Joe Morales, Terry Crowley

Oakland's other younger brother of a more famous active veteran (in this case, of Milwaukee's Richie), Jemile Weeks is a unique prospect in that he's a toolsy 23-year-old with the kind of rawness normally associated with a teenager. He needs a lot of repetition to develop his skills, but a steady stream of injuries has limited him to just 99 games in the year and a half since he was drafted. He has a solid approach, some power potential, and loads of speed, but he remains a bit of a mess at second base. The whole package might end up working out better in center field. Fortunately, his bat will be good enough to play anywhere.

PITCHERS

Brett Anderson

Bats: L   Throws: L   Height: 6' 4"   Weight: 215   Born: February 1, 1988   Age: 22

YEAR	TEAM	LVL	AGE	W	L	SV	G	GS	IP	H	HR	BB	SO	GB%	BABIP	STUFF	WHIP	ERA	SIERA	DERA	EqH9	EqHR9	EqBB9	EqSO9	VORP	SN/WX
2007	SBN	A	19	8	4	0	14	14	81¹	76	3	10	85	60%	.323	35	1.06	2.21	2.60	4.24	9.9	1.2	1.8	6.0	10.5	0.69
2007	VIS	A+	19	3	3	0	9	9	39	50	6	11	40	47%	.379	20	1.56	4.85	3.29	5.75	13.3	2.0	3.0	6.5	-1.0	-0.02
2008	STO	A+	20	9	4	0	14	13	74	68	5	18	80	61%	.309	33	1.16	4.14	2.87	5.07	9.3	1.4	2.8	6.3	3.4	0.23
2008	MID	AA	20	2	1	0	6	6	31	27	3	9	38	67%	.324	29	1.16	2.61	2.45	3.41	8.7	1.2	2.8	8.7	6.7	0.43
2009	OAK	MLB	21	11	11	0	30	30	175¹	180	20	45	150	57%	.309	30	1.28	4.06	3.61	4.54	9.0	1.0	2.0	6.7	18.4	3.86
2010	OAK	MLB	22	8	9	0	28	28	151	160	20	48	119	53%	.313	27	1.37	4.47	3.97	4.66	9.4	1.2	2.6	6.6	14.2	2.81

Breakout: 9% Improve: 49% Collapse: 9% Attrition: 8%   MLB: 100%   Comparables: Renyel Pinto, Scott Olsen, Jaime Garcia, Glendon Rusch

The son of a pitching coach, Anderson was always a mature product with above-average stuff and command, so it wasn't a big surprise to see him handle his own as a 21-year-old in the big leagues. What was surprising was how much of a forward leap he took during the year, as he now looks like a potential All-Star. His curve and changeup were always advanced for his years, but it was with his fastball that he took the largest step forward in 2009, because during the second half of the season, the big lefty was parked at 93-94 mph while touching 97. There was much debate going into the year as to whether Anderson or Trevor Cahill was the better prospect, but one year later, it's less of an argument, as Anderson has upgraded from good to great.

Andrew Bailey

Bats: R   Throws: R   Height: 6' 3"   Weight: 220   Born: May 31, 1984   Age: 26

YEAR	TEAM	LVL	AGE	W	L	SV	G	GS	IP	H	HR	BB	SO	GB%	BABIP	STUFF	WHIP	ERA	SIERA	DERA	EqH9	EqHR9	EqBB9	EqSO9	VORP	SN/WX
2007	KNC	A	23	1	4	0	11	10	51	42	6	22	74	49%	.319	8	1.25	3.35	2.34	5.79	9.8	2.3	4.8	8.9	-1.5	-0.40
2007	STO	A+	23	3	4	0	11	11	66	56	8	31	72	38%	.300	3	1.32	3.82	3.47	4.68	9.7	2.0	4.7	6.9	5.5	0.30
2008	MID	AA	24	5	9	0	37	15	110¹	99	13	56	110	50%	.287	-8	1.40	4.32	3.85	5.67	8.4	1.5	4.7	6.6	-2.0	-1.16
2009	OAK	MLB	25	6	3	26	68	0	83¹	49	5	24	91	46%	.217	36	0.88	1.84	2.72	1.91	5.1	0.5	2.2	8.3	33.7	4.26
2010	OAK	MLB	26	4	5	14	61	1	69	64	8	34	66	42%	.300	5	1.41	4.39	3.93	4.48	8.0	1.0	4.1	8.0	7.8	1.20

Breakout: 27%   Improve: 57%   Collapse: 9%   Attrition: 18%   MLB: 82%   Comparables: Jonathan Papelbon, Rick Huisman, Mark Eichhorn, Bill Dawley

If you've been bragging that you had Bailey in your Rookie of the Year pool going into the year, you are a genius or, more likely, a liar. Taking over the closer's role from Brad Ziegler in June, Bailey's combination of a mid-90s fastball and deceptive cutter proved to be unhittable. Opposing batters averaged just .167 against him, and to make things even scarier, he started throwing strikes in the second half, walking just five batters after the All-Star break. Based on his minor-league numbers, this all seems like a bit of an anomaly, but the scouts think he has the ability to keep it up.

Jerry Blevins

Bats: L   Throws: L   Height: 6' 6"   Weight: 175   Born: September 6, 1983   Age: 26

YEAR	TEAM	LVL	AGE	W	L	SV	G	GS	IP	H	HR	BB	SO	GB%	BABIP	STUFF	WHIP	ERA	SIERA	DERA	EqH9	EqHR9	EqBB9	EqSO9	VORP	SN/WX
2007	DAY	A+	23	1	0	6	15	0	23²	13	0	5	32	—	.250	23	0.76	0.38	1.69	1.39	6.0	0.4	2.4	9.1	10.4	1.45
2007	TEN	AA	23	2	2	3	23	0	29¹	23	1	8	37	36%	.301	18	1.06	1.53	2.30	2.25	8.7	0.6	2.6	8.0	10.1	0.78
2007	MID	AA	23	1	3	1	17	0	21²	18	2	5	29	42%	.327	20	1.06	3.32	1.81	4.72	8.6	1.4	2.3	9.9	1.7	-0.30
2007	OAK	MLB	23	0	1	0	6	0	4²	8	1	2	3	—	.368	-28	2.14	9.64	6.27	10.80	14.4	1.8	3.6	5.4	-2.9	-0.21
2008	SAC	AAA	24	2	2	10	28	0	32¹	31	3	6	36	48%	.308	1	1.14	2.78	2.69	5.01	9.2	1.4	1.7	7.0	1.8	1.11
2008	OAK	MLB	24	1	3	0	36	0	37²	32	2	13	35	42%	.291	11	1.19	3.11	3.62	3.34	8.2	0.5	2.7	7.7	8.7	0.97
2009	SAC	AAA	25	5	3	2	45	0	63¹	65	5	18	62	48%	.328	-10	1.31	3.84	3.35	4.88	10.5	1.5	2.7	6.8	4.2	0.51
2009	OAK	MLB	25	0	0	0	20	0	22¹	19	2	6	23	37%	.288	13	1.12	4.84	3.04	4.50	7.4	0.8	2.0	8.2	2.4	0.21
2010	OAK	MLB	26	4	5	2	64	0	73²	78	9	26	60	36%	.318	-2	1.42	4.61	4.20	4.85	9.5	1.1	3.0	6.8	5.4	1.69

Breakout: 17%   Improve: 40%   Collapse: 32%   Attrition: 14%   MLB: 44%   Comparables: Rodney Windes, Ben Julianel, Tom Gorman, Gene Walter

As a 6-foot-6 lefty with above-average velocity, Blevins surprisingly hasn't established himself in the big leagues. The problem is that beyond his heater, the rest of his arsenal falls short. He tried to convert his slurvy breaking ball into a true slider in 2009, but that was met with mixed results, as more often than not, the pitch would still flatten out. Unless something suddenly works out for him, he's probably headed back to Triple-A, but his size, left-handedness, and radar-gun readings will provide for plenty of opportunities.

Dallas Braden

Bats: L   Throws: L   Height: 6' 1"   Weight: 195   Born: August 13, 1983   Age: 26

YEAR	TEAM	LVL	AGE	W	L	SV	G	GS	IP	H	HR	BB	SO	GB%	BABIP	STUFF	WHIP	ERA	SIERA	DERA	EqH9	EqHR9	EqBB9	EqSO9	VORP	SN/WX
2007	MID	AA	23	1	0	0	2	2	12	5	2	3	13	47%	.125	11	0.67	2.25	2.35	2.45	4.9	1.6	2.5	8.2	3.7	0.31
2007	SAC	AAA	23	2	3	0	11	11	64	51	4	18	74	47%	.285	26	1.08	2.95	2.68	3.61	8.1	1.2	2.7	7.7	13.1	1.50
2007	OAK	MLB	23	1	8	0	20	14	72¹	91	9	26	55	43%	.342	-10	1.62	6.72	4.42	6.91	11.2	1.2	2.9	6.0	-11.3	0.24
2008	SAC	AAA	24	3	1	0	11	9	53¹	49	7	11	54	50%	.302	6	1.12	2.36	2.85	3.67	9.7	2.0	2.0	6.8	9.9	1.37
2008	OAK	MLB	24	5	4	0	19	10	71²	77	8	25	41	43%	.307	-10	1.42	4.14	4.96	4.45	10.4	1.2	3.0	4.9	7.7	1.65
2009	OAK	MLB	25	8	9	0	22	22	136²	144	9	42	81	41%	.297	13	1.36	3.89	4.86	3.95	8.9	0.6	2.3	4.6	23.8	3.50
2010	OAK	MLB	26	7	9	0	29	24	132¹	143	17	46	86	44%	.306	1	1.42	4.65	4.61	4.84	9.6	1.1	2.9	5.4	9.8	2.30

Breakout: 11%   Improve: 46%   Collapse: 15%   Attrition: 14%   MLB: 87%   Comparables: Noah Lowry, Bob Shirley, Ken Brett, Mike Mason

Your classic crafty left-hander, Braden throws a fastball that sits at just 86-88 mph, but he gets by with a lot of movement and deception, as well as a very good changeup. Given this profile and some fly-ball tendencies, he's in exactly the right park to succeed. There's no reason to expect him to get better, but he has such a thin margin for error that not only could he get worse, but he could get much, much worse. Braden's season was cut short by a rash on his foot that turned into an infection and ultimately caused some nerve damage. He should be 100 percent for spring training, however, and will be expected to eat up some innings. Nice tidbit: he's a latter-day Mulholland, because after seven pickoffs in 2008, he didn't allow a single steal in 2009.

Craig Breslow

| | | | | | | | | | | | | Bats: L | Throws: L | | Height: 6' 0" | | Weight: 185 | | Born: August 8, 1980 | | Age: 29 |

YEAR	TEAM	LVL	AGE	W	L	SV	G	GS	IP	H	HR	BB	SO	GB%	BABIP	STUFF	WHIP	ERA	SIERA	DERA	EqH9	EqHR9	EqBB9	EqSO9	VORP	SN/WX
2007	PAW	AAA	26	2	3	1	49	1	68²	70	6	25	73	47%	.328	-3	1.38	4.06	3.33	5.41	9.8	1.1	3.3	7.5	0.6	-0.76
2008	CLE	MLB	27	0	0	0	7	0	8¹	10	1	5	7	40%	.333	-6	1.80	3.24	4.86	3.12	10.4	1.0	4.2	6.2	2.3	-0.02
2008	MIN	MLB	27	0	2	1	42	0	38²	24	0	14	32	45%	.233	15	0.98	1.63	3.85	2.13	5.4	0.0	2.8	6.9	14.2	0.94
2009	MIN	MLB	28	1	2	0	17	0	14¹	11	3	11	11	35%	.211	-6	1.53	6.28	5.58	6.28	6.9	1.9	6.3	6.3	-1.2	-0.42
2009	OAK	MLB	28	7	5	0	60	0	55¹	37	5	18	44	34%	.216	8	0.99	2.60	4.12	3.13	5.8	0.8	2.6	6.3	14.4	1.40
2010	OAK	MLB	29	3	4	0	60	0	59	56	7	23	48	41%	.292	1	1.34	4.25	4.17	4.37	8.3	1.1	3.4	6.7	7.4	0.35

Breakout: 16% Improve: 39% Collapse: 22% Attrition: 9%   MLB: 80%   Comparables: Will Ohman, Alan Embree, Joe Klink, Scott Ruskin

A solid free-talent find for the A's, because while Breslow has bounced around a bit, he's been a surprisingly effective reliever and much more than just a situational soldier, as he's nearly as good against righties as he is against lefties. Primarily a fastball/slider type who hits 89-92 mph with his heater, Breslow has above-average command and attacks hitters. While his ceiling is probably as a seventh-inning type, teams need those guys, too.

Trevor Cahill

| | | | | | | | | | | | | Bats: R | Throws: R | | Height: 6' 3" | | Weight: 195 | | Born: March 1, 1988 | | Age: 22 |

YEAR	TEAM	LVL	AGE	W	L	SV	G	GS	IP	H	HR	BB	SO	GB%	BABIP	STUFF	WHIP	ERA	SIERA	DERA	EqH9	EqHR9	EqBB9	EqSO9	VORP	SN/WX
2007	KNC	A	19	11	4	0	20	19	105¹	85	3	40	117	59%	.306	37	1.19	2.73	3.06	4.37	9.1	1.0	4.4	6.7	12.0	0.68
2008	STO	A+	20	5	4	0	14	13	87¹	52	3	31	103	64%	.246	57	0.95	2.78	2.66	3.71	6.5	1.0	3.9	7.3	16.2	1.19
2008	MID	AA	20	6	1	0	7	6	37	24	2	19	33	70%	.234	35	1.16	2.19	3.65	4.20	6.4	1.0	4.8	6.1	5.1	0.34
2009	OAK	MLB	21	10	13	0	32	32	178²	185	27	72	90	58%	.272	10	1.44	4.63	5.09	4.69	8.9	1.3	3.2	4.0	15.9	3.73
2010	OAK	MLB	22	8	10	0	30	28	157²	155	20	71	99	48%	.283	17	1.43	4.60	4.89	4.73	8.6	1.1	3.8	5.2	13.4	2.99

Breakout: 6% Improve: 43% Collapse: 13% Attrition: 13%   MLB: 100%   Comparables: Kyle Davies, Homer Bailey, Javier Vazquez, Yovani Gallardo

On the surface, Cahill's rookie campaign went pretty well; unless you're a Dwight Gooden–level hurler of lightning bolts, making 32 big-league starts at 21 years old and having slightly below-average results is meeting expectations. Delving deeper into his season reveals some disturbing trends, most of which revolve around walk and strikeout rates that were, respectively, much higher and lower than expected. As Cahill's command was going downhill, he all but abandoned his curve, which had been a go-to offering during his minor-league days. Limited to being a fastball/change pitcher, he just stopped missing bats. The curve has to return to being an integral part of his package if he's going to enjoy continued success.

Santiago Casilla

| | | | | | | | | | | | | Bats: R | Throws: R | | Height: 6' 0" | | Weight: 200 | | Born: June 25, 1980 | | Age: 30 |

YEAR	TEAM	LVL	AGE	W	L	SV	G	GS	IP	H	HR	BB	SO	GB%	BABIP	STUFF	WHIP	ERA	SIERA	DERA	EqH9	EqHR9	EqBB9	EqSO9	VORP	SN/WX
2007	SAC	AAA	27	2	1	3	22	0	24	18	1	14	29	57%	.293	10	1.33	4.12	3.31	4.76	7.9	0.8	5.6	8.3	1.9	0.57
2007	OAK	MLB	27	3	1	2	46	0	50²	43	6	23	52	33%	.270	4	1.30	4.44	3.80	4.21	7.5	1.2	3.7	8.1	7.4	1.06
2008	OAK	MLB	28	2	1	2	51	0	50¹	60	5	20	43	49%	.348	-5	1.59	3.93	4.13	3.92	11.1	1.1	3.3	6.9	8.6	0.89
2009	OAK	MLB	29	1	2	0	46	0	48¹	61	6	25	35	55%	.335	-19	1.78	5.96	4.82	6.30	10.6	1.1	4.0	5.4	-4.4	-0.14
2010	OAK	MLB	30	2	4	2	54	0	53	59	7	24	43	44%	.325	-9	1.56	5.36	4.40	5.53	9.8	1.2	3.9	6.7	-0.2	0.69

Breakout: 15% Improve: 44% Collapse: 18% Attrition: 15%   MLB: 82%   Comparables: Vinnie Chulk, Jerry Johnson, Brian Holton, Cris Carpenter

Casilla can bring it in around 94-98 mph with his fastball, but that also represents the sum of his abilities. Now pushing 30, the pitcher formerly known as Jairo Garcia has yet to throw strikes consistently, and that, along with an always inconsistent breaking pitch, leaves him far more hittable than a guy with his velocity should be. The A's expressed their confidence in Casilla's likelihood of figuring things out by removing him from the 40-man roster to make room for Rule 5 pick Bobby Cassevah.

Joey Devine

Bats: R   Throws: R   Height: 5′ 11″   Weight: 205   Born: September 19, 1983   Age: 26

YEAR	TEAM	LVL	AGE	W	L	SV	G	GS	IP	H	HR	BB	SO	GB%	BABIP	STUFF	WHIP	ERA	SIERA	DERA	EqH9	EqHR9	EqBB9	EqSO9	VORP	SN/WX
2007	MIS	AA	23	2	4	16	33	0	35	26	1	13	51	54%	.338	17	1.11	2.06	2.07	3.09	8.7	0.8	3.7	9.3	8.6	-0.21
2007	RIC	AAA	23	3	0	4	17	0	22	15	1	6	27	48%	.259	22	0.95	1.64	2.36	2.66	6.5	0.8	2.5	8.6	6.9	0.92
2007	ATL	MLB	23	1	0	0	10	0	8¹	7	0	8	7	54%	.292	8	1.80	1.08	5.36	1.08	7.6	0.0	7.6	6.5	4.1	0.23
2008	OAK	MLB	24	6	1	1	42	0	45²	23	0	15	49	40%	.217	32	0.83	0.59	2.80	1.62	4.9	0.0	2.6	8.7	19.1	2.36
2010	OAK	MLB	26	3	3	3	45	1	55¹	55	6	24	45	45%	.303	0	1.43	4.36	4.28	4.48	8.6	1.0	3.7	6.7	6.3	1.18

Breakout: 13%   Improve: 31%   Collapse: 39%   Attrition: 10%   MLB: 52%   Comparables: Scott Strickland, Chad Orvella, Jay Tessmer, Brad Clontz

The A's seem to always find some kind of reliever who goes nuts on the league without having given any prior notice that he was about to do so, and in 2008, it was Devine. Unfortunately, Devine's elbow went pop at the end of March, and after Tommy John surgery, he now has a 2009 stat line with no actual numbers next to it. His stuff was closer-worthy during his breakout, and with Bailey's emergence, there will be less pressure on him to reestablish that stuff quickly upon his return. He'll be throwing this spring, but the jury is still out on his readiness for Opening Day.

Justin Duchscherer

Bats: R   Throws: R   Height: 6′ 2″   Weight: 200   Born: November 19, 1977   Age: 32

YEAR	TEAM	LVL	AGE	W	L	SV	G	GS	IP	H	HR	BB	SO	GB%	BABIP	STUFF	WHIP	ERA	SIERA	DERA	EqH9	EqHR9	EqBB9	EqSO9	VORP	SN/WX
2007	OAK	MLB	29	3	3	0	17	0	16¹	18	3	8	13	64%	.294	-11	1.59	4.96	4.28	4.86	9.7	1.6	3.8	5.9	1.2	0.04
2008	OAK	MLB	30	10	8	0	22	22	141²	107	11	34	95	47%	.235	25	1.00	2.54	4.12	2.97	7.1	0.8	2.0	5.5	38.6	5.77
2010	OAK	MLB	32	3	3	0	15	0	52	52	6	18	34	44%	.290	4	1.34	4.34	4.57	4.42	8.6	1.0	2.8	5.4	6.3	1.34

Breakout: 8%   Improve: 38%   Collapse: 24%   Attrition: 23%   MLB: 69%   Comparables: Johnny Lanning, Jose Bautista, Bob Miller, Tom Brennan

After he'd had an excellent 2008 season that included an All-Star appearance, Duchscherer's elbow began acting up early in spring training. It seemed as if every time he'd report a positive throwing session, he'd get shut down again within a week because of the pain. While he made a handful of minor-league rehab appearances, he never got back to Oakland and was shut down in August with what was originally announced as a "nonbaseball issue" and later revealed to be clinical depression. He received treatment and is reportedly good to go for 2010, having inked an incentive-laden one-year deal to remain with the A's. He's a good reminder that these are human beings we're dealing with here, and it's hard not to root for a big comeback.

Dana Eveland

Bats: L   Throws: L   Height: 6′ 0″   Weight: 240   Born: October 29, 1983   Age: 26

YEAR	TEAM	LVL	AGE	W	L	SV	G	GS	IP	H	HR	BB	SO	GB%	BABIP	STUFF	WHIP	ERA	SIERA	DERA	EqH9	EqHR9	EqBB9	EqSO9	VORP	SN/WX
2007	TUC	AAA	23	1	0	0	7	5	27²	29	0	10	15	63%	.309	-3	1.41	1.95	4.65	2.44	8.5	0.3	3.3	3.6	9.4	0.92
2007	ARI	MLB	23	1	0	0	5	1	5	8	0	5	3	76%	.400	-26	2.60	14.40	5.38	12.66	13.5	0.0	6.8	5.1	-4.2	-0.29
2008	SAC	AAA	24	3	0	0	3	3	21	23	2	4	21	64%	.328	13	1.29	2.57	3.04	4.29	10.3	1.3	1.7	6.0	2.8	0.39
2008	OAK	MLB	24	9	9	0	29	29	168	172	10	77	118	56%	.312	9	1.48	4.34	4.62	4.34	9.7	0.6	3.8	5.8	20.8	4.28
2009	SAC	AAA	25	8	6	0	21	21	124	133	12	51	92	63%	.312	-26	1.48	4.94	4.24	6.85	10.9	1.8	3.8	5.0	-17.5	-0.42
2009	OAK	MLB	25	2	4	0	13	9	44	70	4	26	22	67%	.391	-25	2.18	7.16	5.37	7.42	13.8	0.8	4.7	3.9	-9.3	-0.53
2010	OAK	MLB	26	6	10	0	35	29	147	168	19	70	94	62%	.318	-9	1.62	5.46	4.71	5.68	10.1	1.2	4.0	5.3	-2.9	1.79

Breakout: 13%   Improve: 61%   Collapse: 9%   Attrition: 10%   MLB: 68%   Comparables: Chris Capuano, Paul Maholm, Steven Hammond, Doug Creek

After making 29 starts for Oakland in 2008, Eveland was slotted into the opening week rotation as the third starter, but was soon relegated to the minors as his substandard control went backward. Meanwhile, his inability to get strikeouts was paralleled by his inability to stay away from the buffet table. His fastball/slider combination should work at least in a bullpen role, but he has to work on fitting into his pants before he can work on getting hitters out.

Pedro Figueroa

Bats: L Throws: L Height: 6' 1" Weight: 164 Born: November 23, 1985 Age: 24

YEAR	TEAM	LVL	AGE	W	L	SV	G	GS	IP	H	HR	BB	SO	GB%	BABIP	STUFF	WHIP	ERA	SIERA	DERA	EqH9	EqHR9	EqBB9	EqSO9	VORP	SN/WX
2007	VAN	A-	21	2	2	1	17	7	44	41	2	31	35	58%	.300	-16	1.64	4.30	4.71	6.80	10.3	1.5	6.6	3.7	-5.9	-0.54
2008	VAN	A-	22	2	5	0	15	15	68²	62	3	32	77	47%	.321	-9	1.37	3.93	3.37	6.64	10.5	2.0	4.7	5.5	-8.1	-0.75
2009	KNC	A	23	10	2	0	16	16	86¹	89	6	31	78	54%	.331	-28	1.39	3.23	3.73	5.62	12.4	2.3	4.4	4.8	-1.0	-0.40
2009	STO	A+	23	3	4	0	11	11	65²	62	3	35	67	47%	.330	1	1.48	3.56	3.83	4.71	10.8	1.4	6.0	5.7	5.1	0.14
2010	OAK	MLB	24	3	9	0	34	20	107	137	18	68	63	47%	.333	-29	1.91	6.82	5.57	7.04	11.2	1.5	5.3	4.9	-18.3	1.98

Breakout: 11% Improve: 39% Collapse: 16% Attrition: 12% MLB: 7% Comparables: Todd James, Carlos Perez, Brian Brewer, Kevin King

A late bloomer, Figueroa ended up earning organizational minor-league pitcher of the year honors in his full-season debut, but there's some concern here, as that full-season debut took place in his fourth pro season. Still, his low-90s fastball touched 95 mph at times, while his slider gives him a second plus pitch. The A's are going to be aggressive with his development, and he could begin 2010 as high as Double-A. Scouts differ as to whether he projects as a starter or reliever, but agree that whichever role best suits him, he will be performing it in the major leagues.

Edgar Gonzalez

Bats: R Throws: R Height: 6' 2" Weight: 210 Born: February 23, 1983 Age: 27

YEAR	TEAM	LVL	AGE	W	L	SV	G	GS	IP	H	HR	BB	SO	GB%	BABIP	STUFF	WHIP	ERA	SIERA	DERA	EqH9	EqHR9	EqBB9	EqSO9	VORP	SN/WX
2007	ARI	MLB	24	8	4	0	32	12	102	110	18	28	62	49%	.283	-5	1.35	5.03	4.56	4.72	9.1	1.2	2.2	5.1	8.8	1.96
2008	ARI	MLB	25	1	3	0	17	6	48	58	8	21	32	46%	.318	-12	1.65	6.00	4.85	5.68	10.2	1.1	3.4	5.2	-1.0	-0.13
2009	SAC	AAA	26	3	2	0	7	7	39²	48	4	16	27	38%	.336	-19	1.61	5.22	4.86	6.27	12.3	1.9	3.9	4.6	-3.2	0.02
2009	OAK	MLB	26	0	4	0	26	6	65¹	76	4	28	39	50%	.324	-8	1.59	5.51	5.03	5.28	10.0	0.5	3.3	4.7	1.6	0.06
2010	OAK	MLB	27	4	6	0	28	14	90¹	102	12	37	53	45%	.309	-10	1.53	5.22	5.01	5.42	10.0	1.2	3.4	4.9	0.8	0.59

Breakout: 16% Improve: 38% Collapse: 21% Attrition: 25% MLB: 77% Comparables: Jim Hannan, Dick Pole, Shohei Tateyama, Julio Santana

One of the oodles of players garnered from Arizona in the Dan Haren trade, Gonzalez is far from an impact talent, but he has spent parts of the last seven seasons in the majors as a utility pitcher of sorts. He's basically one of those guys who is a team's 13th- or 14th-best pitcher, so he bides his time at Triple-A until the need arrives. He has a deep arsenal, with four unspectacular but usable pitches, and the versatility to start or relieve, so he'll probably keep banging around for a while.

Gio Gonzalez

Bats: R Throws: L Height: 5' 11" Weight: 185 Born: September 19, 1985 Age: 24

YEAR	TEAM	LVL	AGE	W	L	SV	G	GS	IP	H	HR	BB	SO	GB%	BABIP	STUFF	WHIP	ERA	SIERA	DERA	EqH9	EqHR9	EqBB9	EqSO9	VORP	SN/WX
2007	BIR	AA	21	9	7	0	27	27	150	116	10	57	185	54%	.297	26	1.15	3.18	2.69	4.35	8.4	1.5	3.6	7.5	18.0	2.04
2008	SAC	AAA	22	8	7	0	23	22	123	106	12	61	128	46%	.293	9	1.36	4.24	3.65	5.36	8.9	1.5	4.4	6.8	1.8	1.34
2008	OAK	MLB	22	1	4	0	10	7	34	32	9	25	34	55%	.250	2	1.68	7.68	4.45	8.61	8.7	2.6	5.7	7.7	-12.1	-0.54
2009	SAC	AAA	23	4	1	0	12	12	61	42	5	34	71	47%	.259	18	1.25	2.51	3.39	3.85	7.7	1.6	5.2	8.2	10.5	1.51
2009	OAK	MLB	23	6	7	0	20	17	98²	113	14	56	109	53%	.360	6	1.71	5.75	3.76	5.79	10.3	1.3	4.5	8.6	-3.1	1.09
2010	OAK	MLB	24	7	10	0	35	27	143²	147	20	78	127	42%	.312	5	1.57	5.04	4.39	5.18	9.0	1.2	4.5	7.3	5.1	2.51

Breakout: 10% Improve: 40% Collapse: 17% Attrition: 14% MLB: 94% Comparables: Mark Langston, Sean Thompson, Ken Dayley, Andy Pratt

Gonzalez has driven his employers to fits of frustration for years now, and his high strikeout rate combined with a high hits-allowed rate speaks to his puzzling combination of swing-and-miss stuff and baffling inconsistency. When he's on, he can be dominant with a low-90s fastball that can get up to 94 mph, a big breaking curveball, and the ability to throw strikes. But he rarely shows up with all three things going for him at once, which at times gets so bad that it seems he couldn't get high-school hitters out. The scouting cliché is that at least he has shown that he can do it, so you have to see if you can get it from him more often. Gonzalez will probably get first crack at the final spot in the 2010 rotation.

Jeff Gray

Bats: R   Throws: R   Height: 6' 2"   Weight: 210   Born: November 19, 1981   Age: 28

YEAR	TEAM	LVL	AGE	W	L	SV	G	GS	IP	H	HR	BB	SO	GB%	BABIP	STUFF	WHIP	ERA	SIERA	DERA	EqH9	EqHR9	EqBB9	EqSO9	VORP	SN/WX
2007	MID	AA	25	2	0	3	8	0	12¹	7	0	2	12	82%	.241	11	0.73	0.00	2.19	1.19	6.4	0.8	1.6	7.1	5.4	0.78
2007	SAC	AAA	25	2	4	12	46	0	55	58	2	22	45	68%	.335	-13	1.45	4.09	3.84	5.08	10.5	0.9	3.9	5.6	2.4	-1.28
2008	SAC	AAA	26	2	7	4	54	0	67²	86	9	23	50	54%	.350	-34	1.61	4.39	4.29	4.95	12.6	2.0	3.3	4.7	3.9	0.72
2008	OAK	MLB	26	0	0	0	5	0	4²	8	1	1	4	51%	.412	-4	1.93	7.71	3.96	7.71	15.4	1.9	1.9	7.7	-1.1	0.00
2009	SAC	AAA	27	2	2	16	37	0	41	30	2	6	22	63%	.222	-8	0.88	1.54	4.09	2.40	7.1	0.9	1.6	3.4	13.5	2.20
2009	OAK	MLB	27	0	1	0	24	0	26¹	30	3	4	19	65%	.307	-1	1.29	3.76	3.81	3.95	9.5	1.0	1.0	5.3	4.7	-0.19
2010	CHN	MLB	28	2	5	6	53	0	59	68	8	22	33	64%	.314	-16	1.53	5.27	4.67	5.62	10.5	1.3	3.0	4.7	-0.8	1.00

Breakout: 16%   Improve: 40%   Collapse: 33%   Attrition: 14%   MLB: 31%   Comparables: Brian Wolfe, Paul Abraham, Yoel Hernandez, Laddie Renfroe

If nothing else, Gray throws hard. His fastball sits in the mid-90s while touching 97, but despite being well into his late 20s, he still spends a lot of his time in the minors. Velocity alone can get minor-league hitters out, but in the big leagues, you need movement and a breaking ball, and in both of those regards, Gray's gifts lag behind his speed-gun readings. The Cubs hope he can figure something out, having acquired him as the name player in the Jake Fox deal.

Vin Mazzaro

Bats: R   Throws: R   Height: 6' 2"   Weight: 190   Born: September 27, 1986   Age: 23

YEAR	TEAM	LVL	AGE	W	L	SV	G	GS	IP	H	HR	BB	SO	GB%	BABIP	STUFF	WHIP	ERA	SIERA	DERA	EqH9	EqHR9	EqBB9	EqSO9	VORP	SN/WX
2007	STO	A+	20	9	12	0	28	28	153²	159	13	71	115	59%	.313	2	1.50	5.33	4.39	6.18	10.7	1.5	4.6	4.4	-10.8	-1.49
2008	MID	AA	21	12	3	0	22	22	137¹	115	3	36	104	54%	.278	43	1.10	1.90	3.85	3.09	7.7	0.6	2.6	5.0	35.6	2.69
2008	SAC	AAA	21	3	3	0	6	5	33²	49	3	9	27	50%	.393	10	1.72	6.15	4.07	7.79	13.9	1.4	2.5	5.0	-8.2	-0.35
2009	SAC	AAA	22	2	2	0	10	9	56²	42	2	17	44	61%	.248	21	1.04	2.38	3.81	3.56	7.5	0.8	2.8	5.1	11.7	1.49
2009	OAK	MLB	22	4	9	0	17	17	91¹	120	12	39	59	46%	.350	-3	1.74	5.32	4.94	5.60	11.5	1.2	3.4	5.1	-1.0	0.92
2010	OAK	MLB	23	6	9	0	29	25	137	153	19	61	82	47%	.309	-4	1.57	5.34	5.04	5.52	9.8	1.1	3.8	5.0	-0.2	2.26

Breakout: 6%   Improve: 53%   Collapse: 10%   Attrition: 17%   MLB: 83%   Comparables: Collin Balester, Kevin Lomon, Fernando Nieve, Jeff Pico

Mazzaro began the year with a dominating showing at Triple-A, but his big-league spin lay somewhere between inconsistent and just downright bad. He delivered 13 ⅔ scoreless innings in his first two starts, but his ERA was 6.51 afterward. A ground-ball pitcher coming up through the system, Mazzaro suddenly stopped getting them in the big leagues, which points to elevation caused by overthrowing. The A's still have a lot of confidence in him and think he's in the big leagues to stay. Others outside the organization aren't so convinced.

Jon Meloan

Bats: R   Throws: R   Height: 6' 3"   Weight: 230   Born: July 11, 1984   Age: 25

YEAR	TEAM	LVL	AGE	W	L	SV	G	GS	IP	H	HR	BB	SO	GB%	BABIP	STUFF	WHIP	ERA	SIERA	DERA	EqH9	EqHR9	EqBB9	EqSO9	VORP	SN/WX
2007	JAX	AA	22	5	2	19	35	0	45¹	24	3	18	70	49%	.253	24	0.93	2.18	1.71	3.56	6.9	1.5	3.9	9.7	9.0	1.18
2007	LVG	AAA	22	2	0	1	14	0	21¹	12	2	9	21	48%	.185	20	0.98	1.69	3.55	2.01	4.0	0.8	3.6	6.9	8.6	0.87
2007	LAN	MLB	22	0	0	0	5	0	7¹	8	1	8	7	43%	.333	7	2.18	11.05	5.54	9.82	9.8	1.2	8.6	7.4	-3.5	-0.07
2008	LVG	AAA	23	5	10	0	21	20	105	119	7	60	99	43%	.358	9	1.70	4.97	4.31	5.64	9.8	0.8	4.9	6.5	-1.6	-0.37
2008	BUF	AAA	23	0	1	0	12	0	14²	12	1	9	12	53%	.268	-10	1.43	4.30	4.61	5.14	7.7	0.6	5.8	5.1	0.6	-0.42
2008	CLE	MLB	23	0	0	0	2	0	2	0	0	1	2	34%	.000	2	0.50	0.00	3.22	0.00	0.0	0.0	5.4	10.8	1.0	0.03
2009	COH	AAA	24	0	0	0	25	2	44	52	6	17	37	53%	.329	-17	1.57	5.52	4.13	5.89	10.2	1.6	3.7	5.7	-1.9	-1.05
2009	DUR	AAA	24	0	0	0	10	0	13¹	13	2	10	15	49%	.306	7	1.72	3.37	4.19	4.15	9.7	1.4	6.9	8.3	1.9	0.47
2009	OAK	MLB	24	0	0	0	6	0	8¹	3	0	2	11	32%	.188	8	0.60	0.00	1.43	1.13	3.4	0.0	2.3	9.0	3.9	0.10
2010	OAK	MLB	25	3	5	3	51	3	71	74	9	39	58	40%	.313	-6	1.59	5.13	4.69	5.23	9.0	1.1	4.6	6.7	2.1	0.91

Breakout: 14%   Improve: 32%   Collapse: 29%   Attrition: 20%   MLB: 40%   Comparables: James Garcia, Joe Norris, Randy Wells, John Trautwein

Meloan pitched for four organizations in 2009, as he was often the player first to be taken off the 40-man roster when a move needed to be made, yet someone else always wanted to pick him up. Oakland received his first successful big-league performance. Teams have always seen potential in his 91-93 mph fastball and power curve, so the A's might have caught lightning in a bottle for their bullpen.

Clayton Mortensen

Bats: R   Throws: R   Height: 6′ 4″   Weight: 180   Born: April 10, 1985   Age: 25

YEAR	TEAM	LVL	AGE	W	L	SV	G	GS	IP	H	HR	BB	SO	GB%	BABIP	STUFF	WHIP	ERA	SIERA	DERA	EqH9	EqHR9	EqBB9	EqSO9	VORP	SN/WX
2007	QUD	A	22	0	2	0	10	10	40¹	44	2	8	45	70%	.372	10	1.29	3.12	2.66	5.38	12.5	1.5	2.8	6.5	0.5	0.09
2007	BAT	A-	22	1	1	0	6	4	20¹	13	0	11	23	70%	.277	16	1.18	1.77	3.10	2.95	7.4	1.0	5.9	6.4	5.2	0.49
2008	SFD	AA	23	3	4	0	11	11	59²	59	6	22	48	67%	.298	-2	1.36	4.22	3.80	5.45	9.6	1.4	3.6	5.4	0.3	-0.08
2008	MEM	AAA	23	5	6	0	15	14	80	87	12	42	57	57%	.307	-23	1.61	5.51	4.69	6.15	10.8	2.0	4.8	4.5	-5.5	-0.36
2009	MEM	AAA	24	7	6	0	17	17	105	103	11	34	82	62%	.295	-16	1.30	4.37	3.91	5.75	10.0	1.9	3.1	5.4	-2.7	0.01
2009	SLN	MLB	24	0	0	0	1	0	3	5	1	1	2	49%	.364	-36	2.00	6.00	4.79	21.00	15.0	3.0	3.0	6.0	-5.2	-0.05
2009	SAC	AAA	24	2	2	0	6	6	32¹	40	2	14	18	55%	.342	-22	1.67	4.45	5.05	6.75	12.3	1.2	4.2	3.6	-4.2	-0.10
2009	OAK	MLB	24	2	4	0	6	6	27²	37	5	12	11	64%	.311	-27	1.77	7.81	5.41	8.63	11.0	1.6	3.1	3.1	-10.0	-0.35
2010	OAK	MLB	25	5	10	0	37	23	130¹	156	22	62	80	57%	.320	-18	1.68	6.16	4.93	6.33	10.5	1.4	4.0	5.1	-12.0	1.53

Breakout: 13%   Improve: 43%   Collapse: 18%   Attrition: 13%   MLB: 100%   Comparables: Greg Perschke, Wilton Chavez, Greg Keagle, Garrett Broshuis

Mortensen was part of the package that Oakland received in the Holliday trade, but after his six major-league games with the A's, there's no clear path to the seventh. He has a big-league sinker, but his strikeout rate has nearly halved as he's moved up the minor-league ladder, and in the majors, it dropped to the point of being absolutely unacceptable. Scouts think Mortensen's one notable skill has a chance of working out in a situational relief role, but his days as a starter could be over.

Josh Outman

Bats: L   Throws: L   Height: 6′ 1″   Weight: 185   Born: September 14, 1984   Age: 25

YEAR	TEAM	LVL	AGE	W	L	SV	G	GS	IP	H	HR	BB	SO	GB%	BABIP	STUFF	WHIP	ERA	SIERA	DERA	EqH9	EqHR9	EqBB9	EqSO9	VORP	SN/WX
2007	CLR	A+	22	10	4	0	20	18	117¹	104	7	54	117	48%	.302	7	1.35	2.45	3.70	3.88	9.8	1.4	4.9	6.5	19.5	1.65
2007	REA	AA	22	2	3	0	7	7	42	38	5	23	34	44%	.273	4	1.45	4.50	4.62	6.19	9.2	1.8	4.9	5.4	-3.1	-0.22
2008	REA	AA	23	5	4	1	33	5	70¹	68	3	37	66	45%	.322	0	1.49	3.20	4.12	4.03	9.7	0.8	4.7	6.3	10.9	-0.22
2008	MID	A-	23	1	0	0	4	4	12²	13	1	3	5	74%	.267	-21	1.26	4.26	4.15	5.54	8.3	1.4	2.1	2.1	-0.1	0.02
2008	SAC	AAA	23	1	0	0	5	2	15¹	9	1	5	15	48%	.211	11	0.91	1.76	3.19	2.45	6.1	1.2	3.1	6.1	5.0	0.62
2008	OAK	MLB	23	1	2	0	6	4	25²	34	1	8	19	41%	.384	8	1.64	4.56	4.37	4.81	12.6	0.4	2.6	6.3	1.9	0.60
2009	OAK	MLB	24	4	1	0	14	12	67¹	53	9	25	53	43%	.233	12	1.16	3.48	4.17	3.84	6.8	1.2	2.9	6.1	12.6	1.82
2010	OAK	MLB	25	4	6	0	35	16	92²	99	13	46	68	44%	.308	-5	1.56	5.11	4.72	5.27	9.4	1.2	4.2	6.2	2.4	1.67

Breakout: 9%   Improve: 38%   Collapse: 24%   Attrition: 22%   MLB: 74%   Comparables: Angel Miranda, Pedro A. Martinez, Jake Woods, Pete Filson

Another player received from Philadelphia for Joe Blanton, Outman began the year in the A's rotation and hit his stride in early June, putting together a seven-start streak in which he went at least six innings every time, posted a 2.80 ERA, and limited hitters to a .182 average. With a 92-94 mph fastball that he can dial up to 96 and good enough secondary offerings, he looked very much like another fixture in the team's young rotation, right up until June 19th, when his fastball tumbled down to the upper 80s after his elbow blew up. After Tommy John surgery, he won't be ready to throw until the second half of 2010.

Brett Tomko

Bats: R   Throws: R   Height: 6′ 4″   Weight: 220   Born: April 7, 1973   Age: 37

YEAR	TEAM	LVL	AGE	W	L	SV	G	GS	IP	H	HR	BB	SO	GB%	BABIP	STUFF	WHIP	ERA	SIERA	DERA	EqH9	EqHR9	EqBB9	EqSO9	VORP	SN/WX
2007	SDN	MLB	34	2	1	0	7	4	27¹	25	5	6	26	51%	.263	9	1.13	4.61	3.19	4.67	9.0	2.3	1.7	7.3	2.5	0.51
2007	LAN	MLB	34	2	11	0	33	15	104	124	13	42	79	49%	.327	-10	1.60	5.80	4.45	6.00	10.1	1.1	3.2	6.0	-5.9	-0.21
2008	KCA	MLB	35	2	7	0	16	10	60²	80	11	13	40	55%	.333	-10	1.53	6.97	4.27	6.53	11.2	1.5	1.6	5.4	-7.0	-0.35
2008	SDN	MLB	35	0	0	0	6	0	9¹	3	0	5	9	36%	.136	5	0.86	1.93	3.98	1.93	2.9	0.0	3.9	6.8	3.7	0.12
2009	NYA	MLB	36	1	2	0	15	0	20²	19	5	7	11	43%	.226	-19	1.26	5.23	5.08	4.95	8.6	2.3	2.7	4.5	1.2	-0.24
2009	OAK	MLB	36	4	1	0	6	6	36²	31	7	6	22	41%	.226	9	1.01	2.95	4.26	2.90	7.3	1.8	1.3	4.8	10.3	1.46
2010	OAK	MLB	37	3	4	1	43	1	57²	66	8	21	39	47%	.323	-9	1.52	5.06	4.54	5.25	10.2	1.2	3.1	5.7	1.6	0.31

Breakout: 12%   Improve: 40%   Collapse: 29%   Attrition: 35%   MLB: 92%   Comparables: Boom-Boom Beck, Ted Power, Steve Renko, Aaron Sele

Veteran mediocrity Tomko regained some cred by pitching extremely well at Triple-A Scranton, but when called up to pitch long relief for the Yankees, his fly-ball tendencies plus a park that punished them made him too vulnerable to the home run to be trusted in key relief situations. Released just as the A's were in need of an extra arm, Tomko prospered when he returned to starting, throwing 92-93 mph strikes and even avenging the indignity of his release with five shutout frames against his former club in his A's debut. (The home runs came along too, however.) Just when it looked as though he was lining himself up for a bit of money as a free agent, his elbow started hurting and he was shut down for the year. Tomko will get another look by someone in 2010, but the paycheck won't be as big as it might have been.

Michael Wuertz

Bats: R   **Throws:** R   **Height:** 6' 3"   **Weight:** 205   **Born:** December 15, 1978   **Age:** 31

YEAR	TEAM	LVL	AGE	W	L	SV	G	GS	IP	H	HR	BB	SO	GB%	BABIP	STUFF	WHIP	ERA	SIERA	DERA	EqH9	EqHR9	EqBB9	EqSO9	VORP	SN/WX
2007	CHN	MLB	28	2	3	0	73	0	72¹	64	8	35	79	50%	.295	15	1.37	3.48	3.48	3.50	8.1	0.8	3.9	9.1	16.0	0.92
2008	IOW	AAA	29	0	1	4	17	0	20	13	2	14	29	64%	.268	18	1.35	3.60	2.91	3.96	7.0	1.4	6.1	9.8	3.3	0.26
2008	CHN	MLB	29	1	1	0	45	0	44²	44	4	20	30	57%	.296	-10	1.43	3.63	4.59	4.46	9.6	0.6	3.6	5.5	4.9	0.16
2009	OAK	MLB	30	6	1	4	74	0	78²	52	6	23	102	49%	.266	32	0.95	2.63	2.09	2.82	6.3	0.7	2.3	9.6	22.9	4.25
2010	OAK	MLB	31	4	3	2	68	0	67¹	61	7	27	64	50%	.299	8	1.32	3.81	3.65	3.97	8.1	0.9	3.5	8.0	11.4	1.21

Breakout: 16%   Improve: 41%   Collapse: 20%   Attrition: 8%   MLB: 93%   Comparables: Mike Timlin, Scot Shields, Greg McMichael, John Habyan

Wuertz was a solid reliever on Chicago's North Side, but the Cubs blithely sent him west for a pair of fringy minor leaguers who are already no longer in their system. Meanwhile, Wuertz delivered the best season of his career, with a WHIP under one and nearly 12 strikeouts per nine. One of the few pitchers you'll find who doesn't rely on his fastball, Wuertz instead relies primarily on a plus slider to set up a low-90s fastball as a reverse change-of-pace pitch. With as many breaking balls as he throws, he's always a risk for injury, but he has also yet to have a bad year. There's little reason to think that he won't continue to be a steal for Oakland.

Brad Ziegler

Bats: R   **Throws:** R   **Height:** 6' 4"   **Weight:** 200   **Born:** October 10, 1979   **Age:** 30

YEAR	TEAM	LVL	AGE	W	L	SV	G	GS	IP	H	HR	BB	SO	GB%	BABIP	STUFF	WHIP	ERA	SIERA	DERA	EqH9	EqHR9	EqBB9	EqSO9	VORP	SN/WX
2007	MID	AA	27	4	0	1	15	0	23²	19	0	4	18	66%	.264	3	0.97	1.14	3.45	2.51	7.3	0.4	1.9	5.0	7.8	0.76
2007	SAC	AAA	27	8	3	1	35	0	54²	46	0	14	44	75%	.291	3	1.10	2.96	3.05	3.86	8.4	0.4	2.6	5.4	9.4	2.26
2008	SAC	AAA	28	2	0	8	19	0	24¹	15	0	4	20	70%	.224	8	0.78	0.37	2.95	1.14	6.1	0.4	1.5	5.3	11.5	1.35
2008	OAK	MLB	28	3	0	11	47	0	59²	47	2	22	30	73%	.259	1	1.16	1.06	4.39	1.42	7.8	0.3	3.2	4.5	24.5	4.61
2009	OAK	MLB	29	2	4	7	69	0	73¹	82	2	28	54	71%	.351	3	1.50	3.07	4.04	3.23	10.2	0.3	3.1	6.1	17.6	1.68
2010	OAK	MLB	30	4	4	9	68	0	70¹	70	6	26	44	73%	.294	-4	1.37	4.10	4.11	4.31	8.8	0.8	3.1	5.1	9.3	2.48

Breakout: 15%   Improve: 46%   Collapse: 26%   Attrition: 13%   MLB: 92%   Comparables: Todd Frohwirth, Mike James, Mike Henneman, Tim Burke

You didn't expect another 1.06 ERA, did you? Ziegler was never going to be that good again, but he still beat last year's PECOTA projection despite a fair amount of bad luck on balls in play. He was more than good enough to make himself one of the rarest of things these days: an established major league side-armer. He might have been even better had Oakland not jerked him around as far as his role or given him consistent work, as manager Bob Geren seemed to never have confidence in him in tighter ballgames, with one bad outing seemingly putting him in the doghouse for weeks. Ziegler is still a ground-ball machine, and as long as you know how to use him right, he will not only remain so, he'll stick around forever.

LINEOUTS

Hitters

PLAYER	TEAM	LVL	AGE	PA	R	2B	3B	HR	RBI	BB	SO	SB-CS	EqBRR	AVG/OBP/SLG	EqAVG/EqOBP/EqSLG	EqA	VORP	WARP
RF M. Carson	SAC	AAA	27	493	68	29	3	25	77	38	94	15-4	3.8	.264/.327/.514	.249/.303/.461	.260	12.7	1.7
	OAK	MLB	27	22	1	0	0	1	5	0	7	0-0	-0.1	.286/.273/.429	.286/.273/.429	.247	0.0	0.0
INF Y. Chen	MID	AA	25	75	12	6	0	0	10	7	9	2-0	0.2	.324/.387/.412	.286/.333/.343	.243	0.7	-0.1
	SAC	AAA	25	103	13	2	0	1	8	10	18	4-0	1.0	.283/.353/.337	.277/.340/.330	.247	1.7	-0.4
OF C. Denorfia	SAC	AAA	28	474	62	18	5	9	49	31	52	15-6	0.6	.271/.317/.398	.259/.298/.361	.232	-3.7	-0.6
C J. Donaldson	MID	AA	23	541	67	37	1	9	91	80	92	7-2	1.5	.270/.379/.415	.243/.336/.379	.254	17.2	2.8
1B S. Doolittle*	SAC	AAA	22	121	17	5	1	4	14	15	23	0-1	-0.5	.267/.364/.448	.262/.352/.439	.271	3.7	0.2
SS J. Horton*	MID	AA	23	585	80	21	6	5	62	65	65	9-3	-0.9	.263/.343/.357	.235/.303/.325	.226	-3.1	-1.7
SS T. Ladendorf	BLT	A	21	65	7	2	0	0	4	4	13	2-1	-0.3	.233/.292/.267	.210/.246/.242	.162	-3.5	-0.6
	ELZ	Rk	21	74	18	7	0	4	17	11	7	1-0	0.9	.410/.500/.721	.323/.392/.492	.304	6.2	1.2
	KNC	A	21	145	13	4	2	2	15	10	19	2-2	-1.1	.231/.301/.338	.209/.259/.299	.193	-4.0	-0.4
OF S. Peterson*	PMB	A+	21	319	32	11	4	6	39	21	52	10-1	-0.7	.298/.367/.428	.290/.342/.427	.268	7.8	1.3
	SFD	AA	21	80	10	4	1	1	7	5	10	2-0	0.8	.284/.338/.405	.253/.300/.373	.236	-0.5	-0.6
	MID	AA	21	172	16	10	0	3	17	13	32	4-0	-0.7	.273/.333/.396	.248/.298/.369	.237	-2.4	-0.7
MI G. Petit	SAC	AAA	24	398	45	18	0	5	32	26	83	0-2	-2.3	.244/.292/.336	.246/.288/.326	.217	-3.7	-0.1
	OAK	MLB	24	31	2	1	0	0	1	0	6	0-0	0.2	.226/.226/.258	.226/.226/.258	.150	-2.1	-0.3
C A. Recker	MID	AA	25	65	11	4	0	3	9	8	22	0-0	0.1	.298/.385/.526	.237/.308/.441	.255	1.1	0.0
	SAC	AAA	25	306	30	11	2	12	45	28	80	2-0	0.4	.261/.333/.449	.249/.315/.412	.252	9.3	1.7
C M. Stassi	VAN	A-	18	53	3	4	0	0	8	2	11	0-0	-0.3	.286/.340/.367	.235/.264/.294	.190	-2.2	-0.5
UT C. Wimberly#	MID	AA	25	336	56	10	3	0	28	24	31	21-8	3.5	.296/.363/.350	.257/.308/.300	.221	-2.4	-1.4

In the Yankee system for what seemed like forever, outfielder **Matt Carson** finally earned a cup of coffee in the big leagues, so, you know, good for him. ⊘ Taiwanese infielder **Yung-Chi Chen** has all the skills to make a nice utility player, except the ability to stay healthy, as he's amassed just 126 games over the last three years. ⊘ Buried in the Oakland system and turning 30 this year, **Chris Denorfia** is hoping that San Diego can provide more of a big-league opportunity. ⊘ **Josh Donaldson** was part of the package received from the Cubs in the Harden trade and survived his jump to Double-A; he's still a rough receiver behind the plate, but strong-armed, killing 40 percent of attempted steals. ⊘ **Sean Doolittle**'s 2009 season was wrecked by knee surgery, and he's been passed by Carter on the first-base depth chart while having many of the same limitations of the Buck/Cunningham types for an outfield corner. ⊘ Former college fielding fiend **Josh Horton** made a clean jump to Double-A, but with Green's selection, his best bet is a move to utility work. ⊘ The return from Minnesota for renting out Orlando Cabrera, toolsy **Tyler Ladendorf** didn't do much on a performance level, but remains intriguing. ⊘ Part of the package received from St. Louis for Matt Holliday, **Shane Peterson** is a line-drive machine with above-average speed, but he needs to improve his power and patience to stick in either outfield corner. ⊘ **Gregorio Petit** is a rock-solid defender who can play anywhere in the infield, but he raps out hits about as frequently as K-Fed. ⊘ **Anthony Recker** has a similar skill set and frame as Landon Powell and could get his chance behind the plate, considering Powell's track record of getting hurt. ⊘ A fourth-round pick who got an over-slot bonus of $1.5 million, catcher **Max Stassi** has above-average potential both at the plate and behind it, but you never know with teenage catchers—once they discover girls, that's it. ⊘ **Corey Wimberly** can play six positions and run like the wind, which might be enough for some kind of bench job down the road.

Pitchers

PLAYER	TEAM	LVL	AGE	W	L	SV	IP	H	HR	BB	SO	GB%	BABIP	STUFF	WHIP	ERA	SIERA	DERA	EqH9	EqHR9	EqBB9	EqSO9	VORP
K. Cameron	SAC	AAA	29	2	1	1	13	7	0	11	14	41%	.233	12	1.38	2.77	4.52	4.38	5.8	0.7	7.3	7.3	1.5
—	OAK	MLB	29	0	0	1	18^1	15	1	6	15	47%	.269	5	1.15	3.44	3.87	3.50	7.0	0.5	2.5	6.5	4.0
A. Capra*	KNC	A	22	4	7	0	100	70	9	40	103	43%	.245	-13	1.10	3.24	3.34	5.15	9.2	2.5	4.8	5.7	3.5
—	STO	A+	22	2	2	0	52	42	6	21	67	37%	.298	11	1.21	3.12	2.63	5.17	9.8	2.3	4.6	7.3	1.7
F. De Los Santos	ATH	Rk	23	0	1	0	11^2	12	0	4	16	—	.444	-8	1.37	3.86	2.24	7.00	15.0	2.0	6.0	7.0	-1.5
S. Demel	MID	AA	23	0	2	11	29^1	23	1	9	26	55%	.259	9	1.09	0.61	3.58	1.95	6.6	0.6	2.7	6.3	11.8
—	SAC	AAA	23	2	3	3	32^1	27	1	21	33	56%	.289	3	1.48	3.62	4.08	4.78	8.2	0.8	5.6	6.8	2.6
D. Giese	OAK	MLB	32	0	3	0	22	22	5	9	11	47%	.246	-18	1.41	5.32	5.32	4.98	8.7	2.1	3.3	4.2	1.2
B. Kilby*	SAC	AAA	26	4	2	2	63^1	40	5	24	77	30%	.243	9	1.01	2.13	2.72	2.85	7.1	1.5	3.6	8.4	17.7
—	OAK	MLB	26	1	0	0	17	10	1	4	20	23%	.225	17	0.82	0.53	2.41	1.04	5.2	0.5	1.6	8.8	8.6
J. Lansford	MID	AA	22	1	2	12	45^2	43	2	20	29	55%	.289	-3	1.38	2.36	4.73	2.84	8.3	0.8	3.9	4.5	13.1
—	SAC	AAA	22	0	1	0	11	13	2	12	1	37%	.250	-52	2.27	9.00	8.58	11.51	11.1	3.2	8.7	0.0	-7.6
J. Marshall*	SAC	AAA	26	5	3	7	50^2	53	2	15	30	69%	.311	-20	1.34	3.20	4.19	4.98	10.3	1.0	2.9	4.0	2.7
—	OAK	MLB	26	0	2	0	7^1	13	1	0	1	62%	.375	-46	1.77	14.73	5.51	13.50	14.7	1.2	0.0	1.2	-6.5
C. Reineke	SAC	AAA	27	9	4	2	125	134	17	52	91	44%	.298	-44	1.49	4.75	4.60	6.29	11.1	2.4	3.9	4.9	-10.5
—	OAK	MLB	27	0	0	0	5	7	2	0	1	24%	.278	-18	1.40	7.20	6.36	6.75	13.5	3.9	0.0	1.9	-0.6
H. Rodriguez	SAC	AAA	22	2	1	4	43^2	38	4	38	71	46%	.362	21	1.74	5.77	3.12	6.75	9.6	1.7	7.7	11.1	-5.8
—	OAK	MLB	22	0	0	0	4	4	0	2	4	51%	.308	4	1.50	2.25	4.07	4.15	8.3	0.0	4.2	6.2	0.6
T. Ross	STO	A+	22	5	6	0	86^1	78	10	33	82	58%	.278	-16	1.29	4.17	3.63	6.34	9.9	2.1	4.2	4.8	-7.6
—	MID	AA	22	5	4	0	50	40	3	20	31	70%	.250	11	1.20	3.96	4.02	4.41	7.1	1.1	3.8	4.5	5.8
J. Simmons	SAC	AAA	22	7	7	0	119^2	139	8	47	81	35%	.326	-15	1.55	5.72	4.92	7.31	11.3	1.3	3.7	4.4	-23.3
J. Souza	WTN	AA	23	6	6	0	78	73	4	18	62	37%	.290	2	1.17	3.35	3.91	4.72	9.4	1.1	2.3	5.3	6.5
—	MID	AA	23	0	2	0	20	32	1	10	13	42%	.403	-31	2.10	10.35	5.22	13.94	13.7	0.9	4.4	4.4	-19.1
M. Storey	KNC	A	23	0	0	9	17^1	5	0	1	23	62%	.147	16	0.35	0.52	1.24	1.41	4.5	0.6	1.1	7.3	7.3
—	STO	A+	23	1	1	9	23^2	19	2	6	35	33%	.321	7	1.06	2.28	1.58	4.78	9.6	1.7	3.3	8.3	1.7

Signed to help in the bullpen, **Kevin Cameron** bounced between Triple-A, the big leagues, and the trainer's room. He signed a minor-league contract with the Giants. ⊘ A fourth-round pick in 2008, **Anthony Capra** has a combination of solid stuff, outstanding baseball intelligence, and a nice changeup, all of which should lead to some kind of big-league role. ⊘ The best prospect (at the time) acquired for Nick Swisher, **Fautino De Los Santos** showed enough in his return from Tommy John surgery to earn a spot on the 40-man roster. ⊘ Short, stocky fireballer **Sam Demel** got to Triple-A, but he needs to find some way to balance his arm strength with better control. ⊘ Journeyman **Dan Giese** landed in the bullpen until Tommy John got him; June surgery means he won't be back anytime soon. ⊘ **Brad Kilby** will get a shot at proving that last year's brief, yet dominant big-league show was for real; scouts aren't convinced. ⊘ **Jared Lansford**'s conversion from starting to the bullpen was deemed a success, giving him a good chance to wear the same uniform daddy Carney did. ⊘ The A's were hoping for a left-handed version of Brad Ziegler when they took **Jay Marshall** in the Rule 5 draft two years ago, but instead they've gotten a double-digit ERA. The Mets claimed him off of waivers in January. ⊘ A 6-foot-6 righty, **Chad Reineke** strikes an imposing figure on the mound, but his stuff fails to back up his physical presence. ⊘ One of the hardest throwers in the game, **Henry Rodriguez** might be dangerous if he had any clue where his pitches were going. ⊘ The full-season debut of 2008's second-round pick **Tyson Ross** was just like his college career, combining lots of promise with a considerable lack of refinement. ⊘ Scouts worried that despite **James Simmons'** outstanding command, his lack of pure stuff would catch up to him at some point; that point was Triple-A. ⊘ The arm acquired from Seattle for Jack Hannahan, **Justin Souza** is a low-level prospect with some middle-relief possibilities. ⊘ Pitching across four levels, **Mickey Storey** struck out more than 12 per nine with a 1.22 ERA, but he depends more on location and deception than raw stuff.

MANAGER: BOB GEREN

YEAR	TEAM	W-L	Pythag +/−	Avg PC	100+ P	120+ P	QS	BQS	REL	REL w Zero R	IBB	Subs	PH	PH Avg	PH HR	SB2	CS2	SB3	CS3	SAC Att	SAC %	POS SAC	Squeeze	Swing	In Play
2007	OAK	76-86	-3	95.8	69	2	80	5	445	276	60	33	64	.175	0	51	17	1	3	31	58.1%	16	1	134	86
2008	OAK	75-86	0	93.6	48	0	69	6	441	289	45	54	91	.203	2	84	19	2	2	55	54.5%	27	2	109	74
2009	OAK	75-87	-6	92.7	50	0	62	3	488	316	30	48	76	.153	0	117	42	16	2	46	67.4%	26	0	117	78

For some, Geren might be a sabermetric paragon of skippering virtue, in that there's not a lot going on here: not much scrabbling after runs with one-run strategies, no matter how horrible the offense, and a good record for operating a bullpen. Consistent with his responsibilities as a caretaker of a host of young arms, Geren was one of only three full-season managers who avoided the temptation of letting a starter go 120 pitches in a turn, joining Dave Trembley (also tasked with a young staff in transition) and sneaky old Ozzie Guillen. Beyond the team's remarkably efficient baserunning exploits and some initial tinkering with a Sweeney/Davis platoon in center, there just isn't a signature move to point to; perhaps consistent with the evaluative exercise the season wound up as, Geren increasingly favored picking groups of regulars and seeing what they'd do for a few weeks at a time. What he'll do if he's ever handed a lineup or a physically mature starting pitcher remains something of a theoretical exercise.

Philadelphia Phillies

When Brad Lidge struck out Eric Hinske to end the 2008 World Series, the city of Philadelphia erupted, basking in the glory of its first championship in 27 long seasons. It would have been easy for the team to rest on its proverbial laurels, but a change in leadership brought a philosophical shift: Pat Gillick was notorious for building up a team and keeping the roster intact, ultimately trusting that his plan would work out. Ruben Amaro Jr. had a different way of going about his job.

The fortuitously timed shift to a younger general manager worked to prevent stagnation in the champions, as Amaro proved to be in favor of the occasional shake-up. When Gillick stepped down, he left a few unsolved roster issues in his wake. It was not a long laundry list, but an important one nonetheless: what to do with Pat Burrell and Jamie Moyer, two valued employees whose contracts were up, as well as what would happen with a multitude of arbitration-eligible players, several of whom were due for substantial raises based on their performance.

Burrell's fate was decided quickly with the quick pursuit and capture of Raul Ibañez just as the Hot Stove League put the writing on the wall in capital letters. Ibañez signed a three-year deal worth $31.5 million rather early in an offseason boasting a glut of similar players. The move drew mixed reviews from both performance and financial standpoints, with supporters making favorable comparisons to Burrell in terms of the former's more consistent power and ability to drive in runners, while detractors noted his age and putrid defense, as well as the team's now heavy lean to the left. Regardless, the move represented Amaro's willingness to move fast and grab "his guy," even if available evidence cast doubt on the object of his affection. Moyer soon signed an incentive-laden two-year deal offered to him in spite of his advanced age. These relatively expensive contracts were supplemented by Amaro's avoidance of arbitration with every candidate, either through one-year settlements or extensions for Cole Hamels, Ryan Howard, Jayson Werth, and Ryan Madson.

Amaro's decisiveness reflected an eagerness to avoid in-season distractions, but fate provided enough other issues to make the team's pennant repeat less than a certainty. The 2009 Phillies serve as an interesting case study in success, as the team often defied both conventional wisdom and key sabermetric tenets. Leadoff batter Jimmy Rollins reached base less than 30 percent of the time. Closer Brad Lidge put together the indisputably worst season by a closer in baseball history. Non-Lidge bullpen members failed to provide much more than comic relief (thanks to their very own reality show on the MLB network), while J. C. Romero missed 50 games due to a suspension and injured himself upon returning. Brett Myers missed over half of the season with a right hip injury and was a non-factor when healthy. In the rotation, post-season hero Cole Hamels battled bouts of poor luck and accusations of unreadiness, while Moyer showed his age.

How did a team under so much duress manage to pull off a 93-69 record? A key external factor was the misfortune of others. Almost every key contributor on the Mets fell prey to the injury bug. The Braves built up an incredible rotation and bullpen but struggled offensively. While the Marlins could rake, they offered little in the way of defense or pitching consistency. But beyond those uncontrollable variables, a key internal factor for

PHILLIES PROSPECTUS
2009 W-L: 93-69, 1st in NL East

Pythag	85-77	5th
RS/G	5.1	1st
RA/G	4.4	6th
EqA	.272	3rd
EqBRR	0.5	6th
SNWP	.504	7th
WXRL	6.8	10th
FRAr	4.28	8th
DE	.694	6th
PADE	0.32	6th
Salary	$113.0	3rd
Attend	3.6	2nd

Ballpark: Citizens Bank Park (3-yr. PF: 1005). A haven for homers that rewards pitchers who avoid cookies

2009: A successfully defended pennant isn't quite as good as a title, but it doesn't suck

2010: Trader Ruben's monster exchange adds Doc to the core for four, so expect more flags

Action Items: Amaro finished his winter early; so hope Polanco, Ibanez, and Halladay age well, and Rollins bounces back

Phillies success was the team's multidimensionality. The club's offense could hit for average and power, it ran as efficiently as ever, and its players covered ground and threw well on defense, the roster serving as a mass embodiment of the fabled five-tool player. The Phillies have ranked among the best defensive teams over the last two seasons, finishing in the league's upper third in PADE, FRAA, UZR, and the Plus/Minus system. On offense, they improved on a seventh-best .267 EqA in 2008 by producing a .272 mark that ranked fourth out of 30 teams, largely the by-product of an uptick in power. Four Phillies hitters—Chase Utley, Howard, Werth, and Ibañez—hit 30 or more home runs, only the 12th occurrence of that feat. Only four of these teams qualified for playoff action, and just two (the 1977 Dodgers and 2009 Phillies) made it to the World Series.

When their boppers did bash, the Phillies had absolutely no trouble scoring runs, recording a high percentage of runs on dingers. Baseball Prospectus calls a team's percentage of runs scored via the home run "the Guillen Number," since Ozzie's White Sox teams generally lead or come close to leading the league in the category in spite of his initial reputation as a small-ball manager. Last year, the Phillies scored 45.1 percent of their runs on homers, topping all the other 29 teams by a fairly large margin; the Rangers finished in second place at 42.1 percent. The Phillies' Guillen Number ranks as the 13th-highest of the 886 teams from 1974 to 2009, and at 93-69, the Phillies stake claim to the second-best record of the baker's dozen atop the list. The 2000 Cardinals and 2008 White Sox preceded the 2009 Phils as the only Guillen Number virtuosos to play October baseball, and the 2008 Sox only got that far via a one-game playoff.

Generally, an overreliance on home runs does not correlate with winning, as the aggregate 993-1,031 record and .491 winning percentage of those 13 teams suggests. The lack of success largely derives from a one-dimensional attack, which does not accurately describe the Phillies' offense. While they scored a high percentage of their runs via the long ball, the team had other weapons at its disposal. Consider their stolen-base efficiency under coach Davey Lopes over the past three seasons: 138 stolen bases against 19 times caught in 2007 (87.9 percent), 136 and 25 in '08 (84.5), and 119 and 28 in '09 (80.9). Since 1960, no team has topped the Phillies' 87.9 success rate in 2007, with the closest competitor being the 84.5 percent posted by the 2008 Phillies. The '07 and '08 teams also ranked among the 10 best teams of the last 55 years in Equivalent Baserunning Runs, meaning that their speed was remarkable in every area that speed could affect run-

scoring. Their 2009 rate for successful steals would pale in comparison to that of the two seasons prior, but they still led the majors last season with a mark that ranks as the 13th-highest over the same span. The Phillies also lost ground on team EqBRR in '09, but still finished a useful 11th in the major leagues.

All of which might have counted for little if not for Amaro's in-season patch-up of a rotation that retaining Moyer had not fixed. Although the Phillies won out over other suitors in enlisting Pedro Martinez for stretch-drive support, the subsequent shrewd deadline deal not only stabilized a teetering rotation but also kept bullpen usage to a subsequent survivable minimum. On July 29th, a package of prospects was shipped to Cleveland in exchange for 2008's AL Cy Young Award winner Cliff Lee and bench-bat Ben Francisco. Lee made his Phillies debut on July 31st in San Francisco and twirled a gem of a complete game, scattering four hits and a run while fanning six hitters. In his two months as a senior circuit pitcher, he compiled a gaudy strikeout/walk ratio of over 7.0 in 12 starts. Before his arrival, the Phillies' rotation had surrendered a collective .276/.331/.471 slash line, the bookends of which ranked 25th and 28th in the majors. Post-Lee, the rotation improved to an opponent's line of .269/.319/.427, all three components of which ranked in the better half of the league and greatly contributed to the club's success over the Marlins and Braves down the stretch.

There might not have been any need for fighting had appropriate in-season actions been taken with Lidge, whose "perfect" 2008 season seemed to grant him unwavering loyalty from the team, even after it became clear that replacing him with the Phanatic might have reaped better results. Lidge endured a unique 11-win swing in value, as he declined from a league-best 7.61 WXRL in 2008 to a league-worst -3.26 in 2009. His 2009 record exceeded that of the next-worst reliever (Kyle Farnsworth, naturally) by approximately -1.75 wins. Prior to his historic horror, the worst single-season mark belonged to Steve Wilson, who had cost his team -2.86 wins in 1992; Lidge proved to be a half-win worse while taking his tumble from previous heights.

Typically, relievers as incredibly bad as Lidge lose their jobs before they can do this much damage. When the save-opportunities filter is applied, parsing out those relievers with 30 or more chances to close out the game in a season, Lidge's -3.26 WXRL dwarfs the -1.79 mark of Shawn Chacon in 2004, making this far and away the worst season for any reliever consistently used in the closer role in baseball history. Unfortunately, Lidge's three-year extension worth $37.5 million inked midway through the 2008 campaign and his place in team history made it tough for management, both in the dugout and in the boardroom, to work up the nerve to replace him. While Amaro has placed an emphasis on improving the bullpen moving into the 2010 season, it has yet to be seen if the team will bring in an insurance policy for Lidge.

As it turned out, despite its many flaws the team was almost good enough, as the Phillies quickly dispatched the Rockies, repeated their handy pennant-winning exploits over the flawed Dodgers in the NLCS, and took the World Series against the Yankees to six games. Lee provided the keys to the Phillies' wins in Games One and Five, but the bullpen and Hamels had little beyond their jerseys in common with the pitching that had won the Series in '08. The team's offense was exposed as they played into the latter weeks of October, not for relying too heavily on the home run, but rather for having trouble reaching base often enough to take full advantage of the balls launched out of their giving stadium. Neither Rollins nor Shane Victorino are on-base luminaries atop the order, which precludes their murderer's row from flourishing as much as it could have if, say, Chone Figgins and Bobby Abreu had led off. (Howard could have made a run at Hack Wilson with more baserunners.)

With an eye toward getting more men on base, one player who will not have a role on the team in which to falter is Pedro Feliz, who became this year's version of Burrell, the most expendable lineup regular on a pennant winner. Amaro replaced him with former Phillie Placido Polanco, signing Polanco to a three-year deal, figuring that similar defense could be had with a much improved offense for a mere $1.5 million more in salary for next season. Feliz provided top-notch defense at the hot corner for two seasons, but was reliably exposed as a black hole in the lineup where on-base success goes to die. While Polanco will hopefully rebound from a poor offensive season, even the diminished version of the infielder on display in 2009 put more runs on the board than Feliz did in any of his last five seasons.

That was more of a cosmetic switch, however. Amaro saved his heavy lifting for the pitching side of the ledger, with another dose of now characteristically quick winter work. Initial plans for 2010 involved a lefty-heavy rotation sporting Lee, Hamels, J. A. Happ, Moyer, and Joe Blanton, but after flirting with the Blue Jays around the July trade deadline, Amaro went back to that well to get the ace he coveted then and now. The GM took the lead role in a combination of trades heard 'round the hot stove, shipping prospects Kyle Drabek, Michael Taylor, and Travis d'Arnaud to the Blue Jays for workhorse Roy Halladay, and then flipping Lee and the one year they had control over him to the Mariners for a

trio of prospects (Phillippe Aumont, Tyson Gillies, and J. C. Ramirez) to notionally restock an increasingly empty farm system. As part of the package, Halladay promptly inked a team-friendly contract extension, possibly leaving anywhere from $60-80 million in guaranteed dollars on the table simply because he really wanted to play for the Phillies for the next four or five seasons.

Thus, in an off-season market that lacked top-tier talent available via free agency, Amaro created a complicated solution to ensure that the staff is stocked with a top starter far into the future. The problem is that the Phillies' stars-and-scrubs farm system may now be down to Domonic Brown and a lot of people who aren't Domonic Brown, underscoring the extent to which this is a win-now franchise whose window extends as far as their present collection of big-league stars can carry them. Pinching pennies from the 2010 budget to unnecessarily trade away Lee after adding Halladay not only significantly diminishes Doc's impact in 2010, but also short-changes this team's present. From what might have been the best rotation in baseball, boasting a front three capable of taking down any titan the American League could run against them, the Phillies settled for the more modest expectation that Halladay will be complemented by the expected leveling out of Hamels' performance, providing a potent duo in front of a good second-rank pairing of Blanton and Happ.

Fickle compartments such as the bullpen and bench may loom large in how far the team goes in the future. The bench hasn't had to play a major role with the lineup's relative stability, but Amaro assiduously assembled a "better" bench by speedily signing up known quantities like Ross Gload, Juan Castro, and Brian Schneider. Of course, "known" is not necessarily the same thing as "good." At least these known quantities provide less mystery than does the wishcast that the pen will be better because Lidge and Chad Durbin will just go back to late-game partying like it's two-thousand-zero-zero-eight—oops, overtime? The hope is that a healthy J. C. Romero and the still-improving Ryan Madson will take up the slack.

Happily for Phillies faithful, there are perhaps just a Mordecai Brown–sized handful of teams that can boast a better core than the Phillies can going into 2010. Amaro probably won't be able to be as aggressive in-season in his second spin of steering the club as he was the first time around, because with little left to barter with, it will be harder to adapt should anything go wrong in-season. Nevertheless, a third pennant isn't hard to envision, another product of the same key players who produced the first two.

HITTERS

Paul Bako   C

Bats: L   Throws: R   Height: 6' 2"   Weight: 205   Born: June 20, 1972   Age: 38

YEAR	TEAM	LVL	AGE	PA	R	2B	3B	HR	RBI	BB	SO	SB	CS	EqBRR	AVG	OBP	SLG	EqAVG	EqOBP	EqSLG	EqA	VORP	WARP	DEFENSE
2007	BAL	MLB	35	174	13	3	1	1	8	15	50	0	1	-0.8	.205	.277	.256	.206	.279	.258	.190	-3.1	-0.7	47-C -2
2008	CIN	MLB	36	338	30	11	2	6	35	34	90	0	2	-1.0	.217	.299	.328	.220	.299	.327	.220	1.3	-0.7	87-C -4
2009	PHI	MLB	37	130	12	4	0	3	9	13	32	0	1	-0.5	.224	.308	.336	.233	.315	.336	.228	1.3	-0.2	33-C -2
2010	PHI	MLB	38	155	12	5	1	2	12	16	45	0	1	-0.3	.206	.291	.299	.209	.289	.294	.203	-2.3	-0.4	40-C -1

Breakout: 9%   Improve: 33%   Collapse: 30%   Attrition: 42%   MLB: 85%   Comparables: Ron Hassey, Jeff Reed, Greg Myers, Chad Kreuter

Bako found himself on a major-league team yet again, despite doing little to warrant the position except convincing Charlie Manuel that he was a more adept defender than Chris Coste and still hits lefty. After the year, the Phillies signed Brian Schneider to get the best player of the type. Let this be a lesson to every parent: if your kid hits lefty, but just not that well, get him some catching gear, because the good-enough bar doesn't get any lower than this.

Quintin Berry   CF

Bats: L   Throws: L   Height: 6' 1"   Weight: 165   Born: November 21, 1984   Age: 25

YEAR	TEAM	LVL	AGE	PA	R	2B	3B	HR	RBI	BB	SO	SB	CS	EqBRR	AVG	OBP	SLG	EqAVG	EqOBP	EqSLG	EqA	VORP	WARP	DEFENSE	
2007	LWD	A	22	581	86	19	4	3	44	61	85	55	18	2.6	.312	.395	.386	.292	.355	.351	.257	13.0	0.9	91-CF -2	32-LF -4
2008	CLR	A+	23	590	63	24	1	3	43	65	103	51	14	-0.4	.272	.360	.341	.252	.322	.314	.233	-0.4	-2.5	128-CF -21	
2009	REA	AA	24	598	89	17	2	5	28	63	118	48	14	5.2	.266	.355	.335	.241	.314	.307	.229	-1.8	-1.7	129-CF -13	
2010	PHI	MLB	25	560	56	20	2	4	32	51	126	19	8	1.2	.250	.323	.320	.253	.324	.327	.231	0.6	-0.6	124-CF -6	

Breakout: 13%   Improve: 44%   Collapse: 20%   Attrition: 4%   MLB: 4%   Comparables: Nyjer Morgan, Freddie Bynum, Sherwin Cijntje, Bradley Coon

A speedy string bean in center, Berry has a solid approach at the plate, but with every step he takes up the ladder, his batting average goes down a bit while his strikeout rate rises. That's not a player who is improving; it's a player treading water. Add in horrible numbers against right-handers (.249/.333/.323), and the picture gets downright bleak. While the plus-plus speed is his ticket to the majors, it's more of a jump-seat in the bulkhead as opposed to a first-class ticket.

Domonic Brown   OF

Bats: L   Throws: L   Height: 6' 5"   Weight: 204   Born: September 3, 1987   Age: 22

YEAR	TEAM	LVL	AGE	PA	R	2B	3B	HR	RBI	BB	SO	SB	CS	EqBRR	AVG	OBP	SLG	EqAVG	EqOBP	EqSLG	EqA	VORP	WARP	DEFENSE	
2007	WPT	A-	19	317	43	11	5	3	32	27	49	14	7	-3.2	.295	.356	.400	.276	.324	.369	.244	1.3	-1.1	43-RF -6	29-CF -2
2008	LWD	A	20	516	77	23	3	9	54	64	72	22	7	-0.7	.291	.382	.417	.270	.349	.376	.259	11.3	0.1	65-CF -1	47-RF -10
2009	CLR	A+	21	280	41	12	3	11	44	34	48	15	8	-1.6	.303	.386	.517	.287	.357	.488	.287	14.0	1.3	64-RF -3	
2009	REA	AA	21	162	20	9	4	3	20	14	37	8	1	0.5	.279	.346	.456	.253	.313	.407	.253	1.8	-0.6	35-RF -7	
2010	PHI	MLB	22	480	57	23	3	10	50	50	94	10	5	-1.0	.267	.346	.408	.269	.345	.414	.263	11.7	0.5	107-RF -7	

Breakout: 20%   Improve: 53%   Collapse: 9%   Attrition: 3%   MLB: 15%   Comparables: Trey Beamon, Nick Markakis, Michael Saunders, Jeremy Hermida

One of the better outfield prospects in the game, Brown is a long, lean athlete with above-average speed and significant power capabilities that the club believes will continue to blossom as he gets older. Whether their expectations are correct will determine whether he turns into a star or simply a nice outfielder to have around. On a pure tools level, Brown has it all, but with his mere three home runs in 147 Double-A at-bats, Darryl Strawberry comparisons are more than a little premature.

Travis d'Arnaud   C

Bats: R   Throws: R   Height: 6' 2"   Weight: 195   Born: February 10, 1989   Age: 21

YEAR	TEAM	LVL	AGE	PA	R	2B	3B	HR	RBI	BB	SO	SB	CS	EqBRR	AVG	OBP	SLG	EqAVG	EqOBP	EqSLG	EqA	VORP	WARP	DEFENSE
2007	PHL	Rk	18	151	18	3	0	4	20	4	23	4	2	0.9	.241	.278	.348	.207	.225	.303	.178	-7.3	-1.9	20-C -3
2008	WPT	A-	19	197	21	13	1	4	25	18	29	1	2	-2.5	.309	.371	.463	.289	.335	.439	.266	9.1	0.8	41-C -4
2008	LWD	A	19	70	12	5	0	2	5	5	10	0	0	-1.8	.297	.357	.469	.277	.329	.431	.261	3.1	-0.3	16-C -6
2009	LWD	A	20	540	71	38	1	13	71	41	75	8	4	-2.1	.255	.319	.419	.232	.281	.362	.225	-0.5	-1.7	98-C -14
2010	TOR	MLB	21	476	54	26	1	13	53	37	83	2	2	-1.9	.247	.309	.399	.251	.311	.394	.242	9.9	0.3	93-C -7

Breakout: 22%   Improve: 50%   Collapse: 23%   Attrition: 0%   MLB: 0%   Comparables: Francisco Cabrera, Damon Hollins, Jim Olander, Mike Diaz

The Blue Jays were thrilled to get d'Arnaud in the Roy Halladay trade, as they were prepared to select him in the 2007 draft but were thwarted when the Phillies grabbed him one pick ahead of them (Toronto settled for Brett Cecil). While his overall numbers don't provoke Wieters-level excitement (either flavor: orgasmic or pragmatic optimism), he did have a big second half, batting .302/.366/.473 after the break, and scouts love his athleticism. He got tested a lot in his full-season debut, allowing 132 steals against 40 baserunner kills, a 23 percent rate that will have to improve, but is expected to. This is a high-ceiling catcher in a world where most teams are just happy to have a prospect at the position who knows how to tie his shoes and projects to play every day.

Greg Dobbs   4C   Bats: L   Throws: R   Height: 6' 1"   Weight: 205   Born: July 2, 1978   Age: 31

YEAR	TEAM	LVL	AGE	PA	R	2B	3B	HR	RBI	BB	SO	SB	CS	EqBRR	AVG	OBP	SLG	EqAVG	EqOBP	EqSLG	EqA	VORP	WARP	DEFENSE			
2007	PHI	MLB	28	358	45	20	4	10	55	29	67	3	0	0.9	.272	.330	.451	.273	.332	.450	.270	10.6	1.2	46-3B	-2	11-1B	1
2008	PHI	MLB	29	240	30	14	1	9	40	11	40	3	1	-3.2	.301	.333	.491	.310	.340	.496	.282	10.5	0.8	37-3B	-3	1-RF	0
2009	PHI	MLB	30	169	15	6	0	5	20	11	29	1	0	-1.6	.247	.296	.383	.253	.300	.396	.244	-1.5	0.0	10-3B	2	9-LF	1
2010	PHI	MLB	31	298	32	14	2	9	42	24	59	2	1	-0.8	.263	.324	.423	.265	.325	.421	.257	6.7	0.7	45-3B	-1		

Breakout: 8%   Improve: 41%   Collapse: 25%   Attrition: 12%   MLB: 90%   Comparables: Irv Noren, Ken Caminiti, Eric Chavez, Robin Ventura

Dobbs battled injuries in 2009, but that probably had less to do with his failings than the general difficulty of sustaining success in the pinch-hitter role. Praised as an elite substitute-swinger after pinch-hitting .355 in 2008, Dobbs suffered the reminder that pinch-hitting success is not a persistent skill, even for those good at it, and slumped to .167. Consider that the man pinch-hit 60 times last year; that's 10 times a month. Enough luck goes into the small number of opportunities that pinch-hitters receive that Dobbs could easily rebound or get even worse. The addition of Ross Gload as another lefty bat bench doesn't help, but Placido Polanco's addition at third means there might be a few spot starts for lefty sock to help Dobbs' bat fresh.

Pedro Feliz   3B   Bats: R   Throws: R   Height: 6' 1"   Weight: 210   Born: April 27, 1975   Age: 35

YEAR	TEAM	LVL	AGE	PA	R	2B	3B	HR	RBI	BB	SO	SB	CS	EqBRR	AVG	OBP	SLG	EqAVG	EqOBP	EqSLG	EqA	VORP	WARP	DEFENSE			
2007	SFN	MLB	32	590	61	28	2	20	72	29	70	2	2	-4.9	.253	.290	.418	.257	.294	.424	.243	2.4	3.2	136-3B	23	4-1B	1
2008	PHI	MLB	33	463	43	19	2	14	58	33	54	0	0	-0.8	.249	.302	.402	.254	.304	.404	.245	3.7	0.7	109-3B	3		
2009	PHI	MLB	34	625	62	30	2	12	82	35	68	0	1	-5.6	.266	.308	.386	.274	.314	.396	.246	8.2	2.2	149-3B	11		
2010	HOU	MLB	35	540	54	22	1	14	68	36	72	1	2	-1.8	.258	.309	.391	.259	.309	.397	.241	3.1	1.0	129-3B	6		

Breakout: 10%   Improve: 34%   Collapse: 23%   Attrition: 21%   MLB: 97%   Comparables: Ron Coomer, Brooks Robinson, Matt Williams, Gary Gaetti

Feliz's defense remains strong, but it may not be able to keep him on the field for much longer, given his declining bat. He showed less home-run power than at any time since he became a regular, this despite playing in a bandbox. Between his terrible baserunning and declining bat, he's not the guy to man the hot corner on a contender anymore. Naturally, Ed Wade took that as his cue to sign Feliz to a one-year deal with the Astros. Perhaps Wade failed to note that in two years with Philadelphia, Feliz hit .268/.310/.414 at home, against .250/.301/.372 on the road. The Crawford Boxes won't save him.

Ben Francisco   OF   Bats: R   Throws: R   Height: 6' 1"   Weight: 190   Born: October 23, 1981   Age: 28

YEAR	TEAM	LVL	AGE	PA	R	2B	3B	HR	RBI	BB	SO	SB	CS	EqBRR	AVG	OBP	SLG	EqAVG	EqOBP	EqSLG	EqA	VORP	WARP	DEFENSE			
2007	BUF	AAA	25	425	60	27	2	12	51	36	66	22	8	-3.0	.318	.382	.496	.298	.356	.470	.283	20.8	2.1	45-CF	-2	29-LF	2
2007	CLE	MLB	25	66	10	5	0	3	12	3	19	0	2	-2.5	.274	.303	.500	.274	.303	.484	.259	0.7	0.4	11-LF	2	3-RF	0
2008	BUF	AAA	26	104	9	3	1	1	6	11	25	3	0	-0.5	.228	.308	.315	.204	.279	.290	.209	-3.5	-0.8	17-LF	-2	6-RF	-1
2008	CLE	MLB	26	499	65	32	0	15	54	40	86	4	3	2.2	.266	.332	.438	.274	.340	.456	.271	15.4	2.0	73-LF	2	26-RF	1
2009	CLE	MLB	27	355	48	21	1	10	33	33	59	13	3	2.6	.250	.336	.422	.261	.346	.431	.274	13.6	0.9	44-LF	-6	30-CF	0
2009	PHI	MLB	27	104	10	9	0	5	13	5	24	1	4	-2.4	.278	.317	.526	.299	.337	.557	.275	3.7	0.7	8-LF	2	7-CF	1
2010	PHI	MLB	28	476	60	24	1	16	53	44	95	9	5	-0.6	.266	.343	.442	.264	.340	.438	.269	14.8	1.6	93-LF	0		

Breakout: 6%   Improve: 50%   Collapse: 13%   Attrition: 9%   MLB: 90%   Comparables: Craig Monroe, Mark Quinn, Matt Mieske, Mike Devereaux

Francisco went almost unnoticed as the add-in to the Cliff Lee blockbuster, but he provided a valuable service to the Phillies as a right-handed bench bat on a team that leans to the left. Having had his chances to start and demonstrating a tweener's blend of a bat that is adequate for the corners and a glove that's no better than that in center, he should now settle in for a valuable stretch of quality fourth outfielding.

Anthony Gose   CF   Bats: L   Throws: L   Height: 6' 1"   Weight: 190   Born: August 10, 1990   Age: 19

YEAR	TEAM	LVL	AGE	PA	R	2B	3B	HR	RBI	BB	SO	SB	CS	EqBRR	AVG	OBP	SLG	EqAVG	EqOBP	EqSLG	EqA	VORP	WARP	DEFENSE
2008	PHL	Rk	17	41	4	2	1	0	3	1	12	3	1	-0.6	.256	.293	.359	.200	.220	.300	.178	-2.2	-0.6	9-CF -1
2009	LWD	A	18	572	72	24	9	2	52	35	110	76	20	-1.5	.259	.323	.353	.235	.281	.323	.219	-8.4	-3.2	117-CF -16 6-LF -2
2010	PHI	MLB	19	642	53	29	8	4	52	41	148	29	12	-0.9	.240	.297	.336	.242	.297	.341	.224	-3.5	-1.5	142-CF -10

Breakout: 37%   Improve: 62%   Collapse: 14%   Attrition: 2%   MLB: 0%   Comparables: Gregory Burtt, Duane Singleton, Engel Beltre, Al Martin

The Phillies love athletes, and Gose is just that, with his 76 steals being the first indication of game-changing speed. He just needs to figure out this pesky hitting portion of the program, or his game-changing speed is going to have scant acquaintance with the basepaths. He did show a better approach as the season wore on, and a few scouts think there's a hint of power hidden somewhere in his frame. Keep in mind he was a teenager in a full-season league. If he can show improved form and the power shows up, he's a big-time prospect. If one or the other does, he's a very good prospect. Without either, it could get dicey as he moves up the ladder.

Ryan Howard   1B   Bats: L   Throws: L   Height: 6' 4"   Weight: 255   Born: November 19, 1979   Age: 30

YEAR	TEAM	LVL	AGE	PA	R	2B	3B	HR	RBI	BB	SO	SB	CS	EqBRR	AVG	OBP	SLG	EqAVG	EqOBP	EqSLG	EqA	VORP	WARP	DEFENSE
2007	PHI	MLB	27	648	94	26	0	47	136	107	199	1	0	-4.9	.268	.392	.584	.263	.389	.570	.318	50.2	5.1	138-1B -3
2008	PHI	MLB	28	700	105	26	4	48	146	81	199	1	1	-3.5	.251	.339	.543	.254	.339	.548	.292	34.0	3.7	157-1B 0
2009	PHI	MLB	29	703	105	37	4	45	141	75	186	8	1	-3.4	.279	.360	.571	.290	.366	.590	.314	46.6	4.8	155-1B -3
2010	PHI	MLB	30	672	91	27	2	37	121	87	188	3	1	-2.0	.249	.351	.494	.253	.351	.507	.286	27.0	2.8	150-1B -1

Breakout: 5%   Improve: 33%   Collapse: 15%   Attrition: 8%   MLB: 97%   Comparables: Jim Thome, Fred McGriff, David Ortiz, Mike Epstein

Howard is one of the game's most dangerous hitters against right-handers, with career rates of .307/.409/.661 and a home run once every 10.4 at-bats, but has huge problems seeing same-side hitters, dropping to .226/.310/.444 with a home run every 17.6 at-bats. He takes a lot of criticism for the latter figures among analysts, but this is still above-average power, equivalent to 37 home runs over a 650 at-bat season. He was a bit worse than this in 2009, hitting .207/.298/.356 with a homer every 37 at-bats against southpaws, but until he shows that he can't rebound to his career levels, talk of platooning him against anyone but the toughest left-handers is premature. Sort of like the slugger he replaced, Jim Thome, Howard tends to hit more home runs to left field than to right, while pulling nearly everything that stays in the yard. Teams could cut down on his average by shifting three infielders to the first-base side, but they'd be limited when there are runners on. He may have one of the weakest throwing arms in the game, but his weight loss in the 2008-2009 offseason produced a more mobile fielder. Howard's path from here on will depend on his ability to stay in shape, and last year's focus on conditioning bodes well for a longer career, instead of a Mo Vaughn–style quick peak and flameout.

Raul Ibañez   LF   Bats: L   Throws: R   Height: 6' 2"   Weight: 225   Born: June 2, 1972   Age: 38

YEAR	TEAM	LVL	AGE	PA	R	2B	3B	HR	RBI	BB	SO	SB	CS	EqBRR	AVG	OBP	SLG	EqAVG	EqOBP	EqSLG	EqA	VORP	WARP	DEFENSE
2007	SEA	MLB	35	636	80	35	5	21	105	53	97	0	0	-1.0	.291	.351	.480	.298	.356	.494	.290	32.7	2.4	126-LF -11
2008	SEA	MLB	36	707	85	43	3	23	110	64	110	2	4	-2.1	.293	.358	.479	.306	.371	.504	.294	39.9	3.4	151-LF -8
2009	PHI	MLB	37	565	93	32	3	34	93	56	119	4	0	-3.0	.272	.347	.552	.282	.352	.574	.304	41.0	5.0	125-LF 4
2010	PHI	MLB	38	520	59	26	2	17	77	49	99	1	1	-0.9	.262	.336	.436	.265	.335	.444	.265	13.6	1.3	111-LF -2

Breakout: 1%   Improve: 19%   Collapse: 33%   Attrition: 19%   MLB: 98%   Comparables: Luis Gonzalez, Ken Griffey Jr., Ken Griffey Sr., John Vander Wal

As virtually his first order of business, Amaro jumped out ahead of the free-agent market last December to sign the 37-year-old Ibañez to a three-year, $31.5 million contract, then looked foolish as a glut of corner outfielders and the cratering national economy saw better players signing for shorter terms and fewer dollars. Ibañez helped him save face by getting out to an MVP-level start, batting .312/.371/.656 with 22 home runs in his first 62 games. An injured left groin helped cool him off; he returned after 22 games on the shelf and hit only .232/.323/.448 in the 72 games remaining. No doubt Ibañez returned to form somewhat, but the unhealed injury also played a part. Ibañez's career high in home runs wasn't simply the result of the transfer from Safeco to Citizens Bank Park, and even his typically mediocre fielding seemed to improve in the weaker league. If healthy for the full season, Ibañez could possibly continue to enjoy his late-career peak, but when dealing with a 38-year-old, it's always smarter to bet the under.

John Mayberry Jr.   OF   Bats: R   Throws: R   Height: 6' 6"   Weight: 230   Born: December 21, 1983   Age: 26

YEAR	TEAM	LVL	AGE	PA	R	2B	3B	HR	RBI	BB	SO	SB	CS	EqBRR	AVG	OBP	SLG	EqAVG	EqOBP	EqSLG	EqA	VORP	WARP	DEFENSE			
2007	BAK	A+	23	277	47	15	1	16	45	28	64	9	1	2.7	.230	.314	.496	.194	.263	.381	.224	-6.0	-1.5	58-RF	-6		
2007	FRI	AA	23	271	35	10	0	14	38	20	62	7	1	2.7	.241	.307	.453	.224	.278	.400	.235	-2.6	-0.6	68-RF	-2		
2008	FRI	AA	24	90	16	8	0	4	13	4	21	4	1	0.0	.268	.322	.512	.238	.278	.417	.239	-0.5	-0.4	19-RF	-3		
2008	OKL	AAA	24	475	49	30	7	16	58	30	85	6	2	-2.5	.263	.316	.474	.242	.289	.410	.240	-1.7	-0.3	90-LF	2	20-RF	-3
2009	LEH	AAA	25	358	44	20	2	13	43	34	94	6	2	0.3	.256	.332	.456	.248	.321	.443	.263	8.3	1.5	65-RF	2	23-LF	2
2009	PHI	MLB	25	60	8	3	0	4	8	2	23	0	0	0.9	.211	.250	.474	.211	.250	.474	.245	-0.5	0.0	11-LF	-1	3-RF	1
2010	PHI	MLB	26	404	41	19	2	13	44	32	108	4	2	0.6	.229	.298	.400	.226	.294	.395	.239	-0.3	-0.3	96-RF	-2		

Breakout: 13%   Improve: 39%   Collapse: 23%   Attrition: 13%   MLB: 19%   Comparables: Todd Dunn, Jimmy Hurst, Jeff Kipila, Lyle Mouton

The large, slugging son of the large, slugging original, Mayberry is an odd fit for an aspiring fourth outfielder. He struggles against northpaws, striking out in 31 percent of his plate appearances against them in Triple-A. He has very real power, so if he can improve his ability to make contact against righties—which probably entails learning how to better identify off-speed pitches—then he would still have some upside. However, at his age and after 553 games, with a .256 average between Double-A and Triple-A, it seems like a stretch. The presence of Francisco and the addition of Gload crowds Mayberry off the active roster, but he's at risk for worse without progress.

Jimmy Rollins   SS   Bats: S   Throws: R   Height: 5' 8"   Weight: 175   Born: November 27, 1978   Age: 31

YEAR	TEAM	LVL	AGE	PA	R	2B	3B	HR	RBI	BB	SO	SB	CS	EqBRR	AVG	OBP	SLG	EqAVG	EqOBP	EqSLG	EqA	VORP	WARP	DEFENSE	
2007	PHI	MLB	28	778	139	38	20	30	94	49	85	41	6	7.9	.296	.344	.531	.301	.349	.535	.298	64.3	7.3	160-SS	1
2008	PHI	MLB	29	625	76	38	9	11	59	58	55	47	3	8.9	.277	.349	.437	.282	.352	.445	.285	43.2	5.9	131-SS	9
2009	PHI	MLB	30	725	100	43	5	21	77	44	70	31	8	1.5	.250	.296	.423	.260	.302	.437	.257	27.8	2.5	152-SS	-6
2010	PHI	MLB	31	688	102	41	10	19	76	54	74	34	9	3.0	.278	.340	.464	.277	.337	.459	.277	37.9	4.2	145-SS	1

Breakout: 9%   Improve: 37%   Collapse: 9%   Attrition: 7%   MLB: 99%   Comparables: Omar Vizquel, Frankie Frisch, Brian Roberts, Don Buford

Rollins' season wasn't spectacularly bad by the standards of leadoff men on pennant winners, not when Johnny Sturm (.239/.293/.300) led off for the 1941 Yankees, but it wasn't good, either. From Opening Day through the end of June, Rollins hit .207/.250/.322, causing Charlie Manuel to occasionally (and very reluctantly) drop him from the leadoff spot. Rollins struggles with the occasional case of Willie Mays Hayes syndrome, when a speedy leadoff guy confuses himself with a slugger and tries too hard to hit home runs, resulting in a hail of popups and shallow flies. Simultaneously, his walk rate, which had risen substantially in 2008, fell back to earth. Rollins corrected his swing and in July stopped trying to pull everything. The result was .285/.333/.505 over the final three months, production much more consistent with his career rates. Rollins is a good enough fielder that he was still an asset last year, and if he can stay within himself, he'll resume his place as one of the game's shortstop stars.

Carlos Ruiz   C   Bats: R   Throws: R   Height: 5' 10"   Weight: 200   Born: January 22, 1979   Age: 31

YEAR	TEAM	LVL	AGE	PA	R	2B	3B	HR	RBI	BB	SO	SB	CS	EqBRR	AVG	OBP	SLG	EqAVG	EqOBP	EqSLG	EqA	VORP	WARP	DEFENSE	
2007	PHI	MLB	28	429	42	29	2	6	54	42	49	6	1	0.3	.259	.340	.396	.259	.340	.390	.260	19.9	2.9	101-C	6
2008	PHI	MLB	29	373	47	14	0	4	31	44	38	1	2	1.9	.219	.320	.300	.220	.319	.295	.224	2.7	0.5	93-C	3
2009	PHI	MLB	30	379	32	26	1	9	43	47	39	3	2	-1.8	.255	.355	.425	.265	.361	.444	.276	23.4	3.0	98-C	3
2010	PHI	MLB	31	370	37	19	1	7	44	43	44	3	2	0.0	.257	.352	.389	.257	.349	.384	.261	14.7	1.8	93-C	2

Breakout: 14%   Improve: 40%   Collapse: 23%   Attrition: 11%   MLB: 99%   Comparables: Rick Dempsey, Mike Lieberthal, Brad Ausmus, Jim Sundberg

It's easy to look at Ruiz's rates and figure he was reaching base effectively and providing some pop, but batting eighth helped produce eight intentional passes, and the pleasures of calling CBP home produced almost all of his pop (.553 SLG, against .313 on the road). Not everyone can do that, of course; we have Paul Bako as evidence. Ruiz had a nifty stretch run from August 2nd to October 3rd, hitting .310/.406/.526 in 140 plate appearances that extended into the playoffs. Add in highly regarded defensive skills, and Ruiz gets to settle for being the nifty little player in a star-studded lineup. He'll pair up with added vet Brian Schneider, but should still get the majority of the starts.

Matt Stairs — PH

Bats: L Throws: R Height: 5' 9" Weight: 210 Born: February 27, 1968 Age: 42

YEAR	TEAM	LVL	AGE	PA	R	2B	3B	HR	RBI	BB	SO	SB	CS	EqBRR	AVG	OBP	SLG	EqAVG	EqOBP	EqSLG	EqA	VORP	WARP	DEFENSE			
2007	TOR	MLB	39	405	58	28	1	21	64	44	66	2	1	-2.7	.289	.368	.549	.287	.368	.551	.304	26.3	2.4	37-1B	1	32-LF	-4
2008	TOR	MLB	40	368	42	11	1	11	44	41	87	1	1	-1.2	.250	.342	.394	.251	.345	.401	.261	4.4	-0.1	7-LF	-3	5-RF	-2
2008	PHI	MLB	40	19	4	1	0	2	5	1	3	0	0	0.1	.294	.316	.706	.294	.316	.706	.323	1.7	0.2	2-RF	0		
2009	PHI	MLB	41	129	15	4	0	5	17	23	30	0	0	0.3	.194	.357	.379	.202	.357	.375	.267	1.7	0.2	6-RF	-3	5-LF	3
2010	PHI	MLB	42	169	15	6	0	5	20	21	44	1	0	-0.3	.227	.326	.365	.226	.325	.382	.244	0.8	-0.3	18-RF	-3		

Breakout: 5% Improve: 22% Collapse: 35% Attrition: 46% MLB: 99% Comparables: Enos Slaughter, Stan Musial, Cy Williams, Mickey Vernon

It feels like ages ago when Phillies fans proudly adorned their "In Case of Emergency, Use Stairs" shirts—could this even be the same Wonder Hamster? Regardless of his sapped power and inability to otherwise record hits, the man can still take a walk with the best of them, as evidenced by his patient plate appearance in Game Four of the NLCS; a home run off Jonathan Broxton would have tied the game in the ninth, but Stairs resisted the urge to offer at poor pitches and coaxed a free pass instead. With absolutely no defensive ability, his days as an effective bench weapon are over, but the threat of the long ball from his Ruthian swings is likely to merit a bench spot somewhere or, at the very least, an invitation to spring training. Cliff Johnson has the major-league pinch-hit home-run record with 20; Stairs needs two to pass him.

Michael Taylor — OF

Bats: R Throws: R Height: 6' 6" Weight: 250 Born: December 19, 1985 Age: 24

YEAR	TEAM	LVL	AGE	PA	R	2B	3B	HR	RBI	BB	SO	SB	CS	EqBRR	AVG	OBP	SLG	EqAVG	EqOBP	EqSLG	EqA	VORP	WARP	DEFENSE			
2007	WPT	A-	21	261	30	14	0	6	33	23	53	8	2	1.3	.227	.300	.365	.212	.264	.328	.208	-9.1	-3.4	43-LF	-10	10-RF	-2
2008	LWD	A	22	288	40	12	3	10	50	31	43	10	3	-2.7	.361	.441	.554	.319	.385	.475	.296	16.5	1.3	46-LF	-3	10-RF	-3
2008	CLR	A+	22	266	36	27	1	9	38	19	46	5	6	-1.1	.329	.380	.560	.304	.346	.514	.286	12.7	1.1	39-LF	-2	13-RF	-2
2009	REA	AA	23	363	59	22	4	15	65	35	51	18	4	3.8	.333	.408	.569	.310	.372	.528	.304	24.5	2.9	36-LF	-4	25-RF	4
2009	LEH	AAA	23	128	15	6	1	5	19	13	19	3	1	0.1	.282	.359	.491	.279	.357	.477	.287	6.4	1.1	23-LF	3	7-RF	0
2010	OAK	MLB	24	479	57	26	3	16	68	42	98	10	4	0.3	.278	.347	.464	.278	.347	.461	.275	18.1	1.5	94-LF	-4		

Breakout: 18% Improve: 55% Collapse: 8% Attrition: 7% MLB: 16% Comparables: Scott Morgan, Billy Lott, Michael Restovich, John Mayberry

Taylor's progress as a prospect has been picking up speed; after putting up solid numbers in the low minors in 2008, he took even larger steps forward in Double-A and Triple-A in 2009. He's a difficult batter to evaluate—despite being built like a pro wrestler, Taylor employs a contact-oriented approach, simply hitting home runs because he's just that strong. Traded to Toronto as part of the Halladay package, he was quickly flipped to Oakland for Brett Wallace in an exchange of right-now readiness for upside. If Taylor fulfills that potential, he could hit .300 with 20-25 home runs annually. He might not make the A's right out of spring training, but given their overly vanilla outfield cast, he should put himself into the picture in short order.

Chase Utley — 2B

Bats: L Throws: R Height: 6' 1" Weight: 200 Born: December 17, 1978 Age: 31

YEAR	TEAM	LVL	AGE	PA	R	2B	3B	HR	RBI	BB	SO	SB	CS	EqBRR	AVG	OBP	SLG	EqAVG	EqOBP	EqSLG	EqA	VORP	WARP	DEFENSE	
2007	PHI	MLB	28	613	104	48	5	22	103	50	89	9	1	3.0	.332	.410	.566	.336	.413	.571	.330	68.2	8.3	130-2B	7
2008	PHI	MLB	29	707	113	41	4	33	104	64	104	14	2	1.1	.292	.380	.535	.297	.381	.543	.311	63.0	8.1	156-2B	8
2009	PHI	MLB	30	687	112	28	4	31	93	88	110	23	0	8.8	.282	.397	.508	.295	.405	.531	.321	67.5	8.7	151-2B	10
2010	PHI	MLB	31	672	100	36	3	25	96	72	107	13	2	2.3	.286	.394	.490	.289	.394	.498	.306	53.6	6.2	153-2B	4

Breakout: 5% Improve: 45% Collapse: 16% Attrition: 7% MLB: 100% Comparables: Eddie Mathews, George Brett, Richie Hebner, Roberto Alomar

Despite never winning any major hardware, Utley has totaled 37.9 WARP3 since 2005, leading not only all Phillies players but also *everyone* not named Pujols. He earns his status as perhaps the second-best overall player in the game by combining defensive wizardry at the keystone, a good eye, gap power, and efficient baserunning. As he displayed during this past World Series, he can turn on any pitch from any pitcher, regardless of opposing handedness. His installation as a full-time starter, delayed until he was 26, precludes our waxing poetic about his Hall of Fame chances, but Utley has been the best player at his position for half a decade by a fairly wide margin. Second basemen tend to decline more rapidly than players at other positions, but it seems that only injuries could derail his dominance for the next few seasons (he ducked one bullet by coming back in good form from hip labrum surgery); even then, Utley could decline for years (à la Sandberg) and wind up being incredibly valuable for almost all of it.

Shane Victorino   **CF**   Bats: S   Throws: R   Height: 5' 9"   Weight: 180   Born: November 30, 1980   Age: 29

YEAR	TEAM	LVL	AGE	PA	R	2B	3B	HR	RBI	BB	SO	SB	CS	EqBRR	AVG	OBP	SLG	EqAVG	EqOBP	EqSLG	EqA	VORP	WARP	DEFENSE			
2007	PHI	MLB	26	510	78	23	3	12	46	37	62	37	4	3.5	.281	.347	.423	.284	.349	.422	.279	19.7	2.9	102-RF	8	2-CF	-2
2008	PHI	MLB	27	627	102	30	8	14	58	45	69	36	11	7.2	.293	.352	.447	.302	.359	.459	.281	32.3	3.7	134-CF	0	5-RF	1
2009	PHI	MLB	28	694	102	39	13	10	62	60	71	25	8	3.8	.292	.358	.445	.305	.368	.466	.287	40.7	4.0	148-CF	-4		
2010	PHI	MLB	29	627	95	32	8	14	59	55	73	26	9	2.2	.289	.358	.446	.288	.356	.440	.279	32.3	3.4	135-CF	-1		

Breakout: 3%   Improve: 36%   Collapse: 8%   Attrition: 5%   MLB: 98%   Comparables: Mookie Wilson, Brian McRae, Brett Butler, Billy North

The Flyin' Hawaiian now has four full major-league seasons under his belt and has increased his on-base percentage in each of them, making the most of his baserunning prowess in the process. That steady production through his peak seasons has made him a perfect patch from the briefly beloved Aaron Rowand. PECOTA effectively nailed him last year, projecting .291/.352/.430, with 25 steals against eight times caught. The signing of Placido Polanco to bat second in the order will bump Victorino down to the seventh spot, but his modus operandi will probably go unchanged: be patient, hit the ball hard, drive opposing pitchers batty.

Jayson Werth   **RF**   Bats: R   Throws: R   Height: 6' 5"   Weight: 225   Born: May 20, 1979   Age: 31

YEAR	TEAM	LVL	AGE	PA	R	2B	3B	HR	RBI	BB	SO	SB	CS	EqBRR	AVG	OBP	SLG	EqAVG	EqOBP	EqSLG	EqA	VORP	WARP	DEFENSE			
2007	PHI	MLB	28	304	43	11	3	8	49	44	73	7	1	0.9	.298	.404	.459	.302	.409	.459	.305	20.3	3.3	50-RF	8	14-LF	1
2008	PHI	MLB	29	482	73	16	3	24	67	57	119	20	1	5.1	.273	.363	.498	.280	.367	.510	.301	33.3	4.8	74-RF	8	26-CF	1
2009	PHI	MLB	30	676	98	26	1	36	99	91	156	20	3	2.6	.268	.373	.506	.280	.379	.526	.307	50.6	5.8	143-RF	2	7-CF	1
2010	PHI	MLB	31	574	82	22	2	28	85	73	137	13	3	1.7	.272	.372	.497	.271	.367	.489	.296	35.4	4.3	125-RF	4		

Breakout: 11%   Improve: 48%   Collapse: 11%   Attrition: 7%   MLB: 98%   Comparables: Jay Buhner, Pat Burrell, Jose Canseco, Dale Murphy

Letting bad pitches go by is one facet of exhibiting patience at the plate, but being able to produce positive results on the better pitches is what transforms a player with a good eye into a good player. Werth has not only led Major League Baseball in pitches seen per plate appearance over the past two seasons—earning the honor of being the DVR FF Man of the Year—but also averaged a .503 slugging percentage and .233 ISO in that span. Werth's combination of power and speed places him in rare company: he is the only player with 60 or more blasts since 2008 to also steal 40 or more bases. Add in a plus arm to go along with the ability to cover an ample amount of ground in the outfield, and Werth fits in as yet another multifaceted offensive weapon in a lineup stocked with them. Injuries, frequent organization changes, and picking the right position all contributed to stalling his career, but Werth's newfound durability represents one of the many quiet triumphs of the Dick Martin Award–winning training staff.

PITCHERS

Antonio Bastardo   Bats: L   Throws: L   Height: 5' 11"   Weight: 168   Born: September 21, 1985   Age: 24

YEAR	TEAM	LVL	AGE	W	L	SV	G	GS	IP	H	HR	BB	SO	GB%	BABIP	STUFF	WHIP	ERA	SIERA	DERA	EqH9	EqHR9	EqBB9	EqSO9	VORP	SN/WX
2007	LWD	A	21	9	0	0	15	15	91²	63	3	42	98	38%	.255	21	1.15	1.87	3.46	3.41	8.1	1.2	4.7	6.0	19.9	1.69
2008	CLR	A+	22	2	0	0	5	5	30²	20	2	10	47	27%	.300	28	0.98	1.17	1.45	2.28	8.1	1.6	3.6	9.8	9.9	0.79
2008	REA	AA	22	2	5	0	14	14	67	56	13	37	62	29%	.242	-3	1.39	3.76	4.51	5.40	8.3	2.4	4.8	6.1	0.7	0.32
2009	REA	AA	23	2	2	3	11	5	36	22	1	7	41	44%	.253	28	0.81	1.75	2.18	2.57	6.8	0.8	2.2	8.1	10.9	0.83
2009	LEH	AAA	23	1	0	0	2	2	13	11	1	3	12	37%	.294	12	1.08	2.08	3.19	3.09	9.3	1.5	2.3	6.9	3.1	0.35
2009	PHI	MLB	23	2	3	0	6	5	23²	26	4	9	19	29%	.306	-1	1.48	6.46	4.54	6.85	9.9	1.5	3.0	6.1	-3.5	-0.06
2010	PHI	MLB	24	4	6	0	22	14	78¹	78	11	44	65	30%	.299	2	1.56	4.97	4.90	5.06	8.7	1.2	4.6	6.8	3.8	1.85

Breakout: 10%   Improve: 26%   Collapse: 32%   Attrition: 22%   MLB: 59%   Comparables: Cary Ammons, Rob Russell, Orlando Lara, Casey Whitten

Bastardo serves as an interesting case study in perception, with many conjuring up the image of a flamethrowing youngster with abysmal control based on his jerky windup and reliance on fastballs—they accounted for 75 percent of his deliveries last year. However, his stuff's barely a tick above average for a lefty, and he will need to better incorporate his effective change and merely "there" curve to make it as a starter; major-league hitters catch up to his heater. He's not far from being as ready as he'll ever be, but will the Phillies take a chance on his developing in the bullpen, as opposed to doling out a few bucks for a more experienced lefty?

Joe Blanton

Bats: R   Throws: R   Height: 6' 3"   Weight: 255   Born: December 11, 1980   Age: 29

YEAR	TEAM	LVL	AGE	W	L	SV	G	GS	IP	H	HR	BB	SO	GB%	BABIP	STUFF	WHIP	ERA	SIERA	DERA	EqH9	EqHR9	EqBB9	EqSO9	VORP	SN/WX
2007	OAK	MLB	26	14	10	0	34	34	230	240	16	40	140	55%	.299	15	1.22	3.95	4.21	3.94	9.3	0.7	1.4	4.9	39.1	6.02
2008	OAK	MLB	27	5	12	0	20	20	127	145	12	35	62	55%	.302	-5	1.42	4.96	4.92	5.13	10.4	0.9	2.2	4.0	5.2	1.89
2008	PHI	MLB	27	4	0	0	13	13	70²	66	10	31	49	44%	.264	1	1.37	4.20	4.73	4.56	8.5	1.3	3.5	5.4	7.3	1.41
2009	PHI	MLB	28	12	8	0	31	31	195¹	198	30	59	163	46%	.291	7	1.32	4.05	3.86	4.11	9.1	1.3	2.3	6.3	30.0	4.31
2010	PHI	MLB	29	11	11	0	31	31	189¹	202	22	56	120	49%	.305	4	1.36	4.32	4.48	4.56	9.5	1.0	2.5	5.2	19.7	2.70

Breakout: 8%   Improve: 44%   Collapse: 10%   Attrition: 14%   MLB: 97%   Comparables: Jeff Suppan, Livan Hernandez, Freddy Garcia, Brian Moehler

Although he saw his ground-ball/fly-ball ratio drop, Blanton struck out 2 ½ more hitters per nine innings than he did in 2008—from 5.1 to 7.5—while dropping his unintentional walk rate from 2.8 to 2.5. The reason? Besides his move to the DH-less league, hitters did much worse making contact with his out-of-zone offerings, from touching 71 percent of them in 2008 to just 57 percent last season, when a higher percentage of his pitches were delivered out of the zone. He also served as the Phillies' most consistent pitcher down the stretch. From May 26th onward, he logged 151 frames in 23 starts with a 3.16 ERA, 3.0 K/UBB and .304 OBP. Entering his final year of arbitration, Blanton will face a big year as he attempts to sustain the strikeout and walk rates from last season and prove he can do more than simply eat innings with league-average production.

Drew Carpenter

Bats: R   Throws: R   Height: 6' 3"   Weight: 225   Born: May 18, 1985   Age: 25

YEAR	TEAM	LVL	AGE	W	L	SV	G	GS	IP	H	HR	BB	SO	GB%	BABIP	STUFF	WHIP	ERA	SIERA	DERA	EqH9	EqHR9	EqBB9	EqSO9	VORP	SN/WX
2007	CLR	A+	22	17	6	1	27	24	163	150	16	53	116	43%	.271	-13	1.25	3.20	4.32	4.95	10.0	2.0	3.6	4.4	9.3	1.08
2008	CLR	A+	23	3	3	0	8	8	52¹	44	2	9	32	38%	.258	0	1.01	2.92	4.27	4.26	8.3	1.3	2.2	3.3	6.9	0.27
2008	REA	AA	23	6	8	0	16	16	93²	114	13	30	69	49%	.334	-23	1.54	5.67	4.28	7.43	11.8	1.8	3.0	4.9	-19.1	-1.75
2009	LEH	AAA	24	11	6	0	25	24	156	162	18	47	120	43%	.307	-13	1.34	3.35	4.08	4.73	10.4	1.7	3.0	5.6	12.5	1.39
2009	PHI	MLB	24	1	0	0	3	1	5²	11	1	4	5	63%	.476	-22	2.65	11.12	4.77	11.12	17.5	1.6	4.8	6.4	-3.5	-0.10
2010	PHI	MLB	25	6	9	0	30	22	135	152	20	56	83	39%	.309	-9	1.54	5.16	5.08	5.40	10.0	1.3	3.4	5.0	1.5	1.91

Breakout: 17%   Improve: 56%   Collapse: 8%   Attrition: 22%   MLB: 40%   Comparables: Mike Garcia, Glenn Spagnola, Frank Herrmann, Steve Olsen

After struggling in Double-A in 2008, Carpenter had a fairly good season last year, but his command still isn't where it needs to be. When called up to the big leagues to make an emergency start, he struggled to find the strike zone, which is the essential prerequisite for making it as a finesse pitcher. Carpenter throws a number of different pitches, but the problem is that none of them are terribly good. He does a good job of striking some hitters out in the minors by hitting his spots, but if he is going to be successful in the big leagues, he'll need to have good control. Even then, his fly-ball rate is tailor-made for self-destruction in Citizens Bank Park, and the upside is that he winds up as fourth starter material, probably elsewhere.

Clay Condrey

Bats: R   Throws: R   Height: 6' 3"   Weight: 215   Born: November 19, 1975   Age: 34

YEAR	TEAM	LVL	AGE	W	L	SV	G	GS	IP	H	HR	BB	SO	GB%	BABIP	STUFF	WHIP	ERA	SIERA	DERA	EqH9	EqHR9	EqBB9	EqSO9	VORP	SN/WX
2007	OTT	AAA	31	1	0	1	10	0	22	19	0	5	10	57%	.279	-11	1.09	2.45	4.68	3.32	7.5	0.4	2.2	3.1	4.9	0.60
2007	PHI	MLB	31	5	0	2	39	0	50	61	4	16	27	52%	.324	-13	1.54	5.04	4.95	5.06	10.3	0.7	2.5	4.4	2.5	1.67
2008	PHI	MLB	32	3	4	1	56	0	69	85	6	19	34	62%	.326	-14	1.51	3.26	4.73	3.41	11.1	0.8	2.3	3.9	15.6	0.24
2009	PHI	MLB	33	6	2	1	45	0	42	37	4	14	25	65%	.254	-8	1.21	3.00	4.33	3.67	7.8	0.9	2.6	4.5	8.5	0.42
2010	MIN	MLB	34	3	5	1	54	0	582	69	7	20	28	55%	.311	-16	1.51	5.13	5.10	5.31	10.4	1.1	2.9	4.0	1.2	0.76

Breakout: 7%   Improve: 34%   Collapse: 39%   Attrition: 18%   MLB: 92%   Comparables: Phil Regan, Ron Kline, Dick Drago, Chuck Taylor

From 2006 to 2009, Condrey appeared in 161 games with the Phillies, posting a 3.65 ERA and a 2.4 K/UBB in 189 ⅔ innings pitched. His performance has always been as nondescript as his raw stuff. In that sense, they're deceiving, but not in a good way. Fair Run Average (FRA) tallies the runs allowed per nine innings but factors in bequeathed runners as scoring at a league-average rate; it pegs Condrey as being at a talent level closer to allowing 4.3 RA/9, putting his efforts much closer to the replacement level than standard numbers would suggest. Non-tendered, he signed a one-year deal with the Twins, who will almost certainly use him in the back-end role for which he is most suited.

Kyle Drabek

Bats: R   Throws: R   Height: 6' 0"   Weight: 185   Born: December 8, 1987   Age: 22

YEAR	TEAM	LVL	AGE	W	L	SV	G	GS	IP	H	HR	BB	SO	GB%	BABIP	STUFF	WHIP	ERA	SIERA	DERA	EqH9	EqHR9	EqBB9	EqSO9	VORP	SN/WX
2007	LWD	A	19	5	1	0	11	10	54	50	9	23	46	61%	.263	-8	1.35	4.33	3.90	6.52	10.9	3.4	4.5	4.7	-5.6	-0.40
2008	WPT	A-	20	1	2	0	4	4	20^1	11	1	6	10	61%	.167	3	0.84	2.21	4.50	4.26	6.2	1.9	3.3	1.9	2.6	0.16
2008	PHL	Rk	20	0	1	0	4	4	12	6	0	6	6	56%	.176	-4	1.00	2.25	5.08	3.38	6.8	1.7	5.9	1.7	2.5	0.11
2009	CLR	A+	21	4	1	0	10	9	61^2	49	0	19	74	45%	.318	33	1.10	2.48	2.56	4.45	9.2	0.8	3.7	7.3	6.5	0.48
2009	REA	AA	21	8	2	0	15	14	96^1	92	9	31	76	48%	.288	16	1.28	3.64	4.01	4.75	9.9	1.6	3.2	5.2	7.6	0.20
2010	TOR	MLB	22	6	8	0	23	23	121^1	130	19	55	78	53%	.297	10	1.52	5.09	4.82	5.39	9.7	1.3	3.8	5.3	1.5	2.31

Breakout: 13%   Improve: 48%   Collapse: 16%   Attrition: 11%   MLB: 2%   Comparables: Roy Oswalt, Felipe Lira, Daniel Gutierrez, Daryl Thompson

Drabek turned a lot of heads in his first full year back from Tommy John surgery, dominating at High-A for a couple of months and then finishing with a strong showing at Double-A. The hard-throwing son of Doug can regularly reach the mid-90s, and like his Cy Young–winning forebear, he spins a dominating curve as well. He still has rough edges to smooth out, as his improved changeup didn't help him enough against Eastern League lefties, who tattooed him at a .322/.359/.564 clip. Because of his small stature, a few scouts see him as a future closer, but so far, he has maintained the ability to dominate for the longer stretches required of a starter, and Amaro denied any interest in moving him to the pen in 2010. That's no longer the Phillies' call to make, because as a key part packaged to Toronto in the Roy Halladay deal, he instantly and decisively became the best prospect in the Jays' system.

Chad Durbin

Bats: R   Throws: R   Height: 6' 2"   Weight: 200   Born: December 3, 1977   Age: 32

YEAR	TEAM	LVL	AGE	W	L	SV	G	GS	IP	H	HR	BB	SO	GB%	BABIP	STUFF	WHIP	ERA	SIERA	DERA	EqH9	EqHR9	EqBB9	EqSO9	VORP	SN/WX
2007	DET	MLB	29	8	7	1	36	19	127^2	133	21	49	66	50%	.269	-14	1.43	4.72	5.16	4.65	9.0	1.3	3.1	4.2	12.0	2.36
2008	PHI	MLB	30	5	4	1	71	0	87^2	81	5	35	63	51%	.295	3	1.32	2.87	4.40	3.46	8.7	0.5	3.2	5.8	18.9	1.72
2009	PHI	MLB	31	2	2	2	59	0	69^2	56	8	47	62	46%	.253	1	1.48	4.39	4.65	4.86	7.3	1.0	5.1	6.7	5.0	1.01
2010	PHI	MLB	32	4	5	1	61	1	72	74	9	35	46	49%	.292	-11	1.50	4.82	4.95	5.05	9.1	1.1	3.9	5.2	3.6	0.90

Breakout: 12%   Improve: 44%   Collapse: 22%   Attrition: 17%   MLB: 95%   Comparables: Storm Davis, Bruce Dal Canton, Dick Drago, Scott Kamieniecki

Is a 4.96 FRA from a reliever on the wrong side of 30 years old really worth a contract that will inevitably fall in the $2.5-$3.0 million range? That isn't exactly the question the Phillies' brass will be asking themselves throughout 2010, but having decided to tender Durbin and not Condrey, they should. Durbin's 5.8 unintentional walks per nine is unacceptably bad, and while he caught lightning in a bottle in '08, he's a standard example of getting overly fond of middling middlemen. For a team potentially strapped for cash after exponential increases in payroll, doling out this kind of money for someone like Durbin may not rise to the level of criminal waste; it's more like petty payroll indifference, which adds up when you're throwing seven figures at basically every reserve.

Sergio Escalona

Bats: L   Throws: L   Height: 6' 0"   Weight: 170   Born: August 3, 1984   Age: 25

YEAR	TEAM	LVL	AGE	W	L	SV	G	GS	IP	H	HR	BB	SO	GB%	BABIP	STUFF	WHIP	ERA	SIERA	DERA	EqH9	EqHR9	EqBB9	EqSO9	VORP	SN/WX
2007	LWD	A	22	1	4	0	7	7	39	51	4	11	32	50%	.364	-15	1.59	4.15	3.95	7.77	14.5	2.5	3.3	4.6	-8.9	-0.49
2007	WPT	A-	22	2	2	0	7	7	27^1	32	2	19	26	61%	.380	-19	1.87	7.57	4.27	11.93	15.3	2.7	7.8	5.1	-16.4	-1.02
2008	LWD	A	23	5	1	2	28	0	44^2	36	1	18	60	62%	.343	1	1.21	3.43	2.42	5.52	10.3	1.2	5.2	7.7	-0.1	0.46
2008	REA	AA	23	0	1	1	15	0	24^1	27	3	14	29	62%	.369	3	1.68	2.22	3.47	5.09	11.3	1.6	5.1	8.2	1.1	-0.14
2009	REA	AA	24	2	1	12	32	0	40^2	31	1	14	38	60%	.268	1	1.11	1.77	3.47	3.58	8.1	0.7	3.2	6.2	8.3	1.20
2009	LEH	AAA	24	0	2	2	15	1	19^2	21	4	8	15	47%	.279	-27	1.47	5.95	4.45	7.91	10.2	2.8	3.7	5.1	-5.2	-0.03
2009	PHI	MLB	24	1	0	0	14	0	13^2	12	0	5	10	43%	.286	-4	1.24	4.61	4.45	4.61	7.9	0.0	2.6	5.3	1.4	0.05
2010	PHI	MLB	25	2	5	2	48	0	59^2	74	9	33	47	51%	.347	-17	1.80	6.21	4.70	6.34	10.7	1.3	4.5	6.3	-5.6	1.04

Breakout: 27%   Improve: 58%   Collapse: 14%   Attrition: 21%   MLB: 100%   Comparables: Derek Stroud, Albert Montoya, Aaron Lane, Paul Kilgus

Escalona is a measuring stick. The Phillies understand he's a serviceable southpaw specialist at the major-league level, so any potential acquisition for the role needs to be markedly better than this in-house option. His strikeout and walk numbers translate nicely to the bigs, but his minor league numbers do not portend any special ability to retire lefties. As organizational filler goes, Escalona is sound, but he's unlikely to become a key part of the staff.

Scott Eyre

Bats: L   Throws: L   Height: 6' 1"   Weight: 220   Born: May 30, 1972   Age: 38

YEAR	TEAM	LVL	AGE	W	L	SV	G	GS	IP	H	HR	BB	SO	GB%	BABIP	STUFF	WHIP	ERA	SIERA	DERA	EqH9	EqHR9	EqBB9	EqSO9	VORP	SN/WX
2007	CHN	MLB	35	2	1	0	55	0	52¹	59	3	35	45	44%	.359	4	1.80	4.13	4.80	4.20	10.9	0.4	5.7	7.5	7.1	-0.62
2008	CHN	MLB	36	2	0	0	19	0	11¹	15	1	4	14	31%	.424	11	1.68	7.15	3.02	6.55	12.3	0.8	2.5	9.8	-1.3	0.52
2008	PHI	MLB	36	3	0	0	19	0	14¹	8	1	3	18	54%	.233	14	0.77	1.88	1.93	1.98	5.9	0.7	2.0	9.2	5.4	0.69
2009	PHI	MLB	37	2	1	0	42	0	30	22	3	16	22	36%	.221	-6	1.27	1.50	5.01	2.05	6.5	0.9	3.8	5.3	11.7	1.50
2010	PHI	MLB	38	2	3	0	36	1	35²	39	4	18	29	40%	.328	-8	1.60	5.22	4.57	5.45	9.8	1.0	4.3	6.8	0.2	0.51

Breakout: 20%   Improve: 41%   Collapse: 32%   Attrition: 14%   MLB: 93%   Comparables: Joe Hoerner, Mike Stanton, Ron Villone, Mike Remlinger

Eyre missed much of 2009 with a calf injury, and his low ERA and FRA (2.17) belied weak peripherals. His strikeout rate took a nosedive and his walk rate surged, both of which suggest that he is running out of gas at 37 years old. He needed surgery to remove loose bodies in his elbow after the year ended, and he has hinted that he may retire if the Phillies don't come calling one last time. His surface numbers might attract several other suitors. One of the better personalities in the game, Eyre is, for a modest stipend, certainly worth employing in a secondary situational role.

Cole Hamels

Bats: L   Throws: L   Height: 6' 3"   Weight: 190   Born: December 27, 1983   Age: 26

YEAR	TEAM	LVL	AGE	W	L	SV	G	GS	IP	H	HR	BB	SO	GB%	BABIP	STUFF	WHIP	ERA	SIERA	DERA	EqH9	EqHR9	EqBB9	EqSO9	VORP	SN/WX
2007	PHI	MLB	23	15	5	0	28	28	183¹	163	25	43	177	48%	.279	32	1.12	3.39	3.12	3.40	7.6	1.1	1.9	7.9	42.6	5.31
2008	PHI	MLB	24	14	10	0	33	33	227¹	193	28	53	196	46%	.259	23	1.08	3.09	3.45	3.60	7.7	1.1	1.8	6.7	47.5	6.99
2009	PHI	MLB	25	10	11	0	32	32	193²	206	24	43	168	47%	.317	13	1.29	4.32	3.51	4.41	9.6	1.1	1.7	6.7	23.1	3.81
2010	PHI	MLB	26	13	11	0	33	33	204	203	24	53	166	49%	.304	19	1.25	3.84	3.71	4.01	8.8	1.0	2.1	6.7	33.7	3.65

Breakout: 5%   Improve: 42%   Collapse: 15%   Attrition: 7%   MLB: 100%   Comparables: Jon Matlack, Jim Merritt, Curt Simmons, Frank Tanana

It is tempting to look at Hamels' hefty 2008 innings total and infer that it was at fault in the inflation of his ERA by a full run from the year before. Indeed, Hamels' 262 ⅓ innings (including playoffs) that year were a lot for a 24-year-old, but that does not always portend regression. He walked batters no more frequently in 2009 than in 2008, struck out as many, and generated more ground balls. The real reason for the uptick in ERA was that his BABIP went from .262 to .321—bounding from very lucky to unlucky. The true Cole Hamels is to be found between both seasons, if not leaning toward the former. Still, it wouldn't hurt Hamels if he added an effective third pitch.

J. A. Happ

Bats: L   Throws: L   Height: 6' 6"   Weight: 200   Born: October 19, 1982   Age: 27

YEAR	TEAM	LVL	AGE	W	L	SV	G	GS	IP	H	HR	BB	SO	GB%	BABIP	STUFF	WHIP	ERA	SIERA	DERA	EqH9	EqHR9	EqBB9	EqSO9	VORP	SN/WX
2007	OTT	AAA	24	4	6	0	24	24	118¹	118	12	62	117	36%	.327	-8	1.52	5.02	4.05	6.23	9.6	1.6	4.7	6.8	-9.1	-0.24
2008	LEH	AAA	25	8	7	0	24	23	135	116	14	48	151	45%	.302	9	1.21	3.60	2.96	4.30	8.2	1.5	3.4	7.3	17.1	1.74
2008	PHI	MLB	25	1	0	0	8	4	31²	28	3	14	26	35%	.266	6	1.33	3.69	4.48	3.76	7.8	0.8	3.3	6.1	6.3	1.08
2009	PHI	MLB	26	12	4	0	35	23	166	149	20	56	119	44%	.266	9	1.23	2.93	4.32	3.10	8.1	1.1	2.6	5.5	43.2	5.39
2010	PHI	MLB	27	7	9	0	32	26	136	141	18	63	103	44%	.305	3	1.50	4.81	4.55	4.95	9.1	1.2	3.8	6.2	8.4	2.29

Breakout: 7%   Improve: 38%   Collapse: 15%   Attrition: 14%   MLB: 73%   Comparables: Dave Williams, Vaughn Eshelman, John Halama, Rich Hill

Happ may have lost out on top rookie hardware to Florida's Chris Coghlan, but settling for the team lead in SNWP (.602, which ranked 12th of the 129 pitchers with 100+ frames) and SNLVAR (5.1) will have to suffice. He also led the Phillies' rotation in ERA and was the most reliable starter on the staff. Did we mention that he was a rookie last season? Yes, Happ benefited from a lofty 85 percent rate of stranding runners when the league generally hovers closer to 72 percent, and he may not strike out enough hitters to make that high walk rate stand up. But with his size and some deception in his delivery, he manages to come on top of hitters with his fastball, mixing in his slider and getting good angles on it, which combine to compensate for the lack of a true out pitch. Happ won't be this good every time out, but he should be a rotation stalwart for years to come.

Kyle Kendrick

Bats: R   Throws: R   Height: 6' 3"   Weight: 190   Born: August 26, 1984   Age: 25

YEAR	TEAM	LVL	AGE	W	L	SV	G	GS	IP	H	HR	BB	SO	GB%	BABIP	STUFF	WHIP	ERA	SIERA	DERA	EqH9	EqHR9	EqBB9	EqSO9	VORP	SN/WX
2007	REA	AA	22	4	7	0	12	12	81^1	82	3	18	50	56%	.299	9	1.23	3.21	4.29	5.03	9.9	0.8	2.3	4.1	4.1	0.18
2007	PHI	MLB	22	10	4	0	20	20	121	129	16	25	49	54%	.281	7	1.27	3.87	5.02	3.77	9.2	1.1	1.7	3.5	22.5	3.30
2008	PHI	MLB	23	11	9	0	31	30	155^2	194	23	57	68	53%	.305	-19	1.61	5.49	5.36	5.88	10.9	1.3	2.9	3.3	-6.6	1.98
2009	LEH	AAA	24	9	7	0	24	24	143	133	9	35	62	59%	.262	-4	1.17	3.34	4.90	4.59	8.8	1.1	2.4	2.9	13.8	1.89
2009	PHI	MLB	24	3	1	0	9	2	26^1	27	1	9	15	64%	.302	-4	1.37	3.42	4.51	3.86	9.1	0.4	2.8	4.6	4.7	0.41
2010	PHI	MLB	25	7	9	0	31	24	148	166	18	51	62	52%	.297	-13	1.47	4.85	5.34	5.11	10.0	1.1	2.8	3.5	6.4	2.07

Breakout: 6%   Improve: 45%   Collapse: 14%   Attrition: 11%   MLB: 63%   Comparables: Joe Niekro, Tim Stauffer, Don Vidmar, Jack Russell

Kendrick will be competing for the fifth spot in the rotation in spring training, but Jamie Moyer probably has dibs until he shows that 2009 was the beginning of the end. He spent much of last year trying to find another pitch to add to his predictable sinker/sinker mix, but lefties continued to belt him around a bit. Teams do not exactly line up to develop or acquire ROOGYs, but it's a role Kendrick will probably need to fall back into if he ever wants to experience major-league success again.

Cliff Lee

Bats: L   Throws: L   Height: 6' 3"   Weight: 190   Born: August 30, 1978   Age: 31

YEAR	TEAM	LVL	AGE	W	L	SV	G	GS	IP	H	HR	BB	SO	GB%	BABIP	STUFF	WHIP	ERA	SIERA	DERA	EqH9	EqHR9	EqBB9	EqSO9	VORP	SN/WX
2007	BUF	AAA	28	1	3	0	8	8	41	32	1	25	50	44%	.292	27	1.39	3.51	3.49	4.25	7.4	0.4	5.2	8.3	5.8	0.48
2007	CLE	MLB	28	5	8	0	20	16	97^1	112	17	36	66	39%	.300	-13	1.52	6.29	4.78	6.25	9.7	1.5	2.9	5.4	-8.3	0.26
2008	CLE	MLB	29	22	3	0	31	31	223^1	214	12	34	170	50%	.301	33	1.11	2.54	3.58	2.82	8.3	0.5	1.2	6.3	64.9	8.12
2009	CLE	MLB	30	7	9	0	22	22	152	165	10	33	107	51%	.318	22	1.30	3.14	4.06	3.00	9.2	0.6	1.7	5.5	42.0	5.55
2009	PHI	MLB	30	7	4	0	12	12	79^2	80	7	10	74	46%	.311	27	1.13	3.39	3.01	3.95	8.9	0.8	0.9	7.0	13.7	2.14
2010	SEA	MLB	31	12	11	0	34	34	205	216	22	56	140	46%	.308	10	1.33	4.13	4.25	4.29	9.2	1.0	2.3	5.7	27.6	3.87

Breakout: 3%   Improve: 32%   Collapse: 20%   Attrition: 11%   MLB: 100%   Comparables: Zane Smith, Denny Lemaster, Tommy John, Jimmy Key

Lee may have been left off the Indians' playoff roster in 2007, but after his winning the Cy Young Award in 2008 and a similarly dominant 2009 that proved the earlier year was no fluke, it makes little sense that he's still undervalued. After the Phillies acquired him for four mediocre farmhands, Lee led them to their third straight division title before they put together an exceptional playoff run. As they realized that he would be asking for full market value as a free agent after 2010, the Phillies literally changed horses. They dealt top prospects for Roy Halladay and then swapped Lee to the Mariners to restock their system, only to acquire prospects of the same mediocre ilk they'd given up to bring him aboard. Lee is going to form a potent one-two punch with Felix Hernandez in Seattle, but he could have been part of an incredibly dominant trio with Halladay and Hamels in Philly. If the club falls short in 2010, management should be prepared to explain why a two-time pennant winner couldn't afford to carry an extra ace for a single season.

Brad Lidge

Bats: R   Throws: R   Height: 6' 5"   Weight: 210   Born: December 23, 1976   Age: 33

YEAR	TEAM	LVL	AGE	W	L	SV	G	GS	IP	H	HR	BB	SO	GB%	BABIP	STUFF	WHIP	ERA	SIERA	DERA	EqH9	EqHR9	EqBB9	EqSO9	VORP	SN/WX
2007	HOU	MLB	30	5	3	19	66	0	67	54	9	30	88	51%	.288	18	1.25	3.36	2.75	3.68	7.4	1.2	3.6	10.0	13.6	2.11
2008	PHI	MLB	31	2	0	41	72	0	69^1	50	2	35	92	51%	.296	31	1.23	1.95	2.80	2.40	6.9	0.3	3.9	9.9	23.9	7.50
2009	PHI	MLB	32	0	8	31	67	0	58^2	72	11	34	61	46%	.355	-18	1.81	7.21	4.08	7.63	11.1	1.7	4.4	7.8	-13.9	-3.26
2010	PHI	MLB	33	3	5	19	61	1	60^1	62	7	30	61	47%	.333	0	1.53	4.92	3.80	5.14	9.1	1.1	4.1	8.2	2.4	1.37

Breakout: 9%   Improve: 37%   Collapse: 36%   Attrition: 12%   MLB: 90%   Comparables: Mike Henneman, Jose Mesa, Rollie Fingers, Andy McGaffigan

Although relief pitchers are a fickle breed, "regression" barely does justice to what happened to Lidge in 2009. His velocity fell for the second year in a row, giving hitters an extra instant to tell his fastball from his slider. His slider remains a strong pitch, but hitters could afford to lay off it more often, instead waiting to pulp his fastball. He managed to post the worst WXRL of all time among relievers with 30 or more save opportunities. Considering he has two very expensive years left on his contract, you'd better believe that Charlie Manuel will use him as frequently as he did this past season. But Lidge will need to completely recover from injuries, change his approach, possibly add another pitch, or all of the above to get back to being an effective major-league pitcher. Otherwise, he's napalm by another name, infamously flammable in a rogue's gallery that already includes Mitch Williams and Jose Mesa.

Ryan Madson

Bats: L   Throws: R   Height: 6' 6"   Weight: 200   Born: August 28, 1980   Age: 29

YEAR	TEAM	LVL	AGE	W	L	SV	G	GS	IP	H	HR	BB	SO	GB%	BABIP	STUFF	WHIP	ERA	SIERA	DERA	EqH9	EqHR9	EqBB9	EqSO9	VORP	SN/WX
2007	PHI	MLB	26	2	2	1	38	0	56	48	5	23	43	54%	.262	6	1.27	3.05	4.27	2.94	7.1	0.6	3.2	6.2	16.1	1.68
2008	PHI	MLB	27	4	2	1	76	0	82^2	79	6	23	67	59%	.300	8	1.23	3.05	3.71	3.25	8.9	0.7	2.2	6.4	20.1	1.99
2009	PHI	MLB	28	5	5	10	79	0	77^1	73	7	22	78	53%	.314	12	1.23	3.26	3.17	3.46	8.7	0.8	2.3	7.8	17.0	2.35
2010	PHI	MLB	29	4	4	3	67	0	66	66	7	25	54	55%	.308	0	1.37	4.20	3.98	4.45	8.8	0.9	3.1	6.7	7.7	1.24

Breakout: 7%   Improve: 36%   Collapse: 36%   Attrition: 10%   MLB: 97%   Comparables: Chad Qualls, Justin Duchscherer, Mike Henneman, Tim Burke

Last year marked Madson's first full season working with the benefit of increased velocity, the result of mechanical adjustments he made during the 2008 season. As a result, he consistently reached 95 mph en route to becoming one of the elite relievers in baseball. As he grows accustomed to throwing harder, expect to see the appropriate adjustments in game-planning take form, resulting in even better numbers moving forward and, if the world is just and the Phillies sensible, more save opportunities as well.

Pedro Martinez

Bats: R   Throws: R   Height: 5' 11"   Weight: 195   Born: October 25, 1971   Age: 38

YEAR	TEAM	LVL	AGE	W	L	SV	G	GS	IP	H	HR	BB	SO	GB%	BABIP	STUFF	WHIP	ERA	SIERA	DERA	EqH9	EqHR9	EqBB9	EqSO9	VORP	SN/WX
2007	NYN	MLB	35	3	1	0	5	5	28	33	0	7	32	33%	.379	29	1.43	2.57	2.98	3.45	10.7	0.0	1.9	8.8	6.5	1.02
2008	NYN	MLB	36	5	6	0	20	20	109	127	19	44	87	51%	.320	-20	1.57	5.61	4.28	5.92	11.1	1.9	3.2	6.1	-5.0	0.87
2009	PHI	MLB	37	5	1	0	9	9	44^2	48	7	8	37	41%	.304	11	1.25	3.63	3.60	3.65	9.5	1.4	1.4	6.3	9.1	1.32
2010	PHI	MLB	38	3	5	0	14	14	66^1	79	11	25	49	45%	.330	-4	1.56	5.61	4.41	5.91	10.7	1.4	3.1	6.0	-3.0	0.73

Breakout: 11%   Improve: 44%   Collapse: 27%   Attrition: 27%   MLB: 85%   Comparables: Syl Johnson, Johnny Niggeling, Charlie Root, Johnny Allen

It turned out that Martinez had something left in the tank after all. With a strikeout/walk ratio of 4.6 in 2009, he dominated the National League for a couple of months. Unfortunately, after throwing 130 pitches in a mid-September start against the Mets, Martinez did not really seem to have the same pizzazz as before, but he did manage an excellent start in the NLCS, a solid Game Two in the World Series, and then a not-so-good Game Six. Time has almost run out on Martinez, but he reportedly wants to pitch an entire season rather than pursue the half-season Rent-a-Hall-of-Famer plan pioneered by Roger Clemens, so the first trick he'll still need up his sleeve will be durability. He'd make a heck of an old-school "Sunday starter" if such a thing could be accommodated on today's rosters.

Scott Mathieson

Bats: R   Throws: R   Height: 6' 3"   Weight: 190   Born: February 27, 1984   Age: 26

YEAR	TEAM	LVL	AGE	W	L	SV	G	GS	IP	H	HR	BB	SO	GB%	BABIP	STUFF	WHIP	ERA	SIERA	DERA	EqH9	EqHR9	EqBB9	EqSO9	VORP	SN/WX
2009	REA	AA	25	2	0	1	13	0	19^1	10	1	7	17	40%	.180	-4	0.88	1.40	3.73	3.86	5.8	1.0	3.4	5.8	3.4	0.34
2010	PHI	MLB	26	2	3	0	25	0	41	42	5	22	24	25%	.291	-11	1.56	4.81	6.03	4.96	9.0	1.1	4.4	4.6	2.4	1.07

Breakout: 20%   Improve: 45%   Collapse: 29%   Attrition: 10%   MLB: 10%   Comparables: Pete Bauer, Darrell Einertson, Jailen Peguero, Dave Latter

The recovery rate from Tommy John surgery is very high at this point, but when Mathieson required a second such operation in May 2008, things did not look good. The fireballing right-hander could already touch the mid- to high 90s when he was given a spot in the Phillies rotation as a 22-year-old in 2006, but it wasn't clear that his stuff would return. On the comeback, however, Mathieson was able to throw the ball past hitters in Double-A, reaching 98 mph. He doesn't have the control he did as a young prospect, but that tends to come back in the second season after surgery. Mathieson has yet to be pushed very hard by the Phillies, who are wisely being careful with him, so he will probably start the season in the minors to build up his arm strength. However, with his excellent velocity and injury problems, Mathieson will probably profile as a reliever from now on. He could end up playing a role in the 2010 bullpen, even if he doesn't start the season there.

Jamie Moyer

Bats: L | Throws: L | Height: 6' 0" | Weight: 185 | Born: November 18, 1962 | Age: 47

YEAR	TEAM	LVL	AGE	W	L	SV	G	GS	IP	H	HR	BB	SO	GB%	BABIP	STUFF	WHIP	ERA	SIERA	DERA	EqH9	EqHR9	EqBB9	EqSO9	VORP	SN/WX
2007	PHI	MLB	44	14	12	0	33	33	199¹	222	30	66	133	48%	.303	1	1.44	5.01	4.52	4.99	9.5	1.2	2.7	5.5	11.2	3.43
2008	PHI	MLB	45	16	7	0	33	33	196¹	199	20	62	123	49%	.286	8	1.33	3.71	4.58	3.93	9.1	0.9	2.5	4.9	33.9	4.85
2009	PHI	MLB	46	12	10	0	30	25	162	177	27	43	94	48%	.286	-9	1.36	4.94	4.65	5.01	9.6	1.5	2.0	4.4	8.7	2.28
2010	PHI	MLB	47	6	9	0	27	24	126¹	146	18	46	72	48%	.312	-10	1.53	5.25	4.94	5.50	10.3	1.2	3.1	4.6	0.0	1.60

Breakout: 9%   Improve: 31%   Collapse: 24%   Attrition: 32%   MLB: 96%   Comparables: Phil Niekro, Tommy John

The two-year, $13 million deal Moyer signed following the World Series win in 2008 drew considerable criticism, and his poor performance last season only made matters worse. There was a silver lining, in that the numbers bear out the theory that Moyer's annoyance over being bumped for Pedro Martinez led to a better performance: from the time Martinez signed until the end of the season, Moyer posted a 3.26 RA/9 in 38 ⅔ innings pitched to go along with a 5.0 K/UBB ratio. Expecting that kind of sustained performance moving forward is silly. He's largely unprojectable due to an extreme dearth of comparables—most pitchers his age are pitching coaches or insurance salesmen. Perhaps he can inch back toward his 2008 performance, but with 258 wins and counting—and 224 after turning 30—the ageless one finally seems to be running out of steam.

Brett Myers

Bats: R | Throws: R | Height: 6' 4" | Weight: 240 | Born: August 17, 1980 | Age: 29

YEAR	TEAM	LVL	AGE	W	L	SV	G	GS	IP	H	HR	BB	SO	GB%	BABIP	STUFF	WHIP	ERA	SIERA	DERA	EqH9	EqHR9	EqBB9	EqSO9	VORP	SN/WX
2007	PHI	MLB	26	5	7	21	51	3	68²	61	9	27	83	55%	.301	19	1.28	4.33	2.91	4.07	7.6	1.0	3.1	9.6	11.1	1.38
2008	PHI	MLB	27	10	13	0	30	30	190	197	29	65	163	53%	.303	5	1.38	4.55	3.85	4.83	9.5	1.4	2.7	6.7	13.9	3.44
2009	PHI	MLB	28	4	3	0	18	10	70²	74	18	23	50	57%	.268	-16	1.37	4.84	4.24	4.80	9.5	2.3	2.5	5.5	5.4	1.21
2010	HOU	MLB	29	6	8	3	38	21	113	118	15	43	94	56%	.315	3	1.43	4.60	3.98	4.89	9.4	1.2	3.2	6.8	7.6	1.58

Breakout: 8%   Improve: 41%   Collapse: 15%   Attrition: 26%   MLB: 89%   Comparables: Ken Johnson, Pete Vuckovich, Chien-Ming Wang, Keiichi Yabu

Thomas Wolfe wrote that if a man has a talent and cannot use it, he has failed. That observation aptly sums up the career to date of Brett Myers, a pitcher with the potential to dominate and who, for one reason or another, has never put it all together in the same season. He has always shown just enough to keep hope alive, but seeing as his ERA has risen every season since 2005, the Phillies parted ways with the temperamental hurler. At 28 years old and with a decent, albeit disappointing, set of skills, Myers could still break out and fulfill his promise, but barring a significant change in approach or in his repertoire, he's destined to be a frustrating league-average pitcher (a FLAP?). Appropriately, he flapped to Ed Wade's Houston Home of Declining Ex-Phillies, where he'll be the third starter.

Chan Ho Park

Bats: R | Throws: R | Height: 6' 2" | Weight: 210 | Born: June 30, 1973 | Age: 37

YEAR	TEAM	LVL	AGE	W	L	SV	G	GS	IP	H	HR	BB	SO	GB%	BABIP	STUFF	WHIP	ERA	SIERA	DERA	EqH9	EqHR9	EqBB9	EqSO9	VORP	SN/WX
2007	NWO	AAA	34	4	4	0	9	9	51²	64	9	16	49	53%	.362	-14	1.55	5.57	3.56	6.65	12.9	2.7	3.0	6.7	-6.1	-0.21
2007	ROU	AAA	34	2	10	0	15	15	84	100	18	24	70	50%	.314	-34	1.48	6.21	3.90	8.18	11.3	2.7	2.7	5.5	-24.4	-1.44
2008	LAN	MLB	35	4	4	2	54	5	95¹	97	12	36	79	60%	.302	-9	1.40	3.40	3.94	4.21	9.5	1.4	3.0	6.3	13.3	1.79
2009	PHI	MLB	36	3	3	0	45	7	83¹	84	5	33	73	49%	.321	6	1.40	4.43	3.96	4.61	9.2	0.5	3.1	6.7	8.1	1.97
2010	PHI	MLB	37	3	5	0	45	5	65¹	82	10	28	47	52%	.346	-17	1.69	5.99	4.58	6.24	11.1	1.4	3.6	5.9	-5.4	0.61

Breakout: 10%   Improve: 40%   Collapse: 25%   Attrition: 33%   MLB: 90%   Comparables: Ted Power, Brian Moehler, Boom-Boom Beck, Shinji Sasaoka

It is safe to say that when it hit the wire that the Phillies had signed Chan Ho Park last offseason, fans did not envision a future in which they eagerly anticipated the much-traveled Korean righty's entry into crucial games. Promised a shot at starting and then given it, Park, in keeping with his career, predictably struggled as a member of the rotation, but having pitched his way out of it, he flourished again in the bullpen, compiling a 2.52 ERA and 3.00 FRA in 50 relief innings. He whiffed 20 percent of his batters faced while issuing unintentional walks to just 8.3 percent and managed to accrue a WXRL that ranked 23rd in the senior circuit, a remarkable feat, considering his service in the relief corps did not commence until the end of May. His strong desire is to remain a starter, motivated in part by his celebrity in his home country, but at some point, you have to hope he'll realize that his bullpen dominance over the last two seasons is a sign of where he should stay.

J. C. Romero
Bats: S   Throws: L   Height: 5' 11"   Weight: 205   Born: June 4, 1976   Age: 34

YEAR	TEAM	LVL	AGE	W	L	SV	G	GS	IP	H	HR	BB	SO	GB%	BABIP	STUFF	WHIP	ERA	SIERA	DERA	EqH9	EqHR9	EqBB9	EqSO9	VORP	SN/WX
2007	BOS	MLB	31	1	0	1	23	0	20	24	2	15	11	75%	.333	-9	1.95	3.15	5.02	2.84	11.4	0.9	6.2	4.7	5.6	0.60
2007	PHI	MLB	31	1	2	0	51	0	36¹	15	1	25	31	70%	.167	18	1.10	1.24	4.14	1.29	3.6	0.3	5.7	7.2	16.4	2.34
2008	PHI	MLB	32	4	4	1	81	0	59	41	5	38	52	69%	.232	8	1.34	2.75	4.07	2.84	6.4	0.8	5.1	6.8	17.4	2.20
2009	PHI	MLB	33	0	0	0	21	0	16²	13	2	13	12	57%	.250	-4	1.56	2.70	5.20	3.45	7.5	1.1	6.3	5.7	3.6	1.14
2010	PHI	MLB	34	2	3	0	42	0	40²	37	4	27	32	63%	.286	-10	1.58	5.11	4.66	5.18	8.0	0.9	5.4	6.2	1.4	1.28

Breakout: 5%   Improve: 29%   Collapse: 41%   Attrition: 17%   MLB: 84%   Comparables: Tony Castillo, Aaron Fultz, Steve Kline, Ramon Hernandez

Romero has been devastating to same-handed hitters throughout his Phillies tenure, and his 2008 season showed the kind of dominance he can bring to the table, as he allowed a measly .102/.189/.193 line to lefties and a raw OPS of 382 against a 698 league average for lefty-on-lefty action. His 2009 campaign, derailed by both a controversial suspension and subsequent injuries, should be written off more than it should be used to develop expectations for the upcoming season. Even with his career-long problem with free passes, Romero should have little trouble reclaiming his tag as one of the best specialists in the league.

Joe Savery
Bats: L   Throws: L   Height: 6' 3"   Weight: 215   Born: November 4, 1985   Age: 24

YEAR	TEAM	LVL	AGE	W	L	SV	G	GS	IP	H	HR	BB	SO	GB%	BABIP	STUFF	WHIP	ERA	SIERA	DERA	EqH9	EqHR9	EqBB9	EqSO9	VORP	SN/WX
2007	WPT	A-	21	2	3	0	7	7	26¹	22	0	13	22	50%	.272	2	1.33	2.73	4.30	4.62	9.2	1.1	5.0	3.9	2.5	0.21
2008	CLR	A+	22	9	10	0	27	24	150¹	171	10	60	122	59%	.343	-21	1.54	4.13	4.08	6.98	11.9	1.8	4.3	4.8	-22.7	-1.73
2009	REA	AA	23	12	4	0	21	20	112¹	111	13	53	77	55%	.285	-22	1.46	4.41	4.67	5.49	10.4	1.8	4.5	4.5	0.2	-0.43
2009	LEH	AAA	23	4	2	0	7	7	39	42	0	24	19	50%	.309	-8	1.69	4.38	5.83	6.33	10.0	0.5	5.7	3.1	-3.5	-0.06
2010	PHI	MLB	24	4	9	0	27	22	119	149	19	68	66	54%	.326	-24	1.82	6.35	5.39	6.53	11.0	1.4	4.7	4.5	-13.6	1.26

Breakout: 14%   Improve: 47%   Collapse: 19%   Attrition: 13%   MLB: 7%   Comparables: Joe Beimel, Buddy Groom, Neal Musser, Justin Thomas

Savery was the Phillies' first-round pick in 2007 and was selected despite a disappointing junior year at Rice. The stuff the Phillies thought would develop just hasn't been there, as his velocity has dropped into the mid-80s and his breaking stuff lacks snap, so his performances in the high minors have left a lot to be desired. His control was poor in Double-A and simply got worse at Triple-A. At this stage, Savery seems more likely to make the majors as a reliever (if anything), and we can safely say that his elite prospect status is deader than Elvis. The Phillies are going to keep him starting in the minors for now, but at this point, everyone's just marking time and wondering if something good will happen.

Tyler Walker
Bats: R   Throws: R   Height: 6' 3"   Weight: 275   Born: May 15, 1976   Age: 34

YEAR	TEAM	LVL	AGE	W	L	SV	G	GS	IP	H	HR	BB	SO	GB%	BABIP	STUFF	WHIP	ERA	SIERA	DERA	EqH9	EqHR9	EqBB9	EqSO9	VORP	SN/WX
2007	FRE	AAA	31	1	2	7	20	0	23	25	5	10	23	49%	.303	-13	1.52	4.70	3.74	5.16	10.3	2.4	4.0	6.8	0.9	-0.19
2007	SFN	MLB	31	2	0	0	15	0	14¹	12	0	4	9	38%	.300	3	1.12	1.26	4.44	1.42	8.5	0.0	2.8	5.7	5.7	0.91
2008	SFN	MLB	32	5	8	0	65	0	53¹	47	7	21	49	54%	.270	1	1.27	4.56	3.75	4.61	7.7	1.2	3.0	7.0	5.3	0.93
2009	LEH	AAA	33	2	1	3	15	0	19¹	8	1	3	20	39%	.156	15	0.57	1.40	2.33	2.61	4.3	0.9	1.4	7.1	6.1	0.44
2009	PHI	MLB	33	2	1	0	32	0	35¹	31	4	9	27	36%	.252	1	1.13	3.06	4.11	3.22	7.4	1.0	2.0	5.7	9.2	0.27
2010	PHI	MLB	34	3	3	3	55	0	54¹	52	7	21	41	46%	.286	-2	1.33	4.20	4.24	4.42	8.6	1.1	3.1	6.2	6.5	0.85

Breakout: 10%   Improve: 40%   Collapse: 34%   Attrition: 18%   MLB: 79%   Comparables: Jay Witasick, Rick White, Don Larsen, Jose Mesa

Hauled up as in-season reinforcement because of the overlapping injuries, suspensions, and bouts of ineffectiveness decimating the Phillies' bullpen, Walker exceeded expectations, producing a 3.68 FRA in 35 ⅓ innings pitched. He's not a good bet to reliably deliver those kinds of numbers; he was available when the Mariners discarded him toward the end of spring training, and that wasn't seen as an unusual development. The Phillies decided against bringing him back, but as someone who's been sporadically effective, he'll wash up somewhere, like the odd shell; somebody will pocket him, and they're as likely as not going to wind up wondering why.

LINEOUTS

Hitters

PLAYER	TEAM	LVL	AGE	PA	R	2B	3B	HR	RBI	BB	SO	SB-CS	EqBRR	AVG/OBP/SLG	EqAVG/EqOBP/EqSLG	EqA	VORP	WARP
UT E. Bruntlett	PHI	MLB	31	118	15	7	0	0	7	5	26	2-0	1.9	.171/.224/.238	.171/.222/.229	.170	-7.3	-1.3
INF M. Cairo	LEH	AAA	35	315	44	12	2	5	33	15	40	8-1	1.0	.287/.325/.392	.268/.303/.359	.233	3.4	-0.4
	PHI	MLB	35	47	6	2	1	1	2	0	4	0-0	0.4	.267/.283/.422	.289/.304/.444	.245	-0.1	-0.1
OF Z. Collier*	LWD	A	18	326	40	16	7	0	32	23	80	13-7	0.0	.218/.275/.319	.198/.244/.281	.181	-18.5	-3.9
	WPT	A-	18	151	21	10	1	1	13	9	42	7-0	2.4	.226/.280/.336	.213/.252/.298	.195	-6.9	-2.1
SS F. Galvis#	CLR	A+	19	272	29	8	2	1	15	10	43	6-3	-1.7	.247/.280/.307	.235/.263/.290	.193	-6.6	-2.1
	REA	AA	19	63	6	0	0	1	5	2	7	0-1	-0.2	.197/.222/.246	.180/.206/.230	.120	-4.5	-1.1
2B H. Garcia#	LWD	A	22	502	64	21	5	8	55	29	100	42-12	-3.5	.291/.350/.414	.254/.294/.356	.231	-0.6	-0.1
3B A. Hewitt	WPT	A-	20	247	25	7	6	7	30	9	77	9-5	0.9	.223/.255/.395	.207/.227/.333	.189	-11.1	-3.3
C P. Hoover	LEH	AAA	33	281	26	16	1	1	28	29	66	1-1	0.7	.253/.329/.339	.230/.300/.310	.221	-0.6	-0.3
3B T. Mattair	LWD	A	20	521	55	27	4	3	39	54	131	12-2	0.9	.236/.326/.333	.215/.287/.290	.209	-12.1	-0.9
OF D. Myers	LWD	A	20	289	41	14	5	2	23	12	62	16-4	1.8	.270/.309/.381	.244/.273/.338	.213	-7.8	-2.5
UT D. Newhan*	LEH	AAA	35	401	42	21	3	6	48	33	73	4-2	-2.9	.275/.335/.402	.256/.310/.367	.240	-1.3	-1.2
UT A. Tracy*	LEH	AAA	35	540	76	23	1	26	96	74	110	7-1	-0.8	.254/.361/.481	.236/.335/.431	.267	4.2	-0.4

If **Eric Bruntlett** had ever had a peak, we would say he was past it. In his youth, he could at least hit lefties and run well, but this past year he had only a 648 OPS against southpaws, admittedly better than his 303 OPS against right-ies. He signed a minors deal with the Nats. ⊘ Willing to play anywhere and do anything, **Miguel Cairo** was called up in September, and his veteran something-ness earned him a spot on the post-season roster as well. ⊘ **Zach Collier** is one of a number of young, toolsy outfielders in the system, but his rawness went beyond sushi grade during his full-season debut. ⊘ **Freddy Galvis** plays excellent defense and has a very strong arm, but he doesn't hit the ball very hard, having the ability to ground out to all fields. ⊘ Venezuelan **Harold Garcia** showed contact-hitting ability and speed in his full-season debut, doing all of his damage against right-handed pitchers (.321/.376/.467); of course, being a Phillies second-base prospect risks redefining "failure to launch." ⊘ The club's 2008 first-round pick, **Anthony Hewitt** put together another disappointing season; at this point, the hope is that a conversion from third base to the outfield will help the bat. ⊘ After 10 seasons at Triple-A, third catcher **Paul Hoover** is used to being dammed up, but there's no hidden torrent of hits waiting if the floodgates were opened. ⊘ A second-round pick in 2007, **Travis Mattair** has been stuck at Low-A without making progress in any phase of his hitting, and a third-base glove won't carry you far. ⊘ Athletic **D'Arby Myers** is only 21 years old, and his poor strike-zone judgment explains why he doesn't get more hype. ⊘ **David Newhan**'s versatility makes for good organizational depth, but whatever combination of injuries was necessary didn't happen, stranding him in the piggery. ⊘ Slugger **Andy Tracy** mashed yet again in his ninth Triple-A season as the junior varsity's edition of Matt Stairs.

Pitchers

PLAYER	TEAM	LVL	AGE	W	L	SV	IP	H	HR	BB	SO	GB%	BABIP	STUFF	WHIP	ERA	SIERA	DERA	EqH9	EqHR9	EqBB9	EqSO9	VORP
Y. Flande*	CLR	A+	23	7	1	0	82	72	2	24	67	58%	.293	-1	1.17	2.52	3.69	4.72	9.8	1.2	3.5	4.7	6.4
—	REA	AA	23	4	4	0	70²	81	5	21	50	59%	.333	-10	1.44	4.58	4.18	6.00	11.9	1.4	3.0	4.6	-3.7
E. Garcia	CLR	A+	21	1	4	0	41²	38	3	9	27	44%	.263	-3	1.13	4.32	4.25	7.67	9.8	2.1	2.7	3.4	-9.5
R. Lopez	LEH	AAA	33	7	5	0	100¹	122	9	14	71	53%	.341	-12	1.36	4.31	3.87	6.16	11.7	1.4	1.5	5.0	-6.9
—	PHI	MLB	33	3	1	0	30	42	3	11	19	42%	.375	-12	1.77	5.70	4.85	7.14	12.7	0.9	2.8	5.0	-5.3
G. Majewski	LEH	AAA	29	0	5	5	62²	73	4	24	43	65%	.333	-24	1.55	4.02	4.36	6.18	11.2	1.1	3.8	4.8	-4.5
T. May	LWD	A	19	4	1	0	77¹	58	3	43	95	41%	.306	16	1.31	2.56	3.20	4.70	9.7	2.0	7.2	6.5	5.8
C. Monasterios	CLR	A+	23	5	6	2	82	71	4	27	71	51%	.286	-23	1.20	3.73	3.74	6.42	9.9	1.7	3.9	5.0	-7.6
D. Naylor	CLR	A+	23	8	11	0	158	162	12	37	115	42%	.304	-35	1.26	4.22	4.05	7.24	11.6	2.3	3.0	4.0	-27.6
J. Sanchez	LWD	A	21	10	6	0	136	137	4	42	120	39%	.331	-10	1.32	3.44	3.70	6.30	11.3	1.7	4.3	4.2	-10.7
J. Taschner*	LEH	AAA	31	0	2	2	21²	16	1	10	15	46%	.238	-15	1.20	2.08	4.72	3.27	7.0	0.9	4.4	4.8	5.1
—	PHI	MLB	31	1	1	0	29¹	38	3	20	19	44%	.354	-18	1.98	4.91	5.55	5.59	11.8	0.9	5.3	5.0	-0.3
V. Worley	REA	AA	21	7	12	0	153¹	163	17	49	100	46%	.299	-7	1.38	5.34	4.54	7.36	11.0	1.8	3.1	4.3	-29.7
M. Zagurski*	REA	AA	26	3	4	8	53	42	7	27	63	46%	.267	-6	1.30	3.57	3.29	5.17	8.6	1.9	4.6	8.1	1.9

Dominican **Yohan Flande** is a strike-throwing changeup specialist who works low, but whose limited stuff might only work in situational relief. ⊘ **Edgar Garcia** lost the bulk of the year to visa issues, but was effective in the AFL and will need to show progress with his fastball command to regain his prospect status. ⊘ **Rodrigo Lopez** threw enough strikes to get called up, but hitters caught up soon enough; he was signed with the Snakes to a minor-league deal. ⊘ Once the bone of contention between the Nats and Reds from the F-Lop deal, **Gary Majewski** is now just trying to avoid the bone yard; he's another Phillies discard you'll now see in Houston. ⊘ The Phillies' 2008 fourth-round draft pick, **Trevor May** showed considerable upside last year; he loses his control and has rough stretches at times, but his fastball gets up to 95 mph and his changeup and curveball improved during the year. ⊘ **Carlos Monasterios** was busy having an excellent season in winter ball when he got snagged in the Rule 5 draft; he'll try to break camp with the Dodgers with a decent fastball/curve mix. ⊘ **Drew Naylor** is a big-bodied Aussie with a beaut of a curve, but slow heat and a slow delivery suggest that a jump to Double-A won't be easy. ⊘ Like Monasterios, **Jesus Sanchez** came over in the ugly Bobby Abreu deal with the Yankees; a catcher who couldn't hit, he converted to pitching in 2009 and showed a surprising amount of command to go with a strong arm. ⊘ If you're a lefty specialist who can't consistently get lefties, chances are your name is **Jack Taschner**. He signed a minors deal with the Pirates. ⊘ **Vance Worley**'s peripherals indicate a performance better than his ERA suggests; he got clobbered with ducks on the pond, so avoiding big innings will be his key going forward. ⊘ Recovering from 2008 Tommy John surgery, **Mike Zagurski** stayed healthy but struggled with both command and control; he was all-or-nothing against fellow lefties, giving up a .479 SLG but striking out 30 percent of them.

MANAGER: CHARLIE MANUEL

YEAR	TEAM	W-L	Pythag +/−	Avg PC	100+ P	120+ P	QS	BQS	REL	REL w Zero R	IBB	Subs	PH	PH Avg	PH HR	SB2	CS2	SB3	CS3	SAC Att	SAC %	POS SAC	Squeeze	Swing	In Play
2007	PHI	89-73	1	92.8	55	1	72	7	498	310	62	121	262	.230	9	126	18	11	2	85	76.5%	26	1	146	113
2008	PHI	92-70	-2	96.0	62	3	86	6	468	319	64	98	281	.253	9	119	22	17	2	102	69.6%	25	1	131	99
2009	PHI	93-69	0	97.5	86	7	82	4	458	298	31	28	271	.186	9	96	19	21	8	84	65.5%	16	0	140	98

The only manager in Phillies history to win two pennants with the club, Manuel prefers to stay out of the spotlight, his light touch endearing him to sabermetricians in the process. He runs because his team can, finishing first in double steals, but among full-season NL skippers, only Ken Macha ordered fewer position-player sac bunts, and only Tony La Russa issued fewer intentional walks. Manuel does not overreact to small sample sizes, letting players work through slumps and changing his lineup only rarely: he consistently has the least lineup variation in the game. Far from perfect, Manuel makes some questionable in-game pitching moves, and his fixation with retaining the struggling Brad Lidge in the closer role was a case of the transcendence of loyalty (and perhaps also dollars) over common sense. He makes his biggest impact with his understanding of hitting, as many hitters have improved under his watch, even since he became manager, and his emphasis on patiently waiting for your pitch has helped a number of talented hitters become major-league run producers.

Pittsburgh Pirates

Neal Huntington inherited the baseball equivalent of a condemned house when he took over as the Pirates' general manager late in the 2007 season. The Pirates did not have a particularly talented major-league roster. Their farm system ranked among the worst in the game. The atmosphere around the organization was one of hopelessness, as former GM Dave Littlefield dragged the franchise further and further away from respectability with a series of bad personnel decisions, whether in the form of trades, free-agent signings, or draft picks. More than two years later, the Pirates are still among the game's biggest losers. They went 62-99 last year, their worst mark since christening PNC Park with a 62-100 record in 2001, and the second-worst record in the major leagues last season behind only the Nationals, who were 59-103. The Pirates have lost at least 94 games in each of the last five seasons. They've been not merely bad, but downright dreadful.

Of course, the Pirates cannot be mentioned without pointing out that they set an ignominious major North American professional team sports record last year with their 17th consecutive losing season. Huntington, however, has now at least had time to raze the house. When last season ended, there remained only five players who were on the Pirates' roster when Huntington was hired: left-handers Zach Duke and Paul Maholm, closer Matt Capps, catcher Ryan Doumit, and first baseman/outfielder Steve Pearce. The final stages of the demolition came in June and July last year, when Huntington made a series of seven trades. Those deals, combined with the trades of Jason Bay and Xavier Nady the previous July, left Doumit as the only player who was a regular as recently as July 30, 2008. The Pirates would also have lis-

tened to offers for Doumit at last year's nonwaiver trading deadline, but there was little interest as he had missed 73 games in the first half of the season because of a broken wrist.

PIRATES PROSPECTUS
2009 W-L: 62-99, 6th in NL Central

Pythag	63-98	16th	**Ballpark:** PNC Park (3-yr. PF: 982). Pretty as a picture and pitcher-friendly, but increasingly empty
RS/G	4.0	15th	
RA/G	4.8	13th	
EqA	.251	15th	
EqBRR	-7.9	11th	**2009:** Offloaded the last of the big-name veterans, McCutchen arrives, Garrett Jones a surprise
SNWP	.483	11th	
WXRL	0.66	16th	**2010:** Will the rebuild from a non-contender teardown show promise, or do the Bucs have Nutting to show for it yet?
FRAr	5.16	14th	
DE	.691	9th	
PADE	-1.37	11th	**Action Items:** Development from Milledge, La-Roche; otherwise, it's all just churn and no butter
Salary	$48.7	14th	
Attend	1.58	15th	

When the last of the trades was made, Huntington addressed the players at a team meeting. He told them the dealing was done and that they were the core the Pirates were going to build around. In other words, the foundation had been laid. Time will tell if the foundation will be strong enough to support a consistent winning team.

The Pirates certainly have not used their annual revenue-sharing check to spend on the major-league roster. The payroll stood at a paltry $23 million at the end of last season, which is $12 million less than the amount of revenue-sharing the Pirates reportedly received in 2009. While the Pirates slept with the fishes at the bottom of the NL Central standings, they also spent like the Fish, as their payroll was even smaller than that of the Marlins. With such low overhead, the Pirates reportedly cleared a $15 million profit despite the 99 losses and the lowest attendance of their nine seasons at PNC Park. The organization counters by saying it is spending its revenue-sharing money to improve the scouting and player development departments, rather than stuffing it in the pockets of owner Bob Nutting.

To their credit, the Pirates have gotten creative internationally and had players from five continents on their Bradenton farm club in the rookie-level Gulf Coast League last season. They did also open a $5 million academy in the Dominican Republic in April. But the enthusiasm this project generated was tempered in September, when the Pirates failed to sign highly touted shortstop prospect Miguel Sano. The Twins landed him

438

instead, and his agent, Rob Plummer, said the deciding factor was that the Pirates' Latin American scouting director, Rene Gayo, did not follow the family's wish that they not be contacted directly during the negotiations.

The Pirates have spent on domestic amateur talent recently after infamously drafting on the cheap during Kevin McClatchy's 11-year tenure as managing partner from 1996 to 2006. The team spent $9.8 million on draft bonuses in 2008 and $8.9 million last year. The combined $18.7 million was the highest in baseball during that span. They have routinely gone over the recommended slot bonus to sign high-school players who seemed to have solid commitments to play in college; quite ironic, since Pirates club president Frank Coonelly devised the slotting system when he worked in the commissioner's office. The downside is that most of the talent that has come into the organization since Huntington took over is young and many years away from helping at the major-league level. That is difficult to sell to a fan base that hasn't enjoyed a winning team since 1992.

The Pirates certainly have some interesting pieces in the major leagues, as well as some promising prospects who should begin this season at Triple-A Indianapolis. Center fielder Andrew McCutchen stepped into the lineup last season on June 4th when the Pirates stunned their fans by trading Nate McLouth, a year removed from playing in the All-Star Game and winning a Gold Glove, and four months removed from signing a three-year, $15.75 million contract that seemed to signal he had become the face of the franchise. Yet McCutchen excelled after arriving from Indianapolis, as he posted a .302 EqA and led the team with 37.9 VORP as a 22-year-old. Right-hander Ross Ohlendorf, in his first full season as a starter last season, contributed 3.9 SNLVAR, second on the team to Duke's 4.1. However, Ohlendorf's 5.6 strikeouts per nine innings was cause for concern because it didn't match up with a 95 mph fastball and sharp slider.

Another player who emerged was first baseman/outfielder Garrett Jones, who did not join the Pirates until June 30th (after outfielder Nyjer Morgan was dealt). Jones had a .322 EqA and hit 21 home runs in 358 plate appearances. It will be interesting to see if it was an aberration, given that he was a 28-year-old rookie who had spent 11 seasons in the minors, including five at Triple-A, though he had long been blocked in the Twins' organization by Justin Morneau and Michael Cuddyer. It would be a major boost if Jones proves to be for real, at least for a few seasons. At the end of last year, he was the only player on the roster who had ever had a 20-homer season in the major leagues, having only just done it.

In addition to McLouth, the Pirates also committed to three-year contracts with Maholm and Doumit before last season to buy out their arbitration years. That decision looked dubious in 2009, as Maholm's SNLVAR dropped from 5.2 to 3.9 while the injury-prone Doumit, his power sapped by the wrist injury, saw his EqA fall from .299 to .255. Both are more complementary players than building blocks.

The Pirates believe three players acquired in last season's flurry of trades can become key pieces to their long-term puzzle: right-hander Charlie Morton, first baseman Jeff Clement, and outfielder Lastings Milledge. All were once highly touted prospects whose stock dropped in their previous organizations. The Braves believed Morton lacked the confidence to be a top-of-the-rotation starter and packaged him with two prospects, center fielder Gorkys Hernandez and left-hander Jeff Locke, in the McLouth trade. The Mariners made Clement the third overall pick in the 2005 draft after an All-American career as a catcher at Southern California, but he never made an impact in 75 games in the majors and was shipped to the Pirates as part of the seven-player trade that saw shortstop Jack Wilson and right-hander Ian Snell go to Seattle. Milledge washed out with both the Mets and the Nationals, who traded him and closer Joel Hanrahan for Morgan and left-handed reliever Sean Burnett. Clement missed a chance to get a leg up on a starting job for this season—he was sent to Indianapolis after being acquired July 29th so he could begin making the conversion from catcher to first baseman, but he strained an oblique muscle late in the International League season, scuttling plans to play every day in September for the Pirates.

Morton and Milledge had their moments after joining the Pirates, but the results were inconclusive as an indication of their near-term futures. Morton contributed 2.3 SNLVAR in his 18 starts and was very inconsistent, though he did provide hope for the future by pitching a four-hit shutout against the Cubs in his final outing. Milledge's EqA was just .264 in 239 plate appearances, but he certainly shook the bad-attitude label that had dogged him; he did so by working hard to hone his craft while assimilating well into the clubhouse.

While it has become a Pirates tradition in this millennium to be effectively eliminated from contention in the NL Central by Mother's Day, an influx of top prospects should at least make things interesting after that date in 2010. Third baseman Pedro Alvarez, right-hander Brad Lincoln, and outfielder Jose Tabata all figure to be promoted from Indianapolis at some point after June (so as to ensure their arbitration clocks would not begin to tick too early, thus giving the Pirates an extra season to have contractual control over them). The coronation of Alvarez, the second overall pick from Vanderbilt in the 2008 draft, as the latest savior of the franchise occurred on September 23, 2008, when he ended protracted and sometimes acrimonious negotiations by becoming the first draftee in Pirates history to sign a major-league contract. Alvarez made his professional debut last season and, after a slow start, hit a combined .288/.378/.535 with 27 home runs in 542 plate appearances between Lynchburg and Altoona. He had a .255 EqA in 248 at-bats at Lynchburg, but increased that to .307 in 229 at-bats with Altoona.

As for the other two, Lincoln was the Pirates' first-round draft pick in 2006, but had to undergo Tommy John surgery on his elbow the following April. He still has a 95 mph fastball and an outstanding curveball. Tabata was a highly touted prospect in the Yankees' farm system, but fell out of favor when he walked out on Double-A Trenton in the middle of a game in 2008. Like Milledge, however, he has rehabilitated his image since joining the Pirates' organization and reached Triple-A just before his 21st birthday.

Huntington is a bright young executive and has shown plenty of guts by being willing to risk further alienating fans who had already been aggrieved for years. In the face of such hostility, Huntington has stuck to his vision of how to pull the Pirates out of their generation-long malaise, doing what predecessors Ted Simmons, Cam Bonifay, and Littlefield did not have the stomach to do, completely rebuilding the roster with young talent rather than continue to keep patching holes with broken-down veterans. The process will take time, though, and it is difficult to see the Pirates being competitive until at least 2011. That might even be an optimistic time frame.

The Pirates have emphasized defense since Huntington became the general manager, and they led the major leagues in fielding percentage last season for the first time since Ronald Reagan's first term. But traditional fielding statistics are not always indicative of a team's true defensive ability. Via Defensive Efficiency, simply the percentage of balls put in play, minus home runs, that are turned into outs, the Pirates ranked just 14th among the major-league teams, with a .691 mark. The defense, however, clearly took a hit after July 27th, the last day the double-play combination of shortstop Wilson and second baseman Sanchez played together. After both were traded two days later, Wilson to the Mariners and Sanchez to the Giants, the Pirates' Defensive Efficiency dropped precipitously. Consider where the Pirates stood among major-league teams on the morning of July 27th, and how their Defensive Efficiency stacked up from then until the end of the season (see Table 1). The Mariners, already good, led the majors after acquiring Wilson, the Giants were third after adding Sanchez, and the Pirates fell to 24th after trading both. Rebuilding the defense will be one of Huntington's main jobs this year.

Table 1. Everything's Better with Leather: Team Defensive Efficiency Rankings

Team	DE on 7/27	7/27 MLB Rank	DE after 7/27	Post 7/27 Rank
Dodgers	.715	1	.713	4
Cubs	.709	2	.690	13
Rangers	.708	3	.685	19
Mariners	.706	4	.723	1
Giants	.703	5	.714	3
Pirates	.702	6	.674	24

Questions abound about Nutting and his true commitment to winning. He admittedly knows little about the business of baseball and has developed the reputation of being tightfisted when it comes to running his other businesses (a ski resort and a chain of newspapers; maybe the Pirates are his hedge against global warming and the Internet). Will he spend the money necessary to contend for a championship if players like Alvarez, McCutchen, and Tabata turn into the nucleus of a contender? After all, it's one thing to spend $5 million on a Dominican academy, but another to spend $15-20 million a year on a superstar. However, that's akin to building a mansion. For now, the Pirates are just trying to move out of their 17-year-old doghouse.

HITTERS

Pedro Alvarez **3B** Bats: L Throws: R Height: 6' 2" Weight: 225 Born: July 18, 1987 Age: 22

YEAR	TEAM	LVL	AGE	PA	R	2B	3B	HR	RBI	BB	SO	SB	CS	EqBRR	AVG	OBP	SLG	EqAVG	EqOBP	EqSLG	EqA	VORP	WARP	DEFENSE	
2009	LYN	A+	21	284	38	14	1	14	55	37	70	1	1	0.4	.247	.342	.486	.229	.310	.430	.255	5.4	0.3	57-3B	-3
2009	ALT	AA	21	258	42	18	0	13	40	34	59	1	0	0.5	.333	.419	.590	.303	.376	.539	.307	19.9	1.6	52-3B	-6
2010	PIT	MLB	22	533	64	23	1	23	78	59	144	3	1	0.4	.249	.332	.447	.245	.327	.443	.269	19.1	1.6	108-3B	-4

Breakout: 11% Improve: 35% Collapse: 22% Attrition: 0% · MLB: 4% Comparables: Dan Pasqua, Greg Blosser, Eric Hinske, Chris Haas

Alvarez's professional career finally began last season in the wake of a long and often contentious holdout in 2008 after he was selected second overall in the '08 draft. He struggled early at high High-A Lynchburg, but after being promoted to Double-A, he showed why he is the most highly touted hitter to come into the Pirates' organization since the 1985 first-round draft pick Barry Bonds. Alvarez will start this season at Triple-A Indianapolis only because the Pirates don't want to start his arbitration clock ticking, but he will probably be in the major leagues by midseason and should eventually blossom into a true power-hitting star. His long-term future at third base is another matter, as he will need to concentrate on conditioning to keep his body limber enough for the hot corner. Most think he'll end up at first base sooner rather than later, but it won't matter with a bat this special.

Brian Bixler **UT** Bats: R Throws: R Height: 6' 1" Weight: 195 Born: October 22, 1982 Age: 27

YEAR	TEAM	LVL	AGE	PA	R	2B	3B	HR	RBI	BB	SO	SB	CS	EqBRR	AVG	OBP	SLG	EqAVG	EqOBP	EqSLG	EqA	VORP	WARP	DEFENSE			
2007	IND	AAA	24	556	77	23	10	5	51	54	131	28	4	6.7	.274	.368	.396	.265	.350	.391	.266	23.6	2.1	111-SS	-9	15-2B	3
2008	IND	AAA	25	364	44	8	5	7	36	27	107	23	7	-0.6	.280	.346	.402	.276	.334	.390	.257	13.3	2.3	73-SS	7	10-2B	-1
2008	PIT	MLB	25	120	16	2	1	0	2	6	36	1	0	0.6	.157	.229	.194	.156	.227	.193	.131	-7.7	-0.3	31-SS	5		
2009	IND	AAA	26	451	71	23	8	9	43	35	128	13	3	4.2	.275	.343	.439	.260	.324	.418	.258	14.9	1.2	59-SS	-5	25-2B	-2
2009	PIT	MLB	26	46	5	5	0	0	3	2	26	1	0	1.2	.227	.261	.341	.227	.261	.341	.218	-0.3	-0.2	9-SS	-2	3-2B	0
2010	PIT	MLB	27	446	55	18	5	7	38	38	127	10	4	1.8	.232	.309	.352	.237	.312	.356	.235	4.4	0.4	101-SS	-1		

Breakout: 10% Improve: 32% Collapse: 27% Attrition: 22% MLB: 28% Comparables: Chris Jones, Kevin Ward, D.J. Dozier, Dave Matranga

If Bixler weren't such a likable fellow, he might have a nickname like the Sultan of Strikeouts or the Wizard of Whiffs, because he has struck out an amazing 62 times in 166 major-league plate appearances over the past two seasons. If you're going to strike out more often than Mark Reynolds, you'd at least better hit home runs like Reynolds, but Bixler clearly doesn't have anything like that kind of power. The Pirates have given up on the idea of Bixler's becoming an everyday shortstop in the majors, but feel he has potential value as a utilityman. Thus, he began playing some center field late last season at Indianapolis to add some versatility, but there may be no space for him with the signing of Bobby Crosby.

Ronny Cedeño **MI** Bats: R Throws: R Height: 6' 0" Weight: 180 Born: February 2, 1983 Age: 27

YEAR	TEAM	LVL	AGE	PA	R	2B	3B	HR	RBI	BB	SO	SB	CS	EqBRR	AVG	OBP	SLG	EqAVG	EqOBP	EqSLG	EqA	VORP	WARP	DEFENSE			
2007	IOW	AAA	24	327	52	15	3	10	37	30	46	6	4	-0.3	.359	.422	.537	.325	.385	.466	.292	23.3	2.6	72-SS	-1		
2007	CHN	MLB	24	80	6	2	0	4	13	3	18	2	1	-0.1	.203	.231	.392	.203	.231	.392	.214	-1.4	0.1	12-SS	0	4-2B	1
2008	CHN	MLB	25	236	36	12	0	2	28	18	41	4	1	-1.1	.269	.328	.352	.267	.326	.346	.240	2.7	0.0	30-2B	-4	20-SS	1
2009	SEA	MLB	26	206	15	4	2	5	17	10	50	3	2	-1.3	.167	.213	.290	.168	.215	.293	.176	-8.8	-0.7	38-SS	4	9-2B	-2
2009	PIT	MLB	26	170	17	4	1	5	21	9	29	2	0	1.3	.258	.307	.394	.268	.315	.401	.253	4.8	0.2	42-SS	-4		
2010	PIT	MLB	27	367	42	15	2	9	41	27	70	5	3	-0.3	.250	.310	.383	.255	.314	.388	.241	5.9	0.7	84-SS	0		

Breakout: 12% Improve: 44% Collapse: 20% Attrition: 9% MLB: 85% Comparables: Chris Snopek, Dave Anderson, Tony Graffanino, Fred Manrique

The Pirates acquired Cedeño from the Mariners as part of their seven-player trade last July 29th, and he became their default shortstop as they sent away veteran Jack Wilson in the deal. Once considered a top prospect with the Cubs, he showed flashes of why with the Pirates, as he hit with some pop and made some spectacular defensive plays. He was, however, also very inconsistent, leaving doubts as to whether he can be an everyday shortstop. Cedeño will begin this season as the starter, and having worked his way down to the Pirates, it's obviously make-or-break time.

Jeff Clement 1B

Bats: L   Throws: R   Height: 6' 1"   Weight: 215   Born: August 21, 1983   Age: 26

YEAR	TEAM	LVL	AGE	PA	R	2B	3B	HR	RBI	BB	SO	SB	CS	EqBRR	AVG	OBP	SLG	EqAVG	EqOBP	EqSLG	EqA	VORP	WARP	DEFENSE	
2007	TAC	AAA	23	530	76	35	3	20	80	61	88	0	0	1.2	.275	.370	.497	.258	.344	.446	.273	24.3	2.2	74-C	-6
2007	SEA	MLB	23	19	4	1	0	2	3	3	3	0	0	-0.1	.375	.474	.813	.375	.474	.813	.407	3.7	0.4		
2008	TAC	AAA	24	211	40	17	0	14	43	35	30	0	0	-1.9	.335	.455	.676	.315	.422	.590	.335	24.1	2.4	29-C	-3
2008	SEA	MLB	24	224	17	10	1	5	23	15	63	0	1	-1.2	.227	.295	.360	.236	.304	.384	.236	1.2	-0.9	33-C	-7
2009	TAC	AAA	25	421	65	33	3	14	68	43	81	1	0	-0.7	.288	.366	.505	.267	.337	.463	.274	9.6	0.7	16-C -2 6-1B	-2
2009	IND	AAA	25	115	16	2	0	7	22	12	27	1	1	-0.1	.224	.313	.459	.222	.310	.455	.262	0.2	-0.2	22-1B	-2
2010	PIT	MLB	26	480	57	23	1	17	64	51	107	1	1	-0.4	.254	.343	.436	.249	.335	.432	.270	10.7	0.7	58-1B	-4

Breakout: 5%   Improve: 33%   Collapse: 19%   Attrition: 16%   MLB: 50%   Comparables: Paul Sorrento, Jeff Liefer, Bob Tumpane, Jim Traber

Clement was the key man among the five players the Pirates received from the Mariners in the deadline trade that dispatched Wilson and Snell Seattle-ward. The Pirates believe the former All-American catcher from USC and third overall pick in the 2005 draft can give them a power-hitting first baseman. He spent all of last season at Triple-A level, as hopes for a September call-up were dashed by a strained muscle in his rib cage. Clement is going to get every opportunity to prove that he can at long last be a mid-order hitter, and starting as first baseman this season, he faces likely his last chance to make a name for himself as a major-league regular rather than as a draft bust.

Luis Cruz UT

Bats: R   Throws: R   Height: 6' 1"   Weight: 215   Born: February 10, 1984   Age: 26

YEAR	TEAM	LVL	AGE	PA	R	2B	3B	HR	RBI	BB	SO	SB	CS	EqBRR	AVG	OBP	SLG	EqAVG	EqOBP	EqSLG	EqA	VORP	WARP	DEFENSE	
2007	SAN	AA	23	256	24	10	0	4	19	13	20	3	0	1.0	.252	.293	.345	.253	.285	.332	.218	-1.1	0.7	66-SS	7
2007	POR	AAA	23	167	15	10	1	5	17	9	24	0	0	0.5	.168	.216	.342	.154	.198	.308	.167	-8.2	-1.0	37-SS 0 4-2B	0
2008	ALT	AA	24	406	41	24	1	6	46	19	34	3	3	-1.2	.264	.303	.381	.241	.273	.339	.213	-2.4	1.9	97-SS 16 3-2B	2
2008	IND	AAA	24	127	19	10	0	3	15	3	14	2	4	-1.7	.325	.347	.483	.322	.344	.479	.269	6.0	0.1	16-SS -5 14-2B	0
2008	PIT	MLB	24	74	6	3	0	0	3	3	2	1	1	-0.7	.224	.278	.269	.235	.288	.279	.197	-1.6	0.4	18-SS	4
2009	IND	AAA	25	237	28	15	0	3	23	6	26	3	3	1.0	.253	.274	.358	.257	.277	.352	.215	-3.4	0.3	26-SS 4 12-3B	0
2009	PIT	MLB	25	78	5	1	0	0	2	6	7	0	0	-0.5	.214	.282	.229	.214	.282	.229	.183	-2.8	0.0	15-SS 3 5-2B	-1
2010	MIL	MLB	26	376	40	19	1	7	36	22	49	3	2	-0.2	.246	.295	.363	.254	.301	.372	.230	1.9	0.7	88-SS	5

Breakout: 25%   Improve: 53%   Collapse: 22%   Attrition: 15%   MLB: 56%   Comparables: Clay Bellinger, Casey Smith, Steve Eddie, Jim Auten

Defensive versatility is Cruz's strength, as he is very good with the glove at both middle infield positions, above average at third base, and passable in the outfield. That may be a plus at the very bottom of a very deep bench, but his lack of any sense of what the wooden thing they hand him in his nonfielding playing time is for undermines even that. To have a career notable for anything other than its brevity, he'll have to hit, and he'll get his next shot at it with the Brewers, who claimed him on waivers for reasons that defy easy explanation.

Chase d'Arnaud MI

Bats: R   Throws: R   Height: 6' 1"   Weight: 175   Born: January 21, 1987   Age: 23

YEAR	TEAM	LVL	AGE	PA	R	2B	3B	HR	RBI	BB	SO	SB	CS	EqBRR	AVG	OBP	SLG	EqAVG	EqOBP	EqSLG	EqA	VORP	WARP	DEFENSE	
2008	SCO	A-	21	183	26	10	5	1	21	11	30	14	2	1.2	.286	.333	.423	.244	.279	.360	.227	1.0	-1.0	35-SS -8 5-3B	1
2009	WVA	A	22	255	32	14	3	3	31	30	31	17	3	4.0	.291	.394	.427	.246	.323	.353	.244	5.5	0.9	59-SS	2
2009	LYN	A+	22	253	45	19	4	4	26	30	41	14	5	4.5	.295	.402	.481	.279	.363	.443	.280	13.7	0.5	26-SS -4 25-2B	-6
2010	PIT	MLB	23	453	48	24	4	6	39	41	80	11	4	3.2	.252	.331	.374	.256	.333	.378	.251	11.5	0.8	101-SS	-4

Breakout: 9%   Improve: 45%   Collapse: 12%   Attrition: 5%   MLB: 2%   Comparables: Kevin Romine, Brett Harrison, Jason Donald, Mark Little

Chase d'Arnaud is the older brother of Travis, a catcher in the Blue Jays' farm system (by way of the Halladay trade), who was considered a better prospect until he was Chase'd down just last season. This former Pepperdine shortstop and fourth-round pick isn't outstanding in one particular area, but he does a lot of things well: hitting for average, getting on base, stealing bases, and playing defense. The only question is if he will develop enough power to be an everyday player in the majors, but after just 1 ½ pro seasons, in this organization d'Arnaud certainly looks like a future regular at shortstop or second base, possibly as soon as 2011.

Argenis Diaz   SS   Bats: R   Throws: R   Height: 5' 11"   Weight: 155   Born: February 12, 1987   Age: 23

YEAR	TEAM	LVL	AGE	PA	R	2B	3B	HR	RBI	BB	SO	SB	CS	EqBRR	AVG	OBP	SLG	EqAVG	EqOBP	EqSLG	EqA	VORP	WARP	DEFENSE	
2007	GRN	A	20	447	62	25	5	2	40	36	92	5	9	-6.3	.279	.342	.380	.244	.295	.326	.216	-2.7	0.4	97-SS	6
2008	LNC	A+	21	282	31	9	6	0	29	20	60	3	2	-0.4	.281	.330	.363	.224	.272	.286	.198	-5.2	-1.5	69-SS	-7
2008	PME	AA	21	153	20	8	2	2	23	10	30	0	1	0.2	.288	.336	.417	.270	.309	.397	.244	3.5	0.5	36-SS	1
2009	PME	AA	22	307	21	14	1	0	24	21	60	7	4	-1.8	.253	.309	.310	.237	.281	.286	.202	-5.0	-1.1	76-SS	-4
2009	IND	AAA	22	158	14	1	0	0	8	8	27	1	1	-0.3	.233	.273	.240	.238	.277	.245	.183	-4.9	-0.7	43-SS	-1
2010	*BOS*	*MLB*	*23*	*452*	*46*	*20*	*3*	*3*	*38*	*30*	*102*	*4*	*4*	*-1.5*	*.245*	*.297*	*.330*	*.242*	*.296*	*.320*	*.208*	*-7.0*	*-0.9*	*110-SS*	*-1*

Breakout: 25%   Improve: 53%   Collapse: 15%   Attrition: 12%   MLB: 1%   Comparables: Luis Cruz, Esteban Beltre, Enohel Polanco, Juan Ciriaco

The Pirates acquired Diaz from the Red Sox last July 23rd in a trade for Adam LaRoche and decided to immediately challenge their shortstop prospect by jumping him from Double-A to Triple-A. He didn't exactly rise to it, posting a negligible 512 OPS in 158 plate appearances. Diaz is an above-average defensive shortstop, and the Pirates, enamored with his glove, will send him back to Indianapolis in the hope that his bat will come around. Nothing in his past, however, suggests that Diaz will hit enough to be a major-league regular, perhaps not even a bench player.

Ryan Doumit   C   Bats: S   Throws: R   Height: 6' 1"   Weight: 215   Born: April 3, 1981   Age: 29

YEAR	TEAM	LVL	AGE	PA	R	2B	3B	HR	RBI	BB	SO	SB	CS	EqBRR	AVG	OBP	SLG	EqAVG	EqOBP	EqSLG	EqA	VORP	WARP	DEFENSE			
2007	PIT	MLB	26	279	33	19	2	9	32	22	59	1	2	-1.2	.274	.341	.472	.287	.355	.494	.280	14.3	1.4	35-RF	4	25-C	-4
2008	PIT	MLB	27	465	71	34	0	15	69	23	55	2	2	0.2	.318	.357	.501	.333	.369	.519	.299	40.5	3.0	101-C	-9		
2009	PIT	MLB	28	304	31	16	0	10	38	20	49	4	0	-0.5	.250	.299	.414	.257	.303	.429	.255	11.7	1.6	70-C	3		
2010	*PIT*	*MLB*	*29*	*403*	*51*	*20*	*1*	*14*	*56*	*31*	*67*	*3*	*2*	*-0.5*	*.282*	*.344*	*.453*	*.285*	*.346*	*.460*	*.274*	*22.3*	*2.2*	*90-C*	*-3*		

Breakout: 9%   Improve: 38%   Collapse: 11%   Attrition: 9%   MLB: 92%   Comparables: Terry Kennedy, Eddie Taubensee, Victor Martinez, Johnny Romano

Doumit landed a three-year, $11.5 million contract after his breakthrough in 2008, but as has been the case throughout his professional career, he fell victim to injury in 2009. He suffered a broken right wrist on April 19th when hit by a pitch, and he did not return until just before the All-Star Game. He was unable to hit for power and did not get into any kind of offensive groove until September, this after being benched for a game in August because of a helmet-slamming incident in the dugout. The switch-hitter has the ability to be one of the better offensive catchers in the majors, and his throwing has improved (reaching 31 percent last year), but the key will be his staying in the lineup, a tough proposition, given that his track record for fragility stretches back into his earliest days in the minors.

Brian Friday   SS   Bats: R   Throws: R   Height: 5' 11"   Weight: 180   Born: December 16, 1985   Age: 24

YEAR	TEAM	LVL	AGE	PA	R	2B	3B	HR	RBI	BB	SO	SB	CS	EqBRR	AVG	OBP	SLG	EqAVG	EqOBP	EqSLG	EqA	VORP	WARP	DEFENSE	
2007	SCO	A-	21	176	31	10	1	2	13	10	33	6	4	-1.0	.295	.371	.410	.262	.309	.372	.236	2.1	-0.1	38-SS	-3
2008	LYN	A+	22	391	59	20	4	2	29	34	56	16	11	-3.1	.287	.365	.387	.267	.329	.352	.241	7.5	1.5	80-SS	5
2009	ALT	AA	23	476	48	22	3	7	46	51	69	7	5	-2.9	.265	.361	.386	.252	.331	.371	.249	11.7	0.6	100-SS	-7
2010	*PIT*	*MLB*	*24*	*406*	*44*	*19*	*2*	*6*	*31*	*35*	*73*	*6*	*4*	*-1.4*	*.246*	*.320*	*.356*	*.250*	*.321*	*.359*	*.239*	*5.5*	*0.5*	*87-SS*	*-1*

Breakout: 12%   Improve: 34%   Collapse: 22%   Attrition: 12%   MLB: 10%   Comparables: Eric Mangham, Justin Turner, Bob Bruzik, Lou Collier

Friday seemed poised for a breakout season at Double-A last year until he was felled by an inner-ear infection in late April. He was never the same and wound up with pedestrian offensive numbers. Friday is a fundamentally sound defensive shortstop who would be able to handle playing the position at the major-league level. The question is whether he will hit enough, and it's one he is going to have to start answering in the affirmative fairly soon if he's going to continue to be considered a prospect, especially with Chase d'Arnaud coming behind him in the farm system.

Gorkys Hernandez   CF   Bats: R   Throws: R   Height: 6' 0"   Weight: 175   Born: September 7, 1987   Age: 22

YEAR	TEAM	LVL	AGE	PA	R	2B	3B	HR	RBI	BB	SO	SB	CS	EqBRR	AVG	OBP	SLG	EqAVG	EqOBP	EqSLG	EqA	VORP	WARP	DEFENSE	
2007	WMI	A	19	533	84	25	5	4	50	36	69	54	11	8.8	.293	.344	.391	.273	.316	.367	.247	7.5	2.4	119-CF	12
2008	MYR	A+	20	467	75	23	6	5	42	48	79	20	4	5.9	.264	.348	.387	.246	.313	.352	.238	1.6	2.9	94-CF	22
2009	MIS	AA	21	228	33	11	2	0	19	15	54	10	8	2.2	.316	.361	.387	.284	.322	.349	.235	0.5	0.5	51-CF	4
2009	ALT	AA	21	374	45	14	2	3	31	24	76	9	8	1.1	.262	.312	.340	.244	.285	.321	.212	-7.6	-1.3	82-CF	-3
2010	PIT	MLB	22	566	68	25	4	6	46	43	113	16	7	3.2	.250	.310	.347	.254	.313	.351	.233	1.5	0.9	125-CF	6

Breakout: 20%   Improve: 50%   Collapse: 20%   Attrition: 12%   MLB: 4%   Comparables: Darrin Jackson, Andrew McCutchen, Austin Jackson, Ed Fully

For a young prospect who has yet to see "The Show," Hernandez is becoming pretty well traveled. The Tigers shipped him to the Braves in their trade for Edgar Renteria after the 2007 season, and he was flipped to the Pirates last June as part of the McLouth trade. Hernandez was a disappointment (and perhaps disappointed) following the trade, as he didn't hit much for Altoona and had to be reprimanded multiple times for attitude problems. He's still very young and gifted with outstanding speed and range in center field, but his baserunning speed isn't being exploited effectively, and his walk rate will need to rebound. He could wind up on the move again at some point, as center field figures to be the domain of McCutchen for years to come, and Hernandez's bat doesn't profile well in a corner.

Jason Jaramillo   C   Bats: S   Throws: R   Height: 6' 0"   Weight: 200   Born: October 9, 1982   Age: 27

YEAR	TEAM	LVL	AGE	PA	R	2B	3B	HR	RBI	BB	SO	SB	CS	EqBRR	AVG	OBP	SLG	EqAVG	EqOBP	EqSLG	EqA	VORP	WARP	DEFENSE	
2007	OTT	AAA	24	496	52	13	4	6	56	50	79	0	1	-1.7	.271	.350	.361	.270	.341	.361	.250	16.6	0.8	108-C	-10
2008	LEH	AAA	25	473	48	20	0	8	39	42	82	1	1	-2.3	.266	.340	.371	.258	.326	.352	.241	10.9	1.1	113-C	-2
2009	PIT	MLB	26	224	20	14	0	3	26	17	33	1	0	-0.2	.252	.309	.364	.261	.314	.382	.243	5.8	-0.3	59-C	-6
2010	PIT	MLB	27	279	26	11	1	5	29	24	53	1	1	-0.5	.251	.322	.361	.252	.322	.361	.240	5.4	0.4	66-C	-2

Breakout: 17%   Improve: 39%   Collapse: 28%   Attrition: 31%   MLB: 70%   Comparables: Jason Varitek, Koyie Hill, Chris Bando, Paul Bako

Jaramillo had an adequate rookie season as the backup catcher, though he proved to be stretched offensively when asked to play semiregularly while Ryan Doumit sat out 2 ½ months with a broken right wrist in the first half of the season. Though a switch-hitter, he struggled to hit lefties in limited exposure against them, which depressed his overall rates. Jaramillo's value lies more on the defensive side, as pitchers like throwing to him and he possesses a strong arm, though his caught-stealing percentage was just average. It is hard to imagine him becoming a regular behind the plate, but he's more than good enough to fashion a nice career as a caddy.

Garrett Jones   RF/1B   Bats: L   Throws: L   Height: 6' 4"   Weight: 245   Born: June 21, 1981   Age: 29

YEAR	TEAM	LVL	AGE	PA	R	2B	3B	HR	RBI	BB	SO	SB	CS	EqBRR	AVG	OBP	SLG	EqAVG	EqOBP	EqSLG	EqA	VORP	WARP	DEFENSE			
2007	ROC	AAA	26	446	57	32	3	13	70	32	83	2	2	-0.5	.280	.334	.472	.259	.306	.432	.255	4.8	0.2	44-LF	-1	30-RF	-2
2007	MIN	MLB	26	84	7	2	1	2	5	6	20	1	1	-0.4	.208	.262	.338	.208	.262	.338	.211	-3.3	-0.5	7-1B	0	2-LF	0
2008	ROC	AAA	27	587	82	33	3	23	92	50	98	9	2	2.3	.279	.337	.484	.252	.307	.423	.253	2.9	-1.0	69-1B	-5	30-RF	-6
2009	IND	AAA	28	299	44	18	0	12	50	18	47	14	4	3.2	.307	.348	.502	.297	.334	.473	.275	10.7	1.2	63-RF	-1	5-LF	0
2009	PIT	MLB	28	358	45	21	1	21	44	40	76	10	2	-0.2	.293	.372	.567	.311	.384	.597	.322	31.6	3.4	39-RF	-4	29-1B	2
2010	PIT	MLB	29	612	69	30	2	22	79	50	126	7	4	0.8	.261	.324	.442	.257	.319	.437	.263	15.2	1.2	108-RF	-4		

Breakout: 9%   Improve: 31%   Collapse: 22%   Attrition: 12%   MLB: 38%   Comparables: Luke Scott, Brooks Kieschnick, Dann Howitt, Ryan Ludwick

Jones was supposedly just another good Quad-A hitter, until he actually got a chance to play last season. After the Pirates traded Nyjer Morgan to the Nationals on June 30th, Jones started hitting as soon as he was called up. While the skeptics waited for major-league pitching to expose his weaknesses, he kept hitting all the way to the end of the season, winding up as the Pirates' leader in homers in just a half-season of play. Now Jones will go to spring training assured of being either their starting first baseman or right fielder, heady stuff for a guy who all but had "minor-league journeyman" tattooed across his back at this time last year. Will he keep hitting? His track record doesn't suggest he's a .550 slugger (few players are), but the Pirates could live quite happily with 100 points less, and given that he's a free-talent find, he's a happy addition.

Andy LaRoche — 3B

Bats: R Throws: R Height: 6' 1" Weight: 210 Born: September 13, 1983 Age: 26

YEAR	TEAM	LVL	AGE	PA	R	2B	3B	HR	RBI	BB	SO	SB	CS	EqBRR	AVG	OBP	SLG	EqAVG	EqOBP	EqSLG	EqA	VORP	WARP	DEFENSE			
2007	LVG	AAA	23	311	55	18	1	18	48	39	42	2	2	1.0	.309	.399	.589	.260	.347	.476	.280	13.5	1.1	64-3B	-2	6-LF	-2
2007	LAN	MLB	23	115	16	5	0	1	10	20	24	2	1	0.7	.226	.365	.312	.228	.368	.304	.252	1.1	0.2	27-3B	0		
2008	LVG	AAA	24	166	35	3	0	5	28	37	14	2	1	2.0	.293	.452	.439	.250	.398	.359	.281	7.4	1.2	25-3B	3	7-2B	0
2008	LAN	MLB	24	69	6	1	0	2	6	10	7	0	0	-0.3	.203	.319	.322	.220	.333	.339	.236	-0.1	0.0	12-3B	0		
2008	PIT	MLB	24	183	11	4	0	3	12	14	30	2	0	1.0	.152	.227	.232	.152	.225	.224	.157	-13.1	-1.5	44-3B	0		
2009	PIT	MLB	25	590	64	29	5	12	64	50	84	3	1	1.2	.258	.330	.401	.273	.342	.423	.265	19.4	3.4	141-3B	10		
2010	PIT	MLB	26	519	63	21	2	14	56	59	76	4	2	0.9	.246	.341	.396	.251	.344	.402	.260	13.3	1.7	120-3B	2		

Breakout: 22% Improve: 46% Collapse: 9% Attrition: 10% MLB: 99% Comparables: Jeff Cirillo, Todd Zeile, Michael Cuddyer, Vance Law

LaRoche was considered one of the Dodgers' top prospects in 2008 when the Pirates landed him in the huge trade that sent Jason Bay from Pittsburgh to the Red Sox and Manny Ramirez from Boston to LA. Unfortunately, like a few too many prospects who become Pirates, he's been another DOA—Disappointment On Arrival—as he has failed to produce in his time as the Pirates' starting third baseman, stretches in May and September 2009 excepted. He will be the starter again at the hot corner to begin this season, but it seems he's just keeping the spot warm until Pedro Alvarez arrives, probably sometime in June. His solid glove, Alvarez's lack thereof, the occasional hot streak, and a leftward tilt in the lineup could earn him additional chances at the corners, but failing that, he's in danger of being recycled.

Andrew McCutchen — CF

Bats: R Throws: R Height: 5' 11" Weight: 175 Born: October 10, 1986 Age: 23

YEAR	TEAM	LVL	AGE	PA	R	2B	3B	HR	RBI	BB	SO	SB	CS	EqBRR	AVG	OBP	SLG	EqAVG	EqOBP	EqSLG	EqA	VORP	WARP	DEFENSE			
2007	ALT	AA	20	498	70	20	3	10	48	44	83	17	1	3.2	.258	.327	.383	.240	.298	.355	.234	0.9	0.7	116-CF	5		
2007	IND	AAA	20	72	7	4	0	1	5	4	11	4	3	1.1	.313	.347	.418	.313	.347	.403	.262	2.2	0.6	15-CF	3		
2008	IND	AAA	21	590	75	26	3	9	50	68	87	34	19	-5.3	.283	.372	.398	.280	.364	.391	.265	18.6	2.2	117-CF	1	7-LF	-1
2009	IND	AAA	22	219	41	10	8	4	20	17	24	10	2	2.6	.303	.361	.493	.307	.364	.510	.295	15.1	1.2	47-CF	-5		
2009	PIT	MLB	22	493	74	26	9	12	54	54	83	22	5	1.5	.286	.365	.471	.306	.379	.502	.302	37.9	5.1	108-CF	7		
2010	PIT	MLB	23	637	84	28	6	13	59	61	105	22	9	0.5	.263	.338	.403	.268	.340	.411	.261	20.6	2.5	141-CF	2		

Breakout: 11% Improve: 36% Collapse: 20% Attrition: 11% MLB: 100% Comparables: Ellis Burks, Rontrez Johnson, Winston Ficklin, Kevin Belcher

McCutchen was the biggest bright spot to lighten up what was otherwise yet another dismal Pirates season. Called up on June 4th, the day after McLouth was traded to the Braves, he immediately showed he was much more talented than his All-Star predecessor, while tying with McLouth for the team's best rate of baserunners driven in, with an OBI percentage of 19.8. He wound up being selected as the team MVP for both Indianapolis *and* the Pirates. McCutchen has all the tools necessary for stardom, including great speed, rapidly emerging power, and the type of range and arm to become an outstanding defensive center fielder. The Pirates have had their share of phenoms fizzle out, but McCutchen is the real deal.

Lastings Milledge — LF

Bats: R Throws: R Height: 6' 0" Weight: 205 Born: April 5, 1985 Age: 25

YEAR	TEAM	LVL	AGE	PA	R	2B	3B	HR	RBI	BB	SO	SB	CS	EqBRR	AVG	OBP	SLG	EqAVG	EqOBP	EqSLG	EqA	VORP	WARP	DEFENSE			
2007	NYN	MLB	22	206	27	9	1	7	29	13	42	3	2	-1.1	.272	.341	.446	.288	.356	.462	.277	8.2	1.2	25-RF	-2	13-CF	4
2008	WAS	MLB	23	587	65	24	2	14	61	38	96	24	9	-0.4	.268	.330	.402	.277	.336	.415	.262	18.4	0.8	133-CF	-9		
2009	WAS	MLB	24	26	1	0	0	0	1	1	10	1	0	0.2	.167	.231	.167	.167	.231	.167	.139	-2.1	-0.5	5-CF	-2		
2009	SYR	AAA	24	83	11	5	0	0	4	3	16	6	1	0.4	.253	.277	.316	.241	.265	.291	.204	-3.1	-0.5	13-LF	-3	5-CF	2
2009	IND	AAA	24	74	7	6	0	0	7	8	10	3	2	-1.7	.333	.425	.433	.328	.411	.426	.294	4.1	0.5	14-LF	0		
2009	PIT	MLB	24	239	20	11	0	4	20	12	37	6	4	-3.1	.291	.333	.395	.308	.347	.421	.264	5.9	0.5	57-LF	-2		
2010	PIT	MLB	25	424	48	19	1	12	46	32	78	12	6	-0.9	.262	.331	.407	.269	.337	.417	.258	8.1	0.6	93-LF	-3		

Breakout: 11% Improve: 45% Collapse: 14% Attrition: 7% MLB: 100% Comparables: Wil Cordero, Jeffrey Hammonds, Pedro Munoz, Rondell White

Milledge came to the Pirates with more baggage than Louis Vuitton when he was acquired from the Nationals last June. He had the reputation of being a hot dog, lazy, aloof, and uncoachable. Perhaps being traded twice before the age of 25 was a wake-up call, because if nothing else, Milledge showed a great work ethic once he joined the Pirates' organization. Once considered a future superstar as a Mets prospect, Milledge is still thought by people on the inside to have the potential to be an above-average player, but you could be forgiven for seeing more than 1,200 big-league personal appearances and a .259 career EqA, and read that out to spell "replacement level." The Pirates feel his power will blossom in 2010, a year removed from a broken finger he suffered last May; perhaps if he adds that and a modicum of plate discipline, the intrigue would have staying power.

Brandon Moss   RF   Bats: L   Throws: R   Height: 6' 0"   Weight: 205   Born: September 16, 1983   Age: 26

YEAR	TEAM	LVL	AGE	PA	R	2B	3B	HR	RBI	BB	SO	SB	CS	EqBRR	AVG	OBP	SLG	EqAVG	EqOBP	EqSLG	EqA	VORP	WARP	DEFENSE			
2007	PAW	AAA	23	559	66	41	2	16	78	61	148	3	5	-1.3	.282	.363	.471	.267	.342	.451	.270	16.3	1.5	99-RF	-4	12-CF	0
2007	BOS	MLB	23	29	6	2	1	0	1	4	6	0	0	0.4	.280	.379	.440	.280	.379	.440	.281	1.3	0.0	6-LF	0	1-RF	-1
2008	PAW	AAA	24	182	29	8	4	8	30	16	47	2	0	-0.8	.282	.346	.528	.268	.330	.494	.279	5.9	1.1	36-1B	2	4-RF	1
2008	BOS	MLB	24	86	7	5	1	2	11	6	25	1	1	-0.4	.295	.337	.462	.299	.341	.468	.272	2.5	0.7	10-RF	2	9-LF	1
2008	PIT	MLB	24	177	12	10	2	6	23	15	45	0	1	-2.3	.222	.288	.424	.229	.294	.433	.250	1.1	-0.5	24-LF	-5	17-RF	-1
2009	PIT	MLB	25	424	47	20	4	7	41	34	84	1	5	-3.9	.236	.304	.364	.249	.314	.383	.237	-3.4	1.0	76-RF	12	19-LF	-1
2010	*PIT*	*MLB*	*26*	*463*	*52*	*23*	*4*	*13*	*56*	*45*	*114*	*2*	*3*	*-1.3*	*.251*	*.327*	*.423*	*.248*	*.322*	*.415*	*.259*	*9.1*	*1.2*	*88-RF*	*2*		

Breakout: 11% Improve: 40% Collapse: 11% Attrition: 8%   MLB: 95%   Comparables: *Michael Tucker, Jacque Jones, Troy O'Leary, Eric Anthony*

Having shown flashes of potential with the Red Sox, Moss finally got the opportunity to be a regular last season when he was named the Pirates' right fielder for Opening Day. He responded by fumbling that chance away, hitting for little power, and with not much of an excuse hiding among his balls-in-play results. Moss proved to be a better defensive right fielder than advertised, but that wasn't enough to keep him in a power-starved lineup. At best, he's a fourth outfielder, though his inability to play center field detracts from his value as a bench player.

Jim Negrych   2B   Bats: L   Throws: R   Height: 5' 10"   Weight: 180   Born: March 2, 1985   Age: 25

YEAR	TEAM	LVL	AGE	PA	R	2B	3B	HR	RBI	BB	SO	SB	CS	EqBRR	AVG	OBP	SLG	EqAVG	EqOBP	EqSLG	EqA	VORP	WARP	DEFENSE			
2007	HIC	A	22	376	57	14	4	2	48	27	48	4	1	4.8	.282	.340	.365	.246	.291	.309	.213	-6.0	-1.6	81-2B	-7		
2008	LYN	A+	23	451	77	36	1	5	62	55	55	7	6	-1.2	.370	.448	.508	.331	.395	.444	.293	26.4	2.9	74-3B	-1	17-2B	-1
2008	ALT	AA	23	102	10	5	0	0	10	11	14	5	1	0.7	.310	.394	.368	.289	.360	.333	.254	1.4	0.2	19-3B	0		
2009	ALT	AA	24	378	51	18	1	3	30	45	37	8	1	3.2	.272	.366	.362	.254	.329	.337	.241	2.6	-0.6	82-2B	-8		
2010	*PIT*	*MLB*	*25*	*407*	*49*	*19*	*1*	*4*	*39*	*37*	*68*	*4*	*2*	*1.2*	*.271*	*.340*	*.360*	*.266*	*.334*	*.358*	*.250*	*7.8*	*0.4*	*87-2B*	*-4*		

Breakout: 7% Improve: 29% Collapse: 28% Attrition: 9%   MLB: 6%   Comparables: *Tim Leiper, Chris DeMetral, Orlando Palmeiro, Joseph Bruno*

After winning the Carolina League batting title and being named the Pirates' minor-league player of the year in 2008, Negrych had a disappointing first full season at Double-A. He had a hard time adjusting to the higher caliber of pitching, and just when his bat began to heat up in July, he suffered a season-ending punctured lung when he collided with shortstop Brian Friday while trying to field a ground ball. As is, Negrych's value lies in his batting average and on-base percentage, as he has little power and is a below-average defender, so his opportunities are going to be limited.

Steve Pearce   1B/RF   Bats: R   Throws: R   Height: 5' 11"   Weight: 215   Born: April 13, 1983   Age: 27

YEAR	TEAM	LVL	AGE	PA	R	2B	3B	HR	RBI	BB	SO	SB	CS	EqBRR	AVG	OBP	SLG	EqAVG	EqOBP	EqSLG	EqA	VORP	WARP	DEFENSE			
2007	LYN	A+	24	85	19	4	1	11	24	8	13	2	0	1.1	.347	.412	.867	.282	.329	.667	.315	6.8	0.8	18-1B	0		
2007	ALT	AA	24	335	57	27	2	14	72	33	45	7	2	0.2	.334	.400	.586	.309	.363	.527	.300	18.9	1.9	78-1B	-3		
2007	IND	AAA	24	131	18	9	1	6	17	6	12	5	0	2.2	.320	.366	.557	.317	.359	.553	.306	8.7	1.1	20-1B	2	9-RF	-1
2007	PIT	MLB	24	73	13	5	1	0	6	5	12	2	1	0.5	.294	.342	.397	.309	.356	.412	.264	1.7	0.4	15-RF	2		
2008	IND	AAA	25	433	47	26	1	12	60	32	75	10	4	-1.1	.251	.312	.417	.249	.305	.405	.248	1.0	-1.0	66-RF	-13	27-1B	3
2008	PIT	MLB	25	119	6	7	0	4	15	5	22	2	0	0.1	.248	.294	.422	.259	.303	.444	.258	2.0	-0.5	25-RF	-6		
2009	IND	AAA	26	317	37	18	1	13	54	34	46	3	7	-4.3	.286	.373	.502	.283	.364	.493	.285	9.1	1.1	63-1B	0		
2009	PIT	MLB	26	186	19	13	1	4	16	21	43	1	0	1.1	.206	.296	.370	.217	.301	.398	.241	-3.6	-0.2	41-1B	2		
2010	*PIT*	*MLB*	*27*	*471*	*51*	*24*	*2*	*14*	*63*	*42*	*82*	*5*	*4*	*0.0*	*.254*	*.328*	*.422*	*.259*	*.331*	*.428*	*.260*	*4.9*	*0.6*	*104-1B*	*1*		

Breakout: 4% Improve: 31% Collapse: 28% Attrition: 25%   MLB: 70%   Comparables: *Tony Brewer, Craig Cacek, Larry See, Mike Reddish*

Pearce hasn't come close to matching his outstanding 2007 season, during which he began the year in Low-A and ended it in the majors while being named the Pirates' minor-league player of the year. He's been stalled out ever since, struggling to make much with his sporadic opportunities in the majors. Heading into his age-27 season, Pearce will go to spring training with a small chance of winning the starting first baseman's job, but he is definitely a long shot behind Jeff Clement and may have to settle for a shot to stick as a right-handed bench bat behind Clement at first and Jones in right.

Tony Sanchez   C

Bats: R   Throws: R   Height: 6' 0"   Weight: 220   Born: May 20, 1988   Age: 22

YEAR	TEAM	LVL	AGE	PA	R	2B	3B	HR	RBI	BB	SO	SB	CS	EqBRR	AVG	OBP	SLG	EqAVG	EqOBP	EqSLG	EqA	VORP	WARP	DEFENSE			
2009	WVA	A	21	188	29	15	1	7	46	21	34	1	0	-0.5	.316	.415	.561	.276	.351	.472	.284	12.1	0.7	37-C	-6		
2010	PIT	MLB	22	382	37	18	1	10	60	38	89	0	1	-1.5	.241	.327	.385	.244	.329	.391	.250	10.9	0.7	74-C	-5		

Breakout: 3%   Improve: 16%   Collapse: 38%   Attrition: 0%   MLB: 1%   Comparables: Stan Holmes, Danny Gil, Aaron Royster, Curtis Thigpen

The Pirates took a lot of heat from draftniks who felt they went cheap by taking Sanchez with the fourth overall pick last year. While Sanchez was very good in his pro debut, showing good power and even better defense, that's what his ultimate projection depends upon. It's not as if scouts killed him; they simply saw him as a plus defender in the big leagues who hits .260-.280 with 15-20 homers a year. That's a very valuable player, but when you get to pick fourth, one is always better served by focusing on elite talent, rather than cost-cutting measures. Sanchez was a mid-first-round talent (or later), but his willingness to sign for a reasonable number apparently trumped most other considerations. Team president Frank Coonelly used to be in charge of enforcing MLB's silly slot system, and now that he's on the other side of the coin, he seems to always think he can beat the system. Pedro Alvarez beat him in his first draft in 2008, and by taking Sanchez in 2009, Coonelly just beat himself.

Jose Tabata   OF

Bats: R   Throws: R   Height: 5' 11"   Weight: 215   Born: August 12, 1988   Age: 21

YEAR	TEAM	LVL	AGE	PA	R	2B	3B	HR	RBI	BB	SO	SB	CS	EqBRR	AVG	OBP	SLG	EqAVG	EqOBP	EqSLG	EqA	VORP	WARP	DEFENSE			
2007	TAM	A+	18	456	56	16	2	5	54	33	70	15	7	-2.3	.307	.371	.392	.282	.336	.360	.247	0.6	-0.2	85-RF	-2		
2008	TRN	AA	19	332	40	9	0	3	36	26	49	10	2	2.1	.248	.320	.310	.250	.308	.307	.225	-6.4	-0.9	67-RF	-1		
2008	ALT	AA	19	97	16	6	2	3	13	8	18	8	0	2.5	.348	.402	.562	.308	.357	.516	.302	7.4	0.6	22-CF	-2		
2009	ALT	AA	20	254	31	15	1	2	25	20	25	7	6	-1.0	.303	.370	.404	.283	.339	.382	.252	3.3	-0.2	34-RF	-1	20-CF	-4
2009	IND	AAA	20	148	21	7	1	3	10	10	18	4	2	0.9	.276	.333	.410	.274	.331	.407	.257	3.0	0.1	18-RF	1	15-CF	-3
2010	PIT	MLB	21	483	57	21	2	8	52	37	77	12	5	0.4	.269	.334	.379	.274	.337	.388	.252	6.1	0.6	100-RF	-1		

Breakout: 30%   Improve: 58%   Collapse: 11%   Attrition: 2%   MLB: 7%   Comparables: Chris Brown, Scott Hunter, Papo Bolivar, Keith Mitchell

Tabata took a major step forward in his development last season, which nobody could have predicted in spring training, given that he had to deal with the major distraction of the arrest of his wife, a woman more than twice his age, for allegedly snatching a baby. Tabata was found not to have been involved and then went on to have a fine season, as he reached Triple-A a few weeks before his 21st birthday and then tore up the Arizona Fall League. The last piece of the puzzle for Tabata is to learn how to hit for power, which is why he will go back to Indianapolis to begin this season. It might sound improbable, given how long Tabata has been on people's radars, but remember, he's heading into his age-21 season. If the home runs come, Tabata will become one of the cornerstones of the Pirates' rebuilding effort; if not, he's going to need a whole lot of everything else to be employable in a corner.

Ramon Vazquez   INF

Bats: L   Throws: R   Height: 5' 11"   Weight: 195   Born: August 21, 1976   Age: 33

YEAR	TEAM	LVL	AGE	PA	R	2B	3B	HR	RBI	BB	SO	SB	CS	EqBRR	AVG	OBP	SLG	EqAVG	EqOBP	EqSLG	EqA	VORP	WARP	DEFENSE			
2007	OKL	AAA	30	161	27	10	2	2	13	24	27	3	1	0.6	.258	.375	.409	.228	.331	.331	.242	2.7	0.7	21-SS	3	13-2B	0
2007	TEX	MLB	30	345	42	13	3	8	28	29	72	1	0	0.1	.230	.300	.373	.229	.300	.380	.238	1.4	-0.1	61-3B	1	13-SS	4
2008	TEX	MLB	31	347	44	18	3	6	40	38	66	0	1	-1.4	.290	.365	.430	.293	.370	.441	.281	17.4	0.8	60-3B	-6	16-SS	-2
2009	PIT	MLB	32	239	17	7	0	1	16	31	47	1	0	-0.5	.230	.335	.279	.240	.339	.294	.233	-0.4	-0.6	22-SS	-5	18-2B	-1
2010	PIT	MLB	33	334	37	14	2	7	31	37	73	1	1	-0.2	.248	.335	.381	.245	.331	.372	.253	9.1	1.0	67-SS	0		

Breakout: 12%   Improve: 38%   Collapse: 19%   Attrition: 23%   MLB: 81%   Comparables: Craig Counsell, Grady Hatton, Dale Mitchell, Todd Walker

Vazquez was the closest thing the Pirates had to a major acquisition in the 2008-2009 offseason, as he signed a two-year, $4 million contract as a free agent. Even with such modest standards in play, he managed to disappoint, which was predictable enough, given his Texas-generated park power and a hip-hoppity career-high .349 BABIP in 2008.

Worse yet, he was found to be so wanting on defense that the Pirates became hesitant to play him at short, and even after dealing away both starting middle infielders, turning to Vazquez as a starter seemed inconceivable. Vazquez's utility as a utilityman who can only play second and third seems decidedly unfascinating, but he's under contract, so he'll stay, if not play.

Neil Walker   **3B**   Bats: S   Throws: R   Height: 6' 3"   Weight: 215   Born: September 10, 1985   Age: 24

YEAR	TEAM	LVL	AGE	PA	R	2B	3B	HR	RBI	BB	SO	SB	CS	EqBRR	AVG	OBP	SLG	EqAVG	EqOBP	EqSLG	EqA	VORP	WARP	DEFENSE	
2007	ALT	AA	21	490	77	30	3	13	66	53	73	9	4	2.0	.288	.362	.462	.269	.333	.426	.264	12.5	0.7	113-3B	-7
2007	IND	AAA	21	69	7	3	0	0	0	2	13	1	1	-0.9	.203	.261	.250	.200	.246	.246	.165	-4.6	-0.7	17-3B	-1
2008	IND	AAA	22	550	69	25	7	16	80	29	102	10	6	-0.9	.242	.280	.414	.241	.276	.404	.235	-1.7	0.5	124-3B	6
2009	IND	AAA	23	390	38	31	2	14	69	26	60	5	2	-0.3	.264	.311	.480	.266	.311	.485	.269	14.3	0.2	90-3B	-13
2009	PIT	MLB	23	40	5	1	0	0	0	4	11	1	0	-0.4	.194	.275	.222	.194	.275	.222	.187	-2.3	-0.3	8-3B	-1
2010	PIT	MLB	24	460	57	25	3	14	62	36	88	5	3	-0.1	.251	.310	.420	.253	.311	.423	.252	8.0	0.6	107-3B	-2

Breakout: 21% Improve: 45% Collapse: 14% Attrition: 14%   MLB: 46%   Comparables: Greg Norton, Jose Fernandez, Kevin Roberson, Donny Leon

The Pirates called Walker up on September 1st with roster expansion to great fanfare, as he was the local kid who had (finally) made good. He had been the team's first-round pick in 2004 after starring as a switch-hitting high-school catcher in Pittsburgh's northern suburbs. But John Russell refused to play Walker ahead of Andy LaRoche, which shows how little faith the manager had in the hometown hero. Beyond picking him in the first place, perhaps the Pirates' biggest mistake with Walker was moving him out from behind the plate in 2007. He lost much of his of-fensive value with the move to third base, and while he has worked hard at it, he's not an asset with the glove there, either. As a hitter, Walker has seen his career already be handicapped by an inability to work for walks or to hit left-ies; that would be less of a problem if he could catch, and his hitting .278/.319/.527 against Triple-A right-handers last year suggests that he'd have had some value as a bat while playing behind the plate.

Delwyn Young   **OF/2B**   Bats: S   Throws: R   Height: 5' 10"   Weight: 210   Born: June 30, 1982   Age: 28

YEAR	TEAM	LVL	AGE	PA	R	2B	3B	HR	RBI	BB	SO	SB	CS	EqBRR	AVG	OBP	SLG	EqAVG	EqOBP	EqSLG	EqA	VORP	WARP	DEFENSE			
2007	LVG	AAA	25	537	107	54	5	17	97	38	105	4	3	-0.3	.337	.384	.571	.279	.324	.463	.268	14.1	-0.3	52-LF	-3	51-RF	-14
2007	LAN	MLB	25	36	4	1	1	2	3	2	5	1	0	0.3	.382	.417	.647	.382	.417	.647	.356	4.6	0.6	5-LF	0		
2008	LVG	AAA	26	56	14	5	1	3	10	7	8	0	0	0.2	.347	.429	.673	.280	.357	.520	.294	3.2	0.5	8-RF	1	3-LF	0
2008	LAN	MLB	26	143	10	9	0	1	7	14	34	0	0	-0.1	.246	.321	.341	.252	.326	.354	.242	-1.1	-0.4	10-LF	-2	8-RF	-1
2009	PIT	MLB	27	388	40	16	2	7	43	29	90	2	0	-0.3	.266	.326	.381	.279	.336	.403	.258	7.7	-0.3	51-2B	-9	25-RF	-2
2010	PIT	MLB	28	380	46	20	2	9	41	32	87	2	1	0.0	.258	.323	.403	.261	.324	.410	.253	8.8	0.3	70-2B	-6		

Breakout: 11% Improve: 41% Collapse: 18% Attrition: 7%   MLB: 75%   Comparables: Keith Ginter, Jim Lefebvre, Brendan Harris, Denny Hocking

Following their dealing Sanchez to the Giants, the Pirates were clearly thinking outside the box when they handed the second-base job to the defensively challenged Young, who had been serving as a reserve outfielder. They felt Young would give them a potent bat in a lineup weakened by their trading away five regulars since Opening Day. Young, however, seemed to get worn out physically and mentally from all the extra pregame defensive work he put in and completely stopped hitting, and he was still nightmarishly inept at the keystone. The Pirates pulled the plug on the experiment in November by trading for Akinori Iwamura, which should push Young back into the pinch-hitting role he's had success with.

PITCHERS

Ramon Aguero

| | | | | | | | | | | | Bats: R | | Throws: R | | Height: 6' 4" | | Weight: 175 | | Born: December 21, 1984 | | Age: 25 |

YEAR	TEAM	LVL	AGE	W	L	SV	G	GS	IP	H	HR	BB	SO	GB%	BABIP	STUFF	WHIP	ERA	SIERA	DERA	EqH9	EqHR9	EqBB9	EqSO9	VORP	SN/WX
2008	SCO	A-	23	1	10	0	15	10	49¹	64	3	22	35	51%	.353	-17	1.74	6.75	4.71	11.61	12.5	2.1	4.9	2.8	-32.4	-2.40
2009	WVA	A	24	1	2	0	20	3	49²	58	5	16	40	50%	.342	-28	1.49	4.71	4.06	8.48	14.2	2.9	4.6	4.0	-14.2	-1.55
2009	LYN	A+	24	1	0	0	11	0	21²	20	1	9	22	55%	.306	12	1.34	2.49	3.57	5.57	9.4	1.3	4.3	5.6	-0.2	0.06
2009	ALT	AA	24	0	2	4	8	0	12²	8	0	6	13	41%	.250	12	1.11	2.84	3.61	3.65	6.6	0.7	4.4	6.6	2.5	0.11
2010	PIT	MLB	22	2	6	8	44	4	72	91	13	38	41	51%	.327	-15	1.80	6.91	5.33	7.47	11.5	1.6	4.5	4.9	-15.8	-0.21

Breakout: 38% Improve: 74% Collapse: 7% Attrition: 7%   MLB: 0%   Comparables: James Foley, Tim Reid, Mickey Torres, Anthony Carter

Aguero was originally known as Samuel Vazquez when he signed with the Pirates, but was caught in the Immigration Department's crackdown on fake birth certificates in 2008. Under any name, he showed no signs of being a prospect starting for short-season State College that year, so the Pirates converted him to relief early last season at Low-A, and he dazzled so much with a fastball that consistently hit 95-97 mph that he wound up being placed on the 40-man roster in November. The Pirates love hard-throwing relievers, and Aguero is a sleeper to make the bullpen out of spring training and possibly make an impact.

Tim Alderson

| | | | | | | | | | | | Bats: R | | Throws: R | | Height: 6' 6" | | Weight: 217 | | Born: November 3, 1988 | | Age: 21 |

YEAR	TEAM	LVL	AGE	W	L	SV	G	GS	IP	H	HR	BB	SO	GB%	BABIP	STUFF	WHIP	ERA	SIERA	DERA	EqH9	EqHR9	EqBB9	EqSO9	VORP	SN/WX
2008	SJO	A+	19	13	4	0	26	26	145¹	125	4	34	124	47%	.292	25	1.09	2.79	3.47	4.42	9.2	1.1	2.8	4.8	16.0	2.11
2009	SJO	A+	20	1	1	0	5	5	26	31	4	3	20	47%	.325	11	1.31	4.15	3.62	6.26	14.1	3.5	2.0	3.9	-1.9	-0.17
2009	NRW	AA	20	6	1	0	13	13	72²	76	5	14	46	48%	.296	15	1.24	3.47	4.25	5.37	11.0	1.8	2.1	3.7	1.0	0.23
2009	ALT	AA	20	3	1	0	7	7	38²	39	4	13	18	53%	.267	9	1.34	4.66	5.13	6.33	9.6	1.7	3.1	2.6	-3.5	-0.50
2010	PIT	MLB	21	6	9	0	26	25	129	141	18	49	64	44%	.294	16	1.48	4.94	5.31	5.36	10.0	1.3	3.2	4.3	-2.0	2.75

Breakout: 21% Improve: 63% Collapse: 10% Attrition: 10%   MLB: 5%   Comparables: Kyle Waldrop, Fausto Macey, John Nicholson, Chris Volstad

The Pirates acquired Alderson from the Giants in the Freddy Sanchez trade. The Giants' first-round draft pick in 2007, Alderson was considered one of the top pitching prospects in baseball coming into the last season. However, his stuff wasn't crisp and his control was lacking after he joined Altoona. When he's right, Alderson has an outstanding curveball that complements an above-average fastball. Considering Alderson's youth, there is no cause for great alarm about his struggles as a Pirate, though it will be interesting to see how he responds to pitching at Triple-A this year. A good minor-league season will certainly get him a September call-up at the very least.

Matt Capps

| | | | | | | | | | | | Bats: R | | Throws: R | | Height: 6' 2" | | Weight: 245 | | Born: September 3, 1983 | | Age: 26 |

YEAR	TEAM	LVL	AGE	W	L	SV	G	GS	IP	H	HR	BB	SO	GB%	BABIP	STUFF	WHIP	ERA	SIERA	DERA	EqH9	EqHR9	EqBB9	EqSO9	VORP	SN/WX
2007	PIT	MLB	23	4	7	18	76	0	79	64	5	16	64	34%	.260	23	1.01	2.28	3.69	2.41	6.5	0.6	1.6	6.4	27.6	4.22
2008	PIT	MLB	24	2	3	21	49	0	53²	47	5	5	39	34%	.262	7	0.97	3.02	3.65	3.27	7.4	0.8	0.7	5.5	13.3	1.91
2009	PIT	MLB	25	4	8	27	57	0	54¹	73	10	17	46	47%	.360	-20	1.66	5.80	3.99	6.00	12.0	1.8	2.3	6.3	-3.0	-1.33
2010	WAS	MLB	26	4	4	19	66	0	66¹	63	7	18	48	40%	.287	2	1.22	3.61	4.13	4.09	8.8	1.0	2.3	6.1	10.4	1.19

Breakout: 15% Improve: 41% Collapse: 24% Attrition: 17%   MLB: 100%   Comparables: Chad Cordero, Turk Farrell, Yhency Brazoban, Esteban Yan

Capps had a miserable 2009 after having established himself as a rising young closer in the previous two seasons. He had showed impeccable control up until last season, when he continually fell behind in the count, producing his spiking walk and homer rates as he missed inside the zone and out. Capps has battled shoulder and elbow problems the last two years, and there's a nagging suspicion that he's paying the toll for being used 161 times by former manager Jim Tracy in 2006 and 2007. Signed to a one-year deal by the Nationals in December, Capps goes from heading up the worst bullpen in the NL to the second-worst (as measured by WXRL). He's young enough to recover his old command and to become a bigger hero in the nation's capital than, say, William Henry Harrison Beadle.

Jesse Chavez

Bats: R   Throws: R   Height: 6' 2"   Weight: 170   Born: August 21, 1983   Age: 26

YEAR	TEAM	LVL	AGE	W	L	SV	G	GS	IP	H	HR	BB	SO	GB%	BABIP	STUFF	WHIP	ERA	SIERA	DERA	EqH9	EqHR9	EqBB9	EqSO9	VORP	SN/WX
2007	IND	AAA	23	3	3	2	46	1	80¹	94	4	17	65	42%	.345	-7	1.38	3.92	3.77	5.51	10.8	0.9	2.1	5.3	-0.1	-0.52
2008	IND	AAA	24	2	6	14	51	0	68²	58	8	22	70	48%	.272	-12	1.17	3.80	3.22	4.73	8.8	1.8	3.0	6.4	5.6	-0.11
2008	PIT	MLB	24	0	1	0	15	0	15	20	2	9	16	58%	.383	-6	1.93	6.60	3.99	6.32	11.5	1.1	4.6	7.5	-1.4	-0.58
2009	PIT	MLB	25	1	4	0	73	0	67¹	69	11	22	47	44%	.283	-17	1.35	4.01	4.41	4.55	9.2	1.6	2.6	5.3	7.0	0.12
2010	ATL	MLB	26	4	5	2	63	0	70¹	76	10	27	45	44%	.303	-13	1.46	4.73	4.78	5.25	10.0	1.3	3.2	5.2	2.0	0.10

Breakout: 15%   Improve: 37%   Collapse: 13%   Attrition: 9%   MLB: 77%   Comparables: Tim Drummond, Mike Henneman, Brian Allen, Chuck Crim

Russell lobbied hard for Chavez to be on the Pirates' Opening Day roster last season, even though the rail-thin right-hander had a miserable spring training. To some extent, the skipper made the right call, as Chavez had an adequate first full season in the majors in a low-leverage role. Chavez is aggressive with a 95 mph fastball and complements it with a solid changeup, although sometimes he gets *too* aggressive and leaves pitches out over the middle of the plate. Traded twice over the winter (to the Rays for Iwamura and then to the Braves for Rafael Soriano), he'll be a live arm trying to get Bobby Cox's attention in camp.

Anthony Claggett

Bats: S   Throws: R   Height: 6' 2"   Weight: 185   Born: July 15, 1984   Age: 25

YEAR	TEAM	LVL	AGE	W	L	SV	G	GS	IP	H	HR	BB	SO	GB%	BABIP	STUFF	WHIP	ERA	SIERA	DERA	EqH9	EqHR9	EqBB9	EqSO9	VORP	SN/WX
2007	TAM	A+	22	9	8	2	32	16	112¹	119	7	31	76	50%	.311	-17	1.34	3.69	4.27	5.62	11.1	1.4	3.1	4.2	-1.4	-0.24
2008	TRN	AA	23	4	2	9	29	0	58²	52	1	30	55	55%	.300	0	1.40	2.15	3.99	3.78	9.6	0.6	4.7	5.8	10.7	1.35
2009	SWB	AAA	24	7	7	4	39	5	82	78	6	32	43	54%	.274	-29	1.34	3.07	5.05	4.70	10.0	1.4	3.9	3.6	6.7	0.03
2009	NYA	MLB	24	0	0	0	2	0	2²	11	2	4	3	41%	.643	-49	5.62	33.75	5.94	33.00	33.0	6.0	9.0	9.0	-9.2	-0.06
2009	PIT	MLB	24	0	0	0	1	0	1	2	1	0	0	66%	.250	-46	2.00	9.00	5.68	9.00	18.0	9.0	0.0	0.0	-0.4	-0.01
2010	PIT	MLB	25	3	5	2	42	2	76	90	11	37	40	52%	.313	-22	1.67	5.57	5.35	6.02	10.8	1.3	4.1	4.5	-4.4	1.08

Breakout: 15%   Improve: 44%   Collapse: 23%   Attrition: 19%   MLB: 7%   Comparables: Jim McCready, Dave Lenderman, Barry Johnson, Charlie Isaacson

It seems like any time the Yankees put a pitcher on the waiver wire, the Pirates claim him; Claggett was yet another instance, grabbed during the final days of last season. The Pirates like his sinker/slider combination enough that they will give him a chance to make the club as a middle reliever in spring training, but he has two minor-league options left, and you know the Bucs are likely to use them if he doesn't give them cause to keep him.

Zach Duke

Bats: L   Throws: L   Height: 6' 2"   Weight: 205   Born: April 19, 1983   Age: 27

YEAR	TEAM	LVL	AGE	W	L	SV	G	GS	IP	H	HR	BB	SO	GB%	BABIP	STUFF	WHIP	ERA	SIERA	DERA	EqH9	EqHR9	EqBB9	EqSO9	VORP	SN/WX
2007	PIT	MLB	24	3	8	0	20	19	107¹	161	14	25	41	63%	.368	-24	1.73	5.53	5.06	5.75	12.8	1.2	1.9	3.2	-2.9	0.75
2008	PIT	MLB	25	5	14	0	31	31	185	230	19	47	87	58%	.315	-4	1.50	4.82	4.88	5.13	10.2	1.0	1.9	3.4	7.7	2.24
2009	PIT	MLB	26	11	16	0	32	32	213	231	23	49	106	55%	.293	-1	1.31	4.06	4.72	4.43	9.6	1.1	1.8	3.8	24.8	4.09
2010	PIT	MLB	27	9	12	0	30	30	180	203	23	48	69	59%	.294	-13	1.39	4.52	5.14	5.09	10.5	1.2	2.2	3.3	8.3	1.84

Breakout: 6%   Improve: 39%   Collapse: 16%   Attrition: 6%   MLB: 95%   Comparables: Rick Honeycutt, Allen Watson, Bruce Hurst, Paul Maholm

During the first half of last season, Duke showed the form that made him a rookie sensation back in 2005 down the stretch, which, combined with the selection process's tokenism, got him selected to his first All-Star Game. He followed it with a disastrous second half, going 3-8 with a 5.17 in 14 starts. Duke's stuff has not been the same since he had elbow problems in 2007; though he has never had surgery, he has lost velocity off his fastball and bite on his curve. He still has value as an innings-eater, but his chances of becoming an above-average starter again are getting slimmer with each year that he's further removed from 2005.

Joel Hanrahan

Bats: R   Throws: R   Height: 6' 4"   Weight: 250   Born: October 6, 1981   Age: 28

YEAR	TEAM	LVL	AGE	W	L	SV	G	GS	IP	H	HR	BB	SO	GB%	BABIP	STUFF	WHIP	ERA	SIERA	DERA	EqH9	EqHR9	EqBB9	EqSO9	VORP	SN/WX
2007	COH	AAA	25	5	4	0	15	15	75¹	65	10	36	71	41%	.263	-5	1.34	3.70	4.02	4.93	8.5	1.8	4.3	6.3	4.7	0.44
2007	WAS	MLB	25	5	3	0	12	11	51	59	9	38	43	37%	.318	-8	1.90	6.00	5.24	6.04	10.8	2.0	6.0	6.6	-3.0	0.77
2008	WAS	MLB	26	6	3	9	69	0	84¹	73	9	42	93	45%	.292	12	1.36	3.95	3.50	3.95	7.8	0.9	3.8	8.5	14.5	0.74
2009	WAS	MLB	27	1	3	5	34	0	32²	50	3	14	35	49%	.431	-4	1.96	7.71	3.73	7.16	13.5	0.8	3.2	7.8	-6.1	-0.63
2009	PIT	MLB	27	0	1	0	33	0	31¹	23	0	20	37	32%	.303	19	1.37	1.72	3.74	3.67	7.0	0.0	5.0	9.1	6.2	1.42
2010	PIT	MLB	28	3	5	8	68	2	70	72	9	35	61	44%	.314	-5	1.53	4.88	4.30	5.22	9.3	1.1	4.2	7.3	2.2	0.63

Breakout: 18%   Improve: 49%   Collapse: 17%   Attrition: 20%   MLB: 85%   Comparables: Dave Burba, Aaron Heilman, Kevin Gregg, Willis Roberts

Hanrahan got off to an awful start with the Nationals last season and was twice removed from the closer's role, a job he qualified for solely due to the fact that he was breathing and that somebody is going to get opportunities to protect leads, even a team that had them as infrequently as the Nats. Traded to the Pirates on June 30th, Hanrahan benefited from the change of scenery, as he was able to relax, cut down on his walks and homers allowed, and avoid continued spontaneous combustion. He has an outstanding sinker that he throws in the low 90s and a good slider; in an odd turn of events, he could wind up closing again while Capps takes his place in Washington.

Kevin Hart

Bats: R   Throws: R   Height: 6' 4"   Weight: 220   Born: November 29, 1982   Age: 27

YEAR	TEAM	LVL	AGE	W	L	SV	G	GS	IP	H	HR	BB	SO	GB%	BABIP	STUFF	WHIP	ERA	SIERA	DERA	EqH9	EqHR9	EqBB9	EqSO9	VORP	SN/WX
2007	TEN	AA	24	8	5	0	18	17	102	100	13	27	92	54%	.296	-13	1.25	4.24	3.50	6.26	10.3	1.8	2.6	5.7	-8.1	-0.44
2007	IOW	AAA	24	4	1	0	9	8	56	56	6	23	39	53%	.292	-3	1.41	3.54	4.50	3.98	8.8	1.3	3.8	4.6	9.2	0.85
2007	CHN	MLB	24	0	0	0	8	0	11	7	0	4	13	51%	.280	10	1.00	0.82	2.62	0.87	7.0	0.0	3.5	9.6	5.3	0.38
2008	IOW	AAA	25	4	2	5	26	10	57²	38	3	20	63	52%	.254	14	1.01	2.81	2.95	3.38	6.8	0.8	3.1	7.4	12.9	1.19
2008	CHN	MLB	25	2	2	0	21	0	27²	39	2	18	23	65%	.385	-13	2.06	6.51	4.59	7.39	12.9	0.6	5.1	6.4	-5.9	-0.64
2009	IOW	AAA	26	3	3	3	22	6	52¹	39	5	20	57	52%	.262	4	1.13	3.10	3.16	4.08	8.0	1.6	3.6	7.8	7.9	-0.27
2009	CHN	MLB	26	3	1	0	8	4	27²	23	3	18	13	43%	.238	-7	1.48	2.60	6.11	2.70	7.8	1.0	5.1	3.7	8.3	0.82
2009	PIT	MLB	26	1	8	0	10	10	53¹	74	8	26	39	51%	.369	-18	1.87	6.92	4.74	8.08	12.6	1.5	3.8	5.5	-15.0	-0.50
2010	PIT	MLB	27	5	8	5	45	17	114²	120	15	50	78	48%	.302	-7	1.49	4.96	4.69	5.41	9.7	1.2	3.7	5.9	1.1	1.23

Breakout: 16%   Improve: 39%   Collapse: 16%   Attrition: 21%   MLB: 53%   Comparables: Chad Reineke, Charles Scott, Rick Ramos, Bryan Clutterbuck

The Pirates put Hart into their starting rotation after acquiring him from the Cubs in their deadline deal last season, and he was generally awful. Watching his starts was agonizing, as he would continually nibble at the edges of the strike zone, fall behind in the count, run up big pitch counts in the early innings, and cause his fielders and the fans to nod off. The Pirates believe he has the ability to be a starter, but many scouts feel he is better suited to a short relief role, where he could use his 95 mph fastball and not worry about pacing himself. Hart will have to fight to reclaim a rotation spot in spring training, but if he disappoints his last few believers in the organization, the bullpen beckons.

Steven Jackson

Bats: R   Throws: R   Height: 6' 5"   Weight: 215   Born: March 15, 1982   Age: 28

YEAR	TEAM	LVL	AGE	W	L	SV	G	GS	IP	H	HR	BB	SO	GB%	BABIP	STUFF	WHIP	ERA	SIERA	DERA	EqH9	EqHR9	EqBB9	EqSO9	VORP	SN/WX
2007	TRN	AA	25	0	1	1	10	0	21	20	1	9	16	62%	.297	-19	1.38	3.86	4.10	6.18	10.1	0.9	4.1	5.0	-1.5	0.50
2007	SWB	AAA	25	4	8	0	18	11	69	93	11	29	50	61%	.350	-42	1.77	5.87	4.45	8.78	13.0	2.3	3.8	4.7	-24.3	-1.44
2008	TRN	AA	26	1	3	2	15	0	31¹	28	2	12	37	57%	.338	-3	1.28	5.74	2.87	7.48	10.7	1.6	3.9	8.1	-6.1	-0.54
2008	SWB	AAA	26	3	0	4	34	1	48¹	44	2	19	54	51%	.323	1	1.30	3.17	3.19	4.24	9.7	0.8	3.7	7.3	6.4	1.91
2009	SWB	AAA	27	0	0	1	7	1	14¹	16	1	3	8	41%	.306	-13	1.33	1.88	4.69	2.63	11.2	1.3	2.0	4.0	4.4	0.16
2009	IND	AAA	27	1	0	0	12	0	18	23	1	5	17	67%	.379	-10	1.56	6.50	3.45	8.05	11.9	1.0	2.6	6.2	-4.9	-0.10
2009	PIT	MLB	27	2	3	0	40	0	43	38	2	22	21	46%	.255	-17	1.40	3.14	5.60	4.43	7.6	0.4	3.9	3.5	5.2	0.09
2010	PIT	MLB	28	3	5	1	48	0	68	76	9	31	45	52%	.315	-12	1.57	5.12	4.78	5.53	10.1	1.2	3.8	5.7	-0.3	0.72

Breakout: 26%   Improve: 58%   Collapse: 12%   Attrition: 21%   MLB: 34%   Comparables: Matt Lindstrom, Greg Mix, Travis Hughes, Bob Taylor

Jackson is one of seemingly 173 pitchers the Pirates have claimed off waivers from the Yankees since Neal Huntington became GM. It's enough to make you think the Yankees were an organization known for producing talented young pitchers, but they're not; if the Pirates can succeed where the Bombers failed with their various acquisitions, perhaps the Yankees should try claiming Pirates pitching instructors on waivers. Jackson began last season in the majors with the Yankees, but never got into a game before being sent down. The Pirates claimed him in May, and he shuttled between minor- and major-league bullpens, though he did little to distinguish himself. He'll be given every chance to make the club in spring training because the Pirates like the idea that he can induce lots of ground balls with his sinker ... and he's a former Yankee, so he has to be good, right?

Jeff Karstens

Bats: R Throws: R Height: 6' 3" Weight: 185 Born: September 24, 1982 Age: 27

YEAR	TEAM	LVL	AGE	W	L	SV	G	GS	IP	H	HR	BB	SO	GB%	BABIP	STUFF	WHIP	ERA	SIERA	DERA	EqH9	EqHR9	EqBB9	EqSO9	VORP	SN/WX
2007	SWB	AAA	24	3	0	0	6	5	31	25	2	9	27	42%	.267	12	1.10	1.74	3.60	2.43	7.9	1.2	2.7	6.1	10.1	1.37
2007	NYA	MLB	24	1	4	0	7	3	14²	27	4	9	5	36%	.371	-46	2.45	11.05	6.71	11.74	15.3	2.3	4.7	2.9	-10.6	-0.65
2008	SWB	AAA	25	6	4	0	12	12	68²	66	8	15	55	44%	.290	-7	1.18	3.80	3.66	4.97	10.2	1.8	2.3	5.3	3.7	0.81
2008	PIT	MLB	25	2	6	0	9	9	51¹	56	7	13	23	45%	.277	-8	1.34	4.03	5.13	5.33	8.9	1.4	1.9	3.3	1.0	0.85
2009	PIT	MLB	26	4	6	0	39	13	108	115	12	45	52	44%	.286	-19	1.48	5.42	5.45	5.61	9.4	1.1	3.2	3.6	-1.3	0.24
2010	PIT	MLB	27	4	6	0	28	17	94	102	13	36	51	44%	.297	-10	1.47	4.85	5.13	5.25	10.0	1.3	3.3	4.6	2.6	1.14

Breakout: 17% Improve: 43% Collapse: 15% Attrition: 17% MLB: 65% Comparables: Jeff Shaw, Mike Williams, Willie Blair, Rich Yett

When a touch-and-feel pitcher loses command of his pitches, the results are about as subtle as a subway grope. Karstens' struggles caused him to be moved out of the rotation in early June; he was generally only used in low-leverage relief situations for the rest of the season. He rarely tops 90 mph with his fastball, and his curveball, slider, and changeup are only average pitches. The Pirates dropped him from the 40-man roster last November when they claimed indy league veteran Chris Jakubauskas off waivers from the Mariners, but fear not, Karstens Korner denizens, they re-signed him to a minor-league contract. He'll get a chance to win the long man's job in the bullpen in spring training.

Brad Lincoln

Bats: L Throws: R Height: 6' 0" Weight: 215 Born: May 25, 1985 Age: 25

YEAR	TEAM	LVL	AGE	W	L	SV	G	GS	IP	H	HR	BB	SO	GB%	BABIP	STUFF	WHIP	ERA	SIERA	DERA	EqH9	EqHR9	EqBB9	EqSO9	VORP	SN/WX
2008	HIC	A	23	5	5	0	11	11	62	72	8	6	46	55%	.323	-21	1.26	4.65	3.59	6.43	12.4	2.4	1.7	3.8	-5.9	-0.81
2008	LYN	A+	23	1	5	0	8	8	41²	42	5	11	29	54%	.285	-11	1.27	4.75	4.11	5.90	10.0	2.0	2.7	4.1	-1.8	-0.46
2009	ALT	AA	24	1	5	0	13	13	75	63	4	18	65	45%	.282	13	1.08	2.28	3.43	3.33	8.6	1.2	2.4	5.8	17.0	1.46
2009	IND	AAA	24	6	2	0	12	12	61¹	72	7	10	42	47%	.330	-16	1.34	4.70	3.99	6.39	11.5	2.1	1.7	4.7	-5.7	-0.01
2010	PIT	MLB	25	5	7	0	25	22	112	126	17	38	62	46%	.303	-10	1.47	4.94	4.96	5.38	10.4	1.3	2.9	4.7	1.4	1.78

Breakout: 10% Improve: 46% Collapse: 12% Attrition: 9% MLB: 10% Comparables: Doug McKenzie, Bill Fultz, David Pauley, Rick Shackle

Two years removed from Tommy John surgery, Lincoln finally showed in 2009 why the Pirates chose him ahead of Tim Lincecum in the first round of the 2006 draft ... well, besides his lower signing-bonus demands. Lincoln has a 95 mph fastball, a curveball with a hard break, and an improving changeup. He is also extremely aggressive, attacking hitters and the zone with all three. That mentality hurt at times following his promotion to Triple-A, because hitters with more experience jumped on the many strikes he threw. Lincoln will go back to Indianapolis to start this season, but you can expect he'll work his way into the major-league rotation at some point before the year is out.

Jeffrey Locke

Bats: L Throws: L Height: 6' 2" Weight: 180 Born: November 20, 1987 Age: 22

YEAR	TEAM	LVL	AGE	W	L	SV	G	GS	IP	H	HR	BB	SO	GB%	BABIP	STUFF	WHIP	ERA	SIERA	DERA	EqH9	EqHR9	EqBB9	EqSO9	VORP	SN/WX
2007	DNV	Rk	19	7	1	1	13	11	61	48	2	8	74	54%	.307	20	0.92	2.66	2.06	5.60	10.5	2.0	2.5	5.8	-0.6	0.04
2008	ROM	A	20	5	12	0	25	24	139²	150	6	38	113	55%	.321	18	1.35	4.06	3.82	6.47	10.3	1.4	3.3	3.9	-14.4	-1.57
2009	MYR	A+	21	1	4	0	10	10	45²	47	1	26	43	56%	.346	11	1.60	5.52	4.14	7.55	10.6	1.1	5.7	5.5	-9.6	-0.83
2009	LYN	A+	21	4	4	0	17	17	81²	98	4	18	56	50%	.349	-4	1.42	4.08	4.12	6.36	12.3	1.3	2.7	3.9	-7.1	-0.66
2010	PIT	MLB	22	4	8	0	27	24	108¹	124	16	48	56	48%	.305	-3	1.59	5.41	5.30	5.98	10.6	1.3	3.8	4.5	-5.8	1.54

Breakout: 15% Improve: 50% Collapse: 12% Attrition: 12% MLB: 5% Comparables: Daniel Scarpetta, Ed Riley, Victor Garcia, Joel Adamson

A second-round pick in 2006, Locke was the third element of the McLouth package received from the Braves. He has the immediate virtue of being left-handed while throwing a low-90s fastball and a good curve. He also has problems with consistency in his delivery and with his mechanics, but his command improved after the trade, and he's one of the Bucs' better prospects by default as much as pedigree.

Paul Maholm

Bats: L   Throws: L   Height: 6′ 2″   Weight: 225   Born: June 25, 1982   Age: 28

YEAR	TEAM	LVL	AGE	W	L	SV	G	GS	IP	H	HR	BB	SO	GB%	BABIP	STUFF	WHIP	ERA	SIERA	DERA	EqH9	EqHR9	EqBB9	EqSO9	VORP	SN/WX
2007	PIT	MLB	25	10	15	0	29	29	177^2	204	22	49	105	63%	.312	1	1.42	5.02	4.43	5.16	9.5	1.1	2.2	4.7	6.7	2.32
2008	PIT	MLB	26	9	9	0	31	31	206^1	201	21	63	139	59%	.290	11	1.28	3.71	4.20	3.77	8.5	1.0	2.5	5.2	38.4	5.06
2009	PIT	MLB	27	8	9	0	31	31	194^2	221	14	60	119	57%	.325	4	1.44	4.44	4.51	4.85	10.3	0.7	2.4	4.7	13.6	3.49
2010	PIT	MLB	28	9	11	0	30	29	178^1	186	21	59	99	59%	.293	-1	1.37	4.36	4.69	4.85	9.7	1.1	2.8	4.8	12.8	2.25

Breakout: 5%   Improve: 39%   Collapse: 15%   Attrition: 12%   MLB: 96%   Comparables: Jim Abbott, Denny Neagle, Mark Buehrle, Scott Karl

"Pirates ace" might sound sort of fearsome, sort of like Blackbeard on his best days as far as scary-good, but sadly, Maholm's current claim on the title is more a function of the youth and the talent level of their staff than his ability. He would be a solid third or fourth starter on most clubs, as his average repertoire of four effective pitches (fastball, curve, slider, change) plays up because he has good control and excellent pitching savvy. He is particularly tough on left-handers and has learned to use PNC Park to his advantage, as its 410-foot gap in left-center makes it a difficult park for right-handed batters. Maholm is one of the few players the Pirates refuse to trade, as they believe his work-manlike approach to the game sets a good example on a young team.

Daniel McCutchen

Bats: R   Throws: R   Height: 6′ 2″   Weight: 195   Born: September 26, 1982   Age: 27

YEAR	TEAM	LVL	AGE	W	L	SV	G	GS	IP	H	HR	BB	SO	GB%	BABIP	STUFF	WHIP	ERA	SIERA	DERA	EqH9	EqHR9	EqBB9	EqSO9	VORP	SN/WX
2007	TAM	A+	24	11	2	0	17	16	101	86	7	21	67	44%	.271	-7	1.06	2.50	4.03	3.78	9.6	1.5	2.6	4.3	17.1	1.30
2007	TRN	AA	24	3	2	0	7	7	41	30	2	12	36	43%	.252	10	1.02	2.41	3.56	3.43	8.3	1.2	2.8	5.9	8.7	1.07
2008	TRN	AA	25	4	3	0	9	9	53	43	4	18	52	49%	.279	5	1.15	2.55	3.34	3.91	9.5	1.7	3.4	6.5	8.5	0.81
2008	SWB	AAA	25	4	6	0	11	11	70^1	73	10	11	58	42%	.303	-10	1.19	3.58	3.44	5.05	11.1	2.2	1.7	5.4	3.2	0.59
2008	IND	AAA	25	3	3	0	8	8	48	49	12	7	41	46%	.272	-16	1.17	4.69	3.32	5.54	11.1	3.6	1.6	5.6	-0.2	0.14
2009	IND	AAA	26	13	6	0	24	24	142^2	145	10	29	110	38%	.305	0	1.22	3.47	3.87	4.81	9.6	1.3	2.1	5.2	10.6	1.00
2009	PIT	MLB	26	1	2	0	6	6	36^1	38	6	11	19	48%	.271	-5	1.35	4.21	4.93	4.38	9.3	1.5	2.3	4.0	4.5	0.74
2010	PIT	MLB	27	6	9	0	31	26	137	156	22	46	83	40%	.307	-9	1.47	5.06	4.86	5.53	10.5	1.5	2.8	5.2	-0.5	2.44

Breakout: 9%   Improve: 37%   Collapse: 20%   Attrition: 25%   MLB: 22%   Comparables: Virgil Vasquez, Kyle Denney, Jae Seo, Dave Osteen

Another former Yankee, McCutchen was acquired in 2008 as part of the package for Xavier Nady and Damaso Marte. McCutchen had a strong second half in 2009 at Indianapolis, which got him his chance to make his first major-league starts after being promoted to the Pirates on August 31st. McCutchen is not dominating, as his fastball tops out at 92 mph and his best pitch is a curve. He does, however, have a good idea of how to pitch, befitting someone who graduated with a degree in international finance from Oklahoma. While he may never get to use that degree to figure out how to invest a $100 million contract, he will compete for the Pirates' fifth spot in the rotation in spring training.

Evan Meek

Bats: R   Throws: R   Height: 6′ 0″   Weight: 220   Born: May 12, 1983   Age: 27

YEAR	TEAM	LVL	AGE	W	L	SV	G	GS	IP	H	HR	BB	SO	GB%	BABIP	STUFF	WHIP	ERA	SIERA	DERA	EqH9	EqHR9	EqBB9	EqSO9	VORP	SN/WX
2007	MNT	AA	24	2	1	1	44	0	67	74	2	34	69	62%	.377	-11	1.61	4.30	3.65	5.93	12.0	0.9	4.9	6.7	-2.9	-0.21
2008	ALT	AA	25	1	1	2	9	0	16	14	0	3	17	68%	.318	12	1.06	2.81	2.68	3.52	8.8	0.6	1.8	7.0	3.4	0.28
2008	IND	AAA	25	0	0	2	23	0	41^1	30	2	14	34	66%	.239	-3	1.06	2.40	3.62	3.35	7.1	0.9	3.1	5.1	9.6	0.21
2008	PIT	MLB	25	0	1	0	9	0	13	11	3	12	7	70%	.211	-22	1.77	6.92	5.51	7.27	7.6	2.1	6.9	4.2	-2.6	-0.38
2009	PIT	MLB	26	1	1	0	41	0	47	34	2	29	42	58%	.262	8	1.34	3.45	4.22	3.67	6.8	0.4	4.8	6.9	9.2	0.36
2010	PIT	MLB	27	3	4	1	46	0	63^1	63	7	32	45	62%	.297	-6	1.50	4.59	4.54	4.95	9.0	1.0	4.3	6.1	3.9	0.61

Breakout: 12%   Improve: 49%   Collapse: 25%   Attrition: 10%   MLB: 55%   Comparables: Gabe Dehoyos, Paul Abraham, Brad Salmon, Todd Jones

Meek is a Rule 5 draft success story for the Pirates. They selected him from the Rays at the 2007 Winter Meetings, then worked out a deal to keep him on a minor-league contract, even after he began 2008 in the majors. Meek was the final cut in spring training last season, but he was called back up before April was over and wound up having a good season. His fastball has been clocked as high as 98 mph, and he vows to reach 100 this year. A Pirate with higher ambitions? Sounds good to us. If he can develop a decent off-speed pitch and better control, he has a chance to be a closer, perhaps sooner rather than later.

Bryan Morris

| | Bats: L | Throws: R | Height: 6' 3" | Weight: 200 | Born: March 28, 1987 | Age: 23 |

YEAR	TEAM	LVL	AGE	W	L	SV	G	GS	IP	H	HR	BB	SO	GB%	BABIP	STUFF	WHIP	ERA	SIERA	DERA	EqH9	EqHR9	EqBB9	EqSO9	VORP	SN/WX
2008	HIC	A	21	0	2	0	3	3	14^1	17	2	12	11	49%	.319	-3	2.02	5.02	5.36	7.09	12.2	2.7	9.4	4.1	-2.4	-0.24
2008	GRL	A	21	2	4	0	17	17	81^2	74	5	31	72	59%	.297	0	1.29	3.20	3.72	5.56	10.0	1.8	4.5	4.6	-0.5	-0.13
2009	LYN	A+	22	4	9	0	15	15	72^2	87	2	34	32	63%	.320	-30	1.67	5.57	5.09	9.37	11.4	1.0	4.8	2.1	-29.9	-2.10
2010	PIT	MLB	23	2	6	0	24	13	70^2	83	11	42	31	58%	.304	-22	1.77	5.99	5.69	6.46	10.8	1.4	5.0	3.8	-7.6	0.56

Breakout: 29% Improve: 56% Collapse: 16% Attrition: 15%   MLB: 2%   Comparables: Michael Saatzer, Craig Hanson, Pete Estrada, Rob Radlosky

Morris was considered to have the most upside of the four players the Pirates received from the Dodgers and Red Sox in the 2008 Jason Bay–Manny Ramirez tricorne swap. However, a combination of injuries to his shoulder and foot, along with mediocre to downright poor performances, have made Morris a disappointment since he came over. Morris has a pedigree, as he was a first-round pick in 2006, and he has stuff, blending low-90s heat with a big-bending curve, but he has had trouble staying on the mound (he also missed the 2007 season following Tommy John surgery). The Pirates still believe in him enough to have placed him on the 40-man roster after last season, but at some point, he has to perform to continue warranting his reputation as a prospect.

Charlie Morton

| | Bats: R | Throws: R | Height: 6' 4" | Weight: 190 | Born: November 12, 1983 | Age: 26 |

YEAR	TEAM	LVL	AGE	W	L	SV	G	GS	IP	H	HR	BB	SO	GB%	BABIP	STUFF	WHIP	ERA	SIERA	DERA	EqH9	EqHR9	EqBB9	EqSO9	VORP	SN/WX
2007	MIS	AA	23	4	6	0	41	6	79^2	80	3	37	67	55%	.325	-15	1.47	4.29	4.18	5.67	10.2	1.0	4.3	4.9	-1.4	0.16
2008	RIC	AAA	24	5	2	0	13	12	79	51	0	27	72	59%	.242	33	0.99	2.05	3.45	2.71	5.7	0.3	3.1	5.9	24.2	2.18
2008	ATL	MLB	24	4	8	0	16	15	74^2	80	9	41	48	61%	.290	-13	1.62	6.15	4.88	6.72	9.5	1.2	4.3	4.8	-10.3	0.45
2009	GWN	AAA	25	7	2	0	10	10	64^2	52	3	16	55	48%	.275	17	1.05	2.51	3.48	3.32	8.4	0.9	2.6	6.2	14.5	1.62
2009	PIT	MLB	25	5	9	0	18	18	97	102	7	40	62	53%	.315	3	1.46	4.55	4.71	4.66	9.7	0.7	3.3	5.0	8.6	2.35
2010	PIT	MLB	26	7	9	0	38	22	133^2	130	15	59	83	54%	.283	-1	1.41	4.44	4.81	4.84	9.0	1.0	3.7	5.3	9.9	2.43

Breakout: 4% Improve: 41% Collapse: 18% Attrition: 13%   MLB: 75%   Comparables: Matt Green, Jason Rakers, Chandler Martin, Frank Seminara

Seemingly everybody believes Morton has the stuff to be a quality major-league starting pitcher ... except Charlie Morton. A lack of confidence is the only knock on the slender starter with a 95 mph fastball that has great movement, along with three other potentially good pitches in his curveball, slider, and changeup. Morton was one of the three players acquired from the Braves in the McLouth trade, and he joined the rotation in short order. He hit his low point in mid-August, when he was tagged for 10 runs by the Cubs in little more than an inning, but he came back to shut the Cubs out on four hits at Wrigley Field in his final start of the season, perhaps giving him a shot of confidence for 2010.

Danny Moskos

| | Bats: R | Throws: L | Height: 6' 1" | Weight: 210 | Born: April 28, 1986 | Age: 24 |

YEAR	TEAM	LVL	AGE	W	L	SV	G	GS	IP	H	HR	BB	SO	GB%	BABIP	STUFF	WHIP	ERA	SIERA	DERA	EqH9	EqHR9	EqBB9	EqSO9	VORP	SN/WX
2007	SCO	A-	21	0	0	1	11	0	12^2	19	1	6	13	48%	.409	-7	1.97	4.26	4.01	7.30	15.3	2.2	5.1	5.1	-2.5	-0.52
2008	LYN	A+	22	7	7	0	29	20	110^1	124	8	43	78	59%	.325	-21	1.51	5.95	4.34	7.70	11.0	1.5	4.0	4.2	-25.5	-2.40
2009	ALT	AA	23	11	10	0	27	25	149	159	11	58	77	64%	.301	-20	1.46	3.74	4.78	5.34	10.6	1.4	3.8	3.2	2.4	-0.44
2010	PIT	MLB	24	4	8	0	30	20	110^2	130	16	55	46	58%	.303	-27	1.68	5.67	5.60	6.26	10.9	1.3	4.2	3.6	-9.3	0.65

Breakout: 16% Improve: 44% Collapse: 13% Attrition: 10%   MLB: 9%   Comparables: Brian Bogusevic, Jon Connolly, Eddie Pierce, Chuck Hensley

Moskos will forever be known in Pittsburgh as the man who was selected one pick ahead of Matt Wieters in the 2007 draft. The selection created such a fan backlash that many observers believe this is what pushed ownership to finally fire general manager Dave Littlefield. It's small consolation that Moskos finally had a decent year at Altoona last season, but his strikeout rate, despite secondhand improvement, was alarmingly low for a purported power pitcher; the Pirates openly admit that his fastball and slider are nowhere near as good as when he was a college standout at Clemson. Moskos's best bet to pitch in the major leagues may be as a situational lefty.

Ross Ohlendorf

Bats: R   Throws: R   Height: 6' 4"   Weight: 235   Born: August 8, 1982   Age: 27

YEAR	TEAM	LVL	AGE	W	L	SV	G	GS	IP	H	HR	BB	SO	GB%	BABIP	STUFF	WHIP	ERA	SIERA	DERA	EqH9	EqHR9	EqBB9	EqSO9	VORP	SN/WX
2007	SWB	AAA	24	3	3	0	21	9	66^1	86	7	24	48	56%	.361	-27	1.66	5.02	4.35	6.21	12.7	1.7	3.5	4.9	-4.9	-0.77
2007	NYA	MLB	24	0	0	0	6	0	6^1	5	1	2	9	60%	.286	6	1.11	2.84	2.08	2.84	7.1	1.4	2.8	9.9	1.9	0.14
2008	SWB	AAA	25	1	1	0	5	5	22^1	28	0	5	25	68%	.406	12	1.48	4.03	2.89	5.27	12.7	0.4	2.1	7.2	0.5	0.23
2008	NYA	MLB	25	1	1	0	25	0	40	50	7	19	36	52%	.347	-8	1.72	6.52	4.19	6.42	10.4	1.3	3.8	7.3	-4.1	-0.57
2008	IND	AAA	25	4	3	0	7	7	46^2	46	7	8	40	42%	.295	-1	1.16	3.47	3.34	4.29	10.5	2.3	1.9	5.7	5.8	0.61
2008	PIT	MLB	25	0	3	0	5	5	22^2	36	3	12	13	49%	.388	-20	2.12	6.35	5.38	6.95	13.5	1.2	4.0	4.4	-3.6	-0.27
2009	PIT	MLB	26	11	10	0	29	29	176^2	165	25	53	109	46%	.264	0	1.23	3.92	4.55	4.21	8.5	1.4	2.4	4.7	24.5	3.93
2010	PIT	MLB	27	7	10	0	38	24	143^2	156	20	50	90	53%	.303	-5	1.43	4.76	4.61	5.20	10.0	1.3	2.9	5.4	4.8	1.29

Breakout: 15%   Improve: 53%   Collapse: 9%   Attrition: 10%   MLB: 83%   Comparables: Steve Shields, Doug Brocail, Nick Blackburn, Jason Bergmann

Ohlendorf became a reliable starting pitcher in his first full major-league season in 2009, consistently giving the Pirates good outings. For most of the season, his fastball sat right around 90 mph, which he complemented with a good slider. But the fastball jumped to 94 mph in the final two months, the same velocity he'd shown as a reliever with the Yankees. Ohlendorf is a quick learner, befitting an Ivy Leaguer from Princeton; he also operates a cattle ranch with his father on the outskirts of Austin, Texas, and is a pretty slick networker. He caught a ceremonial first pitch from Department of Agriculture Tom Vilsack last season at PNC Park and turned the meeting into an off-season internship in Washington. Note that SIERA predicts some regression, bringing to mind Casey Stengel's quip about Mike Marshall: "He has wonderful stuff and wonderful control and throws strikes, which shows he's educated. But then, say you're educated and you can't throw strikes; they don't leave you in too long."

Jeff Sues

Bats: R   Throws: R   Height: 6' 4"   Weight: 230   Born: June 8, 1983   Age: 27

YEAR	TEAM	LVL	AGE	W	L	SV	G	GS	IP	H	HR	BB	SO	GB%	BABIP	STUFF	WHIP	ERA	SIERA	DERA	EqH9	EqHR9	EqBB9	EqSO9	VORP	SN/WX
2007	HIC	A	24	3	2	0	8	8	31^1	37	9	19	26	29%	.308	-32	1.79	7.18	5.05	8.79	12.6	4.1	6.3	4.7	-10.5	-0.87
2008	LYN	A+	25	1	1	2	13	0	21^1	11	3	6	17	46%	.151	-10	0.80	2.11	3.62	3.15	5.4	2.3	3.2	4.9	5.2	0.33
2008	ALT	AA	25	3	1	1	24	0	43	35	3	20	55	42%	.302	6	1.28	3.77	2.92	4.71	8.6	1.1	4.1	8.6	3.7	-0.16
2009	ALT	AA	26	2	6	2	40	0	78^2	66	7	37	74	42%	.269	-14	1.31	4.46	3.96	5.78	8.5	1.5	4.2	6.1	-2.4	-1.35
2009	IND	AAA	26	0	0	0	8	0	12	13	1	8	12	44%	.353	-1	1.75	6.00	4.35	8.59	11.5	1.6	6.5	7.4	-3.8	0.03
2010	PIT	MLB	27	3	5	1	40	0	66	67	10	35	49	35%	.295	-9	1.55	5.15	5.00	5.57	9.4	1.3	4.5	6.4	-0.5	0.44

Breakout: 21%   Improve: 56%   Collapse: 18%   Attrition: 22%   MLB: 9%   Comparables: Marcus Gwyn, Rodney Ormond, Ryan Houston, Beau Vaughan

Sues created some buzz in 2008 when he was named the Pirates' minor-league pitcher of the year after struggling for three previous seasons to recover from shoulder surgery. For an encore, however, Sues delivered another disappointment in '09, as his strikeout rate dipped and his velocity was down after he had routinely touched 96-97 mph with his fastball in '08. The Pirates haven't given up on him, but he lost some of his luster last season and is at an age where he needs to take another step forward. Failing that, Sues can always take legal action.

Ronald Uviedo

Bats: R   Throws: R   Height: 6' 1"   Weight: 160   Born: October 7, 1986   Age: 23

YEAR	TEAM	LVL	AGE	W	L	SV	G	GS	IP	H	HR	BB	SO	GB%	BABIP	STUFF	WHIP	ERA	SIERA	DERA	EqH9	EqHR9	EqBB9	EqSO9	VORP	SN/WX
2007	LYN	A+	20	0	0	0	4	0	11	9	2	3	7	45%	.219	10	1.09	4.09	4.39	5.23	8.7	2.6	2.6	3.5	0.3	-0.11
2007	SCO	A-	20	2	0	12	21	0	20^2	16	4	3	26	36%	.267	18	0.92	3.92	1.71	5.35	10.7	4.6	2.0	7.6	0.3	0.56
2008	HIC	A	21	3	1	5	33	0	71^2	70	8	15	76	40%	.308	-8	1.19	3.01	2.86	5.13	10.7	2.2	2.8	5.8	2.7	-0.41
2008	LYN	A+	21	0	0	0	7	0	16	5	1	5	12	46%	.100	15	0.62	2.25	3.85	2.87	3.4	1.1	2.9	4.6	4.6	0.09
2009	LYN	A+	22	5	5	3	23	18	101^2	98	12	28	79	45%	.283	-20	1.24	3.36	3.94	5.04	10.2	2.3	3.1	4.5	4.9	0.15
2010	PIT	MLB	23	3	7	2	35	13	90^2	105	16	37	52	38%	.306	-12	1.57	5.49	5.24	5.95	10.6	1.6	3.5	5.0	-4.6	1.77

Breakout: 7%   Improve: 38%   Collapse: 25%   Attrition: 11%   MLB: 3%   Comparables: Ernesto Frieri, Ralph Diaz, Charles McHugh, T.J. Nall

Uviedo was a surprise addition to the 40-man roster following the 2008 season after spending most of the year relieving at Low-A. The Pirates converted Uviedo to a starter last season at Lynchburg, and he did quite well until being sidelined for six weeks at midseason with shoulder tendinitis. Uviedo has a 94 mph fastball and a very good changeup, and he throws strikes. His ability to add a breaking pitch as he heads to Double-A will ultimately determine whether he remains a starter or goes back to the bullpen.

Virgil Vasquez

Bats: R   Throws: R   Height: 6' 3"   Weight: 205   Born: June 7, 1982   Age: 28

YEAR	TEAM	LVL	AGE	W	L	SV	G	GS	IP	H	HR	BB	SO	GB%	BABIP	STUFF	WHIP	ERA	SIERA	DERA	EqH9	EqHR9	EqBB9	EqSO9	VORP	SN/WX
2007	TOL	AAA	25	12	5	0	25	25	155	139	18	33	127	40%	.275	-9	1.11	3.48	3.60	4.71	9.5	1.9	2.1	5.6	12.7	1.60
2007	DET	MLB	25	0	1	0	5	3	16²	27	7	5	7	54%	.328	-31	1.92	8.64	5.33	8.10	14.0	3.8	2.2	3.2	-4.8	-0.29
2008	TOL	AAA	26	12	12	0	27	27	159	179	27	37	115	41%	.304	-30	1.36	4.81	4.15	5.91	10.8	2.4	2.3	4.5	-7.0	0.15
2009	IND	AAA	27	7	4	0	19	19	107²	116	14	16	72	50%	.298	-24	1.23	3.93	3.98	5.06	10.5	2.3	1.6	4.5	5.0	0.65
2009	PIT	MLB	27	2	5	0	14	7	44²	58	6	18	29	44%	.347	-17	1.70	5.84	4.88	6.08	11.7	1.2	3.1	4.9	-2.8	0.35
2010	PIT	MLB	28	5	9	0	32	22	127	146	22	43	76	45%	.307	-12	1.48	5.27	4.78	5.74	10.5	1.5	2.8	5.2	-3.4	1.45

Breakout: 10%   Improve: 51%   Collapse: 20%   Attrition: 20%   MLB: 31%   Comparables: Hugh Kemp, Kennie Steenstra, Jeremy Cummings, Derek Botelho

Vasquez traveled the waiver-wire circuit from the Tigers to the Red Sox to the Padres to the Pirates in the 2008-2009 offseason. The shaggy-headed Vasquez lost out to Karstens in the fight for the fifth starter's job in spring training, but he was back up for a midseason spin in the rotation, logging three quality starts in seven. A soft touch with an epic poem, his stuff is a little short for a full-time starter to spin in the majors. His fastball rarely touches 90 mph, and his curveball, slider, and changeup are adequate. He's the classic "Quad-A" starter, ready at Triple-A to temporarily plug a hole in the big-league rotation when the need arises, but even the Pirates didn't need that for much more than a month.

Donnie Veal

Bats: L   Throws: L   Height: 6' 4"   Weight: 215   Born: September 18, 1984   Age: 25

YEAR	TEAM	LVL	AGE	W	L	SV	G	GS	IP	H	HR	BB	SO	GB%	BABIP	STUFF	WHIP	ERA	SIERA	DERA	EqH9	EqHR9	EqBB9	EqSO9	VORP	SN/WX
2007	TEN	AA	22	8	10	0	28	27	130¹	126	11	73	131	46%	.316	-1	1.53	4.97	4.02	6.59	10.3	1.3	5.1	6.4	-14.8	-1.04
2008	TEN	AA	23	5	10	0	29	29	145¹	150	19	81	123	49%	.316	-18	1.59	4.52	4.45	6.30	10.7	1.8	5.0	5.8	-12.0	-0.65
2009	ALT	AA	24	0	0	0	7	5	13¹	5	0	10	18	54%	.192	13	1.12	1.35	3.26	2.13	5.0	0.7	6.4	9.2	4.7	0.47
2009	IND	AAA	24	0	1	0	9	1	14	6	0	16	13	67%	.182	11	1.57	6.43	5.10	7.76	4.1	0.7	10.8	6.1	-3.4	-0.03
2009	PIT	MLB	24	1	0	0	19	0	16¹	18	2	20	16	38%	.340	1	2.33	7.16	5.85	7.02	10.3	1.1	9.2	7.0	-2.8	-0.08
2010	PIT	MLB	25	3	6	0	44	13	73	76	10	46	55	45%	.307	-13	1.68	5.50	4.99	6.02	9.8	1.2	5.3	6.5	-4.2	0.80

Breakout: 20%   Improve: 52%   Collapse: 16%   Attrition: 26%   MLB: 34%   Comparables: Terry Wells, Rich Scheid, Sherman Corbett, Don Vesling

The Pirates knew the fireballing Veal was going to be a project when they selected him in the Rule 5 draft from the Cubs after he led the Southern League in walks and wild pitches in 2008. They did their best to hide Veal, using him only in blowouts last season (the ones they were losing, leads being too rare to waste on development opportunities) and finding two injuries during the course of the season that allowed him to get sent away on extended rehabilitation assignments to Indianapolis and Altoona. He spent plenty of hours working on the side with pitching coach Joe Kerrigan last season, and the lessons began paying off in the Arizona Fall League, where Veal was dominant. He'll begin this season in the Triple-A rotation, and if his AFL performance was real, then the Pirates might have something to brag about.

LINEOUTS

Hitters

PLAYER	TEAM	LVL	AGE	PA	R	2B	3B	HR	RBI	BB	SO	SB-CS	EqBRR	AVG/OBP/SLG	EqAVG/EqOBP/EqSLG	EqA	VORP	WARP
C R. Diaz	IND	AAA	25	162	18	4	0	3	15	9	12	0-1	-1.6	.262/.308/.349	.260/.306/.340	.226	-0.9	-0.6
	PIT	MLB	25	138	9	7	0	1	19	3	9	0-1	-0.8	.279/.307/.357	.287/.312/.372	.239	2.7	-0.3
2B S. Ford#	ALT	AA	24	117	12	6	0	2	17	12	18	2-0	1.1	.233/.325/.350	.217/.291/.311	.215	-1.8	-0.2
	IND	AAA	24	321	34	11	2	4	27	14	58	8-1	2.3	.188/.240/.279	.190/.239/.280	.182	-15.4	-2.8
CF R. Grossman#	WVA	A	19	535	83	21	2	5	42	75	164	35-12	0.1	.266/.373/.355	.217/.310/.288	.219	-8.4	-0.9
C E. Kratz	IND	AAA	29	353	45	30	0	11	43	31	72	7-0	-3.8	.273/.337/.470	.264/.323/.444	.266	17.7	1.8
C S. Lerud*	ALT	AA	24	363	31	17	0	4	26	38	53	2-1	-2.8	.240/.339/.336	.228/.304/.307	.222	1.7	-0.5
OF S. Marte	WVA	A	20	247	41	9	5	3	34	12	55	24-7	2.8	.312/.377/.439	.252/.296/.357	.231	-1.2	-0.3
OF J. Salazar*	IND	AAA	28	351	43	7	3	10	39	30	57	16-0	1.8	.270/.334/.406	.260/.319/.382	.253	5.4	-0.1
	PIT	MLB	28	26	1	0	0	0	1	3	7	1-0	0.3	.043/.154/.043	.087/.192/.087	-.139	-3.6	-0.5

Robinson Diaz did a decent job filling in as the backup catcher last season when Jaramillo moved into the starting lineup, but the Pirates dropped him from the 40-man roster in November; he signed a minor-league contract with the Tigers. ⊘ **Shelby Ford** was considered a top Pirates prospect going into last season, made a favorable impression in his first big-league spring training, and then had a god-awful year that put his future in limbo. ⊘ The athletic sixth-rounder from the '08 draft for whom the Pirates paid far over slot, **Robbie Grossman** made his full-season debut and showed some quality leadoff man's talents, but will need to work on his strikeouts. ⊘ Known as an organizational player good at handling pitchers, big **Erik Kratz** has hit well enough to earn consideration for some major-league time. ⊘ **Steve Lerud**'s prospect status took an Altoona curve after his previous progress in 2008, which got him outrighted off the 40-man roster at season's end. ⊘ Dominican **Starling Marte** made an excellent stateside debut, flashing the strong arm and athleticism that led the Bucs to sign him in 2006; his OBP was boosted by his taking one for the team as frequently as he drew walks. ⊘ Journeyman **Jeff Salazar** was called up last July to serve as the backup to McCutchen, but he rarely played and was brutal when he did.

Pitchers

PLAYER	TEAM	LVL	AGE	W	L	SV	IP	H	HR	BB	SO	GB%	BABIP	STUFF	WHIP	ERA	SIERA	DERA	EqH9	EqHR9	EqBB9	EqSO9	VORP
J. Ascanio	IOW	AAA	24	2	4	0	51¹	47	1	18	47	58%	.313	9	1.27	3.16	3.64	4.68	9.0	0.6	3.3	6.4	4.4
—	CHN	MLB	24	0	1	0	15¹	18	1	9	18	47%	.395	10	1.76	3.52	3.69	3.60	11.4	0.6	4.8	9.0	3.2
—	PIT	MLB	24	0	1	0	2²	4	0	0	2	33%	.400	-2	1.50	6.75	3.83	6.75	13.5	0.0	0.0	6.8	-0.4
D. Bautista	IND	AAA	28	2	3	1	48	54	2	34	58	40%	.382	3	1.83	4.87	3.96	6.46	10.8	1.0	6.6	8.1	-5.0
—	PIT	MLB	28	1	1	0	13²	15	1	7	15	34%	.378	4	1.61	5.27	3.71	5.54	10.4	0.7	4.2	8.3	-0.1
V. Black	SCO	A-	21	1	2	1	31¹	26	0	15	33	51%	.286	-3	1.31	3.45	3.65	8.13	10.1	1.2	5.5	4.9	-8.6
K. Bloom*	ALT	AA	26	6	9	0	104¹	92	3	57	71	47%	.276	-1	1.43	4.05	4.99	6.01	8.6	0.8	4.9	4.3	-5.8
M. Crotta	ALT	AA	24	7	8	0	143²	181	7	33	97	64%	.345	-13	1.49	4.76	4.10	6.56	11.8	1.0	2.3	4.2	-16.5
M. Dubee	LYN	A+	23	2	0	6	34¹	22	1	3	52	53%	.304	30	0.73	1.05	0.87	2.32	7.8	0.9	1.5	9.6	10.9
—	ALT	AA	23	3	0	1	34	39	5	10	28	52%	.306	-20	1.44	2.91	3.99	6.55	11.0	2.1	2.6	5.0	-4.0
P. Dumatrait*	PIT	MLB	27	0	2	0	13	13	4	11	7	51%	.214	-27	1.85	6.92	6.09	7.71	8.4	2.6	5.8	3.9	-3.4
E. Hacker	TRN	AA	26	1	1	0	15¹	16	0	7	8	69%	.308	-23	1.50	4.11	4.71	7.85	10.7	0.6	4.4	3.1	-3.7
—	SWB	AAA	26	0	1	0	16	19	3	4	12	62%	.327	-14	1.44	7.87	3.95	10.05	13.2	3.1	2.5	5.7	-7.2
—	IND	AAA	26	5	5	0	116¹	135	6	46	82	49%	.345	-12	1.56	4.02	4.57	5.33	11.1	1.1	3.9	4.8	2.1
—	PIT	MLB	26	0	0	0	3	4	0	2	1	70%	.364	-42	2.00	6.00	5.61	6.75	13.5	0.0	6.8	3.4	-0.4
C. Hansen	PIT	MLB	25	0	0	0	6¹	6	1	4	5	28%	.263	-15	1.58	5.68	5.40	5.40	8.1	1.4	4.1	5.4	0.1
J. Hughes	ALT	AA	23	1	6	3	46¹	55	1	16	36	55%	.355	-11	1.53	3.88	4.18	6.90	11.6	0.6	3.2	5.1	-6.9
J. Machi	ALT	AA	26	2	3	6	34²	28	2	13	25	56%	.255	-13	1.18	2.08	4.23	3.78	8.1	1.1	3.5	4.6	6.4
—	IND	AAA	26	1	1	6	17	8	1	6	12	61%	.163	-8	0.82	2.12	3.98	2.81	4.5	1.1	3.4	5.1	4.8
D. Molleken	LYN	A+	24	3	1	1	41¹	36	2	8	42	50%	.304	-2	1.06	3.48	2.85	4.93	9.4	1.2	2.3	6.1	2.4
—	ALT	AA	24	1	1	1	37	37	5	16	26	39%	.274	-28	1.43	4.62	4.80	5.94	9.7	2.2	4.0	4.5	-1.8
R. Owens*	WVA	A	21	10	1	0	100²	71	8	15	91	37%	.235	5	0.85	1.70	3.00	3.49	9.0	2.3	2.5	4.6	20.2
—	LYN	A+	21	1	1	0	23¹	29	3	2	22	45%	.366	18	1.33	3.86	2.95	5.06	13.1	2.5	1.3	5.5	1.0
T. Yates	PIT	MLB	31	0	2	0	12	14	2	7	9	49%	.324	-25	1.75	7.50	4.88	8.87	10.8	1.5	4.6	5.4	-4.4

The Pirates never really got the chance to see what they had in **Jose Ascanio** after acquiring him from the Cubs before he landed on the DL with a shoulder that eventually required surgery in October to repair his rotator cuff; he won't be able to return to game action until at least June. ⊘ **Denny Bautista** generates plenty of velocity on his fastball with his incredibly long legs, but his 4.9 BB/9 keep him from sticking. The Giants will give him a try. ⊘ Hard-throwing **Victor Black** was taken in the supplemental first round of last year's draft from Dallas Baptist, and many scouts feel he could reach the majors quickly if the Pirates make him a reliever. ⊘ **Kyle Bloom** failed to make the Tigers as a Rule 5 pick last spring and was returned to the Bucs, who should consider making him a situational lefty, considering his strong splits. ⊘ Big **Michael Crotta** can dial his fastball up to 94 mph, but tends to get hit much harder his second time through the lineup, two factors that could make him a successful relief candidate. ⊘ **Michael Dubee**, son of Phillies pitching coach Rich Dubee, has an outstanding enough curve to be seen as a fringe prospect. ⊘ A decade since **Phil Dumatrait** was a first-round pick, scouts still cling to the idea that he can someday live up to it, but a career 7.06 ERA and 1.81 WHIP argue against. ⊘ **Eric Hacker** spent eight years in the Yankees' system, getting derailed by Tommy John and shoulder surgeries before getting to pitch for the Pirates in September. ⊘ **Craig Hansen** did not pitch after April 19th because of a rare nerve condition in his neck that caused him to lose strength in his right shoulder; the nerve finally began to regenerate last fall, but there's doubt he'll be strong enough to throw from a mound by the time spring training starts, making his future cloudier than ever. ⦸ **Jared Hughes** seemed to be turning the corner, with a 1.91 ERA through seven starts, but was then sidelined for three months by a strained shoulder and struggled as a reliever afterward; he'll return to Altoona for a third straight season. ⦸ Beefy reliever **Jean Machi** has been a pro for 10 years without reaching the majors, but had such a good season last year the Bucs quickly re-signed him as a minor-league free agent. ⦸ **Dustin Molleken** logged just 108 innings in his first five pro seasons through 2007 because of a variety of arm ailments, but he has kept on plugging and can be considered a fringe relief prospect. ⦸ **Rudy Owens** came out of nowhere to win the Pirates' minor-league pitcher of the year award, along with the Sally League's most outstanding pitcher prize. ⦸ **Tyler Yates** was the primary set-up man in 2008, but Tommy John surgery at the break last season got him dropped from the 40-man; he won't be able to pitch anywhere until June.

MANAGER: JOHN RUSSELL

YEAR	TEAM	W-L	Pythag +/−	Avg PC	100+ P	120+ P	QS	BQS	REL	REL w Zero R	IBB	Subs	PH	PH Avg	PH HR	SB2	CS2	SB3	CS3	SAC Att	SAC %	POS SAC	Squeeze	Swing	In Play
2008	PIT	67-95	1	92.5	57	1	59	4	497	307	31	21	289	.224	3	52	18	5	1	104	63.5%	36	1	92	72
2009	PIT	62-99	-3	93.3	52	1	82	4	456	293	37	9	247	.267	1	81	29	9	2	90	66.7%	27	0	108	83

In a city with passionate sports fans, no manager or coach has flown under the radar in Pittsburgh quite like John Russell in his two seasons as the Pirates' skipper. The fans neither love nor hate Russell; they're just ambivalent. Much of that has to do with Russell's low-key personality. He does nothing to draw attention to himself and rarely shows any emotion, having been ejected from just two games in two years. Russell had the respect of his players during his rookie season of 2008, but things seemed to change once the Pirates made sweeping roster changes in 2009 and went with a young team. Russell's players looked as if they had quit on him during a dreadful September that included 23 losses in 26 games. Russell doesn't do a whole lot to distinguish himself as a strategist other than his tendency to stick with the starting pitchers too long after they have clearly lost their effectiveness; he is clearly wary of burning out the bullpen. The man is very much a delegator, as he puts a lot of trust in his staff, particularly bench coach Gary Varsho and pitching coach Joe Kerrigan. Although Russell's contract expires at the end of this season, his job does not appear to be in jeopardy, especially after he was left with the equivalent of an expansion team following all of general manager Neal Huntington's wheeling and dealing.

St. Louis Cardinals

You have a team. You have the best hitter, arguably the best player, in all of baseball. You have two of the three best starters in the league, two of the best five in baseball. Your mission, which you cannot refuse, is to win a pennant with that as your starting point.

For the Cardinals, that's been the whole ball of wax, waiting for that combination. In Albert Pujols, they have the game's greatest position player, a man at his peak now. In Adam Wainwright and Chris Carpenter, they have past and (perhaps) future Cy Young–level talent. The 2009 season was their first real spin with all three in action over a full season, mostly because of Carpenter's fragility, but Wainwright's finger injury in 2008 didn't help matters any. And beyond that, for as much support as the Cardinals get from the game's best fans, there is apparently only so far that ownership is willing to go. They've afforded themselves three of the game's best, and it's up to management, both in the front office and down in the dugout, to make the rest of the plan add up.

Unfortunately, this hasn't really added up to much, and not all that much has been invested. It's easy to second-guess their December 2006 decision to tear up the contract they already had with Carpenter—a contract that would pay him $15 million for 2007-2008—and hand him $65 million more for the next five. However, it was equally easy to first-guess it at the time. Carpenter was already widely seen as an unreliable commodity, the kind of gamewide great who's either excellent or absent. When Carpenter effectively missed both of those seasons, perhaps there was some solace in the suggestion that at least they still had him under contract for $43.5 million through 2011, with a $15 million club op-

tion for 2012. But the math doesn't really work out on that, either, because his brilliant bum wing went bust in both seasons, which ought to have led to a pretty good discount. No matter, it's only money, right? After all, it worked in 2006, before they were clear on how fully Wainwright would blossom and into what sort of bloom he'd even become.

Having squeaked into the postseason in 2006, the Cards weren't the kind of team with which you could just let it ride and hope that the best players would drag the rest into October action. Yet, the Cardinals have hardly extended themselves to retain their perch. Throwing money at Braden Looper isn't a solution, and the decisions to haul in Adam Kennedy in 2007, Cesar Izturis in 2008, or Khalil Greene in 2009 reflect a willingness to settle for patchwork solutions in the middle infield. Middling plans begat middling results. It would be hard to ascribe the development of Rick Ankiel as a hitter to any master plan, any more than fishing Ryan Ludwick out of the free talent pool represents more than good fortune. Trading away Scott Rolen for Troy Glaus before the 2008 season has subsequently looked both good and bad. Unsurprisingly, given such modest activity, in 2007 and 2008, they were an also-ran club.

The situation has encouraged a certain amount of adaptive activity and creativity derived from more than one source. It's no surprise that this approach comes in part from a front office that, since the abrupt dismissal of Walt Jocketty in 2007, is the product of a generation where creativity is a given, with general manager John Mozeliak providing an arc between "baseball people" and the analysis-oriented types, like scouting director Jeff Luhnow or house quant Sig Mejdal. Yet, perhaps

CARDINALS PROSPECTUS
2009 W-L: 91-71, 1st in NL Central

Pythag	86-76	4th	**Ballpark:** Busch Stadium (3-yr. PF: 963). One of the most pitcher-friendly parks not named Petco
RS/G	4.5	7th	
RA/G	4.0	3rd	
EqA	.265	6th	**2009:** Tremendous front three starters, Pujols, plus a late Holliday dominate in-season, falls flat in October
EqBRR	5.0	3rd	
SNWP	.542	3rd	
WXRL	8.15	8th	**2010:** Stars/scrubs divide might be crippling if Holliday, Pineiro aren't replaced
FRAr	4.02	4th	
DE	.694	5th	
PADE	-0.21	8th	**Action Items:** A bat to keep Albert company, sorting out who the infield and bullpen regulars are
Salary	$88.5	7th	
Attend	3.34	3rd	

paradoxically, the Cardinals also get results from a skipper who has seen his place in the game change from former revolutionary to present-day old-school reactionary, with that transmogrification being almost purely a function of time, not change. Thirty years ago, Tony La Russa was the guy with a computer who had gone to law school. Twenty years ago, some considered him a player's manager and a great communicator. Ten years ago, you could consider him one of the game's enablers of the Performance-Enhanced Era.* And now? We may be no further from the man who was skippering the Winning Ugly White Sox of 1983, complete with pitching coach Dave Duncan by his side.

The La Russa/Duncan combination has been responsible for almost innumerable successful retreading and salvage operations with veteran hurlers. Even as the rotation was struggling to find bodies during Carpenter's operation, Mozeliak was able to haul in veterans like Todd Wellemeyer and Joel Pineiro at negligible cost in 2007, and sign Kyle Lohse before 2008, with expectations that the Cards might get better results than the Twins, Reds, or Phillies had with the fourth starter. By whatever means, Duncan and La Russa take pitchers others can't use and extract outsized value—hook that up to a front office willing to seek out worthwhile subjects for experimentation, and you've got an organization that can afford a little more risk than most when it comes to sorting out the balance of the rotation beyond Wainwright and Carpenter.

But what really is La Russa's legacy as a manager? His present-day signatures are more subtle than the headline moves. Perhaps the more reliable tactical legacy La Russa gets associated with is hyperspecialization in the bullpen, but even then, he's more poster child than sole inventor. He may have given us Rick Honeycutt a little more than 20 years ago, but Honeycutt began his journey to LOOGY-dom at a time when Jesse Orosco and Tony Fossas were well down that path as well, while pitching for other skippers. Even then, several managers had by the late 1980s already been dabbling with situational lefties. But just to pick one of many examples, nobody's going to put Chuck Cottier in the Hall of Fame for using Ed Vande Berg as a situational specialist with the Mariners 25 years ago. If anything, La Russa should be credited with being the eventual recognized thought leader in what was more generally an industry-wide example of multiple discovery. As much as it has become fashionable in sabermetric circles to bash La

Russa for the inevitable late-game tedium, here again it's worth pointing out that the caricature doesn't reflect the reality. In the last five years, La Russa hasn't finished higher than fifth in his own league in relievers used in any one season. In practical terms, the net benefit is that La Russa has consistently rated among the least likely skippers to issue an intentional pass, never getting out of the bottom third in total intentional walks in any of the last five years.

Situational specialization on defense is taken for granted as a necessity in football (pass-rush specialists and nickelbacks) and basketball (shot blockers or designated coolers to ice the hot shooters) and generates its share of stars. We're now more than 20 years into specialization as a fundamental element of how teams operate, and save for the fascination with finding, nominating, and liberally overcompensating the guy who gets to generate save tallies, it has helped transform relief pitching into cohesive units. This is arguably a tactical maladaptation, committing too much of the roster to stunted specialists with limited responsibilities, but teams have long since stopped treating the 25 roster spots as set for any given length of time beyond any individual ballgame, series, or road trip. With the contemporary advantages of modern communication and travel, any general manager worth his salt is going to rotate a half-dozen players through the last couple of slots every fortnight. There is no great counteradaptation that will get the industry out of this tactical cul-de-sac. Expanding rosters to 27 will only provide better job security for second and third left-handers and more space for equally situational righties, not necessarily create jobs for the right-handed bench bats who might potentially make the pitchers' lives more difficult.

What about on offense? Having the pitcher hit eighth is a cute enough gambit, but it's also entirely disposable. And when the lineup is weak enough overall, as the Cards' attack was in 2009, fidgeting over whether Albert Pujols can help make a big inning a fraction bigger becomes a lot less important than the problem of operating a short bench when you're carrying seven or sometimes eight relievers. In 2009, La Russa employed the lineup tactic just 55 times on 156 possible lineup cards (thanks to interleague play, the six games played with the DH in AL ballparks can't be counted). He didn't use it once in September, *after* roster expansion. Even more interesting, in 70 of the 74 Cardinals playoff games that La Russa skippered the Cards and the pitcher has had to bat, the starting pitcher has *never* batted anywhere but ninth. All of which puts the tactic in its proper place. Yes, it's cute and interesting, but per-

---

*There's an appropriate acronym in that era, considering how it came to an end.

haps only interesting for its own sake. Practically speaking, it serves little effective purpose, beyond broadcasting an ability to zag in a ziggy universe.

This last suggestion points to La Russa's great merit. Creative thought doesn't always have to involve practical, meaningful results, but creativity applied to problems produces unusual solutions. When La Russa tries, as George Will documented 20 years ago, to put players in a position to succeed, that doesn't automatically mean that he's been risk-averse. Consider last year's solution to the persistent problem with staffing the middle infield. Before the Cardinals had any idea that Khalil Greene's issues transcended simple on-field concerns, their fix for second base was to turn to Skip Schumaker and attempt a difficult conversion of the fourth outfielder. Though Schumaker was athletic and strong-armed enough to pitch in college, the conversion was a controversial enough proposition for a position player headed into his age-29 season. It's nevertheless worth remembering that Davey Lopes made his conversion from outfielder to second baseman at 26, and it didn't prevent him from having a fine career; it gave him one.

The results were mixed. On defense, Schumaker's season scored a miserable 88 by Clay Davenport's league-adjusted Rate2. He tied for 57th worst among the 817 second basemen who played in 100 games or more in any one season from 1969 to the present and tied for 74th worst, with -14 Fielding Runs below average. So, it was bad, but also better than quite a few seasons from Lopes, or Steve Sax, or Delino DeShields, or a lot of other people who were second basemen playing second base. Collectively, the Cards' keystone contingent wasn't even the worst in the NL in 2009, rating better than the Padres and Pirates. Consequently, the conversion was a survivable tradeoff, endurable because it gave the lineup a better hitter at the position. What's more, although Schumaker's ability to deliver an EqA above .270 doesn't rate better than average in the outfield corners, it was much better than that at second base, where the 2009 average was .267. As a move made from depth, it created lineup space for Colby Rasmus to take over in center, with Chris Duncan, Ankiel, and Ludwick rotating through the corners. It also created the tactical oddity of providing in the outfield a late-game defensive replacement that La Russa could rotate out of the infield, but the manager's love of multiposition regulars goes back to Tony Phillips, if not earlier.

Lurching into fixes might be the best way to characterize most of the other solutions. The messy left side of the infield was resolved by an in-season decision to commit to organizational soldier Brendan Ryan at

shortstop, as well as a trade for Mark DeRosa to paper over the Cards' patchwork of nonanswers at third base. Their decision to make the most of their shot in 2009 was signaled by trading for Matt Holliday, as it became clear that Carpenter's health was reliable enough. The path to victory seemed clear, with the Cubs' injury woes becoming debilitating and the Brewers' pitching proving unsurvivable. It was a sensible play for not simply settling for a division win with the lineup they had. With Wainwright and Carpenter getting the initial assignments in any post-season series, there was cause for confidence about October outcomes. It didn't work, of course, but it was a worthwhile plan to have fallen into.

The question is how long the window is open for this club. Unless they strike a deal with Holliday (and Scott Boras), they're back to relying upon the big three. Their adjusted wins tally for 2009 suggests a squad that should have won 86 games, not 91. They should be competitive with a healthier Cubs club and the reloading Brewers, but that hardly speaks to any real advantage. Moreover, the team's trinity isn't set as permanent features on the roster-scape. It might seem like just yesterday, but Albert Pujols signed his contract extension in February 2004, wiping out his pre-free-agency arbitration years on a deal that, with the club's 2011 option for $16 million, has two more years to go. Think on that—an eight-year contract that has not only paid off, but will also wind up costing the Cardinals considerably less than its on-paper $107 million, because $12 million is deferred to annual interest-free payments of $1.2 million per year from 2020 to 2029.*

Whether the club gets Pujols to agree to a subsequent bargain remains to be seen, but it's hard to imagine the Cardinals' future without him, because they have so little to work with beyond him. It isn't that the Cardinals are entirely a stars-and-scrubs squad; it's that their second rank is made up of so many second bananas who will never graduate to anything more than complementary excellence, whether it be Ludwick or Schumaker or Yadier Molina. There's hope that Rasmus can develop into a star, but without adding a top bat at third base or an outfield corner, the team is in danger of fielding another merely adequate attack, not unlike its 2006, 2007, or pre-Holliday 2009 teams. To round out the rotation after Pineiro's departure via free agency, the Cards have launched another single-season salvage operation similar to the one they made with Lohse,

*Given that more than two-thirds of the industry's present owners have owned their teams for less time than the decade away such payments are, this might not even be Bill DeWitt Jr.'s debt to pay.

hauling in Brad Penny on the proposition that nobody can do better at teaching an old dog some new tricks than they.

With Carpenter seemingly as healthy as you can hope for, the challenge for management—Mozeliak and La Russa alike—will be to take these next two years with all three elements of their big three completely under contractual control and make them count for something. While last season's result was disappointing, it also represented the franchise's first real spin with its three best players in action, and the Cards

should get a minimum of two more turns around this wheel. The 2010 Cubs don't look like a 95-win team, and the next edition of the Brewers even less so, so the minimum opportunity that's here is for the Cardinals to stick with the low-stakes gambles of the last several years and have a great shot at winding up in the playoffs again. But as the Holliday trade represented, they've been willing to try for something more than that. If ownership will commit to something more than just the odd veteran add-on, there's more to be won than just another division title.

HITTERS

Bryan Anderson   C   Bats: L   Throws: R   Height: 6' 1"   Weight: 200   Born: December 16, 1986   Age: 23

YEAR	TEAM	LVL	AGE	PA	R	2B	3B	HR	RBI	BB	SO	SB	CS	EqBRR	AVG	OBP	SLG	EqAVG	EqOBP	EqSLG	EqA	VORP	WARP	DEFENSE
2007	SFD	AA	20	431	51	15	1	6	53	32	77	0	1	-4.2	.298	.350	.388	.277	.319	.355	.239	10.6	0.2	99-C -9
2008	SFD	AA	21	86	12	5	0	2	14	4	12	0	0	-0.4	.387	.412	.525	.333	.353	.457	.279	5.0	1.0	16-C 3
2008	MEM	AAA	21	275	27	13	2	2	27	32	46	2	0	-2.9	.281	.367	.379	.270	.346	.349	.252	8.8	1.1	66-C 0
2009	MEM	AAA	22	174	22	7	3	4	11	10	42	1	0	0.0	.245	.293	.399	.238	.282	.378	.228	0.7	-0.3	41-C -3
2010	SLN	MLB	23	344	36	14	2	5	32	30	80	1	1	-1.4	.256	.324	.357	.254	.319	.359	.244	8.0	0.7	81-C -2

Breakout: 20%   Improve: 45%   Collapse: 21%   Attrition: 13%   MLB: 7%   Comparables: Marty Pevey, Robin Jennings, Kevin Aitcheson, Brian Schneider

A particularly nasty home-plate collision separated Anderson's shoulder, ending his season in June and deferring for a year the question of whether his future is as a bargaining chip or a backup to Yadier Molina. Given the abbreviated season, there aren't a lot of conclusions to draw. To the positive, he hit right-handers well (.285/.335/.454) and threw out 28 percent of basestealers. He has hit lefties in the past, so the only major obstacle preventing his taking on some team's catching chores is that he needs more reps to improve his receiving skills; doing so would push him into starting consideration somewhere.

Rick Ankiel   CF   Bats: L   Throws: L   Height: 6' 1"   Weight: 210   Born: July 19, 1979   Age: 30

YEAR	TEAM	LVL	AGE	PA	R	2B	3B	HR	RBI	BB	SO	SB	CS	EqBRR	AVG	OBP	SLG	EqAVG	EqOBP	EqSLG	EqA	VORP	WARP	DEFENSE	
2007	MEM	AAA	27	423	62	15	3	32	89	25	90	4	3	-1.3	.267	.314	.568	.236	.277	.467	.250	6.9	1.1	86-CF 2	10-RF 0
2007	SLN	MLB	27	190	31	8	1	11	39	13	41	1	0	0.3	.285	.328	.535	.298	.339	.561	.297	13.0	1.3	22-RF -1	16-CF -1
2008	SLN	MLB	28	463	65	21	2	25	71	42	100	2	1	-0.7	.264	.337	.506	.278	.348	.525	.291	28.6	2.5	85-CF -4	15-LF -2
2009	SLN	MLB	29	404	50	21	2	11	38	26	99	4	3	0.4	.231	.285	.387	.242	.292	.406	.239	0.9	0.1	52-CF -1	21-RF -3
2010	SLN	MLB	30	502	65	22	2	22	72	41	117	3	2	-0.2	.250	.317	.450	.252	.316	.465	.267	19.7	2.1	106-CF -1	

Breakout: 8%   Improve: 47%   Collapse: 11%   Attrition: 7%   MLB: 97%   Comparables: Jim Edmonds, Geoff Jenkins, Rick Monday, Ryan Church

The game's real-life answer to *The Natural*, Ankiel suffered an obvious setback in 2009, but the year was also the first time he was trying to overcome injuries as a hitter, in just his fourth full season as a hitter at any level. Given La Russa's decision to start him in barely more than half of the team's games after he returned from injuries he suffered colliding with a wall in early May, combined with Ankiel's own comments indicating he still wasn't feeling right a couple of months later, he clearly was at less than his best. Ankiel's career path was guaranteed to be unusual at the outset, and good luck separating whether last season's declining rates of pitches per plate appearance and homers to fly balls was due to his injuries, his reserve role, or pitchers adapting to a relative neophyte of batsmanship. Ankiel is a free agent as we go to press (changing from pitching to hitting didn't reset his service time, after all), so somebody is going to take the chance. Given his fly-ball tendencies, a move to a homer haven would put wind beneath his wings.

Allen Craig   4C

Bats: R   Throws: R   Height: 6' 2"   Weight: 190   Born: July 18, 1984   Age: 25

YEAR	TEAM	LVL	AGE	PA	R	2B	3B	HR	RBI	BB	SO	SB	CS	EqBRR	AVG	OBP	SLG	EqAVG	EqOBP	EqSLG	EqA	VORP	WARP		DEFENSE		
2007	PMB	A+	22	468	77	25	2	21	77	35	79	8	3	-5.1	.312	.370	.530	.295	.345	.495	.284	21.9	2.0		83-3B	-5	15-1B 0
2008	SFD	AA	23	568	84	30	0	22	85	48	87	2	1	2.2	.304	.373	.494	.271	.329	.433	.263	14.8	1.9		104-3B	2	15-LF -1
2009	MEM	AAA	24	521	78	26	1	26	83	37	95	3	0	-2.6	.322	.374	.547	.312	.359	.526	.298	29.8	3.0		67-LF	1	40-1B -5
2010	SLN	MLB	25	503	62	22	1	17	60	38	109	2	1	-0.9	.258	.320	.423	.267	.327	.443	.262	11.7	1.3		106-LF	0	

Breakout: 5%   Improve: 27%   Collapse: 26%   Attrition: 7%   MLB: 14%   Comparables: Jason Felice, Marty Cordova, Jerry Lomastro, Mike Edwards

Star of the coming roster adventure *DeRosa on a Dime* (or perhaps *Thirstless for Thurston*), Craig figures to get a long look in camp, perhaps taking over the hot corner after a career of roving. He played the middle infield in college and in the lower minors, but he's sort of the Birds' answer to Jake Fox while playing a better third base. His name won't join Boyer or Pendleton in the organization's history of defensive excellence, but his ability to make contact and hit for power to all fields makes him an excellent patch at a position the club can't Glaus over, and La Russa loves having multiposition flexibility on his in-game options menu.

Mark DeRosa   UT

Bats: R   Throws: R   Height: 6' 1"   Weight: 205   Born: February 26, 1975   Age: 35

YEAR	TEAM	LVL	AGE	PA	R	2B	3B	HR	RBI	BB	SO	SB	CS	EqBRR	AVG	OBP	SLG	EqAVG	EqOBP	EqSLG	EqA	VORP	WARP		DEFENSE		
2007	CHN	MLB	32	574	64	28	3	10	72	58	93	1	2	0.4	.293	.371	.420	.291	.371	.415	.275	24.2	2.6		79-2B	-5	32-3B 4
2008	CHN	MLB	33	593	103	30	3	21	87	69	106	6	0	3.8	.285	.376	.481	.286	.372	.478	.295	38.0	4.8		74-2B	1	30-RF 2
2009	CLE	MLB	34	314	47	13	0	13	50	29	63	1	1	-0.9	.270	.342	.457	.282	.351	.469	.280	14.5	1.4		40-3B	-2	15-LF 0
2009	SLN	MLB	34	262	31	10	1	10	28	18	58	2	1	2.2	.228	.291	.405	.241	.299	.430	.250	4.4	0.8		58-3B	3	
2010	SFN	MLB	35	528	71	23	2	15	68	52	109	2	2	0.9	.256	.339	.410	.259	.342	.413	.261	14.2	1.8		102-3B	2	

Breakout: 4%   Improve: 27%   Collapse: 17%   Attrition: 16%   MLB: 99%   Comparables: Ken Boyer, Casey Blake, Mike Lowell, Doug DeCinces

In retrospect the missing ingredient that took the spice out of the Cubs' life, DeRosa was enjoying a year consistent with his recent standards before tearing up his wrist after his midyear trade to the Cards. He soldiered through the torn tendon sheath, still contributing the same power. Off-season surgery should have him in fine fettle for spring with the Giants, though the signing of Aubrey Huff may place him in left field more often than is ideal; DeRosa's multipositional usefulness lies not in his ability to hit a ton, but in his ability to hit well enough to make spotting him in the outfield corners an acceptable proposition when he isn't your starter at second or third. Space saving of that sort is especially valuable in the age of the 12-man pitching staff.

Daniel Descalso   2B

Bats: L   Throws: R   Height: 5' 10"   Weight: 190   Born: October 19, 1986   Age: 23

YEAR	TEAM	LVL	AGE	PA	R	2B	3B	HR	RBI	BB	SO	SB	CS	EqBRR	AVG	OBP	SLG	EqAVG	EqOBP	EqSLG	EqA	VORP	WARP		DEFENSE		
2007	BAT	A-	20	283	29	7	5	0	31	26	37	12	3	2.0	.268	.346	.336	.236	.293	.297	.213	-6.3	-1.6		45-3B	-4	21-2B 1
2008	PMB	A+	21	456	57	24	2	8	50	33	53	7	7	-2.1	.243	.313	.372	.234	.288	.348	.223	-2.5	-2.9		101-2B	-14	11-SS -8
2008	SFD	AA	21	42	6	1	1	0	4	3	2	1	1	-0.5	.351	.405	.432	.316	.372	.395	.271	1.8	0.7		9-2B	4	
2009	SFD	AA	22	324	46	26	5	8	51	31	41	0	1	0.6	.323	.396	.531	.288	.350	.485	.282	17.4	2.3		73-2B	2	
2009	MEM	AAA	22	172	23	4	0	2	17	16	21	3	0	2.6	.253	.327	.320	.248	.314	.307	.227	-2.5	0.0		28-2B	2	6-1B 1
2010	SLN	MLB	23	446	51	22	3	7	51	38	69	5	3	0.5	.258	.326	.381	.259	.325	.386	.253	10.5	1.0		105-2B	-1	

Breakout: 22%   Improve: 51%   Collapse: 14%   Attrition: 9%   MLB: 4%   Comparables: Brian Kowitz, Felix Molina, Luis Valbuena, Sam Taylor

An infield grinder from UC Davis taken in the third round of the 2007 draft, Descalso improved his bid to escape the marginalization so many organizational second-base types suffer by adding power for a second straight season. Because Schumaker's conversion to the keystone seems unlikely to be a permanent feature of future Cardinals infields, Descalso has an opportunity to slip into the mix, perhaps as soon as the second half. He'll need to retain last year's gains at the plate, because he won't help a lineup with much besides hitting them where they ain't, having little patience or speed.

David Freese   3B

Bats: R   Throws: R   Height: 6' 2"   Weight: 220   Born: April 28, 1983   Age: 27

YEAR	TEAM	LVL	AGE	PA	R	2B	3B	HR	RBI	BB	SO	SB	CS	EqBRR	AVG	OBP	SLG	EqAVG	EqOBP	EqSLG	EqA	VORP	WARP	DEFENSE		
2007	LEL	A+	24	592	104	31	6	17	96	69	99	6	1	3.5	.302	.400	.489	.261	.336	.390	.256	10.0	0.9	125-3B	-3	
2008	MEM	AAA	25	510	83	29	3	26	91	39	111	5	2	0.1	.306	.361	.550	.276	.325	.471	.270	17.8	2.3	113-3B	1	
2009	MEM	AAA	26	225	34	15	0	10	37	22	51	1	0	-0.9	.300	.369	.525	.271	.333	.458	.272	7.9	0.7	43-3B -1	9-1B	-1
2009	SLN	MLB	26	34	3	2	0	1	7	2	7	0	0	-0.2	.323	.353	.484	.355	.382	.516	.300	2.2	0.3	5-3B	0	
2010	SLN	MLB	27	412	47	20	1	10	49	35	99	2	1	0.4	.247	.316	.387	.253	.321	.398	.250	6.4	0.6	91-3B	-1	

Breakout: 6%   Improve: 23%   Collapse: 28%   Attrition: 13%   MLB: 10%   Comparables: Scott McClain, Marshall McDougall, Earl Snyder, Fritzie Connally

Remember those answers to multiple-choice questions that seemed really close to the right answer, but weren't exactly right? Welcome to Freese's world, as his shot at being last season's third baseman got skipped. Freese was bumped from the roster early as La Russa went with Thurston and Barden, and a May ankle injury that shelved him for six weeks perhaps inspired the decisions to first try Khalil Greene before trading for DeRosa. Once Freese returned to action for August, he slugged .620 for Memphis in 140 plate appearances; this got him one September start in the majors. As possible answers go, he's been recycled; he'll contend with Allen Craig in camp, but he's not young and his defense isn't such that it makes selecting him easy.

Troy Glaus   3B/1B

Bats: R   Throws: R   Height: 6' 5"   Weight: 240   Born: August 3, 1976   Age: 33

YEAR	TEAM	LVL	AGE	PA	R	2B	3B	HR	RBI	BB	SO	SB	CS	EqBRR	AVG	OBP	SLG	EqAVG	EqOBP	EqSLG	EqA	VORP	WARP	DEFENSE		
2007	TOR	MLB	30	456	60	19	1	20	62	61	102	0	1	-4.3	.262	.366	.473	.261	.366	.473	.288	24.0	3.2	104-3B	5	
2008	SLN	MLB	31	637	69	33	1	27	99	87	104	0	1	-1.8	.270	.372	.483	.286	.383	.506	.301	44.7	4.7	139-3B -1	3-1B	0
2009	MEM	AAA	32	65	10	0	0	3	8	12	17	1	0	0.3	.216	.369	.392	.208	.338	.340	.252	1.2	-0.1	13-3B	-2	
2009	SLN	MLB	32	32	2	2	0	0	2	3	8	0	0	-0.1	.172	.250	.241	.172	.250	.241	.167	-2.2	-0.2	5-3B	0	
2010	ATL	NL	33	363	37	15	1	12	48	46	78	1	1	-0.9	.248	.350	.417	.253	.351	.429	.275	15.4	1.7	79-3B	0	

Breakout: 9%   Improve: 31%   Collapse: 20%   Attrition: 19%   MLB: 77%   Comparables: Wil Cordero, Dave McCarty, Glenn Davis, Mike Sweeney

In the Rolen-for-Glaus exchange with the Jays, the birds of a redder feather had to settle for getting first the best and then the worst season either of them have had in the last two years. Last year's back injury is cause for concern about how effectively he'll be able to mount another year like 2006 or 2008, but even if he was forced to first base, he could help a club on a one-year, make-good deal, because the options are that he'll hit or have to sit, unable to play. Signed to a one-year, $2 million contract with the Braves, he's a fly-ball hitter who shouldn't struggle in Ted's playplace, and he adds the additional flexibility of possibly playing some third if (and when) Chipper Jones needs to be sat down.

Khalil Greene   INF

Bats: R   Throws: R   Height: 5' 11"   Weight: 185   Born: October 21, 1979   Age: 30

YEAR	TEAM	LVL	AGE	PA	R	2B	3B	HR	RBI	BB	SO	SB	CS	EqBRR	AVG	OBP	SLG	EqAVG	EqOBP	EqSLG	EqA	VORP	WARP	DEFENSE		
2007	SDN	MLB	27	659	89	44	3	27	97	32	128	4	0	1.3	.254	.291	.468	.270	.306	.493	.271	34.7	3.3	153-SS	-5	
2008	SDN	MLB	28	423	30	15	2	10	35	22	100	5	1	-1.4	.213	.260	.339	.225	.267	.357	.220	0.4	-0.5	104-SS	-4	
2009	MEM	AAA	29	57	9	3	0	4	10	2	4	0	0	0.1	.345	.368	.618	.327	.351	.527	.293	4.1	0.5	7-3B 0	7-SS	0
2009	SLN	MLB	29	193	21	7	0	6	24	15	35	2	1	0.6	.200	.272	.347	.212	.281	.365	.226	-1.4	-0.3	27-SS -2	11-3B	0
2010	TEX	AL	30	417	52	21	2	17	60	30	85	3	1	0.2	.255	.315	.457	.247	.304	.433	.249	10.0	0.9	99-SS	-2	

Breakout: 18%   Improve: 40%   Collapse: 13%   Attrition: 16%   MLB: 89%   Comparables: Bucky Dent, Alex Gonzalez, Joe Cronin, Bret Boone

The game's history of dealing well with any flavor of mental illness isn't great, but Greene's career-altering case of social-anxiety disorder doesn't have to be a career-ending affliction of the sort that derailed the careers of Tony Horton or Alex Johnson. What's more, we have the more current example of Zack Greinke to provide some optimism that at least the industry is handling these things better. Because we don't know to what extent this experience has changed Greene's ability to produce, you may as well chuck the projection. He's a lottery ticket: if you think he'll recover his career, he's a shortstop with power, and if you don't, that's cold of you, but understandably cautious. In a world that makes space for Adam Everett, we can hope he'll come back to produce a .180 ISO and earn his keep at short. The Rangers will give him a chance to get back on the beam as a utility-man.

Tyler Greene   SS

Bats: R   Throws: R   Height: 6' 2"   Weight: 180   Born: August 17, 1983   Age: 26

YEAR	TEAM	LVL	AGE	PA	R	2B	3B	HR	RBI	BB	SO	SB	CS	EqBRR	AVG	OBP	SLG	EqAVG	EqOBP	EqSLG	EqA	VORP	WARP	DEFENSE	
2007	SFD	AA	23	247	41	17	2	8	25	16	62	10	2	1.9	.244	.309	.448	.230	.283	.412	.241	4.1	1.5	59-SS 8	
2008	SFD	AA	24	408	62	15	4	16	41	22	99	14	6	2.1	.259	.307	.449	.223	.262	.373	.220	-0.4	-1.5	89-SS -11	4-3B -1
2008	MEM	AAA	24	128	17	7	0	0	7	11	35	6	0	2.4	.234	.325	.297	.219	.294	.263	.212	-0.9	0.6	28-SS 6	
2009	MEM	AAA	25	388	70	10	5	15	42	38	86	31	3	8.7	.291	.369	.482	.271	.341	.444	.276	21.9	3.3	79-SS 4	6-3B 2
2009	SLN	MLB	25	116	9	5	0	2	7	4	32	3	0	0.7	.222	.270	.324	.229	.276	.321	.219	-1.0	-0.1	21-SS 2	7-3B -2
2010	SLN	MLB	26	427	51	18	3	9	31	32	119	10	4	2.7	.226	.291	.358	.232	.296	.372	.233	3.1	0.5	100-SS 2	

Breakout: 12% Improve: 39% Collapse: 21% Attrition: 8%   MLB: 68%   Comparables: Scott Little, Alonzo Powell, Rod Hobbs, Jay Knoblauh

It's worth wondering if the future will ever arrive for the former first-rounder. He has some power and some speed, hard work on his approach has yielded slightly better patience, and he has the range and arm for short. He's still hack-happy, however, and on a team where so many guys caught breaks that translated into jobs, somebody had to be left out. Even the utility role was filled with the acquisition of Julio Lugo. Greene is error-prone at short, which won't help, but put in a smaller park, he could start for someone and have his moments.

Mark Hamilton   1B/LF

Bats: L   Throws: L   Height: 6' 3"   Weight: 220   Born: July 29, 1984   Age: 25

YEAR	TEAM	LVL	AGE	PA	R	2B	3B	HR	RBI	BB	SO	SB	CS	EqBRR	AVG	OBP	SLG	EqAVG	EqOBP	EqSLG	EqA	VORP	WARP	DEFENSE
2007	PMB	A+	22	244	31	12	0	13	49	20	48	1	0	1.2	.290	.348	.520	.272	.324	.478	.272	5.8	0.3	36-1B -3
2007	SFD	AA	22	276	32	15	0	6	41	24	54	1	1	0.2	.250	.318	.383	.234	.292	.345	.223	-8.0	-1.8	62-1B -7
2008	SFD	AA	23	281	27	11	0	8	29	35	67	0	0	-0.2	.241	.338	.384	.211	.298	.327	.221	-8.6	-1.1	60-1B 0
2009	SFD	AA	24	195	26	11	0	8	28	28	46	0	1	-3.5	.307	.421	.521	.259	.354	.447	.275	3.1	0.0	32-1B -3
2009	MEM	AAA	24	144	22	11	0	6	19	13	34	0	0	-1.1	.308	.375	.531	.288	.352	.485	.284	3.9	0.2	23-1B -2
2010	SLN	MLB	25	416	40	17	0	11	46	40	111	1	1	-0.6	.233	.310	.365	.234	.308	.378	.241	-4.0	-0.7	78-1B -3

Breakout: 7% Improve: 36% Collapse: 26% Attrition: 11%   MLB: 11%   Comparables: Dernell Stenson, Jay Kirkpatrick, Mark Merchant, Travis Ishikawa

The game has a place for its "but-for" prospects, as in "but for the presence of the best player in baseball at the position I play, I coulda been something." Hamilton is a good-but-not-great prospect, mashing enough against right-handed pitching to suggest he might at least be a second-division starter, and time lost to a pulled groin didn't stall him much at Memphis. The Cards are exploring their options; Hamilton played left for Tulane as an amateur, and he was back there in winter ball. He could create a role for himself similar to that of former Cardinal Chris Duncan, but he'll have to do it with his bat.

Matt Holliday   LF

Bats: R   Throws: R   Height: 6' 4"   Weight: 235   Born: January 15, 1980   Age: 30

YEAR	TEAM	LVL	AGE	PA	R	2B	3B	HR	RBI	BB	SO	SB	CS	EqBRR	AVG	OBP	SLG	EqAVG	EqOBP	EqSLG	EqA	VORP	WARP	DEFENSE
2007	COL	MLB	27	713	120	50	6	36	137	63	126	11	4	3.3	.340	.405	.607	.331	.397	.587	.323	66.3	7.8	153-LF 6
2008	COL	MLB	28	623	107	38	2	25	88	74	104	28	2	8.1	.321	.409	.538	.317	.403	.524	.319	52.9	6.2	138-LF 4
2009	OAK	MLB	29	400	52	23	1	11	54	46	58	12	3	-0.2	.286	.377	.454	.296	.385	.458	.296	23.7	3.1	91-LF 4
2009	SLN	MLB	29	270	42	16	2	13	55	26	43	2	4	-0.6	.353	.419	.604	.380	.437	.658	.347	34.1	3.6	61-LF -1
2010	SLN	MLB	30	646	89	36	2	23	98	67	114	10	5	1.8	.289	.372	.478	.298	.378	.499	.298	41.7	4.7	145-LF 2

Breakout: 2% Improve: 25% Collapse: 15% Attrition: 16%   MLB: 99%   Comparables: Dave Winfield, Vladimir Guerrero, Moises Alou, Albert Belle

A brief introduction to the stronger league didn't diminish Holliday's reputation that badly; it simply highlighted the extent to which his blend of power and contact takes a hit in a park like the Coliseum. His BABIP in Oakland dipped to .301, normal for most but a steep drop for someone with a career .351 rate. His performance as an Athletic and as a Cardinal suggests you can expect .200 points of ISO from him in any environment, which, added to that base of power-on-contact and a solid walk rate, equals a dangerous hitter. As good as he's been, though, he isn't one of the game's great players; he's one of its very, very good ones. His baserunning value was hit where it most obviously hurts, on steals and hit advancement, and is a portent of what his 30s threaten to bring: little bits of his game getting cut away with age. His defense isn't slipping, which is why he makes the better bet than Jason Bay to deliver on his multiyear deal.

Jon Jay OF Bats: L Throws: L Height: 5' 11" Weight: 200 Born: March 15, 1985 Age: 25

YEAR	TEAM	LVL	AGE	PA	R	2B	3B	HR	RBI	BB	SO	SB	CS	EqBRR	AVG	OBP	SLG	EqAVG	EqOBP	EqSLG	EqA	VORP	WARP	DEFENSE	
2007	PMB	A+	22	134	19	8	0	2	10	5	25	5	2	0.5	.286	.321	.397	.273	.299	.383	.239	-1.5	-0.1	8-LF	1
2007	SFD	AA	22	117	17	4	2	2	11	11	19	4	1	2.3	.235	.333	.373	.219	.293	.352	.229	-1.4	-0.1	21-LF 1 3-CF	0
2008	SFD	AA	23	427	57	17	3	11	47	39	46	10	7	-1.0	.306	.379	.457	.270	.332	.395	.254	8.5	2.1	91-CF	9
2008	MEM	AAA	23	64	8	4	1	1	10	6	10	0	1	0.0	.345	.406	.500	.322	.375	.475	.285	3.5	0.7	15-CF	2
2009	MEM	AAA	24	564	72	23	2	10	54	34	64	20	8	1.8	.281	.338	.394	.278	.329	.385	.251	7.7	1.5	52-CF 1 52-LF	4
2010	SLN	MLB	25	493	54	22	2	9	43	38	78	8	5	0.7	.269	.333	.387	.268	.329	.390	.258	14.1	1.9	94-CF	4

Breakout: 12% Improve: 35% Collapse: 17% Attrition: 5%   MLB: 3%   Comparables: Terrmel Sledge, Pedro Swann, Quinn Mack, Carl Loadenthal

Not to be confused with the least-valuable Founding Father, in the Cards' constellation of near-ready outfield possibilities, Jay might be the one whose star burns both the most steadily and the least brightly. He can play a fine center field, but not so well as to move Rasmus, and nothing about his batting or baserunning gets him beyond backhanded compliments like, "He'll be a good fourth outfielder." Jay may indeed get to be exactly that, assuming Skip Schumaker doesn't wind up back in what was, after all, his old job.

Daryl Jones LF Bats: L Throws: L Height: 5' 11" Weight: 180 Born: June 25, 1987 Age: 23

YEAR	TEAM	LVL	AGE	PA	R	2B	3B	HR	RBI	BB	SO	SB	CS	EqBRR	AVG	OBP	SLG	EqAVG	EqOBP	EqSLG	EqA	VORP	WARP	DEFENSE	
2007	QUD	A	20	481	71	15	3	4	31	41	94	22	12	1.8	.217	.304	.296	.202	.271	.277	.198	-20.2	-5.0	58-RF -8 33-LF	-6
2008	PMB	A+	21	352	43	11	7	7	35	33	67	18	5	-1.2	.326	.406	.476	.293	.357	.438	.277	13.5	1.2	70-LF 0 13-CF	-4
2008	SFD	AA	21	151	19	6	1	6	14	22	30	6	1	0.9	.290	.409	.500	.256	.360	.434	.277	5.5	0.9	30-LF	2
2009	SFD	AA	22	336	50	14	3	3	29	33	65	7	4	0.3	.279	.360	.378	.245	.313	.334	.231	-4.3	-1.6	67-LF	-9
2010	SLN	MLB	23	409	47	17	3	6	31	39	98	8	4	0.3	.243	.322	.358	.241	.317	.363	.246	2.6	0.0	86-LF	-3

Breakout: 23% Improve: 46% Collapse: 11% Attrition: 9%   MLB: 4%   Comparables: Charles McGehee, Cliff Gonzalez, Bruce Fields, Rod Myers

Last year's Lasik-aided breakout set the stage for this year's disappointment as Jones struggled through a nagging quad injury; he wound up losing a good six weeks in the second half. Even if you're inclined to give him a pass, he did little to help himself in the Arizona Fall League, striking out a quarter of the time. Because of concerns that his arm might restrict him to left, the disappearing power is another worry. He's one of the best talents left in a thin system, but he'll have to regroup and deliver power to regain top prospect status in this or any other organization.

Jason LaRue C Bats: R Throws: R Height: 5' 11" Weight: 205 Born: March 19, 1974 Age: 36

YEAR	TEAM	LVL	AGE	PA	R	2B	3B	HR	RBI	BB	SO	SB	CS	EqBRR	AVG	OBP	SLG	EqAVG	EqOBP	EqSLG	EqA	VORP	WARP	DEFENSE	
2007	KCA	MLB	33	195	14	9	0	4	13	17	66	1	0	-0.4	.148	.240	.272	.149	.241	.280	.184	-3.9	0.0	54-C	4
2008	SLN	MLB	34	189	17	8	1	4	21	15	20	0	0	0.4	.213	.296	.348	.218	.298	.352	.233	2.8	0.6	46-C	2
2009	SLN	MLB	35	112	10	3	0	2	6	3	22	1	0	-0.4	.240	.288	.327	.248	.295	.324	.224	0.6	0.1	29-C	-1
2010	SLN	MLB	36	129	10	4	0	3	11	10	32	0	0	-0.1	.193	.276	.299	.201	.284	.317	.203	-1.9	-0.1	34-C	1

Breakout: 13% Improve: 37% Collapse: 34% Attrition: 31%   MLB: 85%   Comparables: Gary Bennett, Steve Yeager, Rick Cerone, Del Crandall

Most backup backstops have the caddying gig figured out: get more attention for yourself by cultivating a relationship with a specific starting pitcher, win friends and influence people as a newly minted Svengali of ignorance's tools, and bank those paychecks. LaRue doesn't have that as an option, because every pitcher would rather throw to Yadier Molina, given the choice. Instead, LaRue takes starts as he can get them, the Cards take him as a known quantity, and he gets to bank paychecks anyway, having been re-upped for 2010.

Ryan Ludwick RF Bats: R Throws: L Height: 6' 3" Weight: 220 Born: July 13, 1978 Age: 31

YEAR	TEAM	LVL	AGE	PA	R	2B	3B	HR	RBI	BB	SO	SB	CS	EqBRR	AVG	OBP	SLG	EqAVG	EqOBP	EqSLG	EqA	VORP	WARP	DEFENSE	
2007	MEM	AAA	28	121	27	8	0	8	36	10	20	1	1	0.3	.340	.380	.642	.306	.339	.528	.291	6.6	1.1	21-LF	3
2007	SLN	MLB	28	339	42	22	0	14	52	26	72	4	4	-3.0	.267	.339	.479	.283	.355	.503	.282	15.0	2.0	37-LF 2 29-RF	-1
2008	SLN	MLB	29	617	104	40	3	37	113	62	146	4	4	2.4	.299	.375	.591	.318	.389	.626	.325	60.8	7.0	107-RF 2 19-LF	-1
2009	SLN	MLB	30	539	63	20	1	22	97	41	106	4	2	1.7	.265	.329	.447	.281	.341	.470	.277	20.6	2.7	120-RF	3
2010	SLN	MLB	31	527	71	26	1	24	88	47	116	4	4	0.2	.271	.345	.481	.281	.352	.506	.286	26.9	3.0	112-RF	1

Breakout: 7% Improve: 46% Collapse: 14% Attrition: 8%   MLB: 99%   Comparables: Juan Gonzalez, Dale Murphy, Richie Zisk, Larry Parrish

On the list of predictable declines from 2008 to 2009, Ludwick may not rank with Milton Bradley, but seeing his line-drive rate plummet from 28 to 21 percent was a big part of why the BABIP fairy didn't leave him anything extra under his pillow. He also put more balls in play (both his walk and strikeout rates dropped), meaning his performance became more dependent on their outcomes. Or, to put it simply, reality had a nasty way of reminding the world that Ludwick is not going to flirt with a .600 SLG all the time. His combination of power and defense should keep him in the mix as a quality component in a semiregular role, but if his future production is going to be more like his first and third years as a Cardinal, as seems likely, he's not a significantly better-than-average everyday player.

Julio Lugo INF Bats: R Throws: R Height: 6' 1" Weight: 175 Born: November 16, 1975 Age: 34

YEAR	TEAM	LVL	AGE	PA	R	2B	3B	HR	RBI	BB	SO	SB	CS	EqBRR	AVG	OBP	SLG	EqAVG	EqOBP	EqSLG	EqA	VORP	WARP	DEFENSE	
2007	BOS	MLB	31	630	71	36	2	8	73	48	82	33	6	1.9	.237	.294	.349	.231	.290	.344	.232	6.1	0.8	138-SS	1
2008	BOS	MLB	32	307	27	13	0	1	22	34	51	12	4	-1.3	.268	.355	.330	.266	.355	.328	.255	10.7	-0.1	75-SS	-11
2009	BOS	MLB	33	123	16	4	1	1	8	12	18	3	0	-0.3	.284	.352	.367	.284	.352	.367	.259	4.3	-0.2	27-SS	-6
2009	SLN	MLB	33	170	24	9	4	2	13	17	27	6	0	2.0	.277	.351	.432	.295	.365	.456	.292	11.8	1.0	19-2B -1 18-SS	-2
2010	SLN	MLB	34	365	38	17	2	5	34	37	62	12	4	0.4	.245	.323	.351	.251	.328	.354	.247	7.9	0.6	83-SS	-3

Breakout: 7%   Improve: 42%   Collapse: 22%   Attrition: 27%   MLB: 94%   Comparables: Chris Speier, Mike Bordick, Bill Russell, Greg Gagne

The man Boston is paying to play in St. Louis might be a worthwhile historical footnote as far as how weird the once apparently forever-expanding market was getting before the downturn; that he would get a four-year, $36 million deal now seems impossible. That's not the Cards' problem. Freed from Fenway's frenzy, Lugo will provide what passes as offense-oriented utility for an infield reserve, and perhaps an in-season solution at second if the Schumaker experiment gets canceled. His walks and power have been consistently useful, he runs well, and if he can't handle short every day, La Russa will have the good sense not to ask him to do so.

Joe Mather OF Bats: R Throws: R Height: 6' 4" Weight: 195 Born: July 23, 1982 Age: 27

YEAR	TEAM	LVL	AGE	PA	R	2B	3B	HR	RBI	BB	SO	SB	CS	EqBRR	AVG	OBP	SLG	EqAVG	EqOBP	EqSLG	EqA	VORP	WARP	DEFENSE			
2007	SFD	AA	24	272	48	17	0	18	46	29	32	4	0	0.0	.303	.387	.607	.274	.343	.506	.287	12.0	0.9	39-1B -5	24-RF 0		
2007	MEM	AAA	24	288	32	10	1	13	31	23	51	6	0	0.9	.241	.329	.443	.226	.304	.397	.246	0.8	0.6	63-RF 3	4-CF 1		
2008	MEM	AAA	25	254	45	14	2	17	41	32	36	7	2	1.0	.303	.411	.630	.281	.375	.544	.306	18.5	2.7	49-RF 2	5-CF 2		
2008	SLN	MLB	25	147	20	7	0	8	18	12	32	1	0	-0.6	.241	.306	.474	.248	.313	.496	.272	5.2	1.1	14-LF 2	8-CF 1		
2009	SFD	AA	26	65	8	3	0	3	11	5	11	0	2	-1.5	.207	.277	.414	.167	.227	.300	.177	-3.8	-0.6	7-RF -1	5-3B 0		
2009	MEM	AAA	26	150	12	6	2	1	14	9	27	7	1	0.3	.176	.233	.272	.174	.225	.254	.172	-9.9	-1.7	34-RF -4	2-1B 0		
2010	SLN	MLB	27	334	37	15	1	11	36	30	68	3	2	0.0	.236	.316	.403	.242	.320	.417	.255	5.2	0.6	69-RF 0			

Breakout: 7%   Improve: 32%   Collapse: 27%   Attrition: 19%   MLB: 15%   Comparables: Todd Trafton, James Betzsold, Mike Hill, Bill Moore

Mather went into camp as one of the club's many options at third base, having been drafted back in 2001's third round as a high school shortstop, but his tendency toward Hobsonian Butch-ery at the hot corner nixed the move. Mather's wrist required season-ending surgery in June after affecting him all season; this followed on the wrist issues that shut him down in 2008. If healthy, he could be a more athletic alternative for left field if the Cards don't add a big-name free agent, but health isn't something you can assume. With wrist injuries, you don't know what you've got until you see the victim's comeback swings.

Yadier Molina C Bats: R Throws: R Height: 5' 11" Weight: 220 Born: July 13, 1982 Age: 27

YEAR	TEAM	LVL	AGE	PA	R	2B	3B	HR	RBI	BB	SO	SB	CS	EqBRR	AVG	OBP	SLG	EqAVG	EqOBP	EqSLG	EqA	VORP	WARP	DEFENSE		
2007	SLN	MLB	24	396	30	15	0	6	40	34	43	1	1	-2.4	.275	.340	.368	.281	.347	.375	.257	16.7	4.3	97-C	16	
2008	SLN	MLB	25	485	37	18	0	7	56	32	29	0	2	-5.0	.304	.349	.392	.315	.356	.403	.266	23.7	4.0	112-C	9	
2009	SLN	MLB	26	544	45	23	1	6	54	50	39	9	3	-5.7	.293	.366	.383	.311	.381	.402	.278	32.8	5.7	132-C 11	1-1B	0
2010	SLN	MLB	27	521	44	21	1	10	61	47	47	3	3	-2.5	.291	.359	.404	.298	.365	.412	.274	27.8	3.8	128-C	7	

Breakout: 25%   Improve: 48%   Collapse: 13%   Attrition: 4%   MLB: 100%   Comparables: Ramon Hernandez, Spud Davis, Bruce Benedict, Shanty Hogan

Given that his value is now more obvious, you can't call the best Molina underrated. He's no longer a player who merely adds value doing "little things" while playing catcher as if born to it—which, as a Molina, he was. He essentially had to learn how to hit at the major-league level, and the last three years reflect what's now an established level as he reaches midpeak. Add in his value as a receiver and how he effectively deters opponents' running games out of existence, and it almost seems a shame to mention one wart: hitting into twin killings. BP's NetDP measures how many additional GIDPs a hitter generated better or worse than average, and Molina's 2009 score (16.4) was the third-highest in the last 55 years (that is, what's covered in the Retrosheet Era: 1955-2009). Jim Rice's 1985 season ranks fifth at 15.9, but topping the list is Brad Ausmus's 2001 (18.1) and Paul Konerko's 2003 (17.1). Though a good baserunning club, the Cardinals weren't fast; Molina spent most of the season batting behind Chris Duncan, Rick Ankiel, and Mark DeRosa, none exactly jackrabbits, which is to say that as prone to the DP as he might be, he had help.

Albert Pujols   1B   Bats: R   Throws: R   Height: 6' 3"   Weight: 230   Born: January 16, 1980   Age: 30

YEAR	TEAM	LVL	AGE	PA	R	2B	3B	HR	RBI	BB	SO	SB	CS	EqBRR	AVG	OBP	SLG	EqAVG	EqOBP	EqSLG	EqA	VORP	WARP	DEFENSE	
2007	SLN	MLB	27	679	99	38	1	32	103	99	58	2	6	-1.3	.327	.429	.568	.342	.442	.588	.338	68.4	10.6	150-1B	27
2008	SLN	MLB	28	641	100	44	0	37	116	104	54	7	3	-0.2	.357	.462	.653	.375	.473	.679	.372	91.7	11.7	135-1B	17
2009	SLN	MLB	29	700	124	45	1	47	135	115	64	16	4	-0.4	.327	.443	.658	.348	.454	.699	.368	92.6	12.7	155-1B	23
2010	SLN	MLB	30	658	98	34	1	34	108	100	64	6	5	-0.3	.317	.427	.564	.327	.434	.589	.340	69.1	8.6	147-1B	11

Breakout: 2%   Improve: 29%   Collapse: 12%   Attrition: 12%   MLB: 99%   Comparables: Jeff Bagwell, Jack Clark, Frank Thomas, Derrek Lee

Even with 44 intentional walks taking the bat out of his hands, Pujols nevertheless managed to finish third in baseball in OBI—Others Batted In—with 88, behind Ryan Howard (96) and Prince Fielder (95), even though he had slightly fewer opportunities. Howard got ordered aboard eight times; Fielder 21. Someday, somebody is going to point out that Pujols has yet to lead the league in RBI, but in the same way that a league-leading tally requires teammates aboard, it also requires an even distribution of opportunities, and no one is arguing that Pujols doesn't cash his in. He also hasn't hit 50 homers; Hank Aaron never did, either, and it isn't hurting Pujols' case for being the best player in the game today. Consider him the symbol of old standards and new coming together. Recognize that he has slugged .600 or better in seven of nine seasons, take your seat, and enjoy every single swing you get to see, every at-bat—they'll still be selling hot dogs afterward, and you don't want to miss what comes next.

Colby Rasmus   CF   Bats: L   Throws: L   Height: 6' 2"   Weight: 195   Born: August 11, 1986   Age: 23

YEAR	TEAM	LVL	AGE	PA	R	2B	3B	HR	RBI	BB	SO	SB	CS	EqBRR	AVG	OBP	SLG	EqAVG	EqOBP	EqSLG	EqA	VORP	WARP	DEFENSE			
2007	SFD	AA	20	556	93	37	3	29	72	70	108	18	3	0.9	.275	.381	.551	.253	.342	.485	.282	29.2	2.5	120-CF	-9		
2008	MEM	AAA	21	387	56	15	0	11	36	49	72	15	3	2.9	.251	.346	.396	.239	.322	.351	.244	4.1	1.0	83-CF	4		
2009	SLN	MLB	22	520	72	22	2	16	52	36	95	3	1	4.3	.251	.307	.407	.264	.317	.432	.256	12.4	2.1	106-CF	7	5-RF	0
2010	SLN	MLB	23	494	66	23	2	15	47	50	103	9	3	1.4	.250	.332	.416	.251	.330	.423	.268	19.4	2.2	107-CF	0		

Breakout: 16%   Improve: 45%   Collapse: 13%   Attrition: 6%   MLB: 100%   Comparables: Carlos Gonzalez, Nick Markakis, Grady Sizemore, Orsino Hill

Anticipation: it's not just for catsup anymore. Like the old Heinz ad, Rasmus' long-awaited arrival ended up being something less than the build-up. However, considering that his walk rates were stronger in the minors, that the power did show up, and that he played through the second half with a painful heel injury that sapped his production, it's easy to anticipate his fulfilling his higher-end PECOTA projections, because he's young, the heel's healthy, and he really has been worth waiting for.

Brendan Ryan   SS   Bats: R   Throws: R   Height: 6' 2"   Weight: 195   Born: March 26, 1982   Age: 28

YEAR	TEAM	LVL	AGE	PA	R	2B	3B	HR	RBI	BB	SO	SB	CS	EqBRR	AVG	OBP	SLG	EqAVG	EqOBP	EqSLG	EqA	VORP	WARP	DEFENSE			
2007	MEM	AAA	25	353	55	9	5	1	15	25	39	17	6	5.4	.272	.328	.341	.257	.307	.315	.224	-0.1	0.0	76-SS	0		
2007	SLN	MLB	25	199	30	9	0	4	12	15	19	7	0	2.3	.289	.347	.406	.298	.355	.414	.277	9.7	1.9	19-SS	4	17-3B	1
2008	MEM	AAA	26	88	13	5	0	3	10	4	17	1	0	-0.3	.237	.279	.412	.222	.256	.346	.213	-1.7	0.2	6-2B	-3	5-RF	3
2008	SLN	MLB	26	218	30	9	0	0	10	16	31	7	2	2.0	.244	.307	.289	.253	.315	.293	.224	-0.3	-0.2	28-SS	0	17-2B	-3
2009	SLN	MLB	27	429	55	19	7	3	37	24	56	14	7	0.8	.292	.340	.400	.311	.355	.429	.270	21.3	6.4	93-SS	31	11-2B	0
2010	SLN	MLB	28	461	63	20	3	5	32	34	70	13	5	1.7	.266	.327	.366	.271	.331	.373	.251	12.1	2.2	94-SS	8		

Breakout: 14%   Improve: 40%   Collapse: 11%   Attrition: 9%   MLB: 86%   Comparables: Adam Everett, Jason Bartlett, Ricky Gutierrez, Julio Franco

When Khalil Greene didn't pan out, the Cardinals needed somebody at shortstop. Nature abhors a vacuum, but that doesn't mean you have to suck. Happily, Ryan turned out to be not just ready, but also one of the biggest surprises of the season, posting an outstanding season afield (31 Fielding Runs is *not* a typo). Working behind Pineiro, Carpenter, and Wainwright helped give him on average more opportunities per game than the average shortstop gets, but not everyone responds to expanded opportunities. Ryan did. His year at the plate benefited from spikes in BABIP and line-drive percentage that are a bit more than you can expect him to repeat. Having made this kind of impression while fielding this well, he won't need a perfect encore to keep his hold on the job.

Skip Schumaker   2B/OF   Bats: L   Throws: R   Height: 5' 10"   Weight: 195   Born: February 3, 1980   Age: 30

YEAR	TEAM	LVL	AGE	PA	R	2B	3B	HR	RBI	BB	SO	SB	CS	EqBRR	AVG	OBP	SLG	EqAVG	EqOBP	EqSLG	EqA	VORP	WARP	DEFENSE			
2007	MEM	AAA	27	264	34	16	0	7	31	27	37	2	3	-2.3	.306	.382	.466	.283	.350	.401	.262	7.4	0.3	46-CF	-5	7-LF	0
2007	SLN	MLB	27	188	19	12	2	2	19	8	20	1	1	-1.9	.333	.358	.458	.345	.367	.469	.288	8.6	0.8	14-LF	1	13-RF	-4
2008	SLN	MLB	28	594	87	22	5	8	46	47	60	8	2	1.1	.302	.359	.406	.315	.371	.424	.277	24.4	1.8	62-CF	-10	38-LF	3
2009	SLN	MLB	29	586	85	34	1	4	35	52	69	2	2	2.6	.303	.364	.393	.320	.378	.414	.277	26.7	1.2	111-2B	-13	9-LF	-3
2010	SLN	MLB	30	567	77	28	2	8	46	50	72	4	3	-0.1	.300	.363	.410	.299	.359	.413	.277	27.6	2.4	101-2B	-6		

Breakout: 9%   Improve: 36%   Collapse: 9%   Attrition: 15%   MLB: 96%   Comparables: Todd Walker, Akinori Iwamura, Marlon Anderson, Jim Gantner

The great infield experiment gave us a fine example of how a merely adequate bat for the outfield can be handy enough at second. Schumaker's athleticism made the proposition viable, and it's possible he'll improve to adequacy with further reps. In the meantime, he's an example of how playing second base in the majors requires more than mere athleticism. He can't hit left-handed pitching, and his bat is shy of good enough for an outfield regular, but La Russa looked at what Schumaker could do (get aboard against righties) and might do, considered what this club needed, and found value. It's a strange thing to have your starting second baseman be your late-game defensive replacement in the outfield, but take that as another reminder that La Russa remains a canny tactician.

Nick Stavinoha   OF/1B   Bats: R   Throws: R   Height: 6' 2"   Weight: 225   Born: May 3, 1982   Age: 28

YEAR	TEAM	LVL	AGE	PA	R	2B	3B	HR	RBI	BB	SO	SB	CS	EqBRR	AVG	OBP	SLG	EqAVG	EqOBP	EqSLG	EqA	VORP	WARP	DEFENSE			
2007	MEM	AAA	25	539	50	17	0	13	49	31	81	7	1	-2.0	.261	.309	.373	.247	.288	.340	.221	-12.2	-3.1	73-LF	-8	50-RF	-6
2008	MEM	AAA	26	453	67	23	3	16	74	20	50	2	1	0.2	.337	.366	.518	.313	.338	.450	.270	13.1	1.2	55-RF	-1	41-LF	-2
2008	SLN	MLB	26	61	4	1	0	0	4	2	11	0	0	0.4	.193	.217	.211	.175	.200	.193	.121	-6.3	-1.1	6-LF	-2	2-RF	-1
2009	MEM	AAA	27	295	39	17	2	11	56	25	48	2	0	-0.2	.282	.353	.490	.268	.328	.442	.267	4.6	-0.8	33-1B	-5	21-RF	-5
2009	SLN	MLB	27	91	6	7	0	2	17	2	15	1	0	1.0	.230	.242	.379	.233	.242	.395	.222	-2.4	-0.6	9-LF	-2	8-RF	-1
2010	SLN	MLB	28	429	40	19	1	9	47	26	78	2	1	-0.1	.250	.300	.371	.257	.306	.382	.237	-5.7	-1.4	88-1B	-7		

Breakout: 7%   Improve: 31%   Collapse: 23%   Attrition: 10%   MLB: 24%   Comparables: Toby Rumfield, Ron Coomer, Mike Eylward, Nate Gold

Among the collection of corner outfield types vying for time before Holliday's acquisition wiped out most of their opportunities, Stavinoha was the extra guy trying to add to the proposition of finding strength in numbers, an odd body asked to chip in against lefties or pinch-hit. Without Ankiel or another lefty hitter in left to platoon with, his value is limited on this roster; the Cardinals don't need a spare at first base, and he doesn't hit well enough against righties to encourage La Russa to get old-school and carry "just" seven relievers.

Joe Thurston   UT   Bats: L   Throws: R   Height: 5' 11"   Weight: 190   Born: September 29, 1979   Age: 30

YEAR	TEAM	LVL	AGE	PA	R	2B	3B	HR	RBI	BB	SO	SB	CS	EqBRR	AVG	OBP	SLG	EqAVG	EqOBP	EqSLG	EqA	VORP	WARP	DEFENSE			
2007	OTT	AAA	27	572	70	29	9	5	59	44	55	16	14	-2.8	.300	.367	.425	.289	.346	.407	.261	17.7	1.1	103-2B	-8	21-LF	-1
2008	PAW	AAA	28	575	84	28	5	11	64	35	75	19	11	-3.4	.316	.367	.456	.286	.332	.404	.256	14.0	1.6	95-2B	-3	17-LF	0
2009	SLN	MLB	29	307	27	17	4	1	25	33	56	4	2	-1.8	.225	.316	.330	.234	.321	.342	.238	0.6	-0.1	52-3B	-1	16-2B	-1
2010	ATL	MLB	30	367	42	17	3	5	36	31	57	5	4	-1.1	.256	.328	.371	.265	.334	.378	.252	6.2	0.6	80-3B	-1		

Breakout: 11%   Improve: 29%   Collapse: 25%   Attrition: 25%   MLB: 32%   Comparables: Chip Hale, Jeff Gardner, Ed Giovanola, Terry Bogener

After seven years at Triple-A with four different organizations, Sloppy Joe finally caught his big break, temporarily winding up atop the depth chart at third base and doing what he could with the opportunity—which predictably had the effect of encouraging the Cards to go get a third baseman. It wasn't for his lack of trying to fill the bill. Thurston started just six games after the All-Star break and, his big breakthrough already over, slipped away to Atlanta on a minor-league deal and presumably another season back in the bushes.

PITCHERS

Mitchell Boggs

Bats: R Throws: R Height: 6' 4" Weight: 215 Born: February 15, 1984 Age: 26

YEAR	TEAM	LVL	AGE	W	L	SV	G	GS	IP	H	HR	BB	SO	GB%	BABIP	STUFF	WHIP	ERA	SIERA	DERA	EqH9	EqHR9	EqBB9	EqSO9	VORP	SN/WX
2007	SFD	AA	23	11	7	0	26	26	152¹	167	15	62	117	55%	.314	-11	1.50	3.84	4.33	5.99	10.5	1.4	3.8	5.0	-8.1	-0.43
2008	MEM	AAA	24	9	3	0	21	21	125¹	107	11	46	81	56%	.261	-3	1.22	3.45	4.44	4.17	8.3	1.3	3.4	4.2	17.4	2.05
2008	SLN	MLB	24	3	2	0	8	6	34	42	5	22	13	60%	.303	-28	1.88	7.41	5.87	7.81	11.1	1.6	5.0	2.9	-8.7	0.00
2009	MEM	AAA	25	6	4	0	14	14	76¹	90	8	32	58	49%	.336	-24	1.60	4.83	4.46	6.13	11.9	1.9	4.0	5.1	-5.0	0.22
2009	SLN	MLB	25	2	3	0	16	9	58	71	3	33	46	60%	.374	-1	1.79	4.19	4.54	4.53	11.9	0.5	4.6	6.1	5.9	0.70
2010	SLN	MLB	26	5	9	0	32	21	118²	135	15	60	73	49%	.318	-13	1.65	5.45	5.11	5.85	10.2	1.2	4.2	5.1	-4.6	1.58

Breakout: 11% Improve: 50% Collapse: 11% Attrition: 25% MLB: 91% Comparables: Dennis Sarfate, Mike Parisi, Darrell Rasner, Ryan Mottl

Prattling about regression can be sort of pointless if you mistake effect for cause; Boggs' results on balls in play aren't going to get better because Yeats was wrong and the center not only holds, but sucks everything toward its general vicinity. It's only going to go down after he finds a pitch that works against left-handed hitters. Until then, he'll be pasted with alarming regularity and be bullpen-bound, no matter how much he or anyone else prays to the BABIP fairy. Majors or minors, his mix of sliders and low-90s heat is only getting right-handed humans out, squelching his bid for the fifth starter's job. Understandably, the Cardinals are talking about a move to the pen.

Chris Carpenter

Bats: R Throws: R Height: 6' 6" Weight: 230 Born: April 27, 1975 Age: 35

YEAR	TEAM	LVL	AGE	W	L	SV	G	GS	IP	H	HR	BB	SO	GB%	BABIP	STUFF	WHIP	ERA	SIERA	DERA	EqH9	EqHR9	EqBB9	EqSO9	VORP	SN/WX
2007	SLN	MLB	32	0	1	0	1	1	6	9	0	1	3	80%	.375	-2	1.67	7.50	4.16	7.50	13.5	0.0	1.5	4.5	-1.3	-0.08
2008	SLN	MLB	33	0	1	0	4	3	15¹	16	0	4	7	63%	.308	-4	1.30	1.76	4.69	3.07	9.8	0.0	1.8	3.7	4.0	0.73
2009	SLN	MLB	34	17	4	0	28	28	192²	156	7	38	144	63%	.269	34	1.01	2.24	3.55	2.66	7.7	0.4	1.6	5.7	58.4	8.01
2010	SLN	MLB	35	7	6	0	24	0	116	114	10	35	71	63%	.290	8	1.28	3.76	4.30	4.08	8.7	0.8	2.5	5.1	18.3	3.14

Breakout: 14% Improve: 32% Collapse: 32% Attrition: 13% MLB: 86% Comparables: Clay Carroll, Jason Grimsley, Julian Tavarez, Tanyon Sturtze

How good was Carpenter's comeback? In the 55 years covered by Retrosheet, it's no surprise that Bob Gibson's 1968 is the all-time franchise high in Support-Neutral Winning Percentage at .732. SNWP is BP's metric for how likely a team is to win a game the man starts. Third in Cards history was John Tudor's '85 season, at .670. And nestled between them? Carpenter's '09, coming in at .673. Gibson won the Cy Young, Tudor didn't, and Carpenter already has one for '05, when his SNWP was .640, which ranks seventh in team history (behind the '69 seasons of Gibson and Steve Carlton and the '67 surprise from Nellie Briles). All of which is the long way around saying Carpenter's place in team history deserves ranking among its all-time greats, and the story isn't even finished yet. He's only guaranteed two more years (2012 is a club option), but after last season's exploits, another bit of greatness or another disappearance onto the DL seem to be the poles he operates from, with little chance of anything in between.

Ryan Franklin

Bats: R Throws: R Height: 6' 3" Weight: 190 Born: March 5, 1973 Age: 37

YEAR	TEAM	LVL	AGE	W	L	SV	G	GS	IP	H	HR	BB	SO	GB%	BABIP	STUFF	WHIP	ERA	SIERA	DERA	EqH9	EqHR9	EqBB9	EqSO9	VORP	SN/WX
2007	SLN	MLB	34	4	4	1	69	0	80	70	8	11	44	55%	.247	1	1.01	3.04	4.26	3.02	7.7	0.9	1.1	4.4	21.8	3.10
2008	SLN	MLB	35	6	6	17	74	0	78²	86	10	30	51	47%	.302	-18	1.47	3.55	4.71	4.02	10.0	1.3	3.0	4.9	12.8	3.16
2009	SLN	MLB	36	4	3	38	62	0	61	49	2	24	44	50%	.263	6	1.20	1.92	4.36	2.26	7.5	0.3	3.0	5.4	21.5	3.81
2010	SLN	MLB	37	3	4	9	61	0	60	63	6	22	32	49%	.296	-11	1.41	4.43	4.98	4.74	9.3	1.0	2.9	4.5	5.0	1.84

Breakout: 15% Improve: 41% Collapse: 34% Attrition: 25% MLB: 94% Comparables: Ron Kline, Kent Tekulve, Clay Carroll, Steve Reed

Per WXRL, Franklin was the fifth-best reliever in the NL, but remember, WXRL is a counting stat; give a guy a lot of save opportunities and a careful usage pattern, and you can find statistical joy. Franklin also ranked seventh in the NL in 2008, when he wasn't getting all the save opportunities. It's more telling when you switch over to a rate metric like Fair Run Average: Franklin led the majors at 1.59 in '09, against a 4.17 mark in '08. We'll never know if further in-season fame awaited him, if only Holliday had caught that ball, but it's in the books now, and finding consistent relief help is like nailing down Jell-O. The billy-goat-bearded one struggled through command issues down the stretch, reflecting his thin line between incandescence and pyromania. Franklin's affordability has made relying on him a minor coup, but three blown saves and another near miss in September suggest they'll need a backup plan.

Jaime Garcia

Bats: L   Throws: L   Height: 6' 2"   Weight: 200   Born: July 8, 1986   Age: 23

YEAR	TEAM	LVL	AGE	W	L	SV	G	GS	IP	H	HR	BB	SO	GB%	BABIP	STUFF	WHIP	ERA	SIERA	DERA	EqH9	EqHR9	EqBB9	EqSO9	VORP	SN/WX
2007	SFD	AA	20	5	9	0	18	18	103¹	93	14	45	97	67%	.281	25	1.34	3.75	3.61	4.91	9.1	1.7	4.1	6.5	6.4	0.21
2008	SFD	AA	21	3	2	0	6	6	35	26	0	16	41	66%	.302	33	1.20	2.06	2.97	3.14	7.9	0.5	4.4	8.2	8.7	0.73
2008	MEM	AAA	21	4	4	0	13	12	71	74	6	26	59	62%	.315	18	1.41	4.44	3.87	5.70	10.0	1.3	3.3	5.2	-1.5	0.05
2008	SLN	MLB	21	1	1	0	10	1	16	14	4	8	8	67%	.208	-5	1.37	5.62	4.87	5.74	8.0	2.3	4.0	4.0	-0.4	0.52
2009	PMB	A+	22	0	1	0	3	2	12²	4	0	4	16	63%	.182	11	0.63	0.71	1.91	1.69	5.1	0.8	4.2	8.4	4.5	0.45
2009	MEM	AAA	22	2	0	0	4	4	21	17	5	9	22	61%	.245	9	1.24	3.86	3.26	6.75	9.6	4.3	4.3	7.7	-2.6	-0.09
2010	SLN	MLB	23	4	5	0	23	10	74²	74	9	39	59	60%	.300	4	1.51	4.86	4.39	5.26	9.0	1.2	4.3	6.4	2.0	1.26

Breakout: 21%   Improve: 56%   Collapse: 20%   Attrition: 18%   MLB: 36%   Comparables: Chi-Hung Cheng, Joel McKeon, Tom Bolton, Tyler Johnson

Garcia lost most of the year recovering from his September '08 Tommy John surgery, but came back in working order to help Memphis down its PCL title–winning stretch, winning a pair of post-season games. He doesn't appear to have lost any of the late hop on his heat or the bend on his big, looping curve, so he's back on the list of interesting pitching prospects. Barring another Brad Penny–level addition, he'll contend for the fifth slot in the rotation, aided in part in that he'd be the lone lefty.

Blake Hawksworth

Bats: R   Throws: R   Height: 6' 3"   Weight: 195   Born: March 1, 1983   Age: 27

YEAR	TEAM	LVL	AGE	W	L	SV	G	GS	IP	H	HR	BB	SO	GB%	BABIP	STUFF	WHIP	ERA	SIERA	DERA	EqH9	EqHR9	EqBB9	EqSO9	VORP	SN/WX
2007	MEM	AAA	24	4	13	0	25	25	129²	150	24	41	88	51%	.309	-42	1.47	5.28	4.42	6.27	11.2	2.6	3.1	4.5	-10.5	-0.06
2008	MEM	AAA	25	5	7	0	18	16	88²	111	12	38	83	59%	.364	-27	1.68	6.09	3.89	7.81	12.2	1.9	3.9	6.1	-21.8	-1.02
2009	MEM	AAA	26	5	4	0	12	12	73	61	3	20	57	51%	.262	11	1.11	3.58	3.89	4.48	8.0	0.9	2.5	5.1	8.2	0.75
2009	SLN	MLB	26	4	0	0	30	0	40	29	2	15	20	58%	.221	-7	1.10	2.02	4.89	2.54	6.7	0.5	3.0	3.7	12.8	1.41
2010	SLN	MLB	27	4	8	0	34	16	95	109	14	42	63	48%	.319	-14	1.59	5.49	4.82	5.91	10.3	1.4	3.7	5.4	-4.3	1.34

Breakout: 17%   Improve: 49%   Collapse: 12%   Attrition: 20%   MLB: 30%   Comparables: Don Heinkel, Dave Tuttle, Jerry Johnson, Greg Perschke

Per FRA, Hawksworth was the second most effective reliever in the Birdpen behind Franklin, at 2.45, but he was also the reliever La Russa preferred to use when the team was down by a few runs. It's not hard to see why: Hawksworth is pure deception material, relying heavily on selling his changeup. Right-handers loaded up and lost, lefties could work him, and there's not a lot to suggest he'll be a reliable contributor until he finds something else to distract hitters with.

Josh Kinney

Bats: R   Throws: R   Height: 6' 1"   Weight: 215   Born: March 31, 1979   Age: 31

YEAR	TEAM	LVL	AGE	W	L	SV	G	GS	IP	H	HR	BB	SO	GB%	BABIP	STUFF	WHIP	ERA	SIERA	DERA	EqH9	EqHR9	EqBB9	EqSO9	VORP	SN/WX
2008	SLN	MLB	29	0	0	0	7	0	7	3	0	1	8	74%	.188	7	0.57	0.00	1.96	0.00	3.9	0.0	1.3	7.7	4.3	0.13
2009	MEM	AAA	30	3	3	1	38	0	44¹	43	6	20	52	58%	.327	-11	1.42	3.86	3.22	5.01	10.5	2.4	4.4	8.3	2.3	0.60
2009	SLN	MLB	30	1	0	0	17	0	15¹	23	2	11	8	56%	.362	-35	2.22	8.80	5.78	8.90	13.2	1.1	5.2	4.0	-5.9	-0.57
2010	SLN	MLB	31	2	4	0	38	0	44²	55	6	23	32	61%	.345	-19	1.74	6.37	4.60	6.75	10.9	1.4	4.2	6.0	-6.2	0.34

Breakout: 13%   Improve: 48%   Collapse: 25%   Attrition: 8%   MLB: 47%   Comparables: Marcus Gwyn, Matt Miller, Dave Borkowski, Will Cunnane

Years removed from some post-season production in '06, Kinney finally came back from Tommy John surgery to earn a spot in the Opening Day pen, but proved to be still dealing with the postsurgical lack of sharpness that can follow the procedure. He tended to nibble against lefties ("Take your base") and miss up to righties ("A cookie, for me?"), a formula for big innings in the big leagues. He should be sharper now, but will have to earn his spot toward the back of the bullpen.

Kyle Lohse

Bats: R   Throws: R   Height: 6' 2"   Weight: 210   Born: October 4, 1978   Age: 31

YEAR	TEAM	LVL	AGE	W	L	SV	G	GS	IP	H	HR	BB	SO	GB%	BABIP	STUFF	WHIP	ERA	SIERA	DERA	EqH9	EqHR9	EqBB9	EqSO9	VORP	SN/WX
2007	CIN	MLB	28	6	12	0	21	21	131²	143	16	33	80	42%	.298	11	1.34	4.58	4.60	4.58	8.8	0.9	2.0	5.0	13.6	2.28
2007	PHI	MLB	28	3	0	0	13	11	61	64	6	24	42	51%	.305	5	1.44	4.72	4.58	4.55	9.1	0.7	3.1	5.7	6.4	1.47
2008	SLN	MLB	29	15	6	0	33	33	200	211	18	49	119	52%	.297	6	1.30	3.78	4.47	4.10	9.6	0.9	2.0	4.6	30.4	5.19
2009	SLN	MLB	30	6	10	0	23	22	117²	125	16	36	77	49%	.287	-9	1.37	4.74	4.48	5.51	9.6	1.5	2.3	4.8	-0.1	1.17
2010	SLN	MLB	31	8	9	0	28	27	141²	153	16	48	80	47%	.303	-2	1.42	4.45	4.86	4.77	9.6	1.1	2.8	4.7	11.4	1.94

Breakout: 2%   Improve: 43%   Collapse: 20%   Attrition: 24%   MLB: 93%   Comparables: Duane Pillette, Todd Ritchie, Steve Trachsel, Bobby Witt

Lohse was supposed to be signed up for the Graybeards Breakthrough Package, same as Pineiro, but a series of injuries—to his nonpitching elbow, his pitching forearm, and later his groin—undermined his effectiveness when it wasn't costing more than a month on the DL. Owed $32.625 million over the next three seasons and equipped with a no-trade clause because the Cardinals bet on their own, as well as Lohse's, ability to perpetuate his 2008 breakout, he has been penciled in as the third starter, one whose only performance tic was a small spike in ratio of homers to fly balls. Healthy, he may not repeat '08, but he should be an asset.

Lance Lynn

Bats: R   Throws: R   Height: 6' 5"   Weight: 250   Born: May 12, 1987   Age: 23

YEAR	TEAM	LVL	AGE	W	L	SV	G	GS	IP	H	HR	BB	SO	GB%	BABIP	STUFF	WHIP	ERA	SIERA	DERA	EqH9	EqHR9	EqBB9	EqSO9	VORP	SN/WX
2008	BAT	A-	21	1	0	0	6	4	18²	12	0	4	22	44%	.261	16	0.86	0.96	2.28	3.89	7.8	1.0	2.6	5.7	3.1	0.25
2009	PMB	A+	22	0	0	0	5	2	15²	16	0	3	17	60%	.364	14	1.21	2.30	2.69	3.54	11.6	0.6	2.6	6.4	3.1	0.13
2009	SFD	AA	22	11	4	0	22	22	126¹	117	5	51	98	48%	.299	18	1.33	2.92	4.26	4.30	9.1	0.9	3.8	5.8	15.9	1.25
2010	SLN	MLB	23	6	9	0	26	24	123¹	135	15	59	90	41%	.319	3	1.58	5.14	4.79	5.46	9.7	1.2	4.0	5.9	0.6	2.62

Breakout: 8%   Improve: 33%   Collapse: 31%   Attrition: 3%   MLB: 5%   Comparables: Cal Eldred, Matt McClendon, Don Sparling, David Mysel

A 2008 supplemental first-rounder picked out of Mississippi with the selection created by Troy Percival's departure, Lynn is one of the organization's typical strike-throwing college pitchers, throwing low-90s heat for strikes while mixing in the standard curve, slider, and change, all with solid command. Sensibly, the Cardinals pushed the polished product to Double-A in his first full season, and they weren't disappointed, as he finished strong. He's already on the radar for 2010, and if the expectations are that he's a modest-ceiling strike-throwing innings-muncher in the making, you can understand why they only gave Brad Penny a one-year deal.

Kyle McClellan

Bats: R   Throws: R   Height: 6' 4"   Weight: 205   Born: June 12, 1984   Age: 26

YEAR	TEAM	LVL	AGE	W	L	SV	G	GS	IP	H	HR	BB	SO	GB%	BABIP	STUFF	WHIP	ERA	SIERA	DERA	EqH9	EqHR9	EqBB9	EqSO9	VORP	SN/WX
2007	PMB	A+	23	4	1	0	16	1	29	22	0	4	24	58%	.268	5	0.90	1.24	3.20	2.03	8.4	0.7	1.7	5.1	10.3	0.87
2007	SFD	AA	23	2	0	0	24	0	30²	24	2	6	30	62%	.275	11	0.98	2.35	2.83	3.45	7.8	0.9	2.2	6.9	6.5	0.82
2008	SLN	MLB	24	2	7	1	68	0	75²	79	7	26	59	56%	.312	-6	1.39	4.04	4.08	4.50	9.6	1.0	2.8	6.0	8.2	1.18
2009	SLN	MLB	25	4	4	3	66	0	66²	56	4	34	51	55%	.264	-2	1.35	3.37	4.50	3.92	7.7	0.7	3.9	5.7	11.7	1.37
2010	SLN	MLB	26	4	4	1	63	0	63²	64	6	25	44	59%	.301	-5	1.40	4.33	4.37	4.59	8.9	1.0	3.2	5.7	6.4	1.19

Breakout: 11%   Improve: 33%   Collapse: 24%   Attrition: 8%   MLB: 87%   Comparables: Jeff Dedmon, Brad Clontz, Elias Sosa, Jeremy Accardo

The son of longtime season-ticket holders, McClellan was clearly born to be a Cardinal, but it doesn't hurt that he's a useful reliever besides. Used as the primary right-handed set-up man, he'd run into the odd bad patch against righties, ulcerating his skipper's gizzards, but he's not really a dominant pen man as much as a useful one. Better alternatives will push him into earlier spots in-game, where he'll remain a useful piece of the puzzle.

Shelby Miller

Bats: R   Throws: R   Height: 6' 5"   Weight: 195   Born: October 10, 1990   Age: 19

YEAR	TEAM	LVL	AGE	W	L	SV	G	GS	IP	H	HR	BB	SO	GB%	BABIP	STUFF	WHIP	ERA	SIERA	DERA	EqH9	EqHR9	EqBB9	EqSO9	VORP	SN/WX
Did Not Play																										
2010	SLN	MLB	19	1	4	0	12	12	46²	73	8	25	0	51%	.337	-37	2.10	7.71	7.28	8.18	13.8	1.8	4.3	0.0	-13.9	0.30

Breakout: 12%   Improve: 36%   Collapse: 29%   Attrition: 2%   MLB: 0%   Comparables: Jake Dittler, Frederick Ludwig, Albert Hartman, Adrian Rosario

Straight from that Texas high-school assembly line known for cranking out big, young power pitchers, Miller was the 19th overall selection in the 2009 draft, as the Cardinals broke with past practice and reached past the college picks they've been known to favor. With low- to mid-90s heat that touches 97 mph and clean mechanics, he's starting from a good place, but he has a lot of polish to add to his off-speed stuff. He's a long way off, but the Cards made a point of getting him under contract to make sure he didn't slip away to Texas A&M.

Trever Miller

Bats: R   Throws: L   Height: 6' 3"   Weight: 200   Born: May 29, 1973   Age: 37

YEAR	TEAM	LVL	AGE	W	L	SV	G	GS	IP	H	HR	BB	SO	GB%	BABIP	STUFF	WHIP	ERA	SIERA	DERA	EqH9	EqHR9	EqBB9	EqSO9	VORP	SN/WX
2007	HOU	MLB	34	0	0	1	76	0	46¹	45	6	23	46	41%	.295	0	1.47	4.86	4.00	4.63	8.3	1.1	3.8	7.7	4.6	0.51
2008	TBA	MLB	35	2	0	2	68	0	43¹	39	2	20	44	37%	.316	9	1.36	4.15	3.77	4.32	8.9	0.4	3.9	8.4	5.5	1.55
2009	SLN	MLB	36	4	1	0	70	0	43²	31	5	11	46	38%	.239	13	0.96	2.06	2.83	2.51	6.9	1.3	1.9	7.7	14.3	1.71
2010	SLN	MLB	19	1	4	0	12	12	46²	73	8	25	0	51%	.337	-37	2.10	7.71	7.28	8.18	13.8	1.8	4.3	0.0	-13.9	0.30

Breakout: 12%   Improve: 36%   Collapse: 29%   Attrition: 2%   MLB: 0%   Comparables: Jake Dittler, Frederick Ludwig, Albert Hartman, Adrian Rosario

In studied contrast to the cherubic Dennys Reyes, Miller is the older, angular, more established southpaw and veteran of postseasons past, and his destiny just as certainly involved his being a Cardinal someday. Technically proficient and born for this work with his sidearm-scything of southpaws, Miller was tasked with protecting eighth-inning leads where Reyes generally got used earlier and in tighter situations, down or up on the scoreboard. That's the Cards' pen for you, with enough subspecialization among specialists that Darwin could have written about them as easily as so many finches' beaks.

Jason Motte

Bats: R   Throws: R   Height: 6' 0"   Weight: 195   Born: June 22, 1982   Age: 28

YEAR	TEAM	LVL	AGE	W	L	SV	G	GS	IP	H	HR	BB	SO	GB%	BABIP	STUFF	WHIP	ERA	SIERA	DERA	EqH9	EqHR9	EqBB9	EqSO9	VORP	SN/WX
2007	SFD	AA	25	3	3	8	44	0	49	36	3	22	63	47%	.303	15	1.18	2.20	2.69	3.08	7.9	1.0	4.4	9.3	12.2	0.62
2008	MEM	AAA	26	4	3	9	63	0	66²	64	6	26	110	38%	.395	12	1.35	3.24	1.70	3.80	10.1	1.3	3.5	10.7	12.1	0.92
2008	SLN	MLB	26	0	0	1	12	0	11	5	0	3	16	43%	.238	10	0.73	0.82	1.33	1.74	5.2	0.0	2.6	10.5	4.3	0.56
2009	SLN	MLB	27	4	4	0	69	0	56²	57	10	23	54	43%	.303	-13	1.41	4.76	3.76	5.22	9.9	2.0	3.1	7.3	1.7	0.56
2010	SLN	MLB	28	3	4	3	64	0	63	67	7	29	64	42%	.341	0	1.53	4.75	3.74	5.06	9.4	1.2	3.8	8.3	3.1	1.13

Breakout: 12%   Improve: 35%   Collapse: 29%   Attrition: 9%   MLB: 48%   Comparables: Jeremy Fikac, Jim Dougherty, Rick Huisman, Mark Williamson

Gifted with velocity that scrapes triple-digit territory, the former catcher was nominated the club's closer for Opening Day. One spectacularly blown opportunity later, Motte learned why they don't carve "established" in granite on most newly minted closers until much later in their careers. La Russa became increasingly disenchanted with Motte as the season progressed, casting him into the bullpen backwater of mop-up work. Motte is still on the list of presumed Franklin replacements in case the veteran implodes, but his galling tendency to make mistakes with the bases empty suggests too much attention to gun readings and strikeouts, and not enough pitching.

Adam Ottavino

Bats: L   Throws: R   Height: 6' 5"   Weight: 215   Born: November 22, 1985   Age: 24

YEAR	TEAM	LVL	AGE	W	L	SV	G	GS	IP	H	HR	BB	SO	GB%	BABIP	STUFF	WHIP	ERA	SIERA	DERA	EqH9	EqHR9	EqBB9	EqSO9	VORP	SN/WX
2007	PMB	A+	21	12	8	0	27	27	143¹	130	10	63	128	52%	.292	4	1.35	3.08	3.97	5.30	10.3	1.8	4.7	5.5	3.0	0.51
2008	SFD	AA	22	3	7	0	24	24	115¹	133	16	52	96	45%	.329	-16	1.60	5.23	4.34	6.69	11.2	1.7	4.2	5.5	-14.7	-1.32
2009	MEM	AAA	23	7	12	0	27	27	144	141	12	82	119	50%	.308	-10	1.55	4.75	4.55	5.81	10.1	1.6	5.3	5.7	-4.7	0.28
2010	SLN	MLB	24	5	9	0	34	25	117	135	17	70	82	39%	.324	-16	1.75	6.01	5.26	6.34	10.2	1.3	4.9	5.8	-10.9	1.49

Breakout: 17%   Improve: 59%   Collapse: 16%   Attrition: 21%   MLB: 12%   Comparables: Nick Maness, Michael Wuertz, Pete Munro, Gary Knotts

One of the system's few upper-level starting prospects who throws hard, Ottavino is still looking for reliable off-speed stuff. The lack of it contributes to his getting hammered the second time through an order, as well as to the disappointment that the club's first-round pick from 2006 (30th overall) hasn't done much since A-ball. He was added to the 40-man because not doing so would expose him to the Rule 5 draft, but he's going to need to regroup and show something to avoid being converted to relief work.

Joel Pineiro

Bats: R   Throws: R   Height: 6' 1"   Weight: 200   Born: September 25, 1978   Age: 31

YEAR	TEAM	LVL	AGE	W	L	SV	G	GS	IP	H	HR	BB	SO	GB%	BABIP	STUFF	WHIP	ERA	SIERA	DERA	EqH9	EqHR9	EqBB9	EqSO9	VORP	SN/WX
2007	BOS	MLB	28	1	1	0	31	0	34	41	3	14	20	61%	.319	-14	1.62	5.03	4.82	4.85	10.7	0.8	3.4	5.0	2.5	-0.38
2007	SLN	MLB	28	6	4	0	11	11	63²	69	11	12	40	53%	.293	0	1.27	3.96	4.19	3.91	10.0	1.8	1.6	5.2	10.8	1.73
2008	SLN	MLB	29	7	7	1	26	25	148²	180	22	35	81	60%	.313	-16	1.45	5.15	4.51	5.46	11.0	1.5	1.9	4.2	0.6	1.47
2009	SLN	MLB	30	15	12	0	32	32	214	218	11	27	105	67%	.290	13	1.14	3.49	4.14	4.22	9.4	0.6	1.0	3.7	29.3	4.63
2010	SLN	MLB	31	10	10	0	41	30	170	188	18	43	84	62%	.303	-5	1.36	4.29	4.64	4.68	10.0	1.1	2.1	4.1	15.4	1.97

Breakout: 10%   Improve: 49%   Collapse: 16%   Attrition: 14%   MLB: 96%   Comparables: Andy Ashby, Ray Washburn, Bryn Smith, Cory Lidle

In some ways, Pineiro's big comeback is like Storm Davis' 19-win season in 1989. Davis and Pineiro both came up as tremendously talented young pitchers, Davis arriving as a 20-year-old with a good Orioles team, Pineiro at 21 with an equally good Mariners organization. Both were initially successful and built up as potential greats. Both disappointed those expectations while creating concerns about their durability. Both had to bounce through another team en route to finally getting put together with Dave Duncan, and both found tremendous success. So when Storm Davis got oodles of cash from the Royals as a free agent, and imploded ... you can see how this isn't helping Pineiro any, especially with his extreme dependence on his defense. Like Davis then, he's not a lock to strike out five guys per nine these days. He was only moderately fortunate in terms of BABIP and line-drives allowed, and the blend of fewer walks and more grounders should make for a very nice fourth starter. Before the downturn, he'd have gotten Suppan money, but teams are understandably wary.

Dennys Reyes

Bats: R   Throws: L   Height: 6' 3"   Weight: 250   Born: April 19, 1977   Age: 33

YEAR	TEAM	LVL	AGE	W	L	SV	G	GS	IP	H	HR	BB	SO	GB%	BABIP	STUFF	WHIP	ERA	SIERA	DERA	EqH9	EqHR9	EqBB9	EqSO9	VORP	SN/WX
2007	MIN	MLB	30	2	1	0	50	0	29¹	34	1	21	21	72%	.351	-5	1.87	3.99	4.71	4.08	10.4	0.3	6.0	6.0	4.5	0.07
2008	MIN	MLB	31	3	0	0	75	0	46¹	40	4	15	39	65%	.281	9	1.19	2.33	3.64	2.40	7.8	0.8	2.6	7.0	15.5	0.75
2009	SLN	MLB	32	0	2	1	75	0	41	35	2	21	33	62%	.273	-4	1.37	3.29	4.26	4.03	7.8	0.4	3.9	5.9	6.8	0.97
2010	SLN	MLB	33	2	3	0	45	0	44¹	45	4	23	34	63%	.312	-7	1.52	4.67	4.38	5.00	8.9	0.9	4.2	6.2	2.5	0.44

Breakout: 16%   Improve: 39%   Collapse: 25%   Attrition: 10%   MLB: 85%   Comparables: Ray King, Steve Kline, Scott Radinsky, Scott Eyre

When a fortune teller speaks of what's to come, he or she can usually win your trust by foreseeing the entirely predictable, like "Dennys Reyes will pitch for Tony La Russa." Insert your own spooky mood music, but we've been expecting this for, what, a decade now? Sure enough, the hefty lefty contributed his usual same-side stifling. Remember when Bill James observed these guys don't work, because they see just as many righties? Guess again: Reyes faced 108 lefties, 72 righties. Anticipating the eight-man bullpen would have been truly oracular, but we always expected that off that way lay madness.

John Smoltz

Bats: R   Throws: R   Height: 6' 3"   Weight: 220   Born: May 15, 1967   Age: 43

YEAR	TEAM	LVL	AGE	W	L	SV	G	GS	IP	H	HR	BB	SO	GB%	BABIP	STUFF	WHIP	ERA	SIERA	DERA	EqH9	EqHR9	EqBB9	EqSO9	VORP	SN/WX
2007	ATL	MLB	40	14	8	0	32	32	205²	196	18	47	197	53%	.303	28	1.18	3.11	3.20	3.47	8.7	0.8	1.9	7.7	46.0	7.21
2008	ATL	MLB	41	3	2	0	6	5	28	25	2	8	36	58%	.324	28	1.18	2.57	2.41	2.89	8.4	0.6	2.3	9.6	8.1	0.75
2009	BOS	MLB	42	2	5	0	8	8	40	59	8	9	33	50%	.383	2	1.70	8.32	3.88	7.25	12.0	1.3	1.8	6.7	-7.9	-0.37
2009	SLN	MLB	42	1	3	0	7	7	38	36	3	9	40	42%	.311	23	1.18	4.26	2.91	4.54	8.8	0.7	1.9	7.9	4.0	0.91
2010	SLN	MLB	43	5	5	0	31	9	81	88	9	25	67	53%	.327	5	1.39	4.36	3.83	4.74	9.6	1.1	2.6	6.9	6.9	1.53

Breakout: 13%   Improve: 37%   Collapse: 30%   Attrition: 40%   MLB: 88%   Comparables: Early Wynn, Mike Timlin, Dazzy Vance, Gaylord Perry

So, the Boston interlude was ugly, but Smoltzie's back now, right? Well, maybe, but underlying that seemingly impressive strikeout rate and its suggestion that he's almost dominating all over again is his highest percentage of called strikeouts—that is, ones where the umps ended the at-bat—since his injury-shortened 2001 season. His velocity was down on everything, and batters swung and missed less frequently. You don't want to count him out, but he managed just three quality starts with the Cardinals and none with Boston. He could endure as a back-end starter, but if he can handle the rigors of more regular work as a reliever, he could still help a club while making a run at 200 saves to build up his Eck-like Hall of Fame campaign.

Brad Thompson

| | Bats: R | Throws: R | Height: 6' 1" | Weight: 190 | Born: January 31, 1982 | Age: 28 |

YEAR	TEAM	LVL	AGE	W	L	SV	G	GS	IP	H	HR	BB	SO	GB%	BABIP	STUFF	WHIP	ERA	SIERA	DERA	EqH9	EqHR9	EqBB9	EqSO9	VORP	SN/WX
2007	SLN	MLB	25	8	6	0	44	17	129^1	157	23	40	53	59%	.297	-33	1.52	4.73	5.22	4.94	10.9	1.7	2.5	3.3	7.9	2.34
2008	SLN	MLB	26	6	3	0	26	6	64^2	72	5	19	32	58%	.313	-14	1.41	5.15	4.82	5.39	10.5	0.9	2.5	3.8	0.8	0.54
2009	SLN	MLB	27	2	6	0	32	8	80	85	8	23	34	61%	.282	-18	1.35	4.84	4.95	5.29	9.8	1.0	2.2	3.2	1.9	-0.20
2010	KCA	MLB	28	3	7	0	41	12	96^1	127	15	33	39	58%	.328	-24	1.66	6.00	5.29	5.89	10.9	1.3	2.8	3.5	-4.2	0.64

Breakout: 12%   Improve: 51%   Collapse: 19%   Attrition: 19%   MLB: 87%   Comparables: Johnny Lanning, Mike Wood, Tomoyuki Uchiyama, Buck Ross

La Russa and Duncan get credit for rotations of retreaded heroes and hyperadaptive reliever usage patterns, but it's worth remembering they also like having an old-fashioned swingman around. Whether it's Gene Nelson or Mark Petkovsek, there's always someone who gets dropped into a utility role; do it well, and you get permanent employment in the People's Republic of Uncle Tony. Thompson is a finesse right-hander who couldn't keep the gig, but he'll give it another shot with the Royals.

Adam Wainwright

| | Bats: R | Throws: R | Height: 6' 7" | Weight: 230 | Born: August 30, 1981 | Age: 28 |

YEAR	TEAM	LVL	AGE	W	L	SV	G	GS	IP	H	HR	BB	SO	GB%	BABIP	STUFF	WHIP	ERA	SIERA	DERA	EqH9	EqHR9	EqBB9	EqSO9	VORP	SN/WX
2007	SLN	MLB	25	14	12	0	32	32	202	212	13	70	136	54%	.304	14	1.40	3.70	4.49	3.90	9.3	0.6	2.8	5.4	35.7	6.03
2008	SLN	MLB	26	11	3	0	20	20	132	122	12	34	91	51%	.272	14	1.18	3.20	4.15	3.63	8.4	0.9	2.1	5.2	27.1	3.93
2009	SLN	MLB	27	19	8	0	34	34	233	216	17	66	212	56%	.296	24	1.21	2.63	3.47	3.20	8.6	0.8	2.2	6.8	58.8	8.52
2010	SLN	MLB	28	13	11	0	34	34	204^2	204	19	63	149	54%	.302	14	1.30	3.83	4.10	4.14	8.9	0.9	2.5	6.0	31.0	4.44

Breakout: 5%   Improve: 45%   Collapse: 13%   Attrition: 8%   MLB: 98%   Comparables: Brad Penny, Kevin Millwood, Mike Krukow, Scott Erickson

Wainwright is now well removed from the injury nexus and niggling suggestions that he might be a great closer. Slow and steady may not have won the race to the Cy Young, but six more starts than Carpenter plus the eighth-best SNWP in Cardinals history since 1955 produced a SNLVAR of 8.5 to Carpenter's 8.0. Add in his other contributions (eight extra-base hits while batting, a Gold Glove for fielding), and you could fairly accuse him of being the best all-around talent on the mound today. Another top-five finish in Cy Young voting in 2010 or 2011 will guarantee the club's 2012-13 option package at $22 million, so if you think last year's vote was controversial because Javier Vazquez got a little bonus for one second-place vote, imagine the stakes this time around.

P. J. Walters

| | Bats: R | Throws: R | Height: 6' 4" | Weight: 200 | Born: March 12, 1985 | Age: 25 |

YEAR	TEAM	LVL	AGE	W	L	SV	G	GS	IP	H	HR	BB	SO	GB%	BABIP	STUFF	WHIP	ERA	SIERA	DERA	EqH9	EqHR9	EqBB9	EqSO9	VORP	SN/WX
2007	QUD	A	22	6	1	1	17	10	68^2	59	2	12	73	63%	.306	14	1.03	2.62	2.71	4.74	9.8	1.1	2.4	6.1	5.4	0.46
2007	PMB	A+	22	3	1	0	5	5	33^2	29	2	6	37	56%	.293	27	1.04	2.67	2.64	3.80	9.6	1.4	2.3	6.8	6.1	0.38
2007	SFD	AA	22	3	4	0	8	8	49^1	42	4	15	37	55%	.260	16	1.16	2.37	4.02	3.09	8.3	1.1	3.0	4.9	12.8	1.38
2008	SFD	AA	23	1	2	0	6	6	36	35	5	8	34	48%	.300	12	1.19	3.25	3.24	4.90	9.8	1.9	2.4	6.6	2.3	0.18
2008	MEM	AAA	23	9	4	0	23	23	122	123	17	62	122	54%	.314	-13	1.52	4.87	3.85	5.73	10.0	1.9	4.5	6.5	-3.0	0.17
2009	MEM	AAA	24	8	10	0	21	20	121	128	6	44	113	57%	.333	0	1.42	4.54	3.71	6.29	10.4	1.0	3.4	6.3	-10.3	0.01
2009	SLN	MLB	24	0	0	0	8	1	16	21	6	9	14	58%	.294	-30	1.87	9.56	4.44	11.07	11.9	3.8	4.3	5.9	-10.3	-0.60
2010	SLN	MLB	25	6	9	0	32	21	126^1	134	16	54	96	48%	.313	0	1.49	4.93	4.40	5.29	9.4	1.2	3.5	6.3	3.0	1.99

Breakout: 21%   Improve: 62%   Collapse: 5%   Attrition: 25%   MLB: 29%   Comparables: Juan Gutierrez, Jason Bell, Rod Imes, Lance Broadway

Walters is another one of the finesse right-handers the system has knocking around, but he complements slow heat with an off-speed pitch variously referred to as a strange change or a screwball. The expectation is that he's an organizational arm, but he might get an audition for the utility pitcher gig, which is sort of the highest aspiration for his type.

Todd Wellemeyer

| | | | | Bats: R | | Throws: R | | Height: 6' 3" | | Weight: 225 | | Born: August 30, 1978 | | Age: 31 |

YEAR	TEAM	LVL	AGE	W	L	SV	G	GS	IP	H	HR	BB	SO	GB%	BABIP	STUFF	WHIP	ERA	SIERA	DERA	EqH9	EqHR9	EqBB9	EqSO9	VORP	SN/WX
2007	KCA	MLB	28	0	1	0	12	0	15²	25	4	11	9	50%	.356	-33	2.30	10.34	5.76	9.72	13.0	2.2	5.4	4.3	-7.8	-0.22
2007	SLN	MLB	28	3	2	0	20	11	63²	52	7	29	51	46%	.250	5	1.27	3.11	4.34	4.12	7.4	1.0	3.7	6.4	9.7	1.56
2008	SLN	MLB	29	13	9	0	32	32	191²	178	25	62	134	43%	.264	4	1.25	3.71	4.38	4.08	8.4	1.3	2.6	5.3	29.9	4.93
2009	SLN	MLB	30	7	10	0	28	21	122¹	160	19	57	78	42%	.349	-36	1.77	5.89	5.09	6.71	12.6	1.7	3.7	5.0	-15.6	-1.32
2010	SLN	MLB	31	5	8	0	30	21	114¹	130	15	50	71	43%	.316	-10	1.57	5.16	5.00	5.51	10.1	1.3	3.5	5.1	-0.1	0.96

Breakout: 7%   Improve: 36%   Collapse: 19%   Attrition: 23%   MLB: 88%   Comparables: Cal Eldred, Dave Burba, Satoru Komiyama, Jimmy Haynes

When spinning some bit of waiver-wire jetsam into gold, it's important to remember that it usually doesn't remain gold. Wellemeyer's rise and fall is sort of the Bottenfield experience redux, but that's the magic: taking something ordinary, making it seem extraordinary, and producing the illusion that convinces batters they're up against a quality pitcher. Duncan's best tricks always go back to ordinariness—it's why they're called tricks. Wellemeyer's fastball lost zip last year; maybe he'll get it back, and maybe his recurring problems getting lefties out will just put him back in somebody's pen as a free agent. From here on out, expect the ordinary.

LINEOUTS

Hitters

PLAYER	TEAM	LVL	AGE	PA	R	2B	3B	HR	RBI	BB	SO	SB-CS	EqBRR	AVG/OBP/SLG	EqAVG/EqOBP/EqSLG	EqA	VORP	WARP
INF B. Barden	MEM	AAA	28	206	26	11	0	4	28	10	44	1-1	0.4	.267/.317/.390	.251/.291/.351	.223	-4.2	-1.1
	SLN	MLB	28	114	13	3	0	4	10	6	21	0-0	-0.4	.233/.286/.379	.240/.292/.385	.240	0.6	0.4
OF A. Chambers*	PMB	A+	22	517	66	17	16	1	46	47	96	21-12	1.0	.283/.370/.400	.270/.340/.393	.256	9.8	-0.2
RF T. Henley*	SFD	AA	24	473	62	31	3	13	63	40	64	9-4	-1.7	.303/.367/.482	.265/.316/.419	.254	4.2	0.3
UT S. Hill	SFD	AA	24	508	62	26	2	19	64	36	106	1-2	-3.7	.282/.333/.470	.241/.281/.400	.234	-4.1	-2.4
2B J. Hoffpauir	MEM	AAA	26	402	53	22	3	14	53	35	28	4-1	-5.3	.291/.357/.486	.279/.336/.449	.270	15.8	1.8
	SLN	MLB	26	16	1	2	0	0	2	4	2	0-0	-1.0	.250/.438/.417	.250/.438/.417	.323	1.1	0.3
SS P. Kozma	PMB	A+	21	84	8	5	0	0	8	8	16	1-0	-0.7	.315/.381/.384	.280/.341/.333	.249	2.3	-0.5
	SFD	AA	21	459	52	15	3	6	37	42	88	4-2	-2.7	.216/.288/.312	.192/.252/.281	.188	-13.0	-0.5
C M. Pagnozzi	MEM	AAA	26	291	21	7	0	5	32	26	78	0-1	-2.4	.221/.299/.308	.219/.286/.292	.205	-2.6	-0.8
RF S. Robinson	MEM	AAA	24	393	46	18	3	5	40	28	42	16-3	4.7	.238/.306/.351	.236/.295/.341	.230	-1.5	0.5
	SLN	MLB	24	26	1	1	0	0	1	0	2	1-0	0.2	.240/.231/.280	.240/.231/.280	.193	-1.5	-0.5
1B C. Smith	PMB	A+	22	399	44	15	3	10	56	15	67	1-3	-1.9	.286/.319/.423	.277/.302/.410	.244	-3.5	-2.2
	SFD	AA	22	70	13	2	1	2	9	3	9	0-0	0.1	.308/.357/.462	.273/.304/.424	.249	-0.9	-0.2
C R. Stock*	JCY	Rk	19	166	25	9	2	7	24	11	28	0-1	-0.4	.322/.386/.550	.271/.313/.413	.251	3.7	0.3

The highlight of **Brian Barden**'s season was starting at third for the Cards on Opening Day, but after he lost to Joe Thurston and got outrighted in August, it's no surprise he went unclaimed and had to settle for a minor-league deal with the Marlins this winter. ⊘ Predictably for a former defensive back from Mississippi State, **Adron Chambers** has speed and no fear of contact (16 HBPs), plus some OBP against righties, but he needs to improve in the field and on the bases. ⊘ Rice alum **Tyler Henley** made a clean jump to Double-A, solidifying his claim to workmanlike "pro" hitter status without graduating to prospect. ⊘ **Steve Hill** got a long look behind the plate in '09 after drifting between the other four corners as the Cardinals try to find a position for his bat and strong arm; a passed ball every fifth game says there's work to be done. ⊘ **Jarrett Hoffpauir** suffered the fate of many organizational soldiers at second base by getting passed over, then placed on waivers, where he was snagged by the Jays; he'll have to convert to a utility role to stick. ⊘ Top 2007 pick **Pete Kozma** has been pushed up the system fast because of his exceptional glove at shortstop, but the youngster's spin in Double-A provided a harsh lesson that there's a long way yet to go for his bat to be endurable. ⊘ **Matt Pagnozzi**'s catch-and-throw skills are up to snuff, but his hopeless hitting handicaps any chance he'll be a good backup backstop. ⊘ Organizational soldier **Shane Robinson** is striving for fifth outfielder's work in a profession that doesn't use them, but he has range and speed going for him. ⊘ Squat Curacao native **Curt Smith** put in four years at the University of Maine before turning pro, but hit in his full-season debut; he's an organizational bat. ⊘ USC's **Robert Stock** was the club's second-round pick in '09; he wants to catch, and the Cardinals will let him, but he can throw mid-90s heat, in case he decides to take matters into his own hands instead of getting shaken off.

Pitchers

PLAYER	TEAM	LVL	AGE	W	L	SV	IP	H	HR	BB	SO	GB%	BABIP	STUFF	WHIP	ERA	SIERA	DERA	EqH9	EqHR9	EqBB9	EqSO9	VORP
N. Additon*	PMB	A+	21	4	3	0	79¹	69	1	37	66	35%	.286	7	1.34	3.06	4.47	6.54	9.1	1.0	5.0	4.4	-8.7
—	SFD	AA	21	2	3	0	48	36	5	21	26	27%	.214	11	1.19	3.19	5.83	4.63	7.3	1.5	3.9	3.9	4.5
R. Castillo	PMB	A+	19	6	13	0	148²	155	4	66	105	42%	.316	9	1.49	3.87	4.73	6.75	11.0	1.3	5.0	3.7	-19.1
S. Freeman*	PMB	A+	22	2	1	1	33	18	0	13	30	50%	.200	1	0.94	1.64	3.69	3.06	5.8	0.8	4.2	4.7	8.8
—	SFD	AA	22	0	1	1	23	19	6	14	17	69%	.220	-7	1.43	3.52	4.39	4.14	9.1	3.5	5.7	5.7	3.1
S. Gorgen	PMB	A+	22	3	5	0	74	50	7	32	73	51%	.230	-9	1.11	2.92	3.56	5.16	8.7	3.0	4.9	5.7	2.5
—	SFD	AA	22	4	5	0	55¹	52	8	36	46	49%	.282	0	1.59	5.20	4.74	7.05	9.6	2.1	5.8	6.2	-9.0
T. Hearne	SFD	AA	25	12	3	0	127²	113	7	43	81	48%	.269	3	1.22	2.82	4.55	3.76	8.6	1.0	3.2	4.6	23.6
—	MEM	AAA	25	2	1	0	26²	23	4	6	16	56%	.221	-8	1.09	3.37	4.36	4.67	8.3	2.3	2.0	3.7	2.5
T. Norrick*	SFD	AA	25	3	1	5	59	48	4	44	78	52%	.314	14	1.56	4.12	3.53	5.93	8.3	1.2	6.4	10.0	-2.8
A. Reifer	PMB	A+	23	4	7	21	48¹	51	2	24	50	45%	.340	-23	1.55	4.47	3.86	7.54	11.5	1.6	5.4	5.8	-10.3
R. Ring*	MEM	AAA	28	5	2	4	47¹	44	4	15	38	54%	.292	-14	1.25	3.04	3.89	4.09	9.6	1.6	3.1	5.5	6.9
F. Salas	SFD	AA	24	1	0	0	11¹	10	0	2	7	34%	.278	-12	1.06	3.18	4.40	4.50	8.2	0.8	1.6	4.1	1.2
—	MEM	AAA	24	3	2	0	27	22	4	10	24	28%	.243	-15	1.19	3.67	4.17	4.85	8.7	2.4	3.5	5.9	1.9
F. Samuel	SFD	AA	22	3	4	22	47²	36	2	46	59	56%	.301	18	1.72	5.66	4.23	6.99	8.0	1.0	8.2	9.3	-7.7
E. Sanchez	PMB	A+	20	0	1	3	25	12	2	5	26	55%	.175	23	0.68	1.44	2.60	2.58	6.8	2.4	2.4	6.0	7.4
—	SFD	AA	20	2	0	10	50	32	4	20	56	59%	.248	46	1.04	2.70	2.97	3.40	6.8	1.4	3.7	8.9	10.8

Nick Additon is a 46th-round junkball artist beating every challenge thrown his way, but working at super slo-mo is a tough way to go at the upper levels. ⊘ Venezuelan import **Richard Castillo** was young for High-A, but he's short and lacks dominating stuff; survival is a skill, Double-A is next. ⊘ A lefty in this organization might go far, and **Sam Freeman** did manage to earn a promotion after an all-star appearance in High-A ... before hurting his elbow. ⊘ **Scott Gorgen** is another example of a short finesse righty who aced college ball, beats up on kids in the lowest levels, and hits a snag at Double-A. ⊘ Give it to control fiend **Trey Hearne**, he has put in four years with the organization and a fifth in Mexico; he didn't miss a beat when pressed into the Double-A rotation. ⊘ **Tyler Norrick**'s bid to be the best pitcher out of Southern Illinois since Dave Stieb is undermined by wildness in every role he's tried. ⊘ **Mike Parisi** spent 2009 recovering from Tommy John surgery, but the Cubs nevertheless selected him via Rule 5, and they're a club that sometimes keeps their picks. ⊘ **Adam Reifer** flashes a plus slider and consistent mid-90s heat, but that was all that was consistent about his full-season debut. ⊘ You'd think a skipper with a taste for operatic tedium in-game would attempt *the* **Royce Ring**, but even TLR has his limits for situational Siegfrieds; Ring spent the year waiting for Miller time to end, and it didn't. ⊘ Mexican league vet **Fernando Salas** hits his spots with excellent command of a curve and low-90s heat, but works high in the zone. ⊘ **Francisco Samuel** had been a thin Dominican with mid-90s velocity and no command, but upon reaching Double-A, he was heavier with even less command. ⊘ Slight Venezuelan **Eduardo Sanchez** has thrived by backing people off the plate and generating scads of ground balls.

MANAGER: TONY LA RUSSA

YEAR	TEAM	W-L	Pythag +/−	Avg PC	100+ P	120+ P	QS	BQS	REL	REL w Zero R	IBB	Subs	PH	PH Avg	PH HR	SB2	CS2	SB3	CS3	SAC Att	SAC %	POS SAC	Squeeze	Swing	In Play
2007	SLN	78-84	8	89.7	44	2	68	4	515	339	25	56	315	.296	5	50	26	6	3	93	73.1%	31	1	140	121
2008	SLN	86-76	-1	93.0	52	1	76	9	506	318	21	78	273	.240	6	63	27	9	3	109	65.1%	33	1	150	120
2009	SLN	91-71	-1	94.5	54	4	83	3	480	335	23	91	280	.221	8	65	25	10	4	109	62.4%	33	0	127	103

La Russa is now historic, if he wasn't already before. Last season, he passed John McGraw for second place in games managed, which for all practical purposes means that he's first all time. What Connie Mack did for the last several years of his career, when his mind had predeceased his body, can hardly be called managing. Moreover, unlike Mack and McGraw, La Russa did not achieve his longevity by owning, in whole or in part, the team that he was coaching.

Nor has he stayed on past the point of effectiveness, serving as a living monument to himself. After all these years, it's fun to see La Russa provide reminders that he's not just the perfunctory human game-delay with his relentless pursuit of platoon advantages with his relief matchups; yes, it's tedious, but at least it means he avoids the intentional pass. When your admirers run from the effete George Will to affected macho man Buzz Bissinger, you're clearly many things to many people at once. His constant tweaking avoided a collapse of any element of a team with plenty of potential problems, especially in the bullpen and the infield, but the team's flaws were obvious by October; repairing them more conclusively to mount a better bid in 2010 isn't entirely La Russa's department, but he's able to adapt to fluid situations with his typical alacrity and competence.

San Diego Padres

Jed Hoyer was the first person to interview for the Padres' general manager vacancy last September. He made quite the impression on CEO Jeff Moorad, arriving armed with a three-ring binder full of information about the Padres. He had done statistical analysis of every player and broken down the organization's personnel from a scouting perspective. Furthermore, the 35-year-old had a detailed plan about how he would go about rebuilding the organization and making the Padres competitive again as they went from losing a 163rd game to the Rockies for the National League Wild Card in 2007 to 63-99 2008 before improving to 75-87 in 2009.

It was an impressive show from a man who did all his research on the side while holding down his day job. Hoyer's main focus was his job as the Red Sox' assistant general manager and Boston's attempt to get into the postseason. If there were such a thing as assistant GM abuse points, Hoyer would have racked up a bunch in the final month of the 2009 season; he worked many days on short rest, staying up until the wee hours of the morning doing research on the Padres once he had completed his day's duties with the Red Sox, and making runs to Kinko's FedEx at odd hours to make copies of his charts and graphs. Moorad interviewed a handful of others for the job of succeeding the popular Kevin Towers after 14 years on the job. He never identified the other candidates, other than to say some had previously been GMs, and some were younger guys like Hoyer, looking for a first-time opportunity. None of the other candidates rivaled Hoyer in Moorad's mind. With each passing interview, Moorad kept thinking back to Hoyer, his binder, and the com-

prehensive plan and knew he was the man to oversee the Padres' baseball operations.

Moorad took control of the Padres last March, the latest step in an interesting baseball career. He first gained renown as a high-profile agent, whose crowning achievement was landing Manny Ramirez an eight-year, $160 million contract from the Red Sox as a free agent following the 2000 season. Moorad then abruptly left the agent business in 2005 to join the Diamondbacks' ownership group and become club president. When owner John Moores was forced to put the Padres up for sale in 2008 while in the midst of an acrimonious divorce, Moorad cobbled together a group of investors to buy the franchise. The purchase began last year, with Moorad's group purchasing 30 percent of the Padres. Under terms of the sale, the group will buy the remaining 70 percent by 2013.

Moorad inherited Towers, who was baseball's longest-tenured GM. Towers certainly had his share of success, winning four NL West titles and the second of the franchise's two pennants. His greatest strength was developing relationships, whether it was with ownership, the players, or other GMs; it's hard to find a person in baseball who will say a bad word about him. Towers, however, was doomed from the time Moorad got to San Diego. When the Diamondbacks were looking for a GM after the 2005 season, Moorad interviewed Towers but did not hire him, instead going with one of the new breed of baseball executives: Red Sox assistant GM Josh Byrnes.

Moorad was looking for someone more contemplative, more strategic in his thinking—someone who

PADRES PROSPECTUS
2009 W-L: 75-87, 4th in NL West

Pythag	74-88	11th
RS/G	3.9	16th
RA/G	4.8	11th
EqA	.260	10th
EqBRR	-6.3	9th
SNWP	.476	14th
WXRL	10.56	3rd
FRAr	4.21	6th
DE	.694	7th
PADE	-1.69	13th
Salary	$43.7	15th
Attend	1.92	12th

Ballpark: PETCO Park (3-yr. PF: 890). Open spaces provide a moundsman's nirvana

2009: Better retreads and new youngsters on the mound got second-half run support, but Peavy had to be sacrificed

2010: 33-25 finish inspired talk of contention, but new drama-free front office should consolidate

Action Items: Barter for the best AGonz deal possible, because they can afford to keep him

could plot the course of the franchise's future. Towers was the opposite, a self-professed gunslinger who lived for the moment and worried about tomorrow when it arrived. When it was time to make player moves, Towers took a cursory glance at the statistics but was more inclined to listen to his scouts, then do what his gut instincts told him. Hoyer, long regarded as a potential GM, had briefly shared the Boston job with fellow front-office wunderkind Ben Cherington for a spell with the Red Sox when Theo Epstein decided to walk away (briefly) after the Red Sox won the World Series in 2004. Leaning on the advice of veteran baseball man Bill Lajoie, Hoyer played a major role in acquiring right-hander Josh Beckett and third baseman Mike Lowell from the Marlins. Becket and Lowell had played key roles when the Red Sox captured another World Series in 2007.

Now Hoyer will have the opportunity to put all the ideas in that three-ring binder into action. He wants to build the Padres through scouting and player development, a familiar tack for a small-market club. Epstein has long said that Boston's success has stemmed from thinking like a small-market club but having big-market resources. The challenge for Hoyer, though, will be to win with a small-market club that actually does have small-market resources. The cash-strapped Moores was forced to slash the payroll from $73 million in 2008 to $43 million at the start of last season. That number was pared down even further when the Padres dealt ace pitcher Jake Peavy, just two seasons removed from winning the NL Cy Young Award, to the White Sox at the July 31st nonwaiver trading deadline, saving at least $52 million over the next three seasons. Towers also fielded deadline offers on first baseman Adrian Gonzalez and closer Heath Bell, but did not pull the trigger, reportedly because he was working on the Peavy deal.

It was quite telling that the Padres did not include Gonzalez in any of the promotional material sent to entice season-ticket holders to renew at the end of the last season, even though he is a local kid, the face of the franchise, and immensely popular with the fan base on both sides of the US-Mexico border. Gonzalez is reasonably priced with a $4.75 million salary this year, and the Padres hold a $5.5 million club option for 2011. The big question Hoyer faces is, does he trade Gonzalez and get multiple players to help the rebuilding cause, or does he build the team around the first baseman? The payroll is expected to be in the $43 million range again this season. The Padres were 29th among the 30 major-league clubs in payroll last season and are unlikely ever to escape the bottom third, because Moorad's group is not as wealthy as most ownerships. Many inside the game suspect that Moorad's bid to buy the Padres was approved as a favor by Major League Baseball to Moores in order to help speed his divorce settlement.

Hoyer, though possibly hamstrung by a lack of financial resources, will at least have his own people executing his plan for building through the draft and international signings. His first order of business was to fire the team's vice president of scouting and player development, Grady Fuson. The Padres had one of the weakest farm systems in the game throughout Towers' tenure, though he often overcame this through his shrewd wheeling and dealing.

In fairness to Fuson, the Padres did bring a great deal of young talent to the major leagues last season, using 24 rookies. Fifteen of them made their big-league debuts. Those youngsters helped the Padres finish strong as they won 37 of their final 62 games, their .597 winning percentage from July 28th until the end of the season ranking fifth in the major leagues in that span.

The strong finish led Towers and manager Bud Black, a cerebral former pitching coach and front-office executive who is held in high regard by Moorad, to believe the Padres might be close to returning to contention in the NL West. That may be a stretch, because the Rockies have a young nucleus and have won the wild card twice in the last three years, while the two-time defending division champion Dodgers also have a good group of core players.

The Padres do at least have many young players in the lineup, but only one offensive star in Gonzalez. The organization believes that right fielder Will Venable (.285 EqA last season), left fielder/third baseman Chase Headley (.280), shortstop Everth Cabrera (.276), and catcher Nick Hundley (.272) are players it can build around, yet none seem capable of carrying the offense if Gonzalez is sent packing for a package of prospects. Cabrera is the one player with considerable potential; he made the jump to the major leagues last season all the way from the Low-A level after the Padres selected him in the Rule 5 draft from the Rockies. Rafael Furcal is a comparison that Padres officials and scouts from other clubs often use in describing Cabrera, although that is just wishcasting at this point. Kyle Blanks (.315) could be a star, but fitting him into the lineup may have to wait until the Padres find a taker for Gonzalez or third baseman Kevin Kouzmanoff; the latter situation would allow them to put Headley at third.

On the pitching side of the ledger, right-hander Kevin Correia led the starting rotation with 4.7 SNLVAR, making for a nice story, as he is a San Diego native who was signed as a low-cost free agent after the Giants nontendered him following the 2008 season. But when

Correia is your ace, you've got a long way to go, as he has been a fourth starter on good teams at best. Chris Young should be ready to begin the season in the rotation after having surgery to remove torn labrum tissue from his shoulder last year. The Padres also have high hopes for the six pitchers they acquired in the Peavy and Hairston trades. Four of them finished last season in the major leagues: left-handers Aaron Poreda and Clayton Richard, and right-handers Adam Russell and Ryan Webb. If there's a homegrown prospect as seemingly ready now as Blanks is in the lineup, it's right-hander Mat Latos, who showed in 10 starts the promise of being the type of pitcher who could anchor the rotation. His numbers weren't overpowering, but the Padres felt he tired out after pitching a combined 122 innings between the majors and minors at the age of 21, more than his career total as a pro in the previous two years.

The Padres also have an effective late-inning relief tandem in closer Heath Bell and set-up man Luke Gregerson. Bell was third in the NL with 3.998 WXRL, as he effectively replaced all-time saves leader Trevor Hoffman; Gregerson was 11th with 2.983. The Padres also have a pair of seemingly useful lefties in Ed Mujica and Joe Thatcher, and fragile fireballer Mike Adams. Bell could be traded if the Padres are out of contention at the July 31st deadline, as could Correia or Young, but much will depend on the offers in play for Hoyer to mull and make do with, with an eye toward stocking his Pads larder with what prospects he can add.

That farm system is much like the major-league roster. The Padres have some interesting prospects but none who obviously stand out as the next Tony Gwynn or Hoffman or, for that matter, even the next Nate Colbert or Randy Jones. It seems likely that the majority of players who will help bring Hoyer's vision of building a championship organization to fruition are not even in the organization and in fact may still be walking the campuses of high schools and colleges around the country. Of course, Hoyer knows that, and he's young enough to invest the time to bring them in. After all, it was all mapped out in the three-ring binder that so intrigued Moorad.

HITTERS

Matt Antonelli 2B Bats: R Throws: R Height: 6' 0" Weight: 200 Born: April 8, 1985 Age: 25

YEAR	TEAM	LVL	AGE	PA	R	2B	3B	HR	RBI	BB	SO	SB	CS	EqBRR	AVG	OBP	SLG	EqAVG	EqOBP	EqSLG	EqA	VORP	WARP	DEFENSE
2007	LEL	A+	22	406	89	14	4	14	54	53	58	18	6	2.0	.314	.409	.499	.284	.362	.432	.278	19.9	0.8	75-2B -14
2007	SAN	AA	22	223	34	11	1	7	24	30	36	10	3	-1.2	.294	.395	.476	.286	.372	.453	.287	13.8	0.9	48-2B -6
2008	POR	AAA	23	540	62	19	4	7	39	76	86	6	4	-0.5	.215	.335	.322	.206	.311	.290	.221	-5.0	-1.9	122-2B -11
2008	SDN	MLB	23	65	6	2	0	1	3	5	11	0	0	0.8	.193	.292	.281	.193	.292	.281	.208	-1.3	-0.6	15-2B -4
2009	POR	AAA	24	219	25	11	2	4	22	26	30	1	1	0.2	.196	.300	.339	.192	.288	.321	.216	-3.9	-0.9	52-2B -4
2010	SDN	MLB	25	392	45	15	2	8	32	43	78	5	3	0.2	.226	.320	.349	.239	.327	.366	.253	9.2	0.4	86-2B -5

Breakout: 5%   Improve: 39%   Collapse: 27%   Attrition: 13%   MLB: 76%   Comparables: Mike Moriarty, Pedro Lopez, Oscar Salazar, Tony Manahan

Antonelli seemed on his way to stardom after being the Padres' first-round draft pick in 2006, but after he reached Triple-A in 2007, nothing has been the same. When Antonelli bulked up before his first season at Portland, it cost him both bat and foot speed, and last season he missed considerable time to leg problems. He has now had two brutal seasons in a row, hitting a combined .209/.336/.306 in 610 at-bats, as he's been tinkering with his swing for so long now that he's parsecs from where he used to be mechanically. He can still draw a walk, but that can't offset his total lack of power. Although he will go back to Triple-A this season, it's difficult to envision him being anything more than a bench player in the major leagues, if that.

Henry Blanco C Bats: R Throws: R Height: 5' 11" Weight: 220 Born: August 29, 1971 Age: 38

YEAR	TEAM	LVL	AGE	PA	R	2B	3B	HR	RBI	BB	SO	SB	CS	EqBRR	AVG	OBP	SLG	EqAVG	EqOBP	EqSLG	EqA	VORP	WARP	DEFENSE
2007	CHN	MLB	35	58	3	3	0	0	4	2	12	0	0	0.0	.167	.193	.222	.167	.193	.222	.128	-4.3	-0.3	12-C 1
2008	CHN	MLB	36	128	15	3	0	3	12	6	22	0	0	-0.2	.292	.325	.392	.289	.323	.380	.247	2.6	1.1	29-C 4
2009	SDN	MLB	37	232	21	12	0	6	16	26	50	0	0	-2.2	.235	.320	.382	.259	.338	.420	.264	10.6	1.8	57-C 3
2010	NYN	MLB	38	160	13	6	0	3	12	14	37	0	0	-0.4	.235	.303	.339	.236	.301	.346	.228	1.1	0.3	37-C 1

Breakout: 11%   Improve: 35%   Collapse: 33%   Attrition: 38%   MLB: 85%   Comparables: Gary Carter, Rick Cerone, Tom Prince, Sandy Alomar Jr.

Blanco has carved out a long career by being the quintessential reserve catcher. He doesn't provide much offense, but isn't a total zero at the plate. On the other hand, Blanco is respected for the way he handles a pitching staff; he throws well and is well liked by his teammates. Although Blanco is getting long in the tooth and doesn't have many more years left, he is still a useful backup for a team that has a solid starting catcher. The Mets do *not* have a solid starting catcher, but they figured they might as well sign Blanco, anyway.

Kyle Blanks   RF/1B   Bats: R   Throws: R   Height: 6' 6"   Weight: 270   Born: September 11, 1986   Age: 23

YEAR	TEAM	LVL	AGE	PA	R	2B	3B	HR	RBI	BB	SO	SB	CS	EqBRR	AVG	OBP	SLG	EqAVG	EqOBP	EqSLG	EqA	VORP	WARP	DEFENSE		
2007	LEL	A+	20	531	94	31	4	24	100	44	98	11	2	-0.2	.301	.380	.540	.272	.333	.456	.271	11.7	1.2	59-1B	-2	
2008	SAN	AA	21	565	75	23	5	20	107	51	90	5	4	-2.2	.325	.404	.514	.308	.372	.478	.291	24.9	2.5	123-1B	-4	
2009	POR	AAA	22	280	35	9	1	12	38	39	63	0	0	-0.7	.283	.393	.485	.273	.371	.471	.291	10.7	1.6	52-1B 3	14-LF	0
2009	SDN	MLB	22	172	24	9	0	10	22	18	55	1	1	-1.0	.250	.355	.514	.289	.384	.584	.315	14.7	1.4	19-RF -4	12-LF	2
2010	SDN	MLB	23	535	64	22	3	21	74	52	127	4	2	-0.7	.254	.339	.447	.269	.348	.470	.288	23.8	2.5	92-1B	-1	

Breakout: 19%   Improve: 46%   Collapse: 16%   Attrition: 14%   MLB: 42%   Comparables: Richie Sexson, Jason Botts, Derrek Lee, Cecil Fielder

Blanks was getting a chance to show he could be a major-league regular and making the most of it when an arch injury caused him to miss the final month of the season. He is beyond large as big men go, with massive power, and is someone who figures to strike out a lot, while showing enough patience to draw some walks. Perhaps most impressive about him is he may be the rare slugger strong enough to challenge Petco's fences, putting six home runs over the walls in 75 at-bats. The .288/.366/.548 he hit on the road may be more indicative of his abilities, but we won't know until we see more of him. Despite his size, Blanks is very athletic and has enough agility to play the corner outfield spots, though his best position is first base, where he'll land if the Padres trade Adrian Gonzalez.

Everth Cabrera   SS   Bats: S   Throws: R   Height: 5' 8"   Weight: 160   Born: November 17, 1986   Age: 23

YEAR	TEAM	LVL	AGE	PA	R	2B	3B	HR	RBI	BB	SO	SB	CS	EqBRR	AVG	OBP	SLG	EqAVG	EqOBP	EqSLG	EqA	VORP	WARP	DEFENSE		
2007	TRI	A-	20	186	29	8	3	1	23	27	24	12	5	-0.1	.300	.432	.413	.270	.360	.368	.260	6.1	0.5	31-2B -1	10-SS	-2
2008	ASH	A	21	550	80	25	6	6	38	51	101	73	16	6.9	.284	.361	.399	.238	.305	.332	.233	3.0	0.7	84-2B 3	34-SS	0
2009	SDN	MLB	22	438	59	18	8	2	31	46	88	25	8	-0.5	.255	.342	.361	.289	.369	.409	.276	25.5	2.5	100-SS	-3	
2010	SDN	MLB	23	457	53	18	5	5	31	49	99	23	8	1.0	.241	.329	.346	.253	.335	.358	.261	17.2	1.7	102-SS	-1	

Breakout: 11%   Improve: 30%   Collapse: 17%   Attrition: 7%   MLB: 89%   Comparables: Jimmy Rollins, Omar Vizquel, Rafael Furcal, Ramon Santiago

While few were paying attention to the Padres in the second half of last season, Cabrera was turning into an interesting story. He'd missed nearly two months in the first half with a broken bone in his hand after the Padres had selected him from the Rockies at the Rule 5 draft at the 2008 Winter Meetings. Tasked with playing because the Pads had nowhere to go but up and because they had nobody else you'd really call a shortstop, he more than held his own despite having never played above Low-A. With his outstanding speed and strong arm, Cabrera is reminiscent of Dodgers shortstop Rafael Furcal, and while he isn't likely to be as good, at the least he should have a solid major-league career.

James Darnell   3B   Bats: R   Throws: R   Height: 6' 2"   Weight: 195   Born: January 19, 1987   Age: 23

YEAR	TEAM	LVL	AGE	PA	R	2B	3B	HR	RBI	BB	SO	SB	CS	EqBRR	AVG	OBP	SLG	EqAVG	EqOBP	EqSLG	EqA	VORP	WARP	DEFENSE
2008	EUG	A-	21	78	9	6	1	2	15	11	12	1	1	0.2	.373	.462	.582	.310	.372	.507	.297	5.1	0.7	16-3B -1
2009	FTW	A	22	283	40	17	2	7	38	57	51	5	5	-3.6	.329	.468	.518	.270	.385	.409	.281	13.8	-0.1	65-3B -15
2009	LEL	A+	22	269	40	18	2	13	43	30	38	3	1	-1.5	.294	.377	.553	.256	.325	.442	.262	7.0	0.4	50-3B -4
2010	SDN	MLB	23	463	46	22	2	10	49	54	99	3	2	-1.8	.242	.332	.384	.254	.338	.405	.268	16.2	1.0	97-3B -7

Breakout: 5%   Improve: 41%   Collapse: 21%   Attrition: 1%   MLB: 3%   Comparables: Mike Edwards, Grant Psomas, Mike Stellern, Bob Bathe

Darnell is part of the Padres' expanding logjam of third basemen, but because of his power and plate discipline, the team will find a place for him somewhere as he moves up the ladder. As exciting as he is at the plate as one of the Padres' best offensive prospects, he's frustrating in the field. While he certainly has the tools and athleticism to succeed at the hot corner, he's just not good there, and scouts have seen little progress. The bat is going to play if and when he gets moved to first base or an outfield corner, but at those positions, he'll be just another player. If he could somehow stay at third, he could be a star.

Jaff Decker · LF

Bats: L   Throws: L   Height: 5' 10"   Weight: 190   Born: February 23, 1990   Age: 20

YEAR	TEAM	LVL	AGE	PA	R	2B	3B	HR	RBI	BB	SO	SB	CS	EqBRR	AVG	OBP	SLG	EqAVG	EqOBP	EqSLG	EqA	VORP	WARP	DEFENSE	
2008	PDR	Rk	18	216	51	11	2	5	34	55	36	9	1	0.9	.352	.523	.541	.270	.401	.399	.287	10.9	1.1	22-CF -2	18-LF -3
2009	FTW	A	19	455	78	25	2	16	64	85	92	10	6	-1.3	.299	.442	.514	.258	.374	.421	.280	17.0	0.3	87-LF -15	
2010	SDN	MLB	20	431	52	17	1	10	42	60	108	4	2	-0.3	.229	.342	.367	.243	.347	.396	.270	13.8	0.7	84-LF -7	

Breakout: 25%   Improve: 50%   Collapse: 19%   Attrition: 4%   MLB: 0%   Comparables: Phil Plantier, Jason Lee, George Cecchetti, Rafael Delima

Decker is a walking conundrum for scouts. On the surface, you have a player who nearly hit .300 while leading the Midwest League in on-base percentage by 37 points and finishing second in slugging, all as *a 19-year-old*. That would normally put him among the top prospects in baseball, but it's hard to look past what he is physically: when he steps to the plate, he more closely resembles a 40-year-old cleanup hitter on the company's softball team than a kid just a year out of high school. That's the kind of thing that gets people wondering, If this is what he looks like at 19, what will he be like when he's in his late 20s? His bat is his only tool, and it's a damn good one, but he might be better off in an American League organization where he can just focus on being the next Billy Butler.

Luis Durango · OF

Bats: S   Throws: R   Height: 5' 9"   Weight: 155   Born: April 23, 1986   Age: 24

YEAR	TEAM	LVL	AGE	PA	R	2B	3B	HR	RBI	BB	SO	SB	CS	EqBRR	AVG	OBP	SLG	EqAVG	EqOBP	EqSLG	EqA	VORP	WARP	DEFENSE	
2007	EUG	A-	21	335	60	6	8	2	32	29	32	17	10	-3.7	.367	.422	.460	.318	.357	.399	.264	9.3	-0.2	40-CF -8	24-LF -3
2008	FTW	A	22	389	56	11	3	1	25	49	43	14	7	1.1	.305	.395	.365	.270	.345	.323	.242	-0.6	-1.8	29-CF -11	20-LF -4
2008	LEL	A+	22	87	20	4	1	0	10	13	7	1	1	-2.3	.431	.506	.514	.378	.455	.459	.323	7.2	0.5	14-LF -3	
2009	SAN	AA	23	560	78	9	2	0	25	81	70	44	17	3.5	.281	.390	.309	.269	.360	.295	.246	3.1	-0.8	73-LF -7	37-CF -3
2009	SDN	MLB	23	14	3	0	0	0	0	2	2	2	1	0.8	.545	.615	.545	.636	.692	.636	.420	2.6	0.2		
2010	SDN	MLB	24	511	62	17	5	3	32	55	77	13	6	-0.1	.263	.343	.342	.278	.351	.353	.262	12.1	0.7	89-LF -6	

Breakout: 10%   Improve: 31%   Collapse: 16%   Attrition: 8%   MLB: 16%   Comparables: Carlos Mendoza, Greg Martinez, Vince Harris, Robbie Katzaroff

Exceptionally speedy, Durango has been clocked at 3.6 seconds from home to first from the left side of the plate. He is willing to play small ball, hitting the ball on the ground, bunting, and working the count. He also has as much power as your Aunt Petunia, the one with the bad hip. Opposing outfielders play him as shallowly as they do most pitchers, because they know he is not an extra-base threat. Luis Castillo has had a long career with this skill set, but it's one thing to be a Punch-and-Judy hitter as a middle infielder, and another as a corner outfielder. Durango's weak arm consigns him to left field despite his speed, and while these kinds of players could often carve out careers in the 1970s and '80s, times have changed. He'll go to Triple-A Portland this season, with hopes of becoming the Padres' leadoff hitter in 2011.

David Eckstein · 2B

Bats: R   Throws: R   Height: 5' 7"   Weight: 175   Born: January 20, 1975   Age: 35

YEAR	TEAM	LVL	AGE	PA	R	2B	3B	HR	RBI	BB	SO	SB	CS	EqBRR	AVG	OBP	SLG	EqAVG	EqOBP	EqSLG	EqA	VORP	WARP	DEFENSE	
2007	SLN	MLB	32	484	58	23	0	3	31	24	22	10	1	-1.7	.309	.356	.382	.320	.365	.398	.274	24.7	2.2	107-SS -5	
2008	TOR	MLB	33	303	27	18	0	1	23	24	27	2	1	-2.6	.277	.354	.358	.284	.361	.370	.261	10.4	0.8	54-SS -4	5-2B 1
2008	ARI	MLB	33	73	5	3	0	1	4	7	5	0	0	0.9	.219	.301	.313	.219	.301	.313	.220	-0.6	0.7	17-2B 6	
2009	SDN	MLB	34	568	64	27	2	2	50	39	46	3	1	0.5	.260	.323	.334	.285	.343	.362	.252	11.6	0.3	122-2B -9	
2010	SDN	MLB	35	450	49	19	1	5	37	35	40	4	2	-0.5	.267	.337	.355	.285	.351	.375	.262	14.7	1.5	101-2B -1	

Breakout: 5%   Improve: 27%   Collapse: 21%   Attrition: 29%   MLB: 96%   Comparables: Jeff Frye, Luis Aparicio, Eric Young, Ted Sizemore

Some statheads ridicule Eckstein for what he isn't, and understandably so. While he has gained an almost mystical reputation because of his scrappiness, his statistics don't measure up to those of most major-league regulars. It's a funny enough development for a player who, earlier in his career, didn't get taken seriously as a shortstop in scouting circles. However, Eckstein did serve as a veteran stabilizer on a very young team last season and as a mentor to rookie Everth Cabrera. These are things that are hard to quantify, but Pads brass thought Eckstein meant enough to the Padres that he was signed to a one-year, $1 million contract for this season last August. Keep in mind that Petco is no hitter's friend; his OBP on the road was .345.

Logan Forsythe — 3B

Bats: R   Throws: R   Height: 6' 1"   Weight: 195   Born: January 14, 1987   Age: 23

YEAR	TEAM	LVL	AGE	PA	R	2B	3B	HR	RBI	BB	SO	SB	CS	EqBRR	AVG	OBP	SLG	EqAVG	EqOBP	EqSLG	EqA	VORP	WARP	DEFENSE
2008	PDR	Rk	21	35	2	0	0	0	0	5	8	0	0	-0.1	.231	.429	.231	.167	.265	.167	.145	-2.6	-0.5	6-3B 0
2009	LEL	A+	22	305	46	13	3	8	30	61	48	6	2	-1.0	.322	.472	.504	.288	.413	.420	.298	19.5	2.0	60-3B -3
2009	SAN	AA	22	290	37	9	3	3	31	41	63	5	0	1.6	.279	.384	.377	.246	.336	.345	.248	3.9	0.5	65-3B 0
2010	SDN	MLB	23	488	52	19	3	8	37	71	114	4	2	0.3	.239	.356	.355	.252	.360	.371	.274	19.8	2.0	102-3B -1

Breakout: 26%   Improve: 50%   Collapse: 16%   Attrition: 7%   MLB: 0%   Comparables: Jamie Allen, Chris Mader, Martin Freeman, Jon Valenti

Forsythe is a fast-rising prospect, making it to Double-A in his first full pro season after being the Padres' second-round draft pick in 2008. Forsythe has shown good plate discipline as a pro, and the Padres believe he can develop more home-run power, but scouts are skeptical. While he seems to be blocked at third base because of the presence of Kevin Kouzmanoff and Chase Headley at the major-league level, Forsythe showed versatility in 2007 for Team USA in the Pan-American Games, playing second, short, and left. He began working on playing second in the Padres' instructional league last fall, and if he can stick there, it would enhance his value dramatically.

Brian Giles — RF

Bats: L   Throws: L   Height: 5' 10"   Weight: 205   Born: January 20, 1971   Age: 39

YEAR	TEAM	LVL	AGE	PA	R	2B	3B	HR	RBI	BB	SO	SB	CS	EqBRR	AVG	OBP	SLG	EqAVG	EqOBP	EqSLG	EqA	VORP	WARP	DEFENSE
2007	SDN	MLB	36	552	72	27	2	13	51	64	61	4	6	1.1	.271	.361	.416	.295	.382	.446	.283	23.0	1.0	117-RF -13
2008	SDN	MLB	37	653	81	40	4	12	63	87	52	2	2	0.7	.306	.398	.456	.342	.426	.506	.319	55.7	4.3	140-RF -15
2009	SDN	MLB	38	253	18	10	1	2	23	26	31	1	0	0.2	.191	.277	.271	.199	.281	.279	.201	-10.2	-2.4	56-RF -11
2010	SDN	MLB	39	314	33	14	1	5	29	39	44	1	2	0.2	.258	.354	.376	.271	.360	.395	.275	11.8	0.8	68-RF -4

Breakout: 6%   Improve: 26%   Collapse: 29%   Attrition: 33%   MLB: 95%   Comparables: Jim Eisenreich, Charlie Gehringer, Enos Slaughter, Gene Woodling

Giles was one of the more underappreciated players in the late '90s and early Aughties when he was putting up good numbers with bad Pirates teams, and then again with the Padres as Petco killed his numbers; he was .298/.397/.478 on the road from 2004 to 2008. However, he's now at the end of the line. Knee problems have robbed him of his power and mobility and, in 2009, of the ability to hit at all. The Padres declined to pick up his option for this season, making him a free agent. Getting out of Petco might help Giles' power numbers a little bit, but at best, he is either a part-time starter or bench player at this point.

Adrian Gonzalez — 1B

Bats: L   Throws: L   Height: 6' 2"   Weight: 225   Born: May 8, 1982   Age: 28

YEAR	TEAM	LVL	AGE	PA	R	2B	3B	HR	RBI	BB	SO	SB	CS	EqBRR	AVG	OBP	SLG	EqAVG	EqOBP	EqSLG	EqA	VORP	WARP	DEFENSE
2007	SDN	MLB	25	720	101	46	3	30	100	65	140	0	0	0.3	.282	.347	.502	.302	.365	.535	.301	42.7	5.4	161-1B 7
2008	SDN	MLB	26	700	103	32	1	36	119	74	142	0	0	-3.2	.279	.361	.510	.307	.383	.555	.312	49.6	5.6	157-1B 1
2009	SDN	MLB	27	681	90	27	2	40	99	119	109	1	1	-3.6	.277	.407	.551	.317	.435	.629	.347	73.6	9.4	152-1B 12
2010	SDN	MLB	28	702	96	33	2	32	104	97	132	1	1	-1.1	.279	.384	.501	.297	.393	.542	.322	59.5	6.7	155-1B 3

Breakout: 9%   Improve: 50%   Collapse: 3%   Attrition: 2%   MLB: 99%   Comparables: Hal Trosky, Fred McGriff, Todd Helton, Justin Morneau

A pretty strong case can be made that Gonzalez was the second-most valuable player to his team in the National League last season, behind only Albert Pujols. Gonzalez presents a difficult decision for new general manager Jed Hoyer: Does he trade the franchise player and get back multiple pieces that might speed up the rebuilding process? Or does he keep Gonzalez and build a team around him? It's a tough call, but because Gonzalez is a native San Diegan, it could be a public relations nightmare if he is traded. Note that Gonzalez has had his candle hidden under the bushel that is Petco; he has hit .264/.362/.443 at home, but .305/.376/.579 on the road. In a hitter's park, he might be so explosive that he would more than earn back the production lost as his league-leading walk total shrinks, as teams no longer opt to pitch around him.

Tony Gwynn Jr. — CF

Bats: L   Throws: R   Height: 5' 11"   Weight: 190   Born: October 4, 1982   Age: 27

YEAR	TEAM	LVL	AGE	PA	R	2B	3B	HR	RBI	BB	SO	SB	CS	EqBRR	AVG	OBP	SLG	EqAVG	EqOBP	EqSLG	EqA	VORP	WARP	DEFENSE	
2007	NAS	AAA	24	138	19	3	3	0	13	9	14	4	3	-0.7	.286	.336	.357	.268	.314	.323	.228	-0.6	-0.2	27-CF -1	
2007	MIL	MLB	24	135	13	3	2	0	10	12	24	8	1	1.2	.260	.326	.317	.260	.326	.317	.244	0.7	0.0	17-CF -1	7-RF 0
2008	NAS	AAA	25	412	47	9	3	2	26	29	54	20	6	-0.4	.275	.328	.331	.260	.306	.299	.221	-5.4	0.2	83-CF 7	7-RF 0
2008	MIL	MLB	25	49	5	1	0	0	1	4	7	3	1	0.7	.190	.271	.214	.190	.271	.214	.196	-2.3	0.0	5-CF 2	
2009	NAS	AAA	26	175	34	8	1	1	9	20	21	15	1	3.7	.309	.387	.395	.297	.364	.381	.274	7.5	1.5	33-CF 5	
2009	SDN	MLB	26	451	59	11	6	2	21	48	65	11	7	-0.2	.270	.350	.344	.301	.374	.386	.269	16.6	3.0	91-CF 6	9-RF 4
2010	SDN	MLB	27	495	63	17	4	3	30	46	82	17	6	0.8	.254	.327	.328	.266	.334	.344	.252	11.2	1.6	103-CF 4	

Breakout: 10%   Improve: 41%   Collapse: 16%   Attrition: 17%   MLB: 96%   Comparables: Tike Redman, Tom Goodwin, Dave Roberts, Jason Tyner

If you can imagine how Edgar Gonzalez felt the last two seasons serving as a utility infielder on the team that his younger brother Adrian was the star of, multiply that by 10, because that's about how Tony Gwynn Jr. must have felt after being swapped for Jody Gerut to the same franchise his father became a Hall of Famer with. (Come to think of it, that must have been how Uncle Chris felt, too.) Little Tony is a solid defensive outfielder; he runs well and has good range. His bat is good enough for a second-division starter as long as he lashes enough singles and walks in 9-10 percent of his plate appearances, but he'd make a fine fourth outfielder on a good team.

Chase Headley — LF/3B

Bats: S   Throws: R   Height: 6' 2"   Weight: 230   Born: May 9, 1984   Age: 26

YEAR	TEAM	LVL	AGE	PA	R	2B	3B	HR	RBI	BB	SO	SB	CS	EqBRR	AVG	OBP	SLG	EqAVG	EqOBP	EqSLG	EqA	VORP	WARP	DEFENSE	
2007	SAN	AA	23	522	82	38	5	20	78	74	114	1	0	-1.9	.330	.437	.580	.302	.393	.528	.312	41.4	4.3	118-3B -5	
2007	SDN	MLB	23	21	1	1	0	0	0	2	4	0	0	0.0	.222	.333	.278	.222	.333	.278	.233	-0.4	-0.3	4-3B -2	
2008	POR	AAA	24	295	49	24	1	13	40	31	65	0	0	-1.0	.305	.383	.556	.280	.351	.489	.285	14.0	1.1	56-LF -4	8-3B -1
2008	SDN	MLB	24	368	34	19	2	9	38	30	104	4	1	-0.5	.269	.337	.420	.296	.359	.456	.281	15.7	1.8	79-LF 0	6-3B 0
2009	SDN	MLB	25	612	62	31	2	12	64	62	133	10	2	1.6	.262	.342	.392	.292	.365	.433	.280	26.7	1.7	110-LF -6	25-3B -4
2010	SDN	MLB	26	619	66	31	3	16	68	68	150	5	2	-0.3	.262	.350	.417	.277	.359	.442	.286	31.7	3.1	141-LF -3	

Breakout: 13%   Improve: 46%   Collapse: 13%   Attrition: 5%   MLB: 95%   Comparables: Bobby Kielty, Jason Giambi, Juan Rivera, Mark Whiten

Headley received a lot of hype after winning the Texas League's MVP award in 2007, but has struggled to meet those expectations the past two seasons. Keep in mind, he's been asked to do a lot of things beyond his best uses, playing left field rather than his natural position at third, because of the presence of Kevin Kouzmanoff. He hasn't hit for the power associated with a corner outfielder, because he doesn't, and playing in Petco hardly helps matters. To his credit, he has hit .301/.368/.437 on the road in roughly a full season's worth of playing time. Heading into what should be his peak seasons, he may have to find a way to beat his home park to earn his full due, although a move back to the hot corner might at least reset expectations somewhat.

Chad Huffman — LF

Bats: R   Throws: R   Height: 6' 1"   Weight: 200   Born: April 29, 1985   Age: 25

YEAR	TEAM	LVL	AGE	PA	R	2B	3B	HR	RBI	BB	SO	SB	CS	EqBRR	AVG	OBP	SLG	EqAVG	EqOBP	EqSLG	EqA	VORP	WARP	DEFENSE	
2007	LEL	A+	22	371	63	19	2	15	76	42	56	0	1	0.7	.307	.402	.522	.277	.352	.438	.274	12.5	1.0	82-LF -4	
2007	SAN	AA	22	197	28	4	1	7	28	22	44	0	0	0.3	.269	.362	.431	.256	.332	.395	.257	2.9	0.1	42-LF -2	
2008	SAN	AA	23	517	68	30	1	9	58	67	83	1	1	-2.6	.284	.383	.419	.269	.352	.389	.264	10.5	1.6	96-LF 2	6-RF 1
2009	POR	AAA	24	540	65	30	2	20	68	57	115	8	5	0.4	.269	.361	.469	.266	.348	.459	.275	17.1	1.9	97-LF -2	15-1B 1
2010	SDN	MLB	25	518	57	21	2	12	55	55	122	2	2	-0.2	.236	.327	.374	.249	.333	.393	.262	12.2	1.2	110-LF -1	

Breakout: 5%   Improve: 28%   Collapse: 20%   Attrition: 10%   MLB: 6%   Comparables: Cole Gillespie, Gary Cooper, Kevin Sliwinski, Mike Berger

Last season, Huffman showed the kind of power that made him the Padres' second-round draft pick out of Texas Christian University in 2006. Still, Huffman is likely to repeat Triple-A after already spending 1 ½ seasons at Double-A, so he's not exactly on the fast track to the majors. The fundamental problem is that the bat is his one tool, and it's useful, but less than great at a position that demands better. He's a below-average fielder and runner, too, which means that his best shot at someday gaining a bench job is to build on a good second half (.296/.385/.508), just to get people's attention.

Nick Hundley — C

Bats: R   Throws: R   Height: 6' 1"   Weight: 210   Born: September 8, 1983   Age: 26

YEAR	TEAM	LVL	AGE	PA	R	2B	3B	HR	RBI	BB	SO	SB	CS	EqBRR	AVG	OBP	SLG	EqAVG	EqOBP	EqSLG	EqA	VORP	WARP	DEFENSE	
2007	SAN	AA	23	422	55	23	1	20	72	42	74	0	2	0.5	.247	.324	.475	.237	.302	.432	.251	15.4	2.0	93-C	1
2008	POR	AAA	24	243	33	13	0	12	39	17	44	0	0	0.1	.232	.285	.451	.220	.264	.396	.226	2.2	0.4	57-C	1
2008	SDN	MLB	24	216	21	7	1	5	24	11	52	0	0	0.4	.237	.278	.359	.250	.287	.372	.234	3.7	0.4	54-C	1
2009	SDN	MLB	25	289	23	15	2	8	30	28	76	5	1	-1.3	.238	.313	.406	.266	.333	.449	.272	16.7	0.2	72-C	-11
2010	SDN	MLB	26	331	32	14	1	11	42	28	83	2	1	0.0	.227	.293	.393	.240	.303	.414	.251	10.6	1.0	80-C	-1

Breakout: 14%   Improve: 34%   Collapse: 20%   Attrition: 16%   MLB: 82%   Comparables: Ozzie Virgil, Jeff Mathis, Joe Girardi, Chris Widger

Hundley had a frustrating first full season in the major leagues, as he missed two months with a badly bruised left wrist suffered after being hit by a pitch on June 8th. He also played with a sports hernia from early May on before having it surgically repaired in November. Hundley is a decent enough hitter for a catcher, but the expectations were higher after he'd put up good power numbers in college at the University of Arizona. His most reliable value lies in his above-average defense, as the Padres are happy with what they've seen of him to look forward to a less dinged-up 2010.

Kevin Kouzmanoff — 3B

Bats: R   Throws: R   Height: 6' 1"   Weight: 210   Born: July 25, 1981   Age: 28

YEAR	TEAM	LVL	AGE	PA	R	2B	3B	HR	RBI	BB	SO	SB	CS	EqBRR	AVG	OBP	SLG	EqAVG	EqOBP	EqSLG	EqA	VORP	WARP	DEFENSE	
2007	SDN	MLB	25	534	57	30	2	18	74	32	94	1	0	-1.8	.275	.329	.457	.294	.345	.487	.283	25.7	3.3	125-3B	4
2008	SDN	MLB	26	668	71	31	4	23	84	23	139	0	0	-0.4	.260	.299	.433	.280	.316	.463	.265	20.2	1.7	153-3B	-4
2009	SDN	MLB	27	573	50	31	1	18	88	27	106	1	0	-1.8	.255	.302	.420	.280	.323	.455	.267	20.7	3.1	133-3B	7
2010	SDN	MLB	28	590	61	27	2	22	87	36	117	1	0	-0.7	.261	.320	.439	.277	.333	.463	.277	27.4	3.1	141-3B	1

Breakout: 15%   Improve: 57%   Collapse: 7%   Attrition: 5%   MLB: 100%   Comparables: Jeff Kent, Tim Wallach, Travis Fryman, Tony Batista

Kouzmanoff has shown good power during his three seasons as the Padres' third baseman, averaging just over 20 bombs a year. But his propensity to swing at everything and rarely take a walk offsets the homers. Kouzmanoff has worked hard to achieve a certain solidity at the corner, setting the National League single-season record for fielding percentage at third last season with a .990 mark, which might seem like trivia, but the major defensive metrics support its suggestion of a solid glove. Considering that Headley is a third baseman playing out of position and the Padres are deep in third-base prospects, Kouzmanoff should be on the trading block, even if his thin OBP wasn't already the sort of thing that Hoyer might see as a problem. Obligatory home/road splits: .239/.290/.394 at Petco, .285/.327/.474 everywhere else. You'd think Padres hitters would be digging tunnels under the walls like Charles Bronson in *The Great Escape*.

Luis Rodriguez — MI

Bats: S   Throws: R   Height: 5' 9"   Weight: 190   Born: June 27, 1980   Age: 30

YEAR	TEAM	LVL	AGE	PA	R	2B	3B	HR	RBI	BB	SO	SB	CS	EqBRR	AVG	OBP	SLG	EqAVG	EqOBP	EqSLG	EqA	VORP	WARP	DEFENSE			
2007	MIN	MLB	27	173	18	5	1	2	12	12	14	1	0	1.5	.219	.281	.303	.221	.282	.305	.212	-4.4	-0.8	26-3B	-1	13-2B	-2
2008	POR	AAA	28	107	10	5	1	1	8	10	3	0	0	-0.9	.302	.368	.406	.286	.340	.378	.252	3.0	0.4	25-SS	0		
2008	SDN	MLB	28	225	22	11	1	0	12	13	13	1	1	0.9	.287	.326	.351	.309	.344	.377	.255	7.7	0.9	44-SS	2	4-2B	-2
2009	SDN	MLB	29	251	18	6	0	2	16	37	23	1	0	0.3	.202	.319	.260	.215	.325	.278	.227	-0.3	-0.2	29-SS	2	25-2B	-4
2010	CLE	MLB	30	303	31	12	2	4	23	29	28	1	1	0.3	.271	.344	.371	.270	.342	.367	.254	8.5	1.0	66-SS	1		

Breakout: 15%   Improve: 42%   Collapse: 21%   Attrition: 12%   MLB: 83%   Comparables: Jose Oquendo, Steve Jeltz, Nick Punto, Mark Lemke

Rodriguez is the type of player who is always one bad year away from being dropped from the 40-man roster, which is exactly what happened to him again following the 2009 season. He has his uses as a switch-hitting utility infielder whose glove plays at second, short, and third, and for an otherwise unimpressive batsman, he manages to squeeze in a decent number of walks. Signed to a minor-league deal by the Indians in the offseason, he could certainly repeat his journeyman's lot by eventually landing on their Opening Day roster.

Oscar Salazar   **PH**   Bats: R   Throws: R   Height: 6' 0"   Weight: 195   Born: June 27, 1978   Age: 32

YEAR	TEAM	LVL	AGE	PA	R	2B	3B	HR	RBI	BB	SO	SB	CS	EqBRR	AVG	OBP	SLG	EqAVG	EqOBP	EqSLG	EqA	VORP	WARP	DEFENSE			
2007	BOW	AA	29	566	73	39	2	22	96	26	77	3	3	-3.1	.289	.324	.494	.238	.262	.355	.211	-16.8	-4.8	74-3B	-15	19-2B	-6
2008	NOR	AAA	30	491	73	42	3	13	85	42	56	8	2	-2.5	.316	.371	.512	.299	.348	.471	.281	16.5	0.7	82-1B	-11	5-3B	0
2008	BAL	MLB	30	94	13	3	0	5	15	12	13	0	1	-0.1	.284	.372	.506	.284	.372	.494	.297	4.5	0.8	9-1B	1	6-3B	1
2009	NOR	AAA	31	213	31	17	1	10	43	13	27	0	3	-2.4	.372	.408	.618	.345	.380	.565	.310	14.0	1.2	30-1B	-2	11-RF	-2
2009	BAL	MLB	31	33	4	0	0	2	6	2	4	0	0	0.2	.419	.455	.613	.419	.455	.613	.355	3.9	0.3	2-3B	-1		
2009	SDN	MLB	31	121	12	8	2	3	19	12	16	0	0	-0.8	.269	.339	.463	.306	.372	.537	.297	7.0	0.4	12-LF	0	4-1B	0
2010	SDN	MLB	32	392	41	21	1	10	51	31	70	2	2	-1.1	.252	.313	.405	.269	.323	.428	.263	5.7	0.3	63-1B	-3		

Breakout: 16%   Improve: 32%   Collapse: 21%   Attrition: 20%   MLB: 16%   Comparables: Tim Tolman, Gene Schall, Alan Knicely, Butch Davis

Kevin Towers engineered one of the season's more curious trades last July when he dealt Cla "No Y" Meredith to the Orioles for Salazar. Thirty-one years old and in his eighth organization, Salazar is primarily a pinch-hitter because there's no defensive position he hasn't tried and been found lacking at. Just as surprisingly, new GM Jed Hoyer kept Salazar on the 40-man roster. Salazar can add some right-handed thump from the bench, and there's some utility to having a guy who can stand at almost position and feel about as equally ready to (not) handle what's hit at him as any of them, but it seems a strange use of a roster spot over the winter.

Donovan Tate   **CF**   Bats: R   Throws: R   Height: 6' 3"   Weight: 200   Born: September 27, 1990   Age: 19

YEAR	TEAM	LVL	AGE	PA	R	2B	3B	HR	RBI	BB	SO	SB	CS	EqBRR	AVG	OBP	SLG	EqAVG	EqOBP	EqSLG	EqA	VORP	WARP	DEFENSE
Did Not Play.																								

Breakout: 16%   Improve: 32%   Collapse: 21%   Attrition: 20%   MLB: 16%   Comparables: NA

The change in philosophy that came with Jeff Moorad's gaining control of the Padres before last season became evident when scouting director Bill "Chief" Gayton was allowed to select the player he wanted with the third overall pick in the amateur draft; the Padres usually drafted on the cheap when John Moores controlled the purse strings. Gayton chose Tate, an ultra-athletic high school player from Cartersville, Georgia, and signed him to a $6.25 million bonus, a record for a prep player, though too late in the summer for Tate to make his pro debut. The son of former NFL running back Lars Tate, Donovan is considered a five-tool player, but he's raw. He also underwent surgery in November to repair a sports hernia. Tate's upside is considerable, but his journey to the major leagues might take a while.

Will Venable   **OF**   Bats: L   Throws: L   Height: 6' 2"   Weight: 205   Born: October 29, 1982   Age: 27

YEAR	TEAM	LVL	AGE	PA	R	2B	3B	HR	RBI	BB	SO	SB	CS	EqBRR	AVG	OBP	SLG	EqAVG	EqOBP	EqSLG	EqA	VORP	WARP	DEFENSE			
2007	SAN	AA	24	572	66	19	3	8	68	38	84	21	2	1.0	.278	.337	.373	.269	.314	.351	.239	-2.3	0.3	95-RF	6	18-CF	-2
2008	POR	AAA	25	496	70	26	4	14	58	44	103	7	3	1.2	.292	.361	.464	.267	.327	.402	.254	8.8	-0.1	98-CF	-10		
2008	SDN	MLB	25	124	16	4	2	2	10	13	21	1	1	0.1	.264	.339	.391	.291	.363	.418	.271	5.0	0.9	26-CF	3		
2009	POR	AAA	26	226	33	10	3	12	30	20	46	1	0	1.8	.260	.329	.520	.250	.310	.475	.267	7.9	-0.7	49-CF	-14		
2009	SDN	MLB	26	324	38	14	2	12	38	25	89	6	1	-0.3	.256	.323	.440	.285	.347	.488	.285	15.7	1.9	55-RF	3	13-CF	-2
2010	SDN	MLB	27	525	54	21	3	10	52	44	127	7	3	0.6	.239	.308	.361	.252	.317	.388	.250	10.9	0.5	109-CF	-7		

Breakout: 6%   Improve: 42%   Collapse: 21%   Attrition: 8%   MLB: 78%   Comparables: Buck Coats, Brant Brown, Mitch Maier, Ryan Church

Venable impressed the Padres so much late last season that he will enter 2010 as a starter. His power and athleticism make him intriguing; some observers believe the son of former major-league outfielder Max Venable has more upside than most 27-year-olds because he did not start playing baseball until his senior year of high school. Moreover, he concentrated on basketball in college, as he was a two-time all–Ivy League guard at Princeton. They would prefer he play right field, but he could wind up as the center fielder if the need arises. Venable has shown good power potential, slugging over .500 against righties and away from Petco, but his plate discipline has been an issue. At worst, he should at least have a career as a solid platoon outfielder.

PITCHERS

Mike Adams

Bats: R   Throws: R   Height: 6' 5"   Weight: 190   Born: July 29, 1978   Age: 31

YEAR	TEAM	LVL	AGE	W	L	SV	G	GS	IP	H	HR	BB	SO	GB%	BABIP	STUFF	WHIP	ERA	SIERA	DERA	EqH9	EqHR9	EqBB9	EqSO9	VORP	SN/WX
2008	POR	AAA	29	3	1	0	12	0	14²	21	0	9	16	56%	.457	-7	2.05	5.52	3.94	7.57	13.8	0.7	5.3	7.2	-3.1	-0.29
2008	SDN	MLB	29	2	3	0	54	0	65¹	49	7	19	74	50%	.264	12	1.04	2.48	2.69	2.79	7.7	1.6	2.4	8.3	19.0	1.80
2009	SDN	MLB	30	0	0	0	37	0	37	14	1	8	45	51%	.159	29	0.59	0.73	2.03	2.51	3.8	0.5	1.7	8.1	12.5	2.34
2010	SDN	MLB	31	4	3	0	62	0	64²	52	7	25	59	49%	.265	7	1.18	3.41	3.65	3.92	7.9	1.1	3.1	7.4	11.4	1.51

Breakout: 7%   Improve: 40%   Collapse: 25%   Attrition: 3%   MLB: 92%   Comparables: Ernie Johnson, Joe Beckwith, Mike Timlin, John Johnstone

The onetime Brewers' closer of the future has put his career back on track during his two seasons with the Padres, despite having arthroscopic shoulder surgery following the 2008 season. Adams has a power sinker that induces ground balls, but he can also get a strikeout when he needs it with his four-seam fastball. Adams has resurrected his career to become a quality set-up man, so he could factor into the closer situation if the Padres do end up trading Heath Bell.

Heath Bell

Bats: R   Throws: R   Height: 6' 3"   Weight: 240   Born: September 29, 1977   Age: 32

YEAR	TEAM	LVL	AGE	W	L	SV	G	GS	IP	H	HR	BB	SO	GB%	BABIP	STUFF	WHIP	ERA	SIERA	DERA	EqH9	EqHR9	EqBB9	EqSO9	VORP	SN/WX
2007	SDN	MLB	29	6	4	2	81	0	93²	60	3	30	102	68%	.252	33	0.96	2.02	2.77	2.29	6.4	0.4	2.7	8.6	32.2	5.79
2008	SDN	MLB	30	6	6	0	74	0	78	66	5	28	71	49%	.281	3	1.21	3.58	3.67	3.85	8.2	0.9	2.8	6.6	13.9	3.20
2009	SDN	MLB	31	6	4	42	68	0	69²	54	3	24	79	49%	.297	18	1.12	2.71	2.83	3.04	7.8	0.7	2.7	8.2	18.2	4.00
2010	SDN	MLB	32	5	4	13	68	0	68¹	58	7	27	63	55%	.283	6	1.24	3.56	3.63	4.10	8.2	0.9	3.2	7.6	10.6	2.46

Breakout: 19%   Improve: 35%   Collapse: 29%   Attrition: 11%   MLB: 98%   Comparables: Todd Jones, Francisco Cordero, Jose Mesa, Dave Veres

Bell took over as the Padres' closer last season and ably filled the shoes of Trevor Hoffman, leading the league in saves and even stranding 12 out of 13 inherited runners. Bell is more of a traditional closer than Hoffman was at the end, in that Bell can throw his fastball as high as 98 mph and mixes in a hard slider, hard stuff that plays well in any park, not just Petco. He held right-handed hitters to just .138/.200/.172. Bell is prime trade-bait, not least because a top-flight closer is a luxury on a rebuilding team.

Greg Burke

Bats: R   Throws: R   Height: 6' 4"   Weight: 204   Born: September 21, 1982   Age: 27

YEAR	TEAM	LVL	AGE	W	L	SV	G	GS	IP	H	HR	BB	SO	GB%	BABIP	STUFF	WHIP	ERA	SIERA	DERA	EqH9	EqHR9	EqBB9	EqSO9	VORP	SN/WX
2007	LEL	A+	24	4	4	0	51	9	96¹	105	11	28	67	58%	.299	-35	1.38	5.23	4.20	6.13	10.1	1.8	2.9	3.7	-6.6	-0.94
2008	SAN	AA	25	2	7	23	59	1	84¹	76	7	17	92	54%	.307	-2	1.10	2.24	2.69	3.54	9.2	1.6	2.1	7.1	17.4	1.56
2009	POR	AAA	26	3	0	7	13	0	16	8	1	4	14	48%	.175	1	0.75	2.25	3.24	2.93	5.3	1.2	2.3	5.9	4.4	1.01
2009	SDN	MLB	26	3	3	0	48	0	45²	48	4	23	33	53%	.308	-19	1.55	4.14	4.69	4.94	10.1	1.2	3.8	5.2	2.8	0.22
2010	SDN	MLB	27	4	5	6	62	0	70	70	9	28	47	53%	.289	-11	1.40	4.37	4.57	5.06	9.7	1.3	3.2	5.4	3.4	1.27

Breakout: 15%   Improve: 48%   Collapse: 20%   Attrition: 16%   MLB: 38%   Comparables: Jay Aldrich, Barry Johnson, Tim Layana, Mike Burns

If nothing else, Burke is a study in perseverance as he took a long road to the major leagues. He went 13-26 in four seasons at Duke, spent a year in the independent Atlantic League, then was signed to a minor-league contract by the Padres out of a tryout camp in 2006. Burke throws a 93-mph fastball and a changeup that is a swing-and-a-miss pitch, giving him enough to be an effective middle reliever, maybe more.

Cesar Carrillo

Bats: R   Throws: R   Height: 6' 3"   Weight: 180   Born: April 29, 1984   Age: 26

YEAR	TEAM	LVL	AGE	W	L	SV	G	GS	IP	H	HR	BB	SO	GB%	BABIP	STUFF	WHIP	ERA	SIERA	DERA	EqH9	EqHR9	EqBB9	EqSO9	VORP	SN/WX
2007	POR	AAA	23	0	2	0	5	5	15²	22	2	14	8	51%	.357	-26	2.30	8.62	6.24	9.39	12.3	1.8	7.6	2.9	-6.6	-0.29
2008	LEL	A+	24	3	5	0	15	14	57¹	69	6	33	32	56%	.318	-38	1.78	5.97	5.29	7.95	11.6	2.2	6.0	2.8	-14.8	-1.19
2009	SAN	AA	25	8	4	0	20	20	121	115	10	37	57	58%	.271	-26	1.26	4.24	4.87	5.63	10.2	1.9	3.1	3.2	-1.6	-0.07
2009	POR	AAA	25	0	3	0	5	5	29¹	37	2	9	26	54%	.376	-1	1.57	5.52	3.76	6.75	12.8	1.3	3.0	6.3	-3.8	-0.11
2009	SDN	MLB	25	1	2	0	3	3	10¹	16	4	12	4	45%	.316	-42	2.71	13.06	7.22	14.40	16.2	5.4	9.0	2.7	-9.9	-0.32
2010	SDN	MLB	26	4	9	0	24	24	111²	135	18	61	47	53%	.308	-35	1.76	6.17	5.81	7.07	11.7	1.5	4.5	3.4	-19.5	1.03

Breakout: 11%   Improve: 51%   Collapse: 19%   Attrition: 9%   MLB: 19%   Comparables: John McMahon, Glenn Carter, Jesse Smith, Darrell Rodgers

Carrillo was once a top prospect as the Padres' first-round draft pick in 2005, a tyro with a fastball that reached 97 mph when he wasn't spinning a curveball with bite. He underwent Tommy John surgery in 2007, however, and is still trying to regain arm strength—sorry folks, not every TJS winds up happily ever after. Carrillo's stuff was OK last season, and the Padres are hopeful that the passage of time will further heal him, but in the meantime, he's close to the bottom of a lengthening list of rotation options.

Simon Castro

Bats: R   Throws: R   Height: 6' 5"   Weight: 203   Born: April 9, 1988   Age: 22

YEAR	TEAM	LVL	AGE	W	L	SV	G	GS	IP	H	HR	BB	SO	GB%	BABIP	STUFF	WHIP	ERA	SIERA	DERA	EqH9	EqHR9	EqBB9	EqSO9	VORP	SN/WX
2007	PDR	Rk	19	2	6	0	14	12	50²	61	4	30	55	48%	.377	-17	1.80	6.22	3.98	10.36	13.3	2.9	6.1	4.9	-25.6	-1.80
2008	EUG	A-	20	2	3	0	15	15	65¹	54	3	29	64	48%	.285	1	1.27	3.99	3.77	7.12	10.2	1.9	4.5	4.7	-10.9	-0.67
2009	FTW	A	21	10	6	0	28	27	140¹	118	9	37	157	43%	.302	0	1.10	3.33	2.72	5.68	10.1	1.9	3.4	6.3	-2.5	-0.63
2010	SDN	MLB	22	5	9	0	27	25	108¹	116	16	58	84	41%	.312	8	1.60	5.55	4.75	6.35	10.3	1.5	4.4	6.3	-10.2	1.76

Breakout: 22% Improve: 61% Collapse: 10% Attrition: 9%   MLB: 3%   Comparables: Robb Welch, Bill Melvin, Kevin Millwood, Joe Young

Seemingly out of nowhere, Castro led the Midwest League in strikeouts last season while leaving scouts scrambling to get another look at the big Dominican whose fastball was sitting at 94-95, touching 97, and—just as importantly—reliably pounding the strike zone. Throw in that he can mix in a plus slider, and no pitcher in the system can now come close to matching his ceiling. If he achieves a better changeup, he could develop into a second starter, with a backup plan of closing out games at the major-league level.

Kevin Correia

Bats: R   Throws: R   Height: 6' 3"   Weight: 200   Born: August 24, 1980   Age: 29

YEAR	TEAM	LVL	AGE	W	L	SV	G	GS	IP	H	HR	BB	SO	GB%	BABIP	STUFF	WHIP	ERA	SIERA	DERA	EqH9	EqHR9	EqBB9	EqSO9	VORP	SN/WX
2007	SFN	MLB	26	4	7	0	59	8	101²	94	9	40	80	53%	.278	8	1.32	3.45	4.21	3.33	8.1	0.7	3.1	6.3	24.7	1.83
2008	SFN	MLB	27	3	8	0	25	19	110	141	15	47	66	42%	.330	-19	1.71	6.05	5.14	6.14	11.0	1.1	3.3	4.5	-8.0	0.57
2009	SDN	MLB	28	12	11	0	33	33	198	194	17	64	142	52%	.294	0	1.30	3.91	4.23	4.52	9.6	1.3	2.6	5.2	20.6	4.65
2010	SDN	MLB	29	9	10	0	48	28	163	162	20	62	101	50%	.286	-5	1.38	4.27	4.73	4.95	9.6	1.2	3.1	5.1	9.9	2.08

Breakout: 5% Improve: 32% Collapse: 9% Attrition: 12%   MLB: 98%   Comparables: Fred Sanford, Kyle Lohse, Mark Clark, Danny Darwin

Correia became the Padres' notional ace last season after Jake Peavy was injured (and later traded to the White Sox). The San Diego native had bounced between the rotation and various relief roles while spending all or parts of six seasons with the Giants, but in the way any middling talent would welcome the chance to pitch in Petco, he found a home with the Padres after signing as a free agent. Although he has always had a live arm with a hard sinker and cut fastball, the biggest difference in 2009 was his better job of throwing his changeup with command. He certainly isn't a true front man in a big-league rotation, but he fits in nicely as the voice of experience among a crew of much younger starters.

Mike Ekstrom

Bats: R   Throws: R   Height: 6' 0"   Weight: 185   Born: August 30, 1983   Age: 26

YEAR	TEAM	LVL	AGE	W	L	SV	G	GS	IP	H	HR	BB	SO	GB%	BABIP	STUFF	WHIP	ERA	SIERA	DERA	EqH9	EqHR9	EqBB9	EqSO9	VORP	SN/WX
2007	SAN	AA	23	7	10	0	27	27	143²	183	6	47	98	54%	.363	-22	1.60	4.76	4.44	6.90	13.2	1.0	3.3	4.4	-20.6	-0.52
2008	SAN	AA	24	11	8	1	41	15	108	137	14	34	101	62%	.363	-43	1.58	4.58	3.59	6.77	12.8	2.3	3.1	5.9	-14.6	-1.13
2008	SDN	MLB	24	0	2	0	8	0	9²	14	2	7	6	61%	.375	-25	2.17	7.45	5.33	7.79	15.6	3.1	6.2	5.2	-2.2	-0.36
2009	POR	AAA	25	4	2	0	42	1	62¹	44	2	16	43	65%	.236	2	0.96	1.73	3.77	2.36	7.0	0.8	2.4	4.7	20.6	2.38
2009	SDN	MLB	25	0	0	0	12	0	18¹	21	3	8	19	48%	.346	-9	1.58	6.38	3.65	7.27	11.9	2.6	3.6	7.8	-3.4	0.16
2010	SDN	MLB	26	3	6	0	51	2	69¹	78	9	32	47	54%	.319	-18	1.60	5.20	4.75	6.03	11.0	1.3	3.8	5.6	-4.1	0.92

Breakout: 33% Improve: 57% Collapse: 15% Attrition: 25%   MLB: 67%   Comparables: Pat Rice, Tim Rodgers, Clay Hensley, Steven Register

Ekstrom, a hometown kid who went to college at Point Loma Nazarene in San Diego, is an easy guy to root for. Unfortunately, he was hit hard during his stints with the Padres in 2008 and 2009, so his giving you cause has been a bit more dicey. He has a good slider and keeps the ball down, but the rest of his stuff is average and he needs pinpoint control to get hitters out. While this works well enough in the minors, it's difficult to pitch that way with any consistent effectiveness against major-league hitters, as they'll jump on mistakes inside the zone.

Ernesto Frieri

Bats: R   Throws: R   Height: 6' 2"   Weight: 190   Born: July 19, 1985   Age: 24

YEAR	TEAM	LVL	AGE	W	L	SV	G	GS	IP	H	HR	BB	SO	GB%	BABIP	STUFF	WHIP	ERA	SIERA	DERA	EqH9	EqHR9	EqBB9	EqSO9	VORP	SN/WX
2007	FTW	A	21	1	2	0	40	0	64²	48	4	23	65	28%	.262	11	1.10	2.64	3.48	3.94	8.5	1.5	4.1	5.8	10.3	-0.15
2007	LEL	A+	21	1	0	1	13	1	21²	11	1	6	27	30%	.227	20	0.78	1.25	2.00	1.83	5.9	0.9	2.7	7.8	8.0	1.10
2008	LEL	A+	22	8	6	0	33	18	123²	125	14	32	108	32%	.306	-20	1.27	4.00	3.73	5.29	10.3	2.3	3.0	5.1	2.7	-0.24
2008	SAN	AA	22	1	0	0	2	2	11	7	3	2	10	33%	.160	10	0.82	4.09	3.04	5.40	8.1	4.5	1.8	6.3	0.1	0.04
2009	SAN	AA	23	10	9	0	27	26	140¹	125	13	62	118	36%	.277	-15	1.33	3.59	4.35	4.90	9.6	2.0	4.1	5.9	8.9	1.09
2009	SDN	MLB	23	0	0	0	2	0	2	0	0	1	2	—	.000	2	0.50	0.00	5.48	0.00	0.0	0.0	4.5	9.0	1.2	0.01
2010	SDN	MLB	24	6	9	0	47	18	127	127	19	62	92	28%	.290	-10	1.49	4.86	5.17	5.56	9.7	1.4	4.0	5.9	-0.8	2.50

Breakout: 8%   Improve: 30%   Collapse: 22%   Attrition: 10%   MLB: 8%   Comparables: Matt Guerrier, Kevin Mulvey, Mark Sievert, Scott May

Signed as an 18-year-old out of Colombia in 2003, Frieri has slowly worked his way through the Padres' farm system, bouncing between starting and relief roles and finally getting a brief taste of the major leagues last September. He has a good slider and curveball and a fastball that sits around 92-94 mph. He'll head back to Portland to make needed refinements to his command and breaking ball, but if all goes well, he'll resurface as a qualified option for service at the back end of a major-league rotation.

Sean Gallagher

Bats: R   Throws: R   Height: 6' 2"   Weight: 235   Born: December 30, 1985   Age: 24

YEAR	TEAM	LVL	AGE	W	L	SV	G	GS	IP	H	HR	BB	SO	GB%	BABIP	STUFF	WHIP	ERA	SIERA	DERA	EqH9	EqHR9	EqBB9	EqSO9	VORP	SN/WX
2007	TEN	AA	21	7	2	0	11	11	61	54	3	24	54	48%	.290	26	1.28	3.39	3.89	4.58	9.3	0.9	3.7	5.6	5.9	0.63
2007	IOW	AAA	21	3	1	0	8	8	40²	33	1	13	37	50%	.294	32	1.13	2.66	3.50	3.05	7.5	0.5	3.1	6.6	10.4	1.27
2007	CHN	MLB	21	0	0	1	8	0	14²	19	3	12	5	37%	.302	-28	2.11	8.59	7.20	8.28	11.7	1.2	6.8	3.1	-4.5	-0.15
2008	IOW	AAA	22	2	2	0	5	5	29	21	2	9	30	58%	.250	29	1.03	3.10	3.07	3.77	6.9	0.9	2.8	6.6	5.5	0.63
2008	CHN	MLB	22	3	4	0	12	10	58²	58	6	22	49	48%	.297	23	1.36	4.45	4.06	4.50	9.2	0.8	2.9	6.7	6.4	0.97
2008	OAK	MLB	22	2	3	0	11	11	56²	60	7	36	54	30%	.317	9	1.69	5.88	4.76	6.47	9.8	1.3	5.1	7.6	-6.2	0.45
2009	SAC	AAA	23	1	0	0	5	5	20²	12	0	6	15	55%	.207	7	0.87	1.74	3.95	2.92	5.8	0.4	2.7	4.9	5.7	0.88
2009	OAK	MLB	23	1	2	0	6	2	14¹	21	1	7	10	45%	.392	-16	1.95	8.16	5.00	9.42	12.6	0.6	3.8	5.7	-6.2	-0.08
2009	SDN	MLB	23	2	0	0	8	0	5¹	5	0	4	4	36%	.313	2	1.87	0.00	6.02	0.00	8.4	0.0	6.8	5.1	3.3	0.48
2010	SDN	MLB	24	5	6	0	30	15	87¹	84	9	45	68	43%	.296	-2	1.48	4.63	4.63	5.26	9.3	1.0	4.1	6.2	2.4	1.61

Breakout: 16%   Improve: 58%   Collapse: 9%   Attrition: 24%   MLB: 90%   Comparables: Mike Morgan, Jim Clancy, Jesus Colome, Eric King

It is easy to assume Gallagher's star has faded after the Cubs traded him in 2008 and the Athletics dealt him to the Padres last season, but Gallagher is still young and heading into his age-24 season. His health is an issue, as he was bothered by shoulder problems in 2008 and knee problems last season. But if he can stay healthy and can consistently throw his hard, slow curveballs for strikes to complement an average fastball, there is no reason he cannot be a midrotation starter. Throwing strikes, though, is the big if.

Luke Gregerson

Bats: L   Throws: R   Height: 6' 3"   Weight: 200   Born: May 14, 1984   Age: 26

YEAR	TEAM	LVL	AGE	W	L	SV	G	GS	IP	H	HR	BB	SO	GB%	BABIP	STUFF	WHIP	ERA	SIERA	DERA	EqH9	EqHR9	EqBB9	EqSO9	VORP	SN/WX
2007	PMB	A+	23	3	4	29	53	0	64	42	0	20	69	66%	.261	12	0.97	1.97	2.78	2.96	7.4	0.6	3.5	6.8	16.8	1.80
2008	SFD	AA	24	7	6	10	57	0	75¹	62	6	26	78	55%	.281	0	1.17	3.35	3.22	4.54	8.2	1.1	3.4	7.1	7.7	-0.16
2009	SDN	MLB	25	2	4	1	72	0	75	62	3	31	93	52%	.314	18	1.24	3.24	2.85	3.83	8.1	0.6	3.2	8.8	13.7	2.98
2010	SDN	MLB	26	4	5	7	65	0	69	60	7	30	63	58%	.290	4	1.31	3.79	3.77	4.30	8.3	1.0	3.6	7.5	9.2	1.69

Breakout: 15%   Improve: 33%   Collapse: 29%   Attrition: 2%   MLB: 73%   Comparables: Jeff Pierce, Doug Piatt, Brian Wood, Milt Hill

Hardly anyone noticed when Gregerson, a rather lightly regarded 28th-round draft picked from St. Xavier, was acquired by the Padres late in spring training last year from the Cardinals to complete the Khalil Greene trade. Then everyone noticed when Gregerson became the primary set-up man to Heath Bell and one of the top relievers in the NL. Gregerson is not the normal sinker/slider reliever, as his sinker has outstanding boring action that breaks bats, while his slider is a true wipeout pitch. Reliever statistics can be very volatile from one season to the next, but Gregerson looks like the real deal and figures to be the first in line to close if Bell is traded.

Craig Italiano

Bats: R   Throws: R   Height: 6′ 4″   Weight: 209   Born: July 22, 1986   Age: 23

YEAR	TEAM	LVL	AGE	W	L	SV	G	GS	IP	H	HR	BB	SO	GB%	BABIP	STUFF	WHIP	ERA	SIERA	DERA	EqH9	EqHR9	EqBB9	EqSO9	VORP	SN/WX
2007	KNC	A	20	0	3	0	6	6	17	32	3	16	24	47%	.558	1	2.82	12.71	4.09	17.27	22.0	3.8	10.7	8.8	-18.7	-1.38
2008	KNC	A	21	7	0	0	14	14	70	43	2	35	79	52%	.241	20	1.11	1.16	3.31	3.22	7.6	1.1	5.6	6.3	16.3	1.26
2008	STO	A+	21	1	4	0	14	5	30	44	7	26	33	45%	.398	-23	2.33	9.90	4.64	12.86	15.1	3.9	9.0	6.4	-22.9	-2.01
2009	STO	A+	22	5	6	0	16	16	76²	83	6	40	75	57%	.347	-18	1.60	5.63	3.96	7.94	12.1	1.8	5.8	5.2	-18.9	-1.89
2009	LEL	A+	22	0	1	0	19	0	31¹	24	0	10	44	78%	.329	13	1.09	1.44	2.00	3.99	8.6	0.9	3.7	7.4	4.9	0.10
2010	OAK	MLB	23	3	7	0	31	16	89¹	107	14	59	68	51%	.335	-12	1.86	6.67	4.99	6.85	10.5	1.4	5.6	6.3	-13.4	0.63

Breakout: 19%   Improve: 63%   Collapse: 6%   Attrition: 9%   MLB: 1%   Comparables: Kelvin Jimenez, Bradley Clapp, Jason Robbins, Tom Wasilewski

The Padres acquired Italiano from the Athletics last season in the July Hairston trade and completely remade him, switching him from starter to reliever and changing his delivery from straight over the top to three-quarters. The moves worked, as he was dominant at High-A Lake Elsinore. Italiano has always had a live arm, but trouble controlling his pitches. The new arm slot helped him gain more command of his pitches and increased the velocity on his changeup and slider. Italiano may not throw his fastball at 97 mph, as he did when he was initially drafted by the Athletics in 2006, but he should have enough talent to pitch out of the Pads' pen as early as 2011.

Mat Latos

Bats: R   Throws: R   Height: 6′ 5″   Weight: 210   Born: December 9, 1987   Age: 22

YEAR	TEAM	LVL	AGE	W	L	SV	G	GS	IP	H	HR	BB	SO	GB%	BABIP	STUFF	WHIP	ERA	SIERA	DERA	EqH9	EqHR9	EqBB9	EqSO9	VORP	SN/WX
2007	EUG	A-	19	1	4	0	16	13	56¹	58	1	22	74	43%	.393	26	1.42	3.83	2.65	5.87	11.6	1.1	4.0	7.0	-2.1	-0.23
2008	EUG	A-	20	2	0	0	3	3	17¹	13	1	3	23	49%	.286	16	0.92	1.04	1.91	2.81	9.6	2.3	2.3	6.8	4.8	0.37
2008	FTW	A	20	0	3	0	7	5	24²	24	3	8	23	48%	.296	10	1.30	3.28	3.59	6.07	10.6	2.3	3.9	5.1	-1.4	-0.12
2009	FTW	A	21	3	0	0	4	2	25¹	10	1	3	27	48%	.164	23	0.51	0.36	1.96	1.19	5.6	1.2	2.0	6.0	10.9	0.76
2009	SAN	AA	21	5	1	0	9	9	47	32	0	9	46	43%	.256	41	0.87	1.91	2.82	3.00	7.0	0.4	2.0	7.0	12.5	1.23
2009	SDN	MLB	21	4	5	0	10	10	50²	43	7	23	39	42%	.252	17	1.30	4.62	4.48	5.55	8.7	2.0	3.5	5.5	-0.3	1.10
2010	SDN	MLB	22	7	7	0	29	25	120²	115	14	50	92	42%	.290	20	1.37	4.22	4.40	4.89	9.3	1.2	3.4	6.2	8.2	3.03

Breakout: 11%   Improve: 49%   Collapse: 9%   Attrition: 10%   MLB: 100%   Comparables: Bill Fulton, Blake Johnson, Jeff Russell, John Ennis

Of all the young pitchers in the Padres' organization, Latos has the best chance of becoming a true number-one starter. He has a fastball that reliably comes into home plate in the mid-90s but touches 97 mph, a true blazer with good late life, along with a slider with a sharp, late break, *and* a big-breaking curveball. Latos pitched well in his first taste of the majors before tiring—the Padres have been extremely, understandably careful with his workloads—and showed he was not scared of pitching on a big stage. In fact, nothing seems to bother Latos. When asked last season what his mother thought about the tattoos covering most of his body, he laughed and said she was jealous she didn't have as many. They'll continue to handle him with care, but the talent is that special, and if they get him past the injury nexus unharmed, he'll be pure power aided by pitchers' heaven.

Wade LeBlanc

Bats: L   Throws: L   Height: 6′ 3″   Weight: 200   Born: August 7, 1984   Age: 25

YEAR	TEAM	LVL	AGE	W	L	SV	G	GS	IP	H	HR	BB	SO	GB%	BABIP	STUFF	WHIP	ERA	SIERA	DERA	EqH9	EqHR9	EqBB9	EqSO9	VORP	SN/WX
2007	LEL	A+	22	6	5	0	16	16	92	72	5	17	90	44%	.268	26	0.97	2.64	2.87	3.64	7.6	1.1	2.0	5.7	18.4	1.62
2007	SAN	AA	22	7	3	0	12	11	57¹	48	8	19	55	47%	.265	5	1.17	3.45	3.40	4.61	9.6	2.4	3.2	6.5	5.2	1.19
2008	POR	AAA	23	11	9	0	26	25	138²	136	21	42	139	37%	.304	-8	1.28	5.32	3.33	5.79	9.5	2.0	2.8	6.6	-4.2	0.72
2008	SDN	MLB	23	1	3	0	5	4	21¹	29	7	15	14	58%	.324	-23	2.06	8.02	5.28	8.47	14.6	4.6	5.9	5.0	-6.5	-0.15
2009	POR	AAA	24	4	9	0	24	20	121	109	15	31	95	50%	.265	-18	1.16	3.87	3.82	4.79	9.2	2.2	2.5	5.3	9.2	1.44
2009	SDN	MLB	24	3	1	0	9	9	46¹	35	6	19	30	41%	.215	-6	1.17	3.69	4.84	4.07	7.5	1.2	3.2	4.6	7.2	1.37
2010	SDN	MLB	25	8	10	0	34	26	142¹	138	21	57	101	38%	.281	-2	1.37	4.47	4.63	5.10	9.3	1.4	3.3	5.8	6.4	3.04

Breakout: 8%   Improve: 43%   Collapse: 20%   Attrition: 19%   MLB: 43%   Comparables: Patrick Misch, Chris Seddon, Matthew Maloney, John Cerutti

LeBlanc pitched so well at the end of last season that he will go to spring training as a favorite to begin 2009 in the Padres' rotation. He is the epitome of the soft-tossing left-hander, his fastball rarely nearing 90 mph. However, he has a devastating changeup that causes plenty of bad swings, as well as a curveball that fools hitters with its late break. He will never be the ace of a staff, but he has enough command and guile to carve out a career as a back-end rotation starter, particularly in a park as forgiving as Petco.

Cory Luebke

Bats: R　Throws: L　Height: 6' 4"　Weight: 200　Born: March 4, 1985　Age: 25

YEAR	TEAM	LVL	AGE	W	L	SV	G	GS	IP	H	HR	BB	SO	GB%	BABIP	STUFF	WHIP	ERA	SIERA	DERA	EqH9	EqHR9	EqBB9	EqSO9	VORP	SN/WX
2007	FTW	A	22	1	2	0	5	5	27	29	2	5	30	46%	.342	13	1.26	3.33	2.75	5.96	11.6	1.8	2.5	6.3	-1.3	-0.25
2007	EUG	A-	22	3	0	0	8	3	24²	18	2	2	26	59%	.246	13	0.81	1.46	2.36	2.85	8.0	1.9	1.5	5.3	7.0	0.43
2008	FTW	A	23	3	3	0	10	10	56	52	6	9	40	54%	.291	-12	1.09	2.89	3.67	4.38	10.4	2.4	2.4	3.9	6.0	0.01
2008	LEL	A+	23	3	6	0	17	15	72¹	97	8	23	60	52%	.374	-37	1.66	6.84	4.00	9.00	13.4	2.3	3.6	4.7	-26.1	-2.04
2009	LEL	A+	24	8	2	0	14	14	88¹	73	3	17	80	60%	.289	7	1.02	2.34	3.10	3.47	8.4	1.2	2.5	4.6	18.4	1.28
2009	SAN	AA	24	3	2	0	9	9	41¹	38	3	15	32	41%	.276	-8	1.28	3.70	4.28	5.63	9.4	1.6	3.4	5.2	-0.6	0.18
2010	SDN	MLB	25	5	7	0	28	18	99¹	109	14	40	59	48%	.301	-15	1.50	4.99	4.92	5.77	10.6	1.4	3.3	4.8	-3.0	1.74

Breakout: 7%　Improve: 39%　Collapse: 21%　Attrition: 13%　MLB: 9%　Comparables: J.R. Mathes, Dave Gassner, Michael Romanovsky, Allen Davis

Luebke, the Padres' supplemental first-round draft pick from Ohio State in 2007, has been making good progress toward justifying the selection. Although he doesn't have one dominant pitch, his sinker and curveball are above-average offerings and his changeup is serviceable. Luebke has a lot of other things going for him, including outstanding athleticism that allows him to consistently repeat his delivery. He followed a fine 2009 season at Double-A San Antonio by pitching for the gold-medal-winning US team at the World Cup, and it looks as if he'll be ready to make the jump to the majors at some point this season.

Edward Mujica

Bats: R　Throws: R　Height: 6' 2"　Weight: 215　Born: May 10, 1984　Age: 26

YEAR	TEAM	LVL	AGE	W	L	SV	G	GS	IP	H	HR	BB	SO	GB%	BABIP	STUFF	WHIP	ERA	SIERA	DERA	EqH9	EqHR9	EqBB9	EqSO9	VORP	SN/WX
2007	BUF	AAA	23	2	1	14	34	0	37²	35	4	9	44	30%	.323	11	1.17	5.02	2.53	5.75	9.0	1.3	2.3	8.5	-1.0	0.68
2007	CLE	MLB	23	0	0	0	10	0	13	19	3	2	7	25%	.333	-17	1.62	8.31	5.22	7.43	12.2	2.0	1.4	4.1	-2.9	0.00
2008	BUF	AAA	24	0	2	4	18	0	26	29	2	10	27	35%	.346	-6	1.50	4.15	3.62	5.26	10.5	1.1	3.5	6.7	0.7	-0.06
2008	CLE	MLB	24	3	2	0	33	0	38²	46	5	10	27	35%	.328	-11	1.45	6.75	4.44	6.46	10.3	1.2	2.1	5.6	-4.1	-1.30
2009	SDN	MLB	25	3	5	2	67	4	93²	101	14	19	76	41%	.306	-27	1.28	3.94	3.68	4.90	10.7	2.2	1.6	5.9	6.0	1.33
2010	SDN	MLB	26	4	6	3	68	0	79	82	11	26	59	37%	.303	-8	1.36	4.33	4.31	5.08	10.1	1.3	2.6	6.1	3.7	0.42

Breakout: 28%　Improve: 52%　Collapse: 9%　Attrition: 11%　MLB: 96%　Comparables: Jose Lima, Heath Bost, Rafael Betancourt, Dick Pole

Mujica was acquired from the Indians in a trade during the latter stages of spring training; he was coming off two awful Tribe seasons in which he'd been hampered by knee problems. Left alone in a role-less role where he was just asked to give the club relief innings, he delivered, relying on a good fastball that he balances against a solid split-finger pitch that induces a lot of swings and misses from right-handed batters. It's an arsenal good enough to make him an effective middle or set-up reliever, although a season-ending experiment with starting lets the Padres ponder that alternative in case they come up short in the rotation.

Luis Perdomo

Bats: R　Throws: R　Height: 6' 0"　Weight: 170　Born: April 27, 1984　Age: 26

YEAR	TEAM	LVL	AGE	W	L	SV	G	GS	IP	H	HR	BB	SO	GB%	BABIP	STUFF	WHIP	ERA	SIERA	DERA	EqH9	EqHR9	EqBB9	EqSO9	VORP	SN/WX
2007	LKC	A	23	4	6	10	56	0	66	43	6	26	81	57%	.242	-3	1.05	3.27	2.74	4.86	7.7	1.7	4.2	7.4	4.4	-0.64
2008	KIN	A+	24	3	1	18	31	0	39	19	0	17	43	50%	.209	8	0.92	0.92	3.12	2.07	5.6	0.7	4.4	6.8	14.1	1.70
2008	SFD	AA	24	2	2	1	15	0	18	18	2	6	22	46%	.327	0	1.33	4.50	2.82	6.75	9.5	1.5	3.0	8.0	-2.5	-0.21
2008	AKR	AA	24	2	0	1	9	0	15¹	12	1	7	17	42%	.289	3	1.24	3.52	3.28	4.40	8.2	1.3	4.4	7.5	1.8	-0.35
2009	SDN	MLB	25	1	0	0	35	0	60	57	11	34	55	59%	.274	-26	1.52	4.80	4.14	5.75	9.8	2.6	4.4	6.6	-1.6	-0.28
2010	SDN	MLB	26	3	5	5	53	0	64²	62	9	35	52	50%	.287	-10	1.49	4.80	4.49	5.46	9.2	1.4	4.4	6.6	0.3	0.69

Breakout: 10%　Improve: 32%　Collapse: 25%　Attrition: 16%　MLB: 83%　Comparables: Jeff Lahti, Julian Heredia, Dean Weese, Joe Ausanio

Perdomo was a popular man last season. The Padres claimed him off waivers from the Giants, who had selected him from the Cardinals in the Rule 5 draft. Despite this magical mystery tour, he had a solid rookie season in middle relief. Perdomo's biggest weakness is his lack of command of his 93 mph fastball, which leads to too many walks. He has an outstanding changeup and a good slider, but his ability to throw the heater for strikes will ultimately determine whether he turns into a top-flight set-up man or even perhaps a closer, or winds up with a short major-league career.

Aaron Poreda

Bats: L   **Throws:** L   **Height:** 6' 6"   **Weight:** 240   **Born:** October 1, 1986   **Age:** 23

YEAR	TEAM	LVL	AGE	W	L	SV	G	GS	IP	H	HR	BB	SO	GB%	BABIP	STUFF	WHIP	ERA	SIERA	DERA	EqH9	EqHR9	EqBB9	EqSO9	VORP	SN/WX
2007	GRF	Rk	20	4	0	0	12	8	46¹	29	1	10	48	61%	.248	34	0.84	1.17	2.45	2.36	6.9	1.1	3.0	5.6	14.7	1.29
2008	WNS	A+	21	5	5	0	12	12	73¹	67	1	18	46	55%	.278	22	1.16	3.31	4.24	4.31	8.7	0.6	2.7	3.7	9.4	0.09
2008	BIR	AA	21	3	4	0	15	15	87²	81	5	22	72	54%	.300	22	1.17	2.98	3.63	4.59	9.6	1.3	2.4	5.2	8.2	1.10
2009	BIR	AA	22	5	4	0	11	11	64¹	47	1	35	69	57%	.284	27	1.27	2.38	3.62	4.15	8.0	0.7	4.9	7.0	9.1	0.83
2009	CHA	MLB	22	1	0	0	10	0	11	9	0	8	12	63%	.321	11	1.55	2.45	3.99	2.53	7.6	0.0	5.9	9.3	3.5	-0.04
2009	POR	AAA	22	0	3	0	7	6	32²	28	3	37	30	54%	.281	9	1.99	7.16	5.47	8.56	9.0	1.7	10.2	6.1	-10.6	-0.97
2009	SDN	MLB	22	0	0	0	4	0	2¹	1	0	5	0	49%	.143	-47	2.57	3.86	10.41	3.86	3.9	0.0	15.4	0.0	0.4	0.00
2010	SDN	MLB	23	6	8	0	28	21	119	109	13	62	79	54%	.272	2	1.44	4.50	4.85	5.07	8.8	1.1	4.2	5.4	5.7	2.27

Breakout: 9%   **Improve:** 37%   **Collapse:** 24%   **Attrition:** 7%   **MLB:** 27%   **Comparables:** Scott Karl, Joe Magrane, Tom Gorzelanny, Errol Simonitsch

As a top prospect, Poreda has the most upside of the four pitchers the Padres acquired from the White Sox in the Peavy trade last summer. Poreda, however, struggled mightily to throw strikes once he joined the Padres' organization. One of the hardest-throwing lefties in the game, with a fastball that has been clocked as high as 100 mph, a sharp slider, and a decent changeup, this big guy's mechanics tend to get out of whack, causing him to lose command, at which point his breaking pitches flatten out. If Poreda can harness his stuff, he certainly has the look of someone who can pitch near the top of a major-league rotation. But he has been this way since he was drafted, and most scouts think he'd be best served by a permanent move to the bullpen. Either way, he clearly needs more time at Triple-A after his rough finish at Portland.

Jackson Quezada

Bats: R   **Throws:** R   **Height:** 6' 3"   **Weight:** 205   **Born:** August 9, 1986   **Age:** 23

YEAR	TEAM	LVL	AGE	W	L	SV	G	GS	IP	H	HR	BB	SO	GB%	BABIP	STUFF	WHIP	ERA	SIERA	DERA	EqH9	EqHR9	EqBB9	EqSO9	VORP	SN/WX
2007	EUG	A-	20	3	2	7	21	0	24	22	0	4	29	56%	.338	23	1.08	3.75	2.39	5.48	9.8	0.8	2.0	5.9	0.1	-0.39
2008	FTW	A	21	2	4	27	59	0	63²	42	1	19	79	45%	.268	20	0.96	2.12	2.36	3.90	7.3	0.9	3.6	6.9	10.7	0.46
2010	SDN	MLB	23	2	3	8	43	0	49	51	6	23	30	47%	.296	-12	1.51	4.83	5.06	5.54	10.0	1.2	3.9	4.9	-0.2	0.85

Breakout: 10%   **Improve:** 28%   **Collapse:** 36%   **Attrition:** 14%   **MLB:** 3%   **Comparables:** Jason Alcala, Troy James, Justin Garza, Rob Kerrigan

Quezada reported to his first major-league spring training with a sore shoulder last February and eventually required season-ending arthroscopic surgery. Although he was able to throw off a mound at instructional league in October the Padres will take it slow with him and may keep him behind in extended spring training as a precaution when the season starts. He has been a dominant reliever at the lower levels of the minors, showing solid command of a 95 mph fastball and a sharp slider. He is not yet close to the major leagues, but his performance so far as a pro and his raw ability make him someone to watch.

Cesar Ramos

Bats: L   **Throws:** L   **Height:** 6' 2"   **Weight:** 190   **Born:** June 22, 1984   **Age:** 26

YEAR	TEAM	LVL	AGE	W	L	SV	G	GS	IP	H	HR	BB	SO	GB%	BABIP	STUFF	WHIP	ERA	SIERA	DERA	EqH9	EqHR9	EqBB9	EqSO9	VORP	SN/WX
2007	SAN	AA	23	13	9	0	27	27	163²	153	15	43	90	49%	.267	-17	1.20	3.41	4.67	5.06	9.9	1.7	2.7	3.4	7.5	1.54
2008	POR	AAA	24	9	11	0	28	27	149²	183	17	57	105	52%	.341	-27	1.60	5.29	4.50	6.78	11.4	1.6	3.5	4.4	-20.4	-0.93
2009	POR	AAA	25	5	6	0	15	15	76²	84	7	31	45	64%	.295	-24	1.50	3.99	4.67	5.79	10.4	1.7	3.7	3.7	-2.5	0.41
2009	SDN	MLB	25	0	1	0	5	2	14²	19	0	4	10	59%	.396	0	1.57	3.07	4.16	3.38	12.8	0.0	2.0	5.4	3.1	0.38
2010	SDN	MLB	26	4	8	0	29	14	97²	109	13	44	50	51%	.300	-21	1.57	5.25	5.30	6.03	10.8	1.3	3.7	4.2	-5.8	1.50

Breakout: 16%   **Improve:** 51%   **Collapse:** 15%   **Attrition:** 30%   **MLB:** 15%   **Comparables:** Paul Ah-Yat, Matt Miller, Andy Van Hekken, Frank Gonzales

"Pitch-to-contact" has become one of baseball's buzz phrases in recent years, and it perfectly describes Ramos's style. His three-pitch arsenal of a fastball, slider, and changeup is average any way you splice it, but he locates each pitch to all quadrants of the strike zone and understands how to attack hitters' weaknesses. The problem is that hitters make too much contact against him, increasing the chances of balls falling in for hits. He'll be a fifth starter in the majors at best, and he looks more like a long reliever who can soak up innings.

Clayton Richard

Bats: L   Throws: L   Height: 6' 5"   Weight: 240   Born: September 12, 1983   Age: 26

YEAR	TEAM	LVL	AGE	W	L	SV	G	GS	IP	H	HR	BB	SO	GB%	BABIP	STUFF	WHIP	ERA	SIERA	DERA	EqH9	EqHR9	EqBB9	EqSO9	VORP	SN/WX
2007	WNS	A+	23	8	12	0	28	27	161^1	159	11	59	99	62%	.290	-14	1.35	3.63	4.39	5.58	10.0	1.4	3.8	3.8	-1.3	-1.15
2008	BIR	AA	24	6	6	0	13	13	83^2	66	2	16	53	54%	.254	11	0.98	2.47	4.05	4.18	7.8	0.8	1.9	3.8	11.7	1.16
2008	CHR	AAA	24	6	0	0	7	7	44	33	3	4	33	61%	.238	18	0.84	2.45	3.28	2.98	7.2	0.9	1.1	4.9	11.9	1.12
2008	CHA	MLB	24	2	5	0	13	8	47^2	61	5	13	29	61%	.333	-4	1.55	6.04	4.48	6.20	10.5	0.7	2.0	5.0	-3.8	0.12
2009	CHA	MLB	25	4	3	0	26	14	89	94	10	37	66	53%	.310	3	1.47	4.65	4.43	4.43	9.3	0.8	3.3	6.1	10.4	1.45
2009	SDN	MLB	25	5	2	0	12	12	64	60	7	34	48	53%	.283	-7	1.47	4.08	4.62	4.72	9.4	1.6	4.3	5.5	5.3	1.55
2010	SDN	MLB	26	8	8	0	33	24	138	131	15	57	83	60%	.277	-2	1.36	4.13	4.67	4.72	9.2	1.0	3.3	4.9	12.0	1.90

Breakout: 14%   Improve: 53%   Collapse: 10%   Attrition: 16%   MLB: 76%   Comparables: Bill Krueger, Joe Saunders, Mark Redman, Kason Gabbard

With a big frame that once allowed him to compete with Chad Henne (now of the Miami Dolphins) for the starting quarterback position in college at Michigan, Richard has the look of a power pitcher. However, Richard is more of a control pitcher, as he throws a sinker, slurve, and changeup. He had outstanding command of all his pitches while with the White Sox, though that largely deserted him after he was dealt to the Padres in the Peavy trade. Perhaps taking his cue from former teammate Mark Buehrle, Richard is an extremely fast worker, which makes him a favorite of his teammates. Between the rhythm, the stuff, and the durability, he should settle in nicely as the Padres' third or fourth starter.

Adam Russell

Bats: R   Throws: R   Height: 6' 8"   Weight: 250   Born: April 14, 1983   Age: 27

YEAR	TEAM	LVL	AGE	W	L	SV	G	GS	IP	H	HR	BB	SO	GB%	BABIP	STUFF	WHIP	ERA	SIERA	DERA	EqH9	EqHR9	EqBB9	EqSO9	VORP	SN/WX
2007	BIR	AA	24	9	11	1	38	20	138^2	159	8	58	95	58%	.332	-29	1.56	4.80	4.55	6.38	11.0	1.3	3.9	3.8	-12.9	-1.15
2008	CHR	AAA	25	3	2	0	25	0	37^1	28	3	19	28	45%	.229	-11	1.26	2.89	4.67	3.65	7.1	1.0	4.6	4.9	7.6	0.32
2008	CHA	MLB	25	4	0	0	22	0	26	30	1	10	22	45%	.349	3	1.54	5.19	4.15	4.61	9.9	0.3	3.1	6.8	2.6	0.10
2009	CHR	AAA	26	2	2	5	34	0	56^1	39	5	18	51	63%	.236	5	1.01	3.20	3.38	3.63	6.8	1.2	3.2	6.8	11.1	1.16
2009	POR	AAA	26	0	0	4	9	0	12	12	1	6	7	61%	.289	-30	1.50	5.25	4.92	6.35	10.3	1.6	4.8	4.0	-1.1	0.93
2009	SDN	MLB	26	3	1	0	15	0	12^1	13	0	11	14	38%	.361	7	1.95	3.65	4.63	4.97	9.9	0.0	6.4	7.8	0.7	-0.29
2010	SDN	MLB	27	4	5	3	54	1	74	74	8	36	47	52%	.289	-13	1.48	4.67	4.92	5.37	9.7	1.1	4.0	5.2	1.0	1.00

Breakout: 12%   Improve: 46%   Collapse: 27%   Attrition: 20%   MLB: 24%   Comparables: Casey Hoorelbeke, Bobby Munoz, Sean Green, Steve Hoeme

Another White Sox player acquired in the Peavy trade, Russell is a mountain of a man who has struggled with his control since being converted from a starter two years ago. Russell has the pitches to be an effective short man, with a 95 mph fastball and plus slider. However, his inability to consistently throw strikes has kept him from breaking through. Some scouts believe Russell's problem stems from changing his arm slot from high three-quarters to almost sidearm, depending on the batter, count, or situation. Regardless, if Russell ever figures it out, the Padres have a potential closer at best, perhaps an effective middle reliever at worst, but with Russell celebrating his 27th birthday not long after the season begins, the time to starting seeing either or anything in between is now.

Tim Stauffer

Bats: R   Throws: R   Height: 6' 1"   Weight: 205   Born: June 2, 1982   Age: 28

YEAR	TEAM	LVL	AGE	W	L	SV	G	GS	IP	H	HR	BB	SO	GB%	BABIP	STUFF	WHIP	ERA	SIERA	DERA	EqH9	EqHR9	EqBB9	EqSO9	VORP	SN/WX
2007	POR	AAA	25	8	5	0	25	20	130^2	147	12	36	96	50%	.318	-6	1.40	4.34	4.14	5.12	9.5	1.3	2.6	4.7	5.6	0.56
2009	SAN	AA	27	1	0	1	12	0	19	13	1	4	12	43%	.207	-10	0.89	1.89	4.23	3.38	6.8	1.4	1.9	4.3	4.4	0.14
2009	POR	AAA	27	2	1	0	4	4	23	16	1	4	16	49%	.221	9	0.87	2.35	3.80	3.57	6.8	0.8	1.6	4.4	4.9	0.64
2009	SDN	MLB	27	4	7	0	14	14	73	71	8	34	53	52%	.292	-9	1.44	3.58	4.57	4.17	9.8	1.7	3.8	5.3	10.2	2.29
2010	SDN	MLB	28	5	6	0	21	13	87^2	86	11	36	54	35%	.281	-5	1.39	4.47	5.10	5.19	9.5	1.3	3.4	5.1	3.0	1.41

Breakout: 17%   Improve: 55%   Collapse: 18%   Attrition: 12%   MLB: 52%   Comparables: Jack Cassel, Nic Ungs, Kiko Calero, Jose Cabrera

Stauffer was the Padres' first-round draft pick in 2003, but his stuff has never been the same in professional baseball after being worked hard during his final two college seasons at Richmond. (Abused college pitchers, throw off your chains; all you have to lose are your scholarships.) Stauffer's fastball now only reaches the low 90s after being routinely clocked at 95 mph in college, so he gets by with changing speeds and throwing strikes with the heater, a curveball, and an above-average changeup. He's not going to be the staff ace the Padres once hoped for, but he has enough smarts to carve out a career as a fourth or fifth starter.

Joe Thatcher

							Bats: L		Throws: L		Height: 6' 2"		Weight: 225		Born: April 10, 1981			Age: 29	

YEAR	TEAM	LVL	AGE	W	L	SV	G	GS	IP	H	HR	BB	SO	GB%	BABIP	STUFF	WHIP	ERA	SIERA	DERA	EqH9	EqHR9	EqBB9	EqSO9	VORP	SN/WX
2007	HUN	AA	26	1	0	0	14	0	16¹	11	0	2	20	43%	.289	15	0.80	0.55	1.70	1.20	7.8	0.6	1.2	7.8	7.2	0.72
2007	NAS	AAA	26	2	1	1	24	0	21²	19	0	7	33	47%	.358	22	1.20	2.08	1.92	2.70	8.7	0.4	2.9	10.0	6.7	0.45
2007	SDN	MLB	26	2	2	0	22	0	21	13	1	6	16	57%	.197	3	0.90	1.29	3.89	2.91	5.8	0.4	2.1	5.4	6.2	0.39
2008	POR	AAA	27	5	2	3	37	0	39	38	2	11	44	59%	.330	5	1.26	2.77	2.90	4.19	9.1	0.9	2.6	7.2	5.6	0.49
2008	SDN	MLB	27	0	4	0	25	0	25²	42	4	13	17	54%	.404	-37	2.14	8.42	4.99	8.94	15.7	2.2	4.0	4.7	-9.4	-0.98
2009	POR	AAA	28	1	2	1	19	0	19	18	1	5	22	51%	.327	8	1.21	1.89	2.75	3.86	9.2	1.0	2.4	7.7	3.4	0.19
2009	SDN	MLB	28	1	0	0	52	0	45	37	2	18	55	46%	.321	16	1.22	2.80	2.82	3.24	8.4	0.6	3.1	9.0	10.8	0.91
2010	SDN	MLB	29	3	4	1	58	0	58²	57	7	22	51	54%	.305	-1	1.34	4.19	3.82	4.79	9.3	1.0	3.1	7.1	4.7	0.78

Breakout: 17%   Improve: 43%   Collapse: 21%   Attrition: 12%   MLB: 61%   Comparables: Tim Hamulack, Chuck McElroy, Neal Cotts, Scott Stewart

Thatcher was one of many pleasant surprises for the Padres in the second half of last season, as he became a lock-down left-hander out of the bullpen. The source of his success? Thatcher moved from the center of the pitching rubber to the far left side, and that helped him on two fronts: it made his sweeping slider almost unhittable to left-handed batters and made his 90 mph fastball a little more deceptive to right-handers. So now Thatcher isn't strictly a left-on-left guy, which makes him that much more valuable as the other lefty in the pen beyond Mujica.

Ryan Webb

							Bats: R		Throws: R		Height: 6' 6"		Weight: 205		Born: February 5, 1986			Age: 24	

YEAR	TEAM	LVL	AGE	W	L	SV	G	GS	IP	H	HR	BB	SO	GB%	BABIP	STUFF	WHIP	ERA	SIERA	DERA	EqH9	EqHR9	EqBB9	EqSO9	VORP	SN/WX
2007	STO	A+	21	4	7	0	15	15	83	83	13	22	71	48%	.286	2	1.27	5.75	3.70	6.95	10.1	2.3	2.8	5.0	-12.8	-1.51
2007	MID	AA	21	0	4	0	5	5	25²	34	10	10	16	46%	.293	-11	1.71	9.12	4.90	10.58	12.4	4.0	3.6	4.0	-13.9	-1.20
2008	MID	AA	22	9	8	0	25	22	130	165	12	44	94	55%	.349	-10	1.61	5.19	4.32	6.54	11.4	1.3	3.3	4.6	-14.7	-1.71
2009	SAC	AAA	23	7	1	2	31	2	45²	57	3	15	39	56%	.375	-14	1.58	4.34	3.89	5.25	12.9	1.3	3.2	6.0	1.2	0.65
2009	SDN	MLB	23	2	1	0	28	0	25²	27	3	11	19	68%	.289	-14	1.48	3.86	4.16	5.37	9.7	1.7	3.1	5.2	0.4	0.23
2010	SDN	MLB	24	4	6	0	46	6	77²	82	10	33	49	46%	.299	-15	1.49	4.84	4.90	5.61	10.3	1.3	3.6	5.1	-1.0	0.53

Breakout: 28%   Improve: 71%   Collapse: 8%   Attrition: 21%   MLB: 100%   Comparables: Jason Johnson, Greg Granger, Mark Poston, Brad Salmon

Webb had a solid major-league debut with the Padres late last season after being acquired from the Athletics in the Scott Hairston trade. Perhaps predictably for a former big-leaguer's son (his father Hank pitched for the Mets and Dodgers in the 1970s), unlike most young hard throwers Webb consistently throws strikes with his 93 mph sinking fastball and big-breaking slider. His performance was subpar in the minor leagues until last season, but he took a big step forward, thanks in part to becoming much more consistent with his mechanics. Webb will almost certainly begin this season in the bullpen and could be a real surprise.

Mark Worrell

							Bats: R		Throws: R		Height: 6' 1"		Weight: 215		Born: March 8, 1983			Age: 27	

YEAR	TEAM	LVL	AGE	W	L	SV	G	GS	IP	H	HR	BB	SO	GB%	BABIP	STUFF	WHIP	ERA	SIERA	DERA	EqH9	EqHR9	EqBB9	EqSO9	VORP	SN/WX
2007	MEM	AAA	24	3	2	4	50	0	67	58	6	25	66	45%	.281	-5	1.24	3.09	3.56	3.82	8.2	1.4	3.4	6.5	12.3	0.43
2008	MEM	AAA	25	3	3	5	53	0	58²	45	2	31	80	35%	.319	16	1.30	2.15	2.79	3.67	8.0	0.6	4.6	9.1	11.4	1.22
2008	SLN	MLB	25	0	1	0	4	0	5²	8	1	4	4	54%	.389	-7	2.12	7.94	5.23	7.20	14.4	1.8	5.4	5.4	-0.9	0.03
2010	SDN	MLB	27	3	4	1	40	0	54¹	53	7	28	41	42%	.294	-9	1.49	4.64	4.72	5.33	9.5	1.1	4.1	6.1	1.0	0.98

Breakout: 12%   Improve: 41%   Collapse: 36%   Attrition: 18%   MLB: 9%   Comparables: Pat Flury, Jeff Kennard, Marty Mason, Howard Hilton

Worrell injured his elbow last March after being acquired from the Cardinals in an off-season trade for Khalil Greene and missed the season recovering from Tommy John surgery. Once he's back in action this spring, check out his delivery: Worrell always pitches from the stretch position, bending over at the waist and then taking a very small step toward the first-base dugout before releasing the pitch with a sidearm motion. Worrell probably won't be ready to pitch on Opening Day, but his success as a reliever in the Cardinals' farm system should help him factor into the Pads' pen later in the season.

Chris Young

| | | | | Bats: R | | Throws: R | | Height: 6' 10" | | Weight: 280 | | Born: May 25, 1979 | | Age: 31 |

YEAR	TEAM	LVL	AGE	W	L	SV	G	GS	IP	H	HR	BB	SO	GB%	BABIP	STUFF	WHIP	ERA	SIERA	DERA	EqH9	EqHR9	EqBB9	EqSO9	VORP	SN/WX
2007	SDN	MLB	28	9	8	0	30	30	173	118	10	72	167	33%	.241	30	1.10	3.12	3.79	3.63	6.7	0.7	3.4	7.4	35.4	6.15
2008	SDN	MLB	29	7	6	0	18	18	102[1]	84	13	48	93	25%	.254	-2	1.29	3.96	4.44	4.35	8.2	1.8	3.8	6.5	12.8	3.01
2009	SDN	MLB	30	4	6	0	14	14	76	70	12	40	50	30%	.250	-25	1.45	5.21	5.53	6.00	9.1	2.3	4.1	4.7	-4.2	1.17
2010	SDN	MLB	31	6	6	0	20	19	97	86	11	46	77	31%	.275	9	1.35	4.11	4.71	4.64	8.5	1.1	3.8	6.4	9.3	1.92

Breakout: 8%   Improve: 35%   Collapse: 19%   Attrition: 27%   MLB: 85%   Comparables: Scott Elarton, Claudio Vargas, Don Larsen, Terry Bross

Thanks to the deception caused by his perceived velocity (thanks to his huge size) and handy helping of home cooking, Young can be appear as one of the better pitchers in the league when he's healthy. Unfortunately, he has logged a combined 178 innings over the last two seasons, because he first suffered multiple fractures of facial bones when struck by a line drive off the bat of Albert Pujols in 2008 (which can hardly count in the "he's fragile" brief) and then missed the second half of last season after arthroscopic shoulder surgery. The Padres expect Young to anchor a young starting rotation this season. Given that he is eligible for free agency at the end of the year if they don't exercise a $8.5 million option for 2011, he'll be a prime candidate to be traded at the July trading deadline.

LINEOUTS

Hitters

PLAYER	TEAM	LVL	AGE	PA	R	2B	3B	HR	RBI	BB	SO	SB-CS	EqBRR	AVG/OBP/SLG	EqAVG/EqOBP/EqSLG	EqA	VORP	WARP
C E. Alfonzo	POR	AAA	30	219	27	11	0	14	36	7	51	1-0	-1.3	.309/.339/.569	.275/.301/.473	.263	10.3	0.8
	SDN	MLB	30	117	6	3	0	2	8	3	34	0-0	0.5	.175/.197/.254	.167/.188/.237	.117	-8.5	-0.6
OF M. Baxter*	SAN	AA	24	229	38	23	1	4	45	23	42	5-2	0.2	.376/.441/.559	.317/.371/.486	.294	12.7	1.3
	POR	AAA	24	345	38	17	4	5	34	38	53	9-5	-3.6	.277/.362/.409	.274/.349/.401	.262	5.9	0.5
SS D. Cumberland*	FTW	A	20	339	57	18	5	2	40	40	36	19-3	4.4	.293/.386/.410	.258/.330/.361	.249	8.8	-0.1
1B A. Dykstra*	FTW	A	22	537	71	22	3	11	60	104	103	1-2	-2.2	.226/.397/.375	.191/.322/.295	.228	-17.9	-3.4
DH C. Floyd*	SDN	MLB	36	17	0	0	0	0	0	1	7	0-0	-0.1	.125/.176/.125	.125/.176/.125	.149	-2.7	-0.4
UT E. Gonzalez	SDN	MLB	31	169	16	8	2	4	18	11	36	1-2	0.5	.216/.278/.373	.235/.294/.412	.239	-1.3	-0.6
C J. Hagerty#	EUG	A-	21	203	34	12	0	6	26	26	47	0-0	0.9	.225/.335/.399	.186/.261/.295	.194	-7.0	-2.1
OF R. Liriano	PDR	Rk	18	216	44	8	1	8	44	15	52	14-5	0.6	.350/.398/.523	.240/.278/.343	.215	-4.9	-2.1
OF D. Macias*	POR	AAA	26	344	43	18	0	5	27	39	56	5-3	-0.7	.232/.329/.343	.227/.311/.322	.227	-3.2	-0.2
	SDN	MLB	26	90	8	6	0	1	7	13	15	0-1	-0.2	.197/.322/.316	.211/.333/.316	.240	-0.4	-0.3
3B E. Rincon	EUG	A-	18	325	47	18	3	7	47	46	60	5-0	-1.5	.300/.415/.468	.255/.335/.381	.255	3.8	-1.1
2B E. Sogard*	SAN	AA	23	530	79	25	3	6	51	58	47	10-6	1.5	.293/.370/.400	.283/.345/.387	.259	13.8	0.5

Eliezer Alfonzo had a nice enough year, but the former PED miscreant is strictly a guy to keep under glass at Triple-A in case of a catching emergency in the majors. ⊘ **Mike Baxter** plays first and left without adding much pop, which doesn't exactly aid his chances of achieving Aldretedom. ⊘ Another injury-wracked season for **Drew Cumberland** didn't prevent the middle-infield prospect from making gains at the plate. ⊘ The full-season debut of 2008 first-rounder **Allan Dykstra** was nothing short of bizarre, as he spent most of it watching pitches, only belatedly hitting for any power at season's end. ⊘ **Cliff Floyd**'s season was short-circuited by knee and shoulder injuries, the latter ultimately requiring surgery to repair the labrum. If this was it, he had a fine career between his frequent injuries, hitting .278/.358/.482 (.288 EqA) in over 1,600 games. ⊘ Adrian's older brother **Edgar Gonzalez** struggled through a year marred by six weeks lost after being hit in the helmet by a Jason Hammel pitch; he opted for free agency after being dropped from the 40-man. ⊘ Former Hurricanes catcher **Jason Hagerty** had a rough pro debut after being the Padres' fifth-round pick in June, but they have high hopes because of his plus power and good plate discipline. ⊘ **Rymer Liriano** has a combination of above-average power and speed, but is still very young and strikes out so much that a European exchange has been set up to trade Liriano whiff emission permits. ⊘ **Drew Macias** was outrighted off the 40-man roster last October after spending parts of three seasons on the Pads and doing little with them; the D'backs will give him another shot at a bench role this spring. ⊘ Dominican **Edinson Rincon** is the newest member of the Padres' third-base cadre, but he might turn out to be the best of them for his plus power and discerning eye. ⊘ A second-round pick in 2007, **Eric Sogard** showed exceptional bat control skills against right-handed pitching in his Double-A debut, hitting .325/.399/.442.

Pitchers

PLAYER	TEAM	LVL	AGE	W	L	SV	IP	H	HR	BB	SO	GB%	BABIP	STUFF	WHIP	ERA	SIERA	DERA	EqH9	EqHR9	EqBB9	EqSO9	VORP
J. Banks	POR	AAA	26	7	7	0	125	120	6	36	95	35%	.300	0	1.25	3.46	4.18	4.47	9.5	1.0	2.7	5.2	13.5
—	SDN	MLB	26	1	1	0	22²	30	6	4	9	44%	.300	-32	1.50	7.15	5.19	7.59	13.5	4.2	1.3	3.0	-5.0
E. De La Cruz	POR	AAA	25	2	6	9	69¹	52	2	44	59	58%	.260	1	1.38	3.12	4.43	4.12	7.4	0.7	5.7	5.7	10.2
S. Garrison*	PDR	Rk	22	0	2	0	20¹	22	1	5	22	—	.344	-24	1.33	6.20	3.06	9.33	12.8	2.9	4.4	4.4	-7.8
J. Geer	POR	AAA	26	2	5	0	52²	60	5	14	21	49%	.299	-24	1.41	4.44	5.28	5.80	11.1	1.8	2.5	2.5	-1.6
—	SDN	MLB	26	1	7	0	102²	116	27	23	54	51%	.270	-67	1.35	5.96	4.70	6.87	11.8	4.0	1.8	3.9	-14.6
S. Hill	SDN	MLB	28	1	1	0	12	15	1	3	7	39%	.318	-9	1.50	5.25	4.85	5.47	10.9	1.5	2.2	3.6	0.0
E. Moreno	POR	AAA	28	3	3	10	45¹	46	7	20	40	55%	.305	-28	1.46	4.17	4.01	5.62	11.0	2.8	4.3	6.3	-0.5
—	SDN	MLB	28	1	3	0	22¹	28	3	15	15	38%	.342	-26	1.93	4.84	5.59	5.70	12.7	2.1	5.5	5.1	-0.5
W. Pelzer	LEL	A+	23	11	8	0	150²	134	6	59	147	63%	.316	-6	1.28	3.94	3.43	5.95	9.3	1.3	4.4	5.0	-6.9
A. Portillo	PDR	Rk	17	1	9	0	52²	67	2	28	44	—	.387	-27	1.80	5.13	4.48	10.51	15.5	2.9	7.8	3.1	-24.3
W. Silva	POR	AAA	32	7	5	0	81¹	98	10	27	56	52%	.335	-39	1.54	6.09	4.43	7.23	12.3	2.3	3.2	4.7	-14.5
—	SDN	MLB	32	0	2	0	24²	34	4	15	11	50%	.330	-39	1.99	8.76	5.92	11.10	12.9	2.2	4.8	3.3	-15.1

Cha-Seung Baek spent the entire 2009 season on the DL with a strained elbow, and the Padres released him at the end of last season. Considering he hasn't established himself 11 years after signing, it's hard to imagine he ever will. ⊘ **Josh Banks** throws eight—count 'em, *eight*—pitches, but has done little in a combined 114 major-league innings over the last three years. Dropped by the Padres, he signed a minor-league deal with the Astros. ⊘ **Eulogio De La Cruz** is living proof that a pitcher can be blessed with a 100 mph fastball but still be unable to succeed in the majors; the absence of control or a second pitch has him leaving for Japan to follow in Marc Kroon's footsteps with the Yakult Swallows. ⊘ **Steve Garrison** blew out his knee late in the AFL season; this after he'd already missed most of 2009 recovering from shoulder surgery, but he's on the 40-man for his effective mix of curves, sliders, and changes to set up an OK sinker. ⊘ **Josh Geer** received an opportunity, but his mid-80s fastballs and sinker/slider control combo is a tough act to pull off in the majors; he has been removed from the 40-man. ⊘ The Pads picked up **Shawn Hill** after the Nats cut him in camp, but he promptly blew out his elbow again, necessitating the fourth arm operation and second Tommy John surgery of his 10-year career and perhaps wrecking what had been one of the game's great sinkers. ⊘ Former Rangers prospect **Edwin Moreno** finally reached the majors last season, but had trouble throwing strikes, was outrighted off the 40-man roster, and did not return. ⊘ One of the better pitching prospects seemingly nobody knows about, **Wynn Pelzer** touches 96 mph with his fastball and complements it with a hard slider. ⊘ **Adys Portillo** set a record for Venezuelan amateur free agents when he received a $2 million signing bonus from the Padres in 2008. With a 95 mph fastball, he's an intriguing prospect despite poor results in his first season in the United States. He was 17 and in a new country, so cut him some slack. ⊘ The Padres beat out the Yankees, of all teams, in a bidding war to sign **Walter Silva**, a veteran Mexican Leaguer, but he made six awful starts and then wasn't much better at Portland.

MANAGER: BUD BLACK

YEAR	TEAM	W-L	Pythag +/–	Avg PC	100+ P	120+ P	QS	BQS	REL	REL w Zero R	IBB	Subs	PH	PH Avg	PH HR	SB2	CS2	SB3	CS3	SAC Att	SAC %	POS SAC	Squeeze	Swing	In Play
2007	SDN	89-74	-1	90.1	47	0	89	5	485	340	48	22	273	.187	3	50	16	5	7	88	72.7%	28	1	114	89
2008	SDN	63-99	-3	91.0	49	3	74	4	490	291	61	31	285	.198	3	34	17	2	0	83	71.1%	18	1	123	93
2009	SDN	75-87	9	91.0	47	1	73	4	527	349	58	43	263	.248	9	72	23	10	5	116	63.8%	38	2	123	90

The one current skipper who's a former pitcher, Black is one of only three men to win at least 100 career games and manage in the major leagues over the last 40 years, joining Roger Craig and Larry Dierker. The Padres began a full-bore youth movement last season, when they used 24 rookies, and Black has the perfect temperament to oversee a young team. Some veteran players tried to push Black as a rookie manager in 2007 by calling him by his given name of Harry; he politely but firmly put an end to that. In terms of game tactics, he bunts a little more than most, but between the talent on hand and the park, it's not extraordinary, and their success rate wasn't good. As a matter of happy outcomes, Black's pinch-hitters tied for the MLB lead in pinch-hit homers, but he also ranked among the pass-happy six in issuing the most intentional walks, ranking behind Joe Torre, Jerry Manuel, Ken Macha, and Fredi Gonzalez. He'd tinker with his batting orders, but not so much with who started where. Black was not affected by the Padres' change of ownership from John Moores to Jeff Moorad last spring, as Moorad quickly became a big fan and extended Black's contract through this season while also adding a club option for 2011.

San Francisco Giants

When is it time to make a change at general manager, even if that GM is the longest-tenured in the game and a respected figure? When do you throw up your hands and admit that the man you have put in charge has no idea how to solve his team's problems within the boundaries you have set for him? The Giants have reached the point where they need to answer that question, because they have been stuck in a terrible rut.

Brian Sabean entered office on September 30th, 1996. For the first few years of his 13-year reign, the Giants were, by their own standards, an offensive powerhouse. In 1999, they scored 872 runs, which was then the fourth-highest total in modern (including New York post-1900) team history. In 2000, the Giants scored 925 runs, the team's second-highest total. After a few relatively fallow years in spite of some historic seasons by Barry Bonds, they came back in 2004 to score 850 runs, the ninth-highest total in team history.

The 2004 team featured the last Ruthian season by Bonds. Since then, despite the presence of a still-potent Bonds for two of the seasons in question, the Giants have been hopeless at the plate. Over the last five years, the Giants rank last among all major league teams in runs, last in EqA, 29th in home runs, 28th in walks, 25th in batting average, 30th in on-base percentage, and tied for 30th in slugging percentage. They have scored fewer than 700 runs in all but one of those seasons, averaging 675 runs a year at a time when the average National League team scored 741. Last season, the Giants took 351 unintentional walks, one of the lowest totals of the last half-century and the fewest in any nonstrike season since the 2002 Tigers drew 341 unintentional walks.

Five years is sufficient time to have the offense declared legally dead; there is no talent on hand for a turn-around, and management clearly doesn't know how to effect repairs. In the immortal words of Monty Python, this is an ex-parrot.

Quality free agents are apparently out of the Giants' budget, which is not necessarily a bad thing, given how Sabean overvalued an average talent like Aaron Rowand, giving him five years and $60 million in December 2007. The farm system has developed some outstanding arms, such as Tim Lincecum, Matt Cain, Jonathan Sanchez, and Brian Wilson, but hitters have been an almost complete miss. A list of homegrown position players who have contributed even 200 games to the franchise in this century is short indeed, rapidly descending past Pedro Feliz, Marvin Benard, and Fred Lewis and quickly reaching the realm of disposable types like Jason Ellison and Calvin Murray. (If you choose to overlook the fact that Rich Aurilia was drafted and largely developed by the Rangers, you can throw him in as well.) Trades have been few, and most have meant dealing from the pitchers who have been developed to acquire the hitters who got away. Thus was born the now-legendary trade of Francisco Liriano, Boof Bonser, and Joe Nathan to the Twins for A. J. Pierzynski, as well as last season's decision to deal pitching prospect Tim Alderson for the mediocre Freddy Sanchez.

Stymied, the Giants, rather than trying to fix the problem, decided to pretend that Bengie Molina was a cleanup hitter and rely on the two Ps—pitchers and "the Panda" (Pablo Sandoval)—to get them through. Superficially, the plan seemed to have worked. Propelled by the best pitching in the league and Sandoval,

GIANTS PROSPECTUS
2009 W-L: 88-74, 3rd in NL West

Pythag	83-79	6th	**Ballpark:** AT&T Park (3-yr. PF: 1009). Neutral as neutral gets, suppresses home runs
RS/G	4.1	13th	
RA/G	3.8	1st	
EqA	.244	16th	**2009:** Quality rotation carries Kung Fu Panda and the slack bats into near-contention
EqBRR	10	1st	
SNWP	.556	1st	
WXRL	10.22	4th	**2010:** Will another Cy season get wasted on inadequate O? Will Lincecum win it? Is Posey ready?
FRAr	3.83	2nd	
DE	.707	2nd	
PADE	2.98	1st	**Action Items:** An offense worthy of the rotation, adding bats at all non-Sandoval corners
Salary	$82.6	8th	
Attend	2.86	7th	

the Giants added 16 wins over their 2008 finish and were alive in the NL West into early August. They would seem to have a base from which to build: just add a third P, offensive production, to the pitchers-and-Panda formula, and they will be all set to race past the Dodgers and the Rockies and win the franchise's first championship since 1954. Well, forget about that. Even if the formula were that simple, finding that third P has escaped Sabean and pals for years and there is no reason to think they're going to start now. More than that, though, the successes of 2009 are built on a foundation of sand. It was transient, and it's all going to crumble away.

The Giants' 2009 campaign was characterized by low-scoring games. The team scored 4.1 runs per game and surrendered only 3.8 runs per game. The 7.8 combined runs per Giants game was the second-lowest in the entire major leagues since 1993 (behind only the 2003 Dodgers' just-under 7.0 R/G mark of 6.98). Whether that was a good thing or bad depends. Although hitters are known to have more stable statistics than pitchers, when you include defense in the equation, run-scoring ability is about as persistent as run-prevention ability; the year-to-year correlation for team runs scored is .46, and for team runs allowed is .47. Given the Giants' lopsided configuration, what needs to be determined is whether they are more likely to start scoring more runs or more likely to start surrendering more runs. Unfortunately for the Giants, the latter seems more likely.

Many things went right for the Giants in 2009. Their offense scored more runs than their batting line suggests. Baseball Prospectus's statistics UEQR and UEQRA estimate how many runs a team should have scored and allowed, respectively, when you ignore the contextual factors surrounding them. Although the Giants were 13th in the National League in runs with 657, their 625 UEQR suggests that they were even lucky to have scored that many. The Giants were fortunate in that they hit better with runners on base than they did with bases empty, allowing them to capitalize on the offense that they did receive, but not in a way that tends to carry over to the following season. With no one on base, the Giants hit .251/.296/.384, but with men on base they hit .265/.327/.397. The NL has an OPS of 25 points higher with men on base; the Giants' winding up 44 points ahead suggests a bit of luck. The team also had surprising extra-base power with the bases loaded: despite slugging .389 overall, they slugged .476 with the bases loaded, putting up an OPS that was 51 points above the NL average in such situations. These elements combined to give the Giants a few more wins

than they would have had with more standard-issue good fortune while hitting.

The pitching staff's record is also deceptive. The defense succeeded to such a high degree that many Giants pitchers simply looked better than they actually were or are likely to be again in the future. The Giants put together an ERA that was 0.22 points below their team's suggested ERA by a number of metrics—good for about four extra wins. The Giants' staff SIERA weighted by innings pitched was 3.77 in 2009, and their actual ERA was 3.55. This is important, because it means that the pitchers got either good defensive support or a good dose of luck, or both.

As it turns out, they did get some good defense. In 2008, the Giants' defense had ranked in the middle of the pack. They were 13th in the majors in Park-Adjusted Defensive Efficiency (PADE), BP's measure of how well a team recorded outs on balls in play after adjusting for its home park. They were 14th in Park-Adjusted Slugging on Balls in Play (PASBP), which is measured similarly. Fast forward to 2009, where the Giants led the entire major leagues in PADE and were first in the National League (second overall) in PASBP. Clay Davenport's Fielding Runs Above Average (FRAA), Mitchel Lichtman's Ultimate Zone Rating (UZR), and Baseball Info Solutions' Total Runs Saved (TRS) approximate the runs added by a defense relative to an average defense. UZR had the Giants saving 35 more runs, going from ninth overall with 16.2 UZR in 2008 up to 51.2 in 2009, which was fourth overall. TRS saw the Giants gaining 40 runs, going from 19th with -7 up to ninth with 33. FRAA saw an even bigger swing, gaining 59 runs. The Giants won about four more games with their defense than they did in 2008, just as the SIERA-to-ERA difference above suggests.

Depending on the metric used, the improved defense can be attributed to different positions. FRAA saw the improvements coming at second base (+24), at third base (+11), and in pitcher fielding (+15); TRS similarly attributed 19 points of the Giants' improvement to pitcher defense, while spreading most of the rest of the defensive improvement around the diamond. UZR saw large gains at first base plus center and left field. Whether they'll retain those improvements in the infield seems more certain at third base with Mark DeRosa than at second with a full season from Freddy Sanchez. However strong their defensive performances in the corners, those have come at the cost of making massive sacrifices on offense, especially last year, with Randy Winn's bat slipping well below replacement level. The Giants may put up strong defensive numbers in 2010, but they are probably not going to lead the league in PADE again. This regression, combined with the anticipated regression in their situational hitting, ought to lead the Giants toward a fall.

Whatever hope they have of avoiding that depends upon their young, talented staff. With several more arms on the way, the Giants' run-prevention abilities should remain strong. Tim Lincecum is quite simply the best pitcher in the National League, and it would be unsurprising to see him add another trophy to his mantle in 2010. Lincecum again put together an extraordinary season in 2009. With a SIERA of 2.86 in 2008 and 2.69 in 2009, he was the only starting pitcher with at least 162 innings to have a SIERA of less than 3.29 in both seasons. In most years, the pitcher who wins the Cy Young is among the league's top 10 who had the most batted-ball luck and run support, but Lincecum won in both 2008 and 2009 with average batted-ball outcomes and poor run support, suggesting both how good he is and how much better he could be if the Giants would surround him with a stronger cast.

The rest of the rotation provides less ample cause for assurance going forward. Barry Zito's climb out of the abyss was real, but re-achieving fourth starter status isn't really front-page news. In contrast to Lincecum's continued dominance, Matt Cain's 2.89 ERA came as a convenient surprise. Most of Cain's improvement was merely a reflection of the Giants' defense. Although the only substantial improvement in his performance was the decline in his walk rate, his batting average on balls in play dropped from .297 to .263. Jonathan Sanchez should be another strong pitcher in the Giants' rotation for 2010, although like many a youngish left-hander, he's still looking for consistency. Just as it seemed as if he was going to drop his season ERA under 4.00, he was hammered in his final five starts of the season, including twice by the Dodgers. Still, his impressive swing-and-miss stuff led him to solid improvement overall, including his no-hitter that was an eighth-inning error away from being a perfect game. Despite his control problems, this high-upside option in the Giants' rotation might be the hurler who takes a big step forward in 2010.

The Giants not only had a higher run differential than their peripheral numbers suggest, but also had more wins than their runs total suggests, as their Pythagenpat win total was two wins behind their overall win total. This was largely because the Giants' bullpen was strong in 2009, but much of that came from good timing as well. Jeremy Affeldt's campaign was especially fortunate; although Affeldt is a strong reliever, he will certainly regress from his 2009 numbers. A majority of this came from happy outcomes on balls in play, because while his .250 BABIP in 2009 is already low, what was more amazing is the rate at which Affeldt recorded double plays. Affeldt is a ground-ball pitcher, but no one can be expected to record double plays in 18 of 64 opportunities (and converting six of 10 double-play opportunities with the bases loaded). The league average would suggest about eight double plays in 64 opportunities.

Consider the picture this paints of the '09 Giants: a team with more wins than their runs suggest, more runs than their hits suggest, and a large spike in defense. Taken together, the Giants are probably unlikely to repeat their 88-win total without a massive overhaul. Furthermore, doing so would certainly require going way over budget or surrendering their young talent, and 88 wins still might not be enough to put them into the playoffs.

As a result, it would have been a mistake for the Giants to overreact to their 88 wins and start making high-priced bids on every Tom, Dick, and Holliday on the free-agent market, but at this writing, the Giants not only are not overreacting, but are barely reacting at all. A full year from Sanchez at second base plus the addition of Mark DeRosa should help the offense, but those are cases of reaching for adequacy, not greatness, especially since the Giants will swap out the at-bats given to their gaggle of weak-hitting first basemen with Sandoval moving across the diamond. The exchange of Bengie Molina for Buster Posey will be a net positive in 2010 if the Eli Whiteside interregnum is short enough ("Nobody thinks he's ready to catch 100-plus games in the big leagues," Sabean said of Posey in December). Young Madison Bumgarner may give the staff a third ace to go with Lincecum and Cain, but that's not going to solve the problem, either—if the offense repeats at the same level, the basic Pythagorean formula suggests that in order for the Giants to reach 95 wins, they would have to allow only 550 runs, something no team has done since 1989, although the 2003 Dodgers came close.

So, if the Giants are the mirage, we're forced to ask again, Who's going to fix this mess? The man who made Barry Zito a bazillionaire? A man whose taste in free-agent hitters reliably runs to the mediocre? As much as the postseason might be a crapshoot, it takes actually getting there to be able to place your faith in what Lincecum and Cain (and perhaps Sanchez and Bumgarner) might do for you in a short series. Spending top dollar on veterans like Sanchez and DeRosa isn't really different from spending top dollar on Randy Winn or Dave Roberts or Aaron Rowand: absent the addition of any premium performers, you wind up with an offense with limited upside. Last season's big bullpen fix-up was effective, but success with relievers has a way of being transient. Given the Giants' failures on Sabean's watch to leverage Barry Bonds when he was the best hitter in the game at his best into reliable post-season participation, the risk now is that they'll do likewise with Lincecum, the best pitcher at his best. Is squandering greatness really a legacy worth bragging about?

HITTERS

John Bowker — OF/1B

Bats: L   Throws: L   Height: 6' 2"   Weight: 200   Born: July 8, 1983   Age: 26

YEAR	TEAM	LVL	AGE	PA	R	2B	3B	HR	RBI	BB	SO	SB	CS	EqBRR	AVG	OBP	SLG	EqAVG	EqOBP	EqSLG	EqA	VORP	WARP	DEFENSE
2007	NRW	AA	23	587	79	35	6	22	90	41	103	3	7	-3.2	.307	.363	.523	.306	.351	.515	.290	31.2	3.0	85-RF -4 23-CF 1
2008	FRE	AAA	24	102	13	3	1	2	9	7	23	2	0	0.9	.237	.304	.355	.223	.284	.340	.223	-2.7	-0.4	13-1B -1 7-LF 0
2008	SFN	MLB	24	350	31	14	3	10	43	19	74	1	1	-2.5	.255	.300	.408	.261	.305	.411	.246	-1.3	-0.4	62-1B -1 10-RF -1
2009	FRE	AAA	25	450	82	22	4	21	83	74	64	10	6	-0.9	.342	.451	.596	.315	.416	.539	.320	37.8	4.6	44-RF -1 39-LF 3
2009	SFN	MLB	25	73	7	2	2	2	7	4	18	1	0	0.4	.194	.247	.373	.194	.247	.373	.220	-2.3	0.0	10-LF 2 3-RF 0
2010	SFN	MLB	26	470	61	23	5	18	67	44	97	4	3	-0.8	.274	.341	.478	.269	.341	.457	.269	14.6	2.1	89-LF 5

Breakout: 11% Improve: 39% Collapse: 14% Attrition: 10%   MLB: 65%   Comparables: Ryan Church, Troy Neel, Mark Sweeney, Mark Leonard

Sometimes, legend transcends real-world terrors beyond all reasonable expectation. James Thurber once invented a monster this terrible, which he called the Todal; it sounds like rabbits screaming and smells of old, unopened rooms. Bowker's defensive rep almost automatically takes the conversation back to his best position (hitter), but for as much help as the offense needed, you'd think his glove work was so Todal-y awful you dared not go looking for him, lest he gleep you. Whether you can risk him at first opposite Sandoval or in either outfield corner behind him was left to the theoretical, but the Giants could paste him into any of those slots and would at least get league-average production.

Emmanuel Burriss — 2B

Bats: S   Throws: R   Height: 6' 0"   Weight: 190   Born: January 17, 1985   Age: 25

YEAR	TEAM	LVL	AGE	PA	R	2B	3B	HR	RBI	BB	SO	SB	CS	EqBRR	AVG	OBP	SLG	EqAVG	EqOBP	EqSLG	EqA	VORP	WARP	DEFENSE
2007	AUG	A	22	405	64	14	4	0	38	28	49	51	15	3.7	.321	.374	.381	.286	.327	.332	.239	6.1	0.0	86-SS -6
2007	SJO	A+	22	160	23	2	0	0	8	12	20	17	3	3.4	.165	.237	.180	.162	.218	.169	.152	-9.4	-0.7	35-SS 4
2008	FRE	AAA	23	64	6	1	1	0	6	2	6	2	2	-0.9	.258	.281	.306	.242	.266	.290	.185	-2.4	-0.4	10-2B 1 4-SS -2
2008	SFN	MLB	23	274	37	6	1	1	18	23	24	13	5	2.9	.283	.357	.329	.293	.365	.339	.256	8.0	0.7	35-SS -2 32-2B -1
2009	FRE	AAA	24	77	9	2	1	1	7	3	4	2	0	0.9	.268	.312	.366	.250	.295	.347	.230	-0.1	-0.1	16-2B -1
2009	SFN	MLB	24	220	18	6	0	0	13	14	34	11	4	1.2	.238	.292	.267	.241	.295	.266	.211	-4.3	-1.1	55-2B -6
2010	SFN	MLB	25	370	44	15	2	2	29	29	53	13	6	1.8	.264	.322	.341	.264	.323	.339	.229	-0.5	-0.4	86-2B -3

Breakout: 20% Improve: 50% Collapse: 17% Attrition: 11%   MLB: 78%   Comparables: Bernie Castro, Larry Reynolds, Rod Lofton, Ramon Sambo

Burriss got dibs among the nonanswers at the keystone, but that really only meant he got to be excused first. Two months in, he was sent to Fresno, where a broken foot shut him down by July, so there was no second act. It's worth wondering whether there will ever be. Rapid advancement hasn't helped him establish any element of his game: he is fast, but doesn't provide that much value on the bases. There is no power, yet he pops up quite a bit, and he's impatient. While he might have the tools to be a good second baseman, he needs reps, having ping-ponged between short and second. Figuring out whether there's something to be recovered should require time in Triple-A.

Matt Downs — UT

Bats: R   Throws: R   Height: 6' 2"   Weight: 190   Born: March 19, 1984   Age: 26

YEAR	TEAM	LVL	AGE	PA	R	2B	3B	HR	RBI	BB	SO	SB	CS	EqBRR	AVG	OBP	SLG	EqAVG	EqOBP	EqSLG	EqA	VORP	WARP	DEFENSE
2007	SLO	A-	23	336	68	33	0	8	48	28	34	16	2	5.7	.338	.410	.537	.280	.323	.407	.256	5.2	-0.3	31-1B -6 26-2B 1
2008	SJO	A+	24	489	74	30	1	17	75	34	57	24	13	-3.3	.304	.357	.494	.277	.321	.414	.254	11.2	1.1	59-2B -4 30-3B 0
2008	FRE	AAA	24	94	10	5	0	3	7	4	10	1	0	-0.1	.244	.298	.407	.218	.266	.333	.212	-2.1	-0.9	11-2B -4 7-LF -2
2009	FRE	AAA	25	467	68	33	3	14	74	25	58	8	2	2.3	.300	.343	.491	.274	.314	.440	.260	13.6	-0.7	88-2B -14 10-3B -4
2009	SFN	MLB	25	60	6	2	0	1	2	6	13	1	0	-0.2	.170	.250	.264	.170	.250	.264	.187	-2.3	-0.1	16-2B 1
2010	SFN	MLB	26	468	56	26	1	11	51	34	73	6	3	0.7	.262	.316	.405	.262	.316	.401	.241	5.3	0.1	91-2B -5

Breakout: 16% Improve: 41% Collapse: 21% Attrition: 12%   MLB: 22%   Comparables: Ruben Santana, Les Norman, Mike Reddish, Alexei Ramirez

Downs is sort of a fair-haired organizational soldier, a scrapper the Giants like for his quick bat, which contains a little bit of power. He's gifted with a strong enough arm that they can ponder his uses at second, at third, or in the outfield. Unfortunately, he lacks the range to stick at second, and his bat doesn't have the power to fix any of the Giants' problems at any position. If he can adapt to the rigors of pinch-hitting, he could have a Dobbs or Norton type of career, but that's not usually a definition you find in the dictionary under "upside."

Kevin Frandsen   INF   Bats: R   Throws: R   Height: 6' 0"   Weight: 185   Born: May 24, 1982   Age: 28

YEAR	TEAM	LVL	AGE	PA	R	2B	3B	HR	RBI	BB	SO	SB	CS	EqBRR	AVG	OBP	SLG	EqAVG	EqOBP	EqSLG	EqA	VORP	WARP	DEFENSE			
2007	FRE	AAA	25	83	13	5	0	1	7	9	6	4	2	1.6	.403	.506	.522	.377	.469	.478	.327	8.6	1.3	10-2B	2	5-SS	1
2007	SFN	MLB	25	296	26	12	1	5	31	21	24	4	3	-1.1	.269	.331	.379	.273	.336	.379	.252	5.7	0.7	38-2B	0	15-SS	-1
2009	FRE	AAA	27	474	67	18	2	13	55	23	34	3	4	-4.6	.295	.352	.438	.268	.316	.388	.244	6.7	-0.1	56-SS	-8	25-2B	0
2009	SFN	MLB	27	54	3	2	0	0	1	3	4	0	0	0.4	.140	.204	.180	.140	.204	.180	.086	-5.0	-0.5	8-2B	-1	5-SS	1
2010	SFN	MLB	28	394	45	18	1	9	39	26	41	3	4	-0.8	.268	.333	.398	.269	.333	.398	.254	11.1	0.9	73-SS	-3		

Breakout: 16%   Improve: 37%   Collapse: 26%   Attrition: 20%   MLB: 54%   Comparables: Luis Rivas, Melvin Mora, Ryan Miller, Steve Smith

With the decision to re-sign Freddy Sanchez, Frandsen's on-again, off-again bid for the second-base job appears to be as permanently turned off as Phyllis Schlafly. It may have been for the best. Since he played all four infield spots for Fresno, maybe he can work his way into becoming a new-model Aurilia type on the bench (fast-forwarding to the modest utility part of that proposition and not getting any of the heavy Aurillary on offense from a decade ago).

Ryan Garko   1B   Bats: R   Throws: R   Height: 6' 2"   Weight: 225   Born: January 2, 1981   Age: 29

YEAR	TEAM	LVL	AGE	PA	R	2B	3B	HR	RBI	BB	SO	SB	CS	EqBRR	AVG	OBP	SLG	EqAVG	EqOBP	EqSLG	EqA	VORP	WARP	DEFENSE			
2007	CLE	MLB	26	541	62	29	1	21	61	34	94	0	1	-8.8	.289	.359	.483	.289	.358	.486	.286	21.3	1.8	118-1B	-5		
2008	CLE	MLB	27	563	61	21	1	14	90	45	86	0	0	-3.8	.273	.346	.404	.280	.352	.412	.271	11.6	0.9	119-1B	-4		
2009	CLE	MLB	28	273	29	10	0	11	39	20	40	0	0	0.5	.285	.362	.464	.294	.371	.466	.291	9.6	0.7	46-1B	1	5-LF	-4
2009	SFN	MLB	28	127	10	3	1	2	12	9	40	0	0	-0.8	.235	.307	.330	.243	.315	.339	.229	-3.9	-0.5	26-1B	0		
2010	SFN	MLB	29	505	54	22	1	18	72	42	83	0	1	-2.3	.274	.356	.448	.277	.359	.448	.278	15.7	1.6	110-1B	-1		

Breakout: 20%   Improve: 58%   Collapse: 9%   Attrition: 13%   MLB: 95%   Comparables: Paul Konerko, Matthew LeCroy, Shea Hillenbrand, Greg Colbrunn

When you want a bottle of wine, do you discriminate between your selections, or are you the Three Buck Chuck type? If the latter, here's your first baseman, the first baseman you trade for because you sort of left that whole first base thing to the last minute, you can't walk in the door empty-handed, and this was all you could get for the dog's least-favorite kidney. Harsh? Sure, but this is a player who's in his prime, and his chief selling point is a modest .170 ISO against lefties, with zero value on defense while being limited to corners (to be generous). Out of desperate need, the Giants traded a pitcher worth having in Scott Barnes, promptly realized General Garko isn't the right pour at a high-offense position, and nontendered him rather than let the arbitration panel get into a tizzy because that's better than they could do against major-league pitching. Of course it is, and there are only a few thousand people on the planet who could do it. Yes, a few thousand, and there are little more than 400 position-playing jobs in the majors. You do the math.

Jesus Guzman   1B   Bats: R   Throws: R   Height: 6' 1"   Weight: 165   Born: June 14, 1984   Age: 26

YEAR	TEAM	LVL	AGE	PA	R	2B	3B	HR	RBI	BB	SO	SB	CS	EqBRR	AVG	OBP	SLG	EqAVG	EqOBP	EqSLG	EqA	VORP	WARP	DEFENSE			
2007	HDS	A+	23	585	102	38	5	25	112	50	85	3	3	0.0	.301	.370	.539	.233	.289	.396	.236	-1.3	-2.4	48-2B	-8	28-3B	-7
2008	MID	AA	24	376	57	21	2	14	76	33	56	5	2	0.9	.364	.419	.560	.313	.362	.480	.287	21.1	0.7	49-3B	-7	30-2B	-9
2008	SAC	AAA	24	65	5	2	0	2	9	4	13	0	2	-1.4	.237	.281	.373	.233	.266	.367	.211	-1.8	-0.6	14-3B	-3		
2009	FRE	AAA	25	500	75	26	5	16	71	37	82	0	2	-1.9	.321	.379	.507	.293	.346	.452	.274	7.5	0.2	107-1B	-6		
2009	SFN	MLB	25	20	0	0	0	0	0	0	3	0	0	0.2	.250	.250	.250	.250	.250	.250	.159	-1.8	-0.2				
2010	SFN	MLB	26	483	55	26	2	12	60	35	96	1	2	-0.3	.254	.311	.403	.256	.313	.402	.246	-2.3	-0.5	88-1B	-2		

Breakout: 6%   Improve: 22%   Collapse: 24%   Attrition: 19%   MLB: 11%   Comparables: Aldo Pecorilli, Jeff Forney, Dan Rohrmeier, Rikkert Faneyte

An A's reject who's slowly worked his way down the defensive spectrum from shortstop toward first base, the Venezuelan Guzman remains what he's been, an aggressive contact hitter with some pop, which really doesn't play that well at first base, but certainly as well as some. If Garko were red-flavored Three Buck Chuck, then Guzman's flavor is purple and weak proof that Brian Sabean is picky when it comes to his Ripple.

Travis Ishikawa   1B

Bats: L   Throws: L   Height: 6' 3"   Weight: 225   Born: September 24, 1983   Age: 26

YEAR	TEAM	LVL	AGE	PA	R	2B	3B	HR	RBI	BB	SO	SB	CS	EqBRR	AVG	OBP	SLG	EqAVG	EqOBP	EqSLG	EqA	VORP	WARP	DEFENSE	
2007	SJO	A+	23	222	35	15	1	13	34	19	78	0	0	-1.8	.268	.342	.551	.230	.288	.436	.246	-1.2	-0.1	38-1B	0
2007	NRW	AA	23	192	17	3	1	3	17	17	48	0	0	-0.9	.214	.292	.295	.216	.281	.295	.202	-9.2	-1.4	48-1B	-2
2008	NRW	AA	24	277	34	16	0	8	48	35	45	10	4	-3.8	.291	.382	.462	.289	.362	.434	.279	8.4	0.7	59-1B	-3
2008	FRE	AAA	24	192	35	19	3	16	46	14	36	0	1	-0.2	.310	.370	.737	.277	.330	.607	.300	11.5	1.4	44-1B	0
2008	SFN	MLB	24	104	12	6	0	3	15	9	27	1	0	0.3	.274	.337	.432	.284	.346	.432	.269	2.2	0.6	24-1B	3
2009	SFN	MLB	25	363	49	10	2	9	39	30	89	2	2	1.3	.261	.329	.387	.269	.333	.404	.254	-2.7	0.4	92-1B	6
2010	SFN	MLB	26	401	43	17	1	12	46	36	112	2	2	-0.7	.237	.312	.390	.240	.314	.399	.244	-2.7	-0.2	92-1B	1

Breakout: 10%   Improve: 39%   Collapse: 18%   Attrition: 19%   MLB: 76%   Comparables: Steve Cox, Scott Thorman, Rico Brogna, Mike Jacobs

Ishikawa is the sort of player you'd see on big-league benches in the '70s, like Mike Squires, Dave Bergman, or Tony Muser, someone whose threat to right-handed pitching rated up there with a girlfriend's mom: inconvenient but unavoidable, so don't slip up while she's in the room. The Giants' attempts to employ other assorted klutzoids at first base kept leaving Ishikawa with playing time, even down the stretch, and even after they'd traded for alternatives. It's freaky fun that his BABIP home/road split was .424/.219. Now, split the difference toward the average in both cases, and what do you get? The same player. The addition of Huff pushes him well back on the bench.

Roger Kieschnick   RF

Bats: L   Throws: R   Height: 6' 3"   Weight: 200   Born: January 21, 1987   Age: 23

YEAR	TEAM	LVL	AGE	PA	R	2B	3B	HR	RBI	BB	SO	SB	CS	EqBRR	AVG	OBP	SLG	EqAVG	EqOBP	EqSLG	EqA	VORP	WARP	DEFENSE	
2009	SJO	A+	22	563	86	37	8	23	110	36	130	9	1	0.7	.296	.345	.532	.260	.298	.436	.252	4.6	0.7	114-RF	1
2010	SFN	MLB	23	538	58	27	3	14	74	34	144	4	1	0.3	.245	.296	.395	.248	.298	.406	.239	-0.8	0.0	110-RF	0

Breakout: 14%   Improve: 39%   Collapse: 21%   Attrition: 1%   MLB: 5%   Comparables: Ralph Bryant, Luke Allen, Brad Bierley, Seth Smith

Toolsy but equipped with a capacity to disappoint (which dropped him into the third round in the '08 draft), the former Texas A&M slugger was allowed to make his regular-season debut at High-A after the Giants let him get wet behind the ears in the Hawaiian Winter League before the '09 season. Predictably for a product of an advanced college program, he hit well in a hitter's league, but the power and the gifts in right field won't add up to a career if he doesn't master the strike zone. Without adjustments, Double-A is going to be hard on him, but the hope is that he's young enough to make them.

Fred Lewis   LF

Bats: L   Throws: R   Height: 6' 2"   Weight: 200   Born: December 9, 1980   Age: 29

YEAR	TEAM	LVL	AGE	PA	R	2B	3B	HR	RBI	BB	SO	SB	CS	EqBRR	AVG	OBP	SLG	EqAVG	EqOBP	EqSLG	EqA	VORP	WARP	DEFENSE			
2007	FRE	AAA	26	191	31	8	6	8	32	19	36	9	1	2.5	.292	.366	.550	.259	.328	.460	.272	7.3	0.3	23-CF	-3	18-LF	-2
2007	SFN	MLB	26	180	34	6	2	3	19	19	32	5	1	0.3	.287	.374	.408	.293	.383	.414	.282	7.6	1.0	23-RF	-1	13-LF	2
2008	SFN	MLB	27	521	81	25	11	9	40	51	124	21	7	5.0	.282	.351	.440	.293	.359	.455	.279	21.3	2.5	102-LF	5	8-CF	-3
2009	SFN	MLB	28	336	49	21	3	4	20	36	84	8	4	2.0	.258	.348	.390	.267	.354	.409	.265	6.7	0.8	66-LF	-1		
2010	SFN	MLB	29	458	67	21	6	9	38	46	108	12	4	1.6	.261	.343	.409	.262	.342	.411	.265	12.2	1.4	87-LF	1		

Breakout: 5%   Improve: 39%   Collapse: 8%   Attrition: 9%   MLB: 97%   Comparables: Daryl Boston, Al Martin, Frank Catalanotto, Brant Brown

To those given modest gifts, modest achievements represent their great deeds. To some extent, Lewis got larded with elaborate expectations because he does some of the things statheads like, and because everyone likes to be the smarty who identifies hidden virtue: he controls the strike zone effectively, runs well, and has value in the field. Unfortunately, he's already in the midst of what are supposed to be a player's best years, and there's no room for growth. Lewis can't blame BABIP, line-drive rates, or gypsy curses for losing his shot at the job in left, just the overlap between his limits and the Giants' dire offensive needs. Losing playing time to Nate Schierholtz, Andres Torres, or Eugenio Velez isn't injustice; it's his lot because that's his level.

Bengie Molina   C   Bats: R   Throws: R   Height: 5′ 11″   Weight: 225   Born: July 20, 1974   Age: 35

YEAR	TEAM	LVL	AGE	PA	R	2B	3B	HR	RBI	BB	SO	SB	CS	EqBRR	AVG	OBP	SLG	EqAVG	EqOBP	EqSLG	EqA	VORP	WARP	DEFENSE
2007	SFN	MLB	32	517	38	19	1	19	81	15	53	0	0	-3.6	.276	.298	.433	.280	.302	.439	.251	20.2	2.7	123-C	6
2008	SFN	MLB	33	569	46	33	0	16	95	19	38	0	0	-7.1	.292	.322	.445	.298	.324	.452	.267	28.7	4.2	127-C	7
2009	SFN	MLB	34	520	52	25	1	20	80	13	68	0	0	-4.5	.265	.285	.442	.270	.288	.453	.252	18.6	2.0	117-C	-2
2010	SFN	MLB	35	440	38	21	1	14	70	20	55	0	1	-2.1	.274	.313	.430	.276	.315	.427	.254	14.8	1.8	104-C	2

Breakout: 15%   Improve: 35%   Collapse: 22%   Attrition: 24%   MLB: 98%   Comparables: Bo Diaz, Mike Lieberthal, Paul Lo Duca, Willie Horton

To be charitable, Molina is a known quantity on offense: he'll post an EqA in the .250-.270 range with modest power and fewer than 20 walks. Maybe if you put someone with that combination of power and reckless indifference to the strike zone in the eight slot, he's a nuisance; on the Giants, that nuisance batted cleanup. Only one player with 100 or more plate appearances had a lower rate of unintentional walks than Molina's 1.9 percent, and that was Jays defensive specialist John McDonald (0.6 percent). Molina is also slipping in his capacity to put the brakes on opponents' running games. Naturally, the expectation is that he'll get zillions as a free agent, because he hit 20 homers and he's an RBI guy. Pity whoever believes that and tries to plug Molina into the middle of his order.

Thomas Neal   LF   Bats: R   Throws: R   Height: 6′ 1″   Weight: 205   Born: August 17, 1987   Age: 22

YEAR	TEAM	LVL	AGE	PA	R	2B	3B	HR	RBI	BB	SO	SB	CS	EqBRR	AVG	OBP	SLG	EqAVG	EqOBP	EqSLG	EqA	VORP	WARP	DEFENSE
2007	GIA	Rk	19	46	7	3	0	1	4	5	7	0	0	0.0	.308	.413	.462	.262	.326	.381	.248	-0.2	0.0		
2008	AUG	A	20	497	69	25	1	15	81	48	103	3	4	-0.4	.276	.359	.444	.245	.313	.380	.244	-3.9	-0.8	38-1B	-3
2009	SJO	A+	21	559	102	41	4	22	90	65	98	3	0	-0.8	.337	.431	.579	.303	.379	.491	.298	32.9	4.2	112-LF	2
2010	SFN	MLB	22	533	67	28	1	15	66	50	121	1	1	-0.3	.259	.337	.417	.259	.338	.418	.263	12.6	1.5	78-LF	1

Breakout: 11%   Improve: 40%   Collapse: 12%   Attrition: 5%   MLB: 10%   Comparables: Corey Kapano, Alonzo Powell, Harvey Pulliam, Shon Ashley

Neal has been around since signing as an 18-year-old draft-and-follow in 2006, so he's young yet. He's a hitting machine with power to all fields, but one limited to left, so he'll go only so far as the bat takes him. Given that his walk rate went up almost half again in the second half as Cal Leaguers tried to avoid throwing him strikes, he's as ready as he'll ever be for the Double-A test; scale those heights, and he's part of the picture for a major-league lineup stocked with various flavors of unsatisfying when it comes to quenching a thirst for offense.

Nick Noonan   2B   Bats: L   Throws: R   Height: 6′ 0″   Weight: 180   Born: May 4, 1989   Age: 21

YEAR	TEAM	LVL	AGE	PA	R	2B	3B	HR	RBI	BB	SO	SB	CS	EqBRR	AVG	OBP	SLG	EqAVG	EqOBP	EqSLG	EqA	VORP	WARP	DEFENSE		
2007	GIA	Rk	18	224	33	11	4	3	40	12	20	18	3	2.2	.316	.357	.451	.263	.291	.371	.234	0.5	0.7	20-2B	1	17-SS	2
2008	AUG	A	19	532	79	27	7	9	68	23	98	29	4	4.7	.279	.315	.415	.248	.279	.360	.225	-3.0	-1.2	116-2B	-7		
2009	SJO	A+	20	530	82	26	8	7	64	48	97	9	5	1.7	.259	.330	.397	.239	.295	.345	.228	-2.1	-1.4	118-2B	-10		
2010	SFN	MLB	21	543	68	26	6	7	55	35	116	9	4	1.7	.248	.300	.367	.250	.301	.367	.233	1.4	-0.3	123-2B	-4		

Breakout: 22%   Improve: 57%   Collapse: 5%   Attrition: 3%   MLB: 1%   Comparables: Brandon Pico, Anthony Lewis, Ben Candelaria, Marcus Lemon

A supplemental first-rounder in the '07 draft—thanks for the memories, Moises Alou, and don't forget to write—the athletic Noonan took another step forward toward adding his name to the crowded post-Sanchez picture at second base. He needs to improve his fielding at the keystone after playing shortstop in high school, but he's acrobatic and promising as a defender. His progress at the plate was masked by his almost desperate struggles against lefties (.198/.262/.270), but to look at the glass as half-full, a guy who hits .282/.355/.444 against right-handers at the age of 20 in High-A is someone who can grow up to do something for you at the plate in the majors.

Buster Posey   C

Buster Posey — C — Bats: R — Throws: R — Height: 6' 2" — Weight: 195 — Born: March 27, 1987 — Age: 23

YEAR	TEAM	LVL	AGE	PA	R	2B	3B	HR	RBI	BB	SO	SB	CS	EqBRR	AVG	OBP	SLG	EqAVG	EqOBP	EqSLG	EqA	VORP	WARP	DEFENSE	
2008	GIA	Rk	21	31	8	3	1	1	4	5	4	0	0	0.1	.385	.484	.692	.321	.387	.500	.302	2.3	0.4	4-C	0
2009	SJO	A+	22	346	63	23	0	13	58	45	45	6	0	1.8	.326	.428	.540	.300	.382	.459	.293	23.9	3.3	62-C	4
2009	FRE	AAA	22	151	21	8	1	5	22	17	23	0	1	-3.5	.321	.391	.511	.301	.364	.481	.288	10.8	1.5	32-C	2
2009	SFN	MLB	22	17	1	0	0	0	0	0	4	0	0	0.0	.118	.118	.118	.176	.176	.176	-.160	-1.5	-0.2	5-C	1
2010	SFN	MLB	23	426	53	20	1	12	52	43	72	2	1	-0.6	.271	.349	.424	.274	.352	.424	.270	21.2	2.6	81-C	3

Breakout: 19% Improve: 42% Collapse: 27% Attrition: 5%   MLB: 100%   Comparables: Tom Magrann, Devin Ivany, Don Slaught, Jeff Banister

Expectations that Posey will be an All-Star catcher lost nothing with his speedy clamber up the chain, rocketing from High-A to the majors in his first full season. The 2008 first-rounder had his rough patches as a receiver, no surprise for a former shortstop and pitcher in his third year of catching, but he threw out 49 percent of stolen-base attempts for San Jose and killed another 38 percent with Fresno. Beyond that, there are few nits to pick, unless you want to quibble over whether he'll be a merely good hitter batting higher than sixth in the order, because he'll obviously be an improvement on the feeble standard set by Molina. The big-league job should be his to lose, though the Giants may opt for more seasoning. Should he come up in time, he's an instant short-list candidate for Rookie of the Year en route to what should be a fine career.

Edgar Renteria   SS

Edgar Renteria — SS — Bats: R — Throws: R — Height: 6' 1" — Weight: 200 — Born: August 7, 1975 — Age: 34

YEAR	TEAM	LVL	AGE	PA	R	2B	3B	HR	RBI	BB	SO	SB	CS	EqBRR	AVG	OBP	SLG	EqAVG	EqOBP	EqSLG	EqA	VORP	WARP	DEFENSE	
2007	ATL	MLB	31	543	87	30	1	12	57	46	77	11	2	4.9	.332	.390	.470	.342	.400	.478	.305	46.5	6.1	113-SS	8
2008	DET	MLB	32	547	69	22	2	10	55	37	64	6	3	-0.5	.270	.317	.382	.273	.321	.387	.249	15.6	0.7	132-SS	-10
2009	SFN	MLB	33	510	50	19	1	5	48	39	69	7	2	-0.3	.250	.307	.328	.255	.309	.338	.231	5.5	1.0	120-SS	3
2010	SFN	MLB	34	455	56	21	1	8	45	39	70	5	3	0.6	.274	.338	.387	.277	.339	.388	.255	13.4	1.5	105-SS	0

Breakout: 6% Improve: 40% Collapse: 24% Attrition: 25%   MLB: 93%   Comparables: Royce Clayton, Scott Brosius, Dickie Thon, Dave Concepcion

A return to the NL was supposed to involve a return to previous standards of success, but Renteria instead wound up playing through pain in his right elbow and later both shoulders before having surgery on the elbow. Whatever the impact, his power dropped to levels he hasn't been at in more than a decade, this after he'd already lost the running game as a significant part of his production before he turned 30. Add in his ranking among MLB's 10 worst for hitting into twin killings via BP's NetDP stat and differing opinions on whatever defensive value remains, and what's left? Two years ago, he was closing in on 2,000 hits and was a 37 percent bet to achieve 3,000 according to Bill James; two of the worst seasons of his career later, and any value he'll have past a 2010 season the Giants will have to pay $9.5 million for (also buying out a $10.5 million option for 2011) seems increasingly speculative.

Ryan Rohlinger   3B

Ryan Rohlinger — 3B — Bats: R — Throws: R — Height: 6' 1" — Weight: 195 — Born: October 7, 1983 — Age: 26

YEAR	TEAM	LVL	AGE	PA	R	2B	3B	HR	RBI	BB	SO	SB	CS	EqBRR	AVG	OBP	SLG	EqAVG	EqOBP	EqSLG	EqA	VORP	WARP	DEFENSE			
2007	AUG	A	23	586	86	31	3	18	78	62	83	3	3	0.2	.235	.332	.415	.198	.270	.321	.207	-18.4	-0.4	132-3B	16		
2008	SJO	A+	24	322	45	16	0	7	46	34	50	5	1	1.2	.285	.368	.419	.262	.330	.360	.247	3.1	-0.3	71-3B	-6		
2008	NRW	AA	24	179	27	12	1	6	19	13	20	1	1	-1.2	.296	.358	.497	.288	.335	.466	.272	6.8	1.3	42-3B	4		
2008	SFN	MLB	24	33	2	1	1	0	2	1	8	0	1	-0.8	.094	.121	.188	.125	.152	.219	-.119	-4.5	-0.4	8-3B	1		
2009	FRE	AAA	25	535	74	37	2	16	78	42	90	4	2	0.8	.281	.351	.468	.259	.321	.425	.258	13.8	2.4	109-3B	5	10-SS	0
2009	SFN	MLB	25	20	0	1	0	0	4	1	6	0	0	-0.3	.158	.200	.211	.158	.200	.211	.104	-1.8	-0.2	3-3B	0		
2010	SFN	MLB	26	512	57	25	2	11	58	42	104	2	2	0.0	.237	.307	.371	.238	.309	.371	.236	0.4	0.4	117-3B	3		

Breakout: 14% Improve: 36% Collapse: 19% Attrition: 11%   MLB: 26%   Comparables: Mike Coolbaugh, Jay Knoblauh, Lee Mitchell, Brian Barden

Rohlinger, a college player added to the system with a sixth-round pick in 2006, had to be pushed by the Giants, and they did so in 2008, getting him through two levels and positioning him for a consolidation year in Fresno last season. However well intentioned, the action didn't spare him his seeming destiny: organizational soldier and a fill-in guy who you don't turn into your everyday third baseman barring a few kidnappings and a permission slip. If he can make the jump to utilityman and adapt to sporadic playing time from the bench, he might make a handy source of some modest sock from the bench. That puts him in a group with Frandsen, Downs, and Velez. You don't get to keep all of them, and Charlotte already spun her web over Velez's locker to let everyone know her favorite to avoid the chopping block.

Aaron Rowand   CF   Bats: R   Throws: R   Height: 6' 0"   Weight: 220   Born: August 29, 1977   Age: 32

YEAR	TEAM	LVL	AGE	PA	R	2B	3B	HR	RBI	BB	SO	SB	CS	EqBRR	AVG	OBP	SLG	EqAVG	EqOBP	EqSLG	EqA	VORP	WARP	DEFENSE	
2007	PHI	MLB	29	684	105	45	0	27	89	47	119	6	3	2.1	.309	.374	.515	.314	.378	.517	.301	51.1	4.8	153-CF	-7
2008	SFN	MLB	30	611	57	37	0	13	70	44	126	2	4	-2.8	.271	.339	.410	.279	.344	.420	.262	18.3	2.9	143-CF	8
2009	SFN	MLB	31	546	61	30	2	15	64	30	125	4	1	1.7	.261	.319	.419	.269	.324	.429	.260	15.6	1.3	126-CF	-3
2010	SFN	MLB	32	534	61	25	1	17	64	40	110	3	3	0.2	.269	.339	.431	.271	.339	.427	.266	19.7	2.1	127-CF	0

Breakout: 4%   Improve: 34%   Collapse: 17%   Attrition: 23%   MLB: 97%   Comparables: Jeffrey Hammonds, Chet Lemon, Derek Bell, Dave Henderson

If you can get past the sticker shock and set aside his 2004 and 2007 seasons as the twin peaks of a career happening in that season-age sweet spot of 25-29, Rowand is much the same player he has been over the bulk of his career, with a pedestrian EqA hovering around .260 and a modest bit of power. Whether that makes him over- or underrated is a matter of how broadly you spread your adjectival values; the real problem is that he's not very good yet not obviously replaceable, with the immovable fact of a contract that owes him $36 million over the next three years coloring any evaluation of his mediocrity. That's on Brian Sabean, not Rowand, but the subsequent problem is figuring out how to afford a lineup that has him in it. It isn't any different from how the Zito deal handicaps the team's ability to afford excellence after paying top dollar for adequacy. The one warning sign that these, the salad days of Rowand's Giants career, might be over is a slowly worsening strikeout rate and a decaying ability to get to a third ball, let alone four.

Freddy Sanchez   2B   Bats: R   Throws: R   Height: 5' 10"   Weight: 190   Born: December 21, 1977   Age: 32

YEAR	TEAM	LVL	AGE	PA	R	2B	3B	HR	RBI	BB	SO	SB	CS	EqBRR	AVG	OBP	SLG	EqAVG	EqOBP	EqSLG	EqA	VORP	WARP	DEFENSE	
2007	PIT	MLB	29	653	77	42	4	11	81	32	76	0	1	-2.3	.304	.343	.442	.313	.351	.453	.277	33.3	3.0	142-2B	-7
2008	PIT	MLB	30	608	75	26	2	9	52	21	63	0	1	0.6	.271	.298	.371	.281	.307	.384	.239	5.2	0.3	126-2B	-3
2009	PIT	MLB	31	382	45	28	3	6	34	20	60	5	1	0.2	.296	.334	.442	.309	.344	.463	.277	19.0	1.4	84-2B	-6
2009	SFN	MLB	31	107	11	1	0	1	7	2	16	0	0	0.7	.284	.295	.324	.291	.302	.330	.221	-1.0	0.3	24-2B	3
2010	SFN	MLB	32	495	58	26	2	8	51	29	75	2	1	-0.2	.277	.325	.394	.278	.325	.396	.250	10.1	0.9	108-2B	-2

Breakout: 8%   Improve: 33%   Collapse: 22%   Attrition: 16%   MLB: 96%   Comparables: Felix Millan, Placido Polanco, Mark Grudzielanek, Deivi Cruz

Whether a team is trading for A. J. Pierzynski or paying too much for the Zitos or the Rowands, there's a track record here for overvaluing adequacy and employing it at extraordinary expense. Trading for Sanchez is the latest example, as he's a nice little player who doesn't kill you or the opposition in any phase of the game and whose perceived value is directly related to the vagaries of BABIP outcomes. His career high in ISO is .138, and his single-season high in unintentional walks drawn is 30. His .266 combined EqA last season was a single tick *below* the position average for second basemen, and while injuries were used to excuse his Giant slump, the other *leitmotif* of Sanchez's career is his getting knicked up. This isn't what you want; it's what you settle for. So of course Sabean elected to give Sanchez a two-year, $12 million extension to decisively secure mediocrity.

Pablo Sandoval   3B/1B   Bats: S   Throws: R   Height: 5' 11"   Weight: 245   Born: August 11, 1986   Age: 23

YEAR	TEAM	LVL	AGE	PA	R	2B	3B	HR	RBI	BB	SO	SB	CS	EqBRR	AVG	OBP	SLG	EqAVG	EqOBP	EqSLG	EqA	VORP	WARP	DEFENSE			
2007	SJO	A+	20	423	56	33	5	11	52	16	52	3	1	1.6	.287	.312	.476	.277	.298	.431	.249	8.9	2.2	58-C	8	39-1B	1
2008	SJO	A+	21	301	61	25	2	12	59	23	39	2	1	-2.1	.359	.412	.597	.343	.389	.556	.315	29.4	3.8	49-C	2	10-1B	1
2008	NRW	AA	21	184	29	13	0	8	37	8	20	0	1	0.6	.337	.364	.549	.339	.359	.531	.296	13.7	2.0	30-C	2	7-1B	1
2008	SFN	MLB	21	154	24	10	1	3	24	4	14	0	0	0.1	.345	.357	.490	.354	.361	.500	.294	9.5	1.1	14-1B	0	10-3B	0
2009	SFN	MLB	22	633	79	44	5	25	90	52	83	5	5	-0.8	.330	.387	.556	.341	.393	.570	.317	56.5	6.0	115-3B	-1	23-1B	0
2010	SFN	MLB	23	601	81	40	2	21	86	39	82	4	3	-0.1	.314	.360	.503	.316	.364	.507	.293	38.0	4.1	124-3B	-1		

Breakout: 17%   Improve: 49%   Collapse: 10%   Attrition: 2%   MLB: 100%   Comparables: David Wright, Carlos Baerga, Michael Barrett, Scott Rolen

"Kung-Fu Panda"? That's the best you've got to describe such a wonderful, unique, fundamentally entertaining ballplayer? That's the standard? For such creativity, we can probably thank the generation that paid top dollar for cookie-cutter townhouses, battlewagon-carriages to cart their sessile four-year-olds around, and, what the hell, a round of minivans with backseat DVD players for everybody. Why not "el Volcan," as the squat power source that erupts with a fierce regularity? "El Osezno," the bear cub? Feh. Sandoval is not the sort of player where pat assertions about regression to leaguewide marks for line-drive rates or BABIP mean much. Like Vladimir Guerrero, his exceptional plate coverage makes him more dangerous because he won't just try to hit your pitch; he *can* hit your pitch. You don't copy it or coach it; you just enjoy it. Rather than live with his immobility at third, the Giants have signed superutility star Mark DeRosa, but a more slender el Volcan's in line to launch lava-hot liners while starting at third after an aggressive off-season conditioning program.

Nate Schierholtz — RF

Bats: L   Throws: R   Height: 6' 2"   Weight: 215   Born: February 15, 1984   Age: 26

YEAR	TEAM	LVL	AGE	PA	R	2B	3B	HR	RBI	BB	SO	SB	CS	EqBRR	AVG	OBP	SLG	EqAVG	EqOBP	EqSLG	EqA	VORP	WARP	DEFENSE	
2007	FRE	AAA	23	439	67	31	7	16	68	17	58	10	4	1.9	.333	.365	.560	.304	.333	.490	.278	16.7	0.9	98-RF	-9
2007	SFN	MLB	23	117	9	5	3	0	10	2	19	3	1	1.3	.304	.316	.402	.306	.316	.405	.255	0.7	-0.1	26-RF	-2
2008	FRE	AAA	24	377	62	22	10	18	73	21	51	9	3	1.9	.320	.363	.594	.288	.326	.508	.279	15.4	0.8	85-RF	-9
2008	SFN	MLB	24	81	12	8	1	1	5	3	8	0	1	0.2	.320	.370	.493	.333	.383	.507	.293	4.8	0.4	18-RF	-1
2009	SFN	MLB	25	308	33	19	2	5	29	16	58	3	1	1.9	.267	.302	.400	.271	.302	.412	.249	1.7	0.4	67-RF	1
2010	SFN	MLB	26	386	46	22	6	10	47	22	65	6	3	1.1	.279	.326	.456	.281	.328	.457	.267	11.5	0.9	88-RF	-3

Breakout: 17%   Improve: 49%   Collapse: 7%   Attrition: 5%   MLB: 81%   Comparables: Troy O'Leary, Robin Jennings, Jeff Wetherby, Andre Ethier

Schierholtz wins brownie points for scrapping, banging into walls, or trying to play through various hurts, but the question is whether he can get away from that and continue to show the kind of adaptive ability he did in cutting down his strikeouts as much as he has as he neared the majors. He's not going to walk, and what pop he delivers depends on his ability to deliver consistent contact. The odds aren't in his favor, but there's a shot at his being the new Nate McLouth if everything goes right and he avoids nagging injuries.

Andres Torres — OF

Bats: S   Throws: R   Height: 5' 10"   Weight: 190   Born: January 26, 1978   Age: 32

YEAR	TEAM	LVL	AGE	PA	R	2B	3B	HR	RBI	BB	SO	SB	CS	EqBRR	AVG	OBP	SLG	EqAVG	EqOBP	EqSLG	EqA	VORP	WARP	DEFENSE				
2007	ERI	AA	29	359	53	15	11	6	35	38	66	17	4	-0.5	.292	.372	.472	.224	.283	.324	.217	-8.6	-1.5	63-LF	-2	11-RF	0	
2007	TOL	AAA	29	188	23	6	9	4	17	11	39	5	6	-6.0	.292	.348	.506	.267	.314	.453	.257	4.2	0.7	28-CF	0	13-RF	2	
2008	IOW	AAA	30	479	91	27	10	11	51	55	103	29	4	6.6	.306	.391	.501	.255	.328	.395	.258	9.4	2.6	46-CF	6	41-LF	3	
2009	FRE	AAA	31	45	7	1	1	1	2	1	18	1	0	0.7	.302	.318	.442	.250	.267	.386	.228	-0.4	0.0	5-CF	0	3-LF	0	
2009	SFN	MLB	31	170	30	6	8	6	23	16	45	6	1	1.7	.270	.343	.533	.281	.353	.549	.299	12.4	2.2	18-LF	2	17-CF	5	
2010	SFN	MLB	32	316	37	13	7	5	26	27	89	6	3	0.3	.234	.304	.378	.235	.305	.381	.238	2.6	0.7	57-CF	3			

Breakout: 11%   Improve: 32%   Collapse: 24%   Attrition: 22%   MLB: 36%   Comparables: Donzell McDonald, Mike Brumley, Quinton McCracken, Eric Fox

A bum hamstring kept Torres shelved for most of the first half, but in the second, when he was finally given his first real opportunity to play in the majors since his participation on the 119-loss Tigers of 2003, he shined as a bench bat. Mostly, he put the hurt on lefties, rapping out 13 extra-base hits in 78 plate appearances against them (including six triples and four homers, making for a hell of a Strat card) while spot-starting at all three positions. He won't slug .500 again, but because he can run and he's always been able to handle center, he may finally settle in as a useful bench weapon.

Juan Uribe — INF

Bats: R   Throws: R   Height: 6' 0"   Weight: 225   Born: March 22, 1979   Age: 31

YEAR	TEAM	LVL	AGE	PA	R	2B	3B	HR	RBI	BB	SO	SB	CS	EqBRR	AVG	OBP	SLG	EqAVG	EqOBP	EqSLG	EqA	VORP	WARP	DEFENSE				
2007	CHA	MLB	28	563	55	18	2	20	68	34	112	1	9	-2.0	.234	.284	.394	.231	.283	.394	.228	3.2	0.4	147-SS	0			
2008	CHA	MLB	29	353	38	22	1	7	40	22	64	1	3	-0.8	.247	.296	.386	.248	.300	.388	.235	0.7	1.9	52-3B	10	41-2B	6	
2009	SFN	MLB	30	432	50	26	4	16	55	25	82	3	1	-0.3	.289	.329	.495	.298	.334	.504	.283	25.5	3.2	36-3B	0	36-SS	-1	
2010	SFN	MLB	31	393	40	19	2	12	46	28	80	2	3	-0.5	.251	.306	.413	.252	.309	.407	.246	4.4	1.1	93-3B	5			

Breakout: 12%   Improve: 38%   Collapse: 24%   Attrition: 9%   MLB: 93%   Comparables: Charlie Hayes, Russ Davis, Dean Palmer, Sean Berry

Where did that come from? In the latest strange turn in an odd career, Uribe's incarnation as a utility bopper was remarkable. While a good chunk of it was a 40-point spike in his BABIP, his home-run rate didn't change much. The other big improvement was cutting his infield flies almost in half from 2007 to 2008. The BABIP will drop, but if he can continue to avoid popping up as much as he had been, he should retain a good chunk of last year's value, plus chip in as a useful part-timer at second and third. Even after the decision to sign Mark DeRosa, Uribe will be back with the Giants, as a worthwhile risk to repeat as an oft-used utilityman.

Eugenio Velez			**UT**									Bats: S		Throws: R		Height: 6' 1"		Weight: 160		Born: May 16, 1982			Age: 28
YEAR	TEAM	LVL	AGE	PA	R	2B	3B	HR	RBI	BB	SO	SB	CS	EqBRR	AVG	OBP	SLG	EqAVG	EqOBP	EqSLG	EqA	VORP	WARP	DEFENSE
2007	NRW	AA	25	411	55	17	9	1	25	26	66	49	17	-0.6	.298	.344	.399	.285	.319	.376	.247	5.7	-1.1	44-CF -1 29-2B -10
2007	SFN	MLB	25	13	5	0	2	0	2	2	3	4	0	1.6	.273	.385	.636	.273	.385	.636	.355	1.7	0.1	1-2B -1
2008	FRE	AAA	26	188	25	11	4	5	15	17	32	13	9	-3.2	.310	.372	.509	.270	.324	.408	.249	2.3	-0.8	24-LF -4 16-2B -5
2008	SFN	MLB	26	292	32	16	7	1	30	14	40	15	6	-1.6	.262	.299	.382	.269	.306	.389	.243	2.6	-1.1	51-2B -11 5-RF -1
2009	FRE	AAA	27	197	30	13	3	3	26	13	26	16	9	-0.6	.297	.340	.451	.266	.305	.391	.237	0.5	-0.3	26-CF 0 7-2B -2
2009	SFN	MLB	27	307	40	13	5	5	31	16	55	11	5	3.5	.267	.308	.400	.276	.316	.413	.252	5.4	0.0	32-LF -1 24-2B 0
2010	SFN	MLB	28	440	53	22	8	6	40	29	84	20	9	0.1	.263	.313	.396	.262	.314	.391	.248	3.8	0.1	71-LF -3

Breakout: 17% Improve: 40% Collapse: 23% Attrition: 19% MLB: 57% Comparables: Mike Ramsey, Stan Jefferson, Nyjer Morgan, Chris Roberson

Aggressive batsmanship and a silly chin beard may a phenomenon make, but happily, the organization doesn't seem caught up in the popular delusion that Velez is anything more than a stopgap. His chief value is getting a few well-hit balls into play against right-handers, and that plus fleetness of foot and playability at second and all three outfield slots make him a handy bench player on a team short of effective regulars. After coming back from a month-long absence with a hamstring injury, he got a two-month window to start regularly down the stretch; he hit .277/.321/.426, which looks good in an outfield corner in roughly the same way that any fluid, however brackish, starts to look thirst-quenching in a desert.

Angel Villalona			**1B**									Bats: R		Throws: R		Height: 6' 3"		Weight: 200		Born: August 13, 1990			Age: 19
YEAR	TEAM	LVL	AGE	PA	R	2B	3B	HR	RBI	BB	SO	SB	CS	EqBRR	AVG	OBP	SLG	EqAVG	EqOBP	EqSLG	EqA	VORP	WARP	DEFENSE
2007	GIA	Rk	16	224	40	12	3	5	37	15	42	1	1	1.8	.285	.344	.450	.238	.276	.376	.226	-3.1	-1.5	48-3B -5
2008	AUG	A	17	500	64	29	0	17	64	18	118	1	2	-2.2	.263	.312	.435	.236	.272	.378	.222	-15.4	-2.6	97-1B -6
2009	SJO	A+	18	310	47	11	0	9	42	9	73	0	1	0.1	.267	.306	.397	.245	.271	.339	.208	-16.8	-2.8	71-1B -6
2010	SFN	MLB	19	403	46	18	1	13	48	18	101	0	1	-0.5	.241	.286	.396	.242	.286	.389	.232	-7.7	-1.2	84-1B -3

Breakout: 44% Improve: 73% Collapse: 12% Attrition: 9% MLB: 1% Comparables: Jose Gonzalez, Gilberto Reyes, Joe Bernhardt, Yorvit Torrealba

The teen phenom had an ugly introduction to High-A play, which, given his youth, didn't seem as though it would put a dent in his future; a strained quad bit into his production before shutting him down in early July, so it could be seen as a learning experience. What *will* alter the course of his career is the murder he was charged with in the Dominican Republic in September, not least because he was subsequently stripped of his visa. Whether he's innocent or guilty, it's hard to know what will come next, let alone whether he'll wind up delivering on his early promise.

Randy Winn			**OF**									Bats: S		Throws: R		Height: 6' 2"		Weight: 195		Born: June 9, 1974			Age: 36
YEAR	TEAM	LVL	AGE	PA	R	2B	3B	HR	RBI	BB	SO	SB	CS	EqBRR	AVG	OBP	SLG	EqAVG	EqOBP	EqSLG	EqA	VORP	WARP	DEFENSE
2007	SFN	MLB	33	653	73	42	1	14	65	44	85	15	3	0.4	.300	.353	.445	.306	.358	.451	.281	28.2	3.1	97-RF -3 32-CF 1
2008	SFN	MLB	34	667	84	38	2	10	64	59	88	25	2	5.7	.306	.363	.426	.314	.367	.435	.286	31.5	5.0	125-RF 13 12-LF 2
2009	SFN	MLB	35	597	65	33	5	2	51	47	93	16	2	4.8	.262	.318	.353	.270	.321	.359	.248	4.1	2.2	86-RF 10 36-LF 5
2010	SFN	MLB	36	527	54	27	2	8	50	44	85	10	5	1.5	.270	.334	.384	.272	.335	.383	.253	7.1	1.2	109-RF 4

Breakout: 6% Improve: 32% Collapse: 24% Attrition: 30% MLB: 99% Comparables: Stan Javier, Bing Miller, B.J. Surhoff, Ken Griffey Sr.

If a rising tide lifts all boats, you can consider the curious case of Randy Winn's compensation as an odd symptom of the go-go Aughties, symbol of an age. He did reasonably good work in the first two years of his three-year, $23.25 million deal, but affording this kind of player that kind of job security was symptomatic of the sort of largesse that preserved baseball's middle class against the chiseling that's now sure to come. The third season, when the Giants had a chance to matter, happened to be the one in which he had the least to contribute. Now he's an unemployed thirtysomething used to a certain rate of compensation, and while he has his uses on the bases and in the field, he's not going to see that kind of money again. Welcome to the new economy.

PITCHERS

Jeremy Affeldt

Bats: L   Throws: L   Height: 6' 4"   Weight: 225   Born: June 6, 1979   Age: 31

YEAR	TEAM	LVL	AGE	W	L	SV	G	GS	IP	H	HR	BB	SO	GB%	BABIP	STUFF	WHIP	ERA	SIERA	DERA	EqH9	EqHR9	EqBB9	EqSO9	VORP	SN/WX
2007	COL	MLB	28	4	3	0	75	0	59	47	3	33	46	61%	.262	9	1.36	3.51	4.45	3.63	7.1	0.3	4.5	6.6	12.1	-0.63
2008	CIN	MLB	29	1	1	0	74	0	78¹	78	9	25	80	65%	.317	11	1.31	3.33	3.19	3.82	8.4	0.9	2.5	7.9	14.8	0.24
2009	SFN	MLB	30	2	2	0	74	0	62¹	42	3	31	55	70%	.250	12	1.17	1.73	3.66	2.17	7.0	0.5	4.0	7.1	21.4	3.86
2010	SFN	MLB	31	3	3	0	57	0	56²	52	5	25	47	63%	.293	1	1.35	3.93	3.95	4.29	8.2	0.8	3.8	6.9	7.6	0.66

Breakout: 17%   Improve: 42%   Collapse: 33%   Attrition: 15%   MLB: 96%   Comparables: Javier Lopez, Mark Guthrie, Mike Stanton, Jeff Fassero

While flogging Sabean on many of his deals can be appropriate (not to mention entertaining), Affeldt lived up to his end of the bargain in the first year of his two-year, $8 million deal, moving straight into a high-leverage role in the newly assembled pen. From the seventh inning on, he was handed 49 leads and came into 16 tied ballgames, and while he notched more appearances than innings, he was once again *not* a situational lefty. The remarkable development was his transmogrification into a ground-balling fiend: all those indicators that he got tremendous defensive support spin from that, but don't convey his 18 double plays induced for a MLB-leading 29.5 percent conversion rate on deuce opportunities (50 IP minimum), the fourth-highest rate on record. No, it's not likely to happen again, but Affeldt's radical change to ground-baller was unusual in the first place.

Madison Bumgarner

Bats: R   Throws: L   Height: 6' 4"   Weight: 215   Born: August 1, 1989   Age: 20

YEAR	TEAM	LVL	AGE	W	L	SV	G	GS	IP	H	HR	BB	SO	GB%	BABIP	STUFF	WHIP	ERA	SIERA	DERA	EqH9	EqHR9	EqBB9	EqSO9	VORP	SN/WX
2008	AUG	A	18	15	3	0	24	24	141²	111	3	21	164	41%	.304	44	0.93	1.46	2.11	3.10	9.5	1.1	2.3	6.6	33.7	3.09
2009	SJO	A+	19	3	1	0	5	5	24¹	20	0	4	23	33%	.282	20	0.99	1.48	3.10	5.79	9.3	0.8	2.3	4.6	-0.7	0.33
2009	NRW	AA	19	9	1	0	20	19	107	80	6	30	69	44%	.236	27	1.03	1.93	4.35	3.56	8.4	1.6	2.8	3.9	21.3	2.36
2009	SFN	MLB	19	0	0	0	4	1	10	8	2	3	10	62%	.240	10	1.10	1.80	3.10	1.86	7.4	1.9	2.8	7.4	3.9	0.20
2010	SFN	MLB	20	8	10	0	32	28	153	160	21	53	100	38%	.296	36	1.39	4.49	4.71	4.79	9.3	1.2	3.0	5.5	12.0	4.63

Breakout: 8%   Improve: 38%   Collapse: 22%   Attrition: 3%   MLB: 59%   Comparables: Sean Burnett, Steve Avery, Jimmy Gobble, Wilson Alvarez

Sometimes, with all the talk of money, we can get away from those times when talent sets its own timetable. The Giants apparently couldn't say no to Bumgarner any more than they could with Posey, putting both on their September roster because it was already obvious that both would be in the big-league picture for 2010. The interesting question is whether the Giants should have worked up the nerve in Bumgarner's case, but he got to make a soft landing, facing the Padres for a team in a pennant race, before they effectively shut him down for the year. Including his big-league work, he wound up with roughly identical workloads in his two seasons in terms of innings and batters faced (548 in '08, 561 in '09). The concern is that he wasn't throwing the heat that touches 97 and sits in the mid-90s in the second half, but his mastering of his off-speed stuff is being interpreted as a positive learning experience. He's a good athlete, holding runners effectively and taking good cuts at the plate (including a Double-A grand slam). His chance to become what we expect should make for some incredible Bumgarner vs. Kershaw duels within the division, but more broadly, the Giants can expect they'll soon have their third man behind Lincecum and Cain.

Matt Cain

Bats: R   Throws: R   Height: 6' 3"   Weight: 245   Born: October 1, 1984   Age: 25

YEAR	TEAM	LVL	AGE	W	L	SV	G	GS	IP	H	HR	BB	SO	GB%	BABIP	STUFF	WHIP	ERA	SIERA	DERA	EqH9	EqHR9	EqBB9	EqSO9	VORP	SN/WX
2007	SFN	MLB	22	7	16	0	32	32	200	173	14	79	163	45%	.278	37	1.26	3.64	4.13	3.63	7.8	0.6	3.2	6.7	40.8	6.62
2008	SFN	MLB	23	8	14	0	34	34	217²	206	19	91	186	38%	.297	22	1.36	3.76	4.19	3.78	8.4	0.8	3.3	6.6	41.1	5.07
2009	SFN	MLB	24	14	8	0	33	33	217²	184	22	73	171	45%	.263	19	1.18	2.89	4.02	3.15	8.2	0.9	2.7	6.2	54.8	7.51
2010	SFN	MLB	25	12	11	0	32	32	209¹	197	21	78	163	44%	.292	16	1.31	3.85	4.19	4.14	8.4	0.9	3.2	6.5	31.6	4.24

Breakout: 5%   Improve: 43%   Collapse: 6%   Attrition: 7%   MLB: 100%   Comparables: Carlos Zambrano, Andy Benes, John Smoltz, Scott Erickson

The numbers have a certain numbing near-reliable quality, as Cain has beaten his SIERA marks all three years above. He's striking out fewer people, giving up a few more homers, while also walking fewer, and he's not generating tons of ground-ball outs, so analysts fidget. Should they, and should you? His BABIPs, rather than regressing, have been significantly below average in three of his four years as a rotation regular, only getting around "normal" in '08; you'll find the same with his line-drive rates, as in the '08 season around normal for everyone else is the abnormal year for Cain. He's throwing more first-pitch strikes, throwing fewer pitches, and seeing fewer three-ball counts. He managed quality starts (through six) in 22 of 33 turns. Predict regression often enough, and eventually you'll be right, but so far, this is looking more like a talented pitcher achieving maturity.

Alex Hinshaw

Bats: L   Throws: L   Height: 6' 4"   Weight: 190   Born: October 31, 1982   Age: 27

YEAR	TEAM	LVL	AGE	W	L	SV	G	GS	IP	H	HR	BB	SO	GB%	BABIP	STUFF	WHIP	ERA	SIERA	DERA	EqH9	EqHR9	EqBB9	EqSO9	VORP	SN/WX
2007	NRW	AA	24	3	1	0	17	5	41¹	22	2	19	50	49%	.217	9	0.99	1.96	2.89	3.96	6.8	1.4	4.4	7.7	6.6	1.13
2008	FRE	AAA	25	0	0	7	13	0	15²	5	0	4	21	44%	.167	15	0.57	0.57	1.52	0.90	3.6	0.6	2.4	9.0	7.7	1.39
2008	SFN	MLB	25	2	1	0	48	0	39²	31	5	29	47	28%	.274	15	1.51	3.40	4.14	3.49	7.2	1.1	5.6	9.0	8.9	-0.37
2009	FRE	AAA	26	1	2	1	46	0	52¹	42	3	32	72	38%	.307	16	1.41	3.96	3.11	4.58	7.6	0.8	5.3	9.5	5.4	0.07
2009	SFN	MLB	26	0	0	0	9	0	6	10	2	7	2	28%	.364	-33	2.83	12.00	8.18	11.12	15.9	3.2	9.5	3.2	-3.5	0.03
2010	SFN	MLB	27	3	4	1	48	0	52²	46	6	31	51	41%	.290	0	1.47	4.42	4.23	4.73	7.9	1.0	5.1	8.0	4.5	1.00

Breakout: 15%   Improve: 28%   Collapse: 30%   Attrition: 12%   MLB: 30%   Comparables: Tim Kubinski, Leo Vasquez, Paul Spoljaric, Jerry Nielsen

Where most lefty relievers tend to be graying caballeros and finesse-dependent magicians, in Hinshaw the Giants have the rare southpaw who simply throws several flavors of nasty, whether it's big-bending breaking stuff or reliable low-90s heat. The problem is command, as well as his frustrations over it. Could he fix matters? Certainly, and last summer's postbreak stretch at Fresno is an interesting reminder of what he's capable of: 17 ⅔ innings pitched in 16 games with a 30/4 K/BB ratio. Hinshaw isn't helped by the fact that neither he nor Affeldt is a LOOGY, so landing in the second lefty's chair isn't really his best possible role.

Bob Howry

Bats: L   Throws: R   Height: 6' 5"   Weight: 220   Born: August 4, 1973   Age: 36

YEAR	TEAM	LVL	AGE	W	L	SV	G	GS	IP	H	HR	BB	SO	GB%	BABIP	STUFF	WHIP	ERA	SIERA	DERA	EqH9	EqHR9	EqBB9	EqSO9	VORP	SN/WX
2007	CHN	MLB	33	6	7	8	78	0	81¹	76	8	19	72	34%	.289	14	1.17	3.32	3.58	3.24	8.5	0.7	1.9	7.4	20.3	3.17
2008	CHN	MLB	34	7	5	1	72	0	70²	90	13	13	59	38%	.344	-11	1.46	5.35	3.69	5.26	11.7	1.4	1.4	6.6	1.9	-0.06
2009	SFN	MLB	35	2	6	0	63	0	63²	50	5	23	46	33%	.234	1	1.15	3.39	4.64	3.74	7.2	0.7	2.6	5.4	12.7	-0.23
2010	ARI	MLB	36	3	4	2	66	0	65²	68	8	19	49	35%	.308	-1	1.33	4.25	4.26	4.48	9.2	1.0	2.5	6.2	7.4	0.58

Breakout: 16%   Improve: 50%   Collapse: 13%   Attrition: 10%   MLB: 93%   Comparables: David Weathers, Tom Ferrick, Steve Reed, Rich Gossage

Add Howry to the list of Sabean's veteran bullpen additions who delivered what he was paid to do. Although he also profited greatly from defensive support, he was also due for a bounce back from a career-high rate of homers to fly balls. Used carefully by Bochy (he was ordered to issue a pen-leading six intentional walks) and with the benefit of a good outfield defense, Howry certainly couldn't have asked for a better circumstance. He took a chance by cashing in on the good year by heading over to the D'backs on another one-year deal. FKA Bob Ballpark is a much less forgiving place for fly-ball pitchers, and he'll be pitching for A. J. Hinch, a manager younger than Howry; the pitcher even struck Hinch out three times in four at-bats, so Howry's the guy who owns skip.

Waldis Joaquin

Bats: R   Throws: R   Height: 6' 2"   Weight: 235   Born: December 25, 1986   Age: 23

YEAR	TEAM	LVL	AGE	W	L	SV	G	GS	IP	H	HR	BB	SO	GB%	BABIP	STUFF	WHIP	ERA	SIERA	DERA	EqH9	EqHR9	EqBB9	EqSO9	VORP	SN/WX
2007	SLO	A-	20	3	0	0	15	5	38	24	2	16	30	59%	.210	18	1.05	2.84	3.85	4.63	7.3	1.5	4.3	3.8	3.5	0.56
2008	AUG	A	21	1	2	2	27	3	52	49	1	20	49	47%	.316	-2	1.33	4.33	3.70	7.89	10.6	1.1	4.8	5.1	-12.6	-1.11
2008	SJO	A+	21	0	1	0	9	4	19¹	20	2	11	23	33%	.367	-2	1.60	4.66	3.56	8.10	12.4	2.7	6.5	7.6	-4.8	-0.05
2009	NRW	AA	22	4	5	1	36	0	54	36	0	28	40	55%	.234	-2	1.19	2.67	4.51	4.21	7.2	0.5	4.7	4.4	7.4	0.94
2009	SFN	MLB	22	0	0	0	10	0	10²	10	1	7	12	80%	.310	11	1.59	4.22	3.40	4.09	9.0	0.8	4.9	8.2	1.7	-0.15
2010	SFN	MLB	23	3	4	0	50	0	62¹	60	7	33	44	50%	.290	-5	1.51	4.65	4.82	5.02	8.8	1.1	4.7	5.8	3.3	1.18

Breakout: 25%   Improve: 55%   Collapse: 15%   Attrition: 6%   MLB: 54%   Comparables: Jeff Bronkey, Greg Mayberry, Francisco Cordova, Travis Bowyer

Joaquin is part of the next wave of relief help, the generation that will come from within to eventually replace last year's veteran patches. The hard-throwing Dominican deserves that kind of confidence, throwing mid-90s fastballs and a plus slider that make for an effective enough combination to eventually put him in the conversation about closing. As you might expect, he needs to improve his command, but having made his big-league debut, he'll be in the mix for one of the supporting slots in camp.

Randy Johnson

Bats: R   Throws: L   Height: 6' 10"   Weight: 225   Born: September 10, 1963   Age: 46

YEAR	TEAM	LVL	AGE	W	L	SV	G	GS	IP	H	HR	BB	SO	GB%	BABIP	STUFF	WHIP	ERA	SIERA	DERA	EqH9	EqHR9	EqBB9	EqSO9	VORP	SN/WX
2007	ARI	MLB	43	4	3	0	10	10	56²	52	7	13	72	42%	.328	40	1.15	3.81	2.17	3.72	8.4	0.8	1.9	10.0	11.0	1.52
2008	ARI	MLB	44	11	10	0	30	30	184	184	24	44	173	42%	.301	25	1.24	3.91	3.34	4.06	8.5	0.9	1.8	7.4	29.7	3.29
2009	SFN	MLB	45	8	6	0	22	17	96	97	19	31	86	52%	.285	-6	1.33	4.87	3.69	5.15	9.6	1.7	2.5	6.9	3.6	1.44
2010	SFN	MLB	46	4	5	0	18	16	83¹	89	11	26	70	47%	.320	10	1.38	4.41	3.82	4.73	9.6	1.1	2.7	7.0	7.1	1.09

Breakout: 10%   Improve: 34%   Collapse: 23%   Attrition: 31%   MLB: 90%   Comparables: Tommy John, Nolan Ryan, Jamie Moyer

Officially retired with his 300th win in the books, the Big Unit pondered whether to pitch at least one more year in the majors before calling it quits. Achieving 5,000 strikeouts wasn't impossible, just 125 third strikes away, a landmark that only Nolan Ryan ever surpassed. There's no begrudging the man his choice; he won't have a problem finding an employer. The question is whether there was much left in the tank, even after he answered that question before with his '03 and '08 campaigns. He provided just six quality starts in the 17 turns when he was able to pitch, and coming back to contribute in relief in September, Johnson was scored on in four of five appearances. And however willing the spirit, the body has contributed its own thought on the subject, as Johnson suffered his first real shoulder injury, a partially torn rotator cuff. He will be the first Diamondback put in the Hall of Fame, or at least he should be, because that 81-win stretch from 1999 to 2002 eliminated any doubt that he was headed for Cooperstown. If this is it, this is ground control to say you've really made the grade.

Tim Lincecum

Bats: L   Throws: R   Height: 5' 11"   Weight: 170   Born: June 15, 1984   Age: 26

YEAR	TEAM	LVL	AGE	W	L	SV	G	GS	IP	H	HR	BB	SO	GB%	BABIP	STUFF	WHIP	ERA	SIERA	DERA	EqH9	EqHR9	EqBB9	EqSO9	VORP	SN/WX
2007	FRE	AAA	23	4	0	0	5	5	31	12	0	11	46	56%	.214	29	0.74	0.29	1.68	0.93	5.0	0.3	3.4	9.9	14.7	1.57
2007	SFN	MLB	23	7	5	0	24	24	146¹	122	12	65	150	53%	.283	35	1.28	4.00	3.54	4.07	7.5	0.7	3.6	8.3	23.2	3.94
2008	SFN	MLB	24	18	5	0	34	33	227	182	11	84	265	50%	.304	45	1.17	2.62	2.86	2.83	7.4	0.4	3.0	9.1	65.9	8.52
2009	SFN	MLB	25	15	7	0	32	32	225¹	168	10	68	261	53%	.282	47	1.05	2.48	2.69	2.94	7.3	0.4	2.3	8.9	62.9	8.25
2010	SFN	MLB	26	14	9	0	32	32	204²	172	16	73	219	53%	.302	38	1.20	3.23	3.10	3.50	7.6	0.7	3.1	8.9	45.6	4.99

Breakout: 5%   Improve: 49%   Collapse: 11%   Attrition: 9%   MLB: 99%   Comparables: Camilo Pascual, Pedro Martinez, Jim Maloney, Jake Peavy

Give Sabean credit where it's due: five of his last six first-round picks look pretty good, with Zach Wheeler ('09) too recently minted to make a guess. Cain and Bumgarner are once and future midrotation hurlers, Posey is going to start, David Aardsma is an All-Star (for somebody else), and Lincecum is on the short list for best pitcher on the planet. In the same way that statheads sometimes like to try to learn something from the outliers, Lincecum is such an extraordinary player from a scouting perspective that it's hard to suggest where his career is headed or what he's capable of. His freakish ability confounds any pat assertions about how power pitchers are supposed to be built, so it isn't as if he's going to inspire a run on people trying to pick the next Lincecum—there's just this one of him. There have been warning signs, with a back injury last September forcing him to miss a turn; the Giants responded carefully, starting him on long rest in three of his last four games, but score another one for Verducci Effect doubters. His fastball velocity dropped significantly, but he achieves devastating separation with his changeup, and an improving ground-ball rate suggests other benefits as well.

Joe Martinez

Bats: L   Throws: R   Height: 6' 2"   Weight: 195   Born: February 26, 1983   Age: 27

YEAR	TEAM	LVL	AGE	W	L	SV	G	GS	IP	H	HR	BB	SO	GB%	BABIP	STUFF	WHIP	ERA	SIERA	DERA	EqH9	EqHR9	EqBB9	EqSO9	VORP	SN/WX
2007	SJO	A+	24	10	10	0	28	28	162²	172	11	36	151	53%	.339	-19	1.28	4.26	3.29	5.85	11.6	1.7	2.6	5.4	-5.8	0.19
2008	NRW	AA	25	10	10	0	27	27	148	131	6	37	112	65%	.277	1	1.14	2.49	3.72	4.68	9.2	1.1	2.4	4.5	12.9	2.32
2009	FRE	AAA	26	0	2	0	7	5	35	39	1	8	22	66%	.322	-1	1.34	4.89	4.11	5.69	10.1	0.5	2.1	4.2	-0.7	0.08
2009	SFN	MLB	26	3	2	0	9	5	30	46	4	12	19	64%	.375	-20	1.93	7.50	4.64	7.95	14.1	1.2	3.0	4.8	-8.2	-0.40
2010	SFN	MLB	27	4	7	0	27	18	98	116	14	35	57	59%	.319	-13	1.54	5.26	4.72	5.68	10.6	1.3	3.1	4.9	-1.9	1.81

Breakout: 9%   Improve: 52%   Collapse: 13%   Attrition: 26%   MLB: 14%   Comparables: Jason Rakers, Jim Magrane, Mike MacDonald, Donne Wall

Martinez seemed to be cruising into his rookie season as a middle reliever with swing-start possibilities when he got his skull fractured in three places by a Mike Cameron line drive in just his second game. It was almost 10 weeks before he returned to a mound at any level, but after "Sadowski" proved to be a wrong answer for Randy Johnson replacement, Martinez got a shot. However heroic the effort, he wasn't much better. As a strike-throwing sinker-baller with below-average velocity who can throw his off-speed stuff for strikes, he'll never be more than a back-end type, either in the pen or as the fifth starter. Still, it beats being chief fry cook.

Brandon Medders

Bats: R   Throws: R   Height: 6' 1"   Weight: 200   Born: January 26, 1980   Age: 30

YEAR	TEAM	LVL	AGE	W	L	SV	G	GS	IP	H	HR	BB	SO	GB%	BABIP	STUFF	WHIP	ERA	SIERA	DERA	EqH9	EqHR9	EqBB9	EqSO9	VORP	SN/WX
2007	TUC	AAA	27	5	3	5	35	0	48	55	3	24	38	43%	.338	-13	1.65	4.69	4.62	5.06	9.6	0.8	4.5	5.4	2.3	0.11
2007	ARI	MLB	27	1	2	0	30	0	29¹	30	9	16	23	33%	.266	-10	1.57	4.30	4.94	4.45	8.9	2.2	4.4	6.7	3.3	-0.42
2008	TUC	AAA	28	1	2	0	26	0	38²	45	4	24	33	58%	.336	-18	1.78	7.45	4.55	7.78	9.8	1.1	5.0	5.5	-10.0	-1.14
2008	ARI	MLB	28	1	0	0	18	0	19²	17	2	11	8	46%	.231	-25	1.42	4.58	6.03	4.43	7.1	0.9	4.4	3.1	2.4	-0.09
2009	SFN	MLB	29	5	1	1	61	0	68²	63	6	32	58	44%	.284	0	1.38	3.01	4.28	3.51	8.7	0.8	3.6	6.5	15.1	1.81
2010	SFN	MLB	30	3	5	1	57	0	62	66	8	31	43	48%	.306	-14	1.56	5.22	4.83	5.63	9.5	1.1	4.4	5.8	-0.9	0.38

Breakout: 16% Improve: 41% Collapse: 29% Attrition: 20%   MLB: 62%   Comparables: Mike Capel, Scott Proctor, Jesus Colome, Darren Hall

Medders was another of the veteran arms Sabean fished out to fix the bullpen, and another who thrived under Bochy's careful use, eventually earning more trust. If you accept that he needs to work around lefties now and again, you've got a reliever who can work well from the stretch and who avoids making mistakes up in the zone, especially now that he's out of the Snakepit.

Justin Miller

Bats: R   Throws: R   Height: 6' 2"   Weight: 200   Born: August 27, 1977   Age: 32

YEAR	TEAM	LVL	AGE	W	L	SV	G	GS	IP	H	HR	BB	SO	GB%	BABIP	STUFF	WHIP	ERA	SIERA	DERA	EqH9	EqHR9	EqBB9	EqSO9	VORP	SN/WX
2007	ABQ	AAA	29	0	0	6	11	0	12	9	0	4	20	48%	.346	12	1.08	1.50	1.47	2.25	7.5	0.0	3.0	11.3	4.3	0.83
2007	FLO	MLB	29	5	0	0	62	0	61²	53	5	24	74	45%	.308	23	1.25	3.65	2.87	3.57	7.0	0.7	3.0	9.3	13.5	1.23
2008	FLO	MLB	30	4	2	0	46	0	46²	46	4	20	43	30%	.318	0	1.41	4.24	4.15	4.80	9.4	0.8	3.4	7.2	3.5	0.39
2009	SFN	MLB	31	3	3	0	44	0	56²	47	7	27	36	46%	.242	-11	1.31	3.18	4.95	3.23	8.1	1.2	3.8	5.0	13.7	0.43
2010	LAN	MLB	32	3	3	1	56	0	55²	55	7	24	49	40%	.307	-1	1.41	4.31	4.07	4.66	8.9	1.0	3.7	7.3	5.2	0.60

Breakout: 18% Improve: 41% Collapse: 24% Attrition: 13%   MLB: 89%   Comparables: Mike Trombley, Joe Boever, Steve Bedrosian, Masafumi Hirai

The illustrated man's latest journey was back to the Bay Area, as the well-traveled former A's farmhand was given a nonroster invite to be part of Sabean's bullpen makeover. The multiply tattooed Miller won a job and earned his keep early, doing his usual situational shut-down work against right-handers, albeit usually with the team trailing. Elbow problems in August derailed and then ended his season, but one quick cleanup surgery later, and he's back on the road, headed for the Dodgers on another nonroster invitation. He will be a tougher sell in a more crowded pen, but don't be surprised if one of the game's great survivors slips back into the picture.

Brad Penny

Bats: R   Throws: R   Height: 6' 4"   Weight: 260   Born: May 24, 1978   Age: 32

YEAR	TEAM	LVL	AGE	W	L	SV	G	GS	IP	H	HR	BB	SO	GB%	BABIP	STUFF	WHIP	ERA	SIERA	DERA	EqH9	EqHR9	EqBB9	EqSO9	VORP	SN/WX
2007	LAN	MLB	29	16	4	0	33	33	208	199	9	73	135	55%	.295	22	1.31	3.03	4.49	3.14	8.4	0.4	2.9	5.3	53.1	7.43
2008	LAN	MLB	30	6	9	0	19	17	94²	112	13	42	51	58%	.312	-25	1.63	6.27	5.04	6.58	11.0	1.5	3.5	4.1	-11.0	0.36
2009	BOS	MLB	31	7	8	0	24	24	131²	160	17	42	89	46%	.327	5	1.53	5.61	4.54	5.23	9.8	0.8	2.4	5.4	4.1	1.32
2009	SFN	MLB	31	4	1	0	6	6	41²	31	5	9	20	57%	.205	6	0.96	2.59	4.59	2.99	7.1	1.1	1.8	3.8	11.4	1.77
2010	SLN	MLB	32	8	10	0	29	28	149²	160	16	57	90	52%	.304	-1	1.45	4.48	4.79	4.82	9.5	1.0	3.1	4.9	11.3	2.23

Breakout: 1% Improve: 43% Collapse: 13% Attrition: 20%   MLB: 92%   Comparables: Rolando Arrojo, Doc Medich, Dave Burba, Kevin Appier

Following the timeless advice to see a Penny and pick it up, the Giants added the veteran after his Boston run had met a necessarily squalid end. Handled carefully by the Sox, he demonstrated how slender the margins can be, managing a dozen quality starts through six innings in his 24 turns (against five "disaster starts," more runs allowed than innings pitched), and not once completing seven innings or having an especially good game. With the Giants, he threw seven or more innings in five of six games against some weak lineups in increasingly meaningless contests. If he had signed anywhere but with the Cardinals (for $7.5 million), you could be dubious about his future, but the expectation is that Dave Duncan will initiate him into whatever mysteries are necessary to fool enough of the people some of the time. Otherwise, the indicators aren't good.

Kevin Pucetas

Bats: R   Throws: R   Height: 6' 4"   Weight: 225   Born: November 27, 1984   Age: 25

YEAR	TEAM	LVL	AGE	W	L	SV	G	GS	IP	H	HR	BB	SO	GB%	BABIP	STUFF	WHIP	ERA	SIERA	DERA	EqH9	EqHR9	EqBB9	EqSO9	VORP	SN/WX
2007	AUG	A	22	15	4	1	27	23	145¹	124	7	21	104	52%	.267	4	1.00	1.86	3.69	3.78	9.4	1.3	1.9	3.9	25.8	1.97
2008	SJO	A+	23	10	2	0	24	24	125¹	115	6	27	102	52%	.301	-10	1.13	3.02	3.55	4.82	10.0	1.5	2.7	4.6	8.6	1.53
2009	FRE	AAA	24	10	6	0	28	28	159	173	15	50	96	48%	.303	-11	1.40	5.04	4.69	5.62	10.1	1.3	2.9	4.2	-2.1	0.17
2010	SFN	MLB	25	6	8	0	31	24	129	144	17	45	69	47%	.304	-10	1.46	4.91	5.01	5.27	10.0	1.2	3.0	4.4	3.2	2.73

Breakout: 13%   Improve: 50%   Collapse: 15%   Attrition: 22%   MLB: 15%   Comparables: Kennie Steenstra, Charles Scott, Randy Phillips, Mike Parisi

The Giants can get aggressive with promotion schedules, and Pucetas was one of the beneficiaries. Last year, the finesse right-hander was pushed up to Triple-A, skipping the Eastern League, and for the first four months, it looked good, as he managed 14 quality starts through his first 21. Unfortunately, there was a fifth month to go, and he finished July with three consecutive 100-pitch games. He got mauled in his final seven turns, giving up 43 runs in 31 innings pitched. Command of a fine curve and change gets his pedestrian fastball to play up, but he was fifth starter material before this bad patch, and that's still his best-case scenario.

Sergio Romo

Bats: R   Throws: R   Height: 5' 11"   Weight: 190   Born: March 4, 1983   Age: 27

YEAR	TEAM	LVL	AGE	W	L	SV	G	GS	IP	H	HR	BB	SO	GB%	BABIP	STUFF	WHIP	ERA	SIERA	DERA	EqH9	EqHR9	EqBB9	EqSO9	VORP	SN/WX
2007	SJO	A+	24	6	2	9	41	0	66¹	35	4	15	106	36%	.256	19	0.75	1.36	0.79	2.46	7.2	1.5	2.5	9.5	20.4	2.29
2008	NRW	AA	25	1	3	11	24	0	27	22	1	7	30	33%	.309	-1	1.07	4.00	2.70	6.39	9.1	1.1	2.6	7.3	-2.4	0.44
2008	SFN	MLB	25	3	1	0	29	0	34	16	3	8	33	32%	.157	18	0.71	2.12	3.07	3.34	4.1	0.8	1.8	7.2	8.4	1.91
2009	SFN	MLB	26	5	2	2	45	0	34	30	1	11	41	33%	.326	20	1.21	3.97	2.72	4.01	8.6	0.3	2.4	9.1	5.6	1.94
2010	SFN	MLB	27	4	3	7	60	0	62	54	6	21	58	37%	.291	11	1.21	3.49	3.55	3.76	7.7	0.9	2.9	7.8	12.0	2.33

Breakout: 14%   Improve: 35%   Collapse: 30%   Attrition: 10%   MLB: 59%   Comparables: Ramon Ramirez, Mark Huismann, Scott Strickland, Darren Holmes

The man of a thousand pitches, master of deception, got a late start on the season, thanks to a sprained elbow, only joining the big-league staff just before the calendar flipped over to June. He wasn't overpowering as much as just difficult to anticipate, and Bochy generally used him as a quick drop-in, drop-out set-up man, usually with the bases empty, usually with the lead, and almost always before or after Affeldt down the stretch. It wasn't your classic lefty/righty set-up combo—a big power ground-ball lefty, a short finesse righty—but it worked in a way that suggests bullpens don't always have to be staffed with certain archetypical relievers.

Dan Runzler

Bats: L   Throws: L   Height: 6' 4"   Weight: 215   Born: March 30, 1985   Age: 25

YEAR	TEAM	LVL	AGE	W	L	SV	G	GS	IP	H	HR	BB	SO	GB%	BABIP	STUFF	WHIP	ERA	SIERA	DERA	EqH9	EqHR9	EqBB9	EqSO9	VORP	SN/WX
2007	GIA	Rk	22	1	2	4	15	0	18¹	15	1	6	24	76%	.333	-3	1.15	3.44	2.29	6.03	12.1	2.9	4.0	6.3	-0.9	-0.24
2008	AUG	A	23	0	1	0	20	0	24²	25	2	19	26	56%	.338	-14	1.78	5.47	4.25	9.14	12.0	2.1	9.1	5.8	-8.8	-0.64
2008	SLO	A-	23	0	1	0	27	0	30	19	1	21	43	65%	.295	10	1.33	2.10	2.86	3.67	8.3	1.7	6.7	8.0	5.5	0.43
2009	AUG	A	24	1	1	11	19	0	26¹	8	0	13	45	75%	.195	23	0.80	0.68	1.68	1.74	5.4	1.2	6.2	10.0	9.8	0.82
2009	SJO	A+	24	1	0	5	19	0	21¹	8	1	4	26	54%	.140	1	0.56	0.84	2.09	2.53	5.1	1.3	2.1	5.9	7.0	0.93
2009	SFN	MLB	24	0	0	0	11	0	8²	6	1	5	11	46%	.250	9	1.27	1.04	3.23	1.04	7.3	1.0	4.2	9.3	4.3	0.37
2010	SFN	MLB	25	2	4	5	54	0	56¹	55	7	34	49	61%	.305	-8	1.59	5.09	4.36	5.40	8.7	1.2	5.3	7.1	0.6	1.87

Breakout: 20%   Improve: 47%   Collapse: 23%   Attrition: 10%   MLB: 100%   Comparables: Brian Partenheimer, Greg Becker, Mark Tranbarger, Al Osuna

It's sort of a foolish exercise to talk about situational relief prospects, and Runzler is a good example of why. A ninth-round pick from UC Riverside in '07, Runzler had control issues on mid-90s heat. The problems didn't seem as though they were just going to go away ... until they did, at which point he was on a rapid tour of the system, shooting up from the lowest full-season affiliate through every stop before arriving in the majors in September. Along the way, he held minor-league lefties to .114/.205/.127 while striking them out 41 percent of the time, and he was no less effective against big-leaguers. The one extra-base hit he allowed to lefties at any level was in his first game of the year (Sean Ratliff of Savannah); nobody scored. So just like that, the Giants have an excellent second lefty to back Affeldt, and the help effectively arrived out of the uttermost depths of a farm system.

Jonathan Sanchez

Bats: L   Throws: L   Height: 6' 2"   Weight: 190   Born: November 19, 1982   Age: 27

YEAR	TEAM	LVL	AGE	W	L	SV	G	GS	IP	H	HR	BB	SO	GB%	BABIP	STUFF	WHIP	ERA	SIERA	DERA	EqH9	EqHR9	EqBB9	EqSO9	VORP	SN/WX
2007	FRE	AAA	24	0	0	0	6	3	20²	15	0	8	27	40%	.306	20	1.11	2.18	2.45	2.70	7.2	0.4	3.6	9.4	6.2	0.90
2007	SFN	MLB	24	1	5	0	33	4	52	57	8	28	62	45%	.363	7	1.63	5.88	3.46	5.42	10.1	1.4	4.4	9.9	0.5	0.43
2008	SFN	MLB	25	9	12	0	29	29	158	154	14	75	157	48%	.317	18	1.45	5.01	3.80	4.84	8.8	0.8	3.7	7.6	11.4	2.80
2009	SFN	MLB	26	8	12	0	32	29	163¹	135	19	88	177	46%	.276	18	1.37	4.24	3.67	4.53	8.1	1.0	4.1	8.3	17.5	2.70
2010	SFN	MLB	27	8	8	0	37	27	148¹	143	17	66	139	48%	.309	15	1.41	4.29	3.85	4.57	8.6	1.0	3.8	7.8	15.3	1.94

Breakout: 8%   Improve: 52%   Collapse: 5%   Attrition: 10%   MLB: 95%   Comparables: Ken Kravec, Bob Ojeda, Pete Richert, Kei Igawa

The frustration with Sanchez is sort of like the Bay Area's answer to the Oliver Perez problem. Is the real problem one of expectations, or inconsistency? Broadly speaking, he appeared to make little or no real progress from his 2008 season, struggling with his command. He can get truly hammered when he falls behind, and he struggles in his second and third passes through a lineup, an ugly combination for a starting pitcher that encourages Bochy to make quick hooks. However, Sanchez's redemptive no-hitter in July against the Padres fended off a challenge to his job security, and his next 10 starts gave a taste of the Perez-like possibilities: six quality starts, 75 strikeouts against 27 unintentional walks in 59 ⅔ innings pitched. Had he turned the corner? In his last five turns, he failed to get out of the sixth inning and allowed 36 baserunners and six homers in 25 innings pitched. If that's a corner turned, it's because he's just going around the same block, over and over.

Ben Snyder

Bats: L   Throws: L   Height: 6' 2"   Weight: 224   Born: July 20, 1985   Age: 24

YEAR	TEAM	LVL	AGE	W	L	SV	G	GS	IP	H	HR	BB	SO	GB%	BABIP	STUFF	WHIP	ERA	SIERA	DERA	EqH9	EqHR9	EqBB9	EqSO9	VORP	SN/WX
2007	AUG	A	21	16	5	1	28	25	151	128	12	32	145	46%	.276	16	1.06	2.09	3.10	4.24	9.7	1.7	2.6	5.6	19.6	1.72
2008	SJO	A+	22	8	3	0	15	14	85²	79	2	18	73	49%	.308	12	1.13	2.00	3.42	3.73	9.8	1.0	2.5	4.8	15.4	1.66
2008	NRW	AA	22	1	6	0	13	12	61²	77	9	23	44	40%	.337	-33	1.62	5.98	4.63	7.83	13.9	3.2	3.7	4.3	-14.6	-1.06
2009	NRW	AA	23	4	4	1	34	5	97	82	4	38	86	37%	.281	-9	1.24	2.88	4.02	4.66	9.2	1.3	3.7	5.4	8.5	1.20
2010	TEX	MLB	24	4	7	0	29	14	96	114	16	42	60	35%	.318	-12	1.62	5.65	5.23	5.62	10.3	1.4	3.5	5.4	-1.3	2.09

Breakout: 13%   Improve: 47%   Collapse: 11%   Attrition: 18%   MLB: 20%   Comparables: Ben Van Ryn, Bryan Harris, Neil Weber, Kurt Birkins

Though he was not on most prospect radars before last season, Snyder's complete dominance of lefty hitters in Double-A put him there. He held them to .146/.198/.197, striking them out in 33 percent of their plate appearances, and with a blend of some deception, a good fastball, and an effective breaking pitch, he could be a big-league LOOGY right now. That's certainly what the Rangers think, having added him via the Rule 5 draft (using the Orioles' pick as part of the Millwood trade). Snyder will be given every opportunity to stick; used carefully, he should be able to handle it.

Henry Sosa

Bats: R   Throws: R   Height: 6' 2"   Weight: 195   Born: July 28, 1985   Age: 24

YEAR	TEAM	LVL	AGE	W	L	SV	G	GS	IP	H	HR	BB	SO	GB%	BABIP	STUFF	WHIP	ERA	SIERA	DERA	EqH9	EqHR9	EqBB9	EqSO9	VORP	SN/WX
2007	AUG	A	21	6	0	1	13	10	62	30	2	25	61	41%	.192	25	0.89	0.73	3.38	2.16	6.2	1.1	4.3	5.9	20.9	2.02
2007	SJO	A+	21	5	5	0	14	14	63²	66	8	36	78	43%	.343	-9	1.60	4.38	3.45	6.25	12.1	2.7	5.5	7.0	-4.9	0.22
2008	SJO	A+	22	3	4	0	12	12	56¹	62	6	18	58	42%	.354	-12	1.42	4.31	3.29	6.16	12.9	2.7	3.8	6.2	-3.6	0.25
2009	NRW	AA	23	6	0	0	14	14	72¹	61	4	25	44	35%	.254	-12	1.19	2.36	4.97	4.06	9.2	1.6	3.3	3.6	10.9	1.04
2010	SFN	MLB	24	3	6	0	27	12	79¹	91	12	42	57	36%	.323	-12	1.67	5.71	5.07	6.05	10.1	1.4	4.5	5.9	-4.9	2.10

Breakout: 19%   Improve: 53%   Collapse: 23%   Attrition: 13%   MLB: 6%   Comparables: Jose Melendez, Colby Miller, Taylor Buchholz, Eric Stone

Sosa keeps making incremental progress toward top prospect status, but combines that and his mid-90s heat with a variety of nagging concerns. He has lost considerable time to injuries the last couple of seasons, but no major, arm-opened-up cut jobs: a knee and a strained pectoral muscle in '08, and an upper back strain in '09 eventually divined from an initially labeled case of arm fatigue. The time lost has kept his off-speed stuff from developing as quickly as the Giants might wish, which is what will make the difference in making up lost ground in his strikeout rate. He's supposed to be fine for '10, but for now, he's a promising arm longer on promises made than promises kept.

Merkin Valdez

Bats: R   Throws: R   Height: 6' 5"   Weight: 230   Born: November 10, 1981   Age: 28

YEAR	TEAM	LVL	AGE	W	L	SV	G	GS	IP	H	HR	BB	SO	GB%	BABIP	STUFF	WHIP	ERA	SIERA	DERA	EqH9	EqHR9	EqBB9	EqSO9	VORP	SN/WX
2008	SFN	MLB	26	1	0	0	17	1	16	14	1	7	13	49%	.283	-1	1.31	1.69	4.25	2.87	8.0	0.6	3.4	6.3	4.6	0.67
2009	SFN	MLB	27	2	1	0	48	0	49¹	57	5	28	38	53%	.338	-16	1.72	5.66	4.72	5.99	11.2	1.0	4.6	6.1	-2.6	-0.87
2010	SFN	MLB	28	2	4	0	48	0	48²	59	6	23	33	46%	.339	-16	1.68	5.64	4.85	6.02	10.7	1.1	4.0	5.7	-2.8	-0.05

Breakout: 18%   Improve: 44%   Collapse: 26%   Attrition: 5%   MLB: 80%   Comparables: Jared Burton, Bob James, Bill Dawley, Toby Borland

For years, the Giants have been waiting for the big Dominican flamethrower to be healthy enough to regularly pour gas in the big leagues, and at long last, he was. The result was self-inflicted napalm, as Valdez struggled to find the strike zone while increasingly getting shunted off to lost causes, appearing in just four Giants wins in his 26 appearances during the season's final three months, and surrendering 24 runs in 26 ⅓ innings pitched. He's out of options, so he either makes the team or visits the waiver wire, and anyone who can dial high-90s heat as often as Valdez does will get claimed. If he's still a Giant by the time you read this, the danger is that he'll be kicked to the end of the pen and stay as stale and ineffective as he was in the second half. He needs to pitch, so something's gotta give.

Brian Wilson

Bats: R   Throws: R   Height: 6' 1"   Weight: 195   Born: March 16, 1982   Age: 28

YEAR	TEAM	LVL	AGE	W	L	SV	G	GS	IP	H	HR	BB	SO	GB%	BABIP	STUFF	WHIP	ERA	SIERA	DERA	EqH9	EqHR9	EqBB9	EqSO9	VORP	SN/WX
2007	FRE	AAA	25	1	2	11	31	0	34¹	24	0	24	37	50%	.270	10	1.40	2.10	4.08	3.74	7.0	0.5	6.1	7.5	6.6	1.59
2007	SFN	MLB	25	1	2	6	24	0	23²	16	1	7	18	59%	.227	8	0.97	2.28	3.84	2.31	6.2	0.4	2.3	6.2	8.3	1.79
2008	SFN	MLB	26	3	2	41	63	0	62¹	62	7	28	67	58%	.325	6	1.44	4.62	3.45	4.38	9.0	1.0	3.5	8.3	7.7	3.46
2009	SFN	MLB	27	5	6	38	68	0	72¹	60	3	27	83	52%	.302	23	1.20	2.74	2.99	3.45	8.0	0.4	2.9	8.8	16.3	3.35
2010	SFN	MLB	28	4	4	31	65	0	64¹	60	6	27	57	53%	.305	3	1.36	4.10	3.89	4.45	8.6	0.9	3.6	7.4	7.5	2.47

Breakout: 13%   Improve: 41%   Collapse: 28%   Attrition: 9%   MLB: 91%   Comparables: Bill Campbell, Jack Baldschun, Dave Schmidt, Ricky Bottalico

In most respects, Wilson enjoyed a better second season than his first full year wearing the closer's cape, at least as far as his rate stats. Combine that with reliable mid-90s velocity, the durability to come into games earlier than the ninth, and a slightly better ground-ball rate than most of his save-generating peers, and he's a fine fireman. Nevertheless, a slightly higher ratio of blown save opportunities kept all of that goodness from showing up in either his saves tally or the WXRL data.

Barry Zito

Bats: L   Throws: L   Height: 6' 4"   Weight: 205   Born: May 13, 1978   Age: 32

YEAR	TEAM	LVL	AGE	W	L	SV	G	GS	IP	H	HR	BB	SO	GB%	BABIP	STUFF	WHIP	ERA	SIERA	DERA	EqH9	EqHR9	EqBB9	EqSO9	VORP	SN/WX
2007	SFN	MLB	29	11	13	0	34	33	196²	182	24	83	131	47%	.260	7	1.35	4.53	4.75	4.53	8.0	1.0	3.4	5.3	21.4	4.35
2008	SFN	MLB	30	10	17	0	32	32	180	186	16	102	120	38%	.295	3	1.60	5.15	5.32	5.40	9.0	0.7	4.4	5.1	2.0	1.81
2009	SFN	MLB	31	10	13	0	33	33	192	179	21	81	154	45%	.285	9	1.35	4.03	4.27	4.20	9.1	1.0	3.3	6.3	26.8	4.47
2010	SFN	MLB	32	9	11	0	32	32	175	180	20	77	110	43%	.296	0	1.47	4.59	4.97	4.90	9.2	1.0	3.8	5.2	11.7	2.19

Breakout: 4%   Improve: 42%   Collapse: 17%   Attrition: 15%   MLB: 98%   Comparables: Doug Davis, Jim Deshaies, Jim Kaat, Kirk Rueter

Zito's re-achievement of mediocrity came with all sorts of nice little side benefits: his best walk rate as a Giant, his highest strikeout rate since his early Cy-winning days, with symptoms like achieving a career high in first-pitch strikes and getting out ahead of people, all while showing better velocity. That said, he wasn't getting people to swing and miss more often; he just got a higher percentage of strikes looking. We'll see if NL batters get used to this more efficient Zito, but his second half was stronger than his first. If he keeps it up, he might at least distract people from a compensation package that makes him an honorary investment banker. At least he has mastery of all the odds and ends you like to find in a fourth starter, holding runners well and even bunting effectively.

LINEOUTS

Hitters

PLAYER	TEAM	LVL	AGE	PA	R	2B	3B	HR	RBI	BB	SO	SB-CS	EqBRR	AVG/OBP/SLG	EqAVG/EqOBP/EqSLG	EqA	VORP	WARP
SS E. Adrianza#	AUG	A	19	448	54	15	3	2	46	42	66	7-1	0.7	.258/.333/.327	.220/.282/.280	.203	-6.9	-2.5
INF R. Aurilia	SFN	MLB	37	133	10	2	0	2	16	8	24	0-0	-1.1	.213/.256/.279	.215/.256/.281	.188	-8.7	-0.6
SS B. Bocock	SJO	A+	24	430	56	25	2	3	48	36	96	6-7	-1.5	.241/.303/.339	.212/.259/.273	.185	-13.3	-1.3
	NRW	AA	24	88	9	1	0	0	3	12	20	2-3	-0.2	.171/.298/.186	.176/.279/.189	.174	-3.4	-0.7
2B B. Bond#	NRW	AA	23	531	93	21	5	1	33	67	69	13-15	0.9	.333/.429/.409	.327/.405/.404	.284	27.5	1.9
SS B. Crawford*	SJO	A+	22	119	21	2	2	6	17	10	32	2-4	-0.6	.371/.445/.600	.321/.378/.495	.292	8.9	0.9
	NRW	AA	22	423	38	26	2	4	31	20	100	11-7	-5.6	.258/.294/.365	.246/.276/.349	.217	-1.5	-0.7
CF D. Ford	SJO	A+	23	441	81	17	9	9	50	49	97	35-12	3.2	.300/.386/.463	.254/.323/.373	.248	6.3	1.9
3B C. Gillaspie*	SJO	A+	21	530	62	31	2	4	67	55	68	2-3	-5.2	.286/.364/.386	.264/.328/.339	.237	0.3	-1.5
CF F. Peguero	AUG	A	21	252	28	12	4	1	34	5	39	15-5	-0.3	.340/.359/.437	.289/.302/.376	.237	1.1	0.0
	SLO	A-	21	76	14	3	1	0	12	3	9	7-0	1.1	.394/.421/.465	.315/.329/.370	.252	1.0	0.3
1B B. Pill	NRW	AA	24	581	71	37	1	19	109	37	72	6-3	-0.2	.298/.348/.480	.296/.333/.460	.272	7.6	-0.6
C E. Whiteside	FRE	AAA	29	126	16	7	1	6	24	8	40	0-0	0.0	.241/.290/.474	.203/.248/.398	.219	0.2	0.1
	SFN	MLB	29	134	15	6	1	2	13	4	30	0-0	0.3	.228/.269/.339	.228/.269/.339	.210	-0.9	0.3
C J. Williams	NRW	AA	23	348	33	20	0	2	24	35	60	1-5	-3.2	.223/.316/.310	.232/.305/.316	.220	1.4	0.2

Ehire Adrianza gets touted for Gold Glove–level potential afield for his plus range at short, and he handled his full-season debut well, showing remarkable patience for a teen. ⌀ In his late-career incarnation as a weak-hitting reserve, **Rich Aurilia** has a name that almost perfectly captured his status as a rich auxiliary. ⌀ **Brian Bocock** is still going to be able to tell his children about the time when he was an Opening Day shortstop in the major leagues. ⌀ Missouri product **Brock Bond** doesn't field well, runs in ways you wish he wouldn't, and lacks power, but this kind of contact and patience while jumping to Double-A is worth noting. ⌀ **Brandon Crawford** was taken in the fourth round in '08 after showing strong-armed flash at short for UCLA, and he made a quick move up to Double-A in his full-season debut. ⌀ Former Brewers prospect **Darren Ford** repeated High-A in his age-23 season and finally made the 40-man in his fifth year as a pro because of those Rule 5 heebie-jeebies. ⌀ **Conor Gillaspie** wangled a September '08 call-up for signing at slot as the club's first-round pick that year and went back down to the Cal League with his first big-league hit already under his belt, but didn't do much there to suggest he'll get a second. ⌀ Dominican prospect **Francisco Peguero** has passed every challenge thrown at him so far, but he's a free-swinging tools guy who will need to stick in center or add power to become more than that. ⌀ Can we vote to make **Brett Pill** an honorary Waner? Merely OK power and an unintentional walk rate below five percent probably makes the question pointless. ⌀ Journeyman **Eli Whiteside** arrived in the general vicinity of the right place and right time to become the notional veteran caddy for Buster Posey; somebody's got to do it. ⌀ The Giants are hoping **Jackson Williams** can develop even enough offensively to be Posey's long-term backup, as he's among the minor leagues' top defensive catchers, throwing out better than 40 percent of stolen-base attempts.

Pitchers

PLAYER	TEAM	LVL	AGE	W	L	SV	IP	H	HR	BB	SO	GB%	BABIP	STUFF	WHIP	ERA	SIERA	DERA	EqH9	EqHR9	EqBB9	EqSO9	VORP
C. Clark*	SJO	A+	24	16	2	0	147²	131	19	36	135	43%	.276	-48	1.13	2.86	3.33	5.01	11.2	3.2	3.2	4.7	7.1
S. Edlefsen	SJO	A+	24	1	1	7	28	15	1	13	40	61%	.233	3	1.00	0.96	2.36	2.60	7.3	1.4	5.2	7.6	8.4
—	NRW	AA	24	2	0	0	11¹	10	1	8	8	61%	.290	-11	1.59	3.18	4.94	4.66	11.2	2.8	7.4	4.7	0.9
—	FRE	AAA	24	5	0	2	30	23	2	16	24	63%	.250	-5	1.30	2.40	4.27	3.10	7.4	0.9	4.7	5.6	7.7
A. King*	AUG	A	20	7	6	0	104²	90	9	52	88	40%	.276	-18	1.36	3.70	4.37	7.14	10.4	2.4	6.4	4.2	-16.8
O. Matos	FRE	AAA	24	3	3	2	54¹	56	7	13	48	34%	.304	-8	1.27	3.48	3.66	4.16	9.7	1.7	2.4	6.3	7.9
—	SFN	MLB	24	0	0	0	6	11	2	1	5	—	.391	-15	2.00	9.00	4.74	9.95	15.6	2.8	1.4	5.7	-3.1
D. Otero	NRW	AA	24	0	3	19	39	40	0	10	31	66%	.333	-7	1.28	1.15	3.61	2.50	10.8	0.5	2.8	5.0	12.0
J. Paterson*	NRW	AA	23	5	6	10	69	47	3	24	69	54%	.251	0	1.03	1.96	3.24	3.53	7.9	1.3	3.4	6.4	13.9
R. Sadowski	FRE	AAA	26	6	3	0	89¹	84	14	43	73	59%	.267	-15	1.42	5.04	4.24	5.71	8.8	1.9	4.3	5.7	-2.0
—	SFN	MLB	26	2	4	0	28¹	28	2	17	17	55%	.286	-5	1.59	4.45	5.24	4.82	9.3	0.6	4.5	4.5	2.1
E. Surkamp*	AUG	A	21	11	5	0	131	129	6	39	169	46%	.369	-1	1.28	3.30	2.40	6.14	12.1	1.8	4.3	7.3	-8.0
C. Tanner*	SJO	A+	21	12	6	0	139¹	132	18	42	121	53%	.289	-34	1.25	3.17	3.65	6.05	11.9	3.2	3.8	4.4	-7.4

Craig Clark was the Cal League's Pitcher of the Year and struck out 10 consecutive batters, but he was an old strike-thrower carving up kids as if he was Freddy Krueger. ⊘ **Steve Edlefsen**'s sinker/slider combo works because of the nasty break on the slider and could propel him into set-up work. ⊘ **Aaron King** slings plus velocity for a lefty, but messy mechanics and dubious affinity for any reliable breaking stuff are hampering his development. ⊘ **Noah Lowry**'s latest comeback attempt was stalled by issues with both major joints and surgery to remove a rib; his return somewhere with somebody isn't quite up there with restoring the czars, but it's not far off. ⊘ **Osiris Matos** hopes to keep out of Set's clutches by throwing enough mid-90s heaters to wind up in the back end of a bullpen, but in the absence of reliable off-speed stuff, he gets predictable with it. ⊘ The latest sleight-of-hand reliever from the farm might be **Dan Otero**, at least if he can keep hitting his spots. ⊘ It may not chap **Joe Paterson**'s hide to have seen Runzler rocket past, but he was dominant against lefties (.112/.194/.147) with slower stuff and figures to get hocked up into somebody's LOOGY role someday. ⊘ **Ryan Sadowski**'s big-league adventure involved two nice starts to prove that strike-throwers can surprise people, then four that showed you need more than that to stick; given an off-season choice between the Astros and Korea, he chose overseas adventure and guaranteed cash. ⊘ **Eric Surkamp** managed to finish strong as a strike-throwing southpaw who uses his height to gain leverage on a mediocre assortment. ⊘ Aussie southpaw **Clayton Tanner** has done well with a modest strike-thrower's assortment so far, making up with aptitude what he lacks in upside. ⊘ Athletic high-school right-hander **Zach Wheeler** was the Giants' first-round pick last June, signing for $3.3 million, but too late to pitch. His fastball is consistently in the low 90s (and touches 95), and his mechanics seem sound, but his off-speed stuff needs work.

MANAGER: BRUCE BOCHY

YEAR	TEAM	W-L	Pythag +/−	Avg PC	100+ P	120+ P	QS	BQS	REL	REL w Zero R	IBB	Subs	PH	PH Avg	PH HR	SB2	CS2	SB3	CS3	SAC Att	SAC %	POS SAC	Squeeze	Swing	In Play
2007	SFN	71-91	-6	98.8	78	8	78	6	495	310	41	83	261	.268	5	106	29	13	2	94	71.3%	31	4	145	115
2008	SFN	72-90	5	99.9	91	8	80	8	478	287	59	60	273	.239	3	99	41	6	1	97	58.8%	26	3	161	133
2009	SFN	88-74	1	97.6	74	5	81	5	457	292	49	76	231	.250	2	69	27	8	0	101	66.3%	18	0	118	99

As a skipper, Bochy exhibits a lack of extremes. This moderation proved commendable, particularly on offense, where beyond a moderate interest in the hit-and-run, he avoided making matters worse with too much in the way of one-run gambits. Instead, he played the hand he was dealt, mixing and matching and substituting in the lineup with a frequency only exceeded by Tony La Russa. This was a tactical response to his roster, but also a symptom of a shortage of enough everyday regulars to rely on. As far as starting pitcher workloads, the freak-out of '08 over Lincecum's load seems to have blown over and was perhaps more a symptom of the increasing lack of pitcher-abuse cases to freak out over these days. Bochy is a little fonder of the intentional walk than most, but in an era where bullpen management is probably the one place where managers can express some individuality, the results he achieved with an odd assortment of talent produced a much improved pen.

Seattle Mariners

No team in baseball last season improved its win total from the year previous by as many games as the Mariners did. The 2008 team won only 61 games, but in 2009, it climbed all the way up to 85 wins. This was no accident, as the team's new general manager, Jack Zduriencik, walked into his first year running the team with a definite strategy for how to improve his baseball team. His plan was to improve his team's defense, and he certainly did so, as can be seen by any number of measures.

The state of defensive statistics available today has expanded radically, giving us several options to measure player and team performance. Not one of them, however, can boast the same sort of accuracy achieved with the most advanced hitting or pitching metrics. Understanding that they all have something to say about defensive performance and rather than relying too heavily on any of them, we'll embrace the wisdom of the statistical crowd, using a variety of metrics to evaluate where the Mariners' defense ranked in 2009.

Let's review the fielding stats we employ in Table 1. First, there's Baseball Info Solutions' Total Runs Saved (TRS), which looks at batted balls with similar trajectories and locations and uses them to compare fielders at different positions. Second, we've got Mitchel Lichtman's Ultimate Zone Rating (UZR), which uses a similar system to that used by Baseball Info Solutions. Third is BP's Park-Adjusted Defensive Efficiency (PADE), which estimates a team's ability to prevent batters from reaching base on balls in play, expressed as a percentage difference above or below average, while adjusting for the difficulty of doing so in a team's home environment. Fourth and last is something that Matt Swartz of Baseball Prospectus worked up on the BP site last fall: Park-

Adjusted Slugging on Balls in Play (PASBP), which does something similar to PADE, but just with power on balls in play.

Reviewing where the 30 teams ranked in these respective metrics, we can come up with some broad conclusions, but there seems to be very little doubt about the evaluation of the Mariners' defense. By TRS, no one even came close to their success, and they led the league in UZR as well. By PADE, they're atop the American League and third overall, and by PASBP, they are first again. Taken together, this quartet suggests an important aspect of why the Mariners were successful: they did not simply prevent batters from reaching base, but also prevented them from getting extra-base hits. When a ball gets by a middle infielder, it may turn into a single, but when it gets by an outfielder or a third baseman, it could be a double or a triple. With strong defenders in the Mariners' outfield and at third base all year long, opposing teams had a difficult time moving into scoring position against the Mariners. Playing strong outfield defense is an area of particular importance to the Mariners because of Safeco Field. A strong defense in a smaller park will not necessarily record that many more outs than an average defense will, but with so many fly balls that could land in the outfield for extra-base hits, replacing those hits with outs was essential to Seattle's radically improved fortunes.

To achieve this product of his first offseason's efforts, Zduriencik significantly changed his roster in very little time, adding, through trades and free agency, players that he and his staff identified as undervalued. This certainly seems to be successful thus far, as the Mariners

MARINERS PROSPECTUS
2009 W-L: 85-77, 3rd in AL West

Pythag	83-79	7th
RS/G	4.0	14th
RA/G	4.3	1st
EqA	.246	14th
EqBRR	-1.7	7th
SNWP	.546	1st
WXRL	11.04	4th
FRAr	4.35	5th
DE	.712	1st
PADE	2.40	1st
Salary	$98.9	5th
Attend	2.2	7th

Ballpark: Safeco Field (3-yr. PF: 966). Hard on extra-base hits of every flavor, making P&D easier to achieve

2009: Jack Z.'s gets defensive and produces immediate results, but still just a short-stack bronze

2010: Fast-morphing M's add Figgins and Lee to put the division in reach

Action Items: Realizing win-now ambition by adding power at 1B, LF; sort out the pen and back end of the rotation

Table 1. Four Scoops of Fielding: 2009 Mariners Defensive Prowess in Four Flavors

Team	TRS	Rank	UZR	Rank	PADE	Rank	PASBP	Rank
Mariners	109	1	85.5	1	2.40	3	7.29	1
Angels	65	2	13.3	10	-0.92	17	-1.68	19
Rays	59	3	69.5	2	-0.51	15	0.28	11
Blue Jays	52	4	-33.3	25	-3.03	30	-4.99	23
Reds	49	5	52.6	3	0.64	6	3.35	5
Rangers	43	6	32.5	6	0.94	5	3.32	6
Tigers	39	7	43.6	5	0.02	10	1.33	7
Diamondbacks	33	8	21.6	9	-0.66	16	-0.94	16
Giants	33	9	51.2	4	2.98	1	7.16	2
Pirates	32	10	30.1	7	-1.37	22	-9.19	29
Dodgers	32	11	-0.1	13	2.55	2	3.99	4
Cardinals	30	12	-17.8	18	-0.21	11	-0.68	15
Mets	18	13	-47.3	29	-1.74	26	-5.88	26
Cubs	17	14	-19.8	21	2.26	4	5.93	3
Rockies	16	15	-14.0	15	0.48	7	0.72	8
Phillies	16	16	27.9	8	0.32	8	0.13	12
Braves	9	17	-18.8	20	-1.12	19	-5.74	24
Nationals	7	18	-26.7	24	-2.20	27	-9.42	30
Yankees	2	19	-18.5	19	-0.39	13	-2.74	20
Astros	-1	20	-17.7	17	-2.46	28	-7.73	28
Indians	-4	21	-33.5	26	-0.32	12	0.13	13
Padres	-5	22	-13.4	14	-1.69	25	-4.08	21
White Sox	-9	23	-35.6	27	-0.40	14	-0.42	14
Orioles	-11	24	-23.6	23	-1.28	20	-4.43	22
Athletics	-12	25	5.2	12	-2.86	29	-7.12	27
Brewers	-23	26	9.9	11	-1.57	23	-5.79	25
Marlins	-28	27	-20.5	22	0.23	9	0.43	9
Twins	-35	28	-37.3	28	-1.33	21	-1.15	17
Red Sox	-52	29	-16.3	16	-1.10	18	0.43	10
Royals	-64	30	-49.9	30	-1.69	24	-1.19	18

are now a young team that turns a lot of batted balls into outs and allows few extra-base hits or other hits. Ichiro Suzuki already provided excellent defense in right field. For center, the Mariners found Franklin Gutierrez under a seat cushion in Cleveland. After the trade and a move to center, he was revealed as perhaps the best outfield glove in baseball, complementing the Mariners' talented mainstay in right field. Depending on your metric, Gutierrez saved 31 more runs (TRS), 29 more runs (UZR), or 23 more runs (BP's Fielding Runs Above Average, or FRAA) than the average center fielder.

In left field, the Mariners struggled to find a bat that would stick, while they resorted to a variety of excellent defenders. Since Safeco is particularly deep in left, recording outs on fly balls headed that way is the difference between doubles and a lot of loud outs. For the first couple of months, Endy Chavez and Wladimir Balentien platooned in left; Chavez's season ended early in mid-June after he needed surgery to repair a knee torn up by a collision with shortstop Yuniesky Betancourt. Up until that point, he had provided as little with the bat as he usually has. He had, however, provided a lot on defense, adding between three and six runs of value, depending on the metric. Balentien was traded away at the end of July, but before this, he did save about five runs with his defense. With Chavez out for the season, the Mariners acquired Ryan Langerhans, another instance of their accepting weak offense in exchange for strong defense. Later in the year, 22-year-old Michael Saunders was called up to see what he could do, and he did little to improve matters on offense, but he saved between four and six runs on defense in just 35 games in left field. All in all, the Mariners' left fielders had saved anywhere from 17 runs (UZR), 12 (FRAA), or eight (TRS). Unfortunately, on offense, the left fielders managed a line of only .219/.276/ .333, a collective .226 EqA, and a VORP of about -27.6. If the Mariners are going to compete in 2010, they'll need to get at least replacement-level production out of left field, a position that teams counted on for the third-most offense in baseball last year, after first base and right field.

When Zduriencik inherited the GM position, Seattle's shortstop was Yuniesky Betancourt, a player with a reputation for being a pretty good defender. The reality, at least as far as it's reflected in the data we have available to us, decisively disagrees, with FRAA, UZR, and TRS all translating his performance in 2009 alone at -19 or worse. These were all near or at the bottom of the league, and Betancourt's purported virtue was his fielding. After Zduriencik traded him away to Kansas City, the Mariners acquired Jack Wilson from the Pirates for the express purpose of playing defense. Wilson's strong defensive reputation is one backed up by the numbers, with endorsements ranging from 27 TRS, 14 UZR combined across the Pirates and Mariners, and 8 FRAA. With an eye toward retaining that defensive value into the future, Zduriencik promptly negotiated a two-year, $10 million extension with Wilson, replacing the $8.4 million club option for 2010.

As a result of the improved defense, the pitching staff had some gaudy ERAs that were not reflective of their true skill level. Already benefiting from a pitcher's park, many Mariners pitchers were also helped out by the safe landing of many balls in play into somebody's leather. The Jarrod Washburn trade to the Tigers was a great example of the front office's identifying and capitalizing on this. Washburn was riding a 2.64 ERA, but with only 5.3 strikeouts per nine and 2.2 walks per nine with a 39 percent ground-ball rate at the time of the trade. His ERA was artificially low, thanks to a mixture of the Mariners' defense behind him and good luck to match: his BABIP at the time of the trade was only .242, low even for a defense-assisted Mariner. The Tigers flipped a couple of prospects over to the Mariners, while Washburn struggled through injuries as he was getting thrashed to the tune of a 7.33 ERA with the Tigers.

By the end of the year, the Mariners' roster bore only a passing resemblance to the one that Bill Basavi had left behind. While Zduriencik couldn't assemble his ideal defense all at once, within his first season he had aggressively targeted the best defenders he could acquire. Mariners pitching was still not amazing, but fielding a quality defense can make up for a lot of limitations. Given that the team improved by 24 wins, it might seem ungrateful to note the reason that the Mariners were not able to improve further: their offense. The Mariners were dead last in the American League in runs scored (by 46 runs) and barely a tick or two better than the Royals in EqA. Plus, Seattle's ambitions are in an entirely different class from Kansas City's.

There wasn't much reason to expect this to change with the players on hand, which is why Zduriencik has moved just as aggressively into the realm of acquiring additional talent in his second winter on the job as he did in the first. With Adrian Beltre departing via free agency, the GM signed the selective player this lineup so clearly lacked, adding Chone Figgins on a four-year, $36 million contract to provide not only better top-of-the-order value and speed, but also a defender with the gifts at the hot corner to keep the left side of the infield shut tight. To add even more OBP, but at considerably less expense, Zduriencik achieved a remarkable feat of roster transubstantiation, taking the inherited sunk cost of employing Carlos Silva's remaining two years and $25 million and repurposing it, swapping Silva and $9 million to the Cubs for mercurial Milton Bradley and the $21 million owed him. In this way, he sent the Cubs the $9 million split between those two seasons to take on the $21 million Bradley is owed over that same span of time. If you start from a position of seeing Silva's salary as money being burned, that's a net addition of just $5 million to the payroll over two years to add a player who, if he's healthy and in his happy place—admittedly both *huge* ifs—can be a major contributor, splitting time between left field and DH. It's far from

guaranteed, of course, but Bradley figures to be a far less prominent personality on a club crowded with stars like Ichiro, King Felix, and even the Kid (however gray Ken Griffey Jr. has gotten).

If Zduriencik merely opened his wallet to get Figgins and showed some creativity and creative accounting skills in unloading a Bavasi mistake (Silva) to add a Jim Hendry mistake (Bradley), then he achieved a general manager's sine qua non in acquiring the ace-level starter to pair with Felix Hernandez atop the rotation. Simply by keeping himself in the conversation as the Phillies tried to get Roy Halladay away from the Blue Jays, he managed to acquire one year of Cliff Lee for three of his predecessor's prospects. The trio—outfielder Tyson Gillies and right-handers Phillippe Aumont and J. C. Ramirez—may well end up having fine careers, but if any of them ever have a year as good as either of Lee's last two or upcoming one, it will be a shock. Lee is a seven- or eight-win player right now, one of the 10 best starting pitchers in the game, being paired up with one of the other 10. It doesn't get any more win-now than acquiring one year of Lee, because it gives you a pair of starters strong enough to contend with any opponent in a post-season series, not unlike the 1987 Twins of Blyleven and Viola, or the 2001 Diamondbacks with Schilling and the Big Unit. In execution, this is the pickup that Erik Bedard was supposed to be and wasn't.

Which puts Zduriencik somewhat in the same position that Bill Bavasi's last successor, Bill Stoneman, faced down in Anaheim when Bavasi was canned for expensive, inept team-building with the Angels after the '99 season. In three seasons, Stoneman had managed to salvage what he could from the wreckage and build a World Series winner in 2002. The Mariners aren't just a team being built to win the AL West during the one year Lee is under contract, or in the two seasons they have Hernandez under contract. Having already massively revamped the club's defense, and now with Figgins, Lee, and even Bradley in the fold and the threat, as we go to press, of further additions to come in the most exciting offseason in Mariners history, Zduriencik is gunning to beat Stoneman's three-year turnaround by a year. With the Angels looking as if they'll tumble from the heights of the AL West's short stack and the Rangers perhaps not yet ready, for the Mariners, the future is now.

HITTERS

Dustin Ackley — OF

Bats: L   Throws: R   Height: 6' 1"   Weight: 185   Born: February 26, 1988   Age: 22

YEAR	TEAM	LVL	AGE	PA	R	2B	3B	HR	RBI	BB	SO	SB	CS	EqBRR	AVG	OBP	SLG	EqAVG	EqOBP	EqSLG	EqA	VORP	WARP	DEFENSE
Did Not Play.																								
2010	SEA	AL	22	445	58	24	3	8	49	37	67	5	3	0.0	.296	.355	.431	.293	.351	.423	.270	18.3	2.0	—

Breakout: 17%   Improve: 49%   Collapse: 9%   Attrition: 6%   MLB: 13%   Comparables: Trey Beamon, Nick Markakis, Brandon Pico, Jon Hamilton

The second overall pick in the 2009 draft, Ackley has the ability to rocket through the system and to make his pro debut as early as this year. His combination of plate discipline, bat speed, and hand-eye coordination has scouts projecting him as a .300 hitter with a .400 on-base percentage annually, and you can throw plus-plus speed into the package as well. There is plenty of debate about his power, but given everything else he does well, power might just be gravy. Limited to first base in college because of arm problems, Ackley looked good in the outfield during his pro debut in the Arizona Fall League, and that's where his future lies.

Adrian Beltre — 3B

Bats: R   Throws: R   Height: 5' 11"   Weight: 225   Born: April 7, 1979   Age: 31

YEAR	TEAM	LVL	AGE	PA	R	2B	3B	HR	RBI	BB	SO	SB	CS	EqBRR	AVG	OBP	SLG	EqAVG	EqOBP	EqSLG	EqA	VORP	WARP	DEFENSE	
2007	SEA	MLB	28	639	87	41	2	26	99	38	104	14	2	-0.7	.276	.319	.482	.283	.327	.499	.279	28.7	3.1	145-3B	0
2008	SEA	MLB	29	612	74	29	1	25	77	50	90	8	2	-2.3	.266	.327	.457	.276	.337	.475	.278	26.6	3.8	136-3B	7
2009	SEA	MLB	30	477	54	27	0	8	44	19	74	13	2	1.5	.265	.304	.379	.272	.310	.382	.246	5.7	2.0	110-3B	11
2010	BOS	AL	31	499	58	27	1	17	62	34	79	9	3	-0.2	.274	.328	.446	.270	.325	.428	.257	11.1	1.5	115-3B	3

Breakout: 7%   Improve: 34%   Collapse: 17%   Attrition: 13%   MLB: 97%   Comparables: Ron Coomer, Shea Hillenbrand, Edgardo Alfonzo, Charlie Hayes

Beltre is an excellent defender and in most seasons an acceptable hitter, but he's not smart enough to wear a cup. The world found out more than it wanted to know about Beltre's privates when a bad-hop grounder, with almost Darwinian precision, scored a bull's-eye on August 12th. Yet, the testicular contusion that cost Beltre 18 games wasn't his most important injury of the season. That was the bone spurs in his left shoulder; they required surgery and not only required 30 games on the DL, but also sapped his power. Pitchers preyed on his weakened condition, challenging him, and his walk rate nearly went the way of his testicles. The Mariners signed Beltre as he came off an outlier of a peak that is as far off the beaten path of his career as Santo Domingo is from Samarkand. Because of this, he is perceived as a disappointment, and there is some truth in that, but it is also true that Safeco Field has a strong prejudice against right-handed hitters. In his four healthy years as a Mariner, Beltre hit .255/.312/.420 with a home run once every 26 at-bats at home, .276/.326/.485 with a home run every 24 at-bats on the road. That's not a huge difference, but it is a significant one, and had the Mariners played in a more equitable ballpark, or even a favorable one, the perception of Beltre might be very different, especially given just how valuable his fielding was to the ballclub. Beltre will never again finish second on an MVP ballot, but he's young enough to recapture some of his old luster playing in Fenway after signing a one-year, $10 million deal with the Red Sox.

Russell Branyan — 1B

Bats: L   Throws: R   Height: 6' 3"   Weight: 195   Born: December 19, 1975   Age: 34

YEAR	TEAM	LVL	AGE	PA	R	2B	3B	HR	RBI	BB	SO	SB	CS	EqBRR	AVG	OBP	SLG	EqAVG	EqOBP	EqSLG	EqA	VORP	WARP	DEFENSE			
2007	SDN	MLB	31	146	16	5	1	7	19	21	48	1	0	-1.2	.197	.322	.426	.215	.338	.471	.273	5.1	0.7	17-3B	4	9-LF	-3
2007	PHI	MLB	31	9	2	0	0	2	5	0	6	0	0	0.0	.222	.222	.889	.222	.222	.889	.320	0.9	0.1				
2007	SLN	MLB	31	39	4	0	0	1	2	7	15	0	0	-0.3	.188	.333	.281	.188	.333	.281	.234	-0.3	0.2	6-3B	2	1-1B	0
2008	NAS	AAA	32	179	24	15	0	12	36	25	49	4	1	0.4	.359	.453	.693	.310	.391	.551	.314	14.9	2.5	31-3B	6		
2008	MIL	MLB	32	152	24	8	0	12	20	19	42	1	0	0.9	.250	.342	.583	.258	.349	.606	.306	12.0	1.4	31-3B	1	3-1B	0
2009	SEA	MLB	33	505	64	21	1	31	76	58	149	2	0	-0.6	.251	.347	.520	.259	.354	.524	.296	21.1	2.8	115-1B	3		
2010	SEA	MLB	34	385	42	15	1	18	49	47	126	3	1	-0.1	.231	.334	.444	.228	.329	.429	.266	6.8	0.9	81-1B	1		

Breakout: 5%   Improve: 31%   Collapse: 19%   Attrition: 21%   MLB: 94%   Comparables: Babe Herman, Vic Wertz, Greg Brock, Paul Sorrento

At 33, Branyan got his first shot at regular playing time since 2002, long after baseball had seemingly dispensed with him as a platoon or reserve player, and a fringe one at that; the Brewers had let him spend a good portion of 2008 at Nashville, after all. It was the strikeouts, you see, the strikeouts! Baseball insiders and fans alike obsess over them like an Edger Allan Poe narrator who has just discovered a black cat with a third eye, and in Branyan's case, this prevented them from seeing that despite his limitations, he still had something to contribute. Branyan's uppercut swing produces home runs and strikeouts and almost nothing else, but he takes his share of walks and has hit into six fewer double plays in his major-league career than Miguel Tejada hit into in 2009 alone. Injuries have shortened his last two seasons, giving him a total of 657 plate appearances in 2008-2009, about one full season's worth. He has hit .250/.346/.535 with 43 home runs, 77 walks, and 191 strikeouts; if you can live with Mark Reynolds (.260/.349/.543 in '09), you can live with Branyan.

Mike Carp — 1B/LF — Bats: L — Throws: R — Height: 6' 2" — Weight: 215 — Born: June 30, 1986 — Age: 24

YEAR	TEAM	LVL	AGE	PA	R	2B	3B	HR	RBI	BB	SO	SB	CS	EqBRR	AVG	OBP	SLG	EqAVG	EqOBP	EqSLG	EqA	VORP	WARP	DEFENSE			
2007	BIN	AA	21	412	55	16	0	11	48	39	75	2	1	0.6	.251	.337	.387	.234	.306	.356	.234	-7.4	-0.6	95-1B	3		
2008	BIN	AA	22	566	67	29	1	17	72	79	88	1	2	-4.9	.299	.403	.471	.276	.364	.426	.276	16.8	1.2	56-1B	-5	49-LF	-2
2009	TAC	AAA	23	490	66	25	1	15	64	58	99	0	1	-2.3	.271	.372	.446	.257	.348	.418	.268	5.3	1.4	80-1B	5	12-LF	1
2009	SEA	MLB	23	65	7	3	1	1	5	8	10	0	0	0.7	.315	.415	.463	.333	.431	.481	.316	4.3	0.6	14-1B	1		
2010	SEA	MLB	24	529	63	23	1	17	63	57	109	1	2	-1.1	.265	.352	.427	.260	.345	.418	.268	9.9	1.2	108-1B	1		

Breakout: 18% Improve: 55% Collapse: 7% Attrition: 4%   MLB: 59%   Comparables: Dan Lewis, Adam LaRoche, Dan Johnson, Rod Brewer

While Carp acquitted himself quite nicely in his big-league debut, he's more of a .270-.280 type who can draw a decent number of walks and smack some doubles. While that's nice, it's not quite up to the standard you'd expect from a major-league first baseman, and Carp's limited athleticism restricts him to that position. He hits righties much better than lefties, so there could be some platoon possibilities in his future, but that's about it. The Mariners will need more than that in a lineup looking for power, and are pretending Casey Kotchman will give it to them.

Ezequiel Carrera — OF — Bats: L — Throws: L — Height: 5' 11" — Weight: 175 — Born: June 11, 1987 — Age: 23

YEAR	TEAM	LVL	AGE	PA	R	2B	3B	HR	RBI	BB	SO	SB	CS	EqBRR	AVG	OBP	SLG	EqAVG	EqOBP	EqSLG	EqA	VORP	WARP	DEFENSE			
2007	BRO	A-	20	77	11	2	0	0	6	4	13	6	1	1.6	.300	.347	.329	.278	.307	.306	.220	-1.7	0.2	8-RF	1	7-LF	1
2007	MTS	Rk	20	209	41	8	3	1	26	26	29	16	5	0.5	.341	.430	.436	.299	.367	.385	.266	7.2	1.0	43-CF	-2		
2008	SLU	A+	21	494	61	11	12	7	29	46	86	28	9	-0.4	.263	.344	.393	.239	.305	.361	.237	0.3	-0.7	94-CF	-6		
2009	WTN	AA	22	405	68	12	4	2	38	59	62	27	13	3.0	.337	.441	.416	.305	.392	.381	.278	17.1	0.8	51-CF	-1	32-LF	-9
2010	SEA	MLB	23	366	45	14	5	4	27	36	74	12	6	0.7	.260	.337	.371	.258	.333	.368	.249	6.8	0.6	74-CF	-2		

Breakout: 15% Improve: 43% Collapse: 18% Attrition: 13%   MLB: 5%   Comparables: Alexis Marte, Troy Thomas, Jason McFarlin, Tony Gwynn

A Venezuelan burner who led the Southern League in batting and on-base percentage, Carrera has no power and an arm than limits him to left, so he's a bench outfielder in the end. Nevertheless, speed, some range in a corner where the front office likes to see it, and a .467 OBP versus right-handed pitching in Double-A as a 22-year-old is worth keeping in mind.

Endy Chavez — OF — Bats: L — Throws: L — Height: 6' 0" — Weight: 170 — Born: February 7, 1978 — Age: 32

YEAR	TEAM	LVL	AGE	PA	R	2B	3B	HR	RBI	BB	SO	SB	CS	EqBRR	AVG	OBP	SLG	EqAVG	EqOBP	EqSLG	EqA	VORP	WARP	DEFENSE			
2007	NYN	MLB	29	165	20	7	2	1	17	9	16	5	2	1.5	.287	.325	.380	.305	.342	.397	.257	3.1	0.7	22-LF	0	11-RF	1
2008	NYN	MLB	30	298	30	10	2	1	12	17	22	6	1	2.1	.267	.308	.330	.275	.314	.337	.235	-2.4	1.7	44-RF	10	22-LF	7
2009	SEA	MLB	31	182	17	3	1	2	13	14	22	9	1	-0.1	.273	.328	.342	.281	.333	.350	.254	2.3	0.7	33-LF	3	8-CF	0
2010	SEA	MLB	32	211	25	9	1	2	16	18	25	5	2	0.5	.281	.341	.370	.277	.334	.368	.250	2.1	0.6	46-LF	3		

Breakout: 10% Improve: 33% Collapse: 17% Attrition: 21%   MLB: 90%   Comparables: Orlando Palmeiro, Greg Gross, Rick Leach, Delino DeShields

As the perception of defense has evolved in recent seasons, there has been a parallel rise in Chavez appreciation. Chavez emphasizes hitting the ball on the ground, but it's tough to make a living that way as one ages and speed ebbs; he doesn't hit the ball hard in enough other situations, nor is he patient enough, to have any offensive value. Still, he's been in some demand in recent years because of his ball-hawking abilities. He missed most of the 2009 season with a torn ACL and MCL after colliding with a firm and unyielding Betancourt. He's expected to recover in time for spring training, but if his speed in the outfield has been affected, then the one reason to tolerate his lack of bat will have vanished, soon to be followed by Endy himself.

Nick Franklin   SS
Bats: S   Throws: R   Height: 6' 1"   Weight: 170   Born: March 2, 1991   Age: 19

YEAR	TEAM	LVL	AGE	PA	R	2B	3B	HR	RBI	BB	SO	SB	CS	EqBRR	AVG	OBP	SLG	EqAVG	EqOBP	EqSLG	EqA	VORP	WARP	DEFENSE	
2009	MRN	Rk	18	44	6	2	0	1	4	1	6	0	0	-0.3	.302	.318	.419	.256	.273	.349	.212	-0.3	-0.3	7-SS	-1
2010	SEA	MLB	19	194	12	10	3	1	9	8	13	0	0	0.3	.245	.277	.344	.249	.281	.348	.207	-3.2	-0.8	10-SS	-4

Breakout: 65% Improve: 73% Collapse: 16% Attrition: 0%   MLB: 0%   Comparables: James Posillico, Glenn Williams, Apostol Garcia, Denio Gabriel

While it was no surprise to see Franklin selected as a supplemental first-rounder last June, it was a bit of a shock to see the Mariners go well over slot at $1.3 million to sign him. Speed and defense are the primary skills he brings to the table; offensively, he projects as a player with a decent batting average and not much else. Still, that's more than enough to be an everyday shortstop in the big leagues, and we live in a world in which there are fewer than 30 men who meet that description.

Tyson Gillies   CF
Bats: L   Throws: R   Height: 6' 2"   Weight: 190   Born: October 31, 1988   Age: 21

YEAR	TEAM	LVL	AGE	PA	R	2B	3B	HR	RBI	BB	SO	SB	CS	EqBRR	AVG	OBP	SLG	EqAVG	EqOBP	EqSLG	EqA	VORP	WARP	DEFENSE			
2007	MRN	Rk	18	101	20	3	2	0	6	6	23	9	6	1.0	.221	.337	.302	.191	.248	.266	.175	-6.5	-0.5	11-LF	2	8-RF	2
2008	HDS	A+	19	33	4	0	1	0	1	1	6	1	1	0.1	.233	.281	.300	.194	.242	.258	.163	-2.6	-0.2	3-RF	1		
2008	EVE	A-	19	242	36	6	5	2	22	35	46	24	7	2.0	.313	.439	.427	.269	.349	.363	.258	5.0	1.0	33-CF	4	11-LF	0
2009	HDS	A+	20	593	104	17	14	9	42	60	81	44	19	0.3	.341	.430	.486	.267	.340	.365	.252	11.8	2.3	123-CF	7		
2010	PHI	MLB	21	505	60	18	6	7	29	46	92	16	7	0.7	.263	.339	.374	.266	.340	.380	.252	11.1	1.6	100-CF	4		

Breakout: 34% Improve: 63% Collapse: 5% Attrition: 4%   MLB: 1%   Comparables: Trent Oeltjen, Brent Bowers, Jeff Clark, Cedric Hunter

The position player thrown in on the Cliff Lee deal, this Canadian flyer becomes a top outfield prospect in the Phillies' system almost by default. Squint, and you can see Brett Butler, because the positives from his first full season are clear: heaping helpings of speed and defense. The question is how much he'll lose by leaving the Cal League's bandboxes and making the move to Double-A. His walk rate of almost 9.4 percent was outstanding for someone so young in a High-A league, but his power was almost entirely a product of his home park; his road ISO was .094. Gillies' youth is his best armor against such considerations, but power is less critical to his game than how much of his OBP he retains against better pitching and how much of his batting average survives against better defenses at higher levels.

Ken Griffey   DH
Bats: L   Throws: L   Height: 6' 3"   Weight: 230   Born: November 21, 1969   Age: 40

YEAR	TEAM	LVL	AGE	PA	R	2B	3B	HR	RBI	BB	SO	SB	CS	EqBRR	AVG	OBP	SLG	EqAVG	EqOBP	EqSLG	EqA	VORP	WARP	DEFENSE	
2007	CIN	MLB	37	623	78	24	1	30	93	85	99	6	1	-4.7	.277	.372	.496	.273	.370	.485	.295	34.7	2.8	130-RF	-9
2008	CIN	MLB	38	425	51	20	1	15	53	61	64	0	1	-2.4	.245	.355	.432	.248	.355	.429	.273	13.5	1.2	85-RF	-3
2008	CHA	MLB	38	150	16	10	0	3	18	17	25	0	0	-2.0	.260	.347	.405	.254	.342	.400	.264	3.6	0.3	28-CF	-2
2009	SEA	MLB	39	454	44	19	0	19	57	63	80	0	0	-2.8	.214	.324	.411	.223	.330	.422	.261	1.3	-0.1	7-LF	-1
2010	SEA	MLB	40	421	45	16	1	16	59	56	80	1	1	-1.5	.248	.349	.428	.243	.342	.416	.267	12.1	0.8	65-LF	-5

Breakout: 2% Improve: 29% Collapse: 23% Attrition: 28%   MLB: 97%   Comparables: Luis Gonzalez, Johnny Mize, Fred McGriff, Rafael Palmeiro

Going into his age-40 season, Griffey still possesses some of the traits of The Kid, who baseball fans fell in love with two decades ago. He still has an excellent batting eye and the same contact skills that he has displayed his whole career. Although he no longer has anywhere near his old power, he still maintains a solid extra-base hit and home-run rate. Griffey ran into a little bad luck on balls in play, however: his hit rate on ground balls was lower than expected, and a few more bloopers falling in could bring his average up. Note his unlikely home-road split as well: .268/.382/.548 at home, .174/.278/.306 on the road. He's not the monster everyday DH worth a big chunk of the Mariners' payroll, but he should be able to justify the one-year, $2.35 million base deal the Mariners gave him in November to stick around, and the rest days you can expect him to take can be filled handily by Milton Bradley.

Franklin Gutierrez CF Bats: R Throws: R Height: 6' 2" Weight: 190 Born: February 21, 1983 Age: 27

YEAR	TEAM	LVL	AGE	PA	R	2B	3B	HR	RBI	BB	SO	SB	CS	EqBRR	AVG	OBP	SLG	EqAVG	EqOBP	EqSLG	EqA	VORP	WARP	DEFENSE			
2007	BUF	AAA	24	138	29	7	0	4	16	8	20	7	3	-1.8	.341	.384	.488	.323	.362	.477	.286	7.2	1.2	15-RF	-1	13-CF	4
2007	CLE	MLB	24	301	41	13	2	13	36	21	77	8	3	0.4	.266	.318	.472	.268	.319	.483	.269	9.3	1.3	64-RF	3	7-LF	0
2008	CLE	MLB	25	440	54	26	2	8	41	27	87	9	3	1.4	.248	.307	.383	.254	.315	.395	.249	2.6	2.4	86-RF	16	11-CF	3
2009	SEA	MLB	26	629	85	24	1	18	70	46	122	16	5	3.7	.283	.339	.425	.294	.349	.432	.271	25.9	6.0	151-CF	25		
2010	SEA	MLB	27	568	81	26	2	18	63	47	120	14	5	0.7	.269	.335	.430	.271	.335	.432	.263	19.2	3.5	132-CF	12		

Breakout: 15% Improve: 54% Collapse: 9% Attrition: 6%   MLB: 93%   Comparables: Dusty Baker, George Hendrick, Jermaine Allensworth, Felipe Alou

There may not be a baseball player who provides more defensive value to his team than Gutierrez. Nearly every metric estimates that in 2009 he saved between 25 and 30 runs more than the average center fielder with the glove. Consequently, many of the Mariners' pitchers had ERAs that exceeded their talent level. So, full credit to Zduriencik and company for acquiring him and recognizing that he was being wasted as a right fielder. Gutierrez's bat is adequate for the position, but with his fielding worth three wins by itself, that's all it has to be. Not too many fielders sustain their performances at this high level, but Gutierrez is young enough to linger in Willie Mays territory for a while longer. He didn't win a Gold Glove, as if we're telling you something you don't already know about how screwed up the selection process for those awards is.

Bill Hall UT Bats: R Throws: R Height: 6' 0" Weight: 210 Born: December 28, 1979 Age: 30

YEAR	TEAM	LVL	AGE	PA	R	2B	3B	HR	RBI	BB	SO	SB	CS	EqBRR	AVG	OBP	SLG	EqAVG	EqOBP	EqSLG	EqA	VORP	WARP	DEFENSE			
2007	MIL	MLB	27	503	59	35	0	14	63	40	128	4	5	-2.4	.254	.315	.425	.262	.322	.436	.258	13.1	1.0	115-CF	-4		
2008	MIL	MLB	28	448	50	22	1	15	55	37	124	5	6	-0.1	.225	.293	.396	.235	.300	.408	.240	1.4	0.2	100-3B	1	4-2B	0
2009	MIL	MLB	29	234	22	12	0	6	24	19	72	1	0	1.0	.201	.265	.341	.210	.270	.350	.219	-4.4	0.9	52-3B	10	4-RF	0
2009	SEA	MLB	29	131	10	8	1	2	12	8	48	1	2	-0.2	.200	.244	.333	.210	.252	.345	.202	-4.9	-1.0	20-LF	-4	8-RF	1
2010	BOS	AL	30	430	48	22	1	14	57	36	112	4	5	-0.6	.240	.308	.408	.236	.305	.395	.235	0.0	0.4	96-3B	3		

Breakout: 16% Improve: 47% Collapse: 8% Attrition: 12%   MLB: 91%   Comparables: Russ Davis, Juan Uribe, Charlie Hayes, Todd Zeile

Hall has played every position except pitcher, catcher, and first base, and he's been a defensive asset at all of them. That versatility has value, but as the old Crazy Horse song goes, his bat is a gone dead train. Over the last three years, he has hit .229/.291/.391 while striking out in over 30 percent of his at-bats. Hall has hit left-handers well enough in his career that he would be an asset to the left-leaning Mariners lineup if he could find any consistency, but last year he lost even that skill, batting only .223/.252/.354 against southpaws. Zduriencik is familiar with Hall, going back to early days together in the Brewers, and the calculation is that maybe returning him to a utility role will get his bat started; after getting traded to the Red Sox for Kotchman, the Brewers will be paying most of his contract to let them find out.

Greg Halman OF Bats: R Throws: R Height: 6' 4" Weight: 190 Born: August 26, 1987 Age: 22

YEAR	TEAM	LVL	AGE	PA	R	2B	3B	HR	RBI	BB	SO	SB	CS	EqBRR	AVG	OBP	SLG	EqAVG	EqOBP	EqSLG	EqA	VORP	WARP	DEFENSE			
2007	WIS	A	19	202	26	5	0	4	15	8	77	15	7	-0.5	.182	.234	.273	.174	.214	.253	.160	-13.5	-2.3	39-CF	-5	9-RF	0
2007	EVE	A-	19	265	37	19	1	16	37	21	85	16	8	-3.2	.307	.371	.597	.263	.307	.486	.265	9.0	0.5	54-CF	-4	4-RF	-2
2008	HDS	A+	20	282	52	15	3	19	53	16	76	23	1	5.1	.268	.320	.572	.218	.263	.452	.248	3.7	-0.1	54-CF	-5		
2008	WTN	AA	20	256	43	14	2	10	30	16	66	8	6	-1.1	.277	.332	.481	.250	.293	.421	.243	2.3	-0.5	57-CF	-7		
2009	WTN	AA	21	506	64	17	2	25	72	29	183	9	7	-1.3	.210	.278	.420	.197	.248	.391	.217	-10.4	-1.3	65-CF	-4	39-RF	4
2010	SEA	MLB	22	514	60	20	2	22	57	34	168	12	7	-0.2	.216	.278	.404	.220	.279	.408	.229	-0.3	-0.6	112-CF	-5		

Breakout: 20% Improve: 63% Collapse: 11% Attrition: 7%   MLB: 3%   Comparables: Keith Kimsey, D.J. Thielen, Chad Hermansen, Chris Jones

If you consider only tools, Halman is not only the top prospect in this system, but one of the best in the game. With his power and speed he *should* project as a 30-30 player. Unfortunately, he has the plate discipline of a six-year-old who just ate a one-pound bag of M&Ms, striking out in 36 percent of his Double-A plate appearances while walking in only six percent. He's so far gone at the plate that some are ready to completely give up on him, but with his raw abilities, he'll get plenty of chances to turn it around.

Jack Hannahan — 3B

Bats: L Throws: R Height: 6' 2" Weight: 205 Born: March 4, 1980 Age: 30

YEAR	TEAM	LVL	AGE	PA	R	2B	3B	HR	RBI	BB	SO	SB	CS	EqBRR	AVG	OBP	SLG	EqAVG	EqOBP	EqSLG	EqA	VORP	WARP	DEFENSE			
2007	TOL	AAA	27	417	56	20	1	13	63	76	92	5	5	-2.0	.295	.422	.476	.269	.385	.439	.288	20.7	3.4	35-2B	2	20-3B	5
2007	OAK	MLB	27	169	16	12	0	3	24	21	39	1	0	-0.5	.278	.369	.424	.287	.377	.434	.287	8.6	1.1	41-3B	1		
2008	OAK	MLB	28	501	48	27	0	9	47	55	131	2	0	-0.5	.218	.305	.342	.224	.312	.353	.238	-0.1	0.9	110-3B	8	9-1B	0
2009	SAC	AAA	29	88	8	7	0	2	11	7	27	0	1	0.4	.222	.284	.383	.207	.261	.354	.207	-2.2	-0.2	15-3B	1	5-2B	0
2009	OAK	MLB	29	134	12	6	2	1	8	13	36	0	0	-0.9	.193	.278	.303	.202	.286	.311	.208	-2.8	0.0	38-3B	3		
2009	SEA	MLB	29	167	15	8	0	3	11	17	35	1	1	-0.1	.230	.311	.345	.236	.317	.338	.237	-1.2	0.5	31-3B	3	10-1B	1
2010	SEA	MLB	30	425	42	18	1	11	47	52	112	2	1	-0.5	.234	.330	.373	.231	.326	.360	.246	4.4	0.9	91-3B	4		

Breakout: 8% Improve: 36% Collapse: 19% Attrition: 25% MLB: 65% Comparables: Mike Pagliarulo, Eric Chavez, Wayne Gross, Greg Norton

Care for a haiku? Jack Hannahan is / Good-field, no-hit third baseman / The crowd snores rainbows. That pretty much describes Hannahan's virtues, as he was acquired in-season after the unsurprising discovery that Chris Woodward wasn't up to the challenge of replacing an injured Adrian Beltre. Batting lefty gives him another weak claim on retention, but the decision to sign Figgins and the presence of Bill Hall limits the applications Hannahan might fulfill on the M's bench, placing his spot on the 40-man at risk.

Rob Johnson — C

Bats: R Throws: R Height: 6' 1" Weight: 210 Born: July 22, 1983 Age: 26

YEAR	TEAM	LVL	AGE	PA	R	2B	3B	HR	RBI	BB	SO	SB	CS	EqBRR	AVG	OBP	SLG	EqAVG	EqOBP	EqSLG	EqA	VORP	WARP	DEFENSE			
2007	TAC	AAA	23	465	57	26	0	6	40	39	62	7	7	-0.3	.268	.331	.372	.258	.315	.349	.232	2.1	-0.3	68-C	-5		
2008	TAC	AAA	24	463	55	30	0	9	49	37	61	7	6	-2.5	.305	.363	.441	.288	.341	.397	.257	16.0	1.3	90-C	-3	9-LF	-2
2008	SEA	MLB	24	32	2	0	0	1	2	0	6	0	0	0.0	.129	.129	.226	.129	.129	.226	.010	-3.7	-0.5	7-C	0		
2009	SEA	MLB	25	290	21	19	2	2	27	26	60	1	1	-1.5	.213	.289	.326	.218	.294	.327	.220	1.3	0.6	76-C	3		
2010	SEA	MLB	26	302	28	13	1	6	27	25	57	2	3	-0.5	.246	.311	.364	.248	.312	.362	.230	2.8	0.2	61-C	-1		

Breakout: 16% Improve: 29% Collapse: 32% Attrition: 24% MLB: 54% Comparables: Steve Decker, Jeff Forney, Trey Lunsford, Chris Heintz

Thanks in part to a strong throwing arm (he threw out 31 percent of base thieves), Johnson has developed a reputation as a strong defensive catcher, but he would have to be quite the defender to make up for his weak bat if he keeps getting regular playing time. Although he put up a strong-seeming offensive performance in Triple-A in 2008, his bat fizzled in the majors, because there just aren't a lot of secondary contributions via walks or power that he'll chip in on offense. With Adam Moore coming up behind him and Josh Bard signed to provide veteran sangfroid, Johnson's days of getting 75 starts at catcher may already be in the past.

Ryan Langerhans — OF

Bats: L Throws: L Height: 6' 3" Weight: 230 Born: February 20, 1980 Age: 30

YEAR	TEAM	LVL	AGE	PA	R	2B	3B	HR	RBI	BB	SO	SB	CS	EqBRR	AVG	OBP	SLG	EqAVG	EqOBP	EqSLG	EqA	VORP	WARP	DEFENSE					
2007	ATL	MLB	27	52	3	1	0	0	1	6	16	0	1	-0.4	.068	.192	.091	.068	.192	.091	-.100	-6.6	-0.9	13-LF	-1				
2007	COH	AAA	27	59	11	3	0	1	2	6	15	1	0	0.7	.275	.351	.392	.250	.316	.365	.244	0.7	-0.3	13-CF	-3				
2007	WAS	MLB	27	187	24	6	2	6	22	22	63	3	0	0.2	.198	.296	.370	.204	.305	.377	.245	1.7	0.5	29-CF	0	13-LF	2		
2008	COH	AAA	28	257	40	16	2	3	31	40	57	12	3	2.7	.310	.418	.446	.266	.367	.367	.267	8.2	0.4	46-CF	-3	11-RF	-2		
2008	WAS	MLB	28	139	17	5	2	3	12	25	31	2	0	0.8	.234	.380	.396	.241	.384	.402	.282	5.2	0.7	16-LF	-1	8-RF	2		
2009	SYR	AAA	29	242	34	16	0	9	40	30	50	7	6	-1.3	.278	.371	.488	.263	.349	.445	.271	6.0	0.1	22-LF	-1	19-1B	-3		
2009	SEA	MLB	29	122	12	6	1	3	10	14	28	0	1	0.1	.218	.311	.386	.220	.311	.390	.249	1.0	0.5	26-LF	4	4-CF	1		
2010	SEA	MLB	30	344	42	15	1	8	40	43	89	4	3	0.5	.233	.334	.375	.230	.329	.369	.247	2.6	0.5	66-LF	2				

Breakout: 13% Improve: 40% Collapse: 15% Attrition: 13% MLB: 48% Comparables: Abraham Nunez, Scott Stahoviak, Dave Clark, Pat Putnam

The Mariners acquired Langerhans in late June for the same reason that they made a lot of acquisitions since Zduriencik became their GM: he plays good defense, and with Endy Chavez's injury, that's what Jack Z. still wanted for his club's left-field mix. Beyond his value on defense, Langerhans has a good eye, but struggles to make contact often enough to use the bit of power in his bat. Nontendered in December, he was quickly re-signed by the Mariners to a one-year contract. Given the increasingly crowded M's outfield, it's likely that Langerhans' primary role as the club's fourth outfielder will be to serve as Milton Bradley's legs in left.

Alex Liddi   **3B**   Bats: R   Throws: R   Height: 6' 4"   Weight: 176   Born: August 14, 1988   Age: 21

YEAR	TEAM	LVL	AGE	PA	R	2B	3B	HR	RBI	BB	SO	SB	CS	EqBRR	AVG	OBP	SLG	EqAVG	EqOBP	EqSLG	EqA	VORP	WARP	DEFENSE			
2007	WIS	A	18	451	41	28	3	8	52	36	123	5	4	-3.6	.240	.308	.385	.226	.283	.356	.224	-7.4	-2.1	104-3B	-10	7-1B	0
2008	WIS	A	19	496	65	26	4	6	53	42	115	17	5	3.8	.244	.313	.360	.224	.281	.327	.215	-11.3	-1.9	113-3B	-4		
2009	HDS	A+	20	565	97	44	5	23	104	53	122	10	6	-2.1	.345	.411	.594	.264	.321	.435	.261	15.5	1.5	120-3B	-4	7-1B	1
2010	SEA	MLB	21	586	65	32	3	14	70	50	151	7	3	-0.4	.240	.309	.388	.244	.310	.388	.239	2.3	-0.2	139-3B	-4		

Breakout: 32%   Improve: 56%   Collapse: 12%   Attrition: 6%   MLB: 2%   Comparables: Brandon Wood, Dale Sveum, Ron Shepherd, Corey Smith

An honest-to-goodness Italian import, Liddi put up massive numbers at High Desert, but scouts think there's more there than just a ballpark that inflates every hitter into something like a gaseous Oliver Hardy. His walk rate jumped in the second half, but how much of that was a league's giving him his due, and how much it represents a fundamentally better approach, will get sorted out with the big jump to Double-A.

Jose Lopez   **2B**   Bats: R   Throws: R   Height: 6' 0"   Weight: 205   Born: November 24, 1983   Age: 26

YEAR	TEAM	LVL	AGE	PA	R	2B	3B	HR	RBI	BB	SO	SB	CS	EqBRR	AVG	OBP	SLG	EqAVG	EqOBP	EqSLG	EqA	VORP	WARP	DEFENSE			
2007	SEA	MLB	23	561	58	17	2	11	62	20	64	2	3	-3.0	.252	.284	.355	.259	.290	.366	.227	-1.0	1.7	139-2B	14		
2008	SEA	MLB	24	687	80	41	1	17	89	27	67	6	3	-2.7	.297	.322	.443	.309	.334	.463	.272	29.6	7.1	139-2B	27	11-1B	3
2009	SEA	MLB	25	653	69	42	0	25	96	24	69	3	3	-3.3	.272	.303	.463	.280	.310	.467	.263	20.7	0.9	138-2B	-13	14-1B	0
2010	SEA	MLB	26	629	69	30	2	20	86	33	68	3	4	-1.6	.281	.324	.438	.285	.326	.442	.257	17.2	2.5	150-2B	5		

Breakout: 19%   Improve: 50%   Collapse: 10%   Attrition: 6%   MLB: 100%   Comparables: Bill Mazeroski, Aaron Hill, Davey Johnson, Rico Petrocelli

Lopez managed the rare feat of having more home runs than walks. He has always swung at a lot of pitches out of the strike zone, but in 2009, he swung at even more of the high and low, the inside and outside, than in previous years. However, a young second baseman who can hit 25 home runs while playing his home games at Safeco Field is not exactly something to sneeze at. His glove is not spectacular (that Mazeroski comp, above, is all about the wood, not the leather), but he gets the job done. At the Winter Meetings, Zduriencik spoke about how Figgins had been signed to play in the infield, creating speculation that Lopez might be moved away from the keystone, so stay tuned.

Adam Moore   **C**   Bats: R   Throws: R   Height: 6' 3"   Weight: 220   Born: May 8, 1984   Age: 26

YEAR	TEAM	LVL	AGE	PA	R	2B	3B	HR	RBI	BB	SO	SB	CS	EqBRR	AVG	OBP	SLG	EqAVG	EqOBP	EqSLG	EqA	VORP	WARP	DEFENSE			
2007	HDS	A+	23	491	74	30	3	22	102	41	84	1	0	2.1	.307	.371	.543	.237	.290	.396	.239	10.6	0.1	98-C	-10	5-1B	0
2008	WTN	AA	24	490	60	34	2	14	71	40	77	0	1	-6.3	.319	.396	.506	.285	.342	.439	.269	24.2	2.0	105-C	-8		
2009	WTN	AA	25	116	14	5	0	3	13	16	21	0	0	-1.2	.263	.371	.411	.240	.319	.360	.245	2.3	0.2	23-C	-1		
2009	TAC	AAA	25	368	41	19	0	9	43	26	51	1	1	-0.3	.294	.346	.429	.276	.323	.395	.249	11.9	1.3	90-C	-1		
2009	SEA	MLB	25	24	4	1	0	1	2	0	7	1	0	0.9	.217	.250	.391	.217	.250	.391	.231	0.3	-0.1	6-C	-1		
2010	SEA	MLB	26	461	47	21	1	13	55	35	96	1	1	-0.7	.248	.312	.393	.251	.314	.404	.240	9.0	0.6	103-C	-3		

Breakout: 16%   Improve: 36%   Collapse: 23%   Attrition: 19%   MLB: 15%   Comparables: Geronimo Gil, Bill Haselman, Mike Amrhein, Shawn Riggans

Moore has always been above average offensively for his position, with a decent batting average and gap power, but his defense has improved dramatically over the last two years. He has become more agile behind the plate while starting to figure out how to turn his plus arm into a legitimate weapon for running-game deterrence. While the signing of veteran placeholder Josh Bard and Rob Johnson's claim on the job might consign Moore to another stretch in Tacoma, it isn't as though Moore is up against Elston Howard and Yogi Berra. So, the right combination of events (injuries, a good camp, managerial preference) could put Moore into the role of first among equals in a group of interchangeably OK receivers.

Michael Saunders   LF   Bats: L   Throws: R   Height: 6' 4"   Weight: 205   Born: November 19, 1986   Age: 23

YEAR	TEAM	LVL	AGE	PA	R	2B	3B	HR	RBI	BB	SO	SB	CS	EqBRR	AVG	OBP	SLG	EqAVG	EqOBP	EqSLG	EqA	VORP	WARP	DEFENSE			
2007	HDS	A+	20	507	91	25	4	14	77	60	116	27	10	2.2	.299	.392	.473	.240	.319	.363	.244	2.2	0.4	52-CF	1	33-RF	-1
2007	WTN	AA	20	60	8	1	2	1	7	7	20	2	1	-0.2	.288	.373	.442	.259	.333	.407	.256	1.2	0.4	11-CF	2		
2008	WTN	AA	21	289	46	18	3	8	30	30	66	11	6	-2.7	.290	.375	.484	.256	.323	.415	.255	5.6	0.4	47-CF	-2	5-RF	0
2008	TAC	AAA	21	105	12	4	1	3	16	9	30	1	2	-1.9	.242	.308	.400	.227	.286	.351	.218	-2.0	-0.2	15-CF	-1	5-LF	1
2009	TAC	AAA	22	282	58	15	2	13	32	25	48	6	3	2.0	.310	.378	.544	.292	.354	.498	.286	15.0	2.4	38-LF	2	22-CF	3
2009	SEA	MLB	22	129	13	1	3	0	4	6	40	4	1	-0.2	.221	.258	.279	.221	.258	.279	.194	-6.3	-0.2	35-LF	4		
2010	SEA	MLB	23	463	61	19	3	13	48	43	120	11	5	-0.1	.249	.325	.400	.247	.320	.393	.250	5.1	1.0	89-LF	4		

Breakout: 16%   Improve: 48%   Collapse: 8%   Attrition: 5%   MLB: 91%   Comparables: Al Chambers, Kelly Johnson, Brian Dubose, Jim Faulk

After being rapidly promoted up through the minors, the athletic Saunders was excellent in the field, but his bat did not show up during his rookie campaign. The bat will come around in time, especially as he'll develop more power as he grows older. The bigger problem will be seeing if he develops a better approach at the plate; Saunders struck out 40 times in 129 plate appearances in the majors last year, not surprising given his high whiff rates in the minors. He's still a big part of Seattle's future, but the acquisition of Milton Bradley takes some pressure off him for 2010. PECOTA's inclusion of Al Chambers, one of the biggest prospect busts in Mariners history, among his comparables shouldn't be taken as an omen or anything ... right?

Ichiro Suzuki   RF   Bats: L   Throws: R   Height: 5' 11"   Weight: 170   Born: October 22, 1973   Age: 36

YEAR	TEAM	LVL	AGE	PA	R	2B	3B	HR	RBI	BB	SO	SB	CS	EqBRR	AVG	OBP	SLG	EqAVG	EqOBP	EqSLG	EqA	VORP	WARP	DEFENSE			
2007	SEA	MLB	33	736	111	22	7	6	68	49	77	37	8	7.2	.351	.396	.431	.359	.405	.442	.299	51.6	7.1	151-CF	11		
2008	SEA	MLB	34	749	103	20	7	6	42	51	65	43	4	12.5	.310	.361	.386	.322	.372	.401	.282	34.6	5.6	89-RF	3	68-CF	11
2009	SEA	MLB	35	678	88	31	4	11	46	32	71	26	9	4.0	.352	.386	.465	.362	.396	.473	.298	41.7	5.6	144-RF	8		
2010	SEA	MLB	36	617	80	26	4	8	46	45	76	21	9	3.4	.322	.375	.426	.320	.372	.420	.278	25.0	3.1	131-RF	3		

Breakout: 5%   Improve: 30%   Collapse: 16%   Attrition: 21%   MLB: 99%   Comparables: Brett Butler, Lou Brock, Bobby Veach, Sam Rice

Despite missing 16 games with a bleeding ulcer and a sore calf, Ichiro put together his ninth straight season of 200 hits in as many major-league campaigns. His unconventional swing produces ground balls (55 percent career rate), but unlike a lot of slap-and-run guys, he hits them hard enough that they find holes. When they stay in the infield, Ichiro is excellent at beating them out: he has 463 career infield hits, and he set a career high last season with 63. This was also the highest infield hit rate of his career—he turned 16 percent of his ground balls into safeties—so Ichiro is showing no signs of slowing down despite his age. When he plays his first game this season, he'll have satisfied the minimum 10-year requirement for the Hall of Fame, and there's little doubt we'll see him in Cooperstown.

Mike Sweeney   DH   Bats: R   Throws: R   Height: 6' 3"   Weight: 225   Born: July 22, 1973   Age: 36

YEAR	TEAM	LVL	AGE	PA	R	2B	3B	HR	RBI	BB	SO	SB	CS	EqBRR	AVG	OBP	SLG	EqAVG	EqOBP	EqSLG	EqA	VORP	WARP	DEFENSE	
2007	KCA	MLB	33	289	26	15	1	7	38	17	29	0	0	0.5	.260	.315	.404	.257	.311	.396	.246	-1.3	-0.2	4-1B	0
2008	OAK	MLB	34	136	13	8	0	2	12	7	6	0	0	-0.1	.286	.331	.397	.294	.338	.413	.263	1.5	0.2	10-1B	0
2009	SEA	MLB	35	266	25	15	0	8	34	17	31	0	0	0.6	.281	.335	.442	.290	.342	.448	.272	3.8	0.3	4-1B	-1
2010	SEA	MLB	36	214	18	10	0	6	27	16	27	0	0	0.1	.262	.326	.405	.264	.325	.401	.250	0.1	0.0	5-1B	0

Breakout: 14%   Improve: 33%   Collapse: 30%   Attrition: 36%   MLB: 94%   Comparables: Eric Karros, Jeff Conine, Frank Thomas, Ron Coomer

After a six-year climb down from hard-earned stardom because of injuries (with the Royals, no less), Sweeney was given a shot to be solid veteran citizen and part-time DH by the new regime. He fulfilled his duties admirably, showing that he still has a little something left, hitting .287/.322/.519 away from a park that punished him and contributing an ISO above .200 against lefties. He could be someone's right-handed Matt Stairs if that was worth a roster spot. Probably not, but we're jes' sayin'.

Carlos Triunfel SS

Bats: R   Throws: R   Height: 5' 11"   Weight: 175   Born: February 27, 1990   Age: 20

YEAR	TEAM	LVL	AGE	PA	R	2B	3B	HR	RBI	BB	SO	SB	CS	EqBRR	AVG	OBP	SLG	EqAVG	EqOBP	EqSLG	EqA	VORP	WARP	DEFENSE	
2007	WIS	A	17	164	18	8	2	0	14	5	23	4	8	-0.3	.309	.342	.388	.286	.311	.364	.231	1.3	-0.9	40-SS -9	
2007	HDS	A+	17	225	32	10	2	0	22	12	31	3	4	-1.7	.288	.333	.356	.227	.266	.270	.185	-7.3	-1.7	49-SS -7	
2008	HDS	A+	18	479	75	20	4	8	49	30	52	30	9	1.3	.287	.336	.406	.229	.273	.328	.215	-4.0	-2.8	72-SS -14	30-2B -6
2010	SEA	MLB	20	433	51	20	4	5	37	27	61	10	6	-0.3	.253	.303	.357	.257	.306	.363	.226	0.6	-0.9	96-SS -9	

Breakout: 46% Improve: 64% Collapse: 16% Attrition: 7%   MLB: 4%   Comparables: Donovan Solano, Luis Ordaz, Luis De Paula, Alcides Escobar

After improving in 2008, the athletic 19-year-old lost the majority of his 2009 season to a fractured fibula and torn ankle ligaments. When he's on the field, Triunfel has a quick bat and an outstanding arm, but between the injuries and consistently being very young for his level, he has never put up big numbers. A healthy season in 2010 should give the Mariners a much better idea of where he stands and how long it will be until he finds his way to Seattle, but with the big-league infield's regulars signed for the next couple of seasons, it's up to Triunfel to heal up and put up or shut up and put himself into the club's long-term plans.

Matt Tuiasosopo INF

Bats: R   Throws: R   Height: 6' 2"   Weight: 223   Born: May 10, 1986   Age: 24

YEAR	TEAM	LVL	AGE	PA	R	2B	3B	HR	RBI	BB	SO	SB	CS	EqBRR	AVG	OBP	SLG	EqAVG	EqOBP	EqSLG	EqA	VORP	WARP	DEFENSE	
2007	WTN	AA	21	548	74	27	5	9	57	76	113	4	8	-2.7	.260	.371	.404	.245	.335	.379	.254	8.3	-0.3	127-3B -11	
2008	TAC	AAA	22	500	87	32	2	13	73	47	104	4	0	0.7	.281	.364	.453	.263	.335	.402	.260	11.4	-1.5	105-3B -25	
2008	SEA	MLB	22	47	1	2	1	0	2	2	16	0	0	-0.6	.159	.213	.250	.159	.213	.250	.150	-3.6	-0.3	12-3B 1	
2009	TAC	AAA	23	269	43	15	0	11	35	36	83	3	1	2.7	.261	.368	.473	.247	.345	.437	.271	9.9	0.4	30-3B 0	21-2B -7
2009	SEA	MLB	23	25	2	1	0	1	2	2	5	0	0	-0.1	.227	.280	.409	.227	.280	.409	.246	0.2	0.2	6-2B 1	
2010	SEA	MLB	24	450	58	21	2	11	49	48	117	3	2	0.0	.239	.329	.383	.240	.328	.386	.247	5.5	-0.1	101-3B -6	

Breakout: 15% Improve: 44% Collapse: 17% Attrition: 9%   MLB: 47%   Comparables: Jose Fernandez, Scott McClain, Garrett Atkins, Tom Evans

A slow-developing player who has already spent six years in the minor-league system, Tuiasosopo may finally have a shot at the majors entering his age-24 season. Originally a shortstop but most often a third baseman in recent seasons, Tuiasosopo played a bit of second base for the first time in his career in 2009 after coming back from an early-season elbow injury that required surgery. Wherever they leave him on the diamond, his hitting .281/.395/.518 for Tacoma after recovering suggests the kind of value he can add. There's not quite the bat to profile as a star, but he has a good approach and hits left-handers well. While the signing of Chone Figgins eliminates his ability to earn a starting role in 2010, he might end up with a bench job.

Jack Wilson SS

Bats: R   Throws: R   Height: 6' 0"   Weight: 200   Born: December 29, 1977   Age: 32

YEAR	TEAM	LVL	AGE	PA	R	2B	3B	HR	RBI	BB	SO	SB	CS	EqBRR	AVG	OBP	SLG	EqAVG	EqOBP	EqSLG	EqA	VORP	WARP	DEFENSE
2007	PIT	MLB	29	535	67	29	2	12	56	38	46	2	5	0.5	.296	.350	.440	.306	.360	.455	.276	29.4	4.7	128-SS 11
2008	PIT	MLB	30	330	24	18	1	1	22	13	27	2	2	-1.3	.272	.312	.348	.283	.322	.358	.238	5.7	2.4	78-SS 14
2009	PIT	MLB	31	286	26	18	1	4	31	15	31	2	1	-1.5	.267	.304	.387	.277	.312	.404	.248	8.1	2.2	74-SS 10
2009	SEA	MLB	31	116	11	5	0	1	8	6	17	1	0	0.5	.224	.263	.299	.226	.265	.292	.202	-2.2	-0.5	30-SS -3
2010	SEA	MLB	32	355	39	18	1	6	38	27	42	2	3	0.0	.279	.340	.394	.281	.340	.402	.252	9.3	1.5	89-SS 4

Breakout: 11% Improve: 41% Collapse: 21% Attrition: 17%   MLB: 94%   Comparables: Ramon Martinez, Johnny Logan, Dick Groat, Bill Russell

Wilson was traded at the deadline from Pittsburgh to Seattle, and while he failed to produce offensively in Seattle, his offense wasn't why he was acquired. He still has a strong arm and solid range, creating a win or two more with his glove than your average shortstop. On the offensive side, Wilson has neither eye nor power, but he does make decent enough contact to maintain his spot in the lineup, and some bad luck as far as his BABIP and line-drive rate suggests he's due for the kind of bounce-back that PECOTA is seeing from him. Signed to a two-year extension, he should continue to be Wilsonian for the duration of the contract and make his special contribution to Zduriencik's re-creation of the 1914 Boston Braves.

PITCHERS

David Aardsma

Bats: R   Throws: R   Height: 6' 4"   Weight: 205   Born: December 27, 1981   Age: 28

YEAR	TEAM	LVL	AGE	W	L	SV	G	GS	IP	H	HR	BB	SO	GB%	BABIP	STUFF	WHIP	ERA	SIERA	DERA	EqH9	EqHR9	EqBB9	EqSO9	VORP	SN/WX
2007	CHR	AAA	25	3	2	15	28	0	35¹	26	7	11	45	33%	.237	6	1.05	4.33	2.34	5.24	7.6	2.4	2.9	9.2	1.0	0.43
2007	CHA	MLB	25	2	1	0	25	0	32¹	39	4	17	36	43%	.376	6	1.73	6.40	3.72	5.79	10.2	0.8	4.1	9.1	-1.0	0.01
2008	BOS	MLB	26	4	2	0	47	0	48²	49	4	35	49	53%	.333	11	1.73	5.55	4.39	5.34	9.2	0.6	5.8	8.6	0.8	-0.06
2009	SEA	MLB	27	3	6	38	73	0	71¹	49	4	34	80	27%	.253	21	1.16	2.52	3.56	2.93	6.9	0.5	3.8	8.8	20.2	5.73
2010	SEA	MLB	28	3	4	15	64	0	62¹	62	7	32	63	39%	.324	3	1.51	4.66	3.89	4.64	8.4	0.9	4.2	8.3	6.0	1.43

Breakout: 12%   Improve: 34%   Collapse: 22%   Attrition: 6%   MLB: 89%   Comparables: Tim Scott, Bobby Ayala, Paul Shuey, Michael Wuertz

It took until he was 27, but former first-round pick Aardsma finally mastered his command, or at least tamed it sufficiently to put together a consistent season. After losing a spring battle for the closer's job to Brandon Morrow, he picked up the job when Morrow got hurt in May, and Aardsma never looked back. He relied almost exclusively on his mid-90s fastball, cutting his use of the slider dramatically. The change in his style meant that he was a more extreme fly-ball pitcher than ever, as he had the fourth-highest fly-ball percentage in the 50+ IP bracket. But just four of them headed over the walls, something not just due to Safeco, as he was even harder to hit on the road, with just one homer allowed. Manager Don Wakamatsu handled him very carefully, bringing him in with runners on base only twice all season. Any of these factors—Aardsma's improved control, flies that don't get out, situations that don't require the closer to pitch under pressure—could change at any time. Aarsdma's 90 percent saves conversion rate may be a onetime thing, headed to the same historical dustbin as Brad Lidge's perfect season.

Phillippe Aumont

Bats: L   Throws: R   Height: 6' 7"   Weight: 220   Born: January 7, 1989   Age: 21

YEAR	TEAM	LVL	AGE	W	L	SV	G	GS	IP	H	HR	BB	SO	GB%	BABIP	STUFF	WHIP	ERA	SIERA	DERA	EqH9	EqHR9	EqBB9	EqSO9	VORP	SN/WX
2008	WIS	A	19	4	4	2	15	8	55²	46	4	19	50	59%	.273	7	1.17	2.75	3.57	5.33	9.4	2.0	4.1	4.6	1.0	0.11
2009	HDS	A+	20	1	2	12	29	0	33¹	24	3	12	35	53%	.247	20	1.08	3.24	3.20	4.50	7.3	1.4	3.9	5.9	3.6	0.58
2009	WTN	AA	20	1	4	4	15	0	17²	21	1	11	24	61%	.408	17	1.81	5.09	3.33	9.09	11.9	1.0	5.2	8.8	-6.9	-1.40
2010	PHI	MLB	21	3	5	13	47	5	62	64	9	34	48	54%	.305	9	1.58	5.27	4.58	5.43	9.1	1.3	4.4	6.3	0.5	0.82

Breakout: 21%   Improve: 49%   Collapse: 14%   Attrition: 10%   MLB: 0%   Comparables: Bill Dodd, Ben Ford, Craig Whitaker, Toby Borland

Scouts always projected the big Canadian as a future reliever, so the Mariners decided not to waste any time and moved their former first-round pick to that role in just his second full season. Aumont is still a bit rough around the edges, but his fastball is truly special, as it combines plus velocity (92-95 mph) with plus-plus heavy sinking movement. He still needs to hone his command, find more consistency with his slider, and harness his emotions (he's the type who slams his glove into the bench after any nonperfect outing), but he's truly closer-worthy in terms of his stuff. He will continue his pursuit of maturity with the Phillies after heading east in the Cliff Lee deal, but he becomes the immediate heir apparent to the closer's crown in the organization that employs the definition of late-game combustion; there's obviously a chance for him to come up quick.

Miguel Batista

Bats: R   Throws: R   Height: 6' 1"   Weight: 200   Born: February 19, 1971   Age: 39

YEAR	TEAM	LVL	AGE	W	L	SV	G	GS	IP	H	HR	BB	SO	GB%	BABIP	STUFF	WHIP	ERA	SIERA	DERA	EqH9	EqHR9	EqBB9	EqSO9	VORP	SN/WX
2007	SEA	MLB	36	16	11	0	33	32	193	209	18	85	133	49%	.310	5	1.52	4.29	4.72	4.49	9.0	1.0	3.5	5.4	21.8	4.44
2008	SEA	MLB	37	4	14	1	44	20	115	135	19	79	73	51%	.306	-28	1.86	6.26	5.49	6.62	10.0	1.7	5.4	5.0	-14.5	-1.28
2009	SEA	MLB	38	7	4	1	56	0	71¹	79	7	39	52	54%	.319	-13	1.65	4.04	4.82	4.57	10.8	0.9	4.4	5.9	7.2	-0.28
2010	SEA	MLB	39	4	8	1	42	14	94²	111	13	53	60	50%	.321	-17	1.72	5.88	5.16	5.94	10.2	1.2	4.6	5.2	-4.6	0.42

Breakout: 3%   Improve: 29%   Collapse: 29%   Attrition: 23%   MLB: 98%   Comparables: Mark Gardner, Tom Seaver, Bob Forsch, Ray Starr

Utility pitcher/poet/novelist Batista spent 2009 in relief, where he again struggled with control and an inability to put hitters away. He allowed eight of 12 inherited runners to score, which made him one of the most permissive relievers in baseball last year and roughly seven runs worse than the average pitcher in that regard. Batista has had a long career mostly filled with average work, but those days are slipping away with time and the tide; he's best relegated to a mop-up role these days, and even then he won't provide anything that a less-expensive Triple-A type cannot—except literary ambition.

Erik Bedard

| | | | | | | | | | | | Bats: L | | Throws: L | | Height: 6′ 1″ | | Weight: 190 | | Born: March 6, 1979 | | Age: 31 |

YEAR	TEAM	LVL	AGE	W	L	SV	G	GS	IP	H	HR	BB	SO	GB%	BABIP	STUFF	WHIP	ERA	SIERA	DERA	EqH9	EqHR9	EqBB9	EqSO9	VORP	SN/WX
2007	BAL	MLB	28	13	5	0	28	28	182	141	19	57	221	56%	.283	42	1.09	3.16	2.56	3.08	7.0	0.9	2.6	9.6	48.3	6.09
2008	SEA	MLB	29	6	4	0	15	15	81	70	9	37	72	46%	.271	14	1.32	3.67	4.07	4.06	7.6	1.1	3.7	7.1	13.0	2.50
2009	SEA	MLB	30	5	3	0	15	15	83	65	8	34	90	52%	.269	28	1.19	2.82	3.27	3.15	7.9	0.9	3.3	8.5	21.2	3.05
2010	SEA	MLB	31	6	6	0	23	17	100[1]	94	11	42	99	49%	.310	22	1.36	4.12	3.58	4.24	8.2	1.0	3.5	8.1	14.1	2.18

Breakout: 3%   Improve: 36%   Collapse: 25%   Attrition: 26%   MLB: 99%   Comparables: Ray Sadecki, Bob Kuzava, Bill Walker, Jack Bentley

Before re-injuring himself last summer, Bedard had at least improved his strikeout rate nearly all the way back up to where it was in 2007. No one doubts his talent, but a torn labrum is a tough injury to come back from. He probably won't be ready for Opening Day, and the team that signs him will tacitly take on a big risk, to both the good and the bad. In mint condition, Bedard is one of the better pitchers in the game, but it's not clear if that version of the southpaw still exists, and nobody is going to repeat a Bavasi-big mistake in offering the sun, moon, and stars to land the lefty. Handled carefully, he could be the perfect add-on for a contending team that doesn't need him immediately, especially if he'll agree to an incentive-laden deal.

Joshua Fields

| | | | | | | | | | | | Bats: R | | Throws: R | | Height: 6′ 0″ | | Weight: 185 | | Born: August 19, 1985 | | Age: 24 |

YEAR	TEAM	LVL	AGE	W	L	SV	G	GS	IP	H	HR	BB	SO	GB%	BABIP	STUFF	WHIP	ERA	SIERA	DERA	EqH9	EqHR9	EqBB9	EqSO9	VORP	SN/WX
2009	WTN	AA	23	2	2	1	31	0	33[1]	33	2	22	36	51%	.330	-9	1.65	6.48	4.06	10.30	10.3	1.1	5.6	7.2	-17.2	-1.75
2010	SEA	MLB	24	2	3	0	44	0	48	51	6	30	41	49%	.322	-9	1.69	5.31	4.63	5.29	9.0	1.0	5.1	7.0	1.1	-1.39

Breakout: 58%   Improve: 78%   Collapse: 9%   Attrition: 4%   MLB: 1%   Comparables: Tony Chavez, Mark Marino, Tracy Allen, John Burden

After not signing with the Braves in 2007 and holding out after Seattle selected him in 2008, Fields entered the year as a 23-year-old with no pro experience, albeit one who could boast a mid-90s heater and wipeout slider. Because of the stuff, he looked as if he could move up quickly. Instead, mechanics that had initially graded out as "poor" deteriorated to "horror movie," resulting in the disturbing combination of less velocity and worse command. He seemed to get a bit of his promise back in the Arizona Fall League, but for now, he's a big disappointment.

Doug Fister

| | | | | | | | | | | | Bats: L | | Throws: R | | Height: 6′ 8″ | | Weight: 200 | | Born: February 4, 1984 | | Age: 26 |

YEAR	TEAM	LVL	AGE	W	L	SV	G	GS	IP	H	HR	BB	SO	GB%	BABIP	STUFF	WHIP	ERA	SIERA	DERA	EqH9	EqHR9	EqBB9	EqSO9	VORP	SN/WX
2007	WTN	AA	23	7	8	0	24	24	131	156	14	32	85	55%	.333	-24	1.44	4.60	4.27	6.18	11.7	1.7	2.5	3.8	-9.1	-0.98
2008	WTN	AA	24	6	14	0	31	23	134[1]	155	12	45	104	50%	.333	-19	1.49	5.43	4.20	6.94	10.8	1.4	3.0	4.9	-20.9	-2.00
2009	TAC	AAA	25	6	4	0	22	17	106[1]	132	10	11	79	50%	.346	-8	1.34	3.81	3.70	4.72	11.4	1.4	1.2	5.2	8.9	0.36
2009	SEA	MLB	25	3	4	0	11	10	61	63	11	15	36	48%	.271	-5	1.28	4.13	4.55	4.17	10.2	1.7	2.0	4.8	8.6	1.65
2010	SEA	MLB	26	6	9	0	35	23	138[2]	168	21	46	84	45%	.325	-10	1.55	5.40	4.78	5.48	10.5	1.3	2.7	4.9	0.3	1.31

Breakout: 9%   Improve: 48%   Collapse: 13%   Attrition: 21%   MLB: 74%   Comparables: Dan Gakeler, Mike Christopher, Curt Hasler, Zach McClellan

Rather than look to a usual suspect like Batista, the Mariners promoted Fister from Tacoma in August to shore up a rotation that had already lost Bedard and shed Washburn. He's a pitch-to-contact type, which works very well pitching in front of this defense. The key step forward in 2009 for Fister was that he cut down on his walks; a contact pitcher will always allow a few base hits, no matter how good his defense is, but if there are no baserunners on at the time, the damage can be minimized. Of course, they also have to keep the ball in the park, something Fister had trouble doing; lefty hitters averaged a home run every 15 at-bats against him. The current plan is to keep him in long relief, but he'll be in the mix for the fifth starter's slot.

Lucas French

Bats: L   Throws: L   Height: 6' 4"   Weight: 220   Born: September 13, 1985   Age: 24

YEAR	TEAM	LVL	AGE	W	L	SV	G	GS	IP	H	HR	BB	SO	GB%	BABIP	STUFF	WHIP	ERA	SIERA	DERA	EqH9	EqHR9	EqBB9	EqSO9	VORP	SN/WX
2007	LAK	A+	21	5	14	0	27	27	149	172	10	47	93	46%	.325	-4	1.47	4.05	4.63	6.59	10.8	1.4	3.4	3.7	-17.2	-1.37
2008	ERI	AA	22	9	11	0	27	26	170	195	16	60	88	55%	.311	-10	1.50	4.02	4.99	5.49	10.9	1.2	3.3	3.4	0.1	-0.27
2009	TOL	AAA	23	4	4	0	13	13	81²	71	6	20	72	52%	.284	16	1.11	2.98	3.41	4.40	8.5	1.2	2.4	6.4	9.5	1.34
2009	DET	MLB	23	1	2	0	7	5	29¹	33	2	11	19	28%	.310	4	1.50	3.37	5.28	3.71	9.5	0.6	3.0	5.0	6.0	0.67
2009	SEA	MLB	23	3	3	0	8	7	38	54	9	17	23	32%	.349	-22	1.87	6.63	5.47	7.32	14.1	2.3	3.8	5.0	-7.2	-0.21
2010	SEA	MLB	24	6	9	0	28	25	130	157	18	56	70	39%	.321	-15	1.64	5.56	5.41	5.71	10.5	1.2	3.5	4.4	-3.1	1.42

Breakout: 14% Improve: 50% Collapse: 11% Attrition: 15%   MLB: 63%   Comparables: Damaso Marte, Andy Pettitte, Chris Seddon, Brad Thomas

Acquired in the Washburn trade, French was an extreme fly-ball pitcher in the majors, which is a tough way to make a living when you don't have the stuff to get a lot of strikeouts: more contact means more flies means more home runs, and that equation proved to be true for French even at pitcher-lovin' Safeco, where he gave up six home runs in 23 innings. Something of an organizational arm with the Tigers before last season, he helped himself significantly by showing a much better slider last year, which gave him a good third offering to mix in with a pedestrian fastball and an effective changeup. French's best bet for continued employment probably involves a conversion to the bullpen, but if he can continue to adapt, he might stay in the mix for the fifth slot.

Felix Hernandez

Bats: R   Throws: R   Height: 6' 3"   Weight: 230   Born: April 8, 1986   Age: 24

YEAR	TEAM	LVL	AGE	W	L	SV	G	GS	IP	H	HR	BB	SO	GB%	BABIP	STUFF	WHIP	ERA	SIERA	DERA	EqH9	EqHR9	EqBB9	EqSO9	VORP	SN/WX
2007	SEA	MLB	21	14	7	0	30	30	190¹	209	20	53	165	72%	.333	29	1.38	3.92	3.42	3.99	9.4	1.1	2.3	7.0	31.5	4.48
2008	SEA	MLB	22	9	11	0	31	31	200²	198	17	80	175	61%	.314	31	1.39	3.45	3.86	3.71	8.7	0.9	3.3	7.1	39.0	5.73
2009	SEA	MLB	23	19	5	0	34	34	238²	200	15	71	217	61%	.278	34	1.14	2.49	3.45	3.11	8.3	0.6	2.4	7.2	61.4	8.74
2010	SEA	MLB	24	13	12	0	33	33	221¹	222	24	75	190	67%	.313	20	1.34	4.12	3.60	4.19	8.7	0.9	2.8	7.1	32.1	4.26

Breakout: 12% Improve: 53% Collapse: 9% Attrition: 8%   MLB: 100%   Comparables: Dwight Gooden, Jeremy Bonderman, Matt Cain, Dean Chance

It's hard to believe, but sometimes we humans do become smarter about the way we go about things. Having reached the majors at the tender age of 19, Hernandez has made the 12th-most starts of any pitcher aged 23 or younger, with 138 (Bert Blyleven is the all-time leader, with 178), but he has thrown only the 27th-most innings. Thus, King Felix is still here for us to enjoy instead of being a name on the list of famous patients of a surgeon TBNL. To his credit, Hernandez has altered his approach as he has matured. When he first surfaced, he had a grounder-oriented approach and put more faith in breaking pitches than he does presently. As he has come to rely more on his fastball, the ratio of grounders and flies has begun to even out. Hernandez couldn't have had better timing, because not only is he now showing better command, but in 2009 those flies were well taken care of by the team's strong defense. He also had some good luck; the defense helped him to a .247 BABIP in high-leverage situations, without which his ERA would have been somewhere in the low 3.00s, but that's the only "negative" here. The best part of all this is that Hernandez is more than three years younger than Justin Verlander, 2 ½ years younger than Zack Greinke, and 22 months younger than Tim Lincecum. He's really only just getting started.

Gaby Hernandez

Bats: R   Throws: R   Height: 6' 3"   Weight: 215   Born: May 21, 1986   Age: 24

YEAR	TEAM	LVL	AGE	W	L	SV	G	GS	IP	H	HR	BB	SO	GB%	BABIP	STUFF	WHIP	ERA	SIERA	DERA	EqH9	EqHR9	EqBB9	EqSO9	VORP	SN/WX
2007	CAR	AA	21	9	11	0	28	28	153²	144	14	56	113	42%	.274	5	1.30	4.22	4.42	6.08	9.6	1.5	3.4	4.3	-9.6	-0.38
2008	WTN	AA	22	1	1	0	6	6	32¹	38	3	15	23	49%	.337	-3	1.64	5.01	4.72	5.81	11.3	1.5	4.1	4.6	-1.1	-0.27
2008	CAR	AA	22	3	0	0	4	4	23	21	3	4	17	48%	.254	10	1.09	4.30	3.81	5.16	8.7	2.0	1.6	4.8	0.9	-0.20
2008	ABQ	AAA	22	2	8	0	13	13	64²	94	14	26	54	49%	.367	-2	1.86	7.24	4.30	7.49	11.4	1.3	3.3	5.6	-14.9	-1.66
2009	TAC	AAA	23	10	9	0	26	26	146¹	158	16	48	98	37%	.303	-12	1.41	5.23	4.69	5.93	10.0	1.5	3.0	4.6	-6.7	-0.23
2010	SEA	MLB	24	5	9	0	33	23	122	138	17	53	76	35%	.313	-8	1.56	5.38	5.18	5.43	9.8	1.2	3.5	5.1	0.9	1.04

Breakout: 23% Improve: 71% Collapse: 10% Attrition: 19%   MLB: 12%   Comparables: Jay Yennaco, Wardell Starling, Steven Matcuk, Pete Munro

Hernandez looked like a future big-league innings-eater a few years back, but his development stalled at Triple-A. Going to Seattle in the Arthur Rhodes deal did little to get the wheels rolling again. He's a big, physical pitcher with decent velocity, a pretty good breaking ball, and the ability to throw strikes, but he's proven to be just too hittable, as he still sometimes pitches as if he's in A-ball, where that kind of combination can just blow hitters away. He needs to start setting up guys and to get smarter. Considering he's just 23, there's still a chance here.

Nicholas Hill

Bats: L   Throws: L   Height: 6' 0"   Weight: 190   Born: January 30, 1985   Age: 25

YEAR	TEAM	LVL	AGE	W	L	SV	G	GS	IP	H	HR	BB	SO	GB%	BABIP	STUFF	WHIP	ERA	SIERA	DERA	EqH9	EqHR9	EqBB9	EqSO9	VORP	SN/WX
2007	EVE	A-	22	1	3	2	18	0	35	24	0	9	45	60%	.289	18	0.94	0.51	2.24	2.34	8.3	0.8	2.8	6.6	11.5	0.68
2008	HDS	A+	23	2	7	1	35	10	94¹	106	10	32	69	60%	.309	-18	1.46	4.48	4.20	6.09	9.2	1.3	3.5	4.2	-6.3	-1.48
2009	WTN	AA	24	5	6	2	36	9	95²	84	5	24	100	66%	.300	6	1.13	3.10	2.95	4.99	9.1	1.1	2.4	7.0	5.2	-0.12
2010	SEA	MLB	25	4	5	1	39	0	83	89	11	34	57	60%	.307	-6	1.49	5.08	4.44	5.23	9.4	1.2	3.4	5.6	2.5	0.73

Breakout: 12%   Improve: 39%   Collapse: 26%   Attrition: 12%   MLB: 5%   Comparables: Paul Gibson, Brian Fitzgerald, Lee Belanger, Jim Boudreau

Scouts first discovered Hill when he was pitching for the Army team at West Point, and he has gone from a nice story to somebody who might just have a big-league future. His fastball has just average velocity, but it plays up due to his ability to add cut and/or sink to the ball while placing it in the strike zone with the accuracy of a laser-guided weapon. Hardly lights-out as prospects go, he needs to find a secondary pitch to depend on, but if he keeps throwing strikes, he could get there as a middle reliever.

Chris Jakubauskas

Bats: R   Throws: R   Height: 6' 2"   Weight: 210   Born: December 22, 1978   Age: 31

YEAR	TEAM	LVL	AGE	W	L	SV	G	GS	IP	H	HR	BB	SO	GB%	BABIP	STUFF	WHIP	ERA	SIERA	DERA	EqH9	EqHR9	EqBB9	EqSO9	VORP	SN/WX
2007	WTN	AA	28	0	4	0	16	3	51	53	3	21	39	55%	.323	-17	1.45	4.94	4.27	6.04	10.4	1.1	4.0	4.7	-2.9	-0.86
2008	WTN	AA	29	3	0	0	6	6	32²	25	1	7	24	53%	.255	14	0.98	0.83	3.76	1.58	7.2	0.9	2.0	4.9	13.6	1.22
2008	TAC	AAA	29	5	1	0	12	9	55²	52	5	14	48	52%	.288	7	1.19	2.59	3.56	3.76	8.3	1.1	2.3	5.6	10.6	1.02
2009	SEA	MLB	30	6	7	0	35	8	93	91	15	27	47	50%	.254	-21	1.27	5.32	4.94	5.60	9.5	1.5	2.3	4.0	-1.0	1.41
2010	PIT	MLB	31	3	5	0	31	4	73	77	10	28	41	54%	.291	-9	1.44	4.62	4.89	5.05	9.7	1.2	3.2	4.8	3.6	1.13

Breakout: 14%   Improve: 38%   Collapse: 19%   Attrition: 21%   MLB: 48%   Comparables: Rob Bell, Ken Ray, Steve Sundra, Roberto Giron

After hanging around the independent leagues until 2007, Jakubauskas finally made "The Show" as a 30-year-old rookie utility pitcher in 2009. His experience was not exactly successful. He got plugged into the rotation in mid-April after Ryan Rowland-Smith got hurt, but handed the opportunity back before the season flipped over to June. He had decent results against right-handed hitters, holding them to a .276 OBP, but lefties had little problem with him, and he couldn't keep either kind of batter in the ballpark. The Pirates claimed him on waivers and will give him a shot at a utility role as an 11th or 12th pitcher, which isn't much, but to his credit, the man did make it when nobody would have expected him to.

Shawn Kelley

Bats: R   Throws: R   Height: 6' 2"   Weight: 215   Born: April 26, 1984   Age: 26

YEAR	TEAM	LVL	AGE	W	L	SV	G	GS	IP	H	HR	BB	SO	GB%	BABIP	STUFF	WHIP	ERA	SIERA	DERA	EqH9	EqHR9	EqBB9	EqSO9	VORP	SN/WX
2007	WIS	A	23	1	1	0	9	0	12	16	1	4	14	47%	.395	-7	1.67	2.25	3.16	4.37	14.3	2.4	4.0	6.4	1.4	-0.17
2008	HDS	A+	24	0	0	3	12	0	12	8	0	3	12	65%	.258	7	0.92	0.00	2.88	0.77	6.2	0.8	3.1	6.2	6.1	0.35
2008	WTN	AA	24	3	1	9	29	0	42²	31	2	17	44	46%	.269	5	1.12	2.11	3.32	2.99	7.3	0.9	3.5	6.9	11.4	1.13
2009	SEA	MLB	25	5	4	0	41	0	46	45	9	9	41	30%	.279	-2	1.17	4.50	3.53	4.36	9.7	1.8	1.6	7.1	5.6	0.97
2010	SEA	MLB	26	3	4	2	45	1	51²	57	7	20	41	39%	.320	-4	1.49	4.85	4.35	4.95	9.5	1.2	3.2	6.5	3.1	1.15

Breakout: 18%   Improve: 28%   Collapse: 24%   Attrition: 4%   MLB: 100%   Comparables: Julio Mateo, Matt Whiteside, Carlos Reyes, Darren O'Day

Kelley's 2009 season is a perfect example of why relievers' statistics are so volatile. A pair of grand slams left Kelley with a decidedly mediocre ERA despite a strong season overall, especially in the control department. Kelly was advance-billed as having good sink on his fastball, but his results were strongly slanted toward flies, something he paid for with a high home-run rate. He struck out 27 percent of the lefty batters he faced, faring better against them than righties, but his minor-league splits were of a more conventional kind. Much about Kelly is confusing, but given that he made the jump from Double-A to the majors and also missed two months with an oblique injury, perhaps we'll get a truer picture of his abilities beginning this spring.

Mark Lowe

				Bats: L		Throws: R		Height: 6′ 3″		Weight: 200		Born: June 7, 1983			Age: 27

YEAR	TEAM	LVL	AGE	W	L	SV	G	GS	IP	H	HR	BB	SO	GB%	BABIP	STUFF	WHIP	ERA	SIERA	DERA	EqH9	EqHR9	EqBB9	EqSO9	VORP	SN/WX
2008	SEA	MLB	25	1	5	1	57	0	63²	78	6	34	55	46%	.353	-12	1.76	5.37	4.51	5.91	10.4	1.0	4.2	6.8	-3.0	-1.58
2009	SEA	MLB	26	2	7	3	75	0	80	71	7	29	69	43%	.274	3	1.25	3.26	3.94	4.31	8.6	0.8	2.8	6.7	10.5	1.77
2010	SEA	MLB	27	3	4	1	59	0	64	71	8	29	49	41%	.325	-7	1.56	5.02	4.55	5.10	9.7	1.1	3.7	6.3	2.8	0.26

Breakout: 19%   Improve: 46%   Collapse: 21%   Attrition: 6%   MLB: 97%   Comparables: Felix Rodriguez, Justin Lehr, Wayne Gomes, Julian Tavarez

Lowe cut down on his changeup usage in 2009 in favor of his slider, and right-handers really struggled to hit him as a result, averaging only .213/.257/.281 as compared with .250/.350/.326. Even better, lefties who had turned into pretty realistic Lou Gehrig facsimiles in '08 shrunk down to a more endurable .253/.335/.466. Lowe pitched primarily in the eighth inning for the Mariners, holding down leads for Aardsma to close out. He also seemed to get all the inherited runners that Aardsma was protected from seeing, but was only moderately successful at stranding them. With a BABIP of only .274, Lowe was clearly helped out by the Mariners' defense, but he also helped himself by cutting 1 ½ walks off his walk rate. Still, his fly-ball tendencies make him a bit dangerous in high-leverage situations, especially on the road.

Brandon Morrow

				Bats: R		Throws: R		Height: 6′ 3″		Weight: 185		Born: July 26, 1984			Age: 25

YEAR	TEAM	LVL	AGE	W	L	SV	G	GS	IP	H	HR	BB	SO	GB%	BABIP	STUFF	WHIP	ERA	SIERA	DERA	EqH9	EqHR9	EqBB9	EqSO9	VORP	SN/WX
2007	SEA	MLB	22	3	4	0	60	0	63¹	56	3	50	66	42%	.314	22	1.67	4.12	4.53	3.98	7.5	0.4	6.4	8.2	10.7	2.39
2008	TAC	AAA	23	1	2	0	6	5	23¹	17	2	11	26	44%	.254	10	1.20	5.01	3.34	5.21	6.6	1.2	3.9	7.3	0.8	0.10
2008	SEA	MLB	23	3	4	10	45	5	64²	40	10	34	75	36%	.205	15	1.14	3.34	3.37	3.53	5.5	1.7	4.2	9.1	14.2	1.80
2009	TAC	AAA	24	5	3	0	10	10	55	50	2	23	40	45%	.284	4	1.33	3.60	4.53	4.25	8.3	0.7	3.8	5.0	7.5	0.80
2009	SEA	MLB	24	2	4	6	26	10	69²	66	10	44	63	41%	.286	-3	1.58	4.39	4.61	4.76	9.4	1.3	5.0	7.1	5.6	0.46
2010	TOR	MLB	25	7	7	5	59	16	121¹	112	15	70	101	41%	.287	1	1.50	4.59	4.62	4.86	8.4	1.0	4.9	6.9	8.7	2.04

Breakout: 8%   Improve: 37%   Collapse: 25%   Attrition: 18%   MLB: 88%   Comparables: Joe Dobson, Eduardo Rodriguez, Nolan Ryan, Ed Whitson

Morrow struggled in the closer role early in 2009, then struggled elsewhere in the bullpen, and then was sent to the minors, where he worked on being a starter. He reemerged with some effectiveness in four starts in September, but he was not necessarily doing anything differently and mostly benefited from logging innings in front of the M's strong defense. Although he threw more first-pitch strikes, he had trouble throwing strikes overall and hitters did not swing and miss as frequently as they did in 2008. The Mariners never really quite knew what they wanted to do with the fifth overall pick of the 2006 draft, and in December, they gave up trying to find out, shipping him to Toronto. The Jays already appear interested in leaving Morrow alone in a rotation role, and while they'll have to cope with his lack of control, the upside for taking the time to see what comes of it should pay off.

Garrett Olson

				Bats: R		Throws: L		Height: 6′ 1″		Weight: 195		Born: October 18, 1983			Age: 26

YEAR	TEAM	LVL	AGE	W	L	SV	G	GS	IP	H	HR	BB	SO	GB%	BABIP	STUFF	WHIP	ERA	SIERA	DERA	EqH9	EqHR9	EqBB9	EqSO9	VORP	SN/WX
2007	NOR	AAA	23	9	7	0	22	22	128	95	13	39	120	48%	.246	4	1.05	3.16	3.36	4.30	8.0	1.9	2.9	6.4	16.0	1.86
2007	BAL	MLB	23	1	3	0	7	7	32¹	42	4	28	28	34%	.380	7	2.16	7.79	5.51	7.11	11.7	1.1	7.1	7.4	-5.6	-0.31
2008	NOR	AAA	24	1	2	0	7	7	36¹	35	1	16	39	53%	.333	11	1.40	2.97	3.46	4.08	9.2	0.5	4.1	6.6	5.6	0.61
2008	BAL	MLB	24	9	10	0	26	26	132²	168	17	62	83	46%	.335	-12	1.73	6.65	5.11	6.26	10.8	1.0	3.7	5.2	-11.2	0.96
2009	TAC	AAA	25	2	3	0	9	9	47¹	38	2	23	38	48%	.271	5	1.29	4.94	4.38	5.26	7.7	0.8	4.4	5.8	1.2	0.41
2009	SEA	MLB	25	3	5	0	31	11	80¹	79	19	34	47	40%	.247	-32	1.41	5.60	5.22	5.61	9.7	2.2	3.5	4.7	-0.9	1.47
2010	SEA	MLB	26	5	8	0	31	22	114	127	15	56	80	45%	.317	-6	1.60	5.38	4.84	5.49	9.7	1.2	4.0	5.7	0.1	1.28

Breakout: 15%   Improve: 49%   Collapse: 15%   Attrition: 25%   MLB: 76%   Comparables: Gustavo Chacin, Tom Gorzelanny, Jeff Johnson, John Cummings

Acquired from the Cubs with Ronny Cedeño in exchange for Aaron Heilman, Olson split his time between Tacoma and Seattle last year, and split his time in Seattle between starting and relieving. He dropped his major-league ERA by more than a run for the second year in a row. Of course, his starting point was at 7.79, so if things hold, it's going to be 2011 before he gets it under 4.00. Olson isn't really fooling anyone, and when you don't get strikeouts or ground balls and have poor control, you don't have much to fall back on except a healthy lifestyle and the love of a good woman. Olson could be in the mix for the fifth starter's job or a back-of-bullpen spot, but unless he finds a new wrinkle, there's little hope of his becoming a significant asset even in those roles.

Juan Ramirez

Bats: R   Throws: R   Height: 6' 3"   Weight: 175   Born: August 16, 1988   Age: 21

YEAR	TEAM	LVL	AGE	W	L	SV	G	GS	IP	H	HR	BB	SO	GB%	BABIP	STUFF	WHIP	ERA	SIERA	DERA	EqH9	EqHR9	EqBB9	EqSO9	VORP	SN/WX
2007	EVE	A-	18	3	7	0	15	15	75¹	61	3	43	73	43%	.271	9	1.38	4.30	4.17	7.33	9.0	1.3	5.3	4.5	-15.0	-0.98
2008	WIS	A	19	6	9	0	25	22	124	112	9	38	113	50%	.293	-3	1.21	4.14	3.58	7.15	10.2	2.0	3.8	4.8	-20.7	-1.76
2009	HDS	A+	20	8	10	0	28	27	142¹	153	18	53	111	48%	.311	-3	1.45	5.12	4.25	6.78	10.2	1.7	4.1	4.2	-19.3	-2.42
2010	PHI	MLB	21	5	9	0	27	25	120¹	134	18	64	73	44%	.305	18	1.64	5.74	5.29	5.96	9.9	1.4	4.4	4.9	-6.2	1.21

Breakout: 15%   Improve: 53%   Collapse: 11%   Attrition: 11%   MLB: 3%   Comparables: Phil Merrell, Marcus Moore, Corey Avrard, Ching Lo

Ramirez's combination of size and 95 mph velocity has always excited scouts, but after more than 400 minor-league innings, he has yet to take the step to graduate from thrower to pitcher. While the heater is enough to be effective at times, his slurvy breaking ball remains unrefined, and his changeup is rudimentary at best. Having seen this rerun a few too many times already, the Mariners bundled Ramirez into the Cliff Lee deal; the Phillies might be best served by just throwing him in the bullpen and seeing if he can dominate in shorter stints.

Ryan Rowland-Smith

Bats: L   Throws: L   Height: 6' 3"   Weight: 240   Born: January 26, 1983   Age: 27

YEAR	TEAM	LVL	AGE	W	L	SV	G	GS	IP	H	HR	BB	SO	GB%	BABIP	STUFF	WHIP	ERA	SIERA	DERA	EqH9	EqHR9	EqBB9	EqSO9	VORP	SN/WX
2007	TAC	AAA	24	3	4	1	25	0	41²	35	2	22	50	38%	.311	6	1.37	3.67	3.35	4.72	7.9	0.9	4.8	8.1	3.6	-0.23
2007	SEA	MLB	24	1	0	0	26	0	38²	39	4	15	42	36%	.333	11	1.40	3.96	3.36	4.19	8.6	1.2	3.0	8.6	5.6	0.20
2008	TAC	AAA	25	2	0	0	3	3	18²	12	1	7	12	38%	.204	1	1.02	2.89	4.76	3.13	5.3	1.0	3.4	3.9	4.9	0.44
2008	SEA	MLB	25	5	3	2	47	12	118¹	114	13	48	77	44%	.276	-4	1.37	3.42	4.81	3.62	8.2	1.1	3.2	5.2	24.6	2.55
2009	TAC	AAA	26	5	3	0	10	10	56¹	61	5	10	38	46%	.308	0	1.26	4.31	4.08	4.86	9.9	1.3	1.8	4.6	3.9	0.68
2009	SEA	MLB	26	5	4	0	15	15	96¹	87	9	27	52	43%	.252	7	1.18	3.74	4.91	3.96	8.7	0.9	2.2	4.3	16.1	2.40
2010	SEA	MLB	27	7	8	1	48	18	132¹	137	16	51	84	40%	.297	-2	1.42	4.57	4.85	4.68	9.0	1.1	3.2	5.2	12.1	1.82

Breakout: 6%   Improve: 41%   Collapse: 17%   Attrition: 14%   MLB: 74%   Comparables: Frank Baumann, Denny Neagle, Joe Crawford, Kei Igawa

Rowland-Smith won the fifth starter's job in spring training but made just one start before triceps tendinitis put him on the DL for more than three months, at which point the Mariners sent him back to Tacoma to work on his command. He wasn't great there, but he succeeded in shaving his walk rate and was called back roughly a month later. In the 14 starts remaining to him, he walked just 2.2 per nine innings and logged 11 quality starts (although two were blown after the sixth inning). That more than filled the bill in what the Mariners were looking for by way of improvement, particularly at home, where the park shielded him from the consequences of his fly-balling ways. The hyphenated Australian is still a bit of an unknown in terms of how good he might be if healthy enough to handle a full season in the rotation, but he showed enough in the second half to merit the benefit of the doubt going into 2010.

Carlos Silva

Bats: R   Throws: R   Height: 6' 4"   Weight: 245   Born: April 23, 1979   Age: 31

YEAR	TEAM	LVL	AGE	W	L	SV	G	GS	IP	H	HR	BB	SO	GB%	BABIP	STUFF	WHIP	ERA	SIERA	DERA	EqH9	EqHR9	EqBB9	EqSO9	VORP	SN/WX
2007	MIN	MLB	28	13	14	0	33	33	202	229	20	36	89	56%	.299	1	1.31	4.19	4.82	4.17	9.8	1.0	1.4	3.6	29.4	5.13
2008	SEA	MLB	29	4	15	0	28	28	153¹	213	20	32	69	51%	.342	-21	1.60	6.46	5.01	6.35	11.9	1.4	1.7	3.6	-14.4	0.59
2009	SEA	MLB	30	1	3	0	8	6	30¹	41	5	11	10	53%	.319	-33	1.71	8.60	5.78	8.38	13.0	1.6	3.1	2.8	-9.3	-0.36
2010	CHN	MLB	31	3	6	0	20	15	80¹	100	11	24	33	51%	.319	-17	1.55	5.27	5.30	5.54	11.0	1.3	2.4	3.4	-0.3	0.69

Breakout: 11%   Improve: 37%   Collapse: 29%   Attrition: 38%   MLB: 75%   Comparables: Ryan Drese, Albie Lopez, John Buzhardt, Jake Westbrook

The four-year, $48 million contract given to Carlos Silva, exemplar of pitch-to-contactism, before the 2008 season seemed questionable at the time and proved to be a disaster. A poor performance in 2008 was followed by a shoulder injury in May 2009. Silva returned from injury in September and got in a couple of relief appearances before the season was over. Zduriencik made Silva the poison pill the Cubs had to swallow to be rid of Milton Bradley, repurposing Bavasi's wasteful commitment to Silva (plus $9 million to help pay him the $25 million already owed to him through 2011). The expectations for him in Wrigleyville are appropriately low, but perhaps pitching in the weaker league might help him survive as the utility pitcher who either slots into the rotation because of injury or soaks up middle-innings assignments, all for the kind of money Warren Brusstar could only enjoy in his wildest dreams of avarice.

Ian Snell

				Bats: R		Throws: R		Height: 5′ 11″		Weight: 200		Born: October 30, 1981		Age: 28							

YEAR	TEAM	LVL	AGE	W	L	SV	G	GS	IP	H	HR	BB	SO	GB%	BABIP	STUFF	WHIP	ERA	SIERA	DERA	EqH9	EqHR9	EqBB9	EqSO9	VORP	SN/WX
2007	PIT	MLB	25	9	12	0	32	32	208	209	22	68	177	52%	.308	19	1.33	3.76	3.83	3.82	8.4	1.0	2.6	6.8	38.7	5.47
2008	PIT	MLB	26	7	12	0	31	31	164¹	201	18	89	135	46%	.351	-5	1.76	5.42	4.61	5.63	10.5	1.0	4.2	6.1	-2.4	1.35
2009	PIT	MLB	27	2	8	0	15	15	80²	87	7	44	52	47%	.313	-5	1.62	5.36	5.13	5.72	9.8	0.8	4.2	4.9	-1.9	0.66
2009	IND	AAA	27	2	2	0	6	6	37¹	28	0	13	47	47%	.315	35	1.10	0.96	2.46	2.42	7.6	0.3	3.3	8.9	12.1	1.28
2009	SEA	MLB	27	5	2	0	12	12	64¹	61	7	39	37	42%	.263	-4	1.55	4.20	5.70	4.36	9.3	1.0	4.9	4.6	8.0	1.50
2010	SEA	MLB	28	8	11	0	32	32	175¹	192	22	81	127	46%	.317	2	1.55	5.03	4.66	5.08	9.5	1.1	3.8	5.9	8.2	2.24

Breakout: 4%   Improve: 42%   Collapse: 17%   Attrition: 13%   MLB: 96%   Comparables: Francisco Cordova, Josh Fogg, Pat Hentgen, Russ Ortiz

Snell had a bizarre season. He began the season looking even more lost than he had in 2008, itself a disappointment following as it did on the heels of his 2007 breakthrough. On the verge of being pulled from the rotation, he requested a demotion instead, citing "too much negativity" in Pittsburgh. As if to prove his point, in his first start at Indianapolis, he struck out 17 batters in seven innings, including 12 in a row. At the same time, Neil Huntington was telling the media that the Pirates had "missed" on the "human element" when they gave Snell a three-year extension in March 2008, and it was clear that Snell wasn't coming back from Indianapolis, no matter how many batters he struck out. A month later, Snell was off to Seattle along with Jack Wilson in a classic "change of scenery" exchange. He pitched superficially better for the M's, but his walk and strikeout rates continued to head in the wrong directions. If he's not hurt, there's still something here to salvage, but the second half proved nothing.

Jason Vargas

				Bats: L		Throws: L		Height: 6′ 0″		Weight: 215		Born: February 2, 1983		Age: 27							

YEAR	TEAM	LVL	AGE	W	L	SV	G	GS	IP	H	HR	BB	SO	GB%	BABIP	STUFF	WHIP	ERA	SIERA	DERA	EqH9	EqHR9	EqBB9	EqSO9	VORP	SN/WX
2007	NWO	AAA	24	9	7	0	24	24	125	141	14	44	108	35%	.328	-21	1.48	4.97	4.11	6.25	11.0	1.7	3.4	5.8	-10.0	0.31
2007	NYN	MLB	24	0	1	0	2	2	10¹	17	4	2	4	22%	.317	-32	1.84	12.19	6.14	12.66	14.3	3.4	1.7	3.4	-8.5	-0.25
2009	TAC	AAA	26	4	3	0	9	9	51²	48	3	15	46	30%	.319	14	1.22	3.14	3.67	3.73	9.2	1.0	2.9	6.7	9.2	0.91
2009	SEA	MLB	26	3	6	0	23	14	91²	98	16	24	54	46%	.285	-18	1.33	4.91	4.62	5.06	10.6	1.7	2.2	4.8	4.3	1.59
2010	SEA	MLB	27	4	7	0	25	18	97¹	118	14	39	65	27%	.332	-9	1.61	5.49	5.22	5.64	10.6	1.3	3.3	5.5	-1.5	1.28

Breakout: 17%   Improve: 53%   Collapse: 6%   Attrition: 20%   MLB: 63%   Comparables: Jason Stanford, Lance Painter, Jeff Fassero, John Cerutti

Despite missing all of 2008 with a torn hip labrum, Vargas was included in the mammoth December 2008 three-team trade between the Mets, Indians, and Mariners. He failed to make the club out of spring training and spent the rest of the season memorizing the countryside along I-5 between Seattle and Tacoma from the window of his car as he was summoned (and returned) on three occasions. Vargas wasn't very successful as a starter (just three quality starts), but did pitch decently in a smattering of relief appearances. He'll head into spring training as one of several not-terribly-appealing choices for the back end of the Mariners' rotation.

Sean White

				Bats: R		Throws: R		Height: 6′ 4″		Weight: 210		Born: April 25, 1981		Age: 29							

YEAR	TEAM	LVL	AGE	W	L	SV	G	GS	IP	H	HR	BB	SO	GB%	BABIP	STUFF	WHIP	ERA	SIERA	DERA	EqH9	EqHR9	EqBB9	EqSO9	VORP	SN/WX
2007	TAC	AAA	26	1	1	0	2	2	10²	11	0	2	7	58%	.314	4	1.22	2.53	4.04	3.80	8.4	0.0	1.7	4.2	2.0	0.33
2007	SEA	MLB	26	1	1	0	15	0	35¹	35	2	20	16	56%	.277	-18	1.56	5.60	5.67	5.70	7.9	0.5	4.5	3.5	-0.8	-0.23
2008	TAC	AAA	27	6	11	0	22	22	125	176	12	43	52	59%	.358	-32	1.75	5.47	5.22	6.20	12.6	1.3	3.2	2.5	-9.3	-0.58
2009	SEA	MLB	28	3	2	1	52	0	64¹	50	3	20	28	56%	.226	-5	1.09	2.80	5.11	3.29	7.6	0.4	2.4	3.4	15.5	2.45
2010	SEA	MLB	29	2	5	0	33	6	60²	82	9	27	24	59%	.333	-29	1.79	6.60	5.53	6.68	11.6	1.3	3.7	3.1	-7.9	0.80

Breakout: 11%   Improve: 39%   Collapse: 33%   Attrition: 27%   MLB: 41%   Comparables: Matt Carnes, Jon Adkins, Craig McMurtry, Keith Glauber

Fantastic luck on balls in play in 2009—a .229 BABIP and just .198 against lefties—belied a performance that was decidedly not major-league quality. White has trouble striking hitters out and doesn't command the strike zone well enough to be effective. Although the Mariners' defense benefited all pitchers, White's performance relies far too much on low BABIP to be anything but a fluke. Expect a significant regression for 2010.

LINEOUTS

Hitters

PLAYER	TEAM	LVL	AGE	PA	R	2B	3B	HR	RBI	BB	SO	SB-CS	EqBRR	AVG/OBP/SLG	EqAVG/EqOBP/EqSLG	EqA	VORP	WARP
C S. Baron	PUL	Rk	18	116	12	6	0	2	13	7	38	0-0	0.2	.179/.241/.292	.147/.190/.211	.108	-9.3	-1.8
C K. Johjima	SEA	MLB	33	258	24	11	0	9	22	12	28	2-2	-1.0	.247/.296/.406	.256/.305/.416	.245	7.3	2.4
1B B. LaHair*	TAC	AAA	26	510	72	28	2	26	85	45	116	0-5	-4.2	.289/.354/.530	.259/.316/.459	.262	8.4	1.5
3B M. Mangini*	WTN	AA	23	469	48	18	5	12	67	38	92	10-2	-0.4	.273/.339/.424	.257/.309/.405	.249	6.6	-0.9
MI O. Navarro	WTN	AA	24	230	23	6	1	1	13	33	44	4-2	-2.7	.258/.376/.316	.236/.330/.291	.228	1.6	0.2
	TAC	AAA	24	175	13	7	0	0	12	8	34	4-1	-0.2	.252/.298/.296	.235/.273/.265	.193	-4.3	-1.7
UT B. Nelson*	TAC	AAA	26	307	35	9	1	15	45	30	56	0-0	-1.9	.247/.322/.451	.222/.290/.387	.234	-7.1	-1.5
SS G. Noriega#	PUL	Rk	18	229	27	14	2	4	26	16	60	8-6	-0.6	.311/.360/.456	.227/.267/.318	.205	-3.3	-1.5
OF J. Owens*	TAC	AAA	28	445	74	10	9	3	37	44	48	23-8	0.6	.323/.390/.418	.295/.353/.375	.259	11.8	1.5
OF C. Peguero*	HDS	A+	22	544	92	21	14	31	98	42	172	3-4	-0.3	.271/.335/.560	.219/.271/.416	.233	-9.5	-1.3
OF P. Redman	TAC	AAA	29	456	84	35	3	21	66	33	77	7-2	2.4	.297/.352/.548	.263/.309/.462	.261	10.1	0.2
1B C. Shelton	TAC	AAA	29	472	71	30	2	15	85	58	86	0-2	0.2	.314/.396/.509	.276/.348/.435	.272	16.2	0.3
	SEA	MLB	29	28	1	2	0	0	4	2	11	0-0	0.2	.231/.286/.308	.231/.286/.308	.210	-1.3	0.0
SS J. Wilson	ARI	MLB	28	30	1	1	0	0	2	3	3	0-0	-0.1	.231/.333/.269	.231/.333/.269	.223	-0.2	0.3
	SDN	MLB	28	43	2	2	0	0	1	3	9	0-0	-0.3	.105/.190/.158	.103/.186/.154	-.092	-3.9	-1.1
	SEA	MLB	28	138	16	8	1	3	10	6	32	1-2	-1.9	.250/.294/.398	.258/.301/.406	.239	2.0	0.0

A supplemental first-round pick last June, **Steve Baron** is a plus-plus defender with power, but his swing might need a total overhaul. ⊘ **Kenji Johjima** went home, forgoing the last two years of his M's contract to sign a four-year deal with the Hanshin Tigers. ⊘ After four seasons at Triple-A, **Bryan LaHair** finally showed some power, hitting 26 homers after never hitting more than 12 in previous seasons. ⊘ **Matt Mangini** is a big third baseman who so far has hit like a little one. ⊘ Slick-fielding **Oswaldo Navarro** never did catch a break with Seattle, but he has moved to an Astros organization that lacks an established shortstop. ⊘ Minor-league vet **Brad Nelson** had been in the Brewers' system for so long that he once babysat for the Seligs, but an escape to Tacoma failed to get his prospectdom back on track. ⊘ Venezuelan shortstop **Gabriel Noriega,** an outstanding defensive prospect who made great strides with the bat in 2009, could be one of the better sleeper prospects in the game. ⊘ **Jerry Owens** had the best year of his career in Tacoma, which was enough to get him a return engagement with the Nationals on a minor-league deal. ⊘ Big Dominican **Carlos Peguero** lit up the scoreboard in High Desert, but will have to prove it wasn't just park-generated fiction at higher levels. ⊘ Journeyman **Prentice Redman** slugged over .500 in Tacoma for the second straight year, but no one bit on what might happen if he were liberated. ⊘ **Chris Shelton** has decent power and is fairly patient, but he has enough trouble making contact that he cannot justify getting regular work; he has been signed to a minor-league contract with the Astros. ⊘ **Josh Wilson** was a waiver-wire floater last year, sailing from team to team like an untethered balloon, but he re-upped with the M's on a minor-league contract.

Pitchers

PLAYER	TEAM	LVL	AGE	W	L	SV	IP	H	HR	BB	SO	GB%	BABIP	STUFF	WHIP	ERA	SIERA	DERA	EqH9	EqHR9	EqBB9	EqSO9	VORP
D. Cortes	NWA	AA	22	6	6	0	80¹	77	3	50	57	50%	.301	4	1.58	3.92	5.04	5.63	9.3	0.9	5.5	5.0	-1.1
—	WTN	AA	22	1	5	0	54²	51	4	35	55	50%	.315	13	1.57	4.94	4.17	6.49	10.0	1.4	5.6	6.8	-5.6
R. Manuel	LOU	AAA	25	3	4	10	46²	37	2	10	38	33%	.257	2	1.01	2.70	3.78	4.04	7.5	0.8	2.2	5.7	7.4
—	TAC	AAA	25	1	1	4	19	13	4	6	11	37%	.167	-22	1.00	3.32	4.94	4.34	6.3	2.4	2.9	3.9	2.4
R. Messenger	TAC	AAA	27	0	2	25	56²	65	4	14	40	45%	.323	-13	1.39	2.86	4.22	4.26	10.3	1.1	2.4	4.8	7.7
—	SEA	MLB	27	0	1	0	10¹	13	3	0	5	37%	.286	-14	1.26	4.35	4.48	4.19	12.1	2.8	0.0	3.7	1.4
R. Orta	WTN	AA	24	3	2	3	41²	29	1	18	41	46%	.257	3	1.13	1.94	3.61	3.83	7.4	0.7	3.8	6.5	7.4
E. Paredes*	HDS	A+	22	8	4	3	71	74	6	22	64	48%	.324	-12	1.35	4.69	3.64	6.51	10.1	1.3	3.6	5.0	-7.6
M. Robles*	WMI	A	20	4	4	0	56¹	45	6	27	71	45%	.300	14	1.28	4.63	2.90	7.26	11.0	3.0	5.8	7.3	-9.5
—	LAK	A+	20	4	2	0	35	34	3	14	40	43%	.341	26	1.37	3.60	3.14	6.10	11.6	2.3	4.6	7.0	-2.1
—	HDS	A+	20	3	2	0	32¹	23	1	19	34	58%	.275	30	1.30	2.78	3.61	4.55	7.6	0.9	6.4	6.1	3.1
S. Shell	WTN	AA	26	3	0	0	21	9	0	6	16	37%	.158	10	0.71	0.43	4.02	1.50	4.3	0.4	2.6	4.7	9.3
—	TAC	AAA	26	3	3	1	40	56	10	15	27	37%	.331	-42	1.77	6.97	4.91	8.28	12.9	3.2	3.4	4.5	-12.3
J. Thomas*	TAC	AAA	25	2	4	6	60¹	67	5	40	53	49%	.328	-13	1.77	4.48	4.70	5.30	10.1	1.2	5.7	6.0	1.4
A. Varvaro	WTN	AA	24	4	3	8	54¹	30	1	44	63	38%	.230	16	1.36	2.82	4.23	4.58	6.3	0.7	6.8	7.8	5.4

Acquired from the Royals in the Yuniesky Betancourt deal, **Dan Cortes** continues to excite scouts with his low-90s heat and plus curve while frustrating them with his performance. ⊘ **Ryan Feierabend** wasn't lighting up any evenings last season, as he was recovering from a March spin with Tommy John surgery on his elbow, but he should resume hurling this spring. ⊘ Acquired from the Reds for Wladimir Balentien, **Robert Manuel** is a trick-pitch righty who depends far more on deception and movement than stuff; Manuel is already lost to the Red Sox on a November waiver claim. ⊘ **Randy Messenger** only got cups of coffee with Seattle the last two years and, having gotten the message, signed with the Hanshin Tigers to take his chances abroad. ⊘ **Ricky Orta** is the rare Venezuelan who's been drafted (fourth round '06; he went to Miami) and has marked time in the minors since, throwing mid-90s heat with spotty command; he was added to the 40-man after a solid AFL performance. ⊘ Dominican **Edward Paredes** might mature into a solid situational southpaw, thanks to a three-quarters delivery and a nasty slider; he can boast of surviving High Desert's mound massacre. ⊘ Mr. French might be the first man received in the Washburn trade to make it to the majors, but little Venezuelan **Mauricio Robles** has a nice fastball/curve mix and command and should be the better prospect. ⊘ **Steven Shell** refused assignment to the Nats' Triple-A squad, so he arranged to take his beatings at Tacoma instead. He has always had a decent arm and showed some signs of life this winter in Venezuela. ⊘ **Justin Thomas** has LOOGY upside, which beats earning beer money as a substitute teacher while trying to figure out what you want to do with the rest of your life; he'll be in the Pirates' camp after a waiver claim. ⊘ **Anthony Varvaro** made an impressive return from Tommy John surgery (his second spin with blowing out his elbow), but he'll need to improve his command beyond the usual case of postsurgical yips.

MANAGER: DON WAKAMATSU

YEAR	TEAM	W-L	Pythag +/−	Avg PC	100+ P	120+ P	QS	BQS	REL	REL w Zero R	IBB	Subs	PH	PH Avg	PH HR	SB2	CS2	SB3	CS3	SAC Att	SAC %	POS SAC	Squeeze	Swing	In Play
2009	SEA	85-77	10	95.8	71	1	77	5	409	268	13	27	58	.216	1	70	24	19	8	80	70.0%	55	6	126	96

In his first season as the Mariners' manager, Wakamatsu endeared himself to several sects. His focus on a strong clubhouse with good chemistry appealed to traditionalists. Wakamatsu also made himself palatable to the hardcore fan, speaking of sabermetrics in his inaugural press conference. He certainly adhered to some basic sabermetric tenets during his first season. No manager issued fewer free passes, and he was careful not to abuse his pitchers. What's more, this former catcher called fewer pitchouts than did any other manager in the league. On the other hand, Wakamatsu sacrificed frequently, leading the majors in sac bunts by position players (and the highest tally in the AL in the last five years), and he wasn't bunting with his scrubs—Franklin Gutierrez led the team with 13. Another tendency of Wakamatsu's may not fall into any strict category: he pinch-hit less than did any other manager in the game.

Tampa Bay Rays

If luck is the residue of design, as Branch Rickey famously cadged from Milton, then the 2009 season provided an object lesson for the Rays. No matter how smart the brain trust or how well-drawn the blueprint behind its sudden success, the franchise will need more good fortune than it saw last year in order to thrive in the game's shark tank, the American League East. The Rays set the game on its ear in 2008. Between owner Stuart Sternberg, team president Matthew Silverman, general manager Andrew Friedman, and manager Joe Maddon, the Rays emerged as one of the game's best-run teams, a textbook example of how to turn the fortunes of an organization around via smart, cutting-edge management. Alas, the Rays fell back in 2009, spending the latter part of their 84-win season well beyond the fray while the division's two power-houses, the Yankees and Red Sox, returned to the playoffs. While the season still ranked as the second-best in franchise history, it was nonetheless a disappointment, raising the question of how the franchise could keep pace in the division's arms race.

The 2008 Rays had improved by 31 games, the majors' fifth-largest turnaround since 1900. They did so on the back of record-setting improvements by their defense and their bullpen. Even with largely the same cast of characters, both areas saw the Rays regress significantly toward the mean. Which really shouldn't be all that surprising. As Bill James observed back in his *Baseball Abstract* days, teams that improve in one season—particularly those that exceed their Pythagorean expectations (as the Rays had, by about five games)—have a strong tendency to fall back in the next. It's what James called the Plexiglas Principle; what looks like a breakthrough is really just the wall giving a little in the short term. In the free-agency era, nearly every team that has made anything close to a comparably large turnaround has fallen back considerably in the following season (see Table 1).

Since 1976, 24 teams have improved by at least 23 wins from one season to the next. Due to player strikes, three of those teams did not play a full schedule the following year. The remaining 21 declined by an average of 11.2 wins. Only the 1978 Brewers and 1991 Braves won even more games the following year. It is something of an irony that those Braves are among the exceptions, because while the Rays might aspire to the kind of continued success that the Bobby Cox/John Schuerholz Atlanta dynasty achieved, Tampa Bay faces much larger obstacles in its path, namely, the Yanks and Sox. As National League West residents at the time of their emergence, the Braves had the good fortune to catch the division's highest-spending teams just as they were headed downward. The 1991 Dodgers, who had the game's second-highest payroll, fell a game short of the division flag in the year of the Braves' big turnaround, then promptly nosedived to a 63-99 record the following year, and managed just an 81-81 record in 1993. The 1991 Reds, carrying the game's 11th-highest payroll after winning the World Series the year prior, slumped to 74-88 in 1991, and while they rebounded to 90-72 the following year, they still finished six games behind the division's new powerhouses.

While the Braves' opponents went quietly into eclipse, the Rays' emergence only redoubled the Yankees' and Red Sox' efforts to remain competitive. Though the Yankees' Opening Day payroll decreased by about $8 million from 2008 to 2009, it still exceeded

RAYS PROSPECTUS
2009 W-L: 84-78, 3rd in AL East

Pythag	92-70	2nd	**Ballpark:** Tropicana Field (3-yr. PF: 985). The last dome causes funny hops, but Rays seek sunshine
RS/G	5.0	5th	
RA/G	4.7	7th	
EqA	.268	2nd	**2009:** Regression's a bitch, the AL East eats its young, but a few nice breakouts and debuts
EqBRR	4.0	3rd	
SNWP	.507	6th	
WXRL	5.69	11th	**2010:** Reinviting themselves to the contention conversation requires steps forward from Upton, Price—which they're capable of making
FRAr	4.64	8th	
DE	.696	4th	
PADE	-0.51	7th	**Action Items:** Get Pat the Bat's mojo back, picking a 2B or RF (you can't clone a Zorilla)
Salary	$63.3	13th	
Attend	1.87	11th	

Table 1. Roller Coaster Rides: Biggest One-Year Gains and Their Aftermaths

Year	Team	W-L	Improve	Next
1999	Diamondbacks	100-62	+35	-15
1989	Orioles	87-75	+33	-11
2008	Rays	97-65	+31	-13
1991	Braves	94-68	+29	+4
2004	Tigers	72-90	+29	-1
1977	White Sox	90-72	+26	-19
1978	Brewers	93-69	+26	+2
1996	Cardinals	88-74	+26	-15
1997	Tigers	79-83	+26	-14
2005	Diamondbacks	77-85	+26	-1
2006	Mets	97-65	+26	-9
1984	Cubs	96-65	+25	-19
1986	Indians	84-78	+24	-23
1986	Rangers	87-75	+25	-12
1990	White Sox	94-68	+25	-7
2001	Mariners	116-46	+25	-23
2002	Angels	99-63	+24	-22
2006	Tigers	95-67	+24	-7
1988	Athletics	104-58	+23	-5
2001	Cubs	88-74	+23	-21
2004	Padres	87-75	+23	-5

Improve = improvement in wins over previous season
Next = change in wins the next season

$200 million after an offseason that saw them commit some $441 million in free-agent contracts to CC Sabathia, A. J. Burnett, and Mark Teixeira. The Red Sox, though not so profligate, did bestow $111 million worth of generous extensions to Dustin Pedroia, Kevin Youkilis, and Jon Lester, maintaining their status as the game's fourth-highest payroll. By comparison, the 2008 Rays left the gate with a $43.8 million payroll, the game's second-lowest, and although it increased to $63.3 million in 2009 primarily due to raises, it was still in the bottom quintile.

It didn't take long to see that the previous year's magic had gone missing for Maddon's squad. Despite outscoring opponents by a total of seven runs in April, the Rays stumbled into the division's basement via a 9-14 record, going just 2-7 in games decided by one or two runs. By comparison, they'd dominated such close contests the year before, with a 52-26 record. They were 5 ½ games out of first place by the time the calendar turned to May; from that point onward, they never drew closer than 3 ½ games or climbed higher than third place in the East. After August 11th, they spent just two days with a division deficit of less than 10 games and remained at least three games out of the wild-card lead.

The Rays' decline from the previous season's dizzying heights owed far more to the pitching-and-defense side

of the equation than the hitting side. Indeed, the offense actually improved. After scoring runs at a league-average clip (4.8 runs per game) in 2008, the Rays saw their production rise to 4.9 runs per game in 2009, a little more than 0.1 better than average, and their EqA rose marginally from .265 to .268. Evan Longoria (.303 EqA) extended his stellar rookie performance—interrupted as it was by injury and minor-league service—over a full season, Carlos Pena (.298) ranked among the league's most productive hitters despite a low batting average, Carl Crawford (.291) rebounded from an injury-wracked campaign, Ben Zobrist (.322) remade his swing and emerged as one of the league's top offensive forces while seeing extensive time in both right field and at second base, and Jason Bartlett (.308) put together a surprisingly strong campaign with the stick. All of that was enough to offset the injury-related downturns of Dioner Navarro (.208, down from .268 due to an elbow problem in his nonthrowing arm), B. J. Upton (.251, down from .289 due to a slow recovery from off-season labrum surgery), and last winter's big free-agent signing, Pat Burrell (.246, down from .299 with the Phillies as a result of neck woes).

As for run prevention, after bettering the league average in 2008 (4.1 to 4.7), the Rays fell back to just barely ahead of average (4.6 to 4.7). The rotation, which had tied for second in the league at 22.9 SNLVAR in 2008, slipped to a still-respectable fourth at 19.4 in 2009, and only thanks to newcomers. While Matt Garza turned in similarly solid numbers, James Shields took a minor step backward, Scott Kazmir a major one, and Andy Sonnanstine, well, he was beaten like he stole something (see Table 2).

The declines of Kazmir and Sonnanstine were partly offset by the emergence of rookies Jeff Niemann (3.94 ERA, 5.0 SNLVAR, and a team-high .559 SNWP) and David Price (4.42 ERA, 2.8 SNLVAR, .501 SNWP). Niemann, a well-regarded prospect limited by arm troubles, made the team in part because he was out of minor-league options, but he nonetheless emerged as a midrotation stalwart. Price entered the year as the game's top pitching prospect following a tantalizing 2008 post-season performance, but he spent the first six weeks of the 2009 season back in Triple-A and couldn't live up to the hype, due to the mysterious disappearance of his vaunted slider.

All told, the rotation's holdovers saw their collective ERAs increase by a full run and their collective SNWP fall nearly 50 points. A good portion of that was due to the team's defense, which after leading the majors at .710 in 2008—setting a Retrosheet-era (1954 onward) record for year-to-year turnaround in the process—fell

Table 2. Rotation Aggravation: Rays Starting Pitcher Performance, 2008 vs. 2009

Pitcher	2008						2009					
	GS	IP	SNLVAR	ERA	QERA	SNWP	GS	IP	SNLVAR	ERA	QERA	SNWP
Shields	33	215	5.4	3.56	3.74	.553	33	219.2	3.9	4.14	4.04	.506
Garza	30	184.2	4.9	3.70	4.58	.540	32	203.0	5.3	3.95	4.14	.545
Kazmir	27	152.1	4.8	3.49	4.11	.565	20	111.0	1.2	5.92	4.93	.450
Sonnanstine	32	193.1	3.0	4.38	4.26	.483	18	99.2	0.1	6.77	5.04	.380
Front Four	122	745.1	18.1	3.79	4.16	.534	103	633.1	10.5	4.80	4.39	.485
Others	40	301.1	4.7	4.60	5.45	.503	59	345.1	8.9	4.10	4.58	.538

to .696 in 2009, still good for fourth in the league, but a substantial fall nonetheless.

The bullpen slumped more drastically, from a league-leading 15.4 WXRL in 2008 to just 5.7 in 2009, 11th in the league. J. P. Howell, Dan Wheeler, and Grant Balfour, Maddon's three mainstays from the prior year, all declined to some extent, with Balfour's fall the most drastic. Relievers, of course, are notoriously volatile from year to year, but it's not as though Friedman didn't work to augment their corps. The Rays replaced departing LOOGY Trever Miller with both Brian Shouse and Randy Choate, brought in Joe Nelson fresh off a strong season with the Marlins, granted Jason Isringhausen a shot at a comeback, and added Russ Springer in August—all to little avail. The Rays simply couldn't get reliable help from their relievers for more than a few weeks at a time (see Table 3).

Table 3. Nothing Constant but Inconsistency: Rays Monthly Pen Performance, 2009

Month	IP	FRAr	WXRL
April	63.1	4.06	0.5
May	101.0	5.12	0.2
June	70.0	1.52	3.2
July	66.1	4.85	1.9
August	74.1	4.90	0.9
Sept/Oct	82.1	6.76	-1.0

FRAr: Fair Run Average, relief-only

Such shaky late-inning work, particularly during the second half, removed any doubt about whether 2009 was going to be the Rays' year, so as the summer went on, the team's efforts to curb its spending took on an air befitting a small-market also-ran. Although the Rays did wind up with a modest 3.4 percent boost in attendance amid an industry-wide six percent decline, as early as June Silverman publicly bemoaned Tropicana Stadium's half-full stands, a subtle dig at their dissatisfaction with their dome-icile as well as an effort to manage the fan base's expectations. The team made no major acquisition prior to the July 31st trade deadline, despite the subpar production of both Burrell and the right-field platoon of Gabe Gross and Gabe Kapler; the club's biggest in-season addition was a waiver-period trade for catcher Gregg Zaun. On August 29th, the Rays shed $22.5 million in future commitments by trading Kazmir, who had started to come around after a wretched first half, to the Angels for three prospects, second baseman Sean Rodriguez, third baseman Matt Sweeney, and pitcher Alex Torres.

The Rays did have more than cost-cutting on their minds in making the Kazmir trade, which opened up a rotation spot for the highly regarded power righty Wade Davis, whose strong September showing probably earned him a spot in the 2010 rotation. As good as he is, Davis isn't even the club's top pitching prospect; that honor now belongs to Jeremy Hellickson, who enjoyed a breakout year at Double-A and Triple-A and who could debut sometime in the coming season. Beyond those two, the farm system appears packed with high-upside arms, including Matt Moore, Alex Colome, Jake McGee, Nick Barnese, and the aforementioned Torres, though McGee is the only one who has even seen Double-A. As the Kazmir trade illustrates, a key facet of the Rays' modus operandi involves peeling off surplus pitching for trade. Not that any team ever has too much pitching, but between the aforementioned stock and the fact that all five starters—all except Garza homegrown, mind you—are under club control for multiple years, the Rays are in an enviable position. Even Shields, the veteran of the group, has a very team-friendly contract through 2011 and then reasonable options thereafter.

So, do the Rays have any chance at conquering the beasts of the East? They do appear to be marshaling their resources and aggressively stretching their budget in the hopes of doing so. They began the winter by greasing the skids toward an obvious spot in the lineup for Zobrist, trading second baseman Akinori Iwamura, who missed much of 2009 with a knee injury, to the Pirates. The move only netted them reliever Jesse Chavez, but it saved the Rays the $550,000 they probably would have spent to buy out Iwamura's rather affordable 2010 option ($4.85 million). A month later, they flipped Chavez to the Braves for Rafael Soriano, who had shocked his soon-to-be-former team by accepting arbitration. Soriano then agreed to a one-year deal worth $7.25 million—ironically, just days after Sternberg had told reporters, "There's no $7 million closer showing up." The move pushed the Rays' payroll toward $70 million even as Silverman sounded an ominous note: "The payroll we had last year isn't one that's sustainable given where we are with revenues. This addition puts us at a level that's even less sustainable, but it's an important move for our organization."

To address other questions in the lineup, the Rays traded yet another one of their lesser pitching prospects, Mitch Talbot, to Cleveland for catcher Kelly Shoppach. While Shoppach is neither a defensive wizard nor an ideal fit with Navarro from a platoon standpoint, he's a bona fide lefty masher. The team appears likely to turn over at least the long half of a right-field platoon—replacing the unproductive Gross—to Matt Joyce, who was acquired in last winter's trade with the Tigers for Edwin Jackson and subsequently spent most of the year honing his plate discipline and marking time in Triple-A. The Rays picked up Crawford's 2010 option of $10 million, and while they paid lip service to a long-term extension, they appear to have an outfield logjam on the horizon between him, a hopefully recovered Upton, and top hitting prospect Desmond Jennings, a speedy center fielder who tore up the Southern League after a lost 2008.

The farm system is primed to keep the talent pipeline flowing. Although the Rays failed to sign either of their top two 2009 draft picks, LeVon Washington and Kenny Diekroeger, the team will receive compensation picks for both in the upcoming draft, as well as supplemental first-round picks for Type B free agents Zaun (who signed with the Brewers) and Shouse (whose return to the majors at 41 is no given, though his left arm remains attached). That could mean as many as six picks prior to the third round, and while the cost-conscious team's desire to avoid too many big bonuses could mean that some of the picks may go unsigned, it's another enviable problem to have.

Stuck in the game's most competitive, biggest-spending division, the Rays are hostage to one of the game's most limited markets, playing in a facility they'd just as soon replace. They'll still need plenty of good fortune, but there's little question that their brain trust has the creativity to put them in the best position to succeed under such circumstances.

HITTERS

Willy Aybar				INF						Bats: S		Throws: R		Height: 5'11"		Weight: 200		Born: March 9, 1983			Age: 27		

YEAR	TEAM	LVL	AGE	PA	R	2B	3B	HR	RBI	BB	SO	SB	CS	EqBRR	AVG	OBP	SLG	EqAVG	EqOBP	EqSLG	EqA	VORP	WARP	DEFENSE
2008	TBA	MLB	25	362	33	17	2	10	33	32	44	2	2	-5.5	.253	.327	.410	.260	.335	.424	.260	7.0	2.5	40-3B 11 17-1B 3
2009	TBA	MLB	26	336	38	12	0	12	41	34	54	1	0	0.7	.253	.331	.416	.258	.334	.410	.264	4.7	-0.3	23-1B -2 16-2B -5
2010	TBA	MLB	27	424	46	19	1	14	51	43	66	2	2	-1.4	.261	.343	.433	.261	.342	.431	.262	5.4	0.7	56-1B 1

Breakout: 17%	Improve: 46%	Collapse: 6%	Attrition: 0%	MLB: 92%	Comparables: David Segui, Todd Benzinger, Joe Kuhel, Scott Spiezio

Aybar filled in at all three infield corners and DH when the injury bug bit in 2009, and while he wound up virtually repeating his overall 2008 performance at the plate, he wasn't as valuable as you'd think. His late-season fade (.219/.279/.323 after August 15th) was ill timed, given that he covered first base once Carlos Pena went down for the year. Aybar's platoon split (.265/.372/.510 vs. lefties, .247/.308/.366 vs. righties) was wide enough to drive a bus through while knocking him down to replacement level more often than not, and where his defense was an asset in 2008, the major systems all viewed it as a liability last year, particularly at the keystone. Bench bats who can hit for league average don't grow on trees, but they do grow kind of like mushrooms: all over the place. You just have to know the difference between the tasty and the poisonous.

Jason Bartlett — SS

Bats: R Throws: R Height: 6' 0" Weight: 185 Born: October 30, 1979 Age: 30

YEAR	TEAM	LVL	AGE	PA	R	2B	3B	HR	RBI	BB	SO	SB	CS	EqBRR	AVG	OBP	SLG	EqAVG	EqOBP	EqSLG	EqA	VORP	WARP	DEFENSE
2007	MIN	MLB	27	570	75	20	7	5	43	50	73	23	3	6.4	.265	.339	.361	.267	.341	.367	.258	19.7	5.0	135-SS 22
2008	TBA	MLB	28	494	48	25	3	1	37	22	69	20	6	0.6	.286	.329	.361	.294	.337	.369	.255	16.7	1.8	122-SS -2
2009	TBA	MLB	29	567	90	29	7	14	66	54	89	30	7	5.1	.320	.389	.490	.331	.399	.500	.308	52.4	4.9	131-SS -8
2010	TBA	MLB	30	551	71	25	4	8	51	47	84	22	6	2.0	.284	.353	.400	.285	.354	.402	.262	20.3	2.5	134-SS 2

Breakout: 11% Improve: 33% Collapse: 5% Attrition: 7% MLB: 98% Comparables: Julio Lugo, Alan Trammell, Alvin Dark, Steve Sax

Bartlett received a great deal of credit for the Rays' defensive turnaround in 2008, with the local Baseball Writers Association of America (BBWAA) chapter even naming him the team's MVP. Nobody hailed him as one of the game's top-hitting shortstops, and rightly so, given that he'd never managed a league-average EqA. That changed in 2009, as Bartlett's line-drive percentage and BABIP both skyrocketed (from 21.3 percent and .332 in 2008 to 27.4 percent and .364). Additionally, he more than doubled his career home-run total and wound up fourth among shortstops in EqA, between Derek Jeter and Troy Tulowitzki, and miles beyond even PECOTA's 90th percentile projection (.281/.340/.386). The reviews of his defense weren't so sunny; while he saved eight runs according to Plus/Minus, both FRAA and UZR (-5.8) saw him as below average after an essentially average 2008 performance. Both the offensive pros and defensive cons owed something to the 15 pounds of bulk Bartlett added last offseason at the Rays' suggestion, though the team had no complaints about his lateral mobility in the field. While the unprecedented nature of his performance suggests that regression is in store for 2010, the breadth of his across-the-board improvements strongly increases the likelihood that he'll be an above-average contributor.

Tim Beckham — SS

Bats: R Throws: R Height: 6' 0" Weight: 188 Born: January 27, 1990 Age: 20

YEAR	TEAM	LVL	AGE	PA	R	2B	3B	HR	RBI	BB	SO	SB	CS	EqBRR	AVG	OBP	SLG	EqAVG	EqOBP	EqSLG	EqA	VORP	WARP	DEFENSE
2008	PRI	Rk	18	197	30	12	0	2	14	13	43	5	1	-0.3	.243	.297	.345	.199	.241	.271	.180	-8.0	-3.1	36-SS -9
2009	BGR	A	19	537	58	33	4	5	63	34	116	13	10	-5.4	.275	.328	.389	.243	.284	.337	.217	-3.2	-2.8	117-SS -20
2010	TBA	MLB	20	505	52	27	2	6	46	34	124	5	3	-1.8	.243	.298	.348	.244	.299	.347	.218	-3.1	-1.4	106-SS -10

Breakout: 47% Improve: 66% Collapse: 13% Attrition: 2% MLB: 1% Comparables: Ellis Burks, Rafael Guerrero, Luis De Paula, Brian Costello

The first overall pick of the 2008 draft struggled mightily in his first taste of pro ball, and the follow-up was nothing to write home about, but Beckham did at least enjoy stretches of productivity. He hit .288/.346/.415 prior to the All-Star break, thanks to a torrid May, but just .263/.310/.365 after the break. He showed an odd reverse platoon split, batting .291/.343/.416 against righties but just .212/.269/.283 against lefties. Scouts still like his athleticism, bat speed, projected power, and ability to hit off-speed pitches. The bigger concern is his defense; after bulking up in the offseason, primarily in his lower body, he lost some range and made 43 errors at shortstop due to inconsistent throws. The consensus is that he'll have to move, though it's likely he remains athletic enough to ward off the calls to invoke the nuclear option of left field or first base.

Reid Brignac — SS

Bats: L Throws: R Height: 6' 3" Weight: 180 Born: January 16, 1986 Age: 24

YEAR	TEAM	LVL	AGE	PA	R	2B	3B	HR	RBI	BB	SO	SB	CS	EqBRR	AVG	OBP	SLG	EqAVG	EqOBP	EqSLG	EqA	VORP	WARP	DEFENSE
2007	MNT	AA	21	596	91	30	5	17	81	55	94	15	5	3.3	.260	.328	.433	.242	.297	.394	.243	11.3	0.6	126-SS -7
2008	DUR	AAA	22	386	43	26	2	9	43	25	93	5	2	0.7	.250	.299	.412	.232	.280	.387	.232	4.5	1.0	89-SS 5 4-2B -1
2009	DUR	AAA	23	453	51	28	2	8	44	27	69	5	5	-1.3	.282	.327	.417	.264	.307	.399	.244	10.2	0.2	88-SS -7 8-2B -2
2009	TBA	MLB	23	93	10	8	2	1	6	3	20	2	2	-0.2	.278	.301	.444	.289	.312	.456	.253	3.1	-0.2	24-SS -4
2010	TBA	MLB	24	507	62	28	3	11	56	37	104	7	4	0.4	.251	.308	.399	.246	.303	.386	.237	6.1	0.4	115-SS -2

Breakout: 14% Improve: 43% Collapse: 19% Attrition: 14% MLB: 42% Comparables: Randy Byers, Joe Deberry, Hector Perez, Troy Fryman

Once considered among the game's top handful of prospects, Brignac has seen his star fade considerably since he won California League MVP honors in 2006. While he has shown decent power for a middle infielder, he has proven quite hacktastic due to a lack of pitch-recognition skills, a vulnerability to chasing balls out of the zone, and a tendency to get pull-happy when he falls into slumps. Even so, both his range and his arm have improved, and the Rays have been impressed with his work ethic. His repeat engagement at Durham represented an incremental improvement over 2008 as he upped his contact rate, showed some pop during an extended look from the Rays, and saw time at second base at both levels. That could open up a utility spot on the big-league roster, though he'll have to stand out in a crowd.

Pat Burrell

Pat Burrell   **DH**   Bats: R   Throws: R   Height: 6' 4"   Weight: 235   Born: October 10, 1976   Age: 33

YEAR	TEAM	LVL	AGE	PA	R	2B	3B	HR	RBI	BB	SO	SB	CS	EqBRR	AVG	OBP	SLG	EqAVG	EqOBP	EqSLG	EqA	VORP	WARP	DEFENSE	
2007	PHI	MLB	30	598	77	26	0	30	97	114	120	0	0	-1.4	.256	.400	.502	.259	.403	.504	.312	45.5	4.0	114-LF	-8
2008	PHI	MLB	31	645	74	33	3	33	86	102	136	0	0	-1.2	.250	.367	.507	.256	.369	.515	.299	40.0	4.4	134-LF	0
2009	TBA	MLB	32	476	45	16	1	14	64	57	119	2	0	-1.9	.221	.315	.367	.226	.319	.370	.246	-7.3	-0.9		
2010	TBA	MLB	33	499	48	18	1	20	69	72	119	1	0	-0.7	.231	.345	.416	.231	.344	.413	.261	5.6	0.6	0- 0	

Breakout: 5%   Improve: 23%   Collapse: 26%   Attrition: 28%   MLB: 91%   Comparables: Greg Luzinski, Dean Palmer, Stan Lopata, Tim Salmon

The Phillies signed Raul Ibañez to a three-year, $30 million deal to replace Burrell after the 2008 season, and when the Rays picked up Burrell via a two-year, $16 million pact, the consensus was that Tampa Bay had gotten the better bargain—particularly given their intention to limit Pat the Bat to the DH role. Alas, while Ibañez flourished in Philly, Burrell never got on track with the Rays, because of a neck strain and a bulging disc, making for his worst major-league season since 2003. Particularly telling regarding Burrell's limitations was his utter futility against lefties (.202/.336/.252 without a homer in 143 PA), given that he had mashed them at a .286/.426/.550 clip from 2005 to 2008, good for the sixth-highest OPS in the game. The Rays explored deals to move Burrell during the winter, but the combination of health questions, defensive shortcomings, and a $9 million salary for 2010 didn't exactly have suitors lining up around the block.

Carl Crawford   **LF**   Bats: L   Throws: L   Height: 6' 2"   Weight: 215   Born: August 5, 1981   Age: 28

YEAR	TEAM	LVL	AGE	PA	R	2B	3B	HR	RBI	BB	SO	SB	CS	EqBRR	AVG	OBP	SLG	EqAVG	EqOBP	EqSLG	EqA	VORP	WARP	DEFENSE	
2007	TBA	MLB	25	624	93	37	9	11	80	32	112	50	10	6.6	.315	.355	.466	.322	.363	.482	.292	35.4	4.2	134-LF	2
2008	TBA	MLB	26	480	69	12	10	8	57	30	60	25	7	4.0	.273	.319	.400	.281	.327	.413	.262	9.9	3.5	102-LF	19
2009	TBA	MLB	27	672	96	28	8	15	68	51	99	60	16	4.2	.305	.364	.452	.318	.375	.467	.291	37.7	5.4	146-LF	10
2010	TBA	MLB	28	630	93	31	10	15	75	45	100	44	15	2.7	.300	.356	.466	.296	.352	.448	.278	26.6	3.5	138-LF	6

Breakout: 6%   Improve: 39%   Collapse: 7%   Attrition: 9%   MLB: 100%   Comparables: Bake McBride, Al Martin, Luis Gonzalez, Terry Puhl

Crawford rebounded from an injury-riddled 2008 to put together the best season of his career according to WARP. Not only did his BABIP shoot up from an atypically low .297 to .342, but improved plate discipline helped him set career highs in walks and OBP. He did so in stolen bases and in caught stealing as well, and although he came out only slightly ahead on that matter (1.11 EqSBR), he still ranked 10th in the league in EqBRR overall. The Rays picked up Crawford's $10 million option for 2010 amid reports that the move upset the outfielder, who allegedly had a handshake agreement that management would renegotiate a long-term deal instead. Andrew Friedman says that the team still intends to work out a multiyear deal, but the situation bears watching, particularly with Desmond Jennings having reached Triple-A.

Gabe Gross   **RF**   Bats: L   Throws: R   Height: 6' 3"   Weight: 220   Born: October 21, 1979   Age: 30

YEAR	TEAM	LVL	AGE	PA	R	2B	3B	HR	RBI	BB	SO	SB	CS	EqBRR	AVG	OBP	SLG	EqAVG	EqOBP	EqSLG	EqA	VORP	WARP	DEFENSE			
2007	MIL	MLB	27	210	28	12	2	7	24	25	37	3	1	1.6	.235	.329	.437	.242	.338	.440	.268	4.7	1.1	32-RF	4	3-CF	1
2008	MIL	MLB	28	54	6	3	0	0	2	10	7	2	0	1.0	.209	.352	.279	.209	.352	.279	.255	0.9	0.2	11-CF	1		
2008	TBA	MLB	28	345	40	13	3	13	38	40	75	2	2	-1.0	.242	.333	.434	.249	.342	.449	.270	10.2	2.9	85-RF	13	3-CF	1
2009	TBA	MLB	29	326	31	16	1	6	36	42	79	6	3	-0.5	.227	.326	.355	.234	.332	.358	.247	0.6	0.9	73-RF	7		
2010	TBA	MLB	30	371	42	17	2	11	42	45	82	4	3	0.3	.247	.341	.420	.243	.338	.407	.259	7.1	1.3	80-RF	4		

Breakout: 8%   Improve: 39%   Collapse: 11%   Attrition: 12%   MLB: 91%   Comparables: Luis Gonzalez, Eric Hinske, Harold Baines, Paul O'Neill

Gross is an above-average defender, but he doesn't bring a whole lot of lumber to the party for a corner outfielder. Considering that Maddon's strict platooning limited him to just 36 plate appearances against lefties, his 32nd rank in EqA among the 35 right fielders with at least 300 plate appearances is nothing short of appalling. Some of it was bad luck, with a .293 BABIP despite a 25.4 percent line-drive rate, but some of it was contact woes, as he had the

28th-highest strikeout rate among the 284 hitters with at least 300 plate appearances. With Matt Joyce the obvious candidate for his role in right field, Gross was nontendered, which makes him a free agent.

Akinori Iwamura — 2B

Bats: L   Throws: R   Height: 5' 9"   Weight: 175   Born: February 9, 1979   Age: 31

YEAR	TEAM	LVL	AGE	PA	R	2B	3B	HR	RBI	BB	SO	SB	CS	EqBRR	AVG	OBP	SLG	EqAVG	EqOBP	EqSLG	EqA	VORP	WARP	DEFENSE	
2007	TBA	MLB	28	559	82	21	10	7	34	58	114	12	8	1.4	.285	.359	.411	.295	.368	.426	.275	21.2	2.4	118-3B	2
2008	TBA	MLB	29	707	91	30	9	6	48	70	131	8	6	-1.3	.274	.349	.380	.282	.358	.391	.264	24.0	2.3	149-2B	-4
2009	TBA	MLB	30	260	28	16	2	1	22	24	44	9	1	1.5	.290	.355	.390	.296	.359	.391	.274	10.9	0.8	63-2B	-4
2010	PIT	MLB	31	489	63	22	5	6	35	54	99	8	5	0.0	.280	.363	.396	.273	.356	.385	.269	19.5	1.9	106-2B	-2

Breakout: 9%   Improve: 45%   Collapse: 15%   Attrition: 13%   MLB: 96%   Comparables: Johnny Pesky, Mickey Morandini, Luis Alicea, Buddy Myer

Iwamura was off to a hot start (.310/.377/.406 through May 24th) when he suffered a torn ACL via a late slide by Chris Coghlan. The injury appeared to be season ending, but by the time doctors operated four weeks later, they discovered that because the ACL hadn't torn to the degree that it needed replacement, he just needed a simple meniscectomy—the difference between 'scoping the knee and opening it, and between a 2009 return and one in 2010. Iwamura rejoined the lineup in late August, but hit just .250/.310/.355 as the team faded from contention. Though hardly a weak link either offensively or defensively, he was rendered expendable by the emergence of Ben Zobrist and shipped off to Pittsburgh for reliever Jesse Chavez so the Rays wouldn't have to pay his option buyout. He'll be a fine OBP source for the Pirates and presumably a deadline flip to the contender looking for help at second base.

John Jaso — C

Bats: L   Throws: R   Height: 6' 2"   Weight: 205   Born: September 19, 1983   Age: 26

YEAR	TEAM	LVL	AGE	PA	R	2B	3B	HR	RBI	BB	SO	SB	CS	EqBRR	AVG	OBP	SLG	EqAVG	EqOBP	EqSLG	EqA	VORP	WARP	DEFENSE	
2007	MNT	AA	23	450	62	24	2	12	71	59	49	2	2	0.1	.316	.408	.484	.296	.374	.457	.288	28.5	3.4	68-C	0
2008	MNT	AA	24	356	51	13	2	7	43	62	33	1	0	-2.3	.271	.408	.405	.246	.352	.362	.258	12.5	0.1	69-C	-12
2008	DUR	AAA	24	118	14	7	0	5	24	10	14	1	1	-0.2	.278	.339	.481	.257	.319	.440	.258	4.4	0.1	25-C	-4
2008	TBA	MLB	24	10	2	0	0	0	0	0	2	0	0	-0.1	.200	.200	.200	.200	.200	.200	.086	-1.2	-0.1		
2009	DUR	AAA	25	387	42	14	2	5	30	46	49	1	0	-0.2	.266	.362	.366	.246	.339	.341	.247	10.1	0.2	87-C	-9
2010	TBA	MLB	26	372	45	17	2	7	44	42	54	1	1	-0.4	.260	.350	.394	.257	.346	.384	.256	12.6	1.0	71-C	-4

Breakout: 9%   Improve: 31%   Collapse: 24%   Attrition: 11%   MLB: 6%   Comparables: Scott Hatteberg, Ray Giannelli, Roy Johnson, Everett Graham

A lefty-hitting, offense-oriented catcher the Rays tabbed in the 12th round in 2003, Jaso had a disappointing year in 2009, his first full season of Triple-A. While he continued to demonstrate solid on-base skills, his already-modest power took month-long vacations; he managed just one extra-base hit in May and July combined. Worse, he failed to progress defensively, throwing out just 17 percent of base thieves, thanks to a shoulder weakened by a history of injuries. Older than Dioner Navarro, he's not simply a ways from establishing himself as a viable big-league catcher; he may as well be viewing the possibility from another planet with no rocket to get from here to there.

Desmond Jennings — CF

Bats: R   Throws: R   Height: 6' 2"   Weight: 180   Born: October 30, 1986   Age: 23

YEAR	TEAM	LVL	AGE	PA	R	2B	3B	HR	RBI	BB	SO	SB	CS	EqBRR	AVG	OBP	SLG	EqAVG	EqOBP	EqSLG	EqA	VORP	WARP	DEFENSE			
2007	CGA	A	20	448	75	21	5	9	37	45	53	45	15	1.4	.315	.401	.465	.289	.356	.413	.269	16.5	2.0	84-CF	0		
2008	VRO	A+	21	102	17	5	1	2	6	14	16	5	2	0.6	.259	.360	.412	.239	.327	.386	.255	2.3	0.4	24-CF	1		
2009	MNT	AA	22	440	69	25	8	8	45	48	52	37	5	8.2	.316	.395	.486	.302	.366	.472	.292	27.3	3.9	85-CF	4	5-RF	1
2009	DUR	AAA	22	137	23	6	2	3	17	19	15	15	2	2.1	.325	.419	.491	.304	.401	.461	.307	10.9	0.9	25-CF	-3		
2010	TBA	MLB	23	471	60	23	5	10	40	46	71	22	7	2.6	.277	.354	.430	.277	.353	.426	.269	19.2	2.2	95-CF	0		

Breakout: 7%   Improve: 42%   Collapse: 17%   Attrition: 9%   MLB: 12%   Comparables: Mike Spidale, Chris James, Alex Ochoa, Lorenzo Cain

Back and shoulder injuries cost Jennings most of 2008, but his rebound was everything the Rays could have hoped for, as he made up for lost developmental time by seamlessly jumping to the upper minors. Healthy for the entire season, he displayed his prodigious talent by winning Southern League MVP honors and making an impressive Triple-A debut as well. The Carl Crawford comparisons are inevitable, but Jennings has a better approach at the plate as well as the ability to play center field. Atop his line-drive swing, gap power, and outstanding speed, he demonstrated improved plate discipline and defense, both in his routes in center field and his throwing arm. He's almost ready for his close-up; the Rays have a year to figure out how he'll fit into their crowded outfield, an enviable dilemma.

Matt Joyce   **RF**   Bats: L   Throws: R   Height: 6' 2"   Weight: 185   Born: August 3, 1984   Age: 25

YEAR	TEAM	LVL	AGE	PA	R	2B	3B	HR	RBI	BB	SO	SB	CS	EqBRR	AVG	OBP	SLG	EqAVG	EqOBP	EqSLG	EqA	VORP	WARP	DEFENSE			
2007	ERI	AA	22	514	61	33	3	17	70	51	127	4	6	-1.2	.257	.333	.454	.230	.298	.400	.240	-2.5	0.3	112-RF	6	4-CF	-1
2008	TOL	AAA	23	227	36	13	2	13	41	24	62	2	3	-0.1	.270	.352	.550	.267	.346	.540	.290	12.6	1.6	41-RF	3	14-CF	-2
2008	DET	MLB	23	277	40	16	3	12	33	31	65	0	2	-0.6	.252	.339	.492	.253	.343	.502	.281	11.9	1.7	46-LF	5	18-RF	-1
2009	DUR	AAA	24	493	73	35	2	16	66	67	98	14	5	-1.0	.273	.373	.482	.255	.354	.451	.279	20.0	2.0	75-RF	0	17-LF	0
2009	TBA	MLB	24	37	3	1	0	3	7	3	7	1	0	-1.0	.188	.270	.500	.188	.270	.500	.266	0.9	0.1	4-RF	0	4-CF	0
2010	TBA	MLB	25	490	62	26	3	19	66	55	128	4	4	-0.6	.240	.328	.446	.235	.324	.428	.258	9.3	1.2	102-RF	2		

Breakout: 9%　Improve: 34%　Collapse: 19%　Attrition: 13%　　MLB: 100%　　Comparables: Ralph Bryant, Ted Wood, Mike Stenhouse, Oreste Marrero

Joyce burst on the major-league scene with nine homers in his first 94 at-bats in 2008, but tailed off after that and then was acquired by the outfield-laden Rays in a deal for Edwin Jackson last December. With Gabe Gross, Gabe Kapler, and (honorary) Gabe Zobrist all putting in claims on time in right field, the Tampa native—who grew up rooting for the Devil Rays, poor lamb—was forced to spend nearly the entire season at Durham despite his likely superiority to Gross, who wound up among the game's least productive right fielders. Joyce's time shooting Bull wasn't entirely wasted; his strikeout and walk rates improved markedly, and he hit .250/.315/.474 with five homers in 130 Durham plate appearances against lefties, compared with .217/.308/.348 with one homer in 52 plate appearances the year before. The Rays love his strong arm and defensive ability and are excited to have six years of him under club control, so expect him to assume the long half of the right-field platoon at the least.

Gabe Kapler   **RF**   Bats: R   Throws: R   Height: 6' 2"   Weight: 190   Born: July 31, 1975   Age: 34

YEAR	TEAM	LVL	AGE	PA	R	2B	3B	HR	RBI	BB	SO	SB	CS	EqBRR	AVG	OBP	SLG	EqAVG	EqOBP	EqSLG	EqA	VORP	WARP	DEFENSE			
2008	MIL	MLB	32	245	36	17	2	8	38	13	39	3	1	1.2	.301	.340	.498	.314	.352	.520	.289	13.7	1.4	28-CF	-1	13-LF	1
2009	TBA	MLB	33	238	26	15	1	8	32	29	39	5	2	-3.4	.239	.329	.439	.245	.333	.446	.270	7.3	0.6	47-RF	2	8-LF	-2
2010	TBA	MLB	34	233	27	12	1	6	31	23	43	4	2	-0.5	.261	.334	.416	.264	.337	.424	.255	3.7	0.5	47-RF	1		

Breakout: 10%　Improve: 36%　Collapse: 25%　Attrition: 23%　　MLB: 97%　　Comparables: Ron Santo, Wally Westlake, Al Cowens, Chet Lemon

The world's most famous Jewish bodybuilding fourth outfielder enjoyed a great 2008 after coming out of a one-year retirement spent managing a Red Sox affiliate, but Kapler didn't fare quite as well in 2009. Which isn't to say he wasn't used as directed; Kapler started 59 of the team's 60 games against lefties and hit a robust .276/.379/.552 in 174 plate appearances against them, but he rusted (.150/.190/.167 in 64 PAs) against righties, where he'd at least been serviceable in the past. He saw much less time in center field than in prior years as well, an area where he could have helped, given Upton's flailings against southpaws (.190/.302/.270). He was signed to a $1.05 million extension for 2010, a nice price, even given the Rays' crowded outfield.

Jose Lobaton   **C**   Bats: S   Throws: R   Height: 6' 0"   Weight: 170   Born: October 21, 1984   Age: 25

YEAR	TEAM	LVL	AGE	PA	R	2B	3B	HR	RBI	BB	SO	SB	CS	EqBRR	AVG	OBP	SLG	EqAVG	EqOBP	EqSLG	EqA	VORP	WARP	DEFENSE	
2007	LEL	A+	22	357	50	15	3	10	47	41	79	0	0	-1.1	.260	.346	.428	.236	.307	.360	.238	8.9	0.5	89-C	-5
2008	SAN	AA	23	342	35	21	0	9	45	39	75	1	1	-3.5	.259	.338	.422	.247	.315	.387	.248	9.9	1.4	80-C	2
2009	MNT	AA	24	102	13	7	0	3	11	15	19	0	0	-0.4	.262	.376	.452	.250	.343	.409	.265	4.8	0.5	24-C	-1
2009	POR	AAA	24	148	14	6	0	3	8	10	35	0	0	-0.5	.241	.292	.353	.237	.283	.333	.217	0.2	-0.2	37-C	-2
2009	SDN	MLB	24	17	0	0	0	0	0	0	5	0	0	-0.2	.176	.176	.176	.176	.176	.176	-.125	-1.5	-0.2	5-C	0
2010	TBA	MLB	25	308	32	13	1	7	31	29	79	1	1	-0.9	.234	.309	.368	.236	.311	.360	.229	2.7	0.2	77-C	-1

Breakout: 16%　Improve: 41%　Collapse: 17%　Attrition: 14%　　MLB: 1%　　Comparables: Jeff McKnight, Mike Yastrzemski, Jim Beswick, Ron Scheer

A nondrafted free agent from Venezuela, Lobaton was once considered the San Diego system's top defensive backstop, but injuries slowed his progress. He got a cup of coffee with the Padres when Henry Blanco went down in July, but was lost in a roster crunch near the trade deadline and sent back to Double-A upon joining the Rays' organization. Nominally a switch-hitter, Lobaton has a bit of patience and pop against righties, but he's best nailed to the bench against lefties (.191 SLG in 2008-2009), and his caught-stealing rates (28 percent in 2009, 27 percent in 2008) are nothing special. His strengths and weaknesses would make him a decent fit as a backup to Kelly Shoppach, but the otherwise superior Dioner Navarro stands—sits? squats?—in his way.

Evan Longoria   3B   Bats: R   Throws: R   Height: 6' 2"   Weight: 210   Born: October 7, 1985   Age: 24

YEAR	TEAM	LVL	AGE	PA	R	2B	3B	HR	RBI	BB	SO	SB	CS	EqBRR	AVG	OBP	SLG	EqAVG	EqOBP	EqSLG	EqA	VORP	WARP	DEFENSE
2007	MNT	AA	21	447	78	21	0	21	76	51	81	4	0	1.3	.307	.403	.528	.289	.367	.487	.292	25.3	2.4	96-3B	-5
2007	DUR	AAA	21	128	19	8	0	5	19	22	29	0	0	0.0	.269	.398	.490	.255	.375	.453	.288	6.5	0.8	27-3B	0
2008	TBA	MLB	22	508	67	31	2	27	85	46	122	7	0	0.3	.272	.343	.531	.279	.348	.546	.300	36.0	5.1	116-3B	9
2009	TBA	MLB	23	671	100	44	0	33	113	72	140	9	0	3.3	.281	.364	.526	.285	.367	.527	.303	50.7	7.9	148-3B	19
2010	TBA	MLB	24	649	95	30	1	35	112	74	139	8	1	1.0	.272	.365	.514	.273	.366	.511	.293	40.3	4.8	147-3B	4

Breakout: 19% Improve: 54% Collapse: 7% Attrition: 2%   MLB: 98%   Comparables: David Wright, Edwin Encarnacion, Aramis Ramirez, Andy LaRoche

Longoria followed up his Rookie of the Year campaign with a nearly MVP-caliber season that combined outstanding play on both sides of the ball, which isn't to say it was devoid of ups and downs. A bat out of hell in April, he homered five times in the season's first six games and batted .327/.396/.623 through May, but spent the next three months in a minor funk (.229/.322/.421) as turf-related hamstring woes and a nagging finger injury took their toll. He closed on a high note even as the Rays faded from contention (.325/.408/.605 in September), winding up fourth in the league in extra-base hits and 13th in EqA. Longoria's excellent performance at the hot corner persisted even when he struggled at the plate, as he ranked among the game's most valuable defenders according to FRAA, UZR, and Plus/Minus, and scooped up a Gold Glove. He's all that and a bag of chips.

Dioner Navarro   C   Bats: S   Throws: R   Height: 5' 9"   Weight: 205   Born: February 9, 1984   Age: 26

YEAR	TEAM	LVL	AGE	PA	R	2B	3B	HR	RBI	BB	SO	SB	CS	EqBRR	AVG	OBP	SLG	EqAVG	EqOBP	EqSLG	EqA	VORP	WARP	DEFENSE
2007	TBA	MLB	23	434	46	19	2	9	44	33	67	3	1	-0.3	.227	.286	.356	.229	.289	.364	.230	7.3	0.2	108-C	-4
2008	TBA	MLB	24	470	43	27	0	7	54	34	49	0	4	-8.1	.295	.349	.407	.304	.358	.426	.268	24.3	5.3	112-C	17
2009	TBA	MLB	25	410	38	15	0	8	32	18	51	5	2	1.0	.218	.261	.322	.223	.265	.322	.208	-2.9	0.4	105-C	5
2010	TBA	MLB	26	409	46	17	1	11	49	34	57	3	3	-1.1	.264	.330	.408	.263	.330	.400	.249	11.5	1.6	103-C	3

Breakout: 22% Improve: 51% Collapse: 14% Attrition: 10%   MLB: 100%   Comparables: Todd Hundley, Yadier Molina, Butch Wynegar, Damon Berryhill

As the 24-year-old, five-win catcher for a pennant winner, Navarro looked like a real steal, but he spent 2009 as a Replacement-Level Killer due to an ulnar nerve problem that required post-season surgery in his left elbow. Passable against lefties (.279/.304/.436), he was such a gaping vortex of suck against righties (.183/.234/.255 in 254 PAs) that he wound up with the lowest EqA of any catcher with more than 155 plate appearances. Defensively, he remained above average despite a caught-stealing rate that fell from 38.4 percent in 2008 to 26.5 percent last year. Given the note from his doctor, he might enjoy a rebound, but the acquisition of lefty-mashing Shoppach suggests playing time is no guarantee.

Carlos Pena   1B   Bats: L   Throws: L   Height: 6' 2"   Weight: 215   Born: May 17, 1978   Age: 32

YEAR	TEAM	LVL	AGE	PA	R	2B	3B	HR	RBI	BB	SO	SB	CS	EqBRR	AVG	OBP	SLG	EqAVG	EqOBP	EqSLG	EqA	VORP	WARP	DEFENSE
2007	TBA	MLB	29	612	99	29	1	46	121	103	142	1	0	-0.8	.282	.411	.627	.285	.414	.639	.341	65.7	7.1	138-1B	0
2008	TBA	MLB	30	607	76	24	2	31	102	96	166	1	1	-5.1	.247	.377	.494	.253	.382	.509	.304	36.5	5.0	130-1B	9
2009	TBA	MLB	31	570	91	25	2	39	100	87	163	3	3	-1.2	.227	.356	.537	.232	.361	.543	.298	25.4	1.7	131-1B	-10
2010	TBA	MLB	32	550	74	23	2	32	94	84	152	1	2	-1.1	.240	.369	.512	.234	.364	.491	.291	25.3	2.7	126-1B	0

Breakout: 0% Improve: 23% Collapse: 18% Attrition: 7%   MLB: 95%   Comparables: Jim Gentile, Willie Stargell, Ted Kluszewski, Fred McGriff

For a guy who tied Mark Teixeira for the league lead in home runs, Pena had one rough season. Contact woes resulted in the highest full-season strikeout rate of his career, and at the same time, his BABIP collapsed from .298 in 2008 to .250, the second-lowest in the majors. That's a product not only of the frequent defensive shifts employed against him, but also of Pena's ability to put the ball in the air more often than any hitter. (On the bright side, he did lead the league with a Three True Outcome percentage of 50.7.) Meanwhile, his defense, which was above-average if not Gold Glove–worthy in 2008, took a turn for the worse, too. Just when he emerged from a dreadful July slump

(.146/.297/.317) by bashing 14 homers in a 33-game span, Pena broke two fingers while being hit on the hand during a check swing on September 7th, ending his season. He heads into the final year of his three-year deal as the highest-paid Ray ($10.125 million), and as much as the team has enjoyed his renaissance, he clearly has to produce to justify his further presence.

Fernando Perez — CF

Bats: S Throws: R Height: 6' 1" Weight: 195 Born: April 23, 1983 Age: 27

YEAR	TEAM	LVL	AGE	PA	R	2B	3B	HR	RBI	BB	SO	SB	CS	EqBRR	AVG	OBP	SLG	EqAVG	EqOBP	EqSLG	EqA	VORP	WARP	DEFENSE			
2007	MNT	AA	24	476	84	24	10	8	33	76	104	32	18	-0.9	.308	.423	.481	.265	.362	.409	.269	18.2	1.7	99-CF	-4		
2008	DUR	AAA	25	579	86	17	11	5	36	58	156	43	12	6.2	.288	.361	.393	.266	.336	.362	.252	10.1	0.9	108-CF	-1	11-RF	0
2008	TBA	MLB	25	72	18	2	0	3	8	8	16	5	0	1.3	.250	.348	.433	.254	.353	.441	.287	4.1	1.2	12-CF	8	4-LF	-1
2009	DUR	AAA	26	43	10	3	0	0	2	7	17	8	1	1.3	.278	.395	.361	.250	.372	.333	.273	1.5	0.4	7-CF	2		
2009	TBA	MLB	26	35	4	0	0	0	2	0	11	0	2	-0.6	.206	.206	.206	.176	.176	.176	.089	-4.3	-0.6	6-CF	-1	4-LF	0
2010	TBA	MLB	27	374	48	15	4	5	22	39	102	14	7	1.2	.240	.322	.358	.239	.320	.348	.236	2.2	0.3	77-CF	1		

Breakout: 9% Improve: 31% Collapse: 29% Attrition: 12% MLB: 20% Comparables: Chris Roberson, Dwaine Bacon, Tommy Murphy, Mike Murphy

A speedy, Ginsberg-quoting, poetry-writing seventh-round 2004 pick out of Columbia University, Perez appeared headed for at least a platoon role with the 2009 Rays after some late-2008 stretch help. Alas, his year was lost as he dislocated his wrist making a diving catch in March, sustaining such ligament damage that he needed the insertion of pins to heal properly. He didn't join the big club until September and then needed surgery to repair his labrum in October. Perez's speed, lefty-mashing skills, ability to play all three outfield positions, and facility with the works of Robert Creeley make him an ideal fourth outfielder, but he'll probably start the year at Triple-A so as to rack up some at-bats.

Sean Rodriguez — INF

Bats: R Throws: R Height: 6' 1" Weight: 215 Born: April 26, 1985 Age: 25

YEAR	TEAM	LVL	AGE	PA	R	2B	3B	HR	RBI	BB	SO	SB	CS	EqBRR	AVG	OBP	SLG	EqAVG	EqOBP	EqSLG	EqA	VORP	WARP	DEFENSE			
2007	ARK	AA	22	587	84	31	2	17	73	54	132	15	8	-2.5	.254	.345	.423	.237	.309	.380	.242	10.0	2.8	125-SS	11	5-CF	2
2008	SLC	AAA	23	289	68	19	1	21	52	29	45	4	1	0.1	.306	.397	.645	.256	.340	.512	.286	17.9	2.0	52-2B	0	8-SS	-1
2008	LAA	MLB	23	187	18	8	1	3	10	14	55	3	1	-0.7	.204	.276	.317	.205	.277	.313	.215	-3.2	0.0	47-2B	1	2-SS	2
2009	SLC	AAA	24	435	81	17	6	29	93	51	119	9	2	3.6	.299	.400	.616	.265	.359	.531	.297	31.9	4.8	74-2B	9	17-SS	0
2009	LAA	MLB	24	29	4	0	0	2	4	3	7	0	0	0.6	.200	.276	.440	.200	.276	.440	.247	0.5	-0.4	4-2B	-3		
2010	TBA	MLB	25	461	63	19	2	16	55	44	121	5	3	0.3	.233	.321	.410	.233	.321	.403	.248	8.1	1.1	103-2B	2		

Breakout: 4% Improve: 33% Collapse: 18% Attrition: 13% MLB: 75% Comparables: Mike Berger, Glenn Murray, Ernie Young, Shon Ashley

A third-round 2003 pick by the Angels, Rodriguez hit well at just about every minor-league stop, but struggled during his extended 2008 major-league look. He continued to compile eye-popping numbers at hitter-friendly Salt Lake City in 2009, including the Pacific Coast League's second-highest homer total, but rode the bench for the better part of his brief big-league stints. Sent to the Rays as the player to be named later in the Kazmir deal, he's probably bound for a utility role given the likely takeover of second base by Ben Zobrist. The keystone is Rodriguez's best position as well, as his arm is a bit stretched at third, and his range limited at shortstop; he does have the ability to play the outfield as well, so he might find enough playing time to make it worth his while.

Justin Ruggiano — OF

Bats: R Throws: R Height: 6' 2" Weight: 205 Born: April 12, 1982 Age: 28

YEAR	TEAM	LVL	AGE	PA	R	2B	3B	HR	RBI	BB	SO	SB	CS	EqBRR	AVG	OBP	SLG	EqAVG	EqOBP	EqSLG	EqA	VORP	WARP	DEFENSE			
2007	DUR	AAA	25	546	78	29	2	20	73	53	151	26	11	-1.7	.309	.386	.502	.288	.358	.473	.284	24.5	3.6	74-RF	2	40-LF	4
2008	DUR	AAA	26	289	49	18	3	11	51	22	77	20	3	1.0	.315	.374	.537	.285	.339	.477	.282	12.8	2.0	38-RF	2	16-LF	0
2008	TBA	MLB	26	81	9	4	0	2	7	4	27	2	0	0.9	.197	.247	.329	.197	.247	.316	.208	-3.4	0.3	10-RF	2	10-LF	3
2009	DUR	AAA	27	532	71	28	1	15	72	51	147	23	4	-3.1	.253	.330	.412	.227	.299	.368	.238	-0.3	0.3	63-CF	-2	30-LF	3
2010	TBA	MLB	28	455	52	20	1	13	51	38	135	11	5	-0.5	.238	.309	.388	.237	.308	.383	.238	3.4	0.2	89-CF	-1		

Breakout: 3% Improve: 35% Collapse: 34% Attrition: 17% MLB: 18% Comparables: Adam Hyzdu, Brad Komminsk, Bo Porter, Tony Chance

An athletic former Dodger farmhand who came to the Rays as the PTBNL in the Dioner Navarro deal in 2006, Ruggiano mashed Triple-A pitching in 2007-2008, but struggled mightily with the big club and complained of problems with his night vision. Because his corneas are too thin for Lasik surgery, he underwent photorefractive keratectomy after the 2008 season; still, the surgery's slower recovery time doesn't explain why he surged in May but flailed for most of the rest of the season. In November, he began working with Jaime Cevallos, the swing mechanic who keyed Ben Zobrist's breakout, but barring drastically positive results in taming his long swing, Ruggiano still faces an uphill battle for a roster spot.

Matthew Sweeney — 3B/1B

Bats: L   Throws: R   Height: 6' 3"   Weight: 210   Born: April 4, 1988   Age: 22

YEAR	TEAM	LVL	AGE	PA	R	2B	3B	HR	RBI	BB	SO	SB	CS	EqBRR	AVG	OBP	SLG	EqAVG	EqOBP	EqSLG	EqA	VORP	WARP	DEFENSE	
2007	CDR	A	19	485	64	29	2	18	72	38	88	7	7	-2.3	.260	.324	.458	.233	.287	.396	.234	-4.6	-2.6	85-3B	-17
2009	RCU	A+	21	241	39	17	1	9	44	26	37	2	0	0.3	.299	.379	.517	.258	.325	.429	.261	3.9	-0.1	33-3B	-5
2010	TBA	MLB	22	375	46	20	1	13	51	31	79	3	2	-0.4	.252	.319	.429	.247	.312	.416	.250	5.9	0.0	60-3B	-6

Breakout: 19%   Improve: 52%   Collapse: 8%   Attrition: 7%   MLB: 7%   Comparables: Al Martin, Chris Haas, Ian Stewart, Greg Blosser

Drafted by the Angels in the eighth round in 2006, Sweeney demonstrated plus raw power during his first two pro seasons, but lost all of 2008 to an ankle injury and missed over two months of 2009 with hip woes. He did hit well prior to getting hurt, demonstrating a fair bit of pop as well as improved plate discipline. Acquired in the Scott Kazmir deal, he's probably bound for first base, given a Hobsonian .860 career fielding percentage and a lack of range and speed, not to mention the imposing presence of Evan Longoria. That raises the offensive bar, of course, but those in the know like his swing and his approach enough to believe he's got the potential to reach it.

B. J. Upton — CF

Bats: R   Throws: R   Height: 6' 3"   Weight: 185   Born: August 21, 1984   Age: 25

YEAR	TEAM	LVL	AGE	PA	R	2B	3B	HR	RBI	BB	SO	SB	CS	EqBRR	AVG	OBP	SLG	EqAVG	EqOBP	EqSLG	EqA	VORP	WARP	DEFENSE			
2007	TBA	MLB	22	548	86	25	1	24	82	65	154	22	8	4.3	.300	.386	.508	.307	.393	.528	.309	46.7	5.0	75-CF	-2	47-2B	1
2008	TBA	MLB	23	640	85	37	2	9	67	97	134	44	16	3.1	.273	.383	.401	.287	.396	.423	.289	38.5	4.7	139-CF	5		
2009	TBA	MLB	24	626	79	33	4	11	55	57	152	42	14	-1.2	.241	.313	.373	.252	.323	.383	.251	12.7	2.1	139-CF	6		
2010	TBA	MLB	25	644	89	30	2	20	77	80	146	37	16	0.8	.272	.366	.437	.273	.367	.437	.275	30.2	3.5	141-CF	2		

Breakout: 11%   Improve: 53%   Collapse: 7%   Attrition: 4%   MLB: 100%   Comparables: Garry Maddox, Ellis Burks, Ben Chapman, Al Kaline

Bossman Junior's monster 2008 postseason offered hope that he could at last blossom into a superstar after surgery for the torn labrum of his nonthrowing shoulder, a repair job that drew comparisons to Hanley Ramirez's post-2007 surgery. Instead, Upton was a disappointment, failing to lift his batting average above the Mendoza Line until May 30th, retreating to the doldrums after a torrid June (.324/.395/.562), and pouting upon being pulled from the leadoff spot in early August, a reminder of the attitude-related complaints that have dogged his career. In September, he conceded that the shoulder wasn't 100 percent, a plausible, frustrating excuse, considering the shape of his season and the substantial decline of his line-drive rate (from 22.9 percent to 17.4 percent). Given another winter to strengthen the shoulder, his chances for a rebound are strong, but with Desmond Jennings on the horizon, this might be a make-or-break year.

Gregg Zaun — C

Bats: S   Throws: R   Height: 5' 10"   Weight: 205   Born: April 14, 1971   Age: 39

YEAR	TEAM	LVL	AGE	PA	R	2B	3B	HR	RBI	BB	SO	SB	CS	EqBRR	AVG	OBP	SLG	EqAVG	EqOBP	EqSLG	EqA	VORP	WARP	DEFENSE	
2007	TOR	MLB	36	391	43	24	1	10	52	51	55	0	0	-2.2	.242	.341	.411	.237	.338	.404	.263	18.7	1.3	94-C	-5
2008	TOR	MLB	37	288	29	12	0	6	30	38	38	2	1	-0.4	.237	.340	.359	.243	.349	.362	.256	10.1	1.2	69-C	1
2009	BAL	MLB	38	197	23	10	0	4	13	27	30	0	0	-1.2	.244	.355	.375	.244	.355	.375	.261	8.2	0.6	49-C	0
2009	TBA	MLB	38	99	11	7	0	4	14	4	18	0	2	-0.8	.287	.323	.489	.298	.333	.479	.269	4.7	0.2	24-C	-2
2010	MIL	MLB	39	222	20	9	0	5	24	27	44	0	1	-0.5	.226	.327	.351	.231	.329	.358	.243	4.7	0.4	54-C	-1

Breakout: 9%   Improve: 29%   Collapse: 32%   Attrition: 50%   MLB: 95%   Comparables: Harmon Killebrew, Wally Schang, Brad Ausmus, Ray Mueller

The Practically Perfect Backup Catcher began his odd year as the Orioles' designated seat-filler, carrying two-thirds of the catching load until Matt Wieters arrived from Triple-A in late May but struggling at the plate (.203/.309/.297). Perhaps not surprisingly, Zaun's bat regained potency (.340/.459/.560) as he spent the next two months serving as Wieters' caddy, and the final two after being swapped splitting time with woeful Dioner Navarro. Signed to a one-year-plus-option $2.15 million deal by the Brewers, he'll again leave the gate as the starter, with the possibility of being joined or displaced by Angel Salome or Jonathan Lucroy before the year is out.

Ben Zobrist UT

| | | | | | | | | | | | | | | Bats: S | | Throws: R | | Height: 6' 3" | | Weight: 200 | | Born: May 26, 1981 | | | Age: 29 |

YEAR	TEAM	LVL	AGE	PA	R	2B	3B	HR	RBI	BB	SO	SB	CS	EqBRR	AVG	OBP	SLG	EqAVG	EqOBP	EqSLG	EqA	VORP	WARP		DEFENSE	
2007	DUR	AAA	26	276	42	14	2	7	22	43	38	8	3	0.4	.279	.403	.455	.258	.371	.428	.282	15.5	1.6	52-SS	-2	
2007	TBA	MLB	26	105	8	2	0	1	9	3	21	2	0	0.6	.155	.184	.206	.156	.186	.208	.130	-7.7	-1.7	26-SS	-7	
2008	DUR	AAA	27	88	15	3	0	4	13	15	16	4	1	0.6	.366	.471	.577	.329	.432	.521	.324	8.7	1.5	7-SS	2	6-3B 2
2008	TBA	MLB	27	227	32	10	2	12	30	25	37	3	0	1.1	.253	.339	.505	.259	.348	.523	.292	16.3	0.8	33-SS	-9	9-LF 2
2009	TBA	MLB	28	599	91	28	7	27	91	91	104	17	6	-0.2	.297	.405	.543	.308	.413	.556	.322	58.4	7.7	81-2B	11	37-RF 7
2010	TBA	MLB	29	512	72	23	4	23	71	66	93	9	4	0.5	.273	.371	.499	.271	.370	.488	.290	32.6	4.3	98-2B	7	

Breakout: 14%   Improve: 52%   Collapse: 9%   Attrition: 7%   MLB: 90%   Comparables: Carlos Guillen, Vance Law, Geronimo Pena, Mark Bellhorn

Zobrist showed a surprising amount of pop while emerging as a superutilityman in 2008, but the work he put in with swing mechanic Jaime Cevallos (which began before the 2008 season) turned him into one of the league's top offensive forces; he blended power, patience, and speed to emerge as ... Zorilla! Zobrist spent nearly the entire first half slugging .600 and wound up ranking seventh in the league on that front, fourth in OBP, and second only to Joe Mauer in EqA. After battling for time in right field, he lucked into the everyday second base job once Akinori Iwamura went down. His UZR of +16 and Plus/Minus of +17 hold Zobrist's work at the keystone in even higher esteem than does his FRAA. Furthermore, he extended his utility to playing every defensive position except catcher. The trade of Iwamura opens up the full-time second base job for Zobrist, but don't be surprised if Joe Maddon takes advantage of his versatility to keep Zorilla on the loose in 2010.

PITCHERS

Grant Balfour

| | | | | | | | | | | | | Bats: R | | Throws: R | | Height: 6' 2" | | Weight: 190 | | Born: December 30, 1977 | | | Age: 32 |

	G	GS	IP	H	HR	BB	SO	GB%	BABIP	STUFF	WHIP	ERA	SIERA	DERA	EqH9	EqHR9	EqBB9	EqSO9	VORP	SN/WX	
2007	HUN	AA	29	0	0	2	8	0	11¹	8	0	4	21	38%	.364	11	1.06	2.38	0.94	3.27	8.2	0.8	3.3	10.6	2.7	-0.14
2007	NAS	AAA	29	1	1	5	24	0	32	17	2	11	47	44%	.246	24	0.87	1.69	1.65	2.28	6.4	0.9	3.3	10.0	10.6	1.37
2007	TBA	MLB	29	1	0	0	22	0	22	26	1	16	27	55%	.424	18	1.91	6.14	3.78	5.40	10.0	0.4	5.8	10.0	0.2	-0.32
2008	DUR	AAA	30	1	0	8	15	0	23²	5	1	10	39	48%	.114	22	0.63	0.38	1.26	0.81	3.2	0.4	4.0	10.1	11.6	1.54
2008	TBA	MLB	30	6	2	4	51	0	58¹	28	3	24	82	31%	.217	36	0.89	1.54	2.06	1.68	5.4	0.5	3.4	10.2	23.9	3.60
2009	TBA	MLB	31	5	4	4	73	0	67¹	59	6	33	69	39%	.296	7	1.37	4.81	3.79	4.75	8.1	0.8	3.9	8.1	5.5	1.32
2010	TBA	MLB	32	3	4	3	59	0	60	57	6	32	63	37%	.322	6	1.48	4.37	3.82	4.40	8.1	0.9	4.5	8.6	7.3	1.42

Breakout: 19%   Improve: 40%   Collapse: 29%   Attrition: 15%   MLB: 86%   Comparables: Steve Reed, Alejandro Pena, John Habyan, Mark Clear

Dominance cometh, and dominance goeth, especially for a reliever with a short track record. Just as the oft-injured journeyman entered the 2008 season with a 5.44 ERA but emerged as a staple of a pennant-winning club's bullpen, so too did he turn back into a pumpkin in 2009. Lost velocity on his fastball was one culprit, as Balfour was hit much harder in 2009 (.235/.326/.355) than in 2008 (.143/.233/.230). Meanwhile, his strikeout, walk, and homer rates all deteriorated, and his Fair Run Average more than quadrupled (0.96 to 4.24). Such volatility is exactly why the Rays keep digging up relievers, though Balfour is still in the mix for a late-inning role.

Randy Choate

| | | | | | | | | | | | Bats: L | | Throws: L | | Height: 6' 1" | | Weight: 195 | | Born: September 5, 1975 | | | Age: 34 |

YEAR	TEAM	LVL	AGE	W	L	SV	G	GS	IP	H	HR	BB	SO	GB%	BABIP	STUFF	WHIP	ERA	SIERA	DERA	EqH9	EqHR9	EqBB9	EqSO9	VORP	SN/WX
2007	TUC	AAA	31	3	1	3	55	0	63¹	68	3	16	61	67%	.339	6	1.33	2.98	3.23	3.80	9.0	0.7	2.4	6.6	12.1	0.67
2008	NAS	AAA	32	0	4	2	26	2	39	42	4	20	31	75%	.314	-21	1.59	5.08	3.90	6.09	10.5	1.4	4.5	5.0	-2.5	-0.60
2009	DUR	AAA	33	3	0	0	21	0	19¹	16	0	9	15	75%	.271	-10	1.29	3.72	3.90	4.26	8.1	0.5	4.3	5.7	2.6	0.01
2009	TBA	MLB	33	1	0	5	61	0	36¹	28	4	11	28	74%	.242	2	1.07	3.47	3.51	3.60	7.2	1.0	2.6	6.2	7.4	1.03
2010	TBA	MLB	34	2	3	1	46	0	45²	51	5	20	32	69%	.326	-10	1.56	5.12	4.22	5.25	9.7	1.0	3.7	5.8	1.3	0.53

Breakout: 21%   Improve: 42%   Collapse: 30%   Attrition: 18%   MLB: 74%   Comparables: Brian Shouse, Rich Sauveur, Paul Mirabella, Gary Lavelle

Virtually absent from the major-league scene since 2006—how'd you like two appearances in which you failed to retire a hitter hanging over your head for two years?—Choate resurfaced in late May when Brian Shouse went down, and did his typical LOOGY act. Righties hit a robust .321/.390/.491 against him, lefties a bare .141/.193/.192; to Maddon's credit, Choate held the platoon advantage 60 percent of the time. With Shouse's departure, he's likely to be the team's primary lefty specialist in 2010, though with J. P. Howell working the high-leverage road and Lance Cormier the low one, that means limited engagements for Choate.

Alex Cobb

Bats: R   Throws: R   Height: 6' 1"   Weight: 180   Born: October 7, 1987   Age: 22

YEAR	TEAM	LVL	AGE	W	L	SV	G	GS	IP	H	HR	BB	SO	GB%	BABIP	STUFF	WHIP	ERA	SIERA	DERA	EqH9	EqHR9	EqBB9	EqSO9	VORP	SN/WX
2007	HUD	A-	19	5	6	0	16	16	81^1	78	4	31	62	52%	.303	6	1.34	3.54	4.20	6.09	11.7	2.0	4.4	3.9	-4.7	-0.30
2008	CGA	A	20	9	7	0	25	25	139^2	113	16	35	97	58%	.245	-5	1.06	3.29	3.92	5.72	9.8	2.7	3.4	3.5	-3.0	-0.16
2009	PCH	A+	21	8	5	0	24	23	124^2	116	6	31	107	57%	.304	12	1.18	3.03	3.51	5.12	10.3	1.4	3.1	5.2	4.8	-0.01
2010	TBA	MLB	22	5	9	0	28	25	119	143	21	54	68	50%	.315	-1	1.65	6.04	5.14	6.08	10.3	1.5	3.8	4.7	-7.7	2.18

Breakout: 16%   Improve: 58%   Collapse: 12%   Attrition: 13%   MLB: 8%   Comparables: Jimmy Barrett, James Parr, Mike Payne, Adam Eaton

A fourth-round 2006 pick from Vero Beach High School, Cobb is an undersized righty with an excellent curveball and a deceptive low-90s heater. His ground-ball rates have always been strong, and though his strikeout rates have been solid, last year he missed more bats. He also did a better job of keeping the ball in the park; from June 12th to September 3rd, he went over 60 innings without allowing a long ball, though the Charlotte ballpark is notoriously homer-suppressing. Although Cobb is well down on this system's list of pitching prospects, the Rays will start to get a better handle on what they have in him as he moves on to Double-A.

Alexander Colome

Bats: R   Throws: R   Height: 6' 2"   Weight: 184   Born: December 31, 1988   Age: 21

YEAR	TEAM	LVL	AGE	W	L	SV	G	GS	IP	H	HR	BB	SO	GB%	BABIP	STUFF	WHIP	ERA	SIERA	DERA	EqH9	EqHR9	EqBB9	EqSO9	VORP	SN/WX
2008	PRI	Rk	19	0	5	0	12	11	46^1	50	5	26	52	40%	.349	-22	1.64	6.80	3.77	13.05	13.5	3.2	7.7	4.9	-33.6	-2.14
2009	HUD	A-	20	7	4	0	15	15	76	46	0	32	94	57%	.267	27	1.03	1.66	2.72	5.23	8.8	1.4	5.4	6.3	1.9	0.33
2010	TBA	MLB	21	3	6	0	20	20	82^2	98	14	53	66	46%	.332	14	1.82	6.48	4.92	6.48	10.2	1.4	5.4	6.5	-9.0	1.17

Breakout: 23%   Improve: 56%   Collapse: 4%   Attrition: 6%   MLB: 0%   Comparables: Ricky Trlicek, Juan Morillo, Duff Brumley, Kyle Cofield

The nephew of former Devil Rays headache Jesus Colome rebounded from a disappointing stateside debut to take a major step forward in 2009. He dominated hitters in the short-season New York-Penn League, topping the circuit in strikeouts while ranking second in ERA; batters hit just .174/.274/.224 against him. Colome's electric arsenal features a 92-94 mph fastball that can touch 96, as well as a late-biting curveball; his changeup is still a work in progress. His upside is as a frontline starter; he'll take the next step toward that goal at Bowling Green.

Lance Cormier

Bats: R   Throws: R   Height: 6' 1"   Weight: 200   Born: August 19, 1980   Age: 29

YEAR	TEAM	LVL	AGE	W	L	SV	G	GS	IP	H	HR	BB	SO	GB%	BABIP	STUFF	WHIP	ERA	SIERA	DERA	EqH9	EqHR9	EqBB9	EqSO9	VORP	SN/WX
2007	RIC	AAA	26	4	2	0	10	10	52	56	4	15	31	72%	.323	-7	1.37	3.46	3.98	4.63	10.8	1.2	2.9	4.2	4.5	0.68
2007	ATL	MLB	26	2	6	0	10	9	45^2	56	16	22	27	67%	.276	-34	1.71	7.09	4.78	7.25	11.3	3.4	4.0	4.8	-8.7	0.03
2008	NOR	AAA	27	1	1	0	9	0	18^2	12	0	5	12	82%	.218	-4	0.91	0.96	3.18	2.21	5.9	0.5	2.5	3.9	6.7	0.70
2008	BAL	MLB	27	3	3	1	45	1	71^2	78	4	34	46	65%	.316	-3	1.56	4.02	4.65	4.23	9.3	0.4	3.8	5.3	10.1	0.66
2009	TBA	MLB	28	3	3	2	53	0	77^1	75	6	25	36	61%	.262	-6	1.29	3.26	4.96	3.45	8.4	0.7	2.5	3.6	17.9	0.70
2010	TBA	MLB	29	4	6	1	51	1	79	94	11	32	43	65%	.317	-17	1.60	5.43	4.76	5.46	10.2	1.2	3.5	4.4	0.3	0.75

Breakout: 9%   Improve: 43%   Collapse: 22%   Attrition: 18%   MLB: 87%   Comparables: John Frascatore, Brian Sikorski, Ricky Stone, Frank Pastore

Nontendered by the Orioles, Cormier moved one stop down the AL East line and did a credible job working primarily as the Rays' long or middle man in low-leverage duty. He was less successful in higher-leverage situational roles later in the year, first because he was still Lance Cormier, and second because his platoon split between righties and lefties was relatively minimal. It wasn't glamorous work, but it was enough for the Rays to re-up Cormier at $1.2 million for 2010, providing him with a rare bit of job security.

Wade Davis

| | | | | Bats: R | | Throws: R | | Height: 6′ 5″ | | Weight: 220 | | Born: September 7, 1985 | | Age: 24 |

YEAR	TEAM	LVL	AGE	W	L	SV	G	GS	IP	H	HR	BB	SO	GB%	BABIP	STUFF	WHIP	ERA	SIERA	DERA	EqH9	EqHR9	EqBB9	EqSO9	VORP	SN/WX
2007	VRO	A+	21	3	0	0	13	13	78¹	54	5	21	88	50%	.262	40	0.96	1.84	2.62	3.02	7.2	1.2	3.0	7.6	20.1	1.37
2007	MNT	AA	21	7	3	0	14	14	80	74	3	30	81	52%	.320	21	1.30	3.15	3.43	5.24	10.0	0.8	3.6	6.3	2.1	0.50
2008	MNT	AA	22	9	6	0	19	19	107²	104	7	42	81	47%	.307	4	1.36	3.85	4.32	4.79	9.9	1.2	3.6	5.0	7.9	0.42
2008	DUR	AAA	22	4	2	0	9	9	53	39	5	24	55	48%	.256	29	1.19	2.72	3.51	3.09	7.1	1.1	4.2	7.1	13.7	1.24
2009	DUR	AAA	23	10	8	0	28	28	158²	139	14	60	140	42%	.276	12	1.25	3.40	3.92	4.46	8.6	1.1	3.6	6.5	17.7	1.23
2009	TBA	MLB	23	2	2	0	6	6	36¹	33	2	13	36	48%	.313	29	1.27	3.72	3.40	4.37	8.5	0.5	2.8	8.0	4.4	1.21
2010	TBA	MLB	24	9	11	3	34	31	168	172	21	75	129	42%	.306	7	1.47	4.71	4.50	4.79	8.8	1.0	3.8	6.3	13.3	3.02

Breakout: 20%   Improve: 43%   Collapse: 14%   Attrition: 13%   MLB: 43%   Comparables: Jason Hammel, Matt Clement, Rod Imes, Andy Hawkins

Davis entered the year as the Rays' second-best pitching prospect behind David Price, and he ended it with the Rays having changed the face of their franchise to accommodate his spot in the rotation. A strapping power pitcher with a 93-94 mph fastball and a plus hard curveball, Davis profiles as a second or third starter, depending upon whether he can improve a third pitch; there's also been some thought to making him a closer. He struggled with his command at Durham to start the year, but wound up overpowering Triple-A hitters with a 3.0 strikeout-to-walk ratio and 9.1 strikeouts per nine innings from June through August. The Rays traded Scott Kazmir at the waiver deadline in part to open up a spot for Davis, who whiffed nine Tigers in his September 6th debut and then tossed a four-hit, 10-strikeout shutout of the Orioles in his third start. He's set to pair with Price in what should become one of the game's best homegrown pitcher tandems.

Matt Garza

| | | | | Bats: R | | Throws: R | | Height: 6′ 4″ | | Weight: 205 | | Born: November 11, 1983 | | Age: 26 |

YEAR	TEAM	LVL	AGE	W	L	SV	G	GS	IP	H	HR	BB	SO	GB%	BABIP	STUFF	WHIP	ERA	SIERA	DERA	EqH9	EqHR9	EqBB9	EqSO9	VORP	SN/WX
2007	ROC	AAA	23	4	6	0	16	16	92	93	5	31	95	48%	.332	17	1.35	3.62	3.34	4.84	10.0	0.8	3.1	7.3	6.6	0.66
2007	MIN	MLB	23	5	7	0	16	15	83	96	8	32	67	47%	.344	8	1.54	3.69	4.21	4.52	10.4	1.0	3.2	6.7	8.8	2.09
2008	TBA	MLB	24	11	9	0	30	30	184²	170	19	59	128	45%	.270	11	1.24	3.70	4.39	4.03	8.8	1.0	2.6	5.8	29.5	5.28
2009	TBA	MLB	25	8	12	0	32	32	203	177	25	79	189	45%	.273	20	1.26	3.95	3.75	3.91	8.0	1.0	3.1	7.3	35.5	5.66
2010	TBA	MLB	26	10	11	0	33	33	187¹	196	23	71	150	47%	.314	11	1.42	4.55	4.14	4.63	9.0	1.0	3.2	6.6	18.0	3.08

Breakout: 5%   Improve: 47%   Collapse: 10%   Attrition: 14%   MLB: 98%   Comparables: Jeff Weaver, Justin Verlander, Wade Miller, Brian Holman

While his won-loss record was the product of a staff-low 3.8 runs per game of support, Garza nevertheless solidified the gains he made in 2008, emerging as a frontline workhorse. He topped 200 innings for the first time and finished 11th in SNLVAR, sixth in strikeout rate, and fourth in hit rate, the latter two marks testament to just how nasty his stuff is. For the first time in his career, he showed a reverse platoon split, holding lefties to a .196/.300/.309 line, compared with .244/.311/.410 in 2008, a result that suggests that his curveball was actually more effective than his vaunted slider despite the general perception and the PITCHf/x micro-accounting. A Super-Two, he'll still be an excellent bargain even with a raise.

Jeremy Hellickson

| | | | | Bats: R | | Throws: R | | Height: 6′ 1″ | | Weight: 185 | | Born: April 8, 1987 | | Age: 23 |

YEAR	TEAM	LVL	AGE	W	L	SV	G	GS	IP	H	HR	BB	SO	GB%	BABIP	STUFF	WHIP	ERA	SIERA	DERA	EqH9	EqHR9	EqBB9	EqSO9	VORP	SN/WX
2007	CGA	A	20	13	3	0	21	21	111¹	87	7	34	106	44%	.270	21	1.09	2.67	3.32	4.17	9.3	1.6	3.5	5.7	14.8	1.46
2008	VRO	A+	21	7	1	0	14	14	76²	64	7	5	83	49%	.289	26	0.90	2.00	2.19	3.23	9.7	1.8	1.2	7.1	17.6	1.05
2008	MNT	AA	21	4	4	0	13	13	75¹	84	15	15	79	48%	.350	5	1.31	3.94	2.80	4.99	12.2	2.8	2.2	7.6	3.7	0.07
2009	MNT	AA	22	3	1	0	11	11	56²	41	4	14	62	38%	.261	26	0.97	2.38	2.70	3.42	7.7	1.3	2.3	7.5	12.5	1.08
2009	DUR	AAA	22	6	1	0	9	9	57¹	31	4	15	70	50%	.213	47	0.80	2.51	2.23	3.42	5.7	0.8	2.6	9.1	12.8	1.27
2010	TBA	MLB	23	6	7	0	29	26	118²	129	18	43	100	37%	.323	12	1.45	4.95	4.08	4.98	9.4	1.3	3.1	6.9	6.8	2.87

Breakout: 3%   Improve: 34%   Collapse: 21%   Attrition: 18%   MLB: 29%   Comparables: Clay Buchholz, Robert Toth, Rusty Meacham, Doug Drabek

Hellickson is the next top prospect headed for the Rays' rotation, following David Price and Wade Davis, and some scouts prefer him to the latter after a breakout 2009. Despite losing seven weeks to an early-season shoulder sprain, Hellickson rebounded from a mediocre late-2008 showing, dominating hitters at both Double-A and Triple-A, thanks to improved command of both his 90-93 mph fastball and a late-fading changeup. He generated the second-highest rate of swings and misses in the International League and drew raves for his ability to mix his pitches. Just as importantly, the consistency with which he worked down in the zone helped pare his home-run rate. The Rays have no opening in their rotation at the moment, but Hellickson could see time there in 2010 if the injury bug bites.

J. P. Howell

Bats: L   Throws: L   Height: 6' 0"   Weight: 175   Born: April 25, 1983   Age: 27

YEAR	TEAM	LVL	AGE	W	L	SV	G	GS	IP	H	HR	BB	SO	GB%	BABIP	STUFF	WHIP	ERA	SIERA	DERA	EqH9	EqHR9	EqBB9	EqSO9	VORP	SN/WX
2007	DUR	AAA	24	7	8	0	21	21	128	110	16	34	145	63%	.289	15	1.12	3.37	2.71	5.12	8.7	1.5	2.5	8.2	5.2	0.84
2007	TBA	MLB	24	1	6	0	10	10	51	69	8	21	49	59%	.374	2	1.76	7.59	3.86	7.00	10.6	1.4	3.2	7.4	-8.9	0.08
2008	TBA	MLB	25	6	1	3	64	0	89¹	62	6	39	92	61%	.245	23	1.13	2.22	3.42	2.94	6.7	0.6	3.5	8.3	25.2	4.89
2009	TBA	MLB	26	7	5	17	69	0	66²	47	7	33	79	58%	.256	20	1.20	2.83	3.15	2.86	6.7	0.8	4.0	9.4	19.3	2.11
2010	TBA	MLB	27	5	5	9	55	3	80²	79	10	33	79	60%	.314	8	1.39	4.43	3.56	4.48	8.4	1.0	3.5	8.0	9.1	1.41

Breakout: 15%   Improve: 43%   Collapse: 10%   Attrition: 13%   MLB: 87%   Comparables: Dave Righetti, C.J. Wilson, Jesse Orosco, Bill Scherrer

Like so many other Rays relievers, Howell wasn't as effective in 2009 as he'd been in 2008, though he was still miles beyond the pitcher who entered last year with a 6.34 career ERA. While Howell set a career high for strikeout rate, his walk and homer rates crept upward, as did his Fair Run Average (2.78 to 3.55). Because Maddon spent half the season using him as the team's primary closer instead of in a multi-inning role, Howell faced lefties less often, and they hit him harder than in 2008 (.280/.372/.400, with a .364 BABIP in 86 plate appearances, compared with .188/.286/.248, with a .244 BABIP in 138 PA). The arrival of Rafael Soriano allows him to move back his previous role, where he'll be more valuable if he can restore his performance against same-side hitters.

Kyle Lobstein

Bats: L   Throws: L   Height: 6' 3"   Weight: 200   Born: August 12, 1989   Age: 20

YEAR	TEAM	LVL	AGE	W	L	SV	G	GS	IP	H	HR	BB	SO	GB%	BABIP	STUFF	WHIP	ERA	SIERA	DERA	EqH9	EqHR9	EqBB9	EqSO9	VORP	SN/WX
2009	HUD	A-	19	3	5	0	14	14	73¹	55	4	23	74	52%	.260	-4	1.06	2.58	3.21	5.63	10.7	3.0	4.4	4.8	-0.9	-0.14
2010	TBA	MLB	20	3	8	0	23	23	98²	125	19	51	59	49%	.328	17	1.79	6.70	5.21	6.82	11.0	1.7	4.4	4.9	-14.5	2.28

Breakout: 13%   Improve: 41%   Collapse: 29%   Attrition: 3%   MLB: 0%   Comparables: Ross Farnsworth, Chris Hill, Kevin Walker, Marc D'Alessandro

Talk about somebody who really should develop an eponymous Eephus pitch. Lobstein entered 2008 as one of the nation's top high-school lefties, but turned off scouts with some mediocre performances and a dip in his velocity. The Rays took the plunge nonetheless, drafting him in the second round and buying him out of a commitment to the University of Arizona with an above-slot $1.5 million bonus. He made a solid pro debut, restoring his velocity into the 89-91 mph range and impressing scouts with his projectable frame and easy delivery while cracking the New York–Penn League's top 10 in both strikeout rate and ERA.

Jake McGee

Bats: L   Throws: L   Height: 6' 3"   Weight: 190   Born: August 6, 1986   Age: 23

YEAR	TEAM	LVL	AGE	W	L	SV	G	GS	IP	H	HR	BB	SO	GB%	BABIP	STUFF	WHIP	ERA	SIERA	DERA	EqH9	EqHR9	EqBB9	EqSO9	VORP	SN/WX
2007	VRO	A+	20	5	4	0	21	21	116²	86	8	39	145	39%	.284	54	1.07	2.93	2.47	4.25	7.7	1.3	3.6	8.4	15.2	0.90
2007	MNT	AA	20	3	2	0	5	5	23¹	19	2	13	30	39%	.315	21	1.37	4.24	3.13	5.27	9.3	1.7	5.1	8.4	0.5	0.37
2008	MNT	AA	21	6	4	0	15	15	77²	65	6	37	65	48%	.273	21	1.31	3.94	4.22	5.09	8.6	1.3	4.2	5.5	3.3	0.22
2009	PCH	A+	22	0	2	0	11	11	22¹	26	2	9	26	55%	.400	-5	1.57	6.45	3.09	8.76	13.7	2.4	4.7	8.1	-6.9	-0.34
2010	TBA	MLB	23	4	5	0	23	19	81	83	11	42	72	38%	.314	11	1.54	4.94	4.33	5.03	8.9	1.2	4.4	7.4	4.2	1.63

Breakout: 10%   Improve: 50%   Collapse: 23%   Attrition: 13%   MLB: 8%   Comparables: Manny Parra, Angel Ortiz, Zach Crouch, Alberto Blanco

Blessed with rare high-90s velocity for a lefty, this 2004 fifth-round pick out of a Nevada high school ranked among the Rays' top pitching prospects before a less-than-dominant showing at Double-A in 2008 led to the discovery that he needed Tommy John surgery. McGee returned to competition in late June, starting games but pitching a maximum of three innings—less if he found trouble, which he did about half the time. McGee's violent delivery and second-rank secondary offerings have the team eying him as a late-game reliever, perhaps his quickest path to the majors given how crowded the team's rotation picture is becoming.

Matt Moore

| | | | | | | | | Bats: L | | Throws: L | | Height: 6' 2" | | Weight: 205 | | Born: June 18, 1989 | | Age: 21 | |

YEAR	TEAM	LVL	AGE	W	L	SV	G	GS	IP	H	HR	BB	SO	GB%	BABIP	STUFF	WHIP	ERA	SIERA	DERA	EqH9	EqHR9	EqBB9	EqSO9	VORP	SN/WX
2007	PRI	Rk	18	0	0	0	8	3	20¹	12	1	16	29	33%	.244	19	1.38	2.66	3.43	4.10	8.7	1.9	8.7	7.2	2.9	-0.09
2008	PRI	Rk	19	2	2	0	12	12	54¹	30	0	19	77	58%	.248	31	0.90	1.66	2.14	5.80	7.8	1.4	4.9	6.5	-1.6	0.26
2009	BGR	A	20	8	5	0	26	26	123	86	6	70	176	51%	.303	8	1.27	3.15	2.70	6.19	10.0	2.3	7.3	7.6	-8.1	-0.63
2010	TBA	MLB	21	3	7	0	22	22	91	101	15	66	80	44%	.326	19	1.84	6.42	4.90	6.48	9.6	1.5	6.2	7.2	-9.9	1.93

Breakout: 9%   Improve: 40%   Collapse: 11%   Attrition: 4%   MLB: 3%   Comparables: Robert Fish, Carl Hamilton, Thomas Melgarejo, Chad Rodgers

This eighth-round 2007 pick from New Mexico is yet another power pitching prospect, the owner of a fastball that sits in the low 90s and can touch 95-96, not to mention a plus power curve and the consistent ability to work down in the zone and produce grounders. Moore dominated Sally League hitters, chalking up the minors' highest strike-out rate and lowest batting average (.195) after doing the same among short-season pitchers in 2008. He did battle control problems early in the year, walking 33 hitters in 35 ⅓ innings in April and May, but overcame them, trimming his walk rate to 3.8 per nine the rest of the way. Obviously, that's a battle he'll have to continue winning in order to reach his frontline starter ceiling.

Joe Nelson

| | | | | | | | | Bats: R | | Throws: R | | Height: 6' 1" | | Weight: 200 | | Born: October 25, 1974 | | Age: 35 | |

YEAR	TEAM	LVL	AGE	W	L	SV	G	GS	IP	H	HR	BB	SO	GB%	BABIP	STUFF	WHIP	ERA	SIERA	DERA	EqH9	EqHR9	EqBB9	EqSO9	VORP	SN/WX
2008	ABQ	AAA	33	1	1	11	19	0	25²	17	1	6	36	53%	.296	25	0.90	2.10	1.68	2.19	6.2	0.4	2.2	9.9	9.1	1.61
2008	FLO	MLB	33	3	1	1	59	0	54	42	5	22	60	47%	.262	16	1.19	2.00	3.22	2.68	7.0	0.8	3.1	8.3	17.3	0.84
2009	TBA	MLB	34	3	0	3	42	0	40¹	32	7	27	36	36%	.225	-2	1.46	4.02	4.89	4.54	6.9	1.5	5.2	6.7	4.5	0.35
2009	DUR	AAA	34	2	2	0	13	0	17¹	22	4	11	14	47%	.333	-18	1.90	6.23	4.93	7.71	12.7	2.8	6.1	6.1	-4.0	-1.08
2010	TBA	MLB	35	3	4	5	53	0	56	55	6	30	50	43%	.312	-3	1.53	4.81	4.34	4.89	8.6	1.0	4.5	7.2	3.8	0.69

Breakout: 17%   Improve: 42%   Collapse: 32%   Attrition: 15%   MLB: 78%   Comparables: Justin Speier, Turk Farrell, Takeo Kawamura, Bob Wells

It took Nelson 13 seasons of toil through seven organizations (including a brief pass through the Devil Rays' system in 2005) and a year lost to labrum surgery before he was able to reach 50 innings in a single major-league season. He finally did so with the Marlins in 2008, and his reward for that effort was a $1.3 million contract with the Rays for 2009. Consistent with last year's expectation that he'd lose ground, Nelson lost more than 2.5 mph on his already slow average fastball and changeup. His strikeout rate suffered, and both his walk and fly-ball rates skyrocketed, with some additional bad luck doubling his home-run rate. His ERA conceals even worse news: his 5.83 Fair Run Average was the highest among Rays relievers with at least 15 innings. Optioned to Triple-A on August 1st, he was DFA'd, outrighted, and ultimately granted free agency at the end of the season. Such is the life of a journeyman reliever.

Jeff Niemann

| | | | | | | | | Bats: R | | Throws: R | | Height: 6' 9" | | Weight: 280 | | Born: February 28, 1983 | | Age: 27 | |

YEAR	TEAM	LVL	AGE	W	L	SV	G	GS	IP	H	HR	BB	SO	GB%	BABIP	STUFF	WHIP	ERA	SIERA	DERA	EqH9	EqHR9	EqBB9	EqSO9	VORP	SN/WX
2007	DUR	AAA	24	12	6	0	25	25	131	144	13	46	123	46%	.337	-4	1.45	3.98	3.71	5.49	10.9	1.2	3.2	6.8	0.1	0.63
2008	DUR	AAA	25	9	5	0	24	24	133	101	15	50	128	52%	.246	13	1.14	3.59	3.52	4.36	7.1	1.2	3.5	6.4	16.4	2.14
2008	TBA	MLB	25	2	2	0	5	2	16	18	3	8	14	48%	.300	-5	1.62	5.06	4.37	6.61	10.5	1.7	3.9	7.2	-2.0	0.06
2009	TBA	MLB	26	13	6	0	31	30	180²	185	17	59	125	47%	.301	11	1.35	3.94	4.42	3.94	9.4	0.8	2.6	5.6	30.4	5.24
2010	TBA	MLB	27	8	10	0	29	28	148²	157	18	58	113	49%	.314	7	1.45	4.72	4.30	4.83	9.2	1.0	3.4	6.3	11.1	2.34

Breakout: 8%   Improve: 44%   Collapse: 16%   Attrition: 16%   MLB: 71%   Comparables: Chris Young, Aaron Harang, Jeff Juden, Brad Penny

The fourth overall pick of the 2004 draft, Niemann has seen his star fall due to shoulder problems that cost him velocity. Out of minor-league options, he earned a rotation spot in a make-or-break spring training and wound up leading all rookies in innings while ranking second in SNLVAR and third in strikeouts and ERA. Niemann is a fairly polished midrotation product, as he should be, considering he's a month older than Andy Sonnanstine. He won't dominate hitters; he's solid across the board but will have to mind the fly balls, as only luck on HR/FB separated him from an ERA much closer to league average.

David Price

| | | | | | | | | | | | | | | Bats: L | | Throws: L | | Height: 6′ 6″ | | Weight: 225 | | Born: August 26, 1985 | | Age: 24 |

YEAR	TEAM	LVL	AGE	W	L	SV	G	GS	IP	H	HR	BB	SO	GB%	BABIP	STUFF	WHIP	ERA	SIERA	DERA	EqH9	EqHR9	EqBB9	EqSO9	VORP	SN/WX
2008	VRO	A+	22	4	0	0	6	6	34²	28	0	7	37	50%	.311	31	1.01	1.82	2.61	2.90	9.3	0.6	2.6	7.3	8.9	0.52
2008	MNT	AA	22	7	0	0	9	9	57	42	7	16	55	56%	.246	24	1.02	1.89	3.16	2.72	7.8	1.9	2.7	6.6	16.4	1.40
2008	DUR	AAA	22	1	1	0	4	4	18	22	0	9	17	63%	.393	12	1.72	4.50	3.79	5.29	11.6	0.5	4.8	6.4	0.4	0.17
2008	TBA	MLB	22	0	0	0	5	1	14	9	1	4	12	49%	.205	14	0.93	1.93	3.63	2.51	5.7	0.6	2.5	6.9	4.8	0.25
2009	DUR	AAA	23	1	4	0	8	8	34¹	28	5	18	35	53%	.261	12	1.34	3.93	3.77	5.79	8.3	1.7	5.0	7.7	-1.0	0.19
2009	TBA	MLB	23	10	7	0	23	23	128¹	119	17	54	102	52%	.268	11	1.35	4.42	4.28	4.73	8.3	1.1	3.3	6.2	11.0	3.02
2010	TBA	MLB	24	8	8	0	29	27	147²	147	17	59	115	52%	.302	11	1.40	4.40	4.21	4.51	8.7	1.0	3.4	6.5	16.3	2.70

Breakout: 9%   Improve: 44%   Collapse: 12%   Attrition: 3%   MLB: 89%   Comparables: Sean Marshall, Britt Burns, Steve Cooke, Chris Nabholz

The first overall pick of 2007 closed 2008 with a tantalizing post-season showing and entered the year ranked behind only Matt Wieters on our Top 101 Prospects list. Unwilling to get caught up in the hype, the Rays sent Price back to Durham during the season's first six weeks, and his initial results upon promotion were underwhelming: a 4.70 ERA and 1.5 strikeout-to-walk ratio prior to the All-Star break. He improved markedly in the second half (4.27 ERA, 2.4 K/BB ratio) by pitching to contact more often; while his strikeout rate fell (9.6 to 5.9), his walk rate plummeted more drastically (6.3 to 2.5), and he produced more ground balls, which allowed him to pitch deeper into games. The most troubling aspect of his season was his struggles with his vaunted slider, which had been considered a plus-plus pitch by scouts. Advertised as a knockout pitch, it generated swings and misses just 4.8 percent of the time, the fourth-lowest rate among pitchers who threw at least 200 sliders. He'll have to restore his feel for that pitch in order to fulfill the lofty expectations set for him.

Aneury Rodriguez

| | | | | | | | | | | | | | | Bats: R | | Throws: R | | Height: 6′ 3″ | | Weight: 180 | | Born: December 13, 1987 | | Age: 22 |

YEAR	TEAM	LVL	AGE	W	L	SV	G	GS	IP	H	HR	BB	SO	GB%	BABIP	STUFF	WHIP	ERA	SIERA	DERA	EqH9	EqHR9	EqBB9	EqSO9	VORP	SN/WX
2007	ASH	A	19	9	9	0	28	28	152	182	19	48	160	41%	.372	10	1.51	5.15	3.28	7.13	11.7	1.8	3.5	6.6	-25.8	-3.00
2008	MOD	A+	20	9	10	0	27	27	156¹	148	12	40	139	40%	.303	13	1.20	3.74	3.53	5.52	10.0	1.7	3.0	5.2	-0.3	-0.06
2009	MNT	AA	21	9	11	0	27	27	142	122	17	59	111	38%	.258	2	1.27	4.50	4.46	6.12	9.1	2.1	3.8	5.1	-9.2	-0.89
2010	TBA	MLB	22	5	9	0	27	26	129²	153	22	56	89	34%	.324	9	1.62	5.72	5.00	5.80	10.2	1.4	3.7	5.6	-4.3	1.39

Breakout: 10%   Improve: 44%   Collapse: 9%   Attrition: 14%   MLB: 17%   Comparables: Eric Hurley, Dan Denham, Arnold Gooch, Chad Durbin

A nondrafted free agent out of the Dominican Republic, Rodriguez spent four years in the Rockies' chain before being traded to Tampa Bay for Jason Hammel in early April. After ranking second in the California League in strikeouts in 2008, the lanky righty struggled with the transition to Double-A and was tagged for a 6.01 ERA and 1.6 HR/9 prior to the All-Star break. Working with pitching coach Neil Allen, he improved the command of his low-90s fastball, tightened his curveball, and worked down in the zone more consistently. The results were impressive; he began the second half by tossing at least five no-hit innings in back-to-back outings, compiling 17 ⅔ consecutive scoreless innings, and finishing with a 2.22 ERA and just 0.3 HR/9 after the break. As he was left off the 40-man prior to the Rule 5 draft, the Rays may have caught a break when he went unselected.

James Shields

| | | | | | | | | | | | | | | Bats: R | | Throws: R | | Height: 6′ 4″ | | Weight: 215 | | Born: December 20, 1981 | | Age: 28 |

YEAR	TEAM	LVL	AGE	W	L	SV	G	GS	IP	H	HR	BB	SO	GB%	BABIP	STUFF	WHIP	ERA	SIERA	DERA	EqH9	EqHR9	EqBB9	EqSO9	VORP	SN/WX
2007	TBA	MLB	25	12	8	0	31	31	215	202	28	36	184	51%	.282	25	1.11	3.85	3.34	3.61	7.2	1.2	1.3	6.7	46.0	5.94
2008	TBA	MLB	26	14	8	0	33	33	215	208	24	40	160	54%	.287	14	1.15	3.56	3.76	3.93	9.3	1.1	1.5	6.2	35.9	5.80
2009	TBA	MLB	27	11	12	0	33	33	219²	239	29	52	167	49%	.308	8	1.32	4.14	3.93	4.35	9.8	1.1	1.9	6.0	27.5	4.21
2010	TBA	MLB	28	13	11	0	32	32	209¹	217	26	46	163	50%	.309	17	1.26	4.03	3.74	4.11	9.0	1.1	1.9	6.4	32.3	3.25

Breakout: 6%   Improve: 43%   Collapse: 10%   Attrition: 9%   MLB: 99%   Comparables: Dan Haren, Dave Bush, Pete Vuckovich, Burt Hooton

The Rays' nominal ace didn't have an awful season by any stretch, but the things he couldn't control—his BABIP, HR/FB, and offensive support—all receded from being just a few hairs better than average in 2008 to a few hairs worse. His walk rate slid in the wrong direction as well, though it was still the sixth-lowest in the league, and his strikeout-to-walk ratio was ninth. Perhaps of more concern was the fact that he was hit considerably harder in the second half (5.16 ERA, 1.5 HR/9, .321 BABIP) than the first (3.42 ERA, 1.0 HR/9, .304 BABIP). Still, over the past three years, Shields' performance has been quite stable and quite good; only six pitchers have higher strikeout-to-walk ratios than his 3.99, and only 20 have a higher SNLVAR than his 15.1. Considering that he'll make just $2.5 million in 2010 and $4.25 million in 2011 (followed by three very reasonable club options at a combined $28 million), he's one of the best bargains in the game.

Brian Shouse

| | | | | Bats: L | | Throws: L | | Height: 5' 10" | | Weight: 195 | | Born: September 26, 1968 | | Age: 41 | |

YEAR	TEAM	LVL	AGE	W	L	SV	G	GS	IP	H	HR	BB	SO	GB%	BABIP	STUFF	WHIP	ERA	SIERA	DERA	EqH9	EqHR9	EqBB9	EqSO9	VORP	SN/WX
2007	MIL	MLB	38	1	1	1	73	0	47²	46	0	14	32	61%	.301	5	1.26	3.02	4.21	3.28	8.1	0.0	2.3	5.4	11.8	1.20
2008	MIL	MLB	39	5	1	2	69	0	51¹	46	5	14	33	71%	.256	-5	1.17	2.81	3.88	3.44	8.3	0.9	2.1	4.9	11.7	0.92
2009	TBA	MLB	40	1	1	0	45	0	28	31	5	7	17	75%	.286	-13	1.36	4.50	4.01	4.50	9.6	1.6	1.9	4.8	3.1	0.63
2010	BOS	MLB	41	3	4	1	54	0	53¹	58	6	16	28	69%	.300	-10	1.40	4.70	4.41	4.83	9.6	1.0	2.7	4.5	4.0	0.78

Breakout: 7%   Improve: 40%   Collapse: 27%   Attrition: 27%   MLB: 92%   Comparables: Kimiyasu Kudoh, Rick Honeycutt, Jeff Fassero, Koji Takagi

Considering he couldn't stick on a major-league roster until his age-34 season, Shouse has enjoyed a nice run, averaging more than 60 appearances per year. His 2009 didn't have many highlights, however, as he spent over two months on the DL due to an elbow strain, returning to a two-homer, four-run greeting at the hands of the Yankees on July 27th. As was the case in 2008 and throughout most of his career, Shouse did his usual good work against lefties (.224/.246/.373), but righties wailed the tar out of him (.356/.442/.622). Unlike the hapless Ned Yost, Maddon was at least able to maneuver such that Shouse had the platoon advantage the majority of the time (57 percent). The Rays declined their $1.9 million option on Shouse, making him a free agent. After all, amid the H1N1 pandemic, is it really all that wise to be harboring stray LOOGYs? Corralled by the Red Sox on a minor-league deal.

Andy Sonnanstine

| | | | | Bats: L | | Throws: R | | Height: 6' 3" | | Weight: 185 | | Born: March 18, 1983 | | Age: 27 | |

YEAR	TEAM	LVL	AGE	W	L	SV	G	GS	IP	H	HR	BB	SO	GB%	BABIP	STUFF	WHIP	ERA	SIERA	DERA	EqH9	EqHR9	EqBB9	EqSO9	VORP	SN/WX
2007	DUR	AAA	24	6	4	0	11	11	71	60	8	13	66	49%	.268	17	1.03	2.66	3.08	3.77	8.5	1.3	1.9	6.8	13.1	1.16
2007	TBA	MLB	24	6	10	0	22	22	130²	151	18	26	97	44%	.326	7	1.35	5.85	3.92	5.21	9.1	1.3	1.6	6.0	4.3	1.36
2008	TBA	MLB	25	13	9	0	32	32	193¹	212	21	37	124	47%	.302	4	1.29	4.38	4.24	4.84	10.3	1.0	1.5	5.3	13.8	3.38
2009	DUR	AAA	26	5	3	0	9	9	57¹	68	4	9	36	47%	.330	1	1.34	4.40	4.21	5.05	11.6	1.0	1.7	4.6	2.7	-0.06
2009	TBA	MLB	26	6	9	0	22	18	99²	131	19	34	60	51%	.326	-27	1.66	6.77	4.83	7.18	11.6	1.6	2.7	4.7	-18.6	0.00
2010	TBA	MLB	27	8	9	0	30	26	154	178	21	43	97	47%	.320	0	1.44	4.81	4.49	4.88	10.0	1.2	2.3	5.2	10.6	1.27

Breakout: 15%   Improve: 52%   Collapse: 4%   Attrition: 17%   MLB: 93%   Comparables: Kyle Lohse, Jeff Weaver, Reggie Cleveland, Joel Pineiro

Sonnanstine is known for pounding the strike zone with his unremarkable arsenal, but last year hitters simply pounded it back out at him at a .311/.364/.525 clip. He wasn't nearly as sharp as in 2008, as his strikeout-to-walk ratio illustrates, and the luck he had at keeping his fly balls in the park ran out; his HR/FB rate shot up from 11.3 percent to 17.3 percent. He finished with the highest ERA of any pitcher making more than 15 starts and, not surprisingly, pitched his way back to Triple-A in the process, surpassed by the young bucks on whose shoulders the team's future rests. With no opening in the rotation for him in 2010 and more live arms on the way, Sonnanstine's future lies at points north of St. Petersburg.

Russ Springer

| | | | | Bats: R | | Throws: R | | Height: 6' 4" | | Weight: 225 | | Born: November 7, 1968 | | Age: 41 | |

YEAR	TEAM	LVL	AGE	W	L	SV	G	GS	IP	H	HR	BB	SO	GB%	BABIP	STUFF	WHIP	ERA	SIERA	DERA	EqH9	EqHR9	EqBB9	EqSO9	VORP	SN/WX
2007	SLN	MLB	38	8	1	0	76	0	66	41	3	19	66	34%	.229	27	0.91	2.18	3.13	2.40	5.6	0.4	2.3	7.9	22.6	2.25
2008	SLN	MLB	39	2	1	0	70	0	50¹	39	4	18	45	33%	.255	7	1.13	2.32	3.88	2.72	7.2	0.7	2.9	6.7	15.4	1.10
2009	TBA	MLB	40	1	3	1	26	0	15¹	16	4	3	11	24%	.261	-7	1.24	4.11	4.49	4.11	9.4	2.3	1.8	5.9	2.4	-0.71
2009	OAK	MLB	40	0	1	0	48	0	41²	52	5	14	47	19%	.376	7	1.58	4.10	3.51	4.01	10.8	1.1	2.5	8.6	7.1	-0.22
2010	TBA	MLB	41	3	3	0	52	0	51	50	6	19	44	30%	.306	3	1.35	4.09	4.14	4.18	8.5	1.0	3.1	7.1	7.5	0.47

Breakout: 8%   Improve: 41%   Collapse: 31%   Attrition: 24%   MLB: 94%   Comparables: Ron Reed, Marv Grissom, Mike Timlin, Don McMahon

Springer was excellent in 2007-08 as a member of the Cardinals' bullpen, but struggled upon moving to the AL in 2009, and as his 5.83 FRA reflects, he did more harm than good upon being claimed off waivers by the Rays in early August. Long balls were a persistent problem, thanks in no small part to his yielding by far the majors' lowest ground-ball rate, at 21.1 percent. At this point in his career, he's best used only against righties; he has held them to a .200/.246/.291 line over the last three years, compared with .291/.370/.474 against lefties, and the latter tagged him at a .350/.430/.550 clip in 93 plate appearances in 2009. A free agent at this writing, he'll have to hope there's a senior circuit team that can afford the luxury of carrying such a specialist.

Mitch Talbot

Bats: R   Throws: R   Height: 6' 2"   Weight: 200   Born: October 17, 1983   Age: 26

YEAR	TEAM	LVL	AGE	W	L	SV	G	GS	IP	H	HR	BB	SO	GB%	BABIP	STUFF	WHIP	ERA	SIERA	DERA	EqH9	EqHR9	EqBB9	EqSO9	VORP	SN/WX
2007	DUR	AAA	23	13	9	0	29	29	161	169	13	59	124	59%	.319	-2	1.42	4.53	4.10	5.79	10.6	1.0	3.5	5.6	-4.9	0.02
2008	DUR	AAA	24	13	9	0	28	28	161	165	9	35	141	59%	.320	15	1.24	3.86	3.45	4.69	9.4	0.7	2.1	5.8	14.1	1.58
2008	TBA	MLB	24	0	0	0	3	1	9²	16	3	11	5	51%	.382	-21	2.79	11.17	6.72	11.00	17.0	3.0	10.0	5.0	-5.5	-0.26
2009	DUR	AAA	25	4	4	0	10	10	54¹	67	3	18	40	59%	.362	-2	1.56	4.47	4.20	5.27	12.3	0.9	3.4	5.5	1.3	-0.15
2009	RAY	Rk	25	0	0	0	4	4	11	5	0	0	21	—	.294	9	0.45	0.82	-0.60	1.93	7.7	1.0	1.0	9.6	3.7	0.25
2010	CLE	MLB	26	5	7	0	26	16	97	106	12	39	67	52%	.314	-4	1.49	4.91	4.53	5.36	9.9	1.1	3.4	5.8	1.5	1.15

Breakout: 14%   Improve: 52%   Collapse: 21%   Attrition: 28%   MLB: 27%   Comparables: Terry Gilmore, Wally Whitehurst, Mike Maddux, Darrell Rasner

Acquired from the Astros in the Aubrey Huff trade along with Ben Zobrist, Talbot—no relation to the *Ball Four* foil, alas—lost the strike zone during his 2008 cup of coffee with the Rays. That wasn't all he lost, as an elbow sprain cost him more than half of the 2009 season. After showcasing his health with six starts in the Arizona Fall League, he was dealt to Cleveland as the PTBNL in the Kelly Shoppach trade; he is out of options and presumably will battle for a rotation spot with the Tribe. The owner of a 90-ish fastball with good movement, a hard slider, and a changeup with a nice fade, he has a usable arsenal, but one thoroughly lost among the high-upside arms in the Rays' system.

Alex Torres

Bats: L   Throws: L   Height: 5' 10"   Weight: 160   Born: December 8, 1987   Age: 22

YEAR	TEAM	LVL	AGE	W	L	SV	G	GS	IP	H	HR	BB	SO	GB%	BABIP	STUFF	WHIP	ERA	SIERA	DERA	EqH9	EqHR9	EqBB9	EqSO9	VORP	SN/WX
2008	RCU	A+	20	3	2	0	10	10	53	52	1	29	62	64%	.370	36	1.53	3.91	3.33	5.25	10.5	0.9	6.0	7.3	1.3	-0.01
2008	ANG	Rk	20	4	0	0	4	4	23¹	11	1	10	24	67%	.213	18	0.90	1.54	2.80	2.70	7.9	2.5	5.4	5.9	5.7	0.33
2009	RCU	A+	21	10	3	0	21	19	121¹	93	4	63	124	66%	.288	23	1.29	2.74	3.47	4.19	8.5	1.1	5.7	5.5	16.0	1.10
2009	ARK	AA	21	3	1	0	5	5	26	23	0	17	25	56%	.329	21	1.54	2.77	4.20	4.56	9.9	0.8	6.1	7.2	2.5	0.32
2010	TBA	MLB	22	4	8	0	22	20	110	123	15	71	73	58%	.313	5	1.76	5.99	5.09	6.09	9.6	1.2	5.5	5.4	-7.2	2.60

Breakout: 10%   Improve: 41%   Collapse: 15%   Attrition: 9%   MLB: 4%   Comparables: Horacio Estrada, Darold Brown, Kevin Spicer, Dan Henrikson

An undersized Venezuelan lefty, Torres blazed through the hitter-friendly California League in his full-season debut, fooling hitters with a variety of arm angles, missing bats, and growing grounders by the bushel. He earned a promotion to Double-A before being sent to the Rays in the Kazmir deal, and he'll probably pick up in 2010 where he left off at Montgomery. Torres has a low-90s fastball and sharp-breaking curve and slider, the latter two having the potential to become plus pitches, but he needs to improve his command and refine his changeup to take the next step.

Dan Wheeler

Bats: R   Throws: R   Height: 6' 3"   Weight: 220   Born: December 10, 1977   Age: 32

YEAR	TEAM	LVL	AGE	W	L	SV	G	GS	IP	H	HR	BB	SO	GB%	BABIP	STUFF	WHIP	ERA	SIERA	DERA	EqH9	EqHR9	EqBB9	EqSO9	VORP	SN/WX
2007	TBA	MLB	29	0	5	0	25	0	25	28	3	10	26	44%	.329	3	1.52	5.76	3.63	6.17	8.3	1.0	3.0	7.7	-2.0	0.21
2007	HOU	MLB	29	1	4	11	45	0	49²	46	8	13	56	42%	.302	13	1.19	5.07	2.72	4.68	8.3	1.5	2.2	9.2	4.4	1.15
2008	TBA	MLB	30	5	6	13	70	0	66¹	44	10	22	53	28%	.190	1	0.99	3.12	4.33	3.41	6.3	1.5	2.6	6.4	15.3	2.36
2009	TBA	MLB	31	4	5	2	69	0	57²	41	11	9	45	40%	.195	3	0.87	3.28	3.47	3.32	6.3	1.6	1.3	6.2	13.8	2.17
2010	TBA	MLB	32	4	4	5	59	0	58²	54	7	19	50	35%	.289	6	1.24	3.86	3.90	3.95	8.0	1.1	2.8	7.1	10.1	1.11

Breakout: 16%   Improve: 40%   Collapse: 19%   Attrition: 18%   MLB: 93%   Comparables: Scott Linebrink, Justin Speier, Doug Henry, Jerry Dipoto

Wheeler didn't spend any time closing for the Rays in 2009 as he had in 2008, but he was the team's most valuable reliever according to WXRL. That isn't saying much, considering that his total would have ranked fourth a year earlier. Because Wheeler works higher in the strike zone than most, he gets opposing hitters to put the ball in the air with a frequency few can match; after finishing with the majors' third-lowest ground-ball rate among pitchers with at least 50 innings in 2008, he ranked 18th in 2009. Unsurprisingly, many of those left the yard, more than the number of guys he walked, which was weird but not unprecedented: 28 others have done that in the wild-card era, one-quarter of them Twins.

LINEOUTS

Hitters

PLAYER	TEAM	LVL	AGE	PA	R	2B	3B	HR	RBI	BB	SO	SB-CS	EqBRR	AVG/OBP/SLG	EqAVG/EqOBP/EqSLG	EqA	VORP	WARP
SS T. Bortnick	HUD	A-	21	255	37	17	4	4	26	27	38	24-8	0.4	.300/.386/.470	.271/.331/.406	.256	7.7	0.8
INF J. Dillon	DUR	AAA	33	147	18	5	0	2	13	14	17	4-0	0.1	.244/.340/.333	.222/.311/.294	.228	-3.0	-0.2
	TBA	MLB	33	35	4	0	0	1	2	3	4	0-0	0.1	.300/.400/.400	.300/.400/.400	.290	1.0	0.1
C M. Hernandez	TBA	MLB	30	107	12	3	1	1	12	7	12	2-1	-0.8	.242/.292/.323	.253/.302/.333	.221	0.9	0.3
UT E. Johnson#	DUR	AAA	25	260	31	9	1	11	35	17	56	7-2	1.3	.262/.319/.451	.247/.299/.430	.251	5.2	-0.1
LF K. Kang*	BGR	A	21	362	42	29	7	5	42	40	74	10-5	-3.7	.307/.390/.491	.262/.331/.406	.257	4.3	-0.3
SS S. O'Malley	PCH	A+	21	447	73	9	2	1	27	58	80	40-14	4.1	.268/.388/.311	.244/.344/.283	.236	5.0	-0.6
1B C. Richard*	DUR	AAA	35	423	56	22	0	24	75	52	83	2-1	-2.5	.263/.364/.521	.232/.326/.442	.263	1.3	0.7
	TBA	MLB	35	23	1	0	0	0	0	4	7	0-0	0.2	.105/.261/.105	.105/.261/.105	.120	-2.5	-0.4
C S. Riggans	PCH	A+	28	45	5	2	0	0	2	4	6	1-0	-0.2	.256/.356/.308	.220/.289/.244	.188	-2.5	-0.4
	DUR	AAA	28	42	4	2	0	1	5	1	7	0-0	0.0	.200/.238/.325	.175/.214/.300	.168	-2.3	-0.3
	TBA	MLB	28	14	2	0	0	1	1	0	3	0-0	0.0	.143/.143/.357	.143/.143/.357	.153	-0.8	-0.2
OF J. Weber*	DUR	AAA	31	518	63	46	0	14	69	56	98	3-7	-5.9	.302/.382/.497	.273/.349/.441	.270	11.8	0.1

A 16th-round 2009 pick out of Coastal Carolina, **Tyler Bortnick** played second base in college but fared well upon being moved back to shortstop during a strong pro debut. His tools aren't outstanding, but he has no glaring weaknesses, either. ⊘ Minor-league masher **Joe Dillon** had a lonely year, moving from the A's to the Rays before being DFA'd and outrighted back to Durham, where he was presumably thrashed to sleep with a belt. ⊘ A third-round pick from a Waco high school where he also played QB, **Todd Glaesmann** was the highest 2009 draftee the Rays signed. He's a five-tool talent with a 6-foot-4, 205-pound frame that offers considerable power projection. ⊘ It took **Michel Hernandez** seven organizations and 12 seasons to wind up a primary backup, which lasted until Gregg Zaun showed up. Hernandez is taking his catch-and-throw act to the O's, leaving the Jays as the only AL East team yet to employ him. ⊘ Best known for a hard slide that touched off a spring 2008 brawl with the Yankees, **Elliot Johnson** has shown improvement at Triple-A in each of the past two seasons, but he's merely organizational depth in a very deep organization. ⊘ No relation to *The Simpsons*' resident aliens from Rigel VII, **Kyeong Kang** is a 15th-round 2006 draft-and-follow who moved from South Korea to Georgia during high school. Power is his only above-average tool, but his hot second half (.328/.427/.513) has people taking notice. ⊘ **Shawn O'Malley** combines fielding skills at short with good baserunning and a nifty OBP to make for an interesting shortstop on his way to Double-A. ⊘ After mashing 95 homers over the past five seasons in Triple-A, **Chris Richard** returned to the majors for the first time since 2003, thanks to Carlos Pena's injury. ⊘ Penciled in as Dioner Navarro's backup, **Shawn Riggans** saw action in just one game (he homered) before going on the DL with shoulder tendinitis and didn't get back to the majors until September; he was nontendered after Kelly Shoppach's arrival. ⊘ A nondrafted free agent who has toiled for six organizations (not to mention a pair of indy-league stints), **Jon Weber** won Durham's team MVP award and made the International League Post-season All-Star team; he'll provide similar organizational depth for the Yankees in 2010.

Pitchers

PLAYER	TEAM	LVL	AGE	W	L	SV	IP	H	HR	BB	SO	GB%	BABIP	STUFF	WHIP	ERA	SIERA	DERA	EqH9	EqHR9	EqBB9	EqSO9	VORP
W. Abreu	DUR	AAA	32	3	1	15	51	23	4	16	77	43%	.207	30	0.76	1.94	1.33	2.45	5.5	0.9	3.0	10.2	16.1
N. Barnese	BGR	A	20	6	5	0	74²	56	3	25	62	52%	.247	13	1.08	2.53	3.86	6.07	9.0	2.0	4.4	3.7	-4.3
J. Bennett	DUR	AAA	29	1	0	0	11¹	14	1	5	8	53%	.342	-11	1.68	4.76	4.67	5.06	11.8	0.8	4.2	5.1	0.5
—	TBA	MLB	29	0	0	0	12²	24	2	11	4	69%	.423	-39	2.76	9.95	6.28	9.00	18.0	1.5	7.5	3.0	-4.7
—	ATL	MLB	29	2	4	0	34	42	2	21	23	64%	.351	-13	1.85	3.18	4.88	3.48	11.2	0.5	4.8	5.1	7.6
C. Bradford	TBA	MLB	34	1	0	0	10¹	22	1	2	6	43%	.457	-15	2.32	4.35	4.86	4.22	18.6	0.8	1.7	4.2	1.5
J. Cruz	BGR	A	20	5	8	0	98	110	5	26	99	49%	.356	-17	1.39	4.04	3.25	8.05	13.4	2.3	3.8	4.9	-24.5
J. Isringhausen	TBA	MLB	36	0	0	1	8	6	0	5	6	36%	.250	-7	1.37	2.25	5.28	2.16	6.5	0.0	4.3	5.4	3.1
E. Morlan	MNT	AA	23	7	5	4	70	67	8	30	62	35%	.291	-21	1.39	3.99	4.21	5.44	9.9	2.0	3.9	5.8	0.4
T. Percival	TBA	MLB	39	0	1	6	11¹	14	3	5	7	29%	.306	-22	1.68	6.35	5.52	5.73	11.5	2.5	3.3	4.9	-0.3
H. Rollins	MNT	AA	24	9	11	0	134	147	9	33	83	55%	.313	-17	1.34	3.83	4.40	5.36	10.9	1.4	2.4	4.0	1.9
D. Thayer	DUR	AAA	28	2	5	17	63¹	59	3	15	44	57%	.281	-3	1.17	2.27	4.06	3.89	9.0	0.7	2.3	5.0	11.0
—	TBA	MLB	28	0	0	1	13²	18	3	1	8	35%	.319	-10	1.39	4.61	4.38	5.27	11.9	2.0	0.7	4.6	0.4

In a surreal series of events only an agate-type junkie could truly appreciate, journeyman **Winston Abreu** spent two weeks on the Rays' roster before being traded to Cleveland for Jon Meloan; a month later, Abreu was released and re-signed by Tampa Bay. ⊘ A third-round 2007 pick out of Simi Valley High School (alma mater of the Weaver brothers), **Nick Barnese** is projectable with a low-90s fastball, two potentially plus off-speed pitches, and a deceptive delivery. He missed the first two months of last year due to shoulder tendinitis, but pitched well upon returning. ⊘ Useful with the Braves in 2008, **Jeff Bennett** was most notable in '09 for breaking a bone in his nonthrowing hand by punching a wall and then going back out to pitch through it. Released after rehabbing, he is re-signed to a minor-league deal. ⊘ Everybody's favorite submariner, **Chad Bradford** underwent elbow surgery in February and was strafed in two stints separated by five weeks on the shelf due to lower-back woes; he's mulling retirement as we go to press, which would end a fascinating 12-year run. ⊘ A 2007 draft-and-follow with a lanky, projectable frame, **Joe Cruz** showed good command with his low-90s fastball and secondary offerings, but was undone by a high BABIP. ⊘ After injury wrecked **Jason Isringhausen**'s 2008 campaign, he rehabbed his way onto the Rays' roster, but lasted a month before tearing up his elbow in June. He'll go through rehab from Tommy John surgery before deciding whether to push for another shot. ⊘ Acquired from the Twins in the same deal that brought Garza and Bartlett, **Eduardo Morlan** lost velocity in 2008 due to shoulder woes; healthy in 2009, his performance has yet to rebound. ⊘ The once-retired **Troy Percival** began the year as the closer, but by late May was back on the DL with shoulder tendinitis; he hasn't officially retired, but he's expected to do so. ⊘ **Heath Rollins** wasn't a tasty Biscuit starting at Montgomery, but he shifted to the bullpen late in the year and missed more bats while generating a plethora of ground balls. ⊘ Mustachioed minor-league closer **Dale Thayer** became a cult figure, thanks to his memorable big-league debut, earning a three-inning save in a 15-2 win *and* taking his hacks against Ross Gload. He's had success at every stop en route to the majors, but scouts have never loved his stuff.

MANAGER: JOE MADDON

YEAR	TEAM	W-L	Pythag +/−	Avg PC	100+ P	120+ P	QS	BQS	REL	REL w Zero R	IBB	Subs	PH	PH Avg	PH HR	SB2	CS2	SB3	CS3	SAC Att	SAC %	POS SAC	Squeeze	Swing	In Play
2007	TBA	66-96	0	97.1	80	0	69	9	483	258	31	16	80	.159	1	114	43	16	4	48	70.8%	33	4	129	92
2008	TBA	97-65	5	96.0	71	0	77	2	448	289	29	50	131	.186	3	113	38	28	10	41	56.1%	20	1	135	94
2009	TBA	84-78	-2	99.4	81	1	72	7	508	323	21	48	138	.160	7	167	49	26	11	45	55.6%	24	9	141	101

Maddon's skills as a motivator received plenty of attention throughout the Rays' 2008 climb from the basement to the World Series, but for all the Camus quotes and "9=8" T-shirts, neither his motivational ability nor his tactical skills were enough to help the team return to the postseason in 2009. Though he did well to find playing time for the versatile and suddenly unstoppable Ben Zobrist and adhered strictly to a right-field platoon, he could do little to coax adequate performances out of the walking wounded Pat Burrell, Dioner Navarro, and B. J. Upton. Indeed, though the offense continued to hum in spite of its struggles, it may have been prudent for Maddon to seek out alternatives, at least in a part-time capacity. As for the pitching staff, though Maddon rode many of the same horses as the year before—always a danger for a successful skipper who feels bound by sentiment to rely on "my guys"—he got considerably less out of those standbys, particularly the ones in his bullpen. After the team's late 2008 success provided at least some amount of vindication for a matchup-based late-inning solution, he vacillated between a desire to rely on a proven closer (Troy Percival early, J. P. Howell later on) and diminishing returns. The addition of Rafael Soriano and his closer-like salary should make Maddon's bullpen machinations one area to keep an eye on in 2010.

Texas Rangers

To solve a problem, you must first understand the issue in need of fixing. For the Rangers, their desired fixes involved run prevention. The team seemed to have no trouble plating runners, but as the Rangers neared the end of a 2008 campaign in which the team finished below .500 for the fourth straight season and the eighth time in nine years, it became clear that improved run prevention was a necessity if they were ever going to amount to much. The front office remained torn between whether the pitchers themselves left much to be desired, or if the below-average performances of the moundsmen ought to be blamed on a lackluster defense. It was the classic conundrum: pitching and defense, where does the one begin and the other end?

When you need more than a little help, Gordian solutions aren't an option. There was no single masterstroke of genius. Instead, the Rangers had to afford to be omnivorous and explore fixing both halves of this equation, and do so systemically, creating a foundation for future success. As the Rays were busily demonstrating over in the AL East en route to a pennant, all the smart kids were going this route. Financial constraints, however, limited the Rangers' potential off-season activities for 2009, precluding the acquisitions of top-tier players or even viable stopgap veterans. With problems as broad and various as the Rangers', opening up the checkbook wouldn't necessarily yield results, anyway. What Texas needed was a combination of talent and ideas, of planning and execution. To the credit of everyone on board and in the front office, they did exactly that, creating the ideas, slowly dropping that talent into place, and providing shape to a future that now isn't merely packed with prospects and frustrations, but instead aims for outright dominance of their division.

To some extent, the wheels were set in motion by the development of Elvis Andrus. Installing the slick-fielding Andrus at shortstop would mean moving Michael Young to the hot corner, because even with a 2008 Gold Glove on his mantelpiece, Young is not seen as the defender Andrus is and will be. Shifting Young over to third base had the additional benefit of solidifying a position previously manned ineffectively by a handful of fielders and allowing Chris Davis to separate from them to cross the diamond and settle into new digs at first base. Factor in the off-season work of Ian Kinsler toward improving his defense, and on paper the Rangers stood to improve their entire infield with the ripple effect created simply by placing their faith in a prospect. Luckily, that winter design stood up to its real-world test during the 2009 season, as the team compiled the fifth-best PADE in all of baseball only a year removed from its dead-last -3.40 mark.

The pitching staff improved as a direct result, lopping a full run off its ERA and even more off its FRA, while almost tripling its prior-year WXRL tally in the bullpen. But while the promotion of Andrus surely bolstered a surprising Rangers team, hiring Mike Maddux as pitching coach paid equal dividends, resulting in improvements in the pitchers themselves so that they could deliver their own contributions toward improved run-prevention. A decreased unintentional walk rate and increased strikeout rate helped confirm Maddux's immediate impact. He worked diligently to develop detailed, individualized game plans, served as an advance

RANGERS PROSPECTUS
2009 W-L: 87-75, 2nd in AL West

Pythag	85-77	5th	**Ballpark:** The Ballpark (3-yr. PF: 1029). With heat, hits, and homers, simply hell on hurlers
RS/G	4.8	7th	
RA/G	4.6	4th	
EqA	.255	8th	**2009:** Getting serious about pitching and defense shapes the talent tidal wave washing in
EqBRR	-2.2	8th	
SNWP	.503	9th	
WXRL	9.94	6th	**2010:** Slow 'n steady should solidify gains, but did the Mariners already set the standard for West success?
FRAr	4.48	6th	
DE	.699	2nd	
PADE	0.94	2nd	**Action Items:** Putting the O back in outfield, picking a role for Neftali Feliz, selecting a rotation from a crowded field
Salary	$68.2	10th	
Attend	2.16	8th	

scout of sorts for his charges, and stressed preparation and communication. This is a marked contrast with what people think pitching coaches do; he did not impose his will by forcing mechanical changes or requiring the addition of new pitches. Instead, he set up guardrails and helped the staff progress past an "Arlington kills pitchers" mind-set, a particularly crucial shift in organizational philosophy for the development of their coming wave of young pitching prospects.

From among those rising, talented hurlers, Derek Holland and Neftali Feliz were the first to be recalled, but neither was immediately added to the starting rotation. The team felt that relief roles at the outset of their careers could help instill confidence and a sense of routine (not to mention familiarize them with game planning), but the practice also represented a latter-day replication of Earl Weaver's rule for breaking in young pitchers in middle relief. The results weren't perfect, with Feliz looking ready for anything the Rangers might ask of him, while Holland produced uneven work both starting and relieving. Neither is guaranteed a spot in the rotation this year, and both will have to earn an increased role, but that's a happy reflection of the new standard in play: prospects have to earn their positions. Both have the talent to shine, and will, but nothing is being handed out to anyone, no matter how blue his blue-chip status. Team president Nolan Ryan preaches the maximization of genetic potential, and strength coach Jose Vazquez has designed personal training regimens based on the team's goal of raising the bar of expectations for young pitchers. The regimens are not cookie-cutter, either, as someone chunky like Tommy Hunter is going to have a regimen different from that of the slender Martin Perez.

With the monumental, teamwide improvement on this side of the ledger, you might have expected a trip to the playoffs. They might have gotten there, save for one big, new problem: the usually reliable offense foundered, badly enough that even park effects couldn't mask the drop-off. Among the culprits were irreplaceable key players such as Ian Kinsler and Josh Hamilton, both of whom had legitimate cases for end-of-season awards a year earlier. Kinsler suffered from homer-itis, swinging for the fences with regularity; this resulted in a severe uptick in fly balls from 43 percent to 54 percent. Hamilton altered his swinging mechanics in the spring, suffered an injury, and reverted to his original mechanics in what was largely a lost year. After producing an aggregate .283/.354/.462 slash line and a league-best .278 EqA in 2008, Rangers bats spiraled downward to a .260/.320/.445 line and a bottom-third .255 EqA in 2009.

Sustained by its ballpark as ever, the offense was still hooked up to its power supply, producing a .185 ISO to last year's .179, but the players' inability to reach base kept the offense on a short-fuse, softball-style attack. The Rangers walked less often, dropping to a 7.3 percent unintentional walk rate from their 8.5 percent clip of the year before, and whiffed even more frequently, at a 20.5 percent rate to the 18.6 percent last season. With 1,253 punch-outs and 472 walks, the Rangers' 2.65 K/BB ratio would have been the worst in the modern era of any playoff team had they managed to stay in the race, narrowly edging the 2006 Tigers, a club that itself had to settle for the AL Wild Card on the final day of the season, with an aggregate 2.63 K/BB ratio. While Davis was the player most readily recognized for producing empty swings, earning a demotion to reassemble his swing and recapture his prospect status, he had plenty of company at the Whiff House: of the key offensive holdovers from 2008 to 2009, only Michael Young improved his strikeout rate.

In addition to struggling to find that same offensive magic they'd received from Hamilton and Milton Bradley in 2008, the team struggled in 2009 with many of its preferred choices for outfield, the DH slot, and catcher, despite a multitude of promising options. Hank Blalock was at long last healthy, but the only benefit, if you could call it that, was that he gave them a year bad enough to finally end the mystery associated with his long litany of repeated disappointments and injuries. If Nelson Cruz finally established himself as their present and future starter in right field, in the other corner David Murphy had a year that, like Blalock's, brings into question what use he has beyond adding to the team whiff total.

The team could not even catch a break behind the plate, where the Rangers expected the pleasure of picking between Taylor Teagarden, Jarrod Saltalamacchia, and perhaps Max Ramirez, and seeing if one would hit well enough to make the choice for them. Ron Washington did indeed wind up not knowing who to start, but not for happy reasons: Ramirez hurt his wrist and never made it to the majors, while Salty and Teagarden could not get into any sort of rhythm. When the husk of Ivan Rodriguez represents an offensive upgrade, it's safe to say that your catching prospects have failed to live up to expectations. Salty was once considered the marquee prospect in the return on Mark Teixeira, but he's been a big disappointment since. Due to their inability, unwilling or not, to settle on a catcher in 2009, the Rangers will have to face the same choice again this year; in this case, progress delayed meant progress denied.

Choosing is at the heart of the Rangers' destiny for 2010. In the rotation, they may have only two set starting pitchers heading into camp: 2009 breakout star Scott Feldman and free-agent addition Rich Harden, the veteran they tacked on after trading away Kevin Millwood at the Winter Meetings. Beyond that duo, they'll be picking from among Holland, Hunter, Brandon McCarthy, Matt Harrison, Feliz, and C. J. Wilson, and that's just as we go to press—more might be added to this mix. Will Washington and Maddux identify the right starters, or will they have to sort this out in-season?

The revival of the offense is similarly going to require picking the right position players, and more successfully than the team did last season. That means not just a return to health and productivity for Hamilton, but a recognition of how badly the lineup needs real production. With Blalock unlamentedly outbound to parts unknown and Marlon Byrd absent from the outfield with his signing up for a three-year dose of Cubbiedom, the Rangers have slots to fill in the lineup. Ideally, they might add the kind of selective performer who will do for their crew of hair-trigger hitters what Bobby Abreu supposedly did for the Angels last season, transmitting to his teammates the obvious benefits of patience by active example. Along those lines, this team could have reaped great benefit from signing a Chone Figgins or Nick Johnson. Those birds have flown, however.

At this stage, perhaps the best they can do for an OBP pick-me-up is to give Justin Smoak every chance to challenge Chris Davis at first base, especially now that DH is manned by Vladimir Guerrero for at least a year and perhaps two. One change in favor of a more dynamic, if not necessarily improved, offense will be the addition of Julio Borbon in place of Byrd. Along with Andrus, Borbon projects to alter the dynamic of the lineup, giving it some additional speed and perhaps some OBP. (It can't get much worse than Blalock.) Hamilton should be healthier, and perhaps Kinsler will regain mastery of the zone; even if Nelson Cruz loses ground, he'll still be a productive corner outfielder.

Overall, the picture is exceptionally promising in the long term. The Rangers fell just short of the playoffs this past season while improving on defense and on the mound in ways they should be able to sustain, while suffering at the plate in ways that are capable of being corrected. Add in one of the top farm systems in the sport, and the Rangers have put themselves in a position to be very tough for a very long time. With the Angels' possible decline, the Mariners' inspired winter might allow them to leapfrog their claim on the division title past the Rangers' for this season. But the storehouse of talent the Rangers are breaking in represents the best bet from among the division's short stack for long-term dominance.

HITTERS

Elvis Andrus SS Bats: R Throws: R Height: 6' 0" Weight: 185 Born: August 26, 1988 Age: 21

YEAR	TEAM	LVL	AGE	PA	R	2B	3B	HR	RBI	BB	SO	SB	CS	EqBRR	AVG	OBP	SLG	EqAVG	EqOBP	EqSLG	EqA	VORP	WARP	DEFENSE
2007	MYR	A+	18	440	59	20	3	3	37	44	88	25	7	1.0	.244	.330	.335	.221	.288	.302	.213	-3.9	-1.0	98-SS	-4
2007	BAK	A+	18	123	19	2	0	2	12	10	19	15	8	-1.7	.300	.369	.373	.274	.328	.336	.237	1.8	0.1	28-SS	-1
2008	FRI	AA	19	535	82	19	2	4	65	38	91	54	16	6.6	.295	.350	.367	.271	.317	.336	.239	8.7	1.6	108-SS	4
2009	TEX	MLB	20	541	72	17	8	6	40	40	77	33	6	4.3	.267	.329	.373	.266	.328	.371	.255	19.0	2.4	140-SS	1
2010	TEX	MLB	21	577	80	24	5	8	56	48	106	30	11	1.8	.264	.330	.374	.258	.321	.358	.238	7.3	0.8	135-SS	0

Breakout: 31% Improve: 58% Collapse: 13% Attrition: 5% MLB: 100% Comparables: Edgar Renteria, Omar Infante, Alcides Escobar, Luis Rivas

Andrus exceeded expectations in 2009, skipping past his 75th percentile PECOTA projection en route to finishing second in the Rookie of the Year tally. That doesn't mean he was drop-dead good, mind you, not with an OPS just over 700. Nor does it mean he won't be good in the future; he's just not there yet. Despite an above-average error total (to be expected), Andrus was a spectacular defender, and for him to do what he did at 20 is a strong indication of future success. The good news is that he's still six to eight years away from his prime. The bad news is that unless the Rangers buy out some of his free-agent years with one of those young-player, extended deals that are fashionable these days, that prime might come elsewhere.

Engel Beltre

OF   Bats: L   Throws: L   Height: 6' 1"   Weight: 169   Born: November 1, 1989   Age: 20

YEAR	TEAM	LVL	AGE	PA	R	2B	3B	HR	RBI	BB	SO	SB	CS	EqBRR	AVG	OBP	SLG	EqAVG	EqOBP	EqSLG	EqA	VORP	WARP	DEFENSE			
2007	RSX	Rk	17	145	20	3	3	5	13	12	44	6	3	1.0	.208	.310	.400	.188	.248	.331	.202	-5.2	-2.1	18-CF	-3	15-RF	-3
2007	RNG	Rk	17	99	19	3	4	4	15	8	21	3	2	-0.8	.310	.388	.583	.244	.286	.433	.246	1.3	-0.1	21-CF	-2		
2007	SPO	A-	17	41	3	0	0	0	1	2	10	2	1	-0.5	.211	.250	.211	.179	.200	.179	.106	-3.8	-1.3	9-CF	-4		
2008	CLN	A	18	598	87	26	9	8	47	15	105	31	11	1.9	.283	.308	.403	.257	.276	.365	.223	-6.8	-1.4	122-CF	-5		
2009	BAK	A+	19	389	44	13	5	3	23	17	77	17	7	2.5	.227	.281	.317	.194	.234	.262	.169	-21.7	-2.5	83-CF	2		
2010	TEX	MLB	20	441	51	21	6	7	31	19	93	10	5	0.9	.242	.279	.370	.243	.281	.362	.210	-8.4	-1.1	94-CF	-2		

Breakout: 45%   Improve: 73%   Collapse: 9%   Attrition: 7%   MLB: 1%   Comparables: Felix Pie, Miguel Negron, Chris Forgione, Darren Riley

Nobody in the system can match Beltre's tools. He's a potentially electrifying player with above-average power and speed to go with a cannon for an arm in the outfield. The problem is that nobody has sat down with the young Dominican and explained to him that there is a rule that allows a player to ignore pitches outside the strike zone and even go to first base should four such offerings cross his path in a single at-bat. His swing-at-everything approach led to some occasional good results at Low-A, but Cal League pitchers are one year older and one year smarter, so they quickly realized that there was no reason to throw Beltre a strike. At this point, it's up to him to make adjustments, or he's going to end up on the scrap pile of players who thought that being a great athlete automatically equaled success.

Hank Blalock

1B   Bats: L   Throws: R   Height: 6' 1"   Weight: 200   Born: November 21, 1980   Age: 29

YEAR	TEAM	LVL	AGE	PA	R	2B	3B	HR	RBI	BB	SO	SB	CS	EqBRR	AVG	OBP	SLG	EqAVG	EqOBP	EqSLG	EqA	VORP	WARP	DEFENSE			
2007	TEX	MLB	26	232	32	16	3	10	33	21	38	4	1	1.7	.293	.358	.543	.290	.355	.551	.299	15.3	1.4	38-3B	-2		
2008	TEX	MLB	27	281	37	19	1	12	38	19	40	1	0	-3.4	.287	.338	.508	.288	.339	.514	.288	13.6	1.3	33-1B	1	30-3B	-3
2009	TEX	MLB	28	495	62	21	4	25	66	26	108	2	0	-1.5	.234	.277	.459	.234	.277	.451	.246	-7.8	-1.5	64-1B	-5		
2010	TEX	MLB	29	417	55	21	3	20	57	33	82	3	1	-0.6	.258	.320	.486	.257	.320	.470	.258	3.5	0.2	70-1B	-1		

Breakout: 13%   Improve: 44%   Collapse: 11%   Attrition: 5%   MLB: 96%   Comparables: Leon Durham, Greg Walker, Vic Wertz, Dave Revering

Once one of baseball's brightest young hitters, Blalock has seen his career become decimated by injuries. While he stayed healthy for most of 2009 for the first time in three seasons, he was slow, stiff, and sluggish, looking like a player nearly a decade older than he was. Pushed to a reserve spot by the end of the year and let go once it was over, he's looking for work with a second-division team hoping for a rebound year, but he'll need a platoon partner. Look at those comps and try to work up some enthusiasm; that's a list of players who would have had careers, but then lots of bad stuff happened, and maybe the Calvinists have a point and they weren't so good in the first place.

Brandon Boggs

LF   Bats: S   Throws: R   Height: 5' 11"   Weight: 205   Born: January 9, 1983   Age: 27

YEAR	TEAM	LVL	AGE	PA	R	2B	3B	HR	RBI	BB	SO	SB	CS	EqBRR	AVG	OBP	SLG	EqAVG	EqOBP	EqSLG	EqA	VORP	WARP	DEFENSE			
2007	BAK	A+	24	108	17	9	1	4	17	14	28	5	1	0.1	.250	.361	.500	.208	.296	.385	.238	-0.4	-0.5	17-LF	-2	5-CF	-2
2007	FRI	AA	24	429	69	21	4	19	55	70	103	10	4	2.1	.266	.385	.508	.238	.340	.429	.268	15.5	1.5	93-CF	-2	6-LF	-1
2008	OKL	AAA	25	76	12	4	3	0	6	7	20	1	1	-0.1	.309	.368	.456	.275	.329	.391	.252	0.8	0.2	13-LF	-1	4-CF	2
2008	TEX	MLB	25	334	30	17	4	8	41	44	93	3	2	-1.2	.226	.333	.399	.231	.339	.413	.262	6.3	0.7	65-LF	-1	1-CF	1
2009	OKL	AAA	26	398	45	15	2	8	47	59	98	9	2	2.4	.268	.380	.398	.238	.339	.346	.249	3.1	-0.7	40-LF	-7	34-RF	-1
2009	TEX	MLB	26	18	0	1	0	0	0	1	8	0	0	-0.1	.059	.111	.118	.118	.167	.176	-.139	-2.6	-0.5				
2010	TEX	MLB	27	397	41	18	3	10	43	47	109	4	3	0.5	.231	.326	.385	.225	.317	.365	.235	-1.8	-0.6	82-LF	-3		

Breakout: 6%   Improve: 32%   Collapse: 27%   Attrition: 18%   MLB: 38%   Comparables: Jason Evans, Skip Kiil, Chris Magruder, Brian Banks

Boggs is somewhere between useful and useless, a chasm that has killed the careers of better fourth-outfielder aspirants. He has never really been a prospect as much as a guy who does enough things well enough to seem potentially useful, someone who can play all three positions, sometimes provide modest power, draw a few walks, switch-hit. Everybody likes those things, right? Step back from the individual greenery to see what you've got, and you realize that what you have isn't a forest, it's a shrubbery.

Julio Borbon — OF

Bats: L   Throws: L   Height: 6' 1"   Weight: 180   Born: February 20, 1986   Age: 24

YEAR	TEAM	LVL	AGE	PA	R	2B	3B	HR	RBI	BB	SO	SB	CS	EqBRR	AVG	OBP	SLG	EqAVG	EqOBP	EqSLG	EqA	VORP	WARP	DEFENSE			
2007	SPO	A-	21	31	1	0	0	0	2	2	3	3	1	-1.3	.172	.226	.172	.133	.161	.133	.000	-3.5	-0.3	7-CF	2		
2008	BAK	A+	22	314	47	20	0	2	36	15	30	36	7	3.3	.306	.346	.395	.275	.308	.356	.240	1.7	-0.1	63-CF	-3		
2008	FRI	AA	22	280	40	12	2	5	22	14	32	17	11	-2.8	.337	.380	.459	.312	.345	.423	.264	8.8	1.7	59-CF	5		
2009	OKL	AAA	23	457	71	12	7	2	34	33	40	25	7	4.4	.307	.367	.386	.294	.349	.366	.257	10.6	0.6	81-CF	-7	15-LF	1
2009	TEX	MLB	23	179	30	4	0	4	20	15	28	19	4	2.2	.312	.376	.414	.314	.378	.410	.284	6.5	0.2	15-LF	-3	3-CF	-1
2010	TEX	MLB	24	538	72	23	4	8	47	34	66	29	10	1.3	.279	.329	.388	.282	.334	.387	.241	5.8	0.5	107-CF	-1		

Breakout: 13%   Improve: 50%   Collapse: 12%   Attrition: 7%   MLB: 90%   Comparables: Kevin O'Connor, Jason Tyner, Dan Arendas, Kenny Lofton

Borbon's comparables suggest the differences between the happier expectations for what he'll be and what he more probably is. Seriously, Kenny Lofton *and* Jason Tyner? That's the difference between the leadoff man who was everywhere and the leadoff man who was never there, but that's the risk for Borbon. His defense in center should be fine, but the Rangers were downright tremulous when it came to working up the nerve to take a look at season's end. The more basic question is whether he'll get on base effectively enough to be a quality leadoff man; his walk rate in the minors was around six percent, but he's not terribly impatient. What's really going to dent his rates is that even as a speed guy, his BABIP is going to come down a lot from last year's .360 clip in the majors. He and Andrus should give the club a running game Mike Scioscia should envy, but if Borbon winds up with an OBP around that projection, he won't be an immediate solution to the club's underwhelming attack.

Marlon Byrd — CF

Bats: R   Throws: R   Height: 6' 0"   Weight: 245   Born: August 30, 1977   Age: 32

YEAR	TEAM	LVL	AGE	PA	R	2B	3B	HR	RBI	BB	SO	SB	CS	EqBRR	AVG	OBP	SLG	EqAVG	EqOBP	EqSLG	EqA	VORP	WARP	DEFENSE			
2007	OKL	AAA	29	195	29	15	2	6	32	13	30	3	2	1.1	.358	.415	.568	.307	.359	.469	.284	8.6	1.3	17-RF	2	12-LF	1
2007	TEX	MLB	29	454	60	17	8	10	70	29	88	5	3	2.9	.307	.355	.459	.306	.355	.464	.279	20.3	2.1	56-CF	-6	35-RF	2
2008	TEX	MLB	30	462	70	28	4	10	53	46	62	7	2	-0.4	.298	.380	.462	.302	.386	.469	.296	27.9	3.6	49-CF	3	31-RF	0
2009	TEX	MLB	31	599	66	43	2	20	89	32	98	8	4	-2.8	.283	.329	.479	.283	.328	.471	.272	24.3	2.0	100-CF	-8	35-LF	1
2010	CHN	MLB	32	551	65	29	3	13	71	45	98	7	4	0.0	.278	.348	.429	.277	.345	.431	.267	20.8	2.0	106-CF	-3		

Breakout: 3%   Improve: 29%   Collapse: 17%   Attrition: 16%   MLB: 96%   Comparables: Jeffrey Hammonds, Baby Doll Jacobson, Shannon Stewart, Torii Hunter

What a difference a few years makes. Having washed up in Texas as a washout, Byrd hit free agency three years later as a 31-year-old regular with a .196 ISO and 65 extra-base hits, just three years after Gary Matthews Jr. hit the market at 31 with a .182 ISO and 69 extra-base hits for the Rangers. Byrd got decent money, but he didn't get $50 million or five years, as Matthews did, and it has nothing to do with justice or stupidity or anything else in between. The industry is operated on the proposition that between expansion of the economy, growth of the product, and inflation, salaries were reliably headed in a particular direction. Economic realities have intruded, so now Byrd is going to get less, while perhaps being worth much the same. In the years to come, we'll be writing about some of the deals of the Aughties the way people used to about Benny Kauff's $30,0000 purchase price going to the Giants from the Federal League. It wasn't that these were the biggest contracts; it was who was getting them, and the proposition that star-level expense equals star-level results. Byrd can be for the Cubs what he has been for the Rangers, an employable placeholder in center, but he may not slug .420 outside Texas, even with the move to the weaker league.

Nelson Cruz — RF

Bats: R   Throws: R   Height: 6' 3"   Weight: 230   Born: July 1, 1980   Age: 29

YEAR	TEAM	LVL	AGE	PA	R	2B	3B	HR	RBI	BB	SO	SB	CS	EqBRR	AVG	OBP	SLG	EqAVG	EqOBP	EqSLG	EqA	VORP	WARP	DEFENSE			
2007	OKL	AAA	26	187	32	9	1	15	45	21	34	1	2	0.4	.352	.428	.698	.309	.380	.588	.314	15.3	1.9	44-RF	1		
2007	TEX	MLB	26	332	35	15	2	9	34	21	87	2	4	-0.9	.235	.287	.384	.235	.290	.392	.229	-4.7	-0.4	69-RF	1	13-LF	1
2008	OKL	AAA	27	448	93	18	3	37	99	56	87	24	8	1.5	.342	.429	.695	.297	.373	.551	.306	32.5	3.7	95-RF	0	2-CF	-1
2008	TEX	MLB	27	133	19	9	1	7	26	17	28	3	1	-0.1	.330	.421	.609	.330	.425	.600	.340	14.7	1.8	31-RF	1		
2009	TEX	MLB	28	515	75	21	1	33	76	49	118	20	4	0.0	.260	.332	.524	.258	.330	.512	.284	24.2	3.9	117-RF	11		
2010	TEX	MLB	29	530	76	24	2	28	82	59	118	11	6	0.2	.273	.359	.516	.263	.345	.485	.279	22.3	2.7	123-RF	2		

Breakout: 11%   Improve: 44%   Collapse: 9%   Attrition: 6%   MLB: 91%   Comparables: Michael Cuddyer, Moises Alou, Tom Brunansky, Preston Wilson

Cruz may be the most presentable, classic example of the Rangers' taking somebody else's former prospect, plugging him in, and enjoying the result. His power is not a ballpark fiction, even slugging 100 points less away from home: a road ISO of .246 is still entirely slug-worthy. His BABIP was a low .278, but he's a fly-ball hitter in a fly-ball-hitting environment finally logging a full season, so you shouldn't invest a ton of hope that he's going to add 20 points and go extra-nuts on the league. Between his strikeouts and fly balls, racking up RBI will depend on his hitting more homers, which is why his OBI% was a surprisingly low 13.9 percent. A fine regular in his prime, he just shouldn't be asked to be the best hitter in a contending lineup.

Chris Davis 1B — Bats: L — Throws: R — Height: 6' 4" — Weight: 235 — Born: March 17, 1986 — Age: 24

YEAR	TEAM	LVL	AGE	PA	R	2B	3B	HR	RBI	BB	SO	SB	CS	EqBRR	AVG	OBP	SLG	EqAVG	EqOBP	EqSLG	EqA	VORP	WARP	DEFENSE		
2007	BAK	A+	21	418	69	28	3	24	93	22	123	3	3	-0.7	.298	.340	.573	.257	.292	.471	.256	7.2	0.0	90-3B	-7	
2007	FRI	AA	21	124	21	7	0	12	25	13	27	0	0	-1.1	.294	.371	.688	.270	.339	.595	.302	9.1	0.6	29-3B	-4	
2008	FRI	AA	22	202	43	14	0	13	42	13	44	5	1	1.6	.333	.376	.618	.296	.335	.545	.292	9.7	0.9	42-1B	-2	
2008	OKL	AAA	22	127	25	7	1	10	31	13	29	2	0	1.0	.333	.402	.685	.301	.362	.593	.314	9.6	1.1	28-1B	0	
2008	TEX	MLB	22	317	51	23	2	17	55	20	88	1	2	0.3	.285	.331	.549	.289	.338	.558	.292	16.9	0.2	45-1B	-4	31-3B -11
2009	OKL	AAA	23	194	27	12	1	6	30	25	39	0	1	-2.7	.327	.418	.521	.304	.390	.488	.300	11.4	0.6	23-3B	-6	10-1B 0
2009	TEX	MLB	23	419	48	15	1	21	59	24	150	0	0	1.7	.238	.284	.442	.238	.284	.433	.244	-6.7	-1.7	93-1B	-4	10-3B -4
2010	TEX	MLB	24	603	82	31	2	33	97	42	171	3	3	0.0	.264	.320	.506	.263	.319	.487	.261	7.4	0.5	136-1B	-3	

Breakout: 15% Improve: 48% Collapse: 6% Attrition: 4% MLB: 100% Comparables: Justin Morneau, Lee Stevens, James Loney, David Ortiz

After a blistering 2008 debut, Davis went into the season as the club's everyday first baseman, but what was once bad plate discipline was ratcheted down to flat-out awful, which led to some pressing, which led to even more bad swings, and ... well, you get the picture. Mercifully sent back to the minors in early July while sporting a .202 batting average with 114 strikeouts in 258 at-bats, Davis took the demotion like a man and proceeded to work with coaches on his approach and rediscovering his swing. Success at Oklahoma did wonders for his confidence, and he was a completely different player after his late August return, batting .308/.338/.496 to stake his claim again as the club's first baseman of the future. With off-the-charts raw power, he has learned the valuable lesson of just hitting balls and letting the home runs come naturally, and all systems should be go for a big 2010.

Josh Hamilton CF — Bats: L — Throws: L — Height: 6' 4" — Weight: 235 — Born: May 21, 1981 — Age: 29

YEAR	TEAM	LVL	AGE	PA	R	2B	3B	HR	RBI	BB	SO	SB	CS	EqBRR	AVG	OBP	SLG	EqAVG	EqOBP	EqSLG	EqA	VORP	WARP	DEFENSE		
2007	CIN	MLB	26	337	52	17	2	19	47	33	65	3	3	-0.8	.292	.368	.554	.293	.370	.549	.302	25.1	3.8	62-CF	8	9-RF 2
2008	TEX	MLB	27	704	98	35	5	32	130	64	126	9	1	1.7	.304	.371	.530	.308	.374	.539	.307	55.5	4.6	103-CF	-9	33-RF -3
2009	TEX	MLB	28	365	43	19	2	10	54	24	79	8	3	0.5	.268	.315	.426	.269	.315	.424	.255	6.3	1.1	53-CF	3	24-RF 0
2010	TEX	MLB	29	480	66	22	2	22	77	44	99	7	3	0.3	.272	.346	.487	.272	.347	.473	.268	18.9	2.1	97-CF	0	

Breakout: 5% Improve: 33% Collapse: 8% Attrition: 10% MLB: 94% Comparables: Jim Edmonds, Ken Griffey Jr., Larry Walker, Cliff Floyd

One of the problems with playing "Gotcha!" is that the guy who says "gotcha" every time out is eventually going to be right. So, Hamilton had a disappointing season, and he struggled through nagging hurts to his groin, abdomen, and back. He lost at least a month to the abdomen alone, and who knows how much his production was affected by injuries. We're far enough out into an unusual career that predicting what comes next is already odd-spot territory. And if he matches his projection, is that success? Put an EqA in the .260s in a corner, as the Rangers will with Hamilton if they take Borbon seriously in center, and you need a lot of offense from places the Rangers aren't getting it: first base and DH in particular, but catcher, too, and center if Borbon reverts to form. At this point, Hamilton could be anything from Comeback Player of the Year to latter-day Joe Charboneau.

Andruw Jones DH — Bats: R — Throws: R — Height: 6' 1" — Weight: 240 — Born: April 23, 1977 — Age: 33

YEAR	TEAM	LVL	AGE	PA	R	2B	3B	HR	RBI	BB	SO	SB	CS	EqBRR	AVG	OBP	SLG	EqAVG	EqOBP	EqSLG	EqA	VORP	WARP	DEFENSE		
2007	ATL	MLB	30	659	83	27	2	26	94	70	138	5	2	-2.5	.222	.311	.413	.228	.317	.422	.257	17.3	2.8	150-CF	7	
2008	LAN	MLB	31	238	21	8	1	3	14	27	76	0	1	0.2	.158	.256	.249	.158	.253	.249	.175	-12.4	-2.0	56-CF	-5	
2009	TEX	MLB	32	331	43	18	0	17	43	45	72	5	1	-1.8	.214	.323	.459	.211	.320	.450	.266	3.8	0.6	11-LF	2	6-RF 0
2010	CHA	MLB	33	367	41	14	1	13	46	42	87	2	2	-0.5	.217	.314	.390	.215	.308	.377	.237	-1.0	0.6	68-LF	6	

Breakout: 8% Improve: 30% Collapse: 21% Attrition: 25% MLB: 93% Comparables: Pete Incaviglia, Raul Mondesi, Kevin McReynolds, Rondell White

Jones is only going to be turning 33 this spring, which is why teams will keep taking him up on the proposition that maybe there's something still there. The Rangers did last year and had no cause for regret. No, he didn't get on base; nor did he stay healthy. His BABIP was well below average for the seventh straight season; so was his line-drive percentage, so Regression obviously doesn't know what zip code he's in. He doesn't have a lot of use for her these days, anyway, having not answered his calls for that long. As he heads to the Cell for the same sort of deal he got from Texas, on a base barely above the minimum, the bet is simple enough. He might be healthy. He might jerk a bunch of pitches down the lines in the Cell and pop 30 homers in 500 plate appearances. He might also eat a metric ton between now and Opening Day, be terrible, and be eminently cut-worthy. For the price, it's a bargain compared with the odds on a lottery ticket and, if something short of living dangerously, certainly worth trying.

Ian Kinsler			2B							Bats: R		Throws: R		Height: 6′ 0″		Weight: 200		Born: June 22, 1982			Age: 28
YEAR	TEAM	LVL	AGE	PA	R	2B	3B	HR	RBI	BB	SO	SB	CS	EqBRR	AVG	OBP	SLG	EqAVG	EqOBP	EqSLG	EqA	VORP	WARP	DEFENSE
2007	TEX	MLB	25	566	96	22	2	20	61	62	83	23	2	6.2	.263	.355	.441	.260	.353	.442	.281	31.3	3.7	129-2B	1
2008	TEX	MLB	26	583	102	41	4	18	71	45	67	26	2	9.1	.319	.375	.517	.323	.379	.529	.310	52.3	5.0	120-2B	-7
2009	TEX	MLB	27	640	101	32	4	31	86	59	77	31	5	5.2	.253	.327	.488	.252	.325	.479	.278	32.6	5.4	142-2B	14
2010	TEX	MLB	28	615	106	32	3	27	85	65	81	26	4	3.7	.280	.364	.500	.271	.352	.476	.283	33.9	3.8	138-2B	1

Breakout: 4%   Improve: 45%   Collapse: 9%   Attrition: 2%   MLB: 100%   Comparables: Don Baylor, Brandon Phillips, Craig Biggio, Edgardo Alfonzo

All of you who thought Kinsler would be healthy, yet put up his worst season yet, give yourselves a star. The fact that he'd struggle *this* badly is perhaps a little more understandable for a fly-ball hitter, but between the venue, that tendency, and his relative youth, he should be able to bounce back. Keep in mind, he has managed to significantly improve in the field as part of a team-level conscious effort to make him a better fielder, he runs the bases like an honorary Phillie, and his walk rate stayed solid. If there was an issue, it was a spike in his pop-up rate, but that seems like something correctable. If he keeps driving balls into play to the pastures, he should be fine, and there's no reason to expect that he shouldn't. It may add up to less than an MVP-level package, but how many middle infielders can rattle off a 31-homer campaign and really call it a relative setback?

Mitchell Moreland			OF							Bats: L		Throws: L		Height: 6′ 2″		Weight: 230		Born: September 6, 1985			Age: 24
YEAR	TEAM	LVL	AGE	PA	R	2B	3B	HR	RBI	BB	SO	SB	CS	EqBRR	AVG	OBP	SLG	EqAVG	EqOBP	EqSLG	EqA	VORP	WARP	DEFENSE
2007	SPO	A-	21	118	10	7	1	2	15	8	25	1	0	-0.7	.259	.308	.398	.216	.248	.351	.206	-5.6	-1.1	21-1B	-1	
2008	CLN	A	22	533	64	37	4	18	99	60	67	2	4	-3.2	.324	.400	.536	.286	.351	.451	.276	15.4	1.5	71-1B	-3	30-RF	0
2009	BAK	A+	23	197	34	19	0	8	26	21	26	1	0	0.0	.341	.421	.594	.288	.354	.458	.280	5.3	-0.1	30-1B	-4	11-RF	-2
2009	FRI	AA	23	327	51	19	3	8	59	23	42	1	1	-1.8	.326	.373	.488	.310	.351	.467	.279	11.9	1.2	55-RF	-3	8-1B	1
2010	TEX	MLB	24	472	55	27	2	13	65	38	81	1	2	-1.2	.277	.337	.441	.278	.339	.436	.253	6.1	0.4	92-RF	-2		

Breakout: 14%   Improve: 43%   Collapse: 13%   Attrition: 5%   MLB: 11%   Comparables: Luke Allen, Brian Stavisky, Seth Smith, Ross Gload

When the Rangers made Moreland a 17th-round pick in 2007, their initial intention was to convert him to the mound due to his strong arm. Moreland resisted the move, convinced he could cut it offensively, and the Rangers acquiesced. He got a chance to hit and hasn't stopped, with a career .321/.387/.518 mark in his first 2 ½ pro seasons. Nothing about his game is pretty, as he's a big, beefy guy with no tools other than the bat and the arm, but he's very close to getting a look in Texas, and it's now clear that he's definitely going to hit.

David Murphy			LF							Bats: L		Throws: L		Height: 6′ 4″		Weight: 205		Born: October 18, 1981			Age: 28
YEAR	TEAM	LVL	AGE	PA	R	2B	3B	HR	RBI	BB	SO	SB	CS	EqBRR	AVG	OBP	SLG	EqAVG	EqOBP	EqSLG	EqA	VORP	WARP	DEFENSE
2007	PAW	AAA	25	444	50	20	5	9	47	41	68	8	1	-1.2	.280	.347	.423	.262	.324	.399	.254	7.5	1.3	51-CF	-4	32-LF	5
2007	TEX	MLB	25	110	16	12	1	2	14	7	19	0	0	0.2	.340	.382	.534	.340	.382	.534	.307	8.2	0.8	11-LF	0	9-RF	0
2008	TEX	MLB	26	454	64	28	3	15	74	31	70	7	2	1.1	.275	.321	.465	.279	.326	.473	.273	15.7	2.6	46-RF	5	46-LF	4
2009	TEX	MLB	27	493	61	24	1	17	57	49	106	9	4	-1.4	.269	.338	.447	.270	.338	.443	.270	14.4	2.8	97-LF	8	8-RF	2
2010	TEX	MLB	28	484	59	25	3	17	64	43	94	5	4	-0.2	.266	.334	.451	.266	.334	.435	.254	7.0	1.3	95-LF	4		

Breakout: 13%   Improve: 43%   Collapse: 15%   Attrition: 14%   MLB: 91%   Comparables: Brad Hawpe, Paul O'Neill, Ryan Church, Brant Brown

Sometimes, strength in numbers reflects the absence of anything that stands out above the ordinary. Consider Murphy, the Rangers' outfielder who wasn't given a big boost by his ballpark; he was merely mediocre everywhere. An attempt to add power as the entire lineup got homer-happy in the second half just led to fewer walks, more strikeouts, and negligible gains in slugging. There's no magical, happy substratum stat that's going to rescue him from a basic replaceability as the latest overrated Red Sox outfield prospect they sensibly elected to not employ. He's a nice reserve if he can adapt to part-time play, but not a starter on a serious contender. Rusty Greer was two wins better at the same age, so any comparison to good modest-power corner outfielders is wasted here without improvement à la Paul O'Neill after 30, and O'Neill was extraordinary.

Max Ramirez — C | Bats: R | Throws: R | Height: 5' 11" | Weight: 175 | Born: October 11, 1984 | Age: 25

YEAR	TEAM	LVL	AGE	PA	R	2B	3B	HR	RBI	BB	SO	SB	CS	EqBRR	AVG	OBP	SLG	EqAVG	EqOBP	EqSLG	EqA	VORP	WARP	DEFENSE			
2007	KIN	A+	22	342	46	20	0	12	62	53	63	1	0	-3.0	.303	.418	.505	.275	.367	.436	.282	22.0	2.3	65-C	-3		
2007	BAK	A+	22	138	16	10	0	4	20	21	39	1	0	-1.3	.307	.420	.500	.277	.370	.429	.282	8.2	1.0	24-C	0		
2008	FRI	AA	23	289	49	16	2	17	50	37	56	2	2	-2.9	.354	.450	.646	.311	.394	.570	.319	28.5	2.4	42-C	-9	8-1B	1
2008	OKL	AAA	23	41	5	1	0	2	6	3	13	0	0	-0.2	.243	.293	.432	.243	.293	.432	.250	1.0	0.0	7-C	-1		
2008	TEX	MLB	23	55	8	1	0	2	9	6	15	0	0	-0.3	.217	.345	.370	.217	.345	.370	.261	1.8	0.1	9-C	-1		
2009	OKL	AAA	24	320	29	13	0	5	43	35	85	1	0	-2.9	.234	.323	.336	.226	.306	.319	.228	-3.0	-0.1	41-C	2		
2010	TEX	MLB	25	352	38	15	1	11	46	40	92	1	1	-1.6	.250	.344	.411	.241	.330	.388	.250	9.8	0.9	60-C	-2		

Breakout: 7%   Improve: 28%   Collapse: 35%   Attrition: 10%   MLB: 11%   Comparables: Jim Olander, Rob Teegarden, George Threadgill, Juan Pautt

After putting up a 1000+ OPS in the minors during the 2008 season, Ramirez just plain stopped hitting in 2009, which is a big problem, as he's a below-average defensive catcher who has to mash to have value. The troublemakers in this case were injuries to both wrists that sapped him of his power and made just swinging a bat an uncomfortable process. The light at the end of the tunnel is that the healthy version of Ramirez showed back up over the winter in Venezuela, where Ramirez smacked 13 home runs in 210 at-bats, leaving the Rangers hoping that 2009 was simply a bump in the road.

Ivan Rodriguez — C | Bats: R | Throws: R | Height: 5' 9" | Weight: 190 | Born: November 30, 1971 | Age: 38

YEAR	TEAM	LVL	AGE	PA	R	2B	3B	HR	RBI	BB	SO	SB	CS	EqBRR	AVG	OBP	SLG	EqAVG	EqOBP	EqSLG	EqA	VORP	WARP	DEFENSE	
2007	DET	MLB	35	515	50	31	3	11	63	9	96	2	2	-2.2	.281	.294	.420	.281	.294	.423	.242	15.4	3.1	118-C	9
2008	DET	MLB	36	328	33	16	3	5	32	19	52	6	1	-1.2	.295	.338	.417	.296	.340	.425	.268	17.0	2.2	79-C	4
2008	NYA	MLB	36	101	11	4	0	2	3	4	15	4	0	1.3	.219	.257	.323	.219	.257	.313	.211	-0.7	-0.3	25-C	-1
2009	HOU	MLB	37	344	41	15	2	8	34	13	74	0	2	2.3	.251	.280	.382	.263	.291	.404	.233	6.3	0.7	85-C	2
2009	TEX	MLB	37	104	14	8	0	2	13	5	18	1	0	1.0	.245	.279	.388	.245	.279	.367	.231	0.7	0.6	24-C	3
2010	WAS	MLB	38	326	28	15	1	6	31	17	66	2	2	0.1	.242	.284	.351	.251	.293	.364	.223	0.8	0.3	79-C	2

Breakout: 9%   Improve: 28%   Collapse: 35%   Attrition: 46%   MLB: 94%   Comparables: Benito Santiago, Joe Girardi, Al Simmons, Birdie Tebbetts

It's time to strip the media-invented layer away: Pudge Rodriguez isn't playing to get another ring, for the challenge, and maybe not even for the money. He's playing because he still can. If there's room for Miguel Olivo or Rod Barajas for seven large, and roles for Henry Blanco, why not Pudge, too? Gary Carter kept on going a good five years or so past the point he was an asset, and nobody begrudged him that when it came time to put him in the Hall of Fame. Of course, Pudge isn't the same player. How could he be? He won't sell tickets in Washington, but that isn't what he's there for. It's notionally to give a young staff the sense that they're playing with somebody with real status in the game. Maybe that isn't worth $6 million over two years. Maybe it helps in ways we can't count. It certainly won't cost the Nationals a shot at the pennant, but if it helps create a sense that the club isn't a Royals-like pit of despair, maybe it's money well spent.

Jarrod Saltalamacchia — C | Bats: S | Throws: R | Height: 6' 4" | Weight: 235 | Born: May 2, 1985 | Age: 25

YEAR	TEAM	LVL	AGE	PA	R	2B	3B	HR	RBI	BB	SO	SB	CS	EqBRR	AVG	OBP	SLG	EqAVG	EqOBP	EqSLG	EqA	VORP	WARP	DEFENSE			
2007	MIS	AA	22	94	18	7	0	6	13	13	17	2	0	-1.2	.309	.404	.617	.301	.383	.578	.318	10.3	1.1	20-C	-1		
2007	ATL	MLB	22	153	11	6	0	4	12	10	28	0	0	-1.4	.284	.333	.411	.291	.340	.426	.263	5.6	0.4	21-C	-1	12-1B	-1
2007	TEX	MLB	22	176	28	7	1	7	21	9	47	0	0	1.0	.251	.290	.431	.251	.290	.425	.245	1.8	-0.3	23-1B	0	21-C	-4
2008	OKL	AAA	23	64	10	3	1	2	13	7	15	0	0	-0.2	.291	.391	.491	.268	.359	.464	.283	4.3	0.5	15-C	0		
2008	TEX	MLB	23	230	27	13	0	3	26	31	74	0	2	-1.6	.253	.352	.364	.254	.357	.360	.258	7.6	0.0	52-C	-5		
2009	TEX	MLB	24	310	34	12	0	9	34	22	97	0	2	-2.2	.233	.290	.371	.234	.291	.362	.227	3.0	-0.2	81-C	-3		
2010	TEX	MLB	25	352	44	15	1	13	42	35	96	1	1	-1.0	.253	.332	.431	.247	.322	.406	.249	9.7	0.8	84-C	-3		

Breakout: 26%   Improve: 55%   Collapse: 11%   Attrition: 12%   MLB: 100%   Comparables: Eddie Taubensee, Ben Davis, Charles Johnson, Lee Stevens

The Rangers have no cause for regret as far as the Teixeira trade, given how Andrus and Feliz are turning out, but Salty's failure to develop isn't something to just write off. As low as the standards are for catchers, striking out 30 percent of the time makes it hard for him to generate much beyond wind. Behind the plate, he's been a worse receiver than expected as well. Surgery to repair his shoulder for 2010 didn't keep him from being shut down during winter ball. That's a lot of bad news, but he's also just heading into his age-25 season, which is why his comps are generally positive. Well, Ben Davis excepted, but if the Rangers wind up with someone who hits like Taubensee or Stevens behind the plate, that's useful.

Justin Smoak   1B   Bats: S   Throws: L   Height: 6' 3"   Weight: 200   Born: December 5, 1986   Age: 23

YEAR	TEAM	LVL	AGE	PA	R	2B	3B	HR	RBI	BB	SO	SB	CS	EqBRR	AVG	OBP	SLG	EqAVG	EqOBP	EqSLG	EqA	VORP	WARP	DEFENSE
2008	CLN	A	21	62	9	3	0	3	6	5	10	0	0	-0.9	.304	.355	.518	.281	.323	.474	.271	1.4	0.2	10-1B	0
2009	FRI	AA	22	227	30	10	0	6	29	39	35	0	0	-1.8	.328	.449	.481	.304	.405	.450	.301	10.2	1.1	44-1B	-1
2009	OKL	AAA	22	237	25	11	0	4	23	35	45	0	0	-0.4	.244	.363	.360	.234	.342	.343	.249	-3.0	-0.5	44-1B	-1
2010	TEX	MLB	23	387	42	16	0	11	41	48	78	0	1	-1.2	.259	.357	.403	.253	.348	.387	.253	1.2	0.0	73-1B	-1

Breakout: 16%   Improve: 42%   Collapse: 20%   Attrition: 5%   MLB: 1%   Comparables: Jon Benick, Chris Pritchett, Terry Tiffee, Jose Birriel

Despite not showing the kind of power that was expected, Smoak was tearing up the Double-A Texas League early in the season, but things went south in a big way following a move up to Triple-A, as he lost his timing while dealing with the aftereffects of a strained oblique. Scouts still love him, as his plate discipline remains exceptional, and there is plenty of reason to think the power will return, as a healthy version of Smoak slugged nine home runs in 14 games for Team USA at the end of the year. His ideal-world projection is as a switch-hitting version of Justin Morneau with better defense, and that's just scary.

Taylor Teagarden   C   Bats: R   Throws: R   Height: 6' 1"   Weight: 200   Born: December 21, 1983   Age: 26

YEAR	TEAM	LVL	AGE	PA	R	2B	3B	HR	RBI	BB	SO	SB	CS	EqBRR	AVG	OBP	SLG	EqAVG	EqOBP	EqSLG	EqA	VORP	WARP	DEFENSE
2007	BAK	A+	23	364	75	25	0	20	67	65	89	2	1	0.8	.315	.448	.606	.260	.371	.471	.289	19.9	2.4	29-C	0
2007	FRI	AA	23	115	19	3	0	7	16	10	39	0	0	0.6	.294	.357	.529	.269	.322	.462	.268	4.3	0.2	14-C	-3
2008	FRI	AA	24	68	6	2	0	2	6	8	23	1	0	0.2	.169	.279	.305	.164	.261	.295	.200	-1.9	-0.1	10-C	1
2008	OKL	AAA	24	218	26	5	3	7	16	28	59	0	1	-2.2	.225	.332	.396	.215	.309	.356	.233	3.6	0.6	55-C	1
2008	TEX	MLB	24	53	10	5	0	6	17	5	19	0	0	0.4	.319	.396	.809	.319	.396	.787	.367	8.6	0.9	11-C	-1
2009	TEX	MLB	25	218	26	13	0	6	24	14	76	0	0	0.2	.217	.270	.374	.218	.270	.371	.223	1.7	1.2	56-C	7
2010	TEX	MLB	26	305	36	13	1	11	36	33	97	1	1	0.0	.225	.314	.400	.218	.303	.382	.234	3.8	0.5	52-C	1

Breakout: 8%   Improve: 23%   Collapse: 28%   Attrition: 17%   MLB: 54%   Comparables: Ozzie Virgil, Bill Schroeder, Tim Laudner, Javier Cardona

If the expectations of Salty's impending greatness have gone unfulfilled, perhaps there's room for schadenfreude because of the elaborate expectations built up around Teagarden. Don't get us wrong: Teagarden is an outstanding player to have if you've got him. He throws exceptionally well, he's a nimble receiver, and he can mash the pitches he catches up to. Get him 300 plate appearances or more, and he'll draw a few more walks than the Barajas types. He might also strike out 100 times in just that many at-bats, but that's the bill you pay if you decide to pick up the check. If you've got a good enough lineup to afford him as a regular, you can win with someone like him behind the plate, in the same way the White Sox could with Ron Karkovice, or the Twins with Tim Laudner. The problem is that the Rangers don't have a lineup (or a rotation) good enough to afford the luxury just yet.

Omar Vizquel   SS   Bats: S   Throws: R   Height: 5' 9"   Weight: 175   Born: April 24, 1967   Age: 43

YEAR	TEAM	LVL	AGE	PA	R	2B	3B	HR	RBI	BB	SO	SB	CS	EqBRR	AVG	OBP	SLG	EqAVG	EqOBP	EqSLG	EqA	VORP	WARP	DEFENSE		
2007	SFN	MLB	40	575	54	18	3	4	51	44	48	14	6	0.9	.246	.305	.316	.250	.309	.318	.226	1.6	3.8	136-SS	28	
2008	SFN	MLB	41	300	24	10	1	0	23	24	29	5	4	-0.2	.222	.283	.267	.220	.280	.265	.196	-6.4	-0.6	74-SS	0	
2009	TEX	MLB	42	195	17	7	2	1	14	13	27	4	0	-2.4	.266	.316	.345	.267	.317	.347	.238	2.3	1.2	22-SS	3	14-2B	2
2010	CHA	MLB	43	166	13	6	1	1	15	16	21	3	2	-0.1	.234	.307	.308	.240	.311	.311	.211	-2.1	0.1	39-SS	3	

Breakout: 10%   Improve: 23%   Collapse: 38%   Attrition: 48%   MLB: 97%   Comparables: Sam Rice, Luke Appling, Graig Nettles, Carl Yastrzemski

You can skip his comps, because having played this long, he's stretching the system for meaningful comparisons, having outlasted Ozzie Smith, Bert Campaneris, and Mark Belanger. At this rate, Little O's active career might encompass a third generation of Bush presidencies, because if all he has to do is live down to the standards of what keeps other utility infielders gainfully employed, perhaps he can do this for years yet. Having given Andrus a practical example and advice for a player young enough to admit to being a childhood fan-boy of his Hall-worthy teammate, the Yoda of the infield has headed to Chicago's South Side to do his sprightly CGI-free acrobatics and mentoring thing for Alexei Ramirez's benefit.

Michael Young   **3B**   Bats: R   Throws: R   Height: 6' 1"   Weight: 200   Born: October 19, 1976   Age: 33

YEAR	TEAM	LVL	AGE	PA	R	2B	3B	HR	RBI	BB	SO	SB	CS	EqBRR	AVG	OBP	SLG	EqAVG	EqOBP	EqSLG	EqA	VORP	WARP	DEFENSE	
2007	TEX	MLB	30	692	80	37	1	9	94	47	107	13	3	-0.2	.315	.366	.418	.313	.366	.420	.275	35.3	3.0	146-SS	-8
2008	TEX	MLB	31	708	102	36	2	12	82	55	109	10	0	4.0	.284	.339	.402	.288	.344	.407	.267	32.6	4.7	145-SS	8
2009	TEX	MLB	32	593	76	36	2	22	68	47	90	8	3	-5.6	.322	.374	.518	.322	.374	.507	.298	41.4	2.9	132-3B	-13
2010	TEX	MLB	33	610	76	31	2	14	74	52	95	7	3	-0.3	.297	.360	.436	.290	.350	.420	.262	16.7	1.1	131-3B	-6

Breakout: 10%   Improve: 34%   Collapse: 24%   Attrition: 12%   MLB: 99%   Comparables: Tim Wallach, Buddy Bell, Al Smith, Ken Boyer

In a lineup loaded with hitters who struggle to make consistent contact, Young is an outstanding complementary player, a hitter with excellent bat-control skills and outstanding line-drive power on contact; he rarely gets cheated in an at-bat, rarely popping up. Despite all this, last year's offensive spike owed a lot to more than doubling his rate of homers per fly ball, and that's going to come back down. While Young has repeatedly shown a willingness to play through assorted nicks, his EqBRR drop-off is a symptom of what happens when you do. He had problems with an ankle early and a hamstring late; he wasn't making mistakes, he was running conservatively. The comparisons to Bell and Wallach seem spot-on, and it's easy to anticipate he'll become a better third baseman; he started 29 double-plays and wasn't error-prone, and a year under his belt and playing alongside Andrus should bring improvement.

PITCHERS

Blake Beavan   Bats: R   Throws: R   Height: 6' 7"   Weight: 210   Born: January 17, 1989   Age: 21

YEAR	TEAM	LVL	AGE	W	L	SV	G	GS	IP	H	HR	BB	SO	GB%	BABIP	STUFF	WHIP	ERA	SIERA	DERA	EqH9	EqHR9	EqBB9	EqSO9	VORP	SN/WX
2008	CLN	A	19	10	6	0	23	23	121²	105	12	20	73	50%	.251	0	1.03	2.37	4.15	4.61	9.8	2.2	2.4	3.0	10.8	0.81
2009	BAK	A+	20	5	4	0	12	12	73¹	75	6	16	51	55%	.297	13	1.24	4.30	4.02	6.75	10.1	1.7	2.7	3.4	-9.6	-1.09
2009	FRI	AA	20	4	4	0	15	15	89²	113	4	13	34	48%	.322	5	1.41	4.01	5.10	5.64	11.7	1.1	1.7	2.3	-1.3	0.09
2010	TEX	MLB	21	6	10	0	28	28	143²	170	25	50	52	42%	.295	3	1.54	5.50	5.80	5.57	10.5	1.4	2.9	3.1	-1.2	2.36

Breakout: 17%   Improve: 50%   Collapse: 11%   Attrition: 3%   MLB: 4%   Comparables: Buddy Carlyle, Bob Keppel, Chris Volstad, Roy Halladay

Beaven was a monster when the Rangers drafted him in the first round of the 2007 draft. A 6-foot-7 Texan with a 95 mph fastball and a mean streak to go with it, he faced only one concern for his future: an ultraviolent delivery. The Rangers worked hard to clean up his mechanics, but after their tinkering, his velocity never returned. Now he's an anomaly as a big, strike-throwing righty who reliably pumps gas at 88-91 mph, doesn't walk anybody, and has a pretty good changeup. His ceiling is still one of a big-leaguer, but now it's more of a back-end rotation type rather than any kind of star.

Scott Feldman   Bats: L   Throws: R   Height: 6' 5"   Weight: 210   Born: February 7, 1983   Age: 27

YEAR	TEAM	LVL	AGE	W	L	SV	G	GS	IP	H	HR	BB	SO	GB%	BABIP	STUFF	WHIP	ERA	SIERA	DERA	EqH9	EqHR9	EqBB9	EqSO9	VORP	SN/WX
2007	OKL	AAA	24	1	1	2	21	0	30	28	1	12	24	59%	.297	-13	1.33	4.50	4.06	6.05	9.0	0.6	3.7	5.3	-1.8	-0.60
2007	TEX	MLB	24	1	2	0	29	0	39	44	3	32	19	64%	.304	-14	1.95	5.77	5.78	5.33	9.5	0.7	6.6	3.9	0.7	-0.41
2008	FRI	AA	25	2	0	0	2	2	12²	11	0	2	4	59%	.244	-12	1.03	4.26	5.01	5.33	7.8	0.7	1.4	1.4	0.2	0.04
2008	TEX	MLB	25	6	8	0	28	25	151¹	161	22	56	74	53%	.284	-4	1.43	5.29	5.17	5.37	8.6	1.1	2.9	4.1	2.2	1.51
2009	TEX	MLB	26	17	8	0	34	31	189²	178	18	65	113	57%	.273	13	1.28	4.08	4.64	3.74	8.5	0.7	2.8	4.9	36.1	5.77
2010	TEX	MLB	27	8	9	0	40	23	153	156	18	67	81	57%	.284	-5	1.45	4.72	5.04	4.82	9.0	1.0	3.6	4.5	11.6	1.52

Breakout: 12%   Improve: 44%   Collapse: 16%   Attrition: 13%   MLB: 91%   Comparables: Charlie Lea, Jake Westbrook, Dick Fowler, Eric King

If anyone under pitching coach Mike Maddux's new program deserves the title "star pupil," it's probably Feldman. His strikeout and ground-ball rates improved and his velocity went up a tick. Critically, the addition of a cutter gave Feldman something he could use to mix lefties up, converting him from a big utility pitcher with an unavoidable problem to a rotation workhorse. That said, he got a lot of help from friends, both from the defense that converted a lot of his outs and from the umpires, who bought Feldman's new, expanded assortment so well they were responsible for an unusually high 39 percent of his strikeouts with called third strikes. SIERA suggests that his improvements weren't quite as significant as his ERA or wins tally says, but even if he's not an ace, he's got a solid claim to being an effective midrotation starter. Credit Maddux, credit Feldman's aptitude, credit the defense, or credit all of the above, you know the Rangers are happy to have found one.

Neftali Feliz

Bats: R   Throws: R   Height: 6' 3"   Weight: 180   Born: May 2, 1988   Age: 22

YEAR	TEAM	LVL	AGE	W	L	SV	G	GS	IP	H	HR	BB	SO	GB%	BABIP	STUFF	WHIP	ERA	SIERA	DERA	EqH9	EqHR9	EqBB9	EqSO9	VORP	SN/WX
2007	DNV	Rk	19	2	0	0	8	7	27¹	18	0	12	28	42%	.269	11	1.10	1.98	3.38	4.70	9.0	1.6	5.9	5.1	2.1	0.20
2007	SPO	A-	19	0	2	0	8	1	15	13	2	12	27	51%	.379	14	1.67	3.60	2.58	5.46	10.9	2.6	7.7	10.3	0.1	-0.21
2008	CLN	A	20	6	3	0	17	17	82	55	2	28	106	58%	.291	45	1.01	2.52	2.36	4.11	8.6	1.1	4.2	7.6	11.2	0.52
2008	FRI	AA	20	4	3	0	10	10	45¹	34	1	23	47	37%	.295	41	1.26	2.98	3.72	4.03	8.1	0.7	5.0	7.2	6.8	1.01
2009	OKL	AAA	21	4	6	0	25	13	77¹	69	2	30	75	53%	.315	27	1.28	3.49	3.55	4.44	8.4	0.6	3.6	6.9	8.7	1.03
2009	TEX	MLB	21	1	0	0	2	20	31	13	2	8	39	39%	.169	31	0.68	1.74	1.99	1.74	4.1	0.6	2.0	9.3	12.9	1.69
2010	TEX	MLB	22	6	7	0	41	23	112²	107	14	58	97	39%	.295	25	1.46	4.67	4.40	4.72	8.3	1.0	4.3	7.3	9.7	2.70

Breakout: 7%   Improve: 43%   Collapse: 15%   Attrition: 18%   MLB: 75%   Comparables: Rich Harden, Angel Guzman, George Ferran, Jose Melendez

Feliz wasn't living up to the high expectations set for him at Triple-A over the first two months of the year, but with the Rangers kinda-sorta in contention and needing bullpen help, they converted him to relief, and—voilà! A star is born. Sitting at 94-98 mph with his fastball and touching triple digits on several occasions, Felix held American League hitters to a minuscule .124 batting average in his 20-game big-league debut, while limiting righties to a remarkable 4-for-47 (.085) mark with 21 strikeouts. The new, "nice problem to have" situation is that the Rangers now have a bit of a Joba Chamberlain situation here. Feliz was just so darn good in the bullpen, but he was raised as a starter, and if he can bring that stuff to the rotation, just imagine what he could be. As the Yankees have learned, that doesn't always work out so well, and the Rangers aren't quite sure what the answer is themselves.

Frank Francisco

Bats: R   Throws: R   Height: 6' 3"   Weight: 230   Born: September 11, 1979   Age: 30

YEAR	TEAM	LVL	AGE	W	L	SV	G	GS	IP	H	HR	BB	SO	GB%	BABIP	STUFF	WHIP	ERA	SIERA	DERA	EqH9	EqHR9	EqBB9	EqSO9	VORP	SN/WX
2007	TEX	MLB	27	1	1	0	59	0	59¹	57	3	38	49	42%	.307	5	1.60	4.55	4.86	4.47	8.2	0.5	5.2	6.8	6.8	1.61
2008	TEX	MLB	28	3	5	5	58	0	63¹	47	7	26	83	37%	.270	27	1.15	3.13	2.59	3.03	6.2	0.8	3.2	9.8	17.9	2.31
2009	TEX	MLB	29	2	3	25	51	0	49¹	40	6	15	57	28%	.274	22	1.11	3.83	2.86	3.44	7.2	0.9	2.4	9.2	11.4	2.59
2010	TEX	MLB	30	4	3	14	61	0	60¹	51	7	27	59	34%	.284	11	1.28	3.80	3.78	3.82	7.4	0.8	3.7	8.4	11.3	1.73

Breakout: 18%   Improve: 41%   Collapse: 21%   Attrition: 3%   MLB: 94%   Comparables: Jason Isringhausen, Trevor Hoffman, Joaquin Benoit, Francisco Cordero

Having paid his dues with two seasons of set-up work, Francisco's move into the closer's role was humming along quite nicely until a midsummer bout of pneumonia cost him three weeks around the All-Star break. There's no real news here: the job is his for the next year, as his leading notional rival, C. J. Wilson, is headed for a shot at rotation work. If there's a danger, it might come in the form of Neftali Feliz, but even then, Feliz's talent is such that Francisco will be applied to other ends. Even half of Francisco's biggest matchup problem may be going away: the Angels' Juan Rivera and Vladimir Guerrero are tied for the most homers allowed by Francisco to opponents with three apiece, and Vladi is almost certainly an ex-Angel.

Jason Grilli

Bats: R Throws: R Height: 6' 5" Weight: 225 Born: November 11, 1976 Age: 33

YEAR	TEAM	LVL	AGE	W	L	SV	G	GS	IP	H	HR	BB	SO	GB%	BABIP	STUFF	WHIP	ERA	SIERA	DERA	EqH9	EqHR9	EqBB9	EqSO9	VORP	SN/WX
2007	DET	MLB	30	5	3	0	57	0	79²	81	5	32	62	50%	.306	3	1.42	4.74	4.32	4.82	8.9	0.6	3.2	6.4	6.1	0.41
2008	DET	MLB	31	0	1	0	9	0	13²	12	1	7	10	42%	.275	-3	1.39	3.29	4.84	3.29	7.2	0.7	4.0	5.9	3.4	-0.05
2008	COL	MLB	31	3	2	1	51	0	61¹	55	1	31	59	47%	.314	17	1.40	2.93	3.94	2.86	7.6	0.1	4.0	7.6	18.0	0.55
2009	COL	MLB	32	0	1	1	22	0	19¹	29	2	13	22	39%	.435	4	2.17	6.05	4.17	5.40	13.1	0.9	4.9	8.6	0.2	-0.63
2009	TEX	MLB	32	2	2	0	30	0	26¹	21	2	14	27	47%	.275	8	1.33	4.78	3.81	4.44	7.2	0.7	4.1	8.2	3.1	0.44
2010	CLE	MLB	33	4	4	0	53	0	64	64	6	31	50	45%	.308	-4	1.48	4.52	4.52	4.90	9.0	0.9	4.1	6.6	4.3	0.17

Breakout: 10% Improve: 38% Collapse: 29% Attrition: 10% MLB: 90% Comparables: Jim Brower, Jose Mesa, Dave Veres, Carl Willis

Apparently, there are no gentlemen's agreements among veteran mop-up men, because after blowing his opportunity with the Rockies, Grilli was sold off to the Rangers two months into the season. As had happened in Denver, he was initially considered a useful add-on, but between an elbow injury that shelved him and his performance, he slowly and surely worked his way back down into the mop-up role, squeezing out Jason Jennings because both of them rated behind Dustin Nippert. Let loose after the season, he finally managed to escape his recent run of affiliations with hitters' parks by signing a nonroster deal with Cleveland. If he sticks there, he might avenge himself with some regularity on Jim Leyland, since the former skipper disposed of the veteran in a bit of a huff in '08.

Eddie Guardado

Bats: R Throws: L Height: 6' 0" Weight: 225 Born: October 2, 1970 Age: 39

YEAR	TEAM	LVL	AGE	W	L	SV	G	GS	IP	H	HR	BB	SO	GB%	BABIP	STUFF	WHIP	ERA	SIERA	DERA	EqH9	EqHR9	EqBB9	EqSO9	VORP	SN/WX
2007	CIN	MLB	36	0	0	0	15	0	13²	16	2	4	8	18%	.298	-17	1.46	7.24	5.75	6.28	8.8	1.3	2.5	4.4	-1.2	0.38
2008	TEX	MLB	37	3	3	4	55	0	49¹	38	3	17	28	29%	.240	0	1.11	3.65	5.36	3.14	6.1	0.6	2.8	4.8	12.7	3.30
2008	MIN	MLB	37	1	1	0	9	0	7	12	1	2	5	27%	.440	-10	2.00	7.71	4.77	6.75	16.2	1.4	2.7	5.4	-0.9	-0.20
2009	TEX	MLB	38	1	2	0	48	0	38¹	39	8	15	20	40%	.256	-21	1.41	4.46	5.37	4.50	8.8	1.4	3.1	4.3	4.2	-0.16
2010	WAS	MLB	39	2	3	0	38	0	38¹	36	5	16	20	32%	.267	-12	1.36	4.15	5.61	4.74	9.1	1.1	3.5	4.4	3.3	0.78

Breakout: 19% Improve: 39% Collapse: 36% Attrition: 22% MLB: 92% Comparables: Mike Stanton, Mike Myers, Grant Jackson, Ron Villone

Formerly famous Everyday Eddie has become something of an oxymoron, as attempts to pitch him on back-to-back days went badly (10.57 ERA with zero days' rest), and his ability to retire lefties with any regularity has also deserted him. As with Pudge Rodriguez, he's taking the formerly famous shtick to DC to provide a sprinkling of gray hair in a clubhouse likely to be stocked with its share of noobs and to help out in a pen counting on Matt Capps and Brian Bruney in one of the chunkiest-looking relief corps of modern memory.

Danny Gutierrez

Bats: R Throws: R Height: 6' 1" Weight: 180 Born: March 8, 1987 Age: 23

YEAR	TEAM	LVL	AGE	W	L	SV	G	GS	IP	H	HR	BB	SO	GB%	BABIP	STUFF	WHIP	ERA	SIERA	DERA	EqH9	EqHR9	EqBB9	EqSO9	VORP	SN/WX
2007	BUR	A	20	1	2	0	7	7	31¹	32	2	12	27	50%	.323	7	1.40	4.88	3.93	7.23	11.6	1.9	4.5	4.8	-5.4	-0.47
2008	BUR	A	21	4	4	0	19	18	90	83	7	25	104	57%	.329	-2	1.20	2.70	2.74	5.71	11.2	2.1	3.6	6.6	-1.8	0.45
2009	WIL	A+	22	1	0	0	8	4	27¹	17	0	7	25	49%	.233	12	0.88	1.65	3.22	3.16	7.0	0.7	2.8	5.3	6.7	0.67
2010	TEX	MLB	23	2	4	0	23	5	58¹	68	10	27	42	50%	.322	-3	1.62	5.74	4.66	5.77	10.1	1.4	3.8	6.0	-1.7	1.27

Breakout: 15% Improve: 43% Collapse: 18% Attrition: 10% MLB: 2% Comparables: Reid Cornelius, Mark Brown, Mike Freitas, Ismael Villegas

Gutierrez has all the talent in the world, starting with a 92-94 mph sinker that he can dial up to 96, a power curveball, and the ability to throw strikes with both pitches. Unfortunately, injuries and a variety of troubling off-field issues have prevented him from ever throwing more than 90 innings in any one season. The complaints about his makeup piled up to the point where the Royals just flat-out sent him away to Texas last summer for a pair of fringe prospects, after which he acquitted himself quite well in the Arizona Fall League to finish up the year. It's more about what's between the ears than what comes out of his hand at this point, and if he can clean up the former, the Rangers could have a good third starter on their hands in return for very little.

Matt Harrison

| | | | | Bats: L | Throws: L | Height: 6' 4" | Weight: 225 | Born: August 16, 1985 | Age: 24 |

YEAR	TEAM	LVL	AGE	W	L	SV	G	GS	IP	H	HR	BB	SO	GB%	BABIP	STUFF	WHIP	ERA	SIERA	DERA	EqH9	EqHR9	EqBB9	EqSO9	VORP	SN/WX
2007	MIS	AA	21	5	7	0	20	20	116²	118	6	34	78	51%	.304	9	1.30	3.39	4.31	4.88	10.0	1.1	2.9	3.9	7.5	0.61
2008	FRI	AA	22	3	2	0	9	9	46	49	3	14	35	48%	.311	3	1.37	3.33	4.12	5.60	10.2	1.2	3.0	4.8	-0.5	0.20
2008	OKL	AAA	22	3	1	0	6	6	38	40	3	14	20	52%	.303	-2	1.42	3.55	4.98	3.95	9.9	1.0	3.6	3.3	6.1	0.36
2008	TEX	MLB	22	9	3	0	15	15	83²	100	12	31	42	47%	.309	2	1.57	5.49	5.25	5.39	9.6	1.2	2.9	4.2	1.0	0.39
2009	TEX	MLB	23	4	5	0	11	11	63¹	81	9	23	34	56%	.335	-6	1.64	6.11	4.98	5.49	11.7	1.0	3.0	4.6	0.1	0.61
2010	TEX	MLB	24	4	7	0	22	19	100¹	117	14	43	51	44%	.311	-12	1.60	5.36	5.40	5.37	10.2	1.2	3.4	4.3	1.5	1.18

Breakout: 11% Improve: 44% Collapse: 13% Attrition: 13%   MLB: 84%   Comparables: Scott Stewart, Kirk Rueter, Chuck Cary, Jeremy Affeldt

One of the forgotten parts of the Mark Teixeira deal, Harrison was getting hammered in the early part of the season before he hit the DL with both shoulder and biceps issues. The problem turned out to be much deeper than that, as he was diagnosed in late July with thoracic outlet syndrome, a dangerous circulatory condition that required season-ending surgery to correct. Healthy enough to pitch in the Arizona Fall League, he reenergized the Rangers' belief in him as a starter by returning to his usual above-average, low-90s velocity, and he'll be given another opportunity this spring to win a spot in the rotation, contending with fellow youngster Tommy Hunter, the oft-disappointing Brandon McCarthy, and C. J. Wilson's experiment with a move out from the pen.

Derek Holland

| | | | | Bats: S | Throws: L | Height: 6' 2" | Weight: 185 | Born: October 9, 1986 | Age: 23 |

YEAR	TEAM	LVL	AGE	W	L	SV	G	GS	IP	H	HR	BB	SO	GB%	BABIP	STUFF	WHIP	ERA	SIERA	DERA	EqH9	EqHR9	EqBB9	EqSO9	VORP	SN/WX
2007	SPO	A-	20	4	5	0	16	14	67	57	7	21	83	34%	.299	21	1.16	3.22	2.59	5.07	9.9	2.1	3.3	6.6	3.0	-0.22
2008	CLN	A	21	7	0	0	17	17	93²	77	2	29	91	52%	.298	23	1.13	2.40	3.27	4.32	9.6	1.1	3.9	5.4	10.9	0.57
2008	BAK	A+	21	3	1	0	5	5	31	20	1	5	37	43%	.271	28	0.81	3.19	1.86	4.02	7.1	1.0	2.3	7.7	4.6	0.19
2008	FRI	AA	21	3	0	0	4	4	26	14	0	6	29	50%	.237	24	0.77	0.69	2.35	2.25	6.0	0.4	2.3	7.9	8.7	1.71
2009	TEX	MLB	22	8	13	0	33	21	138¹	160	26	47	107	49%	.314	4	1.50	6.12	4.21	5.68	10.2	1.3	2.7	6.3	-2.8	0.74
2010	TEX	MLB	23	6	8	0	29	24	122²	131	17	55	88	40%	.306	7	1.51	5.06	4.74	5.04	9.3	1.2	3.6	6.1	6.3	1.92

Breakout: 12% Improve: 51% Collapse: 14% Attrition: 10%   MLB: 100%   Comparables: Jon Lester, Mark Langston, Zach Crouch, John Danks

As a left-hander whose heat sits at 93-96 mph, Holland has true star potential, but his rookie campaign in the big leagues showed that there is still plenty of work to be done to get him there. He occasionally dominated, including a three-hitter against the first-place Angels in a crucial August series. More often than not, however, he was forced to rely overmuch on the heater, as his slider just disappeared completely from his repertoire at times. At just 23, he's still a way from the upswing of his career path, and pitchers with his raw abilities are hard to find, so he's guaranteed a rotation spot in 2010 despite last year's six-plus ERA.

Tommy Hunter

| | | | | Bats: R | Throws: R | Height: 6' 3" | Weight: 255 | Born: July 3, 1986 | Age: 23 |

YEAR	TEAM	LVL	AGE	W	L	SV	G	GS	IP	H	HR	BB	SO	GB%	BABIP	STUFF	WHIP	ERA	SIERA	DERA	EqH9	EqHR9	EqBB9	EqSO9	VORP	SN/WX
2007	SPO	A-	20	2	3	1	10	0	17²	15	0	1	13	54%	.273	17	0.91	2.55	3.36	3.97	8.5	0.5	1.1	3.7	2.9	0.13
2008	BAK	A+	21	5	4	0	9	9	58¹	63	6	8	50	52%	.326	17	1.22	3.55	3.30	4.64	10.9	1.8	1.8	5.1	5.2	0.10
2008	FRI	AA	21	4	2	0	8	8	52¹	52	5	17	28	52%	.285	2	1.32	3.78	4.83	5.21	10.1	1.7	3.4	3.4	1.5	0.28
2008	OKL	AAA	21	4	2	0	8	8	53	55	6	9	28	55%	.278	11	1.21	2.89	4.43	3.46	9.3	1.4	1.7	3.3	11.8	1.21
2008	TEX	MLB	21	0	2	0	3	3	11	23	4	3	9	34%	.422	-4	2.36	16.36	4.51	15.69	15.3	2.9	2.2	5.8	-14.0	-0.63
2009	FRI	AA	22	1	0	0	5	3	21²	30	1	4	16	54%	.358	1	1.57	4.98	4.05	7.46	12.1	1.2	2.0	4.8	-4.9	-0.16
2009	OKL	AAA	22	3	2	0	8	8	49¹	53	5	16	35	48%	.316	6	1.40	3.83	4.32	4.82	10.0	1.5	3.1	5.0	3.5	0.49
2009	TEX	MLB	22	9	6	0	19	19	112	113	13	33	64	45%	.275	18	1.30	4.10	4.81	3.99	8.9	0.8	2.3	4.6	18.7	2.69
2010	TEX	MLB	23	8	11	0	32	27	162¹	182	24	54	89	46%	.302	-1	1.45	4.99	4.94	5.10	9.9	1.2	2.8	4.7	7.1	2.65

Breakout: 10% Improve: 46% Collapse: 9% Attrition: 4%   MLB: 100%   Comparables: Mike Ziegler, Tim Dillard, Ron Chiavacci, Blaine Boyer

Even among the number of big men you'll find on the mound, Hunter stands out for being one who isn't remotely gangly; walking around on a pair of tree trunks that appear proportional for his mass, he just seems to be the textbook definition of *big* in pitcher form. He's not a power pitcher, instead relying on a pedestrian fastball and an increasing number of cutters and mixing in breaking stuff as needed. Basically, he focuses on throwing strikes and relies on his defense. Big-league lefties weren't fooled much, as his strikeout rate and performance flagged down the stretch; he managed quality starts in six of his first nine MLB turns, then just two in his last 10. All of which goes toward why he isn't guaranteed a rotation job, although he may have the inside track on a spot.

Jason Jennings

															Bats: L		Throws: R		Height: 6' 2"		Weight: 235		Born: July 17, 1978			Age: 31

YEAR	TEAM	LVL	AGE	W	L	SV	G	GS	IP	H	HR	BB	SO	GB%	BABIP	STUFF	WHIP	ERA	SIERA	DERA	EqH9	EqHR9	EqBB9	EqSO9	VORP	SN/WX
2007	HOU	MLB	28	2	9	0	19	18	99	119	19	34	71	42%	.313	-15	1.55	6.45	4.51	6.14	10.3	1.7	2.7	5.7	-7.1	0.83
2008	TEX	MLB	29	0	5	0	6	6	27[1]	35	8	18	12	56%	.281	-24	1.94	8.56	5.93	8.07	9.6	2.2	5.0	3.4	-8.3	-0.56
2009	TEX	MLB	30	2	4	1	44	0	61	67	7	28	44	55%	.314	-7	1.56	4.13	4.61	4.13	9.9	0.8	3.6	5.8	9.2	0.36
2010	TEX	MLB	31	3	5	0	31	4	63[1]	71	9	30	40	50%	.312	-11	1.60	5.37	4.98	5.46	9.9	1.2	3.9	5.3	0.3	0.18

Breakout: 22%   Improve: 57%   Collapse: 16%   Attrition: 17%   MLB: 88%   Comparables: Yuuya Andoh, Storm Davis, Doug Brocail, Scott Sanders

It was sort of a successful comeback, but only sort of. Jennings managed to do good work early on as a middle reliever, albeit one generally when the club was up or down by three runs or more, and snapped off enough sinkers to keep the ball in the yard and himself on the roster. That came to an end in the second half, as he started having a hard time keeping fewer than half of opposing batters from getting on base, which led to his late-August release. His heyday as a Rockies workhorse is now more than three years gone, and he was never the most efficient of strike throwers out there. He'll have to settle for following the Kip Wells Trail of Travail, bouncing from one extra-dude gig to the next on only the very worst ballclubs.

Kasey Kiker

															Bats: L		Throws: L		Height: 5' 10"		Weight: 170		Born: November 19, 1987			Age: 22

YEAR	TEAM	LVL	AGE	W	L	SV	G	GS	IP	H	HR	BB	SO	GB%	BABIP	STUFF	WHIP	ERA	SIERA	DERA	EqH9	EqHR9	EqBB9	EqSO9	VORP	SN/WX
2007	CLN	A	19	7	4	0	20	20	96[1]	84	10	41	112	38%	.315	11	1.30	2.90	3.10	4.66	10.9	2.4	5.0	7.2	7.8	0.61
2008	BAK	A+	20	5	5	0	23	21	121[2]	138	14	37	111	47%	.348	-3	1.44	4.73	3.63	6.08	11.9	2.1	3.6	5.5	-7.1	-1.52
2009	FRI	AA	21	7	7	0	25	23	126	108	9	66	120	40%	.286	11	1.38	3.86	4.13	5.43	8.9	1.6	4.7	6.7	0.9	0.54
2010	TEX	MLB	22	4	8	0	27	23	108[1]	128	19	60	82	37%	.328	9	1.74	6.45	5.01	6.32	10.2	1.4	4.5	6.4	-9.9	1.71

Breakout: 11%   Improve: 39%   Collapse: 14%   Attrition: 12%   MLB: 10%   Comparables: John Kilner, Lindsay Gulin, Steve Garrison, Kelvin Villa

The second high-school pitcher selected in the 2006 draft (and the 12th selection overall), Kiker is another name on the long list of players who never throw as hard as a pro as they did in high school. Nonetheless, he's far from being a soft tosser, as his 91-93 mph velocity is well above average for a southpaw, but he has a tendency to overthrow the pitch, leading to occasional control issues. Combine that with his smallish stature and fly-ball tendencies, and his future might be in the bullpen, as the fastball and his nifty power curve limited left-handed hitters to a .178/.341/.244 mark last year.

Warner Madrigal

															Bats: R		Throws: R		Height: 6' 0"		Weight: 200		Born: March 21, 1984			Age: 26

YEAR	TEAM	LVL	AGE	W	L	SV	G	GS	IP	H	HR	BB	SO	GB%	BABIP	STUFF	WHIP	ERA	SIERA	DERA	EqH9	EqHR9	EqBB9	EqSO9	VORP	SN/WX
2007	CDR	A	23	5	4	20	54	0	61	44	3	23	75	54%	.283	1	1.10	2.07	2.68	3.94	8.4	1.3	4.3	7.2	9.7	1.67
2008	FRI	AA	24	1	0	10	14	0	15[2]	11	1	8	18	44%	.270	8	1.21	1.72	3.26	3.07	7.4	1.2	4.9	8.0	4.0	0.95
2008	OKL	AAA	24	0	0	4	17	0	20[1]	20	2	8	25	48%	.321	3	1.38	3.98	2.97	4.79	9.1	1.3	3.5	7.8	1.6	-0.06
2008	TEX	MLB	24	0	2	1	31	1	36	36	4	14	22	41%	.281	-10	1.39	4.75	4.97	4.91	7.9	1.0	2.9	4.9	2.4	-0.70
2009	OKL	AAA	25	2	2	17	42	0	49	42	5	11	48	46%	.276	3	1.08	2.57	3.04	3.09	7.9	1.5	2.1	6.8	12.8	1.87
2009	TEX	MLB	25	0	0	0	13	0	12[2]	18	2	12	5	42%	.340	-34	2.37	9.95	7.08	8.53	12.8	1.4	7.1	3.6	-4.3	-0.16
2010	TEX	MLB	26	3	4	7	59	0	65	68	10	29	48	43%	.301	-7	1.49	4.88	4.59	4.93	9.1	1.2	3.7	6.2	4.1	1.72

Breakout: 8%   Improve: 28%   Collapse: 27%   Attrition: 6%   MLB: 69%   Comparables: Keith Fleming, Scott Medvin, Julio Strauss, Marino Salas

Coming into the year, the Rangers appeared to have mined a nice find in Madrigal, a strong-armed converted outfielder stolen from the Angels when Anaheim tried to sneak him through waivers. Unfortunately, Madrigal suffered a velocity dip in 2009, as his 92-95 mph fastball turned into something coming in around 90-92, and for an inexperienced arm, the corresponding troubles were predictable. He has only been pitching for three years, and his mid-80s power slider and command showed considerable improvement back in Triple-A, so there is still room for optimism here. Even so, 2010 could be his last chance to avoid a career of Triple-A wandering.

Doug Mathis

Bats: R   Throws: R   Height: 6' 3"   Weight: 220   Born: June 7, 1983   Age: 27

YEAR	TEAM	LVL	AGE	W	L	SV	G	GS	IP	H	HR	BB	SO	GB%	BABIP	STUFF	WHIP	ERA	SIERA	DERA	EqH9	EqHR9	EqBB9	EqSO9	VORP	SN/WX
2007	FRI	AA	24	11	7	0	22	22	131^2	140	7	40	92	64%	.320	-4	1.37	3.76	4.06	4.89	10.8	1.0	3.1	4.7	8.3	0.59
2007	OKL	AAA	24	0	3	0	3	2	12^2	21	2	6	8	52%	.404	-36	2.13	10.66	5.04	12.75	15.8	2.3	4.5	4.5	-9.7	-0.87
2008	OKL	AAA	25	5	1	0	10	10	53^2	51	7	14	36	60%	.268	-6	1.21	3.35	4.07	5.02	8.8	1.6	2.4	4.3	2.8	0.51
2008	TEX	MLB	25	2	1	0	8	4	22^1	37	3	14	9	48%	.395	-30	2.28	6.85	6.19	7.16	13.9	1.2	4.9	3.3	-4.1	0.13
2009	OKL	AAA	26	4	2	0	11	10	57	64	3	15	38	61%	.328	1	1.39	2.84	4.17	3.93	10.1	1.0	2.5	4.6	9.6	0.84
2009	TEX	MLB	26	0	1	1	24	2	42^2	39	4	10	25	61%	.267	1	1.15	3.16	4.32	3.27	8.3	0.7	2.0	4.8	10.3	0.39
2010	TEX	MLB	27	4	6	0	26	13	84	96	12	33	51	56%	.313	-8	1.54	5.26	4.76	5.40	10.1	1.2	3.3	5.2	0.9	1.04

Breakout: 18%   Improve: 55%   Collapse: 12%   Attrition: 19%   MLB: 46%   Comparables: Mike Lincoln, Kane Davis, Zach Miner, Dan Smith

After getting nontendered following the 2008 season, Mathis re-signed with the Rangers and managed to get sucked into middle-innings mop-up work, usually in games the Rangers were losing by four runs or more. He'll never blow you away on a stuff level, as he's a bit of a generic sinker/slider righty whose heat is in the 89-92 mph range, but he knows how to hit his spots, set up hitters, and generally keep the ball on the ground. There's nothing sexy about it, but it can work as the eleventh guy on a staff until big-league hitters figure him out, because his inability to miss many bats means there's a great chance of their catching up to him.

Brandon McCarthy

Bats: R   Throws: R   Height: 6' 7"   Weight: 205   Born: July 7, 1983   Age: 26

YEAR	TEAM	LVL	AGE	W	L	SV	G	GS	IP	H	HR	BB	SO	GB%	BABIP	STUFF	WHIP	ERA	SIERA	DERA	EqH9	EqHR9	EqBB9	EqSO9	VORP	SN/WX
2007	TEX	MLB	23	5	10	0	23	22	101^2	111	9	48	59	37%	.300	1	1.56	4.87	5.45	4.89	9.1	0.7	3.8	4.7	6.9	1.99
2008	OKL	AAA	24	1	1	0	5	5	26^2	21	2	8	23	51%	.253	9	1.09	3.37	3.63	3.76	7.2	1.0	2.7	5.5	5.1	0.57
2008	TEX	MLB	24	1	1	0	5	5	22	20	3	8	10	28%	.239	-6	1.27	4.09	6.07	3.77	6.8	1.2	2.8	3.6	4.4	0.79
2009	OKL	AAA	25	0	1	0	5	5	21^2	20	1	9	22	53%	.317	9	1.34	4.15	3.53	4.50	8.6	0.9	3.9	7.3	2.3	0.37
2009	TEX	MLB	25	7	4	0	17	17	97^1	96	13	36	65	46%	.274	8	1.36	4.62	4.65	4.56	8.6	0.9	2.9	5.3	10.2	1.70
2010	TEX	MLB	26	6	7	0	23	23	119^1	119	14	50	72	42%	.286	3	1.42	4.52	5.03	4.61	8.8	1.0	3.5	5.2	11.8	1.95

Breakout: 8%   Improve: 47%   Collapse: 13%   Attrition: 7%   MLB: 86%   Comparables: Paul Hartzell, Bob Walk, Jeff Karstens, Roger Erickson

"Ill-starred" can be applied to a lot of things: monarchies, the Cubs, Gretchen Mol, you name it. But McCarthy may have them beat, at least in terms of having a career that has seemed to be an unending litany of misfortune. Last season, he lost nearly three months to a stress fracture in his right shoulder blade, but before and after, he managed to deliver about what you'd hope for from a back-end starter, managing quality starts almost half of the time. Never appearing to be the best match for this park, given his homer-happy proclivities, he has nevertheless managed to allow 4.4 runs per nine in the ballpark (and 1.2 HR/9) on his punctuated career. McCarthy heads into camp with a fight on his hands for one of the last two open rotation slots, with Harrison, Hunter, and C. J. Wilson also in the lists; the pen is no less crowded. He may finally be on the cusp of a deal someplace where he isn't "the guy traded for John Danks" or "the guy who's always hurt," but he could also finally become the guy who settled into a back-end slot and was just OK. When you're as unlucky as McCarthy has been, even that qualifies as a reversal of fortune.

Kevin Millwood

Bats: R   Throws: R   Height: 6' 4"   Weight: 230   Born: December 24, 1974   Age: 35

YEAR	TEAM	LVL	AGE	W	L	SV	G	GS	IP	H	HR	BB	SO	GB%	BABIP	STUFF	WHIP	ERA	SIERA	DERA	EqH9	EqHR9	EqBB9	EqSO9	VORP	SN/WX
2007	TEX	MLB	32	10	14	0	31	31	172^2	213	19	67	123	54%	.340	1	1.62	5.16	4.51	5.14	10.5	0.9	3.1	5.8	6.9	1.69
2008	TEX	MLB	33	9	10	0	29	29	168^2	220	18	49	125	48%	.355	9	1.59	5.07	4.25	4.86	10.4	0.8	2.2	6.0	12.2	1.80
2009	TEX	MLB	34	13	10	0	31	31	198^2	195	26	71	123	51%	.273	9	1.34	3.67	4.71	3.64	8.7	0.9	2.8	5.0	40.5	5.31
2010	BAL	MLB	35	8	11	0	31	31	167^2	194	23	59	101	49%	.317	-3	1.51	5.13	4.76	5.18	10.0	1.1	3.1	5.1	6.0	1.74

Breakout: 6%   Improve: 30%   Collapse: 10%   Attrition: 12%   MLB: 97%   Comparables: Kevin Gross, Esteban Loaiza, Ed Whitson, Mike Torrez

It might offend some sensibilities that before last season, Millwood, a man with $38 million still coming to him on a five-year, $60 million deal, refamiliarized himself with off-season conditioning, toning up his legs to avoid repeating the hamstring injury that hampered him in 2008. Whether it does or doesn't, as a component of the team's new focus on conditioning for its pitchers, it counted as a success, and Millwood gave the club his best year as a Ranger, producing 17 quality starts and another four quality spins blown after the sixth inning for a total of 21, and logging a .547 Support-Neutral Winning Percentage after marks of just .514, .443, and .452 in the first three years. Keep in mind, both his strikeout and walk rates got worse, and per ISO, he wasn't giving up any less power; the improved defense meant innings were ending earlier, preventing big innings from getting bigger. The Rangers didn't look the gift horse in the mouth; they flipped that fifth year on the contract to the Orioles to get back some of the payroll commitment, converting it into a bet that Rich Harden will do better. It's not a bad choice, and while Millwood might provide veteranosity to the wee ones in the rotation, those declining peripherals and a move away from the defense won't do him many favors in his walk year; PECOTA obviously suggests he'll party like it's 2008.

Guillermo Moscoso

Bats: R Throws: R Height: 6' 1" Weight: 160 Born: November 14, 1983 Age: 26

YEAR	TEAM	LVL	AGE	W	L	SV	G	GS	IP	H	HR	BB	SO	GB%	BABIP	STUFF	WHIP	ERA	SIERA	DERA	EqH9	EqHR9	EqBB9	EqSO9	VORP	SN/WX
2007	ONE	A-	23	8	2	0	14	14	79²	75	3	15	68	38%	.309	-1	1.13	2.37	3.39	4.02	10.5	1.4	2.5	4.9	11.8	0.62
2008	LAK	A+	24	2	3	1	15	6	52	36	4	13	72	37%	.281	15	0.94	2.42	1.72	4.13	8.3	1.7	2.8	9.0	7.3	0.48
2008	ERI	AA	24	3	1	0	6	6	34²	24	4	8	50	33%	.274	33	0.92	3.12	1.43	4.99	7.3	1.4	2.2	9.7	1.9	0.15
2009	FRI	AA	25	3	1	0	9	7	42¹	41	1	14	36	33%	.305	3	1.30	4.46	4.06	5.83	9.1	0.9	3.0	5.8	-1.5	-0.01
2009	OKL	AAA	25	5	4	0	12	11	70	56	2	15	60	38%	.274	25	1.01	2.31	3.44	2.91	7.3	0.7	2.1	6.0	19.6	1.68
2009	TEX	MLB	25	0	0	0	10	0	14	15	1	6	12	38%	.318	0	1.50	3.21	4.36	4.08	9.4	0.6	3.1	6.9	2.3	0.06
2010	TEX	MLB	26	5	6	0	31	15	99	99	13	38	76	35%	.297	8	1.38	4.42	4.44	4.49	8.8	1.1	3.1	6.6	11.1	2.13

Breakout: 11% Improve: 43% Collapse: 23% Attrition: 14%   MLB: 20%   Comparables: Vicyohandry Odelin, Mark Clemons, Jose Melendez, Brian Warren

The primary player received from the Tigers in return for Gerald Laird, Moscoso has struck out more than a batter per inning in the minors, but not because of a power arsenal. He's more of a trick pitcher, with an 89-92 mph fastball that plays up due both to its natural movement and to a highly deceptive delivery that prevents batters from picking up the ball out of his hand. A checkered health record and smallish frame always had scouts projecting him for a bullpen role once he got to the big leagues, and that was the case when he performed admirably in a pair of auditions with the Rangers. Still, the pitching depth chart is deep in Texas, and he goes into the spring with no guarantees.

Dustin Nippert

Bats: R Throws: R Height: 6' 8" Weight: 225 Born: May 6, 1981 Age: 29

YEAR	TEAM	LVL	AGE	W	L	SV	G	GS	IP	H	HR	BB	SO	GB%	BABIP	STUFF	WHIP	ERA	SIERA	DERA	EqH9	EqHR9	EqBB9	EqSO9	VORP	SN/WX
2007	TUC	AAA	26	0	3	0	10	8	36	23	3	23	46	39%	.267	28	1.28	4.75	3.23	4.63	6.1	1.1	5.8	9.5	3.3	0.64
2007	ARI	MLB	26	1	1	0	36	0	45¹	48	5	16	38	45%	.314	2	1.41	5.56	4.01	5.16	9.1	0.8	2.8	6.9	1.7	0.69
2008	OKL	AAA	27	6	2	0	12	10	63¹	65	8	16	43	49%	.295	-7	1.28	3.98	4.19	4.30	9.8	1.7	2.4	4.5	8.0	0.47
2008	TEX	MLB	27	3	5	0	20	6	71²	92	10	37	55	40%	.345	-8	1.80	6.40	4.88	5.69	10.2	1.1	4.0	6.2	-1.6	0.21
2009	TEX	MLB	28	5	3	0	20	10	69²	64	7	29	54	45%	.277	10	1.33	3.88	4.39	3.63	8.2	0.6	3.2	6.2	14.4	1.80
2010	TEX	MLB	29	4	5	0	29	13	83²	87	11	39	59	46%	.302	-1	1.50	4.88	4.69	4.99	9.2	1.1	3.8	6.1	4.7	1.18

Breakout: 13% Improve: 37% Collapse: 18% Attrition: 15%   MLB: 68%   Comparables: Rick Bauer, Craig McMurtry, Kevin Gregg, Gary Waslewski

After missing the first half with a back injury, the big swingman swung back into action in July, bouncing back and forth between the rotation and pen as needed and never really struggling in either role. A prospect once upon a time in his own right equipped with solid enough stuff, he isn't a forgotten man as much as a handy utility pitcher. He's not someone especially likely to wind up in a high-leverage role in the pen or win a rotation spot, but is very likely to wind up contributing to both units. Between the ever-fragile Harden and lefties Holland, Wilson, and Harrison, it's easy to envision him sponging up a few middle-inning assignments while providing an effective in-game change of pace.

Darren O'Day

Bats: R Throws: R Height: 6' 4" Weight: 225 Born: October 22, 1982 Age: 27

YEAR	TEAM	LVL	AGE	W	L	SV	G	GS	IP	H	HR	BB	SO	GB%	BABIP	STUFF	WHIP	ERA	SIERA	DERA	EqH9	EqHR9	EqBB9	EqSO9	VORP	SN/WX
2007	RCU	A+	24	4	0	11	24	0	24	10	1	6	26	58%	.161	9	0.67	0.75	2.61	1.52	4.6	0.8	2.7	6.5	10.5	1.57
2007	ARK	AA	24	3	4	10	29	0	29¹	27	3	14	22	57%	.282	-18	1.40	3.99	4.44	4.77	9.5	1.6	4.6	4.9	2.2	-0.61
2008	SLC	AAA	25	2	2	7	21	0	33	29	3	7	30	49%	.292	7	1.09	3.27	3.19	3.45	8.0	0.9	2.0	6.6	7.1	0.37
2008	LAA	MLB	25	0	1	0	30	0	43¹	49	2	14	29	64%	.324	-1	1.45	4.57	4.33	4.53	9.7	0.4	2.5	5.6	4.7	0.12
2009	NYN	MLB	26	0	0	0	4	0	3	5	0	1	2	28%	.385	-17	2.00	0.00	5.22	5.40	13.5	0.0	2.7	5.4	0.0	-0.45
2009	TEX	MLB	26	2	1	2	64	0	55²	36	3	17	54	46%	.239	25	0.95	1.94	3.19	1.83	6.0	0.3	2.5	8.0	22.0	2.93
2010	TEX	MLB	27	3	4	8	61	0	60	56	7	24	44	52%	.284	-1	1.32	4.33	4.33	4.45	8.4	0.9	3.2	6.3	7.0	1.22

Breakout: 12% Improve: 32% Collapse: 35% Attrition: 12%   MLB: 74%   Comparables: Bob Howry, Matt Turner, Mike Henneman, Jared Burton

As if the Mets didn't have enough problems, they'd had the good sense to add O'Day via the Rule 5 draft before the season, but decided they couldn't keep him, at which point Jon Daniels filched the big-league-ready ROOGY on a waiver claim. A submariner with a nice slider, O'Day provided a reminder that it's easier to pick your spots with a situational righty: Washington got him the platoon advantage 69 percent of the time against the people O'Day held to .164/.259/.195. None of the three homers he allowed to lefties radically altered the ballgames he was in, in part because Washington was willing to roll the dice in those spots. Take the one he gave up on May 15th, facing Kendry Morales in the ninth up by five runs with two on and two out. That isn't managerial malpractice; it's a worthwhile risk and an exercise in trying to avoid using somebody else in a game you've very nearly won. Wilson did have to enter to lock down the game, but the decision tree is defensible enough.

Martin Perez
Bats: L   Throws: L   Height: 6' 0"   Weight: 165   Born: April 4, 1991   Age: 19

YEAR	TEAM	LVL	AGE	W	L	SV	G	GS	IP	H	HR	BB	SO	GB%	BABIP	STUFF	WHIP	ERA	SIERA	DERA	EqH9	EqHR9	EqBB9	EqSO9	VORP	SN/WX
2008	SPO	A-	17	1	2	0	15	15	61²	66	3	28	53	57%	.330	-9	1.52	3.65	4.06	6.67	13.2	2.0	4.7	4.2	-7.2	-0.49
2009	HIC	A	18	5	5	1	22	14	93²	82	3	33	105	55%	.317	16	1.23	2.31	3.00	4.91	10.5	1.5	4.8	6.0	5.4	0.10
2009	FRI	AA	18	1	3	0	5	5	21	29	2	5	14	52%	.365	7	1.62	5.57	4.33	8.10	13.5	1.8	2.3	4.5	-5.8	-0.28
2010	TEX	MLB	19	4	9	0	29	25	117	154	22	62	71	52%	.341	17	1.85	6.77	5.19	6.69	11.4	1.5	4.3	5.2	-15.5	2.13

Breakout: 21% Improve: 55% Collapse: 14% Attrition: 2%   MLB: 0%   Comparables: Darren Hursey, Ricardo Palma, Bob Kipper, Jacob McGee

The best arm in the farm system now that Feliz is a big-leaguer, Perez was pushed to Double-A as an 18-year-old, where he held his own, because everything about his game is well beyond his years. Beyond the 91-94 mph fastball that can get up to 96, Perez already has two plus secondary offerings in his curve and changeup, while his command and control are already advanced. He might be back in Double-A as a teenager in 2010, but he should be in the big leagues before he turns 21; most scouts project true stardom. The only real knock against him is his size, but with this kind of stuff and performance, scouts and observers alike just don't give a damn.

Tanner Scheppers
Bats: R   Throws: R   Height: 6' 4"   Weight: 200   Born: January 17, 1987   Age: 23

YEAR	TEAM	LVL	AGE	W	L	SV	G	GS	IP	H	HR	BB	SO	GB%	BABIP	STUFF	WHIP	ERA	SIERA	DERA	EqH9	EqHR9	EqBB9	EqSO9	VORP	SN/WX

Did Not Play.

Breakout: 21% Improve: 55% Collapse: 14% Attrition: 2%   MLB: 0%   Comparables: NA

Scheppers was one of the best arms available in the 2008 draft, but concerns over a shoulder injury were too much for the Pirates to come to terms with him, so he pitched in independent ball last spring. His medical situation still dropped him out of the first round, with the Rangers finally taking him and signing him to a $1.25 million bonus. Signing too late to make his affiliated pro debut, he pitched in the Arizona Fall League and blew away scouts and batters with a swing-and-miss slider and an upper-90s fastball that got up to 99. He could be in the big leagues as soon as this summer if his move to the bullpen is permanent. Many feel that's the best idea, as every pitch he throws in the minors could be a waste of an investment; between his shoulder issues and ugly mechanics, the expectation is that there are only so many miles on his arm. There's a good chance here for one of those supernova careers, a bright, overwhelming flash of light, and then, just as quickly, he's gone.

C. J. Wilson
Bats: L   Throws: L   Height: 6' 1"   Weight: 210   Born: November 18, 1980   Age: 29

YEAR	TEAM	LVL	AGE	W	L	SV	G	GS	IP	H	HR	BB	SO	GB%	BABIP	STUFF	WHIP	ERA	SIERA	DERA	EqH9	EqHR9	EqBB9	EqSO9	VORP	SN/WX
2007	TEX	MLB	26	2	1	12	66	0	68¹	50	4	33	63	54%	.257	17	1.21	3.03	3.92	2.99	6.4	0.5	4.0	7.6	18.9	2.40
2008	TEX	MLB	27	2	2	24	50	0	46¹	49	8	27	41	55%	.301	-7	1.64	6.02	4.41	6.00	8.4	1.3	4.5	7.1	-2.7	1.41
2009	TEX	MLB	28	5	6	14	74	0	73²	66	3	32	84	65%	.318	25	1.33	2.81	3.21	3.27	8.1	0.2	3.4	9.1	18.4	1.71
2010	TEX	MLB	29	4	4	14	66	0	65	60	6	32	61	55%	.304	6	1.41	4.37	3.89	4.34	8.0	0.9	4.0	8.0	8.3	1.21

Breakout: 14% Improve: 40% Collapse: 24% Attrition: 7%   MLB: 92%   Comparables: Gary Lavelle, Jesse Orosco, Chuck McElroy, Sparky Lyle

After more years of using Wilson as one of their key relievers, the Rangers plan to move him into the rotation, replacing him in the pen with Darren Oliver. This isn't that outlandish; Wilson came up as a starting prospect and started 22 games between the majors and minors in 2005, and he's not a classic two-pitch reliever, but one gifted with a full spread that he can throw for strikes. The Rangers can even point to Kenny Rogers' conversion to full-time rotation work four years into his career in '93. It's important to remember that player talents are mutable, and just because Wilson was molded into a late-game reliever doesn't mean this role was set in cement. Nevertheless, he's got a big platoon split on his career, with right-handers hitting him at a .281/.367/.430 clip, and that's with only three instances of right-handed batters getting a second at-bat against him in a single game in the past four years: A-Rod in '07, and Jorge Cantu and Richie Sexson in '06. Wilson got them out each time.

LINEOUTS

Hitters

PLAYER	TEAM	LVL	AGE	PA	R	2B	3B	HR	RBI	BB	SO	SB-CS	EqBRR	AVG/OBP/SLG	EqAVG/EqOBP/EqSLG	EqA	VORP	WARP
SS J. Arias	OKL	AAA	24	537	63	14	3	5	52	20	47	24-3	6.6	.266/.295/.335	.253/.279/.316	.215	-3.9	-1.9
OF M. Bianucci	HIC	A	23	297	50	21	2	15	49	24	50	8-5	-1.3	.331/.401/.600	.265/.316/.438	.258	4.9	-0.8
	BAK	A+	23	218	35	8	1	15	41	14	69	1-0	2.1	.232/.289/.510	.197/.239/.394	.215	-8.1	-1.6
CF C. Gentry	FRI	AA	25	588	100	21	7	8	53	49	64	49-6	9.9	.303/.378/.418	.279/.334/.380	.258	14.3	-0.4
	TEX	MLB	25	19	4	1	0	0	1	2	5	0-0	-0.2	.118/.211/.176	.118/.211/.176	.112	-1.9	-0.2
UT E. German	OKL	AAA	31	472	63	15	5	4	59	65	63	35-9	-0.8	.319/.419/.414	.293/.380/.367	.273	19.1	0.5
	TEX	MLB	31	50	9	4	0	0	4	4	7	1-0	0.6	.304/.360/.391	.304/.360/.391	.267	1.7	0.1
OF G. Golson	OKL	AAA	23	500	46	17	8	2	40	29	114	20-4	0.8	.258/.299/.344	.240/.277/.315	.214	-11.9	-0.7
MI M. Lemon*	FRI	AA	21	510	56	19	5	1	41	42	70	7-4	-3.5	.262/.326/.333	.249/.301/.318	.220	-5.2	-3.0
3B T. Mendonca*	BAK	A+	21	46	5	3	0	0	2	1	12	1-0	0.5	.209/.261/.279	.182/.217/.227	.134	-3.6	-0.1
	SPO	A-	21	205	33	12	2	9	26	9	66	0-0	-0.7	.309/.361/.537	.224/.254/.383	.216	-3.6	-1.6
C K. Richardson	OKL	AAA	28	281	33	10	1	13	36	19	105	0-0	-0.5	.216/.281/.416	.181/.237/.338	.196	-5.7	-1.6
OF R. Sierra Jr.*	RNG	Rk	18	118	14	3	0	0	10	8	47	7-4	-1.1	.202/.254/.229	.152/.186/.170	.058	-13.4	-3.8

Although he was once a top prospect in the system, injuries and plate discipline issues got **Joaquin Arias** passed by Andrus, but Arias might still have some value in a utility role. ⊘ After leading all Rangers minor-leaguers with 30 home runs, **Mike Bianucci** now needs to prove he's more than just a polished college player beating up on A-ball pitchers. ⊘ **Craig Gentry** is a contact-oriented burner willing to take a pitch (16 HBPs) with fourth outfielder upside. ⊘ **Esteban German** spent most of the year as an insurance policy at Triple-A, doing what he does there: hit .300, steal bases, draw walks, wonder what Emilio Bonifacio has that he doesn't. ⊘ Still one of the toolsiest players in the game, **Greg Golson** has no plate discipline and a very long swing and seems to be just treading water. ⊘ Chet's son, **Marcus Lemon** can play second base or shortstop effectively and draw a few walks, which might be enough for a bench job down the line. ⊘ A second-round pick last June, third baseman **Tommy Mendonca** has a propensity for striking out a lot, but also for absolutely crushing balls when he makes contact. ⊘ Eight years into being a Rangers farmhand, **Kevin Richardson** finally got a spin in "The Show," but he's back off the 40-man and re-signed for further organizational soldiery. ⊘ The son of the former Rangers MVP, **Ruben Sierra Jr.** is a dead ringer for his dad in size and athleticism, but he's a long way from being that kind of baseball player.

Pitchers

PLAYER	TEAM	LVL	AGE	W	L	SV	IP	H	HR	BB	SO	GB%	BABIP	STUFF	WHIP	ERA	SIERA	DERA	EqH9	EqHR9	EqBB9	EqSO9	VORP
K. Benson	OKL	AAA	34	4	5	0	68²	78	5	23	49	48%	.327	-6	1.47	5.24	4.38	6.25	10.2	1.2	3.1	4.8	-5.6
—	TEX	MLB	34	1	1	0	22¹	33	6	12	11	34%	.329	-32	2.01	8.46	6.13	8.22	12.5	2.0	3.9	3.9	-6.9
R. Bermudez	SPO	A-	24	1	2	3	32¹	20	1	18	44	46%	.275	5	1.18	1.67	2.79	3.14	8.2	1.6	6.3	7.5	7.5
W. Boscan	HIC	A	19	6	8	0	105¹	105	7	19	59	50%	.278	-12	1.18	3.59	4.44	6.75	10.7	2.0	2.8	2.3	-13.6
W. Eyre	OKL	AAA	30	0	0	2	34¹	24	1	12	25	54%	.242	0	1.05	2.10	4.12	2.34	6.3	0.6	3.3	5.2	11.5
—	TEX	MLB	30	0	0	0	18	18	0	6	8	39%	.310	-15	1.33	4.50	5.52	3.86	9.9	0.0	2.8	3.9	3.0
W. Font	HIC	A	19	8	3	0	108¹	93	4	59	105	39%	.293	-2	1.40	3.49	4.12	6.04	10.0	1.7	6.7	4.9	-5.8
M. Kirkman*	BAK	A+	22	4	1	0	48	43	1	18	54	44%	.336	16	1.27	2.06	3.07	3.92	9.9	1.0	4.3	6.2	7.7
—	FRI	AA	22	5	7	0	96²	93	9	43	64	47%	.282	-13	1.41	4.19	4.80	6.01	9.8	1.9	4.1	4.5	-5.2
M. Main	BAK	A+	20	4	6	0	58	72	9	37	49	48%	.350	-23	1.88	6.83	4.74	9.25	13.1	2.9	6.8	4.2	-22.1
L. Mendoza	OKL	AAA	25	6	7	0	111¹	130	4	50	78	55%	.344	-8	1.62	4.53	4.66	5.29	10.6	0.8	4.1	4.8	2.5
Y. Nam*	HIC	A	21	9	1	0	88¹	76	8	34	102	46%	.296	-19	1.25	3.77	3.04	6.52	10.4	2.4	5.1	6.1	-9.0
Z. Phillips*	BAK	A+	22	2	3	2	44	19	1	11	46	60%	.164	19	0.68	1.23	2.73	2.25	4.7	0.8	2.9	5.3	15.9
—	FRI	AA	22	0	0	2	33²	27	1	19	29	54%	.255	3	1.37	1.60	4.39	3.76	7.5	0.8	4.7	5.7	6.7
C. Pimentel	HIC	A	19	5	4	1	123	120	15	35	101	44%	.292	-29	1.26	2.93	3.83	5.23	11.6	3.0	4.1	4.2	3.2
O. Poveda	FRI	AA	21	11	5	0	130¹	133	11	48	73	52%	.286	-4	1.39	4.14	4.90	6.01	10.1	1.7	3.5	3.8	-7.0
N. Ramirez	HIC	A	20	3	6	0	66¹	58	8	41	56	31%	.269	-22	1.49	4.75	4.93	7.67	10.7	3.1	7.7	4.1	-14.1
J. Rupe	OKL	AAA	26	5	7	1	89	115	5	41	62	58%	.365	-23	1.75	6.67	4.66	7.98	11.9	1.1	4.2	4.7	-23.6
—	TEX	MLB	26	0	0	0	4²	12	2	5	2	51%	.455	-47	3.64	15.43	6.74	14.40	21.6	3.6	7.2	3.6	-4.9
P. Strop	FRI	AA	24	5	5	4	51¹	48	1	29	48	53%	.315	-3	1.50	4.38	4.17	5.89	9.2	0.7	5.1	6.5	-2.1
—	OKL	AAA	24	1	1	1	12²	13	2	4	13	44%	.324	-8	1.34	7.82	3.27	8.25	9.8	2.3	3.0	7.5	-3.7
—	TEX	MLB	24	0	0	0	7	6	0	4	9	47%	.353	7	1.43	7.71	3.12	6.75	8.1	0.0	4.1	10.8	-0.9

Joaquin Benoit missed the 2009 season recovering from surgery to repair a torn rotator cuff and will be trying to latch on in somebody's camp to restart his career. ⊘ After not pitching in the big leagues for two years, Kris Benson made eight god-awful appearances for the Rangers and spent the winter looking for another spring training invite. ⊘ It's hard to get too worked up about a 24-year-old dominating a short-season league, but Cuban defector Rainer Bermudez showed 94-97 mph gas with Spokane and could move up quickly. ⊘ Venezuelan Wilfredo Boscan has immaculate control and a deep arsenal, but scouts are still looking for a true big-league out pitch from him. ⊘ Middle reliever Willie Eyre came back from 2008 Tommy John surgery, but a groin injury contributed to his being crowded out of the pen picture repeatedly. ⊘ Wilmer Font is an imposing figure on the mound and one of the hardest throwers in the system, but he's still much more thrower than pitcher. ⊘ Once one of the top arms in the system, but someone who stalled at the upper levels, righty Eric Hurley took another step backward by missing all of 2009 following shoulder surgery. ⊘ Plagued by injuries and severe control problems in the past, tall lefty Michael Kirkman suddenly found the strike zone with his 90-94 mph fastball, which got him added to the 40-man roster. ⊘ One of the highest high-ceiling arms in the system, athletic righty Michael Main suffered through most of 2009 with an undiagnosed illness, but he's healthy and expected to be back to form this spring. ⊘ Luis Mendoza is an unspectacular sinker specialist who will struggle to get chances, especially in this pitching-packed system. ⊘ Korean lefty Yoon-Hee Nam only throws in the mid- to upper 80s, but his curveball can sometimes be a thing of beauty, giving him some sort of shot at a bullpen job in the future. ⊘ Moved to the bullpen in 2009, Zach Phillips is a low-velo lefty with a good breaking ball that he used to compile a 1.39 ERA across two levels; he has been added to the 40-man roster. ⊘ Another young arm in the system, but one with the command and polish of a veteran, Carlos Pimentel has average velocity, quality secondary stuff, and a bit of projection. ⊘ Venezuelan control artist Omar Poveda has regressed the last couple of years while trying to find a pitch to miss bats at the more advanced levels. ⊘ Former first-round pick Neil Ramirez had a troubling full-season debut due to injuries and command issues. ⊘ Having taken their spin to see if there was anything there with Josh Rupe (there wasn't), the organization got him through waivers and inflicted him on Oklahoma; The Weather Channel reports that he's headed north toward Kansas City, with a chance of projectile showers on whatever trailer park is closest to Omaha. ⊘ A converted shortstop, Pedro Strop has a mid-90s fastball, but the list of positive things to say about him pretty much ends there.

MANAGER: RON WASHINGTON

YEAR	TEAM	W-L	Pythag +/−	Avg PC	100+ P	120+ P	QS	BQS	REL	REL w Zero R	IBB	Subs	PH	PH Avg	PH HR	SB2	CS2	SB3	CS3	SAC Att	SAC %	POS SAC	Squeeze	Swing	In Play
2007	TEX	75-87	-3	89.8	43	0	48	4	467	290	38	64	89	.215	4	76	23	12	2	82	69.5%	54	1	121	101
2008	TEX	79-83	4	91.3	54	1	52	7	457	261	44	38	117	.250	0	71	23	10	2	62	59.7%	33	0	132	93
2009	TEX	87-75	1	96.7	67	5	66	10	436	283	14	12	48	.119	0	117	31	32	3	55	72.7%	35	4	128	96

Washington's coaching staff still isn't exactly stocked with his selections, with pitching coach Mike Maddux being a deliberate acquisition by higher authority and new hitting coach (and former pennant-winning Rockies skipper) Clint Hurdle brought in to replace highly regarded hitting coach Rudy Jaramillo after the Cubs bought away the latter. That shouldn't be an instance of hauling in a stalking horse, but you never know, as "Wash" has been in hot water before. The pen was a better unit and the rotation came along extremely well, and there's no harm in sharing credit to Washington's benefit; an improved infield defense that helped create this success bore some of his stamp as a former instructor. On offense, he's becoming more and more willing to let loose with the running game, ranking third in stolen-base attempts and first in attempted and successful double steals (17-for-19); those kinds of numbers figure to go up if Borbon is starting in center. The other added kink was a few squeezes, which you can again interpret as exploiting the addition of people who can run. If there's an area of complaint, it might be the amount of time he took to decide that maybe Josh Hamilton is not really a center fielder, but it's a minor complaint at most.

Toronto Blue Jays

We had such high hopes for the J. P. Ricciardi–led Blue Jays when Ricciardi took over as Toronto's general manager after the 2001 season. Formerly Billy Beane's head of player development with the A's and a longtime Oakland scout, Ricciardi arrived in Toronto with an exciting mix of scouting and development experience, faith in advanced statistical analysis (one of his first hires, Keith Law, came from our ranks), and exposure to winning on limited means. This seemed to be exactly the combination Toronto required to compete with the mighty Yankees and Red Sox in the American League East.

Early on, we praised Ricciardi for running the Jays like a business, cutting loose sunk costs, shedding bad contracts, scaling back the team's tendency to take excessive financial gambles on largely unknown Latin American amateurs, and focusing on restocking the farm system with developmentally advanced college players from the domestic draft. It soon became apparent, however, that while Ricciardi was good at eliminating the inefficiencies left over from the Gord Ash administration, his team-building skills were sorely lacking. The first sign came after the 2004 season, when Ricciardi signed a declining and injury-prone Corey Koskie, a Type-A free agent, to a three-year, $17.5 million contract while simultaneously failing to offer departing free-agent Carlos Delgado arbitration, punting three top draft picks in the process. With the one remaining pick he had among the top 85 slots in the 2005 draft—a protected pick, due to the team's 94-loss season the previous year—Ricciardi chose left-handed college pitcher Ricky Romero over slugging shortstop Troy Tulowitzki.

The year prior, Ricciardi had used a third-round pick received as compensation for Kelvim Escobar from the Angels to select Adam Lind, who emerged as the team's best hitter in 2009, but the success of Lind has proven to be more the exception than the rule for Ricciardi. The GM failed to adjust his draft philosophy in his eight years in Toronto, almost completely undermining his player-development reputation in the process. In the top 15 rounds of his first four drafts, Ricciardi drafted just three high-school players, none above the seventh round, and thus far 2006 first-rounder Travis Snider, who should prove to be Ricciardi's best pick in eight drafts, has been the only high-school player drafted by Ricciardi to reach the major leagues. Almost pathologically averse to high-risk, high-reward prep picks, Ricciardi wound up filling the Jays' system not with championship-level players but with mediocrities (Table 1). Mostly he chose low-ceiling college pitchers and unathletic underpowered infielders who will take a walk. Though these players are capable of fleshing out a major-league roster, they are unable to help balance the scales against the spending power of the Yankees and Red Sox as the Rays' (admittedly higher) picks would soon do.

Soon after the 2005 draft fiasco, team owner Ted Rogers, with his company, Rogers Communications, flush with money from the wireless boom, greatly expanded the team payroll. Ricciardi spent the newfound cash on players who were fragile, overrated, or both: B. J. Ryan, A. J. Burnett, Bengie Molina, and, via trade, Troy Glaus, Lyle Overbay, and Shea Hillenbrand. He then later sank the remainder into outsize extensions

BLUE JAYS PROSPECTUS
2009 W-L: 75-87, 4th in AL East

Pythag	85-77	6th
RS/G	4.9	6th
RA/G	4.8	11th
EqA	.264	6th
EqBRR	9.7	2nd
SNWP	.505	8th
WXRL	4.82	12th
FRAr	4.53	7th
DE	.682	10th
PADE	-3.03	14th
Salary	$80.5	8th
Attend	1.88	10th

Ballpark: Rogers Centre (3-yr. PF: 981). Favors lefty power, and the turf generates extra XBHs

2009: J.P.'s final ride went nowhere, but Hill's comeback and retooled rotation provide watch-worthy play

2010: Trading Doc hurts, keeping ahead of O's tough, but adding the Walrus to Hill, Snider, and Lind equals fun Fab Four

Action Items: New management's made its big moves. Sunshine *and* turf? Sod the Centre!

Table 1. Don't Get Excited: Notable Draft Picks of the Ricciardi Era

Year	Player (Round), Preps Picks in Bold
2002	SS Russ Adams (1), RHP David Bush (2)
2003	SS Aaron Hill (1), RHP Shawn Marcum (3)
2004	LHP David Purcey (1), LHP Zach Jackson* (1), C Curtis Thigpen (2), 1B Adam Lind* (3), RHP Casey Janssen (4), RHP Jesse Litsch (24)
2005	LHP Ricky Romero (1), RHP Robert Ray (7), RHP Reidier Gonzalez (19)
2006	**OF Travis Snider (1)**, C Brian Jeroloman (6), 2B Scott Campbell (10)
2007	**3B Kevin Ahrens* (1)**, C J. P. Arencibia (1), LHP Brett Cecil* (1A), **SS Justin Jackson* (1A)**, RHP Trystan Magnuson* (1A), LHP Brad Mills (4), LHP Marc Rzepczynski (5), 2B Brad Emaus (11), 2B Darin Mastroianni (16)
2008	1B David Cooper (1), **CF Kenny Wilson (2)**, OF Eric Thames (7), RHP Daniel Farquhar (10), RHP Robert Bell (18), LHP Chuck Huggins (23)
2009	RHP Stephen Jenkins (1), **LHP James Paxton* (1A)**

*Compensation picks: Jackson and Lind from the Angels for Kelvim Escobar, Ahrens and Jackson from the Rangers for Frank Catalanotto, Cecil from the Angels for Justin Speier, Magnuson from the Cubs for Ted Lilly, Paxton from the Yankees for A. J. Burnett (Paxton didn't sign).

for Ash-era draft picks Vernon Wells and Alex Rios, contracts that remain among the worst in the game. (At least the White Sox's Kenny Williams mercifully relieved the Jays of the $59.7 million owed to Rios over the next five years via a waiver claim last August.) Law jumped ship in May 2006, and by the 2008 edition of this book, we were calling for Ricciardi's dismissal, describing the 2008 Blue Jays as "more former GM Gord Ash's Jays supplemented by Ted Rogers' dollars than ... a team built by J. P. Ricciardi."

The axe finally came down on the penultimate day of the 2009 season, but mirroring Ricciardi's habit of replacing his discarded managers with one of these managers' own coaches, team president and CEO Paul Beeston announced that Ricciardi's permanent replacement would be Ricciardi's assistant, Alex Anthopoulos. The 32-year-old Montreal native and former scouting coordinator had been with the team for six of Ricciardi's eight years and had been part of a player personnel triumvirate with Ricciardi and scouting director Tony LaCava, who in turn was promoted to be Anthopoulos's assistant. Given Ricciardi's failures in the draft, replacing him with two of his former scouting directors seems more than a little problematic, though it suggest that Beeston believed that it wasn't the front office's intelligence that was the problem in the draft and beyond, but the head that was making the final decisions.

Indeed, after taking over as GM, Anthopoulos said that he intends to rebuild the team around a talented core of players in their early 20s, which will mean taking more risks in the draft. He quickly armed himself to ex-

ecute such a plan by making risky arbitration offers to Type-A free-agent shortstop Marco Scutaro and Type-B free-agent catcher Rod Barajas (both of whom declined), netting a pair of early 2010 picks when Scutaro signed a two-year deal with the rival Red Sox. Anthopoulos has also stated his intent to overhaul the Jays' scouting and development process, more evidence that he was dissatisfied with his old boss's way of doing things.

In his first major transaction as Toronto GM, Anthopoulos began his rebuild by succeeding where Ricciardi had failed, trading veteran ace Roy Halladay for three minor-leaguers who instantly took over the top three spots on the organizational prospect list. Halladay was due to become a free agent after 2010, but Ricciardi's efforts to trade him at the 2009 deadline, when his value was highest due to his ability to influence two pennant races under his existing contract, were the last in a series of public relations disasters the Jays endured during Ricciardi's tenure. Though Ricciardi generated a ton of grist for the rumor mill, he ultimately came up empty-handed after asking too much from all comers, leaving Halladay, the team's fans, and his fellow GMs all feeling used and dissatisfied. The eventual National League champion Phillies opted instead to trade a quartet of prospects in a deal for Indians ace Cliff Lee, who had helped lead them to the World Series, but the Phillies interest in Halladay had been so strong that they were willing to trade Lee in December in order to restock their system so that they could spend three more of their top prospects on Halladay.

Of the three players acquired from Philadelphia, righty Kyle Drabek and catcher Travis d'Arnaud are former first-round picks who project as potential above-average starting players. Drabek could open 2011 in the major-league rotation and mature into a front-end rotation starter, while d'Arnaud is further away but has athleticism behind the plate and power at it. The third player acquired from Philadelphia was Michael Taylor, a massive corner outfielder with power and speed who makes contact and hits for average and hit well after a late-season promotion to Triple-A last year. Anthopoulos, however, immediately flipped him to Oakland for Brett Wallace, a third-base prospect whose profile trends toward the sort of infielders preferred by Ricciardi. Indeed, Ricciardi had tried to draft Wallace out of high school in 2005, though Wallace had already committed to ASU.

Wallace's prospect bona fides are solid. He was one of the top college hitters in the nation at Arizona State and the Cardinals' first-round pick in 2008 (13th overall), but he's a thick-bodied, unathletic player (cruelly nicknamed "the Walrus" by scouts) who will be moved to first base by the Jays. Though he arrived in the pros as an accomplished hitter, he doesn't have the power profile to be an above-average first baseman in the game's toughest division. There's some chance that Wallace might turn into the next Kevin Youkilis, but compared with Taylor, he's the low-risk/low-reward alternative to a player who could prove to be a true offensive force in the American League in the coming decade. To paraphrase Pete Townshend, meet the new Overbay, same as the old Overbay.

Anthopoulos gave up another high-ceiling right-field prospect when he traded Yohermyn Chavez to the Mariners with frustrating reliever Brandon League for frustrated starter Brandon Morrow. Morrow is a pitching talent worth the divestment of a significant prospect. But as a 25-year-old whose service clock is already ticking, he seems a bit of an odd addition for a Jays team that is a long way from making waves in their division, particularly with the Rays now among the league's best teams and the Orioles finally beginning to coalesce around some young talent of their own.

Not that he had an alternative, but Anthopoulos has clearly surrendered 2010 to rebuilding, something telegraphed by the stopgap signings of Alex Gonzalez to fill in for Scutaro at shortstop and John Buck to help replace Barajas behind the plate, but one wonders just how deep he's willing to dig to rebuild the franchise's foundations. When he acquired Wallace, Anthopoulos publicly fantasized about Wallace and Aaron Hill becoming institutions on the right side of Toronto's infield. Good as he is, Hill is a player with his share of faults. His reasonable contract (which pays him $9 million over the next two seasons followed by a trio of club options worth a combined $26 million) would be better employed in a trade following an age-27 career year, all the better to bring in multiple prospects capable of contributing to the next contending Jays team.

The Jays do have one small but significant advantage over their US counterparts in rebuilding: the world economic situation has broken in their favor. With the Canadian dollar strong against the US dollar, the Jays currently enjoy the equivalent of a five percent discount on any contract they sign.

There's little doubt that in just three months Anthopoulos has been a significant improvement over his predecessor, but whatever long-term goals he can pursue face the same challenge that Ricciardi was forever up against: the bar for contention is alarmingly high in this division. There can be no quick fixes in the AL East. The Rays spent the better part of the last decade building their 2008 pennant winners, and the roots of the Orioles' current resurgence already date back several years and have yet to effect meaningful change in the standings. After a decade and a half of mismanagement, the Blue Jays cannot be rebuilt in a year or two. It will take time, diligence, and more blood than Anthopoulos might be willing to let and more treasure than he might be allowed to spend.

HITTERS

J. P. Arencibia   C   Bats: R   Throws: R   Height: 6' 1"   Weight: 215   Born: January 5, 1986   Age: 24

YEAR	TEAM	LVL	AGE	PA	R	2B	3B	HR	RBI	BB	SO	SB	CS	EqBRR	AVG	OBP	SLG	EqAVG	EqOBP	EqSLG	EqA	VORP	WARP	DEFENSE
2007	AUB	A-	21	249	31	17	1	3	25	14	56	0	0	-0.6	.254	.309	.377	.226	.261	.336	.206	-2.2	-1.0	54-C -4
2008	DUN	A+	22	262	38	22	0	13	62	11	46	0	0	1.3	.315	.344	.560	.287	.312	.494	.270	14.0	1.6	54-C -1
2008	NHP	AA	22	275	32	14	0	14	43	7	55	0	0	-0.7	.282	.302	.496	.261	.279	.447	.246	5.9	0.6	49-C -1
2009	LVG	AAA	23	500	67	32	1	21	75	26	114	0	1	-1.8	.236	.284	.444	.211	.254	.391	.219	-1.0	-0.8	103-C -6
2010	TOR	MLB	24	431	50	20	1	17	58	24	109	0	1	-0.3	.237	.284	.420	.239	.285	.413	.235	6.5	0.5	88-C -2

Breakout: 19%   Improve: 46%   Collapse: 16%   Attrition: 10%   MLB: 6%   Comparables: Stine Poole, Giuseppe Chiaramonte, Nick Hundley, Jeff Hall

A 2007 supplemental first-round pick out of the University of Tennessee, Arencibia was supposed to be the Jays' catcher of the future, but despite spending all of his third pro season in Triple-A last year, he looks far from ready. Arencibia has power, but his plate discipline is a disaster, as he struck out once every 4.4 plate appearances in Las Vegas last year while walking once every 19.2, a strikeout-to-walk ratio of 4.1. He's athletic behind the plate, and his throwing is seen as an asset behind the plate, but his kill rate on stolen-base attempts dropped to 25 percent; all in all, his defense is still a work in progress. Taken all together and barring improvements to his approach at the plate, he's little better than a latter-day incarnation of the man he might eventually replace.

Rod Barajas — C

Bats: R Throws: R Height: 6' 2" Weight: 245 Born: September 5, 1975 Age: 34

YEAR	TEAM	LVL	AGE	PA	R	2B	3B	HR	RBI	BB	SO	SB	CS	EqBRR	AVG	OBP	SLG	EqAVG	EqOBP	EqSLG	EqA	VORP	WARP	DEFENSE			
2007	PHI	MLB	31	146	16	8	0	4	10	21	24	0	1	-0.5	.230	.352	.393	.230	.356	.402	.261	6.6	1.2	34-C	3		
2008	TOR	MLB	32	377	44	23	0	11	49	17	61	0	0	-4.8	.249	.294	.410	.253	.299	.417	.247	10.9	2.7	88-C	10	3-1B	0
2009	TOR	MLB	33	460	43	19	0	19	71	20	76	1	0	-1.6	.226	.258	.403	.230	.261	.404	.230	5.6	0.9	109-C	3		
2010	TOR	MLB	34	342	37	15	1	13	48	25	66	1	1	-1.3	.242	.306	.421	.244	.305	.407	.247	8.9	1.3	83-C	3		

Breakout: 15% Improve: 42% Collapse: 23% Attrition: 16% MLB: 95% Comparables: Damian Miller, Lance Parrish, Jose Molina, Dan Wilson

If all Arencibia does is improve his defense, he'll be Rod Barajas. Barajas doesn't have as much power as Arencibia, but he doesn't strike out as much, either, and the pop he has is enough to separate him from his catch-and-throw brethren. If you're going to start a defense-first catcher like Barajas, who has thrown out 34 percent of opposing basestealers in each of the last two years, it doesn't hurt to have one who can pop 15 to 20 homers. Still, any team that has to start Barajas's career .284 on-base percentage will have to win despite him.

Jose Bautista — UT

Bats: R Throws: R Height: 6' 0" Weight: 195 Born: October 19, 1980 Age: 29

YEAR	TEAM	LVL	AGE	PA	R	2B	3B	HR	RBI	BB	SO	SB	CS	EqBRR	AVG	OBP	SLG	EqAVG	EqOBP	EqSLG	EqA	VORP	WARP	DEFENSE			
2007	PIT	MLB	26	614	75	36	2	15	63	68	101	6	3	-3.0	.254	.339	.414	.264	.350	.425	.270	19.8	0.6	119-3B	-13	15-RF	0
2008	PIT	MLB	27	363	38	15	0	12	44	38	77	1	1	-4.3	.242	.325	.404	.253	.331	.421	.261	8.6	1.1	81-3B	1		
2008	TOR	MLB	27	61	7	2	0	3	10	2	14	0	0	-0.1	.214	.237	.411	.218	.241	.418	.224	-1.4	0.0	5-3B	2	3-1B	-1
2009	TOR	MLB	28	404	54	13	3	13	40	56	85	4	0	3.5	.235	.349	.408	.243	.355	.416	.273	14.2	2.3	36-LF	0	32-RF	5
2010	TOR	MLB	29	516	68	24	2	18	66	63	107	4	2	-0.6	.249	.346	.433	.253	.346	.425	.269	15.8	1.7	106-LF	0		

Breakout: 14% Improve: 33% Collapse: 2% Attrition: 4% MLB: 99% Comparables: Bob Nieman, Marty Cordova, Dustan Mohr, Candy Maldonado

In addition to giving Barajas and his .258 OBP 110 starts in 2009, the Blue Jays started Jose Bautista at a corner position 89 times. Like Barajas, Bautista has some value as a reserve, but he's woefully overextended as a starter. Bautista has played everywhere but shortstop and catcher, will take his walks, and has 15-homer power. These skills are undermined by his complete inability to hit for average (.238 career) and his inability to be particularly good defensively anywhere, though he has at least made significant strides at third, his "natural" position. With Joe Inglett in Texas and the new Jays administration unwilling to use Bautista to fill one of their corner outfield vacancies, Bautista may finally this year assume the roving utility role for which he's best suited.

Scott Campbell — 3B

Bats: L Throws: R Height: 6' 0" Weight: 200 Born: September 25, 1984 Age: 25

YEAR	TEAM	LVL	AGE	PA	R	2B	3B	HR	RBI	BB	SO	SB	CS	EqBRR	AVG	OBP	SLG	EqAVG	EqOBP	EqSLG	EqA	VORP	WARP	DEFENSE			
2007	LNS	A	22	468	68	17	4	7	43	68	56	4	5	-3.7	.279	.390	.397	.250	.344	.351	.250	9.9	0.7	102-2B	-4		
2008	NHP	AA	23	487	70	21	2	9	46	66	63	2	6	-4.4	.302	.398	.427	.280	.361	.394	.265	17.0	1.2	105-2B	-7		
2009	NHP	AA	24	213	31	8	1	3	19	28	26	4	0	-0.5	.269	.373	.374	.255	.340	.351	.249	0.9	-0.4	26-3B	-4	3-2B	0
2009	LVG	AAA	24	113	17	3	1	0	6	14	9	0	0	0.3	.229	.327	.281	.204	.297	.255	.201	-3.2	-1.0	22-3B	-4	4-2B	-1
2010	TOR	MLB	25	424	51	19	2	6	33	47	70	2	2	-1.4	.248	.332	.356	.253	.338	.354	.241	2.6	-0.5	86-3B	-7		

Breakout: 7% Improve: 26% Collapse: 27% Attrition: 12% MLB: 5% Comparables: Mike Hart, Tim Leiper, Marc Marini, Michael McCain

With Aaron Hill making a strong comeback from a 2008 concussion, Campbell was shifted from second to third in his fourth pro season. Theoretically, that clears Campbell's path a bit, but his lack of power is likely to be more problematic at the hot corner than it would have been at the keystone. Campbell has a tremendous plate approach that has seen him draw more walks than strikeouts every year of his career, but he struggled in his Triple-A debut last year, he's already 25, and he isn't particularly athletic. His hopes of becoming the first native of New Zealand to make the majors are most likely to be realized in some sort of utility role.

Yohermyn Chavez   RF

Bats: R   Throws: R   Height: 6' 3"   Weight: 220   Born: January 26, 1989   Age: 21

YEAR	TEAM	LVL	AGE	PA	R	2B	3B	HR	RBI	BB	SO	SB	CS	EqBRR	AVG	OBP	SLG	EqAVG	EqOBP	EqSLG	EqA	VORP	WARP	DEFENSE		
2007	BLJ	Rk	18	203	29	12	2	6	21	20	50	7	2	0.0	.301	.389	.494	.247	.309	.398	.246	0.8	-0.8	45-LF	-5	
2008	LNS	A	19	439	40	20	2	7	39	25	128	9	5	-3.8	.211	.272	.323	.197	.242	.294	.183	-25.1	-5.6	101-LF	-21	
2009	LNS	A	20	569	87	22	6	21	89	40	137	10	6	-2.2	.283	.346	.474	.246	.292	.398	.239	-2.0	-1.9	110-RF	-9	20-LF -5
2010	SEA	MLB	21	576	62	25	2	14	60	38	161	5	4	-1.7	.222	.282	.354	.226	.282	.359	.215	-14.1	-2.2	135-RF	-6	

Breakout: 27%   Improve: 54%   Collapse: 19%   Attrition: 6%   MLB: 1%   Comparables: Andrew Vessel, Jorge Padilla, Matthew Allegra, Jason Place

This big Venezuelan profiles as a classic, power-hitting right fielder. He's not much in the field, but that doesn't matter, given his bat. Last year, he had a breakout season while repeating A-ball as a 20-year-old, giving us a good idea of what his skills might look like in full bloom. He has a bit of speed, draws just enough walks, and strikes out a lot, but will hit for a respectable average with a lot of power. He's still young and raw, and he'll start out in High-A this year. Having been flipped to Seattle in the Brandon Morrow trade, he gives the Mariners a legitimate middle-of-the-order prospect.

David Cooper   1B

Bats: L   Throws: L   Height: 6' 0"   Weight: 175   Born: February 12, 1987   Age: 23

YEAR	TEAM	LVL	AGE	PA	R	2B	3B	HR	RBI	BB	SO	SB	CS	EqBRR	AVG	OBP	SLG	EqAVG	EqOBP	EqSLG	EqA	VORP	WARP	DEFENSE	
2008	LNS	A	21	106	15	10	0	2	17	10	14	0	0	-0.7	.354	.415	.521	.316	.368	.449	.282	3.6	0.4	21-1B	0
2008	DUN	A+	21	102	10	9	0	1	13	10	16	0	0	-1.1	.304	.373	.435	.277	.333	.383	.251	0.0	-0.1	21-1B	-1
2008	AUB	A-	21	95	10	10	1	2	21	10	16	0	1	-1.8	.341	.411	.553	.295	.347	.489	.283	3.4	0.4	17-1B	-1
2009	NHP	AA	22	538	62	32	0	10	66	59	92	0	0	-3.3	.258	.340	.389	.248	.317	.375	.243	-10.0	-1.8	92-1B	-5
2010	TOR	MLB	23	504	52	26	1	12	65	47	100	0	1	-2.1	.253	.323	.394	.257	.327	.395	.247	-1.8	-0.4	91-1B	-2

Breakout: 15%   Improve: 47%   Collapse: 16%   Attrition: 6%   MLB: 1%   Comparables: Joe DeSa, Billy McMillon, Jason Friedman, Tim Raley

The 17th overall pick in 2008, Cooper had a terrific debut in 2008, hitting .333/.399/.502 across three levels, but Double-A threw cold water on his fast dash to the big leagues. He maintained a strong plate approach, but as an offense-only first baseman (and we mean *only*), he still has a lot to prove. The key to his major-league potential is his power, or lack thereof. Cooper has 61 doubles in 841 minor-league plate appearances, and he needs to start turning those into home runs. If he can do that without suffering a spike in his strikeouts or collapsing his batting average, he'll pull out a career as a major-league starter, but that's a mighty big if. His poor showing in the Arizona Fall League wasn't encouraging, and he has since been blocked by the acquisition of Brett Wallace.

Brian Dopirak   1B

Bats: R   Throws: R   Height: 6' 4"   Weight: 235   Born: December 20, 1983   Age: 26

YEAR	TEAM	LVL	AGE	PA	R	2B	3B	HR	RBI	BB	SO	SB	CS	EqBRR	AVG	OBP	SLG	EqAVG	EqOBP	EqSLG	EqA	VORP	WARP	DEFENSE		
2007	DAY	A+	23	379	49	23	0	17	64	23	91	1	1	0.0	.277	.325	.490	.241	.280	.419	.239	-5.1	-1.2	33-1B	-5	
2007	TEN	AA	23	81	2	1	0	1	4	3	19	0	0	-0.3	.218	.247	.269	.203	.222	.253	.148	-7.3	-1.1	18-1B	-1	
2008	DUN	A+	24	463	77	25	2	27	88	47	100	0	0	-3.0	.308	.382	.577	.258	.317	.460	.265	7.0	-0.6	84-1B	-11	5-LF -1
2008	NHP	AA	24	91	5	6	0	2	13	2	10	1	1	-0.9	.287	.297	.425	.264	.275	.379	.226	-2.5	-0.7	17-1B	-3	
2009	NHP	AA	25	366	44	29	1	19	68	35	75	1	3	-6.4	.308	.374	.576	.270	.324	.484	.271	4.6	-0.3	50-1B	-7	
2009	LVG	AAA	25	232	33	13	1	8	34	13	44	0	0	-0.1	.330	.366	.509	.286	.319	.441	.260	-0.2	-0.1	41-1B	-1	
2010	TOR	MLB	26	538	55	25	1	19	68	38	147	1	2	-2.3	.241	.298	.411	.245	.299	.405	.239	-6.1	-1.2	84-1B	-5	

Breakout: 14%   Improve: 33%   Collapse: 20%   Attrition: 11%   MLB: 9%   Comparables: Lyle Mouton, Chris Kirgan, Leo Daigle, Shelley Duncan

Since being salvaged from the Cubs' system prior to 2008, Dopirak has done nothing but rake across three levels of the Jays' system over the last two years. He was rewarded with a spot on the 40-man roster in November. He could keep first base warm for Wallace if the Jays manage to flip Lyle Overbay, who is in the final year of his contract, but given that he's still just 26, Dopirak deserves a longer look from one organization or another.

Brad Emaus 2B
Bats: R Throws: R Height: 5' 11" Weight: 200 Born: March 28, 1986 Age: 24

YEAR	TEAM	LVL	AGE	PA	R	2B	3B	HR	RBI	BB	SO	SB	CS	EqBRR	AVG	OBP	SLG	EqAVG	EqOBP	EqSLG	EqA	VORP	WARP	DEFENSE			
2007	AUB	A-	21	152	21	6	0	2	14	12	26	2	0	-0.7	.228	.298	.316	.206	.257	.270	.185	-7.7	-0.7	26-3B	4	4-2B	0
2008	DUN	A+	22	543	87	34	3	12	71	60	56	12	4	0.4	.302	.380	.463	.278	.343	.423	.267	19.0	1.2	97-2B	-12	13-3B	3
2009	NHP	AA	23	581	67	28	2	10	67	59	69	10	3	-1.3	.253	.336	.376	.244	.310	.368	.242	5.3	1.8	129-2B	10		
2010	TOR	MLB	24	498	62	25	1	12	58	46	76	5	2	-0.4	.252	.325	.390	.256	.326	.389	.249	9.3	1.0	108-2B	0		

Breakout: 14% Improve: 48% Collapse: 18% Attrition: 6%   MLB: 6%   Comparables: Richard Lewis, Manny Martinez, Brad Dandridge, Steve Springer

With Campbell at the hot corner, Emaus would be in line to take over second base should the Jays decide to cash in Aaron Hill as part of their rebuilding, or he would have been, had he done anything to embolden the Jays in 2009. Struggling after making the leap to Double-A last year, Emaus let his frustration show in his play, which is problematic for a player whose hard-nosed style is a large part of his appeal. Emaus is a solid but unspectacular defender with a bit of speed and an excellent approach at the plate, but he'll need to recoup the power and intensity he lost in 2009 and survive Triple-A before he becomes a viable candidate for the big club.

Edwin Encarnacion 3B
Bats: R Throws: R Height: 6' 1" Weight: 215 Born: January 7, 1983 Age: 27

YEAR	TEAM	LVL	AGE	PA	R	2B	3B	HR	RBI	BB	SO	SB	CS	EqBRR	AVG	OBP	SLG	EqAVG	EqOBP	EqSLG	EqA	VORP	WARP	DEFENSE	
2007	CIN	MLB	24	556	66	25	1	16	76	39	86	8	1	0.8	.289	.356	.438	.289	.356	.436	.276	21.5	1.0	131-3B	-11
2008	CIN	MLB	25	582	75	29	1	26	68	61	102	1	0	1.1	.251	.340	.466	.257	.344	.475	.279	26.5	0.7	139-3B	-18
2009	CIN	MLB	26	165	10	6	1	5	16	24	38	1	1	-2.8	.209	.333	.374	.221	.339	.407	.257	4.3	0.0	40-3B	-4
2009	TOR	MLB	26	173	25	5	1	8	23	13	29	1	0	2.1	.240	.306	.442	.248	.312	.451	.263	5.3	0.9	41-3B	2
2010	TOR	MLB	27	567	73	25	1	27	81	56	99	4	1	0.2	.263	.348	.477	.265	.347	.465	.281	27.8	2.3	137-3B	-6

Breakout: 15% Improve: 52% Collapse: 10% Attrition: 3%   MLB: 92%   Comparables: Doug Rader, Tim Wallach, Tony Batista, Puddin' Head Jones

After a slow start, Encarnacion fractured his wrist 19 games into the 2009 season, sat out two months, and then, after a strong return in July, was flipped to Toronto in the deal that brought Scott Rolen closer to home in Cincinnati. His two months in Toronto followed a similar pattern minus the injury: bad August, strong September. Thus, entering his age-27 season, Encarnacion is no closer to realizing his potential. He might actually be further away, given that he'll no longer be playing his home games at the Gap (.274/.368/.476 career vs. .250/.320/.427 elsewhere). A brutal fielder, Encarnacion has survived thus far on the promise in his bat, but he's in danger of breaking that promise.

Aaron Hill 2B
Bats: R Throws: R Height: 5' 11" Weight: 205 Born: March 21, 1982 Age: 28

YEAR	TEAM	LVL	AGE	PA	R	2B	3B	HR	RBI	BB	SO	SB	CS	EqBRR	AVG	OBP	SLG	EqAVG	EqOBP	EqSLG	EqA	VORP	WARP	DEFENSE	
2007	TOR	MLB	25	657	87	47	2	17	78	41	102	4	3	-0.3	.291	.333	.459	.292	.335	.460	.271	29.2	6.7	158-2B	28
2008	TOR	MLB	26	229	19	14	0	2	20	16	31	4	2	1.9	.263	.324	.361	.270	.330	.363	.248	3.6	-0.3	54-2B	-7
2009	TOR	MLB	27	734	103	37	0	36	108	42	98	6	2	1.4	.286	.330	.499	.294	.337	.503	.283	41.6	5.6	153-2B	8
2010	TOR	MLB	28	627	84	31	1	27	88	48	99	5	4	0.6	.280	.338	.477	.283	.340	.470	.275	29.6	3.9	144-2B	6

Breakout: 15% Improve: 53% Collapse: 11% Attrition: 7%   MLB: 99%   Comparables: Hubie Brooks, Bill Mazeroski, Davey Johnson, Mike Lansing

Hill seemed due for a breakout entering 2008, but an infield collision on May 29th of that year resulted in a season-ending concussion. That significantly dampened expectations for his 2009 season, but Hill instead delivered on the promise of 2007 last year, leading the majors in plate appearances, finishing second in the AL in total bases and third in home runs, starting the All-Star Game, winning the Silver Slugger, and even picking up some down-ballot MVP votes. He also finished second in the AL in outs and posted a .288 on-base percentage over 81 games from late May through the end of August. Hill is signed to a very reasonable deal that, with three option years, could last through 2014, but he's on the other side of 27 and is unlikely to ever have a better season. The rebuilding Jays should cash him in for prospects before he has a chance to be exposed.

Joe Inglett — UT

Bats: L Throws: R Height: 5' 10" Weight: 185 Born: June 29, 1978 Age: 32

YEAR	TEAM	LVL	AGE	PA	R	2B	3B	HR	RBI	BB	SO	SB	CS	EqBRR	AVG	OBP	SLG	EqAVG	EqOBP	EqSLG	EqA	VORP	WARP	DEFENSE			
2007	BUF	AAA	29	455	45	15	9	4	57	40	62	7	12	-4.8	.253	.327	.367	.229	.292	.336	.221	-4.9	-0.8	56-2B	-4	25-LF	2
2008	SYR	AAA	30	62	12	2	2	1	6	7	7	1	2	-0.5	.407	.484	.574	.364	.435	.527	.322	5.9	0.7	9-2B	-2	4-LF	2
2008	TOR	MLB	30	385	45	15	7	3	39	28	43	9	2	2.5	.297	.355	.407	.304	.364	.412	.275	16.7	1.8	61-2B	-2	10-RF	-1
2009	LVG	AAA	31	186	29	14	1	3	25	16	18	4	2	0.5	.360	.422	.516	.307	.363	.434	.275	8.2	0.6	26-2B	0	5-SS	-1
2009	TOR	MLB	31	99	11	4	1	0	6	8	21	3	1	-0.3	.281	.347	.348	.292	.357	.348	.256	1.0	0.1	13-LF	1	9-RF	-1
2010	TEX	MLB	32	331	37	14	4	4	39	28	52	4	3	-0.3	.261	.329	.379	.265	.334	.380	.234	1.3	0.0	58-2B	-2		

Breakout: 11% Improve: 30% Collapse: 23% Attrition: 20% MLB: 63% Comparables: Keith Lockhart, Don Blasingame, Stuart Pederson, Mike Kingery

A utility man with a surprisingly consistent ability to hit for solid averages, Inglett has hit below .280 just once in his 10 professional seasons. That's important, because he doesn't have the power and walks to keep him in the majors at .260. Indeed, a career built on batting average is one built on a shaky foundation, particularly when it's a career as a thirtysomething second baseman/outfielder. Claimed off waivers by the Rangers, Inglett could find it even harder to crack their 25-man roster in 2010 than he did last year with the Jays.

Brian Jeroloman — C

Bats: L Throws: R Height: 6' 0" Weight: 200 Born: May 10, 1985 Age: 25

YEAR	TEAM	LVL	AGE	PA	R	2B	3B	HR	RBI	BB	SO	SB	CS	EqBRR	AVG	OBP	SLG	EqAVG	EqOBP	EqSLG	EqA	VORP	WARP	DEFENSE	
2007	DUN	A+	22	382	32	14	0	3	39	85	57	0	0	-3.1	.259	.421	.338	.237	.385	.307	.264	16.9	1.0	92-C	-9
2008	NHP	AA	23	285	30	15	0	6	31	47	47	0	0	0.1	.270	.396	.416	.255	.361	.391	.270	14.0	0.8	64-C	-7
2008	SYR	AAA	23	88	5	2	0	0	5	11	17	0	0	0.1	.200	.302	.227	.197	.299	.224	.193	-1.8	-0.2	22-C	0
2009	NHP	AA	24	432	32	16	1	6	32	62	120	1	0	-0.8	.217	.330	.316	.210	.302	.300	.218	0.9	0.5	108-C	3
2010	TOR	MLB	25	392	29	14	0	6	35	53	96	1	0	-0.6	.218	.327	.315	.222	.330	.320	.229	3.3	0.1	96-C	-2

Breakout: 8% Improve: 36% Collapse: 20% Attrition: 10% MLB: 3% Comparables: Todd Takayoshi, Scott Hatteberg, Jed Morris, Dan Moylan

It was a bad year for the Jays' top two catching prospects. Projected as Arencibia's eventual backup, Jeroloman got a taste of Triple-A in 2008, but spent all of 2009 in Double-A, where his average plummeted and his strikeouts spiked. Jeroloman is a superlative defender who threw out 43 percent of opposing basestealers in 2009, but his utter lack of power at the plate made his strong plate approach the key to his becoming a viable major leaguer. He needs a big rebound this year, though his glove will eventually get him a big-league chance either way.

Adam Lind — DH

Bats: L Throws: L Height: 6' 1" Weight: 205 Born: July 17, 1983 Age: 26

YEAR	TEAM	LVL	AGE	PA	R	2B	3B	HR	RBI	BB	SO	SB	CS	EqBRR	AVG	OBP	SLG	EqAVG	EqOBP	EqSLG	EqA	VORP	WARP	DEFENSE	
2007	SYR	AAA	23	190	20	8	2	6	28	14	42	0	0	-0.5	.299	.353	.471	.280	.332	.451	.268	5.1	0.1	38-LF	-4
2007	TOR	MLB	23	311	34	14	0	11	46	16	65	1	2	0.3	.238	.278	.400	.239	.279	.398	.232	-4.2	-0.2	73-LF	2
2008	SYR	AAA	24	213	24	17	2	6	50	19	36	1	1	-0.6	.328	.394	.534	.314	.376	.503	.298	12.6	1.3	37-LF	-2
2008	TOR	MLB	24	349	48	16	4	9	40	16	59	2	0	3.6	.282	.316	.439	.286	.319	.449	.264	7.3	0.8	66-LF	0
2009	TOR	MLB	25	654	93	46	0	35	114	58	110	1	1	-1.0	.305	.370	.562	.312	.376	.567	.312	44.7	4.1	53-LF	-8
2010	TOR	MLB	26	625	80	32	3	27	102	49	109	2	2	0.3	.282	.343	.492	.286	.348	.492	.281	27.9	2.8	99-LF	-2

Breakout: 17% Improve: 54% Collapse: 2% Attrition: 4% MLB: 96% Comparables: Geoff Jenkins, Vic Wertz, Luis Gonzalez, Harold Baines

Lind was by far the Jays' best hitter in 2009, finally delivering in full on the potential he showed in the minors and in his cup of coffee in 2006. Though he shed more than 200 points of OPS against his fellow lefties and was awful in his limited opportunities afield, Lind battered righties enough to remain valuable, and his split against lefties was hardly disastrous (.275/.318/.461). Still, it's damning that the only two under-27 hitters who J. P. Ricciardi left the Jays to build around (Lind and Travis Snider) barely register on the defensive spectrum.

John McDonald — SS

Bats: R Throws: R Height: 5' 10" Weight: 175 Born: September 24, 1974 Age: 35

YEAR	TEAM	LVL	AGE	PA	R	2B	3B	HR	RBI	BB	SO	SB	CS	EqBRR	AVG	OBP	SLG	EqAVG	EqOBP	EqSLG	EqA	VORP	WARP	DEFENSE			
2007	TOR	MLB	32	353	32	20	2	1	31	11	48	7	2	0.5	.251	.279	.333	.253	.281	.336	.219	-2.7	0.7	89-SS	2	10-3B	6
2008	TOR	MLB	33	207	21	8	0	1	18	10	25	3	1	-0.8	.210	.255	.269	.212	.258	.277	.193	-5.5	-1.5	54-SS	-7	3-3B	1
2009	TOR	MLB	34	156	18	7	0	4	13	1	18	0	2	-1.0	.258	.271	.384	.267	.279	.380	.223	-2.6	-0.1	22-SS	0	9-3B	-1
2010	TOR	MLB	35	181	19	8	0	2	16	9	28	2	2	-0.2	.239	.282	.325	.248	.291	.334	.204	-3.4	-0.5	49-SS	-1		

Breakout: 7% Improve: 28% Collapse: 32% Attrition: 41% MLB: 90% Comparables: Alvaro Espinoza, Ossie Bluege, Rey Sanchez, Juan Castro

McDonald's power spike last year, including a career high in home runs, resulted in his second-best EqA in a season in which he had more than 10 plate appearances. What? That EqA was still just .223? And the career high in homers was four? And his defense at age 34 was unexceptional? So, why did the Jays give him another two-year deal worth $3 million? What do you mean you read this book to get the answers to questions like that? Look, this is *Baseball Prospectus*, not *Crazy Prospectus*.

Kevin Millar 1B Bats: R Throws: R Height: 6' 0" Weight: 215 Born: September 24, 1971 Age: 38

YEAR	TEAM	LVL	AGE	PA	R	2B	3B	HR	RBI	BB	SO	SB	CS	EqBRR	AVG	OBP	SLG	EqAVG	EqOBP	EqSLG	EqA	VORP	WARP	DEFENSE		
2007	BAL	MLB	35	562	63	26	1	17	63	76	94	1	1	-2.5	.254	.365	.420	.253	.365	.424	.276	15.3	1.4	98-1B	-2	
2008	BAL	MLB	36	610	73	25	0	20	72	71	93	0	1	-4.8	.234	.323	.394	.235	.326	.398	.255	2.0	0.8	128-1B	4	
2009	TOR	MLB	37	283	29	14	0	7	29	31	49	0	0	-1.8	.223	.311	.363	.231	.318	.367	.241	-5.6	-0.9	43-1B	-2	2-3B 0
2010	TOR	MLB	38	286	31	11	0	10	35	34	56	0	1	-0.9	.232	.329	.394	.235	.327	.386	.250	0.0	0.0	54-1B	0	

Breakout: 9%   Improve: 25%   Collapse: 37%   Attrition: 34%   MLB: 93%   Comparables: Todd Zeile, Harmon Killebrew, Gil Hodges, Roy Sievers

As a right-handed caddy for Lyle Overbay, Millar hit a weak .250/.333/.390 against lefties, which still greatly outpaced his production against righties (.191/.285/.330), but is far short of keeping a bench player in beer and skittles if that's his primary responsibility. He also played a poor first base. Now 38, he'll probably get another shot at another second-division platoon job somewhere, but his career looks deader than the pharaohs.

Lyle Overbay 1B Bats: L Throws: L Height: 6' 2" Weight: 230 Born: January 28, 1977 Age: 33

YEAR	TEAM	LVL	AGE	PA	R	2B	3B	HR	RBI	BB	SO	SB	CS	EqBRR	AVG	OBP	SLG	EqAVG	EqOBP	EqSLG	EqA	VORP	WARP	DEFENSE	
2007	TOR	MLB	30	476	49	30	2	10	44	47	78	2	0	-0.8	.240	.315	.391	.239	.315	.392	.247	-1.7	0.5	109-1B	6
2008	TOR	MLB	31	627	74	32	2	15	69	74	116	1	2	-1.5	.270	.358	.419	.275	.364	.425	.277	16.7	4.3	152-1B	20
2009	TOR	MLB	32	500	57	35	1	16	64	74	95	0	0	0.4	.265	.372	.466	.273	.378	.469	.293	18.4	2.8	118-1B	6
2010	TOR	MLB	33	493	50	25	2	13	55	59	95	1	1	-0.3	.253	.345	.411	.258	.350	.410	.262	6.5	1.3	118-1B	5

Breakout: 5%   Improve: 42%   Collapse: 15%   Attrition: 15%   MLB: 95%   Comparables: J. T. Snow, Daryle Ward, Boog Powell, Lee Stevens

Overbay's increased production in 2009 was largely the result of his being platooned with Millar, which is to say, he wasn't necessarily any more productive; he just sat out the at-bats in which he was least likely to contribute. Overbay hit .282/.396/.509 against righties in 2009 and .291/.384/.481 against them in 2008. The biggest difference between the two seasons was that he had almost twice as many at-bats against lefties in 2008. Entering the final year of his contract, he's a 33-year-old platoon first baseman whose defense is now no better than average. If the Jays haven't traded him by the time you read this, they probably missed their chance.

Randy Ruiz DH Bats: R Throws: R Height: 6' 3" Weight: 235 Born: October 19, 1977 Age: 32

YEAR	TEAM	LVL	AGE	PA	R	2B	3B	HR	RBI	BB	SO	SB	CS	EqBRR	AVG	OBP	SLG	EqAVG	EqOBP	EqSLG	EqA	VORP	WARP	DEFENSE		
2007	ALT	AA	29	185	20	9	1	7	30	18	32	0	1	-0.3	.290	.362	.488	.229	.281	.347	.220	-5.8	-1.1	15-1B	-3	3-LF 0
2007	NRW	AA	29	165	25	6	3	8	27	11	40	0	0	-0.1	.291	.352	.530	.237	.279	.378	.225	-4.5	-0.7	9-1B	-1	
2007	REA	AA	29	89	16	10	0	3	12	6	21	1	0	-0.9	.378	.427	.610	.271	.311	.400	.245	0.0	-0.1	13-LF	-1	4-1B 0
2007	OTT	AAA	29	88	11	4	0	4	11	9	23	0	0	-0.1	.215	.295	.418	.200	.273	.350	.216	-3.0	-0.3	9-1B	2	5-LF -1
2008	ROC	AAA	30	456	58	33	3	17	68	23	116	1	2	-3.9	.320	.366	.536	.277	.318	.460	.265	6.8	0.4	40-1B	-4	
2008	MIN	MLB	30	68	13	2	0	1	7	6	21	0	0	1.0	.274	.338	.355	.274	.338	.355	.250	-0.4	0.0			
2009	LVG	AAA	31	521	81	43	2	25	106	47	99	0	0	2.1	.320	.392	.584	.269	.332	.470	.273	7.5	-0.1	60-1B	-9	
2009	TOR	MLB	31	130	25	7	0	10	17	10	35	1	1	0.7	.313	.385	.635	.322	.392	.635	.332	11.5	1.3			
2010	TOR	MLB	32	541	62	28	2	17	66	39	146	1	1	-0.2	.242	.307	.411	.246	.309	.406	.244	-3.2	-0.7	51-1B	-3	

Breakout: 9%   Improve: 32%   Collapse: 17%   Attrition: 21%   MLB: 13%   Comparables: Russ Morman, Gene Schall, Russ McGinnis, Joe Vitiello

An 11-year minor-league veteran with a career .304/.378/.531 line in the bush leagues and a positive performance-enhancing drug test on his record, Ruiz finally got a long major-league look with his ninth organization, doing some late-season crushing for the Jays while briefly pushing Lind into the field. Unfortunately, when you already have a core player who can't play defense like Lind, adding a second one means that someone has to play the field. Baseball doesn't allow you two designated hitters, even in Canada, where they otherwise do some pretty strange things, like putting gravy and cheese curds on their french fries. Lind won that particular battle, natch, as Ruiz's playing time decreased in September, due not to a drop in production, but to the Jays' need to get Lind out of the outfield.

Ruiz has little plate judgment and was a huge double-play threat last year, yet he has the pop to benefit a team in a platoon or pinch-hitting role. But as someone both slow and positionless, he's the equivalent of human roster coagulant.

Marco Scutaro   SS

Bats: R   Throws: R   Height: 5' 10"   Weight: 185   Born: October 30, 1975   Age: 34

YEAR	TEAM	LVL	AGE	PA	R	2B	3B	HR	RBI	BB	SO	SB	CS	EqBRR	AVG	OBP	SLG	EqAVG	EqOBP	EqSLG	EqA	VORP	WARP	DEFENSE			
2007	OAK	MLB	31	379	49	13	0	7	41	35	40	2	1	0.2	.260	.332	.361	.264	.337	.368	.251	7.1	1.2	39-SS	-1	33-3B	-2
2008	TOR	MLB	32	592	76	23	1	7	60	57	65	7	2	-0.1	.267	.341	.356	.273	.347	.365	.257	17.0	5.9	53-SS	14	40-2B	3
2009	TOR	MLB	33	680	100	35	1	12	60	90	75	14	5	2.9	.282	.379	.409	.292	.387	.420	.286	44.8	6.5	140-SS	12		
2010	BOS	MLB	34	560	78	26	1	11	58	62	68	7	4	0.5	.274	.360	.395	.272	.359	.384	.257	17.1	2.5	106-SS	6		

Breakout: 9%   Improve: 47%   Collapse: 18%   Attrition: 24%   MLB: 97%   Comparables: Luke Appling, Orlando Cabrera, Pee Wee Reese, Mike Bordick

Scutaro is an easy player to root for. An undersized late-bloomer, he doesn't excel at any particular facet of the game, but he does almost everything well. He's a solid defensive shortstop with a bit of speed, a ton of hustle, and a good plate approach that makes him more valuable than your typical hacktastic scrappy infielder. Though he has started the majority of his teams' games every year for the last six years, 2009 was the first season that he entered with a job as a major-league starter, and he ran with it, setting career highs in nearly every offensive category, and not just because of the added playing time. Scutaro also set career highs in all three slash stats and drew more walks than strikeouts for the first time. Those walks will be the key to his continued success in Boston, where he's a nice fit as a budget solution to the Red Sox's perennial shortstop problem.

Travis Snider   LF

Bats: L   Throws: L   Height: 5' 11"   Weight: 245   Born: February 2, 1988   Age: 22

YEAR	TEAM	LVL	AGE	PA	R	2B	3B	HR	RBI	BB	SO	SB	CS	EqBRR	AVG	OBP	SLG	EqAVG	EqOBP	EqSLG	EqA	VORP	WARP	DEFENSE			
2007	LNS	A	19	517	72	35	7	16	93	49	129	3	10	-1.9	.313	.377	.525	.262	.321	.443	.260	8.8	-1.3	108-RF	-20		
2008	DUN	A+	20	66	15	5	0	4	7	5	22	1	0	-0.1	.279	.333	.557	.242	.288	.500	.264	1.0	0.1				
2008	NHP	AA	20	423	65	21	0	17	67	52	116	1	1	0.8	.262	.357	.461	.242	.322	.419	.257	5.1	0.0	37-RF	-5	21-LF	0
2008	SYR	AAA	20	70	9	5	0	2	17	4	16	1	0	0.0	.344	.386	.516	.328	.371	.484	.296	4.0	0.4	13-LF	1	4-RF	-2
2008	TOR	MLB	20	80	9	6	0	2	13	5	23	0	0	0.4	.301	.338	.466	.306	.342	.458	.282	2.8	0.3	11-LF	-1	7-RF	0
2009	LVG	AAA	21	204	32	13	1	14	40	28	47	2	3	-3.1	.337	.431	.663	.298	.387	.573	.312	15.9	1.0	37-LF	-8	5-RF	1
2009	TOR	MLB	21	276	34	14	1	9	29	29	78	1	1	-0.3	.241	.328	.419	.250	.337	.425	.263	6.5	-0.2	49-LF	-3	19-RF	-5
2010	TOR	MLB	22	539	71	27	2	21	76	54	146	3	3	-0.7	.253	.332	.449	.255	.335	.447	.265	14.7	1.1	104-LF	-4		

Breakout: 19%   Improve: 50%   Collapse: 4%   Attrition: 2%   MLB: 100%   Comparables: Dee Brown, Jack Cust, Ricky Ledee, Rich Becker

The Jays' top prospect entering the 2009 season, Snider opened the year in a left-field platoon with Bautista, but a cool month got him demoted in late May, and eight games later, he landed on the DL with a back injury. After returning to action in July, he hit .354/.453/.743 with 14 homers in 170 Triple-A plate appearances, but again underwhelmed once he was promoted back to "The Show," hitting .239/.351/.437 the rest of the way. Then again, that last line isn't terrible for a 21-year-old rookie. We're still expecting big things from him sooner rather than later.

Vernon Wells   CF

Bats: R   Throws: R   Height: 6' 1"   Weight: 235   Born: December 8, 1978   Age: 31

YEAR	TEAM	LVL	AGE	PA	R	2B	3B	HR	RBI	BB	SO	SB	CS	EqBRR	AVG	OBP	SLG	EqAVG	EqOBP	EqSLG	EqA	VORP	WARP	DEFENSE	
2007	TOR	MLB	28	642	85	36	4	16	80	49	89	10	4	1.5	.245	.304	.402	.244	.304	.404	.246	9.2	2.0	143-CF	8
2008	TOR	MLB	29	466	63	22	1	20	78	29	46	4	2	-1.2	.300	.343	.496	.306	.349	.511	.288	28.1	2.3	100-CF	-6
2009	TOR	MLB	30	684	84	37	3	15	66	48	86	17	4	1.8	.260	.311	.400	.269	.319	.407	.254	15.4	-0.1	152-CF	-15
2010	TOR	MLB	31	611	77	32	3	19	76	49	85	9	4	0.4	.263	.324	.434	.267	.326	.426	.259	18.2	1.7	136-CF	-2

Breakout: 10%   Improve: 43%   Collapse: 13%   Attrition: 10%   MLB: 96%   Comparables: Marquis Grissom, Aaron Rowand, Juan Encarnacion, Torii Hunter

The extension that J. P. Ricciardi signed Wells to after his strong 2006 season kicks into high gear in 2010 with his salary jumping from the $1.5 million he was paid in 2009 to $12.5 million. (That's not counting the last installment of his signing bonus, $8.5 million per year once a year in 2008-2010.) We say "was paid" as opposed to "earned" because Wells was a subreplacement player in 2009, perhaps in part due to some bad luck on balls in play, but more significantly due to his dreadful play in center: -15 by FRAA, and 18.2 runs below average per UZR, ranking among the worst major-league starting center fielders. Wells' performance at the plate last season looked an awful lot like what he did in 2007, which suggests that there was more than just bad luck to blame. Having a center fielder who is a detriment in the field and at the plate is problematic enough, but over the final four years of his contract, 2011 through 2014, Wells will be paid an almost comically outlandish $86 million, or an annual average of $21.5 million, which is a little bit more than the Phillies will be paying Roy Halladay per year.

PITCHERS

Jeremy Accardo

Bats: R Throws: R Height: 6' 2" Weight: 190 Born: December 18, 1981 Age: 28

YEAR	TEAM	LVL	AGE	W	L	SV	G	GS	IP	H	HR	BB	SO	GB%	BABIP	STUFF	WHIP	ERA	SIERA	DERA	EqH9	EqHR9	EqBB9	EqSO9	VORP	SN/WX
2007	TOR	MLB	25	4	4	30	64	0	67¹	51	4	24	57	53%	.250	14	1.11	2.14	3.83	2.57	7.0	0.5	2.8	6.9	21.7	3.38
2008	TOR	MLB	26	0	3	4	16	0	12¹	15	1	4	5	42%	.311	-28	1.54	6.57	5.61	6.93	10.9	0.7	2.9	3.6	-2.0	-0.36
2009	LVG	AAA	27	2	1	13	27	0	30	32	1	8	27	59%	.333	4	1.33	3.00	3.53	3.45	9.3	0.6	2.4	6.6	6.8	1.24
2009	TOR	MLB	27	0	0	1	26	0	24²	23	2	17	18	55%	.309	-2	1.62	2.55	5.06	2.78	8.7	0.8	6.0	6.4	6.9	1.39
2010	TOR	MLB	28	3	4	16	61	0	61	60	7	25	41	52%	.287	-7	1.39	4.39	4.60	4.72	9.0	1.0	3.5	5.7	5.3	1.83

Breakout: 10% Improve: 39% Collapse: 31% Attrition: 11% MLB: 72% Comparables: Mike Garman, Clay Carroll, Bill Koch, Yasuhiro Oyamada

Having lost nearly all of 2008 to a forearm strain, the man who was the Blue Jays' closer in 2007 started the 2009 season closing games for Las Vegas, finally returning to the major-league pen when Scott Downs hit the DL in mid-June. Accardo was reasonably effective over the next two months, but an excess of walks put his opponents on base in 37 percent of their plate appearances and got him farmed out in mid-August. Though he again walked too many in a late-September return, Accardo has not been prone to wildness in the past, and his Triple-A peripherals were strong last year, so there's little reason to doubt his ability to contribute going forward.

Shawn Camp

Bats: R Throws: R Height: 6' 0" Weight: 205 Born: November 18, 1975 Age: 34

YEAR	TEAM	LVL	AGE	W	L	SV	G	GS	IP	H	HR	BB	SO	GB%	BABIP	STUFF	WHIP	ERA	SIERA	DERA	EqH9	EqHR9	EqBB9	EqSO9	VORP	SN/WX
2007	DUR	AAA	31	0	1	4	12	0	15¹	13	0	2	16	64%	.317	14	0.98	1.17	2.55	1.88	8.8	0.0	1.3	7.5	5.8	1.09
2007	TBA	MLB	31	0	3	0	50	0	40	63	7	18	36	76%	.418	-15	2.02	7.20	3.87	6.53	12.8	1.5	3.5	7.1	-4.6	-0.82
2008	TOR	MLB	32	3	1	0	40	0	39¹	40	2	11	31	67%	.317	4	1.30	4.12	3.73	4.14	9.5	0.5	2.4	6.6	5.7	0.36
2009	TOR	MLB	33	2	6	1	59	0	79²	73	7	29	58	67%	.281	4	1.28	3.50	4.07	3.89	7.8	0.8	2.9	5.7	14.1	1.56
2010	TOR	MLB	34	3	4	2	62	0	63²	66	7	23	47	63%	.308	-5	1.40	4.60	4.08	4.95	9.5	1.0	3.2	6.2	3.9	0.72

Breakout: 14% Improve: 37% Collapse: 29% Attrition: 14% MLB: 91% Comparables: Paul Quantrill, Dick Drago, Julian Tavarez, Gene Garber

A nonroster invitee prior to the 2008 season, Camp has settled in nicely as an adequate and utterly indistinct middle reliever for the Blue Jays after suffering through some bad luck and bad fielding with the Royals and Devil Rays. His relative success has also been aided by an improved changeup, which last year he threw more often than his slider, which had always been his primary breaking pitch. Credit Camp for learning a new pitch in his early 30s, but even with the change, the only thing that keeps Camp from being perfectly average is the excess of ground balls he induces.

Jesse Carlson

Bats: L Throws: L Height: 6' 1" Weight: 160 Born: December 31, 1980 Age: 29

YEAR	TEAM	LVL	AGE	W	L	SV	G	GS	IP	H	HR	BB	SO	GB%	BABIP	STUFF	WHIP	ERA	SIERA	DERA	EqH9	EqHR9	EqBB9	EqSO9	VORP	SN/WX
2007	NHP	AA	26	8	2	6	58	0	70¹	77	4	18	81	44%	.369	1	1.35	4.86	2.76	5.53	10.3	1.1	2.5	7.8	-0.2	1.16
2008	TOR	MLB	27	7	2	2	69	0	60	41	6	21	55	41%	.230	13	1.03	2.25	3.59	2.48	6.5	0.9	2.9	7.6	19.4	2.28
2009	TOR	MLB	28	1	6	0	73	0	67²	67	7	21	51	48%	.287	-1	1.30	4.66	4.17	4.57	8.2	0.9	2.3	5.7	7.2	0.20
2010	TOR	MLB	29	3	4	1	62	0	61¹	61	9	22	49	43%	.298	-3	1.36	4.43	4.12	4.67	9.1	1.2	3.0	6.6	5.7	1.21

Breakout: 17% Improve: 34% Collapse: 29% Attrition: 16% MLB: 75% Comparables: Erasmo Ramirez, Scott Ruskin, Willie Hernandez, Dave Tomlin

After his opponents hit just .232 on balls in play in 2008, Carlson suffered a significant and wholly expected BABIP correction in 2009. That his ERA more than doubled from 2008 can be explained by this, a few missing strikeouts, and the fact that he was still used as a LOOGY despite a slight reverse split (lefties hit .272/.333/.421 against him).

Carlson is no specialty pitcher. If anything, he's a younger, left-handed version of Camp minus those extra grounders, which is to say that he's an utterly average relief pitcher.

Brett Cecil

Bats: R   Throws: L   Height: 6' 3"   Weight: 220   Born: July 2, 1986   Age: 23

YEAR	TEAM	LVL	AGE	W	L	SV	G	GS	IP	H	HR	BB	SO	GB%	BABIP	STUFF	WHIP	ERA	SIERA	DERA	EqH9	EqHR9	EqBB9	EqSO9	VORP	SN/WX
2007	AUB	A-	20	1	0	0	14	13	49²	36	1	11	56	66%	.278	36	0.95	1.27	2.44	2.82	8.4	1.2	2.7	6.2	13.8	1.57
2008	NHP	AA	21	6	2	0	18	18	77²	66	4	23	87	65%	.302	36	1.15	2.55	2.84	3.35	7.7	0.9	2.7	7.4	18.4	1.71
2008	SYR	AAA	21	2	3	0	6	6	30²	28	1	16	31	67%	.310	21	1.43	4.11	3.65	5.64	8.3	0.6	4.7	6.5	-0.5	0.36
2009	LVG	AAA	22	1	5	0	9	9	49	53	2	19	32	67%	.313	6	1.47	5.69	4.34	6.80	9.2	0.6	3.5	4.6	-7.1	-0.71
2009	TOR	MLB	22	7	4	0	18	17	93¹	116	17	38	69	50%	.338	-2	1.65	5.30	4.50	5.30	10.8	1.6	3.2	5.9	2.0	1.60
2010	TOR	MLB	23	7	8	0	30	29	127¹	128	17	55	90	59%	.294	6	1.44	4.74	4.43	4.99	9.2	1.1	3.6	5.9	7.2	2.64

Breakout: 6%   Improve: 37%   Collapse: 21%   Attrition: 8%   MLB: 99%   Comparables: Errol Simonitsch, Tom Gorzelanny, Eddie Guardado, Joe Magrane

The Jays' top pitching prospect entering the season, Cecil replaced David Purcey in the rotation in early May and began his major-league career with three quality starts before giving up five home runs in 4 ⅔ innings to the Red Sox in his fourth and being sent back to Vegas when Ricky Romero returned from the DL. Cecil returned to stay after Roy Halladay hit the DL in late June, but was erratic, turning in just five more quality starts in 13 tries while posting a 1.6 K/BB and 1.74 WHIP. Bad luck on balls in play and fly balls leaving the yard played a part, so trust his minor-league track record more than that rookie performance. With Halladay in Philadelphia, Cecil should remain in the Jays' rotation and continue to develop, though it remains to be seen if he can leverage his solid repertoire, which features a low- to mid-90s fastball and a plus slider, into something more than a career as a league-average innings eater.

Tim Collins

Bats: L   Throws: L   Height: 5' 7"   Weight: 155   Born: August 29, 1989   Age: 20

YEAR	TEAM	LVL	AGE	W	L	SV	G	GS	IP	H	HR	BB	SO	GB%	BABIP	STUFF	WHIP	ERA	SIERA	DERA	EqH9	EqHR9	EqBB9	EqSO9	VORP	SN/WX
2008	LNS	A	18	4	2	14	39	0	68¹	36	3	32	98	48%	.250	42	1.00	1.58	2.22	3.06	7.2	1.3	5.5	8.7	16.4	1.28
2009	DUN	A+	19	7	4	3	40	0	64²	47	2	28	99	45%	.326	48	1.16	2.37	2.03	4.45	8.6	1.2	4.8	9.7	7.0	0.13
2009	NHP	AA	19	2	3	0	9	0	12²	12	1	7	17	34%	.355	12	1.50	5.68	3.03	7.88	10.5	1.5	5.3	9.0	-3.2	-0.49
2010	TOR	MLB	20	4	5	3	49	0	75¹	72	11	43	72	46%	.305	39	1.53	4.87	4.14	5.09	8.8	1.2	4.7	7.8	3.4	1.55

Breakout: 16%   Improve: 45%   Collapse: 15%   Attrition: 1%   MLB: 6%   Comparables: Arnie Munoz, Edgar Alfonzo, Alex Leon, Fabio Castro

Since being signed out of a tryout camp as a 17-year-old in 2007, this little lefty has struck out 13.1 men per nine innings in his two-plus minor-league seasons. He doesn't do anything special to get those Ks, just whips in low-90s fastballs with good location, mixes them up with a solid curve, and hides the ball well in his delivery. It could be that no one is expecting major-league-quality stuff from a Lilliputian (the height and weight above are surely rounded up), but whatever he's doing, it's working. He even struck out 17 men in 12 ⅔ Double-A innings after making the leap late last year. It's hard to imagine that he can keep it up all the way into the majors, but the Jays owe it to Collins and themselves to find out.

Scott Downs

Bats: L   Throws: L   Height: 6' 2"   Weight: 210   Born: March 17, 1976   Age: 34

YEAR	TEAM	LVL	AGE	W	L	SV	G	GS	IP	H	HR	BB	SO	GB%	BABIP	STUFF	WHIP	ERA	SIERA	DERA	EqH9	EqHR9	EqBB9	EqSO9	VORP	SN/WX
2007	TOR	MLB	31	4	2	1	81	0	58	47	3	24	57	71%	.286	17	1.22	2.17	3.30	2.33	7.7	0.5	3.5	8.2	19.7	2.43
2008	TOR	MLB	32	0	3	5	66	0	70²	54	3	27	57	77%	.256	16	1.15	1.78	3.52	2.01	7.1	0.4	3.1	6.6	26.9	4.01
2009	TOR	MLB	33	1	3	9	48	0	46²	46	4	13	43	67%	.304	10	1.26	3.09	3.40	3.40	8.1	0.8	2.1	7.0	11.1	0.71
2010	TOR	MLB	34	3	3	3	48	1	48¹	46	5	19	39	66%	.294	-1	1.34	4.14	3.86	4.47	8.7	0.9	3.4	6.7	5.5	1.27

Breakout: 10%   Improve: 34%   Collapse: 42%   Attrition: 15%   MLB: 92%   Comparables: Terry Forster, Tug McGraw, Paul Assenmacher, Arthur Rhodes

Downs had a palindromic season in 2009. After starting the season as B. J. Ryan's set-up man, he assumed the closer's job when Ryan hit the DL. After converting eight of nine save opportunities, he hit the DL himself in mid-June with a sprained big toe. He returned as closer three weeks later, but three bad outings in late July handed the job to Jason Frasor, returning Downs to the set-up job. Having come full circle, he settled back in as his usual, dominant self. The increase in Downs' ERA last year was simply a BABIP correction and masked the fact that despite his circuitous season, he posted a career-low walk rate.

Jason Frasor

Bats: R Throws: R Height: 5′ 10″ Weight: 180 Born: August 9, 1977 Age: 32

YEAR	TEAM	LVL	AGE	W	L	SV	G	GS	IP	H	HR	BB	SO	GB%	BABIP	STUFF	WHIP	ERA	SIERA	DERA	EqH9	EqHR9	EqBB9	EqSO9	VORP	SN/WX
2007	TOR	MLB	29	1	5	3	51	0	57	47	3	23	59	53%	.284	16	1.23	4.58	3.43	4.42	7.6	0.5	3.3	8.4	6.8	0.70
2008	TOR	MLB	30	1	2	0	49	0	47¹	36	4	32	42	47%	.248	6	1.44	4.18	4.64	4.28	7.0	0.8	5.3	7.2	6.4	-0.10
2009	TOR	MLB	31	7	3	11	61	0	57²	43	4	16	56	42%	.262	20	1.02	2.50	3.17	2.53	6.5	0.6	2.2	7.6	18.8	3.58
2010	TOR	MLB	32	3	3	5	53	0	52¹	46	5	24	47	44%	.286	4	1.33	4.05	3.99	4.25	7.9	0.9	3.9	7.4	7.3	0.86

Breakout: 18% Improve: 40% Collapse: 31% Attrition: 10%   MLB: 96%   Comparables: Micheal Nakamura, Enrique Romo, Jeff Montgomery, Cliff Politte

Frasor has flirted with the Blue Jays' closer job several times. As a rookie in 2004, he picked up 17 saves but was replaced after a poor August. Three years later, he opened 2007 as the Jays' last line of defense but lost the job with one ugly outing in late April. Last year, he took over the ninth inning from Downs on July 22nd and converted eight of nine chances the rest of the way, posting a 2.66 ERA with strong peripherals (4.2 K/BB, 9.5 K/9, 1.01 WHIP). Given that performance, he'll keep the job entering 2010, though his low BABIPs and middling track record suggest his grip is anything but firm. The most impressive facet of Frasor's game is his dominance of his fellow righties, who have hit .158/.245/.244 against him over the last two seasons. It seems that opposing managers are catching on; lefties had more plate appearances against Frasor than righties in 2009.

Reidier Gonzalez

Bats: R Throws: R Height: 5′ 10″ Weight: 215 Born: November 1, 1985 Age: 24

YEAR	TEAM	LVL	AGE	W	L	SV	G	GS	IP	H	HR	BB	SO	GB%	BABIP	STUFF	WHIP	ERA	SIERA	DERA	EqH9	EqHR9	EqBB9	EqSO9	VORP	SN/WX
2007	LNS	A	21	9	7	0	20	20	114²	121	4	30	71	62%	.310	1	1.32	3.53	4.20	5.98	10.2	1.2	3.2	3.2	-5.7	-0.86
2008	DUN	A+	22	12	4	1	27	20	137²	155	6	30	74	60%	.318	-13	1.34	3.14	4.40	5.25	11.2	1.2	2.6	3.0	3.5	-0.14
2009	NHP	AA	23	4	6	0	17	17	93	82	4	25	67	57%	.275	5	1.15	2.90	4.00	4.60	8.9	1.0	2.6	4.6	8.9	0.98
2010	TOR	MLB	24	4	6	0	23	14	85¹	98	13	35	41	56%	.301	-16	1.55	5.24	5.20	5.57	10.4	1.2	3.5	4.0	-0.6	1.25

Breakout: 12% Improve: 42% Collapse: 17% Attrition: 20%   MLB: 7%   Comparables: Albert Bustillos, Woody Williams, Mike Bovee, Brett Walters

A midround prep pick in 2005, the Cuban-born Gonzalez survived the leap to Double-A in 2009 and, despite a midseason groin strain that made him miss the Eastern League all-star game, turned in his best professional season yet. He was added to the 40-man roster in November. A small, strike-throwing sinkerballer, Gonzalez doesn't project as much more than a middle reliever, but getting even that out of the 566th pick in the draft is a nice trick.

Roy Halladay

Bats: R Throws: R Height: 6′ 6″ Weight: 225 Born: May 14, 1977 Age: 33

YEAR	TEAM	LVL	AGE	W	L	SV	G	GS	IP	H	HR	BB	SO	GB%	BABIP	STUFF	WHIP	ERA	SIERA	DERA	EqH9	EqHR9	EqBB9	EqSO9	VORP	SN/WX
2007	TOR	MLB	30	16	7	0	31	31	225¹	232	15	48	139	62%	.301	15	1.24	3.71	4.14	3.95	9.7	0.6	1.8	5.2	37.2	6.86
2008	TOR	MLB	31	20	11	0	34	33	246	220	18	39	206	63%	.284	31	1.05	2.78	3.30	3.30	8.3	0.7	1.3	6.9	58.9	8.34
2009	TOR	MLB	32	17	10	0	32	32	239	234	22	35	208	61%	.306	30	1.13	2.79	3.20	3.03	8.4	0.8	1.1	6.9	64.9	8.60
2010	PHI	MLB	33	14	11	0	32	32	218¹	223	23	48	160	61%	.306	15	1.24	3.80	3.78	4.05	9.1	0.9	1.8	6.0	35.2	4.70

Breakout: 8% Improve: 35% Collapse: 22% Attrition: 13%   MLB: 97%   Comparables: Kevin Brown, Paul Derringer, Mike Mussina, Darryl Kile

Setting aside the merits and machinations of the trade(s) that brought him to Philadelphia, taking Roy Halladay out of the AL East and putting him on the only team in the NL East with a dominating offense has "CC Sabathia on the Brewers"-level potential, doesn't it? Maybe, but how much better can he really get? Against the Yankees and Red Sox over the last two seasons, Halladay has gone 13-6 with a 2.59 ERA and 0.99 WHIP. The Rays have given him a bit more trouble, but not much (3.69 ERA, 1.15 WHIP). Halladay was fifth in the majors in the opposition-adjusted SNLVAR last year; Cliff Lee was ninth, the difference between the two being less than a win. In 2008, Halladay and Lee were just a tenth of a win apart. What the Phillies have acquired by dealing one ace in Lee and acquiring another in Halladay is stability. While Lee seemed likely to test the free-agent market after the coming season, Halladay signed a three-year extension with the Phillies that includes an innings-based vesting option for 2014—an option that would take him through his age-37 season. Halladay also has the more convincing track record; Lee was an average pitcher with a worrisome fly-ball rate prior to 2007 and actually spent some time in the minors trying to sort things out in '07. Halladay has been great when healthy since 2002, and save for a mild groin strain in June of last year, he has been healthy since 2006.

Dirk Hayhurst

| | | | | Bats: L | | Throws: R | | Height: 6' 3" | | Weight: 200 | | Born: March 24, 1981 | | | Age: 29 |

YEAR	TEAM	LVL	AGE	W	L	SV	G	GS	IP	H	HR	BB	SO	GB%	BABIP	STUFF	WHIP	ERA	SIERA	DERA	EqH9	EqHR9	EqBB9	EqSO9	VORP	SN/WX
2007	LEL	A+	26	0	1	0	13	0	20	23	0	6	16	66%	.359	-15	1.45	1.80	3.80	5.45	10.9	0.5	3.3	4.7	0.1	-0.03
2007	SAN	AA	26	4	1	2	32	1	59¹	54	6	9	55	55%	.282	-9	1.06	3.19	3.08	4.87	9.7	1.8	1.8	6.1	3.9	-0.10
2008	POR	AAA	27	2	3	2	46	2	84	84	7	28	98	43%	.341	0	1.33	3.75	2.90	4.13	9.6	1.2	3.0	7.6	12.4	0.50
2008	SDN	MLB	27	0	2	0	10	3	16²	27	2	10	14	57%	.431	-20	2.22	9.72	4.64	10.05	16.1	1.7	5.2	6.3	-7.9	-0.56
2009	LVG	AAA	28	4	6	0	25	6	57²	69	6	12	48	50%	.348	-4	1.40	3.75	3.64	5.22	10.6	1.1	2.1	6.1	1.7	0.46
2009	TOR	MLB	28	0	0	0	15	0	22²	23	2	9	13	45%	.296	-9	1.41	2.78	5.06	2.86	8.6	0.8	3.3	4.5	6.4	-0.07
2010	TOR	MLB	29	3	5	1	47	3	73²	86	10	26	52	49%	.328	-11	1.53	5.22	4.44	5.59	10.7	1.2	3.0	5.8	-0.8	0.65

Breakout: 17%　Improve: 54%　Collapse: 21%　Attrition: 25%　　　MLB: 22%　　　Comparables: Miguel Alicea, Greg Mix, Jeromy Palki, John Ennis

A Kent State product out of the Padres' system, author/humorist/after-dinner speaker/swingman Hayhurst was a nice free-talent find for the Jays last year. Though he's always been old for his leagues, Hayhurst has strong minor-league peripherals (8.2 K/9, 2.6 BB/9, 3.2 K/BB), good control, a four-pitch assortment, and a good sense of how to use it and has added some movement on his fastball. Called up in June, he gave the Jays some solid low-leverage work before taking a few more trips on the Las Vegas shuttle. A grand slam by Michael Aubrey in his final outing of the season sullied his major-league ERA, which had been 1.31 entering that game. One would hope that he gets as much mileage out of that home run as he did out of the 2008 shot he gave up to Manny Ramirez, which happened, as he explained in a *Baseball America* essay, on the same night a windstorm dropped a tree on his car.

Casey Janssen

| | | | | Bats: R | | Throws: R | | Height: 6' 4" | | Weight: 220 | | Born: September 17, 1981 | | | Age: 28 |

YEAR	TEAM	LVL	AGE	W	L	SV	G	GS	IP	H	HR	BB	SO	GB%	BABIP	STUFF	WHIP	ERA	SIERA	DERA	EqH9	EqHR9	EqBB9	EqSO9	VORP	SN/WX
2007	TOR	MLB	25	2	3	6	70	0	72²	67	4	20	39	52%	.273	-1	1.20	2.35	4.72	2.71	8.7	0.5	2.3	4.5	21.6	2.77
2009	DUN	A+	27	0	0	0	4	3	13	6	0	2	10	73%	.176	4	0.62	0.69	2.82	1.46	5.1	0.7	2.2	4.4	5.5	0.41
2009	NHP	AA	27	1	0	0	6	1	15	12	0	5	12	54%	.273	-7	1.13	2.40	3.90	4.71	8.2	0.6	3.1	5.0	1.3	0.21
2009	TOR	MLB	27	2	4	1	21	5	40	59	5	14	24	65%	.367	-18	1.82	5.85	4.68	6.15	12.1	1.1	2.6	4.6	-2.9	-0.07
2010	TOR	MLB	28	4	4	2	40	2	64¹	67	8	22	35	37%	.289	-10	1.39	4.40	5.20	4.78	9.7	1.1	2.9	4.4	5.1	1.16

Breakout: 9%　Improve: 33%　Collapse: 32%　Attrition: 16%　　　MLB: 72%　　　Comparables: Jose Santiago, Todd Coffey, Gary Majewski, Dave Frost

After rehabbing in the minors following a 2008 season lost to labrum surgery, Janssen rejoined the Blue Jays' crumbling rotation in late May with a couple of quality starts, but after being roughed up in two of three June outings, he was shut back down with inflammation in his repaired shoulder. He returned in mid-August as a reliever with more strikeouts, but also more walks and, despite an early save, spent most of his time in low-leverage sixth-inning work. As a utility groundballer, Janssen should remain a modest asset capable of plugging emerging holes, but seems unlikely to ever become a full-time solution to any of them.

Chad Jenkins

| | | | Bats: R | | Throws: R | | Height: 6' 4" | | Weight: 225 | | Born: December 22, 1987 | | Age: 22 |

Did Not Play.

Breakout: 9%　Improve: 33%　Collapse: 32%　Attrition: 16%　　　MLB: 72%　　　Comparables: NA

The Blue Jays have had some rough drafts of late, as they've been positioned in each of the last two years just outside where the elite talent ends. Picking from the best of the Plan B players in 2009, they selected Jenkins, a physical beast of a right-hander with a pure power arm. With his fastball sitting at 93-94 mph and touching 96 consistently, Jenkins has the ability to blow hitters away and complements it with a plus slider. What kept him out of the upper tier of the first round was a shallow arsenal (his changeup is as rarely seen as the ivory-billed woodpecker) and a body that walks the fine line between big and just plain soft. Before the Halladay trade, he might have been the best prospect in the Toronto system, which is more of an indictment of the talent level in the organization than an affirmation of Jenkins' own skill.

Brandon League

				Bats: R		Throws: R		Height: 6' 2"		Weight: 200		Born: March 16, 1983		Age: 27							

YEAR	TEAM	LVL	AGE	W	L	SV	G	GS	IP	H	HR	BB	SO	GB%	BABIP	STUFF	WHIP	ERA	SIERA	DERA	EqH9	EqHR9	EqBB9	EqSO9	VORP	SN/WX
2007	SYR	AAA	24	0	0	0	11	0	12	12	0	6	10	72%	.324	-14	1.50	3.00	4.07	7.13	9.0	0.0	4.5	5.3	-2.2	0.00
2007	TOR	MLB	24	0	0	0	14	0	11²	19	1	7	7	81%	.419	-15	2.23	6.17	4.50	5.73	15.5	0.8	4.9	4.9	-0.3	-0.17
2008	SYR	AAA	25	2	3	2	20	0	34¹	36	2	10	32	75%	.321	-4	1.34	3.93	3.24	5.53	9.0	0.8	2.6	5.7	-0.1	0.29
2008	TOR	MLB	25	1	2	1	31	0	33	28	2	15	23	77%	.265	-1	1.30	2.18	3.99	2.51	7.8	0.6	3.6	5.8	10.8	0.64
2009	TOR	MLB	26	3	6	0	67	0	74²	72	8	21	76	68%	.318	12	1.25	4.58	3.10	4.54	8.5	1.0	2.2	8.1	7.8	0.05
2010	SEA	MLB	27	3	4	1	60	0	62²	62	7	26	52	72%	.305	0	1.40	4.56	3.73	4.66	8.6	0.9	3.4	6.7	5.8	0.40

Breakout: 15%   Improve: 48%   Collapse: 14%   Attrition: 6%   MLB: 79%   Comparables: Brian Wilson, Hipolito Pichardo, Danny Patterson, Luis Ayala

At 26, the hard-throwin' Hawaiian finally had a full, healthy season in the majors, but despite putting up the sort of peripherals his stuff would suggest (9.2 K/9, 2.5 BB/9, and fewer hits than innings pitched despite a slightly inflated BABIP), he was barely useful according to WXRL. It seems League's right wing was made of wax in 2009, and the hotter the situation, the more likely he was to melt. Opposing batters hit .257/.325/.411 against him overall, but when the game was tied or within one run, they hit .317/.368/.533 with seven homers in 190 plate appearances. Similarly, in situations with a leverage index below 0.7 (1.0 being average), they hit .219/.296/.349, but with leverage marks of 0.7 or above, they hit .299/.347/.478. With his trade to Seattle in the Brandon Morrow deal, it's now up to the Mariners to figure out what to make of him.

Jesse Litsch

				Bats: R		Throws: R		Height: 6' 1"		Weight: 215		Born: March 9, 1985		Age: 25							

YEAR	TEAM	LVL	AGE	W	L	SV	G	GS	IP	H	HR	BB	SO	GB%	BABIP	STUFF	WHIP	ERA	SIERA	DERA	EqH9	EqHR9	EqBB9	EqSO9	VORP	SN/WX
2007	NHP	AA	22	7	2	0	10	10	61¹	51	5	14	46	60%	.251	18	1.06	2.35	3.79	3.96	7.3	1.2	2.2	4.7	10.5	0.63
2007	SYR	AAA	22	1	0	0	2	2	15	12	0	3	10	71%	.267	14	1.00	1.80	3.51	2.20	6.9	0.0	1.9	4.4	5.3	0.44
2007	TOR	MLB	22	7	9	0	20	20	111	116	14	36	50	56%	.275	0	1.37	3.81	5.13	4.38	9.8	1.2	2.7	3.8	13.5	3.07
2008	SYR	AAA	23	1	1	0	3	3	20	18	1	4	18	70%	.298	16	1.10	3.60	3.09	5.12	8.4	0.9	1.9	6.1	0.8	-0.01
2008	TOR	MLB	23	13	9	0	29	28	176	178	20	39	99	55%	.278	8	1.23	3.58	4.50	4.03	9.3	1.0	1.8	4.7	28.1	5.09
2009	TOR	MLB	24	0	1	0	2	2	9	14	4	1	8	46%	.357	3	1.67	9.00	3.44	8.50	13.0	4.0	1.0	7.0	-3.0	-0.29
2010	TOR	MLB	25	5	6	0	19	15	88	90	12	27	52	52%	.287	0	1.33	4.51	4.63	4.79	9.3	1.1	2.7	4.9	6.9	1.48

Breakout: 9%   Improve: 46%   Collapse: 17%   Attrition: 26%   MLB: 72%   Comparables: Julio Valera, Chad Durbin, Jay Hook, David Hooten

The third of the trio of established young Toronto starters to suffer a severe, season-erasing injury over a 12-month period, Litsch left the fourth inning of his second start of 2009 with elbow pain and never returned. Tommy John surgery in June wiped out his season and is likely to keep him on the shelf for the first half, if not all of the 2010 season. He's young enough to get his career back on track after he returns, but one imagines the gains he made in his sophomore season will have been lost in the interim.

Shaun Marcum

				Bats: R		Throws: R		Height: 6' 0"		Weight: 185		Born: December 14, 1981		Age: 28							

YEAR	TEAM	LVL	AGE	W	L	SV	G	GS	IP	H	HR	BB	SO	GB%	BABIP	STUFF	WHIP	ERA	SIERA	DERA	EqH9	EqHR9	EqBB9	EqSO9	VORP	SN/WX
2007	TOR	MLB	25	12	6	1	38	25	159	149	27	49	122	48%	.267	-2	1.25	4.13	4.04	4.13	8.8	1.6	2.6	6.4	23.4	4.50
2008	TOR	MLB	26	9	7	0	25	25	151¹	126	21	50	123	49%	.245	15	1.16	3.39	3.94	3.56	7.7	1.3	2.6	6.6	32.4	4.88
2010	TOR	MLB	28	5	6	0	24	9	86¹	85	12	33	67	51%	.294	6	1.36	4.51	4.18	4.78	8.9	1.2	3.3	6.4	7.0	1.68

Breakout: 5%   Improve: 40%   Collapse: 32%   Attrition: 30%   MLB: 84%   Comparables: Mike Gardiner, Greg Cochran, Jim Hardin, Hiroki Kuroda

Having undergone Tommy John surgery in September 2008, Marcum made five minor-league rehab starts late last season with encouraging results. Prior to the surgery, Marcum was a control pitcher with enough guts and guile to keep his strikeout rates above league average, and that control seemed to be uncompromised in those rehab innings. Marcum is expected to be in the Jays' Opening Day rotation in April. He'll be the "veteran" in the group, despite having never made more than 25 starts or thrown 160 innings in a single major-league season and having just 64 big-league starts to his name.

Dustin McGowan

Bats: R   Throws: R   Height: 6' 3"   Weight: 230   Born: March 24, 1982   Age: 28

YEAR	TEAM	LVL	AGE	W	L	SV	G	GS	IP	H	HR	BB	SO	GB%	BABIP	STUFF	WHIP	ERA	SIERA	DERA	EqH9	EqHR9	EqBB9	EqSO9	VORP	SN/WX
2007	TOR	MLB	25	12	10	0	27	27	169²	146	14	61	144	60%	.273	23	1.22	4.08	3.78	4.13	8.0	0.8	3.0	7.0	25.4	4.39
2008	TOR	MLB	26	6	7	0	19	19	111¹	115	9	38	85	50%	.315	12	1.37	4.37	4.17	4.72	9.8	0.8	2.8	6.5	9.2	2.15
2010	TOR	MLB	28	4	5	0	20	2	71²	72	8	30	54	52%	.302	4	1.42	4.47	4.34	4.75	9.1	1.0	3.5	6.3	6.0	1.13

Breakout: 19%   Improve: 50%   Collapse: 17%   Attrition: 24%   MLB: 87%   Comparables: Paul Moskau, Mac Suzuki, Ken Forsch, Jose Silva

McGowan was the first of the three Jays starters to go under the knife, having a frayed labrum repaired in July 2008. As a result, he was expected back ahead of Marcum, but he didn't throw a pitch all of last year and is not expected to be ready to start the 2010 season. July 2009 surgery to repair cartilage in his left knee is the official culprit, but his rehab wasn't going well before he injured the knee during running drills (he hadn't advanced beyond playing catch), and there are some doubts about what he'll have left when (and if) he does return this year. The Jays were willing to bet $500,000 on McGowan's age-28 season, but that's not big money even for a cash-strapped team like Toronto.

Brad Mills

Bats: L   Throws: L   Height: 6' 0"   Weight: 185   Born: March 5, 1985   Age: 25

YEAR	TEAM	LVL	AGE	W	L	SV	G	GS	IP	H	HR	BB	SO	GB%	BABIP	STUFF	WHIP	ERA	SIERA	DERA	EqH9	EqHR9	EqBB9	EqSO9	VORP	SN/WX
2007	AUB	A-	22	2	0	0	6	2	18	9	0	6	21	48%	.214	17	0.83	2.00	2.64	2.91	6.4	0.5	3.7	6.4	4.9	0.30
2008	LNS	A	23	6	3	0	15	15	81¹	71	3	28	92	56%	.319	1	1.22	2.55	2.97	5.11	10.0	1.3	4.1	6.3	3.2	0.13
2008	DUN	A+	23	4	0	0	6	6	33¹	25	2	12	35	35%	.274	11	1.11	1.35	3.21	3.82	8.2	1.5	3.8	6.8	5.7	0.67
2008	NHP	AA	23	3	2	0	6	6	32²	24	2	12	32	33%	.262	17	1.10	1.10	3.53	3.59	6.9	1.1	3.4	6.6	6.6	0.75
2009	LVG	AAA	24	2	8	0	14	14	84¹	83	6	35	72	50%	.314	10	1.40	4.06	4.05	4.65	8.9	0.9	3.8	6.3	7.7	0.45
2009	TOR	MLB	24	0	1	0	2	2	7²	14	4	6	9	24%	.435	-4	2.61	14.09	4.64	14.09	16.4	4.7	5.9	9.4	-7.3	-0.30
2010	TOR	MLB	25	4	6	0	14	14	81	83	12	39	61	43%	.298	3	1.51	5.05	4.65	5.29	9.3	1.2	4.0	6.2	1.9	1.50

Breakout: 7%   Improve: 33%   Collapse: 25%   Attrition: 10%   MLB: 15%   Comparables: Bob Gunnarsson, Jim Boudreau, Lance Painter, Doug Swearingen

A slim lefty with average stuff who relies heavily on his command, this University of Arizona product tore through the lower levels in his first two pro seasons, but began to look a bit ordinary in Triple-A last year. He looked even worse when he was given two major-league starts in late June and, after one more turn in Triple-A, had his season ended by injury. He's nonetheless in the mix for the back of the rotation this spring.

David Purcey

Bats: L   Throws: L   Height: 6' 5"   Weight: 230   Born: April 22, 1982   Age: 28

YEAR	TEAM	LVL	AGE	W	L	SV	G	GS	IP	H	HR	BB	SO	GB%	BABIP	STUFF	WHIP	ERA	SIERA	DERA	EqH9	EqHR9	EqBB9	EqSO9	VORP	SN/WX
2007	NHP	AA	25	3	5	0	11	11	62	67	4	16	55	47%	.337	3	1.34	5.37	3.58	6.52	9.9	1.0	2.5	5.8	-6.8	-0.73
2008	SYR	AAA	26	8	6	0	19	19	117	97	8	34	121	47%	.293	22	1.12	2.69	3.03	3.67	7.9	1.0	2.8	6.9	22.7	2.15
2008	TOR	MLB	26	3	6	0	12	12	65	67	9	29	58	33%	.307	5	1.48	5.54	4.30	5.48	9.6	1.3	3.7	7.3	0.1	1.09
2009	LVG	AAA	27	9	6	0	24	24	139¹	132	7	78	109	46%	.302	11	1.51	4.46	4.72	5.37	8.4	0.7	5.0	5.7	1.9	0.39
2009	TOR	MLB	27	1	3	0	9	9	48	54	6	30	39	35%	.327	1	1.75	6.19	5.08	6.19	9.6	1.1	4.9	6.4	-3.7	-0.03
2010	TOR	MLB	28	7	10	0	30	27	149¹	151	18	74	114	45%	.303	3	1.50	4.99	4.59	5.27	9.2	1.0	4.1	6.3	3.8	1.80

Breakout: 13%   Improve: 48%   Collapse: 16%   Attrition: 19%   MLB: 57%   Comparables: Sean Lawrence, Tim Lollar, Omar Daal, Buddy Groom

The 16th overall pick in 2004 out of the University of Oklahoma, Purcey has been a source of constant frustration for the Jays. After appearing to finally get his act together in 2008, the big lefty opened the 2009 season in the major-league rotation but didn't survive April. He didn't return to the big club until mid-September. In between, he failed to impress with the Jays' Triple-A team, which had relocated from Syracuse to the hitting-friendly Las Vegas. Perhaps most problematically, Purcey returned to his pre-2008 wildness, walking five men per nine innings. Purcey is a lefty who can throw in the mid-90s, and the Jays rotation is built out of popsicle sticks and chewing gum, but even then, he'll be 28 in April, and his mechanics are inconsistent. As far as other applications, he's too often behind in the count, and he lacks a relief-friendly platoon split. Unless he makes a big leap forward, Purcey seems like a long shot to get an extended second audition.

Robert Ray

| | | | Bats: R | Throws: R | Height: 6' 5" | Weight: 190 | Born: January 21, 1984 | Age: 26 |

YEAR	TEAM	LVL	AGE	W	L	SV	G	GS	IP	H	HR	BB	SO	GB%	BABIP	STUFF	WHIP	ERA	SIERA	DERA	EqH9	EqHR9	EqBB9	EqSO9	VORP	SN/WX
2007	DUN	A+	23	3	3	1	18	15	66²	83	3	24	57	55%	.374	-16	1.60	4.86	3.98	6.57	12.7	1.2	3.9	5.5	-7.3	-0.77
2008	DUN	A+	24	5	3	0	13	13	70²	71	6	18	60	56%	.310	-14	1.26	4.20	3.62	6.65	10.6	1.8	2.9	5.2	-8.4	-0.83
2008	NHP	AA	24	8	6	0	16	16	96¹	108	6	27	72	54%	.330	1	1.40	3.18	4.09	4.53	9.9	1.0	2.7	4.8	10.1	0.64
2009	TOR	MLB	25	1	2	0	4	4	24¹	23	4	6	13	56%	.250	1	1.19	4.44	4.65	5.18	7.8	1.5	1.8	4.1	0.9	0.25
2010	TOR	MLB	26	3	5	0	24	11	73²	83	10	30	44	56%	.308	-11	1.52	5.35	4.78	5.74	10.3	1.2	3.4	5.0	-2.0	0.93

Breakout: 13% Improve: 51% Collapse: 19% Attrition: 23%   MLB: 26%   Comparables: Dustin Moseley, Zach Miner, Khalid Ballouli, Ben Burlingame

A bum shoulder shut down Ray in late May of last year, just four starts into his major-league career, but that didn't come as a surprise to anyone who heard the lanky righty grunt through his delivery prior to that. Those four big-league turns were a mixed bag, but he made a solid comeback in the Arizona Fall League and is expected to be ready to open the season in the Triple-A rotation. Ray has good control and can keep the ball on the ground often enough to have a future as a back-end starter, though the Jays might ultimately decide to move him into the bullpen, from which his high-effort delivery can be confined to short outings.

Scott Richmond

| | | | Bats: R | Throws: R | Height: 6' 5" | Weight: 225 | Born: August 30, 1979 | Age: 30 |

YEAR	TEAM	LVL	AGE	W	L	SV	G	GS	IP	H	HR	BB	SO	GB%	BABIP	STUFF	WHIP	ERA	SIERA	DERA	EqH9	EqHR9	EqBB9	EqSO9	VORP	SN/WX
2008	NHP	AA	28	5	8	0	16	16	89²	89	14	30	84	48%	.290	-11	1.33	4.92	3.63	6.17	8.8	2.0	3.0	6.0	-6.7	-0.91
2008	SYR	AAA	28	1	3	0	8	8	48	44	6	13	40	43%	.277	4	1.19	3.56	3.72	4.27	8.4	1.6	2.5	5.4	6.3	0.66
2008	TOR	MLB	28	1	3	0	5	5	27	32	2	2	20	43%	.345	18	1.26	4.00	3.59	3.98	11.1	0.7	0.7	6.2	4.4	0.68
2009	TOR	MLB	29	8	11	0	27	24	138²	147	27	59	117	44%	.295	-6	1.49	5.52	4.23	5.48	9.0	1.7	3.3	6.5	0.4	1.28
2010	TOR	MLB	30	7	9	0	28	25	136¹	140	20	52	99	44%	.297	3	1.41	4.65	4.42	4.93	9.4	1.3	3.2	6.0	8.7	1.18

Breakout: 6% Improve: 48% Collapse: 7% Attrition: 6%   MLB: 83%   Comparables: Claudio Vargas, Matt Kinney, Shane Bowers, Kevin Gross

This British Columbia native was an independent-league find in 2008 and a regular part of the Jays' rotation in 2009, though it's unclear if that is more a credit to Richmond or an embarrassment to the Jays. Richmond had solid peripherals in 2009, but was beaten about the head and neck by lefties (.292/.377/.550, 17 homers in 378 PAs) and had an acute case of gopheritis (1.8 HR/9), the latter the result of an extreme fly-ball rate and a lot of hard contact. Things only got worse as the season went along: in his final eight starts, Richmond allowed 11 homers, struck out just five more men than he walked, posted a 9.40 ERA, and averaged less than 4 ⅔ innings per start. If he's still a major-league starter two years from now, we'll be shocked.

Josh Roenicke

| | | | Bats: R | Throws: R | Height: 6' 3" | Weight: 200 | Born: August 4, 1982 | Age: 27 |

YEAR	TEAM	LVL	AGE	W	L	SV	G	GS	IP	H	HR	BB	SO	GB%	BABIP	STUFF	WHIP	ERA	SIERA	DERA	EqH9	EqHR9	EqBB9	EqSO9	VORP	SN/WX
2007	SAR	A+	24	2	1	16	27	0	27²	23	1	15	41	61%	.361	18	1.37	3.25	2.53	4.26	9.2	1.1	5.7	10.3	3.5	0.57
2007	CHT	AA	24	1	1	8	19	0	19	12	0	6	15	53%	.235	-5	0.95	0.95	3.77	2.04	6.1	0.5	3.1	5.1	6.8	0.70
2008	CHT	AA	25	4	2	10	22	0	22	21	2	12	28	47%	.328	5	1.50	3.27	3.22	4.70	9.0	1.2	4.5	8.2	1.9	-0.34
2008	LOU	AAA	25	2	0	3	35	0	39	34	2	14	43	49%	.314	6	1.23	2.54	3.05	3.04	8.8	0.7	3.4	7.5	10.1	1.18
2008	CIN	MLB	25	0	0	0	5	0	3	6	0	2	6	—	.667	3	2.67	9.00	2.54	9.00	18.0	0.0	6.0	15.0	-1.2	-0.21
2009	LOU	AAA	26	1	0	12	27	0	28	30	0	6	32	62%	.366	14	1.29	2.57	2.76	3.62	10.2	0.3	2.3	8.2	5.7	0.55
2009	CIN	MLB	26	0	0	0	11	0	13¹	13	0	4	14	51%	.361	12	1.27	2.70	3.03	2.92	10.2	0.0	2.2	8.8	3.5	-0.03
2009	TOR	MLB	26	0	0	0	13	0	17²	19	2	12	19	61%	.340	1	1.75	7.13	4.05	7.00	9.0	1.0	5.0	8.0	-3.0	-0.02
2010	TOR	MLB	27	3	5	8	60	0	59¹	61	7	27	53	54%	.318	-3	1.49	4.67	4.02	4.97	9.3	1.0	3.9	7.4	3.5	1.13

Breakout: 14% Improve: 41% Collapse: 30% Attrition: 9%   MLB: 34%   Comparables: Steve Reed, Mark Huismann, Mike Timlin, Todd Stephan

Ron's kid has a mid-90s fastball that's straight and a slider that's nothing special. He also got off to a late start after spending four full years as an outfielder at UCLA; thus he has just three full professional seasons under his belt at age 27, and they comprise the vast majority of his pitching experience. Roenicke flat-out dominated the International League over 27 appearances last year, walking just six and not allowing a home run while striking out 32 in 28 innings, but got a little wild after being flipped to Toronto in the Scott Rolen deal. He'll try to fight his way up the Jays' bullpen hierarchy this year, but he'll need a pitch that moves to have any sustained success in the majors.

Ricky Romero

Bats: R   Throws: L   Height: 6' 1"   Weight: 195   Born: November 6, 1984   Age: 25

YEAR	TEAM	LVL	AGE	W	L	SV	G	GS	IP	H	HR	BB	SO	GB%	BABIP	STUFF	WHIP	ERA	SIERA	DERA	EqH9	EqHR9	EqBB9	EqSO9	VORP	SN/WX
2007	NHP	AA	22	3	6	0	18	18	88¹	98	9	51	80	49%	.336	-4	1.69	4.89	4.39	6.44	10.4	1.6	5.2	6.0	-8.9	-0.95
2008	NHP	AA	23	5	5	0	21	21	121²	139	9	55	78	61%	.332	-13	1.59	4.96	4.67	5.78	10.4	1.2	4.1	4.1	-3.6	-1.22
2008	SYR	AAA	23	3	3	0	7	7	42²	42	3	20	38	63%	.322	10	1.45	3.37	3.91	4.02	9.4	0.9	4.5	6.0	6.6	0.57
2009	TOR	MLB	24	13	9	0	29	29	178	192	18	79	141	65%	.333	9	1.52	4.30	4.16	4.20	9.6	0.9	3.6	6.4	24.6	4.24
2010	TOR	MLB	25	7	11	0	31	29	156²	171	21	78	107	58%	.310	-6	1.59	5.29	4.71	5.59	9.9	1.1	4.1	5.6	-1.6	1.64

Breakout: 10% Improve: 45% Collapse: 15% Attrition: 15%   MLB: 100%   Comparables: Matt Young, Jeff Johnson, Kason Gabbard, Paul Maholm

With the rest of the Toronto rotation falling to pieces around him, Romero emerged as a pleasant surprise four years after being infamously drafted ahead of Troy Tulowitzki. Romero made the rotation out of spring training and, save for an oblique injury that disabled him early in the season, remained there as the default number-two starter behind Halladay. Still, Romero exhibited some of same the worrisome trends that Richmond did, including a .297/.348/.531 line by opposing lefties and a rough second half in which his team went 6-10 in his starts while he posted a 5.54 ERA, a 1.77 WHIP, and a weak 1.5 K/BB. In response, Romero spent the offseason working on a cutter and reviewing his mechanics as well as those of intradivision lefties Andy Pettitte and Jon Lester. That sort of dedication bodes well for an improved sophomore season, as does his youth, solid ground-ball rate, and the inflated BABIP from his rookie campaign.

Marc Rzepczynski

Bats: L   Throws: L   Height: 6' 3"   Weight: 205   Born: August 29, 1985   Age: 24

YEAR	TEAM	LVL	AGE	W	L	SV	G	GS	IP	H	HR	BB	SO	GB%	BABIP	STUFF	WHIP	ERA	SIERA	DERA	EqH9	EqHR9	EqBB9	EqSO9	VORP	SN/WX
2007	AUB	A-	21	5	0	0	11	7	45²	33	2	17	49	67%	.272	11	1.09	2.76	2.90	5.66	8.7	1.5	4.1	6.1	-0.7	0.17
2008	LNS	A	22	7	6	0	22	22	121	100	2	42	124	69%	.311	12	1.17	2.83	3.01	4.75	9.6	1.0	4.3	5.9	8.9	0.35
2009	NHP	AA	23	7	5	0	14	14	76²	80	1	36	88	66%	.367	14	1.51	2.93	3.26	5.76	10.9	0.6	4.3	7.7	-2.1	0.30
2009	LVG	AAA	23	2	0	0	2	2	11¹	7	0	4	16	55%	.280	11	0.97	0.79	2.07	1.19	5.6	0.0	3.2	9.5	5.4	0.52
2009	TOR	MLB	23	2	4	0	11	11	61¹	51	7	30	60	64%	.270	24	1.32	3.67	3.69	3.79	7.2	1.0	3.8	7.6	11.7	1.94
2010	TOR	MLB	24	6	8	0	29	25	125²	129	15	62	102	60%	.312	4	1.52	4.92	4.24	5.19	9.3	1.0	4.2	6.7	4.4	2.45

Breakout: 7% Improve: 43% Collapse: 20% Attrition: 9%   MLB: 100%   Comparables: Ken Holubec, Paul Maholm, Matthew Maloney, Jeff Johnson

In just his second full professional season after being drafted in the fifth round after four years at the University of California at Riverside, Rzepczynski (pronounced zep-CHIN-ski) skipped over High-A completely and joined the big-league rotation in early July. He didn't come out until September (after a run of four quality starts), because he had hit his limit of 150 innings for the year. A lefty with a heavy sinker who doesn't give up much against righties, Rzepczynski has a bit of BABIP correction coming his way, but as PECOTA suggests, he should be a midrotation stalwart in 2010 and beyond.

Zach Stewart

Bats: R   Throws: R   Height: 6' 2"   Weight: 205   Born: September 28, 1986   Age: 23

YEAR	TEAM	LVL	AGE	W	L	SV	G	GS	IP	H	HR	BB	SO	GB%	BABIP	STUFF	WHIP	ERA	SIERA	DERA	EqH9	EqHR9	EqBB9	EqSO9	VORP	SN/WX
2008	DYT	A	21	1	2	3	11	0	16¹	10	0	3	13	62%	.227	11	0.80	0.55	3.26	2.15	7.4	0.6	2.5	4.3	5.5	0.08
2008	SAR	A+	21	0	2	2	13	0	16²	16	0	11	23	38%	.400	15	1.62	1.62	3.19	3.90	10.8	0.6	6.6	9.0	2.7	0.08
2009	SAR	A+	22	1	1	0	7	7	42¹	47	1	8	32	67%	.341	5	1.30	2.13	3.54	5.05	11.7	1.2	2.6	4.5	1.9	0.06
2009	CAR	AA	22	3	0	0	7	7	37	29	1	10	31	64%	.275	23	1.05	1.46	3.45	2.65	8.5	0.8	2.6	5.8	10.8	1.10
2009	LOU	AAA	22	0	0	2	9	0	12¹	11	0	8	16	60%	.355	12	1.54	0.73	3.30	2.31	9.3	0.0	6.2	9.3	4.1	0.79
2009	LVG	AAA	22	0	0	0	11	0	13¹	18	1	6	14	66%	.415	6	1.80	3.37	3.56	5.54	12.5	0.7	4.2	7.6	-0.1	-0.36
2010	TOR	MLB	23	4	7	1	40	1	85²	94	12	40	60	55%	.314	-6	1.57	5.18	4.63	5.55	10.1	1.1	3.9	5.8	-0.4	1.67

Breakout: 8% Improve: 27% Collapse: 41% Attrition: 4%   MLB: 6%   Comparables: Anthony Claggett, Juan Guzman, Matt Torra, Joe Silkwood

The better of the two righty relievers acquired in the Rolen trade, Zach Stewart was taken out of Texas Tech by the Reds in the third round of the 2008 draft. He started 2009 as a starter in High-A and remained in the role in Double-A, posting a combined 1.82 ERA with a 3.5 K/BB. He nonetheless returned to relief in Triple-A, dominating the International League despite a few too many walks and continuing to pitch well (with fewer walks, but also fewer strikeouts) in the Pacific Coast League after the trade. Just 23, he has above-average velocity and is a contender for the major-league pen this year.

Brian Tallet

| | | | | | | Bats: L | | Throws: L | | Height: 6' 7" | | Weight: 215 | | Born: September 21, 1977 | | Age: 32 |

YEAR	TEAM	LVL	AGE	W	L	SV	G	GS	IP	H	HR	BB	SO	GB%	BABIP	STUFF	WHIP	ERA	SIERA	DERA	EqH9	EqHR9	EqBB9	EqSO9	VORP	SN/WX
2007	TOR	MLB	29	2	4	0	48	0	62¹	49	1	28	54	44%	.270	14	1.24	3.47	4.15	3.68	7.2	0.1	3.6	7.1	12.6	-0.07
2008	TOR	MLB	30	1	2	0	51	0	56¹	52	4	22	47	52%	.289	6	1.31	2.88	4.04	3.07	8.6	0.6	3.1	6.8	15.0	0.31
2009	TOR	MLB	31	7	9	0	37	25	160²	169	20	72	120	44%	.299	0	1.50	5.32	4.64	5.18	8.8	1.0	3.5	5.7	5.8	2.16
2010	TOR	MLB	32	6	7	0	81	11	110²	104	12	55	80	45%	.285	-3	1.44	4.42	4.76	4.69	8.6	0.9	4.2	5.9	10.0	0.50

Breakout: 8%   Improve: 42%   Collapse: 23%   Attrition: 20%   MLB: 93%   Comparables: Scott Radinsky, Mark Guthrie, Cliff Melton, Pete Schourek

Tallet's career ERA as a starter is more than a run higher than his career ERA as a reliever. That makes him something less than the handy utility pitcher the Jays believed he was last year when they gave him 25 starts and got a 5.41 ERA, 1.53 WHIP, and 1.6 K/BB in return. Not that they had many alternatives. Entering 2010, Tallet should be back in the long-relief role that worked so well for him the previous three years, though one worries that he'll be among the first names called should a rotation hole emerge.

LINEOUTS

Hitters

PLAYER	TEAM	LVL	AGE	PA	R	2B	3B	HR	RBI	BB	SO	SB-CS	EqBRR	AVG/OBP/SLG	EqAVG/EqOBP/EqSLG	EqA	VORP	WARP
3B K. Ahrens#	DUN	A+	20	423	35	17	2	4	36	37	76	1-1	-1.4	.215/.282/.302	.198/.258/.279	.189	-19.1	-3.8
C M. Barrett	TOR	MLB	32	19	3	0	0	1	2	1	5	0-0	0.0	.167/.211/.333	.167/.211/.333	.170	-0.6	-0.2
C R. Chavez	TOR	MLB	36	168	10	8	0	2	15	6	23	1-1	-0.7	.258/.285/.346	.266/.293/.342	.222	0.9	1.0
CF B. Coats*	LVG	AAA	27	553	82	33	3	6	56	47	64	25-7	6.1	.302/.361/.416	.262/.315/.356	.239	3.5	-0.4
SS J. Jackson	DUN	A+	20	294	44	12	1	0	17	39	87	17-4	2.6	.213/.321/.269	.195/.289/.246	.200	-5.2	-1.5
OF A. Loewen*	DUN	A+	25	391	47	22	4	4	31	50	114	5-2	-0.9	.236/.340/.355	.195/.276/.275	.196	-18.7	-3.6
CF D. Mastroianni	DUN	A+	23	274	55	11	2	0	26	37	38	32-7	2.9	.325/.426/.390	.293/.379/.347	.266	7.8	0.7
	NHP	AA	23	292	39	10	2	1	25	39	45	38-8	4.9	.271/.372/.340	.259/.345/.325	.255	6.7	0.7
C C. Perez	BLJ	Rk	18	163	17	11	3	1	21	16	23	2-5	-1.2	.291/.364/.433	.257/.309/.365	.234	1.0	0.2
C K. Phillips*	NHP	AA	25	43	1	0	0	1	1	3	8	0-0	0.0	.175/.233/.250	.171/.209/.244	.138	-3.3	-0.4
	LVG	AAA	25	316	37	13	0	8	29	29	53	0-0	-4.3	.300/.372/.433	.265/.331/.378	.251	6.0	0.5
	TOR	MLB	25	18	1	3	0	0	2	0	4	0-0	0.0	.278/.278/.444	.278/.278/.444	.246	0.7	-0.2
LF E. Thames*	DUN	A+	22	220	33	15	5	3	38	21	40	1-1	-2.3	.313/.386/.487	.276/.341/.432	.266	4.4	-0.2
CF K. Wilson	LNS	A	19	373	51	12	3	4	27	35	99	37-12	1.8	.212/.306/.305	.194/.261/.278	.197	-13.0	-3.2

Drafted with the compensation pick the Jays received from Texas for Frank Catalanotto in 2007, **Kevin Ahrens** is a strong-armed third baseman who went from "isn't hitting" to "can't hit" in his High-A debut last year. ⊘ **Michael Barrett** was the most productive catcher in the NL in 2006, but injuries and a bad attitude have derailed his career since, as he has hit .232/.276/.355 in 138 big-league games. ⊘ **Raul Chavez** has never hit, but keeps getting minor-league contracts and major-league opportunities because of his veteran catch-and-throw reputation. ⊘ **Buck Coats** is no prospect, but he does a little bit of everything well, is a solid organizational player, and would be of some value as a stopgap center fielder if not for Vernon Wells' immovable contract. ⊘ Drafted with the other compensation pick received for Catalanotto in 2007, **Justin Jackson** is the shortstop version of Ahrens, a toolsy, slick fielder whose bat washed out at Dunedin in 2009, taking his prospect status with it. ⊘ After a promising major-league introduction, Orioles southpaw **Adam Loewen** suffered an elbow fracture that ultimately forced him to give up pitching and try hitting, but year one of the experiment revealed that he's no Rick Ankiel, even if some scouts see power potential in his bat. ⊘ A speedy, hard-nosed center fielder out of the University of Southern Indiana, **Darin Mastroianni** gets the most out of his limited talent with the added advantage of having been old for his leagues thus far. ⊘ Venezuelan catcher **Carlos Perez** showed some facility with the bat in his stateside debut last year, making his upcoming full-season debut worth watching—the Jays may have an actual prospect! ⊘ Since being picked off the scrap heap by the Blue Jays, **Kyle Phillips** has hit .299/.358/.431 across their top three levels in the minors while spending more time at the infield corners than behind the plate. ⊘ A seventh-round pick out of Pepperdine in 2008, **Eric Thames** hit well in his pro debut, but as a left fielder without much power, he's unlikely to amount to much after making the leap to Double-A. ⊘ A second-round pick out of a Tampa high school in 2008, **Kenny Wil-**

son is a toolsy center fielder with a ton of speed, but is just shy of a total disaster at the plate. He's young enough and athletic enough to get sorted out, but he'll be a project.

Pitchers

PLAYER	TEAM	LVL	AGE	W	L	SV	IP	H	HR	BB	SO	GB%	BABIP	STUFF	WHIP	ERA	SIERA	DERA	EqH9	EqHR9	EqBB9	EqSO9	VORP
H. Alvarez	LNS	A	19	9	6	0	124¹	121	1	19	92	53%	.302	32	1.13	3.47	3.72	5.44	9.0	1.0	2.2	3.5	0.7
R. Bell	DUN	A+	23	4	1	0	96¹	66	5	22	112	53%	.264	6	0.91	2.43	2.39	4.16	7.8	1.5	2.8	7.2	13.2
B. Bullington	TOR	MLB	28	0	0	0	6	7	0	6	5	32%	.350	-3	2.17	3.00	6.09	2.84	9.9	0.0	7.1	5.7	1.9
—	LVG	AAA	28	3	1	3	38¹	42	2	7	43	58%	.370	14	1.28	3.52	2.67	4.94	9.9	0.7	1.9	8.4	2.3
B. Buzachero	NHP	AA	28	1	2	2	31	18	3	4	22	49%	.174	-3	0.71	1.74	3.54	3.00	6.0	1.8	1.5	4.5	8.3
—	LVG	AAA	28	4	2	8	41¹	29	4	10	34	52%	.219	3	0.94	3.05	3.58	4.00	5.8	1.1	2.2	5.8	7.0
F. Castro*	NHP	AA	24	2	0	0	21²	15	0	3	24	33%	.288	20	0.83	0.83	2.08	1.60	7.8	0.5	1.8	7.8	8.5
—	LVG	AAA	24	7	6	0	142¹	148	7	64	81	49%	.298	0	1.49	4.49	5.14	4.98	8.9	0.7	4.0	4.0	8.2
D. Farquhar	DUN	A+	22	1	0	7	17	10	0	11	23	57%	.263	16	1.24	0.53	3.08	3.38	6.8	0.6	6.8	8.4	3.8
—	NHP	AA	22	1	4	15	45²	31	1	30	51	52%	.268	13	1.34	2.36	3.81	4.02	7.4	0.6	5.8	7.4	7.2
C. Huggins*	LNS	A	23	1	1	0	34¹	24	1	11	40	30%	.280	12	1.02	1.57	2.65	2.73	7.8	1.4	3.7	6.6	9.6
—	DUN	A+	23	5	3	0	99²	90	12	30	83	45%	.281	-30	1.20	3.25	3.78	5.06	10.3	2.8	3.6	5.1	4.4
R. Lewis*	NHP	AA	26	2	4	1	42	35	2	22	45	31%	.306	1	1.36	2.57	3.80	3.58	9.2	1.2	4.8	7.4	8.3
—	LVG	AAA	26	2	3	0	24	23	1	9	20	56%	.301	-3	1.33	3.37	4.01	3.75	8.3	0.8	3.4	6.0	4.7
L. Perez*	NHP	AA	24	9	11	0	162¹	145	11	67	112	64%	.273	-11	1.31	3.55	4.30	5.62	9.3	1.4	3.9	4.4	-2.0

Henderson Alvarez is a righty control artist with a good changeup who pitched well starting for the Lugnuts last year as a 19-year-old; he could have a future as a back-end big-league starter. ⦸ A midround pick out of Rice in 2008, **Robert Bell** exceeded expectations by dominating at Dunedin last year, starting the year in the pen and finishing it in the rotation. Though he'll continue to start in the minors, he projects as a power reliever in the majors and should move swiftly. ⦸ Though the Pirates were to blame, **Bryan Bullington** will forever bear the scarlet letter B for "bust" as the top overall pick in 2002. His conversion to relief last year resulted in some impressive peripherals after an abbreviated stint in the majors in late April. ⦸ Would-be ROOGY **Bubbie Buzachero** returned to the Jays last year after a spin with the Tribe, having been dealt for Brian Tallet. ⦸ Pint-sized Dominican lefty **Fabio Castro** is now on his fifth organization at age 25, having signed a minor-league deal with the Red Sox. A hard thrower, he's built for relief, but last year's reverse split as a starter complicates things. ⦸ A 10th-round pick out of the University of Louisiana in 2008, **Daniel Farquhar** spent most of his first pro season closing in Double-A and dominating, but his swollen walk rate is a sign of trouble to come. ⦸ A late-round pick out of UC Santa Barbara, **Chuck Huggins** acquitted himself well in the High-A rotation in his first full pro season. ⦸ Plucked out of the Orioles' system, 27-year-old former prospect **Rommie Lewis** is a big lefty with a low, three-quarters delivery and the accompanying severe platoon split. ⦸ A 25-year-old sinkerballer who was unexceptional at Double-A last year, **Luis Perez** does happen to be left-handed, which may be why he continues to cling to a 40-man roster spot.

MANAGER: CITO GASTON

YEAR	TEAM	W-L	Pythag +/−	Avg PC	100+ P	120+ P	QS	BQS	REL	REL w Zero R	IBB	Subs	PH	PH Avg	PH HR	SB2	CS2	SB3	CS3	SAC Att	SAC %	POS SAC	Squeeze	Swing	In Play
2008	TOR	51-37	-4	99.9	47	3	47	2	215	153	16	34	36	.333	0	26	4	7	0	44	63.6%	27	0	61	46
2009	TOR	75-87	-9	97.5	84	1	77	9	445	284	26	20	48	.289	2	54	20	19	3	36	66.7%	22	0	112	83

In the first 129 games of Gaston's second stint as manager, the Blue Jays went 78-51, a .605 clip that would have, over a full single season, put them among the two best teams in the American League and made them a postseason shoo-in. In the 121 games that followed, Gaston's Jays went 48-73, a .397 clip that, over a full single season, would have ranked them among the worst two teams in the AL. Gaston didn't suddenly get stupid on May 19th of last year. Though tales of clubhouse discontent stemming from Gaston's alleged aloofness seeped out as the season drew to a close, such problems are as likely to be the result of losing as the cause. Rather, Gaston's luck ran out before his personality did. The Jays were a sub-.500 team under John Gibbons in 2008, and that was back when Dustin McGowan,

Shawn Marcum, and Jesse Litsch were in the rotation. Gaston made some logical upgrades to the lineup by making Adam Lind and Marco Scutaro regulars and platooning Lyle Overbay, but even those improvements could only go so far, with the non-Halladay members of the Jays' rotation posting a 5.28 ERA while averaging less than 5 ⅔ innings per start. Gaston announced in early December that he would step down after the 2010 season, the second on the two-year extension he signed following the 2008 season, and would take an advisory role with the organization that has employed him for 26 of the last 28 years. That makes it easy for first-year general manager Alex Anthopoulos to hire his own man for 2011 without having to fire a member of the franchise's Level of Excellence.

Washington Nationals

On April 17th, the 1-7 Nationals took on the Marlins with the hopes of distancing themselves from league laughingstock status. Unfortunately, Majestic Apparel was not careful enough, leaving Ryan Zimmerman and Adam Dunn to take the field with misspelled uniforms, "Natinals" emblazoned across the front. If ever there was a portent that a team would struggle to be taken seriously, this error certainly qualified. Sure enough, mocking shirts soon surfaced, printing the slogan "Natinals: No 'O' In Here," a double entendre serving as a potshot toward either the crosstown foe Baltimore Orioles and/or the perceived anemic offense.

Perhaps alone among the team's features, knocking the lineup wasn't merited. As the Nationals sank to the league's bottom in every conceivable category, at least their offense performed relatively well. Their struggles in the field, rotation, and bullpen negated their offense's contributions and firmly planted the Nats in the cellar, but a better offense did point toward how the 2009 Nationals squad was a much different animal from its prior incarnations.

One different aspect involved roster construction, as Nick Johnson finally seemed healthy, Jesus Flores and Ryan Zimmerman were bound to continue their evolution toward expected stardom, and Adam Dunn and Josh Willingham were brought in from the outside to solidify the attack. Joining Willingham in DC would be his fellow former Marlin Scott Olsen, who, if healthy, was supposed to help a teetering and tattered rotation. The team also made a bevy of low-risk pitching moves, signing players like Daniel Cabrera, Kip Wells, Julian Tavarez, Jorge Sosa, and, later, Josh Towers. Par for former GM Jim Bowden's constant pursuit of the next fourth-starter find in the free-talent pool, none of these players were expected to contribute all that much, but all were deemed worthy of fliers. Unfortunately, none of them provided any utility, and Olsen looked like a completely different pitcher before it was learned he had torn his labrum.

Olsen's failings and the inability for any of the fliers to work out left the pitching staff, already headed for limited success because of a putrid defense, in shambles. In fact, the Nationals ranked no higher than 12th in any meaningful pitching or defensive category, be it ERA, FRA, WXRL, SO/UBB, WHIP, or PADE. Aside from a solid half-season from Zimmermann, the key contributors were John Lannan and various disappointing auditions from Collin Balester, Shairon Martis, J. D. Martin, Garrett Mock, and Craig Stammen; things got so bad that in-season addition Livan Hernandez was actually viewed as a savior and stabilizing force.

Making matters worse was how, despite a very solid aggregate on-base percentage, the Nationals ranked among the worst baserunning teams in the league, with limited slugger productivity due to an almost lineup-wide case of lead-foot syndrome. The offense was further reduced when Jesus Flores suffered a season-ending injury requiring the extended use of Josh Bard. Exacerbating matters, Cristian Guzman decided that his .319/.354/.446 over the last 18 months was but an act to secure a contract extension, while the perpetually raging Elijah Dukes became a milquetoast at the dish. As a result, a whole lot of ugly emerged. A full season of Flores, Guzman's repeat of his recent performances, and Dukes' development were expected to add to the potent core of Zimmerman, Johnson, Dunn, and Will-

NATIONALS PROSPECTUS
2009 W-L: 59-103, 5th in NL East

Pythag	70-92	14th
RS/G	4.4	10th
RA/G	5.4	16th
EqA	.262	9th
EqBRR	-11.6	14th
SNWP	.441	15th
WXRL	1.83	15th
FRAr	5.64	16th
DE	.686	14th
PADE	-2.20	15th
Salary	$60.3	13th
Attend	1.82	13th

Ballpark: Nationals Park (2-yr. PF: 1012). Neutral, as RFK's helping hand missed by poor pitching

2009: Skimming scandal and on-field disaster tarnishes brass, heads roll, another Bowdastrophe

2010: The worldwide Strasburg Watch started last June; office pools form to pick debut dates

Action Items: Are the Lerners the new Clan Angelos, or will the grownups get to run their plaything?

ingham, creating a fearsome offense. That simply did not happen, and the pitching and defense only exacerbated the situation.

Everything above describes what happened on the field, however, while so much of the Nationals' last campaign dealt with off-field issues. Two separate but related scandals rocked the nation's capital in February, both of which involved the front office. Bowden resigned after allegations were aired that he had been skimming money off the bonuses signed by Latin American prospects. Though nothing concrete was proven at the time, Bowden felt—or was told to say this was how he felt—that the situation had become an unwanted distraction for the team. Assistant GM Mike Rizzo took over on an interim basis. A week earlier, special assistant Jose Rijo lost his job after it was discovered that prospect Esmailyn Gonzalez, a 19-year-old shortstop who had signed a $1.4 million signing bonus after training at Rijo's facility in the Dominican Republic, was actually Carlos Lugo, a 23-year-old born in November 1985 and not September 1989. Suddenly, his .343/.431/.475 performance in rookie ball in 2008 did not seem as impressive.

Scandals involving the skimming of bonuses paid to Latin American prospects have become much more commonplace in recent years, primarily due to the rising stipends doled out to the youngsters. At the beginning of the decade, signing bonuses for such players rarely rose above $10,000, meaning there was little to skim, but a recent study indicated that the average signing bonus, which was $29,272 in 2004, had risen to $108,130 in 2008. Though there are various ways to achieve such schemes, the underlying idea is similar. Someone in the front office or scouting department of the major league team inflates the value of the player and receives some of the "excess" when the player inevitably signs with the team. In a sense, the scout involved in the fraudulent act serves as a broker or an agent, causing more money to be paid to a player so that, in actuality, the money goes to both player and scout; the scout will act dishonestly to get the player $1.1 million when he might normally receive $450,000 if say $100,000 off the top is returned to the player.

Sometimes, the money isn't demanded, but rather offered as a gift by the player or his relatives as a means of issuing a wink-wink thanks for garnering such a lucrative signing bonus, but the act is illegal in any event. The problem is widespread in large part because Major League Baseball, up until the Mitchell Report's suggestions, had not established any sustained investigative branch. Once such an investigative unit was formed and its explorations began, reports surfaced that several teams had personnel involved in similar scandals, with an estimation that six teams and 20 employees would be implicated, with the caveat that further research and investigation could uncover even more wrongdoing. The Nationals were only the first team to be implicated and the first to have the taint of corruption bring down its front-office management.

Add to that the minor controversy involving Odalis Perez, who had signed a minor-league deal but reneged on the contractual stipulations upon deciding he instead desired a guaranteed contract, and the Nationals had plenty working against them before spring training began. During the season, the team dealt with further distractions such as the drawn-out firing of manager Manny Acta as the field-results fall guy, as well as the buildup to picking and then eventually signing first-round draft pick Stephen Strasburg to a four-year, $15.1 million deal.

Though these situations off the field hogged much of the spotlight, Rizzo has inherited some very real personnel issues. The interim executive would eventually be instated on a permanent basis and exhibited considerable patience in his first year on the job, opting to change the makeup of the big-league club as well as unload assets with little current utility for the best prospects he could acquire. With a player-development background going back to his days as a scout and later as the D'backs' director of scouting, he was very much in his element.

Trading Ronnie Belliard to the Dodgers and shipping Lastings Milledge to the Pirates fit within the goal of achieving a clubhouse makeover, while prospects of some value were added with the acquisitions of Aaron Thompson, Ryan Mattheus, and Robinson Fabian in separate deals for Nick Johnson and reliever Joe Beimel. Throughout the in-season trading period, many analysts questioned why Adam Dunn stayed put, when a player of his offensive caliber could provide a huge boost to playoff hopefuls like the Giants or Braves. Though Dunn was undoubtedly shopped, there were factors working against the Nationals' ability to extract a commensurate return. Specifically, his contract was back-loaded, whereby he earned $8 million in 2009 but $12 million in 2010, which probably meant that the team would need to send some funds in addition to the Big Donkey in exchange for other middling prospects, a proposition they decided against. Without making this move, the Nationals still managed to bring back pitching prospects that added both depth and at least a suggestion of upside.

Upside in the pitching department was more than welcome in this organization. Strasburg has yet to throw a minor-league pitch—though he did whiff 23 hitters in 19 innings in the Arizona Fall League—and Jordan Zimmermann will not return until the later stages of the 2010 season at the earliest after undergoing Tommy John surgery. This left John Lannan, a nice enough midrotation starter, as the only sure thing on the staff, flanked by a slew of hurlers projecting as either relievers or back-of-the-rotation options.

To add stability beyond Lannan, Rizzo decided to pursue an innings-eater and inked Jason Marquis to a two-year, $15 million deal after souring on Jon Garland's contractual requests. Marquis' track record is spotty at best, but the Nationals are holding out hope that he'll be the league-average innings-eater they need to reduce the bullpen's workload; if they aren't sure of rebuilding it, they can at least try to ensure that they see less of it. There's a long list of ifs, but if Scott Olsen is healthy, if Marquis can pitch to an ERA of no higher than 4.50, if Lannan retains his gains, if the club gets a combined 20 starts or so from Strasburg, and if improved contributions from whichever of last year's sacrificial chuck-and-duck lambs can be salvaged, then the Nats could see a major improvement in the pitching staff. They won't have an upper-echelon rotation, by any means, but they'll certainly have a better unit than last year's sad-sack doormat.

Admittedly, signing Marquis and several other free agents is a questionable move. The one-year, $3.5 million contract given to Matt Capps, the two-year, $6 million deal bringing Pudge Rodriguez into the fold, and the trade of a Rule 5 pick for arbitration-eligible reliever Brian Bruney invite a discussion of cellar-dwelling philosophy: to spend, or not to spend? In some situations, signings such as these make sense, either to signify a step in the right direction to the fans, to aid marketing the product, or even to potentially flip any or several of the players to another team at or near the trading deadline. While Dunn and Marquis conceivably fit as deadline-swap options, Capps and Rodriguez raise eyebrows. Capps signed a much more reasonable contract than the deals other teams doled out to mediocrities such as Brandon Lyon, John Grabow, and Fernando Rodney, but that's akin to justifying a D on a test by pointing out how all the other kids failed. One benefit of being in the Nationals' position, though, is being able to install just about anyone in the closer role—be it Capps or Bruney—as a means of inflating their value before a trade. In that regard, even the Capps deal makes some sense. Signing Rodriguez, however, makes little sense, considering that he can no longer hit, has seen his defensive ability wane, and makes too much guaranteed money to attract any suitor at any deadline.

With Flores shelved for a while, Pudge Rodriguez will undertake everyday duty, but the lineup will look a bit different. Dunn will move to first base permanently, and Guzman will shift to the keystone, with prospect Ian Desmond taking his place at shortstop. The new infield alignment should improve the team's defense, even if that improvement is marginal, while adding a power/speed bat to the lineup in the form of young Desmond. Several wild cards in the rotation and the bullpen could improve the pitching staff, but the point of gambling is that you never know if you'll win.

In short, there is plenty to like on the Nationals' current roster, but a lot has to go right for them to reach a modest goal of even 70 wins. They may not be the worst team in the senior circuit next season, and that's a first step in the right direction. More than that will have to wait.

HITTERS

Josh Bard			C							Bats: S	Throws: R	Height: 6' 3"		Weight: 225		Born: March 30, 1978			Age: 32

YEAR	TEAM	LVL	AGE	PA	R	2B	3B	HR	RBI	BB	SO	SB	CS	EqBRR	AVG	OBP	SLG	EqAVG	EqOBP	EqSLG	EqA	VORP	WARP	DEFENSE
2007	SDN	MLB	29	443	42	27	2	5	51	50	58	0	1	-4.2	.285	.364	.404	.302	.380	.429	.282	30.7	1.9	102-C -7
2008	SDN	MLB	30	198	11	9	0	1	16	18	25	0	0	-0.3	.202	.279	.270	.207	.283	.263	.195	-4.4	-1.5	46-C -6
2009	WAS	MLB	31	301	20	18	0	6	31	24	50	0	1	-5.1	.230	.293	.361	.240	.300	.375	.233	3.7	-0.6	72-C -7
2010	*SEA*	*MLB*	*32*	*294*	*25*	*14*	*1*	*5*	*30*	*29*	*49*	*0*	*1*	*-1.4*	*.252*	*.328*	*.369*	*.254*	*.327*	*.374*	*.241*	*5.7*	*0.3*	*68-C -3*

Breakout: 18% Improve: 41% Collapse: 29% Attrition: 23%   MLB: 85%   Comparables: Michael Barrett, Mike Matheny, Gus Triandos, John Flaherty

Jesus Flores' latest breakdown left Bard punching in as the Nats' primary backstop for much of the season. Underwhelmed by his impotent bat and nondescript glove work, they issued him his walking papers at season's end, but Bard's ability to at least masquerade as a switch-hitting catcher was attractive to the Mariners, who lacked veteran gravitas in their catching options. The days when Bard was considered likely to produce a beneficial on-base percentage are long gone, however, and the little value he'll provide involves giving Don Wakamatsu a different flavor of "Eh" in making out the tail end of his daily lineup.

Roger Bernadina   **OF**   Bats: L   Throws: L   Height: 6' 1"   Weight: 190   Born: June 12, 1984   Age: 26

YEAR	TEAM	LVL	AGE	PA	R	2B	3B	HR	RBI	BB	SO	SB	CS	EqBRR	AVG	OBP	SLG	EqAVG	EqOBP	EqSLG	EqA	VORP	WARP	DEFENSE			
2007	HAR	AA	23	415	58	15	2	6	36	38	80	40	13	-0.2	.270	.340	.369	.249	.308	.344	.236	1.1	-0.1	84-CF	-4	7-RF	2
2007	COH	AAA	23	53	6	3	0	0	1	9	11	0	1	-0.6	.167	.327	.238	.163	.308	.233	.198	-1.6	-0.2	12-CF	0		
2008	HAR	AA	24	303	47	11	7	5	38	31	64	26	9	4.0	.323	.398	.474	.270	.333	.387	.255	6.3	0.4	56-CF	-4	7-RF	1
2008	COH	AAA	24	215	33	13	3	4	16	16	37	15	2	-0.8	.351	.404	.513	.330	.381	.479	.297	14.9	1.2	45-CF	-5		
2008	WAS	MLB	24	86	10	1	1	0	2	9	21	4	3	0.0	.211	.294	.250	.221	.302	.260	.202	-3.2	-0.8	12-CF	-4	6-LF	0
2009	WAS	MLB	25	5	1	1	0	0	0	1	1	1	0	0.3	.250	.400	.500	.250	.400	.500	.340	0.6	0.1				
2010	WAS	MLB	26	296	29	13	3	4	19	28	68	9	5	0.4	.235	.312	.347	.239	.313	.340	.238	-3.7	-0.4	0-	0		

Breakout: 13% Improve: 29% Collapse: 32% Attrition: 25%   MLB: 6%   Comparables: Blane Fox, Tommy Dunbar, Darrell Sherman, Dave Krynzel

A broken ankle put Bernadina on the shelf for most of 2009, though he's scheduled to attend the Nationals' reserve outfielder casting call this spring. He has speed to burn but an inconsistent bat, with his lone productive minor-league season (2008) built on the fault line of a BABIP over .400. His wheels makes him look like a solid outfielder, but he has been stretched as a center fielder. And while some in the organization have highlighted Bernadina as a break-out candidate, Justin Maxwell is a more useful player and is (or should be) a better bet to go north with the big club.

Mike Burgess   **RF**   Bats: L   Throws: L   Height: 5' 11"   Weight: 195   Born: October 20, 1988   Age: 21

YEAR	TEAM	LVL	AGE	PA	R	2B	3B	HR	RBI	BB	SO	SB	CS	EqBRR	AVG	OBP	SLG	EqAVG	EqOBP	EqSLG	EqA	VORP	WARP	DEFENSE	
2007	NAT	Rk	18	154	22	6	3	8	32	25	37	1	2	-2.1	.336	.442	.617	.259	.344	.459	.273	4.8	-0.2	33-RF	-6
2007	VER	A-	18	81	10	1	1	3	10	10	23	1	1	-0.8	.286	.383	.457	.247	.321	.411	.249	0.4	-0.4	18-RF	-3
2008	HAG	A	19	460	60	26	4	18	60	46	136	5	1	-1.6	.249	.335	.469	.221	.292	.389	.238	-2.7	-1.5	109-RF	-10
2008	POT	A+	19	83	12	3	0	6	19	9	26	0	2	-1.7	.225	.325	.521	.219	.293	.452	.249	0.5	-0.3	17-RF	-3
2009	POT	A+	20	545	63	23	2	19	71	54	135	12	8	-5.8	.235	.325	.410	.217	.289	.364	.228	-8.7	-1.0	120-RF	1
2010	WAS	MLB	21	505	54	22	3	17	55	46	142	4	3	-2.2	.222	.300	.394	.225	.301	.397	.245	2.6	-0.1	116-RF	-3

Breakout: 29% Improve: 59% Collapse: 10% Attrition: 3%   MLB: 1%   Comparables: Xavier Paul, John Drennen, George Cecchetti, Greg Blosser

Burgess is a prototypical right fielder with a cannon arm and prodigious raw power, but his all-or-nothing approach at the plate leads to inconsistent production and low batting averages that aren't quite compensated for by his solid walk rate, and he loses a lot of his sock while facing lefties (.230 ISO vs. RHPs, .080 vs. LHPs). He's young and already scheduled this year to enroll in Double-A, baseball's classic weeder class, but Burgess will need to make more consistent contact if he wants to graduate to the productive big-league career that his tools will support.

Kory Casto   **4C**   Bats: L   Throws: R   Height: 6' 2"   Weight: 205   Born: December 8, 1981   Age: 28

YEAR	TEAM	LVL	AGE	PA	R	2B	3B	HR	RBI	BB	SO	SB	CS	EqBRR	AVG	OBP	SLG	EqAVG	EqOBP	EqSLG	EqA	VORP	WARP	DEFENSE			
2007	COH	AAA	25	472	56	20	2	11	55	54	106	4	4	-3.2	.246	.334	.384	.235	.315	.372	.242	0.4	-1.3	59-3B	-10	46-LF	-2
2007	WAS	MLB	25	57	1	2	0	0	3	2	17	0	0	0.1	.130	.158	.167	.130	.158	.167	-.097	-7.5	-1.0	10-LF	-1		
2008	COH	AAA	26	149	19	5	0	6	26	19	27	1	2	0.8	.308	.396	.485	.288	.369	.447	.278	5.4	0.5	29-RF	-1	3-1B	0
2008	WAS	MLB	26	182	15	10	0	2	16	19	36	1	0	-0.1	.215	.297	.313	.221	.302	.319	.219	-4.6	-0.5	20-1B	-2	12-3B	2
2009	SYR	AAA	27	504	57	22	1	8	58	44	85	4	4	-2.3	.271	.334	.378	.255	.313	.355	.237	-2.1	-0.6	54-3B	4	39-RF	-4
2010	WAS	MLB	28	464	49	20	1	9	50	46	106	2	2	-0.8	.231	.309	.350	.236	.312	.352	.237	0.7	-0.2	90-3B	-2		

Breakout: 13% Improve: 35% Collapse: 20% Attrition: 9%   MLB: 25%   Comparables: Jeff Wetherby, Tom Grant, Greg Dobbs, Dan Grunhard

Being a third base prospect in Ryan Zimmerman's organization is tough duty to begin with, but lately, Casto hasn't done himself any favors. His Double-A breakout in 2006 has been followed by a cumulative .265/.342/.395 line in Triple-A and two forgettable stints with the big club, and the organization's opinion of his future was demonstrated last spring when they chose to go north with three catchers while exposing Casto to waivers. Casto, typically described as a gamer, boasts four-corner flexibility and a lefty bat, but he's been hopeless against same-side pitching and will be hard-pressed to beat out Mike Morse for a utility role, even if Riggleman likes some multipositional sock on his benches. The Dobbs comp seems appropriate, but to his credit, Casto is a better glove.

Leonard Davis — UT

Bats: L | Throws: R | Height: 5' 10" | Weight: 195 | Born: December 24, 1983 | Age: 26

YEAR	TEAM	LVL	AGE	PA	R	2B	3B	HR	RBI	BB	SO	SB	CS	EqBRR	AVG	OBP	SLG	EqAVG	EqOBP	EqSLG	EqA	VORP	WARP	DEFENSE			
2007	HAG	A	23	385	47	29	4	16	56	25	86	7	6	-4.4	.290	.344	.534	.240	.280	.413	.236	-1.5	-2.0	56-3B	-12	18-2B	-2
2007	POT	A+	23	87	8	4	0	4	10	1	22	0	2	-1.1	.262	.267	.452	.235	.241	.365	.203	-3.3	-1.0	20-3B	-5		
2008	POT	A+	24	247	47	14	2	14	37	23	47	7	5	-0.9	.332	.403	.608	.280	.336	.476	.274	9.6	0.3	53-3B	-7		
2008	HAR	AA	24	48	8	1	0	4	10	6	5	2	0	0.3	.488	.553	.805	.429	.489	.667	.381	7.8	0.9	8-3B	0		
2008	COH	AAA	24	190	21	13	3	7	29	5	48	1	1	0.5	.239	.266	.461	.232	.259	.436	.234	-1.0	-0.5	26-LF	-1	10-2B	0
2009	HAR	AA	25	434	47	19	5	14	51	32	95	14	2	0.0	.281	.340	.462	.248	.295	.400	.241	1.0	-0.5	46-LF	-5	20-RF	1
2009	SYR	AAA	25	53	4	1	1	2	4	4	13	0	0	-0.3	.208	.269	.396	.208	.269	.396	.228	-0.8	-0.1	13-LF	0		
2010	WAS	MLB	26	445	42	21	4	13	44	30	122	4	3	-1.0	.231	.286	.394	.235	.287	.388	.238	-1.0	-0.4	79-LF	-3		

Breakout: 7%   Improve: 29%   Collapse: 31%   Attrition: 16%   MLB: 7%   Comparables: Quinn Mack, Doug Loman, Beau Allred, Pedro Swann

The Nationals have finally decided that the appropriate position for Davis is "everywhere," as he again saw time in the outfield as well as second and third base last year. His lefty bat produces middling power (he socked Eastern League right-handers at a .307/.380/.529 clip), and he displayed a new ability to steal the odd base. If Willie Harris had a younger sibling with slightly more power and slightly less speed, it might be Davis, but fitting both of them on the big-league roster would require some sort of shoehorn, as well as blinders to look past how brutal Davis's infield play has been. At some point with the organizational soldiers on the rosters sprinkled with the odd prospect, you sum them up with, "They also played."

Ian Desmond — SS

Bats: R | Throws: R | Height: 6' 2" | Weight: 185 | Born: September 20, 1985 | Age: 24

YEAR	TEAM	LVL	AGE	PA	R	2B	3B	HR	RBI	BB	SO	SB	CS	EqBRR	AVG	OBP	SLG	EqAVG	EqOBP	EqSLG	EqA	VORP	WARP	DEFENSE			
2007	POT	A+	21	536	69	30	4	13	45	57	99	27	11	-7.4	.264	.357	.432	.241	.312	.382	.245	11.5	0.2	127-SS	-10		
2008	HAR	AA	22	364	42	14	0	12	44	31	78	12	8	-1.1	.251	.318	.406	.230	.287	.364	.227	3.0	-0.2	91-SS	-5		
2009	HAR	AA	23	189	29	12	1	6	18	16	40	13	4	1.5	.306	.372	.494	.276	.330	.454	.269	9.6	1.6	43-SS	4		
2009	SYR	AAA	23	205	25	12	2	1	14	20	31	8	1	2.3	.354	.428	.461	.330	.403	.436	.297	15.8	1.2	52-SS	-6		
2009	WAS	MLB	23	89	9	7	2	4	12	5	14	1	0	0.3	.280	.318	.561	.293	.330	.610	.298	8.2	0.6	16-SS	-2	5-2B	0
2010	WAS	MLB	24	454	46	21	2	10	36	39	107	10	5	-0.8	.238	.310	.373	.246	.317	.392	.246	9.4	0.7	112-SS	-3		

Breakout: 12%   Improve: 38%   Collapse: 19%   Attrition: 15%   MLB: 53%   Comparables: Juan Delarosa, Jim Olander, Jack Ayer, Erick Almonte

A toolsy former third-round pick out of a Florida high school, Desmond apparently has a very slow-burning fuse after making merely fitful progress in his five years while climbing the organizational ladder. A combined .330/.401/.477 line in the upper minors last season earned him a successful 21-game tryout with the big club, and the Nationals seem committed to shifting Cristian Guzman's overpriced carcass to the other side of the keystone and installing Desmond as their starting shortstop this year. If Desmond sticks, he should provide double digits in homers and steals as well as adequate glove work. Last year's offensive breakout was a bit of a mirage produced by a BABIP north of .400, and his nondescript walk rate precludes any chance he'll become a valuable table-setter, but a broad-based tool set gives him a good chance to become more than just a standard middle-infield filler.

Elijah Dukes — RF

Bats: R | Throws: R | Height: 6' 1" | Weight: 240 | Born: June 26, 1984 | Age: 26

YEAR	TEAM	LVL	AGE	PA	R	2B	3B	HR	RBI	BB	SO	SB	CS	EqBRR	AVG	OBP	SLG	EqAVG	EqOBP	EqSLG	EqA	VORP	WARP	DEFENSE			
2007	TBA	MLB	23	220	27	3	2	10	21	33	44	2	4	-1.1	.190	.318	.391	.197	.327	.415	.250	3.3	0.4	38-CF	-1		
2008	COH	AAA	24	57	8	3	1	1	6	8	17	2	2	-0.6	.234	.368	.404	.229	.362	.396	.260	0.9	0.0	8-LF	-1		
2008	WAS	MLB	24	334	48	16	2	13	44	50	79	13	4	-0.1	.264	.386	.478	.275	.392	.496	.303	22.4	3.0	68-RF	2	7-LF	1
2009	SYR	AAA	25	80	8	8	0	3	10	9	9	5	1	-0.2	.279	.387	.529	.275	.375	.493	.298	4.8	0.8	15-RF	2		
2009	WAS	MLB	25	416	38	20	4	8	58	46	74	3	10	-3.6	.250	.337	.393	.266	.346	.416	.256	7.9	0.6	62-RF	3	31-CF	-6
2010	WAS	MLB	26	494	56	21	3	16	63	67	96	10	10	-1.3	.246	.358	.423	.254	.364	.438	.276	19.4	2.4	101-RF	2		

Breakout: 15%   Improve: 55%   Collapse: 6%   Attrition: 2%   MLB: 96%   Comparables: Austin Kearns, Carmelo Martinez, Derek Bell, Dave Henderson

Is it a positive development when "oft-injured" and "disappointing" overtake "troubled" as the adjective of choice to describe a young player? Dukes started the season in center and posted a .277/.347/.473 line before a hamstring problem put him on the DL in May. He scuffled badly after his return and spent a month in Syracuse. His overall numbers and plate approach took a big step back from 2008, as he took more big hacks, walked less, and hit more popups and warning-track fly balls—trends he'll need to address. To his credit, there were no major off-field distractions, and the Nats went out of their way last fall to praise Dukes' new maturity, though the tragic death of his father this winter, shortly after he was released from a long prison sentence, serves only to heap more misery and stress on an already troubled life. Dukes should be set to enter the season as Washington's right fielder, and he may finally deliver on the patience/speed/power combination that has teased his employers for years, but time is no longer on his side.

Adam Dunn   **1B**   Bats: L   Throws: R   Height: 6' 6"   Weight: 275   Born: November 9, 1979   Age: 30

YEAR	TEAM	LVL	AGE	PA	R	2B	3B	HR	RBI	BB	SO	SB	CS	EqBRR	AVG	OBP	SLG	EqAVG	EqOBP	EqSLG	EqA	VORP	WARP	DEFENSE	
2007	CIN	MLB	27	632	101	27	2	40	106	101	165	9	2	1.5	.264	.386	.554	.262	.386	.547	.312	49.5	4.3	133-LF	-9
2008	CIN	MLB	28	464	58	14	0	32	74	80	120	1	1	-2.0	.233	.373	.528	.239	.373	.542	.304	32.4	1.7	103-LF	-16
2008	ARI	MLB	28	187	21	9	0	8	26	42	44	1	0	-0.7	.243	.417	.472	.234	.406	.448	.303	11.1	0.8	21-RF -4	15-1B -4
2009	WAS	MLB	29	668	81	29	0	38	105	116	177	0	1	-1.9	.267	.398	.529	.279	.403	.550	.319	51.5	3.4	61-1B -6	57-LF -10
2010	WAS	MLB	30	641	83	24	1	35	97	107	157	3	2	-0.5	.244	.375	.491	.247	.375	.493	.303	39.1	3.5	125-1B	-6

Breakout: 6%   Improve: 34%   Collapse: 15%   Attrition: 9%   MLB: 97%   Comparables: Jim Thome, Carlos Delgado, Mo Vaughn, Boog Powell

Baseball's version of the Lego block, the shape of Dunn's production never changes. His patience and power make him a solid base upon which to snap together a productive lineup, his strikeouts and low batting averages make him seem less valuable than he really is, and his inanimate defense erodes a large portion of his value. Dunn's first season in Washington on a two-year, $20 million contract saw him fall short of 40 home runs for the first time since 2003, but a career-high batting average and OBP and continued power in a less hitter-friendly park led to his best EqA. The Nationals have permanently shifted his iron glove to first base, where they feel it will do less damage, and the Big Donkey is taking jujitsu to improve his agility. If that works, Washington will have even less chance to re-sign him at year's end, since even a hint of glove-liness will add NL teams to a list of suitors already likely to include everyone in the market for a boppin' DH.

Danny Espinosa   **SS**   Bats: S   Throws: R   Height: 6' 0"   Weight: 190   Born: April 25, 1987   Age: 23

YEAR	TEAM	LVL	AGE	PA	R	2B	3B	HR	RBI	BB	SO	SB	CS	EqBRR	AVG	OBP	SLG	EqAVG	EqOBP	EqSLG	EqA	VORP	WARP	DEFENSE
2008	VER	A-	21	87	8	2	0	0	4	17	17	2	2	-1.0	.328	.476	.359	.261	.381	.275	.251	2.1	0.2	16-SS -1
2009	POT	A+	22	576	90	31	4	18	72	74	129	29	11	3.3	.264	.375	.460	.245	.335	.414	.263	23.9	3.9	125-SS 8
2010	WAS	MLB	23	473	51	21	2	11	44	52	125	9	5	0.9	.226	.319	.370	.233	.324	.379	.249	11.3	1.5	105-SS 3

Breakout: 9%   Improve: 46%   Collapse: 14%   Attrition: 6%   MLB: 4%   Comparables: Drew Sutton, Jerome Nelson, Tim Vannaman, Kevin Stocker

Espinosa's full-season debut was an unqualified success, as the former Long Beach State star drew walks and showed impressive power in the Carolina League, capping off his year with a fine run in the Arizona Fall League. The organization loves the makeup of this switch-hitter with a solid glove and is already dreaming of a slick-fielding, productive, and low-cost Desmond/Espinosa middle infield in the seasons to come.

Jesus Flores   **C**   Bats: R   Throws: R   Height: 6' 0"   Weight: 230   Born: October 26, 1984   Age: 25

YEAR	TEAM	LVL	AGE	PA	R	2B	3B	HR	RBI	BB	SO	SB	CS	EqBRR	AVG	OBP	SLG	EqAVG	EqOBP	EqSLG	EqA	VORP	WARP	DEFENSE
2007	WAS	MLB	22	197	21	9	0	4	25	14	48	0	1	-0.4	.244	.310	.361	.256	.320	.372	.240	4.5	0.8	44-C 2
2008	COH	AAA	23	69	8	3	0	1	7	8	20	0	0	-0.7	.153	.275	.254	.150	.271	.233	.181	-2.1	-0.6	15-C -3
2008	WAS	MLB	23	324	23	18	1	8	59	15	78	0	1	-2.9	.256	.296	.402	.260	.298	.403	.243	7.6	-0.2	76-C -6
2009	WAS	MLB	24	106	13	3	2	4	15	11	26	0	0	-1.1	.301	.371	.505	.312	.381	.548	.305	9.8	1.1	23-C 0
2010	WAS	MLB	25	317	29	14	1	8	48	26	79	0	1	-1.2	.243	.315	.386	.251	.322	.400	.248	8.8	0.8	72-C -2

Breakout: 22%   Improve: 53%   Collapse: 11%   Attrition: 13%   MLB: 100%   Comparables: Yadier Molina, Shanty Hogan, Javy Lopez, Kelly Stinnett

The future was set to arrive for Flores in 2009, but shoulder woes culminating in September labrum surgery limited him to 29 games, during which he continued to give tantalizing hints of what may be in store. The former Rule 5 pickup has always been a solid defensive catcher with power and had started to improve on a few of his offensive weaknesses by drawing more walks and hitting righties (.313/.384/.547) before being shelved (small-sample caveats apply). Flores is scheduled to be ready sometime in spring training, although there is some concern that his throwing arm might take longer to recover. The late-career shadow of Ivan Rodriguez is on hand just in case, but since

Flores has the tools to be an above-average big-league backstop, any time he spends both healthy and on the bench will be a waste.

Alberto Gonzalez — 2B

Bats: R   Throws: R   Height: 5' 11"   Weight: 160   Born: April 18, 1983   Age: 27

YEAR	TEAM	LVL	AGE	PA	R	2B	3B	HR	RBI	BB	SO	SB	CS	EqBRR	AVG	OBP	SLG	EqAVG	EqOBP	EqSLG	EqA	VORP	WARP	DEFENSE			
2007	NYA	MLB	24	15	3	0	0	0	1	1	1	0	1	-0.3	.071	.133	.071	.143	.200	.143	-.153	-1.5	-0.1	4-SS	1		
2008	NYA	MLB	25	58	4	2	0	0	1	4	8	0	0	0.8	.173	.232	.212	.176	.236	.216	.153	-3.7	-0.5	7-SS	-1	6-3B	0
2008	WAS	MLB	25	54	9	6	0	1	9	4	6	0	1	-0.1	.347	.407	.531	.347	.407	.510	.314	4.6	0.5	10-SS	-1		
2009	WAS	MLB	26	316	31	16	3	1	33	14	27	1	1	-3.4	.265	.299	.351	.272	.305	.362	.235	2.2	-0.8	41-2B	-2	32-SS	-8
2010	WAS	MLB	27	396	43	21	3	4	38	26	54	4	3	0.1	.255	.312	.359	.264	.320	.368	.239	5.5	0.5	89-SS	-1		

Breakout: 15%   Improve: 42%   Collapse: 18%   Attrition: 15%   MLB: 74%   Comparables: Al Pedrique, Adam Everett, Rod Correia, Rafael Santana

Peruse the 2009 numbers produced by the Attorney General at your peril, as they have been known to cause nausea, headaches, and an extreme feeling of sympathy for both the player who suffered through such a difficult season and the fans forced to witness it. Uncharacteristically bad defense, poor baserunning, and a pestilential .228/.262/.281 line against right-handed pitching led to the National League's lowest WARP. Gonzalez isn't quite as bad as all that, and his glove at least should bounce back, but the arrival of Ian Desmond and a front office keen on adding another veteran infielder should preclude him from anything but a token role on the 2010 club. In layman's terms, this is referred to as progress.

Cristian Guzman — MI

Bats: S   Throws: R   Height: 6' 0"   Weight: 215   Born: March 21, 1978   Age: 32

YEAR	TEAM	LVL	AGE	PA	R	2B	3B	HR	RBI	BB	SO	SB	CS	EqBRR	AVG	OBP	SLG	EqAVG	EqOBP	EqSLG	EqA	VORP	WARP	DEFENSE	
2007	WAS	MLB	29	192	31	6	6	2	14	15	21	2	0	3.0	.328	.380	.466	.347	.396	.486	.306	16.7	1.2	42-SS	-6
2008	WAS	MLB	30	612	77	35	5	9	55	23	57	6	5	-3.0	.316	.345	.440	.324	.350	.446	.273	32.6	5.0	132-SS	10
2009	WAS	MLB	31	555	74	24	7	6	52	16	75	4	5	3.5	.284	.306	.390	.296	.317	.404	.245	12.6	2.0	113-SS	4
2010	WAS	MLB	32	481	64	24	4	7	43	26	60	5	4	0.6	.292	.334	.409	.300	.340	.419	.263	18.6	2.2	103-SS	1

Breakout: 10%   Improve: 37%   Collapse: 12%   Attrition: 5%   MLB: 96%   Comparables: Mark Grudzielanek, Luis Castillo, Rich Aurilia, Jose Offerman

Talk about doubling down: after already getting a four-year, $16.8 million deal from Jim Bowden before the 2005 season, Guzman managed to parlay 18 months of relatively useful production into a two-year, $16 million extension signed during the 2008 season. The ink was hardly dry before the veteran shortstop reverted to his prodigiously out-making ways. His ephemeral offensive value had been constructed on a short-term jump in his line-drive rates and the concurrently higher BABIPs they produced, but walking in fewer than three percent of his plate appearances last year—a rate only surpassed in the NL by the swingin' comedy team of Miggy and Bengie—guaranteed that he would once again show up on most "OBP sinkhole" lists. The Nationals are considering a move across the keystone to mask his ever-decreasing range. It's safe to say that last year was his true level of production, and the only good news here is that Guzman is likely to be someone else's problem come 2011.

Willie Harris — UT

Bats: L   Throws: R   Height: 5' 9"   Weight: 185   Born: June 22, 1978   Age: 32

YEAR	TEAM	LVL	AGE	PA	R	2B	3B	HR	RBI	BB	SO	SB	CS	EqBRR	AVG	OBP	SLG	EqAVG	EqOBP	EqSLG	EqA	VORP	WARP	DEFENSE			
2007	ATL	MLB	29	391	56	20	8	2	32	40	71	17	11	0.2	.270	.349	.392	.289	.366	.411	.266	10.6	1.7	69-LF	3	12-CF	1
2008	WAS	MLB	30	424	58	14	4	13	43	50	66	13	3	0.4	.251	.344	.417	.257	.348	.428	.272	14.4	2.4	63-LF	6	15-CF	1
2009	WAS	MLB	31	393	47	18	6	7	27	57	62	11	4	-1.3	.235	.364	.393	.248	.371	.411	.279	17.5	1.6	53-CF	0	20-LF	-1
2010	WAS	MLB	32	381	53	19	5	7	34	44	64	11	6	-0.1	.259	.354	.410	.262	.354	.405	.274	17.8	2.0	70-CF	1		

Breakout: 8%   Improve: 27%   Collapse: 17%   Attrition: 16%   MLB: 96%   Comparables: Marvin Benard, Matt Lawton, Vada Pinson, Brady Anderson

The speedy Harris has surprisingly carved out a niche for himself as a useful superutility player, moving between center field and second base, stealing a few bases, and posting big-league career highs last season in EqA and VORP—and it's all due to a radical change in his approach. The AL version of Harris had used a "slap it and run" style, but in the senior circuit, his fly-ball rate has climbed from just under 30 percent to 38.3 percent in 2008 to 46.7 percent last year. Consequently, he has increased his isolated power and made up for the inevitable drop in batting average by drawing considerably more walks. Last year, his home-run rate sank despite the extra fly balls, his line-drive rate plunged, and his career-high OBP was boosted by nine HBPs, so a reduced number of prodigious hacks is definitely in order. If he can manage that, he'll be in line for a nice little raise when he hits the free-agent market at season's end.

Destin Hood				OF							Bats: R		Throws: R		Height: 6' 1"		Weight: 180		Born: April 3, 1990			Age: 20		
YEAR	TEAM	LVL	AGE	PA	R	2B	3B	HR	RBI	BB	SO	SB	CS	EqBRR	AVG	OBP	SLG	EqAVG	EqOBP	EqSLG	EqA	VORP	WARP	DEFENSE
2008	NAT	Rk	18	98	18	6	1	0	14	8	19	5	2	0.6	.256	.333	.349	.200	.258	.289	.191	-5.0	-2.1	22-LF -6
2009	VER	A-	19	159	12	4	1	2	24	11	45	2	1	-1.1	.246	.302	.333	.215	.252	.285	.194	-7.7	-1.6	23-RF -3 9-LF 1
2009	NAT	Rk	19	98	18	10	3	3	24	8	19	3	0	2.3	.330	.388	.614	.264	.306	.484	.268	2.6	-0.1	20-LF -3
2010	WAS	MLB	20	223	15	9	0	4	23	15	67	1	0	-0.8	.212	.272	.309	.218	.278	.312	.205	-7.5	-1.2	47-RF -3

Breakout: 47% Improve: 65% Collapse: 20% Attrition: 0%   MLB: 0%   Comparables: Joe Secoda, Danny Oyas, Dorian Daughtry, Ronnie French

More of an athlete than a baseball player when the Nationals signed him away from a Crimson Tide football scholarship after the 2008 draft, Hood remains much more projection than production. He lacks the instincts and blazing speed to play center field, and he has yet to flash much in the way of power, patience, or hitting ability; on the other hand, he has yet to play 100 professional baseball games, so it's way too early to start writing him off. Hood is a seed that may take a lot of time to germinate.

Austin Kearns				RF							Bats: R		Throws: R		Height: 6' 3"		Weight: 240		Born: May 20, 1980			Age: 30		
YEAR	TEAM	LVL	AGE	PA	R	2B	3B	HR	RBI	BB	SO	SB	CS	EqBRR	AVG	OBP	SLG	EqAVG	EqOBP	EqSLG	EqA	VORP	WARP	DEFENSE
2007	WAS	MLB	27	674	84	35	1	16	74	71	106	2	2	1.2	.266	.355	.411	.280	.368	.427	.278	24.3	4.6	154-RF 17 2-CF -1
2008	WAS	MLB	28	357	40	10	0	7	32	35	63	2	2	0.8	.217	.311	.316	.224	.315	.323	.227	-5.6	-0.6	82-RF 0
2009	WAS	MLB	29	211	20	6	2	3	17	32	51	1	1	0.4	.195	.336	.305	.206	.341	.314	.241	-0.5	0.2	41-RF 3
2010	CLE	AL	30	407	50	17	1	11	46	48	77	2	2	0.4	.253	.351	.397	.251	.348	.392	.265	10.7	1.5	92-RF 3

Breakout: 11% Improve: 45% Collapse: 14% Attrition: 12%   MLB: 91%   Comparables: Wil Cordero, Jermaine Dye, Michael Cuddyer, Al Cowens

After one final year of injury and almost comically bad offensive production, a necessary August thumb surgery mercifully brought an end to the Washington run of "Austin Kearns: Nationals Man of Misery." For $17.5 million over three years, Kearns produced one solid season followed by two vastly inferior efforts—not unlike the Mike Myers film series. The Nats kept writing his name in the lineup, hoping against hope for a transient return of his offensive mojo to dupe some contender into a midseason swap, but corner outfielders that can't outhit corner shopkeepers aren't in high demand. PECOTA is mildly optimistic that he could hit well enough to stick as a reserve, and he might, if healthy, but there have been few extended stretches when Kearns has been healthy.

Chris Marrero				1B							Bats: R		Throws: R		Height: 6' 3"		Weight: 210		Born: July 2, 1988			Age: 21		
YEAR	TEAM	LVL	AGE	PA	R	2B	3B	HR	RBI	BB	SO	SB	CS	EqBRR	AVG	OBP	SLG	EqAVG	EqOBP	EqSLG	EqA	VORP	WARP	DEFENSE
2007	HAG	A	18	243	31	14	0	14	53	14	39	0	4	0.2	.293	.337	.545	.257	.292	.447	.249	1.4	-0.9	35-LF -8 10-RF -1
2007	POT	A+	18	290	40	11	3	9	35	32	63	0	0	-4.7	.259	.338	.431	.233	.297	.366	.233	-3.2	-0.6	53-LF -2 4-RF 0
2008	POT	A+	19	289	40	15	2	11	38	25	55	0	0	2.0	.250	.325	.453	.232	.291	.392	.237	-4.5	-0.9	68-1B -3
2009	POT	A+	20	469	58	21	2	16	65	42	97	2	3	-3.8	.287	.360	.464	.264	.322	.417	.256	-2.3	-1.5	104-1B -10
2009	HAR	AA	20	84	9	6	0	1	11	8	18	0	1	-1.6	.267	.345	.387	.247	.318	.351	.232	-2.6	-0.7	21-1B -3
2010	WAS	MLB	21	548	58	24	2	16	65	44	126	1	2	-1.6	.242	.308	.392	.249	.314	.408	.247	-1.5	-0.7	120-1B -5

Breakout: 24% Improve: 53% Collapse: 13% Attrition: 7%   MLB: 1%   Comparables: Wes Bankston, David Winfree, Marc Newfield, Chris Brown

The slugging first-base prospect bounced back from the broken leg that shortened his 2008 season to put up solid numbers during his second spin through the Carolina League, but never unleashed his power stroke during a late-season stint in Double-A. Marrero has moved to the bottom of the defensive spectrum, but remains a liability in the field. He strikes out too often to produce high batting averages, and his power and patience are notable but not elite-level good. Only 21 as he enters the high minors, Marrero has time to work on his game and will need to amp up the power, or he'll fall far short of the high offensive standards set by major-league first basemen.

Justin Maxwell — CF

Bats: R Throws: R Height: 6' 5" Weight: 245 Born: November 6, 1983 Age: 26

YEAR	TEAM	LVL	AGE	PA	R	2B	3B	HR	RBI	BB	SO	SB	CS	EqBRR	AVG	OBP	SLG	EqAVG	EqOBP	EqSLG	EqA	VORP	WARP	DEFENSE			
2007	HAG	A	23	244	51	12	2	14	40	26	57	14	3	2.4	.301	.389	.579	.247	.314	.429	.258	5.6	0.6	36-CF	-2	9-RF	0
2007	POT	A+	23	260	35	13	0	13	43	24	65	21	5	1.3	.263	.338	.491	.237	.292	.407	.245	3.2	0.4	54-CF	0		
2007	WAS	MLB	23	27	5	0	0	2	5	1	8	0	0	0.2	.269	.296	.500	.269	.296	.500	.275	0.6	0.4	5-CF	2		
2008	HAR	AA	24	180	35	6	3	7	28	31	28	13	4	0.5	.233	.367	.459	.211	.322	.388	.255	2.7	0.6	15-LF	1	12-RF	0
2009	SYR	AAA	25	448	68	10	5	13	42	54	136	35	8	2.2	.242	.344	.396	.229	.327	.379	.254	9.4	1.1	83-CF	1	15-LF	-1
2009	WAS	MLB	25	102	13	4	1	4	9	12	32	6	1	0.7	.247	.343	.449	.258	.353	.461	.287	5.6	0.7	23-CF	0		
2010	WAS	MLB	26	437	51	15	3	13	43	46	129	14	6	1.3	.217	.307	.373	.224	.312	.383	.246	7.0	0.8	89-CF	0		

Breakout: 11% Improve: 38% Collapse: 17% Attrition: 15% MLB: 44% Comparables: Mark Smith, Derrick Gibson, Lyle Mouton, Jeff Deardorff

Always a physical specimen but only occasionally healthy, Maxwell provides a lunch-menu version of Mike Cameron's more filling entree: speed, power, patience, strikeouts, and center-field defense, but somewhat less of each. Injuries have slowed his development so that he only just reached Triple-A, but his disappointing numbers there may have been overshadowed by a .292/.370/.554 line after rosters expanded and that has him vying for a big-league bench job this spring. He's best cast as a fourth outfielder, where his right-handed bat and solid makeup can help alleviate Nyjer Morgan's platoon issues and Elijah Dukes' Elijah Dukes issues, but a team that makes him an everyday corner outfielder would be settling.

Nyjer Morgan — CF

Bats: L Throws: L Height: 6' 0" Weight: 175 Born: July 2, 1980 Age: 29

YEAR	TEAM	LVL	AGE	PA	R	2B	3B	HR	RBI	BB	SO	SB	CS	EqBRR	AVG	OBP	SLG	EqAVG	EqOBP	EqSLG	EqA	VORP	WARP	DEFENSE			
2007	IND	AAA	26	184	30	4	2	0	10	15	28	26	7	3.6	.305	.374	.354	.293	.352	.341	.256	3.9	0.4	32-CF	-2	9-LF	1
2007	PIT	MLB	26	118	15	3	4	1	7	9	19	7	3	-1.1	.299	.359	.430	.318	.376	.449	.281	6.0	1.9	25-CF	9		
2008	IND	AAA	27	352	54	13	4	1	33	18	47	44	8	4.7	.298	.349	.373	.287	.330	.355	.251	3.6	0.2	60-LF	3	16-CF	-5
2008	PIT	MLB	27	175	26	13	0	0	7	10	32	9	5	1.4	.294	.345	.375	.313	.362	.394	.263	3.6	1.2	19-LF	2	11-CF	3
2009	PIT	MLB	28	321	39	6	5	2	27	29	49	18	10	1.5	.277	.351	.356	.296	.365	.389	.265	8.4	2.8	60-LF	13	8-CF	2
2009	WAS	MLB	28	212	35	9	2	1	12	11	25	24	7	0.6	.351	.396	.435	.368	.411	.456	.303	16.6	2.9	45-CF	8		
2010	WAS	MLB	29	468	65	21	6	4	35	36	73	27	12	1.9	.283	.349	.391	.289	.353	.385	.269	14.7	2.3	101-LF	6		

Breakout: 7% Improve: 39% Collapse: 12% Attrition: 12% MLB: 81% Comparables: Milt Thompson, Kerry Robinson, Alex Cole, Endy Chavez

A prototypical speed-and-defense player, Morgan was traded last year from the Pirates for the perennially disappointing Lastings Milledge and became an instant hit in DC. Fans loved his infectious enthusiasm and overly daring play on the basepaths, pitchers relished his ability to run down their mistakes in the center pasture, while in the clubhouse his prankster-ish "Tony Plush" alter ego helped keep teammates loose. Although he'd been previously criticized for sloppy outfield play and bad routes, Morgan's dramatic defensive improvement and high on-base percentage unexpectedly made him a five-win player last year. As wonderful as all that is, and as much fun as it is to root for someone with Morgan's back story (he's a former junior-league hockey player and 33rd-round pick out of Walla Walla Community College), the enchantment is not likely to last. Morgan's low walk rate and nonexistent power make his offensive value too reliant on a slap-and-dash approach to maintain high batting averages, a recipe that rarely turns out well every time, hence that list of very comparable comps according to PECOTA. Morgan is already 29, but his speed and defense should age well and he has shown he can be a starting center fielder. But if Nationals fans expect an All-Star, he's not the droid they're looking for.

Mike Morse — UT

Bats: R Throws: R Height: 6' 4" Weight: 230 Born: March 22, 1982 Age: 28

YEAR	TEAM	LVL	AGE	PA	R	2B	3B	HR	RBI	BB	SO	SB	CS	EqBRR	AVG	OBP	SLG	EqAVG	EqOBP	EqSLG	EqA	VORP	WARP	DEFENSE			
2007	TAC	AAA	25	324	48	26	0	6	39	26	47	5	3	-1.0	.309	.368	.460	.295	.347	.420	.267	10.6	0.2	52-3B	-5	19-SS	-4
2007	SEA	MLB	25	20	1	2	0	0	3	1	4	0	0	0.0	.444	.500	.556	.444	.500	.556	.376	2.7	0.4	3-1B	0		
2008	SEA	MLB	26	11	0	1	0	0	0	1	4	0	0	0.1	.222	.364	.333	.222	.364	.333	.266	0.1	0.0	3-RF	0		
2009	TAC	AAA	27	289	38	14	0	10	52	20	50	0	0	-3.9	.312	.370	.481	.283	.334	.423	.263	10.1	-1.4	25-SS	-12	18-2B	-6
2009	SYR	AAA	27	183	21	12	3	6	34	15	27	2	1	-0.6	.339	.404	.558	.317	.377	.527	.302	10.8	0.5	26-1B	-2	15-3B	-3
2009	WAS	MLB	27	55	4	3	0	3	10	3	16	0	0	0.2	.250	.291	.481	.269	.309	.481	.265	0.6	0.3	5-1B	1		
2010	WAS	MLB	28	409	40	20	1	9	49	30	84	2	2	-1.2	.258	.320	.391	.268	.329	.407	.252	1.1	0.0	61-1B	-1		

Breakout: 8% Improve: 27% Collapse: 21% Attrition: 10% MLB: 15% Comparables: Brick Smith, Greg Wells, Julio Zuleta, Todd Trafton

Morse came over from Seattle last year in exchange for Ryan Langerhans and spent a month slugging in the International League before getting a brief look as Dunn's defensive replacement at first. The polar opposite of fellow utilitarian Wee Willie Harris in size, handedness, speed, and plate approach, at first glance Morse's four-corner skill set seems to mesh well with Harris's to complete some sort of Utility Player 3-D Cube Puzzle, but Morse's missing piece is power. He has never consistently produced the sort of thunder you'd hope for from an infield corner, even in a reserve role, which presages a short shelf-life, even with the talent-starved Nationals.

Wil Nieves C Bats: R Throws: R Height: 5' 11" Weight: 185 Born: September 25, 1977 Age: 32

YEAR	TEAM	LVL	AGE	PA	R	2B	3B	HR	RBI	BB	SO	SB	CS	EqBRR	AVG	OBP	SLG	EqAVG	EqOBP	EqSLG	EqA	VORP	WARP	DEFENSE	
2007	NYA	MLB	29	66	6	4	0	0	8	2	9	0	0	0.0	.164	.190	.230	.167	.194	.233	.133	-3.6	-0.8	19-C	-3
2008	WAS	MLB	30	196	15	9	1	1	20	13	29	0	1	-0.6	.261	.309	.341	.266	.311	.345	.231	2.8	0.0	51-C	-1
2009	WAS	MLB	31	249	20	6	0	1	26	17	45	1	0	-2.8	.259	.313	.299	.265	.313	.309	.229	2.8	0.3	63-C	-1
2010	WAS	MLB	32	201	16	8	1	2	23	14	35	1	0	-0.9	.240	.297	.323	.248	.305	.329	.222	0.4	0.0	54-C	0

Breakout: 13% Improve: 35% Collapse: 31% Attrition: 21%   MLB: 80%   Comparables: Jerry Grote, Gary Bennett, Rick Cerone, Joe Kmak

Not so long ago, the Nats seemed determined to corner the market in replacement-level middle infielders (e.g., Anderson Hernandez, Alberto Gonzalez, Emilio Bonifacio), but it appears their new hobby is collecting backup backstops. Injuries to Jesus Flores left Nieves unexpectedly spending much of last season splitting time behind the plate with Josh Bard, making the former Yankee afterthought an accomplice to Washington's pitching disaster. Spending so much time just inches away from hitters making consistently hard contact didn't help the perennially punchless Nieves at the plate, yet the Nationals inexplicably offered him arbitration even after signing Ivan Rodriguez to work with a now-healthy Flores, then signed fellow-IBBC member Jamie Burke to a minor-league contract. Can Alberto Castillo be far behind?

Derek Norris C Bats: R Throws: R Height: 6' 0" Weight: 210 Born: February 14, 1989 Age: 21

YEAR	TEAM	LVL	AGE	PA	R	2B	3B	HR	RBI	BB	SO	SB	CS	EqBRR	AVG	OBP	SLG	EqAVG	EqOBP	EqSLG	EqA	VORP	WARP	DEFENSE	
2007	NAT	Rk	18	151	16	6	2	4	15	25	38	2	1	-2.6	.203	.344	.382	.168	.272	.298	.205	-4.6	-1.7	13-C	-4
2008	VER	A-	19	302	42	12	0	10	38	63	56	11	9	-2.7	.278	.444	.463	.246	.380	.389	.274	14.0	2.1	46-C	-1
2009	HAG	A	20	540	78	30	0	23	84	90	116	6	3	-2.0	.286	.413	.513	.241	.349	.407	.267	22.0	0.7	97-C	-17
2010	WAS	MLB	21	487	53	18	1	15	54	69	117	4	4	-1.4	.231	.346	.387	.240	.353	.398	.265	21.8	1.8	84-C	-5

Breakout: 16% Improve: 47% Collapse: 22% Attrition: 1%   MLB: 1%   Comparables: Carmelo Martinez, Mike Napoli, Wilson Ramos, Chris Brown

Here's a top-flight catching prospect equipped with an almost-complete Mickey Tettleton accessory kit; the dealership shorted him the switch-hitting option, but everything else is here. Norris used a mature approach and impressive raw power to lay waste to the South Atlantic League. As a converted third baseman, he has adapted quickly in some regards, showing the ability to control the running game with a strong arm and a quick release, but his other receiving skills are still a work in progress. Catchers with his offensive potential are rare, however, and while it's a long road from Hagerstown to Washington (figuratively), if Norris can stay behind the dish, he'll be a star.

Josh Willingham LF Bats: R Throws: R Height: 6' 2" Weight: 215 Born: February 17, 1979 Age: 31

YEAR	TEAM	LVL	AGE	PA	R	2B	3B	HR	RBI	BB	SO	SB	CS	EqBRR	AVG	OBP	SLG	EqAVG	EqOBP	EqSLG	EqA	VORP	WARP	DEFENSE			
2007	FLO	MLB	28	604	75	32	4	21	89	66	122	8	1	1.6	.265	.364	.463	.275	.374	.475	.293	33.7	2.5	132-LF	-10		
2008	FLO	MLB	29	416	54	21	5	15	51	48	82	3	2	-2.1	.254	.364	.470	.265	.371	.487	.291	22.2	3.0	96-LF	5		
2009	WAS	MLB	30	502	70	29	0	24	61	61	104	4	3	-1.5	.260	.367	.496	.273	.375	.521	.300	32.7	3.2	79-LF	-3	30-RF	0
2010	WAS	MLB	31	519	66	24	3	20	65	57	105	5	3	-0.3	.256	.355	.452	.265	.362	.472	.286	25.9	2.6	118-LF	-2		

Breakout: 11% Improve: 46% Collapse: 10% Attrition: 8%   MLB: 99%   Comparables: Jay Buhner, Wally Post, Jim Rice, Moises Alou

As any bluegrass musician can attest, there ain't no ham like Willingham. The Marlins sent him north to DC on the Orange Blossom Special prior to the 2009 season, and the slugging outfielder provided his new employers with exactly the solid season we've come to expect from him, with a dash of power, a dollop of patience, and a smattering of subpar defense. Willingham seems like a late bloomer, but like so many others, being associated with the Marlins obscured his fundamental goodness; entering 2009, he was a career .280/.373/.510 hitter on the road. Washington was little more to his liking, as he hit just .233/.347/.406 at home, and .284/.384/.578 with 17 of his 24 home runs in other places. He is still two years from free agency, and Willingham's consistent production should be especially valuable in an outfield set to rely on the more speculative feats of Nyjer Morgan and Elijah Dukes, but as he's on the verge of becoming expensive, the Nationals have been shopping him—a decision they would be likely to regret. He's not a star, but players like Willingham are often harder to replace than you'd think.

Ryan Zimmerman **3B** Bats: R Throws: R Height: 6' 3" Weight: 230 Born: September 28, 1984 Age: 25

YEAR	TEAM	LVL	AGE	PA	R	2B	3B	HR	RBI	BB	SO	SB	CS	EqBRR	AVG	OBP	SLG	EqAVG	EqOBP	EqSLG	EqA	VORP	WARP	DEFENSE
2007	WAS	MLB	22	722	99	43	5	24	91	61	125	4	1	1.5	.266	.330	.458	.280	.343	.478	.279	31.7	5.0	160-3B 13
2008	WAS	MLB	23	466	51	24	1	14	51	31	71	1	1	-2.2	.283	.333	.442	.290	.337	.450	.269	16.5	1.4	102-3B -2
2009	WAS	MLB	24	693	110	37	3	33	106	72	119	2	0	5.6	.292	.364	.525	.303	.369	.548	.306	56.0	7.1	152-3B 8
2010	WAS	MLB	25	675	94	34	3	28	93	62	110	2	1	1.1	.276	.345	.480	.286	.355	.498	.288	39.1	4.6	150-3B 4

Breakout: 11% Improve: 59% Collapse: 1% Attrition: 2%   MLB: 100%   Comparables: Travis Fryman, Cal Ripken, Edwin Encarnacion, Scott Rolen

A walking, talking Web Gem, Zimmerman has finally stepped up his offensive game to the elite level that's long been anticipated, which combined with his ever-artistic leatherwork gives Washington one of baseball's most valuable and most entertaining commodities. His gains at the plate don't look like a fluke: the increased walk rate looks like sustainable progress, and a seven percent increase in his fly-ball rate points to his finally taking full advantage of his raw power potential. Perhaps most importantly, he overcame a career-long struggle by posting a .298/.361/.545 line against right-handed pitching. Now that Zimmerman has just turned 25, these improvements coupled with David Wright's power outage make identifying the National League's best young third baseman a much more interesting topic of conversation.

PITCHERS

Collin Balester Bats: R Throws: R Height: 6' 5" Weight: 195 Born: June 6, 1986 Age: 24

YEAR	TEAM	LVL	AGE	W	L	SV	G	GS	IP	H	HR	BB	SO	GB%	BABIP	STUFF	WHIP	ERA	SIERA	DERA	EqH9	EqHR9	EqBB9	EqSO9	VORP	SN/WX
2007	HAR	AA	21	2	7	0	17	17	98²	103	9	25	77	50%	.306	18	1.30	3.74	3.91	4.77	10.1	1.3	2.5	5.2	7.8	0.23
2007	COH	AAA	21	2	3	0	10	10	51²	49	3	23	40	38%	.293	20	1.39	4.18	4.57	5.40	9.2	0.9	4.0	5.2	0.6	0.00
2008	COH	AAA	22	9	3	0	15	15	78²	79	14	23	64	50%	.286	-3	1.30	4.00	3.86	4.74	9.6	2.2	2.9	5.3	6.3	0.58
2008	WAS	MLB	22	3	7	0	15	15	80	92	12	28	50	43%	.305	3	1.50	5.51	4.81	5.48	10.1	1.2	2.7	4.9	0.2	0.29
2009	SYR	AAA	23	7	10	0	20	20	107¹	129	5	37	71	48%	.349	-6	1.55	4.44	4.60	5.80	11.1	0.8	3.4	4.6	-3.4	-0.12
2009	WAS	MLB	23	1	4	0	7	7	30¹	34	10	14	20	43%	.264	-15	1.58	6.82	4.96	6.75	9.9	2.7	3.6	5.1	-4.2	-0.08
2010	WAS	MLB	24	6	8	0	31	25	129¹	136	17	52	80	38%	.298	-6	1.46	4.68	5.03	5.23	9.8	1.2	3.4	5.2	3.8	1.15

Breakout: 20% Improve: 61% Collapse: 15% Attrition: 14%   MLB: 100%   Comparables: Jason Olsen, Don August, Nick Green, Michael Wuertz

Balester's performance as a big-league starter over the last two seasons—a .386 SNWP in 22 starts—meets the expectations of a replacement-level hurler pried from the scrap heap rather than someone once considered an upper-echelon prospect. Seeing as his struggles derive from facing a lineup more than once while relying too heavily on his fastball (heat accounted for 70 percent of his deliveries last year), a move to the bullpen is in store for the young righty.

Jason Bergmann Bats: R Throws: R Height: 6' 4" Weight: 215 Born: September 25, 1981 Age: 28

YEAR	TEAM	LVL	AGE	W	L	SV	G	GS	IP	H	HR	BB	SO	GB%	BABIP	STUFF	WHIP	ERA	SIERA	DERA	EqH9	EqHR9	EqBB9	EqSO9	VORP	SN/WX
2007	COH	AAA	25	2	1	0	5	5	24	20	0	6	22	35%	.303	19	1.08	1.50	3.32	2.01	8.5	0.4	2.4	6.4	8.6	0.94
2007	WAS	MLB	25	6	6	0	21	21	115¹	99	18	42	86	37%	.244	-2	1.22	4.45	4.44	4.54	8.1	1.7	2.9	5.9	12.1	3.27
2008	COH	AAA	26	2	2	0	5	5	29	26	2	11	27	38%	.289	7	1.28	3.72	3.79	4.55	8.2	0.9	3.5	6.0	3.0	0.24
2008	WAS	MLB	26	2	11	0	30	22	139²	153	25	47	96	34%	.288	-10	1.43	5.09	4.72	5.57	9.4	1.5	2.6	5.2	-1.1	1.76
2009	SYR	AAA	27	1	1	2	19	0	23¹	18	1	8	15	41%	.246	-8	1.11	1.16	4.66	1.79	6.8	0.8	3.2	4.4	9.4	0.49
2009	WAS	MLB	27	2	4	0	56	0	48	50	7	25	40	42%	.312	-12	1.56	4.50	4.51	4.95	9.7	1.4	4.1	6.6	2.8	0.76
2010	WAS	MLB	28	6	6	0	42	15	102	101	13	41	69	39%	.289	-3	1.40	4.31	4.76	4.76	9.2	1.2	3.4	5.7	8.3	1.55

Breakout: 8% Improve: 47% Collapse: 14% Attrition: 22%   MLB: 85%   Comparables: Rob Bell, Ken Forsch, Brett Tomko, John Maine

Having been unsuccessful in a variety of roles over the last several seasons, Bergmann is probably on his last legs with the Nationals' organization. He is a poor starter, having compiled the second-lowest SNWP of any pitcher to make 20 or more starts over 2008-2009, and despite average rates in the controllable-skills group (walks, strikeouts, and the like), he is not a world beater in the bullpen, either; his relief-only FRA in the same span is an uninspiring 4.29. He isn't awful if used sparingly from the back of a roster as a swingman, but Bergmann represents the type of pitcher who should be kept around while under team control and dismissed when arbitration makes for raises beyond his value. There just isn't enough here to merit a guaranteed roster spot, let alone a well-defined role on a pitching staff.

Sean Burnett

Bats: L   Throws: L   Height: 6' 1"   Weight: 200   Born: September 17, 1982   Age: 27

YEAR	TEAM	LVL	AGE	W	L	SV	G	GS	IP	H	HR	BB	SO	GB%	BABIP	STUFF	WHIP	ERA	SIERA	DERA	EqH9	EqHR9	EqBB9	EqSO9	VORP	SN/WX
2007	IND	AAA	24	4	5	0	15	15	70¹	83	4	39	31	53%	.325	-23	1.73	4.48	5.73	6.00	11.2	1.1	5.0	2.9	-3.7	0.09
2008	IND	AAA	25	1	1	3	12	0	17¹	9	1	8	15	68%	.186	-4	0.98	1.04	3.60	1.65	5.5	1.1	4.4	5.5	7.0	0.70
2008	PIT	MLB	25	1	1	0	58	0	56²	57	7	34	42	59%	.298	-13	1.61	4.76	4.72	4.77	8.9	1.3	4.7	5.7	4.5	0.65
2009	PIT	MLB	26	1	2	1	38	0	32¹	22	3	15	23	50%	.213	-6	1.14	3.06	4.58	3.52	6.2	0.8	3.7	5.3	7.1	0.50
2009	WAS	MLB	26	1	1	0	33	0	25¹	14	3	13	20	64%	.162	-3	1.07	3.20	4.13	3.08	4.8	1.0	3.8	5.8	7.1	0.80
2010	WAS	MLB	27	3	5	1	61	1	61	60	8	33	35	51%	.279	-16	1.52	4.77	5.24	5.31	9.1	1.1	4.6	4.9	1.3	0.81

Breakout: 9%   Improve: 33%   Collapse: 25%   Attrition: 14%   MLB: 61%   Comparables: Wally Ritchie, Craig Lefferts, Pat Gomez, Len Whitehouse

A survivor of multiple arm injuries finally coming into his own as a reliever, Burnett was acquired from the Pirates in a midseason trade. His ERA belied weaker peripherals, a common theme with relief pitchers, but eight intentional free passes inflated his walk rate. When these walks are removed, the stats reveal a much sunnier scenario for the situational southpaw. A 2.2 K/UBB ratio is nice for a reliever, as is an ability to generate grounders. Burnett took real strides forward in 2009, but he still relies on hitters chasing junk. His skill set may not portend an ERA in the low 3.00s moving forward, but if nothing else, more utility is likely to be gained by calling his name than doling out expensive contracts to "established" relievers.

Matt Chico

Bats: L   Throws: L   Height: 5' 11"   Weight: 220   Born: June 10, 1983   Age: 27

YEAR	TEAM	LVL	AGE	W	L	SV	G	GS	IP	H	HR	BB	SO	GB%	BABIP	STUFF	WHIP	ERA	SIERA	DERA	EqH9	EqHR9	EqBB9	EqSO9	VORP	SN/WX
2007	COH	AAA	24	1	1	0	2	2	11	9	1	5	7	25%	.258	-7	1.27	3.27	5.48	3.60	8.1	1.8	4.5	4.5	2.1	0.22
2007	WAS	MLB	24	7	9	0	31	31	167	183	26	74	94	37%	.286	-22	1.54	4.63	5.44	5.09	10.3	1.7	3.6	4.5	7.5	3.10
2008	WAS	MLB	25	0	6	0	11	8	48	63	10	17	31	42%	.331	-15	1.67	6.19	4.78	5.89	11.6	1.7	2.9	5.1	-2.1	0.03
2009	HAG	A	26	0	0	0	3	3	11	11	2	0	8	40%	.281	-12	1.00	2.45	3.25	3.72	12.1	3.7	0.9	3.7	1.9	0.06
2009	HAR	AA	26	2	4	0	12	12	50¹	54	2	28	36	39%	.333	-12	1.63	4.29	5.05	6.07	10.6	1.0	5.2	4.6	-3.0	-0.29
2010	WAS	MLB	27	3	6	0	18	15	75¹	88	11	36	40	37%	.313	-18	1.65	5.57	5.65	6.22	10.9	1.3	4.1	4.5	-6.0	0.77

Breakout: 18%   Improve: 45%   Collapse: 21%   Attrition: 27%   MLB: 59%   Comparables: Bruce Chen, Angel Miranda, Eddie Oropesa, Pat Underwood

A finesse lefty, Chico has struggled with command in 42 big-league outings, a performance characteristic he will need to master if his goal is to succeed as a starter with an 86-88 mph fastball. His development was stunted by Tommy John surgery in the middle of the 2008 season, and although he recovered in time to pitch in the second half last year, there is no guarantee that he will stick as a starter, even with a successful rehab. Chico has struggled equally against batters from both sides of the plate—his 852 OPS against lefties ranks fifth-worst among southpaws facing 200 or more of them since 2007; his 854 OPS against right-handed hitters ranks as the sixth-worst (750 batters faced). Given that Chico's numbers worsen exponentially multiple times through the order, and barring a change in approach or an improvement in command, he seems destined to become a long reliever or specialist.

Tyler Clippard

Bats: R   Throws: R   Height: 6' 3"   Weight: 200   Born: February 14, 1985   Age: 25

YEAR	TEAM	LVL	AGE	W	L	SV	G	GS	IP	H	HR	BB	SO	GB%	BABIP	STUFF	WHIP	ERA	SIERA	DERA	EqH9	EqHR9	EqBB9	EqSO9	VORP	SN/WX
2007	TRN	AA	22	2	1	0	6	6	26²	22	5	12	28	25%	.258	4	1.27	5.40	3.92	7.69	10.1	3.4	4.5	7.1	-5.8	-0.06
2007	SWB	AAA	22	4	4	0	14	14	69¹	82	7	35	55	36%	.346	-10	1.69	4.15	4.75	6.20	11.7	1.7	4.7	5.4	-5.1	-0.08
2007	NYA	MLB	22	3	1	0	6	6	27	29	6	17	18	36%	.277	2	1.70	6.33	5.58	5.67	9.3	2.0	5.0	5.3	-0.5	0.28
2008	COH	AAA	23	6	13	0	27	27	143	129	15	66	125	40%	.284	-2	1.36	4.66	4.18	5.57	8.6	1.4	4.3	5.7	-1.1	0.61
2008	WAS	MLB	23	1	1	0	2	2	10¹	12	2	7	8	22%	.323	10	1.84	4.35	5.78	4.05	10.8	1.8	5.4	6.3	1.6	0.01
2009	SYR	AAA	24	4	1	1	24	0	39	20	2	15	42	45%	.200	15	0.90	0.92	3.00	2.51	5.0	0.7	3.6	7.6	12.5	1.74
2009	WAS	MLB	24	4	2	0	41	0	60¹	36	9	32	67	32%	.197	13	1.13	2.69	3.58	2.91	5.5	1.3	4.0	8.4	17.4	1.30
2010	WAS	MLB	25	4	6	0	46	10	85²	81	11	44	69	38%	.291	-2	1.47	4.57	4.63	5.04	8.8	1.2	4.5	6.8	4.4	1.21

Breakout: 11%   Improve: 41%   Collapse: 18%   Attrition: 28%   MLB: 68%   Comparables: Jonah Bayliss, Steve Bedrosian, Dave Veres, Doug Bochtler

Clippard doesn't throw very hard, just 90-91 mph. He's also very fly-ball-oriented, but last season, he induced more swings on his pitches than the year before, up from 39 to 45 percent, the vast majority of which were empty, with an opposing contact rate reduced from 82 percent to 69. The credit goes to a new slider that gave batters fits, though Clippard had trouble controlling it, so his walk rate went up even as his ERA went down. If he can harness the pitch, he could become even more effective and work his way into more important game situations than the mop-up responsibilities he was usually entrusted with. The one caveat is that he benefited greatly from a .197 BABIP, a rate that bested everyone with at least 60 innings pitched and not named Tim Byrdak. This is going to regress, but since dingers are excluded from the formula and Clippard is an extreme fly-ball pitcher, the regression may not be as severe as it would be for other pitchers (fly balls are generally outs, lucky or not).

Ross Detwiler

Bats: R   Throws: L   Height: 6' 5"   Weight: 185   Born: March 6, 1986   Age: 24

YEAR	TEAM	LVL	AGE	W	L	SV	G	GS	IP	H	HR	BB	SO	GB%	BABIP	STUFF	WHIP	ERA	SIERA	DERA	EqH9	EqHR9	EqBB9	EqSO9	VORP	SN/WX
2007	NAT	Rk	21	0	0	0	4	4	12	11	1	3	15	45%	.323	11	1.17	2.25	2.47	3.18	10.3	2.4	3.2	6.4	2.9	0.17
2007	POT	A+	21	2	2	0	5	4	21¹	27	1	9	13	51%	.351	-6	1.69	4.22	4.93	6.07	12.6	1.4	4.5	3.6	-1.3	-0.21
2008	POT	A+	22	8	8	0	26	26	124	140	8	57	114	56%	.354	-16	1.59	4.86	3.94	6.55	12.1	1.5	4.7	5.7	-13.3	-1.06
2009	HAR	AA	23	0	3	0	6	6	27¹	28	2	10	28	47%	.321	5	1.39	2.96	3.49	5.76	9.5	1.3	3.3	6.6	-0.8	0.11
2009	SYR	AAA	23	4	2	0	10	10	49¹	56	2	20	42	55%	.346	4	1.54	3.10	4.08	5.12	10.2	0.7	3.9	6.0	2.0	0.59
2009	WAS	MLB	23	1	6	0	15	14	75²	87	3	33	43	47%	.323	3	1.59	5.00	5.16	4.82	10.1	0.4	3.3	4.3	5.7	0.97
2010	WAS	MLB	24	5	10	0	30	27	121²	143	16	60	75	48%	.323	-18	1.67	5.61	5.10	6.32	11.0	1.3	4.2	5.2	-11.1	1.59

Breakout: 11%   Improve: 39%   Collapse: 28%   Attrition: 14%   MLB: 100%   Comparables: Kris Johnson, Bryan Oelkers, Ryan Mullins, Pete Roberts

Once considered the second-best prospect in the organization, Detwiler had taken a few steps backward in his development in 2008 before an extended audition at the big-league level last season. The reviews of his performance were mixed. Some looked forward to being electrified by his mid-90s fastball and were shocked to see the lanky lefty rarely even register 92 mph on the gun, walking too many and whiffing too few in the process. Others saw a young pitcher with plenty of promise who may still project as a second or third starter. Fewer fastballs and a more varied spread could counteract an inevitable regression in the HR/FB department; there's no way he can sustain a 3.7 percent rate of homers on fly balls. He managed to post the third-highest SNWP on the team, but except for Lannan, that's a "tallest dwarf" competition.

Jesse English

Bats: L   Throws: L   Height: 6' 3"   Weight: 220   Born: September 13, 1984   Age: 25

YEAR	TEAM	LVL	AGE	W	L	SV	G	GS	IP	H	HR	BB	SO	GB%	BABIP	STUFF	WHIP	ERA	SIERA	DERA	EqH9	EqHR9	EqBB9	EqSO9	VORP	SN/WX
2007	SLO	A-	22	5	0	0	10	0	26	14	0	5	46	42%	.311	23	0.73	0.69	0.42	1.74	7.7	0.8	2.3	9.6	9.8	0.94
2008	SJO	A+	23	13	7	0	26	26	135¹	121	12	51	135	49%	.301	-27	1.27	3.19	3.45	5.36	10.5	2.4	4.3	5.8	1.9	0.89
2009	NRW	AA	24	7	7	0	26	19	100²	98	9	57	71	44%	.289	-41	1.54	4.20	5.02	6.63	11.1	2.3	5.4	4.3	-11.6	-0.74
2010	SFN	MLB	25	3	7	0	26	15	82	100	14	46	54	40%	.328	-21	1.78	6.38	5.29	6.75	10.9	1.6	4.8	5.5	-11.4	1.61

Breakout: 8%   Improve: 30%   Collapse: 27%   Attrition: 12%   MLB: 3%   Comparables: Mike Remlinger, Len Manning, Chuck Crowder, David Purcey

English performed well in High-A in 2008, but he was too old for the level at 24, having struggled to advance through the Giants' farm system, thanks to frequent injuries. His control fell by the wayside last season, a devastating blow to a lefty relying predominantly on a fastball and changeup. The Nationals claimed him off waivers on September 11th and see him as a relief specialist. He has shown signs of promise in the past, but the injuries and struggles with command and control are concrete reasons for his waiver availability.

Marco Estrada

Bats: R Throws: R Height: 6' 0" Weight: 180 Born: July 5, 1983 Age: 26

YEAR	TEAM	LVL	AGE	W	L	SV	G	GS	IP	H	HR	BB	SO	GB%	BABIP	STUFF	WHIP	ERA	SIERA	DERA	EqH9	EqHR9	EqBB9	EqSO9	VORP	SN/WX
2007	HAG	A	23	1	5	0	8	8	36	39	4	17	35	47%	.330	-11	1.56	5.25	3.91	6.95	10.7	1.8	4.7	5.5	-5.5	-0.66
2007	POT	A+	23	5	3	0	11	11	58^1	67	7	17	54	53%	.351	-15	1.44	4.94	3.50	6.45	12.6	2.6	3.3	6.0	-5.5	-0.86
2008	HAR	AA	24	6	3	0	13	13	74^1	62	5	32	67	54%	.274	8	1.26	2.66	3.88	3.94	8.1	1.1	3.9	6.0	12.5	1.12
2008	COH	AAA	24	3	3	0	12	12	65^1	73	3	21	52	48%	.348	2	1.44	3.58	4.03	4.33	10.6	0.7	3.1	5.3	8.0	0.74
2008	WAS	MLB	24	0	0	0	11	0	12^2	17	4	5	10	45%	.310	-18	1.74	7.82	4.48	8.44	11.5	2.7	2.7	6.1	-4.4	-0.25
2009	SYR	AAA	25	9	5	0	27	25	136^1	133	10	33	98	48%	.294	1	1.22	3.63	4.03	4.87	8.9	1.1	2.4	5.0	9.3	1.66
2009	WAS	MLB	25	0	1	0	4	1	7^1	6	1	4	9	45%	.263	6	1.36	6.14	3.33	7.04	7.0	1.2	3.5	9.4	-1.3	-0.21
2010	WAS	MLB	26	6	8	0	33	25	119^2	129	17	51	76	48%	.302	-9	1.50	4.94	4.85	5.51	10.0	1.3	3.6	5.4	-0.1	1.80

Breakout: 6% Improve: 36% Collapse: 17% Attrition: 19%   MLB: 29%   Comparables: Bill Long, Kevin McGehee, Scott Cassidy, Joe Edelen

A slow-developing sixth-rounder out of Long Beach State from the 2005 draft, Estrada has made a steady rise up through the system with his solid, low-90s fastball and a plus changeup. At the very least, he might have middle-relief possibilities (not least because of a good move to first base), but both of his introductions to the big-leagues have been a bit rough.

Livan Hernandez

Bats: R Throws: R Height: 6' 2" Weight: 245 Born: February 20, 1975 Age: 35

YEAR	TEAM	LVL	AGE	W	L	SV	G	GS	IP	H	HR	BB	SO	GB%	BABIP	STUFF	WHIP	ERA	SIERA	DERA	EqH9	EqHR9	EqBB9	EqSO9	VORP	SN/WX
2007	ARI	MLB	32	11	11	0	33	33	204^1	247	34	79	90	46%	.303	-11	1.60	4.93	5.54	4.49	10.4	1.2	3.1	3.7	22.7	3.25
2008	MIN	MLB	33	10	8	0	23	23	139^2	199	18	29	54	52%	.345	-20	1.63	5.48	5.22	5.73	12.4	1.2	1.6	3.2	-3.6	1.21
2008	COL	MLB	33	3	3	0	8	8	40^1	58	7	14	13	51%	.342	-25	1.79	8.03	5.75	7.21	12.1	1.1	2.7	2.5	-7.5	-0.33
2009	NYN	MLB	34	7	8	0	23	23	135	164	16	51	75	47%	.329	-16	1.59	5.47	5.03	5.51	11.5	1.3	3.0	4.3	-0.1	1.83
2009	WAS	MLB	34	2	4	0	8	8	48^2	56	3	16	27	51%	.317	2	1.48	5.36	4.87	5.03	10.1	0.6	2.4	4.3	2.5	0.68
2010	WAS	MLB	35	7	11	0	31	31	156	187	22	54	63	49%	.308	-22	1.55	5.23	5.48	5.85	11.2	1.3	3.0	3.4	-6.1	1.14

Breakout: 8% Improve: 36% Collapse: 8% Attrition: 17%   MLB: 98%   Comparables: Jack Billingham, Kevin Appier, Esteban Loaiza, Don Robinson

In Hernandez's eight turns, the Nationals got exactly what they had hoped for: over six innings per start, and results above the replacement level. As low-risk, low-reward signings go, Livan makes more sense than Daniel Cabrera, but that comparison really should not be made outside 2005 Strat-o-Matic replays, especially for a cellar-dweller with a surplus of young and untested hurlers. On the whole, a .454 SNWP in 31 starts pegs Livan's season as thoroughly replaceable. For a team looking to pay next to nothing for 180-200 frames to avoid speeding up the development of young hurlers, Hernandez is the pitching equivalent of a Yellow Pages emergency fill-in, but that's essentially the limit of his usefulness.

Logan Kensing

Bats: R Throws: R Height: 6' 1" Weight: 185 Born: July 3, 1982 Age: 27

YEAR	TEAM	LVL	AGE	W	L	SV	G	GS	IP	H	HR	BB	SO	GB%	BABIP	STUFF	WHIP	ERA	SIERA	DERA	EqH9	EqHR9	EqBB9	EqSO9	VORP	SN/WX
2007	FLO	MLB	24	3	0	0	9	0	13^1	11	0	7	13	35%	.297	11	1.35	1.35	4.17	1.32	6.6	0.0	4.0	7.9	6.4	0.60
2008	ABQ	AAA	25	1	0	3	13	0	12^2	8	3	12	17	37%	.185	11	1.58	6.39	4.13	6.59	4.6	1.3	7.2	9.2	-1.6	-0.48
2008	FLO	MLB	25	3	1	0	48	0	55^1	50	7	33	55	33%	.277	0	1.50	4.23	4.37	4.05	8.1	1.1	4.6	7.5	9.1	-0.71
2009	FLO	MLB	26	0	1	0	6	0	7^1	14	1	5	7	49%	.481	-16	2.59	9.82	4.68	9.20	17.2	1.2	4.9	7.4	-3.0	-0.30
2009	SYR	AAA	26	2	1	17	31	0	33^1	28	2	6	35	45%	.292	10	1.02	2.97	2.63	3.76	7.8	0.8	1.9	7.5	6.3	1.67
2009	WAS	MLB	26	1	1	1	26	0	28	40	7	12	12	52%	.327	-40	1.86	8.68	5.55	8.13	12.7	2.3	3.3	3.3	-8.1	-0.22
2010	WAS	MLB	27	3	5	3	55	0	61	61	8	30	48	43%	.301	-7	1.49	4.68	4.54	5.14	9.3	1.1	4.1	6.6	2.4	0.38

Breakout: 17% Improve: 47% Collapse: 29% Attrition: 11%   MLB: 64%   Comparables: Carlos Reyes, Eddie Gaillard, Sandy Wihtol, Tom Dukes

It *feels* as if Kensing has been around forever. He's one of the nondescript relievers who happens to stick around for a while, but he has just three full seasons under his belt out of the six in which he has appeared. He joined the Nationals at the end of April and proceeded to make Kip Wells look like Johan Santana, posting an 8.68 ERA and 10.23 FRA in 26 outings. Known more for his hobby of hunting hogs and coyotes from helicopters, Kensing transformed last year from a high-strikeout, high-walk reliever with a plus fastball into a pitcher with nothing to his name aside from poor control. He signed a minor-league deal with the Nationals after the season ended, but should he even break camp with the team, his role will be limited to low-leverage, mop-up duty.

John Lannan   Bats: L   Throws: L   Height: 6' 4"   Weight: 225   Born: September 27, 1984   Age: 25

YEAR	TEAM	LVL	AGE	W	L	SV	G	GS	IP	H	HR	BB	SO	GB%	BABIP	STUFF	WHIP	ERA	SIERA	DERA	EqH9	EqHR9	EqBB9	EqSO9	VORP	SN/WX
2007	POT	A+	22	6	0	0	8	8	50²	31	3	15	35	59%	.206	12	0.91	2.13	3.86	3.30	6.6	1.6	3.1	4.3	11.3	0.82
2007	HAR	AA	22	3	2	0	6	5	36	31	2	15	20	62%	.261	2	1.28	3.25	4.79	3.88	8.6	1.1	4.0	3.7	6.1	0.54
2007	COH	AAA	22	3	1	0	7	6	38	30	1	12	19	55%	.240	8	1.11	1.66	4.85	2.43	7.3	0.5	2.9	3.2	12.6	1.08
2007	WAS	MLB	22	2	2	0	6	6	34²	36	3	17	10	55%	.273	-11	1.53	4.15	6.09	4.32	9.7	1.1	4.1	2.4	4.4	0.97
2008	WAS	MLB	23	9	15	0	31	31	182	172	23	72	117	62%	.266	9	1.34	3.91	4.45	4.08	8.3	1.0	3.1	5.0	28.6	4.65
2009	WAS	MLB	24	9	13	0	33	33	206¹	210	22	68	89	59%	.272	0	1.35	3.88	5.08	4.16	8.9	0.9	2.5	3.3	30.3	4.68
2010	WAS	MLB	25	11	11	0	32	32	189¹	182	21	71	88	63%	.268	-4	1.33	4.14	4.94	4.68	9.1	1.0	3.2	3.9	17.2	3.61

Breakout: 8%   Improve: 34%   Collapse: 15%   Attrition: 10%   MLB: 91%   Comparables: Andy Pettitte, Scott Karl, Tom Gorzelanny, Larry Jaster

Because somebody has to be best, even on the Nationals, Lannan bore the burden of being the team's nominal ace. Ground-ballers can get away with lower strikeout rates, but his 4.8 K/9 since 2008 is much too low relative to his 3.1 UBB/9, both of which are more appropriate for a pitcher competing for the final spot in a rotation, not its top starter. Although his .519 SNWP has led all Nationals over the last two seasons, it ranks 62nd out of the 140 hurlers to make 30 or more starts in the same span. Lannan might be a pitcher whose worth can be artificially inflated by virtue of his modest status in an attempt to extract a great return in a trade, because as he gets closer to arbitration, it isn't best practice to pay big money to a fourth starter whose upside is that he'll remain a fourth starter.

Mike MacDougal   Bats: S   Throws: R   Height: 6' 4"   Weight: 175   Born: March 5, 1977   Age: 33

YEAR	TEAM	LVL	AGE	W	L	SV	G	GS	IP	H	HR	BB	SO	GB%	BABIP	STUFF	WHIP	ERA	SIERA	DERA	EqH9	EqHR9	EqBB9	EqSO9	VORP	SN/WX
2007	CHA	MLB	30	2	5	0	54	0	42¹	50	3	33	39	65%	.359	0	1.96	6.80	4.60	6.80	10.0	0.6	6.3	7.5	-6.2	-0.08
2008	CHR	AAA	31	0	4	4	38	2	49¹	48	2	30	65	62%	.359	12	1.58	3.83	3.22	4.50	9.8	0.6	5.4	8.8	5.3	-0.18
2008	CHA	MLB	31	0	0	0	16	0	17	16	0	12	12	54%	.308	4	1.65	2.12	5.23	2.16	8.6	0.0	5.9	5.9	6.2	-0.02
2009	CHA	MLB	32	0	0	0	5	0	4¹	7	0	7	3	64%	.467	-8	3.23	12.46	6.71	11.25	15.8	0.0	13.5	6.8	-2.6	-0.22
2009	WAS	MLB	32	1	1	20	52	0	50	45	3	31	31	72%	.275	-8	1.52	3.60	4.65	4.29	8.2	0.5	4.7	4.7	6.6	1.59
2010	WAS	MLB	33	2	4	7	54	0	53²	55	6	35	40	65%	.308	-16	1.68	5.43	4.67	6.03	9.5	1.0	5.5	6.4	-3.2	0.46

Breakout: 9%   Improve: 42%   Collapse: 27%   Attrition: 25%   MLB: 78%   Comparables: Tom Murphy, Dan Osinski, Mike Henneman, Pat Zachry

The artist formerly known as "Mac the Ninth" during his long-ago days as a Royals closer has always been an unpredictable commodity: skinny but a power arm, a ground-ball pitcher who gets strikeouts, a closer who has no control. That last trait was ascendant in 2009, and he survived it only because of his very low home-run rate. He was a literal savior for a bullpen that had been blasted like Keith Moon after a case of Jack Daniels, closing out 20 of 21 save opportunities, but to their credit, the Nats simply thanked him for the pick-me-up and then declined to tender him a contract. In any context other than absolute desperation, he's just too wild to trust.

J. D. Martin   Bats: R   Throws: R   Height: 6' 4"   Weight: 195   Born: January 2, 1983   Age: 27

YEAR	TEAM	LVL	AGE	W	L	SV	G	GS	IP	H	HR	BB	SO	GB%	BABIP	STUFF	WHIP	ERA	SIERA	DERA	EqH9	EqHR9	EqBB9	EqSO9	VORP	SN/WX
2007	AKR	AA	24	2	3	0	9	9	42¹	42	4	16	23	53%	.273	-18	1.37	4.25	4.99	5.49	9.4	1.3	3.5	3.3	0.1	0.14
2008	AKR	AA	25	11	3	0	31	8	79²	73	5	19	71	47%	.304	2	1.15	2.49	3.39	3.53	9.4	1.1	2.4	6.2	16.2	1.61
2009	SYR	AAA	26	8	3	0	16	15	88	75	4	10	63	44%	.274	18	0.97	2.66	3.57	4.18	7.8	0.8	1.3	5.0	12.3	1.48
2009	WAS	MLB	26	5	4	0	15	15	77	85	14	24	37	39%	.273	-13	1.42	4.44	5.35	4.40	9.5	1.5	2.3	3.6	9.5	1.37
2010	WAS	MLB	27	6	7	0	32	20	118²	121	15	37	66	48%	.286	-4	1.33	4.36	4.79	4.87	9.5	1.1	2.7	4.7	8.3	2.30

Breakout: 7%   Improve: 37%   Collapse: 26%   Attrition: 13%   MLB: 40%   Comparables: Doug Welenc, Brian Denman, Justin Mallett, Terry Clark

A former Indians supplemental first-rounder from 2001, Martin had been reduced to journeyman status and was signed to provide pitching depth in the minors. Then he tore through the International League, and given their dire need, the Nats couldn't ignore the performance. His approach relies more heavily on changeups than his fastball, which doesn't generally translate into big-league success, but Martin held his own and is certainly worthy of another extended look. He probably won't get to enjoy a lengthy career in the bigs, but the dominance he displayed in the minors did not happen by chance. Every rotation needs its back-end starters, so why not a strike-throwing survivor who put in nine years to make it?

Shairon Martis

Bats: R   Throws: R   Height: 6' 1"   Weight: 175   Born: March 30, 1987   Age: 23

YEAR	TEAM	LVL	AGE	W	L	SV	G	GS	IP	H	HR	BB	SO	GB%	BABIP	STUFF	WHIP	ERA	SIERA	DERA	EqH9	EqHR9	EqBB9	EqSO9	VORP	SN/WX
2007	POT	A+	20	14	8	0	27	26	151	150	9	52	108	34%	.299	6	1.34	4.23	4.55	6.42	10.1	1.5	3.6	4.2	-14.5	-1.48
2008	HAR	AA	21	4	4	0	14	14	74²	73	5	28	57	43%	.300	19	1.35	3.98	4.30	4.98	9.5	1.1	3.4	5.0	4.1	-0.01
2008	COH	AAA	21	1	2	0	7	7	41²	42	2	17	42	33%	.333	26	1.42	3.02	3.72	4.20	9.3	0.7	3.8	6.4	5.9	0.52
2008	WAS	MLB	21	1	3	0	5	4	20²	18	5	12	23	41%	.250	21	1.45	5.66	3.76	5.70	7.6	2.1	4.2	8.4	-0.5	0.18
2009	SYR	AAA	22	4	4	0	13	13	74¹	90	9	18	40	37%	.318	-12	1.45	4.96	5.01	6.03	11.1	1.8	2.4	3.6	-4.2	-0.08
2009	WAS	MLB	22	5	3	0	15	15	85²	83	11	39	34	43%	.249	-1	1.42	5.25	5.92	5.12	8.3	1.0	3.4	3.0	3.7	0.78
2010	WAS	MLB	23	6	10	0	30	25	137¹	149	19	62	72	35%	.293	-9	1.54	5.10	5.65	5.64	10.1	1.3	3.9	4.5	-2.1	1.43

Breakout: 5%   Improve: 47%   Collapse: 14%   Attrition: 26%   MLB: 74%   Comparables: Scott Mathieson, Collin Balester, James Parr, Mark Cahill

Martis got off to a misleading start, putting together a 5-0 record and 4.10 ERA in his first seven games, becoming a veritable fantasy baseball darling in the process. Due diligence would have prevented the horde of fant-league waiver activity, as his ugly strikeout and unintentional walk rates portended a decline in the near future. Sure enough, in his next eight starts Martis posted a 6.34 ERA, with 2.7 K/9 and 4.1 UBB/9, earning a trip back to glorious upstate New York in time for July. While it would be easy to write him off as having little upside beyond that of a fifth starter, his problems at the major-league level were with his control, and he has had great command in the minors. He won't be an ace, but if he can regain his control, most teams could do worse than to employ Martis as a back-end rotation starter. The Nats' problem is that they have more candidates for the fifth slot than the third or fourth.

Ryan Mattheus

Bats: R   Throws: R   Height: 6' 3"   Weight: 215   Born: November 10, 1983   Age: 26

YEAR	TEAM	LVL	AGE	W	L	SV	G	GS	IP	H	HR	BB	SO	GB%	BABIP	STUFF	WHIP	ERA	SIERA	DERA	EqH9	EqHR9	EqBB9	EqSO9	VORP	SN/WX
2007	TUL	AA	23	9	11	0	26	26	158²	182	13	55	102	58%	.325	-16	1.49	5.56	4.52	6.67	11.4	1.2	3.4	4.3	-19.5	-1.94
2008	TUL	AA	24	2	5	17	58	0	57²	50	5	27	56	64%	.290	-9	1.34	3.28	3.60	4.72	8.9	1.3	4.5	6.6	4.7	-0.45
2009	CSP	AAA	25	1	1	0	13	0	16²	19	3	8	20	74%	.364	9	1.62	4.32	3.06	4.41	9.9	1.7	4.4	9.4	2.0	-0.15
2010	WAS	MLB	26	3	5	5	41	0	64¹	70	8	33	40	54%	.308	-15	1.60	5.17	4.98	5.74	10.1	1.2	4.3	5.3	-1.7	0.35

Breakout: 22%   Improve: 47%   Collapse: 17%   Attrition: 17%   MLB: 15%   Comparables: Jarrett Grube, Jamie Brisco, Justin Lehr, Matt Skrmetta

Acquired from the Rockies in the Joe Beimel deal, Mattheus is a high-risk, high-reward asset, a power arm who underwent Tommy John surgery while he was a Colorado farmhand. The Nationals immediately placed him on the 60-day DL, enabling the future reliever with a plus sinker to rehab in new digs. He isn't going to crack prospect leaderboards anytime soon, but his upside as a back-end reliever offers some hope of utility received for Beimel's even briefer National engagement.

Garrett Mock

Bats: R   Throws: R   Height: 6' 3"   Weight: 240   Born: April 25, 1983   Age: 27

YEAR	TEAM	LVL	AGE	W	L	SV	G	GS	IP	H	HR	BB	SO	GB%	BABIP	STUFF	WHIP	ERA	SIERA	DERA	EqH9	EqHR9	EqBB9	EqSO9	VORP	SN/WX
2007	HAR	AA	24	1	5	0	11	11	51¹	66	5	28	41	55%	.345	-19	1.83	5.79	4.66	7.96	11.8	1.4	4.8	5.0	-14.2	-1.20
2008	COH	AAA	25	6	3	0	19	17	104²	98	9	25	96	52%	.297	10	1.18	3.01	3.37	4.01	8.7	1.1	2.3	5.9	16.8	1.31
2008	WAS	MLB	25	1	3	0	26	3	41	37	4	23	46	48%	.308	13	1.46	4.17	3.61	4.06	8.1	0.9	4.4	8.6	6.6	0.24
2009	SYR	AAA	26	5	1	2	13	8	51	36	2	13	48	53%	.258	19	0.96	2.65	3.16	3.42	6.7	0.7	2.6	6.8	11.2	1.41
2009	WAS	MLB	26	3	10	0	28	15	91¹	114	9	44	72	55%	.355	-10	1.73	5.62	4.46	6.03	11.3	0.9	3.7	6.1	-5.3	-0.27
2010	WAS	MLB	27	6	8	0	38	15	115	114	13	48	89	54%	.301	4	1.40	4.37	4.23	4.85	9.2	1.0	3.5	6.6	8.3	1.01

Breakout: 22%   Improve: 61%   Collapse: 13%   Attrition: 17%   MLB: 69%   Comparables: Brian Bass, Tim Belcher, Jason Grimsley, Doug Brocail

Consistently inconsistent when he hasn't been just fragile, Mock has now spent two years in the majors. A groundballer with decent command and the ability to whiff almost a batter per frame, he nevertheless suffers from a lack of command. The constant shuffling of his roles looms large in his struggles to date, especially as he'd already struggled to achieve consistency in the minors before serious knee problems. If the Nats can steel themselves for a bumpy ride, Mock should simply be given every opportunity to just seize a spot in the starting rotation. His upside looks a lot better than those of most alternatives, and if he can finally settle into a groove, he could still be a keeper.

Scott Olsen

Bats: L   Throws: L   Height: 6' 5"   Weight: 215   Born: January 12, 1984   Age: 26

YEAR	TEAM	LVL	AGE	W	L	SV	G	GS	IP	H	HR	BB	SO	GB%	BABIP	STUFF	WHIP	ERA	SIERA	DERA	EqH9	EqHR9	EqBB9	EqSO9	VORP	SN/WX
2007	FLO	MLB	23	10	15	0	33	33	176²	226	29	85	133	43%	.341	-9	1.76	5.81	4.76	6.17	10.3	1.4	3.7	5.9	-13.4	-0.07
2008	FLO	MLB	24	8	11	0	33	33	201²	195	30	69	113	40%	.258	-3	1.31	4.20	5.04	4.55	8.7	1.4	2.7	4.3	21.0	3.87
2009	WAS	MLB	25	2	4	0	11	11	62²	83	11	25	42	43%	.341	-13	1.72	6.03	4.80	6.06	11.7	1.4	3.0	5.1	-3.9	0.05
2010	WAS	MLB	26	6	8	0	24	23	124²	131	16	51	77	43%	.296	-4	1.45	4.58	4.92	5.14	9.8	1.2	3.5	5.2	5.0	0.77

Breakout: 16%   Improve: 48%   Collapse: 12%   Attrition: 22%   MLB: 96%   Comparables: Bob Owchinko, John Smiley, Randy Lerch, George Stone

After showing promise in 2006, Olsen has lost velocity, become more fly-ball prone, and missed time due to injuries, most recently with a small tear in his left labrum. His laundry list of suspensions, legal woes, and insubordination is much longer than the list of his accolades. The hope is that if he's fully healed, he still has some potential to shore up the rotation; proper recovery from the shoulder injury could restore some of the missing velocity. The Nationals wisely nontendered him, opting to bring him back on a cheaper deal as a means of mitigating the inherent risk. Only heading into his age-26 season, he's more than worth a flier or two, given that he looked like a quality midrotation option not so long ago, and considering that the Nats have so very few of those knocking around.

Saul Rivera

Bats: S   Throws: R   Height: 5' 10"   Weight: 185   Born: December 7, 1977   Age: 32

YEAR	TEAM	LVL	AGE	W	L	SV	G	GS	IP	H	HR	BB	SO	GB%	BABIP	STUFF	WHIP	ERA	SIERA	DERA	EqH9	EqHR9	EqBB9	EqSO9	VORP	SN/WX
2007	WAS	MLB	29	4	6	3	85	0	93	88	1	42	64	57%	.301	6	1.40	3.68	4.60	3.75	8.9	0.1	3.7	5.5	17.5	2.64
2008	WAS	MLB	30	5	6	0	76	0	84	90	3	35	65	58%	.327	4	1.49	3.96	4.25	4.05	9.6	0.3	3.2	6.0	13.4	1.62
2009	SYR	AAA	31	2	5	2	30	0	45²	57	1	25	32	66%	.364	-15	1.80	3.55	4.68	6.03	11.3	0.6	5.1	4.9	-2.6	-0.50
2009	WAS	MLB	31	1	3	0	30	0	38¹	48	7	14	21	65%	.313	-25	1.62	6.10	4.70	6.22	11.0	1.6	2.8	4.2	-3.1	-0.43
2010	CLE	MLB	32	4	5	1	69	0	72²	80	8	34	44	54%	.312	-16	1.58	4.98	4.99	5.42	10.0	1.0	4.1	5.1	0.6	0.64

Breakout: 17%   Improve: 41%   Collapse: 26%   Attrition: 20%   MLB: 84%   Comparables: Bob Humphreys, Roger McDowell, Takashi Ishii, Mark Williamson

A workhorse middle reliever who got his big break via outright need and a bit of Acosta-inspired subtlety in his usage patterns, the diminutive Rivera imploded in the early going in 2009, doing his unhappy part in undermining the man who'd done so much to employ him as a relief stalwart in the first place. It comes as no surprise that now that Acta has landed in Cleveland, Rivera wasn't far behind, signing as a minor-league free agent with a NRI for spring training. He has had great peripherals in the past, his HR/FB ratio figures to come back down from last season's stratosphere, and he should get every opportunity to settle back in as a rubber-armed middle-innings sponge.

Craig Stammen

Bats: R   Throws: R   Height: 6' 3"   Weight: 210   Born: March 9, 1984   Age: 26

YEAR	TEAM	LVL	AGE	W	L	SV	G	GS	IP	H	HR	BB	SO	GB%	BABIP	STUFF	WHIP	ERA	SIERA	DERA	EqH9	EqHR9	EqBB9	EqSO9	VORP	SN/WX
2007	POT	A+	23	8	6	0	28	22	125	156	9	54	96	57%	.365	-36	1.68	4.18	4.31	7.34	13.0	1.8	4.5	4.7	-23.3	-2.13
2008	POT	A+	24	4	2	1	15	9	69¹	59	6	17	62	51%	.275	-4	1.10	2.21	3.37	4.13	9.2	1.7	2.7	5.6	9.8	0.94
2008	HAR	AA	24	3	1	0	6	6	38¹	22	1	11	31	61%	.208	19	0.86	1.64	3.51	2.45	5.6	0.7	2.7	5.4	12.4	1.10
2008	COH	AAA	24	1	4	0	9	8	43	62	3	16	35	60%	.415	-15	1.81	7.33	4.10	8.05	13.8	1.1	3.6	5.4	-11.3	-1.03
2009	SYR	AAA	25	4	2	0	7	7	40	33	4	8	14	67%	.213	-6	1.02	1.80	4.79	2.99	6.9	1.3	2.0	2.2	11.4	0.95
2009	WAS	MLB	25	4	7	0	19	19	105²	112	14	24	48	55%	.273	-4	1.29	5.11	4.88	5.35	9.1	1.1	1.7	3.4	1.8	1.16
2010	WAS	MLB	26	6	9	0	30	21	123²	136	18	49	65	58%	.298	-13	1.50	4.93	4.98	5.47	10.2	1.3	3.4	4.5	0.4	1.35

Breakout: 9%   Improve: 47%   Collapse: 19%   Attrition: 15%   MLB: 87%   Comparables: Chien-Ming Wang, David Pauley, Tim Burke, Cam Reimers

Another of the low-strikeout, low-walk, grounder-generating pitchers in the system, Stammen was sucked into the rotation vortex for a half-season of work last year. A tacit decision to gear down and rely more on slower-velocity sinkers rather than try to blow people away has been the calling card for his limited success so far, but throwing fastballs 70 percent of the time won't fly for a rotation regular without a better curve and change. Pitchers with this kind of GB/FB ratio with few walks are always worth a look, but Stammen is going to have to adapt to survive in the majors, or he'll face a career path that diverts him to the pen or an endless round of demotions and reassignments.

Drew Storen

														Bats: S	Throws: R	Height: 6' 1"		Weight: 170		Born: August 1, 1987		Age: 22

YEAR	TEAM	LVL	AGE	W	L	SV	G	GS	IP	H	HR	BB	SO	GB%	BABIP	STUFF	WHIP	ERA	SIERA	DERA	EqH9	EqHR9	EqBB9	EqSO9	VORP	SN/WX
2009	HAG	A	21	0	1	0	11	0	14²	11	2	0	26	29%	.310	14	0.75	3.68	-0.06	5.60	9.9	3.3	1.3	9.9	-0.1	-0.30
2009	HAR	AA	21	1	0	9	10	0	12¹	3	0	6	12	37%	.111	12	0.73	0.00	3.67	0.75	3.0	0.8	4.5	6.8	6.3	0.89
2010	WAS	MLB	22	4	4	8	49	0	60	55	8	22	46	38%	.278	13	1.29	3.92	4.33	4.37	8.5	1.2	3.1	6.5	7.5	2.31

Breakout: 4%   Improve: 19%   Collapse: 54%   Attrition: 4%   MLB: 1%   Comparables: Mark Zamarripa, R.J. Rodriguez, Pedro Strop, Brad Guy

The less heralded of the Nationals' first-round picks last year, Storen was drafted to be a future closer after impressing Bob Boone and Bob Hamelin, members of the Nationals' scouting department, with an eight-whiff relief performance against Oregon State. Storen also has connections to the franchise, rooming with fellow prospect Jack McGeary at Stanford and serving as an Expos bat boy in 2003. Storen has said that he hopes to develop as quickly as his friend Chad Cordero, who made it to the majors only a few months after being drafted. The Nationals are leaving his fate in 2010 in his own hands, and if he can build on his stellar pro debut, he should have little trouble pushing his way into an accelerated timetable and a 2010 big-league debut.

Stephen Strasburg

														Bats: R	Throws: R	Height: 6' 4"		Weight: 220		Born: July 20, 1988		Age: 21

Did Not Play.

YEAR	TEAM	LVL	AGE	W	L	SV	G	GS	IP	H	HR	BB	SO	GB%	BABIP	STUFF	WHIP	ERA	SIERA	DERA	EqH9	EqHR9	EqBB9	EqSO9	VORP	SN/WX
2010	WAS	MLB	21	6	8	0	30	18	126²	128	19	53	122	42%	.316	36	1.43	4.56	3.73	5.06	9.4	1.4	3.6	8.2	6.2	—

Breakout: 13%   Improve: 52%   Collapse: 10%   Attrition: 6%   MLB: 14%   Comparables: Jeremy Hellickson, David Pauley, Candy Sierra, Wade Davis

The number of amateur players ever hyped as much as Strasburg has already been can be counted on one hand, but then again, a collegian who can hit the upper 90s with ease while throwing a devastating slider that registers 91-94 mph, and who can control both pitches ... well, damn straight, that guy *should* turn heads. His line as a senior at San Diego State is simply amazing: 109 IP, 59 H, 19 BB, 195 K, and a 1.32 ERA. He signed a four-year, $15.1 million deal after being selected first overall in the amateur draft and is on the fast track to the big leagues. In 19 innings in the Arizona Fall League, he whiffed 23 batters, and while his 4.26 ERA isn't all that impressive, only one bad outing palled the overall performance. He may take his lumps, but Strasburg is unique and worthy of the accelerated promotion schedule to come. His heat sits at 97-99 mph and touches 101, and he throws it with command that rates as a 70-80 on the 80-point scouting scale. Not only has no college pitcher come along with these qualities before, but no *major-league* pitcher can boast them, either. The way some evaluators talk about him, perhaps Strasburg shouldn't be allowed to pitch; he should be put out to stud so that his genes can found a new race of super-pitchers. More pragmatically, he should have no trouble serving as the ace of the Nationals' rotation as soon as 2011, if not sooner. He could be on the Mark Prior plan—nine minor-league starts and up.

Ron Villone

														Bats: L	Throws: L	Height: 6' 3"		Weight: 245		Born: January 16, 1970		Age: 40

YEAR	TEAM	LVL	AGE	W	L	SV	G	GS	IP	H	HR	BB	SO	GB%	BABIP	STUFF	WHIP	ERA	SIERA	DERA	EqH9	EqHR9	EqBB9	EqSO9	VORP	SN/WX
2007	SWB	AAA	37	0	1	1	17	0	23²	21	0	10	27	56%	.328	9	1.31	1.90	3.18	3.13	8.6	0.4	3.9	7.8	6.1	0.50
2007	NYA	MLB	37	0	0	0	37	0	42¹	36	5	18	25	42%	.248	-10	1.28	4.25	5.08	3.95	7.5	1.1	3.5	5.0	7.1	0.22
2008	SLN	MLB	38	1	2	1	74	0	50	45	4	37	50	48%	.301	4	1.64	4.68	4.46	4.89	8.5	0.7	5.8	7.4	3.4	0.78
2009	WAS	MLB	39	5	6	1	63	0	48²	54	6	29	33	44%	.304	-17	1.71	4.25	5.23	4.47	9.7	1.1	4.4	5.1	5.6	0.01
2010	WAS	MLB	40	2	4	0	50	0	50	52	7	28	34	45%	.301	-17	1.61	5.18	5.08	5.76	9.7	1.2	4.8	5.8	-1.4	0.42

Breakout: 16%   Improve: 40%   Collapse: 38%   Attrition: 26%   MLB: 87%   Comparables: Mike Stanton, Mike Remlinger, Chris Hammond, Ken Takahashi

Cut by the Mets during spring training, Villone signed an incentive-laden minor-league contract with the Nats in early April, when it was already clear that their bullpen would need all the help it could get. Reaching the majors on May 7th, Villone was the team's best reliever for a little over a month, not allowing a run in 19 appearances. The peripherals were poor, so it was clear that the ice would soon break, and from June 10th on, Villone was pounded to the tune of .344/.439/.588 and a 6.54 ERA in 44 games. The long-ago first-round draft pick is 40 years old this year. He has never had good control, and at his age, he's not going to find it, but lefties get a million chances, even old ones. Villone, however, got hit by lefties at a .293/.386/.414 clip after holding them to .204/.310/.310 from 2004 to 2008; he might have at long last reached the end of the line.

Jordan Zimmermann

| | | | | | | | Bats: R | | Throws: R | | Height: 6' 2" | | Weight: 200 | | Born: May 23, 1986 | | | Age: 24 |

YEAR	TEAM	LVL	AGE	W	L	SV	G	GS	IP	H	HR	BB	SO	GB%	BABIP	STUFF	WHIP	ERA	SIERA	DERA	EqH9	EqHR9	EqBB9	EqSO9	VORP	SN/WX
2007	VER	A-	21	5	2	0	13	11	53	45	2	18	71	50%	.344	26	1.19	2.38	2.30	3.54	10.5	1.3	3.8	8.2	10.2	0.66
2008	POT	A+	22	3	1	1	5	4	27^1	15	1	8	31	55%	.237	24	0.84	1.65	2.46	3.00	6.8	1.1	3.4	7.9	6.7	0.76
2008	HAR	AA	22	7	2	0	20	20	106^2	89	9	39	103	53%	.281	19	1.20	3.21	3.48	4.26	8.3	1.3	3.4	6.6	13.9	1.30
2009	WAS	MLB	23	3	5	0	16	16	91^1	95	10	29	92	52%	.332	22	1.36	4.63	3.33	4.79	9.6	0.9	2.4	7.8	7.1	0.98
2010	WAS	MLB	24	6	7	0	27	25	119	116	15	51	98	47%	.299	8	1.40	4.37	4.18	4.84	9.1	1.1	3.6	7.0	8.7	2.46

Breakout: 9%   Improve: 39%   Collapse: 14%   Attrition: 12%   MLB: 100%   Comparables: Alan Fowlkes, Rick Huisman, Doug Bochtler, Jeff Peterek

One of the only pitchers in the Nationals' treasury projected to be a front-end rotation starter in anybody's rotation, Zimmermann posted an impressive strikeout-to-walk rate, inducing plenty of worm beaters in the process. Poised and in possession of good command and control and four quality pitches (including a four-seam fastball in the 92-95 mph range), he looked to headline the Nationals' rotation this season before learning that he would need Tommy John surgery. The team will look to be as conservative in his rehabilitation as possible, hoping for a late-2010 return, by which point he might potentially form a dynamic duo atop the rotation with Stephen Strasburg. Consider the PECOTA above Zimmermann's telegram of what might have been.

LINEOUTS

Hitters

PLAYER	TEAM	LVL	AGE	PA	R	2B	3B	HR	RBI	BB	SO	SB-CS	EqBRR	AVG/OBP/SLG	EqAVG/EqOBP/EqSLG	EqA	VORP	WARP
C J. Burke	SEA	MLB	37	43	1	0	0	1	1	2	13	0-0	-0.1	.122/.163/.195	.122/.163/.195	-.042	-3.8	-0.4
	WAS	MLB	37	13	0	0	0	0	1	1	5	0-0	0.1	.100/.167/.100	.100/.167/.100	.105	-1.0	-0.1
2B J. Kobernus	VER	A-	21	44	8	1	0	0	2	2	5	4-0	1.2	.220/.273/.244	.190/.209/.214	.132	-3.7	-0.8
2B Lombardozzi#	HAG	A	20	576	90	26	7	3	58	62	80	16-7	4.9	.296/.375/.395	.254/.321/.341	.238	3.5	-0.6
OF M. Lowrance*	HAR	AA	24	408	47	22	2	15	45	41	89	1-2	-3.2	.241/.323/.438	.221/.287/.383	.232	-7.4	-1.8
INF P. Orr*	SYR	AAA	30	464	50	13	5	9	50	27	77	18-8	-1.5	.245/.305/.367	.230/.281/.335	.220	-3.9	0.2
	WAS	MLB	30	81	5	2	1	1	10	3	15	2-1	-0.6	.253/.272/.347	.270/.284/.365	.228	-0.3	0.3
UT J. Padilla	SYR	AAA	29	350	58	18	3	4	21	24	32	14-11	-5.8	.367/.424/.482	.345/.397/.456	.290	17.5	1.7
	WAS	MLB	29	26	3	0	0	0	0	1	8	0-0	-0.1	.120/.154/.120	.160/.192/.160	-.136	-4.6	-0.6
LF J. Ramirez*	VER	A-	19	314	35	18	6	4	39	14	45	6-9	-5.6	.264/.306/.407	.229/.258/.346	.204	-12.8	-3.5
PH D. Young#	HAR	AA	35	34	4	2	0	0	2	3	4	0-0	-0.1	.241/.324/.310	.226/.286/.290	.210	-1.8	-0.5

Veteran backstop **Jamie Burke** has been re-upped as a nonroster invitee, apparently to spend time teaching Stephen Strasburg his interview clichés and reminding him never to punch a drunk with his pitching hand. ⊘ Washington's second-round pick in last year's draft, **Jeffrey Kobernus** was limited by minor knee surgery to 10 games in his pro debut. Scouts speak favorably of his good approach, gap power, and speed, though his defense is still an open question. ⊘ The son of the Twins' 1987 World Series hero of the same name, **Stephen Lombardozzi** is a similarly slick-fielding second baseman who flashed solid on-base skills in his full-season debut. ⊘ Not to be confused with the star of *Big Momma's House*, **Marvin Lowrance** turned 25 in Double-A, slumped at the plate, and will be hard-pressed to avoid being typecast as an organizational soldier. ⊘ Former Brave **Pete Orr** has managed to leverage 150 not-quite-horrible plate appearances in 2005 into 450 quite-horrible plate appearances in the years since; time to stop the madness. ⊘ Minor-league vet **Jorge Padilla** achieved one life goal by making his big-league debut before turning 30, but there's little chance he'll still be playing there at 31. ⊘ Texas prep star **J. P. Ramirez** disappointed at the plate in his short-season debut, and as his bat is his only tool, that's quite a problem. ⊘ Another unfortunate Bowden contract that's finally coming off the books, **Dmitri Young** earned $5 million last year while rehabbing hip and back problems; concern that his diabetes may lead to further health issues means Young will probably soon need to find something other than baseball to fill his summers with.

Pitchers

PLAYER	TEAM	LVL	AGE	W	L	SV	IP	H	HR	BB	SO	GB%	BABIP	STUFF	WHIP	ERA	SIERA	DERA	EqH9	EqHR9	EqBB9	EqSO9	VORP
L. Atilano	HAR	AA	24	7	8	0	114²	143	12	27	61	61%	.332	-33	1.48	4.16	4.54	5.77	12.0	1.8	2.4	3.3	-3.2
—	SYR	AAA	24	2	0	0	11	11	2	1	5	65%	.257	-4	1.09	2.45	4.29	3.48	9.6	2.6	0.9	3.5	2.3
T. Engles	HAG	A	23	4	2	0	51	50	5	12	60	63%	.346	-8	1.22	3.53	2.50	5.73	11.9	2.6	3.7	6.5	-1.1
—	POT	A+	23	4	3	0	49	43	2	17	48	62%	.308	4	1.22	3.12	3.30	4.97	9.9	1.2	3.9	6.1	2.6
C. Everts	POT	A+	24	3	0	2	20	14	2	5	26	58%	.273	9	0.95	0.90	2.17	2.95	8.8	2.0	2.9	8.3	5.2
—	HAR	AA	24	3	1	4	29¹	21	0	11	31	61%	.280	7	1.09	1.53	3.16	3.05	7.4	0.6	3.5	7.1	7.6
—	SYR	AAA	24	2	0	0	10²	14	1	10	11	54%	.406	6	2.25	3.37	4.85	4.50	12.6	1.8	9.0	7.2	1.1
M. Frias	HAG	A	20	9	5	0	126²	124	6	30	112	45%	.314	0	1.22	2.91	3.50	5.84	10.7	1.7	3.4	4.4	-4.3
V. Garate*	CHT	AA	24	0	1	4	53	36	1	23	56	35%	.259	9	1.11	2.04	3.49	2.82	7.2	0.5	3.9	7.2	15.2
—	WAS	MLB	24	0	0	0	2	5	1	3	0	16%	.400	-59	4.00	22.50	9.77	21.21	19.3	3.9	11.6	0.0	-4.1
J. Jaime	HAG	A	21	3	1	0	31²	22	2	16	40	44%	.274	8	1.20	2.27	2.99	6.19	8.6	1.9	6.4	7.0	-2.2
—	VER	A-	21	2	1	0	24	15	0	15	36	46%	.319	20	1.25	1.87	2.59	4.05	9.4	1.4	7.7	8.6	3.2
J. McGeary*	HAG	A	20	0	6	0	55²	58	4	45	44	55%	.331	-10	1.85	6.79	5.04	11.09	12.3	2.5	10.2	4.0	-29.0
—	VER	A-	20	2	6	0	56¹	61	5	41	45	45%	.320	-25	1.81	4.31	5.11	10.80	14.0	3.5	8.8	3.7	-28.5
Z. Segovia	HAR	AA	26	1	3	1	44	57	2	19	39	53%	.387	-16	1.73	3.68	4.10	4.97	12.7	1.1	4.1	5.8	2.5
—	SYR	AAA	26	2	2	5	28¹	18	1	8	27	41%	.236	7	0.92	2.54	3.26	3.29	5.9	0.7	2.6	6.9	6.7
—	WAS	MLB	26	1	0	0	10¹	11	1	6	4	47%	.278	-37	1.65	7.84	6.12	8.27	9.6	0.9	4.4	2.6	-3.2
A. Severino*	POT	A+	24	4	0	13	46	35	4	14	39	60%	.240	-16	1.07	2.54	3.58	4.05	8.5	1.9	3.3	5.0	7.0
—	HAR	AA	24	6	0	2	22²	19	1	14	27	61%	.321	8	1.46	2.78	3.49	4.15	8.7	0.8	5.4	7.9	3.2
J. Sosa	SYR	AAA	32	1	2	3	48¹	40	3	13	53	53%	.301	15	1.10	2.79	2.77	3.52	8.0	1.0	2.7	8.0	10.1
—	WAS	MLB	32	2	1	2	22¹	28	5	12	17	36%	.333	-19	1.79	6.45	4.96	6.02	11.6	2.1	4.2	5.8	-1.3
J. Tavarez	WAS	MLB	36	3	7	1	35	34	1	27	32	56%	.308	-1	1.74	4.89	4.71	6.50	8.3	0.2	5.6	6.6	-4.1
A. Thompson*	JAX	AA	22	5	9	0	114	121	7	43	75	54%	.302	-19	1.44	4.11	4.63	7.06	11.5	1.6	3.5	4.0	-18.7
—	HAR	AA	22	0	3	0	32²	32	3	11	27	44%	.299	6	1.32	3.31	3.96	6.18	9.5	1.7	3.2	5.5	-2.4
J. Wilkie	HAR	AA	24	5	2	3	49¹	48	2	13	40	56%	.303	-5	1.24	2.37	3.75	3.44	9.1	0.9	2.6	5.2	11.0
—	SYR	AAA	24	2	3	2	22¹	19	0	4	25	75%	.328	17	1.03	3.22	2.42	4.01	8.0	0.4	1.7	8.0	3.5

A former Braves first-round pick, **Luis Atilano** throws a ton of strikes, but his mediocre stuff leads to few strikeouts and a ton of hits allowed. ⊘ A low-upside righty with good control, **Terrence Engles** was lost to the Mariners in the Rule 5 draft. ⊘ A 2002 first-rounder who saw his career derailed by injuries, **Clint Everts** showed some signs of life last year, so the Mets (run by Omar Minaya, who originally drafted him) signed him to a major-league deal and will take a long look in camp. ⊘ Gifted with great command and an ability to locate in spite of average stuff, **Marcos Frias** projects to be a viable back-end rotation option. ⊘ The PTBNL received in the Ronnie Belliard deal, southpaw **Vic Garate** depends more on deception than stuff, but he gets hitters out consistently. ⊘ Added to the 40-man roster despite only eight career games in a full-season league, **Juan Jaime** has mid-90s velocity that had the Nationals afraid someone might go fishing in the Rule 5 draft, despite his sushi-grade rawness. ⊘ **Jack McGeary** matched whiffs and walks en route to an underwhelming first full season, meaning that his formerly high upside has probably gone the way of the Go-Go's: "Fading Fast." ⊘ **Zack Segovia** keeps the ball on the ground, but his secondary offerings are well below average and his heater isn't fast enough for him to get by as a one-pitch reliever. ⊘ **Atahualpa Severino** throws hard from the left side, and despite being a tad old for his minor-league levels, there's an Inca-ling he'll be a decent specialist. ⊘ **Jorge Sosa** defines disposability for pitchers by throwing hard without control or command, always turning up to replace someone somewhere before being replaced. ⊘ **Julian Tavarez** altered his approach, throwing sliders 51 percent of the time to post one of the highest strikeout rates of his career, but the highest walk rate as well, producing his unemployment. ⊘ A Fish fry received in the Nick the Stick trade, **Aaron Thompson** touches the low 90s with his fastball and has some upside if he can develop with his assortment. ⊘ **Josh Wilkie** went undrafted out of college, but he has tremendous control and an ability to keep the ball on the ground, both of which bode well despite his average-to-below repertoire.

MANAGER: MANNY ACTA

YEAR	TEAM	W-L	Pythag +/–	Avg PC	100+ P	120+ P	QS	BQS	REL	REL w Zero R	IBB	Subs	PH	PH Avg	PH HR	SB2	CS2	SB3	CS3	SAC Att	SAC %	POS SAC	Squeeze	Swing	In Play
2007	WAS	73-89	4	88.2	28	0	59	3	587	372	43	102	291	.198	5	59	20	10	2	90	70.0%	26	0	121	92
2008	WAS	59-102	-2	92.9	53	0	64	5	517	314	44	55	288	.237	7	74	36	7	7	106	60.4%	22	1	97	73
2009	WAS	26-61	-7	93.3	21	0	32	3	280	152	26	29	145	.215	2	31	15	5	2	48	64.6%	10	0	78	65

MANAGER: JIM RIGGLEMAN

YEAR	TEAM	W-L	Pythag +/–	Avg PC	100+ P	120+ P	QS	BQS	REL	REL w Zero R	IBB	Subs	PH	PH Avg	PH HR	SB2	CS2	SB3	CS3	SAC Att	SAC %	POS SAC	Squeeze	Swing	In Play
2008	SEA	36-54	-3	93.0	39	0	37	1	272	158	25	37	75	.235	0	32	15	6	2	37	56.8%	19	1	84	75
2009	WAS	33-42	1	87.9	16	1	29	3	250	137	33	38	114	.282	2	32	18	5	2	50	66.0%	14	1	55	46

Manny Acta wound up being sacrificed, but in the same way that everybody can use a change of scenery, it was perhaps for the best that he got his walking papers and an opportunity to land in Cleveland. The bullpen Acta had managed to run so desperately and well went from a charming collection of functional castoffs to an increasingly awful mishmash of no-trick ponies and formerly famous people. Having ditched the "interim" tag applied to him in consecutive seasons, Riggleman is getting a merited opportunity at a job. He has his virtues as a skipper, and it wasn't as if he was handed the best opportunities in San Diego and Chicago in the '90s. He's open to building platoons when he can find them and has the need, and as much as you can infer how a skipper solves problems by how he sets up his roster, he has identified and put to good use multipositional bench players (Jose Hernandez in particular). He also finds ways of using backup catchers who do more than just catch (Phil Clark, Tyler Houston). Riggleman was as aggressive in using the intentional walk in the '90s as he appeared to be in his brief work with the Nats, so you can anticipate a lot of La Russian machinations with whatever group he's got. Having had to work through the controversies of Sammy being Sammy and a Ryne Sandberg comeback, Riggleman has been able to handle the limelight; the real question might be if the misfortune of pushing Kerry Wood a start too far in '98 will inform his handling of Strasburg, but only time will tell.

The Baseball Prospectus Top 101 Prospects

Kevin Goldstein

I'm not going to lie here. I have a love-hate relationship with rankings. They are definitely a must-do in my job, and I love doing them, but more for the process than the result, as what you see below is the product of hundreds of hours of phone calls with scouts and front-office executives. Their insight into the talent they see on the fields is invaluable, as knowing what a player is doing is just one part of the equation; understanding *how* a player is doing it is the real key and the pleasurable part of the work.

The reason I'm less inclined to love the list that comes after the conversations is that any ranking is highly subjective. In making this list, I spent a lot of time moving players around, shuffling them again, stepping away for a night, and then coming back to make sure things still looked right (they often did not). Now they're locked in print, yet still liquid in my mind. I hardly have all 101 names and positions memorized, so if you asked me today (and again the next day), chances are good that upward of 90 percent of those named would remain the same, but the rankings themselves would be greatly altered. That guy in the 50s might move up or down 10 spots, as perhaps I've already had a conversation with a scout who saw him this spring and the scout was moved to something like poetry in describing his improvement, or the player's farm director, who is suddenly less confident than he was over the winter that his top prospect can stay at his current position. It's the ever-changing nature of prospects and the constant stream of new talent that draws me to this aspect of the game; as long as my e-mail, phone, and instant-message clients are working, the target never stops moving. It's the most exciting beat there is, but it's hell on static lists.

1. Stephen Strasburg, RHP, Nationals

Not just the best college pitcher in the 2009 draft, maybe the best college pitcher in baseball history. His combination of top-of-the-line velocity and command is found once in a generation, if that, and Strasburg adds to the package with a well-above-average slider and changeup. Only an injury or a meteor strike will prevent him from being a perennial Cy Young contender.

2. Jason Heyward, OF, Braves

The top position prospect in the game flirted with .400 at Double-A ... as a teenager. Every tool is there: the 6-foot-4, 220-pound beast is an above-average runner and even has outstanding plate discipline. The Braves are going to give him a long look this spring, and even if he doesn't hook on then, he'll be the starting right fielder before his 21st birthday.

3. Neftali Feliz, RHP, Rangers

The thing about Feliz is just how easy he makes it look: 96-100 mph velocity explodes out of his hand, but he has the ease of someone who is just warming up. Brought up as a starter, he might spend at least another year in the bullpen in 2010, but while the desire to use him in the late innings is understandable, a Pedro Martinez trajectory of 100 long relief innings might be best for his development.

4. Jesus Montero, C, Yankees

He's almost assuredly not a catcher in the end, and it's almost assuredly not going to matter. In terms of pure hitting ability, no prospect matches Montero, whose ability to put up big numbers in horrible hitting environments at levels a player at his age has no right to be in has everyone projecting him as a monster force in the big leagues.

5. Mike Stanton, OF, Marlins

If power is the last tool to develop, then what is Stanton going to be in six years? He has slugged 67 home runs over the last two seasons, including 16 in half a season at Double-A at the age of 19. If you're betting on one prospect in the game to put up a 50-home-run season, then Stanton is your guy.

6. Pedro Alvarez, 3B, Pirates

The best hitter in the 2008 draft showed during the second half of the year why he has this label, as Alvarez hit for average and power and drew a truckload of walks. His big body has him rapidly growing out of third base, but the Pirates need a first baseman, too. Worst-case scenario is Mo Vaughn, but if Alvarez gets in shape, he could move into a special category.

7. Desmond Jennings, OF, Rays

Jennings didn't just have a good return from injuries in 2009; he got better in every way, earning Double-A Southern League MVP honors. With hitting ability, burner-level speed, good plate discipline, and developing power, he basically could be Carl Crawford with walks—a scary proposition indeed.

8. Carlos Santana, C, Indians

If Santana was a first baseman, he'd still rank highly, but once you put his kind of bat together with the game's toughest position, he becomes elite. While he'll never win a Gold Glove award back there, he's more than good enough to stay at the position while batting third for a first-division lineup.

9. Buster Posey, C, Giants

Posey brings the athleticism of a middle infielder and a cannon arm to a position normally designed for the big and husky. He's also a tremendous threat at the plate, with the natural ability to hit .300 with 15-20 home runs a year.

10. Chris Carter, 1B, Athletics

After leading the minor leagues in total bases in 2008, Carter merely tied for the honors in 2009, but he also closed a lot of the holes in his swing, giving scouts more confidence in his ability to hit for average. Some big-league total-bases titles could be in his future as well.

11. Dustin Ackley, OF/2B, Mariners

The second overall pick in the 2009 draft, Ackley isn't like most top college hitters, as he's loaded with tools beyond his ability to work the count and lace line drives to all fields. Everyone thinks he can hit .300 and put up on-base percentages near .400. The only subject of debate is just how much power he has, an unanswered question that prevents him from ranking higher.

12. Jeremy Hellickson, RHP, Rays

Hellickson's ability to carve up hitters like a surgeon with pinpoint control often overshadows the excellence of his raw stuff. Dr. Hellickson throws a low-90s fastball that gets up to 95, an excellent changeup, and a good curve. One scout commented, "I know he's a guy I'm not allowed to compare prospects to, but every time I see him pitch, I see Greg Maddux."

13. Ryan Westmoreland, OF, Red Sox

Given a well over-slot $2 million bonus in 2008, Westmoreland enjoyed a pro debut that was one of the biggest coming-out parties of the year. The multifaceted outfielder showed all five tools to go with an approach at the plate that rivals that of any big-league veteran. He's quite similar to Grady Sizemore, except the Cleveland star wasn't anywhere near this good a hitter at the same age.

14. Martin Perez, LHP, Rangers

When an 18-year-old holds his own at Double-A, you know you have something special. With a low- to mid-90s fastball and two plus secondary offerings (including an outstanding changeup), Perez' stuff is so good that scouts are happy to look past his smallish frame and project him as an All-Star.

15. Kyle Drabek, RHP, Blue Jays

After refusing to include him in a deal for Roy Halladay last summer, the Phillies finally acquiesced in December, and now the Jays suddenly have a new top prospect and potential impact arm. Returning from Tommy John surgery, Drabek showed 96 mph heat to go with the outstanding hammer curve learned from his father, Kyle.

16. Justin Smoak, 1B, Rangers

Although a strained oblique hampered Smoak at Triple-A in 2009, he was healthy and mashing for Team USA in September, hitting nine home runs in 14 games. A switch-hitter with power from both sides, lots of walks, and above-average defense, the comparisons to Mark Teixeira are inevitable and appropriate.

17. Brian Matusz, LHP, Orioles

It surprised no one to see Matusz reach the big leagues in his first full season. His greatest strength is a lack of weaknesses, as he has four offerings that rate as average or above and the ability to throw any of them for strikes. On a team loaded with exciting young hitters, Matusz and Chris Tillman will give Baltimore the pitching they need to get out of the lower half of the AL East.

18. Alcides Escobar, SS, Brewers

Escobar's .304 batting average in 38 big league games is what made J. J. Hardy expendable. Even though it's an empty .300, without power and patience, it's more than enough to make him an above-average everyday player. Did we mention that he's the best defensive shortstop in the minors?

19. Michael Taylor, OF, Athletics

Taylor presents a strange dichotomy for scouts, as he's a 6-foot-6, 250-pound monster with a contact-oriented approach, leading to a .300-plus batting average and 20-plus home runs annually just because he's so big and strong. He still has room for improvement, as he abandoned the Stanford Swing only two years ago and continues to make adjustments.

20. Madison Bumgarner, LHP, Giants

Bumgarner was the best pitcher in the minor league in 2008, and although his numbers were good in 2009, including a brief big-league audition, scouts noted a consistent velocity drop that by the end of the year had amounted to a full 5 mph. His ability to succeed with average velocity is a tribute to everything else he brings to the table. If the velocity comes back, and it should, he'll make this ranking look conservative.

21. Christian Friedrich, LHP, Rockies

A late first-round pick in 2008, Friedrich rocketed up the charts by putting up a 2.41 ERA and striking out 12 batters per nine while pitching in a pair of hostile offensive environments. With above-average velocity and one of the best curveballs in the minors, Friedrich could be less than 100 innings away from the big leagues.

22. Tyler Matzek, LHP, Rockies

On a pure stuff level, Matzek blows Friedrich away. He's a 6-foot-3 lefty who got up to 97 mph this spring for his high-school team while also showing the ability to spin a breaking ball. The only thing preventing him from ranking higher is the fact that he has yet to throw a pitch as a pro.

23. Domonic Brown, OF, Phillies

The Darryl Strawberry comps are ludicrous and lazy, but that doesn't mean Brown isn't one of the best outfield prospects in the game. Long and left-handed with plenty of speed, Brown has been tapping into his raw power a bit more each year, and many feel that 2010 is the season when he'll hit the mother lode.

24. Jacob Turner, RHP, Tigers

Seen by many as the best high-school righty in the 2009 draft, Turner is everything the Tigers look for in a pitcher: he is big and throws very hard (up to 98 mph).

With his above-average breaking ball and smooth arm action, he's seen by Detroit as having a Justin Verlander starter kit; he could be in the big leagues within three years.

25. Aaron Hicks, OF, Twins

At a Midwest League game I attended with a scout in August, Hicks smacked a mammoth home run and then made one of the best catches I saw all year—all within the span of 20 minutes—leading the scout to turn to me and say, "Well, I'm sold." Ignore the numbers; Hicks is one of the toolsiest players in the game, and his ability to already understand the strike zone will work in his favor.

26. Dee Gordon, SS, Dodgers

In his full-season debut, Gordon hit .301 with 73 stolen bases for Low-A Great Lakes. He did this on sheer athleticism while seemingly having little idea what he's doing out there: his inexperience and rawness led to 34 errors and 25 caught stealing. Scouts shudder at what he can be once he figures things out, as he's got Jimmy Rollins' tool set.

27. Derek Norris, C, Nationals

Norris led the Sally League with a .413 on-base percentage while finishing fifth in slugging (.513), and that was only because he had a bad final month; he had an outside shot at a Triple Crown before the slump hit. Oh yeah, he's a catcher, too. Not a great catcher, mind you, but he projects as at least average, and an everyday catcher who can hit in the middle of a lineup is a rare commodity.

28. Donovan Tate, OF, Padres

The son of a former NFL running back, Tate was not only the best athlete in the 2009 draft, but one of the best available in years. The problem is that he's not a very refined baseball player, and he has already had more than his share of injuries before stepping to the plate once as a pro. One front-office executive put it best before the draft: "He could be Mickey Mantle, and he could never get out of A-ball."

29. Casey Kelly, RHP, Red Sox

For this two-way star in high school, the Red Sox have been extremely patient in allowing Kelly to split his roles so far, but after a 2.08 ERA as a pitcher and a .642 OPS as a shortstop, his future is now firmly on the mound. With two plus pitches to go with sublime command, he could move quickly, now that he's focusing only on getting outs instead of making them.

30. Josh Vitters, 3B, Cubs

Vitters had arguably the best hot streak in the minors last year. In late May, the 2007 first-round pick reeled off 16 games for Low-A Peoria in which he went 29-for-67 with 10 home runs. His swing might be the prettiest in the minors, but his ability to make contact might also be his undoing: he swings at too many bad pitches because he can hit anything, anywhere.

31. Casey Crosby, LHP, Tigers

After missing all of 2008 while recovering from Tommy John surgery, Crosby showed why he earned a seven-figure bonus out of high school. A 6-foot-5 lefty with plus-plus velocity and a good curve, he has excited the Tigers about what he can do next year with a significantly increased workload.

32. Julio Teheran, RHP, Braves

Signed out of Panama in 2007, Teheran has a career ERA of 4.11 as a pro, but don't be fooled. Just 19 years old and so skinny he provokes thoughts of Twiggy and Kate Moss, Teheran has as much projection as anyone else in the game. Blessed with silky smooth mechanics, he already throws a fastball that gets up to 96. Some in the Braves' organization see a resemblance to another Latin American arm once in the Atlanta system, Neftali Feliz.

33. Wade Davis, RHP, Rays

Davis was dominant at times after replacing Scott Kazmir in the Tampa rotation, but like his minor-league career, he was also inconsistent. With a classic power-pitching frame, 92-95 mph heat, and a plus curveball, Davis can dominate when he's on, but the command and off-speed stuff has to improve for him to become a go-to asset.

34. Miguel Sano, SS, Twins

One of the best hitters to come out of the Dominican Republic in years, Sano is only a shortstop in name, probably projecting as a strong-armed right fielder by the time he gets to the big leagues, but we're talking about a 16-year-old who already has big-league average power and a feel for hitting. The Twins tend to be conservative with the development of young talents, but Sano might end up challenging their usual timetable.

35. Mike Montgomery, LHP, Royals

A 6-foot-5 left-hander with off-the-charts athleticism, a smooth delivery, and power stuff? Sign us up. Montgomery possesses a heater that sits at 92-94 mph with movement and a very good breaking ball. He has com-piled a 2.06 ERA in his first 33 professional games, and those kinds of numbers should continue all the way up the ladder.

36. Starlin Castro, SS, Cubs

Assigned to High-A for his full-season debut, Castro surprised, not only holding his own, but earning MVP honors in the Florida State League All-Star game and continuing to hit after a promotion to Double-A. Heady stuff for a 19-year-old, but his tools prevent a star-level projection; secondary skills are lacking, while his average-at-best speed makes him a dependable but unspectacular shortstop. The total package is still that of an above-average regular.

37. Shelby Miller, RHP, Cardinals

Miller was one of the top high-school arms in the 2009 draft and has a low- to mid-90s fastball with tons of movement as his calling card, along with a promising breaking ball. With all the trades the Cardinals made to secure a 2009 title (whoops), their system is completely bereft, making Miller their top prospect by a Grand Canyon–sized margin.

38. Josh Bell, 3B, Orioles

Sent by the Dodgers to Baltimore in the George Sherrill deal, Bell had already taken a step forward during the first half of the year, but his brief showing at Double-A Bowie had scouts convinced that he's Baltimore's third baseman of the future, given his plus power and considerable defensive improvements. The Orioles are looking for no more than a hot corner stopgap for 2010 in order to accommodate Bell.

39. Chris Withrow, RHP, Dodgers

Healthy for the first time since being a first-round pick in 2007, Withrow went from well behind on the developmental curve to ahead by reaching Double-A (and succeeding there) as a 20-year-old. The best arm in the system, he has a mid-90s fastball that touches 98 and a power curve, and if he can throw more strikes, he has true star potential.

40. Matt Moore, LHP, Rays

Moore led the minors with 176 strikeouts in 2009, a feat made all the more impressive by the low pitch count that limited him to just 123 innings. His fastball is above average, but it's his hammer curve that generates the majority of swings and misses, with some scouts seeing him as a bigger, stronger version of former Rays lefty Scott Kazmir.

41. Alex Colome, LHP, Rays

No player in the short-season leagues took a bigger step forward than Colome, who led the New York-Penn League in strikeouts while compiling a 1.66 ERA in 15 starts. Just as impressive was an explosive mid-90s fastball that got up to 98 and a long, lanky frame that's loaded with projection. Look out for this one.

42. Lonnie Chisenhall, 3B, Indians

Some teams were surprised to see Cleveland take Chisenhall with their first-round pick in 2008, but one year later, those same teams were wondering why they missed on him. His quick, quiet swing is designed for a high average, but he adds the natural loft and backspin for 20-25 home runs as well, and his transition to the hot corner was an unquestioned success.

43. Brett Wallace, 1B, Blue Jays

An on-base machine with solid power, Wallace is already with his third organization, primarily because teams have decided that his big, sluggish body just isn't going to work at third base. As a first-base-only type, he needs to hit .300 to have value because of his average power for the position, but everyone thinks he will.

44. Arodys Vizcaino, RHP, Braves

The top young arm in the Yankees system, Vizcaino, not Melky Cabrera, was the key to the Javier Vasquez deal. Vizcaino's low- to mid-90s fastball touches 97, and his curveball is already big-league average. Few teams have as many young Latin arms as the Braves do, and Vizcaino just adds to their riches.

45. Ben Revere, OF, Twins

A career .337 hitter in the minors, Revere is a true burner who rarely strikes out, and in 2009, he greatly improved his approach at the plate, working the count more in order to reach base and take advantage of his speed. Despite just three career home runs in 254 games, scouts think he's a good enough pure hitter to end up with 8-12 a year when he gets to the big leagues, which will help keep pitchers honest down the road.

46. Simon Castro, RHP, Padres

Castro had a low profile entering the season, but after leading the Low-A Midwest League in strikeouts and showing low- to mid-90s velocity with plus command, he's now the best pitching prospect in the system. A dead ringer for Jose Contreras physically, Castro has the frame and stamina to be a rotation stalwart, and some improvements in his secondary offerings could make him much more than that.

47. Jennry Mejia, RHP, Mets

One of the most exciting arms to come through the Mets' system in the last decade, Mejia reached Double-A as a teenager, thanks to a 93-96 mph fastball that can get close to triple digits at times. The pitch is made all the more deadly by the sinking or cutting action he adds to it. Mejia can be a spectacular mess at times, with command issues and a messy breaking ball, but this is a rare arm.

48. Austin Jackson, OF, Tigers

The trade of Curtis Granderson made Jackson Detroit's center fielder of the future, and that future probably begins on Opening Day. His tools aren't elite as much as they are solid across the board, but a .280-.300 hitter with good defense and speed should help ease Tigers fans' feelings after the loss of a star.

49. Logan Morrison, 1B, Marlins

If you are a big fan of the walk, then Morrison is your man, as he drew 64 against just 289 at-bats in an injury-hampered 2009 season. The good news is that he can hit for average as well, although his power might be a bit under what is normally expected for a first baseman—think a more athletic John Olerud.

50. Freddie Freeman, 1B, Braves

If his first name were Gordon, we'd be the happiest people on earth, but even without that little touch of geek heaven, we just like him for being a very good first base prospect. Playing nearly his entire career in the shadow of Justin Heyward, Freeman also reached Double-A at 19, and while he met with his first pro struggles there, scouts love the bat and see plenty of power to come out of his 6-foot-5, 220-pound frame.

51. Jarrod Parker, RHP, Diamondbacks

Were it not for the Tommy John surgery that will cost Parker all of 2010, he'd be in the top 20, as he's one of just a handful of minor-leaguers with two plus-plus offerings, his 93-97 mph fastball and wipeout slider.

52. Mike Trout, OF, Angels

Trout could have gone off the 2009 draft board in the top 20, and now plenty of teams are wishing they pulled the trigger on him after he showed a surprising amount of polish to go with his impressive tools, which include above-average power and speed.

53. Aaron Crow, RHP, Royals

Crow still didn't get the money he was looking for when he didn't sign with Washington after the 2008 draft, but then his slider wasn't quite as sharp as it was, either, after nearly a year off. He still has a power arm and could move quickly through the system on his way to becoming an above-average starter.

54. Dan Hudson, RHP, White Sox

Hudson arguably took the single biggest leap forward of any minor-leaguer in 2009, beginning the season as a nondescript fifth-round pick in Low-A and finishing it in the majors. With plus velocity and plus-plus command, he might start 2010 in the big-league bullpen until a starting opportunity arises.

55. Tim Beckham, SS, Rays

The top pick in the 2008 draft didn't exactly set the world on fire in his full-season debut, but scouts still see the tools and believe that plenty of his 33 doubles will turn into home runs down the road. However, they are less sanguine than ever as to his ability to stay up the middle.

56. Scott Sizemore, 2B, Tigers

The favorite to win the Tigers' second base job out of spring training, Sizemore could end up being a dead ringer for Placido Polanco offensively, a high-average hitter with tons of doubles and 8-12 home runs a year. He comes a lot cheaper as well (for now).

57. Josh Reddick, OF, Red Sox

With the Mike Cameron signing, Reddick has no avenue to anything more than a bench job in Boston, but his power bat, big-time arm, and ability to play all three outfield positions could make him an attractive trade candidate.

58. Mike Leake, RHP, Reds

The eighth overall pick last June, Leake had numbers that would have been the talk of college baseball had it not been for that Strasburg guy. While he's a bit undersized, there's an outside shot at his becoming the next Tim Hudson.

59. Drew Storen, RHP, Nationals

Though he was the best college reliever in the draft, many scouts didn't see Storen as more than a set-up man, but he gained velocity throughout the spring and was sitting at 95-97 mph in the Arizona Fall League. He could be closing games in Washington by July.

60. Jared Mitchell, OF, White Sox

Had the draft taken place after the College World Series instead of shortly before, Mitchell would have gone up to 10 picks higher than number 23 after earning Most Outstanding Player honors in Omaha. Although he's the best athlete available among college players, his power hasn't translated to wood bats yet, but everything else has.

61. Michael Saunders, OF, Mariners

Overmatched in his big-league debut, Saunders needs to rediscover the plate discipline that served him so well in the minors; when he's swinging at good pitches, he's a classic corner outfielder with the ability to hit for average and power.

62. Hak-Ju Lee, SS, Cubs

Signed out of Korea for more than seven figures, Lee has the speed to steal 30 bases, the bat speed to hit .300, and a surprisingly refined approach. His defensive tools are just as impressive. He could move way up the list with an equally impressive showing in this year's full-season debut.

63. James Darnell, 3B, Padres

In 142 pro games, Darnell has hit .319 with 41 doubles, 22 home runs, and 98 walks. If scouts were convinced that he could stay at third base, he'd rank higher on this list. He has the tools to stay there, but we said the same thing about Ryan Braun, another player who frustrated in his inability to translate physical skill into defensive performance.

64. Wilson Ramos, C, Twins

Ramos has everything you look for in a catcher except good health, with above-average power and a good arm—too bad he's a Twin and stuck behind Joe Mauer. If Mauer leaves for free agency ... Nah, don't even think about it, Twins fans. Don't imagine Mauer in Yankees pinstripes, in Red Sox red, or hiding his head under a haloed Angels A. Well, if you must, but afterward, console yourself with the knowledge that while Ramos is no Mauer, he might be pretty good.

65. Michael Ynoa, RHP, Athletics

One of the best, if not *the* best raw arm to ever come out of the Dominican Republic, Ynoa never showed up in a box score last year, as the A's were very cautious about some elbow soreness. That downgrades him from well ahead of schedule to merely ahead, and gives him an injury history before he has thrown an inning.

66. Grant Desme, OF, Athletics

After barely playing in his first two seasons due to injuries, Desme quickly made up for lost time by slugging

31 home runs and stealing 40 bases in 45 attempts between Kane County and Stockton, then earning MVP honors in the Arizona Fall League. He still has some more time to make up and a strike-out rate that needs to be cut down.

67. Todd Frazier, 2B, Reds
After being tried at five different positions, Frazier may have finally found a home at the keystone. The Reds dream of Frazier's becoming a Jeff Kent–like offensive presence at second; too bad their best player, Brandon Phillips, currently resides there.

68. Tanner Scheppers, RHP, Rangers
With a fastball that threatens to reach triple digits, Scheppers wins the award for "Most Likely to Save 40 Games." But with a history of shoulder problems and a violent delivery, he's also the most likely to undergo surgery before he reaches the big leagues.

69. Reid Brignac, SS, Rays
Brignac is a strange prospect who has gone from an offense-first shortstop who might need to move to third to a defensive whiz who has power but needs to pick up the other aspects of his batting game. With Jason Bartlett's equally strange transformation from stopgap to star, it's hard to figure out Brignac's future in Tampa.

70. Jake Arrieta, RHP, Orioles
Arrietta's fastball might be the best in a system loaded with young arms, but he depends on the pitch far too much, and it caught up to him at Triple-A. Without some improvement of his other pitches—his curve and change are unexceptional—his ceiling will be no higher than third starter.

71. Kyle Gibson, RHP, Twins
A surefire top 10 pick before suffering a stress fracture in his forearm, Gibson has the potential to be a steal. Even before the injury, his stuff was good but not of ace quality. Still, if his low-90s velocity returns, his journey to Minnesota could be a short one.

72. Tyler Flowers, C, White Sox
While Flowers offers plenty to like offensively as a massive catcher with power and patience, it was the strides he made defensively in 2009 that made him the clear White Sox catcher of the future once A. J. Pierzynski's contract is up after this season.

73. Zach Britton, RHP, Orioles
Possessing one of the best sinkers in the minors, along with well-above-average velocity and movement, Britton can miss bats with both his fastball and his slider, but it was the nearly 5-to-1 ground-ball ratio in the second half that had some brave scouts making Brandon Webb comparisons.

74. Jaff Decker, OF, Padres
Decker reminds many scouts of John Kruk. He could easily hit .300 with decent power and 100 walks a year, but at 19, he already has Kruk's body, leaving many to wonder if he'll be able to play any position other than designated hitter by the time he's in his mid-20s.

75. Tony Sanchez, C, Pirates
No matter what the Pirates say, Sanchez was a severe overdraft as the fourth overall pick of the 2009 draft, but he was also better than the late first-rounder many projected him to be. Sanchez is a well-above-average defender who could hit .260-.275 with 15 home runs a year. That's not an impact player, but it is an occasional All-Star.

76. Ryan Kalish, OF, Red Sox
What a difference a year makes. With a healthy wrist, Kalish finally began to tap into his power, which combines with speed a tick above average to make him a potentially dynamic outfielder. As with Reddick, there's no real room for him in Boston.

77. Alex White, RHP, Indians
While the Indians talked about grooming White as a closer after they drafted him, they've come to their senses, realizing they can get 200 innings a year out of him. They'll focus on improving his secondary pitches, as his fastball/splitter combination is already dominating.

78. Phillippe Aumont, RHP, Phillies
Aumont's conversion to the bullpen was a success, as the 20-year-old handled Double-A with aplomb. His intensity on the mound worked against him as a starter, but it's an asset in shorter stints, and he's a stronger pitcher now that he can junk his weaker offerings and pitch solely off his bowling-ball sinker and improving slider.

79. Mike Moustakas, 3B, Royals
Having spent the last two years in brutal hitting environments, Moustakas has yet to really blow up a stat sheet, but scouts still see one of the minor leagues' fastest bats, and his power and arm give him two elite tools.

80. Fernando Martinez, OF, Mets

In four full seasons, Martinez has played just 303 games, and just when it seemed as if he was growing into his tools with a fine start at Triple-A Buffalo, the Mets jerked him up to the big leagues; he lasted about a month before requiring knee surgery. The Jason Bay signing makes him the odd man out with the Mets, but at just 21, he has plenty of time.

81. Hank Conger, C, Angels

Conger has solid power and the hand-eye coordination to flirt with .300 in the big leagues, but the most important aspect of his 2009 performance was his improvement on defense. It was once taken for granted that Conger would have to move out from behind the plate, but he has improved to the point that he can legitimately be called that rare thing, an offense-oriented backstop.

82. Jason Knapp, RHP, Indians

Acquired from the Phillies in the Cliff Lee deal, Knapp was the talk of the Sally League in the first half of the season, getting consistent mid- to upper-90s velocity out of his massive 6-foot-5 frame. Scouts were concerned about his messy delivery, correctly as it turned out, given that he required season-ending arthroscopic shoulder surgery. The Indians will try to clean that up for 2010.

83. Wil Myers, C, Royals

Given a $2 million bonus as a third-round pick, all Myers did was reach base 41 times and rack up 57 total bases in his 22-game pro debut. Nobody questions his bat, but he has a long way to go before people believe in his ability to stay behind the plate.

84. Wilmer Flores, SS, Mets

Sure, Flores didn't do much in his full-season debut, but he was also still younger than most 2009 high-school draftees. Scouts see considerable potential in his bat; the bigger concern is a rapidly thickening body that will have him moving from shortstop sooner than later.

85. Brandon Allen, 1B, Diamondbacks

With power and patience, Allen looked like the Arizona first baseman of the future after the Diamondbacks acquired him from the White Sox for reliever Tony Pena, but his struggles to make contact during a big-league audition mean there are no guarantees for 2010.

86. Grant Green, SS, Athletics

Seen as a top three pick before the 2009 college season began, Green struggled in his junior year and fell to 13th overall. He's going to hit and steal bases, and he should end up with double-digit power down the road, but arm issues might end up making him a second baseman as opposed to a shortstop.

87. Ike Davis, 1B, Mets

Unfairly written off after his powerless pro debut, Davis made a lot of people look stupid by reaching Double-A last year and slugging 13 home runs in 55 games there. He still struggles against lefties, but his ability to hit 25-30 home runs a year gives the Mets a Carlos Delgado replacement that wasn't there before.

88. Zach Wheeler, RHP, Giants

Every year, one or more big talents come out of Georgia's famous East Cobb program, and in 2009, that talent was Wheeler. He's a 6-foot-4 pure athlete who already touches 95 mph with command and tons of movement, so it will be the development of his secondary pitches that dictates his future.

89. Jordan Walden, RHP, Angels

Walden simply wasn't himself in 2009, struggling through a strained forearm before being shut down in July. When healthy, he's a 6-foot-5 beast with a fastball that gets up to 98 mph, and the Angels are hoping for a return to form in 2010.

90. Jose Tabata, OF, Pirates

It's quite easy to project Tabata as a .300 hitter in the big leagues, but the question remains as to whether it will be enough, as he offers little on a secondary level. The existence of Andrew McCutchen and average-at-best speed limits him to a corner in the big leagues, which places further pressure on his bat.

91. Nick Hagadone, LHP, Indians

Traded from Boston as part of the Victor Martinez deal, Hagadone made an impressive return from Tommy John surgery in 2009, but he hasn't really been tested yet as far as workload goes. Few lefties in the game can match his velocity, and if starting doesn't work out, Cleveland envisions him as a bigger version of Billy Wagner.

92. Trevor Reckling, LHP, Angels

Reckling reached Double-A in 2009 as a teenager. While his fastball features merely average velocity, both his breaking ball and downright outstanding changeup generate plenty of swings and misses. Command issues are the only bugaboo in his game.

93. Tim Melville, RHP, Royals

Given a seven-figure deal in the fourth round last year, Melville is part of a cadre of young arms in the Royals' system, and while he's not spectacular, everything about his scouting profile is at least good, with a power frame, 94-mph heat, and a quality breaking ball.

94. Gabriel Noriega, SS, Mariners

Like so many young Venezuelan shortstops, Noriega is a defensive whiz, but it was his showing with the bat in the Appy League that really got scouts excited. His big, athletic frame and surprising power make him one of the better sleepers in the game.

95. Fabio Martinez, RHP, Angels

The best pitcher in the Arizona League last summer, Martinez used a mid-90s fastball (up to 98 mph) and an impressive slider to strike out 92 batters in just 60.2 innings. He's a raw product who is much more of a thrower than a pitcher at this point, but his ceiling is sky high.

96. Brett Jackson, OF, Cubs

Jackson's tools were worthy of a top-15 pick last June, but concerns over the amount of swing-and-miss in his game dropped him to the end of the first round. He showed power, speed, defense, and arm strength in his pro debut, and many teams now question why they didn't take him when they had the chance.

97. Jio Mier, SS, Astros

Nearly every kid drafted out of high school is a shortstop, as that's where the best athletes play, but Mier is going to stay there; he has a chance to be a spectacular defender. Add to that the speed, plate discipline, and almost shocking power he showed in his pro debut, and he could rank much higher on next year's list.

98. Ethan Martin, RHP, Dodgers

After a blistering start, Martin ran out of gas during the second half of his full-season debut, resulting in a velocity dip and flattened breaking ball. When he's on, his stuff ranks with that of any other pitcher in the Dodgers' system, but after 2009, some folks are wondering if he'd be better off in the bullpen.

99. Brett Lawrie, 2B, Brewers

The Canadian product showed plenty of promise in his full-season debut, profiling as a true power threat, but the ground ball to the face that broke his nose has many scouts convinced that the Brewers should just stop asking him to play a skill position.

100. Jason Castro, C, Astros

Castro hits for a decent average, draws some walks, has gap-to-average power, and plays solid defense, and while none of it is good enough to turn him into a big-league star, he should be a solid, dependable everyday catcher, and there aren't 30 of those in the big leagues.

101. Danny Espinosa, SS, Nationals

Espinosa has rare secondary skills for a shortstop, as demonstrated by his 18 home runs, 29 stolen bases, and 74 walks in 2009. That should more than make up for a low batting average. Defensively, it's the same story, as he rarely makes the spectacular play, but converts every ball he gets to into an out.

Team Name Codes

Code	Team	League	Affiliation	Name
Code	Team	League	Affiliation	Name
ABE	Aberdeen	NYP	Orioles	IronBirds
ABQ	Albuquerque	PCL	Marlins, Dodgers	Isotopes
AGU	Aguascalient	MEX	—	Rieleros
AKR	Akron	EAS	Indians	Aeros
ALT	Altoona	EAS	Pirates	Curve
ANG	AZL Angels	AZL	Angels	—
ARI	Arizona	NL	D'backs	D'backs
ARK	Arkansas	TXS	Angels	Travelers
ASH	Asheville	SAL	Rockies	Tourists
AST	GCL Astros	GCL	Astros	—
ATH	AZL Athletics	AZL	Athletics	—
ATL	Atlanta	NL	Braves	Braves
AUB	Auburn	NYP	BlueJays	Doubledays
AUG	Augusta	SAL	Giants	GreenJackets
BAK	Bakersfield	CLF	Rangers	Blaze
BAL	Baltimore	AL	Orioles	Orioles
BAT	Batavia	NYP	Cardinals	Muckdogs
BGR	BowlingGreen	SAL	Rays	Hot Rods
BIL	Billings	PIO	Reds	Mustangs
BIN	Binghamton	EAS	Mets	Mets
BIR	Birmingham	SOU	WhiteSox	Barons
BLJ	GCL BlueJays	GCL	BlueJays	—
BLT	Beloit	MDW	Twins	Snappers
BLU	Bluefield	APL	Orioles	Orioles
BNC	Burlington NC	APL	Royals	Royals
BOI	Boise	NWN	Cubs	Hawks
BOS	Boston	AL	RedSox	RedSox
BOW	Bowie	EAS	Orioles	BaySox
BRA	GCL Braves	GCL	Braves	—
BRI	Bristol VA	APL	WhiteSox	WhiteSox
BRO	Brooklyn	NYP	Mets	Cyclones
BRR	AZL Brewers	AZL	Brewers	—
BRV	BrevardCnty	FSL	Brewers	Manatees
BUF	Buffalo	INT	Indians, Mets	Bisons
BUR	Burlington IA	MDW	Royals	Bees
CAR	Carolina	SOU	Marlins, Reds	Mudcats
CAS	Casper	PIO	Rockies	Rockies
CAv	CiegoD'Avila	CBA	—	Tigres
CCH	CorpusChristi	TXS	Astros	Hooks
CDR	CedarRapids	MDW	Angels	Kernels
CGA	Columbus GA	SAL	Rays	Catfish
CHA	ChiWhiteSox	AL	WhiteSox	WhiteSox
CHB	ChibaLotte	JPL	—	Marines
CHH	Chihuahua	MEX	—	Dorados
CHN	ChiCubs	NL	Cubs	Cubs
CHR	Charlotte	INT	WhiteSox	Knights
CHT	Chattanooga	SOU	Dodgers, Reds	Lookouts
CHU	Chunichi	JCL	—	Dragons
CIN	Cincinnati	NL	Reds	Reds
CLE	Cleveland	AL	Indians	Indians
CLN	Clinton	MDW	Mariners, Rangers	LumberKings
CLR	Clearwater	FSL	Phillies	Threshers
CMP	Campeche	MEX	—	Piratas
COH	Columbus OH	INT	Nats, Indians	Clippers
COL	Colorado	NL	Rockies	Rockies
CRD	GCL Cards	GCL	Cardinals	—
CSC	Charleston SC	SAL	Yankees	RiverDogs
CSP	ColoSprings	PCL	Rockies	SkySox
CUB	AZL Cubs	AZL	Cubs	—
Cfg	Cienfuegos	CBA	—	Camaroneros
Cmg	Camaguey	CBA	—	Ganaderos
DAY	Daytona	FSL	Cubs	Cubs
DEL	Delmarva	SAL	Orioles	Shorebirds
DET	Detroit	AL	Tigers	Tigers
DGR	GCL Dodgers	GCL	Dodgers	—
DNV	Danville	APL	Braves	Braves
DUN	Dunedin	FSL	BlueJays	BlueJays
DUR	Durham	INT	Rays	Bulls
DYT	Dayton	MDW	Reds	Dragons
ELZ	Elizabethton	APL	Twins	Twins
ERI	Erie	EAS	Tigers	SeaWolves
EUG	Eugene	NWN	Padres	Emeralds
EVE	Everett	NWN	Mariners	AquaSox
FKU	Fukuoka	JPL	—	Hawks
FLO	Florida	NL	Marlins	Marlins
FRD	Frederick	CRL	Orioles	Keys
FRE	Fresno	PCL	Giants	Grizzlies
FRI	Frisco	TXS	Rangers	RoughRiders
FTM	FtMyers	FSL	Twins	Miracle
FTW	FtWayne	MDW	Padres	TinCaps
FTW	FtWayne	MDW	Padres	Wizards
GIA	AZL Giants	AZL	Giants	—
GRB	Greensboro	SAL	Marlins	Grasshoppers
GRF	GreatFalls	PIO	WhiteSox	WhiteSox
GRL	GreatLakes	MDW	Dodgers	Loons
GRN	Greenville	SAL	RedSox	Drive
GRV	Greeneville	APL	Astros	Astros
GWN	Gwinnett	INT	Braves	Braves
Gra	Granma	CBA	—	Alazanes
Gtm	Guantanamo	CBA	—	Indios
HAG	Hagerstown	SAL	Nationals	Suns
HAR	Harrisburg	EAS	Nationals	Senators
HDS	HighDesert	CLF	Mariners	Mavericks
HEL	Helena	PIO	Brewers	Brewers
HIC	Hickory	SAL	Pirates, Rangers	Crawdads
HNS	Hanshin	JCL	—	Tigers
HOU	Houston	NL	Astros	Astros
HRO	Hiroshima	JCL	—	Carp
HUD	HudsonValley	NYP	Rays	Renegades

630

Code	Team	League	Affiliation	Name	Code	Team	League	Affiliation	Name
HUN	Huntsville	SOU	Brewers	Stars	NHP	NewHampshire	EAS	BlueJays	FisherCats
Hab	LaHabana	CBA	—	Vaqueros	NIP	NipponHam	JPL	—	Fighters
Hol	Holguin	CBA	—	Sabuesos	NOR	Norfolk	INT	Orioles	Tides
IDA	IdahoFalls	PIO	Royals	Chukars	NRW	Connecticut	EAS	Giants	Defenders
IDN	GCL Indians	GCL	Indians	—	NVL	NuevoLaredo	MEX	—	Tecolotes
IJv	IslaJuventud	CBA	—	Toronjeros	NWA	NWArkansas	TXS	Royals	Naturals
IND	Indianapolis	INT	Pirates	Indians	NWO	NewOrleans	PCL	Mets, Marlins	Zephyrs
IOW	Iowa	PCL	Cubs	Cubs	NYA	NYYankees	AL	Yankees	Yankees
Ind	Industriales	CBA	—	LeonesAzules	NYN	NYMets	NL	Mets	Mets
JAM	Jamestown	NYP	Marlins	Jammers	OAK	Oakland	AL	A's	A's
JAX	Jacksonville	SOU	Dodgers, Marlins	Suns	OAX	Oaxaca	MEX	—	Guerreros
JCY	JohnsonCity	APL	Cardinals	Cardinals	OGD	Ogden	PIO	Dodgers	Raptors
JUP	Jupiter	FSL	Marlins	Hammerheads	OKL	Oklahoma	PCL	Rangers	Redhawks
KAN	Kannapolis	SAL	WhiteSox	Intimidators	OMA	Omaha	PCL	Royals	Royals
KCA	KansasCity	AL	Royals	Royals	ONE	Oneonta	NYP	Tigers	Tigers
KIN	Kinston	CRL	Indians	Indians	ORI	GCL Orioles	GCL	Orioles	—
KNC	KaneCounty	MDW	A's	Cougars	ORM	Orem	PIO	Angels	Owlz
KNG	Kingsport	APL	Mets	Mets	ORX	Orix	JPL	—	Buffaloes
LAA	LAAngels	AL	Angels	Angels	OTT	Ottawa	INT	Phillies	Lynx
LAK	Lakeland	FSL	Tigers	Flying Tigers	PAW	Pawtucket	INT	RedSox	RedSox
LAN	LADodgers	NL	Dodgers	Dodgers	PCH	Charlotte	FSL	Rays	StoneCrabs
LEH	LehighValley	INT	Phillies	IronPigs	PDR	AZL Padres	AZL	Padres	—
LEL	LakeElsinore	CLF	Padres	Storm	PEO	Peoria	MDW	Cubs	Chiefs
LEX	Lexington	SAL	Astros	Legends	PHI	Philadelphia	NL	Phillies	Phillies
LKC	LakeCounty	SAL	Indians	Captains	PHL	GCL Phillies	GCL	Phillies	—
LNC	Lancaster	CLF	Astros	JetHawks	PIR	GCL Pirates	GCL	Pirates	—
LNC	Lancaster	CLF	RedSox	JetHawks	PIT	Pittsburgh	NL	Pirates	Pirates
LNS	Lansing	MDW	BlueJays	Lugnuts	PMB	PalmBeach	FSL	Cardinals	Cardinals
LOU	Louisville	INT	Reds	Bats	PME	Portland ME	EAS	RedSox	SeaDogs
LOW	Lowell	NYP	RedSox	Spinners	POR	Portland OR	PCL	Padres	Beavers
LTu	LasTunas	CBA	—	Lenadores	POT	Potomac	CRL	Nationals	Nationals
LVG	LasVegas	PCL	Dodgers, BlueJays	51s	PRI	Princeton	APL	Rays	Rays
LWD	Lakewood	SAL	Phillies	BlueClaws	PUE	Puebla	MEX	—	Pericos
LYN	Lynchburg	CRL	Pirates	Hillcats	PUL	Pulaski	APL	BlueJays	BlueJays
MCD	MexicoCityD	MEX	—	Diablos Rojo	PZA	Minatitlan	MEX	—	Petroleros
MCL	Monclova	MEX	—	Acereros	PdR	PinarDelRio	CBA	—	Vegueros
MCT	MexicoCityT	MEX	—	Tigres	QUD	QuadCities	MDW	Cardinals	RiverBandits
MEM	Memphis	PCL	Cardinals	Redbirds	QUR	QuintanaRoo	MEX	—	Tigres
MHV	MahoningValley	NYP	Indians	Scrappers	RAK	Rakuten	JPL	—	GoldenEagles
MID	Midland	TXS	A's	Rockhounds	RAY	GCL Rays	GCL	Rays	—
MIL	Milwaukee	NL	Brewers	Brewers	RCU	RCucamonga	CLF	Angels	Quakes
MIN	Minnesota	AL	Twins	Twins	RDS	GCL Reds	GCL	Reds	—
MIS	Mississippi	SOU	Braves	Braves	REA	Reading	EAS	Phillies	Phillies
MNT	Montgomery	SOU	Rays	Biscuits	REY	Reynosa	MEX	—	Broncos
MOB	Mobile	SOU	D'backs	BayBears	RIC	Richmond	INT	Braves	Braves
MOD	Modesto	CLF	Rockies	Nuts	RNG	AZL Rangers	AZL	Rangers	—
MRL	GCL Marlins	GCL	Marlins	—	RNO	Reno	PCL	D'backs	Aces
MRN	AZL Mariners	AZL	Mariners	—	ROC	Rochester	INT	Twins	RedWings
MSO	Missoula	PIO	D'backs	Osprey	ROM	Rome	SAL	Braves	Braves
MTR	Monterrey	MEX	—	Sultanes	ROU	RoundRock	PCL	Astros	Express
MTS	GCL Mets	GCL	Mets	—	ROY	AZL Royals	AZL	Royals	—
MYR	MyrtleBeach	CRL	Braves	Pelicans	RSX	GCL RedSox	GCL	RedSox	—
Met	Metropolitanos	CBA	—	Guerreros	SAC	Sacramento	PCL	A's	RiverCats
Mtz	Matanzas	CBA	—	Cocodrilos	SAN	SanAntonio	TXS	Padres	Missions
NAS	Nashville	PCL	Brewers	Sounds	SAR	Sarasota	FSL	Reds	Reds
NAT	GCL Nationals	GCL	Nationals	—	SAV	Savannah	SAL	Mets	SandGnats
NBR	NewBritain	EAS	Twins	RockCats	SBN	SouthBend	MDW	D'backs	SilverHawks

Code	Team	League	Affiliation	Name	Code	Team	League	Affiliation	Name
SBR	InlandEmpire	CLF	Dodgers	66ers	TRI	TriCity	NWN	Rockies	DustDevils
SCO	StateCollege	NYP	Pirates	Spikes	TRN	Trenton	EAS	Yankees	Thunder
SCu	SantiagoCuba	CBA	—	Avispas	TUC	Tucson	PCL	D'backs	Sidewinders
SDN	SanDiego	NL	Padres	Padres	TUL	Tulsa	TXS	Rockies	Drillers
SEA	Seattle	AL	Mariners	Mariners	TWI	GCL Twins	GCL	Twins	—
SEI	Seibu	JPL	—	Lions	VAN	Vancouver	NWN	A's	Canadians
SFD	Springfield	TXS	Cardinals	Cardinals	VAQ	VaqLaguna	MEX	—	Vaqueros
SFN	SanFrancisco	NL	Giants	Giants	VCl	VillaClara	CBA	—	Naranjas
SJO	SanJose	CLF	Giants	Giants	VER	Vermont	NYP	Nationals	LakeMonsters
SLC	SaltLake	PCL	Angels	Bees	VIS	Visalia	CLF	D'backs	Oaks/Rawhide
SLM	Salem VA	CRL	Astros	Avalanche	VRC	Veracruz	MEX	—	Rojos
SLM	Salem VA	CRL	RedSox	RedSox	VRO	VeroBeach	FSL	Rays	Rays
SLN	StLouis	NL	Cardinals	Cardinals	WAS	Washington	NL	Nationals	Nationals
SLO	SalemKeizer	NWN	Giants	Volcanoes	WIC	Wichita	TXS	Royals	Wranglers
SLT	Saltillo	MEX	—	Seraperos	WIL	Wilmington	CRL	Royals	BlueRocks
SLU	StLucie	FSL	Mets	Mets	WIS	Wisconsin	MDW	Brewers, Mariners	TimberRattlers
SPO	Spokane	NWN	Rangers	Indians	WMI	WMichigan	MDW	Tigers	Whitecaps
SSp	SanctiSpiritus	CBA	—	Gallos	WNS	WinstonSalem	CRL	WhiteSox	Dash
STA	StatenIsland	NYP	Yankees	Yankees	WPT	Williamsport	NYP	Phillies	Crosscutters
STO	Stockton	CLF	A's	Ports	WTN	WTennessee	SOU	Mariners	DiamondJaxx
SWB	Scranton/WB	INT	Yankees	Yankees	WVA	WVirginia	SAL	Brewers, Pirates	Power
SYR	Syracuse	INT	BlueJays, Nats	SkyChiefs	YAK	Yakima	NWN	D'backs	Bears
TAB	Tabasco	MEX	—	Olmecas	YAN	GCL Yankees	GCL	Yankees	—
TAC	Tacoma	PCL	Mariners	Rainiers	YKL	TokyoYakult	JCL	—	Swallows
TAM	Tampa	FSL	Yankees	Yankees	YKO	Yokohama	JCL	—	BayStars
TBA	TampaBay	AL	Rays	Rays	YOM	Yomiuri	JCL	—	Giants
TCV	TriCity	NYP	Astros	ValleyCats	YUC	Yucatan	MEX	—	Leones
TEN	Tennessee	SOU	Cubs	Smokies	gcr	GrandCanyon	AFL	—	Rafters
TEX	Texas	AL	Rangers	Rangers	jav	PeoriaJ	AFL	—	Javalinas
TGR	GCL Tigers	GCL	Tigers	—	msa	Mesa	AFL	—	Solarsox
TIJ	Tijuana	MEX	—	Potros	phx	Phoenix	AFL	—	DesertDogs
TOL	Toledo	INT	Tigers	MudHens	sag	PeoriaS	AFL	—	Saguaros
TOR	Toronto	AL	BlueJays	BlueJays	sco	Surprise	AFL	—	Scorpions

PECOTA Leaderboards

Compiled by Marc Normandin

HITTERS

Batting Average

RANK	NAME	TEAM	BA
1.	Ichiro Suzuki	SEA	.322
2.	Hanley Ramirez	FLO	.321
3.	Joe Mauer	MIN	.318
4.	Albert Pujols	SLN	.317
5.	Pablo Sandoval	SFN	.314
6.	Dustin Pedroia	BOS	.311
T7.	Nick Markakis	BAL	.303
T7.	David Wright	NYN	.303
T9.	Miguel Cabrera	DET	.302
T9.	Martin Prado	ATL	.302
T11.	Carl Crawford	TBA	.300
T11.	Skip Schumacher	SLN	.300
T13.	Carlos Lee	HOU	.299
T13.	Howie Kendrick	LAA	.299
15.	Ryan Braun	MIL	.298
T16.	Jacoby Ellsbury	BOS	.297
T16.	Yunel Escobar	ATL	.297
T16.	Michael Young	TEX	.297
T16.	Alberto Callaspo	KCA	.297
20.	James Loney	LAN	.296

Home Runs

RANK	NAME	TEAM	HR
1.	Prince Fielder	MIL	51
2.	Miguel Cabrera	DET	40
3.	Ryan Braun	MIL	39
4.	Ryan Howard	PHI	37
T5.	Mark Teixeira	NYA	35
T5.	Evan Longoria	TBA	35
T5.	Adam Dunn	WAS	35
8.	Albert Pujols	SLN	34
9.	Chris Davis	TEX	33
T10.	Adrian Gonzalez	SDN	32
T10.	Carlos Pena	TBA	32
12.	Alex Rodriguez	NYA	31
13.	Justin Morneau	MIN	30
T14.	Joey Votto	CIN	29
T14.	Dan Uggla	FLO	29
T16.	Ryan Zimmerman	WAS	28
T16.	Nelson Cruz	TEX	28
T16.	Jayson Werth	PHI	28
T16.	Curtis Granderson	NYA	28
T16.	Jason Bay	NYN	28
T16.	Mark Reynolds	ARZ	28
T16.	Nick Swisher	NYA	28
T16.	Jack Cust	OAK	28

Runs Batted In

RANK	NAME	TEAM	RBI
1.	Prince Fielder	MIL	140
2.	Miguel Cabrera	DET	125
3.	Ryan Howard	PHI	121
4.	Ryan Braun	MIL	119
T5.	Mark Teixeira	NYA	115
T5.	Justin Morneau	MIN	115
7.	Evan Longoria	TBA	112
T8.	Albert Pujols	SLN	108
T8.	Nick Markakis	BAL	108
10.	David Wright	NYN	105
11.	Adrian Gonzalez	SDN	104
12.	Brian McCann	ATL	103
T13.	Adam Lind	TOR	102
T13.	James Loney	LAN	102
15.	Carlos Lee	HOU	100
T16.	Matt Holliday	SLN	98
T16.	Jeff Francoeur	NYN	98
T18.	Adam Dunn	WAS	97
T18.	Chris Davis	TEX	97
T20.	Troy Tulowitzki	COL	96
T20.	Chase Utley	PHI	96

Runs

RANK	NAME	TEAM	RUNS
T1.	Ryan Braun	MIL	110
T1.	Dustin Pedroia	BOS	110
T3.	Prince Fielder	MIL	109
T3.	Hanley Ramirez	FLO	109
5.	Jacob Ellsbury	BOS	107
6.	Ian Kinsler	TEX	106
7.	Curtis Granderson	NYA	104
8.	Nick Markakis	BAL	103
9.	Jimmy Rollins	PHI	102
T10.	Chase Utley	PHI	100
T10.	Brian Roberts	BAL	100
12.	Albert Pujols	SLN	98
13.	Grady Sizemore	CLE	97
T14.	Mark Teixeira	NYA	96
T14.	David Wright	NYN	96

T14.	Adrian Gonzalez	SDN	96
T17.	Evan Longoria	TBA	95
T17.	Shane Victorino	PHI	95
T17.	Chone Figgins	SEA	95
20.	Miguel Cabrera	DET	94

Stolen Bases, Major Leaguers

RANK	NAME	TEAM	SB
1.	Jacoby Ellsbury	BOS	55
T2.	Carl Crawford	TBA	44
T2.	Michael Bourn	HOU	44
4.	Jose Reyes	NYN	43
5.	B. J. Upton	TBA	37
T6.	Brian Roberts	BAL	36
T6.	Chone Figgins	SEA	36
8.	Jimmy Rollins	PHI	34
T9.	Hanley Ramirez	FLO	30
T9.	Elvis Andrus	TEX	30
T11.	Matt Kemp	LAN	27
T11.	Carlos Gomez	MIN	27
T11.	Nyjer Morgan	WAS	27
T14.	Ian Kinsler	TEX	26
T14.	Shane Victorino	PHI	26

Stolen Bases, Minor Leaguers

RANK	NAME	TEAM	SB
1.	Anthony Gose	PHI	29
T2.	Michael Brantley	CLE	26
T2.	Derrick Robinson	KCA	26
4.	Tyler Pastornicky	TOR	23
T5.	Devaris Strange-Gordon	LAN	19
T5.	Quintin Berry	PHI	19
T7.	Wilkin Ramirez	DET	18
T7.	Darin Mastroianni	TOR	18
9.	Che-Hsuan Lin	BOS	17
10.	Tyson Gillies	PHI	16

On-Base Percentage

RANK	NAME	TEAM	OBP
1.	Albert Pujols	SLN	.427
2.	Nick Johnson	NYA	.421
3.	Joe Mauer	MIN	.412
4.	Hanley Ramirez	FLO	.409
T5.	Prince Fielder	MIL	.402
T5.	Todd Helton	COL	.402
7.	David Wright	NYN	.397
T8.	Milton Bradley	SEA	.395
T8.	Mark Teixeira	NYA	.395
10.	Chase Utley	PHI	.394

Isolated Power

RANK	NAME	TEAM	ISO
1.	Prince Fielder	MIL	.311
2.	Carlos Pena	TBA	.272
3.	Ryan Braun	MIL	.264
4.	Alex Rodriguez	NYA	.250

5.	Miguel Cabrera	DET	.249
T6.	Mark Teixeira	NYA	.247
T6.	Adam Dunn	WAS	.247
T6.	Albert Pujols	SLN	.247
9.	Jay Bruce	CIN	.246
10.	Ryan Howard	PHI	.245

Equivalent Average

RANK	NAME	TEAM	EqA
1.	Albert Pujols	SLN	.340
2.	Prince Fielder	MIL	.333
3.	Adrian Gonzalez	SDN	.322
4.	Hanley Ramirez	FLO	.315
5.	David Wright	NYN	.314
6.	Ryan Braun	MIL	.313
7.	Mark Teixeira	NYA	.309
8.	Miguel Cabrera	DET	.307
T9.	Chase Utley	PHI	.306
T9.	Joe Mauer	MIN	.306

Wins Above Replacement Player, American League

RANK	NAME	TEAM	WARP
1.	Joe Mauer	MIN	5.9
2.	Grady Sizemore	CLE	5.4
3.	Mark Teixeira	NYA	5.0
4.	Dustin Pedroia	BOS	4.9
T5.	Miguel Cabrera	DET	4.8
T5.	Evan Longoria	TBA	4.8
T7.	Alex Rodriguez	NYA	4.4
T7.	Curtis Granderson	NYA	4.4
9.	Ben Zobrist	TBA	4.3
10.	Nick Markakis	BAL	4.2

Wins Above Replacement Player, National League

RANK	NAME	TEAM	WARP
1.	Albert Pujols	SLN	8.6
2.	Prince Fielder	MIL	7.1
T3.	Adrian Gonzalez	SDN	6.7
T3.	Hanley Ramirez	FLO	6.7
5.	Ryan Braun	MIL	6.3
6.	Chase Utley	PHI	6.2
7.	David Wright	NYN	6.1
T8.	Matt Kemp	LAN	5.2
T8.	Troy Tulowitzki	COL	5.2
10.	Brian McCann	ATL	5.1

Value Over Replacement Player, All Hitters

RANK	NAME	TEAM	VORP
1.	Prince Fielder	MIL	71.7
2.	Albert Pujols	SLN	69.1
3.	Hanley Ramirez	FLO	64.0
4.	Adrian Gonzalez	SDN	59.5
5.	Ryan Braun	MIL	58.9
6.	David Wright	NYN	57.9
7.	Chase Utley	PHI	53.6
8.	Joe Mauer	MIN	51.9

| 9. | Brian McCann | ATL | 49.2 |
| 10. | Grady Sizemore | CLE | 47.0 |

Value Over Replacement Player, Catcher

RANK	NAME	TEAM	VORP
1.	Joe Mauer	MIN	51.9
2.	Brian McCann	ATL	49.2
3.	Russell Martin	LAN	34.3
4.	Victor Martinez	BOS	30.5
5.	Carlos Santana	CLE	28.1
6.	Yadier Molina	SLN	27.8
7.	Matt Wieters	BAL	26.1
8.	Kurt Suzuki	OAK	22.5
9.	A. J. Pierzynski	CHA	13.6
10.	Ronny Paulino	FLA	13.0

Value Over Replacement Player, First Base

RANK	NAME	TEAM	VORP
1.	Prince Fielder	MIL	71.7
2.	Albert Pujols	SLN	69.1
3.	Adrian Gonzalez	SDN	59.5
4.	Miguel Cabrera	DET	45.8
5.	Mark Teixeira	NYA	43.3
6.	Adam Dunn	WAS	39.1
7.	Joey Votto	CIN	33.8
8.	Lance Berkman	HOU	32.9
9.	Justin Morneau	MIN	29.8
10.	James Loney	LAN	28.7

Value Over Replacement Player, Second Base

RANK	NAME	TEAM	VORP
1.	Chase Utley	PHI	53.6
2.	Dustin Pedroia	BOS	39.9
3.	Ian Kinsler	TEX	33.9
4.	Dan Uggla	FLO	33.3
5.	Ben Zobrist	TBA	32.6
6.	Rickie Weeks	MIL	32.5
7.	Brandon Phillips	CIN	32.0
8.	Brian Roberts	BAL	30.6
9.	Aaron Hill	TOR	29.6
10.	Martin Prado	ATL	28.8

Value Over Replacement Player, Third Base

RANK	NAME	TEAM	VORP
1.	David Wright	NYN	57.9
2.	Evan Longoria	TBA	40.3
3.	Alex Rodriguez	NYA	39.4
T4.	Chipper Jones	ATL	39.1
T4.	Ryan Zimmerman	WAS	39.1
6.	Pablo Sandoval	SFN	38.0
7.	Aramis Ramirez	CHN	29.1
8.	Edwin Encarnacion	TOR	27.8
9.	Kevin Kouzmanoff	SDN	27.4
10.	Chone Figgins	SEA	24.3

Value Over Replacement Player, Shortstop

RANK	NAME	TEAM	VORP
1.	Hanley Ramirez	FLO	64.0
2.	Jose Reyes	NYN	42.2
3.	Yunel Escobar	ATL	40.8
4.	Troy Tulowitzki	COL	39.9
5.	Jimmy Rollins	PHI	37.9
6.	Asdrubal Cabrera	CLE	31.6
7.	J. J. Hardy	MIN	24.6
8.	Rafael Furcal	LAN	23.0
9.	Stephen Drew	ARI	20.8
10.	Alexei Ramirez	CHA	20.3

Value Over Replacement Player, Center Field

RANK	NAME	TEAM	VORP
1.	Grady Sizemore	CLE	47.0
2.	Matt Kemp	LAN	43.3
3.	Nate McLouth	ATL	36.1
4.	Curtis Granderson	NYA	35.2
5.	Carlos Beltran	NYN	35.1
6.	Shane Victorino	PHI	32.3
7.	B. J. Upton	TBA	30.2
8.	Jacoby Ellsbury	BOS	29.2
9.	Cody Ross	FLO	27.9
10.	Denard Span	MIN	26.3

Value Over Replacement Player, Left Field

RANK	NAME	TEAM	VORP
1.	Ryan Braun	MIL	58.9
2.	Matt Holliday	SLN	41.7
3.	Jason Bay	NYN	35.8
4.	Carlos Lee	HOU	31.8
5.	Chase Headley	SDN	31.7
6.	Adam Lind	TOR	27.9
7.	Carlos Quentin	CHA	26.7
8.	Carl Crawford	TBA	26.6
9.	Josh Willingham	WAS	25.9
10.	Chris Coghlan	FLO	20.4

Value Over Replacement Player, Right Field

RANK	NAME	TEAM	VORP
1.	Andre Ethier	LAN	45.5
2.	Jayson Werth	PHI	35.5
3.	Nick Markakis	BAL	35.4
4.	Hunter Pence	HOU	33.5
5.	Shin-Soo Choo	CLE	32.2
6.	Milton Bradley	SEA	27.6
7.	Ryan Ludwick	SLN	26.9
8.	Nick Swisher	NYA	26.2
9.	Jack Cust	OAK	26.0
10.	Jason Heyward	ATL	25.9

Value Over Replacement Player, Rookies

RANK	NAME	TEAM	VORP
1.	Jesus Montero	NYA	32.4
2.	Carlos Santana	CLE	28.1
3.	Jason Heyward	ATL	25.9
4.	Mike Stanton	FLO	24.6
5.	Tyler Flowers	CHA	23.4
6.	Derek Norris	WAS	21.8
7.	Logan Forsythe	SDN	19.8
8.	Desmond Jennings	TBA	19.2
9.	Pedro Alvarez	PIT	19.1
10.	Michael Taylor	OAK	18.1

Value Over Replacement Player, Top Risers

RANK	NAME	TEAM	2009 VORP	2010 PREDICTED	CHANGE
1.	Jose Reyes	NYN	9.5	42.2	32.7
2.	Grady Sizemore	CLE	18.0	47.0	29.0
3.	Brian Giles	SDN	-14.8	11.8	26.6
4.	Kelly Johnson	ARI	1.0	27.5	26.5
5.	Russell Martin	LAN	8.0	34.3	26.3
6.	Garrett Atkins	BAL	-8.4	17.1	25.5
7.	Dioner Navarro	TBA	-13.4	11.5	24.9
8.	J. J. Hardy	MIN	0.2	24.6	24.4
9.	B. J. Upton	TBA	6.2	30.2	24.0
10.	Rick Ankiel	SLN	-4.2	19.7	23.9
11.	Edwin Encarnacion	TOR	4.2	27.8	23.6
12.	Jody Gerut	MIL	-3.3	19.3	22.6
13.	Rickie Weeks	MIL	10.0	32.5	22.5
14.	Conor Jackson	ARI	-7.1	14.3	21.4
15.	Mike Aviles	KCA	-10.5	9.9	20.4
T16.	Aubrey Huff	DET	-13.4	6.8	20.2
T16.	Elijah Dukes	WAS	-0.8	19.4	20.2

Value Over Replacement Player, Greatest Declines

RANK	NAME	TEAM	2009 VORP	2010 PREDICTED	CHANGE
1.	Derek Jeter	NYA	71.2	20.0	-51.2
2.	Joe Mauer	MIN	89.1	51.9	-37.2
3.	Jason Bartlett	TBA	57.1	20.3	-36.8
4.	Michael Young	TEX	51.0	16.7	-34.3
5.	Derrek Lee	CHN	51.9	19.3	-32.6
6.	Albert Pujols	SLN	100.1	69.1	-31.0
7.	Adam Lind	TOR	57.2	27.9	-29.3
8.	Kevin Youkilis	BOS	52.3	23.7	-28.6
9.	Pablo Sandoval	SFN	65.4	38.0	-27.4
10.	Ben Zobrist	TBA	59.7	32.6	-27.1
T11.	Miguel Tejada	HOU	44.4	17.5	-26.9
T11.	Kendry Morales	LAA	39.1	12.2	-26.9
13.	Ichiro Suzuki	SEA	51.8	25.0	-26.8
14.	Raul Ibañez	PHI	38.9	13.6	-25.3
15.	Todd Helton	COL	41.8	18.3	-23.5
16.	Marco Scutaro	BOS	38.9	17.1	-21.8
T17.	Torii Hunter	LAA	40.3	18.6	-21.7
T17.	Hideki Matsui	NYA	32.6	10.9	-21.7
T17.	Juan Uribe	SFN	26.1	4.4	-21.7

20.	Robinson Cano	NYA	49.4	27.8	-21.6
T21.	Ryan Howard	PHI	48.4	27.0	-21.4
T21.	Casey McGehee	MIL	27.1	5.7	-21.4
T23.	Casey Blake	LAN	32.5	11.3	-21.2
T23.	Mark Reynolds	ARI	43.4	22.2	-21.2
25.	Troy Tulowitzki	COL	60.3	39.9	-20.4

PITCHERS

Wins

RANK	NAME	TEAM	W
1.	CC Sabathia	NYA	15
T2.	Dan Haren	ARI	14
T2.	Javier Vazquez	NYA	14
T2.	Roy Halladay	PHI	14
T2.	Tim Lincecum	SFN	14
T6.	Cole Hamels	PHI	13
T6.	Felix Hernandez	SEA	13
T6.	Adam Wainwright	SLN	13
T6.	James Shields	TBA	13
T10.	Jair Jurrjens	ATL	12
T10.	Josh Beckett	BOS	12
T10.	John Lackey	BOS	12
T10.	Justin Verlander	DET	12
T10.	Zack Greinke	KCA	12
T10.	Chad Billingsley	LAN	12
T10.	Scott Baker	MIN	12
T10.	Cliff Lee	SEA	12
T10.	Matt Cain	SFN	12
T19.	Jon Lester	BOS	11
T19.	Ubaldo Jimenez	COL	11

Strikeouts

RANK	NAME	TEAM	K
1.	Tim Lincecum	SFN	219
2.	Felix Hernandez	SEA	190
3.	CC Sabathia	NYA	183
4.	Dan Haren	ARI	181
5.	Javier Vazquez	NYA	180
T6.	Justin Verlander	DET	179
T6.	Zack Greinke	KCA	179
T8.	Chad Billingsley	LAN	175
T8.	A.J. Burnett	NYA	175
T10.	Cole Hamels	PHI	166
T10.	Josh Beckett	BOS	166
T12.	James Shields	TBA	163
T12.	Matt Cain	SFN	163
T14.	Roy Halladay	PHI	160
T14.	Scott Kazmir	LAN	160
16.	Ubaldo Jimenez	COL	159
17.	Yovani Gallardo	MIL	155
18.	Jon Lester	BOS	152
T19.	Matt Garza	TBA	150
T19.	Joba Chamberlain	NYA	150

Earned Run Average (min. 125 IP)

RANK	NAME	TEAM	ERA
1.	Tim Lincecum	SFN	3.23
2.	Dan Haren	ARI	3.40
3.	CC Sabathia	NYA	3.66
4.	Zack Greinke	KCA	3.71
5.	Roy Halladay	PHI	3.80
6.	Ricky Nolasco	FLO	3.82
T7.	Adam Wainwright	SLN	3.83
T7.	Josh Beckett	BOS	3.83
9.	Cole Hamels	PHI	3.84
T10.	Matt Cain	SFN	3.85
T10.	Javier Vazquez	NYA	3.85
12.	Jair Jurrjens	ATL	3.90
13.	Ted Lilly	CHN	3.91
T14.	Scott Baker	MIN	3.94
T14.	Clayton Kershaw	LAN	3.94
T16.	Johan Santana	NYN	3.96
T16.	Josh Johnson	FLO	3.96
T18.	Justin Verlander	DET	3.99
T18.	Clay Buchholz	BOS	3.99
T18.	Tommy Hanson	ATL	3.99

Walks plus Hits per Inning Pitched (min. 125 IP)

RANK	NAME	TEAM	WHIP
1.	Dan Haren	ARI	1.16
2.	CC Sabathia	NYA	1.19
3.	Tim Lincecum	SFN	1.20
4.	Javier Vazquez	NYA	1.22
5.	Roy Halladay	PHI	1.24
T6.	Ricky Nolasco	FLO	1.25
T6.	Cole Hamels	PHI	1.25
T6.	Scott Baker	MIN	1.25
T9.	Zack Greinke	KCA	1.26
T9.	Josh Beckett	BOS	1.26
T9.	Johan Santana	NYN	1.26
T9.	James Shields	TBA	1.26
T13.	Ted Lilly	CHN	1.28
T13.	John Lackey	BOS	1.28
T13.	Kevin Slowey	MIN	1.28
16.	Roy Oswalt	HOU	1.29
T17.	Adam Wainwright	SLN	1.30
T17.	Justin Verlander	DET	1.30
T17.	Jered Weaver	LAA	1.30
T17.	Gavin Floyd	CHA	1.30
T17.	Jake Peavy	CHA	1.30

Saves

RANK	NAME	TEAM	SV
1.	Joakim Soria	KCA	43
2.	Jose Valverde	HOU	37
3.	Bobby Jenks	CHA	34
4.	Francisco Rodriguez	NYN	33
5.	Jonathan Papelbon	BOS	32
6.	Brian Wilson	SFN	31
7.	Joe Nathan	MIN	30
8.	Francisco Cordero	CIN	26
9.	Huston Street	COL	24
10.	Mariano Rivera	NYA	22
11.	Trevor Hoffman	MIL	22
12.	Matt Capps	PIT	21
T13.	Brad Lidge	PHI	19
T13.	Brian Fuentes	LAA	19
15.	Jonathan Broxton	LAN	18
T16.	Kevin Gregg	CHN	17
T16.	George Sherrill	LAN	17
T16.	J. J. Putz	CHA	17
T19.	Jeremy Accardo	TOR	16
T19.	Kerry Wood	CLE	16

Win Expectancy over Replacement, Lineup-adjusted

RANK	NAME	TEAM	WXRL
1.	Joakim Soria	KCA	3.76
2.	Jonathan Papelbon	BOS	3.08
3.	Joe Nathan	MIN	3.06
4.	Mariano Rivera	NYA	2.96
5.	Carlos Marmol	CHN	2.73
6.	Phil Hughes	NYA	2.52
7.	Brad Ziegler	OAK	2.48
8.	Brian Wilson	SFN	2.47
9.	Heath Bell	SDN	2.46
10.	Francisco Rodriguez	NYN	2.37

Equivalent Strikeouts per Nine Innings

RANK	NAME	TEAM	SO/9
T1.	Jonathan Broxton	LAN	9.3
T1.	Octavio Dotel	CHA	9.3
3.	Jason Bulger	LAN	9.2
T4.	Jonathan Papelbon	BOS	9.0
T4.	Edwar Ramirez	NYA	9.0
T6.	Chris Perez	CLE	8.9
T6.	Tim Lincecum	SFN	8.9
T8.	Joe Nathan	MIN	8.6
T8.	Billy Wagner	ATL	8.6
T8.	Carlos Marmol	CHN	8.6
T8.	Grant Balfour	TBA	8.6
T8.	Rich Harden	TEX	8.6

Stuff Score

RANK	NAME	TEAM	STUFF
1.	Tim Lincecum	SFN	38
T2.	Rich Harden	TEX	30
T2.	Clayton Kershaw	LAN	30
T4.	Zack Greinke	KCA	27
T4.	Dan Haren	ARI	27
T4.	Brett Anderson	OAK	27
T7.	Tommy Hanson	ATL	25
T7.	Javier Vazquez	NYA	25
T7.	Neftali Feliz	TEX	25
T7.	CC Sabathia	NYA	25

Value Over Replacement Pitcher

RANK	NAME	TEAM	VORP
1.	Tim Lincecum	SFN	45.6
2.	Dan Haren	ARI	44.3
3.	CC Sabathia	NYA	41.8
4.	Zack Greinke	KCA	39.6
5.	Roy Halladay	PHI	35.2
6.	Javier Vazquez	NYA	35.0
7.	Cole Hamels	PHI	33.7
8.	Josh Beckett	BOS	33.2
9.	James Shields	TBA	32.3
10.	Felix Hernandez	SEA	32.1
11.	Matt Cain	SFN	31.6
12.	Justin Verlander	DET	31.2
13.	Adam Wainwright	SLN	31.0
T14.	John Lackey	BOS	29.8
T14.	Scott Baker	MIN	29.8
16.	Ubaldo Jimenez	COL	29.6
17.	Cliff Lee	SEA	27.6
18.	Ricky Nolasco	FLO	27.5
19.	Jered Weaver	LAA	27.1
20.	Ted Lilly	CHN	27.0

Value Over Replacement Pitcher, Rookies

RANK	NAME	TEAM	VORP
1.	Alex Wilson	BOS	22.3
2.	Casey Kelly	BOS	16.7
3.	Paul Smyth	OAK	14.1
4.	Wade Davis	TBA	13.3
5.	Matt Maloney	CIN	12.9
6.	Madison Bumgarner	SFN	12.0
7.	Daniel Hudson	CHA	11.4
8.	Kevin Mulvey	ARI	11.3
9.	Guillermo Moscoso	TEX	11.1
10.	Michael Bowden	BOS	11.0

Contributors

Will Carroll is called "the industry standard" by Peter Gammons, and that's good enough for us. He lives near Indianapolis.

Clifford J. Corcoran is a freelance writer, a regular contributor to SportsIllustrated.com, and the coauthor of Alex Belth's Bronx Banter blog, now part of the SNY.tv network. He was a coauthor of the Baseball Prospectus books *It Ain't Over* and *Mind Game* and is contributing to the annual for the third time. He was Plume's editor for the 2007 and 2008 editions of the annual and edited Howard Bryant's *Juicing the Game* and Brad Snyder's *A Well-Paid Slave,* among others. Formerly a music critic and lead singer, he is now the stay-at-home dad to both an infant daughter and an agility border spaniel in northern New Jersey.

Clay Davenport is a meteorologist for the National Oceanic and Atmospheric Administration (NOAA), for which he develops products to track rainfall from satellites so as to get an earlier jump on flash-flood warnings. He is one of the founding five of Baseball Prospectus and lives in Maryland with his wife, Susan.

Ken Funck manages various computer systems for the University of Wisconsin, while by night he pens his "Changing Speeds" column for BaseballProspectus .com and bemoans his unrequited love for the Chicago Cubs. This is his first year contributing to the annual. He lives outside Madison, Wisconsin (America's greatest small city), with his ever-supportive wife Stephanie, their children Max and Abby, and a wide array of snow-removal equipment.

Steven Goldman is a contributing editor to Baseball Prospectus. In addition to writing the historical analysis column "You Could Look It Up" for BaseballProspectus.com, he has edited the BP-authored books *Mind Game* and *It Ain't Over 'Til It's Over,* and contributed to *Baseball Between the Numbers.* Steven is also the author of the biography *Forging Genius: The Making of Casey Stengel.* He has contributed to the BP annual since 2005 and has been co-editor of the last five editions. He is the creator of the long-running "Pinstriped Bible" column for the YES Network and has appeared on several of the network's television programs. He was a baseball columnist for the *New York Sun* from 2004 to 2008, and his work has appeared in *Yankees Magazine,* the *Village Voice, Commentary, American Heritage,* and other publications. He blogs about politics and history at www.wholesomereading.com. Steven lives in New Jersey with his wife Stefanie, daughter Sarah, and son Clemens.

Kevin Goldstein is the Managing Partner of Prospectus Entertainment Ventures as well as Baseball Prospectus's national writer on scouting and player development. A recognized leader in his field, he is in constant contact with front-office executives, talent evaluators, and scouts from around the world. In his spare time, he plays obscure Japanese video games and wonders what the record is for most minutes used on a cell phone over a seven-day period, as he's quite sure he's in the top ten. He lives in DeKalb, Illinois (where much corn is grown), with the love of his life, Margaret, their two kids Cameron and Xander, cats Henry and Pickles, and Otto the Pit Bull, who is the official mascot of Baseball Prospectus, no matter what Christina Kahrl and her dog think.

Shawn Hoffman analyzes MLB's business and technology on BaseballProspectus.com. He has consulted for major-league teams on both the baseball and the business sides and served as an in-house sabermetrician for the University of Michigan's baseball program from 2004 to 2007. He also blogs about baseball, business, statistics, and whatever else crosses his mind at SquawkingBaseball.com. In real life, he runs a technology consulting start-up out of New York City and hasn't missed a Pittsburgh Steelers game in sixteen years.

Jay Jaffe is the founder of the nine-year-old Futility Infielder Web site (www.futilityinfielder.com), one of the oldest baseball blogs. In addition to covering the annual Hall of Fame ballot for BaseballProspectus.com, he writes the weekly "Prospectus Hit List" and "Prospectus Hit and Run" during the season. In recent years, he has contributed work to *It Ain't Over 'Til It's Over, Mind Game,* Will Carroll's *The Juice, Bombers Broadside,* and *Fantasy Baseball Index.* A graduate of

Brown University who works as a graphic designer in New York City, he's married to Andra, the most supportive gal in the world, and once came in third in the famous Milwaukee Brewers sausage race.

Christina Kahrl is one of the founding five of Baseball Prospectus, is a member of the Baseball Writers' Association of America, and is now the Executive Editor of BaseballProspectus.com. Beyond her regular writing on the site and on ESPN.com, she has written about baseball and football all over the place, including gigs with *Playboy* and Playboy.com, SportsIllustrated.com, and for *Pride;* she has also contributed to *Mind Game, It Ain't Over 'Til It's Over,* and the *ESPN Pro Football Encyclopedia.* Happily settled on Chicago's North Side in the city she's loved since she first arrived in 1985 to attend the University of Chicago, she's bemused that the White Sox (not the Cubs) helped spruce up the local diamonds. In her spare time, she volunteers and works in state and local civil rights organizations, and plays with the world's best dog, Argentina.

Tim Kniker is a principal in an operations engineering consulting firm (read "mathematically grounded 'efficiency experts'"). He was one of the top three finalists in the inaugural Baseball Prospectus Idol competition and continues to contribute articles to Baseball Prospectus.com. This is his first year contributing to the annual. A lifelong Royals fan, he currently resides in the heart of Red Sox nation with his wife, Kara, and their twin sons, Sammy and Freddy.

Marc Normandin writes the "Fantasy Beat" and "Player Profile" columns at BaseballProspectus.com and is in his fourth year of contributing to the annual. He writes about video games as the Gaming Editor at Blast-Magazine.com. He lives in Northampton, Massachusetts, which helps with his love of music and affinity for microbrews, but sadly is just a few miles closer to Petco Park and the Padres than his past residences.

John Perrotto is the Editor in Chief of BaseballProspectus.com. He has covered the major leagues since 1988, written for Baseball Prospectus since 2007, and lives in Beaver Falls, Pennsylvania, with his beautiful and patient wife Brenda.

Eric Seidman writes the "Checking the Numbers" column for BaseballProspectus.com, applying sabermetric methods to a variety of topics ranging from historical research to PITCHf/x evaluations. In addition to his weekly articles, Eric is the author of *Bridging the Statistical Gap,* an introductory book designed to introduce advanced statistical methods to sabermetric novices through conducted studies and careful explanations. He has been published in the quarterly SABR newsletter *By the Numbers* as well as *The Baseball Research Journal.* Eric lives in his mother's basement in Philadelphia as he completes his MBA and works as an accountant.

Matt Swartz is the author of the weekly column "Ahead in the Count" at BaseballProspectus.com. A government economist, Matt received his Ph.D. in economics from the University of Pennsylvania. In his dissertation, he applied economic theory to study dating and marriage as a metaphor for how learning and matching work together. Meanwhile, he married his wife Laura while working on said dissertation, evidence that he knew what he was talking about. Further cementing the case, Matt wrote a supplemental chapter to his dissertation discussing interviewing for jobs and was hired at his current job while writing that chapter. Matt's baseball analysis applies economic insight and statistical methods as well. He and Eric Seidman co-created SIERA, the luck-neutral ERA estimator you find in the pitcher statistics on each page of this book. Prior to writing at Baseball Prospectus, Matt wrote for the Phillies' blog "The Good Phight" and the sabermetric blog "Statistically Speaking."

Acknowledgments

Manny Acta
Sean Ahmed
R. J. Anderson
Andy Andres
Chris Antonetti
Andrew Baharlias
Kevin Baker
Peter Baker
Lois Bates
Tom Ballentine
Billy Beane
Heath Bell
Alex Belth
Peter Bendix
Tommy Bennett
Stephanie Bee
Tony Blengino
Joe Bohringer
Paul Bonanos
Kent Bonham
Scott Boras
Nancy Boyajy
Corey Brock
Craig Brown
Josh Boyd
Larry Burke
William Burke
Josh Byrnes
Craig Calcaterra
Jim Callis
Alex Carnevale
Brian Cartwright
Steve Canter
Russell A. Carleton
Jason Carr
Jay Catalano
James Click
David Cohen
Jared Cohen
Ben Cherington
Mike Chernoff
Jason Collette
John Coniff
John Coppolella
Jon Daniels

Rocco DeMarro
Mike DeMars
Neil deMause
John Dewan
Bobbie Dittmeier
Scott Drucker
Bob Dutton
Sagiv Edelman
Jeff Euston
Bryan Evans
Dan Evans
Ned Fabian
Gennaro Felice
Mike Ferrin
David Fischer
Oneri Fleita
Sean Forman
David Forst
Scott Free
Lee Froehlich
Brent Gambill
San Geaney
Chase Gharrity
Mike Gilberg
Gary Gillette
Jeff Goldman
Reuven and Eliane Goldman
Stefanie, Sarah, and Clemens
    Goldman
Theodore Q. Goldman
Jeremy Gottschalk
Rich Hahn
Joe Hamrahi
Jeff Hem
Charlie Hepp
Perry Husband
Mike Janes
Rany Jazayerli
Argentina T. D. Kahrl
Bill and Kathy Kahrl
Sky Kalkman
David Kaplan
Jonathan Kaplow
Dan Kaufman
Jonah Keri

Ted Keith
Matt Klotche
Danny Kopelson
Sydelle Kramer
Eric Kubota
Josh Kusnick
Sean Lahman
John Lalonde
Jon Lane
Tony Lastoria
June LaTrobe
David Laurila
Keith Law
Matt Leach
Keith Leippman
Ian Levin
Ben Lindbergh
Gordon and Linda Lorig
Rebecca Lorig
Benny Looper
Scott Lucas
Jacob Luft
Pete Macheska
Dan Malkiel
Erik Manning
Ben Mathis-Lilly
Dr. Mike Marshall
Jason McClelland
Jim McLennan
Kiley McDaniel
Will McDonald
Matt Melzak
Rob Miller
John Mirabelli
Bill Mitchell
Dr. Richard Mohring
Adam Morris
Eddit Motl
Chris Needham
Jamey Newberg
Mark Newman
Rob Neyer
Reid Nichols
Jack O'Connell
Jared Odom

Keith Olbermann
Jason Pare
Brian Parker
Grant Paulsen
Harry Pavlidis
David Pease
Jeff Pease
Caleb Peiffer
Susan Petrone
J. J. Piccolo
Nick Piecoro
Rick Reilly
Alex Reimer
Ned Rice
Doug Ross
SABRen beyond count
John Sanders
Eno Sarris
Bill Savage
Jon Scher
Keith Schloss
Casey Schwartz
Cory Schwartz
Alan Schwarz

Dan Scotto
Corey Seidman
Tom Shafer
Stu Shea
Nate Silver
Eric Simon
David W. Smith
Kate Sosin and the GqC Crew
Ken Spindler
Vern Stenman
Nick Stone
Steve Stone
Kevin Sullivan
Patrick Sullivan
Paul Sullivan
Laura Swartz
Joel Swartz
Nancy Swartz
Walter Sylvester
Bruce Taylor
Rick Telander
C. J. Thieleke
Shawn Touney
Dan Turkenkopf

Chris Villani
John Vuch
Richard Wade
Norm Wamer
Charley Wanamaker
Dejon Watson
Steve Wilson
Kathy Woolner
Keith Woolner
Serena Worthington
Colin Wyers
Josh Yates
John Zajc
Brad Ziegler

Special thanks to Our Man at Wiley, Eric Nelson, for his enthusiasm, patience, and knowledgeability, and to Christine Marra of *Marra*thon Editorial Production Services for what has become an annual habit of making the very complicated business of putting this book together seem simple.

Index